Western Europe

on a shoestring

Mark Balla
Rob van Driesum
Richard Everist
Helen Gillman
Mark Honan
Leanne Logan
Daniel Robinson
Lynn Seldon
David Stanley
Robert Strauss
Tony Wheeler

Western Europe on a shoestring

1st edition

Published by
    Lonely Planet Publications
    Head Office: PO Box 617, Hawthorn, Vic 3122, Australia
    Branches: PO Box 2001A, Berkeley, CA 94702, USA
                    12 Barley Mow Passage, Chiswick, W4 4PH, UK

Printed by
    Colorcraft Ltd, Hong Kong

Front Cover
    Neuschwanstein Castle in Bavaria (© Tony Stone Worldwide)

First Published
    January 1993

National Library of Australia Cataloguing in Publication Data

    Western Europe on a shoestring

    Includes index.
    ISBN 0 86442 149 4.

    1. Europe – Guidebooks. I. Wheeler, Tony, 1946- . (Series:
    Lonely Planet on a shoestring)

914

Mark Balla

Mark wrote the Spain chapter and updated part of the Germany chapter. He started travelling at the tender age of three months, and in the 25-odd years since then he hasn't found the time to stop. Somewhere along the way he managed to pick up half a dozen languages and a degree before joining Lonely Planet as our first phrasebook editor. After writing our *Brazilian phrasebook*, he departed for life in Europe, where he is living somewhere in the north of Germany bound for the south of France via Mexico, Albania or Australia.

Rob van Driesum

Rob coordinated the Germany chapter and updated part of it, and wrote much of this book's introductory material. He grew up in several Asian and African countries before moving to Holland, where he studied Modern History at the University of Amsterdam and worked as a teacher, bartender and freelance journalist to finance his travels to more than 100 countries (54 of them by motorcycle). A round-the-world motorcycle tour was cut short in Australia, where he worked as a labourer, flower salesman, truck driver and motorcycle magazine editor before joining Lonely Planet.

Richard Everist

Richard wrote the Great Britain chapter. He grew up in Geelong, Australia, has travelled a bit and had a wide variety of jobs. He worked full time in Lonely Planet's Melbourne office before jumping the fence to become a freelance writer. He has co-written travel survival kits to *Nepal* and *South Africa*, as well as updating *Papua New Guinea*, and has contributed to shoestring guides of *West Asia*, *Africa* and *Mediterranean Europe*.

Helen Gillman

Helen wrote the Italy chapter. She worked as a journalist and editor in Melbourne, Australia, for 12 years, including three years as the editorial manager of 10 suburban newspapers. Trying to manage journalists is not easy, so Helen decided to 'retire' in 1990, at the age of 31, and go to live in Italy. She has decided that her new incarnation as a Lonely Planet travel writer is far preferable to sitting behind a desk in a newspaper office. Helen is now working on Lonely Planet's forthcoming travel survival kit to *Italy*.

Mark Honan

Mark wrote the Austria, Liechtenstein and Switzerland chapters, updated part of the Germany chapter, and wrote this book's Getting Around chapter. After a university degree in Philosophy opened up a glittering career as an office clerk, he decided the 'meaning of life' lay elsewhere and set off on a two-year trip around the world. As a freelance travel writer, he then went camper vanning around Europe to write a series of articles for a London magazine. When the magazine went bust Mark joined a travel-agent from where he was rescued by Lonely Planet. Mark is now working on the forthcoming Lonely Planet guide to *Switzerland*.

Leanne Logan

Leanne wrote the Belgium, Luxembourg and Netherlands chapters. First experiencing Europe at the age of 12, she has long been lured by travel. From Brisbane on Australia's east coast, she explored her homeland while reporting for newspapers and the national news agency, and then set off through Asia and the Middle East. Her journey led via London, and work on a travel magazine, to Africa, and a quest to help save its decimated elephant population. Returning to Europe to cover the Benelux for this book, she also made a personal discovery of Belgium's famous beers and is now working on Lonely Planet's forthcoming travel survival kit for *France*.

Daniel Robinson

Daniel wrote the France and Andorra chapters. Raised in the San Francisco Bay Area and Glen Ellyn, Illinois in the USA, and in Israel, he graduated from Princeton University with a BA in Near Eastern Studies (Arab and Islamic history and the Arabic language). Daniel has travelled extensively in the Middle East and South, South-East and East Asia and currently lives in Tel Aviv. His previous work for Lonely Planet includes the Vietnam and Cambodia chapters in our award-winning *Vietnam, Laos & Cambodia – a travel survival kit*. He is currently working on the new LP guide to *France*.

Lynn Seldon

Lynn laid the groundwork for the western half of the Germany chapter. He is a full-time freelance travel writer and photographer, specialising in adventure travel and sports. After graduating from a military university and serving in the army, he discovered his true love was exploring the world. He currently lives in Richmond, Virginia, and travels at least eight months each year. He lived and worked in Germany for three years and has returned often since.

David Stanley

David is the author of Lonely Planet's *Eastern Europe on a shoestring*; its Eastern Germany chapter was updated to form part of the Germany chapter in this book. A quarter century ago, his right thumb carried him out of Toronto, Canada, and onto a journey which has so far wound through 137 countries. David studied at the universities of Barcelona and Florence before settling down to a degree in Spanish literature from the University of Guelph, Canada. From his base in Amsterdam he makes frequent trips to Eastern Europe and farther afield and has also written guidebooks to Micronesia and the South Pacific.

Robert Strauss

Robert wrote the Portugal chapter. In the early 1970s he left Britain to take the overland route to Nepal and then studied, taught and edited in England, Germany, Portugal and Hong Kong. For Lonely Planet he has worked on travel survival kits to *China, Tibet* and *Japan* and he has also written *The Trans-Siberian Rail Guide*. He has contributed photos and articles to other books, magazines and newspapers in the USA, Australia and Asia.

Tony Wheeler

Tony wrote the Ireland chapter. He was born in England but grew up in Pakistan, the Bahamas and the USA. He returned to England to do a degree in engineering at Warwick University, worked as an automotive design engineer, returned to university to complete an MBA in London, then dropped out on the Asian overland trail with his wife Maureen. Eventually settling down in Australia they've been travelling, writing and publishing guidebooks ever since, having set up Lonely Planet Publications in the mid-1970s. Travel for the Wheelers is considerably enlivened by their daughter Tashi and their son Kieran.

This Book

Western Europe on a shoestring, Lonely Planet's biggest ever new title, is part of a new *Europe on a shoestring* series that includes *Eastern Europe, Mediterranean Europe* and *Scandinavian & Baltic Europe*; each guide is complemented by a phrasebook covering the languages of that region – more details can be found in the back pages of this book.

Many experienced authors were involved in the exhaustive two-stage production process. In round one the authors researched and wrote their chapters which were then edited and the maps were drawn. In round two the authors returned to Europe to check prices, test the maps and tie up loose ends so that the information contained in these pages would be as thorough and up to date as possible.

From the Authors

Mark Balla Special thanks to Reyes and José, Miguelangel, Isabel & friends, Kate Cohen, Loli Sanchez, Pilar & Johnny (San Sebastián), and Bill Asbell. Thanks to the tourist office staff who were so helpful in Spain and the north of Germany. Special thanks to Hanna, Rainer, Gerard, Karin, Katia, Mario, Juanxie, Dolores and Nicola.

Rob van Driesum Thanks to Liesbeth Blomberg, Ulrike Böhme (Meissen), Marita Diehl, Sabine Keller, Rainer Lohrig (Saarbrücken), Brigitte Lübeck (Weimar), Dagmar Peter (Dresden), Dr Carsten Pollnick, Maria Antoinette Ritter (Köln), Dr Peter Roth (DZT Frankfurt), Gisela Schenk, Josef Schmenk (Bonn), Jarka & Milan

Schmiedt, Dr Christa Sommer (Leipzig), and last but certainly not least, Manfred Stäuber (GNTO Sydney).

Richard Everist Thanks to Angela Phillips who helped update the first draft of the Britain chapter, and David Morley who road-tested it. The following organisations also gave valuable assistance: the British Tourist Authority, in particular Val Austin; Britrail, in particular Richard Todman; and Driveaway Holidays, Sydney.

Helen Gillman Dedications to my friend Daniela and to Stefano, for making it an adventure. Thanks to Signor Valentino Paparelli (Terni), Paola Alunno and the staff at ENIT in Rome for their invaluable assistance. Also my wonderful parents, who continue to support me in all my follies.

Mark Honan Thanks to the Austrian, German and Swiss tourism authorities for their help, and special thanks to Wolfgang Kaiser from Kümmerly & Frey.

Leanne Logan Thanks to Sonja Tholl from the Luxembourg National Tourist Office and Els Wamsteeker from the Amsterdam Tourist Office; Philip Eikelboom (Delft); Math Stroes (Maastricht); Fred Witte ('s-Hertogenbosch); Sissi Puttaert and Tina Vanhoye from the Brussels Tourist Information Office; KLM Royal Dutch Airlines; David & Ria for the Amsterdam attic; Corry & An for Arnhem hospitality; Philip & Dee – the 'computer literates'; Sixy & BB – Trunks Rule!; and especially thank you to Geert Cole.

Daniel Robinson Thanks to George Whitman of Shakespeare & Co, Maurice & Eliane Bebe, Rabbi Pauline Bebe, Antoine Bebe, Mary Guggenheim, Gérard Boulanger, Guillaume Boulanger, the ever-helpful Georges, Sylvia Star, Cressida Reese, Richard Hallward, Nathalie Zend, John O'Brien, Julia Wilson, Benjamin Schmidt, Beth Reisberg, James King, Andrew Singer, Liza Hall, Allison Bigelow, Richard Everist, Cathy Karnow, Thierry di Costanzo, Sarinah Kalb, Miel de Botton, Sylvia & Robert Nathusius, Annette, Jean-Pierre, Agatte & Valerie Berman, Julien & Béatrice Ben Simon, Suzette Slama, Jacob & Mireille Berdugo, David & Simone Assayag and Rabbi Hayik of Toulouse. And finally, thanks to my parents, Rabbi Bernard & Yetta Robinson, for their love, support and friendship over the past 27 years.

Lynn Seldon Thanks to the staff at the GNTO, Lufthansa, AYH and Lonely Planet's San Francisco folks. Special thanks to all my friends in Richmond who support my travels and dreams.

Robert Strauss For help, advice, companionship and hospitality, many thanks go to: Rui Coelho, Sergio Tinoco and José & Fátima Abreu (Oporto), Ana Almeida Pinheiro (Tourist Office, Lisbon), and Joãozinho. Special thanks to Deanna Swaney (Alaska) for changing the tunes and keying in the notes.

Tony Wheeler Thanks to the Irish Tourist Board (particularly Gordon Stepto at their Australian office) and the Northern Ireland Tourist Board (particularly Jim Paul in London), to Terry & Gillian Dixon in Belfast, to Sean Sheehan for an amusing night at Kilcrohane and to the many interesting and helpful people I met all over the island.

From the Publisher
This book was edited at the Lonely Planet headquarters in Melbourne, Australia, by Adrienne Costanzo and Rob van Driesum (who also coordinated the project), with help from Diana Saad, Tom Smallman, Sally Steward, Alan Tiller, Jeff Williams and Caroline Williamson. Special thanks go to Sue Mitra for her patient support, to LP's computer whiz, Dan Levin, for keeping things running smoothly, to Sharon Wertheim for indexing, and to Adrienne Costanzo and Frith Pike for their contributions to the introductory chapters.

The language sections were coordinated by Sally Steward and written by Chris Andrews (French), Rob van Driesum (Dutch), Jim Jenkin (German), Isabelle Moutinho (Portuguese & Spanish) and Sally Steward (Italian).

The input from Lonely Planet's art department was coordinated by Chris Lee Ack, who drew the maps with help from Rachel Black, Jane Hart, Sandra Smythe, Sally Woodward and several other LP cartographers. Vicki Beale designed the book and helped put together the tables in the appendix, Sandra Smythe designed the cover, and Ann Jeffree illustrated the title page.

Additional thanks go to the authors for their cooperation and enthusiasm.

Warning & Request
Things change – prices go up, schedules change, good places go bad and bad places go bankrupt – nothing stays the same. So if you find things better or worse, recently opened or long since closed, please write and tell us and help make the next edition better. We're particularly interested to hear your reactions to this book, our first guide to Western Europe.

Your letters will be used to help update future editions and, where possible, important changes will also be included in a Stop Press section in reprints.

We greatly appreciate all information that is sent to us by travellers. Back at Lonely Planet we employ a hard-working readers' letters team to sort through the many letters we receive. The best ones will be rewarded with a free copy of the next edition or another Lonely Planet guide if you prefer. We give away lots of books, but, unfortunately, not every letter/postcard receives one.

Contents

Map Legend

BOUNDARIES

— ·· — ·· — ··	International Boundary
— · — · — ·	Internal Boundary
+++++++++	National Park or Reserve
- - - - - - - - -	The Equator

SYMBOLS

◉ NEW DELHI	National Capital
● BOMBAY	Provincial or State Capital
● Pune	Major Town
◆ Barsi	Minor Town
■	Places to Stay
▼	Places to Eat
≜	Post Office
✈	Airport
i	Tourist Information
⊖	Bus Station or Terminal
66	Highway Route Number
☽ ✝ 🕌 ⛪	Mosque, Church, Cathedral
∴	Temple or Ruin
✚	Hospital
※	Lookout
Å	Camping Area
⊼	Picnic Area
⌂	Hut or Chalet
▲	Mountain or Hill
⛛⛛⛛⛛	Stairway
⊢●⊣	Railway Station
🚇	Metro Station, Tube Station
+++++	Road Bridge
⇒ ⇐	Railway Bridge
→) (←	Road Tunnel
	Escalator Tunnel
⌣	Cliff
⊓⊔⊓⊔	Ancient or Historic Wall

Note: not all symbols displayed ...

ROUTES

	Major Road or Highway
- - - - - - - - -	Unsealed Major Road
	Sealed Road
- - - - - -	Unsealed Road or Track
≡≡≡	City Street
+++++++++	Railway
⊙	Subway
++++++++++	Tram
··············	Walking Track
- - - - - -	Ferry Route
+++-+-+-+-+	Cable Car or Funicular

HYDROGRAPHIC FEATURES

	River or Creek
⬭ ⬭	Lake, Intermittent Lake
	Coast Line
⟶	River Flow
⇟	Waterfall
⅏ ⅏ ⅏ ⅏	Swamp
	Salt Lake or Reef
	Glacier

OTHER FEATURES

	Park, Garden or National Park
⊠	Built Up Area
	Pedestrian Mall
⊠	Plaza or Town Square
+ + + +	Cemetery

book

Introduction

Western Europe is many things to many people. Some marvel at the diversity of cultures and languages crammed into such a small area; the wealth of museums, theatre and architecture unmatched anywhere in the world; or the shopping, restaurants and nightlife in the bustling cities. Others are attracted to Western Europe's varied scenery, from sun-drenched beaches and dense forests to snow-capped peaks. Residents of the Americas and Australasia see Western Europe as the source of their culture and civilisation, while almost all visitors are pleased with the minimal bureaucracy, well-developed tourist facilities and efficient transport, which make it possible to explore the region with a minimum of fuss.

Western Europe is often considered to be the hub of the developed world, at least historically. Although other regions may be changing faster today, Western Europe is still an economic powerhouse and a leader in art, literature and music. For the visitor to the region the biggest problem is simply choosing what to do and see; which dishes to select from an overloaded table. There are magnificent museums and galleries like the British Museum in London, the Louvre in Paris and the Pergamon Museum in Berlin. There are architectural set pieces like the ancient Colosseum in Rome, Gaudí's fantastic church in Barcelona, or fantasy German castles like Neuschwanstein in Bavaria (pictured on the cover of this book). There are superb natural features like the soaring Swiss Alps, the magnificent stretches of coastline in Ireland or the dense forests of Germany. For the energetic, there are walking trails from the Circuit of Mt Blanc to the Cotswolds Way in England; ski runs from Albertville to Zermatt; and water sports all along the Atlantic, Baltic and Mediterranean coasts. And there are places where it's simply fun to be, whether it's after dark in Amsterdam, pub-crawling through Dublin or watching the world go by from a sidewalk café in Paris.

Western Europe on a shoestring covers this diverse collection of countries with an insight into their history, people and culture as well as practical information to help you make the most of your time and money. It takes you through Western Europe from pre-departure preparations to packing your bag for the return home. There's information on how to get to Europe and how to get around once you're there. There are extensive details on what to see, when to see it and how much it all costs. The thousands of recommendations about places to stay range from Spanish camp sites, German youth hostels and French pensions to Irish bed & breakfasts. Cafés, restaurants and bars are covered in equally exhaustive detail with suggestions ranging from the cheapest cheap eats to the ideal place for that long-awaited big splurge. There are even recommendations on what to buy and where to buy it.

Western Europe is a great place; there's lots out there waiting to be enjoyed. All you have to do is go.

Western Europe

0   300   600 km

Approximate North Only

FAROE ISLANDS
Shetland Islands
Orkney Islands
SWEDEN
NORWAY
Oslo
Stockholm

NORTH SEA

Belfast
Edinburgh
IRELAND
Dublin

DENMARK
Copenhagen
BALTIC SEA

ATLANTIC OCEAN

NETHERLANDS
Amsterdam
GREAT BRITAIN
Cardiff
London
Berlin
GERMANY
POLAND

English Channel
Brussels
Bonn
BELGIUM
LUXEMBOURG
Luxembourg
Prague
CZECH & SLOVAK REPUBLIC

To Lisbon 1500 km
Ponta Delgada
Azores (Portugal)

Bay of Biscay

Paris
LIECHTENSTEIN
Vienna
Bratislava
AUSTRIA
Budapest
HUNGARY
FRANCE
Bern
SWITZERLAND
Mt Blanc
The Alps
SLOVENIA
CROATIA
BOSNIA–HERCEGOVINA

Pyrenees
ANDORRA
Monaco
ITALY
Corsica
Apennines
Adriatic Sea

PORTUGAL
Madrid
Rome

Lisbon
SPAIN
Sardinia
Tyrrhenian Sea

Gibraltar
Balearic Islands

MEDITERRANEAN SEA

Madeira (Portugal)
Funchal
To Lisbon 1000 km
Canary Islands (Spain)
Las Palmas

Algiers
Tunis
SICILY
Valletta
MALTA
Tripoli
LIBYA
TUNISIA
ALGERIA

Facts for the Visitor

There are those who say that Europe is so well developed that you don't have to plan a thing, since anything can be arranged on the spot. As any experienced traveller knows, the problems you thought about at home often turn out to be irrelevant, or will sort themselves out once you get going.

This theory is fine if you've decided to blow the massive inheritance sitting in your bank account; but if your financial status is more modest, some prior knowledge and a bit of careful planning can make your hard-earned travel budget stretch further than you thought. You'll also want to make sure that the things you plan to see and do will be possible at that particular time of the year.

PLANNING

Maps

You can't plan without maps. The maps in this book will help you to get an idea of where you might want to go and will be a useful first reference when you arrive in a city. Good maps of various descriptions are easy to come by once you're in Europe, but you might want to buy a few beforehand, especially if you know that you're going to spend a lot of time in a particular place or want to plan your trip in greater detail. Proper road maps are essential if you're driving or cycling.

You can't go wrong with Michelins, and because of their soft covers, they fold up easily so you can stick them in your pocket. Some people prefer the meticulously produced Freytag & Berndt, Kümmerly & Frey or Hallwag maps. The British AA maps are also good – as a rule, maps published by automobile associations in Europe are excellent, and they're sometimes free if membership of your local association gives you reciprocal rights.

Tourist offices are another good source of maps. Generally, one of the most sensible things to do when you arrive in a town is to head straight for the local tourist information office to stock up on maps and brochures.

When to Go

Any time can be the best time to visit Europe, depending on what you want to do. Summer lasts roughly from June to September, and offers the most pleasant climate for outdoor pursuits in the northern half of Europe. In the southern half (along the Mediterranean coast and in the Iberian Peninsula), where the summers tend to be hotter, you can extend that period by one or even two months either way, when temperatures may also be more agreeable.

Unfortunately, you won't be the only tourist during summer – all of France and Italy, for instance, goes on holidays in August. Prices can be high, accommodation fully booked, and the sights packed. You'll find much better deals, and less crowds, in the shoulder seasons either side of summer; in April and May, for instance, flowers are in bloom and the weather can be surprisingly mild, and indian summers are not uncommon in September and October.

On the other hand, if you're keen on winter sports, resorts in the Alps and the Pyrenees begin operating in November and move into full swing after the New Year, closing down again when the snows begin to melt in March or April.

The Climate & When to Go sections in the individual country chapters explain what to expect and when to expect it, and the Climate Charts appendix in the back of the book will help you compare different destinations. As a rule, spring and autumn tend to be wetter and windier than summer and winter. The temperate maritime climate along the Atlantic seaboard is relatively wet all year, with moderate extremes in temperature; the Mediterranean coast is hotter and drier, with most rainfall during the mild winter; the continental climate in eastern Germany and the Alps tends to show much stronger extremes between summer and winter.

The climate will have a bearing on the clothes you bring along. Don't bring too much – you can always buy whatever you need along the way. Insulation works on the principle of trapped air, and several layers of thin clothing are warmer than only one that is thick (and will be easier to dry, too). You'll also be much more flexible if the weather suddenly turns warm on you. Just be prepared for rain at any time of year.

How Long?

The amount of time you spend in Europe is entirely up to you and your bank account. The more time you spend in one place, the lower your daily expenses are likely to be as you get to know your way around. But remember, you're not on some sort of travelling economy run – being tight with your money can mean you lose the whole purpose of being there. See the Money section that follows for an indication of expenses.

If you have a rail pass, you'll have to stay on the move to make the best use of it. Even so, you should be able to save money by timing your arrivals and departures so that you sleep on the train. See Move or Stay? in the following section.

What Kind of Trip?

Travelling Companions Travelling alone is not a problem in Europe, if that's what you want to do. The region is well developed and relatively safe, so you don't really need the support of a team.

If you decide to travel with others because you prefer to share the experience, keep in mind that travel can put relationships to the test like few other experiences can. It has been said that if you plan to marry, you should go travelling with that person first. Many a long-term friendship has collapsed under the strains of constant negotiations about where to stay and eat, how much to spend, what to see and where to go next. But many friendships have also become closer than ever before. You won't find out until

you try, but make sure you agree on itineraries and routines beforehand.

If travel is a good way of testing a friendship, it's also a great way of meeting new people. Hostels and camping grounds are good places to meet other travellers with whom to team up or simply share experiences. Even if travelling alone, you need never be lonely.

The Getting Around chapter has information on organised tours with groups. The young, the elderly and the inexperienced tend to appreciate such tours because they take the daily hassles and uncertainties out of travel. Just sit back and enjoy. Long tours, however, can become experiments in social cohesion since not everybody always gets on well with everybody else, and frictions can develop.

Move or Stay? 'If this is Thursday, it must be Zürich.' Though often ridiculed, the mad dash that crams six countries into a month does have its merits. If you've never visited Europe, you won't know which areas you'll like, and a quick 'scouting tour' will give an overview of your options. With a rail pass that offers unlimited travel within a set period of time, why not do just this?

But if you know where you want to go, or find a place you like, the best advice is to stay for a while and 'blend in'. Discover some of the lesser known sights; make a few local friends and settle in to a different way of life.

With your own transport, or buying train and bus tickets as you go along, you can stay in a place long enough to get a bit of a feel for it and then move on. You'll probably finish where you started; but rather than follow the same itinerary back, take a different route and see twice as much – or better still, make it a circuit and keep your options open.

Working Holiday European countries aren't keen to hand out jobs to foreigners. Officially, an EC (European Community) citizen is allowed to work in any other EC country, but the paperwork isn't always straightforward for longer term employment. Other country/nationality combinations require special work permits that can be almost impossible to arrange, especially for temporary work. That doesn't prevent enterprising travellers from topping up their funds occasionally, and they don't always have to do this illegally either.

Britain, for example, issues special 'working holiday' permits to Commonwealth citizens aged between 17 and 27, and Switzerland has a system of work permits allocated by employers. Your national student exchange organisation may be able to arrange temporary work permits to several countries through special programmes. For more details on working as a foreigner, see Work in the Facts for the Visitor sections of the individual country chapters.

If you have a parent or grandparent who was born in an EC country, you may have certain rights you never knew about. Get in touch with that country's embassy and ask about dual citizenship and work permits – if you go for citizenship, also ask about any obligations, such as military service... Not all countries allow dual citizenship, so a work permit may be all you can get. Do your homework. Ireland is particularly easygoing about granting citizenship to people with Irish ancestry, and with an Irish passport, the EC is your oyster.

If you do find a temporary job, the pay is likely to be less than that offered to locals. The only exceptions appear to be jobs teaching English, but these are hard to come by. Other typical tourist jobs (picking grapes in France, washing dishes in Alpine resorts) often come with board and lodging and the pay is little more than pocket money, but you'll have a good time partying with other travellers.

Work Your Way Around the World by Susan Griffith (paperback) gives good, practical advice on a wide range of issues. The same publisher, Vacation Work, has a book titled *The Au Pair and Nanny's Guide to Working Abroad* by Susan Griffith & Sharon Legg (paperback), which is useful if you're after that kind of work.

If you play an instrument or have other artistic talents, you could try working the streets. It's fairly common in many major cities (especially in Britain, Ireland and Italy), but not common in Switzerland, while the Portuguese seem to lack the means to support street artists altogether. Beware: it's illegal in Switzerland and Austria, and illegal but more or less tolerated in Germany and Belgium; most other countries require municipal permits that can be hard to obtain. Talk to other street artists before you boogie.

Selling goods on the street is generally frowned upon and can be tantamount to vagrancy apart from at flea markets. It's also a hard way to make money if you're not selling something special. Austria, Italy and Luxembourg require permits for this sort of thing. It's fairly common, though officially illegal, in Britain, Germany and Spain.

What to Bring

As little as possible is the best policy. It's very easy to find almost anything you need along the way, and since you'll inevitably buy things as you go, it's better to start with too little rather than too much.

A backpack is still the most popular method of carrying gear as it is convenient and the only way to go if you have to do any walking. On the debit side, a backpack doesn't offer too much protection for your valuables, the straps tend to get caught on things and some airlines may refuse to be responsible if the pack is damaged or broken into.

Travelpacks, a combination of backpack and shoulder bag, have become very popular. The backpack straps zip away inside the pack when not needed so you almost have the best of both worlds. Some packs have sophisticated shoulder-strap adjustment systems and these can be used comfortably even for long hikes. Packs are always much easier to carry than a bag. Another alternative is a large, soft zip-bag with a wide shoulder strap so it can be carried with relative ease if necessary. Backpacks or travelpacks can be reasonably thief-proofed with small padlocks. Forget suitcases unless you're travelling in style.

As for clothing, begin light and buy local clothes that take your fancy as you go along. See the following Appearances & Conduct section for a rundown on dress standards in Europe. Bearing in mind that you can buy virtually anything on the spot, a minimum packing list could include:

• underwear, socks & swimming gear
• a pair of jeans and maybe a pair of shorts
• a few T-shirts & shirts
• a warm sweater
• a solid pair of shoes
• sandals or thongs for mouldy showers
• a coat or jacket
• a raincoat or umbrella, or waterproof jacket
• a medical kit and a sewing kit
• a padlock
• a Swiss Army knife
• soap & towel
• toothpaste, toothbrush & toiletries

A tent and sleeping bag are vital if you want to save money by camping. Even if you're not camping, a sleeping bag is still very useful. It can double as a cushion on hard train-seats, a seat for long waits at bus or railway stations, and a quilt in cold hotels. A sleeping sheet with pillow cover is necessary if you plan to stay in youth hostels – you'll have to hire or purchase one if you don't bring your own. In any case, a sheet that fits into your sleeping bag is easier to wash than the bag. Make one yourself out of old sheets (including the built-in pillow cover), or buy one from your youth hostel association.

A padlock is useful to lock your bag to a train or bus luggage rack, and may also be needed to secure your youth hostel locker. A Swiss Army knife is useful for all sorts of things (any pocket knife is fine, so long as it includes a bottle opener and strong cork-screw). You could need waterproof gear at any time of the year. Soap, toothpaste and toilet paper are readily obtainable almost anywhere, but you'll need your own supply of paper in many public toilets and camping ground amenity blocks. In some countries, toilets in public areas cost a bit of small change, so have that handy. Tampons are available at pharmacies and supermarkets in

all but the most remote places. Condoms are widely available, even in Ireland.

Optional items include a compass (to help orient yourself in large cities), a flashlight (torch), an alarm clock (if you're a heavy sleeper, otherwise a watch with alarm function will do), an adapter plug for electrical appliances (such as a cup water heater to save on expensive tea and coffee), a universal bath/sink plug (a film canister sometimes works, too), sunglasses and a few clothes pegs. During city sightseeing, a small day-pack is better than a shoulder bag at deterring snatch thieves (see the Dangers & Annoy-ances section).

There are two final considerations. The secret of successful packing is plastic carry bags or garbage bags inside your backpack: they not only keep things separate and clean but also dry if the bag gets soaked. Airlines do lose bags from time to time, but you've got a much better chance of it not being yours if it is tagged with your name and address *inside* the bag as well as outside. Outside tags can always fall off or be removed.

Appearances & Conduct

Europeans are tolerant of eccentric fashions and behaviour, but attention to your appear-ance will help. Although dress standards are fairly informal in northern Europe, your clothes may well have some bearing on how you're treated in Italy, Spain and Portugal – where the locals will try to dress neatly and cleanly even in the poorer areas.

By all means dress casually, but keep it clean, and ensure sufficient body cover (trousers or knee-length dress) if your sight-seeing includes churches, synagogues or mosques. Wearing shorts away from the beach is not very common among men in Europe. Some nightclubs and fancy restau-rants may refuse entry to people wearing jeans; men might consider packing a tie as well, just in case. For more information on female dress codes, see Female Travellers in the Special Needs section.

Europeans have 'been there, done that' with hair length. The process has come full circle, and long hair appears to be making a bit of a comeback among men. Nevertheless, the 'long hair equals despicable hippy' syndrome still survives in remote areas, especially with hair that's unkempt and greasy.

Most border guards and immigration officials are too professional to judge people entirely by their appearance, but some will be ambitious types who think they are on to a drug-smuggling ring when they spot a 'hippy'. Officials are always paranoid of potential 'vagrants' without means of support. This can be particularly true of the police in rural areas, though perhaps not so much in northern Europe. At the risk of stating the obvious, first impressions do count, and you'll find life easier if you're well presented when dealing with officialdom.

On the beach, nude bathing is usually limited to restricted areas, but topless bathing is very common in many parts of Europe – indeed, in France, Germany, the Netherlands and Scandinavia it can seem *de rigueur*, and in Greece many tourists do it. But women should be wary of taking their tops off as a matter of course. The rule is, if nobody else seems to be doing it, don't. You're not there to educate the locals.

You'll soon notice that Europeans are heavily into shaking hands and even kissing when they greet one another. If you can't handle the kissing, that's fine, but at least get into the habit of shaking hands with virtually everyone you meet. It's an important ritual, and your handshake could mean a lot to how the other person gauges you. If you're male, make it firm without crushing your opponent.

It's also customary to greet the proprietor when entering a shop, café or quiet bar, and to say goodbye when you leave.

The Top 10

There is so much to see in Western Europe, that compiling a top 10 is almost impossible. But we asked the authors involved in this book to list their personal highlights, and the results are as follows:

1. Paris
2. Rome
3. London
4. Berlin
5. Amsterdam
6. The Alps
7. Venice
8. Scotland
9. Tuscany
10. Munich

Other nominations included Barcelona, the Algarve, Florence, Umbria, Provence and the Pyrenees. A visit to any of these places could be rewarding.

The Bottom 10

The writers were also asked to list the 10 worst 'attractions' of the region:

1. Spanish coasts
2. Paris
3. Frankfurt Airport
4. Traffic jams in Paris, London and Rome
5. The *Sound of Music* tour in Salzburg
6. The French north coast
7. The Munich *Bierfest*
8. The Monte Carlo casino
9. British coastal resorts
10. Bullfights in Spain

Other nominations included the English weather, drunken Scandinavian tourists, Madame Tussaud's, the Scottish east coast, Milan, Rotterdam and Palma de Mallorca. A visit to any of these places could leave you feeling that you've wasted your time. Note that Paris is almost as good at repelling our authors as attracting them.

PASSPORT & VISAS
Passport

Your most important travel document is a passport, which should remain valid until well after your trip. If it's just about to expire, renew it before you go – having it done by your embassy in Rome (or wherever) can be tedious and inconvenient. Some countries, like Belgium, insist that your passport remain valid for a specified minimum period (usually three months) after your visit; even if they don't insist on this, expect questions from immigration officials if it's due to expire in a matter of days.

If you don't have a passport, you'll have to apply for one, which can be an involved process. A renewal or application can take anything from a few days to several months, depending on many factors, so don't leave it till the last minute (it can sometimes be speeded up with a good excuse, though this may attract a higher fee). Bureaucracy usually grinds faster if you do everything in person at the actual passport issuing office if possible, rather than relying on the mail or agents. Check first what you need to bring: passport photos, birth certificate, population register extract, signed statements, exact payment in cash, whatever.

Australian citizens can apply at a post office or the passport office in their state capital; Britons can get application forms from travel agents and major post offices, and the passport is issued by the regional passport office; Canadians can apply at regional passport offices; New Zealanders can apply at any district office of the Department of Internal Affairs; US citizens must apply in person (but may usually renew by mail) at a US Passport Agency office or some courthouses and post offices.

Once you start travelling, carry your passport at all times and guard it carefully. The locals in some countries are required by law to carry personal identification, and the same applies to foreigners. Camping grounds and hotels sometimes insist that you hand over your passport for the duration of your stay, which is very inconvenient, since you won't be able to cash travellers' cheques or arrange visas. They tend to be a bit more flexible about this if you pay in advance, but a Camping Carnet usually solves the problem (see the Documents section).

See Theft in the Dangers & Annoyances section about photocopying your passport and other important documents.

Europeans Citizens of many European countries don't always need a valid passport to travel within the region. A national identity card or something like the British Visitor's Passport may be sufficient; this can often work out cheaper and usually involves less paperwork and processing time. An expired passport may be all right, too. An EC citizen travelling to another EC country will generally face the least problems. *Important:* If you want to exercise any of these options, check with your travel agent or the embassies of the countries you plan to visit.

Visas

A visa is a stamp in your passport permitting you to enter the country in question and stay for a specified period of time. The word is Latin for 'seen', and means that a consular official of that country has seen your passport and decided that it's OK for you to visit. In 99.9% of cases, the procedure is a mere formality, but one that you must go through if your passport requires a visa for the country in question. Often you can get the visa at the border or at the airport of arrival, but not always, especially not if you're travelling by train or bus and the procedure is likely to hold everybody up – check first with the embassies or consulates of the countries you plan to visit.

There's a wide variety including tourist, transit and business visas. Transit visas are usually cheaper than tourist or business visas, but only allow a very short stay of one or two days and can be difficult to extend.

Most readers of this book, however, will have very little to do with visas. With a valid passport they'll be able to visit most European countries for up to three (sometimes even six) months, provided they have some sort of onward or return ticket and/or 'sufficient means of support' (money!). Except at international airports, it's unlikely that immigration officials will give you and your passport more than a cursory glance if you look OK – see the previous Appearances & Conduct section.

Border checks are likely to become even more relaxed: the Schengen accord signed by eight of the 12 EC countries (the exceptions are the UK, Ireland, Denmark and Greece) aims to abolish passport controls within the EC altogether. Border procedures between EC and non-EC countries remain a bit more thorough.

There are a few important exceptions to these easy visa rules. Holders of diplomatic or official passports face different requirements to ordinary passport holders, and should check with the embassies of the countries they wish to visit. South Africans have little joy travelling on their 'Green Mamba', though restrictions may gradually be eased. Hong Kong residents may need visas to several countries depending on their (UK) passport endorsements. Australians still need a visa to visit France – it may not be checked when entering the country overland, but major problems can arise if it is requested on departure and can't be shown.

Although European countries are tolerant of the nationalities they allow in, it pays to beware of 'unpopular' passport markings if you do any further travelling. Greece denies entry to people who have a northern Cyprus stamp in their passport; Morocco may turn

back people whose passports show that they've visited Israel; South Africans have had trouble in the past getting into Yugoslavia and Scandinavia; visa stamps from Cuba, Vietnam or North Korea could cause delays at some borders while reference lists are consulted (Germany can be thorough in this sort of thing). 'Unpopular' countries will often provide a loose-leaf visa if you ask for one.

Visa requirements can change, and you should always check with the individual embassies or a reputable travel agent before travelling. In most cases, visas are available on the spot at the border, but it pays to check that too. It's generally easier to get your visas as you go along, rather than arranging them all beforehand. Carry plenty of spare passport photos (you'll need one to four every time you apply for a visa). The chart below lists visa requirements for some nationalities.

DOCUMENTS

Apart from your passport, there are a number of documents worth considering.

Visas Requirements

	Country of Origin								
	Aust	Can	HK	Ire	N Z	Sing	S Afr	UK	USA
Andorra	–	–	–	–	–	–	–	–	–
Austria	–	–	–	–	–	–	✓	–	–
Belgium	–	–	✗	–	–	–	✓	–	–
France	✓	–	✓	–	–	✓	✓	–	–
Germany	–	–	✗	–	–	–	✓	–	–
Ireland	–	–	–	–	–	–	–	–	–
Italy	–	–	✗	–	–	–	✓	–	–
Luxembourg	–	–	–	–	–	–	✓	–	–
Netherlands	–	–	–	–	–	–	✓	–	–
Portugal	–	2	✗	–	–	✓	✓	–	2
Spain	1	–	✗	–	–	–	✓	–	–
Switzerland/Liech	–	–	✗	–	–	–	–	–	–
United Kingdom	–	–	–	–	–	–	–	–	–

✓ Tourist visa required
✗ Depends on endorsements in passport. Check with embassy.
1 Maximum stay without visa: one month (with two entries/exits) every six months
2 Maximum stay without visa: two months

International Health Certificate

You'll need this yellow booklet only if you're coming into the region from areas, such as Africa and South America, where cholera or yellow fever are prevalent – see Immunisation in the Health section for more details. Europe is free of such diseases, and the authorities like to keep it that way.

International Driving Permit (IDP)

If you hold a non-European driving licence and plan to drive in the region, obtain one of these permits from your local automobile association before you leave – you'll need a passport photo and a valid licence. They are usually inexpensive and valid for one year only. An IDP helps Europeans make sense of your unfamiliar local licence (make sure you take that with you, too) and can make life much simpler, especially when hiring cars and motorbikes.

While you're at it, ask your automobile association for a Card of Introduction. This entitles you to services offered by sister organisations in Europe, usually free of charge (touring maps and information, help with breakdowns, technical and legal advice etc). See the Getting Around chapter for more details.

Camping Carnet

Your local automobile association also issues a Camping Carnet, which is basically a camping ground ID. Carnets are also issued by your local camping federation, and sometimes on the spot at camping grounds. They incorporate third party insurance for damage you may cause, and many camping grounds offer a small discount if you sign in with one. Some hostels and hotels also accept carnets for signing-in purposes, but won't give discounts.

International Youth Hostel Card

An IYHF (International Youth Hostel Federation) card is useful if you're staying at youth hostels. Some European hostels don't require that you be a YHA (Youth Hostel Association) member, but often charge less if you have a card. Many youth hostels will issue one on the spot or after a few stays, though this costs a bit more than getting it in your home country.

Student & Youth Cards

The most useful of these is the International Student Identity Card (ISIC), a plastic ID-style card with your photograph. It can perform all sorts of wonders, particularly discounts on many forms of transport (including airlines and local public transport). Even if you have your own transport, the card will soon pay for itself through cheap or free admission to museums and sights, and cheap meals in some student restaurants.

It's no surprise that there is a worldwide industry in fake student cards, and many places now stipulate a maximum age for student discounts or, more simply, they've substituted a 'youth discount' for a 'student discount'. If you're aged under 26 but not a student, you can apply for a Federation of International Youth Travel Organisations (FIYTO) card which gives much the same discounts as an ISIC.

Both types of card are issued by student unions or 'alternative-style' travel agencies. They don't automatically entitle you to discounts, and some companies and institutions refuse to recognise them altogether, but you won't find out until you flash the card.

MONEY

Bring as much of this fine stuff as you can. You will generally find that US dollars, Deutschmarks, pounds sterling, and French and Swiss francs are the most easily exchanged, followed by Italian lire and Dutch guilders, but you may well decide that other currencies suit your purposes better. You lose out through commissions and customer exchange rates every time you change money, so if you only visit Portugal, for example, you may be better off buying escudos straight away if your bank at home can provide them.

All Western European currencies are fully convertible, but you may have trouble exchanging some of the more obscure ones in small banks, while currencies of countries with high inflation face unfavourable exchange rates. Try not to have too many leftover Portuguese escudos, Spanish pesetas, Irish punts, Belgian or Luxembourg francs, or Austrian Schillings. Get rid of Scottish pounds before leaving Scotland: nobody outside the UK will touch them. The same goes for Northern Irish pounds.

Banks are closed on public holidays, which are listed in the individual country chapters. If you get caught out, remember that most airports, central train stations, some fancy hotels and many border posts have banking facilities outside normal office hours, sometimes on a 24-hour basis. Post offices in Europe often perform banking tasks, tend to be open longer hours, and outnumber banks in remote places.

If you visit several countries, the constant currency conversions can drive you up the wall. Buy a cheap pocket calculator, cut out the list of exchange rates from a newspaper before you leave, and stick it to the back for easy reference. The best exchange rates are usually at banks. Bureaux de change usually (but not always) offer worse rates or charge higher commissions. Hotels are almost always the worst places to change money. American Express and Thomas Cook offices usually do not charge commission for changing their own cheques, but may offer a less favourable exchange rate than banks.

How Much Money?

The answer is simple: as much as possible. Europe is seldom cheap, and you can easily throw hundreds of dollars down the drain on a daily basis. But the continent also has its fair share of people whose surname isn't Rockefeller, and they manage to travel there quite well without spending a fortune.

The secret is cheap accommodation. Europe has a highly developed network of camping grounds, some of them quite luxurious, and they're great places to meet people. The youth hostel network, too, is well developed, but the clientele might make those aged over 30 feel a bit old at times.

Other money-saving strategies include a

student card (worthwhile discounts on museum admissions and transport – see the previous Documents section); various rail and public transport passes (see the Getting Around chapter); applying for consumer tax rebates on large purchases (see Consumer Taxes in the introductions to the individual countries); and, generally, following the advice in this book on food and accommodation. Hitchhiking, preparing your own meals and avoiding alcohol are other good ways of saving money.

Your budget depends on how you live and travel. If you're moving around fast, going to lots of places, spending time in the big cities, then your day-to-day living costs are going to be quite high; if you stay in one place and get to know your way around, they're likely to come down.

Including transport but not private motorised transport, your daily expenses could work out to around US$20 to US$30 a day if you're operating on a rock-bottom budget. This means camping or staying in hostels, eating as economically as possible and using a transport pass. In Spain and Portugal you could probably get the daily cost down to under US$20 a day.

Travelling on a moderate budget, you should be able to manage on US$50 to US$75 a day. This would allow you to stay at cheap hotels, guesthouses or bed & breakfasts (B&Bs). You could afford meals in economical restaurants and even a few beers! Again, Spain and Portugal would be somewhat cheaper, while Switzerland and Britain (London!) would be pricier. If you really want to exercise that gold card, you can begin to live well in Europe for US$100 a day.

Tipping

In Europe, tipping is much less prevalent than in North America, but much more than in Australia, New Zealand or Asia. In many countries, it's common for a service charge to be added to restaurant or hotel bills, in which case no tipping is necessary. In others, simply rounding up the bill is sufficient. See the individual country chapters for more details.

Cash

Nothing beats cash for convenience... or risk. If you lose it, it's gone forever and very few travel insurers will come to your rescue.

It's still a good idea, though, to bring some local currency in cash, if only to tide you over until you get to an exchange facility. The equivalent of, say, US$100 should usually be enough. Some extra cash in an easily exchanged currency is a good idea, too. Often, it is much easier to change just a few dollars (when leaving a country, for example) in cash rather than cheques – and more economical.

Remember that banks will always accept paper money but very rarely coins in currencies other than their own. Before you leave one country for the next, spend your last coins on a cup of coffee, fuel if travelling by car, or whatever.

Travellers' Cheques

American Express, Visa or Thomas Cook travellers' cheques are probably the best to carry because of their wide acceptance and 'instant replacement' policies. The main idea of carrying cheques rather than cash is the protection they offer from theft, but it doesn't do a lot of good if you have to go back home first to get the refund. Ask about European representatives and telephone hotline numbers when you buy your cheques.

Keeping a record of the cheque numbers and the initial purchase details is vital when it comes to replacing lost cheques. Without this, you may well find that 'instant' is a very long time indeed. You should also keep a record of which cheques you have cashed. Keep these details separate from the cheques themselves. If you're going to remote places, it's worth sticking to American Express since small local banks may not always accept other brands. American Express has offices in most of the major cities.

Cheques are available in various currencies. American Express, for instance, offers

US dollars, pounds sterling, Deutschmarks, French and Swiss francs, Japanese yen and Canadian dollars. Unless you live in the USA, however, there's little point using US$ cheques in Europe, since you'll lose on the exchange rate when you buy the cheques and again each time you cash one in. Choose the currency you're likely to need most – say, pounds sterling if you're going to spend a lot of time and money in Britain. The trick is to ensure that you only convert currencies once, not twice. You actually pay for the cheques in two ways when you buy them: not only does the vendor make a margin on the exchange rate but there is also a commission on the sale, usually 1%.

When you change cheques, don't look at just the exchange rate; ask about fees and commissions as well. Some places charge a per-cheque service fee, so changing US$100 in US$20 cheques can end up more expensive than a single US$100 cheque. Other places charge a flat transaction fee instead, or a percentage of the total amount, irrespective of the number of cheques, and you might want to take advantage of this by changing a few small cheques at once. Some banks charge fees to cash some brands of travellers' cheques but not others. In most countries these days, the exchange rate for travellers' cheques is slightly better than the exchange rate for cash, but it's often better to settle for a worse exchange rate if it's balanced by lower fees or commissions.

Take most of the cheques in large denominations, say US$100s or £100s. It's only towards the end of a stay that you may want to change US$20 or US$10 cheques to make sure you don't get left with too much local currency.

International Transfers

If you run out of money or need more for whatever reason, you can instruct your bank back home to send you a draft (always assuming you've got money back home to send). Specify the city, the bank and the branch to which you want your money directed. If you don't know a bank to transfer money to, ask your home bank to tell you where a suitable one is, and make sure you get the details right.

The whole procedure will be easier if you've authorised someone back home to access your account. Also, a transfer to a tiny bank in a remote village in the Pyrenees is obviously going to be more difficult than to a head office in Paris. If you have the choice, find a large bank and ask for the international division.

Money sent by telegraphic transfer (there will be costs involved, typically US$20 or more, but ask) should reach you within a week; by mail, allow at least two weeks. When it arrives, it will most likely be converted into local currency – you can take it as it is or buy travellers' cheques.

You can also transfer money by American Express or Thomas Cook. Americans can also use Western Union although it has fewer offices in Europe from which to collect. If you have an American Express card, you can cash up to US$1000 of personal cheques at American Express offices in any 21-day period.

Credit Cards & ATMs

If you're financially sound, a credit card is an ideal travelling companion. If you're not familiar with credit cards, ask your bank to explain the workings and relative merits of credit, credit/debit, debit and charge cards. Make sure you know what to do in case of theft (telephone hotline numbers etc).

It's always amusing to see how many backpackers also have their credit cards. With one of these you can put a lot of things (like airline tickets) on your account and save carrying so much with you. Another major advantage is that they allow you to withdraw cash at selected banks or to draw money from automated teller machines (ATMs).

Though still not as widespread in Europe as they are in other parts of the world, ATMs are now linked up internationally in many countries and you can shove your credit card in, punch in a personal identification number (PIN) and get instant cash. But ATMs aren't fail-safe, especially if the card was issued outside Europe, and you may be better off withdrawing cash at the bank counter. If an ATM swallows your card abroad it can be a major headache. Credit cards usually aren't hooked up to ATM networks unless you specifically ask your bank to do this and request a PIN number.

You should also ask which ATMs abroad will accept your particular card. Note that many European ATMs won't accept PIN numbers of more than four digits. Cash cards, which you use at home to withdraw money directly from your bank account or savings account, are slowly becoming more widely linked internationally – ask your bank at home for advice.

If you use a credit card to get money from an ATM, you pay interest on the money from the moment you get it. You can get around that by leaving the card in credit when you depart, or by having somebody at home pay money into the card account from time to time. On the plus side, you don't have money tied up in travellers' cheques in a currency that might be diving, you don't pay commission charges or transaction fees, you don't have cash or cheques to lose (you could of course lose the card), you can get money after hours and on weekends, and the exchange rate is at a better interbank rate than that offered for travellers' cheques or cash exchanges. Bear in mind that if you use a credit card for purchases, exchange rates may have changed by the time your bill is processed, which can work out to your advantage or disadvantage.

Charge cards like American Express and Diners Club have offices in most countries, and will generally replace a lost card within 24 hours. That's because they treat you as a customer of the company, rather than of the bank that issued the card. In theory, the credit they offer is unlimited and they don't charge interest on outstanding accounts, but they do charge fees for joining and annual membership, and payment is due in full within a few days of the account statement date. Their major drawback is that they're not widely accepted beyond the beaten track of mainstream travel. Charge cards can also be hooked up to ATM networks on request.

Credit and credit/debit cards like Visa and MasterCard are more widely accepted because they tend to charge lower commissions to merchants. Their major drawback is that they have a credit limit based on your regular income, and this limit is usually too low to cover major expenses like long-term car hire or long-distance airline tickets. You can get around this by leaving your card in credit when you leave home. Other drawbacks are that interest is charged on outstanding accounts, either immediately or after a set period (always immediately on cash advances), and that the card can be very difficult to replace if lost abroad.

Don't put all your eggs in one basket. If you want to rely heavily on bits of plastic, go for two different cards – for instance, an American Express or Diners Club with a Visa or MasterCard. Better still is a combination of credit card and travellers' cheques so you have something to fall back on if an ATM swallows your card or the banks in the area don't accept your card.

Europe has only recently embraced credit cards in a major way, and quite a few shops, restaurants and service stations may still only accept cash. Visa and MasterCard are the most popular brands all-round. MasterCard (also known as Access in the UK) is linked to Europe's extensive Eurocard system, which makes it widely accepted and thus a convenient card to carry. Visa is sometimes called Carte Bleue in France, where it's particularly strong.

One problem that can arise with credit cards, is that you can run out of credit even though you're sure that you haven't spent that much. This is because of authorisations that haven't been cancelled. What happens is that when you leave an imprint of your credit card as security with your hotel or car rental agency, they can contact your card agency and ask that a certain amount of your credit be set aside ('authorised') to cover your expected bill. If the eventual bill is lower and the hotel or rental agency forgets to cancel its authorisation with your card agency, you won't be able to delve into the remaining portion of the credit that was set aside.

Contact your card agency if you think this may have happened.

A final word of warning: fraudulent shopkeepers have been known to quickly make several charge-slip imprints with your credit card when you're not looking, and they then simply copy your signature from the one that you authorise. Always check your statements.

Other Methods

As Europeans may know, guaranteed personal cheques are another way of carrying money or obtaining cash. While countries like the USA, Canada and Australia went from unguaranteed personal cheques straight to electronic banking in the form of credit cards and ATM cash cards, Europe replaced bouncing personal cheques with cheques guaranteed to a certain limit per cheque.

The most popular of these is the Eurocheque system. To get Eurocheques, you need a European bank account; depending on the bank, it takes at least two weeks to apply for the cheques, which may be too long for most visitors. It's a neat system, though. Throughout Europe, when paying for something in a shop or withdrawing cash from a bank or post office, you write out a Eurocheque (up to its maximum limit, otherwise simply write out two or more cheques) and show the accompanying guarantee card with your signature and registration number. You may also have to show your passport. Once the shopkeeper or bank clerk has checked the cheque's signature with that on the card and copied your registration number onto the cheque, it's guaranteed by the issuing bank, who will deduct the amount from your account when the paperwork comes through. The card can double as an ATM card, and should obviously be kept separate from the cheques for safety.

Some countries have similar systems operating nationally. The most advanced of these is the Dutch 'postgiro' system, with cheques issued to postal account holders. The cheques are only valid for purchases within the Netherlands, but allow cash withdrawals at post offices in 40 countries.

COMMUNICATIONS & MEDIA

Post

Details of the main post offices are given in the city Information sections. From major European centres, airmail typically takes about a week to North American or Australasian destinations. Postage costs do vary from country to country, and so does post office efficiency – the Italian post office is notoriously unreliable.

You can collect mail from post office *poste restante* sections. Ask people writing to you to print your name clearly and underline your surname. When collecting mail, your passport may be required for identification and you may have to pay a small fee. If an expected letter is not waiting for you, ask to check under your given name: letters do get misfiled. Post offices usually hold mail for about a month, but sometimes less (in Germany, for instance, they only hold mail for a fortnight), so plan your mail drops carefully. Unless the sender specifies otherwise, mail will always be sent to the city's main post office or GPO. The lines of travellers collecting mail are favourite meeting points in many European cities.

You can also have mail (but not parcels) sent to you at American Express offices so long as you have an American Express card or travellers' cheques. When you buy American Express cheques, ask for a booklet listing all its office addresses worldwide.

Telephone

The telephone system in Europe generally works very well. You can ring abroad from most phone booths if you have sufficient coins; otherwise, use the phone cards that are becoming increasingly popular, or ring from a booth inside a post office or telephone centre and settle your bill at the counter – if you ring from a hotel room, the bill can be astronomical. Reverse-charge (collect) calls are often possible, but not always – for a start, you'll have to be able to communicate with the local operator, who might not always speak English. From many countries, however, you can dial direct to your home operator, which solves the problem. See the

Telephones appendix in the back of this book for more details.

Newspapers & Magazines

If you want to keep up with the news in English, you'll have no trouble in England or Ireland, and in larger towns in the rest of Europe you can get the surprisingly interesting *Herald Tribune* or the colourful but very superficial *USA Today*. The British *Guardian* and *Financial Times* are also produced in widely available European editions. Other British papers are often available but are more expensive and likely to be out of date. In the news-magazine category, *Time*, *Newsweek* and the *Economist* are widely available.

Radio & TV

Close to the English Channel, you can pick up British radio stations, particularly BBC Radio 4. Otherwise, the BBC World Service can be found on short wave at 6195, 9410, 12095, 15070 and 15575 kHz, the appropriate frequency depending on where you are and the time of day. The Voice of America (VOA) can usually be found on 1197 kHz. There are also numerous English-language broadcasts (or even BBC World Service rebroadcasts) on local AM radio stations.

Cable and satellite TV have spread across Europe with much more gusto than radio. Sky TV can be found in better hotels all over Europe, as can CNN and other networks. You can also pick up many cross-border TV stations, including British stations close to the Channel.

ELECTRICITY

By all means bring along the electrical appliances that you feel you can't live without. If they're battery operated, so much the better, but hotels almost always have power points, and these are also pretty widespread in hostels and camping grounds. Voltage and plug design will be your main problems.

Voltage & Cycle

Most of Europe runs on 220 V, 50 Hz AC. The exceptions are Britain, which has 240 V, and Spain, which usually has 240 V but sometimes still the old 125 V depending on the network (some houses can have both). Some old buildings and hotels in Italy might still have 125 V as well. In the mid-1990s, the EC countries should become standardised at 230 V.

Check the voltage and cycle (usually 50 Hz) used in your home country. Most appliances that are set up for 220 V will handle 240 V quite happily without modifications (and vice versa); the same goes for 110 and 125 V combinations. It's always preferable to adjust your appliance to the exact voltage if you can (some modern battery chargers and radios will do this automatically). Just don't mix 110/125 with 220/240 V without a transformer, which will be built in if the appliance can be adjusted.

Several countries outside Europe (the USA and Canada, for instance) have 60 Hz AC, which will affect the speed of electric motors even after the voltage has been adjusted to European values, so record players and tape recorders (where motor speed is all-important) will be useless. But things like electric razors, hair driers, irons and radios will be fine.

Plugs & Sockets

Britain, Ireland and Malta use a design with three flat pins – two for current and one for earth. The rest of Europe uses two round pins. Many Continental plugs and some sockets don't have provision for earth, since most local home appliances are double-insulated; when provided, earth usually consists of two contact points along the edge, although Italy and Switzerland use a third round pin in such a way that the standard two-pin plug still fits the sockets (though not always in Italy).

If your plugs are of a different design, you'll need an adapter. Get one before you leave, since the adapters available in Europe usually go the other way.

Video Systems

If you want to record or buy video tapes to play back home, you won't get a picture if the image registration systems are different.

Europe generally uses PAL (France, SECAM), which is incompatible with the North American and Japanese NTSC system. Australia uses PAL.

HEALTH

Europe is a healthy place. Your main risks are likely to be sunburn, foot blisters, insect bites, and upset stomachs from eating and drinking too much. You might experience mild gut problems in southern Europe if you're not used to copious amounts of olive oil (you'll get used to it after a while, and current research says the stuff is good for you).

If you plan to visit North Africa or the remoter parts of Turkey, health risks increase and you'll want to come a bit better prepared than we outline here. Especially if you're going to be roughing it. Discuss your plans with your physician or travellers' health agency, and ask about hepatitis, typhoid and malaria (there's no malaria in Tunisia). Discussion of these diseases is beyond the scope of this book, so get your physician to explain them. Water purification tablets also become a good idea in these countries.

Travel health depends on your predeparture preparations and fitness, your day-to-day health care while travelling, and how you handle any medical problem or emergency that does develop. If you're reasonably fit, the only things you should organise before departure are a visit to your dentist to get your teeth in order, and travel insurance with good medical cover (see the following Predeparture Preparations section).

Travel Health Guides

There are a number of books on travel health, most of them geared towards the tropics where health is a major issue. Worth considering are:

Travellers' Health, Dr Richard Dawood, Oxford University Press. Comprehensive, easy to read, authoritative and also highly recommended, although it's rather large to lug around.

Travel with Children, Maureen Wheeler, Lonely Planet Publications. Includes basic advice on travel health for younger children.

Predeparture Preparations
Health Insurance A travel insurance policy to cover theft, loss and medical problems is a must. There is a wide variety of policies and your travel agent will have recommendations. The international student travel policies handled by STA or other student travel organisations are usually good value. Some policies offer lower and higher medical-expense options – go as high as you can afford, especially if you're visiting Switzerland, Germany or any of the Scandinavian countries, where medical costs can be astronomical. Check the small print:

- Some policies specifically exclude 'dangerous activities' which can include scuba diving, motorcycling, skiing, mountaineering, even trekking. If such activities are on your agenda, you don't want that sort of policy.
- You may prefer a policy that pays doctors or hospitals directly rather than you having to pay on the spot and claim later. If you have to claim later, make sure you keep all documentation. Some policies ask you to call back (reverse charges) to a centre in your home country where an immediate assessment of your problem is made.
- Check if the policy covers ambulances or helicopter rescue, and an emergency flight home. If you have to stretch out you will need two seats and somebody has to pay for them!

Citizens of EC countries are covered for emergency medical treatment throughout the EC on presentation of an E111 form. Enquire about this at your national health service or travel agent well in advance. Similar reciprocal arrangements exist between the Nordic countries. Australian Medicare covers emergency treatment in Italy, Malta, the Netherlands, Sweden and the UK. You may still have to pay on the spot but you'll be able to reclaim these expenses back home (keep all documentation). However, travel insurance is still advisable because of the flexibility it offers in where and how you're treated, as well as covering expenses for ambulance and repatriation.

Medical Kit A small, straightforward medical kit is a wise thing to carry. A possible kit list includes:

- Aspirin or Panadol – for pain or fever
- Antihistamine (such as Benadryl) – useful as a decongestant for colds, allergies, to ease the itch from insect bites or stings or to help prevent motion sickness
- Kaolin preparation (Pepto-Bismol), Imodium or Lomotil – for possible stomach upsets in southern Europe
- Antiseptic, Mercurochrome and antibiotic powder or similar 'dry' spray – for cuts and grazes
- Calamine lotion – to ease irritation from bites or stings
- Bandages and Band-aids – for minor injuries
- Scissors, tweezers and a thermometer (note that mercury thermometers are prohibited by airlines)
- Insect repellent, sunscreen, suntan lotion, chapstick, perhaps water purification tablets

When buying medicines over the counter, especially in southern Europe, make sure that correct storage conditions have been followed and that the expiry date has not passed.

Health Preparations If you wear glasses, take a spare pair and your prescription. Losing your glasses can be a problem, but you can usually get new spectacles made up quickly, cheaply and competently.

If you require a particular medication, take an adequate supply, as it may not always be available in remote places. The same applies for your specific oral contraceptive. Take prescriptions, with the generic rather than the brand name (which may not be locally available), as it will make getting replacements easier.

It's a wise idea to have a prescription and a letter from your doctor to show you legally use the medication – it's surprising how often over-the-counter drugs from one place are illegal without a prescription or even banned in another. Keep the medication in its original container. If you're carrying a syringe for some reason, have a note from your doctor to explain why you're doing so.

A Medic Alert tag is a good idea if your

medical condition is not always easily recognisable (heart trouble, diabetes, asthma, allergic reactions to antibiotics etc).

Immunisations In Europe, jabs are not necessary, but they may be an entry requirement if you're coming from an infected area – yellow fever and cholera are the most likely requirements. If you're going to Europe with stopovers in Asia, Africa or Latin America, check with your travel agent or with the embassies of the countries you plan to visit.

There are, however, a few routine vaccinations that are recommended whether you're travelling or not, and this Health section assumes that you've had them: polio (usually administered during childhood), tetanus and diphtheria (usually administered together during childhood, with a booster shot every 10 years), and sometimes measles. See your physician or nearest health agency about these. You'll also need a malaria prophylactic and protection against hepatitis and typhoid if you plan to rough it in North Africa and Turkey.

All vaccinations should be recorded on an International Health Certificate, which is available from your physician or government health department. Don't leave this till the last minute, since the vaccinations may have to be spread out a bit.

Basic Rules

Care in what you eat and drink is the most important health rule in North Africa and the remoter parts of Turkey and southern Europe; stomach upsets are the most likely travel health problem here but the majority of these upsets will be relatively minor. Don't become paranoid – after all, trying the local food is part of the experience of travel.

Water Tap water is almost always safe to drink in Europe. In southern Europe, it may contain certain organisms that your body wants to get used to first, so only drink small amounts the first few days and see how you go. Tap water is usually *not* safe in North Africa or Turkey, so stick to bottled water

(also for brushing teeth) and avoid ice cubes, fresh salads and reconstituted fruit juices.

Dairy products are fine throughout Europe, but should be treated with suspicion in North Africa and Turkey as milk is often unpasteurised. Boiled milk is fine if it is kept hygienically, and yoghurt is always good. Tea or coffee should also be OK, since the water should have been boiled.

Always beware of natural water. The burbling Alpine stream may look crystal clear and very inviting, but before drinking it you want to be absolutely sure there are no people or cattle upstream.

Water Purification This section is only relevant if you're going to spend some time in North Africa or Turkey, or are planning extended hikes in Europe where you have to rely on natural water.

The simplest way of purifying water is to boil it thoroughly. Technically this means boiling for 10 minutes, something which happens very rarely. Remember that at high altitude water boils at lower temperature, so germs are less likely to be killed.

Simple filtering will not remove all dangerous organisms, so if you cannot boil water it should be treated chemically. Chlorine tablets (Puritabs, Steritabs or other brand names) will kill many but not all pathogens. Iodine is very effective in purifying water and is available in tablet form (such as Potable Aqua), but follow the directions carefully and remember that too much iodine can be harmful.

If you can't find tablets, tincture of iodine (2%) or iodine crystals can be used. Two drops of tincture of iodine per litre or quart of clear water is the recommended dosage; the treated water should be left to stand for 30 minutes before drinking. Iodine crystals can also be used to purify water but this is a more complicated process, as you have to prepare a saturated iodine solution first. Iodine loses its effectiveness if exposed to air or damp so keep it in a tightly sealed container. Flavoured powder will disguise the taste of treated water and is a good idea if you are travelling with children.

Food Salads and fruit should be safe throughout Europe, but elsewhere they should be washed with purified water or peeled where possible. Ice cream is usually OK, but beware of street vendors in North Africa and Turkey, and of all ice cream that has melted and been refrozen. Take great care with fish or shellfish (for instance, cooked mussels that haven't opened properly can be dangerous), and avoid undercooked meat.

If a place looks clean and well run and if the vendor also looks clean and healthy, then the food is probably safe. In general, places that are packed with travellers or locals will be fine. Be careful with food that has been cooked and left to go cold.

Mushroom-picking is a favourite pastime in Europe as autumn approaches, but make sure you don't eat any mushrooms that haven't been positively identified as safe.

Nutrition If you don't vary your diet, if you're travelling hard and fast and therefore missing meals, or if you simply lose your appetite, you can soon start to lose weight and place your health at risk – just as you would at home.

If you rely on fast foods, you'll get plenty of fats and carbohydrates but little else. Remember that overcooked food loses much of its nutritional value. If your diet isn't well balanced, it's a good idea to take vitamin and iron pills (women lose a lot of iron through their periods). Fruit and vegetables are good sources of vitamin, but also very expensive in Scandinavia where they're seldom served in large quantities – vitamin pills may be a good idea there, too.

In hot climates make sure you drink enough – don't rely on feeling thirsty to indicate when you should drink. Not needing to urinate or very dark-yellow urine is a danger sign. Carry a water bottle on long trips. Excessive sweating can lead to loss of salt and therefore muscle cramping. Salt tablets are not a good idea as a preventative, but in places where salt is not used much, adding salt to food can help.

Everyday Health A normal body temperature is 98.6°F or 37°C; more than 2°C higher is a 'high' fever. A normal adult pulse rate is 60 to 80 per minute (children 80 to 100, babies 100 to 140). You should know how to take a temperature and a pulse rate. As a general rule, the pulse increases about 20 beats per minute for each °C rise in fever.

Respiration (breathing) rate is also an indicator of illness. Count the number of breaths per minute: between 12 and 20 is normal for adults and older children (up to 30 for younger children, 40 for babies). People with a high fever or serious respiratory illness (like pneumonia) breathe more quickly than normal. More than 40 shallow breaths a minute usually means pneumonia.

Many health problems can be avoided by taking care of yourself. Wash your hands frequently. Clean your teeth. Avoid climatic extremes: keep out of the sun when it's hot, dress warmly when it's cold. Minimise insect bites by covering bare skin when insects are around, or by using insect repellents.

Medical Treatment

Local pharmacies or neighbourhood medical centres are good places to visit if you have a small medical problem and can explain what the problem is. Hospital casualty wards will help if it's more serious, and will tell you if it's not. Major hospitals and emergency numbers are indicated on the maps in this book and mentioned in the text. Tourist offices and hotels can put you on to a doctor or dentist, and your embassy or consulate will probably know one who speaks your language.

Climatic & Geographical Considerations

Sunburn In southern Europe, and anywhere on water, ice, snow or sand, you can get sunburnt surprisingly quickly, even through cloud. Use a sunscreen and take extra care to cover areas that don't normally see sun – eg your feet. A hat provides added protection, and it may be a good idea to use zinc cream or some other barrier cream for your nose and lips. Calamine lotion is good for mild sunburn.

Remember that too much sunlight can damage your eyes, whether it's direct or reflected (glare). If your plans include water, ice, snow or sand, then good sunglasses are doubly important. Make sure they're treated to absorb ultraviolet radiation – if not, they'll actually do more harm than good by dilating your pupils and making it easier for ultraviolet light to damage the retina.

Prickly Heat Prickly heat is an itchy rash caused by excessive perspiration trapped under the skin. It usually strikes people who have just arrived in a hot climate and whose pores have not yet opened sufficiently to cope with greater sweating. Keeping cool but bathing often, using a mild talcum powder or even resorting to air-conditioning may help until you acclimatise.

Heat Exhaustion Dehydration or salt deficiency can cause heat exhaustion. Take time to acclimatise to high temperatures and make sure you get sufficient liquids (nonalcoholic). Salt deficiency is characterised by fatigue, lethargy, headaches, giddiness and muscle cramps, and in this case salt tablets may help. Vomiting or diarrhoea can deplete your liquid and salt levels.

Anhydrotic heat exhaustion, caused by an inability to sweat, is quite rare. Unlike the other forms of heat exhaustion, it is likely to strike people who have been in a hot climate for some time, rather than newcomers.

Heat Stroke This serious, sometimes fatal, condition can occur if the body's heat-regulating mechanism breaks down and the body temperature rises to dangerous levels. Long, continuous periods of exposure to high temperatures can leave you vulnerable to heat stroke. You should avoid excessive alcohol or strenuous activity when you first arrive in a hot climate.

The symptoms are feeling unwell, not sweating very much or at all, and a high body temperature (39°C to 41°C). Where sweating has ceased, the skin becomes flushed and red. Severe, throbbing headaches and lack of coordination will also occur, and the sufferer

may be confused or aggressive. Eventually the victim will become delirious or convulse. Hospitalisation is essential, but meanwhile get patients out of the sun, remove their clothing, cover them with a wet sheet or towel and then fan continually.

Fungal Infections Hot-weather fungal infections are most likely to occur on the scalp, between the toes or fingers (athlete's foot), in the groin (jock itch or crotch rot) and on the body (ringworm). You get ringworm (a fungal infection, not a worm) from infected animals or by walking on damp areas, like shower floors.

To prevent fungal infections, wear loose, comfortable clothes, avoid artificial fibres, wash frequently and dry carefully. Always wear plastic sandals or thongs in showers you can't completely trust. If you do get an infection, wash the infected area daily with a disinfectant or medicated soap and water, and rinse and dry well. Apply an antifungal powder like the widely available Tinaderm. Try to expose the infected area to air or sunlight as much as possible and wash all towels and underwear in hot water as well as changing them often.

Cold Too much cold is just as dangerous as too much heat, particularly if it leads to hypothermia. Cold combined with wind and moisture (ie soaking rain) is particularly risky. If you are trekking at high altitudes or in a cool, wet environment, be prepared.

Hypothermia occurs when the body loses heat faster than it can produce it and the core temperature of the body falls. It is surprisingly easy to progress from very cold to dangerously cold due to a combination of wind, wet clothing, fatigue and hunger, even if the air temperature is above freezing. It is best to dress in layers – silk, wool and some of the new artificial fibres are all good insulating materials. A hat is important, as a lot of heat is lost through the head. A strong, waterproof outer layer is essential, as keeping dry is vital. Carry basic supplies, including food that contains simple sugars to generate heat quickly, and lots of fluid to drink.

Symptoms of hypothermia are exhaustion, numb skin (particularly toes and fingers), shivering, slurred speech, irrational or violent behaviour, lethargy, stumbling, dizzy spells, muscle cramps and violent bursts of energy. Irrationality may take the form of sufferers claiming they are warm and trying to take off their clothes.

To treat hypothermia, first get the patient out of the wind and/or rain, remove their clothing if it's wet and replace it with dry, warm clothing. Give them hot liquids – not alcohol – and some high-kilojoule, easily digestible food. This should be enough for the early stages of hypothermia, but if it has gone further, it may be necessary to place victims in warm sleeping bags and get in with them. Do not rub patients, place them near a fire or remove their wet clothes in the wind. If possible, place a sufferer in a warm (not hot) bath.

Altitude Sickness Acute Mountain Sickness or AMS occurs at high altitude and can be fatal. There is no hard and fast rule as to how high is too high: AMS can strike at altitudes of 3000 metres, although 3500 to 4500 metres is the usual range. Very few treks or ski runs in the Alps and Pyrenees reach heights of 3000 metres or more, so it's unlikely to be a major concern.

Headaches, nausea, dizziness, a dry cough, insomnia, breathlessness and loss of appetite are all signs to heed. Mild altitude problems will generally abate after a day or so, but if the symptoms persist or become worse the only treatment is to descend – even 500 metres can help.

Motion Sickness Eating lightly before and during a trip will reduce the chances of motion sickness. If you are prone to motion sickness, try to find a place that minimises disturbance – near the wing on aircraft, close to midships on boats, near the centre on buses. Fresh air and a steady reference point like the horizon usually help, whereas reading or cigarette smoke don't. Commercial antimotion-sickness preparations, which can cause drowsiness, have to be taken before the trip commences – when you're feeling sick, it's too late. Ginger is a natural preventative and is available in capsule form.

Diseases of Insanitation
Diarrhoea A change of water, food or climate can all cause the runs; diarrhoea caused by contaminated food or water is more serious. Despite all your precautions, you may still have a bout of mild travellers' diarrhoea if you travel beyond the relatively safe confines of Europe, but a few rushed toilet trips with no other symptoms is not indicative of a serious problem.

Moderate diarrhoea, involving half-a-dozen loose movements in a day, is more of a nuisance. Dehydration is the main danger with any diarrhoea, particularly for children, so fluid replenishment is the number one treatment. Weak black tea with a little sugar, soda water, or soft drinks allowed to go flat and diluted 50% with water are all good.

With any diarrhoea more severe than this, go straight to the casualty ward of the nearest hospital and have yourself checked. You may need a rehydrating solution to replace minerals and salts. Stick to a bland diet as you recover.

Viral Gastroenteritis This is caused not by bacteria but, as the name suggests, by a virus. It is characterised by stomach cramps, diarrhoea, and sometimes by vomiting and/or a slight fever. All you can do is rest and drink lots of fluids.

Worms These parasites are most common in rural areas outside Europe, and a stool test when you return home is not a bad idea. They can be present on unwashed vegetables or in undercooked meat and you can pick them up through your skin by walking in bare feet. Infestations may not show up for some time, and although they are generally not serious, they can cause severe health problems if left untreated. A stool test is necessary to pinpoint the problem, and medication is often available over the counter.

Diseases Spread by People & Animals

Rabies Though nonexistent in Britain and rare in the rest of Europe, where it's usually dealt with swiftly and decisively by the authorities, rabies is found in many countries and is caused by a bite or scratch by an infected animal. Dogs are a noted carrier, but cats, foxes and bats can also be affected. Any bite, scratch or even lick from a mammal should be cleaned immediately and thoroughly. Scrub with soap and running water, and then clean with an alcohol solution. If there is any possibility that the animal is infected, particularly if it froths at the mouth and behaves strangely, medical help should be sought immediately. Even if it is not rabid, all bites should be treated seriously as they can become infected or can result in tetanus.

Tuberculosis (TB) Although this disease is widespread in many developing countries and used to be a scourge in Europe, it is not a serious risk to healthy travellers and is no longer a problem in Western Europe. Young children are more susceptible than adults, and vaccination is a sensible precaution for children aged under 12 travelling in endemic areas. TB is commonly spread by coughing or by unpasteurised dairy products from infected cows. Milk that has been boiled is safe to drink; the souring of milk to make yoghurt or cheese also kills the bacilli.

Sexually Transmitted Diseases (STDs) Sexual contact with an infected partner spreads these diseases. While abstinence is the only 100% preventative, using condoms is also effective. Gonorrhoea and syphilis are the most common of these diseases: sores, blisters or rashes around the genitals, discharges, or pain when urinating are common symptoms. Symptoms may be less marked or not observed at all in women. Syphilis symptoms eventually disappear completely but the disease continues and can cause severe problems in later years. The treatment of gonorrhoea and syphilis is by antibiotics. STD clinics are widespread in Europe. Don't be shy about visiting them if you think you may have contracted something.

There are numerous other STDs, for most of which effective treatment is available, though as yet there is no cure for herpes or HIV/AIDS. The latter has become a considerable problem in Europe. HIV, the Human Immunodeficiency Virus, may develop into AIDS, Acquired Immune Deficiency Syndrome. Apart from abstinence, the most effective preventative is always to practise safe sex using condoms. It is impossible to detect the HIV-positive status of an otherwise healthy-looking person without a blood test.

HIV/AIDS can also be spread through infected blood transfusions; most developing countries cannot afford to screen blood for transfusions. It can also be spread by dirty needles – vaccinations, acupuncture, tattooing and ear or nose piercing can potentially be as dangerous as intravenous drug use if the equipment is not clean. If you do need an injection outside Europe, it may be a good idea to buy a new syringe from a pharmacy and ask the doctor to use it.

Cuts, Bites & Stings

Cuts & Scratches Skin punctures can easily become infected in hot climates and may be difficult to heal. Treat any cut with an antiseptic solution and Mercurochrome. Where possible, avoid bandages and Band-aids, which can keep wounds wet. Coral cuts are notoriously slow to heal, as the coral injects a weak venom into the wound. Avoid coral cuts by wearing shoes when walking on reefs, and clean any cut thoroughly.

Bites & Stings Bee and wasp stings are usually painful rather than dangerous. Calamine lotion will give relief, or ice packs will reduce the pain and swelling. There are some spiders with dangerous bites (rare in Europe), but antivenins are usually available. Scorpion stings are notoriously painful, but the small scorpions occasionally found in southern Europe are not considered fatal. Scorpions often shelter in shoes or clothing – always give your shoes a good shake-out before donning them in the morning, especially when camping.

There are various fish and other sea creatures that can sting or bite dangerously or that are dangerous to eat. Seeking local advice is the best way of avoiding problems.

Jellyfish Local advice will help prevent you coming into contact with these sea creatures and their stinging tentacles. Stings from most jellyfish are merely painful. Dousing in vinegar will de-activate any stingers which have not 'fired'. Calamine lotion, antihistamines and analgesics may reduce the reaction and relieve the pain. The Portuguese man-of-war jellyfish with its sail-like float and long tentacles has been fatal on rare occasions, but is seldom found in colder waters or close to shore, though the North Atlantic Gulf Stream may carry the odd few as far north as Britain and Ireland.

Mosquitoes Mosquitoes can be a nuisance in southern Europe, but can almost drive you insane during the summer months in northern Europe and Scandinavia (Finland, with its many lakes, is particularly notorious). They can also cause sleepless nights in a swampy country like the Netherlands (one author of this book lived in a student house in Amsterdam where the tenants slept under mosquito nets five months of the year).

The subsoil in much of Scandinavia remains frozen throughout the year (the so-called permafrost), and when snow and ice begin to melt in spring the water can't sink away, thus turning the countryside into one huge swamp. This is an ideal breeding ground for billions of hyperactive insects that only have a three-month 'window' in which to do their thing. Early summer is the worst period, and hikers will have to cover exposed skin and may even need special mosquito hats with netting to screen their faces. Seek local advice, as regular mosquito repellents and green coils are hardly effective against the ravenous hordes that home in on you 24 hours a day. A mosquito-proof tent is absolutely essential at night.

Fortunately, mosquito-borne diseases like malaria are unknown in this part of the world, and the main risks are mental (people

have been driven literally insane by the incessant buzzing and itching). Most people get used to mosquito bites after a few days as their bodies adjust, and the itching and swelling will become less severe. An antihistamine cream may help alleviate the symptoms.

Midges – small, blood-sucking flies related to mosquitoes – are a major problem in some parts of Europe (eg Scotland) during summer.

Snakes Snakes tend to keep a very low profile, but to minimise your chances of being bitten, always wear boots, socks and long trousers when walking through undergrowth where snakes may be present. Tramp heavily and they'll usually slither away before you come near. Don't put your hands into holes and crevices, and be careful when collecting firewood (scorpions also like dead wood).

Snake bites do not cause instantaneous death and antivenins are usually available. Keep the victim calm and still, wrap the bitten limb tightly, as you would for a sprained ankle, and then attach a splint to immobilise it. Then seek medical help, if possible with the dead snake for identification. Don't attempt to catch the snake if there is even a remote possibility of being bitten again. Tourniquets and sucking out the poison are now comprehensively discredited.

Bedbugs & Lice Bedbugs live in various places, but particularly in dirty mattresses and bedding. Though rare in Europe, they are not uncommon in cheap hotels in North Africa and Turkey. Spots of blood on bedclothes or on the wall around the bed can be read as a suggestion to find another hotel. Bedbugs leave itchy bites in neat rows. Calamine lotion may help to soothe the itching.

All lice cause itching and discomfort. They make themselves at home in your hair (head lice), your clothing (body lice) or in your pubic hair (crabs). You catch lice through direct contact with infected people or by sharing combs, clothing and the like.

Powder or shampoo treatment will kill the lice, and infected clothing should then be washed in very hot water.

Women's Health

Some women experience irregular periods when travelling, due to the upset in routine. Don't forget to take time zones into account if you're on the pill; if you run into intestinal problems, the pill may not be absorbed. Ask your physician about these matters.

Gynaecological Problems Poor diet, lowered resistance due to the use of antibiotics for stomach upsets, and even contraceptive pills, can lead to vaginal infections when travelling in hot climates. Maintaining good personal hygiene, and wearing skirts or loose-fitting trousers and cotton underwear will help to prevent infections.

Yeast infections (thrush), characterised by a rash, itch and discharge, can be treated with a vinegar or even lemon-juice douche or with yoghurt. Nystatin suppositories are the usual medical prescription. Trichomonas is a more serious infection; symptoms are a discharge and a burning sensation when urinating, and if a vinegar-water douche is not effective, medical attention should be sought. Flagyl is the prescribed drug. In both cases, male sexual partners must also be treated.

DANGERS & ANNOYANCES

Europe is as safe or unsafe as any other part of the developed world. If you can handle Toronto, Sydney or Hong Kong, you'll have little trouble dealing with the less pleasant aspects of Europe. If you come from Los Angeles or New York, you may even be able to teach the locals a thing or two.

Whatever you do, don't leave friends and relatives back home worrying about how to get in touch with you in case of emergency. Work out a list of places where they can contact you – see the previous Post section for where to collect mail. Best of all is to phone home now and then – see the Telephones appendix for how and where to make

phone calls most efficiently and economically.

Theft

As a traveller, you're often fairly vulnerable and when you do lose things it can be a real hassle. Theft is definitely a problem in Europe (more so in the south than in Scandinavia), and it's not just other travellers you have to be wary of. The most important things to guard are your passport, papers, tickets and money. It's best always to carry these next to your skin or in a sturdy leather pouch on your belt. Train station lockers or luggage storage counters are useful places to store your luggage (but not valuables) while you get your bearings in a new town. Be very suspicious about people who offer to help you operate your locker. Carry your own padlock for hostel lockers.

You can further lessen the risks by being careful of snatch thieves. Cameras or shoulder bags are great for these people, who sometimes operate from motorcycles or scooters and expertly slash the strap before you have a chance to react. A small daypack is better, but watch your rear. Pickpockets are most active in dense crowds, especially in busy train stations and peak-hour public transport. A common ploy is for one person to distract you while another zips through your pockets (some of these types would make great magicians!). Beware of gangs of dishevelled-looking kids, particularly in Italy and France, waving newspapers and demanding attention. In the blink of an eye, a wallet or camera can go missing.

Be careful even in hotels; don't leave valuables lying around in your room. Also be wary of sudden friendships – you never know what they may be after. Parked cars are prime targets for petty criminals in most cities, and cars with foreign number plates and/or rental agency stickers in particular. Remove the Avis or Hertz stickers (or cover them with local football club stickers or something similar), leave a local newspaper on the seat and generally try to make it look like a local car. Don't ever leave valuables in the car, and remove all luggage overnight, even (some would say especially) if it's in a parking garage. Many Europeans also remove their car radios, which fit into special contact sleds in the dashboard (removable radio control panels are the latest gimmick). In some places, freeway service centres have become unsafe territory: in the time it takes to drink a cup of coffee, your car can be broken into and cleared out.

Another ploy, common in Spain, is for muggers to pull up alongside your car and point to the wheel; when you get out to have a look, you become one more robbery statistic. While driving in cities, beware of snatch thieves when you pull up at the lights – keep doors locked and windows rolled up high. In case of theft or loss, always report the incident to the police and ask for a statement, or your travel insurance won't pay out.

There are many other ways of losing things apart from straightforward theft and robbery. Over the years, Lonely Planet has received letters from unfortunate travellers who have been the victims of just about every scam imaginable. Two favourites have been airline-ticket rackets and 'bargain' antiques. Gambling rackets (such as the one where an operator shuffles matchboxes, one of them containing the token, amidst a cheering crowd of helpers), 'losing' travellers' cheques, guaranteeing loans – they're all scams on which unfortunate or foolish travellers have lost their shirts. Keep your wits about you.

Photocopies The loss of your passport is a real hassle, but it can be made a little easier if, somewhere else, you've got a record of its number and issue date, or even better, photocopies of the relevant data pages. A photocopy of your birth certificate can also be useful.

While you're compiling that information, add the serial numbers of your travellers' cheques (cross them off as you cash them in) and photocopies of your credit cards, airline ticket and other travel documents. Keep all this emergency material totally separate from your passport, cheques and other cash, and leave extra copies with someone you can

rely on back home. Add some emergency money, say US$50, to this separate stash as well. If you do lose your passport, notify the police immediately to get a statement, and contact your nearest consulate.

Drugs
Always treat drugs with a great deal of caution. There is a fair bit of dope available in the region, sometimes quite openly, but that doesn't mean it's legal. Even a little harmless hashish can cause a great deal of trouble. Also, as soon as you try to export it or start messing with heavier stuff they'll land on top of you.

Authorities in the Netherlands and Denmark unofficially tolerate 'soft' drugs so the police can concentrate on the harder stuff. But whatever you may have heard, it's still illegal there, despite the proliferation of 'coffee shops' and discos with 'house dealers' that sell hash and grass, complete with price lists and choice of brands. Getting caught with a small amount for personal use in those countries might earn you no more than an angry rap over the knuckles, but could make life very difficult if you're already in trouble over something else; and larger amounts (the distinction is murky) put you in the much more serious drug-trafficking category. Authorities in surrounding countries often take a dim view of such tolerance, and may well single you out for special attention at the border.

The situation becomes even riskier in dope-producing countries like Morocco and Turkey, despite that impressive cannabis field opposite the police station. Different rules seem to apply to locals and foreigners, and sellers have been known to tip off the police after making a sale. The days of paying off a few cops and then making a speedy exit have pretty much disappeared.

Don't bother bringing drugs home with you either. With 'suspect' stamps in your passport (including one from Amsterdam Airport!), energetic customs officials could well decide to take a closer look.

ACTIVITIES

Europe offers countless opportunities to indulge in activities other than sightseeing. The varied geography and climate allow the full range of outdoor pursuits: windsurfing, skiing, fishing, trekking, cycling, mountaineering – you name it, Europe will have several great places to do it. If your interests are more cerebral, you can enlist in courses on anything from language to alternative medicine. For more local information, see the individual country chapters.

Windsurfing & Surfing

Of the many water sports on offer in Europe, windsurfing could well be the most popular after swimming and fishing. Its growth has been explosive in recent years; if you haven't visited Europe in the past decade, you'll be surprised at the transformation that the 'poor people's sailing boats' have caused to the weekend appearance of lakes and coastal resorts. Wetsuits enable the keener windsurfers to continue throughout the colder months. It's easy to rent sailboards in many tourist centres, and courses are usually on offer for beginners.

Believe it or not, you can also go surfing in Europe. Forget the shallow North Sea and Mediterranean, and the calm Baltic Sea, but there can be excellent surf, and an accompanying surfie scene, in south-west England and west Scotland (wetsuit advisable!), along the Irish west coast, the Atlantic coast of France, in Portugal, and along the north and south-west coasts of Spain. The Atlantic seaboard of Morocco, too, has some excellent waves and deserted beaches.

Skiing

During winter, snow skiing is the activity of choice of many Europeans as they flock to hundreds of resorts in the Alps and Pyrenees. Most still opt for downhill skiing, though cross-country has become very popular – skiing in Scandinavia is usually cross-country, with some of the world's best trails.

Skiing is quite expensive due to the costs of ski lifts, accommodation and the inevitable après-ski drinking sessions. Equipment hire (or even purchase), on the other hand, can be relatively cheap if you follow the tips in this book, and the hassle of bringing your own skis may not be worth it. As a rule, a skiing holiday in Europe will work out twice as expensively as a summer holiday of the same length. Cross-country skiing costs less than downhill because you don't rely as much on ski lifts.

The skiing season generally lasts from early December to late March, though at higher altitudes, it may extend an extra month either way. Snow conditions can vary greatly from one year to another and from region to region, but January and February tend to be the best (and busiest!) months.

Ski resorts in the French and Swiss Alps offer great skiing and facilities but are also the most expensive. Expect high prices, too, in the German Alps, though Germany has cheaper (but far less spectacular) options in the Black Forest and Harz. Austria is generally slightly cheaper than France or Switzerland, especially in Carinthia. Prices in the Italian Alps are similar to Austria (with up-market exceptions like Cortina d'Ampezzo), and can work out relatively cheaply with the right package. Cheaper still are the Julian Alps in Slovenia, across the border from Austria and Italy, which is once again open to tourism and is luring back skiers with attractive deals.

Possibly the cheapest skiing in Europe is to be found in the Pyrenees in Spain and Andorra, and in the Sierra Nevada mountain range in the south of Spain. Greece and Scotland also boast growing ski industries – good value in Greece, disappointing in Scotland. See the individual country chapters for more information.

Hiking

Keen hikers can spend a lifetime exploring Europe's many exciting trails. Probably the most spectacular are to be found in the Alps and Italian Dolomites, which are littered with well-marked trails (some complete with duration indicators) during the summer months, with food and accommodation available along the way. The equally sensational Pyrenees are less developed, which can add to the experience as you often rely on remote mountain villages for rest and sustenance. Hiking areas that are less well known but nothing short of stunning are Corsica and Sardinia.

In Britain, the Ramblers' Association (☎ 071-582 6878) is a London charity that promotes long-distance walking in Britain and can help with maps and information. The European Rambling Association has similar aims Europe-wide, and is hot on environmental concerns – contact the Europäische Wandervereinigung eV (☎ 0681-39 00 70), Reichsstrasse 4, Saarbrücken, Germany. The British-based Ramblers Holidays (☎ 0707-33 1133) offers hiking-oriented trips in Europe and elsewhere. A good guide for hiking in the Alps is *Walking in the Alps* by Brian Spencer (paperback).

Every country in Europe has national parks and other interesting areas that may qualify as a trekker's paradise, depending on your preferences. Guided treks are often available for those who aren't sure about their physical abilities or who simply don't know what to look for. Read the Hiking information in the individual country chapters in this book and take your pick. Also see the Getting Around chapter.

Cycling

Along with hiking, cycling is the best way to really get close to the scenery and the people, keeping yourself fit in the process. It's also a good way to get around many cities and towns.

Much of Europe is ideally suited to cycling. In the north-west, the flat terrain ensures that bicycles are a popular form of everyday transport, though rampant headwinds often spoil the fun. In the rest of the continent, hills and mountains can make for heavy going, but this is offset by the dense concentration of things to see. Cycling is a great way to explore many of the Mediterranean islands, though the heat can get to you after a while (make sure you drink enough).

Popular cycling areas include the Belgian Ardennes, most of Ireland, the upper reaches of the Danube in southern Germany, the coasts of Sardinia and Apulia, anywhere in the Alps (for those fit enough), and the south of France. The French in particular take their cycling very seriously, and the country almost grinds to a halt during the annual Tour de France marathon.

If you come from outside Europe, you can often bring your own bicycle along on the plane for a surprisingly reasonable fee. Alternatively, this book lists many places where you can hire one (make sure it has plenty of gears if you plan anything serious), though apart from Ireland they might take a dim view of rentals lasting more than a week.

See the Getting Around chapter for more information on bicycle touring, and the individual country chapters and city/town sections for rental agencies and tips on places to go to.

Boating

Europe's many lakes, rivers and diverse coastlines offer a variety of boating options unmatched anywhere in the world. You can canoe in Finland, raft down rapids in Slovenia, charter a yacht in the Aegean, hire a Hobie Cat in Holland, row on a peaceful Alpine lake, join a luxurious Rhine River cruise from Basel all the way down to Rotterdam (see the Getting Around chapter), rent a sailing boat on the Côte d'Azur, dream away on a canal boat along Britain's extraordinary canal network – the possibilities are endless. The country chapters have more details.

Courses

Apart from learning new physical skills with something like a diving course in the south of France or a mountaineering course in Italy, you can enrich your mind in a variety of structured ways. Language courses are often available to foreigners through universities or private institutions, and these are justifiably popular since the best way to learn a language is in the country where it's spoken. But you can also take courses in art, literature, architecture, drama, music, cooking, alternative energy, photography, organic farming – you name it, and chances are that there will be a course somewhere that suits you.

The individual country chapters in this book give pointers on where to start looking. But in general, the best sources of information are the cultural institutes maintained by many European countries around the world; failing that, try their embassies. Student exchange organisations, student travel agencies, and organisations like the YMCA/YWCA and the YHA can also put you on the right track. Ask about special holiday packages that include a course in something or other.

SPECIAL NEEDS
If you're a traveller with special requirements, national tourist offices can often provide information on facilities for particular groups. There are local organisations in Europe that cater for students, women travelling solo, gays, disabled travellers and so on. The country chapters in this book list addresses and phone numbers of some of these local organisations.

Women Travellers
Women often travel alone or in pairs around Europe. While this is usually quite safe, women do tend to attract more unwanted attention than men, and common sense is the best guide to dealing with potentially dangerous situations like hitchhiking, walking alone at night etc.

Slightly conservative dress and toned-down make-up can help to avoid attention, and dark sunglasses help to avoid unwanted eye contact. Women are more likely to experience problems in rural Spain and southern Italy, particularly Sicily. Marriage, however, is highly respected in southern Europe, and a wedding ring (on the left ring finger) sometimes helps, along with talk about 'my husband'. Hitchhiking alone in these areas is asking for trouble.

In Muslim countries like Morocco, Turkey and, to a lesser degree, Tunisia, a Western woman without a male companion will have a trying time coping with constant attention from males. The only sexual contacts available to most single men in such societies are with prostitutes and with each other. Though the women's movement has begun to make its presence felt in the major cities, the average Muslim woman is still bound to very strict codes of behaviour and dress, so it's not surprising that her Western sister is seen as being freer of moral or sexual constraints.

Dress conservatively, taking care to show as little skin as possible and to minimise body contours – tight trousers are a no-no. It's best to wear a long, loose skirt or dress with a loose, long-sleeved, high-necked shirt. Although head cover is not compulsory in Morocco, Tunisia or Turkey, it's a good idea to wear a headscarf if you're visiting mosques and so on. Recommended reading is the *Handbook for Women Travellers* by M & G Ross, published by Judy Piatkus Publishers (London).

Student Travellers
There are no specific problems facing students travelling in Europe, apart from the obvious ones, like shortage of money and wanting to take the maximum advantage of money-saving opportunities open to students. Your local student travel agency is a great source of information on discounts and special deals for students and other young people – make it your first port of call, since it might well help determine what you're going to do in the first place. Ask for any pamphlets and books that seem useful.

Travel with Children
Successful travel with young children can require some special effort. Don't try to overdo things; even for adults, packing too much into the time available can cause problems. And make sure the activities include the kids as well – balance that day at the Louvre with a day at Euro Disney. Include children in the trip planning; if they've helped to work out where you will be going, they will be much more interested when they get there. See Lonely Planet's *Travel with*

Children by Maureen Wheeler for much more information.

Disabled Travellers
If you have a physical disability, get in touch with your national support organisation (preferably the 'travel officer' if there is one) and ask about the countries you plan to visit. You'll be surprised how much they can tell you about travelling independently or on package tours. They often have complete libraries devoted to travel, and can put you in touch with travel agents who specialise in tours for the disabled.

The British-based Royal Association for Disability and Rehabilitation (RADAR) publishes a useful guide titled *Holidays and Travel Abroad: A Guide for Disabled People*, which gives a good overview of facilities available to disabled travellers in Europe. Contact RADAR (☎ 071-637 5400) at 25 Mortimer St, London W1N 8AB.

Gay & Lesbian Travellers
Gays and lesbians should also get in touch with their national organisation. This book lists several contact addresses and gay and lesbian venues in Europe, but your organisation should be able to give you much more comprehensive information. The *Spartacus Guide for Gay Men*, published by Bruno Gmünder (Berlin), is a good international directory of gay entertainment venues in Europe. It's best used in conjunction with listings in local papers. For lesbians, the international *Gaia's Guide* is recommended; the book lists publications that will offer specific local information.

Senior Travellers
Senior citizens are entitled to many discounts in Europe on things like public transport, museum admission fees etc, provided they show proof of their age. In some cases they might need a special pass. The minimum qualifying age is generally 60 to 65 for men, and 55 to 65 for women. In your home country, a lower age may already entitle you to all sorts of interesting travel packages and discounts (on car hire, for instance) through organisations and travel agents that cater for senior travellers. Start hunting at your local senior citizens advice bureau.

Special Diets
If you have dietary restrictions – you're a vegetarian or you require kosher food, for example – tourist organisations may be able to advise you or provide lists of suitable restaurants. Some vegetarian restaurants are listed in this book. See also the Food section later in this chapter.

ACCOMMODATION
The cheapest places to stay in Europe are camping grounds, followed by hostels and student accommodation. Cheap hotels are virtually unknown in the northern half of Europe, but guesthouses, pensions, private rooms and B&Bs often present good value. Self-catering flats and cottages are worth considering with a group, especially if you plan to stay somewhere for a while.

The Facts for the Visitor sections in the country chapters give an overview of the local accommodation options and how they work. During peak holiday periods, accommodation can be hard to find, and unless you're camping, it's advisable to book ahead. Even camp sites can fill up, particularly popular big-city ones.

Reservations & Bookings
If you arrive in a country by air, there is often an airport hotel-booking desk, although it rarely covers the lower strata of hotels. Tourist offices often have extensive lists of accommodation, and the more helpful ones will really go out of their way to find you something suitable. In most countries the fee for this service is very low, and if accommodation is tight, it can save you a lot of running around and phone calls. This is also an easy way to get around any language problems. Agencies offering private rooms can be good value if you don't mind staying with a local family.

Sometimes people will come up to you on the street offering a private room or a hostel bed. This can be good or bad, there's no hard and fast rule – just make sure it's not way out in a suburb somewhere, and that you negotiate a clear price. As always, be careful when someone offers to carry your luggage: they might carry it away altogether.

Camping

Camping is immensely popular in Europe and is the cheapest way to stay. There's usually a charge per tent or site, per vehicle and per person. National tourist offices generally have booklets or brochures listing camp sites all over their country. See the previous Documents section for information on Camping Carnets.

Although there are some camp sites commendably close to city centres, in most cases they will be some distance out from the centre in larger cities. For this reason, camping is most popular for people who have their own vehicles. If you're on foot, the money you save by camping can quickly be outweighed by the money you spend on commuting to and from a town centre. You also need a tent, sleeping bag, cooking equipment and other bits and pieces, all of which is easier to cart around if you have a vehicle.

Camping other than on designated camping grounds is difficult because the population density makes it hard to find a suitable spot to pitch a tent away from prying eyes. It is also illegal without permission from the local authorities (the police or local council office) or from the owner of the land (don't be shy about asking – you may be pleasantly surprised by the response).

In some countries, such as Austria, Britain and Germany, free camping is illegal on all but private land, and in Greece it's illegal altogether. This doesn't prevent hikers from occasionally pitching their tent for the night, and they'll usually get away with it if they keep a low profile (don't disturb the locals, and don't build a fire or leave rubbish). At worst, they'll be woken up by the police and asked to move on. Beware of camping freelance near camping grounds.

Hostels & Youth Hostels

Hostels offer the cheapest roof over your head in Europe. Most hostels are part of the national YHA (Youth Hostel Association), which is affiliated with the IYHF (International Youth Hostel Federation). There are also some privately run hostels, although it's only in Ireland that private backpacker hostels have really taken off like they have in Australia or New Zealand. Technically you're supposed to be a YHA/IYHF member in order to use affiliated hostels, but you can often stay by simply paying an extra charge and this will often be set against future membership. Stay enough nights as a nonmember and you're automatically a member.

Bavaria in Germany is the only place with an age limit for IYHF members, but some places elsewhere may give members under 27 years of age priority if space is limited. To join the IYHF, ask at any hostel or contact your national or local YHA office. The offices for each European country are covered in this book. Other national YHA offices include:

Australia
Each state has its own Youth Hostel Association. The National Administration Office is at Australian Youth Hostels Association, Level 3, 10 Mallett St, Camperdown, NSW 2050 (☎ 02-565 1699)

Canada
Canadian Hostelling Association, 1600 James Naismith Drive, Suite 608, Gloucester, Ontario K1B 5N4 (☎ 613-748 5638)

England & Wales
Youth Hostels Association, Trevelyan House, 8 St Stephen's Hill, St Albans, Herts AL1 2DY (☎ 0727-55215)

New Zealand
Youth Hostels Association of New Zealand, PO Box 436, 173 Gloucester St, Christchurch 1 (☎ 03-799 970)

Northern Ireland
Youth Hostel Association of Northern Ireland, 56 Bradbury Place, Belfast BT7 1RU (☎ 0232-324733)

Scotland
Scottish Youth Hostels Association, 7 Glebe Crescent, Stirling FK8 2JA (☎ 0786-51181)

USA
American Youth Hostels Inc, PO Box 37613, Washington, DC 200013-7613 (☎ 202-783 6161)

At a hostel, you get a bed for the night, plus use of communal facilities which often include a kitchen where you can prepare your own meals. You are usually required to have a sleeping sheet – simply using your sleeping bag is not permitted. If you don't have your own approved sleeping sheet, you can usually hire one.

Hostels vary widely in character, but the growing number of young people travelling and the increased competition from other forms of accommodation (particularly private 'backpacker hostels') have prompted many hostels to improve their facilities and cut back on rules and regulations. Increasingly, hostels are open all day, curfews are disappearing and 'wardens' with a sergeant-major mentality are an endangered species. In some places, particularly Scandinavia and northern Europe, you'll even find hostels with single and double rooms. Everywhere the trend has been towards smaller dormitories with just four to six beds.

The IYHF *Guide to Budget Accommodation* details hostels throughout Europe. There are other hostel guides available, including cooperatively produced guides to the Irish backpacker hostels. Many hostels accept reservations by phone but usually not during peak periods; they'll often book the next one for you for a small fee. You can also book hostels through national hostel offices. Popular hostels can be heavily booked in summer and sometimes limits are placed on how many nights you can stay.

Student Accommodation
Some university towns rent out student accommodation during holiday periods. This is quite popular in France (see the France chapter for more details). These will often be single rooms and may have cooking facilities available. Enquire at the college or university, at student information services or at local tourist offices.

B&Bs, Guesthouses & Hotels
There's a huge range of accommodation above the hostel level. In Britain and Ireland the myriad B&Bs are the real bargains in this

field where you get a room and breakfast in a private home. In some areas every other house will have a B&B sign out front. In other countries similar private accommodation may go under the name of pensions, guesthouses, *Gasthäuser, Zimmer frei* and so on. Although the majority of B&Bs are simple affairs, there are more expensive ones where you will find attached bathrooms and other luxuries.

Above this level are hotels, which at the bottom of the bracket may be no more expensive than B&Bs or guesthouses while at the other extreme they extend to luxury five-star hotels with price tags to match. Although categorisation varies from country to country, the hotels recommended in this book will generally range from no stars to one or two stars. In any town, you'll generally find hotels clustered around the bus and train station areas – always good places to start hunting.

Check your hotel room and the bathroom before you agree to take it, and make sure you know what it's going to cost – discounts are often available for longer stays. Ask about breakfast: sometimes it's included but other times you may be required to have it and to pay extra for it (which can be a real rip-off). If the sheets don't look clean, ask to have them changed right away. Check where the fire exits are.

If you think a hotel is too expensive, ask if they have anything cheaper. Often they may have tried to steer you into more expensive rooms, or may simply have been trying it on a bit. In southern Europe in particular, hotel owners may be open to a little bargaining if times are slack (don't try this if prices are clearly listed). If you're with a group or plan to stay for a reasonable length of time, it's always worth trying to negotiate a special rate.

FOOD
Few regions in the world offer such a variety of cuisines in such a small area. Dishes can be completely different from one country to the next. Sampling the local food is one of the most enjoyable aspects of travel.

The Facts for the Visitor sections in the individual country chapters contain details of local cuisine, and there are many suggestions on places to eat in the chapters themselves. If you've tried several dishes and not found one to your taste, the best advice is to persevere – there will always be something that's right up your taste buds. There often are alternatives – Chinese, Indian, North African and the wide range of American-inspired fast-food places.

Restaurant prices vary enormously. The cheapest places for a decent meal are often the self-service restaurants in department stores. Official student mensas are dirt cheap, but the food tends to be bland and it's not always clear whether you'll be allowed in if you're not a local student. Kiosks often sell cheap snacks that can be as much a part of the national cuisine as the fancy dishes.

Self-catering – buying your ingredients at a shop or market and preparing them yourself – can be a cheap and wholesome way of eating. Most campers will prepare at least some of their meals (Camping Gaz replacement canisters are widely available), and hostels and student accommodation often have cooking facilities. Even if you don't cook, a lunch on a park bench with a fresh stick of bread, some local cheese and salami and a tomato or two, washed down with a cheap bottle of local wine, can be one of the recurring highlights of your trip. Recommended.

Vegetarians won't have to go hungry. Vegetarianism has taken off in a big way in Europe, though not everywhere to the same extent and more so in the north than in the south. Tourist offices can supply lists of vegetarian restaurants, and some are recommended in this book. Many standard restaurants have one or two vegetarian dishes, or at least a few items on the menu that don't contain meat. Some restaurants will prepare special dishes on request (approach them about this in advance), and you can always ask the waiter to talk with the cook on your behalf. If all else fails, you can put together your own meals from shops and markets.

Getting There & Away

Step one is to get to Europe and, in these days of severe competition between the airlines, there are plenty of opportunities to find cheap tickets to a variety of 'gateway' cities.

Forget shipping, unless by 'shipping' you mean the many ferry services between Europe and North Africa. Only a handful of ships still carry passengers across the Atlantic; they don't sail often and are very expensive even compared with full-fare air tickets. See the Sea section at the end of this chapter for more details.

Some travellers still arrive or leave overland – the options being Africa, the Middle East and Asia, and what used to be the Soviet Union. The trans-Siberian and Mongolian express trains could well begin to carry more people to and from Europe as Russia opens up to tourism. See the following Train and Land sections for more details.

Whichever way you're travelling, make sure you take out travel insurance. This not only covers you for medical expenses and luggage theft or loss, but also for cancellation or delays in your travel arrangements (you might fall seriously ill two days before departure, for example). Cover depends on your insurance and type of ticket, so ask both your insurer and your ticket issuing agency to explain where you stand. Ticket loss is also covered by travel insurance. Make sure you have a separate record of all your ticket details – or better still, a photocopy (see Photocopies under Dangers & Annoyances in the earlier Facts for the Visitor chapter). Buy travel insurance as early as possible. If you buy it the week before you fly, you may find, for example, that you're not covered for delays to your flight caused by strikes or other industrial action that may have been in force before you took out the insurance.

Paying for your ticket with a credit card often provides limited travel accident insurance, and you may be able to reclaim the payment if the operator doesn't deliver. In the UK, for instance, credit card providers are required by law to reimburse consumers if a company goes into liquidation and the amount in contention is more than £100. Ask your credit card company what it's prepared to cover.

AIR

Remember always to reconfirm your onward or return bookings by the specified time – usually 72 hours before departure on international flights. Otherwise there's a real risk that you'll turn up at the airport only to find that you've missed your flight because it was rescheduled, or that you've been reclassified as a 'no show' (see the Air Travel Glossary elsewhere on these pages), with all the problems that involves if your flight happens to be full. Lonely Planet has received several letters from people who've found themselves in this embarrassing predicament, so be warned.

Buying a Plane Ticket

The plane ticket will probably be the single most expensive item in your budget, and buying it can be an intimidating business. There is likely to be a multitude of airlines and travel agents hoping to separate you from your money, and it's always worth putting aside some time to research the current state of the market. Start early: some of the cheapest tickets have to be bought months in advance, and some popular flights sell out early.

Talk to other recent travellers, as they may be able to stop you from making some of the same old mistakes. Look at the ads in newspapers and magazines (not forgetting the press of the ethnic group whose country you plan to visit), and watch for special offers.

Cheap tickets are available in two distinct categories: official and unofficial. Official ones are advance-purchase tickets, budget fares, Apex, super-Apex or whatever other brand name the airlines care to tack on them in order to put, as it is so succinctly expressed, 'bums on seats'.

Unofficial tickets are simply discounted tickets that the airlines release through selected travel agents. Don't go looking for discounted tickets straight from the airlines: they are only available through travel agents. Airlines can, however, supply information on routes and timetables, and their low-season, student and senior citizens' fares can be very competitive.

Return tickets usually work out cheaper than two one-ways – often *much* cheaper: in some cases, a well-planned return ticket can even be cheaper than a one-way. Beware that immigration officials often insist on return or onward tickets, and that if you can't show either, you might be asked to provide proof

---

Air Travel Glossary

Apex Apex ('advance purchase excursion') is a discounted ticket which must be paid for in advance. There are penalties if you wish to change it.

Baggage Allowance This will be written on your ticket: usually one 20-kg item to go in the hold, plus one item of hand luggage.

Bucket Shop An unbonded travel agency specialising in discounted airline tickets.

Bumped Just because you have a confirmed seat doesn't mean you're going to get on the plane – see Overbooking.

Cancellation Penalties If you have to cancel or change an Apex ticket there are often heavy penalties involved – insurance can sometimes be taken out against these penalties. Some airlines impose penalties on regular tickets as well, particularly against 'no show' passengers (see No Shows).

Check In Airlines ask you to check in a certain time ahead of the flight departure (usually 1½ hours on international flights). If you fail to check in on time and the flight is overbooked, the airline can cancel your booking and give your seat to somebody else.

Confirmation Having a ticket written out with the flight and date you want doesn't mean you have a seat until the agent has checked with the airline that your status is 'OK' or confirmed. Meanwhile, you could just be 'on request'. It's also wise to reconfirm onward or return bookings directly with the airline 72 hours before departure (see Reconfirmation).

Discounted Tickets There are two types of discounted fares: officially discounted (see Promotional Fares) and unofficially discounted. The lowest prices often impose drawbacks like flying with unpopular airlines, inconvenient schedules, or unpleasant routes and connections. A discounted ticket can save you other things than money – you may be able to pay Apex prices without the associated Apex advance booking and other requirements. Discounted tickets only exist where there is fierce competition.

Full Fares Airlines traditionally offer 1st-class (coded F), business-class (coded J) and economy-class (coded Y) tickets. These days there are so many promotional and discounted fares available from the regular economy class that few passengers pay full economy fare.

Lost Tickets If you lose your airline ticket, an airline will usually treat it like a travellers' cheque and, after enquiries, issue you with another one. Legally, however, an airline is entitled to treat it like cash and if you lose it then it's gone forever. Take good care of your tickets.

No Shows No shows are passengers who fail to show up for their flight, sometimes due to unexpected delays or disasters, sometimes due to simply forgetting, sometimes because they made more than one booking and didn't bother to cancel the one they didn't want. Full fare passengers who fail to turn up are sometimes entitled to travel on a later flight. The rest of us are penalised (see Cancellation Penalties).

On Request An unconfirmed booking for a flight (see Confirmation).

of 'sufficient means of support', which means you have to show a lot of money.

Round-the-World (RTW) tickets have become very popular in recent years. The airline RTW tickets are often real bargains, and can work out to be no more expensive or even cheaper than an ordinary return ticket. Prices start at about UK£850, A$1800 or US$1300 depending on the season. The official airline RTW tickets are usually put together by a combination of two airlines, and permit you to fly anywhere you want on their route systems so long as you don't backtrack. Other restrictions are that you (usually) must book the first sector in advance and cancellation penalties then apply. There may be restrictions on how many stops you are permitted, and usually

---

Open Jaws A return ticket where you fly out to one place but return from another. If available, this can save you backtracking to your arrival point.

Overbooking Airlines hate to fly empty seats, and since every flight has some passengers who fail to show up (see No Shows), airlines often book more passengers than they have seats. Usually the excess passengers balance those who fail to show up but occasionally somebody gets bumped. If this happens, guess who it is most likely to be? The passengers who check in late.

Promotional Fares Officially discounted fares like Apex fares which are available from travel agents or direct from the airline.

Reconfirmation At least 72 hours prior to departure time of an onward or return flight you must contact the airline and 'reconfirm' that you intend to be on the flight. If you don't do this the airline can delete your name from the passenger list and you could lose your seat. You don't have to reconfirm the first flight on your itinerary or if your stopover is less than 72 hours. It doesn't hurt to reconfirm more than once.

Restrictions Discounted tickets often have various restrictions on them – advance purchase is the most usual one (see Apex). Others are restrictions on the minimum and maximum period you must be away, such as a minimum of 14 days or a maximum of one year. See Cancellation Penalties.

Standby A discounted ticket where you only fly if there is a seat free at the last moment. Standby fares are usually only available on domestic routes.

Tickets Out An entry requirement for many countries is that you have an onward or return ticket – in other words, a ticket out of the country. If you're not sure what you intend to do next, the easiest solution is to buy the cheapest onward ticket to a neighbouring country or a ticket from a reliable airline which can later be refunded if you do not use it.

Transferred Tickets Airline tickets cannot be transferred from one person to another. Travellers sometimes try to sell the return half of their ticket, but officials can ask you to prove that you are the person named on the ticket. This is unlikely to happen on domestic flights, but on international flights, tickets may be compared with passports. Also, if you're flying on a transferred ticket and something goes wrong with the flight (hijack, crash), there will be no record of your presence on board.

Travel Agencies Travel agencies vary widely and you should ensure you use one that suits your needs. Some simply handle tours while full-service agencies handle everything from tours and tickets to car rental and hotel bookings. A good one will do all these things and can save you a lot of money, but if all you want is a ticket at the lowest possible price, then you really need an agency specialising in discounted tickets. A discounted ticket agency, however, may not be useful for other things, like hotel bookings.

Travel Periods Some officially discounted fares, Apex fares in particular, vary with the time of year. There is often a low (off-peak) season and a high (peak) season. Sometimes there's an intermediate or shoulder season as well. At peak times, when everyone wants to fly, not only will the officially discounted fares be higher but so will unofficially discounted fares, or there may simply be no discounted tickets available. Usually the fare depends on your outward flight – if you depart in the high season and return in the low season, you pay the high-season fare. ■

the tickets are valid for 90 days up to a year. An alternative type of RTW ticket is one put together by a travel agent using a combination of discounted tickets.

Generally, you can find discounted tickets at prices as low as or lower than the Apex or budget tickets. Phone around the travel agents for bargains. Find out the fare, the route, the duration of the journey, the stopovers allowed, and any restrictions on the ticket (see Restrictions in the Air Travel Glossary). Ask about cancellation penalties.

You may discover that those impossibly cheap flights are 'fully booked, but we have another one that costs a bit more...' Or the flight is on an airline notorious for its poor safety standards and leaves you in the world's least favourite airport in mid-journey for 14 hours – where you're confined to the transit lounge because you don't have a visa. Or the agent claims to have the last two seats available for that country for the whole of July, which he will hold for you for a maximum of two hours. Don't panic – keep ringing around.

If you are travelling from the USA or South-East Asia, or trying to get out of Europe from the UK, you will probably find that the cheapest flights are being advertised by obscure agencies whose names haven't yet reached the telephone directory. Many such firms are honest and solvent, but there are a few rogues who will take your money and disappear, to reopen elsewhere a month or two later under a new name. If you feel suspicious about a firm, don't give them all the money at once – leave a deposit of 20% or so and pay the balance when you get the ticket. If they insist on cash in advance, go somewhere else or be prepared to take a very big risk. And once you have the ticket, ring the airline to confirm that you are actually booked onto the flight.

You may decide to pay more than the rock-bottom fare by opting for the safety of a better-known travel agent. Firms such as STA, which has offices worldwide, Council Travel in the USA or Travel CUTS in Canada offer good prices to most destinations, and are unlikely to disappear overnight leaving you clutching a receipt for a nonexistent ticket.

Use the fares quoted in this book as a guide only. They are approximate and based on the rates advertised by travel agents at the time of going to press, and are likely to have changed by the time you read this.

Travellers with Special Needs

If you have special needs of any sort – you've broken a leg, you're vegetarian or require a special diet, travelling in a wheelchair, taking the baby, terrified of flying, whatever – let the airline people know as soon as possible so that they can make arrangements. Remind them when you reconfirm your booking (at least 72 hours before departure) and again when you check in at the airport. It may also be worth ringing around the airlines before you make your booking, to find out how they can handle your particular needs.

Children aged under two travel for 10% of the standard fare (or free on some airlines) as long as they don't occupy a seat. They don't get a baggage allowance either. 'Skycots', baby food and diapers should be provided by the airline if requested in advance. Children aged between two and 12 can usually occupy a seat for half to two-thirds of the full fare, and do get get a baggage allowance.

To/From the USA

The North Atlantic is the world's busiest long-haul air corridor and the flight options are bewildering. The *New York Times*, the *LA Times*, the *Chicago Tribune* and the *San Francisco Chronicle Examiner* all produce weekly travel sections in which you'll find any number of travel agents' ads. Council Travel and STA Travel have offices in major cities nationwide. Access International in New York offers discounts to Europe from 50 cities in the USA. You should be able to fly New York-London return for US$350-450 low season, US$550-650 high season.

One-way fares can work out to about half this on a stand-by basis. Airhitch (☎ 212-864 2000) specialises in this sort of thing, and can get you to Europe one-way for US$160/269/ 229 from the east coast/west coast/elsewhere in the USA.

An interesting alternative to the boring New York-London flight is offered by Icelandair (☎ 800-223 5500), which has competitive year-round fares to Luxembourg with a stopover in Iceland's capital, Reykyavík – a great way of spending a few days in an unusual country that's otherwise hard to get to.

Another option is a courier flight, where you accompany a parcel or freight to be picked up at the other end. A New York-London return through one of these can be had for about US$250/500 low/high season or less (about US$100 more from the west coast). You can also fly one-way. The drawbacks are that your stay in Europe may be limited to one or two weeks, that your luggage is usually restricted to hand luggage (the parcel or freight you carry comes out of your luggage allowance), and that you may have to be a resident and apply for an interview before they'll take you on (dress conservatively, preferably in a business suit). Find out more about courier flights from Council Travel in New York (☎ 212-661 1450) and Los Angeles (☎ 310-208 3551), Discount Travel International in New York (☎ 212-362 3636), and Way to Go in Los Angeles (☎ 213-466 1126) and San Francisco (☎ 415-292 7801). Call two or three months in advance, at the very beginning of the calendar month.

The *Travel Unlimited* newsletter, PO Box 1058, Allston, MA 02134, publishes details of the cheapest air fares and courier possibilities for destinations all over the world from the USA and other countries including the UK. It's a treasure trove of information. A single monthly issue costs US$5, and a year's subscription, US$25 (US$35 abroad).

To/From Canada

Travel CUTS has offices in all major cities. Scan the budget travel agents' ads in the *Toronto Globe & Mail*, the *Toronto Star* and the *Vancouver Province*.

See the previous To/From the USA section for general information on courier flights. For courier flights originating in Canada, contact FB On Board Courier Services (☎ 514-633 0740 in Montreal or Toronto, or ☎ 604-338 1366 in Vancouver). A courier return flight to London or Paris will set you back about C$350 from Toronto or Montreal, C$425 from Vancouver.

To/From Australia

STA and Flight Centres International are major dealers in cheap air fares. Check the travel agents' ads in the Yellow Pages and ring around.

The Saturday travel sections of Sydney's *Sydney Morning Herald* and Melbourne's *The Age* newspapers have many ads offering cheap fares to Europe, but don't be surprised if they happen to be 'sold out' when you contact the agents: they're usually low-season fares on obscure airlines with conditions attached. With Australia's large and well-organised ethnic populations, it pays to check special deals in the ethnic press – Olympic Airways sometimes has good deals to Athens.

Discounted return fares on mainstream airlines through a reputable agent like STA cost between A$1600 (low season) and A$2500 (high season). Flights to/from Perth are a couple of hundred dollars cheaper.

To/From New Zealand

As in Australia, STA and Flight Centres International are popular travel agents in New Zealand. Not surprisingly, the cheapest fares to Europe are routed through the USA, and a Round-the-World ticket can be cheaper than a return.

To/From Africa

Nairobi is probably the best place in Africa to buy tickets to Europe, thanks to the many bucket shops and the strong competition between them. A typical one-way/return fare to London would be about US$550/800. Several West African countries such as Burkina Faso and The Gambia offer cheap charter flights to France, and charter fares from Morocco can be incredibly cheap if you're lucky enough to find a seat. If you are thinking of flying to Europe from Cairo, it's often cheaper to fly to Athens and to proceed with a budget bus or train from there.

To/From Asia

Hong Kong is the discount plane-ticket capital of Asia, and its bucket shops are at least as unreliable as those of other cities. Ask the advice of other travellers before buying a ticket. Many of the cheapest fares from South-East Asia to Europe are offered by Eastern European carriers. STA has branches in Hong Kong, Tokyo, Singapore, Bangkok and Kuala Lumpur.

To/from India, the cheapest flights tend to be with Eastern European carriers like LOT and Aeroflot, or with Middle Eastern airlines such as Syrian Arab Airlines and Iran Air. Bombay is the air transport hub, with many transit options to/from South-East Asia, but tickets are slightly cheaper in Delhi. Try Delhi Student Travel Services in the Imperial Hotel, Janpath.

From the UK

If you're looking for a cheap way out of Europe, London is Europe's major centre for discounted fares. The Trailfinders head office in west London is an amazing place complete with travel library, bookshop, visa service and immunisation centre. STA also has branches in the UK. Campus Travel is helpful and has many interesting deals. See the London Information section in the Great Britain chapter for addresses and phone numbers of these and other discount travel agencies. Ask them about courier flights organised by Polo Express, Courier Travel Service and Shades International Travel. See also the Air section in the following Getting Around chapter.

The listings magazines *Time Out* and *City Limits*, the Sunday papers, the *Evening Standard* and *Exchange & Mart* carry ads for cheap fares. Also look out for the free magazines and newspapers widely available in London, especially *TNT* (recommended), *Southern Cross* and *Trailfinder* – you can

often pick them up outside the main train and tube stations.

Most British travel agents are registered with the ABTA (Association of British Travel Agents). If you have paid for your flight to an ABTA-registered agent who then goes out of business, ABTA will guarantee a refund or an alternative. Unregistered bucket shops are riskier but sometimes cheaper.

The Globetrotters Club (BCM Roving, London WC1N 3XX) publishes a newsletter called *Globe* which covers obscure destinations and can help in finding travelling companions.

From Continental Europe

Though London is the discount capital of Europe, there are several other cities in the region where you'll find a wide range of good deals. Athens is one of them: shop around the travel agents in the backstreets between Syntagma and Omonia squares. Amsterdam is another good centre for cheap tickets (see the Amsterdam section for more details).

Across Europe, many travel agents have ties with STA, where cheap tickets can be purchased and STA tickets can be altered free of charge (first change only). Outlets in important transport hubs include: Voyages et Découvertes (☎ 1-42.61.00.01), 21 Rue Cambon, Paris; SRID Reisen (☎ 069-43 01 91), Berger Strasse 118, Frankfurt; and ISYTS (☎ 01-32 21 267), 2nd Floor, 11 Nikis St, Syntagma Square, Athens.

The Belgian newsletter for 'passionate travellers', *Farang* (☎ 019-69 98 23), La Rue 8, 4261 Braives, Belgium, deals with obscure destinations. So does the French club, Aventure du Bout du Monde (☎ 1-43.35.08.95), 11bis Rue Maison Dieu, 75014 Paris.

TRAIN

Morocco and most of Turkey lie outside Europe, but the rail systems of both countries are still covered by Inter-Rail. If you don't have an Inter-Rail pass, the price of a cheap return train ticket from London to Morocco compares favourably with equivalent bus fares – worth keeping in mind.

To/from central and eastern Asia, a train can work out more cheaply than flying depending on how much time and money you spend along the way. You can choose from four different trains, three of which (the trans-Siberian, trans-Mongolian and trans-Manchurian) follow the same route to/from Moscow across Siberia but have different eastern railheads. The fourth, the trans-Kazakhstan, runs between Moscow and Ürümqi (north-western China) across central Asia. Prices can vary enormously, depending on where you buy the ticket and what is included – the prices quoted here are a rough indication only.

The trans-Siberian takes 8½ days from Moscow via Khabarovsk to Nakhodka, from where there is a boat to Japan (Yokohama) or Hong Kong. The boats only run from May to September. The complete rail/boat journey from Moscow to Yokohama costs upwards of US$640 per person, for a 2nd-class sleeper in a four-berth cabin.

The trans-Mongolian passes through Mongolia to Beijing and takes about 5½ days. A 2nd-class sleeper in a four-berth compartment would cost upwards of US$530 in Moscow. In Europe, cheaper tickets can be purchased from some travel agents in Budapest or Warsaw. In Beijing, CITS sells the cheapest tickets, starting at US$150. Tickets take about a week to organise, but if you need to prebook accommodation for Russia (depending on your visa), Intourist takes about four weeks to organise this.

The trans-Manchurian passes through Manchuria to Beijing and takes six days, costing the same as the trans-Mongolian.

The trans-Kazakhstan runs via Alma Ata (Kazakhstan). CITS at the moment will not book the ticket in Beijing, so you'll have to travel to Ürümqi first, where the ticket to Moscow is about US$95.

There are countless travel options between Moscow and the rest of Europe. Most people will opt for a train, usually to/from Berlin, Helsinki, Munich or Vienna.

LAND

After the heady 1970s, the overland trail to/from Asia lost much of its popularity in the 1980s as the Islamic regime in Iran made life hard for travellers from certain countries, while the war in Afghanistan closed that country to all but the most foolhardy. Now that Iran is rediscovering the merits of tourism, the Asia route has begun to pick up again, though unsettled conditions in Afghanistan and southern Pakistan could prevent the trickle of travellers turning into a flood for the time being.

A new overland route through what used to be the Soviet Union could become important over the next few years. At this stage the options are more or less confined to the trans-Siberian/Mongolian railway lines to/from Moscow (see the previous Train section), but other modes of transport are likely to become available beyond the Urals as the newly independent states open up to travellers.

Going to/from Africa will involve a Mediterranean ferry crossing (discounting the complicated Middle East route). Ferry details are provided in the following Sea section and, in more detail, in the France, Spain and Italy chapters of this book. Due to political problems in Africa (war between Morocco and the Polisario in the west, civil war in Sudan in the east), the most feasible Africa overland routes run through Algeria and its southern neighbours.

Travelling by private transport beyond Europe requires plenty of paperwork and other preparations. A detailed description is beyond the scope of this book, but the following Getting Around chapter tells you what's required within Europe.

SEA

Mediterranean Ferries

There are many ferries across the Mediterranean between Europe and Africa. The ferry you take will depend on your travels in Africa, but in order of cheapness they are: Spain-Morocco, Italy-Tunisia, Greece-Egypt and France-Algeria. Some of the Greece-Egypt ferries actually start from

Venice but are, of course, much more expensive from there. Ferries are often filled to capacity in summer, especially to/from Algeria and Tunisia, so book well in advance if you're taking a vehicle across. See the relevant country chapters in this book for more details.

Passenger Ships

The days of earning your passage on a freighter to or from Europe have well and truly passed. Even if you have a mariner's ticket, a shipping company is unlikely to want to sign you up for a single trip.

Regular, long-distance passenger ships disappeared with the advent of cheap air travel, to be replaced by a small number of luxury cruise ships. The grand lady of them all, Cunard's *Queen Elizabeth 2*, sails between New York and Southampton 20 times a year; the trip takes five nights each way and a return ticket can be had from UK£1255, though there are also one-way and 'fly one way' deals. Your travel agent will have more details. The standard reference for passenger ships is the *ABC Passenger Shipping Guide* published by the Reed Travel Group (☎ 0582-60 0111), Church St, Dunstable, Bedfordshire LU5 4HB, Great Britain.

A more adventurous (though not necessarily cheaper) alternative is as a paying passenger on a freighter. Freighters are far more numerous than cruise ships and there are many more routes from which to choose. With a bit of homework, you'll be able to sail between Europe and just about anywhere else in the world, with stopovers at exotic ports which you may never have heard of. The previously mentioned *ABC Shipping Guide* is a good source of information, or contact the Freighter Travel Club of America, 3524 Harts Lake Rd, Roy, WA 98580 – included in the US$18 yearly membership is a monthly bulletin, *Freighter Travel News*.

Passenger freighters typically carry six to 12 passengers (more than 12 would require a doctor on board) and, though less luxurious than dedicated cruise ships, give you a real taste of life at sea. Schedules tend to be flexible and costs vary, but seem to hover around US$95 a day; vehicles can often be included for an additional fee.

One of the better known passenger freighter operators is Polish Ocean Lines. Its popular Atlantic routing (weekly service) is Bremerhaven, Le Havre, Halifax, New York, Baltimore, Wilmington, New York, Le Havre, Rotterdam, Bremerhaven, which costs UK£1375 for the 28-day round voyage or US$1010 for New York-Le Havre one-way (prices per person in a double cabin). Contact Gdynia America Line (☎ 212-952 1280), 39 Broadway, 14th Floor, New York, NY 10006.

DEPARTURE TAXES

Some countries charge you a small fee for the privilege of leaving from their airports. Some also charge port fees when leaving by ship. Such fees are usually included in the price of your ticket, but it pays to check this when purchasing your ticket. If not, you'll have to have the fee ready when you leave. Details of departure taxes are given in the individual country chapters.

WARNING

This chapter is particularly vulnerable to change – prices for international travel are volatile, routes are introduced and cancelled, schedules change, special deals come and go, and rules and visa requirements are amended. Airlines and governments seem to take a perverse pleasure in making price structures and regulations as complicated as possible. You should check directly with the airline or travel agent to make sure you understand how a fare (and ticket you may buy) works. In addition, the travel industry is highly competitive and there are many lurks and perks. The upshot of this is that you should get opinions, quotes and advice from as many airlines and travel agents as possible before you part with your hard-earned cash. The details given in this chapter should be regarded as pointers and are not a substitute for careful, up-to-date research.

Getting Around

AIR

At the beginning of 1993 the skies over the EC were deregulated, ending the virtual monopoly of some airlines within their home countries. Though the details are still being worked out, the likely result will be a slight drop in fares and a great increase in the choice of airlines on which to fly.

The different classes of cheap air tickets mentioned in the previous Getting There & Away chapter are also available on European routes. London is a good centre for picking up cheap, restricted-validity tickets through bucket shops (see also the Getting There & Away section in the Great Britain chapter). Amsterdam is another good place for bucket-shop tickets (see the Netherlands chapter).

Across Europe many travel agents have ties with STA, where cheap tickets can be purchased and STA tickets can be altered free of charge (first change only). Outlets in important transport hubs include: Voyages et Découvertes (☎ 1-42.61.00.01), 21 Rue Cambon, Paris; and SRID Reisen (☎ 069-43 01 91), Berger Strasse 118, Frankfurt.

For longer journeys, you can sometimes find air fares that beat on-the-ground alternatives in terms of cost. A restricted return (valid for one month maximum) from London to Zürich, for example, is available through discount travel agents for upwards of £90. A two-month return by rail between the same cities costs £123. Getting between airports and city centres is rarely a problem in Europe thanks to ever improving subway networks and good bus services.

The main drawback with flying is that you don't see very much of Europe from the air. It's the best way to go if you're very pushed for time, but if you really want to tour Europe properly you should do it at ground level. You can't very well hop off the London-to-Zürich aeroplane to take a day out in Paris, but you can if you take the train. Air travel is best viewed as a means to get you to the starting point of your itinerary rather than as

your main means of travel. Also, if you start taking aeroplanes for relatively short hops it gets extremely expensive, particularly as special deals are rarely available on internal flights.

Open Jaw returns, by which you can travel into one city and out of another, provide some measure of flexibility. In London, Trailfinders (☎ 071-937 5400) and STA (☎ 071-937 9921) can both give you tailor-made versions of these tickets. Your chosen cities needn't necessarily be in the same country.

If you are travelling alone, it might be worth looking into courier flights. You get cheap passage in return for accompanying an urgent package through customs and delivering it to a representative at the destination airport. Polo Express (☎ 081-759 5383) in London has the most options within Europe. Routes are subject to change every six months and you are committed to returning on a set date, usually within two weeks. Examples of return fares from London are Berlin £49, Barcelona £59, Lisbon £35 and Athens £65 to £75.

BUS

International Buses

International bus travel tends to take second place to going by train. The bus has the edge in terms of cost, sometimes quite substantially, but is generally slower, less comfortable and more cramped. Eurolines (☎ 071-730 0202), 52 Grosvenor Gardens, Victoria, London SW1, is the main international carrier and has representatives across Europe. See the Getting There & Away section in the Great Britain chapter for further details.

Eurolines' European representatives include: Eurolines/Budgetbus (☎ 020-627 51 51), Rokin 10, Amsterdam; Eurolines (☎ 1-43.54.11.99), 55 Rue Saint Jacques, 75005 Paris; Deutsche Touring (☎ 089-59 18 24), Arnulfstrasse 3, Munich; and Lazzi

Express (☎ 06-841 74 58), via Tagliamento 27R, Rome. These may also be able to advise you on other bus companies and deals.

Eurolines Capital Trippers offer a return ticket from London taking in two capital cities from £59. Eurolines Bus Circuits offer a variety of tours of cities. One version allows you to travel from London to Munich, Barcelona, Rome, Paris and back to London for £215. Tickets are valid for two months and there are no reductions for students or young people.

On ordinary return trips, youth fares are around 10% less than the ordinary full fare, eg a London-Munich return ticket (valid six months) costs £99 for adults or £87 for youths up to 25 years old. Onward or return journeys must be reserved prior to departure for all tickets.

Europabus is the motor coach system of the European railways and has information offices in Brussels (☎ 02-217 66 60), Frankfurt (☎ 069-7 90 30), Paris (☎ 1-40.38.93.93), Rome (☎ (06-481 82 77), and Vienna (☎ 0222-501 80).

Local Buses

Buses provide a viable alternative to the rail network in most countries. Again, compared to trains they are usually slightly cheaper and, with the exception of Spain and Portugal, slightly slower. Buses tend to be best for shorter hops such getting round cities and reaching remote rural villages. They are often the only option in mountainous regions where rail tracks fear to tread. Advance reservations are rarely necessary. Many city buses operate on a pay-in-advance and punch-your-ticket-in-the-slot system. See the individual country chapters and city sections for more details.

TRAIN

Trains are a popular way for backpackers of getting around: they are good meeting places, comfortable, frequent, and generally on time. In some countries, such as Italy, Spain and Portugal, fares are heavily subsidised; in others, European rail passes make travel affordable. Supplements and reserva-

tion costs are not covered by passes, and pass holders must always carry their passport on the train for identification purposes.

If you plan to travel extensively by train, it might be worth getting hold of the *Thomas Cook European Timetable*, which gives a complete listing of train schedules and indicates where supplements apply or where reservations are necessary. It is updated monthly and is available from Thomas Cook outlets worldwide.

Paris, Amsterdam, Munich, Milan and Vienna are all important hubs for international rail connections. See the relevant city sections for details and budget ticket agents.

Express Trains

Fast trains can be identified by the symbols EC (EuroCity) or IC (InterCity). The French TGV and the German ICE are even faster trains. Supplements can apply on fast trains, and it is a good idea (sometimes obligatory) to make seat reservations at peak times and on certain lines.

Overnight Trains

Overnight trains will usually offer a choice of couchette or sleeper if you don't fancy sleeping in your seat with somebody else's elbow in your ear. Again, reservations are advisable as sleeping options are allocated on a first-come, first-served basis. Couchettes are bunks numbering four (1st class) or six (2nd class) per compartment and are comfortable enough, if lacking a bit in privacy. A bunk costs a fixed price of around US$16 for international travel irrespective of the length of the journey.

Sleepers are the most comfortable option, offering beds for one or two passengers in 1st class, and two or three passengers in 2nd class. Charges vary depending upon the journey but they tend to be significantly more expensive than couchettes. Most long-distance trains have a dining car or an attendant who wheels a drink-and-snack-laden trolley through carriages, but prices tend to be steep.

Security

People often tell horror stories about train journeys, ranging from whole carriages being gassed through the ventilation system by bandits and the occupants divested of their belongings, to individual travellers being drugged and robbed with the collusion of the railway staff. This sort of thing can happen, although it's not nearly as widespread as some people make out. The overwhelming chances are that you will only have fond memories of being on the train. Nevertheless, it pays to take basic precautions. Don't leave your stuff unattended, and make sure you lock compartment doors overnight. Some people make a point of leaving a window open to maintain a flow of fresh air (possibly to protect themselves against less sinister gaseous emissions from those mentioned above!).

Eurail Passes

These passes can only be bought by residents of non-European countries, and are supposed to be purchased before arriving in Europe. However, Eurail passes can be purchased within Europe so long as your passport proves you've been there for less than six months, but the outlets where you can do this are limited. French National Railways (071-493 9731), 179 Piccadilly, London, is one such outlet. If you've lived in Europe for more than six months, you are eligible for an Inter-Rail pass, which is a better buy.

Eurail passes are valid for unlimited travel on national railways and some private lines in Austria, Belgium, Denmark, Finland, France (including Monaco), Germany, Greece, Hungary, Italy, Luxembourg, the Netherlands, Norway, Portugal, Ireland, Spain, Sweden and Switzerland (including Liechtenstein). Britain is not covered.

Eurail is also valid for ferries between Ireland and France (but not between Britain and France), between Italy and Greece, and from Sweden to Finland, Denmark or Germany. In addition, reductions are given on steamer services in various countries.

Eurail passes offer reasonable value to people aged under 26. A Youthpass is valid for 2nd-class travel for 15 days (£188), one month (US$470 or £294) or two months (US$640 or £384). The Youth Flexipass, also for 2nd class, is valid for seven days' travel in two months (£128) or 15 days in two months (US$420 or £254). A journey commencing after 7 pm counts as the next day's travel but there is no leeway beyond midnight at the end of a day's travel. The traveller must fill out in ink the relevant box in the calendar before starting a day's travel. Some people try to sneak extra days by 'forgetting' to fill in the box or using an erasable pen and hoping the ticket isn't stamped for that day. However, conductors are getting wise to such dodges and if caught you are liable to pay a fine of US$100 in local currency.

The corresponding passes for those aged over 26 are available in 1st class only. The Flexipass (five versions) costs from US$280 (£168) for five days in a 15-day period up to US$610 (£366) for 14 days within one month. The standard Eurail Pass (also five versions) costs from US$430 (£270) for 15 days' unlimited travel up to US$1150 (£726) for three months. Two or more people travelling together (minimum three people between 1 April and 30 September) can get good discounts on a Saverpass, which works like the standard Eurail Pass.

If you lose your Eurail pass before you get to Europe, you cannot claim a refund. If your pass is lost or stolen once you are in Europe, you may apply for a duplicate, but only if the original pass was already validated and you can prove it by showing a validation slip. A police report is also necessary and a US$25 reissuance fee applies. The catch with losing a Flexipass is that they assume you've been travelling every day since the validation (even if you haven't), so if your number of flexible days is equal to or is exceeded by the number of days since the pass was validated, you won't be able to claim anything at all. There is at least one Eurail Aid Office (where duplicates are issued) in each country participating in the scheme; addresses are listed in the Eurail Traveller's Guide which comes with the pass.

Inter-Rail Passes

Inter-Rail passes are available to residents of European countries. The normal Inter-Rail card is limited to travellers under 26 years of age and costs £180 for one month. Terms and conditions vary slightly from country to country but in all cases it applies that in the country of origin there is only a discount of around 50% on normal fares. Within Great Britain, Inter-Rail passes can only be purchased by people who have been resident in Britain for at least six months, and passport identification is required. Inter-Rail cards should be treated like cash, as you can make no claims in the event of loss or theft.

Cards are valid for free 2nd-class rail travel in all countries covered by Eurail, plus Bulgaria, Czechoslovakia, Morocco, Poland, Romania, Turkey and former Yugoslavia. If bought in Britain, the card is also valid for 34% to 50% discounts on train travel in Britain and Northern Ireland, as well as 30% to 50% discounts on various ferry routes (many more than covered by Eurail) and certain river and lake services. It also gives free travel (barring port tax) on shipping routes from Brindisi (Italy) to Patras (Greece).

There is also an Inter-Rail card for people aged 26 or over, imaginatively called the Inter-Rail 26+. This is nowhere near as good a deal. Not only are the costs higher (£180 for 15 days or £260 for one month), but the card is also more restricted: it is not valid in Britain or Spain and it gets discounts on fewer ferry routes. On certain trips, though, it can still be very good value.

The national rail organisations of France, Italy, Portugal and Spain have indicated that they want to pull out of the Inter-Rail accord by the beginning of 1993, which would seriously undermine the attraction of an Inter-Rail pass. As this book went to press, the issue was still under negotiation. One compromise being discussed was the charging of supplements to Inter-Rail pass holders travelling in these countries.

Cheap Tickets

European Rail Passes are only worth buying if you plan to do a reasonable amount of travelling within a short space of time: Eurail itself reckons its passes only start saving money above 2400 km of travel within a two-week period – a long distance in Europe, equivalent to a one-way trip from London to the south of Spain, or not quite from London to Athens. Some people tend to overdo it and spend every night they can on the train, and end up too tired to enjoy the sightseeing the next day.

When weighing up options, you should consider the cost of other cheap ticket deals. Travellers aged under 26 can pick up BIJ (Billet International de Jeunesse) tickets which cut fares by up to 50%. Unfortunately, you can't always bank on a substantial reduction: the £115 return from London to Zürich represents just an £8 saving on the normal fare; similarly, London to Munich return saves £10 on the full fare of £146. Various agents issue BIJ tickets in Europe, including Eurotrain (071-730 3402), 52 Grosvenor Gardens, London SW1. Eurotrain also sells circular Explorer tickets for those aged under 26, allowing a different route for the return trip: London to Madrid, for instance, takes in Barcelona, Paris and numerous other cities. The fare for this 'Spanish Explorer' ticket is £185, valid for two months. British Rail International (071-834 2345) and Wasteels (071-834 7066) also sell BIJ tickets.

If you intend to travel extensively within one country, it might be worth getting a national rail pass which allows unlimited travel in that country within a set period. All Western European countries offer their own version of this sort of deal, although to make them pay you may have to travel even more slavishly to a tight schedule than with the pan-European passes. Details can be found in the Getting Around sections in the individual country chapters. You need to plan ahead if you intend to take this option, as some passes can only be purchased prior to arrival in the country concerned.

Other passes that allow ticket discounts are the Rail Europe Family Card and the Rail

Europe Senior Card, worth investigating for families or travellers aged over 60.

TAXI

Taxis in Europe are generally an avoidable and ill-affordable luxury. They are metered and rates are high (watch your savings ebb away), plus there are supplements (depending on the country) for things like luggage, the time of day, the location from which you were picked up, and the presence in the cab of extra people. Good bus, rail and underground railway networks make the taking of taxis all but unnecessary, but if you need one in a hurry they can usually be found idling like a gang of street urchins by train stations. In Spain and Portugal, lower fares make taxis more viable.

CAR & MOTORBIKE

Travelling in your own vehicle is the best way to get to those remote places and it gives you the most flexibility. An added bonus is that, compared to North America or Australia, it is not necessary to spend very long on the road between places of interest. Unfortunately, the independence you enjoy does tend to isolate you to some extent from the local people. Cars are usually inconvenient in city centres, where it is generally worth ditching your trusty chariot and relying on public transport.

Paperwork & Preparations

Proof of ownership of a private vehicle should always be carried (Vehicle Registration Document for British-registered cars) when touring Europe. A British or other European driving licence is acceptable for driving throughout Europe (but not in Turkey). However, to complicate matters, old-style green UK licences are no good for Spain and should be backed up by a Italian translation in Italy. If you have any other type of licence (or even a European one if you're going to Turkey), you should obtain an International Driving Permit from your motoring organisation (see Documents in the earlier Facts for the Visitor chapter).

Third party motor insurance is a minimum requirement in Europe. Most UK motor insurance policies automatically provide this for EC countries and some others. Get your insurer to issue a Green Card (which may cost extra), an internationally recognised proof of insurance, and check that it lists all the countries you intend to visit. Though seldom checked at borders, a Green Card is compulsory, and you'll need it if you're involved in an accident. Also ask your insurer for a European Accident Statement form, which can simplify things if worst comes to worst. Never sign statements you can't read or understand – insist on a translation and sign that only if it's acceptable.

If you want to insure a vehicle you've just purchased (see the following Purchase section) and have a good insurance record, you might be eligible for considerable premium discounts if you can show a letter to this effect from your insurance company back home.

Taking out a European breakdown assistance policy is a good investment, such as the AA Five Star Service or the RAC Eurocover Motoring Assistance. Both of these include a bail bond for Spain, which is also recommended. Ask your motoring organisation for a Card of Introduction, which entitles you to free services offered by sister organisations around Europe (see Documents in the earlier Facts for the Visitor chapter).

Every vehicle travelling across an international border should display a nationality plate of its country of registration (see the International Country Abbreviations appendix in the back of this book). A warning triangle, to be used in the event of breakdown, is compulsory almost everywhere. Recommended accessories are a first-aid kit (compulsory in Austria and Greece), a spare bulb kit, and a fire extinguisher (compulsory in Greece and Turkey). Contact the RAC (☎ 081-686 0088) or the AA (☎ 0256-20123) in the UK for more information.

Road Rules

With the exception of Britain and Ireland, driving is on the right. Vehicles brought over from either of these countries should have their headlights adjusted to avoid blinding oncoming traffic at night (a simple solution on older headlight lenses is to cover up the triangular section of the lens with tape). Priority is usually given to traffic approaching from the right in countries that drive on the right-hand side. The RAC annually brings out its *European Motoring Guide*, which gives an excellent summary of regulations in each country, including parking rules. Motoring organisations in other countries have similar publications.

Take care with speed limits, as they vary significantly from country to country. You may be surprised at the apparent disregard of traffic regulations in some places (particularly in Italy) but as a visitor it is always best to err on the side of caution. Many driving infringements are subject to an on-the-spot fine in all countries except Britain and Ireland. Always ask for a receipt.

Europeans are particularly strict on drink-driving laws. The blood-alcohol concentration (BAC) limit when driving is either 0.05% or 0.08%, but in some areas (eastern Germany, Eastern Europe, Scandinavia) it can be *zero* per cent. See the introductory Getting Around sections in the country chapters for more details on traffic laws.

Roads

Conditions and types of roads vary across Europe, but it is possible to make some generalisations. The fastest routes are four or six-lane dual carriageways, ie two or three lanes either side (motorway, autobahn, autoroute, autostrada etc). These tend to skirt cities and plough though the countryside in straight lines, often avoiding the most scenic bits. Some of these roads incur tolls, often quite hefty (eg in Italy and France, or Switzerland which has a one-off yearly charge for visitors), but there will always be an alternative route you can take. Motorways and other primary routes are universally in good condition.

Road surfaces on minor routes are not so reliable in some countries (eg Portugal) although normally they will be more than adequate. These roads are narrower and

progress is generally much slower. To compensate, you can expect much better scenery and plenty of interesting villages along the way.

Rental

The variety of special deals and terms and conditions attached to car rental can be mind-boggling. However, there are a few pointers that can help you through. The multinationals – Hertz, Avis, Budget Car, and Europe's largest rental agency, Europcar – will give you reliable service and a good standard of vehicle. Usually you will have the option of returning the car to a different outlet at the end of the rental period.

Unfortunately, if you walk into an office and ask for a car on the spot, you will pay over the odds, even allowing for special weekend deals. If you want an on-the-spot deal like this, look to national or local firms, which can often undercut the big boys by up to 40%. Nevertheless, you need to be wary of the neighbourhood cowboy who will take your money and point you towards some clapped-out wreck. Additionally, the rental agreement you sign might be bad news if you have an accident or the car is stolen – a cause for concern if you can't even read what you sign.

If you plan ahead, the multinationals might have the deal for you. Prebooked and prepaid rates are always cheaper, and there are fly/drive combinations and other programmes that are worth looking into. No matter where you rent, make sure you understand what is included in the price (unlimited km, tax, insurance, collision damage waiver etc) and what your liabilities are. The minimum rental age is either 21 or 23, and you'll probably need a credit card (life will certainly be easier with one).

Motorbike and moped rental is common in some countries, such as Italy, Spain and Greece, but it is all too common to see inexperienced riders leap on bikes and very quickly fall off them again. Take care!

Purchase

The purchase of vehicles in some European

countries is illegal for nonresidents of that country. Britain is probably the best place to buy: second-hand prices are good and, whether buying privately or from a dealer, the absence of language difficulties will help you establish exactly what you are getting for your money and what guarantees you can expect in the event of a breakdown. See the Great Britain Getting Around section for information on purchase-paperwork and European insurance.

Bear in mind that you will be getting a left-hand drive car (ie steering wheel on the right) in Britain. If you want right-hand drive and can afford to buy new, prices are low in Belgium, the Netherlands and Luxembourg. Paperwork can be tricky wherever you buy, and many countries have compulsory roadworthiness checks on older vehicles.

Camper Van

A popular way to tour Europe is for three or four people to band together to buy or rent a camper van. London is the usual embarkation point. Look at the adverts in London's free magazine *TNT* if you wish to form or join a group. *TNT* is also a good source for purchasing a van, as is *Loot* newspaper and the Van Market in Market Rd, London N7 (near Caledonian Rd tube station), where private vendors congregate on a daily basis. Some second-hand dealers offer a 'buy-back' scheme for when you return from Europe, but buying and re-selling privately should be more advantageous if you have the time.

Camper vans usually feature a fixed high-top or elevating roof and two to five bunk beds. Apart from the essential camping gas cooker, professional conversions may include a sink, fridge and built-in cupboards. You will need to spend at least £1000 to £1500 (US$1800 to US$2700) for something reliable enough to get you around Europe.

The most common camper van is the VW based on the 1600 cc or 2000 cc Transporter. It has a deserved reputation for reliability and durability, and the additional advantage that spares are widely available throughout Europe. Ford and Bedford camper vans are slightly roomier despite returning a similar fuel consumption to the VW of approximately nine km per litre (25 mpg).

The main advantage of going by camper van is flexibility: with transportation, eating and sleeping requirements all taken care of in one unit, you are tied to nobody's timetable but your own. You don't always need to rely on camping grounds, either. Discrete free camping is not overly encouraged in some countries but it is rarely a problem; however, you may be moved on by the police occasionally in built-up areas. The golden rule is to act responsibly. Don't stop where you will be a nuisance to other road users, and don't damage the countryside or leave litter. Autobahn rest areas are convenient, if not very pleasant, stopover sites.

Camper vanning can work out very cheaply: a group, predominantly free-camping and eating in the van, can get by on under US$30 per person per day. When planning your budget, remember to set some money aside for emergency repairs.

The main disadvantage of camper vanning is that you are in a confined space for much of the time. Four adults in a small van can soon get on each other's nerves, particularly if the group has been formed at short notice. It is not unknown for van members to split up and go their separate ways once in Europe. Tensions can be minimised if you agree on itineraries and daily routines before setting off. When planning your trip, bear in mind that travelling 250 km per day is the maximum with which most people feel comfortable in Europe.

Another disadvantage of camper vans is that they're expensive to buy in spring and hard to sell in autumn. As an alternative, consider a car and tent.

Motorcycle Touring

Europe is made for motorcycle touring, with winding roads of good quality, stunning scenery to stimulate the senses, and an active motorcycling scene. Just make sure your wet-weather gear is up to scratch.

The motorcycle often puts you at a psychological advantage with the locals, and elderly people will often come up and chat enthusiastically about the bikes they used to own (especially in Britain). Sometimes, though, it can have an adverse effect due to the *Easy Rider* image, but motorcyclists so affected often have themselves to blame for living up to it.

The wearing of crash helmets for rider and passenger is compulsory everywhere in Europe nowadays. Austria, Belgium, France, Germany, Luxembourg and Spain also require that motorcyclists use headlights during the day; in other countries it is recommended (it's compulsory throughout Scandinavia and former Yugoslavia).

Motorcycles are often parked on pavements (sidewalks) in Europe. Though this is illegal in some countries, the police usually turn a blind eye so long as the vehicle doesn't obstruct pedestrians. Don't try this in Britain, however. Another advantage is that you very rarely have to book ahead with ferries. Unless you're very unlucky, you can turn up an hour before departure, buy the ticket and they'll usually be able to squeeze you in.

Anyone considering a motorcycle tour from Britain might benefit from joining the International Motorcyclists Tour Club (£14 per annum plus £2 joining fee). It organises European (and worldwide) biking jaunts, and members regularly meet to swap information. Contact Ken Brady, Membership Secretary, Cornerways, Chapel Rd, Swanmore, Southampton, Britain SO3 2QA.

Fuel

Fuel prices can vary enormously from country to country, and savings may be be made by filling up in the right place. For instance, Luxembourg has the cheapest fuel in Europe but prices are much higher in neighbouring Germany (25% more), Belgium (45% more) and France (55% more).

Prices also sometimes bear little relation to the general cost of living in each country. Switzerland, for example, is one of the most expensive countries in Europe yet one of the cheapest when it comes to fuel. The reverse is true for Portugal. Italy used to stand out there on its own by having the most expensive fuel in Europe by far, but prices began to come down after they were deregulated in 1992.

The relative cost of unleaded, super (premium) and diesel is fairly consistent within each country with the exception of Greece, where diesel is very much cheaper. Unleaded petrol is not widely available yet in Portugal or Spain.

BICYCLE

Cycling as a means of getting around is gaining in popularity, but contemplating a tour of Europe on a bike is rather daunting. One organisation that can help is the Cyclists' Touring Club (☎ 0483-417 217), Cotterell House, 69 Meadrow, Godalming, Surrey GU7 3HS, Britain. It can supply information to members on cycling conditions in Europe as well as detailed routes, itineraries and cheap insurance. Membership costs £24 per annum, or £12 to people aged under 18.

A worthwhile book is *Europe by Bike* by Karen & Terry Whitehall (paperback), available in the USA or selected outlets in the UK. It has good descriptions of 18 cycling tours of up to 19 days' duration, although city information should be taken with a pinch of salt.

A primary consideration on a cycling tour is to travel light, but you should take a few tools and spares including a puncture repair kit and and a spare inner tube. Panniers are essential to balance your possessions on either side of the bike frame. A bike helmet is also a very good idea. Take a good bike lock and always use it when you leave your machine unattended.

Seasoned cyclists can average 80 km a day but there's no point in overdoing it. The slower you travel, the more locals you're likely to meet. If you get weary of pedalling or simply want to skip a boring transport section, you can put your feet up on the train. On slower trains, bikes can usually be taken on board as luggage, subject to a small supplementary fee. Fast trains (IC, EC etc) can rarely accommodate bikes: they need to be sent as registered luggage and may end up on a different train from the one you take (the cost varies, from London to Zürich it is £7).

For more information on cycling, see the Activities sections in the earlier Facts for the Visitor chapter and the individual country chapters.

Rental

Cycling doesn't have to be an endurance test; it can be a relaxing (and quiet) means of exploring the countryside. It is easy to hire bikes throughout Europe (except in Portugal) on a half-day, daily or weekly basis. Often it is possible to return the machine at a different outlet so you don't have to double back. Many train stations have bike rental counters, some of which are open 24 hours a day. See the country chapters for more details.

Bringing Your Own

If you want to bring your own bicycle to Europe, you should be able to take it along with you on the plane relatively easily. You can either take it to pieces and pack everything in a bike bag or box, or simply wheel it to the check-in desk, where it should be treated as a piece of baggage. You may have to remove the pedals and turn the handlebars sideways so that it takes up less space in the aircraft's hold; check all this with the airline well in advance, preferably before you pay for your ticket. If your bicycle and other luggage exceed the allowable weight limit, ask about alternatives or you may suddenly find yourself being charged a fortune for excess baggage.

HITCHING

Hitching can be the most rewarding and frustrating way of getting around. Rewarding, because you get to meet and interact with the locals, and are forced into unplanned detours that may yield unexpected treasures off the beaten track. Frustrating, because you may get stuck on the side of the road to nowhere with nowhere (or nowhere cheap) to stay.

Hitchers can end up making good time, but obviously your plans need to be flexible in case a trick of the light makes you appear invisible to passing motorists. A man and woman travelling together is probably the best combination. Two or more men must expect some delays; two women together will make good time and will be reasonably safe. A woman hitching on her own is taking a risk, particularly in Italy and Spain.

Don't try to hitch from city centres: take public transport to suburban exit routes. Hitching is usually illegal on motorways (freeways) – stand on the slip roads, or approach drivers at petrol stations and truck stops. Look presentable and cheerful and make a cardboard sign indicating your intended destination in the local language. Never hitch where drivers can't stop in good time or without causing an obstruction. At dusk, give up and think about finding somewhere to stay. If your itinerary includes a ferry crossing (for instance, across the Channel), it might be worth trying to score a ride before the ferry rather than after, since vehicle tickets sometimes include a number of passengers free of charge.

Dedicated hitchers may wish to invest in *Europe – a Manual for Hitch-hikers* by Simon Calder (paperback), even though it's getting a bit ancient by now. It is sometimes possible to arrange a lift in advance: scan student noticeboards in colleges, or contact car-sharing agencies. Such agencies are particularly popular in France (Allostop-Provoya) and Germany (Mitfahrzentrale). See the relevant country chapters.

Although many travellers hitch many rides in Europe, this is not a totally safe way of getting around. Just because we explain how it works doesn't mean we recommend it.

WALKING

Many city centres are compact enough to enable major tourist sights to be seen on a walking tour, but walking really comes into its own in rural areas. Hikes are an excellent way to leave behind the wail of car horns and the opaque logic of train schedules. For more information, see the Activities section in the earlier Facts for the Visitor chapter, as well as the individual country chapters.

BOAT
Ferries

Several different ferry companies compete on all the main ferry routes. The resulting service is comprehensive but complicated. The same ferry company can have a whole host of different prices for the same route, depending upon the time of day or year, the validity of the ticket, or the length of your vehicle. Vehicle tickets may sometimes cover up to five passengers free of charge. It is worth planning (and booking) ahead where possible as there may be special reductions on off-peak crossings. On English Channel routes, apart from one-day or short-term excursion returns, there is little price advantage in buying a return ticket as against two singles.

The Sealink-Stena Line is the largest ferry company in the world and services British, Irish and Scandinavian routes. The shortest cross-Channel routes (Dover to Calais, or Folkestone to Boulogne) are also the busiest. Italy (Brindisi or Bari) to Greece (Corfu, Igoumenitsa, Patras or Piraeus) is also a popular route. Rail-pass holders are entitled to discounts or free travel on some lines (see the earlier Train section).

Food is often expensive on ferries, so it is worth bringing your own when possible. It is also worth knowing that if you take your vehicle on board, you are usually denied access to it during the voyage. For further information, see the Getting There & Away sections in the relevant country chapters.

Steamers

Europe's main lakes and rivers are serviced by steamers, and not surprisingly, schedules are more extensive in the summer months. Rail-pass holders are entitled to some dis-

counts (see the earlier Train section). Extended boat trips should be considered as relaxing and scenic excursions; viewed merely as a functional means of transport, they can be grotesquely expensive.

It is possible to take a cruise up the Rhine all the way from the Netherlands to Switzerland but you'll need a boatload of money to do so. The main operator along the Rhine is the German Köln-Düsseldorfer Line (☎ 0221-2 08 82 88) based in Cologne.

TOURS

Young people who like travelling in a group with like-minded revellers may consider joining one of the youth-oriented tour buses which are based on hotel or camping accommodation. In London, Contiki (☎ 081-290 6422) offers a variety of tours starting from 14 days for £420 (plus food fund). Tracks (☎ 071-937 3028) can work out slightly cheaper. Top Deck (☎ 071-370 6487) has the added novelty of tours where you travel and sleep in a converted double-decker bus. Student or youth travel agencies in other countries have similar deals.

For people aged over 60, Saga Holidays (☎ 0800-300 500), Saga Building, Middelburg Square, Folkstone, Kent CT20 1AZ, Britain, offers holidays ranging from cheap coach tours to luxury cruises. Saga also operates in the USA (☎ 617-451 6808), 120 Boyleston St, Boston, MA 02116; and Australia (☎ 02-957 4222), Level 4, 20 Alfred St, Milsons Point, Sydney 2061.

National tourist offices in most countries offer organised trips to points of interest. These may range from two-hour city tours to several-day circular excursions. They often work out more expensively than going it alone, but are sometimes worth it if you are pressed for time. A short city tour will give you a quick overview of the place and can be a good way to begin your visit.

Andorra

The Catalan-speaking Principality of Andorra (population 52,000), whose mountainous territory comprises only 468 sq km, is nestled between France and Spain in the middle of the Pyrenees. Except for the novelty of visiting such a tiny political anomaly, it's hard to think of a compelling reason to come to Andorra unless you need to do some duty-free shopping.

Facts about the Country

Andorra is officially a 'co-principality' because its sovereignty is invested in the persons of two 'co-princes', the President of the French Republic (who inherited the job from France's pre-Revolutionary kings, to whom the position had passed from the Counts of Foix in the 16th century) and the Catholic bishop of the Spanish town of La Seu d'Urgell. This arrangement dates from the late 13th century.

When it comes to day-to-day affairs, the country is ruled by the Consell General (General Council), a parliament whose forerunner was established in 1419. It has 28 members, four from each parish. Women were given the right to vote in 1970. Andorra is not a member of the EC (European Community).

LANGUAGE

The official language is Catalan, which is closely related to *Castellano* (Castilian Spanish) and, to a lesser extent, French. Numerous trilingual restaurant menus provide a good opportunity to compare Catalan with Spanish and French.

See the language sections in the France and Spain chapters in this book.

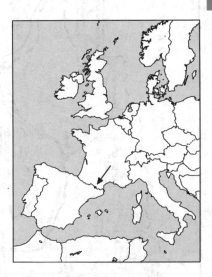

Facts for the Visitor

VISAS & EMBASSIES

You do not need a visa to visit Andorra – the Andorran authorities figure that if Spain or France have let you in, that's good enough for them. The principality does not have any diplomatic legations abroad. There are no embassies in the capital, Andorra la Vella.

MONEY

Andorra, which has no currency of its own, uses the French franc and the Spanish peseta (see the chapters on France and Spain for details). Except in Pas de la Casa (on the French frontier), prices are usually marked in pesetas. If you opt to pay in francs, the exchange rate selected by the merchant may not be the most favourable.

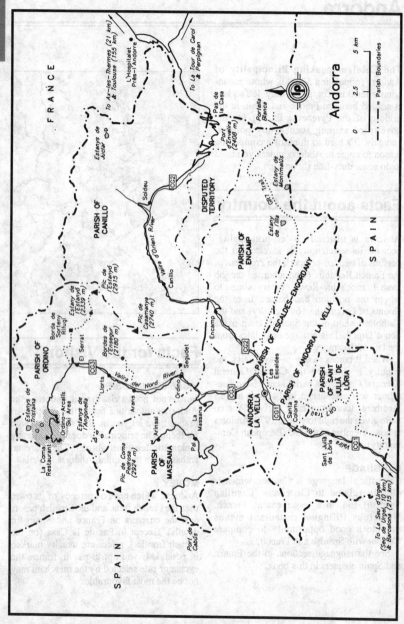

Andorra

FRANCE

To La Tour de Carol & Perpignan

L'Hospitalet Près-l'Andorre

To Ax-les-Thermes (21 km) & Toulouse (155 km)

Estanys de Juclar

Pas de la Casa

Port d'Envalira (2408 m)

Portella Blanca

CG2

Soldeu

PARISH OF CANILLO

DISPUTED TERRITORY

Estany de Montmalús

CG1 Trail

PARISH OF ENCAMP

Estany de l'Illa

SPAIN

Canillo

Valira d'Orient River

Pic de l'Estanyó (2915 m)

Estany de l'Estanyó (2339 m)

Pic de Casamanya (2740 m)

Borda de Sorteny Rifugi

El Serrat

Bordes de l'Ensegur (2180 m)

PARISH OF ORDINO

Estanys de Tristaina

Ordino–Arcalís Ski Area

Estanys de l'Angonella

La Coma Restaurant

Llorts

Arans

Segudet

Ordino

CG3

Valira del Nord River

PARISH OF ESCALDES–ENGORDANY

CG2

Encamp

Les Escaldes

PARISH OF ANDORRA LA VELLA

CG3

La Massana

ANDORRA LA VELLA

Arinsal

PARISH OF MASSANA

Pal

Pic de Coma Pedrosa (2924 m)

Santa Coloma

CG1

CG1 Trail

PARISH OF SANT JULIÀ DE LÒRIA

Sant Julià de Lòria

Valira River

Port de Cabús

SPAIN

To La Seu d'Urgell (Seo de Urgel, 3 km) & Barcelona (215 km)

0   2.5   5 km

· – · – · = Parish Boundaries

Exchange Rates

US$1	=	5FF	=	105 pta
UK£1	=	8.5FF	=	178.9 pta
A$1	=	3.6FF	=	71 pta
1FF	=			19.7 pta
100 pta	=	5.1FF		

POST & TELECOMMUNICATIONS

Post

The postal systems of France and Spain each operate separate networks of post offices in Andorra. Andorran stamps printed, issued, sold and – attached to letters – delivered by the French post office are in francs, while those printed, issued, sold and delivered by the Spanish system are in pesetas. Andorran stamps of both types are valid only for items posted within Andorra and are necessary only for international mail – letters mailed in Andorra to destinations inside the principality are free and do not need stamps. Regular French and Spanish stamps cannot be used in the principality.

International postal rates are the same as those of the issuing country. For overseas mail, the French tariffs are slightly cheaper, and locals advise that you are better off routing all international mail (except letters to Spain) via France by using French stamps. There are two kinds of postboxes – one for each postal system – but if you use the 'wrong' one your letter will be transferred to the other system for processing.

Telephones

To call Andorra from France, dial 628 (16 628 in Paris) before the five-digit local number. From Spain, dial 9738 before the local number. To call Andorra from other countries, dial the international access code, 34 (Spain's country code), 738 (Andorra's Spanish regional code), and then the five-digit local number. You can also dial the international access code, 33 (France's country code), 628 and then the local number.

To call France from Andorra, dial 7 (71 for the Paris area) and then the eight-digit local number. For Spain, dial 9 and then the regional prefix followed by the local number. To call other countries, dial 0 followed by the country code, area code and local number.

Except for a few older phones that take pesetas (or, at Pas de la Casa, francs), public telephones use Andorran *tele-tarjas*, which operate on the same principle as the télé-cartes (telephone cards) used in France (see the Facts for the Visitor section in the France chapter for details). Tele-tarjas can be purchased at post offices, tobacconists and tourist offices. Telephone rates are 50% cheaper between 10 pm and 8 am and all day on Sunday and public holidays. Reverse-charges (collect) calling is not available except to Spain, and then only from the STA calling offices in Andorra la Vella (see Information in the Andorra la Vella section) and Sant Julià de Lòria.

TIME

Andorra is one hour ahead of GMT/UTC in winter and two hours ahead during summer.

ELECTRICITY

The electric current is either 220V or 125V, both at 50 Hz.

ACTIVITIES

Hiking

There are some beautiful hiking areas in the north-west of the country (see the Parish of Ordino section). The GR-7 trail, which traverses the Pyrenees from the Mediterranean to the Atlantic, crosses the southern part of Andorra. Hikers can sleep for free in the numerous *refugi* (mountain huts for use by shepherds and hikers).

A 1:50,000 scale *mapa topogràfic* of the country costs 475 pta in bookshops. Maps in 1:10,000 scale (10 cm = 1 km) are also available.

Skiing

For information on Andorra's five ski areas (*estació d'esquí*), enquire at one of the capital's tourist offices. Two of the largest are Ordino-Arcalís (see the Parish of Ordino section) and Pal (☎ 36236). Ski passes cost about 2500 pta a day.

ACCOMMODATION

There are no youth hostels in Andorra. The 26 refugi, most of which have bunks, fireplaces and sources of potable water, are free and do not require reservations. Tourist offices have maps indicating the location of each refugi.

By law, you must present a passport or national identity card when registering at a hotel.

Getting There & Away

LAND

Short-Haul Bus

The Societat Franco-Andorrana de Transports and La Hispano Andorrana (☎ 21372 for both) handle bus transport from Andorra la Vella (Plaça Guillemó, to be exact) to La Seu d'Urgell (also known as Seo de Urgel; 230 pta; 45 minutes) in Spain, L'Hospitalet Près-l'Andorre (630 pta or 34FF; two to three hours) in France and, between May and October, Ax-les-Thermes (780 pta or 42FF; 2¼ to 3¼ hours), also in France. The runs to France cross Port d'Envalira, which, at an elevation of 2408 metres, is the highest pass in the Pyrenees. The company's office at 14 Carrer La Llacuna, around the corner from Plaça Guillemó, is open Monday to Saturday from 9.30 am to 1.30 pm and 3 to 7 pm and on Sunday from 9.30 am to 2 pm. The left-luggage room, open the same hours as the office, charges only 50 pta a day.

Long-Haul Bus

Alsina Graells (☎ 26567, 27379), at 24 Carrer Prat de la Creu in Andorra la Vella, has four buses a day (the last at 2.30 pm) to Barcelona. The trip costs 1815 pta and takes either 3½ hours, via the Cadí Tunnel, or 4½ hours. Its Barcelona office (☎ 302 4086, 302 6545) is at 4 Ronda Universitat.

A number of other companies (☎ 26289), also at 24 Carrer Prat de la Creu, handle long-distance transport to Spain and southeastern France. Cities served include Madrid (☎ 468 4236), Murcia (☎ 968-29 1911) and Tuy (☎ 968-63 0375) in Spain, and Toulouse (☎ 61.58.14.53) and Nice (☎ 93.80.08.70) in France. The office is closed on Friday.

Train

The train station in Spain nearest the Andorran border is at Puigcerdà, whence it's a one-hour bus trip to La Seu d'Urgell (10 km south of the Andorran frontier). The closest French train stations to Andorra are at L'Hospitalet Près-l'Andorre (bus connections all year) and Ax-les-Thermes (bus connections from May to October only). For information on bus transport from these railheads, see the Short-Haul Bus section. You might want to call the relevant bus company in order to synchronise your train travel with the bus schedules.

Getting Around

BUS

The Cooperativa Interurbana (☎ 20412) is responsible for bus transport within Andorra. It has three lines from Andorra la Vella: to Sant Julià de Lòria (75 pta; from Plaça Guillemó), to Encamp (75 pta; from Plaça Princep Benlloch), and to Ordino (85 pta; from Plaça Princep Benlloch). All three services operate every day about twice an hour from 7 am (7.30 am on Sunday) to 9.30 pm (8.30 pm to Ordino). The company's office is at 21 Avinguda Princep Benlloch; go into the shopping arcade, up the stairs and to the left.

Andorra la Vella

Andorra la Vella (Vella is pronounced 'Vey-yah'; population 17,000), the capital of the principality and its largest town, is situated at an elevation of 1000 metres in the Valira River valley. The town is given over almost entirely to the retailing of tax-free electronics and luxury goods. Unless you love to shop, there isn't much to do in this overgrown duty-free bazar. If they put a roof over the area, added a few fountains and spruced things up a bit, they could call it a shopping mall... Andorra La Malla, perhaps!

Orientation

Andorra la Vella is strung out along the main drag, Avinguda Meritxell and its continuation, Avinguda Princep Benlloch. The Historic Quarter (Barri Antic) is between Plaça Princep Benlloch and the area around Casa de la Vall.

Information

Tourist Office The helpful municipal tourism office (Caseta d'Informació i Turisme; ☎ 27117), across the street from 44 Avinguda Meritxell, is open Monday to Saturday from 9 am to 1 pm and 4 to 7 pm and on Sunday from 9 am to 5 pm. During July and August, it's open daily from 9 am to 9 pm (7 pm on Sunday). The office has maps, all sorts of brochures, postage stamps and telephone cards. An excellent booklet entitled *The Parish of Andorra la Vella* (50 pta) gives lots of background on the capital and includes a number of hiking suggestions.

The National Tourist Office (Sindicat d'Iniciativa Oficina de Turisme; ☎ 20214) is at the top of Carrer Doctor Vilanova between Plaça del Poble and Plaça Rebés. It is open Monday to Saturday from 10 am (9 am in July and August) to 1 pm and 3 to 7 pm. On Sunday, hours are 10 am to 1 pm.

Money Banks are open weekdays from 9 am to 1 pm and 3 to 5 pm and on Saturday from 9 am to noon. There are banks every 100 metres or so along Avinguda Meritxell (at Nos 32, 40, 61, 80 and 96), at Plaça Princep Benlloch (next to No 2) and on Avinguda Princep Benlloch (No 25). The Banc Internacional (☎ 20043) at 32 Avinguda Meritxell has a 24-hour automatic teller machine that processes Visa and MasterCard cash advances. Crèdit Andorrà, next to the river at 80 Avinguda Meritxell, has a 24-hour currency exchange machine.

Post The main French post office (☎ 20408), La Poste Correus Francesos, is at 1 Carrer Pere d'Urg. It is open weekdays from 9 am to noon and 3 to 6 pm and on Saturday from 9 am to noon. During July and August, weekday hours are 9 am to 7 pm. All purchases must be made with French francs.

The main Spanish post office, Correus Espanyols (☎ 20657), is three blocks away at 10 Carrer Joan Maragall. It is open weekdays from 9 am to 1 pm and 3 to 5 pm and on Saturday from 9 am to 1 pm. They accept pesetas only.

Telephone International calls (non-reverse charges *only*, except to Spain) can be placed at the Servei de Telecomunicacions d'Andorra (STA; ☎ 21021) at 110 Avinguda Meritxell, which is open every day from 9 am to 9 pm.

Things to See

Casa de la Vall Casa de la Vall (☎ 21234), built in 1580 as the private home of a wealthy family, has served as Andorra's parliament since 1702. Downstairs is the only courtroom in the whole country, Sala de la Justicia. There are free guided visits in Catalan, French, Spanish and sometimes English about once an hour from 9.30 am to noon and 4 to 6 pm on weekdays and every other Saturday morning. The **Museu Filatèlic** (Philatelic Museum; ☎ 29129) on the 2nd floor is open Monday to Saturday from 9 am to 1 pm and 3 to 7 pm (mornings only in July and August).

Places to Stay

Camping *Camping Valira* (☎ 22384), which is at the southern edge of town off Avinguda de Salou, charges 400 pta per person, 400 pta for a tent and 400 pta for a car. It is open all year and always has space in the morning.

Hotels There are a number of hotels in the centre of town around Plaça Guillemó. Two

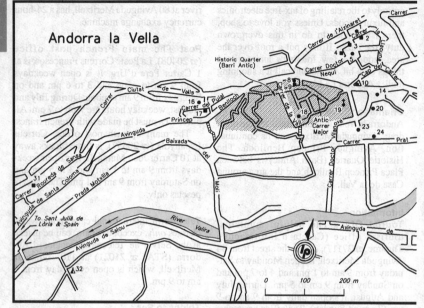

Andorra la Vella

Historic Quarter
(Barri Antic)

	PLACES TO STAY	13	Restaurant Marti	16	Plaçeta del Puial
2	Residència Benazet	21	Pizzeria La Mossegada	18	Casa de la Vall &
3	Hostal del Sol	30	McDonald's		Philatelic Museum
4	Hotel des Arcades			19	Sant Esteve Church
6	Hotel Residència Albert		OTHER	20	National Tourist Office
7	Hotel El Roure	1	Short-Haul Bus Compa-	22	Crèdit Andorrà 24-hour
9	Pensió La Rosa		nies		Currency Exchange
13	Hotel Costa	5	Plaça Guillemó		Machine
17	Residència Baró	8	Cooperativa Interurb-	23	Plaça del Poble
31	Hotel Enclar		ana (Domestic	24	Public Lift
32	Camping Valira		Buses)	25	Alsina Graells & Long-
		10	Plaça Princep Benlloch		Haul Bus Companies
▼	PLACES TO EAT	12	Municipal Tourism	26	Police
			Office	27	French Post Office
11	Pyrénées Department	14	Plaça Rebés	28	Spanish Post Office
	Store & Supermarket	15	Banc Internacional	29	STA Telephone Office

other groups of hotels are found north-east and south-west of the centre of town.

Centre *Residència Benazet* (☎ 20698) is at 21 Carrer La Llacuna, around the corner from Plaça Guillemó, the terminus for many buses from Spain and France. Large, service-able rooms for one to four people cost 1200

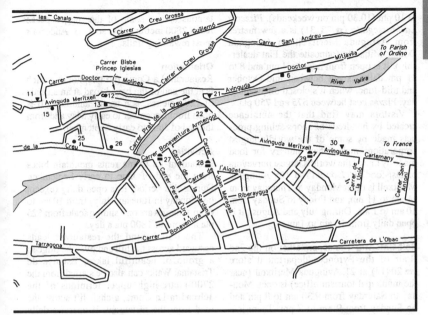

pta per person. The *Hostal del Sol* (☎ 23701) at 3 Plaça Guillemó has tiny, utilitarian doubles/triples from 3000/4000 pta (perhaps a bit less in the off season). Quads cost 4500 to 6000 pta depending on the time of year. The hotel is closed in November. Not far away, at 5 Plaça Guillemó, is the *Hotel des Arcades* (☎ 26693, 21355), which has doubles/triples including breakfast from 3000/4000 pta.

Pensió La Rosa (☎ 21810) at 18 Antic Carrer Major, not far from Casa de la Vall, has nondescript singles/doubles for 1600/2800 pta and triples/quads for 3300/4400 pta. The *Hotel Costa* (☎ 21439) at 44 Avinguda Meritxell has basic but clean singles, doubles, triples and quads for 1200 pta per person. Reception is on the 3rd floor; take the stairs on the left of the ground-floor shopping arcade.

South *Residència Baró* (☎ 21484), also known as Habitacions Baró, is at 21 Carrer del Puial, which is at the top of the stairs opposite 53 Avinguda Princep Benlloch. This place, one of the cheapest in town, *may* have rooms for 1350 to 1600 pta. Nearby, the *Hotel Enclar* (☎ 20310) at 18 Carrer Roureda de Sansa has doubles/quads for 2700/4400 pta. Doubles/quads with shower and toilet cost 3200/5850 pta.

North *Hotel El Roure* (☎ 25483) at 24 Avinguda Doctor Mitjavila has doubles for 3100 pta. *Hotel Residència Albert* (☎ 20156), down the block at 16 Avinguda Doctor Mitjavila, has singles/doubles for 1500/3000 pta. This place does not accept telephone reservations.

Places to Eat

Restaurants *Restaurant Marti* (☎ 20946), hidden at the back of the 1st floor of the building at 44 Avinguda Meritxell, has *menus* for 38 and 55FF. It is open daily from noon to 3.30 pm (4 pm on weekends) and 8 to 10 pm (10.30 pm on weekends). *Pizzeria La Mossegada* (☎ 23131) is a few metres from Avinguda Meritxell on Avinguda Doctor Mitjavila (opposite the Fiat dealership). It is open from noon to 4 pm and 8 to 11 pm daily except between mid-October and mid-June, when it's closed on Wednesday. Pizzas cost between 575 and 750 pta.

Visitors may find that the ambience created by hundreds of shops selling products made by some of the world's largest corporations makes them hungry for food made by one of the world's largest purveyors of fast-food. *McDonald's* at 105 Avinguda Meritxell is open Monday to Thursday from 11 am to 11 pm, and Friday to Sunday from 10 am to 1 am. During July and August, it is open daily from 10 am to 1am.

Self-Catering The supermarket on the 2nd floor of the Pyrénées department store (☎ 20414) at 21 Avinguda Meritxell (near the municipal tourism office) is open Monday to Saturday from 9.30 am to 8 pm and on Sunday from 9 am to 7 pm. There is a *Godiva* chocolate shop near the checkout counters but expect to pay at least 4500 pta per kg!

Getting There & Away
International bus lines and domestic buses to Sant Julià de Lòria leave from Plaça Guillemó (in front of the Hostal del Sol); buses to Ordino and Encamp depart from Plaça Princep Benlloch. For more information, see the Getting There & Away and Getting Around sections at the start of this chapter.

The Parish of Ordino

ORDINO-ARCALÍS SKI AREA
The Ordino-Arcalís ski area (☎ 64500, 36320), one of Andorra's largest, is at the far north-western corner of the principality. During the winter, there are 11 lifts (mostly tow lines) and 16 ski runs of all levels of difficulty. In summer, this beautiful mountainous area – some of the rugged peaks reach 2800 metres – has some of Andorra's most rewarding trails.

Orientation
Restaurant La Coma (no telephone), which is at the end of the paved road at an altitude of 2200 metres, is a useful landmark. It is open from December to early May and from the end of June to early September.

Activities
Restaurant La Coma rents mountain bikes from the end of June to early September. During this period, it is open daily (except on Monday in June and July) from 10 am to 6 pm. Charges are on a sliding scale from 525 pta an hour to 1800 pta a day.

The trail behind the restaurant leads eastward across the hill and over the ridge to a group of beautiful lakes, Estanys de Tristaina. Walks can also be started from the 2700-metre-high upper terminus of the Telecadira La Coma, a chair lift across the road from the restaurant. It operates daily during July and August from 10 am to 5 pm. In summer, fees are 350/500 pta one-way/return.

Getting There & Away
The only way to get up here is to drive or hitchhike.

LLORTS
The tiny mountain village of Llorts (pronounced 'Yorts'; population 99; 1413 metres) has retained its traditional architecture, tobacco fields and near-pristine mountain setting. This is one of the most unadulterated spots in the whole country.

Things to See & Do
A trail leads up the valley west of town (along Riu de l'Angonella) to a group of lakes, Estanys de l'Angonella. Count on it taking 3½ hours to get up there.

From slightly north of the village of El Serrat (population 53; 1600 metres), which is four km up the valley from Llorts, a secondary road leads to the Borda de Sorteny refugi. From there, a trail continues on to Estany (lake) de l'Estanyó (2339 metres) and Pic (mountain) de l'Estanyó (2915 metres).

From Arans (population 72; 1360 metres), a village which is a couple of km south of Llorts, a trail goes north-eastward to Bordes de l'Ensegur (2180 metres), where there is an old shepherds' hut.

Places to Stay
Some 200 metres north of Llorts is *Camping Els Pradassos* (☎ 37142, proprietor's home ☎ 22550), perhaps the most beautiful camping ground in all of Andorra. It's open from the end of June to early September. This place, named after the cow pasture in which it is located (every field in Andorra has a proper name), is also surrounded by forested mountains and has its very own spring. It costs 175 pta per person, 175 pta for a tent and 175 pta for a vehicle. Bring your own food.

The *Hotel Vilaró* (☎ 35225), 200 metres south of the village limits, has doubles with washbasin and bidet for 2800 pta. It is open all year except from mid-November to Christmas (25 December).

Getting There & Away
There may be a bus down to Andorra la Vella around 8 am; it drives back up to Llorts in the evening. Otherwise, the nearest bus stop is at Ordino, five km down the valley.

ORDINO
Ordino (population 743; 1298 metres) is much larger than Llorts but, despite recent development, has also kept its Andorran character.

Orientation & Information
The tourist office kiosk (Ofici de Turisme; ☎ 36963) is on highway CG3. There are a number of banks at the Plaça, which is 50 metres up the hill from the tourist office.

Things to See & Do
The **Casa d'Areny de Plandolit** (☎ 36908) is a 17th century house of typically Andorran design that has been turned into a museum.

There is a trail from Ordino via the village of Segudet northward up the mountainside towards the top of Pic de Casamanya (2740 metres).

Places to Stay & Eat
Just off the Plaça, in the alley behind Crèdit Andorrà, is the *Hotel Quim* (☎ 35013), which is run by a friendly older woman. Doubles/triples with shower cost 3000/3500 pta.

There is a food shop, *Commerç Fleca Font,* which also sells bread, at the Plaça near the Banc Internacional. It is open from 7 am to 2 pm and 4 to 8 pm daily except Sunday afternoon. Spring water flows from two spouts right outside the door.

Getting There & Away
The bus from Andorra la Vella (85 pta), which departs from Plaça Princep Benlloch, runs daily about every 30 minutes from 7 am (7.30 am on Sunday) to 8.30 pm.

Austria

Austria (Österreich) is situated at the crossroads of Europe. Surrounded on its eastern borders by what used to be socialist countries, politically and economically it has always belonged very much to the West. Today it is one of the most popular destinations in Europe. Its rich cultural heritage, winter sports and stunning scenery are a hard combination to beat. In Vienna it has one of the great capital cities anywhere, in Salzburg a living Baroque museum, in Innsbruck a city set in a perfect panorama of peaks. And everywhere you go, the country moves to the rhythm of its unrivalled musical tradition.

Facts about the Country

HISTORY

In its early years the land that became Austria was constantly invaded by tribes and armies approaching particularly by way of the Danube Valley. The Romans, Vandals, Visigoths, Huns, Avars and Slavs all made their mark and were beaten back by successive invaders. Charlemagne established a territory in the Danube Valley known as the Ostmark in 803, which was later undermined by invading Magyars and ultimately re-established by Otto I in 955. In 962 Pope John XII crowned Otto as Holy Roman Emperor of the German princes.

A period of growth and consolidation followed under the Babenbergs, during which time trade and prosperity increased and the territory acquired the status of a duchy. Influence in what is now Lower Austria expanded and the duchy of Styria came under central control in 1192. The last Babenberg died in battle in 1246. A time of uncertainty followed until the territory fell into the hands of the Habsburgs in 1278. One of the most powerful dynasties in history, their influence was to extend to the 20th century.

Under the rule of the Habsburgs, Austrian

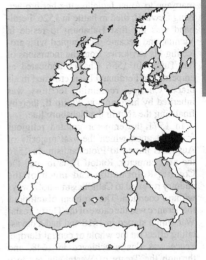

territory gradually extended. Carinthia (Kärnten) and Carniola were annexed in 1335, followed by Tirol in 1363. Generally, however, the Habsburgs preferred to extend their lands without force. Much of Vorarlberg was purchased from bankrupt lordships, but by far the most significant gains were achieved by politically motivated marriages. The intermarriage policy was extremely effective although it did have a genetic side-effect: a distended lower jaw became an increasingly visible family trait, albeit discreetly ignored in official portraits.

In 1477 Maximilian gained control of Burgundy and the Netherlands by marriage to Maria of Burgundy. His eldest son, Philip, was married to the infanta of Spain in 1496. The person who gained most was Philip's son Charles. He became Charles I of Spain in 1516 (which included control of vast overseas territories) and also Charles V of the Holy Roman Empire in 1519.

All these acquisitions were too diverse for

one person to rule effectively. Charles handed over the Austrian territories to his younger brother Ferdinand in 1521, who also inherited Hungary and Bohemia through his marriage to Anna Jagiello after her brother, King Lewis II, died in battle in 1526. Ferdinand was the first Habsburg to reside in Vienna, and became preoccupied with protecting his territories from the incursions of the Turks. In 1556 Charles abdicated as emperor and Ferdinand I was crowned in his place. Charles' remaining territory was inherited by his own son, Philip II, thereby finalising the split in the Habsburg line.

In 1571 the emperor granted religious freedom, upon which the vast majority of Austrians turned to Protestantism. In 1576 the new emperor, Rudolf II, embraced the Counter-Reformation and much of the country reverted to Catholicism – not always without coercion. The problem of religious intolerance was the cause of the Thirty Years' War which started in 1618 and had a devastating effect on the whole of central Europe. Peace was finally achieved in 1648, and through the Treaty of Westphalia territory was lost to France. For much of the rest of the century, Austria was preoccupied with halting the advance of the Turks into Europe and towards Vienna in particular.

In 1740 Maria Theresa ascended to the throne, despite the fact that as a woman she was ineligible to do so. A war followed to ensure that she stayed there. Her rule lasted 40 years, and is generally acknowledged as a golden era in which Austria developed as a modern state. Centralised control was established along with a civil service. The army and economy were reformed and a public education system was introduced. But progress was halted with the appearance of Napoleon, who defeated Austria at Austerlitz in 1805 and forced the dissolution of the title of Holy Roman Emperor. European conflict dragged on until the settlement at the Congress of Vienna in 1814-15, which was dominated by the Austrian foreign minister, Klemens von Metternich. Austria was left with control of the German Confederation until forced to relinquish it in the Austro-Prussian War in 1866. Thereafter Austria had no place in the new German Empire unified by Bismarck.

In the meantime Metternich and the Austrian emperor had been ousted in the revolutions of 1848. The new emperor, Franz Josef, became head of the dual Austro-Hungarian monarchy, created in 1867, under which there was a common defence, foreign and economic policy. Nevertheless, unity was not complete, as two separate parliaments remained. Another period of prosperity began during which Vienna in particular developed. The situation changed in 1914 when the emperor's nephew was assassinated in Sarajevo on 28 June. A month later Austria-Hungary declared war on Serbia and WW I began.

In 1916 Franz Josef died. His successor abdicated at the conclusion of the war in 1918 and the Republic of Austria was created on 12 November. The new state was much smaller than that before the war. In 1919 Austria was forced to recognise the independent states of Czechoslovakia, Poland, Hungary and Yugoslavia, which, along with Romania and Bulgaria, had previously been largely under the control of the Habsburgs. The loss of so much land caused severe economic difficulties which in turn caused political and social unrest. More problems were to be created by the rise of the Nazis in Germany. They tried to start a civil war in Austria and succeeded in killing Chancellor Dolfuss. Hitler was then able to manipulate the new chancellor to increase the power of the National Socialists. He was so successful that German troops met little resistance when they invaded Austria in 1938 and incorporated it into the German Reich. A national referendum in April of that year actually supported the annexation.

Austria was subjected to bombing during WW II, and in 1945 the victorious Allies restored Austria to its 1937 frontiers. There began a period of occupation by the four powers – the USA, the Soviet Union, Britain and France. The whole country was divided into four zones. Vienna, within the Soviet zone, was itself divided into four zones.

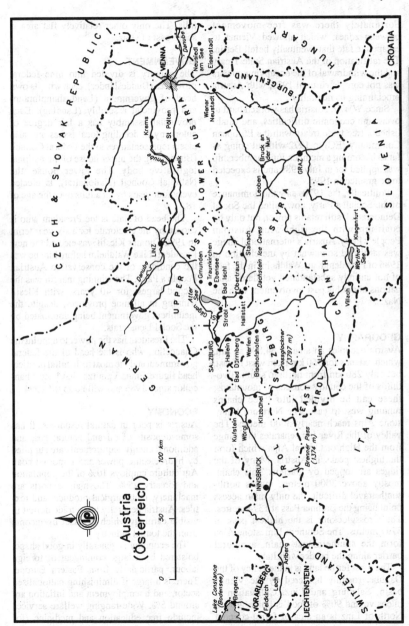

Austria
(Österreich)

0   50   100 km

Lake Constance
(Bodensee)

SWITZERLAND

Bregenz

VORARLBERG
Feldkirch Lech
Arlberg

LIECHTENSTEIN

GERMANY

CZECH & SLOVAK REPUBLIC

Danube

Krems

St Pölten

Melk

Danube

LINZ

UPPER AUSTRIA

Alter See

Traunkirchen Gmunden
Ebensee
Bad Ischl
Obertraun
Strobl
Hallstatt
IS
SALZBURG

Hallein Dürrnberg
Werfen
Bischofshofen
Bad Dürrnberg

Kitzbühel

Kufstein
Wörgl

INNSBRUCK

TIROL

Brenner Pass
(1374 m)

Gschütt

Dachstein Ice Caves
Stainach

Grossglockner
(3797 m)

Lienz

EAST TIROL

ITALY

VIENNA

Danube

Neusiedl
am See Eisenstadt

Wiener
Neustadt

LOWER AUSTRIA

BURGENLAND

Bruck an
der Mur

Leoben

STYRIA

GRAZ

SLOVENIA

CARINTHIA

Klagenfurt

Wörther
See

Villach

HUNGARY

CROATIA

AUSTRIA

Fortunately there was free movement between zones, which allowed Vienna to escape the fate that eventually befell Berlin. The ratification of the Austrian State Treaty and the withdrawal of the occupying powers was not completed until 1955, with Austria proclaiming its neutrality.

Since WW II, Austria has worked hard to overcome economic difficulties, and established a free trade treaty with the European Community (EC) in 1972 without going as far as becoming a member. Full membership was applied for in July 1989 and is expected to be granted in 1995.

Politically, the 1970s saw the dominance of the Socialist Party, now called the Social Democrats. It still retains power, but only by coalition with the right-wing Austrian People's Party. Austria's international image was tarnished somewhat by the election in 1986 of President Kurt Waldheim in the face of not entirely substantiated yet fierce allegations about his past involvement with the Nazis.

GEOGRAPHY

Austria occupies an area of 84,800 sq km, which extends for 560 km from west to east, but only 280 km from north to south. Two-thirds of the country consists of mountains; these can be divided into three chains running west to east. The Northern Limestone Alps reach nearly 3000 metres. The valley of the River Inn separates this range from the High or Central Alps which form the highest peaks in Austria. Many of the ridges are topped by glaciers. This chain, mostly above 3000 metres, makes north-south travel difficult, the only main access point being the Brenner Pass at 1374 metres. The Grossglockner is the highest peak at 3797 metres. The Southern Limestone Alps form the southernmost chain, a natural barrier along the border with Italy.

The most fertile land is in the valley of the Danube, roughly bordered by the Vienna basin, Salzburg and Linz. Cultivation is intensive and 90% of food is home-grown. North of Linz is an area of forest-covered hills. The only other relatively flat area is south-east of Graz.

GOVERNMENT

The country is divided into nine federal provinces (Bundesländer), each with its own head of government (Landeshauptmann) and provincial assembly (Landtag). Each provincial assembly has a fair degree of autonomy in deciding local issues and also elects representatives to the Federal Council (Bundesrat), the upper house of the national legislative body. The lower house, the National Council (Nationalrat), is elected every four years by all adults over the age of 18.

The head of state is the President who is chosen by the electorate for a six-year term. In 1992 Thomas Klestil was elected the new President. Like Waldheim before him he was the candidate of the conservative Austrian People's Party. The winning margin was the second-largest for 40 years, with Klestil winning in all nine provinces, despite the incumbent government being dominated by the Social Democrats.

The President has the power to appoint the Chancellor, who is the head of the federal government and the most influential political head figure. Franz Vranitzky has been Chancellor since 1986 and will be so till 1994.

ECONOMY

Austria is poor in natural resources. It has some deposits of oil and natural gas, and additional energy requirements are supplied by hydroelectric power and imported coal. Agriculture employs 10% of the population and forestry 25%. The main exports are machinery, metallurgical products and textiles. Austria generally has a trade deficit in visible earnings which is offset by income from the tourist industry.

The economy is generally in good shape, bolstered by a large contingent of foreign labour, particularly from Eastern Europe. There is a large if diminishing nationalised sector, and unemployment and inflation are around 5%. Wide-ranging welfare services include free education and medicine (for locals) and a good pensions and housing policy.

POPULATION & PEOPLE

The north-east is the most densely populated region. The five main cities of Vienna, Linz, Salzburg, Innsbruck and Graz account for 30% of the 7.5-million population. Overall there are only 90 inhabitants per sq km. Native Austrians are almost entirely of Germanic origin. National service is compulsory, but men may opt out of the military in favour of civil-service duties. Women are not conscripted and cannot even volunteer to join the armed services.

ARTS

Above all else, Austria is known for music. Composers throughout Europe were drawn to Austria and especially Vienna in the 18th and 19th centuries by the willingness of the Habsburgs to patronise this medium. The various forms of classical music, symphony, concerto, sonata, opera and operetta were explored and developed by the most eminent exponents of the day. The waltz originated in Vienna in the 19th century and was perfected as a musical genre by the father and son who shared the same name, Johann Strauss. The musical tradition continued in the 20th century with the innovative work of Arnold Schönberg. Today, Austrian orchestras have a worldwide reputation, and important yearly musical festivals are held in Vienna, Salzburg and Graz.

Architecture is also important in Austria's cultural heritage. The Gothic style was popular in the 14th, 15th and 16th centuries. The next major influence in buildings was Baroque. Learning from the Italian model, Fischer von Erlach developed a national style called Austrian Baroque, as typified in the National Library and Church of St Charles in Vienna.

CULTURE

Traditional Lifestyle

Traditional costumes are still worn in rural areas of Tirol, but all varieties of local costume can be seen during celebrations and processions. Typical dress for men is shorts with wide braces, and jackets without collars or lapels. The best known form of dress for women is the *Dirndl:* pleated skirt, apron, and white, pleated corsage with full sleeves.

Many festivals act out ancient traditions, such as welcoming the spring with painted masks and much ringing of bells. The departure of herders and cattle to high Alpine pastures in early summer and their return in autumn are the cause of much jollity in village life.

Avoiding Offence

Austrians tend to dress up when going to the opera or theatre, so the wearing of jeans and trainers is tolerated but not wholly appreciated. Attitudes to homosexuality are less tolerant than in most other European countries.

It is customary to greet people, even shop assistants, with the salute *Grüss Gott.*

Sport

Skiing, soccer, tennis, mountaineering, hiking, cycling and water sports are popular activities.

RELIGION

Roman Catholicism is embraced by 90% of the population; most of the rest are Protestants, who are mainly concentrated in Burgenland and Carinthia. Religion plays an important part in the lives of many Austrians. It is not unusual to see small roadside shrines decorated with fresh flowers.

LANGUAGE

The Austrians speak German. In the eastern province of Burgenland about 25,000 people speak Croatian, while in the southern province of Carinthia about 20,000 people speak Slovene. For a rundown on German, turn to the Germany chapter in this book.

English is widely understood in the main cities and tourist resorts. Even in smaller places, hotel and railway-counter staff usually know some English, but don't bank on it. Knowledge of some German phrases would be an asset and would help to endear you to the local population.

Facts for the Visitor

AUSTRIA

VISAS & EMBASSIES
Visas are not required for EC, US, Canadian, Australian or New Zealand citizens. Visitors may stay a maximum of three months although passports rarely receive an entry stamp. British and Japanese nationals may stay six months. South African and some Third World and Arab nationals require a visa.

Austrian Embassies
Austrian embassies abroad include:

Australia
   12 Talbot St, Forrest, Canberra, ACT 2603 (☎ 06-295 1376)
Canada
   445 Wilbrod St, Ottawa, Ont K1N 6M7 (☎ 613-563 1444)
New Zealand
   Austrian Consulate, 4 Ponui Place, Mt Wellington, Auckland (☎ 09-276 17 35). Does not issue visas or passports. Contact the Australian office for these services.
UK
   18 Belgrave Mews West, London SW1 8HU (☎ 071-235 3731)
USA
   2343 Massachusetts Ave NW, Washington, DC 20008 (☎ 202-483 4474)

Foreign Embassies in Austria
See the Vienna section for details. There are consulates in most major towns.

DOCUMENTS
British people may travel on a one-year British Visitors passport. For drivers, there is no problem with EC licences but other nationalities should carry an International Driving Permit. A Green Card is compulsory. The vehicle registration documents should be carried.

CUSTOMS
Travellers from European countries may bring in 200 cigarettes or 50 cigars or 250 grams of tobacco. Visitors from non-European countries may bring in twice as much. The allowance for the importation of alcohol is the same for everyone: 2.1 litres of wine and one litre of spirits. Tobacco and alcohol may only be brought in by those aged 17 or over.

MONEY
Currency
The Austrian Schilling (AS, or ÖS in German) is divided into 100 Groschen. Banknotes come in denominations of AS20, AS50, AS100, AS500, AS1000 and AS5000. There are coins to the value of 500, 100, 50, 25, 10, 5, and 1 Schillings, and for 50, 10, 5 and 2 Groschen. There is no limit on the value of currency that can be brought in, but you may export no more than AS100,000 without special permission. Visa, MasterCard, American Express and Diners Club credit cards are equally acceptable, although a surprising number of shops and restaurants refuse to accept any credit cards at all. It is usually possible to get a cash advance with a Visa card. American Express and Thomas Cook are the best known travellers' cheques.

Exchange rates hardly vary between banks. Changing cash attracts a negligible commission but the exchange rate is about 2% lower than for cheques. Commission at American Express offices for their own travellers' cheques is AS40 on the first US$245. Otherwise, the post office always charges the lowest commission rate: AS40 for any number of cheques up to a total of AS10,800, with no commission for cash. Train stations charge around AS60 minimum for cheques, up to AS10 for cash. Banks charge a minimum of AS45 to AS80, comprising a basic commission plus a sum per cheque. In other words, don't change a lot of low-value cheques (although for some reason, banks usually charge you for a minimum of three to five cheques even if you're only cashing one).

You can cash your cheques into any hard

currency, so Austria is a good place to stock up on US dollars if you're travelling on into Eastern Europe. To get money sent to Austria, a direct transfer of funds through a bank is possible but an international money order is cheaper.

Exchange Rates

A$1	=	AS7.4
C$1	=	AS8.3
DM1	=	AS7.0
NZ$1	=	AS5.6
Sfr1	=	AS8.0
UK£1	=	AS17.7
US$1	=	AS10.4

Costs

Austria can be reasonably cheap away from the big cities and main tourist resorts. Budget travellers can get by on as little as AS300 a day, but it is hard work, especially if you do a lot of travelling.

Ice cream, coffee and alcoholic drinks are subject to a refreshment tax on top of the inevitable value-added tax (VAT), called the *Mehrwertsteuer* (MWST), which makes them expensive. Prices are always displayed inclusive of all taxes, even (usually) service charges in hotels and restaurants.

It is customary to tip an extra 5% in restaurants if the service has been good. Taxi fares do not include an element for tips and the driver will expect around 10% extra. Prices are fixed, so bargaining for goods is not an option.

Consumer Taxes

For purchases over AS1000 in 'Tax Free' shops, the MWST can be reclaimed, either upon leaving Austria or subsequently. A U-34 form must be filled out at the time of purchase and presented to customs on departure. The form will be signed and stamped. You then post it to the shop, which will send the refund to the address given. The airports at Vienna, Salzburg, Innsbruck, Linz and Graz have counters for instant refunds, as do some land crossings.

CLIMATE & WHEN TO GO

Austria has a central European climate but temperatures vary according to altitude. Average rainfall is 71 cm per year. Maximum temperatures in Vienna are: January 1°C, April 14°C, August 23°C and October 13°C. Minimum temperatures are typically 9°C lower in spring and summer and 4°C lower in autumn and winter. Salzburg and Innsbruck match the maximum temperature of Vienna very closely, but night-time temperatures are 6°C lower than Vienna's in late summer and slightly higher in late winter. Some people find the *Föhn*, a hot, dry wind which sweeps down from the mountains, rather uncomfortable. A combination of summer sightseeing and winter sports make Austria a year-round destination. July and August are peak times and crowded, November is between seasons.

WHAT TO BRING

Pack warm clothing for nights at high altitude. Sleeping bags are occasionally required in youth hostels; sometimes they simply save you the cost of renting sheets.

SUGGESTED ITINERARIES

Depending on the length of your stay, you might want to see and do the following things:

Two days
  Vienna – see the central sights and visit the Opera and a few *Heurigen* (wine taverns).
One week
  Spend four days in Vienna, two days in Salzburg and one day visiting the Salzkammergut lakes.
Two weeks
  Spend five days in Vienna, two days in Salzburg (with a one-day trip to the Wergen ice caves), two days at the Salzkammergut lakes, two days in Innsbruck and two days at a ski resort.
One month
  Visit the same places as the two-week scenario but spend a bit more time here and there. It's worth including a tour of the south, taking in Graz, Klagenfurt and Lienz.
Two months
  Visit all the places mentioned in this chapter.

AUSTRIA

TOURIST OFFICES

Local tourist offices (called *Verkehrsverein* or *Verkehrsamt*) are efficient and helpful. A centrally situated office can be found in any town or village that tourists are likely to visit. Someone always speaks English and most offices have a room-finding service, often without commission. Maps are always available and usually free. Each region has a provincial tourist board.

Local tourist offices in some resorts organise a Guest Card with the intention of enticing visitors to stay an extra couple of days (and spend an extra few hundred Schillings). Cards are issued either by the tourist office or hotels, but they must be stamped by your hotel in order to be valid. They are good for various discounts – sometimes useful things like reductions on cable cars – but entitlement depends on a minimum stay, usually three nights.

Tourist Offices Abroad

Austrian National Tourist Office (ANTO) branches abroad include:

Australia
    1st Floor, 36 Carrington St, Sydney, NSW 2000 (☎ 02-299 3621)
Canada
    2 Bloor St East, Suite 3330, Toronto, Ont M4W 1A8 (☎ 416-9673 381)
New Zealand
    7th Floor, 76 Symonds St, Auckland (☎ 09-373 4078)
UK
    30 St George St, London W1R OAL (☎ 071-629 0461)
USA
    500 Fifth Ave, Suite 2009-2022, New York, NY 10110 (☎ 212-944 6880)

There are also tourist offices in Los Angeles, Montreal, Paris, Zürich, Milan, Rome and Frankfurt.

USEFUL ORGANISATIONS

The following organisations might prove useful:

Youth Hostel Association
    (*Österreichischer Jugendherbergsverband*)
    Gonzagagasse 22 or Schottenring 28 (the office is on the corner of the two), A-1010 Vienna (☎ 0222-53 35 353)
Austrian Camping Club
    (*Österreichischer Camping Club*)
    An der Au, A-3400 Klosterneuburg (☎ 0904-85 877)
Austrian Automobile Club
    (*Österreichischer Automobil, Motorrad- und Touring Club, ÖAMTC*)
    Schubertring 1-3, A-1010 Vienna (☎ 0222-711 99; dial ☎ 120 for emergency assistance)
24-hour Breakdown Assistance
    Schanzstrasse 44-50, A-1150 Vienna (☎ 0222-927 651)
Austrian Alpine Club
    (*Österreichischer Alpenverein, ÖAV*)
    Wilhelm-Greil-Strasse 15, A-6010 Innsbruck (☎ 0512-231 71)
Club Handicap
    Wattgasse 96-98, A-1170 Vienna (☎ 0222-467 1045). Handles travel arrangements for the disabled.

BUSINESS HOURS & HOLIDAYS

Shops are open Monday to Friday from 8 am to 6.30 pm and Saturdays to 1 pm. They generally close for up to two hours at noon except in big cities. Banking hours vary but are commonly from 9 am to 3 pm Monday to Friday with later closing on Thursday. Public holidays are 1 and 6 January, Easter Monday, 1 May, Ascension Day, Whit Monday, Corpus Christi, 15 August, 26 October, 1 November, and 8, 25 and 26 December.

CULTURAL EVENTS

Most events take place only on a local basis, so it is worth checking with local tourist offices. The national tourist office compiles a list of annual and one-off events taking place in the current year. Vienna has almost continuous music festivals. Salzburg has an Easter festival and one of Austria's most important music festivals lasting from the end of July to the end of August. Linz has the Bruckner Festival in September.

There are fairs in Vienna, Innsbruck and Graz in September. General celebrations take place at New Year and on religious

AUSTRIA

holidays, when you can expect colourful processions. Also look out for *Fasching* (Shrovetide carnival) week in early February, maypoles on 1 May, midsummer night's celebrations on 21 June, the autumn cattle roundup at the end of October and St Nicholas Day parades on 5 and 6 December. Expect much flag-waving on national day (26 October).

POST & TELECOMMUNICATIONS
Postcards and letters within Austria cost AS4 and AS5 respectively. To Europe they cost AS5 and AS6; elsewhere the cost is AS7.50 and AS11.

Poste restante is *Postlagernde Briefe* in German. Mail can be sent care of any post office and is held for a month; a passport must be shown to collect. American Express will also hold mail for a month for customers who have its card or cheques.

Post office hours vary: typical hours are Monday to Friday from 8 am to noon and 2 to 6 pm, and Saturday from 8 to 11 am, but a few main post offices in big cities are open 24 hours. Stamps are available in tobacco *(Tabak)* shops as well as post offices.

Telephone calls within Austria are 33% cheaper on weekends and between 6 pm and 8 am on weekdays. The minimum charge is AS5 for very short calls. An annoying feature of Austrian phones is that Schillings tick away at the local rate while you're waiting for the dialled party to pick up the receiver. International direct-dialling is nearly always possible, otherwise dial ☎ 09 for the operator. Post offices invariably have telephones. Be wary of using telephones in hotels, as they can cost up to twice as much as post office phones.

You can save money and avoid messing around with change by buying a phone card *(Telefon-Wertkarte)*. For AS48 you get A50 worth of calls and for AS95 and AS190 you gain AS5 and AS10 respectively.

TIME
Austrian time is GMT/UTC plus one hour. If it's noon in Vienna it is 7 pm in New York and Toronto, 4 am in San Francisco, 10 pm in Sydney and midnight in Auckland. Clocks go forward one hour on the last Saturday in March and back again on the last Saturday in September.

LAUNDRY
Look out for *Wäscherei* for self-service or service washes. Minimum cost is around AS80 to AS90 to wash and dry. Many youth hostels have laundry facilities.

WEIGHTS & MEASURES
The metric system is used. Like other Continental Europeans, Austrians indicate decimals with commas and thousands with points.

ELECTRICITY
The current used is 220 V AC, 50Hz, and the socket used is the two-pin variety.

BOOKS & MAPS
A useful volume is *Mountain Walking in Austria* by Cecil Davies (paperback). *Off the Beaten Track 'Austria'* (various authors, paperback) concentrates on less well-known regions. See also the Switzerland chapter for other suggestions. Freytag & Berndt of Vienna publishes good maps in varying scales. Its 1:100,000 series is popular with hikers, as is its new 1:50,000 blue series. Extremely detailed maps are produced by the Austrian Alpine Club.

MEDIA
Austria Radio broadcasts the news in English daily at 8.05 am. The strongest signals are around 90 and 98 FM. Blue Danube Radio (103.8 FM) is a news and information station for visitors in English, Spanish and French. English-language newspapers are widely available for around AS30.

HEALTH
No inoculations are required for entry. There is a charge for emergency hospital treatment and medication, and for doctor consultations, so private medical insurance is advised. Treatment is cheaper than in Swit-

zerland. Many Viennese get their dental treatment in Budapest where costs are lower and the work reliable. Chemist shops (*Apotheken*) operate an out-of-hours service in rotation.

WOMEN TRAVELLERS

Women should experience no special problems. Attacks and verbal harassment are less common than in many countries. Austrian women do not enjoy equal social status to men in conservative areas, but this should not affect travellers. Sanitary products are widely available: DM (a drugstore chain) outlets have a good selection.

DANGERS & ANNOYANCES

Dial ☎ 133 for the police, ☎ 144 for an ambulance, or ☎ 122 in the event of a fire. Take care in the mountains: helicopter rescue is expensive unless you are covered by insurance (that's assuming they find you in the first place!). Austrian train stations are a habitual haunt of drunks and dropouts. They can be annoying and occasionally intimidating.

FILM & PHOTOGRAPHY

Film is widely available and there are no special restrictions as to what to photograph. Vienna is the cheapest place to buy film in Austria, but it is still more expensive than in Switzerland.

WORK

The official line is that no foreigner may enter Austria in order to look for work. Jobs and permits must be obtained prior to arrival. The rules are not so strictly applied in ski resorts, where there are often vacancies for jobs with unsociable hours. Check with tourist offices, as it might be possible to arrange a Volunteer Work Permit. Otherwise, you may be able to find casual work in return for free board and lodging and pocket money. Likely opportunities are in snow clearing, chalet cleaning, restaurants and ski equipment shops.

ACTIVITIES

Skiing

Skiing is generally slightly cheaper than in France or Switzerland. Vorarlberg and Tirol are the most popular areas, although there is also skiing in Salzburgerland, Upper Austria and Carinthia, where prices can be lower still. Equipment can always be hired in resorts. You may initially get some strange looks if you ask in hire shops to buy ex-rental stock, but great bargains can be picked up this way. Also keep your eyes open for discarded equipment that may still be perfectly usable.

Ski coupons for ski lifts can sometimes be bought, but more usually there are general passes available for complete or partial days. Count on at least AS220 for a day's ski pass, AS150 for downhill rental and AS75 for cross-country skiing. The skiing season starts in December and lasts well into April in some higher resorts. Year-round skiing is possible at the Stubai Glacier near Innsbruck.

Hiking & Mountaineering

Walking and climbing are popular with visitors and locals alike. Mountain paths are marked with direction indicators, and most tourist offices have free maps of hiking routes. Mountaineering is also popular but should not be undertaken without proper equipment and some previous experience. Tirol province has many mountain guides and mountaineering schools; these are listed in the *Mountains* booklet from the tourist office.

Spa Resorts

A relatively relaxed activity is putting your feet up at a spa or health resort. There are many of these throughout the country, identified by the prefix *Bad* ('Bath'), eg Bad Ischl. Leisurely long walks and much wallowing in hot springs are typical ingredients of these salubrious locations.

ACCOMMODATION

Advance reservations are recommended at the peak times of Christmas and Easter and in July and August. Be careful particularly at Christmas and New Year as many hotels and hostels close at this time. Reservations are binding on either side and compensation may be claimed if you do not take a reserved room or the room is unavailable. Instant hotel reservations can be made from Britain via Austria On-Line (☎ 0345-581126 – the call is free). Prices are lower out of season.

A cheap and widely available option is taking a room in a private house (AS110 to AS200 per person). Look out for *Zimmer frei* ('room(s) available') signs. Tourist offices can supply listings of all types of accommodation, and often make reservations for little or no commission. Sometimes accommodation costs more for the first night's stay.

Camping

There are over 400 camp sites but most close in the winter. Cost is around AS30 to AS50 per person plus the same again for a tent and for a car. Free camping in camper vans is officially permitted except in Vienna and protected rural areas, as long as camping equipment is not set up outside the van.

Alpine Huts

These are maintained by the Austrian Alpine Club. Members of the club take priority and are sometimes entitled to a discount. Huts are rarely full, however, and not too expensive. Most are situated between 900 and 2700 metres in hill-walking regions, and meals or cooking facilities are often available.

Hostels

Austria has an excellent network of private and IYHF-affiliated hostels. Membership cards are always required except in a few private hostels. Nonmembers pay a guest surcharge of AS30 per night for a guest card; after six nights the guest card counts as a full membership card. Most hostels accept reservations by telephone. Some hostels have a fax reservation service: you pay AS7 for the fax and AS70 deposit which you get back when you claim your bed at the new hostel. Prices are around AS120 including breakfast

and showers, and usually sheets. Youth hostel in German is *Jugendherberge*.

Hotels & Pensions

With very few exceptions, rooms are clean and adequately appointed. Expect to pay from AS200/350 for a single/double. Use of hall showers sometimes incurs a charge of around AS20. In low-budget accommodation, a room with a private shower may mean a room with a shower cubicle rather than a proper *en suite* bathroom. Breakfast is usually included. Prices in main cities are significantly higher than in rural areas, particularly in Vienna. A small country inn *(Gasthaus)* or a guesthouse *(Pension)* tends to be more intimate than a hotel. Self-catering accommodation is available in ski resorts.

FOOD

The main meal is taken at midday. Most restaurants have a set meal or menu of the day *(Tagesteller* or *Tagesmenu)* which gives the best value for money. The cheapest deal around is in university restaurants *(mensas)*; these are only mentioned in the text if they are open to all. Wine cellars are fairly cheap places to eat, and some food shops have tables for the consumption of produce on the premises.

Soups are good, often with dumplings *(Knödl)* and pasta added. A great variety of sausages *(Würste)* are available. *Wiener Schnitzel* is a veal (occasionally pork) cutlet coated in breadcrumbs. Paprika is used to flavour several dishes including *Goulasch* (beef stew) and *Paprikahuhn* (paprika chicken). Look out for regional dishes such as *Tiroler Bauernschmaus*, a selection of meats served with sauerkraut, potatoes and dumplings. Overall, Austrians tend to eat a lot of meat – vegetarians will have a fairly tough time finding varied dishes. Famous desserts include the *Strudel* (baked dough filled with a variety of fruits) and *Salzburger Nockerl* (an egg, flour and sugar pudding); pancakes are also popular. Good supermarket chains are Billa, Hofer and Sparmarkt.

DRINKS

Nonalcoholic Drinks

Tea and coffee are expensive. Luckily, bottled water isn't, and tap water is fine to drink. Apple juice (*Apfelsaft*) is widely available. Coffee houses are an established part of Austrian life, particularly in Vienna. Strong Turkish coffee is popular. Linger over a cup (from AS20) and read the free newspapers.

Alcohol

Austria (especially in the east) specialises in producing white wines. *Österreichischer Weingütesiegel* on the label designates a wine of high quality, *Wein aus Österreich* is standard table wine. Wine bought by the carafe is cheaper. Austria is also well known for beer, particularly of the lager variety. Some well-known makes include Gösser, Schwechater, Stiegl and Zipfer. Beer is served by the half litre (*Krügel*) and 0.35 litre (*Seidel*).

ENTERTAINMENT

Cinemas usually show films in the original language; advertising posters will state if the film is dubbed or subtitled.

The main season for opera, theatre and concerts is September to June. Cheap, standing-room tickets are often available shortly before performances begin and they represent excellent value.

Gamblers can have fun at over a dozen casinos around the country, including in Vienna, Graz, Linz and Salzburg. The admission fee is AS170 but you are immediately presented with AS200 worth of gambling chips. Smart dress is required; opening hours are typically 3 pm to midnight.

It isn't hard to find bars or taverns featuring traditional or rock music. Nightclubs throughout Austria are listed in *Disco Digest*, available at bookstalls. Admission and drinks prices generally aren't too frightening. Late opening is common in the cities: in Vienna you can party all night long.

THINGS TO BUY

Popular souvenirs are local craft products such as textiles, pottery, painted glassware, woodcarving and wrought-iron work.

Getting There & Away

AIR

The airports at Vienna, Linz, Graz, Salzburg, Innsbruck and Klagenfurt all receive international flights. Vienna is the busiest airport with several daily nonstop flights to all major transport hubs such as Amsterdam, Berlin, Frankfurt, Paris, Zürich and London Heathrow. There is at least one flight daily from Frankfurt and Zürich to all the other airports. No airport departure tax applies when leaving Austria.

LAND

Bus

International bus connections to/from Austria are minimal. Vienna does have some services to Eastern Europe – see the Vienna Getting There & Away section for details. There is one bus a week (Friday) to Vienna from London Victoria Station, which takes 24 hours.

Train

Austria benefits from its central location within Europe by having excellent rail connections to all important transport centres. Vienna has express services to Prague (AS360), Budapest (AS266) and Bucharest (AS1149). Most connections to former Yugoslavia and Greece go via Villach or Graz. Salzburg has at least hourly trains to Munich with onward connections to Frankfurt (AS898), Hamburg (AS1516) and Paris (AS1388). Express sleepers from Vienna stop at Salzburg (AS360) and Innsbruck (AS620) on the way to Zürich (AS964) and Basel. Express services to Italy go via Innsbruck or Villach. Supplements sometimes apply on international trains.

Reserving train seats in 2nd class within Austria (either on national IC or international EC trains) costs AS30; in 1st class, IC costs AS30 and EC AS50. The German ICE is a special case where the charge depends upon the distance travelled.

Car & Motorbike

There are numerous entry points from Germany, Czechoslovakia, Hungary, Slovenia, Italy and Switzerland. All main border crossing points (ie those served by main roads) are open 24 hours a day.

RIVER

Steamers and hydrofoils operate along the Danube in the summer. See the Vienna and Danube Valley sections for details.

Getting Around

AIR

Vienna has several flights a day to Graz, Klagenfurt and Innsbruck and at least one a day to Salzburg and Linz. The main carrier is Austrian Air Services which has nonstop flights from each of the airports to most of the others. It is worth checking schedules, as they vary according to the season.

BUS

The yellow postbus service is mainly used as a backup to the rail network. It is complemented by orange buses run by Austrian Railways, but the distinction is not a significant one for the traveller. The term 'postbus' has been used throughout this chapter for convenience. Some rail routes are duplicated by buses, but mostly they operate in the more inaccessible mountainous regions. Buses are clean, efficient and on time. Advance reservations are possible, but sometimes you can only buy tickets from the drivers. Fares work out at around AS120 per 100 km.

TRAIN

Trains are efficient and frequent. The whole country is well covered by the state network, with only very few private lines. Eurail and Inter-Rail passes are valid on the former. Many stations have information centres where the staff speak English. Tickets can be purchased on the train but they cost around AS10 extra. Couchettes (six beds) cost a fixed rate of AS170 on top of the normal fare.

In this chapter, fares are always quoted for 2nd class.

Trains are expensive but the cost can be reduced by special passes. The best is the Rabbit Card which allows four days' unlimited travel within 10; the price is AS1070 or AS660 for those aged under 26 (identity card needed). The Kilometerbank allows up to six people to travel on journeys over 71 km; the cost is AS1800 for 2000 km, AS2700 for 3000 km, AS3600 for 4000 km and AS4500 for 5000 km. Regional Passes *(Regional-Netzkarte)* give four days' unlimited travel in 10, but only within one of 18 regions; the fare is AS400. Ordinary return tickets (over 70 km) are valid for two months and you can break your journey as many times as you like, but you should warn the conductor of your intentions.

'Corridor' trains are trains where part of a journey passes through a neighbouring country, but disembarkation is not possible and there are no passport controls. The two main corridor routes are Innsbruck to Salzburg (AS300) and Innsbruck to Lienz (AS224).

Fast trains from Vienna take about 3½ hours to Salzburg and 5½ hours to Innsbruck. In German, *Bahnhof* means train station, whereas *Hauptbahnhof* denotes the main train station. Sometimes, reduced fares are available for those aged under 26: wave your passport and ask. Normal fares are AS134 for the first 100 km, reducing over longer distances. The *Bundes-Netzkarte*, valid for the whole of Austria for one month, costs AS3400 in 2nd class. In the larger towns, train information can be obtained on ☎ 1717.

CAR & MOTORBIKE

Roads are generally good, but sufficient respect should be given to difficult mountain routes. There are toll charges for some of the tunnels through the mountains. The tourist office has full details, as well as lists of the few roads and passes which are closed in winter.

On mountain roads, postbuses always have priority, otherwise priority lies with uphill traffic. Drive in low gear on steep downhill stretches. Give priority to vehicles coming from the right. The penalty for drink-driving (over 0.08% BAC) is a hefty on-the-spot fine and confiscation of driving licence. Speed limits are 50 km/h in towns, 130 km/h on motorways and 100 km/h on other roads. Snow chains are recommended in winter. Cars can be transported by train: Vienna is linked by a daily motorail service to Salzburg, Innsbruck, Feldkirch and Villach. Motorbikes must have their headlights on during the day.

Rental

Car rental can be arranged prior to arrival through travel agents or direct through the main operators. Within Austria, Europcar offers unlimited-km rates of AS900 per day, AS583 per day over seven days or AS1260 for a weekend (noon Friday to 9 am Monday). The head office (☎ 0222-597 00 41) is at Linke Wienzeile 120-2, Vienna, and it has offices in all cities with international airports. Local hire firms usually have cheaper rates; the local tourist office will be able to supply details.

BICYCLE

As in Switzerland, bicycles can be hired from train stations and returned to any other station with a rental office, which is nearly all of them. The rate is AS90 per day, or AS45 if you can show a train ticket for arrival that day. Cycling is popular even though minor roads can be steep with sharp bends. There is a fixed fare of AS40 for transporting a bike on a train.

HITCHING

For the most part, hitching is not too bad – it is even institutionalised. *Mitfahrzentrale* companies link hitchers with car drivers who have spare seats. Hitchers pay approximately half the equivalent train fare, which is passed on to the driver after the agency takes a cut. See the Vienna, Linz and Bregenz sections for details.

Trying to hitch rides on trucks is often the best bet: check border customs posts and

truck stops. *Autohof* indicates a parking place able to accommodate trucks. Always carry a sign showing your destination.

BOAT

Services along the Danube are scenic excursions rather than functional transport, as they are slow and expensive. Nevertheless, a boat ride is definitely worth it if you like lounging on deck and having the scenery come to you rather than the other way round. The larger Salzkammergut lakes have ferry services.

MOUNTAIN TRANSPORT

See the Switzerland chapter introduction for an account of the different modes available.

LOCAL TRANSPORT
Public Transport

Buses, trams and underground railways are efficient and reliable. Most towns have an integrated system and offer excellent value one-day or 24-hour tickets (AS20 to AS45) available in advance from Tabak shops. Even single tickets can sometimes only be purchased in advance. On-the-spot fines apply to people caught travelling without tickets, although you'll find more than a few locals prepared to take the risk.

Taxi

Taxis are metered and expensive, only to be used if there is no other choice. Look for them round train stations.

TOURS

These vary from two-hour walks in a city centre to all-inclusive packages to ski resorts. Arrangements are made through tourist offices.

Vienna

The character of modern Vienna (Wien) owes much to its colourful political and cultural past. There's so much to see and do that you could still feel pressed for time if you allow yourself a week to see the city. It

AUSTRIA

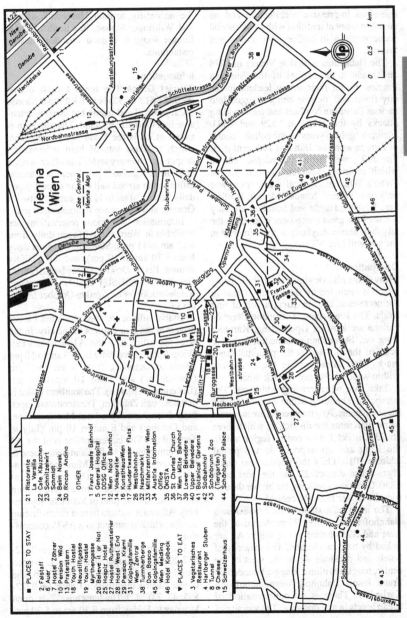

Vienna (Wien)

PLACES TO STAY
- 2 Falstaff
- 6 Auer
- 7 Hostel Zöhrer
- 10 Pension Wild
- 13 Praterstern
- 18 Youth Hostel
- 19 Youth Hostel Myrthengasse
- 20 Believe it or Not
- 25 Hospiz Hotel
- 27 Hostel Ruthensteiner
- 28 Hotel West End
- 29 Pension Kraml
- 31 Kolpingsfamilie Wien Zentral
- 38 Turmherberge Don Bosco
- 45 Kolpingsfamilie Wien Meidling
- 46 Hotel Kolbeck

▼ PLACES TO EAT
- 3 Vegetarisches Restaurant
- 4 Hartberger Stuben
- 8 Tunnel
- 9 Chelsea
- 15 Schweizerhaus

- 21 Ristorante La Versilia
- 22 Cafe Käuzchen
- 23 Schmidt
- 24 Beim Novak
- 30 Rincon Andino

OTHER
- 1 Franz Josefs Bahnhof
- 5 General Hospital
- 11 DDSG Office
- 12 Wien Nord Bahnhof
- 14 Volksprater
- 16 KunstHausWien
- 17 Hundertwasser Flats
- 26 Westbahnhof
- 32 Naschmarkt
- 33 Mitfahrzentrale Wien
- 34 Austria Information Office
- 35 ÖKISTA
- 36 St Charles Church
- 37 Wien Mitte Bahnhof
- 39 Lower Belvedere
- 40 Upper Belvedere
- 41 Botanical Gardens
- 42 Südbahnhof
- 43 Schönbrunn Zoo (Tiergarten)
- 44 Schönbrunn Palace

combines impressive architecture and an enviable musical tradition with a busy social scene centred in coffee bars, clubs and taverns.

The Habsburgs settled in Vienna in 1278 and made it the capital of the Austrian Empire. Under their strong leadership the city flourished, despite being dragged into various European conflicts and withstanding attacks by the Turks in 1529 and 1683. Vienna's 'golden years' as the cultural centre of Europe were the 18th and 19th centuries. For 200 years Vienna played the tune to which aspiring musicians danced. In the 'Who's Who' of classical music there was only one 'Where'. Strauss, Mozart, Beethoven, Brahms, Haydn and Schubert are only a few of the great composers who made the city their home. Anybody with an interest in the arts will love Vienna.

Orientation

Many of the historic sights are in the old city, which is encircled by the Danube Canal to the north-east, and the Ring, a belt of ring roads. The Ring changes its name along its various sections, eg Opern Ring, Kärntner Ring etc. St Stephen's Cathedral is in the heart of the city and is the principal landmark. Most attractions in the centre are within walking distance of each other.

Take care when reading addresses. The number of a building within a street follows the street name. Any number before the street name represents the district, of which there are 23. District 1 is the central region within the Ring and corresponds to the postal address 1010. Only the middle two digits alter, hence district 23 has the post code 1230. Generally speaking, the higher the district the farther from the centre.

The main train stations are Franz Josefs Bahnhof to the north, Westbahnhof to the west and Südbahnhof to the south. All are linked by tram or U-Bahn. The majority of hotels and pensions are to the west of the centre, roughly within a triangle bounded by Franz Josefs Bahnhof, Westbahnhof and Karlsplatz. There is no concentration of cheap hotels in any one area. The vicinity of

the university, around Universitätsstrasse and Währinger Strasse, just north of Dr K Lueger Ring, is a good area for cheaper restaurants.

Information

Tourist Office The main tourist office (☎ 0222-513 88 92) is at 1 Kärntner Strasse 38. It is small and hectic but there is extensive free literature on hand. The city map is excellent, as is the *Youth Scene* magazine, which contains lots of hard information despite the chummy style. The office is open daily from 9 am to 7 pm. There is a tourist office in the arrival hall of the airport (open daily from 8.30 am to 11 pm, except between October and May when it closes at 10 pm).

Information and room reservations are available in Westbahnhof (open daily from 6.15 am to 11 pm); Südbahnhof (open daily from 6.30 am to 10 pm); and the quaintly named Erste Donau Dampfschiffahrts-Gesellschaft (DDSG) boat-landing stage, Reichsbrücke (open April to October from 9 am to 7 pm).

Tourist offices are specially sited for car drivers at the four corners of the city. In the west the office is at the A1 autobahn exit Wien-Auhof, open daily from 8 am to 10 pm (April to October), from 9 am to 7 pm (November) and from 10 am to 6 pm (December to March). The southern office is at the A2 exit Zentrum, Triesterstrasse, open daily from 9 am 7 pm (mid-March to June, and October) and 8 am to 10 pm (July to September). The eastern office is at the A4 exit Simmeringer Haide, Landwehrstrasse 6, open from 8 am to 6 pm (March to September). The office in the north is at Floridsdorfer Brücke/Donauinsel, open from 8 am to 6 pm (end of March to September). All tourist offices have a room-finding service which is subject to a AS35 commission.

The Austrian Information Office (☎ 0222-587 20 00), 4 Margaretenstrasse 1, is open Monday to Friday from 9 am to 5.30 pm. The Lower Austria Information Centre (☎ 0222-533 47 73) at 1 Heidenschuss 2 is open Monday to Friday from 8.30 am to 5.30 pm.

The Youth Info centre (☎ 0222-526 46 37), 1 Dr Karl Renner Ring, Bellaria Passage, can get tickets for a variety of events at reduced rates for those aged between 14 and 26. It is open from Monday to Friday from noon to 7 pm, and Saturday and school holidays from 10 am to 7 pm.

Money Banks are open Monday to Friday from 8 am to 3 pm, with late opening on Thursday until 5.30 pm. Visa cash advances are widely available, including at the 128 branches of Zentralsparkasse. The lowest commission is at post offices. Train stations have extended hours for exchange.

Post & Telecommunications The main post office is at 1 Fleischmarkt 19. There are also post offices open 24 hours daily at Südbahnhof, Westbahnhof and Franz Josefs Bahnhof. Stamps are sold in Tabak shops. The telephone code for Vienna is 0222, or 1 if you're ringing from outside the country.

Foreign Embassies Most embassies are either in the Ring or very close to it. The British Embassy (☎ 713 15 75) is at 3 Jauresgasse 12. The US Embassy (☎ 31 55 11) is at 9 Boltzmanngasse 16. The Canadian Embassy (☎ 533 36 91) is at 1 Dr Karl Lueger Ring 10. The Australian Embassy (☎ 512 85 80) is at 4 Mattiellistrasse 2-4, by St Charles' Church. The New Zealand Embassy (☎ 512 66 36) is at 1 Lugeck 1.

Vienna is becoming an increasingly important jumping-off point for Eastern Europe. Visa requirements are being relaxed all the time. The Hungarian Embassy (☎ 533 26 31), 1 Bankgasse 4-6, is open Monday to Friday from 8.30 am to 12.30 pm. Visas are issued within one hour for those who still require them (none of the above nationalities require visas). The Czechoslovak Embassy (☎ 894 62 136), 14 Penzingerstrasse 11-13, is open Monday to Friday from 8 am to 11 am. Get there early for visa issue within half an hour; the cost varies although the minimum charge is AS60. Australian and New Zealand citizens may still require a visa

for Czechoslovakia; these cost AS90 and AS200 respectively.

Travel Agencies American Express (☎ 515 40), 1 Kärntner Strasse 21-23, is open Monday to Friday from 9 am to 5.30 pm, and Saturday from 9.30 am to noon. The Österreichisches Komitee für Internationalen Studentenaustausch (ÖKISTA), whose head office (☎ 401 480) is at 9 Garnisongasse 7, is a student travel agency that nonstudents can also use and is open Monday to Friday from 9.30 am to 5.30 pm. Other offices are at 9 Türkenstrasse 4-6 and 4 Karlsgasse 3 (☎ 505 01 28).

Bookshops Two to try are the British Bookshop (☎ 512 19 45), 1 Weihburggasse 8, and Shakespeare & Co Booksellers (☎ 535 50 53), 1 Sterngasse 2. Freytag & Berndt (☎ 52 24 21/2), 1 Kohlmarkt 9, stocks a vast selection of maps.

Museum Tickets There is free entry to national museums on presentation of a Eurocard or a MasterCard. Municipal museums are free on Friday morning, usually from 9 am till noon.

Theatre Tickets Standing-room tickets for the Staatsoper and the Theater an der Wien go on sale at around 6 pm on the evening of the performance, but check for starting times as some are earlier. For major productions, stand in line around 4 pm; for less important works, you can often get tickets with minimal queuing. Don't join the queue for student tickets by mistake. Same-day tickets for students (from AS50) are available for most theatres. Staatsoper, Volksoper, Burgtheater and Akademietheater need to see a university ID rather than an ISIC card.

Emergency Dial ☎ 144 for an ambulance, ☎ 141 for medical emergencies and ☎ 133 for the police. For out-of-hours dental treatment, call ☎ 512 20 78. Get medical treatment at the general hospital (☎ 48 00) at 9 Alser Strasse 4.

AUSTRIA

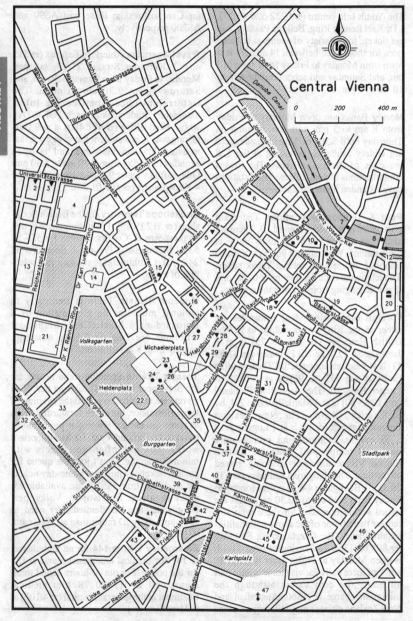

Central Vienna

0   200   400 m

AUSTRIA

■ PLACES TO STAY

1   Hotel Am Schottenpoint
6   Pension Solderer
17 Pension Nossek
38 Pension Am Operneck
43 Hotel-Pension Schneider

▼ PLACES TO EAT

2   Mensa
3   Zwillings Gewölb
5   China Restaurant Peking
18 Wrenkh
19 Alt Wien
28 Adonies
39 Restaurant Smutny

OTHER

4   University
7   Marienbrücke
8   Schwedenbrücke
9   Shakespeare & Co Booksellers
10 Bermuda Triangle area
11 Krah Krah
12 DDSG Canal Tour Landing
    Stage
13 City Hall (Rathaus)
14 National Theatre (Burgtheater)
15 Café Central
16 Esterházykeller
20 Main Post Office
21 Parliament
22 Hofburg
23 Spanish Riding School
24 Royal Chapel
25 Imperial Treasury
26 State Apartments
27 Freytag & Berndt
29 Café Bräunerhof
30 St Stephen's Cathedral
    (St Stephan)
31 American Express
32 Volkstheater
33 Natural History Museum
34 Museum of Fine Arts
35 Albertina
36 Hotel Sacher
37 Main Tourist Office
40 State Opera
41 Academy of Fine Arts
42 Café Museum
44 Secession Building
45 Musikverein
46 Konzerthaus
47 St Charles' Church

Things to See & Do

Walking Tour Walking is the best way to see the centre. Architectural riches confront you at nearly every corner, testimony to the power and wealth of the Habsburgs' rule. Grandiose public buildings and statues line both sides of the Ring. Those that stand out include the neo-Gothic **Rathaus** (City Hall), the Greek Revival-style Parliament (particularly the Pallas Athene statue), the 19th-century National Theatre and the Baroque St Charles' Church. Carefully tended gardens and parks break up the brickwork.

To the west of the city, the rolling hills and marked trails to the **Wienerwald** (Vienna Woods) are perfect for walkers; brochures are available from the information office in the City Hall (open Monday to Friday from 8 am to 6 pm).

See Museum Tickets in the previous section for information on entry to some of the following sights.

St Stephen's Cathedral The latticework spire of this 13th century Gothic masterpiece at 1 Stephansplatz rises high above the city. Interior walls and pillars are decorated with fine statues. Particularly impressive is the **stone pulpit**: at the centre of the intricate design are two clerics with hunched shoulders, wringing their hands, ambiguously expressive.

Go for a walk round the outside too; at the rear of the cathedral the agony of the crucifixion is well captured, although some irreverent souls attribute Christ's pained expression to toothache. Take the lift up the north tower (AS40) or the stairs up the higher south tower (AS20) for an impressive view.

In the catacombs (open daily, AS30) reside the internal organs of the Habsburgs. The hearts of the Habsburgs are in the Church of the Augustinian Friars, 1 Augustinerstrasse 3, which is open weekdays. The rest of their bits are in the Imperial Burial Vaults in the Church of the Capuchin Friars, 1 Neuer Markt.

Hofburg The Imperial Palace, at 1 Helden-platz, was begun in 1530 and consistently extended, resulting in the current mixture of architectural styles. The grand complex houses the Royal Chapel and the Spanish Riding School (see the following Entertainment section) as well as government offices and conference rooms.

The **Imperial Apartments** cost AS25 to visit (AS10 for students aged under 27), but limit yourself to those in Schönbrunn if you're pressed for time (see the following section). The **Imperial Treasury** is also here in Hofburg (AS60, students AS30) and contains treasures and relics spanning 1000 years, including the crown jewels. Allow up to one hour to get round.

Schönbrunn Palace The palace can be reached by U-Bahn No 4. Daily guided tours take in 40 of its 1440 rooms (AS50, students aged under 27 years AS25); the final tour of the day in English leaves at 4.30 pm. The interior is suitably majestic with frescoed ceilings, crystal chandeliers and gilded ornaments. The pinnacle of finery is reached in the Great Gallery. The Mirror Room is where Mozart played his first concert aged six in the presence of Maria Theresa and the royal family. Extensive formal gardens are enlivened by several fountains. Up the hill is an excellent view from the Gloriette monument. The attractively laid-out zoo (Tiergarten) is also worth a look (entry AS35, students AS10).

Belvedere Palace Within walking distance of the Ring, this Baroque palace contains two art collections in the two main buildings on either side of its spacious gardens. Lower (Untere) Belvedere (entrance Rennweg 6A) contains some interesting Baroque pieces, but more important is the Upper (Obere) Belvedere with instantly recognisable works by Gustav Klimt and other Austrian artists from the 19th and 20th centuries (entrance Prinz Eugen Strasse 27). There is also a good view of the city. Open Tuesday to Sunday from 10 am to 5 pm, entry for both is AS60, or AS30 for students.

Art History Museum You should not miss this museum, known as the Kunsthistorisches Museum. The building itself is a delight and holds a huge collection of 16th and 17th century paintings, ornaments and glassware plus Greek, Roman and Egyptian antiquities.

The huge extent of the Habsburgs' domains led to many important works of art being funnelled back to Vienna. Rubens was appointed to the service of a Habsburg governor in Brussels, so it is not surprising that the museum has one of the best collections of his works in the world. There is also a great collection of paintings by Peter Brueghel the Elder as well as Vermeer's *Allegory of Painting*. Look out for Cellini's stunning saltcellar and the unbelievably lavish clocks from the 16th and 17th centuries. The composite paintings by Archimboldo in room No 29 predate some of the work of Salvador Dali and the surrealists by nearly 400 years.

The museum is open Tuesday to Sunday from 10 am to 6 pm. Entry is AS45 (students AS20). Guided tours in English at 3 pm cost AS30 extra.

Secession Building Built in 1898 as a 'temple of art', this building, at 1 Friedrich-strasse 12, is the Art-Nouveau answer to the Viennese architecture as typified by the Baroque work of Fischer von Erlach. It bears a golden dome that looks like an enormous Ferrero Rocher chocolate wrapper. The 1902 exhibition here featured the famous *Beethoven Frieze* by Klimt. Although this 34-metre-long work has been restored and can be seen in the basement, the building primarily houses contemporary art. 'Sometimes people just walk past the art, they think they're in empty rooms,' the lady at the desk told me. You have been warned! It's open Tuesday to Friday from 10 am to 6 pm, and Saturday and Sunday to 4 pm; entry costs AS60, students AS30.

KunstHausWien This newly built gallery, at 3 Untere Weissgerberstrasse 13, looks like something out of a toyshop. It was designed by Friedensreich Hundertwasser to house his own works of art. It features coloured ceramics, uneven floors, irregular corners and grass on the roof. His vivid paintings are equally distinctive and there are some interesting models of other building projects. It is open daily from 9 am to 7 pm and costs AS50 to get in (AS40 for students). When you are in the area, walk down the road to see a block of residential flats built by Hundertwasser on the corner of Löwengasse and Kegelgasse. It is now one of Vienna's most prestigious addresses.

Other Museums Architecturally, the **Museum of Natural History**, at 1 Maria Theresien Platz, is the mirror image of the Art History Museum and contains minerals, meteorites and an assortment of animal remains in jars. It also puts on special exhibitions (closed Tuesday, AS30, students AS15). However, if you're going to Salzburg, the equivalent museum there is superior.

You can certainly overdose on art in Vienna. The **Albertina**, 1 Augustinerstrasse 1, has a world-renowned collection of around 220,000 etchings and drawings. Unfortunately only a fraction are on display at any one time, so you can get round in only an hour (AS45, students AS20). Further important collections are housed in other museums dotted around the city, notably in the **Museum of Modern Art**, 9 Fürstengasse 1, and the **Academy of Fine Arts**, 1 Schillerplatz 3. The former homes of the great composers are also open to the public.

Cemeteries Numerous famous composers have memorial tombs in the **Central Cemetery**, 11 Simmeringer Hauptstrasse 232-244, including Beethoven, Schubert, Brahms and Schönberg. Mozart also has a monument here, but he was actually buried in an unmarked grave in the **Cemetery of St Mark**, 3 Leberstrasse 6-8. Nobody quite knows where. It was only many years after the true location had been forgotten that gravediggers cobbled together a poignant memorial from a broken pillar and a discarded stone angel.

Volksprater This large amusement park, commonly referred to as the Prater, is dominated by the Giant Wheel built in 1897. It featured in the film *The Third Man*. Rides in the park cost AS10 to AS30 and it is a great place to have a wander. As you walk, you're liable to bump into one of the colourful metal sculptures depicting humans caught up in strange hallucinogenic happenings. The park adjoins a complex of sports grounds and a large forested area ideal for rambles.

Market The best known market is the Naschmarkt along 6 Linke Wienzeile, open Monday to Friday from 8 am to 6 pm and Saturday morning. It mainly consists of food stalls, but there are some stalls selling clothes and curios. It's also a good place to eat cheaply in snack bars.

Organised Tours Several companies offer tours of the city and surroundings, including walking and cycling tours. DDSG conducts tours along the Danube Canal departing from Schwedenbrücke in the Ring. Get the details, as ever, from the tourist office. See also the Boat information in the following Getting There & Away section.

Festivals
The cycle of musical events is unceasing. Mozart features heavily, as he had his most productive years in Vienna, from 1781 to 1791, but all varieties of music get a look-in. The Vienna International Festival (from mid-May to mid-June) has a wide-ranging programme of the arts. Contact Wiener Festwochen (☎ 586 16 76), Lehárgasse 11, A 1060 Vienna, for details as early as January. Vienna's Summer of Music (from mid-July to mid-August) fills an otherwise flat spot in the musical calendar. Contact Wiener Musik Sommer (☎ 4000 8400), Friedrich Schmidt Platz 1, A 1082 Vienna, to reserve tickets in writing before 30 April. Student tickets are available from 1 June at

the box office, 1 Friedrich Schmidt Platz 1, Monday to Friday from 10 am to 6 pm.

On a different theme, Vienna's traditional Christmas market takes place in front of the City Hall from mid-November to 24 December. Trees in the vicinity are decorated and shaped by artists and there are many original handicrafts for sale. Other seasonal events include New Year concerts and gala balls (January and February), the Vienna Spring Marathon (March/April), Vienna trade fairs (March and September), the Spring Festival in the Prater (May), a Flower Parade also in the Prater (June) and the Schubert Festival (November). The tourist office sells no tickets but has full details.

Places to Stay

Vienna can be a nightmare for accommodation. Hotels are expensive and often full, especially in the summer. Reserve ahead or at least use the telephone before you trek round everywhere.

Several agencies can help with accommodation. ÖKISTA (see Travel Agencies in the Vienna Information section) concentrates on finding cheaper rooms and charges no commission. The Mitwohnzentrale (☎ 402 60 61), 8 Laudongasse 7, can find private rooms from AS150 and apartments from AS500 (both types of accommodation are for a minimum stay of three days); the office is open Monday to Friday from 10 am to 6 pm but it does charge a commission. The tourist office also has lists of private rooms as well as the useful *Jugendherbergen* pamphlet detailing youth hostels and camp sites. Breakfast is included in the price of hostels and hotels unless stated otherwise.

Camping Vienna has several camp sites out into the suburbs. *Wien West II* (☎ 94 23 14), Hüttelbergstrasse 80, is open all year. Down the road is *Wien West I* (☎ 94 14 49) at No 40, open in July and August. Both cost AS55 per person and AS50 per tent. To get there, take U4 or S45 to Hütteldorf, then bus No 152. *Camping Neue Donau* (☎ 94 23 14), 22 Am Kleehäufel, is the same price, open from

the end of April to mid-September. Take the U1 to Kaisermühlen, then the No 91A bus.

Hostels near the Centre There are two linked IYHF *hostels*, at 7 Myrthengasse 7 (☎ 93 63 16) and round the corner at 7 Neustiftgasse 85 (☎ 93 74 62). Both are well run with new facilities and knowledgeable staff. Enjoy the good showers, lockers and personal bedside light (sheer luxury!). Beds are AS140, lunch or dinner AS60 and laundry is AS50 per load. Dorms are closed from 9 am to 2 pm, curfew is 12.45 am, and you can check in any time during the day.

Believe it or Not (☎ 526 46 58), Apartment 14, 7 Myrthengasse 10, is a small private hostel. There's no clue on the main door that it's anything other than a private house. Some people like it, others find the triple-level bunks 'like a sauna'. No breakfast is available, but you cán make use of kitchen facilities. Beds are AS160 in summer or AS110 during winter and you get your own key for late entry. *Hostel Zöhrer* (☎ 43 07 30), 8 Skodagasse 26, is a private hostel with four to six-bed dorms, and the price is AS150 per night. Kitchen facilities are available. Reception is open from 8 am to 10 pm.

The only hostel inside the Ring is *City Hostel* (☎ 512 84 63), 1 Seilerstätte 30, open 24 hours a day but only from 1 July to 30 September. Singles/doubles are AS260/360 for the first night and AS220/330 for subsequent nights. Students and IYHF members get the lower rate on the first night.

Hostels away from the Centre Near Westbahnhof, *Hostel Ruthensteiner* (☎ 83 46 93), 5 Robert Hamerling Gasse 24, has the advantage of being open 24 hours. Dorms are AS119 and singles/doubles are AS199 per person. Kitchen facilities are available and breakfast costs AS25. *Kolpinghaus Meidling* (☎ 83 54 87), 12 Bendlgasse 10-12, is near the U4 stop south of Westbahnhof. Beds start at AS90 (AS110 for non-IYHF members) in different-size dorms. Breakfast costs AS40, curfew is 11 pm. *Turmherberge Don Bosco* (☎ 713 14 94), 3 Lechnerstrasse 12, south-east of the

Ring, has the cheapest beds in town (AS55 without breakfast) and a tendency to attract impoverished locals.

Out in the suburbs, but with lots of beds, are two IYHF hostels. *Brigittenau* (☎ 338 29 40), 20 Friedrich Engels Platz 24 (take the U4 north), has a midnight curfew and the doors are locked from 9 am to 4 pm. *Hütteldorf-Hacking* (☎ 877 02 63), 13 Schlossberggasse 8 (take the U4 west), has large dorms, locked doors from 9 am to 4 pm and a 11.45 pm curfew. Both cost AS140 per night.

Student Dorms These are mostly open from 1 July to 30 September and provide cheap beds while students are on holiday. If you're stuck for somewhere to stay in summer, ring round the following *Studentenheime*: ☎ 432 54 90, 1 Auerspergstrasse 9; ☎ 34 72 82, 8 Porzellangasse 30; ☎ 505 53 84, 4 Mayerhofgasse 3; ☎ 43 16 61, 8 Pfeilgasse 4-6; ☎ 310 31 30, 9 Bolzmanngasse 10; ☎ 34 25 85, 9 Nussdorferstrasse 75; ☎ 433 23 17, 9 Alserstrasse 33; and ☎ 36 53 77, Säulengasse 17.

Pensions inside the Ring Inevitably you pay more for the convenience of a central location. *Pension Solderer* (☎ 63 81 56), 1 Heinrichsgasse 2, has singles/doubles from AS380/600 with a free shower in the hall. Rooms with private shower/WC are also available and reception is open from 7 am to 10 pm. *Pension Nossek* (☎ 533 70 41), 1 Graben 17, is good value considering it's a stone's throw from Stephansplatz. Clean, comfortable singles/doubles with shower start from AS550/900 and there are a few cheaper rooms without a private shower. *Pension Am Operneck* (☎ 512 93 10), 1 Kärntner Strasse 47, opposite the tourist office, has singles/doubles for AS530/800 with own shower and WC.

Hotels & Pensions near the Centre
Pension Wild (☎ 43 51 74), 8 Langegasse 10, is quieter than the name suggests. Singles/doubles start from AS350/520 and there are some triples/quads from

AS710/960. Make use of the free hall shower or indulge in the novelty of a sauna and steam bath for AS80. The reception is open 24 hours. Kitchen facilities are a bonus.

Kolpingsfamilie Wien Zentral (☎ 587 56 31), 6 Gumpendorfer Strasse 39, has singles without shower for AS230 and doubles with shower for AS720. *Auer* (☎ 43 21 21), 9 Lazarettgasse 3, is small and pleasant with a helpful owner. Singles/doubles start from AS290/410 with use of a free shower in the hall, or there are doubles with private shower for AS500.

Falstaff (☎ 34 91 27), 9 Müllnergasse 5, has singles/doubles without shower for AS320/520 and with shower for AS420/610. The rooms are long but lack the width to make them spacious. The dodgy 'sauna' establishment in the basement of the building merely adds to the atmosphere. It is convenient for tram D to the Ring and Nussdorf.

Hotels & Pensions near Westbahnhof
Hospiz Hotel (☎ 93 13 04), 7 Kenyongasse 15, has singles/doubles for AS300/520 with a free shower in the hall and a pool table in the lobby. Triples, quads and rooms with private shower are also available. Prices are around AS40 lower in winter and reception is open from 8 am to 10 pm. *Hotel West End* (☎ 597 67 29), 6 Fügergasse 3, has reasonable singles/doubles for AS300/540 in a nice building with a rather grand stairway. Reception is open 24 hours.

Pension Kraml (☎ 587 85 88) is at 6 Brauergasse 5. Small and friendly, it has singles/doubles for AS250/540 and large doubles with a private shower from AS620. *Praterstern* (☎ 24 01 23), 2 Mayergasse 6, east of the Ring, has singles/doubles for AS240/445 without breakfast and it costs AS40 to use the hall shower.

Hotels & Pensions away from the Centre
Zum Goldenen Stern Gasthof (☎ 804 13 82), at 12 Breitenfurter Strasse 94, has singles/doubles for AS180/350 with free use of a hall shower. To get there, take the train or the S Bahn No 1 or 2 to Hetzendorf. Breitenfurter

AUSTRIA

Strasse is two minutes' walk to the south. Ten minutes' walk from Südbahnhof is *Hotel Kolbeck* (☎ 604 17 73), 10 Laxenburger Strasse 19. Singles without shower are AS340 and singles/doubles with shower and WC are AS500/900. Reception is open 24 hours.

Mid-Range Hotels Located in a typically grand Viennese building, the *Hotel Altanta* (☎ 42 12 30), 9 Währinger Strasse 33, next to Hartberger Stuben, is probably the best mid-range hotel. Rooms are reasonably spacious and well furnished with elegant touches. Each has a large walk-in wardrobe, TV and bath or shower. It is especially good value in the low season (November to March) when singles/doubles are AS700/900 and triples are AS1150. The rest of the year prices go up around AS250 per person.

Also good but without quite the same style is *Hotel Am Schottenpoint* (☎ 310 87 87), Währinger Strasse 22. The entrance is through a small gallery with murals and a stucco ceiling. Singles/doubles are AS700/980 rising to AS800/1160 in the high season.

Close to the Theatre an der Wien, the theatrical connection of *Hotel-Pension Schneider* (☎ 588 38 0), Getreidemarkt 5, is obvious when you enter the lobby and see the signed photos of the actors and opera stars who have stayed here. Singles are AS880 to AS1180 and doubles are AS1430, and there are excellent self-contained two-person apartments for AS1850. Prices do not go up in the summer.

Places to Eat
Supermarkets are shut Saturday afternoon and Sunday, but you can stock up on groceries during these times at the stations. Westbahnhof has a shop in the main hall open daily from 6 am to 11 pm. There is a wider selection in *Gerngross* supermarket in Franz Josefs Bahnhof, which also has a restaurant section with menus from AS59 (open daily to 10.30 pm). Wurst stands are scattered around the city and provide a quick snack of sausage and bread for around AS30.

Vienna's best known dish, the Wiener schnitzel, is difficult to miss, served up as it is everywhere from top restaurants to takeaway shacks in subways. Goulash is also widely available. Vienna is well known for its excellent pastries and desserts, which are best avoided if your money belt is emptier than your stomach.

Inside the Ring The *Adonies*, 1 Habsburgergasse 1A, is a small restaurant that offers a reasonable selection of food. Lunch and evening menus cost around AS60 and AS80 and include soup. The food is good, the taste in music distinctly dubious, and it is open daily.

Wrenkh (☎ 533 15 26), 1 Bauernmarkt 10, is a rather up-market specialist vegetarian restaurant. Meticulously prepared dishes start at AS95 and it's open Monday to Friday from 11.30 am to 3 pm and 6 pm to midnight. There is another branch at 15 Hollergasse 9.

Vienna has many different nationalities of restaurants. *China Restaurant Peking*, 1 Färbergasse 3, is open daily from 11.30 am to 2.30 pm and 6 to 11.30 pm. Lunch-time specials start from AS53, salads from AS25 and other dishes from AS73. Try the excellent Hunan spicy duck.

Outside the Ring *Schnitzelwirt Schmidt* (☎ 93 37 71), 7 Neubaugasse 52, is the best place for schnitzels. It prides itself on its enormous portions (from AS55). Salads start at AS16. It's informal, hectic and very popular, open Monday to Saturday from 10 am to 10 pm.

The *Tunnel* (☎ 42 43 65), 8 Floriangasse 39, is a pub with a lively atmosphere, popular with students. The food is satisfying and amazingly cheap, eg breakfast AS29, lunch specials AS45, spaghetti from AS38, pizza from AS48 and salads from AS20. Bottled beer is AS23 for half a litre. There is a cellar bar with live music nightly from 9 pm; entry is from AS30 to AS100 depending on the artist and whether it's the weekend or not. Tunnel is open daily from 9 am to 2 am.

Also very cheap is the university *mensa*, 9 Universitätsstrasse 7, open Monday to Friday from 11 am to 2 pm. Dishes start from just AS25. Take the continuous lift to the top from the foyer. The adjoining snack bar is open weekdays from 8 am to 7 pm.

Look in *Youth Scene* for details of several other cheap student cafeterias. *Café Bierkeller Zwillings Gewölb*, by the mensa on Universitätsstrasse, is also popular with students. It features many different daily dishes from AS55 in many different subterranean rooms. It's open Monday to Friday from 8 am to 1 am and Saturday from 9.30 am to 11 pm.

On Währinger Strasse there are two vegetarian restaurants. *Hartberger Stuben* (☎ 43 33 35) at No 33-35 has vegetarian dishes from AS70, as well as pizzas and standard Austrian food. It's open Tuesday to Saturday until midnight and for Sunday lunch. Farther along, at No 57, *Vegetarisches Restaurant* (☎ 425 06 54) has a daily menu for AS92. Other specialities include cheese schnitzel (AS69) and it's open lunch times Sunday to Friday. The restaurant is run by the adjoining health food shop, open Monday to Friday from 9 am to 6 pm and Saturday to noon.

For a complete contrast, head down to *Schweizerhaus* in the Prater, Strasse des Ersten Mai 116. It's famous for its roasted pork hocks. A meal consists of a massive chunk of meat on the bone (AS79 for 500 grams, usually 700 to 800 grams minimum), served with mustard and horseradish sauce. Chomping your way through vast slabs of pig is almost a medieval experience but very tasty when washed down with draught Budweiser (the Czech stuff). There are many outside tables and it's open daily from 10 am to midnight.

Restaurant Smutny (☎ 587 13 56), 1 Elisabethstrasse 8, serves typical Viennese food in a typical Viennese environment. Dishes are filling and reasonably priced and it's open daily from 10 am to midnight.

Mid-Range Restaurants Situated in the new and controversial building right by Stephansdom, *DO & CO* (☎ 535 39 69), 1 Stephansplatz 12, has good food to match the good views. It specialises in fish and Oriental dishes around the AS200 mark and is open Monday to Saturday from noon to midnight. There's also an adjoining café.

The friendly and solicitous *Beim Novak* (☎ 93 32 44), 7 Richtergasse 12, has Austrian food (AS65 to AS225) with good explanations of each dish in the English menu. Speciality of the house is *Überbackene Fledermaus* (Gratinated Bat) for AS130. The 'bat wings' are actually cuts of beef. It's closed on Sundays and holidays, and Saturdays during summer.

A cut above the usual Italian restaurant is *Ristorante La Versilia* (☎ 96 19 21), 7 Neustiftgasse 47. It has elegant clientele, plush surroundings, and dishes for AS70 to AS240 (closed Sunday). *Steirereck* (☎ 713 31 68), 8 Rasumofskygasse 2, is a quality restaurant that does its best to draw a younger crowd. There are sometimes special prices for young people on Sunday.

Coffee Houses The coffee house is an integral part of Viennese life. The story goes that the tradition started after retreating Turkish invaders left behind their supplies of coffee beans in the 17th century. Today Vienna has around 15,000 coffee houses. They are a great place for observing the locals in repose and recovering after a hard day's sightseeing. Small coffees cost at least AS20 and the custom is to take your time. Most places have lots of newspapers including British and other foreign titles; as these would cost over AS30 to buy, a coffee is an excellent investment.

Coffee houses basically fall into two types, though the distinction is becoming increasingly blurred nowadays. A *Kaffeehaus*, traditionally preferred by men, offers games such as chess and billiards and serves wine, beer, spirits and light meals. The *Café Konditorei* attracts more women and typically has a salon look with Rococo mouldings and painted glass. A wide variety of cakes and pastries is usually on offer.

Café Museum, 1 Friedrichstrasse 6, is open daily from 7 am to 11 pm and has chess, billiards, a TV room, many newspapers and outside tables. *Café Bräunerhof*, 1 Stallburggasse 2, offers free classical music on the weekends from 3 to 6 pm, and British newspapers. It's open weekdays to 7.30 pm (8.30 pm in winter) and weekends to 6 pm.

Café Central, 1 Herrengasse 14, has a fine ceiling and pillars, and piano music from 4 to 6 pm. Trotsky came here to play chess. Opening hours are Monday to Saturday from 8.30 am to 10 pm. The *Hotel Sacher*, 1 Philharmonikerstrasse 4, behind the State Opera, is a picture of opulence with chandeliers, battalions of waiters and rich, red walls and carpets. It's famous for its chocolate peach cake, *Sachertorte* (AS45 a slice). Inevitably it is one of the more expensive cafés, with coffee costing at least AS30.

Heurigen *Heurigen* are wine taverns that only sell 'new' wine produced on the premises, a concession first allowed during the reign of Maria Theresa. They can be identified by a green wreath or branch hanging over the door. Outside tables are common and you can bring your own food or make a selection from inexpensive hot and cold buffet counters. Heurigen usually have a relaxed atmosphere which gets more and more lively as the customers and mugs of wine get drunk. Many feature live music of a traditional, folksy variety; these can be a bit touristy but great fun nonetheless. Native Viennese tend to prefer a music-free environment. Opening times are approximately 4 to 11 pm, and wine is around AS100 a litre.

Heurigen are concentrated in the wine-growing suburbs to the north, south and west of the city. Taverns are so close together that it is best to pick a region and explore once there. The Heurigen areas of Nussdorf and Heiligenstadt are near each other at the terminus of tram D.

The food and wine are good in *Schübel Auer*, Kahlenberger Strasse 22, Nussdorf. In 1817 Beethoven lived in the *Beethovenhaus*, Pfarrplatz 3, Heiligenstadt, which has a big hall with music and many annexes. Down the road (bus No 38A from Heiligenstadt or tram 38 from the Ring) is Grinzing, a large, lively

area favoured by tour groups (count the buses lined up outside at closing time), with several good Heurigen in a row along Cobenzlgasse and Sandgasse. Stammersdorf (tram No 31) and Strebersdorf (tram No 32) are cheaper regions.

Entertainment

Nightclubs & Bars Vienna has no shortage of good spots for a night out. The most well-known area is around Ruprechtsplatz, Seitenstettengasse and Rabensteig in the Ring. This area has been dubbed the 'Bermuda Triangle' as drinkers can disappear into the numerous pubs and clubs and be lost to the outside world for hours at a time. Most places are lively and not expensive; some have live music which is either free or subject to a low cover charge.

Krah Krah, 1 Rabensteig 8, has 50 different brands of beer and is open daily until 2 am. Draught beer *(Bier vom fass)* is AS27 and bottled beer is around AS33 for half a litre. Opposite is *Roter Engel*, 1 Rabensteig 5, which has live music daily (the cover charge is around AS40 to AS70) and is open until 2 or 4 am.

Alt Wien, 1 Bäckerstrasse 9, is a coffee house by day and a good drinking hall by night. Beer is AS30 for a Krügel. Also well known for its goulash (AS70 large, AS45 small), it is open daily from 10 am to 4 am. Earlier in the evening, try *Esterházykeller*, Haarhof 1, off Naglergasse, a busy wine cellar with cheap wine from AS20 for a quarter litre, and meals and snacks, open daily from 11 am (4 pm weekends) to 10 pm. Several places stay open all night. *Youth Scene* lists a selection.

Late-night bars are by no means limited to the city centre. *Chelsea*, 8 Piaristengasse 1, has a DJ or live music, open daily from 7 pm to 2 am. *Café Käuzchen*, Garde Gasse 8, has interesting décor, including part of an old VW Kombi bursting out of one wall. It's open daily and is good for late-night conversation to 2 or 4 am. *Rincon Andino* (☎ 56 72 06), 6 Münzwardeingasse 2, is a Latin-American bar with live rock or Latin jazz music daily upstairs (free or up to AS200 for

AUSTRIA

big-name bands). It has lively murals, a limited menu and is open daily from 10.30 am to 2 or 4 am.

One of the most well-known discos in Vienna is *U4* (☎ 85 83 18), 12 Schönbrunner Strasse 222, open daily from 11 pm to 4 or 5 am. Cover charge is from AS50, beer is AS38 a Krügel. Friday (new music) and Sunday ('60s and '70s music) are popular nights; Thursday is gay night.

Performances See Theatre Tickets in the previous Information section on how to procure tickets to some of the following events.

Classical music is not to everyone's taste, but it is so much a part of what Vienna is all about that you really should make an effort to sample some. In fact it is difficult to avoid it, as many of the buskers playing along Kärntner Strasse and Graben are classical musicians. Check with the tourist office for free events around town. In the summer there are sometimes free concerts in front of the Rathaus in the afternoon.

Lavish productions can be heard and viewed in the state opera building (Staatsoper), near the tourist office. Advance tickets for performances are expensive at AS150 to AS600 but standing-room tickets are only AS15 or AS20; the AS20 tickets are in a good position at the back of the stalls, whereas AS15 puts you way up in the heavens. The Viennese take their opera very seriously and dress up accordingly. Wander around the foyer and the refreshment rooms in the interval to fully appreciate the gold and crystal interior. There are no performances in July and August. The Vienna Philharmonic Orchestra performs in the Musikverein.

The Vienna Boy's Choir (Wiener Sängerknaben) sings every Sunday (except during July and August) at 9.15 am in the Royal Chapel in the Hofburg. Tickets are expensive, but standing room is free. Queue by 8.30 am to find a place inside the open doors, but you can get a flavour of what's going on from the TV in the foyer. Just as interesting is the scrum afterwards when everybody struggles to photograph and be photo-graphed with the serenely patient choir members. The choir also regularly sings a mixed programme of music in the Konzerthaus.

Spanish Riding School Famous Viennese performers with a difference are the Lipizzaner stallions who strut their stuff in the Spanish Riding School. Reservations are booked up months in advance, but it's worth asking about cancellations as these tickets are sold two hours before performances. Write to the Spanische Reitschule, Michaelerplatz 1, A 1010 Wien.

You need to be pretty keen on horses to be happy about paying AS200 to AS700 for seats or AS150 to AS160 for standing room, although a few of the tricks, such as seeing a stallion bounding along on only its hind legs like a demented kangaroo, do tend to stick in the mind. Tickets to watch them train can be bought the same day (AS70, students AS20) at gate No 2, Josefsplatz in the Hofburg. Training is from 10 am to noon, Tuesday to Saturday, from mid-February to the end of October, except in July and August when they go on their summer holidays (seriously!) to Lainzer Tiergarten, west of Vienna. Queues are very heavy early in the day, but if you try around 11 am most people have gone and you can get in fairly quickly – indicative of the fact that training is relatively dull except for isolated high points.

Cinema & Theatre Check local papers for listings. Many cinemas show films in English – *OF (Original Fassung)* means it's shown in the original language, *OmU (Original mit Untertiteln)* means it's shown in the original language with subtitles. There are performances in English at the English Theatre and the International Theatre, and mime shows at the Serapionstheater. See the previous Festivals section for seasonal cultural events. Full details of all activities, including where to get tickets, are in *Summer Scene, Winter Scene* and the monthly list of events issued by the tourist office.

Things to Buy

Local specialities include porcelain, ceramics, handmade dolls, wrought-iron work and leather goods. Selling works of art is big business; check the art auctions at the state-owned Dorotheum, 1 Dorotheergasse 19. Lots can be inspected in advance with their opening prices marked. Don't forget form U34 if you splash out (see the information about Consumer Taxes under Money in the Facts for the Visitor section at the beginning of this chapter).

Getting There & Away

Air Regular scheduled flights link Vienna to Linz, Salzburg, Innsbruck, Klagenfurt and Graz. There are daily nonstop flights to all major European destinations. Austrian Airlines (☎ 505 57 57) has a city office at 1 Kärntner Ring 18.

Bus Buses to Prague leave from 1 Dr Karl Lueger Ring 8 at 7 am and arrive at Prague's Florenc bus station at noon. Departures are daily except Sunday, and the cost is AS280. On Sunday, Monday, Thursday and Friday a bus also leaves at 3 pm. Contact Bus Tours (☎ 53 41 10) for information.

Train Not all destinations are exclusively serviced by one station, so check with train information centres for the best way to go. It's worth doing this anyway as all schedules are subject to change.

Westbahnhof is the main station for trains to Greece (two a day to Athens via Zagreb), the UK, Belgium, Netherlands, France, Germany, Switzerland, Hungary, Bulgaria, Poland, Romania and western Austria. There are seven departures a day to Budapest (AS266, takes 3½ hours) and four a day to Zürich. Approximately hourly services head to Salzburg, some continue to Munich and terminate in Paris Est.

Südbahnhof has trains to Yugoslavia, Italy, Czechoslovakia and Hungary. Trains depart from there every two hours to Graz. There are three a day to Rome via Venice and Florence. Südbahnhof has three departures a day to Budapest and four a day to Bratislava

(the journey takes approximately two hours and costs AS118). Franz Josefs Bahnhof handles local trains. It also has four trains a day to Prague (AS360), two of which continue to Berlin. Wien-Mitte is used for local trains, including the airport service (AS30).

Car & Motorbike Beyond the inner Ring there is an outer ring road, the Gürtel, which joins up with the A22 on the north bank of the Danube and the A23 south-east of town. All the main road routes hit this system, including the A1 from Linz and Salzburg and the A2 from Graz.

Hitching Mitfahrzentrale Wien (☎ 587 42 25), 5 Franzensgasse 11, links up hitchhikers and drivers and is open Monday to Friday from 9 am to 6 pm and Saturday to 2 pm. Examples of fares are Salzburg AS200, Innsbruck AS260 and Munich AS290. It is not worth going to the office without telephoning first to check availability. Lifts across Austria are limited, but there are usually many cars going into Germany. Mitzfahrzentrale Kuk (☎ 408 22 10), 8 Daungasse 1A, has similar rates.

Boat DDSG operates boats along the Danube. Its Vienna office (☎ 21 75 00) is at Handelskai 265, by the Reichsbrücke bridge. Fast hydrofoils travel eastwards to Bratislava and Budapest.

The trip to Bratislava costs AS210 one-way and AS330 return; the journey takes one hour with four departures a day in the high season and two in the low season. Budapest costs AS790 one-way, AS1200 return and takes four hours 40 minutes; there are daily departures at 8.10 am in the high season, but only around two a week in the low season. High season lasts from the end of April to mid-September; low season starts at the end of March and ends early in November.

Steamers ply the Danube from Vienna to Passau, on the German border, every day from mid-May to the end of September. Limited services start in mid-April. See the Danube Valley section for details.

Getting Around

To/From the Airport Wien Schwechat Airport is 19 km from the city centre. There are buses every 30 minutes from 6 am to 7 pm between the airport and Westbahnhof and Südbahnhof (AS60 one-way). There are also frequent train and underground connections which work out cheaper.

If taking a taxi is the only option, negotiate the fare first. AS300 to AS400 is the usual price but you're better off calling the CK Airport service (☎ 68 40 46) for a car at the fixed price of AS250.

Public Transport Vienna has a comprehensive and unified public transport network. Flat-fare tickets are valid for trains, trams, buses, the underground ('U' lines) and the rapid transport system ('S' lines). Routes are given in the free tourist office map, or for a more detailed listing, buy a map (AS10) from a Vienna Transit window. Single tickets cost AS20 from ticket machines, or AS15 each in multiples of four or five from Transit windows or Tabak shops. You may change lines on the same trip.

Daily passes (Stunden-Netzkarte) give a better deal. Costs are AS45 (valid 24 hours from first use) and AS115 (valid 72 hours). Validate the ticket in the machine at the beginning of your first journey. An eight-day, multiple-user pass (Acht-Tage-Streifenkarte) costs AS235. The validity depends upon the number of people travelling on the same card: one-person validity, eight days, two-people validity, four days, and so on. Validate the ticket once per day per person. A photo is required for weekly tickets, valid Monday to Sunday, and they cost AS125. Ticket inspections are not very frequent, but fare dodgers pay an on-the-spot fine of AS390 plus the fare, if caught. Public transport finishes by midnight.

Taxi Taxis are metered for city journeys (AS22, then AS2 per 200 metres) but the rate for longer trips must be negotiated. There is an AS10 surcharge for phoning a radio taxi.

Car & Motorbike Parking places are very limited in the city centre and there is an irksome system of one-way streets. The tourist office encourages visitors to use public transport for sightseeing and it might be worth heeding their advice. Blue parking zones allow a maximum stop of 30, 60 or 90 minutes. Parking vouchers can be purchased in Tabak shops.

Bicycle Bikes can be hired from the main train stations, open 24 hours daily. Pick up the tourist office's leaflet, *See Vienna by Bike*.

Fiacres Strictly for the well-heeled tourist are the ponies and traps lined up at St Stephen's. Commanding prices of AS400 for 20 minutes' trot, these ponies must be among Vienna's richest inhabitants.

AROUND VIENNA

Eisenstadt

Orientation & Information The provincial capital of Burgenland lies 50 km south of Vienna. The train station is 10 minutes' walk from the centre. Walk straight ahead down Bahnstrasse until it intersects Hauptstrasse, the main shopping and restaurant street. Turn right to get to the tourist office in the town hall (☎ 02682-2507) at No 35. Free maps are available and opening hours are Monday to Friday from 8.30 am to 4 pm.

Back the other way, you get to Esterházy Palace, which houses the tourist office for the whole province (☎ 02628-3384), open daily from 9 am to 4 pm (weekdays only from October to May). The main post office and postbus ticket office are by the cathedral.

Things to See & Do Joseph Haydn lived and worked in Eisenstadt for 31 years, and although he died in Vienna his remains were transferred here to the **Haydn Church**, Kalverienburg, where they lie in a white marble tomb. His skull was actually stolen from a temporary grave shortly after he died in 1809, and 154 years passed before it was reunited with the body. The church itself is remarkable for its unique cavalry display round the other side. Life-sized figures depict the stations of the cross in a series of suitably austere, dungeon-like rooms. It's well worth a visit, but is only open between 1 April and 31 October; opening hours are from 9 am to noon and 2 to 5 pm every day; entry is AS15 (students AS10) and includes the mausoleum. The Kalverienburg can be viewed in winter but only by prior appointment (☎ 02682-2638).

The Baroque **Esterházy Palace** features the frescoed Haydn Hall, open the same hours as the Burgenland tourist office. Entry costs AS20, or AS10 for students. Behind the palace is a large, relaxing park. There are several museums in the town, most of which shut on Monday.

Places to Stay & Eat The nearest IYHF *youth hostel* (☎ 02167-2252), Herbergsgasse 1, is 30 minutes away by train at Neusiedl, itself a pleasant town on the shores of a lake. Beds are AS79 (AS63 for those aged under 19) without breakfast. The hostel is open from March to October. *Gasthof Kutsenits Ludwig* (☎ 02682-3511), Mattersburgerstrasse 30, has the cheapest doubles (AS400) in Eisenstadt, excluding rooms in private houses.

Schnitzer's Café, opposite the Haydn Church, has a daily menu for AS65 and a good choice of Austrian food. It's open daily to midnight, except Monday when it closes at 2 pm. *Gasthof Zum Haydnhaus*, Joseph Haydngasse 24, has dishes from AS55. Near the cathedral is a *Billa* supermarket.

Getting There & Away Trains depart from Vienna Südbahnhof every two hours from 6.20 am, and cost AS124 one-way. The total journey takes as long as 90 minutes, as some time is wasted changing trains in Neusiedl. Buses take 70 minutes and depart from Wien-Mitte. Wiener Neustadt is on the Vienna-Graz train route; buses from there take 30 minutes.

The Danube Valley

The historical importance of the Danube (Donau) Valley as a corridor between east and west ensured that control of the area was hotly contested. As a result there are some 550 castles and fortresses in Lower Austria alone. This includes the many monasteries and abbeys which have defences to match conventional castles. The Wachau section of the Danube, between Krems and Melk, is considered to be the most scenic with wine-growing villages, forested slopes, vineyards and imposing fortresses at nearly every bend.

DDSG operates steamers along the river west of Vienna from mid-April to the end of October. It has an office in the German border town of Passau (☎ 08351-330 35), Im Ort 14A, Dreiflusseck; see the Vienna and Linz Getting There & Away sections for offices in Austria. The Vienna Getting There & Away section also has details about the high season and eastern services. The Danube flows from west to east and you need to be prepared for longer sailing times when travelling upstream. Return fares are approximately 50% more than the one-way fares quoted here.

The route by road is also scenic. Highway 3 links Vienna and Linz and stays close to the north bank of the Danube for much of the way. There is a cycle track along the south bank from Vienna to Krems, and along both sides of the river from Krems to Linz.

St Pölten has recently become the state capital of Lower Austria, and will in due course take over the information and administration functions for the region currently located in Vienna.

KREMS

The historic town of Krems reclines on the north bank of the Danube, surrounded by terraced vineyards.

Orientation & Information

The town centre is 300 metres in front of the train station, stretching along Obere and

Untere Landstrasse. To the left it leads to the main city gate, Steinertor, off Südtiroler Platz. The main post office is to the left of the station on Brandströmstrasse 4 (Postamt 3500) and it's open for money exchange until 7 pm on weekdays and until 11 am on Saturday. Two km west of the station is the suburb of Stein. The tourist office (☎ 02732-82676) is halfway between the two, at Undstrasse 6. It is open Monday to Friday from 8 am to 5 pm. Between mid-April and 31 October it is also open Saturday and Sunday from 10 am to 5 pm and weekdays to 7 pm.

Things to See & Do
There's little to do in Krems except relax and enjoy the peaceful ambience. Take your time and wander round the cobbled streets, adjoining courtyards and ancient city walls. The most interesting streets are Landstrasse in Krems and Steiner Landstrasse in Stein. There are several churches worth a look, including the **St Viet** high on the hill, and the **Dominican Church**, which contains a collection of religious and modern art and wine-making artefacts. The street plan from the tourist office details points of interest.

Places to Stay & Eat
Camping Donau (☎ 02732-84 455) at Wiedengasse 7, near the boat station, is open from mid-April to 31 October and costs AS35 per person, from AS20 for a tent and AS35 for a car.

The IYHF *youth hostel* (☎ 02732-84 217), Kasernenstrasse 6, off Südtiroler Platz, has large, imposing dorms in the corner of a large, imposing building, in which beds cost AS90 per night and breakfast is AS20. Doors are locked from 9 am to 5 pm and curfew is at 10 pm. The hostel is closed from 16 December to 31 January. A brand-new *youth hostel* (☎ 02732-83 452) is at Ringstrasse 77, the first of its kind in Austria: it is designed especially for cyclists (although noncyclists can stay) and has a garage and an on-site repair service. Beds are for IYHF members only and cost AS145 including breakfast in four or six-bed dorms.

Many hotels have a 10% surcharge for a single-night stay. The best value is *Frühstückspension Einzinger* (☎ 2732-82 316) at Steiner Landstrasse 82, with singles/doubles for AS240/400 with shower and TV. *Hotel Restaurant Alte Poste* (☎ 02732-82 276), Obere Landstrasse, has good singles/doubles from AS290/520 including breakfast and private shower, and an excellent courtyard round the back. It's a good place to eat too, with daily menus from AS70 and local wine from AS18 per quarter litre.

The popular restaurant *Zur Wiener Brücke* (☎ 02732-82 143), Wienerstrasse 2, has a wide selection of main dishes from AS70 and terrace seating overlooking the canal. It is open daily from 7 am to midnight. There is a large *Hofer* supermarket in Sparkassegasse, off Obere Landstrasse.

Getting There & Away
The boat station (Schiffsstation) (☎ 02752-82 050) is 20 minutes' walk from the train station towards Stein on Donaulände. There are up to four departures a day to Melk between 10.30 am and 4 pm. It costs AS228 and takes three hours (Eurail passes are valid, Inter-Rail gets 50% off). Bike rental is available here for AS70 per day or AS30 with a boat ticket. Four buses a day (three a day on weekends) to Melk leave from outside the train station. The fare is AS56 and it takes 65 minutes. Trains to Vienna cost AS114 and take about an hour to Franz Josefs Bahnhof.

MELK
Lying in the lee of its imposing monastery-fortress, Melk is an essential stop on the Wachau stretch.

Orientation & Information
The train station is 300 metres from the town centre. Walk straight ahead for 50 metres down Bahnhofstrasse to get to the post office (Postamt 3390), where money exchange is available to 6 pm on weekdays and 10 am on Saturday. Turn next right for the youth hostel or carry straight on to Hauptstrasse for the centre. From there the tourist office (☎ 02752-23 07) is to the right at Babenbergerstrasse 1, open Monday to Friday from

9 am to noon and 3 to 6 pm and Saturday and Sunday from 10 am to 2 pm. Hours are subject to alteration depending on demand.

Things to See & Do

The **Benedictine Monastery** dominates the town from the hill and provides an excellent view. Guided tours (up to two a day in English) explain its historical importance and are well worth the extra money.

The huge monastery church is Baroque gone mad, with endless prancing angels and gold twirls, but is very impressive nonetheless. The fine library and the mirror room both have an extra tier painted on the ceiling to give the illusion of greater height. The ceilings are slightly curved to aid the effect.

It is open from the Saturday before Palm Sunday to All Saints' Day from 9 am to 5 pm, except between May and September when it closes at 6 pm. Entry costs AS45, or AS20 for students aged up to 27 years, and the guided tour is AS10 extra. During winter the monastery may only be visited by guided tour (☎ 02752-2312 for information).

There are other interesting buildings around town. Try following the walking route outlined in the tourist office pamphlet. Also well worth a visit is **Schallaburg Castle**, five km south of Melk by bus, a 16th century Renaissance palace with marvellous terracotta arches. It is open from mid-May to the end of October and costs AS50, or AS15 for students. A reduced combination ticket with the monastery is available.

Places to Stay & Eat

Camping Melk is on the west of the canal where it joins the Danube, and is open from April to October. Charges are AS35 per person, AS35 per tent and AS25 for a car. The reception is in the restaurant *Melker Fähr-haus* (☎ 02752-3291), Kolomaniau 3, open Wednesday to Monday (daily in summer) from 8 am to midnight. When it is closed, just camp and pay later. The restaurant has good lunch-time menus including soup from AS65.

The IYHF *youth hostel* (☎ 02752-2681), Abt Karl Strasse 42, looks unappealing from the outside but has good showers and four-bed dorms. Beds are AS138 (AS110 for those aged under 19) including breakfast. Reception is closed from 10 am to 5 pm when the doors are also locked, but during the day you can reserve a bed and leave your bags behind the door to the left of the entrance. Curfew is 10 pm and the hostel is closed from November to February.

Gasthof Baumgartner (☎ 02752-2419), Bahnhofstrasse 12 by the station, has singles/doubles for AS150/280 including breakfast. Its restaurant is good and cheap and open from 7 am to midnight every day. Wiener schnitzel, chips and salad will set you back AS70 and beer is AS23 a Krügel.

Gasthof Goldener Hirsch (☎ 02752-27 52), at Rathausplatz 13 in the centre of town, offers newly renovated singles/doubles with private shower from AS280/480. The restaurant has a good range of daily menus with soup for AS45 to AS95.

There is a *Spar* supermarket at Rathausplatz 9.

Getting There & Away

Boats leave from the canal by Pionierstrasse, 400 metres to the rear of the monastery. The 5½-hour boat journey from Melk to Vienna costs AS510; Krems is reached along the way after less than two hours. Bicycle rental is available in the train station and at the boat station. Trains to Vienna Westbahnhof (AS124) travel via St Pölten and take around 75 minutes.

LINZ

Despite all the heavy industries based in Linz, the provincial capital of Upper Austria retains a picturesque old-town centre. It's just a pity about the belching smokestacks on the outskirts that smudge your view of the Alps.

Orientation & Information

Most of the town is on the south bank of the Danube. The tourist office (☎ 0732-2393 1778), Hauptplatz 34, is on the main square and has a free room-finding service and a worthwhile walking tour pamphlet. It is open

Monday to Saturday from 9 am to noon and 1 to 7 pm and Sunday from 2 to 7 pm, except from 1 October to 30 April when it is only open Monday to Friday from 9 am to noon and 1 to 6 pm. To get there from the train station, walk right, then turn left at the far side of the park and continue along Landstrasse for 10 minutes.

There is also an information office in the station, and 24-hour bike rental. The main post office is opposite the station on the left, and is open 24 hours. American Express (☎ 0732-669 013) is at Bürgerstrasse 14. The provincial tourist office (☎ 0732-663 021), with information on Salzkammergut, is at Schillerstrasse 50. Opening hours are Monday to Thursday from 8 am to noon and 1 to 5 pm, and Friday from 8 am to 1 pm.

Things to See & Do

The large, Baroque **Hauptplatz** has at its centre the Pillar of the Holy Trinity, sculpted in Salzburg marble in 1723. From Hauptplatz, turn into Hofgasse and climb the hill to **Linz Castle**. The castle has been periodically rebuilt since 799 AD and provides a good view of the many church spires in the centre. It also houses the **Schlossmuseum** which has interesting alternating exhibitions. The museum is open daily and admission is AS25, but exhibitions cost extra.

The neo-Gothic **New Cathedral**, built in 1855, has an incredible array of stained-glass windows including one depicting the history of the town. Walk or take the special tram up **Pöstlingberg**, on the north bank, recognised by the twin-spired church at the summit of the hill. There is a great view from the top. Also on the north bank is the **Neue Galerie**, Blütenstrasse 15, featuring modern German and Austrian art. Entry is AS20 and it's open daily except Sunday. The *Posthof* (☎ 0732-770 548), Posthofstrasse 43, is a centre for contemporary music, dance and theatre.

Places to Stay

The nearest *camping* (☎ 0732-30 53 14) is out of town at Wiener Bundesstrasse 937, Pichlinger See.

There are three youth hostels in Linz. The *Jugendgästehaus* (☎ 0732-66 44 34), at Stanglhofweg 3 near Linz Stadium, has two-bed rooms for AS180 per person, and four-bed rooms for AS130, including breakfast. The *Jugendherberge* (☎ 0732-78 27 20), Kapuzinerstrasse 14, near the centre, has beds for AS100 without breakfast. The *Landes-Jugendherberge* (☎ 0732-23 70 78), Blütenstrasse 23, on the north bank, has beds from AS105 including breakfast.

Hotels start at AS180 per person, but these cheaper places aren't convenient for the centre. *Wilder Mann* (☎ 0732-56 0 78), Goethestrasse 14, off Landstrasse, has singles/doubles from AS290/480, or AS360/580 with private bath. *Goldener Anker* (☎ 0732-77 10 88), Hofgasse 5, off Hauptplatz, has rooms from AS260 per person excluding breakfast.

Places to Eat

A good place for eating in a lively bar environment is *Schwarzer Bär* (☎ 0732-77 24 77 0), Herrenstrasse 9-11, with meals starting at AS59. It also has comfortable rooms from AS330 per person. Mainly young people crowd into *Café Ex-Blatt*, on the corner of Steingasse and Waltherstrasse, for pizza (AS64) and beer (AS33). It's open daily to midnight.

One of the cheapest places to sit down and eat is *Goldenes Kreuz*, Pfarrplatz 11, behind the parish church. It has typical Austrian food plus fish, spaghetti and grilled dishes and is closed Saturday. *Klosterhof*, on the corner of Bischofstrasse and Landestrasse, is large and popular in a 17th century building. It has midday menus from around AS70 and is open daily from 9 am to midnight. Evening dishes are in the range of AS85 to AS140. There are plenty of cheap Wurst stalls around the park on Landstrasse, and a *Mondo* supermarket at the station end of Landstrasse in Blumauerplatz.

Getting There & Away

The DDSG Schiffsstation (☎ 0732-771 090) is at Untere Donaulände 1, on the south bank just east of Nibelungen Bridge. Services to

Melk (AS316, takes 5¾ hours) and Passau (AS198, takes 6½ hours) only operate from mid-May to the end of September. There is just one departure daily in either direction. Linz is on the main rail route between Vienna and Salzburg.

There is a Mitfahrzentrale (☎ 0732-78 27 20) for hitchers at Kapuzinerstrasse 14, open Monday to Friday from 7.30 am to 8 pm.

The South

The two principal states in the south, Styria (Steiermark) and Carinthia (Kärnten) are less visited by foreigners, yet they offer the usual mountains and lakes as well as influences from the neighbouring countries of Italy, Slovenia and Hungary.

GRAZ

Graz is the capital of Styria, a province characterised by mountains and dense forests. In former times, Graz was an important bulwark against invading Turks. Today, it is fast becoming an essential stop on the tourist trail.

Orientation

Graz is dominated by the Schlossberg, the castle hill which rises over the medieval town centre. The river Mur cuts a north-south path just to the west of the hill. The main train station is 1.5 km west of the river. Tram Nos 3 and 6 leave from the station and continue along Annenstrasse to the town centre.

Hauptplatz is the central point of the old town. Leading off it are a number of streets including Sporgasse, an important shopping street, and Herrengasse, the main pedestrian thoroughfare.

Information

There is an information office (☎ 0316-91 68 37) in the main train station on platform 1, open daily from 9 am to 7 pm. Closing times are brought forward to 5 pm on Saturday and

4 pm on Sunday and holidays. Also in the station, bike rental and ticket counters for money exchange are open 24 hours daily.

The main tourist office (☎ 0316-83 52 41), Herrengasse 16, is open Monday to Saturday from 9 am to 7 pm, and Sunday and holidays from 10 am to 3 pm. The main post office is at Neutorgasse 46 (Hauptpostamt Graz, A-8010), open 24 hours for international telephones and for money exchange. American Express (☎ 81 70 70) is at Hamerlingasse 6. The telephone code for Graz is 0316.

Things to See & Do

Paths wind up the **Schlossberg** from all sides. The hike up takes less than 30 minutes and rewards walkers with excellent views. At the top is an open-air theatre, a small military museum and the bell tower which dates from 1588. Unusually, the larger hand on the clock face shows the hours. The townsfolk paid the French not to destroy it during the Napoleonic Wars.

The nearby **Stadtpark** (City Park) is a relaxing place to sit and wander. The impressive Baroque **Mausoleum** is the resting place of Ferdinand II and several other related Habsburgs. It is open Monday to Saturday from 11 am to noon and in the summer from 2 to 3 pm and costs AS15 for admission. The next-door **cathedral**, at the corner of Hofgasse and Bürgergasse, is also worth a look.

Don't miss the **Landeszeughaus** (Armoury), Herrengasse 16, an incredible array of gleaming armour and weapons, enough to equip nearly 30,000 soldiers. Most of it dates from the 17th century when the original Armoury was built. Those two-handed swords look too heavy to even lift, let alone wield with any accuracy. If you're short of time, head straight for the upper floors where the best stuff is stored. The Armoury is open between 1 April and 31 October, Monday to Friday from 9 am to 5 pm, Saturday and Sunday to 1 pm. Entry costs AS25, or free if you're a student. Students get free entry to several other museums around town.

A good activity for those with kids is the

AUSTRIA

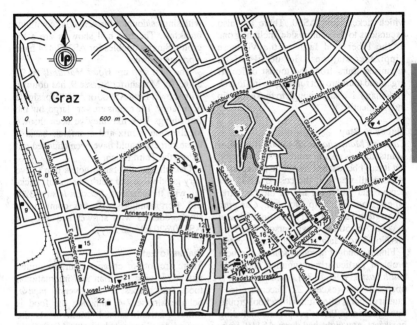

1	Schmid Greiner	12	Mangolds Vollwert Restaurant
2	Pension Iris	13	American Express
3	Schlossberg	14	Opera
4	Mensa	15	Hotel Strasser
5	Hotel Goldener Engel	16	Landhaus Keller
6	Café Art Scherbe	17	Tourist Office & Landeszeughaus
7	Gasthaus Goldene Kugel	18	Operncafé
8	Train Station	19	Post Office
9	Kügerl Lukas	20	Restaurant Gösser Bräu
10	Hotel Mariahilf	21	Restaurant Schweizerhof
11	Kommod	22	Youth Hostel

Schlossberg Cave Railway, Sackstrasse, the longest grotto railway in Europe, which winds its two-km-way around scenes from fairy tales. It is open daily and admission prices are: one adult AS30, two adults AS55, children free with adults.

Eggenberg Castle, Eggenbergen Allee 90, is three km west of the centre and can be reached by tram No 1. The interior of this sumptuous 17th century residence can be visited by guided tour; it also has two museums and extensive parkland in which to roam around. Entry to the building is AS25, or free for students. The park (AS2 entry) is open daily all year; the state rooms are open between 31 March and 31 October from 10 am to 1 pm and 2 to 5 pm every day.

Organised Tours There are a variety of guided walks of the city in the summer, for which tickets cost AS50. There are also excursions to the countryside, including one to the Piber stud farm of the Viennese Lippizaner stallions. Get details of all organised tours from the tourist office. If organised tours are not running owing to lack of demand, it's easy enough to make the trip independently.

Places to Stay

Camping Mantscha (☎ 28 43 80), Riederhof Mantscha 1, is six km south-west of the city, but it can't be reached by public transport. It is open all year and the cost is AS35 per person and AS55 for use of the car park. Open from April to October, *Camping Strassgang* (☎ 28 18 31), Martinhofstrasse 3, costs AS150 for a two-person site. Take bus No 32 from Jakomini Platz in the centre.

Finding budget accommodation can be a problem, particularly in summer. The IYHF *youth hostel* (☎ 91 48 76), Idlhofgasse 74, is open all year (except 22 December to 7 January), but is often full with school groups during summer. Prices per person, including breakfast, are: eight-bed dorm AS110, four-bed dorm AS170 and double room AS220, all with a AS10 surcharge for the first night's stay. Dorms are closed from 9 am to 5 pm but the downstairs section of the hostel stays open. Curfew is at 10 pm. It's 15 minutes' walk from the station: head right along Bahnhofgürtel, turn left into Josef Huber Gasse then take the first right.

On the way to the youth hostel, you'll pass *Hotel Strasser* (☎ 91 39 77), Eggenberger Gürtel 11. It has functional singles/doubles for AS260/460 without shower, or AS320/560 with private shower. Breakfast is included in the price.

Around the back of the station, pension *Kügerl Lukas*, (☎ 52 5 90), Waagner Birò Strasse 8, has fairly drab singles/doubles from AS210/370, without breakfast. Much nicer is the cosy pension *Schmid Greiner* (☎ 68 14 82), Grabenstrasse 64, north of Schlossberg. Singles/doubles with breakfast are AS250/380, plus AS20 to use the hall shower. Convenient for the centre is *Hotel Goldener Engel* (☎ 91 37 57), Lendplatz 1,

with singles/doubles for AS247/424 without breakfast. The free hall showers are a bit grotty. Singles/doubles for AS277/474 have a private shower.

The next step up, *Hotel Mariahilf* (☎ 91 31 63 0), Mariahilfer Strasse 9, has doubles with shower from AS980 or AS690 for single occupancy. The rooms are very large, but the furnishings look like they've been thrown together on a mix-and-mismatch basis – those carpets should have been chucked out before the Third Reich.

Overall, the mid-range hotels don't give very good value and you're better off sticking with the pensions. *Pension Iris* (☎ 32 0 81), Bergmanngasse 10, has comfortable singles/doubles with shower and WC for AS420/620 (closed July).

Places to Eat

There are lots of cheap restaurants dotted around, serving Austrian and international food. The cheapest is the university *mensa*, Schubertstrasse 2-4, although the food is rather institutionalised. Main meals are around AS40 and salads start at AS18. Food is served Monday to Saturday from 11 am to 2.30 pm. The adjoining café is open extended hours. There are several other cheap places in the vicinity of the university which are popular with students, such as *Café Harry* on Harrachgasse (open weekdays to 10 pm).

Restaurant Schweizerhof, Josef Huber Gasse 24, is near the youth hostel. The best deals are the wonderful three-course lunchtime menus from AS50, but also good value is the spaghetti from AS48, local and Austrian specialities from AS75 and beer for AS25 a Krügel. It is open weekdays and (except June and July) Saturday lunch time.

For a splurge, head to the 16th century *Landhaus Keller* (☎ 83 02 76) at Schmiedgasse 9. A meal with soup will cost around AS200 to AS260 plus drinks, but the quality is excellent and the white wines served in ice-filled buckets on stands by the tables add to the pose value. It is open Monday to Saturday from 11 am to midnight. For somewhat cheaper fodder, there is a large *Billa* supermarket at Annenstrasse 23, five minutes from the Hauptbahnhof.

A good place to try local cooking is *Gasthaus Goldene Kugel* at Leonhardstrasse 32. Midday menus are AS55 and AS65, evening dishes are around AS80 and it's open Sunday to Friday from 9 am to midnight. Open the same hours, *Restaurant Gösser Bräu*, Neutorgasse 48, also has a good choice of regional dishes from AS60, and more important, an excellent selection of local Gösser beer (from AS28). There are many different rooms in this large place, and a garden terrace.

Cafeteria-style vegetable heaven can be found at *Mangolds Vollwert Restaurant*, Griesgasse 11. Salad is AS12 per 100 grams, a plate with five different vegetables is AS45 and there are various healthy desserts.

Entertainment

Graz has several traditional coffee houses; a good one is *Operncafé*, Opernring 22, open daily from 8 am (9 am Sunday) to midnight. In the centre of town, Mehlplatz and Prokopigasse are full of lively and crowded bars which are not too expensive for wine or beer. Many offer snacks or full meals until late.

Burggasse is another good street to explore: some of the bars along it have live music. *Kommod*, at No 15, is bright and busy and serves pizza and pasta from AS55; it's open daily from 5 pm to 2 am. *Café art Scherbe* (☎ 91 73 22), Stockergasse 2, off Lendl Platz, is a very relaxed bar with amusing art objects and temporary displays of paintings (which are for sale). Beer is AS27 a Krügel and it's open Monday to Saturday from 10 am to 3 am, Sunday from 11 am to midnight.

Graz is an important cultural centre with various musical events taking place throughout the year. The *Tageskasse* (☎ 8000), Kaiser Josef Platz 10, sells theatre and opera tickets; students aged under 27 pay half price. Students can also get cheap tickets at the door an hour before performances.

For information about performances, telephone the theatre (Schauspielhaus) on ☎ 8005 and the opera house (Opernhaus) on ☎ 8008.

Getting There & Away

Direct IC trains to Vienna Südbahnhof depart every two hours. The fare is AS256 and the journey takes two hours 40 minutes. There are four direct trains a day to Salzburg (AS360) and two a day to Zagreb (AS200, takes four hours). Several trains a day also go to Budapest via Szombathely. Trains to Klagenfurt go via Leoben. The A2 autobahn from Vienna to Klagenfurt passes a few kilometres south of the city.

Getting Around

Individual public transport tickets cost AS15 each or AS60 for a block of six. The Schlossbergbahn (castle hill railway) runs from Sackstrasse up the castle hill. The fare is AS15 up, AS10 down and AS20 return. The Touristenkarte costs AS42 and is valid for 24 hours, including rides on the Schlossbergbahn.

KLAGENFURT

The capital of Carinthia since 1518, Klagenfurt is not so well known as a tourist destination yet it is not without its attractions.

Orientation & Information

The main train station is one km south of Neuer Platz, the heart of the city. To get there from the station, walk straight ahead down Bahnhofstrasse and take a left at Paradieser Gasse. The tourist office (☎ 0463-537 295) is in the Rathaus on Neuer Platz. Opening hours are Monday to Friday from 8 am to 8 pm, and Saturday to Sunday from 10 am to 5 pm, except from October to mid-May when hours are reduced to Monday to Friday from 8 am to 6 pm. The staff reserves rooms (no commission), and rents bikes cheaply at a low rate of AS30 for three hours or AS70 for the day. The Hauptbahnhof also rents bikes, and the counters are open 24 hours. The main post office is on Dr Hermann Gasse (Postamt 9010), one block to the west of Neuer Platz.

AUSTRIA

Things to See & Do

The **Neuer Platz** (New Square) is dominated by the Dragon Fountain, the emblem of the city, and also by a statue of Maria Theresa dating from 1765. **Alter Platz** (Old Square) is the oldest part of the city and an interesting street to explore. In the 16th century **Landhaus** is the Hall of Arms (Wappensaal), the walls of which are covered in paintings of 655 coats of arms. More impressive than the walls is the roof, which has an extra gallery painted on it, giving the illusion that it is vaulted and higher than it is. It is actually 10 metres high and perfectly flat. Stand in the centre of the room for the best effect. It is open between 1 April and 31 September, Monday to Friday from 9 am to 4 pm. Entry costs a nominal AS6, or AS3 for students.

Lake Wörther is four km west of the city centre. Owing to the presence of subterranean thermal springs, it is one of the warmer lakes in the region and ideal for water sports. STW (☎ 0463-211 55), St Veiter Strasse 31, runs steamers on the lake from early May to mid-October. A one-day circular tour costs AS130 for adults and there's a four-week holiday ticket for AS400 (children AS200). One-day family cards (two adults and three children) cost AS330 or AS300 in advance. Boats also travel up the canal to the city centre (AS30).

At the lakeside **Strandbad** by the boat station there is swimming, boating and waterskiing in the summer. Telephone ☎ 0463-211 69 for information. The adjoining **Europa Park** has various attractions, such as tennis courts, crazy golf, a reptile zoo and a 'plantarium'. The most touristy offering in the park is **Minimundus**, displaying 150 models of famous international buildings on a 1:25 scale. It is open daily from late April to mid-October and costs AS65 for adults and AS20 for children. Take bus S or K from Heiligen Geist Platz.

Klagenfurt is ringed by castles and stately homes. The tourist office has a free map detailing routes, ideal if you have your own transport. It also has a *Radwandern* cycling map listing sights and distances. The longest tour is 34 km.

Places to Stay & Eat

Camping Strandbad (☎ 0463-211 69) is in a good location in Europa Park by the lake. Cost is AS58.50 per person and AS25 for a car.

Within 10 minutes' walk of Neuer Platz is *Jugendgästehaus Kolping* (☎ 0463-569 65), Enzenbergstrasse 26, but it's only open in July and August. The brand-new IYHF *Jugendgästehaus Klagenfurt* (☎ 0463-23 00 20), Neckheimgasse 6, near Europa Park, has gleaming facilities and inexperienced management. Four-bed dorms with breakfast cost AS150 or AS140 for three days or more. Half-board is AS200. The hostel closes from mid-December to mid-February.

Lodging is pretty cheap near the inner ring roads. For B&B, try *Lindenkeller* (☎ 0463-51 32 01), Villacher Ring 9, from AS190 per person, or *Liebetegger* (☎ 0463-56 9 35), Völkermarkter Strasse 8, from AS220 per person. *Klepp* (☎ 0463-32 2 78), Platzgasse 4, has beds without breakfast for AS200 per person. For more style overlooking the lake, go to *Hotel Wörther See* (☎ 0463-21 1 58), Villacher Strasse 338. It has well-presented rooms, some with balcony, with cable TV and bath or shower. Singles/doubles start at AS590/880 with prices rising around 10% in summer. Extra beds for kids are AS260.

Eating cheaply in the centre isn't too hard, either. There are several *Imbiss* (snack) stands dotted around, or you can stock up at the *Spar* supermarket in Adlergasse or Dr Hermann Gasse. *Gasthof Pirker* on the corner of Adlergasse and Lidmanskygasse has typical meat-and-potatoes fare from AS50. It's open daily (except Saturday) to midnight. The *Restaurant Am Dom*, Lidmanskygasse 10, has tasty lunch and evening menus with soup from AS90 to AS120. There is a good selection of other dishes from AS70 and beer is a palatable AS26 a Krügel.

Getting There & Away

Just three buses a day (bus A) go direct to the airport from the city bus terminal which is off Dr Hermann Gasse, but many more (bus F) go via Annabichl. There are five flights a day to Vienna and two a day to Zürich and

Frankfurt. Trains to Graz depart every one to two hours; the fare is AS278 and it takes around three hours. Trains to west Austria, Italy and Germany go via Villach, to which there are several departures an hour (takes 30 to 40 minutes).

City buses cost AS15 for one journey (including changes) or AS36 for a day pass.

Salzburg

The city that delivered Mozart to the world has much to recommend it, despite the fact that in more recent years the nearby hills were alive to the *Sound of Music*. The influence of Mozart is everywhere. There is Mozartplatz, the Mozarteum, Mozart House and the Mozart Museum, to name but a few of the attractions that bear his name. He even has chocolate bars and liqueurs named after him.

But Mozart himself must take second place to the powerful bishop-princes who shaped the skyline and the destiny of the city since 798 AD. The Hollywood musical, meanwhile, is remembered in one of the most popular city tours around.

Orientation
The centre of the city is split by the River Salzach. The old part of town is on the south bank, with the unmistakable Hohensalzburg Fortress dominant on the hill above. Most of the attractions are on this side of the river. Opposite, on the north bank, the new town is the centre of business activity and the site of most of the cheaper hotels.

Information
Tourist Offices The central office (☎ 0662-84 75 68 or 88 98 7-331) is at Mozartplatz 5. Its opening hours are April to October daily from 9 am to 7 pm, and November to March from 9 am to 6 pm Monday to Saturday. Hours vary according to demand: it sometimes closes as late as 10 pm in July and August. The provincial information section in the same building shuts at 6 pm.

Other information offices open all year are in the Hauptbahnhof (☎ 0662-871 712 or 873 638) on platform 10; and Mitte (☎ 0662-432 228 or 433 110), Münchner Bundesstrasse 1. Offices only open from 1 April to 31 October are: South (☎ 0662-20 966 or 889 87-335) at Park & Ride Parkplatz, Alpensiedlung Süd, Alpenstrasse; North (☎ 663 220) at Autobahnstation Kasern; and West (☎ 0662-85 24 51) at the airport by the BP petrol station, Bundesstrasse 95.

Money Banks are open Monday to Friday from 8 am to noon, and from 2 to 4.30 pm. Currency exchange at the Hauptbahnhof is available from 7 am to 10 pm daily in the summer and 7.30 am to 9 pm daily in the winter. At the airport the exchange booth is open daily from 8 am to noon and from 12.30 to 4 pm. Between 4 and 8 pm the information counter in the airport will exchange money.

Post & Telecommunications At the train station, the post office (Bahnhofspostamt A 5020) is open 24 hours daily, but poste restante and money exchange shut at 10 pm. In the town centre, the main post office at Residenzplatz 9 is open Monday to Friday from 7 am to 7 pm, and Saturday from 8 to 10 am. The telephone code for Salzburg is 0662.

Foreign Consulates The British Consulate (☎ 84 81 33) is right in the centre of the old town at Alter Markt 4. The US Consulate (☎ 28 601) is at Giselakai 51. South of old town is the Swiss Consulate (☎ 22 530) at Alpenstrasse 85. The German Consulate (☎ 84 15 91) is near the Mönchsberg lift at Bürgerspitalplatz 1-II. The Italian Consulate (☎ 25 233) is at Alpenstrasse 102-II.

Travel Agents American Express (☎ 84 25 01), Mozartplatz 5, is open Monday to Friday from 9 am to 5.30 pm and Saturday to noon. The office is next door to the tourist office. ÖKISTA (☎ 88 32 52), Wolf Dietrich Strasse 31, is open Monday to Friday from 9 am to 5.30 pm. Young Austria (☎ 213 570), Alpenstrasse 108A, is open Monday to

AUSTRIA

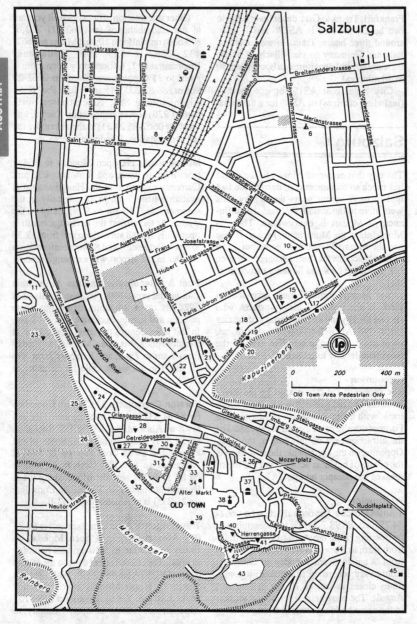

Salzburg

■ PLACES TO STAY

1   Youth Hostel Haunspergstrasse
5   Sandwirt
6   Stadt Camping
7   Elizabeth Pension
9   International Youth Hotel
17 Youth Hostel Glockengasse
19 Junger Fuchs
20 Goldene Krone
26 Naturfreundehaus
27 Blaue Gans
35 Zur Goldenen Ente
44 Hinterbrühl
45 Youth Hostel Salzburg

▼ PLACES TO EAT

8   Café-Bistro Tabasco
10 Restaurant Wegscheidstuben
12 Vollwertkost Spezialitäten
14 Michael Haydn Stube
16 Hotel Restaurant Hofwirt
23 Schloss Mönchstein
28 Sternbräu
29 Fabrizi Espresso
40 Weisses Kreuz
41 St Paul's Stuben
42 Stieglkeller

OTHER

2   Railway Station Post Office
3   Postbus Station
4   Hauptbahnhof
11 Augustiner Braustübl
13 Mirabell Castle & Gardens
15 Hofer Supermarket
18 St Sebastian Church
21 Schnaitl Musik Pub
22 Mozart's Residence
24 Museum of Natural History
25 Mönchsberg Lift
30 Mozart's Birthplace
31 Collegiate Church
32 Festival Houses
33 Café Tomaselli
34 Residenz Gallery &
     State Rooms
36 Main Tourist Office &
     American Express
37 Main Post Office
38 Cathedral
39 St Peter's Abbey &
     Catacombs
43 Hohensalzburg Castle

Friday from 9 am to 6 pm and Saturday to noon.

Emergency The Medical Emergency Centre (☎ 141), Paris-Lodron-Strasse 8a, is open without break from Saturday 7 am to Monday 7 am and on public holidays. St John's Hospital (☎ 44 820) is at Müllner Hauptstrasse 48 on the south bank. The police can be contacted on ☎ 133.

Things to See & Do

Walking Tour The whole of the old town is a Baroque masterpiece set amid the Kapuzinerberg and Mönchsberg mountains, both of which have a good network of footpaths. Take time to wander round the many plazas, courtyards and fountains.

Start at the vast **cathedral** (Dom) on Domplatz, with its three bronze doors symbolising faith, hope and charity. Nearby is **St Peter's Abbey**, dating from 847 AD. The interesting graveyard contains the catacombs which have 20-minute guided tours every hour (AS10, students AS7). There are several other impressive churches in the town centre. Fisher von Erlach's **Collegiate Church**, Universitätsplatz, is considered an outstanding example of Baroque. Most of it is, but the cherubs and clouds above the altar are a bit ridiculous, and the gold figures below look like something cheap and nasty given away with a few litres of petrol.

Hohensalzburg Castle In many ways this is the high point of a visit to Salzburg. Walk up in 30 minutes or take the Festungbahn (AS18 up, AS28 return) from Festungsgasse 4. It is almost like a separate village within the castle walls. Admission is AS20 (students AS10), but it's worth paying the extra for the guided tour (25AS, students 15AS) which allows entrance to the torture chambers, state rooms, the tower and two museums. The view from the castle over the city is stupendous. Look also at the view on the south side: the isolated house in the middle of the big field is reputed to have once belonged to the official executioner. He wasn't allowed to live within the city and nobody else wanted to live anywhere near him.

Museums At Museumsplatz 5, the **Museum of Natural History** (Haus der Natur) is stunning. You could spend most of the day wandering round its diverse and well-presented exhibits. On top of the usual flora, fauna and mineral displays there are good hands-on sections on physics and astronomy, plus bizarre oddities such as the stomach-churning display of deformed human embryos. There are also many tropical fish and an excellent reptile house with lizards, snakes and alligators. It even has a cheap terrace café with menus from AS68. It is open daily from 9 am to 5 pm, and admission costs AS35, or AS20 for students.

The other museums don't take too long to get round. In the **Residenz**, Residenzplatz 1, you can visit the Baroque state rooms of the archbishop's palace (by guided tour only) and the gallery which houses some good 16th and 17th century Dutch and Flemish paintings. A combined ticket costs AS60. The **Rupertinium**, Wiener Philharmoniker Gasse 9, has 20th century works of art and temporary exhibitions. Entry costs AS35, or AS20 for students.

Mozart's Birthplace (Geburtshaus) (admission AS50, students AS35), Getreidegasse 9, and **Residence** (Wohnhaus) (AS35, students AS25), Makartplatz 8, are popular but overrated and contain musical instruments, sheet music and other memorabilia of the great man. A combined ticket for the two Mozart museums costs AS70, or AS45 for students.

Mirabell Castle The castle was built by the worldy prince-archbishop Wolf Dietrich for his mistress in 1606, with attractive gardens that many will recognise from the *Sound of Music*. It is a great place to sit down and relax. 'Musical Spring' concerts are held in the castle. Take a look inside at the marble 'angel' staircase, bedecked in Baroque sculptures.

Mausoleum of Wolf Dietrich This is in the

graveyard of the 16th century Sebastian Church on Linzer Gasse. It is newly restored and has some interesting epitaphs. In a wonderful piece of arrogance, the archbishop commands the faithful to 'piously commemorate the founder of this chapel' (ie himself) and 'his close relations', or expect 'God Almighty to be an avenging judge'. Mozart's father and widow are buried in the graveyard.

Organised Tours One-hour walking tours of the old city leave from the main tourist office (AS80). Other tours of the city and environs leave from Mirabellplatz and Residenzplatz, including the *Sound of Music* tour. The film was a flop in Austria, but this is the most popular tour by far with English-speaking visitors. Tours last three to four hours, cost around AS280 and take in major city sights featured in the movie and include a visit to Salzkammergut.

A bit of pot luck is involved: tour itineraries and emphasis can vary even within the same tour operator depending upon the guide, and you do need to be in good company. If you go with a group with the right mix of tongue-in-cheek enthusiasm, it can be brilliant fun. It is hard to forget memories of loutish youths skipping in the summer house, chanting 'I am 16 going on 17', or manic Julie Andrews impersonators flouncing in the fields, screeching 'the hills are alive' in voices to wake the dead. On the other hand, if you go with a serious, earnest group, it can be quite dull.

Festivals
The Summer International Festival takes place from the end of July to the end of August and predominantly features Mozart's music. Several events take place per day in different locations. Prices are steep (AS150 to AS3600!) but most things still sell out months in advance. Write for information as early as September to: Kartenbüro der Salzburger Festspiele, Postfach 140, A 5010 Salzburg.

Sometimes, standing-room tickets are sold 45 minutes before performances –

concert tickets go for AS50 and opera tickets for AS200. Enquire at the ticket office, Hofstallgasse 1, which is open all year but not every day. The opening hours are extended to 9.30 am to 5 pm daily only in July and August.

Places to Stay

Accommodation is at a premium during the festival. Ask for the tourist office's list of private rooms and apartments, and the *Hotelplan* map which, as well as hotels and pensions, lists six youth hostels and seven camp sites.

Camping *Stadt Camping* (☎ 871 169), Bayerhamerstrasse 14A, is the largest site in the centre. Charges are AS60 per person including a tent, AS35 for a car or AS45 for a camper van. There are free hot showers, the shop/buffet is open daily and reception shuts at 8 pm. The site is closed from 1 October to 30 April. Open the same months is *Camping Kasern* (☎ 50 576), Kasern 1, just north of the A1 Nord exit.

Hostels, North Bank If you're travelling for the purpose of partying, head for the *International Youth Hotel* (☎ 87 96 49), Paracelsusstrasse 9. Loud music, cheap beer (AS20 a Krügel), cheap food (meals from AS40) and dancing on the tables add up to a fun time. The staff are almost exclusively young North Americans. Not surprisingly it is very popular, but phone reservations are accepted no earlier than the day before. Beds per person are AS110 (eight-bed dorm), AS120 (four-bed dorm, own key) and AS150 (double room, own key). There is no curfew and it's open all day, showers cost AS10, lockers AS10 and sheets (if required) are AS20. It's not the cleanest place, but most people are too drunk to notice. The hotel also organises outings and shows the *Sound of Music* daily.

The IYHF *youth hostel* (☎ 876 241) at Glockengasse 8 is a bit old, with a tendency to be overrun by noisy school groups, but it is the cheapest hostel in town. Beds in large dorms are AS110 (AS100 per night for two

or more nights) including breakfast. Dinner is AS60, curfew is at midnight and doors are locked from 9 am to 3.30 pm. The hostel is open from 1 April to 15 October and is conveniently situated for excursions on Kapuzinerberg. The IYHF *youth hostel* (☎ 875 030), Haunspergstrasse 27 near the train station, is only open in July and August. The price per night of AS130 includes breakfast.

If everywhere is full in town, try the IYHF *youth hostel* (☎ 232 48), Aignerstrasse 34 in the southern suburb of Aigen. It's open all year, and dorm beds with breakfast cost AS125.

Hostels, South Bank The *Naturfreundehaus* (☎ 84 17 29), Mönchsberg 19, is clearly visible high on the hill between the fortress and the casino. Take the footpath up from near Max Reinhardt Platz or the Mönchsberg lift (AS11 up, AS19 return) from A Neumayr Platz. It has new management and is newly renovated, and offers dorm beds for AS100 without breakfast. Showers cost AS10 and it's open all day, but there is an 11 pm curfew. The views from the top are marvellous. The café has breakfast for AS45 and light meals from AS58. Phone ahead in winter, as it may be closed.

The IYHF *youth hostel Salzburg* (☎ 84 26 70 or 84 68 57), Josef Preis Allee 18, is large, modern and busy. Dorms are AS135, four-bed rooms are AS180 per person and two-bed rooms are AS225 per person. Prices are AS10 lower for two or more nights' stay. It has good showers, free lockers and bike rental for AS70 per day. *Sound of Music* tours are available at the discounted price of AS230 and the film is shown daily. South of town is an IYHF *youth hostel* (☎ 25 976), at Eduard Heinrich Strasse 2, where beds are AS110 including breakfast. The hostel is only open in July and August.

Pensions & Hotels *Sandwirt* (☎ 874 351), Lastenstrasse 6A, is round the back of the station but there is no noise from the trains. Singles/doubles are AS240/360 with a free shower in the hall. Triples/quads with own

AUSTRIA

shower are AS600/700. The hallways are slightly musty, but the rooms are clean and it represents good value. Breakfast is included.

Elizabeth Pension (☎ 871 664), Vogelweiderstrasse 52, has singles/doubles with own shower for AS280/460, and doubles with free use of a hall shower for AS360. Breakfast is included but the rooms are slightly cramped, and it is by a noisy street. On the plus side, however, the building is just around the corner from the Breitenfelderstrasse stop of bus No 15, which goes every 15 minutes to the town centre.

Junger Fuchs (☎ 875 496), Linzer Gasse 54, has singles/doubles/triples for AS220/360/460 without breakfast. The rooms are better than the dingy corridors would suggest and it's in a convenient location. Hall showers cost AS15 in summer but are free in winter. Room rates don't change in the high season. More expensive, but merited by its position in the old town, is *Hinterbrühl* (☎ 84 67 98), Schanzlgasse 12. Singles/doubles are AS400/550 which includes breakfast and free use of the hall shower. Reception is in the restaurant downstairs, open daily from 10 am to 11 pm.

Mid-Range Hotels On the north bank, *Goldene Krone* (☎ 87 23 009), Linzer Gasse 48, has singles/doubles with private shower for AS500/850 or AS400/70 without. Most of the rooms have groined vaults (curved ceilings common in Romanesque churches) which add a bit of character. Virtually opposite is *Amadeus* (☎ 87 14 01), at No 43-45, with similar comfort and prices: it costs AS580/920 for singles/doubles with shower, AS400/600 without.

All the rooms in *Zur Goldenen Ente* (☎ 84 56 22), Goldgasse 10, have private bath/shower and TV but prices vary depending upon size and situation, starting at AS520/780 per single/double. The atmospheric restaurant offers dishes such as the exotic-sounding 'Fillet of Wildboar' (AS178). Also in the old town is *Blaue Gans* (☎ 84 13 17), Getreidegasse 43, where standard singles/doubles start at AS400/800 with

shower and AS350/600 without. It has a good restaurant with three-course menus from AS80 and Mexican specialities from AS60.

Places to Eat

North Bank *Michael Haydn Stube*, Aicher Passage, 1 Mirabellplatz, is unbelievably good value. Lunch specials cost AS40 to AS60, spaghetti bolognese or napoli is AS48, and other dishes start from AS35. It also has cheap beer, pastries and coffee, and is open Monday to Friday from 9.30 am to 6 pm. Just down the passage is the small *Café Gelateria San Marco*, Dreifaltigkeitsgasse 13, which is good for cheap Italian food. It's open Monday to Saturday from 9 am to 10 pm. *Restaurant Wegscheidstuben* (☎ 874 618), Lasserstrasse 1, has a three-course menu for AS105, available lunch time and evening. It offers traditional Austrian cooking which is popular with locals, and it's open Tuesday to Saturday from 8 am to midnight and Sunday lunch time.

Hotel Restaurant Hofwirt (☎ 8753 300), Schallmooser Hauptstrasse 1, has good lunch-time three-course menus for AS75. Evening eating is more expensive, however, but there are English menus. One of the few vegetarian places in town is *Vollwertkost Spezialitäten* (☎ 875 746), Schwartzstrasse 33, a shop and snack bar with a salad buffet (AS30 to AS50) and other vegetable ingredients. It is open Monday to Friday from 10.30 am to 6 pm. There is a fruit-and-vegetable market at Mirabellplatz on Thursday mornings. A large *Billa* supermarket is at Schallmooser Hauptstrasse 16. Just down the road at No 5 is a *Hofer* supermarket.

Café-Bistro Tabasco, Rainerstrasse 25, attracts a fairly affluent clientele with its tempting array of international and Austrian dishes (AS130 to AS230). It has a hot midday buffet including soup for AS95, as well as a lunch and evening salad buffet (AS62 per bowl). It's open daily to midnight.

South Bank It's almost as if they're trying to keep *St Paul's Stuben*, Herrengasse 16, a secret from the tourists. It looks completely anonymous from the outside but for the hanging sign overhead. Pasta and tasty wholewheat pizzas are served upstairs until late and it has a good, intimate atmosphere for drinking and meeting locals. It is open daily from 6 pm to 1 am.

Sternbräu, in a courtyard between Getreidegasse 36 and Griegasse 23, is a bit touristy, but has a nice garden and many different rooms. Good standard Austrian food with grill and fish specialities are served, and daily dishes start from AS62. Opening hours are 8 am to midnight daily. *Fabrizi Espresso*, Getreidegasse 21, is a small café in another pleasant courtyard and has lunch-time Tagesmenus for AS70/80 including soup. It is also open daily (to 6 or 7 pm).

For a good, strong coffee for just AS7, nip into *Eduscho*, Getreidegasse 34, but be prepared to stand. The southern end of Kaigasse is a good place for cheapish restaurants near the old town. On Universitätsplatz there are market stalls and fast-food stands.

A bit higher up the scale is *Weisses Kreuz* (☎ 84 56 41), Bierjodlgasse 6, with Austrian food from AS100 and some interesting Balkan specialities (from AS60). It's a small place so reservations are advised (it's closed Tuesday). Right at the top of the range is the restaurant in *Schloss Mönchstein* (☎ 848 55 50), Mönchsberg Park 26. Enjoy lavishly prepared food in an opulent setting, all shining silverware and soft classical music. Inevitably you have to pay for it, with most dishes topping AS300.

Entertainment

The *Augustiner Bräustübl*, Augustinergasse 4-6, proves that monks can make beer as well as anybody. The quaffing clerics have been supplying the lubrication for this huge beer hall for years. Meat, bread and salad ingredients are available in the delicatessen shops in the foyer. Eat inside or in the large, shady beer garden. It is very atmospheric, with cheap beer served in litre mugs (AS42), and it's open daily from 3 to 11 pm.

Stieglkeller, Festungsgasse 10, is another large beer hall. It's rather touristy, as indi-

cated by the summer folklore show, but there is a good garden overlooking the town. Daily menus in the restaurant are in the range of AS80 to AS170. Opening hours are 10 am to 10 pm daily. The *Schnaitl Musik Pub*, on Bergstrasse 5, has a young and lively local clientele and live rock music every second Wednesday from September to May. Cover charge is around AS50 on music nights. The pub is open daily in the summer from 7.30 pm to 2 am and in the winter from 6.30 pm to 1 am. Imbergstrasse and Steingasse are good streets to explore for late-night bars.

As in Vienna, coffee houses are a well-established tradition. *Café Tomaselli* and *Café Konditorei Fürst* face each other in an ideal central position overlooking Alter Markt. Both have newspapers, lots of cakes and outside tables.

Things to Buy

Not many people leave without sampling some Mozart confectionery. Chocolate-coated combinations of nougat and marzipan cost AS4 to AS6 per piece and are available individually or in souvenir presentation packs. Getreidegasse is the main shopping street.

Getting There & Away

Air There are regular scheduled flights to London, Paris, Brussels, Frankfurt and Zürich. Austrian Airlines (☎ 875 544) has an office at Makartplatz 9, and British Airways (☎ 842 108) has one at Griesgasse 29.

Bus Postbuses depart from outside the Hauptbahnhof. A timetable is displayed in the ticket office. There are five departures a day to Kitzbühel (AS110) between 7.30 am and 4.30 pm, and one to Kufstein (AS156) at 4.30 pm. Buses to Lienz run only in the summer. Numerous buses leave for the Salzkammergut region: 13 daily to Bad Ischl (AS86), 19 to Mondsee (AS46), 17 to St Gilgen (via Fuschl, AS54) and 12 to St Wolfgang (AS80). The first bus leaves around 6.30 am and the last around 8 pm.

Train Salzburg is connected by fast trains to Vienna via Linz every hour. The express service to Klagenfurt goes via Villach. The quickest way to Innsbruck is by the 'corridor' train via Rosenheim in Germany (no passport required) and Kufstein. Departures are every two hours and the fare is AS300. There are around 20 trains a day to Munich. The fare is AS242 and it takes 90 minutes to two hours. Some Munich trains (approximately eight) continue to Karlsruhe via Stuttgart.

Car & Motorbike Three motorways converge on Salzburg and form a ring road round the city: the A1 from Linz and Vienna and the east, the E11 from Munich and the west, and the A10 from Villach and the south. Heading south, you cross over a series of mountain ranges. The A10 has a long toll section from Altenmarkt to Rennweg. The scenic Grossglockner route to Lienz is only open from about mid-May to mid-November.

Getting Around
To/From the Airport Salzburg airport is just four km west of the city centre. Bus No 77 stops near the airport tourist office and terminates at the Hauptbahnhof.

Public Transport Single tickets cost AS18, available from the bus driver, but it is worth buying tickets in advance from Tabak shops. A book of five costs AS60. The 24-hour pass valid for all city buses (including those to/from Hellbrunn) is excellent value at AS23. Passes which are also valid for the castle funicular and the Mönchsberg lift cost AS48/96 for 24/72 hours. All passes are half price for children (aged six to 15 years, free for those aged under six).

Car & Motorbike Driving in the city centre is hardly worth the effort. Parking places are limited and much of the old town is pedestrian access only. The largest car park near the centre is the Altstadt Garage under the Mönchsberg. Attended car parks cost around AS25 per hour. Rates are lower on streets with automatic ticket machines, where a 90-

minute or three-hour maximum usually applies.

Other Transport Taxis cost AS30, plus AS10 per km inside the city or AS18 per km outside the city. To book a radio taxi, call ☎ 874 400. Bike rental in the Hauptbahnhof is open 24 hours, or try VELOrent (☎ 45 65 00) at Franz Josef Strasse 15. Rates for a pony-and-trap (fiacre) for up to four passengers are AS350 for 25 minutes and AS680 for 50 minutes.

AROUND SALZBURG
Hellbrunn
Eight km south of Salzburg's old-town centre is the popular **Hellbrunn Palace** built in the 17th century by bishop Marcus Sitticus, Wolf Dietrich's nephew. The main attraction is the ingenious trick fountains and water-powered figures installed by the bishop and activated today by the tour guides. Expect to get wet! This section of the gardens is open daily from April to October, with the last tour at 4.30 pm, or later in the summer. Tickets cost AS48, or AS24 for students, and include entry to the palace and the small Folklore Museum up on the hill (open from 9 am to 5 pm). There is no charge to stroll round the attractive palace gardens, open from February to November and as late as 9 pm in summer.

The **Hellbrunn Zoo** is as naturalistic and as open-plan as possible: less-dangerous animals are hardly caged at all. From April to September, it is open daily from 8.30 am to 6 pm, and from October to March it is open daily from 9 am to 4 pm. Admission costs AS40, or AS25 for students.

Getting There & Away Bus No 55 stops directly outside the palace every half-hour. Pick it up from Salzburg's Hauptbahnhof or Rudolfskai in the old town. The last bus back to the city is at 9.10 pm.

Hallein
Hallein is primarily visited for the **salt mine** at Bad Dürrnberg, on the hill above the town. Much of Salzburg's past prosperity was

dependent upon salt mines, and this one is the closest to the city and most convenient to visit. The mine stopped production in 1989 and now concentrates on guided tours. Many people rave about the experience but some find the one-hour tour disappointing and overpriced (AS105, students AS95). Careering down the wooden slides in the caves is fun, but there's little to see and technical information is limited, especially for English speakers who receive commentary via a tape recorder. It is open daily from the end of April to mid-October, and the last tour leaves around 5 pm, depending upon demand. Miner's overalls are supplied for the tour.

The tourist office in Hallein (☎ 06245-53 94), Unterer Markt 1, is open Monday to Friday from 9 am to 4.30 pm. In July and August it is also open on Saturday from 9 am to noon.

Getting There & Away Hallein is easily reached from Salzburg by bus or train in about half an hour. To Bad Dürrnberg there are several options. Ten minutes' walk from the station (signposted) you can take the cable car. The AS170 (students AS160) return fare includes entry to the mines and the Celtic and Mining museums. A cheaper option, unless you want to see the museums, is the 15-minute bus ride from outside the station (AS20, departures linked to train arrivals). Hiking is also possible in around 40 minutes, but it is steep: from the tourist office, head straight on, turn left just beyond the church, follow the road round and look for the sign pointing up to the right by the white school building.

Werfen

Werfen is a more rewarding day trip from Salzburg. The **Hohenwerfen Fortress** stands on the hill above the village. Originally built in 1077, the present building dates from the 16th century and can be visited daily from Easter to 31 October. Entry costs AS25, or AS50 with a guide (AS45 for students). The walk up from the village takes 20 minutes.

A greater attraction is the **Eisriesenwelt Höhle**, the largest accessible ice caves in the world. It's like entering another world with its amazing ice formations. The 90-minute tour costs AS65. Take warm clothes as it can get cold inside. The caves are open from 1 May to early October.

The tourist office (☎ 06468-388) in the village main street is open Monday to Friday from 9 am to 5 pm, except in July and August when it's open Monday to Friday from 9 am to 7 pm and weekends from 5 to 7 pm.

Getting There & Away Werfen (and Hallein) can be reached from Salzburg by highway 10. By train it takes an hour. The village is a couple of minutes' walk from Werfen station. Getting to the caves is more complicated. A minibus service (AS60 return) from the station operates along the steep, six-km road to the car park, the limit of road traffic. A 15-minute walk brings you to the cable car (AS85 return) after which it is a further 15-minute walk to the caves. Allow five hours return from the station, or three hours from the car park. The whole route can be hiked – allow around four hours from the village up to the caves.

Salzkammergut

Salzkammergut is the holiday region of mountains and lakes to the east of Salzburg, popular throughout the year with both Austrians and tourists. It is an area where you can simply relax and take in the scenery, or get involved in the numerous sports and activities on offer. In the summer, hiking and water sports are favoured pursuits. In the winter, some hiking paths stay open but downhill and cross-country skiing are more important.

A winter ski pass is available for the Salzkammergut-Tennengau region, which includes 140 cable cars and ski lifts in 21 ski resorts. It costs AS1125 for five days. Six, seven and 10-day passes are also available.

FACTS FOR THE VISITOR
Orientation

The largest lake is Attersee to the north. West

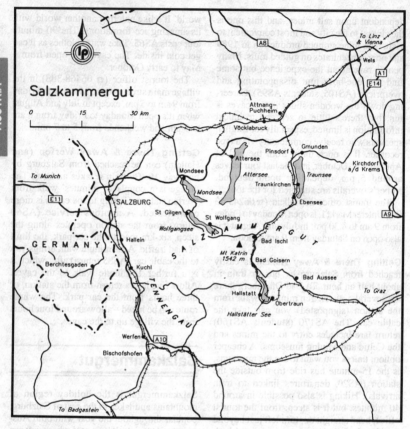

Salzkammergut

0   15   30 km

To Linz & Vienna

To Munich

SALZBURG

GERMANY

Berchtesgaden

To Badgastein

of it is Mondsee, a picturesque lake with warm water making it a favoured swimming spot. The village of Mondsee has an attractive church where the wedding scenes in the *Sound of Music* were filmed. To the east of Attersee is Traunsee with its three main resorts: Gmunden (famous for twin castles linked by a causeway on the lake), Traunkirchen and Ebensee. South of Traunsee is Bad Ischl, the geographical centre of Salzkammergut. Most of the lakes south of Bad Ischl are much smaller, the largest being Hallstätter See. West of Bad Ischl is the Wolfgangsee.

Information

The Salzburg tourist office holds a great deal of information on the area, including bus and train schedules and a list of camp sites. Most of Salzkammergut is in Upper Austria, so the Linz provincial tourist office is also a good source of information. The Salzkammergut tourist association (☎ 06132-69 09) is at Kreuzplatz 23, Bad Ischl. Styria stretches up to claim the area around Bad Aussee: contact the Graz tourist office (☎ 0316-40 30 330), Herrengasse 16, for further information.

The whole area is dotted with youth hostels, and hotels are also generally affordable, but the best deal is probably rooms in private houses even though a single-night surcharge often applies. Tourist offices can supply lists of these, as well as details of Alpine huts at higher elevations. Most resorts offer a holiday/guest card which is useful for a variety of discounts. This must be stamped by the place where you are staying.

GETTING AROUND

The main rail routes pass either side of Salzkammergut, but the region can be crossed by regional trains on a north-south route. You can get on this route from Attnang Puchheim on the Salzburg-Linz line. The track from here connects Gmunden, Traunkirchen, Ebensee, Bad Ischl, Hallstatt and Obertraun. After Obertraun the railway continues east via Bad Aussee before connecting with the main Bischofshofen-Graz line at Stainach Irdning. Attersee can also be reached from the Salzburg-Linz line prior to the Attnang Puchheim stop.

Regular bus services connect all towns and villages in the area. Timetables are displayed at stops, and tickets can be bought from the driver or sometimes in advance. See the Salzburg Getting There & Away section for more bus information. Passenger boats ply the waters of the Attersee, Traunsee, Mondsee, Hallstätter See and Wolfgangsee.

To reach Salzkammergut from Salzburg by private transport, take the A1 or highway 158. You can explore Salzkammergut by bicycle, but roads can be steep, and don't expect to find many separate cycling tracks. Hitching is not particularly widespread.

BAD ISCHL

This spa town's reputation snowballed after Princess Sophie took a treatment to cure her infertility in 1828. Within two years she had given birth to Franz Josef (the penultimate Habsburg emperor). Two other sons followed.

Orientation & Information

The centre of town is compactly contained within a bend of the River Traun.

The tourist office (☎ 06132-35 200) is close to the station (ahead and to the left) at Bahnhofstrasse 6. It is open Monday to Friday from 8 am to noon and 2 to 5 pm, and Saturday from 9 am to noon. Between 1 June and 30 September hours are extended to Monday to Friday from 8 am to 6 pm, Saturday to 4 pm and Sunday from 9 am to noon. Not far along Bahnhofstrasse is the post office (Postamt 4820), which has money-exchange facilities. Bike rental in the station is open daily from 5 am to 9.10 pm.

Things to See & Do

Salzkammergut became popular in the mid-19th century when Emperor Franz Josef I began spending his summers in Bad Ischl in the **Kaiservilla**. He used to get up every day at 3.30 am for his bath, and also signed the declaration of war here that started WW I. The villa was his hunting lodge and contains an obscene number of hunting trophies. It can be visited only by guided tour which is given in German, but there are written English translations. The tour takes 40 minutes and costs AS63. It costs an extra AS25 to get into the Kaiserpark grounds. The nearby small **Photomuseum** in the park has some interesting old photos and cameras (entry AS15, students AS10).

Free 'spa concerts' take place two to three times a day during the summer. The tourist office has a list of venues and times. It also has information on health treatments available in this health resort. An operetta festival takes place in July and August; for details and reservations, call ☎ 06132-3839.

Bad Ischl has downhill skiing from **Mt Katrin** (a winter day pass costs AS190) and a variety of cross-country skiing routes. In summer the Mt Katrin cable car costs AS140 return but there is a reduction with the guest card (AS125). There is a **salt mine** to the south of town for which tours cost AS100 (AS90 with guest card).

Places to Stay & Eat

The IYHF *youth hostel* (☎ 06132-65 77) is at Am Rechensteg 5, in the town centre behind Kreuzplatz. Beds are AS120 including breakfast. The youth hostel *Pfarrheim* (☎ 06132-34 83), Auböckplatz 6C, costs AS50 for beds in 20-bed dorms but it's only open from mid-June to mid-September.

There are also many private rooms: the woman at Stiegengasse 1 (☎ 06132-46 072) has four singles and two doubles for around AS120 per person including breakfast. Baths cost AS20 and it's excellent value with TVs in many rooms. *Haus Kurpark* (☎ 06132-77 35), Wiesingerstrasse 5, has spacious rooms with own bath and WC from AS220 per person, with breakfast an extra AS30. In the summer, prices rise by AS50 per person.

Reception is in the adjoining *Pizzeria Don Camillo*, which has pizza and spaghetti dishes from AS55 and salads from AS35. It is open daily from 11 am to 2 pm and 5 to 11 pm. For hotel reception in the afternoon, just knock on the restaurant door. For uninspiring but cheap filler food, go to *Traunnreiter-stuben* restaurant, Pfarrgasse 5, with daily menus from AS60.

Getting There & Away
Postbuses leave from outside the station. There are hourly departures to St Wolfgang between 6.45 am and 8.10 pm (fare AS36) and to Salzburg between 5.05 am and 6.20 pm (fare AS86). Many buses a day go to Hallstatt; the fare is AS42 and it takes 50 minutes. Three buses a day go to Mondsee and four a day to Obertraun.

Train departures are every one to two hours. To Hallstatt costs AS30 but you must add the cost of the boat (see the Hallstatt Getting There & Away section), whereas the bus goes direct into the village. The fare to Salzburg by train is AS154 (via Attnang Puchheim).

HALLSTATT
Hallstatt has a history stretching back 4500 years. In 50 AD the Romans came here, attracted by the rich salt deposits. Today the village is prized mainly for its picturesque location.

Orientation & Information
Seestrasse is the main street. From the ferry,

turn left for the tourist office (☎ 06134-208), Seestrasse 169. It is open daily in summer and Monday to Friday in winter, although the hours are subject to change. Around the corner is the post office (Postamt 4830), which changes money. The postbus stop is by the stream at the southern end of the road tunnel. From there, walk left (as you face the lake) for the tourist office. The youth hostel is not far from the base of the cable car.

Things to See & Do
Hallstatt is set in idyllic, picture-postcard scenery between the mountains and the lake. Consequently it is invaded by crowds of day trippers, particularly tour groups from Czechoslovakia. But don't let that put you off: they only stay a few hours and then the village returns to its natural calm.

Above the village are the **Saltworks**, open daily from 9.30 am. From May to October the last tour is at 3 pm and in the summer it is at 4.30 pm. Admission costs AS115, or AS100 with the holiday card. The cable car to the top costs AS85 return (AS70 with holiday card), but there are two scenic hiking trails you can take instead. Near the mine, 2000 flat graves were discovered dating from 1000 to 500 BC. Don't miss the macabre **Bone House** by the village parish church, containing rows of decorated skulls. Around the lake at Obertraun are the **Dachstein Giant Ice Caves**, open May to mid-October, which cost AS68 to view.

Places to Stay & Eat
Campingplatz Höll (☎ 06134-329), Lahnstrasse 6, costs AS35.50 per person, AS27 per tent and AS23 per car. It's open from 1 May to 30 September.

The IYHF *youth hostel* (☎ 06134-681 or 279), Salzbergstrasse 50, is open from 1 May to 15 October, depending on the weather. Beds cost AS72, breakfast is AS25, sheets (if required) are AS25 and, unusually, there is no surcharge for nonmembers. It is friendly and relaxed, with new showers. Reception shuts at 8 pm and a key is available for late nights beyond the 10 pm closing time.

TVN Naturfreunde Herberge (☎ 06134-

318), Kirchenweg 36, has dorm beds for AS150 including sheets, showers and breakfast. The cheap restaurant (closed on Wednesday) has pizzas from AS58 and Austrian dishes from AS55. Some private rooms are only available during the busiest months of July and August, some others require a minimum three-night stay.

Go to *Bräugasthof*, Seestrasse 120, for typical Austrian food in a homely atmosphere. Lunch-time specials start from AS85, other dishes from AS60, and it's open daily, but only from 1 May to mid-October. Double rooms with private WC and shower are available all year for AS660, including breakfast. *Gasthof Hallberg* (☎ 06134-286), Seestrasse 113, is popular with locals for pizzas and drinking, especially the back room. It is also the base for the diving and ski school, as well as offering rooms for AS380 per person including breakfast and private WC and shower.

Getting There & Away

There are around six buses a day to Obertraun and Bad Ischl, but none after 6 pm. The train station is across the lake. The boat service from there to the village (AS18) coincides with train arrivals (eight a day from Bad Ischl).

WOLFGANGSEE

The ease of access from Salzburg means this lake can become crowded in summer, but its scenery and lakeside villages make it well worth a visit.

Orientation & Information

The lake is dominated by the Schafberg (1783 metres) on the northern shore. Next to it is the most important resort, St Wolfgang. The tourist office (☎ 06138-22 390) is on the main street near the bus stop, open Monday to Friday and Saturday morning. St Gilgen, on the western shore, provides easy access to Salzburg 29 km away. Its tourist office (☎ 06227-348), Mozartplatz 1 in the Rathaus, is open Monday to Friday in the winter and daily in July and August.

Things to See & Do

The most important sight in St Wolfgang is the **Pilgrimage Church**, built in the 14th and 15th centuries. This incredible church is virtually a museum of altars – nine in all! The best is the winged altarpiece made by Michael Pacher from 1471 to 1481, with astonishing detail on the carved figures and Gothic designs. The church wardens used to be so protective of this piece that the wings were kept closed except for important festivals. Now, thankfully, they are always open (except at Easter). The double altar by Thomas Schwanthaler is also excellent. The church is open daily from 7.30 am to 6 pm.

The **White Horse Inn** in the village centre was the setting for a famous operetta. Ascend the **Schafberg** for good hikes and views. The Schafberg cog-wheel railway runs from May to early October approximately every 90 minutes during the day, and reaches 1734 metres. The cost is AS110 up, AS90 down and AS200 return. Eurail passes and the Rabbit Card allow a free ride, and Inter-Rail gets 50% off. Buy picnic materials at the Konsum supermarket 100 metres from the ticket office towards the village centre.

St Gilgen has good views of the lake, but little else of interest, unless you count the birthplace of Mozart's mother. In the winter there is downhill and cross-country skiing. Get information from the St Gilgen tourist office or the director of the ski school, Pepi Resch (☎ 06227-275), Liam 136, St Gilgen.

Places to Stay & Eat

Camping Appesbach (☎ 06138-2206), Au 99, is one km from St Wolfgang on the lakefront in the direction of Strobl. It is open from Easter to 30 September and costs AS55 per person, plus tax.

St Gilgen has a modern IYHF *youth hostel* (☎ 06227-365) at Mondseestrasse 7. Dorms are AS108 including breakfast. One to four-bed rooms are also available for AS118 to AS168. Curfew is at 11 pm but it doesn't close during the day.

Both St Wolfgang and St Gilgen have a good selection of pensions (from AS150 per person) and private rooms (from AS120 per person). Lists are available from the respective tourist offices. At the cheaper end, places to try are: *Gästehaus Raudaschl* (☎ 06138-2561), Deschbühel 41, St Wolfgang, with singles/doubles from AS170/280; and *Café Nannerl* (☎ 06227-368), at Kirchenplatz 2, St Gilgen, with singles/doubles from AS170/340.

There are lots of places to eat down St Wolfgang's main street. *Schlosswirt*, Pilgerstrasse 33, open daily from 10 am to 11 pm, has pizzas and grilled dishes from AS65. In St Gilgen, *Gasthof Rosam*, Frontfestgasse 2, has menus from AS80 with good portions. It is open daily from 8 am to 9 pm.

Getting There & Away

An hourly ferry service operates from Strobl to St Gilgen between May and early October, stopping at various points en route. Services are more frequent during the high season from mid-June to mid-September. The journey from St Wolfgang to St Gilgen takes 40 minutes, and the service starts at 8 am and stops at 6.22 pm (7.30 pm in the high season). The fare is AS44. In the reverse direction from St Gilgen, the ferry operates from 9.08 am to 7.05 pm (8.40 pm in the high season). Rail-card validity for these services is as for the Schafberg cog-wheel railway.

Buses from St Wolfgang to Salzburg and to St Gilgen go via Strobl on the east side of the lake. St Gilgen is less than 50 minutes from Salzburg by bus, with hourly departures until 8 pm. The fare is AS54.

Tirol

The province of Tirol (sometimes spelled Tyrol) has some of the best mountain scenery in Austria. It is an ideal playground for skiers, hikers, mountaineers and anglers, and the tourist office releases plenty of glossy material to promote these pursuits. It is a province in two parts: East Tirol has been isolated from the main part of the state ever since prosperous South Tirol was ceded to Italy at the conclusion of WW I.

1	Jugendherberge St Nicholas
2	Goldenes Brünnl
3	Cathedral
4	Landestheater
5	Restaurant Dom Stub'n
6	Golden Roof
7	Gasthaus Goldenes Dachl
8	Hofburg
9	City Tower
10	Don Camillo
11	Club Filou
12	Main Tourist Office
13	Hofkirche
14	Treibhaus
15	Tiroler Landesmuseum Ferdinandeum
16	MK Jugendzentrum
17	Mensa
18	Andrä Hörtnagl
19	Café Central
20	Bosner Platz
21	American Express
22	Main Post Office
23	Triumphal Arch
24	Tirol Information Office
25	Hauptbahnhof
26	Restaurant Philippine
27	Utopia
28	Westbahnhof
29	Riese Haymon

INNSBRUCK

Innsbruck has been an important trading post since the 12th century, thanks in part to the Brenner Pass, the gateway to the south. It wasn't long before the city found favour with the Habsburgs, particularly Maria Theresa and Emperor Maximilian who built many of the important buildings that still survive in the well-preserved old town centre. More recently, the capital of Tirol has become an important winter sports centre, and staged the Winter Olympics in 1964 and 1976.

Orientation

Innsbruck is in the valley of the River Inn, scenically squeezed between the northern chain of the Alps and the Tuxer mountain range to the south. Extensive mountain transport facilities surround the city and provide ample hiking and skiing opportuni-

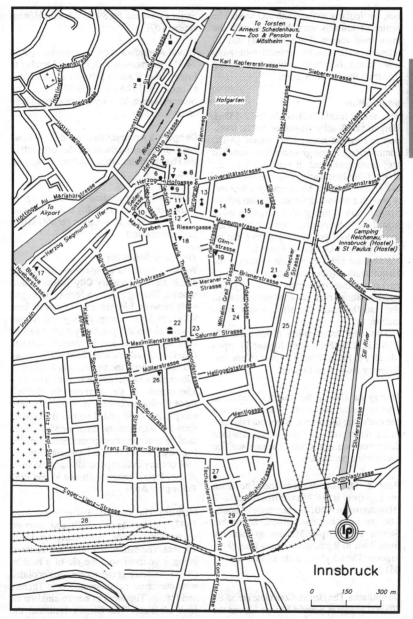

Innsbruck

0   150   300 m

ties, particularly to the south and west. The centre of town is very compact, with the main train station (Hauptbahnhof) just 10 minutes' walk from the pedestrian-only old town centre (Altstadt), which has Herzog Friedrich Strasse at its heart.

Information
The main tourist office (☎ 0512-5356), Burggraben 3, sells ski passes, public transport tickets and books hotel rooms (AS30 commission). It also gives out free maps like they were going out of fashion. Ask here about 'Club Innsbruck' if you intend to stay at least three nights. Membership is free and is good for various discounts; it also allows participation in free guided mountain hikes from June to September. Opening hours are from 8 am to 7 pm every day (to 6 pm on Sunday from 1 October to Easter).

There are hotel reservation centres in the Hauptbahnhof (open daily from 9 am to 10 pm) and at motorway exits for the city. The youth waiting room (*Jugendwarteraum*) in the Hauptbahnhof also offers useful information.

The Tirol Information office (☎ 0512-5320) is at Wilhelm Greil Strasse 17, open Monday to Friday from 8.30 am to 6 pm, and Saturday from 9 am to noon.

Money As always, the lowest commission rates are in the post office. The train station has exchange facilities to 8 pm, but take care as the ticket counters offer worse rates than the station exchange office. The tourist office also exchanges money.

Post & Telecommunications The main post office is at Maximilianstrasse 2 (Hauptpostamt A 6010), open daily 24 hours. The train station post office, Brunecker Strasse 1-3, is open Monday to Saturday from 7 am to 9 pm, and Sunday from 9 am to noon. The telephone code for Innsbruck is 0512.

Consulates The British Consulate (☎ 58 83 20) is at Matthias Schmid Strasse 12, and the Swiss Consulate (☎ 89 22 20) is at Höhenstrasse 107.

Travel Agencies American Express (☎ 58 24 91), Brixnerstrasse 3, is open Monday to Friday from 9 am to 5.30 pm and Saturday to noon. ÖKISTA (☎ 58 89 97), Josef Hirn Strasse, is open Monday to Friday from 9.30 am to 5.30 pm.

Dangers & Annoyances Avoid the bellowing and staggering drunks in the main hall of the Hauptbahnhof: they can become aggressive.

Emergency For medical treatment, try the University Clinic (☎ 5040) at Anichstrasse 35, or St Lukas Day Clinic (☎ 590 90) at Leopoldstrasse 1.

Things to See & Do
Walking Tour For an overview of the city, climb the 14th century **City Tower** (Stadtturm) in Herzog Friedrich Strasse. It is open daily between 1 March and 31 October from 10 am to 5 pm, except in July and August when it closes at 6 pm. Entry costs AS18, or AS9 for students and children. Combined tickets are available with the small **Olympic Museum** across the square, which displays videos of the winter games hosted by the city. The outside of the museum, the **Golden Roof** (Goldenes Dachl), is of more interest, comprising 2657 gilded copper tiles dating from the 16th century. Emperor Maximilian used to observe street performers from the balcony. Take note of the elegant 15th and 16th century buildings on all sides and stroll down Maria Theresien Strasse to the 1767 **Triumphal Arch**.

Hofburg The Imperial Palace dates from 1397, but has been rebuilt and restyled several times since, particularly by Maria Theresa. The half-hourly 'tour' is a matter of doing it yourself with the aid of a booklet (AS5). Suitably grand rooms are decorated with numerous paintings of Maria Theresa and family. The faces of her 16 children all look identical. The Giant's Hall and the chapel are highlights. It is open daily from 9 am to 4 pm (except from mid-October to mid-May when it closes on Sunday and holidays), and admission costs AS30 (students AS10).

Hofkirche On the other side of Burggraben from the palace, the Hofkirche (Imperial Church) contains the massive tomb of Maximilian, decorated with scenes of his life. The twin rows of 28 giant bronze figures of the Habsburgs are memorable. The intricate detail on the clothing contrasts with the dullness of the metal, yet certain parts of the statues are shiny where many hands have touched them. A certain intimate part of Kaiser Rudolf is very shiny indeed! It is open daily to 5 pm and it costs AS20 (students AS14) to get in. Combined tickets are available with the adjoining **Folk Art Museum** (Volkskunst Museum).

Ambras Castle Located east of the centre (take tram No 3 or 6), this 16th century castle features the Renaissance Spanish Hall, fine gardens, and collections of art and armour. Opening hours are Wednesday to Monday from 10 am to 5 pm, but only from May to September. Entry charges are AS30 for adults, AS10 for children and students.

Alpine Zoo The zoo is north of the River Inn on Weiherburggasse and features a comprehensive collection of Alpine animals including amorous bears and combative ibexes. It is open daily from 9 am to 6 pm except between November and February when it closes at 5 pm. Admission costs AS50 for adults and AS25 for students and children. Walk up the hill to get there or take the Hungerburgbahn which is free if you buy your zoo ticket at the bottom (it's AS12 each way otherwise).

Tiroler Landesmuseum Ferdinandeum This museum, at Museumstrasse 15, houses a good collection of art and artefacts, particularly the Gothic statues and altarpieces. There's a relief map of Tirol in the basement. Opening hours are May to September daily

from 10 am to 5 pm (Thursday also from 7 to 9 pm); October to April, Tuesday to Saturday from 10 am to 1 pm and 2 to 5 pm; and Sunday and holidays from 10 am to 3 pm. Entry costs AS50, or AS30 for students.

Market A large indoor market selling flowers, meats and vegetables is by the river in Markthalle, Herzog Siegmund Ufer.

Skiing Most of the ski runs around Innsbruck are intermediate or easy with a few difficult ones thrown in. Many areas, such as Seefeld, were used in Olympic competitions. A one-day ski pass is around AS280 depending on the area, and there are several versions of multi-day tickets available. Equipment rental starts at AS150.

A popular excursion is to the **Stubai Glacier**, where skiing is possible all year. The journey there takes 90 minutes by bus No 1 from the train station. The last bus back is at 5.30 pm and you buy your ticket on board (AS130 return). Many places offer complete packages to the glacier, which are not much more expensive than doing it yourself. The cheapest is through the tourist office: AS620 includes transport, passes and equipment rental.

Places to Stay
The tourist office has lists of private rooms in Innsbruck and Igls in the range of AS140 to AS240 per person. Igls is south of town and you can get there by tram No 6 or bus J.

Camping *Camping Innsbruck Kranebitten* (☎ 28 41 80), Kranebitter Allee 214, is west of the town centre and open from May to September. Prices are AS55 per person, AS35 for a tent and AS35 for a car. There is a restaurant on site.

Hostels A convenient hostel for the centre is *Jugendherberge St Nicholas* (☎ 28 65 15), Innstrasse 95. Reception is also here for the hostel *Glockenhaus* at Weiherburggasse 3 up the hill. Dorm beds are AS115 for the first night and AS100 for additional nights, including sheets. Shower tokens are AS10 each and there are no closed hours or curfew (get the key for late returns). Some singles/doubles are available for AS190/300. Reception is open from 8 to 10 am and 5 to 8 pm. The attached restaurant is open to all and is a good place for socialising. The food is cheap but mediocre, comprising standard fare such as spaghetti bolognese (AS55), Wiener schnitzel and bacon-and-egg breakfasts.

Two hostels down Reichenauerstrasse are accessible by bus No O from the station. *Innsbruck* (☎ 46 179) at No 147, by the camp site, costs AS121 the first night, AS91 thereafter (AS6 less if you're aged under 18), including breakfast. Curfew is at 11 pm and the place is closed from 10 am to 5 pm. Kitchen facilities are available and it costs AS45 for laundry. *St Paulus* hostel (☎ 44 291) at No 72 has large dorms for AS75 (AS10 extra for nonmembers) and sheets for AS20. Breakfast also costs AS20, although kitchen facilities are available. Curfew is at 10 pm and the doors are locked from 9 am to 5 pm. The hostel is only open from 18 June to 18 August.

Two other hostels to try in the summer are: *MK Jugendzentrum* (☎ 571 311), Sillgasse 8A (open from July to mid-September) with beds for AS130 including breakfast, and sheets at AS10; and *Torsten Arneus Schwedenhaus* (☎ 585 814) at Rennweg 17B (open July and August), where beds cost AS90 the first night and AS80 thereafter, breakfast is AS40 and sheets are AS20.

Hotels & Pensions Not far from the station is *Riese Haymon* (☎ 589 837), Haymongasse 4. It has long, spacious rooms with a sofa, stucco work on the ceiling and lots of character. The rooms do vary in quality so ask to see a selection. The best rooms are mostly in the older part of the building. Singles/doubles sharing the hall shower cost AS250/440, and doubles with own shower start at AS500, including breakfast. Reception is open between 7 am and 11 pm in the adjoining restaurant. On Saturday, when the restaurant is closed, look for the cleaner on the 1st floor.

Ferrarihof (☎ 580 968), Brennerstrasse 8, is south of town just off the main road, with lots of parking space. Singles/doubles are AS220/440 with use of a shower in the corridor, breakfast included. Reception is in the bar downstairs from 7 am to midnight.

Pension Möslheim (☎ 67 134), Oberkoflerweg 8, Mühlau, has singles/doubles for AS180/360, but charges AS20 extra for a single night's stay. It's a quiet, family-run place 10 minutes' walk from the zoo. Hall showers and breakfast are included in the price. Reception is next door at No 4. The other side of the river from old town, *Goldenes Brünnl* (☎ 28 35 19), St Nikolaus Gasse 1, has reasonable singles/doubles for AS340/460 with showers down the corridor. Breakfast is AS60 and reception is in the restaurant, open to midnight (closed Tuesday).

The pick of the hotels in the Altstadt is *Weisses Kreuz* (☎ 59 4 79), Herzog Friedrich Strasse 31, with singles/doubles from AS360/660 or AS600/900 with private shower/WC, including breakfast buffet. This 500-year-old inn played host to Mozart when he was 13, and all the rooms are spacious, well presented and comfortable. Prices rise around 10% from June to September. If it's full, try the *Hotel Happ* (☎ 58 29 80) across the street at No 14. It's slightly cheaper and almost as atmospheric. The reception is closed on Sunday.

Places to Eat
There are various Wurst stands and Imbiss shops for fast, cheap snacks around the city, and two supermarkets are close together on Museumstrasse. *Andrä Hörtnagl*, Maria Theresien Strasse 5, is a supermarket with a café area serving snacks from AS26 and main dishes from AS52, open weekdays to 6.30 pm and Saturday morning. The university *mensa*, Herzog Siegmund Ufer 15, on the 1st floor, serves good lunches between 11 am and 2 pm from Monday to Friday. For AS30 to AS50 you can get a main dish, soup and salad. Sometimes it opens on Saturday but you can't rely on it. The mensa closes for

holidays from mid-August to mid-September.

The only specialist vegetarian place in town is *Restaurant Philippine* (☎ 589 157), Müllerstrasse 9. It has a wide selection of main dishes in the range of AS86 to AS130 and features dishes from different nationalities on a weekly basis. It is open Monday to Saturday from 10 am to midnight (the kitchen closes at 10.30 pm).

Café Central, Gilmstrasse 5, is a typical Austrian coffee house popular with students. It has English newspapers, menus for AS86 and AS125, and opens daily from 8 am to 11 pm.

Altstadt Area *Don Camillo* bar and café, on the corner of Marktgraben and Seilergasse, has pizza and pasta from AS58, and cheap Austrian food. The quality is good and represents the best value in the Altstadt. Opening hours are Monday to Saturday from 11 am to 1 am, and Sunday from 5 to 11 pm. *Dom Café-Bar*, Pfarrgasse 3, is a busy, dimly lit drinking establishment with good pizzas and other dishes from AS75. It's open daily from 5 pm.

For a change of pace, go down the street to *Gasthaus Goldenes Dachl* (☎ 58 93 70), Hofgasse 1. Soothing classical music will help you digest Austrian and Tirolean specialities such as *Tiroler Bauergröstl*, a beef-and-potatoes concoction for AS96. It is open daily from 8 am to midnight.

Neuböck, a delicatessen shop on Herzog Friedrich Strasse, is a good place to sit down and chomp cheap, hot and cold snacks.

For more up-market eating, *Restaurant Altstadtstüberl*, Riesengasse 13, is one of the best places to try typical Tirolean food. Main dishes are in the range of AS160 to AS240, and it's closed on Sundays and holidays. *Restaurant Stiftskeller* on Burggraben is another good place to consume a wide range of local and Austrian specialities. Dishes start at AS90 and it's open daily to 10 pm.

Entertainment
Ask the tourist office about 'Tirolean evenings' (brass bands, folk dancing, yodel-

ling) and summer classical concerts. The *Landestheater* has year-round performances ranging from opera and ballet to drama and comedy. Get information and tickets from the tourist office.

Utopia (588 587), Tschamlerstrasse 3, is a good venue staging theatre and especially live music (entry AS60 to AS120). It has a café which is open Monday to Saturday from 5 pm to midnight. Downstairs is a beer cellar, open Tuesday to Saturday from 8 pm or later to around 1.30 am, where beer is AS28 a Krügel. *Treibhaus* (☎ 58 68 74), Angerzellgasse 8, has live music during the week. Admission to see the bands varies but it's around AS100 and it shuts at 1 am. On Sunday there is free jazz from 10.30 am to 1 pm. *Club Filou*, Stiftsgasse 12 in the old city, is a bright, chic disco and restaurant open daily from 6 pm to 4 am. There's a cover charge to go downstairs to the disco on Friday and Saturday but that includes some free drinks.

Cinematograph, Museumstrasse 31, shows non-mainstream films in their original language. Tickets are around AS50. Some cinemas around town are cheaper on Monday.

Getting There & Away
Air Tyrolean Airlines flies daily all year to Vienna, Zürich, Paris and Frankfurt, and daily in the summer to Linz and Amsterdam.

Bus Postbuses leave from the Hauptbahnhof. The bus ticket office is near the youth waiting room in the smaller of the two station halls.

Train Fast trains depart every two hours for Bregenz and Salzburg. Regular express trains head north to Munich (via Kufstein) and south to Verona. There are departures every hour to Kitzbühel, and the fare is AS134. Three trains a day go to Lienz (AS224) passing through Italy. The noon train is an international train, which means you'll need to show your passport. The fare for this train is only AS196, as part of the journey is priced on lower Italian rates.

AUSTRIA

However, if you're travelling on an Austrian Rail Card, you must pay for the Italian section (AS82). The 6.55 am and 5.02 pm trains are 'corridor' trains on which no passport is necessary. For train information, call ☎ 1717.

Car & Motorbike The A12 and the parallel highway 171 are the main roads to the west and east. Highway 177, to the west of Innsbruck, heads north to Germany and Munich. The A13 motorway is a toll road southwards through the Brenner Pass to Italy; it includes the impressive Europabrücke ('Europe Bridge') several km south of the city. Toll-free highway 182 follows the same route, passing under the bridge.

Getting Around

To/From the Airport The airport is four km to the west of the centre. To get there, take bus F which leaves every 20 minutes from Maria Theresien Strasse (AS17).

Public Transport Tickets on buses and trams cost AS17, or AS42 for a block of four. Four-day passes cost AS88 and are not valid for the Hungerburgbahn, but up to four people can use the same pass (thereby reducing the validity to one day). A seven-day pass costs AS100, valid Monday to Sunday.

Other Transport It's hardly worth using private transport in the compact city centre. It's OK to park in unmarked streets but you'll be lucky to find a space. Marked parking zones allow a maximum 60-minute stay. Get tickets from pavement dispensers. The charge is AS10 per half-hour, except on weekends and holidays when it's free.

Taxis cost AS25, plus AS12 per km. Bike rental in the Hauptbahnhof is open daily 24 hours, but only in the summer.

KITZBÜHEL

Kitzbühel, if you believe the tourist brochures, is 'a sun-kissed, joyful little town, filled with bustle'. True or not, it is definitely a fashionable and prosperous winter resort

offering some excellent skiing and a variety of other sports.

Orientation & Information

The main train station is one km from the centre. Turn left from Bahnhofstrasse into Josef Pirchl Strasse. Take the right fork (no entry for cars), which is still Josef Pirchl Strasse, and continue past the post office (Postamt 6370). The tourist office (☎ 05356-2155 or 2272), Hinterstadt 18, is in the centre, open every day (except Sunday in the low season). Maps, copious information and free room-finding (not reservations) are available. Ask about the summer guest card which can be used to get various discounts.

Things to See & Do

There are good intermediate ski runs on Kitzbüheler Horn to the north and Hahnenkamm to the south. A one-day ski pass costs AS300 to AS320, covers the whole area and includes bus transport to neighbouring villages. Partial-day and several-day passes are also available. A day's equipment rental is around AS155 for downhill or AS75 for cross-country skiing. The three-day summer pass costs AS260 (children AS130) and is valid for use on the main cable cars. The Hahnenkamm professional downhill ski race takes place in January.

Dozens of summer walking trails surround the town and provide a good opportunity to take in the scenery. Get a free map showing routes from the tourist office. There is an Alpine flower garden with free admission on the slopes of the Kitzbüheler Horn.

Places to Stay & Eat

Kitzbühel is well fixed for accommodation, although many places shut in April and November. A single-night surcharge (AS20 to AS30) usually applies, but try to negotiate. Prices tend to be higher in the high season which occurs over Christmas, from February to early March, and in July and August. Prices peak in the winter high season.

Pension *Schmidinger* (☎ 05356-31 34), Ehrenbachgasse 13, has singles/doubles from AS150/260 plus AS20 to use the showers down the corridor. Pension *Neuhaus* (☎ 05356-22 00), Franz Reisch Strasse 23, is also well situated near the centre of the resort and has singles/doubles from AS220/400 with free use of the hall showers. Both include breakfast and are usually open in the off season. Many private rooms are available and there is a year-round *camp site* (☎ 05356-28 06) near Schwarzsee lake.

For more comfort, try *Gasthof Eggerwirt* (☎ 05356-24 55), Untere Gänsbachgasse 12, with its painted façade, conveniently located down the steps from the three churches. Singles/doubles with shower and WC start at AS590/1040, and parking is available. This place is also recommended for good-quality food from AS100 to AS200.

For excellent if pricey vegetarian food, head westwards out of town to the *Hotel Schloss Lebenberg* (☎ 05356-43 01) on Lebenbergstrasse. It's closed from mid-October to early December.

Huberbräu Stüberl (☎ 05356-56 77), Vorderstadt 18, offers good Austrian food and an AS80 menu. After the kitchens close at 9.30 pm it remains popular with beer drinkers taking advantage of the low price of AS24 a Krügel. It is open daily until midnight. By the post office are two cheap pizzerias which are open in the off season: *Adria* is open daily and *Karaffe* is shut Monday; both have main dishes starting around AS60. There is a *supermarket* behind the tourist office on Franz Reisch Strasse.

Getting There & Away

By train Kitzbühel is one to 1½ hours from Innsbruck (AS134) and around 2½ hours from Salzburg (AS194). There are approximately hourly departures. If your train stops at Kitzbühel-Hahnenkamm, get off as it is closer to the centre than the main Kitzbühel stop.

Getting to Lienz is awkward by train: two changes are required and it takes over four hours. The bus is much easier. It leaves from outside the main train station at 10.35 am and 5 pm and takes two hours. The fare is AS154 and you get the ticket on the bus from the driver. Heading south to Lienz you pass through some marvellous scenery. Highway 108 (the Felber Tauern Tunnel) and highway 107 (the Grossglockner mountain road, closed in winter) both have toll sections.

KUFSTEIN

Near the German border, Kufstein receives its fair share of tourists drawn by the surrounding lakes and the 13th century castle. The tourist office (☎ 05372-62207), at Münchner Strasse 2, is by the train station, open Monday to Friday from 8 am to noon and 1 to 5 pm, and Saturday from 9 am to noon. The office may be open additional times too, as hours are subject to change depending on demand. It makes room reservations without charge.

Across the River Inn is the main square, Unterer Stadtplatz, where there are several reasonable restaurants and a Spar supermarket. The **fortress** dominates from a hill in the centre of town. There is a lift (AS12 return), but the 15-minute walk up is not demanding. The **Heimat Museum** in the castle has a bit of everything and can only be visited by guided tour, which lasts around 80 minutes. Entry costs AS25 for adults or AS20 for students, and there are five tours a day. It is open Tuesday to Sunday from March to October, except in July and August when it's open daily (and there are tours every half-hour).

The **lakes** around Kufstein make an ideal cycling destination and you can rent bikes in the train station. Buses do go there but they are only regular in the summer season. Buses leave from the Bahnhof and from the post office on Unterer Stadtplatz.

Places to Stay

If you decide to stay overnight, there is a *camp site* by the river (☎ 05372-62229), Salurner Strasse 36, which charges AS30 per person, AS25 for a tent and AS25 for a car. The *Gasthof Traube* (☎ 05372-64520), Karl Kraft Strasse 5, overlooking the river, has singles/doubles from AS200 per person.

Getting There & Away

Kufstein is on the main Innsbruck-Salzburg 'corridor' train route. Getting to/from Kitzbühel involves changing at Wörgl. Allow one hour to 90 minutes each way depending upon connections. The fare is AS72 one-way or AS112 return. The easiest road route is also via Wörgl.

LIENZ

The capital of East Tirol combines winter sports and summer hiking in an Alpine setting with a relaxed, small-town ambience. Even so, many headline rock bands find their way to Lienz. You may be quite surprised at who's sharing the resort with you if you check the posters around the centre.

Orientation & Information

The town centre is within the junction of the rivers Isel and Drau. The pivotal Hauptplatz is directly in front of the train station and is the location of the the post office (Postamt 9900, money exchange available). The tourist office (☎ 04852-65 265) is just off Hauptplatz at Europaplatz 1. It is open Monday to Friday from 8 am to noon and 2 to 6 pm. Between mid-December and mid-April it is also open on Saturday from 8 am to noon and 2 to 6 pm, and on Sunday from 9 am to noon. These hours are subject to change.

Things to See & Do

Overlooking the town, **Bruck Castle** contains varied folklore displays as well as several rooms devoted to local turn-of-the-century artist Albin Egger. Between Palm Sunday and 31 October it is open Tuesday to Sunday from 10 am to 5 pm, except between mid-June and mid-September when it is open daily from 10 am to 6 pm. Admission costs AS28 for adults or AS20 for students. There are good hikes in the mountains and to surrounding villages.

Most of the downhill skiing takes place on the **Zettersfeld** peak north of town (mostly medium to easy runs), and there are several cross-country trails in the valley. **Hockstein** is another skiing area. One-day ski passes are

AS260 and the ski lifts are open from November to April. Downhill equipment rental is AS160 and cross-country rental is AS75. The Hockstein and Zettersfeld cable cars operate in the summer from approximately June to early October.

North of Lienz is the **Grossglockner** (3797 metres), the highest mountain in Austria, which also affords some excellent hiking. To get there, take the bus to the Franz Josefs Höhe hotel, the limit of road travel. The fare is AS89 one-way and there are departures at 6.45, 8 and 11.15 am on weekdays. In winter, buses only go as far as Heiligenblut as the road beyond is closed. This region is part of the Nationalpark Höhe Tauern, where flora and fauna are protected. If you drive yourself, you must pay a toll for the north-south Grossglockner Hochalpenstrasse (Highway 107): AS280 per car for a single journey or AS340 for a day card. For more information, contact the Glockner Aktive office (☎ 04824-22 22), Heiligenblut.

Places to Stay

Camping Falken (☎ 04852-64 022), Eichholz 7, is south of the town, closed from November to mid-December.

The IYHF *youth hostel* (☎ 04852-33 10), Linker Iselweg 22, overlooking the river west of the centre, has beds for AS85 but it's only open in July and August. There's another *youth hostel* (☎ 04824-22 59) on highway 107 to the Grossglockner and Zell am See, about 15 km away at Hof 36, Heiligenblut, which is closed in October and November.

Pension *Lugger* (☎ 04852-62 104), Andrä Kranz Gasse 7, is a bit basic but right in the centre and only costs AS180/300 for singles/doubles. Breakfast is not available and use of the hall showers costs AS20. *Gästehaus Masnata* (☎ 04852-65 536), Drahtzuggasse 4 to the rear of the main tourist office, is excellent value with a friendly owner. Modern, spacious rooms are AS250 per person with private WC and shower, or AS260 with own bath. Breakfast is included and there are also apartments available.

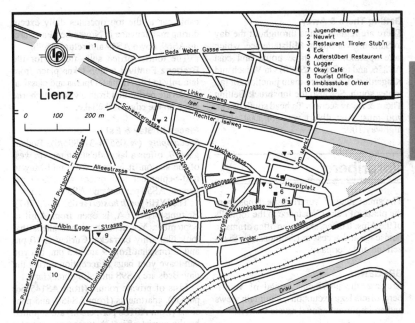

1 Jugendherberge
2 Neuwirt
3 Restaurant Tiroler Stub'n
4 Eck
5 Adlerstüberl Restaurant
6 Lugger
7 Okay Café
8 Tourist Office
9 Imbissstube Ortner
10 Masnata

AUSTRIA

The *Hotel Garni Eck* (☎ 04852-23 263), has been run by the same family for 500 years. It has large rooms with high ceilings, shower/WC, sofa and comfy chairs, nicely decorated corridors, big breakfasts and an excellent location on Hauptplatz, all for just AS380/700 a single/double.

Private rooms in and around the town start at AS120 per person. They are excellent value and a single night's stay is often possible. The tourist office will make reservations free of charge.

Places to Eat
Imbissstube Ortner, Albin Egger Strasse 5, has the best grilled chicken in Austria and is open daily from 10 am to 10 pm. The smell of the chickens sizzling on the spit outside is enough to make vegetarians join Meat-Eaters Anonymous; a half chicken *(Hendl)* and chips is AS50. The *Adlerstüberl Restaurant*, Andrä Kranz Gasse 5, is a good place to try Tirolean specialities from AS88. It's

popular and is open daily from 8 am to midnight.

Restaurant Tiroler Stub'n, Südtiroler Platz 2, has tasty food topping AS100, like the filling *Tiroler Stub'n Platte* (AS390 for two). *Gasthof Neuwirt*, at Schweitzer Gasse 22, offers a good selection of local and grilled dishes from AS85, including vegetarian options. Choose one of the many different rooms that suits your mood, such as the Fischerstube. Could the stuffed fish, mouths agape, mounted on the walls, be daily specials that went wrong?

Entertainment
The *Okay Café* in the CreativCentre off Zwergergasse is a dark and smoky meeting place for local young people. In the back room there are jazz and avant-garde concerts every week, for which entry costs around AS100. It is open daily from 5 pm (7 pm Friday and Saturday) to 1 am.

Getting There & Away
There are regular trains throughout the day to Salzburg via Spittal Millstättersee, which take approximately three hours and cost AS256, and to Graz (AS420) via Villach and Klagenfurt. Villach is a main junction for rail routes south. See also the Innsbruck Getting There & Away section. To head south by car, you must first divert west or east along highway 100.

Vorarlberg

The small state of Vorarlberg extends from the plains of Lake Constance to the foothills of the Alps. It offers skiing, an often dramatic landscape and access to Liechtenstein, Switzerland and Germany.

BREGENZ
Bregenz, the provincial capital of Vorarlberg, offers lake excursions, mountain views and an important annual music festival.

Orientation & Information
The town is on the east shore of Lake Constance (Bodensee). Turn left down Bahnhofstrasse as you exit the station for the town centre and the tourist office (☎ 05574-433 910), which is on Anton Schneider Strasse 4A. It is open Monday to Friday from 9 am to noon and 2 to 6 pm, and Saturday to noon, except in July and August when hours are extended. The State Tourist Board Vorarlberg (☎ 05574-425 250) is at Römerstrasse 7. The post office is on Seestrasse (Postamt 6900). Bike rental in the station is open daily from 7 am to 10 pm. Postbuses leave from outside the station.

Things to See & Do
The old town is worth a stroll. Its centrepiece and the town emblem is the bulbous, Baroque **St Martin's Tower** built in 1599. Follow the walking route described in the tourist office leaflet.

The **Pfänder** mountain offers an impressive panorama over the lake and beyond. A cable car to the top operates daily except during maintenance in November. Fares are: up AS69, down AS49 and return AS98.

The tourist office sells tickets for the **Bregenz Festival** which takes place from late July to late August. Operas and classical works are performed from a vast waterborne stage on the edge of the lake.

Places to Stay & Eat
Seecamping (☎ 05574-31 895/6), Bodangasse 7, offers a lakeside site three km west of the station. It is open from mid-May to mid-September and prices are AS50 per person, AS50 per tent and AS50 per car.

The IYHF *youth hostel* (☎ 05574-22 867), Belruptstrasse 16A, is open from April to September. Yes, it is those two sheds that look like army barracks. Curfew is 10 pm and dorms shut from 9 am to 5 pm, but you can leave your bags in reception during the day. Beds are AS98 including breakfast.

Lists of private rooms (from AS145 per person), apartments (from AS450) and pensions (from AS180 per person) are supplied by the tourist office. A surcharge normally applies for a single night's stay. Cheap and in the centre is *Pension Günz* (☎ 05574-43 657), Anton Schneider Strasse 38, with rooms from AS190 per person. It's only open from Easter to 1 October. *Pension Traube* (☎ 05574-42 401), Anton Schneider Strasse 34, has rooms from AS240 per person.

For Austrian food, try *Gasthaus Maurachbund*, Maurachgasse 11, with main dishes from AS75 to AS185, or the more expensive but more atmospheric *Alte Weinstube Zur Ilge*, Maurachgasse 6. Both are closed Sunday.

One of the cheapest eating-houses in town is *Restaurant Charly* (☎ 05574-459 59), Anton Schneider Strasse 19, which serves pizza and pasta from AS60. It is open daily (except Thursday) to midnight. It's so popular you may even need to reserve a table.

Getting There & Away
Trains to Munich go via Lindau and to Constance (AS136) via the Swiss shore of the

lake. There are also regular departures to St Gallen (AS92) and Zürich. To Innsbruck, trains depart every one to two hours and take around three hours. The fare is AS236. Feldkirch is on the same line and the fare from Bregenz is AS46.

Boat services operate from June to late September, with reduced services in May. For information, call ☎ 05574-42 868. Bregenz to Constance by boat (via Lindau) takes 3½ hours with up to six departures per day.

There is a Mitfahrzentrale for hitchers near Bregenz: Mario Theurl (☎ 05574-611 00), Bildsteiner Strasse 7, A-6960 Wolfurt, open weekdays from 10 am to 6 pm, and Saturday from 10 am to 3 pm.

FELDKIRCH

Feldkirch is the gateway to Liechtenstein. Vorarlberg's oldest town, it has a **game park** (free admission) with 100 species and good views from the 12th century **Schattenburg castle.**

There are ski slopes just half an hour away by car at Laterns, for which a three-day ski pass costs AS705 to AS735. Alternatively, there is a ski bus (calling at the town, the station and the youth hostel) which is free if you buy that day's ski pass (AS260) from the driver.

The tourist office (☎ 05522-23 467), Herrengasse 12, is open Monday to Friday from 8 am to noon and 2 to 6 pm, and Saturday from 9 am to noon. It reserves rooms free of charge.

Places to Stay & Eat

The IYHF *youth hostel* (☎ 05522-73 181), Reichsstrasse 111, is beyond the train station, 1.5 km from the centre. In a historic old building, it has been completely modernised inside with good facilities. Beds are AS140 including breakfast. Reception is closed from 9.30 am to 5 pm, when the doors are locked. Curfew is 10 pm and the hostel shuts from 1 November to early January and at Easter.

Gasthof Engel (☎ 05522-22 0 62), Liechtensteiner Strasse 106, a few km south-west

of the centre in Tisis, has rooms from AS220 per person.

For cheap eating in town, go to *Löwen City*, Neustadt 17, with self-service meals from AS50. It's open Monday to Friday from 9 am to 6 pm.

Getting There & Away

At least one bus an hour (usually 14 minutes past) departs to Liechtenstein from in front of the train station. The capital, Vaduz, is just 40 minutes away; the fare is AS28 and you must change buses in Schaans. Trains to Buchs on the Swiss border pass through Schaans, but only a few stop there. Buchs has connections to major destinations in Switzerland including Zürich and Chur.

ARLBERG REGION

The Arlberg region, shared by Vorarlberg and neighbouring Tirol, comprises a number of resorts and is considered to have some of the best skiing in Austria.

St Anton is the largest resort, enjoying an easy-going atmosphere and vigorous nightlife. It has good, medium-to-advanced runs as well as nursery slopes on Gampen and Kapall. Get full information from the tourist office (☎ 05446-22690), A-6580 St Anton, Tirol. Accommodation and food prices are reasonable, and the village plays host to a fairly large population of Australasian 'ski bums' who like to crack open the crates of beer outside the tourist office in the early evening.

There are nearly 200 B&B places in and around St Anton; the tourist office brochure has a full listing. In the main street, try *Ludwig* (☎ 05446-26 10) or *Mallaun* (☎ 05446-33 90). For eating, look to the *IFEA* supermarket, the takeaway stands, or the pizzas at *Pomodoro*. Good après-ski bars include *Krazy Kanguruh* on the slopes and *Piccadilly* in the village.

Lech, the most up-market resort, is a favourite with royalty and film stars. Runs are predominantly medium to advanced. For details, contact the tourist office (☎ 05583-21 610), A-6764 Lech, Vorarlberg.

Despite its sophisticated profile, Lech has

AUSTRIA

a *youth hostel* (☎ 05583-24 19), two km from the main resort in the village of Stubenbach. It is closed in May, June, October and November.

A three-day ski pass valid for 77 ski lifts in Lech, Zürs, Stuben, St Anton and St Christoph costs AS940 to AS1040. Rental starts at AS160 for skis and sticks, and AS40 to AS70 for shoes.

Getting There & Away

St Anton is on the main railway route from Bregenz to Innsbruck. From Bregenz, the train takes around 90 minutes and costs AS134.

The village is close to the eastern entrance of the Arlberg Tunnel, the toll road connecting Vorarlberg and Tirol. The tunnel toll is AS150 for cars and minibuses. You can avoid the toll by taking the B197, but no vehicles with trailers are allowed on this winding road. Lech is 40 minutes by bus from St Anton (AS40 one-way).

Belgium

Think of Belgium (België in Flemish, Belgique in French) and it's 'Bruges, beer and chocolate' that generally spring to mind. While certainly exceptional, they are hardly the whole. Yet surprisingly little else is commonly known about this much-embattled country which spawned Western Europe's first great towns, and whose early artists are credited with inventing the oil painting.

Perhaps it's a lack of fervent nationalism – the result of many dominant cultures integrating here over the centuries – which has kept Belgium's spotlight dim on the European stage. Rarely boastful, the country has in fact plenty to fascinate the visitor – from rich historical art towns to the serenity of the hilly Ardennes, and everywhere wonderful bars and cafés where Belgians feel at home. You'll rapidly feel the same.

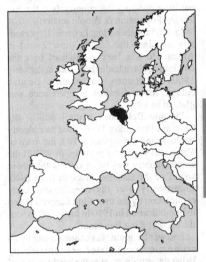

Facts about the Country

HISTORY

Belgium's position between France, Germany and England has long made it one of Europe's main battlegrounds. Prosperous throughout the 13th and 14th centuries, the Flemish towns of Ypres, Bruges and Ghent were the first major cities, booming on the manufacturing and trading of cloth. Their craftspeople established powerful guilds (organisations to stringently control arts and crafts) whose elaborate guildhalls you'll see in many cities. Alas the cloth industry faded and with it these towns, trade moving east to Antwerp which soon became the greatest port in Europe.

When Protestantism swept Europe in the 16th century, the Low Countries (present-day Belgium, the Netherlands and Luxembourg, often referred to as the Benelux) embraced it, much to the chagrin of their ruler, the fanatically Catholic Philip II of Spain. He sent the cruel Inquisition to enforce Catholicism, thus flaming the smouldering religious tensions. The eruption came with the Iconoclastic Fury, in which Protestants ran riot, ransacking the churches. Philip retaliated with a force of 10,000 soldiers, and thousands were imprisoned or executed before war broke out in 1568. The 'Revolt of the Netherlands' lasted 80 years, and in the end roughly laid the present-day borders – Holland and its allied provinces victoriously expelling the Spaniards while Belgium and Luxembourg stayed under their rule.

For the next 200 years, Belgium remained a battlefield for successive foreign powers. After the Spaniards, the Austrians came and in turn the French. Napoleon's defeat at the Battle of Waterloo near Brussels led in 1814 to the creation of the United Kingdom of the Netherlands, incorporating Belgium and Luxembourg into the Netherlands. But the Catholic Belgians revolted, winning independence from the Netherlands in 1830 and forming their own kingdom.

The ensuing years saw the start of Flemish nationalism, with tension growing between the Flemish (Dutch) and French speakers which would eventually lead to a language partition dividing the country (see the following Population & People section).

In 1885 the then king, Leopold II, personally acquired the Congo (now Zaïre) in Africa. He was later scandalised over the continuing slave trade there, and in the early 1900s the country was made a Belgian colony. Much-disputed independence was granted in 1960.

Despite Belgium's neutral policy, the Germans invaded in 1914. Used as a bloody battleground throughout WW I, the town of Ypres was wiped off the map. In WW II the whole country was taken over within three weeks of the surprise attack in May 1940. Controversy over the questionably early capitulation by the then King Leopold III led to his abdication in 1950 in favour of his son, the present King Baudouin.

Postwar Belgium was characterised by an economic boom, later accentuated by Brussels' appointment as the headquarters of the European Community (EC) and the North Atlantic Treaty Organisation (NATO).

GEOGRAPHY

Occupying just 30,000 sq km, Belgium is one of Europe's smallest nations, sandwiched between the Netherlands, Germany, Luxembourg and France. The north is flat, the south dominated by the high, forested Ardennes, and the 65-km North Sea coastline monopolised by resorts, save for a few patches of windswept dunes.

GOVERNMENT

A constitutional parliamentary monarchy is led by King Baudouin I. Up until 1980 the government was centralised, but the longstanding division between the two language communities led to the national government being partially regionalised. There are now three regions – Flanders, Wallonia and the capital, Brussels – each with its own government. The political scene is dominated by the (Catholic) Christian Democrats, Socialists

and Liberals, but in recent years there has been increasing support for the Green parties and the ultra-right-wing Vlaams Blok (Flemish Bloc).

POPULATION & PEOPLE

While spread over nine provinces, Belgium's population is basically split in two: the Flemish and the Walloons. Language is the dividing factor, made official in 1962 when an invisible line – or Linguistic Divide as it's called – was drawn across the country, cutting it almost equally in half. To the north lies Flanders, whose Flemish speakers make up 60% of the 10-million population. To the south is Wallonia with the 40%, French-speaking Walloons. To further complicate matters, Brussels is officially bilingual but predominantly French speaking, and lies within the Flemish region but is governed separately from both. There's also a tiny German-speaking enclave in the far east.

The language issue stems from discrimination against the Flemish when the Belgian constitution was drawn up – French was official, Flemish banned – and over the years has caused many political and social conflicts. Before WW II, the Flemish north was economically poorer than the Walloon south, but the situation has since been reversed, adding new fuel to the controversy.

As a traveller, the Linguistic Divide will cause few problems as many people speak at least a smattering of English. The most confusing part will be on the road, when the sign you're following to Mons (as it's known in French) disappears and the town of Bergen (the Flemish name) appears. A list of alternative place names is included in the back of this book.

ARTS

The arts first flourished in Belgium as early as the 15th century, starting with the realist paintings of the Flemish Primitives, whose leading figure, Jan van Eyck, is said to have invented oil painting. The mid-16th century gave way to Pieter Brueghel with his depictions of peasant life. In the 17th century followed greats such as Pieter Paul Rubens

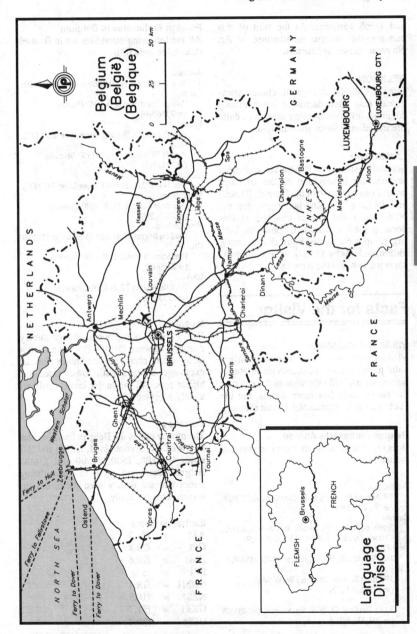

Belgium
(België)
(Belgique)

LP

0   25   50 km

NORTH SEA

Ferry to Dover
Ferry to Dover
Ferry to Felixstowe
Ferry to Hull

NETHERLANDS

GERMANY

FRANCE

FRANCE

LUXEMBOURG

Zeebrugge
Ostend
Bruges
Ypres
Courtrai
Tournai
Ghent
Antwerp
Mechlin
BRUSSELS
Louvain
Mons
Charleroi
Namur
Dinant
Hasselt
Tongeren
Liège
Spa
Champlon
Bastogne
Martelange
Arlon
LUXEMBOURG CITY

ARDENNES

Western Scheldt
Meuse
Scheldt
Lys
Sambre
Meuse
Lesse
Meuse

BELGIUM

Language
Division

FLEMISH

Brussels

FRENCH

and Jacob Jordaens. At the turn of this century, the sinuous architecture of Art Nouveau started in Brussels.

RELIGION
Long a Catholic stronghold, church attendances may have decreased but traditions continue, influencing many aspects of daily life including politics and education.

LANGUAGE
See the History and Population & People sections for information on the language issue. For a rundown of the Flemish (Dutch) and Walloon (French) languages, see the Netherlands and France chapters in this book. English is widely, if somewhat haltingly, spoken throughout the country, although less frequently in the French-speaking east and the Ardennes.

Facts for the Visitor

VISAS & EMBASSIES
Visitors from many countries need only a valid passport for three-month visits. Regulations are basically the same as for entering the Netherlands (for more details, see the Facts for the Visitor section in that chapter).

Belgian Embassies Abroad
Belgian embassies in other countries include:

Australia
    19 Arkana St, Yarralumla, Canberra, ACT 2600 (☎ 06- 273 2501/2)
Canada
    Suite 601-604, 85 Ranch Rd, Sandringham, Ottawa, Ont KIN 8J6 (☎ 613-236 2767/9)
New Zealand
    1-3 Willston St, Wellington (☎ 04-72 9558/9)
UK
    103 Eton Square, London SW1W 9AB (☎ 071-235 5422)
USA
    3330 Garfield St, NW Washington DC 20008 (☎ 202-333 6900)

Foreign Embassies in Belgium
All the following embassies are in Brussels (telephone code 02):

Australia
    Rue Guimard 6, B-1040 Brussels (☎ 2310500)
Canada
    Ave de Tervueren 2, B-1040 Brussels (☎ 7356040)
France
    Rue Ducale 65, B-1000 Brussels (☎ 2200111)
Germany
    Ave de Tervueren 190, B-1150 Brussels (☎ 7741911)
Luxembourg
    Rue Noyer 211, B-1040 Brussels (☎ 7339977)
Netherlands
    Rue de la Science 35, B-1040 Brussels (☎ 2303020)
New Zealand
    Blvd du Régent 47, B-1000 Brussels (☎ 5121040)
UK
    Rue Marie Thérèse 1, B-1040 Brussels (☎ 2179000)
USA
    Blvd du Régent 27, B-1000 Brussels (☎ 5133830)

MONEY
Banks are the best place to change money, charging between f50 and f100 commission on travellers' cheques. Out of hours there are exchange bureaus with lower rates and higher fees. All the major credit cards are widely accepted.

Currency
The money unit is the Belgian franc, written as f or Bf. Coins come in f1, f5, f20 and f50, notes in f100, f500, f1000 and f5000. Belgian francs are equal to Luxembourg francs and are widely used there, but the reverse does not apply.

Exchange Rates

A$1	=	f21.7
C$1	=	f24.4
DM1	=	f20.6
FF1	=	f6
Nethf1	=	f18.4
NZ$1	=	f16.5
UK£1	=	f51.7
US$1	=	f30.4

Costs

Travelling modestly – hostels and cheap restaurants – you can get by on about f750 a day. Tipping is not obligatory, and due to the country's size, getting around is not a major outlay.

Consumer Taxes

Value-added tax, or VAT (BTW in Flemish, TVA in French), is calculated at 20%. To get a rebate, you must fly out of the country, getting your purchase invoice stamped by customs as you leave. You then send it back to the shop and they'll forward the refund.

CLIMATE & WHEN TO GO

The country generally has a mild, maritime climate. July and August are the warmest months. They are also the wettest, although precipitation is spread pretty evenly over the year. The Ardennes are often a few degrees colder than the rest of the country, with snow in winter.

SUGGESTED ITINERARIES

Depending on the length of your stay, you might want to see and do the following things:

Two days
Spend one day each in Brussels and Bruges.
One week
Spend two days each in Brussels and the Ardennes, and one day each in Antwerp, Bruges and Ypres.
Two weeks
Spend three days in Brussels and surrounds, two days each in Antwerp and the Ardennes, two days in Bruges and Ypres, two days in Ostend and other coastal resorts, and one day each in Ghent, Namur and Liège.
One month
This should give you plenty of time to explore the above-mentioned places and to discover a few new places of your own.

TOURIST OFFICES

The head office of the Flemish and Walloon tourist authorities is at Rue du Marché aux Herbes 61, B-1000 Brussels (☎ 02-5040391).

Tourist Offices Abroad

Belgian tourist offices abroad include:

UK
Belgian Tourist Office, Premier House, 2 Gayton Rd, Harrow, Middlesex, HA1 2XU (☎ 081-8613300)
USA
Belgian Tourist Office, 745 Fifth Ave, New York, NY 10151 (☎ 212-7588130)

USEFUL ORGANISATIONS

The following organisations in Belgium may prove useful:

FWH – gay/lesbian information centre – Vlaanderenstraat 22, 9000 Ghent (☎ 091-236929)
Gîtes de Wallonie – rural accommodation service in Wallonia – Rue de Millénaire 53, 6941 Durbuy (☎ 086-499531)
Help Line – 24-hour English-speaking crisis line based in Brussels – ☎ 02-6484014
Infor-Jeunes – young peoples' information service – Rue du Marché aux Herbes 27, 1000 Brussels (☎ 02-5123274)
Les Auberges de Jeunesse – youth hostels in Wallonia – Rue Van Oost 52, 1030 Brussels (☎ 02-2153100)
Touring Club de Belgique – motoring club – Rue de la Loi 44, 1040 Brussels (☎ 02-2332211)
Vlaamse Jeugdherbergcentrale – youth hostels in Flanders – Van Stralenstraat 40, 2060 Antwerp (☎ 03-2327218)

BUSINESS HOURS & HOLIDAYS

Shops are open weekdays from 8.30 or 9 am to 6 pm – often closing for lunch – with similar hours on Saturdays. Banks are open weekdays from 9 am to noon or 1 pm, and 2 to 4 or 5 pm, and Saturday mornings; in large cities, they often don't close for lunch.

Public holidays are: New Year's Day, Easter Monday, Labour Day (1 May), Ascension Day, Whit Monday, National Day (21 July), Assumption (15 August), All Saints' Day (1 November), Armistice Day (11 November), Christmas Day (25 December).

CULTURAL EVENTS

There's a swarm of local and national, artistic or religious festivals – pick up the tourist office's free brochure.

POST & TELECOMMUNICATIONS

Post offices are open weekdays from 9 am to 5 pm and in cities on Saturday mornings. Letters (under 20 grams) cost f15 within Europe, or f32 to the USA, Canada, Australia and New Zealand. They average a week to nine days to reach places outside Europe, two to three days inside. Poste restante attracts a f12 fee, often not demanded.

Local phone calls cost f10 for about three minutes. Call boxes take f5 and f20 coins, or f200 and f1000 phone cards available from post offices. International calls can be made from public boxes, the post office or telephone centres, but they're expensive and there are no cheap off-peak rates to Australia or New Zealand. Rates from hotels, including youth hostels, are exorbitant – ask before you dial.

For making international telephone calls to Belgium, the country code is 32. To telephone abroad, the international access code is 00. Within Belgium, telephone codes for the main cities and towns include Antwerp 03, Bruges 050, Brussels 02, Dinant 082, Ghent 091, Liège 041, Namur 081 and Ypres 057.

TIME

Belgium runs on Central European Time. Noon is 11 am in London, 6 am in New York, 3 am in San Francisco, 6 am in Toronto, 9 pm in Sydney, and 11 pm in Auckland. Daylight-saving time comes into effect at midnight on the last Saturday in March, when clocks are moved an hour forward; they're moved an hour back again at midnight on the last Saturday in September. The 24-hour clock is commonly used.

LAUNDRY

Self-service laundries (wassalon, laverie) on average charge f100 for a five-kg wash and f5 per dryer cycle. Take plenty of f5 and f20 coins.

WEIGHTS & MEASURES

The metric system is in force. Like other Continental Europeans, Belgians indicate decimals with commas and thousands with points. In Flemish shops, 250 grams is called a half-pond and 500 grams a pond.

MEDIA

The English-language Bulletin magazine (f75) comes out Thursdays and has national news and a comprehensive entertainment guide. The BBC's World Service is on 648 kHz medium wave.

HEALTH

There are reciprocal health arrangements only with EC and other European countries (bring your formula E111 card). For others, it's wise to have travel insurance.

FILM & PHOTOGRAPHY

Prices are reasonable: a Kodak 64 (36-exposure) slide film costs f465, while developing averages f18 per photo plus f100 for film processing.

WORK

For non-EC nationals it's officially illegal, but it's possible to pick up work in hostels and in resorts along the coast.

ACCOMMODATION

Hostels and camping grounds are plentiful, low-budget hotels scarce, and in summer everything's heavily booked. The national tourist office will book accommodation for free and also has camping and hotel leaflets, and a handy Budget Holidays brochure. TaxiStop (see Travel Agency in the Brussels Orientation & Information section) has a free, useful, Benelux B&B booklet.

In the Wallonian countryside, B&Bs (chambres d'hôtes in French) and rural houses available for weekly rental (gîtes ruraux) are becoming increasingly popular. The national tourist office has lists of both (a list of the latter costs f100), or contact Gîtes de Wallonie (See the previous Useful Organisations section).

There are two official youth hostel groups, charging between f320 and f360 per night in a dorm including breakfast. In cities, you'll also find private hostels. Camping rates vary widely, but on average you'll be looking at f50 per adult, tent and vehicle in a basic ground. The cheapest hotels charge f900/1300 for singles/doubles in a room without facilities but with breakfast; B&Bs average the same.

FOOD

Belgian cuisine is highly regarded throughout Europe – some say it's second only to the French while in others' eyes it's equal. Combining French style with German portions, you'll rarely have reason to complain. Meat and seafood are abundantly consumed and then of course there are *frites* – chips or French fries – which the Belgians swear they invented and which, judging by availability, is a claim few would contest.

Cafés & Bars

One of the country's true joys, there are sidewalk terraces, old tobacco-stained brown pubs or enticing Art-Nouveau cafés everywhere. Some serve hundreds of varieties of beer and many dish up reasonably priced snacks and a *dagschotel* or *plat du jour* (dish of the day).

Snacks

The popularity of frites cannot be understated. Every village has at least one *friture* where frites are served up in a paper cone or dish, smothered until almost unrecognisable with large blobs of thick mayonnaise and eaten with a small wooden fork in a mostly futile attempt to keep your fingers clean.

On the sweet side, waffles (*wafels* or *gaufres*) are eaten piping hot from market stalls. Then there are filled chocolates (*pralines*) whose fame rivals Belgian beer. The most exclusive is Godiva, where you'll pay for the white gloves they wear to hand-pick each piece, or there's the poor person's delicious equivalent, the elephant-emblazoned Côte d'Or.

Main Dishes

Meat, poultry and hearty vegetable soups are high on menus, but it's *mosselen* (mussels) cooked in white wine and served with a mountain of frites, that's known as the national dish. Grown mainly in the Delta region in the Netherlands, the rule of thumb for mussels is: eat them during the months which include an 'r', and don't touch the ones that haven't opened properly when cooked.

Eating out is rarely cheap: pizzas start at f140, while the cheapest dagschotel or plat du jour costs f200 to f225.

DRINKS

Beer rules...and deservedly so. The quality is excellent and the variety incomparable – somewhere upwards of 350 types, from standard lagers to specialist brews. The most noted are the traditionally abbey-brewed *Trappist* beers, dark in colour, grainy in taste and dangerous in quantity (from 6% to 10% alcohol by volume). Then there's *lambic*, a spontaneously fermented beer which comes sweet or sour depending on what was added during fermentation: *gueuze* is the sour alternative, and *kriek* (with cherries) or *framboise* (with raspberries) two of the sweet varieties. Prices match quality, with a 250 ml lager costing f35, and a 330 ml Trappist f70.

ENTERTAINMENT

Nightlife almost uniformly centres around the ubiquitous bars and cafés. On the whole, cinemas screen films in their original language and are cheaper on Mondays.

THINGS TO BUY

Chocolate, lace and beer are the specialities, but the first two don't come cheap. Five individual Godiva pralines will set you back f140, a lace handkerchief anywhere from f130 to f700.

Getting There & Away

AIR

Belgium has two international airports. The main one is Zaventem, 14 km north-east of Brussels and the hub for international flights. The departure tax from here is f340. The other airport, Deurne, is close to Antwerp and has less-frequent flights to Amsterdam and London only. Prices from both airports to Amsterdam are the same but, depending on when you leave, flights to London can be cheaper from Deurne. The departure tax from Deurne is f180.

The national airline, Sabena, has offices in both Brussels and Antwerp (see the Getting There & Away sections in those cities) and often has good deals to West African destinations.

LAND
Bus
Eurolines and Hoverspeed Citysprint operate international bus services to and from Belgium. Tickets can be bought for Eurolines in its offices in Antwerp, Brussels or Liège. Alternatively, many travel agencies sell tickets for both companies. Reduced fares for people aged under 26 are offered by both lines.

Eurolines has regular buses to many Western, Eastern, Mediterranean and central European destinations as well as Scandinavia and North Africa. Depending on the destination, its buses stop in Antwerp, Bruges, Brussels, Ghent, Liège and Namur.

Hoverspeed runs several services, but only between London, Belgium and the Netherlands. Routes include via Antwerp, Bruges, Brussels and Ghent. All its buses go via Calais in France, using either the SeaCat or Hovercraft to cross the Channel – intending travellers should check whether a French visa is needed.

For more detailed information on these services, see the Getting There & Away section in the relevant city.

Train
Belgium Railways – symbolised by a 'B' surrounded by an eye-shaped oval – has frequent international services. Eurail and Inter-Rail tickets are valid throughout the country. Brussels is the central international hub, with lines in all directions. Large train stations have information offices, usually open until about 9 pm, or you can ask at the ticket windows. Travellers under 26 years get a 20% to 35% reduction on international fares – for other special fares, see the following Getting Around section.

Brussels has three main train stations. All international services pass through two of them – Gare du Nord and Gare du Midi – but some trains (such as to Amsterdam, Cologne and London) also stop at Gare Centrale. Examples of one-way, 2nd-class, adult fares and journey times from Brussels to some destinations on the main neighbouring routes are as follows:

Trains going north pass Antwerp en route to Amsterdam (f940, three hours, hourly trains). Southwards, the line goes via Mons (Bergen in Flemish) to Paris' Gare du Nord (f1320, three hours, six per day). Heading south-east, trains run via Namur to Luxembourg City (f790, 2¾ hours, hourly), while east, the line passes Liège to Cologne (f620, four hours, hourly). To London (f2670, eight hours), trains connect with ferries or jetfoils in Ostend; there are about six services per day. If you go via the quicker jetfoil, there's a f480 supplement.

SEA
Two companies operate car/passenger ferries to Britain from either Ostend or Zeebrugge. Tickets can be bought from most travel agencies. For information on train/ferry or jetfoil services, see the previous Train section.

P&O has services from Ostend to Dover with either the ferry (four hours, seven per day) or the jetfoil (1⅔ hours, four per day). One-way fares for cars (excluding driver and passengers) start at f4600 but rise dramatically depending on the time of the day (and the month) you cross. Foot passengers are charged f2650, with an extra f400 to f550 surcharge (it varies depending on the month) if you take the jetfoil. P&O also has two ferries per day from Zeebrugge to Felixstowe (5¾ hours) – prices are the same as above. P&O has offices in Brussels (☎ 02-2190709) at Madouplein 1, in Ostend (☎ 059-559955) at Natiënkaai 5, and at the car ferry terminal in Zeebrugge (☎ 050-542222).

North Sea Ferries sails overnight from Zeebrugge to Hull (14 hours) and charges from f3540 for a car, and f2700 for a foot passenger. It has an office (☎ 050-543430) at the Zeebrugge terminal.

For quicker Channel crossings, you can go from Calais in France – for details, see the France chapter in this book.

HITCHING

It's illegal on motorways but there are plenty of secondary roads. TaxiStop agencies match drivers with travellers on the road for a reasonable fee.

LEAVING BELGIUM

Airline passengers departing from Brussels pay a f340 departure tax, from Antwerp, f180.

Getting Around

Belgium's transport system is dominated by its efficient rail network, supplemented by buses and trams in cities with buses and trams. In the Ardennes, buses are often the only option.

TRAIN

The fastest services are the InterCity (IC) trains, backed up by InterRegional (IR) and local trains. Depending on the line, there will be an IC and an IR train every half-hour or hour. Most train stations have a few luggage lockers, but mainly it's up to the luggage rooms. They are generally open from 5 am until midnight, and charge f60 per article.

Tickets & Passes

On weekends, return tickets are reduced by 40% for the first passenger, 60% for the rest of the group (to a maximum of six people). Those aged under 26 years get 20% to 25% off standard adult fares.

There are several rail passes. The 'Benelux Tourrail', which gives five days' travel in 17 in Belgium, the Netherlands and Luxembourg, costs f4620/3080 1st/2nd class for adults and f3440/2290 for those aged under

26. This pass can no longer be bought in the Netherlands, but passes bought in either Belgium or Luxembourg are valid for all three countries.

The 'Belgian Tourrail' pass gives five days' travel in 17 within Belgium for f1800, or f1350 for those aged under 26. A 'Half-Fare' card for f550 is valid for one month.

CAR & MOTORBIKE

Drive on the right and give way to the right! The speed limit in towns is 50 km/h, outside, 90 km/h and on motorways, 120 km/h. The permissible blood alcohol concentration level is 0.05%. Fuel prices per litre are f31 for super, f30 for lead-free and f25 for diesel. More motoring information can be obtained from the Touring Club de Belgique (see the previous Useful Organisations section).

BICYCLE

Popular in the flat north, many roads have separate cycle lanes, and bikes can be hired from 62 railway stations for f130 a day if you have a train ticket (including Eurail and Inter-Rail passes), f250 without. They can be returned to any station and can be taken on trains for f175.

LOCAL TRANSPORT

With such a good train network, buses and trams (and small metro systems in Brussels and Antwerp) are used mainly for inner-city hopping. Each city has its own fare system, but generally, single tickets cost about f40. Often you can buy a multistrip ticket – eight strips for f175, for example – which works out cheaper. Services generally run until about 11 pm or midnight. For more information, you'll find public-transport ticket kiosks in or near most train stations.

Brussels

Not a capital that sets out to seduce, Brussels (Bruxelles in French, Brussel in Flemish) is an unpretentious mix of grand edifices and modern skyscrapers. Its character largely

BELGIUM

Brussels
(Bruxelles)
(Brussel)

0   125   250 m

■ PLACES TO STAY

5   CHAB Hostel
6   Jacques Brel Hostel
8   Hotel Sabina
9   Sleep Well Hostel
10 Hotel Madou
19 Hotel la Madeleine
35 Bruegel Hostel
39 Hotel Windsor

▼ PLACES TO EAT

17 Le Savarin
37 L'Orféo
38 Bocca d'Oro

    OTHER

1   Gare du Nord
2   De Ultieme Hallucinatie
3   Laundry
4   L'Aiglon
7   City 2 Shopping Centre
11 Comic Strip Museum
12 Place de Brouckère
13 À la Mort Subite
14 St Michel Cathedral
15 Post Office
16 Telephone Office
18 Galeries St Hubert
20 Sabena Office
21 Bourse
22 National Tourist Office
23 Gare Centrale
24 Grand Place
25 Falstaff
26 Tourist Office Brussels (TIB)
27 Blues Corner
28 Connections Travel
29 Goupil le Fol
30 Acotra Travel
31 Place Royal
32 Royal Palace
33 Manneken Pis
34 Ancient & Modern Art Museums
36 Laundry

reasons), the bilingual city is now headquarters of the EC and NATO, and home to Europe's most impressive central square.

Orientation

The city reverberates around the Grand Place, its imposing 15th century market square. A meeting place for tourists and locals alike, it sits dead centre in the Petit Ring, a pentagon of boulevards enclosing central Brussels and within which are many of the sights. But there's also plenty to see outside the Ring, where you'll also find much of the budget accommodation, often about 20 minutes' walk from the Grand Place but accessible by tram, bus or metro.

There are three main railway stations: Gare du Nord in the north, Gare du Midi in the south, and Gare Centrale about five minutes' walk from the Grand Place. (Brussels streets are written in French and Flemish – we have used the French versions here.)

Information

Tourist Offices There are two offices: one for Brussels, the other for national information. The Tourist Information Brussels (TIB) (☎ 02-5138940), in the town hall on the Grand Place, has city guff and is open daily from 9 am to 6 pm (in October and November Sundays from 10 am to 2 pm, from December to 28 February closed Sundays). The national office (☎ 02-5040391), nearby on Rue du Marché aux Herbes 61, is open June to September weekdays from 9 am to 8 pm, weekends until 7 pm, and October to May daily from 9 am to 6 pm (except November to February Sundays from 1 to 5 pm). Up the road at No 27 there's Infor-Jeunes (☎ 02-5123274), a youth information service, open weekdays from noon to 5 pm.

Money Outside banking hours, there are exchange bureaus at the airport, Gare Centrale (until 9 pm), Gare du Nord and Midi (until 11 pm). On the Grand Place, Kredietbank at No 17 is open weekdays from 9 am to 4.30 pm. Nearby, Paul Laloy Agent de Change at Rue de la Montagne 6 is open weekdays until 6 pm, Saturday from 10.30

follows that of the nation it governs: modest, confident, but rarely striving to overtly impress. This said, its drawing cards are significant. Having grown from a 6th century, marshy village on the banks of the River Senne (filled in long ago for sanitary

BELGIUM

am to 6 pm and Sunday from 11 am to 1 pm. Thomas Cook (☎ 02-5132844) is at Grand Place 4, American Express (☎ 02-5121740) at Place Louise 2.

Post & Telecommunications The main post office is on the 2nd floor of the Centre Monnaie near Place de Brouckère on Blvd Anspach, open Monday to Thursday 9 am to 6 pm, Friday until 7 pm, Saturday 9 am to noon. Use the branch office near Gare Centrale at Blvd l'Impératrice 17 for international phone calls between 7 am and 10 pm. More centrally, there's a telephone house at Rue du Lombard 30a, open daily from 10 am to 10 pm.

Brussels' telephone code is 02.

Foreign Embassies See the Facts for the Visitor section earlier in this chapter.

Travel Agencies Some of the more useful agencies include:

Acotra, Rue de la Madeleine 51 (☎ 5128607) – student travel agency

Connections Travel Shop, Rue du Marché-au-Charbon 13 (☎ 5125060)

TaxiStop, Rue du Marché aux Herbes 27 (☎ 5121015) – paid rides in cars going to other European cities. It also operates AirStop, which organises 40% to 60% off seats on charter flights to southern Europe (you must be a member – three months costs f600)

Bookshops W H Smith (☎ 2192708), Blvd Adolphe Max 71, has English-language novels, travel guides and maps.

Laundry Outside the Petit Ring to the northeast, the self-service Ipsomat at Place Hauwaert is open daily from 7 am to 10 pm. Around the corner from Bruegel youth hostel there's the steamy Salon Lavoir de la Chapelle on Rue Haute, open weekdays from 8 am to 4.30 pm.

Emergency The national emergency numbers are police, ☎ 101, and fire/ambulance, ☎ 100. For medical emergencies in

Brussels, 24 hours, ☎ 6488000 or 4791818, and for dental problems, ☎ 4261026.

Things to See & Do
There's little fanfare to Brussels' sights, and unlike towns such as Bruges, it's not a city for idly wandering. Maybe that's partly due to the 220 days a year the city gets rain. But if so, shelter can be found in 70 museums or the beautiful glass-covered arcades which stretch through the centre, the finest of which is Galeries St Hubert, Europe's oldest.

Walking Tour The **Grand Place** is the obvious start for exploring within the Petit Ring. Formerly home to the craft guilds, their rich guildhouses line the square, topped by golden figures which glisten by day, and which are fanfared with a sound-and-light show by night (from mid-April to 30 September – check with the TIB for times).

Off the Grand Place to the south on Rue Charles Buls is one of the first glimpses of the city's once-famous Art-Nouveau cult: an 1899 gilded plaque dedicated to the city from its appreciative artists. It's beside a reclining 14th century hero whose gleaming arm passers-by rub for good luck. A couple of blocks farther is **Manneken Pis**, the statue of a small boy weeing on the corner of Rue du Chêne and Rue de l'Étuve.

One block north-east of the Grand Place is the covered Galeries St Hubert. Farther north, the **Comic Strip Museum** at Rue des Sables 20 is a favourite for fans of the quiffed Tintin, Belgium's most famous cartoon character. Alternatively, head east up the hill past Gare Centrale to Rue Royale and the refinement of the upper town, where near the **Palace** you'll find the Modern and Ancient art museums.

Museums The choice of museums is staggering – ranging from traditional topics to more specialised tastes, such as a Sewer Museum or one on the local police. The TIB has a list of them all.

One of the most central – and perhaps for Belgium the most appropriate to start with – is the **Brewery Museum** in the Maison des

Brasseurs at Grand Place 10. It's not much more than a collection of everything associated with the consumption of beer (and if you prefer to participate rather than observe, you'd be better off at the Gueuze Museum detailed below), but it's a good way to see inside one of the guildhouses. Admission is f50 and it's open weekdays from 10 am to noon and 2 to 5 pm (also on Saturday morning from 1 April to 31 October).

Also on the Grand Place, in the Maison du Roi, is the **City of Brussels Museum**, which gives a historical rundown on the city and exhibits every piece of clothing ever worn by Manneken Pis. It's open weekdays from 10 am to 12.30 pm and 1.30 to 5 pm (until 4 pm from 1 October to 31 March), and weekends from 10 am to 1 pm; entry costs f80.

The **Ancient Art Museum**, Rue de la Régence 3, has works by Flemish Primitives, Brueghel and Rubens. It's open Tuesday to Sunday from 10 am to noon and 1 to 5 pm. For contemporary Belgian works, head to the **Modern Art** section at Place Royale 1, open Tuesday to Sunday from 10 am to 1 pm and 2 to 5 pm. Admission to both is free.

There are several museums to draw you out of the Petit Ring. The **Horta Museum**, Rue Américaine 25 in St Gilles, was the house of Victor Horta who founded Art Nouveau at the turn of the century – open daily except Monday from 2 to 5.30 pm, admission f150, tram No 92.

To the east, **Cinquantenaire** is a large museum conglomerate – art, history, military and motor vehicles together in a huge park. Take the metro to Merode.

A few minutes' walk from Gare du Midi is the **Gueuze Museum** at Rue Gheude 56 in Anderlecht – a working brewery still using traditional methods, and where you can sample the real thing. It's open weekdays from 8.30 am to 4.30 pm and Saturday from 10 am to 6 pm (9.30 am to 1 pm from June to mid-October); entry is f60.

Atomium This space-age leftover from the 1958 World Fair, at Blvd du Centenaire in the suburb of Laeken, has virtually become a symbol of the city. It's open daily from 9.30 am to 6 pm and costs f150. Get tram No 18 or 19 to Heysel.

Market The biggest is Sunday morning's food and general goods market around Gare du Midi.

Organised Tours Chatterbus (☎ 6731835) has three-hour walking/minibus tours led by native Brusselians. They start daily at 10 am from 1 June to 15 September, and cost f250; meet at Galeries St Hubert. For specialised tours – Horta and Art Nouveau, or Brussels in the Art-Deco era, for example – contact Arau (☎ 5134761) at 37 Rue Henri Maus.

Around Brussels A huge stone lion and nearly a million visitors a year look out over the plains where Napoleon was defeated and European history changed course at the Battle of **Waterloo**, south of Brussels. There's a visitor's centre (☎ 3851912) at Route du Lion 252 – take bus W from Place Rouppe.

Not quite as big is the elephant that marks the entrance to the **Central African Museum** at Tervuren, 20 km to the east. It's old and in parts musty but with an impressive range of Zaïrese artefacts. It's open daily from mid-March to mid-October from 9 am to 5.30 pm, the rest of the year from 10 am to 4.30 pm; admission is f50. Take the metro to Montgomery, then tram No 44.

Festivals

The most prestigious annual event is Ommegang, a 16th century-style procession staged within the illuminated Grand Place in early July. Just as popular is the biennial flower carpet that colours the square every second year (even numbers) in August.

Places to Stay

There's no shortage of hotels for f2500 and upwards, but the budget class is a different story. A handful of hostels are dotted within or just outside the Petit Ring.

Camping The most central option is the back yard at *Maison Internationale* (see the following Hostels section); it's f220, but for cyclists only. Alternatively there are plenty of grounds outside the Petit Ring. *Paul Rosmant* (☎ 7821009), at Warandeberg 52 in Wezembeek-Oppem to the east, charges f200 for an adult and a tent, and is open from April to September; take the metro to Stockel and then tram No 39 to the Marcelisstraat stop.

To the north in Grimbergen forest, *Veldkant* (☎ 2692597) at Veldkantstraat 64 is open from January to 31 October, and costs f150 per adult and tent; take bus No G from Gare du Nord to the end of the line and then it's a 15-minute walk. Heading south, there's *Beersel* (☎ 3310561) at Steenweg op Ukkel 75, or closer to Waterloo, *Camp Paul Charles* (☎ 6536215) at Ave Albert 1er 114 in Genval; both are open all year.

Hostels The most centrally located youth hostel is *Bruegel* (☎ 5110436) at Rue du St Esprit 2, an official hostel with singles/doubles/dorms for f590/970/360 per person. Otherwise, to the north, *Sleep Well* (☎ 2185050), Rue de la Blanchisserie 27, is oppressively crowded but with extensions due to be finished. Singles/doubles/dorms cost f480/820/290, and in July and August there's the multi-bed sleep-in for f240.

The other official hostel, *Jacques Brel* (☎ 2180187) at Rue de la Sablonnière 30, is 15 minutes from the centre, impersonal but with parking; a single/double/dorm costs f485/940/360. Just north is *CHAB* (☎ 2170158) at Rue Traversière 8, popular with backpackers, with singles/doubles /dorms for f580/960/340 and a summer sleep-in for f280. Otherwise, *Maison Internationale* (☎ 6489787), at Chaussée de Wavre 205, has singles/doubles for f350/600, but it's a hike from the centre – get bus No 34, 95 or 96 from Bourse.

Hotels The streets near Gare du Nord and Gare du Midi have cheap, but sometimes seedy, options. Alternatively, *Sabina* (☎ 2182637), at Rue du Nord 78 near metro Madou, is popular with weekend travellers and weekday Eurocrats. Rooms, all with shower, start at f1400 and there's street parking. Two blocks south, *Hôtel Madou* (☎ 2188375), Rue du Congrès 45, has decent singles/doubles from f1300/1550 but breakfast is f125 extra.

Farther north, behind St Maria church, is *Hôtel Albert* (☎ 2179391) at Rue Royal Sainte-Marie 27 with singles/doubles from f1180/1540, and parking for f100 a day. In front of St Maria, *Hotel International* (☎ 2173344) at Rue Royale 344 has singles/doubles from f1130/1350, while centrally, *La Madeleine* (☎ 5132973) at Rue de la Montagne 22 has singles/doubles from f1145/2495. Farther south, heading towards Gare du Midi, the little *Hotel Windsor* (☎ 5112014) at 13 Place Rouppe has affordable singles/doubles/triples from f1220/ 1580/1900, and there's parking on the square in front.

Places to Eat

If you've got money to burn, the question is where, amongst 2000 restaurants, to blow it. Most reasonably priced fare is outside the Petit Ring. However, if you're just after frites or a pitta bread, take your pick of the swarm of places along Rue Marché aux Fromages off the southern corner of the Grand Place.

City Centre Brussels' dining heart, although it more resembles a stomach, is Rue des Bouchers ('Butcher's Street') near the Grand Place. If you can't afford the lobsters and crabs awaiting conspicuous consumption, there's *Le Savarin* (☎ 5117483) at No 7 specialising in mid-priced Belgian cuisine.

Alternatively, *'t Kelderke* (☎ 5137344), in a 16th century cellar at Grand Place 15, has a lunch-time plat du jour for f295. *Bocca d'Oro* (☎ 5112469) at Rue de Rollebeek 15 is a pleasant but pricey pizzeria in a quaint street lined with art shops and international cuisine. Around the corner, *L'Orféo* (☎ 5126041) on Rue Haute 18 has huge stuffed pitta breads from f140 until 1 am.

For self-caterers, there's a *GB* supermarket in the basement of the City 2 shopping centre near Rogier metro.

Outside the City Centre For authentic moussaka and retsina, try *Le Cheval de Troie* (☎ 5383095) at Rue d'Argonne 32, near Gare du Midi. For equally delicious Turkish fare, head to one of the cheap *pide* (Turkish pizza) saloons in St Josse to the north. The *Metin* at Chaussée de Haecht 94 is popular with the locals and has complimentary *locum* (Turkish delight). For vegetarian food, *Le Paradoxe* (☎ 6498981) at Chaussée d'Ixelles 329 is Buddhist-run, with a plat du jour for f300.

Entertainment
The *Bulletin's* what's-on guide – free from the city tourist office – lists the live-music and cinema scenes. Otherwise there are enough bars and cafés to keep you on a long pub crawl.

Falstaff, by the stock exchange at Rue Henri Maus 17, is an Art-Nouveau showpiece, trendy with the fashionable young and eccentric old. Alternatively, the auspiciously named *De Ultieme Hallucinatie* at Rue Royale 316 has more subtle Art-Nouveau tones and live music late Fridays. *L'Aiglon* at Place Houwert 2 is a tiny African bar, while *À la Mort Subite* (literally, 'instant death') at Rue Mont-aux-Herbes-Potagères 7 has one of the many brews named after it. For specialist beers, try *Toone*, a puppet theatre/tavern off Petite rue des Bouchers, or for loud live rock, the *Blues Corner* off the Grand Place at Rue des Chapeliers 12. One street away at Rue de la Violette 22 there's ample French ambience at *Goupil le Fol* ('Crazy Folk').

Capricorne is a weekends-only, lesbian bar at Rue d'Anderlecht 8. *Le Garage* at Rue Duquesnoy 16 is a loud, Friday/Saturday gay and lesbian nightclub, or for men only, there's *Why Not* at Rue des Riches-Claires 7.

Getting There & Away
Air Airline offices in Brussels include the following:

Air Canada
    Zaventem Airport (☎ 7253981)

American Airlines
    Troonstraat 98 (☎ 5087700)
British Airways
    Centre Rogier (☎ 7253000)
KLM
    Ave Marnix 28 (☎ 5077070)
Sabena
    Rue Cardinal Mercier 35 (☎ 7233111)

Bus Eurolines (☎ 2170025) has an office at Place de Brouckère 50, where services leave for cities throughout Europe and Scandinavia. To London (f1690, 9½ hours) there's an overnight bus via Antwerp and Ghent, arriving at London's Victoria Station about 6 am. Other destinations include Amsterdam (f600, four hours), Cologne (f600, four hours) and Paris (f950, four hours).

Hoverspeed (☎ 5139340) Citysprint buses to London (f1700, 9½ hours) pick up at the office at Rue Antoine Dansaert 101. It's a daytime service (depending on the time of year, it also goes through Bruges) via Calais in France (check if you need a French visa), arriving at Victoria Station about 7.45 pm.

Train The train information office (☎ 2192640) at Gare Centrale is open daily from 6.30 am to 9 pm. There's a much quieter branch office (☎ 2190040) on Blvd Adolphe Max 142, which is open regular business hours.

For prices and journey times from Brussels to other Belgian cities and towns, check the Getting There & Away section in those places. For international services, see the Getting There & Away section at the beginning of this chapter.

Hitching North to Antwerp or Amsterdam, get tram No 52 or 92 to Heysel for the A12 motorway; east towards Liège or Cologne, take tram No 90 to metro Diamant for the E40; south-east to Namur and Luxembourg, get the metro (line 1) to Station Delta for the E411; south to Mons and Paris, get tram No 52 to Rue de Stalle and follow it to the E19; west to Ghent, Bruges or London, get bus No 85 to one stop before the terminus, and then follow the E40 signs.

Getting Around
Brussels' transport network consists of
buses, trams and a small, two-line metro.
Transport maps are handed out from the
tourist offices or metro information kiosks.

To/From the Airport The national airport,
Zaventem, lies 14 km to the north-east and
is connected to all three central stations by
three trains per hour (20 minutes, f75). Taxis
charge f900 to f1000.

Bus, Tram & Metro Single rides cost f45,
five-journey cards f200, 10-journey tickets
cost f275, and a 24-hour card f180. Valid on
all transport, tickets can be bought from the
metro stations or bus drivers, the 24-hour
card from tourist offices. Public transport
runs until about midnight.

Taxi There are plenty of ranks, or phone ATR
(☎ 6472222) or Taxis Orange (☎ 5136200).

Car Car rental starts at about f940 a day or
f6000 a week, with local operators such as
ABC offering some of the cheapest rates.
Rental firms include the following:

ABC
  Rue d'Anderlecht 133 (☎ 5131954)
Avis
  Rue Américaine 145 (☎ 5371280)
Budget
  Ave Louise 93 (☎ 5388075)
Europcar
  Ave Louise 235 (☎ 6409400)
Hertz
  Blvd Lemonnier 8 (☎ 513886)

Antwerp

Second in size to the capital and often more
likeable, Antwerp (Antwerpen in Flemish,
Anvers in French) is perhaps Belgium's most
underrated tourist city. It's compact and
heavily beautified by many Baroque edifices, and once home to 17th century artist
Pieter Paul Rubens.

With a prime spot on the Scheldt River,

Antwerp came to the fore as Western
Europe's greatest economic centre in the
early 16th century. But the times of prosperity were relatively short-lived. When the
city's Protestants smashed up a cathedral in
1566 as part of the Iconoclastic Fury, the
Spanish ruler Philip II sent troops to take
control. Ten years later the unpaid garrison
mutinied, ransacking the city and in three
nights massacring 8000 people in the
Spanish Fury. The final blow came in 1648
when the Dutch closed the Scheldt to all
non-Dutch ships, blocking Antwerp's vital
link to the sea. It wasn't until Napoleon
arrived and the French rebuilt the docks that
Antwerp got back on its feet.

Today it's brimming with a self-confi-
dence that is rarely extolled outside its
boundaries. As a world port, its air is international but at times seedy, while from
behind the discreet façades of the Jewish
quarter runs the world's largest diamond
industry.

Orientation
Easily navigated, Antwerp is bordered by the
Scheldt and the 'Ring', a highway built on a
16th century moat which encircled the city.
Most of the sights are concentrated between
the recently restored Centraal Station (CS)
and the old centre – a 15-minute walk away,
based around the Grote Markt. To get there,
head straight up Keyserlei and along the
newly pedestrianised Meir. At the end, turn
right into the Eiermarkt and head to the huge
Onze Lieve Vrouwe (Our Lady's) cathedral
which towers above the Grote Markt.

Information
Tourist Office At Grote Markt 15, the tourist
office (☎ 03-2320103) is open Monday to
Saturday from 9 am to 6 pm, Sunday to 5 pm,
and has f30 walking guides and the *Blaazuit*
events guide.

Money There's a Kredietbank in the base of
the tower (Europe's first skyscraper) on
Eiermarkt 20, open weekdays from 9 am to
4.30 pm (until 5.15 pm on Thursday) and
Saturday from 9.15 am to 12.15 pm. Other-

wise, the best rate you'll find around CS is at Leo Stevens & Cie on Vestingstraat 70. It doesn't charge commission, but is only open weekdays from 9 am to 4.30 pm. The exchange bureau inside CS has low rates but is open daily from 8 am to 11 pm. Thomas Cook (☎ 2263257) is across the road at Koningin Astridplein 33, open until 9 pm. American Express (☎ 2325920) at Frankrijklei 21 is open normal business hours.

Post & Telecommunications The main post office is at Groenplaats 43. There's a telephone centre at Jezusstraat 1, open daily from 8 am to 8 pm.

Antwerp's telephone code is 03.

Bookshops De Slegte (☎ 2316627) at Wapper 5 next to Rubens' House has a reasonable range of second-hand English novels. For an excellent variety of travel guides and maps, there's the VTB Boekhandel (☎ 2203369) at St Jakobsmarkt 45.

Laundry Near the New International Youth Home (see Hostels in the Places to Stay section that follows) there's Was-o-Was at Plantin en Moretuslei 77, open daily from 7 am to 8 pm.

Emergency The national emergency numbers are police, ☎ 101, and fire/ambulance, ☎ 100.

Things to See & Do

To its favour, Antwerp is a city for wandering, its former canals filled in long ago leaving an old centre with many wide squares and narrow, cobbled streets. Many buildings and city sections were face-lifted before Antwerp became the Cultural Capital of Europe for 1993.

Museums You'll find a host of museums. The major ones mostly charge f75, or you can buy a three-museum discount ticket for f150. All those listed below are, unless stated otherwise, open Tuesday to Saturday from 10 am to 5 pm.

Rubens' House at Wapper 9 tops most visitors' lists although his most noted works are in the cathedral. Admission is f75. Another fine 17th century home is the **Rockox House** at Keizerstraat 10, admission free. For more Rubens, as well as Flemish Primitives and contemporary works, there's the **Royal Art Gallery** at Leopold de Waelplaats (free entry); take tram No 8.

The 16th century home and workshop of a prosperous printing family, the **Plantin-Moretus** house showcases antique presses and splendid old globes. It's at Vrijdagmarkt 22 and costs f75. The **Steen**, the city's medieval riverside castle, houses a maritime museum at Steenplein, admission f75. The **Diamond Museum** at Lange Herentalsestraat 31 is open daily from 10 am to 5 pm, with cutting demonstrations on Saturday between 2 and 5 pm; entry is free.

To get a glimpse of the amount of diamonds and golds being traded in Antwerp, just wander along Pelikaanstraat, to the left out of CS, any time during the day.

Cathedral With its 120-metre spire, Onze Lieve Vrouwe is Belgium's largest Gothic cathedral and home to Rubens' *Descent from the Cross*. Entry is from Groenplaats 21; it's open weekdays from 10 am to 5 pm, Saturday from 10 am to 3 pm, Sunday from 1 to 4 pm, and costs f30/10 for adults/children.

Cogels Osylei This is a radical street of turn-of-the-century houses built in eclectic styles from Art Nouveau to classical or neo-Renaissance. It's away from the centre but well worth a wander – tram No 11 runs along it, or get a train to Berchem.

Boat Trips The NV Flandria (☎ 2313100) near the castle on Steenplein has cruises around the port – a 50-minute trip costs f220/120 for adults/children, or there are 2½-hour voyages for f350/200. Day trips to towns such as Bruges cost f1800/1200.

Markets On Friday mornings, the Vrijdagmarkt has second-hand goods. On Saturday

BELGIUM

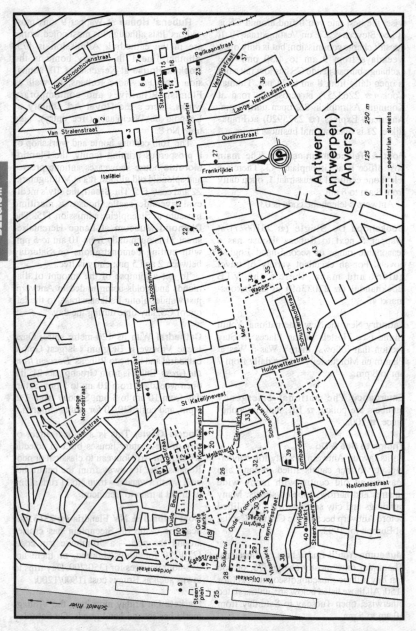

Antwerp
(Antwerpen)
(Anvers)

0   125   250 m

- - - = pedestrian streets

the Vogelmarkt (Bird Market), held on the square in front of the Schouwburg (Theatre) a block south of Wapper, is a lively food market; on Sunday it's birds, pets and general stuff.

Places to Stay
For its size, Antwerp is well covered with hostels but none are central. Conversely, cheap hotels are few, the main ones clumped on the square next to CS.

Camping There are two camp sites, both open from April to September and charging f35 for each adult/child/tent/car. *De Molen* (☎ 2196090) is north at St Annastrand – get bus No 81 or 82. *Vogelzang* (☎ 2385717) is at Vogelzanglaan near the Bouwcentrum, easily reached by tram No 2.

Hostels The cheapest option is the modern, official *youth hostel* (☎ 2380273) at Eric Sasselaan 2, about 10 minutes by tram No 2 or bus No 27 from CS – get off at Bouwcentrum and follow the signs. Open all year, it costs f320, and there are parking and laundry facilities.

The closest private hostel to CS is the friendly *New International Youth Home* (☎ 2300522) at Provinciestraat 256. It's 10 minutes' walk through the Jewish neighbourhood – turn left out of the station, follow Pelikaanstraat to the Plantin and En Moretuslei intersection, left through the tunnel and it's the third street on the right. There are singles/doubles/triples for f720/1040/1500 or dorms for f360.

Near the Royal Art Gallery, the laid-back, mural-splashed *Boomerang* (☎ 2384782) has dorms for f340 – get bus No 23 or tram No 8. Four blocks south, the *Sleep Inn* (☎ 2373748) at Bolivarplaats 1 has singles/doubles/triples for f470/940/1410, and laundry facilities; take bus No 1 from Frankrijklei.

Hotels The sage budget choice is *Rubenshof* (☎ 2370789) at Amerikalei 115, with singles/doubles/triples from f800/1500/1600 – get bus No 1, or tram No 12 or 24. Otherwise, on the square next to CS there's *Billiard Palace* (☎ 2334455) at Koningin Astridplein 40 with basic singles/doubles from f950/1400, or *Hotel Monico* (☎ 2250093) at No 34 with rooms from f1070/1390. On the other side of CS, the *Tourist Hotel* (☎ 2325870) at Pelikaanstraat 20 has pricey singles/doubles starting at f2050.

Places to Eat

Antwerp's old centre is well endowed with cafés and restaurants where you can eat well without blowing the budget. One of the best known is *Pelgrom* (☎ 2319335) on Pelgrimstraat 15, a cavernous, candle-lit cellar which before you descend offers sweeping views of the cathedral. For vegetarian lunches, or dinner Saturdays only, try *Elixir* (☎ 2317321) a few streets farther south at Steenhouwersvest 57.

North-east of Grote Markt there's *'t Hart* (☎ 2252692) at Wolstraat 3, which has mussels for f360, or the popular *Domus Eethuisje* (☎ 2251506) at No 11, with spaghetti or lasagne from f210. Two streets south, there are roasted or fried horse steaks for f445, and other similarly priced mains, at *De Peerdestal* (☎ 2319503), Wijngaardstraat 8. Down another two streets, you'll come to *Paros* (☎ 2262618) at Korte Nieuwstraat 8, a great-value Greek taverna, closed Tuesday, and full every other night. Next door is the vegetarian *Atlantis* (☎ 2340517), to its regulars as legendary as its namesake (closed Tuesday).

Pitta-bread places reign in the streets in front of CS, where you'll also find the *Mosselhuis* (☎ 2310028), one of Antwerp's oldest mussel restaurants, at Statiestraat 32.

Self-caterers will find a *Midi* supermarket at Jezusstraat 22, open weekdays from 8 am to 6.30 pm, Saturday from 9 am to 6 pm.

Entertainment

Antwerp's nightlife consists of its 2500 bars and cafés. Terraces line the cobbled streets around the cathedral, one of the most popular being the angel-adorned *'t elfde Gebod* (the 11th Commandment) at Torfbrug 10. *Cartoons* at Kaasstraat 6 is full of smoke and conversation, located under a cinema of the same name which screens alternative films.

Den Engel on Grote Markt is a lively local haunt, as are *De Herk* and the brown café-style *De Ware Jacob*, both on Reyndersstraat. On the same street, *De Vagant* at No 21 serves more than 150 *genevers* (Belgian gins), while the *Taverna Bierland* on Korte Nieuwstraat 28 is a tourist stronghold boasting 465 beers. The cosy *De Negen Vaten* (The Nine Barrels) at Zand 1 specialises in fine port authentically poured straight from wooden barrels.

Near the waterfront, *Muziekdoos* at Van Dijckkaai 12 has regular live bands or a succession of buskers. *De Trein der Traagheid* at Lange Noordstraat 33 is an old wooden train carriage converted into a lively café where on Thursday and Saturday nights budding vocalists take the microphone and act like nightingales. For a more classical atmosphere, there's the glass-domed *De Foyer* upstairs in the restored city theatre on Komedieplaats.

Alternatively, the streets off Keyserlei near CS blaze with clubs and discos, while the riverside quarter north of Grote Markt is home to a red-light district. A few gay bars dot Van Schoonhovenstraat off Koningin Astridplein.

Getting There & Away

Air Deurne Airport is eight km south-east of Antwerp, connected by bus No 16 from CS. Sabena has an office in Antwerp (☎ 2316825) at Keyserlei 74 just up from CS, or at the airport (☎ 2395960). For details on flights from here, see the Getting There & Away section at the beginning of this chapter.

Bus Eurolines (☎ 2338662) has an office at Van Stralenstraat 20, with buses from here to Amsterdam (f600, three hours), Cologne (f600, four hours) and Paris (f1050, five hours). There are two services per day to London (f1690) – the daytime bus takes about 7½ hours, the overnight run nine hours.

Hoverspeed (☎ 2188828) has no office in Antwerp, but tickets can be bought from American Express (see Money in the previous Information section) and other travel agents. The daytime Citysprint bus to London (f1700, seven hours) leaves from Cogels Osylei 88 near Berchem station. It goes via Calais in France (check if you need a French visa), and depending on the time of year, it stops in Bruges.

Train Depending on their destination, international trains stop at either CS and/or Berchem Station to the south-east (from where there are regular train connections to CS). Trains to Paris (f1440, 3½ hours, 12 per day) leave from Berchem only. To Amsterdam (f800, 2¼ hours, hourly) and London (f2690, six per day), they pass through both stations. London trains go via Ostend where they connect with a ferry or jetfoil. The total journey takes eight hours with the ferry, or four hours with the jetfoil.

National connections include IC trains to Bruges (f335, 70 minutes), Brussels (f165, 35 minutes) and Ghent (f215, 45 minutes). The CS train information office (☎ 2333915) is open Monday to Saturday from 7 am to 10 pm and Sunday from 9 am to 7 pm. The Berchem office is open 24 hours.

Getting Around
There's a good network of buses, trams and a tiny metro – pick up the f50 public transport map from metro kiosks at Diamant (in front of CS), open weekdays from 8.30 am to 12.30 pm and 1.30 to 4 pm, or Groenplaats (near Grote Markt), open the same weekday hours and also Saturday from 9 am to noon. The main bus hubs are Koningin Astridplein next to CS and Franklin Rooseveltplaats two blocks west. Single tickets cost f37, eight-strip cards f185, or a 24-hour unlimited card f180.

Bruges

Known as the 'perfect' tourist attraction, Bruges (Brugge in Flemish) is one of Europe's best preserved medieval cities and,

hardly surprising, Belgium's most visited town. Its richly ornate 13th century centre was suspended in time five centuries ago (and has remained that way because of strict building regulations) due largely to the silting of the Zwin River. At that time, Bruges was a prosperous cloth manufacturing town and the centre of Flemish Primitive art. When the river silted, Bruges died, its wealthy merchants abandoning it for Antwerp, leaving unoccupied homes and deserted canals.

That air has long gone. Today, particularly in summer, this 'living museum' is smothered with people. Go out of season or stay around late on summer evenings, when the carillon chimes seep through the cobbled streets and local boys cast their fishing rods into willow-lined canals, and Bruges will show its age-old beauty.

Orientation
Neatly encased by an oval-shaped canal, Bruges is an amblers' ultimate dream, its sights sprinkled within leisurely walking distance around its compact centre. There are two central squares, the Markt and the Burg. Many local buses stop at the former, while the more impressive latter is home to the tourist office. The train station is 20 minutes' walk south of the Markt – buses shuttle regularly between the two.

Information
Tourist Information The tourist office (☎ 050-448686) at Burg 11 is open summer (1 April to 30 September) weekdays from 9.30 am to 6.30 pm and weekends from 10 am to noon and 2 to 6.30 pm. In winter it's open Monday to Saturday from 9.30 am to 12.45 pm and 2 to 5.45 pm. In the foyer there's a handful of luggage lockers, accessible during these hours. A small bureau at the station is open weekdays from 7 am to 7 pm and weekends from 9.30 am to 5.30 pm.

Money There's a BBL Bank on the Markt. Out of hours, the exchange bureau at the tourist office is open daily from 9.30 am to 6.30 pm (from 1 November to 31 March on

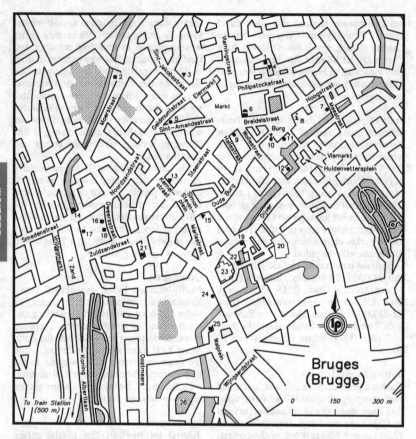

**Bruges
(Brugge)**

0   150   300 m

To Train Station
(500 m)

Saturdays only – same hours as the tourist office). Alternatively, you can change money, with lower rates, at the train station ticket counters from 5 am to 11 pm.

Post & Telecommunications The post office is at Markt 5. The telephone office at Meestraat, two blocks west of the Burg, is open Monday to Thursday from 8.30 am to 4 pm and Friday until 6 pm.

Bruges' telephone code is 050.

Laundry North of the Markt, next door to Snuffel Travellers Inn (see Hostels in the

following Places to Stay section), there's a wassalon open daily from 7 am to 10 pm.

Emergency For police, ring ☎ 101, and for ambulance, ☎ 100. To contact a doctor on weekends, ☎ 813899.

Things to See & Do
There are many sights but also a wealth of things to do, from climbing the Belfry to cruising the canals.

Walking Tour The **Markt** and neighbouring **Burg** are the dual medieval cores. From the

PLACES TO STAY

1 Hotel Cordoeanier
2 B&B
14 Speelmanshuys
16 Imperial Pension
18 Bruno's Passage Hostel
21 Salvators
25 Rembrandt-Rubens Hotel

PLACES TO EAT

3 In den Wittenkop
4 Lotus
13 De Hobbit
15 't Koffiehuisje

OTHER

5 Chagall
6 Post Office
7 Telephone Office
8 Tourist Office
9 Belfry
10 Holy Blood Basilica
11 Town Hall
12 Canal Cruises
17 l'Obcéolé
19 Brangwyn Museum
20 Groeninge Museum
22 Gruuthuse Museum
23 Church of Our Lady
24 Memling Museum
26 Begijnhof

Markt rises the 90-metre-high **Belfry** with its 47-bell carillon, while the Burg, connected by a lace-lined alley next to the post office, is home to Belgium's oldest **City Hall** as well as the **Basilica of the Holy Blood** where a few coagulated drops of Christ's blood are said to be stored.

From the Burg, go through the tunnelled Blinde Ezelstraat (Blind Donkey Street) to the **Fish Market** and Huidenvettersplein, where canal boats leave. It's the start of the Dijver, along which you'll find the **Groeninge Museum**. The Dijver also leads past the **Brangwyn** and **Gruuthuse** museums – the former housing artwork including lace, the latter a 15th century lord's mansion. Nearby, the **Church of Our Lady** is home to Michelangelo's *Madonna and*

Child – his only sculpture to leave Italy during his lifetime – while across from the church on Mariastraat is the **Memling Museum**, housing works by Hans Memling, one of the early Flemish Primitives. Farther down Mariastraat, signs lead to the **Begijnhof**.

Museums There's a f250 discount ticket available if you're visiting the Groeninge, Memling, Gruuthuse and Brangwyn museums. The **Groeninge Museum** at Dijver 12 houses Flemish art, from early Primitives through to contemporary. It's open daily in summer from 10 am to 5.30 pm, in winter from 10 am to noon and 2 to 4.30 pm, and costs f100/50 for adults/students.

Belfry The view from the top of the 366 steps is rosy at sunset. It's open daily in summer from 10 am to 5 pm, in winter from 10 to 11.45 am and 1.30 to 4 pm, and costs f80/40 for adults/children.

Begijnhof Once home to unmarried women and widows, this serene 13th century grassy square, enclosed by modest, whitewashed houses, is today inhabited by Benedictine nuns. It's about 10 minutes' walk south of the Markt.

Organised Tours Bruges by boat, bike, bus, foot or horse-drawn carriage – name it and you can tour by it. The tourist office has copious details. Alternatively, Quasimodo's (☎ 370470) day tours, set up for travellers by a Belgian/New Zealand couple, will take you either to Ypres and around the battlefields of Flanders, for a Flemish beer binge or through Bruges and to the coast – prices start at f1100.

Around Bruges The famous, poppy-filled **battlefields of Flanders** draw many people south for a day or longer (see the Ypres section). In the opposite direction, the former fishing village of **Damme** is just five km away, connected by the Noorweegse Canal, and popular as a lunch-time destination for day trippers. A gaudy-coloured paddle wheeler plies between the two towns (30 minutes one-way), leaving from Noorweegse Kaai 31, a good 45-minute walk from the Markt (or take bus No 4). A one-way voyage costs f130/90 for adults/children, and f190/130 return.

Places to Stay

Bruges' attractiveness has resulted in a mass of accommodation – all oppressively booked in summer.

Camping East at St Kruis, *Memling* (☎ 355845) at Veltemweg 109 is open all year and charges f85/70 per person/tent. Get bus No 58a from the station. The slightly more expensive *St Michiel* (☎ 380819), Tillegemstraat 55, is reached by bus No 7.

Hostels There are three unofficial hostels, all with lively, traveller-filled bars, less than 10 minutes' walk from the Markt. *Bruno's Passage* (☎ 340232) at Dweersstraat 26 has instruments for travelling musicians, and offers 5% off its rates – f325/375 for a dorm/four-bed room – if you arrive towing a guidebook in which it's mentioned. *Snuffel Travellers Inn* (☎ 333133) at Ezelstraat 49 is popular and smoky, with a café serving a small range of hearty meals for f260 from 7 to 9 pm. Dorms/doubles cost f325/f900 – from the Markt, head up St Jakobsstraat. *Bauhaus International Youth Hotel* (☎ 341093) at Langestraat 135 is big, bustling with a wide range of meals until midnight, and charges f320/950 for dorms/doubles – get bus No 6 from the Markt or follow Hoogstraat from the Burg.

Alternatively, there's the tranquil little *Kilroy's Garden* (☎ 389382) at Singel 12, which charges f325 per person (f50 extra for sheets). You're guaranteed a warm welcome, but there's only one four-bed room and three doubles, so ring ahead. The official *youth hostel* (☎ 352679), Baron Ruzettelaan 143, has dorms/four-bed rooms for f320/405, and a car park. It's closed between 10 am and 1 pm. Get bus No 2 from the station to the second stop.

Hotels Most of the cheaper hotels are away from the centre but rarely more than a 15-minute walk. The cosy *'t Keizershof* (☎ 338728), at Oostmeers 126 opposite the train station, has singles/doubles from f850/1150, and a car park. Next door, *Breugelhof* (☎ 343428) has singles/doubles for f1100/1400, and triples/quads for f1600/2000. The *Rembrandt-Rubens Hotel* (☎ 336439), on the horse-and-carriage route at Walplein 38, has singles/doubles from f900/1300, and parking; it's closed from 1 October to 1 April.

On the restaurant-lined Vrijdagmarkt, *'t Speelmanshuys* (☎ 339552) at No 3 has rooms from f950/1550 single/double. The *Imperial Pension* (☎ 339014) on Dweersstraat 28 has singles/doubles for f900/f1400. Nearby, the stained-glass entry to *Salvators* (☎ 331921) at St Salvatorskerkhof 17 hides good-value singles at f840, doubles for f1580. Very central but on a quiet backstreet is *Hotel Cordoeanier* (☎ 339051) at Cordoeanierstraat 16, which has singles/doubles/triples from f1300/1500/2000. More intimately, there's Mrs Nyssen's little *B&B* (☎ 343171) at Moerstraat 50, where singles/doubles cost f800/1200.

Places to Eat

Mainly geared for big budgets, Bruges has a sprinkling of reasonable restaurants, backed up by the hostels (see the previous section) which offer traveller-sized meals. Otherwise, *De Hobbit* (☎ 335520) on Kemelstraat has charcoal-grilled spare ribs for f390, and complimentary wholemeal bread. On Simon Stevinplein, *'t Koffiehuisje* (☎ 337950) serves mussels in white wine for slightly less (f450) than its Markt counterparts.

Toermalijn (☎ 340194) wholefood restaurant in the Alfa Dante Hotel at Coupure 29, 10 minutes' walk from the Burg, has a mouth-watering vegetarian menu (closed Sunday and Monday). For cheaper, more central vegetarian fare, try *Lotus* at Wapenmakersstraat 5. It's open daily for lunch, but dinner Saturday night only.

Popular and affordable, with a smooth jazz atmosphere, is the two-tiered bistro *In*

den Wittenkop (☎ 332059) at St Jacobstraat
14. A variety of mains start from f300. Out
of the centre, there's a small *supermarket* on
Smedenstraat off the north-west corner of 't
Zand.

Entertainment
Besides the lively hostel bars, *De Versteende
Nacht* at Langestraat 11 (follow Hoogstraat
until it changes name) is a jazz café open
nightly, except Monday, from 7 pm. Farther
along at No 121, the spacious *Cactus Café*
draws a hip crowd.

In the centre, there's a throng of noisy bars
on the Eiermarkt, and a pair of beer houses
on Kemelstraat. *Chagall* at St Amandsstraat
40 is a laid-back pub, and *l'Obcéolé* on 't
Zand is a lively bar with a band playing on
Thursday.

Getting There & Away
Bus The overnight Eurolines bus to London
(f1690, seven hours) leaves from the train
station. Hoverspeed's Citysprint daytime
bus to London (f1700, six hours) departs
from Spoorwegstraat through the tunnel
immediately behind the train station. It goes
via Calais in France (check if you need a
visa). Tickets for both can be bought from
the BBL Bank travel agent on the Markt.

Train The station information office
(☎ 382406) is open weekdays from 7 am to
7 pm and weekends from 9.30 am to 5.30 pm.
There are IC trains to Antwerp (f335, 70
minutes), Brussels (f320, one hour), Courtrai
(f175, 40 minutes, from where there are
hourly connections to Ypres), Ghent (f145,
20 minutes) and Ostend (f90, 15 minutes).

Getting Around
There's a small network of buses, most
leaving from the Markt, and many pass by
the train station. The boards outside the
tourist office list the routes and timetables,
or you can ring ☎ 382382.

Bicycle The train station shop (☎ 385871),
open daily from 7 am to 8.30 pm, has the
cheapest rental rates. Rent-a-Bicycle

(☎ 338027), next to the Belfry at Hallestraat
4, charges f250 a day.

Ypres

The stories have long been told about the
WW I battlefields of Flanders. There were
the tall red poppies which rose over the flat,
flat fields; the soldiers who disappeared
forever in the quagmire of battle; and the
little town of Ypres (Ieper in Flemish) which
was wiped off the map.

Sitting in the country's south-west corner,
Ypres and its surrounding land were the last
bastion of Belgian territory unoccupied by
the Germans in WW I. As such, the region
was a barrier to a German advance towards
the French coastal ports around Calais. More
then 500,000 Allied soldiers were killed here
during four years of fighting that left the
medieval town flattened. Convincingly
rebuilt, its outlying farmlands are today
dotted with cemeteries, and in early spring,
the poppies still grow.

Orientation & Information
The town's hub is the Grote Markt. It's about
five minutes' walk from the train station –
head straight up Stationsstraat, and at the
end, turn left into Tempelstraat and then right
into Boterstraat. Three blocks on, at the
beginning of the Markt, rises the Renais-
sance-style town hall.

Inside here is the tourist office (☎ 057-
200724) at Grote Markt 34, open daily
between 1 April and 30 September from 9.30
am to 5.30 pm; the rest of the year, it's open
Monday to Saturday from 9 am to 5 pm, and
Sunday from 11 am to 4 pm.

At the opposite end of the Markt sits the
elegant courthouse, a former 12th century
hospital.

Things to See
Ypres ranked alongside Bruges and Ghent as
an important cloth town in medieval times,
and its postwar reconstruction holds true to
its former prosperity. On the 1st floor of the

town hall, the **Ypres Salient '14-'18 Museum** details the wartime destruction of the town, open 1 April to 31 October from 9.30 am to noon and 1.30 to 5.30 pm (entry f30).

Around the town, in outlying fields and hamlets, are 150 British cemeteries and row upon row of white crosses. The tourist office sells a car/bike map (f20) known as the *'14-'18 Route* which winds for 40 km around the north-eastern battlefields past many of these cemeteries. But within the town itself stands perhaps the saddest reminder: the **Menin Gate**, inscribed with the names of 55,000 British and Commonwealth troops who were lost in the quagmire of the trenches and who have no graves. A bugler sounds the last post here every evening at 8 pm. It's about 300 metres from the tourist office – up Meensestraat to the right of the courthouse.

Places to Stay & Eat

For camping, there's *YPRA* (☎ 057-444631) at Pingelarestraat 2 in Kemmel, 10 km south. The closest (unofficial) hostel is *De Lork* (☎ 057-445970) at Lindestraat 1, also in Kemmel. Otherwise, heading towards the coast, the official *youth hostel* (☎ 057-400901) is at Veurnestraat 4 in Vleteren, 15 km away.

One of the most affordable central hotels, *Gasthof 't Zweerd* (☎ 200475) at Grote Markt 2 next to the courthouse, has good-value singles/doubles from f750/1250. Alternatively, *Hostellerie St Nicolas* (☎ 200622) at G de Stuersstraat 6 (two blocks west of the Grote Markt towards the train station) has rooms with shower from f1100/1600.

Restaurants line the Grote Markt, but alternatively, *Pita Pyramide* at Tempelstraat 7, halfway to the train station, has stuffed pitta breads for f140. *De Wyngaard* (☎ 204230) at M Fochlaan 8, immediately to the left out of the train station, has hearty meals such as steaks from f380.

Getting There & Away

Bus Regional buses leave to the left out of the train station. To Kemmel, take bus No

743 which runs until 6.55 pm on weekdays, 5.15 pm on weekends. To Vleteren, take the 'Veurne' bus and get off halfway.

Train The station information office is open weekdays from 5.30 am to 8.45 pm and weekends from 6.30 am to 9.45 pm. There are hourly trains to Courtrai (f120, 30 minutes) and direct to Ghent (f260, one hour); for Bruges, Antwerp and Brussels, you have to change in Courtrai.

Bicycles can be rented from the luggage room at the station (open until 11 pm).

Ghent

Medieval Europe's largest city outside Paris, Ghent's glory lives in its industrious and rebellious past. Sitting on the junction of the Leie and Scheldt Rivers, by the mid-14th century it had become Europe's largest cloth producer, importing wool from England and employing thousands of people. The townsfolk were well known for their armed battles for civil liberties and against the heavy taxes imposed on them. Today home to many students, it's grey and somewhat begrimed, not picturesque like Bruges, but ultimately more realistic. Ghent is known as Gent in Flemish, Gand in French.

Orientation

Unlike many Belgian cities, Ghent does not have one central square. Instead, the medieval core is a row of large open squares connected by three imposing edifices: St Nicholas' church, the Belfry and St Baaf's cathedral, their line of towers long the trademark of Ghent's skyline. The Korenmarkt is the westernmost square, technically known as the town centre and a 25-minute walk from the main railway station, St Pieters-station, but regularly connected by tram Nos 1, 10 and 11.

Information

Tourist Information Housed in the City Hall crypt next to the Belfry, the tourist office

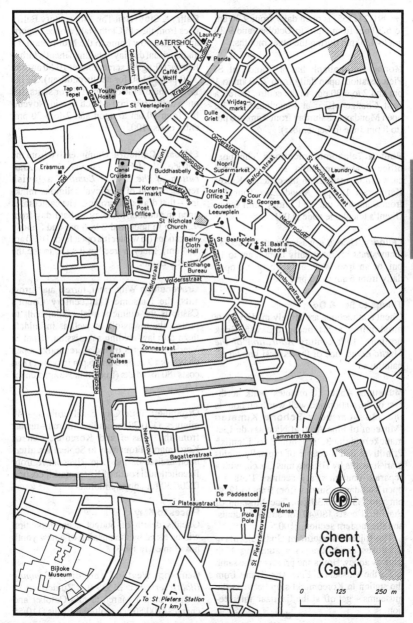

(☎ 091-241555) is open daily from 9.30 am to 6.30 pm from April to October, and 9.30 am to 4.30 pm during the other months.

Money Europabank has a branch at St Pietersstation, open daily from 7.30 am to 1 pm and 2 to 6.30 pm. In the centre, there's a Best Change office at Mageleinstraat 36, open Monday to Saturday from 9 am to 6 pm (to 8 pm June to September).

Post & Telecommunications The post office is at Korenmarkt 16. International calls can be made from the office at Keizer Karelstraat 1, open Monday to Thursday from 8 am to 4 pm, and Friday until 6 pm. Ghent's telephone code is 091.

Laundry There's a wassalon at St Jacobsnieuwstraat 85, open daily from 8 am to 10 pm, or an Ipso Wash at Oudberg 25, open daily from 6 am to 10 pm.

Things to See & Do

Ghent's attractions are largely medieval, its most noted sight being the van Eyck brothers' 15th century *Adoration of the Mystic Lamb*, one of the earliest known oil paintings.

Museums About 10 minutes' walk northeast of the station and well worth an hour is the **Museum voor Schone Kunsten** (Museum of Fine Arts) at Nicolaas de Liemaeckereplein 3. It's home to Flemish Primitives and a couple of typically nightmarish works by Hieronymus Bosch, with a separate contemporary section. Both are open Tuesday to Sunday from 9 am to 12.30 pm and 1.30 to 5.30 pm. The Museum of Fine Arts costs f80/40 for adults/students, and the modern section, f100/50.

The **Bijloke Museum** at Godshuizenlaan 2 houses antiquities in a stunning 13th century abbey. Hours and prices are the same as for the Museum of Fine Arts. Trams from the station to Korenmarkt stop between the museums – get off at the Ijzerlaan intersection.

Belfry & Cloth Hall The 14th century Belfry rises from the old Cloth Hall, a once important edifice now home to the Multivision, an audio-visual display detailing Ghent's turbulent past (English screenings at 10.50 am and 3.20 pm, f80/30 for adults/children). To the Belfry, there's the option of lift or stairs. It's open daily from mid-March to mid-November from 10 am to noon and 2 to 5.30 pm; entry costs f100.

St Baaf's Cathedral Unimpressive from the outside, it's Hubert & Jan van Eyck's *Adoration of the Mystic Lamb* – a lavish representation of medieval religious thinking – that draws the crowds. The cathedral is open in summer Monday to Saturday from 9.30 am to noon and 2 to 6 pm and Sunday afternoons (in winter it's open from 10.30 am to 4 pm). Entry is free but it's f50 to see the Mystic Lamb.

Gravensteen With moat, turrets and arrow slits, the fearsome 12th century Count's Castle is the quintessential castle, built to protect the townsfolk as well as intimidate them into law-abiding submission. It's at St Veerleplein north of the Korenmarkt, open daily from 9 am to 6 pm (5 pm in winter) and costs f80 for adults (free for those aged under 12).

Organised Tour City canal cruises – 40 minutes, f120/70 for adults/children – depart from the Graslei and Korenlei, east of Korenmarkt. From May to September, afternoon cruises on the Leie River leave from Recollettenlei south of Korenmarkt, costing f220/130 for adults/children.

Places to Stay

Ghent's dearth of budget accommodation will be eased by the opening of a new youth hostel in early 1993.

Camping West of the city, *Camping Blaarmeersen* (☎ 215399) at Zuiderlaan 12 is open from 1 March to mid-October and charges f100/50 per adult/child, plus f110/55 per tent/car. Take bus No 38 from the centre or the station.

Colleges From mid-July to late September a single room in one of the four southside university colleges costs f500 including breakfast. To book, contact Mrs K van den Broeck (☎ 220911) at Stalhof 6, 9000 Ghent.

Hostel An official *youth hostel* is expected to open in February 1993 in a renovated old warehouse at St Widokaai, across the canal behind the Gravensteen, entry off Gewad. Prices in a double or four-bed room will cost f400.

Hotels Most of the budget options are clustered around St Pietersstation. In Prinses Clementinalaan to your right out of the station is *La Lanterne* (☎ 201318) at No 140, with singles/doubles without breakfast but with parking for f900/1200. To the left out the station's rear entrance, *Adoma* (☎ 226550) at Sint Denijslaan 19 has doubles for f1300; breakfast is f170 extra and the hotel is closed the last two weeks in July. *Trianon II* (☎ 204840) to the right on Voskenslaan 34 has doubles with parking for f2100.

In the centre, everything's pricey. Across from the tourist office, *Cour St Georges* (☎ 242424) at Botermarkt 2 has singles/doubles starting at f2600/3000. In a more serene surrounding is *Erasmus* (☎ 242195) at Poel 25, with elegant rooms from f2450/3000.

Places to Eat
The student ghetto, about 10 minutes' walk south-east of the Korenmarkt, is the best area for well-priced meals. Here on St Pietersnieuwstraat and Overpoortstraat you'll find plenty of cheap cafés and bars. There's also a vegetarian lunch-time café, *De Paddestoel* (☎ 251330), at Guinardstraat 9. Otherwise, the best value eateries are the two student restaurants: the *Octopus* cafeteria/restaurant complex at Overpoortstraat 49 is open weekdays for lunch between 11.30 am and 2 pm; alternatively, on St Pietersnieuwstraat 45

there's another university mensa open weekdays from noon to 2.30 pm and 6 to 9 pm.

In the centre, *Buddhasbelly* (☎ 251732) on Hoogpoort 30 is open until 9 pm (closed Sunday) and has eat-in or takeaway vegetarian fare. The spacious *Caffé Wolff* (☎ 330157) on Kraanlei 29 near the Count's Castle has snacks, while farther along at Oudburg 38, the *Panda* (☎ 250786), at the back of a large health food shop, has biologically sound, three-course vegetarian specialities for f425.

In a thicket of cobbled lanes west of here is the recently restored Patershol quarter. The choice of restaurants here is ample, but the old-world ambience means prices are high. Across the bridge on the Vrijdagmarkt, once the city's forum for public meetings and executions, *Keizershof* (☎ 234446) tavern at No 47 has snacks.

Self-caterers have a *Nopri* supermarket at Hoogpoort 42, behind the tourist office, open Monday to Saturday from 9 am to 6 pm, and *Grimsel*, a health food shop on Prinses Clementinalaan to the right out of the train station.

Entertainment
As always, there are plenty of atmospheric bars in which to while away the evenings. The student quarter has a lively selection – the *Pole Pole* (Swahili for 'Slowly Slowly') at St Pietersnieuwstraat 158 has an African ambience and is open nightly from 8 pm to 2 am. Behind the Gravensteen, the *Tap en Tepel* at Gewad 7 is dark and mysteriously inviting, while on Vrijdagmarkt, the *Dulle Griet* specialises in Trappist beers.

Getting There & Away
Bus Eurolines and Hoverspeed buses leave from in front of St Pietersstation. Tickets can be bought from the BJK travel shop (☎ 210805) at Prinses Clementinalaan 205 immediately to the right out of the station. Eurolines has buses to London (f1690, 8½ hours, overnight), Cologne (f600, four hours) and Bonn (f1000, six hours). Hoverspeed's bus to London (f1700, six hours,

daytime) from Brussels stops in Ghent in summer only.

Train The station information office (☎ 224444) is open daily from 7 am to 9 pm. There are IC trains to Antwerp (f215, 45 minutes), Bruges (f145, 20 minutes), Brussels (f200, 45 mintues) and direct to Ypres (f260, one hour).

Getting Around

The public transport information kiosks at the station and on the Korenmarkt sell tickets and f25 tram/bus maps.

Liège

Compared with other cities in Belgium, it's hard to rave about Liège (Luik in Flemish). Sprawled along the Meuse River in the eastern part of Wallonia, this noisy city is seemingly forever shrouded in an atmosphere of grey. Its two main drawing cards are its many museums – 17 at the last count – and its position as the northern gateway to the forested Ardennes (see the following section). To the south-east gurgles the famous old resort of Spa, while farther east still rises the Hautes-Fagnes park. About 15 km north-west, across the language divide in the Flemish province of Limburg, is Belgium's oldest town, Tongeren.

Orientation

The 'central' district is strewn along the western bank of the Meuse River, which splits in two here creating the island of Outremeuse. There are several main squares, the most central being Place St Lambert in front of the Palais des Princes Evêques. Most of the major museums lie north-west of here, while directly to the south is the shopping and nightlife hub around Place de la Cathédrale. The main railway station, Gare Guillemins, is about two km south of Place Lambert.

Information

The main Office du Tourisme (☎ 041-223578) is at Féronstrée 92, about 2.5 km from Gare Guillemins. It's open weekdays from 9 am to 6 pm and weekends from 10 am to 4 pm (to 2 pm on Sunday). At Gare Guillemins there's a small bureau (☎ 041-524419) open daily from 9.30 am to 6 pm.

Regional information can be picked up from the Fédération du Tourisme de la Province de Liège (☎ 041-224210) at Boulevard de la Sauvenière 77, open weekdays from 8.30 am to 6 pm and Saturday from 9 am to 1 pm.

Money There's a BBL Bank one block straight up Rue des Guillemins from the train station. Alternatively, 24-hour exchange is available at the international ticket windows at the station.

Post & Telecommunications The main post office is at Rue de la Régence 61, or there's a branch to the left out of Gare Guillemins open Monday to Saturday from 8 am to 8 pm. The main telephone office is at Rue de l'Université 32, open daily from 8 am to 7 pm, but international calls can also be made between 8 am and 4.15 pm from the bureau at Gare Guillemins (under the post office).

Liège's telephone code is 041.

Laundry Two blocks north of Gare Guillemins on Rue des Guillemins, the Hypernet laundry is open daily from 8 am to 9 pm.

Emergency The national emergency numbers are police, ☎ 101, and fire/ambulance, ☎ 100.

Things to See & Do

Liège has a diverse range of museums, from glass or weapons to public transport and the conventional arts. Their common denominator is that they're all staunchly local. Admission for each is f50/20 for adults/children.

Above the city sits the **citadelle**, a half-hour walk straight up the Montagne de

BELGIUM

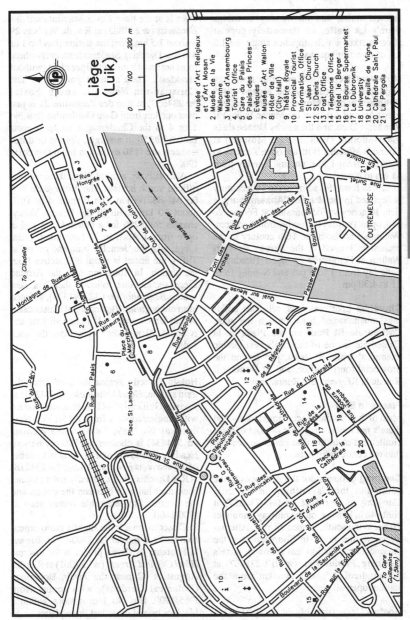

Liège (Luik)

0   100   200 m

1 Musée d'Art Religieux
   et d'Art Mosan
2 Musée de la Vie
   Wallonne
3 Musée d'Ansembourg
4 Tourist Office
5 Gare du Palais
6 Palais des Princes–
   Evêques
7 Musée d'Art Wallon
8 Hôtel de Ville
   (City Hall)
9 Théâtre Royale
10 Provincial Tourist
   Information Office
11 St Jean Church
12 St Denis Church
13 Post Office
14 Telephone Office
15 Hotel le Berger
16 La Bourse Supermarket
17 Le Dubrovnik
18 University
19 La Feuille de Vigne
20 Cathédrale Saint Paul
21 La Pergola

Bueren stairs, and on Sunday mornings there's **La Batte**, an immensely popular street market which stretches along the 1.5 km of riverfront quays.

Museums Depending on your taste, the highlights are probably the **Musée d'Art Religieux et d'Art Mosan** (Museum of Religious Art and Art from the Meuse Valley) at Rue Mère Dieu, and the nearby **Musée de la Vie Wallonne** (Walloon Life Museum) at Cour des Mineurs. Both are open Tuesday to Saturday from 1 to 6 pm and Sunday from 11 am to 4 pm.

Life as it was for some in the 18th century is depicted in the **Musée d'Ansembourg**, a rich, Regency-styled mansion at Féronstrée 114, open Tuesday to Sunday from 1 to 5 pm. Wallonian art from the 16th century to the present is housed in the **Musée de l'Art Wallon** at Féronstrée 86, open Tuesday to Saturday from 1 to 6 pm and Sunday from 11 to 4.30 pm.

Churches Like museums, religious buildings mushroomed here through the ages. **Cathédrale St Paul** on the Place de la Cathédrale is one of the city's best Gothic examples, while **St Jean**, just behind the provincial tourist office, and **St Denis**, off Rue de la Régence, are Romanesque.

Places to Stay

Most of the affordable accommodation – and there's not much – is either in front of Gare Guillemins or in the first km or so heading into the centre from here.

Camping Grounds dot the Ardennes to the south but there's nothing in the city. *Camping an der Hill* (☎ 087-744617) at Hütte 46 in Esneux, on the railway line about 20 km to the south, is open all year. Alternatively, to the north in Tongeren (see the Around Liège section that follows), there's *Camping Pliniusbron* (☎ 012-231607) at Fonteindreef 3, about two km from the station, open all year.

Hostels Unquestionably the cheapest bed in town is at the busy *Foyer International des Étudiants* (☎ 233885) at Rue du Vertbois 29 – about 1.5 km from the station (bus No 1 or 4 to Rue Darchis). Students from everywhere roost here as it's only f150 per night (without breakfast). There's an 11 pm curfew. The Christian-run *New Val* youth hostel (☎ 234653) at Rue des Augustins 21 is just over one km from Gare Guillemins (bus No 1 or 4 to the Charlemagne stop). It costs f550/850/350 in a single, double or dorm – sheets are f150 extra and breakfast costs f90.

Alternatively, around Liège there are two official youth hostels. The *Auberge de Tilff* (☎ 041-882100) at Rue Blandot 4 in Tilff, about 10 km south in the Ourthe Valley, charges f690/295 for a double/dorm and is open from 1 April to 30 September. From Liège, take the 'Jemelle' train and get off at Tilff – the hostel is about 800 metres from the station. In Tongeren (see the Around Liège section that follows) there's a new hostel, *Begeinhof* (☎ 012-391370), situated in an old *begijnhof* (grouping of almshouses) at Sint Ursulastraat 1. It's open all year and is about 10 minutes' walk from the train station.

Hotels Directly across the road from the train station, *Hôtel Métropole* (☎ 524293) at Rue des Guillemins 141 is clean and modern with singles/doubles from f915/1355. Next door at No 139, *Pension des Nations* (☎ 524434) is cheaper at f500 per person. Heading into town, and preferable to either of the above, is *Pension Darchis* (☎ 234218) at Rue Darchis 18. It's friendly and on a quiet backstreet halfway between the station and the centre. Single/double rooms start at f900/1400.

Closer to town is the slightly more expensive *Hôtel le Berger* (☎ 230080) at Rue sur la Fontaine 41. Even pricier is the discrete *Hôtel Cygne d'Argent* (☎ 237001) at Rue des Augustins 42 near the Jardin Botanique (Botanical Gardens), with rooms from f965/1900. Bus No 1 or 4 stops within a block or two of these last three places.

Places to Eat

The best-value haunts are along Rue des Guillemins in front of the station. *Pension des Nations* (see the previous Hotels section) has a menu of the day for f280, while just along at No 119, *Crommen* (☎ 524203) charges f180 to pick from the self-service salad bar. One-and-a-half blocks on, *Le Stendhal* (☎ 522209) at No 46 also has a three- course menu including a glass of wine for f300.

In the centre, the pedestrianised streets around the cathedral – particularly Rue d'Amay and Rue Saint Paul – are filled with restaurants and brasseries. To pick from the many, *Le Dubrovnik* (☎ 236192) at Rue de la Sirène 12 has a dish of the day for f250. Nearby, *La Feuille de Vigne* (☎ 222010) at Rue Soeurs de Hasque 12 is a little vegetarian restaurant open weekdays only from noon to 3 pm.

For more serene surroundings, cross the river to Outremeuse where there's an old cobbled street, En Roture, lined with little restaurants offering a smorgasbord of cuisines. *La Pergola* (☎ 425708), an Italian joint at No 46, is one of the reasonable options.

For self-caterers there's a small supermarket, *La Bourse* at Place de la Cathédrale 5, open Monday to Saturday from 9 am to 6.30 pm.

Getting There & Away

Bus Eurolines (☎ 526949) has an office at Rue des Guillemins 77, from where a nightly bus departs to London (f1830, 11 hours). There are also less frequent buses from here to a pick of destinations including Austria, Czechoslovakia, Greece, Morocco, Poland, Portugal and Spain.

Train There are two train stations: the virtually defunct Gare du Palais, and the principal hub, Gare Guillemins, two km from Place St Lambert but connected by bus No 1 or 4. The train information office (☎ 529450) is open daily from 7 am to 10 pm.

Major connections include to Brussels (f335, 1¼ hours, two trains per hour),

Maastricht (f200, 30 minutes, hourly trains), Cologne (f570, 1½ hours, 11 per day) and Luxembourg City (f600, 2½ hours, seven per day). Locally there are hourly trains to Namur (f200, 50 minutes), Spa (f120, 50 minutes) and Tongeren (f105, 30 minutes).

Getting Around

Inner-city buses leave to the right out of Gare Guillemins. Bus No 1 or 4 plies between here and the centre, heading along the main Boulevard d'Avroy (which becomes Boulevard de la Sauvenière), and stopping near the tourist office and most of the major museums.

AROUND LIÈGE
Tongeren

The oldest town in Belgium, Tongeren is as opposite in atmosphere to Liège as you can get. A peaceful little place, it's not outstandingly quaint or picturesque, but at the same time it gives a good idea at how many Belgian towns – those that aren't on the main tourist route – look today.

Settled in 15 BC as a base for Roman troops, the town has an important collection of Gallo-Roman remains (displayed in the provincial museum which is closed until 1994) and is surrounded by Roman and medieval walls. In a different historic vein, Belgium's largest antique market draws about 6000 people here every Sunday.

For more information, the tourist office (☎ 012-232961) sits in the shadow of the square-towered Onze Lieve Vrouwe basilica at Stadhuisplein 9 about 10 minutes' walk from the train station, and is open weekdays from 9 am to noon and 1 to 4.30 pm, and from Easter to 30 September also on weekends from 10 am to noon and 1 to 5 pm.

Spa

The town whose name gave the English language a new word, Spa was for centuries the luxurious retreat for royalty and the wealthy who came to drink, bathe and cure themselves in the mineral-rich waters which bubble forth here. But like Vichy, its French thermal counterpart, Spa had its day in the

18th and 19th centuries, only to appear now as a rather rundown reminder of what was. The waters are still drinkable though (f7 per cup), and you can try the more modern therapeutic cure of being coated in peat dug from the nearby Hautes-Fagnes park.

The town is about 35 km south-east of Liège, connected by regular trains (see the Liège Getting There & Away section). For more information, the local Office du Tourisme (☎ 087-771700) is at Place Royale 41, open daily from 9 am to 12.30 pm and 2 to 6 pm (from 10 am on weekends).

Centre Nature à Botrange

Located within the boundary of the swampy Hautes-Fagnes park, the Centre Nature à Botrange (Botrange Nature Reserve Centre) (☎ 080-445781) sits on the highest point in Belgium – 694 metres. About 50 km east of Liège, this is where Belgians come to walk, cycle, study nature, and in winter, to ski. Admission to the centre costs f70/40 for adults/children and equipment can be hired here – bikes f360 per day, skis f280. It takes about 1¼ hours to get there with public transport from Liège – take the train to Verviers and then bus No 106 (on Sunday it's bus No 102).

Namur & the Ardennes

Home to deep river valleys and high forests, Belgium's south-east corner is often overlooked by travellers hopping between the old art towns and the capital. But here, in the provinces of Namur, Liège and Luxembourg, you'll find tranquil villages nestled into the grooves of the Meuse and Lesse valleys or sitting atop the verdant Ardennes. Hiking, canoeing, cycling, skiing and exploring underground caves are popular pursuits. Historically, this is where the Battle of the Bulge once raged.

The town of Namur (Namen in Flemish) is the best base for exploring much of the region – well positioned on the rail line to Luxembourg and with rail and bus connec-

tions to some of the more inaccessible spots. However, if you don't have transport, getting around once you're 'inaccessible' can take time.

Orientation

Just 50 km south-east of Brussels, Namur is a picturesque town, towered over by its 15th century citadel, and with a pleasant, riverfront youth hostel that travellers use as a base for wandering farther afield. From Namur the railway line forks north to Liège, east through the Ardennes in Belgium's Luxembourg province and on to Luxembourg itself, and south to Dinant from where the Lesse and Meuse rivers wind away.

Information

The tourist office (☎ 081-222859) in Namur is on Ave de la Gare, 200 metres to the left out of the station. It's open daily from 8.30 am to 5 pm, later in summer.

There are smaller offices in Dinant (☎ 082-222870) at Rue Grande 37, in Rochefort (☎ 084-212537) at Rue de Behogne 2, in Han-sur-Lesse (☎ 084-377576) at Place Lannoy, and in Bastogne (☎ 062-213715) at Place McAuliffe.

Things to See & Do

Namur Perched dramatically above the town, the **citadel** is easily reached either by a 15-minute cablecar ride (adults/children f170/130 return) starting at Rue Notre Dame, or by car along the Route Merveilleuse. Open from April to 31 October, admission to the citadel costs f180/120 for adults/children.

There are several museums, including the **Félicien Rops** at Rue Fumal 12, which has works by the 19th century Namur-born artist who fondly illustrated debauched and erotic life styles; it's open daily from 10 am to 5 pm, closed Tuesday, and costs f100/50 for adults/children.

Dinant A heavy, distinctive town, Dinant's bulbous cathedral competes for attention with the cliff-front citadel, while below, a hive of boat operators compete for the Meuse

River day trippers or the Lesse Valley kayakers. The **citadel** is open all year and accessible by cable car – a combined ticket costs f160/120 for adults/children.

For kayaking, several companies have trips leaving in the morning upriver from Houyet, ending in Anseremme next to Dinant several hours later. Try Kayaks Ansiaux (☎ 082-222325) at 15 Rue du Velodrome, or Libert Frères (☎ 082-222478) at Quai de Meuse 1, both in Anseremme.

More sedate are the boat cruises down the Meuse, which spans out south of Anseremme to expose dramatic rocky escarpments, a wide expanse of water and a tranquil western bank dotted by chateau-style houses. Companies include Bayard (☎ 082-23042) at Rue Caussin 13, which has voyages ranging in destination and price from the 45-minute trip to Anseremme (f150/100 for adults/children) to the nine-hour haul to Givet over the French border and back (f480/350). Mountain bikes can be hired from Bayard for f650/1100 a day/week.

Han-sur-Lesse & Rochefort The millennium-old underground limestone **grottoes** are the drawing card of these two villages. The Han caves are a little way out of town – a tram takes you to the entrance and a boat brings you back. Open from 1 March to 31 December from 9.30 am to 5 pm, they cost f265/185 for adults/children. Rochefort's grottoes are of equal magnitude but the presentation is more low-key. Open from April to mid-November, hour-long tours start at 9.45 am and cost f150/105 for adults/children.

Bastogne North of Arlon near the Luxembourg border, it was here where thousands of soldiers and civilians died during the Battle of the Bulge in the winter of 1944-45. A huge, star-shaped American memorial, on

BELGIUM

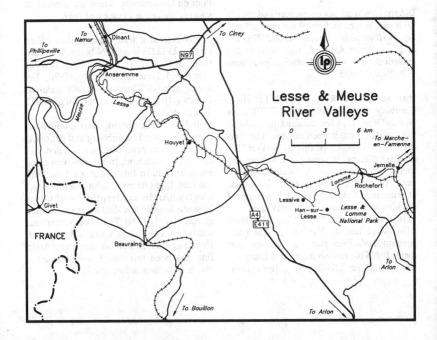

Lesse & Meuse River Valleys

the hill two km out of town, is next to the Bastogne Historical Centre, open daily from mid-February to November.

Places to Stay
The tourist offices in these towns have lists of B&Bs that offer singles/doubles from f700/800. The region is lightly covered with hostels and, naturally, thick with camping grounds.

Namur If you're camping, try *Camping des 4 fils Aymon* (☎ 081-588313) on Chaussée de Liège about eight km east – get bus No 8 from the station. The *youth hostel* (☎ 081-223688) is at Ave F Rops 8, 30 minutes' walk from the train station, or jump on bus No 3 or 4. *Queen Victoria Hotel* (☎ 081-222971) on Ave de la Gare 11, left out of the train station and next to the McDonald's, has singles/doubles/triples from f1000/1400/2050. Just up at No 22, *Taverne de Rome* (☎ 081-230424) has rooms from f1200.

Dinant Hotels are not cheap here and there's no hostel to turn to. One of the most affordable is *Hôtel de la Citadelle* (☎ 082-223543) at Place Reine Astrid 5, right next to the cathedral, with singles/doubles/triples from f1200/1350/1900.

Han-sur-Lesse & Rochefort In Han, *Camping de la Lesse* (☎ 082-377290), on Rue du Grand Hy a few hundred metres from the tourist office, is open all year. The *Gîte d'étape* youth hostel (☎ 084-377441) at Rue du Gîte d'étape 10, one block behind the tourist office, charges f300 and is open all year. Alternatively, there's *Hôtel le Central* at Rue des Grottes 20 which has singles/doubles with bathroom for f1050/1250.

In Rochefort, *Le Vieux Moulin* (☎ 084-214604) at Rue de Hableau 25 has half-pension deals (bed plus breakfast and one meal) for f510. Just up the road is *Camping Communal* (☎ 084-211900), open from Easter to 31 October. Otherwise, *Hôtel la Fayette* (☎ 084-214273) at Rue Jacquet 87 has singles/doubles from f800/1100.

Bastogne *Camping de Renval* (☎ 061-212985), about 500 metres from the tourist office on Rue de Marche, is open all year. There are two *youth hostels* in the vicinity of Bastogne: one is 23 km north-west at Champlon (☎ 084-455292), Rue de la Gendarmerie 4, and the other at Martelange (☎ 063-600956) at Route d'Arlon 14, 21 km south on the Luxembourg border. As for hotels, there are two of them near the tourist office: *le Borgès* (☎ 061-211100) at Place McAuliffe 10 with cheap singles/doubles from f600/980, and *Hôtel du Sud* (☎ 061-211114) at Rue de Marche 39 with rooms from f790/1090.

Getting There & Away
Bus Eurolines buses stop in Namur at Place St Nicolas to the east of the train station near Pont du Luxembourg. There are services to various regions in France and Italy.

Train Namur's train information office (☎ 081-252222) is open 24 hours. There are trains to Brussels (f200, one hour, two per hour) and Luxembourg City (f590, 1¾ hours, hourly). There are hourly trains to Dinant (f105, 30 minutes) and Liège (f200, 50 minutes).

To Han and Rochefort, take the train from Namur towards Luxembourg and get off at Jemelle. From here, bus Nos 166 and 951 connect to Rochefort, from where you catch buses to Han. In July and August the GLT (Guided Light Transit) – an electric/diesel bus/tram/train contraption – shuttles between Jemelle and the two towns; adults/children pay f100/60. To Bastogne, continue south-east and change trains at Libramont. However, the Libramont-Bastogne train line has been threatened with closure – check at Namur before leaving.

France

For first-time and veteran visitors alike, France's most salient characteristic is its exceptional diversity. The largest country in Western Europe, France stretches from the rolling plains of the north to the jagged ridges of the Pyrenees, from the rugged coastline of Brittany to the clear, blue lakes and icy crags of the Alps, and from the limestone plains of Bordeaux, home to millions of grape vines, to the west bank of the Rhine, another area whose climate is perfect for cultivating grapes. There are sand dunes and glaciers, cliff-lined canyons and seemingly endless beaches, thick forests and near-desert salt marshes. And with the country's superb train system, you can – during most of the year – go skiing one day and sunbathing the next. Of course, you'll have to decide whether to go skiing in the Alps or the Pyrenees, and whether you'd like to take a dip in the English Channel, the Atlantic or the Mediterranean, but a glance through this chapter can help solve such dilemmas.

Over the centuries, France has received more immigrants than any other country in Europe. The groups that have made France their home range from the Celts (Gauls), Greeks and Romans, all of whom arrived in the centuries BC, to the mid-20th century immigrants from France's former colonies in Indochina, sub-Saharan Africa and North Africa. In each case, elements of the culture, cuisine and artistic sense of the new arrivals were assimilated into one of the many streams of French culture. France's incredible variety of cheeses (over 400 by some accounts), sauces and other gourmet specialities are a small part of a centuries-old legacy of cultural assimilation, fusion and metamorphosis that, in conjunction with the country's varied geographical conditions, have created out of many traditions the unique – and uniquely diverse – civilisation that is France.

At one time, France was on the western edge of Europe, the last stop for migrants

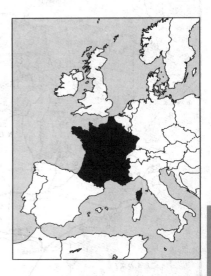

seeking a bit of land on the frontier of the known world. Today, as Europe moves towards unification of one sort or another, France is at the crossroads: between England and Italy, between Belgium and Spain, between North Africa and Scandinavia. Of course, this is exactly how the French have always thought of France – at the very centre of things – which is one of the reasons why they are among the most enthusiastic supporters of European unification.

Facts about the Country

HISTORY
Gaul

The Gauls, a Celtic people, moved into what is now France between 1500 and 500 BC. By about 600 BC, they had established trading links with the Greeks, whose colonies on the Mediterranean coast included Marseilles

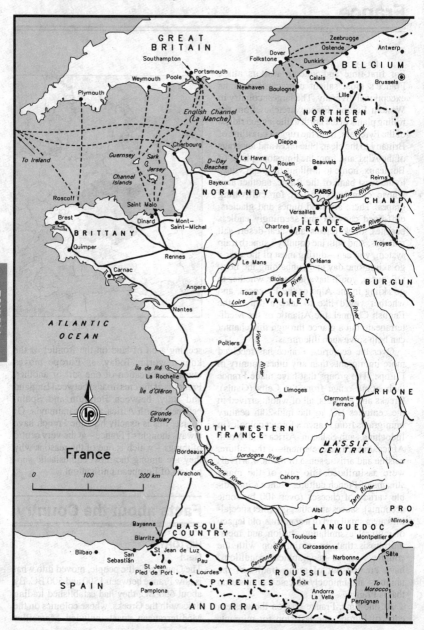

(then called Massilia). After several centuries of conflict between Rome and the Gauls, the Roman legions of Julius Caesar took control of Gaul around 52 BC, when a revolt led by the Gallic chief Vercingétorix was crushed. Christianity was introduced to Roman Gaul early in the 2nd century AD, and by 250 the country had been partly Christianised.

Despite a series of civil wars and barbarian invasions, France remained under Roman rule until the 5th century, when the Franks (from whom the name 'France' is derived) and other Germanic groups, including the Visigoths, Burgundians and Alemanni, took over the country. These groups adopted important parts of Gallo-Roman civilisation – including Christianity – and their eventual assimilation resulted in a fusion of Germanic culture with that of the Celts and the Romans.

The Middle Ages

Two Frankish dynasties, the Merovingians and the Carolingians, ruled from 476 to 986. The Frankish tradition by which the king was succeeded by *all* of his sons, each of whom was given a piece of the kingdom, gave rise to a virtually endless series of power struggles, insurrections and invasions and led to the eventual disintegration of the kingdom into a collection of small, feudal states. In 732, Charles Martel, grandfather of Charlemagne, defeated the Moors at Poitiers, thus ensuring that France would not come under Muslim rule, as had Spain.

Charlemagne, who ruled from 768 to 814, significantly extended the boundaries of the kingdom and, because of France's preeminent political position in Europe, was crowned Holy Roman Emperor (Emperor of the West) in 800.

During the 9th century, the Scandinavian Vikings (also known as the Normans, ie Northmen) began raiding France's western coast and later ravaged large areas of the country. They eventually settled in the lower Seine Valley and formed the Duchy of Normandy.

FRANCE

The Capetians

The Capetian dynasty was founded in 987, when the nobles elected Hugh Capet as their king. At the time, the domains under direct royal control were quite modest, consisting mostly of bits of land around Paris and Orléans.

Under William the Conqueror, Duke of Normandy, Norman forces conquered England in 1066, making Normandy – and later, Plantagenet-ruled England – a formidable rival of the kingdom of France. A further one-third of France came under the control of the English crown in 1154, when Eleanor of Aquitaine, whose marriage to the French king Louis VII had been annulled, married Henry of Anjou (later King Henry II of England). The subsequent battle between France and England for control of Aquitaine and the vast English territories in France lasted for three centuries.

Between 1209 and the 1240s, the Cathar sect (an ascetic Christian sect in Provence who believed the material world was evil) was suppressed by a papal inquisition and a holy war accompanied by wholesale atrocities, including mass burnings of unrepentant Cathars. The bloody work of the Albigensian Crusade (so named because the town of Albi was a major Cathar stronghold) was completed by Louis IX (ruled 1226-70), better known as Saint Louis.

The Hundred Years' War

The struggle between the Capetians and the English king Edward III (a member of the Plantagenet family) over who would ascend to the throne of France – the most powerful kingdom in Europe – set off the Hundred Years' War, which was fought on and off from 1337 to 1453 and brought suffering and devastation to much of the country. The Black Death ravaged the country in 1348, killing about a third of the population, but interrupted the warfare only temporarily.

Just when it seemed that the Plantagenets had pulled off a dynastic union of England and France on their own terms, a 17-year-old peasant girl known to history as Jeanne d'Arc (Joan of Arc) appeared in 1429 and rallied the French soldiery at Orléans. She was later captured by the Burgundians and turned over to the English, who convicted her of heresy and burned her at the stake in Rouen in 1431. However, her efforts helped to turn the war in favour of the French, and the English were finally expelled from French territory (except Calais) in 1453.

The Reformation

Lutheranism arrived in France in about 1519. By the 1530s the position of the Reformation in France had been strengthened by the ideas of John Calvin, a French exile resident in Geneva. Tolerance alternated with repression until the Edict of January (1562), which afforded the Protestants certain rights, was met by violent opposition from the ultra-Catholic House of Guise and other noble families, whose fidelity to Catholicism was mixed with a desire to strengthen their power base in the provinces.

The Wars of Religion (1562-98) were a series of religious and political wars involving three parties: the Huguenots (French Protestants); the Catholic League, led by the Guises; and the Catholic-led monarchy. The war, a confusing series of persecutions, assassinations, massacres, battles and treaties, inflicted general lawlessness on the countryside, severely weakened the position of the king and brought the French state close to disintegration. The most outrageous massacre took place in Paris in 1572, when some 3000 Huguenots who had come to Paris to celebrate a wedding were slaughtered in the notorious Saint Bartholemew's Day Massacre (24 August).

Eventually, Henry of Navarre, a Huguenot and member of the House of Bourbon, became King Henry IV, but not before he had embraced Catholicism. Regarding his conversion, he is reported to have commented that *'Paris vaut bien une messe'* (Paris is well worth a mass). In 1598, Henry IV promulgated the Edict of Nantes, which guaranteed the Huguenots freedom of conscience and many civil and political rights. It was revoked by Louis XIV in 1685.

Louis XIV & the Ancien Régime

Le Roi Soleil (the Sun King) ascended to the throne in 1643 at the age of five and ruled until 1715. Throughout his 72-year reign, he sought to project the power of the French monarchy – bolstered by claims of divine right – both at home and abroad. Internationally, he involved the country in a long series of costly wars that managed to fulfil many French territorial ambitions but terrified France's neighbours and nearly bankrupted the treasury. Domestically, Louis XIV put huge sums of money into building his extravagant palace at Versailles, a vastly expensive architectural extension of the king's authority – and his insatiable ego.

Louis XIV was followed by Louis XV (ruled 1715-74) who, like his great-grandfather, came to power at the age of five. He was succeeded by the incompetent – and, later in his reign universally despised and powerless – Louis XVI. As the 18th century progressed, new economic and social circumstances rendered the old order (the ancien régime) dangerously out of sync with the needs of the country. The regime was further weakened by the anti-Establishment and anticlerical ideas of the Enlightenment, whose leading lights included Voltaire, Rousseau and Montesquieu. But entrenched vested interests, a cumbersome power structure and royal lassitude prevented change from starting until it was too late.

The Seven Years' War (1756-63), fought by Britain and Prussia against France and Austria, was one of a series of ruinous wars pursued by Louis XV and it caused France to lose its flourishing colonies in Canada, the West Indies and India to the English. It was in part to avenge these losses that Louis XVI sided with the colonists in the American War of Independence. By and large, French military forces acquitted themselves successfully, and naturally it warmed many a French heart to see the English humiliated. But the war also had two unintended results: it cost a fortune, tripling annual debt repayments at a time when the necessary revenue-enhancing measures proved politically impossible; and it helped to disseminate in France the radical democratic ideas which the American Revolution had thrust on the world stage.

The French Revolution

By the late 1780s, Louis XVI and his queen, Marie-Antoinette, had managed to alienate virtually every segment of society. More enlightened groups were angered by the lack of effective reforms, while conservatives were enraged that the king was not making any attempt to change the status quo. When the king tried to neutralise the power of the more reform-minded delegates at a meeting of the Estates General in 1789 – convened to deal with the huge national debt – the urban masses took to the streets and, on 14 July of that year, a Parisian mob stormed the Bastille prison – the ultimate symbol of the despotism of the *ancien régime* (France's pre-Revolutionary political and social system).

At first, the Revolution was in the hands of relative moderates. France was declared a constitutional monarchy and various enlightened changes were made, including the adoption of the Declaration of the Rights of Man. But as the masses armed themselves to do battle with the external threat to the Revolution posed by Austria, Prussia and the many French nobles who had sought asylum abroad, patriotism and nationalism mixed with revolutionary fervour, thereby popularising and radicalising the Revolution. It was not long before the moderate, republican Girondists (Girondins in French) lost power to the radical Jacobins, led by Robespierre, Danton and Marat, who set up the notorious Committee of Public Safety. This body virtually had dictatorial control over the country during the Reign of Terror (September 1793 to July 1794).

In January 1793, Louis XVI was guillotined in what is now Place de la Concorde in Paris. By autumn, the Reign of Terror was in full swing, and by the middle of 1794 some 17,000 people in every part of the country had had their heads lopped off. In the end the Revolution turned on its own, and many of its leaders, including Robespierre, followed their victims to the guillotine.

During the Reign of Terror, stability was threatened by a popular movement known as de-Christianisation: churches were closed and desecrated, religious freedoms were revoked and Notre Dame Cathedral and other cathedrals around the country were reconsecrated as Temples of Reason.

Napoleon

In the chaos that reigned as the Revolution spent itself, the leaders of the French military began disregarding instructions from the increasingly corrupt and tyrannical Directory (as the executive power in Paris was then called), pursuing instead their own ambitions on the battlefield. One dashing, daring young general by the name of Napoleon Bonaparte was particularly successful in the Italian campaign of the war against Austria, and the personal prestige brought by his victories soon turned him into an independent political force. In 1799, when it appeared that the Jacobins were again on the ascendancy in the legislature, Napoleon – just back from defeat in Egypt and Ottoman Palestine – overthrew the discredited Directory and assumed power himself.

In the beginning, Napoleon took the title of First Consul. In 1802, a referendum declared him 'consul for life' and his birthday became a national holiday. The following year, his face began to appear on coinage. By 1804, when he had himself crowned Emperor of the French by Pope Pius VII in a ceremony held in Paris' Notre Dame Cathedral, the scope and nature of Napoleon's ambitions were quite obvious. But to consolidate and legitimise his authority, Napoleon needed more victories on the field of battle. So began a seemingly endless series of wars in which France came to control most of Europe. But in 1812, in an attempt to do away with his last major rival on the continent, the tsar, Napoleon invaded Russia. This time, however, his military genius failed, and although his Grande Armée (Grand Army) captured Moscow, it was wiped out shortly thereafter by the brutal Russian winter. Prussia and Napoleon's other enemies quickly recovered from their earlier defeats, and less than two years after the fiasco in Russia, the Allied armies entered Paris. Napoleon abdicated and left France for his tiny Mediterranean island-kingdom of Elba.

At the Congress of Vienna (1814-15), the Allies restored the Bourbons to the French throne by installing Louis XVI's brother as Louis XVIII. But in March 1815, Napoleon escaped from Elba, landed in southern France and gathered a large army as he marched northward towards Paris. But his 'Hundred Days' back in power ended when his forces were defeated at Waterloo in Belgium. Napoleon surrendered to the English, who – to make sure he never pulled a similar stunt again – exiled him to the remote South Atlantic island of Saint Helena, where he died in 1821.

Although reactionary in some ways – he re-established slavery in the colonies, for instance – Napoleon instituted a number of important reforms, including a reorganisation of the judicial system and the promulgation of a new legal code, the Code Civil, also known as the Napoleonic Code, which forms the basis of the French legal system to this day. More importantly, he preserved the essence of the changes wrought by the Revolution. For this, along with his many victories and the dramatic denouement to his extraordinary career, he came to be remembered by the French as a great hero.

The 19th Century

The 19th century was a chaotic one for France. Louis XVIII's reign (1815-24) was dominated by the struggle between extreme monarchists, who wanted to return to the *ancien régime*, and people who saw the changes wrought by the Revolution as irreversible. Charles X (ruled 1824-30) handled the struggle between reactionaries and liberals with great ineptitude and was overthrown in the July Revolution of 1830. Louis-

Philippe (ruled 1830-48), an ostensibly constitutional monarch of upper bourgeois sympathies and tastes, was then chosen by parliament to head what became known as the July Monarchy.

Louis-Philippe was in turn overthrown in the February Revolution of 1848, in whose wake the Second Republic was established (the First Republic had been set up in 1792 after Louis XVI proved unreliable as a constitutional monarch). In presidential elections held the same year, Napoleon's undistinguished nephew Louis-Napoleon Bonaparte, whose greatest (and virtually only) asset was his name (which conveyed to the masses an aura of power, law and order and the glory of empire), was overwhelmingly elected. Legislative deadlock led Louis-Napoleon to lead a coup d'état in 1851, after which he was proclaimed Napoleon III, Emperor of the French.

The Second Empire (the First Empire was led by the original Napoleon) lasted from 1852 until 1870. During this period, France enjoyed significant economic growth. But as his uncle had done, Napoleon III embroiled France in a number of conflicts, including the Crimean War (1853-56), which proved a fiasco to all involved, and a bizarre attempt to make Maximilian, archduke of Austria, emperor of Mexico. But it was the Prussians who ended the Second Empire. In 1870, Bismarck, Prussia's prime minister, goaded Napoleon III into declaring war on Prussia. Within months the thoroughly unprepared French army had been defeated and the emperor himself taken prisoner.

When news of the debacle reached the French capital, the Parisian masses took to the streets and demanded that a republic be declared. The Third Republic began as a provisional government of national defence – the Prussians were, at the time, advancing on Paris. But in the National Assembly elections of February 1871 – required by the armistice which had been signed after a four-month siege of Paris, so that the Prussians would have a government to negotiate a final peace treaty with – the republicans, who had called on the nation to continue resistance,

lost to the monarchists, who had campaigned on a peace platform.

As expected, the monarchist-controlled National Assembly ratified the Treaty of Frankfurt (1871). However, when ordinary Parisians heard of its harsh terms – France had agreed to pay a 5000 million franc war indemnity and give up the provinces of Alsace and Lorraine – they revolted against the government that had accepted such a dishonourable peace. The Communards, as the supporters of the Paris Commune were known, took over the city, but were slowly pushed back in bloody fighting in which several thousand rebels were killed. A further 20,000 or so Communards, mostly from the working class, were summarily executed.

The greatest moral and political crisis of the Third Republic was the infamous Dreyfus Affair, which began in 1894 when a Jewish army officer named Captain Alfred Dreyfus was framed as a German spy, court-martialled and sentenced to life imprisonment on Devil's Island, the notorious prison off the northern coast of South America. Despite bitter opposition from the army command, right-wing politicians and many Catholic groups, the case was eventually reopened after evidence of Dreyfus' innocence came to light. In the end Dreyfus was vindicated, but the army and the Church were greatly discredited by the affair, leading to more rigorous civilian control of the military, and, in 1905, the legal separation of church and state.

WW I

The German defeat in WW I, which got Alsace and Lorraine back for France, was achieved at an unimaginable human cost. Of the eight million French men who were called to arms, 1.3 million were killed and almost one million crippled. The war was officially ended by the Treaty of Versailles in 1919, whose severe terms (Germany was to pay US$33 billion in reparations) were heavily influenced by French prime minister Georges Clemenceau, the most uncompromising of the Allied leaders when it came to postwar dealings with Germany.

WW II

During the 1930s the French, like the British, did their best to appease Hitler, but two days after the 1939 German invasion of Poland, the two countries reluctantly declared war on Germany. By June of the following year, France – whose generals had, as usual, been caught completely unprepared – had capitulated. The British expeditionary force sent to help the French barely managed to avoid capture by retreating to Dunkirk (Dunkerque) and crossing the English Channel in small boats. The hugely expensive Maginot Line (named after a French minister of war), a supposedly impregnable line of fortifications along the the Franco-German border, had proved useless: the German armoured divisions had simply outflanked it by going through Belgium.

The Germans divided France into a zone under direct German occupation (in the north and along the west coast) and a puppet state based in the spa town of Vichy, which was led by General Philippe Pétain, an ageing WW I hero. Pétain's collaborationist government, whose leaders and supporters assumed that the Nazis were Europe's new masters and had to be accommodated, also believed that an ideology that had proved so successful on the battlefield shouldn't be dismissed out of hand. The Vichy government was, as were the French police forces in occupied areas, very helpful to the Germans in rounding up French Jews for deportation to Auschwitz.

After the capitulation, General Charles de Gaulle, France's undersecretary of war, fled to London and set up a French government-in-exile. The underground movement known as the *Résistance* (Resistance), which never included more than perhaps 5% of the population (the other 95% either collaborated or did nothing), slowly grew to include people fleeing German conscript labour, Jewish refugees, and members of the Communist Party (who joined only after Hitler attacked the Soviet Union). The Resistance engaged in such activities as railway sabotage (intended in part to slow the massive flow of valuable foodstuffs and raw materials to Germany),

collecting intelligence for the Allies, helping Allied airmen who had been shot down and publishing anti-German leaflets.

The liberation of France began with the US, British and Canadian landings in Normandy on D-Day, 6 June 1944. On 15 August, Allied forces also landed in southern France. After a brief insurrection by the Resistance, Paris was liberated on 25 August by an Allied force spearheaded by General Leclerc's Free French units, sent in ahead of the Americans so that Free French forces would have the honour of liberating the French capital.

The Fourth Republic

De Gaulle soon returned to Paris and set up a provisional government, but in January 1946 he resigned as its president, miscalculating that such a move would create a popular outcry for his return. A few months later, a new constitution was approved by referendum. The Fourth Republic was a period of unstable coalition cabinets that followed one another with bewildering speed (on average, once every six months). It was characterised by slow economic recovery helped immeasurably by massive US aid, an unsuccessful war to reassert French colonial control of Indochina and an uprising by Arab nationalists in Algeria, which was legally part of France and whose population included over one million French settlers.

The Fifth Republic

The Fourth Republic came to an end in 1958, when extreme right-wingers, furious at what they saw as defeatism rather than 'tough' action in dealing with the uprising in Algeria (one can only wonder what could be 'tougher' than the wholesale massacres of Algerian civilians carried out by French paratroops), began conspiring to overthrow the government. De Gaulle was brought back to power to prevent a military coup d'état and, perhaps, civil war. He soon drafted a new constitution that gave considerable powers to the president at the expense of the National Assembly.

The Fifth Republic (which continues to

this day) was rocked in 1961 by an attempted coup staged in Algiers by a group of right-wing military officers. When it failed, the Organisation de l'Armée Secrète (OAS; a group of French settlers and sympathisers opposed to Algerian independence) turned to terrorism, trying several times to assassinate De Gaulle (the book and film *The Day of the Jackal* portray a fictional account of an OAS attempt on De Gaulle's life). In 1962, De Gaulle negotiated an end to the war in Algeria. Some 750,000 *pieds noirs* (as Algérian-born French people are known in France) flooded into France. In the meantime, almost all of the other French colonies and protectorates in Africa had demanded and achieved independence. Shrewdly, the French government began a programme of economic and military aid to its former colonies in order to bolster France's waning importance in international affairs by helping to create a bloc of French-speaking nations in the Third World.

The crisis of May 1968 took the government, and much of the country, by total surprise. A seemingly insignificant incident, in which police broke up yet another in a long series of protests by Paris university students, sparked a violent reaction on the streets of Paris: students occupied the Sorbonne, barricades were erected in the Latin Quarter and unrest spread to other universities. Workers then joined in the protests. About nine million people participated in a general strike, virtually paralysing the country. But just as the country seemed on the brink of revolution and an overthrow of the Fifth Republic, De Gaulle defused the crisis by successfully appealing to people's fear of anarchy. When stability was restored, the government made a number of important changes, including a reform of the higher education system.

In 1969, De Gaulle was succeeded as president by the Gaullist leader Georges Pompidou, who was in turn succeeded in 1974 by Valéry Giscard d'Estaing. François Mitterand, a Socialist, was elected president in 1981 and re-elected for a second seven-year term in 1988. In the 1986 parliamentary

elections, the right-wing opposition led by Jacques Chirac received a majority in the National Assembly. For the next two years, Mitterand was forced to work with a prime minister and cabinet from the opposition, an unprecedented arrangement which became known as *cohabitation*.

In recent years, in part because of the economic situation and in part because of prejudice, there has been increasing hostility towards France's immigrant communities, especially those from North Africa. These sentiments have been encouraged and exploited by the anti-Semitic and racist National Front, led by Jean-Marie Le Pen, which polls about 14% nationwide. The Front National has particularly strong support in cities such as Nice, Cannes, Marseilles and Avignon.

GEOGRAPHY

France covers an area of 551,000 sq km and is the largest country in Europe after Russia and the Ukraine. It is shaped like a hexagon, with either mountains or water on the north-west (the English Channel), west (the Atlantic), south (the Pyrenees), south-east (the Mediterranean) and east (the Alps and the Jura). France has repeatedly been invaded across its relatively flat north-east frontier, which abuts Germany, Luxembourg and Belgium.

The territory of modern-day France was assembled by centuries of conquests, treaties and carefully planned royal marriages. Despite a long tradition of highly centralised government, the country remains linguistically and culturally heterogeneous, and in some areas there's less than complete acceptance of control by Paris. There are groups demanding complete independence from France in the Basque Country, Brittany and Corsica.

GOVERNMENT

France has had 11 constitutions since 1789. The present constitution, which was instituted by Charles de Gaulle in 1958, established what is known as the Fifth Republic (see the History section). It gives considerable power to the President of the Republic, a position presently held by François Mitterand of the Socialist Party.

Parliament is made up of two houses: the Assemblée Nationale (National Assembly) and the Sénat (Senate). The 577 members of the National Assembly are directly elected in single-member constituencies for five-year terms. The 317 members of the rather powerless Senate, who serve for nine years, are indirectly elected. The president of France is elected by direct election for a seven-year term. Women were given the right to vote in 1944.

Executive power is shared by the president and the Council of Ministers, whose members, including the prime minister, are appointed by the president but responsible to parliament. The president, who resides in the Élysée Palace (Palais de l'Élysée) in Paris, makes all major policy decisions.

France is one of the five permanent members of the UN Security Council. France, which left NATO's joint military command in 1966, has maintained an independent arsenal of nuclear weapons since 1960. Until recently, the French government has insisted upon testing such weapons in the South Pacific despite opposition from all the countries in the region. In July 1985, French agents blew up the Greenpeace ship *Rainbow Warrior* in Auckland harbour in an attempt to derail the organisation's protests against French nuclear tests on Mururoa atoll. In April 1992 the prime minister, Pierre Bérégovoy, announced that France was suspending all nuclear tests until at least the end of the year.

Local Administration

Historically, France was divided into about two dozen regions. Their names are still widely used, but for administrative purposes the country has, since 1790, been divided into units called *départements* (departments). At present, there are 96 departments in metropolitan France and a further five overseas. Most are named after geographical features, especially rivers. The government in Paris is represented in each department by a *préfet* (prefect). A department's main town, where the departmental government and the prefect are based, is known as the *préfecture* (prefecture).

POPULATION & PEOPLE

France has a population of 55.8 million, one-sixth of whom reside in the Paris metropolitan area. The percentage of French people living in rural and mountain areas has been declining since the 1950s. For much of the last two centuries, France has had a considerably lower rate of population growth than its neighbours, in part because the use of birth control for family planning began in France at the end of the 18th century, much earlier than anywhere else in the world.

During the last 150 years, France has received more immigrants than any other European country, including significant numbers of political refugees. From 1850 to WW II, most immigrants to France came from other parts of Europe (especially Italy, Spain, Belgium, Switzerland, Poland and Russia), but the post-WW II economic boom attracted several million workers – most of them unskilled – and their families from North Africa and French-speaking sub-Saharan Africa. In recent years, there has been a racist backlash against France's non-White immigrant communities, especially Muslims from North Africa.

During the late 1950s and early 1960s, as the French colonial empire came to an end, over one million French settlers returned to metropolitan France from Algeria, Morocco, Tunisia and Indochina.

ARTS
Architecture

A religious revival in the 11th century led to the construction of a large number of Romanesque churches, so called because their architects adopted many architectural elements from Gallo-Roman buildings still standing at the time. Romanesque buildings typically have round arches, heavy walls that let in very little light and a lack of ornamentation bordering on the austere.

The Gothic style originated in northern

France during the mid-12th century and subsequently spread to the rest of Europe. Gothic churches have pointed arches and, to let in more light, large stained-glass windows. Since the windows themselves could not support the roof, thick stone buttresses were placed between the panels of stained glass. It was soon found that removing the middle part of the buttresses made for a lighter, airier building but did not compromise their structural integrity. This discovery gave rise to flying buttresses. Over time, Gothic decoration became more and more ornate, culminating in the 15th century Flamboyant Gothic style, so named because its wavy stone carving was said to resemble flames.

Painting

An extraordinary flowering of artistic talent took place in France during the late 19th and early 20th centuries. The Impressionists, who dealt with colour as a property of light (rather than of objects) and endeavoured to capture the ever-changing aspects of reflected light, included Edgar Degas, Edouard Manet, Claude Monet, Camille Pissarro and Pierre-Auguste Renoir. They were followed by a diverse but equally creative group of artists known collectively as the postimpressionists, among whose ranks were Paul Cézanne, Paul Gauguin, Vincent Van Gogh and Georges Seurat. A bit later, the Fauves (literally, wild beasts), the most famous of whom is Henri Matisse, became known for employing especially vivid colours. In the years before WW I, Pablo Picasso, who was living in Paris, and Georges Braque pioneered cubism, a school of art which concentrated on the analysis of form through abstract and geometric representation.

CULTURE

Many visitors to France conclude that France would be a lovely country if it weren't for the people who live there. As in other countries, however, the more tourists a particular town or neighbourhood attracts, the less patience the locals tend to have for them. All you have to do to find friendly, helpful French people is to get away from places like Paris, Versailles and Mont-Saint-Michel.

Avoiding Offence

By being generally civilised and following a number of simple rules, you can avoid offending nearly everyone.

A few don'ts:

1. When buying fruits and vegetables anywhere except at supermarkets, do not touch the produce. Show the shopkeeper what you want and he or she will choose the vegetables or fruit for you.

2. In a restaurant, do not summon the waiter by shouting *garçon*, which means 'boy'. Saying *s'il vous plaît* is the way it's done nowadays.

3. When dining, keep your hands above the table or people will wonder what you are doing with them.

4. Money is a subject that is simply not discussed in France. Never ask how much someone earns, especially if it's a lot. In general, children don't even know how much their parents earn, and co-workers haven't a clue what their colleagues take home.

5. French lawn *(pelouse)* is meant to be looked at and praised for its greenness, not touched. Except in wide open areas suitable for playing Frisbee, walking on the grass or even placing one's behind upon it for a picnic is not only forbidden by some bylaw – the inspiration for the signs reading *pelouse interdite* – but will be looked upon by locals as hardly better than doing callisthenics on a flower bed.

6. The French police are very strict about security, especially at airports. Do *not* leave baggage unattended – they're serious when they warn that suspicious objects will be summarily blown up.

A few dos:

1. The easiest way to improve the quality of your casual relations with French people you come into contact with is always to say *'Bonjour, Monsieur/Madame/Mademoiselle'*

when you walk into a shop. Before you turn to leave, say *'Merci, Monsieur/Madame/ Mademoiselle, au revoir'*. *Monsieur* means 'sir' and can be used with any male person who isn't a child. Addressing women is a bit trickier. *Madame* is used where 'Mrs' would apply in English, whereas *Mademoiselle* is supposed to be used when talking to unmarried women. When in doubt, use 'Madame'.

2. It is customary for people who know each other to exchange kisses as a greeting. Women kiss women, men and women exchange kisses and in many circles men also exchange kisses with men. The usual ritual is one kiss on each cheek, but some people go for three or even four kisses. The French do *not* hug each other unless they're romantically involved.

3. When you go out for the evening, it is highly recommended that you follow the local custom of being well dressed and well groomed. Not to do so merely invites unfriendly reactions in discos (eg from bouncers), restaurants, etc. Torn jeans may be the height of fashion at home, but in France you're liable to be mistaken for a bum and treated accordingly.

4. If invited to someone's home or a party, always bring some sort of gift. Wine is fine, but not some 10FF red *vin de table*, which everyone will know came from the grocery's discount shelf.

RELIGION

Some 80% of French people say that they are Catholic, but although most have been baptised very few ever attend church. Church attendance is least unpopular among the middle classes. The French Catholic church is generally very progressive and ecumenically minded.

Protestants, who were severely persecuted during much of the 16th and 17th centuries, now number about one million. They are concentrated in Alsace, the Jura, the southeastern part of the Massif Central and along the Atlantic coast.

France now has at least three million Muslims, making Islam the second-largest religion in the country. The vast majority are immigrants (or the children of immigrants) who came from North Africa during the 1950s and 1960s.

There has been a Jewish community in France for most of the time since the Roman period. About 75,000 Jews resident in France were killed during the Holocaust. The country's Jewish community, which now numbers some 700,000, grew substantially during the 1960s as a result of immigration from Algeria, Tunisia and Morocco.

LANGUAGE

Modern French developed from the Langue d'Oïl, a group of dialects spoken north of the Loire River that grew out of the vernacular Latin used during the late Gallo-Roman period. The Langue d'Oïl eventually displaced the Langue d'Oc (from which the Mediterranean region of Languedoc got its name), the dialects spoken in the south of the country.

Standard French is taught and spoken everywhere, but its various accents and dialects are an important source of identity in certain regions. In addition, some of the peoples subjected to French rule many centuries ago have preserved their traditional languages. These include Flemish in the far north; Alsatian in Alsace; Breton (a Celtic tongue) in Brittany; Basque (a language unlike anything spoken anywhere in Western Europe) in the Basque Country; Catalan in Rousillon; Provençal in Provence; and Corsican on the island of Corsica.

At least 200 million people worldwide speak French, which is an official language in Belgium, Switzerland, Luxembourg, Quebec and over two dozen other countries, most of them former French colonies in Africa. It is also spoken in the Val d'Aosta region of north-western Italy. Various creoles are used in Haiti, French Guiana and parts of Louisiana. France has a special government ministry, the Ministère de la Francophonie, to deal with the country's relations with the French-speaking world.

Unlike some countries, where everyone is extremely impressed if you learn 10 words of the language, the French tend to take it for granted that all human beings should speak French. Your best bet is always to approach people politely in French, even if the only words you know are *'Pardon, Monsieur/ Madame/Mademoiselle, parlez-vous anglais?'* (Excuse me Sir/Madam/Miss, do you speak English?).

Pronunciation

French has a number of sounds which are notoriously difficult to produce for Anglophones. The main causes of trouble are:
1. The distinction between the 'u' sound (as in *tu*) and 'oo' sound (as in *tout*). For both sounds, the lips are rounded and projected forward, but for the 'u' the tongue is towards the front of the mouth, its tip against the lower front teeth, whereas for the 'oo' the tongue is towards the back of the mouth, its tip behind the gums of the lower front teeth.
2. The nasal vowels. During the production of nasal vowels the breath escapes partly through the nose and partly through the mouth. There are no nasal vowels in English; in French there are three, as in *bon vin blanc*, 'good white wine'. These sounds occur where a syllable ends in a single 'n' or 'm'; the 'n' or 'm' in this case is not pronounced, but indicates the nasalisation of the preceding vowel.

The standard 'r' of Parisian French is produced by moving the bulk of the tongue backwards to constrict the air flow in the pharynx while the tip of the tongue rests behind the lower front teeth. It is quite similar to the noise made by some people before spitting, but with much less friction.

Greetings & Civilities

Hello.	*Bonjour.*
Goodbye.	*Au revoir.*
Yes.	*Oui.*
No.	*Non.*
Please.	*S'il vous plaît.*
Thank you.	*Merci.*
That's fine. You're welcome.	*Très bien. Je vous en prie.*
Excuse me.	*Excusez-moi.*

Sorry. (excuse me, forgive me)	*Pardon.*
Do you speak English?	*Parlez-vous anglais?*
Does anyone speak English?	*Est-ce qu'il y a quelqu'un qui parle anglais?*
I understand.	*Je comprends.*
I don't understand.	*Je ne comprends pas.*
Just a minute.	*Attendez une minute.*
Please write that down.	*Est-ce-que vous pouvez l'écrire?*
How much is it ?	*C'est combien?*

Signs

Camping Ground	*Camping*
Entrance	*Entrée*
Exit	*Sortie*
Full/No Vacancies	*Complet*
Residential Hotel	*Pension de Famille*
Hotel	*Hôtel*
Information	*Renseignements*
Open/Closed	*Ouvert/Fermé*
Police	*Police*
Police Station	*(Commissariat de) Police*
Prohibited	*Interdit*
Rooms Available	*Chambres Libres*
Toilets	*Toilettes, W.C.*
Train Station	*Gare SNCF*
Youth Hostel	*Auberge de Jeunesse*
Ferry Terminal	*Gare Maritime*
Bus Station	*Gare Routière*

Getting Around

What time does the next boat leave/ arrive?	*À quelle heure part/arrive le prochain train?*
the boat	*le bateau*
the bus (city)	*l'(auto)bus*
the bus (intercity)	*l'(auto)car*
the tram	*le tramway*
the train	*le train*
next	*prochain* (m) *prochaine* (f)

FRANCE

first	*premier* (m)
	première (f)
last	*dernier* (m)
	dernière (f)
I would like ...	*Je voudrais ...*
a one-way ticket	*un billet aller simple*
a return ticket	*un billet aller-retour*
1st class	*Première classe*
2nd class	*Deuxième classe*
Where is the bus/tram stop?	*Où est l'arrêt d'autobus/de tramway?*
I want to go to ...	*Je veux aller à ...*
I am looking for ...	*Je cherche ...*
Can you show it to me (on the map)?	*Est-ce que vous pouvez me le montrer (sur la carte)?*
far/near	*loin/proche*
Go straight ahead.	*Continuez tout droit.*
Turn left ...	*Tournez à gauche ...*
Turn right ...	*Tournez à droite ...*

Around Town

I'm looking for ...	*Je cherche ...*
a bank	*une banque*
the city centre	*le centre-ville*
the ... embassy	*l'ambassade de ...*
my hotel	*mon hôtel*
the market	*le marché*
the police	*la police*
the post office	*le bureau de poste*
a public toilet	*des toilettes*
the railway station	*la gare*
a public telephone	*une cabine téléphonique*
the tourist information office	*l'office de tourisme/le syndicat d'initiative*

Where is (the) ...?	*Où est ...?*
beach	*la plage*
bridge	*le pont*
castle, mansion, vineyard	*le château*
cathedral	*la cathédrale*
church	*l'église*
hospital	*l'hôpital*
island	*l'île*
lake	*le lac*
main square	*la place centrale*
mosque	*la mosquée*
old city	*la vieille ville*
palace	*le palais*
quay/bank	*le quai/la rive*
ruins	*les ruines*
sea	*la mer*
square	*la place*
tower	*la tour*

Accommodation

Where can I find a cheap hotel?	*Où est-ce que je peux trouver un hôtel bon marché?*
What is the address?	*Quelle est l'adresse?*
Could you write the address, please?	*Est-ce vous pouvez écrire l'adresse, s'il vous plaît?*
Do you have any rooms available?	*Est-ce que vous avez des chambres libres?*
I would like ...	*Je voudrais ...*
a single room	*une chambre pour une personne*
a double room	*une chambre double*
a room with a shower and toilet	*une chambre avec douche et W.C.*
to stay in a dormitory	*coucher dans un dortoir*
a bed	*un lit*
How much is it per night/per person?	*Quel est le prix par nuit/par personne?*
Can I see it?	*Je peux la voir?*

Where is the bathroom/shower?	*Où est la salle de bain/douche?*

Food

bakery	*boulangerie*
cake shop	*pâtisserie*
cheese shop	*fromagerie*
delicatessen	*charcuterie*
grocery	*épicerie*
restaurant	*restaurant*
breakfast	*petit déjeuner*
lunch	*déjeuner*
dinner	*dîner*
I would like the set lunch, please.	*Je prends le menu.*
I am a vegetarian.	*Je suis végétarien* (m)/ *végétarienne* (f).

Time & Dates

today	*aujourd'hui*
tomorrow	*demain*
yesterday	*hier*
in the morning	*le matin*
in the afternoon	*l'après-midi*
in the evening	*le soir*
Monday	*lundi*
Tuesday	*mardi*
Wednesday	*mercredi*
Thursday	*jeudi*
Friday	*vendredi*
Saturday	*samedi*
Sunday	*dimanche*
January	*janvier*
February	*février*
March	*mars*
April	*avril*
May	*mai*
June	*juin*
July	*juillet*
August	*août*
September	*septembre*
October	*octobre*
November	*novembre*
December	*décembre*

Numbers

0	*zéro*
1	*un*
2	*deux*
3	*trois*
4	*quatre*
5	*cinq*
6	*six*
7	*sept*
8	*huit*
9	*neuf*
10	*dix*
11	*onze*
12	*douze*
13	*treize*
14	*quatorze*
15	*quinze*
16	*seize*
17	*dix-sept*
18	*dix-huit*
19	*dix-neuf*
20	*vingt*
21	*vingt-et-un*
22	*vingt-deux*
30	*trente*
40	*quarante*
50	*cinquante*
60	*soixante*
70	*soixante-dix*
80	*quatre-vingts*
90	*quatre-vingt-dix*
100	*cent*
1000	*mille*
one million	*un million*

Health

I'm ...	*Je suis ...*
diabetic	*diabétique*
epileptic	*épileptique*
asthmatic	*asthmatique*
anaemic	*anémique*
I'm allergic ...	*Je suis allergique ...*
to antibiotics	*aux antibiotiques*
to penicillin.	*à la pénicilline.*
I am constipated.	*Je suis constipé(e).*
antiseptic	*antiseptique*
aspirin	*aspirine*

FRANCE

condoms	*préservatifs*
contraceptive	*contraceptif*
diarrhoea	*diarrhée*
medicine	*médicament*
sunblock cream	*crème (solaire) haute protection*
tampons	*tampons hygiéniques*

Emergencies

Help!	*Au secours!*
Call a doctor!	*Appelez un médecin!*
Call the police!	*Appelez la police!*
Go away!	*Laissez-moi tranquille!*

Facts for the Visitor

VISAS & EMBASSIES

Citizens of the USA, Canada, most European countries and a handful of other countries can enter France for up to three months without a visa. Sometimes, the official at the airport will just glance at your passport and hand it back without stamping the date of entry. Australians, on the other hand, must have visas to visit France, even as tourists. The usual length of a tourist visa is three months.

If you plan to stay in France for over three months to study or work (including as an au pair – see the following Work section), apply to the French consulate nearest where you live for the appropriate sort of long-stay visa. It is extremely difficult to get a visa that will permit you to work in France; one of the few exceptions is the provision that people with student visas can apply for permission to work part-time. For any sort of long-stay visa, begin the paperwork several months before you plan to leave. If you'll be in France for over six months, you must, within eight days of arrival, report to either the Préfecture de Police in Paris or, in the provinces, the nearest departmental prefecture, to receive a *carte de séjour* (temporary residence permit).

French Embassies

French embassies abroad include:

Australia
    20th floor, 31 Market St, Sydney, NSW 2000 (☎ 02-261 5931, 261 5779)
Canada
    42 Sussex Promenade, Ottowa, Ontario K1M 209 (☎ 613-232 1795)
New Zealand
    Robert Jones House, 1-3 Willeston St (PO Box 1695), Wellington (☎ 04-72 0200)
UK
    21 Cromwell St, London SW7 2DQ (☎ 071-581 5292). The visa section is at 6A Cromwell Place, London SW7 2EQ (☎ 071-823 9555)
USA
    934 Fifth Ave, New York, NY 10021 (☎ 212-606 3688)

Visa Extensions

If you qualify for an automatic three-month stay upon arriving in France, you'll qualify for a visa that will allow you to stay a further three months if you exit France and then re-enter. The fewer French entry stamps you have in your passport, the easier this is likely to be.

If you needed a visa to enter France you can apply for an extension from either Paris' Préfecture de Police (Rue de Lutèce, 4ème) or, in the provinces, the nearest departmental prefecture.

Foreign Embassies in France

You will find the embassies for the following countries in Paris.

Australia
    4 Rue Jean Rey, 15ème (☎ 1-40.59.33.00; metro Bir Hakeim). The consular section, which deals with Australian nationals, is open Monday to Friday from 9.30 am to 12.15 pm and 2 to 4 pm.
Canada
    35 Ave Montaigne, 8ème (☎ 1-47.23.01.01; metro Alma Marceau or Franklin D Roosevelt).
New Zealand
    7ter Rue Léonard de Vinci, 16ème (☎ 1-45.00.24.11; metro Victor Hugo)
UK
    35 Rue du Faubourg Saint Honoré, 8ème (☎ 1-42.66.91.42; metro Concorde or Madeleine). The visa section is around the corner at 16 Rue d'Anjou, 8ème. The consular section (☎ 1-42.66.38.10) is at 9 Ave Hoche (8ème; metro Courcelles).

USA
  2 Rue Saint Florentin, 1er (☎ 1-42.96.12.02;
  metro Concorde). The American Services section
  is open Monday to Friday from 9 am to 4 pm. Be
  prepared for extremely tight security.

DOCUMENTS

By law, everyone in France, including tourists, must carry identification with them at all times. For visitors from abroad, this means a passport or, in the case of most EC nationals, a national identity card.

MONEY

You'll get a better exchange rate for travellers' cheques than for cash. The most useful travellers' cheques are those issued by American Express in US dollars or French francs, which can be exchanged at many post offices.

Do not bring travellers' cheques in Australian dollars as they are hard to change, especially outside of Paris. US$100 dollar bills are also hard to change because there are so many counterfeits around.

Visa (Carte Bleue) is more widely accepted than MasterCard (Eurocard). Credit-card holders can get cash advances from certain banks and from some automatic teller machines. American Express cards are not very useful except to get cash at an AmEx office or to pay for things in up-market establishments. To have money sent from abroad, have it wired to either Citicorp's Paris office (see Money in the Paris section for details) or to a specific branch of a specific French or foreign bank. You can also have money sent via American Express.

Currency

The currency of France is the franc (FF); one franc is worth 100 centimes. French coins come in denominations of 5, 10 and 20 centimes and ½, 1, 2, 5 and 10FF. The old 10FF pieces, which are larger than the new two-tone type and made of solid copper, are no longer legal tender. Banknotes are issued in denominations of 20, 50, 100, 200 and 500FF. The higher the denomination, the larger the bill. It is sometimes difficult to get

change for a 500FF bill. Beware of counterfeits – it's a good idea to glance at the watermark.

Exchange Rates

A$1	=	3.6FF
C$1	=	4.0FF
NZ$1	=	2.7FF
UK£1	=	8.5FF
US$1	=	5.0FF

The Banque de France, France's central bank, offers by far the best exchange rate, especially for travellers' cheques and they do not charge any commission (except 1% for travellers' cheques in French francs). There are Banque de France bureaus in the prefectures (capitals) of each department.

In areas frequented by foreign tourists, many post offices perform exchange transactions at a very good rate. Post office exchange counters accept banknotes in a variety of currencies as well as travellers' cheques issued by American Express, but *only* if the cheques are denominated in US dollars or French francs.

In large cities, especially Paris, *bureaux de change* (currency exchange offices) are faster, easier, have longer opening hours and give better rates than the banks – unless you go to an exchange bureau whose business strategy is to milk clueless tourists who can't multiply or divide (eg Checkpoint or Exact Change). As always, your best bet is to compare the rates offered by various banks, which usually charge 22 to 30FF per transaction, and exchange bureaus, which are not allowed to charge commissions.

If your American Express traveller's cheques or credit card are lost or stolen, call ☎ 05.90.86.00, AmEx's 24-hour toll-free number.

Costs

If you stay in hostels (or, if there are two or more of you, the cheapest hotels) and have picnics rather than dining at restaurants, it is possible to tour France for about US$30 a day per person (US$40 in Paris). Eating out, lots of travel or treating yourself to France's

FRANCE

many little luxuries can increase this figure dramatically. A student card can significantly reduce the price of getting into museums, cinemas, etc.

Tipping

It is not necessary to leave a tip *(pourboire)* in restaurants, hotels, etc as, according to French law, the bill must already include a 15% service charge. Some people leave the copper change or a few francs on the table for the waiter but this is neither necessary nor expected. At truly posh restaurants, however, a more generous gratuity will be anticipated. For a taxi ride, the usual tip is only 2 or 3FF no matter what the fare.

Consumer Taxes

France's VAT (value-added tax, ie sales tax) is known in French as TVA *(taxe sur la valeur ajoutée)*. The TVA is 18.6% on most goods except food, medicine and books, for which you pay only 5.5%. There's a special 21% rate for noncommercial vehicle rental. Prices that include VAT are often marked TTC *(toutes taxes comprises,* which means 'all taxes included').

It is possible (though rather complicated) to get a reimbursement for TVA provided you meet three conditions: 1) you are not an EC national; 2) you buy more than 2000FF worth of goods at a single store; and 3) that store is familiar with the paperwork. Basically, you get some coloured forms in triplicate stamped at your port of exit, thereby proving that you have taken the goods out of the country. The store then reimburses you for the TVA you've paid. For this to work, you must fill out the proper *bordereau* (export sales invoice) at the time you make your purchase.

CLIMATE & WHEN TO GO

Weather-wise, France is at its best in spring, though winter-like relapses are not unknown and the beach resorts only begin to pick up in May. Autumn is pleasant, too, but later on it gets a bit cool for sunbathing, even along the Côte d'Azur. Winter is great for snow sports in the Alps and Pyrenees, but Christ-mas, New Year's and the February school holidays create surges in domestic and foreign tourism that can make it very difficult to find accommodation. On the other hand, Paris always has all sorts of cultural activities going on during the winter.

In summer, the weather is warm and even hot, especially in the south, which is one reason why the beaches, beach resorts and camping grounds are packed to the gills. Another reason is that uncounted millions of French people all take their annual month-long holiday *(congé)* during August. In areas upon which France's holidaying urban masses descend like a locust storm, hotel rooms and camp sites are in extremely short supply, while in the half-deserted cities – only partly refilled by the zillions of foreign tourists – many shops, restaurants, cinemas, cultural institutions and even hotels simply shut down. If at all possible, avoid travelling in France during August.

WHAT TO BRING

English-language books, including used books, cost about twice as much in France as in the UK or North America, so voracious readers might want to bring along a supply. A pocketknife and silverware are invaluable for picnicking. Bikini tops are not used much in France – neither, in some places, are bathing suits – and, as a weight-saving measure, can be left at home. Many people strongly suggest that you bring lots of money, and some even go so far as to recommend spending less money elsewhere in Europe (or even forgetting about the rest of Europe) so you can spend it in France on the pastries...

SUGGESTED ITINERARIES

Depending on the length of your stay, you might want to see and do the following things:

Two days
    Paris or one other city.
One week
    Paris plus something not too far away, such as the Loire Valley, Alsace and Lorraine or Normandy.

Two weeks
  As above, plus one area in the west or south, such as Brittany, the Alps or the Côte d'Azur.
One month
  As above, but spending more time in each place and visiting more of the west or south.
Two months
  In summer, hiking in the Alps or Pyrenees; hanging out in one of the beach areas on the English Channel, Atlantic coast or the Mediterranean coast; and spending some time in more remote areas (eg in Brittany, the southern Alps or the Pyrenees foothills).

TOURIST OFFICES
Local Tourist Offices
Virtually every French city, town and one-chateau village has a tourist office. See Information under each town or city for details.

French Tourist Offices Abroad
French Government Tourist Offices are located in the following countries and can provide tourist information of all sorts, much of it in the form of brochures.

Australia
  BNP Building, 12 Castlereagh St, Sydney, NSW 2000 (☎ 02-231 5244)
Canada
  30 Saint Patrick St, suite 700, Toronto, Ontario M5T 3A3 (☎ 416-593 4723)
UK
  178 Piccadilly, London W1V OAL (☎ 071-629 1272)
USA
  610 Fifth Ave, New York, NY 10020 (☎ 212-257-1125)

USEFUL ORGANISATIONS
For details on a few budget travel agencies, see Travel Agencies under Information in the Paris section.

Most of France's hostels belong to one of three Paris-based organisations: the Fédération Unie des Auberges de Jeunesse (FUAJ; ☎ 1-46.07.00.01; metro La Chapelle), which has 220 youth hostels and is headquartered at 27 Rue Pajol (18ème); the Ligue Française pour les Auberges de la Jeunesse (LFAJ; ☎ 1-45.48.69.84; metro Sèvres Babylone), which has 100 youth

hostel affiliates and is based at 38 Blvd Raspail (7ème); and the Union des Centres de Rencontres Internationales de France (UCRIF; ☎ 1-42.60.42.40; metro Louvre Rivoli), which is based at 4 Rue Jean-Jacques Rousseau (1er).

The Paris branch of the Centre Régional des Œuvres Universitaires et Scolaires (CROUS; ☎ 1-40.51.37.10; metro Port Royal), an organisation whose purpose is to improve the quality of student life (eg by running restaurants and providing information on matters of interest to students), is at 39 Ave Georges Bernanos (5ème). This is an excellent source of information on the institutional side of student life in Paris. Each French university has a CROUS office. The headquarters of the Automobile Club de France (☎ 1-42.65.34.70; metro Concorde) is at 8 Place de la Concorde (8ème). You might also contact the Automobile Club de l'Île de France (☎ 1-43.80.68.58; metro Argentine), the Automobile Club de France's Paris-area affiliate, at 14 Ave de la Grande Armée (17ème).

The Fédération Française de Naturisme (French Nudist Federation; ☎ 1-42.80.05.21; metro Trinité) at 53 Rue de la Chaussée d'Antin (9ème) can provide information on *au naturel* leisure activities – many of them family-oriented – all over France.

BUSINESS HOURS & HOLIDAYS
Most museums are closed on either Monday or Tuesday and on *jours feriés* (public holidays), though during the summer some stay open seven days a week, especially in the south of France. Most small businesses are open from 9 or 10 am to 6.30 or 7 pm daily except Sunday and perhaps Monday, with a midday break between noon and 2 pm or 1 and 3 pm. In the south, midday closures tend to resemble siestas and may continue until 3.30 or 4 pm.

Many food shops are open daily except Sunday afternoon and Monday. As a result, Sunday morning may be your last chance to stock up on provisions until Tuesday. Many restaurants are closed all day Sunday.

In August, lots of establishments simply close so that their owners and employees alike can take their annual month-long holiday.

CULTURAL EVENTS

Most French cities have at least one major cultural festival each year. For details about what's on when (dates change from year to year), contact the Paris tourist office or, abroad, a French Government Tourist Office.

POST & TELECOMMUNICATIONS

Postal services in France are fast and reliable – and expensive. After spending the 1950s and 1960s with one of the worst telephone systems in Western Europe, France leap-frogged into the era of high-tech telecommunications during the last two decades. Today, you can direct-dial almost anywhere in the world from any telephone in France.

Postal Rates

Postcards and letters up to 10/20 grams cost 2.50/2.50FF within the EC, 3.70/4.00FF to the USA and Canada and 4.10/4.80FF to Australasia. Aerograms cost 4.50FF to all destinations. All overseas packages are now sent by air, which is very expensive; sea mail services have been discontinued.

Receiving Mail

All mail to France *must* include the area's five-digit postcode, which begins with the two-digit number of the department. In Paris, all postcodes begin with 75, are followed by a 0 and end with the two-digit arrondissement number, eg 75004 for the 4th arrondissement (see Orientation in the Paris section for details). The local postcode appears in each listing under Information or Post & Telecommunications.

Since poste restante mail is held alphabetically by the last name, it is important that you follow the French practice of having your family name written in capital letters. In case your friends back home forget, have the post office check under your first name as well.

Poste restante mail not specifically sent to a particular branch post office ends up at the town's main post office *(recette principale)*. In Paris, this means it goes to the post office (☎ 1-40.28.20.20; metro Sentier or Les Halles) at 52 Rue du Louvre (1er). See Post & Telecommunications in the Paris section for details. There is a 2.50FF charge for every poste restante mail item you receive.

It is also possible to receive mail in care of American Express offices, although if you do not have an AmEx card (or at least AmEx travellers' cheques) there is a 5FF charge each time you check to see if you have received any mail.

Telephones

Public Telephones Most public telephones in France require telephone cards, known as *télécartes*, which are on sale at post offices, tobacconists' shops *(tabacs)*, Paris metro ticket counters and elsewhere. Cards worth 50 units cost 40FF, and those worth 120 units cost 96FF. Each unit is good for one six-minute local call. Rates for overseas calls vary according to the time of day, so you will need to ask the French operator (see International Dialling). To make a phone call with a télécarte, pick up the receiver, insert the card and dial when the second line of the LCD screen reads *Numérotez*. The number that appears on the first line of the screen after the word *solde* is the number of units you have left on your card.

All telephone cabins can take incoming calls, so if you want someone to call you back, just give them the eight-digit number (preceded by a 1 in the case of Paris numbers) written after the words *ici le* on the information sheet that should be posted right next to the telephone.

Domestic Dialling For telecommunications purposes, France is divided into two regions: the Paris area; and the rest of France (the 'provinces'). A '1' written before the eight-digit subscriber number indicates that it is in the Paris area. To make calls within either region, just dial the eight-digit phone number. To call Paris from the provinces, dial 16, wait for the dial tone, then add 1 and the eight digits. To call the provinces from Paris, dial 16; when you hear the tone, dial the eight-digit local number.

Toll-free numbers *(numéros verts, or green numbers)*, which have eight digits and begin with 05, can be dialled without an area code from anywhere in France. From public phones, you do not need to insert a telephone card or deposit any money.

For directory assistance *(service des renseignements)*, dial 12. This service is free from public phones but costs 3.65FF from subscribers' phones.

International Dialling To call Paris from outside France, dial the international access code, then 33 (France's country code), then 1 and finally the eight-digit number. To call anywhere else in France from abroad, dial the international access code, 33 and then the eight-digit local number.

Direct-dial calls to almost anywhere in the world can be placed using a telephone card. Just dial 19, wait for the tone, and then add the country code, area code and local number. Be prepared for your telephone card's value to be counted down at an alarming rate. If you're calling a country whose code does not appear on the information sheet posted in phone cabins, consult a telephone book or dial 12 (directory assistance).

To make a reverse-charges call *(en PCV)* or person-to-person *(avec préavis)* from France to other countries, dial 19 (the international operator), wait for the tone and then dial 33 plus the country code of the place you're calling. If you're using a phone cabin, you must insert a telephone card (or, in the case of coin telephones, deposit 1FF) to place reverse-charges calls through 19.

For directory enquiries outside of France, dial 19, and when the tone sounds, dial 33, then 12, and finally the country code. You often get put on hold for quite a while.

Home Direct Calls With home direct you can dial the number for your country and be automatically connected to a local operator. You then choose how you want to pay and are connected to your correspondent. For the USA you have various home direct services. For AT&T, dial 19, wait for the tone, and then dial 0011. MCI's number is 19 (tone) then 0019. For Sprint, dial 19 (tone) followed by 0087. See the Telephones appendix for more information.

TIME
France is one hour ahead of GMT/UTC in winter and two hours ahead in summer. The 24-hour clock is widely used in France.

ELECTRICITY
The electric current in France is 220 volts, 50 Hz, and plugs have two round pins.

LAUNDRY
To find an unstaffed, self-service launderette *(laverie libre service)*, ask at the front desk of your hotel or hostel. Be prepared to pay 15 to 17FF per load and around 2FF for six minutes of drying.

WEIGHTS & MEASURES
France uses the metric system, which was invented by the French Academy of Sciences and adopted by the French government in 1795.

BOOKS & MAPS
Nonfiction
There are so many excellent books on French history that it's hard to choose just a few to recommend, though the task was made somewhat easier by limiting the selection to those available in paperback. *Citizens*, a highly acclaimed and truly monumental work by Simon Schama, looks at the first few years after the Revolution of 1789. The three volumes of Alfred Cobban's *A History of Modern France* cover the period from Louis XIV to 1962. *Petain's Crime* by Paul Webster examines the collaborationist Vichy government that ruled part of the country during WW II. You might also take a look at any of the books by the military historian Alistair Horne, which include *The Fall of Paris* (on the Commune of 1870-71), *The Price of Glory* (on the WW I Battle of

Verdun) and *To Lose a Battle* (on the French defeat in 1940).

France Today by John Ardagh provides excellent insights into the way French society has evolved during the postwar period.

Fiction

To get a bit of a sense of France and its literature in the 19th century, you might pick up a translation of one of the novels by Victor Hugo (eg *Les Misérables* or *The Hunchback of Notre Dame*), Stendahl (born Henri Beyle), Honoré de Balzac, Émile Zola or Charles Baudelaire.

France has long attracted expatriate writers from the UK, North America and even Australasia, most of whom spent at least part of their sojourn in France writing something. *A Moveable Feast* by Ernest Hemingway portrays Bohemian life in prewar Paris. Henry Miller also wrote some pretty dramatic stuff set in Paris, including *Tropic of Cancer* and *Tropic of Capricorn*. A more recent favourite is *A Year in Provence* by the English expatriate Peter Mayle, which takes a witty, insightful and very English look at life in modern-day Provence. The sequel is called *Toujours Provence*.

Travel Guides

Michelin's hardcover red guide to France (125FF), published annually, has over 1200 pages of maps and information on hotels, restaurants, garages for car repairs, etc in every corner of the country, but it's best known for rating France's greatest restaurants with one, two or three stars. Most of the information in the red guide is indicated with little icons whose meaning is explained in English at the front of the book.

Michelin's green guides (47 to 52FF each), covering all of France in 24 regional volumes (10 of which are available in English), are full of generally interesting historical information, though the editorial approach is very conservative and the prose can hardly be called lively. The green guide to all of France (about 50FF), with brief entries on the most touristed sights, is now

available in English. Guide du Routard has a very popular guide to France purely listing restaurants and accommodation.

Maps

If you're going to be driving around France, the best road map is Michelin's *Atlas Routier France*, which covers the whole country in 1:200,000 scale (1 cm = 2 km) and costs about 95FF. If you'll only be in one or several regions of France, you might prefer to use Michelin's yellow-jacketed 1:200,000 scale sheet maps.

Éditions Didier & Richard's series of 1:50,000 scale trail maps (about 67FF each) are adequate for most hiking and cycling excursions. The Institut Géographique National (IGN) publishes maps of France in both 1:50,000 and 1:25,000 scale. Topo-Guides are little booklets for hikers that include trail maps and information (in French) on trail conditions, flora, fauna, villages en route, etc. They usually cost 30 or 35FF and can be purchased at bookshops and, in areas where walking and hiking are popular, at some tourist offices.

Abbreviations commonly used on city maps include *R* for *rue* (street), *Boul, Bould* or *Bd* for boulevard, *Av* for avenue, *Q* for *quai* (quay), *Cr* for *cours* (avenue), *Pl* for *place* (square), *Pte* for *porte* (gate), *Imp* for *impasse* (dead-end street), *St* for saint (masculine) and *Ste* for saint (feminine). When a new building is added in a location where they've run out of consecutive street numbers, they fuse the number of an adjacent building with the notations *bis* (twice) or *ter* (thrice). Thus, the street numbers 14bis or 92ter are the equivalent of 14A or 92B.

MEDIA

The excellent *International Herald Tribune*, published six times a week and distributed around the globe, is edited in Paris. It is sold at many news kiosks for 8.50FF.

Radio

The BBC World Service can be picked on 195 kHz long wave and 6195 kHz, 9410 kHz, 9760 kHz and 12,095 kHz short wave.

In northern France, BBC for Europe is on 648 kHz AM.

HEALTH

Public Health System France has an extensive public health care system. Anyone (including foreigners) who is sick, even mildly so, can receive treatment in the emergency room *(service des urgences)* of any public hospital. Such treatment costs much less in France than in many other countries, especially the USA. Hospitals usually ask that visitors from abroad settle accounts right after receiving treatment.

Condoms Many pharmacies have 24-hour automatic condom *(préservatif)* dispensers near the door. Some brasseries and discothèques also have condom vending machines.

WOMEN TRAVELLERS

In general, women need not walk around in fear of passers-by – women are rarely physically attacked on the street. However, you are more likely to be left alone if you have about you a purposeful air that implies that you know exactly where you're going, even if you haven't a clue.

If you are subject to catcalls or are hassled in any way while walking down the street, the best strategy is usually to carry on and completely ignore the macho lowlife who is disrupting your holiday. Trying to make a cutting retort is ineffective in English and risky in French if your slang isn't extremely proficient.

France's national rape crisis hotline, which is run by a women's organisation called Viols Femmes Informations, can be reached toll-free from any telephone by calling ☎ 05.05.95.95. It is staffed by volunteers Monday to Friday from 10 am to 6 pm.

DANGERS & ANNOYANCES

France is generally a very safe place to travel. The biggest crime problem for tourists is theft, including theft from, and of, cars. Pickpockets are a problem, and women are a common target because of their handbags. Be especially careful at airports and on crowded public transport.

France's laws regarding even small quantities of drugs are very strict. Thanks to the Napoleonic Code, the police have the right to search anyone they want at any time, whether or not there is probable cause, and they have been known to stop and search charter buses solely because they are coming from Amsterdam.

If stopped by the police for any reason, your best course of action is to be polite – even deferential – and to remain calm. It is a very bad idea to be overly assertive, and being rude or disrespectful is asking for serious trouble. The French police have wide powers of search and seizure, and if they take a dislike to you, they may opt to use them. Emergency telephone numbers in use all over France include:

Police	☎ 17
Fire Brigade	☎ 18
Ambulance (SAMU)	☎ 15

The rise in support for the extreme right-wing National Front in recent years reflects the growing racial intolerance in France, particularly against Muslim North Africans and, to a lesser extent, blacks from sub-Saharan Africa and France's former colonies and overseas territories in the Caribbean. In many parts of France, especially in the south (eg Provence and the Côte d'Azur), entertainment places such as bars and discos are, for all intents and purposes, segregated: owners and their ferocious bouncers make it abundantly clear what sort of people are 'invited' to use their public facilities and what sort are not.

FILM & PHOTOGRAPHY

Be prepared to have your camera and film forced through the ostensibly film-safe x-ray machines at airports and when entering sensitive public buildings. Arguing almost never works; you're most likely to get an affirmative response if all you ask is that they hand check your film, if not your whole camera (which could, after all, conceal a bomb...).

WORK

Getting a *carte de séjour* (temporary residence permit), which in most cases lets you work in France, is almost automatic for EC citizens (contact the Préfecture de Police in Paris or, in the provinces, the nearest prefecture) and almost impossible for anyone else. However, the government seems to tolerate undocumented workers helping out with some agricultural work, especially the harvests. The apple harvest takes place in the autumn, beginning in the south and then moving northward into cooler regions, where the apples ripen later. It's hard work, and they usually put you up in barracks, but it's work. The grape harvest, another source of agricultural work for the paperless, also takes place in autumn.

Working as an au pair is very common in France, especially (but not exclusively) in Paris. Single young people – particularly women – receive board, lodging and a bit of money (400FF per week is the going rate) in exchange for taking care of the kids and doing housework. Basically, you are paid to be a cheap, live-in housekeeper and babysitter. Knowing at least a bit of French may be a prerequisite. Even US and other non-EC citizens, who find it almost impossible to get a carte de séjour, can become au pairs, but they must be studying something (eg a recognised language course) and have to apply for an au pair's visa before leaving home.

For information on au pair placement, contact a French consulate or the Paris tourist office. Most private agencies charge the au pair about 700FF and collect an additional fee from the family. Some agencies check the family and the living conditions they are offering, whereas others are less thorough. In any case, be assertive and even pushy in dealing with the agency to make sure you get what you want. Ask *lots* of questions, especially about living conditions.

ACTIVITIES

Skiing

The French Alps have some of the finest skiing in Europe. Smaller, lower-altitude stations are much cheaper than their larger, classier and higher-altitude cousins. There are quite a few low-altitude ski stations in the Pyrenees.

Surfing

The best surfing in France (and some of the best surfing in all of Europe) is on the Atlantic coast around Biarritz.

Hiking

France has thousands of km of hiking trails in every region of the country and through every imaginable kind of terrain. These include *sentiers de grande randonnée*, long-distance hiking paths whose alphanumeric names begin with the letters GR and which may be many hundreds of km long.

Courses

Language See Language Courses under Activities in the Paris section for details. Information on studying in France is available from French consulates and French Government Tourist Offices abroad, and, in the USA, the French Cultural Service (☎ 212-439 1400) at 974 Fifth Ave, New York, NY 10021.

HIGHLIGHTS

Beaches

The Côte d'Azur, also known as the French Riviera, has some of the best known beaches in the world, but you'll also find lovely beaches farther west on the Mediterranean coast, on the island of Corsica, along the Atlantic coast (eg Biarritz, La Rochelle) and even along the English Channel (eg Dinard).

Museums

Every city and town in France has at least one museum, but a good number of the country's most exceptional museums are in Paris. In addition to the rather overwhelming Louvre, not-to-be-missed Parisian museums include the Musée d'Orsay (late 19th and early 20th century art), the Pompidou Centre (modern and contemporary art), the Musée Rodin and the Petit Palais. Other cities renowned for their museums include Nice, Bordeaux, Strasbourg and Lyons.

Chateaus

The royal palace at Versailles is merely the largest and most grandiose of hundreds of chateaus located all over the country. Many of the most impressive chateaus, including Chambord, Cheverny, Chenonceau and Azay-le-Rideau, are in the Loire Valley (around Blois and Tours).

ACCOMMODATION
Camping

France has thousands of seasonal and year-round camping grounds, many of which are situated near streams, rivers, lakes or the ocean. Facilities and amenities, which are reflected in the number of stars the site has been awarded, determine the price. At the less fancy places, two people with a small tent should expect to pay 25 to 40FF a night. Another option in some rural areas is *camping à la ferme* (camping on a farm). Tourist offices should have details.

Camping grounds near cities and towns covered in this guide are detailed under Places to Stay for each city or town. For information on other camping grounds, enquire at a tourist office or consult the *Guide Officiel Camping/Caravaning*, or *Camping Caravaning France*, which is published by Michelin. Both are updated annually.

Campers who arrive at a camping ground without a vehicle can usually get a spot, even late in the day – but not in July and especially not in August, when most camping grounds are completely packed with families on their annual holiday.

If you'll be doing overnight backpacking, remember that in national and regional parks, camping is permitted only in proper camp sites. Camping elsewhere, eg in a road or trailside meadow *(camping sauvage)*, is tolerated to varying degrees except in Corsica; you probably won't have any prob-

lems with the police if you're not on private land, have only a small tent, are discreet, stay only one night and are at least 1500 metres from a camping ground.

Refuges & Gîtes d'Étape

Refuges (mountain huts or shelters) are basic dorm rooms established and operated by national park authorities, the Club Alpin Français and other private organisations along trails in uninhabited mountainous areas frequented by hikers and mountain climbers. They are marked on hiking and climbing maps. Some are open all year, whereas others are open only during the warm months.

In general, *refuges* are equipped with mattresses and blankets but not sheets, which you have to bring yourself. Charges average 50 to 60FF per night per person. Meals, prepared by the *gardien* (attendant), are sometimes available. Most *refuges* are equipped with a telephone, so it's a good idea to call ahead and make a reservation.

For details on *refuges*, contact a tourist office near where you'll be hiking or consult one of the books that list *refuges*, such as *Guide des Refuges et Gîtes des Alpes* (published by Grenoble-based Glénat) for the Alps or, for the Pyrenees, *Hébergement en Montagne* (published by Saint Girons-based Éditions Randonnées Pyrénéennes). These books should be available in bookshops or a *maison de la presse* (newsagency).

Gîtes d'étape, which are usually better equipped and more comfortable than *refuges* (some even have showers), are found in less remote areas, often in villages. They also cost around 50 or 60FF per person.

Hostels

In the provinces, youth hostels *(auberges de jeunesse)* generally charge from 40FF (for out-of-the-way places with basic facilities) to 60FF for a bunk in a single-sex dorm room. A few of the nicer places that aren't officially auberges de jeunesse charge up to 75FF. The simple, usually optional, breakfasts served at the auberges de jeunesse are not a bad deal at around 15FF. In Paris,

FRANCE

expect to pay 90 to 100FF a night, including breakfast.

In the cities, especially Paris, you will also find *foyers*, student dorms converted for use by travellers during summer. Information on youth hostels and foyers is available from tourist offices.

Cheap Hotels

Staying in an inexpensive hotel often costs less than a hostel when two or more people sleep in the same room. Unless otherwise indicated, prices quoted in the France chapter refer to rooms in no-star or one-star hotels equipped with a sink (and usually a bidet, too) but without a toilet or shower. Most doubles, which generally cost the same as, or only marginally more than, singles, have only one bed. Taking a shower *(douche)* in the hall bathroom usually costs between 10 and 15FF per person.

Reservations If you'll be arriving after noon (or after 10 am during peak tourism periods, eg July and August in many areas), it is a good idea to call ahead and make reservations. For advance reservations, most hotels require that you send them a deposit *(des arrhes)* by post. But if you call on the day you'll be coming and sound credible, many hotels will hold a room for you until a set hour; however, this is rarely later than 6 or 7 pm and often much earlier. Local tourist offices will also make reservations for you.

FOOD

A fully fledged traditional French dinner – usually begun quite late in the evening (8.30 pm is average) – has quite a few distinct courses:

An apéritif
A first course *(entrée)*
The main course *(plat principal)*
Salad *(salade)*
Cheese *(fromage)*
Dessert *(dessert)*
Fruit *(fruit)*
Coffee *(café)*
A *digestif*

French meals are always accompanied by wine (see the Drinks section that follows).

France has lots of restaurants where several hundred francs gets you excellent French cuisine, but inexpensive French restaurants are in short supply. Fortunately, delicious and surprisingly inexpensive ethnic cuisine is available from the many immigrant-owned restaurants specialising in dishes from France's former colonies in North Africa, West Africa, Indochina, India, the Caribbean and the South Pacific. One of the most delicious of the North African dishes is couscous – steamed semolina onto which you ladle vegetables and a meat-based sauce right before digging in. It is usually eaten with lamb shish kebab, *merguez* (North African sausage), *mechoui* (lamb on the bone), chicken or some other meat.

Restaurants & Brasseries

There are two principal differences between restaurants and brasseries: restaurants usually specialise in a particular cuisine (eg French, North African, Vietnamese, etc), whereas brasseries – which look very much like cafés – serve quicker meals of more standard fare (eg steak and chips, omelettes). Restaurants are usually open only at lunch time (11.30 am or noon to 2 or 3 pm) and dinnertime (6 or 7 pm to 9.30 or 10.30 pm); brasseries, on the other hand, serve meals (or at least something solid) at all times of the day.

Most restaurants offer at least one fixed-price, multicourse meal known in French as a *menu, menu à prix fixe* or *menu du jour*. In general, *menus* cost much less than ordering each dish separately (à la carte) but may not be available after 9 pm or so. When you order the *menu*, you usually get to choose a first course (eg salad, pâté, soup); a main dish; and a last course (cheeses or desserts). Drinks *(boissons)* and wine *(vin)* cost extra unless the *menu* says *boisson comprise* (a drink is included). Except at vegetarian restaurants (see Marais under Places to Eat in the Paris section), *menus* almost always include a meat or fish dish.

Cafés

Sitting in a café to read, write, talk with friends or just daydream is an integral part of everyday life in France. People see café-sitting as a way of keeping in touch with their neighbourhood, maximising the chances that they'll run into friends and acquaintances, and generally participating in the public social life of their town or city.

Three factors determine how much you'll pay in a café: where the café is; where you are sitting within the café; and when you come. A café located on a grand boulevard (such as Blvd du Montparnasse or the Champs Élysées in Paris) will charge considerably more than a place that fronts a semianonymous side street. Once inside, progressively more expensive tariffs apply at the counter (*comptoir* or *zinc*), in the table area (*salle*) and on the outside terrace (*terrasse*), the best vantage point from which to see and be seen. The price of drinks goes up at night, usually after 8 pm. However, ordering one cup of coffee (or anything else) earns you the right to sit there for as long as you like.

Self-Catering

France is justly renowned for its extraordinary chefs and restaurants, but one of the country's premier culinary delights – especially for vegetarians, who will find France's restaurants obsessed with meat and seafood – is to stock up on amazingly fresh breads, cheeses, fruit, vegetables, prepared dishes, etc and have a picnic. Although prices are likely to be much more expensive than you're used to, you will find that the food is of excellent quality.

Although there are supermarkets (*supermarchés*) and slightly more expensive grocery shops (*épiceries*), most people buy their food from small neighbourhood shops, each with its own speciality. At first, having to go to four shops and stand in four lines to assemble a picnic may seem rather a waste of time, but the whole ritual is an important part of the way the French live their day-to-day lives. And since each merchant specialises in purveying only one type of food, he or she can almost always provide all sorts of useful tips: which round of Camembert is young, ripe or extra ripe, what inexpensive wine would complement a certain kind of sandwich, and so on. The whole setup is geared towards people buying small quantities of fresh food each day, so it's completely acceptable to purchase very small quantities (eg a few slices (*tranches*) of meat for a sandwich, or 100 grams of seafood salad).

The following information describes some of the speciality shops you'll encounter. Fresh baguettes and bread are baked and sold at a *boulangerie*. Often, boulangeries also have baguette sandwiches, quiche slices and small, bad pizzas. Mouthwatering pastries are available from a *pâtisserie*. For chocolate and sweets, look for a *confiserie*. Boulangeries, pâtisseries and confiseries are often combined. For a selection of superb cheeses, such as *chèvre* (goat's-milk cheese) and a whole or half-round of perfectly ripe Camembert, go to a *fromagerie*, also known as a *crémerie*. Fruit and vegetables are sold by a *marchand de légumes et de fruits*. Wine is sold by a *marchand de vin*, such as the shops of the Nicolas chain.

A general butcher is a *boucherie*, but for specialised poultry you have to go to a *marchand de volaille*, and a *boucherie chevaline* will sell you horsemeat. Fish is available from a *poissonnerie*. A *charcuterie* is a delicatessen offering pricey but delicious sliced meats, seafood salads, pâtés and ready-to-eat main dishes. Most supermarkets have a *charcuterie* counter. If the word *traiteur* (trader) is written on a sign, it means that the establishment sells ready-to-eat takeaway dishes. In most towns and cities, many of the aforementioned products are available one or more days a week at open-air markets (*marchés découverts*) or their covered equivalents (*marchés couverts*).

DRINKS

Nonalcoholic Drinks

Despite the warnings of some squeamish guidebooks, the tap water in France is safe to drink, so there is no medical reason to buy expensive bottled water. If you prefer to lubricate your meal with tap water rather than some exorbitantly priced soft drink or wine, don't be put off if the waiter scowls – French law mandates that restaurants must serve tap water to clients who so request. Make sure you ask for *une carafe d'eau* (a jug of water) or *de l'eau du robinet* (tap water) or you may get pricey mineral water (*eau de source*).

A small cup of espresso is called either *un café noir*, *un express* or simply *un café*. You can also ask for a large (*grand*) version. *Un café crème* is espresso with steamed cream. *Un café au lait* is espresso served in a large cup with lots of steamed milk. The French consider American coffee to be undrinkably dishwatery but they will serve it (or something similar) if you ask for *un café américain* or, because it has been 'lengthened' by adding extra hot water, *un café allongé* or *un café long*. Decaffeinated coffee is *un café décaféiné* or *un déca*.

Other hot drinks that are widely available include tea (*thé*), which is unlikely to be up to the English standard but will be served with milk if you ask for *un peu de lait frais* (a little fresh milk); herbal tea (*infusion* or *tisane*); and hot chocolate (*chocolat chaud*), which is usually of excellent quality.

Alcohol

The French almost always take their meals with wine – red (*rouge*), white (*blanc*) or rosé (*rosé*), chosen to complement what's being eaten. The least expensive wines cost less per litre than soft drinks.

Wines that meet stringent government regulations governing where, how and under what conditions the grapes are grown, fermented and bottled, bear the abbreviation AOC (*Appellation d'Origine Contrôlée*, which means 'mark of controlled place of origin'). The cheapest wines have no AOC certification and are known as *vins ordinaires* or *vins de table* (table wines). They sell for as little as 5FF a litre in wine-producing areas and closer to 10FF a litre in supermarkets, but spending an extra 5 or 10FF per bottle can make the difference

between drinkability and undrinkability (the headache you'll get after one glass of truly bad wine will convince you...).

Alcoholic drinks other than wine include apéritifs, such as *kir* (dry white wine sweetened with cassis – blackcurrant liqueur), *kir royale* (champagne with cassis), and *pineau* (cognac and grape juice); and *digestifs* such as brandy or Calvados (brandy made from apple cider). Beer is usually either from Alsace or imported. A *demi* (about 250 ml) of beer is cheaper on draught (*à la pression*) than from a bottle.

ENTERTAINMENT

If you don't want to see your favourite star slurring away in some colloquial form of French, look in the film listings and on the theatre marquis for the letters 'v.o.' (*version originale*) or 'v.o.s.t' (*version originale sous-titrée*), which mean the film retains its original foreign soundtrack but has been given French subtitles. If 'v.o.' is nowhere to be seen, or if you notice the letters 'v.f.' (*version française*), it means the film has been dubbed into French.

THINGS TO BUY

France is renowned for its luxury goods, including *haute couture* fashion, expensive apparel (eg Hermès scarves), perfume and such alcoholic beverages as champagne and brandy. Purchases of over 2000FF by people who live outside the EC are eligible for a rebate of the 18.6% value added tax (TVA) – ask at the store for the forms for making your purchase *détaxé*.

Getting There & Away

AIR

Air France and scores of other airlines link Paris with every part of the globe. Other French cities with direct international air links include Nice, Lyons and Marseilles. Discount tickets and inexpensive charters to Paris are available in North America, South-East Asia and elsewhere. For details on agencies selling discount international tickets in Paris, see Travel Agencies in the Paris section.

For information on Paris' two international airports, Orly and Charles de Gaulle, see Getting There & Away in the Paris section. Information on how to get from the airports into Paris (and vice versa) is given under Getting Around in the Paris section.

To/From the UK

Flights between Paris' Charles de Gaulle Airport and London start at 920FF return to Gatwick or Stanstead and 945FF return to Heathrow on Dan-Air, Air UK and British Midland. You must stay over a Saturday night. A 590FF one-way fare to Gatwick is also available. In Paris, contact Transchannel (☎ 1-40.34.71.50; metro Gare du Nord) at 24 Rue de Saint Quentin (10ème). Call SOS Charters (☎ 1-49.59.09.09) for information on various round-trip packages and a 500FF one-way fare.

To/From Europe

One-way discount charter fares available for flights from Paris include 550 to 700FF to Rome; 700FF (or a bit less) to Athens; 550FF (or even 450FF) to Dublin; 600FF to Istanbul and 600FF to Madrid. The cheapest fares apply only in the off season (early spring and late autumn). Contact a travel agent or call SOS Charters (☎ 1-49.59.09.09) for more information.

LAND
To/From the UK

When the Channel Tunnel (Chunnel) is finished in late 1993 or early 1994, special trains will whisk cars and people from near Folkstone to near Calais in just 37 minutes. The privately financed project, originally budgeted at US$8700 million, is now expected to cost at least US$14,700 million.

To/From Europe

Bus For information on bus services between France and other parts of Europe, see Getting There & Away in the Paris and Avignon sections.

Train France's main rail hub, Paris, is linked with every part of Europe. Depending on where you're coming from, you may have to transit through Paris to get to the provinces. For details on Paris' six railway stations, each of which handles traffic to/from different parts of France and Europe, see Train under Getting There & Away in the Paris section.

BIJ (Billet International Jeunes) tickets, which are available to people under 26, cost about 20% or 25% less than regular tickets on international 2nd-class train travel started during blue or white periods (see Discounts under Train in the following Getting Around section for details).

BIJ tickets are not sold at SNCF ticket windows; you have to go to an office of Transalpino, Frantour Tourisme or Voyages Wasteels. There's usually one in the vicinity of major train stations but it may be open only during working hours on weekdays.

SEA
To/From the UK

The fastest way across the Channel is the 30 to 35-minute trip by hovercraft (aéroglisseur). Hoverspeed (☎ 05.26.03.60 in France, 0304-24 0241 in Dover and 071-554 7061 in London) runs both giant catamarans (SeaCats) and hovercraft from Calais to Dover (Douvres), Boulogne to Dover and Boulogne to Folkstone. Passage costs 230FF (190FF for people over 60) one-way; various cheap excursion fares are also available. A small car with four passengers costs at least 670FF on a SeaCat and at least 1100FF on a hovercraft. Bus-boat combos from Victoria Coach Station in London to 135 Rue La Fayette (10ème; metro Gare du Nord) take about eight hours and cost 290FF one-way (270FF for people under 25 or over 60). Train-boat combos start at 520FF and are sold at train stations. Hovercrafts cannot operate in rough weather, so if a storm is brewing you might get there sooner by booking passage on a car ferry.

Sealink (☎ 1-47.42.86.87 in Paris, 21.34.55.00 in Calais and 0304-20 3203 in Dover) has car ferries from Calais to Dover

(230FF one-way for pedestrians and cyclists; 1½ hours), Dieppe to Newhaven (260FF one-way; four hours) and Cherbourg to Southampton (220FF one-way; six/eight hours during the day/night). Cars cost from 700 to 1050FF one-way on the Calais-Dover route and from 530 to 880FF on the Dieppe-Newhaven route. Tickets for train-ferry packages are available at train stations.

P&O European Ferries (☎ 1-42.66.40.17 in Paris, 0304-223 000 in Dover) runs car ferries from Calais to Dover (1¼ hours), Boulogne to Dover (1¾ hours), Le Havre to Portsmouth (5¾ hours) and Cherbourg to Portsmouth (3¾ hours). Their Paris office is at 9 Place de la Madeleine (8ème; metro Madeleine). If you're going to far northern France, you might consider the company's Dover-Oostende (Belgium) and Dover-Zeebrugge (Belgium) routes.

To/From the Channel Islands
For information on ferries from Saint Malo to Jersey, Guernsey (Guernesey) and Sark (Sercq), see Ferry under Getting There & Away in the Saint Malo section.

To/From Ireland
Irish Ferries (☎ 1-42.66.90.90 in Paris, 01-61 0714 in Dublin), formerly known as Irish Continental Ferries, links Le Havre with Cork and Rosslaire and Cherbourg with Rosslaire. The trip takes about 20 hours. There are only two or three ferries a week from October to March but daily runs the rest of the year. Pedestrians pay 413 to 836FF one-way, depending on when they travel, and students get a small discount. The cheapest couchette is an extra 45FF. Irish Ferries' Paris office is at 8 Rue Auber (9ème; metro Auber). Eurail passes are valid on these ferry services.

To/From Italy
For information on ferry services between Italy and Corsica, see Getting There & Away in the Corsica section. You can purchase tickets from many French travel agents.

To/From North Africa
The Société Nationale Maritime Corse Méditerranée (SNCM) and its Algerian counterpart, Algérie Ferries, operate ferry services from Marseilles to the Algerian ports of Algiers (Alger), Annaba, Bejaia, Oran and Skikda. Passage takes 18 to 24 hours, and slightly more to Oran. SNCM also has service from Marseilles to Tunis (Tunisia) and Porto Torres (Sardinia). See Ferry under Getting There & Away in the Marseilles section for details.

The Compagnie Marocaine de Navigation (☎ 91.56.32.00 in Marseilles) runs ferries from Sète (near Montpellier) to the Moroccan cities of Tangier (Tanger) and Nador. The trip takes about 36 hours.

Getting Around

AIR
Air Inter (☎ 1-45.46.90.00 in Paris) handles domestic passenger flights. In general, flying within France is quite expensive, but people under 25 (and students under 27) can get discounts of 50% and more on certain Air Inter flights. The most heavily discounted flights may be cheaper than long-distance rail travel. Details are available from travel agents.

BUS
Because the French train network is state-owned and the government prefers to operate a monopoly, the country has only extremely limited intercity bus service. Buses are widely used, however, for short-distance intra-departmental routes, especially in rural areas with relatively few train lines (eg Brittany, Normandy).

Costs
In some areas (eg along the Côte d'Azur), you may have the choice of going by either bus or train. For longer trips, buses tend to be much slower but slightly cheaper than trains, whereas on short runs they are both slower and more expensive.

TRAIN

France's excellent rail network, operated by
the state-owned and state-subsidised SNCF
(Société Nationale des Chemins de Fer),
reaches almost every part of the country.
Places not served by train are linked with
major railheads by bus.

France's most important train lines radiate
out from Paris like the spokes of a wheel,
rendering rail travel between provincial
towns and cities located on different radii
infrequent and rather slow. In some cases,
you have to transit through Paris, which may
require transferring from one of Paris' six
train stations to another (see Train under
Getting There & Away in the Paris section
for details).

The pride and joy of the SNCF is the
world-famous TGV (train à grande vitesse),
which means 'high-speed train'. There are
three TGV lines: the TGV Sud-Est, which
links Paris' Gare de Lyon with Lyons,
Valence and – via non-TGV tracks – the
south-east; the TGV Atlantique, which runs
from Paris' Gare Montparnasse to the Loire
Valley, Bordeaux and the south-west; and the
new TGV Nord, which will eventually go
from Paris' Gare du Nord to Calais and
London. Although it usually travels at 300
km/h, the TGV Atlantique has, in test runs,
reached 515.3 km/h, the world speed record
for trains. The TGV Sud-Est goes up to 270
km/h. Going by TGV costs the same as travelling on regular trains except that you must
pay a reservation fee (see Costs & Reservations) of 16 to 94FF, depending on when you
travel.

Most larger SNCF stations have a consigne manuelle (left-luggage office), which
charges 30FF per bag for 24 hours, as well
as a consigne automatique (left-luggage
lockers), which is no bargain either. It's
much cheaper, however, to pay to lock up
your bag while you sleep on the Nice beach
than it is to wake up and find all your stuff
gone.

Information

Most train stations have both ticket windows
(guichets) and an information and reservation office or desk. For details, including
local telephone numbers for getting train
information and making reservations, see
Train under the Getting There & Away
section of each listing. For train information
in English, call ☎ 1-45.82.08.41 in Paris.

Formalities

Before boarding the train on each leg of your
journey, you must validate your ticket *and*
your reservation card by time-stamping them
in one of the *composteurs*, postbox-like
orange machines that are located somewhere
between the ticket windows and the tracks.
Eurail passes and France Railpasses *must* be
time-stamped before you begin your first
journey to initiate the period of validity.
Always keep your ticket and reservation card
with you until the end of the journey: if you
are caught travelling without a ticket (or with
one that hasn't been time-stamped), you will
be heavily fined.

Costs & Reservations

Train fares consist of two parts: the cost of
passage, which is calculated according to the
number of km you'll be travelling; and a
reservation fee. The reservation fee is
optional unless you'll be travelling by TGV,
or if you want a couchette or special reclining
seat. In addition, on especially popular trains
(eg on holiday weekends) you may have to
make advance reservations in order to get a
seat. Eurail pass holders should bear in mind
that they must pay any applicable reservation
fees. Since some overnight trains are
equipped only with couchettes – eg most of
the overnight trains on the Paris-Nice run –
there's no way for Eurail pass holders to
avoid the reservation fee except by taking a
day train with a supply of nonreserved seats.

Discounts

For the purpose of granting discounts, SNCF
divides train travel into three periods
(périodes): blue (bleue), when the largest
discounts are available; white (blanche),
when moderate discounts are available; and
red (rouge), when there are almost no discounts. To be eligible for a given discount,

your journey must begin during a period of the appropriate colour. For a chart of blue, white and red periods, ask for a *Calendrier Voyageurs* at any SNCF information counter.

Discounts Available Only Overseas The France Railpass lets you travel by rail within France for any four days within a 15-day period (US$119 if you buy the pass in the USA) or any nine days during a 30-day period (US$209 in the USA). Like the Eurail pass, the France Railpass must be purchased overseas – contact a travel agent before you leave home for details.

Discounts Available in France The new Carrissimo card, valid for travel within France *only*, grants the holder (who must be 12 to 25 years old) and from zero to three travelling companions (who must also be aged 12 to 25) a 50% discount for journeys begun during blue periods and a 20% discount for travel begun during white periods. A Carrissimo card costs 190FF for four trips or 350FF for eight trips and is available from SNCF information offices.

For travel within France, students aged 12 to 25 can purchase BSE (Billet Scolaire et Étudiants) tickets, which cost 20% to 25% less than regular one-way or return fares. Like BIJ tickets, they cannot be purchased directly from SNCF – you have to go to an agency of Wasteels, Transalpino or Frantour Tourisme. You'll find one of these agencies in or near all major train stations.

No matter what age you are, the Billet Séjour excursion fare gives you a 25% reduction for round-trip travel within France if you meet three conditions: the total length of your trip is at least 1000 km; you'll be spending at least part of a Sunday at your destination; and you begin travel in both directions during blue periods. It is available at either ticket counters or the station's information and reservation office. With a Carte Couple – which is available to any two people who are living together – one of the two people who appear on the card pays full fare and the other gets 50% off on travel undertaken together provided it's begun during blue periods. To get a Carte Couple, which is free, bring both of your passports, proof of cohabitation and passport-size photos to the SNCF information office of any major train station.

People aged 60 or over can get a Carte Vermeil Plein Temps, which entitles the bearer to a 50% reduction for 1st or 2nd-class travel begun during blue periods. It costs 230FF, is valid for one year in most parts of Europe and is available from the information offices of major train stations in most parts of Europe. A four-journey version, the Carte Vermeil Quatre Temps, costs 130FF.

TAXI
France's cities and larger towns all have 24-hour taxi service. French taxis are equipped with meters; prices range from about 3FF per km in Paris to almost 10FF per km in Corsica. Tariffs are always quite a bit higher at night (after 7 or 8 pm) and on Sunday and public holidays. There are often surcharges (5FF or so) for each piece of luggage or if you are picked up or dropped off at a train station or airport. Passengers always sit in the back seat. No matter what the fare is, the usual tip is about 3 or 4FF.

CAR & MOTORBIKE
There's nothing quite like the feeling of exploring the backroads of the Loire Valley or the Alps on your own, free of train and bus schedules...Unfortunately, travelling around France by car or motorbike is expensive, as petrol is exorbitant, tolls can reach hundreds of francs a day if you're going cross-country in a hurry, and there's a special 21% VAT on the rental of noncommercial vehicles. Given how expensive all transport is in France, however, three or four people travelling together may find that renting a car is cheaper than taking the train, especially if the savings from being able to stay a bit out of town (eg at less well-situated camping grounds) are taken into account.

Road Rules
To drive in France, you must carry with you at all times a passport or EC national identity

card, a valid driver's licence, proof of insurance and car ownership papers.

Unless otherwise posted, speed limits are 130 km/h (110 km/h in the rain) on the *autoroutes* (dual carriageways whose alphanumeric names begin with A); 110/90 km/h on the *routes nationales* (highways whose names begin with N) with or without a dividing strip down the middle; and 90 km/h on the *routes départementales* (rural highways whose names start with D). The moment you pass a sign indicating that you've entered the boundaries of a town, village or hamlet, the speed limit automatically becomes 50 km/h (unless it's posted as being less) and stays 50 km/h until you pass an identical sign with a red bar across it.

If you drive below or at the speed limit, expect to have lots of cars coming up to within two metres of your rear bumper, flashing their lights and then whizzing past at the first opportunity.

The most idiosyncratic – and, for tourists, dangerous – traffic law in France is the notorious *priorité à droite* rule, under which any car entering an intersection from a road to your right has the right-of-way no matter how small the road it's coming from is. On roads where *priorité à droite* has been suspended, there will be a sign indicating that this is the case.

The maximum permissible blood-alcohol level in France is 0.08%. The police will sometimes set up roadblocks and give Breathalyzer tests to everyone who drives past.

Expenses

Regular leaded petrol (*essence*) with an octane rating of 97, usually sold as *super*, costs about 5.29FF per litre. It is a bit more expensive than unleaded (*sans plomb*) petrol with an octane rating of 98, which costs around 5.14FF per litre. Diesel fuel (*gasoil* or *gazole*) is about 3.45FF per litre. Fuel (*carburants*) is most expensive at the rest stops along the autoroutes and cheapest in small rural petrol stations. Tolls are another major expense: by autoroute, the trip from

Paris to Nice costs about 270FF for tolls alone.

Rental

Renting a car in France is extremely expensive, especially if you do it through one of the big, international car hire companies. In the Getting Around sections for many cities, the Car & Motorbike entry supplies details on the cheapest places to rent cars.

Before you sign anything or hand over any cash or credit cards (the latter may be a prerequisite to renting), always check what the excess (*franchise*) is (ie how much money you will forfeit if there's an accident and it's your fault). You can usually pay a bit extra (ie a collision damage waiver) and have the excess reduced to zero or a lesser amount. If you get into a minor accident, fill out a Constat Aimable d'Accident Automobile (joint automobile accident report) – there should be one in the glove compartment or the driver's side door shelf – along with the other driver. You both sign and each of you gets a copy. If you were not at fault, make sure all the facts reflecting this are included on the form, which, unless your French is really fluent, should be filled out with the assistance of someone who can translate all the French automobilese.

Purchase/Repurchase Plans

If you'll be needing a car in France for between 23 and 180 days, it is usually cheaper to 'purchase' one from the manufacturer and later 'sell it back' than it is to rent. In reality, you only pay for the number of days you use the vehicle, but the purchase/repurchase (*achat/rachat*) aspect of the paperwork, none of which is your responsibility, lets you save France's 21% VAT on car rentals.

Renault's purchase/repurchase plan is known as the Formule Eurodrive. A Renault Clio, which has a tiny 1.1-litre engine, costs 5320FF for 23 days, 5600FF for 33 days and 70FF for each day thereafter (up to 15,890FF for six months), including comprehensive insurance, unlimited km and 24-hour towing and breakdown service (☎ 05.05.15.15 from anywhere in France). It is 20% to 30% cheaper to arrange your purchase/repurchase car outside of France, where various discounts are available, than in France, where they charge the full, official price. Renault's Paris office (☎ 1-40.40.33.27) at 186 Ave Jean Jaurès (19ème; metro Porte de Pantin) can arrange a car within a day or two. In Australia, call ☎ 02-229 3344; in Canada, call ☎ 514-461 1149; in the USA, call ☎ 212-532 3190. Abroad, it's best to contact Renault three or four weeks before your trip. Citroën also has a purchase/repurchase plan – contact the dealer in your country.

BICYCLE

Most towns have at least one cycling shop that hires out bicycles by the hour, day or week. You can still get 10-speeds (*vélos à 10 vitesses*) or low-tech one and three-speeds for 50 to 80FF a day, but in some areas such antiquated contrivances are fast going the way of the penny-farthing, at least in the rental business. A growing number of shops only have mountain bikes (*vélos tout-terrain*, known as VTTs), which generally cost 70 to 120FF a day. Most places, especially those renting expensive mountain bikes, require a substantial deposit.

HITCHING

Hitching in France is more difficult than in Germany, Switzerland or almost anywhere else in Europe. Getting out of the big cities (eg Paris, Lyons, Marseilles) or travelling around the Côte d'Azur by thumb is well nigh impossible. Remote rural areas are your best bet, but few cars are likely to be going farther than the next large town. Women should not hitch alone, but two women will probably be all right.

To maximise your chances of being picked up, look unobtrusive, nonthreatening and respectable; orient your backpack so it looks as small as possible to oncoming drivers; and make eye contact with the people driving by. It is an excellent idea to hold up a sign with your destination followed by the letters *s.v.p.*, short for *s'il vous plaît* (please), written on it. One traveller reports

that a destination sign reading *n'importe où* ('it doesn't matter where') works well if you aren't going to any particular place.

Some people have reported good luck hitching with truck drivers from truck stop to truck stop. It is illegal to hitch on autoroutes and other major expressways but you can stand near the entrance ramps.

Allostop-Provoya (☎ 1-42.46.00.66; metro Château d'Eau) at 84 Passage Brady (10ème) in Paris can put you in touch with a driver who is going where you're going. If you are not a member (220FF for up to eight journeys over two years), there is a per-trip fee of between 27FF (for distances under 200 km) and 67FF (for distances over 500 km). In addition, you have to pay the driver 0.18FF per km for expenses.

Paris

Paris has just about exhausted the superlatives that can reasonably be applied to cities, at least in the form of neat travel clichés. Notre Dame and the Eiffel Tower – at sunrise, at sunset, at night – have been described ad nauseam. So have the Seine, and the subtle, and not-so-subtle, differences between the Left Bank and the Right Bank. But what writers have been unable to capture is the grandness and even magic of strolling along the city's broad avenues – a legacy of the 19th century – which lead from impressive public buildings and exceptional museums to parks, gardens and esplanades galore. With the metro, all this is readily accessible – you can whizz around under the traffic and pop up wherever you choose.

Orientation

In central Paris, the Rive Droite (Right Bank) is north of the Seine, while the Rive Gauche (Left Bank) is south of the river. For administrative and other purposes, Paris is divided into 20 *arrondissements* (districts), which spiral out clockwise from the centre of the city. Paris addresses always include the arrondissement number. In this chapter, arrondissements are listed in parentheses immediately after the street address, using the French abbreviations, eg, *1er* for *premier* (1st), *4ème* for *quatrième* (4th), 19ème for *dix-neuvième* (19th). When an address includes the full five-digit postcode, the last two digits indicate the arrondissement: 75001 for the 1st, 75019 for the 19th, and so forth.

As there is nearly always a metro station within 500 metres of wherever you want to go in Paris, we've included the station nearest each hotel, museum, etc immediately after the telephone number or the arrondissement number.

Maps The best map of Paris is the 1:10,000 scale *Paris Plan* published by Michelin. It comes in both booklet form *(Paris Plan 11)* and sheet form *(Paris Plan 10)* and is available in many bookshops and some stationery stores.

Information
Tourist Offices Paris' main tourist office (☎ 47.23.61.72; metro George V) is 200 metres east of the Arc de Triomphe at 127 Ave des Champs Élysées (8ème). It is open every day of the year except 1 January, 1 May and 25 December from 9 am to 8 pm. This is the best source of information in English on the city's museums, concerts, expositions, theatre performances and the like. Brochures on other parts of France are available on request. For a small fee and a deposit, the office can find you a place to stay in Paris (for the night of the day you come in) or the provinces (up to eight days in advance).

There are tourist office annexes (open Monday to Saturday from 8 am to 8 pm, or to 9 pm in summer) in all of Paris' train stations except Gare Saint Lazare. From May to September, the tourist office annexe at the Eiffel Tower (7ème) is open from 11 am to 6 pm. Both international airports have Aéroports de Paris (ADP) tourist information desks. The one at Orly is in the Orly-Sud terminal on the ground floor opposite Gate H; it is open daily from 6 am to 11.45 pm. At Charles de Gaulle, there's a tourist informa-

tion bureau (☎ 48.62.27.29) on the arrival level of Aérogare 1 and an ADP *banque information* in each of the three terminals of Aérogare 2.

For recorded information in English on cultural and other events taking place in Paris, call ☎ 47.20.88.98 any time of the day or night.

Money All of Paris' six major train stations have exchange bureaus open seven days a week until at least 8 pm (7 pm for Gare Montparnasse), but what you gain in convenience you pay for in the less-than-optimal rates. The exchange places at Orly (Orly-Sud terminal) and Roissy-Charles de Gaulle (both Aérogares) are open until 10 or 11 pm.

Unless you want to get about 10% less than a fair rate, avoid the big exchange bureau chains like Chequepoint and Exact Change.

Banque de France By far the best rate in town is offered by the Banque de France, France's central bank, whose headquarters (☎ 42.92.22.27; metro Palais Royal-Musée du Louvre) is three blocks north of the Louvre at 31 Rue Croix des Petits Champs (1er). The exchange service is open Monday to Friday from 9.30 am to noon and 1.30 to 4 pm. The Banque de France branch (☎ 42.61.15.33; metro Bastille) at 5 Place de la Bastille (4ème), which is directly across from the Opéra Bastille, is open weekdays from 9 am to noon and 1.30 to 3.30 pm.

American Express Paris' landmark American Express office (☎ 47.77.70.07; metro Auber or Opéra) at 11 Rue Scribe (9ème) faces the west side of Opéra Garnier. It is open Monday to Friday from 9 am to 5.30 pm and – for poste restante, refunds, currency exchange and cash advances *only* – on Saturday from 9 am to 5 pm. Since you can get slightly better exchange rates elsewhere and this office is often plagued by long lines of impatient US tourists, it should be avoided if at all possible.

Citibank Money wired from abroad by or to

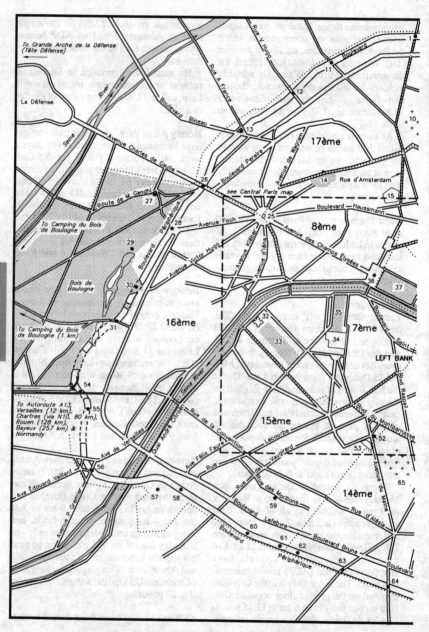

To Grande Arche de la Défense
(Tête Défense)

La Défense

1

11

12

13

17ème

Boulevard

Rue V Hugo

Boulevard Bineau

Avenue Charles de Gaulle

Seine River

Boulevard

Avenue de Wagram

10

Boulevard Pereire

26

Route de M Gandhi

27

To Camping du Bois
de Boulogne

28

Boulevard Périphérique

Avenue Foch

14

Rue d'Amsterdam

15

see Central Paris map

Boulevard — Haussmann

8ème

0 25

Avenue Kléber

Avenue des Champs Elysées

29

Avenue Victor Hugo

Avenue d'Iéna

To Camping du Bois
de Boulogne (1 km)

30

Bois de
Boulogne

16ème

31

36

37

32

33

35

34

7ème

Seine River

LEFT BANK

54

To Autoroute A13,
Versailles (12 km),
Chartres (via N10, 80 km),
Rouen (128 km),
Bayeux (257 km) &
Normandy

55

Quai André Citroën

Rue de la Convention

15ème

Blvd Raspail

Blvd du Montparnasse

52

53

56

Ave de Versailles

Ave Félix Faure

Rue Lecourbe

Rue Vaugirard

Ave Édouard Vaillant

57

58

Rue des Morillons

Rue d'Alésia

Avenue du Maine

65

14ème

Avenue P Grenier

59

Boulevard Lefebvre

60

Boulevard Brune

61

62

63

64

Boulevard
Périphérique

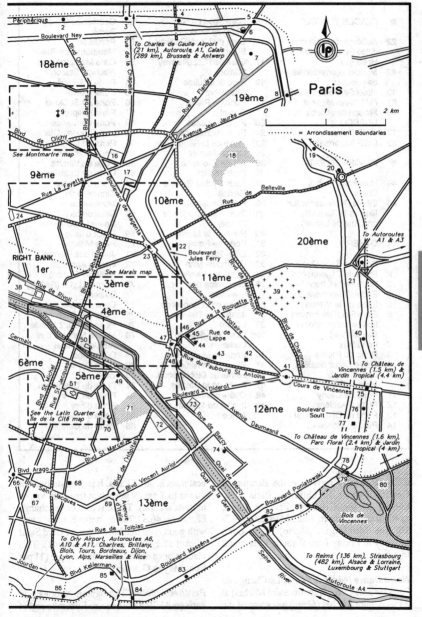

Périphérique
Boulevard Ney
18ème
To Charles de Gaulle Airport
(21 km), Autoroute A1, Calais
(289 km), Brussels & Antwerp
19ème

Paris

0   1   2 km

= Arrondissement Boundaries

See Montmartre map

Blvd de Clichy

9ème
Rue La Fayette
10ème
Rue de Belleville
20ème

To Autoroutes
A1 & A3

RIGHT BANK
1er
Boulevard Jules Ferry
See Marais map
3ème
11ème
Boulevard de Ménilmontant
39

4ème
Rue de la Roquette
Rue de Lappe
Rue de la Voltaire
Rue du Faubourg St Antoine

6ème
5ème
See the Latin Quarter &
Ile de la Cité map

To Château de
Vincennes (1.5 km) &
Jardin Tropical (4.4 km)

Cours de Vincennes
12ème
Boulevard Soult

To Château de Vincennes (1.6 km),
Parc Floral (2.4 km) & Jardin
Tropical (4 km)

Blvd Arago
Blvd Saint Jacques
13ème
Rue de Tolbiac

To Orly Airport, Autoroutes A6,
A10 & A11, Chartres, Brittany,
Blois, Tours, Bordeaux, Dijon,
Lyon, Alps, Marseilles & Nice

Bois de
Vincennes

To Reims (136 km), Strasbourg
(482 km), Alsace & Lorraine,
Luxembourg & Stuttgart

Autoroute A4

Blvd Kellermann
Boulevard Masséna
Jourdan

Seine River

FRANCE

Citibank usually arrives at the Banque de Gestion Privée du Citibank Paris (also known as the Citibank Private Bank; ☎ 40.70.00.80; metro Alma Marceau) at 17-19 Ave Montaigne (8ème). It is open Monday to Friday from 9 am to 1 pm and 2 to 4 pm.

Notre Dame (4ème & 5ème) Le Change de Paris (☎ 43.54.76.55; metro Saint Michel) at 2 Place Saint Michel (6ème) has some of the best rates in all of Paris. It is open daily from 10 am to 7 pm (9 pm when there are lots of tourists around). There is another exchange bureau (☎ 46.34.70.46; metro Saint Michel) with good rates one block west of Blvd Saint Michel at 1 Rue Hautefeuille (6ème). This place is open daily from 9 am to 9 pm (11 pm from May to October).

Panthéon (5ème) The Banque Nationale de Paris (☎ 43.29.45.50; metro Luxembourg) at

7 Rue Soufflot exchanges foreign currency Monday to Friday from 9 to 11.45 am and 1 to 5 pm.

Champs Élysées (8ème) Thanks to fierce competition, the Champs Élysées is an excellent place to change money. The Bureau de Change (☎ 42.25.38.14; metro Franklin D Roosevelt) at 25 Ave des Champs Élysées has some of the best rates in the city and is an especially good bet on weekends. It is open every day of the year from 9 am to 8 pm.

Montmartre (18ème) There's a bureau de change (☎ 42.52.67.19; metro Abbesses) at 6 Rue Yvonne Le Tac, which is two blocks east of Place des Abbesses. It is open Monday to Saturday from 10 am to noon and 12.30 to 7 pm and on Sunday from 10.30 am to noon and 12.30 to 2.30 pm.

Post & Telecommunications The main post office (☎ 40.28.20.20; metro Sentier or Les Halles) at 52 Rue du Louvre (1er) is open 24 hours a day all week. Services include sending mail, poste restante, telegrams, telephones (phone-card calls only) and currency exchange, which is available only on weekdays from 8 am to 7 pm and Saturday from 8 am to noon. This is where poste restante mail not specifically addressed to a particular branch post office ends up. At the post office (☎ 43.59.55.18; metro George V) at 71 Ave des Champs Élysées (8ème), you can place telephone calls (with phonecards), pick up poste restante mail and send letters and telegrams Monday to Saturday from 8 am to 10 pm and on Sunday and public holidays from 10 am to noon and 2 to 8 pm. All other branch post offices in Paris are open Monday to Friday from 8 am to 7 pm and on Saturday from 8 am to noon.

The telephone code for Paris is 1. See Orientation for an explanation of Paris' postcodes.

Foreign Embassies See the Facts for the Visitor section at the start of this chapter.

Cultural Centres The American Church (☎ 47.05.07.99; metro Pont de l'Alma) at 65 Quai d'Orsay (7ème) functions as something of a community centre for English speakers and is an excellent source of information on all sorts of subjects, including job openings and apartments for rent. Reception is staffed daily from 10 am to 10 pm (8 pm on Sunday).

The American Centre (☎ 44.73.77.77), which sponsors cultural events of all sorts, will move to its huge and striking new home at 51 Rue de Bercy (12ème; metro Bercy) in late 1993. It will be equipped with a theatre, a cinema, a restaurant, a bookshop and 23 apartments for resident artists and scholars.

The British Council (☎ 49.55.73.00; metro Varenne) at 9-11 Rue de Constantine (7ème) has a lending library (230FF a year for membership) and a free reference library. The bulletin board outside the entrance has information on the British Council's many cultural activities, most of which are co-sponsored by French institutions and do not take place in the council's building.

Travel Agencies Nouvelles Frontières (☎ 46.34.55.30) at 66 Blvd Saint Michel (6ème) specialises in discount long-distance plane tickets. Another agent, Selectour Voyages (☎ 43.29.64.00; metro Saint Michel) at 29 Rue de la Huchette (5èmc), is open weekdays from 9.45 am to 6.30 pm. Council Travel (☎ 42.66.20.87; metro Quatre Septembre), the American student travel agency, has its main Paris office at 31 Rue Saint Augustine (2ème). It is open Monday to Friday from 9.30 am to 6.30 pm and on Saturday from 10 am to 2 pm. From June to August, Saturday hours are 10 am to 1 pm and 2 to 5 pm. Expect long lines during the summer.

Bookshops Paris' most famous English-language bookshop is Shakespeare & Company (no phone; metro Saint Michel) at 37 Rue de la Bûcherie (5ème), which is right across the Seine from Notre Dame. The shop has a varied and unpredictable collection of new and used English books in English, but even the second-hand stuff doesn't come cheap. It's generally open daily from 10 am to about midnight.

Paris' largest English-language bookshop, W H Smith (☎ 42.60.37.97; metro Concorde) at 248 Rue de Rivoli (1er), is a block east of Place de la Concorde. Its orientation is more English than American. It is open Monday to Saturday from 9.30 am to 7 pm, and there is free tea and coffee for browsers. At 27 Rue de la Parcheminerie (5ème), the mellow Abbey Bookshop (☎ 46.33.16.24; metro Cluny-La Sorbonne) is something of a gathering place for Canadian expats. It is open Monday to Thursday from 11 am to 10 pm, on Friday from 11 am to midnight, on Saturday from 10 am to midnight and on Sunday from noon to 10 pm.

Lonely Planet books (and other travel guides of all sorts) are available for about double the Australian or North American price from a number of shops on the Left Bank, including the FNAC Librairie Internationale (☎ 44.41.31.50; metro Cluny-La Sorbonne) at 71 Blvd Saint Germain (5ème); Gabelli Adventure (☎ 46.33.80.06; metro Cluny-La Sorbonne) at 14 Rue Serpente (6ème); and Gibert Jeune (☎ 43.25.70.07; metro Saint Michel), which is on the east side of Place Saint Michel on the corner of Rue de la Huchette (5ème).

Lost & Found Paris' infamous Bureau des Objets Trouvés (Lost Property Office; ☎ 45.31.14.80; metro Convention), run by the Préfecture de Police, is at 36 Rue des Morillons (15ème). The only lost-and-found objects that do not make their way here are those found in the SNCF train stations. Since telephone enquiries are impossible, you have to come out here and fill out some forms to see if what you've lost has been located. The office is open on weekdays from 8.30 am to 5 pm (Monday and Wednesday), 5.30 pm (Friday) or 8 pm (Tuesday and Thursday). In July and August, it closes at 5 pm every day.

Emergency Paris has about 50 Assistance Publique (public health service) hospitals. The Hôtel Dieu hospital (☎ 42.34.82.34; metro Cité), on the north side of the square in front of Notre Dame Cathedral (4ème), is very easy to find. The emergency room *(service des urgences)*, which treats everything from stomach upsets to really serious illnesses, is open 24 hours a day. See Health in the Facts for the Visitor section at the start of this chapter for general information on France's public health care system.

Dangers & Annoyances In general, Paris is a safe city, especially when compared to any large or medium-sized urban area in the USA. You should, of course, always use common sense – avoid the Bois de Boulogne and Bois de Vincennes after nightfall – but there is no reason not to use the metro until it stops running (around 12.45 am). As you'll notice, women do travel alone on the metro late at night – at least in most areas. Metro stations that are probably best avoided late at night, by both women and men, especially if you are alone, include Châtelet (1er) and its many seemingly endless tunnels to Les Halles and Châtelet-Les Halles stops; Blanche, Pigalle and Château Rouge in the vicinity of Montmartre (18ème); Gare du Nord (10ème); and Strasbourg-Saint Denis (2ème & 10ème).

Things to See
Museum Hours & Discounts Paris has about 70 museums of all sizes; a comprehensive list is available from the tourist office. The *musées nationaux* (museums run by the French government) in Paris and the Île de France (eg the Louvre, the Musée de Cluny, the Musée Picasso, the Musée de l'Orangerie) are open daily except Tuesday. The only exceptions are the Musée d'Orsay, the Musée Rodin and Versailles, which are open daily except Monday. The musées nationaux are free for people 17 or younger and are half-price if you're aged 18 to 25 or over 60. Paris' municipal museums *(musées de la Ville de Paris*; ☎ 42.78.73.81 for information) are open daily except Monday.

The Carte Musées et Monuments (☎ 44.78.45.81) gets you into more than 60 museums and monuments in Paris and the Île de France without having to queue for a ticket. The card costs 55/110/160FF for one/three/five consecutive days. It is on sale at the museums and monuments it covers, at some metro ticket windows and at the tourist office.

Things to See – Left Bank

Île de la Cité (1er & 4ème) Paris was founded sometime during the 3rd century BC, when members of a tribe known as the Parisii set up a few huts on Île de la Cité. By the Middle Ages, the city had grown to encompass both banks of the Seine, but Île de la Cité remained the centre of royal and ecclesiastical power. The middle part of the island was demolished and rebuilt during the 19th century.

Notre Dame Notre Dame (☎ 43.26.07.39; metro Cité or Saint Michel), Paris' cathedral, is one of the most magnificent achievements of Gothic architecture. Its construction was begun in 1163 and completed around 1345. Exceptional features include the three spectacular rose windows, especially the window on the north side of the transept, which has remained virtually unchanged since the 13th century. One of the best views of Notre Dame is from the lovely little park behind the cathedral, where you can see the mass of ornate flying buttresses that encircle the chancel and hold up its walls and roof.

Notre Dame is open daily from 8 am to 7 pm. There is no entry charge. Free concerts are held every Sunday at about 5 or 5.30 pm. The **Trésor** (treasury) at the back of the cathedral, which contains precious liturgical objects, is open Monday to Saturday from 9.30 am to 6 pm; admission is 15FF (10FF for students). The top of the west façade, from which you can view many of the cathedral's most ferocious gargoyles – not to mention a good part of Paris – is open from 9.30 am to noon and from 2 pm until 4.30 pm (in winter) or 5.30 pm (in summer). The entrance is at the base of the north tower. Entry is 31FF (17FF if you're 18 to 24 or over 60).

Sainte Chapelle The gem-like Sainte Chapelle (☎ 43.54.30.09; metro Cité), illuminated by a veritable curtain of luminous 13th century stained glass, is inside the **Palais de Justice** (Law Courts), which are on the west side of Blvd du Palais (1er). Consecrated in 1248, Sainte Chapelle was built in only 33 months to house the Crown of Thorns (believed to be the thorny crown worn by Jesus) and other relics purchased by King Louis IX (Saint Louis) earlier in the 13th century. From October to March, it is open daily from 10 am to 4.30 pm. The rest of the year, hours are 9.30 am to 6 pm. Tickets cost 25FF (14FF reduced rate). A ticket valid for both Sainte Chapelle and the nearby Conciergerie (☎ 43.54.30.06; metro Cité) costs 40FF. The visitors' entrance to the Palais de Justice is directly across from 7 Blvd du Palais (1er). Be prepared to pass through airport-type security.

Conciergerie The Conciergerie was a luxurious royal palace when it was built in the 14th century but later lost favour with the kings of France and was transformed into a prison and place of torture. During the Reign of Terror (1793-94), the Conciergerie was used to incarcerate presumed enemies of the Revolution before they were brought before the tribunal, which met next door in what is now the Palais de Justice. Among the 2600 prisoners held here before being sent in tumbrels to the guillotine were Queen Marie-Antoinette and the Revolutionary radicals Danton and Robespierre. The Conciergerie is open daily from 10 am to 5 pm (9.30 am to 6 pm from April to September). The entrance is at 1 Quai de l'Horloge (1er) and tickets cost 25FF (14FF reduced rate).

Île Saint Louis (4ème) Île Saint Louis, the smaller of Paris' two islands, is just upstream from Île de la Cité. The 17th century houses of grey stone and the small-town shops that line the streets and *quais* impart an almost provincial calm on the neighbourhood, making it a great place for a quiet stroll. If circumnavigating the island makes you hungry, you might want to join the line in front of Bertillon (☎ 43.54.31.61; metro

FRANCE

Central Paris

Pont Marie) at 31 Rue Saint Louis en l'Île (4ème), which is reputed to have Paris' best ice cream. On foot, the shortest route between Notre Dame and the Marais passes through Île Saint Louis.

Latin Quarter (5ème & 6ème) This area is known as the Quartier Latin because all communication between students and their professors took place in Latin up until the Revolution. The 5ème has become increasingly touristy in recent years but still has a

large population of students and academics affiliated with the University of Paris and other institutions of higher learning. Shop-lined **Blvd Saint Michel**, known as the 'Boul Mich', runs along the border of the 5ème and the 6ème.

Panthéon The Latin Quarter landmark now known as the Panthéon (☎ 43.54.34.51; metro Luxembourg or Cardinal Lemoine), which is at the eastern end of Rue Soufflot (5ème), was commissioned as an abbey church in the mid-18th century. In 1791, the Constituent Assembly converted it into a mausoleum for the 'great men of the era of French liberty'. Permanent guests of the Panthéon include Victor Hugo, Voltaire and Rousseau. The Panthéon's ornate marble interior is gloomy in the extreme, but you get a great view of the city from around the colonnaded dome, which is visible from all over Paris. From October to March, the Panthéon is open daily from 10 am to 12.30 pm and 2 to 4.45 pm. The rest of the year, it is open from 10 am to 5.15 pm. Entry costs 25FF (12FF reduced rate).

Sorbonne Paris' most famous university, the Sorbonne, was founded in 1253 as a college for 16 poor theology students. After centuries as France's major theological centre, it was closed in 1792 by the Revolutionary government but reopened under Napoleon. Today, the Sorbonne's main campus complex (bounded by Rue Victor Cousin, Rue Saint Jacques, Rue des Écoles and Rue Cujas) and other buildings in the vicinity house several of the 13 autonomous universities created when the Université de Paris was reorganised after the violent student protests of 1968. **Place de la Sorbonne** links Blvd Saint Michel with Église de la Sorbonne, the university's domed church, which was built in the mid-17th century.

Jardin du Luxembourg When the weather is warm (or even just slightly sunny), Parisians flock to the Luxembourg Gardens (6ème; metro Luxembourg) in their thousands to sit in the chairs and read, write, relax, talk, sunbathe and sail toy boats in the fountains. Hemingway claimed that as an impoverished young writer, he would come to the Jardin du Luxembourg and, when the police were distracted with other matters, catch pigeons in order to eat them. The gardens' main entrance is across the street from 65 Blvd Saint Michel.

The **Palais du Luxembourg**, fronting Rue Vaugirard at the northern end of the Jardin du Luxembourg, was built for Maria

de' Medici (Marie de Médicis in French), queen of France from 1600 to 1610, in the early 17th century. It now houses the Sénat, upper house of the French parliament. During WW II, it served as a German headquarters.

Musée de Cluny The Musée de Cluny (☎ 43.25.62.00; metro Cluny-La Sorbonne) is Paris' premier museum of the Middle Ages. Its greatest masterpiece is a series of six late 15th century tapestries from the southern Netherlands known as **La Dame à la Licorne** (the Lady and the Unicorn). The museum is housed in two structures: the frigidarium (cold room) and other remains of Gallo-Roman baths from around the year 200 AD; and the late 15th century residence of the abbots of Cluny.

The Musée de Cluny, whose entrance is across the street from the park next to 31 Rue du Sommerard (5ème), is open from 9.30 am to 5.05 pm daily except Tuesday. Entry is 17FF (9FF reduced rate). On Sunday, everyone pays 8FF.

Paris Mosque (5ème) Paris' central mosque (*mosquée*; metro Monge) was built between 1922 and 1926 in an ornate North African style. There are tours from 10 am to noon and 2 to 6 pm daily except Friday. The mosque complex includes a salon de thé (open daily from 10 am to 9.30 pm; 9FF for mint tea, Arab coffee or a North African pastry) and a public bath (*hammam*; ☎ 43.31.18.14). The hammam is open from 10 or 11 am to 8 or 9 pm on Monday, Wednesday, Thursday and Saturday for women and Friday and Sunday for men and costs 63FF (plus 50FF for an optional massage). The entrance to the salon de thé and the hammam is at 39 Rue Geoffroy Saint Hilaire (5ème).

The mosque is opposite the western end of the **Jardin des Plantes** (Botanical Gardens), which includes a small **zoo**. The **Muséum National d'Histoire Naturelle** (☎ 40.79.30.00; metro Monge) has a fascinating display of giant crystal rocks and lots of skeletons.

Institut du Monde Arabe (5ème) Set up by
20 Arab countries to showcase Arab and
Islamic culture and to promote cultural contacts between the Arab world and the West,
this institute (☎ 46.34.25.25; metro Cardinal
Lemoine) at 23 Quai Saint Bernard occupies
one of the most graceful and highly praised
public buildings constructed in Paris in
recent decades. The 7th-floor museum of 9th
to 19th century Muslim art and artisanship is
open daily except Monday and costs 20FF
(15FF reduced rate).

Catacombs (14ème) In 1785, it was
decided to solve the hygienic and aesthetic
problems posed by Paris' overflowing cemeteries by exhuming the bones and storing
them in the tunnels of three disused quarries.
One such ossuary is the Catacombes
(☎ 43.22.47.63; metro Denfert Rochereau),
in which the bones and skulls of millions of
Parisians from centuries past are neatly
stacked along the walls. During WW II, these
tunnels were used by the Resistance as a
headquarters.

The route through the Catacombs begins
at Place Denfert Rochereau. The entrance is
in a small green building from which you can
see in perfect profile the left side of the head
of the lion statue. The site is open Tuesday
to Friday from 2 to 4 pm and on weekends
from 9 to 11 am and 2 to 4 pm. Tickets cost
16FF (10FF for students and children aged 7
to 16). I'm not sure why people over 60 get
in for free, but a series of unpleasant specu-
lations come to mind... The exit, where a
guard will check your bag for stolen bones,
is south-west of Place Denfert Rochereau on
Rue Remy Dumoncel.

Musée d'Orsay to the Eiffel Tower (7ème)
This part of the Left Bank has quite a few
governmental buildings scattered among the
museums and apartment buildings.

Musée d'Orsay The Musée d'Orsay
(☎ 40.49.48.14; metro Musée d'Orsay),
along the Seine at 1 Rue de Bellechasse,
showcases paintings, sculptures, *objets d'art*
and other works of art produced between

1848 and 1914, including the fruits of the
Impressionist, postimpressionist and Art-
Nouveau movements. It thus fills in the
chronological gap between the Louvre and
the Musée d'Art Moderne at the Centre Pompidou. The Musée d'Orsay is spectacularly
housed in a former train station built in 1900
and re-inaugurated in its present form in
1986. It is open daily, except Monday, from
10 am (9 am on Sunday and in summer) to
5.15 pm (9.15 pm on Thursday). Entry costs
31FF (16FF reduced rate).

Musée Rodin The Musée Auguste Rodin
(☎ 47.05.01.34; metro Varenne) at 77 Rue
Varenne (7ème) is many people's favourite
Parisian museum. Rodin's extraordinarily
vital bronze and marble sculptures are on
display both inside the Hôtel Biron and in the
delightful garden out the back. The Musée
Rodin is open from 10 am to 5 pm (5.45 pm
from April to September) daily except on
Monday. Entry costs 21FF (11FF reduced
rate). On Sunday, everyone gets in for 10FF.

Invalides The **Hôtel des Invalides** (7ème;
metro Invalides for the Esplanade, metro
Varenne or La Tour Maubourg for the main
building) was built in the 1670s by Louis
XIV to provide housing for 4000 *invalides*
(disabled ex-soldiers). On 14 July 1789, the
Paris mob forced its way into the building
and, after fierce fighting, took 28,000 rifles
before heading on to the Bastille prison.

The **Église du Dôme**, so named because
of its gilded dome, was built between 1677
and 1735 and is considered one of the finest
religious edifices erected during the reign of
Louis XIV. The church began its career as a
mausoleum for military leaders in 1800, and
in 1861 received the remains of Napoleon,
encased in six concentric coffins. The buildings on either side of the **Cour d'Honneur**
(main courtyard) house the **Musée de
l'Armée** (☎ 45.55.37.70), a huge military
museum. The Musée de l'Armée and the
Tombeau de Napoléon 1er (Napoleon's
tomb) are open daily from 10 am to 6 pm (7
pm from April to September). Entry costs

FRANCE

30FF (20FF for students under 30 and people over 60).

Eiffel Tower The Tour Eiffel (☎ 45.50.34.56, 45.55.91.11; metro Champ de Mars-Tour Eiffel) faced massive opposition from Paris' artistic and literary elite when it was built for the Exposition Universelle (World's Fair) of 1889, held to commemorate the Revolution. It was almost torn down in 1909 but was spared for purely practical reasons – it proved an ideal platform for the transmitting antennae needed for the new science of radiotelegraphy.

The Eiffel Tower is 320 metres high, including the television antenna at the very tip. This figure can vary by as much as 15 cm as the tower's 7000 tonnes of steel, held together by 2.5 million rivets, expands in warm weather and contracts when it's cold. When you're done peering upwards through the girders, you can choose to visit any of the three levels open to the public. The lift costs 17FF for the 1st platform (57 metres above ground), 34FF for the 2nd (115 metres) and 51FF for the 3rd (276 metres). Walking up the stairs to the 1st or 2nd platforms costs 8FF. The tower is open every day from 9.30 am to 11 pm (midnight in summer). You can walk up from 9 am to 6.30 pm (11 pm from early July to early September and on Friday, Saturday and public holiday nights from late May to early June).

Champ de Mars The Champ de Mars, the grassy area south-east of the Eiffel Tower, was originally a parade ground for the **École Militaire** (France's military academy), the huge, 18th century building at the south-east end of the lawns.

Things to See – Right Bank
Trocadéro to Bois de Boulogne (16ème)
This area includes a few museums and Paris' most famous park, the Bois de Boulogne.

Jardins du Trocadéro The Jardins du Trocadéro (metro Trocadéro), whose fountain and nearby statue garden are grandly illuminated at night, are across Pont d'Iéna

(7ème & 16ème) from the Eiffel Tower. The two colonnaded wings of the **Palais de Chaillot**, built in 1937, house a number of museums, including the Musée de la Marine (☎ 45.53.31.70), the Musée du Cinéma (☎ 45.53.74.39) and the Musée des Monuments Français (☎ 47.27.35.74), all of which are closed on Tuesday. The view from the terrace between the two wings is one of the most impressive in Paris.

Musée Guimet The Musée Guimet (☎ 47.23.61.65; metro Iéna) at 6 Place d'Iéna (16ème), which is about midway between the Eiffel Tower and the Arc de Triomphe, displays antiquities and works of art from South Asia (Afghanistan, India, Nepal, Pakistan and Tibet), South-East Asia (Cambodia) and East Asia (China, Japan and Korea). It is open daily except Tuesday from 9.45 am to 5.15 pm. Entry costs 26FF (13FF reduced rate).

Bois de Boulogne The 8.65 sq km Bois de Boulogne, located on the western edge of the city, is endowed with meandering trails, gardens, forested areas, cycling paths and Belle Époque-style cafés. Rowing boats can be rented at the **Lac Inférieur** (metro Ave Henri Martin), the largest of the park's lakes and ponds. At night, the park is taken over by prostitutes (most of whom have AIDS, according to a recent study) and people of unusual sexual tastes. Locals advise both men and women not to walk alone in the Bois de Boulogne at night.

Paris Cycles (☎ 47.47.76.50) rents one-speed bicycles at two locations: on Route du Mahatma Gandhi (metro Les Sablons), opposite the Porte Sablons entrance to the Jardin d'Acclimatation amusement park; and near the Pavillon Royal (metro Ave Foch) at the northern end of the Lac Inférieur. Charges are 26FF an hour or 80FF a day. From mid-April to mid-October, bicycles are available daily (unless it rains) from 10 am to sundown. During the rest of the year, you can rent them on Wednesday, Saturday and Sunday *only*. Bicycles can be hired every day during school holidays.

Louvre Area (1er & 8ème) This area includes many important historical, architectural and artistic sights, most notably the Louvre Museum.

Musée du Louvre The Louvre Museum (☎ 40.20.53.17, 40.20.51.51; metro Palais Royal-Musée du Louvre), constructed around 1200 as a fortress and rebuilt in the mid-16th century as a royal palace, began its career as a public museum in 1793. The paintings, sculptures and artefacts on display were assembled by French governments over the past five centuries and include works of art and artisanship from all over Europe as well as important collections of Assyrian, Egyptian, Etruscan, Greek, Coptic, Roman and Islamic art and antiquities. The Louvre's most famous work is undoubtedly Leonardo da Vinci's *Mona Lisa*. Since it takes several serious visits to get anything more than the briefest glimpse of the offerings, your best bet – after seeking out a few things you really want to see (eg masterpieces such as the *Winged Victory of Samothrace* or *Venus de Milo*) – is to choose a period or section of the museum and pretend the rest is somewhere across town.

The Louvre's main entrance is covered by a 21-metre-high glass pyramid designed by American architect I M Pei. Commissioned by François Mitterand and completed in 1990, the design generated bitter opposition in the mid-1980s but is now generally acknowledged as a brilliant success.

The Louvre is open daily except Tuesday. From Thursday to Sunday, it is open from 9 am to 5.45 pm. On Monday and Wednesday, it is open from 9 am to 9.45 pm, but on Monday only part of the museum stays open after 5.30 pm. Ticket sales end 30 minutes before closing time. The entry fee is 31FF (16FF reduced rate), but on Sunday everyone gets in for 16FF. In summer, be prepared for long queues.

Free brochures with rudimentary maps of the museum are available at the information desk in Hall Napoléon, where you can also get details on guided tours. Cassette tours *(acoustiguides)* in six languages can be rented for 25FF on the mezzanine level (one floor up from the main reception level, or *niveau accueil*). Detailed explanations in a variety of languages, printed on heavy plastic-coated pages, are stored on racks in each display room.

Place Vendôme The square and the arcaded buildings around Place Vendôme (1er; metro Tuileries) were designed in the 17th century to showcase a giant statue of Louis XIV that was later destroyed during the Revolution. The present 44-metre column in the middle of Place Vendôme consists of a stone core wrapped in a spiral of bronze made from 1250 cannons captured by Napoleon at the Battle of Austerlitz (1805). The shops around the square are among the most fashionable and expensive in Paris.

Musée de l'Orangerie The Musée de l'Orangerie (☎ 42.97.48.16; metro Concorde), which is in the south-east corner of Place de la Concorde, displays important Impressionist works, including a series of Monet's *Nymphéas* (water lilies) and paintings by Cézanne, Matisse, Modigliani, Picasso, Renoir and Soutine. It is open daily except Tuesday from 9.45 am to 5.15 pm. The entry fee is 26FF (14FF reduced rate).

Place de la Concorde Vast, cobbled Place de la Concorde (8ème), set between the Jardin des Tuileries and the eastern end of the Champs Élysées, was laid out between 1755 and 1775. Louis XVI was guillotined here in 1793, and during the next two years, another 1343 people were beheaded here, including Marie-Antoinette and Robespierre. The 3300-year-old Egyptian **obelisk** in the middle of Place de la Concorde was given to France in 1829 by the ruler of Egypt, Muhammad Ali. It is from Luxor in upper Egypt.

La Madeleine The church of Saint Mary Magdalen (☎ 42.65.52.17; metro Madeleine), known to everyone as La Madeleine, is 350 metres north of Place de la Concorde along Rue Royale. Built in the style of a Greek temple, it was consecrated in 1842 after almost a century of design changes and construction delays. The front porch affords a superb view of Place de la Concorde and, across the river, the 18th century **Palais Bourbon**, whose façade dates from the very early 19th century. It is now the home of the Assemblée Nationale.

Fauchon (☎ 47.42.60.11; metro Madeleine) at 26 Place de la Madeleine, Paris' most famous luxury food shop, is open daily except Sunday from 9.40 am to 7 pm.

Champs Élysées (8ème) The two-km-long Ave des Champs Élysées (8ème) links Place de la Concorde with the Arc de Triomphe. Once popular with the aristocracy as a stage on which to parade their wealth, it has, in recent decades, been partly taken over by fast-food restaurants, overpriced tourist cafés and other establishments well suited to separating enthralled but hungry tourists from their money. The nicest part is the park between Place de la Concorde and Rond Point des Champs Élysées.

Musée du Petit Palais The Petit Palais (☎ 42.66.96.24, 42.65.12.73; metro Champs Élysées-Clemenceau), built for the Exposition Universelle (World Fair) of 1900, is on Ave Winston Churchill (8ème), which runs between Ave des Champs Élysées and the Seine. The museum it houses specialises in medieval and Renaissance porcelain, clocks, tapestries, drawings and 19th century French painting and sculpture from the collections of the City of Paris. It is open from 10 am to 5.40 pm daily except Monday. The entry fee is 15FF (8.50FF for students and people over 60). Temporary exhibitions usually cost 30 or 35FF extra (20FF if you qualify for the reduction).

The **Grand Palais**, which is across Ave Winston Churchill from the Petit Palais, was also built for the World Fair of 1900. It is now used for various temporary exhibitions.

Arc de Triomphe The Arc de Triomphe (☎ 43.80.31.31; metro Charles de Gaulle-Étoile) is 2.2 km north-west of Place de la Concorde in the middle of Place Charles de

Gaulle (Place de l'Étoile), the world's largest traffic roundabout and the meeting point of 12 avenues (and three arrondissements: the 8ème, 16ème and 17ème). It was commissioned in 1806 by Napoleon to commemorate his imperial victories but remained unfinished when he started losing first battles and then whole wars. It was finally completed between 1832 and 1836. Among the armies to march triumphally through the Arc de Triomphe were the victorious Allies in 1919, the victorious Germans in 1940 and the victorious Allies in 1944. Since 1920, an Unknown Soldier from WW I has rested under the arch, his fate and that of countless others like him commemorated by a memorial flame that is lit each evening sometime between 5 and 7 pm.

The platform atop the arch is open from 10 am to 5 pm (5.30 pm from April to September) daily except on public holidays . It costs 31FF (17FF reduced rate). The only sane way to get to the base of the arch is via the underground passageways from its perimeter – trying to cross the traffic on foot is suicidal.

From the Arc de Triomphe, the **Voie Triomphale** (Triumphal Way) – the Louvre-Arc de Triomphe axis – stretches 4.5 km north-west along Ave de la Grande Armée and beyond to the new skyscraper district of **La Défense**, whose best known landmark, the **Grande Arche** (Grand Arch), also known as the Tête Défense, is a hollow cube 112 metres to a side. The Grand Arch is almost, but not quite, parallel to the Arc de Triomphe.

Centre Pompidou Area (4ème, 1er & 3ème) The highly animated neighbourhood between the Centre Pompidou and Les Halles is crowded with restaurants, cafés and fast-food places. Sex-shop-lined Rue Saint Denis, an integral part of the area, gets seedier as you move north.

Centre Georges Pompidou This centre (☎ 44.78.12.33; metro Rambuteau), also known as the Centre Beaubourg, is dedicated to displaying and promoting modern and

contemporary art. Thanks in part to its vigorous schedule of outstanding temporary
exhibitions, it is by far the most visited sight
in Paris. The square between the Pompidou
Centre and 123 Rue Saint Martin (4ème)
attracts street and mime artists, musicians,
jugglers and, Parisians complain, pickpockets and drug dealers.

The design of the Centre Pompidou has
not ceased drawing wide-eyed gazes and
critical comment since it was built between
1972 and 1977. In order to keep the exhibition halls as spacious and uncluttered as
possible, the architects – one Italian, the
other British – put the building's 'insides' on
the outside. The purpose of each of the ducts,
pipes and vents that enclose the building's
glass walls can be divined from the paint job:
escalators and elevators are red, electrical
circuitry is yellow, the plumbing is green and
the air-conditioning system is blue.

The Centre Pompidou consists of several
sections, each with its own opening hours
and fees. The **Musée National d'Art
Moderne** (MNAM), which displays the
national collection of modern and contemporary (ie 20th century) art, is open daily except
Tuesday from noon (10 am on weekends and
public holidays) to 10 pm. Entry costs 28FF
(18FF reduced rate), but everyone gets in for
free on Sunday from 10 am to 2 pm. The free
Bibliothèque Publique d'Information
(BPI; same opening hours as the MNAM) is
a huge, nonlending library equipped with the
latest high-tech information retrieval
systems. The entrance is on the 2nd floor.

If you'll be visiting several parts of the
complex in the same day, the one-day pass
(Forfait Journalier), which costs 55FF (50FF
if you're 13 to 25 or over 60), is a good deal,
especially if you take a guided tour. Tours in
English leave at 4 pm daily except Tuesday
from the Accueil Général information desk.
Unless you've got a one-day pass, the cost
of the tour alone, which lasts 1½ hours, is
35FF (28FF reduced rate).

Les Halles Paris' central food market, Les
Halles, occupied this site from around 1110
until 1969, when it moved out to the suburb

of Rungis. A huge (and, many would say,
horribly ugly) underground shopping mall,
known as Forum des Halles, was built in its
place and has proved highly popular with
Parisian shoppers, especially those in search
of reasonable prices. Just north of the grassy
area on top of Les Halles is one of Paris' most
attractive churches, the mostly 16th century
Église Saint Eustache.

Hôtel de Ville Paris' city hall (☎ 42.76.40.40;
metro Hôtel de Ville) at Place de l'Hôtel de
Ville (4ème) was burned down during the
Paris Commune of 1871 and rebuilt in the
neo-Renaissance style between 1874 and
1882. There are guided tours in French every
Monday at 10.30 am except on public holidays and when official functions
(manifestations officielles) are taking place.
The visitors' entrance is at 29 Rue de Rivoli.

Marais (4ème) The Marais (literally, the
marsh), the part of the 4ème east of the
Centre Pompidou and north of Île Saint
Louis, was in fact a marsh until the 13th
century, when it was converted to agricultural use. During the 17th century this was
the most fashionable part of the city, and the
nobility erected luxurious but discreet mansions known as hôtels particuliers. When the
aristocracy moved to trendier pastures, the
Marais was taken over by ordinary Parisians.
By the time renovation was begun in the
1960s, the Marais had become a poor but
lively Jewish neighbourhood centred around
Rue des Rosiers (see Marais under the
following Places to Eat section). In the
1980s, the area underwent serious gentrification and is today one of the trendiest
neighbourhoods for young professionals to
live and shop in.

Place des Vosges In 1605, King Henri IV
decided to turn the Marais into Paris' most
fashionable district. The result of this initiative, completed in 1612, was the Place
Royale – now Place des Vosges (metro Bastille or Chemin Vert) – a square ensemble of
36 symmetrical houses with ground-floor
arcades, steep slate roofs and large dormer

windows on the south side of Rue des Francs Bourgeois. Duels were once fought in the elegant park in the middle. Today, the arcades around Place des Vosges are occupied by up-market art galleries, pricey antique shops and elegant places where you can sip tea.

Victor Hugo lived at 6 Place des Vosges from 1832 to 1848. The **Maison de Victor Hugo** (☎ 42.72.10.16; metro Bastille or Chemin Vert), now a municipal museum, is open daily except Monday from 10 am to 5.40 pm. The entry fee is 12FF (6.50FF for students, free for people over 60).

Musée Picasso The Picasso Museum (☎ 42.71.25.21; metro Saint Sébastien Froissart), housed in a mid-17th century residence, is a few hundred metres north-east of the Marais at 5 Rue de Thorigny (3ème). Paintings, sculptures, ceramic works, engravings and drawings that the heirs of Pablo Picasso (1881-1973) donated to the French government in lieu of huge inheritance taxes are on display, as is Picasso's personal art collection, which includes works by Braque, Cézanne, Matisse, Rousseau and others. The museum is open daily except Tuesday from 9.15 am to 5.15 pm (until 10 pm on Wednesday). The entry fee is 26FF (14FF reduced rate).

Bastille (4ème, 11ème & 12ème) The **Bastille** is the most famous monument in Paris that doesn't exist – the notorious prison was demolished shortly after the mob stormed it on 14 July 1789 and freed all seven prisoners held inside. Today, the site where it stood is known as Place de la Bastille. **Opéra de la Bastille** (☎ 40.01.19.71; metro Bastille) at 2-6 Place de la Bastille (12ème), Paris' giant new opera house, is one of the huge public buildings which each French president (Mitterand, in this case) constructs in Paris in order to immortalise himself.

Opéra Garnier (9ème) Paris' renowned opera house (☎ 40.01.19.70; metro Opéra) at Place de l'Opéra, designed in 1860 by Charles Garnier to display the splendour of Napoleon III's France, is one of the most impressive monuments erected during the Second Empire. The extravagant **entrance hall**, with its grand staircase, is decorated with multicolored marble and a gigantic chandelier. The **ceiling** of the auditorium was painted by Marc Chagall in 1964.

Opéra Garnier is open to visitors from 11 am to 4.30 pm daily except Sunday. Entry is 28FF (15FF for children aged 10 to 16). Opera performances now take place at Opéra Bastille, but Opéra Garnier is still used for concerts and ballets.

Montmartre (18ème) During the 19th century – and especially after 1871, when the Communard uprising began here – Montmartre's Bohemian life style attracted artists and writers, whose presence turned the area into Paris' most important centre of artistic and literary creativity. In English-speaking countries, Montmartre's mystique of unconventionality has been magnified by the notoriety of the **Moulin Rouge** (☎ 46.06.00.19; metro Blanche) at 82 Blvd de Clichy, a nightclub founded in 1889 and known for its nearly naked chorus girls.

Basilique du Sacré Cœur Perched at the very top of Butte de Montmartre, the Sacré Cœur (☎ 42.51.17.02; metro Lamarck Caulaincourt), was built to fulfil a vow taken by many Parisian Catholics after the disastrous Franco-Prussian War of 1870-71. On warm evenings, groups of people gather on the steps below the church to contemplate the view, play guitars and sing. Although the basilica's domes are a well-loved part of the Parisian skyline, the architecture of the rest of the building, which is typical of the exceptionally garish taste of the late 19th century, is hardly graceful. Some describe it as hideous, though behind the vehemence and contempt there's usually more than a little affection.

The basilica is open daily from 6.45 am to 11 pm. The **Dome** and the **Crypt**, which cost 15FF (8FF for students) each or 25FF (13FF for students) for both, are open daily from 9 am to 6 pm (7 pm from about April to September). The recently rebuilt *funiculaire* (funicular railway), up the hill's southern slope, costs one metro/bus ticket each way; daily, weekly and monthly passes are also accepted.

Place du Tertre Slightly west of **Église Saint Pierre**, the only building left from the great abbey of Montmartre, is Place du Tertre. The square is as animated as an amusement park – it's filled with cafés, restaurants, portrait artists and excited tourists – but hardly more authentic. The real attraction of Montmartre, apart from the view, is its quiet, twisting streets and shaded parks, such as Rue de l'Abreuvoir, Rue Saint Vincent, Place Constantin Pecqueur and Place Émile Goudeau.

Pigalle Pigalle, only a few blocks south-west of the tranquil, residential areas of Montmartre, is one of Paris' two major sex districts (the other is along Rue Saint Denis in the 1er and 2ème). Although the area along Blvd de Clichy between the Pigalle and Blanche metro stops is lined with neon-lit sex shops and striptease parlours, the area also has plenty of legitimate nightspots, including La Locomotive discothèque (see the following Entertainment section) and several all-night cafés.

Cimetière du Père Lachaise (20ème) Cimetière du Père Lachaise (☎ 43.70.70.33; metro Philippe Auguste, Père Lachaise or Gambetta), final resting place of such famous people as Chopin, Delacroix, Oscar Wilde, Édith Piaf and Sarah Bernhardt, may be the most visited cemetery in the world. The best known tomb (and the only thing most visitors come to see) is that of 1960s rock star Jim Morrison, lead singer for the Doors, who died in 1971. It is in Division 6. Maps indicating where various famous people are buried are posted around the cemetery.

Cimetière du Père Lachaise is open daily from 8 am to 5.30 pm (7.30 am to 6 pm from mid-March to early November). On Saturdays, it opens at 8.30 am, and on Sundays

and public holidays at 9 am. The cemetery has five entrances, including one opposite 23 Blvd de Ménilmontant.

Bois de Vincennes (12ème) Paris' other large English-style park, the 9.29 sq km Bois de Vincennes, is in the far south-eastern corner of the city. Highlights include the **Parc Floral** (Floral Garden; metro Château de Vincennes) on Route de la Pyramide; the Parc Zoologique de Paris (Paris Zoo; ☎ 43.43.84.95; metro Porte Dorée) on Ave Daumesnil, 250 metres east of the Blvd Périphérique; and, at the park's eastern edge, the **Jardin Tropical** (Tropical Garden; RER stop Nogent-sur-Marne) on Ave de la Belle Gabrielle.

Château de Vincennes The Château de Vincennes (☎ 43.28.15.48; metro Château de Vincennes), at the northern edge of the Bois de Vincennes, is a bona fide 14th century royal chateau complete with massive fortifications and a moat. You can walk around the grounds for free, but the only way to see the more interesting sights – the Gothic **Chapelle Royale**, built between the 14th and 16th centuries, and the 14th century Donjon (keep), with its small historical museum – is to take a guided tour (in French with an information booklet in English). Tickets cost 25FF (14FF reduced rate) and are on sale in the Donjon. Tours begin daily between 10 am and 4.15 pm (6 pm from April to September). The main entrance, which is opposite 18 Ave de Paris in the inner suburb of Vincennes, is right next to the Château de Vincennes metro stop, the eastern terminus of line 1.

Musée National des Arts Africains et Océaniens This museum (☎ 43.43.14.54; metro Porte Dorée) at 293 Ave Daumesnil specialises in art from the South Pacific, North Africa and western and central Africa. It is open weekdays except Tuesday from 9.45 am to noon and 1.30 to 5.20 pm and on weekends from 12.30 to 6 pm. The entry fee is 24FF (16FF reduced rate).

FRANCE

Euro Disney It took US$4000 million to turn the beet fields 32 km east of Paris into the much heralded Euro Disney theme park (☎ 64.74.43.06), which opened in April 1992 amid much moaning from France's intellectuals. The park is open daily from 9 am to 9 pm (11 pm on Friday, Saturday, Sunday and public holiday nights). All-day entry costs 225FF for everyone aged 12 and over (150FF for children aged three to 11). Three-day passes are also available. To get to Euro Disney, which is just east of Paris, take RER line A4 to Marne-la-Vallée Chessy, the end-of-the-line stop. Check the destination boards to make sure you get a train that goes all the way. Trains, which take 35 minutes from the Nation stop, run every 10 or 15 minutes or so.

Activities
Language Courses The Alliance Française (☎ 45.44.38.28; metro Saint Placide) has its Paris headquarters at 101 Blvd Raspail (6ème). Month-long French courses usually begin during the first week of each month – you can register during the five business days before the start of each session. If there is space, it is possible to enrol for only two weeks of study. The registration office is open Monday to Friday from 9 am to 6 pm. The monthly, month-long French courses offered by the Accord Language School (☎ 42.36.24.95; metro Les Halles) at 72 Rue Rambuteau (1er) get high marks from students. A one-month, 10 hour a week course costs 1500FF.

For information on cooking and other courses in and around Paris, contact the tourist office.

Organised Tours For bicycle tours, see under Getting Around later in this section.

The Bateaux Mouches company (☎ 42.25.96.10, 42.25.22.55; metro Alma Marceau), which is based on the north bank of the Seine just east of Pont de l'Alma (8ème), runs the biggest tour boats on the Seine. The cost for a 1¼-hour cruise is 30FF (no student discount). Vedettes du Pont Neuf (☎ 46.33.98.38; metro Pont Neuf), whose home port is on the northern side of the far western tip of Île de la Cité (1er), operates one-hour boat circuits for 40FF.

Places to Stay
Accommodation Services Accueil des Jeunes en France (AJF) can always find you accommodation in a hostel or hotel, even in summer. It works like this: you come in on the day you need a place to stay and pay AJF for the accommodation, plus a 10FF fee, and they give you a voucher to take to the hostel or hotel. The earlier in the day you come, the better – the convenient and cheap places always go first. AJF's main office (*bureau d'accueil*, ☎ 42.77.87.80; metro Rambuteau) is at 119 Rue Saint Martin (4ème), right across the square from the entrance to the Centre Pompidou. It is open Monday to Saturday from 9 am to 5.30 pm (6.30 pm from June to September). Be prepared for long queues during the summer. The AJF annexe (☎ 42.85.86.19; metro Gare du Nord) at the Gare du Nord train station (10ème) is open daily from June to mid or late September from 7.30 am to 9.30 pm.

The tourist office (☎ 47.23.61.72; metro George V) at 127 Ave des Champs Élysées (8ème) can also find you accommodation for the evening of the day you visit their office. There is a 7FF charge for a spot at a hostel and a 17FF charge for reservations at a one-star hotel. For information on the tourist office and its annexes, see Tourist Offices under Information at the start of the Paris section.

Camping *Camping du Bois de Boulogne* (☎ 45.24.30.00) on Allée du Bord de l'Eau (16ème), the only camping ground actually within the Paris city limits, is along the Seine at the far western edge of the Bois de Boulogne. Two people with a tent pay 40 to 70FF a night depending on the season. From April to September, privately operated shuttle buses from the Porte Maillot Metro Station (16ème & 17ème) run daily from 8.30 am to 1 pm and 5 pm to sometime between 11 pm and 1 am. During July and August, the shuttles run every half-hour from 8.30 am to 1 am. Throughout the year, you can take either bus No 244 from the Porte Maillot metro stop or bus No 244C from the Porte d'Auteuil metro stop (16ème). Both lines run from 6 am to about 8 pm.

Hostels & Foyers Many hostels allow guests to stay for only three nights, especially in summer. Places that have age limits (eg up to 30) tend not to enforce them very rigorously. Only official auberges de jeunesse require that guests present IYHF cards. Curfews at Paris hostels tend to be 1 or 2 am. Few hostels accept reservations by telephone, but those that do are noted in the text.

Louvre Area (1er) The newly renovated *Centre International BVJ Paris-Louvre* (☎ 42.36.88.18; metro Louvre-Rivoli) at 20 Rue Jean-Jacques Rousseau is only a few blocks north-east of the Louvre. Beds in single-sex rooms cost 100FF, including breakfast. There is a second BVJ hostel, the *Centre International BVJ Paris-Les Halles* (☎ 40.26.92.45), around the corner at 5 Rue du Pélican.

Marais (4ème) The Maison Internationale de la Jeunesse et des Étudiants, better known as MIJE, runs three *hôtels de jeunes* (young people's hostels) in attractively renovated 17th and 18th century residences in the Marais. A bed in a single-sex dorm with shower costs 100FF, including breakfast. Individuals can make reservations up to five days in advance by coming to the hostel and paying in full. *MIJE Fourcy* (☎ 42.74.23.45; metro Saint Paul) is at 6 Rue de Fourcy, 100 metres south of Rue de Rivoli. *MIJE Fauconnier* (☎ 42.74.23.45; metro Saint Paul or Pont Marie) is two blocks away at 11 Rue du Fauconnier. *MIJE Maubisson* (☎ 42.72.72.09; metro Hôtel de Ville) is half a block south of the Mairie (town hall) du 4ème Arrondissement at 12 Rue des Barres.

Panthéon Area (5ème) The clean and friendly *Y & H Hostel* (☎ 45.35.09.53; metro

Monge), whose name is short for 'young and happy', is at 80 Rue Mouffetard, a hopping, happening street known for its numerous restaurants, pubs and the like. A bed in a cramped room with a sink costs 95FF. This place gives priority to people who fall under the 'young' category. Reservations can be made only if you leave a deposit for the first night.

11ème Arrondissement The *Auberge de Jeunesse Jules Ferry* (☎ 43.57.55.60; metro République or Oberkampf) is at 8 Blvd Jules Ferry. This youth hostel is a bit institutional but the atmosphere is fairly relaxed and – an added bonus – they don't accept large groups. A bed costs 92FF, including breakfast.

The friendly *Hôtel Sainte Marguerite* (☎ 47.00.62.00; metro Ledru Rollin) at 10 Rue Trousseau, 700 metres east of Place de la Bastille, is run like a youth hostel and attracts a young, international crowd. Beds in rooms for two, three or four people cost 90FF per person, including breakfast and use of the shower.

The *Maison Internationale des Jeunes* (MIJPC; ☎ 43.71.99.21; metro Faidherbe Chaligny) at 4 Rue Titon is 1.3 km east of Place de la Bastille. A bed in a spartan dorm room for two, three, five or eight people costs 100FF, including breakfast. If you don't have your own sheets, there's a 15FF rental charge. Telephone reservations are accepted only the same day you arrive.

12ème Arrondissement The *Centre International de Séjour de Paris Ravel* (☎ 43.43.19.01; metro Porte de Vincennes), better known as CISP Ravel, is on the south-western edge of the city at 4-6 Ave Maurice Ravel. A bed in a 12-person dormitory is 93FF. Rooms for two to five people cost 117FF per person, and singles are 136FF. All prices include breakfast. Reservations are accepted from individuals no more than 24 hours in advance.

13ème & 14ème Arrondissements The *Foyer International d'Accueil de Paris Jean*

FRANCE

FRANCE

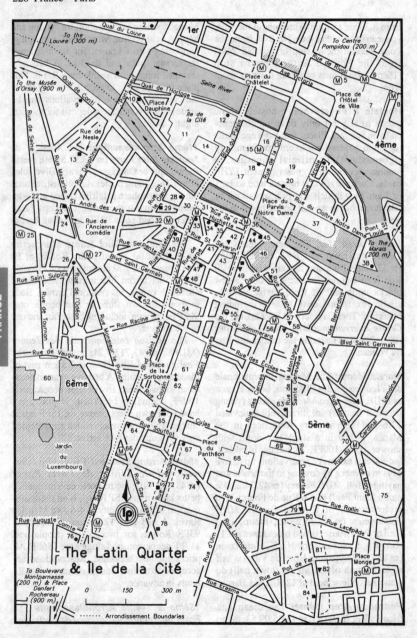

The Latin Quarter & Île de la Cité

■	PLACES TO STAY				
10	Hôtel Henri IV				
13	Hôtel de Nesle				
23	Hôtel Petit Trianon				
29	Hôtel Saint Michael				
45	Hôtel Esmerelda				
49	Hôtel du Centre				
71	Hôtel de Médicis				
78	Hôtel Gay Lussac				
84	Y & H Hostel				

■ PLACES TO STAY
- 10 Hôtel Henri IV
- 13 Hôtel de Nesle
- 23 Hôtel Petit Trianon
- 29 Hôtel Saint Michael
- 45 Hôtel Esmerelda
- 49 Hôtel du Centre
- 71 Hôtel de Médicis
- 78 Hôtel Gay Lussac
- 84 Y & H Hostel

▼ PLACES TO EAT
- 22 Food Shops
- 24 24-Hour Boulangerie
- 41 Restaurants (bacteria alley)
- 42 L'Année du Dragon Chinese Restaurant
- 48 McDonald's
- 49 Le Cloitre Pub and Polly Maggoo Pub
- 50 Au Coin des Gourmets Cambodian Restaurant
- 51 Boulangerie
- 52 Pâtisserie Viennoise
- 57 Food Shops
- 59 Pâtisserie des Carmes (Boulangerie) & Fromagerie
- 63 Le Violon Dingue Pub
- 64 McDonald's
- 72 Food Shops
- 73 Tashi Delek Tibetan Restaurant
- 74 Boulangerie
- 79 Restaurant Cous-Cous
- 81 Restaurants
- 82 Crêpes Stand

OTHER
- 1 Vedettes du Pont Neuf (Boat Tours)
- 2 Samaritaine Department Store
- 3 Châtelet Metro Station
- 4 Noctambus (all-night bus stops)
- 5 Hôtel de Ville Metro Station
- 6 Hôtel de Ville Metro Station
- 7 City Hall
- 8 Hôtel de Ville Metro Station
- 9 Musée de la Monnaie (Coin Museum)
- 11 Law Courts & Conciergerie
- 12 Conciergerie Entrance
- 14 Sainte Chapelle
- 15 Cité Metro Station
- 16 Flower Market
- 17 Préfecture de Police (Police Headquarters)
- 18 Entrance to the Préfecture de Police
- 19 Hôtel Dieu (Hospital)
- 20 Entrance to Hospital
- 21 Banque Rivaud
- 25 Mabillon Metro Station
- 26 Carrefour de l'Odéon
- 27 Odéon Metro Station
- 28 La Change de Paris (Currency Exchange)
- 30 Place Saint Michel
- 31 Saint Michel Metro Station
- 32 Place Saint André des Arts & Saint Michel Metro Station
- 33 Gibert Jeune Bookshop
- 34 Selectour Voyages (Travel Agent)
- 35 Caveau de la Huchette Jazz Club
- 36 Saint Michel Metro Station (RER Exit)
- 37 Cathédrale Notre Dame
- 38 WW II Deportation Memorial
- 39 Exchange Bureau
- 40 Gabelli Aventure Travel Bookshop
- 43 Église Saint Séverin
- 44 Shakespeare & Co Bookshop
- 46 Square R Viviani
- 47 Abbey Bookshop
- 53 Cluny-La Sorbonne Metro Station
- 54 Musée de Cluny
- 55 Eurolines Bus Office
- 56 Maubert Mutualité Metro Station
- 58 Place Maubert
- 60 Palais du Luxembourg (French Senate Building)
- 61 Sorbonne (University of Paris)
- 62 Église de la Sorbonne
- 65 Post Office
- 66 Luxembourg Metro Station
- 67 Banque Nationale de Paris
- 68 Panthéon
- 69 Église Saint Étienne du Mont
- 70 Cardinal Lemoine Metro Station
- 75 Arènes de Lutèce
- 76 Nouvelles Frontières Travel Agent
- 77 Luxembourg Metro Station
- 80 Place de la Contrescarpe
- 83 Monge Metro Station

FRANCE

Monnet (☎ 45.89.89.15; metro Glacière), known as FIAP Jean Monnet for short, is at 30 Rue Cabanis (14ème), a few blocks southeast of Place Denfert Rochereau. A bed costs 110/130FF (including breakfast) in modern rooms for eight/four people. Singles/doubles cost 220/150FF per person. Rooms specially outfitted for disabled people *(handicapés)* are available. Telephone reservations are accepted only on the same day you arrive.

The *Centre International de Séjour de Paris Kellermann* (☎ 45.80.70.76; metro Porte d'Italie), usually referred to as CISP Kellermann, is at 17 Blvd Kellermann

(13ème). A bed in an attractive dorm for eight costs 93FF, and staying in a double or quad will cost 116FF per person. Singles are 136FF. All prices include sheets and breakfast. This place also has facilities for disabled people. Telephone reservations are accepted if you call the same day you'll be arriving.

The rather institutional *Maison des Clubs UNESCO* (☎ 43.36.00.63; metro Glacière) is at 43 Rue de la Glacière (13ème), midway between Place Denfert Rochereau and Place d'Italie. A bed in a large, unsurprising room for three or four people is 105FF; singles/doubles cost 140/120FF per person.

15ème Arrondissement The friendly, down-to-earth *Three Ducks Hostel* (Hostal Trois Canards; ☎ 48.42.04.05; metro Félix Faure), a favourite with young backpackers, is at 6 Place Étienne Pernet, near Rue du Commerce. A bunk bed costs 85FF, and if you don't have your own sheets, there is a one-time charge of 12FF. Telephone reservations are accepted. For information on the mountain bike tours that are run from here, see Bicycle under the Getting Around section that follows. The *Aloha Hostel* (☎ 42.73.03.03; metro Volontaires) at 1 Rue Borromée is about a km west of Gare Montparnasse. It is run by the same people who run the Three Ducks Hostel. Beds cost 75FF and sheets, if you don't have your own, cost 12FF.

Hotels A veritable plague of renovations, redecorations and other improvements has turned many of Paris' finest fleabag hotels into quaint and spotless two-star places where the sheets are changed daily and the receptionists aren't rude. But the guests, who aren't backpackers and students (such people can't afford the new rates), no longer get to meet each other on the landing while waiting for the shower.

Marais (4ème) One of the best deals in town is the *Hôtel Rivoli* (☎ 42.72.08.41; metro Hôtel de Ville) at 44 Rue de Rivoli. Room rates range from 100FF (for singles with running water) to 200FF (for doubles with

bath and toilet). The *Grand Hôtel du Loiret* (☎ 48.87.77.00; metro Hôtel de Ville) is two buildings away at 8 Rue des Mauvais Garçons. Singles/doubles start at 120/140FF. Rooms with shower are 200FF. The friendly *Hôtel de Nice* (☎ 42.78.55.29; metro Hôtel de Ville) at 42bis Rue de Rivoli is a step up in comfort and price. Doubles with a wash-basin cost 220FF, 250FF with a shower and 310FF with a shower and toilet. There is a 16FF charge to use the hall showers.

The *Hôtel Moderne* (☎ 48.87.97.05; metro Saint Paul) at 3 Rue Caron has singles/doubles for 130/150FF with running water, 190FF with a bath and 220FF with both shower and toilet. It does not accept telephone reservations. The *Hôtel Pratic* (☎ 48.87.80.47; metro Saint Paul) is round the corner at 9 Rue d'Ormesson. Rooms cost 120FF with a washbasin, 150 to 160FF with a washbasin and bidet, 180 to 200FF with a bath and 200 to 280FF with both a toilet and a bath. The old but well-maintained and clean *Grand Hôtel Mahler* (☎ 42.72.60.92; metro Saint Paul) is at 5 Rue Mahler. Doubles start at 120FF and cost 150FF with a washbasin and bidet, 200FF with two beds, and 320FF with shower and toilet.

Notre Dame Area (5ème) The run-down *Hôtel du Centre* (☎ 43.26.13.07; metro Saint Michel) at 5 Rue Saint Jacques has very basic singles/doubles starting at 80/110FF. Doubles with shower cost 130 to 180FF, and hall showers are 20FF. They do not accept reservations but reception is open 24 hours a day.

The *Hôtel Esmerelda* (☎ 43.54.19.20; metro Saint Michel) is at 4 Rue Saint Julien le Pauvre, right across the Seine from Notre Dame. Their three 130FF singles are almost always booked up months in advance – other singles/doubles (with shower and toilet) start at 290FF.

Panthéon Area (5ème) The *Hôtel de Médicis* (☎ 43.54.14.66 for reception, 43.29.53.64 for the public phone in the hall; metro Luxembourg), which is at 214 Rue Saint Jacques, is exactly what a dilapidated, cockroach-infested, Latin Quarter dive for impoverished students should be like. Very basic singles start at 75FF, but the cheapest rooms are usually occupied. Basic doubles/triples are 130/210FF. The *Hôtel Gay Lussac* (☎ 43.54.23.96; metro Luxembourg) at 29 Rue Gay Lussac has small singles from 165FF and doubles/triples with shower or toilet for 400/475FF.

Saint Germain des Prés (6ème) The unique and somewhat eccentric *Hôtel de Nesle* (☎ 43.54.62.41; metro Odéon or Mabillon) at 7 Rue de Nesle is a favourite with students and young people from all over the world. Singles cost 200FF, and a bed in a double is 125FF. If you come alone, they'll find you a roommate. The only way to get a place here is to stop by in the morning – 10 or 11 am at the latest, especially in summer. The *Hôtel Petit Trianon* (☎ 43.54.94.64; metro Odéon) at 2 Rue de l'Ancienne Comédie also attracts lots of young travellers. Singles start at 160FF. Doubles/triples with shower and toilet are 350/390FF.

The exceptional *Hôtel Henri IV* (☎ 43.54.44.53; metro Cité or Saint Michel), the only hotel on Île de la Cité, is at 25 Place Dauphine (1er), a quiet square at the western end of the island near Pont Neuf. Perfectly adequate singles without toilet or shower are 125FF, doubles are 155 to 185FF, and hall showers are 14FF. This place is usually booked up months in advance, but the odd cancellation makes it worth giving them a call.

The *Hôtel Saint Michel* (☎ 43.26.98.70; metro Saint Michel) is a block west of Place Saint Michel and a block south of the Seine at 17 Rue Gît le Cœur. Singles/doubles with running water are 195/220FF, including breakfast. A double with shower is 315FF, including breakfast.

Montmartre (18ème) The *Idéal Hôtel* (☎ 46.06.63.63; metro Abbesses) at 3 Rue des Trois Frères has simple but acceptable singles/doubles starting at 120/150FF. A shower is 20FF. The *Hôtel Bonséjour* (☎ 42.54.22.53; metro Abbesses), a block

north of Rue des Abbesses at 11 Rue Burcq, has basic but pleasant singles from 110 to 140FF and doubles for 170FF. The *Hôtel Audran* (☎ 42.58.79.59; metro Abbesses) is on the other side of Rue des Abbesses at 7 Rue Audran. Singles/doubles start at 90/120FF.

The *Hôtel Tholozé* (☎ 46.06.74.83; metro Abbesses) is at 24 Rue Tholozé. Doubles cost 170FF with running water, while doubles/triples with shower and toilet are 240/300FF. The friendly *Hôtel des Arts* (☎ 46.06.30.52; metro Abbesses), which was completely rebuilt in 1991, is down the block at 5 Rue Tholozé. This two-star place has singles/doubles with shower and toilet starting at 310/390FF.

Places to Eat
Restaurants Most of Paris' thousands of restaurants (except those in touristy areas, eg in the Notre Dame Area, near the Louvre and along the Champs Élysées) are, by Parisian standards, pretty good value for the money – the intense competition tends to rid the city quickly of places with bad food or prices that are out of line.

Around Forum des Halles *Léon de Bruxelles* (☎ 42.36.18.50; metro Les Halles) at 120 Rue Rambuteau (1er), which is on the northern side of Forum des Halles, is dedicated to only one thing: the preparation of mussels *(moules)*. Meal-size bowls of mussels start at 59FF. This place is open daily from 11.45 am to midnight (1 am on Friday and Saturday nights). A favourite with *branchés* ('with-it') young Parisians is *Batifol* (☎ 42.36.85.50; metro Les Halles or Étienne Marcel), a bistro at 14 Rue Mondétour (1er), half a block north of Forum des Halles, which is open daily from 11 am to 1 am. Their specialities include *pot au feu* (beef and vegetables cooked in a special kind of pot).

Opéra Area (2ème & 9ème) *Le Drouot* (☎ 42.96.68.23; metro Richelieu Drouot) is on the 1st floor at 103 Rue de Richelieu (2ème), which is 500 metres east of Opéra

FRANCE

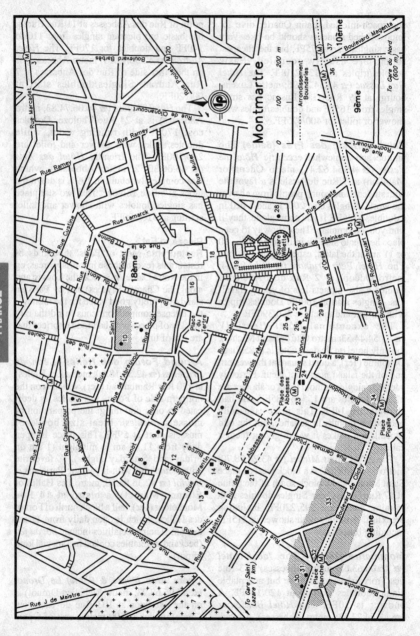

Montmartre

Arrondissement
Boundaries

0   100   200 m

FRANCE

	PLACES TO STAY	2	Museum of Jewish Art	20	Château Rouge Metro
		3	Marcadet Poissonniers		Station
12	Hôtel Tholozé		Metro Station	23	Abbesses Metro Station
13	Hôtel des Arts	5	Place Constantin	24	Post Office & 24-Hour
14	Hôtel Bonséjour		Pecqueur		Currency Exchange
21	Hôtel Audran	6	Cimetière St Vincent		Machine
29	Idéal Hôtel	7	Cimetière de	26	Bureau de Change
			Montmartre		(Exchange Bureau)
▼	PLACES TO EAT	8	Moulin de la Galette	28	Museum of Naive Art
			(Windmill)	30	La Locomotive
4	Franprix Supermarket	9	Moulin Radet (Windmill)		Discothèque
22	Food Shops	10	Vineyard	31	Moulin Rouge Nightclub
25	Refuge des Fondus	11	Museum of Old	32	Blanche Metro Station
	Restaurant		Montmartre	33	Pigalle Sex & Entertain-
27	Raz South Indian Res-	15	Place Émile Goudeau		ment District
	taurant	16	Église Saint Pierre	34	Pigalle Metro Station
		17	Sacré Cœur Basilica	35	Anvers Metro Station
	OTHER	18	Place du Parvis du	36	Barbès Rochechouart
			Sacré Cœur		Metro Station
1	Lamarck Caulaincourt	19	Funicular Railway	37	Barbès Rochechouart
	Metro Station				Metro Station

Garnier. Its décor and ambience haven't changed since the late 1930s. A three-course traditional French meal with wine only costs about 70FF. Le Drouot is open daily from 11.45 am to 3 pm and 6.30 to 10 pm. *Chartier* (☎ 47.70.86.29; metro Rue Montmartre) at 7 Rue du Faubourg Montmartre (9ème), which is under the same management, is famous for its ornate, late 19th century dining room. The prices and fare are similar to Le Drouot. It is open daily from 11 am to 3 pm and 6 to 9.30 pm.

Marais (4ème) The heart of the old Jewish neighbourhood, Rue des Rosiers, has quite a few kosher *(cacher)* and kosher-style restaurants; most are closed on Friday evening, Saturday and Jewish holidays. *Société Rosiers Alimentation* (☎ 48.87.63.60; metro Saint Paul) at 34 Rue des Rosiers has Israeli takeaway food and Middle Eastern snacks such as shwarma *(chawarma)* and felafel. It is open Sunday to Thursday from 10 am (noon for felafel) to 10 pm and on Friday from 10 am until one hour before sunset. The *kosher pizza place* (☎ 48.87.17.83; metro Saint Paul) at 11 Rue des Rosiers is open Monday to Thursday from noon to 4 pm and

7 to 11 pm and on Friday from noon until about 3 pm. A slice costs 14FF.

Paris' best known Jewish restaurant is *Restaurant Jo Goldenberg* (☎ 48.87.20.16, 48.87.70.39; metro Saint Paul) at 7 Rue des Rosiers, founded in 1920. The food is kosher-style but not actually kosher according to Jewish law. The main dishes cost about 70FF. Jo Goldenberg is open from 8.30 am until about midnight daily (including Saturday) except on Yom Kippur (Day of Atonement). The bullet holes in the window date from 1982, when Palestinian gunmen attacked this place, killing six people, including the son of the proprietor.

Marais Plus (☎ 48.87.01.40; metro Saint Paul) at 20 Rue des Francs Bourgeois is a mellow *salon de thé* (tearoom) that specialises in quiches (45FF) and pies (30FF). It is open daily from 10 am to 6.30 pm.

Le P'tit Gavroche (☎ 48.87.74.26; metro Hôtel de Ville) at 15 Rue Sainte Croix de la Bretonnerie, also known as the Bistro du Marais, is a favourite with crowds of raucous working-class regulars. It is open for meals daily except Sunday from noon to 2.30 pm and from 7 pm to midnight. The daily *menu,*

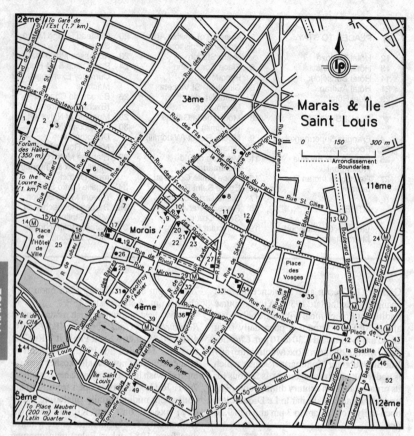

available until about 10 pm or whenever they run out, costs 45FF. Main dishes are also about 45FF.

For vegetarian food, a good bet is *Aquarius* (☎ 48.87.48.71; metro Rambuteau) at 54 Rue Sainte Croix de la Bretonnerie, which has a calming, airy atmosphere that makes you think of fresh bean sprouts. It is open Monday to Saturday from noon to 9.45 pm but the plat du jour is available only from noon to 2 pm and 7 to 9.45 pm. They have a two-course *menu* for 51FF.

Bastille (4ème, 11ème & 12ème) Lots of

ethnic restaurants line Rue de la Roquette (11ème) and Rue de Lappe (11ème), which intersects Rue de la Roquette 200 metres north-east of Place de la Bastille. Among the pizza joints and Chinese, North African and Korean places, you'll find Paris' only fish-and-chip shop, *Hamilton's Fish & Chips* (☎ 48.06.77.92; metro Ledru Rollin) at 51 Rue de Lappe (11ème), which gets good reviews from homesick English expats. It is open Monday to Friday from noon to 2.30 pm and 6.30 pm to midnight (1 am Friday) and on Saturday evening till 1 am.

	PLACES TO STAY	38	Ethnic Restaurants	26	Town Hall of the 4ème Arrondissement
		48	Food Shops		
17	Grand Hôtel du Loiret	49	Bertillon Ice Cream	29	Saint Paul Metro Station
18	Hôtel Rivoli				
19	Hôtel de Nice		OTHER	31	Memorial to the Unknown Jewish Martyr
27	Grand Hôtel Mahler				
28	MIJE Maubisson (hostel)	1	Accueil des Jeunes en France (AJF)	35	Victor Hugo's House
30	Hôtel Pratic	2	Place Georges Pompidou	37	Bastille Metro Station
32	MIJE Fourcy (hostel)			39	Pont Marie Metro Station
34	Hôtel Moderne	3	Centre Pompidou	40	Bastille Metro Station
36	MIJE Fauconnier (hostel)	4	Rambuteau Metro Station	41	Bastille Metro Station
		5	Musée Picasso	42	Banque de France
▼	PLACES TO EAT	8	Musée Cognacq-Jay	43	Bastille Metro Station
		12	Musée Carnavalet	44	Cathédrale Notre Dame
6	Aquarius Vegetarian Restaurant	13	Chemin Vert Metro Station	45	Bastille Metro Station
7	Le P'tit Gavroche Restaurant	14	Hôtel de Ville Metro Station	46	Entrance to Opéra Bastille
9	Finkelsztajn Bakery	15	Hôtel de Ville Metro Station	47	WW II Deportation Memorial
10	Société Rosiers Alimentation	16	Hôtel de Ville Metro Station	50	Sully Morland Metro Station
11	Marais Plus	22	Jewish Neighbourhood	51	Port de Plaisance Paris-Arsenal (Pleasure Boat Port)
20	Finkelsztajn Bakery	24	Bréguet Sabin Metro Station		
21	Kosher Pizza Place			52	Opéra de la Bastille
23	Restaurant Jo Goldenberg	25	City Hall		
33	Food Shops				

FRANCE

Notre Dame Area (4ème, 5ème & 6ème)

The Greek, North African and Middle Eastern restaurants in the area bounded by Rue Saint Jacques, Blvd Saint Germain, Blvd Saint Michel and the Seine attract mainly foreign tourists, unaware that some people refer to Rue de la Huchette (and nearby streets such as Rue Saint Séverin and Rue de la Harpe) as 'bacteria alley' because of the high incidence of food poisoning among those who yield to the blandishments of the door attendants. Although you'll probably be better off if you give a miss to the establishments that ripen their meat and seafood in the front window, it is still possible to get a cheap, decent meal around here.

L'Année du Dragon (☎ 46.34.23.46; metro Saint Michel) at 10 Rue Saint Séverin (5ème), which serves Chinese and Vietnamese food, has *menus* for as little as 35FF. It is open daily from noon to 2.30 pm and 6.30 to 11 pm. Sandwich shops sell baguette halves and thirds with various fillings for around 17FF, and there's always *McDonald's* (metro Cluny-La Sorbonne) at the corner of Blvd Saint Germain and Rue de la Harpe (5ème).

East of Rue Saint Jacques, *Au Coin des Gourmets* (☎ 43.26.12.92; metro Maubert Mutualité) at 5 Rue Dante (5ème) serves superb Cambodian food, much of it gently seasoned with lemon grass *(citronelle)* and coconut milk *(lait de coco)*. This place is open daily except Tuesday from noon to 2.30 pm and 7 to 10.30 pm. Reservations are recommended.

For a delightful selection of scrumptious Central European pastries and *tourtes* (quiche-like pies), drop by *Pâtisserie Viennoise* (☎ 43.26.60.48; metro Cluny-La Sorbonne) at 8 Rue de l'École de Médicine (6ème), which is on the other side of Blvd Saint Michel from the Musée de Cluny. It is open Monday to Friday from 9 am to 7.15 pm but is closed from mid-July to the end of August.

Panthéon (5ème) The area around Rue Mouffetard is filled with dozens of places to eat and is especially popular with students. Some of the best discount *crêpes* in Paris are sold in a little stall across the street from 68 Rue Mouffetard, which is open from 11 am to 2 am. A delicious crêpe full of cheese is only 12FF.

Restaurant Cous-Cous (☎ 43.26.66.43; metro Monge) at 6 Rue Mouffetard, also known as La Rose Mouffetard, serves some of the cheapest sit-down food in town, including generous portions of tasty couscous starting at only 25FF. This place is open daily from 11 am to midnight.

For Tibetan food, a good choice is *Tashi Delek* (☎ 43.26.55.55; metro Luxembourg) at 4 Rue des Fossés Saint Jacques, which is open from noon to 2.30 pm and 7 to 10.00 pm daily except Sunday (all day) and Monday (midday). Lunch/dinner *menus* cost 55/105FF.

Montmartre (18ème) There are dozens of cafés and restaurants around Place du Tertre but they tend to be touristy and overpriced.

An old Montmartre favourite is *Refuge des Fondues* (☎ 42.55.22.65; metro Abbesses) at 17 Rue des Trois Frères, whose speciality is fondues. For 80FF, you get wine (in a baby bottle) and a good quantity of either fondue Savoyarde (cheese) or fondue Bourguignonne (meat). It's open daily from 7 pm to 2 am. Make reservations a couple of days in advance. *Raz* (☎ 42.59.88.80; metro Abbesses), a South Indian restaurant at 11 Rue des Trois Frères, is open daily from 5.30 pm to 2 am. This place has *menus* for 59 and 75FF.

University Restaurants The Centre Régional des Œuvres Universitaires et Scolaires, or CROUS (☎ 40.51.37.10), runs 17 *restaurants universitaires* (student cafeterias) around Paris. Tickets (on sale at mealtimes) for institutional but filling cafeteria meals cost 11.50FF for students and 21.40FF for nonstudents. Some of the restaurants also have à la carte brasseries. In general, CROUS restaurants have rather confusing opening times that change according to rotational agreements among the restaurants and school holiday schedules (eg most are closed on weekends and during July and August).

Restaurant Universitaire Bullier (metro Port Royal) is in the Centre Jean Sarrailh at 39 Rue Bernanos (2nd floor; 5ème). Lunch and dinner are served Monday to Friday and, during some months, on weekends as well (days and times are posted). The ticket window, which is up one flight of stairs, is open from 11.30 am to 2 pm and 6 to 8 pm. One of the nicest CROUS restaurants in town is on the 7th floor of the Faculté de Droit et des Sciences Économiques (Faculty of Law and Economics; metro Vavin), which is south of the Jardin du Luxembourg at 92 Rue Assas (6ème). The ticket window is on the 6th floor. For security reasons, you may have to present student identification at the building entrance.

Pubs *Le Cloître* (☎ 43.25.19.92; metro Saint Michel) at 19 Rue Saint Jacques (5ème) is an unpretentious, relaxed place whose mellow background music seems to please the young Parisians who congregate here. It is open daily from 3 pm to 2 am. Informal, friendly *Polly Maggoo* (☎ 46.33.33.64; metro Saint Michel), up the street at 11 Rue Saint Jacques (5ème), was founded in 1967 and still plays music from that era. It is open daily from 3 pm to 4 or 5 am – it's one of the few nightspots with a police licence to stay open after 2 am.

Another favourite with Anglo-Saxons is a rather loud and dirty American-style bar named *Le Violon Dingue* (☎ 43.25.79.93; Maubert-Mutualité), which is at 46 Rue de la Montagne Sainte Geneviève (5ème). It is open daily from 6 pm to 2 am.

Self-Catering Buying your own food is one of the best ways to keep the cost of staying in Paris down. Supermarkets are always cheaper than small grocery shops.

Food Markets The very freshest and best-quality fruits, vegetables, cheeses and meats at the lowest prices in town are on offer at Paris' neighbourhood food markets. The city's dozen covered marketplaces are open from 8 am to sometime between 12.30 and 1.30 pm and from 3.30 or 4 to 7.30 pm daily except Sunday afternoon and Monday. The open-air markets – about 60 of which are scattered throughout the city – are set up two or three mornings a week in public squares and are open from 7 am to 1 pm. For details on the market nearest your hotel or hostel, ask anyone who lives in the neighbourhood.

Notre Dame Area (5ème) On Île Saint Louis, there are boulangeries, fromageries and fruit and vegetable shops on Rue Saint Louis en l'Île and Rue des Deux Ponts (4ème).

Fresh bread and superb pastries are available two blocks south of Notre Dame at the boulangerie (metro Maubert-Mutualité) at 10 Rue Lagrange (5ème). It is open Tuesday to Sunday from 7.15 am to 8 pm.

There is a cluster of food shops in the vicinity of Place Maubert (5ème; metro Maubert-Mutualité), which is 300 metres south of Notre Dame, and on Rue Lagrange. On Tuesday, Thursday and Saturday from 7 am to 1 pm, Place Maubert is transformed into an outdoor produce market. The excellent fromagerie (metro Maubert-Mutualité) at 47 Blvd Saint Germain (5ème) is open daily except Sunday afternoon and Monday from 7 am to 1 pm and 3.30 to 7.30 pm.

Saint Germain des Prés (6ème) The largest cluster of food shops in the neighbourhood is one block north of Blvd Saint Germain around the intersection of Rue de Buci and Rue de Seine. There are also food shops along Rue Dauphine and the two streets that link it with Blvd Saint Germain, Rue de l'Ancienne Comédie and Rue de Buci. The boulangerie (metro Odéon) at 10 Rue de l'Ancienne Comédie is open 24 hours a day every day of the week except from 6 am to 9 pm on Sunday.

Panthéon Area (5ème) There are several food shops (metro Luxembourg) along Rue Saint Jacques between No 172 and No 218 (the area just south of Rue Soufflot). At 198 Rue Saint Jacques, there's a fromagerie and a *Nicolas* wine shop. There's a boulangerie nearby at 16 Rue des Fossés Saint Jacques.

Marais (4ème) Fresh breads and Jewish-style Central European pastries are available at the two *Finkelsztajn* bakeries (metro Saint Paul), which are at 27 Rue des Rosiers and across the street from 32 Rue des Rosiers. One or the other is open daily except Tuesday.

There are quite a few food shops on Rue de Rivoli and Rue Saint Antoine around the Saint Paul metro stop. There's a boulangerie at 109 Rue Saint Antoine (closed Sunday), a fruit and vegetables shop at 97-99 Rue Saint Antoine, and a wine shop at 95 Rue Saint Antoine.

Louvre Area (1er) You'll find a number of food shops one block north of where the western part of the Louvre meets the eastern end of Jardin des Tuileries. There's *Félix Potin* grocery (closed Sunday; metro Tuileries) at 205 Rue Saint Honoré (1er) and a boulangerie (closed Tuesday; metro Tuileries) at 302 Rue Saint Honoré.

Arc de Triomphe Area (8ème, 16ème & 17ème) *Fromager de l'Étoile* (closed Sunday and Monday; metro Charles de Gaulle Étoile, Grande Armée exit) is one block north-west of the Arc de Triomphe at 11 Ave de la Grande Armée (16ème). The boulangerie (metro Argentine) a couple blocks farther west at 36 Ave de la Grande Armée (17ème) is open daily except Friday.

Montmartre (18ème) Most of the food shops in this area are along Rue des Abbesses, which is about 500 metres south-west of Sacré Cœur. *Fromagerie Tissot* (metro Abbesses) at 32 Rue des Abbesses is open from 8.30 am to 1 pm and 4 to 8 pm daily except Monday afternoon and Sunday.

FRANCE

Entertainment

Information in French on cultural events, concerts (classical, jazz, etc), theatre performances, films, museum exhibitions, festivals, circuses, etc is listed in three publications that come out each Wednesday: *Pariscope* (3FF), *L'Officiel des Spectacles* (2FF) and *7 à Paris* (7FF). All are available at newspaper kiosks.

Tickets Reservations and ticketing for all sorts of cultural events are handled by the ticket outlets in the FNAC stores at 136 Rue de Rennes (6ème; ☎ 49.54.30.00; metro Saint Placide) and on the -3 Level of the Forum des Halles shopping mall (1er; ☎ 40.41.40.00; metro Châtelet-Les Halles).

Cinemas The fashionable cinemas on Blvd du Montparnasse (6ème & 14ème; metro Montparnasse Bienvenue) and nearby streets show mostly dubbed *(v.f.)* feature films. There's another cluster of cinemas near Carrefour de l'Odéon (6ème; metro Odéon) and lots more movie theatres along the Ave des Champs Élysées (8ème; metro George V) and along Blvd Saint Germain (6ème; metro Saint Germain des Prés). The *Cinémathèque* (☎ 47.04.24.24; metro Trocadéro), which is in the north-eastern tip of the Palais de Chaillot (the end nearest Ave Albert de Mun) almost always leaves its foreign offerings undubbed.

Parisian movie-going is rather pricey. Expect to pay around 40FF for a ticket. Students and people under 18 and over 60 usually get discounts of about 25% except on Friday, Saturday and Sunday nights. On Monday, most cinemas give discounts to everyone.

Discothèques A *discothèque*, as distinct from a 'disco' in English, is just about any sort of place where music leads to dancing. The discothèques favoured by the Parisian 'in' crowd change frequently, and many are officially private, which means that the (often thug-like) bouncers can refuse entry to whomever they don't like the look of. Single men may not be admitted simply because they're single men, even if they are properly dressed. Women, on the other hand, get in free on some nights. Get the picture? None of this comes cheap: expect to pay at least 50FF on weekdays and 100FF on weekends.

Le Balajo (☎ 47.00.07.87; metro Bastille), a mainstay of the Parisian dance-hall scene since the time of Edith Piaf, is at 9 Rue de Lappe (11ème), two blocks north-east of Place de la Bastille. It offers accordion music on Monday, Friday, Saturday and Sunday afternoons from 3 to 6.30 pm and dancing on Monday, Thursday, Friday and Saturday nights from 11 pm to 5 am. During the day it costs 50/20FF with an alcoholic/nonalcoholic drink. At night admission is 100FF and includes one drink. Women get in for free on Monday and Thursday from 11 pm to 12.30 am.

La Locomotive (☎ 42.57.37.37; metro Blanche) at 90 Blvd de Clichy (18ème), which is in Pigalle next to the Moulin Rouge nightclub, occupies three floors, each offering a different ambience and a different kind of music (especially rock). It is open from 11 pm until 6 am nightly except Monday. Entry costs 60FF from Tuesday to Thursday and 100FF on Friday and Saturday nights, including one drink. On Sunday nights men pay 60FF and women get in for free.

Jazz For the latest on jazz happenings in town, check the listings (see Information at the beginning of the Paris section). *Caveau de la Huchette* (☎ 43.26.65.05; metro Saint Michel) at 5 Rue de la Huchette (5ème) is an old favourite which has live jazz. It is open every night from 9.30 pm to 2.30 am (Sunday to Thursday nights), 3 am (Friday night) or 4 am (Saturday and holiday nights). From Sunday to Thursday, entry costs 55FF (50FF for students), 60FF on Friday and 65FF on Saturday and public holidays.

Concerts & Opera Paris always has all sorts of orchestra, organ and chamber music concerts, especially during the warmer half of the year. Some are even free, such as the Sunday afternoon organ concerts at Notre

Dame (see Île de la Cité under Things to See).

Opéra Bastille (☎ 43.43.96.96; metro Bastille) at 2-6 Place de la Bastille (12ème) has been Paris' main opera house since its opening in 1989. The old opera house, *Opéra Garnier* (☎ 40.01.19.70 for information, 47.42.53.71 for reservations; metro Opéra) at Place de l'Opéra (9ème) now stages concerts and ballets. The cheapest regular tickets, which get you a seat with an obstructed view high above the stage, cost as little as 15 to 30FF. Subject to availability, people under 25 and over 65 may be able to purchase decent seats 15 minutes before the curtain rises for the 60FF *tarif spécial*.

Things to Buy

Fashionable Shopping Streets For fashionable clothing and accessories, some of the fanciest shops in Paris are along Ave Montaigne (1er) Rue Saint Honoré (1er), Rue du Faubourg Saint Honoré (8ème) and Rue de Rivoli (1er), and around Place Vendôme (1er). Rue de Rivoli gets less expensive as you move east into the 4ème. Rue Bonaparte (9ème) offers a good choice of mid-range boutiques.

Department Stores Right behind Opéra Garnier are two of Paris' largest department stores. Printemps (metro Havre Caumartin) at 64 Blvd Haussmann (9ème) is open Monday to Saturday from 9.35 am to 7 pm. Galeries Lafayette (metro Auber or Chaussée) at 40 Blvd Haussmann (9ème) is housed in two adjacent buildings linked by a pedestrian bridge. It is open Monday to Saturday from 9.30 am to 6.45 pm. The third of Paris' 'big three' department stores, Samaritaine (☎ 40.41.20.20; metro Pont Neuf), consists of four buildings between Pont Neuf and Rue de Rivoli. It is open from 9.30 am to 7 pm (10 pm on Thursday) daily except Sunday. There is an amazing view of the city centre from the 9th and 10th floor terraces of Building 2 at 19 Rue de la Monnaie.

Getting There & Away

Air Paris has two major international airports. Aéroport d'Orly is 16 km south of central Paris. For flight and other information, call ☎ 49.75.15.15 between 6 am and 11.45 pm. Aéroport Charles de Gaulle, also known as Roissy-Charles de Gaulle because it is in the Paris suburb of Roissy, is 27 km north of central Paris. Flight and other information is available from 6 am to 11.30 pm on ☎ 48.62.22.80.

See Travel Agencies under Information at the start of the Paris section for details on where to buy discounted air tickets. Paris' airline offices include:

Air France	☎ 45.35.61.61
Air Inter, the domestic carrier	☎ 45.46.90.00
American Airlines	☎ 05.23.00.35
British Airways	☎ 47.78.14.14
Continental Airlines	☎ 42.25.31.81
Delta Air Lines	☎ 47.68.92.92
Northwest Airlines	☎ 42.66.90.00
Qantas Airways	☎ 42.66.53.05
Singapore Airlines	☎ 45.53.90.90
Thai Airway International	☎ 44.20.70.80
Tower Air	☎ 40.13.80.80
TWA	☎ 47.20.62.11
United Airlines	☎ 48.97.82.82
UTA	☎ 40.17.44.44

Bus The Gare Routière Internationale (international bus terminal; ☎ 40.38.93.93; metro Porte de la Villette), Eurolines' Paris headquarters, is at 3-5 Ave de la Porte de la Villette (19ème) in the city's north-eastern corner. It is open daily from 9 am to 7 pm. Eurolines has bus service to Amsterdam (240FF one-way; eight hours), Istanbul (805FF one-way; 69 hours), London (310FF one-way; nine hours), Madrid (485FF; 17 hours), Rome (570FF one-way; 26 hours) and many other European cities. Students or people aged under 26 receive a discount of 30%. The Eurolines ticketing office (☎ 43.54.11.99; metro Cluny-La Sorbonne) at 55 Rue Saint Jacques (5ème) is open Tuesday to Saturday from 9.30 am to 1 pm and 2.30 to 7 pm.

There is no domestic intercity bus service to or from Paris.

FRANCE

Train Paris has six major train stations (gares), each of which handles traffic to different parts of France and Europe. For information on trains departing from any of the stations, call ☎ 45.82.08.41 (English) or 45.82.50.50 (French). For reservations (French), call ☎ 45.65.60.60. The switchboards are staffed from 8 am to 9 pm. All the stations have exchange bureaus and there is a tourist office annexe at each of the stations except Gare Saint Lazare. The metro station attached to each train station bears the same name as the train station.

Paris' major train stations are:

1. Gare d'Austerlitz on Blvd de l'Hôpital (13ème; metro Gare d'Austerlitz): trains to the Loire Valley, Spain and Portugal and non-TGV trains to south-western France (Bordeaux, the Basque Country, etc).

2. Gare de l'Est at the northern end of Blvd de Strasbourg (10ème; metro Gare de l'Est): trains to parts of France east of Paris (Champagne, Alsace, Lorraine, Troyes), Luxembourg, parts of Switzerland (Basel, Lucerne, Zürich), southern Germany (Frankfurt, Munich) and points further east.

3. Gare de Lyon on Blvd Diderot (12ème; metro Gare de Lyon): regular and TGV Sud-Est trains to points south-east of Paris, including Dijon, Lyons, Provence, the Côte d'Azur, the Alps, parts of Switzerland (Bern, Geneva, Lausanne), Italy and points beyond.

4. Gare Montparnasse at the intersection of Ave du Maine and Blvd de Vaugirard (15ème; metro Montparnasse Bienvenue): trains to Brittany and places on the way (Chartres, Angers, Nantes); and the TGV Atlantique, which serves Tours, Bordeaux and other places in south-western France.

5. Gare du Nord on Rue de Dunkerque (10ème; metro Gare du Nord): trains to northern France (Lille, Calais), the UK, Belgium, northern Germany, Scandinavia, Moscow, etc; and the new TGV Nord, which will serve Calais and, via the Chunnel, London. Be especially vigilant here for pickpockets, con artists and thieves.

6. Gare Saint Lazare at 13 Rue d'Amsterdam (8ème; metro Saint Lazare): trains to Normandy (and, via the Channel ports and in coordination with ferries, to England). The SNCF information office, which is 50 metres behind Voie 2 (track 2), also tries to help tourists with nontrain matters in the absence of a municipal tourist office annexe.

Getting Around
Paris' public transit system, RATP, is one of the most efficient in the world. It's also one of the Western world's great urban transport bargains (see Metro/Bus Tickets). Free metro/RER/bus maps are available at the ticket windows of metro/RER stations and at tourist offices. For information on metros and RER commuter trains and buses, call ☎ 43.46.14.14 between 6 am and 9 pm.

To/From the Airports There is a variety of quick and reasonably priced ways to get from the airports into the city and vice versa.

Orly Orly Rail is the quickest way to get to the Left Bank and the 16ème. Take the free shuttle bus to the Pont de Rungis-Aéroport d'Orly RER (commuter rail) station, which is on the C2 line, and get on a train (25FF) heading into the city. A faster (and much more expensive) way into town is to hop on the Orlyval shuttle train (55FF, including the 24FF RER fare); it stops near Orly Sud's Porte F and links Orly with the Antony RER station, which is on line B4. Orly Bus (23FF or six bus/metro tickets), takes you to the Denfert-Rochereau Metro Station (14ème). Air France buses charge 32FF to take you to Gare Montparnasse (15ème) or the Aérogare des Invalides, which is next to Esplanade des Invalides (7ème). Jet Bus, which costs 17FF, takes you to the Villejuif Louis Aragon metro stop. RATP bus No 183 (four tickets) goes to Porte de Choisy (13ème) but is very slow.

All the services between Orly Airport and Paris run every 15 minutes or so (less frequently late at night) from early in the morning (sometime between 5.30 and 6.30 am) to 11 or 11.30 pm.

Charles de Gaulle (CDG) The fastest way to get to/from the city is by Roissy Rail. Free shuttle buses take you from the airport terminals to the Roissy-Aéroport Charles de Gaulle RER (commuter rail) station. You can buy tickets to CDG (33FF) at RER stations. If you get on at an ordinary metro station you have three options: you can buy a ticket when you change to the RER; pay at the other end or on the train if you get caught; or jump the barrier once there (as the locals do). Air France buses (48FF) go to Porte Maillot (16ème & 17ème; metro Porte Maillot) and the corner of Ave Carnot near the Arc de Triomphe (17ème). RATP bus No 350 goes to Gare du Nord (10ème) and Gare de l'Est (10ème). Until 9.15 pm (heading into the city) and 8.20 am (towards the airport), RATP bus No 351 goes to Ave du Trône (11ème & 12ème), on the eastern side of Place de la Nation. Both RATP buses require six tickets.

Unless otherwise indicated, the buses and trains from CDG to Paris run from sometime between 5 and 6.30 am until 11 or 11.30 pm.

Bus Paris' extensive bus network tends to get overlooked by visitors, in part because the metro is so quick, efficient and easy to use. Bus routes are indicated on the RATP map *Grand Plan de Paris*, which is available for free at many metro stations.

Short trips cost one bus/metro/RER ticket (see Metro/Bus Tickets), while longer rides require two. Special tickets valid only on the bus can be purchased from the driver. Whatever kind of ticket you have, you must cancel *(oblitérer)* it in the *composteur* (cancelling machine) next to the driver. The fines are hefty if you're caught without a ticket or without a cancelled ticket. If you have a Carte Orange, Formule 1 or Paris Visite pass (see the following Metro/Bus Tickets section), just flash it at the driver when you board – do *not* cancel your *coupon* (ticket).

After the metro shuts down at around 12.45 am, the Noctambus network, whose symbol is a black owl silhouetted against a yellow circle (the moon), links the Châtelet-Hôtel de Ville area (4ème) with lots of places on the Right Bank (served by lines A to H) and a few destinations on the Left Bank (served by lines J and R). Buses begin their runs from the even-numbered side of Ave Victoria (4ème), which is between the Hôtel de Ville and Place du Châtelet, every hour on the half-hour from 1.30 to 5.30 am. A ride requires three tickets (four tickets if your journey involves a transfer).

Metro & RER Paris' underground rail network consists of two separate but linked systems: the Métropolitain, known as the metro, which has 13 lines and over 300 stations, many marked by Hector Guimard's famous noodle-like Art-Nouveau entrances; and the suburban commuter rail network, the RER, which, along with certain SNCF lines, is divided into eight concentric zones. The term 'metro' is used in this chapter to refer to the Métropolitain and any part of the RER system within Paris proper. Free metro maps are available at metro ticket windows.

The whole system has been designed so that no point in Paris is more than 500 metres from a metro stop; some places in the city centre are within a few hundred metres of up to three stations. You may be able to reduce the number of transfers you'll have to make (and thus get there faster) by going to a station a bit farther on from your destination.

For metro stations to avoid late at night, see Dangers & Annoyances earlier in the Paris section.

How It Works Each metro train is known by the name of its end-of-the-line terminal stop, which means that trains on the same line have different names depending on which direction they are travelling in. For instance, trains on the line that links Porte de Clignancourt with Porte d'Orléans are known as *direction Porte de Clignancourt* when heading one way and *direction Porte d'Orléans* when going in the opposite direction. On metro lines that split into several branches and thus have more than one end-of-the-line station, the final destination of each train is indicated on the front, sides and interior of the train cars, usually by illuminating the relevant panel. In the stations, white-on-blue *sortie* signs indicate exits and black-on-orange *correspondance* signs show how to get to connecting trains.

The last metro train sets out on its final run at 12.30 am. Plan ahead so as not to miss your connecting train(s). After about midnight, metro travel becomes free – the authorities open the gates next to the turnstiles and stop checking for invalid tickets. The metro resumes functioning at 5.30 am.

Metro/Bus Tickets The same blue 2nd-class tickets are valid on the metro, the bus and, for travel within the Paris city limits, the RER's 2nd-class carriages (1st-class carriages have the numeral 1 painted next to the doors). They cost 6FF if bought separately and 36.50FF for a *carnet* (booklet) of 10. For children aged four to nine a carnet of 10 costs 18FF. One ticket lets you travel between any two metro stations, including stations outside of the Paris city limits, no matter how many transfers are required. You can also use it on the RER commuter rail system for travel within Paris (within zone 1). For travel on the RER to destinations outside the city, purchase a special ticket *before* you board the train or you won't be able to get out of the station and could be fined when you arrive at your destination. Always keep your ticket until you reach your destination and exit the station; if you're caught without a ticket, or with an invalid one, you'll be fined.

A weekly and monthly bus/metro/RER pass, known as the Carte Orange, is available for travel in two to eight urban and suburban zones. The weekly ticket *(coupon semaine)*, which costs 57FF for travel in zones 1 and 2 (which cover all of Paris proper plus a few RER stops in the inner suburbs), is valid all week. Another weekly ticket *(carte hébdomadaire; 37FF)* gets you two journeys a day for six days of the week. The validity of the monthly *(mensuel)* ticket (201FF for zones 1 and 2), begins on the first day of each calendar month. By law, you *must* write your name on the Carte Orange and the number of your Carte Orange on your weekly/monthly ticket *(coupon)*. The Carte Orange and the weekly/monthly tickets are nontransferable.

The Formule 1 and Paris Visite passes, designed to facilitate bus, metro and RER travel for tourists, are on sale in many metro stations, all six train stations and both international airports. The Formule 1 card and its *coupon* allow unlimited travel for one day in two to four zones. The version valid for zones 1 and 2 costs 25FF. The four-zone version (47FF) lets you go all the way out to Versailles and both airports. Paris Visite passes are valid for three consecutive days of travel in either three or four zones. The 1-to-3 zone version costs 85/135FF (three/five days). Paris Visite is much dearer than a weekly two-zone Carte Orange ticket.

Taxi Paris' 15,000 taxis have a reputation for paying little heed to riders' convenience or the official taxi regulations. People often report being refused a ride because the driver didn't feel like going to the destination they wanted. Another common complaint is that it can be difficult to find a taxi late at night (after 11 pm) or in the rain. The meter begins at 10FF; within the city, it costs 2.62FF per km between 7 am and 7.30 pm Monday to Saturday. On nights, Sunday and holidays, it's 4.08FF per km. Tips are not obligatory, but no matter what the fare is, usual tips range from a minimum of 2FF to a maximum of 5FF; the average tip is 3 or 4FF.

It is possible to try to flag down a taxi anywhere, but the easiest way to find one is to walk to the nearest *tête de station* (taxi stand), indicated on any of the Michelin 1:10,000 maps of Paris. Radio-dispatched taxis include Taxis Bleus (☎ 49.36.10.10); G7 Radio (☎ 47.39.47.39); Alpha Taxis (☎ 45.85.85.85); Taxis-Radio Étoile (☎ 42.70.41.41); and Artaxi (☎ 42.41.50.50). If you order a taxi by phone, the meter is switched on as soon as the driver gets word of your call, wherever that may be, which is usually not too far from where you are.

Car & Motorbike Driving in Paris is nerve-racking but not impossible by any means except for the insecure, faint-hearted or indecisive. Most side streets are one-way *(sens unique)* and, without a good map, trying to get around town by car will make you feel like a rat in a maze crowded with other rats. In general, the best way to get across the city is via one of the major boulevards, unless, of course, it's rush hour and traffic has come to a standstill. Then all you can do is find a parking and take the metro, except that if you're in one of the central arrondissements of the city it won't be easy finding a parking, and, even if you do, you'll have to come back within two hours to plug the meter...

The ultimate test of Parisian driving is the 10-lane roundabout that swirls around the Arc de Triomphe in utter anarchy, especially at rush hour. Don't forget to give priority to cars approaching from the right *(priorité à droite)*. Except when it's clogged by traffic, the fastest way to get all the way across Paris is usually the Blvd Périphérique, the ring road (beltway) that encircles the city.

Rental A car (☎ 43.79.76.48; metro Porte de Vincennes) at 77 Rue de Lagny (20ème) has Fiat Pandas with 100 free km for 218FF (with a 3500FF excess) or 253FF (with a 500FF excess) a day, including comprehensive insurance. Weekly rates are 1523FF with 700 free km, including 35FF a day to reduce the excess to 500FF. Additional km cost 1.15FF each. Acar's office is open Monday to Saturday from 8 am to 7 pm. It's a good idea to reserve in advance, especially for public holiday weekends and during the summer. Rent A Car (☎ 43.45.98.99), whose offices are at 79 Rue de Bercy (12ème; metro Bercy) and 84 Ave de Versailles (16ème; metro Mirabeau), has Fiat Pandas with unlimited km for 268FF a day, including insurance and a 69FF-a-day charge to bring the excess down to 1200FF. The weekly rate is 1495FF. The Rue de Bercy office is open Monday to Friday from 8 am to 7 pm and on Saturday from 9 am to 1 pm and 2 to 7 pm.

Avis (☎ 45.50.32.31) has offices at all six train stations, both airports and several other locations around the Paris area. Europcar (☎ 30.43.82.82) has bureaus at both airports and almost 20 other places around the city. Hertz (☎ 47.88.51.51) also has offices at the airports and at many other locations around Paris.

For information on purchase/repurchase plans, see the Getting Around section at the start of this chapter.

Bicycle Paris, with its heavy traffic and impatient drivers, is not particularly suited to cycling. Except in the Bois de Boulogne (see Bois de Boulogne under Things to See in the Paris section), very few places rent bicycles.

Mountain Bike Trip (☎ 48.42.57.87; metro Félix Faure), based in the Three Ducks Hostel (☎ 48.42.04.05) at 6 Place Étienne Pernet (15ème), runs well-reviewed six-hour mountain bike tours of Paris in English for 118FF, including rental. Phone to reserve a place between 8 am and 9 pm the day before you'd like to go. Mountain Bike Trip also rents mountain bikes for 90FF a day.

Around Paris

The region surrounding Paris is known as the Île de France (Island of France) because of its position between four rivers: the Aube, the Marne, the Oise and the Seine. It was from this relatively small area that, starting around 1100, the kingdom of France began to expand. Today, the region's proximity to Paris and a number of remarkable sights, including Versailles and Chartres, make it an especially popular day-trip destination for people staying in Paris.

VERSAILLES
Versailles, site of the grandest and most famous chateau in all of France, served as the country's political capital and the seat of the royal court for almost the entire period from 1682 until 1789, when Revolutionary mobs massacred the palace guard and dragged Louis XVI and Marie-Antoinette off to Paris, where they were later guillotined. After the Franco-Prussian War of 1870-71, the victorious Prussians proclaimed the establishment of the German empire from the chateau's Galerie des Glaces (Hall of Mirrors), the same room where, in 1919, the Treaty of Versailles officially ended WW I

and imposed harsh conditions on a defeated Germany.

Because many people consider Versailles one of those must-see destinations, the chateau is often overrun with tourists, especially in summer and most especially on summer Sundays. During the summer tourist season, the best way to avoid the lines is to arrive first thing in the morning.

Information

The tourist office (☎ 39.50.36.22) is at 7 Rue des Réservoirs, just north of the northern end of the chateau's façade. From October to April, it is open Monday to Saturday from 9 am to 6.15 pm. During the rest of the year, it is open daily from 9 am to 7 pm. From May to September, the tourist office has a *stand d'information* (☎ 30.84.76.61) in two tents pitched in the Place d'Armes near the chateau gates. The tents are staffed from 9 am to 7 pm.

Books Unless you have some sense of the historical and aesthetic context of what you're seeing, Versailles can seem like little more than a series of gaudy, gilded rooms. If you opt not to take a tour (see Guided Tours), a chateau guidebook – several of which are on sale near the ticket counters – is an excellent investment, especially if a number of people will be using it. The Michelin green guide to the Île de France, which is available in English, has a detailed entry on Versailles.

Château de Versailles

The enormous Château de Versailles (☎ 30.84.74.00) was built in the mid-17th century during the reign of Louis XIV, the Sun King, to project both at home and abroad the absolute power of the French monarchy, then at the height of its autocratic splendour. Among the advantages of Versailles was its distance from the political intrigues of Paris – out here, away from the city, it was much easier for the king to keep an eye on his scheming nobles. The plan worked brilliantly, all the more so because court life turned the nobles into sycophantic courtiers

who expended most of their energy vying for royal favour.

The chateau consists of four main parts: the main palace building, which is a classical structure with innumerable wings, sumptuous bedchambers and grand halls; the vast 17th century gardens, laid out in the formal French style; and two out-palaces, the late 17th century Grand Trianon and the mid-18th century Petit Trianon.

Opening Hours & Tickets The main building is open daily except Monday from 9 am to 5.30 pm (6.30 pm from May to September). It does not close on public holidays except for 1 January, 1 May, 8 May and 25 December.

Entrance to the **Grands Appartements** (State Apartments), which include the 73-metre-long **Galerie des Glaces** (Hall of Mirrors) and the **Appartement de la Reine** (Queen's Suite), costs 31FF (16FF reduced rate). Everyone pays 16FF on Sunday. Tickets are on sale at Entrée A (Entrance A; also known as Porte A), which, as you approach the building, is off to the right from the equestrian statue of Louis XIV. You won't be able to visit other parts of the main palace unless you take one of the guided tours (see Guided Tours, below).

Entrée H has facilities for the handicapped, including a lift.

The Grand Trianon, which costs 17FF (9FF reduced rate), is open daily except Monday. From October to April, opening hours are 9.45 am to noon and 2 to 5 pm. During the rest of the year, hours are 11 am to 6.30 pm. The Petit Trianon, also open daily except Monday, costs 12FF (7FF reduced rate). From October to April, it is open from 2 to 5.30 pm; during the rest of the year, hours are 11 am to 6.30 pm.

The gardens are open every day of the week (unless it's snowing) from 7 am to nightfall (ie sometime between 5.30 and 9.30 pm, depending on the season). Entry is free *except* on Sundays from May to September when the fountains are in operation (the Grandes Eaux show takes place from 3.30 to 5 pm). Admission then costs 18FF.

It may be worthwhile purchasing a Carte Musées et Monuments (55/110/160FF for one/three/five consecutive days), which allows you to visit the main building and the Trianons as well as more than 60 other museums and monuments in Paris and the Île de France. See Museum Hours & Discounts under Things to See in the Paris section for details.

Guided Tours Guided tours *(visites guidées)* in English of the **Appartement du Roi** (King's Suite) leave from Entrée C and cost 37FF (29FF reduced rate and on Sunday). Most of the time there are guides, but because of a shortage of staff some guests have to make do with recorded commentary. Given the layout of the building, it's probably best to take this tour before exploring the Grands Appartements.

Seven other smaller tours *(petites visites)*, three of which (including the **Opéra**) are available in English, begin at Entrée F. Each one costs 20FF in addition to the regular entry fee. To buy tickets and make advance reservations for the petites visites, go to Entrée D.

A cassette-guided tour of the Grands Appartements is available at Entrée A for 25FF (in addition to the entry fee).

Other Sights
The city of Versailles is filled with all sorts of beautiful and interesting buildings from the 17th and 18th centuries. The tourist office has a brochure of *promenades historiques* (historic walks) indicating the location of over two dozen of these structures, including the **Jeu de Paume** (open on Saturday during July and August only from 2 to 4.30 pm) on Rue du Jeu de Paume, where the representatives of the Third Estate constituted themselves as a National Assembly in June 1789; the **Musée Lambinet** (☎ 39.50.30.32) at 54 Blvd de la Reine (open Tuesday to Sunday from 2 to 6 pm); and mid-18th century **Cathédrale Saint Louis** at Place Saint Louis.

Getting There & Away
Bus Bus No 171 takes you from the Pont de Sèvres metro stop in Paris all the way to Place d'Armes, right in front of the chateau.

Train Versailles, which is 23 km south-west of central Paris, has three train stations: Versailles-Rive Gauche, Versailles-Chantiers and Versailles-Rive Droite. Each is served by one of the three rail services that link Versailles with Paris. For schedule information, contact RER or SNCF in Paris (see Getting There & Away and Getting Around in the Paris section).

RER line C5 takes you from Paris' Gare d'Austerlitz and various other RER stations on the Left Bank (including Saint Michel and Champ de Mars-Tour Eiffel) to Versailles-Rive Gauche, which is 700 metres south-east of the chateau on Ave Général de Gaulle. Check the electronic destination lists on the platform to make sure you take a train that goes all the way to Versailles. There are SNCF trains from Paris' Gare Montparnasse to Versailles-Chantiers, which is 1.3 km south-east of the chateau out Ave de Sceaux. SNCF trains also run from Paris' Gare Saint Lazare to Versailles-Rive Droite, 1.2 km north-east of the chateau. Many of the trains from Gare Montparnasse to Versailles continue on to Chartres. Eurail pass holders can travel free on the SNCF trains but not on those operated by the RER.

CHARTRES
The magnificent 13th century cathedral of Chartres rises abruptly from the cornfields 86 km south-west of Paris. Crowned by two soaring spires – one Gothic, the other Romanesque – it dominates the medieval town clustered around its base.

The present cathedral has been attracting pilgrims for almost eight centuries, but the city has been a site of pilgrimage for over two millennia: the Gallic Druids may have had a sanctuary here, and the Romans apparently built a temple dedicated to the Dea Mater (mother-goddess), who was later interpreted by Christian missionaries as prefiguring the Virgin Mary.

FRANCE

Orientation

The medieval sections of Chartres are situated along the Eure River and on the hillside west of the river. The cathedral, which is visible from almost everywhere in town, is about 500 metres east of the train station.

Information

The tourist office (☎ 37.21.50.00) is one block from the front of the cathedral at Place de la Cathédrale. It is open Monday to Friday from 9.30 am to 6, 6.30 or 6.45 pm, depending on the season. Saturday hours are 9.30 am to 5 pm (6 pm from March to October). From May to September, the office is also open on Sunday from 10 am to noon and 3 to 6 pm. Hotel reservations in the Chartres area cost 20FF (plus a 50FF deposit).

Banks are usually open Tuesday to Saturday. The Banque de France (☎ 37.91.59.03) at 32 Rue du Docteur Maunoury is open from 8.45 am to 12.30 pm and 1.45 to 3.30 pm daily except Sunday and Monday.

Chartres' postcode is 28000.

Things to See

Cathédrale Notre Dame Chartres Cathedral (☎ 37.21.56.33) was built in the first quarter of the 13th century and, unlike so many of its contemporaries, has not been significantly modified since then. Built to replace an earlier structure devastated by fire in 1194, construction of this early Gothic masterpiece took only 25 years, a fact to which the cathedral owes its high degree of architectural unity.

The cathedral is open daily from 7 am to 7 pm (7.30 pm from April to September). From Easter to November (and sometimes during winter as well), Malcolm Miller, the Englishman who has been leading tours here since 1958, gives fascinating lectures on the cathedral's history and architecture at noon and 2.45 pm every day except Sunday. The tour costs 30FF (20FF for students). The 105-metre **Clocher Vieux** (old bell tower), the tallest Romanesque steeple still standing, is to the right as you face the Romanesque **Portail Royal** (the main entrance). The **Clocher Neuf** (new bell tower), the Gothic spire of which dates from 1513, can be visited daily, except Sunday morning, from 9.30 or 10 to 11.30 am and 2 to 4 or 4.30 pm (October to March) or 5.30 pm (April to September). The fee is 20FF (12FF reduced rate).

Inside, the cathedral's most exceptional feature is the extraordinary **stained glass**, almost all of which consists of 13th century originals. The three exceptional windows over the main entrance date from around 1150. The depth and intensity of the blue tones – the famous 'Chartres blue' – are renowned. The **trésor** (treasury) displays a piece of cloth given to the cathedral in 876 and said to have been worn by the Virgin Mary. It is open every afternoon from Monday to Saturday and, from Easter to October, in the morning as well. The early 11th century Romanesque **crypt**, the largest in France, can be visited only if you join a half-hour guided tour (in French), which costs 10FF (7FF for students). Tours depart from the cathedral's gift shop, La Crypte, which is outside the south entrance at 18 Rue du Cloître Notre Dame, every day at 11 am, 2.45 pm, 3.30 pm and 4.30 pm and – from mid-June to mid-September – at 5.15 pm as well.

Centre International du Vitrail The International Centre of Stained Glass Art (☎ 37.21.65.72), partly housed in the Cellier de Loëns, a 13th century underground storehouse, has exhibits on stained glass production, restoration, history and symbolism. There are also exhibitions of works by contemporary stained-glass artists from around the world. The centre, which is down the hill from the cathedral's north entrance at 5 Rue du Cardinal Pie, is open daily from 9.30 am to 12.30 pm and 1.30 to 6 pm (9.30 am to 7 pm from April to September). The entry fee is 15FF (12FF reduced rate).

Musée des Beaux-Arts The fine arts museum (☎ 37.36.41.39), which is behind the cathedral at 29 Cloître Notre Dame, is housed in the 17th and 18th century **Palais Épiscopal** (Bishop's Palace). Its collections include paintings from the 16th to 19th centuries, wooden sculptures from the Middle Ages, a number of 17th and 18th century harpsichords and some tapestries. The museum is open daily, except Tuesday, from 10 am to noon and 2 to 5 pm (10 am to 6 pm from April to October. Entry is 7FF (3.50FF reduced rate).

Old City During the Middle Ages, the city of Chartres grew and developed along the banks of the Eure River. Among the many buildings remaining from that period are private residences, stone bridges, tanneries, wash houses and a number of churches. Streets with buildings of interest include **Rue de la Tannerie**, which stretches along the Eure, and **Rue des Écuyers**, which is midway between the cathedral and the river. **Église Saint Pierre** at Place Saint Pierre has a bell tower dating from around 1000 and some fine late 13th and early 14th century stained glass.

Walking Tour Self-guided cassette-tape tours of the old city can be rented at the tourist office for 35FF.

Places to Stay

Camping *Les Bords de l'Eure* camping ground (☎ 37.28.79.43), which is about 2.5 km south-east of the train station on Rue de Launay, is open from Easter to the second week of September. Two adults with a tent and vehicle pay 41FF. To get there from the train station take bus No 8 to the Vignes stop.

Hostel The pleasant, calm *Auberge de Jeunesse* (☎ 37.34.27.64) at 23 Ave Neigre is about 1.5 km east of the train station via the ring road (Blvd Charles Péguy and Blvd Jean Jaurès). By bus, take line No 3 from the train station and get off at the Rouliers stop. Reception is open daily from the early morning until 10 am and from 6 to 10 pm (11 pm in summer). A bed costs 56FF, including breakfast. Guests must have a hostelling card. The hostel is closed from the Monday before Christmas until the first Monday in February.

Hotels The cheapest hotel in town is the *Hôtel du Nord* (☎ 37.21.11.78) at 17 Rue Nicole, which is 200 metres to the right as you exit the train station. Simple singles/doubles/triples with communal showers and toilets are 80/90/120FF. Hall showers cost 15FF. Reception, which is at the bar, is closed on Sunday morning. The *Hôtel de l'Ouest* (☎ 37.21.43.27), a two-star place across the street from the train station at 3 Place Pierre Sémard, has clean, carpeted doubles for 120FF (with washbasin and bidet), 160FF (with shower) and 210FF (with shower and toilet). Singles are slightly cheaper; triples cost 50FF more than doubles.

Places to Eat

Restaurants *Café Serpente* (☎ 37.21.68.81), a brasserie and salon de thé across from the south porch of the cathedral at 2 Rue du Cloître Notre Dame, has main dishes for 50 to 60FF and large salads for 40 to 60FF. It is open daily from 10 am to 1 pm. *La Reine du Saba* (☎ 37.21.89.16), down the block at 8 Rue du Cloître Notre Dame, is a casual restaurant specialising in traditional French food. *Menus* cost 70 and 90FF. It is open daily from 9.30 am to 6 or 7 pm (8.30 am to 11 pm from April to September).

Self-Catering There is a boulangerie about 200 metres south-west of the cathedral at 19 Rue Sainte Meme. It is open daily except Sunday and Wednesday from 7.30 am to 12.30 pm and 3 to 7 pm. There is another boulangerie next to 5 Rue Noël Ballay. The *Monoprix* supermarket at 21 Rue Noël Ballay is open Monday to Saturday from 9 am to 7 pm.

Getting There & Away

Train The train station (☎ 37.28.50.50) is at Place Pierre Sémard. The trip from Paris' Gare Montparnasse (61FF one-way) takes only 50 to 70 minutes. The last train back to Paris leaves Chartres at around 9 pm on weekdays and an hour or so later on weekends. There is also direct rail service to/from

FRANCE

Brest, Nantes, Quimper, Rennes and Versailles.

Taxi For a taxi, call ☎ 37.36.00.00. They're open 24 hours a day.

Alsace

Alsace, the easternmost part of northern France, is nestled between the Vosges Mountains and, about 30 km to the east, the Rhine River – the final resting place of the long-disputed Franco-German border. The area owes its unique language, architecture, cuisine and atmosphere to centuries of interplay between local Alsatian culture, which is similar in many ways to what you find on the German side of the Rhine, and French civilisation.

Most of Alsace became part of France in 1648, although Strasbourg, the region's largest city, retained its independence until 1681. But over two centuries of French rule did little to dampen 19th and early 20th century German enthusiasm for a foothold on the west bank of the southern Rhine, and Alsace was twice annexed by Germany: between 1871 and 1918 (from the Franco-Prussian War until the end of WW I); and again between 1939 and 1944.

Language
The Alsatian language, a Germanic dialect similar to that spoken in nearby parts of Germany and Switzerland, is still used by many Alsatians, especially older people in rural areas. Alsatian is known for its singsong intonations, which also characterise the way some Alsatians speak French.

Food
Alsace is famed for its foie gras (fattened goose liver pâté) and *choucroute* (sauerkraut) served with sausage, pork or ham and, usually, a cold, frothy beer or a local wine. The pâtisseries are particularly well stocked, with scrumptious pastries and the most irresistible chocolate pralines.

STRASBOURG
Cosmopolitan Strasbourg (population 252,000), located just a couple of km west of the Rhine, is Alsace's great metropolis and its intellectual and cultural capital. Towering above the restaurants, pubs and *bars à musique* of the lively old city is the cathedral, a medieval marvel in pink sandstone near which is clustered one of the finest ensembles of museums in France. Strasbourg's distinctive architecture, including the centuries-old half-timbered houses, and its exemplary orderliness impart on the city an unmistakably Alsatian ambience.

When it was founded in 1949, the Council of Europe (Conseil de l'Europe) – which now has 23 members – decided to base itself in Strasbourg, hoping that the city would become a symbol of postwar European cooperation and friendship. The organisation's huge headquarters, Palais de l'Europe, is used for one week each month (except during July and August) by the European Parliament, the legislative branch of the European Community.

Orientation
The train station is 350 metres east of the old city, which is an island delimited by the Ill River to the south and the Fossé du Faux Rempart to the north. The main public square in the old city is Place Kléber, which is 400 metres north-west of the cathedral. The quaint Petite France area is in the old city's south-west corner.

Information
Tourist Office The well-informed and efficient tourist office (☎ 88.32.51.49) is in front of the train station; it will move to a new, underground home when the tramway construction at Place de la Gare (the square in front of the station) is finished in 1994 or 1995. It is open daily from 9 am to 12.30 pm and 1.45 to 6 pm (June to September from 8 am to 7 pm). This is a good place to pick up bus tickets and a free bus map. The tourist office annexe (☎ 88.52.28.22) at Place de la Cathédrale is open daily from 9 am to 6 pm (7 pm from June to September).

Money The Banque de France, whose public entrance is on Impasse de Birschheim (the alley next to 9 Place Broglie), is open Monday to Friday from 9 am to 12.30 pm and 1.30 to 3.30 pm. The Banque CIAL bureau (☎ 88.23.35.99) in the train station is open Monday to Friday from 9 am to 1 pm and 2 to 7.30 pm and Saturday, Sunday and public holidays from 9 am to 8 pm. The commission is 15FF and the exchange rate is not too bad. There's a 24-hour exchange machine outside the Sogenal bank at Place Gutenberg, near which are a number of other banks. American Express (☎ 88.75.78.75) at 31 Place Kléber is open Monday to Friday from 8.45 am to noon and 1.30 to 6 pm.

Post The main post office, which is opposite 8 Ave de la Marseillaise, is open Monday to Friday from 8 am to 7 pm and on Saturday from 8 am to noon. The branch post office next to the train station (to the left as you exit) has the same opening hours. Both do exchange operations.

The postcode of central Strasbourg is 67000.

Things to See

Walking Tour Strasbourg is a great place for an aimless stroll. The bustling **old city** is filled with pedestrian malls, up-market shopping streets and bustling public squares. There are watery views from the quais and paths along the **Ill River** and the **Fossé du Faux Rempart**. In **Petite France**, the old city's south-west corner, half-timbered houses line the narrow streets and canals. The city's parks provide a welcome respite from the traffic and bustle – see the following Parks section for details.

Cathédrale Strasbourg's impossibly lacy Gothic cathedral was begun in 1176 after an earlier cathedral had burnt down. The west façade was completed in 1284, but the spire (whose southern companion was never built) was not in place until 1439. Following the Reformation and a long period of bitter struggle, the cathedral came under Protestant control and was not returned to the Catholic

Church until 1681. Many of the statues decorating the cathedral are copies – the originals can be seen in the Musée de l'Œuvre Notre-Dame (see the following Museums section).

The cathedral (☎ 88.37.33.12) is open daily, except during masses (ie Sunday and public holiday mornings), from 7 to 11.40 am and 12.45 to 6.30 pm. The three-storey-high, half-Gothic, half-Renaissance contraption just inside the south entrance is the **horloge astronomique**, a 16th century clock (the mechanism dates from 1842) that strikes noon every day at precisely 12.30 pm. To pay for the clock's upkeep, there is a 4FF charge to see the carved wooden figures do their thing, which is why between 11.40 am and the end of the show only the cathedral's south entrance is open.

The 66-metre-high platform above the façade – from which the tower and its spire soar another 76 metres – can be visited daily from 9 am (8.30 am in July and August) to 4.30 pm (November to February), till 5.30 pm (March and October), till 6.30 pm (April to June and September) or till 7 pm (July and August). The entrance (☎ 88.32.59.00) is at the base of the tower that was never built. Tickets cost 10FF (7FF for students). While visiting the platform, it is recommended that you do not think about earthquakes and the fact that the whole cathedral consists of little more than millions of stones delicately placed one on top of the other.

Église Saint Thomas This Protestant church on Rue Martin Luther, built in the late 12th century and turned into a Lutheran church in 1529, is best known for the mausoleum of Marshal Maurice of Saxony, which is considered a masterpiece of 18th century French sculpture. Erected on the order of Louis XV, it depicts Maurice (elector of Saxony from 1547 to 1553) – in full dress uniform – stepping boldly into a coffin held open by a shrouded figure of Death while a grieving, bare-breasted France tries to hold Death at bay. To the Marshal's right lie the defeated heraldic animals of

FRANCE

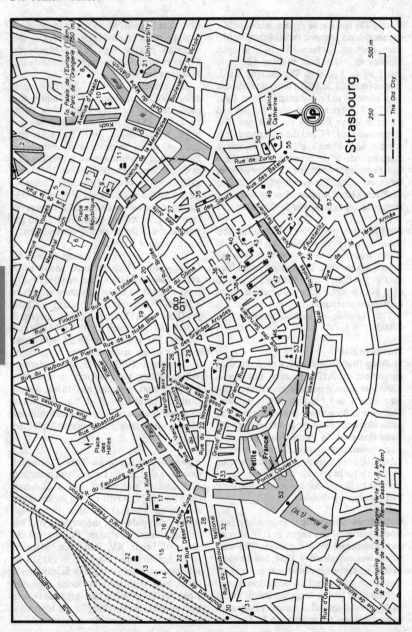

Strasbourg

- - - = The Old City

To Palais de l'Europe (1 km)
& Parc de l'Orangerie (750 m)

21 University

Boulevard de la Victoire

Rue Sainte Catherine

Rue de Zurich

Rue des Bateliers

Rue des Saurs

R des Saurs

Rue Brûlée

Rue du Dôme

OLD CITY

Rue des Grandes Arcades

Avenue de la Marseillaise

Quai Koch

Quai Finkwiller

Petite France

Ponts Couverts

Quai St Nicolas

Quai des Bateliers

Quai des Pêcheurs

R d'Austerlitz

R de la 1ère Armée

Rue de la 1ère Armée

Place de la République

Avenue des Vosges

Avenue du Maréchal Foch

Avenue de la Paix

Rue du Faubourg de Pierre

Rue des Bonnes Gens

Rue Finkmatt

Rue de la Fonderie

Quai Kléber

Rue de la Nuée Bleue

Marché aux Vins

R des Enfants

Grand Rue

Rue du Vieux

Rue du 22 Novembre

Rue Sébastopol

Place des Halles

Boulevard Président Wilson

Rue Kuhn

R du Maire Kuss

Rue Déserte

Rue du Faubourg National

Boulevard de Metz

Boulevard de Saverne

Ill River (1.2 km)

To Camping de la Montagne Verte (1.8 km)
& Auberge de Jeunesse René Cassin (1.2 km)

Rue d'Obernai

Rue de Molsheim

500 m

250

0

■ PLACES TO STAY	OTHER	35	Bar des Aviateurs
		36	Tourist Office Annexe
3 CIARUS (Hostel)	1 Main Synagogue	37	Place Gutenberg & 24-
17 Hôtel de Bruxelles	2 Contades Park		Hour Exchange
18 Hôtel Jura	4 Law Courts		Machine (Sogenal
23 Hôtel Le Colmar	5 Prefecture Building		Bank)
31 Hôtel Weber	6 Palais du Rhin	38	Place de la Cathédrale
41 Hôtel Michelet	7 Library	39	Cathédrale
46 Hôtel Patricia	8 US Consulate	40	Place du Château
49 Hôtel de l'Ill	9 Theatre	42	Musée d'Art Moderne
	10 Église Saint Paul	43	Musée de l'Œuvre
▼ PLACES TO EAT	11 Main Post Office		Notre Dame
	12 Post Office	44	Château des Rohan
16 Restaurant Le	13 Railway Station		(Museums)
Cappodoce	14 Tourist Office	47	Place de la Grande
27 Aldo Pizzeria	15 Place de la Gare		Boucherie
28 Boulangerie	19 Banque de France	50	Café des Anges (live
32 Alder Supermarket	20 Place Broglie		music)
34 Suma Supermarket	21 Place de l'Université	51	Festival Bar Américain
(Nouvelles Galeries-	22 Euro Rent Car Rental	52	Barrage Vauban
Magmod Store)	24 Cinéma Club	53	Église Saint Thomas
45 Au Pont Saint Martin	25 Cinéma Star	55	Place de Zurich
Restaurant	26 American Express	56	Musée Alsacien
48 Winstub Strissel	29 Place Kléber	57	Place d'Austerlitz
54 Bierstub Le Trou	30 Budget Car Rental		
	33 L'Académie de la Bière		

FRANCE

Austria (the eagle), England (the leopard) and Holland (the lion). Notice that the church is arranged so that all the members of the congregation sit facing the altar, placed in what was once the transept crossing.

Museums Strasbourg's most important museums are in the immediate vicinity of the cathedral (see map). All are open daily except Tuesday *except* the Musée de l'Œuvre Notre Dame and the Musée d'Art Moderne, which are open seven days a week. Hours are 10 am to noon and 2 to 6 pm (10 am to 6 pm on Sunday from April to October). Each museum costs 15FF (8FF for students under 26). Entry is free if you're under 18, over 65 or a teacher (ID required).

The **Musée de l'Œuvre Notre-Dame** (☎ 88.32.88.17), housed in a group of 14th and 15th century buildings at 2 Place du Château, is Strasbourg's single most outstanding museum. It displays one of France's finest collections of Romanesque, Gothic and Renaissance sculpture (in both stone and

wood), including many of the cathedral's original statues, brought here for preservation and display. The celebrated figures of a downcast and defeated **Synagoga** (representing Judaism) and a victorious **Église** (the Church triumphant), which date from around 1230 and once flanked the south entrance to the cathedral, are in Room VI.

The **Château des Rohan** (also known as the Palais Rohan; ☎ 88.32.48.95) at 2 Place du Château, was built between 1732 and 1742 as a residence for the city's prince-bishops. It now houses three museums, each with its own 15FF entry fee. The **Musée Archéologique** in the basement covers the period from 1 million BC to 800 AD. The **Musée des Arts Décoratifs**, which takes up the ground floor, includes a series of grand chambers decorated in the style of the 18th century. Louis XV and Marie-Antoinette each slept here once (in 1744 and 1770, respectively). The **Musée des Beaux-Arts**, which displays paintings from the 14th century to 1870, is on the 1st floor. The

Musée d'Art Moderne (☎ 88.32.48.95) at 5 Place du Château (2nd floor) specialises in painting and sculpture from the Impressionists (circa 1870) to the present.

The **Musée Alsacien** (☎ 88.35.55.36) at 23 Quai Saint Nicolas, housed in three 16th and 17th century houses, has two dozen rooms of truly fascinating Alsatian folk art. Displays range from kitchen utensils (biscuit cutters, stoves, ceramics) and children's toys to a tiny, 18th century synagogue.

Parks The shaded paths, flower beds, children's playgrounds and swan-filled lake of **Parc de l'Orangerie**, two km north-east of the cathedral, are a favourite with local families, especially on sunny Sunday afternoons. To get there from the train station or Place Broglie, take bus No 15. **Place de la République** is a round, flower-filled formal garden encircled by some of Strasbourg's most important public buildings.

Places to Stay

Many of the city's hotel rooms are reserved up to a year in advance on Monday, Tuesday, Wednesday and Thursday nights during the one week each month from September to June when the European Parliament is in session. The tourist office will tell you the parliament's schedule.

Place de la Gare and nearby Rue du Maire Kuss are literally lined with two and three-star hotels.

Camping The municipal *Camping de la Montagne Verte* (☎ 88.30.25.46; open from March to October) at 2 Rue Robert Forrer, is a wide expanse of grass partly shaded by young trees. It costs 10.50FF to pitch a tent and park your car; plus each adult is charged 10.50FF. The *Auberge de Jeunesse René Cassin* (see the next section) has a place to pitch tents at the back. The charge, including breakfast, is 38FF per person. Both the camping ground and the auberge de jeunesse are served by the same bus (see the next section for details).

Hostels The shiny, modern *Centre Interna-* *tional d'Accueil et de Rencontre Unioniste de Strasbourg* (CIARUS; ☎ 88.32.12.12), a 200-bed Protestant-run hostel at 7 Rue Finkmatt, is about one km north-east of the train station. Per-person tariffs, including breakfast, range from 75FF in a room with six or eight beds to 170FF in a single. CIARUS also has facilities for the handicapped. To get to CIARUS from the train station, take bus No 10 and get off at the Place de Pierre stop.

The 286-bed *Auberge de Jeunesse René Cassin* (☎ 88.30.26.46) is two km south-west of the train station at 9 Rue de l'Auberge de Jeunesse. A bed costs 62FF (in a room for four to six people), 88FF (in a double) or 136FF (in a single), including breakfast. The hostel is linked with the city centre (Rue du Vieux Marché aux Vins) and the train station (Quai Altorffer) by bus Nos 3, 13 and 23, which run every 10 to 15 minutes from 6 am to 11.30 pm (less frequently but the same hours on Saturday and Sunday). Get off at the Auberge de la Jeunesse stop.

Hotels Strasbourg's cheapest hotels are to be found near the train station but the old city also offers several good options.

Train Station Area The *Hôtel Le Colmar* (☎ 88.32.16.89) at 1 Rue du Maire Kuss (1st floor) may have linoleum floors and sound-tiled ceilings, but it's cheap and convenient and the rooms are clean and serviceable. Singles/doubles/triples start at 105/125/150FF with sink and bidet. Rooms for one/two people with shower and toilet cost 160/175FF. Hall showers are 17FF. The *Hôtel Weber* (☎ 88.32.36.47) is at 22 Blvd de Nancy. This is hardly the nicest part of Strasbourg, but it's convenient if you arrive by rail. Nondescript singles/doubles cost 95 to 105FF (with sink) or 180/220FF (with shower and toilet). Triples and quads with shower and toilet are 270FF. Hall showers are 12FF.

The older two-star *Hôtel de Bruxelles* (☎ 88.32.45.31) at 13 Rue Kuhn has clean and fairly large singles/doubles/triples/

quads with shower, toilet and TV for 215/235/300/340FF.

Old City The small, family-run *Hôtel Michelet* (☎ 88.32.47.38) is at 48 Rue du Vieux Marché aux Poissons (literally, street of the old fish market). Double rooms cost 105FF with sink, 150FF with shower and 175FF with shower and toilet. Hall showers are 12FF. An extra bed is only 20 or 25FF, and breakfast in your room costs a mere 15FF. From the train station, take bus No 1 or 11 and get off at Place Gutenberg. The *Hôtel Patricia* (☎ 88.32.14.60) at 1a Rue du Puits, a few blocks farther west, has very ordinary singles/doubles with sink for 105/130FF and doubles with shower and toilet for 180FF. There is a 12FF charge to use the hall shower.

The friendly, one-star *Hôtel Jura* (☎ 88.32.12.72) at 5 Rue du Marché is about equidistant from the train station and the cathedral. Old-fashioned but cosy doubles cost 130FF (with sink and bidet) and 180FF (with shower). Room 7 has a sexy, red neon 'hôtel' sign right outside the window, but it's equipped with two twin beds! Triples with shower and toilet cost 200FF. Hall showers are free. The hotel is closed between noon and 2 pm. The two-star *Hôtel de l'Ill* (☎ 88.36.20.01), across the Ill from the cathedral at 8 Rue des Bateliers, has singles/doubles for 145/170FF (with sink), 180/210FF (with shower) and 215/250FF (with shower and toilet). Hall showers are free.

Places to Eat

Local specialities can be sampled at two uniquely Alsatian kinds of eating establishments. *Winstubs* ('VEEN-shtub') serve both wine and hearty Alsatian fare, much of it prepared with wine. Typical winstub fare includes choucroute (sauerkraut) served with meat and *baekeoffe* (also spelled *backehofe* and *baeckeoffe*), pork, beef and lamb marinated for two days before being cooked with vegetables in a *baekeoffe* (baker's oven). Some places serve baekeoffe only on certain days (eg Friday).

As you would expect, *Bierstubs* ('BEER-shtub') primarily serve beer – the selection may include dozens, scores, even hundreds of kinds! Although they do have food (such as *tarte flambée*, a pastry base with cream, onion, bacon and sometimes other ingredients), they don't usually serve multicourse meals.

Restaurants *Au Pont Saint Martin* (☎ 88.32.45.13) at 15 Rue des Moulins in Petite France specialises in Alsatian dishes, including choucroute (62FF) and baekeoffe (available daily for 78FF). Vegetarians can order the *fricassée de champignons* (mushroom fricassee; 42FF). The lunch *menu* costs 52FF. Au Pont Saint Martin is open every day from noon to 2.30 pm and 6 to 11 pm.

The relaxed and hugely popular *Aldo Pizzeria* (☎ 88.36.00.49, or 88.37.95.15 for home delivery) at 8 Rue du Faisan has design-it-yourself pizzas (29 toppings) for 40FF, huge salads (36 ingredients) for 39FF, tartes flambées, pasta and ice-cream desserts. It is open daily from 11.30 am to 2 pm and 6.30 to 11.30 pm.

Restaurant Le Cappadoce (☎ 88.23.00.25, 88.32.88.95) at 15 Rue Kuhn serves excellent, freshly prepared Turkish food in an informal dining room. Main meat or chicken dishes are 45 to 70FF, and salads are 15 to 25FF. Meals are served from noon to 2.30 pm and 6 pm to midnight daily except Sunday at midday.

Winstubs *Winstub Strissel* (☎ 88.32.14.73), near the cathedral at 5 Place de la Grande Boucherie, has a typical winstub ambience, with wooden floors, benches and panelling and colourful stained-glass windows. A quarter-litre of wine will set you back 14 to 26FF. *Menus* are available for 53 and 66FF. Strissel is open daily, except Sunday and Monday, from 10 am to 11 pm, though hearty Alsatian meals are served only from 11.45 am to 2 pm and 6.30 to 9.30 pm.

Bierstubs *Le Trou* (☎ 88.36.91.04), housed in a vaulted brick cellar at 5 Rue des Couples, serves the usual bierstub munchies as well as 100 to 150 kinds of beer. Prices for a demi on tap start at 14FF. Le Trou is open daily

FRANCE

from 9 pm (8 pm from mid-September to March) to 4 am. At *L'Académie de la Bière* (☎ 88.32.61.08, 88.23.21.83) at 17 Rue Adolphe Seyboth, you can sit at rough-hewn wooden tables and sip your beer (10FF, or 15FF after 8 pm) every day from 8 pm (11 am on Saturday and Sunday) to 4 am.

Self-Catering There is an excellent selection of picnic food at the *Suma* supermarket on the 3rd floor of the Nouvelles Galeries-Magmod store at 34 Rue du 22 Novembre, which is just off Place Kléber. It's open Monday to Saturday from 9 am to 7 pm.

Near the train station, the *Alder* supermarket opposite 42 Rue du Faubourg National is open Monday to Friday from 8 am to 12.30 pm and 2.30 to 7 pm and on Saturday from 8 am to 1 pm and 2.30 to 6 pm. There's a boulangerie-pâtisserie with extraordinary chocolates (about 2FF each) down the block at 30 Rue du Faubourg National. It is open Monday to Saturday from 7 am to 7 pm and on Sunday from 8 am to 6 pm.

Bars The *Festival Bar Américain* (% 88.36.31.28), a fashionable and rather up-market, American-style bar at 4 Rue Sainte Catherine, is open daily from 6 pm (9 pm from October to March) to 4 am. A demi of beer costs 20FF. Check out the ceiling fans, which are all run by, well, a single fan belt. *Bar des Aviateurs* (☎ 88.36.52.69) at 12 Rue des Sœurs, whose poster and photo-covered walls and long wooden counter impart a '40s sort of atmosphere, is open every day from 6 pm to 3 am (4 am on Friday and Saturday nights). Beers are always 20FF.

Entertainment
Live Music *Café des Anges* (☎ 88.37.12.67) at 5 Rue Sainte Catherine, whose extreme informality positively oozes mellowness, is a bar à musique that puts on live concerts of anything from salsa to North African raï almost every night at around 9.30 or 10 pm. Tickets generally cost 30 to 40FF, but the entry fee to the *bœufs* (jam sessions) held on Monday (blues) and Tuesday (jazz) is just 10FF. Beers are 9FF (15FF after 10 pm). The

Café des Anges is open Monday to Friday from 11 am until very late, on Saturday from 3 pm to 1 am or later, and every other Sunday from 7 pm to 11 pm or midnight.

Cinemas Strasbourg has two movie houses that screen nondubbed (v.o.) flicks. The five-screen *Cinéma Club* (☎ 88.32.01.48, or 88.32.12.30 for their answering machine message) at 32 Rue du Vieux Marché aux Vins charges 42FF (31FF concession except on weekends). The four-screen *Cinéma Star* (☎ 88.22.66.42), which is nearby at 27 Rue du Jeu des Enfants, charges 40FF (30FF for people under 18, students and people over 60 except on Saturday evening and all-day Sunday). At both places, everyone gets in for the reduced price on Monday.

Getting There & Away
Bus Strasbourg's municipal bus No 21 goes from the train station via Place Kléber to Kehl, Germany, which is just across the Rhine.

Train In the train station (☎ 88.22.50.50), the information office is open Monday to Friday from 8 am to 8 pm and on Saturday, Sunday and public holidays from 9 am to 7 pm. Strasbourg is well connected by rail with Basel (Bâle; 95FF), Colmar (51FF; about half an hour; a dozen a day); Munich (332FF) and Paris (247FF; four to 4½ hours; at least 10 a day). There are also trains to Amsterdam (406FF), Chamonix (307FF) and Nice (435FF). Certain trains to/from Paris (but not other destinations) require payment of a *supplément* of up to 32FF in 2nd class.

BIJ tickets are available from Wasteels (☎ 88.32.40.82) at 13 Place de la Gare, which is open Monday to Saturday from 9 am to 7 pm (6 pm on Saturday).

Car Euro Rent (☎ 88.75.07.75) at 14 Rue Déserte rents small cars with unlimited km for 400FF a day. It charges 500FF for a two-day weekend and 650FF for a three-day weekend. The office is open from 8 am to noon and 2 to 6 pm daily except Saturday afternoon and Sunday.

Budget (☎ 88.75.68.29) at 31 Ave de Nancy charges 395FF for 24 hours, insurance and unlimited km included.

Getting Around

The tourist office has bus maps, carnets of five tickets (24FF) and Tourpasses (20FF), which are good for 24 hours of travel from the moment you time-stamp them. Buses from Strasbourg's city centre run until about 11.30 pm.

There are taxi ranks in front of the train station and at Place Kléber. To order a cab, call ☎ 88.36.13.13.

COLMAR

Colmar (population 64,000) is famous for the typically Alsatian architecture of its older neighbourhoods and the unparalleled Issenheim Altarpiece in the Musée d'Unterlinden. Colmar makes a great day trip from Strasbourg.

Orientation

Ave de la République stretches from one block in front of the train station to the Musée d'Unterlinden. The streets of the old city are south-east of this museum. Petite Venise (little Venice), a neighbourhood of old, half-timbered buildings, runs along the Launch River at the southern edge of the old city.

Information

Tourist Office The efficient and helpful tourist office (☎ 89.20.68.92) is at 4 Rue d'Unterlinden, which is opposite the Musée d'Unterlinden. The tourist office is open Monday to Saturday morning from 9 am to noon and 2 to 6 pm. From Easter to mid-November, it is also open on Saturday from 9 am to noon and 2 to 5 pm and Sunday from 9.30 am to 12.30 pm.

Money Banque de France (☎ 89.41.25.78) at 46 Ave de la République is open Monday to Friday from 8.45 am to 12.10 pm and 1.50 to 3.30 pm. The tourist office will change

money whenever it's open but the rate is terrible.

Post The main post office (☎ 89.41.19.19) at 36 Ave de la République is open Monday to Friday from 8 am to 6.30 pm and Saturday from 8 am to noon. Exchange operations are available.

Colmar's postcode is 68000.

Things to See

Unterlinden Museum This museum (☎ 89.20.15.58) is world-famous for the **Issenheim Altarpiece** (Rétable d'Issenheim), one of the most dramatic and pathos-filled works of art ever created. The carved and gilded wooden figures were made by Nicolas of Hagenau in the late 15th century, and the wooden wings – which originally closed over each other to form a three-layered altarpiece – were painted by Grünewald between 1511 and 1516. The Musée d'Unterlinden also displays several other medieval altarpieces, an Alsatian wine cellar, 15th and 16th century armour and weapons, pewter ware and Strasbourg faïence (decorated earthenware).

From November to March, the Musée d'Unterlinden is open from 9 am to noon and 2 to 5 pm daily except Tuesday; during the rest of the year it is open daily from 9 am to noon and 2 to 6 pm (and perhaps between noon and 2 pm as well). Ticket sales end half an hour before closing time in both the morning and the afternoon. Tickets cost 25FF (15FF for students under 30, 20FF for people over 65).

Musée Bartholdi This museum (☎ 89.41.90.60) at 30 Rue des Marchands – the house in which Frédéric Auguste Bartholdi (1834-1904), creator of the *Statue of Liberty*, grew up – displays some of the sculptor's work and his personal memorabilia from the Statue of Liberty project. From April to October, the museum is open daily from 10 am to noon and 2 to 6 pm; it may also stay open at midday. During the rest of the year, it is open *only* on Saturday and

Sunday from 10 am to noon and 2 to 5 pm. The fee is 15FF (5F for students).

Église des Dominicains This desanctified church at Place des Dominicains is known for its 14th and 15th century stained glass and Martin Schongauer's celebrated painting, *Vierge au Buisson de Roses (The Virgin and the Rosebush)*. It is open from 10 am to 6 pm daily from mid-March to November *only* .

Old City The medieval streets of the old part of Colmar, including **Rue des Marchands** and much of **Petite Venise**, are lined with half-timbered buildings. **Maison Pfister**, which is opposite 36 Rue des Marchands, was built in 1537 and is remarkable for its exterior decoration (frescoes, medallions and a carved wooden balcony). The **Maison des Têtes** at 19 Rue des Têtes, whose façade is crowded with all manner of carved stone heads and faces, was built in 1609. It is now home to a wine shop run by a local vintners' cooperative.

Places to Stay
Camping *Camping de l'Ill* (☎ 89.41.15.94; open from February to November) is four km from the train station in Horbourg-Wihr. It costs 14FF to park and pitch a tent plus 12FF per adult. To get to the camping ground from the train station, take bus No 1.

Hostels The *Maison des Jeunes et de la Culture* (MJC; ☎ 89.41.26.87) is five minutes' walk from the train station at 17 Rue Camille Schlumberger. A bed costs 39FF. Curfew is 11 pm. The *Auberge de Jeunesse* (☎ 89.80.57.39) is at 2 Rue Pasteur, which from the train station is a bit over two km north along the railway tracks and then west on Route d'Ingersheim. From the train station or the Unterlinden stop, take bus No 4 and get off near the Lycée Technique. You can't check in between 10 am and 5 pm. A bed costs 56FF, including breakfast. There is a midnight curfew.

Hotels The one-star *Hôtel La Chaumière*

(☎ 89.41.08.99) at 74 Ave de la République, Colmar's cheapest hotel, has simple and rather small rooms for 150FF. Singles/doubles with shower, toilet and TV are 200/220FF. Hall showers cost 15FF. Reception is closed on Sunday from 2 to 5 pm. The *Hôtel Rhin et Danube* (☎ 89.41.31.44), a two-star place at 26 Ave de la République, has old-fashioned doubles with high ceilings for 200FF (with shower) or 250FF (with shower and toilet). A triple/quad with bath and toilet is 330/390FF.

The *Hôtel Primo* (☎ 89.24.22.24) at 5 Rue des Ancêtres is two blocks from the Musée d'Unterlinden. The rooms, which are accessible by lift, are modern in a tacky sort of way and cost 175FF (with a sink and TV) or 250FF (with a shower, toilet and TV). Hall showers are free.

Places to Eat
Restaurants Reasonably priced restaurants are not Colmar's forte, but one good bet is *La Maison Rouge* (☎ 89.23.53.22) at 9 Rue des Écoles, which specialises in Alsatian cuisine, including ham cooked on a spit (53FF). The four-course *menu* costs 73FF. This place is open from noon to 2.30 pm and 6.30 to 9.30 pm daily except Sunday evening and Monday at midday. The inexpensive *Flunch cafeteria* (☎ 89.23.56.56) at 8 Ave de la République is open daily from 11.30 am to 2.30 pm and 5.30 to 9.30 pm.

Self-Catering There is a *Monoprix* supermarket with an in-house boulangerie directly across the square from the entrance to the Musée d'Unterlinden. It is open Monday to Saturday from 8.30 am to 7.30 pm (8 pm on Friday). *Fromagerie Saint Nicolas* at 18 Rue Saint Nicolas, which sells only the finest traditionally made cheeses, is open daily except all-day Sunday and Monday morning from 9 am to 12.30 pm and 2 to 7 pm.

For exotic fish and seafood, including fresh, ready-to-eat *crevettes* (prawns) and various seafood salads, try *Poissonnerie Colmarée*, which is in Petite Venise at 13 Quai de la Poissonnerie. It is open from 7 am to 12.15 pm and 2.15 to 7.15 pm (5 pm on Saturday) daily except Sunday and Monday.

Getting There & Away
The train trip to/from Strasbourg takes 29 to 43 minutes and costs 51FF each way.

Getting Around
All nine of Colmar's bus lines – which operate Monday to Saturday until 7.30 or 8 pm – serve the Unterlinden (Point Central) stop, which is next to the tourist office and the Musée d'Unterlinden. To get to the museum from the train station, take bus Nos 1, 2 or 3. On Sunday, lines A and B operate about once an hour between 1 and 6.30 or 7 pm.

Normandy

The former duchy of Normandy (Normandie) stretches from just west of the Paris basin to the Cotentin Peninsula, which divides the Baie de la Seine (where the Seine River empties into the English Channel) from the Golfe de Saint Malo (Gulf of St Malo), famed for its extraordinary tides and the abbey of Mont-Saint-Michel. The region derives its name from the Vikings (Norsemen, or Northmen), who took control of the area in the 9th century.

The city of Rouen is especially well endowed with medieval architecture, including a spectacular cathedral. Bayeux is home to the 11th century Bayeux Tapestry and is only about 12 km from the D-Day landing beaches. Because it has the closest coastline to Paris (only a couple of hours by train), the Normandy littoral is lined with beach resorts, including the fashionable twin towns of Deauville and Trouville. Rural Normandy is famed for its cheeses and dairy products.

Ferries link southern England with three Norman ports: Cherbourg, Dieppe and Le Havre.

Getting Around
Given how attractive Normandy's rural areas are and how limited the region's public transport is, renting a car will add more to your visit here than almost anywhere else in France.

ROUEN
The city of Rouen (population 105,000), for centuries the farthest downriver you could cross the Seine by bridge, is known for the many spires and church towers that dominate its skyline. The old city is graced with over 700 half-timbered houses, quite a few of which have rough-hewn beams, posts and diagonals that were probably off-kilter when they were built and have become even more so over the centuries. Rouen also has a renowned Gothic cathedral and a number of excellent museums. The city can be visited as an overnight trip (or even a day trip) from Paris.

Orientation
The passenger train station (Gare Rouen-Rive Droite) is at the northern terminus of Rue Jeanne d'Arc, the major thoroughfare in the city centre. The old city is centred around Rue du Gros Horloge.

Information
Tourist Office The tourist office (☎ 35.71.41.77) is in a wonderful early 16th century building at 25 Place de la Cathédrale, opposite the façade of Cathédrale Notre Dame. It is open Monday to Saturday from 9 am to 12.30 pm and 2 to 6.30 pm. From May to September, opening hours are Monday to Saturday from 9 am to 7 pm and on Sunday and holidays from 9.30 am to 12.30 pm and 2.30 to 6 pm.

Money Banque de France (☎ 35.52.78.08) at 32 Rue Thiers is open weekdays from 8.45 am to 12.30 pm and 1.30 to 3.30 pm. There is a bureau de change (☎ 35.88.00.65) offering a good rate near the cathedral at 9 Rue des Bonnetiers. It is open from 10 am to 7 pm daily except Sunday. There are half a dozen banks along Rue Jeanne d'Arc between the Théâtre des Arts (Arts Theatre)

FRANCE

FRANCE

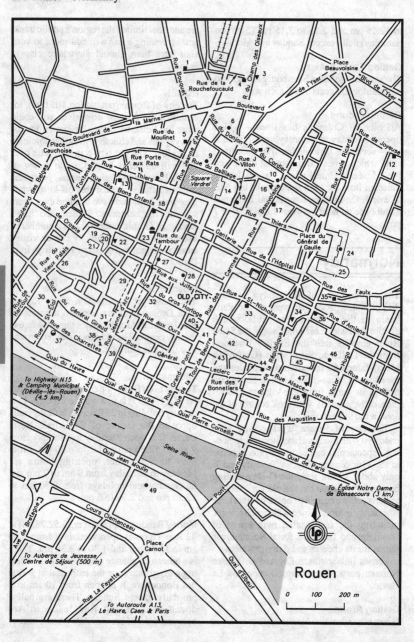

Rouen

0   100   200 m

To Highway N15
& Camping Municipal
(Déville-lès-Rouen)
(4.5 km)

To Auberge de Jeunesse/
Centre de Séjour (500 m)

To Autoroute A13,
Le Havre, Caen & Paris

To Église Notre Dame
de Bonsecours (3 km)

Seine River

OLD CITY

Square Verdrel

Place
Beauvoisine

Place
Cauchoise

Place
Carnot

Place
du Général
de Gaulle

Rue Bouquet

Rue de la
Rouchefoucauld

R. du Champ des Oiseaux

Boulevard de l'Iser

Blvd de l'Yser

Boulevard de la Marne

Rue du Moulinet

Rue Jeanne d'Arc

Rue du Donjon

Rue du Cordier

Rue de Joyeuse

Rue Louis Ricard

Rue Porte
aux Rats

Rue de Fontenelle

Rue Thiers

Rue des Bons Enfants

Rue J
Villon

Rue du
Bailliage

Beauvoisine

Rue Thiers

Place
du Général
de Gaulle

Rue de l'Hôpital

Boulevard des Belges

Rue de Crosne

Rue du Vieux Palais

Rue du Tambour

Canterie

Carmes

Rue des

Rue St-Nicholas

Rue des Faulx

Rue d'Amiens

Rue aux Juifs

Rue du Gros Horloge

Rue de Harcourt

Rue St Eloi

Rue du Général Giraud

Rue des Charrettes

Rue Jeanne d'Arc

Rue aux Ours

Rue Général

Pont de la Tour de Beurre

Rue Grand-Pont

Quai du Havre

Quai de la Bourse

Quai Pierre Corneille

Pont Jeanne d'Arc

Quai Jean Moulin

Cours Clemenceau

Ave de Bretagne

Rue La Fayette

Rue des
Bonnetiers

Leclerc

Rue de la République

Rue Alsace-Lorraine

Rue des Augustins

Rue Victor Hugo

Rue Martainville

Pont Corneille

Quai de Paris

Quai d'Elbeuf

■ PLACES TO STAY	31	Bar Charles (Pub)	27	Law Courts
	34	Alimentation Générale	28	Law Courts Courtyard
1 Hôtel des Familles		(Grocery)		& Monument Juif
4 Hôtel de la	47	Boulangerie	29	Banks
Rouchefoucauld	48	Mini-Club Grocery	30	Rouen Cycles (Bicycle
5 Hôtel du Square				Rental)
7 Hôtel Normandya		OTHER	32	Gros Horloge
11 Hôtel Sphinx				(Medieval Clock)
12 Hostellerie du Vieux	2	Gare Rouen-Rive	36	Laundrette
Logis		Droite (Railway	37	Bus Station
13 Hôtel Jacqueline		Station)	38	Le Bus (Local Bus
17 Hôtel Napoléon	6	Tour Jeanne d'Arc		Information)
18 Hôtel des Flandres	8	Banque de France	39	Théâtre des Arts
33 Modern' Hôtel	9	Musée de la	40	Tourist Office
35 Hôtel Saint Ouen		Céramique	41	Place de la Cathédrale
	10	Laundrette	42	Cathédrale Notre
▼ PLACES TO EAT	14	Musée des Beaux-Arts		Dame
	15	Musée le Secq des	43	Place de la Calende
3 Boulangerie		Tournelles	44	Currency Exchange
16 Food Shops	19	Place du Vieux Marché		Office
20 Covered Food Market	21	Église Jeanne d'Arc	45	Église Saint Maclou
22 La Tarte à Papa	23	Main Post Office	46	Aitre Saint Maclou
(Boulangerie)	24	City Hall	49	Prefecture
26 Restaurants	25	Église Saint Ouen		

and the Palais de Justice (see the Things to See section).

Post The main post office (☎ 35.08.73.83), where you can also change foreign currency, is at 45bis Rue Jeanne d'Arc. It is open weekdays from 8 am to 7 pm and on Saturday from 8 am to noon.

Rouen's postcode is 76000.

Things to See

Old City Like the rest of Rouen, the old city suffered enormous damage during WW II but has since been painstakingly restored. The main street is **Rue du Gros Horloge**, which runs from Notre Dame Cathedral to **Place du Vieux Marché**, where 19-year-old Jeanne d'Arc (Joan of Arc) was burned at the stake in 1431 after being convicted of heresy. The striking church (Église Jeanne d'Arc) marking the site was completed in 1979. There is a covered food market (see the Places to Eat section) next to the church.

Rue du Gros Horloge is spanned by an early 16th century gatehouse holding aloft the **Gros Horloge**, a large medieval clock with only one hand. The late 14th century belfry of the Gros Horloge, which is open *only* from sometime in late March or early April to September, can be visited from 10 am to noon and 2 to 6 pm daily except Wednesday morning, Tuesday and public holidays.

The incredibly ornate **Palais de Justice** (law courts), which was left a shell at the end of WW II, has been restored to its early 16th century Gothic glory, though the 19th century façade along Rue Jeanne d'Arc still shows extensive bullet and shell damage. The extraordinary Flamboyant courtyard, entered through a gate on Rue aux Juifs, is well worth a look. Under the courtyard is the **Monument Juif**, a stone building used by Rouen's Jewish community in the early 12th century. For information on tours of the Monument Juif, enquire at the tourist office.

Cathédrale Notre Dame Rouen's cathedral, which was painted repeatedly by Monet, is considered one of the masterpieces of French Gothic architecture. Built between 1201 and 1514, it suffered extensive damage during WW II and has been undergoing restoration for decades. The Romanesque **crypt** was part of a cathedral completed in 1062 and destroyed by fire in 1200. There are guided visits (10FF) to the **Chapelle de la Vierge** (Chapel of the Virgin), the final resting place of many important church officials. The cathedral is open daily from 8 am to noon and 2 to 7 pm (6.30 pm on Saturday, 6 pm on Sunday). Masses are held on Sunday morning, so it's best not to visit then.

Musée Le Secq des Tournelles This fascinating museum (☎ 35.71.28.40) of the blacksmith's craft displays some 12,000 locks, keys, scissors, tongs, pocketknives and other utensils made of wrought iron between the 3rd and 19th centuries. Located on Rue Jacques Villon (opposite 27 Rue Thiers), it is open from 10 am to noon and 2 to 6 pm daily except Wednesday morning and Tuesday. The entry fee is 11FF (free for students with identification).

Other Museums The **Musée des Beaux-Arts** (☎ 35.71.28.40) at 35 Rue Thiers features paintings from the 16th to 20th centuries. Some parts of the building may be closed until renovations are completed in 1994 or 1995. The **Musée de la Céramique** (☎ 35.07.31.74), whose speciality is 16th to 19th century faïence, most notably that produced in Rouen, is behind Square Verdrel on Rue du Bailliage. Opening hours and ticket prices at both these museums are the same as at the Musée Le Secq des Tournelles.

Aitre Saint Maclou This curious (and almost unique) ensemble of half-timbered buildings, built between 1526 and 1533, is decorated with macabre 16th century carvings of skulls, crossbones, grave-diggers' tools, and the like. As late as 1780, the courtyard was used as a burial ground for victims of the plague. It is now the municipal École des Beaux-Arts. The courtyard, whose entrance is behind **Église Saint Maclou** at 186 Rue Martainville, can be visited for free every day from 8 am to 8 pm.

Places to Stay
Camping *Camping Municipal* (☎ 35.74.07.59)

in the suburb of Déville-lès-Rouen is five km north-west of the train station on Rue Jules Ferry. From the train station, take bus No 2 and get off at the mairie of Déville-lès-Rouen. Two persons with a tent are charged 46FF. The camping ground is open all year except during February.

Hostel Rouen's *Auberge de Jeunesse/Centre de Séjour* (☎ 35.72.06.45) is at 17 Rue Diderot, 2.5 km south of the train station. It is served by bus No 5 (from Rue Jeanne d'Arc) and bus No 12 (from the train station), both of which run until about 11 pm. Get off at the Diderot stop. Beds cost 53.50FF, including breakfast and sheets.

Hotels Most of the budget hotels are north of the city centre, but there are some good, though slightly more expensive, places in the city centre as well.

North of the Centre The spotless *Hôtel Normandya* (☎ 35.71.46.15), a pleasant, family-run place at 32 Rue du Cordier, is on a quiet street 300 metres from the train station. Singles (some with shower) are 90 to 130FF, doubles are 10 or 15FF more; an additional bed costs 40FF and a bath or shower costs 15FF. The quiet *Hôtel du Square* (☎ 35.71.56.07) at 9 Rue du Moulinet, a few hundred metres south of the train station, is quite pleasant. Singles are 80 or 90FF and doubles start at 120FF, or 165FF with shower and toilet.

The *Hôtel de la Rouchefoucauld* (☎ 35.71.86.58) is at 1 Rue de la Rouchefoucauld, only a block from the train station. Singles start at 90FF, doubles with one or two beds range from 120 to 150FF, and two-bed triples are 160FF. Showers are 15FF (10FF each for two or more people). The *Hôtel Sphinx* (☎ 35.71.35.86) at 130 Rue Beauvoisine is a family-run hotel with doubles from 80 to 90FF; an additional bed is 50FF. Showers cost 16.50FF (10FF if you stay for a while). The *Hôtel Napoléon* (☎ 35.71.43.59), a small, comfortable place at 58 Rue Beauvoisine, has singles for 85 to

95FF and doubles for 130 to 140FF. Showers are 15FF.

The very French *Hostellerie du Vieux Logis* (☎ 35.71.55.30) at 5 Rue de Joyeuse, almost a km west of the train station, has a relaxed and pleasantly derelict atmosphere. There is parking next to the beautiful garden out the back. Singles/doubles start at 100FF, two-bed triples cost 140FF. You can shower for free for up to five minutes. The ground-floor restaurant is quite good.

City Centre The attractive *Hôtel Saint Ouen* (☎ 35.71.46.44) is opposite the garden of Église Saint Ouen at 43 Rue des Faulx. Simple singles/doubles cost from 80/90FF to 95/105FF. Only one block from Notre Dame Cathedral, at 59 Rue Saint Nicolas, the *Modern' Hôtel* (☎ 35.71.14.42) has singles starting at 75FF and basic doubles from 75 to 90FF.

At 16 Rue Porte aux Rats, the basic *Hôtel Jacqueline* (☎ 35.89.26.09) has the cheapest rooms in the city, with singles/doubles for 55/80FF to 90FF. There are no hall showers. This place is often full-up with long-term guests and no reservations are accepted. The *Hôtel des Flandres* (☎ 35.71.56.88), nearby at 12 Rue des Bons Enfants, has doubles for 100FF (with washbasin and bidet), 140FF (with shower) and 160FF (with shower and toilet).

Places to Eat

Restaurants Near Place du Vieux Marché, *La Galetteria* (☎ 35.88.98.98), opposite 17 Rue du Vieux Palais, has crêpes for around 30FF. It is open from noon to 2.30 pm and 7 to 10.30 pm daily except all day Sunday and Saturday at midday. For Lebanese food, try *La Phenicia* (☎ 35.88.46.22), which is opposite 23 Rue du Vieux Palais. It is open from noon to 2.15 pm and 7 to 11 pm daily except Sunday lunch time and Monday evening. *Pizzeria Pépé* (☎ 35.07.44.94) at 19 Rue du Vieux Palais is open from noon to 2 pm and 7 to 11.30 pm daily except Monday at lunch time and Sunday.

A number of unexciting but cheap restaurants are on Rue des Bons Enfants (near the main post office) and on Rue d'Amiens (one block south of Église Saint Ouen). There are more cheap places to eat on Rue de la République between the Hôtel de Ville and the river.

Self-Catering There is a boulangerie 150 metres to the left as you exit the train station at 24 Rue du Champ des Oiseaux. It is open from 7 am to 8 pm daily except Sunday.

Dairy products, fish and fresh produce are on sale from 7 am to 7 pm daily except Monday at the covered market at Place du Vieux Marché. *La Tarte à Papa*, a boulangerie at 6 Place du Vieux Marché, is open from 7 am to 8 pm daily except Monday.

Near Église Saint Maclou, there is a *Mini-Club* grocery (closed Sunday) at 13 Rue Alsace-Lorraine; a boulangerie (closed Wednesday) across the street at 14 Rue Alsace-Lorraine and a grocery (open daily) at 78 Rue de la République.

North of the centre, you will find a number of food shops between No 63 and No 73 Rue Beauvoisine. The boulangerie at 65 Rue Beauvoisine is open from 6.30 am to 1 pm and 2.30 to 8 pm daily except Sunday afternoon. The fruit store next door at 67 Rue Beauvoisine is open Monday to Saturday from 8 am to 1 pm and 2.30 to 8 pm.

Getting There & Away

Bus Bus service to Dieppe and Le Havre is expensive and much slower than the train. The bus station (gare routière; ☎ 35.71.23.29 or 35.71.81.71) is on Rue des Charrettes near the Théâtre des Arts.

Train Rouen is only 70 minutes by express train from Paris' Gare Saint Lazare. There are 24 trains a day in each direction, the latest at about 9 pm (towards Paris) and 10 pm (towards Rouen). At Rouen's train station (Gare Rouen-Rive Droite; ☎ 35.98.50.50 for information, 35.15.30.30 for reservations), which is at the northern end of Rue Jeanne d'Arc, the information office is open Monday to Saturday from 8 am to 6.30 pm.

FRANCE

Getting Around

Bus The local bus network is operated by TCAR. Tickets cost 4.20FF if bought on board. A carnet of 10 tickets is available for 31.40FF at the Le Bus counters in the train station and in front of the Théâtre des Arts.

Bicycle Rouen Cycles (☎ 35.71.34.30) at 45 Rue Saint Eloi rents mountain bikes and 10-speeds for 120FF a day (320FF a week). The store is open Tuesday to Saturday from 8.30 am to 12.15 pm and 2 to 7.15 pm.

BAYEUX

Bayeux (population 13,000) was made famous by two trans-Channel invasions: the conquest of England by the Normans (under William the Conqueror) in 1066, an event graphically depicted on the world-famous Bayeux Tapestry; and the Allied D-Day landings of 6 June 1944, which began the liberation of Nazi-occupied France. On the day after D-Day, Bayeux became the first town in France to be freed by the Allies.

These days, Bayeux is an attractive place with several worthwhile museums. It also serves as an excellent base for visits to sites associated with the Allied landings. For information on the landing beaches, see the D-Day Beaches section.

Orientation

Cathédrale Notre Dame, the major landmark in the centre of Bayeux, is one km north-west of the train station.

Information

Tourist Office The tourist office (☎ 31.92.16.26) is in a 14th century building at 1 Rue des Cuisiniers. It is open Monday to Saturday from 9 am to 12.30 pm and 2 to 6.30 pm. During July and August it is also open on Sunday from 10 am to 12.30 pm and 3 to 6.30 pm.

Money Banks are open Tuesday to Saturday. There is a Société Générale at 30 Rue Saint Malo and a Caisse d'Épargne down the road at 60 Rue Saint Malo. The tourist office changes money when the banks are closed.

Post The main post office (☎ 31.92.04.35) is at 29 Rue Larcher, opposite the Hôtel de Ville. It is open weekdays from 8 am to 7 pm and on Saturday from 8 am to noon. You can exchange foreign currency here.

Bayeux's postcode is 14400.

Things to See

A *billet jumelé* (multipass ticket) valid for all four museums listed here costs 50FF (26FF for students).

Bayeux Tapestry The world-famous Bayeux Tapestry – actually a 68.5-metre-long strip of coarse linen decorated with woollen embroidery – was commissioned by Odo, Bishop of Bayeux and half-brother of William the Conqueror (Guillaume le Conquérant), sometime between 1066 (when the Norman invasion of England took place) and 1082, when Odo was disgraced for raising troops without William's permission. The tapestry, which was probably made in England, recounts the dramatic story of the Norman invasion and the events that led up to it – from the Norman perspective, of course – in a sequence of 58 panels presented like a modern comic strip, with action-packed scenes following each other in quick succession. The events are accompanied by written commentary in rather bad Latin. The scenes themselves are filled with depictions of 11th century Norman dress, food, tools, cooking and weapons. Halley's Comet, which passed through our part of the solar system in 1066, also makes an appearance.

The tapestry is housed in the **Musée de la Tapisserie de Bayeux** (☎ 31.92.05.48), part of the Centre Guillaume le Conquérant on Rue de Nesmond. It is open daily from 9 or 9.30 am to 12.30 pm and 2 to 6 or 6.30 pm. From mid-May to mid-September, the museum does not close at midday and stays open until 7 pm. The entry fee is 25FF (12FF for students). The excellent taped commentary (available in six languages), which visitors listen to while viewing the tapestry itself, renders the roomful of explanations upstairs somewhat unnecessary.

Cathédrale Notre Dame Bayeux's cathedral is considered an exceptional example of Norman-Gothic architecture. Most of the rather austere building dates from the 13th century, although the crypt, the arches of the nave and the lower portions of the towers on either side of the main entrance are Romanesque (late 11th century). The cathedral is open Monday to Saturday from 8 am to noon and 2 to 7 pm and on Sunday from 9 am to 12.15 pm and 2.30 to 7 pm.

Musée Diocésain d'Art Religieux Also known as the Musée d'Art Sacré (Museum of Sacred Art; ☎ 31.92.14.21), this museum is just south of the cathedral on Rue Lambert Leforestier. It is open daily from 10 am to 12.30 pm and 2 to 6 pm (till 7 pm from July to mid-September). The entry fee is 10FF (5FF for students). The section dedicated to sacred art is not especially gripping unless you're a fan of altar implements and clerical garb. But the **Conservatoire de la Dentelle** (☎ 31.92.73.80), which is dedicated to the preservation of traditional lace-making techniques, is fascinating. The more intricate pieces require dozens of bobbins and hundreds of pins.

Musée Baron Gérard This pleasant museum (☎ 31.92.14.21), next to the cathedral at Place de la Liberté, specialises in porcelain (including local products), lace and 15th to 19th century painting. Out front there is a huge plane tree known as the Arbre de la Liberté (Tree of Freedom), which was planted in 1797. The museum is open daily from 9.30 or 10 am to 12.30 pm and 2 to 6 or 6.30 pm. From June to September, it is open from 9 am to 7 pm. The entry fee is 15FF (8FF for students).

Musée Mémorial 1944 Bataille de Normandie Bayeux's municipal war museum (☎ 31.92.93.41) on Blvd Fabien Ware rather haphazardly displays thousands of photos, uniforms, weapons, newspaper clippings, etc associated with D-Day and the Battle of Normandy. It is open daily from 9.30 or 10 am to 12.30 pm and 2 to 6 or 6.30 pm. From June to August, the opening hours are 9 am to 7 pm. Entry costs 20FF (10FF for students). A 30-minute film in English is screened two to five times a day.

Bayeux War Cemetery This British cemetery, located on Blvd Fabien Ware a few hundred metres west of the war museum, is the largest of the 18 Commonwealth military cemeteries in Normandy. It contains the tombs of 4648 soldiers from 11 countries, including the graves of 466 Germans. There is an explanatory plaque in the small chapel to the right as you enter the grounds.

Places to Stay

Camping The *Camping Municipal de Bayeux* (☎ 31.92.08.43) is 1.6 km north of the centre of town just off Blvd d'Eindhoven. It's open from mid-March to mid-November. A tent site costs 6FF and guests pay 11.10FF each.

Hostels The *Family Home* youth hostel and guesthouse (☎ 31.92.15.22) at 39 Rue du Général de Dais is an excellent place to meet other travellers. A bed in a dorm room costs 80FF (73FF if you've got a YHA card), including breakfast. Singles are available for 125FF and telephone reservations are accepted. The hostel is open all day, but curfew is (theoretically) 11 pm. Multicourse French dinners prepared by the proprietor herself – 'incredible feasts' according to travellers – cost only 55FF, including wine. Vegetarian dishes are available on request.

The *Centre d'Accueil Municipal* hostel (☎ 31.92.08.19) at 21 Rue des Marettes, one km south-west of the cathedral, is housed in a large, modern building that nevertheless manages to be both efficient and friendly; however, don't count on meeting people here. Antiseptic but comfortable singles (all they have) are a great deal at 75FF, including breakfast at 8 am. They usually accept reservations by telephone. A YHA card is not necessary.

Hotels The old but well-maintained *Hôtel de*

FRANCE

FRANCE

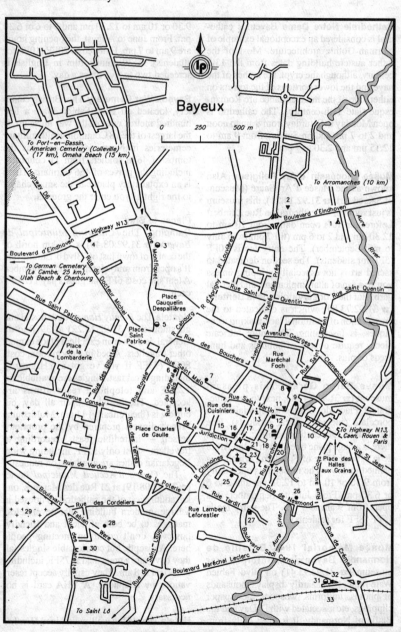

Bayeux

0   250   500 m

To Port-en-Bessin,
American Cemetery (Colleville)
(17 km), Omaha Beach (15 km)

To Arromanches (10 km)

Boulevard d'Eindhoven

Aure River

Highway N13

Boulevard d'Eindhoven

To German Cemetery
(La Cambe, 25 km),
Utah Beach & Cherbourg

Rue du Docteur Michel

Rue Montfiquet

Rue Saint
Quentin

R d'Abrigny

Rue des Prés

Rue Saint Quentin

Place
Gauquelin
Despallières

R Cabourg

Rue des Bouchers

Avenue Georges

Avenue de la Vallée des Prés

Rue Saint Laurent

Place
Saint
Patrice

Rue Saint Patrice

Place de la
Lombarderie

Rue des Bluettes

Rue Royale

Rue Saint Malo

Rue du Général de Dais

Rue Maréchal
Foch

Rue Clemenceau

Avenue Conseil

Rue Saint Martin

Rue des Terres

R de la Juridiction

Rue des
Cuisiniers

To Highway N13,
Caen, Rouen &
Paris

Place Charles
de Gaulle

Rue St Jean

Rue de Verdun

R de la Poterie

R Chanoines

Rue Larcher

Place des
Halles
aux Grains

Rue aux Coqs

Boulevard
Fabien
Ware

Rue des Cordeliers

Rue des Marettes

Rue de Nesmond

Aure River

Rue Tardif

Rue Lambert
Leforestier

Rue de Saint-Loup

Boulevard Sadi Carnot

Rue de Crémel

Boulevard Maréchal Leclerc

To Saint Lô

■ PLACES TO STAY	10	Wednesday Food	13	Tourist Office
		Market	18	City Hall
1 Camping Municipal de	11	Boulangerie	19	Main Post Office
Bayeux	15	Crêperie Notre Dame	21	Musée Baron Gérard
12 Hôtel des Sports	17	Boulangerie La	22	Notre Dame Cathedral
14 Family Home Youth		Cathédrale	23	Place de la Liberté
Hostel & Guesthouse	24	Le Petit Normand	25	Musée Diocésain d'Art
16 Hôtel Notre Dame		Restaurant		Religieux
20 Hôtel La Tour d'Argent			26	Museum of the Bayeux
27 Relais des Cèdres		OTHER		Tapestry
30 Centre d'Accueil			28	Musée Mémorial 1944
Municipal	3	Bus Fly (to Omaha		Bataille de
32 Hôtel de la Gare		Beach)		Normandie
	4	Lefebvre Car Rental	29	Bayeux War Cemetery
▼ PLACES TO EAT	5	Bus Stops	31	Bus Verts Office
	6	Caisse d'Épargne Bank	32	Normandy Tour Buses
2 Champion Supermarket	7	Société Générale Bank	33	Railway Station
8 Point Coop Grocery	9	Laundrette		

la Gare (☎ 31.92.10.70) at 26 Place de la Gare is opposite the railway station. Singles/doubles start at 85/100FF. Two-bed triples/quads are 160FF and showers are free.

The *Hôtel Notre Dame* (☎ 31.92.87.24) at 44 Rue des Cuisiniers is a two-star establishment opposite the front of the cathedral. They have half a dozen cheaper rooms, including eminently serviceable doubles from 130FF. Showers cost 20FF. This is an excellent deal given the location and amenities. The *Hôtel La Tour d'Argent* (☎ 31.92.30.08), which is two blocks away at 31 Rue Larcher, has large, quiet singles/doubles starting at 110FF. An extra bed is only 45FF. Unfortunately, this place is not equipped with showers. They do not accept telephone reservations, and from October to May reception is closed on Mondays.

If you can afford something more up-market, you might try the *Relais des Cèdres* (☎ 31.21.98.07), which is in an early 20th century mansion at 1 Blvd Sadi Carnot. Doubles cost 120 or 160FF with washbasin and 180 to 260FF with shower and toilet. The *Hôtel des Sports* (☎ 31.92.28.53) at 19 Rue Saint Martin has tastefully appointed singles/doubles (most with shower) starting at 160/180FF.

Places to Eat

Le Petit Normand (☎ 31.22.88.66) at 35 Rue Larcher specialises in traditional Norman food prepared with apple cider. *Menus* start at 49FF. The restaurant is open from noon to 2 pm and 7 to 10 pm daily except Sunday and Thursday evenings. It is open Thursday night from May to mid-November and every day of the week in July and August. *Crêperie Notre Dame* (☎ 31.21.88.70), half a block from the cathedral at 8 Rue de la Juridiction, is open Monday to Sunday from noon to 2 pm and 7 to 9 pm (and often later).

There is an open-air market along Rue Saint Jean on Wednesday mornings and at Place Saint Patrice on Saturday mornings. *Teurgoule*, a sweet cinnamon-flavoured rice pudding typical of the Bayeux region, is usually available at the market. There are lots of food shops along Rue Saint Martin and Rue Saint Jean between the tourist office and Place des Halles aux Grains, including a boulangerie at 32bis Rue Saint Martin (closed Thursday). *Boulangerie La Cathédrale* (closed Wednesday) at 37 Rue du Bienvenu has excellent chocolate and custard pastries. The *Point Coop* grocery at 23 Rue du Maréchal Foch is open Tuesday to Saturday from 8.30 am to 12.15 pm and 2.30 to 7.15 pm and on Sunday from 8.30 am to noon or 12.30 pm.

FRANCE

Getting There & Away
Train The train station (☎ 31.92.80.50 or 31.83.50.50 for information, 31.34.14.05 for reservations) is open Monday to Saturday from 6 am to 9 pm (10.30 pm on Friday) and on Sunday from 7.30 am to 8 pm. Trains from here serve Paris' Gare Saint Lazare (via Caen), Cherbourg, Rennes and points beyond.

Getting Around
See the D-Day Beaches section for information on car rental and transport to places in the vicinity of Bayeux. Taxis can be ordered 24 hours a day by calling ☎ 31.92.92.40.

D-DAY BEACHES
The D-Day landings, codenamed Operation Overlord, were the largest military operation in history. Early on the morning of 6 June 1944, swarms of landing craft (part of a flotilla of 6939 boats and ships of all sorts) hit the beaches and tens of thousands of soldiers from the USA, UK and Canada (with small contingents from other countries) began pouring onto French soil. Most of the 135,000 Allied troops who were transported to France that day stormed ashore or disembarked along 80 km of beaches along the coast north of Bayeux codenamed (from west to east) Utah and Omaha (in the American sector) and Gold, Juno and Sword (in the British and Canadian sector). The landings on D-Day (Jour J in French) were followed by the start of the 76-day battle of Normandy.

Things to See
Arromanches To make it possible to unload the vast quantities of cargo necessary to prosecute the war, the Allies established two prefabricated ports codenamed (and known to this day) as **Mulberry Harbours**. One of them, Port Winston, can still be seen at Arromanches, a seaside town 10 km northeast of Bayeux. The harbour consists of 146 massive cement caissons towed over from England and sunk to form a semicircular breakwater inside which floating piers were moored. In the three months after D-Day,

2½ million men, four million tonnes of equipment and 500,000 vehicles where unloaded here. At low tide you can walk out to many of the caissons. The best view of Port Winston is from the hill east of town.

The well-regarded **Musée du Débarquement** (D-Day Landing Museum; ☎ 31.22.34.31) in Arromanches explains the logistics and importance of the establishment of Port Winston and makes a good first stop before visiting the beaches. It is open daily from 9 to 11.30 am and 2 to 5.30 pm. From May to early September, museum hours are 9 am to 6.30 pm; the entry fee is 25FF (12FF for students). The last guided tour (in French, with a written text in English) leaves 45 minutes before closing time (both at midday and in the evening).

Omaha Beach The most brutal fighting of 6 June was fought 15 km north-west of Bayeux along seven km of coast codenamed Omaha. As you stand on the beach, try to imagine how the US soldiers must have felt running up the sand towards the German positions along the nearby ridge... A memorial marks the site of the first US military cemetery on French soil, where soldiers killed right on the beach were initially buried. Today, Omaha Beach is lined with holiday cottages and is popular with swimmers and sunbathers. Little evidence of the war remains except a single concrete boat which was used to carry tanks ashore.

American Military Cemetery The remains of the Americans who lost their lives during the Battle of Normandy were either sent back to the USA (if their families so requested) or buried in the American military cemetery (☎ 31.22.40.62) at Colleville, 17 km north-west of Bayeux, which contains the graves of 9386 American soldiers and a memorial to 1557 others whose remains were never found. The huge, immaculately tended expanse of white crosses and Stars of David, set on a hill overlooking Omaha Beach, testifies to the extent of the killing which took place around here in 1944. The cemetery is open from 8 am to 5 pm (9 am to 6 pm from

FRANCE

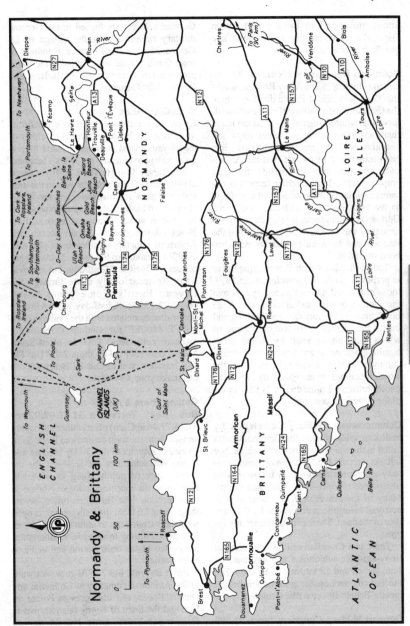

Normandy & Brittany

about mid-April to September). From Bayeux, it can be reached by Bus Verts' line No 70, but service is infrequent.

Pointe du Hoc Ranger Memorial At 7.10 am on 6 June, 225 US Army Rangers scaled the 30-metre cliffs at Pointe du Hoc, where the Germans had a battery of mammoth artillery guns whose range of up to 20 km made them a serious threat to Allied ships and beachheads. The guns, as it turns out, had been transferred elsewhere, but the American commandos captured the gun emplacements (huge circular cement structures) and the German command post (next to the two flagpoles) and then fought off German counterattacks for two days. By the time they were relieved on 8 June, 77 of the Rangers had been killed and 58 more had been wounded.

Today, the site, which France turned over in perpetuity to the US government in 1979, looks much as it did half a century ago, and the ground is still pockmarked with huge bomb craters. Visitors can walk among and inside the German fortifications, some of which were blown apart by Allied aerial bombing and naval artillery. In the German command post, you can still see where the wooden ceilings were charred by American flame-throwers. Pointe du Hoc is 12 km west of the American cemetery.

Commonwealth Military Cemeteries By tradition, soldiers from the Commonwealth killed in the war were buried near where they fell. As a result, the 18 Commonwealth military cemeteries in Normandy follow the line of advance of British and Canadian troops. Many of the gravestones are adorned with personal inscriptions composed by the families of the dead. These cemeteries are always open.

There is a Canadian military cemetery at Bény-sur-Mer, which is a few km south of Juno Beach and 18 km east of Bayeux. See the Bayeux section for information on the mostly British Bayeux War Cemetery.

German Military Cemetery Some 21,000 German soldiers are buried in the German military cemetery near the village of La Cambe, 25 km west of Bayeux. Hundreds of other German dead were buried in the Commonwealth cemeteries, including the Bayeux War Cemetery.

Organised Tours
Given the limitations posed by other forms of transport, a bus tour offered by either of the Bayeux-based companies listed here is an excellent way to see the D-Day beaches.

Normandy Tour (☎ 31.92.10.70) is based at Hôtel de la Gare, which is next to the train station. Times and itineraries are very flexible and will basically be adapted to whatever the clients want. Tours that stop at Juno Beach, Arromanches, Omaha Beach, the American cemetery and Pointe du Hoc cost 100FF a person. Bus Fly (☎ 31.22.00.08) has offices at 24 Rue Montfiquet but reservations are most easily made through the Bayeux Family Home youth hostel (☎ 31.92.15.22). A half-day guided tour to major sites associated with the landings costs 120FF (100FF for students), including museum entry fees. Trips to Mont-Saint-Michel cost 150FF. For about 25FF Bus Fly will transport you to Omaha Beach so you can make your way back.

Getting There & Away
Bus Bus Verts (☎ 31.92.02.92, or 31.44.77.44 in Caen) offers rather infrequent service from the train station and Place Saint Patrice in Bayeux to the D-Day beaches and Caen. The schedules are arranged for the convenience of pupils going to school in Bayeux in the morning and going home in the afternoon. The Bus Verts office, across the parking lot from the train station, is open weekdays from 9 am to noon and 2 to 5 pm. It is closed during most of July. Timetables are posted in the train station and at Place Saint Patrice.

From Bayeux, bus No 70 goes westward to the American cemetery at Colleville and Omaha Beach, and also goes to Pointe du Hoc and the town of Isigny (also known as Isigny-sur-Mer). Line No 74 serves

Arromanches, Gold and Juno beaches and Courseulles. During July and August only, the Ligne Côte de Nacre goes to Caen via Arromanches, Gold, Juno and Sword beaches, and the town of Ouistreham.

Car For three or more people, renting a car can actually be cheaper than a tour. Lefebvre Car Rental (☎ 31.92.05.96) on Blvd d'Eindhoven (at the Esso petrol station) charges 300FF for one day with 100 free km (about the distance of a circuit to the beaches) and 500FF for two days with 300 free km. If you're in an accident and it's your fault, there is a 2000FF excess (deductible). The office is open from 8 am to 8 pm daily except Sunday afternoon, and every day of the week from July to mid-September.

Bicycle Ten-speeds are available at the Bayeux Train Station for 50FF a day. One-speeds cost 50FF a day at the Family Home youth hostel. For mountain bikes, try Pitard (☎ 31.92.27.85) at 29 Rue Saint Jean.

MONT-SAINT-MICHEL

No matter how many pictures you've seen, it is difficult not to be at least slightly overwhelmed by your first glimpse of Mont-Saint-Michel. Around the base are the ancient ramparts and a jumble of buildings that house the 120 people who live here. Completely covering the summit is the massive abbey, a soaring ensemble of buildings in a hotchpotch of architectural styles. The abbey is topped by a slender spire at the very tip of which – 152 metres above the sea – is a gilded statue of Saint Michel (the Archangel Michael) and the dragon.

Mont-Saint-Michel's fame derives in part from the area's extraordinary tides, which are in many ways even more amazing than the abbey itself. Depending on the orbits of the moon and, to a lesser extent, of the sun, the difference in the level of the sea between low tide and high tide can reach 15 metres! At low tide, the Mont looks out on bare sand stretching many km off into the distance. At high tide – only about six hours later – this huge expanse of tideland will be under water.

It is said that when the tide comes in, seawater races across the sand at the clip of a galloping horse. Because of progressive siltation, the Mont and causeway (constructed in 1879) are completely surrounded by the sea only during the highest of tides (those given a grade of 90 or more).

History

According to Celtic mythology, Mont-Saint-Michel was one of the sea tombs to which the souls of the dead were conveyed. In 708 AD Saint Michel appeared to Aubert, Bishop of Avranches, and told him to build a devotional chapel at the top of the Mont. In 966, Richard I, Duke of Normandy, transferred Mont-Saint-Michel to the Benedictines, who turned it into an important centre of learning, and, later, into something of an ecclesiastical fortress, with a military garrison at the disposal of the abbot – and the king.

In the early 15th century, during the Hundred Years' War (waged between England and France from 1337 to 1453), the English blockaded and besieged Mont-Saint-Michel three times and, for a while, even occupied Tombelaine, the tiny island two km north of the Mont. But the fortified abbey withstood these assaults and managed to remain the only place in all of western and northern France not to fall into English hands. All this martial activity turned the abbey into a base for powerful and ambitious churchmen, rather than a place of reflection and scholarship.

Orientation

There is only one opening in the ramparts, Porte de l'Avancée. The only street, the Grande Rue, is lined with touristy shops. Pontorson, the nearest town, is nine km south along D976.

Information

The tourist office (☎ 33.60.14.30) is up the stairs to the left as you enter Porte de l'Avancée. It is open Monday to Saturday from 9 am to noon and 2 to 6 pm. From Easter to sometime in autumn, it is open on Sunday from 9.30 am to noon and 1 to 6.30 pm. In

July and August hours are 9 am to 7 pm daily. If you are interested in what the tide will be doing during your visit, ask for a copy of the *horaire des marées*.

Things to See

Walking Tour When the tide is out, it's possible to walk all the way around Mont-Saint-Michel, a distance of about one km. Straying away from the Mont can be risky: you could get stuck in quicksand (from which Norman soldiers are depicted being rescued in one scene of the Bayeux Tapestry) just as the tide comes rushing in...

Abbaye du Mont-Saint-Michel The Mont's major attraction is the renowned abbey (☎ 33.60.04.52), which is open daily except on holidays from 9.30 to 11.45 am and 1.45 to 5 pm (4.15 pm during January and the first half of February). From mid-May to mid-September, it is open from 9.30 am to 6 pm. To get there, walk all the way to the top of the Grande Rue and then climb the stairway.

A few rooms can be visited without a guide, but given the Mont's rich history and the remarkable diversity of its architectural features, it's well worth taking a guided tour. One-hour tours in English, available all year except in winter, cost 32FF (18FF if you're aged 18 to 24). From June to September, eight English tours are held each day. The last tour in English leaves at least half an hour before closing time.

The **Église** (abbey church) was built at the rocky tip of the mountain. To be more precise, the transept rests on solid rock while the nave, choir and transept arms are supported by the massively built rooms below. The church is famous for its mixture of architectural styles: the nave (11th-12th century) is Romanesque (Norman) while the choir (late 15th century) is Flamboyant-Gothic.

The buildings on the north side of the Mont are known as the **Merveille** (marvel). The famous **Cloître** is surrounded by a double row of delicately carved arches resting on granite pillars. The early 13th century **Réfectoire** (dining hall) is illuminated by a wall of recessed windows,

a remarkable arrangement given that the sheer drop-off precluded the use of flying buttresses. The High Gothic **Salle des Hôtes** (Guest Hall), which dates from 1213, has two giant fireplaces. It's easy to imagine the king and his entourage seated at huge tables, dining sumptuously with some of the most powerful monks in all of France.

Places to Stay

Camping *Camping du Mont-Saint-Michel* (☎ 33.60.09.33) is on D976 (the road to Pontorson) only two km from the Mont. This grassy, shaded camping ground is open from mid-February to mid-November and charges 12FF per person, 11FF for a tent and 11FF for a car. There are several other camping grounds a couple of km farther towards Pontorson.

Hostel *Centre Duguesclin* (☎ 33.60.18.65) in Pontorson operates as a hostel from June to September. You don't need a YHA card to stay here. A bed in a three-bunk room costs 38FF a night, but you must bring your own sheets. There are kitchen facilities on the ground floor. The hostel is closed from noon to 5 pm, but there is no curfew. If you arrive when reception is closed, you can leave your luggage in the common room.

The hostel is about one km from the train station. At the Courriers Bretons office, turn right onto Rue du Docteur Tizon, go left onto Rue du Couësnon and then right onto Rue du Général Patton. The hostel is on the left in a three-storey stone building.

Hotels Across Place de la Gare from the Pontorson train station, there are a number of cheap hotels. The *Hôtel de France* (☎ 33.60.29.17) at 2 Rue de Rennes has singles/doubles from 75/110FF and triples/quads from 130/140FF. Showers are free. Telephone reservations are not accepted during July and August. The *Hôtel Le Rénové* (☎ 33.60.00.21) at 4 Rue de Rennes has simple doubles for 130 to 170FF (140 to 180FF in July and August). Triples or quads cost 230FF. The *Hôtel de l'Arrivée* (☎ 33.60.01.57) at 14 Rue du Docteur Tizon has doubles for 80FF (with washbasin) and 145FF (with shower). Triples/quads with washbasin are 145/160FF. Hall showers are 15FF.

Places to Eat
The tourist restaurants around the base of the Mont are not bargains. A few places along the Grande Rue sell sandwiches.

The supermarket nearest the Mont is next to Camping du Mont-Saint-Michel, which is on D976, two km south of the Mont. The store is open mid-February to October from 8 am to 8 pm (10 pm in July and August).

In Pontorson, there is a boulangerie (closed Monday) near the train station at 12 Rue du Docteur Tizon. There is a *Supermarché Champion* down the block from the Centre Duguesclin hostel.

Getting There & Away
Bus STN (☎ 33.58.03.57 in Avranches) bus No 15 runs from the Pontorson Train Station to Mont-Saint-Michel all year long. There are nine buses a day in July and August (six on weekends and holidays) and fewer during the rest of the year. Most of the buses connect with the departure or arrival of trains to/from Paris, Rennes and Caen.

For information on bus transport from Saint Malo to Mont-Saint-Michel, a distance of 52 km, see Getting There & Away in the Saint Malo section. The Pontorson office of Courriers Bretons buses (☎ 33.60.11.43, or 99.56.79.09 in Saint Malo) is 60 metres to the left as you exit the train station. It is open weekdays from 10 am to noon and 5.30 to 7 pm. Courriers Bretons buses on their way *to* Mont-Saint-Michel do not pick up passengers in Pontorson.

Train There are trains to the Pontorson-Mont-Saint-Michel train station (☎ 33.60.00.35 or 33.57.50.50 for information) from Caen (via Folligny) and Rennes (via Dol). From Paris, take the train to Caen (from Gare Saint Lazare) or Rennes (from Gare Montparnasse). Schedules are posted at the station.

Bicycle Bikes can be rented at the Pontorson train station and from E Videloup (☎ 33.60.11.40) at 1bis Rue du Couësnon,

which is halfway between the train station and the Centre Duguesclin hostel. Three or 10-speeds are 30FF a day and mountain bikes are 50FF a day. This place is open from 8.30 am to 12.30 pm and 2 to 7 pm daily except Monday morning and Sunday.

Brittany

Brittany (Bretagne), the westernmost region of France, is a land celebrated for its rugged countryside and wild coastline. The area is also known for its long list of saints unrecognised by Rome and its many colourful religious celebrations (*pardons*). Traditional costumes, including various versions of the extraordinary lace headdresses worn by the women, can still sometimes be seen at *pardons* and local festivals.

Breton customs are most in evidence in Cornouaille, the area at the south-western tip of the Breton peninsula, whose largest town is Quimper. Saint Malo is a popular tourist destination and seaside resort on Brittany's north coast.

Breton Identity
The people of Brittany, driven from their homes in what is now Great Britain by the Anglo-Saxon invasions, migrated across the English Channel in the 5th and 6th centuries, bringing with them their Celtic language and traditions. For centuries a rich and powerful duchy, Brittany became part of France in 1532. To this day, many Bretons have not abandoned the hope that their region will one day regain its independence.

Language
The indigenous language of Brittany is Breton, a Celtic language related to Welsh and, more distantly, to Irish and Scottish Gaelic. Breton can sometimes still be heard in western Brittany and especially Cornouaille, where perhaps a third of the population understands the language. However, only a tiny fraction of the people speak Breton at home.

FRANCE

Getting Around

Brittany's lack of convenient, intercity public transport and the appeal of exploring out-of-the-way destinations make renting a car or motorbike worth considering.

QUIMPER

Situated at the confluence (kemper in Breton) of two rivers, the Odet and the Steïr, Quimper (pronounced cam-PAIR), with a population of 60,000, has successfully preserved its Breton architecture and atmosphere and is considered by many the cultural and artistic capital of Brittany. Some even refer to the city as the 'soul of Brittany'. It is the prefecture of the department of Finistère.

The Festival de Cornouaille, a showcase for the traditional music, costumes and culture of Brittany, is held here every year between the third and fourth Sundays in July.

Orientation

The old city is to the west and north-west of Cathédrale Saint Corentin, which is a block north of the Odet River. The train and bus stations are 700 metres east of the old city. Mont Frugy overlooks the city centre from the south bank of the Odet River.

Information

The tourist office (☎ 98.53.04.05) at Place de la Résistance is generally open Monday to Saturday from 9 am to noon and 2 to 6 pm. From May to June and during the first half of September, afternoon hours are from 1.30 to 6.30 pm (till 7 pm in June). During July and August, the office is open from 8.30 am to 8 pm. From May to mid-September, Sunday and holiday hours are 9.30 am to 12.30 pm.

Money The Banque de France (☎ 98.90.70.00) is 150 metres from the train station at 29 Ave de la Gare. It is open Tuesday to Saturday from 8.45 am to noon and 1.30 to 3.30 pm. There are a number of banks on Rue Amiral Ronarc'h and another few across Place Saint Corentin from the cathedral. Most are open Tuesday to Saturday, although the Crédit Agricole (☎ 98.95.46.33) at 14 Place Saint Corentin is open Monday to Saturday from 8.30 or 9 am to 12.30 pm and 2 to 5.40 pm (4.40 pm on Monday and Saturday).

Post The main post office (☎ 98.95.65.85) at 17 Blvd de Kerguélen, which offers currency exchange services, is open weekdays from 8 am to 7 pm and on Saturday from 8 am to noon.

Quimper's postcode is 29000.

Things to See

Walking Tour Strolling along the quays that run along both banks of the Odet River is a fine way to get a feel for the city. The old city is known for its centuries-old houses, which are especially in evidence on **Rue Kéréon**. To scale 70-metre-high **Mont Frugy**, from where much of the city can be viewed, take the path near the tourist office.

Cathédrale Saint Corentin Quimper's cathedral, built between 1239 and 1515 (with spires added in the 1850s), incorporates many Breton elements, including – on the west façade between the spires – an equestrian statue of King Gradlon, the mythical 5th century founder of Quimper. The early 15th century nave is out of line with the choir, built two centuries earlier. The cathedral's patron saint is Saint Corentin, who was the town's first bishop and who, according to legend, ate half of a miraculous fish each morning and threw the rest back in the river. The following morning the fish would reappear whole and again offer itself to the saint.

Museums The **Musée Départemental Breton** (☎ 98.95.21.60), which is next to the cathedral in the former bishop's palace, houses exhibits on the history, furniture, costumes, crafts and archaeology of the Finistère area. It is open from 9 am to noon and 2 to 5 pm daily except Sunday morning and Monday. From June to September it is open daily from 9 am to 6 pm. The entry fee is 20FF (10FF for students) but is slightly

FRANCE

PLACES TO STAY
4 Hôtel Celtic
33 Hôtel de l'Ouest
34 Hotels

▼ **PLACES TO EAT**
5 Euzen Traiteur
  (Prepared Foods)
6 Boulangerie Louis
  Tandé
11 Monoprix Supermarket

12 Covered Market
24 Aux Jardins du Midi
  Supermarket
30 Crêperies du Frugy
31 Crêperies
32 Restaurants

OTHER
1 Torch' VTT
  (Bicycle Rental)
2 Place de la Tourbie
3 Place de Locronan

7 Église Saint Mathieu
8 Place Au Beurre
9 Musée des Beaux-Arts
  & City Hall
10 Place Laennec
13 Crédit Agricole Bank
14 Place Saint Corentin
15 Ar Bed Keltiek &
  François Villec Shops
16 Cathédrale Saint
  Corentin
17 Musée Départemental
  Breton

18 Cathedral Garden
19 Main Post Office
20 Prefecture Building
21 Police Station
22 Theatre
23 Laundrette
25 Banque de France
26 Bus Station & Biciclub
  (Bicycle Rental)
27 Railway Station
28 Place de la Résistance
29 Tourist Office
35 Faïenceries HB Henriot

Rue de Missilien

Rue Henri de Bournaze

Rue de Kerfeunteun

Rue de Pen Ar-Steir

Rue de la Providence

Rue de Locronan

Rue du Moulin du Duc

Steir River

Rue du Pichery

Rue Élie Fréron

Rue de Kerustin

Rue Saint Marc

Rue des Gentilshommes

Rue des Douves

Rue de Brest

Route de Brest

Allée de Kerfily

Rue du Couedic

Rue du Chapeau Rouge

Rue Kéréon

Rue Verderet

Rue Étienne Gourmelen

Rue de l'Hippodrome

Pl. de la Tour d'Auvergne

Rue Laennec

Rue du Frout

Rue des Réguaires

Rue Jacques Cartier

Impasse de l'Odet

Rue du Parc

Blvd A de Kerguélen

Blvd Dupleix

Rue Aristide Briand

Ave. de la Gare

Rue Sainte Thérèse

Rue Théodore Le Hars

Rue J-P Calloch

Rue Le Déan

Rue Jean Jaurès

To Concarneau (24 km) & Lorient

Allées de Locmaria

Odet River

Quai de l'Odet

Mont Frugy

Rue de Pen-Ar-Stang

Rue Haute

Rue Alfred de Musset

Rue du 19 Mars

Route de Bénodet

To Camping Municipal (700 m)

To Highway D34, Bénodet (17 km), Concarneau (24 km)

Quimper

0   250   500 m

higher during the summer. The **Musée des Beaux-Arts** (☎ 98.95.45.20), in the Hôtel de Ville near the cathedral, has paintings – French, Breton, Flemish, Dutch, Spanish and Italian – from the 16th to early 20th centuries.

Faïencerie Tour Faïenceries HB Henriot (☎ 98.90.09.36), founded in 1690, have frequent tours of their factory, which is on Rue Haute, on weekdays from 9 or 9.30 to 11.30 am and 1.30 or 2 to 4.30 pm (3 pm on Friday). The cost is 13FF (7FF for students).

Places to Stay

It is extremely difficult to find accommodation between the third and fourth Sundays in July, when the Festival de Cornouaille is held.

Camping *Camping Municipal* (☎ 98.55.61.09; open all year) is very cheap: 7FF per person, 5FF for a shower, 2FF for a tent emplacement and 4FF for a car. It is slightly over one km west of the old city; to get there, take Rue de Pont l'Abbé north-westward from Quai de l'Odet and keep walking straight ahead when Rue de Pont l'Abbé veers left. From the train station, take bus No 1 (which runs Monday to Saturday only) and get off at the Chaptal stop.

Hotels The friendly *Hôtel de l'Ouest* (☎ 98.90.28.35) at 63 Rue Le Déan, up Rue Jean-Pierre Calloch from the train station, has large, pleasant singles/doubles from 95/140FF and triples/quads from 170/210FF; showers are 15FF. The *Hôtel Pascal* (☎ 98.90.00.81) at 17bis Ave de la Gare has a few doubles for 100 or 120FF. Singles/doubles with shower, toilet and TV are 155/180FF. You might also try the *Hôtel Café Nantaïs* (☎ 98.90.07.84) at 23 Ave de la Gare, whose doubles (with washbasin and bidet) are 118FF.

The *Hôtel Celtic* (☎ 98.55.59.35), 100 metres north of Saint Mathieu Church at 13 Rue Douarnenez, has doubles without/with shower for 90/140FF. Doubles with shower and toilet are 200FF.

Places to Eat

Restaurants Crêpes, a Breton speciality, are your best bet for a cheap and filling meal. They are usually eaten with *cidre* (cider), which comes either *doux* (sweet) or *brut* (dry). Along Rue Sainte Catherine, which is right across the river from the cathedral, there are crêperies at No 11, No 15 and No 16. *Crêperie du Frugy* (☎ 98.90.32.49) at No 9 Rue Sainte Thérèse is open from noon to 2.30 pm and 6.30 to 10.30 pm daily except Sunday lunch time and Monday. Crêpes cost 6 to 38.50FF.

In the train station area, you'll find several restaurants on Rue Le Déan and Rue Jean Jaurès. These include a Vietnamese place at 53 Rue Le Déan and a Moroccan restaurant (☎ 98.53.04.13) at 37 Rue Le Déan.

Self-Catering *Boulangerie Louis Tandé* at 15 Rue du Chapeau Rouge, three blocks west of the cathedral, has outstanding wholegrain and multicereal breads. It is open from 7 am to 7.30 pm Tuesday to Saturday and one Monday in three (in rotation with nearby boulangeries). Except in summer, it is closed for a half-hour between 1.30 and 2 pm. Just down the block at 10 Rue du Chapeau Rouge is *Euzen Traiteur*, which has meats, prepared dishes and especially tasty gnocchi (dumplings). It is open from 8 am to 7.30 pm daily except Sunday. The *Monoprix* supermarket on Quai du Port au Vin (near the covered market) is open from 9 am to 12.30 pm and 2 to 7 pm daily except Sunday.

The *Aux Jardins du Midi* supermarket, open daily from 8 am to 8 pm, is two blocks from the train station at 41 Ave de la Gare. There is a boulangerie at 47 Ave de la Gare.

Things to Buy

Ar Bed Keltiek (☎ 98.95.42.82) at 2 Rue du Roi Gradlon has a wide selection of Celtic music, books, pottery and jewellery. The store is open Tuesday to Saturday from 10 am to noon and 2 to 7 pm. During July and August it is open Monday to Saturday from 8.30 or 9 am to 7.30 pm and on Sunday from 10 am to 1 pm and 2.30 to 6 pm. For faïence and high-quality textiles, decorated with traditionally inspired original designs, go to the excellent shop of François le Villec (☎ 98.95.31.54) at 4 Rue du Roi Gradlon. It is open Monday to Saturday from 9 am to noon and 2 to 7 pm (daily with no midday break in summer).

Getting There & Away

Bus The bus station is in the building to the right as you exit the train station. Schedules are posted on the station building and on the uprights around the parking lot. The office (☎ 98.90.17.83) serving two bus companies, Castric and Le Cœur (☎ 98.54.40.15 in Pouldreuzic, 15 km west of Quimper), is open from 9 or 9.30 am to noon and 2 or 2.30 to 6.30 pm daily except Saturday afternoon and Sunday. There is reduced service on Sunday and during the off season. CAT (☎ 98.44.46.73 in Brest), whose office is at 5 Blvd de Kerguélen, has buses to Brest, Pointe du Raz, Roscoff (from where there are ferries to Plymouth, England) and other destinations. Caoudal (☎ 98.56.96.72 in La Forêt-Fouesnant, near Concarneau) has service to Concarneau and Quimperlé (east of Concarneau). For information on SNCF buses to Douarnenez, Camaret-sur-Mer, Concarneau and Quiberon, enquire at the train station.

Train The train station (☎ 98.90.50.50 for information, 98.90.26.21 for reservations) is east of the centre of town on Ave de la Gare. The information counters are open daily from 8.30 am to 6.30 or 7 pm (8 am to 7 pm in July and August). A one-way ticket to Paris' Gare Montparnasse costs 283FF (plus TGV reservation fee if applicable); TGV trains can be picked up in Rennes. The trip takes about five hours. You can also reach Saint Malo by train.

Getting Around

Bus The company that runs Quimper's bus network, QUB, has an information booth near the tourist office at Place de la Résistance. Buses stop around 7 pm and do not operate on Sunday.

Bicycle Possible cycling destinations from Quimper include Bénodet, Concarneau and even Pointe du Raz. Torch' VTT (☎ 98.53.84.41) at 58 Rue de la Providence rents mountain bikes for 100FF a day and 69FF for half a day (69 and 49FF respectively from October to April). This shop, which is open from 9.30 am to 7 pm daily except Sunday, is a good source of information on cycling routes. Biciclub (no phone), across the parking lot from the train station, has three-speeds for 60FF a day, 10-speeds for 80FF and mountain bikes for 100FF. It is open from 9 am to 7 pm every day but *only* during the summer.

CONCARNEAU

Concarneau (population 18,000), France's third most important trawler port, is 24 km south of Quimper. Much of the tuna brought ashore here is caught in the Indian Ocean and off the coast of Africa. The town is slightly scruffy and at the same time a bit touristy, but it's refreshingly unpretentious and is near several decent beaches.

Information

The tourist office (☎ 98.97.01.44) is on Quai d'Aiguillon, 100 or so metres north of the west gate to the Ville Close (see below). It is open Monday to Saturday from 9 am to 6 pm and, from mid-May to June, on Sunday from 9 am to 12.30 pm. During July and August, it's open daily from 9 am to 8 pm.

Concarneau's postcode is 29900.

Things to See

The **Ville Close** (walled city), built on a 350-metre-long island that was fortified between the 14th and 17th centuries, is reached from Quai Peneroff by a bridge. It is jam-packed with touristy shops and restaurants but there are nice views of the town, the port and the bay from the **ramparts** *(remparts)*, which are open for strolling every day from Easter to September from 10 am to noon or 12.30 pm and 2 to sometime between 6 and 7.30 pm. There is no midday closure during July and August. The entry fee is 4FF; the ticket

FRANCE

office is up the stairs to the left just inside the west gate.

The **Musée de la Pêche** (☎ 98.97.10.20), on Rue Vauban not far from the west gate, has interesting exhibits and dioramas on everything you didn't know you wanted to know about the fishing industry over the centuries. The aquariums contain mostly edible varieties of marine life. The museum is open daily from 9.30 am to 12.30 pm and 2 to 6 pm (9.30 am to 7 pm from mid-June to mid-September). The entry fee is 30FF (no student discount).

Beaches There are two beaches around Concarneau. **Plage des Sables Blancs** is 1.5 km north-west of the tourist office on Baie de la Forêt. To get there, take bus No 1. **Plage du Cabellou**, several km south of town, can be reached by bus No 2.

Places to Stay

Camping Concarneau's half a dozen camping grounds include *Camping Moulin* (☎ 98.50.53.08 or 98.97.09.37), which is 600 metres south-east of the Ville Close at 49 Rue de Tregunc. It is open from Easter to September. It costs 17FF per person plus 15FF for a tent emplacement and a place to park. Take bus No 2 to get there. *Camping Lanadan* (☎ 98.97.17.78), about 100 metres north of the Plage des Sables Blancs on Route de la Forêt, is open from mid-June to mid-September. It is served by bus No 1.

Hostel The *Auberge de Jeunesse* (☎ 98.97.03.47) is right on the water at Place de la Croix, next to the small granite church. To get there from the tourist office, walk south to the end of Quai Peneroff and turn right. A bed is 40FF and breakfast is 16FF. Reception is open from 9 to noon and 6 to 8 pm, but the dining room, where you can leave your bags, is open all day.

Hotels At 9 Place Jean Jaurès, across Quai Peneroff from the Ville Close, the *Hôtel Les Voyageurs* (☎ 98.97.08.06) has doubles for 125FF with washbasin and bidet and 160FF with shower.

Places to Eat

There are lots of restaurants near the west gate to the Ville Close at Place Jean Jaurès and along Ave Docteur Nicolas.

The alimentation générale (grocery store; ☎ 98.97.28.14) at 8 Ave Docteur Nicolas is open Monday to Saturday from 7.30 am to 9.30 pm (8 pm on Saturday) and on Sunday from 7.30 am to 1 pm and 6 to 8.30 pm. The *Rallye Super* supermarket on Quai Carnot, 50 metres north and then 120 metres east of the tourist office, is open Monday to Saturday from 9 am to 7.30 pm and, during most of July and August, on Sunday from 9.30 am to 12.30 pm.

Getting There & Away

Bus The Concarneau bus terminal is next to the tourist office. Caoudal (☎ 98.97.35.31 in Concarneau, 98.56.96.72 in La Forêt-Fouesnant) runs five buses a day between Quimper and Quimperlé via Concarneau. There may be reduced service on Sunday. The trip from Quimper to Concarneau costs 18.60FF. In Quimper, the bus stops at Place Saint Corentin (near the cathedral) and opposite the bus station at Café Nantaïs (23 Ave de la Gare).

Getting Around

Bus Concarneau's two rather infrequent bus lines, Nos 1 and 2, run from 7.20 am until about 6.30 pm daily except Sunday. Both stop at the bus terminal (next to the tourist office).

SAINT MALO

The Channel port of Saint Malo (population 47,000) is one of the most popular tourist destinations in Brittany, and with good reason. Situated at the mouth of the Rance River, it is famed for its walled city and nearby beaches. The Saint Malo area has some of the highest tidal variations in the world – depending on the lunar and solar cycles, the high-water mark is often 13 metres or more above the low-water mark. The tide comes in and goes out twice every 24 hours.

Saint Malo is an excellent base from

which to explore the Côte d'Émeraude (Emerald Coast), the section of the northern Breton coast between Pointe du Grouin and Le Val André. Mont-Saint-Michel – technically part of Normandy – can be visited as a day trip from Saint Malo.

Saint Malo reached the height of its importance during the 17th and 18th centuries, when it was one of France's most active ports for both merchant ships and privateers (in effect, government-sanctioned pirates), whose favourite victims were the English.

Orientation

The commune of Saint Malo consists of the contiguous resort towns of Saint Servan, Saint Malo, Paramé and Rothéneuf. Saint Malo's old city, signposted as 'Intra-Muros' (literally, between the walls) and also known as the Ville Close (walled city), is connected to Paramé by the Sillon Isthmus. Esplanade Saint Vincent, where the tourist office and bus station are located, is a giant parking lot just outside one of the old city gates, Porte Saint Vincent. The train station is 1.2 km south of Esplanade Saint Vincent.

Information

Tourist Office Saint Malo's efficient tourist office (☎ 99.56.64.48) is just outside the old city on Esplanade Saint Vincent. It is open Monday to Saturday from 9 am to noon and 2 to 6 or 6.30 pm, and, from Easter to September, on Sunday from 10 am to noon and 2 to 5 or 5.30 pm. During July and August, it is open Monday to Saturday from 8.30 am to 8 pm and on Sunday from 10 am to 6.30 pm.

Money There are half a dozen banks near the train station, along Blvd de la République and at Place de Rocabey. All are open on weekdays during approximately the same hours: 8.30 am to 12.15 pm and 1.30 to 5 pm. In the old city, the Caisse d'Épargne at 14 Rue de Dinan (three blocks up from Porte de Dinan) is open weekdays from 8.45 am to noon and 1.30 to 5.30 pm (5 pm on Friday). The Change (☎ 99.40.21.10) at 2 Rue Saint Vincent is open for business from mid-

March to mid-November only. It gives a miserable rate but stays open every day of the week from 10 am to 7 pm (9 am to 10 pm from June to September).

Post Saint Malo's main post office (☎ 99.20.51.78) is near Place de Rocabey at 1 Blvd de la Tour d'Auvergne. It is open weekdays from 8 am to 7 pm and on Saturday from 8 am to noon. Currency exchange services are available.

In the old city, the post office at Place des Frères Lamennais, which also changes foreign currency, is open weekdays from 8.30 am to 12.30 pm and 1.30 to 6.30 pm and on Saturday morning. During July and August, there is no midday closure.

Saint Malo's postcode is 35400.

Things to See

Walking Tours Suggested walks include the following:

1. From Porte de Dinan on the south side of the old city, walk southward via Plage des Bas Sablons to Fort de la Cité and the Corniche d'Aleth, a footpath which circumnavigates the peninsula.
2. Head north-east from the old city along the Sillon Isthmus and the Grande Plage to Plage de Rochebonne and the thriving beach resort of Paramé, a distance of three km. Rothéneuf is 1.5 km farther north.
3. Walk from Saint Malo via the Château de Solidor in Saint Servan via the Barrage de la Rance (see the Dinard section) to Dinard, a distance of about 10 km.

Old City In August 1944, in the course of the battle that drove the Germans from Saint Malo, 80% of the old city (Intra-Muros) was destroyed. After the war, the old city's principal historical monuments were faithfully reconstructed but the rest of the area was rebuilt in the *style* of the 17th and 18th centuries, with allowances made for the needs of a modern city. **Cathédrale Saint Vincent**, begun in the 11th century, is noted for its medieval and modern stained-glass windows.

The **ramparts**, which were built between

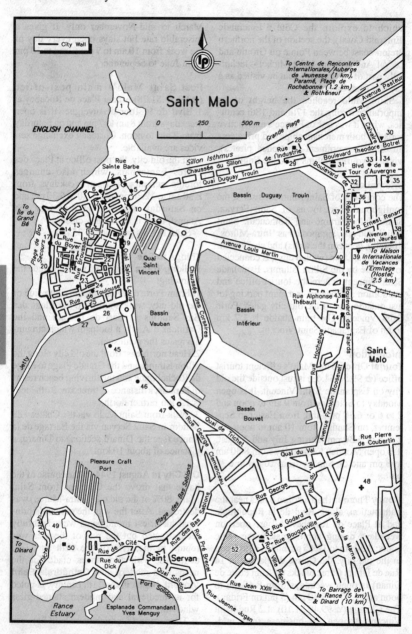

Saint Malo

ENGLISH CHANNEL

City Wall

0   250   500 m

To Centre de Rencontres
Internationales/Auberge
de Jeunesse (1 km),
Paramé, Plage de
Rochebonne (1.2 km)
& Rothéneuf

Avenue Pasteur

Grande Plage

Sillon Isthmus

Rue Sainte Barbe

Chaussée du Sillon

Quai Duguay Trouin

Rue de l'Industrie

Boulevard Theodore Botrel

Boulevard de la Tour d'Auvergne

Blvd de la République

R Ernest Renan

Avenue Jean Jaurès

Bassin Duguay Trouin

To Île du Grand Bé

Plage de Bon Secours

Rue du Boyer

Rue Broussais

Quai Saint Louis

Quai Sainte Vincent

Avenue Louis Martin

Chaussée des Corsaires

Rue de Toulouse

Bassin Vauban

Bassin Intérieur

Rue Alphonse Thébault

Boulevard des Talards

Rue Hochelaie

Avenue Franklin Roosevelt

Saint Malo

To Maison Internationale de Vacances de l'Ermitage (Hostel; 2.5 km)

Bassin Bouvet

Quai de Trichet

Rue George Clemenceau

Quai du Val

Rue Pierre de Coubertin

Jetty

Pleasure Craft Port

Plage des Bas Sablons

Rue des Bas Sablons

Rue Pré Brécel

Rue George

Rue Godard

Rue Bougainville

Rue Ville Pépin

Rue de la Marne

To Dinard

Conche d'Aleth

Rue de la Cité

Rue du Dick

Saint Servan

Quai Solidor

Port Solidor

Rue Jean XXIII

Rue Jeanne Jugan

To Barrage de la Rance (5 km) & Dinard (10 km)

Rance Estuary

Esplanade Commandant Yves Menguy

■ PLACES TO STAY		2	Aquarium	25	Porte de Dinan (City Gate)
7	Hôtel Port Malo	3	Wax Museum	26	Esplanade de la Bourse
16	Hôtel Le Victoria	4	Château de Saint Malo	27	Émeraude Lines Ferries to Dinard
18	Hôtel Armoricaine	5	Musée de la Ville	29	Diazo Vélocation (Bicycle Rental)
21	Hôtel Au Gai Bec	6	Exotarium Malouin	31	Main Post Office
28	Hôtel Le Neptune	8	Porte Saint Vincent (City Gate)	32	Place de Rocabey
34	Hôtel de l'Avenir	9	Bureau de Change (on Rue St Vincent)	33	Laundrette
36	Hôtel Le Vauban	10	Esplanade Saint Vincent	35	Église de Rocabey
38	Hôtel de Moka	11	Tourist Office & Bus Station	37	Banks
40	Hôtel de l'Europe & Hôtel de la Petite Vitesse	13	Place des Frères Lamennais	41	Place de la Grande Hermine
43	Hôtel Suffren	14	Post Office	42	Railway Station
50	Camping Municipal Cité d'Aleth	15	Cathédrale Saint Vincent	45	Ferry Terminal
		17	Porte des Bés (City Gate)	46	Car Ferry Terminal
▼ PLACES TO EAT		19	Change (Currency Exchange) & Grande Porte (Gate)	47	Car Ferry Vehicle Entrance
12	Tourist Restaurants	20	Porte Saint Pierre (Gate)	48	Hospital
22	Food Shops	23	Caisse d'Épargne (bank)	49	Fort de la Cité
30	Intermarché Supermarket	24	Musée de Poupées et de Jouets	51	Place Saint Pierre
39	Boulangerie			52	Parc de Bel Air
44	Boulangerie			53	Post Office
OTHER				54	Musée International du Long Cours Cap-Hornier & Château de Solidor
1	Fort National				

the 12th and 18th centuries, survived the war and are largely original. They afford superb views in all directions: the freight port, the interior of the old city, the English Channel. There is free access to the **ramparts walk** at Porte de Dinan, the Grande Porte, Porte Saint Vincent and elsewhere.

Old City Museums The **Musée de la Ville** (☎ 99.40.71.11), in the Château de Saint Malo next to Porte Saint Vincent, specialises in the history of the city and the Pays Malouin (the area around Saint Malo). From April to October, it is open daily from 9.30 am to noon and 2 to 6.30 pm. During the rest of the year, it is open daily except Tuesday from 10 am to noon and 2 to 5.30 pm. The entry fee is 16FF (8FF for students).

The **Musée de Cire** (Wax Museum; ☎ 99.40.80.26) across the courtyard has taped commentaries to guide you through eight rooms illustrating famous moments in

Saint Malo's history. The exact same text takes 35 minutes in English, 40 minutes in French and 55 minutes in German!

The **aquarium** (☎ 99.40.91.86), which has about 100 tanks filled with some of the world's most colourful and extraordinary fish, is built into the walls of the old city, next to Place Vauban. The smaller and less impressive **Exotarium Malouin**, which displays all sorts of live reptiles and some huge spiders, is across the street. Both are open daily from 9 am to noon and 2 to 6 or 7 pm. From July to mid-August, they are open from 9 am to 10 or 11 pm. The entry fee is 19FF (14FF for students) for each or 33FF (28FF for students) for both.

Île du Grand Bé You can reach the Île du Grand Bé, where the writer and statesman Chateaubriand is buried, at low tide via the Porte des Bés and the nearby old city gates. When the tide comes in, the submersible causeway remains impassable for about six hours.

Saint Servan Saint Servan's fortress, **Fort de la Cité**, was built in the mid-18th century and served as a German base during WW II. The German pillboxes of thick steel flanking the fortress walls were heavily scarred by Allied shells in 1944. The interior of the fort is now used by caravanners and is theoretically closed to visitors, but no-one will stop you if you walk into the camping ground (Camping Municipal Cité d'Aleth) via the main entrance (see map).

The **Musée International du Long Cours Cap-Hornier** (☎ 99.40.71.56) is housed in the **Château de Solidor**, built in 1382, on Esplanade Menguy. The museum has nautical instruments, ship models and other exhibits on the sailors who, between the early 17th and early 20th centuries, sailed around Cape Horn, the southern tip of South America. There is a great view from the top of the tower. The museum is open from 10 am to noon and 2 to 5.30 pm daily except Tuesday. From May to September, it is open daily from 9.30 am to noon and 2 to 6.30 pm. Tickets cost 16FF (8FF for students).

Beaches Saint Servan's **Plage des Bas Sablons** has a cement wall that keeps the sea from receding all the way to the yacht harbour at low tide. It is popular with older sunbathers. The **Grande Plage**, which stretches north-eastward from the Sillon Isthmus, is lined with vertical tree trunks stuck there to serve as wave-breaks. **Plage de Rochebonne** is farther to the north-east. There are a number of nice beaches in and around Dinard (see the Dinard section).

Places to Stay

Camping Sleeping on the beach is a sure way to get wet if not drowned. *Camping Municipal Cité d'Aleth* (☎ 99.81.60.91), at the northern tip of Saint Servan, next to Fort de la Cité, has an exceptional view in all directions. This place stays open all year and always has room for another small tent. People pay 14.50FF each, a tent site costs

7.40FF and the charge per car is 5.75FF. In summer, take bus No 1. During the rest of the year, your best bet is bus No 6.

Hostels There are two good youth hostels in Saint Malo. The *Centre de Rencontres Internationales/Auberge de Jeunesse* (☎ 99.40.29.80) is at 37 Ave du Père Umbricht, which is in Paramé, a bit over two km north-east of the train station. A bed in a four or six-person room is 57FF, doubles cost 67FF per person, and singles with shower and toilet are 100FF, all including breakfast. The hostel is closed from 10 am to 5 pm, but you can check in at any time of the day or night. From the train station, take bus No 5.

The *Maison Internationale de Vacances l'Ermitage* (☎ 99.56.22.00), which is at 13 Rue des Écoles in Paramé, is very laid-back as hostels go. Rooms are open all day, there is no curfew and they accept telephone reservations. A dorm bed costs only 42FF (54FF with breakfast), although sheets (if you need them) are 21FF. In the summer, you can stay in a large tent they set up in the yard for 32FF (44FF with breakfast). The hostel is 2.5 km east of the train station and 1.3 km south-east of Plage de Rochebonne. To get there from the train station, take bus No 2 or 4.

Hotels It is often difficult to find a hotel room during July and August. Among the cheaper places, the noisy and charmless hotels near the train station are the first to fill up. If you're looking for a bargain, the hotels around Place de Rocabey are probably your best bet, though there are also a few good deals in the old city.

Place de Rocabey The *Hôtel Le Vauban* (☎ 99.56.09.39) at 7 Blvd de la République is one of the cheapest places in town, with very basic singles/doubles for 80/100FF (100/120FF from April to September). Showers are free. Passing traffic and the bells of the nearby church may bother people sensitive to noise. The small *Hôtel de l'Avenir* (☎ 99.56.13.33) at 31 Blvd de la Tour d'Auvergne has singles and doubles for

100FF (130FF with a shower in the room). Hall showers cost 15FF.

Hôtel l'Embarcadère (☎ 99.40.39.58) at 53 Quai Duguay Trouin is on the Sillon Isthmus a few hundred metres west of Place de Rocabey. Modest but comfortable singles/doubles start at 105FF, a two-bed quad is 180FF and showers cost 10FF. The *Hôtel Le Neptune* (☎ 99.56.82.15), an older, family-run place at 21 Rue de l'Industrie, has adequate doubles from 115FF. Doubles with shower and toilet cost 160FF. Hall showers are free.

Train Station Area The *Hôtel de Moka* (☎ 99.56.29.86) at 49 Ave Jean Jaurès has quiet rooms with high ceilings, large windows and old-fashioned furniture. Singles/doubles cost 100/110FF and triples/quads go for 130FF. Showers are free. This place does not have any rooms with shower and they might not accept telephone reservations in July and August.

The *Hôtel de l'Europe* (☎ 99.56.13.42) is at 44 Blvd de la République, across the roundabout from the train station. Modern, nondescript doubles start at 110FF (130FF from mid-April to August). Shower-equipped rooms without/with toilet are 170/195FF (195/220FF from mid-April to August). There are no hall showers. Like other places in this area, it is somewhat noisy.

The *Hôtel de la Petite Vitesse* (☎ 99.56.31.76), next door at 42 Blvd de la République has good-sized but noisy doubles from 90FF (130FF with shower) and two-bed quads for 160FF. Hall showers are 20FF. Telephone reservations are not accepted in summer. The *Hôtel Suffren* (☎ 99.56.31.71) at 4 Blvd des Talards has unsurprising doubles without/with use of a shower from 110/130FF. A bath costs 20FF. A two-bed quad costs 180FF including use of a shower.

Old City The friendly, family-run *Hôtel Au Gai Bec* (☎ 99.40.82.16) is in the hopping heart of the old city at 4 Rue des Lauriers or 9 Rue Thévenard, depending on how you look at it. Singles/doubles start at 100FF

(160FF with shower); hall showers are free. They won't accept telephone reservations unless you are at the train station and about to head over there. The hotel is closed from mid-November to mid-December.

The *Hôtel Le Victoria* (☎ 99.56.34.01) at 4 Rue des Orbettes has doubles from 130FF. Showers are free. The *Hôtel Armoricaine* (☎ 99.40.89.13) at 6 Rue du Boyer (near the post office) has decent doubles from 130FF (220FF with shower and toilet). Showers are 12FF.

The *Hôtel Port Malo* (☎ 99.20.52.99), which was completely renovated in 1991, is a medium-sized place 150 metres from Porte Saint Vincent at 15 Rue Sainte Barbe. Singles/doubles with shower and toilet are 180/240FF (200/260FF from May to September).

Places to Eat
Restaurants The old city has lots of tourist restaurants, crêperies and pizzerias in the area between Porte Saint Vincent, the cathedral and the Grande Porte. There are several crêperies just inside Porte de Dinan. More tourist restaurants line the streets nearest the Plage de Bon Secours.

Self-Catering The cheapest food in town is available at the *Intermarché* supermarket two blocks from Place de Rocabey on Blvd Théodore Botrel. It is open Monday to Saturday from 9 am to 12.15 pm and 3 to 7.15 pm. On Saturday, the store does not close at midday. During July and August, it is also open on Sunday morning.

In the old city, you'll find a number of food shops along Rue de l'Orme, including a cheese shop (closed Sunday and Monday) at No 9, a fruit and vegetable shop (closed Sunday) at No 8 and two boulangeries. There is a small boulangerie (closed Sunday) just inside the Grande Porte at 1 Grande Rue.

Near the train station, there is a boulangerie (closed Thursday) at 6 Ave Jean Jaurès and another (closed Wednesday) at 26 Blvd des Talards.

Getting There & Away

Bus The bus station is at Esplanade Saint Vincent, next to the tourist office. Many buses that depart from here also stop at the train station. All of the bus companies mentioned here have their offices at the bus station.

Les Courriers Bretons (☎ 99.56.79.09) has regular service to destinations such as Cancale (33FF return), Fougères (Monday to Saturday only) and Mont-Saint-Michel (87FF return, 1¼ hours each way). The daily bus to Mont-Saint-Michel leaves in the late morning and returns around 7 pm. During July and August, there are four return trips a day. The Courriers Bretons' office is open from 8.30 am to 12.15 pm and 2 to 6.15 pm daily except Saturday afternoon and Sunday (daily except Sunday in summer).

Tourisme Verney (☎ 99.40.82.67), which is closed on Saturday afternoon (except during July and August) and Sunday, handles TIV's regular service to Cancale, Dinan, Dinard, Rennes and Saint Jacut. During July and August, they run excursions to various destinations, including Mont-Saint-Michel (120FF).

Voyages Pansart (☎ 99.40.85.96), whose office is open Monday to Saturday (daily in July and August), offers various excursions. All-day tours to Mont-Saint-Michel (87FF, or 78FF for students) operate daily from June to mid-September and three times a week in April and May.

Train The train station (☎ 99.65.50.50 for information, 99.65.18.65 for reservations) is one km east of the old city along Ave Louis Martin. The information counters are open daily from 9 am to 12.30 pm and 1.30 to 6.30 pm. The left-luggage room closes from 1 to 2 pm and stays open until 7.30 pm (7 pm on Sunday, 9.30 pm on Friday). There is direct service to Paris' Gare Montparnasse (222FF one-way, 4¼ hours) in summer only. During the rest of the year, you have to change trains at Rennes but the trip takes as little as three hours. You can also get to Quimper by train.

Ferry Saint Malo has two ferry terminals.

Hydrofoils, catamarans and the like depart from Gare Maritime de la Bourse. Car ferries use Gare Maritime du Naye, also known as the Terminal Ferries. Shuttles to Dinard (see the Dinard section for details) depart from just outside the old city's Porte de Dinan.

Gare Maritime de la Bourse, where the following ferry companies have their offices, is a few hundred metres south of the old city. There is service from here to the Channel Islands (les Îles Anglo-Normandes) and England.

Hydroglisseurs Condor (☎ 99.56.42.29) has service to the islands of Jersey (248FF one-way), Guernsey (Guernesey, 285FF one-way) and Sark (Sercq) from mid-March to October. Same-day excursion fares to the islands cost about the same as one-way fares. Condor's service to Weymouth, England (500FF one-way, 5½ hours) operates daily from April to September.

Between early March and December, Brittany Ferries (☎ 99.82.41.41) has boats to Portsmouth, England, once or twice a day (except Sunday during some months). One-way fares are 200 to 338FF per passenger and 456 to 786FF for a car.

Émeraude Lines (☎ 99.40.48.40) has ferries to Jersey, Guernsey, Sark and the resort town of Poole in England. Service is most regular between late March and mid-November. Car ferries to Jersey and Poole run all year long but are rather infrequent in winter.

Getting Around

Bus Saint Malo Bus has seven lines, but line No 1 runs only during the summer. Tickets cost 6.50FF and can be used as transfers for one hour after they're time-stamped. Saint Malo Bus tickets are also valid on Courriers Bretons buses for travel within Saint Malo. Buses usually operate until about 7.15 pm, but in summer certain lines keep running until about midnight (a bit before midnight on Sunday and holidays). The company's information office at Esplanade Saint Vincent (☎ 99.56.06.06) is open from 8.30 or 9 am to noon and 2 to 6.15 or 6.30 pm daily except Saturday afternoon and Sunday (daily except Sunday in summer).

Esplanade Saint Vincent, where the tourist office and bus station are, is linked with the train station by bus Nos 1, 2, 3 and 4.

Taxi Taxis can be ordered from Taxis Malouin (☎ 99.81.30.30) and Taxi Ameline (☎ 99.82.92.57).

Bicycle Diazo Vélocation (☎ 99.40.31.63) at 47 Quai Duguay Trouin is open Monday to Saturday from 9 am to noon and 2 to 6 pm. At the train station, bicycles can be hired from Bicyclub, whose office is near the station exit (follow the *sortie* signs). Three-speeds cost 60FF a day, 10-speeds are 80FF and mountain bikes are 100FF.

DINARD

While Saint Malo's old city and beaches are oriented towards middle-class family tourism, Dinard (population 10,000) sets out to attract the sort of well-heeled clientele – especially from the UK and the USA – who have been coming here since the town first became popular with the English aristocracy in the mid-19th century. Indeed, Dinard retains something of the air of a turn-of-the-century English beach resort, especially in the summer, when the atmosphere is vivified by striped bathing tents, beachside carnival rides, spiked *belle époque* mansions perched above the turquoise waters and sea-view promenades with elderly English couples adorning each bench. Dinard is living proof of how well wealthy French and English people at play get along.

Staying in Dinard can be a bit hard on the budget, but since the town and its many delights are right across the Rance Estuary from Saint Malo, you can easily enjoy Dinard by coming over by bus or boat for the day.

Orientation

Plage de l'Écluse (also known as the Grande Plage), which is right down the hill from the tourist office, runs along the northern edge of town between Pointe du Moulinet and

Pointe de la Malouine. To get there from the Embarcadère (the pier where boats from Saint Malo dock), walk 200 metres north-west along Rue Georges Clemenceau. Place de la Gare, where the disused train station stands, is one km south-west of the tourist office.

Information

The tourist office (☎ 99.46.94.12) is in a round, colonnaded building at 2 Blvd Féart. It is open Monday to Saturday from 9 am to noon and 2 to 6 pm. During July and August, it is open every day from 9.30 am to 7.30 pm.

Things to See

Walking Tours Beautiful seaside trails extend along the coast in both directions from Dinard. The tourist office sells a topoguide with maps and information (in French) on coastal trails entitled *Sentiers du Littoral du Canton du Dinard*. The cost is 5FF.

Dinard's famous **Promenade du Clair de Lune** (moonlight promenade) runs along the Baie du Prieuré south-west from the Embarcadère. What may be the town's most civilised walk links the Promenade du Clair de Lune with **Plage de l'Écluse** by following the rocky coast of **Pointe du Moulinet**, from where Saint Malo's old city can be seen across the water. This trail continues westward along the coast, passing **Plage de Saint Énogat** on its way to Saint Briac, some 14 km away.

If you are in the mood for a bit of a hike, you might take the bus or ferry over from Saint Malo and walk the 10 km back via the Barrage de la Rance (see following).

Beaches Wide, sandy **Plage de l'Écluse**, is surrounded by fashionable hotels. Next to the beach there is an Olympic-sized swimming pool filled with heated seawater (☎ 99.46.22.77). **Plage du Prieuré**, one km to the south along Blvd Féart, isn't as smart but it is less crowded. **Plage de Saint Énogat** is a km west of Plage de l'Écluse on the other side of Pointe de la Malouine.

St Bartholemew's British-American Church This Anglican church, built from contributions in 1871, is on Rue Faber, 50 metres up the hill from 25 Ave George V. Like other such bits of England overseas, this structure is more impossibly English than anything on the London side of the Channel could possibly be. Look out for the pigeon-proof swinging screen doors.

Barrage de la Rance People driving or walking between Saint Malo and Dinard on the D168 pass over the Rance Tidal Power Station (☎ 99.46.21.89), a hydroelectric dam across the estuary of the Rance River that uses Saint Malo's extraordinarily high tides to generate 8% of the electricity consumed in Brittany. The 750-metre-long dam, built between 1963 and 1967, has 24 turbines that are turned at high tide by sea water flowing into the estuary and at low tide by water draining into the sea. Near the lock on the Dinard side is a small, subterranean visitor's centre *(circuit de visite)*, open daily from 8.30 am to 8 pm, which has recorded explanations in French, English and German on how the power station works. A worthwhile stop if you've got any interest in nonpolluting sources of electrical power.

Places to Stay
A number of less expensive hotels can be found around Place de la Gare. The *Hôtel de la Gare* (☎ 99.46.10.84) at 28 Rue de la Corbinais has doubles with washbasin and bidet for 105 to 150FF. Reception (closed on Sunday after 3 or 3.30 pm) is inside Restaurant l'Épicurien. The *Hôtel de l'Arrivée* (☎ 99.46.13.05) at 5 Place de la Gare has singles/doubles for 130/180FF; showers are 25FF. *Hôtel du Commerce* (☎ 99.46.11.19) at 52 Rue de la Gare has singles/doubles from 100/120FF. It is closed on Sunday.

The *Hôtel du Parc* (☎ 99.46.11.39), a bit closer to the centre of town at 20 Ave Édouard VII, is a medium-sized hotel with half a dozen cheap rooms starting at 130FF for one or two people. Doubles with shower and toilet are 230FF.

Getting There & Away
Bus TIV buses (☎ 99.82.26.26) from Saint Malo begin their journey at Esplanade Saint Vincent and pick up passengers at Saint Malo Railway Station before continuing on via the Barrage de la Rance to Dinard, where they stop at two places: the old train station (Place de la Gare) and next to the tourist office (this stop is called Le Gallic). The buses run slightly less often than once an hour until about 7 pm. On Friday nights, buses to Dinard connect with two late trains that arrive in Saint Malo around 10 pm and a bit after 11 pm.

Boat From April to September, the Bus de Mer (ferry) run by Émeraude Lines links Saint Malo with Dinard. The trip costs 20FF one-way (30FF return) and takes 10 minutes. In Saint Malo, the dock is right outside the old city's Porte de Dinan (☎ 99.40.48.40); in Dinard the dock is at 27 Ave George V (☎ 96.46.10.45). There are eight to 14 trips a day from 9 or 10 am to around 6 pm.

Loire Valley

During the 15th to 18th centuries, the Loire Valley (Vallée de la Loire) was the playground of kings, princes, dukes and nobles, who expended the wealth of the nation and family fortunes to turn it into a vast neighbourhood of lavish (and not-so-lavish) chateaux. Today, the region is a favourite destination of tourists seeking architectural testimony to the glories of the Middle Ages and the Renaissance.

The earliest chateaux in the Loire Valley were medieval fortresses *(châteaux forts)*, some constructed hastily in the 9th century as a defence against the marauding Vikings. These structures were built on high ground and, from the 11th century, when stone came into wide use, were often outfitted with fortified keeps, massive walls topped with battlements, loopholes (arrow slits) and moats spanned by drawbridges.

As the threat of invasion lessened – and

the cannon (in use by the mid-15th century) rendered castles almost useless for defence – the architecture of new chateaux (and the new wings added to older ones) began to reflect a different set of priorities, including aesthetics and comfort. Under the influence of the Italian Renaissance, whose many innovations were introduced to France at the end of the 15th century, the defensive structures so prominent in the early chateaux metamorphosed into whimsical, decorative features (eg Azay-le-Rideau, Chambord, Chenonceau). Instead of being built on an isolated hilltop, the Renaissance chateaux were placed near a body of water or in a valley and proportioned to harmonise with their surroundings. Most chateaux from the 17th and 18th centuries are grand country houses built in the neoclassical style and set amid formal gardens.

BLOIS

The medieval town of Blois (population 50,000), whose name is pronounced 'Blwah', was a major centre of court intrigue between the 15th and 17th centuries. Much of the action, involving some of the most important personages of French history (kings Louis XII, François I and Henri III among them), took place inside the city's outstanding attraction, the Château de Blois. The old city, seriously damaged by German attacks in 1940, retains its steep, twisting medieval streets. Blois is quiet at night, but if you're not exhausted from a day of touring, there's always the bowling alley...

Several of the most rewarding chateaux in the Loire Valley, including Chambord and Cheverny, are within a 20-km radius of the city. See later in this section for details.

Orientation

Blois, which is on the north bank of the Loire River, is quite compact and almost everything is within a few minutes' walk of the train station. The old city is the area south and east of the Château de Blois, which towers over Place Victor Hugo.

Information

Tourist Office The local tourist office (☎ 54.74.06.49) is at 3 Ave Jean Laigret in an early 16th century outbuilding of the Château de Blois. From October to March, it is open Monday to Saturday from 9 am to noon and 2 to 6 pm. From April to September, it's open Monday to Saturday from 9 am to 7 pm and on Sunday and holidays from 10 am to 1 pm and 4 to 7 pm.

Money The Banque de France is down the block from the train station at 4 Ave Jean Laigret. It is open Tuesday to Saturday from 8.45 am to 12.15 pm and 1.45 to 3.45 pm. There are a number of banks along Quai de la Saussaye near Pont Jacques Gabriel. The tourist office changes money whenever it is open, but their commission is 23FF.

Post The post office (☎ 54.78.08.01), which has a currency exchange service, is near Place Victor Hugo on Rue Gallois. It is open weekdays from 8 am to 7 pm and on Saturday from 8 am to noon.

Blois' postcode is 41000.

Things to See

Château de Blois The Château de Blois (☎ 54.78.06.62 or 54.74.16.06) is not the most impressive in the valley, but it has a compellingly bloody history, and its mixture of architectural styles is extraordinary. The chateau's four distinct sections date from medieval times (13th century), the reign of Louis XII (around 1500), the early part of the reign of François I (1515 to 1524) and towards the end of the reign of Louis XIII (1630s), when the classical style was in vogue. In the Louis XII section, look for the many porcupines (Louis XII's symbol) carved into the stonework. The Italianate François I wing, which includes the famous **spiral staircase**, is decorated with repetitions of François I's insignia, the royal 'F' and the salamander.

The most infamous episode in the history of the Château de Blois occurred during the chaotic 16th century, a period of violence

FRANCE

FRANCE

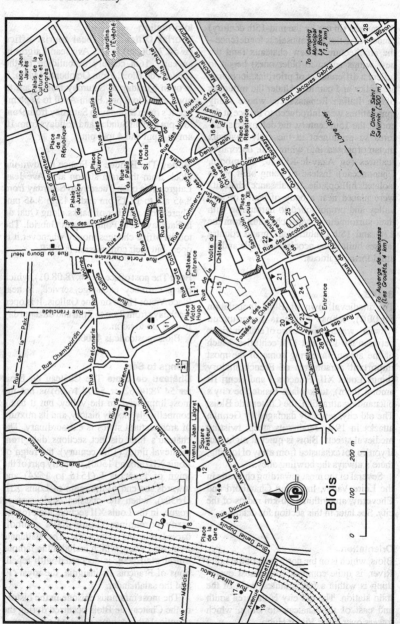

Blois

0   100   200 m

■ PLACES TO STAY		21	Restaurant Le Maïdi	7	Cathédrale Saint Louis
		22	Boulangerie-Pâtisserie	8	Railway Station
1	Hôtel L'Étoile d'Or		Blond	10	Tourist Office
2	Hôtel du Bellay	23	Boulangerie	11	Église Saint Vincent
9	Hôtel François 1er	25	Covered Market	12	Banque de France
18	Hôtel Saint Jacques	26	Boulangerie	13	Point Bus (Bus
27	Hôtel Saint Nicolas				Information)
28	Hôtel Le Pavillon		OTHER	14	Hertz Car Rental
				15	Château de Blois
▼ PLACES TO EAT		3	Laundrette	16	Sports Motos Cycles
		4	Bus Station (Gare		(Bicycle Rental)
19	Intermarché		Routière)	17	Bowling de Blois
	Supermarket	5	Post Office	24	Église Saint Nicolas
20	Pizzarella Pizzeria	6	Maison des Acrobates		

between the Huguenots and Catholics. On 23 December 1588 at about 8 am, King Henri III summoned the Duke of Guise, a leader of the Catholic League (which threatened the authority of the king, himself a Catholic), to his Salle du Conseil (study). When the duke reached the *chambre du roi*, he was set upon by 20 royal bodyguards, some armed with daggers, others with swords. When the violence was over, the king, who had been hiding behind a tapestry, stepped into the room to survey the duke's perforated body. Henri, overjoyed by the success of the assassination, informed his mother, Catherine de' Medici, of what had transpired and went merrily to mass. Henri III was himself assassinated eight months later.

The chateau houses a small **archaeological museum**, the **Musée des Beaux-Arts** and the **Musée Robert Houdin**, which displays clocks and other objects invented by the magician Houdin (1805-71) after whom the great Houdini (1874-1926) named himself. All three museums have the same opening hours as the chateau but close between noon and 2 pm.

From November to mid-March, the Château de Blois is open daily from 9 am to noon and 2 to 5 pm. From mid-March to October, opening hours are from 9 am to 6 pm. The entry fee is 30FF (15FF if you are aged 7 to 25 or over 60). Free guided tours in English can usually be arranged upon request.

Old City The brown explanatory signs tacked up around the old city are both informative and in English. Part of the area, many of whose buildings in the old city have blue-slate roofs, red-brick chimneys and white façades, has been turned into a pedestrian mall.

Cathédrale Saint Louis is named after Louis XIV, who assisted in rebuilding it after a devastating hurricane in 1678. The crypt dates from the 10th century. The cathedral may be closed between noon and 3 pm and after 6 pm. There is a great view of Blois and both banks of the Loire River from the **Jardins de l'Évêché** (garden of the bishop's palace), which is at the back of the cathedral.

The **Maison des Acrobates** at 3 Place Saint Louis, across the square from the façade of the cathedral, is one of the few medieval houses in Blois not destroyed during WW II. The building, which dates from the late 15th century, is so named because its exposed timbers are decorated with characters taken from medieval farces, including acrobats.

Places to Stay
Camping *Camping Municipal La Boire* (☎ 54.74.22.78), open from March to November, is 2.5 km east of the train station on the south bank of the Loire River. It is on Blvd du Docteur Alexis Carrel near the *hélistation* (heliport) and Pont Charles de Gaulle, a highway bridge over the river. Two

people with a tent are charged 33FF. There are no buses to get out here.

Hostels The *Auberge de Jeunesse* (☎ 54.78.27.21), open from March to mid-November, is 4.5 km south-west of the Blois Train Station in the village of Les Grouëts. The street address is 18 Rue de l'Hôtel Pasquier. Call before heading out there as it is often full. Beds are 39FF and breakfast (optional) is 16FF. Renting a sleeping bag costs 14FF, and kitchen facilities are available. The hostel is completely closed from 10 am to 6 pm. To get to the hostel, take bus No 4, which runs until 7 or 7.30 pm.

Hotels Near the train station, your best bet is the *Hôtel Saint Jacques* (☎ 54.78.04.15) at 7 Rue Ducoux, just off Place de la Gare. The rooms are ordinary but the staff go out of their way to be friendly. Doubles start at 115FF; doubles with shower, toilet and TV are 195FF. The *Hôtel François 1er* (☎ 54.78.97.86) is at 39 Ave Jean Laigret, 120 metres east of the station. Their cheaper doubles start at 120FF. Doubles/triples/quads with shower and TV (no toilet) cost 200/250/280FF.

The *Hôtel du Bellay* (☎ 54.78.23.62) at 12 Rue des Minimes is open from mid-March to mid-November. This place has a few very pleasant doubles for 115FF; hall showers are free. Rooms with shower and toilet are 180FF for two people. Nearby, the *Hôtel L'Étoile d'Or* (☎ 54.78.46.93) at 7 Rue du Bourg Neuf has doubles from 140FF (240FF with shower and toilet). Showers cost 10FF.

The *Hôtel Saint Nicolas* (☎ 54.78.05.85 or 54.78.41.09) is in the old city at 33 Rue des Trois Marchands. Simple, old-fashioned singles/doubles start at 90/125FF. The *Hôtel Le Pavillon* (☎ 54.74.23.27) is across the river from the old city at 2 Ave Wilson. Ordinary doubles with high ceilings start at 95FF, and triples/quads are 160/200FF. Hall showers cost 15FF. Doubles/triples/quads with shower and toilet are 200/240/320FF.

Places to Eat
Restaurants In general, Blois' restaurants, such as those along the pedestrian mall in the centre of town, are expensive and middling. One place you might try is *Restaurant Le Maïdi* (☎ 54.74.38.58), a North African place in the old city at 42 Rue Saint Lubin. It is open from noon to 2 pm and 6.30 to 10 or 11 pm daily except Thursday (daily in July and August). Couscous starts at 50FF. *Pizzarella* (☎ 54.78.05.07), a pizzeria at 15 Rue des Trois Marchands, is open from noon to 1.30 pm and 7.15 to 9.30 or 10 pm daily except Monday and Tuesday.

Self-Catering The *Intermarché* supermarket, west of the train station on Ave Gambetta, has an in-house boulangerie. It is open Monday to Saturday from 9 am to 12.15 pm and 2.30 or 3 to 7.15 pm.

The *Marché Couvert Halle Louis XII* (covered market) off Quai de l'Abbé Grégoire is, for the most part, open daily except Sunday and Monday from 7 am to 12.30 pm and 3 to 7 pm. *Boulangerie-Pâtisserie Blond* at 11 Rue Anne de Bretagne has a good variety of breads. It is open Monday to Saturday from 6.45 am to 2 pm and 3.30 to 8 pm. There is a boulangerie opposite 23 Rue des Trois Marchands and another at 29 Rue des Trois Marchands (closed Monday).

Entertainment
Towns don't come much quieter than Blois. Even the pedestrian mall in the old city is almost dead after nightfall. One of the few nightspots here is a bowling alley, Bowling de Blois (☎ 54.42.42.27), which is right across the tracks from the train station at 6 Rue Alfred Halou. It is open daily from 3 pm to 2 am (in August, weekday hours are 8 pm to 2 am). Games cost 17 to 30FF per person, depending on when you go to play (nights and weekends are the most expensive) and shoe rental is 7FF. Billiards costs 10FF per game.

Getting There & Away
Train The train station (☎ 47.20.50.50 in Tours for information) is at the western terminus of Ave Jean Laigret. The information

office is open daily except Sunday from 9 am to 7 pm. Service from Blois to Paris' Gare d'Austerlitz (111FF) takes 1¾ to 2½ hours by direct train but only one hour via Orléans. Tours (46FF) is 20 to 60 minutes away and Bordeaux (211FF) is five hours by direct train but less if you change to a TGV at Saint Pierre des Corps (near Tours).

Getting Around
Bicycle See Getting There & Away in the next section for information on renting a bike in Blois.

BLOIS AREA CHATEAUX
Chateaux in the Blois area include the spectacular Château de Chambord, the magnificently furnished Château de Cheverny, the castle-like Château de Chaumont (also accessible from Tours) and the more modest Beauregard. The town of Amboise (see the Tours Area Chateaux), can also be reached from Blois.

Organised Tours
Given the state of bus transport (see the next section) and depending on how pressed you are for time, your best bet to see more than one chateau on the same day may be to take a tour. Blois-based TLC (☎ 54.78.15.66) bus company, offers two itineraries (prices do not include admission fees): Chambord and Cheverny (50FF return, 35FF for students); and Chaumont, Chenonceau and Amboise (100FF, or 70FF if you're a student). Both operate daily (or almost daily) from mid-June to mid-September, on weekends between late May and mid-June, and on the days around Easter, Pentecost and Ascension Day. It is possible to pick up the Chaumont tour at the youth hostel in Les Grouëts.

Getting There & Away
Bus The TLC bus system is set up to transport school kids into Blois in the morning and get them home after school. As a result, afternoon service from the countryside to Blois is limited on some lines. There is reduced service during the summer school holidays and on Sunday. All times quoted in

this chapter are approximate and should be verified with the company before you make plans.

Your best source of bus information is the Point Bus office (☎ 54.78.15.66) at 2 Place Victor Hugo in Blois. It is open from 8 am to 12.10 pm and 1.30 to 6 pm weekdays except Monday morning and from 9 am to 12.10 pm and 1.30 to 4.30 pm Saturday. In July and August, opening hours are from 8.30 am to 12.10 pm and 1.30 to 5.30 pm weekdays except Monday morning and from 9 am to noon Saturday .

TLC buses to destinations in the vicinity of Blois depart from Place Victor Hugo (in front of the Point Bus office) and the gare routière. The latter, which functions mostly as a bus stop, is next to the brasserie that is next to the train station.

Bicycle The countryside around Blois, with its many quiet country backroads, is perfect for cycling. Unfortunately, Chambord, Cheverny and Chaumont are each about 20 km from Blois. An excursion to both Chambord and Cheverny, which are 20 km from each other, is a 60-km proposition – quite a bit for one day if you're not in shape. A 1:200,000 scale Michelin road map or a 1:50,000 scale IGN is indispensable to find your way around the rural backroads.

The Hôtel Saint Jacques (☎ 54.78.04.15), which is near the train station at 7 Rue Ducoux, rents three-speed bikes for 60FF a day (50FF in winter). Sports Motos Cycles (☎ 54.78.02.64) at 6 Rue Henry Drussy rents 10-speeds (35FF a day). The store is open Tuesday to Saturday from 9 am to noon and 2 to 6.30 pm.

Château de Chambord
The Château de Chambord (☎ 54.20.31.32), the construction of which was begun in 1519 by King François I (reigned 1515-47), is the largest and most spectacular chateau in the entire Loire Valley. Its Renaissance architecture and decoration, grafted onto a feudal ground plan, may have been inspired by Leonardo da Vinci who, at the invitation of François I, lived in Amboise (45 km south-

west of here) from 1516 until his death three years later. If you're going to see more than one chateau, leave 440-room Chambord for last or the rest may seem unlivably small by comparison.

Chambord is the creation of François I, whose emblems – a royal monogram of the letter F and salamanders of a particularly fierce disposition – adorn many parts of the building. Though forced by liquidity problems to leave his two sons as hostages in Spain and to help himself to both the treasuries of his churches and his subjects' silver, the king kept 1800 workers and artisans at work on Chambord for 15 years. At one point he even suggested that the Loire River be rerouted so it passed by Chambord; eventually, a smaller river, the Cosson, was diverted instead. Molière first staged two of his most famous plays at Chambord to audiences that included Louis XIV.

The chateau's famed **double-helix staircase**, attributed by some to Leonardo himself, consists of two spiral staircases that wind around the same central axis but never meet. The rich ornamentation is in the style of the early French Renaissance. It's not too hard to imagine mistresses and lovers chasing one another up and down the stairs while their sweating consorts and assorted servants give chase...

The royal court used to assemble on the Italianate **roof-top terrace**, reached via the double-helix staircase, to watch military exercises, tournaments and the hounds and hunters returning from a day of stalking deer. As you stand on the terrace (once described as resembling an overcrowded chessboard), you will see all around you the towers, cupolas, domes, chimneys, dormers, mosaic slate roofs and lightning rods that create the chateau's imposing skyline.

Tickets to the chateau are on sale daily from 9.30 to 11.45 am and 2 to 4.45 pm (October to March), till 5.45 pm (April to June and September) and till 6.45 pm (July and August). Guests already in the chateau can stay there for half an hour after ticket sales end. Chambord does *not* close at midday from mid-June to the second week

of September and during certain holiday periods. The entry fee is 31FF (17FF for people aged 18 to 24). A brochure available in various languages is on sale for 3FF behind the ticket counters. The maps are its most useful feature.

Getting There & Away Chambord is 16 km east of Blois and 20 km north-east of Cheverny. During the school year, TLC line No 2 averages three daily return trips from Blois to Chambord (17.20FF one-way). The first bus out to Chambord leaves Blois a bit after noon on Wednesday and Saturday and around 2 pm on other days. The last bus back to Blois leaves Chambord at 5.30 pm on weekdays and at 4.30 pm on weekends and holidays. There is no good way to get there by public bus during July and August.

Getting Around The Centre d'Information Touristique (☎ 54.20.34.86) is open from mid-April to mid-October daily from 10 am to 7 pm. It is at Place Saint Michel (the parking lot surrounded by tourist shops) and rents bicycles for 25FF an hour, 40FF for two hours and 80FF a day.

Château de Cheverny
The Château de Cheverny (☎ 54.79.96.29), the most magnificently furnished of the Loire Valley chateaux, was built between 1604 and 1634. After entering the building through its finely proportioned, neoclassical façade, visitors are treated to room after sumptuous room outfitted with the finest of period appointments: furniture, canopied beds, tapestries (note the *Abduction of Helen* in the Salle d'Armes, the former armoury), paintings, mantelpieces, parquet floors, painted ceilings and walls covered with embossed Córdoba leather.

Cheverny is open daily from 9.15 or 9.30 am to noon and 2.15 to 5 pm (November to February), till 5.30 pm (October and March), and till 6 pm (the last half of September) or 6.30 pm (April and May). From June to mid-September, the chateau stays open every day from 9.15 am to 6.45 pm. The entry fee is 28FF (19FF for students).

Getting There & Away Cheverny is 16 km south-east of Blois. Bus No 4 from Blois to Romorantin stops at Cheverny (14.40FF). Throughout the year, buses leave Blois daily except Sunday at 6 or 6.30 am and noon. Heading back to Blois, the last buses depart at 7.30 pm from Monday to Saturday and at 8.15 pm (6.30 pm during July and August) on Sunday and holidays.

Château de Chaumont

The Château de Chaumont (☎ 54.20.98.03), set on a bluff overlooking the Loire River, looks as much like a feudal castle as any chateau in the area. The luxurious **stables** (*Écuries*) are Chaumont's most famous feature (present your entry ticket from the main building to get in). In the years after American independence, Benjamin Franklin, then serving as American ambassador to France, was a frequent guest at Chaumont.

Tickets to this state-owned chateau are on sale daily from 9.15 to 11.35 am and 1.45 to 3.45 pm (5.35 pm from April to September). There is no midday closure in July and August. The chateau stays open for half an hour after ticket sales end. The entry fee is 25FF (14FF for people aged 18 to 24 and over 60). The park around the chateau, with its many cedar trees, is free and open daily from 9 am to 5 pm (7 pm from April to September).

Wine Tasting From Easter to September, there is free wine tasting in the small building 50 metres up Rue du Village Neuf from the beginning of the path up to the chateau. Wine producers from the Touraine area take turns displaying and selling their products, especially premium AOC wines, the quality of which is guaranteed by strict laws (see the Bordeaux Vineyard Visits section in this chapter for more information). Opening hours depend on the preferences of each vineyard's representative.

Getting There & Away The Château de Chaumont is 20 km south-west of Blois and 20 km north-east of Amboise in the village of Chaumont-sur-Loire, which is on the south bank of the Loire River. The path leading up to the park and the chateau begins at the intersection of Rue du Village Neuf and Rue Maréchal Leclerc (highway D751). If you're coming by bicycle, you're best off taking the quiet backroads on the south (left) bank of the river. By rail, take a local train on the Blois-Tours line and get off at Onzain, which is two km from the chateau. Cross the bridge over the Loire River to reach the chateau.

Château de Beauregard

Beauregard (☎ 54.70.40.05 or 54.70.46.64), the closest chateau to Blois, is relatively modest in size, demonstrating the limitations of being a fabulously wealthy noble rather than a prince or king. Built in the mid-16th century and enlarged 100 years later, it is set in the middle of a large, forested park. The count and countess who own the place still live in one wing, which is why only a few rooms are open to the public.

From April to September, Beauregard is open daily from 9.30 am to noon and 2 to 6.30 pm; there is no closure at midday during July and August. During the rest of the year (except from mid-January to mid-February, when it's closed), the chateau is open from 9.30 am to noon and 2 to 5 pm daily except Wednesday. Tariffs are 20FF (15FF for students under 25 and people over 60).

Getting There & Away The Château de Beauregard, only six km south of Blois, makes a good destination for a short bike ride (or as a stop on the way to Cheverny). There is access to the chateau from both D765 (the Blois-Cheverny road) and D936 (turn left at the village of Cellettes, which is one km south-west of the chateau).

Bus No 5B from Blois towards the town of Saint Aignan stops at the village of Cellettes. The first bus from Blois to Cellettes leaves on weekdays and Saturday at noon. Unfortunately, there is no afternoon bus back apart from one operated by Transports Boutet (☎ 54.34.43.95), which passes through Cellettes at about 6.30 pm from

FRANCE

Monday to Saturday and at about 6 pm on Sunday (except during August).

TOURS

Whereas Blois remains essentially medieval in layout and small-townish in atmosphere, Tours (population 136,000) has the cosmopolitan and bourgeois air of a miniature Paris, with wide 18th century avenues, public spaces built around formal gardens, café-lined boulevards and a major university. It also has a number of worthwhile museums. The city was devastated by German bombardment and an accompanying fire in June 1940. Locals believe that the French spoken here is the purest in all of France. Tours is the only town in the Loire Valley with much nightlife.

Like Blois, Tours makes a good base for forays out to nearby chateaux.

Orientation

Tours' focal point is Place Jean Jaurès, where the city's major thoroughfares – Rue Nationale, Blvd Heurteloup, Ave de Grammont and Blvd Béranger – meet. The train station is 300 metres to the east along Blvd Heurteloup. The old city, centred around Place Plumereau, is 400 metres west of Rue Nationale.

Information

Tourist Office The tourist office (☎ 47.05.58.08) is in the Hôtel de Ville at Place Jean Jaurès. In late 1993 it will move to the new Centre International de Congrès (International Convention Centre), which is being built across Blvd Heurteloup from the train station. From May to September, the office is open Monday to Saturday from 8.30 am to 7.30 pm and on Sunday from 10 am to 12.30 pm and 3 to 6 pm. From October to April, it is open daily except Sunday from 8.30 am to 12.30 pm and 2 to 6 pm.

Money Most banks in Tours are closed on Sunday and Monday. The Banque de France (☎ 47.20.73.41) at 2 Rue Chanoineau is open Tuesday to Saturday from 8.45 am to noon and 1.30 to 3.30 pm. Cross the verandah and

go through the doors under the sign reading 'Bureaux'. Crédit Agricole (☎ 47.20.84.85), next to the train station at 10 Rue Édouard Vaillant, is open Monday to Friday from 9 am to 12.30 pm and 1.30 to 5.15 pm (4.15 pm on Friday). There are a number of banks around Place Jean Jaurès.

Post The main post office is 200 metres west of Place Jean Jaurès on Blvd Béranger. It is open weekdays from 8 am to 7 pm and on Saturday from 8 am to noon. Currency exchange is available.

Tours' postcode is 37000.

Things to See

Walking Tour Tours is a great city for strolling. Areas worth exploring include the **old city** (the area around Place Plumereau, which is surrounded by half-timbered houses) and **Rue Nationale**. Also of interest is the neighbourhood around the Musée des Beaux-Arts which includes **Cathédrale Saint Gatien** (built between 1220 and 1547 and renowned for its stained glass).

Museums The **Musée Archéologique de Touraine** (☎ 47.66.22.32) is at 25 Rue du Commerce in the Hôtel Gouïn, a splendid Renaissance residence completed around 1510. Its Italian-style façade, all that was left after the conflagration of June 1940, is worth seeing even if the eclectic assemblage of artefacts inside doesn't interest you.

The **Musée du Campagnonnage** (Museum of Craftsmen's Societies; ☎ 47.61.07.93) at 8 Rue Nationale displays the products of crafts rendered obsolete by the Industrial Revolution. It is open from 9 am to noon and 2 to 5 pm (6 pm from April to mid-June) daily except Tuesday. From mid-June to mid-September, it's open daily from 9 am to 6.30 pm. Tickets cost 20FF (10FF for students). The **Musée des Vins de Touraine** (Museum of Touraine Wines; ☎ 47.61.07.93), which is a few metres away at 16 Rue Nationale, is in the 13th century wine cellars of Saint Julien Abbey. They do not give out wine samples but the museum does have a roomful of displays on the sig-

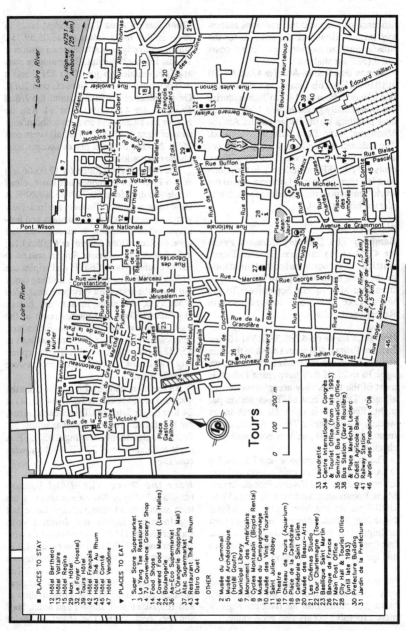

FRANCE

PLACES TO STAY
12 Hôtel Berthelot
13 Hôtel Voltaire
15 Hôtel Regina
29 Mon Hôtel
32 Le Foyer (Hostel)
39 Tours Hôtel
42 Hôtel Français
43 Hôtel Thé Au Rhum
45 Hôtel Comté
47 Hôtel Vendôme

PLACES TO EAT
1 Super Score Supermarket
3 Le Yang Tse Restaurant
4 7J Convenience Grocery Shop
14 Food Shops
24 Covered Food Market (Les Halles)
25 Boulangerie
36 Atac Supermarket
 (As-Eco Supermarket
 L'Orangerie Shopping Mall)
37 Atac Supermarket
43 Restaurant Thé Au Rhum
44 Bistro Quet

OTHER
2 Musée du Gemmail
5 Musée Archéologique
 (Hôtel Goüin)
6 Municipal Library
7 Monument des Américains
8 Cycles Montaubin (Bicycle Rental)
9 Musée du Campagnonage
10 Musée des Vins de Touraine
11 Saint Julien Abbey
16 Theatre
17 Château de Tours (Aquarium)
18 Place de la Cathédrale
19 Cathédrale Saint Gatien
21 Musée des Beaux-Arts
22 Les Cinémas Studio
23 Tour Charlemagne (Tower)
23 Basilique Saint Martin
26 Banque de France
27 Main Post Office
28 City Hall & Tourist Office
 (until late 1993)
30 Préfecture Building
31 Jardin de la Préfecture
33 Laundrette
34 Centre International de Congrès
 & Tourist Office (from late 1993)
35 Semitrat Bus Information Office
38 Bus Station (Gare Routière)
 & Place Maréchal Leclerc
40 Crédit Agricole Bank
41 Railway Station
46 Jardin des Prebendes d'Oé

nificance of wine and the traditions associated with it. Hours are the same as for the Musée du Campagnonnage. Entry costs 10FF (5FF for students).

Musée des Beaux-Arts (☎ 47.05.68.73) at 18 Place François Sicard has a fine collection of works from the 14th to 20th centuries but is especially proud of two 15th century altar paintings by the Italian painter Andrea Mantegna, taken from Italy by Napoleon. The museum is open from 9 am to 12.45 pm and 2 to 6 pm daily except Tuesday. Entry costs 30FF (15FF for students). In the courtyard is a superb cedar of Lebanon, one of the world's most majestic varieties of tree. It was planted here in 1804.

Places to Stay

Camping The *Camping Édouard Péron* (☎ 47.54.11.11) at Place Édouard Péron, which is 2.5 km north-east of the train station on the north bank of the Loire River, is open from mid-May to mid-September. To get there, take bus No 7 towards Sainte Radegonde Ermitage.

Hostel *Le Foyer* (☎ 47.05.38.81) at 16 Rue Bernard Palissy, 400 metres north of the train station, is a dorm for workers of both sexes aged 16 to 25. If they have space (which is most of the time), they accept travellers of all ages. Doubles cost 65FF per person per night. Reception is open for check-in on weekdays from 8 am to 7 pm and on Saturday from 8 am to 2.30 pm. It is not possible to check in on Sunday.

The *Auberge de Jeunesse* (☎ 47.25.14.45) is five km south of the train station and two km south of the Cher River in Parc de Grand-Mont. Rooms are closed from 10 am to 5 pm. Until 8 pm you can take bus No 1 or 6 from Place Jean Jaurès. Between 10 pm and about midnight, take the Semitrat Bleu de Nuit Sud line (represented by a yellow crescent moon) and get off at the Monge stop.

Hotels Most of the cheapest hotels – those very close to the train station – are pretty basic. The places near the river are slightly more expensive but are also good value.

Train Station Area The cheapest hotel in town is the *Tours Hôtel* (☎ 47.05.59.35), which is directly opposite the train station at 10 Rue Édouard Vaillant. Basic singles start at 61FF, doubles go for 70 to 85FF and a two-bed quad is 110FF. Showers cost 10FF. On the other side of the station, the *Hôtel Français* (☎ 47.05.59.12) at 11 Rue de Nantes has singles and doubles without/with shower from 100/120FF. Hall showers cost 20FF. Neither of these places accepts telephone reservations.

The *Hôtel Thé Au Rhum* (☎ 47.05.06.99) at 4-6 Place des Aumônes has basic, clean singles/doubles from 60/75FF to 80/95FF. A large triple is 130FF. Showers are free. New guests cannot check in on Sundays and holidays, when reception is closed. Another good choice is *Hôtel Comté* (☎ 47.05.53.16) at 51 Rue Auguste Comte. Singles cost 66 to 99FF, doubles start at 83FF, and triples are 115 to 132FF. The rooms are nothing fancy but given the price are a very good deal. *Mon Hôtel* (yes, the name means 'my hotel', ☎ 47.05.67.53) is 500 metres north of the train station at 40 Rue de la Préfecture. Singles/doubles with a oversize bed start at 85/95FF. Showers are 15FF. The reception area is a bit dank and dark but the rooms were recently redone.

An excellent choice a bit farther from the station is *Hôtel Vendôme* (☎ 47.64.33.54) at 24 Rue Roger Salengro. This cheerful place, run by a friendly older couple, has simple but decent singles/doubles starting at 85/95FF. A triple with shower is 200FF. Hall showers cost 15FF.

Near the River The *Hôtel Voltaire* (☎ 47.05.77.51) is 900 metres north of the train station at 13 Rue Voltaire. Basic but comfortable singles and doubles with shower start at 115FF. A two-bed triple with shower costs 175FF. Hall showers are 12FF. Overall, this is a good deal. The *Hôtel Regina* (☎ 47.05.25.36) is down the block at 2 Rue Pimbert. Neat, well-maintained singles/doubles start at 93/115FF without shower and 165/205FF with shower and toilet. Hall showers cost 15FF. The *Hôtel Berthelot*

(☎ 47.05.71.95), a block away at 8 Rue Berthelot, has clean, basic doubles of decent size for 100/120FF without/with shower. Showers are 10FF. Two-bed triples with shower cost 145FF. The rooms at the back are the quietest.

Places to Eat

Restaurants In the old city, Place Plumereau and Rue du Commerce are filled with places to eat and drink (cafés, crêperies, pâtisseries, etc). Just east of Place Plumereau at 83bis Rue du Commerce is *Le Yang Tse* (☎ 47.61.47.59), a Chinese/Vietnamese restaurant whose main dishes cost 20 to 35FF. It is open daily from noon to 2.30 pm and 5.30 to 11.30 pm or midnight. There is a sandwich shop, *Le Petit Gourmand*, at 86 Rue du Commerce.

Near the train station, the simple *Restaurant Bistro Quet* (☎ 47.05.12.76) at 17 Rue Blaise Pascal has French menus from 49FF. Their speciality is *paella*, a Spanish rice dish made with seafood, chicken and pork. This place is open from noon to 1.30 pm and 7.30 to 9.30 pm daily except Friday evening and Sunday. *Thé Au Rhum*, on the ground floor of the Hôtel Thé Au Rhum, has traditional French food, including crêpes (14 to 30FF) and meat dishes (25 to 50FF). There are *menus* for 45 and 65FF.

Self-Catering There is an *Atac* supermarket with an in-house boulangerie in front of the train station at 5 Place du Maréchal Leclerc. It is open Monday to Saturday from 8.30 am to 8 pm and Sunday from 9.30 am to 12.30 pm. At 19bis Place Jean Jaurès, inside the Orangerie shopping mall, there is an *As-Eco* supermarket with its own bakery and a nice selection of prepared salads. It is open Monday to Saturday from 9 am to 8 pm and Sunday from 9 am to 12.30 pm.

The covered market, *Les Halles*, is 500 metres west of Rue Nationale at Place Gaston Pailhou. It is open Monday to Saturday from 6 am to 7 pm and on Sunday from 6 am to 1 pm. The boulangerie at 30 Place Gaston Pailhou is open daily except Monday from 7 am to 7.30 pm.

In the old city, there are several boulangeries along Rue du Grand Marché. East of Rue Nationale, there are food shops along Rue Colbert.

Entertainment

Les Cinémas Studio (☎ 47.05.22.80 for a recorded message), whose entrance is opposite 17 Rue des Ursulines, shows subtitled (rather than dubbed) films. Tickets cost 30FF.

Getting There & Away

Bus Les Rapides de Touraine (☎ 47.46.06.60) handles service to other parts of the department of Indre-et-Loire. Schedules are posted at the gare routière, which is in front of the train station at Place du Maréchal Leclerc. See each chateau entry for details.

Train The train station (☎ 47.20.50.50 or 47.05.60.60) is off Blvd Heurteloup at Place du Maréchal Leclerc. The information office is open Monday to Saturday from 8.30 am to 6.30 pm. Paris' Gare Montparnasse is only 55 minutes away by TGV (149FF). There is also service to Paris' Gare d'Austerlitz, Bordeaux (196FF, 2½ hours) and Nantes (127FF, two hours). Some of the chateaux around Tours can be reached by train or SNCF bus, both of which accept Eurail passes. See each Getting There & Away section under Tours Area Chateaux for details.

Getting Around

Bus The bus network serving Tours and its suburbs is known by its acronym, Semitrat. Almost all lines stop at Place Jean Jaurès. Three Bleu de Nuit lines operate nightly from about 9.30 pm to just after midnight. Tickets, which cost 6FF, are valid for one hour after being time-stamped. A carnet of 10 tickets costs 46FF.

Semitrat has an information office (☎ 47.66.70.70), known as Espace Bus, at Place Jean Jaurès. It is open daily except Sunday from 7.30 am to 7 pm (6.30 pm on Saturday).

Taxi Call Taxi Radio (☎ 47.20.30.40) at 13 Rue de Nantes (next to the train station) to order a taxi.

Bicycle See Tours Area Chateaux for information on renting a bike in Tours.

TOURS AREA CHATEAUX

Tours, with its many cheap hotels, makes a good base for visits to some of the most interesting of the Loire chateaux, including Chenonceau (which you can also visit by tour from Blois), Azay-le-Rideau, Amboise (also accessible from Blois) and Chaumont (listed under Blois Area Châteaux). If you have a Eurail pass, more chateaux can be reached from Tours than from any other railhead in the region.

Organised Tours

Three companies offer organised chateau tours in English. Reservations can be made at the tourist office in Tours or you can phone the company yourself. Prices quoted here include entry fees, which are a major expense if you go on your own.

Marques Dos Santos (☎ 47.37.15.60) at 16 Rue de l'Hospitalité charges 95 to 180FF for minibus tours. Touraine Évasion (☎ 47.66.52.32 on weekdays, 47.66.63.81 on Sunday morning and Saturday), which also uses minibuses, charges about the same. Services Touristiques de Touraine (☎ 47.05.46.09), based in the train station, charges about 125FF for a half-day and 170FF for a full-day trip by tour bus.

Getting There & Away

Bus Les Rapides de Touraine (☎ 47.46.06.60) has limited bus service to the area around Tours. The company's buses, which stop at the bus station and, in some cases, Place Jean Jaurès as well, do *not* run on Sunday. Getting out to the chateaux by bus is fairly expensive – an organised tour might work out not only faster and simpler but also cheaper. All times quoted here are approximate, so verify them before making plans.

Train Some of the chateaux (including Azay-le-Rideau, Chenonceau and Chaumont) can be reached from Tours by train or SNCF buses. Certain trains allow you to take a bicycle along free of charge, letting you cycle either there or back. For up-to-date schedules, ask for the brochure *Les Châteaux de la Loire en Train* at the Tours Train Station.

Bicycle Cycles Montaubin (☎ 47.05.62.27), in Tours at 2 Rue Nationale (near the river), rents 10-speeds for 70FF a day and 100FF for a three-day weekend (Saturday to Monday). Mountain bikes cost 100FF a day and 200FF for a three-day weekend. The store is open Tuesday to Saturday from 9.15 am to noon and 2 to 7 pm. Make sure you have a detailed Michelin road map before heading out of the city.

Château de Chenonceau

Castles don't get much more fairy-tale-like than 16th century Chenonceau (☎ 47.23.90.07), which comes complete with stylised (rather than defensive) moat, drawbridge, towers and turrets. The interior is filled with period furniture, tourists, paintings, tourists, tapestries, tourists and tourists, all of only moderate interest.

One of the series of remarkable women who created Chenonceau, Diane de Poitiers, mistress of King Henri II, planted the garden to the left (east) as you approach the chateau down the avenue of plane trees. After the death of Henri II in 1559, she was forced to give up her beloved Chenonceau to the vengeful Catherine de' Medici, Henri II's wife. Catherine then applied her own formidable energies to the chateau, and, among other works, laid out the garden to the right (west) as you approach the castle. In the 18th century, Madame Dupin, the owner at the time, brought Jean-Jacques Rousseau to Chenonceau as a tutor for her son.

The 60-metre-long **Galerie** (gallery) over

the Cher River, built by Catherine de' Medici, was converted into a hospital during WW I. Between 1940 and 1942, the demarcation line between Vichy-ruled France and the German-occupied zone ran down the middle of the Cher: the castle itself was under direct German occupation but the Galerie's southern entrance was in the area controlled by Maréchal Pétain. For many people trying to escape to the Vichy zone, this room served as a crossing point.

Chenonceau is open all year from 9 am until sometime between 4.30 pm (mid-November to mid-February) and 7 pm (mid-March to mid-September. The entry fee is 35FF (25FF for students).

Getting There & Away The Château de Chenonceau, situated in the town of Chenonceaux (with an 'x' at the end), is 34 km east of Tours, 10 km south-east of Amboise and 40 km south-west of Blois.

Milk-run local buses *(omnibus)* on the Tours-Vierzon rail line stop at Chisseaux, which is two km east of Chenonceaux. A couple of trains a day also go from Tours to Chenonceaux Station, which is only 500 metres from the chateau. From Monday to Saturday during July and August, certain runs (two a day) of Les Rapides de Touraine's bus No 10 from Tours stop at Chenonceaux (33.50FF one-way, 57FF return).

Château d'Azay-le-Rideau
Azay-le-Rideau (☎ 47.45.42.04), built on an island in the Indre River and surrounded by a quiet pool dotted with lily pads, is one of the most harmonious and elegant of the Loire chateaux. It is adorned with stylised fortifications and turrets intended both as decoration and to indicate the owners' rank.

The bloodiest incident in the chateau's history – a subject of invariable fascination for modern-day chateau-goers – occurred in 1418. During a visit to Azay, then a fortified castle, the crown prince (later King Charles VII) was insulted by the Burgundian guard.

Enraged, he executed some 350 soldiers and officers and had the town burned down. The present chateau was begun exactly a century later by Giles Berthelot, one the the king's less-than-selfless financiers. When the prospect of being audited and hanged drew near, he fled abroad and never completed the structure. The chateau's finishing touches weren't put on until the 19th century.

From October to March, the chateau's interior can be visited daily from 10 am to 12.30 pm and 2 to 4.30 pm. From April to June and in September, it is open from 9.30 am to 5.30 pm. During July and August, hours are from 9 am to 6.30 pm. The park stays open half an hour later than the interior. Tickets cost 25FF (14FF if you're aged 18 to 24 or over 60).

Getting There & Away Azay-le-Rideau, which is in the town of the same name, is 26 km south-west of Tours. SNCF has year-round service from Tours to Azay (the station is 2.5 km from the chateau) by either train or bus. There are two or three runs a day. The last train/bus back to Tours leaves Azay at about 6 pm (9 pm on Sunday).

Amboise
The picturesque hillside town of Amboise (population 11,400), whose chateau reached the pinnacle of its importance around the turn of the 16th century, is an easy day trip from Tours.

Tourist Office The tourist office (Accueil d'Amboise; ☎ 47.57.01.37) is along the river opposite 7 Quai Général de Gaulle.

Château d'Amboise The rocky outcrop overlooking the town on which the Château d'Amboise (☎ 47.57.00.98) was built has been fortified since Gallo-Roman times. King Charles VIII, who grew up here, began work to enlarge the chateau in 1492 after a visit to Italy, where he had been deeply impressed by the Italians' artistic creativity and luxurious lifestyle. King François I, who also grew up here, lived in the chateau for the first few years of his reign, a wild period marked by balls, masquerade parties, tournaments and festivities of all sorts.

Today, only a few of the 16th century structures are extant. The chateau's ramparts afford a panoramic view of the town and the Loire Valley. The best way to exit the chateau is via the souvenir shop: the side door leads to the **Tour Hurtault** (begun in 1495), whose interior consists of a circular ramp decorated with sculptured faces.

The entrance to the chateau is a block south along Rue François 1er from the quay along the Loire River. It is open daily from 9 am to noon and from 2 pm until sometime between 5 and 6.30 pm, depending on the season. During July and August, the hours are 9 am to 6.30 pm. The entry fee is 28FF (18FF for students aged 24 or younger).

Le Clos Lucé At the invitation of François I, Leonardo da Vinci came to Amboise in 1516. Until his death at the age of 67, three years later, Leonardo lived and worked in Le Clos Lucé (☎ 47.57.62.88), a brick manor house 400 metres up Rue Victor Hugo from the chateau. The building now contains restored rooms and scale models of some of Leonardo's multifarious inventions. It is open daily from 9 am to 6 or 7 pm except in January. The entry fee is 31FF (25FF for students). The road to Le Clos Lucé passes troglodytic dwellings – caves in the limestone hillside – in which local people still live.

Wine Tasting The Caveau de Dégustation (wine-tasting cellar; ☎ 47.57.23.69), opposite 14 Rue Victor Hugo (below the chateau), is open from April to September daily from 10 am to 7 pm. The tasting is free but you have to pay 1FF to use the toilets next door!

Getting There & Away Amboise is 23 km upstream (east) of Tours. A few trains a day between Tours and Blois stop right across the river from Amboise (21FF one-way from Tours). The last train back to Tours departs sometime between 6 and 7 pm. From Tours, you can also take Les Rapides de Touraine's bus No 10 (21.40FF one-way, 36.50FF return).

South-Western France

The south-western part of France includes a number of diverse regions, ranging from the Bordeaux wine-growing area near the beach-lined Atlantic coast to the Basque Country and the Pyrenees Mountains in the far south. There is convenient rail transport from this part of the country to Paris, Spain and even the Côte d'Azur.

LA ROCHELLE

La Rochelle (population 78,000) is a laid-back but lively city midway down France's Atlantic seaboard. Lots of tourists come here, but most of them are of the domestic, middle-class variety: unpretentious families or young people on holiday. A major university is being built here which promises to attract even more young people. The nearby Île de Ré is encircled by tens of km of fine-sand beaches.

La Rochelle was one of the first places in France where Protestantism took root, incurring the wrath of Catholic authorities during the Wars of Religion that plagued France during the latter half of the 16th century. In 1628 the city, a Huguenot stronghold, surrendered to Louis XIII's forces after all but 5000 of its 28,000 residents had starved to death during a 15-month siege directed personally by Cardinal Richelieu, the principal minister of Louis XIII.

Orientation

The old city is north of the northern end of Quai Valin, which runs more or less north-south along the Old Port. Quai Valin is linked to the train station, which is 500 metres south-east of the port, by Ave du Général de Gaulle. To get to Place du Marché, walk 250 metres north along Rue des Merciers from the old city's Hôtel de Ville.

Information

The tourist office (☎ 46.41.14.68) is in Le Gabut, the area just west of where Quai Valin and Ave du Général de Gaulle meet. It is open Monday to Saturday from 9 am to 12.30 pm and 2 to 6 pm. From June to September, opening hours are Monday to Saturday from 9 am to 7 pm (8 pm during July and August) and Sunday from 11 am to 5 pm.

La Rochelle's postcode is 17000.

Things to See

To protect the harbour at night and defend it in times of war, a chain used to be stretched between the two stone towers at the harbour entrance, **Tour de la Chaîne** and **Tour Saint Nicolas**, both of which were built in the late 14th century. Visitors can climb to the top of Tour Saint Nicolas. West along the old city wall is **Tour de la Lanterne**, also known as Tour des Quatre Sergents (Tower of the Four Sergeants), which was used for a long time as a prison. It now houses a museum (☎ 46.41.56.04), which is open daily except Tuesday (daily in July and August). The English graffiti on the walls was carved by English privateers held here during the 18th century. **Tour de la Grosse Horloge**, the imposing clock tower on Quai Duperré, was built in the 18th century. From July to mid September, the archaeological museum inside is open every afternoon (and until midnight on Saturday). There's a good view of the city from the roof. The **Hôtel de Ville** at Place de l'Hôtel de Ville in the old city was begun in the late 15th century and is still used to house the municipal government. Guided tours of the interior are held on Saturday and Sunday afternoons; they are held daily from June to September and during school holidays.

The sober, austere architecture of the **Temple Protestant** at 2 Rue Saint Michel, 150 metres east of the Hôtel de Ville, is remarkable for its contrast to most Catholic churches. An earlier building on this site served La Rochelle's Protestant community from 1563 until the siege of 1628. The current building, which dates from the late 17th century, became a Protestant church after the Revolution. The interior took on its present form during the last 75 years of the 19th century.

Île de Ré The Île de Ré, a 30-km-long island whose eastern tip is nine km west of the centre of La Rochelle, is reached by a three-km toll bridge completed in 1988. In summer, the island's many beaches (and the seasonal camping grounds nearby) are a favourite destination for families with young children, in part because the water is shallow and safe and the sun less harsh than along the Mediterranean coast. The island is accessible from Quai Valin and the train station by STCR bus No 1, which goes to Sablanceaux (the narrow bit of the island nearest La Rochelle). The whole island is served by Ré Bus, whose La Rochelle stops include Place de Verdun and the train station. If you decide to drive, be prepared for the 110FF bridge toll.

Places to Stay

During July and August, most places are full by noon.

Camping During the warm season, many camping grounds open up in the La Rochelle area, especially on the Île de Ré. The closest camping ground to town is *Camping du Soleil* (☎ 46.44.42.53), also known as Camping Municipal Les Minimes, which is on Ave des Minimes (Ave de Marillac on some maps) about a km south-west of the town centre. It is open from May to September and is often completely full. Two people with a tent are charged 40FF. From Quai Valin or the train station, take bus No 10.

Hostel The *Centre International de Séjour/ Auberge de Jeunesse* (☎ 46.44.43.11) is two km south-west of the centre of town on Ave des Minimes in Les Minimes, a beachside neighbourhood of La Rochelle. Beds are 62FF, double rooms cost 154FF and sheets are 15FF. The hostel is closed from 10 am to 12.30 pm. To get there, take bus No 10 from Quai Valin or the train station and get off at the Lycée

Hôtelier stop (next to the bowling alley). Bus service ceases at 7.15 pm.

Hotels The *Hôtel Henri IV* (☎ 46.41.25.79) is in the middle of the old city at Place de la Caille. The official address is 31 Rue des Gentilshommes. Doubles start at 120FF. For 170FF you can get a room for two with shower, toilet and TV. Breakfast (25FF per person) is obligatory in July and August. From Quai Valin, go east on Quai Maubec and take an immediate left onto Rue Saint Sauveur, which leads to Place de la Caille.

A number of cheap hotels can be found in the vicinity of Place du Marché, which is one km north of the train station and 250 metres north of the old city. The *Hôtel Le Perthus* (☎ 46.41.10.16) is next to the covered market at 17 Rue Gambetta. Singles/doubles start at 95FF; showers are free. Doubles with shower and toilet are 135FF and quads with shower are 180FF. During July and August guests must take their meals at the hotel. The slightly dilapidated *Hôtel Printania* (accent on the last syllable; ☎ 46.41.22.86) is at 9 Rue du Brave Rondeau. Singles/doubles start at 120FF, and triples/quads with shower are 170FF. Hall showers cost 6FF. Breakfast (16FF) is obligatory from July to September.

The *Hôtel de la Paix* (☎ 46.41.33.44), housed in an 18th century building at 14 Rue Gargoulleau, has a few doubles for 130FF and triples/quads with shower for 210FF (230FF from Easter to October). A double with shower and toilet is 180FF (200FF in the high season). Hall showers are free.

BORDEAUX

Bordeaux (population 211,000) is known for its 18th century grandeur: neoclassical architecture, wide avenues and well-tended public squares and parks. The city may give the impression that it has seen better (or at least more prosperous) times, but its ethnic diversity, excellent museums and un-touristed atmosphere make it much more than just a convenient stop for travellers going between Paris and Spain.

Bordeaux was founded by the Romans in the 3rd century BC. From 1154 to 1453, it

prospered under the rule of the English, whose fondness for the region's red wines (known across the Channel as claret) gave impetus to the local wine industry. The city's single most important economic activity is still the marketing and export of Bordeaux wines.

Orientation

Cours de la Marne stretches from the train station to Place de la Victoire, which is linked to Place de la Comédie by the Rue Sainte Catherine pedestrian mall. The city centre lies between Place Gambetta and the Garonne River. Cours de l'Intendance is the city's fanciest shopping street. Rue de la Porte Dijeaux has been turned into a pedestrian mall.

Information

Tourist Office The main tourist office (☎ 56.44.28.41) at 12 Cours du 30 Juillet is open daily from 9 am to 7 pm (8 pm from June to September). The tourist office annexe at the train station is open daily from 9 am (10 am on off-season Sundays) to 7 pm.

Money Most banks are open Monday to Friday, and some also stay open on Saturday mornings. The Banque de France, around the corner from the tourist office at 13 Rue Esprit des Lois, is open weekdays from 9 am to noon and 1 to 3.30 pm. There are lots of commercial banks nearby on Rue Esprit des Lois, Cours de l'Intendance and Cours du Chapeau Rouge. American Express (☎ 56.52.40.52) at 14 Cours de l'Intendance is open Monday to Friday from 8.45 am to noon and 1.30 to 6 pm. The rate at the Thomas Cook bureau (☎ 56.91.58.80) in the train station is 5% worse than that of the banks, but its services are available seven days a week from 8 am to 8 pm. During July and August, the office is open until 9 pm.

Post The main post office (☎ 56.96.62.30), west of the centre at 36 Rue du Château d'Eau, is open Monday to Friday from 8 am to 7 pm and on Saturday from 8 am to noon.

Central Bordeaux's postcode is 33000.

Foreign Consulates Bordeaux has some 40 consulates, including:

UK
> 353 Blvd Président Wilson (☎ 56.42.34.13); open Monday to Friday from 9 am to 12.30 pm and 2.30 to 5 pm

USA
> 22 Cours du Maréchal Foch (☎ 56.52.65.95); the American Services section is open weekdays from 9 am to noon and, by appointment, from 2 to 4 pm.

Things to See

The most prominent feature of the **Esplanade des Quinconces**, laid out in 1820, is a towering (and somewhat grandiose) fountain-monument to the Girondists, a group of moderate, bourgeois legislative deputies during the French Revolution, 22 of whom were executed in 1793 for alleged counter-Revolutionary activities. Don't miss the horses' nostrils, which squirt water. The **Jardin Public**, a 19th century park laid out in the English style, is along Cours de Verdun. It includes Bordeaux's **botanical garden** and **natural history museum**.

The much praised, neoclassical **Grand Théâtre** at Place de la Comédie was built in the 1770s. It is surrounded by a Corinthian colonnade decorated with 12 huge figures of the Muses and Graces. **Place de la Bourse**, flanked by the old Hôtel de la Douane (customs house) and the Bourse du Commerce (stock exchange), was built between 1731 and 1755. The riverside area nearby is fairly lifeless.

Porte Dijeaux, which dates from 1748 and was once one of the city's gates, leads to **Place Gambetta**, a beautiful garden by a pond. Today it is an island of calm in the midst of the city centre's hustle and bustle, but during the Reign of Terror that followed the Revolution, a guillotine emplaced here severed the heads of 300 alleged counter-Revolutionaries.

Cathédrale Saint André was where the future King Louis VII was married to Eleanor of Aquitaine in 1137. The cathedral's 15th century belfry, **Tour Pey-Berland**, stands behind the choir, whose chapels are nestled among the flying buttresses. The cathedral is open Monday to Saturday from 7.30 to 11.30 am and 2 to 6.30 pm and on Sunday from 8 am to 12.30 pm and 2.30 to 5.30 pm.

Bordeaux' impressive **Synagogue** (☎ 56.91.79.39), inaugurated in 1882, is between Nos 6 and 18 Rue du Grand Rabbin Joseph Cohen. Its architecture is a mixture of Sephardi and Byzantine styles. During the Holocaust, the synagogue's interior was ripped apart by the Nazis, who turned the complex into a prison. After the war, it was painstakingly rebuilt according to the original plans. Visits are possible Monday to Thursday from 3 to 5 pm. Just ring the side entrance bell, which is around the corner at 213 Rue Sainte Catherine.

Museums Most museums are open daily except Tuesday, although the Musée d'Art Contemporain and the Musée d'Aquitaine are open daily except Monday. On Wednesday, most museums are free.

The outstanding **Musée d'Aquitaine** (☎ 56.10.17.10) at 20 Cours Pasteur illustrates the history and ethnography of the Bordeaux area from 25,000 years ago to the 19th century. The prehistoric period is represented by, among other artefacts, a number of stone carvings of women. The exhibits are exceptionally well designed. Unfortunately, when archaeologists dig up the ruins of this place a few thousand years from now, they'll probably conclude that the absence of signs in any language but French constitutes conclusive evidence that French proficiency was universal during the late 20th century. The museum is open daily except Monday from 10 am to 6 pm. The entry fee is 150FF (8FF if you're a student), but on Wednesday it's free.

At 20 Cours d'Albert, the **Musée des Beaux-Arts** (☎ 56.10.16.93, 56.10.17.49) occupies two wings of the Hôtel de Ville (built in the 1770s), between which is an attractive public garden, Jardin de la Mairie. The museum houses a large collection of paintings, including Flemish, Dutch and Italian works from the 17th century and a

FRANCE

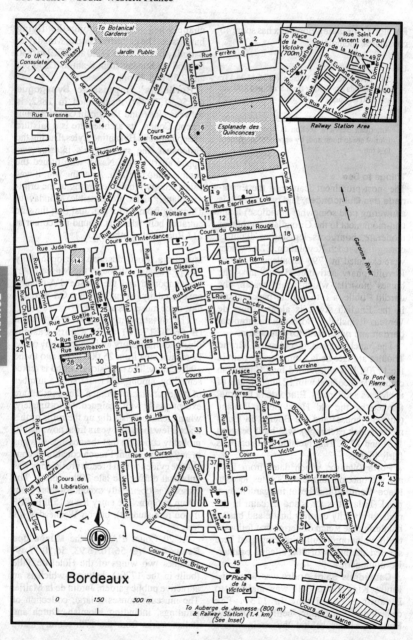

Bordeaux

0   150   300 m

To Auberge de Jeunesse (800 m)
& Railway Station (1.4 km)
(See Inset)

■	PLACES TO STAY	46	Marché des Capucins (Wholesale Food Market)	19	Place de la Bourse
15	Hôtel d'Amboise			20	Hôtel de la Douane (Customs)
24	Hôtel Boulan			21	Main Post Office
25	Hôtel de Lyon		OTHER	23	Place du Colonel Raynal
26	Hôtel de la Boëtie				
36	Maison des Étudiants (Summer Hostel)	1	Natural History Museum	27	Musée des Arts Décoratifs
37	Hôtel Le Pavillon	2	Museé d'Art Contemporain	28	Musée des Beaux-Arts
39	Hôtel Helvetic	3	US Consulate	29	Jardin de la Mairie
47	Auberge de Jeunesse	4	CITRAM Bus Station	30	City Hall
48	Hôtel Noël, Hôtel Les Deux Mondes &	5	Place de Tourny	31	Cathédrale Saint André
		6	Monument des Girondins	32	Tour Pey Berland
	Hôtel La Terrasse			33	Musée d'Aquitaine
49	Hôtel de Dijon	7	Maison du Vin de Bordeaux	34	Porte de la Grosse Cloche (Clock Tower)
▼	PLACES TO EAT	8	Place des Grands Hommes	35	Porte des Salinières (Gate)
8	Marché des Grands Hommes	9	Tourist Office	38	Synagogue
22	Auchan Supermarket & Centre Commercial Mériadeck	10	Banque de France	41	Cycles Pasteur (Bicycle Rental)
		11	Place de la Comédie	42	Tour Saint Michel
		12	Grand Théâtre	43	Église Saint Michel
25	Café Freedom	13	Place Jean Jaurès	45	Porte d'Aquitaine (Gate)
40	Lagrue Supermarket	14	Place Gambetta		
44	La Dakaroise African Restaurant	16	Porte Dijeaux (Gate)	50	Railway Station (Gare Saint Jean)
		17	American Express		
		18	Bourse de la Commerce		

FRANCE

major painting by Delacroix. The museum is open from 10 am to 6 pm daily except Tuesday. Entry costs 150FF (8FF for students) but is free on Wednesday.

At 39 Rue Bouffard, the **Musée des Arts Décoratifs** (☎ 56.10.15.62) specialises in faïence, porcelain, silverware, glassware, furniture and the like. It is open daily except Tuesday from 2 to 6 pm. Temporary exhibits stay open from 10 am to 6 pm. Entry costs 150FF (8FF for students) but on Wednesday it's free.

The **Musée d'Art Contemporain** (☎ 56.44.16.35), whose entrance is opposite 16 Rue Ferrère, hosts temporary exhibits by contemporary artists. It is open from 11 am to 7 pm (10 pm on Wednesday) daily except Monday. Tickets cost 30FF (20FF for students 25 and under), but entry is free if you arrive between noon and 2 pm. The museum is housed in the Entrepôts Lainé, built in 1824 as a ware-

house for the rare and exotic products of France's colonies: coffee, cocoa, peanuts, vanilla, etc.

Places to Stay

Camping *Camping Beausoleil* (☎ 56.89.17.66; open all year) charges 50FF for two people with their own tent. It is about 10 km south-west of the city centre at 371 Cours du Général de Gaulle (also known as Highway RN10) in Gradignan. To get there, take bus G from Place de la Victoire towards Gradignan Beausoleil and get off at the last stop.

Camping Les Gravières (☎ 56.87.00.36; open all year) charges 16FF for a tent and 17FF per person. This place is 10 km south-east of central Bordeaux at Place de Courréjean in Villenave d'Ornon. Take bus B from Place de la Victoire towards Courréjean and get off at the end of the line. Both camping grounds carry a three-star rating.

Hostels The *Maison des Étudiantes* (☎ 56.96.48.30) at 50 Rue Ligier, a dorm for women students during the academic year, accepts female and male student travellers (with an international student card) from July to September. If there's space, you can check in at any time of the day or night. A bed costs 47FF, including sheets and use of the showers and kitchen. The rooms are simple and a bit run-down but the atmosphere is friendly. To get there from the train station, take bus No 7 or 8 to the Bourse du Travail stop and walk 400 metres west on Cours de la Libération.

The charmless *Auberge de Jeunesse* (☎ 56.91.59.51) at 22 Cours Barbey is 650 metres west of the train station. A spot in a utilitarian, eight-bed room is only 39FF (44FF if you don't have an IYHF card). The 1st floor (the women's section) and the 2nd floor (the men's section) are reached by separate staircases! The hostel is theoretically closed from 9.30 am to 6 pm, but they'll let you sleep in later. More of a problem is the Draconian curfew of 11 pm. Talk to the manager in advance if you'll be staying out late for a concert, etc. On the brighter side, they accept telephone reservations. Reception is open daily from 8 to 9.30 am and 6 to 11 pm.

Hotels Hotels in the area around the train station are convenient for rail passengers, but in terms of both price and value, you're much better off staying around Place Gambetta or Place de la Victoire.

Place Gambetta There are a number of excellent deals in the area between Place Gambetta and the Musée des Beaux-Arts. From the train station, take bus No 7 or 8 and get off at Place du Colonel Raynal (for the Hôtel d'Amboise and the Hôtel de Lyon, get off at Place Gambetta).

The quiet *Hôtel Boulan* (☎ 56.52.23.62) at 28 Rue Boulan has modest singles/doubles with high ceilings for 90/95FF (110/120FF with shower). Hall showers cost 15FF. The *Hôtel de la Boétie* (☎ 56.81.76.68) at 4 Rue La Boétie has modern singles/doubles with TV, toilet, telephone and shower from 120/135FF. Triples/quads are 180FF.

The *Hôtel d'Amboise* (☎ 56.81.62.67) at 22 Rue de la Vieille Tour is through Porte Dijeaux from Place Gambetta. The rooms are small, dark and have carpeted walls, but the location is excellent and the price is right: 65/90FF to 100/110FF for a single/double. Singles/doubles with shower and toilet are 110/120FF. Hall showers cost 10FF for 10 minutes. There is free locked parking for two-wheeled vehicles. The friendly *Hôtel de Lyon* (☎ 56.81.34.38), 31 Rue des Remparts, has singles/doubles with shower, toilet and TV for 120/135FF. Try not to get one of the small, 3rd-floor rooms.

Place de la Victoire To get to this area from the train station, take bus No 7 or 8 and get off at Place de la Victoire.

The family-run *Hôtel Le Pavillon* (☎ 56.91.75.35) at 6 Rue Honoré Tessier, a block from the Musée d'Aquitaine, is one of the best deals in town. Large, slightly dilapidated singles/doubles without shower start at 85 to 90FF, and two-bed doubles are 95FF. Another good bet is the *Hôtel Helvetic* (☎ 56.91.54.61) at 1 Rue André Dumercq. Huge, plain singles/doubles cost 80 to 90FF. Two-bed doubles and rooms for three or four people cost 125FF. Showers are 10FF.

Train Station Area There is a rather seedy neighbourhood of sex shops, X-rated cinemas, restaurants and legitimate hotels in the immediate vicinity of the train station.

The popular *Hôtel La Terrasse* (☎ 56.91.42.87) at 20 Rue Saint Vincent de Paul has clean singles/doubles from 95FF. Doubles with shower cost 140FF; hall showers are 15FF. The *Hôtel Les Deux Mondes* (☎ 56.91.63.09), nearby at 10 Rue Saint Vincent de Paul, is a decent place with lots of foreign guests during the summer. Rates are 105/126FF for singles/doubles with showers and 189FF for two-bed triples. The *Hôtel Noël* (☎ 56.91.62.48) at 8 Rue Saint Vincent de Paul has doubles/triples with shower starting at 98/120FF.

One of the last places to fill up (for good

reason) is the musty, run-down *Hôtel de Dijon* (☎ 56.91.76.65), which is directly opposite the station at 22 Rue Charles Domercq. Singles/doubles start at 85/95FF, and showers cost 10FF. Telephone reservations are not accepted.

Places to Eat
Restaurants The cafés, ethnic restaurants and sandwich shops opposite the train station stay open until late at night. The *Café Freedom* (☎ 56.01.00.97) at 37 Rue des Remparts (near Place Gambetta) serves salads, omelettes and other light dishes. It is open Monday to Saturday from 8.30 am to 2 am, but meals are available only from noon to 3 or 4 pm and 6 to 11 pm. *La Dakaroise* (☎ 56.92.77.32) at 9 Rue Gratiolet specialises in dishes from Senegal and other parts of West Africa. It is open daily from 7 to 11.30 pm.

Self-Catering The mirrored, marbled *Marché des Grands Hommes* at Place des Grands Hommes, 100 metres north of Cours de l'Intendance, has up-market stalls of fruit, vegetables, cheese, bread, pastry and sandwiches in the basement. It is open Monday to Saturday from 7 am to 7.30 pm.

There is a huge, cheap *Auchan* supermarket in the Centre Commercial Mériadeck, whose eastern entrance is opposite 58 Rue du Château d'Eau. Opening hours are Monday to Saturday from 8.30 am to 10 pm. The *Lagrue* supermarket at 190 Rue Sainte Catherine is open from 8.30 am to 8 pm daily except Sunday.

In the neighbourhoods around the Église Saint Michel, the aroma of bulk spices emanates from the scattered food shops that cater to the North Africans, sub-Saharan Africans, Spanish, Portuguese, Vietnamese and other immigrant groups who live here.

Things to Buy
Bordeaux wine in all price ranges is on sale at three speciality shops near the main tourist office: Vinothèque at 8 Cours du 30 Juillet, L'Intendant at 2 Allées de Tourny and Bordeaux Magnum at 3 Rue Gobineau.

Getting There & Away
Bus Buses to places all over the Gironde and nearby departments leave from the CITRAM Bus Station (☎ 56.43.04.04), whose two entrances are at 14 Rue de Fondaudège and opposite 69 Rue La Faurie de Monbadon. The information office is open Monday to Friday from 9 am to 12.30 pm and 1.30 to 6 pm (5 pm on Friday). On Saturday you can call ☎ 56.44.93.59. Destinations include Soulac (on the coast near the mouth of the Gironde River) and Cap Ferret (south-west of Bordeaux near the Bassin d'Arachon, a bay on the coast west of Bordeaux). There is year-round service to the medieval vineyard town of Saint Émilion. Trips cost 34.50FF each way; there are five round trips from Monday to Friday and one round trip on Sunday – see the Bordeaux Vineyard Visits section.

Train Bordeaux's train station, Gare Saint Jean (☎ 56.92.50.50 for information or 56.92.60.60 for reservations), is about three km from the city centre at the southern terminus of Cours de la Marne. It is one of France's major rail transit points – there are trains from here to almost everywhere. The station's information office is open weekdays from 9 am to 7 pm, Saturday from 9 am to 6.30 pm and Sunday and holidays from 10 am to 12.30 pm and 2 to 7 pm. If you take the TGV Atlantique, Bordeaux is only about three hours from Paris' Gare Montparnasse. Non-TGV trains use Paris' Gare d'Austerlitz.

Getting Around
Bus Single tickets on Bordeaux's urban bus network, CGFTE (☎ 57.57.88.88), cost 7FF and are valid for one hour after being time-stamped. Bus information bureaus *(espaces accueil)* at the train station and Place Gambetta have easy-to-use route maps. The remarkably cheap Carte Bordeaux Découverte, which allows unlimited bus travel for one day (19FF) or three days (45FF), can be purchased at the tourist office or at CGFTE bureaus.

As you exit the train station, the bus stops

are to the left – take bus No 7 or 8 to get to the city centre.

Bicycles Cycles Pasteur (☎ 56.92.68.20) at 42 Cours Pasteur (near Place de la Victoire) has 10-speeds and mountain bikes for 50FF a day. It is open Monday to Friday from 9 am to noon and 2 to 6.30 pm. A 1600FF deposit is required.

BORDEAUX VINEYARD VISITS

The Bordeaux wine-producing region is subdivided into 53 *appellations* (production areas whose climate and soil impart distinctive characteristics upon the wine produced there) grouped into six *familles* (literally, families). The majority of the region's diverse wines (reds, rosés, sweet and dry whites, sparkling wines, etc) have earned the right to include the abbreviation AOC on their labels, indicating that the contents have been grown, fermented and aged according to strict regulations which govern such matters as the number of vines permitted per hectare. The region's production averages 660 million bottles of wine a year.

The Bordelais has many thousands of chateaux, a term that in this context refers not to palatial residences but rather to properties where grapes are raised, fermented and then matured. The smaller chateaux often accept walk-in visitors, but many of the larger and better known ones (eg Château Mouton-Rothschild) accept visitors only by appointment. Most of the chateaux are closed in August. Each vineyard has different rules about tasting *(dégustation)* – at some it's free, others make you pay, and others do not serve wine at all.

Information

Opposite Bordeaux's main tourist office at 3 Cours du 30 Juillet, the Maison du Vin de Bordeaux (☎ 56.00.22.66), has lots of information on visiting vineyards. First you have to decide which growing area you would like to visit, a decision the maison's colour-coded map of *appellations* can help with. The staff will then give you the address of the local *maison du vin* (a sort of tourist office for

wine-growing areas), which has details on which chateaux are open and when. The Maison du Vin de Bordeaux is open weekdays from 8.30 am to 6 pm. From mid-June to mid-October it is open on Saturday from 9 am to 12.30 pm and 1.30 to 5 pm. There is free wine tasting here at 10.30 am, 11.30 am, 2.30 pm and 4.30 pm.

Organised Tours

From mid-June to mid-October, bus tours to various chateaux in the Bordeaux area are a possible solution to transport difficulties. Afternoon excursions, which take place daily from mid-June to mid-September and last from 1.30 to 6.30 pm, cost 130FF (110FF for students). All-day trips, available a couple of days a week, cost 240FF (220FF for students). Commentary is in French and English and there is a different itinerary each day. Make reservations at the tourist office a day in advance.

Saint Émilion

If you'll be going vineyard visiting on your own, one destination to consider is the medieval village of Saint Émilion, 38 km east of Bordeaux, which is in an area famous for its full-bodied, deeply coloured red wines. The local tourist office (☎ 57.24.72.03; open daily) is at Place des Créneaux. From Bordeaux, Saint Émilion is relatively accessible by train (via Libourne, which is also a TGV stop) and CITRAM bus (see Getting There & Away under Bordeaux). Bus service on Sundays and holidays is very limited.

BAYONNE

Bayonne (population 43,000) is the most important city in the French part of the Basque Country (Pays Basque in French), a region straddling the French-Spanish border with its own history, language, culture and identity. Unlike the up-market beach resort of Biarritz, a short bus ride away, Bayonne retains much of its Basqueness: the architecture, for instance, is typical of the region, and you're quite likely to hear locals speaking Basque among themselves. Most of the graffiti you see around town is the work of nationalist groups seeking an independent Basque state. The city is famous for its ham, chocolate and marzipan. The latter two products were introduced in the late 15th century by Jews fleeing the Spanish Inquisition.

Bayonne's most important festival is the annual Fête de Bayonne, which begins on the first Wednesday in August. The festival includes a 'running of the bulls' like the one in Pamplona except that here they have cows rather than bulls and usually it's the people – dressed in white with red scarves around their necks – who chase the cows rather than the other way around. The festival also includes Basque music, *corrida* (bullfighting), a float parade, and rugby matches (rugby is a favourite sport in this area).

Orientation

The Adour and Nive rivers, which merge at Bayonne, split the town into three areas: Saint Esprit, the area north of the Adour River, where the train station is located; Grand Bayonne, the oldest part of town, on the west bank of the Nive River; and Petit Bayonne, east of the Nive River. The suburban area known as Anglet (the final 't' is pronounced) is sandwiched between Bayonne and the beach resort of Biarritz, eight km to the west.

Information

Tourist Office The tourist office (☎ 59.59.31.31) is at Place de la Liberté in the Hôtel de Ville building. It is open weekdays from 9 am to 12.30 pm and 1.30 to 6.30 pm and Saturday 9 am to noon. In July and August, it is open 9 am to 7 pm daily except Sunday. There are plans to move the tourist office to Place des Basques, 400 metres west of the Hôtel de Ville. The many cultural and sporting activities held from June to October are listed by date in the brochure *Programme des Fêtes en Pays Basque*.

Money Banks in Bayonne are open from Monday to Friday (those in Anglet are open from Tuesday to Saturday). The Banque de France (☎ 59.59.02.29) at 18 Rue Albert 1er is open weekdays from 9 am to noon and

1.35 to 3.35 pm. There are lots more banks in Grand Bayonne near the Hôtel de Ville, along Rue Thiers and on Rue du 49ème (behind the post office). Near the train station, there are a Banque Populaire (☎ 59.55.00.54) at 20 Place de la République and a Crédit Agricole at 26 Place de la République.

Post The post office (☎ 59.59.32.00) at 11 Rue Jules Labat is open weekdays from 8 am to 6.30 pm and Saturday 8 am to noon. Address post restante mail to 64100 Bayonne-Labat. Foreign currency can be exchanged here. Bayonne's postcode is 64100.

Things to See & Do

Cathédrale Sainte Marie This Gothic cathedral at the southern end of the Rue du Port Neuf pedestrian mall is in the heart of the oldest part of town. Construction of the cathedral was begun in the 13th century, when Bayonne was ruled by the English, and completed after the area came under French control in 1451. These political changes are reflected in the cathedral's ornamentation, which includes both the English arms, three leopards, and that most French of emblems, the fleur-de-lis. Many of the statues that once graced the church's crumbly exterior were smashed during the Revolution. Sainte Marie is open daily from 7 am to 12.30 pm and 2.30 to 7.30 pm.

Museums The **Musée Bonnat** (☎ 59.59.08.52) at 5 Rue Jacques Laffitte in Petit Bayonne has a diverse collection of works, including a whole room of paintings by Peter Paul Rubens (1577-1640). It is open from 10 to 11.30 am and either 2.30 to 6 pm or 3 to 6.30 pm (8.30 pm on Friday) daily except Tuesday and public holidays. From mid-September to mid-June, opening hours on Friday are 3 pm to 8.30 pm only. The entry fee is 15FF (5FF for students).

The highly regarded **Musée Basque** (☎ 59.59.08.98) on Rue Marengo in Petit Bayonne has been under renovation since the late 1980s. If funding comes through, it may reopen sometime in the mid-1990s. Nearby

FRANCE

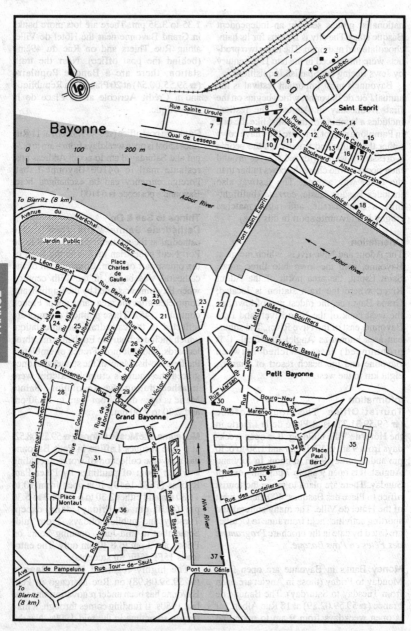

Bayonne

0   100   200 m

Saint Esprit

Rue Maubec

Rue Sainte Ursule

Quai de Lesseps

Rue Neuve

Rue Hugues

Rue Sainte Catherine

Boulevard d' Alsace-Lorraine

Quai Amiral Bergeret

Adour River

To Biarritz (8 km)

Avenue du Maréchal Leclerc

Jardin Public

Place Charles de Gaulle

Ave Léon Bonnat

Rue Bernède

Rue Jules Labat

Rue du 49ème

Rue Albert 1er

Rue Thiers

Rue du Port Neuf

Rue Victor Hugo

Rue Lormand

Avenue du 11 Novembre

Rue des Gouverneurs

Rue de la Monnaie

Grand Bayonne

Rue du Rempart Lachepaillet

Rue de la Salle

Place Montaut

Rue d'Espagne

Rue des Basques

Ave de Pampelune

Rue Tour-du-Sault

Pont du Génie

Nive River

Pont Saint Esprit

Adour River

Allées Boufflers

Rue Frédéric Bastiat

Rue Lafitte

Rue Jacques

Rue Marsan

Petit Bayonne

Bourg-Neuf

Rue Marengo

Rue des Lisses

Place Paul Bert

Rue Pannecau

Rue des Cordeliers

To Biarritz (8 km)

■	PLACES TO STAY	11	Restaurant Koskera	18	Distillerie de la Côte Basque
		14	Small Restaurants		
2	Hôtel Paris Madrid	29	Monoprix Supermarket	19	City Hall
5	Hôtel de la Gare	32	Les Halles (Food Market)	20	Tourist Office
7	Hôtel Vauban			21	Place de la Liberté
8	Hôtel La Crémaillère	36	Restaurant Dacquois	22	Place du Réduit
9	Hôtel Monte Carlo	37	Temporary Food Market	23	Bus Information & Ticket Kiosk
13	Hôtel Côte d'Argent			24	Post Office
15	Hôtel Beausoleil		OTHER	25	Banque de France
16	Hôtel San Miguel			27	Musée Bonnat
17	Hôtel du Moulin	1	Railway Station	28	Château Vieux
26	Hôtel des Arceaux	3	Synagogue	30	Musée Basque (closed)
34	Hôtel des Basques	4	Bus Station	31	Cathédrale Sainte Marie
		6	Place de la Gare		
▼	PLACES TO EAT	12	Place de la République	33	Zabal Diffusion
				35	Château Neuf
10	Restaurant Maisterrena				

is the Nive River, lined with traditional houses.

Izarra Tasting Izarra, a local liqueur made with dozens of exotic herbs, is produced at the **Distillerie de la Côte Basque** (☎ 59.55.09.45), which is in Saint Esprit at 9 Quai Amiral Bergeret. Half-hour free tours (an English text is available) with a tasting at the end take place on weekdays from 9 to 11.30 am and 2 to 5 pm. From mid-July to August, the distillery is open daily except Sunday from 9 to 11.30 am and 2 to 6 pm.

Pelote *Pelote Basque* (sometimes rendered in English as 'pelota') is the name given to a group of games native to the Basque Country which are played with a *chistera* (a curved leather or wicker racquet strapped to the wrist) and a *pelote* (a hard ball with a rubber centre). The best known variety of pelote in the Basque Country is *cesta punta*, the world's fastest game played with a ball. Matches are held on a court with three walls known as a *jaï-alaï* (hence the English name of one type of pelote played by two or four players). For information on championship tournaments, which take place in Biarritz, Saint Jean de Luz and elsewhere during the summer months, enquire at one of the area's tourist offices. Introductory 1½-hour cesta

punta lessons (100FF per person including equipment, minimum four people) are available in Biarritz – contact the Biarritz Athlétique Club (☎ 59.23.91.09) a few days in advance.

Bullfights *Corrida*, Spanish-style bullfighting in which the bull is killed, has its devotees all over the south of France, including Bayonne. Tournaments are held about half a dozen times each summer. Advance reservations are usually necessary – information is available at the tourist office. The matadors are either French or Spanish.

Places to Stay
Accommodation is most difficult to find from mid-July to mid-August, especially during the five-day Fête de Bayonne in August.

Camping There are several camping grounds in Anglet. The one-star *Camping du Fontaine Laborde* (☎ 59.03.89.67), open June to September, is on Blvd des Plages not far from the youth hostel. It often fills up in July and August. To get there, follow the instructions for taking the bus to the Auberge de Jeunesse (see the next section) but get off at the Fontaine Laborde stop. You might also try *Camping de la Chambre d'Amour*

(☎ 59.03.71.66), open from May to September, which is off Route de Bouney. It costs 17FF to pitch a tent and 17FF per adult (20% less in May and June). The nearest bus stop on line No 6 is Chapelle.

Hostel The *Auberge de Jeunesse* (☎ 59.63.86.49) nearest Bayonne is at 19 Route des Vignes in Anglet. It is open from February to November and charges 60FF for a bed. One-week sports courses (golf, sailing, surfing, diving, horse riding, etc) are available. To get there from the Bayonne Train Station, take bus No 2 (to Nuit de Mai in Biarritz) or No 1 (to Le Palais in Biarritz) and change to the northward-bound No 6 (or, during July and August, the Navette des Plages shuttle bus). Get off at the Auberge de Jeunesse stop.

Hotels There are a number of hotels right around the train station. The *Hôtel Paris Madrid* (☎ 59.55.13.98) is to the left as you exit the station. The cheapest singles cost 80FF. Big, pleasant singles and doubles without/with shower cost 110/130FF. Doubles with shower and toilet are 150FF. The *Hôtel de la Gare* (☎ 59.55.06.63), which is in the train station building under the clock tower, has singles/doubles with shower starting at 90/120FF. Triples/quads cost 200FF.

The *Hôtel du Moulin* (☎ 59.55.13.29) at 12 Rue Sainte Catherine may be the best deal in town. Singles/doubles cost from 75/95FF to 90/105FF, and triples/quads cost anywhere from 115 to 180FF. Showers are 10FF. The ground-floor restaurant serves excellent meals. The recently renovated *Hôtel Beausoleil* (☎ 59.55.00.10), up the block at 23 Rue Sainte Catherine, has doubles starting at 130FF; showers are free. The nicer *Hôtel San Miguel* (☎ 59.55.17.82) at 8 Rue Sainte Catherine has spacious doubles with big beds for 130/170FF without/with shower. Hall showers are 20FF.

The *Hôtel Monte Carlo* (☎ 59.55.02.68), owned by the same people as the Hôtel de la Gare, is opposite the train station at 1 Rue Sainte Ursule. Singles/doubles start at 80FF (130FF with shower). Hall showers are free.

Telephone reservations are not accepted. The *Hôtel Vauban* (☎ 59.55.11.31) at 13 Rue Sainte Ursule has average singles/doubles with shower for 140/180FF. A two-bed quad with shower is 180FF. You might also try the *Hôtel La Crémaillère* (☎ 59.55.12.35) at 3 Rue Sainte Ursule, which has doubles from 72 to 115FF. Showers are 10FF. The *Hôtel Côte d'Argent* (☎ 59.55.17.68) at 5 Blvd d'Alsace-Lorraine has singles/doubles/triples from 100/120/150FF. Reception is closed on Sunday except from mid-July to August.

In the centre of Grand Bayonne, the *Hôtel des Arceaux* (☎ 59.59.15.53) at 26 Rue du Port Neuf has doubles from 120FF (190FF with shower, toilet and TV). The least expensive hotel in Petit Bayonne is the *Hôtel des Basques* (☎ 59.59.08.02), which is next to 3 Rue des Lisses at Place Paul Bert. Large, nondescript singles/doubles start at 80FF (135FF with two beds). Showers cost 10FF.

Places to Eat
Restaurants Bayonne is an excellent place to sample Basque cuisine. *Restaurant Maisterrena* (☎ 59.55.15.13), which is open for meals from noon to 2 or 2.30 pm and 7 to 8 or 9 pm daily except Sunday evening, is near the train station at 3 Place de la République (next to the Hôtel Loustau on Rue Neuve). The sign, intended for the local clientele, just says 'Hôtel, Restaurant, Bar'. *Menus* start at 40FF. *Restaurant Koskera* (☎ 59.55.20.79), not far away at 3 Rue Hugues, has *plats du jour* (daily special) for 35FF and *menus* from 65FF. It is open Monday to Saturday from noon to 2 pm only (daily from noon to 2 pm and 8 to 10.30 pm from mid-June to September). In Grand Bayonne, a good bet is the unpretentious *Restaurant Dacquois* (☎ 59.59.29.61) at 48 Rue d'Espagne. It is open Monday to Saturday from 8 am to 8.30 pm and serves breakfast, lunch and dinner. *Menus* with a choice of main dishes and hors d'oeuvres costs 52FF.

Near the train station, there are a number of small restaurants along Rue Sainte Catherine, including a pizza place at No 11 and a crêperie at No 7.

Self-Catering Rue Sainte Catherine, which is not far from the train station, has a boulangerie, a fruit and vegetable shop (at No 29), and other food shops. The central market, *Les Halles*, is in Grand Bayonne on the west quay of the Nive River, but while the present building – a concrete monstrosity built in 1963 – is knocked down and replaced, the market will be located on the east side of the river near Pont du Génie. Les Halles is open Tuesday to Saturday from 6 am to 1 pm and Thursday, Friday and Saturday from 3.30 to 6.30 or 7 pm (6 pm in winter).

The *Monoprix* supermarket at 8 Rue Orbe is open Monday to Saturday from 8 or 8.30 am to 7 pm. The food section is at the back.

Things to Buy

Zabal Diffusion (☎ 59.25.43.90) at 52 Rue Pannecau has a large selection of cassettes (55 to 90FF) and CDs of Basque music. They also carry lots of books (including a few in English) on Basque history and culture and hiking in the Basque country. The shop is open from 9.15 am to 12.30 pm and 2.30 to 7.30 pm daily except Monday morning and Sunday.

Getting There & Away

Bus The bus station (☎ 59.55.17.59) is next to the train station at Place de la Gare. It is open weekdays from 9 am to noon and 2 to 6 pm. RDTL serves destinations in Les Landes, the department north of the Pyrénées Atlantiques (the department in which Bayonne is located). To get to the beaches along the coast north of Bayonne, take the line (which runs all year) to the beachside town of Vieux Boucau.

Train The train station (☎ 59.55.50.50 for information, 59.55.11.88 for reservations) is in Saint Esprit at Place de la Gare. The information office is open Monday to Saturday from 9 am to noon and 2 to 6.30 pm. During July and August it is open daily from 9 am to 7.30 pm. TGVs to/from Paris (340FF plus TGV reservation fee) take five hours and go to Gare Montparnasse. Other trains take about eight hours and stop at Paris' Gare d'Austerlitz. There are also trains to Bordeaux (134FF, two hours), Lourdes (86FF), Pau (67FF, one hour), Saint Jean de Luz and Saint Jean Pied de Port. For travel to Spain, change trains at Irun. Night trains go via Lourdes, Marseilles and the Côte d'Azur to the Italian border town of Ventimiglia.

Getting Around

Bus The bus network serving Bayonne, Biarritz and Anglet is known as STAB. Tickets cost 6.50FF if bought on board or 5.25FF if purchased in carnets of five or 10. Tickets remain valid for an hour after they are time-stamped.

In Bayonne, STAB has an information and ticket kiosk (☎ 59.59.04.61) at Place du Réduit, which is across the Nive River from the tourist office. It is open Monday to Saturday from 7.30 am to 6.30 pm.

Line No 1 links Bayonne's train station with the centre of Biarritz. Line No 2 starts at Bayonne's train station and passes through the centre of Biarritz before continuing on to the Biarritz-La Négresse Railway Station. Bus No 6 links the centre of Biarritz with the coast of Anglet (to the north) and the airport (to the south-east). During July and August *only*, the Navette des Plages shuttle bus connects the beach-lined Anglet coast with central Biarritz and, farther south, Plage de la Côte des Basques.

BIARRITZ

The classy Basque Coast (Côte Basque) town of Biarritz (population 26,000), which is eight km west of Bayonne, got its start as a resort in the mid-19th century, when Emperor Napoleon III and his Spanish-born wife, the Empress Eugénie, began coming here. In later decades, Biarritz became popular with wealthy Britons and was visited by Queen Victoria and King Edward VII, both of whom have streets named in their honour. These days, the Biarritz area is known for its fine beaches and some of the best surfing in Europe.

The wealth assembled in Biarritz is given a cosmopolitan aspect by assorted incongruous imports: Southern California-style surf shops, a blue-domed Russian church, feet shod in boating shoes à la New England. But even more than the town itself, it's the summer visitors who exude prosperity – and the sense of entitlement that comes with it. It can be vastly entertaining just to people-watch.

Biarritz can be a real budget-buster, but you can enjoy most of what people pay lots of money for on inexpensive day trips from Bayonne or the youth hostel in Anglet.

Information

The tourist office (☎ 59.24.20.24) is one block east of Ave Édouard VII at Square d'Ixelles. It is open daily from 9 am to 12.30 pm and 2 or 2.15 to 6.15 pm (3 to 6 pm on Saturday and Sunday afternoons). From mid-June to mid-September, opening hours are 8 am to 8 pm every day. There are lots of banks around Place Clemenceau. Many businesses close for a siesta between noon and 3 or 3.30 pm.

Biarritz' postcode is 64200.

Things to See & Do

The **Grande Plage**, lined in season with striped white-and-primary-colour bathing tents, stretches from the Casino Bellevue to the grand old Hôtel du Palais, built in the mid-19th century as a villa by Napoleon III and the Empress Eugénie. North of the Hôtel du Palais is Plage Miramar, bounded on the north by **Pointe Saint Martin** and the **Phare de Biarritz** (lighthouse). At low tide (when there are more than rocks above the water line), there is **nude bathing** at the northern end of Plage Miramar (beyond the boulders). There are four km of beaches north of Pointe Saint Martin in Anglet.

Heading southward from the Grande Plage, you can walk along the coast past the old fishing port and around the mauve cliffs of **Rocher de la Vierge**, a stone island reached by a bridge and so named because it

has a white statue of the Virgin on top. There is a small beach just south of Rocher de la Vierge at the **Port Vieux** (old port). The long **Plage de la Côte des Basques** begins a few hundred metres farther down the coast.

Places to Stay

Most hotels raise their rates substantially in summer, sometimes by almost 100%. All in all, you're much better off staying in Bayonne.

The *Château Silhouette* (☎ 59.24.20.83), a gem of an old-fashioned hotel, is at 30 Rue Gambetta, which is two blocks up Rue Gambetta from Place Clemenceau. By decision of the feisty proprietor, it is *only* open from June to October. Large, simply furnished singles/doubles cost 125 to 150FF. Hall showers are 15FF. The friendly *Hôtel Fandango* (☎ 59.24.23.42) at 13 Ave Maréchal Joffre is only open from May to September. Simple singles/doubles of a good size start at 160/190FF with washbasin and bidet and 190/250FF with shower. Hall showers are free. To get there from Place Clemenceau, walk 600 metres south on Rue Victor Hugo, which becomes Ave Maréchal Joffre.

Places to Eat

Les Halles, a large food market two blocks south along Rue Gambetta or Ave Victor Hugo from Place Clemenceau, is open seven days a week from 5 am to 1.30 pm. There are lots of food shops in the immediate vicinity.

Things to Buy

For Basque music and crafts and guidebooks to the Basque Country, try Eki (☎ 59.24.79.64) at 21 Ave de Verdun, 300 metres east of Place Clemenceau. It is open daily except Monday morning and Sunday from 9 am to noon and 3 to 7 pm.

Getting There & Away

Bus For information on STAB buses to/from Bayonne and Anglet, see Getting Around in the Bayonne section. The STAB information office in Biarritz is across Square d'Ixelles from the tourist office.

Train The Biarritz-La Négresse Railway Station is three km south of the centre of Biarritz at the southern terminus of Ave du Président John F Kennedy (the southern continuation of Ave du Maréchal Foch). In Biarritz proper, SNCF information and tickets are available at Frantours Tourism travel agency (☎ 59.24.00.94), which is 200 metres south of Place Clemenceau at 13 Ave du Maréchal Foch. It is open Monday to Friday from 9 am to noon and 1.30 to 6.30 pm, and on Saturday from 9 am to noon. From April to September it is also open on Saturday afternoon from 2 to 5 pm.

Getting Around
Bicycle & Motorbike Two-wheeled conveyances of all sorts can be rented from Sobilo (☎ 59.24.94.47) at 24 Rue Peyroloubilh.

AROUND BAYONNE
Saint Jean Pied de Port
The walled Pyrenean town of Saint Jean Pied de Port (population 1700), 55 km south-east of Bayonne, was once the last stop in France for pilgrims on their way south to the Spanish city of Santiago de Compostela, the most important Christian pilgrimage site after Jerusalem and Rome in the Middle Ages. Today, the town, which is in a hilly rural area, retains much of its Basque character.

The tourist office (☎ 59.37.03.57) is at 14 Place Charles de Gaulle. Half the reason for coming to Saint Jean Pied de Port is the scenic train trip from Bayonne, which takes about an hour. The cost from Bayonne is 82FF return or 41FF one-way. There are about six trains a day.

Saint Jean de Luz
The seaside town of Saint Jean de Luz (population 13,000), 20 km south-west of Bayonne, is an attractive beach resort with a colourful history of whaling and piracy. The richly decorated **Église Saint Jean Baptiste**, a mid-17th century church built in the traditional Basque manner, was the scene in 1660 of the marriage of King Louis XIV to the Spanish princess Marie-Thérèse, only an infant at the time.

The tourist office (☎ 59.26.03.16) is at Place Foch. Frequent trains and buses go to Saint Jean de Luz from Bayonne and Biarritz. The trip takes about 20 minutes.

LOURDES
Lourdes (population 17,000) was just a sleepy market town in 1858 when Bernadette Soubirous (1844-79), an illiterate, 14-year-old peasant girl, saw the Virgin Mary, dressed in white, in a series of 18 visions that took place in a cave near the town. The girl's account of the apparition was investigated first by the diocese and later by the Vatican and confirmed as a bona fide miracle. Bernadette, who lived out her short life as a nun, was beatified in 1925 and canonised eight years later, thus becoming Saint Bernadette.

These events set Lourdes on the path to becoming one of the world's most important pilgrimage sites. Some five million pilgrims from all over the world converge on Lourdes annually, and the number is growing every year. Among the faithful are many sick people seeking a miraculous cure to their afflictions. But whatever their reasons for being in Lourdes, the pilgrims tend to be remarkably good-natured – after all, they may be on a religious mission, but they're also on holiday in France! On summer nights, groups of pilgrims wander in and out of the brightly lit souvenir shops and restaurants, making the whole town seem like a giant carnival.

Accompanying the fervent, almost medieval piety of the pilgrims is an astounding display of commercial exuberance that is reminiscent of the bazaars of the Middle East. If your sense of propriety and good taste is governed by the Anglo-Protestant preference for understatement, it can all seem unspeakably tacky. Granted, the souvenir wall thermometers on sale all over town are tawdry by any standard. But the choice of materials – affordable and flashy things like cast plastic and blinking Christmas lights – makes it too easy to discount the significance of these knick-knacks to the people who spend their life savings to come here.

Orientation

Lourdes' two main east-west streets – both lined with souvenir shops – are Rue de la Grotte and, 300 metres north, Blvd de la Grotte. Both lead to the Sanctuaires Notre Dame de Lourdes, but Blvd de la Grotte takes you to the main entrance. The principal north-south thoroughfare, known as Chaussée Maransin where it passes over Blvd de la Grotte, connects Ave de la Gare (which runs by the train station) with Place du Champ Commun, where the tourist office is.

Information

The municipal tourist office (☎ 62.94.15.64) at Place du Champ Commun is open Monday to Saturday from 9 am to noon and 2 to 6 pm (7 pm from Easter to mid-October). From Easter to mid-October, it is also open on Sunday and public holidays from 10 am to noon. During July, August and September, it is open daily and there is no midday closure except on Sunday and holidays, when hours are 10 am to 12.30 pm and 1.30 to 6 pm. To get to the tourist office from the train station, walk 250 metres west on Ave de la Gare and then 600 metres south on Chaussée Maransin, whose name changes several times along the way.

For information (eg brochures in a variety of languages) on the Sanctuaires Notre Dame de Lourdes, drop in on the Forum Information (☎ 62.42.78.78) which is in the sanctuaries complex on the Esplanade next to the statue of the Crowned Virgin. It is open every day from 9 am to noon and 2 to 6 pm. Summer hours are 8.30 am to 6.30 pm.

Lourdes' postcode is 65100.

Things to See

The **Sanctuaires Notre Dame de Lourdes**, the huge religious complex that has grown up around the cave where Bernadette's visions took place, are west across the Gave de Pau (a small river) from the city centre. Development of this area began within a decade of the events of 1858, and the expan-sion has gone on ever since. You won't be alone if you find it difficult to understand how the gaudy architecture, much of it built in the debatable taste of the late 19th century and more reminiscent of Disneyland than the majesty of a Gothic cathedral, inspires awe and devotion. But clearly it does.

The more noteworthy sites in the complex include the **grotte**, where Bernadette had her visions and which today is hung with the crutches of cured cripples, and the **Basilique de la Rosaire** (Basilica of the Rosary), which was built in 1889 in an overwrought pseudo-Byzantine style. The grounds can be entered 24 hours a day via the Entrée des Lacets, which is on Rue Monseigneur Theas, the continuation of Blvd de la Grotte. Proper dress is required: at the very least, don't wear short shorts or skirts or sleeveless shirts.

From the Sunday before Easter to at least mid-October, there are **torch-light processions** nightly at 8.45 pm. The **Procession Eucaristique** (Blessed Sacrament Procession), in which groups of pilgrims carrying banners march along the Esplanade des Processions, takes place daily during the same period at 4.30 pm. In case of rain, it is held inside the bunker-like **Basilique Souterraine Saint Pie X** (Underground Basilica of Saint Pius X), described by some as a cross between a football stadium and an underground parking garage. It was built in 1959 (in case you didn't guess) in the Fallout Shelter style, then at the height of its popularity.

Other attractions in Lourdes include the **wax museum** (☎ 62.94.33.74) at 87 Rue de la Grotte, where you can see life-size dioramas of important events in the lives of both Jesus Christ and Bernadette Soubirous, and **Saint Bernadette's home** (*maison paternelle*), down the alley next to 55 Blvd de la Grotte. The free, self-guided tour ends up at Saint Bernadette's bedroom, whose only exit leads into a souvenir shop. Between April and mid-October, the same two films about Saint Bernadette are always playing at the **Cinéma Pax** (☎ 62.94.52.01), which is down the small street opposite 64 Rue de la Grotte.

The rather grim, medieval **Château Fort**, most of whose present buildings date from the 17th or 18th centuries, houses the **Musée Pyrénéen** (☎ 62.94.02.04). The entrances to the château, which are opposite 42 Rue du Fort and off Rue du Bourg, are open from 9 to 11 am and 2 to 5 pm (6 pm from April to September) daily except Tuesday and public holidays (daily from April to September). The museum and chateau close at noon and 6 pm (7 pm from April to September). The entry fee is 26FF (no student discount).

Places to Stay
Lourdes has over 350 hotels, more than any city in France except Paris. Indeed, there are probably more hotels per sq km here than anywhere else on the face of the earth. Even in winter, when many places close, it is no problem to find a relatively cheap room. The camping ground nearest the centre of town is *Camping de la Poste* (☎ 62.94.40.35) at 26 Rue de Langelle, a few blocks east of the main post office. It is open from Palm Sunday (late April or early May) to late October.

Places to Eat
There are lots of undistinguished restaurants scattered around town. *Les Halles*, the covered market next to the tourist office, is open daily from 7 am to 1 pm.

Burgundy & the Rhône Region

The Dukedom of Burgundy (Bourgogne in French), situated on the great trade route between the Mediterranean and northern Europe, waxed wealthier and more powerful than the Kingdom of France during the 14th and 15th centuries. These days, the region of Burgundy and its capital, Dijon, are known for their medieval architecture, multi-coloured tile roofs, great gastronomy and the production of quality wine.

By far the most important urban centre in the Rhône region, which lies south of Burgundy, is Lyons, France's second-largest city in terms of area. Lyons' centuries of commercial and industrial prosperity, made possible by the mighty Rhône River and its tributary the Saône, have created an appealing city with superb museums, an attractive centre, shopping to rival that of Paris and a flourishing cultural life.

DIJON
Dijon (population 146,000), prosperous capital of the dukes of Burgundy for almost 500 years, reached the height of its brilliance during the 14th and 15th centuries under Philippe le Hardi (Philip the Bold), Jean sans Peur (John the Fearless) and Philippe le Bon (Philip the Good). During this period, Dijon was a great centre of European art, and the Burgundian court was one of the continent's most illustrious.

Modern Dijon is one of France's most appealing provincial cities, with an inviting city centre graced by elegant residences built during the Middle Ages and the Renaissance. Despite its long history, Dijon has a distinctly youthful air, in part because of the major university situated here. The city is a good starting point for visits to the nearby vineyards of Burgundy, among the most renowned in France.

Orientation
Dijon's main thoroughfare runs from the train station to Église Saint Michel. Ave Maréchal Foch links the train station with the tourist office. Rue de la Liberté, a pedestrian mall that serves as the main shopping street, runs between Porte Guillaume (a triumphal arch erected in 1788) and the Palais des Ducs (Ducal Palace).

Information
Tourist Office The tourist office (☎ 80.43.42.12) is at Place Darcy. From mid-November to mid-April it is open daily from 9 am to noon and 2 to 7 pm. During the rest of the year, hours are 9 am to 8 pm (9 pm from June to mid-September). There is a

FRANCE

FRANCE

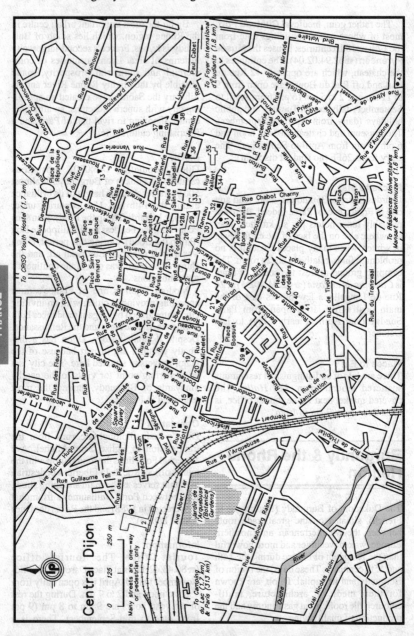

Central Dijon

0   125   250 m

Many streets are one-way
or pedestrian only

Blvd Voltaire

Rue Alfred de Musset

43

Rue de Mirande

Rue Jean Baptiste Baudin

To Foyer International
d'Étudiants (1.8 km)

Paul Cabet

Rue de Mulhouse

Boulevard Thiers

Georges Clemenceau

Rue Marceau

Lycée

Rue du

Rue Diderot

Rue Jeannin

38

37

36

35

Rue Chancellerie
de l'Hôpital

Boulevard de la Côte
d'Or

Rue Prieur

Carnot

Rue d'Auxonne

Rue Devosge

Place de la
République

Rue
du Nord

J Rousseau

Rue d'Assas

de la Préfecture

Rue Vannerie

Rue de la
Sainte Chapelle

Chouinnerie

Rue Berbier

Rue Buffon

Rue Chabot Charny

42

Place
Wilson

To Résidences Universitaires
Mansart & Montmuzard (1.6 km)

To CRISD Youth Hostel (1.7 km)

La Tremouille

Rue
de la Préfecture

Place de
la Banque

Rue de la
Chouette

28

34

Rue Vaillant

33

32

31

30

29

Rue des
Bons Enfants

Rue Amiral Roussin

Rue Pasteur

Rue Turgot

Rue de Tivoli

Rue du Transvaal

Blvd de la Trémouille

2

Blvd Bannelier

Rue Quentin

Rue des Forges

25

24

23

27

26

Rue Musette

22

Rue Jules Mercier

Rue Rameau

Place
des
Cordeliers

Rue Charrue

40

41

Rue de la Manutention

Place Saint
Bernard

Rue des Brosses

Rue du Château

Rue des Godrans

Rue Bossuet

Rue Chaudronnerie

Rue de la
Liberté

Rue du
Chapeau
Rouge

Rue Piron

8

10

Rue Michelet

21

Place
Bossuet

39

Berbisey

Rue Sainte Anne

Rue des Fleurs

Rue Jacques Cellerier

Rue Audra

Blvd de Temple

Rue de
la Poste

18

19

20

17

16

Rue Danton

Rue Monge

Rue de la
Manutention

Rue Devosge

Ave de la 1ère Armée

Square
Davey

5

6

7

Dr Chaussier

Dr Maret

15

Rue Condorcet

Rue de la
Manutention

Rue Victor Hugo

Ave Victor Hugo

Blvd Maréchal Foch

14

3

Rue
Mariotte

Rue de Séville

Rempart

Rue Miséricorde

Rue de l'Hôpital

To l'Hôpital

Rue Guillaume Tell

Rue des Perrières

Ave Albert 1er

Rue de l'Arquebuse

Jardin de
l'Arquebuse
(Botanical
Gardens)

Rue du Faubourg Raines

Ouche River

1

2

To Camping
du Lac (1.1 km)
& Paris (313 km)

Quai Nicolas Rolin

■ PLACES TO STAY	18	Restaurant	17	Place Saint Bénigne
		Universitaire Maret	19	Musée Archéologique
14 Hôtel de la Gare (Hôtel	21	Prisunic Supermarket	20	Cathédrale Saint
Bossuet)	23	Food Shops		Bénigne
27 Hôtel Confort (Hôtel	36	Brunet Alimentation &	22	Place François Rude
Lamartine)		Boulangerie	24	Tourist Office Annexe
32 Hôtel du Théâtre	39	Restaurant Marrakech		(Hôtel Chambellan)
37 Hôtel Diderot			25	Église Notre Dame
38 Hôtel du Lycée		OTHER	26	Palais des Ducs et des
39 Hôtel Monge				États de Bourgogne
	1	Bus Station (Gare	28	Place des Ducs de
▼ PLACES TO EAT		Routière)		Bourgogne
	2	Gare Dijon-Ville	29	Musée des Beaux-Arts
3 Brasserie Foch &		(Railway Station)	30	Place de la Libération
Boulangerie	4	Tourist Office	31	Musée Magnin
5 L'Orient Express	6	Place Darcy	33	Theatre
Lebanese Restau-	7	Porte Guillaume (arch)	34	Musée François Rude
rant & Boulangerie	8	Main Post Office	35	Église Saint Michel
11 Halles du Marché	9	STRD Kiosque	40	Musée d'Art Sacré
(Food Market)		Centrale (Bus	41	Musée de la Vie
13 Casino Supermarket		Information)		Bourguignonne
15 Café Au Carillon	10	Place Grangier	42	Synagogue
16 Café La Cathédrale	12	Banque de France	43	Cinéma Eldorado

tourist office annexe (☎ 80.30.35.39) at 34 Rue des Forges.

Money The tourist office will change money whenever it's open. The Banque de France (☎ 80.40.41.50), at 2 Place de la Banque (just north of the covered market), is open weekdays from 8.45 am to noon and 1.15 to 3.30 pm. There are quite a few banks along Rue de la Liberté, including a Crédit Lyonnais at 6 Rue de la Liberté. There are a couple of exchange bureaus at Place Grangier.

Post The main post office (☎ 80.50.62.14), which is at Place Grangier, is open weekdays from 8 am to 7 pm and on Saturday from 8 am to noon. Exchange services are available.

Dijon's postcode is 21000.

Things to See & Do
Dijon's Hôtel de Ville occupies most of the **Palais des Ducs et des États de Bourgogne** (Palace of the Dukes and States-General of Burgundy), whose classical appearance is the result of rebuilding in the 17th and 18th centuries. The mid-15th

century **Tour Philippe le Bon** affords a great view of the city. The Musée des Beaux-Arts (see the following Museums section), founded in 1783, is in the east wing. Between May and October, you can go up the **Tour de Bar**, a tower off the Cour de Bar (the courtyard next to the museum). Nearby are the vaulted **Cuisines Ducales** (Ducal Kitchens) built in 1445, a fine example of Gothic civic architecture. The front of the palace looks out on the semicircular **Place de la Libération**, a gracious, arcaded public square laid out in 1686.

Some of the finest of Dijon's many medieval and Renaissance *hôtels particuliers* (aristocratic mansions) are along **Rue Verrerie** and **Rue des Forges**, Dijon's main street until the 18th century. The splendid courtyard of the **Hôtel Chambellan** (1490) at 34 Rue des Forges, now home to a branch of the tourist office, is worth at least a peek. There's some remarkable vaulting at the top of the spiral staircase. **Rue de la Chouette**, where there are more old residences, runs along the north side of Église Notre Dame (see the next section). It is named for the small stone owl (*chouette*) carved into the corner of one of the church's chapels, which people stroke to gain happiness and wisdom. The social centre of Dijon is **Place François Rude**, a popular hang-out in good weather.

Churches The Burgundian-Gothic **Cathédrale Saint Bénigne**, built in the late 13th century over what may be the tomb of Saint Benignus (who by tradition is believed to have brought Christianity to Burgundy in the 2nd century), is open daily from 8.45 am to 7 pm. Many of the great figures of Burgundy's history are buried here. The multicoloured tile roof is typically Burgundian.

Église Saint Michel, begun in 1499, is a Gothic church with an impressive Renaissance façade that was added in 1661. Also of architectural interest is **Église Notre Dame**, built in the Burgundian-Gothic style during the first half of the 13th century. The three friezes of the façade are decorated with lots of false gargoyles (false because they aren't there to throw rainwater clear of the building). The **Horloge à Jacquemart** (mechanical clock) on the right tower dates from the late 14th century.

Museums The Carte d'Accès aux Musées, a combo ticket that gets you into each of Dijon's seven major museums, costs only 13FF (6.50FF for students and people over 60). You can purchase it at museum ticket counters. All the museums are closed on Tuesday except the Musée Magnin (closed Monday).

The fine **Musée des Beaux-Arts** (☎ 80.74.52.70), one of the most renowned fine arts museums in the provinces, is at Place de la Sainte Chapelle in the east wing of the Palais des Ducs. It is worth a visit just for the magnificent **Salle des Gardes** (Room of the Guards), rebuilt after a fire in 1502, which houses the extraordinary, 15th century Flamboyant Gothic sepulchres of two of the first Valois dukes of Burgundy. The museum is open from 10 am to 6 pm daily except Tuesday. On Sunday, it closes from 12.30 to 2 pm and may do so every day

during the winter. The entry fee is 10FF, but students get in for free as does anyone who comes on Sunday.

Next to the cathedral at 5 Rue du Docteur Maret is the **Musée Archéologique** (☎ 80.30.88.54), whose collections include a number of rare Celtic and Gallo-Roman artefacts. It is open from 9 am to noon and 2 to 6 pm daily except Tuesday. There is no midday closure during June, July and August. Entry costs 9FF, but the museum is free on Sunday and holidays.

The **Musée Magnin** (☎ 80.67.11.10) is just off Place de la Libération at 4 Rue des Bons Enfants. This mid-17th century residence, the ancestral home of Jeanne Magnin and her brother Maurice Magnin, houses a collection of 2000 assorted works of art assembled by the two around the turn of the century. It is open from 10 am to noon and 2 to 6 pm daily except Monday. From June to September, it does not close at midday. The admission fee is 12FF (7FF for students under 25).

Vineyards around Dijon Dijon is just north of one of the world's foremost wine-growing regions. The town of Beaune (population 21,127), a major wine-making centre about 40 km south of Dijon, makes an excellent day trip. The tourist offices in Dijon, Beaune (☎ 80.22.24.51) and nearby towns can provide details on *caves* (wine cellars) that offer tours and *dégustation* (wine tasting).

You can get from Dijon to Beaune either by train (35FF, about 30 minutes) or by bus (35FF, one hour). Transco bus No 44 is a good bet if you want to stop along the way (there are wineries at virtually every stop). It runs about 10 times a day except on Sunday and holidays, when service is drastically reduced.

Places to Stay
Camping Camping du Lac (☎ 80.43.54.72) at 3 Blvd Chanoine Kir is 1.7 km west of the train station, behind the psychiatric hospital. It is open from April to mid-November. Guests pay 8FF each, a tent emplacement is 4FF and parking for a car costs 4FF. To get

here from the train station, take bus No 12 and get off at the Hôpital des Chartreux stop.

Hostels The *Foyer International d'Étudiants* (☎ 80.71.51.01) at 6 Rue Maréchal Leclerc, 2.5 km east of the centre of town, accepts travellers throughout the year if there's space (which is most of the time, even in summer). Single rooms are 55FF a night. To get there, catch bus No 4 (towards Apollinaire) along Ave Victor Hugo or on Rue de la Liberté and get off at the Billardon stop. The *Centre de Rencontres Internationales et de Séjour de Dijon* (CRISD; ☎ 80.71.32.12), Dijon's large, institutional youth hostel, is 2.5 km north-east of the centre of town at 1 Blvd Champollion. Prices range from 62FF (for a bed in a dorm room) to 130FF (for a single). The hostel is closed from 10 am to 4 or 5 pm but there's no curfew. To get to CRISD, take bus No 5 from Place Grangier.

From late May to sometime in September, travellers can stay at the *Résidence Universitaire Mansart* (☎ 80.66.18.22), a dorm 2.5 km south-east of the centre of town on the main university campus. The address is 94 Rue Mansart (also spelled 'Mansard'). The reception (*secrétariat*) is in a building made of green glass. If you have an international student card, it costs 56FF per person, otherwise, the charge is 75FF. If Mansart is full, you might try the *Résidence Universitaire Montmuzard* (☎ 80.39.68.01), behind the Faculté de Droit (Law Faculty), a five-minute walk north. To get out here, catch bus No 9 (towards the terminus called Facultés) either at the train station or along Rue de la Liberté; get off at the Mansard stop.

Hotels *Hôtel de la Gare* (☎ 80.30.46.61), also known as the Hôtel Bossuet, is 300 metres from the train station at 16 Rue Mariotte. Nondescript, smallish singles/doubles with toilet and shower start at 143/161FF, including breakfast. On Sundays, reception is closed from noon to 5 pm.

The *Hôtel du Théâtre* (☎ 80.67.15.41) at 3 Rue des Bons Enfants is an old place only a block from the Palais des Ducs. Large, simple rooms, some with lots of light, start

at 85FF. Singles/doubles with shower are 95 to 112FF, and quads with shower cost 200FF. There are no hall showers. The small *Hôtel Confort* (☎ 80.30.37.47), also known as the Hôtel Lamartine, is also right in the centre of town at 12 Rue Jules Mercier, an alley off Rue de la Liberté. Decent singles/doubles start at 115FF (165FF with shower and toilet). Hall showers are 23FF. On Sunday, reception is closed from noon to 5 pm.

The friendly, accommodating *Hôtel Monge* (☎ 80.30.55.41) at 20 Rue Monge has singles/doubles starting at 115/125FF (190/200FF with shower, toilet and TV). Showers are 15FF.

West of the centre, the *Hôtel Diderot* (☎ 80.67.10.85) at 7 Rue du Lycée has singles and doubles from 100FF. The large rooms have high ceilings and are furnished in the prewar style. Triples with two beds cost 180FF and showers cost 15FF. Reception may be closed on Sunday afternoon. The *Hôtel du Lycée* (☎ 80.67.12.35) at 28 Rue du Lycée has ordinary but adequate rooms from 100FF; showers are free. Reception is closed on Sundays from noon to 5 pm.

Places to Eat

Restaurants You'll find a number of reasonably priced brasseries along Blvd Maréchal Foch, including the café-style *Brasserie Foch* (☎ 80.41.27.93) at 1bis Blvd Maréchal Foch, which is open daily except Sunday from 11 am to 10 pm. There is a small Lebanese place, *L'Orient Express* (☎ 80.30.22.44), at 3 Blvd de Sévigné. It is open from noon to 2.30 pm and 6 pm to midnight daily except Sunday at midday. *Restaurant Marrakech* (☎ 80.30.82.69) at 20 Rue Monge has huge portions of excellent couscous starting at 35FF. Food is served every evening from 5.30 pm to midnight and from Thursday to Sunday from 10.30 am to 2.30 or 3 pm.

The *Restaurant Universitaire Maret* (☎ 80.40.40.34) at 3 Rue du Docteur Maret, next to the Musée Archéologique, has cheap cafeteria food for students. Except during July and August, it is open weekdays and one weekend a month. Lunch is served from

11.45 am to 1.15 pm, dinner from 6.45 to 7.45 pm. Tickets, which cost 11.50FF for students, are sold on the ground floor whenever the restaurant is open.

Self-Catering The cheapest place to buy food is the *Halles du Marché*, a 19th century covered market 150 metres north of Rue de la Liberté. It is open Tuesday, Friday and Saturday from 6 am to 1 pm. There are a number of food shops in the immediate vicinity, including a cheese shop (closed Sunday afternoon) at 10 Rue François Rude, a *Nicolas* wine shop (closed Monday morning and Sunday) at 6 Rue François Rude and several boulangeries. There is a *Prisunic* supermarket south of Rue de la Liberté at 11-13 Rue Piron. The food section is upstairs. It is open Monday to Saturday from 8.45 am to 8 pm.

Near the tourist office, there is a boulangerie at 1 Blvd de Sévigné. It is open from 7 am to 7 pm (6.30 pm on Saturday) daily except Sunday. During July and August, it's closed on Saturday afternoon.

Brunet Alimentation at 83 Rue Vannerie (right near Église Saint Michel) is one of the only places in Dijon where you can get food on Sunday afternoon. It is open Monday to Saturday from 8 am to 10 pm and on Sunday from 9 am to 1 pm and 3.30 to 9 pm. Nearby are two boulangeries, one at 81 Rue Vannerie (closed Sunday afternoon and Saturday) and the other at 57 Rue Vannerie.

Entertainment

The *Cinéma Eldorado* (☎ 80.66.51.89, or 80.66.12.34 for a recorded message in French) at 21 Rue Alfred de Musset specialises in movies that are subtitled rather than dubbed. Regular tickets cost 38FF. The 29FF student rate is not available all day Saturday and on Sunday before 8 pm. The cinema is closed from mid-July to mid-August.

The *Café Au Carillon* (☎ 80.30.63.71), which is opposite the cathedral at 2 Rue Mariotte, is extremely popular with young locals. It is closed during August. Hours are Monday to Saturday from 6.30 am to 12.30

or 1 am (2 am in summer). Also popular is the *Café La Cathédrale* (☎ 80.30.42.10), which is across the street at 4 Place Saint Bénigne.

Getting There & Away

Bus The gare routière (☎ 80.42.11.00) is next to the train station. There is excellent service from here to points all over the department of Côte d'Or, including the wine town of Beaune. The information counter is open from 8.30 am to 12.30 pm and 2.30 to 6.30 pm daily except Saturday afternoon and Sunday.

Train The train station (☎ 80.41.50.50 for information, 80.43.52.56 for reservations), Gare Dijon-Ville, was built to replace an earlier structure destroyed in 1944. The information office is open from 8.30 am to 7.15 pm (6.45 pm on Saturday) daily except Sunday. By TGV, going to/from Paris' Gare de Lyon (184FF plus the reservation fee) takes about 1½ hours. Non-TGV trains to Lyons (127FF) take about two hours. The trip to Nice (353FF) takes around seven hours. The Dijon-Nice line is served by TGV trains but reservations are required.

Getting Around

Bus Dijon's extensive urban bus network is run by STRD (☎ 80.30.60.90). Single trips cost 4.90FF and a carnet of five tickets is 15.50FF. Seven different bus lines stop along Rue de la Liberté and five more stop at Place Grangier. Most STRD buses run Monday to Saturday from 6 am to 8 pm. Sunday service lasts from 1 to 8 pm. STRD's Kiosque Centrale (information office) at Place Grangier is open daily except Sunday.

LYONS

The grand city of Lyons (Lyon), with a population of 418,000, is part of a prosperous urban area of almost two million people, making it the second-largest conurbation in the country. Founded by the Romans over 2000 years ago, it has spent the last 500 years as a commercial, industrial and banking powerhouse. Present-day Lyons is endowed with outstanding museums, a dynamic cultural life, classy shopping, lively pedestrian malls (great for strolling) and excellent cuisine – it is, after all, one of France's gastronomic capitals, even for people on a budget.

Lyons, founded under the name Lugdunum in 43 BC, served as the capital of the Roman territories known as the Three Gauls under Augustus. The 16th century marked the beginning of the city's extraordinary prosperity. Banks were established, great commercial fairs were held, and trade flourished. Printing arrived before the end of the 15th century; within 50 years Lyons was home to several hundred printers. The city became a major silk-weaving centre in the mid-1700s. The famous *traboules*, a network of covered passageways in Croix Rousse and Old Lyons (see further), originally built to facilitate the transport of silk during inclement weather, proved very useful to the Resistance during WW II. In 1944, the retreating Germans blew up all but one of the city's two dozen bridges.

Orientation

The city centre area is in the middle of the Presqu'île, a long, thin peninsula bounded by the Rhône and Saône rivers. The elevated area north of Place des Terreaux is known as Croix Rousse. Place Bellecour is one km south of Place des Terreaux and one km north of Place Carnot, which is next to one of Lyons' train stations, Gare de Perrache. The city's other train station, Gare de la Part-Dieu, is two km east of the Presqu'île in a huge, modernistic commercial district known as La Part-Dieu. Old Lyons (Vieux Lyon) is on the west bank of the Saône River between the city centre and Fourvière Hill.

Information

Tourist Office The main tourist office (☎ 78.42.25.75) is in the south-east corner of Place Bellecour. It is open weekdays from 9 am to 6 pm (7 pm in summer) and on weekends until 5 pm (6 pm in summer). The SNCF desk, which has train information and sells tickets, is open Monday to Saturday from 9 am to 6 pm (5 pm on Saturday). The tourist office annexe at Gare de Perrache (on the upper level of the Centre d'Échange) is open Monday to Friday from 9 am to 12.30 pm and 2 to 6 pm and Saturday from 9 am to 5 pm.

Money The Banque de France (☎ 72.41.25.25) is on Rue de la République at Place de la Bourse. There is a Caisse d'Épargne de Lyon (open Tuesday to Friday and on Saturday mornings) at 2 Place Ampère, and there are other banks on Rue Victor Hugo just north of Place Ampère. Near Place des Terreaux, there are a number of banks on Rue du Bât d'Argent. American Express (☎ 78.37.40.69), which is near Place de la République at 6 Rue Childebert, is open weekdays from 9 am to noon and 2 to 6 pm and, from May to September, on Saturday morning also. At Gare de la Part-Dieu, Thomas Cook (☎ 72.33.48.55) is open daily from 9.30 am to 6.30 pm.

Post The main post office (☎ 72.40.65.22) at 10 Place Antonin Poncet has foreign currency services and is open Monday to Friday from 8 am to 7 pm and on Saturday from 8 am to noon. The post office at 3 Rue du Président Édouard Herriot, near Place des Terreaux, can also change money. It has the same opening hours as the main post office. There is a branch post office at 8 Place Ampère.

Lyon's postcodes follow a similar system to that of Paris. They consist of the digits 6900 plus the number of the arrondissement (one to nine). For the Presqu'île, the postcode is 69001 north of the Banque de France and 69002 south of the Banque de France.

Foreign Consulates The UK Consulate (☎ 78.37.59.67) is at 24 Rue Childebert (4th floor). It is open weekdays from 10 am to 12.30 pm and 2.30 to 5 pm. The US Consulate (☎ 78.24.68.49) is across the Rhône River from Place des Terreaux at 7 Quai du Général Sarrail (4th floor). The American services section is open weekdays from 9 am to noon and 2 to 5 pm (4 pm on Friday).

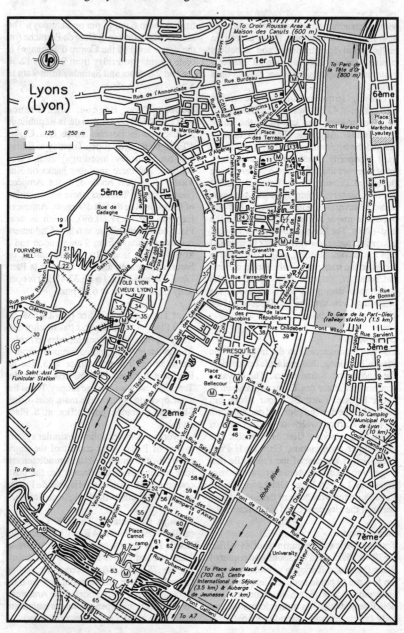

Lyons
(Lyon)

0   125   250 m

To Croix Rousse Area &
Maison des Canuts (600 m)

To Parc de
la Tête d'Or
(800 m)

1er

6ème

Rue Burdeau

Rue de l'Annonciade

Rue de la Grande Côte

Rue Terme

Rue des Capucins

Place
du
Maréchal
Lyautey

Rue de la Martinière

Pont Morand

Rue d'Algérie

Place
des Terreaux

Rue de la Pêcherie

5ème

Rue de Gadagne

Quai Général Sarrail

Quai de la Pêcherie

Rue St-Antoine

Rue du Président Édouard Herriot

Rue de la République

Rue Mercière

Rue du Garet

FOURVIÈRE
HILL

Montée Saint Barthélemy

Rue du Bœuf

Saint Jean

Rue des Trois Maries

Rue de Brest

Rue de la Bourse

Rue Grenette

Rue du Président Carnot

Rue
de Bonnel

Rue Roger Radisson

Rue
Cléberg

OLD LYON
(VIEUX LYON)

Rue Ferrandière

To Gare de la Part-Dieu
(railway station) (1.5 km)

To Saint Just
Funicular Station

Saône River

Quai des Célestins

Place
des
Jacobins

Place
de la
République

Rue Childebert

Pont Wilson

3ème

Rue Servient

Quai Victor Augagneur

Cours de la Liberté

PRESQU'ÎLE

Rue Émile Zola

Quai Tilsitt

Quai du Piet

Place
Bellecour

Rue de la Barre

To Camping
Municipal Porte
de Lyon
(10 km)

To Paris

Rue Victor Hugo

Rue Sala

Rue de la Charité

2ème

Rue Jarente

Rue Sainte Hélène

Rue des
Remparts d'Ainay

Rue Franklin

Rue de Condé

Rue Duhamel

Place
Carnot
ramp

Rue d'Enghien

Rue Auguste Comte

Pont de l'Université

Pont de
l'Université

Rhône River

Cours Gambetta

Rue Pasteur

Quai Claude Bernard

7ème

University

Rue de l'Université

Rue Pasteur

A6

To A7

To Place Jean Macé
(700 m), Centre
International de Séjour
(3.5 km) & Auberge
de Jeunesse (4.7 km)

Pont Galliéni

FRANCE

	PLACES TO STAY		OTHER		
4	Hôtel Le Terme	1	Amphithéâtre des	31	Minimes Funicular Stop
5	Hôtel Croix Pâquet		Trois Gauls (Roman	32	Place Saint Jean
49	Hôtel Vaubecour		Amphitheatre)	33	Saint Jean Metro
54	Hôtel Le Beaujolais	7	Croix Pâquet Metro		Station
55	Hôtel Chez Soi		Station	34	Cathédrale Saint Jean
56	Hôtel d'Ainay	8	Musée des Beaux-Arts	35	Place Édouard Comm-
		9	Musée d'Art Con-		ette
	PLACES TO EAT		temporain	38	American Express
		10	City Hall	39	UK Consulate
2	Food Market	11	Post Office	40	Église Saint Georges
3	Chouette! Un Tonneau!	12	Hôtel de Ville Metro	41	Eton English Bookshop
6	Crémerie Savoyarde		Station	42	Louis XIV Statue
14	Chez Georges	13	Opéra	43	Bellecour Metro Station
15	Le Garet	17	Banks	44	Main Tourist Office
16	Alyssaar Syrian Res-	18	US Consulate	45	Place Antonin Poncet
	taurant	19	Tour Métallique (Tower)	46	Main Post Office
36	Express Market &	20	Fourvière Funicular	47	Police
	Boulangerie		Station	48	Guillotière Metro
37	MorningFood Market	21	Panoramic View		Station
50	Food Shops (along	22	Basilique Notre Dame	51	Post Office
	Rue Vaubecour)		de Fourvière	52	Place Ampère
53	McDonald's	23	Musée Gadagne	58	Musée des Arts
57	Fromagerie Victor	24	Église Saint Nizier		Décoratifs
	Hugo	25	Musée de l'Imprimerie	59	Musée Historique des
60	Unico Supermarket	26	Banque de France		Tissus
		27	Place de la Bourse	61	Société Générale Bank
		28	Cordeliers Metro	62	Laundrette
			Station	63	Centre d'Échange &
		29	Musée Gallo-Romain		Bus Station
		30	Roman Theatres	64	Perrache Metro Station
				65	Gare de Perrache
					(Railway Station)

FRANCE

Bookshops The Eton English Bookshop (☎ 78.92.92.36) at 1 Rue du Plat has lots of new paperbacks as well as some Lonely Planet titles. It is open on Monday from 2 to 7 pm and Tuesday to Saturday from 10 am to 12.30 pm and 1.30 to 7 pm. Students and people with a copy of this book get a 5% discount.

Things to See

Old Lyons Old Lyons (Vieux Lyon), whose narrow streets are lined with over 300 medieval and Renaissance (15th to 17th century) houses, lies at the base of Fourvière Hill. The area underwent urban renewal two decades ago and has since become a trendy place in which to live and socialise. Many of the most interesting **old buildings** are along Rue du Bœuf, Rue Juiverie, Rue des Trois Maries

and Rue Saint Jean. There are a number of pleasant cafés around **Place Saint Jean**, which is next to **Cathédrale Saint Jean**, begun in the late 12th century. Don't miss the 14th century astronomical clock in the north transept. The west façade was damaged by the Huguenots and, later, during the French Revolution. The cathedral can be visited from 8 am to noon and 2 to 7.30 pm (5 pm on weekends and holidays).

The **Musée Gadagne** (☎ 78.42.03.61) at 12 Rue de Gadagne has two sections: the **Musée de la Marionette**, which has puppets of all sorts, including *guignol* (a French Punch-and-Judy type puppet), which was created by the museum's founder, Laurent Mourguet (1769-1844) and has become one of the city's symbols; and the **Musée Historique**, which illustrates the history of

Lyons. Both are open from 10.45 am to 6 pm (until 8.30 pm on Friday) daily except Tuesday and on some bank holidays. The entry fee is 20FF (10FF for students).

Fourvière Two millenniums ago, the Romans built the city of Lugdunum on the slopes of Fourvière. Today, the hill – topped by the Tour Métallique, a sort of stunted Eiffel Tower erected in 1893 and now used as a TV transmitter – affords spectacular views of Lyons and its two rivers.

Several paths lead up the slope, but the easiest way to get up to the top is to take the *funiculaire* (funicular railway) from next to the Saint Jean metro stop in Old Lyons. The Fourvière line, which stops right behind the basilica of Notre Dame de Fourvière, operates daily until 8.30 pm. You can either use a bus/metro ticket or purchase a special return ticket for 9.50FF, which is valid all day long. Time-stamp your ticket before boarding.

Musée Gallo-Romain The exceptional Musée de la Civilisation Gallo-Romaine (☎ 78.25.94.68) at 17 Rue Cléberg in Fourvière is well worth seeing even if you don't consider yourself a fan of Roman history. Among the museum's extraordinary artefacts, almost all of which were found in the Rhône Valley area, are the remains of a four-wheeled vehicle from around 700 BC, several sumptuous mosaics and lots of Latin inscriptions, including the bronze text of a speech made by the Lyons-born Roman emperor Claudius in 48 AD. The two rebuilt Roman theatres next to the museum are still used for concerts. The museum is open from 9.30 am to noon and 2 to 6 pm daily except Monday, Tuesday and on bank holidays. The entry fee is 20FF (10FF for students).

Basilique de Notre Dame de Fourvière Like Sacré Cœur in Paris, this monstrosity, completed in 1896, was built by subscription to fulfil a vow taken during the disastrous Franco-Prussian War of 1870-71. The august and rather stuffy *Blue Guide* declares it 'hideous...in a depraved taste which should

be seen to be believed', and indeed, its ornamentation is a superb example of the exaggerated enthusiasm for embellishment that convulsed French church architecture during the late 19th century. If overwrought marble and mosaic are not your cup of tea, the panoramic view from the nearby terrace still merits a visit. From November to March, the basilica is open from 6 am to noon and 2 to 6 pm; during the rest of the year, opening hours are 6 am to 7 pm.

Presqu'île The four horses of the fountain at **Place des Terreaux** signify rivers galloping seaward. Fronting the square is the **Hôtel de Ville**, built in 1655 but given its present façade in 1702. There are up-market shops along and around **Rue de la République**, known for its 19th century buildings. The southern half of Rue de la République is a pedestrian mall, as is Rue Victor Hugo, which runs southward from **Place Bellecour**, one of the largest public squares in Europe. Laid out in the 17th century, it has an equestrian statue of Louis XIV in the middle. Adjacent areas were razed during the Reign of Terror (early 1790s) by radicals furious at the city's resistance to *la Convention* (the National Convention), the assembly that governed France (September 1792 to October 1795) during the Revolution's most critical period. Thousands of Lyonnais were executed before Robespierre's fall saved the city from even greater devastation.

Musée Historique des Tissus The Lyonnais are especially proud of their Museum of the History of Textiles (☎ 78.37.15.05) at 34 Rue de la Charité, whose collections include extraordinary Lyonnais silks and fabrics from around the world. The museum is open from 10 am to 5.30 pm daily except Monday and holidays. The 20FF fee (10FF for students aged 18 to 25) also gets you into the **Musée des Arts Décoratifs**, down the street at 30 Rue de la Charité. The latter institution closes between noon and 2 pm. Entry is free on Wednesdays.

Musée de l'Imprimerie The history of printing, a technology which established itself in Lyons in the 1480s (less than 40 years after its invention) is illustrated by the Musée de l'Imprimerie (☎ 78.37.65.98) at 37 Rue de la Poulaillerie. Among the exhibits are some of the first books ever printed, including a page of a Gutenberg Bible (1450s) and several incunabula (books printed before Easter in the year 1500). The museum is open from 9.30 am to noon and 2 to 6 pm daily except Monday and Tuesday. The entry fee is 20FF (10FF for students).

Musée des Beaux-Arts Lyons' outstanding fine arts museum (☎ 78.28.07.66), whose 90 rooms house sculptures and paintings from every period of European art, is next to the Hôtel de Ville at 20 Place des Terreaux. It is open from 10.30 am to 6 pm daily except Monday and Tuesday. The entry fee is 20FF (10FF for students age 18 to 25).

Musée d'Art Contemporain The museum of contemporary art (☎ 78.30.50.66), which specialises in works produced after 1960, is round the corner from the Musée des Beaux-Arts at 16 Rue du Président Édouard Herriot. It is open from noon to 6 pm daily except Tuesday and public holidays. Entry costs 20FF (10FF for students).

Maison des Canuts Set up by the Guild of Silk Workers, who are known as *canuts* in French, this museum (☎ 78.28.62.04) traces the history of Lyons' silk-weaving industry. Weavers are usually on hand to demonstrate the art of operating traditional silk looms. The maison is open weekdays from 8.30 am to noon and 2 to 6.30 pm and on Saturday from 9 am to noon and 2 to 6 pm. Tickets cost 6FF. It is at 10-12 Rue d'Ivry, 300 metres north of the Croix Rousse metro stop (walk along Rue du Mail).

Places to Stay

Camping *Camping Municipal Porte de Lyon* (☎ 78.35.64.55) is about 10 km east of Lyon in Dardilly. This attractive and well-equipped camping ground is open from March to October and charges 45FF to park

and pitch a tent. To get there by car, take highway N6, the continuation of Cours Gambetta. By bus, take No 19 from the Hôtel de Ville towards Ecully-Dardilly.

Hostels The *Auberge de Jeunesse* (☎ 78.76.39.23) is 5.5 km south-east of Gare de Perrache at 51 Rue Roger Salengro in Vénissieux. Beds are 43FF and breakfast costs 16FF. The hostel is closed from 10 am to 5 pm; curfew is 11.30 pm. To get to the hostel, take bus No 35 from Place Bellecour (get off at the Georges Levy stop), No 53 from Gare de Perrache (get off at États-Unis-Viviani) or No 36 from Gare de la Part-Dieu (get off at Viviani-Joliot-Curie).

The *Centre International de Séjour* (☎ 78.01.23.45 or 78.76.14.22) is 4.3 km south-east of Gare de Perrache at 46 Rue du Commandant Pégoud, which is behind 101 Blvd des États-Unis. Students/nonstudents pay between 70/77FF (for a bed in a quad) and 113/121FF (for a single), including breakfast and sheets. From the train stations, take the same buses you would to get to the Auberge de Jeunesse.

Hotels The clean, newly renovated *Hôtel Vaubecour* (☎ 78.37.44.91) at 28 Rue Vaubecour has singles for 95 and 106FF and doubles for 117FF. Two-bed doubles are 170FF; showers cost 12FF. The *Hôtel d'Ainay* (☎ 78.42.43.42) at 14 Rue des Remparts d'Ainay (2nd floor) is just off Place Ampère. Simply furnished singles/doubles cost 120/127FF without shower and 178/185FF with shower and toilet. Hall showers are 18FF.

The recently renovated *Hôtel Le Terme* (☎ 78.28.30.45) at 7 Rue Catherine, a few blocks north-west of the Hôtel de Ville metro stop, has simply furnished singles from 110FF and doubles for 165FF (240FF with shower and toilet). Lonely Planet readers (with a copy of this book) get a 6% discount. The pricier rooms come with TV. Showers are free. *Hôtel Croix Pâquet* (☎ 78.28.51.49) is 300 metres north-east of Place des Terreaux at 11 Place Croix Pâquet, which is not far from the Croix Pâquet metro stop. This friendly, family-operated place is old and run-down on the outside but well kept and cheerful on the inside. Take lift B to the 3rd floor. Singles/doubles start at 100/110FF. Two-bed doubles are 180FF.

The neighbourhood around Place Carnot, which is just north of Gare de Perrache, is a bit on the seedy side, but the hotels here are convenient if you're travelling by train. The cheapest place in town is the very basic *Hôtel Le Beaujolais* (☎ 78.37.39.15) at 22 Rue d'Enghien. Singles/doubles cost between 91 and 152FF; the more expensive rooms come with shower. On Sunday, reception, which is at the bar, is closed until 2 pm. The *Hôtel Chez Soi* (☎ 78.37.18.30) at 4 Place Carnot has singles/doubles from 131/142FF (161/171FF with shower and toilet).

Places to Eat
Restaurants There are two *bouchons* – small, friendly, unpretentious restaurants that serve traditional Lyonnais cuisine – near Place des Terreaux. At 8 Rue du Garet, *Chez Georges* (☎ 78.28.30.46), with main dishes from 29 to 61FF, is open weekdays and Saturday evening from noon to 2 pm and 7.30 to 10 pm. *Le Garet* (☎ 78.28.16.94) at 7 Rue du Garet is open Monday to Friday from noon to 2 pm and 7.30 to 10 pm. *Alyssaar* (☎ 78.29.57.66), a Syrian restaurant specialising in dishes (39 to 49FF) from Aleppo, is at 29 Rue du Bât d'Argent. It is open Monday to Saturday from 7.30 pm to midnight.

Chouette! Un Tonneau! (☎ 78.27.42.42) at 17 Rue d'Algérie serves excellent French food daily nonstop from 11.30 am to midnight. Quite a few other restaurants are in the immediate vicinity.

There are lots of places to eat, including several hamburger joints, along the Rue Victor Hugo pedestrian mall. At Place Ampère, the *McDonald's* is open daily from 10 am to midnight.

Self-Catering The Presqu'île has lots of food shops along Rue Vaubecour, including a boulangerie (closed Saturday afternoon and Sunday) at No 26 and another (closed

Sunday afternoon and Monday) at No 8. *Fromagerie Victor Hugo* is a particularly fine cheese shop at 26 Rue Sainte Hélène. It is open Tuesday to Saturday from 8.30 am to 1 pm and 3.30 to 8 pm. On the other side of the peninsula, there is a boulangerie (closed Sunday afternoon and Monday) at 27 Rue de la Charité and an *Unico* supermarket (closed Sunday) at 60 Rue de la Charité.

In the old city, there are a number of food shops on Rue du Doyenné, including a North African boulangerie (closed Monday) and an *Express Market* grocery (closed Sunday afternoon and Monday), both at No 11. There's another grocery (open Monday to Saturday from 6.30 am to 10 pm) at 1 Ave du Doyenné (next to Place Édouard Commette). The outdoor food market along the Saône River (Quai Saint Antoine and Quai des Célestins) on the Presqu'île is open from 7 am to 12.30 pm daily except Monday.

North of Place des Terreaux, there is a superb fromagerie, *Crémerie Savoyarde* at 26 Rue des Capucins. It is open daily except Saturday afternoon and Sunday from 6 am to 1 pm and 3 to 7.30 pm. Their Saint Marcellin is fantastic. For bread, try the *Boulangerie Parisienne* (closed Sunday) nearby at 3 Rue Romarin. This place also has great *pain aux raisins* (raisin swirl pastry).

Entertainment
Enquire at the tourist office for up-to-date information on Lyons' lively cultural life, which includes theatre, opera, dance, classical music, jazz, variety shows, sporting events and films.

Getting There & Away
Bus Intercity buses (of which there are relatively few) depart from the bus terminal under the Centre d'Échange (the building next to Gare de Perrache). Timetables and other information are available from the information office of Lyons' mass transit authority, TCL (☎ 78.71.70.00 for intercity bus information), which is on the lower level of the Centre d'Échange. Tickets for travel on buses run by private companies are sold by the driver.

Train Lyons has two train stations: Gare de Perrache and Gare de la Part-Dieu. There are lots of exceptions, but in general, trains which begin or end their runs in Lyons use Perrache, whereas trains passing through the city stop at Part-Dieu. As you would expect, trains to/from Paris (258FF) use the capital's Gare de Lyon. Some trains, including all the Lyons-Paris TGVs, stop at both stations. For travel between the stations, you can go by metro (change at Charpennes), but if there happens to be an SNCF train going from one station to the other you can take it without buying an additional ticket. Fares from Lyons include Marseilles (200FF), Nice (279FF) and Bordeaux (300FF; 7½ hours).

The complex that includes Gare de Perrache (☎ 78.92.50.50 for information, 78.92.50.70 for reservations) consists of two main buildings: the Centre d'Échange, whose bowels serve as a bus terminal and metro station; and, southward over the pedestrian bridge, the gare SNCF (train station) itself. In the gare, the information office on the lower level is open Monday to Saturday from 8 am to 7.30 pm.

Gare de la Part-Dieu (same phone number as Perrache), part of a huge complex of modern office blocks and shopping areas, is two km east of Place de la République. The information counters are open Monday to Saturday from 9 am to 7 pm; to find them, walk out the exit signposted as 'Sortie Vivier-Merle' and go right for 20 metres.

Getting Around
Bus & Metro Lyons' mass transit authority is known as TCL (☎ 78.71.80.80). The metro's three lines start operating at 5 am; the last trains begin their final run at about midnight. Tickets, which cost 7FF if bought individually, are valid for one-way travel on buses, trolleys, the funicular and the metro for an hour after time-stamping. A carnet of six tickets, valid on both the metro and buses and available from bus drivers and at metro stations, costs 36FF (29FF for students aged 25 or younger). On the metro, tickets have to be validated before you enter the platform.

TCL has information bureaus on the lower level of the Centre d'Échange, at 43 Rue de la République (on the Presqu'île) and at 19 Blvd Marius Vivier-Merle (near Gare de la Part-Dieu).

Taxi Taxi Lyonnais (☎ 78.26.81.81) operates 24 hours a day.

Bicycle Except in winter, mountain bikes can be rented for 120FF a day (or 430FF a week) from Locasport (☎ 78.61.11.01), which is at 62 Rue du Colombier, one block east of Place Jean Macé. The shop is open from 9 am to noon and 2 to 7 pm daily except Monday morning and Sunday.

The French Alps

The French Alps, a land where fertile valleys meet soaring peaks with craggy, snowbound summits, are without doubt one of the most awe-inspiring mountainscapes in the world. In summer, visitors can take advantage of hundreds of km of magnificent hiking trails and engage in all sorts of warm-weather sporting activities. In winter, the area's profusion of fine ski resorts attracts snow-sport enthusiasts from around the world. Albertville and nearby towns hosted the 1992 Winter Olympics.

If you're going skiing, expect to pay at least 150FF a day (including equipment hire, lifts and transportation) at lower-altitude stations, which usually operate from December to March. The larger, high-altitude stations cost 250 to 300FF a day (plus lodgings). The cheapest time to go skiing is in January, between the school holiday periods. Tourist offices have up-to-the-minute information on ski conditions, hotel availability and prices.

GRENOBLE
Grenoble (population 160,000), host of the 1968 Winter Olympics, is the undisputed intellectual and economic capital of the French Alps. Set in a broad valley surrounded by the Alps on all sides, this

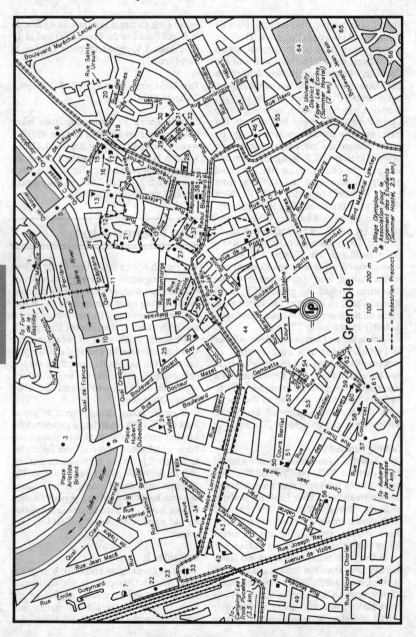

■ PLACES TO STAY		31	La Panse Restaurant	18	Place Notre Dame
20	Foyer de l'Étudiante (Summer Hostel)	34	Boulangerie	19	Cathédrale Notre Dame
26	Hôtel Beaulieu	36	McDonald's	21	Place d'Agier
29	Hôtel du Moucherotte	37	Prisunic Supermarket	22	Railway Station
42	Hôtel Alize	41	Restaurant Indochinois	23	Place de la Gare
45	Hôtel de la Poste	43	Grocery	25	Banque de France
48	Hôtel Saint Bruno	50	Boulangerie	27	Place Grenette
51	Hôtel des Doges	52	Produce Shop	32	Maison de la Randonnée
53	Hôtel Victoria	60	Food Shops	33	Post Office & Gare Europole Tram Station
54	Hôtel Beau Soleil	62	Chouette! Un Tonneau!		
56	Hôtel Colbert				
58	Hôtel Condorcet		OTHER	35	Lyonnaise de Banque
59	Hôtel Lakanal	1	Musée Dauphinois	38	Post Office
		2	Pont de la Citadelle	39	Tourist Office (Maison du Tourisme)
▼ PLACES TO EAT		3	Jardin des Dauphins	40	Église Saint Louis
		4	Mountain Bike Grenoble	44	Place Victor Hugo
8	University Restaurant	5	Pont St Laurent	46	Place de Verdun
13	Namastay Indian Restaurant	6	Musée de Grenoble (opening late 1993)	47	Place Vaucanson
15	Le Tunis Restaurant	7	Bus Station	49	Place Saint Bruno
16	Le Tonneau de Diogène	9	Pont de la Porte de France	55	Prefecture
17	Los Tacos	10	Pont Marius Gontard	57	Place Condorcet
24	La Chandelle Pizzeria	11	Téléphérique to Fort de la Bastille	61	Place Championnet
28	Les Halles Food Market	12	Place St André	63	Main Post Office
30	Cheese & Wine Shop	14	Place Aux Herbes	64	Jardin des Plantes
				65	City Hall
				66	Parc Paul Mistral

FRANCE

spotlessly clean city has something of a Swiss feel to it, perhaps because of the ultra-modern electric tram system. The city makes a good base and transit point for exploring much of the southern Alps.

Orientation
The old city is centred around Place Grenette, with its many cafés, and Place Notre Dame. Both are about a km east of the train and bus stations. There are quite a few inexpensive hotels in the vicinity of Place Condorcet.

Information
Tourist Office The Maison du Tourisme at 14 Rue de la République houses the tourist office (☎ 76.54.34.36), a counter for information on the local bus network (known as TAG) and an SNCF train information counter. All are open from 9 am to 6 pm daily

except Sunday. The tourist office stays open until 6.30 pm from about mid-May to mid-June and till 7 pm from mid-June to mid-September. The Maison du Tourisme is served by both tram lines (see the following Getting Around section).

Money The Banque de France is on the corner of Blvd Édouard Rey and Ave Félix Viallet. The Lyonnaise de Banque (☎ 76.28.79.76) at 11 Blvd Édouard Rey is open weekdays from 8 am to noon and 1.15 to 5 pm. There are several other banks along Blvd Édouard Rey. The Banque de la Région Dauphinoise at Place Notre Dame is open Tuesday to Friday from 8 am to noon and 1.30 to 5.30 pm and on Saturday from 8 am to noon and 1 to 4 pm.

Post The branch post office next door to the

tourist office is open weekdays from 8 am to 6 pm and on Saturday from 8 am to noon. Grenoble's postcode is 38000.

Things to See

Fort de la Bastille Fort de la Bastille, built in the 16th century (and expanded in the 19th) to control the approaches to the city, sits on the north side of the Isère River, 263 metres above the old city. The fort affords spectacular views of Grenoble and the surrounding mountain ranges. A sign near the disused Mont Jalla chair lift (300 metres beyond the arch next to the toilets) indicates the hiking trails that pass by here. To reach the fort you can take the Téléphérique (cable car) de Grenoble Bastille (☎ 76.44.33.65) from Quai Stéphane Jay, which costs 18.50/29FF one-way/return (10/15.50FF for students).

Musée Dauphinois The Musée Dauphinois (☎ 76.87.66.77), at 30 Rue Maurice Gignoux (near the bottom of the hill at the top of which sits Fort de la Bastille), has displays on the crafts and history of the Dauphiné region, which corresponds to the modern departments of Isère, Drôme and Hautes Alpes. It is open from 9 am to noon and 2 to 6 pm daily except Tuesday. Tickets cost 15FF (10FF for students and people over 60).

Musée des Beaux-Arts Grenoble's Musée des Beaux-Arts, which has a fine collection of painting and sculpture, including a well-regarded modern section, will move to new quarters at Place de Lavalette in the old city in late 1993.

Activities

Skiing Downhill skiing *(ski de piste)* and cross-country skiing *(ski de fond)* are possible at a number of relatively inexpensive, low-altitude ski stations near enough to Grenoble for you to stay in town and take buses out to the slopes. These include **Col de Porte** and **Le Sappey** (both north of Grenoble) and **Saint Nizier du Moucherotte, Lans-en-**

Vercors, Villard-de-Lans and **Méaudre** (west of the city).

Summer skiing, which is relatively expensive, is possible during June and July (and even into August) at several high-altitude ski stations east of Grenoble. These include **l'Alpe d'Huez** (tourist office ☎ 76.80.35.41), which offers skiing (during July) on glaciers at elevations of 2530 to 3350 metres, and **Les Deux Alpes** (tourist office ☎ 76.79.22.00), the largest summer skiing area in Europe, where you can hit the slopes from mid-June to early September.

Hiking A number of beautiful trails can be picked up in Grenoble or very nearby (eg from Fort de la Bastille). The northern part of the **Parc Naturel Régional du Vercours** (☎ 76.95.40.33) is just west of town.

The place in Grenoble to go for hiking information is La Maison de la Randonnée (☎ 76.51.76.00) at 7 Rue Voltaire. This office, which is open on weekdays from 9 am to 6 pm and on Saturday from 10 am to noon and 2 to 6 pm, has a large selection of hiking maps (40 to 67FF), topo-guides and day-hike guides and has information on places you can stay overnight when hiking *(gîtes d'étape* and *refuges)*. The friendly staff can help with itineraries and they also organise group hikes.

Places to Stay

Camping *Camping Les Trois Pucelles* (☎ 76.96.45.73), which is open all year, is at 58 Rue des Allobroges (one block west of the Drac River) in Grenoble's western suburb of Seyssins. To get there from the train station, take the tramway towards Fontaine and get off at the Maisonnat stop. Then take bus No 51 to Mas des Îles and walk east on Rue du Dauphiné. A place to camp and park costs 43FF for two people.

Hostels The *Auberge de Jeunesse* (☎ 76.09.33.52) is at 10 Ave du Grésivaudan in Échirolles, 5.5 km south of the train station. To get there from Cours Jean Jaurès, take bus No 8 (which runs until about 9 pm) and get off at the Quinzaine stop (look for the Casino supermarket). Reception is open from 7.30 to 11 pm. The cost is 60FF per person, including breakfast.

Hotels Near the train station, the *Hôtel Alize* (☎ 76.43.12.91), recently redecorated in ultramodern style, is at 2 Rue Amiral Courbet. Singles/doubles start at 100/150FF. If you're looking for a very quiet place, try the *Hôtel Saint Bruno* (☎ 76.96.32.49), down the alley at 6 Rue Michelet. Airy, recently renovated doubles begin at 100FF. They also have two-bed triples (170FF) and three-bed quads (200FF).

Quite a few cheap hotels are within a few blocks of Place Condorcet, which is a bit under a km south-east of the train station. The *Hôtel Lakanal* (☎ 76.46.03.42) at 26 Rue des Bergers attracts a young, friendly crowd. Singles/doubles start at 95/120FF (150/180FF with shower and toilet); hall showers are 14FF. A block away, the *Hôtel Condorcet* (☎ 76.46.20.64) at 8 Rue Condorcet has doubles from 120FF. The *Hôtel des Doges* (☎ 76.46.13.19) at 29 Cours Jean Jaurès has singles/doubles from 100/120FF. Showers are 15FF.

The *Hôtel Victoria* (☎ 76.46.06.36), a quiet, comfortable place at 17 Rue Thiers, has doubles for as little as 116FF (188FF with shower, toilet and TV); hall showers cost 18FF. Guests with cars can park in the courtyard for 15FF. The relaxed *Hôtel Beau Soleil* (☎ 76.46.29.40) at 9 Rue des Bons Enfants has singles/doubles from 105/125FF (10FF more with a TV). There is a 15FF charge for showers. The *Hôtel Colbert* (☎ 76.46.46.65) is on the west side of Cours Jean Jaurès at 1 Rue Colbert (2nd floor). Singles/doubles with high ceilings start at 95/125FF; showers are 15FF. Doubles with shower and toilet are 175FF.

Hôtel du Moucherotte (☎ 76.54.61.40) at 1 Rue Auguste Gaché has huge, well-kept rooms and a great central location. With showers, singles/doubles start at 114/154FF and triples/quads cost 208/256FF. Singles/doubles without showers begin at 100/134FF but there's a 20FF charge to use the hall showers. The pleasant and friendly

Hôtel de la Poste (☎ 76.46.67.25) at 25 Rue de la Poste has singles/doubles from 80/130FF and triples for 180FF. Showers are free. Overall, this is an excellent deal. The *Hôtel Beaulieu* (☎ 76.46.30.90) at 14 Rue Saint François is a clean, modern place with singles from 100FF and doubles from 110FF. Showers cost 15FF for two.

Places to Eat
Restaurants For excellent French food at very reasonable prices, try *Le Tonneau de Diogène* (☎ 76.42.38.40) at 6 Place Notre Dame, which attracts a young, lively crowd. It's open daily from 7 to 11.30 am for breakfast and from 11.30 am to midnight for lunch and dinner. Their other Grenoble location, *Chouette! Un Tonneau!* (☎ 76.46.92.36), is a few blocks east of Place Condorcet at 5 Rue Aubert Dubayet (open Monday to Saturday from 10.30 am to 10.30 pm).

Los Tacos (☎ 76.42.25.96), very close to Le Tonneau de Diogène on Place Notre Dame, sells tacos (a good bit of food for 15FF) that look a lot more like crêpes than the North American version. They're open on Monday from 7 pm to midnight and Tuesday to Saturday from noon to 10.30 pm. *La Panse* (☎ 76.54.09.54) at 7 Rue de la Paix offers traditional French cuisine from noon to 1.30 pm and 7.15 to 10 pm daily except Sunday. Their 65FF lunch *menu* is especially good value.

You can get vegetarian and nonvegetarian main dishes for 30 to 55FF at the *Namastay Indian Restaurant* (☎ 76.54.29.89) at 2 Rue Renauldon. This place is open from Monday evening to Saturday from noon to 1.15 pm and 7.15 to 11.15 pm. *Le Tunis Restaurant* (☎ 76.42.47.13) at 5 Rue Chenoise, open daily from noon to 2 pm and 6 to 10.30 pm, has excellent Tunisian couscous from 38FF. There are more North African places along and around Rue Renauldon and Rue Chenoise. The area around Place Condorcet has lots of places to eat, including several Chinese restaurants.

Self-Catering *Les Halles* food market, which is near the tourist office, is open every day except Monday from 6 am to 1 pm. The boulangerie nearest Les Halles is at 4 rue Auguste Gaché (closed Sunday afternoon and Monday). There are boulangeries that do not close at midday at 3 Place Notre Dame (closed Monday) and nearby at 8 Rue Barnave (closed Sunday). There's a particularly well-stocked cheese and wine shop a block away at 17 Rue Bayard. It is open Tuesday to Saturday from 6 am to 12.30 pm and 3 to 7.30 pm. The *Prisunic* at 22 Rue Lafayette, one block west of the tourist office, has a supermarket in the basement and an in-house boulangerie on the ground floor. It is open from 8.30 am to 7 pm daily except Sunday.

In the Place Condorcet area, there is a boulangerie at 31bis Cours Berriat (closed Monday) and a produce shop with high-quality cheese, fruit and vegetables at 15 Cours Berriat (open Tuesday to Saturday from 6 am to 12.30 pm and 3.30 to 7.30 pm). There are a number of food shops (closed on Sunday) around 2 Rue Turenne.

Getting There & Away

Bus The bus station is next to the train station. VFD (☎ 76.47.77.77), which is open daily from 6.45 am to 7 pm, has service to Geneva, Nice, Annecy, Chamonix, Gap, Albertville and many places in the Isère region (including quite a few ski stations). Unicar (☎ 76.87.90.31) handles tickets to Aéroport Lyon-Satolas (the international airport for Lyons and the Alps; 120FF), Marseilles (134FF), Gap (south-east of Grenoble), Valence (south-west of Grenoble), etc. It is open Monday to Saturday from 6.30 am to 6.30 pm and on Sunday from 7.30 am to noon and 1.30 pm to 6.30 pm.

Train The train station (☎ 76.47.50.50 for information, 76.47.54.27 for reservations) on Rue Émile Gueymard is served by both tram lines (get off at the Gares Europole stop). The information office is open daily from 8.30 am to 7.15 pm. There is an SNCF information and reservations office inside the tourist office building. By TGV, the trip to Paris' Gare de Lyon (303FF) takes about

3½ hours. There is also service to Lyons (94FF), Nice (273FF) and Chamonix (153FF).

Getting Around

Bus & Tram The buses and trams (there are two tram lines, A and B) take the same tickets (6.50FF), which are sold by bus (but not tram) drivers and by ticket machines at tram stops. They are valid for transfers (but not return trips) within one hour of time-stamping, which must be done either on board the buses or in the little blue machines at each tram stop. Most buses cease running rather early, some time between 7 and 9 pm. TAG (☎ 76.20.66.66), the local bus company, has an information desk inside the tourist office building.

Taxi Radio-dispatched taxis can be ordered by calling ☎ 76.54.42.54.

Bicycle Mountain Bike Grenoble (☎ 76.87.44.45) at 6 Quai de France has mountain bikes for 130FF a day (less a day for two or more days). It's open Tuesday to Saturday from 9 am to noon and 2 to 7 pm.

CHAMONIX

The town of Chamonix (elevation 1035 metres; population 10,000), site of the 1924 Winter Olympiad, sits in a valley surrounded by far and away the most spectacular scenery in the French Alps. The area is almost Himalayan in its awesomeness: the tongues of deeply crevassed glaciers many km long ooze down the valley in the gullies between the icy spikes and needles around Mont Blanc, which soars 3.8 vertical km above the valley floor. In late spring and summer, the glaciers and high-altitude snow serve as a glistening, white backdrop for meadows and hillsides carpeted with flowering plants, bushes and trees.

There are some 310 km of hiking trails in the Chamonix area. In winter, Chamonix and its environs offer superb skiing, with dozens of ski lifts and 200 km of downhill and cross-country ski runs.

Orientation

The mountain range to the east of the Chamonix Valley, the Aiguilles de Chamonix, is characterised by lots of glaciers. It includes the mind-boggling mass of Mont Blanc (4807 metres), the highest mountain in the Alps. The almost-glacierless Aiguilles Rouges range, whose highest peak is Le Brévent (2525 metres), runs along the western side of the valley.

Information

Tourist Office The tourist office (☎ 50.53.00.24) at Place de l'Église is open daily from 8 or 8.30 am to 12.30 pm and 2 to 7 pm. During July and August, it is open from 8.30 am to 7.30 pm. They have all sorts of useful brochures on ski-lift hours and costs, *refuges*, camping grounds, parapente schools, etc. During the winter, they sell a two-day ski pass, valid for bus transport and all the ski lifts in the valley (except Les Grands Montets), for 310FF (280FF during discount periods). The seven-day version costs 930FF (840FF during discount periods).

Maison de la Montagne Maison de la Montagne, near the tourist office at 109 Place de l'Église, houses the Office de Haute Montagne (2nd floor; ☎ 50.53.22.08), which has information for walkers, hikers and mountain climbers on routes, hiking conditions, the weather, *refuges* (they can help non-French speakers make reservations) and more. They also sell all sorts of maps. The office is open from 8.30 am to 12.30 pm and 2 or 2.30 to 6 or 6.30 pm daily except Saturday afternoon and Sunday. From mid-June to September, it is open every day of the week until 6.30 pm.

Money There are quite a few places to change money in the area between the tourist office and the post office. The Change (☎ 50.55.88.40) at 21 Place Balmat offers a decent rate and is open daily from 9 am to 1 pm and 3 to 7 pm (8 am to 8 pm from July to early September and around Christmas). Outside is a 24-hour exchange machine that accepts banknotes in any of 15 flavours. The exchange service at the tourist office is open on weekends and bank holidays and, during July and August, every day during their regular hours.

Post The post office (☎ 50.53.15.90) at Place Balmat is open weekdays from 8 am to noon and 2 to 6 pm and on Saturday from 8 am to noon. During July and August, their weekday hours are 8 am to 7 pm.

Chamonix' postcode is 74400.

Climate Any time of the year, the success of a visit to Chamonix depends in part on the vagaries of the weather. Clouds, for instance, can turn a spectacular vista into something resembling what you see through the aeroplane window when flying inside a cloud. Bulletins from the meteorological service *(la météo)* are posted in the window of the tourist office and at Maison de la Montagne; the latter may have English translations. It's a good idea to bring warm clothing, as even in summer it can get pretty cool at night.

Things to See

Aiguille du Midi The Aiguille (pronounced 'eh-gweey') du Midi (3842 metres), a lone spire of rock eight km across glaciers, snowfields and rocky crags from the summit of Mont Blanc, is unique in its accessibility to people whose interest in scaling sheer cliffs is limited. The views in all directions are truly breathtaking and, if at all possible, should not be missed just to save a few francs...In general, visibility is best and rain least likely early in the morning.

The téléphérique (☎ 50.53.30.80) from Chamonix to the Aiguille du Midi is the highest aerial tramway in the world. From July to September, you can continue on from the Aiguille du Midi to **Pointe Helbronner** (3466 metres) on the Italian border (where there's some summer skiing) and the Italian resort town of **Courmayeur**. Return tickets to the Aiguille du Midi cost 150FF; it's an extra 70FF return for the spectacular transglacial ride to Pointe Helbronner. One-way

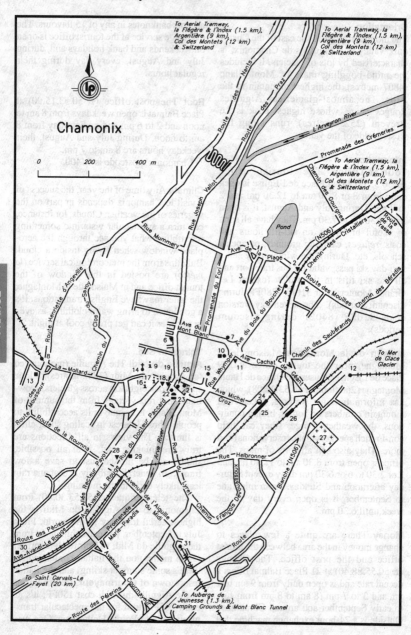

Chamonix

To Aerial Tramway,
la Flégère & l'Index (1.5 km),
Argentière (9 km),
Col des Montets (12 km)
& Switzerland

To Aerial Tramway, la
Flégère & l'Index (1.5 km),
Argentière (9 km),
Col des Montets (12 km)
& Switzerland

To Aerial Tramway, la
Flégère & l'Index (1.5 km),
Argentière (9 km),
Col des Montets (12 km)
& Switzerland

L'Arveyron River

Promenade des Crémeries

Chemin des Cristalliers

Promenade des Gournes

Pond

Route des Nants

Route des Praz

Route Joseph Vallot

Rue Mummery

Ave de la Plage

Route de Flasse

(N506)

Chemin des Mouilles

Route des Mouilles

Route des Bérâdis

Chemin des Bérâdis

Chemin des Saubrands

Route Henriette d'Angeville

Chemin du Clos

Chemin du Savoy

Rue Joseph Vallot

Promenade du Fori

Ave du Mont Blanc

Ave du Bois du Bouchet

Ave Cachat

Rue Whymper

Ave Michel Croz

Chemin de Géant

To Mer
de Glace
Glacier

La Mollard

Route des Moussoux

Route de la Roumna

Rue du Docteur Paccard

Arve River

Rue du Lyret

Rue Helbronner

Route Blanche (N506)

Chemin François Devouassoux

Allée Recteur Payot

Ave-Avanel-Le Rouge

Ave-Avanel-Le Rouge

Promenade Marie-Paradis

Ave de l'Aiguille du Midi

Ave de Courmayeur

Route des Pêcles

Route des Pèlerins

To Saint Gervais-Le
Fayet (20 km)

To Auberge de
Jeunesse (1.3 km),
Camping Grounds & Mont Blanc Tunnel

0   200   400 m

	PLACES TO STAY	19	Fruit & Vegetable Shop	16	Tourist Office
1	Gîte Le Chamoniard Volant (Hostel)	28	Le Croissant d'Or	17	Chamonix Bus Information Office
5	Les Grands Charmoz Guesthouse		OTHER	20	Exchange Bureau & 24-Hour Currency Exchange Machine
10	Hôtel Le Stade	3	Ice-Skating Rink	21	Chamonix Mountain Bike & Ski Location Guy Perillat
13	Chalet Ski Station (Hostel)	4	Au Grand Bi (Bicycle Rental & Cross-Country Skis)		
29	Hostellerie du Lion d'Or	7	Place du Mont Blanc	22	Place Balmat
30	Hôtel Valaisanne	8	Télécabine/Téléphérique to Planpraz & Le Brévent	23	Post Office
	PLACES TO EAT	9	Maison de la Montagne	24	SAT Bus Office
		10	Azur Bike	25	Chamonix-Mont Blanc Railway Station
2	Le Fond des Gires Restaurant	12	Ski Lift (Télésiège des Planards) & Summer Luge Track	26	Gare du Montenvers (Train to Mer de Glace)
6	Payot-Pertin Supermarket	14	Église Saint Michel	27	Cemetery
11	Le Fer à Cheval	15	Musée Alpin	31	Aiguille du Midi Téléphérique
18	Boulangerie				

prices are only 20% to 25% less than those for a return trip. A ride from Chamonix to the tramway's halfway point, Plan de l'Aiguille (2308 metres), an excellent place to start hikes during the summer, costs 47FF one-way. No student discounts are available. Prices are a bit higher during July and August.

The téléphérique, which operates all year (except during repair work), begins running at 8 am (6 am in July and August). The last ride up is at 4.45 pm. Be prepared for long queues – the earlier you get there the better. You can make advance reservations 24 hours a day by calling ☎ 50.53.40.00.

Le Brévent Le Brévent (2525 metres), the highest peak on the west side of the valley, is known for its great views of Mont Blanc and the rest of the east side of the valley. It can be reached from Chamonix by a combination of télécabine and téléphérique (☎ 50.53.13.18) for 48FF one-way and 68FF return. Service begins at 8 am (9 am in winter). The last trips up/down are at 5/5.45 pm in summer and an hour or so earlier in winter. Quite a few hiking trails (including various routes back to the valley) can be

picked up at Le Brévent or at the aerial tramway's midway station, Planpraz (1999 metres; 40FF one-way).

Mer de Glace Glacier The heavily crevassed Mer de Glace (sea of ice), the second-largest glacier in the Alps, is 14 km long, 1950 metres wide at its widest point and up to 400 metres deep. It has become a popular tourist destination thanks to a crémaillère cog-wheel rail line built between 1897 and 1908. The upper terminus is at an altitude of 1913 metres.

The train, which runs from mid-May until the first snow, leaves from Gare du Montenvers (☎ 50.53.12.54) in Chamonix. A one-way/return trip costs 40/53FF. A combined ticket valid for the train, the cable car to the ice cave (12FF return) and entry to the ice cave (Grotte de la Mer de Glace) costs 71FF. There are often long queues for the train during July and August. The ride takes 20 minutes each way.

The Mer de Glace can also be reached on foot from Plan de l'Aiguille (take the Grand Balcon Nord – see under Activities) and Chamonix. The uphill trail, which takes about two hours, begins near the summer luge track. Traversing the glacier, with its many crevasses, is dangerous without a guide and proper equipment.

Musée Alpin This museum (☎ 50.53.25.93) on Ave Michel Croz in Chamonix displays artefacts, lithographs and photos illustrating the history of mountain climbing and other Alpine sports. From June to mid-October, it's open daily from 2 to 7 pm, and between Christmas and Easter hours are 3 to 7 pm. It's closed the rest of the year. The entry fee is 15FF.

Activities

Hiking In late spring and summer (mid-June to October), the Chamonix area has some of the most spectacular hiking trails anywhere in the Alps. In general, the more rewarding trails and the more dramatic views are to be found at higher elevations, which can be reached in minutes by aerial tramway. In June and July there is enough light to hike until at least 9 pm.

The *Carte des Sentiers de Montagne en Été* (summer trails map), available for 20FF from the tourist office and Maison de la Montagne, is adequate for straightforward day hikes. It includes lots of trails and the locations of *refuges*. The best map of the area is the 1:25,000 scale IGN map entitled *Massif du Mont Blanc*, which can be purchased at Maison de la Montagne.

The fairly flat **Grand Balcon Sud** trail along the Aiguilles Rouges (western) side of the valley, which stays up around 2000 metres, offers great views of Mont Blanc and the glaciers along the east side of the valley. If you prefer to avoid a vertical km of uphill walking, take either the Planpraz lift (40FF one-way) or the La Flégère lift (30FF one-way).

From Plan de l'Aiguille (47FF one-way), the midway point on the Aiguille du Midi téléphérique, the **Grand Balcon Nord** takes you to the Mer de Glace, whence you can hike down to Chamonix. There are a number of other trails from Plan de l'Aiguille.

There are trails to **Lac Blanc** (2350 metres), a turquoise lake surrounded by mountains, from either the top of Les Praz-

L'Index aerial tramway (44FF one-way) or La Flégère (30FF one-way), the line's midway transfer point.

Cycling Many of the trails around the valley (eg the Petit Balcon Sud) are perfect for mountain cycling. See the following Getting Around section for information on bike rentals.

Skiing The Chamonix area has 160 km of marked ski runs, 40 km of cross-country trails and 62 ski lifts of all sorts. These include *téléskis* (tow lines), *télésièges* (chair lifts), *télécabines* (lots of little cabins suspended from a cable) and *téléphériques* (one large cabin suspended from a cable). The tourist office has all the information you could ever want on downhill runs and their lifts.

Many sports shops around Chamonix rent out skiing equipment. Count on paying 35/235FF a day/week for regular skis and 30/200FF a day/week for shoes. Ski Location Guy Perillat (☎ 50.53.54.76) at 138 Rue des Moulins rents skis daily from 9 am to noon and 2 to 7 pm. Cross-country skis are available from Au Grand Bi (☎ 50.53.14.16) at 240 Ave du Bois du Bouchet.

During the summer, there is limited (but expensive) skiing from Pointe Helbronner on the Italian frontier, which is accessible by aerial tramway (see Aiguille du Midi in the Things to See section for details). The runs, which are down a glacier, are only about 800 metres long and have four tow lines.

Parapente Parapente is the sport of floating down from somewhere high – the top of an aerial tramway line, for instance – suspended from a wing-shaped, steerable parachute that allows you, if you're both lucky and skilled, to catch updraughts and fly around for quite a while. An initiation flight (*baptême de l'air*) with an instructor (*moniteur*) costs 450FF. A five-day beginners' course (*stage d'initiation*) costs 2500 to 2900FF. For information on parapente schools, contact the tourist office.

Places to Stay

Camping *L'Île des Barrats* (☎ 50.53.51.44), near the base of the Aiguille du Midi téléphérique, is open from June to September. Three-star *Camping Les Deux Glaciers* (☎ 50.53.15.84) on the Route des Tissières in Les Bossons, three km south of Chamonix, is open all year except mid-November to mid-December. Two people with a car and tent pay 52FF. To get there, take the train to Les Bossons or Chamonix Bus to the Tremplin-le-Mont stop. There are a number of camping grounds a couple of km south of Chamonix in the village of Les Pèlerins (near the turn-off to the Mont Blanc Tunnel to Italy). These include *Camping Le Mazot* (☎ 50.53.41.02; open from late May to September) at 1400 Route des Pèlerins and *Camping Les Arolles* (☎ 50.53.14.30; open from late June to September) at 281 Chemin du Cry.

Another option is *Camping Glacier d'Argentière* (☎ 50.54.17.36), open from June to mid-September. It is 700 metres towards Switzerland from the Argentière Railway Station (nine km north of Chamonix) at 58 Chemin des Moilettes. Campers pay 16FF each plus 7FF for their tent.

Refuges Most mountain *refuges*, whose dorm beds cost 40 to 50FF a night (some have double rooms at higher prices), are accessible to hikers, though a few can be reached only by mountain climbers.

Among the easier-to-reach *refuges* is one (☎ 50.53.55.60) at Plan de l'Aiguille (2308 metres), the intermediate stop on the Aiguille du Midi téléphérique, and another (☎ 50.53.06.13) at La Flégère (1877 metres), the midway station on the Les Praz-L'Index aerial tramway. It is advisable to call ahead to reserve a place. Breakfast and dinner, prepared by the *gardien* (attendant), are often available. For information on other *refuges*, contact Maison de la Montagne (see the preceding Information section).

Hostels *Chalet Ski Station* (☎ 50.53.20.25 is a gîte d'étape at 6 Route des Moussoux in Chamonix (next to the Planpraz/Le Brévent télécabine station). Beds cost 45FF a night, there's a 15FF charge for sheets (in other words, bring your own), and showers are 5FF. This place is closed from mid-May to late June and from mid-September to mid-December. Semirustic *Gîte Le Chamoniard Volant* (☎ 50.53.14.09) is on the north-eastern outskirts of town at 45 Route de la Frasse. A bunk in a cramped, functional room of four, six or eight costs 60FF; sheets are 15FF. Reception is open from 10 am to 10 pm. The nearest bus stop is La Frasse.

The *Auberge de Jeunesse* (☎ 50.53.14.52) is a couple of km south-west of Chamonix at 103 Montée Jacques Balmat in Les Pèlerins. By bus, take the Chamonix-Les Houches line and get off at the Pèlerins École stop. Beds in rooms of four or six cost 70FF; doubles are 80FF per person. The youth hostel is closed during October and November.

The relaxed (open all day) and exceptionally friendly *Gîte d'Étape Le Belvédère* (☎ 50.54.02.59) is at 501 Route du Plagnolet in Argentière (nine km north of Chamonix). It is 250 metres down the hill from the Argentière Railway Station (near the Argentière Sud bus stop). In summer, a dorm bed costs 37FF (40FF per person in a quad). Spartan rooms for two, three and four persons are 116FF, 159FF and 184FF respectively. The *Gîte du Moulin* (☎ 50.54.05.37) is one km north of Argentière at 32 Chemin du Moulin. The closest railway station is Montroc, 200 metres away. If coming by bus, ask the driver to stop near the gîte. A dorm bed costs 45FF and you must bring your own sheets. Another decent gîte in the area is the *Chalet Refuge La Boerne* (☎ 50.54.05.14), which is in Tréléchamps, two km towards Vallorcine and the Swiss border from Argentière. A bed costs 42FF in summer and 60FF in winter, including use of the kitchen; a sleeping sheet is 10FF. During the summer, they strongly prefer that guests take on *demi-pension* (dinner and breakfast) for 135FF per person. From the Montroc Railway Station, follow the signs (it's a 700-metre walk). By bus, get off at Montroc.

FRANCE

Hotels *Les Grands Charmoz Guesthouse* (☎ 50.53.45.57) at 468 Chemin des Cristalliers, next to the railway tracks 600 metres north of the train station, is run by a friendly, easy-going American couple. Doubles cost 150FF including use of the shower and sheets (but not towels); dorm beds are 55FF. This place is closed from late September to November. The central *Hôtel Le Stade* (☎ 50.53.05.44) at 79 Rue Whymper (the entrance is around the back on the 1st floor) has simple but pleasant doubles from 204FF (289FF with shower and toilet); triples are 291FF. The *Hôtel Valaisanne* (☎ 50.53.17.98) is a small family-owned place at 454 Ave Ravanel le Rouge, 900 metres south of the centre of town. Doubles cost 140FF. At the *Hostellerie du Lion d'Or* (☎ 50.53.15.09) at 255 Rue du Docteur Paccard, doubles start at 175FF; showers are free.

Places to Eat

Restaurants *Le Fer à Cheval* restaurant (☎ 50.53.13.22) at 118 Rue Whymper is reputed to have the best fondue Savoyarde (cheese fondue) in town. During the summer and skiing seasons, it is a good idea to reserve a day in advance.

Le Fonds des Gires (☎ 50.55.85.76) is a self-service restaurant on the north side of town at 350 Route du Bois du Bouchet. This place, a favourite with people staying at the nearby gîtes, is open daily for lunch (noon to 2 pm) all year long (except during January) and for dinner (7 to 9 pm) during July and August. Their three plats du jour cost 30 to 42FF, vegetables are 7 to 18FF and desserts cost just 6 to 12FF.

Countless restaurants offering pizza, fondue, etc can be found in the centre of town (in all directions from the post office).

Self-Catering The *Payot-Pertin* supermarket at 117 Rue Joseph Vallon is open Monday to Saturday from 8.15 am to 12.30 pm and 2.30 to 7.30 pm and on Sunday from 8.30 am to 12.15 pm. There's a boulangerie (open daily) opposite the tourist office at 31 Place de l'Église. The fruit and vegetable shop nearby at 23 Place de l'Église is closed on Sunday.

Getting There & Away

Bus Chamonix' bus station is next to the train station. SAT Autocar (☎ 50.53.01.15) has buses to Annecy, Courmayeur (Italy; 46FF; 40 minutes), Geneva (135FF; 1½ to two hours), Grenoble, Turin (130FF; three hours) and elsewhere. Opening hours are posted on the door.

Train The narrow-gauge train line from Saint Gervais-Le Fayet (20 km west of Chamonix) to Martigny, Switzerland (42 km north of Chamonix) stops at 11 towns in the Chamonix Valley. There are nine to 12 return trips a day. You have to switch trains at the Swiss border (at Châtelard or Vallorcine) because the track gauge changes. Le Fayet serves as a railhead for long-haul trains to destinations all over France.

Chamonix-Mont Blanc Railway Station (☎ 50.53.00.44) is in the middle of Chamonix. The information counters are open Monday to Saturday from 9 am to noon and 2 to 6.30 pm. From June to September and December to April, they're open on Sunday as well. Major destinations include Paris' Gare de Lyon (324FF plus TGV reservation fee; six to seven hours; five trains a day), Lyons (165FF; four to 4½ hours; four to five trains a day) and Geneva (75FF; two to 2½ hours via Saint Gervais, or longer via Martigny).

Getting Around

Bus Bus transport in the valley is handled by Chamonix Bus, whose stops are marked by black-on-yellow roadside signs. During the winter (mid-December to mid-May), there are 13 lines to all the ski lifts in the area. During the rest of the year, there are only two lines, both of which leave from Place de l'Église and pass by the Chamonix Sud stop. Chamonix Bus summer lines do not run after about 7 pm (6 or 6.30 pm in June and September).

The Chamonix Bus information office (☎ 50.53.05.55) at Place de l'Église (opposite the tourist office) is open daily in winter from 8 am to 7 pm. The rest of the year, hours are 8 am to noon and 2 to 6.30 pm (7 pm from June to August).

Taxis There is a taxi stand (☎ 50.53.13.94) outside the train station.

Bicycles Chamonix Mountain Bike (☎ 50.53.54.76) at 138 Rue des Moulins, run by an Aussie and an Englishman, is open daily from 9 am to noon and 2 to 7 pm. They charge 50FF for two hours and 120FF a day. The prices are similar at Azur Bike (☎ 50.53.50.14) at 79 Rue Whymper, which is open daily from 9 am to 7 pm during the biking season. Between April and October, Au Grand Bi (☎ 50.53.14.16) at 240 Ave du Bois du Bouchet has three-speeds or 10-speeds for 60FF a day, mountain bikes for 100FF, tandems for 150FF and helmets for 30FF. This place is open Monday to Saturday from 8.30 am to noon and 2 to 7 pm.

ANNECY
Annecy (elevation 448 metres, population 50,000), situated at the northern tip of incredibly blue Lac d'Annecy, is the perfect place to spend a tremendously relaxing holiday. Visitors in a sedentary mood can sit along the lakefront and feed the swans or mosey around the geranium-lined canals of the old city. For once, there's no pressure to see yet another art museum or chateau – mercifully, the city has only one of each.

For the athletically inclined, the town is an excellent base for water sports, hiking and biking. In winter, there is bus transport to low-altitude ski stations located only a few tens of km away.

Orientation
The train and bus stations are 500 metres north of the the old city, which is centred around the canalised Thiou River. The modern town centre is between the main post office and the Centre Bonlieu complex, home of the tourist office. The lakefront town of Annecy-le-Vieux is just east of Annecy.

Information
The tourist office (☎ 50.45.00.33), between Rue Président Favre and Rue Jean Jaurès in the Centre Bonlieu, is open Monday to Saturday from 9 am to noon and 1.45 to 6.30 pm. During July and August, it does not close at midday. It is open on Sunday from 9 am to noon and 1.45 to 6 pm except from October to mid-May, when Sunday hours are 3 to 6 pm.

Money The Banque de Savoie (☎ 50.51.43.19) at 4 Rue Saint François de Sales (opposite the main post office) is open Tuesday to Saturday. There are several other banks in the vicinity. The Banque de Savoie (☎ 50.52.80.05) opposite the tourist office at 2 Rue du Pâquier is open weekdays from 9 am to 12.25 pm and 1.30 to 5.30 pm. From mid-July to mid-September, it is also open on Saturday from 9 am to 4 pm. There is a 24-hour currency exchange machine outside the Crédit Lyonnais in the Centre Bonlieu. In the old city, the Change (☎ 50.45.79.91) at 20 Rue Perrière is open Tuesday to Saturday from 9.30 am to noon and 2 to 6 pm. In July and August, it is open Monday to Saturday from 8.30 am to 7.30 pm and on Sunday from 10 am to 1 pm. It is closed in January and February.

Post The main post office (☎ 50.33.68.20) at 4bis Rue des Glières is open weekdays from 8 am to 7 pm and on Saturday from 8 am to noon. Foreign exchange services are available.

Annecy's postcode is 74000.

Things to See
Walking Tour Just walking around, taking in the water, flowers, grass and quaint buildings, is the essence of a visit to Annecy. The old city can be viewed to best advantage (as a 19th century guidebook would have put it) from both sides of the restaurant-lined Canal du Thiou.

Just east of the old city, behind the Hôtel de Ville, are the flowery **Jardins de l'Europe**, shaded by giant redwoods brought all the way from California. The grassy

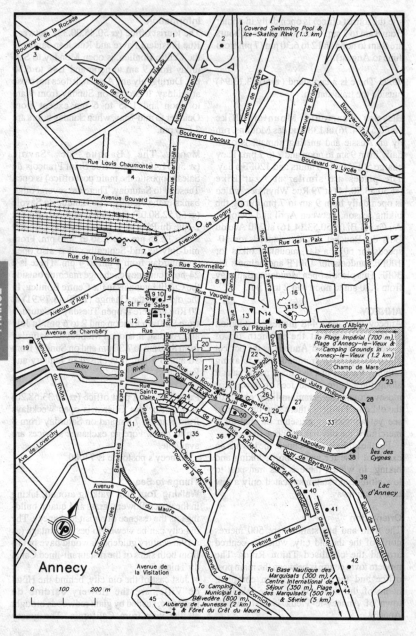

Annecy

Covered Swimming Pool &
Ice-Skating Rink (1.3 km)

Boulevard de la Rocade

Boulevard de Cran

Rue de Narvik

Avenue du Stand

Avenue de Genève

Boulevard de Brogny

Boulevard Teine

Rue de Brogny

Boulevard Decouz

Boulevard du Lycée

Rue Louis Chaumontel

Avenue Berthollet

Avenue Bouvard

Avenue de Brogny

Rue de la Paix

Rue Guillaume Fichet

Rue Louis Revon

Rue de l'Industrie

Rue Sommeiller

Rue de la Poste

Rue Vaugelas

R St F de Sales

Rue Carnot

Rue Président Favre

Avenue d'Alery

Avenue de Chambéry

Rue Royale

R du Pâquier

Avenue d'Albigny

To Plage Impérial (700 m),
Plage d'Annecy-le-Vieux &
Camping Grounds in
Annecy-le-Vieux (1.2 km)

Champ de Mars

Avenue de Loverchy

Thiou

Rue de la Gare

River

Rue de la République

Rue J J Rousseau

Rue Grenette

Quai Chapouis

Rue Joseph Blanc

Quai Jules Philippe

Quai Napoléon III

Îles des
Cygnes

Lac
d'Annecy

Quai de la Tournette

Rue Sainte Claire

Passage Nemours

Tour de la Reine

Chemin de la

Quai de l'Évêché

R de l'Isle

Quai de l'Isle

Rue Perrière

Quai de Bayreuth

Rue de la Providence

Rue des Marquisats

Avenue du Crêt du Maure

Faubourg des Balmettes

Avenue de la Visitation

Boulevard de la Corniche

Avenue de Trésun

To Camping
Municipal Le
Bélvédère (800 m),
Auberge de Jeunesse (2 km)
& Fôret du Crêt du Maure

To Base Nautique des
Marquisats (300 m),
Centre International de
Séjour (350 m), Plage
des Marquisats (500 m)
& Sévrier (5 km)

0   100   200 m

■ PLACES TO STAY		OTHER		28	Boat Rental
				29	Place de l'Hôtel de Ville
1	Hôtel Plaisance	2	Place des Romains	30	Musée d'Histoire
3	Hôtel Savoyard	5	Bus Station & Voyages		d'Annecy
4	Hôtel Les Terrasses		Crolard Office	31	Porte du Sépulcre
19	Maison de la Jeunne	6	Railway Station		(Gate)
	Fille (Summer	7	Place de la Gare	32	Eglise Saint François
	Hostel)	10	Banque de Savoie	33	Jardins de l'Europe
40	Hôtel Rive du Lac	11	Main Post Office	34	Place du Château
		12	Ebur Stationery Shop	35	Château d'Annecy
▼ PLACES TO EAT		14	Banque de Savoie	37	Change (Currency
		15	Tourist Office & SIBRA		Exchange)
8	Le Danay Boulangerie		Office	38	Boat Rental
9	Provencia	16	Centre Bonlieu	39	Boat Rental
	Supermarket	17	24-Hour Currency	41	Police Station
13	Boulangerie Rouge		Exchange Machine	42	Stade Nautique des
22	Pomme de Pain	18	Place de la Libération		Marquisats (Swim-
	Sandwich Shop	20	Église Notre Dame de		ming Pools)
24	Morning Food Market		Liesse	43	Sports Évasion (Bike
25	Food Shop	21	Cathédrale Saint		Rental)
36	Boulangerie		Pierre	44	Regate Service (Snow-
		23	Boat Rental		board Rental)
		26	Église Saint Maurice	45	Basilique de la
		27	City Hall		Visitation

FRANCE

expanse of the **Champ de Mars**, across the Canal du Vasse from the redwoods, is perfect for playing Frisbee. It's great to stroll from Jardins de l'Europe along Quai de Bayreuth and Quai de la Tournette to the Base Nautique des Marquisats and beyond. Another fine promenade begins at the Champ de Mars and goes eastward around the lake towards **Annecy-le-Vieux**.

Old City The Vieille Ville, an area of narrow streets on either side of the Canal du Thiou, retains much of its 17th century appearance despite recent quaintification and touristification. On the island in the middle, the Palais de l'Île (a former prison) houses the **Musée d'Histoire d'Annecy et de la Haute Savoie** (☎ 50.51.02.33), which is open Monday to Saturday (daily from July to September) from 10 am to noon and 2 to 6 pm. Entry is free.

Château d'Annecy The **Musée d'Annecy** (☎ 50.45.29.66), housed in the 13th to 16th century chateau overlooking the town, puts on innovative temporary exhibitions and has

a varied permanent collection that includes examples of local artisanship and miscellaneous objects relating to the region's natural history. The museum (20FF, 10FF for students) is open from 10 am to noon and 2 to 6 pm daily except Tuesday (every day of the week in July and August). The climb up to the chateau is worth it just for the view.

Activities
Sunbathing & Swimming In the warm months, you can choose any of several grassy areas along the lakefront to hang out, have a picnic, sunbathe and swim. There is a free beach, **Plage d'Annecy-le-Vieux**, a km east of the Champ de Mars. Slightly closer to town is the **Plage Impérial**, which costs 15FF and is equipped with changing rooms and other amenities. Perhaps Annecy's most pleasant stretch of lawn-lined swimming beach is the free **Plage des Marquisats**, which is one km south of the old city along Rue des Marquisats, just past the Centre International de Séjour.

Hiking The Forêt du Crêt du Maure, the

forested area behind the Centre International de Séjour, has lots of walking trails. It is conveniently close to town but can hardly be called a pristine wilderness. There are nicer hiking areas in and around two nature reserves: **Bout du Lac** (20 km from Annecy at the southern tip of the lake) and the **Roc de Chère** (10 km from town on the east coast of the lake). Both can be reached by Voyages Crolard buses (see the Getting There & Away section that follows). A 1:25,000 scale map of the Lac d'Annecy area is on sale at the tourist office.

Cycling There is a bike path (*piste cyclable*) – totally closed to motorised traffic – along the west coast of the lake. It starts 1.5 km south of Annecy (out Rue des Marquisats) and goes all the way to the lakeside town of Duingt, 12 km to the south.

Bicycles can be rented from Sports Évasion (☎ 50.51.21.81) at 30 Rue des Marquisats, which is open Monday to Saturday from 9 am to noon and 2 to 7 pm. Mountain bikes cost 80FF a day (50FF for a half-day).

Pedal Boats From March to November, pedal boats (47FF an hour) and small boats with outboard motors (*moteurs hors-bord*) can be hired along the shore of the Jardins de l'Europe and the Champ de Mars. The boats are available daily unless it's raining from 9 am until some time between 6 pm (in March) and 9 pm (in July and August).

More Serious Boats The Base Nautique des Marquisats, 800 metres south of the old city (opposite the Centre International de Séjour), is a centre for all sorts of aquatic activities. The various clubs based here rent kayaks, canoes, sailboats, sailboards, rowing hulls and skin-diving equipment.

Swimming Pools The **Stade Nautique des Marquisats** (☎ 50.45.39.18) at 29 Rue des Marquisats has four swimming pools (including one for children) and lots of lawn. The complex is open from mid-May to early September from 9 am (10 am on Sundays and holidays) to 7 pm (8 pm from mid-June to mid-August). The entry fee is 16FF. If you leave, you have to pay again to get back in. There are showers, changing rooms, a free place to check your stuff and a snack bar.

The **covered pool** (☎ 50.57.56.02) at 90 Chemin de Fins (on the corner of Blvd du Fier) is open from mid-August to June. The entry fee is 16FF. The pool is served by bus Nos 2, 3 and 8. There is an **ice-skating rink** (*patinoire*; ☎ 50.57.56.02) in the same complex. The entry fee is 16FF; skate rental is 10FF.

Miniature Golf There is a miniature golf course (☎ 50.66.04.99) at 2 Ave du Petit Pont in Annecy-le-Vieux, which is 500 metres east along Ave d'Albigny from the Champ de Mars (near the Plage Impériale). From April to October, it's open daily from 1 to 10 pm (10 am to 11 pm in July and August). The cost is 19FF per person.

Parapente Col de la Forclaz, the huge ridge overlooking Lac d'Annecy from the east, is a perfect spot from which to descend by parapente. For details on parapente and hang-gliding (*delta-plane*) schools, ask at the tourist office.

Winter Sports Not much snow falls in Annecy itself, but there's lots of cross-country skiing at **Le Semnoz** (about 15 km from town) and both downhill and cross-country skiing at **La Clusaz** (tourist office ☎ 50.02.60.92) and **Le Grand Bornand** (tourist office ☎ 50.02.20.33), both of which are 32 km east of Annecy. Count on 110FF a day for lift tickets. All three can be reached by Voyages Crolard buses (see the following Getting There & Away section for details).

In Annecy, skis can be rented from Sports Évasion (see Cycling earlier). Snowboards (*surfs de neige*) are available from Regate Service (☎ 50.45.74.75) at 34 Rue des Marquisats (closed Sunday and perhaps Monday).

Places to Stay
Camping *Camping Municipal Le Belvédère*

(☎ 50.45.48.30) is 2.5 km south of the train station in the Forêt du Crêt du Maure. To get there, turn off Rue des Marquisats onto Ave de Trésun, take the first left and follow Blvd de la Corniche. From mid-June to early September you can take bus No 91 (the Ligne des Vacances – Holiday Line) from the train station. Tent emplacements are 12.80FF and campers pay 14.80FF each.

There are several other camping grounds near the lake in Annecy-le-Vieux, just east of Annecy. *Le Pré d'Avril* (☎ 50.23.64.46; open all year) at 56 Rue du Pré d'Avril, charges 21FF for a place to camp and park, and 15FF per person (67FF for two people with a tent and car in the summer).

Hostels The modern *Centre International de Séjour* (☎ 50.45.08.80), on a superb lakeside site at 52 Rue des Marquisats, has beds in antiseptic singles, doubles and quads (all with shower, toilet and sheets) for 113FF, 78FF and 57FF respectively. Rooms are open all day and there is no curfew. Places usually become available each morning. Reservations can be made by telephone between 8 am and 5 pm. The *Auberge de Jeunesse* (☎ 50.45.33.19) is four km from town at 16 Route du Semnoz in the Forêt du Semnoz. From mid-June to early September, bus No 91 runs out there seven times a day. During the rest of the year, you have to hoof it or hitchhike. From Camping Municipal Le Belvédère, follow Route du Semnoz. In 1994 the hostel will move to a new location at the end of Route du Semnoz nearest Annecy.

Hotels The small *Hôtel Rive du Lac* (☎ 50.51.32.85), superbly located near the old city and the lake at 6 Rue des Marquisats, has modestly furnished rooms with one/two beds for 130/170FF.

The *Hôtel Savoyard* (☎ 50.57.08.08), a sterile, dorm-like (and, some say, spooky) place at 41 Ave de Cran (north-west of the modern town centre), is the cheapest hotel in town, with singles/doubles starting at 110FF (180FF with shower and toilet). Showers are 10FF. The *Hôtel Plaisance* (☎ 50.57.30.42) at 17 Rue de Narvik has simple but neat and

well-lit singles/doubles from 110/130FF. The pleasant *Hôtel Les Terrasses* (☎ 50.57.08.98) at 15 Rue Louis Chaumontel, 300 metres north of the train station, has singles/doubles from 140/160FF. From June to September, guests must take their meals here, which gets expensive. This place is closed from November to January.

Places to Eat

Restaurants In the old city, the streets on both sides of the Canal du Thiou are lined with tourist restaurants, most of which look remarkably like their neighbours. There are a number of cheap, hole-in-the-wall sandwich shops in the old city along Rue Perrière and Rue de l'Île. Farther north, *Pomme de Pain* (☎ 50.45.19.27) on Rue Joseph Blanc has decent sandwiches for 14 to 21FF. It is open daily from 11 am to 8.30 pm (11 pm in summer).

Self-Catering In the old city, there is a food market along Rue Sainte Claire on Sunday, Tuesday and Friday from 6 am to 12.30 pm. The boulangerie nearby at 16 Rue Perrière has excellent *pain campagnard* (country loaf); it is open from 7 am to 1 pm and 2.30 to 8 pm daily except Thursday (daily in summer). Fancy vegetables, fruit, cheese and wine are on sale at the food shop at 7 Rue Jean-Jacques Rousseau, which is open daily from 8 am to 8 pm.

In the town centre, there is a small *Provencia* supermarket opposite the main post office at 10 Rue des Glières. It is open from 8.15 am to 12.15 pm and 2.45 to 7.15 pm Monday to Saturday. *Le Danay*, a boulangerie-pâtisserie-confiserie at 27 Rue Carnot, has a good selection of nonwhite breads (closed Monday).

Getting There & Away

Bus The bus station, Gare Routière Sud, is on Rue de l'Industrie next to the train station. Voyages Crolard (☎ 50.45.08.12) has an office at the bus station that is open from 6.15 am to noon and 1.15 to 7.20 pm daily except Sunday. The company has regular service to points around Lac d'Annecy; there are lines

FRANCE

to Roc de Chère on the east shore and Bout du Lac at the far southern tip as well as to places east of Annecy, including ski stations such as La Clusaz and Le Grand Bornand and the towns of Albertville and Chamonix. Service on shorter runs ceases around 7 pm (earlier on Sunday and holidays). Autocars Frossard (☎ 50.45.73.90), open from 7.45 am to 12.30 pm and 1.45 to 7 pm daily except Sunday and holidays, sells tickets to Geneva, Grenoble, Nice and elsewhere. Autocars Francony (☎ 50.45.02.43, or 79.54.81.23 at their head office in Le Châtelard) has buses to Chamonix. Most do not run on Sunday or holidays. Their office at the bus station is open weekdays from 7.15 to 11 am and 2.15 to 6.15 pm.

Train The train station (☎ 50.66.50.50 for information, 50.51.50.60 for reservations) is a modernistic structure at Place de la Gare. The information counters are open daily from 8.30 am (9 am on Sunday) to 7 pm. There are frequent trains, not all of them direct, to Paris' Gare de Lyon (287FF plus TGV reservation fee; 3¾ hours), Nice (224FF via Lyons, 308FF via Grenoble; eight to nine hours, faster with a change of train), Lyons (102FF; two hours), Chamonix (80FF; 2½ to three hours) and Aix-les-Bains (30 to 60 minutes; about 15 trains a day). The night train to Paris' Gare de Lyon, which is often full on Friday and Saturday nights, leaves at 10.30 or 11.20 pm and arrives around 7 am. Sleepers cost 82FF extra, even for Eurail pass holders.

Getting Around
Bus SIBRA (☎ 50.51.72.72), the bus company responsible for transportation within Annecy, has an information bureau (☎ 50.51.70.33) across the covered courtyard from the tourist office. It is open Monday to Saturday from 8.30 am to 7 pm. Annecy's buses run Monday to Saturday from 6 am to 8 pm. On Sundays, 20-seat minibuses – identified by letters rather than numbers – provide limited service. Bus No 91 (the Ligne des Vacances), runs only from mid-June to early September.

Taxi Taxis based at the bus station can be ordered by calling ☎ 50.45.05.67.

Provence

Provence stretches along both sides of the Rhône River from a bit north of Orange down to the Mediterranean and along France's southern coast from the Camargue salt marshes in the west to Marseilles and beyond in the east. The spectacular Gorges d'Ardèche, created by the often-torrential Ardèche River, are west of the Rhône, and to the east are the region's famous upland areas: 1909-metre Mount Ventoux, the Vaucluse Plateau, the Lubéron Range and the chain of hills known as the Alpilles. East of Marseilles is the Côte d'Azur and its hinterland, which, though often considered part of Provence, is treated as a separate region in this guide.

Provence was settled by the Ligurians, the Celts and the Greeks, but it was after its conquest by Julius Caesar in the mid-1st century BC that the region really began to flourish. Many exceptionally well-preserved amphitheatres, aqueducts (particularly Pond du Gard) and other buildings from the Roman period can still be seen in such towns as Arles, Nîmes and Orange.

During the 14th century, the Catholic Church, then led by a series of French-born popes, moved its headquarters from feud-riven Rome to Avignon, thus beginning the most resplendent period in that city's history.

Language
A thousand years ago, *oïl* and *oc* were the words for 'yes' in the Romance languages of what is now northern and southern France, respectively. As Paris-based influence and control spread, so did the northern French language, the *Langue d'Oïl*, and thus the *Langue d'Oc* – the language of Provence – was gradually supplanted. The Provençal language is not spoken much these days, but it has left the world a rich literary legacy: the Langue d'Oc was used by the medieval trou-

badours, whose melodies and poems were motivated by the ideal of courtly love. It was also used by the winner of the 1904 Nobel Prize for literature, Frédéric Mistral (1830-1914).

Climate
Provence's weather is bright and sunny for much of the year, and the extraordinary light has attracted quite a number of painters, including Van Gogh, Cézanne and Picasso. The cold, dry winds of the *mistral*, which gain surprising fury as they careen down the Rhône valley can, however, with little warning, turn a fine spring day into a bone-chilling wintry one.

MARSEILLES
The cosmopolitan and much maligned port of Marseilles (Marseille), France's second-largest city (with a population of 878,000) and third most populous urban area (population 1,100,000), is not in the least bit prettified or quaintified for the benefit of tourists. Its urban geography and atmosphere are a function of the diversity of its inhabitants, the majority of whom are immigrants (or the descendants of immigrants) from the Mediterranean basin, West Africa and Indochina. Although Marseilles is notorious for organised crime and racial tensions (the extreme right polls about 25% citywide), the city has more to reward the visitor who likes exploring on foot than almost any other city in France.

Orientation
The city's main street, La Canabière, stretches eastward from the old port (Vieux Port). The train station is north of La Canabière at the northern end of Blvd d'Athènes. The city centre is around Rue Paradis, which gets more fashionable as you move south.

Information
The tourist office (☎ 91.54.91.11), next to the old port at 4 La Canabière, is open Monday to Saturday from 9 am to 7.30 pm and on Sunday from 10 am to 5 pm. From mid-June to September, opening hours are 8.30 am to 8 pm daily. The tourist office annexe (☎ 91.50.59.18) at the train station (on the right as you exit the station's main doors) is open weekdays from 9 am to 12.30 pm and 2 to 6.30 pm. From mid-June to September, it is open daily except Sunday from 9 am to 7 pm.

Money Banque de France (☎ 91.04.10.27) at Place Estrangin Pastré, a block west of the prefecture, is open weekdays from 8.45 am to 12.30 pm and 1.45 to 3.30 pm. There are a number of banks on La Canabière near the tourist office. Change de la Bourse (☎ 91.54.10.13), at 3 Place du Général de Gaulle, open weekdays from 8.30 am to 6.30 pm and on Saturday from 8.30 am to noon and 2 to 6 pm, will exchange dozens of currencies.

American Express (☎ 91.91.41.72) at 39 La Canabière is open weekdays from 8 am to 6 pm and on Saturday from 8 am to noon and 2 to 5 pm. The Comptoir de Change Méditerranéen (☎ 91.84.68.88) at the train station will exchange foreign currencies every day from 8 am to 6 pm.

Post The main post office (☎ 91.95.47.32) at 1 Place de l'Hôtel des Postes is open weekdays from 8 am to 7 pm and on Saturday from 8 am to noon. Exchange services are available.

Marseilles' postcode consists of the digits 130 plus the arrondissement number (01 to 16). The areas covered by the Marseilles map in this book are in 13001 except the area south of Rue Grignan, which is in 13006.

Foreign Consulates There is a UK Consulate (☎ 91.53.43.32) at 24 Ave du Prado (near Place Castellane and the Castellane metro stop). It is open Monday to Friday from 9 am to noon and 2 to 5 pm. The US Consulate (☎ 91.54.92.00) is next to the prefecture building on Blvd Paul Peytral. The American services section is open weekdays from 8.30 am to noon and 1 to 5.30 pm.

Dangers & Annoyances Despite its fearsome reputation for underground crime

FRANCE

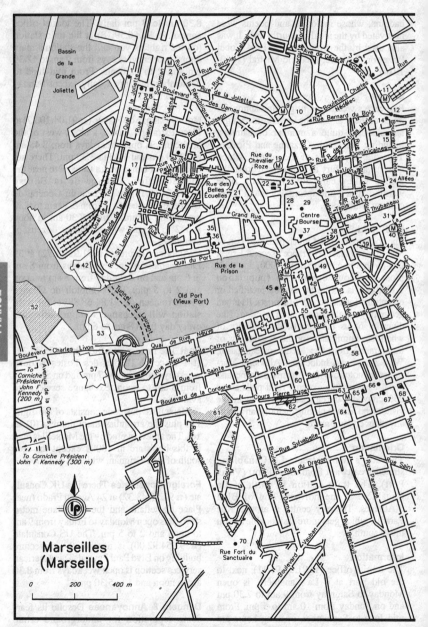

FRANCE

Marseilles
(Marseille)

0   200   400 m

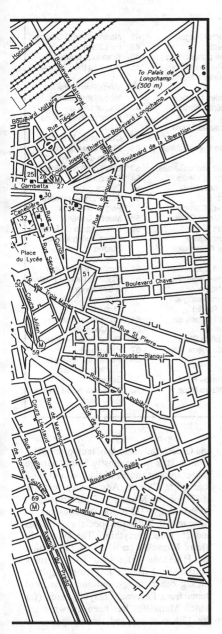

Marseilles is probably no more dangerous than other French cities. As elsewhere, street crime (bag-snatching, pickpocketing) is best avoided by keeping your wits about you and your valuables hard to get at. Guard your luggage very carefully, especially at the train station, and *never* leave anything inside a parked motor vehicle.

It is probably a good idea for lone visitors – especially women and, as one policeman put it, men who are not 'musclemen gorillas' – to avoid the Belsunce area at night. This is the poor, immigrant neighbourhood southwest of the train station bounded by La Canabière, Cours Belsunce and Rue d'Aix, Rue Bernard du Bois and Blvd d'Athènes.

Things to See
Walking Tour Marseilles grew up around the **old port**, where Greeks from Asia Minor established a settlement around 600 BC. The quarter north of Quai du Port (around the Hôtel de Ville) was blown up by the Germans in 1943 and rebuilt after the war. The lively **Place Thiars** pedestrian zone, with its many late-night restaurants and cafés, is south of the Quai de Rive Neuve. To get from one side of the harbour entrance to the other, you can walk through the Saint Laurent Tunnel, which surfaces in front of the cathedral (near Fort Saint Jean) and, on the south side, just east of Fort Saint Nicolas. Also worth a stroll is the more fashionable **6ème arrondissement**, especially the area between La Canabière and the prefecture building, and the Rue Saint Ferréol pedestrian mall.

Corniche Président John F Kennedy runs along the coast from 200 metres west of the **Jardin du Pharo,** a park with good harbour views, to the Plages Gaston Defferre (Plage du Pharo), 4.5 km to the south. Along its entire length, the corniche is served by bus No 83, which goes to the Quai des Belges (the old port) and the Rond-Point du Prado metro stop.

If you like great panoramic views or over-wrought mid-19th century architecture, consider a walk up to the **Basilique Notre Dame de la Garde**, which is one km south of the old port on a hilltop 154 metres above

■	**PLACES TO STAY**	4	Place Victor Hugo	40	Noailles Metro Station
		5	Taxi Stand	42	Fort Saint Jean
8	Hôtel Terminus des Ports	6	Palais de Longchamp	43	American Express
		7	SNCM Ferries Office	45	Boats to the Château d'If
15	Hôtel Beaulieu	9	Jules Guesde Metro Station		
25	Hôtel Gambetta			46	Vieux Port-Hôtel de Ville Metro Station
26	Hôtel de Dijon & Hôtel de Bourgogne	10	Place Jules Guesde		
		11	Gare Saint Charles (Railway Station) & Saint Charles Metro Station	47	Tourist Office
33	Hôtel de Nice			48	Place du Général de Gaulle
34	Hôtel Ozea & Hôtel Pied-à-Terre				
		12	Staircase from Railway Station	49	Change de la Bourse
41	Hôtel Titanic			51	Place Jean Jaurès
56	Hôtel Le Provençal	14	Place des Marseillaises	52	Jardin du Pharo
68	Hôtel Salvator	16	Centre de la Vieille Charité (Museum)	53	Bas Fort Saint Nicolas
				54	Place Thiars
▼	**PLACES TO EAT**	17	Cathédrale	55	Opera
		18	Place Sadi Carnot	57	Fort d'Entrecasteaux & Fort St Nicholas
13	Roi du Couscous	19	Colbert Metro Station		
21	Auberge 'In' (Vegetarian Restaurant)	20	Place des Moulins	58	Musée Cantini
		22	Main Post Office	59	Notre Dame du Mont-Cours Julien Metro Station
31	McDonald's	23	Place de l'Hotel des Postes		
32	Restaurant La Dent Creuse				
		24	Place des Capucines	60	Law Courts
37	Supermarket	27	Reformés-Canebière Metro Station	61	Jardin Pierre Puget
39	Takeaway Restaurants			63	Place Estrangin-Pastré & Estrangin Préfecture Metro Station
44	Marché des Capucins (Food Market)	28	Jardin des Vestiges (Roman Ruins)		
50	Ethnic Restaurants	29	Musée d'Histoire de Marseille		
62	Fruit & Vegetable Morning Market			64	Banque de France
		30	Square Léon Blum	65	US Consulate
		35	Musée du Vieux Marseille	66	Place de la Préfecture
	OTHER			67	Prefecture
		36	City Hall	69	Place Castellane & Castellane Metro Station
1	Passenger Ferry Terminal	38	Espace Infos-RTM (Bus & Metro Information)		
2	Joliette Metro Station			70	Basilique Notre Dame de la Garde
3	Bus Station				

sea level, the highest point in the city. The basilica and the crypt are open from 7.30 am to 5.30 pm (7 am to 7.30 pm in the summer). Bus No 60 will get you back to the old port.

Museums Except where noted, the museums listed here are open daily from 10 am to 5 pm (from June to September, hours are 11 am to 6 pm). All of them admit students and teachers for half the regular price.

The **Centre de la Vieille Charité** (☎ 91.56.28.38), which used to be a charity centre and is housed in a workhouse and hospice built between 1671 and 1745, has superb permanent exhibits on ancient Egypt and Greece and all sorts of temporary exhibitions. It is in the mostly North African Panier quarter (north of the old port) at 2 Rue de la Charité. Adult entry fees are 10FF for the Museum of Mediterranean Archaeology, 10FF for the Museum of African Art, 20FF for special exhibitions and 25FF for everything. The **Musée du Vieux Marseille** (☎ 91.55.28.72), behind the Hôtel de Ville in a 16th century mansion at 2 Rue de la Prison, displays, among other things, antique household items from Provence, playing cards (for which Marseilles has been known since the 17th century) and the equipment to make them, and photos of the city under German occupation. Admission costs 10FF.

The **Musée Cantini** (☎ 91.54.77.75), off Rue Paradis at 19 Rue Grignan, has changing exhibitions of modern and contemporary art. The entry fee is usually 15FF. The museum is closed on Monday.

Roman history buffs might want to visit the **Musée d'Histoire de Marseille** (☎ 91.90.42.22) on the ground floor of the Centre Bourse shopping mall (just north of La Canabière), whose exhibits include the freeze-dried remains of a merchant ship that plied the waters of the Mediterranean in the late 2nd century AD. It is open Monday to Saturday from noon to 7 pm. The entry fee is 10FF. Roman buildings, uncovered by accident during construction of the shopping mall, can be seen nearby in the **Jardin des Vestiges**, which is between the Centre Bourse and Rue Henri Barbusse.

Château d'If Château d'If (☎ 91.59.02.30), the 16th century island fortress-turned-prison made infamous by Alexandre Dumas' *The Count of Monte Christo*, can be visited daily from 9 am until 6 pm (or whenever the last boat of the day departs). The entry fee is 25FF (14FF for people aged 18 to 24). The island is not particularly interesting unless you've read the book or love either islands or prisons. Boats (35FF return, 20 minutes each way) leave from the Quai des Belges (old port) and continue on to the nearby **Îles du Frioul**.

Beaches Marseilles' nicest beach, the **Plages Gaston Defferre** (formerly the Plage du Prado), is four km south of the city centre. To get there, take bus No 19, 72 or 83 from the Rond-Point du Prado metro stop or bus No 83 from the Quai des Belges. You can walk there along the Corniche Président John F Kennedy.

Places to Stay

Camping All of Marseilles' municipal camping grounds are presently closed, although *Camping de Bonneveine* at 187 Ave Clot Bey (about 4½ km south of the city

centre) may be reopened. To get out there, take bus No 44 from the Rond-Point du Prado metro stop. Travellers with tents can camp at the Auberge de Jeunesse de Bois Luzy (see the next section).

Hostels The *Auberge de Jeunesse de Bonneveine* (☎ 91.73.21.81) is at 47 Ave Joseph Vidal, which is about 4.5 km south of the old port. To get to the youth hostel, take bus No 44 from the Rond-Point du Prado metro stop and get off at Place Louis Bonnefon. A bed in a six-person room is 71FF for the first night and 56FF for subsequent nights, including breakfast. Valuables should be kept in the lockers (5FF each time you open them). There's another youth hostel, the *Auberge de Jeunesse de Bois Luzy* (☎ 91.49.06.18), 4.5 km east of the city centre at 76 Ave de Bois Luzy (in the Montolivet neighbourhood). To get out there, take bus No 6 from near the Réformés Canabière metro stop or No 9 from the Centre Bourse. Beds are 40FF and breakfast is 16FF. It costs 22FF per person to camp here.

Hotels The good news is that Marseilles has some of France's cheapest hotels – you can still find rooms for 50FF a night! The bad news is that most of these establishments are filthy dives in unsafe areas whose main business is renting out rooms by the hour. Some of them don't even have any showers! I've mentioned where such 'bargains' can be found, but all of the places listed by name in this section (except one) are reputable and relatively clean.

Train Station Area The *Hôtel Beaulieu* (☎ 91.90.70.59) is down the grand staircase from the train station at 3 Place des Marseillaises. Plain but clean singles/doubles are 110/120FF with washbasin and bidet and 184/198FF with shower and toilet; hall showers cost 15FF. There is a cluster of small, extremely cheap hotels of less-than-pristine reputation along Rue des Petites Maries.

The *Hôtel Gambetta* (☎ 91.62.07.88) at

49 Allées Léon Gambetta has singles without showers for 90FF and singles/doubles with showers from 120/150FF. Hall showers are 15FF, but if you stay a few days the friendly proprietor will throw one in free. The *Hôtel de Dijon* (☎ 91.62.62.22) at 33 Allées Léon Gambetta has fairly large, pleasant singles and doubles for 92 or 104FF and doubles/triples with shower from 140/180FF. Hall showers cost 20FF. The *Hôtel de Bourgogne* (☎ 91.62.19.49) at 31 Allées Léon Gambetta has singles/doubles from 100FF and triples for 160FF; showers are free and an extra bed (if there's space) is only 30FF.

The *Hôtel Ozea* (☎ 91.47.91.84) is at 12 Rue Barbaroux (the 'x' is pronounced), which is across Square Léon Blum from the eastern end of Allées Léon Gambetta. This place, which welcomes new guests 24 hours a day (if you arrive late at night just ring the bell three times to wake up the night clerk), has clean, old-fashioned doubles without/ with shower for 100/130FF. There are no showers in the hallways. The *Hôtel Pied-à-Terre* (☎ 91.92.00.95) is down the street at 18 Rue Barbaroux. The well-kept singles and doubles, which cost 100/130FF without/ with shower, are a bit on the small side. Hall showers cost 20FF. You can check in until 1 am.

South of La Canabière There are lots of rock-bottom hotels, many specialising in short-time business, along Rue Sénac and around Place du Lycée. There are a number of one-star hotels along Rue des Feuillants.

The down-market *Hôtel Titanic* (☎ 91.48.01.56) at 27 Rue Sénac, considerably less luxurious than its namesake (but much less likely to strike an iceberg), has singles/doubles for 70/100FF and two-bed triples with shower for 150FF. The rooms are dilapidated and not the cleanest, but you can certainly sleep in them, whatever the neighbours may be doing. The *Hôtel de Nice* (☎ 91.48.73.07), down the block at 11 Rue Sénac, is a step up from most other places in the area. Doubles without/with shower are 120/140FF; hall showers cost 20FF per

person. Both these places will register guests 24 hours a day.

Rue Paradis Area The *Hôtel Salvator* (☎ 91.48.78.25) at 6 Rue Salvator is in a decent area half a block east of the prefecture. Doubles with high ceilings and almost-antique furniture cost 85/120FF without/with showers. The shower in the hall costs 20FF. A few blocks from the old port at 32 Rue Paradis, the *Hôtel Le Provençal* (☎ 91.33.11.15) has singles/doubles from 90FF and doubles/triples with shower for 120/180FF. Hall showers are 15FF.

Places to Eat

Restaurants There are lots of cheap takeaway places selling pizza, Middle Eastern sandwiches of various sorts, etc on Rue des Feuillants, which intersects La Canabière just east of Cours Saint Louis. Cours Belsunce is lined with inexpensive food kiosks.

Restaurants along Cours Julien, which is a few blocks south of La Canabière, offer an incredible variety of cuisines: Antillean, Pakistani, Thai, Lebanese, Tunisian, Italian and so on. If you'd rather have something French, try *Restaurant La Dent Creuse* (☎ 91.42.05.67), just south of La Canabière at 14 Rue Sénac. Lunch/dinner *menus* cost 50/79FF. This place is open from noon to 2 or 2.15 pm and 7.30 pm to midnight daily except Saturday and Sunday at midday and Monday evening.

Countless sandwich shops, cafés and restaurants line the pedestrian streets around Place Thiars, which is on the south side of the old port. Many offer bouillabaisse, a rich fish soup (made with onions, herbs, saffron and several kinds of fish) for which Marseilles is famous. Avoid the touristy restaurants on the Quai de Rive Neuve.

The *Auberge 'In'* (☎ 91.90.51.59) is a vegetarian restaurant a few hundred metres north of the old port at 25 Rue du Chevalier Roze. Giant salads cost 40 to 44FF. Meals are served from noon to 2 pm and 7 to 10 pm daily except Sunday. The attached food shop and salon de thé (closed at meal times) are open from 8 am to 11 pm. The *Roi du Cous-cous* (☎ 91.91.45.46) at 63 Rue de la République serves couscous for 40 to 60FF. This place is open from noon to 2.30 or 3 pm and 7.30 to 10.30 pm daily except Monday. There is a Chinese place (closed Tuesday) next door and many other restaurants along Rue de la République.

Self-Catering There is an up-market super-market, open Monday to Saturday from 9 am to 7 pm, in the Nouvelles Galeries, a depart-ment store a block north of La Canabière in the Centre Bourse shopping mall complex. The most convenient entrance is at 28 Rue de Bir Hakeim. At the *Marché des Capucins*, one block south of La Canabière on Rue Longue des Capucins, you can purchase fruit and vegetables from 7 am to 7 pm daily except Sundays and holidays.

Getting There & Away
Bus The bus station (*gare des autocars*; ☎ 91.08.16.40) at Place Victor Hugo, 150 metres to the right as you exit the train station, offers service to Aix-en-Provence, Arles, Avignon, Cannes, Carpentras, Nice (direct and via the coast), Nice airport, Oranges and Salon. The buses, which are slower than rail travel, cost more or less the same as the trains unless you're a student aged 25 or under, in which case you may qualify for a discount of around 30%. The information counter and the left-luggage office are open Monday to Saturday from 7.45 am to 6.30 pm and on Sunday from 9 am to noon and 2 to 6 pm. Tickets are sold on the bus.

Train Marseilles' passenger train station, Gare Saint Charles (☎ 91.08.50.50 for infor-mation, 91.08.84.12 for reservations), is served by both metro lines. Trains from here go everywhere, including Paris' Gare de Lyon (200FF plus TGV reservation fee if needed; five to eight hours), Bordeaux (321FF; five to six hours), Toulouse (229FF; three to four hours) and Nice (143FF; 1½ to two hours). The information office, one floor under the platforms, is open Monday to Sat-

urday from 9 am to 8 pm. The SNCF desk (☎ 91.95.14.31) in the tourist office at 4 La Canabière is open from 9.15 am to 12.30 pm and 2 to 5.30 pm weekdays except holidays.

Ferry The Société Nationale Maritime Corse-Méditerranée (SNCM; ☎ 91.56.30.10 for information ☎ 91.56.30.30 for reserva-tions) at 61 Blvd des Dames offers ferry service from the gare maritime (at the foot of Blvd des Dames) to Corsica, Sardinia (Sardaigne in French), Tunisia (see the intro-ductory Getting There & Away section in the Tunisia chapter for further details) and Algeria. Discounts of up to 30%, some limited to the off season or applicable only if you're a student or under 25 (or both), are available. The SNCM office is open week-days from 8 am to 6 pm and on Saturday from 8.30 am to noon and 2 to 5.30 pm.

Getting Around
Bus & Metro Marseilles has two beautiful, new metro lines (look for the white-on-brown signs bearing an angular letter 'M') and an extensive bus network. Numbered buses run until 9 pm; lines identified with letters, known as the *autobus de nuit*, run from 9 pm to 12.30 am. Tickets (7.50FF) are valid for travel on both the bus and the metro for 70 minutes after they've been time-stamped. Exact change is needed to buy a ticket on the bus. When you buy a carnet of six tickets (available in metro stations for 34FF) you get two coupons (*talons*) with the same serial number as your tickets; to use a ticket as a transfer you must show one of the coupons. For more information, visit the Espace Infos-RTM (☎ 91.91.92.10) at 6-8 Rue des Fabres, which is open weekdays from 8.30 am to 5.30 pm (closed from noon to 2 pm during July and August).

Taxi Marseille Taxi (☎ 91.02.20.20) and the Maison du Taxi (☎ 91.95.92.50) will dis-patch a taxi 24 hours a day.

AVIGNON
Avignon acquired its ramparts and its repu-tation as a city of art and culture during the

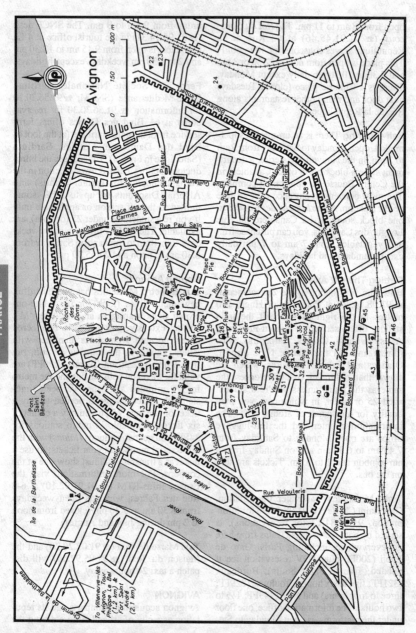

Avignon

■ PLACES TO STAY		OTHER		26	Cinéma Utopia (one
1	Camping Bagatelle & Auberge Bagatelle	2	Entrance to Pont Saint Bénézet		screen) & Institute for American Universities
14	Hôtel Mignon	3	Musée du Petit Palais	27	Musée Calvet (closed
23	Avignon Squash Club (Hostel)	4	Cathédrale Notre Dame des Doms	29	until 1995) Musée Lapidaire
31	Hôtel Innova	5	Palais des Papes	33	Tourist Office
35	Hôtel du Parc		(Popes' Palace)	34	Square Agricol
39	Hôtel Saint Roch	6	Music Conservatory		Perdiguer
46	Hôtel Monclar	7	Banque de France	37	Place des Corps Saints
		8	Place Campana	38	Peugeot 84 (Bicycle
▼ PLACES TO EAT		9	Opéra d'Avignon		Rental)
		10	City Hall	40	Main Post Office & Bus
15	Casino Grocery	11	Place de l'Horloge		No 10 (to Villeneuve-
16	Boulangerie	12	Porte de l'Oulle (City		lès-Avignon)
18	Restaurant Song Long		Gate)	41	Porte de la République
22	Casino Supermarket	13	Place Crillon		(City Gate)
28	Restaurant Le Petit	17	Musée Louis Voland	42	Local Bus Information
	Bedon	19	Place Carnot		Office (in the city
30	Snack (Sandwich	20	Place Jérusalem		wall)
	Shop)	21	Synagogue	43	Railway Station
32	Brasserie Le Palais	24	French Army Barracks	44	Locarplus & Other Car
36	Koala Bar	25	Cinéma Utopia (two		Rental Places
			screens)	45	Bus Station
				46	Location Vélos Minibus

14th century, when, fleeing political turmoil in Rome, Pope Clement V and his court established themselves at Avignon. From 1309 to 1377, the Holy See was based in Avignon, and huge sums of money were invested in building and decorating the popes' palace and other important church edifices. Even after the pontifical court returned to Rome – amid bitter charges that Avignon had become a den of criminals and brothel-goers and was unfit for papal habitation – Avignon, which remained under Vatican rule until the Revolution, continued to serve as an important cultural centre.

Today, Avignon maintains its tradition as a patron of the arts, most notably through its annual performing arts festival. The city's other attractions include a bustling (if slightly touristy) walled town and a number of interesting museums, including several across the Rhône in Villeneuve-lès-Avignon. Avignon is a good base for day trips to other parts of Provence.

The world-famous **Festival d'Avignon**, held every year during the last three weeks of July, attracts many hundreds of performers (actors, dancers, musicians, etc) who put on some 300 *spectacles* (performances) of all sorts each day. There are, in fact, two simultaneous events: the prestigious, expensive and government-subsidised official festival; and the *festival 'off'*, which consists of performers who, on their own initiative (and at their own expense), just decided to show up. The festival attracts incredible numbers of people, creating major accommodation and transportation headaches.

Orientation
The walled city's main avenue runs northward from the train station all the way to Place de l'Horloge; it's called Cours Jean Jaurès south of the tourist office and Rue de la République north of the tourist office. Place de l'Horloge is 200 metres south of Place du Palais, which is next to the Palais

des Papes (the Palace of the Popes). The island that runs down the middle of the Rhône between Avignon and Villeneuve-lès-Avignon is known as Île de la Barthelasse.

Information

Tourist Office The tourist office (☎ 90.82.65.11) is 300 metres north of the train station at 41 Cours Jean Jaurès. It is open Monday to Saturday from 9 am to 1 pm and 2 to 6 pm (5 pm on Saturday). See Places to Stay for information on the departmental hotel reservation service.

Money There is a Banque de France (☎ 90.86.56.64) is at the northern end of Place de l'Horloge. It is open Monday to Friday from 8.35 am to 12.05 pm and 1.55 to 3.35 pm.

Post The main post office (☎ 90.86.78.00) is on Cours Président Kennedy, which is through Porte de la République from the train station. It is open Monday to Friday from 8 am to 6 pm and on Saturday from 8 am to noon. Currency exchange stops at 5 pm on weekdays and 11 am on Saturday.

Avignon's postcode is 84000.

Things to See

Avignon's most interesting areas are within the walled city (*intra-muros*). The ramparts were restored during the 19th century but the original moats were not re-excavated, leaving the crenellated fortifications looking rather less imposing than they once did.

Palais des Papes Avignon's leading tourist attraction is the Palace of the Popes (☎ 90.27.50.71/3) at Place du Palais, built during the 14th century as a fortified palace for the pontifical court. Six centuries ago, the seemingly endless halls, chapels, corridors and staircases were sumptuously decorated with frescoes, tapestries, paintings, etc but these days, except for a few damaged frescoes, they are nearly empty. As a result, the palace is of interest more because of the dramatic events that took place here than

because of the inherent beauty of its undecorated stone halls. If you know a bit about medieval Catholic history, you might try to imagine what the rooms were like when cardinals and royal emissaries paraded purposefully about, attended by armies of servants, clerks and factotums...

The Palais des Papes is open daily from 9 am to 12.45 pm and 2 to 6 pm. From April to October, hours are 9 am to 6, 7 or 8 pm. When the palace closes at midday, morning ticket sales end at 11.45 am; in the evening, the ticket window closes 45 minutes to an hour before the palace does. You can have a look at the main courtyard for free, but entry to the palace's interior costs 27FF (19FF concession, available to students and people over 60). One-hour guided tours (35FF, or 27FF concession) are available in English from April to October *only*, usually at 10 am and 3 pm. Occasionally, especially during summer, special exhibits may raise the entry fees by 10FF or so.

Around Place du Palais The **Musée du Petit Palais** (☎ 90.86.44.58), at the far northern end of Place du Palais, houses an outstanding collection of 13th to 16th century Italian religious paintings. It is open from 9.30 to 11.50 am and 2 to 6 pm daily except Tuesday. Tickets cost 16FF (8FF concession). Just up the hill is **Rocher des Doms**, a delightful bluff-top park that affords great views of the Rhône, Pont Saint Bénézet, Villeneuve-lès-Avignon, the Alpilles, and so on; a semicircular viewing table tells you what you're looking at. There's also a playground for children. This is a perfect spot for a picnic in a town singularly lacking in public benches.

Pont Saint Bénézet (☎ 90.85.60.16) was built in the 12th century to link Avignon with Villeneuve-lès-Avignon. The 900-metre-long structure was repaired and rebuilt several times before but four of its 22 spans were washed away once and for all in the mid-1600s. Yes, this is the Pont d'Avignon mentioned in the French nursery rhyme. If you want to stand *on* the bridge (not look at it from a distance), you can do so – in exchange for 10FF (5FF concession) – from 9 am to 1 pm and 2 to 5 pm every day except Monday (from April to September, daily from 9 am to 6.30 pm).

Synagogue The synagogue (☎ 90.85.21.24) at 2 Place Jérusalem was established on this site in 1221. A 13th century oven used to bake unleavened bread for Passover is still in place, but the rest of the present dome-topped, neo-Classical structure dates from 1846. You can visit the synagogue Monday to Friday from 10 am to noon and 3 to 5 pm. Visitors must be modestly dressed (no short pants or sleeveless shirts) and men must cover their heads.

Museums The **Musée Lapidaire** (no tel) at 27 Rue de la République is the archaeological annexe of the **Musée Calvet** (☎ 90.86.33.84), which is closed for repairs until about 1995. It displays Gallo-Roman, Romanesque and Gothic stone carvings. It is open from 10 am to noon and 2 to 6 pm daily except Tuesday. Entry is free.

At 17 Rue Victor Hugo, the **Musée Louis Vouland** (☎ 90.86.03.79) exhibits a fine collection of faïence and some superb pieces of 18th century French furniture. It is open from 2 to 6 pm (and, from June to September, from 10 am to noon as well) daily except Sunday and Monday. Entry costs 20FF (10FF for students and people over 65).

Villeneuve-lès-Avignon Avignon's sister-city, Villeneuve-lès-Avignon, has a number of sights as interesting (if not more so) than those offered by Avignon itself. The **Chartreuse du Val de Bénédiction** (☎ 90.25.05.46) at 60 Rue de la République, a Carthusian Charterhouse founded in the 14th century, is open daily from 9.30 am to 5.30 pm (9 am to 6.30 pm from April to September). The **Musée Pierre de Luxembourg** (☎ 90.27.49.66) on Rue de la République near Place Jean Jaurès has a fine collection of religious paintings, many of them from the 15th, 16th and 17th centuries. The museum is open from 10 am to noon and 2 to 5 pm (April to September from 10 am to

12.30 pm and 3 to 7.30 pm) daily except Tuesday. The **Tour Philippe le Bel** (☎ 90.27.49.68), a defensive tower built in the 14th century at what was then the western end of Pont Saint Bénézet, affords great views of Avignon's walled city, the river and the surrounding countryside. Another place to visit for a wonderfully Provençal panorama is 14th century **Fort Saint André**.

From Avignon, Villeneuve can be reached by bus No 10, which you can catch in front of the main post office. Unless you want to take the grand tour of the Avignon suburb of Les Angles, take a bus marked 'Villeneuve puis (then) Les Angles' (rather than 'Les Angles puis Villeneuve').

Places to Stay
Camping The attractive, shaded *Camping Bagatelle* (☎ 90.86.30.39, 90.85.78.45), which is open all year, is on Île de la Barthelasse slightly north of Pont Édouard Daladier. Charges are 15FF per adult, 6.50FF to pitch a tent and 6.50FF to park a car. To get to the camping ground by public transport, take bus No 10 from in front of the main post office and get off at the stop called La Barthelasse.

Hostels The new, 210-bed *Auberge Bagatelle* (☎ 90.86.30.39, 90.85.78.45) and its many amenities are part of a large, parklike area on Île de la Barthelasse that includes Camping Bagatelle. A bed costs 49FF. Rooms are locked from 1 to 5 pm, but there's no curfew. See the previous section for bus directions.

The friendly *Avignon Squash Club* (☎ 90.85.27.78) at 32 Blvd Limbert is both a place for people to play squash and a travellers' hostel. A bunk in a converted squash court costs only 45FF; renting a squash court costs 40FF for 40 minutes (if you don't travel with your squash racquet, you can borrow one from the management). Travellers can check in daily except Sunday from 9 am to 10 pm, but from June to October reception is open seven days a week from 8 to 11 am and 5 to 11 pm. To get there by bus, take No 2 from the main post office and get off at the Thiers stop.

Hotels During the festival (the last three weeks of July), it is nearly impossible to find accommodation in Avignon unless you've booked many months in advance.

At the train station, hotel reservations anywhere in the department of Vaucluse (of which Avignon is the capital) can be made through Vaucluse Tourisme Hébergement (☎ 90.82.05.81). The charge for a booking in a one/two-star hotel is about 15/25FF. The office is open Monday to Friday from 9 am to 6 pm and, from Easter to September, on Saturday from 10 am to 5 pm. Public holiday hours are also 10 am to 5 pm.

Walled City The very proper *Hôtel du Parc* (☎ 90.82.71.55) at 18 Rue Agricol Perdiguier, which is only 300 metres from the train station, has rather ordinary single and double rooms for 110FF (without shower) and 140FF (with shower). A quad with shower costs 200FF. Hall showers are 10FF; toilets are in the hallway. The friendly *Hôtel Innova* (☎ 90.82.54.10) at 100 Rue Joseph Vernet has doubles without/with shower for 130/150FF; rooms for two with shower and toilet cost 180FF. Hall showers are free.

The *Hôtel Mignon* (☎ 90.82.17.30), which is three blocks west of Place de l'Horloge at 12 Rue Joseph Vernet, has spotless, well-kept singles/doubles with shower for 130/165FF and doubles with shower and toilet for 195FF. To get there by bus, take No 10 from in front of the main post office and get off at Porte de l'Oulle.

Outside the Walls The family-run *Hôtel Monclar* (☎ 90.86.20.14) is across the tracks from the train station at 13 Ave Monclar. Eminently serviceable doubles cost 150FF with sink and bidet, 170FF with shower and 200FF with shower and toilet. This place has its own parking lot. The *Hôtel Saint Roch* (☎ 90.82.18.63) at 9 Rue Paul Mérindol has large, airy doubles with shower and toilet for 180 to 195FF.

Places to Eat
Restaurants The *Brasserie Le Palais* (☎ 90.82.53.42) at 36 Cours Jean Jaurès (opposite the tourist office) has menus starting at 55FF. Meals are served every day of the year from noon to 3 pm and 7 pm to midnight. *Snack* (☎ 90.82.48.92), the signless sandwich shop at 26 Rue de la République, has remarkably cheap crêpes (6 to 10FF) and sandwiches (10 to 16FF). It is open daily from 7 am to 1 am.

Restaurant Song Long (☎ 90.86.35.00) at 1 Rue Carnot (next to Place Carnot) offers a wide variety of excellent Vietnamese dishes, including 16 *plats végétariens* (vegetarian soups, salads, first courses and main dishes). Lunch/dinner *menus* start at 42/60FF. Song Long is open daily from 11 am to 2.15 pm and 7 to 11.30 pm.

If you're in the mood to splurge on French cuisine, you might try *Le Petit Bedon* (☎ 90.82.33.98) at 70 Rue Joseph Vernet, whose specialities include frogs' legs and escargots. The *menus* (there's no à la carte service) cost 95FF (lunch only) and 145FF.

Self-Catering Near Place de l'Horloge, there is a boulangerie (open Monday to Saturday from 7.45 am to 7.30 pm) at 17 Rue Saint Agricol and a *Casino* grocery (open Monday to Saturday, closed 12.30 to 3.30 pm) at 22 Rue Saint Agricole. Avignon's fanciest food shops are along Rue Joseph Vernet and Rue Saint Agricol.

Bar The Australian-run *Koala Bar* (☎ 90.86.80.87), an extremely popular hangout for English speakers (including Aussie rugby league players brought in to play for Avignon), is at 2 Place des Corps Saints (literally 'square of the holy bodies', a name not intended to refer to the prostitutes who ply their trade around here). A demi on tap usually costs 9 to 11FF, but the price drops to an incredible 5FF during happy hour (9 to 10 pm on Wednesday, Friday and Saturday).

Entertainment
The only movie theatre in town with non-dubbed (v.o.) movies is Cinéma Utopia

(☎ 90.82.65.36), which has two screening halls at 15 Rue Galante and another one at 5 Rue Figuière. Tickets cost 29FF. *La Gazette Utopia*, the cinema's free booklet of schedules and film reviews, includes the films' original (ie untranslated) names. It is available at the tourist office, bookshops and other places around town.

The Opéra d'Avignon (☎ 90.82.42.42) at Place de l'Horloge stages operas, operettas, theatre, symphonic concerts, chamber music and ballet from October to June. Performance prices in the 4th gallery/orchestra range from 30/120FF to 90/360FF, depending on what's playing. The ticket office is open Monday to Saturday from 11 am to 6 pm except during August.

Getting There & Away

Bus The bus station (*halte routière*; (☎ 90.82.07.35) is down the ramp to the right as you exit the train station. The information windows are open Monday to Friday from 8 am to noon and 2 to 6 pm (5 pm on Friday), but don't count on getting much information. Tickets are sold on the buses, which are run by 19 different companies.

Places you can get to by bus include Aix-en-Provence (about 12 a day), Arles (four direct a day), Carpentras (about 15 a day), Nice (one a day), Nîmes (five a day), Orange (about 20 a day) and Marseilles (seven a day). Most lines run on Sunday, but much less frequently than during the rest of the week. A schedule is posted in the waiting room.

Train The train station (☎ 90.82.50.50) is across Blvd Saint Roch from Porte de la République, the gate to the walled city at the southern end of Cours Jean Jaurès. The information counters are open from 9 am to 6.45 pm daily except Sunday and public holidays. There are frequent trains to Arles (33FF; 20 to 25 minutes; 18 a day), Nice (196FF), Nîmes (41FF; 30 minutes; 15 a day) and Paris (342FF).

Car & Motorbike Location Vélos Minibus (☎ 90.85.56.63) at 11 Ave Monclar offers Renault R5s with unlimited km for 380FF a day and 600FF a weekend, including insurance. The office is open Monday to Friday from 9.30 am to noon and 3 to 6 pm. Locarplus (☎ 90.85.81.61) at 2A Ave Monclar has similar prices.

Getting Around

Municipal buses run from 7 am to about 7.40 pm. On Sunday, buses are less frequent, and most lines run only between 8 am to 6 pm.

AROUND AVIGNON

The Provençal cities of Arles and Nîmes, famed for their well-preserved Roman antiquities, are only a short train or bus ride from Avignon – see Getting There & Away under Avignon for transport details.

Arles

Arles (population 51,000), situated on the northern edge of the Camargue alluvial plain, began its ascent to prosperity and political importance in 49 BC, when Caesar (to whom the city had given its support) captured and despoiled Marseilles (which had backed Pompey). It soon became a major trading centre, the sort of place that, by the late 1st century AD, needed a 20,000-seat amphitheatre and a 12,000-seat theatre. Now known as the **Arènes** and the **Théâtre Antique** respectively, the two structures are still used to stage bullfights and cultural events. Arles is also known for its **Cathédrale Saint Trophime** and **Cloître Saint Trophime** – significant parts of both date from the 12th century and are in the Romanesque style.

Nîmes

The city of Nîmes (population 130,000) has some of the best preserved Roman structures in all of Europe. The **Arènes** (amphitheatre), which, unlike its counterpart at Arles, retains its upper storey, dates from around 100 AD. The rectangular **Maison Carrée** (literally, square house), a 26 by 15-metre Greek-style temple, looks much as it did in the late 1st century BC.

FRANCE

Côte d'Azur

The Côte d'Azur, also known as the French Riviera, stretches along France's Mediterranean coast from Toulon to Menton and the Italian border. Many of the towns along the coast – Saint Tropez, Cannes, Antibes, Nice, Monaco – have become world-famous thanks to the recreational activities of the rich, famous and tanned, especially as portrayed in films and in the tabloids. The reality is rather less glamorous than reputation alone would imply, but the Côte d'Azur still has a great deal to attract visitors: sun, 40 km of beaches, amazingly bronze people, all sorts of cultural activities and, sometimes, even a bit of glitter.

Unless you'll be camping or hostelling, your best bet is to stay in Nice, which has a generous supply of cheap hotels, and take day trips to other places in the area. Trains run between Ventimiglia (just across the border in Italy) and Saint Raphaël – via Menton, Monaco, Nice, Antibes, Cannes and many smaller towns – every few minutes from early morning until late at night. See Getting There & Away in the Nice section for details.

The Côte d'Azur includes many seafront and hillside towns: Toulon, Saint Tropez, the Massif of Esterel, Grasse (renowned for its perfume production), Antibes, Vence, Saint Paul de Vence, and so on. Unfortunately, there is not enough space to describe them in this chapter. You can easily explore them by hopping on a train or bus in Nice or Cannes.

Media

Radio The English-language Riviera Radio, based in Monte Carlo, can be heard on 106.3 MHz FM (in Monaco) and 106.5 MHz FM (along the rest of the Côte d'Azur). They broadcast BBC World Service news pretty much every hour.

Dangers & Annoyances

Theft from backpacks, pockets, cars and even launderettes is a serious problem along the Côte d'Azur. To avoid unpleasantness, keep a sharp eye on your bags, especially at train and bus stations; keep your wallet in a front pocket and handbags shielded from passers-by; use the lockers at train and bus

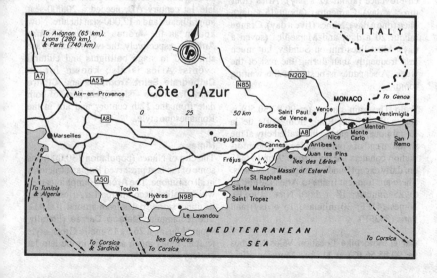

stations if you'll be sleeping outside (say, on the beach); and *never* leave anything in a parked vehicle. If you have any problems in Nice, call the police on (☎ 93.92.62.22) or stop by their headquarters at 1 Ave Maréchal Foch.

Getting Around

The Côte d'Azur is notorious for its traffic jams, so if you'll be driving along the coast, especially in summer, be prepared for slow going. Around Saint Tropez, for instance, it can sometimes take hours to move just a few km, which is why some of the truly wealthy have taken to reaching their seaside properties by helicopter.

NICE

Known as the capital of the Riviera, the fashionable but fairly relaxed city of Nice (population 338,000) makes a great base from which to explore the entire Côte d'Azur. The city, which became part of France in 1860, has plenty of relatively cheap accommodation and is only a short train or bus ride away from the rest of the Riviera. Nice's beach may be nothing to write home about, but the city is blessed with as fine an ensemble of museums as you'll find outside of Paris. And most of them are free!

Orientation

Ave Jean Médecin runs from near the train station to Place Masséna. The Promenade des Anglais (literally, the Promenade of the English) follows the curved beachfront from the city centre all the way to the airport, six km to the west. Old Nice (Vieux Nice) is the area delineated by the Quai des États-Unis, Blvd Jean Jaurès and the 92-metre hill known as Le Château. The neighbourhood of Cimiez, home of several very good museums, is north of the centre of town.

Information

Tourist Offices From July to September, the tourist office (☎ 93.87.07.07) at the train station is open Monday to Saturday from 8.45 am to 7 pm and on Sunday from 8.45 am to 12.30 pm and 2 to 6 pm. During the rest of the year, it's open Monday to Saturday from 8.45 am to 12.30 pm and 2 to 6 pm. The tourist office annexe (☎ 93.87.60.60) at 5 Ave Gustave V is open on weekdays from February to October from 8.45 am to 12.30 pm and 2 to 6 pm. During July and August, it is open on Saturday as well.

Travel Agencies Council Travel (☎ 93.82.23.33) is one block from the train station at 37bis Rue d'Angleterre. It's open weekdays from 9.30 am to 6.30 pm and Saturday from 9.30 am to 12.30 pm.

USIT Voyages (☎ 93.87.34.96), the Irish student travel outfit, is nearby at 10 Rue de Belgique.

Money Banque de France (☎ 93.13.54.00) at 14 Ave Félix Faure is open Monday to Friday from 8.45 am to 12.15 pm and 1.30 to 3.30 pm. There are numerous places where you can change money along Ave Jean Médecin near Place Masséna. The Banque Niçoise de Crédit at 17 Ave Jean Médecin has a 24-hour currency exchange machine. The Office Provençal Change (☎ 93.88.56.80) at 17 Ave Thiers (to the right as you exit the train station) offers less-than-optimal rates but is open every day of the year from 7 am to midnight.

American Express (☎ 93.87.29.82) at 11 Promenade des Anglais is open weekdays from 9 am to noon and 2 to 6 pm. During the summer (May to August) it is open weekdays from 9 am to 1 pm and 2 to 6 pm and on Saturday from 9 am to 1 pm.

Post The main post office, which will exchange foreign currency, is at 23 Ave Thiers, one block to the right as you exit the train station. It is open weekdays from 8 am to 7 pm and on Saturday from 8 am to noon. In the old city, there is a branch post office (☎ 93.80.71.00) at 2 Rue Louis Gassin.

Nice's postcode is 06000 north of Ave Jean Jaurès (including the train station area) and 06300 south and south-east of there (including the old city).

FRANCE

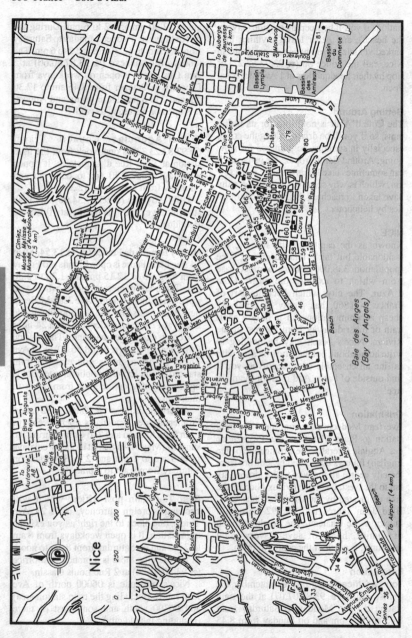

FRANCE

Nice

To Cimiez &
Musée Matisse &
Musée d'Archéologie
(1.5 km)

To Auberge de Jeunesse
(2.5 km)

To Monaco

To Autoroute

To Airport (4 km)

To Cannes

Baie des Anges
(Bay of Angels)

Beach

0   250   500 m

Bassin
Lympia

Bassin
des
Amiraux

Bassin
du
Commerce

Le Château

■	**PLACES TO STAY**	29	Prisunic Supermarket	35	Musée des Beaux-Arts
		31	Casino Supermarket	37	Public Showers &
1	Hôtel Jean Marie	50	Häagen Dazs Ice		Toilets
5	Let's Go Guest House		Cream	39	Musée Masséna
	Number 2	60	Express Minimarket	40	Cinéma Rialto
7	Let's Go Guest House	63	Hole-in-the-Wall	42	Rent-a-Car Système
8	Hôtel Astrid		Restaurant	43	American Express
9	Hôtel Regency	64	Nissa Socca	44	Anglican Church
10	Hôtel Pastoral		Restaurant	45	Tourist Office Annexe
11	Hôtel Darcy	65	Maison de La Pizza	46	Jardin Albert 1er
20	Hôtel Belle Munière	71	Food Shops (along	47	Place Grimaldi
21	Hôtel Les Orangers		Rue Pairolière)	48	Cycles Arnaud (Bicycle
24	Hôtel Idéal Bristol	72	Paul Michèle		Rental)
25	Hôtel Novelty			51	Place Masséna
32	Hôtel Soleil d'Or		**OTHER**	52	Banque de France
33	Les Collinettes			54	Local Bus Information
	University Dorms	2	Place Général de	55	Station Central (Local
	(Summer Hostel)		Gaulle		Bus Terminal)
36	Centre Hébergement	3	Gare du Sud (Railway	56	Square Général Leclerc
	Jeunes (Summer		Station)	57	Espace Masséna
	Hostel)	4	Musée Chagall	59	Opéra
38	Hôtel Negresco	12	Council Travel	60	Post Office
41	Hôtel Mimosa	15	Tourist Office	62	Place Pierre Gautier
49	Hôtel Little Masséna	16	Gare SNCF Nice Ville	66	Jonathan's Bar
53	Hôtels Acanthe &		(Railway Station)	67	William's Pub-Biererie
	Chauvain	17	Russian Orthodox	69	Place Saint François
58	Hôtel Meublé Genevois		Cathedral	70	Bus Station
61	Hôtel Meublé Confort	18	Main Post Office	73	Theatre
68	Hôtel Saint François	19	Office Provençal	74	Musée d'Art Moderne
			Change (Currency	75	Place Garibaldi
▼	**PLACES TO EAT**		Exchange)	76	Cinémas Mercury
		22	Nicea Location Rent	77	Cinémas Mercury
6	Les Cèdres du Liban		(Bike Rental)	78	Place Île de Beauté &
	Restaurant	23	USIT Travel Agency		Buses to Town
13	Cafétéria Casino	28	Église Notre Dame		Centre
14	Flunch Cafétéria	30	24-Hour Currency	79	Parc du Château
26	Restaurant Le Toscan		Exchange Machine	80	Lift
27	La Baraka Grocery	34	Musée des Beaux-Arts	81	Ferry Terminal

FRANCE

English Church The Anglican Church (☎ 93.87.19.83) at 11 Rue de la Buffa, which has a mixed American and English membership, functions as something of an Anglophone community centre. There are masses at 11 am on Sundays.

Things to See

Walking Tour The **Promenade des Anglais**, which runs along the Baie des Anges (Bay of Angels), provides a fine stage for a beachside stroll. Other attractive places to walk around include the Jardin Albert 1er, Espace Masséna (with its fountains) and Ave Jean Médecin (Nice's main commercial street).

On top of the 92-metre-high hill at the eastern end of the Quai des États-Unis is **Parc du Château** (open 8 am to 7 pm), a forested public park where local families come to walk, admire the panoramic view, visit the artificial waterfall and munch on snacks. There is a lift (3FF one-way, 4.40FF return) up the hill from under the Bellanda Tower. It runs from 9 am to 6.45 pm.

Musée d'Art Moderne One block northwest of Place Garibaldi, this museum (full name: Musée d'Art Moderne et d'Art Contemporain; ☎ 93.62.61.62) specialises in eye-popping French and American avant-garde works from the 1960s to the present. The building, inaugurated in 1990, is itself a work of modern art. The museum is open from 11 am to 6 pm (10 pm on Friday) daily except Tuesday. Admission is free. It is served by bus Nos 3, 5, 7, 16 and 17.

Musée Chagall The main exhibit of the Musée National Message Biblique Marc Chagall (☎ 93.81.75.75), across the street from 4 Ave Docteur Ménard, is a series of incredibly vivid paintings illustrating stories from the Old Testament. It is open from 10 am to 12.20 pm and 2 to 5.20 pm daily except Tuesday. From July to September, hours are 10 am to 6.50 pm. Entry costs about 25FF in summer (when there are special exhibits) and 17FF during the rest of the year. If you're 18 to 25, the fee is 15FF in summer and 9FF the rest of the year.

Musée Masséna The Musée Masséna (☎ 93.88.11.34), also known as the Musée d'Art et d'Histoire, has entrances at 35 Promenade des Anglais and 65 Rue de France. The eclectic collection of paintings, furniture, icons, ceramics and religious art can be viewed for free from 10 am to noon and 2 to 5 pm daily except Monday. From May to September, afternoon hours are 3 to 6 pm.

Musée des Beaux-Arts The Musée des Beaux-Arts (☎ 93.44.50.72) at 33 Ave des Baumettes, housed in a late 19th century villa just off Rue de France, is open from 10 am to noon and 2 to 5 pm daily except Monday. From May to September, afternoon hours are 3 to 6 pm. Admission is free.

Musée Matisse The newly renovated Musée Matisse (☎ 93.53.17.70), with its fine collection of works by Henri Matisse (1869-1954), is at 164 Ave des Arènes de Cimiez in Cimiez, 2.5 km north-east of the train station. It is open from 10 am to 6 pm daily except Monday. Entry is free. To get there, take bus

No 15, 17, 20 or 22 and get off at the Arènes stop.

Musée d'Archéologie The new Musée d'Archéologie (☎ 93.81.59.57) and the nearby **Gallo-Roman Ruins** (which include public baths and an ampitheatre) are near the Musée Matisse at 160 Ave des Arènes de Cimiez. The museum (free) and the baths (5FF or 2.50FF) are open from 10 am to noon and 2 to 5 pm (6 pm from May to September) daily except Sunday morning and Monday.

Russian Cathedral Saint Nicolas Russian Orthodox Cathedral (☎ 93.96.88.02), crowned by six onion domes, was built between 1903 and 1912 in the style of the early 17th century. Step inside and you'll be transported to Imperial Russia, a world of Cyrillic characters and gilded icons. The cathedral, opposite 17 Blvd Tzaréwitch, is open from 9 or 9.30 am to noon and 2.30 to 5 pm (5.30 pm in spring and autumn, from May to September). The entry fee is 12FF (8FF for students). Short shorts or skirts and sleeveless shirts are forbidden.

Activities

Nice's **beach** is great if you hate sand since it is covered with smooth little rocks, many of them the size and shape of hamburgers. Between mid-April and mid-October, the sections of beach open to the public without charge alternate with private beaches (40 to 60FF a day) offering all sorts of amenities (mattresses, showers, changing rooms, parasols, a reduced chance of theft, etc). Along the beach you can hire catamaran paddle boats (80FF an hour), sailboards (80FF an hour) and jet skis, and go parasailing (220FF for 10 minutes) and water skiing (120FF for 10 minutes). There are indoor showers (12FF) and toilets (2FF) open to the public opposite 50 Promenade des Anglais.

Places to Stay

In summer, lots of young people sleep on the beach, some because the hotels are full, others because it's free. This is theoretically illegal, but the Nice police usually look the other way.

Hostels The friendly and clean *Let's Go Guest House* (☎ 93.13.97.92), a favourite with backpackers, is on the 3rd floor at 22 Rue Pertinax. (It is upstairs from the peculiar *Abadie Guest House* (☎ 93.85.81.21 or 93.52.62.87), whose garrulous owner personally selects 'nice, smiling, clean' guests each morning at the train station). Dorm beds in Let's Go's mixed sex rooms cost 50FF; a double with shower is 110FF. The hostel is closed from noon to 6 pm (unless it's raining) but there's no curfew. Telephone reservations are not accepted. The same people run another *guesthouse* (☎ 93.80.98.00) with the same unfortunate name two blocks away in an unmarked building at 26 Blvd Raimbaldi (1st floor). Both places may be closed from mid-December to mid-January. The crowded and haphazardly managed *Hôtel Novelty* (☎ 93.87.51.73), near the train station at 26 Rue d'Angleterre, has dorm beds for 70FF.

The *Auberge de Jeunesse* (☎ 93.89.23.64) is five km east of the train station on the Route Forestière du Mont Alban. Beds cost 57FF and sheets are 15FF. There is an 11 pm curfew (midnight in summer). It's often full so call ahead before coming all the way out here; in summer, arrive by 10 am. If you don't want to walk, take bus No 14 from Square Général Leclerc, which is linked to the train station by bus Nos 5 and 17.

From mid-June to mid-September the *Centre Hébergement Jeunes* (☎ 93.86.28.75) serves as a hostel. It is at 31 Rue Louis de Coppet, half a block from 173 Rue de France. A bed in a six-bed room costs only 45FF, but if you don't have a YHA or student card you must buy an MJC card for 25FF. This place has several disadvantages: rooms are closed from 10 am to 6 pm, there is a midnight curfew and bags must be stored in the luggage room during the day.

Les Collinettes University Dorms (☎ 93.97.10.33) at 3 Ave Robert Schuman, 1.5 km west of the train station, will put up travellers of all ages during July and August.

A single (all they have) costs 90FF. This place is often full so phone ahead. Check-in is possible 24 hours a day. To get there from Rue de France, walk north on Ave Émile Henriot, which becomes Ave Robert Schuman. From the train station, take bus No 10, 23 or 24.

Hotels There are quite a few cheap hotels near the train station and lots of places in a slightly higher price bracket along Rue d'Angleterre, Rue d'Alsace-Lorraine, Rue de Suisse, Rue de Russie and Rue Durante, also near the station. For a good part of the year (Easter to September) the inexpensive places fill up by late morning – come by or call ahead by 10 am. Most overnight trains will get you in just in time to start looking.

Train Station Area The *Hôtel Idéal Bristol* (☎ 93.88.60.72), a friendly place popular with backpackers, is a block and a half southeast of the train station at 22 Rue Paganini. Doubles start at 134FF (174FF with shower and toilet). Rooms with shower and toilet for four/five people are 328/385FF. There's no charge for showers. You can lounge around or have a picnic on the rooftop terrace. The *Hôtel Belle Meunière* (☎ 93.88.66.15) at 21 Ave Durante, a clean, friendly place that attracts lots of young people, is also an excellent bet. Dorm beds are 50 to 77FF. Large doubles/triples with high ceilings, some with century-old décor or kitchenette, start at 114/171FF (169/251FF with shower and toilet). This place is closed in December and January. Down the block, the *Hôtel Les Orangers* (☎ 93.87.51.41) charges 80 to 85FF per person in large, plain rooms with shower, hotplate and fridge. The *Hôtel Darcy* (☎ 93.88.67.06) at 28 Rue d'Angleterre has singles/doubles for 130/160FF (175/210FF with shower and toilet). Prices are slightly higher from May to September.

The *Hôtel Pastoral* (☎ 93.85.17.22) is just off Ave Jean Médecin at 27 Rue Assalit (the 't' is pronounced). Large, simple singles/doubles with fridge start at 95/100FF; showers cost 10FF. Doubles with shower and

FRANCE

toilet are 160FF. Reception is open daily from 8 am to 3 pm and 6 to 8 pm.

The *Hôtel Astrid* (☎ 93.62.14.64), above the kosher restaurant at 26 Rue Pertinax, has clean, pleasant doubles/triples/quads with fridge for 140/210/280FF. Showers cost 10FF. Reception closes at 8 pm.

The *Hôtel Regency* (☎ 93.62.17.44) at 2 Rue Siagre has tacky but large, two-level studios with shower, toilet, kitchenette and fridge for two/three people for 150/180FF (180/260FF from May to September).

Old Nice The *Hôtel Saint François* (☎ 93.85.88.69 or 93.13.40.18) at 3 Rue Saint François has small singles from 75FF, doubles with one/two beds for 120/150FF and triples from 210FF. Showers cost 15FF.

Hôtel Meublé Genevois (☎ 93.85.00.58), in an unmarked building at 11 Rue Alexandre Mari (3rd floor), has 1950s-style singles/doubles with kitchenette from 90/110FF. Huge studios with shower and toilet are 130 to 200FF for three or four people. The *Hôtel Meublé Confort* (☎ 93.85.00.58), which is run by the same people and whose prices are similar, is down the block in an unmarked building at 17 Rue Alexandre Mari (4th floor). Both these places are near the Station Centrale local bus terminal – take No 5 (or any of several other lines) from the train station.

Elsewhere in Town The pink-domed *Hôtel Negresco* (☎ 93.88.39.51), along the water at 37 Promenade des Anglais, is Nice's fanciest hostelry. In the off season, rooms without a sea view start at 1200FF. A continental breakfast costs 100FF.

The *Hôtel Little Masséna* (☎ 93.87.72.34) is right in the centre of things at 22 Rue Masséna. Reception, which stays open until 7 pm, is on the 5th floor (yes, there's a lift). Doubles with hotplate and fridge range from 105 to 170FF; showers are free. The relaxed, family-style *Hôtel Mimosa* (☎ 93.88.05.59) is at 26 Rue de la Buffa (2nd floor), a block north of the Musée Masséna. Depending on the season, good-sized, utilitarian rooms cost 100 to 130FF for one person and 120 to

160FF for two. Showers cost 10FF. You can check in here 24 hours a day.

The *Hôtel Acanthe* (☎ 93.62.22.44) is half a block north of Espace Masséna at 2 Rue Chauvain. Half of their 50 rooms are singles/doubles costing 160/170FF; the other half have shower and toilet and cost 250FF. Hall showers are free. The *Hôtel Chauvain* (☎ 93.85.34.01) is nearby at 8 Rue Chauvain. Big, old-fashioned doubles start at 130FF, and showers cost 12FF. Reception stays open until 1 am.

The *Hôtel Soleil d'Or* (☎ 93.96.55.94) is 1.3 km south-west of the train station at 16 Ave des Orangers. Simple singles with high ceilings cost 75FF, doubles start at 104FF, and an extra bed costs 40FF. A shower will set you back 12FF. Doubles with shower and toilet are 180FF. This place is closed in November. The *Hôtel Jean Marie* (☎ 93.84.87.23) is 600 metres north of the train station at 15-17 Rue André Theuriet. The inconvenient location means that they may have rooms when other places are full. Dim but serviceable doubles (all they have) without/with shower start at 110/135FF. There are no hall showers, but you may be able to take a shower in an unrented room. Buses from Ave Jean Médecin include Nos 4 and 18.

Places to Eat
Restaurants Cheap places near the train station include the *Flunch Caféteria* (☎ 93.88.41.35), which is to the left as you exit the station building and is open daily from 11 am to 10 pm, and, across the street at 7 Ave Thiers, the *Caféteria Casino* (☎ 93.82.44.44), which serves breakfast from 7 to 11 am, lunch from 11 am to 2.30 pm and dinner from 6 to 10 pm.

In the same vicinity, *Restaurant Le Toscan* (☎ 93.88.40.54), a family-run Italian place at 1 Rue de Belgique, offers large portions of home-made ravioli, pasta or tripe from noon to 2 pm and 6.45 to 10 pm daily except Sunday. Both the 55 and 90FF *menus* let you choose from a wide selection of dishes. There are over a dozen Vietnamese and Chinese restaurants on Rue Paganini, Rue d'Italie and Rue d'Alsace-Lorraine. *Les Cèdres du Liban* (☎ 93.80.35.37) on the other side of Ave Jean Médecin, at 27 Blvd Raimbaldi, serves inexpensive Lebanese food in an informal atmosphere. It is open from 9 am to 10 pm daily except all-day Sunday and Friday before 4 pm.

In the old city, a perennial favourite with locals is *Nissa Socca* (☎ 93.80.18.35) at 5 Rue Sainte Reparate. Their Niçois specialities include *socca*, whose ingredients include chickpea flour and olive oil. Spaghetti and pasta dishes are 32 to 38FF. Nissa Socca is open daily except all day Sunday and Monday at midday. It is closed during January. Nearby streets, such as Rue de l'Abbaye, are lined with restaurants. *Maison de la Pizza* (☎ 93.85.45.39) at 12 Rue Mascoïnat (30 metres from Église Sainte Reparate) serves pizza, pasta and lasagna Monday to Saturday from noon to 3 pm and 7 to 11 pm. Their *menu* costs 60FF. For Niçois-style sandwiches (10 to 17FF), pizza (6 to 10FF per piece) and other takeaway dishes, you can't beat *Paul-Michèle* at 1 Rue Pairolière, which is open daily except Monday from 8 am to 9 pm.

The *Häagen Dazs* ice-cream place (☎ 93.88.64.69) at 2 Place Magenta, whose hours are daily from 11 am to at least 10 pm, dares to charge 13.50FF for one scoop.

Self-Catering The *Prisunic* supermarket across the street from 33 Ave Jean Médecin is open Monday to Saturday from 8.30 am to 7.15 pm (9 pm during July and August). Farther west, there is a *Casino* supermarket at 27 Blvd Gambetta. A few blocks southeast of the train station, *La Baraka* grocery at 10 Rue de Suisse is open daily except Tuesday from 3 pm to midnight.

In Old Nice, there are a number of food shops along Rue Pairolière, including a fromagerie (closed Sunday and Monday) at No 37, a boulangerie (closed Sunday afternoon and Monday) at No 30 and another boulangerie (closed Monday) at No 10. For fruit and vegetables, try the shop (closed Sunday afternoon) at No 26. The *Express Minimarket* at 2 Rue Louis Gassin is open

from 7 am to 12.30 pm and 4 to 7.30 pm daily except Sunday afternoon (and holiday afternoons).

Entertainment

Two cinemas offer v.o. films, many of them in English. The 10-screen *Cinémas Mercury* (☎ 93.55.32.31 for a recorded message in French) are in contiguous buildings at 12 and 16 Place Garibaldi. Regular tickets are 35 or 37FF. Students pay 25FF from Tuesday to Friday. Everyone gets in for 25FF on Monday. *Cinéma Rialto* (☎ 93.88.08.41) at 4 Rue de Rivoli, is slightly more expensive.

William's Pub-Biererie (☎ 93.85.84.66), opposite the bus station at 4 Rue Centrale, has live rock music every night except Sunday starting at around 10 pm. The pub itself is open Monday to Saturday from 6 pm to 2.30 am. There's pool, darts and chess in the basement. A demi on tap costs 15FF. *Jonathan's*, another bar à musique just down Rue Centrale from Ave Jean Jaurès, has live music (country, boogie-woogie, Irish folk, etc) every night except Monday. Bottles of beer and soft drinks are 22 to 30FF.

Hole-in-the-Wall Restaurant at 3 Rue de l'Abbaye is both a place to eat and a place to hear live music. Open from 8 pm to midnight nightly except Monday, this place has main dishes for 35 to 65FF and the famous salade niçoise for 38FF. Beer (in bottles) is 22 to 28FF.

Getting There & Away

Air Nice's airport, Aéroport International Nice-Côte d'Azur, six km west of the centre of town, is the second-busiest in France. To get there from the bus station or the Promenade des Anglais, take the bus which has as its symbol an airplane with its nose pointed upwards (20FF). From the train station or Rue de France, take bus No 23 (8FF).

Bus Lines operated by some two dozen bus companies stop at the bus station, which is opposite 10 Blvd Jean Jaurès. The helpful information counter (☎ 93.85.61.81) is open Monday to Saturday from 8 am to 6.30 pm. There is slow but frequent service every day

FRANCE

until about 7.30 pm to Cannes (26FF one-way; 1½ hours), Antibes (22FF one-way; 1¼ hours), Monaco (18.50FF return; 45 minutes), Menton (24FF return; 1¼ hours) and Grasse (31FF one-way). Student discounts are not applicable for travel within the Alpes Maritimes department.

Train The train station, Gare SNCF Nice Ville (☎ 93.87.50.50), is on Ave Thiers about 1.2 km from the beach. There is fast, frequent service (up to 40 trains a day in each direction) to points all along the coast, including Monaco (15FF, 20 to 25 minutes), Antibes (19FF, 24 minutes) and Cannes (28FF, 35 minutes). From June to September there are trains every 20 minutes between 5 am and 11 or 11.30 pm. The rest of the year trains run at least once an hour. Two of the three overnight trains to Paris (Gare de Lyon) are sleepers, for which a 82FF supplement must be paid even if you have a Eurail pass. Second-class tickets cost 250FF to Rome and 337FF to Barcelona.

Ferry The fastest and least expensive ferries from mainland France to Corsica depart from Nice (see Getting There & Away in the Corsica section). The SNCM office (☎ 93.13.66.66) on Quai du Commerce (at the ferry port) is open from 8 am to noon and 2 to 5.45 pm daily except Saturday afternoon and Sunday. From mid-June to September, weekday hours are 6 am to 8 pm and Saturday hours are 6 am to noon. SNCM tickets can be purchased at many travel agencies. To get to the ferry port from Ave Jean Médecin, take bus No 1 or 2 and get off at Quai Cassini.

Getting Around

Bus Local buses cost 8FF for a single ride. Bus No 12 links the train station with the beach. To go from the train station to Old Nice and the bus station, take bus No 17. Bus information and one, five and seven-day passes are available at the Centre d'Information (☎ 93.62.08.08), 10 Ave Félix Faure (next to the Station Central, the main terminal for municipal buses).

Taxi Call ☎ 93.80.70.70 to order a taxi.

Car Rent-a-Car Système (☎ 93.87.87.37) at 25 Promenade des Anglais rents Fiat Pandas for 268FF a day, including insurance and unlimited km. The excess is 900FF (for 199FF a day, the excess is an outrageous 8000FF!). The office is open daily from 8 am to 12.30 pm and 1.30 to 7 pm.

Bicycle & Motorbike Bicycles (120FF a day), mopeds (from 150FF a day), scooters and motorcycles can be hired from Nicea Location Rent (☎ 93.82.42.71) at 9 Ave Thiers, which is open daily from 9 am to 6.30 pm. From November to February, it's closed on Sunday. Cycles Arnaud (☎ 93.87.88.55) at 4 Place Grimaldi has bicycles for 90FF a day and 80 cc scooters for 250FF a day. It is open Monday to Friday from 9 am to 6.30 pm.

CANNES

It is the money of the affluent, spent with fashionable nonchalance, that keeps Cannes' many expensive hotels, fancy restaurants, exorbitant boutiques and yachts the size of ocean-liners afloat. It may be true that the well-heeled are, for the most part, boring (or at least predictable), especially when they are on holiday, but watching people whose lunch hors-d'oeuvre cost more than this guidebook has its fascinations. In any case, the harbour, the bay, Le Suquet Hill, the beachside promenade, the beaches and the people sunning themselves provide more than enough natural beauty to make at least a day trip well worth the effort.

Cannes is famous for its many festivals and cultural activities, the most renowned of which is the International Film Festival, which runs for two weeks in mid-May. People come to Cannes all year long but the season runs from May to October.

Orientation

Rue Jean Jaurès, which runs in front of the train station, is four or five blocks north of the huge Palais des Festivals et des Congrès, to the west of which is the old port (vieux port). Place de l'Hôtel de Ville is at the north-west corner of the old port. Cannes' most famous promenade, the magnificent, hotel-lined Blvd de la Croisette, begins at the Palais des Festivals and continues eastward around the Baie de Cannes to Pointe de la Croisette.

Information

Tourist Office The main tourist office (☎ 93.39.24.53) is on the ground floor of the Palais des Festivals, which is at the western end of Blvd de la Croisette. It is open Monday to Saturday from 9 am to 6.30 pm and, during festivals and conventions, on Sunday as well. During July and August, the office is open daily from 9 am to 8 pm. The tourist office annexe (☎ 93.99.19.77) at the train station is open from 9 am to 12.30 pm and 2 to 6 pm. In July and August, it opens half an hour earlier and closes half an hour later. To get there, go left as you exit the terminal building and then walk up the stairs next to Frantour Tourisme. Be prepared for long queues in the summer.

Money There are banks along Rue d'Antibes (two blocks towards the beach from Rue Jean Jaurès) and on Rue Buttura (across Blvd de la Croisette from the main tourist office). American Express (☎ 93.38.15.87) at 8 Rue des Belges (two blocks north-east of the Palais des Festivals) is open from 9 am to noon and 2 to 6 pm daily except Saturday afternoon and Sunday.

Post The post office at 22 Rue Bivouac Napoléon (two blocks inland from the Palais des Festivals) is open weekdays from 8 am to 7 pm and on Saturday from 8 am to noon. It will exchange foreign currency.

Cannes' postcode is 06400.

Things to See

Walking Tour Since people-watching is the main reason to come to Cannes, and people are best watched while you're strolling, and strolling is one of the few activities in Cannes that doesn't cost anything, taking a leisurely

walk is highly recommended. The best places to walk are not far from the water.

Some of the largest yachts you've ever seen are likely to be sitting in the **old port**, which was once a fishing port but is now given over to pleasure craft. The streets around the old port are particularly pleasant on a summer's night after dark, when the many cafés and restaurants – overflowing with smiling, laughing patrons in fashionable casual wear – light up the whole area with coloured neon signs.

The hill just west of the old port, **Le Suquet**, affords spectacular views of Cannes, especially in the late afternoon and on clear nights. Musée de la Castre (see following) is at the summit.

The pine and palm-shaded walkway along **Blvd de la Croisette** is probably the classiest promenade on the whole Riviera.

Beaches Each of the fancy hotels that line Blvd de la Croisette has its own private section of the beach, where the beachside equivalent of room service is available for those willing to pay 60FF to have a serving of fresh melon delivered to their deck chair! From the promenade you can catch glimpses of people so bronzed by the sun that they'd be perfectly camouflaged among the red rocks of the Corniche de l'Esterel. Unfortunately, this arrangement leaves only a small strip of sand near the Palais des Festivals for the bathing pleasure of the public.

Free public beaches, the **Plages du Midi** and **Plages de la Bocca**, stretch for several km westward from the old port along Blvd Jean Hibert and Blvd du Midi.

Musée de la Castre The Musée de la Castre (☎ 93.38.55.26), housed in the chateau atop Le Suquet hill, has a diverse collection of Mediterranean and Middle Eastern antiquities as well as objects of ethnographic interest from all over the world. The museum, which costs only 3FF (and is free on Sunday and Wednesday), is open from 10 am to noon and 2 to 5 pm daily except Tuesday. In May, June and September, after-

FRANCE

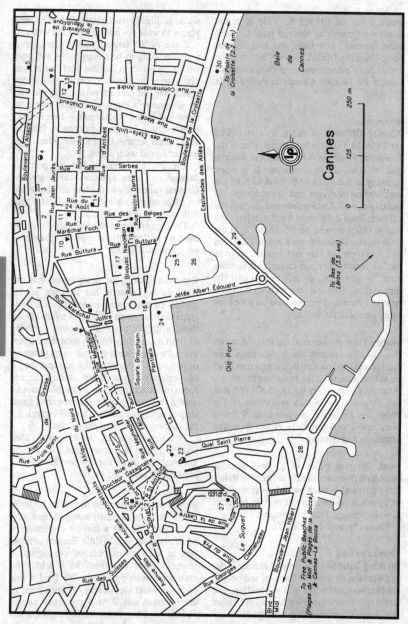

Cannes

Baie de Cannes

To Pointe de la Croisette (2.2 km)

To Îles de Lérins (3.5 km)

Boulevard de la République

Boulevard d'Alsace

Rue Commandant André

Rue Chabaud

Rue Macé

Rue Hoche

Rue Jean Jaurès

Rue d'Antibes

Rue des Serbes

Boulevard de la Croisette

Rue des États-Unis

Rue du 24 Août

Rue Notre Dame

Rue des Belges

Rue Maréchal Foch

Rue Buttura

Rue Bivouac Napoléon

Esplanades des Alliés

Jetée Albert Édouard

Old Port

Square Brougham

Rue Maréchal Joffre

Rue Pantiero

Avenue de Grasse

Rue du Nord

Rue Louis Blanc

Avenue Louis Blanc

Rue Félix Faure

Rue Meynadier

Quai Saint Pierre

Rue des Combattants en Afrique

Rue Docteur Gazagnaire

Rue St-Antoine

Rue du Suquet

Rue Louis Perissol

Le Suquet

Rue de la Castre

Rue du Pré

Clemenceau

Rue Georges

Avenue des Suisses

Rue des Suisses

Boulevard Jean Hibert

Blvd du Midi

To Free Public Beaches (Plages du Midi & Plages de la Bocca) & Cannes–La Bocca

0   125   250 m

■	**PLACES TO STAY**	13	Morning Food Market	18	American Express
		15	Marché Forville	19	Post Office
5	Pension Les Glycines	21	Restaurants	22	Place de l'Hôtel de Ville
9	Hôtel National			23	Bus Station (to Nice)
11	Hôtel de Bourgogne		**OTHER**	24	Société Cannoise Maritime (Ferries to the Îles de Lérins)
14	Hôtel Atlantis				
20	Hôtel Chanteclair	1	Place du 18 Juin		
		2	Railway Station	25	Tourist Office
▼	**PLACES TO EAT**	3	Tourist Office Annexe	26	Palais des Festivals et des Congrès
		4	Bus Station (to Grasse)		
6	Boulangerie	12	Place Gambetta	27	Musée de la Castre
7	Food Shops	16	Place Général de Gaulle	28	Square Jean Hibert
8	Champion Supermarket			29	Public Beach
10	Monoprix Supermarket	17	Cannes English Bookshop	30	Plages de la Croisette (Private Beaches)

noon hours are 2 to 6 pm; during July and August, they're 3 to 7 pm.

Îles de Lérins The eucalyptus and pine-covered **Île Sainte Marguerite**, where the Man in the Iron Mask (made famous in the novel by Alexandre Dumas) was held during the late 17th century, lies 1.1 km from the mainland. The island, which measures 3.2 by 0.95 km, is criss-crossed and circumnavigated by many trails and paths. The smaller **Île Saint Honorat** (1.5 by 0.4 km) was once the site of a renowned and powerful monastery founded in the 5th century.

The Société Cannoise Maritime (SCM; ☎ 93.99.62.01) runs ferries to Île Saint Honorat (40FF return, 20 minutes) and Île Sainte Marguerite (35FF return, 20 minutes). Both islands can be visited for 50FF. The ticket office, which is at the old port across Jetée Albert Édouard from the Palais des Festivals, is open daily from 8.30 am to 12.15 pm and 2 to 6 pm. From early May to August, it is open from 8.30 am to 6 pm (9.30 pm three nights a week in July and August).

Places to Stay
Hotel prices in Cannes fluctuate wildly according to seasonal demand. Tariffs can be up to 50% higher and in July and August – when you'll be lucky to find a room at any price – than in the dead of winter. There are no hostels in Cannes. During the film festival

(mid-May), all the hotels are booked up to a year in advance.

Hotels Cannes should have more places like the *Hôtel Chanteclair* (☎ 93.39.68.88) at 12 Rue Forville. This friendly hotel, a favourite with backpackers, has singles/doubles for between 130/150FF (mid-October to mid-April) and 160/220FF (during the film festival and from mid-July to mid-August). Showers are free. Two-wheeled conveyances can be parked in the courtyard. To get there, walk north-west from Place de l'Hôtel de Ville on Rue Docteur Gazagnaire and take the second left. The *Hôtel National* (☎ 93.39.91.92) at 8 Rue Maréchal Joffre has doubles starting at 150FF (220FF in the high season). To get there from the train station, follow Rue Jean Jaurès to the right until you get to Place du 18 Juin and turn left onto Rue Maréchal Joffre.

The large *Hôtel Atlantis* (☎ 93.39.18.72) is half a block south of the train station at 4 Rue du 24 Août. Despite their two-star rating, they have singles/doubles with TV for only 147/168FF in the low season. The price of a double shoots up to 210FF during festival periods and in July and August. The *Hôtel de Bourgogne* (☎ 93.38.36.73) at 13 Rue du 24 Août has singles/doubles for 170FF in the summer and 154/176FF in the off season. Showers cost 20FF.

Pension Les Glycines (☎ 93.38.41.28) at

32 Blvd d'Alsace, an old place across the train tracks from the train station, has singles/doubles from 120/150FF. A huge triple/quad costs 170/300FF from September to April and 300FF the rest of the year. Showers are 7FF.

Places to Eat

Restaurants Cheap dining is not Cannes' strong point. There are a few small, cheap restaurants around the Marché Forville (a block north of Place de l'Hôtel de Ville) and many little (but not necessarily cheap) restaurants along Rue Saint Antoine, which runs north-west from the Place de l'Hôtel de Ville.

Self-Catering Square Brougham, next to the old port, is a great place for a picnic.

There's a *Monoprix* supermarket with an in-house bakery at 9 Rue Maréchal Foch, half a block towards the beach from the train station. As you exit the terminal building, turn right and then left onto Rue Maréchal Foch. It is open from 8.45 am to 7 pm (till 7.30 pm from June to September) daily except Sunday. If you turn left along Rue Jean Jaurès as you exit the train station you soon get to Place Gambetta, where there is a morning food market every day except Monday (and daily during the summer). A number of food shops are in the immediate vicinity, including a boulangerie (closed Tuesday) at 9 Rue Jean Jaurès.

There is a *Champion* supermarket, open Monday to Saturday from 8.30 am to 7.45 pm, at 6 Rue Meynadier, a pedestrian mall two blocks inland from the old port. Other food shops along Rue Meynadier include boulangeries at No 18 and No 48 and fromageries at No 22 and No 56. One block north of Place de l'Hôtel de Ville along Rue Gazagnaire is the *Marché Forville*, a fruit and vegetable market which is open every morning except Monday.

Getting There & Away

Bus Buses to Nice (26FF one-way; 1½ hours), Nice's airport (65FF one-way; 40 minutes) and other destinations, most of them operated by Rapides Côte d'Azur, leave from Place de l'Hôtel de Ville. The bus information office (☎ 93.39.11.39) is open Monday to Saturday from 8 am to noon and 2 to 6 pm and on Sunday from 8 am to 2 pm. No student discounts are available.

Buses to Grasse (line No 600), Vallauris, Valbonne and elsewhere depart from the bus station, which is to the left as you exit the train station. The information counter (☎ 93.39.31.37) is open from 9 am to noon and 2 to 6.30 pm daily except Wednesday, Sunday and holidays.

Train The train station (☎ 93.99.50.50 for information, 93.88.89.93 for reservations) is five blocks inland from the Palais des Festivals on Rue Jean Jaurès. The information office (on the 1st floor over the left-luggage office) is open daily from 8.30 am to noon and 2 to 6 pm. Opening hours are 8.30 am to 6.45 pm from mid-July to mid-September.

Getting Around

Bus Bus Azur buses serve Cannes and destinations up to about seven km from town. Their office (☎ 93.39.18.71) at Place de l'Hôtel de Ville, in the same building as Rapides Côte d'Azur, is open daily from 7 am to 7.30 pm.

Taxi Call ☎ 93.38.30.79 to order a taxi.

MENTON

Menton, reputed to be the warmest spot on the Côte d'Azur (especially during the winter), is only a few km from the Italian frontier. In part because of the weather, Menton is popular with older vacationers, whose life style and preferences have made the town a particularly tranquil – some would say boring – and well-heeled corner of the Riviera.

Menton is renowned for its production of lemons and holds a two-week Lemon Festival (Fête des Citrons) that begins every year on Shrove Tuesday (sometime between mid-February and early March).

Orientation

The Promenade du Soleil runs more or less east-west along the beach. The train tracks run more or less east-west about 400 metres inland. Ave Boyer and Ave de Verdun (on either side of the wide centre strip) run perpendicular to both the Promenade du Soleil and the railway tracks. The old city (Vieille Ville) is on and around the hill at the eastern end of the Promenade du Soleil. The port is east of the old city.

Information

The tourist office (☎ 93.57.57.00) is in the Palais de l'Europe at 8 Ave Boyer. It is open Monday to Saturday from 8.30 am to 12.30 pm and 2 to 6.30 pm. From sometime in June to mid-September, the office is open from 8.30 am to 7.30 pm every day except Sunday, when the hours are 9.30 am to 12.30 pm.

Things to See

The **beach** along the Promenade du Soleil is public and, like Nice's, is carpeted with smooth little rocks. More beaches lie east of the old city in the pleasure port area.

Église Saint Michel, the grandest Baroque church in this part of France, sits perched in the centre of the **old city**, with its many narrow and winding passageways. The church is open from 10 am to noon and 3 to 6 pm except on Saturday mornings. The ornate interior is Italian in inspiration. Farther up the hill is the cypress-shaded **Cimetière du Vieux Château**, which is open from 7 am to 6 pm (8 pm from May to September). Graves of English, Irish, North Americans, New Zealanders and other foreigners who died here during the 19th century can be seen in the cemetery's southwest corner (along the road called Montée du Souvenir). The view is worth the climb. The **Musée Jean Cocteau** (☎ 93.57.72.30) is near the old city on Quai de Monléon. It is open from 10 am to noon and 2 to 6 pm daily except Tuesday; afternoon hours are 3 to 7 pm from mid-June to mid-September. Entry is free.

Places to Stay

Camping Menton's *Camping Saint Michel* (☎ 93.35.81.23; open from April to October) on Route des Ciappes de Castellar is best reached by walking eastward from the bus and train stations along Chemin des Terres Chaudes, which runs along the north side of the train tracks; turn left at the end. Tariffs are 12FF per person, 12FF for a tent and 12FF for a car.

Camping Fleur de Mai (☎ 93.57.22.36) at 67 Vallée de Gorbio, two km west of the train station, is open from late March or early April to September. The charge for two people with a car and a small tent is 68FF. The simplest way to get there is to walk westward on the street one block inland from the Promenade du Soleil, and then turn right onto Ave Florette, which becomes Route de Gorbio. Both camping grounds have a two-star rating and are open from April to sometime in October.

Hostels The *Auberge de Jeunesse* (☎ 93.35.93.14) on Plateau Saint Michel (the hill north-east of the train station) is reached by Route des Ciappes de Castellar. There may be a minibus from the bus station. Beds cost 60FF with breakfast. Daytime closure is from 10 am to 5 pm. The hostel is closed between mid-December and mid-January. There is a midnight curfew. Between 7 am and 7 pm, you can get to the hostel from the train station by minibus. This privately run service operates something like a shared taxi.

Hotels *Hôtel Le Terminus* (☎ 93.35.77.00) at Place de la Gare (opposite the train station) has a few basic singles/doubles for 112/120FF. Showers are free. Reception is closed after 11 am on Saturday and after 5 pm on Sunday. The hotel is closed from mid-October to mid-November. The *Hôtel de Belgique* (☎ 93.35.72.66) at 1 Ave de la Gare has singles/doubles from 167/241FF, including the obligatory breakfast. This place is closed in November.

Places to Eat

The *Marché Municipal*, also known as Les

Halles, is in the old city on Quai de Monléon. Food of all sorts is on sale daily from 5 am to 1 pm.

Getting There & Away

Bus The bus station is next to 12 Promenade Maréchal Leclerc, the northern continuation of Ave Boyer. The information office is open from 8 am to noon and 2 to 6 pm daily except Saturday afternoon and Sunday.

Train The information desk at the train station, which is at Place de la Gare, is open on weekdays from 8 am to noon and 2 to 6.30 pm and on weekends from 8.30 am to noon and 2 to 6 pm. See Getting There & Away in the Nice section for more information.

Ave Édouard VII links the train station with the beach. Ave Boyer, where the tourist office is, is 200 metres west of the station along Ave de la Gare.

Monaco

The Principality of Monaco, which has been under the rule of the Grimaldi family for most of the period since 1297, is a sovereign state whose territory, surrounded by France, covers only 1.95 sq km. It has been ruled since 1949 by Prince Rainier III (born in 1923), whose sweeping constitutional powers make him far from merely a figurehead. The citizens of Monaco (Monégasques in French), of whom there are only about 4500 (out of a total population of 28,000), pay no taxes. The official language is French, although efforts are being made to revive the country's traditional dialect. The official religion is Catholicism. There are no border formalities upon entering Monaco.

Despite all of the things people always complain about – the border-to-border highrises, the huge number of tourists, the principality's unabashed preference for wealthy visitors – there's still something magical and exhilarating about walking around Monaco and watching it twinkle at night. Given the principality's undeniable charms and the quality of several of its museums, a visit to Monaco makes a perfect day trip from Nice.

Orientation

Monaco consists of four principal areas: Monaco Ville, a 60-metre-high outcrop of rock 800 metres long (also known as the old city and the Rocher de Monaco), located south of the Port of Monaco; Monte Carlo, famed for its casino and annual Grand Prix motor race (held in late May), located north of the port; La Condamine, the flat area around the port; and Fontvieille, an industrial area south-west of Monaco Ville and the Port of Fontvieille. The French town of Beausoleil is just north of Monte Carlo.

Information

Tourist Office The Office National de Tourisme (☎ 93.50.60.88) is at 2a Blvd des Moulins, which is across the public gardens from the casino. It is open Monday to Saturday from 9 am to 7 pm, and Sunday 10 am to noon. From mid-June to mid-September, there are several tourist office kiosks around the principality, including one at the railway station, another next to the Jardin Exotique and another on the Quai des États-Unis, which runs along the north side of the port.

Money The currency of Monaco is the French franc. Both French and Monégasque coins are in circulation but the latter are not widely accepted outside the principality.

In Monte Carlo, you'll find lots of banks in the vicinity of the casino (along Ave Princesse Alice, for instance). In La Condamine, try Blvd Albert 1er. American Express (☎ 93.25.74.45) is near the tourist office at 35 Blvd Princesse Charlotte. It is open on weekdays from 9 am to noon and 2 to 6 pm and on Saturday from 9 am to noon.

Post & Telecommunications Monégasque stamps, one of the principality's few symbols of independence, are valid only within Monaco. Postal rates are the same as in

France. Monaco's public telephones accept either Monégasque or French télécartes.

The main post office (☎ 93.25.11.11) is in Monte Carlo at 1 Ave Henri Dunant (inside the Palais de la Scala). It is open weekdays from 8 am to 7 pm and on Saturday from 8 am to noon. They do not exchange foreign currency. Other post offices are at Place de la Visitation in Monaco, near the Musée Océanographique, and near the train station (look for the sign of the Hôtel Terminus).

Monaco's French postcode is 98000.

Things to See

Palais du Prince The changing of the guard takes place outside the Palais du Prince de Monaco (☎ 93.25.18.31) every day at precisely 11.55 am. The guards, who carry out their duties of state in spiffy dress uniforms (white in summer, black in winter), are apparently resigned to the comic-opera nature of their circumstance. From June to October *only*, about 15 rooms in the palace are open to the public every day from 9.30 am to 6.10 pm (10 am to 5 pm in October). The entry fee is 25FF (12FF for children and students). Thirty-minute guided visits in English leave every 15 or 20 minutes.

Musée des Souvenirs Napoléoniens Located in the south wing of the Palais du Prince, this museum displays some of Napoleon's personal effects (handkerchiefs, a sock, etc) and a fascinating collection of the sort of bric-a-brac (medals, coins, swords, uniforms) that princely dynasties collect over the centuries. The museum, which costs 15FF (7FF for children and perhaps students), is open daily except Mondays. Tickets are sold from 10.30 am to 12.30 pm and 2 to 4.30 pm. From June to September, they're on sale are from 9.30 am to 6.30 pm.

Musée Océanographique If you're going to go to one aquarium on your whole trip, the world-renowned Musée Océanographique de Monaco (☎ 93.15.36.00) should be it. The fish living in the sea-water aquariums (about 90 of them) can only be described in super-

latives: the bluest, the spiniest, the frilliest, the pink-and-yellowest, the one you'd least like to meet in a back alley in Chicago at 2 am... Upstairs are all sorts of exhibits on ocean exploration. The museum, which is on Ave Saint Martin in Monaco Ville, is open daily from 9 or 9.30 am to 7 pm (9 pm in July and August). The entry fee (brace yourself!) is 50FF (25FF for students).

Walk around the Rock The touristy streets and alleys facing the palace are surrounded by beautiful, shaded gardens affording great views of the entire principality (as well as a good bit of France and some of Italy too).

Jardin Exotique The steep slopes of the wonderful Jardin Exotique (☎ 93.30.33.65), which is at one end of the No 2 bus line, are home to some 7000 varieties of cacti and succulents from all over the world. The spectacular view is worth at least half the admission fee of 32FF (16FF for students), which also gets you into the **Musée d'Anthropologie Préhistorique** (part of the Jardin Exotique) and also includes a half-hour guided visit to the **Grottes de l'Observatoire**, stalactite and stalagmite caves located 279 steps down the hillside. The garden is open daily from 9 am until 5 pm (in December), 5.30 pm (in November and January), 6 pm (in October, February and March), 6.30 pm (in September and April) and 7 pm (from May to August).

Casino The drama of watching people risk their money in Monte Carlo's spectacularly ornate casino (☎ 93.50.69.31), built between 1878 and 1910, makes visiting the gaming rooms almost worth the stiff entry fees: 50FF for the Salon Ordinaire (which has French roulette and trente-quarante) and 100FF for the Salons Privés (which offer baccarat, blackjack, craps, American roulette, etc). You must be at least 21 to enter. Short shorts are forbidden in the Salon Ordinaire. For the Salons Privés, men must wear tie and jacket after 9 pm. Income from gambling accounts for 4.3% of Monaco's total state revenues.

FRANCE

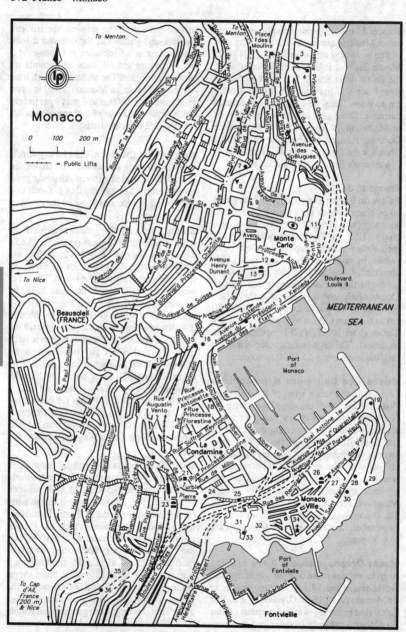

Monaco

0   100   200 m

= Public Lifts

To Menton

To Menton

Place des Moulins

Beausoleil (FRANCE)

To Nice

Monte Carlo

Avenue Henry Dunant

MEDITERRANEAN SEA

Port of Monaco

Rue Augustin Vento

La Condamine

Quai Albert 1er

Quai Antoine 1er

Monaco Ville

To Cap d'Ail, France (200 m) & Nice

Port of Fontvieille

Fontvieille

1	Plage du Larvotto (Beach)	13	Main Post Office	25	Rampe Major (Path to Palais du Prince)
2	Public Lift	14	CAM (Local Bus Company) Office	26	Post Office
3	Musée National (Dolls & Automatons Museum)	15	Public Lift	27	Place de la Visitation
		16	Place Sainte Dévote	28	Public Lift to Parking des Pêcheurs
4	Public Lift	17	Public Lift	29	Parking des Pêcheurs
5	Hôtel Cosmopolite (Beausoleil)	18	Monaco Market Super-market	30	Musée Océanographique
6	Public Lift	19	Fort Antoine	31	Palais du Prince
7	American Express	20	Youth Hostel	32	Place du Palais
8	Codec Top Supermar-ket	21	Hôtel Cosmopolite (La Condamine) & Hôtel de France	33	Musée des Souvenirs Napoléoniens
9	Tourist Office	22	Railway Station	34	Cathedral
10	Place du Casino	23	Post Office	35	Jardin Exotique & Musée Préhistorique
11	Casino of Monte Carlo	24	Place d'Armes & Food Market	36	Public Lift
12	Square Beaumarchais				

Places to Stay

There are no cheap places to stay in Monaco. Less expensive accommodation is scarce and often full. Over three-quarters of Monaco's hotel rooms are classified as 'four-star deluxe'.

Hostel The *Centre de la Jeunesse Princesse Stéphanie* (☎ 93.50.83.20), Monaco's youth hostel, is at 24 Ave Prince Pierre, 120 metres up the hill from the train station. You must be aged between 16 and 30 to stay here, and officially anyone over 26 must also be a student. The cost is 60FF per person, including breakfast and sheets. Stays are usually limited to one night during the summer. Beds are given out each morning on a first-come first-served basis – numbered tickets are distributed from 9 am or even earlier. Registration begins at 10.30 am.

Hotels The clean, pleasant *Hôtel Cosmopolite* (☎ 93.30.16.95) at 4 Rue de la Turbie in La Condamine was recently renovated. It still has some of the cheapest rooms in the principality, though the prices are a lot more than you would pay in Nice. Singles/doubles with shower, toilet and TV cost 240/270FF at another, unrelated *Hôtel Cosmopolite* (☎ 93.78.36.00), at 19 Blvd Maréchal Leclerc in Beausoleil, which is up the hill

from the casino. The even-numbered side of the street is in Monaco and is called Blvd de France. The nearest bus stop is Crémaillère, which is served by bus Nos 2 and 4.

The *Hôtel de France* (☎ 93.30.24.64) at 6 Rue de la Turbie has singles/doubles/triples with shower, toilet and TV for 255/310/370FF.

Places to Eat

There are a few cheap restaurants in La Condamine along Rue de la Turbie.

The *Codec Top* supermarket opposite 33 Blvd Princesse Charlotte, a block from the main tourist office, is open from 8.30 am to 12.15 pm and 3 to 7.15 pm daily except Sunday. It has an in-house bakery. In La Condamine, there is a morning food market every day at Place d'Armes and a *Monaco Market* supermarket on Blvd Albert 1er at the corner of Rue Princesse Antoinette. It is open Monday to Thursday from 8.45 am to 12.30 pm and 2.45 to 7.30 pm, on Friday from 8.45 am to 7.30 pm and on Saturday from 9 am to 7 pm.

Getting There & Away

Bus There is no single bus station in Monaco – intercity buses leave from various points around the city.

Train The train station, which is part of the French national railway network, is on Ave Prince Pierre. See Getting There & Away in the Nice section for more information.

Getting Around

Bus Monaco's urban bus system has six lines. You're most likely to use line No 2, which links Monaco Ville with Monte Carlo and then loops back to the Jardin Exotique. Rides cost 7.50FF, which is pretty steep given how small the country is. Four/eight-ride magnetic cards are on sale from bus drivers for 16.50/26.50FF. The bus system operates every day until 8.45 or 9 pm; bus maps are available at the tourist office. The bus company, Compagnie des Autobus de Monaco (CAM; ☎ 93.50.62.41 for information), has offices at 3 Ave Président John F Kennedy, on the north side of the port.

Lifts Six large public lifts (ascenceurs publics) run up and down the hillside (see the Monaco map). They operate from 6 am to 10 pm.

Taxis Taxis can be ordered by calling ☎ 93.15.01.01 or 93.50.56.28.

Corsica

Corsica (Corse) is the most mountainous and geographically diverse of all the islands of the Mediterranean. Though only 8720 sq km in extent, it in many ways resembles a miniature continent, with 1000 km of coastline, soaring granite mountains that stay snow-capped until July, a huge national park (the Parc Naturel Régional de Corse), flatland marshes (along the east coast), an uninhabited desert (the Désert des Agriates) and a 'continental divide' running down the middle of the island – depending on where it falls, rain ends up flowing into the Mediterranean on either the east coast or the west coast. Much of the island is covered with that typically Corsican form of vegetation, the maquis, whose, low, dense shrubs and

bushes provide many of the spices used in Corsican cooking.

Corsica was ruled by Genoa from the 13th century until the Corsicans, led by the extraordinary Pasquale Paoli (Pascal Paoli in French), declared the island independent in 1755. But the Corsican independence was short-lived. France took over Corsica in 1769 and has ruled it ever since – except for the period from 1794 to 1796, when it came under English rule, and during WW II. Despite having spent only 14 years as a self-governed country, the people of Corsica (who now number some 240,000) have retained a fiercely independent streak. Only a minority, however, support the separatist Front de Libération National de la Corse (FLN), whose initials are spray-painted all over the island, especially on road signs.

Language

The Corsican language, which is almost exclusively oral, became gradually Latinised after the arrival of the Romans. Starting in the 9th century, it absorbed many elements of the Tuscan language.

When to Go

Corsica is overrun with holidaymakers (mostly Germans and Italians) during the summer, especially during July and August and most especially between mid-July and mid-August. It is highly recommended that you avoid Corsica during this period.

Dangers & Annoyances

When Corsica makes the newspapers in English-speaking countries, it's usually because nationalist militants have placed a bomb next to some public building or mainlander's holiday villa. But such attacks are *not* targeted at tourists or, generally, at people, and there is no reason for visitors to the island to be concerned about their safety.

Activities

Hiking Corsica has some superb hiking trails, including three *mare à mare* (sea-to-sea) trails that cross the island from east to west and the celebrated Grande Randonnée

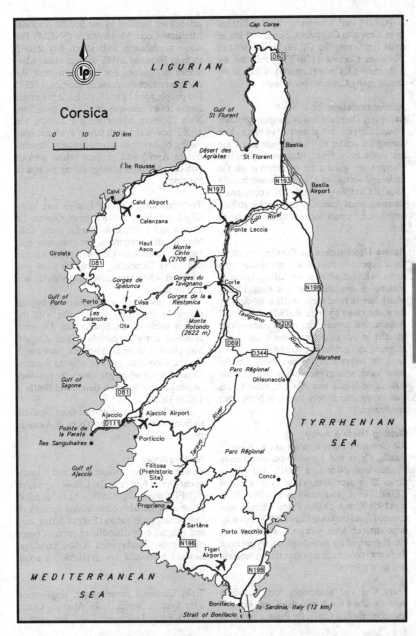

Corsica

0   10   20 km

LIGURIAN SEA

Cap Corse

D80

Gulf of St Florent

Désert des Agriates

St Florent

Bastia

N193

Bastia Airport

l'Île Rousse

N197

Calvi

Calvi Airport

Calenzana

Golo River

Ponte Leccia

Girolata

D81

Haut Asco

▲ Monte Cinto (2706 m)

Gorges du Tavignano

Corte

N198

Gulf of Porto

Gorges de Spelunca

Evisa

Gorges de la Restonica

Porto

Les Calanche

Ota

▲ Monte Rotondo (2622 m)

Tavignano River

N200

D69

D344

Marshes

Gulf of Sagone

D81

Parc Régional

Ghisonaccia

Ajaccio

Ajaccio Airport

D111

TYRRHENIAN SEA

Pointe de la Parata

Îles Sanguinaires

Porticcio

Taravo River

Parc Régional

Gulf of Ajaccio

Filitosa (Prehistoric Site)

Conca

Propriano

Sartène

Porto Vecchio

N196

Figari Airport

N198

MEDITERRANEAN SEA

Bonifacio

To Sardinia, Italy (12 km)

Strait of Bonifacio

FRANCE

'20 (GR20) trail, which stretches for 220 km from Conca to Calenzana. Some 600 km of trails (including the GR20) are covered in *Walks in Corsica* (100FF), published by Robertson McCarta (London), which is on sale in many Corsican bookshops.

Accommodation
Camping There are lots of camping grounds around Corsica, but almost all of them close during the colder half of the year and some are open only from June to September. Charges are quite a bit higher than on the mainland – a rate of 22FF per person is quite usual. Camping outside of recognised camping areas *(camping sauvage)* is strictly prohibited, in part because of the danger of fires.

Hotels Hotel rooms on Corsica are much more expensive than on the mainland: for a room without shower or toilet, virtually nothing is available for less than 120FF. Many hotels raise their tariffs considerably (in some cases by over 200%!) in July and August, but unless you make reservations months in advance (or arrive early in the morning and get lucky) you probably won't have the opportunity to pay them. On the other hand, wintertime visitors will find that outside of Bastia and Ajaccio, most hotels shut down completely between November and Easter.

Getting There & Away
Air Corsica's main airports are at Ajaccio, Bastia, Calvi and Figari (near Bonifacio). Flights from Nice cost 393FF, but people under 25 or over 60 may qualify for a fare of 273FF. The regular one-way fare from Paris is 1195FF, but charters and certain discounted fares cost as little as 500FF one-way, depending on when you go, how old you are, etc. If you qualify for a discount, flying from Paris may cost much less than taking the train and then a ferry.

Ferry Car and passenger ferry services between the French mainland and Corsica (Ajaccio, Bastia, Calvi, Île Rousse and Pro-

priano) are handled by the Société National Maritime Corse-Mediterranée (SNCM). For one-way passage, individuals pay 220FF to/from Nice and 245FF to/from either Marseilles or Toulon. For overnight trips, the cheapest couchette costs an additional 70FF. For people aged 12 to 25, the basic passenger fare is 160FF one-way on all sailings to/from Nice. To/from Marseille and Toulon, the 180FF one-way youth fare is available only during blue periods (approximately November to April) and perhaps white periods (which cover most sailings during the rest of the year).

To/From Italy Corsica Ferries has year-round car ferry service from Genoa, La Spezia and Livorno to Bastia. From mid-May to mid-September, the company also runs ferries between Genoa and both Ajaccio and Calvi. Depending on which route you take and when you travel, individuals pay 145 to 200FF.

From mid-April to October, Mobylines (formerly Navarma) links Bastia with the Italian ports of La Spezia and Livorno. Between early or mid-June and August, Mobylines' car ferries also link Bastia with Genoa, Piombino and Porto Santo Stefano. Depending on when you travel, the one-way passenger fare between Genoa and Bastia is 150 to 185FF.

For information on ferries from Sardinia to Bonifacio, see Getting There & Away in the Bonifacio section.

Getting Around
Bus Bus transport around the island is infrequent (one to four run a day), slow, expensive (100FF from Ajaccio to Bastia) and handled by an unfathomably complicated network of independent companies. Except during July and August, only a handful of intercity buses operate on Sunday and public holidays. Student discounts are available on some routes.

Train Corsica's metre-gauge, single-track train system, which links Ajaccio, Corte, Bastia, Ponte Leccia and Calvi, has more in common with the Kalka-Simla line through the Himalayan foothills of northern India than it does with the TGV. The two and four-car trains make their way unhurriedly through the stunning scenery (and a not inconsiderable number of tunnels), stopping at tiny rural stations and, when necessary, for sheep and cows. This is definitely the most interesting (and the most comfortable) way to get around the island.

Corsica's train system uses a different system of tariffs than SNCF's mainland operations and does *not* accept Eurail passes or give any discounts except to holders of Inter-Rail passes, who get 50% off. It costs 105FF to go from Ajaccio to Bastia and 80FF to travel from Bastia to Calvi.

Car Travelling by car is a fantastic way to see the island, especially given the difficulties (and significant expenses) of getting around by train or bus. The best car rental deals in Corsica are listed under Getting There & Away in the Ajaccio and Bastia sections.

AJACCIO

The port city of Ajaccio (pronounced ah-ZHAK-syo; population 55,000), birthplace of Napoleon Bonaparte (1769-1821), is a great place to begin a visit to Corsica. This pastel-shaded, Mediterranean town is eminently strollable, but spending some time here can also be educational: Ajaccio's several museums (and many statues) dedicated to Bonaparte (who, local people will neglect to mention, never came back to visit after becoming emperor) speak volumes, not about Napoleon himself, but about how the people of his native town prefer to think of him.

Orientation

Ajaccio's main street is Cours Napoléon, which stretches from Place du Général de Gaulle northward to the train station at Square Pierre Griffi and beyond. The old city is east of Place de Gaulle and south of Place Foch.

Information

Tourist Office The less-than-outstandingly helpful tourist office (☎ 95.21.40.87, 95.21.53.39) at 1 Place Foch is open Monday to Friday from 8.30 am to 6 pm and on Saturday from 8.30 am to noon. From mid-June to mid-September, it is open daily from 8 am to 8 pm.

Hiking Information The Informations Randonnées office (☎ 95.21.56.54) at 4 Rue Fiorella (just north of Place de Gaulle) has lots of information on the Parc Naturel Régional de Corse (Corsica's huge national park) and its many hiking trails. It is open Monday to Friday from 9 am to noon and 3 to 6 pm.

Money & Post The Banque de France (☎ 95.21.00.05) is at 8 Rue Sergent Casalonga. The main post office, which is at 5 Cours Napoléon, is open Monday to Friday from 8 am to 6.30 pm and on Saturday from 8 am to noon. Exchange services are available.

Ajaccio's postcode is 20000.

Things to See & Do

Museums The house where Napoleon was born and raised, the **Maison Bonaparte** (☎ 95.21.43.89) on Rue Saint Charles, was sacked by Corsican nationalists in 1793 but rebuilt (with a grant from the government in Paris) at the end of the 1790s. It is open from 9 am (10 am from October to April) to noon and 2 to 6 pm (5 pm from October to April) daily except Sunday afternoon and Monday morning. The entry fee of 17FF (9FF for people aged 18 to 25 and over 60) includes a guided tour in French.

The **Salon Napoléonien** (☎ 95.21.90.15), which exhibits memorabilia of the emperor, is on the 1st floor of the Hôtel de Ville at Place Foch. It is usually open Monday to Friday from 9 am to noon and 2 to 5 pm. The fee is only 2FF, but visitors must be properly dressed.

The **Musée Fesch** (☎ 95.21.48.17) at 50-52 Rue du Cardinal Fesch has a fine collection of 14th to 19th century Italian

FRANCE

FRANCE

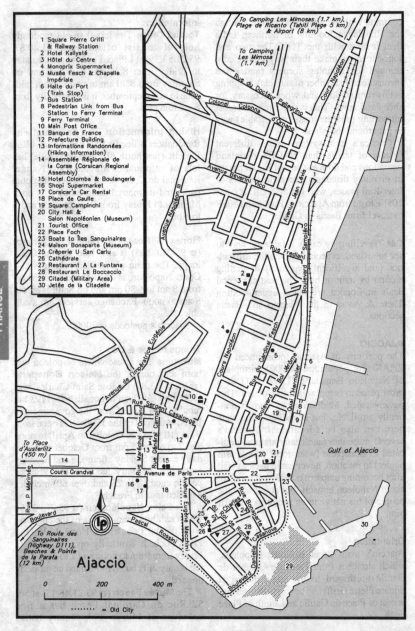

1 Square Pierre Griffi
  & Railway Station
2 Hotel Kallysté
3 Hôtel du Centre
4 Monoprix Supermarket
5 Musée Fesch & Chapelle
  Impériale
6 Halte du Port
  (Train Stop)
7 Bus Station
8 Pedestrian Link from Bus
  Station to Ferry Terminal
9 Ferry Terminal
10 Main Post Office
11 Banque de France
12 Prefecture Building
13 Informations Randonnées
  (Hiking Information)
14 Assemblée Régionale de
  la Corse (Corsican Regional
  Assembly)
15 Hotel Colomba & Boulangerie
16 Shopi Supermarket
17 Corsicar's Car Rental
18 Place de Gaulle
19 Square Campinchi
20 City Hall &
  Salon Napoléonien (Museum)
21 Tourist Office
22 Place Foch
23 Boats to Îles Sanguinaires
24 Maison Bonaparte (Museum)
25 Crêperie U San Carlu
26 Cathédrale
27 Restaurant A La Funtana
28 Restaurant Le Boccaccio
29 Citadel (Military Area)
30 Jetée de la Citadelle

To Camping Les Mimosas (1.7 km),
Plage de Ricanto (Tahiti Plage 5 km)
& Airport (8 km)

To Camping
Les Mimosa
(1.7 km)

Rue du Docteur Pellegrino

Avenue Colonel Colonna d'Ornano

Cours Napoléon

Avenue Beverini Vico

Avenue Jean Lévie

Boulevard Sampiero

Rue Frediani

Cours Napoléon

Rue du Cardinal Fesch

Rue du Bel Verdure

Boulevard du Roi Jérôme

Quai l'Herminier

Avenue Napoléon III

Rue de l'Impératrice Eugénie

Rue Sergent Casalonga

Rue Maréchal d'Ornano

Rue Général Campi

Avenue de l'Impératrice Eugénie

To Place
d'Austerlitz
(450 m)

Cours Grandval

Cours Grandval   Avenue de Paris

Rue P Mérimée

Boulevard

Pascal Rossini

Avenue Eugène Macchini

Rue St Charles

Rue St Roch

Rue Bonaparte

Rue de Rome

Rue Danielle Casanova

Boulevard Danielle

Gulf of Ajaccio

To Route des
Sanguinaires
(Highway D111),
Beaches & Pointe
de la Parata
(12 km)

Ajaccio

0   200   400 m

········· = Old City

primitive art paintings, and an exhibit of Napoleonia in the basement. It is open from 9.30 am to noon and 2.30 to 6 pm (3 to 6.30 pm from May to September) daily except Sunday, Monday and public holidays. During July and August, it is also open on Friday night from 9 pm to midnight. Entry costs 25FF (15FF for students aged 18 to 25 and people over 60). There is a fee of 10FF (5FF if you qualify for the reduction) to get into the museum's **Chapelle Impériale**, built in 1857 as a sepulchre for the Bonaparte family.

Cathédrale Ajaccio's late 16th century cathedral is in the **old city** on the corner of Rue Forcioli Conti and Rue Saint Charles. It is known for Napoleon's marble baptismal font, which is to the right of the entry, and the painting *Vierge au Sacré-Cœur* by Eugène Delacroix (1798-1863), which is situated – as you face the altar – in the back, left-hand corner of the nave. The cathedral is open from 7 to 11.30 am and 3 to 6.30 pm (6 pm in winter) daily except Sunday afternoon.

Pointe de la Parata This wild, black granite promontory, 12 km west of the city out Route des Sanguinaires (Highway D111), is famed for its sunsets, which you can watch from the base of a crenellated, early 17th century Genoan watchtower. Bus No 5 links Ajaccio with the Pointe.

The **Îles Sanguinaires**, which are visible offshore, can be visited on three-hour boat excursions (70FF) between May and October (more or less). Boats to the Îles Sanguinaires leave from the quayside opposite Place Foch.

Beaches Ajaccio's beaches are nothing to write home about. Plage de Ricanto, popularly known as Tahiti Plage, is about five km east of town on the way to the airport. As with the airport, it can be reached by taking bus No 1 (see the following Getting There & Away section). The small, segmented beaches between Ajaccio and Pointe de la

Parata (Ariadne, Neptune, Palm Beach and Marinella) are served by bus No 5.

Places to Stay

Camping The *Camping Les Mimosas* (☎ 95.20.99.85; open April to October), is about three km north of the centre of town on Route d'Alata. To get there, take bus No 4 to the roundabout at the western end of Cours Jean Nicoli and walk up Route d'Alata for about one km. A tent emplacement and a place to park cost 9FF each. It costs 22FF per adult.

Hotels The best deal in town is the tiny *Hôtel Colomba* (☎ 95.21.12.66) at 8 Ave de Paris (3rd floor). Clean, pleasant singles and doubles cost 130 to 150FF, and triples are 200FF. Toilets are down the hall. The friendly *Hôtel Kallysté* (☎ 95.51.34.45) at 51 Cours Napoléon has eminently serviceable singles/doubles with air-conditioning for 200/235FF (15% to 25% more from May to mid-November). Studios with kitchenettes for one/two people range from 225/260FF to 300/350FF, depending on the season. The *Hôtel du Centre* (☎ 95.21.62.02) at 45 Cours Napoléon (1st floor) has old-fashioned singles and doubles with shower for 200FF and triples with bath and toilet for 350FF.

Places to Eat

Restaurants *Le Boccaccio* (☎ 95.21.16.77) at 19 Rue Roi de Rome specialises in Italian cuisine. It is open from noon to 2.30 pm and 7 to 9 pm all year except January. Main dishes cost 50 to 60FF; the summer-season *menu* is about 90FF. *A La Funtana* (☎ 95.21.78.04), an up-market French restaurant at 9 Rue Notre Dame (near the cathedral), is open from noon to 3 pm and 7 pm to midnight daily except Saturday at midday and all-day Sunday. A La Funtana's *menu* costs 120FF.

Crêperie U San Carlu (☎ 95.21.30.21) at 16 Rue Saint Charles has crêpes of all descriptions for 10 to 50FF. It is open April to September from 11 am to 9.30 or 10 pm.

Self-Catering The *Shopi* supermarket oppo-

FRANCE

site 4 Cours Grandval is open Monday to Saturday from 9 am to 12.30 pm and 3.15 to 7.30 pm. The boulangerie at 8 Ave de Paris, which is just down the block, is open every day from 7.30 am to 1 pm and 3 to 8 pm.

Getting There & Away

Air Aéroport d'Ajaccio-Campo dell'Oro is eight km east of the city out Cours Napoléon and its continuation. Public bus No 1 links Place de Gaulle and Cours Napoléon with the airport (15FF).

Bus Ajaccio's gare routière is on Quai l'Herminier next to the ferry terminal. Except on Sunday and public holidays, about a dozen companies operate buses from here to Bastia (100FF; twice a day), Bonifacio (105FF; twice a day), Calvi (110FF; via Ponte Leccia), Corte (55FF; twice a day), Porto (55FF; twice a day), Sartène (62FF; twice a day), Propriano and many other destinations. Eurocorse (formerly Ollandini; ☎ 95.21.06.30, 95.70.13.83), which handles most of the 'long-distance' lines, keeps its kiosk open Monday to Saturday from 8 to 11 am and 2 to 6.30 pm (7 am to 6.30 pm in July and August). The bus station's information booth (☎ 95.21.28.01), which can provide schedules for all routes, is open Monday to Saturday from 7 am to 6.30 or 7 pm. From mid-June to mid-September, it is open daily and often stays open later in the evening.

Train The train to Corte, Bastia, Calvi and intermediate destinations can be caught either at the train station (at Square Pierre Griffi) or at the Halte du Port (train stop), which is a few metres north of the bus station. See Train under Getting Around at the start of the Corsica section for more information.

Car & Motorbike The best car rental prices in town are offered by Corsicar's (☎ 95.21.87.12), whose office is on the ground floor of the building at 6 Place de Gaulle. Office hours are Monday to Saturday from 8 am to noon and 2 to 6 pm (7 pm from late April to September). During the warm months, they're often open on Sundays as

well. With unlimited km, a Peugeot 106 or a Citroën AX costs 290FF a day (340FF from June to September), including insurance.

About a dozen car rental companies have bureaus at the airport, but the least expensive is probably Aloha (☎ 95.20.52.00). For a Fiat Panda, they charge 975FF for three days, including insurance and unlimited km.

Ferry The ferry terminal (*gare maritime*) is on Quai l'Herminier next to the bus station. SNCM's ticketing office (☎ 95.29.66.99), across the street at 3 Quai l'Herminier, is open Monday to Friday from 8 to 11.45 am and 2 to 6 pm and on Saturday from 8 to 11.45 am. Whenever there's an evening ferry, the SNCM bureau in the ferry terminal opens two or three hours before the scheduled departure time.

BASTIA

Bastia (population 45,000), Corsica's most important business and commercial centre, is served by more ferries from France and Italy than any other port on the island. Unfortunately, there's not all that much to do or see here, and most visitors simply pass through. Bastia does, however, make a good base for exploring **Cap Corse**, the 40-km-long peninsula north of Bastia.

Orientation

The focal point of the city centre is 300-metre-long Place Saint Nicolas, which, like the coastline, is oriented north-to-south. Bastia's main avenues are east-west oriented Ave Maréchal Sebastiani, which runs westward from the gare maritime past the northern end of Place Saint Nicolas to the train station; and north-south oriented Blvd Paoli, which is parallel to and one block west of Place Saint Nicolas.

Information

Tourist Office The tourist office (☎ 95.31.00.89) is at the northern edge of Place Saint Nicolas. It is open Monday to Saturday from 8 am to 6 pm (during July and August, daily from 7 am to 10 pm).

Money Banque de France (☎ 95.31.24.09) is at 2bis Cours Henri Pierangeli, half a block south of the southern end of Place Saint Nicolas. It is open Monday to Friday from 8.45 am to 12.10 pm and 1.55 to 3.30 pm.

Post The main post office is on the even side of Ave Maréchal Sebastiani, a block west of Place Saint Nicolas. It is open Monday to Friday from 8 am to 7 pm and on Saturday from 8 am to noon. Exchange services are available.

Bastia's postcode is 20200.

Things to See
Tree-lined **Place Saint Nicolas**, a huge esplanade as long as three football pitches, was laid out in the late 19th century. The narrow streets and alleyways of **Terra Vecchia**, which is centred around Place de l'Hôtel de Ville, begin a bit south of Place Saint Nicolas. The **Oratoire de l'Immaculée Conception**, opposite 3 Rue Napoléon, was given its rich interior decoration during the 18th century.

The picturesque, horseshoe-shaped **Vieux Port** is between Terra Vecchia and the **Citadelle** (also known as Terra Nova), which can be reached by climbing the stairs through the **Jardin Romieu**, the hillside park on the south side of the port. Inside the Citadelle, built by the Genoans between the 15th and 17th centuries, is the **Ancien Palais des Gouverneurs** (former Genoan governors' palace). It houses a less-than-scintillating anthropology museum, but the views from the gardens behind the submarine conning tower are worth the climb. **Église Sainte Marie**, whose entrance is on Rue de l'Évêché, was begun in 1495 and became a cathedral at the end of the 16th century. Its interior ornamentation is in the Baroque style that was fashionable during the 17th and 18th centuries.

Places to Stay
Camping In Miomo, about five km north of Bastia, you'll find the *Camping Casanova* (☎ 95.33.91.42; open from June to October). To get there, take the bus towards Erbalunga

from Rue du Nouveau Port, opposite the north-west corner of Place Saint Nicholas. Charges are 22FF per person and 9FF for a place to pitch your tent.

Hotels The eight-room *Hôtel du Cap* (☎ 95.31.18.46) at 11 Rue du Commandant Luce de Casabianca, run by an elderly woman dressed all in black, is 250 metres north and one block inland from the ferry terminal building. Small, simply furnished doubles with shower and toilet in the hall cost 120FF.

The most convenient (but hardly the most salubrious) hotel in Bastia is the *Hôtel de l'Univers* (☎ 95.31.03.38) at 3 Ave Maréchal Sebastiani. Singles/doubles/triples cost 120/150/180FF with washbasin and bidet, 180/200/250FF with shower and 220/240/300FF with shower and toilet. Prices are 10% to 20% higher in August and September. The one-star *Hôtel Le Riviera* (☎ 95.31.07.16) at 1bis Rue du Nouveau Port is 100 metres north of the northern end of Place Saint Nicolas. Fairly large rooms with shower cost 150FF (250FF from July to mid-September) for either one or two people. Singles/doubles with shower, toilet and TV are 230/260FF (420FF from July to mid-September).

Places to Eat
Restaurant Fesch Pâtes (☎ 95.31.23.94) at 18 Ave Émile Sari (400 metres north of Place Saint Nicolas) specialises in fresh, Italian-style pasta. They have a *menu* for 85FF.

There are a number of boulangeries along Rue César Campinchi, two blocks west of Place Saint Nicolas. *Timy Supermarché* at 2 Rue Campanelle (one block north of Ave Maréchal Sebastiani) is open Monday to Saturday from 8.30 am to 12.30 pm and 3.30 to 7.30 pm

Getting There & Away
Air Aéroport de Bastia-Poretta, the 5th busiest airport in France, is 20 km south of the city. Municipal buses to the airport (32FF) depart from in front of the prefecture building (which is across the roundabout from the train station) about an hour before

each flight's departure. A timetable is available at the tourist office.

Bus Rapides Bleus, whose buses serve Porto Vecchio (100FF) – and, with a transfer at Porto Vecchio, Bonifacio – has a ticket office (☎ 95.31.03.79) at 1 Ave Maréchal Sebastiani. Eurocorse's twice-daily bus to Corte and Ajaccio, which runs on Sunday and holidays from July to mid-September only, stops in front of the Hôtel de l'Univers, which is at 3 Ave Maréchal Sebastiani. The bus to Calvi leaves from a short way up the block. Short-haul buses serving the Bastia area stop along Rue du Nouveau Port, which is opposite the north-west corner of Place Saint Nicolas.

Train The train station (☎ 95.32.60.06) is across the roundabout from the northern end of Ave Maréchal Sebastiani. See Getting Around at the start of the Corsica section for information on the train system.

Car & Motorbike The cheapest place in Bastia to rent a car is ADA Location de Véhicules (☎ 95.31.09.02) at 35 Rue César Campinchi, the street two blocks west of Place Saint Nicolas. It is open Monday to Saturday from 8 am to noon and 2 to 7 pm. Small cars (eg the Peugeot 106) cost 285FF a day, 450FF for the weekend and 1799FF a week, including unlimited km and insurance.

Ferry The gare maritime is at the quayside end of Ave Maréchal Sebastiani. SNCM's office is across the roundabout from the ferry terminal. It's open from 8 to 11.30 am and 2 to 5.30 pm daily except Saturday afternoon and Sunday. The SNCM counter in the ferry terminal is open two hours before each sailing (three hours before on Sunday).

Mobylines' office (☎ 95.31.46.29) is 200 metres north of Place Saint Nicolas at 4 Rue du Commandant Luce de Casabianca. It is open Monday to Saturday from 8 am to noon and 2 to 6 pm. From mid-April to October, the company's bureau (☎ 95.31.46.29) in the ferry terminal is open daily from 10 am until the boat leaves. Corsica Ferries' office

(☎ 95.31.18.09) is 250 metres north of the ferry terminal at 5 Rue Chanoine Leschi (right behind the Mobil petrol station).

CALVI

The citadel-town of Calvi (population 3600), set at the western end of a beautiful, half-moon shaped bay, is the largest settlement in the Balagne, a fertile region on Corsica's north-west coast. The coast between Calvi and Île Rousse (see Beaches) is dotted with beaches – in the spring, seaside sunbathers may catch a few rays reflected from the snowy summits of the towering mountains only 20 or so km inland.

Orientation

The Haute Ville (upper city), also known as the citadel, is north-east of the port. Calvi's major thoroughfare is known as Blvd Wilson between Place Christophe Colomb (just west of the upper city) and the post office, and as Ave de la République as it passes the train station. It becomes Ave Christophe Colomb and then Highway N197 as it heads south-eastward out of town.

Information

The tourist office (☎ 95.65.16.67) is upstairs from the Capitainerie (harbour master's office); from the train station, cross the tracks and go out the back gate. It is open Monday to Friday from 9 am to noon and 2 to 6 pm (from mid-June to mid-September, the hours are 9 am to 1 pm and 3 to 7.30 pm). Ask for a map and the free *Historical Tour* brochure which lets you guide yourself around the citadel.

Calvi's postcode is 20260.

Things to See & Do

The **Haute Ville**, set atop an 80-metre-high granite promontory and enclosed by Genoan ramparts, affords great views of the whole Calvi region: the sea, the coast, the Balagne and the mountains. **Église Saint Jean Baptiste** was built in the 13th century and rebuilt in 1570. You can also visit the site where, according to local tradition, Christopher Columbus (Christophe Colomb) was born. The imposing **former palace of the Genoan governors**, built in the 13th century and enlarged in the mid-16th century, is above the entrance to the citadel. Now known as Caserne Sampiero, it serves as a barracks and mess hall for officers of the French Foreign Legion. The last tourist who wandered inside was subsequently seen wearing a kepi in a former French colony so remote that no Lonely Planet guide even mentions it...

Beaches Calvi's famous, four-km-long beach begins just east of the marina and stretches around the Golfe de Calvi. West of town, there are a number of other nice beaches, including one at **Algajola**. The port and resort town of **Île Rousse** (red island), 24 km east of Calvi, is also endowed with a long, sandy beach. Île Rousse was founded by the Corsican nationalist leader Pasquale Paoli in 1758 to compete with fiercely pro-Genoan Calvi.

Between late April and October, many of the beaches between Calvi and Île Rousse can be reached by shuttle train (see the following Getting There & Away section for details).

Places to Stay
Camping & Bungalows *Camping Les Castors* (☎ 95.65.13.30; open from April to October), is 800 metres south-east of the centre of town on Route de Pietra Maggiore (turn right off Ave Christophe Colomb a few hundred metres past L'Arche supermarket). Campers pay 20FF per adult, 8FF for a camp site and 7FF to park their car. Rustic, two-person bungalows with communal showers and toilets cost only 80FF a night (160FF a night in July and August). Studios with shower, toilet and kitchenette cost 185FF (290FF in July and August).

Hostel The friendly, 136-bed *Youth Hostel/Hôtel de Jeunes* (☎ 95.65.14.15; open from late March to October) on Ave de la République, is 70 metres to the left as you leave the train station. Beds in rooms for two to eight people cost 105FF per person,

including a filling breakfast. No reservations are accepted and guests do not need a hostelling card.

Hotels The *Hôtel du Centre* (☎ 95.65.02.01) at 14 Rue Alsace-Lorraine (parallel to and one block down the hill from Blvd Wilson) is open from late May or early June to mid-October. Doubles/triples start at 200/250FF; prices are higher in the middle of summer. *Hôtel Le Belvédère* (☎ 95.65.01.25) at Place Christophe Colomb is open all year. Small, cheaply appointed doubles with shower and toilet cost 200 to 250FF (350FF in August).

Getting There & Away
Air Aéroport Calvi-Sainte Catherine is seven km south-east of Calvi. There is no bus service from Calvi to the airport. Taxis cost 60 to 70FF (85 to 90FF on Sunday, public holidays and at night).

Bus From Monday to Friday, the bus to Bastia leaves from Place de la Porteuse d'Eau. During summer, one bus a day goes to/from Porto.

Train The most scenic way to get to Calvi from Ajaccio, Corte or Bastia is by rail. Calvi's train station is between the port and Ave de la République.

From late April to October, one-car shuttle trains *(navettes)* make 19 stops between Calvi and Île Rousse. The line is divided into three sectors and it costs one ticket (8FF, or 36FF for a carnet of six) for each sector you travel in.

Ferry SNCM ferries sail to Calvi from Nice and Marseille, but during winter they are very infrequent (once every two weeks). Between June and mid-September, Corsica Ferries links Calvi with Genoa.

PORTO
The seaside town of Porto, on Corsica's wildly beautiful west coast, is about midway between Ajaccio and Calvi. Nestled among huge outcrops of red granite, it is famous for its sunsets. The **marina** is across the Porto

FRANCE

River from an old eucalyptus grove and a small **beach**.

Porto is an excellent base for visits to a number of Corsica's natural wonders. **Les Calanche** (Les Calanques de Piana in French), a truly spectacular mountain landscape of red-and-orange granite forms resembling both nightmarish and fairly normal people, animals, fortresses, etc, towers above the deep-blue waters of the Mediterranean slightly south of Porto along Highway D81. The **Gorges de Spelunca**, one of Corsica's most famous river gorges, stretch from the town of Evisa almost to **Ota**; the latter is five km east of Porto's pharmacy and two km west of the gorges.

Orientation & Information

The marina is about 1.5 km down the hill from Highway D81, where you'll find Porto's pharmacy (where the bus from Ajaccio makes its first stop) and a big, new Bravo supermarket.

The tourist office (syndicat d'initiative; ☎ 95.26.10.55) is 500 metres towards the port from Highway D81.

Porto's postcode is 20150.

Places to Stay

Camping The *Camping Sole e Vista* (☎ 95.26.18.03), which is open from mid-April to late October, is behind the Bravo supermarket near the pharmacy.

Hostels There are two hostels in the nearby village of Ota. *Gîte d'Étape Chez Félix* (☎ 95.26.12.92) and *Gîte d'Étape des Chasseurs* (☎ 95.26.11.37) are open all year. Both charge 50FF for a bed in a dormitory room. Chez Félix has doubles and triples for 150FF and a room for five for 300FF.

Hotels At the marina, the *Hôtel Monte Rosso* (☎ 95.26.11.50) has doubles with shower and toilet for 220FF (260FF in July and August).

Getting There & Away

Except on Sunday, two buses a day run between Porto and Ajaccio (55FF). During summer, one bus a day goes to/from Calvi (60FF). Several buses a day link the village of Ota to both Ajaccio and Porto, but unfortunately there are no buses between Evisa and either Ota or Porto.

CORTE

When Pasquale Paoli led Corsica to independence in 1755, one of his first acts was to make Corte (population 5500) – which lies in a mountain valley right in the middle of the island – the country's capital. To this day the town remains a potent symbol of Corsican independence. In 1765, Paoli founded a national university here, but it was closed when his shortlived republic was taken over by France in 1769. The Università di Corsica was reopened in 1981 and now has about 3000 students, who make Corte Corsica's youngest-feeling and liveliest town. You can thank the students for the late-night sandwich shops and inexpensive pizzerias.

Information

The tourist office *(bureau d'information touristique*; ☎ 95.46.24.20, 95.61.01.62) is at the far end of the long building up the vehicle ramp directly opposite the entrance to the Citadelle. It is open Monday to Friday from 9 am to noon and 1.30 to 5 pm. From May to October, when the office moves to the building on the left as you walk into the Citadelle, it is open daily from 9 am to noon and 2 to 6 pm (9 am to 8 pm from mid-June to mid-September).

Corte's postcode is 20250.

Things to See & Do

The **Citadelle** (☎ 95.46.24.20, 95.61.01.61), built in the early 15th century and largely reconstructed during the 18th and 19th centuries, is perched on top of a hill, with the steep and twisted alleyways and streets of the **Ville Haute** (upper city) to one side and the Tavignanu and Restonica river valleys on the other. In every tourist brochure, the Citadelle's **Belvédère** is described as resembling an eagle's nest, and with good reason.

A staircase from the Belvédère leads down to the river.

Occupied by the Foreign Legion from 1962 until 1983, Corte's Citadelle is now open to the public, though only from May to October. It houses an anthropological museum (scheduled to open in 1993), the **Musée de la Corse** (☎ 95.61.00.61), and the **Font Régional d'Art Contemporain** (☎ 95.46.22.18), which puts on temporary exhibitions of contemporary art.

The **Gorges de la Restonica**, a deep valley cut through the mountains by the Restonica River, is a favourite with hikers. The river passes right by Corte, but some of the choicer trails begin about 16 km from town at the Bergeries Grotelle sheepfolds.

Places to Eat
The *Restaurant Le Bip's* (☎ 95.46.06.26, 95.46.04.48) at 14 Cours Paoli specialises in Corsican cuisine. The daily *menu* costs 70FF. Except during summer, Le Bip's is closed on Saturday.

Places to Stay
Camping *Camping Alivetu* (☎ 95.46.11.09; open from Easter to mid-October), is just south of Pont Restonica, the bridge on Allée du Neuf Septembre over the Restonica River.

Hostel The quiet and very rural *Gîte d'Étape U Tavignanu* (☎ 95.46.16.85), which is open all year, charges 45FF per person. To get there from Pont Tavignano (the bridge on Allée du Neuf September over the Tavignano River), walk westward along Chemin de Baliri and follow the signs. It's about 250 metres from the end of the narrow road.

Hotels The large *HR Hôtel* (☎ 95.61.01.21), housed in a complex of converted apartment blocks at 6 Allée du Neuf Septembre, is 300 metres to the left as you exit the train station. Utilitarian rooms for one or two people cost 135FF (with shower and toilet in the hall) or 155FF (with shower and toilet in the room). Prices are slightly higher from mid-July to .

mid-September. This place almost always has rooms available, even in the summer.

The *Hôtel de la Poste* (☎ 95.46.01.37) is a few blocks north of the centre of town at 2 Place du Duc de Padoue. A spacious, simply furnished double with shower costs 135 to 175FF, depending on how big it is.

Getting There & Away
Eurocorse buses to Bastia and Ajaccio stop in front of Bar Colonna at 3 Ave Xavier Luciani.

The train station (☎ 95.46.00.97) is about a km south-east of the town centre along Ave Jean Nicoli.

SARTÈNE
The town of Sartène (population 3200), whose unofficial slogan is 'the most Corsican of Corsica's towns', is a delightful place to spend a morning or afternoon. Local people chatting in Corsican gather in **Place de la Libération**, the town's main square, next to which is **Église Sainte Marie** and the **Hôtel de Ville**, once the Genoan governors' palace. The **Musée de Préhistoire Corse** (☎ 95.77.15.40) is up the hill. It's open Monday to Friday from 10 am to noon and 2 to 4 or 5 pm.

Getting There & Away
Given Sartène's dearth of reasonably priced hotels (or any hotels at all in winter), your best bet is to stop off here on your way from Ajaccio to Bonifacio, or to make a day trip from Ajaccio. Buses operated by Eurocorse stop at the Ollandini travel agency (☎ 95.77.18.41), which is 50 metres down Cours Gabriel Péri from the roundabout at the bottom of Cours Sœur Amélie.

BONIFACIO
Bonifacio's famed **citadel**, also known as the old city, sits 60 metres above the turquoise waters of the Mediterranean atop a long, narrow and eminently defensible promontory. On all sides, white cliffs sculpted by the wind and the waves – topped in places with precariously perched apartment houses – drop almost vertically to the

FRANCE

sea. The north side of the promontory looks out on 1.6-km-long Bonifacio Sound, at the eastern end of which is Bonifacio's **marina**, and the southern ramparts of the citadel afford views of the coast of Sardinia, 12 km to the south.

Information

The tourist office (☎ 95.73.11.88) is in the old city at Place de l'Europe – go in through the ground-floor side entrance of the Mairie. From mid-June to mid-September, there is a tourist office annexe at the marina.

Bonifacio's postcode is 20169.

Places to Stay

Camping Araguina (☎ 95.73.02.96; open from mid-March to October) is 400 metres north of the marina on Ave Sylvere Bohn (the road to Porto Vecchio). Camping here doesn't come cheap: it costs 10FF for a camp site, 10FF to park and 24FF per person.

Bonifacio has no really cheap hotels and relatively few hotels of any sort. Your best bet for budget accommodation is the *Hôtel des Étrangers* (☎ 95.73.01.09), which is on Ave Sylvere Bohn a bit up the hill from Camping Araguina. Plain doubles with shower and toilet cost 180 to 210FF; from July to September, prices are 40 or 50FF higher.

Getting There & Away

Bus From Monday to Saturday, Rapides Bleus' buses to Porto Vecchio (three times a day) and Bastia (once a day) and Eurocorse buses to Ajaccio via Sartène (twice a day) leave from the parking lot across the street from the eastern end of the marina.

Ferry Saremar (☎ 95.73.00.96) offers year-round car ferry service from Bonifacio's ferry port (in Bonifacio Sound, right below the citadel) to Santa Teresa, Sardinia. One-way pedestrian passage costs 49FF (54FF from June to September). If you want to get a vehicle across, make sure you have reservations at least a week in advance.

Germany

Perhaps no other country in Western Europe provides such a fascinating past, as well as history in the making. The reunification of West and East Germany in 1990 was the beginning of another chapter in Germany's long and rich history. Much of this old and more recent history is easily explored by visitors today, in a country packed with sheer beauty and many outdoor opportunities. Most things are extremely well organised (at least in the western part of the country, though the east is rapidly catching up), accommodation and food are often good value by Western European standards, and the beers and wines are second to none.

Though it's now officially one country, the cultural, social and economic differences between the two Germanys will take several years to disappear. In this book, the two are referred to as western Germany and eastern Germany when the distinction is relevant. The Germans themselves speak of the *Alte Bundesländer* (Old Federal States) and the *Neue* (New) *Bundesländer*, and their inhabitants commonly refer to each other as *Wessis* and *Ossis* ('Westies' and 'Easties').

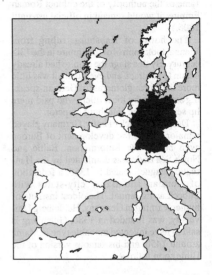

Facts about the Country

HISTORY

Events in Germany often dominated the history of central Europe, and in recent years they had a major influence on that of Europe as a whole. For many centuries, however, Germany was a patchwork of semi-independent principalities and city-states, preoccupied with internal quarrels and at the whim of foreign conquerors. In the 18th and 19th centuries, these gradually came under the control of Prussia, a state of eastern Baltic origins that had been brought into the German fold by crusaders of the Teutonic order and incorporated firmly into German affairs by the rulers of Brandenburg (the area

around Berlin). Germany only became a nation-state in 1871, and despite the momentous events that have occurred since then, many Germans still retain a strong sense of regional identity.

Ancient & Medieval History

Germany west of the Rhine and south of the Main rivers was part of the Roman Empire, but Roman legions never managed to subdue the proud warrior tribes beyond. With the collapse of Roman power, the Frankish conqueror Charlemagne forged a huge empire that covered most of Christian Western Europe. He held court in Aachen, from where he introduced the hierarchical state structure known as feudalism that held sway in Europe for many centuries.

Charlemagne's empire inevitably broke up after his death in 814 AD. Its eastern branch developed into the Holy Roman Empire, organised under Otto I 'the Great' in 962 AD, which included much of present-day Germany, Austria, Switzerland, the Benelux and northern Italy. (The term 'Holy Roman' was coined in an effort to assume some of the authority of the defunct Roman Empire; it would remain in official use until 1806.)

The house of Habsburg, ruling from Vienna, took control of the empire in the 13th century. By this stage the empire had already begun to contract, and eventually it was little more than a conglomerate of German-speaking states run by local rulers who paid mere lip service to the Habsburg emperor.

Despite this lack of unity, Germany played a major role in the development of Europe even before the Reformation. Baltic and North Sea trade was dominated by the Hanseatic League created in 1358, a federation of German and Baltic city-states with Lübeck as its capital. The oldest institute of higher learning in Germany, Heidelberg University, was founded in 1386. Gutenberg is said to have invented movable type in Mainz around 1450, and his famous version of the Bible soon followed.

The Reformation

Things would never be the same in Europe after Martin Luther, a monk from the monastery in Erfurt, nailed his 95 'theses' to the church door in Wittenberg in 1517, proclaiming his opposition to a Church racket involving the selling of documents ('indulgences') that absolved sinners from temporal punishment. In 1521 he was condemned by the Diet ('Parliament') of Worms and went into exile in Wartburg Castle in Eisenach. There he translated the Bible from Church Latin into German – in itself a revolutionary act.

The emerging class of merchants and wealthy townsfolk had long been irritated by Church arrogance, and Luther's efforts at reforming the Church gained widespread support. In 1529, tensions came to a boil. Six German princes and representatives from 14 towns met in Speyer in protest at the Church crackdown on Luther (thus, the term 'Protestant'). The *Confession of Augsburg*, drawn up by Luther supporter Philipp

Melanchton, became the charter of the later Lutheran churches. The Peace of Augsburg in 1555 declared that the religion of a state would be determined by its ruler *(cuius regio, eius religio)*.

Meanwhile the 'official' Church, which some people began to refer to as the (Roman) Catholic Church, recovered its composure and began striking back with methods like the Inquisition to root out the 'heresy' of the Reformation (the movement aimed at reforming the Church). This Church campaign against the spread of Protestantism in its many forms, known as the Counter-Reformation, led to the Thirty Years' War (1618-48), which developed into a full-scale European war. The German countryside was the scene of much of the fighting and lost almost a third of its population.

The Peace of Westphalia in 1648 established the rights of both faiths in Germany once and for all, and in so doing, sealed the political division of Germany as a patchwork of independent states and principalities within the loose framework of the Holy Roman Empire.

Prussia Unites Germany

In the 18th century, the Kingdom of Prussia, with its capital in Berlin, became one of Europe's strongest powers thanks to the organisational talents of Frederick William I, the 'Soldier King', and his son, Frederick II 'the Great'. It expanded eastwards at the expense of Poland, Lithuania and Russia. Westwards expansion was slower: the other German states could not afford to antagonise Prussia, but Prussia could not annex them until Austria and France offered the opportunity.

In the early 19th century, the fragmented German states proved easy pickings for invading French forces led by Napoleon. The Austrian emperor, Francis II, relinquished his crown as Holy Roman Emperor in 1806 following his defeat at Austerlitz. But though the French occupied Berlin, they never quite managed to subdue Prussia, and it became the centre of stubborn German resistance. When French fortunes turned with

Germany
(Deutschland)

GERMANY

Napoleon's disastrous foray into Russia, Prussia led the war of liberation that put an end to Napoleon's German aspirations in a decisive battle at Leipzig in 1813. Bonapartist megalomania met its final defeat at Waterloo in 1815.

In 1814, with Napoleon temporarily banished to Elba as a result of his Leipzig defeat, the Congress of Vienna began to redraw the map of Europe that he had so strongly altered, and restored the old order he had toppled. The Holy Roman Empire was replaced with a German Confederation of 35 states; it had a parliament in Frankfurt and was led by the Austrian chancellor and Congress of Vienna architect, Klemens von Metternich. The Confederation felt the tremors of the liberal revolutions that shook Europe in 1830 and 1848, but the old order remained basically intact, with the Austrian monarchy continuing to dominate a divided Germany.

The well-oiled Prussian civil and military machine eventually smashed this cosy arrangement. In 1862, Prince Bismarck was appointed chancellor (prime minister) of Prussia, and took it to war against Austria in 1866. With lightning speed, the 'Iron Chancellor' annexed or otherwise shackled northern Germany. When France declared war, the superior Prussian army pursued French troops all the way to Paris. The Catholic, anti-Prussian states in southern Germany had no choice but to negotiate with Bismarck.

As payback for the humiliation suffered under Napoleon, the Prussians proclaimed the German Empire in the Mirror Hall in Versailles, near Paris, on 18 January 1871. The Prussian king, Wilhelm I, became German emperor, or *Kaiser*.

WW I & the Rise of Hitler

Wilhelm II succeeded his father in 1888 and dismissed Bismarck in 1890. But Germany's rapid industrialisation and explosive population growth overtaxed the Kaiser's modest talents, particularly in international affairs. His efforts to earn Germany a 'place under the sun' led to mounting tensions with England, Russia and France. When these tensions erupted into war after the assassination of Austrian Archduke Franz Ferdinand in Sarajevo on 28 June 1914, Germany's only ally was a weakened Austria-Hungary.

Germany maintained the upper hand in the war in the east, leading to revolution in Russia, but lost it through attrition in the trenches in the west. On the home front, mounting dissatisfaction with senseless sacrifice and deprivation resulted in a full-scale uprising led by the Spartakus League, the forerunner of the German Communist Party. Its leaders, Karl Liebknecht and Rosa Luxemburg, organised revolutionary workers' and soldiers' councils, or soviets, modelled on the self-ruling bodies that were busy consolidating their power in Russia.

The Kaiser, backed into a corner, had no choice but to agree to an armistice on 11 November 1918, followed by his abdication and exile to Holland. The Social Democratic chancellor, Friedrich Ebert, immediately moved troops to Berlin to crush the fledgling revolution, and Liebknecht and Luxemburg were murdered. On 11 August 1919 Germany became a republic, with Ebert as president.

The Treaty of Versailles in 1919 chopped huge areas off Germany to allow for the re-creation of Poland and the establishment of Czechoslovakia. The victorious powers imposed heavy reparation payments on Germany that were virtually impossible to meet, and when France and Belgium occupied the Rhineland to ensure continued payments, the subsequent hyperinflation and miserable economic conditions provided fertile ground for political extremists.

One of these was Adolf Hitler, an Austrian drifter and German army veteran who joined the German Workers' Party, which became the National (or 'Nazi') Socialist German Workers' Party. As head of its propaganda arm and soon its president, he staged an abortive coup (the 'Beer Hall Putsch') in Munich in 1923, which landed him in prison for nine months. Revolutionary anarchists and extraparliamentary communists usually received much harsher sentences.

A short period of economic growth in the late 1920s came to an abrupt end in 1929 when the worldwide economic depression set in. It hit Germany particularly hard, leading to massive unemployment, strikes and demonstrations. The Communist Party under Ernst Thälmann gained strength, a development that fed the anti-Communist paranoia of the leading Social Democrats. Wealthy industrialists funnelled money to the Nazi party; the police turned a blind eye to Nazi street thugs, yet came down heavily on their Communist counterparts.

The Nazis went from strength to strength in general elections and in 1933 replaced the Social Democrats as the largest party, with 230 seats in the 670-seat Reichstag (parliament). Hitler was appointed chancellor by President von Hindenburg, amassed greater powers after a convenient fire in the Reichstag building in Berlin, and a year later assumed absolute control as *Führer* (leader) of what he called the Third Reich (the 'third empire', the previous two being the Holy Roman Empire and Wilhelm I's German Empire).

WW II & the Division of Germany

In March 1935 Germany reintroduced military service, while its industry shifted into gear and the country marched its way out of the depression with Hitler's policy of rearmament and strategic public works (such as the autobahns, or expressways, which allowed troops to move around quickly). Hitler reoccupied the demilitarised Rhineland in March 1936, signed pacts with Japan and Italy in 1936 and 1937, and sent fascist troops to Spain from 1936 to 1939. Austria was annexed in March 1938, the Czech Lands in 1938, and finally, in September 1939, after signing a pact with Stalin that allowed both a free hand in the east of Europe, Hitler invaded Poland, leading to war with Britain and France.

The ensuing cataclysm unleashed death and destruction on a scale not yet experienced by the industrialised world. It also saw the first 'assembly-line' genocide in history, with extermination camps designed specific-

ally to rid Europe of Jews and other people who were considered undesirable in perverted Nazi minds.

Germany itself did not exactly survive the horror years to 1945 unscathed. It lost an estimated 10% of its population, many of them conscripts sent to the eastern front to engage the Red Army in battles on a scale the world had never seen, involving hundreds of thousands of soldiers at a time. Systematic bombing by Allied air forces reduced Germany's industrial centres to rubble, and many great cities, such as beautiful Dresden and Cologne, had been all but wiped off the map by the time Germany accepted unconditional surrender in May 1945.

At conferences in Yalta and Potsdam, the Allies agreed on their respective spheres of influence in postwar Europe and Germany. They redrew the borders of Germany, making it a quarter smaller than it had already become after the Treaty of Versailles 26 years earlier. Some 6.5 million ethnic Germans migrated or were expelled to Germany from their homes in Poland, Czechoslovakia, the Soviet Union and the Baltic states, where some of them had lived for centuries – thus countering the population loss suffered by Germany during the war. Germany was divided into four occupation zones and Berlin was occupied jointly by the four victorious powers pending the reunification of the country, which was not destined to occur any time soon.

In April 1946 the Social Democratic Party in the Soviet zone was forced to merge with the Communist Party to form the Socialist Unity Party (SED), which won the elections there later that year. It began nationalising industry, and by 1948 more than 60% of production in the Soviet zone came from the public sector.

In June 1948 the Soviet Union interrupted land traffic between Germany's western zones and Berlin, after a new currency linked to the dollar was introduced in the western sectors of the city. The Western allies countered this with a military airlift operation that supplied West Berlin by plane. The Soviet Union lifted the blockade in May 1949, after

GERMANY

the SED had expropriated the financial institutions in East Berlin. In September 1949 the Federal Republic of Germany (FRG) was created out of the three western zones; in response, the German Democratic Republic (GDR) was founded in the Soviet zone the following month, with Berlin as its capital.

From Division to Détente

Mindful of the disastrous consequences of the heavy reparation payments imposed after WW I, the USA took the opposite approach this time and pumped US$4 billion of Marshall Plan money into West Germany from 1945 to 1955. An offer also to invest in East Germany was turned down by Stalin – instead, East Germany had to pay US$10 billion in war reparations to the Soviet Union, and Soviet agents looted anything of potential value; East Germany had to rebuild itself completely from scratch. In contrast, the renewal of war-torn Western Europe was enhanced by the Marshall Plan, and West Germany experienced rapid economic development under the leadership of Konrad Adenauer.

The division between east and west continued to grow on many fronts. So long as the border between East and West Germany remained relatively open (many East Berliners, for example, worked in West Berlin), the promise of a better life in the West kept luring people away from the miserable economic conditions in the East. These migrants included doctors, engineers and talented students – the sort of people East Germany could ill afford to lose. Until the Berlin Wall was built and the rest of the border hermetically sealed in 1961, more than a fifth of the population had left East Germany.

Construction of the Wall allowed the GDR to proceed with its development without further interference. From 1964, the GDR's economy began to improve. But West Germany was unwilling to accept the establishment of the GDR, desiring reunification and even the return of territories annexed by Poland and the Soviet Union in 1945. Until the early 1970s, the Federal Republic was able to prevent the GDR from being recognised in the West.

The far-sighted *Ostpolitik* of West German chancellor Willy Brandt changed this. In 1970 West Germany signed a treaty with the Soviet Union recognising the territorial integrity of all the states of Europe within their existing boundaries – the start of a thaw in East-West relations, known as détente.

In 1971, with détente in full swing, a Quadripartite Agreement was signed by the Soviet Union, the USA, the UK and France, normalising the status quo in Berlin. With this agreement in place, many Western countries recognised the GDR and established diplomatic relations. In 1972 the FRG and the GDR reached agreement on how to run their bilateral affairs, although full recognition was prevented by the West German constitution.

From Détente to Unity

In May 1971 the GDR's postwar leader, Walter Ulbricht, a hardline 'Moscow' Communist who had spent WW II in the Soviet Union, was removed from power for opposing détente. He was replaced by Erich Honecker, a 'national' Communist imprisoned by the Nazis from 1935 to 1945. Honecker emphasised consumer production, yet despite living standards better than those of any other Eastern European country, the GDR only attained levels half as high as West Germany. With European unity just over the horizon and the Western technological lead increasing, the country seemed likely to fall behind even further.

After March 1985, when Mikhail Gorbachev took over in the Soviet Union, the East German Communists no longer had full Soviet backing. The GDR's identity was undermined by West German TV programmes accessible to 85% of East Germans, leading to increasing alienation between people and state. Accusations that the results of local elections in May 1989 were falsified gave people the feeling of being unrepresented in government.

Meanwhile, the West German government

was offering instant citizenship and emergency benefits to any East German who made it across the border, and many took the first opportunity to escape. Most of the 340,000 East Germans who eventually left in 1989 were well-educated people aged between 20 and 30.

In May 1989 Hungary began dismantling its border controls, creating a gap in the security net which had held the Eastern bloc together for 40 years. By August, 5000 East Germans a week were reaching West Germany via Hungary, and when the Hungarian government opened its border with Austria on 10 September, 12,000 East Germans crossed within 72 hours.

The failure of the Soviet Union to intervene at this point, sent the East German public the signal that Soviet troops would not be used to prop up the Communist regime, and on 25 September mass demonstrations against the government began in Leipzig. The protesters were encouraged by political changes elsewhere in Eastern Europe. In August 1989 a non-Communist government had taken office in Poland, and moves towards reform were well advanced in Hungary. An informal opposition had already existed in the GDR for several years in the form of a 'peace movement' centred around the Lutheran Church. The East German government countered by prohibiting travel to Hungary, and would-be defectors began taking refuge in the West German Embassy in Prague, where 5000 were soon camped.

In October 1989, Gorbachev visited East Berlin for the 40th anniversary celebrations of the foundation of the GDR. He urged the ruling Politburo to take the lead in reform, a course strongly resisted by Honecker, who feared destabilisation. West Germany had promised Gorbachev DM10 billion in economic aid if he didn't try to prop up East Germany's Communist government. Monday-evening demonstrations continued in Leipzig throughout October, with the number of participants doubling each time and the unrest spreading to other cities.

Honecker ordered a crackdown on the Leipzig protesters, but his internal security chief, Egon Krenz, wavered and cancelled the order. As things slipped out of control, Honecker resigned and was replaced by Krenz, who was unpopular due to his long association with the regime. On 5 November 1989, a million people gathered in East Berlin's Alexanderplatz to demand change.

In a desperate bid to keep pace with events, Krenz reshuffled the Politburo, promised free elections and, on 9 November 1989, opened the Berlin Wall. The choice of that particular date, the 51st anniversary of the *Kristallnacht* in 1938, when the Nazis conducted a notorious pogrom against German Jews, was a brilliant final ploy by the Communists which has prevented the day from being celebrated as a German national holiday.

Krenz had gambled that giving East Germans the freedom to travel to the West (a major demand of the protesters) would convince most of them to stay home, but the opening of the Wall only increased the mass emigration, and by early 1990 as many as 2000 a day were departing. After televised revelations of the lavish perks enjoyed by the Communist leadership, Krenz and his Politburo resigned. Hans Modrow, the reformist Dresden party leader, took over.

New Forum, the original opposition group founded in September 1989, and others such as Democracy Now, United Left and Democratic Awakening, contained a strong leftist element interested in 'democratic dialogue' with the regime and preserving 'the real and successful socialist achievements of the GDR' (wording from the draft programme of Democracy Now). The Social Democratic Party, re-established in the GDR in October 1989, also favoured gradual change.

But in November 1989, West German chancellor Helmut Kohl entered the fray with a 10-point plan for German reunification, and the popular mood began swinging away from mere reform. After a meeting with Gorbachev in February 1990, even Modrow came out in favour of reunification.

Elections were slated for 18 March 1990, and only two weeks before them, the Social

GERMANY

Democratic Party was leading the polls with a programme of gradual change and preserving positive elements of East Germany's identity. Then Kohl intervened again by campaigning for quick reunification and a one-for-one currency exchange (at this time one Deutschmark was trading for 10 Ostmarks on the black market).

Bundesbank president Karl Otto Pöhl warned that a one-for-one exchange rate would lead to economic collapse in the east, but Kohl claimed that the mass emigration (120,000 East Germans left the GDR in the first two months of 1990) made gradual change impossible, and played on the long-standing desire for reunification on both sides of the border. Kohl reassured West German voters that taxes would not have to be increased to pay for reunification.

These generous promises swung the election in favour of Kohl's Christian Democratic Union (CDU), which received 41% of the popular vote in East Germany; the Social Democrats got 22% and the Socialists (ex-Communists) just 16%. The groups that had spearheaded the November 1989 'revolution' were completely sidelined.

Christian Democrat Lothar de Mazière became prime minister and formed a conservative alliance which implemented the economic and monetary union of the two Germanys on 1 July 1990. East Germans were given one week to convert 4000 Ostmarks each into Deutschmarks at the one-to-one rate; the rest of their savings and debts were converted at a two-to-one rate. Prices were also converted one-to-one, dooming the inefficient East German industries to certain bankruptcy.

In September 1990, representatives of the two Germanys and the four wartime Allies signed the Two-Plus-Four Treaty in Moscow, ending the postwar system of occupation zones. On 3 October 1990, the East German parliament voted itself out of existence, and the German Democratic Republic became part of the Federal Republic of Germany amid scenes of mass jubilation throughout the country – and much sadness among those who had devoted their produc-tive lives to a lie. The date of 3 November is now celebrated as a national holiday, and German reunification is widely regarded as the 'official' end of the Cold War between the Soviet empire and the West.

Reunification had nothing to do with a negotiated merger of the two states: West Germany in effect simply annexed East Germany, and in the general euphoria Kohl's CDU easily won the all-German elections of 2 December 1990.

Disillusionment & Optimism

Wild celebrations are often followed by heavy hangovers. So, too, in Germany, when the realisation began to sink in that incorporating eastern Germany into the western framework was going to take more time and money than most people expected – or than Kohl had promised.

The sudden liquidation of uncompetitive and highly polluting eastern German industries was only partly matched by new investments from the west. Up to 50% of eastern Germans lost their jobs or were put on short-time, and the government had to break its promise not to raise taxes. A net total of DM140 billion (US$85 billion) was transferred to the east in 1991 to pay for welfare and badly needed investments; in 1992 this figure climbed to DM180 billion (US$110 billion), or a quarter of all public spending.

As western Germany's economic miracle came under threat from rising inflation and budget deficits, western Germans began to feel the costs of reunification in their own wallets. Kohl's failure to issue a 'blood, sweat and tears' speech towards the end of 1990, when most Germans might have been receptive to the idea of sacrifice to make reunification work, was a major political mistake that came to haunt him when the government announced belt-tightening measures in the middle of 1992. Disgusted by broken promises and faced with the lack of real wage increases, western Germans took to the streets and brought the country to a standstill with the largest series of strikes since the early 1930s. Compromise solutions worked out between trade unions, employers and the government will place further strains on the German economy.

In eastern Germany, however, the future looks promising. Despite high levels of unemployment and major upheavals to established social patterns, the development of new industries continues apace. Eastern Germans, in their optimistic moments, seem to agree that the hardships are temporary – which is more than can be said for their reforming neighbours across the eastern and southern borders, who don't have a rich uncle to bail them out. With a bit of luck, eastern Germany could be well and truly on its feet by the end of the decade. With new, high-tech industries, some of which are already more advanced than those in western Germany, it might even be able to lead the way.

GEOGRAPHY

Germany is a country of 356,866 sq km. The area along the North Sea coast is flat and protected by dykes. The Frisian Islands dot the coastline and offer miles of deserted sandy beaches and dunes. In contrast to the wild North Sea coast, at the mercy of the elements, the tideless Baltic coast is calm, featuring fine, sandy beaches, wooded surroundings and a favourable climate.

South of the Baltic and North Sea coasts, the German-Polish Plain is relatively flat, but still has a unique landscape with peat bogs, wet pastureland and farmland.

The Harz Mountains around Wernigerode are known as an area of old traditions and scenic beauty. The Weser River and Harz Mountains dominate the 'heart' of Germany.

Picturesque Thuringia to the south, the 'green heart' of Germany, has rolling hills and valleys and is a magnificent hiking area. In Saxon Switzerland, between Dresden and Bad Schandau along the River Elbe, are picturesque rocks *(Steine)* and gorges, sandstone cliffs and bizarre landforms.

The Rhineland Schist Massif is a mountainous area in the west, marked by deep schisms. South of these mountain ranges lies the Swabian-Franconian Basin, with vineyards and rolling countryside. To the southwest sits the Black Forest, stretching for 170 km and full of fresh woods and streams, tourists and cuckoo clocks.

Along the Swiss and Austrian borders are the Bavarian and Allgau Alps. The mountains offer incredible vistas, culminating at the Zugspitze, at 2966 metres the highest peak in Germany.

GOVERNMENT

With reunification, eastern Germany adopted the governmental structure of western Germany, and the two areas now generally operate as one governmental unit. In many ways it's the most decentralised government structure in Europe.

From 1952 to 1990, what was then the German Democratic Republic consisted of 14 districts *(Bezirke)*, but with reunification these were scrapped and regional government was reorganised on the basis of the six original (ie pre-1952) states, or *Länder*: Berlin, Brandenburg, Mecklenburg-Vorpommern (Mecklenburg-Pomerania), Sachsen (Saxony), Sachsen-Anhalt and Thüringen (Thuringia). In the context of the German Federal Republic they are now referred to as *Bundesländer*, or Federal States. The Bundesländer in western Germany are Schleswig-Holstein, Hamburg, Niedersachsen (Lower Saxony), Bremen, Nordrhein-Westfalen (North Rhine-Westphalia), Hessen, Rheinland-Pfalz (Rhineland-Palatinate), Saarland, Baden Württemberg and Bayern (Bavaria).

The Bundesländer have a large degree of autonomy in internal affairs, and exert influence on the central government through the upper house, or *Bundesrat*. The lower house, or *Bundestag*, is elected by direct universal suffrage with proportional representation, though a party must have at least 5% of votes to gain seats. Federal government has alternated between the Christian Democrats (CDU) and the Socialists (SPD), with the balance of power generally held by the small but influential Liberal party (the Free Democrats, or FDP).

Although Berlin is officially the capital of

GERMANY

the new Germany, the seat of government remains in Bonn. In June 1991 the Bundestag in Bonn voted to move to Berlin within four years. Government ministries are to follow before the year 2003.

ECONOMY

The Marshall Plan contributed much to the rapid postwar economic recovery of what was then West Germany. This economic miracle *(Wirtschaftswunder)* occurred in the 1950s and 1960s and turned the FRG into the third-largest economy in the world. Throughout this period and into the 1980s, the powerful trade unions and huge industrial corporations developed a unique 'economic contract' by which the workers shunned strikes in return for some of the highest wages, longest holidays and generally best working conditions in the world. Thanks to a well-developed apprenticeship system, the labour force was also highly skilled. Important industries then and now include electrical manufacturing, precision and optical instruments, chemicals, vehicle manufacturing, and domestic and foreign trade.

While the West German economic miracle received wide publicity in the 1960s, East Germany's recovery was even more remarkable considering the wartime destruction, postwar looting by the Soviet Union, loss of skilled labour, and isolation from Western markets. Careful economic planning built the GDR into the largest industrial and trading nation in Eastern Europe and, by some dubious counts, one of the world's top-10 industrial nations. Important industries included metallurgy, electric power, chemicals, and general and electrical engineering.

When the two Germanys merged, western Germans enjoyed an annual gross domestic product of DM38,000 (US$23,500) per head; the figure in eastern Germany was about one-third of that. But rather than improve, the eastern German gross domestic product dropped by 10% in 1990 and another 20% in 1991. A major blow was the collapse of Comecon (the trading bloc of the Soviet

Union and Eastern European states), brought about by the introduction of world prices for goods rather than the fancy-paperwork 'accounting roubles'. At a stroke, eastern Germany lost 40% of its export market, and by mid-1991 it was facing a severe economic crisis with 50% unemployment and stagnant industry, unable to compete on Western markets due to the one-to-one exchange rate and the relatively low quality of its goods. Things seemed worse than during the economic depression of the 1930s. Industrial production dropped by 53%. Even blue chips such as Interflug, Carl Zeiss, Wartburg, Trabant and the shipbuilding industry were liquidated.

Eastern Germany went from Stalinist Communism to Thatcherite capitalism in one jump. Many eastern Germans thought that by becoming part of unified Germany they would immediately get all the consumer goods they saw on TV. Many bought cars on credit and then lost them together with their jobs. Eastern Germans seemed to become the poor relations in a capitalist Germany. With little or no chance of finding new jobs, the middle-aged and elderly languished on welfare while many of their children migrated to western Germany in search of work, only to be cheated by unscrupulous employers.

In the course of 1992, however, things have begun to look up. The astute government agency in charge of privatising the eastern German economy, the Treuhandanstalt, has sold about half of the 12,000 enterprises on its hands, many of them on condition that the new owners take responsibility for existing employees. Massive government investments ensure that roads are being fixed, that telephones are beginning to work, and that households are switching from brown coal to much more environmentally friendly natural gas. Buildings are being cleaned and restored, often by former owners who've reclaimed their properties, and colourful advertising is transforming the formerly drab appearance of streets.

The average eastern German wage is now

a bit more than half that in the west, and a fifth of workers are on contracts promising parity by 1994. Unemployment and short-time are down to about 30%. Some 200,000 small, private firms have sprung up all over eastern Germany, many of them in the restaurant and hotel industries.

It will probably take a decade before the eastern German economy matches its western counterpart. Before WW II, northern Germany was the richest part of the country, but after the war Germany's wealth moved south, with the big car makers (Mercedes and BMW), electronics (IBM) and the armaments industries all based there. The same thing may eventually happen in the east (market economists swear it will), but the generation that made the changes possible may be sacrificed somewhere along the way.

POPULATION & PEOPLE

There are 62 million people in western Germany and 16.5 million in eastern Germany, making the unified country by far the most populous European country apart from Russia-in-Europe. Unlike western Germany, which has 4,400,000 foreign residents, Prussians and Saxons comprise 99.7% of the eastern German population, with a small Slavonic minority, the Sorbs and Wends, in the south-eastern corner. The southern half of eastern Germany is much more densely populated and industrialised than the north. In all, 75% of the population live in urban areas.

Berlin is the largest city in Germany and one of the 10 biggest cities in Europe. Former West Berlin, with 2.2 million inhabitants, occupies 480 sq km, while 1.3 million people live in what used to be East Berlin (403 sq km). By the year 2005 the population of reunified Berlin could double to about six million.

Prior to the building of the Wall, some 60,000 East Berlin workers held jobs in West Berlin and crossed daily. Once the border was closed, their places were taken by immigrants. There are a quarter million non-German residents in West Berlin, about half of them Turkish. The others are mostly Yugoslavs, Poles, Greeks and Italians. More than a quarter of the population of Kreuzberg is foreign. As for the rest of the country, the collapse of Communism in Eastern Europe and the civil war in Yugoslavia have led to a large influx of asylum-seekers in the early 1990s, thanks to Germany's economic wealth and generous asylum policy – a development that has led to increased social tension in inner-city areas around the country.

Tens of thousands of foreign troops are still present in eastern Germany, though the occupation system was suspended in October 1990. The withdrawal of 12,000 US, British and French troops and dependents from West Berlin, and a much larger number of Soviet troops from the rest of eastern Germany, is to be completed by 1994.

The entire area has suffered through an identity problem since WW II. The people lost vast territories to the Soviet Union and Poland and had the rest divided between Eastern and Western bloc countries. The ramifications of the Nazi regime can be seen in the actions of the people: much protest, rather than submissiveness, a genuine interest in peace, and a constant concern for the environment.

Throughout unified Germany, WW II is no longer the taboo topic of discussion that it used to be. Today's Germans understand that the past cannot and must not be forgotten. Many make pilgrimages to Dachau, Belsen and other former concentration camps. Despite a fair amount of press, neo-Nazism has little genuine support beyond a vocal minority of unemployed youth in the east.

The stereotypical German doesn't exist. Many visitors used to view Germans as too disciplined, overbearing and conforming. Today's Germans are generally much more relaxed, personable and interested in enjoying life. It's easy for travellers to find much in common with Germans and to strike up conversations throughout the country. This relaxed attitude is increasing as a result of reunification. It also appears to be spreading east.

GERMANY

ARTS
Architecture, Painting & Literature

The scope of German art is such that it could be the focus for an entire visit. Much of the artistic progress revolved around the church, and this can be seen in artistic works and architecture. The first blossoming of the arts occurred during the Romanesque period (800-1200). Examples can be found at the Stiftskirche at Gernrode, St Michael's Church in Hildesheim, the National Germanic Museum in Nuremberg, the Trier Cathedral, and many others.

The Gothic style (1200-1500) is best viewed at the Freiburg Minster, the Minden Cathedral, or the Paderborn Cathedral. Gothic painting and sculpture featured famous works, such as those produced by artists from the Cologne School of painters, and sculptors Peter Vischer and his sons.

The Renaissance was slower to develop in Germany than in Italy, but painting and graphic art flourished once it took hold. One of Germany's most famous draughtsmen, Albrecht Dürer of Nuremberg (1471-1528), became one of the world's finest portraitists (try to see his *Four Apostles* in the Nuremberg town hall). Another renowned visual artist was Lucas Cranach the Elder (1472-1553). During his 45 years in Wittenberg, Cranach's studio turned out hundreds of paintings and woodcuts. Though best known for his portraits, Cranach initiated the Lutheran school of painting.

The 18th century Baroque period brought great sculpture, including works by Andreas Schlüter and Rococo artists Johan Baptist Straub and Ignaz Günther in Munich. Franz Anton Bustelli made his contribution through porcelain, at the Nymphenburg manufacturing plant in Munich.

Goethe & Schiller During the 18th century Enlightenment, the Saxon court at Weimar attracted figures of European stature. Though born in Frankfurt-am-Main and educated at Leipzig, Johann Wolfgang von Goethe (1749-1832) moved to Weimar in 1775, spending the rest of his life there despite an invitation from Napoleon to reset-

tle in Paris. Arguably the greatest of German writers, Goethe the poet, dramatist, novelist, critic, painter, statesman, teacher, scientist and philosopher was perhaps the last European to achieve the Renaissance ideal of excellence in many fields. His greatest work, the drama *Faust*, is a masterful compendium of all that went before him, as the archetypical Western human strives relentlessly for meaning. Goethe characterised his literary works as 'fragments of a great confession'. The ghost of Goethe lives throughout Germany.

Goethe's closest friend was the poet, dramatist and novelist Friedrich Schiller (1759-1805). His most famous work is the dramatic cycle, *Wallenstein* (translated by Samuel Taylor Coleridge), based on the life of a treacherous Thirty Years' War general who plotted to make himself arbiter of the empire until his murder in 1634. If *Wallenstein* demonstrated the corrupting effects of power, Schiller's other great play, *William Tell*, dealt with the right of the oppressed to rise against tyranny. Large museums to both Schiller and Goethe exist in Weimar today.

The 19th & Early 20th Centuries Berlin too produced remarkable individuals like Alexander von Humboldt (1769-1859), a precursor of modern environmentalism through his studies of the relationship of plants and animals to their physical surroundings. Son of an important Berlin family, Humboldt set out in 1799 on a five-year exploration of Latin America including a three-month journey on foot through the Amazon rainforest and the ascent of Andean peaks around Quito. He was among the first to connect geological faults with volcanoes and earthquakes.

Humboldt's contemporary, Georg Wilhelm Friedrich Hegel (1770-1831), came to Berlin in 1818 to occupy the chair of philosophy at Berlin University, becoming rector in 1830 just prior to his death from cholera. Hegel created an all-embracing classical philosophy still influential today. His dialectical system in which thesis and antithesis are resolved by a higher synthesis inspired existentialists, Marxists and positivists alike.

The neoclassical period in Germany was led by painter Friedrich Schinkel and the Munich neoclassical school. The Romantic period looked even further back, to the Middle Ages, and is best exemplified by the works of Caspar David Friedrich.

The reaction to all of this looking back was Impressionism, which developed in France, and the popularity of Max Liebermann. Even further new developments occurred through Art Nouveau, which saw great contributions in German architecture. Wonderful examples include August Endell's Haus Elvira in Munich and Alfred Messel's Wertheim department store in Berlin.

Next came expressionism, with great names like Paul Klee and the Russian painter Wassily Kandinsky. This period also saw the development of the famous Bauhaus movement, founded in 1919 by Walter Gropius in an attempt to meld the theoretical concerns of architecture with the practical problems faced by artists and craftspeople. The Nazis closed the School of Design founded by Gropius in Weimar, and he emigrated to Cambridge, Massachusetts, becoming the chairman of Harvard University's department of architecture. Other Bauhaus directors were Ludwig Mies van der Rohe, who established the department of architecture at the Illinois Institute of Technology, and László Moholy-Nagy, who founded the Chicago Institute of Design.

Brecht In the 1920s, Berlin was the theatrical capital of Germany, and its most famous practitioner was the poet and playwright Bertolt Brecht (1898-1956). Brecht moved to Berlin from Munich in 1924 and was here converted from cynical anarchism to the controlled didactic Marxism of his mature period. Brecht's experience in WW I made him a lifelong pacifist, and in Marxism he thought he had found a scientific alternative to the moral dilemmas of a mass society and capitalist selfishness. Yet it was the poetic simplicity of his moral parables, the precise language and sharp characterisation which

lifted his work above dogmatic concerns. Brecht revolutionised the theatre by detaching the audience from what was happening on stage to permit them to observe and judge without illusion or involvement. Viewed from the 1990s, Brecht's works are a stirring rebuttal to fascism and war, woven with music and song which make even German-language productions appealing to non-German speakers.

In 1933 Brecht fled the Nazis and eventually settled in Santa Monica, California. He attempted to write for Hollywood, until 1947 when he was compelled to appear before the notorious 'Committee on Un-American Activities' of the US Congress. The next day, Brecht sailed for Europe, and after a time in Switzerland, accepted the directorship of the Berliner Ensemble in East Berlin in 1949, where his work has been performed ever since. He died of a heart attack in 1956.

WW II & Beyond During the Third Reich, the arts sadly were devoted mainly to propaganda, with grandiose projects and realist art extolling the virtues of Germanhood. Max Ernst, resident in France and the USA, was a prominent exponent of Dada and surrealism, who developed the technique of collage.

Eastern Germany's leading contemporary novelist, Christa Wolf (1929-) maintained her independence while living and publishing in the GDR. Her *Der geteilte Himmel* (1963), or 'Divided Heaven', is the story of a young woman whose fiancé abandons her for life in the West. In *Nachdenken über Christa* (1968), or 'Thinking About Christa', based on the early death of a female friend, Wolf ponders individual self-realisation in a collective society. Her novel *Kindheitsmuster* (1976), or 'Patterns of Childhood', traces her own childhood under fascism and poses the question, 'How have we become the way we are?'

Wolf's preoccupation with the role of women in history and society found its highest expression in *Kassandra* (1983), in which she creates a utopic female counterpart for the aggressive thought/action male model. The incapacity of humanity to

GERMANY

prevent nuclear self-destruction is the theme of *Störfall* (1986), Wolf's literary response to Chernobyl. Long before 1989, Wolf bridged the gap between the two Germanys and won high esteem on both sides of the Wall.

Music

Few countries can claim the impressive musical heritage of Germany. Much of the early music revolved around the church, but developed rapidly in the 18th century. A partial list of household names includes Johann Sebastian Bach, Georg Friedrich Händel, Ludwig van Beethoven, Richard Wagner, Richard Strauss, Felix Mendelssohn-Bartholdy, Robert Schumann, Johannes Brahms and Gustav Mahler. More recently, German contributions have included works by Paul Hindemith and many others.

It's significant indeed that the two greatest Baroque composers should have been born in Saxony in the same year. Johann Sebastian Bach (1685-1750) was born at Eisenach into a prominent family of musicians. From 1708 to 1717 he served as court organist at Weimar, moving to Leipzig in 1723 where he spent his remaining 27 years as city musical director. Bach's duties at Leipzig involved conducting services at St Thomas and St Nikolai, supplying music and training boys to sing in the Thomas Choir. During his life, Bach produced some 200 cantatas, plus masses, oratorios, passions and other elaborate music for the Lutheran service, and sonatas, concertos, preludes and fugues for secular use. Though regarded as a conservative by his contemporaries, the Bach revival which began 50 years after his death continues today.

At the age of 18, Georg Friedrich Händel (1685-1759) left his native Halle for Hamburg. During his three years in Italy he mastered the Italian opera. Händel's first visit to England was in 1710, and the highly successful performance of his opera *Rinaldo* there the next year encouraged him to spend most of the rest of his life in that country. Händel composed 40 operas before the public lost interest in the genre in 1741. At this, Händel switched to oratorios – his *Messiah* (1742) is still regularly performed. Händel democratised court music by performing before a large audience in churches, parks and gardens – an aspect of lasting influence. The birthplaces of both Händel and Bach are now large museums.

In the 19th century, the musical traditions of Saxony continued unabated with the song writer Robert Schumann (1810-56), born at Zwickau. In 1843 Schumann opened a music school at Leipzig in collaboration with composer Felix Mendelssohn (1809-47), director of Leipzig's famous Gewandhaus Orchestra. From 1848 to 1861 the famous Hungarian composer and piano virtuoso, Franz Liszt (1811-86), lived at Weimar where he wrote his *Dante* and *Faust* symphonies, a piano sonata, two piano concertos, the *Totentanz* and other illustrious works. In 1869 the Grand Duke invited Liszt to return to Weimar to found a music school which still exists today.

These musical traditions continue to thrive: the Dresden Opera and Leipzig Orchestra are known around the world, and musical performances are hosted almost daily in every major theatre in the country.

The Studio for Electronic Music in Cologne is a centre for cutting-edge developments in this field. Contemporary music is also popular: jazz, folk, rock and roll, new wave, and much more can be found in every large city – the emphasis is often on beat and volume rather than melody. And traditional German oompah music is still popular with locals and tourists.

Porcelain

Germany has long been a world leader in porcelain production. The Meissen factory was the first in Europe to make white hard-paste porcelain. Factories in Fürstenberg and Nymphenburg gained a reputation for their vases, tableware and figurines. Excellent porcelain exhibits can be found in Munich's Palace Museum, Frankfurt's Museum of Applied Arts, and Berlin's Museum of Decorative Arts.

CULTURE

Germany is a highly organised nation. But don't be fooled by its relative wealth and outward signs of materialism: Germans have a great respect for culture and tradition. After all, Germany could never have made its major contributions to European culture if the soil hadn't been fertile.

Traditional Lifestyle

Even as modern times engulf the country, there are still strong traditions. Hunters still wear green, master chimney sweeps still wear their top hats, Bavarian women sometimes wear the *Dirndl* skirt and blouse, and many men in Bavaria will find suitable occasions to wear leather shorts, a *Loden* (short jacket), and felt hat.

In daily life, locals often meet at the *Lokal* (local pub) over a beer to discuss things; many households still shop daily along pedestrian streets.

Taboos

There are few great taboos left in modern Germany. There is, perhaps, still a reluctance on the part of some people to discuss the Nazi regime, though reunification has brought the subject more into the open. Some Germans are also sensitive to their stereotypical portrayal as too disciplined and overbearing, and will bear you down with arguments as to why this is not the case.

Avoiding Offence

Formal manners are still important, though perhaps less so than a decade ago. Except for very close friends, most Germans still use *Herr* and *Frau* in daily discussion. In fact, the transition from the formal *Sie* to the informal *du* is often celebrated. Similarly, professional titles are almost always used instead of a surname (eg *Herr Professor*). Germans always shake hands when greeting or leaving. Cheek kissing is standard between males and females who know one another.

Eastern Germans are socially more conservative than western Germans, though the only place you really have to wear a tie is to a wedding or funeral. Nude bathing is very common in eastern Germany – in fact, it's one of the few freedoms these people were formerly allowed. Nude beaches are marked 'FKK'.

Sport

The Germans love their sports for participation and watching – one in three Germans belongs to some sort of sports club. The most popular sport is, of course, football (soccer). Gymnastics, swimming, skiing and, more recently, tennis (thanks to Boris Becker, Steffi Graf and Michael Stich) are increasingly popular.

With renewed interest in the environment, outdoor activities and sports, ever popular in Germany, are experiencing astounding growth. The possibilities can range from hiking to white-water rafting.

RELIGION

Most Germans belong to a church, and membership is almost equally divided between the Catholic and Protestant persuasions – roughly speaking, Catholics predominate in the south, Protestants in the north. A majority of citizens pay contributions to their church, which the government collects along with their taxes (a bone of contention). These funds mean huge budgets, which are used for buildings, schools, hospitals and welfare operations. In practice, less than 5% of the Protestants and 25% of the Catholics are active churchgoers.

The long history of conflict between Catholics and Protestants in Germany is generally nonexistent these days, but conflict *within* the two churches is great. Catholics are concerned with old and new problems, like abortion. Protestants are struggling with the church's involvement in political issues, like the environment.

In eastern Germany, the Protestant church, which claims support among 80% of the population there, played a major role in the overthrow of German Communism by providing a gathering place for antigovernment protesters. Some of the leaders of the first opposition groups were Protestant pastors.

In 1933 there were 160,000 Jews in Berlin alone. Some 6500 live in Berlin today.

LANGUAGE

It might be a surprise to know that German is a close relative of English. English, German and Dutch are all known as West Germanic languages. This means that you know lots of German words already – *Arm, Finger, Gold* – and you'll be able to figure out many others – *Mutter*, 'mother', *trinken*, 'drink', *gut*, 'good'. A primary reason why English and German have grown apart is that when the Normans invaded England in 1066 they brought in many non-Germanic words. It's meant that English has lots of synonyms, with the more basic word being Germanic, and the more literary or specialised one coming from French; for instance, 'start' and 'green' as opposed to 'commence' and 'verdant'.

German is spoken throughout Germany and Austria and in much of Switzerland. It is also extremely useful in Eastern Europe, especially with older people. Although you may hear different dialects, there is a strong tradition of a prescribed official language, used here, which will always be understood. In some tourist centres, English is so widely spoken that you may not have a chance to use German, even if you want to! However, as soon as you try to meet ordinary people or move out of the big cities, especially in what was East Germany, the situation is totally different. Your efforts to speak the local language will be very much appreciated and will make your trip much more enjoyable and fulfilling.

Words that you'll often encounter on maps and throughout this chapter include: *Altstadt* (old city), *Bahnhof* (station), *Brücke* (bridge), *Hauptbahnhof* (main train station), *Markt* (market, often the central square in old towns), *Platz* (square) and *Rathaus* (town hall). One distinctive feature of German is that all nouns are written with a capital letter.

Pronunciation

Unlike English or French, German does not have silent letters: you pronounce the **k** at the start of the word *Knie*, 'knee', the **p** at the start of *Psychologie*, 'psychology', and the **e** at the end of *ich habe*, 'I have'.

Vowels As in English, vowels can be pronounced long, like the 'o' in 'pope', or short, like the 'o' in 'pop'. As a rule, German vowels are long before one consonant and short before two consonants: the **o** is long in the word *Dom*, 'cathedral', but short in the word *doch*, 'after all'.

a	short, as the 'u' sound in 'cut', or long, as in 'father'
au	as in 'vow'
ä	short, as in 'act', or long, as in 'hair'
äu	as in 'boy'
e	short, as in 'bet', or long, as in 'day'
ei	as the 'ai' in 'aisle'
eu	as in 'boy'
i	short, as in 'in', or long, as in 'see'
ie	as in 'see'
o	short, as in 'pot', or long, as in 'note'
ö	as the 'er' in 'fern'
u	as the 'u' in 'pull'
ü	like the 'u' in 'pull' but with stretched lips

Consonants Most German consonants sound similar to their English counterparts. One important difference is that **b**, **d** and **g** sound like 'p', 't' and 'k', respectively, at the end of a word.

b	normally the English 'b', but 'p' at end of a word
ch	the *ch* in Scottish *loch*
d	normally as the English 'd', but 't' at end of a word
g	normally as the English 'g', but 'k' at the end of a word, and *ch*, as in the Scottish *loch*, at end of a word and after **i**
j	as the 'y' in 'yet'
qu	'k' plus 'v'
r	as the English 'r', but rolled at the back of the mouth
s	normally as the 's' in 'sun'; as the 'z' in 'zoo' when followed by a vowel
sch	as the 'sh' in 'ship'

sp, st	's' sounds like the 'sh' in 'ship' when at the start of a word
tion	the **t** sounds like the 'ts' in 'hits'
ß	as in 'sun' (written as **ss** in this book)
v	as the 'f' in 'fan'
w	as the 'v' in 'van'
z	as the 'ts' in 'hits'

Greetings & Civilities

Hello (Good day).	*Guten Tag.*
Goodbye.	*Auf Wiedersehen.*
Yes.	*Ja.*
No.	*Nein.*
Please.	*Bitte.*
Thank you.	*Danke.*
That's fine. You're welcome.	*Bitte sehr.*
Sorry. (excuse me, forgive me)	*Entschuldigung.*

Some Useful Phrases

Do you speak English?	*Sprechen Sie Englisch?*
Does anyone here speak English?	*Spricht hier jemand Englisch?*
I (don't) understand.	*Ich verstehe (nicht).*
Just a minute.	*Ein Moment!*
Please write that down.	*Können Sie es bitte aufschreiben?*
How much is it ?	*Wieviel kostet es?*

Useful Signs

Camping Ground	*Campingplatz*
Entrance	*Eingang*
Exit	*Ausgang*
Full, No Vacancies	*Voll, Besetzt*
Guesthouse	*Pension , Gasthaus*
Hotel	*Hotel*
Information	*Auskunft*
Open/Closed	*Offen/Geschlossen*
Police	*Polizei*
Police Station	*Polizeiwache*
Rooms Available	*Zimmer Frei*
Toilets	*Toiletten (WC)*
Train Station	*Bahnhof (Bf)*
Youth Hostel	*Jugendherberge*

Getting Around

What time does... leave?	*Wann fährt...ab?*
What time does... arrive?	*Wann kommt...an?*
What time is the next boat?	*Wann fährt das nächste Boot?*
next	*nächste*
first	*erste*
last	*letzte*
the boat	*das Boot*
the bus (city)	*der Bus*
the bus (intercity)	*der (Überland)bus*
the tram	*die Strassenbahn*
the train	*der Zug*
I would like...	*Ich möchte...*
a one-way ticket	*eine Einzelkarte*
a return ticket	*eine Rückfahr- karte*
1st class	*erste Klasse*
2nd class	*zweite Klasse*
Where is the bus stop?	*Wo ist die Bushaltestelle?*
Where is the tram stop?	*Wo ist die Strassen- bahnhaltestelle?*
Can you show me (on the map)?	*Können Sie mir (auf der Karte) zeigen?*
I'm looking for...	*Ich suche...*
far/near	*weit/nahe*
Go straight ahead.	*Gehen Sie geradeaus.*
Turn left...	*Biegen Sie...links ab.*
Turn right...	*Biegen Sie...rechts ab.*

Around Town

I'm looking for...	*Ich suche...*
a bank	*eine Bank*
the city centre	*die Innenstadt*
the...embassy	*die...Botschaft*
my hotel	*mein Hotel*
the market	*den Markt*
the police	*die Polizei*
the post office	*das Postamt*

GERMANY

a public toilet	*eine öffentliche Toilette*
the telephone centre	*die Telefonzentrale*
the tourist information office	*das Verkehrsamt*

beach	*Strand*
bridge	*Brücke*
castle	*Schloss*
cathedral	*Dom*
church	*Kirche*
hospital	*Krankenhaus*
island	*Insel*
lake	*See*
main square	*Hauptplatz*
market	*Markt*
monastery	*Kloster*
mosque	*Moschee*
old city	*Altstadt*
palace	*Palast*
ruins	*Ruinen*
sea	*Meer*
square	*Platz*
tower	*Turm*

Accommodation

Where is a cheap hotel?	*Wo ist ein billiges Hotel?*
What is the address?	*Was ist die Adresse?*
Could you write the address, please?	*Könnten Sie bitte die Adresse aufschreiben?*
Do you have any rooms available?	*Haben Sie noch freie Zimmer?*

I would like...	*Ich möchte...*
a single room	*ein Einzelzimmer*
a double room	*ein Doppelzimmer*
a room with a bathroom	*ein Zimmer mit Bad*
to share a dorm	*einen Schlafsaal teilen*
a bed	*ein Bett*

| How much is it per night/per person? | *Wieviel kostet es pro Nacht/pro Person?* |
| Can I see it? | *Kann ich es sehen?* |

| Where is the bathroom? | *Wo ist das Bad?* |

Food

bakery	*Bäckerei*
grocery	*Lebensmittelgeschäft*
delicatessen	*Delikatessengeschäft*
restaurant	*Restaurant, Gaststätte*
breakfast	*Frühstück*
lunch	*Mittagessen*
dinner	*Abendessen*

I would like the set lunch, please.	*Ich hätte gern das Tagesmenü bitte.*
Is service included in the bill?	*Ist die Bedienung inbegriffen?*
I am a vegetarian.	*Ich bin Vegetarierin (f) Vegetarier. (m)*

Time & Dates

today	*heute*
tomorrow	*morgen*
in the morning	*morgens*
in the afternoon	*nachmittags*
in the evening	*abends*

Monday	*Montag*
Tuesday	*Dienstag*
Wednesday	*Mittwoch*
Thursday	*Donnerstag*
Friday	*Freitag*
Saturday	*Samstag, Sonnabend*
Sunday	*Sonntag*

January	*Januar*
February	*Februar*
March	*März*
April	*April*
May	*Mai*
June	*Juni*
July	*Juli*
August	*August*
September	*September*
October	*Oktober*
November	*November*
December	*Dezember*

Numbers

0	*null*
1	*eins*
2	*zwei*
	(zwo on the telephone)
3	*drei*
4	*vier*
5	*fünf*
6	*sechs*
7	*sieben*
8	*acht*
9	*neun*
10	*zehn*
11	*elf*
12	*zwölf*
13	*dreizehn*
14	*vierzehn*
15	*fünfzehn*
16	*sechzehn*
17	*siebzehn*
18	*achtzehn*
19	*neunzehn*
20	*zwanzig*
21	*einundzwanzig*
22	*zweiundzwanzig*
30	*dreissig*
40	*vierzig*
50	*fünfzig*
60	*sechzig*
70	*siebzig*
80	*achtzig*
90	*neunzig*
100	*hundert*
1000	*tausend*
one million	*eine Million*

Health

I'm...	*Ich bin...*
diabetic	*Diabetikerin* (f)
	Diabetiker (m)
epileptic	*Epileptikerin* (f)
	Epileptiker (m)
asthmatic	*Asthmatikerin* (f)
	Asthmatiker (m)

I'm allergic to antibiotics/penicillin.	*Ich bin gegen Antibiotika/Penizillin allergisch.*
antiseptic	*Antiseptikum*

aspirin	*Aspirin*
condoms	*Kondome*
constipation	*Verstopfung*
contraceptive	*Verhütungsmittel*
diarrhoea	*Durchfall*
medicine	*Medizin*
nausea	*Übelkeit*
sunblock cream	*Sunblockcreme*
tampons	*Tampons*

Emergencies

Help!	*Hilfe!*
Call a doctor!	*Holen Sie einen Arzt!*
Call the police!	*Rufen Sie die Polizei!*
Go away!	*Gehen Sie weg!*

Facts for the Visitor

VISAS & EMBASSIES

Americans, Australians, Britons, Canadians, New Zealanders and Japanese require only a valid passport (no visa) to enter Germany. Citizens of the European Community (EC) and many other Western European countries can enter on an official identity card. Unless you're a citizen of a Third World country you can probably stay up to three months. Many documents will be required if you decide to get married, otherwise a valid passport will suffice.

German Embassies

German embassies abroad include:

Australia
  119 Empire Circuit, Yarralumla, ACT 2600 (☎ 06-270 1911)
Canada
  1 Waverley St, Ottawa, Ont K2P 0T8 (☎ 0613-232 1101)
New Zealand
  90-92 Hobson St, Wellington (☎ 04-736 063)
South Africa
  180 Blackwood St, Arcadia, Pretoria 0083 (☎ 012-344 3854)
UK
  23 Belgrave Square, London SW1X 8PZ (☎ 071-235 5033)

USA
    4645 Reservoir Rd, NW Washington, DC 20007-
    1998 (☎ 202-298 8140)

Foreign Embassies in Germany

German government bodies are gradually moving from Bonn to Berlin, but so long as the foreign ministry remains in Bonn, the main diplomatic missions of other countries will remain there too. Many former embassies in East Berlin have closed down or have been demoted to the status of consulates. See the Berlin Information section for details on some consulates there. Embassies in Bonn (telephone code 0228) include:

Australia
    Godesberger Allee 105-107, 5300 Bonn 1
    (☎ 8 10 30)
Austria
    Johanniterstrasse 2, 5300 Bonn 1 (☎ 5 33 00 60)
Canada
    Friedrich-Wilhelm-Strasse 18, 5300 Bonn 1
    (☎ 23 10 61)
France
    Kapellenweg 1a, 5300 Bonn 2 (☎ 36 20 31)
New Zealand
    Bundeskanzlerplatz 2-10, 5300 Bonn 2
    (☎ 22 80 70)
Switzerland
    Gotenstrasse 156, 5300 Bonn 2 (☎ 81 00 80)
UK
    Friedrich-Ebert-Allee 102-104, 5300 Bonn 2
    (☎ 23 40 61)
USA
    Deichmannsaue 29, 5300 Bonn 2 (☎ 33 91)

CUSTOMS

Most items needed for personal use during a visit are duty-free. When entering Germany from another EC country, visitors can bring: 300 cigarettes, 75 cigars, or 400 grams of tobacco; 1.5 litres of liquor more than 22% by volume or three litres of less than 22% by volume; five litres of wine; 75 grams of perfume and ⅓ litre of toilet water; and other products to a value of DM780.

From a non-EC country (eg Switzerland, Austria or Poland), duty-free allowances are: 200 cigarettes, 50 cigars, or 250 grams of tobacco; one litre of liquor more than 22% by volume or two litres of less than 22% by volume; two litres of wine; 50 grams of perfume and ¼ litre of toilet water; and other products to a value of DM115.

When entering from a non-European country, visitors can bring: 400 cigarettes, 100 cigars, or 500 grams of tobacco; one litre or liquor more than 22% by volume or two litres less than 22% by volume; two litres of wine; 50 grams of perfume and ¼ litre of toilet water; and other products to a value of DM115.

Tobacco products and alcohol may only be brought in by people aged 17 and over.

MONEY

The German Mark, or Deutschmark (DM), consists of 100 Pfennig (Pf). Germans refer to it as the Mark or D-Mark ('day-mark'). The German economy is generally cash-based and, though this is changing, it's best to plan to use cash much of the time. The easiest places to change money in Germany are banks and bank-operated booths at airports and railway stations. Post offices often have money-changing facilities as well, where rates tend to be better than at the bank.

Travellers' cheques are widely used and accepted, especially if issued in Deutschmark denominations. If that's the case, you'll usually get the full amount, though bank branches at borders often charge a small commission regardless, and post offices charge a flat DM3 per-cheque fee for any cheques outside the postal financial system. A commission of DM3 to DM10 (ask first!) is charged every time you change foreign currency into Deutschmarks.

The most popular travellers' cheques are American Express, Barclays and Thomas Cook. American Express offices charge no commission on their own cheques, but the exchange rates aren't great if the cheques have to be converted into DM – it might be worth cashing larger cheques at post offices despite the DM3 fee, because rates there are better.

Credit cards are not widely accepted outside major cities, but are handy for emergencies. Hotels and restaurants often accept MasterCard, Visa and American Express. German banks prefer Eurocard, which is linked with Access and MasterCard; in small-town banks, you may have difficulty drawing cash with cards other than these three.

Having money sent to Germany is fairly straightforward. American Express is a good bet, but transfers to large commercial banks are also easy. The only hassle is that you may have to open an account at the German branch.

Currency

Coinage includes 1, 2, 5, 10, and 50 Pf, as well as 1, 2, and 5 Marks. There are banknotes of DM5, 10, 20, 50, 100, 200, 500 and 1000. In 1989 new banknotes were issued, though the larger 1980 series is still widely circulated. Beware of confusing the old DM5 and DM20 banknotes, which are the same colour and have similar designs, although the DM20 note is larger, and watch out for counterfeit banknotes made on colour photocopy machines!

Exchange Rates

A$1	=	DM1.05
C$1	=	DM1.18
NZ$1	=	DM0.80
UK£1	=	DM2.50
US$1	=	DM1.47

Costs

Because of the strong economy, the DM has been a healthy currency for decades – a great source of pride for Germans. Combined with low inflation, it has become the cornerstone of the European Monetary System. Since reunification, however, inflation has been on the increase and the DM is losing some of its shine. Rising interest rates, on the other hand, have begun to push up the value of the DM in relation to other currencies, which could make Germany's relatively cheap food and accommodation more expensive for visitors. On the whole, eastern Germany is still a bit cheaper than western Germany in small towns and villages, but prices have almost reached western levels in the cities.

Tipping

Tipping is not overly prevalent in Germany. In restaurants, service *(Bedienung)* is usually included but it is normal to round the bill up a bit if you're satisfied with the service. Taxi drivers, too, expect a slight tip. A tip of 10% is considered generous and is gratefully received.

Bargaining

Bargaining rarely occurs in this country, but when paying cash for largish purchases of more than, say, DM100, you could try asking for *Skonto*, which is a 3% discount. This doesn't apply to services like hotel and restaurant bills, however.

Consumer Tax Refunds

Most German goods and services include a value-added tax *(Mehrwertsteuer)* which generally runs at 14%, although the EC is working on a flat rate of 15% for all its members and Germany has promised to follow suit. Non-EC residents leaving the EC can have this tax refunded for goods (not services) bought, which is definitely worth it for large purchases.

Check that the shop where you're buying has the necessary customs forms which, together with the bills, must be stamped by German customs as you're leaving the country. You're not allowed to use the items purchased until you're out of Germany. Bus drivers and railway conductors aren't likely to want to wait at the border while you're getting your paperwork stamped, so if you're travelling this way, ask the shop (or the tourist office) for the nearest customs authority that can do this beforehand. If you're leaving by air, have the paperwork stamped at the airport before you check in (you have to show the articles). The stamped forms, together with the bills, must be returned to the shop where the goods were bought. The shop will mail the refund, minus costs, to your home address.

Some 17,000 shops, including the biggest department stores, are affiliated with the Tax-Cheque Service, which makes the procedure a lot easier. The shop will issue you

GERMANY

with a cheque for the amount of value-added tax to be refunded, which you can cash in when leaving the country for a non-EC destination. Get details at German tourist offices, major hotels, airports and harbours.

CLIMATE & WHEN TO GO

It can always be a good or bad time to be in Germany, depending on mother nature. Winters can be very cold or quite mild, while summers can be quite hot or cool and rainy. It's best to be prepared for all types of weather throughout the year.

That said, the best time for predictable weather is May to October. This, of course, coincides with the standard tourist season (except for skiing). The shoulder periods can bring less people and surprisingly nice weather.

Eastern Germany lies in a transition zone between the temperate maritime climate of Western Europe and the rougher continental climate of Eastern Europe – continental and Atlantic air masses meet here. The mean annual temperature in Berlin is 11°C, the average range of temperatures varying from -1°C in January to 18°C in July. The average annual precipitation is 585 mm and there is no special rainy season. The camping season is May to September.

WHAT TO BRING

If you forget to bring it, you can probably find and buy it in Germany. It's best to travel light and then purchase needed items than carry something never used.

Standard dress can be casual, but conservative. A layering system is best in Germany, where weather can change drastically from region to region and day to night. Jeans are generally accepted throughout the country. Swimming pools usually require bathing caps. Youth hostels require that you use a sleeping bag sheet, and if you don't have one, you'll have to rent or buy it off them – they supply the blankets.

SUGGESTED ITINERARIES

Depending on the length of your stay, you might want to see and do the following things:

Two days
   Depending on where you enter the country, try and spend at least two days in either Berlin or Munich.
One week
   Divide your time between Berlin and Munich, and throw in a visit to Dresden or the Alps.
Two weeks
   Berlin (including Potsdam), Dresden, Meissen, the Bavarian Forest, Munich and the Alps.
One month
   Berlin (including Potsdam), Dresden, Meissen, Leipzig, the Bavarian Forest, Munich, the Alps, Lake Constance and the Black Forest.
Two months
   As for one month, plus Weimar, the Harz Mountains, the Danube, the Romantic Road, the Moselle and Rhine valleys, Cologne, Hamburg, Lübeck and the Frisian Islands.

TOURIST OFFICES

Tourism in Germany runs like the train system: very efficiently. Small and large tourist offices are incredibly helpful and well informed. Don't hesitate to make use of their services.

Local Tourist Offices

The German National Tourist Office (Deutsche Zentrale für Tourismus, DZT) is headquartered at Beethovenstrasse 69, D-6000 Frankfurt-am-Main (☎ 069-7 57 20, fax 75 19 03). For local information, the office to head for in cities and towns in eastern and western Germany alike is the *Verkehrsamt* (tourist information office) or *Kurverwaltung* (resort administration).

East Germany's internal travel agency was known as *Reisebüro*, and the division serving East Germans travelling abroad was *Reisewelt*. Young people were catered for by *Jugendtourist*. Since reunification, these government monopoly organisations have been taken over by western German travel agents, most notably TUI, ITS and Neckermann, but in many cases the old offices and billboards remain. They might still be able to help you out with train and bus tickets, but their main focus these days consists of sunny package tours to travel-hungry eastern Germans.

Tourist Offices Abroad

DZT representatives abroad include:

Australia
German National Tourist Office, Lufthansa House, 12th Floor, 143 Macquarie St, Sydney, NSW 2000 (☎ 02-367 3890)

Canada
German National Tourist Office, 175 Bloor St East, North Tower, 6th floor, Toronto, Ont M4W 3R8 (☎ 416-968 1570)

New Zealand
Represented by Lufthansa: Level 10, Lufthansa House, 36 Kitchener St, Auckland 1 (☎ 09-3031 529)

South Africa
German National Tourist Office, c/o Lufthansa German Airlines, 22 Girton Rd, Parktown, Johannesburg 2000 (☎ 011-643 1615)

UK
German National Tourist Office, Nightingale House, 65 Curzon St, London W1Y 7PE (☎ 071-495 39 90/91)

USA
German National Tourist Office, 122 East 42nd St, 52nd Floor, New York, NY 10168-0072 (☎ 212-661 7200)
German National Tourist Office, 11766 Wilshire Blvd, Suite 750, Los Angeles, CA 90025 (☎ 310-575 9799)

There are also offices in Amsterdam, Brussels, Copenhagen, Madrid, Milan, Paris, Stockholm, Tokyo, Vienna and Zürich, and agencies in Chicago, Helsinki, Hong Kong, Ljubljana, Mexico City, Moscow, Oslo, São Paulo and Tel Aviv.

USEFUL ORGANISATIONS

The following organisations might come in useful:

ADZ Room Reservation Service
Corneliusstrasse 34, D-6000 Frankfurt/Main 1 (☎ 069-74 07 67) – accommodation-booking service run by the German National Tourist Board

Allgemeiner Deutscher Automobil Club (ADAC)
Am Westpark 8, D-8000 Munich 70 (☎ 089-7 67 60) – Germany's main motoring organisation, with offices in all major cities

Deutsche Camping Club (DCC)
Mandlstrasse 28, D-8000 Munich 40

Deutsches Jugendherbergswerk
Bismarckstrasse 8, D-4930 Detmold (☎ 05231-7 40 10) – German youth hostel federation, with a listing of all German youth hostels for DM6 plus postage

Deutsche Touring GmbH
Am Römerhof 17, D-6000 Frankfurt/Main 90 (☎ 069-7 90 30) – a good contact for bus tours run by Europabus and the German railway and post office transport group

Deutsche Bundesbahn
Rhabanusstrasse 3, D-6500 Mainz 1 (☎ 06131-15 55 35) – German Federal Railway, the former West German train system, merged with the former East German Deutsche Reichsbahn

Verband Deutscher Gebirgs- und Wandervereine
Reichsstrasse 4, D-6600 Saarbrücken (☎ 0681-39 00 70) – German Climbing & Hiking Association, provides information about trails, shelters, huts etc, and addresses of local hiking associations

BUSINESS HOURS & HOLIDAYS

Shopping hours are generally from 8 or 9 am to 6.30 pm Monday to Friday, and from 9 am to 2 pm on Saturdays, though times can vary in different parts of the country. On the first Saturday of each month, shops generally stay open until 4 or 6 pm ('long Saturday').

For a country known for its hard-working mentality, business hours are surprisingly short. Banking hours are generally from 8.30 am to 1 pm and 2.30 to 4 pm on Monday through Friday (many stay open until later on Thursdays). Government offices close for the weekend at 1 or 3 pm on Friday. Museum hours vary greatly, but they're generally closed Mondays.

The main restaurants are open from 10 am to midnight, with varying closing days. Many of the cheap restaurants are closed on Saturday afternoons and Sundays, although fast-food stands and places in the railway stations are open daily. Night bars are open from 9 pm to 4 am.

Germany has many holidays, some of which vary from state to state. Public holidays include: New Year's Day; Good Friday through Easter Monday; 1 May (Labour Day); Ascension Day and Corpus Christi (10 days before and after Pentecost, respectively); Whit Monday (the eighth day after Easter); 3 October (Day of German Unity); 1 November (All Saints Day); 18 November (Day of Prayer and Repentance); and usually Christmas Eve through the day after Christmas. All shops and banks are closed on public holidays.

CULTURAL EVENTS
There are many festivals, fairs and cultural events throughout the year. Famous and/or worthwhile ones include:

January
The carnival season (Shrovetide, known as 'Fasching' in Bavaria) begins, with many carnival events in large cities, most notably Cologne, Munich, Düsseldorf and Mainz; the partying peaks just before Ash Wednesday. International Green Week Agricultural Fair in Berlin.
February
International Toy Fair in Nuremberg. Frankfurt International Fair of Consumer Goods kicks off the trade show season. International Film Festival in Berlin.
March
Frankfurt Music Fair and Frankfurt Jazz Fair. Thuringian Bach Festival. Many spring fairs throughout Germany. Sommergewinn Festival in Eisenach.
April
Stuttgart Jazz Festival. Munich Ballet Days. Mannheim May Fair. Walpurgis Festivals – the night before May Day in Harz mountain towns.
May
International Mime Festival in Stuttgart. International May Festival in Wiesbaden. Red Wine Festival in Rüdesheim. Dresden International Dixieland Jazz Festival. Dresden Music Festival (last week of May into first week of June).
June
Moselle Wine Week in Cochem. Händel Festival in Halle. Sailing regatta in Kiel. Munich Film Festival. International Theatre Festival in Freiburg.
July
Folk festivals throughout Germany. Munich Opera Festival. Richard Wagner Festival in Bayreuth. German-American Folk Festival in Berlin. Kulmbach Beer Festival. International Music Seminar in Weimar.
August
Heidelberg Castle Festival. Wine festivals throughout the Rhineland area.

September
Munich's Oktoberfest, the world's biggest beer festival. Berlin Festival of Music & Drama (last week in September and first two weeks in October).
October
Frankfurt Book Fair. Berlin International Marathon. Bremen Freimarkt. Gewandhaus Festival in Leipzig. Berlin Jazzfest.
November
St Martin's Festival throughout Rhineland and Bavaria.
December
Many Christmas fairs throughout Germany, most famously in Munich, Nuremberg, Berlin, Essen and Heidelberg.

POST & TELECOMMUNICATIONS
Post offices are generally open from 8 am to 6 pm Monday through Friday and to noon on Saturday. Many railway station post offices stay open later. Mail-sorting facilities are still somewhat antiquated in eastern Germany, so do all of your mailing in western Germany or West Berlin if you want to be sure of some of the fastest mail deliveries in Europe.

Postal Rates
Air-mail letter rates are DM1 (20 grams) within Europe, DM1.65 (five grams) to North America and DM1.85 (five grams) to Australia; 10-gram letters are DM1.90 to North America and DM2.30 to Australia. Postcards cost DM0.60 within Europe, DM1.05 to North America and DM1.25 to Australia. Aerogrammes cost DM1.65 to anywhere but you have to buy them in stationery shops.

Receiving Mail
Mail can be sent poste restante (Postlagernde Briefe) to the city of your choice, where you can pick it up at the main post office (no fee). German post offices only hold mail for two weeks, so plan your drops carefully.

You can also have your mail addressed c/o American Express Travel Service in any large city. It holds mail for 30 days but won't accept registered mail or parcels. This service is free if you have an American

Express card or travellers' cheques, otherwise it's DM2 each time you come in. Mail will be forwarded for a flat DM8 fee.

Telephones

The telephone infrastructure in eastern Germany used to be decades behind that of western Germany, but the federal government has given this problem top priority and the situation is improving rapidly. The eastern area codes have all been changed, although the dates of their introduction vary as local networks are updated. Many subscriber numbers are changing, too. New area codes have been used throughout this chapter, and new subscriber numbers have been given where possible. If your call doesn't go through, try dialling local information.

Meanwhile, to call from western Germany to eastern Germany, dial 03 followed by the area code (dropping the initial zero). So, Cologne to Leipzig would be 0341 followed by the subscriber number. To call from eastern Germany to western Germany, dial 00049 followed by the area code (dropping the initial zero). So, Leipzig to Cologne would be 00049221 followed by the subscriber number. You don't have to wait for a dialling tone between area code and subscriber number.

To call from eastern Germany to elsewhere in eastern Germany, dial 0 followed by the area code (*including* the initial zero). The area codes may still differ depending on the areas you're ringing from, but they should be fixed for the major cities. To ring from Leipzig to Dresden, for instance, dial 0051 and then the subscriber number. West and East Berlin are 030 from anywhere.

To ring abroad from western Germany, dial 00 followed by the country code and the rest; from eastern Germany (preferably from main post offices), dial 000 followed by the country code and the rest. All post offices have public telephones, but you might not always be able to access them outside opening hours. You don't have to wait for a dialling tone after the area code or international access code.

If you want to talk to someone back home, you can call them from a pay phone and quickly give them your number so they can call you right back; this is much cheaper than calling reverse charges (collect call, *R-Gespräch*), which from Germany is only possible to a limited number of countries anyway. People can ring to phone booths indicated with a bell sign, but it's a bit hit-and-miss whether the number is actually indicated somewhere in the booth.

An increasing number of pay phones in Germany accept telephone cards, not coins. These cards (available at any post office) can be used throughout the country and are a good investment if you're making many calls or ringing abroad. (They carry all sorts of interesting illustrations, and the rarer ones have become hot collectors' items.) The DM12 card only gets you DM12 worth of calls (the standard DM0.30 per unit) but the DM50 card is good for DM60 worth of calls (DM0.25 per unit).

Fax, Telex & Telegraph

The best bets for faxing and telexing are main post offices, followed by large hotels. Beware: faxes (sending or receiving) are expensive. Some shops also provide these services. Telegrams can be sent through the post office, from many hotels, or by calling ☎ 1131.

TIME

Germany is on Central European Time (GMT/UTC plus one hour), the same time used from Madrid to Warsaw. Daylight-saving time comes into effect at the end of March when clocks are turned one hour forward. At the end of September they're turned an hour back again. Times are usually indicated with the 24-hour clock, eg 6.30 pm is 18.30.

LAUNDRY

You'll find a laundry (*Wäscherei*) in almost every town in western Germany and in West Berlin. A coin-operated laundry is called a *Münzwäscherei*. Some camping grounds and youth hostels also have them. They're still a bit of a rarity in eastern Germany, however, and your best bet is to ask your ho(s)tel or camp site proprietor. If you're staying in a private room, chances are your host will take care of your washing for a reasonable fee. Most major hotels provide laundering services for fairly steep fees, but only for guests.

WEIGHTS & MEASURES

Electricity is 220 volts AC, 50 Hz. Germany uses the metric system. Like other Continental Europeans, Germans indicate decimals with commas and thousands with points. Cheese and other food items are often sold per *Pfund*, which means 500 grams.

BOOKS & MAPS

The German literary tradition is strong and there are many works that provide excellent background into the German experience. These include Günter Grass' *The Tin Drum* and Thomas Mann's *Buddenbrooks*. Many spy novels are also based in Germany, including John Le Carré's *A Small Town in Germany*, Leon Uris' *Armageddon: A Novel of Berlin*, and Alistair MacLean's *Where Eagles Dare*. Mark Twain's *A Tramp Abroad* is recommended for his comical observations of German life.

The most complete German guidebook available to eastern Germany is *Baedeker's Deutschland – Ost* (Verlag Karl Baedeker). Though good on culture, it ignores the needs of the flesh. Similar story with the *Michelin Green Guide* to Germany. *The Real Guide: Berlin* by Jack London (Prentice Hall Press, New York) covers the entire city in detail, and is useful if you're spending a couple of months in Berlin; in Britain it's called *The Rough Guide: Berlin*. A good collection of motoring itineraries is presented in *German Country Inns & Castles*, written by Karen Brown and published by Harrap, but it only concentrates on upmarket accommodation.

Maps of and produced in Germany are among the best in the world. Most tourist offices have an excellent supply of free city maps (if they're closed, try the classy hotels). The automobile clubs ADAC and AvD produce excellent road maps. More detailed maps can be obtained at most bookshops. The best city maps are made by Falkplan, with a patented folding system that's a joy to use once you've mastered it.

MEDIA

Information is easily available through various media sources. If anything, Germany suffers from information overload, but away from major train stations and airports it's often difficult to obtain reading material of any kind in English.

Newspapers & Magazines

The most-read newspapers in western Germany are *Die Welt*, *Bild*, *Frankfurter Rundschau*, *Frankfurter Allgemeine*, Munich's *Süddeutsche Zeitung*, and the green-leaning *Die Tageszeitung (Taz)*. The most popular magazines are *Der Spiegel*, *Die Zeit* and *Stern*. The *International Herald Tribune* is available in most major cities, as are the international editions of *Time* and *Newsweek*.

The Berlin newspaper *Zweite Hand* (Second Hand) comes out three times a week and carries classified listings of jobs *(Arbeit & Mehr)*, vehicles for sale *(Fahrzeuge & Zubehör)*, apartments for rent *(Wohnen & Immobilien)*, lonely hearts *(Ich & Andere)* etc. Throughout the paper, the word *biete* lists things being offered while *suche* indicates ads placed by people looking for something. In Hamburg, the weekly magazine *Avis* is similar.

Of special interest to Berlin visitors are the fortnightly magazines *Tip* and *Zitty*, which cover virtually everything that's happening on the entertainment scene, both alternative and mainstream, in Berlin. The magazines come out on alternate weeks. In Hamburg, the weekly *Szene* magazine is similar. Although in German, these publications are fairly easy to follow.

Radio & TV

Germany's two main channels are ARD and ZDF, while a third, *Drittes Programm*, features regional fare. German radio is great for weather reports, if you can understand them, but the best bets are the BBC World Service and AFN (American Forces Network) on varying AM and FM wavelengths (depending on the part of the country you're in).

Germany has Europe's highest density of private satellite receiver dishes, so if you're staying in hotels or with friends, chances are you'll be able to watch all sorts of European channels and even some from the USA and Japan.

HEALTH

Germany is a clean and healthy nation, with no peculiar health concerns. No vaccinations are required to visit Germany, except for the usual ones if you're coming from certain Third World areas. Tap water is safe to drink everywhere; south of Berlin it may taste terrible but there's no particular health problem with it.

Most major hotels have doctors available. The best bet for emergencies is to look in the telephone book under *Ärztlicher Notdienst* (Emergency Doctor Service). Emergency health care is free for EC citizens with an E111 form, but otherwise, any form of treatment can be very expensive, so make sure you have travel insurance.

DANGERS & ANNOYANCES

Theft and other crimes against travellers are relatively rare. In the event of problems, the police are incredibly helpful and efficient. In most areas, the emergency number for the police is ☎ 110.

Be careful in crowded Berlin railway stations, where pickpockets are often active (foreign pickpockets, not locals). Don't allow anyone to help you put your luggage in a coin locker, especially at West Berlin's Zoo Station. They may switch keys as they're closing the locker, and later come back to pick up your things.

Blacks, Asians and southern Europeans may encounter racial prejudice, such as not getting served in a restaurant, especially in eastern Germany, where they have been singled out by neo-Nazi youth as convenient scapegoats for economic hardship. People in eastern Germany are only slowly getting

used to foreigners in general, and can still feel a bit awkward in their presence.

Women should not encounter any major difficulties. There is, however, some sexism as the male still rules the German household and office, though this is changing rapidly.

FILM & PHOTOGRAPHY

Germany is a photographer's dream, from the Alps to the picturesue old towns. Alpine shots are generally better in the morning and with as much blue sky as possible; a polarising filter will help.

German film and photography equipment is among the best in the world – it's a great place to buy any needed camera bodies, lenses or accessories. Expect to pay about DM14 for a roll of 36-exposure slide film and DM6 for developing – shop around.

WORK

Reunification has made what was very difficult virtually impossible. With unemployment running at 35% in some parts of eastern Germany and eastern Germans moving west for work, the whole country is not what you'd call a prime job-hunting area. Legally, only EC citizens may work in Germany, and temporary work permits are not available. The average income in western Germany is about DM2500 a month, and about half that in the east. Playing music and selling things on the street is widespread in the cities, though strictly speaking it's not legal. Street vendors are supposed to have a permit, though few do.

To get an idea of the sort of jobs available, check the *Stellenmarkt* (Employment Market) section in the classified sections of major city newspapers. Many of the positions offered are unskilled, and the sort of advertisers appearing here are mainly interested in finding cheap labour and not overly concerned whether you're legally authorised to work in Germany. Jobs are offered under the heading *biete*, while people looking for work advertise themselves under *suche*.

ACTIVITIES

The Germans are active outdoors people,

GERMANY

which means there's plenty for visitors to pursue.

Cycling

Bicycling is a favoured form of transport and recreation, as it is in many other parts of Europe. Popular biking areas include the Moselle and Danube rivers, and the Harz and Black Forest nature areas, where you'll often find marked cycling routes. Eastern Germany has much to offer cyclists in the way of lightly travelled back roads and a well-developed hostel network, especially in the flat, less populated north. Offshore islands like Poel and Rügen are ready made for pedal-powered travellers.

Germanrail offers a 'Bicycle at the Station' programme at more than 300 stations throughout the country. Bikes can be rented at these stations, along with maps and recommendations. They can then be returned to any participating station that's open. The charge is DM12 per day, or DM8 for German Rail Pass holders.

See also the Cycling heading in the following Getting Around section, and check the cycling information given in various sections throughout this chapter. Get a good lock for your bike.

Hiking

Walking, hiking and climbing are among the most popular participant sports in the country. There are more than 100,000 km of marked trails throughout Germany and they are often filled with hikers on nice weekends.

The leading hiking group is the Verband Deutscher Gebirgs- und Wandervereine eV (☎ 0681-39 00 70), Reichsstrasse 4, 6600 Saarbrücken 3. It has lots of information on various itineraries, guides, other clubs and much more.

The Alps are the most popular area, and for good reason. With more than 10,000 km of trails and 50 mountain huts with varying amenities, hiking the German Alps could be the focus of any trip. The best source of information is the Deutsche Alpenverein (☎ 089-23 50 90 0), Prater-Insel 5, 8000 Munich 22.

In eastern Germany, the Rennsteig, a ridge path through the Thuringian Forest (Thüringer Wald), stretches 168 km, with youth hostels along the way at Tabarz, Tambach-Dietharz and Oberhof; the Hohe Sonne restaurant near Eisenach is the trailhead. Other fine hiking areas are Saxon Switzerland (Sächsische Schweiz) south-east of Dresden, and the Harz Mountains south of Wernigerode. There are many other possibilities. See also Hiking in the following Getting Around section.

Skiing

The German Alps are by far the most popular area for downhill and cross-country skiing, but there are other possibilities off the beaten path. In the Alps, Garmisch-Partenkirchen is the most popular base of operations (if you notice lots of English being spoken, it's because there's a large US military recreation facility there). Those who wish to avoid the glitz and glamour (and prices) of the Alps may want to try the Black Forest or the Harz Mountains.

In general, it's much cheaper, though usually impractical, to take your own equipment. All winter resorts have full rental equipment.

The skiing season generally runs from early December to late March. It's possible to ski in April at higher altitudes (eg the Zugspitze near Garmisch-Partenkirchen). In the shoulder season, discounted ski package weeks can be found by looking for *Weisse Wochen* signs in tourist offices, hotels and ski resorts.

Windsurfing

This sport has exploded on bodies of water throughout Germany. On almost any weekend, cars and vans can be seen loaded with boards and sails. This popularity makes it an easy sport for visitors to pursue, with courses and board rental available at many resorts. The Bavarian lakes are the current hot spot, but there are other excellent spots, as well as the North Sea and Baltic coast.

Swimming

The proliferation of indoor and outdoor pools must offer the highest per-capita public pool density in the world. Swimming is big business and it's a convenient way to stay in shape or relax while on the road in Germany. Most of the pools are public and there is a per-visit charge of DM2 to DM5. Of course, this does not include the elaborate German spas. Bathing caps are required at almost every pool, but they can be purchased or rented. Other swimming options include many Bavarian lakes, other natural or artificial lakes, and the brisk seas in the north.

HIGHLIGHTS
Museums & Galleries

Germany is a museum-lovers dream country. In western Germany, Munich features the Alte Pinakothek and the huge Deutsches Museum. Hamburg offers the Kunsthalle. Cologne's Römisch-Germanisches Museum is one of the finest of its type in the world. Frankfurt's Museumsufer (Museum Bank) has enough museums to overdose a hardened addict.

Eastern Germany has dozens of illustrious museums, such as the Dahlem and Pergamon museums in Berlin and the Neue Meister Gallery in Dresden. Lesser known are the excellent special-interest museums including the Oceanic Museum & Aquarium in Stralsund and the Karl May (Indian) Museum in Dresden. Among the many historical museums, the Imperial Court Museum in Leipzig focuses on the Reichstag fire trial.

Castles

Western Germany has so many castles, they even have a tourist route called the 'Castle Road'. If you're into castles, make sure to hit Heidelberg, Neuschwanstein, the Rhine's Burg Rheinfels and the Moselle's Burg Eltz.

Eastern Germany has castles from every epoch including medieval Königstein and Wartburg castles, Renaissance Wittenberg Castle, Baroque Jagdschloss Moritzburg and romantic Wernigerode Castle.

Historic Towns

Time stands still in much of Germany, and some of the best towns in which to find this flavour in western Germany include Rothenburg, Goslar and Passau. The old parts of many large cities also impart this historic feel.

In eastern Germany, there are many historic towns, of which Meissen and Quedlinburg have a fairy-tale air, Stralsund has a salty taste of the sea, Weimar is *the* repository of German culture, and Berlin is a historic city of European stature.

Hotels & Restaurants

Given the relative price of things in western Germany, you're better off splurging on meals and budgeting on accommodation. Some sleeping highlights include the hostels along the Rhine and Moselle; camping at 'the Tent' in Munich; and hiking and camping in the Alps, Bavarian Forest, Black Forest or Harz Mountains. Eating highlights include huge meals in Frankfurt's Sachsenhausen district; beer-hall eating and drinking in Munich; and fresh seafood in Hamburg.

The hotel scene in eastern Germany is changing fast as privatisation proceeds, but the church-operated Christliches Hospiz chain will remain good. The Touristenhaus Grünau in East Berlin is a privatised youth hostel, now an excellent (though somewhat pricey) youth hotel. Quedlinburg's Hotel Zum Bär is just the old German inn you expected.

The restaurants in eastern Germany are changing even faster as some go broke and the others scramble to upgrade their service and food to Western standards. Auerbachskeller is such a Leipzig institution that things wouldn't be the same without it. Kreuzberg's Rathaus Casino and Schwarzes Café are two West Berlin eateries you'll enjoy.

ACCOMMODATION

Accommodation in Germany, like the rest of its tourism, is extremely well organised, though in eastern Germany the situation remains a bit confused with privatisation. If you're after a hotel or private room, the best

GERMANY

bet when arriving in town is to head straight for the tourist information office and use the room-finding service, which usually costs DM2 or DM3. Most staff will go out of their way to find something in the price range you specify. Private rooms are often excellent value but may not always be available in the bigger cities in western Germany. Private rooms and cheap hotels rarely supply soap, and even a decent towel may be asking for a bit much.

If you arrive when the tourist information office is closed, you might have trouble finding cheap accommodation, especially in eastern Germany where privatisation and renovation have temporarily limited the options. In that case, it's always worth asking around in shops, restaurants, pubs and hotels whether they know anyone in the area who rents private rooms.

Accommodation in all but camping grounds usually includes breakfast (a boiled egg, bread, butter, marmalade, sliced meats and cheeses, coffee or tea), but ask first. A sign that says *Heute Ruhetag* (Rest Day Today) means it's their day off and you'll have to move on.

Camping

With more than 2000 camping possibilities, the options for tenting it are excellent. Most camp sites are open from April to September, but several hundred stay open throughout the year. Local tourist information sources can help, but the best overall source of information is the DCC (German Camping Club), Mandlstrasse 28, D-8000 Munich 40.

The range of facilities varies greatly, from quite primitive to ridiculously packed with amenities (and people). For camping on private property, permission from the landowner is required and often granted. If you can't find the landowner, check with the local police.

Many camping grounds in eastern Germany rent small bungalows, convenient if it's raining. But if you want to make camping your main form of accommodation, you'll probably need your own transport,

since camping grounds tend to be far from city centres.

Hostels

The youth hostel (*Jugendherberge*) situation in Germany is arguably the best in the world, which is to be expected of the country that pioneered the concept. There are more than 600 of them conveniently located throughout the country, from big-city properties to excellent locations for the outdoors enthusiast. Almost all of them are open all year.

Visitors must be a member of an IYHF-affiliated organisation. If not, they must pay DM5 per night for a guest card and after six nights they receive full membership – not too bad a deal, considering that full membership for a German national costs DM26.

Priority is given until 6 pm to visitors aged under 27, and to families; in Bavaria, the maximum age limit for anyone except group leaders is 27. Prices depend on facilities and standards of comfort, but they generally run from DM11 to DM30 in western Germany. In eastern Germany, they generally cost DM13 to DM15 for juniors aged 26 and under, and DM15 to DM18 for seniors, depending on the category of the hostel (the West Berlin hostels are more expensive). Camping at a hostel (where permitted) is usually half-price. For more information, contact the Deutsches Jugendherbergswerk (☎ 05231-7 40 10), Bismarckstrasse 8, D-4930 Detmold.

If you don't have a youth hostel-approved sleeping sheet, it's usually DM6 extra to rent one, though some hostels insist you rent one even if you bring your own. Breakfast is usually included in the overnight price (a pot of coffee may be DM2 extra). A lunch-time or evening dinner could cost anywhere from DM4.50 to DM8.

Generally, you can only check in after 3 or 4 pm and must be out by 9 am. If there's a room key, always leave it at the reception when you go out. You don't need to do chores at the hostels and there are few rules.

Guesthouses

German guesthouses offer the best way to

immerse oneself in the country's unique culture, while not spending too much money – look for *Gasthof, Gasthaus, Fremdenheim, Zimmer frei* or *zu vermieten* signs. Many of these properties are country inns that specialise in serving food, but also rent rooms. Others are private houses with rooms to rent. If a place is full, you'll see *besetzt* ('occupied') posted. Another sign to watch out for is *Metzgerei* ('butcher's shop'): in small towns these often rent rooms at very decent prices, sometimes include a restaurant, and serve the best value breakfasts around.

Longer term rentals are also very popular in Germany. Look for *Ferienwohnungen* or *Ferien-apartments*, which usually house more than two people. Rates vary dramatically, but are typically lower than most hotels and decrease with the length of stay.

Cheap Hotels

Budget hotel rooms can be a bit hard to come by in Germany during the summer months. In eastern Germany, cheap hotels are very hard to find at any time due to privatisation and recent renovations, though the situation is likely to improve once things settle down. The cheapest hotels only have rooms with shared toilets and showers in the corridor.

Expensive Hotels

Expensive hotels in Germany provide few advantages for the often extremely high prices. Don't splurge on them unless you plan to take advantage of a package deal.

FOOD

Germans are hearty eaters, and it's easy for visitors to enjoy this aspect of their culture rather inexpensively. Locals often eat out, and there are many options from which to choose.

Each region has its own specialities, but this is truly a meat-and-potatoes kind of country. Though vegetarian and health-conscious restaurants are starting to sprout up, it's best to stop counting calories and cholesterol levels while in Germany. Vegetarians will have a hard time especially in eastern Germany, where even confirmed carnivores might wonder if they're getting enough vitamins. Many restaurants are more than happy to prepare something vegetarian if you give fair warning.

Restaurants always post their menu outside (in German) with prices listed, though drink prices are often *not* listed and these can add up. Watch for daily specials chalked onto blackboards. Beware of early closing hours, and of the Ruhetag (Rest Day) in country areas. Tipping is not necessary, although you're expected to 'round up' the bill as you're paying. Lunch is the main meal of the day; getting a main meal in the evening is never a problem, but you may find that the dish or menu of the day only relates to lunch time.

A *Gaststätte* is somewhat less formal than a *Restaurant*, while a *Weinkeller* or *Bierkeller* would be fine for a lighter meal. Many town halls, especially in eastern Germany, have an atmospheric restaurant, or *Ratskeller*, in the basement, serving traditional German dishes at reasonable prices. The *Gastmahl des Meeres* chain specialises in seafood. If you're on a low budget, you can get German sausages and beer at stand-up food stalls *(Schnell-Imbiss* or simply *Imbiss)* in all the towns. A *Konditorei* or café is the place to indulge in that sinful German habit of coffee and cakes.

A good German breakfast usually includes hearty bread and rolls, butter, jam, cheese, several types of sliced meat, a hard-boiled egg, and coffee or lemon tea. (Note that the German word for jam is *Marmelade,* and that marmalade is usually referred to as *Orangenmarmelade.)*

Chain and fast-food restaurants are not too popular in eastern Germany (yet) and it's best to go with local guesthouses. Germans at home tend to eat their heaviest meal at midday and then have lighter evening fare *(Abendbrot* or *Abendessen,* consisting of cheeses and bread).

Cafés & Bars

Much of the German daily and social life revolves around these two institutions. It's a

GERMANY

great way to meet locals without spending too much money.

Snacks

Schnell-Imbisses continue to be the best bet for snacks and quick meals. These places can range from mobile units to fixed buildings with tables. The food is usually quite reasonable and filling.

Main Dishes

Sausage *(Wurst)* is by far the most popular main dish, in its hundreds of forms. Regional favourites include *Bratwurst* (spiced sausage), *Weisswust* (veal sausage), *Bauernwurst* (farm sausage), *Blutwurst* (blood sausage) and many others. In Berlin, *Eisbein* (pickled pork knuckles) is the dish of choice. Other standbys include *Rippenspeer* (spare ribs), *Rotwurst* (black pudding), *Rostbrätl* (grilled meat) and many forms of *Schnitzel* (breaded pork or veal cutlet).

Fish is also abundant from the North and Baltic seas, and the lakes and rivers. Herring is a popular choice and a bargain for budget diners. Chinese, Italian, Indonesian, Polish and many other exotic cuisines are often interesting and inexpensive.

Potatoes feature prominently in most German meals, either fried *(Bratkartoffeln)*, mashed *(Kartoffelpüree)*, grated and then fried (the Swiss *Rösti*), or as French fries *(Pommes Frites)*; a Thuringian speciality is *Klösse*, a ball of mashed and raw potato which is then cooked (a bit like a dumpling). In Baden-Württemberg, potatoes are often replaced by *Spätzle* – wide, flattened noodles, the German equivalent of *fettuccine*.

Desserts

Germans are keen on rich desserts. A popular choice is the *Schwarzwälder Kirschtorte* (Black Forest cherry cake), which is one tourist trap that is worth it. Desserts and pastries are also often enjoyed during another German tradition, the 4 pm coffee break.

Fruit

As can be expected with a meat-and-potatoes society, fruit is not overly abundant, but most groceries and markets have a fairly good, if expensive, fruit section.

Self-Catering

It's very easy and relatively cheap to put together picnic meals in any town. Simply head for the local supermarket and stock up on breads, sandwich meats, cheeses, wine and beer.

DRINKS

Buying beverages can get to be very expensive. Be very careful at restaurants, and if you like lots of liquids, make a point of buying your beverage of choice in supermarkets.

Nonalcoholic Drinks

Though their love of beer is legendary, Germans occasionally drink other brews. The most popular choices are mineral water and international and local soft drinks. Nonalcoholic beers are becoming more popular and are quite good. Löwenbräu makes an especially tasty nonalcoholic beer that is also frequently served on tap.

Alcohol

Beer is the national beverage and it's one cultural phenomenon that must be adequately explored. The beer is excellent and still relatively cheap compared with other beverages. Each region and brewery has its own distinctive taste and body.

Beer-drinking in Germany has its own vocabulary. *Vollbier* is 4% by volume, *Export* is 5% and *Bockbier* is 6%. *Helles Bier* is light, while *dunkles Bier* is dark. Export is similar to, but much better than, typical international brews, while the *Pils* is more bitter. *Alt* is darker and more full-bodied. A speciality is *Weizenbier*, which is made with wheat instead of hops and served in a tall, half-litre glass with a slice of lemon.

Eastern Germany's best beers hail from Saxony, especially Radeberger Pils from near Dresden and Wernesgrüner from the

Erzgebirge on the Czech border. In East Berlin, Berliner Pilsner is the local brew, whereas Schultheiss is brewed in West Berlin. *Berliner Weisse*, or 'white beer', is a foaming, low-alcohol wheat beer mixed with red or green fruit syrup.

German wines are increasing in popularity throughout the world, and for good reason. German wines are typically white, light and relatively sweet. As with beer, the cheaper wines are almost as cheap as bottled water or soft drinks, and quite good. Germans usually ask for a *Schoppen* of whatever – a solid wine glass holding 200 or 250 ml. A *Weinschorle* or *Spritzer* is white wine mixed with mineral water. Wines don't have to be drunk with meals.

ENTERTAINMENT

Germans are highly cultured, and the standard of theatre performances, concerts and operas is among the best in Europe. In eastern Germany, performances are still heavily subsidised, and you can often get good seats at almost unbelievable prices (don't expect this situation to last, however). Berlin is unrivalled when it comes to concerts and theatre, while Dresden is synonymous with opera.

Cinemas

The film scene in Germany is excellent, but English-language, subtitled options are limited to large cities like Munich, Hamburg and Frankfurt. There are, however, often English-language cinemas where there is a large American or British military presence – eg Berlin, Frankfurt, Kaiserslautern, Garmisch-Partenkirchen or Heidelberg.

Discos

The German disco scene is quite lively. Ask any young local where the hottest places are. There are usually only cover charges on Fridays and Saturdays, but drinks are often expensive. The crowds tend to be young, and the atmosphere and dress standards casual.

Nightclubs

Because of the huge number of German guesthouses offering beer and conversation, nightclubs are not overly popular except in large cities. Many of these clubs tend to be in international hotels, patronised by foreigners with money to burn. There are, however, exceptions, and any young local or tourist office can point you in the right direction.

Spectator Sports

Soccer is the sport of choice for those who like to watch, rather than participate. Almost every city or town has at least one team and stadium. Games are easy to find and attend. Not many foreigners attend games, and it's an excellent way to meet Germans. Plan to spend some time drinking a few beers after a rough day of spectating.

THINGS TO BUY

Because of the general high costs in Germany, there are no true bargains, but there are certain regional items that could be worth purchasing. Of particular interest are cuckoo clocks in the Black Forest, wine from the regional wineries, woodcarved pieces in Bavaria, and optical equipment in the east. German books and maps are among the best in the world. Art reproductions, books, posters, catalogues and magazines are sold in museums and speciality shops.

Getting There & Away

AIR

The major arrival/departure points for Germany are Frankfurt, Munich and Berlin – Frankfurt is Europe's second-busiest airport after Heathrow. Flights are priced competitively among all major airlines, but Germany's national carrier, Lufthansa, offers the most flexibility. The German charter company, LTU, also does regular scheduled flights.

Flights to Frankfurt are usually cheaper than to other German cities, irrespective of whether you're flying from London or from outside Europe. Regular flights from

Western Europe to Germany are usually more expensive than the train or bus but not always: discount tickets from London can be as low as £90 return. Lufthansa alone has 40 flights a day from the UK to Germany. It also flies from North America and Australia, but not from New Zealand. Munich's new airport is the hub for Lufthansa flights to southern Germany. Lufthansa ticket offices in Germany include: Am Hauptbahnhof 2, Frankfurt (☎ 069-23 06 21); and Lenbach-platz 1, Munich (☎ 089-5 11 38).

It might be worth looking into various fly/drive or flight/accommodation packages put together by travel agents or the airlines. Lufthansa often has special deals, particularly from the USA. If you plan to hire a car, prices can be very attractive. If you're flying with Lufthansa out of Frankfurt, there's a special Rail & Fly setup that allows you to check-in your luggage and travel by train from six stations between Cologne and Nuremberg.

To/from the former Soviet Union, Lufthansa has regular connections with the Baltic states, Belorussia, the Ukraine, Moscow and St Petersburg – a return Frankfurt-Minsk, for instance, can be had from DM788. It also flies Düsseldorf-Prague and from Berlin to Prague, Budapest or Warsaw; there are many discount options.

For other information on cheap flights to far places, check with travel agencies. Individuals offering plane tickets they no longer require, at very cheap prices, advertise in the *Urlaub & Reisen (biete)* section of major city newspapers.

An airport departure tax of DM6 is included in ticket prices.

LAND
Bus
If you're already in Europe, it's generally cheaper to get to Germany by bus than it is by train or plane, though some discount plane fares can work out cheaper. Long bus rides can be tedious, so bring along a good book. Some of the coaches are quite luxurious with toilet, air-conditioning and snack bar.

Advance reservations may be necessary, and any German travel agency should be able to tell you where to go for them. A convenient West Berlin travel agency handling bus tickets is Reisebüro Zoo, Hardenbergplatz 2 opposite Zoo Station. Return fares are notably cheaper than two one-ways.

Eurolines has a youth fare for those aged under 26, which saves around 10%. It also has a daily service from London to Frankfurt which costs £49/83 for an adult one-way/return, and four times a week (Thursday, Friday, Saturday and Monday) to Munich which costs £60/99. Eurolines buses also run from Frankfurt to Warsaw and Prague, and from Munich to Prague, Zagreb, Istanbul and Athens. There are many other connections. In London, contact Eurolines (☎ 071-730 0202) at 52 Grosvenor Gardens, London SW1. The buses leave from Victoria Coach Station. In Germany, Eurolines is represented by Deutsche Touring GmbH (☎ 069-7 90 30), Am Römerhof 17, 6000 Frankfurt 90, though any major travel agent should be able to help you with tickets (see Bus in the Getting Around section that follows).

Train
The train is a good way to get to Germany if you're already in Western Europe, and is a lot more comfortable (if a bit more expensive) than the bus.

Train tickets to any city with an S-Bahn system (see Local Transport in the following Getting Around section) are also valid on that S-Bahn until you've reached your destination, even if it happens to be the youth hostel in the outer suburbs. In the opposite direction, you can take the S-Bahn to the train station from which your train is leaving. This only applies on actual journeys – you cannot get off for a few hours and then hop back on the S-Bahn, for instance. Train passes are also valid on S-Bahns. Beware: you cannot use other local transport (including U-Bahns) in this way.

The German word for train station is *Bahnhof*, often abbreviated *Bf;* the main train station is *Hauptbahnhof*, often abbreviated *Hbf*.

Driving & Hitchhiking

Germany is serviced from the rest of Western Europe by an excellent highway system. If you're coming from the UK, the cheapest route by car is the car ferry or hovercraft from Dover, Folkestone or Ramsgate to Boulogne or Calais in France. You can be in Germany three hours after the ferry docks.

Hitchhikers should not have too many problems getting to Germany by the main highways. If coming from the UK, it's probably easier to aim for the Belgian rather than the French ports.

Ride Services

Aside from hitchhiking, the cheapest way to get to Germany from elsewhere in Europe is as a paying passenger in a private car. Leaving Germany, or travelling within the country, such rides are arranged by *Mitfahrzentrale* agencies in many German cities. You pay a reservation fee to the agency and your share of petrol to the driver. The local tourist information office will be able to direct you to several such agencies, or you can check the entry 'Mitfahrzentrale' in the Yellow Pages phone book. Some of the ones mentioned in this chapter belong either to the large Arbeitsgemeinschaft Deutscher Mitfahrzentralen (66 members throughout Germany – dial the local telephone code plus 1 94 40), or the computer-equipped City-Netz Mitfahrzentrale (12 members in most of the major cities – dial the local telephone code plus 1 94 44).

There are organisations offering ride services in a number of other European countries, including Austria (Daungasse 1a, Vienna, ☎ 01-408 2210), Belgium (Marché aux Herbes 27, Brussels, ☎ 02-512 1015), the Netherlands (Nieuwezijds Voorburgwal 256, Amsterdam, ☎ 020-620 5121), and Switzerland (Leonhardstrasse 15, Zürich, ☎ 01-261 68 93).

SEA

In western Germany, the two best port bets

for coming/going by sea are Hamburg and Bremerhaven, but this really only makes sense if you're heading to/from the UK or Scandinavia. The Puttgarden-Rødbyhavn ferry is popular among those heading to Copenhagen (see the Hamburg Getting There & Away section for details). There are also ferries to a number of Scandinavian ports from Kiel (see the Kiel Getting There & Away section for details).

In eastern Germany, there are five large ferries in each direction daily all year between Trelleborg, Sweden, and Sassnitz Hafen near Stralsund (DM27 one-way from Sunday to Thursday, DM34 on Friday and Saturday, four hours). Trelleborg is just south of Malmö, Sweden, near Copenhagen in Denmark. From April to October, ferries also run several times a week between the Danish island of Bornholm and Sassnitz Hafen (DM30 one-way from Monday to Thursday, DM36 from Friday to Sunday, 3½ hours). Car-ferry service is also good from Gedser, Denmark, to Warnemünde near Rostock (DM15 one-way, two hours, all year). See the Rostock, Warnemünde, Stralsund and Rügen Island Getting There & Away sections for more details.

Getting Around

AIR

There are lots of flights within the country, but costs can be prohibitive compared to the train. Lufthansa is the frequent flyer within Germany, as well as the charter company, LTU. Foreign airlines also offer services between major cities. There are several small airlines that offer services to/from northern cities, as well as the Frisian Islands.

BUS

As with the train system, the bus network in Germany is excellent and comprehensive. For trips of any distance, however, the train is faster and generally as cheap. Buses are better geared towards regional travel in areas where the terrain makes rail travel more difficult.

Europabus, the motor coach system of Europe's railways, operates within Germany under the banner of Deutsche Touring GmbH, a subsidiary of the German Federal Railways (Deutsche Bundesbahn, DB). Europabus services include the Romantic and Castle Road buses in southern Germany, and a seven-day 'Eastern Germany' tour that leaves from Frankfurt and visits key historic cities like Weimar, Eisenach, Erfurt, Dresden, Leipzig, Berlin and Magdeburg for DM2377. See the Frankfurt and Romantic Road sections for details, or contact the Deutsche Touring GmbH main booking office (☎ 069-7 90 30), Römerhof 17, 6000 Frankfurt 90.

TRAIN

The German train system (Germanrail) is one of the best in the world. Travellers will mainly deal with *Inter-City* (IC) trains, which offer express service at least hourly from more than 50 major cities. The IC trains are supplemented by *Fern-Expresszüge* (FD), which are the express long-distance trains, as well as the *Schnellzüge* (D), the regular fast trains, and the slower *Eilzüge* (E). For E trains and local services, no supplementary charge is added, thus making it cheaper to avoid fast trains for short trips.

More than 200 east-west connections have been added to the Germanrail timetable to link the Deutsche Bundesbahn (west) with the Deutsche Reichsbahn (east). The two will eventually be merged, though tickets are already valid on both.

Germanrail's *Inter-City Express* (ICE) began in mid-1991. Travelling at speeds of up to 275 km/h, the ICE service has cut travel time between destinations by 30% to 50%. The ICE's initial route is Hamburg-Frankfurt-Munich (no stop at Frankfurt Airport), as well as a shorter, more direct line from Hamburg to Munich via Würzburg.

Reservations are recommended when possible, even when travelling with some sort of pass. Many night trains are equipped with couchettes, which attract a surcharge of DM24 or DM34 (six or four people per compartment); more expensive sleeping-car tickets are available for three or two-bed compartments, and also one-bed compartments in 1st class.

In almost all cases, the least expensive and most convenient way to travel within Germany is with some sort of train pass. The German Rail Pass is available to anyone who is not a resident in Germany, and entitles you to unlimited 1st, 2nd or 3rd-class travel for five, 10 or 15 days within a one-month period. It costs US$128, US$192 and US$240 respectively (2nd class). A similar setup is the German Rail Youth Pass, limited to 2nd-class travel by those aged between 12 and 25, which costs US$110, US$145 and US$180 respectively. The German Rail Twin Pass for couples costs US$160, US$240 and US$300 respectively (2nd class). These passes can be obtained in the USA, Canada, or from many train stations in Germany itself (passport required). They are valid on all trains, DB buses, and some river services operated by the Köln-Düsseldorfer Line. Of course, Inter-Rail and Eurail passes are also good within Germany.

Germanrail offers other options that can be purchased at train stations within Germany (enquire at train information counters). Apart from youth, student and senior discounts on some tickets, there are reduced-rate return tickets if you limit your travel to particular days of the week. Enquire about the 'Super-Sparpreis Ticket', a return ticket between any two stations in Germany (including Salzburg in Austria) for DM140. It's valid for 30 days and stopovers are allowed, and a second person can be included for only DM70. You cannot use it on Fridays, Sundays or public holidays unless you pay a DM50 supplement, in which case it becomes a 'Sparticket'.

If you're buying single tickets, you might have to rely on ticket-vending machines when the booths are closed (or the queues are long). They're simple to operate but will only calculate fares for destinations less than 50 km away. If you're travelling farther than that, press 'X' for maximum fare and contact the conductor when you board the train. If you don't buy a ticket before contacting the conductor, you'll pay a DM5 administration fee.

Train tickets and passes are also valid on local S-Bahns (see Train in the previous Getting There & Away section).

CAR & MOTORBIKE

German roads are excellent, and motorised transport can be a great way to tour the country. Fuel costs about DM1.50 per litre – try to avoid the more expensive autobahn filling stations.

The autobahn system of motorways (blue signs with A numbers) runs throughout the country and connects Germany with the rest of Europe (recognised with a green E number). Though very efficient, the autobahns are often busy, and literally present life in the fast lane. The advisory speed limit of 130 km/h is often ignored (though German insurers are trying through the courts to stop paying out people who have accidents while driving faster). Tourists often have trouble coping with the very high speeds and the dangers involved in overtaking – don't overestimate the time it takes for a car in the rear-view mirror to close in at 180 km/h... Also beware of eastern Germans still unaccustomed to the capabilities of their new Western cars – reunification has pushed the accident rate up to one of the highest levels in Europe. Secondary roads are easier on the nerves, much more scenic, and still present a very efficient way of getting from A to B.

In the cities and towns, cars are less practical due to one-way streets and extensive pedestrian zones in the old town centres. Your best bet is to head for a central parking garage (Parkhaus) and proceed on foot. Most cities have an efficient system of parking garages, complete with electronic signs indicating which ones in the area still have space. They tend to be expensive and are often automated (keep your ticket and pay, usually at a machine, before collecting your car). Motorbikes can generally be parked on pavements (sidewalks) so long as they don't obstruct pedestrians.

Road Rules

Road rules are easy to understand and generally displayed with international road signs. The usual speed limits are 50 km/h in built-up areas (in effect as soon as you see the yellow name-board of the town), 100 km/h on the open road, and unlimited on the autobahns; exceptions are clearly signposted. In eastern Germany, the limits are 50, 80 and 100 km/h respectively. The maximum permissible blood-alcohol concentration is 0.08% in western Germany and zero per cent in eastern Germany. Obey the road rules carefully: the German police are very efficient and issue heavy on-the-spot fines; speed and red-light cameras proliferate, and notices are sent to the car's registration address wherever that may be.

Rental

All of the major car rental firms operate in Germany. There are many lower priced packages, as well as smaller budget rental companies. It's best to shop around upon arrival rather than making advance reservations (unless picking up the rental car at the airport through a fly/drive deal).

Purchase

The costs and paperwork hassles make car purchase and possible resale an unwise option in Germany, especially since the bargains have already been snapped up by eager eastern Germans and Polish entrepreneurs. It's much easier in other Western European countries, unless you're willing to buy it 'as is', which is often with an expired inspection sticker, insurance, and unpaid taxes.

Berlin is probably the best place in Germany to pick up a cheap used car (especially if you're heading east from there, and the paperwork is less important). The classified newspaper Zweite Hand has a section listing cars available for less than DM500 (PKW bis 500,- biete). You may be able to snap up a Trabant for as little as DM100! A Czech-made Škoda or Soviet-made Lada would be ideal, as servicing for these is readily available throughout Eastern Europe. Motorcycles for sale are listed under

Motorräder – biete. Beware of ads including the words *ohne TÜV*, as these are vehicles whose roadworthiness certificate has expired and therefore cannot be registered. Before agreeing to anything, make sure the ownership can be legally transferred to you. You can often buy a car with the roadworthiness certificate (TÜV) just about to expire for an incredibly low price, and this may be no problem if you're able to drive it out of Germany (and the EC) before the deadline (officials in Poland or Czechoslovakia may not scrutinise the registration papers that closely).

What you *will* require is insurance, and agencies arranging it are listed in the yellow pages of the phone book under *Auto Versicherung*. If you have a German friend who will help with all this, so much the better.

CYCLING

Bicycle touring is quite popular in Germany, especially in the southern sections (the Danube River in particular) and along the Rhine and Moselle rivers. There are often separate cycling routes so you don't have to use the highways, and cycling is of course strictly *verboten* on the autobahns. It's easy to bring your own or to purchase everything needed upon arrival. There are bike shops in almost every town, and a fairly active market for used touring bikes.

Bikes can also be rented at many major train stations (DM12 per day, or DM8 for German Rail Pass holders), and are frequently seen on trains (except IC trains). A separate ticket (DM6.50) must be purchased for each journey. Germanrail also offers a 30-day 'Tramper Ticket' for DM234, which allows bikes on board for free. Bikes can also be rented at hundreds of train stations. A great source of information is the railways brochure, *Fahrrad am Bahnhof*. See also Activities in the previous Facts for the Visitor section.

HITCHING

Hitchhiking *(Weg-Wandern)* is quite prevalent in Germany, and getting rides is relatively easy. Don't waste time hitching in urban areas: take public transport to the main exit routes. It's illegal to hitchhike on autobahns or their entry/exit roads. Make sure to prepare a neat sign for your destination in German (eg 'München', not 'Munich'). You can save yourself a lot of trouble by arranging a ride through a Mitfahrzentrale (see Ride Services in the previous Getting There & Away section).

HIKING

In the less urban areas, long-distance walking is enjoyable and quite feasible. There a numerous marked trails and enjoyable long-distance routes all over Germany, especially in the Black Forest, Bavarian Alps, Bavarian Forest, the Harz, Eifel, Spessart and Thuringian Forest. See also Activities in the previous Facts for the Visitor section, and the hiking information given in various sections throughout this chapter.

Wanderparkplätze (walkers' car parks) are ideal starting points for drivers wishing to embark on circular hikes. There is usually a trail map on display.

BOAT

The two times boats are likely to be used for transport will be when travelling to or between the Frisian Islands, and when taking a boat tour along one of the rivers – the Rhine and Moselle being the obvious candidates. The boats on Lake Constance are frequent, but, except for the Constance-Meersburg car ferry, are generally meant more for tourist excursions than as a transport option.

From April to October, Weisse Flotte excursion boats ply the lakes, rivers and coastline of eastern Germany – an excellent, inexpensive way of seeing the country. In the north, trips on the Baltic are possible, and the big paddle-wheel steamers operating out of Dresden are a fine way to tour the Elbe and see much of the area around Dresden. The Weisse Flotte is also very active at Berlin, Potsdam, Rostock, Schwerin, Stralsund, Warnemünde and Wismar. See the relevant sections for details.

LOCAL TRANSPORT

Local transport is excellent within big cities and small towns. The options revolve around buses, trams, suburban trains *(S-Bahn)*, and underground railways *(U-Bahn)*. S-Bahns are part of Germanrail, so train tickets and train passes are valid (see Train in the previous Getting There & Away section).

Ticketing for local transport is often based on a zonal system, and a ticket will almost always be valid on all forms of transport. Usually there are special deals available, such as multi-ticket strips or day passes; these are much more economical than buying single tickets. See the individual Getting Around sections in this chapter for details.

Bus & Tram

Most cities and towns operate their own local bus and/or tram services, though trams are not as ubiquitous as buses. Electric buses (trolleybuses) are a regular sight in eastern Germany. It's best to get schedules and maps at the local tourist office or a public transport information/ticket booth. Buy bus and tram tickets before boarding, and validate your own ticket once aboard. Bus drivers usually sell single-trip tickets as a service to forgetful passengers, but these are more expensive than tickets bought in advance.

Train

Most large cities have a system of suburban train lines called the S-Bahn. They tend to cover a wider area than buses or trams, but are less frequent. They're often linked to the national rail network, and rail cards or tickets are valid on these services.

Underground

A few large cities have an underground rail system known as the U-Bahn, a very efficient way of getting around town once you've seen what you want to see and know where you want to go.

Taxi

Taxis are expensive and, given the excellent public transport system, not recommended unless you're in a screaming hurry (they can actually be slower if you're going to or from the airport). The taxis are often diesel-powered Mercedes, though Fords and Opels are also common. Except at airports and recognised pick-up points, taxis are not generally hailed on the street. They are all metered and usually cost DM2 to DM4 per km; fares may be higher at night, and trips out of town are double fare. If you order a taxi by telephone, you must pay for its return trip. The standard tip is to round up to the nearest DM, though 5% to 10% is gratefully received.

TOURS

Local tourist offices often have many options, from one-hour city sightseeing tours to multiday adventure, spa-bath, wine-tasting and other packages. Apart from city tours, other good sources for organised tours in and around Germany are Europabus and Germanrail.

There are many other international and national tour operators with specific options. Your travel agent should have some details, but it's worth contacting the German National Tourist Office in your home country if you wish to pursue this further. Keep in mind that many airlines also offer tour packages (eg fly/drive, fly/rail or city hotels and tours) with their tickets.

Berlin

Berlin, the largest city in Germany, has more to offer visitors than almost any city in Europe. Sliced in half by a 162- km-long Wall until as recently as mid-1990, East and West Berlin retain their individual characters despite a common city-wide government. Berliners on both sides of the former divide still speak in terms of East Berlin and West Berlin and it will be years before the wounds of the Cold War are fully healed.

For decades, capitalism and socialism

GERMANY

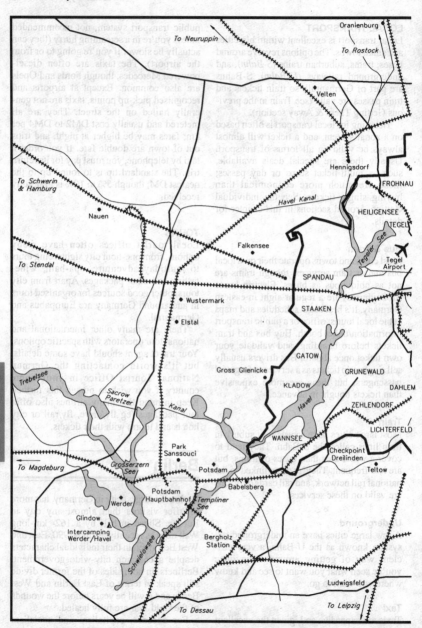

To Neuruppin

To Rostock

Oranienburg

Velten

To Schwerin
& Hamburg

Hennigsdorf

FROHNAU

Havel Kanal

HEILIGENSEE

Nauen

TEGEL

Falkensee

Tegeler See

To Stendal

Tegel
Airport

SPANDAU

Wustermark

STAAKEN

Elstal

Trebelsee

GATOW

Gross Glienicke

GRUNEWALD

Sacrow
Paretzer

KLADOW

DAHLEM

Kanal

Havel

ZEHLENDORF

Grosserzern
See

WANNSEE

LICHTERFELD

To Magdeburg

Park
Sanssouci

Checkpoint
Dreilinden

Teltow

Potsdam

Babelsberg

Potsdam
Hauptbahnhof

Templiner
See

Werder

Glindow

Intercamping
Werder/Havel

Bergholz
Station

Schielowsee

Ludwigsfeld

To Dessau

To Leipzig

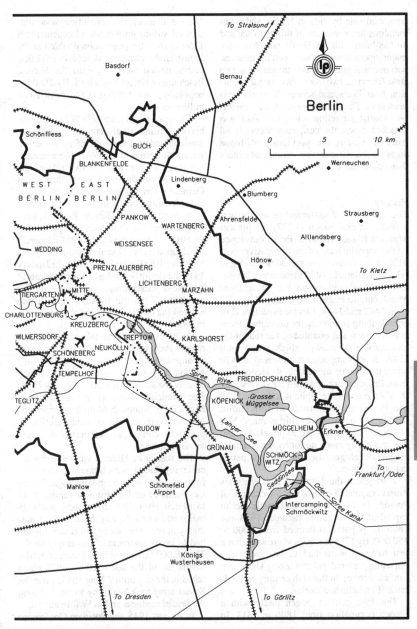

GERMANY

competed side by side in Berlin, and a tremendous infrastructure of things to see and do has been built up. Berlin now has three major opera houses, two operetta theatres, two national galleries, two universities, two state libraries, two zoos, two major excursion boat fleets and scores of world-class museums. Though the city lost its number-one tourist attraction when the Wall was knocked down, the new, easy access to all parts of the city and previously off-limits areas in the surrounding countryside more than compensate.

History

The first recorded settlement on the site was a place named Kölln (1237) on present Museum Island. Medieval Berlin developed on the opposite bank of the Spree River near St Nicholas Church and spread north-east to Alexanderplatz. In 1432 these minor Hanseatic trading centres on the route from Magdeburg to Poznán were merged.

In 1442 and 1448, Elector Frederick II of Brandenburg conquered the previously independent town and established the rule of the Hohenzollern dynasty, which lasted until 1918. Berlin's importance increased in 1470 when the elector moved his residence here from Brandenburg and built a palace where the Palace of the Republic is today. In 1539 the Protestant Reformation took hold. During the devastating Thirty Years' War (1618-48) Berlin lost half its population, but this was partly made up for by thousands of Huguenot refugees fleeing religious persecution in France.

Throughout the 17th and 18th centuries Prussia expanded eastward at the expense of Poland. In 1701 Frederick I made Berlin capital of the kingdom. Between 1648 and 1800 the population jumped from 6000 to 150,000. By 1734 the city had grown so large that the city walls had to be razed. The imposing restored palaces along Unter den Linden went up in the 18th century as Frederick II embellished Berlin.

The 19th century began badly with a French occupation from 1806 to 1813. In 1848 a democratic revolution was suppressed, stifling political development. From 1850 to 1870 the population doubled as the Industrial Revolution took hold. In 1871 Bismarck united Germany into the Second Reich under Kaiser Wilhelm I. By 1890 the population was 1,600,000 and passed two million in 1905.

The years leading up to WW I saw Berlin become an industrial giant, but power was concentrated in the hands of an autocracy which blundered into WW I. The senseless wartime violence and the example of the Russian Revolution led to revolt throughout Germany. On 9 November 1918 Philipp Scheidemann, leader of the Social Democrats, proclaimed the German Republic from a balcony of the Reichstag (the parliament building). A few hours later Karl Liebknecht proclaimed a Free Socialist Republic from a balcony of the Berlin City Palace. In January 1919 the Berlin Spartakists, Karl Liebknecht and Rosa Luxemburg, were murdered by remnants of the old imperial army which entered the city and drowned the revolution in blood.

On the eve of the Nazi takeover, the Communist Party under Ernst Thälmann was the strongest single party in 'Red Berlin', polling 31% of the votes in 1932 (almost exactly the same as the 30% they got in the free municipal elections in East Berlin in May 1990). Although Munich spawned the Nazi movement, Hitler made Berlin its political centre as Germany marched towards disaster.

The results of Hitler's vicious plans for enslaving Europe came home to Berlin in the form of Anglo-American bombings. During the 'Battle of Berlin', from November 1943 to March 1944, British bombers made 35 major attacks on the city. Most of the buildings you see today along Unter den Linden had to be reconstructed from empty shells. The 18,000 Soviet soldiers buried in Berlin remind us of the last terrible battle which raged in the city until 2 May 1945, when the Soviet army took Berlin by storm, bringing the fascist madness and WW II to an end.

In August 1945, the Potsdam Conference

sealed the fate of the city by agreeing that each power would occupy a separate zone. In June 1948 the city was split in two when the three Western Allies introduced West German currency and established a separate administration in the western sectors. The Soviets blockaded West Berlin because of this, but an airlift kept it in the Western camp.

In October 1949 East Berlin became the capital of the GDR and an integral part of East Germany. Construction of the Wall in August 1961 was almost inevitable as East Germany could no longer support the drain of skilled labour lured west by higher wages. Between 1945 and 1961 some three million East Germans left.

When Hungary decided to breach the Iron Curtain in May 1989, the East German government was back where it had been in 1961, this time without Soviet backing. On 9 November 1989 the Wall opened, but border controls continued until 1 July 1990 when West German currency was adopted in what was then still East Germany.

The Unification Treaty between the two Germanys designated Berlin the official capital of Germany, and in June 1991 the German parliament (Bundestag) voted to move the seat of government from Bonn to Berlin over the next decade at a cost of DM60 billion to DM80 billion.

Orientation

Berlin, in the centre of Europe, halfway between Amsterdam and Warsaw, sits on the great plain of the northern German lowlands. Roughly a third of Berlin is made up of parks, forests, lakes and rivers. There are more trees here than in Paris and more bridges than in Venice. Much of this natural beauty of rolling hills and quiet shorelines is on the south-eastern and south-western sides of the city.

The Spree River winds across the city for over 30 km from the Grosser Müggelsee to Spandau, where it joins the Havel River. North and south of Spandau the Havel widens into a series of lakes from Tegel to Potsdam. From Potsdam the Havel flows on into the Elbe and past Hamburg before reaching the North Sea. A dense network of canals links the other waterways and there are beautiful walks along some of them.

The tourists' haunt centres on Unter den Linden, the fashionable avenue of aristocratic Berlin. Together with its continuation, Karl Liebknecht Strasse, they extend east from the Brandenburg Gate to Alexanderplatz, one-time heart of socialist Germany. Between these two streets are some of Berlin's finest museums, on an island in the Spree River. The theatre district revolves around Friedrichstrasse, which crosses Unter den Linden just south of Friedrichstrasse Railway Station.

The ruin of Kaiser Wilhelm Memorial Church on Breitscheidplatz, a block away from Zoo Station, is your best central reference point in West Berlin. The tourist office and hundreds of shops are in the Europa Centre at the end of the square farthest away from the station. The Kurfürstendamm (Ku'damm), West Berlin's most fashionable avenue, runs 3.5 km south-west from Breitscheidplatz. North-east between Breitscheidplatz and the Brandenburg Gate is Tiergarten, a vast city park which was once a royal hunting domain.

While in Berlin, keep in mind that the street numbers usually (but not always) go up one side of the street and down the other. Be aware too that a continuous street may change names several times as it goes along. Some street names have been changed for political reasons and more will follow, so be prepared.

Information

Tourist Offices The Berlin-Information tourist office (☎ 030-2 42 46 75) below the TV tower near Alexanderplatz Railway Station is open daily from 8 am to 8 pm. The helpful, patient staff can give you a map and answer questions.

The more crowded Berlin Tourist Information Office (Verkehrsamt Berlin) (☎ 030-2 12 34), at Budapester Strasse 45 by

GERMANY

the Europa Centre in West Berlin, is open daily from 8 am to 10.30 pm.

The Informationszentrum Berlin is also near Zoo Station, on the 2nd floor of Hardenbergstrasse 20, behind the Deutsche Bundesbahn ticket office (open weekdays from 8 am to 7 pm, Saturday to 4 pm). It's less oriented towards consumer tourism and supplies two excellent free booklets in English: *Berlin for Young People* and *Berlin – Outlook*.

If you want to make contact with Berlin's political counterculture, try the café in the rear courtyard at Mehringhof, Gneisenaustrasse 2 (U-Bahn: Mehringdamm); it's closed Saturday.

Foreign Tourist Offices Tourist information on Eastern European countries is available from Balkantourist (Bulgaria), Unter den Linden 40; Čedok (Czechoslovakia), Strausbergerplatz 8 (U-Bahn: Strausbergerplatz); Ibusz (Hungary), Karl Liebknecht Strasse 9 (S-Bahn: Alexanderplatz); and Orbis (Poland), Warschauer Strasse 5 (U-Bahn: Frankfurter Tor).

Money The DVB Bank has an exchange office with a large yellow sign opposite the ticket windows in Friedrichstrasse Railway Station (open weekdays from 8 am to 8 pm, and weekends from 9 am to 5 pm). It will change travellers' cheques for DM3 commission (up to DM100 value) or DM7.50 commission (up to DM750 value) or 1% commission (over DM750 value).

American Express at Kurfürstendamm 11 (open weekdays from 9 am to 5 pm, Saturdays to noon) cashes its own travellers' cheques without charging commission, but gives a lousy rate. American Express has a second office at Friedrichstrasse 171. Only the first of these offices offers a clients' mail service.

If you're embarking on a major trip through Eastern Europe, you'll need lots of small denomination travellers' cheques. American Express will break its US$100 or US$50 travellers' cheques down into US$20s at no additional charge.

The Europa Centre Wechselstube, by the fountain on the opposite side of Breitscheidplatz from American Express, buys and sells banknotes of all countries without any commission charge. It gives a better rate than the bank at Zoo Station.

Post & Telecommunications Mail is still sorted by hand in East Berlin, so post your letters in West Berlin. It may also be a little while yet before the telephone connections in East Berlin attain the same standard as those in West Berlin, so go to West Berlin if you have any international telephone calls to make.

Postamt 12, Goethestrasse 3 a couple of blocks west of Zoo Station (open weekdays from 8 am to 6 pm, Saturday to 1 pm), is an uncrowded place to make international calls.

The telephone code for all of Berlin is 030.

Consulates The Australian Consulate General (☎ 3 92 21 09), Markgrafenstrasse 46 (S-Bahn: Friedrichstrasse), is open from 9 am to noon and 2 to 4 pm. New Zealand has no representation in Berlin as yet, and the Australian Consulate General will only help what they call 'stressed New Zealanders' (lost or stolen passport, money, luggage etc).

The British Consulate General (☎ 3 09 52 92), Uhlandstrasse 7-8 near Zoo Station, opens weekdays from 9 am to noon and 2 to 4 pm. The Canadian Consulate is on the 12th floor of the Europa Centre (open weekdays from 9 am to noon). The French Embassy is at Unter den Linden 40.

The US Consulate (☎ 8 32 40 87), Clay Allee 170 (U-Bahn: Oskar-Helene-Heim), is open weekdays from 8.30 to 11.30 am and 1.30 to 3 pm, closed Wednesday afternoon. For 'American citizen services' it's better to go in the afternoon when visa applications are not accepted and there is no queue.

The Polish Consulate is at Richard Strauss Strasse 11 on the far western side of the city (bus No 119 from the Ku'damm to Lassenstrasse). It is open weekdays from 9 am to 1 pm but closed Wednesday (tourist visas, if required, cost DM40, or DM50 for British passport holders, issued on the spot). Visas are not issued by the Polish Embassy, Unter den Linden 72.

The Hungarian Consulate, Toleranzstrasse 6 (S-Bahn: Unter den Linden, open Monday, Wednesday and Friday from 9 am to 1 pm), charges DM35 for visas (if required). At the Czechoslovak Consulate, Toleranzstrasse 21 (U-Bahn: Mohrenstrasse, open Monday to Friday from 8.30 am to 11 pm), visas are DM20 (if required). The Bulgarian Embassy is at Leipziger Strasse 20.

Cultural Centres The Centre Culturel Français, Unter den Linden 37 (open weekdays from 11 am to 7 pm), includes a good French library and organises cultural events listed on a poster outside.

The British Council Library, 1st floor, Hardenbergstrasse 20 near Zoo Station, is open Monday, Wednesday and Friday from noon to 6 pm, Saturday to 7 pm. Amerika Haus, Hardenbergstrasse 22-24, is open Monday, Wednesday and Friday from 11.30 am to 5.30 pm, Tuesday and Thursday to 8 pm.

Travel Agencies The Europäisches Reisebüro, in the tall building on the east side of Alexanderplatz, is a large travel agency (open Monday to Saturday) offering a variety of services. At Berlin-Tourist downstairs you can make room reservations, book local sightseeing tours and buy theatre tickets. Counter No 5 in the back office makes train reservations, while the adjacent counter No 6 sells international railway tickets.

Reisewelt, Charlottenstrasse 45 just off Unter den Linden, is a good place to buy international train tickets or make reservations as it's not too crowded. Youth-fare international train tickets are available from Jugendtourist, Friedrichstrasse 79a (open weekdays from 10 am to 6 pm, Saturday from 9 am to noon).

If you want a regular return railway ticket, check with the Deutsches Reisebüro (DER), Kurfürstendamm 17 near Zoo Station, which will tell you about special discount offers

that the railway station ticket office won't bother to mention.

SRS Studenten Reise Service, at Marienstrasse 23 (U-Bahn and S-Bahn: Friedrichstrasse), offers flights at student (aged 34 or less) or youth (aged 25 or less) fares. It also sells the FIYTO youth and ISIC student cards (DM10 and one photo) and can answer questions about travel around eastern Germany.

Reisebüro Zoo, Hardenbergplatz 2 opposite Zoo Station, sells bus tickets to western Germany, Holland, the UK etc.

Travel agencies offering cheap flights advertise in the *Reisen* classified section of *Zitty* (see Media in the Facts for the Visitor section earlier in this chapter). One of the better ones is Alternativ Tours (☎ 8 81 20 89), Wilmersdorfer Strasse 94 (U-Bahn: Adenauerplatz), which specialises in unpublished, discounted fares to anywhere in the world.

Laundry The Wasch Center, Wexstrasse 34 (U-Bahn: Bundesplatz), is a self-service laundrette which charges DM6 to wash six kg, soap included. Drying is DM1 for 15 minutes. It's open from 6 am to midnight daily. The Bio-wasch Center, Uhlandstrasse 53 (U-Bahn: Hohenzollernplatz, open from 6 am to 11 pm), is similar.

Bookshops For paperbacks in English, try the Marga Schoeller Bücherstube, Knesebeckstrasse 33-34. It carries mostly fiction. A smaller but more interesting selection of books in English, both new and second-hand, is at Wordsworth Books, Goethestrasse 69. Both of these should have something in English by local writer Christa Wolf.

East Berlin's biggest bookshop is Das Internationale Buch Bouvier, Spandauer Strasse 4 (S-Bahn: Marx-Engels-Platz), which has glossy art books, German travel guidebooks and some maps, but only cheap novels in English.

There are two travel bookshops in West Berlin: Kiepert, Knesebeckstrasse 2 at Hardenbergstrasse (U-Bahn: Ernst Reuter

GERMANY

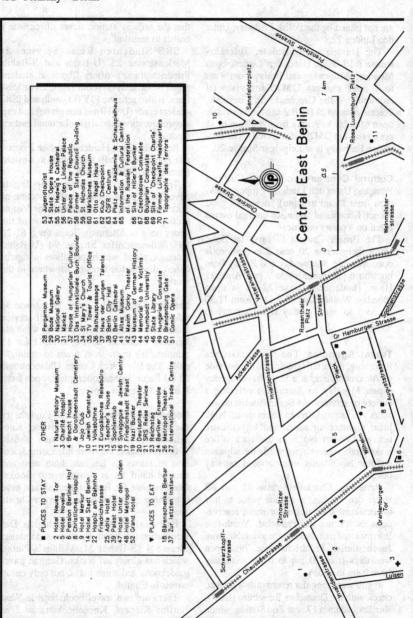

Central East Berlin

PLACES TO STAY
1 Hotel Neues Tor
5 Hotel Novalis
6 Pension Berliner Hof
8 Christliches Hospiz
9 Hotel Merkur
14 Hotel Stadt Berlin
25 Adria Hotel
39 Palast Hotel
47 Hotel Unter den Linden
48 Hotel Metropol
52 Grand Hotel

PLACES TO EAT
18 Bärenschenke Bierbar
37 Zur letzten Instanz

OTHER
1 Natural History Museum
2 Charité Hospital
3 Brecht House
4 Dorotheenstadt Cemetery
 & Dorotheenstadt Cemetery
7 Jojo Club
10 Jewish Cemetery
13 Hausvogtei
 Friedrichstrasse
11 Europäisches Reisebüro
12 Haus der Jungen Talente
13 Teacher's House
15 Sophienklub
16 Synagogue & Jewish Centre
17 Friedrichstadt Palast
19 Nazi Bunker
20 Deutsches Theater
21 SRS Reise Service
23 Reichstag
24 Berliner Ensemble
26 Metropol Theater
27 International Trade Centre

28 Pergamon Museum
29 Bode Museum
30 National Gallery
31 Market
32 House of Hungarian Culture
33 Das Internationale Buch Bouvier
35 St Mary's Church
35 TV Tower & Tourist Office
36 Rathauspassage
38 Berlin City
40 Berlin Cathedral
41 Altes Museum
42 Maxim Gorky Theater
43 Memorial to the Victims
44 Humboldt University
46 State Library
49 Hungarian Consulate
50 Brandenburg Gate
51 Comic Opera

53 Jugendtourist
54 State Opera House
55 St Hedwig's Cathedral
56 Unter den Linden Palace
57 Palace of the Republic
58 Former State Council building
59 St Nicholas Church
60 Märkisches Museum
61 Otto Nagel Haus
62 Berlin Checkpoint
63 CSR Centrum
64 Platz der Akademie & Schauspielhaus
65 Information & Cultural Centre
 of the Russian Federation
66 Site of Hitler's Federation
67 Czechoslovak Consulate
68 Bulgarian Consulate
69 Site of 'Checkpoint Charlie'
70 Former Luftwaffe Headquarters
71 Topographie des Terrors

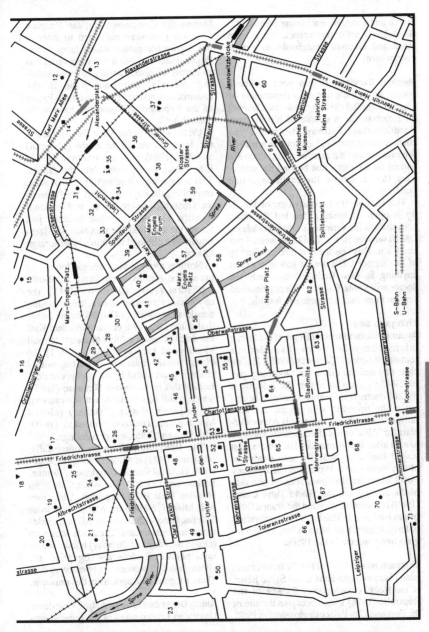

GERMANY

Platz), and Schropp, Potsdamer Strasse 100 (U-Bahn: Kurfürstenstrasse). They have maps and German guidebooks to almost everywhere.

Medical Services If you need to see a doctor, go to the emergency department of Charité Hospital *(Rettungstelle der Charité)* on Luisenstrasse a couple of blocks from Friedrichstrasse Railway Station. As you come from the station, look for an unmarked driveway where a couple of ambulances are parked on the right, just beyond the underpass that is below the main high-rise building.

This Humboldt University-operated facility is open 24 hours a day but the basic consultation fee varies: it's DM6 weekdays, DM18 weekends, and DM25 between 7 pm and 8 am. This was the best medical facility of the former GDR and is just as good as anything in West Berlin, though only the doctor will speak English. The personalised service more than compensates for this.

Things to See
Around Alexanderplatz Begin at the tourist information office below East Berlin's soaring 365-metre **TV tower** (1969). If it's a clear day and the queue isn't too long, pay the DM3 to go up the tower. The Telecafé at the 207-metre level revolves once an hour.

On the opposite side of the elevated railway station from the tower is Alexanderplatz (or 'Alex' as it is affectionately known), named after Tsar Alexander I of Russia who visited Berlin in 1805. The area was completely rebuilt in the 1960s, and the 39-storey **Hotel Stadt Berlin** now stands on one side of the square, and the **World Time Clock** (1969) on the other. Beyond the domed **Congress Hall** beside Teacher's House stretches orderly, lifeless Karl Marx Allee, faced with glass and concrete in the 1950s.

Museum Island West of the TV tower, on an island between two arms of the Spree River, is the sleek, contemporary **Palace of the Republic** (1976) which occupies the site of the Baroque City Palace demolished in 1950.

During the Communist era, the People's Chamber (Volkskammer) used to meet in this showpiece palace which faces Marx-Engels-Platz. In 1990 it was discovered that an excess of cancer-causing asbestos building material had been used in the construction, and the 180-metre-long Palace of the Republic will probably have to be demolished!

On the south side of Marx-Engels-Platz is the former **Council of State** (Staatsrat) building (1964), with a portal from the old City Palace incorporated into the façade. This body acted as a collective head of state, controlling the Supreme Court, the Prosecutor General, foreign policy and national security. The modern white building just across the canal on the east side of Marx-Engels-Platz housed the ministry of foreign affairs.

North across the busy avenue looms the great neo-Renaissance dome of **Berlin Cathedral** (1904, admission DM2), the city's main Protestant church. The imposing neoclassical edifice (1829) beside the cathedral is the early 19th century architect Karl Friedrich Schinkel's **Altes Museum** (closed Monday and Tuesday, admission DM1), the oldest public museum in Berlin, where changing art exhibitions are presented. Behind this is the **Neues Museum** (1855), which is still being rebuilt, but you can visit the adjacent **National Gallery** (closed Monday and Tuesday, admission DM1), with 19th and 20th century paintings.

The **Pergamon Museum** (open daily, admission DM1) is a feast of antiquity, especially classical Greek, Babylonian, Roman, Islamic and Oriental. The Ishtar Gate from Babylon (580 BC), Pergamon Altar from Asia Minor (160 BC) and Market Gate from Miletus, Greece (2nd century AD) are world-renowned monuments. The **Bode Museum** (closed Monday and Tuesday) houses sculpture, paintings, coins and Egyptian art, although not all sections are open every day. There's a good café upstairs in this museum.

Along Unter den Linden A stroll west down Unter den Linden takes in the greatest surviving monuments of the former Prussian capital. All the captions may be in German at the **Museum of German History** in the former Armoury (1706) opposite the Unter den Linden Palace (1732), but the extensive collection of objects, maps and photos is fascinating. Be sure to see the building's interior courtyard with its 22 heads of dying warriors by Andreas Schlüter.

Next to this museum is Schinkel's **Neue Wache** (1818), now the Memorial to the Victims of Fascism & Militarism. **Humboldt University** (1753), the next building west, was originally a palace of the brother of Frederick II, and was converted to a university in 1810. Beside this is the massive **State Library** (1914). An equestrian statue of Frederick II stands in the middle of the avenue in front of the university.

Across the street from the university, beside the Old Library (1780) with its curving Baroque façade, is the 18th century architect Wenzeslaus von Knobelsdorff's **German State Opera** (1743). On Bebelplatz, the square between these buildings, the Nazis staged a notorious book burning on 10 May 1933. A decade later in scores of concentration camps, they fulfilled Heinrich Heine's terrible prophecy: 'Where books are burned, people too are burned in the end.' Behind this site is the Catholic **St Hedwigs Cathedral** (1773), modelled on the Pantheon in Rome.

Around Tiergarten At the west end of Unter den Linden (S-Bahn: Unter den Linden) is the **Brandenburg Gate** (1791), a symbol of Berlin and once the boundary between East and West Berlin. The route of the Wall south from here to Potsdamer Platz is plain to see. The winged victory goddess and four-horse quadriga atop the gate was taken to Paris by Napoleon as a spoil of war, only to be returned to Berlin by the victorious Prussians a few years later. At the open-air flea market around the gate you can buy East German and Soviet military caps, belts, helmets, binoculars, army manuals, hammer & sickle emblems, flags, painted pieces of the Wall,

Soviet pocket watches etc. Compare prices before buying anything, and bargain.

Beside the Spree River just north of the Brandenburg Gate is the **Reichstag** (1894), the German parliament until it was burned by the Nazis on the night of 27-28 February 1933 as a pretext for rounding up their opponents. At midnight on the night of 2-3 October 1990 the reunification of Germany was enacted here. The restored Reichstag contains an excellent exhibition covering German history from 1800 to the present (closed Monday, admission free). All of the captions are in German, but a kiosk upstairs near the entrance to the exhibition rents a Walkman with a 45-minute guided tour in English, French or German for DM2. Downstairs, there's a good café for a coffee, and a cafeteria with goulash soup and Bockwurst. Between the Reichstag and the river is a small memorial to some of the 191 people who died trying to cross the Wall.

Berlin's huge inner-city park, **Tiergarten**, stretches west from here towards Zoo Station. Once a private hunting ground of the prince electors, it became a park in the 18th century, and from 1833 to 1838 it was landscaped with streams and lakes. Strasse des 17. Juni, which leads west from the Brandenburg Gate through the park, was known as the East-West Axis during the Nazi era, Hitler's showplace entrance to Berlin. On the north side of this street, just west of the gate, is a **Soviet War Memorial** flanked by the first Russian tanks to enter the city in 1945. German police with dogs defend the memorial against desecration by neo-Nazi skinheads.

Turn left (south) on Entlastungsstrasse just beyond the memorial and continue straight ahead till you see the **Philharmonie** (1963), designed by Hans Scharoun, diagonally across the street. This striking modern concert hall is unique in that the orchestra is completely surrounded by rows of seats. The **Musical Instruments Museum** (1984), Tiergartenstrasse 1 beside the Philharmonie (closed Monday, admission free), has a rich collection that is beautifully displayed.

Red-brick **St Matthew Church** (1846)

GERMANY

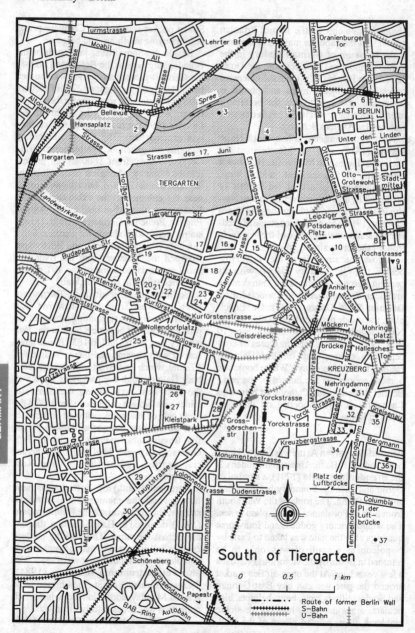

South of Tiergarten

0   0.5   1 km

Route of former Berlin Wall
S-Bahn
U-Bahn

stands just south of the abovementioned buildings in the centre of Berlin's new 'Kulturforum', and beyond it is the **New National Gallery**, Potsdamer Strasse 50 (closed Monday, permanent collection downstairs free, special exhibitions DM6), with 19th and 20th century paintings. This sleek, ultramodern gallery (1968) is a creation of the famous architect Mies van der Rohe. The **State Library** (1976) across the street contains reading, periodical and exhibition rooms (closed Sunday).

From the New National Gallery, walk west along the Landwehrkanal (without crossing it) past the Bewag building, or 'Shell House' (1932), to the **Museum for Design**, Klingelhofer Strasse 13-14 (closed Tuesday, admission DM3.50, free on Monday). This museum dedicated to the Bauhaus school (1919-33), which laid the basis for much contemporary architecture, is housed in a building designed by its founder, Walter Gropius.

North up Hofjäger Allee from this museum is the **Victory Column** (1873), topped by a gilded statue of the Roman victory goddess, Victoria, visible from much of Tiergarten, which commemorates 19th century Prussian military adventures. Just north-east is **Schloss Bellevue** (1785), built for Prince Ferdinand, brother of Frederick II the Great, and now an official residence of the President of Germany.

East along the Spree River is the **Kongresshalle** (1957), nicknamed the 'pregnant oyster' for its shape. The arched roof collapsed in 1980 but has since been rebuilt. The photo and art exhibits (often with Third World themes) inside are worth a look (closed Monday, admission free), but the main attraction are the soft seats where you can take a rest. You can board an excursion boat behind the building.

Along the U6 U-Bahn Line The house at Chausseestrasse 125 (U-Bahn: Zinnowitzer Strasse or Oranienburger Tor), where the famous playwright **Bertolt Brecht** lived from 1953 until his death in 1956, can be visited Tuesday to Friday from 10 to 11.30 am, Thursday from 5 to 6.30 pm and Saturday from 9.30 am to 1 pm in groups of eight people maximum with a German-speaking guide (admission free). Go into the rear courtyard and up the stairs to the right. The entrance is upstairs.

Next to Brecht House is **Dorotheenstadt**

GERMANY

Cemetery (1762) with tombs of the illustrious, such as the architect Schinkel, the philosopher Hegel, the poet Johannes R Becher and Brecht himself. There are two adjacent cemeteries here: you want the one closer to Brecht's house. The **Natural History Museum** (1810) nearby at Invalidenstrasse 43 (closed Monday, U-Bahn: Zinnowitzer Strasse) has a good collection of dinosaurs and minerals, plus an interesting exhibit on Charles Darwin.

All of the stations along the U6 U-Bahn line from Schwarzkopffstrasse south to Stadtmitte (excepting Friedrichstrasse) were below East Berlin and tightly sealed until mid-1990, although the U6 still rumbled through. Nothing remains of the famous **Checkpoint Charlie**, but if you want to see where it stood, get off at Kochstrasse Station and walk north on Friedrichstrasse. The abandoned multi-million-dollar structure at Friedrichstrasse 207-208 was, until 1990, the headquarters of all Western intelligence organisations in Berlin, and from here, or from the now-removed Allied guard trailer in the middle of the street nearby, photos were taken of everyone crossing the border. The Cold War rhetoric of this period is perpetuated across the street in the **Haus Am Checkpoint Charlie**, a commercial museum charging DM7.50 (DM4.50 for students) admission (open daily from 9 am to 10 pm).

Just west on Zimmerstrasse is the site of the former SS/Gestapo headquarters where the **Topographie des Terrors** exhibition (open daily) documents Nazi crimes. A platform atop a high mound of rubble from the ruined buildings provides a good view of this desolate area.

The massive grey government office block at the north-west corner of Zimmerstrasse and Toleranzstrasse used to be the headquarters of Hermann Göring's Luftwaffe. Diagonally opposite the Czechoslovak Consulate just north on the corner of Toleranz Strasse and Vossstrasse is the site of **Hitler's bunker**. The Chancellery built here by Albert Speer in 1938 was demolished after the war, and the bunker below it (where Hitler shot himself on 30 April 1945) was

completely effaced in the late 1980s when the Communists built the apartment complex which presently occupies the site.

West Berlin The stark ruins of neo-Romanesque **Kaiser Wilhelm Memorial Church** (1895) in Breitscheidplatz (S and U-Bahn: Zoologischer Garten), engulfed in the roaring commercialism all round, marks the heart of rebuilt West Berlin. The British bombing attack of 22 November 1943 left standing only the broken west tower. The former entry hall below the tower and the modern church (1961) may be visited. (As you're standing beside the church, look west across the street and you'll see a yellow Eduscho sign at Tauentzienstrasse 13. On weekdays you can get a nice cup of coffee in there for DM1.10.)

By the **Globe Fountain** (1983) next to the tower, assorted street artists and musicians play to the crowd. Just beyond rises the gleaming **Europa Centre** (1965) with a rotating Mercedes symbol on top. You can pay DM3 to stand on the 20th floor observation deck, but you can get a view almost as good for free from the 18th floor. North-east of the Europa Centre on Budapester Strasse is the elephant gate to West Berlin's **aquarium & zoo**, but it's a stiff DM12 (students DM6) to see both (open daily). This first zoo in Germany opened in 1844.

KaDeWe Department Store (1907), or Kaufhaus des Westens, on Wittenbergplatz a few blocks south, has been the main temple to German consumerism since the turn of the century; it's still the largest department store in Europe.

Along the Wall At Wittenbergplatz or Zoo Station, board the U1 U-Bahn line towards Schlesisches Tor. The movie, *Linie 1*, was made about this line and you'll get some great views of Berlin after the U1 escapes from its tunnel east of Kurfürstenstrasse Station and carries you up onto an elevated trestleway. Your fellow passengers will be as colourful as those who appeared in the film, because the U1 rolls right through counterculture **Kreuzberg**. Stay on to Schlesisches

Tor, heart of the largest Turkish community outside Turkey, and then follow the overhead U-Bahn line east a block to the Spree River. The longest surviving stretch of the **Berlin Wall** is just across the bridge.

As the Wall was being demolished in mid-1990, this 300-metre section was turned over to artists who created a permanent open-air art gallery along the side facing Mühlenstrasse (the side facing the river is sprayed with graffiti). Walk along the median strip as far as Berlin-Hauptbahnhof Railway Station where you can pick up the S-Bahn.

The Wall only existed for two-thirds of the life of the German Democratic Republic – from 1945 to 1961 there was no Wall. It's hard to visualise the Wall from this isolated fragment, but Ian Walker captures the mood in his fascinating book, *Zoo Station*:

The Wall was epic, beautiful in its way, the white concrete, the metal crosses, the watchtowers standing like toy soldiers. We had loved that snowy night when we scaled the wooden watchtower in Spandau.

Retracing the GDR Several interesting sights are accessible on East Berlin's two U-Bahn lines, which intersect at Alexanderplatz. Take a train to Märkisches Museum Station. The collection of the **Märkisches Museum** (closed Monday and Tuesday) is intended to illustrate the history of Berlin, and special features include a scale model of Berlin in 1750 and drawings by Heinrich Zille. Bears housed in a pit in the park behind the museum are the official mascots of the city.

Otto Nagel Haus, Märkisches Ufer 16-18 on the Spree Canal nearby (closed Friday and Saturday, admission DM0.50), exhibits the work of Berlin painter Otto Nagel (1894-1967) and his contemporaries. Many of the paintings here have social themes popular under the old regime. The good little café inside serves beer and liqueurs produced in eastern Germany.

Continue by U-Bahn in the direction of Hönow to Magdalenenstrasse Station and the former headquarters of the East German Stasi (secret police). In Haus 1 at Rusche-strasse 59 (from the station around the corner to the right) is **Antistalinistische Aktion**, a museum of GDR memorabilia housed in the former executive suite of Erich Mielke, the Minister of State Security (open Wednesday to Sunday from 2 to 5 pm, admission DM5). On the evening of 15 January 1990, some 50,000 demonstrators gathered outside this complex to protest ongoing Stasi activities. As they entered the compound, the crowd was attracted to the modern building with the gold-coloured windows near Haus 1, the only brightly lit building at the time. Stasi agents incited the mob to break into the building by throwing thousands of old currency declaration forms collected from tourists out the upper windows. Inside, the demonstrators found stocks of imported liquor and cigarettes, the Stasi bowling alley and recreational facilities etc. Meanwhile, Stasi officers in the foreign intelligence centre, the tall, well-protected buildings directly above the U-Bahn station, had time to destroy their documents. There isn't a lot to see in the museum but it's fun to wander around this complex, until recently one of the most tightly guarded of its kind in the world.

Charlottenburg Built as a country estate for Queen Sophie Charlotte, **Schloss Charlottenburg** (1699) is an exquisite Baroque palace on Spandauer Damm three km northwest of Zoo Station (U-Bahn: Richard Wagner Platz). The palace was bombed in 1943 but has been completely rebuilt. Before the entrance is a Baroque equestrian statue of Sophie's husband, Frederick I (1700). Along the Spree River behind the palace are extensive French and English gardens (free admission), while inside the many buildings are an important group of museums.

In the central building below the dome are the former living quarters of Sophie and Frederick, which may only be seen on a 45-minute tour with a German-speaking guide (closed Monday, admission DM7). The winter chambers of Frederick William II, upstairs in the New Wing (1746) to the east, may be visited individually on the same ticket. The **Romantic Art Collection**

GERMANY

GERMANY

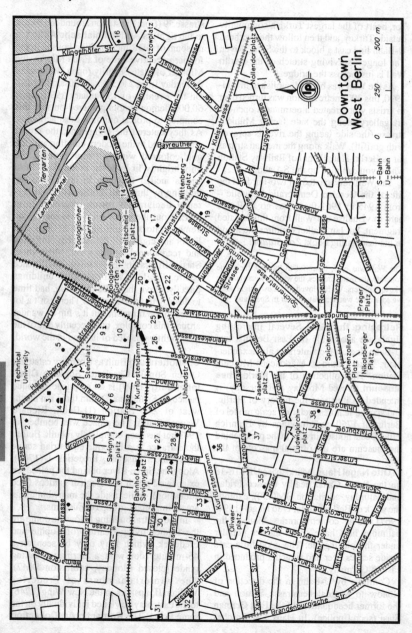

Downtown
West Berlin

0   250   500 m

━━━ S-Bahn
╫╫╫╫ U-Bahn

of the National Gallery is housed downstairs in this wing (closed Monday, admission free).

The combined palace ticket includes three buildings in the gardens. The **Schinkel Pavilion** (1825) was the summer house of Frederick William III. Farther back by the river is the **Belvedere** (1790), a Rococo teahouse which now houses a collection of Berlin porcelain. The neoclassical **Mausoleum** (1810) on the other side of the gardens contains the tombs of several kings and queens (closed in winter).

In addition to these sights, three branches of the State Museum at Charlottenburg should not be missed (all have free admission but are closed on Friday). The **Museum of Prehistory** occupies the west wing of the palace. Across the street at the beginning of Schlossstrasse are the Egyptian and Antiquities museums. The **Egyptian Museum** has a superb collection, including the 14th century BC bust of Queen Nefertiti from Tell el-Amarna. The **Museum of Antiquities** (1859) has objects from ancient Greece and Rome displayed on four floors.

Huge crowds are often waiting for the guided tour of Charlottenburg Palace and it may be difficult to get a ticket. This is especially true on weekends and holidays. If you can't get into the main palace, content yourself with the façades, gardens and free museums. Though the all-inclusive ticket is good value, there's plenty to see without paying.

West of the Centre Four km west of Zoo Station at a major crossroads is the **International Congress Centre** on Messedamm (U-Bahn: Kaiserdamm). This striking complex, nicknamed *das Superding* (the Super Thing), cost a billion Deutschmarks to erect in 1979. In the fairgrounds across the road from the ICC is the **Funkturm** (1926), a 138-metre-high tower you may ascend for DM5. Only the police and taxi radios still use this tower.

Three stops west on the U1 towards Ruhleben is the **Olympic Stadium** (U-Bahn: Olympia-Stadion) where Hitler watched Black American Jesse Owens steal the show at the 1936 Olympic Games (open daily, admission DM1).

Dahlem Museum One Berlin museum worth all the others combined is the **Dahlem**

GERMANY

Museum, Lansstrasse 8 (U-Bahn: Dahlem-Dorf); it's closed Monday, and admission is free. Here is kept the better part of the former Prussian art collections amassed by Frederick the Great, evacuated from Museum Island during WW II and never returned to East Berlin. This fantastic museum full of old master paintings, sculpture, ethnographical exhibits, and Indian, Oriental and Islamic art will knock you over. Arrive early in the morning and plan to spend the day there. There's a cafeteria downstairs in the museum, or you can have a picnic lunch on the grass outside.

A couple of blocks away is the **Botanical Garden**, Königin Luise Strasse 6-8 (open daily, DM2.50 admission), which opened in 1903. The **Botanical Museum** (closed Monday, admission free) is just outside the garden.

Activities

Central Berlin may be crowded with roads, office buildings and apartments, but the south-east and south-west sections of the city are surprisingly green with forests, rivers and lakes. From April to October, tourist boats cruise the waterways, calling at picturesque villages, parks and castles. If you're looking for an organised tour of Berlin, skip all the bus tours (which aren't much different from those offered in dozens of other European cities) and board one of the many excursion boats unique to Berlin. Food and drink are sold aboard but they're moderately expensive, so take along something to nibble or sip.

Spree River Cruises The Spree River crosses Berlin from east to west, connecting with an extensive network of lakes and canals. Take the S-Bahn in the direction of Königs-Wusterhausen or Schönefeld to Treptower Park Station, which is directly opposite Treptow Hafen, six km south-east of Alexanderplatz. The Weisse Flotte (☎ 2 71 20), or Stern und Kreis Schifffahrt as it is sometimes known, is based here.

Daily at 11 am and 3 pm from April to October the big boats operate from Treptow

to the Grosser Müggelsee and back, a trip called the *Müggelseefahrt* (three hours, DM8.50). An even better trip is the five-hour *Seerundfahrt* (DM12.50) at 11.30 am daily, a complete circuit of south-eastern Berlin via the Spree and Dahme rivers, the Langersee, the Seddinsee, the Müggelspree and the Grosser Müggelsee. One of the prettiest areas is the Müggelspree between the Dämeritz-See and the Grosser Müggelsee, covered during this trip. There's also a four-hour return trip to Charlottenburg daily at 2 pm (DM12.50).

Same-day tickets are sold at the ticket office labelled 'Tagesverkauf' (offerings are listed on a board); the 'Vorverkauf' ticket windows sell advance tickets only. These big excursion boats carry hundreds of passengers, so you should have no trouble getting on. All these trips are a great introduction to Berlin as you lounge on deck – highly recommended.

Canal & River Boats Spreefahrt (☎ 3 94 49 54), in a kiosk by the riverside behind the Kongresshalle in Tiergarten (S-Bahn: Unter den Linden), offers circular cruises around Berlin daily from mid-April to September. The morning cruise at 9.30 am circles central Berlin via the Spree River and Landwehrkanal (three hours, DM10). At 1 pm the boat sails right up the Spree River to the Grosser Müggelsee and back (four hours, DM12). A 1½-hour evening trip at 6 pm (DM8) passes Westhafen and Schloss Charlottenburg. A commentary is provided in German, and refreshments are sold on board.

Similar trips are offered by Reederei Heinz Riedel (☎ 6 93 46 46) whose kiosk is just downstream from the Kongresshalle. From April to October its boat travels down the Spree to the Landwehrkanal, then east through a lock and 'under the bridges' to Kreuzberg two or three times daily (three hours, DM14).

Lake Boats From Tegel to Potsdam, the Havel River widens between the forests into a picturesque series of lakes. Most of the large tour boats are based at Wannsee (S-

Bahn: Wannsee) and Tegel (U-Bahn: Tegel), although it's also possible to board at Kladow, Spandau and Potsdam.

Stern und Kreisschiffahrt (Weisse Flotte) (☎ 2 71 20) operates three lines several times daily all summer. Line 1 runs from Wannsee to Potsdam via Pfaueninsel and Glienicker Brücke from April to October (one hour, DM6.50). Line 2 operates from April to October from Wannsee on a seven-lake return trip (two hours, DM9). Line three is a grand tour between Tegel and Wannsee (from mid-April to September, two hours, DM8.50).

Other companies such as Reederverband (☎ 3 31 50 17), Reederei Bruno Winkler (☎ 3 91 70 10) and Reederei Triebler (☎ 3 31 54 14) also operate on these routes and their schedules and prices are sometimes more convenient, so check.

Places to Stay

Camping The camping facilities in Berlin are not good. There are several camping grounds in West Berlin charging DM6.40 per person plus DM5 per tent, but they're far from the centre, crowded with caravans and often full. They cater almost exclusively to permanent residents who live in their caravans all year, and although you may be admitted if you're polite and persistent, they aren't really set up to receive casual tourists. For more information, call the German Camping Club (☎ 2 18 60 71) during business hours.

The only camping ground convenient to public transport is *Campingplatz Kohlhasenbrück* (☎ 8 05 17 37), which is on Stubenrauchstrasse in a peaceful location overlooking the Griebnitzsee in the far south-west corner of Berlin. Bus No 118 from Wannsee S-Bahn Station runs directly there. If the gate is locked when you arrive, just hang around until someone with a key arrives, and then search for the manager in the caravan near the gate. It is open from 1 May to 30 September.

If Kohlhasenbrück is full, you'll have to walk two km east along the Teltowkanal to *Campingplatz Dreilinden* (☎ 8 05 12 01) at Albrechts-Teerofen (open from 1 May to 30 September).

Campingplatz Haselhorst (☎ 3 34 59 55) is near Spandau, two km north-west of Haselhorst U-Bahn Station. Walk north on Daumstrasse to Pulvermühlenweg and then west to the canal.

Krossin Lake Intercamping (☎ 6 75 86 87), two km beyond Schmöckwitz in the far south-east corner of East Berlin, is another option worth considering.

The best camping around Berlin is at Potsdam, so turn to that section if you're keen to unroll the tent.

Hostels – East Berlin The two youth hostels in East Berlin are now privately run and no longer connected with the IYHF, but their prices are about the same as those charged by the hostels in West Berlin, and your chances of getting a bed without reserving weeks in advance are infinitely better. You don't need a YHA card and everyone is welcome. For an advance reservation at either of the two, write to: Jugend-, Touristik- und Sport-Hotel GmbH, Franz-Mett-Strasse 7, 1136 Berlin (☎ 5 10 01 14, fax 5 12 40 40).

The 747-bed *Jugendhotel 'Am Tierpark'* (☎ 51 00 11 41), Franz-Mett-Strasse 7 (U-Bahn: Tierpark), offers rooms at DM45/90 single/double without bath, DM70/110 with bath, or DM40 per person in a four-bed dormitory, breakfast included. It's open all year and usually has beds available. Across the street is the East Berlin zoo.

One of the nicest places to stay in Berlin is the *Touristenhaus Grünau* (☎ 6 76 44 22), Dahmestrasse 6 in a quiet, attractive location beside the Dahme River in the quaint little town of Grünau. Take the S-Bahn to Berlin-Grünau, then any tram two stops towards Köpenick. It offers 150 beds in two, three, four and five-bed rooms at DM30 per person including breakfast. Though on the far south-east side of Berlin, transport to the city centre from here is good and there are hiking possibilities in the nearby Berlin City Forest (Berliner Stadtwald). There's usually space,

GERMANY

though groups occasionally book out the whole place, so try calling first.

Hostels – West Berlin The three youth hostels in West Berlin fill up fast on weekends and all summer, so call before going out. Until early July, the hostels are often fully booked by noisy school groups. Although the hostels are open to anyone, priority is given to those under 27 years of age, and you'll have to be an IYHF member (or become one through the guest-card scheme). None of the hostels offer cooking facilities but breakfast is included in the overnight charge; lunch is DM5.90, dinner DM7.50. The hostels stay open all day throughout the year.

The only hostel within walking distance of the city centre is the 364-bed *Berlin Youth Guest House* (☎ 2 61 10 97), Kluckstrasse 3 (U-Bahn: Kurfürstenstrasse), which costs DM25 for juniors, DM30.50 for seniors.

The ultramodern, 264-bed *Wannsee Youth Guest House* (☎ 8 03 20 34), Badeweg 1 on the corner of Kronprinzessinenweg, is in a pleasant lake-front location on Grosse Wannsee near the beach. Although 15 km south-west of the centre, this hostel is only an eight-minute walk from Nikolassee S-Bahn Station, with fast commuter trains to Zoo Station and Friedrichstrasse. It's also DM25 for juniors, DM30.50 for seniors, and a DM20 key deposit is required.

The *Ernst Reuter Youth Hostel* (☎ 4 04 16 10), Hermsdorfer Damm 48, is in the far north of West Berlin. Take the U-Bahn to Tegel, and then bus No 125 right to the door. The 110 beds are DM20 for juniors, DM24.50 for seniors. Try here first if you're arriving without a reservation.

The only sure way of getting into one of the West Berlin hostels is to write to the Deutsches Jugendherbergswerk (☎ 2 62 30 24), Tempelhofer Ufer 32, 1000 Berlin 61, several weeks in advance. State precisely which nights you'll be in Berlin and enclose an International Postal Reply Coupon (available at any post office) so they can send back confirmation. You must give an address where the confirmation can be sent to. Oth-

erwise you could just try calling a hostel to ask if they'll reserve a place for you.

The *Jugendgästehaus Am Zoo* (☎ 3 12 94 10), Hardenbergstrasse 9a, three blocks from Zoo Station, charges DM47/80 single/double, DM35 dormitory, DM6 extra for breakfast. It's limited to people aged under 27, but the location is great if you get in.

The *Jugendhotel International* (☎ 2 62 30 81), Bernburger Strasse 28 (S-Bahn: Anhalter Bahnhof), has rooms at DM50/90 single/double including breakfast. When things are busy you could have to share a three, four or five-bed room at about DM38 per person. It's often fully booked by school groups.

Hotel Transit (☎ 7 85 50 51), Hagelberger Strasse 53-54 (U-Bahn: Mehringdamm), a youth hotel crowded with young travellers, offers 120 beds at DM55/85 single/double, or DM30 per person in a six-bed dorm, a big breakfast included. All rooms have a shower. The Transit sometimes fills up with school groups from March to May and in September and October, but in the other months it should have beds available.

The *Studenthotel Berlin* (☎ 7 84 67 20), Meininger Strasse 10 (U-Bahn: Schöneberg), operates like a youth hostel but you don't need a card. Bed and breakfast is DM36 per person in a double, DM32 per person in a quad. Call first as it's often full.

From mid-July to mid-September you can sleep in a big tent at the *International Jugendcamp Fliesstal* (☎ 4 33 86 40) in northern West Berlin. From U-Bahn Tegel take bus No 222 (towards Lübers) four stops to the corner of Ziekowstrasse and Waldmannsluster Damm. The tents are behind the Jugendgästehaus Tegel, a huge, red-brick building opposite the bus stop. Beds in large communal tents are DM7 per person (blankets and foam mattresses provided) and check-in is after 5 pm (no curfew). Officially this place is only for those aged 14 to 23, but they don't turn away foreigners who are a little older. The maximum stay is three nights. Food can be purchased at the camp and a cheap breakfast is sold in the morning. Sit around the campfire at night.

If all else fails there's the *Bahnhofsmission* at Zoo Station, which provides dorm beds for DM15 (no breakfast). The office is on Jebensstrasse below the train tracks just outside the station. It's there mostly to help down-and-outs and should not be used by travellers except as a last resort. Ring the bell beside the door.

Private Rooms Your best bet for private rooms is the 'Zimmervermittlung' counter at Berlin-Tourist (open weekdays from 10 am to 6 pm, Saturdays to 5 pm) in the Europäisches Reisebüro on Alexanderplatz. It has rooms in East Berlin for DM15 to DM35 per person and can also reserve hotel rooms throughout eastern Germany.

Berlin-Information at the TV tower (U and S-Bahn: Alexanderplatz) sometimes has private rooms at DM30 per person, though they're often full.

The Verkehrsamt Berlin tourist office in the Europa Centre (U and S-Bahn: Zoologischer Garten) will find you a private room for DM45 per person (minimum stay two nights) plus DM3 commission.

If these fail, you can turn to one of the Mitwohnzentrale agencies listed in the following section, which will always be able to arrange a private room for you.

Long-Term Rentals If you'd like to spend some time in Berlin, look for someone willing to sublet their apartment. Many Berliners take off for extended holidays and are only too happy to have the bills paid while they're gone. Check the *Wohnungen* classified section in *Zitty* or *Zweite Hand*, or visit one of the Mitwohnzentrale agencies, which arrange private subrentals for periods as short as a day. They charge 10% of the monthly rental rate, or DM3 per person per day for short stays. If you're staying for under a month, you'll end up sharing a flat with others, a good way to meet people.

Take the escalator up to the *Mitwohnzentrale* (☎ 88 30 51) on the 2nd floor of the Ku'damm-Eck shopping arcade at Kurfürstendamm 227 near Zoo Station. It has apartments which cost DM35/60/80 single/double/triple per day, plus longer-term, cheaper rooms.

Mitwohnzentrale Charlottenburg (☎ 3 24 30 31), Sybelstrasse 53 (U-Bahn: Adenauerplatz), has rooms from DM35 a day per person (minimum stay two nights) or DM500 a month. It's open Monday from 9 am to 8 pm, Tuesday to Friday from 9 am to 7 pm and Saturday from 10 am to 6 pm.

Mitwohnzentrale Kreuzberg (☎ 7 86 20 03), 3rd floor, Mehringdamm 72 (U-Bahn: Platz der Luftbrücke), has rooms for DM20 to DM50 daily per person. The monthly rate for a room in a shared flat is DM250 to DM500 or more per person. Whole flats are almost impossible to locate (starting at DM500 plus 20%). It's open weekdays from 10 am to 7 pm, Saturday from 11 am to 4 pm.

Cheaper Hotels – East Berlin There's a cluster of relatively inexpensive hotels on the streets just north of Friedrichstrasse Railway Station. It's usually easier to get a room at these than at similar establishments in West Berlin, and the location is great, just minutes on foot from the theatres and museums around Unter den Linden.

The friendly *Christliches Hospiz* (☎ 28 49 70), Auguststrasse 82, has 70 rooms at DM70/110 single/double without bath, DM90/170 with bath, breakfast included. This clean, five-storey hotel run by the Verband Christlicher Hospize of the Protestant church is perhaps the nicest in East Berlin, if you get a room.

Part of the same chain is the 110-room *Hospiz Am Bahnhof Friedrichstrasse* (☎ 2 40 31 10), Albrechtstrasse 8, which is DM70/120 single/double with shared bath, breakfast included.

The 70-room *Adria Hotel* (☎ 2 82 54 51), Friedrichstrasse 134, was closed for a complete overhaul in mid-1992, and the management had no idea how long the whole thing would take.

The family-operated, nine-room *Hotel Merkur* (☎ 2 82 82 97), at Wilhelm Pieck Strasse 156, is DM78/114 single/double with bath and breakfast. It's a little overpriced for what you get, but should have rooms.

GERMANY

Other places to try include: the *Hotel Neues Tor* (☎ 2 82 38 59), Invalidenstrasse 102 (U-Bahn: Zinnowitzer Strasse); *Hotel Novalis* (☎ 2 82 40 08), Novalisstrasse 5 off Wilhelm Pieck Strasse; *Hotel-Pension Berliner Hof* (☎ 2 82 74 78), Friedrichstrasse 113a at Oranienburger Strasse; and *Hotel Märkischer Hof* (☎ 2 82 71 55), directly across the square from the Berliner Hof. If you're staying in this area, you can get a good stand-up breakfast weekdays at the *Bäckerei Jürgen Lange*, Linienstrasse 130 (U-Bahn: Oranienburger Tor).

Though rather out of the way, *Gästehaus 19, ARWOGE* (☎ 439 4103), Storkower Strasse 14 (S-Bahn to Ernst Thälmann Park, then walk 10 minutes), is a modern, eight-storey tourist hotel with 128 rooms that cost DM40/60 single/double including breakfast. The toilet and shower are shared by each cluster of four rooms in this former workers' residence. The tourist office below the TV tower can book you in here.

Cheaper Hotels – West Berlin Inexpensive *Hotel Pensionen* do exist in West Berlin but they're all small, plain and uncommercial, so expect no luxury and try calling first. Prices begin around DM65/90 single/double for a room with shared bath. Breakfast is usually DM8 to DM15 extra, although a light breakfast of tea or coffee, bread, butter and jam is sometimes included in the rate. The tourist office in the Europa Center will refuse to book any of the places mentioned here, so you'll just have to start calling or walking.

There are several budget places west of Zoo Station and north of the Ku'damm: *Pension Knesebeck* (☎ 31 72 55), Knesebeckstrasse 86-87 just off Savignyplatz (singles/doubles for DM70/120); *Pension Centrum* (☎ 31 61 53), Kantstrasse 31 (DM45/85); *Pension Alt-Lietzow*, Mommsenstrasse 11; *Pension Bachmann* (☎ 3 24 44 88), Mommsenstrasse 27; and *Hotel Pension Majesty* (☎ 3 23 20 61), Mommsenstrasse 55 (DM75/98).

The *Hotel Charlottenburger Hof* (☎ 3 24 48 19), Stuttgarter Platz 14 above Café Voltaire (open 24 hours) outside Charlottenburg

S-Bahn Station, is larger and farther away and thus more likely to have space (singles/doubles for DM65/95).

Two similar hotels south of the Ku'damm are *Hotel-Pension Pariser Eck* (☎ 8 81 21 45), Pariser Strasse 19 (singles/doubles for DM75/98), and *Pension Elton* (☎ 8 83 61 55), Pariser Strasse 9 (DM55/65).

There are five budget pensions in the building at Lietzenburger Strasse 76 on the corner of Uhlandstrasse. These establishments have no connection with the sordid sex clubs downstairs. *Hotel-Pension May* on the 4th floor is well above the action.

Three places just south of Breitscheidplatz are *Pension Riga* (☎ 2 11 12 23), Rankestrasse 23, *Hotel-Pension Nürnberger Eck* (☎ 2 18 53 71), Nürnberger Strasse 24a (singles/doubles for DM57/100), and *Pension Fischer* in the same building as the Nürnberger Eck.

If you'd rather stay out in Kreuzberg (U-Bahn: Mehringdamm), try *Hotel-Pension Südwest* (☎ 7 85 80 33), Yorckstrasse 80 (singles/doubles for DM40/80), or *Pension Kreuzberg* (☎ 2 51 13 62), Grossbeerenstrasse 64 (DM40/65).

Expensive Hotels If you want a luxury hotel, you'll do better at one of the Interhotels in East Berlin which are closer to the museums, theatres, and mass transit. If you don't mind socialist-modern architecture, their prices are also lower than those asked at Western chain hotels such as West Berlin's Inter-Continental.

The 305-room *Hotel Unter den Linden* (☎ 2 20 03 11), near Friedrichstrasse Railway Station, charges DM170/250 single/double, while the 880-room *Hotel Stadt Berlin* (☎ 2 38 90) on Alexanderplatz – the largest hotel in Berlin – is DM200/265. The 346-room *Hotel Berolina* (☎ 2 40 95 41), at Karl Marx Allee 31 (U-Bahn: Schillingstrasse), charges DM135/170 for a small room, DM190 double for a large room. This three-star hotel is less comfortable and convenient than the other two (both four-stars). Prices at all these include bath and breakfast.

One up-market West Berlin hotel deserves special attention. The 22 rooms at *Riehmers Hofgarten* (☎ 78 10 11), Yorckstrasse 83 in Kreuzberg (U-Bahn: Mehringdamm), cost DM196/236 single/double, including a big breakfast. Bus No 119 from the Ku'damm passes the door. This elegant, eclectic edifice erected in 1892 will delight romantics, and it's a fun area in which to stay.

Places to Eat

There's a restaurant for every cuisine under the sun in Berlin – literally thousands of them. Greek, Yugoslav and Italian restaurants serve good food at reasonable prices. Most restaurants post their menu outside and daily specials are listed on a blackboard. A cooked lunch or dinner at an unpretentious restaurant will cost DM17 if you order carefully. The price includes tax and service. Tipping is not obligatory although you can round your bill up to the next DM. Do this as you pay, rather than leave money on the table.

At those prices, it's unlikely you'll wish to sit down to a meal more than once a day. Substantial snacks are available at the many *schnell Imbiss* stands around the city. In addition to German stand-bys like *Rostbratwurst* and *Currywurst*, most Imbiss stands also have *döner kebab*, a filling Turkish sandwich of lamb cut from a vertical spit and stuffed into a big piece of pitta bread with lots of salad (DM4). Many Imbiss also offer half, barbecued chickens (DM5).

One Berlin treat to get acquainted with right away is a hot cup of DM1.10 coffee dispensed by a coin-operated machine at many Eduscho and Tchibo outlets around Berlin. You have to drink standing up, and this deal isn't offered on evenings or weekends (even though the shop itself may be open), but the throngs of local people tell you you're onto something good. You'll soon learn to recognise the Eduscho and Tchibo trademarks from afar, but not all outlets offer this service.

Breakfast Breakfast cafés are a Berlin institution catering to the city's late risers. In addition to canned music in a genteel setting, you can get a filling brunch of yoghurt, eggs, meat, cheese, bread, butter and jam for around DM10.50 (coffee extra). Some of the breakfasts are huge, so consider sharing one between two people. They also make a good lunch.

Typical of the genre are *Café Bleibtreu*, Bleibtreustrasse 45 (S-Bahn: Savignyplatz; breakfast from 9.30 am to 2 pm), and *Schalander*, Olivaerplatz 4 (U-Bahn: Adenauerplatz; breakfast until 5 pm). The *Zillemarkt*, Bleibtreustrasse 48, also does breakfasts and has a special lunch menu from noon to 1 pm on weekdays.

Schwarzes Café, Kantstrasse 148 near Zoo Station, serves breakfast any time and is open around the clock from 11 am Wednesday until 3 am Monday. This is one place to get off the street if you happen to roll into Berlin in the middle of the night.

On weekdays from 7 to 11 am you can get breakfast at the *Kleine Konditorei Am Metropol Theater* opposite the exit from Friedrichstrasse Railway Station.

Eating Cheaply There are lots of places to eat near Alexanderplatz. Next to the tourist office below the TV tower is a basic cafeteria (open daily from 7 am to 6 pm). Better meals with regular table service can be had at *Gaststätte Alextreff* (daily from 11 am to 4 pm), upstairs between the elevated tracks and the Rathauspassage. There are many places to consume a quick snack standing up below the Rathauspassage.

Substantial, inexpensive meals are consumed in the food halls of the large West Berlin department stores, *KaDeWe* and *Wertheim*. At KaDeWe (U-Bahn: Wittenbergplatz), the top floor is the 'gourmet floor'. At the *Club Culinar* in the basement at Wertheim, Kurfürstendamm 232 near the Ku'damm-Eck, you can get a good bowl of soup or half a chicken for a lower-than-average price. There's also a supermarket, café and a small wine bar with half a dozen Berliners in very good spirits down there.

Pizzeria Amigo, Joachimstaler Strasse 39-40 near Zoo Station (open daily from 11 am

448 Germany – Berlin

to 1 am), serves a wicked plate of spaghetti napoli or a pizza margherita for only DM5. It's self-service but the food is good and there's a fine place to sit down.

The *Athener Grill*, Kurfürstendamm 156 (U-Bahn: Adenauerplatz), has spaghetti, pizza, steaks, salads, Greek dishes and big mugs of draught beer at the lowest prices in town. It's also self-service but there are plenty of tables. It's open daily from 11 am to 4 am.

Subsidised Meals If even these cheap places are too expensive, you can enjoy a hot subsidised meal (DM5 to DM10) in a government cafeteria. They're open weekdays only and you clear your own table.

If you have a valid student card there's the *mensa* of the Technical University, Hardenbergstrasse 34 three blocks from Zoo Station (open weekdays from 8 am to 5 pm).

The *Kantine* downstairs in Rathaus Charlottenburg, Otto-Suhr-Allee 100 close to Schloss Charlottenburg (U-Bahn: Richard Wagner Platz), serves nonemployees from 2 to 2.30 pm only. It's in the basement inside the building, not the expensive Ratskeller outside. What's available is written on a blackboard at the far end of the counter. This is a good place to have lunch after seeing Schloss Charlottenburg.

The *Rathaus Casino* on the 10th floor of Rathaus Kreuzberg, Yorckstrasse 4-11 (U-Bahn: Mehringdamm), is open weekdays from 7.30 am to 3 pm and offers cheap lunch specials and great views. Everyone is welcome. (Nearby at Yorckstrasse 14 is an Eduscho outlet dispensing cheap coffee on weekdays.)

Also good is the *Kantine* in the unemployment insurance office (Arbeitsamt) at Charlottenstrasse 90 (U-Bahn: Kochstrasse); it's open weekdays from 9 am to 1 pm. Just walk straight in and take the lift on the left up to the 5th floor.

Another unemployment office with a *Kantine* on the 5th floor (open weekdays from 8.30 am to 12.30 pm) is at Müllerstrasse 16 just outside Wedding U-Bahn Station. (In fact, almost any Arbeitsamt you see in West Berlin will have a cheap *Kantine*.)

The *cafeteria* in the State Library (closed Sunday) opposite the New National Gallery in Tiergarten offers soup, salad and sandwiches, plus hot specials. You have to check your bag (free) to get in.

There's a reasonable self-service restaurant straight back inside the office building at Unter den Linden 38 (open weekdays from 8 am to 2 pm) – convenient for sightseers.

East Berlin One of the easiest places to experience a typical German meal is the *Ratskeller* (daily from 11 am to 1 am) below Berlin City Hall just south of the TV tower (S/U-Bahn: Alexanderplatz). Prices are reasonable but the service tends to be slow.

More expensive is the *Gastmahl des Meeres* on the corner of Spandauer Strasse and Karl Liebknecht Strasse (S-Bahn: Marx-Engels-Platz), which specialises in seafood such as whole trout (charged by weight) and eel.

Zur letzten Instanz, Waisenstrasse 14-16 (U-Bahn: Klosterstrasse), is a typical Berlin tavern (built in 1525) on a backstreet behind the Haus der jungen Talente south-east of Alexanderplatz. Meals are served. The place got its present name 150 years ago when a newly divorced couple came in from the nearby courthouse with their witnesses for a few drinks. By the time they were ready to leave they'd made up and decided to remarry the next day, at which one of those present exclaimed, 'This is the court of last resort!'

The *Bärenschenke Bierbar*, Friedrichstrasse 124 (U-Bahn: Oranienburger Tor), is an unpretentious local pub serving meals from 10 am to 11 pm (closed Monday). Specialities include *Schlachteplatte mit Blut und Leberwurst* (a mixed meat plate typical of Berlin), *Wildsuppe* (venison soup) and *Gebackener Camembert* (fried cheese). There's a nice long bar here where you can chat with Berliners as you swill your beer.

West Berlin Since most West Berlin restaurants offer exotic cuisine, finding authentic German fare takes a little doing. *Beiz*,

Schlüterstrasse 38 off the Ku'damm (open daily from 6 pm to 2 am), is rather expensive. *Dicke Wirtin*, Carmerstrasse 9 off Savignyplatz, is an old German pub offering goulash soup and beer. In summer, make for *Loretta's Biergarten*, Lietzenburger Strasse 89 behind the ferris wheel. Stein of pils in hand at a long wooden table out the back, you'd swear you were in Bavaria.

More out of the way but full of atmosphere is *Zum Ambrosius*, Einemstrasse 14 (U-Bahn: Nollendorfplatz). The specials are marked on blackboards outside this rustic pub/restaurant. If Zum Ambrosius fails to please, try *Spatz*, a block away at Kurfürstenstrasse 56, a basement pub and steakhouse (opens at 6.30 pm daily except Sunday). There's a second Zum Ambrosius at Kurfürstenstrasse 40 just outside Kurfürstenstrasse U-Bahn Station.

Cafés *The* place for coffee and cakes is *Café Kranzler* (open daily till midnight), on the corner of Kurfürstendamm and Joachimstaler Strasse near Zoo Station. Look for the circular pavilion up on the roof.

Berlin's most elegant literary café is *Café Einstein*, Kurfürstenstrasse 58 (U-Bahn: Kurfürstenstrasse); it's open daily from 10 am to 2 am. This is a good place to go with friends if you want to talk.

The *Café zum Trichler*, Schiffbauer Damm 7 around the corner from the Berliner Ensemble (U and S-Bahn: Friedrichstrasse), is a favourite hang-out for actors and the literary crowd. It opens at 5 pm.

A café for women only is *Extra Dry*, Mommsenstrasse 34 off Lewishamstrasse (U-Bahn: Adenauerplatz).

A counterculture café with a real earthy atmosphere is *Seifen und Kosmetik*, Schliemannstrasse 21 (S-Bahn: Prenzlauer Allee). *Café Anfall*, Gneisenaustrasse 64 (S-Bahn: Südstern) has pretty wild décor and good, but loud, music.

A late-evening place to visit is *Café 'Arkade'*, Französische Strasse 25 near Platz der Akademie (U-Bahn: Französische Strasse), which stays open until midnight daily. Here you can get excellent Viennese coffee, ice cream or drinks in a pleasant, relaxed atmosphere.

Entertainment

Musical Theatres East Berlin beats West Berlin hands down as far as opera and operetta go, and the best theatres are conveniently clustered near Friedrichstrasse Railway Station. The productions are lavish with huge casts, and the best seats cost less than half the same tickets in West Berlin. Some theatres (such as the Metropol) give students and pensioners a 50% discount on unsold tickets 30 minutes before the performance. All performances are listed in the monthly *Berlin Programm Magazin*, available at newsstands, hotels and tourist offices. Tickets to special events are available from the Festspielgalerie, Budapester Strasse 48 across from the Kaiser Wilhelm Memorial Church (open daily from noon to 7 pm). Many of the theatres take Monday evening off and close from mid-July to late August.

Good seats for performances on the same evening are usually obtainable, and unclaimed tickets are made available an hour before the performance. The best way to get in is simply to start making the rounds of the box offices at about 6 pm. If there's a big crowd of people waiting at one theatre, hurry on to the next. You're allowed to move to unoccupied, better seats just as the curtain is going up. Berlin's not stuffy, so you can attend theatre and cultural events dressed as you please.

East Berlin's two opera houses are the *State Opera House*, Unter den Linden 7 (the box office is open Monday to Saturday from noon to 6 pm, Sunday from 2 to 6 pm, tickets DM5 to DM75), and the *Comic Opera* (Komische Oper), Behrenstrasse 55-57 at the corner of Glinkastrasse (U-Bahn: Französische Strasse); the box office across the street opens Tuesday to Saturday from noon to 6 pm, and tickets cost DM5 to DM60.

West Berlin's *Deutsche Oper* (1961), Bismarckstrasse 35 (U-Bahn: Deutsche Oper), is all glass and steel. Its box office opens Monday to Saturday from 11.30 am to

GERMANY

5.30 pm, Sunday from 10 am to 2 pm (tickets DM10 to DM125).

Musicals and operettas are presented at the *Metropol Theater*, Friedrichstrasse 101-102 directly in front of Friedrichstrasse Railway Station (box office opens Monday to Saturday from 10 am to 6 pm). It's not as famous as the State Opera or Comic Opera, so tickets are easier to obtain – highly recommended! (Don't confuse this Metropol theatre with the Metropol disco in West Berlin.)

Seats at West Berlin's *Theater des Westens*, Kantstrasse 12 near Zoo Station, cost DM15 to DM70. The box office across the street is open Tuesday to Saturday from noon to 6 pm, Sunday from 3 to 6 pm. Though this beautiful old theatre (1896) has style and often features excellent musicals, it's hard to see much from the cheap seats.

The new *Friedrichstadt Palast* (1984), Friedrichstrasse 107, offers vaudeville musical revues but it's often sold out (box office opens Tuesday to Saturday from noon to 3.30 pm and 4 to 6.30 pm).

Concert Halls East Berlin's wonderfully restored *Schauspielhaus* is on Platz der Akademie (U-Bahn: Stadtmitte). The box office opens Tuesday to Saturday from 2 to 6 pm.

All seats at West Berlin's *Philharmonie*, Matthaikirchstrasse 1 (U-Bahn: Kurfürstenstrasse, then bus No 148), are excellent, so just take the cheapest. Do try to hear at least one concert at the Philharmonie.

Other musical programmes are offered at the *School of Art Concert Hall*, Hardenbergstrasse 33 near Zoo Station (tickets sold Tuesday to Friday from 3 to 6.30 pm, Saturday from 11 am to 2 pm).

Other Theatres Even if your German is nonexistent, the *Berliner Ensemble*, Bertolt Brecht's original theatre, near the Friedrichstrasse Railway Station (box office opens Tuesday to Saturday from 11 am to 3.30 pm and 4 to 6.30 pm), is worth attending for both the architecture and classic Brecht plays. Most of Brecht's works include music. *The Threepenny Opera*, Brecht's first great popular success, premiered here in 1928.

Share the joys and fantasies of childhood at the *Puppentheater*, Greifswalder Strasse 81-84 just outside Ernst Thälmann Park S-Bahn Station. Performances are often held on weekdays at 10 am and 3 pm, but check. Tickets are usually available at the door.

East Berlin's ultramodern *Zeiss Grossplanetarium* near Prenzlauer Allee S-Bahn Station offers programmes daily from Wednesday to Sunday at 3.30, 5 and 6.30 pm (admission DM4, Sunday half-price).

Cinemas If you want to see a movie, go on Wednesday ('Cinema Day', or *Kinotag*), when tickets are half-price (DM6). The *Filmzentrum Zoo Palast*, Hardenbergstrasse 29a near Zoo Station, contains nine cinemas (the film festival is held here). There are many other movie houses along Kurfürstendamm, but foreign films are dubbed into German. (If the film is being shown in the original language with German subtitles it will say 'O.m.U.' on the advertisement. If it's in English the ad will be marked 'engl. OF'.)

See movies in the original English at the *Odeon Theatre* (☎ 7 81 56 67), Hauptstrasse 116 (U-Bahn: Innsbrucker Platz, or S-Bahn: Schöneberg). There are three shows daily.

The *Kurbel Cinema* (☎ 8 83 53 25), Giesebrechtstrasse 4 off Kurfürstendamm (U-Bahn: Adenauerplatz), also usually has at least one film in English.

The *Original Version*, Sesenheimer Strasse 17 (U-Bahn: Deutsche Oper), hires out movie videos in English if you have access to a video recorder.

Youth Centres The nightlife scene in East Berlin is less slick but more authentic than that in West Berlin. Your best bets are the various youth cultural centres which offer a variety of entertainment possibilities under one roof. All are good places to meet people and they're relatively drug-free compared to West Berlin.

The *Haus der jungen Talente*, Klosterstrasse 68-70 south-east of Alexanderplatz (U-Bahn: Klosterstrasse), offers films (at 7 pm, DM3), pantomime (at 7 pm, DM3), folk dancing (at 7 pm, DM5), cabaret (at 8 pm, DM10), jazz (at 9 pm, DM8), blues (at 9 pm, DM5), a disco (at 9 pm, DM3), café entertainment etc. What's on varies daily, so pick up a copy of the monthly programme at the door.

A more counterculture place is *Jojo* (☎ 2 82 46 56), Wilhelm Pieck Strasse 216 (U-Bahn: Oranienburger Tor), which includes a cinema, bookshop, theatre, music room, bar, disco and café. The DM5 entry price admits you to everything, but it's only open in the evening and things don't start moving until 11 pm.

Checkpoint, Leipziger Strasse 55 (U-Bahn: Spittelmarkt), puts on a nightly programme of video, jazz, disco, cinema, theatre, dance, art gallery, bar, café and live music. Not everything is offered every night, so check the programme.

Discos West Berlin has a reputation for its nightlife, and nothing happens until 10 pm. That's the time to stroll down the Ku'damm amid all the glitter. A disco tout will hand you an invitation to *Big Eden*. Before you get sucked into any of the tourist joints along the strip, take a look up Bleibtreustrasse and around Savignyplatz where the locals go.

West Berlin discos are wild and you have to put a big effort into keeping up with the scene. The favourite tourist disco is *Big Eden*, Kurfürstendamm 202 (open daily from 7 pm). Other than Friday and Saturday nights there's no cover charge, but they make up for it in the price of the drinks. *Society*, Budapester Strasse 42 opposite the Europa Centre, is similar.

If you'd rather dance with Berliners it's *Far Out*, Kurfürstendamm 156 (U-Bahn: Adenauerplatz). The entrance to this Bhagwan disco is beneath the bowling alley around the side of the building. It's open from 10 pm, closed Monday, with a DM10 cover charge on Friday and Saturday, DM5 other nights. Drinks are normally priced.

For a slightly offbeat trip, try the *Metropol*, Nollendorfplatz 5 (U-Bahn: Nollendorfplatz), popular with gays and

straights. The big disco operates Friday and Saturday nights from 10 pm, the small disco Sunday to Thursday from 10 pm. Rock concerts unroll at the Metropol (☎ 2 16 41 22) around 7 pm, but they're often sold out.

One disco with live 'independent underground' music (hard rock or punk) is *Madhouse Ecstasy*, Hauptstrasse 30 in Schöneberg (U-Bahn: Eisenacher Strasse). It has top bands playing from 9 pm to dawn every Friday and Saturday night (DM10 to DM20 cover charge depending on the fame of the group, student discounts available). On other nights, you can dance in its Madhouse or Funhouse discos (DM5 cover charge) after 10 pm. For information on what's happening in Ecstasy, call its business office on ☎ 781 1865 weekdays from noon to 4 pm, or the disco direct on ☎ 782 0649 at other times (they speak English). Fascist skinheads are not admitted.

In East Berlin, try the disco below the TV tower (S or U-Bahn: Alexanderplatz), which opens at 8 pm Friday and Saturday. Entry is free but there's a DM10 minimum consumption charge. It's upstairs above the tourist office.

The music scene in Berlin is constantly changing, and for up-to-date information it's best to check the fortnightly magazines *Zitty* and *Tip*, which carry complete listings of what's happening.

Pubs There are thousands of pubs, or *Kneipen*, in Berlin, and in the absence of licensing hours they're open day and night (usually from 7 pm to 4 am). Many pubs offer live music and food. A cover charge of DM4 to DM15 may be asked if there's live music, although some places only charge admission on Friday and Saturday nights.

The *Sophienklub*, Sophienstrasse 6 off Rosenthaler Strasse (S-Bahn: Weinmeisterstrasse), has jazz nightly from 9 pm, with a special programme on Tuesday and Saturday nights.

Quasimodo, Kantstrasse 12a near Zoo Station (open from 9 pm, music from 10 pm), is a Jazzkeller with live jazz, blues or rock

GERMANY

every night. The cover charge varies from free to DM20 depending on who is playing.

For folk music, try *Go In*, Bleibtreustrasse 17 (S-Bahn: Savignyplatz); it's open daily from 8 pm. *Salsa*, Wielandstrasse 13, features Latin American and Caribbean music. It opens at 8 pm, has live music from 10.30 pm and offers free admission Sunday to Thursday. *Madow*, at Pariser Strasse 23-24 (open Wednesday, Friday, Saturday and Sunday from 10 pm), features music from the 1970s. There's a DM4 cover charge and you can dance.

The *Djungel Club*, Nürnberger Strasse 56 (U-Bahn: Wittenbergplatz), is a late-night place for the super cool (closed Tuesday). If you're too old, fat, poorly dressed or not with it you won't get past the doorkeeper. It's such an insiders' scene, they don't even have a sign outside, but look for the tropical vegetation in the window of the place next to the Alles für den Hund canine paraphernalia shop.

A typical Berlin pub is *E & M Leydicke*, Mansteinstrasse 4 (S or U-Bahn: Yorckstrasse). This oldest pub in Berlin (founded in 1877) bottles its own liqueurs on the premises. Open daily from 4 pm to midnight, it's primarily a drinking place.

Spectator Sports There's trotting at *Trabrennbahn Karlshorst* (Karlshorst Race Track) near Karlshorst S-Bahn Station after 6 pm Tuesdays and 2 pm Saturdays throughout the year (admission DM2). Even if you're not a regular horse racing fan, this is a wonderfully informal place to see local people enjoying themselves. Buy the programme (DM2) at the gate if you intend to wager. There are dozens of stands here dispensing cheap food and drink, so come hungry and thirsty.

From September to June, you can see soccer (European football) every other Saturday at 3 pm at the *Friedrich Ludwig Jahn Sportpark* (U-Bahn: Dimitroffstrasse) or the *Olympic Stadium* (U-Bahn: Olympia-Stadion). The matches alternate between the two stadiums on successive weeks, so check.

On weekends, you're welcome to join in soccer and volleyball games in the field in front of the Reichstag.

Things to Buy
Tauentzienstrasse is the main shopping street for affluent West Berlin consumers. At the Wittenbergplatz end of this street is KaDeWe (Kaufhaus des Westens), an amazing, six-storey, turn-of-the-century department store which sells just about everything you can name. Wertheim, Kurfürstendamm 232, West Berlin's second department store, is less pretentious and less expensive.

Shops selling discount cameras are along Augsburger Strasse near the Ku'damm.

The largest camping goods store in West Berlin, with a good selection of top-quality tents and backpacks, is Alles für Tramper, Bundesallee 88 (U-Bahn: Walther Schreiber Platz).

Good, inexpensive, second-hand clothes of all descriptions can be found at Made in Berlin, Potsdamer Strasse 106 (U-Bahn: Kurfürstenstrasse). You can find some pretty funky attire there!

The Kunstsalon, Unter den Linden 41, has German art books, reproductions, sheet music, records and cassettes. Meissner Porzellan, Unter den Linden 39, sells the famous Meissen porcelain.

There's an open-air flea market (Trödelmarkt) every Saturday and Sunday morning on Strasse des 17. Juni at Tiergarten S-Bahn Station. Don't buy any GDR paraphernalia here, as you can get it much cheaper at the street market around the Brandenburg Gate.

Eastern European Products Several countries have cultural centres in Berlin (open weekdays), which sell their books, maps, records, handicrafts and souvenirs. The House of Hungarian Culture (☎ 2 10 91 46), Karl Liebknecht Strasse 9, and the Polish Cultural Centre (☎ 2 12 32 68), Karl Liebknecht Strasse 7, are opposite St Mary's Church near Alexanderplatz. The Bulgarian Cultural Centre (☎ 2 00 23 80) is at Unter den Linden 10, and the Czechoslovak Cultural Centre (ČSFR Centrum) (☎ 2 00 09 60) is at Leipziger Strasse 60.

Getting There & Away
Bus The Funkturm Bus Station (U-Bahn: Kaiserdamm) is open from 5.30 am to 10 pm. Westkreuz S-Bahn Station is within walking distance from this bus station.

Bayern Express (☎ 87 01 81) has buses to Amsterdam, Frankfurt/Main, Hanover, Munich, Nuremberg and many points in southern Germany. Sperling GmbH (☎ 33 10 31) has services to Bremen, Düsseldorf, Goslar, Hamburg, Kiel, Lübeck and other cities in northern Germany. Tickets are available from most travel agencies in West Berlin.

Train Information on all railway services in Eastern Europe is available from counters No 5 & 6 downstairs in the back office of the Europäisches Reisebüro on Alexanderplatz. They sell international train tickets and make reservations for the same price as the counters in the railway stations but without the queues. The ticket and reservation offices at Berlin-Friedrichstrasse, Berlin-Alexanderplatz, Berlin-Hauptbahnhof and Berlin-Lichtenberg railway stations are also far less congested than the one in Berlin-Zoo Station.

With the opening up of Russia, elderly Germans have begun to visit the Russian territory of Kaliningrad, an area that equates roughly to the northern half of what used to be East Prussia. What's now the city of Kaliningrad used to be the East Prussian capital of Königsberg, the home of the famous philosopher, Immanuel Kant. Rail Tours Mochel Reisen (☎ 07821-4 30 37), Georg-Vogel-Strasse 2, W-7630 Lahr im Schwarzwald, offers a return train trip from Berlin plus a week in Kaliningrad or Svetlogorsk for US$600 to US$1050, or a lightning in-and-out trip with just 12 hours in Kaliningrad for US$185 to US$570.

East Berlin's main railway station is Bahnhof Berlin-Lichtenberg, with trains to all parts of Germany and Eastern Europe. This station is easily reached by S-Bahn (direction Wartenberg, Ahrensfelde or Strausberg Nord) or on the Hönow U-Bahn line. The reservation office opens on weekdays from 6 am to 8 pm, on weekends from 8 am to 6 pm, and international tickets are easily purchased. The helpful attendants in the station information office speak good English and there's no crowd! The left-luggage room is open nonstop (DM2 per piece per *calendar* day) and there are plenty of coin lockers.

Trains to Poland and points farther east depart from Berlin-Hauptbahnhof as well as Berlin-Lichtenberg. The left-luggage office at the Hauptbahnhof only closes from 1.30 to 3 am.

Many trains to Dresden, Leipzig, Halle, Chemnitz, Gera, Erfurt and Magdeburg also leave from Bahnhof Berlin-Schöneweide. All trains travelling to the south and west of eastern Germany stop at Flughafen Berlin-Schönefeld.

Bahnhof Berlin-Zoologischer Garten (Zoo Station) on Hardenbergplatz is the main railway station in West Berlin, although some trains to/from western Germany also stop at Berlin-Wannsee or Berlin-Spandau. This overcrowded station features plenty of coin lockers (DM2 or DM3 depending on the size of the locker), a reservation office (long, slow queue), a railway information office (*Zugauskunft*), a 24-hour post office with public telephones opposite, and a tourist information office which makes (expensive) hotel reservations for DM3 commission. The currency exchange office of the Deutsche Verkehrs-Kredit Bank (open until 9 pm Monday to Saturday, and 6 pm Sunday) is just outside.

Trains between Poland and Western Europe pass through West Berlin, so you can get on or off at Zoo Station. Trains to Berlin from Czechoslovakia and Hungary, however, terminate at Lichtenberg Railway Station in East Berlin. From there you can take the S-Bahn to Alexanderplatz or Berlin-Zoo.

Train tickets to/from Berlin are valid for all railway stations in the city (*Stadtbahn*), which means that on arrival you may use the S-Bahn network (but not the U-Bahn) to proceed to your destination; conversely, you can use the S-Bahn to go to the station from where your train leaves. It's always best to board trains leaving Berlin at the originating station mentioned on your ticket.

Hitchhiking You can hitchhike to Dresden, Hanover, Leipzig, Munich, Nuremberg and beyond from Checkpoint Dreilinden at Wannsee, which used to be the entrance to the transit highway between Berlin and western Germany. Take the S-Bahn to Wannsee, then walk less than a km up Potsdamer Chaussee and follow the signs to Raststätte Dreilinden. There's always a bunch of hitchhikers here, but everyone gets a ride eventually. Bring a small sign stating your destination, and consider waiting until you find a car going right where you want to go.

There are numerous Mitfahrzentrale agencies in West Berlin, which tend to charge DM10 to DM17 commission. One office is on the platform of the U1 U-Bahn line towards Schlesisches Tor at Zoologischer Garten underground station (☎ 31 03 31), open daily from 8 am to 9 pm. Another office (☎ 8 82 76 04), also open daily from 8 am to 9 pm, is on the 2nd-floor shopping arcade at Kurfürstendamm 227 (Ku'damm-Eck). Other Mitfahrzentrale agencies are listed in the 'Mitfahrer' classified section of *Zitty*. The people answering the phone in these offices always speak good English, so don't hesitate to call around.

If you arrange a ride a few days in advance, be sure to call the driver the night before and again on departure morning to make sure he/she is still going.

Getting Around

To/From the Airport Most Eastern European and Third World carriers fly from Berlin-Schönefeld Airport (SXF), next to Flughafen Berlin-Schönefeld Railway Station just outside the southern city limits, 25 km south-east of Alexanderplatz. The S-Bahn from Zoo Station and Alexanderplatz runs to Schönefeld every 20 minutes from 4 am to 1 am. Otherwise take bus No 171 to/from U-Bahn Rudow direct to/from the terminal, also every 20 minutes.

Flughafen Tegel (TXL), West Berlin's main commercial airport, six km north-west of Zoo Station, receives most flights from Western Europe. Regular BVG transit buses run to gate No 8 upstairs at the terminal – bus No 128 from Kurt Schumacher Platz U-Bahn Station, and bus No 109 from the Inter-Continental Hotel via Zoo Station. These buses operate every 15 minutes from 5 am to midnight. Near the tourist office in the main hall at Tegel is a baggage storage office (open from 5.30 am to 10 pm) and a bank.

Tempelhof Airport (THF) receives mostly domestic and US military flights (U-Bahn: Platz der Luftbrücke). Flugplatz Gatow west of the Havel River is a UK air-force base.

Public Transport The Berliner Verkehrs-Betriebe (BVG) operates an efficient suburban railway (S-Bahn), underground (U-Bahn), ferry and bus system which reaches every corner of Berlin and the surrounding area. Trams exist only in East Berlin. The BVG ferry from Kladow to Wannsee operates hourly all year (except when there's ice or fog), with regular tickets, passes and transfers accepted. System maps are posted in all stations and most vehicles, and are available free from all ticket or information windows. You'll find the whole system easy to use.

A single DM3 ticket allows unlimited transfers on all forms of public transport within two hours, and return trips are allowed. A four-ride *Sammelkarte* works out slightly cheaper at DM10.40, while a 24-hour ticket costs DM12. You validate your own ticket in a red automat *(Entwerter)* at the entrances to the S and U-Bahn stations. There's no ticket control, but if you're caught by an inspector without a valid ticket, there's a DM60 fine (no excuses accepted). The S-Bahn (but not the U-Bahn) is part of the German railway system, so Eurail and Inter-Rail passes are valid on it.

You can carry a bicycle in specially marked cars on the S or U-Bahn, but a 2nd-class half-fare must be paid. Daily, weekly and monthly tickets allow you to take a bicycle with you free. You're not allowed, however, to take a bike on the West Berlin

U-Bahn weekdays from 2 to 5.30 pm, or on the East Berlin S-Bahn weekdays from 6 to 7.30 am and 3.30 to 6 pm.

The S-Bahn differs from the U-Bahn in that more than one line uses the same track. Destination indicators on the platforms tell you where the next train is going. All trains from Friedrichstrasse run to Alexanderplatz. For Treptow Park, you want a train going to Schönefeld or Königs Wusterhausen. For Karlshorst or Köpenick, look for the Erkner train. To go to Bahnhof Berlin-Lichtenberg, you want the Ahrensfelde or Strausberg trains. The Oranienburg and Bernau trains go north through Pankow. The system is easy to use and route maps are posted in all carriages, but you have to pay attention.

The double-decker buses offer great views from the upstairs front seats. One of the most popular double-decker routes is bus No 119, which runs from Grunewald to Kreuzberg via the Ku'damm. It's fun just to get on it in either direction and trace your route from above with the help of a good map.

The bus numbers of all Berlin city buses changed in 1991. In this book we give the new numbers, but be aware that older publications may still have the former numbers.

The S and U-Bahn lines close down between 1 and 4 am, but night buses run every 30 minutes all night from Zoo Station to key points such as Rathaus Spandau, Alt Tegel, Hermannplatz, Rathaus Steglitz, Mexikoplatz etc. Regular fares apply.

Special Tickets The best transportation deal in Berlin is a seven-day, DM28 ticket which entitles you to use the whole BVG network during any seven-day period. A slight variation on this is the Monday-to-Saturday *6-Tage-Wertmarke* ticket (DM26), and the 24-hour, unlimited-travel Berlin Ticket (DM12). Since the latter is good for 24 hours, it will overlap the morning or evening of another day, allowing an extra ride. A monthly ticket, *Monatswertmarke Umweltkarte* ('environment ticket'), is DM65. All transit passes except the seven-day ticket are transferable and can be shared between several people.

Bus drivers sell single tickets, but multiple, 24-hour, seven-day or monthly tickets must be purchased in advance. The seven-day ticket can only be purchased at the BVG Information kiosk (open daily from 10 am to 6 pm) in front of West Berlin's Zoo Station; the other passes are available from automats in mass transit stations.

Taxi There's a taxi stand beside all main railway stations. The basic flagfall tariff is DM3.60, then an additional DM1.70 per km. On Sunday and holidays it's DM1 extra, and oversized luggage is DM0.50 apiece. All taxis have meters, and they're no more expensive in the middle of the night.

Car & Motorcycle Rentals All of the large car rental chains are represented in Berlin, and their rates for the cheapest car begin around DM198 daily or DM952 weekly with unlimited km. Collision insurance begins at DM28 a day extra. Rental cars are often fully booked in Berlin, so advance reservations are advisable, and you may even get a better rate by booking from abroad.

Among the large chains, only Hertz (☎ 2 61 10 53), Budapester Strasse 39 at the Europa Center, allows its cars to be driven into Poland (check first), but only if you hire a steering-wheel lock at DM5 daily.

A good independent car rental company is Minibus Service, Zietenstrasse 1 (U-Bahn: Nollendorfplatz). Its cheapest cars are DM59 a day including 100 km, DM119 a day including 800 km or DM145 a weekend including 1500 km. It's open weekdays from 9 am to 6 pm, Saturdays from 9 am to 1 pm.

Eurorent (☎ 20 96 21 75), Clara Zetkin Strasse 30 (U and S-Bahn: Friedrichstrasse), offers a 'super spar Tarif' of DM102 a day or DM374 weekly with unlimited km for the cheapest car (collision insurance is DM25 a day extra). Payment is only possible by credit card. It has a branch at Schönefeld Airport.

Small companies offering discount car rentals advertise in the *'PKW – Vermietung'* section of the classified newspaper *Zweite Hand*.

GERMANY

Budget/Sixt Rent-a-Car (☎ 2 61 13 57), Budapester Strasse 18 near the Europa Center, has Harley-Davidson motorcycles such as the Low Rider Custom (DM77 daily), the Heritage Softail Classic (DM88 daily) and the Electra Glide Classic (DM99 daily). Rates include 70 km, and weekly and monthly rentals are possible, but reservations must be made well in advance as the bikes are usually all taken.

Bicycle Rentals Zweirad Bahrdt (☎ 3 23 81 29), Kantstrasse 89 (S-Bahn: Charlottenburg), rents bicycles at DM15 a day, DM50 for a week, DM100 for two weeks, and DM120 for a month. A deposit of DM100 must be paid and they'll want to see your passport. Do use the lock provided with the cycle. This is also a good place to buy a bicycle. It's open weekdays from 9 am to 6 pm, Saturdays to 1 pm.

Bicycles can also be rented at the Fahrrad Büro-Berlin (☎ 7 84 55 62), Hauptstrasse 146 (U-Bahn: Kleist Park), It charges DM12 a day, DM60 a week, DM50 deposit, and is open Monday, Tuesday, Wednesday and Friday from 10 am to 6 pm, Thursday from noon to 7 pm, and Saturday from 10 am to 2 pm.

Most other bicycle shops in West Berlin will also rent bikes, but not for less than 24 hours.

Brandenburg

The State of Brandenburg surrounds Berlin and includes the former districts of Potsdam, Frankfurt (Oder) and Cottbus. It's a watery region of lakes, marshes and rivers, and canals connecting the Oder and Elbe rivers utilise the Havel and Spree rivers, which meet at Spandau in Berlin. The Spreewald, a marshy area near Cottbus, was inhabited by Slavonic Sorbs right up until WW II.

Brandenburg played a central role in German history. The electors of Brandenburg acquired the eastern Baltic duchy of Prussia in 1618, merging the two states into a powerful union called the Kingdom of Prussia. This kingdom eventually brought all of Germany under its control, leading to the establishment of the German Empire in 1871.

POTSDAM

Potsdam, on the Havel River just beyond the south-west tip of Berlin, became important in the 17th century as the residence of the Elector of Brandenburg. Later, with the creation of the Kingdom of Prussia, Potsdam became a royal seat and garrison town, and in the mid-18th century Frederick the Great built many of the marvellous palaces in Sanssouci Park which visitors come to see today. Hitler exploited Potsdam's prestige by organising a lavish ceremony here on 21 March 1933 to proclaim to President Hindenburg 'the union between the symbols of the old greatness and the new strength'.

Twelve years later, on 14 April 1945, just a week before the war's end, British bombers devastated the historic centre of Potsdam, but fortunately most of the palaces escaped undamaged (only the City Palace was badly hit). To make a point of their victory over German militarism, the victorious Allies chose the city for the Potsdam Conference of August 1945, which set the stage for the division of Berlin and Germany into four occupation zones.

Orientation

If you arrive by S-Bahn from Berlin-Wannsee and you want to go directly to the centre of town, get out at Potsdam-Stadt Railway Station, just south-east across the Havel River. The next stop after Potsdam-Stadt is Potsdam-West which is closer to Sanssouci Park; most trains also stop at Bahnhof Wildpark (ask), closer still. The Wannsee trains usually continue on to Potsdam-Hauptbahnhof Station, off Zeppelinstrasse five km south-west of the centre of town. The centre and Sanssouci Palace are both reached from here by tram or bus (buy your ticket in advance at a kiosk). If you need a cloakroom for luggage storage (DM2 per piece), you'll find one open from 8 am to 6 pm at Potsdam-Hauptbahnhof.

Information

Potsdam-Information (☎ 0331-2 11 00), Friedrich Ebert Strasse 5 on Alter Markt next to the Nikolaikirche, sells a variety of maps and brochures but is incredibly crowded in summer (open daily from 9 am to 6 pm). If it's closed, try the reception of the nearby Hotel Potsdam.

Potsdam's telephone code is 0331.

Things to See

Sanssouci Park This large park is open from dawn till dusk with no admission charge, but the various palaces and galleries scattered through it cost DM2 to DM6 each to enter. Begin with Knobelsdorff's **Schloss Sanssouci** (1747), a famous Rococo palace with glorious interiors (open daily all year, closed the first and third Mondays of the month). Arrive early and avoid weekends and holidays, or you may not get a ticket (DM6).

The late-Baroque **Neues Palais** (1769), summer residence of the royal family, is by far the largest and most imposing building in the park, and the one to see if your time is limited. It is open daily all year, except on the second and fourth Monday of the month. Admission costs DM6.

Schinkel's **Schloss Charlottenhof** (1826) must be visited on a German-language tour, but don't wait around too long if the crowds are immense. The exterior of this Italian-style mansion is more interesting than the interior (open daily from May to October, DM4).

Central Potsdam The Baroque **Brandenburg Gate** on Platz der Nationen bears the date 1770. From this square a pleasant pedestrian street, Brandenburger Strasse, runs directly east to **Sts Peter & Paul Church** (1868). The Bassinplatz Bus Station is next to this church. From near here, Friedrich Ebert Strasse runs north to **Nauener Tor** (1755), another monumental arch.

Follow Friedrich Ebert Strasse south and

you'll come to the great neoclassical dome of Schinkel's **Nikolaikirche** (1849, open daily from 2 to 5 pm) on Alter Markt. To the left of the Nikolaikirche is the **Hans Marchwitza Kulturhaus** in Potsdam's old town hall (1755), which today contains several art galleries upstairs (open daily, free) and two elegant restaurants in the cellar. The **Film Museum** (closed Monday) housed in the royal stables (1685) is across the street from Alter Markt.

Neuer Garten This winding park along the west side of Heiliger Lake is a fine place to relax after all the high art in Park Sanssouci. The **Marble Palace** (1792) is right on the lake.

Farther north is **Cecilienhof Palace**, an English-style country manor built in 1913-16 for Princess Cecilie, a daughter of Kaiser Wilhelm II. It's quite a contrast to the Rococo palaces and pavilions in Sanssouci Park. Cecilienhof is remembered as the site of the 1945 Potsdam Conference, and large photos of the participants – Stalin, Truman and Churchill – are displayed inside (open daily all year, closed the second and fourth Monday of each month, admission DM3).

You can walk from Cecilienhof Palace to Glienicker Brücke (and bus No 116 back to Wannsee) in about 10 minutes.

Activities

Excursion Boats Weisse Flotte excursion boats operate on the lakes around Potsdam, departing from the dock below the soaring Interhotel Potsdam regularly between 9 am and 5.30 pm from April to September. There are frequent boats to Wannsee (DM10) with some boats continuing on to Tegel (DM16 from Potsdam). Other frequent trips are to Werder.

The 'Romantische Schlossrundfahrt' (Romantic Castle Tour) is a scenic four-hour loop right around Potsdam passing a number of outlying palaces (operates daily from May to September, DM14). Saturday at 8.30 am (from mid-May to mid-September) there's a boat down the Havel all the way to the town

GERMANY

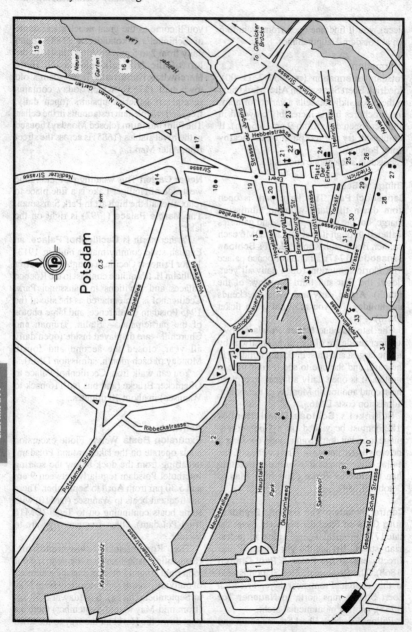

Potsdam

■ PLACES TO STAY

13 Hotel am Jägertor
17 Youth Hostel
27 Interhotel Potsdam

▼ PLACES TO EAT

3   Brolier Beer Garden
10 Gaststätte Charlottenhof
30 Cafeteria

OTHER

1   Neues Palais
2   Orangerie
4   Schloss Sanssouci
5   Bildergalerie
6   Chinese Teahouse
7   Bahnhof Potsdam-West
8   Schloss Charlottenhof
9   Roman Baths
11 Hans Otto Theater
12 Kabarett am Obelisk
14 Russian Colony
15 Cecilienhof Palace
16 Marble Palace
18 Town Hall
19 Nauener Tor
20 Schwarzer Adler Pub
21 Sts Peter & Paul Church
22 Bassinplatz Bus Station
23 Hospital
24 Post Office
25 Nikolaikirche
26 Potsdam-Information
27 Weisse Flotte
28 Stadium
29 Film Museum
31 Potsdam Museum
32 Platz der Nationen
33 Mosque
34 Bahnhof Wildpark

of Brandenburg (DM28 single or return, four hours).

Places to Stay

Camping *Intercamping D-139 Werder/ Havel*, Riegelspitze, is eight km south-west of Potsdam. There are small bungalows, but they're booked solid in July and August. Bus No D-31 Werder from platform No 2 at

Potsdam's Bassinplatz Bus Station passes within a five-minute walk of this camping ground every couple of hours. One bus departs from Bassinplatz daily at 6 pm. The bus goes down Zeppelinstrasse within a few hundred metres of Potsdam-Hauptbahnhof but doesn't stop right in front of the station, so make certain you're waiting at the right bus stop.

There's also the *Gaisberg-Geltow D-125 Campground* right on the Templiner Lake, two km from Potsdam-Hauptbahnhof along a pleasant road through the forest. It is open from April to October.

Hostel The 48-bed *Am Neuen Garten* youth hostel (☎ 2 25 15), Eisenhardstrasse 5 between central Potsdam and the Neuer Garten, is in a large mansion between Neuer Garten and the centre. It's DM14 for juniors, DM17 for seniors, plus DM7 for sheets (compulsory) and DM4 for breakfast (tea).

Private Rooms The Zimmernachweis office in Potsdam-Information, Friedrich Ebert Strasse 5 (open in summer on weekdays from 1 to 8 pm, weekends and holidays from 9 am to 6 pm), arranges private rooms in Potsdam at DM20 to DM35 per person. If you can get a room near the centre, this is your best bet.

Hotels The 222-bed *Hotel Am Schwielowsee* (☎ 28 50), Am Schwielowsee 110, is in a modern, three-storey building by Schwielow Lake, not far from the Intercamping D-139 listed earlier (same bus to get there). Rooms with shared bath cost only DM37 to DM44 per person, but the remote location makes it convenient only if you have your own transport.

The functional, 25-room *Hotel Am Jägertor* (☎ 2 18 34), Hegelallee 11 in the centre, is overpriced at DM80/110 single/double with shared bath, DM110/170 with private bath. The breakfast buffet is DM15 extra.

The 187-room, five-star *Hotel Potsdam* (☎ 46 31), Lange Brücke, is the place to stay if you have money (DM155/245 single/ double, bath and breakfast included).

GERMANY

The 42 rooms at the three-star *Hotel Schloss Cecilienhof* (☎ 2 31 41) in the Neuer Garten begin at DM130/250 single/double with bath and breakfast, and you get to sleep in one of Potsdam's most famous buildings. If you don't mind the price, have a travel agent book your room well in advance.

Places to Eat

The cheapest self-service in town is *Schnell Sicher Rationell Cafeteria* at the DV Zentrum Potsdam, the building with the mosaics on the wall at the corner of Breite Strasse and Dortustrasse. It serves breakfast from 8 to 9.30 am and lunch from 11.30 am to 1 pm, weekdays only.

Just behind the triumphal arch on Platz der Nationen is the *Gastmahl des Meeres*, which specialises in seafood.

The *Klosterkeller*, Friedrich Ebert Strasse 94 on the corner of Gutenbergstrasse, includes a grill bar (open weekdays from 8 am to 9 pm, weekends to 3 pm), a regular restaurant (daily from 11.30 am to midnight), a beer garden (May to September) and a night bar (Tuesday to Saturday from 9 pm to 3 am, erotic show at midnight, cover charge for men). Prices are moderate and the place combines modern German décor with a traditional menu.

The *Badische Weinstube*, Gutenbergstrasse 90, often has good weekday lunch specials as advertised in the window.

The *Gaststätte Charlottenhof*, just outside Park Sanssouci near Schloss Charlottenhof, offers much more elegant dining in this area, if you have time.

For afternoon coffee and cakes, *Café Heider*, Friedrich Ebert Strasse 28 just across from the Nauener Tor, is good.

Entertainment

The Besucherservice, Brandenburger Strasse 18 (closed Sunday and Monday), has tickets for performances at the *Hans Otto Theater*, Zimmerstrasse 10, and the *Schlosstheater* in the Neues Palais. Wednesdays at 7.30 pm from July to mid-September, there are organ concerts at various churches in Potsdam. Potsdam-Information, Friedrich Ebert Strasse 5, will know which churches.

The *Film Museum* opposite Alter Markt shows films for children in the morning and afternoon, quality films for adults in the evening.

The *Potsdamer Kabarett am Obelisk*, Schopenhauerstrasse 27, presents drama (in German) on contemporary themes at 8 pm from Wednesday to Sunday. Its ticket office (open weekdays from 8 am to 4.30 pm) is in the rear courtyard.

A local pub with a real earthy atmosphere is the *Schwarzer Adler*, Gutenbergstrasse 91 (closed Tuesday).

Getting There & Away

Potsdam's Bassinplatz Bus Station is accessible from West Berlin on bus No 138 from Rathaus Spandau (hourly from 6 am to 8 pm) and bus No 113 from Wannsee (every 20 minutes from 5 am to 1 am).

Bus No 113 takes a roundabout route through Babelsberg, so if you're headed for Cecilienhof Palace it would be much faster to take bus No 116 from Wannsee to the Glienicker Brücke and walk from there.

Hourly S-Bahn trains run from Berlin-Wannsee to Potsdam-Stadt, Potsdam-West and Potsdam-Hauptbahnhof, the most direct route by rail.

You can also travel on the double-decker S-Bahn from Berlin-Karlshorst Station to Potsdam-Hauptbahnhof every hour. It's possible to pick this train up at Flughafen Berlin-Schönefeld. The S-Bahn takes only 50 minutes to travel from Schönefeld to Potsdam. All Berlin transit passes are valid for the trip to Potsdam by either S-Bahn or BVG transit bus, and for local trams and buses around Potsdam.

From April to October, large excursion boats ply between Wannsee and Potsdam (DM6.50 one-way). This service operates six times a day from April to October, 11 times a day from May to mid-September.

All fast trains between Berlin-Karlshorst and Magdeburg stop at Potsdam-Hauptbahnhof. Trains between Hanover and Berlin-Zoo also stop at Potsdam-Stadt. For

Schwerin, take a train from Potsdam-Hauptbahnhof to Stendal.

Rail connections from Potsdam south to Leipzig or Dresden are poor. A couple of trains a day call at Potsdam-Hauptbahnhof between Rostock and Leipzig, but they pass in the night. You may be able to pick up an infrequent train to Dessau by changing at Bergholz Station (check with the information office), but to travel between Potsdam and Saxony, it's usually simpler to change at Berlin-Schönefeld.

Saxony

The Free State of Saxony (Sachsen) includes the former districts of Dresden, Leipzig and Chemnitz (Karl-Marx-Stadt in Communist times). The Germanic Saxon tribe originally occupied Lower Saxony and Holstein in north-western Germany, from where groups migrated to England in the 5th century. In the late 8th century the Saxons were conquered by Charlemagne and converted to Christianity, and expanded south-eastward into the territory of the pagan Slavs in the 10th century.

The medieval history of the various Saxon duchies and dynasties is complex, but in the 13th century the Duke of Saxony at Wittenberg obtained the right to participate in the election of Holy Roman emperors. Involvement in Poland weakened Saxony in the 18th century, and ill-fated alliances, first with Napoleon and then with Austria, led to the ascendancy of Prussia over Saxony in the 19th century.

In the south, Saxony is separated from Bohemia by the Erzgebirge, Eastern Germany's highest mountain range. The Elbe River cuts north-west from the Czech border through a picturesque area known as the 'Saxon Switzerland' towards the old capital, Dresden. Leipzig, a great educational and commercial centre on the Weisse Elster River, rivals Dresden in historic associations. Quaint little towns like Bautzen, Görlitz and Meissen punctuate this colour-ful, accessible corner of Germany. Colditz, between Meissen and Leipzig, is well known in Britain for its 16th century castle where Allied prisoners were held during WW II and whose daring escapes later became the subject of a British TV series.

DRESDEN

In the 18th century the Saxon capital Dresden was famous throughout Europe as 'the Florence of the north'. During the reigns of Augustus the Strong (ruled 1694-1733) and his son Augustus III (ruled 1733-63) Italian artists, musicians, actors and master craftsmen, particularly from Venice, flocked to the Dresden court. The Italian painter Canaletto depicted the rich architecture of the time in many paintings which now hang in Dresden's Alte Meister Gallery alongside countless masterpieces purchased for Augustus III with income from the silver mines of Saxony.

The great Baroque palaces with their priceless art treasures were restored following devastation in 1945, and the city's brilliant musical traditions still live on today. In February 1945 much of Dresden was destroyed by Anglo-American bombings ordered by Churchill. Some 35,000 people died in this atrocity which happened at a time when the city was jammed with refugees and the war almost over.

The Elbe River cuts a curving course between the low, rolling hills, and in spite of modern rebuilding in concrete and steel, Dresden holds visitors' affection. There are numerous museums, and with the many fine palaces and outstanding excursions, there is ample reason to spend some time in the area. Fortunately, the facilities are good. Three nights are the bare minimum required to do Dresden justice.

Orientation

There are two main railway stations: Dresden-Hauptbahnhof on the south side of town and Dresden-Neustadt on the north. Both stations have all facilities, but the Hauptbahnhof is more convenient. Take tram No 11 (under the tracks beside the

GERMANY

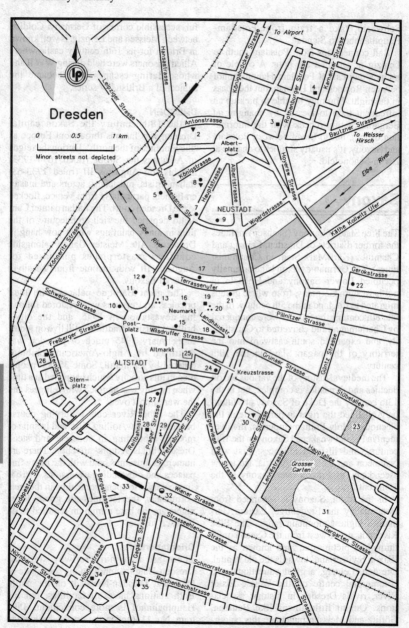

Dresden

0   0.5   1 km

Minor streets not depicted

■ PLACES TO STAY

3 Hotel Rothenburger Hof
4 Hotel Stadt Rendsburg
6 Maritim Hotel Bellevue
19 Dresden Hilton
26 Touristenhotel Haus der Kultur
   und Bildung
28 Hotel Königstein
34 Jugendherberge Dresden

▼ PLACES TO EAT

2 Winzerstube Alt Dresden
8 Kügelgenhaus Restaurant
30 Café Vitanova

OTHER

1 Dresden-Neustadt
5 Japanisches Palais
7 Goldener Reiter Statue
8 Museum of Early Romanticism
9 Folk Art Museum
10 Staatsschauspiel
11 Zwinger
12 Semperoper
13 Royal Palace Remains
14 Hofkirche
15 Palace of Culture
16 Museum of Transport
17 Weisse Flotte
18 City Historical Museum
20 Frauenkirche Ruins
21 Albertinum
22 Kupferstichkabinett
   (copperplate engravings)
23 Botanical Gardens
24 Neues Rathaus
25 Kreuzkirche
27 Karstadt Department Store
29 Dresden-Information
30 Hygiene Museum
31 Zoo
32 Bus Station
33 Dresden-Hauptbahnhof
35 Russian Church

station) to get to Postplatz near the Zwinger (see the following Things to See section). Otherwise walk to town along Prager Strasse, the pedestrian mall directly in front of the station.

Information

Dresden-Information (☎ 051-495 5025), at Prager Strasse 10 on the east side of the mall in front of the Hauptbahnhof, sells maps and theatre tickets and has an accommodation service (private rooms only). It's open Monday to Saturday from 9 am to 8 pm (Saturday to 2 pm in the low season), Sunday to 1 pm.

A branch of Dresden-Information is in the underpass below the Goldener Reiter statue in Neustadt (open Monday to Friday from 9 am to 6 pm, Saturday and Sunday to 4 pm).

Dresden's telephone code is 051.

Things to See

Dresden Altstadt A 10-minute walk north along Prager Strasse from the Hauptbahnhof brings you into the Altmarkt area, the historic hub of Dresden until the 1945 bombings. On the right you'll see the rebuilt **Kreuzkirche** (1792), famous for its boys' choir, and behind it the **Neues Rathaus** (1912).

Cross busy Wilsdruffer Strasse to the **City Historical Museum** (closed Friday) in a building erected in 1776. North-west up Landhausstrasse is Neumarkt and the massive ruins of the **Frauenkirche** (1738), once Germany's greatest Protestant church, now a reminder of the 1945 destruction (there are plans to rebuild it). The figure of Martin Luther keeps watch. On this same square is the interesting **Museum of Transport** (closed Monday, DM4, students DM2, half-price Friday).

Leading north-west from Neumarkt is Augustus Strasse with a 102-metre-long *Procession of Princes* mural depicted on the outer wall of the old royal stables. This street brings you directly to the Catholic **Hofkirche** (1755) where the organ is played each Saturday at 4 pm from May to October. The remains of the Renaissance **Royal Palace** directly behind the Hofkirche are slowly being restored as part of a long-term programme.

Most of Dresden's priceless art treasures are in two large buildings, the Zwinger and the Albertinum, about three blocks apart below a majestic bend of the Elbe. To reach

GERMANY

the **Albertinum** on Brühlsche Garten just off Terrassenufer, stroll east along the terrace overlooking the river. Here you'll find the **Neue Meister Gallery** with renowned 19th and 20th century paintings (closed Monday, DM5, students DM2.50) and the **Grünes Gewölbe**, or 'Green Vault', one of the world's finest collections of jewel-studded precious objects (closed Thursday). You can enter the Grünes Gewölbe through a door on the west side of the building down some stairs, but the ticket office is inside the main entrance.

On the west side of the Hofkirche is Theaterplatz, with Dresden's glorious opera house, the neo-Renaissance **Semperoper**. The first opera house on the site opened in 1841 but burned down in 1869. Rebuilt in 1878, it was again destroyed in 1945 and only reopened in 1985 after the Communists invested millions in the restorations. The Dresden opera has a tradition going back 350 years, and many works by Richard Strauss, Carl Maria von Weber and Richard Wagner premiered here.

The south side of Theaterplatz is filled by the Baroque **Zwinger** (1728), which houses no less than five major museums. The most important are the **Alte Meister Gallery** (closed Monday), with old master paintings including Raphael's *Sistine Madonna*, and the **Historisches Museum** (closed Wednesday), with a fantastic collection of ceremonial weapons. There's also the **Mathematics Saloon** with old instruments and timepieces (closed Thursday), the **Museum für Tierkunde** (closed Thursday and Friday) with natural history, and the **Porcelain Collection** (closed Friday), all housed in opposite corners of the complex with separate entrances. The grey porcelain bells of the clock on the courtyard's east gate chime hourly on the hour (you'll see the crowd waiting). However, the Zwinger is undergoing extensive renovations and several of its museums could still be closed.

Anyone with even the slightest interest in the human body and health will enjoy the unique **Hygiene Museum** (closed Monday), Lignerplatz 1, with fascinating interactive displays and transparent models of humans and animals.

Dresden Neustadt At the north end of the Augustus Bridge, the **Goldener Reiter** statue (1736) of Augustus the Strong beckons us to visit Neustadt. The Hauptstrasse beyond the statue is a pleasant pedestrian mall with the **Museum of Early Romanticism** (closed Monday and Tuesday) at No 13. In Albertplatz at its north end there's an evocative marble monument to the poet Schiller.

Other museums in the vicinity of the Goldener Reiter include the **Museum für Volkskunst** (Museum of Folk Art, closed Monday) at Grosse Meissner Strasse 1, and the **Japanisches Palais** (1737), Palaisplatz, with Dresden's famous Ethnological Museum (closed Friday).

Greater Dresden A surprising attraction is the **Karl-May-Museum**, Karl-May-Strasse 5 in Radebeul, eight km north-west of Dresden Neustadt (tram No 4 or 5). The museum occupies the house of adventure writer Karl May (1842-1912), whose tales of the Wild West, such as *The Treasure of Silver Lake* and *Old Surehand*, captured the imagination of several generations of young Germans. You'll see a huge collection of authentic North American Indian clothing and artefacts.

From 1765 to 1918, **Pillnitz Palace** on the Elbe, east of Dresden, was the summer residence of the kings and queens of Saxony. The most romantic way to get there is by Weisse Flotte excursion boat from near Dresden's Augustus Bridge. Otherwise, take tram No 14 from Wilsdruffer Strasse or tram No 9 from in front of the Hauptbahnhof east to the end of the line, then walk a few blocks down to the riverside and cross the Elbe on a small ferry operating throughout the year. The museum at Pillnitz (open from May to mid-October) closes at 5 pm, but the gardens, which stay open till 8 pm, and the palace exterior with its Oriental motifs are far more interesting than anything inside (which must be visited on a boring German-language tour), so don't worry if you arrive too late to get in. In summer the Dresden Philharmonic Orchestra sometimes holds concerts here.

Museum Tickets The ticket office at the Albertinum sells a combined ticket to many Dresden art museums for DM8 (students DM4) for one day or DM10 (students DM7.50) for one year! This not only saves you money but allows you to bypass the long ticket queues. The museums which accept it are listed on the back of the ticket.

Around Dresden Like a French Renaissance chateau, **Jagdschloss Moritzburg** rises impressively from its lake 14 km north-west of Dresden. Erected as a hunting lodge for the duke of Saxony in 1546, the palace was completely rebuilt in Baroque style in 1730. Try to come during visiting hours (open Tuesday to Sunday from 10 am to 5 pm, shorter opening hours in winter, closed Monday all year) as it has an impressive interior.

Behind the palace a huge park stretches out, and a walk through the woods is just the thing to clear a travel-weary head. Get a map from the information office (open in summer only) near the palace entrance and hike to **Fasanenschlösschen** (1782), a former hunting villa which is now a natural history museum (open daily from May to October). Then backtrack through the forest to the camping ground on Mittelteich where you can rent a rowing boat to tour the lake (see the Places to Stay section that follows). The bus service between Dresden and Moritzburg is fairly good. Check platform No 4 at the bus station beside Dresden-Hauptbahnhof.

Activities
Elbe River Excursions From mid-April to mid-October the Weisse Flotte (White Fleet) runs daily paddle-wheel steamers upriver from Dresden to Schmilka in the Sächsische Schweiz (Saxon Switzerland) near the Czech border. Shorter trips terminate at Pirna and Bad Schandau. The boats are big and depar-

tures frequent, so you shouldn't have difficulty getting a ticket even in midsummer. Local trains return to Dresden from Schmilka-Hirschmühle opposite Schmilka about every half-hour until late in the evening, with stops all along the river.

Between Pirna and Bad Schandau the scenery climaxes at medieval **Königstein Castle** (1241) on a hilltop to the west. Here the Elbe River has cut a deep valley through the hills with striking sandstone formations protruding from the banks. Three such rock pinnacles are Lilienstein (415 metres) and Pfaffenstein (427 metres), north and south of Königstein, and Bastei (305 metres) downstream near Rathen, all of which can be climbed.

Bad Schandau, a quaint resort town on the river's right bank, 40 km south-east of Dresden, is the starting point for the Kirnitzschtalbahn which runs the eight km to tiny Lichtenhainer Waterfall. From May to mid-October this narrow-gauge tram runs hourly; during the rest of the year it runs every couple of hours on school days only. Hiking trails lead south from the falls up onto the ridge above the river, then west back to Bad Schandau through the Schrammsteine, a lovely walk of a couple of hours.

Places to Stay
Camping There are two camping grounds near Dresden. The closest is *Camping Mockritz* (☎ 4 71 82 26, open March to December) five km south of the city. Take bus No 76 towards Mockritz from behind Dresden-Hauptbahnhof (frequent). This will take you directly there. There are bungalows but they're often full and in summer this camping ground can be very crowded.

A more appealing choice, if more distant, is *Camping Mittelteich Moritzburg* (☎ 05207-4 23; open April to October) on a lake called Mittelteich, a 10-minute walk beyond Schloss Moritzburg (see the previous Around Dresden section). The camping ground is spacious, there's a restaurant and there are even small caravans (camping trailers – often full). The lake is too murky to swim in but rowing boats are available and

GERMANY

the nearby park offers hours of restful walks – recommended.

Hostels The 75-bed *Jugendherberge Dresden* (☎ 4 71 06 67), Hübnerstrasse 11, is a nine-minute walk from the south exit of the Hauptbahnhof. The overnight charge is DM14/17 for juniors/seniors.

An excellent alternative is the 82-bed *Jugendherberge Radebeul* (☎ 7 47 86), Weintraubenstrasse 12, Radebeul. This hostel is 10 km north-west of Dresden, but access is easy as Radebeul-Weintraube Station on the S-Bahn line from Dresden to Meissen (hourly service or better) is only a few minutes' walk away. You can also get there on tram Nos 4 and 5 from central Dresden but it's easier to come by train the first time. The hostel has its own bar, but the best feature is the double rooms available at normal YHA prices (DM13.50/16 juniors/ seniors). Breakfast is also good here.

Private Rooms Dresden-Information, Prager Strasse 10, has private rooms at DM20-35/30-90 for singles/doubles, plus a hefty DM5 per-person room-finding fee. It also keeps a list of inexpensive pensions (from DM40/50 single/double), but none of them is in the city centre, so be sure to have the staff there phone before trekking out somewhere.

Cheaper Hotels A short walk north-west of the Hauptbahnhof, *Touristenhotel Haus der Kultur und Bildung* (☎ 4 84 52 04 or 4 84 55 00), Maternistrasse 17, has rooms from DM65 to DM140. It's housed in a large complex with cinema, theatre etc, all of which are former Communist party training facilities.

Two inexpensive old hotels within walking distance of Bahnhof Dresden-Neustadt survive in a picturesque old quarter of Dresden unaffected by the wartime bombings. Both, however, are usually full. The 33-room *Hotel Rothenburger Hof* (☎ 5 02 34 34), Rothenburger Strasse 15-17, is DM65/110 single/double with shared bath and breakfast. The 20-room *Hotel Stadt*

Rendsburg (☎ 5 15 51), built in 1884, Kamenzer Strasse 1, is DM55/85, also with shared bath and breakfast.

Weisser Hirsch, a suburb east of Dresden and north of the Elbe, is full of small pensions but most have *besetzt* (full) notices on the door and the others don't answer. Try the 15-room *Hotel-Pension Haus Sonneneck* (☎ 3 64 30), Plattleite 43, and the nine-room *Pension Steiner* (☎ 3 73 76), Plattleite 49. If you're told they're full, always ask if they know anyone in the neighbourhood who rents private rooms (*privat Zimmer*). This would be a great area in which to spend a few days if you manage to find something.

Expensive Hotels Of the four gleaming, 300-room hotels on Prager Strasse near the Hauptbahnhof, the 'cheapest' are *Hotel Königstein* (☎ 4 85 66 69) and *Hotel Lilienstein* (☎ 4 85 63 72), which both have singles/doubles from DM125/150. *Hotel Bastei* (☎ 4 85 63 85) has rooms for DM165 to DM210, and the flashy *Hotel Newa* (☎ 4 96 71 12) next door charges DM165/190 or more for singles/doubles.

The spanking new *Dresden Hilton* (☎ 4 84 10) next to the Frauenkirche ruins, a six-storey blend of architecture old and new, charges DM290/365 single/double, including use of the fitness club but without breakfast. Bourgeois decadence is also catered for at the five-star *Maritim Hotel Bellevue* (☎ 5 66 20), at a cost of DM250/ 350 facing the street, DM330/430 facing the river, breakfast not included. It's at Grosse Meissner Strasse 15 near the Goldener Reiter.

Dresden's most interesting up-market hotel by far is the *Hotel Schloss Eckberg* (☎ 5 25 71), Bautzner Strasse 134 between Dresden Neustadt and Weisser Hirsch (tram No 11). This romantic castle (1861) in a lovely park overlooking the Elbe has singles/doubles from 175/190. Be aware that many of the rooms are in a modern annexe called 'Haus Eckberg', so if you want to stay in the castle itself be sure to ask for a room in the *'Schloss'*. Under the Communists the Eckberg was a youth hostel and the castle was restored by young volunteers in their spare time, though there's nothing spartan about it today.

Places to Eat

Nowhere in eastern Germany is the restaurant scene as fluid as in Dresden, with long-established eateries closing down for renovations or for good, the survivors struggling under uncertain ownership, and countless newcomers opening up.

For something special, dine at the *Kügelgenhaus Restaurant* (open from 11 am to 11 pm daily), Hauptstrasse 13 below the Museum of Early Romanticism in Neustadt. There's a beer cellar (open from 5 to 11 pm) below the restaurant.

For a small, student-type place with piano music, simple fare and great atmosphere, join the locals at *Winzerstube Alt Dresden*, Antonstrasse 19. For a good meal and an even better view, head to *Weinrestaurant Laterne*, Albertplatz, on the top floor of a new apartment house. *Trompeter*, Bautzner Landstrasse 83, serves good cheap food. *Gaststätte Zur Keule* on Sternplatz is a lively beer hall where you can have Weizen beer and solid meals. The only place in Dresden that caters well for vegetarians is *Café Vitanova* in the Hygiene Museum.

Restaurant Prager 1 at the up-market Hotel Bastei is surprisingly affordable. The *restaurant* on the 2nd floor of the Karstadt department store, on the corner of Prager Strasse and Waisenhausstrasse, isn't bad either.

Entertainment

Dresden's two largest theatres, the *Semperoper* and *Staatsschauspiel*, stand on opposite sides of the Zwinger. The *Staatsoperette*, Pirnaer Landstrasse 131, is in Leuben in the far east of the city (tram No 9, 12 or 14). You can buy tickets for all three theatres at the Zentrale Vorverkaufskasse in the Altstadler Wache, the stone building on Theaterplatz opposite the Semperoper, between the equestrian statue and the palace ruins (open Monday to Friday from noon to 5 pm, Saturday from 10 am to 1 pm). Many theatres

close for holidays from mid-July to the end of August.

Dresden is, of course, synonymous with opera. Dresden-Information has Semperoper tickets for DM25 to DM50 (plus a DM1 booking fee), but they're often booked well in advance. You can always make a last attempt at the Abendkasse (box office) in the theatre itself an hour before the performance, or stand outside the door with a small sign reading *Ich möchte eine Karte haben* (I'd like to have a ticket). If you do get a chance for tickets to the Semperoper, take them with profuse thanks, for the performances are brilliant and the opera house is Dresden's architectural highlight.

The Staatsoperette is hardly ever sold out, as less tourists go there. A ticket at the entrance should set you back about DM10 (students get 50% discount), which is embarrassingly cheap for the lavish performances and means they'll never be able to afford desperately needed air-conditioning.

A variety of musical events is presented in the *Palace of Culture* with a change of programmes daily (admission DM10 to DM40). The *Tonne Jazz Club* on Tzschirnerplatz behind the Albertinum often offers live jazz Friday and Saturday at 8.30 pm; tickets are available at Dresden-Information. Dresden's International Dixieland Festival takes place every year in the first half of May.

Getting There & Away

Dresden is just over two hours south of Berlin-Lichtenberg Railway Station by fast train (189 km). The Leipzig-Riesa-Dresden service (120 km, 1½ hours) operates hourly. Trains from Erfurt (253 km, five hours) travel via Chemnitz and Gera. The double-decker S-Bahn runs 27 km north-west to Meissen every half-hour.

Direct trains go to/from Prague (194 km, four hours), Nuremberg (391 km, six hours), Munich (542 km, 8½ hours), Stuttgart (581 km, 9½ hours) and Wrocław (known as Breslau in German, 160 km, four hours). All trains between Berlin and Prague stop here. A slightly adventurous way to go to Poland is to take a local train to Görlitz (106 km),

GERMANY

and then walk across the Neisse River bridge to Zgorzelec, where you'll find onward Polish trains to Jelenia Góra (76 km) and Wrocław (163 km).

Dresden-Klotzsche Airport can be contacted on ☎ 58 31 41. For train enquiries, call ☎ 47 06 00 or 47 15 02; for bus enquiries, call ☎ 47 52 25. The Mitfahrzentrale (☎ 5 12 16) is at Königstrasse 10.

Getting Around

Buy a strip of 11 bus and tram tickets (DM6) at a machine or kiosk as soon as you arrive. Public transport operates on a zonal system and you'll usually have to stamp off two strips. One of the most useful trams is No 11 which runs between the two railway stations via Postplatz and on to Weisser Hirsch in the far north-eastern suburbs.

MEISSEN

Meissen is a perfectly preserved old German town, the centre of a rich wine-growing region. In Albrechtsburg, the medieval quarter crowning a ridge high above the Elbe River, is the former ducal palace and Meissen Cathedral, a magnificent Gothic structure. Augustus the Strong of Saxony created Europe's first porcelain factory here in 1710. Unlike Dresden, Meissen was undamaged in WW II and the winding, cobbled streets of the lower town are fun to explore. With its inexpensive accommodation, you might consider spending a night here instead of simply seeing the town as a day trip from Dresden or as a stop between Dresden and Leipzig.

Orientation & Information

Meissen straddles the Elbe, with the old town on the western bank. The bus station is behind the train station on the eastern bank, a five-minute walk from the old town. As you leave the train station (which has a left-luggage office), turn left and follow Bahnhofstrasse, where you'll soon be presented with a picture-postcard view of the Elbe River bridge and the old town. Elbstrasse, straight ahead over the bridge, leads you to Markt.

Meissen-Information (☎ 0521-44 70), An der Frauenkirche 3, is in the old Brauhaus (1571) just off Markt. It's open Monday to Friday from 10 am to 6 pm, and in summer also on Saturday and Sunday from 10.30 am to 3 pm. The staff are very helpful, which makes it all the more sad that the office's future is under a cost-cutting cloud.

Meissen's telephone code is 0521.

Things to See

On Markt are the **Rathaus** (1472) and the 15th century **Frauenkirche** (open May to September from 2 to 5 pm). You can climb the church tower (1549) Tuesday to Thursday from 1 to 4 pm (DM2), and by the door is the schedule of the tower's porcelain carillon, which chimes every quarter-hour regardless.

The way up to **Albrechtsburg** begins beside the Vincenz Richter Restaurant on Markt. Albrechtsburg's towering 13th century Gothic **cathedral** (open daily, DM2.50) is visible from afar, but unfortunately the only way to visit it and see the altarpiece by Lucas Cranach the Elder is with a German-speaking guide, though you do get an English translation sheet. The Renaissance **palace** (1471) beside the cathedral is now a major museum (closed Monday and in January, DM3, students DM2). Below Albrechtsburg all Meissen stretches out like a painting by Cranach himself, the old buildings completely unmarred by the sort of block concrete edifices that now dominate Dresden.

Meissen has long been famous around the world for its 'White Gold' chinaware with the blue crossed-swords insignia. The original **porcelain factory** was in the castle; the present factory, at Talstrasse 9, one km south-west of town, can be visited. There are often impossibly long queues for the porcelain demonstrations (DM4, students DM3) but you should be able to get into the museum (another DM4, students DM3, closed Monday) without difficulty. Unless you're really interested, don't waste your time on it and settle for the porcelain display that you can see for free in the shop at Markt 8.

Places to Stay

Campingplatz Scharfenberg (☎ 26 80, open mid-April to November) is in a beautiful forest at Scharfenberg on the bank of the Elbe, three km south-east of Meissen along the main road to Dresden; in spring, the blossoming orchards over the hill are a sight to behold. Two-bed cabins cost DM15 per person for the first night and DM10 thereafter. There's a small shop, and a reasonable restaurant next door – recommended.

The 54-bed *youth hostel* (☎ 30 65) is at Wilsdruffer Strasse 28, just south of town. It's DM13/15.50 for juniors/seniors.

Meissen-Information has an abundance of private rooms from DM20 per person (no room-finding fee).

The hotel situation is constantly changing while privatisation runs its course, and the selection is modest. One survivor is the 19-room *Hotel Mitropa* (☎ 5 58) right inside Meissen Railway Station itself (through the restaurant). It costs DM50 to DM55 per person with shared bath, but is run-down and very noisy, caught as it is between the railway lines and a major road.

A much more pleasant option is *Landhaus Nassau* (no telephone yet), an old farmhouse at Nassauweg 1, about three km east of the station. It costs DM62.50 to DM95 per person – expensive for Meissen, but the clean rooms and quiet, rural setting at the edge of a nature reserve are worth it.

As a last resort, try *Pension Plossen-schänke* (☎ 22 54) at Wilsdruffer Strasse 35, about 15 minutes' walk south of the Markt. It's a former school holiday barracks with very basic rooms at an all-but-basic price of DM47 per bed.

Places to Eat

The *Mitropa Restaurant* in the railway station is reasonable, but there are better places. Check the stand-up buffet in the middle of Kleinmarkt, a square just down from Markt; if it's operating you'll get a very nice snack for a low price.

Weinschänke Vincenz Richter, an expensive wine restaurant in a wood-beamed house built in 1523 beside the Frauenkirche on Markt, has a very short menu but the wine list is many pages long. The place is like a living museum (check the torture chamber), and is open Tuesday to Saturday from 4 to 11 pm. The *Ratskeller* across the square at Markt 1 serves standard meals from DM10 to DM19, and you can sample the local wines there as well.

If Vincenz Richter is beyond your budget, try *Weinschänke Winkelkrug*, up the hill to the north at Schlossberg 13 (closed Monday and Tuesday). Up the hill west of Markt, *Monasterium* at Freiheit 10 is a former monastery dining hall (closed Saturday and Sunday) that serves cheap meals in great surroundings and lays claim to being Meissen's oldest eatery.

Meissner Hof, Lorenzgasse 7, is cheap and simple (closed Saturday and Sunday). A small place with great atmosphere is the *Domkeller* on Domplatz (closed Sunday and Monday). Eat from Meissen porcelain for DM15 to DM25 at *Bauernhäusel*, Oberspaarer Strasse 20 in the south-eastern suburbs. Finally, if you have a huge appetite, you'll get meals to match in the excellent *Probierstuben der Sächsischen Winzergenossenschaft*, seven minutes' walk north-east of the train station, at Bennoweg 9; it's small and often full, so you had better ring ahead on ☎ 32 93.

Entertainment

Meissen is a sleepy place at night, and apart from hanging around in a restaurant or wine hall for a few drinks after your meal, there's not much to do. You could check for programmes at the cute *Stadttheater*, an old building (1545) on Theaterplatz. The young, alternative crowd heads for the *Soziokulturelles Zentrum* at Hafenstrasse 28, near the bridge on the east bank, for a changing programme of films, videos, poetry readings and sometimes bands.

Getting There & Away

Meissen is easily accessible as a half-day trip

from Dresden by riverboat (mid-May to September) or train. Meissen is on the railway line from Dresden to Leipzig via Döbeln, less than an hour from Dresden by double-decker S-Bahn. The regular express trains are faster but several times more expensive. The Leipzig-Meissen train service (107 km) is far less frequent than Dresden-Meissen (27 km). A direct bus runs from Meissen to Moritzburg from stand No 1 at the bus station.

LEIPZIG

Leipzig, eastern Germany's second-largest city, is right in the middle of the southern half of the region. This, together with its musical traditions and trade fairs, puts Leipzig on many German itineraries. Aside from its business-oriented present, Leipzig is a city with a past. Here Bach worked from 1723 until his death in 1750, Napoleon met with defeat in 1813 and Georgi Dimitrov stood up to the Nazis in 1933 during the Reichstag Fire trial. Leipzig was always a major publishing and library centre; the city's Deutsche Bücherei houses almost seven million volumes, including every book published in German since 1913.

Leipzig was never as badly bombed as Dresden, so a lot of old buildings remain in the city centre. The camping ground at Auen Lake is convenient and you can spend a full day doing the round of museums.

Orientation

Leipzig-Hauptbahnhof (1915), with 26 platforms, is one of the largest terminal stations in Europe. The main luggage room won't accept backpacks and the coin lockers are often full, so take your pack to the oversized-luggage room just inside the far west exit of the station, beside the stairs going down.

To enter the city centre, which is next to the station, use the underpass to cross wide Platz der Republik. Most of Leipzig's tram lines stop in the centre of this square, and historic Markt with the old town hall is just a couple of blocks south-west. Here you'll find museums and churches, inviting restaurants and cafés. The ring roads around the old

city centre more or less follow the lines of the former city walls.

Giant Augustusplatz (formerly Karl-Marx-Platz), three blocks east of Markt, is ex-socialist Leipzig, with the space-age lines of the university (1975) and concert hall (1983) juxtaposed against the functional opera house (1960). Leipzig's famous International Fairgrounds are about three km south-east along Prager Strasse. The massive Battle of Nations Monument looms just beyond.

Information

Leipzig-Information (☎ 041-7 95 90, open from 9 am to 7 pm weekdays, and to 2 pm Saturday) is at Sachsenplatz 1, between the Hauptbahnhof and the old town hall. Bear right after going through the underpass. It gives away free city maps and sells theatre tickets.

Bavaria Studentenreisebüro (☎ 041-7 19 22 67), in the tall university building at Augustusplatz 9, sells youth/student train and plane tickets and is a generally useful travel agency.

If you have come for the Leipzig Fair and don't have a Fair Card, you can buy one at the Messe stand at Leipzig-Information.

Leipzig's telephone code is 041.

Things to See

Old Leipzig The Renaissance **old town hall** (1556) on Markt, one of Germany's largest town halls, houses the City History Museum (closed Monday). Behind it is the **Alte Börse** (1687) with a monument to Goethe (1903) in front. Goethe, who studied law at Leipzig University, called the town a 'little Paris' in his drama *Faust*. **St Nikolai Church** (1165), between Markt and Augustusplatz, has a remarkable interior.

Just south-west of Markt is **St Thomas Church** (1212), with the tomb of composer Johann Sebastian Bach in front of the altar. The Thomas Choir which Bach once led is still going strong. Opposite the church at Thomaskirchhof 16 is **Bach's house**, now a museum (closed Monday, DM2, or DM1 for students).

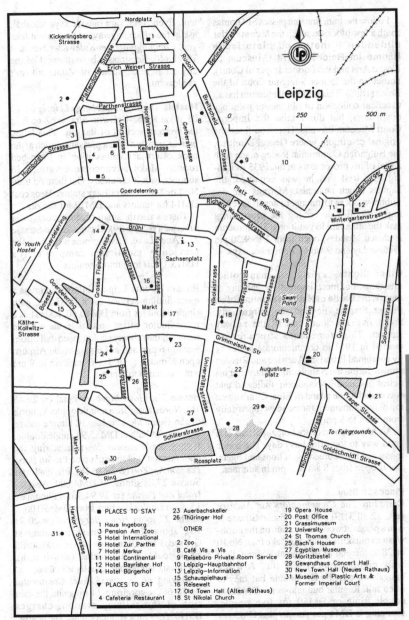

Leipzig

0   250   500 m

PLACES TO STAY
1 Haus Ingeborg
3 Pension Am Zoo
5 Hotel International
6 Hotel Zur Parthe
7 Hotel Merkur
11 Hotel Continental
12 Hotel Bayrisher Hof
14 Hotel Bürgerhof

▼ PLACES TO EAT
4 Cafeteria Restaurant

23 Auerbachskeller
26 Thüringer Hof

OTHER
2 Zoo
8 Café Vis a Vis
9 Reisebüro Private Room Service
10 Leipzig–Hauptbahnhof
13 Leipzig–Information
15 Schauspielhaus
16 Reisewelt
17 Old Town Hall (Altes Rathaus)
18 St Nikolai Church

19 Opera House
20 Post Office
21 Grassimuseum
22 University
24 St Thomas Church
25 Bach's House
27 Egyptian Museum
28 Moritzbastei
29 Gewandhaus Concert Hall
30 New Town Hall (Neues Rathaus)
31 Museum of Plastic Arts &
   Former Imperial Court

GERMANY

Follow the tram line that passes St Thomas south a few blocks to reach the **Museum der bildenden Künste und historische Räume im Reichsgericht** (Museum of Plastic Arts and the Former Imperial Court), housed in the former Supreme Court of the Reich (1888). This important museum has an excellent collection of old master paintings downstairs, but don't miss the Imperial Court Museum upstairs. Here you'll see the original courtroom where Georgi Dimitrov, the Bulgarian Communist leader, made such a fool of his prosecutors in the 1933 Reichstag Fire trial that he was acquitted; the hapless Dutch anarchist, Marinus van der Lubbe, was less fortunate. Listen to a recording in English describing the proceedings (ask the attendant to put it on). The museum is closed Monday, open from 1 to 9.30 pm Wednesday and 9 am to 5 pm other days.

Other Sights Leipzig has many other museums, but more impressive than any of them is the **Battle of Nations Monument** on Prager Strasse, beyond the fairgrounds, about five km south-east of the railway station. This tremendous structure was erected in 1913 to commemorate a victory by combined Prussian, Austrian and Russian armies during the Napoleonic wars. After his defeat at Leipzig, Napoleon abdicated and was exiled to the island of Elba. Climb up on top of the monument for the view (open daily from 9 am to 5 pm).

An afternoon visit to Leipzig's **zoo** is a good way to top off a busy day. The zoo is renowned for its breeding of lions and tigers, and is open from 8 am to 7 pm in summer.

Places to Stay

Camping The *Campingplatz Am Auensee* (☎ 2 12 30 31/91), Gustav-Esche-Strasse 5, is in a pleasant wooded location on the north-western outskirts of the city (take tram No 10 or 28 to the end of the line at Wahren, then walk eight minutes). On-site, A-frame bungalows cost DM20 double but they're often full. Regular bungalows are DM30/45 double/triple or DM50 for five people. Camping is DM4 per person plus DM3 per

tent. Even if the sign outside says 'closed', ask at the office anyway, as they might take you. *Campingplatz Am Kulkwitzer See* (☎ 4 78 21 68), Seestrasse, is south-west of the city centre in the suburb of Miltitz but isn't as pleasant.

Hostels The *Jugendherberge Leipzig* (☎ 47 05 30) at Käthe-Kollwitz-Strasse 62-66 is in the western section of the city. This large, prewar mansion with a pleasant garden at the back offers accommodation in three-bed rooms. Make advance reservations in summer, as it fills quickly. Get there on tram No 1 or 2 from the railway station. Beds cost DM14 for juniors and DM17 for seniors.

There's also the small *Jugendherberge Am Auensee* (☎ 5 71 89), Gustav-Esche-Strasse 4 on Auen Lake, a five-minute walk from the previously mentioned camp site. It's DM13/15.50 for juniors/seniors.

Private Rooms Leipzig-Information runs a room-finding service for a DM5 fee, with singles/doubles from DM40/60. It also has a room-finding office upstairs in the western corner of the railway station, open daily from 9 am to 6 pm, and at Leipzig-Halle Airport, open Monday to Friday from 7 am to 9 pm and weekends to 6 pm.

Hotels The *Haus Ingeborg* hotel (☎ 29 48 16), Nordstrasse 58, a couple of blocks north of the Hotel Merkur, has 10 simple rooms with shared bath at DM55/94 single/double. If they don't answer downstairs, ring the door marked 'Feldmann' up on the 3rd floor. *Pension Am Zoo* (☎ 29 18 38), Pfaffendorfer Strasse 23, is similar at DM45/80. Also try *Hotel Zur Parthe* (☎ 29 94 90), Löhrstrasse 15, with singles/doubles from DM65/100.

The 27-room *Hotel Bürgerhof* (☎ 20 94 96), above the Vietnamese restaurant at Grosse Fleischergasse 4, is DM60/85 single/double with breakfast (shared bath), but the six singles are usually all taken.

Moving up in price, *Hotel Continental* (☎ 75 66), Georgiring 14 opposite the east side of the railway station, charges DM159/199 for a single/double. The nearby,

45-room *Hotel Bayrischer Hof* (☎ 20 92 51), Wintergartenstrasse 13, is cheaper at DM85/130 with shared bath.

As a major trade fair city, Leipzig has a number of top-class hotels. The soaring, five-star *Hotel Merkur* (☎ 79 90), a palatial, Japanese-built landmark at Gerberstrasse 15 near the station, is top of the line at DM240/325 single/double. All of Leipzig's other deluxe hotels face noisy tram lines.

Former East German government ministers used to stay at the elegant *Gästehaus Am Park* (☎ 3 93 90), Schwägrichenstrasse 14, south-west of the old city gate, with singles/doubles from DM250/270. Its freestanding status in park surroundings guaranteed security.

Places to Eat

Privatisation is drastically altering the restaurant scene, and the choice is expanding by the week. Ever since 1525, however, Leipzig's most famous eatery has been *Auerbachskeller*, downstairs in the Mädler-Passage just south of the Altes Rathaus. Look for the statues depicting scenes from Goethe's *Faust* near the entrance. (After carousing with students at Auerbachskeller, Mephistopheles and Faust left riding on a barrel.)

The nearby *Naschmarkt Buffet*, Grimmaische Strasse 10, is a cheap cafeteria that closes at 6 pm on weekdays, 1 pm Saturdays. Two large *Mitropa* restaurants are at platform level in the railway station: *Restaurant West* is a cheap self-service, whereas *Restaurant Ost* offers full service. A good, old pub with great meals and atmosphere is *Thüringer Hof*, Burgstrasse 19-23 (open from 11 am to 11 pm Sunday to Thursday, till 4 pm Friday and Saturday).

If you're staying at the youth hostel, a great little pub nearby is the *Am Johanna Park*, Sebastian Bach Strasse 13. The beer is on tap, they serve good meals and even have a pool table and dartboard. If you're staying at the Auensee camping ground, try *Haus Auensee* across the street. It has a pleasant terrace restaurant overlooking the lake.

Entertainment

Ask Leipzig-Information about tickets to the *Opernhaus* and the ultramodern *Gewandhaus Concert Hall*, both on Augustusplatz. Established in 1743, the Gewandhaus Orchestra is Europe's oldest – the composer Mendelssohn was once its conductor. The *Schauspielhaus* at Bosestrasse 1 is a few blocks west of Markt. All of these theatres close for holidays during July and August.

Leipzig's *Musical Comedy Theatre*, Dreilindenstrasse 30-32, is on the far west side of the city (take tram No 15, 17, 27 or 57 from Platz der Republik to Lindenauer Markt, then ask).

Soundbar U2, Grosse Fleischergasse 12, is a popular drink-and-dance establishment in the former East German secret police headquarters, open daily from 9 pm. *Café Vis a Vis*, Rudolf Breitscheid Strasse 33, a block north from the west exit of the Hauptbahnhof, is a lively bar/café with a friendly young clientele. For blues, jazz, disco and anything else, head for *Moritzbastei*, Universitätsstrasse 9, a three-storey, subterranean complex in the old city wall at the university, with its own, monthly what's-on pamphlet.

Leipzig Fairs Leipzig's fairs are the only medieval fairs to survive into our times. The tradition goes back to medieval markets at the crossing of the Via Regia from Western Europe to Poland and the Via Imperii from the Baltic Sea to Nuremberg. In the 16th century, spices, wines and metal goods from the south were traded for wool, canvas and hides from the north. Chartered in 1165, the original fair was held on the market square in front of the Altes Rathaus.

Today, the grand spring and autumn fairs of the postwar years have made way for more modest fairs spread out over the year, and the famous spring book fair is no longer a match for its autumn counterpart in Frankfurt/Main. Nevertheless, during fairs, the hotels are full and restaurants hike their prices.

Getting There & Away

Finding a train to or from almost anywhere

else is not a problem at Leipzig's huge station. For train information, ring ☎ 7 02 11 (national connections) or ☎ 20 08 04 (international). For bus connections, ring the train station (middle building) on ☎ 29 17 77.

Leipzig/Halle Airport is halfway between the two cities. For flight information, call ☎ 2 24 11 55.

For advance train, bus or air tickets, go to Reisewelt (☎ 7 92 10), Katharinenstrasse 1-3. The Mitfahrzentrale (☎ 2 11 42 22) is at Rudolf-Breitscheid-Strasse 39.

Getting Around

Leipzig's city transport system is based on trams; buy single tickets or a strip of tickets at machines and validate them once aboard.

Thuringia

The State of Thuringia (Thüringen) occupies a basin cutting into the heart of Germany between the Harz Mountains and the hilly Thuringian Forest. The Germanic Thuringians were conquered by the Franks in 531 and converted to Christianity by St Boniface in the 8th century. The duke of Saxony seized the area in 908 and for the next 1000 years the region belonged to one German principality or another. Only in 1920 was Thuringia reconstituted as a state with something approaching its original borders. Under the Communists the state was split into the districts of Erfurt, Suhl and Gera, but since 1990 it has been a single unit once again.

WEIMAR

Not a monumental city, or a medieval one, Weimar appeals to more refined tastes. As a respository of German humanistic traditions it's unrivalled, but these can be difficult to assimilate by a foreign visitor in a rush. The parks and small museums are meant to be savoured, not downed in one gulp.

Many famous men lived and worked here, including Lucas Cranach the Elder, Johann Sebastian Bach, Christoph Martin Wieland,

Friedrich Schiller, Johann Gottfried von Herder, Johann Wolfgang von Goethe, Franz Liszt, Friedrich Nietzsche, Walter Gropius, Lyonel Feininger, Vasili Kandinsky, Gerhard Marcks and Paul Klee. The Bauhaus (Staatliches Bauhaus), which laid the foundations of modern architecture, functioned in the city from 1919 to 1925. Today Weimar is a prominent centre for architecture and music studies.

■	PLACES TO STAY
4	Hotel Russischer Hof
20	Hotel Elephant
24	Christliches Hospiz
26	Am Poseckschen Garten Youth Hostel
32	Tourist Hotel Am Wilden Graben

▼	PLACES TO EAT
6	Scharfe Ecke
8	Gastmahl des Meeres
23	Alt-Weimar

	OTHER
1	City Historical Museum
2	Goethe-Schiller Archive
3	Post Office
5	Students' Club 'Kasseturm'
7	Parish Church
9	Schlossmuseum
10	Weimar-Information
11	Kunsthalle
12	Wittums Palace
13	German National Theatre
14	Bus Station
15	Studentenclub Schütze
16	Schillerhaus
17	Museum Ticket Office
18	Rathaus
19	Lucas Cranach's House
21	Franz Liszt Music School
22	Goethe Museum
25	Museum of Prehistory
27	Goethe-Schiller Mausoleum
28	Academy of Architecture
29	Liszthaus
30	Goethe's Cottage
31	Römisches Haus
33	Märzgefallenen Monument

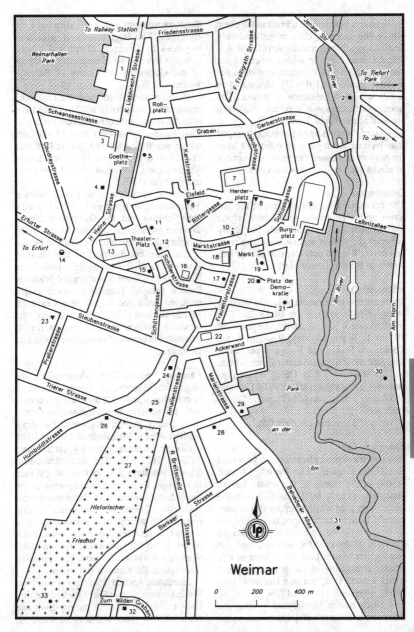

To Railway Station
Friedensstrasse
Weimarhallen Park
1
K Liebknecht Strasse
Roll-platz
Schwanseestrasse
Graben
F Freiligrath Strasse
Ilm River
To Tiefurt Park
2
Gerberstrasse
To Jena
3
Goethe-platz
5
Karlstrasse
Jakobstrasse
7
Coudraystrasse
4
Eisfeld
6
Herder-platz
8
Schlossgasse
9
Leibnizallee
H Heine Strasse
11
Rittergasse
10
Burg-platz
Erfurter Strasse
To Erfurt
14
Theater-Platz
12
13
Schillerstrasse
15
16
Marktstrasse
18
Markt
19
17
20
Platz der Demo-kratie
Am Horn
Ilm River
21
23
Steubenstrasse
Prellerstrasse
Frauentorstrasse
22
Ackerwand
24
Amalienstrasse
30
Trierer Strasse
25
Marienstrasse
Park
29
Humboldtstrasse
26
28
an der
27
Historischer
R Breitscheid Strasse
Ilm
Friedhof
Berkaer Strasse
Belvederer Allee
31
lp
Weimar
33
Zum Wilden Graben
32
0   200   400 m

GERMANY

Weimar is best known abroad as the place where the German constituent assembly drafted a republican constitution after WW I. The German republic which preceded the rise of fascism was therefore known as the Weimar Republic (1919-33), although you won't see much reference to it here. The horrors of Buchenwald concentration camp are well remembered, however.

A lot of German money is being pumped into Weimar these days, so it doesn't have the run-down, Eastern European atmosphere of places such as Eisenach and Halle.

Orientation

The centre of town is just west of the Ilm River and a 20-minute walk south of the railway station. Buses run fairly frequently between the station and Goetheplatz, from where you'll wend your way east along small streets to Herderplatz or Markt.

Information

There are two information offices in Weimar. Weimar-Information (☎ 0643-21 73), Marktstrasse 4 just off Markt, is open from 10 am to 6 pm Monday, 9 am to 6 pm Tuesday to Friday, and 9 am to 4 pm Saturday. Ask about tickets to cultural events here.

The Museum Ticket Office, Frauentorstrasse 4, sells a ticket that is valid for eight of Weimar's museums (DM15, or DM10 for students).

Weimar's telephone code is 0643.

Things to See

City Centre A good place to begin your visit is on Herderplatz. The **Parish Church** (1500) in the centre of the square has an altarpiece (1555) by Lucas Cranach the Elder, who died while painting it. His son, Lucas Cranach the Younger, completed the work and included a portrait of his father (to the right of the crucifix, between John the Baptist and Martin Luther). In front of this church is a statue of the philosopher and writer Johann Gottfried von Herder (1744-1803), who settled here in 1776.

A block east of Herderplatz towards the Ilm River is Weimar's major art museum, the

Schlossmuseum (closed Monday) on Burgplatz. This large collection, with masterpieces by Cranach, Dürer and others, occupies three floors of the former residence of the elector of the Duchy of Saxony-Weimar.

Platz der Demokratie with the renowned music school founded in 1872 by Franz Liszt is up the street running south from the castle. This square spills over into Marktplatz, where you'll find the neo-Gothic **Rathaus** (1841) and the house in which Lucas Cranach the Elder spent his last two years and died (in 1553).

West of Markt via some narrow lanes is Theaterplatz, with statues (1857) of Goethe and Schiller and the **German National Theatre**, where the constituent assembly, escaping the revolutionary climate in Berlin, drafted the constitution of the German Republic in 1919. Also on this square is the **Kunsthalle** (closed Monday) and **Wittums Palace** (closed Tuesday), now a major museum dedicated to the poet Christoph Martin Wieland (1733-1813). Wieland, who moved to Weimar in 1772, was the first to translate Shakespeare's complete works into German.

Famous People From Theaterplatz, the elegant Schillerstrasse curves around to **Schillerhaus** at No 12, now newly restored, with the modern **Schillermuseum** (1988) immediately behind it (closed Tuesday). Schiller lived in Weimar from 1799 to 1805.

Goethe, his contemporary, spent the years 1775 to 1832 here. The **Goethemuseum** (closed Monday) is a block ahead and then to the right, by far the most important of the many home-museums of illustrious former residents. There are two parts to this museum: to the right the personal quarters where Goethe resided, and upstairs an exhibition on his life and times. The immortal work *Faust* was written here. The appealing little café in the museum is a bonus.

Liszthaus (closed Monday) is south on Marienstrasse by the edge of Park an der Ilm. Liszt resided in Weimar during 1848 and from 1869 to 1886, and here he wrote his

Hungarian Rhapsody and *Faust Symphony*. In the yellow complex across the road from Liszt House, Walter Gropius laid the groundwork for all modern architecture. The buildings themselves were erected by the famous architect Henry van de Velde between 1904 and 1911 and now house the **Academy of Architecture**.

The tombs of Goethe and Schiller lie side by side in a neoclassical crypt in the **Historischer Friedhof** (Historical Cemetery), two blocks west of Liszt House. Behind the mausoleum is an onion-domed Russian Orthodox church (1862). Continue south through the cemetery, past a church and over a small bridge. Here you'll find the **Monument 'Den Märzgefallenen 1920'**, designed in 1922 by Walter Gropius, destroyed by the Nazis in 1933 and re-erected in 1945. The monument honours workers murdered by the military during the November 1918 revolution.

Parks & Palaces Weimar boasts three large parks, each replete with monuments, museums and attractions. Most accessible is **Park an der Ilm** which runs right along the east side of Weimar and contains Goethe's cottage. Goethe himself landscaped the park.

A km or two farther south is **Belvedere Park** with a Baroque palace, viewpoints, an orangery with a coach museum etc. The palace and museum are open from April to October (closed Monday). The palace itself may still be closed for renovations but the main attraction here is the beautiful park which could absorb hours of your time. To get to Belvedere Park, take bus No 11 from Goetheplatz towards 'Ehringsdorf' as far as Café Hainfels, then walk 15 minutes. Coming back, get on the bus going in the same direction as the one that brought you here – bus No 11 makes a big circle.

Tiefurt Park, a few km east of the railway station, is similar but smaller (palace closed Monday, also Tuesday from November to March). Duchess Anna Amalia organised famous intellectual 'round-table gatherings' here in the late 18th century. Get there on bus No 3 from Goetheplatz hourly.

Buchenwald The Buchenwald museum and memorial are on Ettersberg Hill, seven km north-west of Weimar beyond what used to be a large Soviet military base. You first pass the memorial (open at any time) with mass graves of some of WW II's 56,500 victims from 18 nations, including German anti-fascists, Jews, and Soviet and Polish prisoners of war. The concentration camp and museum (closed Monday and after 4.30 pm other days) are a km beyond the memorial. Many prominent German Communists and Social Democrats, Ernst Thälmann and Rudolf Breitscheid among them, were murdered here. On 11 April 1945, as US troops approached, the prisoners rose in armed rebellion at 3.15 pm (the clock tower above the entrance still shows that time), overcame the SS guards and liberated themselves.

The Soviet occupation forces turned the tables after the war, and until the camp's closure in 1950 thousands of anti-Communists and former Nazis were worked to death here as slave labourers. Weimar residents knew about this 'Special Camp No 2', but it was not the sort of thing anyone dared to talk about until the Communists' fall from power in 1990.

Buses run to Buchenwald from Weimar Hauptbahnhof (bus platform No 31) every hour or so. Pay the driver.

Places to Stay
Unlike many other eastern German cities, which fill up during the week with business travellers but are quiet on weekends, Weimar is a popular travel destination on weekends and public holidays. Arrive early if you want to find something reasonable.

Camping The closest camping ground is *Campingplatz Oettern* (☎ 06453-264, open mid-April to November) in Oettern, seven km south-east of Weimar. It's in a scenic part of the Ilm Valley, with many walking trails.

Hostels The *Jugendherberge Germania* (☎ 20 76) is near the railway station at Carl August Allee 13, the street that runs straight into town. It charges DM15/18.50 for juniors/seniors and has lunch-time meals for DM7. The *Am Poseckschen Garten* youth hostel (☎ 6 40 21), at Humboldtstrasse 17 near the Historischer Friedhof, has identical prices though it charges less for sheets (DM5 instead of DM6.50).

The *Tourist Hotel Am Wilden Graben* (☎ 34 71) is on the opposite side of the Historischer Friedhof at Zum Wilden Graben 12 (bus No 5 from the station). It charges DM16.50/20.50 for juniors/seniors.

Private Rooms The tourist office's room-finding service *(Zimmervermittlung)* (☎ 6 53 84) is open Monday to Friday from 10 am to 7.30 pm, and Saturday from 9 am to 4 pm. For a DM3 fee, it has rooms for DM20 to DM30 per bed.

Hotels On the square in front of the railway station, the 27-room *Hotel Thüringen* (☎ 36 75), Brennerstrasse 42, has singles/doubles from DM50/90 with breakfast, but as it's going to be renovated, prices are sure to change. Across the square, at Carl August Allee 17, the *Hotel Kaiserin Augusta* (☎ 21 62) has singles/doubles from DM45/78 but it is also due for renovations.

South-west of the city centre, at Liszt-strasse 3, *Hotel-Pension Liszt* (☎ 6 19 11) is a good choice with singles/doubles from DM50/90. All rooms have bath, toilet and TV but the catch is that there are only eight of them.

The *Hotel Russischer Hof* (☎ 77 40) at Goetheplatz 2 has been in business since 1805; it offers singles/doubles with bath and breakfast from DM100/150. For the ultimate in style, *Hotel Elephant* (☎ 6 53 10), right in the heart of town at Markt 19, has rooms from DM95/135 (you'd be lucky to get them at those prices). It's a characterful old building quite appropriate for Weimar – perfect if you can afford it.

Not far away is the *Christliches Hospiz*, Amalienstrasse 2 near Goethehaus. It was being completely rebuilt as this book was researched, and nobody seemed to know what the story was. It used to be a good choice, so could be worth trying.

Places to Eat

The *Gastmahl des Meeres* (☎ 6 45 21), Herderplatz 16, serves seafood at reasonable prices in a Renaissance house dating back to 1566.

The restaurants in the Thüringen and Kaiserin Augusta hotels in front of the railway station are unpretentious, accessible, inexpensive and good, but things could change with the pending renovations. The Russischer Hof and Elephant hotels have good restaurants where a meal should set you back no more than DM20. Slightly cheaper is the *Ratskeller* (☎ 6 41 42) below the Reisebüro at Markt 10 (closed Sunday and Monday).

The *Felsenkeller* (☎ 6 19 41) at Humboldtstrasse 37, a few minutes' walk up the road from the Am Poseckschen Garten youth hostel, is run by the Felsenbräu brewery. The atmosphere is great, the beer is cheap, the food is good and reasonably priced – no wonder it's often full. *Alt-Weimar* (☎ 20 56) at Prellerstrasse 2 has filling German meals (closed Sunday and Monday). At Eisfeld 2, *Scharfe Ecke* (☎ 24 30) offers Thuringian cuisine and a wide range of beers (closed Tuesday). For an enjoyable splurge, Weimar's best restaurant is *Zum weissen Schwan* (☎ 6 17 15, closed Monday), next to the Goethemuseum on Frauenplan. Goethe, Schiller, Liszt and many other greats ate here, and you can do likewise. A three-course meal costs DM65 (book ahead).

There's a lively *market* on Markt square from Monday to Saturday.

Cafés The poorly marked *Goethe Café*, Wielandstrasse 4 between Goetheplatz and Theaterplatz, is the place for afternoon coffee and cakes (closed Sunday). *Café Sperling*, Schillerstrasse 18, also serves meals (daily).

Entertainment

The *German National Theatre* on Theaterplatz is the city's main theatre. To buy tickets to this theatre and other events, try the Besucherabteilung office (☎ 75 53 21/2) in the adjacent street. Organ music is performed in the Herder Church every Sunday at 6 pm from June to mid-September (DM4).

Despite Weimar's students there's not much nightlife, though this could change as more private enterprises fire up. On weekends there's sometimes a disco at the students' club *Kasseturm* in the round tower on Goetheplatz – not a bad place for a cheap drink or two. An all-out student pub is *Studentenclub Schütze* on Schützengasse 2.

Getting There & Away

There are direct trains to Weimar from Berlin-Lichtenberg (264 km, 3½ hours), Eisenach (78 km, 1½ hours), Frankfurt/Main (293 km, five hours), Halle (86 km, 1½ hours) and Leipzig (82 km, 1½ hours). Trains from Dresden (232 km, five hours) arrive via Chemnitz and Jena. There are frequent services between Erfurt and Weimar, which is a 22-km, 20-minute trip. For practical travel arrangements, go to the Reisebüro, Markt 10, or Jugendtourist, Erfurter Strasse 1 next to the bus station.

ERFURT

This trading and university centre, founded as a bishop's residence by St Boniface in 742, is the capital of Thuringia. Erfurt University, dating back to 1392, counted Martin Luther among its students. Only slightly damaged during the war, Erfurt is a town of towers and flowers, with colourful burgher mansions gracing the well-preserved medieval quarter. Fortunately, industry has kept to the modern suburbs. Each summer the Erfurt Garden Exhibition (EGA) takes place in the south-western section of the city.

Orientation

As you come out of the railway station, turn left, then right and walk straight up Bahnhofstrasse. In a few minutes you'll reach the Anger, a large square in the heart of the city. Continue straight ahead and follow the tram tracks along Schlösserstrasse past the Rathaus till you come to Domplatz, Erfurt's most impressive sight.

Information

Erfurt-Information (☎ 0361-2 62 67), Bahnhofstrasse 37, is on the corner of Bahnhofstrasse and Juri Gagarin Ring, halfway between the station and the Anger. It's open Monday to Friday from 9 am to 6 pm, Saturday from 10 am to 3 pm. You can buy theatre tickets here.

Erfurt's telephone code is 0361.

Things to See

Begin by visiting the **Anger Museum** (closed Monday and Tuesday), Anger 18 on the corner of Bahnhofstrasse, and then take Schlösserstrasse north-west to Fischmarkt, the medieval city centre. Historical buildings such as the **Rathaus** (1873), **Haus Zum Breiten Herd** (1584) and the **House of the Red Ox** (1562) surround this square.

The 13th century Gothic **Dom St Marien** and adjacent **Severikirche** (closed) crown a hilltop just west of the old town. The wooden stools (1350) and stained glass (1410) in the choir, and figures on the portals, make the Dom one of the richest medieval churches in Germany (open until 5 pm Monday to Saturday, till 4 pm Sunday).

From Fischmarkt, the eastbound street beside the Rathaus leads to the medieval **Krämerbrücke** (1325), which has now been completely restored and is lined on each side with timber-framed shops. This is the only such bridge north of the Alps.

Continue east on Futterstrasse for a block till it terminates at Johannesstrasse; the **City Historical Museum** (closed Friday and Saturday) is around the corner at number 169. From the historical museum, go south on Johannesstrasse to a large church, on the opposite side of which is the Anger.

Places to Stay

Because of the many business people who visit Erfurt, accommodation is expensive and it can be difficult to get a hotel room or even a private room during the week. Weekends are usually not a problem.

Hostels & Private Rooms The 80-bed *Jugendherberge Erfurt* (☎ 2 67 05), Hochheimer Strasse 12, is on the western side of the city (tram No 5 southbound to the terminus). It costs DM15/18.50 for juniors/seniors.

Erfurt-Information has private singles/doubles for about DM25/50, but the number of singles is limited.

Hotels The 167-room, four-star *Hotel Erfurter Hof* (☎ 53 10), Bahnhofsvorplatz 1-2 in front of the train station, has great atmosphere but you pay for it (from DM175/240 single/double, breakfast included).

A much cheaper option is the 49-room *Hotel Bürgerhof* (☎ 6 42 13 07), Bahnhofstrasse 35-36 beside Erfurt-Information. This older hotel near the station charges DM70/100 single/double with shared bath, breakfast included.

The high-rise *Hotel Am Ring* (☎ 6 46 55 20), Juri Gagarin Ring 148, is a former workers' residence with two-bedroom apartments that can accommodate up to four people; one room in an apartment is DM65/95 single/double.

Nearby at Juri Gagarin Ring 154-156 is the *Hotel Thüringen* (☎ 6 46 55 12), a former youth tourist hotel that now operates as a regular hotel. Its prices (from DM110/150 single/double) reflect its good reputation.

Getting There & Away

Erfurt is well connected by train to Eisenach (56 km, one hour), Dresden (253 km, five hours), Leipzig (104 km, 1½ hours), Nordhausen (80 km, 1½ hours), Sömmerda (25 km, 30 minutes), Suhl (65 km, 1½ hours), Weimar (22 km, 20 minutes) and most other cities in Germany.

Erfurt is midway between Berlin and Frankfurt/Main, and the main line from Berlin-Lichtenberg (286 km, four hours) reaches Erfurt via Halle. To/from the Baltic coast you may have to change at Magdeburg, although some trains run straight through. The TUI Reisebüro Reise Welt at Anger 62 has train tickets and times.

EISENACH

Eisenach is a picturesque medieval town on the edge of the Thuringian Forest. From Romanesque Wartburg Castle overlooking Eisenach, the landgraves ruled medieval Thuringia. Richard Wagner based his opera *Tannhäuser* on a minstrel's contest which took place in the castle in 1206-07. Martin Luther was kept in protective custody here by the elector under the assumed name 'Junker Jörg' after being excommunicated and put under the ban of the empire by the pope.

The first country-wide proletarian party, the Social Democratic Workers' Party, was founded at Eisenach by August Bebel and

■ PLACES TO STAY

10	Thüringer Hof Hotel
14	Bahnhofs Hotel
15	Hotel Burghof
19	'Erich Honstein' Youth Hostel
25	Stadt Eisenach Hotel

▼ PLACES TO EAT

8	Alt Eisenach
9	Restaurant Karlshalle
17	Gaststätte am Johannisplatz
18	Café-Bistro Marianne
20	Hotel-Restaurant Glockenhof
21	Gaststuben Alt Nürnberg
23	Mičik's Restaurant
26	Pizzeria Da Angelo

OTHER

1	Predigerkirche Museum
2	Post Office
3	Lutherhaus
4	Residenzhaus
5	Georgenkirche
6	Thuringian Museum
7	Rathaus
11	Nikolaikirche
12	Eisenach-Information
13	Railway Station
16	Gaststätte Carré
22	Bachhaus
24	Automotive Museum
27	Gedenkstätte Parteitag 1869
28	Reuter-Wagner Museum
29	'Wartburg Express'

Wilhelm Liebknecht in 1869. Another first was the first automobile produced in Eisenach in 1896. The sturdy Wartburg cars, until recently assembled in the local factory, were the only East German alternative to the fibreglass Trabants, whose indestructible shells are causing such headaches for disposal experts in the new Germany.

Orientation

The railway station and medieval Wartburg are on opposite sides of town. If time is short, take a bus or taxi to the Wartburg and walk back through the forest. To walk to the castle from the station, follow Bahnhofstrasse west under the arch, cross the square and continue west on Karlstrasse to Markt. Two blocks west of Markt is Schlossberg, with the Predigerkirche Museum (closed Monday) on the corner. Follow Schlossberg directly south-west (another two km uphill) and you'll come to the castle.

Information

Eisenach-Information (☎ 0691-48 95) is at Bahnhofstrasse 3 near the station, and is

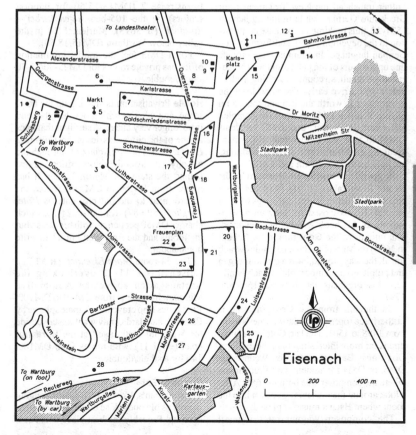

Eisenach

open Monday from 10 am to 6 pm, Tuesday to Friday from 9 am to 6 pm, and Saturday from 9 am to 3 pm. It sells hiking maps and literature (in German) on the Rennsteig hiking trail. Its room-finding service (private rooms only) costs DM3. The monthly *Eisenach-Information* pamphlet is a good investment at DM1; even though it's in German, it's fairly easy to understand.

Eisenach's telephone code is 0691.

Things to See

Most tourists come to Eisenach to see the old fortress of **Wartburg** on a hilltop overlooking the Thuringian forests and hills. Martin Luther translated the New Testament from Greek into German while in hiding here in 1521-22, thus making an immense contribution to the development of a uniform written German language. In summer huge crowds line up for tours of the palace and its Romanesque great hall, so count on waiting a while unless you arrive early. The view from the tower alone is worth the trip and there's no queue. You pay DM1 to enter the complex and climb the tower, and DM7 (students DM3) to tour the castle with a German-speaking guide. It's open all year, and tours are held between 8.30 am and 4 pm.

In town the **Thuringian Museum** in the former Town Palace (1751), Markt 24, has a collection of ceramics and paintings of local interest. It was closed for long-term renovations as this book was being researched. The interior of the **Georgenkirche** (rebuilt in 1676) on Markt has three balconies which run all the way around, plus a glorious organ and pulpit. Four members of the Bach family served as organists here between 1665 and 1797.

Up the hill from the Georgenkirche is **Lutherhaus** (open daily), the reformer's home from 1498 to 1501. The late-Gothic architecture is far more interesting than the exhibits. Don't miss **Bachhaus** (closed Wednesday, DM5, or DM4 for students) on Frauenplan, where the composer was born in 1685. After a look around the museum, go down into the room where Bach's music is played.

The composer Wagner rates a small display in the **Reuter-Wagner Museum** (closed Monday) on Reuterweg, leading up to Wartburg. The **Gedenkstätte Parteitag 1869** (closed Wednesday, Saturday and Sunday) nearby at Marienstrasse 57 has a fascinating exhibit on the 19th century workers' movements in Germany. It's now also the regional SPD office. The adjacent **Kartausgarten** with its 1825 teahouse (closed for long-term renovations) is a relaxing contrast to it all.

Places to Stay

Hostels & Private Rooms Try the 52-bed *Erich Honstein Youth Hostel* (☎ 2012), Bornstrasse 7 (DM13/15.50 for juniors/seniors), or the 105-bed *Jugendherberge Eisenach* (☎ 3613), Mariental 24 in the valley below Wartburg (DM15/18.50).

For a DM3 fee, the tourist information office has private rooms for DM25-30/35-70 single/double.

Hotels Privatisation is shaking up the hotel scene, and what's coming out the other end is no longer very cheap. A survivor that rates as one of the city's classics is the *Thüringer Hof* (☎ 31 31) on Karlsplatz 11, through the old city gate from the tourist office and just behind the statue of Martin Luther. It has rooms from DM60 to DM130. Across the square, next to the old city gate, is *Hotel Burghof* (☎ 33 87), Karlsplatz 24-26, which charges DM50 per person with breakfast, but the rooms and the food aren't much to write home about.

The 54-room *Stadt Eisenach* (☎ 53 71), Luisenstrasse 11-13 overlooking the Kartausgarten above the Automotive Museum, has rooms from DM60 to DM100. Romantics who crave the ultimate splurge by Eisenach standards, may want to stay beside the Wartburg castle itself at the *Wartburghotel* (☎ 51 11), with rooms from DM100/140 for a single/double.

Places to Eat

The restaurants, like the hotels, are changing rapidly as old ones close down and new ones open up. Probably the best place to eat at is

Alt Eisenach (☎ 7 60 88), Karlstrasse 51; the food is good, the surroundings are stylish, and most meals are under DM20. Many shoppers drop in for a coffee during the day.

The Thüringer Hof hotel's restaurant is good but a bit on the pricey side. Virtually next door, at Karlsplatz 7, is *Restaurant Karlshalle*, where locals eat filling meals at Eastern European prices (by far the most expensive item on the menu is rump steak with mushrooms for DM13) – the sort of place that cannot last in the new climate. *Gaststätte Am Johannisplatz*, Johannisplatz 16 next to the library, is similar.

Café-Bistro Marianne (☎ 7 53 66), Frauenberg 1, serves snacks from DM4.50 to DM12 in pleasant surroundings. The rather stately *Hotel-Restaurant Glockenhof* (also known as Christliches Hospiz) (☎ 52 16/8), Grimmelsgasse 4, is good but expensive (three-course menus cost about DM33). Better bets are the lively *Gaststuben Alt Nürnberg* (☎ 7 21 77), Marienstrasse 7, with lunch-time menus for DM15 to DM18, and *Mičik's Specialitäten-Restaurant* (☎ 7 63 85), Marienstrasse 4, which specialises in creative home cooking for under DM20.

A local pizza favourite is *Pizzeria Da Angelo* (☎ 20 38), Marienstrasse 51, with nothing over DM10.

Entertainment

There are plays or musicals almost every night at the *Landestheater*, Theaterplatz 4-7. For information or bookings, contact the Visitor Service Office (☎ 53 61) at Querstrasse 34 (open Monday to Friday from 10 am to 5 pm, till noon on Saturday).

Apart from that, Eisenach nightlife centres around the bar/restaurants – see the previous Places to Eat section for some possibilities. Young pool players head for *Gaststätte Carrée* at Löbersstrasse 3.

Getting There & Away

Train connections to Erfurt (56 km) are good, and through-trains running between Frankfurt/Main and Berlin-Lichtenberg also stop here. ITS, Bahnhofstrasse 5 next to

Eisenach-Information, has train tickets and information.

Getting Around

Eisenach is eminently walkable. The Wartburg Express, made up of a couple of wagons pulled by a jeep, shuttles up Wartburgallee to the castle for DM2.50 each way.

NORDHAUSEN

Nordhausen, a large railway junction just south of the Harz Mountains, is interesting primarily as the southern terminus of the narrow-gauge railway over the forested hills to/from Wernigerode (60 km, three hours, four trains a day). There's an old town centre a little over a km from the station if you get stuck here.

Nordhausen's telephone code is 03631.

Places to Stay & Eat

The *Hotel Handelshof* (☎ 51 21) directly in front of the railway station has singles/ doubles from DM40/56 with shared bath and breakfast (70 rooms), but the 28 singles are often all taken. If they're full, try the 12-room *Gaststätte 'Zur Sonne'* (6 44 33), in Halleschestrasse 8, which is about one km away (ask directions). Singles/doubles cost DM80/160.

If you don't like those prices, take the toy train 11 km to Ilfeld, where there are cheaper pensions and a forest where you could camp for free. In fact, almost any of the stations between Ilfeld and Wernigerode offer good hiking and unofficial camping possibilities.

The nearest Intercamping is Kelbra-Kyffhäuser on Kelbra Dam, five km south-west of Berga-Kelbra Railway Station (17 km east of Nordhausen on the line to Halle).

Getting There & Away

The narrow-gauge station adjoins the main railway station, where connections are available to/from Halle (97 km, 2½ hours by local train), Erfurt (80 km, 1½ hours) and Kassel (119 km, 2½ hours).

GERMANY

Saxony-Anhalt

The State of Saxony-Anhalt (Sachsen-Anhalt) comprises the former East German districts of Magdeburg and Halle. Originally part of the duchy of Saxony, medieval Anhalt was split into smaller units as the sons of various princes divided the region among themselves. The plethora of minor dukes made it easy for Prussia to dominate the area from the 17th century onwards. In 1863 Leopold IV of Anhalt-Dessau united the three existing duchies, and in 1871 his realm was made a state of the German Reich.

The mighty Elbe River flows north-west across Saxony-Anhalt past Lutherstadt Wittenberg, Dessau and Magdeburg on its way to the North Sea at Hamburg. Wittenberg is a charming small town full of history, and Magdeburg would also be a fascinating city had it not been bombed out in WW II. On the Saale River south of Magdeburg is Halle, a dynamic industrial city with enough sights to justify a visit, and farther south, the Romanesque cathedral of Naumburg.

The Harz Mountains fill the south-west corner of Saxony-Anhalt and spread across into Lower Saxony to Goslar (see the Harz Mountains section for further information on the Harz Mountains in Lower Saxony, as well as a map of the region). Mt Brocken (1142 metres) is Saxony-Anhalt's highest peak. Quaint little towns like Quedlinburg and Wernigerode hug the gentle, wooded slopes, while a network of narrow-gauge railways makes getting into the back country fun. Genuine steam locomotives puff their way up, around and over the Harz Mountains, climbing from 234 metres at Wernigerode to 540 metres at Drei Annen Hohne, five km south. The wood-framed Berghotel overlooks Drei Annen Hohne Station, and from here hiking trails lead north to Ottofels (600 metres) and the Steinerne Renne waterfalls on the way back to Wernigerode.

WERNIGERODE

Surrounded by verdant hills, Wernigerode is a quaint little town at the very foot of the Harz Mountains. A romantic ducal castle rises above the medieval town centre. Here you find the northern terminus of the steam-operated, narrow-gauge Harzquerbahn, which has chugged 60 km south to Nordhausen for almost a century. In summer this is a busy tourist centre attracting large throngs of German holiday-makers. Nevertheless, Wernigerode is still well worth a visit.

Orientation & Information

The bus and railway stations are adjacent on the north side of town. A large map is posted in front of the train station. If you follow Rudolf Breitscheid Strasse and Bahnhofstrasse south-east a couple of blocks, you'll reach Breite Strasse, which runs straight south-west into Marktplatz.

Wernigerode-Information (☎ 03943-3 30 35) is at Breite Strasse 12. Wernigerode's telephone code is 03943.

Things to See

Wander through the streets, admiring the medieval brick-and-wood houses. The **Town Hall** (1544) on Marktplatz, with its pair of pointed black-slate towers, is a focal point, and the **Harz Museum** (closed Sunday) on Klintstrasse, a block behind, features local history and natural history.

On Marktstrasse south of the town hall, you can get in a string of wagons towed by a tractor (DM2.50 one-way) and ride up to Wernigerode's fairy-tale neo-Gothic **castle**, though it's also easy to walk (the castle is visible from most parts of town – follow the crowd). Built from 1862 to 1885 by Count Otto of Stolberg-Wernigerode, the castle's Schlossmuseum (closed Monday, entry DM4) is worth visiting to see the chapel and great hall. You don't need to go around with a guide, so you shouldn't have to wait too long to get in. The views of all Wernigerode from the castle terrace are free.

Places to Stay

Wernigerode-Information arranges private rooms. These can also be rented at Harz Tourist Service, Burgberg 9b on the road up to the castle (open weekdays from 2 to 5 pm, weekends from 10 am to 3 pm).

Your first choice for a hotel room should be the 16-room *Hotel Weisser Hirsch* (☎ 3 24 34), Marktplatz 5, at DM70/90 single/double with shared bath, breakfast included. The adjacent *Gotisches Haus Hotel* (☎ 37 50) was recently rebuilt and is expensive (DM115/200).

The 11-room *Hotel Zur Post* (☎ 3 24 36), Marktstrasse 17, is great value at DM35 per person with breakfast. The 18-room *Hotel Schlossblick* (☎ 3 40 49), Burgstrasse at Schöne Ecke, has rooms for DM45/65. If all these are full, try the 11-room *Hotel Zur Tanne* (☎ 3 25 54), Breite Strasse 59, which charges only DM25 per person (closed Wednesday and Thursday).

Places to Eat

The 'in' place to eat is the *Ratskeller* in the basement of the town hall on Marktplatz. Another typical German restaurant is the *Zur bunten Stadt*, Breite Strasse 49 (open from 10 am to 8 pm, closed Monday). Cheaper meals are served at the *Gaststätte Zur Sonne*, Johannisstrasse 27 on Neuer Markt between the railway station and town (open weekdays from 9 am to 11 pm, weekends to 3 pm). There is nothing on the menu over DM10.

Getting There & Away

There are four buses daily from Wernigerode to Bad Harzburg (22 km), where you can connect with trains to Goslar, Hanover and other cities in western Germany.

Wernigerode is on a dead-end railway line 24 km south-west of Halberstadt. In Halberstadt, connect for Quedlinburg, Magdeburg or Berlin-Schöneweide, though some trains run straight through. The Reisebüro, Breite Strasse 39, has train tickets and information.

The narrow-gauge railway runs south from Wernigerode to Nordhausen (60 km, three hours) about four times daily all year. Tickets are available at the station, and normal railway tariffs apply.

Wernigerode is connected by bus with the town of Bad Harzburg in Lower Saxony.

From Bad Harzburg, you can take a train to Goslar from where you can reach most of the important destinations in Lower Saxony's Harz. See the Harz Mountains section for more details on these connections.

QUEDLINBURG

Unspoiled Quedlinburg, a medieval German town at the edge of the Harz Mountains, is so quaint you expect to meet Hansel and Gretel around every corner. Almost all the buildings in the centre are of timber-framed brick, street after cobbled street of them. It's a little more off the beaten track than Wernigerode, so it gets far fewer tourists than its neighbour.

Orientation & Information

The centre of the old town is a 10-minute walk from the train station. Go straight ahead on Kurt Dillge Strasse and follow the signs once you pass the post office.

Quedlinburg-Information (☎ 03946-28 66) is at Markt 12. Quedlinburg's telephone code is 03946.

Things to See

A statue of the medieval epic hero Roland (1427) stands before Quedlinburg's Renaissance **Town Hall** (1615) on Markt, the main square.

On a rocky hill just south-west is the old castle district, Schlossberg, containing the Romanesque **Church of St Servatii** (1129), or 'Dom' (closed Monday, DM1). The crypt dates back to the 10th century. In 1938 the Nazi SS confiscated the Dom to use it for their meetings as a 'Germanic solemn shrine'. The adjacent **Schlossmuseum** (closed Monday, admission DM2.50) in the 16th century castle has a good historical collection. The view of Quedlinburg from the castle is one of the most evocative in Germany.

To get in some hiking, take a bus or train 10 km south-west to Thale at the mouth of the lovely **Bode Valley** in the Harz Mountains south of Quedlinburg. Here you'll find a cable car (closed Monday in winter) to Hexentanzplatz (the 'Witches' Dancing

Ground' mentioned in Goethe's *Faust)*, a trail up the valley and several caves.

Places to Stay

Quedlinburg-Information has some private rooms and is eager to rent you one. Unless you come in mid-winter, it is a good idea to book ahead.

There is one hotel and one motel in Quedlinburg. The 30-room *Hotel Zum Bär* (☎ 22 24), Markt 8 (DM65/90 single/double), is in an old building right in the centre of town. *Motel Quedlinburg* (☎ 28 55), Wipertii Strasse 9, has singles/doubles for DM90/120. There are moves afoot to build more hotels or pensions, but it will probably take some time before anything actually happens.

Getting There & Away

Quedlinburg is connected to Halberstadt (19 km) by rail, with connections there for Wernigerode and Magdeburg. For Halle (95 km), change at Wegeleben. For tickets and times, ask at the Reisebüro, Steinbrücke 9.

If you want to explore the Harz in Lower Saxony as well, you will need to go to Wernigerode and take a bus from there. See the Wernigerode and Harz Mountains sections for more information on these connections.

MAGDEBURG

Magdeburg, by the Elbe River at a strategic crossing of transport routes from Thuringia to the Baltic and Western Europe to Berlin, was severely damaged by wartime bombing. It was rebuilt in steel and concrete, and only merits a brief visit. Before 1989, Magdeburg was a bulwark of Eastern Europe, and large numbers of Soviet soldiers and civilians were stationed here. Now it's the capital of Saxony-Anhalt.

Train connections with western Germany are good, and although Magdeburg works fine as a gateway city to the region, it's better to have only a quick look around and then continue to Quedlinburg or Wernigerode, picturesque towns in the Harz Mountains south-west of Magdeburg where there are cheaper hotels and a nicer atmosphere.

Orientation

From the broad square in front of the station, Wilhelm Pieck Allee leads east to a bridge over the Elbe, with Alter Markt a block back on the left.

Information

Magdeburg-Information (☎ 0391-3 16 67) is at Alter Markt 9. No free maps are offered although a perusal of the one posted in the office should suffice. The telephone code for Magdeburg is 0391.

Things to See

The centre of the old town is Alter Markt, with a copy of the bronze *Magdeburg Rider* figure (1240) of King Otto the Great facing the **Rathaus** (1698). Behind the Rathaus are the ruins of the 15th century **Johanniskirche** (open from mid-April to mid-October, closed Monday and Tuesday), with a fascinating collection of photos of Magdeburg before WW II. For your DM1 admission you may climb the tower for a sweeping view of the rebuilt city.

South two blocks is the 12th century Romanesque convent, **Unser Lieben Frauen**, now a museum (closed Monday, DM2). On some evenings, concerts are given here. South again is the soaring 13th century Gothic **Dom**, with its fine sculptures. Entry to the Dom is from the cloister. The **Historical Museum** (closed Monday) is on Otto von Guericke Strasse at the corner of Danzstrasse, just west of the Dom. The original 'Rider' statue is kept here.

Places to Stay

There's no camping ground nearby but you can get a private room through Magdeburg-Information.

The 44-room *Hotel Grüner Baum* (☎ 3 21 66), Wilhelm Pieck Allee 40 on the north side of the square in front of the railway station, to the left as you exit, offers Magdeburg's least expensive hotel rooms (DM50/93 for a single/double with shared bath, breakfast included).

The 355-room, four-star *Maritim Hotel* (☎ 38 40), Otto von Guericke Strasse 87 directly across the square from the station, is very expensive with singles/doubles for DM200/260. Around the corner from the Maritim Hotel, at Leiterstrasse 10, is *Magdeburger Hof* (☎ 3 38 81), a reasonable deal at DM65/70 without breakfast. The 113-room *Hotel Zur Ratswaage* (☎ 5 83 71), Julius Bremer Strasse 1 a block behind Markt, is overpriced at DM135/180 with bath and breakfast.

Getting There & Away

Most trains between Hanover and Berlin-Zoo call at Magdeburg. Between Magdeburg and Berlin-Zoo (139 km), these trains stop at Potsdam-Stadt. Trains from Cologne (470 km, seven hours) are frequent. Trains from East Berlin leave from a variety of stations but all pass Schönefeld Airport and Potsdam-Hauptbahnhof, carrying on to Halberstadt (58 km).

Magdeburg is on the main route of trains from Rostock and Schwerin to Leipzig or Erfurt. Trains from Leipzig to Magdeburg run via either Halle or Dessau. The Reisebüro at Wilhelm Pieck Allee 14 has train times and tickets.

HALLE

Halle, a pleasant, untouristed town 40 km north-east of Leipzig, is the chemical capital of eastern Germany. Despite this, a few churches and museums in the old town justify a brief visit. During the last years of Communism, many new apartments were built in the historic centre of Halle near the Händel Museum, and the tasteful way this was done demonstrates how far the science of city planning has come since Berlin and Dresden were rebuilt.

Orientation

Trams in Halle follow a roundabout route, so to get to the centre from the Hauptbahnhof, walk through the underpass and straight down the shopping mall, Leipziger Strasse, past the 15th century Leipziger Turm to Markt.

Information

Halle-Information (☎ 0345-2 33 40) is im-

possible to miss. It is situated in an elevated gallery wrapped around the Rote Turm in the middle of the Markt (see the following Things to See section).

Jugendtourist is at Leipziger Strasse 27, behind the Leipziger Turm. SRS Studenten Reiseservice, Franckeplatz 1, sells student/youth train and plane tickets and is a good budget travel agency if you need help making arrangements. It also sells ISIC student cards.

Halle's telephone code is 0345.

Things to See

In the centre of Markt, Halle's central square, is a statue (1859) of the great composer George Frederick Händel. You can't miss **Marktkirche** (1529) with its four tall towers dominating the square. It's worth going inside to see the exquisitely decorated Gothic interior.

Also on Markt is the **Roter Turm** (1506), a great red tower which is now an art gallery. Just south, at Grosse Märker Strasse 10, is the **City Historical Museum** (closed Friday).

Composer George Frederick Händel was born in Halle in 1685, and his home at Grosse Nikolai Strasse 5 has been converted into a major museum, the **Händel Haus** (closed Monday), with a large collection of musical instruments. Händel left Halle in 1703 and, after stays in Hamburg, Italy and Hanover, spent the years from 1712 to 1759 in London where he achieved great fame.

On Friedemann Bachplatz, a few blocks beyond Händel Haus, is the 15th century **Moritzburg Castle** with its art museum and Gothic chapel.

Places to Stay

Camping The closest *Intercamping* is at Seeburg on the northern shore of the Süsser See, 20 km west of Halle (last bus from Halle at 8.30 pm). The Seeburg bus departs from stand No 7 at the bus station near the Moritzkirche in the centre of Halle. It's an additional 15-minute walk from the bus stop to the camping ground.

GERMANY

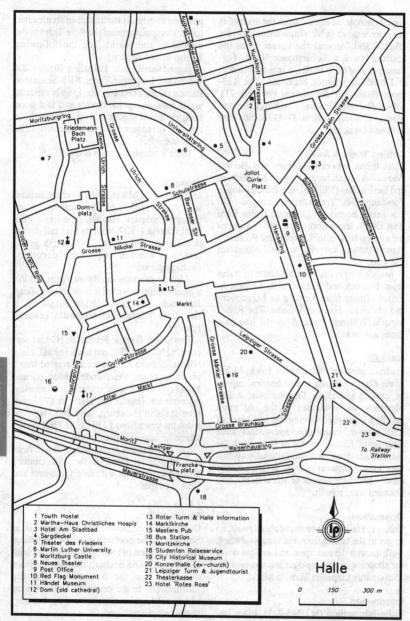

1 Youth Hostel
2 Martha–Haus Christliches Hospiz
3 Hotel Am Stadtbad
4 Sargdeckel
5 Theater des Friedens
6 Martin Luther University
7 Moritzburg Castle
8 Neues Theater
9 Post Office
10 Red Flag Monument
11 Händel Museum
12 Dom (old cathedral)
13 Roter Turm & Halle Information
14 Marktkirche
15 Masters Pub
16 Bus Station
17 Moritzkirche
18 Studenten Reiseservice
19 City Historical Museum
20 Konzerthalle (ex-church)
21 Leipziger Turm & Jugendtourist
22 Theaterkasse
23 Hotel 'Rotes Ross'

Halle

0   150   300 m

Hostel & Hotels The 44-bed *Halle Youth Hostel* (☎ 2 47 16), August-Bebel-Strasse 48a, charges DM14 and serves the full range of meals. Halle-Information, at the Rote Turm, can help with private rooms.

The 345-room, four-star *Hotel Stadt Halle* (☎ 88 80), Ernst Thälmann Platz 17 near the Hauptbahnhof, is expensive at DM200/300 for a single/double. A better bet price-wise, location-wise and atmosphere-wise is the older, 47-room *Hotel Rotes Ross*, Leipziger Strasse 76 between the station and centre of town (DM70/100 with shared bath, breakfast included).

The very friendly 21-room *Martha-Haus Christliches Hospiz* (☎ 2 44 11), Adam Kuckhoff Strasse 5-8, is DM50/80 single/double without bath or breakfast. If the Martha-Haus is full, the newly renovated *Hotel Am Stadtbad* (☎ 3 84 71), Grosse Stein Strasse 64-65, has singles/doubles for DM80/120.

Places to Eat

The food in the *Masters Pub* (open weekdays from 11 am to 8 pm) on Hallorenring is very good value. The restaurant in the *Hotel Am Stadtbad* is reasonable and open daily.

Entertainment

You can find out what's happening in Halle at the Theaterkasse, Leipziger Strasse 82. The *Theater des Friedens* on Joliot Curie Platz is Halle's main stage, but there's also the *Neues Theater* at Grosse Ulrich Strasse 51. Concerts are sometimes held at the Händel Haus.

The best little bar in town is *Sargdeckel*, Marthastrasse 28 near Theater des Friedens (open Monday to Friday from 3 to 11 pm). It's the perfect place to go after the show.

Getting There & Away

Halle is on the route of fast trains from Rostock and Magdeburg to Leipzig or Erfurt, and also from Berlin-Lichtenberg or Berlin-Schöneweide to Erfurt and Eisenach. If you're coming from Dresden, you may have to change at Leipzig. Between Lutherstadt Wittenberg and Halle, you may have to take a local train (68 km, one hour).

NAUMBURG

Naumburg is one of those pretty little medieval towns for which Germany is famous. It is strategically located between Halle or Leipzig and Weimar and has frequent train services. The scenic Unstrut Valley lies to the north-west. There are several youth hostels and camping grounds in the area, all of which makes this town well worth including in a German itinerary.

Orientation & Information

The railway station is 1.5 km north-west of the old town, but there are frequent buses, and trams will start running again once the roads are fixed; Theaterplatz is a good place to get off. If you'd rather walk, just follow Rossbacher Strasse and visit Naumburg's famous cathedral on your way into town.

Naumburg-Information (☎ 0454-2514) is at Markt 6, and is open from 9 am to 6 pm Monday to Friday, to noon Saturday, and to noon Sunday in summer.

Naumburg's telephone code is 0454.

Things to See & Do

Naumburg is picturesque, its **Old Town Hall** (1528) and Gothic **St Wenzel Church** (built between 1218 to 1523) rising above the central marketplace. The **City Historical Museum** (closed Monday) is beyond the polyclinic on the east side of Naumburg at Grochlitzer Strasse 49-51. Though closed for renovations, it should be open again by the time you read this.

In the ancient western quarter of the town stands the magnificent Romanesque **Cathedral of Sts Peter & Paul** with the famous 13th century statues of Uta and Ekkehard in the west choir. The cloister, crypt, sculpture and four tall towers of this great medieval complex are unique. Unfortunately, the cathedral (Dom) can only be visited on a boring German-language tour, though you might be able to latch on to an English-language tour group if you're lucky. If it's quiet, they'll let you walk around on your own. Admission costs DM3.50 (DM2 for students).

GERMANY

Freyburg Eight km north-west of Naumburg and easily accessible by train or bus, Freyburg is picturesquely situated in the Unstrut Valley; a large medieval castle sits on the wooded hilltop directly above. The castle will be closed for restoration for many years to come, but the adjacent tower (closed Monday) offers a splendid view.

Freyburg's vineyards are almost the most northerly in Europe (the most northerly are in England), and during the second weekend in September the town hosts eastern Germany's largest wine festival.

Places to Stay

Private enterprise has caught on that accommodation in Naumburg is scarce and often full, so you can expect improvements in the future. Meanwhile, try *Camping Blutengrund* (☎ 27 11) in Blutengrund, at the confluence of the Saale and Unstrut rivers, 1.5 km north-east of Naumburg Station. *Camping Am Waldschwimmbad* is in Bad Bibra, 19 km north-west of Naumburg (the last bus there from Naumburg Railway Station leaves at 7.30 pm). The closest railway station to Bad Bibra is Laucha, five km east of the camping ground.

The 161-bed *Youth Tourist Hotel* (☎ 53 16), Am Tennisplatz 9, charges DM19 per bed. It's four km on the opposite side of Naumburg from the train station, but may no longer be open when you read this. *Jugendherberge Freyburg* (☎ 04464-2 95), Schlossstrasse 21a on the road up to the castle in Freyburg, has beds for DM14.50/17.50 juniors/seniors; the bus to Bad Bibra passes Freyburg. In Bad Kösen, five km south-west of Naumburg, the *Jugendherberge Bad Kösen* (☎ 04463-5 97), Bergstrasse 3, has beds for DM13.50/16.

Ask Naumburg-Information about private rooms (there's a DM1 per night room-finding fee). Expect to pay at least DM30 per person.

Five minutes' walk north-east of the cathedral, *Hotel Deutscher Hof* (☎ 27 12), Franz-Ludwig-Rasch-Strasse 10, has rooms ranging from DM25 single to DM85 double; the cheap singles are being renovated and

will become more expensive. Just north of Markt, *Pension Wenzelsblick* (☎ 35 01), Fischstrasse 23, has one single and three doubles for DM20 and DM35 respectively. The only other option is *Hotel Toscana* (☎ 38 62), Topfmarkt 16, which is always full despite prices of DM135/190 for a single/double.

Getting There & Away

There are fast trains to Naumburg from Halle (45 km, one hour), Leipzig (54 km, one hour), Jena (37 km, 45 minutes) and Weimar (42 km, 45 minutes), and a local line to Artern via Laucha and Freyburg. The new InterCity Berlin-Munich also passes through Naumburg. Reisewelt, which for the time being also handles Naumburg-Information at Markt 6, will have train tickets and times.

LUTHERSTADT WITTENBERG

Wittenberg is best known as the home of Martin Luther, but the Renaissance painter Lucas Cranach the Elder also lived here for 45 years. Wittenberg was a famous university town and the seat of the Elector of Saxony until 1547, when the Protestant princes were defeated by Catholic emperor Charles V and the elector moved to Weimar. It was at Wittenberg Castle in 1517 that Luther launched the Reformation, an act of the greatest cultural importance to all of Europe.

You can see most of Wittenberg during a three-hour stopover, though it's also a nice place to spend the night.

Orientation

There are two railway stations. You'll probably arrive at Bahnhof Lutherstadt Wittenberg on the main line from Berlin to Leipzig/Halle. Bahnhof Wittenberg-Elbtor is a minor stop on a secondary line from Dessau. The main station is a pleasant 10-minute walk from the centre of town. From the station exit, walk straight ahead between the two railway lines and then go right under the tracks. Continue straight up on the street that cuts across the park into Collegien-

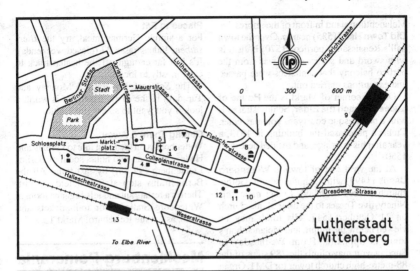

Lutherstadt
Wittenberg

1 Wittenberg Castle & Youth Hostel
2 Lucas Cranach's House
3 Old Town Hall
4 Hotel Goldener Adler
5 St Mary's Church
6 Wittenberg-Information
7 Bierstuben
8 Post Office
9 Bahnhof Lutherstadt
   Wittenberg
10 Lutherhaus
11 Hotel Wittenberg Hof
12 Melanchthon Museum
13 Bahnhof Wittenberg-Elbtor

strasse. This will bring you to the Luther-haus.

Information

Wittenberg-Information (☎ 03491-25 37) is at Collegienstrasse 29. Check for cultural events and tickets at the Theatre Service office, Markt 10 (closed weekends). Wittenberg's telephone code is 03491.

Things to See

The **Lutherhaus**, Collegienstrasse 54 (closed Monday, admission DM4, Sunday free), contains an original room furnished by Luther in 1535. Luther moved into this monastic building in 1508 when he came to teach at Wittenberg University. After dissolution of the monastery in 1522, the building was considered Luther's property and

remained so until his death in 1546. Since 1883 it has been a Luther Museum. The home of Luther's friend, the humanist Philipp Melanchthon, nearby at Collegienstrasse 60, is also a museum (closed Friday, entry DM2).

In Gothic **St Mary's Church** is a large altarpiece, begun by Lucas Cranach the Elder and finished by his son in 1555, containing portraits of Luther, Melanchthon and many other townspeople, plus a self-portrait of Cranach the Elder. Luther married Katherina von Bora, a former nun, in St Mary's in June 1525 and often preached here. In this church was celebrated the first mass in the German language in 1526. The baptismal font and marble tombstones in this church are also remarkable.

Imposing monuments to Luther and

Melanchthon stand in front of the impressive **Old Town Hall** (1535) nearby. Over the town hall's Renaissance portico (1570) is Justitia with sword and scales, for it was from the portico balcony that sentences were passed and executions carried out.

On one corner of Markt is the **House of Lucas Cranach the Elder**, Schlossstrasse 1, with a picturesque courtyard you may enter. Cranach purchased the building in 1513, a year after his marriage, and resided here until 1550.

At the west end of town is **Wittenberg Castle** (1499) with its huge, rebuilt, Gothic church (closed Monday). Luther nailed his Ninety-five Theses to the door of this church on 31 October 1517. His tomb may be viewed below the pulpit, and Melanchthon's tomb is opposite. From Wednesday to Sunday, you may climb the 289 steps of the 88-metre-high church tower for DM1. Organ concerts are advertised at the church entrance.

If you still have some time, the **Stadt Park** near the castle contains a very enjoyable children's zoo. If you want to see the Elbe River, walk south a short distance on the road that goes under the railway tracks near Wittenberg-Elbtor Station.

Places to Stay
There's no camping ground near Wittenberg. Wittenberg-Information has private rooms from DM25 per person (closed weekends). The 104-bed *Otto Plättner Youth Hostel* (☎ 32 55) is housed in Wittenberg Castle (DM13.50 for juniors, DM16 for seniors).

There are two attractive hotels. The 20-room *Hotel Wittenberger Hof* (☎ 35 94), Collegienstrasse 56 beside the Lutherhalle, used to be the cheapest place but after renovations in 1990 it became much more expensive. Singles/doubles/triples with breakfast cost DM62/82/106.

The 40-room *Hotel Goldener Adler* (☎ 20 53), Markt 7, is DM65/80 single/double without bath, DM100 double with bath, breakfast not included.

Places to Eat
For a simple German meal, try the *Bierstuben*, Jüdenstrasse 27 (closed weekends). It's just far enough off the beaten track to cater mostly to locals.

The *Schlosskeller* (closed Monday and Tuesday) in the castle basement is worth a look if you want to splash out a little.

Getting There & Away
Wittenberg is on the main line to Leipzig and Halle – less than two hours south of Berlin-Lichtenberg (99 km) by fast train. All the Berlin trains stop at Schönefeld Airport. There's a restaurant and left-luggage room at Wittenberg Station. For train tickets and times, ask at the Reisebüro, Markt 12.

Mecklenburg-Pomerania

The State of Mecklenburg-Pomerania (Mecklenburg-Vorpommern) comprises the former East German districts of Schwerin, Rostock and Neubrandenburg. This low-lying, postglacial region of lakes, meadows, forests and Baltic (Ostsee) beaches stretches across northern Germany from Schleswig-Holstein to Poland, just south of Denmark and Sweden. Most of the state is historic Mecklenburg, and only Rügen Island and the area from Stralsund to the Polish border traditionally belong to Western Pomerania, or Vorpommern. The rest of Pomerania went to Poland in 1945.

By the 7th century, Slavonic tribes had displaced the original Germanic inhabitants of Mecklenburg, but in 1160 the duke of Saxony, Henry the Lion, conquered the region under the guise of introducing Christianity and made the local Polish princes his vassals. Germanisation gradually reduced the Slavonic element, and in 1348 the dukes of Mecklenburg became princes of the Holy Roman Empire. Tall, red-brick churches remain from the medieval period when the towns were members of the Hanseatic League. In the 16th century, Lutheranism was adopted. Sweden became involved in the area during the Thirty Years' War and held Wismar and environs from 1648 to 1803, and Stralsund and Rügen from 1648 to 1815. In 1867 the whole region joined the North German Confederation and in 1871 the German Reich.

Bismarck once remarked that when the world came to an end, he would move to Mecklenburg because everything was 20 years behind the times there. That about sums up the atmosphere here even today, and since eastern Germans now have a much wider choice of summer holiday destinations, it's far less crowded than it used to be. Dazzled by the attractions in adjacent areas, few English-speakers venture this way, which is unfortunate as Germany's Baltic coast has a lot to offer. The offshore islands of Poel, Hiddensee and Rügen are still undiscovered paradises for outdoors people. Just keep in mind the very short swimming season (July and August only, unless you're a member of the Polar Bears Club). Spring and autumn can be cold.

SCHWERIN

Almost surrounded by lakes, Schwerin is perhaps the most picturesque town in eastern Germany. The town gets its name from a Slavonic castle known as 'Zaurin' (animal pasture) on the site of the present Schloss. This former seat of the Grand Duchy of Mecklenburg and contemporary capital of Mecklenburg-Pomerania is an interesting mix of medieval and 19th century architecture. It's small enough to get around, and packed with attractions – an OK place to stop on the way north to the Baltic coast.

Orientation & Information

As you come out of the railway station, you'll see a large hotel on your right. Go towards it, then down the hill to Pfaffenteich, a lake where you turn right again. The city centre focuses on Markt beyond the south end of this lake. Farther south, around Schlossinsel on the Schweriner See, are the museums, parks and tour boats which will keep you entertained.

Schwerin-Information (☎ 0385-86 45 09)

is at Am Markt 11. Schwerin's telephone code is 0385.

Things to See

Above Markt rises the tall 14th century Gothic **Dom**, a superb example of north German red-brick architecture. On Wednesdays in summer there are organ concerts at 8 pm in the Dom. Climb the 19th century church tower (DM1) for the view. The winding medieval streets of the old town complement well the verdant parks and gardens along the lakes.

Schwerin's neo-Gothic **Schloss** (closed Monday) is on an island connected to the lakeside promenades by causeways. Entry costs DM3 (DM1.50 for students). At the end of the causeway on the city side is the **State Museum** (closed Monday, entry DM2, students DM1) with an excellent collection of old Dutch masters including Frans Hals, Rembrandt, Rubens and Brueghel. The other causeway leads to the 18th century **Schlossgarten**. Schwerin's **zoo** (open daily from 8 am to 7 pm) is three km south-east of here.

Activities

From May to September, Weisse Flotte excursion boats operate on the Schweriner See from Schlossbucht, the landing beside the museum opposite the castle. The cruises depart daily in season at 10 am and 2 pm (DM15). A ferry trip south from the same landing to Zippendorf, a lakeside resort near the zoo, runs six times daily in midsummer. Departure times are posted.

Places to Stay

Camping *Seehof Intercamping*, 10 km north of Schwerin on the west shore of the Schweriner See, is easily accessible on bus No 8 from the bus station, or take any northbound tram from the railway station to the end of the line at KGW (Klement Gottwald Werk) and catch bus No 8 there. Buses run hourly as late as 10.30 pm daily. There aren't any bungalows and in summer it's crowded, but there's a snack bar that stays open till 9 pm, and of course the lake for swimming and rowing.

GERMANY

GERMANY

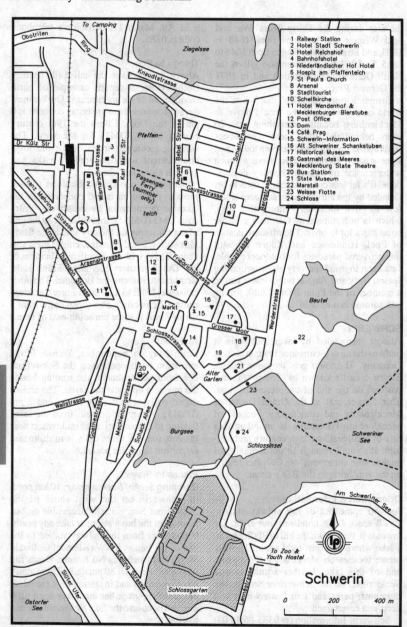

1 Railway Station
2 Hotel Stadt Schwerin
3 Hotel Reichshof
4 Bahnhofshotel
5 Niederländischer Hof Hotel
6 Hospiz am Pfaffenteich
7 St Paul's Church
8 Arsenal
9 Stadttourist
10 Scheifkirche
11 Hotel Wendenhof &
   Mecklenburger Bierstube
12 Post Office
13 Dom
14 Café Prag
15 Schwerin–Information
16 Alt Schweriner Schankstuben
17 Historical Museum
18 Gaststrah des Meeres
19 Mecklenburg State Theatre
20 Bus Station
21 State Museum
22 Marstall
23 Weisse Flotte
24 Schloss

Schwerin

0   200   400 m

Hostel Schwerin's 63-bed *Kurt Bürger Youth Hostel* (☎ 21 30 05) is on Waldschulenweg just opposite the entrance to the zoo, about four km south of the city centre (bus No 15 from the bus station on Hermann Matern Strasse). It's DM13.50 for juniors, DM16 for seniors.

Private Rooms Schwerin-Information, Am Markt 11, has private rooms. Stadt Tourist, Körnerstrasse 18, also rents private rooms (open daily after 4 pm).

Hotels The cheapest hotels in town are the 23-room *Bahnhofshotel* (☎ 8 37 78) opposite the railway station (DM40/69 single/double, without private bath or breakfast), and the 16-room *Hotel Wendenhof* (☎ 8 34 93), Wismarsche Strasse 104 a couple of blocks south of the station (singles/doubles for DM30/60). The Wendenhof is usually full.

If you would like a room with a private bath, two hotels on Grunthalplatz in front of the station can supply it: the 24-room *Reichshof* (☎ 86 40 45) (DM75/100 single/double) or the seven-storey, 166-room *Hotel Stadt Schwerin* (from DM87/124 including breakfast).

Hospiz Am Pfaffenteich (☎ 8 33 21), Gaussstrasse 19 near the far landing of the small ferry which crosses Pfaffenteich from near the station, is worth trying though usually closed or full.

Best of all, try for one of the 27 rooms at the tasteful old *Niederländischer Hof Hotel* (☎ 8 37 27), Karl Marx Strasse 13-14 right on Pfaffenteich, a block down from the Hotel Stadt Schwerin. At DM70/110 single/double with breakfast but only shared bath it is not exactly cheap, but it is Schwerin's best deal and it's also free of the tram noise you get in the places along Wismarsche Strasse.

Places to Eat
Mecklenburger Bierstube, Wismarsche Strasse 104 in the same building as the Hotel Wendenhof, serves half and quarter barbecued chickens. The *Grill Station* fast-food place across the street has the same for less if you're in a hurry and don't need table service. For seafood, it's the *Gastmahl des Meeres*, Grosser Moor 5 (expensive).

The moderately expensive *Alt Schweriner Schankstuben*, on the Schlachtermarkt behind Schwerin-Information in the old town, serves excellent-value meals till 10 pm and wine till midnight. *Café Prag*, on the corner of Puschkinstrasse and Schlossstrasse, is a great place to get a coffee during the day and a drink at night.

Getting There & Away
Fast trains arrive regularly from Rostock (87 km, 1½ hours), Magdeburg (194 km, three hours), Halle (280 km, 4½ hours), Leipzig (318 km, five hours) and Berlin-Lichtenberg (238 km, 3½ hours). From Weimar and Erfurt, you may have to change at Magdeburg. From Wismar, it's often faster to change trains in Bad Kleinen than to wait for a through service. Trains from Hamburg and Lübeck travel via Bad Kleinen. For train tickets and times, ask at the Reisebüro, Grosser Moor 9.

Reservations for the afternoon Sonnenschein Reisen coach to West Berlin (mid-April to October, DM33) are available from Reisebüro Schwerin Plus, Schmiedestrasse 21. People aged 26 and under get a 50% discount.

WISMAR
Wismar, about halfway between Rostock and Lübeck, became a Hanseatic trading city in the 13th century. For centuries Wismar belonged to Sweden, and traces of Scandinavian rule can still be seen. It's less hectic than Rostock or Stralsund, a pretty little town worth seeing for itself. It's also the gateway to Poel Island.

Information
Wismar-Information (☎ 03841-29 58) at Am Markt 11 has maps, brochures, stickers etc. Wismar's telephone code is 03841.

Things to See
Like many other German cities, Wismar was a target for Anglo-American bombers just a few weeks prior to the end of the war. Of the

GERMANY

three great red-brick churches that once rose above the rooftops, only **St Nikolai** (closed Sunday and Monday) is intact. The massive red shell of **St George's** has been left as a reminder of the April 1945 raids. Cars now park where 13th century **St Mary's Church** once stood, although the great brick steeple (1339) still towers above.

Apart from this, it's hard to believe that Wismar's gabled houses were seriously bombed. Nearby in a corner of Markt are the graceful old **Waterworks** (1602) and the **Rathaus** (1819). The **City Historical Museum** (closed Monday) at Schweinsbrücke 8 near St Nikolai has many interesting exhibits.

Activities

To get out onto the Baltic, board a Weisse Flotte or private excursion boat to Kirchdorf on Poel Island, a very popular summer bathing resort for Germans. The trips operate from May to September (one hour, DM6). You can also get to Poel by bus several times a day from the bus station near the corner of Lübsche and Bahnhofstrasse. Otherwise the Weisse Flotte offers 90-minute cruises (DM7) out to sea from Wismar three times a day.

Places to Stay

Zierow Intercamping is on the coast eight km north-west of Wismar. The bus service to Zierow from beside Wismar Railway Station finishes at 5 pm, after which you'll either have to take a taxi (just under DM20) or a highway bus to Gägelow from where it's a four-km walk downhill to Zierow. There's a shop at Zierow but no bungalows.

Wismar-Information arranges private rooms from around DM25 per person.

Wismar has four hotels, with more in planning. The best situated hotel is *Alter Schwede* (☎ 35 52), Am Markt right next door to the Italian restaurant, Il Restaurante. Singles/doubles cost DM85/140. *Hotel Altes Brauhaus* (☎ 32 23), Lübschestrasse 95, has rooms for DM90/140, and *Hotel Reingard* (☎ 49 72), Weberstrasse 18, has rooms for DM110/145. The picturesque, 18-room *Hotel Wismar* at Breite Strasse 10, erected in

1896, has been closed for major renovations, and will certainly be expensive when it eventually reopens.

Places to Eat

For some local seafood, try the *Fischrestaurant 'Seehase'*, at Altböterstrasse 6 (open weekdays from 10.30 am to 8 pm). *Café Lissi* on Grossschmiederstrasse just off the Markt has a good choice of cakes, and the coffee smells great. *Il Restaurante*, Am Markt 22, serves large portions of spaghetti bolognese for DM7.

Getting There & Away

Trains arrive from Rostock (57 km, 1½ hours) every couple of hours, and from Berlin-Lichtenberg (270 km, 5½ hours) twice a day. Between Schwerin and Wismar (32 km) it's often quicker to change trains at Bad Kleinen than to wait for a through service. Trains to/from Lübeck and Hamburg travel via Bad Kleinen. For train tickets and times, try the Reisebüro, An der Hegede 1 on the corner of Lübschestrasse.

There are daily buses to/from Lübeck, Kiel, Rendsburg and Hamburg from beside the railway station.

Large motor vessels and hydrofoils link Wismar to Neustadt in Schleswig-Holstein (DM10 one-way).

ROSTOCK

Rostock, the largest city in lightly populated north-eastern Germany, is a major Baltic port and shipbuilder. The giant Warnow shipyards on the estuary of the Warnow River were built from scratch after 1957. In 1992, Rostock caught the world's attention when neo-Nazi youth staged violent demonstrations outside a hostel for Vietnamese and Gypsy immigrants, who had to be evacuated to ensure their safety.

In the 14th and 15th centuries, Rostock was an important Hanseatic city trading with Riga, Bergen and Bruges. Rostock University, founded in 1419, was the first in northern Europe. The salty city centre along Kröpeliner Strasse retains the flavour of this period. It's a popular tourist centre with the beach resort of Warnemünde only 12 km north.

Orientation & Information

Rostock-Information (☎ 0381-2 26 19), Lange Strasse 5, is about two km from the train station. To get there, take tram No 11 or 12 outside the station and get off at the next stop after the Rathaus and St Mary's Church in the centre of town. Jugendtourist is at Kröpeliner Strasse 10, above the fabric shop.

Rostock's telephone code is 0381.

Things to See

Rostock's greatest sight is 13th century **St Mary's Church** (closed Monday), which survived the war unscathed. This great medieval brick edifice contains a functioning astronomical clock (1472), a Gothic bronze baptismal font (1290), a Renaissance pulpit (1574) and a Baroque organ (1770) – all artistic treasures. Ascend the 207 steps of the 50-metre-high church tower for the view.

Kröpeliner Strasse, a broad pedestrian mall lined with 15th and 16th century burgher houses, runs west from the **Rathaus** on Neuer Markt to the 14th century **Kröpeliner Tor** (closed Thursday) on the city walls. Halfway along, off the south-west corner of Universitätsplatz, is the **Kloster 'zum Heiligen Kreuz' Museum** (closed Monday) in an old convent (1270).

Rostock also has a good **Maritime Museum** (closed Friday) on August Bebel Strasse opposite the tower at the entrance to town from the railway station.

If you've got a little spare time, Rostock's **zoo** on the south-west side of town (tram No 11) is pleasant and there's a large beer garden opposite the entrance.

Places to Stay

The 84-berth *'Traditionsschiff' Youth Tourist Hotel* (☎ 71 62 02) is in a converted freighter on the harbour at Schmarl-Dorf between Rostock and Warnemünde (S-Bahn to Lütten Klein Station, then walk 25 minutes). It is more expensive than most youth hostels at DM26.50/30.50 for juniors/seniors, but the setting is worth paying a little extra for. The closest camping grounds are at Wismar and Stralsund.

Rostock-Information does not rent private rooms. For these, you must go to its other office (☎ 2 52 60), at Schnickmannstrasse 13 (open weekdays from 8 am to 10 pm, Saturdays to 8 pm, Sundays to 2 pm), or to Reisebüro Zwerg (☎ 2 23 86) at Lange Strasse 19. Prices generally start at around DM30 per person.

Of the hotels, the eight-storey, 82-room *Hotel Am Bahnhof* opposite the train station is overpriced at DM112/134 single/double for a room with shared bath and breakfast. Even more expensive is the nine-storey, four-star *Interhotel Warnow*, Hermann Duncker Platz 4, at DM120/190 with bath and breakfast. *Hotel Nordland* (☎ 2 37 06), Steinstrasse 7 beside the post office on Neuer Markt, was closed in 1992 for a major overhaul; it may be worth calling to see if it is open again.

Places to Eat

The plush *Ostseegaststätte*, Lange Strasse 9 near Rostock-Information, specialises in seafood in the upstairs dining room, and there's a pizzeria downstairs. The service is good but it's not the cheapest place in town.

The *Gastmahl des Meeres* opposite the Maritime Museum on August Bebel Strasse also specialises in seafood and is equally expensive.

For a late lunch, don't miss the *Rostocker Ratskeller* in the Rathaus building on Neuer Markt. Everything is half-price between 3 and 5 pm from Monday to Friday.

Getting There & Away

There are direct trains to Rostock from Berlin-Lichtenberg (231 km, three hours), Schwerin (87 km, 1½ hours), Magdeburg (281 km, four hours), Erfurt (475 km, seven hours) and Leipzig (via Halle 407 km, 6½ hours). Trains run to Stralsund, Wismar and Schwerin every couple of hours. Overnight trains with sleepers are available to/from Leipzig via Potsdam. The Reisebüro at Hermann Duncker Platz 2 in front of Hotel Warnow sells train tickets and books sleepers.

GERMANY

There are two car-ferry trains a day between Berlin-Zoo Station and Copenhagen via Rostock. These trains connect with the international ferry service from Warnemünde to Gedser, Denmark. The ferry terminal is a few minutes' walk from Warnemünde Railway Station, and the crossing takes only two hours. There is also a ferry (from Rostock, not Warnemünde) once a week to Rønne on the Danish island of Bornholm. Departures are on Saturday evening at 9 pm, the crossing takes around 11 hours and costs DM90/180 one-way/return (DM68/136 for students).

There is at least one ferry departure every day from Rostock to Trelleborg, Sweden. The crossing takes eight hours and costs DM42/84 one-way/return (students DM38/76). A car can be transported for DM60 one-way, and a bicycle costs DM10 one-way.

WARNEMÜNDE

Warnemünde, at the mouth of the Warnow River on the Baltic Sea just north of Rostock, is eastern Germany's most popular beach resort. Trying to find a room here in midsummer used to be a hopeless task, but now that eastern Germans are able to spend their holidays wherever they like, it's not nearly as crowded as it used to be.

Regular commuter trains connect Warnemünde to Rostock every 15 minutes and the town can easily be used as a base for day trips to Rostock, Wismar, Stralsund and even Schwerin. It's a good choice if you want to enjoy the comforts of city life while staying in what is ostensibly a small fishing village on the beach.

Warnemünde has the same telephone code as Rostock: 0381.

Things to See

From the railway station, turn left and cross the small bridge over **Alter Strom**, the old harbour. This picturesque inlet is still lined with quaint fishermen's cottages, one of which has been converted into a **museum** (open daily except Wednesday and Sunday, or Monday in July and August, DM2). It's

next to the Imbiss straight ahead from the bridge, a block back from Alter Strom.

After a brief visit, return to Alter Strom and follow the crowded promenade north to the sea where German tourists congregate. Warnemünde's broad, sandy beach stretches west from the lighthouse (1898), chock-a-block with bathers on a hot summer's day.

Activities

Throughout the year (weather permitting), boats depart from near the mouth of Alter Strom on harbour cruises. Numerous private fishing boats tied up along Am Alter Strom also offer one-hour harbour cruises for DM6 to DM10 per person. Generally, those boats which are moored nearer to the train station are more expensive.

Places to Stay & Eat

The 65-bed *Erwin Fischer Youth Hostel* (☎ 5 23 03), Parkstrasse 31, is DM13.50 for juniors, DM16 for seniors.

For a private room in Warnemünde, go to the 'Kurverwaltung' or 'Urlauberanmeldung' office on the corner of Wachtler and Heinrich Heine streets, three blocks back from the Strand Hotel. The sign outside the building says 'Kur- und Erholungswesen' – it's in a corner of the park not far from the Kaufhalle supermarket. Not only are the name and location confusing but the office hours are capricious: Monday, Thursday and Friday from 8.30 to 11.30 am and 2 to 3.30 pm, Tuesday 8.30 to 11.30 am and 2 to 6 pm, and Wednesday 8.30 to 11.30 am only. You enter through a back door. Good luck!

If you can't fit in with those hours, there are loads of private rooms for rent along Parkstrasse. Just look for the 'Zimmer frei' signs in the windows.

The functional, 24-room *Promenade Hotel* (5 27 82), Seestrasse 5, has rooms beginning at DM92/104 single/double with shared bath, breakfast included; on weekends the rate drops to DM72/94 per night. A better bet is the cheerful, 48-room *Strand Hotel*, Seestrasse 12, with singles/doubles from DM46/82. Both hotels have a nice seaside atmosphere.

The 15-storey, 350-room *Neptune Hotel* overlooking the beach at Warnemünde is DM239/319 single/double with private bath and breakfast, fine for those with five-star wallets and Sheraton tastes.

Eating in Warnemünde is very expensive. In an emergency, you might try *Café Zur Traube* at Alexandrinenstrasse 72 (one street back from where the tour boats are anchored). The food is uninspiring, but the prices are right. If the price is not important, then try the *restaurant* run by the Hotel Neptune (next to the hotel). It offers an interesting mixture of Hungarian, Cuban, Vietnamese and Russian food.

Getting There & Away

It's easy to get to Warnemünde on the double-decker S-Bahn. Trains depart every 15 minutes from Rostock Station (DM1). The 20-minute trip takes you past row after row of modern apartment blocks to the Baltic coast.

There is a car and train ferry service between Warnemünde and Gedser in Denmark (DM15 one-way, two hours, all year). The ferry fits in with the Berlin-Copenhagen train schedule.

STRALSUND

Stralsund, an enjoyable city on the Baltic north of Berlin, is nearly surrounded by lakes and the sea, which once contributed to its defence. A Hanseatic city in the Middle Ages, Stralsund later formed part of the Duchy of Pommern-Wolgast. From 1648 to 1815, Stralsund was under Swedish control. Today it's an attractive old town with fine museums and buildings, pleasant walks and a restful, uncluttered waterfront. Rügen Island is just across the Strelasund, and the ferry to Hiddensee leaves from here.

Orientation & Information

From the main railway station, cross the causeway to the right and you're in the old town. Continue up Tribseer Strasse to Neuer Markt, and you'll have St Mary's Church on the right and the museums of Mönchstrasse on the left.

Stralsund-Information (☎ 03831-5 92 15)

is at Alter Markt 15. Stralsund's telephone code is 03831.

Things to See

First, visit 14th century **St Mary's Church**, a massive red-brick edifice typical of north German Gothic church architecture. Recitals on the 1659 organ are offered every other Wednesday in summer at 8 pm. Climb the 345 steps of the tower for a sweeping view of all of Stralsund.

Nearby on Mönchstrasse are two excellent museums. The **Historical Museum** (closed Monday, DM3, students DM1) has a large collection housed in the cloister of an old convent. Stralsund's highlight is the adjoining 13th century convent church, now a fantastic **Oceanic Museum & Aquarium** (closed Monday and Tuesday in winter, DM3, students DM1). There's a large natural history section and much information on the fishing industry. Aquariums on the ground floor contain tropical fish while those in the basement display creatures of the Baltic Sea, North Sea and North Atlantic Ocean.

From these museums, make your way north through the old city to Alter Markt with the medieval **Rathaus**, itself a delightful sight, and impressive **St Nikolai Church** (1350). Long-term restoration work at St Nikolai is continuing, but part of the church is now open weekdays from 2 to 4 pm, Saturday from 9 to 11 am and Sunday from 11 am to noon.

There are many gabled Baltic houses on the small streets just north of Alter Markt, and the old harbour is close by. You'll want to stroll out along the sea wall, then walk west along the waterfront park for a great view of Stralsund's skyline.

Activities

From May to September, Weisse Flotte ships depart from the old harbour for Hiddensee Island (DM20 return trip). Alternatively, consider just taking the regular ferry across the Strelasund to Altefähr on Rügen Island. It operates eight times a day from May to early October (DM0.50 one-way).

GERMANY

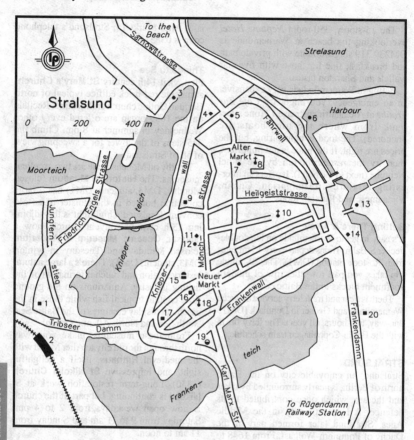

Places to Stay

The closest *Intercamping* is at Stahlbrode on the coast, about 19 km south-east of Stralsund and four km from Reinberg off the main road to Berlin.

Stralsund's excellent 180-bed *Grete Walter Youth Hostel* (☎ 21 60) is in the old waterworks (1690) at Am Kütertor 1 near the Oceanographic Museum. It's DM14 for juniors, DM17 for seniors.

Reisebüro Zwerg (☎ 29 21 51), Ossenreyerstrasse 23, has private rooms but few singles.

Stralsund doesn't have an Interhotel, so

the best on offer is the rather grim, 34-room *Hotel Baltic* (☎ 53 81) (DM54/108 single/double), a monolithic, Stalin-era building at Frankendamm 17 in an ugly neighbourhood south of the harbour.

Hotel Norddeutscher Hof (☎ 31 61), Neuer Markt 22, has singles/doubles from DM90/180, while the *Good Morning Hotel Astoria* (☎ 1 31 46 37), Fährbrücke 1, is at the top of the pyramid with singles/doubles for DM125/150, and DM25 per extra person thereafter.

A number of hotels are in planning in Stralsund, and others have been closed for

1 Hotel Am Bahnhof
2 Railway Station
3 Rowboat Rentals
4 Stralsund Theatre
5 Kniepertor
6 Weisse Flotte
7 Rathaus
8 St Nikolai's Church
9 'Grete Walter' Youth Hostel
10 St Jacob's Church
11 Oceanic Museum & Aquarium
12 Historical Museum
13 Fish Market
14 Heilgeistkirche
15 Post Office
16 Hotel Schweriner Hof
17 Nordland Hotel
18 St Mary's Church
19 Bus Station
20 Hotel Baltic

major renovations. Among those are *Hotel Am Bahnhof*, Tribseer Damm 4 right opposite the train station, *Nordland Hotel* on Platz der Solidarität just across the causeway, and *Hotel Schweriner Hof*, Neuer Markt 2-3 beside St Mary's Church. It may be worth passing by to see if they have reopened. One thing is certain: they will be expensive.

Places to Eat
The *Ratskeller* below the town hall on Alter Markt is open daily from 9 am to 10 pm. The *Ratscafé*, Alter Markt 9, is a great place for a cup of tea or coffee, and its meal prices are lower than those of many other local restaurants (closed Monday).

Getting There & Away
Express trains arrive from Rostock (73 km, 1½ hours), Magdeburg (354 km, 5½ hours), Leipzig (429 km, 5½ hours) and Berlin-Lichtenberg (247 km, three hours). Some of the Berlin trains run straight through from Leipzig to Stralsund.

International trains between Berlin-Zoo and Stockholm or Oslo use the car ferry between Sassnitz Hafen and Trelleborg, Sweden. Some trains to/from Sassnitz Hafen

don't stop at Stralsund's main railway station but instead call at Stralsund-Rügendamm, another station on the south-east side of the city.

For train tickets and times, try the Reisebüro, Alter Markt 10 next to the Rathaus.

In summer, enquire at the Weisse Flotte office about ships from Sassnitz to Świnoujście (Swinemünde), Poland, which generally leave at 8.30 am from Wednesday to Saturday (DM25 return).

HIDDENSEE ISLAND
Hiddensee is a narrow island about 17 km long off Rügen's west coast north of Stralsund. No cars are allowed on Hiddensee. At last report there were no camping grounds, youth hostels or hotels either, only a couple of tiny guesthouses, so check the latest accommodation situation with Stralsund-Information before planning an overnight trip.

The Weisse Flotte runs regular passenger boats from Stralsund to Neuendorf (DM7.50/10 one-way/return), Vitte or Kloster villages (both DM10/18 one-way/return) on Hiddensee several times a day from May to September. In winter this service also operates on most days. If you want to take a bicycle on this boat, check beforehand as it may not be allowed.

There are also ferries from Schaprode on Rügen's west coast across to Hiddensee. Although it is a shorter and cheaper crossing (DM5/8 one-way/return), this is only a realistic option if you have your own transport. Hitching is slow and unreliable.

RÜGEN ISLAND
Rügen Island, just north-east of Stralsund and connected by causeway, is Germany's largest island. At Stubnitz, six km north of Sassnitz, is the highest point on the island (118 metres), and steep chalk cliffs tower above the sea. The main resort area is around Binz, Sellin and Göhren on a peninsula on Rügen's east side.

Places to Stay
Rügen has 18 camping grounds, the largest

GERMANY

concentration of them at Göhren. For information about the individual sites, contact C & W Rohrdantz A Dirks KG (☎ 03838-2 22 05), Industriegebiet Teschenhagen in Teschenhagen. The building is on route B96 about three km from Bergen.

In Binz, there's a 108-bed *youth hostel* (☎ 038393-24 23) at Strandpromenade 35. It's DM14.50 for juniors, DM17.50 for seniors.

Several small hotels exist, such as the 15-room *Gaststätte Zentralhotel*, Hauptstrasse 13, Binz; the 19-room *Gaststätte Mecklenburger Hof*, Bahnhofstrasse 67, Bergen; and the 10-room *Hotel Am Markt*, Am Markt, Putbus. The only place you'll be reasonably certain of finding a room is at the 116-room, four-star *Rügenhotel*, Seestrasse 1, Sassnitz.

Getting There & Away

Local trains run every couple of hours from Stralsund to Sassnitz (52 km) or Binz (52 km) on Rügen's north-east side. Both services pass Lietzow, 13 km before Sassnitz, where you may have to change trains (ask). From Binz, a narrow-gauge railway continues to Göhren (14 km) at Rügen's eastern tip. There are eight ferries per day from Sassnitz to Trelleborg, Sweden. The crossing takes four hours and costs DM27/54 one-way/return (DM17/34 if you are aged under 25). For information and bookings, call ☎ 038392-2 22 67.

Tickets for the luxury afternoon coach from Sassnitz to West Berlin (mid-April to October, DM58) are handled by Reisebüro Rügentourist, Hauptstrasse 50, Sassnitz. People aged 26 and under pay DM30.

See the Hiddensee Island section regarding transport from Rügen to Hiddensee.

Bavaria

For many visitors to Germany, Bavaria (Bayern) is a microcosm for the whole country. Here you will find fulfilled the Germanic stereotypes of *Lederhosen*, beer halls, oompah bands and romantic castles. Yet the Bavarians themselves are proudly independent and pursue a separate course from the rest of Germany in a number of ways, not least in the refusal of its youth hostels to accept any guests over the age of 26.

Bavaria was ruled for centuries as a duchy under the line founded by Otto I of Wittelsbach, and eventually graduated to the status of a kingdom in 1806. The region suffered amid numerous power struggles between Prussia and Austria and was finally brought into the German empire in 1871 by Bismarck. The last king of Bavaria was Ludwig II (1845-86), who earned the epithet the 'mad monarch' for his obsession with building crazy castles at great expense. He was found drowned in Lake Starnberg in suspicious circumstances, and left no heirs.

Bavaria draws visitors all year. If you only have time for one part of Germany after Berlin, this is it. Munich is its capital and the heart and soul of the area. The Bavarian Alps, Nuremberg and the medieval towns on the Romantic Road are other important attractions. Try getting off the beaten track in a place like the Bavarian Forest for a taste of Germany away from the tour buses.

MUNICH

Munich (München) is the Bavarian mother lode. But this beer-belching, sausage-eating city can be as cosmopolitan as anywhere in Europe. Munich residents have figured out how to enjoy life and they're usually happy to show visitors. Just head to the Hofbräuhaus (or some other beer hall) and ask for advice on the Munich way of life.

There's much more to Munich, however, than beer halls. Decide on one of the many fine museums and take a leisurely look. Head to the Viktualienmarkt (food market) for a snack, linger over coffee at Café Extrablatt, go eat some Weisswurst and drink some Weizen beer.

The city is an ideal base for day trips to the great outdoors. On a clear day anywhere in Munich, the Bavarian Alps beckon. If the weather's good, head for the mountains;

much of Munich can be seen on a rainy day, but clouds don't do the Alps justice.

Munich has been the capital of Bavaria since 1503, but really achieved eminence under the guiding hand of Ludwig I in the 19th century. It has seen many turbulent times, but the last century has been particularly rough. WW I practically starved the city, and WW II brought more than 200,000 deaths and much shame to its citizens by their early acceptance of Hitler's Nazi movement.

Orientation

The Hauptbahnhof is less than one km west of the centre of town. Though there's an extensive subway system, old-town Munich is enjoyable for walking. Head east along Bayerstrasse, through Karlsplatz, and then along Neuhauser Strasse and Kaufingerstrasse to Marienplatz, the hub of Munich.

To the north of Marienplatz are the Residenz (the former royal palace), Schwabing (the famous student section), and the Englischer Garten grounds. To the east is the Platzl quarter for beer houses and restaurants, as well as Maximilianstrasse, a fashionable street that's fun for strolling and window-shopping.

Information

The main tourist information office (☎ 089-23 91 256) is at the Hauptbahnhof, beside the south entrance near track No 11. Its hours are 8 am to 10 pm from Monday to Saturday and 11 am to 7 pm Sunday. Despite the efficiency of the staff, you must expect to stand in line during summer. The room-finding service costs DM5. Pick up one of the most helpful city pamphlets in the country, *Munich for Young People* (DM1), which will be worth its weight in Deutschmarks saved.

The train station also features another excellent source of information in English at EurAide (☎ 089-59 38 89), across from track No 11. It's an information office run by Germanrail, but has more than just train information and seems more inclined than the tourist office to find the right accommo-

dation at the right price. It's only open from May to October.

Other useful information sources are Amerika-Haus (☎ 089-59 53 67) at Karolinenplatz 3, and the British Council (☎ 089-40 18 32) at Rosenheimerstrasse 116b.

Money The main post office has lower commission rates than the Sparkasse bank at the Hauptbahnhof's main entrance.

Post & Telecommunications Munich's main post office and telephone exchange is directly opposite the station at Bahnhofplatz 1, and is open 24 hours for all services. Munich's telephone code is 089.

Consulates Among the many consulates in the city are the British Consulate (☎ 381 62 80) at Amalienstrasse 62, the US Consulate (☎ 28 881) at Königinstrasse 5, and the Canadian Consulate (☎ 22 26 61) at Tal 29-III.

Travel Agencies American Express (☎ 21 990) is at Promenadeplatz 6. Student travel information and services are available at ASTA-Reisen (☎ 50 06 05 40, extension 544), Amalienstrasse 73.

Bookshops Munich is the best German city for stocking up on English-language reading material. Try the Anglia English Bookshop at Schellingstrasse 3, in the university area on a street filled with bookshops. Its Penguin collection is excellent. Just down the street, you might also try Words' Worth Books at No 21a.

Emergency Medical help is available at the Medical Emergency Service (Kassenärztlicher Notfalldienst) on ☎ 55 86 61. The police is on ☎ 110.

Dangers & Annoyances Crime and staggering drunks leaving the beer halls are major problems in Munich. Watch valuables carefully around touristy areas and the seedy streets south of the Hauptbahnhof. A

GERMANY

GERMANY

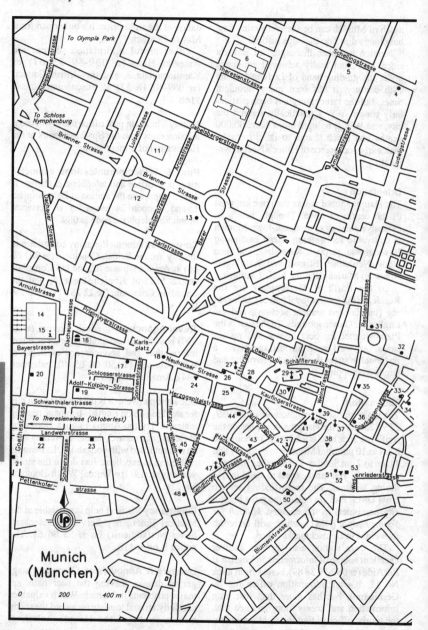

To Olympia Park

To Schloss Nymphenburg

Schleissheimerstrasse

Schellingstrasse
5
4

Theresienstrasse
6

7

Luisenstrasse

Gabelsbergerstrasse

Arcisstrasse

Amalienstrasse

Ludwigstrasse

Brienner Strasse

11

Brienner Strasse

12

Meiserstrasse

13

Karlstrasse

Barer Strasse

Strasse

Dachauer Strasse

Arnulfstrasse

Dachauerstrasse

Pfefferstrasse

14

15

Bayerstrasse

16

Karlsplatz

18 Neuhauser Strasse

Löwengrube
Ettstrasse

Schäfflerstrasse

31

32

17

Schlosserstrasse

Sonnenstrasse

24

27
26

28

29

Kaufingerstrasse

Weinstrasse

35

33

34

Adolf–Kolping–Strasse

19

20

Schwanthalerstrasse

25

30

36

To Theresienwiese (Oktoberfest)

Landwehrstrasse

Herzogspitalstrasse

Herzog Strasse

44

Farbergraben

39
40

41

37

Sparkassenstrasse

22
23

21

Pettenkofer-strasse

Goethestrasse

45

46

43

47

42

38

48

Sendlinger Strasse

Kreuzstrasse

Wilhelm–Strasse

Oberanger

49

50

51
52

53

Wesenriederstrasse

Blumenstrasse

Residenzstrasse

Munich
(München)

0   200   400 m

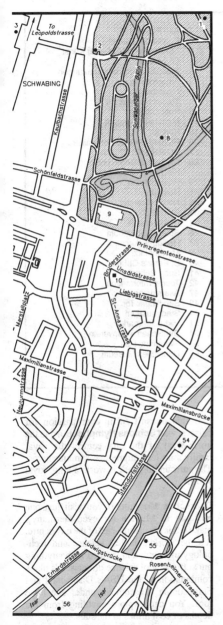

common trick is to steal your gear if you strip off in the Englischer Garten.

Things to See

The pivotal **Marienplatz** contains the towering neo-Gothic **Altes Rathaus** (Old Town Hall) and the often photographed **Glockenspiel** (carillon), which does its number at 11 am, noon and 5 pm (only at 11 am from 1 November to 30 April). Many other attractions are within easy walking distance.

Walking Tour Start at the Marienplatz. Two important churches are on this square: **St Peter's** and, behind the Altes Rathaus, the **Heiliggeistkirche**. Head along the shopping street, Kaufingerstrasse, to the late-Gothic **Frauenkirche** (Church of Our Lady), the landmark church of Munich; the monotonous red brick is very Bavarian in its simplicity. Continue west on Kaufingerstrasse to **St Michael's**, Germany's grandest Renaissance church.

Farther west is the **Richard Strauss fountain** and then the medieval **Karlstor**. Double back towards Marienplatz and turn right onto Eisenmannstrasse which becomes Kreuzstrasse and Herzog-Wilhelm-Strasse. This all ends at the medieval gate of Sendlinger Tor. Go down the right side of the shopping street, Sendlinger Strasse, to the **Asamkirche**. This remarkable church was totally designed by the Asam brothers and contains a unity rarely found in churches, which typically involve the input of many people in their development. It could have inspired some of Dame Edna Everage's less suitable outfits: with barely an unembellished surface to be found, it takes late Baroque to its almost bizarre extreme – Rococo run wild.

Next, continue along Sendlinger Strasse, turn right on Hermann-Sack-Strasse and onto St Jakobs Platz and the **Stadtmuseum**, one of the better city museums in the country (great exhibits on beer and brewing for adults, puppets for kids and photography for Fuji fanatics). Walk around the left side of the museum and veer left onto Sebastiansplatz and Prälat-Zistl-Strasse. The

GERMANY

■ PLACES TO STAY

10 Pension Beim Haus der Kunst
19 Pension Schiller
20 Jugendhotel Marienherberge
21 Hotel Gebhardt
22 Pension Marie-Luise
23 CVJM
44 Hotel Arosa
50 Hotel Blauer Bock
53 Hotel-Pension am Markt

▼ PLACES TO EAT

24 Augustinerbräu
25 Zum Pschorrbräu
30 Nürnberger Bratwurst Glöckl
    am Dom
35 Alois Dallmayr
38 Tong Shinh
43 Altes Hackerhaus
45 Art + Tart Vitamin Buffet
46 Bella Italia
52 Löwenbräu Stadt Kempten

OTHER

1 Chinesischer Turm
2 Bike Rental
3 University
4 Anglia English Bookshop
5 Words' Worth Books
6 Neue Pinakothek

7 Alte Pinakothek
8 Englischer Garten
9 Staatsgalerie Moderner Kunst
11 Glyptothek
12 Staatliche Antikensammlungen
13 Amerika-Haus
14 Hauptbahnhof
15 Tourist Information
16 Post Office
17 Mathäser Bierstadt
18 Karlstor
26 Richard Strauss Fountain
27 St Michael's Church
28 Deutsches Jagd- und
    Fischereimuseum
29 Frauenkirche
31 Residenz
32 Nationaltheater
33 Platzl Bühne
34 Hofbräuhaus
36 Spielzeugmuseum
37 Heiliggeistkirche
39 Marienplatz
40 St Peter's Church
41 Sport Schuster
42 Tourist Information
47 Asamkirche
48 Sendlinger Tor
49 Stadtmuseum
51 Viktualienmarkt
54 Deutsches Alpenverein
55 Swimming Hall
56 Deutsches Museum

Viktualienmarkt (food market), one of Europe's great markets, is nearby, as is our starting point, the Marienplatz.

Residenz Easily found at Max-Joseph-Platz 3, this huge palace housed Bavarian rulers from 1385 to 1918 and features more than 500 years of architectural history. Along with the house, restored after WW II, visit the **Residenz Museum's** 100 rooms of Wittelsbach belongings, and the **Schatzkammer** (Treasure Room) for a look at a ridiculous amount of jewels, crowns and ornate gold. Admission to the Residenz is DM3.50 and it's open Tuesday to Sunday from 10 am to 4.30 pm; the Treasure Room costs another DM3.50.

If this doesn't fulfil your passion for palaces, visit **Schloss Nymphenburg** to the north-west of the city centre, the royal family's no less impressive summer home. The surrounding park is worth a long, royal stroll.

Deutsches Museum If you visit just one museum in Munich (or even Germany), make it this one, south-east of the city centre. It's the world's largest science and technology museum, and is filled with anything but stuffy school science projects. It's like a combination of the USA's Disneyland and Smithsonian Museum all under one huge roof. You can explore anything from the depths of coal mines to the stars.

It's definitely too large to see everything (at 55,000 sq metres, it covers a whole island on the Isar and would require over 13 km of walking to see it all), so pursue specific interests. There's an excellent brochure, *Information for Your Visit*, which details times of free demonstrations. The museum's hours are 9 am to 5 pm daily (closed on important holidays) and admission is DM8 for adults and DM2.50 for students and children (free for those aged under six). A visit to the planetarium costs DM1.50 extra. Parking is very limited. Take the S-Bahn to Isartor, U-Bahn 1 or 2 to Fraunhoferstrasse, or Tram 18 to Deutsches Museum.

Alte Pinakothek At Barer Strasse 27, this is one of the largest painting museums in Europe and is simply overwhelming in scale and contents. Everywhere you turn there's another recognisable artist or work. The best floor is upstairs where you'll find Dürer's Christ-like *Self-Portrait* and his *Four Apostles*, Rogier van der Weyden's *Adoration of the Magi*, and Botticelli's famous *Pietà*. Next door, the **Neue Pinakothek** concentrates on the 19th century. Combined entrance costs DM7 (free on Sunday) and they are closed on Monday.

Other Museums On Königsplatz, two museums are worth a look. The **Glyptothek** at No 3 and the **Staatliche Antikensammlungen** at No 1 feature Germany's best antiquities collection (mostly Greek and Roman stuff).

Also interesting is the **Staatsgalerie Moderner Kunst** at Prinzregentenstrasse 1. This gallery offers some of the great German and international contributions to modern art, including wild paintings by Munch, Picasso and Magritte, as well as funky sculpture and some pop art.

Schwabing Lying to the north of the city centre, but still within a pleasant walk, Schwabing is a student stomping ground. The bar, café and restaurant scene can be electric, trendy, sociable and surprisingly expensive. Unwind here after a visit to the

Englischer Garten (see the following Activities section).

BMW Factory In the north is BMW's Munich factory at Peutelring 130. The excellent free tour (in English) takes visitors from raw metal to completed cars, and is conducted at 9.30 am and 1 pm on weekdays. The somewhat self-congulatory museum is open daily from 9 am to 5 pm (DM4.50). Take the U3 or U8 to Olympiazentrum.

Olympia Park The complex was built for the 1972 summer Olympics and is still an active sporting facility. You can swim in the same pool where the USA's Mark Spitz won seven gold medals, or simply admire the various arenas and the tent-roof covering 75,000 sq metres. The Olympic tower provides one of the best views of Munich. Since you're already in the area, head for Dachau.

Dachau Don't miss this. Dachau was the very first concentration camp, and the Germans detail the sordid business with admirable frankness. The gruesome concentration camp was built by Himmler in March 1933 and processed more than 200,000 prisoners, though it's not known exactly how many of these died. In 1933 Munich had 10,000 Jews. Only 200 survived the war.

A visit to Dachau includes camp relics, a memorial, and a very sobering museum. There's a film in English at 11.30 am, 2 and 3.30 pm. It's open from 9 am to 5 pm every day except Monday, and admission is free. Take the S2 to Dachau and then bus No 722 (DM1.30), which departs from Dachau S-Bahn station.

Activities
Adventure Munich is the perfect place to plan adventurous outings. The Deutscher Alpenverein (German Alpine Club) headquarters (☎ 23 50 90 0) is at Praterinsel 5 and can be very helpful with planning and information for mountain trips.

The Sport Schuster sporting goods store (☎ 23 70 77) at Rosenstrasse 1-6 has five floors of everything imaginable for the adventurer, from simple camping gear to expedition wear, plus an excellent bookshop. It has a travel service on the 1st floor, offering various adventure outings under its Club Alpin Extra programme, such as white-water rafting on the Salzach River for around DM60, and a five-day kayak school for DM499.

Cycling With Munich's many parks and pedestrian zones, the city is ideal for biking. The Radius Touristik company (☎ 59 61 13) near platform No 35 in the Hauptbahnhof charges DM16 to DM27 per day. It can also suggest specific routes. Ask for the brochure *Radl-Touren* (DM0.50) at any tourist office, which gives four very specific routes. The directions are in German, but the maps are clear. The 15 km 'Isar-Tour' is one of the best near Munich; it's generally traffic-free and easy, scenic pedalling.

The Englischer Garten also has bike rental (☎ 39 70 16) on summer weekends at Veterinärstrasse. The first hour is DM6 with additional hours costing DM3.50, or DM18 for the whole day.

Englischer Garten One of the largest city parks in Europe, this is a great place for strolling, especially along the Schwabinger Bach. Take liquid refreshment at the Chinesischer Turm beer garden or the nearby, less crowded Hirschau beer garden along the banks of the Kleinhesseloher See. The Englischer Garten is also the place to head for nude sunbathing with lots of company. It's not unusual for hundreds of naked people to be in the park on a normal business day, with their coats, ties and dresses stacked primly on the grass.

Like almost everything else that's green in Germany, the park is in trouble. Since 1977, the trees (especially elms) have been in declining health.

Festivals
Oktoberfest Try to get to Munich for one of the continent's biggest and best parties, lasting from the last Saturday in September to the first Sunday in October. Reserve accommodation well ahead. The Oktoberfest takes place at the Theresienwiese grounds south-west of the Hauptbahnhof. There's no entrance fee, but most of the fun costs something. There are incredibly crazy carnival rides, food stands and, best of all, lots of beer tents.

Places to Stay
No-one older than 26 (unless travelling with children aged under 18) can stay in Bavarian IYHF hostels. This puts extra pressure on budget hotels and pensions, of which there are precious few in Munich. Reserve ahead when possible and arrive early in the day.

Camping The most central location is *Campingplatz Thalkirchen* (☎ 7 23 17 07), south-west of the city centre at Zentralländstrasse 49, close to the hostel on Miesingstrasse. Camping costs DM5 per person (DM2 for children aged 6 to 14), DM3.50 to DM5 per tent and DM6 per car. It can be incredibly crowded in summer (it's closed from November to mid-March), but there's seemingly always room for one more tent. Take the U3 to Thalkirchen and bus No 57 to the last stop, 'Thalkirchen' (about 20 minutes from the centre).

A bit farther from the city centre, but also more Bavarian, are *Waldcamping Obermenzing* (☎ 8 11 22 35) and *Langwieder See* (☎ 8 64 15 66); the latter has a great location but can only be reached by car on the autobahn towards Stuttgart.

Hostels The most central hostel is the *DJH Jugendherberge* (☎ 13 11 56), north-west of the city centre at Wendl-Dietrich Strasse 20 (U-Bahn: Rotkreuzplatz). It's one of the largest in Germany and is relatively loud and busy. Theft can be a problem but it's a great place to meet people. Dorms cost from DM18.80.

Still decently close, and a better deal, is the more modern *DJH Jugendgästehaus München* (☎ 7 23 65 50/60), south-west of the city centre in the suburb of Thalkirchen, at Miesingstrasse 4. Take the U1 or U2 to Sendlinger-Tor-Platz, change to the U3 for

Thalkirchen, and then follow the signs. Per-person costs are DM22 in dorms, DM24 in triples and quads, DM26 in doubles, and DM30 in singles. Both hostels have a 1 am curfew.

DJH Jugendherberge Burg Schwaneck (☎ 7 93 06 43) at Burgweg 4-6 is in the southern suburbs, conveniently close to the Pullach stop on S-Bahn No 7. Dorms cost just DM12.50 and it's in a great old castle. Unfortunately for evening revellers, the 11.30 pm curfew means catching a train from the centre at around 10.30 pm.

The Munich hostel mecca (non-IYHF) is the *Jungendlager Am Kapuziner Hölzl* (☎ 1 41 43 00) on In den Kirschen, near the Botanical Garden north of Schloss Nymphenburg. Nicknamed 'the Tent', it's only open from late June to early September, and there's an under-24 age limit that's rarely enforced. Take U-bahn No 1 to Rotkreuzplatz and change to tram No 12 for the Botanischer Garten. It costs DM6 for a mattress, blanket, cooking facilities and some hot tea in the morning. More than 20,000 people take the Tent experience each summer.

The *Christlicher Verein junger Menschen* (CVJM) (☎ 55 59 41) at Landwehrstrasse 13 is near the Hauptbahnhof and takes females as well as males. Singles/doubles are DM43/76 and triples are DM105. Prices are 15% higher for those aged over 27. Women aged under 26 should try the *Jugendhotel Marienherberge* (☎ 55 58 91) at Goethe-strasse 9, starting at DM25 and featuring singles for only DM29.

Hotels Prices are higher than in most other parts of Germany. Accommodation services (see the earlier Information section) can help, but even if you insist on the lowest price range, they won't find you anything cheaper than DM50 for a single or DM80 for a double.

There are tons of fairly cheap, if seedy, options near the station. The best one is *Hotel Gebhardt* (☎ 53 94 46) at Goethestrasse 38, with singles/doubles starting at DM60/90. For a bed without breakfast, head for *Pension Schiller* (☎ 59 24 35) at Schiller-

strasse 11. Acceptable singles/doubles start at DM45/70 and triples at DM96. The cramped *Marie-Luise* (☎ 55 42 30) at Landwehrstrasse 37-IV offers rooms from DM40/78. Phone for vacancies at the 11 am check-out time.

An ideal compromise of location, price and cleanliness is *Pension Haydn* (☎ 53 11 19) at Haydnstrasse 9. It's near the Goetheplatz U-Bahn station and within walking distance of the Hauptbahnhof (head south down Goethestrasse). Rooms start at DM60/80 for singles/doubles. If they're full, head around Kaiser-Ludwig-Platz to *Pension Schubert* (☎ 53 50 87) at Schubert-strasse 1-I. Bathless singles/doubles are DM45/85, while a fully equipped double isn't bad for DM95.

Munich's best location for the money is *Hotel-Pension Am Markt* (☎ 22 50 14) at Heiliggeiststrasse 6, just off the Viktualien-markt. Check the many photos of concert stars. Rooms start at DM54/94. Also good, especially if you fall in love with life at the Englischer Garten, is *Pension beim Haus der Kunst* (☎ 22 21 27) at Bruderstrasse 4-I. Singles/doubles are DM55/80. Ask about the small apartment.

Clean, comfortable, central and reason-ably spacious rooms can be found at *Hotel Blauer Bock* (☎ 23 17 80), Sebastiansplatz 9. Singles/doubles with private shower and WC start at DM90/130, or DM65/90 with communal facilities. Breakfast buffet is included and garage parking is available for DM8. Of a similar standard and price is *Hotel Arosa* (☎ 26 70 87), Hotterstrasse 2.

The best mid-price deal is the *Hotel Petri* (☎ 58 10 99), Aindorferstrasse 82. Rooms have distinctive old wooden furniture and a TV, plus there is a garden and a small indoor swimming pool, free for guests. Rooms with private shower and WC start at DM112/134, and breakfast costs DM8. It's 10 minutes' walk from the Laimer Platz stop on U-Bahn No 4 or 5.

Rental Lengthy stays are a bit uncommon in the centre of the city, but are more popular in the smaller Bavarian resort towns outside

Munich. Check with the tourist office about stays of more than six days, and expect to pay DM250 per week or more. Rates are much more expensive in Munich itself. The *Stollberg Plaza Boardinghouse* (☎ 23 50 40) in the centre of the city at Stollbergerstrasse 2-4 has 35 apartments for monthly rental, ranging in size from 45 sq metres (DM4400 per month) to 100 sq metres (DM8000 per month).

Places to Eat

Eating cheaply in Munich is much like anywhere else in Germany. Go where the locals go – mostly to the less touristy beer halls and restaurants, or one of the many markets.

Student card holders can fill up for just DM2.70 to DM3.80 at one of the university *mensas*, such as the busy site at Leopoldstrasse 13. Cheap eating is also available in various department stores in the centre. More refined dining can be undertaken in the *Altes Hackerhaus*, Sendlinger Strasse 75, a 400-year-old traditional inn. Main meals are DM10 to DM25. Eat Chinese at *Tong Shinh*, Hochbrücken Strasse 3; splash out on the set meals from DM22.50, or go there Monday to Friday lunch times for specials at around DM10.

The beer halls like the *Hofbräuhaus* at Am Platzl are not particularly appetising or cheap for eating, unless just munching on a pretzel or a few sausages. Instead, head to one of the local Bavarian beer restaurants, where the company is just as lively, the beer just as cold, and the food generally much better in taste and quantity. On the Viktualienmarkt, find *Löwenbräu Stadt Kempten* at No 4 (closed Sunday). There, you'll get a half-litre of Löwenbräu for DM4.10 and food for DM10 to DM20. Try the excellent *Jägerschnitzel*, French fries and mixed salad for DM16.80. The place to try for sausages, especially if you don't plan to make it to Nuremberg, is the *Nürnberger Bratwurst Glöckl Am Dom* at Frauenplatz 9, in the shadow of the Frauenkirche. Here, the small Nuremberg sausages are served by the thousands day and night. Expect to pay about DM20 for eight sausages, sauerkraut and a

couple of beers. It's closed on Sundays and holidays.

Munich picnicking can help you balance your diet. A good place to go for making your own meal is the open-air *Viktualienmarkt*, just south of Marienplatz. Make sure you figure out the price before buying, and don't be afraid to move on to another stall. There's also a large branch of the seafood chain restaurant, *Nordsee*, and an excellent beer garden.

For a special picnic that's lots more expensive, call at the legendary *Alois Dallmayr* at Dienerstrasse 14, one of the world's great delicatessens. Try a little bit (100 grams should suffice) of anything from its huge international selection. The upstairs restaurant (☎ 21 35 100) is expensive, but if you can afford it, you can expect the best. Daily specials are DM25 to DM40 and there is an impressive cold buffet. The gourmet menu is a culinary treat at DM80 for five courses. Reservations are advised, especially at lunch time. Another good place for a blowout is the *Ambiente Restaurant* (☎ 5 19 60) in the Arabella Westpark Hotel, Garmischer Strasse 2. It has all-you-can-eat lunch-time buffets every day except Saturday. A drink, soup, main dishes and dessert will set you back DM42.

Vegetarianism is catching on in this cosmopolitan, red-meat city. For a vegetable splurge, try *Art + Tart Vitamin-Buffet* at Herzog-Wilhelm-Strasse 25. It has an incredible platter for two at DM59, as well as lots of salads and creative concoctions that sell for DM2.60 per 100 grams to eat inside, and DM2.30 to take out. It's open Monday to Saturday to 10 pm. Also recommended for vegetarian food is *Jahreszeiten*, Sebastianplatz 9.

Italian food is also a good deal in Munich. There are at least six *Bella Italia* restaurants in the city, including one at Sendlinger Strasse 66. They offer pasta for less than DM10, and pizza from DM5.50 to DM15. On the other side of the Isar is *Al Macarone* at Franziskanerstrasse 15, near the Rosenheimer Platz S-Bahn stop. It has large salads, pizza (DM6 to DM10 for one, DM11.50 to

DM19 for two), and excellent pasta dishes for DM6 to DM12.

Cafés Though not the rival of a city like Paris, Munich has an excellent café scene. With the exception of the ideally situated *Café Am Dom*, stay away from the touristy cafés around Marienplatz. *Café Extrablatt*, at Leopoldstrasse 7 in Schwabing, is by far the best place to head for that caffeine fix. This is the ideal place to spend a leisurely morning; the food is good and relatively inexpensive, and there's a large breakfast menu. It's open daily to midnight (1 pm Saturday).

Entertainment

Munich is one of the cultural capitals of Germany. Opportunities revolve around the *Nationaltheater* on Max-Joseph-Platz. It's the home of the Bavarian State Opera and the site of many cultural events.

Munich is also a hot scene for jazz, and the place to go is *Jazzclub Unterfahrt* (☎ 448 27 94) at Kirchenstrasse 96, near the Ostbahnhof station. It has live music every night starting at 9 pm, jam sessions open to everyone on Sunday nights, and a popular jazz brunch on Sundays from October to April at 10.30 am. The best two English-language cinemas are the *Europa-Kino* at Schwanthalerstrasse 2-6, and the *Cinema* at Nymphenburger Strasse 31.

A bit on the unusual side, *Circus Krone* (☎ 55 81 66), Marsstrasse 43, features a circus from late December to early March and varied entertainment the rest of the year. For other events and locations, pick up the *Monatsprogramm* for DM2 at any tourist office.

Beer Halls Beer drinking is the main form of entertainment in this city, and for good reason. Germans drink an average of 250 litres of beer each per year, while Munich residents average 350. Eight major breweries run their own beer halls around the city. The *Hofbräuhaus*, Am Platzl 9, is rightfully the most famous and the most filled with tourists. It can really be good fun and a great

chance to meet travellers and locals. Try at least one large, frothy, litre-mug (called a *Mass)* of beer for DM8.50 before heading off to another beer hall. This is the hall where Hitler publicly announced his programme at a meeting on 20 February 1920.

Just across the plaza, check *Platzl Bühne* at Am Platzl 1. It features a Bavarian show every night except Sunday at 8 pm, for which it charges DM12, and it's about the best value in the city for this type of entertainment.

There are two beer halls along Neuhauserstrasse, and both are much more subdued than the Hofbräuhaus. *Augustinerbräu* at No 16 is quiet and dark, but with decent food, while *Zum Pschorrbräu* at No 11 has loud entertainment, a wine cellar and probably the best food of the beer-hall scene.

Munich's blue-collar beer hall is the *Mathäser Bierstadt* at Bayerstrasse 5. This is the Löwenbräu brewery's beer hall and it's a favourite with locals. Head upstairs to the beer hall in the back right-hand corner. It's just as lively as the Hofbräuhaus, but somehow more genuine. There's also a separate cellar for Weizen beer.

A bit farther afield is the *Löwenbräukeller* (☎ 52 60 21) at Nymphenburger Strasse 2. Call ahead to ask about any special Bavarian evenings. For a more peaceful (and possibly romantic) drinking session, head for the historic *Weinschenke Am Markt* on Dreifaltigkeitsplatz 1, near the Viktualienmarkt.

Things to Buy

Many shops line the pedestrian street between Karlsplatz and Marienplatz. Most shoppers look for optical goods (Leica cameras and binoculars), handicrafts from throughout the country, and beer steins. It's best to buy steins directly from your favourite brewery or beer hall.

The *Christkindlmarkt* (Christmas Market) on Marienplatz in December is large and well stocked but often expensive. The *Auer Dult*, a huge flea market on Mariahilfplatz, has great buys and takes place during the last weeks of April, July and October, always

GERMANY

commencing on a Saturday. It includes a small fairground for the kids.

Getting There & Away

Air Munich is second in importance only to Frankfurt for international and national connections. Flights will take you to all major destinations including London, Paris, Rome, Athens, New York and Sydney. Main German cities are serviced by at least half-a-dozen flights daily. The main carrier is Lufthansa (☎ 5 11 30), Lenbachplatz 1. Examples of one-way fares from Munich are: Frankfurt (DM256), Berlin (DM355), Hamburg (DM399) and Düsseldorf (DM353).

Bus Munich is linked to the Romantic Road (see the Romantic Road section that follows) by the Europabus Munich-Frankfurt service (daily from mid-March to late October). Eurail and German Rail passes are valid for the bus, as is a Frankfurt-Munich train ticket; Inter-Rail gets a 50% discount. Enquire at Deutsche Touring GmbH (☎ 59 18 24) in Starnberger Bahnhof, by track 26 of the Hauptbahnhof. This is also the agent for Eurolines bus services to Prague and northern Germany. Buses to London depart three times a week; they take 24 hours and cost DM168.

Train Train services to/from Munich are excellent. There are hourly services to every major city in western Germany, as well as many European connections. Frankfurt is 3½ hours from Munich with the ICE (DM108). To Vienna takes around five hours (DM84). Other fares are: Paris (DM168), Rome (DM115), Salzburg (DM35) and Prague (DM85 to DM100, depending upon the route).

Car & Motorbike Munich has autobahns radiating outwards on all sides. Take the A9 to Nuremberg, the A92 to Passau, the A8 to Salzburg, the A95 to Garmisch-Partenkirchen and the A8 to Ulm or Stuttgart. For information or help, contact the ADAC

(☎ 51 950) at Ridlerstrasse 35. The Mitfahrzentrale (☎ 28 01 24) is at Amalienstrasse 87.

Getting Around

To/From the Airport Munich's new airport, Franz Josef Strauss Flughafen, opened in 1992, replacing the old Riem airport. It is connected to the Hauptbahnhof by S-Bahn No 8 (DM10 one-way).

Bus & Train Getting around is easy on the excellent public transport network. Tickets are valid on the S-Bahn, U-Bahn, trams and buses and must be validated before use. Single rides cost DM2.50, but it's cheaper to buy a series of tickets *(Streifenkarte)* for DM10. Validate at least two strips on the adult ticket for journeys over four stops. A day pass for the inner zone *(Innenraum)* costs DM8 and covers most places of interest (except Dachau). The *Gesamttarifgebiet* day pass for DM16 covers the whole of Munich. The same day pass can be used by up to two adults and three children aged under 18, subject to time limits. For longer stays, consider the transferable monthly season ticket for DM49.

The subway ends around 12.30 am on weekdays and 1.30 am on weekends, but there are some later buses. Rail passes are valid on S-Bahn trains.

Car & Motorbike It's not worth driving in the city centre. The tourist office map shows city parking places. Car rental (DM129 per day, unlimited km) is available from Sixt AG (☎ 614 14 480), Dr Carl von Linde Strasse 2.

Taxi Taxis are expensive (DM7 flagfall, plus DM1.90 per km) and not much more convenient than public transport. In an emergency, check for taxis outside a major hotel, the train station, or call for a radio-dispatched one (☎ 2 16 10).

ROMANTIC ROAD

The Romantic Road (Romantische Strasse) is a marketing concept linking a series of picturesque villages. Nevertheless, this is one occasion where it is well worth falling for the sales pitch and taking time to explore the area. The trip is one of the most popular in Germany. It's just a pity that the very thing that attracts everyone in the first place (peaceful countryside, unspoiled medieval village centres) is undermined by the presence of so many visitors. Avoid claustrophobic summer weekends and try to take in some of the lesser known villages.

Orientation & Information

The Romantic Road runs north-south through western Bavaria, from Würzburg to Füssen near the Austrian border, passing through many villages such as Rothenburg, Dinkelsbühl and Augsburg. It is possible to cover the route by car or local bus but most people take the Europabus. Reservations are only necessary on peak-season weekends, but it doesn't hurt to ask in advance. For information and reservations, contact Deutsche Touring GmbH (☎ 069-23 07 35), Mannheimer Strasse 4, Frankfurt, or its main office (☎ 7 90 30) at Am Römerhof 17. The best places for information about the Romantic Road are the tourist offices in Rothenburg (☎ 09861-4 04 92) at Marktplatz 1, and in Dinkelsbühl (☎ 09581-9 02 40), Marktplatz.

Things to See

Rothenburg Rothenburg (full name: Rothenburg ober der Tauber) is the main tourist attraction along the route. Granted the status of a 'Free Imperial City' in 1274, it's one of the oldest towns on the Romantic Road and is packed with paved streets and picturesque old houses straight out of the history books.

Start a walking tour at the **Town Hall**, commenced as Gothic in the 14th century but completed in Renaissance style (facing the Marktplatz). Climb to the top of the tower for a majestic view of the roofs and ramparts of the town. According to legend, the town was saved during the Thirty Years' War when the mayor won a challenge by downing three litres of wine in a single gulp. The scene is re-enacted by the figures round the three clocks on the Marktplatz. All the streets in

the centre are worth exploring, although **Plönlein**, a corner on Untere Schmiedgasse which joins descending and ascending streets, each ending at a fortified gate, is particularly attractive.

The fascinating **Kriminal Museum** details crimes from medieval times (in English). In the 16th century, for example, it was an offence to wear clothes that were too fashionable for your social class. Punishments were a devious mixture of ridicule and torture. The museum is open daily (DM4, students DM3). Also interesting is the **Puppen und Spielzeugmuseum** (Doll & Toy Museum) at Hofbronnengasse 13. It's the largest private collection in Germany.

If peace and quiet away from the massed tourists and souvenirs is possible in Rothenburg, it's found in the **Burggarten** (Castle Garden), a fortified castle area that juts out into a bend in the Tauber River. Even better, stroll north along the Tauber for two km to the small village of Detwang.

Dinkelsbühl South of Rothenburg, this town is another treasure trove of cobbled streets and half-timbered houses. In mid-July it celebrates the **Kinderzeche** (Children's Festival), commemorating another legend from the Thirty Years' War, which states that the children of the town successfully begged the invading Swedish troops to leave Dinkelsbühl unharmed. The festivities include a pageant, re-enactments, lots of music and other entertainment.

Nördlingen The town is completely circled by the original 14th century walls, three km long. Climb the church tower for a bird's-eye view. Nördlingen is also within the basin of the Ries, a huge crater created by a meteor more than 15 million years ago. It's one of the largest in existence (25 km in diameter) and was used by US astronauts to train for the exploration of the moon. The **Rieskrater Museum** gives details.

Füssen Although it has a castle of its own, Füssen is primarily visited for the two castles in nearby Schwangau associated with King

GERMANY

Ludwig II. Historians agree that Ludwig was a couple of wursts short of a Bavarian breakfast, and these castles provide a fascinating glimpse into his state of mind. Both are beautifully situated, overlooking mountains and lakes, and can only be visited by guided tour (35 minutes). Go early to avoid the crowds.

Hohenschwangau is where Ludwig lived as a child. More interesting is his own creation, **Neuschwanstein**, which was unfortunately unfinished at the time of his death in 1886. Even so, there is plenty of evidence of his twin obsessions: swans and Wagnerian operas. The fantastic mishmash of Romanesque and other architectural styles inspired Walt Disney's Fantasyland castle.

From Füssen, take the bus from the train station (DM1.90) or walk five km. Both castles are open daily from 8.30 am to 5.30 pm (from 10 am to 4 pm between 1 November and 31 March) and entry costs DM8 (students DM5) for each. There's a great view of Neuschwanstein from the Marienbrücke, south of the castle up Pöllat Gorge. From here you can hike up Tegelberg for even better panoramas.

Places to Stay

Tourist offices in most towns are very efficient at finding accommodation in almost any price range, although private rooms are rarely available for just a single night's stay. All the youth hostels listed below only accept people aged under 27.

Rothenburg For camping, walk to the village of Detwang and follow the signs to *Camping Tauber-Idyll* (☎ 09861-31 77). It's open from March to November.

Rothenburg has two excellent youth hostels, *Rossmühle* (☎ 09861-45 10) at Mühlacker 1, and *Spitalhof* (☎ 09861-78 89), just down the street. Check-in for both is at Rossmühle and beds start at DM13.

Pensions in Rothenburg don't come cheaply, but one pleasant exception is *Pension Hofmann* (☎ 09861-33 71) at Stollengasse 29. Singles/doubles with shower start at DM38/65. *Pension Raidel*

(☎ 09861-31 15), Wenggasse 3, has the cheapest rooms in the old town, for DM30/54 without shower.

Dinkelsbühl Check the IYHF *youth hostel* (☎ 09851-95 09) at Koppengasse 10 for beds at DM14.50. *Pension Lutz* (☎ 09851-94 54), Schäfergässlein 4, has a cheerful owner, excellent breakfasts, and singles/doubles from DM28 per person. The front façade of the *Deutsches Haus* (☎ 09851-60 59), Weinmarkt 3, is one of the town's attractions; singles/doubles start at DM85/120.

Nördlingen The IYHF *youth hostel* (☎ 09081-8 41 09) is at Kaiserwiese 1 and costs DM14.50. Two hotels by the church with singles/doubles for DM25/50 are *Walfisch* (☎ 09081-31 07), Hallgasse 15, and *Zum Goldenen Lamm* (☎ 09081-42 06), Schäfflesmarkt 3. Both these places are OK for food, too, with Walfisch being slightly cheaper.

Füssen The IYHF *youth hostel* (☎ 08362-77 54), Mariahilferstrasse 5, is by the railway tracks, 10 minutes from the station. Dorms cost DM15.50 and curfew is at 10 pm. *Hotel Bayerischer Hof* (☎ 08362-61 88), Bahnhofstrasse 3, is good value with singles/doubles for DM36/60. *Pension Josef Kössler* (☎ 08362-73 04), Kemptener Strasse 42, has beds from DM35 per person.

Places to Eat

Except for the smallest towns, this is one area where it pays to picnic. Most restaurants cater to the hordes of tourists and set their prices accordingly.

Rothenburg Rothenburg really takes this to the extreme, with one exception being the large plates of pasta and pizza (DM8 to DM12) at *Pizzeria Roma*, Galgengasse 19. It's open daily to midnight. Virtually opposite is *Gasthof Zum Ochsen* at No 26; fill up on standard German fare for DM6.50 to DM15.50 (closed Thursday). *Bräustüble*, Alter Stadtgraben 2 near the Kriminal Museum, has daily specials comprising soup, main dish and salad for DM13.50, DM15.50 and DM20.50.

Dinkelsbühl The *Fränkischer Hof* (☎ 09851-23 71), Nördlinger Strasse 10, is acknowledged to be the best place to eat, although it is expensive. At the other end of the scale is the self-service *Königsgrill*, Nördlinger Strasse 27, where nothing is over DM10. For good local food and atmosphere, try *Goldenes Lamm*, Lange Gasse 26-28.

Füssen Grab fast food at *Pic Nic*, Bahnhofstrasse 2. *Pizzeria La Perla*, Drehengasse 44 in the pedestrian zone, has pizza and pasta from DM7 and is popular with families (closed Wednesday). *Gasthaus Torschänke*, Augsburger Tor Platz 2, is not bad for local food (closed Wednesday evening and Thursday).

Getting There & Away
Though Frankfurt is the most popular port of embarkation, Munich is a better choice if you decide to take the bus. The buses heading south are often much more crowded than the ones heading north, making photography and sightseeing less comfortable. The Munich bus joins the Romantic Road proper at Friedberg. To start at the southern end, take the hourly train from Munich to Füssen (2½ hours, DM30).

Getting Around
The Europabus service leaves daily in each direction between Frankfurt and Munich (from mid-March to late October, DM92), and between Würzburg and Füssen (from mid-May to early October, DM85). Each route takes 11 hours and includes short stops in some towns, but it's silly to do the whole thing in one go, particularly as there is no charge for breaking the journey and resuming the next day. Eurail and German Rail passes are valid and Inter-Rail gets 50% discount. Tickets are available for short segments of the trip; alternatively, you can duplicate the route on less crowded local buses.

Driving gives much more flexibility. Car drivers just need to follow the special 'Romantische Strasse' signs. The most popular driving stretches are between Bad Mergentheim and Rothenburg, and Landsberg and Füssen. Parking is very limited in most town centres; many are pedestrian-only.

The distances between towns make walking prohibitive, except for shorter stretches and hikes into the countryside. Biking, however, is perfectly viable; machines can be rented from the train stations in Rothenburg and Füssen. Hitching is not very popular and is fairly frustrating compared to the rest of the country.

NUREMBERG
Nuremberg (Nürnberg) is the capital of the Franconia (Franken) region of northern Bavaria. Though this quintessential medieval German town never seems to cease in its flood of tourists, it's still worth the trip. The funding fathers of the city completely rebuilt Nuremberg after Allied bombs reduced it to rubble on the night of 2 January 1945. That includes the castle and the three old churches in the Altstadt, which were painstakingly rebuilt using the original stone.

Orientation & Information
The train station is right outside the city walls of the old town; the tourist office (☎ 0911-23 36 0) is in the main hall, open Monday to Saturday from 9 am to 7 pm. There's another tourist office at Hauptmarkt 18. The main post office, Bahnhofplatz 1, is by the station. The telephone code for Nuremberg is 0911.

Things To See & Do
The scenic **Altstadt** (old town) is easily covered on foot. The **Handwerkserhof**, a re-creation of the crafts of old Nuremberg, is in front of the station (open from March to December). It's about as quaint as they can possibly make it, but the goods are overpriced. Walk down the main artery, Königstrasse, to the **Lorenzkirche**, noted for the 15th century tabernacle which curls

GERMANY

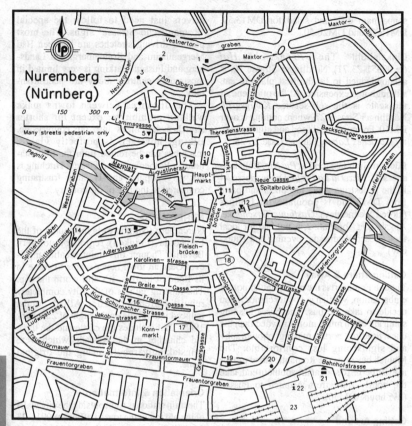

Nuremberg (Nürnberg)

0   150   300 m

Many streets pedestrian only

against a column like a vine, all the way up to the curve of the ceiling.

Continue north to the bustling **Hauptmarkt**. This is the site of the most famous Christmas market *(Christkindlmarkt)* in Germany, lasting from the Friday before Advent to Christmas Eve. The church here is the **Frauenkirche**; the figures around the clock go walkabout at noon.

Near the Rathaus is the **Sebalduskirche**, Nuremberg's oldest church (13th century). Near the altar is the bronze tomb of St Sebaldus; note the giant snails under the platform which for some reason represent resurrection. Next, climb up Burgstrasse to the **Kaiserburg** (Emperor Castle). This location offers one of the best views of the city, and the area near the **Tiergärtnertor** is great for sitting and people-watching.

Head just a bit downhill to the **Dürerhaus**, where Germany's version of the Renaissance Man, Albrecht Dürer, lived from 1509 to 1528. This house made it through WW II and features a ton of stuff from the life of the great painter and man of many other talents (entry DM3, students DM1).

Dürer is also featured in the **Germanisches Nationalmuseum** on Kornmarkt,

1	Youth Hostel
2	Kaiserburg
3	Tiergärtnertor
4	Dürerhaus
5	Alte Küch'n
6	St Sebalduskirche
7	Bratwurst Haüsle
8	Spielzeugmuseum
9	Mensa
10	Tourist Information
11	Frauenkirche
12	Heilig Geist Spital
13	Altstadt & Pizzeria Majorka
14	Café Treibhaus
15	Irish Castle Pub
16	Amaranth
17	Germanisches Nationalmuseum
18	Lorenzkirche
19	Zum Schwänlein
20	Handwerkserhof
21	Post Office
22	Tourist Information
23	Hauptbahnhof

which houses a stunning collection of works by German painters and sculptors. It's open Tuesday to Friday from 9 am to 5 pm (to 9.30 pm Thursday), and Saturday and Sunday from 10 am to 5 pm; entry costs DM4 (students DM1.50) except on Thursday and Sunday evening, when it's free. At Karlstrasse 13-15, the **Spielzeugmuseum** (Toy Museum) offers an enormous display of toys throughout the ages.

Much more sobering is a look at the role of Nuremberg during and after WW II. The city was a hotbed of Nazi activity and rallies before 1945. After the war, it was the site of the trials of Nazi war criminals. Ask the tourist office for the informative pamphlet, *Nürnberg 1933-45*. Nazi rallies were held in the eerily named Zeppelin Field and Mars Field, where nowadays a tourist board-produced film, *Fascination and Force*, is shown between July and October. Get there by S-Bahn or U-Bahn to Dutzendteich, or tram No 9 to Luitpoldhain.

Places to Stay

December is difficult for accommodation because of the Christmas market. Prices are sometimes lower in August when there are no conventions.

Campingplatz Am Stadion (☎ 81 11 22), Hans Kalb Strasse 56, is near the Dutzendteich lakes in the Volkspark, south-east of the centre beyond the B4 ring road – take the U1 from the main train station to Messezentrum, which gets you fairly close. It costs DM6 per person, DM5 per tent and DM5 per car, and is open from 1 May to 30 September.

The excellent IYHF *youth hostel* (☎ 24 13 52) is in the Kaiserburg. Dorms including sheets cost DM23, and reception is open long hours, from 7 am to 1 am. The cheapest option for those aged over 27 is the *Jugend-Hotel Nürnberg* (☎ 521 60 92), Rathsbergerstrasse 300, north of town via tram No 3. Dorm beds start at DM17 and breakfast is DM5. The brand-new *Jugend Economy Hotel* (☎ 92 62 0), south-west of the city centre at Gostenhofer Hauptstrasse 47, has reasonable facilities including games rooms and disco-reject dining room chairs. All rooms are double, starting at DM58, although it's possible to share and just pay half. There is a surcharge for a single night's stay, and prices leap in the high season. Breakfast costs DM4.

The most reasonable pension in the centre is *Altstadt* (☎ 0911-22 61 02), Hintere Ledergasse 2, with singles/doubles for DM45/80. A better deal is the *Hotel Garni Royal* (☎ 53 32 09), Theodorstrasse 9, just outside the eastern edge of the old city. This grand old building has a mock-marble hallway, ample parking round the corner, and spacious rooms, many with TV. Singles/doubles are DM35/70 with free use of hall shower, DM53/89 with shower cubicle in the room, and DM65/105 with *en suite* shower and WC. Extra beds cost DM35 and breakfast is included. Reception shuts at noon on Sunday and holidays, so call ahead. Near the station is *Zum Schwänlein* (☎ 20 51 62), Hintere Sterngasse 11, with functional rooms for DM40/70, including free hall shower.

GERMANY

Places to Eat

The eating and drinking scene in Nuremberg is quite lively. Ask the tourist office for the excellent *Grossstadtdschungel* booklet detailing cafés, bars, restaurants and discos.

Nuremberg is a student town. The university *mensa*, Maxplatz 8, offers lunch daily for DM2.80. Ask a student to buy you a ticket if you have no ID. *Café Treibhaus*, Karl Grillenberger Strasse, is a popular student bar, verging on the arty. Pick up a copy of *Doppelpunkt* here, a free magazine of cultural events. The *Irish Castle Pub*, Schlehengasse 31, has pub food and is small and crowded with live music most nights.

Try Nuremberg's famous sausages at *Bratwurst Häusle*, Rathausplatz 1 (closed Sunday). Interesting potato dishes (DM8.50 to DM19.50) can be chomped at *Alte Küch'n*, Albrecht Dürer Strasse 3. *Pizzeria Majorka*, Hintere Ledergasse 2, has a wide menu including steaks, schnitzels, salads, fish dishes and good pizza and pasta from DM7.50 (closed Monday). Sample more up-market food at *Heilig Geist Spital* (☎ 22 17 61), Spitalgasse 16 Am Hauptmarkt. It offers civilised dining in an excellent spot over the river. There's an extensive wine list (from DM18.50 a bottle), and German main dishes are in the range of DM19 to DM35.

The most interesting and varied place to eat is *Amaranth* at Färberstrasse 11, on the 4th floor. This cavernous modern joint is the city's *gesunde Alternative* (healthy alternative), with lots of creative eating options, and good company. It has specials every day for around DM7.40, and salads at DM1.89 per 100 grams.

Getting There & Away

More-or-less hourly trains run to most towns including Frankfurt (2½ hours, DM55), Stuttgart (2½ hours, DM46) and Berlin (seven hours, DM81). There are two an hour to Munich (1½ hours, DM46) and eight a day to Prague (six hours, DM58.30). Several autobahns converge on Nuremberg, but only the north-south A73 joins the B4 ring road.

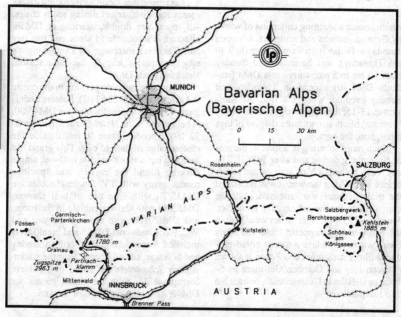

Tickets on the efficient city transport system cost DM2.80 per journey or DM6.10 for a day pass (in the central zone). Family cards are DM7.50.

BAVARIAN ALPS

Though not as tall as some of their sister summits to the south in Austria, the Alpine peaks are just as inspiring on the German side of the border. The Bavarian Alps (Bayerische Alpen) also tend to be a bit less crowded.

Orientation & Information

The Bavarian Alps stretch from Garmisch-Partenkirchen in the west to Berchtesgaden in the east, with lots of open space for exploration in between. It's probably best to use one of these two fairly touristy towns as a base and then head for the mountains. Another possible base is Füssen, west of Garmisch-Partenkirchen; for information on Füssen, see the Romantic Road section.

Garmisch-Partenkirchen is Germany's most visited Alpine resort during all seasons. The tourist office (☎ 08821-18 06), Richard Strauss Platz, is open Monday to Saturday from 8 am to 6 pm, and Sunday and holidays from 10 am to noon. It has excellent brochures and maps of the city and surrounding skiing and hiking areas. For skiing information and schools, try the Skischule Garmisch-Partenkirchen (☎ 08821-49 31), Am Hausberg 8. For mountain climbing and ski touring (cross-country) information, contact Bergsteigerschule Zugspitze (☎ 08821-58 99 9), Dreitorspitzstrasse 13.

In the eastern section of the Alps, popular Berchtesgaden's tourist office is directly opposite the train station (☎ 08652-50 11) on Königsseer Strasse, open Monday to Friday from 8 am to 5 pm, and Saturday from 9 am to noon (daily in the summer).

Things to See

Bavaria's Alpine villages are generally more of a base for four seasons' worth of sports than they are for sightseeing.

Garmisch-Partenkirchen The huge ski stadium on the slopes right outside town has two ski jumps and a slalom course; it hosted more than 100,000 people for the Winter Olympics of 1936. Take a peek at the pink-and-silver chapel of **St Anton**, at the edge of Partenkirchen, and then walk along **Philosophenweg** for incredible Alpine views.

Garmisch can also be used as a base for exploring crazy King Ludwig II's extravagant castles. **Hohenschwangau**, and **Neuschwanstein** are most easily visited from Füssen (see the Romantic Road section for details), although a bus does run from Garmisch (two hours each way, DM21 return fare). **Schloss Linderhof** (open daily, DM7, students DM4) is about equidistant from the two towns. The grounds of this residence are the big draw, particularly the lake with the ludicrous Wagner-inspired golden conch-boat. The return bus fare is DM9.60, or it's 20 km by car.

Mittenwald A great excursion from Garmisch, or an alternative base, is Mittenwald, 18 km towards the Austrian border. It has good hiking possibilities, particularly on Mt Karwendel (2384 metres). Just 100 metres down Bahnhofstrasse from the station sits the lively **Erlebnisbad**. It's a typical German pool setup with a sauna, steam bath and whirlpool. A bit farther along Bahnhofstrasse on the right is the Rathaus and the tourist office (☎ 08823-33 98 1), open Monday to Friday and Saturday morning.

Berchtesgaden In Berchtesgaden, don't miss a tour of the **Salzbergwerk** (☎ 08652-60 02 0). Visitors get to wear the almost doctorlike protective gear of a typical miner before descending into the depths of the salt mine for a tour. It's open from 1 May to 15 October from 8.30 am to 5 pm daily, or 12.30 to 3.30 pm Monday to Saturday during the rest of the year. Admission is DM14 for adults and DM7 for children.

Outside of Berchtesgaden is Hitler's former headquarters at **Obersalzberg**. The six-km bus ride to the **Kehlstein** summit, also known as the 'Eagle's Nest', is one of the most scenic in Germany. Hitler wrote *Mein Kampf* at Haus Wachenfels and turned it into a holiday house ('Berghof') for Nazi leaders. He then built Eagle's Nest as an elaborate retreat (open from late May to early October). It's reached from Berchtesgaden by getting to Obersalzberg-Hintereck (DM5.50 return by bus), taking a special bus to the Kehlstein car park (DM18 return) and then riding an elevator 120 metres to the summit (DM4). For strong walkers, it's only a half-hour walk from the Kehlstein car park to the summit. Once there, the views and walking tours are worth the hassle.

The other great destination out of Berchtesgaden is the **Königssee**, an Alpine lake only five km to the south. It's an enjoyable hour's walk or quick drive (well signposted) out of town, or you can take the bus (DM2.60). Call ☎ 08652-40 26 for information about good boat tours (DM18). The mountains almost enclose the lake and a hiking tour around the perimeter is difficult. However, the hike to Obersee on the far side is worth the sweat.

Activities

Both Garmisch-Partenkirchen and Berchtesgaden are ideal for outdoor pursuits, but Garmisch seems better prepared and organised for the serious adventurer.

Information Garmisch's tourist office offers an incredible number of activities through its *Ferienprogramm* (Holiday Programme) brochure. Seven days of climbing, biking, canoeing and parachuting are in the range of DM500 to DM700. Contact the Garmisch Verkehrsamt at Postfach 1562, D-8100 Garmisch-Partenkirchen.

Another good source is the Olympia Sporthaus at Bahnhofstrasse 8-12. It has an excellent selection of gear and is the base for the Olympia Bergschule (☎ 08821-72091), which offers a popular year-round series of courses and outings, including hiking, mountain climbing, ice climbing, mountain biking and rafting. The well-travelled staff add considerably to the fun of any trip.

Relatively new to Europe, mountain biking is catching on quickly. The Mountain-Bike-Schule Garmisch-Partenkirchen (☎ 08821-7 12 48) at Ludwigstrasse 22 rents bikes and provides information.

Hiking One of the best short hikes directly out of Garmisch is to the Partnachklamm Gorge. It lies between the peaks of Hausberg and Graseck and features a well-trodden path along a ledge, winding above a raging stream and underneath several waterfalls. Take the cable car to the first stop on the Graseck route and follow the signs.

An excursion to the Zugspitze summit, Germany's highest peak (2966 metres), is understandably the most popular outing from Garmisch. There are various ways to get there, including a return trip by rack-railway, summit cable car and Eibsee cable car for DM48; but the best way is by hiking (two days).

Some other summits deserve consideration for hiking, such as Wank, Eckbauer and Hausberg. All are accessible by cable car. The tourist office has an excellent brochure and map for all three, with specific hikes recommended. One of the best hikes (about four hours) is over Gschwandtnerbauer to the Talstation, with incredible views on clear days. For information about the weather up there, call ☎ 08821-7 16 17.

Skiing Garmisch is Germany's ski centre and this is an ideal way to see the Bavarian Alps. There are two major ski areas outside of town: the Zugspitze plateau and the Wank/Eckbauer area. The Zugspitze is less crowded in early November and December and in late spring (April/May). One great trail is the three-km run from the Schnee-fernerkopf at 2874 metres.

Regional daily ski passes cost between DM24 (Eckbauer) and DM48 (Zugspitze). The Happy Ski Card covers the whole area and is available for a minimum of three days (DM116). Rental equipment (about DM28 per day) is available all over town and on the slopes.

For the Zugspitze, the most friendly and inexpensive place is Sepp Hohenleitner's

(☎ 08821-5 06 10), located conveniently at the Zugspitze station. For children, the ski kindergarten (☎ 08821-5 27 29) costs DM7 for half a day.

Places to Stay
Garmisch-Partenkirchen and Berchtesgaden are the best bases for overnighting, but it's also possible to find interesting accommodation in the smaller Alpine villages in between. Most towns have small tourist information offices near the train station that can help with finding rooms, and 'Zimmer frei' signs abound. One problem may be renting a room for less than three nights during busy winter and summer seasons.

Garmisch-Partenkirchen
The nearest Garmisch camping, *Zugspitze* (☎ 08821-31 80), is along highway B24. Take the blue-and-white bus outside the station in the direction of the Eibsee. Rates start at DM6.50 per person and DM8.50 per site, but autumn, winter and spring camping can be pretty harsh. There are six other beautifully situated camping grounds in nearby towns. Ask for the brochure *Camping-Urlaub im Werdenfelser Land* from the tourist office.

The IYHF *youth hostel* (☎ 08821-29 80), Jochstrasse 10 in the suburb of Burgrain, offers kitchen facilities, smelly toilets, an 11.30 pm curfew and beds for DM15. It's closed in November and December. Take bus No 6 or 7 from the station to Burgrain (DM1).

Garmisch is packed with relatively inexpensive pensions and private rooms. Try *Haus Buchwieser* (☎ 08821-20 84) at Mitterfeldstrasse 2, or *Haus Cenci* (☎ 08821-47 15), next door at No 4. Both places have great balconies and friendly people, and cost around DM30 per person. There is a minimum stay of at least two days. Most guesthouses that accept single-nighters bump up the price. A good exception is *Haus Lichtenstern* (☎ 08821-37 77), Herbststrasse 15, which has rooms for DM30 per person with free hall shower.

For convenience to the station, ignore the inhospitable *Vier Jahreszeiten* and veer to the right for the much friendlier *Alpengruss* (☎ 08821-26 16), Gehfeldstrasse 10. It has attractive rooms with private shower for DM55 per person. The tourist office has a list of *Ferienwohnungen* (holiday homes) for longer stays.

Mittenwald
Try *Gästehaus Franz Brandtner* (☎ 08823-16 50) at Mauthweg 7, or his brother *Manfred Brandtner* (☎ 03323-58 32) next door. The former offers skiing and hiking tours and the latter has horse stables. They both start at DM35 per person.

Berchtesgaden
In-town camping is available, but a more natural option is to head for the Königssee's two camping grounds: *Grafenlehen* (☎ 08652-41 40) and *Mülleiten* (☎ 08652-45 84); both cost around DM8 per person and DM7 per place.

The IYHF *youth hostel* (☎ 08662-21 90) is in the Strub part of town, at Gebirgsjägerstrasse 52. It costs DM15 and closes in November and December.

Like Garmisch, Berchtesgaden has lots of private rooms. One of the friendliest is *Haus Bergwald* (☎ 08652-25 86) at Duftbachweg 3-5, which costs DM35 per person with shower, or DM26 without. *Watzmann*, a family-run inn on Franziskanerplatz 2, by the single-spire church, has doubles with private shower for DM98 (DM136 in summer), and singles without for DM36. It closes in November and December. *Betriebe* (☎ 08652-50 46), Seestrasse 29, in nearby Königssee, has singles/doubles from DM46/90.

Places to Eat
Garmisch-Partenkirchen
Because it's a tourist town, Garmisch can be expensive. However, Germans and Americans alike head to what they call *'The Cheap Chicken'*, behind Marienplatz at Griesstrasse 1 (open daily to 8 pm). This otherwise nameless, often crowded cafeteria (there's more seating upstairs) serves grilled chicken for DM5.50, French fries for DM2.70, and 0.5 litres of draught Löwenbräu for only DM2.90. Opposite at No 4 is *Schranne*, with

GERMANY

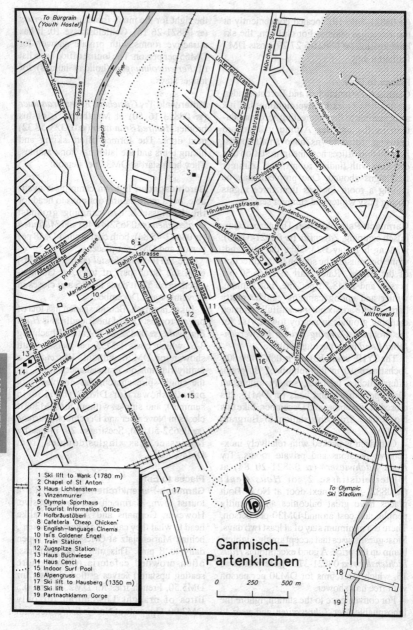

1   Ski lift to Wank (1780 m)
2   Chapel of St Anton
3   Haus Lichtenstern
4   Vinzenmurrer
5   Olympia Sporthaus
6   Tourist Information Office
7   Hofbräustüberl
8   Cafeteria 'Cheap Chicken'
9   English-language Cinema
10 Isi's Goldener Engel
11 Train Station
12 Zugspitze Station
13 Haus Buchwieser
14 Haus Cenci
15 Indoor Surf Pool
16 Alpengruss
17 Ski lift to Hausberg (1350 m)
18 Ski lift
19 Partnachklamm Gorge

To Burgrain
(Youth Hostel)

Garmisch–
Partenkirchen

To Olympic
Ski Stadium

To Mittenwald

0   250   500 m

good local cuisine and a daily salad buffet (DM5.90). It's closed Thursday.

One of the best restaurants in town is *Isi's Goldener Engel* (☎ 08821-56 67 7), Bankgasse 5, complete with outside frescoes and stags' heads. Even at DM15 to DM40 per dish it's good value (open daily).

For picnics, call at *Vinzenmurrer* on Bahnhofstrasse at the Rathausstrasse corner. Assemble your own sandwich or salad at the deli counter or use the cheap cafeteria section. It's open weekdays to 6 pm, and Saturday morning. After a day's activity, go to the *Hofbräustüberl* at Bahnhofstrasse 59. Its grilled platter for two at DM38 will replace any calories burned, and the Löwenbräu at DM3.90 won't hurt either (open daily to 11 pm).

Mittenwald At Hockstrasse 14 is the cheap *Grill Shop*, opposite at No 11 is a kebab shop, and two doors down is *Osteria* for pizza and pasta from DM7. On the corner is a supermarket.

Berchtesgaden Over in Berchtesgaden, prices are as high as the Alps. Assemble a picnic, or fill up on fast food at *Express Grill*, Maximilianstrasse 8 (open daily to 7 pm). *Watzmann* (see the previous Places to Stay section) serves large portions of local fare for around DM15. *Gasthaus Bier-Adam*, Marktplatz 22, offers Bavarian specialities for DM12 to DM27, and a three-course daily special for DM19.

Getting There & Away

Garmisch-Partenkirchen is serviced from Munich by hourly trains (1½ hours, DM23). There's a special same-day return fare of DM30 on Tuesday, Thursday, Saturday and Sunday. The A95 is the direct road route. Trains from Garmisch to Innsbruck (DM14.10) pass through Mittenwald.

Hourly trains also connect Munich and Berchtesgaden (2½ hours), although Berchtesgaden is more easily reached from Salzburg, from where there are buses, trains, and even organised half-day tours. By road,

Berchtesgaden is south of the Munich-Salzburg A8 autobahn.

Getting Around

If not driving already, the Bavarian Alps might be the perfect place in Germany to rent a car for a few days. Both hub towns have several car rental agencies. Avis (☎ 08821-55 06 6), Hindenburgstrasse 35, Garmisch, has Opel Corsas at DM50 per day with unlimited km. Also in Garmisch, try Traffic (☎ 08821-50 16 8), St Martin Strasse 6. The public transport system in this region, however, is also excellent, and various organised tours are available. Owing to the mountain geography, the bus network is more extensive than the train service.

BAVARIAN FOREST

Like the Harz Mountains to the north, the Bavarian Forest (Bayerischer Wald) is mostly visited by Germans, even though it's the largest continuous mountain forest in all of Europe. Near the Czechoslovak border, a trip here has the feel of a new frontier compared to the rest of Germany. Go out of your way to get in some hiking, but don't get too excited about the downhill skiing possibilities. English is not very widely understood.

For information on Regensburg and Passau, see the Danube River section in Baden-Württemberg.

Orientation & Information

Most Germans agree that the traditional and ideal base for exploring the heart of the Bavarian Forest is Zwiesel, a valley town devoted to the forest surrounding it. Zwiesel's Kurverwaltung (☎ 09922-96 23) is in the centre of town, about one km from the station at Stadtplatz 27. It has lots of free brochures, maps and helpful hints for the entire area.

The tourism headquarters (☎ 08552-20 85) for the Bavarian Forest is in Grafenau at Freyungerstrasse 2. Another excellent information source is in Neuschönau at the Hans-Eisenmann Haus (☎ 08558-13 00) at Böhmstrasse 35. Ask them (or almost anyone else) about the effects of acid rain.

GERMANY

Things to See & Do

Zwiesel With 10,000 inhabitants, Zwiesel sits on the banks of the rushing Schwarzer Regen (Black Rain) River, between the Great Arber (1456 metres), the Falkenstein (1313 metres) and the Rachel (1453 metres).

It has an excellent **Waldmuseum** (Forest Museum) that covers the area's forests and its wood and glass products. Entry costs DM3 (students DM2, children DM1) and opening times are Monday to Friday from 9 am to 5 pm, and Saturday and Sunday from 10 am to noon and 2 to 4 pm. Hours are slightly reduced in winter.

An essential excursion for the tour buses is to the **Bayerwald-Bärwurzerei Hieke** (☎ 09922-15 15), two km out on Frauenauer Strasse at No 80. It has no less than 26 Bavarian schnapps specialities that you can try as well as buy. There's also a background film in three languages, music cassettes and souvenirs. *Die lustige Opa* (The merry Grandfather) and the female version, *Die lustige Oma*, are popular, potent brews (25% to 40% by volume).

Along with schnapps, glass is also an important product of the area. You can see locals blowing glass and purchase the wares

in many places, such as at Zwieseler Kunst-glasbläserei Gerhard Krauspe, Frauener Strasse 10, right in the centre of town.

Hiking & Skiing South of Zwiesel is a 130-sq-km national park. It's a paradise for the outdoors enthusiast and a refreshing respite from the more touristy Bavarian Alps or Black Forest.

The hiking is always good. Aside from tourist offices, a good place for planning is Sport Schmatz (☎ 09922-14 74) at Regener-strasse 4, Zwiesel. Besides selling gear, it can provide lots of information and programmes for hiking (or skiing, though that is always unpredictable) throughout the Bavarian Forest.

There are several long-distance hiking routes, with mountain huts along the way. The most famous (and most difficult) is the Nördliche Hauptwanderlinie, a 180-km trek from Furth im Wald to Dreisesselberg. It's gorgeous and worth the 10 days it takes. The Südliche Hauptwanderlinie is its shorter sister at 105 km, while the 50-km trek from Kötzting to Bayerisch-Eisenstein is the quickest way to see lots of the Bavarian Forest.

Cross-country skiing is available almost everywhere. Zwiesel's tourist office details routes leaving directly from town. For fairly sedate downhill skiing, the Breitenau area, with the Geisskopf at 1100 metres and the Einödriegel at 1150 metres, has six lifts and lots of support facilities.

Places to Stay
Zwiesel is an ideal overnight base for excursions into the Bavarian Forest. *AZUR Camping* (☎ 09922-18 47) is one km from the train station, near public pools and sports facilities. Head left from the station down Äussere Bahnhofstrasse and follow the signs. The small IYHF *youth hostel* (☎ 09922-10 61), Hindenburgstrasse 26, costs DM13. If you want to stay in the middle of the Bavarian Forest, try the IYHF *Wald-häuser* (☎ 08553-3 00) at Herbergsweg 2, 17 km out of Grafenau.

As with any German sporting town,

Zwiesel is packed with pensions and apartments. One unique possibility is *Pension Waldeck* (☎ 09922-32 72) at Ahornweg 23 (they'll pick you up at the train station), near Zwiesel's sports complex and with a nice view. This health-conscious pension features vegetarian cooking, no smoking and a child-friendly environment. It's a great place for exploring the Hennenkobel mountains, and costs DM44 to DM50 per person for half board.

If you want some flexibility, head to *Pension Bergfeld* (☎ 09922-95 53), Hock-strasse 45, which charges around DM50 per person. Nearby, the *Ferienhaus Bergfeld* (☎ 09922-26 36), Kolpingstrasse 9, charges DM51 to DM110 per person for apartments accommodating two to six people. Solicitous and excellent value is *Pension Haus Inge*, (☎ 09922-10 94), Buschweg 34, offering comfortable rooms with balcony and private shower/WC for DM35 per person. Dinner (three courses) is just DM6 extra.

Places to Eat
Zwiesel has a genuine bargain in *The Big Chicken* at Bergstrasse 1. It's family oriented, friendly and cheap. Burgers are DM2.90 to DM8.95, and full meals are DM7 to DM12. It's closed on Fridays. *Pfeffer Bräustüberl*, Regener Strasse 6 (closed Tuesday), has Bavarian food and cheap beer (the brewery is opposite) for DM2.80 per half-litre.

Try Balkan specialities at *Restaurant Nepomuk*, Stadtplatz 30. Dishes are DM7 to DM17 and it has a salad buffet (DM2.50 to DM5 per plate). *Zwieseler Hof Hotel-Restaurant*, Regener Strasse 5, has a comfortable ambience despite the plastic plants. The extensive menu (DM9 to DM24) includes fish, lamb and Bavarian dishes.

Getting There & Away
Only one railway line runs through the region, providing local trains approximately hourly. From Zwiesel, trains go south to Plattling (DM12.60) with connections to Munich, Nuremberg and Passau. The direct bus from Zwiesel to Passau (DM9) is much

cheaper than the train. Less frequent trains go north to Bayerisch-Eisenstein on the Czechoslovak border (DM4.20), with connections to Prague. Various travel agents in Zwiesel offer cheap bus excursions to Prague. From Plattling, the A92 goes directly to Munich.

Getting Around

Other than private transport, the bus is the way to get around. Most routes, however, are only covered a couple of times daily. It's a conservative area and hitching is not very widespread.

Baden-Württemberg

With recreational centres like the Black Forest (Schwarzwald) and Lake Constance (Bodensee), and towns like the medieval jewel of Heidelberg and the health spa of Baden-Baden, prosperous Baden-Württemberg is one of Germany's main regions for tourism.

The modern state of Baden-Württemberg was created in 1951 out of three smaller regions: Baden, Württemberg and Hohenzollern. Baden was first unified and made a grand duchy by Napoleon Bonaparte, the person also responsible for making Württemberg a kingdom in 1806. Both areas, in conjunction with Bavaria and 16 other states, formed the Confederation of the Rhine under French protection, part of Napoleon's plan to undermine the might of Prussia. Baden and Württemberg sided with Austria against Prussia in 1866, but were ultimately drafted into the German Empire in 1871.

STUTTGART

Stuttgart enjoys the clout of being Baden-Württemberg's state capital and the hub of its industries. Lacking historical monuments, Stuttgart nevertheless attracts visitors with its impressive museums and air of relaxed prosperity. At the forefront of Germany's economic recovery from the

■ PLACES TO STAY	
8	Youth Hostel
12	Pension Märklin
14	Alte Mira
15	Hotel Wartburg
16	Schwarzwaldheim

▼ PLACES TO EAT	
4	Le Buffet (Hertie Department Store)
5	Mensa
6	Restaurant Marché
9	Urban Stuben
13	Stuttgarter Kellerschenke
16	Schwarzwaldheim
18	Zur Kiste
19	Weinhaus Stetter
20	Iden
21	Taverna Litfass bei Ali

OTHER	
1	Hauptbahnhof
2	Omnibusbahnhof
3	Tourist Office
7	Staatsgalerie Stuttgart
10	Neues Schloss
11	Post Office
17	Altes Schloss

ravages of WW II, Stuttgart started life somewhat less auspiciously, as a stud farm.

Orientation & Information

The Hauptbahnhof and the adjoining Omnibusbahnhof are immediately to the north of the central pedestrian shopping street, Königstrasse. The tourist office (☎ 2 22 80), Königstrasse 1, is opposite the station. Opening hours are Monday to Saturday from 8.30 am to 9 pm, and Sunday from 11 am to 6 pm (1 to 6 pm from October to April). Room reservations incur no fee. The main post office is at Lautenschlagerstrasse 17, and there is a branch at the train station with longer hours (to 10 or 11 pm daily). American Express (☎ 2 08 90) is at Lautenschlagerstrasse 3.

The telephone code for Stuttgart is 0711.

Stuttgart

0   200   400 m

Stadtgarten

Oberer Schloss-garten

Mittlerer Schloss-garten

To Nuremberg

Schloss-platz

Akademie-garten

Schiller-platz

Karls-platz

Markt-platz

To Karlsruhe

To Munich

Things to See & Do

Stuttgart is where 'the ordinary meets with the unusual, the profane with the poetic, and where down-to-earth common sense and the fiery impatience of the adventurous mind meet in a harmonious manner to form a perfect union.' That's according to the *Stuttgart '92* booklet from the tourist office. You can try looking for this strange synthesis (sorry, 'perfect union') in the **Schloss-garten**, an area of parkland and ponds in the city centre, complete with swans, street entertainers and modern sculptures. At the north end it stretches beside the railway

tracks to the **Wilhelma** zoo & botanical gardens (open daily, DM8, students DM4). At the south end it emcompasses the sprawling Baroque **Neues Schloss** (now government offices), and the Renaissance **Altes Schloss**, housing the **Württemberg-isches Landesmuseum** (free, closed Monday).

Adjoining the park, at Konrad-Adenauer-Strasse 30, is the city's best art gallery, the **Staatsgalerie Stuttgart** (free, closed Monday). The new section concentrates on modern art and has a good selection of Picassos; the old section (closed until around April

1993) has works from the Middle Ages to the 19th century.

Motor Museums The motor car was first developed by Gottlieb Daimler and Carl Benz at the end of the 19th century. The impressive **Mercedes-Benz Museum** (☎ 172 25 78) tells the story of their partnership and achievements via recorded commentary and numerous gleaming vehicles. It's open Tuesday to Sunday from 9 am to 5 pm (free entry). Take S-Bahn No 1 to Neckarstadion. It's larger and more fun than the equivalent **Porsche Museum**, open Monday to Friday from 9 am to noon and 1.30 to 5 pm (free). Take S-Bahn No 6 to Neuwirkshaus.

Better than either museum is a factory tour where you can view the whole production process from unassembled components to completed cars. Porsche does two each weekday in English (free) which you may be able to join at short notice (☎ 827 53 84), but it's best to reserve six weeks ahead. Write to: Dr Ing hc F Porsche, Besucherservice, Frau Schlegl, Postfach 400640, D-7000 Stuttgart. The Mercedes-Benz tour is easier to get on as it's out of the city at the Sindelfingen factory. Contact the museum for information.

Places to Stay

Camp at *Campingplatz Stuttgart* (☎ 55 66 96), by the river at Mercedesstrasse 40, 500 metres from Bad Cannstatt S-Bahn station. The IYHF *youth hostel* (☎ 24 15 83), Haussmannstrasse 27, is a signposted, 15-minute walk east of the main station. Beds cost DM17.50/22.50 for juniors/seniors, reception is shut from 9 am to noon, and there is an 11.30 pm curfew. The *Jugendwohnheim* (☎ 24 11 32), north of the centre at Richard-Wagner-Strasse 2, charges DM35/60 for singles/doubles.

Hotels & Pensions Breakfast is included unless stated. Near the U-14 'Mineralbäder' stop is *Gästehaus garni Bronni* (☎ 33 52 66), Stierlenstrasse 2, with basic singles/doubles for DM35/60. Book ahead for the plain but

central *Pension Märklin* (☎ 29 13 15), Friedrichstrasse 39. Singles/doubles start at DM35/80 with free hall shower and no breakfast. Also without breakfast are the double rooms for DM80 in *Schwarzwaldheim* (☎ 29 69 88), Fritz-Elsas-Strasse 20. There's a rough-and-ready restaurant downstairs with daily specials for DM7 to DM13.

More comfortable yet still lacking any frills are the rooms at *Alte Mira* (☎ 29 51 32), Büchsenstrasse 24. Singles/doubles with shower unit in the room start at DM75/125, or with free use of hall shower from DM55/90. Look for Balkan specialities in the restaurant downstairs. *Hotel Wartburg* (☎ 204 54 50), Lange Strasse 49, is a mid-range, comfortable hotel. All rooms have TV and radio, and parking is no problem. Singles/doubles for DM67/112 are a bargain – until, that is, you feel the need to take a nonexistent shower. Rooms with private bath or shower start at DM98/225.

Places to Eat

Look out for the Swabian speciality, *Maultaschen* (meat and spinach inside pasta envelopes). The cheapest food is at the student *mensas*, Holzgartenstrasse 11 and Pfaffenwaldring 45. Lunches are DM2.90 and student ID is not rigorously checked.

Le Buffet, with main dishes from DM8 and salad at DM1.79 per 100 grams, is the best of the department-store *restaurants* along Königstrasse. It's inside the Hertie department store, where there's also a supermarket. The Mövenpick *Restaurant Marché*, Königstrasse 16, is another good buffet-style restaurant, open daily from 8 am to 11 pm. Vegetarian self-service fare can be found at *Iden*, Eberhardstrasse 10, open Monday to Friday from 11 am to 8 pm and Saturday from 10 am to 4 pm.

Stuttgarter Kellerschenke, Theodor-Heuss-Strasse 2A, is downstairs in an anonymous grey block. It's unpretentious and friendly and offers Swabian specialities from DM9. Daily specials including soup cost DM8.90, DM10.90 and DM12.50, and it's open Monday to Friday from 10 am to midnight. The unassuming exterior of

Weinstube Zur Kiste (☎ 24 40 02), Kanalstrasse 2, belies the wholehearted attention to quality within. It's small, busy and open weekdays and Saturday lunch time. Main meals are DM15 to DM28. *Urban Stuben*, on the corner of Urbanstrasse and Eugenstrasse, is a dark and cosy wine place with predominantly vegetarian dishes (DM15 to DM30).

Head to *Weinhaus Stetter*, Rosenstrasse 32, for light meals and a wide selection of wines from DM3.10 per 0.25 litre (closed Sunday). *Taverna Litfass bei Ali*, Eberhardstrasse 35, has a young clientele and live music on Friday and Saturday. Food costs DM6 to DM25 and it's open daily from 11.30 am to 5 am.

Getting There & Away

Stuttgart has an international airport south of the city. There are frequent trains to all German cities and many international destinations. Every two hours trains leave for Milan (8½ hours) via Zürich (three hours, DM100). Of the more than 30 daily trains to Munich (2½ hours, DM61), most continue to Salzburg (four hours). Two to three trains an hour run to Frankfurt (DM54).

The A8 from Munich to Karlsruhe passes by Stuttgart, as does the A81 from Würzburg south to Lake Constance. There is a Mitfahrzentrale (☎ 6 36 80 36) at Lerchenstrasse 65.

Getting Around

Bus A runs from the train station to the airport every 20 minutes (DM6.10, children DM2) between 5 am and 11.30 pm. On city transport, normal singles start at DM2.30, though very short journeys (check this on the ticket machine) are DM1.40. One-day passes are a hefty DM13, the same price as a one-day family card valid for up to four adults (two children count as one adult). Rail passes are valid on suburban S-Bahn lines.

HEIDELBERG

The magnificent castle and medieval old town of Heidelberg are magnets drawing hordes of tourists. Add a sizeable student population (attending the oldest university in the country) and a huge American military presence (the USA's European headquarters is just outside the city centre), and you soon get an idea of what a sardine feels like. If you have a choice, avoid visiting in July and August.

Heidelberg has always been a popular haunt, although it was all but destroyed by invading French troops in 1693. The USA's Mark Twain began his European travels here and recounted his comical observations in *A Tramp Abroad*. Britain's J M W Turner loved Heidelberg and it inspired him to produce some of his greatest landscape paintings.

Orientation

Arriving in Heidelberg's Hauptbahnhof is a bit of a letdown. Expectations of a quaint medieval town don't jive with the modern western side of the city where the train station sits. That changes by heading down Kurfürsten-Anlage to the old town. Romantic Heidelberg is now in session.

The Hauptstrasse is the main street in the centre, stretching from Bismarckplatz to Karlsplatz, two km east. It's a nice orientation walk past old buildings, shops, bars and restaurants. Yet wherever you are in the city, the castle seems to loom in the distance, drawing an endless stream of tourists.

North of the Neckar River is the Philosophenweg ('Philosopher's Way'). It's great for pictures and pondering. Hegel got quite philosophic while roaming these paths.

Information

The tourist information office (☎ 06221-2 77 35) is directly outside the Hauptbahnhof. Its room-finding service costs DM3. The staff are very helpful when they're not busy, and quite curt when they are (July and August). Opening hours are 9 am to 7 pm Monday to Saturday throughout the year, plus Sunday from 10 am to 6 pm March to October and 10 am to 3 pm in November and December.

There's a smaller tourist information office at the funicular railway station up at the castle, open from 10 am to 5 pm daily.

GERMANY

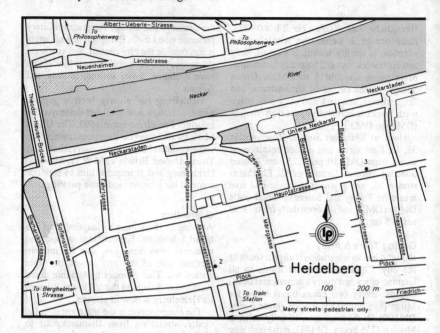

PLACES TO STAY

17 Jeske Hotel
19 Zum Ritter
28 Hotel Zum Pfalzgrafen

PLACES TO EAT

5 Weisser Bock
8 Schnookeloch
10 Südpfanne
11 Zum Roter Ochsen
12 Zum Sepp'l
21 Café Journal
25 Mensa

OTHER

1 Bismarckplatz
2 Institute of Natural Sciences
3 Palatinate Museum
4 Marstall
6 Zum Mohren
7 Kleiner Mohr
9 Neckarmünzplatz
13 Karlsplatz
14 Kornmarkt
15 Rathaus
16 Marktplatz
18 Church of the Holy Ghost
20 Jürgen Belz
22 Students' Jail
23 Old University
24 Universitätsplatz
26 University Library
27 Jesuit Church & Former
    Seminary
29 Castle Funicular Railway
30 Castle
31 Schloss Station & Tourist
    Information

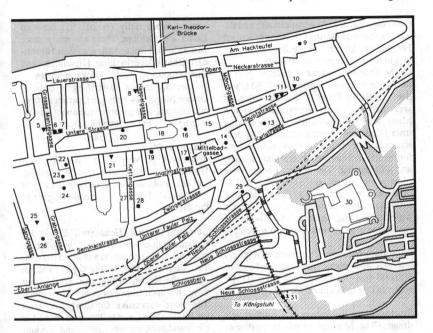

Money You can change money in the train station, but rates are better at the post office. Many money-changing facilities in the city centre offer rip-off tourist rates.

Post & Telecommunications The main post office is just outside the station and to the right. Heidelberg's telephone code is 06221.

Dangers & Annoyances Be careful with belongings around the Hauptbahnhof and the crowded Hauptstrasse and castle. The police can be reached on ☎ 52 00.

Things to See & Do
Castle The large castle (Schloss) is Heidelberg's big draw and for good reason. It's one of Germany's finest examples of a Gothic-Renaissance castle, even if it's mostly in ruins. You can take the funicular railway from the Kornmarkt (DM3.50 return), or it's an undemanding 10-minute walk.

Admission is free if you just want to roam the grounds and explore the **Rondell** (great view) and the gardens. There is a fairly dull guided tour of the interior (DM4, students DM2), but do see the **Grosses Fass** (Great Vat), an enormous 18th century keg holding 221,726 litres (DM1, students DM0.50, or part of the guided tour). The **Deutsches Apothekenmuseum** (German Pharmaceutical Museum) does a good job of recalling earlier times (DM3, students DM1.50). All parts of the castle are open daily.

Farther up the mountain from the Schloss is the **Königstuhl** funicular station, where there's a **children's park** (Märchenparadies) with figures from *Grimm's Fairy Tales*, and much more. It's a great outing.

University The **Universitätsplatz** is dominated by the 18th century **Alte Universität** (Old University) and the **Neue Universität** (New University). Head south down Grabengasse to the **University Library** and

GERMANY

then down Plöck to Akadamiestrasse and the old **Institute of Natural Sciences**. Robert Bunsen, the inventor of the Bunsen burner, taught here for more than 40 years.

The **Studentenkarzer** (students' jail) is on Augustinergasse, open daily (DM1, students DM0.70). From 1778 to 1914 this jail was used for overly uproarious students. Many 'convicts' passed their time by carving inscriptions and drawing on the walls. Sentences (usually two to 10 days) were earned for heinous crimes such as drinking, singing and womanising. The drinking bouts were often at one of the student taverns still in existence (see the Places to Eat section that follows). Other popular student pastimes were fencing and duelling. The **Marstall** is the former arsenal, now a student refectory.

Palatinate Museum This contains regional artefacts and works, plus the jawbone of 600,000-year-old Heidelberg Man (DM3, students DM1.50, closed Monday).

Photography Heidelberg is a shutterbug's dream. The Marktplatz offers postcard-perfect photo opportunities, containing the 15th century Church of the Holy Ghost and the Rathaus. The Schloss is at a nice angle looking up from the Kornmarkt; if there is a full or nearly full moon, this is a great spot in the early evening. For a more panoramic shot of the city, try the Philosophenweg, the northern quays of the river, or up on the Königstuhl's TV tower.

Hiking Heidelberg's tourists can wear you down, but it's easy to escape. The Philosophenweg is the perfect retreat, offering great views of the Altstadt and the Schloss. There are also many hiking excursions in the nearby mountains. Ask for maps at the tourist office. The Hohlerkästenbaumweg hike from Königstuhl is highly recommended.

Around Heidelberg Excursions to the Neckar Valley are popular. One great way to begin exploration of the area is to visit **Neckarsteinach** and its four castles. Boats (DM14 return) leave from Heidelberg

several times daily (☎ 201 81) between Easter and October. There are many more castles in the Neckar Valley, such as **Hirschorn Castle** overlooking Hirschorn, and **Burg Homberg** outside Neckarzimmern.

Sporting goods store Jürgen Belz at Untere Strasse 24 sells gear, arranges trips and courses, and gives advice about adventure travel in the surrounding area.

Places to Stay
You don't get very good value for your Deutschmarks here, and finding anything can be a problem. Arrive early in the day or book ahead. Prices are generally higher in the summer.

Camping Camping Haide (☎ 06223-21 11) is about eight km east of the city by the river, and costs DM5 per person and DM5 per tent. Take bus No 35 from Bismarckplatz and get off at the second orthopaedic clinic from town. It's open from Easter to 1 November. The more expensive Camping Neckartal (☎ 80 25 06) is across the river from the clinic and back towards town about one km; the owner is unfriendly.

Hostels The IYHF youth hostel (☎ 41 20 66), Tiergartenstrasse 5, is often packed with young students getting down in the disco room. Dorms are DM15.50/18.50 for juniors/seniors. The doors are locked from 9 am to 1 pm, and there's an 11.30 pm curfew. Its cheap snackbar is open to 11 pm. Take bus No 33 from the station or Bismarckplatz. After 8 pm, you need to take tram No 1 to the Chinese clinic and then bus No 330.

More a hostel than a hotel, the legendary Jeske Hotel (☎ 2 37 33) is ideally situated at Mittelbadgasse 2. The moody Frau Jeske crams two to five beds in smallish rooms at DM20 per person without breakfast.

Pensions & Hotels All places listed here include breakfast.
Astoria (☎ 4 52 64), Rahmengasse 30, is in a quiet residential street north of the river. Singles/doubles start at DM55/100. Cheap and in the centre is Weisser Bock (☎ 2 22 31),

Grosse Mantelgasse 24, with rooms from DM50/85, though the owner could use some lessons in how to smile. Also good value in the centre is *Hotel Zum Pfalzgrafen* (☎ 2 04 89), Kettengasse 21. Rooms are DM85/115 with private shower, DM50/80 without. The ageing *Hotel Elite* (☎ 2 57 34), Bunsenstrasse 15, has reasonable rooms from DM50/75, but expect prices to be at least DM10 higher after renovations are completed. Just down the road, *Kohler* (☎ 2 43 60), Goethestrasse 2, has better appointed rooms from DM60/82.

With base prices so high, you don't need to pay much extra for a higher standard of accommodation. *Hotel Anlage* (☎ 2 64 25), Friedrich Ebert Anlage 32, has good singles/doubles from DM85/125, all with shower/WC, cable TV and comfortable chairs. Private parking is available. The 16th century *Hotel Zum Ritter* (☎ 2 42 72), Hauptstrasse 178, is the most attractive building on Marktplatz. Rooms start at DM115/200 with private bath or shower and WC. It has definite charm, and the corridors and lift areas contain interesting objects to divert the attention.

Places to Eat

One would think a student town would mean cheap eating, but unfortunately, free-spending tourists outweigh frugal scholars. Unless you can bluff your way into the *mensa* (meals DM2.90), try the self-service restaurant in the *Horten* department store on Bismarckplatz or look for the fast-food joints along Hauptstrasse. For sit-down food, Bergheimer Strasse, west of Bismarckplatz, is a much cheaper street than Hauptstrasse. *Tengelmann* supermarket is at Bergheimer Strasse 57.

Zum Roter Ochsen at Hauptstrasse 217, and *Zum Sepp'l* at No 213 next door, are historic student dens that have been usurped by tourists. They are entertaining and lively, but the food and drink are a bit pricey. *Schnookeloch* at Haspelgasse 8 is similar but better. It opened in 1407 and has been serving big plates of food ever since. It's usually crowded, so expect to share a table and a song or two with the piano player. The 'Schnookeloch-Platte' at DM73 for two should keep you full for at least two days. Another place to try for filling food is *Südpfanne* at Hauptstrasse 223. All these student pubs are open daily to around midnight, except Roter Ochsen which is closed Sunday.

Try international and Italian dishes in the informal environment of *Stadt Bergheim*, Bergheimer Strasse 23 (open daily to midnight); pizzas with generous toppings start at DM7. *City China Restaurant*, Bergheimer Strasse 41 (open daily), has excellent-value midday specials for DM8, and evening dishes for around DM15. More up-market, the brasserie of the plush *REGA Hotel*, Bergheimer Strasse 63, has well-prepared local and international dishes in the range of DM24 to DM31. Starve yourself for three days prior to pigging out at the all-you-can-eat Sunday brunch (DM39) in the *Atrium Restaurant* of the Holiday Inn Crowne Plaza, Kurfürsten-Anlage 1.

Thanks to the large student population, you'll see lots of vegetarian entrées on menus. The *Weisser Bock* at Grosse Mantelgasse 24 has some meatless dishes starting at DM9. Open weekdays only is the *Vegetarisches Restaurant*, Kurfürsten-Anlage 9.

Entertainment

Along with any of the student pubs mentioned above, the best place to head in the evening is Untere Strasse. Cafés and bars line the street, which gets and stays active late into the night. One of the best spots is *Gasthaus Zum Mohren* at No 5-7, or its little sister, *Kleiner Mohr*, next door.

Cafés filled with readers, talkers, thinkers and posers also abound. One of the best is *Café Journal* at Hauptstrasse 162. You can linger for hours over a cup of coffee, read the English-language magazines, and fill up on decent food. It's open daily from 8.30 am to midnight.

Getting There & Away

Heidelberg is on the Castle Road route from

Mannheim to Nuremberg. Buses run daily in summer. Enquire at Deutsche Touring GmbH (☎ 069-7 90 30), Am Römerhof 17, Frankfurt. Train connections are excellent, with at least hourly departures to: Frankfurt (DM21, takes one hour), Stuttgart (DM26, 45 minutes), Baden-Baden (DM18.60, one hour), Munich (DM82, three hours) and Nuremberg (DM60, 3½ hours). The north-south A5 connects Heidelberg to Frankfurt and Karlsruhe.

Getting Around

Bismarckplatz is the main transport hub. The bus and tram system in and around Heidelberg is extensive and efficient. Single tickets are DM2.40; a better deal is the 24-hour pass for DM7 within the city or DM11 and DM15 to include the outskirts. For car rental, try AVM (☎ 2 13 77), Bergheimer Strasse 125, which has weekend rates from DM119 (including 1000 km). Bicycle rental is available in the station (from April to October).

Car parking can be a nightmare in Heidelberg. The tourist office map gives the locations of city parking garages, which are clearly signposted and open 24 hours daily but often full in summer.

BADEN-BADEN

Taking a cure in affluent Baden-Baden is one of those splurges all visitors to Germany should consider. But plan on much more than a quick sit in some therapeutic water. This is a fully fledged health spa, offering lots of sports and other healthy activities.

Baden-Baden became fashionable in the 19th century when it attracted the likes of Victor Hugo and King Edward VII of Britain. Even today it boasts more resident millionaires than any other German town.

Orientation

The train station is an inconvenient four km north-west of town, but buses run frequently to Leopoldsplatz, the heart of Baden-Baden. Almost everything is within walking distance of this square. Sophienstrasse leads east to the more historic part of town. North of Sophienstrasse are many baths, the

Stiftskirche and the Neues Schloss. Across the river to Goetheplatz, it's a short stroll to the Kurhaus with the Spielbank (casino), and the Trinkhalle (pump room).

Information

The Kurverwaltung (☎ 07221-27 52 00), Augustaplatz 8, is one of the best tourist offices in the country. Set in appropriately elegant park surroundings, the friendly staff members are really into promoting the spa facilities. It even has a TV room and reading room with English-language newspapers. Opening hours are Monday to Saturday from 9 am to 10 pm, Sunday and holidays from 10 am.

Ask about the various programmes on offer, such as the three-day 'Caracalla-Therme' package starting at DM163, including spa visits and accommodation. Other packages, worthwhile for longer stays, include dancing, hiking, tennis, horse riding, golf, gymnastics, wine tasting, ballooning and yoga. There is a visitors' spa tax (*Kurtaxe*) of DM4 (central zone) or DM1.50, entitling you to a *Kurkarte* from your hotel which is good for various discounts. It doesn't apply to the youth hostel.

Money Deutschmarks (and lots of them) rule this town, and it's easy to change money or just use credit cards. The train station has a small money-changing office.

Post & Telecommunications The main post office is on Leopoldsplatz. Baden-Baden's telephone code is 07221.

Emergency Call the police on ☎ 69 00 – they could use a little excitement. Call ☎ 2 22 22 for medical emergencies.

Dangers & Annoyances The biggest danger in this subdued town is spending too much money.

Things to See & Do

For a real taste of Baden-Baden, head for the **Trinkhalle** at Kaiserallee 3. Here, in an ornate setting, the springs of Baden-Baden dispense curative drinking water (DM2, open from Good Friday to 1 November). Next door is the **Kurhaus** from the 1820s, which houses the obscenely opulent **Casino** (guided tours daily, DM3). The **Neues Schloss**, on the hill, offers a good view and a small historical museum (open from April to October, closed Monday, DM2).

Spas Baden-Baden's water was renowned back in Roman times. On Römerplatz are the **Römische Badruinen** (Roman Bath Ruins). Don't bother with the boring tour, just peer in through the glass. Either side are

the two leading places where you can currently take the waters: the **Friedrichsbad** (☎ 27 59 21) at Römerplatz 1, and the **Caracalla-Therme** (☎ 27 59 40) at Römerplatz 11. A visit to one (or both) is an experience not to be missed.

The 19th century Friedrichsbad is ornately Roman in style and operates under a set programme called 'The Roman Irish Bath', that leaves you feeling scrubbed, lubed and loose as a goose. Your two hours of bliss consist of a timed series of hot and cold showers, saunas, steam rooms and baths. One highlight is the all-too-short, eight-

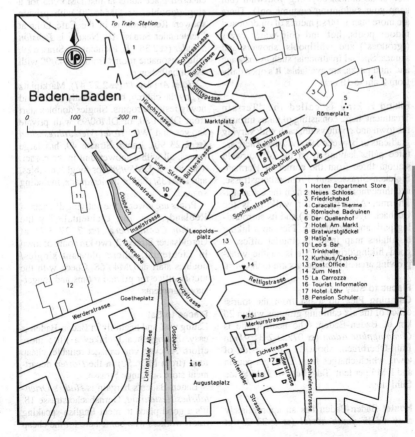

Baden–Baden

0   100   200 m

To Train Station

1 Horten Department Store
2 Neues Schloss
3 Friedrichsbad
4 Caracalla–Therme
5 Römische Badruinen
6 Der Quellenhof
7 Hotel Am Markt
8 Bratwurstglöckel
9 Hatip's
10 Leo's Bar
11 Trinkhalle
12 Kurhaus/Casino
13 Post Office
14 Zum Nest
15 La Carrozza
16 Tourist Information
17 Hotel Löhr
18 Pension Schuler

GERMANY

minute, soap-and-brush massage. At the end of the session they wrap you in a blanket for a half-hour of rest.

No clothing is allowed inside, and several of the bathing sections are mixed on most days, so leave your modesty at the reception desk. It costs DM38, or DM34.20 with the Kurkarte. If you tell them you're staying at the hostel, it costs DM32. The baths are open Monday to Saturday from 9 am to 10 pm. Mixed bathing is on Wednesday and Saturday and from 4 pm on Tuesday and Friday.

The Caracalla-Therme opened in 1985. You pay DM18 for a two-hour visit and are free to do almost anything you want (but keep your swimming costume on!). There are more than 1700 sq metres of outdoor and indoor pools, hot and cold-water caves ('grottoes') and whirlpools, showers and saunas. Special treatments, such as massage and mud packs, are available. It's open daily from 8 am to 10 pm.

Hiking Hiking is called the 'Terrain Treatment' here, consisting of paths through the town and countryside, each with varying gradients of between 1% and 20%. There are three paths leaving from the Merkurwald station, three from the corner of Herman-Sielcken-Strasse and Fremersbergstrasse, and three more departing near the Caracalla-Therme. Also good for walking is the Oosbach river (the 'Oos') and its surrounding park and promenade. Pick up a hiking highlights map from the tourist office. A good hiking/driving tour is to the wine-growing area of Rebland, six km to the west.

Places to Stay

Camping Pick up a list from the tourist office of the six camping grounds within 25 km of Baden-Baden. The nearest site is *Campingplatz Adam* (☎ 07223-2 31 94) in Bühl-Oberbruch, about 12 km outside of town, which charges from DM5 per person and DM5 per tent. Take bus No 7135 to the Bühl stop.

Hostel Baden-Baden has an appropriately ritzy IYHF *youth hostel* (☎ 5 22 23) at Hardbergstrasse 34. From the station, take bus No 1 to Grosse-Dollen- Strasse and walk up the hill. It's about two km from the town centre and costs DM17/22.50 for juniors/seniors. The main hassle is the restricted check-in time: between 5 and 6 pm, and at 8 or 10 pm on the dot. The nearby outdoor pool is a bargain for DM3.

Hotels & Pensions Spa paradise isn't cheap and this is really seen in the hotel prices. Breakfast is usually included.

The best bet in town is *Hotel Löhr* (☎ 2 62 04) at Adlerstrasse 2, off Augustaplatz. This cheerful place starts at just DM35/65 for a single/double, or DM45/70 with private shower. Reception is in the Café Löhr at Lichtentaler Strasse 19. Nearby is *Pension Schuler* (☎ 2 36 19), Lichtentaler Strasse 29, with reasonable rooms from DM45/90 with use of hall shower.

Hotel Am Markt (☎ 2 27 47), Marktplatz 17, by the church, has a friendly owner and newly restored rooms. Singles/doubles start from DM44/80, or DM60/95 with private shower and WC. *Hotel Vier Jahreszeiten* (☎ 2 23 90), Lange Strasse 49, has large rooms, all with a shower unit in the corner. The cost is DM59/98 for singles/doubles, and DM135/188 for triples/quads, including spa tax.

Prices are lower in the outlying districts of Rebland, Oos and Lichtental. Try the *Gasthof Cäcilienberg* (☎ 7 22 97) at Geroldsauer Strasse 2, two km south of town in Lichtental, where pleasant singles/ doubles start at DM40/68. Check with the tourist office for private rooms and longer-stay apartments.

Places to Eat

Eating well and healthily in Baden-Baden is easy. Eating cheaply takes a little more effort. As ever, you can get reliable, cheap food (from MD6.50) in the *Horten* department store on Lange Strasse.

Baden-Baden's bargain is *Hatip's Orientalishes Restaurant*, Gernsbacherstrasse 18. It's a good place to meet English-speaking resort workers who come here for the cheap beer (DM3.50 for half a litre). Smallish portions of spaghetti bolognese or curry are just DM6.50, plus there are kebabs and various vegetarian dishes.

At Rettigstrasse 1 is *Zum Nest* (☎ 2 30 76), one of Baden-Baden's few secret gourmet splurges (closed Tuesday). It features three menus daily for DM18 to DM25 which are creative, well prepared and well presented; in season, the asparagus ranks with any in the region. The Best Western *Der Quellenhof* restaurant on Sophienstrasse has a good salad bar: DM8.50 for a small plate or DM9.50 for a large plate. For good Italian food in a family restaurant, wander over to *La Carrozza*, Merkurstrasse 3, where dishes start at DM8. It's open to midnight (closed Sunday).

A youngish clientele gathers at *Warsteiner Brasserie*, Kaiserallee 4, with its colourful, stained-glass ceiling and loud background music. Daily specials are DM9 to DM12 and it's open daily to 1 am. *Bratwurstglöckel*, Steinstrasse 7, offers typical German food (DM10 to DM20) in a much quieter environment. It's open to midnight (closed Tuesday).

Entertainment
Baden-Baden isn't exactly a partying town, but there are the expensive discos *La Fontaine* and *Tiffany* on Luisenstrasse. People-watching is fun along Lichtentaler Allee and the Oos, or in the chic confines of *Leo's Bar* at Luisenstrasse 8.

Getting There & Away
Baden-Baden is on the main north-south corridor. Trains leave every hour to most important destinations, including Freiburg (DM24), Basel (DM38), Stuttgart (DM28) and Heidelberg (DM19, direct or via Karlsruhe). The town is also close to the north-south A5 autobahn. Access the westward A8 at Karlsruhe.

The hub for city transport is Augustaplatz. One-zone, single rides are DM2, or it's DM5 for a 24-hour pass.

BLACK FOREST
Yes, there are lots of tourists roaming the Black Forest (Schwarzwald), but it's easy to leave the busy areas far behind. Home of the cuckoo clock, the moniker 'Black Forest' comes from the dark canopy of evergreens. It's an ideal hiking region. The fictional Hansel and Gretel encountered their wicked witch here, but 20th century hazards are rather more ominous. The Black Forest looks as lush as ever, but experts will tell you it is slowly being destroyed by acid rain. Enjoy it while you can.

Orientation & Information
The Black Forest lies east of the Rhine between Karlsruhe and Basel. It's roughly triangular in shape, about 160 km long and 50 km wide. Baden-Baden, Freudenstadt and Freiburg act as the unofficial capitals for Black Forest information and excursions. Most of the towns in the area have excellent tourist information offices. Freudenstadt's tourist office (☎ 07441-86 40) is at Lauerbadstrasse 5. See also the previous Baden-Baden section and the Freiburg section that follows. Some regions, such as Glottertal, offer a Guest Card which is good for local discounts.

Things to See
Though taking advantage of the countryside will be the main focus, there's still lots of history and culture to explore in the region. For Baden-Baden and Freiburg, check the individual sections for recommendations.

Halfway between Baden-Baden and Freudenstadt along the Schwarzwald-Hochstrasse, the first major tourist sight is the **Mummelsee** south of the Hornisgrinde peak. It's a small, deep lake steeped in folklore (legend has it that an evil sea king inhabits the depths). If you want to escape the busloads, hike down the hill to the peaceful and inappropriately named **Wildsee**.

Farther south, the friendly town of **Freudenstadt** is mainly used as a base for excursions into the countryside. Be sure to visit the central marketplace, which is the largest in Germany and great for photos.

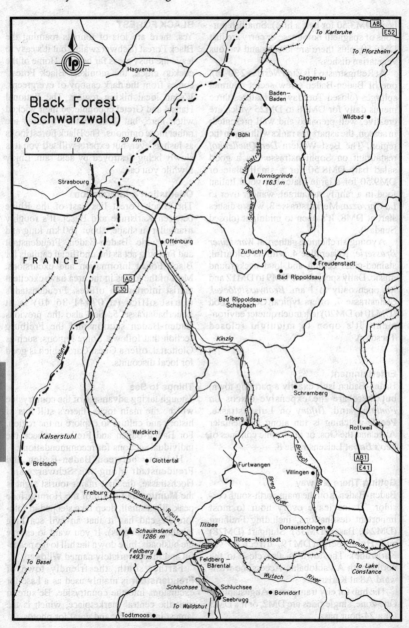

Black Forest (Schwarzwald)

0   10   20 km

Haguenau

Gaggenau

Baden-Baden

Wildbad

Bühl

Hornisgrinde 1163 m

Strasbourg

FRANCE

Offenburg

Zuflucht

Freudenstadt

Bad Rippoldsau

Bad Rippoldsau–Schapbach

Kinzig

Kaiserstuhl

Waldkirch

Schramberg

Breisach

Glottertal

Triberg

Rottweil

Freiburg

Höllental Route

Furtwangen

Villingen

Rhine

Schauinsland 1286 m

Titisee

Feldberg 1493 m

Titisee-Neustadt

Donaueschingen

Danube

Feldberg–Bärental

To Basel

Schluchsee

Wutach River

Schluchsee

Bonndorf

Seebrugg

To Waldshut

To Lake Constance

Todtmoos

To Karlsruhe

To Pforzheim

A8 E52

A5 E35

A81 E41

Hochstrasse

Schwarzwald

Breg

Breg River

Brigach

To Basel

GERMANY

The area between Freudenstadt and Freiburg is cuckoo clock-country, and a few popular stops are **Schramberg, Triberg** and **Furtwangen**. If you simply must have a cuckoo clock, this is the area in which to buy one. In Furtwangen, visit the **Deutsches Uhrenmuseum** (German Clock Museum) for a fascinating look at the traditional Black Forest skill of clockmaking.

Triberg has many clock shops along Hauptstrasse, including the extensive **Haus der 1000 Uhren** (House of 1000 Clocks). The town's **Schwarzwald-Museum** (Black Forest Museum) at Wallfahrtstrasse gives a vivid introduction to history and life in the region (open daily except mid-November to mid-December, DM4). Triberg's famous **waterfall** is worth the trek from the parking area near Gutach Bridge. The pretty falls hurtle down 162 metres over seven stages. In the summer you're charged DM2 to see it, but you can avoid this by entering from the hiking trails above and to the sides.

Activities
Four-season outdoor sports are as organised here as anywhere in Europe. Allow enough time to do the area justice. Tourist offices can provide maps and further information.

Hiking The possibilities are almost endless, but there are a few hikes especially worth pursuing. In the north, the popular **Westweg** is a trail marked by red diamonds that runs parallel with the Schwarzwald-Hochstrasse. Take this trail from Baden-Baden to Freudenstadt. The entire Westweg (280 km) actually goes all the way to Basel. Other popular long-distance trails include the **Mittelweg** (220 km) and the **Ostweg** (240 km).

The southern Black Forest is best in the **Feldberg** area. Small hiking towns dot the landscape and many are used as bases by knowledgeable Germans getting off the well-worn Black Forest trails. Head for Todtmoos or Bonndorf for a true Black Forest hiking holiday. The 10-km gorge outside Bonndorf, the **Wutachschlucht**, is justifiably famous.

Winter Sports The area around the **Titisee** is a major centre for winter sports. The Feldberg (1493 metres) features fairly uncrowded downhill skiing (day pass DM30). There are 18 lifts in the area. Cross-country skiing is basically anywhere you can find snow, but many Germans take cable cars to higher ground and then start from there. For skiing information, contact the tourist information office in Feldberg (☎ 07655-80 19) at Kirchgasse 1. If you just need area conditions and understand German, call ☎ 07676-12 14.

Places to Stay
Camping Some of the best camp sites in Germany can be found here. Particularly recommended spots include: *Campingplatz Weiherhof* (☎ 07652-14 68) on the Titisee; the *Wolfsgrund* camping ground (☎ 07656-77 39) on the Schluchsee; *Camping Langenwald* (☎ 07441-28 62), three km outside of Freudenstadt; and *Schwarzwald-Camping-Alisehof* (☎ 07839-2 03) in the centre of the Black Forest near Bad Rippoldsau-Schapbach.

Hostels The youth hostel situation is equally impressive in the south, though there's less choice in the north. Some convenient hostels include: the *Jugendherberge* (☎ 07667-76 65), Rheinuferstrasse 12, Breisach, in the Kaiserstuhl region; *Hebelhof* (☎ 07676-2 21), Passhöhe 14, on the Feldberg; the non-IYHF *Europäisches Jugendgästehaus* (☎ 07674-4 10) in tiny Todtmoos; the very receptive IYHF *Triberg* (☎ 07722-41 10) at Rohrbacher Strasse 37 (unfortunately closed for renovations from spring 1993 to summer 1994); and the sterile *Jugendherberge Freudenstadt* (☎ 07441-77 20) at Eugen-Nägele-Strasse 69 in Freudenstadt.

If you're hiking the Westweg, be sure to include a stay at the *Naturfreundehaus* (☎ 07226-238) in Plättig/Bühlerhöhe, or the *Jugendherberge* (☎ 07804-611) in Zuflucht. Both places are an ideal base for exploring the area.

Hotels The problem with the hotel industry

GERMANY

in the Black Forest is that it caters for mid
and top-range budgets. Some exceptions are:
Seebrugg's *Pension Berger* (☎ 07656-2 38)
along the Schluchsee (DM25 per person);
Triberg's *Hotel Bären* (☎ 07722-44 93),
Hauptstrasse 10 (DM30 per person), and
Gasthaus Schwarzwaldstüble (☎ 07722-33
24), Ober-Vogt-Huberstrasse 25A (DM37
per person); and Freudenstadt's friendly
Gasthof See (☎ 07441-26 88) at Forststrasse
15 (DM36 per person), near the Stadt-
bahnhof train station. Also in Freudenstadt,
try the similarly priced *Hotel Gasthof
Jägerstüble* (☎ 07441-23 87), Marktplatz
12.

The Black Forest is ideal for longer stays,
with holiday apartments and private rooms
available in almost every town. Enquire at
tourist offices.

Places to Eat
Black Forest treats include ham *(Schwarz-
wälderschinken)* and the famous cherry
cake. But restaurants are often expensive,
something you can offset by picnicking
whenever possible.

In the Kaiserstuhl region north-west of
Freiburg, splurge on the regional feasts of
venison (DM12 to DM45 per person) at the
Hotel Post, Neutorstrasse 1, Breisach. Along
the main Talstrasse in the Glottertal region is
the *Goldenen Engel*, which serves a *Stu-
dentenschüssel* ('student bowl') for
DM14.50, comprising a huge plate of local
grub. Virtually opposite, *Hirschen* has a
similar deal (DM12.50).

In ultra-touristy Titisee, check *Hirsch-
stüble* (☎ 07651-84 86), tucked away near
the church on Im Winkel. It has evening
specials for DM12.50 (and double rooms for
DM65). Farther north in Triberg, try *Krone*,
Schulstrasse 37, for German dishes from
DM12, or go Italian at *Sonne*, Hauptstrasse
27.

Gasthof See (see the previous Places to
Stay section) is one of Freudenstadt's best
eating deals (shut Wednesday). Also good is
Gasthof Kaiser, Schulstrasse 9, just off the
main square, with lunch-time specials from
DM10 (shut Saturday).

Getting There & Away
The north-south train route makes entering
and leaving the region very easy. Trains run
hourly between Karlsruhe and Basel, calling
at Baden-Baden and Freiburg en route. There
are also easy rail connections to some of the
hub towns from Strasbourg, Stuttgart and
Constance. Road access is good too, with the
A5 skirting the western side of the forest and
the A81 the eastern side.

Getting Around
Rail connections are excellent for a
mountainous area. Lines run between
Baden-Baden, Freudenstadt and Freiburg.
The prettiest stretch (called the 'Höllental
Route') runs from Freiburg to the lake at
Titisee. It's fun but a bit overrated.

Where the rail fails to go, the bus system
usually provides the way. Distances can have
little to do with travel time, due to rugged
terrain, and buses don't run as frequently as
in the rest of the country. Get schedules and
ask about regional passes if you're going to
be in a certain area for more than a couple of
days. Cycling is a good way to get about,
despite the hills (rental in Baden-Baden and
Freiburg train stations).

Drivers enjoy flexibility in an area that
rewards it. The main tourist road, the
Schwarzwald-Hochstrasse (B500), runs
from Baden-Baden to Freudenstadt and
Triberg to Waldshut. Other thematic roads to
explore are the Schwarzwald-Bäderstrasse
(spa town route), Schwarzwald-Panor-
amastrasse (good views) and Badische
Weinstrasse (wine route).

FREIBURG
The centre of the southern Black Forest,
Freiburg (full name: Freiburg im Breisgau)
has a modern, relaxed feel, yet retains many
traditional features, such as the monumental
13th century cathedral. Freiburg was ruled
by the Austrian Habsburgs for many centuries, and suffered severe bombing damage in
WW II. Besides being a gateway to the Black
Forest, one of the city's most alluring features is the large, thriving university
community.

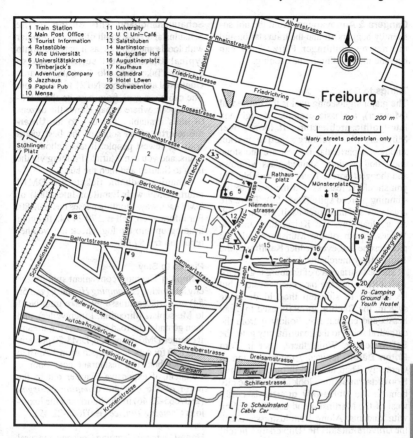

Freiburg

0   100   200 m

Many streets pedestrian only

1 Train Station
2 Main Post Office
3 Tourist Information
4 Ratsstüble
5 Alte Universität
6 Universitätskirche
7 Timberjack's
   Adventure Company
8 Jazzhaus
9 Papula Pub
10 Mensa
11 University
12 U C Uni–Café
13 Salatstuben
14 Martinstor
15 Markgräfler Hof
16 Augustinerplatz
17 Kaufhaus
18 Cathedral
19 Hotel Löwen
20 Schwabentor

To Camping
Ground &
Youth Hostel

To Schauinsland
Cable Car

GERMANY

Orientation

The train station is a convenient 10 minutes' walk west of the city centre which is dominated by the red cathedral. All the sights are within walking distance. Take Eisenbahnstrasse to the tourist information office and the bustling pedestrian zone.

Information

The tourist information office (☎ 0761-36 89 00), Rotteckring 14, is open Monday to Saturday from 9 am to 9.30 pm, and Sunday and holidays from 10 am to 2 pm. Closure times from 1 November to 30 April are brought forward to 6 pm weekdays, 3 pm Saturday and noon Sunday. Pick up the excellent official guide (DM4). The office has a free room-finding service, or you can use the information board at the entrance.

Money The train station has an extended-hours bank, but the rates are better at the post office (money exchange to 6 pm).

Post & Telecommunications The main post office, Eisenbahnstrasse 58-62, is open daily from 8 am to 8 pm. Freiburg's telephone code is 0761.

Dangers & Annoyances Avoid the not-so-friendly beggars around the train station and the nearby Stühlinger Platz. They can become intimidating in the evening.

Things to See

The major sightseeing goal is the **cathedral** (Münster), a classic example of high and late-Gothic architecture. It looms over Münsterplatz, Freiburg's active market square. Of particular interest are the stone and wood carvings, stained-glass windows and the west porch. Tours are available, but you should at least ascend the tower to the stunning pierced spire (DM1.50). There are great views of the church itself, Freiburg and, on a clear day, the Kaiserstuhl and the Vosges. South of the Münster stands the picturesque and even redder **Kaufhaus**, the 16th century merchants' hall.

The pedestrian area of Freiburg is great for walking. Notice the pavement mosaics but be careful to sidestep the old drainage system, the **Bächle**, formerly used to clean beasts and combat fire. Follow it from the cathedral south to the beautiful city gate, the **Schwabentor**. While there, peer in **Zum Roten Bären**, reputedly the oldest inn in Germany. Then head north on the restored **Konviktstrasse** for a look at some fine city homes. The **University quarter** is northwest of the Martinstor and usually bustling with students. Along Bertoldstrasse, check the **Universitätskirche** (University Church) and then walk round the back to the picturesque Rathausplatz.

The Museum of Modern Art, the Museum of Ethnology, the Museum of Natural History and the Augustiner Museum are all in the vicinity of Augustinerplatz. They're free, closed on Monday, and worth a wander on a rainy day.

Activities

After a tour of the city, the Black Forest beckons. Timberjack's Adventure Company (☎ 37934), Moltkestrasse 5, is a good source of camping equipment, courses and Black Forest information.

Schauinslandbahn This outing to the Schauinsland Peak south of town is popular with locals and tourists, as it gets them into typical Black Forest surroundings so quickly. Take tram No 2 south towards Günterstal and then bus No 21 to Talstation. The cable car goes from here up the 1286-metre peak, where a map shows the dozens of trails available. The trek to the **Untermünstertal** offers some of the best vistas with the fewest people. It takes about five hours, and you can return to Freiburg via the train to Staufen and then the bus.

Schauinslandbahn tickets are DM14 return (DM9 with Eurail or Inter-Rail) or DM8 each way. Monthly passes cost DM80. For information, call ☎ 2 79 24 24. To avoid heading up into the fog, check the weather report on ☎ 1 97 03.

Places to Stay

Camping The most convenient spot for the city and hiking is *Camping Hirzberg* (☎ 3 50 54) at Kartäuserstrasse 99. Take tram No 1 to Messeplatz (direction: Littenweiler), and then go under the road and across the stream. It charges DM6 per person, DM3.50 per tent, DM3.50 for cars, and is open from 1 April to mid-October. The restaurant next door is excellent, if expensive. Farther out to the north of the city are *Camping Breisgau* (☎ 07665-23 46) in Hochdorf, and the luxurious *Camping Tunisee* (☎ 07665-22 49).

Hostel Out near Camping Breisgau, the rural IYHF *youth hostel* (☎ 6 76 56), Kartäuserstrasse 151, is often full with groups of German students, so phone ahead. Take tram No 1 to Römerhof (direction: Littenweiler) and follow the signs down Fritz-Geiges-Strasse. Beds cost DM17/22.50 for juniors/seniors. Reception is open all day and there is an 11.30 pm curfew.

Hotels & Pensions You need to pay extra for a convenient location. The cheapest central option is *Pension Schemmer* (☎ 27 24 24), Eschholzstrasse 63 behind the train station, where singles/doubles cost DM40/66, or it's DM70 for a double with a shower. If you can spend more, go to *Hotel Restaurant Löwen* (☎ 331 61), Herrenstrasse 47. Rooms have character and it's right in the middle of town. Rooms with private shower are DM75/120, or DM60/90 without. The double for DM150 is huge.

Several viable places are on Breisgauer Strasse (take tram No 1 to Padua-Allee in the direction of Landwasser). *Gasthaus Hirschen* (☎ 821 18) at No 47 has immaculate singles/doubles for DM40/70, or DM65/90 with private shower. The owner's brother runs *Hirschengarten Hotel* (☎ 803 03) at No 51. Rooms with private shower and cable TV start at DM75/95. Both places share off-road car parking. Down the road at No 62 is *Hotel Löwen* (☎ 846 61) with rooms from DM40/70.

Perhaps the best deal is at *Lydia Kalchtaler's* (☎ 671 19), Peterhof 11 in Kappel. Friendly Lydia charges DM18/36 for singles/doubles without breakfast (but there is a kitchen) in her typical Black Forest farmhouse. Take tram No 1 to Littenweiler and then bus No 17 to Peterhof.

Places to Eat

Because it's a university town, Freiburg can mean cheap eats. Pasta and pretzels are popular. Take advantage of the numerous cheap street-side takeaways while you can, as Black Forest food is more expensive.

Try at least one filling meal at the university *mensas*: Rempartstrasse (Monday to Saturday lunch times) and Hebelstrasse (dinners). Meal tickets cost DM3.50 and no-one seems to worry if you're not a German student.

For more exciting fare and company, try trendy *Brasil* at Wannerstrasse 21 (open daily to at least midnight). It has dozens of salads and creative, pseudo-South American dishes ranging from DM6 to DM15. The Pasta Loco for only DM7.50 is especially tasty.

Freiburg has its share of vegetarian restaurants. The *Salatstuben*, Loewenstrasse 1, has a wide choice of salads for DM1.89 per 100 grams. It's open to 8 pm on weekdays and 4 pm on Saturday. For reliable German food in typical surroundings (despite the green neon sign), go to *Ratsstüble*, Universitätsstrasse 4. Daily specials are around DM14 to DM19 (closed Sunday).

With money to spend, go to *Markgräfler Hof* (☎ 325 40), Gerberau 22. The unassuming exterior conceals a bacchanalian bonanza for wine buffs. Prices start at DM25 for a bottle, but there are hundreds of vintages dating back to 1934, topped off by a 1961 Bordeau Château Pétrus for a mere DM3300. The food is German prepared in a French style, with main dishes for DM25 to DM45. It's open Tuesday to Saturday from noon to 3 pm, and 7 to 10pm; reserve ahead.

If you want a typical Freiburg student hang-out, head for the *Papula Pub* at Moltkestrasse 30. It offers a special of pizza and beer (DM6.50) every day from 3 to 5.30 pm, and excellent plates of pasta only cost DM6.50 to DM10.

There are other good student joints all around the university. The *UC Uni-Café*, on the corner of Universitätsstrasse and Niemanstrasse, is bright and popular, serving drinks, snacks and build-your-own breakfasts.

Entertainment

The *Jazzhaus* at Schnewlinstrasse 1 is one of Germany's hottest jazz clubs, with live jazz every night (from DM10) and appearances by internationally acclaimed artists. Get schedules from the tourist office or call the Jazzhaus on ☎ 3 49 73.

Freiburg is a great place to buy and taste the local wines of the Baden region. The best times for this are late June for the five days of *Weintagen* (Wine Days), or mid-August for the nine days of *Weinkost* (Wine Fare).

Getting There & Away

The nearest airport is at Mulhouse in France (take the A36). Because it's directly on the north-south train corridor, getting to and from Freiburg is easy. Frequent trains depart for Basel (DM14.80), Baden-Baden (DM24), Freudenstadt (DM31) and Donaueschingen (DM16.80).

The north-south A5 autobahn linking

Frankfurt and Basel passes by Freiburg. This is an easy hitching route, though you could also resort to the Mitfahrzentrale (☎ 367 49) at Belfortstrasse 55.

Getting Around

The bus-and-tram network is very efficient. Single rides cost DM2.50 but it makes sense to get a 24-hour ticket (valid for two adults and four children) for DM6.50, or a 48/72-hour pass for DM9/12. Freiburg also has an excellent 'environmental protection ticket' valid for a calendar month on regional and city transport. It costs just DM49 and is transferable.

DANUBE RIVER

The Danube (Donau), one of Europe's great rivers, rises in the Black Forest. In Austria, Hungary and Romania it is a mighty, almost intimidating waterway, but in Germany it is narrower and more tranquil, making it ideal for hiking, biking and motoring tours.

Orientation & Information

The Danube flows from west to east through central Europe, finally finding an outlet in the Black Sea. Donaueschingen is recognised as being the source of the river proper, though Furtwangen, on the Breg River, claims to be the source of its water – a rivalry that helps stimulate tourism to both places.

Donaueschingen has a tourist office (☎ 0771-38 34) at Karlstrasse 58, open weekdays, plus Saturday morning in summer. Another good information source is Southern Cross Travel in the Donaueschingen hostel (see the following Places to Stay & Eat section). The Danube leads northeast to attractive Regensburg; its tourist office (☎ 0941-5 07 21 41) is in the Altes Rathaus, open daily. The river then sweeps south-east and exits Germany at Passau, which has a tourist office (0851-3 51 07) at Rathausplatz 3 (open weekdays and summer weekends), as well as an information centre for the town and Upper Austria in the Hauptbahnhof.

Things to See & Do

Donaueschingen To mark the source of the Danube, the town has a **Donauquelle** (Danube Source) monument in the park of the Fürstenberg Schloss. This arbitrarily positioned pool points out that it's 2840 km to the Black Sea. However, the two tributaries that meet one km down the path, the Brigach and the Breg, rise farther from the Black Sea. Both these rivers are worth exploring.

Regensburg Medieval Regensburg has less impact than some of the towns on the Romantic Road, yet it also lacks the packaged feel of those places. Dominating the skyline is the vast, twin-spired **cathedral** with fine stained-glass windows, statues and stonework balconies around the windows. Guzzle some free beer on the brewery tour of the **Fürstliches Brauerei Thurn und Taxis** (☎ 0941-504 80), Galgenbergstrasse 14, open Monday to Friday – reserve ahead.

Passau Situated at the confluence of the Danube, Inn and Ilz rivers, Passau is a delight. Admire the view from the 13th century **Oberhaus** fort, which also contains the **Cultural History Museum** (closed Monday and all February, DM3, students DM1.50). The Baroque **St Stephan's Cathedral** is very impressive and houses the world's largest church organ (17,388 pipes). Recitals can be heard at noon between mid-May and October, except Sunday (DM3, students DM1).

Cycling The most popular activity is to follow the course of the river. This can be done by car or on foot, but perhaps the most enjoyable way is by bicycle. There is a cycle track *(Donauradweg)* running the entire way from Ulm to Passau and beyond into Austria. The sections from Donaueschingen to Ulm are either complete or under construction. Ordinary roads can easily be used where the cycle track is not finished.

Bikes can be rented in the summer from the train stations in Ulm, Regensburg and Passau and returned to any of the others. It's

possible to send your pack ahead on the train.
Bikes can also be rented for DM12 per day
from Donaueschingen's Southern Cross
Independent Hostel (see the following
Places to Stay & Eat section), which can also
arrange car and camper van rental at low
rates.

Places to Stay & Eat
Donaueschingen The excellent *Southern
Cross Independent Hostel* (☎ 0771-3327),
Josefsstrasse 13, is newly opened and run by
an ex-traveller who knows what people want
and is prepared to provide it cheaply. Beds
cost DM15 including a light breakfast, and
the dorms are always open. There are kitchen
facilities, a common room with a bar, and
various organised outings. The owner,
Martin, also runs Southern Cross Travel on
the premises, offering cheap worldwide
flights.

The best place for those seeking a greater
level of comfort is *Hotel-Restaurant Ochsen*
(☎ 0771-4044), Käferstrasse 18. Good
singles/doubles including shower, WC, TV,
radio, breakfast and use of the swimming
pool are DM65/95.

Eat cheap snacks (Wurst DM3) and meals
(spaghetti bolognese DM6.50) at *SB Restaurant*, Käferstrasse 16, open Monday to
Friday. Traditional Black Forest cooking can
be sampled at *Hotel Schützen* on Josef-
strasse. The three-course menu starts at
DM12, a better bargain than the double
rooms for DM135. The eat-all-you-can
Sunday brunch at the plush, modern *Carlton
Hotel*, Hagelrainstrasse 15-23, is a good deal
at DM35.

Regensburg Camp at the *Campingplatz*
(☎ 0941-268 39), am Weinweg 40 (adults
DM5, tent and car DM6.50). The IYHF
youth hostel (☎ 0941-574 02), Wöhrdstrasse
60, costs DM15 for juniors only (closed in
December). *Stadlerbräu* (☎ 0941-856 82),
Stadtamhof 15, has singles/doubles for
DM24/48, some with private shower (otherwise it's DM2 for the shower key). It's also
a good place to eat, with German dishes for
DM8 to DM15. The restaurant and hotel are

closed on Sunday. By the river is the
Wurstküche, Goldene-Bärenstrasse, a 12th
century hut with a frantic turnover of grilled
Wurst and sauerkraut (from DM4.80, open
daily to 7 pm).

Passau There's camping at the *Zeltplatz*
(☎ 0851-414 57), Halser Strasse 34. The
IYHF *youth hostel* (☎ 0851-413 51) is in the
castle; dorms are DM15 for juniors only.
Pension Weisses Lamm (☎ 0851-22 19),
Theresienstrasse 10, has the cheapest
singles/doubles in town at DM27/47.
Gasthof zum Hirschen (☎ 0851-362 38), Im
Ort 6, has rooms for DM30/55, and good
local dishes in the restaurant from DM10.50.
Beer is just DM3 for half a litre.

The *Kaufhalle* department store on
Bahnhofstrasse has a cheap restaurant and
takeaway. For refined dining within
muralled walls, go to the *Passauer Ratskeller* (☎ 0851-26 30), Rathausplatz 2
(dishes from DM12 to DM25, open daily).

Getting There & Away
Donaueschingen is on the Constance-
Freiburg train route. Regensburg has good
rail connections to Munich (DM46), Frankfurt (DM55) and Prague (DM58.30). Hourly
trains run from Linz to Regensburg via
Passau.

The Danube is shadowed by a series of
roads, most notably the B311 (Tuttlingen to
Ulm), the B16 (Ulm to Ravensburg) and the
B8 (Regensburg to Passau). North-south
autobahns intersect at various points.

For information about boat services
between Regensburg and Passau, contact the
tourist offices, or Ludwig Wurm (☎ 09424-
13 41), Donaustrasse 71, Irlbach. For
services to Austria, contact DDSG (☎ 0851-
330 35), Im Ort 14a, Passau.

LAKE CONSTANCE
Lake Constance (Bodensee) is a perfect cure
for travellers in landlocked southern
Germany. The German side of this giant
bulge in the sinewy course of the Rhine
offers a choice of water sports, relaxation or
cultural pursuits. The southern side of the

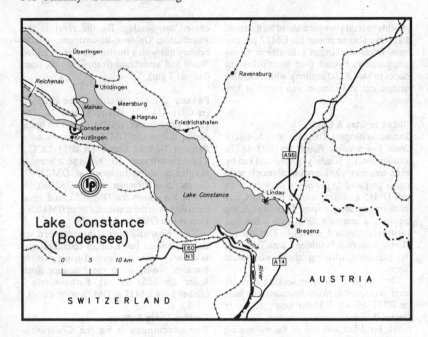

Lake Constance
(Bodensee)

SWITZERLAND

AUSTRIA

lake provides access to Switzerland and Austria.

The town of Constance (Konstanz) achieved historical significance in 1414 when the Council of Constance convened to try to heal huge rifts in the Church. The consequent burning at the stake of the religious reformer, Jan Hus, as a heretic, and the scattering of his ashes over the lake, failed to block the impetus of the Reformation.

Orientation & Information

The German side of Lake Constance features three often crowded tourist centres in Constance, Meersburg and the island of Lindau. It's a summer area, too often foggy or at best hazy in winter. In the off season, the pre-Lent Fasnacht celebrations can be lively, helped along by Constance's large student population.

In the west, Constance straddles the Swiss border, good fortune that helped it avoid Allied bombing in WW II. The adjoining

Swiss town of Kreuzlingen can be reached with minimal border controls. The tourist information office (☎ 07531-28 43 76) is to the right from the train station and is not overly helpful. The Bodensee-Verkehrsdienst (☎ 07531-28 13 89), Hafenstrasse 6, by the Platz 4 boat berth on the lakefront, is the information and sales office for ship travel, and is much more enthusiastic about helping you plan outings (closed in winter).

Meersburg lies across the lake from Constance and is an ideal base for exploring the long north shore. The friendly tourist information office (☎ 07532-8 23 83) is up the steep hill on the Schlossplatz at Kirchstrasse 4. It's open Monday to Friday from 9 am to noon, and 2.30 to 5 pm.

Most of the German part of Lake Constance lies within Baden-Württemberg, but Lindau in the east is just inside Bavaria, near the Austrian border. The tourist information office (☎ 08382-2 60 00) for the island and environs is directly opposite the station, open weekdays and Saturday mornings in summer.

Things to See
The lake itself is the major attraction of most of the resorts; explore its shores by boat and on foot.

Constance The town's most visible feature is the Gothic spire of the **cathedral**, added only in 1856 to a church that was started in 1052. The views from the top are excellent. Follow the walking tour of the historic centre prescribed in the tourist office leaflet, lingering in the **Stadtgarten** and the bohemian **Rheingasse** quarter. If you have time, head across the footbridge to **Mainau Island**, a peaceful tropical garden that was established by the royal house of Sweden (DM12).

Meersburg Meersburg is the prettiest town on the lake, with terraced streets and vineyard-patterned hills. The **Marktplatz** offers great vistas and leads to **Steigstrasse**, one of the classic streets of Germany, with two lines of beautiful half-timbered houses. The 17th century **Altes Schloss** is the oldest inhabited castle in Germany, and houses ancient weaponry (open daily, DM6, students DM5). The adjoining **Neues Schloss** is classic Baroque and contains a wonderful staircase (open daily from April to October; DM3, students DM1.50).

Lindau This island village spills over onto the adjoining north shore. If you decide to join the crowds, take a walking tour along **Maximilianstrasse**, **Ludwigstrasse**, and the **harbour** with its Bavarian Lion monument and lighthouse. Also note the muralled **Altes Rathaus** at Reichsplatz. There's a great **Modelbahn** (model railway) at Seeparkplatz Insel, with 500 metres of track, but unfortunately it's due to close in 1994.

Elsewhere There is a wide choice of excursions around the lake. Count Zeppelin was born in Constance, but first built his overgrown balloons across the lake in Friedrichshafen, an endeavour commemor-

ated in that town's **Zeppelin Museum**. Überlingen features the astonishing **Cathedral of St Nicholas**, which boasts a dozen side altars and a wooden, four-storey central altar dating from the 17th century, bedecked in intricate carvings. Another impressive Baroque church can be found at Birnau.

Activities
Water Sports In season, the lake offers plenty of possibilities. In Constance, head to the hot little sports shop, 3 UP (☎ 07531-2 31 17), Münzgasse 10, for gear, information and instruction packages. Constance has a public beach at Strandbad Horn, open from May to September.

Overall, Meersburg is a better base for watery pursuits. The active windsurfing school (☎ 07532-53 30) at Uferpromenade 37 is one of the best organised on the lake, and some of the best boardsailors hang out here.

In nearby Hagnau, there's another school called RePa Yachtschule-Windsurfing Hagnau (☎ 07545-62 93). It offers an unhurried, seven-day beginner's windsurfing course for DM220.

For sailing, contact the Bodensee-Yachtschule in Meersburg on ☎ 07532-55 11. Rudi Thum and his crew run lots of courses, starting at DM250 for one week. Call Motorboot-Charter (☎ 07532-3 64) for sailing boat and motorboat rental.

Lindau's water isn't as crowded as the land; Hermann Kreitmeir (☎ 08382-2 33 30) has windsurfing schools and equipment rental at Strandbad Eichwald.

Places to Stay
The thriving tourist industry means hotels and pensions can be a bit pricey; fortunately there are excellent hostel and camping facilities around the lake. Tourist offices have lists of apartments and cheap private homes (three days minimum).

Camping Though there are many others along the shore, recommended camping grounds include: *Camping Hagnau* (☎ 07545-64 13), four km east of Meersburg (one of three camping grounds side-by-side); *Camping Seeperle* (☎ 07556-54 54) in Uhldingen-Seefelden, five km west of Meersburg; and *Campingplatz Lindau-Zech* (☎ 08382-7 22 36), three km south-east of Lindau proper. Constance doesn't have any convenient camping.

Hostels The *Jugendherberge* (☎ 07531-3 32 60) at Allmannshohe 18 in Constance is closed during winter and costs DM15.50/20.50 for juniors/seniors. Take bus No 1 or 4 from the station. The *Jugendherberge* (☎ 07551-42 04), Alte Nussdorfer Strasse 26 in Überlingen, 15 km west of Meersburg, costs DM17/22.50. The *Jugendherberge* (☎ 08382-58 13) at Herbergsweg 11 in Lindau is closed until 1994 (juniors only). Friedrichshafen's *Jugendherberge* (☎ 07321-420 45) is at Liststrasse 15 (DM16.50/21).

Hotels In Constance, check the accommodation board outside the tourist office. The central *Pension Gretel* (☎ 07531-2 46 35), Zollernstrasse 6-8, has rooms for DM40 per person. Unfortunately the management can be unreliable and unfriendly; telephone reservations may not be honoured. Also central, but more amenable, is *Pension Graf* (☎ 07531-2 14 86), Wiesenstrasse 2, with singles/doubles for DM47/70, and triples/quads for DM99/105.

In Meersburg, head up the steep hill to *Gasthaus zum Letzten Heller* (☎ 07532-61 49), Daisendorfer Strasse 41, for singles/doubles at DM35/65 (great food, too). For splurging windsurfers who want to stay where they can overlook the action, the hot spot to sleep and eat is the *Hotel-Café Off* (☎ 07532-3 33) on the water at Uferpromenade 51. At DM90/140 for singles/doubles it's not cheap, but the people, location and balconies are great.

In Lindau, the best deal on the island is at *Gästehaus Limmer* (☎ 08382-58 77), In der Grub 16, with singles/doubles for DM32/60. *Gästehaus Tannheim* (☎ 08382-37 36) is near the water on the mainland at Bregenzer Strasse 16. Rooms are DM40/70.

Places to Eat

If you eat anywhere overlooking the water, including from a ship, you're paying for the view and the food rarely lives up to the prices.

In Constance, make a habit of eating and drinking at *Seekuh* at Konzilstrasse 4, a student-type bar that dishes up great food and company. Salads, pasta and pizza cost DM5 to DM10, and the conversation is free and easy. It's open every evening until 1 am. Another good place in a similar mould is *Sedir*, Hofhalde 11, serving tasty bowls of pasta (open daily). Also visit the university *mensa* for cheap lunches. *Gasthaus Burengeneral*, Brotlaube 4, is the place to try fish from the lake for around DM20 (closed Thursday).

The best place to eat in Meersburg is *Gasthof zum Bären*, at Marktplatz 11 in the story-book centre of town. The Gilowsky-Karrer clan prepares huge portions of food (and has singles/doubles for DM58/110). *Winzerstube zum Becher* (☎ 07532-60 19), Höllgasse 4, is highly recommended if you can afford to pay for top quality. Main dishes start at DM30, and it's closed on Monday; reserve ahead for the balcony seating.

In nearby Hagnau, try the cheerful *König-Stüble* at Seestrasse 10. Otto Denzinger specialises in creative personal pizzas from DM7.50 to DM13.50.

Life in Lindau isn't easy when it comes to food, but the friendly *Früchtehaus Hannes* at In der Grub 36 makes up for all of the bland tourist eateries. It offers fruit, vegetables, meats, fish, pastas and prepared salads, all sold by weight. Put together a picnic to eat outside or in the small café in the rear (open weekdays to 6 pm and Saturday to 1 pm). The touristy *Goldenes Lamm Restaurant* on Paradiesplatz has a good three-course menu for DM20, other specialities from DM16 and occasional live music.

Getting There & Away

Constance has train connections every one to two hours to Zürich, Donaueschingen (DM21) and Stuttgart (DM48). Meersburg is most easily reached by bus from Friedrichshafen, or by the car ferry from Staad at Constance (every 15 minutes all year, DM2). Lindau can be reached by hourly trains from Bregenz (takes 15 minutes), Ulm (via Friedrichshafen) and Munich (2½ hours). Access to the lake by road is also good.

Getting Around

Although trains link Lindau, Friedrichshafen and Constance, buses provide the easiest land connections. By car, the B31 hugs the northern shore of the lake but it can get busy. The most enjoyable way to get around is by boat. Ferries ply a circular route round the lake several times a day in summer; rail passes get 50% off.

Constance is a good base for cycling. Aktiv-Reisen Velotours (☎ 07531-5 20 85) at Mainaustrasse 34 rents good bikes (DM20 per day or DM100 per week), and runs popular bike trips around the lake. Constance and Lindau train stations also rent bikes.

Rhineland-Palatinate

Rhineland-Palatinate (Rheinland-Pfalz) has a rugged topography characterised by thinly populated mountain ranges and forests cut by deep river valleys. Created after WW II from parts of the former Rhineland and Rhenish Palatinate regions, its turbulent history saw the area settled by the Romans and later hotly contested by the French and a variety of German states. The capital city is Mainz.

This land of wine and great natural beauty is still a secret spot for many travellers willing to get off the busy Rhine River tourist route. Instead of just riding the Rhine wave, head for the Moselle Valley, or become one of the few English-speaking travellers who visit the Ahr Valley, famous for its light and fruity red wines.

THE MOSELLE VALLEY

Exploring the vineyards of the Moselle (Mosel) Valley is an ideal way to get a taste of German culture, the people and, of course, the wonderful wines. Take the time to slow down and do some sipping.

Orientation & Information

The German part of the Moselle Valley runs 195 km from Trier in the south-west to Koblenz in the north-east. For much of the way, the river banks are packed with quaint towns and steeply sloping vineyards – they say locals are born with one leg shorter than the other so that they can work the vines. Though the entire route is a tourist attraction, and is packed with visitors from June to October, it is possible to get off the beaten path very quickly. Cochem is the tourist centre of the Moselle and gets more than 2.5 million visitors a year.

Before heading into the Moselle region, the best places for tourist information are in Koblenz (☎ 0261-31304) in the small round building adjoining the bus area opposite the train station, or in Trier (☎ 0651-97 80 80) at An der Porta Nigra (not the most helpful of tourist offices). In the Moselle Valley proper, the staff in Cochem's tourist office (☎ 02671-39 71/72), on Endertplatz next to the bridge, are especially keen to please. Almost every other town has some sort of friendly visitor information centre. If not, people at the vineyards are usually full of ideas.

There's lots more to the Moselle than wine. Heading south-west from Koblenz to Trier, there are many small towns with historical significance and sights.

Things to See

Burg Eltz One of the more popular destinations is Burg Eltz (pictured on the DM500 note), the queen of the German castles, at the end of the beautiful Eltz Valley near Moselkern. It's open from April to November, and can be reached by a steep climb out of the hamlet of Müden or a longer, but more gradual, walk from Moselkern. Alternatively, you can drive up to the car park and take the bus to the entrance for DM1.50 return. The property is packed with towers and pinnacles overlooking everything

GERMANY

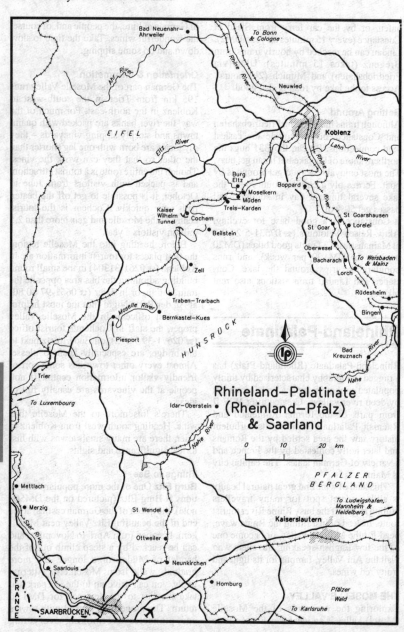

To Bonn & Cologne

Bad Neuenahr-Ahrweiler

Ahr River

EIFEL

Elz River

Neuwied

Koblenz

Lahn River

Burg Eltz
Moselkern
Müden
Treis-Karden

Kaiser Wilhelm Tunnel
Cochem

Beilstein

Boppard

St Goarshausen
Lorelei
St Goar
Oberwesel
Bacharach
Lorch

To Weisbaden & Mainz

Rüdesheim

Zell

Traben-Trarbach

Moselle River

Bernkastel-Kues

Piesport

HUNSRÜCK

Bingen

Rhine River

Trier

To Luxembourg

Idar-Oberstein

Nahe River

Bad Kreuznach

Nahe

Rhineland–Palatinate
(Rheinland–Pfalz)
& Saarland

0   10   20 km

PFALZER BERGLAND

Mettlach
Merzig

St Wendel

Kaiserslautern

To Ludwigshafen,
Mannheim &
Heidelberg

Saar River

Ottweiler

Neunkirchen

Homburg

Pfälzer
Wald

Saarlouis

FRANCE

SAARBRÜCKEN

To Karlsruhe

below. The tour (DM6.50, students DM4.50) includes lots of frescoes, paintings, furniture and ornately decorated rooms.

Cochem Cochem is one of those picture-postcard German towns with narrow alleyways and gates, and is a good base for hikes into the hills. For a great view, head up to the **Pinnerkreuz** with the chair lift on Endertstrasse. This costs DM5 up and DM7.50 return, but you can take the trip up and walk back down through the vineyards.

Cochem has its own famous castle, the **Reichsburg**, about 15 minutes' walk uphill from town. Forty-minute tours are conducted daily on the hour from 9 am to 5 pm and cost DM4, or DM3.50 for students; you get an English translation sheet, or you can enquire about an English-speaking guide on ☎ 02671-255 one day in advance.

Beilstein, Traben-Trarbach & Bernkastel-Kues A bit farther upstream, visit Beilstein, Traben-Trarbach or Bernkastel-Kues for a look at typical Moselle towns that survive on more than just the tourist trade. Just south of Traben-Trarbach is **Bad Wildstein**, a lesser known health resort with thermal springs.

Trier By all means spend some time in Trier, even if it's just a day. It is touted as Germany's oldest town, with origins dating back to 400 BC. Founded in 15 BC, Augusta Treverorum was the capital of Gaul and second in importance only to Rome in the Western Roman Empire. Though there are few clear reminders of its golden age in the 4th century AD, you'll find more Roman ruins here than anywhere else north of the Alps. There's a university too, and Trier can get pretty lively.

The town's star attraction is the **Porta Nigra**, the imposing city gate on the northern edge of the town centre, whose origins date back to the 2nd century AD. You can pay DM2 (students DM1) to go inside, or better still, invest DM6 (students DM3) in a combined ticket to many of the city's Roman sights. There's a good view of the old city from the upper terrace.

Don't miss the **Rhineland Museum** (Rheinisches Landesmuseum), Weimarer Allee 1 (same place as Ostallee 44 in the brochures, which was the address before the street name was changed), one of Germany's finest museums. It has a collection of Moselle artefacts and works of art dating from Palaeolithic to modern times, with understandable emphasis on the Roman period (admission free, open from 10 am to 4 pm Monday, from 9.30 am Tuesday to Friday, 9.30 am to 1 pm Saturday, and 9 am to 1 pm Sunday).

Trier has an impressive, mainly Romanesque, **cathedral** with a 1600-year history. Also worth visiting is the **Karl Marx Museum**, in the house where the prophet was born on Brückenstrasse 10. The Nazis published their party organ here from 1933 to 1945. The museum is open daily from 10 am to 6 pm (admission DM3, students DM2). You may have trouble following some of the exhibits if you can't read German, but history buffs and socialist torchbearers will find much of interest.

Activities
Wine Tasting The main activities along the Moselle Valley centre around eating, drinking and being merry. Wine tasting and buying are why most people visit – just pick out a vineyard and head inside.

Wine tasters speak an international language, but a few tasting tips might help: indicate whether you like a dry *(trocken)* or sweet *(süss)* wine; smell the wine while swishing it around in the glass; taste it by swishing it around in your mouth before swallowing; and don't drink too much without buying.

Though almost any town will have many tasting options, Cochem is big enough for some flexibility, yet small enough for friendliness. H H Hieronimi (☎ 02671-2 21) at Stadionstrasse 1-3 just east of the river, is a friendly, family-run vineyard that offers very good tours of the facilities. On the west side of the river, Weingut Rademacher (☎ 02671-41 64) at Pinnerstrasse 10, diagonally behind the train station, runs tours of its vineyards,

GERMANY

cellar (which served as a WW II bunker) and winery, and then leads you through a fun tasting. All of this for DM2 plus DM1 for each small glass of wine that you taste.

If you want to taste wines in another town, the tourist offices can recommend vineyards to visit and give details about the many festivals throughout the summer. It's worth the time and effort to attend at least one of these festivals, which can become a miniature Moselle version of Munich's Oktoberfest.

Hiking The Moselle Valley is especially scenic walking country, but plan on some

steep climbs if you venture away from the river. The views are worth the sore muscles. Most tourist information offices carry the beautifully drawn, '3-D' *Moselle with Saar Valley* map (DM5), which shows walking routes but is really a driving map; proper *Wanderkarte* hiking maps cost DM6.50 each.

If you do want to explore the Moselle on foot, contact the Cochem tourist office for the week-long Mosel-Wein-Wanderung, an all-inclusive tour from Cochem to Bernkastel-Kues and back. It costs DM655, the walking is fairly easy (no more than 15 km

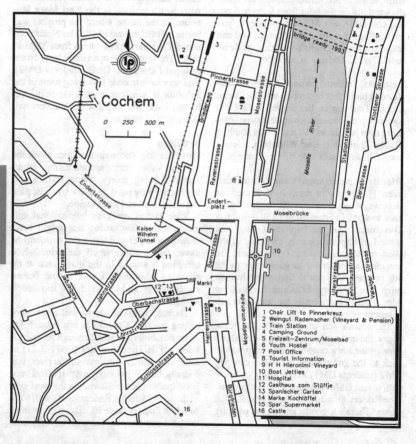

1   Chair Lift to Pinnerkreuz
2   Weingut Rademacher (Vineyard & Pension)
3   Train Station
4   Camping Ground
5   Freizeit–Zentrum/Moselbad
6   Youth Hostel
7   Post Office
8   Tourist Information
9   H H Hieronimi Vineyard
10 Boat Jetties
11 Hospital
12 Gasthaus zom Stüffje
13 Spanischer Garten
14 Marke Kochlöffel
15 Spar Supermarket
16 Castle

a day) and the experienced tour guide speaks English. You're asked to book a month in advance; write to Verkehrsamt Cochem, Postfach 1550, 5590 Cochem.

Other Activities For a fitness fix, head for Cochem's Freizeit-Zentrum/Moselbad at Klottener Strasse 17 on the east side of the river. This pool palace, typical of many such places throughout Germany, is a perfect place to experience the unique German way of swimming and exercise. It costs DM7.20 for use of all the facilities for two hours, or DM3.50 if you just want to swim in the heated pool. Discounts are available if you're staying at the camping ground or youth hostel.

Places to Stay
As usual, the local tourist offices operate great room-finding services. If you understand German, there's a 24-hour hotline service for the Moselle area which will tell you which hotels have rooms available and how much they cost: dial ☎ 1 94 12, preceded by the area code for your target town if you aren't already there.

Koblenz Although it's an interesting city if you put your mind to it, Koblenz is not the sort of place where you want to spend too much time when the Moselle beckons. It does, however, feature a wonderful *youth hostel* (☎ 0261-7 37 37) in the old fortress across the river near the Ehrenbreitstein bus stop (bus No 7, 8, 9 or 10). It's a steep, 15-minute walk up the hill from there; alternatively, the daytime chair lift gives discounts to youth hostel card holders and will even take luggage. The view is great and the price is right: DM16.90 to DM18.50, depending on the breakfast you choose. Other meals are also available and there's a reasonable coffee shop. Call before heading out there in summer.

The *Rhein Mosel* camping ground (☎ 0261-80 24 89, April to mid-October) is on Schartwiesenweg, on the confluence of the Moselle and Rhine rivers opposite 'Deutsches Eck', the German unity park at

the north-eastern corner of the city centre. The daytime passenger ferry across the Moselle puts the camping ground within five minutes' walk of town.

Cochem Though there are three other camping spots in the vicinity, Cochem's municipal *camp site* (☎ 02671-12 12, Easter to November) on Stadionstrasse sits right on the river at the downstream end of town. It's especially well situated, with the Freizeit-Zentrum/Moselbad (see the previous Activities section) just up the hill. From the train station, cross the Moselle Bridge, turn left and head back down to the river, and keep walking.

Along the same route but one street up from the river is Cochem's *Jugendherberge* (☎ 02671-86 33) at Klottener Strasse 9, with a commanding view of the valley (DM14.30). The new northern bridge near the train station, which should be ready in early 1993, will considerably cut back the walk to either place – the youth hostel sits right at its eastern base, the camping ground 100 metres downstream.

Despite the hordes of tourists, hotels in Cochem are still reasonably priced, and with a bit of luck you should be able to get something for about DM35/60 single/double. The previously mentioned *Weingut Rademacher* has five pleasant rooms starting at DM30/52, including a free tour of the vineyard. The tourist office will probably find you a private room in the centre of town for less (no service fee, but a DM2 deposit on the room), but forget about any bargains on summer weekends and especially when the wine harvest starts in mid-September.

Trier The *Trier-City* municipal camping ground (☎ 0651-8 69 21, all year) is nicely positioned on the Moselle at Luxemburger Strasse 81. The *Jugendherberge* (☎ 0651-2 92 92) is at Maarstrasse 156 along the river. There are only a handful of cheap hotels, and the pick of the bunch is *Handelshof* (☎ 7 39 33), Kellner-Strasse 1, next to the Rathaus in the south-western corner of the old town,

GERMANY

554 Germany – Rhineland-Palatinate

with singles/doubles for DM35/70 (forget about the restaurant).

Elsewhere Elsewhere in the Moselle Valley, there are lots of camping grounds, hostels and rooms with great views. Recommended camping grounds include: *Camping Schenk* (☎ 06531-81 76; open Easter to November) near Bernkastel-Kues in Wehlen, and Traben-Trarbach's *Rissbach* (☎ 06541-31 11; open April to mid-October) at Rissbacher Strasse 170. Especially good hostels include the *Jugendherberge* (☎ 06531-23 95) in Bernkastel-Kues at Jugendherbergsstrasse 1, and Traben-Trarbach's *Jugendherberge* (☎ 06541-92 78) at Am Letzten Hirtenpfad.

The Moselle also offers perfect opportunities to stay at a vineyard or some wine-related pension. Just ask any tourist office or any vineyard where you're tasting wines. Then, after a long tasting session, you shouldn't have to worry about finding your way home.

Places to Eat
Good wine often means good food and this is true all along the Moselle, with dozens of inexpensive family places from which to choose.

There are reasonably priced eateries in Cochem and Trier. Elsewhere along the valley, check food and wine prices very carefully before entering. The Moselle is perfect for buying picnic items and wine, and just enjoying the peaceful river and countryside.

Cochem Some tiny streets lead to some big meals. Though not listed on the comprehensive tourist-office map, locals head for the *Gasthaus zom Stüffje* at Branntweingäsche 14 (up Oberbachstrasse from Markt on your right) for regional fare at reasonable prices (DM10 to DM20). Just before that establishment, you'll find a fruit-and-vegetable shop, *Spanischer Garten*, where you can put together a picnic. A good fast-food choice is *Marke Kochlöffel* opposite the town hall on the Markt; it has fresh salads from DM3.75, and half a chicken with French fries for only DM5.90. The *Spar* supermarket on Herren-

strasse 3, just off Markt, has a large selection of wines.

Trier This is a great place to sample some French-German cooking, and one of the best places to do it is *Zum Christophel* at Simeonstrasse 1, next to the Porta Nigra. It has creative and filling omelettes for DM10.50 – other dishes are far more expensive, though good. A favourite student hang-out is *Astarix*, down an arcade at Karl-Marx-Strasse 11. Food is good value here, with salads ranging from DM3 to DM6.90, large pizzas for about DM6.60, and main dishes for about DM7.90; there's also a good selection of reasonably priced drinks. Pick up a copy of the monthly what's on booklet at the entrance. Otherwise, head for the *daily market* at the Hauptmarkt, or try one of the *restaurants* at the Kaufhof or Karstadt department stores along Simeonstrasse (Nos 53 and 46 respectively).

Getting There & Away
Begin your trip along the Moselle Valley in either Trier or Koblenz. This is much easier than trying to get to a starting point somewhere midway. But if you have private transport and you're coming from the north, you can head up the Ahr Valley and cut through the High Eifel mountain area, past the stunningly located Nürburgring motor racing track (which you can drive around for a fee), to Cochem. This is a scenic route, but cyclists will find the going tough.

Getting Around
Exploring the Moselle can be accomplished on foot or by bike, car, boat and other public transport. Each is different and enjoyable.

River Cruises One of the best ways to explore the Moselle is by boat, and there are many options, ranging from two-hour excursions to multiday wine-tasting packages. The Köln-Düsseldorfer Line does special Trier-Cologne trips that take two days (from DM416/520 in the low/high season, all-inclusive), and also sails daily between Koblenz and Cochem (DM31.40 one-way).

Normal runs (not the all-inclusive cruises or the hydrofoil) are free with Eurail and German Rail passes and also on your birthday, or cost 50% if you hold a normal train ticket for that stretch. Ring the K-D Line head office (☎ 0221-2 08 82 88) in Cologne for details.

Train The trains running along the Moselle are frequent and convenient, even to the smallest towns, but won't let you enjoy much of the beautiful scenery. Trivia department: the 4.2-km Kaiser Wilhelm Tunnel between Eller and Cochem was opened in 1877 and is still the longest tunnel in Germany.

Bus Unfortunately, there are no regular bus services along the Moselle (the many buses that you see are all tour buses), but a private bus runs daily between Trier and Bullay, about three-fifths of the way to Koblenz. It leaves the main train station in Trier and costs DM13 one-way, DM18.40 return. For details, contact Moselbahn GmbH (☎ 0651-2 10 75), Schönbornstrasse 7, 5500 Trier.

Car & Motorbike Driving along the Moselle is also ideal, though drivers will risk cramped necks (not to mention nervous passengers) from looking up at the majestic slopes. One possibility is to rent a car in either Koblenz or Trier and drop it off at the other end.

Hitchhiking is good, especially during summer, when the roads are crowded with friendly drivers. Just make sure that whoever picks you up hasn't spent too much time at one of the vineyards.

Cycling Many train stations will rent bikes at DM8 a day for rail pass and ticket holders, or DM12 otherwise. The Moselle is a very popular cycling route and there's even a separate cycling track for much of the way (follow the 'Moselroute' cycling signs). You can send luggage ahead on the train and drop off bikes at other stations for a DM5 'return transport' fee; however, luggage handling and bicycle drop-off are only available at the larger stations.

RHINE VALLEY – MAINZ TO KOBLENZ

Some sort of trip along the Rhine is on almost every traveller's itinerary. The section between Mainz and Koblenz offers the best scenery, especially the narrow tract from Bingen onwards. Try to visit here in the spring or autumn, when there are less tourists. And by all means try some of the local wines.

Orientation & Information

The best places for information are the tourist information offices in Mainz (☎ 06131-28 62 10, down Bahnhofstrasse diagonally to your right as you exit the station, on the corner of Parcusstrasse) and Koblenz (☎ 0261-3 13 04, the small round building adjoining the bus area opposite the train station). However, any town along the Rhine Valley tourist trail will have its own office, with specific recommendations for sightseeing and other activities in the area.

Things to See

Where the slopes of the Rhine aren't covered with vines, you can bet they built a castle there. One of the most impressive is **Burg Rheinfels** in St Goar – worth visiting. Across the river, just south of St Goarshausen, is the most famous sight along the Rhine: the **Lorelei Cliff**. Legend states that a maiden sang sailors to their deaths against its base. The cliff juts out into the river, and even today St Goar does a lively trade in pilots who guide the many Rhine barges through this treacherous passage. It's worth the trek to the top of the Lorelei for the view, but try to get up there early in the morning before the hordes ascend – follow the 'Loreley Felsen' signs.

Rüdesheim This town is drunk on tourism, but you should still take the time to see the **Rheingau-und Weinmuseum** in Brömserburg castle for a better perspective of the area and the wines you'll be tasting. The museum includes a history of wine-making, wine glasses, wine-making equipment and much more. One of the most touristy streets in the country is Rüdesheim's **Drosselgasse**, a

GERMANY

tourist trap of shops, and eating and drinking establishments.

Mainz A half-hour ride from Frankfurt's main strain station with the S-14, Mainz is worth visiting for the following sights: the **Gutenberg Museum of World Printing** at Liebfrauenplatz 5 (open Tuesday to Saturday from 10 am to 6 pm, Sunday to 1 pm, admission free); the massive **St Martin's Cathedral** (entrance off Markt square); and **Marc Chagall's stained-glass windows** in St Stephen's Church on Stephansplatz (daily from 10 am to noon and 2 to 5 pm).

Activities

Wine Tasting As with the Moselle Valley, the Mainz-to-Koblenz section of the Rhine Valley is great for wine tasting. Although Rüdesheim is justifiably famous as a wine and tourism haven, the two best towns for a true Rhine wine experience are Oberwesel and Bacharach, both about 45 km south of Koblenz. For wine tasting in other towns, ask for recommendations at the tourist offices or just follow your nose.

Hiking Though the trails here may be a bit more crowded with day-trippers than those along the Moselle, hiking along the Rhine is also excellent. The slopes and trails around Bacharach are justly famous and offer a great way to work off Rhine wine and cooking.

Places to Stay

Camping facilities line the Rhine, but amenities and views vary greatly. Good possibilities include: Oberwesel's *Schönburg* (☎ 06744-2 45, open April to October) directly on the river; Bacharach's *Sonnenstrand* camp site (☎ 06743-17 52, open all year) on the river at the southern end of town (can get windy); and St Goarshausen's *Auf der Loreley* (☎ 06771-430, open April to October) on the legendary rock.

There are excellent *hostels* at Lorch (☎ 06726-3 07), Schwalbacherstrasse 54; Oberwesel (☎ 06744-70 46), Auf dem Schönberg; St Goarshausen (☎ 06771-26 19), Auf der Loreley; Bacharach (☎ 06743-

12 66), a legendary facility housed in Burg Stahleck castle; and Rüdesheim (☎ 06722-27 11), Am Kreuzburg. The hostel in St Goarshausen is on the Lorelei, 100 metres from the lookout point; at DM9.50 (or DM15.50 including meals) it's always full, so book ahead.

Hotels and pensions feed off the tourist trade, and a cheap bed is sometimes as hard to find as a cold beer in this wine-crazed region. Out of season you should have far less problems. If your hotel or guesthouse overlooks the Rhine, trains may often pass at arm's length, so ask for a room at the back if that's the case.

If you decide to base yourself in Bacharach for a few days (not a bad choice, even if you don't go hiking), try the beautiful *Hotel Kranenturm* (☎ 06743-13 08), Langstrasse 30. It's above an old town gate overlooking the Rhine, and the singles/doubles with toilet and shower from DM35/70 are only a small step above the very cheapest alternatives. Try to avoid spending the night in Rüdesheim.

For accommodation in Koblenz, see Places to Stay in the previous Moselle Valley section.

Places to Eat

This is picnic country and the locals oblige with many markets and shops. Most of the hotels and wine halls serve good food, sometimes at reasonable prices – check the menus posted outside.

If you've been waiting for a big splurge, one great choice for food, wine and merriment is the *Rüdesheimer Schloss* on the Drosselgasse in Rüdesheim. It has a huge selection of wines, a live and lively band, and great food. Avoid almost any other restaurant in Rüdesheim, and under normal circumstances don't even think about eating along the Drosselgasse.

Getting There & Away

Get to Koblenz or Mainz and head into the Rhine Valley from there. The area is also easily accessible from Frankfurt on a long day trip, but that won't do justice to the region.

Getting Around

Each mode of transport has its own advantages and all are equally enjoyable. Try combining several of them by going on foot one day, cycling the next, and then taking a ship for a view from the river.

River Cruises The Köln-Düsseldorfer Line (☎ 0221-2 08 82 88) earns its bread and butter on the Rhine, with many slow and fast boats daily between Koblenz and Mainz. The most scenic portion is between Koblenz and Bingen; it takes about 3½ hours to head downstream (Bingen-Koblenz, DM51.40) and about 5½ hours upstream (DM42.60 – the K-D Line says it's cheaper because it's more popular...). See Getting Around in the previous Moselle Valley section for discounts. Some of the boats stop at small villages along the way.

Train & Bus Train and bus services are excellent on each side of the river. Make sure you travel during the day and sit at a window facing the water. A train trip along the Rhine is one of Europe's classics, and if you combine it with a visit to Cologne, you can get out under the shadow of the magnificent cathedral and see the surrounding sights within a few hours – a perfect setup.

Car Touring the Rhine Valley by car is also ideal. The route between Koblenz and Mainz is short enough for a car to be rented and returned to either one of these cities. There are no bridge crossings between Koblenz and Bingen, but there are frequent ferries.

Saarland

In the late 19th century, Saarland's coal mines and steel mills fed the burgeoning German economy. Since WW II, however, the steady economic decline of coal and steel has made Saarland the poorest region in western Germany.

Though distinctly German since the early Middle Ages, Saarland was ruled by France for several periods during its turbulent history. Again occupied by the French after WW II, it only joined the German Federal Republic in 1959, after the population rejected French efforts to turn it into an independent state.

Germany's forgotten sister shouldn't be forgotten by travellers. Though mainly industrial and not particularly attractive along the major transport routes, this area does offer the city of Saarbrücken, a charming place that most travellers ignorantly skip.

SAARBRÜCKEN

This city of 200,000 has both a French and German feel, a mix that gives it an interesting atmosphere. Lacking in major tourist sights, Saarbrücken is a 'real' place where people go about their daily business of living and working in a friendly manner, and where tourists are treated as individuals. Make a point of spending at least a day here when heading south from Trier or east from France.

Orientation & Information

The main train station is in the north-western corner of the old town, which stretches out on both sides of the Saar River.

The tourist information office (☎ 0681-3 51 97) is to your left on the square as you exit the station, and is open from 7.30 am to 8 pm Monday to Friday, and to 4 pm Saturday. The staff don't seem to get many English-speaking visitors and this novelty makes them even more helpful. The room-finding service costs DM3. The main tourist office (☎ 0681-3 69 01) is at Grossherzog-Friedrich-Strasse 1, past the parking garage next to the Rathaus, but isn't really geared up for nonstop visitor queries and keeps normal office hours (from 7.45 am to 6 pm Monday to Friday).

There's a bank just outside the train station exit on your left. It's open Monday to Friday from 7 am to 7.45 pm, Saturday 8.30 am to

4 pm, Sunday 9 am to 3 pm. The Kaiser-strasse leading into town is lined with banks and international automatic teller machines.

The main post office is at Trierer Strasse 33, to your right as you go out of the station. There's another branch at Dudweilerstrasse 17, opposite the corner with Kaiserstrasse, near the centre of town.

If you need to do any washing, there's a laundry at Nauwieserstrasse 22, open from 7 am to 10 pm every day.

Saarbrücken's telephone code is 0681.

Things to See & Do

Besides strolling and sitting around the lively **St Johanner Markt**, there aren't many obvious things to see or do in the city. It's the sort of place that you have to go out and conquer, and then it slowly grows on you.

If you're interested in architecture, the stately **Ludwigsplatz** across the river is a fine example of Baroque, entirely designed by King Wilhelm Friedrich's court architect, Friedrich Joachim Stengel, in the 18th century. The square is dominated by the **Ludwigskirche**, an odd combination of a Lutheran church in a Baroque setting. It keeps hopeless opening hours, but you can see all you need to see through the glass wall in the entrance.

The nearby **Schloss Saarbrücken**, the former palace on Schlossplatz, was Stengel's first major work. A modern central section was completed in 1989 and now houses the Museum of Regional History. A more interesting museum, however, is the **Abenteuer Museum** (Adventure Museum), on the 2nd floor of the old Rathaus opposite the palace (not to be confused with the current grand Rathaus on the eastern side of the river). It's a hotchpotch of weird souvenirs and photos collected since 1950 by the solo adventurer extraordinaire, Heinz Rox-Schulz. At the entrance, the dramatic photo of a cobra slithering away from a dead child would be etched in your mind for weeks if you didn't know it was posed. Unfortunately, opening hours are rather limited: from 9 am to 1 pm Tuesday and Wednesday, 3 to 9 pm Thursday and Friday, and 10 am to 2 pm on 'long

Saturdays'. Admission costs DM2, and is worth every Pfennig.

There are some beautiful little towns around Saarbrücken that you can reach easily on a day trip. **Ottweiler** and **St Wendel** might provide the Saarland quaint-ness that Saarbrücken is too big to offer.

Places to Stay

The camping ground *Am Spicherer Berg* (☎ 5 17 80, open April to October), Am Spicherer Berg, is out on the French border, south of the city; take bus No 12 to the ZF Gewerbegebiet or the Mercedes tower. The *Jugendherberge* (☎ 3 30 40) is at Meer-wiesertalweg 31, a half-hour walk east of the train station – take bus No 19 to the Prinzenweiher stop. It costs DM16.20/19.70 for juniors/seniors.

There are no private rooms in Saar-brücken, and because of the many French day and weekend trippers, hotels are not cheap. Count on at least DM45/90 for a single/double if you want to stay in the city (only marginally cheaper otherwise). Use the tourist information office's accommodation-booking service. The best choice is *Hotel Schlosskrug* (☎ 3 54 48), Schmollerstrasse 14, not only because it offers among the cheapest rooms in town from DM42/90 single/double, but also because it's close to the lively Nauwieserplatz area (see the following section).

Places to Eat & Drink

Your taste buds can visit France with German servings at many of Saarbrücken's eateries. Take a look at the menus in any of the restaurants and cafés on and around St Johanner Markt. *Zum Stiefel* at Am Stiefel 2 is especially recommended for a splurge.

But, as the local students say, the St Johan-ner Markt area represents 'culture', whereas the 'subculture' resides across Grossherzog-Friedrich-Strasse in the area around Nauwieserplatz. Here, in Saarbrücken's modest red-light district, is where most of the student pubs and restaurants (usually the same thing) are to be found. *Ubu Roi*, on the corner of Cecilienstrasse and Försterstrasse, serves French breakfasts for DM5.50 at outdoor tables. *Café Max* at Nauwieserplatz 3 has vegetarian dishes and salads from DM5.50 to DM13, and steak dishes for around DM18.

A proper vegetarian restaurant (open only at meal times) is *La Carotte* (☎ 3 14 11), upstairs at Karcherstrasse 15. Though slightly up-market, you can eat good, creative food for under DM20.

There's a *market* on St Johanner Markt every Monday, Wednesday and Friday morning, and on Ludwigsplatz every Thursday and Saturday morning. St Johanner Markt also hosts an interesting flea market every second Saturday.

Getting There & Away

Saarbrücken has a small international airport just 12 km from the city centre. There are hourly trains to the connecting cities of Mannheim, Koblenz, Mainz and Karlsruhe.

If you arrive by private transport, Saarbrücken has a nerve-racking system of one-way streets, and ongoing building projects to create even more confusion. Head for one of the many (expensive) parking garages, sort out your accommodation, and dump your vehicle there for the duration of your stay.

Getting Around

Unless you decide to stay outside the city at the camping ground or youth hostel, or pursue some day trips, Saarbrücken is fairly easy to explore on foot. Public transport consists of buses, and near the station there's a ticket/information booth on the corner of Trierer Strasse and Faktoreistrasse – head straight down Reichsstrasse out of the station, and if you look carefully, you'll see it on the right. Another booth lives in the shopping arcade under the big Karstadt department store on Betzenstrasse. If you're staying at the youth hostel, you're still in the city area and a single ticket costs DM2.50 (DM2.30 in batches of four); a 24-hour pass costs DM6, and a weekly pass costs DM15 (students DM11).

Taxis are expensive at DM4 flagfall plus DM2.10 per km. There are several taxi stands around the city, or ring ☎ 4 19 19 or ☎ 3 30 33.

Hesse

The Hessians, a Frankish tribe, were among the first people to convert to Lutheranism in the early 16th century. Apart from a brief period of unity in that same century under Philip the Magnanimous, Hesse (Hessen) remained a motley collection of principalities and, later, of Prussian administrative districts until it was proclaimed a state in 1945. Its main cities are Frankfurt, Kassel and the capital, Wiesbaden.

Along with being a transportation hub, the city of Frankfurt can also be used as a base to explore some of the smaller towns in Hesse that remind you that you're still in Germany. One possibility is Marburg, halfway between Frankfurt and Kassel, with its splendid St Elizabeth's Church and Europe's first Protestant university (the Philipps-Universität), founded in 1527. The beautiful Taunus and Spessart regions offer quiet village life and hours of scenic walks.

FRANKFURT/MAIN

They call it 'Bankfurt' and 'Mainhattan' and much more. It's on the Main (pronounced 'mine') River, and is often referred to as Frankfurt-am-Main, or Frankfurt/Main, since there's also a fairly large city called Frankfurt in eastern Germany, on the Oder River (Frankfurt/Oder).

Frankfurt/Main is the financial and geographical centre of what used to be West Germany, and is the site of important trade fairs, including the largest book, consumer goods and musical instruments fairs in the world. Frankfurt's 650,000 inhabitants produce 8% of Germany's GNP and it's a wealthy city – even the students seem rich! But regardless of the expensive cars and haute couture, 11% of the city's taxes are devoted to culture, and you'll find the richest collection of museums in the country.

GERMANY

GERMANY

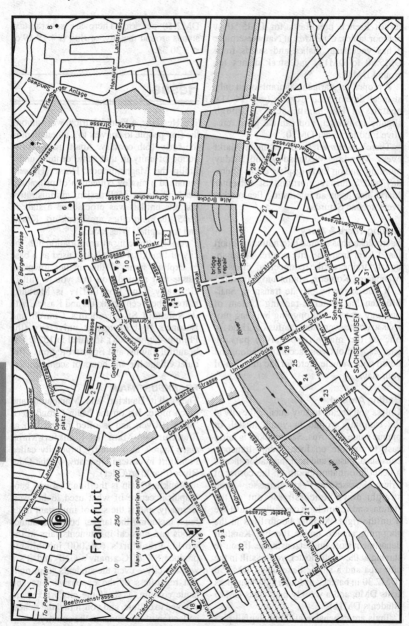

Frankfurt

0   250   500 m

Many streets pedestrian only

■ PLACES TO STAY

1   Hotel-Pension Gölz &
    Pension Sattler
17 Hotel Adler
18 Hotel Glockshuber
22 Pension Wal
28 Haus der Jugend Youth Hostel

▼ PLACES TO EAT

9   Mozart Café
10 Kleinmarkthalle
16 China-Restaurant Panda
29 Lorsbacher Tal
30 Zum Gemalten Haus
31 Wagner Adolf

    OTHER

2   Jazzkeller
3   Hauptwache & Tourist
    Information
4   Main Post Office
5   Sinnkasten
6   Zeil 10
7   Plastik
8   Zoo
11 Museum of Modern Art
12 Dom
13 Römerberg
14 Römer & Tourist Information
15 Goethehaus
19 Tourist Information
20 Hauptbahnhof
21 Mitfahrzentrale
23 Städel Museum
24 Bundespostmuseum
25 Architecture Museum
26 Film Museum
27 Negativ
32 Südbahnhof

Because Frankfurt has an enormous train station and airport, not to mention the largest autobahn intersection in the country, you'll probably end up here at some point. Don't be surprised if you find this cosmopolitan melting-pot much more interesting than you expected.

Orientation

The airport is about 15 minutes by train south-west of the city centre. The Haupt-bahnhof is on the western side of the city, but within walking distance of the old city centre.

The best way to walk into the old city from the train station is to head east along Taunusstrasse. This leads you to Goetheplatz and then to a large square called the Hauptwache, the unofficial city centre. Most major attractions are within walking distance of this square.

The Main River runs to the south of the Altstadt. Several bridges lead to the liveliest part of the city, Sachsenhausen. Its north-eastern corner, behind the youth hostel (see the Places to Stay section that follows), is known as Alt Sachsenhausen, and is full of picturesque old houses and narrow alley-ways. Sachsenhausen and especially Alt Sachsenhausen are easily covered on foot (which can't be said for most of the rest of Frankfurt), and are recommended as centres of operations.

Information

The head office of Germany's National Tourist Board (☎ 069-75 72 0) is north of the Hauptbahnhof at Beethovenstrasse 69 (open Monday to Thursday from 9 am to 4 pm, to 1 pm Friday), and is one of the least crowded and least frazzled tourist offices in the country.

The tourist office itself (☎ 069-212 388 49/51) is in the main train station, at the head of track No 24. It's open Monday to Saturday from 8 am to 10 pm (9.30 am to 8 pm Sundays and holidays). It is efficient at finding (pricier) rooms and handing out bro-chures, but that's about it; the room-finding service costs a hefty DM5 plus a DM8 deposit on the room. The *Frankfurt Live* brochure shows good walking tours.

In the centre of the city, the tourist office (☎ 069-212 387 08/09) at Römerberg 27 (in the north-west corner of the square) is open from 9 am to 7 pm Monday to Friday, and 9.30 am to 6 pm weekends and holidays. The Hauptwache shopping mall also has a tourist information centre on Level B (☎ 069-2 12 87 08/9).

The airport has no tourist information

GERMANY

office as such, but there are general information booths in the arrival and departure halls B, on levels 1 and 2 respectively. Rooms for a limited number of expensive hotels can be booked at the hotel-booking service in arrival hall B. For more information on Frankfurt Airport, see the Getting There & Away section that follows.

Money The main train station has a branch of the Deutsche Verkehrs-Kredit Bank (☎ 069-2 64 82 01) near the southern exit at the head of track No 1, which is open daily from 6.30 am to 10 pm; otherwise, use the money-exchange machine at the head of track No 15. There are several banks at the airport, most of them open till about 10 pm, and exchange and automatic teller machines are dotted around the various arrival and departure halls.

Post & Telecommunications The main post office (☎ 069-44 40) is near the Hauptwache at Zeil 108-110. It's open Monday to Friday from 8 am to 6 pm, Saturday till noon; the telephone office next door is open from 8 am to 8 pm Monday to Friday, to 6 pm Saturday, and from 11 am to 4 pm Sunday. There's a 24-hour post office in the main train station (above the tourist office); the one at the airport (in the waiting lounge in departure hall B) is open from 6 am to 10 pm.

Frankfurt's telephone code is 069.

Bookshops Stock up on international magazines and newspapers at the Internationale Presse shop in the train station, at the head of track No 15.

Emergency For police and ambulance, call ☎ 110; for fire, ☎ 112. There's a 24-hour medical clinic (☎ 69 06 67 67) at the airport near gate 12 on Level 1 – the entry is down the stairs through departure hall C on Level 2; the pharmacy in departure hall B stays open till 9 pm. Another 24-hour clinic is the Uni-Clinic (☎ 6 30 11) at Theodor Stern Kai 7 in Sachsenhausen. For medical queries, contact either of these clinics, or the 24-hour doctor service on ☎ 1 92 92.

Dangers & Annoyances As with any large transportation hub, there can be crime problems in and around the train station. Thanks to an effective policing campaign, however, it's not the major concern it used to be.

Things to See & Do
Eighty per cent of the old city was wiped off the map by two Allied bombing raids in March 1944, and postwar reconstruction was subject to the demands of the new age. Rebuilding efforts were more thoughtful, however, in the **Römerberg**, the old central square of Frankfurt, west of the cathedral, where restored 14th and 15th century buildings provide a glimpse of the beautiful city this once was. The old town hall, or **Römer**, is in the north-western corner of Römerberg, and consists of three 15th century houses topped with Frankfurt's trademark stepped gables.

East of the Römerberg, behind the Historical Garden (remains of Roman and Carolingian foundations), is the **Dom** (Cathedral), the coronation site of German emperors from 1562 to 1792. It's dominated by the elegant, 15th century Gothic **tower** (completed in the 1860s) – one of the few structures left standing in the 1944 raids. The Dom is closed for renovations till 1994, but you can visit the small **Wahlkapelle** (Voting Chapel) on the south side, where the seven electors of the Holy Roman Empire chose the emperor from 1356 onwards, and the adjoining **choir** with its beautiful wooden stalls.

Aficionados of German literature and philosophy should visit the **Goethe-Haus**, Grosser Hirschgraben 23-25. Goethe, arguably the last person to master all fields of human knowledge, was born in this house in 1749. The adjoining museum contains a library, manuscripts and art relating to his work. It's open Monday to Saturday from 9 am to 6 pm, Sunday from 10 am to 1 pm, and costs DM3 (students DM2), which is worth it if there aren't too many tour buses out the front.

Frankfurt has more interesting museums than any other German city. The latest addition is the **Museum of Modern Art**, north of the cathedral at Domstrasse 10, featuring work by Joseph Beuys, Claes Oldenburg and many others; admission is free. A string of other museums lines the south bank of the Main River along the so-called **Museum Row** (Museumsufer). Pick of the crop is the **Städel Museum** at Schaumainkai 63, with a world-class collection of art from the Renaissance to the 20th century, including Botticelli, Dürer, van Eyck, Rubens, Rembrandt, Vermeer, Cézanne and Renoir, among many other greats. It costs DM3 (DM1.50 for students, free on Sundays and public holidays). Other popular possibilities along the way include the **Deutsches Architekturmuseum** (Architecture Museum), the **Deutsches Filmmuseum**, and the **Bundespostmuseum** (Postal Museum). The museums are generally open Tuesday to Sunday from 10 am to 5 pm, Wednesday to 8 pm.

After some museum time, head for one of Sachsenhausen's **apple-wine taverns** (see the Places to Eat section that follows) and try the unique *Ebbelwei* (Frankfurt dialect for *Apfelwein)* that resembles spiked apple juice; it tastes much weaker than cider but contains well over 5% alcohol by volume – beware!

A bit farther afield, the **Palmengarten** (extensive botanical gardens) and the creative **Frankfurt Zoo** are perfect reliefs from the metropolitan madness.

Places to Stay

Camping The only camp site is *Heddernheim* (☎ 57 03 32, open all year) at An der Sandelmühle 35, in the Heddernheim district north-west of the city centre. It charges DM10 for a site and DM9 per person, and is 15 minutes with the U-1, 2 or 3 from the Hauptwache (one zone) – get off at the Heddernheim stop.

Hostels The *Haus der Jugend* youth hostel (☎ 61 90 58), on the south side of the Main River at Deutschherrnufer 12, D-6000 Frankfurt 70, is within easy walking distance of the city centre and Sachsenhausen. It's big, bustling and fun. A dorm bed costs DM18.50/22.50 for those aged under/over 20, including breakfast; additional meals cost DM7. It also has singles/doubles for DM40/65, but these have to be booked in writing. From the train station, take bus No 46 to Frankensteiner Platz; from the airport, take the S-14 to Lokalbahnhof. Check-in begins at 1 pm and it can get crowded.

Hotels Forget about cheap hotels in Frankfurt if you want something reasonably central. When fairs are on, forget about anything cheap within a radius of 80 km!

Most of the affordable stand-bys near the train station have either gone up in flames or been given over to government housing for Eastern European immigrants and asylumseekers. One survivor is *Pension Wal* (☎ 25 35 45), Stuttgarter Strasse 9, which charges DM52/85 for claustrophobic singles/doubles (add DM10/20 when fairs are on). A more cheerful option is the *Hotel Glockshuber* (☎ 74 26 28/29), on the 4th and 5th floors of Mainzer Landstrasse 120, where sunny rooms for DM75/130 include bacon-and-egg breakfasts. *Hotel Adler* (☎ 23 34 55), on the 4th floor at Niddastrasse 65, is just north of the station (shoot through the arcade next to Restaurant Panda), and has reasonable rooms for DM70/105 (DM85/170 during fairs); the doubles come with toilet and shower, the singles with toilet (shower in the hallway).

Close to the quieter Palmengarten area, along Beethovenstrasse at No 44 and No 46 respectively, try *Hotel-Pension Gölz* (☎ 74 67 35) or *Pension Sattler* (☎ 74 60 91) for singles/doubles starting at DM60/95, though you'd be lucky to get in at those prices. Alternatively, use the room-finding service at the Hauptbahnhof and be firm about your maximum price.

Places to Eat

The Hauptbahnhof is a good place to pick up a snack. Otherwise, the budget dining options in the city are slim. *China-Restaurant Panda* (☎ 25 12 90), Düsseldorfer Strasse 10, across the road north of the train

GERMANY

station, is a straightforward Chinese restaurant where a surprising number of Chinese eat; meals cost under DM20. The locals' best kept secret is the *Kleinmarkthalle* off Hasengasse. It's an active little city market with picturesque displays of fruit, vegetables, meats, fish and hot food. The *Mozart Café* (☎ 29 19 54) at Töngesgasse 23-25 serves good breakfasts for DM5 to DM10.

The Kalbächer Gasse and Grosse Bockenheimer Strasse area, between Opernplatz and Rathenauplatz, is known to the locals as *Fressgasse* ('Chomp-Alley') and has many cheap fast-food places with outdoor tables (weather permitting). It's at the north-eastern edge of the bank district and is favoured by the lunch-time pinstripe brigade.

In Alt Sachsenhausen, the area directly behind the hostel is filled with cosmopolitan eateries and pubs. The apple-wine taverns in Sachsenhausen are good places to try some typical Frankfurt snacks like *Handkäse mit Musik* (literally, 'hand-cheese with music', a round cheese soaked in oil and vinegar with lots of onions – the music comes later), and *Grüne Sosse* ('green sauce', a mixture of yoghurt, mayonnaise, sour cream and plenty of herbs served with potatoes and meat or eggs – Goethe's favourite food). A particularly good apple-wine tavern in Alt Sachsenhausen is *Lorsbacher Tal* (☎ 61 64 59), Grosse Rittergasse 49.

In Sachsenhausen proper, head for Schweizer Strasse, the main shopping street, where you'll find plenty of snack bars and other eateries. Two worthwhile apple-wine taverns in this area are *Wagner Adolf* (☎ 61 25 65), Schweizer Strasse 71, and *Zum Gemalten Haus* (☎ 61 45 59), Schweizer Strasse 67, a lively place full of paintings of old Frankfurt.

Back on the north shore, a good hunting ground is Berger Strasse, the artery of the trendy Bornheim area north of the zoo. At No 6 is *Café Gegenwart* (☎ 4 97 05 44), a stylishly funky bar/restaurant with good traditional German food for DM13.50 to DM20; good breakfasts are prepared there too, and if the weather cooperates you can sit outside.

Some of the pubs mentioned in the following Entertainment section also serve meals. There's a fruit-and-vegetable *market* every Friday at Südbahnhof.

Entertainment

With 30,000 students and many more visitors, there's plenty of evening entertainment. Frankfurt's jazz scene is second to none, and the top acts perform at the *Jazzkeller* (☎ 28 85 37), Kleine Bockenheimer Strasse 18a, which is open Tuesday to Saturday from 9 pm to around 3 am; concerts begin at 9.30 pm. The second choice, which is a bit less commercial, is the *Jazzkneipe* (☎ 28 71 73) at Berliner Strasse 70.

You'll inevitably find something worthwhile if you stroll around Sachsenhausen at night, but young and trendy Frankfurters shun the area a bit these days, declaring it run-down and swamped by tourists and US service personnel. They prefer Bornheim and Nord End.

In the Bornheim area (see the previous Places to Eat section), you'll find several interesting pubs at the beginning of Berger Strasse. Another popular hang-out is *Mousonturm* (☎ 40 58 95 20), Waldschmidtstrasse 4, a converted soap factory that offers dance performances and politically oriented cabaret as well as a lively coffee shop. The New Wave/punk scene (or whatever it's called this month) congregates at *Harveys* on Friedberger Platz, or closer to the city centre at *Zeil 10*, which is also the address. Another popular venue is the appropriately named *Negativ*, close to the youth hostel at Walter Korb Strasse 1, where there are regular band performances.

The Nord End area, west of Bornheim, also attracts students and trendoids. *Grössenwahn* (☎ 59 93 56), Lenaustrasse 97, is a lively pub with good creative food for less than DM20. *Paulaner* (☎ 43 15 10), Rotlintstrasse 28, is a pub that's always packed, though the food is only so-so. The young disco crowd goes to the up-market *Plastik* at Seilerstrasse 34 (open from 9 pm to 4 am, closed Tuesday and weekends).

Top bands perform at *Sinnkasten* (☎ 23 08

85), just north of the city centre at Brönner-strasse 5. It is open daily except Monday from 9.30 pm to 2 or 3 am (disco Friday and Saturday). You can play pool there, too.

Opera and theatre are other strong points of Frankfurt's entertainment scene. For information and bookings, ring the Municipal Opera on ☎ 23 60 61 (Theaterplatz 1-3), or the Hertie concert and theatre-booking service on ☎ 29 48 48 (Zeil 90). There's a recorded information service in German on ☎ 1 15 17.

Things to Buy

There aren't any special things you should buy in Frankfurt, but the shopping is excellent and it's an ideal place to satisfy any souvenir needs before boarding the train or aeroplane home. Frankfurt's main shopping street is the Zeil, particularly the section between the Hauptwache and the Konstablerwache. It's reputed to do more business than any other shopping district in Europe yet it is generally expensive. A better option is the huge Kaufhalle department store at the Hauptwache.

For much more pleasant shopping, however, stroll down Schweizer Strasse, Sachsenhausen's main shopping street, or Berger Strasse north-east of the city centre. The latter has a friendly, small-town atmosphere and is lined with little art galleries and odd shops selling all sorts of weird and wonderful stuff. There's a great flea market along Museumsufer every Saturday till the early afternoon.

Getting There & Away

Air The airport, Flughafen Frankfurt/Main, is Germany's largest airport and has the second-highest passenger turnover in Europe. It's a complete town in itself and a claustrophobic maze. Departure halls A, B and C are on Level 2; arrival halls A, B and C, as well as bus connections, are on Level 1; check-in counters and train connections are on Level 0 (ground floor); and the U-Bahn lives on Level -1. Departure and arrival halls A are for domestic flights, whereas halls B and C are for international flights. Good

luck! For airline information, ring ☎ 6 90 30 51.

Bus Long-distance buses congregate on the southern side of the main train station, where there's a Europabus office (☎ 23 07 35/6) open Monday to Friday from 7.30 am to 6 pm, weekends to 2.30 pm. It caters for most European destinations, but the most interesting possibility is the Romantic Road bus (rail passes accepted), which leaves daily at 8.15 am and costs DM104/187 one-way/return for the full 11½-hour trip to Füssen; a one-day excursion to Rothenburg would set you back DM43/77. The Europabus head office is Deutsche Touring GmbH (☎ 7 90 30), Römerhof 17. For Germanrail bus information, call ☎ 1 94 19.

Train The Hauptbahnhof digests more trains than any other station in Germany (1450 a day, with more than a quarter of a million travellers), so finding a train to/from almost anywhere is not a problem. The information office for train connections, tickets etc is at the head of track No 9, and you can stock up on supplies in the many shops above and below ground. For train information, call ☎ 1 94 19.

Car & Motorbike Frankfurt features the famed Frankfurter Kreuz, the biggest autobahn intersection in the country. The Mitfahrzentrale (☎ 1 94 40) is at Baseler Strasse 7, three minutes' walk south of the train station. It's open Monday to Friday from 8 am to 6 pm, Saturday till noon. Examples of fares are: DM28 to Amsterdam, DM20 to Basel, DM24 to Munich, DM40 to London and DM46 to Milan, plus DM3 to DM25 agency costs, depending on the destination.

Getting Around

To/From the Airport The S-Bahn No 15 travels between the airport and the main train station every 10 minutes (takes 11 minutes and costs DM5, or DM3.70 outside peak hours); the S-14 continues to the Hauptwache every 20 minutes (takes 15 minutes, same price). Bus No 61 runs to/from the Südbahnhof in Sachsenhausen. Taxis charge about DM35 for the trip into town but are slower than the train.

Car & Motorbike Traffic flows smoothly in Frankfurt, but the extensive system of one-way streets makes it extremely frustrating to get to where you want to go. You're better off parking your vehicle in one of the many (expensive) parking garages and proceeding on foot. Motorbikes can be parked on the pavement so long as they don't obstruct pedestrians.

Public Transport The bus system is OK, but the rail system (tram, S-Bahn and U-Bahn) is almost as comprehensive and much faster. Tickets are valid for all forms of transport and are based on a zone system – one zone will get you around most of town, but to get to/from the airport you need a two-zone ticket. Most tickets are dispensed from machines taking DM5 coins and less. A single trip costs DM2.60/5 for one/two zones, or DM1.90/3.70 outside peak hours. Trips of up to two km, irrespective of the zones, cost DM1.40 outside peak hours (DM2.10 otherwise). If you plan to do much travelling, buy a single-zone, 24-hour ticket for DM5, which is also valid for the airport (available from blue FVV machines or from bus drivers). The three-day version costs DM12, and a seven-day ticket costs DM23.50 (DM17.50 for students). There are many other options.

Major ticket/information offices can be found in the main train station (in the shopping arcade under the tourist office, open Monday to Friday from 6.30 am to 7 pm, Saturday 8 am to 5 pm, Sunday 9 am to 4 pm); the Hauptwache and Konstablerwache shopping arcades (open Monday to Friday from 7 am to 7 pm, Saturday 9 am to 3 pm); and the airport, next to exit No 5 in arrival hall B (open daily from 6 am to 10.30 pm). Ask for the informative *Discover Frankfurt by Train & Bus* brochure (also available from the tourist offices), which tells you how to get to the major sights. For further informa-

tion, call ☎ 26 94 62 (Monday to Friday from 8.30 am to 4.30 pm).

Taxi Taxis are slow compared with public transport and quite expensive at DM3.60 flagfall plus DM2.05 per km. There are taxi ranks throughout the city, or ring ☎ 23 00 01/33, ☎ 25 00 01 or ☎ 54 50 11.

North Rhine-Westphalia

North Rhine-Westphalia (Nordrhein-Westfalen) was formed in 1946 from a hotchpotch of principalities and bishoprics, most of which had belonged to Prussia since the early 19th century. A quarter of Germany's population lives here. The Rhine-Ruhr industrial area is the country's economic powerhouse and one of the most densely populated conurbations in the world. The capital is Düsseldorf.

Though the area is dominated by barren industrial cities connected by a maze of autobahns, the forested highlands of Sauerland and the northern Eifel region offer ample scope for outdoor recreation, thanks in part to an extensive network of dams and artificial lakes that form the Ruhr's water supply. Some of the cities are steeped in history and possess countless sights and other attractions that warrant an extensive visit.

COLOGNE
Because of its location on a major crossroads of European trade routes, Cologne (Köln) was an important city even in Roman times. It was then known as Colonia Agrippinensis, the capital of the province of Germania, and had no less than 300,000 inhabitants. In later years it remained one of northern Europe's major cities (the largest in Germany until the 19th century), and is still the centre of the German Roman Catholic church. Though almost completely destroyed in WW II, it was soon rebuilt and many of its old churches were meticulously restored.

It's worth making an effort to visit this city, if only for the cathedral (Dom), which gets more visitors than any other attraction in Germany. It's even worth just jumping off at the convenient train station for an hour or two. Once there, though, you might want to stay, because there's much more to see.

Orientation

Situated on the Rhine, the skyline of Cologne is dominated by the Dom. The pedestrianised Hohe Strasse runs straight through the middle of the old town from north to south and is Cologne's major shopping street. The main train station is just north of the Dom, within walking distance of almost everything. The main bus station is immediately behind the train station, on Breslauer Platz.

If you arrive by private transport, head for one of the many underground parking garages in the city centre; a neat system of electronic signs indicates exactly how many parking spaces are left, and where they are.

Information

The tourist office (☎ 0221-2 21 33 45) is conveniently located opposite the Dom's main entrance, at Unter Fettenhennen 19. It's open Monday to Saturday from 8 am to 10.30 pm, Sundays and public holidays from 9 am; from November to May, opening hours are from 8 am to 9 pm, and 9.30 am to 7 pm respectively. Expect to stand in line, and have your questions ready, because the staff can act like assembly-line workers. Browse through the chained booklets before deciding which to buy. *Monatvorschau*, the monthly what's-on booklet, is a good investment at DM2. The room-finding service, at DM3, is a bargain when the city is busy with trade fairs.

Money The bank at the train station is open from 7 am to 9 pm, seven days a week. The station post office (open from 7 am to 10 pm Monday to Friday, 11 am to 8 pm Saturday, and 10.30 am to 10 pm Sunday) cashes travellers' cheques but won't exchange cash.

Post & Telecommunications The main post office (☎ 0221-1400) is just opposite the train station at An den Dominikanern. It's

open from 8 am to 6 pm Monday to Friday, to 1 pm Saturday.

Cologne's telephone code is 0221.

Bookshops The train station has an Internationale Presse shop with newspapers and magazines from all over the world. Female travellers can get additional reading matter from the Women's Cultural Centre (☎ 52 92 08) at Moltkestrasse 66, which has a bookshop with a great selection of feminist publications. It's open Monday to Friday from 10 am to 6.30 pm, Saturday to 2 pm.

Emergency You can call the police on ☎ 110; for fire and ambulance, ring ☎ 112. An on-call doctor can be contacted on ☎ 72 07 72.

Dangers & Annoyances The train station is usually quite safe, as it stays busy from early in the morning to late at night. Watch your valuables, however, during the crazy days of the Cologne Carnival (see the Festivals section that follows).

Things to See

Cologne has one of the most extensive old town centres in the country, and the Dom is its heart, soul, and tourist draw. Combined with the excellent museums next door, plan to spend at least one full day inside and around the cathedral.

Dom First, head around to the south side of the Dom for an overall view. The structure's sheer size, with spires rising to a height of 157 metres, is the first shock to the system. Building began in 1248 in the French Gothic style. The huge project was stopped in 1560, but was started again in 1842, in the style originally planned, as a symbol of Prussia's drive for unification. It was finished in 1880, an impressive feat that is almost unimaginable in these days of cost-surveillance bureaucrats. On the square in front of the Dom, check the life-size copy of the finial that crowns each of the spires – they look like little flowers way up there, but they are actually 9.5 metres high.

GERMANY

GERMANY

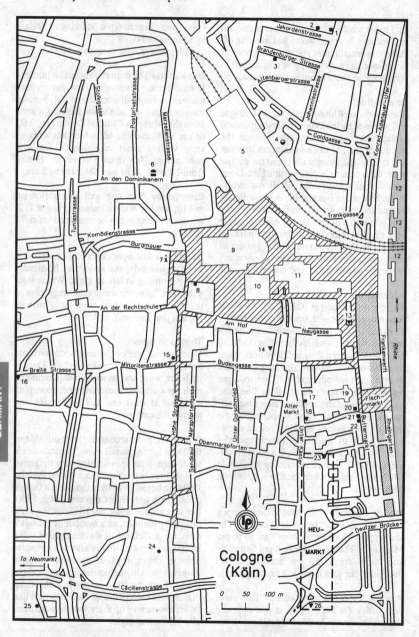

Cologne
(Köln)

0   50   100 m

To Neumarkt

HEU-
MARKT

■ PLACES TO STAY

1 Hotel Einig
2 Hotel Rossner
3 Hotel Berg
20 Stapelhäuschen

▼ PLACES TO EAT

13 Op d'r Woosch-Eck
14 Brauhaus Sion
16 Rauchermacher
18 Gaffel-Haus
23 Päffgen
26 Zur Malzmühle

OTHER

4 Bus Station
5 Train Station
6 Main Post Office
7 Tourist Office
8 4711 Ferdinand Mühlens
9 Cathedral (Dom)
10 Römisch-Germanisches Museum
11 Wallraf-Richartz & Ludwig Museum
12 Rhine Boat Jetties
15 Kaufhalle Department Store
17 Papa Joe's Klimperkasten
19 Gross St Martin Church
21 Biermuseum
22 Papa Joe's Em Streckstrump
24 Kaufhof Department Store
25 Schnütgen Museum

The Dom is open daily from 7 am to 7 pm. Invest DM1 in the informative *Cologne Cathedral* booklet sold at the tourist office and head inside the cathedral by the west door, the main entrance. When you reach the transept, you'll be overwhelmed by the sheer size and magnificence of it all. The five **stained-glass windows** along the north aisle depict the lives of the Virgin and St Peter. Behind the high altar, check the **Magi's Shrine**, attributed to the Flemish enamellist and goldsmith, Nicholas of Verdun (circa 1150-1210). On the south side, in a chapel off the ambulatory, is the **Adoration of the Magi altarpiece**, painted by Stefan Lochner (circa 1400-51).

If you understand German, the free guided tours are excellent and get you into places that other people can't reach. They are held at 10 and 11 am, and 2.30, 3.30 and 4.30 pm Monday to Friday, 10 and 11 am Saturday, and 2.30 and 3.30 pm Sunday; groups meet to the right inside the entrance. Contact the tourist office to see if you can join an English-language tour. But most of all, simply walk around this awe-inspiring building.

For a fitness fix, pay DM3 (students DM1.50) to climb 509 steps up the Dom's south tower to the base of the stupendous steeple, which used to tower over all of Europe until the Eiffel Tower took over. Check the 24-tonne **Peter Bell** on your way up: tuned in C-minor, it's the largest working bell in the world. At the end of your climb, the view from the vantage point, 98.25 metres off the ground, is absolutely stunning: with clear weather you can see all the way to the Siebengebirge mountains beyond Bonn. The cathedral treasury, just inside the north entrance (open from 9 am to 5 pm Monday to Saturday, 1 to 4 pm Sunday, DM3/1.50 adults/students entry fee) is pretty average. Kids all head for the crypt a few steps farther, where Cologne's archbishops are interred.

Other Churches Back in the city streets, there are many other, smaller, churches worth a look. Though many were destroyed in WW II (Allied bombers were instructed to spare the Dom but not much else), they were soon rebuilt and Cologne now has 12 interesting Romanesque churches, all within walking distance. The most handsome from the outside is **Gross St Martin**, Cologne's riverside signature before the Dom was completed, while the best interior has to be that of **St Gereon** on Christophstrasse, with its incredible four-storey decagon.

Museums The **Römisch-Germanisches Museum**, next to the cathedral at Roncalliplatz 1, has an inspired collection of artefacts from the original Roman settlement. It's one of Europe's finest archaeological museums, with exhibits on architecture, travel, river

GERMANY

use, cults, coins, statuary, entertainment and much more. On the 2nd floor, you can see artefacts from the Rhine Valley.

The **Wallraf-Richartz & Ludwig Museum** at Bischofsgartenstrasse 1 is one of the country's finest art galleries and makes brilliant use of natural light. The 1st floor is devoted to the Cologne Masters of the 14th to 16th centuries, known for their distinctive use of colour. Farther along, look for familiar names like Rubens, Frans Hals, Rembrandt and Munch. On the 2nd floor, the contemporary art collection provides a wonderful contrast. Catch some prime Kirchner, Kandinsky, Max Ernst, as well as pop-art works by Rauschenberg and Andy Warhol. The building also houses the Cologne Philharmonic Orchestra, and a unique photography collection from the former Agfa Museum in Leverkusen.

At Cäcilienstrasse 29, the former church of St Cecilia houses the **Schnütgen Museum**, an overwhelming display of church riches, including many religious artefacts and early ivory carvings.

The old town centre also has many other museums worth visiting, depending on your interests. One lesser known museum is actually in a bank branch and thus keeps bank hours. The **Käthe Kollwitz Museum** at Neumarkt 18-24 displays the work of one of Germany's great socialist female artists. Though some of her sculpture is here as well, it's her black-and-white graphics that steal the show.

Organised Tours

The tourist office has all sorts of organised tours and city walks. The standard, two-hour bus tour of the city (in German and English) leaves from the tourist office every hour on the hour between 10 am and 3 pm, takes two hours and costs DM20.

Festivals

Carnival Try to time a visit to Cologne during the wild and crazy period of carnival, rivalled only by Munich's Oktoberfest. People dress in creative costumes, clown suits, as popular personalities, and whatever else their alcohol-numbed brains may invent. The streets explode with activity beginning on the Thursday before the seventh Sunday prior to Easter. Friday and Saturday are relatively normal during the day, but the streets pep up in the evening. Sunday is like Thursday, but Monday's *Rosenmontag* celebration is unique. There are formal and informal parades, much spontaneous singing and celebrating, and general merriment. Check with the tourist office for specific events and ticket information. Accommodation will be booked out, so come early or make reservations.

Places to Stay

Apart from the camp sites and youth hostels, cheap accommodation in Cologne is nonexistent. You'd be lucky to find a reasonably central hotel room for under DM60/90 single/double. Private rooms – great alternatives elsewhere in Germany – are reserved for exhibitors at Cologne's huge fairs and aren't rented out to mere mortals.

Camping The most (though not very) convenient camping grounds are the municipal camp site *Cologne-Poll* (☎ 83 19 66, open May to October) on Weidenweg in Poll, five km south-east of the city centre; and *Camping Berger* (☎ 39 24 21, open March to November) in Cologne-Rodenkirchen at Uferstrasse 53a, south of Poll in Rodenkirchen. *Camping Waldbad* (☎ 60 33 15), on Peter-Baum-Weg in Dünnwald, is 15 km from the city centre but open all year.

Hostels Cologne has two youth hostels. The first *Jugendherberge* (☎ 81 47 11) is at Siegesstrasse 5 in Deutz, a 15-minute walk from the station across the Rhine over the Hohenzollernbrücke; it's convenient and relatively cheap (DM19.20), but crowded and not very pleasant. The second *Jugendherberge* (☎ 76 70 81) is a half-hour walk north along the river, in Riehl at An der Schanz. It's much more enjoyable (DM26.20, meals DM7.50). Take U-Bahn No 5, 16 or 18 to the Boltensternstrasse stop.

Hotels Hotels in Cologne are expensive and prices increase by at least 20% when fairs are on. The cheapest rooms are usually taken, so count on paying DM10 to DM15 above the prices quoted here. Several of the more up-market hotels, on the other hand, often slash their prices when things are quiet. If you have private transport, enquire about parking – a night in a parking garage will set you back DM25 (beware: not all garages operate 24 hours). The tourist office room-finding service is your best bet for hotel rooms in the lower price range.

If you insist on hunting around yourself, try *Stapelhäuschen* (☎ 21 20 43) at Fischmarkt 1-3, right in the middle of the Altstadt. Pleasant singles/doubles start at DM60/95, but you'd be lucky to get in at those prices. There's a good but expensive restaurant downstairs.

In the area behind the train and bus stations, try *Hotel Rossner* (☎ 12 27 03), Jakordenstrasse 19, with singles/doubles from DM50/65. *Hotel Berg* (☎ 12 11 24), Brandenburger Strasse 6, has rooms from DM45/75. *Hotel Einig* (☎ 12 21 28), Johannisstrasse 71, offers rooms from DM55/75. All these cheap rooms have toilet and shower facilities out in the corridor.

Places to Eat & Drink
A cosmopolitan range of restaurants lines the Rhine bank south of the cathedral, all of them good but none of them particularly cheap. The Italian restaurants are the best value, so long as you stick to pizza and pasta.

As is the rule in Germany, pubs tend to be the most interesting places to eat. The majority serve decent meals for under DM20 if you don't get carried away by the menu. Cologne's beer halls serve cheap and filling (though often bland) meals to go with their home brew (see the Beer Halls section that follows). *Brauhaus Sion* at Unter Taschenmacher 9 is a big beer hall, packed most nights and for good reason: you'll eat your fill for well under DM20, including a couple of beers. *Zur Malzmühle*, at Heumarkt 6 beyond the Deutzer Brücke feeder roads, is smaller but similar. Slightly more up-market

and much more of a cosy pub, *Päffgen* at Heumarkt 62 (another location at Friesenstrasse 64-66) serves meals for about DM20. It's not uncommon to see the same crowd for lunch and dinner day after day. *Gaffel-Haus*, Alter Markt 20-22, is similar.

The *Kaufhalle* department store on Hohe Strasse, a minute or two from the cathedral, on your right, has a self-service cafeteria downstairs where you can get a dish of the day for around DM9. Cologne's largest department store, *Kaufhof*, towards the end of Hohe Strasse on your right, has a self-service restaurant on the 3rd floor where breakfast costs DM4.95 and main meals cost around DM13.

Snack bars and other eateries are dotted throughout the city. There's a particularly good batch of them in the shopping arcade on the corner of Breite Strasse and Krebsgasse; the *Rauchermacher* butchery here serves great sausage dishes. *Op d'r Woosch-Eck*, on the corner where Neugasse meets the greenery along the Rhine, is another worthwhile target: a generous serving of sausage, sauerkraut and mashed potatoes will set you back DM8.50.

To put together a picnic, there is inevitably a *market* going in one of the squares; the biggest is on Friday in Alter Markt. There are also plenty of supermarkets, though you may have to hunt for them a bit in the city centre.

Entertainment
Evenings and weekends in the Altstadt are like miniature carnivals, with bustling crowds and lots to do. Beer is the beverage of choice and there are lots of places to enjoy it.

For excellent jazz, head for either *Papa Joe's Klimperkasten* at Alter Markt 50, or *Papa Joe's Em Streckstrump* at Buttermarkt 37. The first is large and lively, with a wonderful old pianola, whereas the second is more intimate.

Zülpicher Strasse and Zülpicher Platz, near the university in the south-western part of town (take U-Bahn No 6, 7, 10, 15 or 19 to Zülpicher Platz, or others to the nearby Barbarossaplatz), is the student centre, known as *Quartier Lateng*. The gay scene congregates in the *Belgisches Viertel* around Bismarckstrasse (there is public transport to Bahnhof West or Friesenplatz).

Cologne's leading venue for rock concerts is *E-Werk*, a converted power station at Schanzenstrasse 28-36 in Mülheim. It turns into a huge disco on Friday and Saturday nights from 10.30 pm. Ring ☎ 62 10 91 to find out what's on (recorded message in German outside office hours).

For theatre programme information, ring ☎ 1 15 17; for concerts, exhibitions, special events, trade fairs etc, call ☎ 1 15 16.

Beer Halls Much as in Munich, beer reigns supreme in Cologne. There are 24 local breweries, all producing a local variety called *Kölsch*, a beer unlike any other in Germany. It's relatively light and slightly bitter. The breweries run their own beer halls and serve their wares in skinny glasses holding a mere 200 ml, and you'll soon agree it's a very satisfying way to drink the stuff.

Though not as large or entertainment-oriented as those in Munich, Cologne's beer halls are packed with locals instead of tourists. Apart from the halls already mentioned in the Places to Eat & Drink section, try *Früh am Cathedral* at Am Hof 12-14. For more of a choice in beers, the *Biermuseum* at Buttermarkt 39 (beside Papa Joe's) serves 32 varieties. Another favourite among beer connoisseurs is *Küppers Kölsch Brauhaus* at Altenberger Strasse 157. It has an interesting museum with guided tours.

Things to Buy
This is not the place to make any major purchases, though a good souvenir might be a small bottle of eau de Cologne, which is still produced in its namesake city. Try the fancy 4711 Ferdinand Mühlens Parfümerie Fabrik at Domkloster 2, or find a cheaper version at the Kaufhof at Hohe Strasse 41. Otherwise, check at an airport duty-free shop when you're heading home.

Getting There & Away
Air Cologne/Bonn Airport, the international airport that Cologne shares with Bonn, is growing quickly. There are many connections within Europe and the rest of the world. For flight information, ring ☎ 02203-40 40 01/2. The Lufthansa office (☎ 82 64) is in the city at Bechergasse 2-8.

Train Trains deposit passengers in the shadow of the cathedral. With over 1100 trains a day (Cologne has Germany's highest turnover of train passengers), it's quite easy to jump off and on for a quick visit. For train enquiries, call ☎ 1 94 19.

Boat One enjoyable way to arrive in and depart from Cologne is by boat. The KD German Rhine Line (☎ 2 08 82 88) has its headquarters in the city at Frankenwerft 15, and has dozens of tours and ways to get to other cities along the Rhine, anywhere from Amsterdam to Basel.

Car & Motorbike The city is on a major north-south autobahn route and is thus easy for drivers and hitchhikers. The Mitfahrzentrale (☎ 19 44 4) is at Saarstrasse 22.

Getting Around
To/From the Airport Bus No 170 runs between Cologne/Bonn Airport and the main bus station, as well as Ottoplatz behind the Siegesstrasse youth hostel, every 15 minutes (DM3.80 for the 20-minute trip).

Public Transport Cologne offers a convenient and extensive mix of buses, trams and local trains – trams go underground in the inner city, and trains handle destinations up to 50 km around Cologne. The main bus station is on Breslauer Platz, directly behind the train station.

Ticketing and tariff structures are complicated. The best ticket option is the one-day pass for DM8 if you're staying near the city (one or two zones), DM12 for most of the Cologne area (three zones), and DM16 including Bonn (six zones) and nonexpress connections between the two. It's DM14/25/28 for the three-day versions, and DM2.50/3.70/5 for one-off trips. A one-day family pass for up to four people costs the same as a one-day pass for a single – an excellent deal.

Taxi Taxis cost DM3 flagfall plus DM2.05 per km; add another DM1 if you order by phone (☎ 28 82). There are taxi ranks on the city's larger squares.

DÜSSELDORF

More than 80% of Düsseldorf's Altstadt was destroyed in WW II, but it was reconstructed to become one of the most elegant and wealthy cities in all of Germany. Though not particularly strong in sights, the city is a charming example of big-city living along the Rhine.

Düsseldorf's telephone code is 0211.

Things to See & Do

The tourist office (☎ 35 05 05) is at Konrad-Adenauer-Platz, in front of the main train station (Hauptbahnhof). Upon arrival, head straight for the Königsallee, or 'Kö', a famed shopping, eating and drinking street that provides a perfect view of Düsseldorf's elegant lifestyle. Stroll north along the 'Kö' to the **Hofgarten**, a large park in the city centre.

Museums The Hofgarten is a good base for exploring one or more of Düsseldorf's interesting museums. Art museums include the **Kunstmuseum** at Ehrenhof 5, with a comprehensive collection of paintings, and the **Kunstsammlung Nordrhein-Westfalen** at Grabbeplatz 5, which has a huge collection of Paul Klee's work and other excellent modern art.

The **Goethe-Museum Düsseldorf** in Schloss Jägerhof, Jacobistrasse 2, pays tribute to the life and work of one of Europe's greatest poet-philosophers. The collection and exhibits are large and complete, with books, first drafts, letters, medals and much more.

German-literature buffs will also want to visit the **Heinrich-Heine-Haus** at Bilker Strasse 14, which documents the native Düsseldorfer's poetic career. Appropriately enough for the traveller, his *Reisebilder*

(Travel Images) are an interesting series of travel sketches in a style of travel writing that has become quite popular, where the writer uses life on the road to express opinions about life, politics and anything else.

Places to Stay

The closest camping grounds are *Unterbacher See* (☎ 8 99 20 38) in Düsseldorf-Unterbacher (bus No 781 to Unterbacher), or *Camping Oberlörick* (☎ 59 14 01) in Düsseldorf-Lörick (U-Bahn No 76, 705 or 717 to Belsenplatz, and then bus No 838). The trek to the Altstadt is very inconvenient from either camping ground.

The *Jugendherberge* (☎ 57 40 41) is at Düsseldorfer Strasse 1, a pleasant walk across the river. This is by far the best compromise of price and convenience. It even offers nice private rooms at only DM28. Düsseldorf's city-centre hotels cater to visiting businesspeople and conference attendants.

There is a *YMCA* (☎ 36 07 64) at Graf-Adolf-Strasse 102. Singles/doubles start at DM52/90. For similar rates, try the centrally located *Hotel Esser* (☎ 32 74 67) at Mertensgasse 1, where rooms start at DM70/90. Another option is *Hotel Amsterdam* (☎ 84 05 89) at Stresemannstrasse 20, with rooms from DM70/125.

Places to Eat

One of the best places for a hearty German meal with atmosphere to boot is *Brauerei im Füchschen* at Ratinger Strasse 28. *Zum Schlüssel* on Bolkerstrasse, mentioned in the following Entertainment section for its beer, also has great food; there are daily specials for DM9 to DM15. Also on Bolkerstrasse, at No 44, is *Im goldenen Kessel*, serving similar food to Zum Schlüssel.

Put together a picnic along Flingerstrasse or Bolkerstrasse. Another street worth taking a look down is Liefergasse, which is lined with drinking and eating places serving very tasty-looking meals.

Entertainment

Besides walking and museum-hopping, one

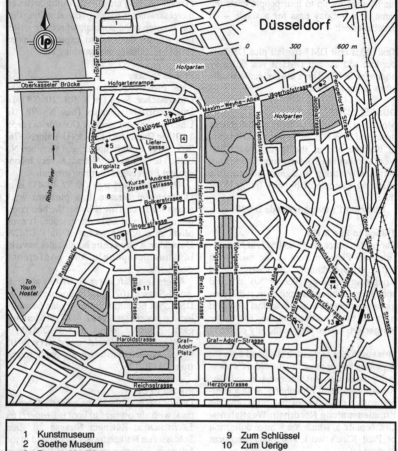

1	Kunstmuseum
2	Goethe Museum
3	Brauerei im Füchschen
4	Kunstsammlung
5	St Lambertus Basilica
6	Kunsthalle
7	Hotel Esser
8	Town Hall

9	Zum Schlüssel
10	Zum Uerige
11	Heinrich Heine Haus
12	Hotel Amsterdam
13	YMCA
14	Main Post Office
15	Tourist Information
16	Hauptbahnhof

of the best things to do in Düsseldorf is (surprise!) drink beer. There are lots of bars (for drinking and eating) in the Altstadt, affectionately referred to as the 'longest bar in the world'. On evenings and weekends,

the best places overflow onto the pedestrian-only streets. Favoured streets include Bolkerstrasse, Kurze Strasse, Andreasstrasse and the surrounding side streets.

The beverage of choice is the Alt beer, a

dark and semisweet brew. Try Gatzweilers Alt in *Zum Schlüssel* at Bolkerstrasse 43-47, and check the sign that says that schnapps is bad for *your* health and *their* business. Even more local in colour, find *Zum Uerige* on Berger Strasse, the only place where you can buy Uerige Alt beer. It charges DM1.90 per glass, and the beer flows so quickly that the waiters just carry around trays and give you a glass when you're ready.

Getting There & Away

Düsseldorf's Lohausen Airport (five minutes by S-Bahn from the city centre) is a major hub for Lufthansa, and is busy with many of its international flights. Lufthansa also offers an express-train service to and from Frankfurt.

Getting Around

To/From the Airport Take the S-Bahn commuter train to and from the Hauptbahnhof, rather than the lengthy and expensive taxi ride. Most visitors, however, take the train into the Hauptbahnhof. It's not at the city centre, but it's a short and pretty walk.

Public Transport Because of its sheer size, Düsseldorf is a difficult city for just walking. But there's an excellent public transport system with an S-Bahn, buses and trams. The 24-hour transport card is a great deal at DM8.50, especially if you opt to camp or sleep outside the expensive city centre.

BONN

This friendly, relaxed city of 310,000 on the Rhine south of Cologne became West Germany's temporary capital in 1949, partly because the leading politician of the time, Konrad Adenauer, happened to live there. Despite being the centre of postwar West German politics, Bonn never lost its provincial feel. Since reunification, it threatens to sink into obscurity once more as the all-German parliament and government ministries shift back to Berlin, where everyone but the Bonn City Council feels they belong. Much to the council's relief, however, the move that was supposed to take four years looks like taking at least twice that long.

Bonn was already settled in Roman times, and celebrated its 2000th anniversary in 1989. In the 18th century, it was the seat of the electors of Cologne, and some of their Baroque architecture survived the ravages of WW II and the postwar demand for modern government buildings. The former court, for instance, is now the university. When the sun and the crowds are out, the old town centre, which is a couple of minutes' walk from the train station, is a lovely area for a stroll.

If you're staying in Cologne, organise a day trip out here and to nearby Bad Godesberg, the spa town that forms one city with Bonn and houses most of its diplomats. Classical music buffs will want to visit Bonn to pay homage to its most famous son, Ludwig van Beethoven, who grew up here before leaving for Vienna at the age of 22.

Information

The modern Bonn Tourist Information Office (☎ 0228-77 34 66) is in an arcade at Münsterstrasse 20. Look carefully, because it's not well signposted. It's open from 8 am to 9 pm Monday to Saturday, 9.30 am to 12.30 pm Sunday (closes at 7 pm weekdays from November to March), and operates a DM3 room-finding service (DM5 for rooms over DM100). The staff, looking like ticket-takers behind their glass screens, enthusiastically promote their city, and the range of brochures and free maps is second to none. Invest DM1 in the *Bonn – Sights & Museums* booklet and, if you understand German, DM1.50 in the excellent monthly *Bonn Information* booklet that lists everything you need to know, including what's happening on the busy cultural scene. Ask about the walking tour.

The bank in the train station operates Monday to Saturday from 7.30 am to 6.30 pm, Sunday 8.30 am to 1 pm. The main post office is on Münsterplatz, and is open Monday to Friday from 8 am to 6 pm, Saturday to 1 pm, and Sunday from 11 am to noon, with extended hours for telephone services.

Bonn and Bad Godesberg's telephone code is 0228.

GERMANY

Foreign Embassies So long as the German foreign ministry remains in Bonn, most of the foreign embassies will remain here too. Those in East Berlin have generally been demoted to the status of consulates or have been closed altogether. See the Facts for the Visitor section at the beginning of this chapter for a list.

Things to See & Do

A key attraction is **Beethoven's House** at Bonngasse 20 (open Monday to Saturday from 10 am to 5 pm, Sunday to 1 pm, DM5, students DM1.50). The composer was born in this house in 1770 and it contains much memorabilia concerning his life and music. In the front room on the 2nd floor, take a look at his last piano, specially made with an amplified sounding board to accommodate his deafness. The ear trumpets will make you wonder what kind of music he could have written with good hearing. If possible, plan your visit to Bonn during the Beethoven Festival, which is held every three years (the next will be in 1995).

In a memorial to another composer, the **Robert Schumann House** at Sebastianstrasse 182 is packed with stuff from Schumann's turbulent life in Bonn. He tried to commit suicide by jumping into the Rhine, and ultimately had himself committed to the sanatorium next door. Admission is free.

Sts Cassius and Florentinus, two martyred Roman officers who became the patron saints of Bonn, are honoured in the **Münster-basilica** on Münsterplatz. It's one of the best examples of the unique Rhenish style of architecture in the transition from Romanesque to Gothic. The interior is mainly Baroque.

The **Bundeshaus**, Germany's parliament building, started off as an education academy in the Bauhaus period but has since been extensively rebuilt and expanded. It's at Göresstrasse 15, south-east of the city centre on the Rhine. You would have to be particularly interested in German politics to take the (excellent) tour, which has to be booked in advance – contact the tourist office, or the Bundestag visitor service direct on ☎ 16 21

52. There are several museums and palaces in Bonn, which you can keep in mind in case it rains.

Places to Stay & Eat

Bonn doesn't have convenient camping, and the *Venusberg* youth hostel (☎ 28 12 00), Haager Weg 42, is inconveniently, but beautifully, located in the woods on Venusberg south of the city. With 257 beds, it tends to cater for visiting school kids and is large and loud. A bunk costs DM26.20 including breakfast, and there is lunch and dinner for DM7.50. Take bus No 621 to the 'Jugendherberge' stop.

For the ultimate in German hostel elegance, head for the 90-bed *Jugendgästehaus Bad Godesberg* (☎ 31 75 16) in Bad Godesberg at Horionstrasse 60. Prices are identical to Venusberg. Take bus No 615 from this pretty town's train station to the 'Jugendgästehaus' stop. At both youth hostels, couples may be able to grab one of the rooms reserved for group leaders.

Perhaps because of the modesty of public servants' expense accounts, Bonn's hotels are not as pricey as you'd expect – DM55/90 should get you a single/double within easy walking distance of the city centre. Try *Kurfürstenhof* (☎ 63 11 66) on Baumschulallee 20 behind the train station; *Eschweiler* (☎ 63 17 60), Bonngasse 7, right in the city centre just off Markt; or *Deutsches Haus* (☎ 63 37 77), Kasernenstrasse 19-21, just north of the centre (with a good, unpretentious restaurant). As usual, the tourist office's room-finding service can save you a lot of aggravation. Hotels in Bad Godesberg are slightly cheaper.

Many pubs in Bonn serve decent food at decent prices. *Zum Gequetschen* at Sternstrasse 6, on the corner with Kasernenstrasse, is a cosy, Cologne-style beer establishment where you'll eat more than you should for under DM20, and that includes a beer or two. Snack bars aren't hard to find, and there's a colourful *food market* on Markt square in front of the Rathaus from 8 am to 6.30 pm Monday to Friday, to 2 pm Saturday.

Getting There & Away

Bonn makes for a pleasant day trip from Cologne or Düsseldorf, and it can even be seen by just jumping off the train for a few hours on your way through. There are 71 trains a day to/from Cologne in the north, and 77 a day to/from Koblenz in the south. The Köln-Düsseldorfer boat line (☎ 65 48 98 for the Bonn office) also runs through Bonn.

Getting Around

Most of Bonn's sights are within an easy and pleasant walk from the station. The Bonn transit system is linked with Cologne's (see the Cologne Getting Around section for a pass covering both). A one-day pass only for Bonn costs DM8 (same price for a whole family); a three-day single pass costs DM14.

AACHEN

This industrial and commercial city of 260,000, within a stone's throw of the point where Germany, the Netherlands and Belgium meet, was already known in Roman times for its thermal springs. The great Frankish conqueror, Charlemagne (Karl der Grosse in German), was so impressed by their revitalising qualities that he settled here and made it the capital of his empire in 794 AD. Ever since, Aachen has held special significance among the icons of German nationhood, and no less than 32 Holy Roman emperors were crowned in its cathedral.

Although Charlemagne and his legacy dominate the city's tourist literature, Aachen's location on the north-western edge of the scenic Eifel Massif makes it a convenient base for hikers and day-trippers in the area. Worth visiting is the fairy-tale town of Monschau, where the law requires that roofs be made from slate cut in the nearby hills.

Aachen is home to the largest technical university in Germany, its 50,000 students adding considerably to the city's charm.

Orientation

Aachen's compact old centre is contained within two ring roads that roughly follow the old city walls. The inner ring road, or Grabenring, has different names all ending in '-graben', and encloses the old city proper. This is mainly a pedestrian zone, although the city planners have done a good job of keeping it accessible to cars, with unobtrusive parking garages. The roads that form the outer ring, or Alleenring, have all sorts of different names and only a few of them end in '-allee'.

The main train station is in the south-eastern corner of the Alleenring. The city centre with the cathedral and the Rathaus is a 10-minute walk away.

Information

The helpful tourist office (☎ 0241-1 80 29 65) is opposite the train station at Bahnhofplatz 4. It's open Monday to Friday from 9 am to 6.30 pm, Saturday to 1 pm, and books hotels and private rooms for a DM3 fee. The main tourist office (☎ 0241-1 80 29 60/1) is at Atrium Eisenbrunnen, just inside the Grabenring east of the cathedral. (The locals head for the arcade next door to recharge their internal batteries with a drink of warm, sulphurous spring water that flows from the spouts 24 hours a day.)

There's a bank with exchange facilities at the train station, to your left at the exit. It is open Monday to Friday from 8.30 am to 12.30 pm and 1.30 to 4.30 pm, and Saturday from 9 am to 1.30 pm. Make sure you obtain some DM beforehand if you're coming across the border outside these hours.

The main post office (☎ 0241-41 20) is at Kapuzinergraben 19, diagonally opposite the main tourist office, back towards the train station. It's open Monday to Friday from 8 am to 6 pm, Saturday to 1 pm. The bus station is at the north-eastern edge of the Grabenring on the corner of Kurhausstrasse and Peterstrasse.

If you need to do any washing, there's a laundrette in an old bus (no kidding!), complete with dummy driver, next to Gaststätte Labyrinth (see the Places to Eat & Drink section) on Pontstrasse.

Aachen's telephone code is 0241.

Things to See & Do

Cathedral Aachen's major drawcard is its

GERMANY

GERMANY

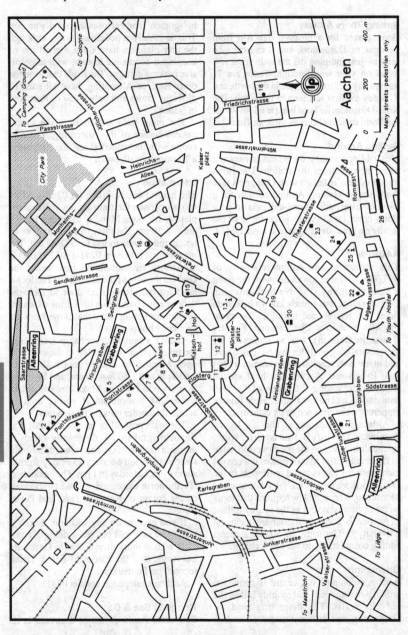

■ PLACES TO STAY

21 Hotel Marx
23 Hotel Rösener
24 Karls-Hotel

▼ PLACES TO EAT

3 Gaststätte Labyrinth
4 Pizzeria La Finestra
5 Katakomben Studentenzentrum
6 Café Kittel
8 Goldener Schwan
10 Aachener Ratskeller &
    Postwagen
11 Goldene Rose

OTHER

1 Ponttor
2 Laundry Bus
7 International Newspaper
   Museum
9 Rathaus
12 Cathedral
13 Tourist information
14 Domkeller
15 Römerbad
16 Bus Station
17 Ludwig Forum for
    International Art
18 Club Voltaire
19 City Theatre
20 Main Post Office
22 Marschiertor
25 Tourist Information
26 Main Train Station

cathedral (Dom, Kaiserdom or Münster), open daily from 7 am to 7 pm. Though not very grand, the cathedral's historical significance and interior serenity make a visit almost obligatory – it's on UNESCO's world cultural heritage list as an 'ensemble of importance to the history of art and architecture'. The Holy Roman emperors were crowned here from 936 to 1531, when the coronation site was moved to Frankfurt.

The heart of the cathedral is formed by a Byzantine-inspired **octagon**, built on Roman foundations, which was the largest vaulted structure north of the Alps when it was inaugurated as Charlemagne's court chapel in 805. It became a site of pilgrimage

after his death, not least because of the religious relics contained therein: Christ's swaddling clothes and loincloth, Mary's gown and the decapitation cloth of St John the Baptist. The Gothic **choir** was added in 1414 – its massive stained-glass windows are impressive even though some date from after WW II. The octagon received its **folded dome** after the city fire of 1656 destroyed the original tent roof. The **western tower**, which crowns the entrance, looks Gothic but dates from the 19th century.

Worth noting are the huge brass **chandelier**, which was added to the octagon by Emperor Frederick Barbarossa in 1165; the **high altar** with its 11th century, gold-plated *Pala d'Oro* frontal depicting scenes of the Passion; and the gilded copper ambo, or **pulpit**, donated by Henry II. Unless you join a German-language tour (DM2, ring ahead on ☎ 4 77 09 27 to see if you can join one in English), you'll only catch a glimpse of Charlemagne's white-marble **throne** on the upper gallery of the octagon where the nobles sat (common people sat downstairs).

When you exit the cathedral, turn right into Klostergasse, and immediately on your right is the entrance to the **Domschatzkammer** ('Cathedral Treasury', DM3 entry fee, or DM2 for students), with one of the richest collections of religious art north of the Alps. It's housed in a well-camouflaged, multi-million-dollar, reinforced-concrete bunker with air-conditioning capable of withstanding outside temperatures of 300°C. Highlights include the gold-and-silver bust of Charlemagne, the beautiful Lotharian Cross (coronation cross of the Holy Roman emperors), a 2nd century AD marble sarcophagus said once to contain Charlemagne's remains, and the shrine of the Virgin, designed to hold the four Aachen relics. A large map on the stairwell wall gives a clear idea of the extent of Charlemagne's empire, which stretched from the Pyrenees and southern Italy to the Elbe.

Other Sights North of the cathedral, the 14th century **Rathaus** overlooks Markt square with its fountain statue of Charlemagne. The eastern tower of the Rathaus, the Granusturm, was once part of Charlemagne's palace. The Rathaus is open Monday to Friday from 8 am to 1 pm and 2 to 7 pm, Saturday and Sunday from 10 am, and admission costs DM2 (DM1 for students). Don't bother if you're pressed for time, but history buffs will no doubt be thrilled to stand in the grand Empire Hall upstairs, where German emperors enjoyed their celebratory feasts after their coronations. There's a good view of the cathedral as you go up the stairs.

There are several museums worth visiting, most notably the **Ludwig Forum for International Art** in a former umbrella factory built in Bauhaus style on Jülicherstrasse 97-109; it has works by Warhol, Lichtenstein, Baselitz and others (closed Monday, admission DM4, students DM2, free on the first Sunday of the month). The **International Newspaper Museum**, Pontstrasse 13, has a collection of 120,000 newspapers with many first, last and other special editions. It's open Tuesday to Friday from 9.30 am to 1 pm and 2.30 to 5 pm (only to 1 pm Saturday), and admission is free.

Thermal Baths You're unlikely to find a thermal bath closer to a city centre anywhere else in Europe. **Römerbad** (☎ 1 80 29 22), Buchkremerstrasse 1, will let you drift off on cloud nine for DM10 (students DM5). It's open Monday to Friday from 7 am to 7 pm, to 9 pm Wednesday, and to 1 pm Saturday and Sunday.

Places to Stay
The *camping ground* (☎ 15 85 02, open May to October) is in a great location just 10 minutes' walk north-east of the city centre, at the edge of the City Park at Passstrasse 85.

The *Colynshof* youth hostel (☎ 7 11 01), Maria-Theresia-Allee 260, is four km south-west of the train station on a hill overlooking the city. Catch bus No 2 to the Ronheide stop, or bus No 12 to the closer Colynshof stop at the foot of the hill (a taxi from the train station will set you back DM8.50). It costs DM15.80/19.30 for juniors/seniors, including breakfast, and other meals are available. It's usually packed with school kids, but couples may be able to score a room normally reserved for teachers.

The tourist information offices have private rooms from DM30/50 single/double, but make sure they give you something that's within walking distance of the city centre, as this is where everything happens.

Hotels are of the usual German standard, ie clean, friendly and efficient. Don't be disappointed if the cheapest rooms are taken, even on a Monday in the low season. *Hotel Marx* (☎ 3 75 41/2/3), Hubertusstrasse 33-35, has singles/doubles from DM55/90, and an inner courtyard where you can park your car (a bonus in Aachen). *Hotel Rösener* (☎ 40 72 15), Theaterstrasse 62, has rooms from DM52/80, but parking can be a problem. Opposite the train station, *Karls-Hotel* (☎ 3 54 49), Leydelstrasse 10, has the same prices.

Places to Eat & Drink
Being a university town, Aachen is full of lively cafés, restaurants and pubs. The distinction between the different categories is murky, since many pubs and cafés double as restaurants and most cafés serve alcohol. A large number are concentrated along Pontstrasse, which runs from Markt north-west to the early 14th century Ponttor, one of Aachen's two remaining city gates (the other is the less impressive Marschiertor, near the train station).

Heading up from Markt, *Café Kittel* (☎ 3 65 60), Pontstrasse 39, is a popular student hang-out that manages to seem warm despite the cold white paint, chrome and mirrors. It serves reasonably priced small meals including vegetarian dishes. *Katakomben Studentenzentrum*, Pontstrasse 74-76, is a mensa-type cafeteria in a horribly modern building; redeeming features are its excellent value and the fact that it also serves breakfast.

For authentic Italian food and a matching ambience, complete with a gaggle of Italian waiters shouting out their orders, head for *Pizzeria La Finestra* (☎ 2 58 45), Pontstrasse

123, where you can get mini pizzas from DM3 and large ones from DM8.50. Diagonally opposite, on Pontstrasse 156-158, next to the Holy Cross Church, is *Gaststätte Labyrinth* (☎ 3 55 95), a rambling beer-hall-type place that lives up to its name. The clientele includes students and nonstudents alike, and it's invariably busy. Good, filling meals range from DM8 to DM15, and the menu also lists several vegetarian dishes.

Back on Markt, *Goldener Schwan* (☎ 3 16 49), Markt 37, is a great old pub with meals from DM10 to DM24, and pizzas for around DM9. The jewel of Aachen's pub/restaurants is the *Aachener Ratskeller & Postwagen* (☎ 3 50 01), a 300-year-old establishment on the eastern side of the Rathaus underneath Charlemagne's Granusturm, with small, wooden rooms up and down several stairs, and a tremendous atmosphere. The Postwagen is a pub as well as a restaurant, whereas the Ratskeller only serves food. Prices are surprisingly reasonable, with a lunch-time dish of the day for DM12.50.

Goldene Rose (☎ 2 87 82), facing the west side of the cathedral on Fischmarkt 1, is busy and boisterous, with more than a touch of style at slightly above-average prices. *Domkeller*, around the other side of the cathedral at Hof 1, is a pub with great atmosphere but, unfortunately, no food.

On Katschhof, the square between the cathedral and the Rathaus, there's a food-and-flower *market* on Tuesdays and Fridays from 8 am to 1 pm. Alternatively, there are many small supermarkets around town where you can put together a picnic meal.

Entertainment

There are several discotheques in Aachen, mainly frequented by the young to the very young. The more mature crowd heads for *Club Voltaire* (☎ 54 34 27), Friedrichstrasse 9, which really starts swinging to funk and other Black music from midnight. *Be-bop* (☎ 2 14 21), Südstrasse 54, plays jazz in its pub but South American and other rhythms on the dance floor, from 10 pm to 2 am Tuesdays to Sundays. *Rotation* (☎ 4 88 74),

Pontstrasse 135, isn't bad either but charges a DM5 entry fee.

Aachen has a lively music scene, with talented buskers playing the streets and squares, and many pubs featuring occasional live performances. The *City Theatre* (☎ 4 78 42 44 for bookings) on Theaterplatz has concerts and opera almost every night; the tourist information offices can tell you what's on, or contact the Culture Office (☎ 4 32 41 09) on the corner of Wilhelmstrasse and Theaterstrasse.

Getting There & Away

Aachen is well served by road and rail. Just north-east of town is the junction of the A4 autobahn between Maastricht/Heerlen and Cologne, and the A44 autobahn between Liège and Düsseldorf. There are fast trains almost every hour to Cologne (55 minutes, DM16.80) and Liège (50 minutes, DM12), and local trains every two hours to Maastricht (45 minutes, DM9.20).

Getting Around

Aachen's points of interest are clustered around the city centre, which is small enough to be covered easily on foot. Those arriving with private transport can dump their cars in one of the many parking garages.

Public transport consists of buses. Tickets bought from the driver cost DM1 or DM2 (usually the latter), depending on the distance. A batch of five 'long-distance' tickets bought in advance (at the main train station, the bus station or tobacconists) costs DM7.50; a day ticket costs DM4.60, and a family day ticket for up to five people costs a mere DM6. If you plan to spend a long time in the area, a monthly pass will set you back DM48 (DM37 for students).

Bremen

Bremen is the smallest federal state in Germany, covering a total area of 404 sq km. The state comprises the two cities of Bremen and Bremerhaven, with Bremen as the state capital. It is, after Hamburg, the most important harbour in Germany, even though the open sea lies 113 km to the north.

In 837 AD, Bremen replaced Hamburg as Europe's most northerly archbishopric. The city was ruled by the church until the 14th century, when a break was made and Bremen joined the Hanseatic League. Bremen was controlled by the French from 1810 to 1813, but went on to join the German Confederation in 1815. In 1871, the city was made a state of the German Reich. Bremen was occupied by British armed forces in 1945, later to be taken over by US forces as a part of their military zone. In 1949 Bremen was officially declared a Bundesland of the Federal Republic of Germany.

BREMEN

Many ignore Bremen in favour of its big sister port city, Hamburg, but there is much to see and do in and around town. While exploring, make sure to drink a few Beck's beers.

Orientation & Information

The heart of the city is the Marktplatz, but the soul is the port, which provides about 40% of local employment. Everything worthwhile is within walking distance of the Marktplatz.

The tourist information office (Verkehrsverein) (☎ 0421-30 80 00) is directly in front of the main train station (Hauptbahnhof). The staff are helpful and can provide an excellent brochure in English. The maps of the city, however, are less useful.

When you get lost (and you will), look down – the city government seems to have put its money into painting directions on the street to major sites, rather than produce bigger and better maps. There is also a booth at the New Town Hall opposite the cathedral.

Bremen's telephone code is 0421.

Things to See & Do

Around the Marktplatz, take a look at the splendid and ornate **Town Hall**, the **St Peter's Cathedral**, and the large statue of **Roland**, erected in 1404 and Bremen's sentimental protector.

Walk down **Böttcherstrasse**, a re-creation of a medieval alley, complete with tall brick houses, shops, galleries, museums and restaurants. The **Paula Becker-Modersohn House** is at No 8, with works of the famous Bremen contemporary painter, and the **Roselius House** is at No 6, with medieval objects.

The nearby **Schnoorviertel** area features fishing cottages that are now a tourist attraction, with shops and restaurants. Make sure to wander off onto the tiny side alleys.

A great walk just blocks from the Marktplatz is along the **Wallanlagen** (Rampart Parks), stretching along the old city walls and moat. They're a peaceful break from the city.

Along with Bremerhaven, 59 km downstream, Bremen sports a large port system. The port tour is excellent and not as crowded or overwhelming as the one in Hamburg. It costs DM10 per person. The **Beck's Brewery** (☎ 5 09 40) is at Am Deich 18-19. It doesn't normally do tours, but you might try calling to see if there are any groups going through that you could join.

One great reference around which to frame a Bremen trip is the Fairy-Tale Road, from Bremen to Hanau, the birthplace of the Brothers Grimm (see the Fairy-Tale Road section).

Places to Stay

The closest camping ground is at *Freie Hansestadt Bremen* (☎ 21 20 02) on Am Stadtwaldsee 1. It's reasonably close to the university – take tram No 5 from the Hauptbahnhof to the terminus, and then bus No 22 or 23 to the university and walk the last couple of km. The city's *youth hostel* (☎ 17 13 69) is at Kalkstrasse 6, across the river from the Beck's Brewery (take bus No 25 from the Hauptbahnhof to Faulenstrasse, then walk).

Hotels in Bremen are expensive, but *Pension Gästehaus Walter* (☎ 55 80 27), Buntentorsteinweg 86-88 (just across the river), charges only DM40/68 for comfort-

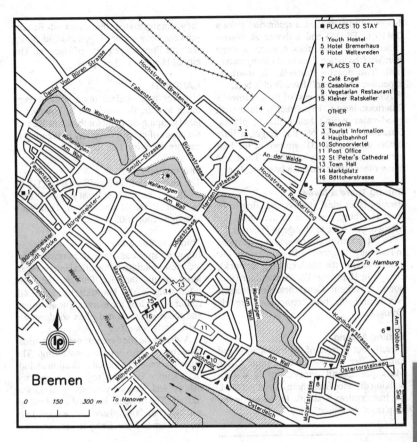

PLACES TO STAY

1 Youth Hostel
5 Hotel Bremerhaus
6 Hotel Weltevreden

PLACES TO EAT

7 Café Engel
8 Casablanca
9 Vegetarian Restaurant
15 Kleiner Ratskeller

OTHER

2 Windmill
3 Tourist Information
4 Hauptbahnhof
10 Schnoorviertel
11 Post Office
12 St Peter's Cathedral
13 Town Hall
14 Marktplatz
16 Böttcherstrasse

Bremen

0   150   300 m

To Hanover

able singles/doubles. Another place worth trying is *Pension Haus Hohenlohe* (☎ 34 23 95), Hohenlohe Strasse 5, which has rooms for DM45/65. *Pension Domizil* (☎ 3 47 81 47) at Graf-Moltke-Strasse 42 is a little farther out but can be recommended. Singles/doubles cost DM50/98. To get there, take bus No 30 or 34 to Holler Allee, then walk. *Hotel Weltevreden* (☎ 7 80 15), Am Dobben 62, has comfortable rooms for DM52/90. A good up-market option is *Hotel Bremerhaus* (☎ 3 29 40), Lönningstrasse 16-20, where comfortable singles/doubles cost DM110/140 including breakfast.

Places to Eat & Drink

The best spot for meals is *Kleiner Ratskeller*, a charming, narrow guesthouse at Hinter dem Schütting 11 (at the head of Böttcherstrasse). Hearty meals usually cost between DM8 and DM12. It's open from 10 am to midnight. It's also a great place for the first of many Beck's. If you'd like to try another popular Bremen beer, the *Schüttinger Brauerei* is next door.

For a good splurge in the Schnoorviertel, head for *Beck's in'n Schnoor*, at Schnoor 35-36. It has large meals in a nice atmosphere from DM15 to DM30. Just off Schnoor, there's a little *vegetarian restaurant* (meals DM10 to DM15) and teahouse at Wüstestätte 1. The Marktplatz features a large *Nordsee* (the national seafood chain) restaurant. The nearby *Ratskeller* is touristy, expensive and doesn't have Beck's beer.

A little way to the east of the old town is Ostertorsteinweg. This street is lined with good-value eating and drinking places. *Casablanca*, at No 59, and *Engel*, a little farther along at No 31, are two of the best known among the city's students. These and many other places are open late, late, late.

Getting There & Away
Bremen is an ideal stopover heading to or from Hamburg, one hour to the north. For Munich, you have to change in Hanover.

To get to Berlin, you have to change trains in Hamburg, Hanover or Braunschweig. For destinations in the north-east (eg Rostock), change in Hamburg. For Amsterdam (four hours), change in Osnabrück. For Brussels (six hours), the best connections are via Cologne.

Getting Around
Directly out in front of the train station and tourist office, follow the tram route to the Marktplatz, and everything is within walking distance from there. If you get tired, the tram system is simple to follow on the map from the tourist office.

Lower Saxony

You won't see nearly as many fellow travellers in this part of the country, dominated as it is by the great North German Plain. But Lower Saxony (Niedersachsen) has much to offer, and it's a quick train ride or autobahn drive from the tourist centres down south. Major drawing cards are the scenic Harz Mountains, the old student town of Göttingen, and the picturesque towns along the legendary Fairy-Tale Road.

The British occupation forces created the federal state of Lower Saxony in 1946, when they amalgamated the states of Braunschweig, Schaumburg-Lippe and Oldenburg with the Prussian province of Hanover. The city of Hanover is the capital.

HANOVER
Hanover is a modern town without very much to offer the tourist. It is, however, a good jumping-off point for those headed into the states of eastern Germany or wanting to explore the Fairy-Tale Road.

Information
The tourist information office (☎ 0511-1 68 23 19) in Hanover is at Ernst August Platz 8 in front of the Hauptbahnhof. Hanover's telephone code is 0511.

Things to See & Do
If you do spend any time in Hanover, there are a few buildings of historical interest scattered around the city. Perhaps the most interesting is the **Marktkirche**, the 14th century church by the market. The altarpiece and the original stained-glass windows are particularly beautiful.

A visit to the **Niedersächsisches Landesmuseum** is also worth considering. The museum contains a varied collection including exhibits covering regional prehistory, history and works by artists from Lower Saxony. The museum is closed on Mondays and bank holidays, otherwise it is open daily from 10 am to 5 pm. Entry is free.

Places to Stay & Eat
Hanover's *youth hostel* (☎ 1 31 76 74) is a little out of town at Ferdinand-Wilhelm-Fricke-Weg 1 (see the Getting Around section that follows). If you want to stay in the centre of the city, you will have to pay for it. One reasonable option is *Hotel Flora* (☎ 34 23 34), Heinrichstrasse 36. Singles/doubles with a private bathroom cost DM60/90, and with shared bathroom they cost from DM45/85.

Restaurant Gilde-Hof, Joachimstrasse 6 near the Hauptbahnhof, has typical German food at very reasonable prices. If you've had your fill of Teutonic fare, try the slightly more expensive Turkish restaurant *Kreuzklappe*, on the corner of Kreuzstrasse and Kreuzkirchhof behind the 14th century Kreuzkirche church.

Getting There & Away
Hanover is at a major intersection of train lines. There are trains virtually every hour from 5 or 6 am to Hamburg, Munich, Frankfurt and Berlin. Approximate travelling times to these four cities are 1¼, 4½, 2¼ and four hours respectively.

If you are driving, Hanover is well positioned for autobahns to the same four cities. There are also good autobahn connections to Bremen, Cologne, Amsterdam and Brussels.

Getting Around
The only time you are likely to use public transport in Hanover is to get out to the youth hostel. Take U-Bahn line No 3 or 7 from the Hauptbahnhof to Fischerhof, then cross the river on the Lodemannbrücke bridge and turn right into Ferdinand-Wilhelm-Fricke-Weg. The hostel is a couple of hundred metres along on the right.

FAIRY-TALE ROAD
The Fairy-Tale Road (Märchenstrasse), so called because of the number of legends and fairy tales which find their roots in this region, is definitely worth spending a day or two exploring. The route begins at Bremen, passes near Hanover and then goes farther south to Göttingen, Kassel and Hanau. The stretch from Hanover to Göttingen is the most historical section of the route. Among the most interesting towns here are Hamelin (Hameln) of Pied Piper fame, Bodenwerder, where the great adventurer, Baron von Münchhausen, was at home, and the surprising town of Bad Karlshafen.

Information
Every town, village and hamlet along the Fairy-Tale Road has an information office of sorts. The office in Hamelin (☎ 05151-20 26 17) is likely to be more helpful than the others. It is at Deister Allee 3, just outside the old town. In Bodenwerder, you will find the

tourist office (☎ 05533-4 05 41) at Brückenstrasse 7. In Bad Karlshafen, you will find it in the Kurverwaltung (☎ 05672-10 91) by the 'harbour'. The office in Hamelin has a colourful map of the entire route.

The telephone codes for Hamelin, Bodenwerder and Bad Karlshafen are 05151, 05533 and 05672 respectively.

Things to See & Do
Hamelin Among the most interesting sights is the so-called **Rattenfängerhaus** (Rat Catcher's, or Pied Piper's, House) on Osterstrasse, the old town's main street. The house was built at the beginning of the 17th century. On the side of the house, in Bungelosenstrasse, is an inscription in Latin which tells how, on 26 June 1284, 150 children of Hamelin were led past this site and out of town by a piper wearing multicoloured clothes, never to be seen again.

Also have a look at the **Rattenfänger Glockenspiel** at the Hochzeitshaus (wedding house) farther down the same street. The **Löwenapotheke** (Lion Pharmacy) on Bäckerstrasse is one of the oldest buildings in the city, in Gothic style. It dates to the beginning of the 14th century.

Bodenwerder The present-day **Rathaus** is said to be the house in which the legendary Baron von Münchhausen was born. The baron's fame was due to his telling of outrageous stories. Perhaps the most famous of these is how he rode through the air on a cannonball; this very cannonball can be seen today in the room dedicated to the baron in the Rathaus. Also interesting is the statue of the baron riding half a horse, in the garden outside the Rathaus. This was, of course, another of his stories.

There is a pleasant walking track along the Weser River in both directions from Bodenwerder.

Bad Karlshafen This place is simply unexpected. After passing through towns like Hamelin and Bodenwerder, the last thing you would expect is this whitewashed, meticulously planned, Baroque village. Originally the city had been planned with an impressive harbour and a canal connecting the Weser River with the Rhine, in the hope of diverting trade away from Hanover and Münden in the north. The plans were laid by a local earl named Carl, with help from Huguenot refugees who had fled religious persecution in France. The earl's death in 1730 prevented completion of this project, but even today his incomplete masterpiece and the influence of the Huguenots is too beautiful to miss.

Places to Stay

There is a *youth hostel* in Hamelin (☎ 34 25) at Fischbeckerstrasse 33. It costs DM16.50/ 20 for seniors/juniors, with breakfast. To get there, take bus No 2 from the Hauptbahnhof to Wehler Weg. In Bodenwerder, the *youth hostel* (☎ 26 85) is on Richard Schirrmann Weg. In Bad Karlshafen, the *youth hostel* (☎ 3 38) is at Winnefeldstrasse 7. There are a number of other hostels along the Fairy-Tale Road, including at Höxter, Holzminden and Uslar.

You can organise a private room through most of the tourist offices, and they can all supply you with a local accommodation list.

Because this region is not on the main tourist trail, there are some surprisingly good hotel deals around. In Hamelin, try *Hotel zur Börse* (☎ 70 80), Osterstrasse 41a, which has singles/doubles from DM55/61; or the luxurious *Christinenhof Hotel Garni* (☎ 4 36 11), Alte Markt Strasse 18, which has singles from DM74. In Bodenwerder, you can't go beyond the three-star *Hotel Deutsches Haus* (☎ 39 25), Münchhausenplatz 4, which has rooms from DM34/62!

Places to Eat

For a delicious, budget-breaking treat in Hamelin, you might try *Gaststätte Rattenfängerhaus* right inside the Rat Catcher's House (see the previous Things to See & Do section). Considerably cheaper, but just as big on atmosphere, is *Pupasch*, on the corner of Emmernstrasse and Pferdemarkt in the heart of the old town.

In Bodenwerder, *Restaurant Münchhausenstube*, at Grosse Strasse 5 in the pedestrian zone, is worth seeking out. In Bad Karlshafen, try *Café Sieberg* next to the Rathaus by the 'harbour'.

Getting There & Away

The main entry points to the Fairy-Tale Road are Bremen, Hanover, Göttingen, Kassel and Hanau, of which only Hanover is not directly on the route.

Getting Around

The easiest way to follow the Fairy-Tale Road is by car. The ADAC map of the Weserbergland covers the area in detail.

If you have to rely on public transport, do not despair. There are a number of direct trains a day from Hanover to Hamelin. From Hamelin's train station, there are about a dozen buses a day to Bodenwerder and on to the town of Holzminden, which is also worth a brief stop. From Bodenwerder, there are also buses to Höxter, from where there are buses to Kassel which pass through Bad Karlshafen. From Holzminden, there are buses to Göttingen.

GÖTTINGEN

This bustling university town is an ideal stopover on your way north or south – it's on the direct train line between Frankfurt and Hamburg. You can make a quick exploration by hopping off and back on the train in the same day (check baggage for DM2 – don't pay DM3 for a locker). Better still, give Göttingen the two days or more it deserves.

Information

The main tourist office (☎ 0551-5 40 00) is just outside the station, and a large post office is just to the left. There is another tourist office in the old Rathaus (at Markt 9), in a side room just off the main hall. Both tourist offices have a very good brochure in English, *A Walk through the City*.

Göttingen's telephone code is 0551.

Things to See & Do

From the train station, take the tunnel to

Goethe-Allee and the city centre. Goethe-Allee leads onto the pedestrian **Prinzenstrasse**, where the student population becomes immediately apparent, with an abundance of bikes and backpacks, as well as dozens of well-stocked bookshops. Turn right off Prinzenstrasse and down Weenderstrasse to the **Markt**.

Make sure you see the beautifully decorated **main hall** in the old Rathaus. Also take time to consider the **statue of the Goose Girl** (Gänseliese), Göttingen's favourite daughter, in the middle of the Markt. Her fame is due to her reputation as the most kissed girl in the world.

Almost one-fourth of Göttingen's population are students. The Brothers Grimm were professors here. The prestigious Max Planck Institute is based here. Connected to Göttingen's university is a carefully presented **Zoological Museum** (☎ 39 54 47), Berliner Strasse 28. It is open on Sundays from 10 am to 1 pm, or by prior arrangement.

Places to Stay
Try camping at *Campingplatz Am Sösestausee* (☎ 05522-33 19) at the Sösetal dam east of Osterode, or *Waldcampingplatz Eulenburg* (☎ 05522-66 11) at Scheerenberger Strasse 100 and closer to town.

The lively *Jugendherberge* (☎ 5 76 22) is at Habichtsweg 2. There is no bus from the train station – head under the tunnel to the right of the station, take the first right and then left to Groner Tor Strasse, and catch bus No 6 to the youth hostel. There is also an excellent *hostel* at nearby Osterode.

Pensions are not cheap in Göttingen and the best bets are up near the university. Try *Hotel zum Schwan* (☎ 4 48 63) at Weender Landstrasse 23, which costs DM39/59 for a single/double.

In the centre of Göttingen, try *Central Hotel* (☎ 5 71 57), Jüdenstrasse 12, which has singles/doubles for DM65/95 including breakfast, and *Hotel Kasseler Hof* (☎ 7 20 81), Rosdorfer Weg 26, with rooms from DM46/80. *Hotel-Restaurant Zur Rose* (☎ 5 70 50), Kurze Geismar Strasse 11, is a small

hotel with pleasant rooms for DM50/100. The restaurant is not too bad either.

Places to Eat
Because it's a student centre, eating in Göttingen is fairly cheap and lively. Though the large *Zentralmensa* off Weender Landstrasse is good for information and cheap food, a better option with lots more flavour is *Zum Altdeutschen* at Prinzenstrasse 16, a student hang-out.

Das Nudel Haus, on the corner of Jüdenstrasse at Rote Strasse 13, has a huge selection of noodle-based dishes at very reasonable prices. It is very popular with local students. Another student hang-out is *Feuerstein* ('Flintstone', as in Fred) at Wendenstrasse 8a, on the corner of Mauerstrasse; you can still order a full meal here after midnight.

If you have an urge to eat a hearty Bavarian meal, you can't go past *Zur Alten Brauerei*. If you are lucky, your eating may be accompanied by live music. The restaurant is in a courtyard next to the florist – the address for both is Düstere Strasse 20.

There is a lively *market* on Tuesdays, Thursdays and Saturdays (head south on Kurze Strasse past the Markt and turn left into the covered alley). If you're not there on market day, put together a small feast at *Wulff Fleischwaren*, Weender Strasse 29-31. It offers cold and hot items.

Getting There & Away
Trains constantly pass through on the Frankfurt-Hamburg line. The Mitfahrzentrale (☎ 4 40 04) is at Obere-Masch-Strasse 18. There are trains from Göttingen to Goslar in the Harz. See the Harz Mountains section for more information.

Getting Around
This is a city easily explored on foot. The map provided by the tourist office also gives the bus numbers and routes.

HARZ MOUNTAINS
Like the Bavarian Forest, the Harz Mountains (Harzgebirge) are one of Germany's

GERMANY

outdoor secrets. Known mostly to Germans and Scandinavians, the Harz Mountains don't have the peaks and valleys of the Alps, but they offer a great four-season sports getaway without some of the Alpine tackiness and tourism – in fact, the area provides one of the best opportunities in Europe to get off the crowded tourist tracks.

Once there were many silver, lead and copper mines in the area, but these have been worked to the stage where many of them are no longer profitable.

The following section deals with the western German part of the Harz. For the even less touristy eastern German Harz, see the sections on Nordhausen, Wernigerode and Quedlinburg earlier in this chapter.

Orientation & Information

Goslar is the centre for Harz tourism activities and is an ideal base. The tourist information office (☎ 05321-28 46) is only 500 metres from the train station straight down Rosentorstrasse and Fischemäkerstrasse at Markt 7. It generally can give information only on Goslar and the north Harz area, but the staff are extremely helpful and can help when the area's accommodation is packed (often the case).

The Harzer Verkehrsverband (☎ 05321-22 00 31) at Marktstrasse 45 is the regional tourist office. It is great for information about Goslar and the entire Harz area. Make sure to pick up the booklet, *Grüner Faden für den Harz-Gast* ('Green Thread for the Harz Guest').

Along with standard tourist offices, many mountain towns also have their own Alpenverein and Harzclub offices, which are ideal places for further information, specific recommendations, itineraries, hiking partners and guided hikes. The Goslar Alpenverein office is in the shoeshop, Deckert Schuhmode & Sport, at Fische-

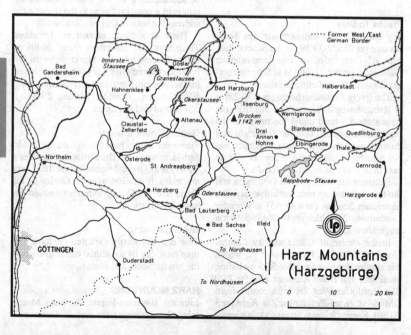

Harz Mountains
(Harzgebirge)

0   10   20 km

mäkerstrasse 1a, and some of the staff can provide excellent guidance on organised hikes and other possibilities.

As well as being interesting in its own right, Goslar is just to the north of the most interesting parts of the Harz. Other towns nearby that are ideal for day trips or as bases on their own are Altenau (20 km south) and Hahnenklee (15 km south-west).

Goslar's telephone code is 05321. For Hahnenklee, the code is 05325, and for Altenau, 05328.

Things to See

Goslar's **Marktplatz** has several photogenic houses. Opposite the town hall there's one with a chiming clock depicting four different scenes of the history of mining in the area. It struts its stuff at 9 am, noon, 3 pm and 6 pm.

Head north-west away from the Marktplatz to the **Schuhhof**, a square surrounded by timber-fronted houses. Then head south to take a look at the outside of the **Kaiserpfalz**, a huge palace now loaded with tour bus visitors. The tour is boring, but the more peaceful gardens in the back are free.

For an excellent review of the history of Goslar and the geology of the Harz Mountains, visit the **Goslarer Museum** at Königstrasse 1, on the corner of Abzuchtstrasse. The DM3.50 admission is worth it, making you a much more knowledgeable hiker. The **Zinnfiguren Museum** (Pewter Statuette Museum), at Münzerstrasse 11, has hundreds of painted figures in many different pretty settings. Entry costs DM2.50, and it's closed on Mondays.

Activities

Hiking The **Naturpark Harz** is well organised for hikers, but its beauty doesn't suffer. Maps and information are abundant. Goslar has many highly recommended hikes just outside town, but the area up to and around the **Granestausee** (four or five km west of Goslar Hauptbahnhof towards the town of Wolfshagen) is particularly scenic. Most of the hikes can be accomplished in a half-day and most are less than 10 km. Ask the tourist office about the Granestausee hike, with

great vistas and a giant playground for children of all ages.

For a smaller base, or a day trip from Goslar, head for **Hahnenklee** or **Altenau**. You can hike the 15 km to Hahnenklee from Goslar without ever leaving the forest.

The excellent *Auto + Wanderkarte Harz* map (DM9.80) gives good information for hikers, as well as being a great driving map. Make sure to ask for the newest version. Most trails are well marked and maintained, but it doesn't hurt to occasionally ask if you're heading the way you think you are. At any time of year and no matter what the current weather, be prepared for almost anything mother nature can throw at you. Snow in the very late spring is not uncommon. Call ☎ 05321-4 01 24 for a local weather report (in German).

Skiing Downhill skiing is below average, due to uninspiring slopes and inconsistent snow conditions. Locals, however, are passionate about cross-country skiing, and this is a better overall option. Most tourist offices have an excellent brochure and map, *Skilanglauf im Naturschutzgebiet Oberharz*. This gives details about 10 different loops, ranging from three to 15 km, with information on elevation, elevation changes, difficulty and trailheads. One of the more consistent and popular downhill resorts is **Hahnenklee**, with five nice runs (two of them 1500 metres long) and three lifts (one a cable car).

Rental equipment for both sports is easy to find. Downhill skis and boots can be had from DM17 per day, cross-country gear from DM16. Lift tickets cost DM21 for half a day and DM29 for the whole day. Hahnenklee-Information (☎ 20 14) is based in the Kurverwaltung at Rathausstrasse 16. For regional snow reports, call the Harz snow line on ☎ 05325-2 00 24.

Spas The Harz Mountains also offer many popular spas, but they don't come cheaply. Hahnenklee and Altenau have many accommodations with spa amenities, but it's best to stay somewhere cheaper and then ask the

GERMANY

tourist office about paying separately to use private or public facilities. Hahnenklee's pump house is great for a splurge, with a sauna, indoor swimming pool and standard spa amenities.

Places to Stay

It's best to stay in Goslar, Hahnenklee or Altenau, but there are many other hostels and camping grounds in the area. Ask the tourist office for maps showing the locations. Many of the camping grounds are open all year, but that doesn't mean the weather is suitable for camping, just that they cater for caravans.

If not camping or hostelling, beware of high tourist prices. For extended stays, ask the tourist office about apartments or holiday homes, which become pretty good deals when staying for a week or more.

Goslar The pretty *Jugendherberge* (☎ 2 22 40) is at Rammelsberger Strasse 25 behind the Kaiserpfalz. From the train station, take the frequent bus No 2434 to the edge of Goslar and then head up the signed path. It charges DM16.50/20 for juniors/seniors, with breakfast. It wouldn't hurt to call ahead from the station, because the hostel is often full with students.

A better option is *Hotel und Campingplatz Sennhütte* (☎ 2 25 02), three km south on Route B241 at Clausthaler Strasse 28. This is also reached by bus No 2434, getting off at the 'Sennhütte' stop. You can camp here if the weather or mood suits (DM3.50 per tent, DM4.50 per person, DM1 for long, hot and clean showers), or pay only DM30/60 for comfortable singles/doubles with nice views. There are many trails leading away from the camping ground and into the mountains, including the one to Hahnenklee. Behind the hotel, look for the tame deer.

In town, a Zimmer frei is the only inexpensive option. Try *Haus Bielitza* (☎ 2 07 44) at Abzuchtstrasse 11, or *Rüland* (☎ 2 51 62) at An der Abzucht 30, for singles starting at DM22 and doubles up to DM44.

Hahnenklee *Campingplatz Am Kreuzeck* (☎ 25 70) is on the road two km north of

Hahnenklee (bus from Goslar). It's nice, but expensive (DM6.50 per person and DM10 per tent). The *Jugendherberge* (☎ 22 56) is at Steigerstieg 1 near the 'Bockwiese' stop on the road from Goslar (DM13.50/16 for juniors/seniors). The tourist information office (☎ 20 14) at Rathausstrasse 16 can help you find a private room.

Altenau *Campingplatz Obertalsperre* (☎ 7 02) is on the B 498 just north of town. The *Jugendherberge* (☎ 6 12) is at Auf der Rose 11. If you would like a private room, the Kurverwaltung (☎ 80 20) can help.

Places to Eat & Drink

It's best to stock up on picnic items before heading out of Goslar, because the countryside is filled with expensive, tourist-oriented restaurants. The Marktplatz features a wonderful *market* every Tuesday and Friday, but make sure to get there by 1 pm. Otherwise, put together a picnic at one of the shops nearby, or stop by *Nordsee* at Fischemäkerstrasse 4. For a splurge and some strong and tasty beer, head to *Gils Bräu Brauhaus Goslar* at Marstallstrasse 1. It offers daily luncheon and dinner specials in a brewery atmosphere, and even has two-litre portions of beer to go.

Getting There & Away

Goslar is best reached by train from Göttingen (about 1¼ hours); eight to 10 trains a day cover the route directly, and there are another 10 or so where you will need to change trains in Kreiens. For information on getting to/from the eastern German Harz region, see the Nordhausen, Quedlinburg and Wernigerode sections earlier in this chapter.

Getting Around

A car is best for heading out of Goslar to hiking trailheads. However, the bus service is excellent and is accustomed to handling hikers. There are eight or nine buses a day from Goslar to Altenau (DM4.50), around half of which pass directly by the youth hostel (if you feel like counting, the youth hostel is the 30th stop and 32 minutes after leaving Goslar Hauptbahnhof). The bus then continues on to the town of **St Andreasberg**, another popular ski resort. Between Goslar and Hahnenklee, there are 11 or 12 buses in each direction every day. The trip takes 25 minutes and costs DM3.90.

However, the only effective public transport connection between the western and eastern German Harz regions is the bus from Bad Harzburg (accessible by train from Goslar) to Wernigerode. Six buses ply the route every day in both directions. The trip takes just under an hour and costs DM9 one-way. The bus stops at the main train stations in both Bad Harzburg and Wernigerode.

Hamburg

The first recorded settlement on the current site of Hamburg was the moated castle of Hammaburg, built in the first half of the ninth century AD. The city which developed around it became the northernmost archbishopric in Europe to facilitate the conversion of the peoples to the north. The city was burned down by Viking raiders in 845 AD, and then another eight times in the following 300 years.

None of this seemed to slow Hamburg's development. In the 13th century, it became the Hanseatic League's gateway to the North Sea, and was second in importance and influence only to Lübeck. With the decline of the Hanseatic League in the 16th century, Lübeck faded into insignificance but Hamburg continued to thrive. By the beginning of the 18th century, Cologne was the only city in Germany with a larger population. The crown on Hamburg's rise was the proclamation of the city as an Imperial City of Germany, which meant that it had only the emperor to answer to.

Hamburg strode confidently into the 20th century, but WW I stopped all incoming and outgoing trade, and the Allies claimed most of Hamburg's merchant shipping fleet

(almost 1500 ships) as part of Germany's postwar reparation payments. In WW II, over half of Hamburg's residential areas and port facilities were demolished and 55,000 people killed in Allied air raids. Twenty-five years later, however, Hamburg was as good as rebuilt.

Today it is a sprawling port city and a separate state of the Federal Republic of Germany, offering much more than the Reeperbahn (one of Europe's largest red-light districts) for which it is so famous. It has a stylish inner city, numerous waterways (with more bridges than Venice), and even a beach in Blankenese, Germany's most exclusive suburb. Give yourself time to get to know Hamburg. You won't be disappointed.

Orientation
The Hauptbahnhof is very centrally located near the Aussenalster (Outer Alster Lake) and is fairly close to most of the sights. These are south of the Aussenalster and north of the Elbe River, which runs all the way from Czechoslovakia to Hamburg before flowing into the North Sea. The city centre features the Rathaus and St Michaelis Church. Two imposing landmarks are the Television Tower and the Köhlbrandbrücke, a huge suspension bridge which spans the Elbe.

Information
This city has made successful efforts to draw and serve travellers. It has (by far) the largest collection of English-language brochures and services in Germany. To receive some of this excellent information ahead of time, contact the Hamburg Tourist Board (☎ 040-30 05 10), Burchardstrasse 14, D-2000 Hamburg 1.

The airport has a tourist information office (☎ 040-30 05 12 40) at arrival hall D in Terminal 3, which is open from 8 am to 11 pm daily. There are also free phones in Terminal 2 to use for selected hotels.

The small tourist information office in the Hauptbahnhof at the Kirchenallee exit offers limited brochures and a room-finding service (DM3). It has great hours (7 am to 11

GERMANY

GERMANY

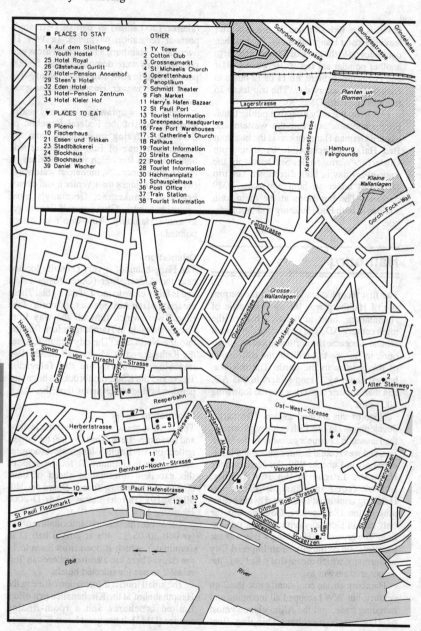

PLACES TO STAY

14 Auf dem Stintfang
   Youth Hostel
25 Hotel Royal
26 Gästehaus Gurlitt
27 Hotel-Pension Annenhof
29 Steen's Hotel
32 Eden Hotel
33 Hotel-Pension Zentrum
34 Hotel Kieler Hof

PLACES TO EAT

8 Piceno
10 Fischerhaus
21 Essen und Trinken
23 Stadtbäckerei
24 Blockhaus
35 Blockhaus
39 Daniel Wischer

OTHER

1 TV Tower
2 Cotton Club
3 Grossneumarkt
4 St Michaelis Church
5 Operettenhaus
6 Panoptikum
7 Schmidt Theater
9 Fish Market
11 Harry's Hafen Bazaar
12 St Pauli Port
13 Tourist Information
15 Greenpeace Headquarters
16 Free Port Warehouses
17 St Catherine's Church
18 Rathaus
19 Tourist Information
20 Streits Cinema
22 Post Office
28 Tourist Information
30 Hachmannplatz
31 Schauspielhaus
36 Post Office
37 Train Station
38 Tourist Information

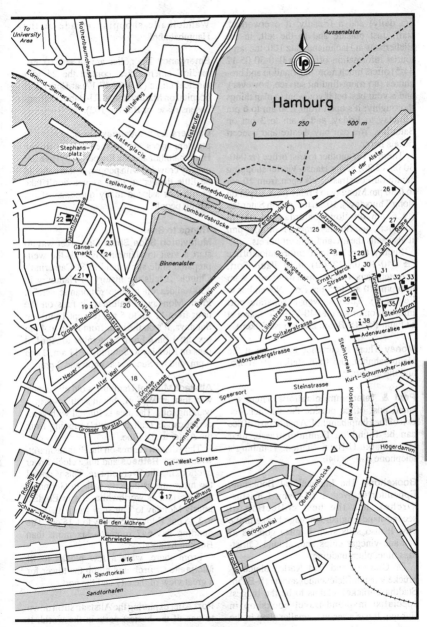

To
University
Area

Rothenbaumchaussee

Edmund-Siemers-Allee

Mittelweg

Alsterglacis

Alsterufer

Aussenalster

Hamburg

0   250   500 m

An der Alster

Stephans-
platz

Esplanade

Kennedybrücke

Lombardsbrücke

Ferdinandstor

26

Holzdamm

25

27

Lange Reihe

Dammtorstrasse

22

Gänse-
markt

23

24

21

Jungfernstieg

20

19

Binnenalster

Ballindamm

Glockengiesser-
wall

29

28

30

Ernst-Merck-
Strasse

31

Kirchenallee

32 33

34

35

Steindamm

36

37

38

Adenauerallee

Grosse Bleichen

Poststrasse

Wall

Neuer

Alter Wall

18

Grosse
Johannisstrasse

Lilienstrasse

39

Spitalerstrasse

Mönckebergstrasse

Speersort

Steinstrasse

Steintorwall

Kurt-Schumacher-Allee

Klosterwall

Högerdamm

Grosser Burstah

Dornstrasse

Ost-West-Strasse

17

Zippelhaus

Oberbaumbrücke

Rödings
markt

Schaar-Kaien

Bei den Mühren

Kehrwieder

16

Am Sandtorkai

Sandtorhafen

Brooktorkai

Brooktor

GERMANY

pm daily) and a friendly, if overworked, staff. Just outside and to the left, in the Bieberhaus at Hachmannplatz 100, the large tourist information office (☎ 040-30 05 12 44/5) offers much more information and brochures (no room-finding service, however), and is your best bet if you want to plan things thoroughly; it's open from 7.30 am to 6 pm Monday to Friday, and 8 am to 3 pm on Saturday. You can buy theatre and concert tickets here.

There is yet another tourist office (☎ 040-30 05 12 20) at the Hanse-Viertel shopping centre on Poststrasse; it's open from 10 am to 6.30 pm Monday to Friday (to 8.30 pm on 'long Thursday'), 10 am to 3 pm on Saturday (to 6 pm on 'long Saturday', 4 pm in summer), and Sunday from 11 am to 3 pm. It also sells theatre and concert tickets.

Finally, there's a small information office (☎ 040-30 05 12 00) at St Pauli Port, between piers 4 and 5, open daily from 9 am to 6 pm (10 am to 5 pm from November to February). There's even a separate port information office (☎ 040-31 97 77), also at St Pauli Port (S-Bahn: Landungsbrücken).

Money There is currency exchange at the Hauptbahnhof, the train station at Altona, and the airport.

Post & Telecommunications There's a small post office outside the Kirchenallee exit of the Hauptbahnhof. A major post office can be found on Dammtorstrasse, near Gänsemarkt U-Bahn Station. Hamburg's telephone code is 040.

Bookshops The International Bookshop, Eppendorfer Weg 1 (U-Bahn Christuskirche), has the best collection of second-hand English language books in the city. It also sells such English goodies as salt-and-vinegar chips and, around Christmas time, plum pudding.

Dr Goetze Land und Karte, Bleichenbrücke 9 in the Bleichenhof arcade (S-Bahn: Stadthausbrücke), claims to be the biggest specialist map-and-travel bookshop in Europe. It has a second, smaller shop in the Wandelhalle shopping arcade at the Hauptbahnhof.

Emergency The police are on ☎ 1 10. For medical emergencies, contact the 24-hour medical clinic (☎ 4 68 47 17) at Eppendorf hospital on Martinistrasse (U-Bahn: Kellinghusenstrasse, or Bus No 102).

Dangers & Annoyances The only two real problem areas are in the vicinity of the Hauptbahnhof and the Reeperbahn. Both are usually crowded with people, so there should be little danger so long as you don't take pictures or ask too many questions of the wrong people.

Things to See

Multivision Slide Show One great way to start a visit to Hamburg is with the well-prepared slide show held at St Catherine's Church. It tells the history of Hamburg in 1300 slides on a huge panoramic screen. From Monday to Saturday, it runs on the hour from 11 am to 5 pm (except 1 pm); on Sundays, it's on the hour from noon to 4 pm (except 1 pm). From September to April, it runs on Monday to Saturday at 11 am, 2 and 3 pm, and on Sundays at noon and 3 pm.

Altstadt Much of Hamburg's old city centre was lost in WW II, but it's still worth a walking tour. The area is filtered with wonderful canals (called 'fleets') running from the Alster to the Elbe.

The Altstadt centres on the Rathausmarkt, with a large **Rathaus** and huge clock tower overlooking the lively square. This is one of the most interesting city halls in Germany, and the tour is worthwhile. It's in English hourly Monday to Thursday from 10.15 am to 3.15 pm, Friday to Sunday to 1.15 pm. The building has 647 rooms – six more than Buckingham Palace.

From there, walk a few blocks to **St Michaelis Church** and climb the tower for a great view of the city and the port.

Port After exploring the Altstadt, stroll down to one of the busiest ports in the world. It boasts the world's largest carpet warehouse complex, and the Free Port Warehouses stockpile most spices from all continents.

The **port cruises** are admittedly touristy, but still worthwhile. Until you take one, you literally have no idea of the immensity of the world's shipping industry. There are many options. Launch tours (DM12, or half-price for children aged from four to 14) run all year for 70 minutes from Pier 3. They depart half-hourly from 9 am to 5 pm from April to October, and hourly from 10 am to 4 pm from November to March. A one-hour HADAG steamer Grand Tour (DM12, children half-price) sails from Pier 2, with sailings half-hourly from 9 am to 6 pm Monday to Saturday, and 8.30 am to 6 pm on Sunday (the winter schedule is more limited). A 1½-hour HADAG steamer Super Grand Tour (DM16, children half-price) runs hourly from Pier 7 on Sundays from March to October from 8 am to 2 pm. Find out about other tour options on ☎ 31 46 44.

If you're in the port area on a Sunday, head for the fish market at St Pauli on the Elbe.

Reeperbahn Though the Altstadt and the port are interesting, Hamburg's biggest tourist attraction is probably the Reeperbahn, one of the world's most famous red-light districts. The Reeperbahn is 600 metres long and is the heart of the St Pauli entertainment district, which includes shows, bars, clubs, a casino and the **Operettenhaus**. The area is generally safe for walking and looking, but try to travel in pairs or more with at least one male.

Trips inside bars or other 'events' can turn out to be more expensive than they at first appear. Be defensive and hard-nosed about all transactions and make sure you understand prices beforehand (ask for the price list, which is required by law). Order only beer, avoiding more expensive mixed drinks and 'champagne'. Expect to pay about DM5 to enter a bar or a show, and then DM15 to DM30 for each drink. Often there's a minimum charge.

If you really want the Reeperbahn experience, turn onto Grosse Freiheit and visit either *Tabu*, *Safari* or *Colibri*, which feature sex shows that may not be for the faint-hearted. The other popular street is Herbertstrasse, cordoned off at each end by a metal wall with small entry ways. This is the infamous street where the prostitutes sit, stand, and lean out the windows offering their wares. The scene is almost surreal.

Panoptikum This is the only waxworks museum in Germany and is one of those unusual museums that seem to be fun for the entire family. It was founded in 1879 and contains more than 100 well-known (at least to Germans) historical, political and show business celebrities. It's at Spielbudenplatz 3, and is open from 11 am to 9 pm Monday to Friday, Saturday to 11 pm, and Sunday from 10 am to 9 pm. It's closed from mid-January to early February. Admission costs DM8 (students DM5).

Other Sights Carl Hagenbeck's **Tierpark** (☎ 54 00 01 47) is the largest privately owned zoo in Europe. All in all, there are around 2000 animals representing over 370 species in 54 enclosures. It's in the suburb of Stellingen a little way to the north-east of the centre. The easiest way to get there is to take the U2 U-Bahn line towards Niendorf; Hagenbeck's Tierpark Station is the ninth stop after leaving the Hauptbahnhof. Entry to the zoo costs a hefty DM15 for adults and DM10 for kids. It is open from 8 am daily.

One popular goal (a mecca for many) is the **Greenpeace headquarters** at Vorsetzen 53 along the port. It's great fun just to stop by the shop or offices, but there's also a weekly discussion every Monday night at 7.30 pm and everyone is invited. The well-stocked shop is open Monday to Friday from 9.30 am to 6.30 pm, Thursday to 8.30 pm, and Saturday to 2 pm (to 4 pm on 'long Saturdays').

One of Hamburg's best kept secrets is **Harry's Hamburger Hafen Basar** (☎ 31 24 82) on Bernhard-Nocht-Strasse near Balduinstrasse (the nearest S-Bahn stations are Reeperbahn and Landungsbrücken). This incredible 'shop' is the life's work of

Harry, a bearded character known to sailors all over the world, who for decades has been buying trinkets and souvenirs from sailors and others. The result is over 2000 sq metres of space absolutely jammed with tens of thousands of articles ranging from Zulu drums to stuffed giraffes and kangaroos. He even has a shrunken head in his collection. It is open seven days a week from 10 am to 6 pm, but it might be safest to call in advance just to be sure. Entry costs DM2 for which you receive a postcard. If you decide to buy something, you return the postcard and the entry fee is deducted from the price of the item you purchase. Incidentally, the shrunken head is not for sale – on the contrary, you must pay an extra DM2 to see it.

Activities
Though exploring the Reeperbahn can be considered an activity in its own right, there are many other things of a physical nature to pursue in Hamburg.

The Bieberhaus tourist office, on Hachmannplatz by the Hauptbahnhof, rents bikes in good shape for DM10 a day (DM100 deposit), and these are great to use around the Alster or in one of the city's parks. They are also available at DM2 per hour or DM20 for the weekend from Friday to Sunday. Officially, bikes are only rented from May to September, but they're usually available earlier and later if you ask.

For a really unique way to look at this unique city and harbour, take a Junkers 52 flight from Fuhlsbüttel airport. These flights are run by Lufthansa – contact the city-centre office (☎ 3 59 52 24) at Dammtorstrasse 14. These wartime planes fly low and slow and give a great 30-minute look at the city for about DM200 (ask about specials). Cessna flights are run by the Alsterflugcenter (☎ 5 08 22 68) at the airport; a 20-minute flight costs DM70, or DM50 for children aged under 10.

Places to Stay
Camping Though inconvenient, the best camping option, *Campingplatz Buchholz* (☎ 5 40 45 32), is at Kieler Strasse 374, but it mainly caters for caravans. It charges DM6 per person and from DM3 per tent. To reach Kieler Strasse from the Hauptbahnhof, take S-Bahn No 2 or 3 to Stellingen or Eidelstedt. It's better to get off the train at the Hamburg-Altona station and then take bus No 183 towards Schelsen. It runs straight down Kieler Strasse. There are several other camping grounds within walking distance along Kieler Strasse.

Hostels Because of the inconvenient camping and the expensive hotel situation, Hamburg's two hostels are the best bet. The first is convenient to the port and the second is convenient to very little. *Auf dem Stintfang* (☎ 31 34 88) is at Albert-Wegener-Weg 5. *Horner-Rennbahn* (☎ 6 51 16 71) is at Rennbahnstrasse 100. Rates at both start at DM17.

Private Rooms Private rooms are hard to come by in Hamburg, and the price is unlikely to be a big saving on the more conveniently located budget accommodation around the Hauptbahnhof. You could try *Agentur Zimmer Frei Jens-Christian Moos* (☎ 41 20 70/79, Heimweg 3, an agency specialising in short-term private accommodation. For longer stays, see the following Rental section.

Pensions & Hotels The best budget bets are along Steindamm, and a few blocks east of the Hauptbahnhof down Bremer Reihe. On Holzdamm, try *Steen's Hotel* at No 43 (from DM63/75 for singles/doubles) or *Hotel Royal* at No 5 (from DM50/80). *Pension Sarah Petersen* (☎ 24 98 26) at Lange Reihe 50 is a very friendly place. Nearby is one of the cheapest places in the area, *Hotel-Pension Annenhof* (☎ 24 34 26), at Lange Reihe 23, with rooms for DM40/70.

A little closer to the Aussenalster, in a quiet street, is *Gästehaus Gurlitt* (☎ 24 30 11), Gurlittstrasse 38. It caters to a somewhat more discerning clientele as its prices would suggest: singles/doubles/triples for DM105/150/195.

Closer to the Hauptbahnhof, *Eden Hotel*

(☎ 24 84 80), Ellmenreichstrasse 20, has comfortable rooms, all with TV and telephone. Singles/doubles with shared bathroom cost DM75/110, or DM120/175 with private shower and toilet. In Bremer Reihe, one street farther along, are a few reasonable-value budget options. *Hotel-Pension Kieler Hof* (☎ 24 30 24) at No 15, has singles/doubles/triples/quads for DM60/96/135/180, breakfast included. At No 23 in the same street is *Hotel-Pension Zentrum* (☎ 2 80 25 28). The rooms are basic and the management is not overly friendly, but the place is clean and efficiently run, and the position and price are right, with singles/doubles for DM60/100 including breakfast.

Rental The Bieberhaus tourist information office can help with long-term rentals, but for more options, contact one of the following: Die Mitwohnzentrale (☎ 39 13 73) at Lobuschstrasse 22; Mitwohnzentrale Rutschbahn (☎ 41 80 18) at Rutschbahn 3; or Mitwohnzentrale Hamburg (☎ 89 51 18) at Haubachstrasse.

Places to Eat
Hamburg is one of the best spots in Germany for fish, but it doesn't come cheaply. For a splurge and a truly fishy Hamburg experience, head to *Fischerhaus* (☎ 31 40 53) at Fischmarkt 14. The food is just as good and the atmosphere almost so at any of the three *Daniel Wischer* locations, with specials costing less than DM10 and almost everything else less than DM15. The most convenient is at Spitalerstrasse 12 (250 metres from the Hauptbahnof).

One of the best kept secrets in this part of town is the *Restaurant im Theaterkeller*, downstairs in the Deutsches Schauspielhaus on Kirchenallee in front of the Hauptbahnhof. Officially it caters for actors and others working in the theatre, but anyone is welcome. With a new menu every day, and main courses from as little as DM7 on the right day, this place is simply too good to miss.

As always, the university area offers some cheap and unique dining options. First, try the *Hindukusch* at Grindelhof 15. This friendly, family-run Afghan restaurant has lots of vegetarian dishes, and almost everything costs less than DM15. Just up the street at No 19, eat some stand-up Indian dishes at the *Curry Hütte*. Most of the curries are under DM7.50, and you can also buy many things off the shelf to try later.

There is a wide variety of eating establishments around Gänsemarkt and Jungfernstieg near the Alster lake. One lunch-time spot popular with locals is *Essen und Trinken*, Gänsemarkt 21, a vaguely buffet-style cooperative setup where you can choose from Greek, Italian, German and other dishes. In general, you should be able to put a meal together (main course and drink) for around DM12.

If you are looking for a more substantial meal, an excellent choice is *Blockhaus*. This is a Hamburg-based chain of steakhouses, which does a roaring trade for both lunch and dinner. The turkey breast *(Putenbrust)* steak is a real treat. The most convenient of its restaurants are on the 2nd floor of the Gänsemarkt Passage at Gänsemarkt, and at Kirchenallee 50, off Hachmannplatz by the Hauptbahnhof. Expect to pay a minimum of DM25 to DM30 per person for a salad, steak and drink.

Also at Gänsemarkt, close to Dammtorstrasse, is the *Stadtbäckerei*, a bakery which has expanded to cater for shoppers and workers in need of a warm drink and a filling, tasty snack. This is a hot tip for breakfast, but it is good at any time.

If you are spending the evening around the Reeperbahn, *Piceno*, Hein-Hoyer-Strasse 8 serves up delicious Italian fare at very reasonable prices. In the evenings it is always full of young people.

The lively Sunday fish market, near Landungsbrücken S-Bahn Station on the banks of the Elbe River, is open from 6 to 9.30 am, with lots more than just fish. After you visit the market, head for one of the taverns with the locals for an early-morning beer.

Entertainment

The Reeperbahn provides more entertainment than most humans can handle. However, there are other, more cultural possibilities in town.

The jazz scene is Hamburg's Germany's best, and it's definitely worth catching a show at the *Cotton Club*, near Grossneumarkt at Alter Steinweg 10. It opens at 8 pm and shows start at 8.30 pm, Monday to Saturday. On Sunday there's a daytime show from 11 am to 3 pm.

For an English-language fix, head for the plays at the *English Theatre* at Lerchenfeld 14. For kids (their language is more international) there's the personably presented *Theater für Kinder* at Max-Brauer-Allee 76 in Altona. *Streits* cinema, on Jungfernstieg near the corner of Grosse Bleichen, shows films in their original version every Sunday at 11 am. Half of Hamburg's expatriate English and American communities seem to show up, so you're well advised to come along a little early to get a ticket.

Hamburg has an excellent alternative and experimental theatre scene. In particular, *Kampnagelfabrik*, Jarrestrasse 20-26 (bus No 172 or 173), is highly thought of. *Schmidt Theater*, Spielbuddenplatz 24 (S-Bahn: Reeperbahn), is much loved for its wild variety shows and a very casual atmosphere.

Andrew Lloyd Webber seems to be all the rage now in Hamburg (isn't he everywhere?). The musical *Cats* is booked at the *Operettenhaus*, Spielbuddenplatz 1 (S-Bahn: St Pauli), for a number of years. And before the controversial *Neue Flora Theater*, on the corner of Alsenstrasse and Stresemannstrasse (S-Bahn: Holstenstrasse), was even built, it was booked to host *Phantom of the Opera* for 10 years.

A cheap way to see cultural events in the city is to check at the last-minute *Kartenshop* (Ticket Shop) in the Hanse-Viertel shopping centre on Poststrasse. It sells tickets for the theatre, concerts and much more for up to 50% off the full price. Same-day tickets are on sale from 3 to 6.30 pm. Normal booking hours are from 10 am to 7 pm Monday to Friday (to 8.30 pm on 'late Thursday'), and 11 am to 7 pm on Saturday. More than 100 of the city's travel agents can also book tickets through the START/KART computer booking service.

Things to Buy

Because it hosts so many tourists, Hamburg is a pretty expensive place to shop. If you're interested in the sea and related products, there are some great shops along the port (see the previous Things to See section for a very special shop). Many shops along the Reeperbahn also sell normal goods that are competitively priced.

Getting There & Away

Air Hamburg's international airport is growing in stature as Lufthansa continues to add services. Commuting businesspeople on expense accounts are the most frequent flyers.

Bus International destinations which are not served directly by train from Hamburg, such as Amsterdam and London, are served by Eurolines buses. You can buy tickets from the travel agent on the 2nd floor of Altona Station.

A very cheap option for getting to London is Rainbow Tours, which offers a weekend trip to London with accommodation included for DM99. Even if you don't use the return portion of the ticket, you will be hard pushed to find a cheaper one-way fare which includes your first night in London.

Train Hamburg lies right on the north-south train corridor, and makes an ideal stopover when heading to/from Scandinavia. Hamburg's Hauptbahnhof is one of the busiest in Germany. There are hourly trains to Lübeck, Kiel, Hanover and Bremen, as well as good, direct connections to Berlin. There are a number of trains a day to Frankfurt, most of which make a stop at the airport (the super-fast ICE trains do not). There is an overnight train to Munich and another to Basel which continues to Milan.

Car & Motorbike Situated right off two

major autobahns, Hamburg is still quite a drive from most other destinations in Germany. The Mitfahrzentrale (☎ 23 41 23) is at Högerdamm 26a. There are a number of other companies offering ride services. Check in the Yellow Pages under 'Mitfahrzentrale'.

Ferry Hamburg is 20 hours by car ferry from the English port of Harwich. Timetables vary according to the time of year, and may be affected by extremes in the weather, but sailings are at least twice a week in either direction. Check with the tourist office, or with the Scandinavian Seaways information line on ☎ 38 90 31 17. The one-way passenger fare varies from DM108 to DM256, depending on the season and the day of the week. A car costs an extra DM52 to DM124, a motorcycle DM42 to DM74, and a bicycle will cost DM20 in the high season but is free the rest of the year. Ferries leave from Landungsbrücken, near the S-Bahn station of the same name, at 4.30 pm.

The busy train, car and passenger ferry from Puttgarden to Rødbyhavn (the quickest way to Copenhagen) goes every half hour 24 hours a day, and takes one hour. If you're travelling by train, the cost of the ferry will be included in your ticket. A car costs DM125/200 one-way/return (DM91/146 on Sunday and Monday) including up to five people. A motorcycle including up to two people costs DM38/61, and a bicycle is DM5/10. A single passenger pays DM16 (DM7 on Monday and Tuesday) for a one-way ticket which is also valid for a return on the same day.

Getting Around
Public transport consists of buses, the U-Bahn and S-Bahn. A day pass for everything is only DM6.30, and a family pass for the day is just DM11. A taxi from the Hauptbahnhof to the airport should cost around DM40. A better option is to take the airport shuttle bus which leaves from Kirchenallee directly in front of the Hauptbahnhof at least once an hour.

Schleswig-Holstein

Schleswig-Holstein is Germany's most northerly state. Covering an area of 16,696 sq km, it borders with Denmark at the lower end of the Jutland Peninsula. Among Schleswig-Holstein's many attractions are the North Frisian Islands, the beautiful lake district known as the Holsteinische Schweiz (Switzerland of Holstein) in the south-east, the state capital Kiel with its world-famous sailing regattas, and last but certainly not least, the historical city of Lübeck.

In the year 1460 AD, the Danish king, Christian I, declared that the the two lands of Schleswig and Holstein should be forever united. Although the eternal union did not hold, both Schleswig and Holstein began the long process of breaking away from Denmark with the help of Sweden in the mid-17th century. Only in 1773 were both finally free of their Danish masters. In 1815, Holstein joined the German Confederation, which resulted in Denmark trying to lure Schleswig back to the motherland.

Ever-increasing tensions finally led to two wars between Germany and Denmark, the first in 1848-50 and the second in 1864. After a short period under combined Prussian and Austrian rule, and yet another war, Austria was forced to accept Schleswig-Holstein's annexation by Bismarck's Prussia in 1866. Under the conditions of the Treaty of Versailles in 1919, North Schleswig was handed over to Denmark. Finally, in 1946, the British military government formed the state of Schleswig-Holstein from the Prussian province of the same name.

LÜBECK
A great excursion from Hamburg, Lübeck is a medieval town known as the Queen of the Hanseatic League. It was the capital of this association of towns that ruled trade on the Baltic Sea from the 12th to the 16th century.

One tourist office is in the train station and another is on the Markt. Lübeck's telephone code is 0451.

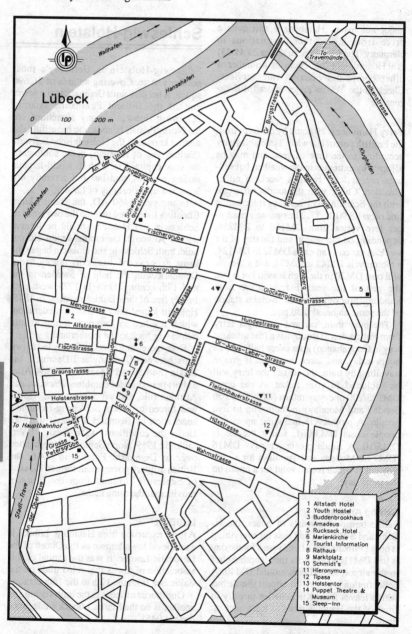

GERMANY

1 Altstadt Hotel
2 Youth Hostel
3 Buddenbrookhaus
4 Amadeus
5 Rucksack Hotel
6 Marienkirche
7 Tourist Information
8 Rathaus
9 Marktplatz
10 Schmidt's
11 Hieronymus
12 Tipasa
13 Holstentor
14 Puppet Theatre & Museum
15 Sleep-Inn

Things to See & Do

The Altstadt is encircled by canals fed by the Trave River. Start a walking tour at the **Holstentor**, a fortified gate with huge twin towers. Then head up Holstenstrasse to the pretty Marktplatz.

The Rathaus covers two full sides of the Marktplatz. The Marienkirche is on another side, with a stark reminder of WW II: a bombing raid brought the church bells crashing to the stone floor and the townspeople have left the bell fragments in place, with a small sign saying, 'A protest against war and violence.'

To the north of the church, the Volksbank occupies **Buddenbrookhaus**, the house where Thomas Mann was born and which he made famous in his novel, *Buddenbrooks*. Then, for a real medieval feel, stroll down **Glockengiesserstrasse**, with its open *Höfe* (courts).

Lübeck's **Marionettentheater** (Puppet Theatre) on Kolkstrasse, on the corner of Kleine Petersgrube, is an absolute must (closed Monday). Usually there is an afternoon performance for children (3.30 pm) and an evening performance for adults (7.30 pm), but times do vary. Entry is DM6. When you pass by to check the time of the next show, visit the **Puppenmuseum** (Doll & Puppet Museum), just around the corner on Kleine Petersgrube. It is open Tuesday to Thursday from noon till 6 pm, Friday to Sunday from 10 am. The entry fee of DM3 is worth every Pfennig.

Places to Stay

Though a bit of a trek, the camping is excellent along the Travemünde shoreline. This area, on the mouth of the Trave River, is an international beach resort. The tourist offices have a list of camping grounds.

For budget accommodation, you can't go past the *Rucksack Hotel* (☎ 70 68 92), Kanalstrasse 70, at DM18 to DM32 per person depending on the room; there are cooking facilities. It only has 29 beds, so you'd be wise to book ahead. To get there, take bus No 1, 3 or 12 from the Hauptbahnhof and ask the driver to let you off at the corner of Glockengiesserstrasse and Kanalstrasse.

Lübeck has two youth hostels: *Jugendgästehaus Lübeck* (☎ 7 03 99), Mengstrasse 33 (bus No 1, 3 or 12 from the Hauptbahnhof), is well situated in the middle of the old town; the other hostel, *Folke-Bernadotte-Heim* (☎ 3 34 33), is at Am Gertrudenkirchhof 4, a little outside the old town (same bus numbers, about five minutes farther along). Both hostels charge DM16/19.50 for juniors/seniors, with breakfast included. The cheapest place in town is the YMCA's *Sleep-Inn* (☎ 7 89 82) at Grosse Petersgrube 11 (DM14 per night, breakfast not included).

For something a little more up-market, try the *Bahnhofs Hotel* (☎ 8 38 83), right by the Hauptbahnhof at Am Bahnhof 21. Singles/doubles cost DM50/75. In the centre of town, *Altstadt Hotel* (☎ 7 20 83) is very well situated at Fischergrube 52. Rooms start at DM60/95.

Places to Eat

The most popular restaurant among Lübeck's student population is *Tipasa*, Schlumacherstrasse 14. For atmosphere it is second to none. The menu includes a variety of meat, fish and vegetarian dishes as well as excellent pizzas. If you need a good brew, there are several beers on tap, including Guinness. Another place that is always crowded is *Schmidt's Gasthaus*, Dr Julius Leber Strasse 60-62. The menu is similar to Tipasa's.

Hieronymus, Fleischhauerstrasse 81, is an enormous restaurant spread over three floors. A meal from the impressive menu can cost anywhere from DM15 to DM50 or more. *Amadeus*, Königstrasse 26, is a great little café with good music. It has a limited menu, but the prices are right: pizzas go from DM5.50. It is also a good place for breakfast (open from 10 am).

Save room for a dessert or a snack of marzipan, which was invented in Lübeck (local legend has it that the town ran out of flour during a long siege and resorted to grinding almonds to make bread). The best

GERMANY

place for marzipan is *J G Niederegger* at Breite Strasse 89, directly opposite the Rathaus.

Getting There & Away

Lübeck is close to Hamburg, with at least one train every hour. The trip takes from 40 minutes to a little over an hour depending on the train. Most people use Hamburg as a base for a one-day trip. Kiel is nearby, and there are numerous trains connecting Kiel with Lübeck every day. All trains from Hamburg to Rostock make a stop in Lübeck.

There is a Mitfahrzentrale (☎ 7 10 74) at Fischergrube 45.

Getting Around

Lübeck is easily walkable. If you plan to go to Travemünde, you'll find lots of transport options during the tourist season. Note that bus Nos 1, 3 and 12 will take you from the Hauptbahnhof past all the budget accommodation spots (hostels, YMCA, Rucksack Hotel).

KIEL

Kiel, the capital of Schleswig-Holstein, was seriously damaged by Allied bombing during WW II, but has since been rebuilt into a vibrant and modern city. Located at the end of a modest fjord, it has long been one of Germany's most important Baltic Sea harbours, and has hosted Olympic sailing events in 1936 and 1972.

Orientation & Information

Kiel's main street is Holstenstrasse, a colourful, pedestrianised street a few hundred metres inland from the sea. It runs from St Nikolai church in the north to the tourist office in the south, although at this end the street is actually an undercover shopping mall. The tourist office is reached by an overpass from the Hauptbahnhof – just follow the signs from within the station.

Kiel's telephone code is 0431.

Things to See & Do

Kiel's most famous attraction is the **Kieler Woche** (Kiel Week) in the last full week in June, a week of festivities revolving around a yachting regatta attended by over 4000 of the world's sailing elite. Even if you're not into sailing, the atmosphere is electric – just make sure you book a room in advance if you want to be in on the fun.

If you want to experience Kiel's love for the sea in a less energetic fashion, you could take a ferry ride to the town of **Laboe** at the mouth of the fjord. Ferries leave every 90 minutes or so from a pier off Kaistrasse, no more than five minutes' walk from the Hauptbahnhof. They take around one hour to reach Laboe, hopping back and forth across the fjord along the way. In Laboe, you can visit **U995**, a wartime U-boat on the beach, which is now a technical museum. Nearby is a **naval war memorial** and a **navigation museum**. The last ferry returning to Kiel leaves Laboe at around 7.30 pm.

Kiel is also the point at which the 99-km-long shipping canal from the North Sea enters the Baltic Sea. Some 60,000 ships pass through the canal every year, and the **locks** (*Schleusen* in German) are well worth a visit.

Finally, do not miss the **Schiffahrts-museum** (Maritime Museum), which contains an interesting collection of models and other maritime artefacts. It is open Tuesday to Sunday from 10 am to 5 pm, and entry is free.

Places to Stay

Kiel's *youth hostel* (☎ 73 57 23) is at Johannesstrasse 1 in the suburb of Gaarden, across the water from the Hauptbahnhof. To get there, you have a couple of options. One is to take the Laboe ferry from near the train station and get off at the first stop ('Gaarden'), from where it's a 10-minute walk. The other option is to take bus No 4, 24 or 34 from Sophienblatt by the tourist office and ask the driver to let you off near the 'Jugendherberge'.

In the budget-hotel range, *Touristhotel Schweriner Hof* (☎ 6 14 16), Königsweg 13, is the most centrally located. It has singles/doubles from DM45/85. *Rabe's Hotel* (☎ 67 60 91) at Ringstrasse 30 is also very central, but a little more expensive with rooms from DM60/95.

In Gaarden, not too far from the youth hostel, is *Hotel Runge* (☎ 73 19 92) at Elisabethstrasse 16. Singles/doubles start at DM40/75. Also in Gaarden is *Motel Karlstal* (☎ 73 16 90) at Karlstal 18-20. After the youth hostel, this is probably the cheapest place in town, with rooms from DM33/64.

Places to Eat

There are plenty of opportunities to eat at very reasonable prices. One of the best places is *Friesenhof*, at Fleethorn 9 in the Rathaus building. It has a daily special (from 11 am to 3 pm) for under DM10, and tasty main courses from around DM15.

The *Klosterbrauerei* at Alter Markt 9 (at the northern end of Holstenstrasse) has a great atmosphere with prices to match. On Sundays from 6 to 10 pm, it has a buffet with all you can eat for DM12.50. Children's rates vary according to their height – those under 80 cm tall eat for free!

A hot dinner at the *youth hostel* costs DM7.10, and a cold meal only DM5.90. Otherwise, there are a number of kebab and pizza places within walking distance.

Getting There & Away

There are numerous trains every day running between Kiel and Hamburg's Altona Station. The trip takes one to 1½ hours and costs DM25/50 one-way/return. To Lübeck, there are trains just about every hour (sometimes more often). The trip takes about 1¼ hours and costs DM17/34.

If you are in a hurry to get to Scandinavia, Kiel may well be the place to go from. There are two or three ferries a day to Bagenkop on the Danish island of Langeland (they do not run in January or the first half of February). The trip takes 2½ hours. The fare is DM6.50/10.50 one-way/return except in July, when it is DM8/15. For bookings and information, call ☎ 9 16 52.

The daily ferry from Kiel to Gothenburg, Sweden, leaves at 7 pm. From the beginning of November to the beginning of April, the fare is DM72/124 one-way/return; from

mid-June to the beginning of August, it costs DM186/294; the rest of the year, DM112/184. Bicycles are carried free. Sleeping berths vary in price from DM28 to DM530! For booking and information, call Stena Line on ☎ 90 99.

Finally, you can also take a ferry from Kiel direct to Oslo, Norway. Ferries leave almost every day from April to December, and generally every second day the rest of the year, although around Christmas there is a five-day break. Departures are at 4.30 pm except on Mondays and Thursdays, when the ferry leaves at 1.30 pm. The trip takes just under 20 hours. Fares start at DM95/190 one-way/return (around 30% extra in summer) for a single bed in a four-bed cabin. For bookings and information, call Color Line on ☎ 97 40 90.

On all these ferries, student discounts are sometimes available.

Getting Around

Kiel has an excellent network of bicycle tracks, and cycling is a very tempting transport option. You can rent bikes at the train station.

The city bus station *(ZOB)* is conveniently located on Auguste-Viktoria-Strasse near the Hauptbahnhof. To get to the North-Baltic Sea Canal and the locks, take the bus to Wik and get off at the end (around five minutes' walk from the locks).

Enquire at the tourist office about a 'Kieler Karte', which allows you unlimited use of buses and ferries for one, three or seven days (DM10/15/25).

FRISIAN ISLANDS

The Frisian Islands reward those who make the trek with sunshine, sand dunes, sea and very pure air.

Friesland itself covers an area stretching from the northern Netherlands along the coast up into Denmark. It is inhabited by farmers who speak Frisian, a language that's very closely related to English but is virtually incomprehensible if you hear it spoken. East Friesland (Ostfriesland) is the patch of Germany north-west of Bremen; North

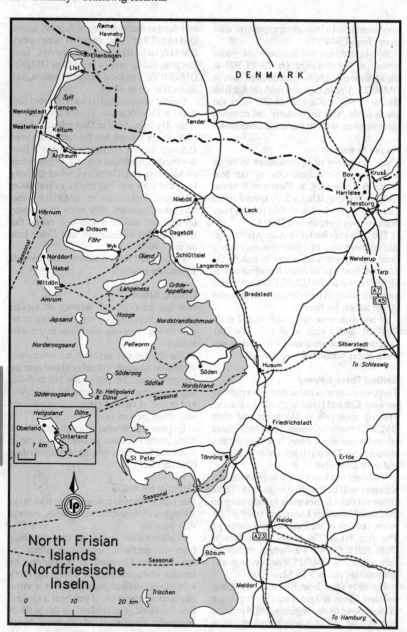

North Frisian
Islands
(Nordfriesische
Inseln)

DENMARK

Friesland (Nordfriesland) is the western coastal area of Schleswig-Holstein up to and into Denmark; West Friesland is in the northern Netherlands, where Frisian is recognised as an official language.

Orientation & Information

The East Frisian Islands are large sand dunes rising up to 30 metres above sea level. The two most popular are Borkum and Norderney, but Wangerooge, Langeoog and Juist are also quite accessible. The most popular of the North Frisian Islands is Sylt, known as a resort with fresh air, spa facilities and water sports, while Föhr and Amrum are far more relaxed and less touristy. And, though not technically part of the Frisian Islands, Heligoland (Helgoland in German) lies 70 km out to sea and serves as a popular outing for its sea, air, water and duty-free port.

Sylt's information office is Tourist Information Westerland (☎ 04651-2 40 01) across from the town's train station. On Amrum, the small tourist office is in one of the harbour car parks; you'll see it to the left as you head out of the harbour.

On Sylt, the telephone code for Westerland is 04651; for List, the code is 04652, and for Hörnum, 04653. For the island of Amrum, the code is 04682.

Things to See

Besides the sea, the beaches and the sun, there's little to see in the North Frisian Islands, but Sylt's **casino** is excellent. To get away from the often stifling summer crowds of Sylt, try Föhr or Amrum instead.

Heligoland is a fun one or two-day excursion from the north coast. The island was used as a submarine base in WW II and it's still possible to tour the strong bunkers and underground tunnels. The island was heavily bombed in the war and all of the houses are new. Take a walk along Lung Wai (Long Way), filled with duty-free shops, and then up the stairway of 180 steps to Oberland for a nice view. There's also a scenic trail around the island, with lots of nature.

To get even farther away from it all, take the ferry from Heligoland to neighbouring

Düne, a small island filled with beaches and nudists. It also has an interesting aquarium dedicated to North Sea life.

Activities

The **spa** facilities of Sylt might be worth a splurge. Other options include golf, tennis, lots of swimming and sunning spots, and much more.

Horse riding is a popular option, particularly on Amrum. However, if you have images of yourself galloping off into the dunes, then you'd better slow down before you start: the only way to go riding is as a member of a guided group (unless you have your own horse with you). The going rate is around DM20 per hour, and the groups usually go out for two hours. If you are interested, contact the tourist offices on Amrum or Sylt.

One of Sylt's best kept secrets is the **beach sauna**. To get there, take the road to Ellenbogen, which branches off the main island road about four km south-west of List. You will see a sign for the sauna on the left. When you've boiled yourself in the sauna, the idea is to run naked into the chilly North Sea. Brrr. It costs DM20 to use the facilities, which are open from 11 am to 5 pm, although the sauna is closed between the end of October and Christmas, and again from mid-January until the end of March.

Places to Stay

Camping is the most enjoyable way to sleep on Sylt. There are many options, but the best is *Sylt-Kampen* (☎ 4 20 86) in the small town of Kampen. Two other options are *Sylt-Wennigstedt* (☎ 4 10 81) and *Sylt-Westerland* (☎ 2 25 12). The *hostel* in the south at Hörnum (☎ 2 94) is OK. The *hostel* at List (☎ 3 97) should be a last resort. Most other options are expensive, although there are a few reasonably priced places around. The tourist office or the Kurverwaltung in every town on the island can supply you with a list of places to stay

In Westerland, *Hotel Garni Niedersachsen* (☎ 70 23), Margarethenstrasse 5, has singles/doubles from DM50/68. Even

GERMANY

606 Germany – Schleswig-Holstein

better value is *Haus Wagenknecht* (☎ 2 30 91), Wenningstedter Weg 59, with rooms for DM48/55 in the low season and DM50/68 in the high season. For a little more class at reasonable prices, try *Hotel Vierjahreszeiten* (☎ 2 30 28), Johann Möller Strasse 40, which has singles/doubles with a good breakfast from DM50/80 in the low season and DM70/100 in the high season.

In List, most places don't have more than five or six rooms available, so things fill up quickly. A reasonable bet might be *Pension Jensen* (☎ 6 68), Am Lister Tor 1, with doubles for DM100/120 in the low/high season.

On Amrum, try *Pension Haus Südstrand* (☎ 27 08) on Mittelstrasse in Wittdün, with singles/doubles for DM35/66 in the low season and DM50/96 in the high season. *Hotel Pension Treffpunkt* (☎ 20 87), also on Mittelstrasse, with rooms for DM48/96, is another possibility.

Places to Eat

Your best bet up here is to picnic. For a splurge, try Westerland's *Alte Friesenstube* at Gaadt 4. It specialises in northern German and Frisian cooking, with full meals starting at DM38. For good, inexpensive fare, try *Toni's Restaurant*, Norderstrasse 3. It has a variety of main courses at around DM11. Another good option is the *Barbecue Steakhouse* in Westerland's pedestrian zone at Sandstrasse 6-8, which has main courses from DM13.50 for chicken and vegetables to around DM30 for some mouth-watering seafood dishes. Farther down the same street is *Schlachter's Stube*, which is a butcher's shop with a stand-up hot food service. Apart from the usual kiosk fare such as burgers and sausages, it has some tasty-looking items from as little as DM10 for a main course.

In List's harbour, there are a number of very colourful-looking kiosks. One of them, *Gosch*, which prides itself on being Germany's northernmost fish kiosk, is an institution, well known even in Hamburg. The food is delicious, and if you are not too hungry, it won't break your budget.

One of the nicest places on Sylt to sit with friends over a cockle-warming drink or a small meal is *Witthüs*. It is on the main island road about two km south of the town of Kampen, directly on the corner of the road which leads to Keitum.

There are not that many restaurants on Amrum, and many of them close out of season. One place which is open all year is *Restaurant Strandvogt* in the Strandhotel Vierjahreszeiten in Wittdün. Everyone on the island over the age of 10 knows where the hotel is. The restaurant specialises in seafood, with main courses starting at DM16 – highly recommended.

Getting There & Away

Since Sylt is such a resort draw, it's fairly convenient to reach. Most people take the train directly from Hamburg's Altona Station to Westerland. Between 13 and 18 trains make the three-hour trip every day. The fare is DM55/110 one-way/return.

If you are travelling by car, you will have to drive to the town of Niebüll near the Danish border and load your car onto a train. There is no need to reserve in advance: just turn up and they will make room for your car. There are around 12 to 15 crossings in both directions every day. The cost is DM106 to DM116 return (one-way is half price) depending on the size of the car. This price includes all passengers.

You can also get from Sylt by ferry to the Danish island of Rømø. There are at least five and as many as 13 crossings each way on any one day. It costs DM4/6 one-way/return (DM5/8 with a bicycle) and takes 55 minutes. Cars cost DM43 or DM48 one-way. For information and reservations, call ☎ 04652-4 75 in List, or ☎ 0045-74 75 53 03 in Havneby, Rømø.

To get to Föhr and Amrum, you take the Sylt-bound train from Hamburg-Altona but get off in Niebüll. From Niebüll, you take a train to Dagebüll Hafen (DM8.50 one-way, no rail passes as it is a private line). From Dagebüll Hafen, there is a fairly frequent ferry service to Föhr and Amrum. A day-return costs DM15 per person. A return ticket valid up to four days costs DM17.50. The ticket allows you to visit both islands. The trip to Amrum takes around two hours, stopping at Föhr on the way.

Heligoland is easy to reach by taking the train to Cuxhaven and then boarding one of the frequent ferries.

Getting Around

There is a reasonable bus service on Sylt, with buses running from Westerland north to List, south to Hörnum and east to Keitum and Archsum around once every hour, although the timetable seems to be pretty flexible. On Amrum, a bus runs from the ferry terminal in Wittdün to Norddorf and back every half to one hour depending on the season.

Cycling is certainly the best way to get around on the islands. It is particularly convenient on Amrum, which is only about 14 km long. There are countless places to rent bicycles on the islands – just look for the signs saying 'Fahrrad Verleih'. Rates begin at around DM7 per day, varying upwards according to the kind of bicycle you rent.

Great Britain

At one stage of its history this small island ruled half the world's population and had a major impact on many of the rest. For those whose countries once lay in the shadow of its great empire a visit may be a cliché, but it is also essential – a peculiar mixture of homecoming and confrontation.

To the surprise of many, Britain remains one of the most beautiful islands in the world. All the words, paintings and pictures that you have read and seen are not just romantic exaggerations. In terms of area it is small, but the more you explore, the bigger it seems to become. Visitors from the New World are often fooled by this magical expansion and try to do too much too quickly. So much is packed into this island that covering it all is impossible. J B Priestley observed of England, 'She is just pretending to be small.'

The United Kingdom comprises Great Britain (England, Wales and Scotland) and Northern Ireland. Its full name is the United Kingdom of Great Britain and Northern Ireland. This chapter confines itself to the island of Great Britain, the largest of the British Isles, and Scotland's outlying islands – the Hebrides in the west and Orkneys and Shetlands in the north-east. For reasons of geographical and practical coherence, Northern Ireland is dealt with alongside the Irish Republic.

Sometimes in summer it seems like the whole world has come to Britain. Don't spend too much time in the big, tourist-ridden towns. Do pick a small area and spend at least a week or so wandering around.

Facts about the Country

HISTORY
Celts & Romans
England had long been settled by hunters when, around 4000 BC, a new group of immigrants arrived from Europe. They

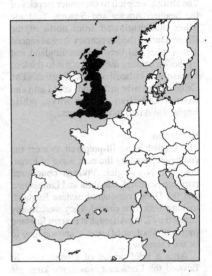

farmed the chalk hills radiating from Salisbury Plain and began the construction of stone tombs, and around 3000 BC, the great ceremonial complexes at Avebury and Stonehenge.

The next great influx of people were the Celts, a people from central Europe who had mastered the smelting of bronze, and later of iron. They brought two forms of the Celtic language: the Gaelic, which is still spoken in Ireland and Scotland, and the Brythonic, which was spoken in England and is still spoken in Wales.

In 43 AD, the Romans arrived in force and despite fierce resistance, established themselves in England. The mountains of Wales and Scotland remained Celtic strongholds, but England was a part of the Roman empire for 350 years. Paved roads radiated from London to important regional centres – Ermine St ran north to Lincoln, York and Hadrian's Wall, and Watling St ran north-west to Chester. Christianity arrived in the 3rd century.

GREAT BRITAIN

English

By the 4th century the empire was in retreat, and in 409 the last Roman troops withdrew. The British were left to the tender mercies of the heathen Angles and Saxons, Teutonic tribes that originated from north of the Rhine. During the 5th century they advanced across what had been Roman England and by the 7th century they had come to think of themselves collectively as English. The Celts, particularly in Ireland, kept Latin and Roman Christian culture alive, while England slid into the Dark Ages.

Northmen

The English were ill-prepared to meet the challenge posed by the next wave of invaders. The Norwegian Vikings conquered northern Scotland, Cumbria and Lancashire, and the Danes conquered eastern England, making York their capital. They were finally stopped by King Alfred, but eastern England (north of Watling St) was acknowledged to be the Danelaw.

After a brief period of Danish rule, St Edward the Confessor was made king. He had been brought up in Normandy – a Viking duchy in France – where he became close friends with his cousin Duke William, the future Conqueror. Edward's death left two contenders for the crown: Harold, Edward's brother-in-law and heir, and William. In 1066 William landed with 12,000 men and defeated Harold at the Battle of Hastings.

The conquest of England by the Northmen/Normans was completed rapidly; English aristocrats were replaced by French-speaking Normans, dominating castles were built, and the feudal system was imposed.

Middle Ages

In the 12th century, after a disastrous civil war fought over the succession to the crown, Henry II, the Count of Anjou, was made king. He had inherited more than half of modern France and clearly surpassed the King of France in the extent of his power. The struggle to retain this Angevin empire was a dominant concern of the Plantagenet and Lancastrian kings – leading to the Hundred Years' War, and finally to English defeat. In order to finance these adventures, the Plantagenet kings conceded a considerable amount of power to Parliament, which jealously protected its traditional right to control taxation.

Further disputes over the royal succession allowed Parliament to consolidate its power. The Wars of the Roses, a dynastic struggle between the houses of York and Lancaster, lasted for 30 years. The final victor in 1485 was Henry VII, the first Tudor king.

The Tudors & Stuarts

Under Henry VIII, the long struggle of the English kings against the power of the pope came to a head. Parliament made Henry the head of the Church of England, and the Bible was translated into English. In 1536 the monasteries were dissolved, the bulk of their enormous wealth being transferred to the king – a largely popular move, because many monasteries were corrupt.

The 16th century was a golden age. Greek learning was rediscovered, the European powers explored the world, trade boomed, Shakespeare wrote his plays, and Francis Bacon laid the foundation for modern science. An age of religious intolerance was beginning, however, and after Elizabeth I the relationship between Parliament and the autocratic Stuart kings deteriorated.

In 1644 the conflict became a civil war. Catholics, traditionalist members of the Church of England and the old gentry supported Charles I, whose power base was the north and west. The Puritans and the Commons, based in London and the towns of the south-east, supported Parliament.

Parliament found its champion in Oliver Cromwell, the royalists were defeated and in 1649 Charles I was executed. Cromwell assumed dictatorial powers, but he also laid the foundation for the British Empire by modernising the army and navy. After his death in 1658, a reconstituted Parliament recalled Charles II from exile.

Empire & Industry

The Restoration was a period of expansion:

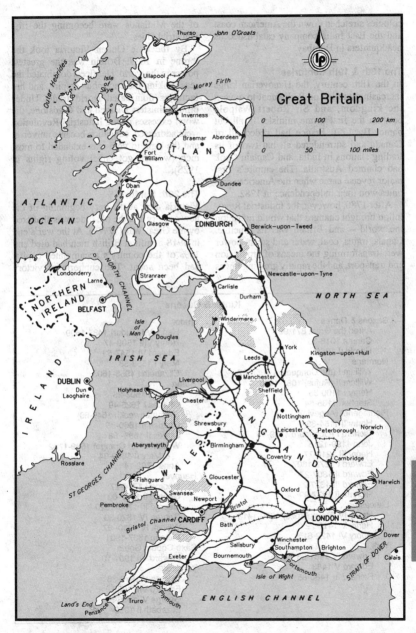

Great Britain

0   100   200 km

0   50   100 miles

ATLANTIC
OCEAN

Thurso   John O'Groats

Ullapool

Isle
of
Skye

Outer Hebrides

Moray Firth

Inverness

SCOTLAND

Braemar   Aberdeen

Fort
William

Dundee

Oban

Glasgow   EDINBURGH

Berwick-upon-Tweed

Stranraer

Newcastle-upon-Tyne

NORTH CHANNEL

Carlisle

Durham

NORTH SEA

Londonderry

Larne

NORTHERN
IRELAND   BELFAST

Windermere

Isle
of
Man   Douglas

IRISH SEA

York

Kingston-upon-Hull

Leeds

DUBLIN

Dun
Laoghaire

Liverpool   Manchester

Holyhead

Chester   Sheffield

IRELAND

Nottingham

Shrewsbury

Leicester   Peterborough   Norwich

Aberystwyth

Birmingham

ENGLAND

Coventry

Cambridge

Rosslare

WALES

Gloucester

Oxford

ST GEORGES CHANNEL

Fishguard

Swansea

Pembroke

Newport

CARDIFF

Bristol

LONDON

Harwich

Bristol Channel

Bath

Dover

Salisbury   Winchester

Exeter   Bournemouth   Southampton   Brighton

Calais

STRAIT OF DOVER

Land's End

Truro   Plymouth

Penzance

Isle of Wight   Portsmouth

ENGLISH CHANNEL

GREAT BRITAIN

colonies stretched down the American coast and the East India company established its headquarters in Bombay.

The 18th & 19th Centuries

In the 18th century, the Hanoverian kings increasingly relied on Parliament to govern the kingdom, and Sir Robert Walpole became the first prime minister in all but name. By 1770 France had ceded all of Canada and surrendered all but two of its trading stations in India, and Captain Cook had claimed Australia. The empire's first major reverse came when the American colonies won their independence in 1782.

After 1780, however, the Industrial Revolution brought changes that would refashion the world – and Britain was its crucible. Canals, trains, coal, water and steam power were transforming the means of production and transport, and the rapidly growing towns of the Midlands were becoming the first industrial cities.

By the time Queen Victoria took the throne in 1837, Britain was the greatest power in the world. Her fleets dominated the seas, linking the enormous empire, and her factories dominated world trade. Under prime ministers Disraeli and Gladstone, the worst excesses of the Industrial Revolution were addressed, education became universal and the right to vote was extended to most men (women got equal voting rights in 1928).

The 20th Century

Victoria died at the very beginning of the new century and the old order was shattered by the Great War (WW I). At the war's end in 1918 a million British men had died and 15% of the country's accumulated capital had been spent. The euphoria of victory

Kings & Queens

Saxons & Danes
  Alfred the Great 871-99
  Canute 1016-35
  Harold II 1066
Normans
  William I (the Conqueror) 1066-87
  William II (Rufus) 1087-1100
  Henry I 1100-35
  Stephen 1135-54
Plantagenet (Angevin)
  Henry II 1154-89
  Richard I (Lionheart) 1189-99
  John 1199-1216
  Henry III 1216-77
  Edward I 1272-1307
  Edward II 1307-27
  Edward III 1327-77
  Richard II 1377-99
Lancaster
  Henry IV (Bolingbroke) 1399-1413
  Henry V 1413-22
  Henry VI 1422-61
York
  Edward IV 1461-83
  Edward V 1483
  Richard III 1483-85

Tudor
  Henry VII (Tudor) 1485-1509
  Henry VIII 1509-47
  Edward VI 1547-53
  Mary I 1553-58
  Elizabeth I 1558-1603
Stuart
  James I 1603-25
  Charles I 1625-49
  (Commonwealth 1649-60)
  Charles II 1660-85
  James II 1685- 88
  William III (of Orange) 1689-1702
    & Mary II 1689-94
  Anne 1702-14
Hanover
  George I 1714-27
  George II 1727-60
  George III 1760-1820
  George IV 1820-30
  William IV 1830- 37
  Victoria 1837-1901
Saxe-Coburg Gotha
  Edward VII 1901-10
Windsor
  George V 1910-36
  Edward VIII 1936
  George VI 1936-52
  Elizabeth II 1953-

didn't last long. In the late 1920s the world economy slumped, ushering in more than a decade of misery and political upheaval. The Labour Party first came to power in 1924, but lasted less than a year. Bitter industrial struggles wracked the country and unemployed hunger marchers converged on London. In 1933 Hitler came to power in Germany.

On 1 September 1939, Hitler finally provoked a new war by invading Poland. By mid-1940, France had surrendered, and Britain, under the extraordinary leadership of Winston Churchill, was virtually isolated. Between July and October 1940 the Battle of Britain was won by the Royal Air Force and Hitler's invasion plans were blocked. Even so, by 1941, 43,000 Britons had been killed by bombs.

The postwar years have been challenging for Britain. The last of its empire became independent – India in 1947, Malaya in 1957, Kenya in 1963 – and traditional industries have collapsed. The nation has had to accept a new role as a partner in the European Community (EC). It is still a wealthy and influential country, but it's no longer a superpower and no longer able to maintain that it is anything more than an island, just off the mainland.

GEOGRAPHY

Britain has an area of 240,000 sq km (93,000 sq miles) and is about the same size as New Zealand or half the size of France. It is less than 1000 km (600 miles) from south to north and under 500 km (300 miles) at its widest point.

There are no great mountains in terms of height, but this does not prevent a number of ranges from being spectacular. The mountains of Snowdonia in north-west Wales, the Cumbrian mountains in north-west England, and the Glenkens in south-west Scotland all reach around 1000 metres. The Grampians form the mountainous barrier between the Scottish Lowlands and Highlands, and include Ben Nevis, the highest mountain on the island at 1343 metres.

The seas surrounding the British Isles are shallow, and relatively warm because of the influence of the warm North Atlantic Current, also known as the Gulf Stream. This creates a temperate, changeable, maritime climate with few extremes of temperature and few cloudless, sunny days!

GOVERNMENT

The United Kingdom does not have a written constitution but operates under a mixture of Parliamentary statutes, common law (a body of legal principles based on precedents that go back to Anglo-Saxon customs) and convention.

The monarch is the head of state with enormous potential power. Over a long period of time, however, the real power has been whittled away to the point where the current Queen acts almost entirely on the advice of 'her' ministers.

Parliament is the supreme legislative authority and there are three separate elements – the Queen, the House of Commons and the House of Lords. In practice, the supreme body is the House of Commons, which is directly elected and has a maximum duration of five years. Voting is not compulsory, and a candidate is elected if they win a simple majority in their constituency. There are 650 constituencies (seats) – 523 for England, 38 for Wales, 72 for Scotland and 17 for Northern Ireland.

The House of Lords consists of the Lords Spiritual (26 senior bishops of the Church of England) and the Lords Temporal (all hereditary and life peers, including the Lords of Appeal or 'law lords'). None are elected by the general population. If the Lords refuse to pass a bill, but it is passed twice by the Commons, it is sent to the Queen for her automatic assent.

The Queen appoints the leader of the majority party in the House of Commons as Prime Minister; all other ministers are appointed on the recommendation of the Prime Minister, most from the House of Commons. Ministers are responsible for government departments. The senior 20 or so ministers make up the Cabinet, which, although answerable to Parliament, meets

GREAT BRITAIN

confidentially and in effect manages the government and its policies.

For the last 150 years a predominantly two-party system has operated. Most winning candidates belong to one of the main parties (a situation that is encouraged by the voting system). Since 1945 either the Conservative Party or the Labour Party has held power, the Conservatives drawing their support from suburbia and the countryside, Labour from urban industrialised areas.

Put crudely, the Conservatives are right-wing, free-enterprise supporters, and Labour is left-wing, in the social-democratic tradition. In practice, under Neil Kinnock the Labour Party has shed most of its socialist credo, and under John Major the Conservatives have softened their hard-right approach.

In the 1992 elections, John Major led the Conservatives to their fourth consecutive victory: despite Labour's moderate policies and a serious economic recession the electorate decided to stick with the devil it knows. The Conservatives won 42% of the vote and 336 seats (down 31 seats from 1987); Labour won 35% of the vote and 271 seats (up 44); the next largest party was the Liberal Democrats with 20 seats.

The United Kingdom is a member of the 12-nation EC, and elects 16% of the European Parliament.

ECONOMY
Up to the 18th century the economy was based on agriculture and the manufacture of woollen cloth. In the late 18th century the empire and the Industrial Revolution allowed Britain to become the first industrialised trading nation. The population of South Wales, the Midlands, Yorkshire and the Scottish Lowlands expanded rapidly. Conditions for workers were appalling, but 19th century Britain dominated world trade.

In the 20th century, a considerable proportion of industry was nationalised (railways, services, coal mines, steel, shipbuilding, even cars), a process that was reversed during the years of Thatcherism. Today the economy is primarily free enterprise, and although manufacturing continues to play an important role (particularly in the Midlands), service industries like banking and finance have grown rapidly (particularly in London and the south-east). A great deal of the traditional mining, engineering and cotton industries (especially in the Midlands and north) have disappeared.

The last 20 years have seen a continuous battle against unemployment and inflation. The latest development has been rising unemployment (9.3%) and dropping inflation (4.3%).

POPULATION & PEOPLE
Britain has a population of over 55 million, which works out to about 236 inhabitants per sq km. The majority are concentrated in and around London (nearly seven million, or 4288 people per sq km), and in the Midlands around Birmingham, Manchester, Liverpool, Sheffield and Nottingham.

The big cities are multicultural, and there has been a highly visible influx of Blacks (from the West Indies) and Indians (from Pakistan and India). Outside London and the big Midlands cities, however, the population is overwhelmingly White (although every town will have its Chinese and Indian restaurant).

ARTS
The greatest artistic contributions of the British have been in theatre, literature and architecture. Apart from a few exceptional individuals there is not a tradition of great painters, sculptors or composers. Perhaps the most distinctive phenomenon, however, was the creation of the extraordinary country palaces that litter the landscape.

The aristocrats of the 18th and 19th centuries certainly knew quality when they saw it. Surrounded by treasures in the most beautiful houses and gardens of Europe, waited on hand and foot, they must have believed they were at the absolute pinnacle of civilisation. Most of their priceless private art collections are now accessible to the public – if not in Britain, in the USA and Japan. Despite the shift in global wealth, Britain is still a treasure house of masterpieces from every age and continent.

Although it would not be difficult to find cynics who would happily proclaim the death of British culture, the major cities (London, Birmingham, Manchester, Edinburgh and Glasgow) are still cultural powerhouses. You can only wonder what they will create next – after house, punk, hippy and mod, after Thatcherism, socialism, industrialisation and imperialism. British publishers still publish over 30,000 books a year, and the theatre has survived the unsupportive Thatcher years.

Only modern architecture has almost totally failed. The heritage is incomparable – country houses, cottages, cathedrals, castles, municipal buildings, and beautiful villages – but the 20th century has failed to add anything more inspiring than motorways, high-rise housing estates and tawdry suburban development (with a couple of notable exceptions).

LANGUAGE

English as it is spoken in Britain is sometimes incomprehensible to overseas visitors – even to those who assume they have spoken it all their lives. It's OK to ask someone to repeat what they have said, but don't laugh.

Facts for the Visitor

VISAS & EMBASSIES

You don't need a visa if you are a citizen of Australia, Canada, New Zealand, South Africa, or the USA. Tourists are permitted to stay for six months. The immigration authorities can be tough; dress neatly and carry some evidence you have sufficient funds. A credit card and/or an onward ticket will help. People have been refused entry because they happened to be carrying documents (perhaps work references) that suggest they intend to work.

EC nationals don't need a work permit, but all other nationalities must have one to work legally. If the *main* purpose of your visit is to work, you must obtain an entry clearance before you go; basically you will need to be sponsored by a British company.

However, if you are a citizen of a Commonwealth country, and aged between 17 and 27 inclusive, you can get a special working holiday permit that allows you to spend up to two years in Britain. In theory you shouldn't work full-time for more than half your stay – the work should be 'incidental' to your holiday. You must satisfy the Immigration Officer that entry clearance is not 'necessary', meaning you must have sufficient funds to make a holiday feasible. Again, a credit card or onward ticket will help.

You don't *have* to get a working holiday visa in advance at a British consulate in your home country, but it is a good idea to do so if possible. Immigration at Heathrow is notoriously difficult.

If you spend any of your two years in other countries, you can apply to the Home Office to have that time added to your original permit. Bear in mind that you may well have to run the immigration gauntlet again when you re-enter the country. If you are returning to a job, make it clear to immigration that although you might be returning to full-time employment your main purpose is to have a holiday and that your job is for a finite period. Don't use up your working holiday visa unless you really do plan to work; you can switch your permission from being a visitor to being a working holiday maker, when and if you do make that decision.

If a parent or grandparent was born in the UK you are eligible for a patriality certificate (you must get this in advance), which allows you to live and work in the UK for an initial period of four years.

Visiting students from the USA can get a work permit allowing them to work for six months; you must be at least 18 years old and a full-time student at a college or university. It costs US$125 and is available through the Council on International Educational Exchange (☎ 212-661 1414), 205 East 42nd St, New York, NY 10017.

If you wish to extend your stay and/or get a working holiday visa (for part-time work!) once you are in the UK, contact the Home

Office (☎ 081-686 0688) before the expiry date in your visa.

UK Embassies Abroad

Some UK embassies abroad are:

Australia – British High Commission
Commonwealth Ave, Canberra, ACT 2600
(☎ 06-270 6666)
Canada – British High Commission
80 Elgin St, Ottawa, Ont KIP 5K7
(☎ 613-237 1530)
New Zealand – British High Commission
Reserve Bank of New Zealand Building, 2 The Terrace, Wellington (☎ 72 6049).
USA
– British Embassy
3100 Massachusetts Ave, Washington, DC 20008
(☎ 202-462 1340)
– British Consulate General
845 Third Ave, New York, NY 10022
(☎ 212-888 2112)

Embassies in the UK

Some foreign embassies in the UK are:

Australian High Commission
Australia House, Strand, London WC2
(☎ 071-379 4334) (tube: Temple)
Canadian High Commission
Macdonald House, 1 Grosvenor Square, London W1 (☎ 071-629 9492) (tube: Bond St)
French Embassy
6A Cromwell Place, London SW7
(☎ 071-823 9555) (tube: South Kensington)
New Zealand High Commission
New Zealand House, Haymarket, London SW1Y 4TQ (☎ 071-930 8422) (tube: Piccadilly Circus)
Spanish Embassy
20 Draycott Place, London SW3
(☎ 071-581 5921) (tube: Sloane Square)
US Embassy
24 Grosvenor Square, London W1
(☎ 071-409 4111) (tube: Bond St)

DOCUMENTS

No special documents are required. Your normal driving licence or an International Driving Permit (recommended for non-EC nationals and available from motoring clubs and associations) is legal for 12 months from the date you last entered the country; you then apply for a British licence at post offices. See the introductory section of this book for information on international student identity

and discount cards. Before buying a ticket or making a purchase always check whether there is a discount for a card holder; members of the Youth Hostel Association (YHA) or International Youth Hostel Federation (IYHF) are also sometimes eligible.

CUSTOMS

You are allowed to import 200 cigarettes or 250 grams of tobacco, two litres of still wine plus one litre of spirits or another two litres of wine (sparkling or otherwise), 60 cc of perfume, 250 cc of toilet water, and other duty-free goods to the value of £32.

MONEY

Currency

The currency is the pound sterling (£). There are 100 pence (p) in a pound. One and 2p coins are copper; 5p, 10p, 20p and 50p coins are silver; and the bulky £1 coin is gold. The word pence is rarely used in common language; like its written counterpart it is abbreviated, and pronounced *pee*.

Notes (bills) come in £5, £10, £20 and £50 denominations and vary in colour and size. There are currently two versions of the £20 and £10 note in circulation – beware, the new £20 looks similar to the £5. You may also come across notes issued by the Bank of Scotland; they are legal tender on both sides of the border, though shopkeepers in England and Wales may be reluctant to accept them.

Exchange Rates

A$1	=	0.42
C$1	=	0.47
DM1	=	0.40
FF1	=	0.12
NZ$1	=	0.32
US$1	=	0.59

Costs

Britain is extremely expensive and London is horrendous. You can expect prices to increase at nearly 10% a year.

While you are in London you will need to budget £15 to £20 a day for bare survival.

Dormitory accommodation alone will cost from £9 to £16 a night, a one-day travel card is £2.50, and drinks and basic sustenance will cost you at least £4. Any sightseeing, restaurant meals or nightlife will be on top of that. There's not much point visiting if you can't participate in some of the city's life, so if possible add another £15. Costs will obviously be even higher if you choose to stay in a central hotel (their rates start at around £20 per person) and eat restaurant meals (around £10).

Once you start moving around the country, particularly if you have a transport pass of some description, or you're walking or hitching, the costs can drop. Fresh food is roughly the same price as in Australia and the US. However, without long-distance transport, and assuming you stay in hostels and an occasional cheap B&B, you'll still need £15 to £20 per day. A country youth hostel will cost from £5 to £7; add £4 for food, £4 for entry fees and/or local buses, and £2 for miscellaneous items like films, shampoo, books, telephone calls...

If you hire a car or use a transport pass, stay in B&Bs, eat one sit-down meal a day, and don't stint on entry fees you'll need £30 to £40 per day (not including long-distance transport). Most basic English B&Bs will be from £12 to £15 per person, and dinner will be from £7 to £14 (depending on whether you're eating in a pub or a restaurant and how much you drink); then add £2 for snacks and drinks, £2 for miscellaneous items, and £5 for entry fees. If you are travelling by car you will probably average a further £6 per day on petrol and parking; if you travel by some sort of pass you will probably need to average a couple of pounds a day on local transport, or hiring a bike.

Bureaux, Banks & Societies

Avoid using *bureaux de change*; they may offer good exchange rates, but they frequently levy outrageous commissions and fees. Make sure you establish the rate, the percentage commission and any fees before you start. The airport bureaus are actually reasonable value; they don't charge commission on sterling travellers' cheques, and on other currencies it's 1.5% with a £2 minimum charge.

Bank hours vary, but you'll be safe if you visit between 9.30 am and 3.30 pm, Mondays to Fridays. Friday afternoons get very busy. Some banks are open on Saturday, generally from 9.30 am till noon.

It's difficult to open a bank account, although if you're planning to work, it may be essential. Building societies tend to be more welcoming. You'll need a (semi) permanent address, and you'll smooth the way considerably if you have a reference or introductory letter from your bank manager at home, *plus* bank statements for the previous year. Owning credit/charge cards also helps.

Cheques are still widely used in England, but they are validated and guaranteed by something that looks similar to a credit card. Look for a current account that pays interest, gives you a cheque book and guarantee card, and access to automatic teller machines.

Cheques & Cards

Your travellers' cheques should ideally be in pounds. Use American Express, Thomas Cook or Diners Club, because they are widely recognised and don't charge for cashing their own cheques. There are variations but as a rule banks charge 1% for cashing sterling cheques (sometimes with a £3 minimum charge), 2% for other currencies (again, sometimes with a £3 minimum charge). The exception is American Express, which will cash cheques of any currency issued by any organisation free of charge.

Visa, MasterCard, Access, American Express and Diners Club cards are widely used and accepted. MasterCard is operated by the same organisation that issues Access and Eurocards and can be used wherever you see one or other of these signs. You can get cash advances using your Visa card at the Midland Bank and Barclays, or using MasterCard at National Westminster (NatWest), Lloyds and Barclays.

If you plan to stay for an extended period, and have a permanent address, it's usually straightforward to change the billing address for your card.

GREAT BRITAIN

Tipping

Taxi drivers and waiters all expect 10 to 15% tips. Some restaurants automatically include a service charge (tip) of 10 to 15% – the fact that there is a service charge should be clearly shown on the menu and on the bill. If the service was satisfactory you must pay the service charge, or explain the reasons for your dissatisfaction to the manager. You do not add a further tip. Some restaurants have been known to quietly include the service charge in the total cost shown on a credit card voucher, but still leave a blank for a further tip/gratuity – this is a scam; you only have to tip once!

Bargaining

Bargaining is expected if you are buying second-hand gear, but is uncommon elsewhere. You can also try your Delhi delivery in the markets. Always check whether there are discounts for students or YHA/IYHF members.

Value-Added Tax (VAT)

VAT is a 17.5% sales tax that is levied on virtually all goods and services, but not on food and books. Restaurant menu prices must by law include VAT.

In some cases it is possible to claim a refund of VAT paid on goods – a considerable saving. If you have spent less than 365 days out of the two years prior to making the purchase living in Britain, and if you are leaving the EC within three months of making the purchase, you are eligible.

Not all shops participate in this Retail Export Scheme, and different shops will have different minimum purchase conditions (normally around £40). On request, participating shops will give you a special form/invoice; they will need to see your passport. This form must be presented with the goods and receipts to customs when you depart. After customs has certified the form, it should be returned to the shop who will send you a refund less an administration fee. These goods cannot be posted home.

There are a number of companies that offer a centralised refunding service to shops in the scheme. Participating shops carry a sign in their window.

You can avoid bank charges usually encountered when cashing pound cheques by using a credit card for purchases and requesting that your VAT refund is credited to your card account.

CLIMATE & WHEN TO GO

Anyone who spends any extended period of time in Britain will soon sympathise with the locals' conversational obsession with the weather. Although in relative terms the climate is mild (London can go through winter without a snowfall) and the rainfall is not spectacular (912 mm, or 35 inches), it can be utterly depressing. Settled periods of sunny weather are rare.

Even in midsummer you can go for days without seeing the sun, and showers (or worse) should be expected. To enjoy England you have to convince yourself that you *like* the rain – after all, that's what makes it so incredibly green! The average July temperature in London is 17.6°C (64°F), the average January temperature is 4°C (39°F).

July and August are the busiest months, and should be avoided if at all possible. The crowds in London and at popular towns like Oxford, Bath and York have to be seen to be believed. You are just as likely to get good weather in spring and autumn, so May/June and September/October are the best times to visit, although October is getting too late for the Scottish Highlands.

WHAT TO BRING

Since anything you think of can be bought in London (including Vegemite), pack light and pick up extras as you go along. A Goretex rainjacket is highly recommended.

SUGGESTED ITINERARIES

Depending on the length of your stay, you might want to see and do the following things:

Two days
   Visit London.
One week
   Visit London, Oxford, the Cotswolds, Bath and
   Wells.
Two weeks
   Visit London, Salisbury, Avebury, Bath, Wells,
   Oxford, York and Edinburgh.
One month
   Visit London, Cambridge, York, Edinburgh,
   Inverness, Kyle of Lochalsh, Fort William, Oban,
   Glasgow, the Lake District, Shrewsbury, the
   Cotswolds, Wells, Bath, Avebury and Oxford
   before returning to London.
Two months
   As for one month, but stay in one or two places
   for a week, and do a week-long walk.

TOURIST OFFICES

The British Tourist Authority (BTA) has a
remarkable, extensive collection of information, quite a lot of it free and relevant to
shoestringers. Make sure you contact BTA
before you leave home, because some materials and some discounts are only available
outside Britain. Overseas, it represents both
the Scottish and Welsh Tourist Boards.

Tourist Information Centres (TICs) can be
found in even small towns. They can give
invaluable advice on accommodation and
cheap ways of seeing the area, often including excellent guided walking tours.

Addresses of some overseas offices are as
follows:

Australia
   4th Floor, Midland House, 210 Clarence St,
   Sydney, NSW 2000 (☎ 02-299 8627, fax 02-262
   1414)
Canada
   Suite 600, 94 Cumberland St, Toronto, Ont M5R
   3N3 (☎ 416-925 6326, fax 416-961 2175)
New Zealand
   3rd Floor, Dilworth Building, Corner Queen and
   Customs Sts, Auckland 1 (☎ 09-303 1446, fax
   09-776 965)
USA – Chicago
   625 North Michigan Ave, Suite 1510, Chicago,
   IL 60611 (☎ 312-787 0490, fax 312-787 7746)
USA – Los Angeles
   350 South Figueroa St, Suite 450, Los Angeles,
   CA 90071 (☎ 213-628 3525, fax 213-687 6621)
USA – New York
   40 West 57th St, New York, NY 10019 (☎ 212-
   581 4700, fax 212-265 0649)

There are also offices in Brussels, Copenhagen, Dublin, Frankfurt, Paris, Rome,
Stockholm and other cities.

USEFUL ORGANISATIONS

Membership of the YHA/IYHF is a must.
There are over 330 youth hostels in Britain
and you are also eligible for an impressive
list of discounts.

Membership of English Heritage and the
National Trust is worth considering, especially if you are going to be in the country
for an extended period and are interested in
historical buildings. Both are nonprofit
organisations dedicated to the preservation
of the environment.

English Heritage has over 350 important
properties; most cost nonmembers around
£1.50 to enter. Adult membership of English
Heritage is £15. This entitles you to free
entry to all English Heritage properties, half
price entry to Historic Scotland and Cadw
(Wales) properties, and an excellent guidebook and map that together sell for £3.95.
You can join at most major sites, or write to
English Heritage Membership Dept, PO Box
1BB, London W1A 1BB.

The National Trust has over 300 historic
buildings, all or a significant part of 59 villages and over 570,000 acres of land –
making it the largest 'private' landowner in
Britain. Most properties cost nonmembers
around £2.50 to enter. Adult membership is
£23, under age 23 is £9. This entitles you to
free entry to all English, Welsh and Northern
Irish properties, to the 100 properties belonging to the National Trust of Scotland, and an
excellent guidebook and map that together
sell for £3.95.

You can join at most major sites, or write
to The National Trust, PO Box 39, Bromley,
Kent BR1 1NH. There are reciprocal
arrangements with the National Trust
organisations in Australia, New Zealand and
Canada.

If you're only going to be in the country
for a short time but still plan to blitz a number
of the major historic sites, you can get a Great
British Heritage Pass, which gives you
access to National Trust, English Heritage

and some of the fiercely expensive private properties. It ain't cheap, but it can easily pay for itself: 15 days is £27, one month is £41. It's available overseas or at the British Travel Centre in London.

The London Walkabout Club (☎ 071-402 7633), 22 Craven Terrace, W2, Deckers London Club (☎ 071-244 8641), 135 Earl's Court Rd, SW5 9RH, and Drifters (☎ 071-262 1292), 10 Norfolk Place, W2 1QL, all offer backup services like mail holding, apartment and employment finding, information, social events and cheap tours. They're mainly aimed at Australians and New Zealanders, but any nationality is welcome – membership is around £15. They all have branches or agents in Australia, New Zealand and North America. There is no hard sell, but their hope is that you will use them if and when you book tours.

The Travellers' Contact Point (☎ 071-925 0783, fax 071-925 0784), 3rd Floor, 2 Bridge St, London SW1A 2JR (tube: Westminster) can be the answer to a prayer, especially if you're trying to find work before you have a settled address. For an annual membership fee of £20 they will keep and/or forward your mail and faxes, take telephone messages, allow you to leave messages for callers (especially useful), and give general advice on accommodation and work. The office is above Grandma Lee's Restaurant opposite Big Ben.

BUSINESS HOURS & HOLIDAYS

Offices are open from 9 am to 5 pm, Mondays to Fridays. Shops may be open for longer hours, and all shops are open on Saturdays from 9 am to 5 pm. In country towns, particularly in Scotland and Wales, there may be an early closing day for shops – usually Tuesday or Wednesday afternoon. Late night shopping is Thursday.

Most banks, businesses and a number of museums and other places of interest are closed on public holidays: New Year's Day; 2 January (bank holiday in Scotland); Good Friday; Easter Monday (not in Scotland); May Day Bank Holiday (first Monday in May); Spring Bank Holiday (last Monday in May); Summer Bank Holiday (first Monday in August in Scotland, last Monday in August outside Scotland); Christmas Day; and Boxing Day.

POST & TELECOMMUNICATIONS
Post
Post office hours can vary, but most are open from 9 am to 5 pm, Monday to Friday, and 9 am to noon on Saturdays. First-class mail is quicker and more expensive (24p per letter) than 2nd-class mail (18p).

Airmail letters to EC countries are 24p, to non-EC European countries 28p, to the Americas and Australasia 39p (up to 10 grams) and 57p (up to 20 grams).

If you don't have a permanent address, mail can be sent to poste restante in the town or city where you are staying. American Express Travel offices will also hold mail free for card holders. Deckers and the London Walkabout Club (see the section on Useful Organisations earlier in this chapter) hold mail for members. Canadians can have mail sent to Canada House.

An airmail letter to the USA or Canada will generally take less than a week; to Australia or New Zealand, around a week.

Telephones
Mrs Thatcher achieved one of her dreams when she privatised British Telecom and broke its traditional monopoly. In 1992 there was only one new kid on the block – Mercury – but more are anticipated. Mercury is a bit cheaper, and it has access to all Telecom's main lines.

The famous red booth (as in *Dr Who*) has almost completely disappeared, replaced by glass cubicles of two types: one takes money, while the other, increasing in numbers, uses prepaid, plastic debit cards.

All phones come with reasonably clear instructions. The old-fashioned ones are the trickiest: you don't insert your money until you're connected.

If you think you're likely to make some calls (especially international) and don't want to be caught out, make sure you buy a Telecom Phonecard (not accepted by

Mercury). These are widely available from all sorts of retailers, including post offices and newsagents. Phonecards can be bought in units of 20 (£2), 40 (£4), 100 (£10) and 200 (£20); the phone gives a progressive display of how many units are left.

Mercury has a similar card, also widely available, including from post offices, in denominations of £2, £4 and £10.

Telecom services are expensive; a wake-up call is £2.50. Make your directory assistance calls from a public telephone – they're free that way.

Local & National Calls Dial 100 for a Telecom operator. Local calls are charged by time, national calls (including Scotland, Wales and Northern Ireland) are charged by time and distance. Peak rates are from 9 am to 1 pm, Monday to Friday; standard rates are from 8 to 9 am and 1 to 6 pm, Monday to Friday; and the cheap rate is 6 pm to 8 am, Monday to Friday, and all weekend. Standard rates can be around 30% less than peak; cheap rates can be around 50% less.

International Calls Dial 155 for the international operator. Direct dialling is cheaper, but some shoestringers have been known to prefer operator-connected reverse charges (collect) calls!

To get an international line (for international direct dialling) dial 010, then the country code, area code (drop the first zero if there is one), and number. Calls to the USA and Canada are most expensive between 3 and 5 pm, Monday to Friday, about 25% cheaper between 8 pm and 8 am, and on Saturdays and Sundays. The cheapest rates (20% off) to Australia and New Zealand are from 2.30 to 7.30 pm and from midnight to 7 am every day. For more details, ☎ 0800-272 172 (free).

TIME
One hundred years ago the sun never set on the British Empire, so the British could perhaps be forgiven for thinking that London, more specifically Greenwich, was the centre of the world. Greenwich is still the location for the prime meridian, which divides the world into eastern and western hemispheres. And wherever you are in the world, the time on your watch is measured in relation to the time in Greenwich – Greenwich Mean Time (GMT). Strictly speaking, GMT is used only in air and sea navigation, and is otherwise referred to as Universal Coordinated Time, which is abbreviated as UTC.

Daylight-saving time confuses the issue, but to give you an idea, New York is five hours behind GMT, San Francisco is eight hours behind, and Sydney is 10 hours ahead of GMT. Phone the international operator on ☎ 155 to find out the exact difference.

LAUNDRY
You'll find a laundrette on every High St. Average cost for a single load is £1.20 for washing, between 60p and £1 for drying.

WEIGHTS & MEASURES
Britain still clings to non-metric weights and measures. Distances are given in miles, yards, feet and inches. Weights are given in stones, pounds and ounces. Liquid is measured in pints and fluid ounces (especially beer), although, strangely, most petrol bowsers show both gallons and litres. For conversion tables, see the back pages of this book.

BOOKS & MAPS
There are countless guidebooks covering every nook and cranny in the British Isles. When you arrive, one of your first stops should be at a good bookshop so you can dig out the book(s) that will suit you best. Stanfords (see the London Bookshop section) has an enormous collection of maps, guidebooks and travel literature. The YHA Adventure Shop, 14 Southampton Row, Covent Garden, has a wide selection of walking guides and maps. The bookshops at the British Travel Centre and at the London Tourist Board's Victoria Station centre are also pretty good (see the London Tourist Offices section).

GREAT BRITAIN

Guidebooks

To get an advance idea of what you will encounter, as well as a pretty good introduction to history and culture, the *Insight Guides* are recommended. They have separate guides to *England*, *Scotland* and *Wales* at £11.95 each.

For detailed information on history, art and architecture, the *Blue Guide* series is excellent. They have a wealth of scholarly information on all the important sites, including good maps. They too have separate guides to *England* (£19.95), *Scotland* (£14.95) and *Wales* (£12.95).

If you are going to spend more than four or five days in London, it is definitely worth buying *The Time Out London Guide* (£9.99) – an outstanding guide. It manages to be densely packed with detail (sights, shops, clubs, pubs, opening hours, prices etc), and to cover the off-beat corners of London that really make the city.

There are numerous books that list B&Bs, restaurants, hotels, country houses, camping and caravan parks, self-catering cottages... The objectivity of most of these books is questionable as the places they cover actually pay for the privilege of being included. However, if you plan a camping holiday, or to use B&Bs, it is worth getting the appropriate publications. Those published by the tourist authorities are reliable and are widely available in information centres; most are around £5.

Walkers will find they are very well catered for. The long distance trails are all covered by the excellent *Countryside Commission National Trail Guide* series published by Aurum Press. Each book in the extensive series is £8.99. For shorter day walks the *Bartholomew Map & Guide* series is recommended. They are spiral bound books with good maps and descriptions; most walks they describe take around two to three hours.

Literature

Anyone who has studied 'English' literature will find that to some extent the landscapes and people they have read about can still be found. Travelling in the footsteps of the great English, Scottish and Welsh writers, and their characters, can be one of the highlights of visiting Britain. There is a phenomenal wealth of books that capture a moment in time, a landscape, or a group of people . This guide can only give a few suggestions of where to start.

In the beginning was Chaucer with his *Canterbury Tales*. This book may be responsible for more boring lectures than any other, but in its natural environment it becomes very interesting, giving a vivid insight into medieval society, in particular into the lives of pilgrims on their way to Canterbury. Neville Coghill has written a good modern translation.

The next great figure to blight school children's lives was Shakespeare. Nonetheless, many will be tempted to follow in his footsteps – to Stratford-on-Avon where he lived and the site of the Globe Theatre in London where he played.

Skipping right along, the most vivid insight into 17th century life, particularly in London, is courtesy of *Samuel Pepys' Diary*. In particular, he gives the most complete account of the plague and the Great Fire of London.

The popular English novel, as we know it, did not really appear until the 18th century with the upsurge of the literate middle class. If you plan to spend time in the Midlands, read Elizabeth Gaskell's *Mary Barton*, which paints a sympathetic picture of the plight of the workers during the Industrial Revolution. This was also the milieu about which Charles Dickens wrote most powerfully. *Hard Times* is set in fictional Coketown and paints a brutal picture of the capitalists who prospered in it.

Jane Austen wrote about a very different social class – a prosperous, provincial middle class. The intrigues and passions boiling away under the stilted constraints of 'propriety' are beautifully portrayed in *Emma* and *Pride and Prejudice*.

If you visit the Lake District, you will find constant references to William Wordsworth, the romantic poet who lived there for the first half of the 19th century. Modern readers may find him difficult, but at his best he has an exhilarating appreciation for the natural world.

More than most writers, Thomas Hardy depended heavily on a sense of place and on the relationship between place and people. This makes his best work an evocative picture of Wessex, the region of England centred on Dorchester (Dorset) where he lived. *Tess of the D'Urbervilles* is one of his greatest novels.

Moving into the 20th century, D H Lawrence chronicled life in the northern coalmining towns in the brilliant *Sons & Lovers*. Joseph Conrad's *The Secret Agent* explores a murky world of espionage in London.

Written in the 1930s in the middle of the depression, George Orwell's *Down & Out in Paris & London* describes Orwell's destitute existence as a temporary vagrant. Shoestringers in the 1990s may find they can identify with him. About the same time, Graham Greene wrote of the seamy side of Brighton in *Brighton Rock*.

Doris Lessing painted a picture of London in the 1960s in *The Four Gated City*, a part of her Children of Violence series.One of the funniest and most vicious portrayals of Britain in the 1990s is by Martin Amis in *London Fields*, but there are many other interesting perspectives. Hanef Kureishi writes of growing up in England's Pakistani community in *The Buddha of Suburbia* and Caryl Phillips writes of the Caribbean immigrants' experience in *The Final Passage*.

There are also some more straightforward modern travelogues. *The Kingdom by the Sea* by Paul Theroux was written in 1982 so it is now a little out of date, but it's still a funny and perceptive book. *Coasting* by Jonathan Raban was written at the same time and describes a slow circumnavigation of the island in an old boat – it's beautifully written.

Maps

The best introductory map to Britain is published by the British Tourist Authority, and is widely available (95p). If you plan to catch a lot of trains Britrail has a useful passenger map (free).

Drivers will find there is a range of excellent road atlases. There really isn't much to separate them in terms of accuracy or price, but the graphics do differ. Pick the one you find easiest to read. If you plan to go off the beaten track you will need one that shows at least three miles to the inch. The spiral bound *Ordnance Survey Motoring Atlas of Great Britain* (£8.99) is recommended.

The Ordnance Survey also caters to walkers with a wide variety of maps at different scales. Their Landranger maps at 1:50,000 or about 1¼ inches to the mile are ideal.

MEDIA

Britain has one of the liveliest, most diverse publishing industries in the world, reasonable radio, and tedious TV. There are four regular TV channels – BBC1, BBC2, ITV and Channel 4 – plus Murdoch's satellite Sky TV. Radio also has a mix of BBC and commercial stations.

There are few countries in the world where you can wake up to such a range of newspapers. The choice of newspaper is an infallible guide to the politics and personality of the buyer – *The Independent* is middle-of-the-road and high quality. The other 'quality' daily papers are *The Guardian, The Telegraph* and *The Times* while at the other extreme Britain has the world's top-selling (and bottom-quality) dailies in the tabloid *Daily Mirror* and *Sun*. Curiously, media magnate Rupert Murdoch, the 'dirty digger', owns *The Times* and the *Sun*.

HEALTH

Aside from the threat posed by Scotch whisky, there are no major health hazards. International Certificates of Vaccination are not required. Reciprocal arrangements with the UK allow Australians, New Zealanders and a number of other nationalities to receive free emergency medical treatment and subsidised dental care through the excellent National Health Service – you can use hos-

GREAT BRITAIN

pital emergency departments, GPs and dentists (check any yellow page phone book). All other holiday-makers have to pay. Make sure you're insured.

Chemists can give advice for minor ailments. Phone ☎ 100 (free call) for a telephone operator who can give you the address of a local doctor or hospital. In an emergency phone ☎ 999 (free call) for an ambulance.

WOMEN TRAVELLERS

Britain is a reasonably enlightened country. Single women should have no problems, although common-sense caution should be observed in big cities. *Spare Rib* is a monthly feminist magazine that lists women's centres and groups, and includes classified ads for accommodation and jobs. The London Rape Crisis Centre (☎ 071-837 1600) is run by women and gives confidential advice and support to women who have been sexually assaulted.

DANGERS & ANNOYANCES

Britain is remarkably safe considering its size and the disparities in wealth. However, city crime is certainly not unknown, so caution, especially at night, is necessary. Pickpockets and bag snatchers operate on London's tube and on crowded streets. At night, lone women should choose a carriage with other people and avoid some of the deserted tube stations in the suburbs; a bus can be a better choice.

Hotel/hostel touts descend on backpackers at underground stations like Earl's Court, Liverpool St and Victoria. Treat their claims with scepticism and don't accept an offer of a free lift (you could end up miles away). By all means take one of their brochures; it might come in handy if the places recommended in this book are full.

In front of some landmarks you may be approached by a friendly local who will offer to take your photograph. Unfortunately, they are only friendly because they con so many tourists into paying a fortune for the privilege.

The big cities, particularly London, have many beggars; if you give, don't wave a full wallet around, carry some change in a separate pocket.

Britain is not without racial problems, particularly in some of the deprived inner suburbs of some of the big cities, but in general tolerance prevails. Visitors are unlikely to have problems associated with their skin colour, although non-Europeans may well feel conspicuous in country villages.

Plumbing is often woefully inadequate. In particular, the British do not understand that a good shower (at least once daily) is one of life's most basic essentials. Particularly in B&Bs or private houses you will be faced either with a bath, or if you are lucky, a dangerous and complicated contraption that will produce a thin trickle of scalding hot or freezing cold water.

Much has been written about the phenomena of the British queue. It can be a neurotically polite and efficient phenomenon, but these days it has a tendency to degenerate into anarchy. The reason for its continued existence is a little puzzling – after all, the war has been over for some time now. Gross inefficiency and greed on the part of those delivering services is part of the answer. Most banks, for instance, are clearly not prepared to jeopardise their profits by either fully computerising their branches or by employing sufficient staff. The other part of the answer is that the long-suffering customers are resigned, unquestioningly, to their fate.

WORK

See the Visas section earlier in this chapter for details on how to go about it legally. The economic downturn has made it difficult to find jobs. However, if you are prepared to do anything and to work long hours for lousy pay, you'll almost certainly find something. It is extremely difficult to save significant amounts. Although you should be able to break even, you are almost certainly better off saving in your country of origin.

Traditionally, visitors have worked in bars and restaurants and as nannies. Both jobs often provide live-in accommodation, but the hours are long, the work is exhausting and the pay is lousy. If you live in, you'll be lucky to get £110 per week; if you have to find your own accommodation, you'll be lucky to get £150.

In better economic times accountants, nurses, medical personnel, computer programmers, lawyers, teachers and clerical workers (with computer experience) quickly found well-paid work. Life has become considerably more difficult; you'll need to have some money to tide you over while you search. Don't forget copies of your qualifications, references and a CV. Teachers should contact London borough councils (they administer separate education departments).

TNT Magazine and *Southern Cross* (see the London Information section) are good starting points for jobs and agencies aimed at travellers. For au pair and nanny work buy the quaintly titled *The Lady*. Also check the *Evening Standard*, national newspapers and the government-operated Jobcentres. Jobcentres are scattered around London; they're listed under the Manpower Services Commission in the telephone book, and have a branch at 195 Wardour St, W1. Whatever your skills, it is worth registering with a number of temporary agencies.

ACTIVITIES
Hiking

Shoestringers are inevitably going to do plenty of walking, but this is also the best way of seeing Britain. In Britain, with the exception of Scotland, you are rarely going to be far away from civilisation, so it is easy to put together walks that connect with public transport and take you from hostel to hostel, village to village. A tent and cooking equipment will not be necessary. Some warm and waterproof clothing and sturdy footwear is all you will need.

The countryside is crisscrossed by a network of countless footpaths, many of them crossing private land. Rights of way which have existed for centuries run through farmyards and fields, and are marked on the

excellent Ordnance Survey maps. Any small town will have day walks around it; look for local guidebooks in newsagents or bookshops. It's possible to spend a pleasant week staying in one place and doing a series of circular walks in the surrounding countryside.

For long-distance walks, the best areas include the Cotswolds, the Exmoor National Park, the North York Moors National Park, the Yorkshire Dales National Park, the Lakes District, the Pembrokeshire Coast National Park, and the Scottish islands. There are many superb long-distance walks in Scotland but, in general, apart from day walks, these require a greater degree of preparation.

The national parks were set up to protect the finest landscapes, but the land remains largely privately owned. It is almost always necessary to get permission from a landowner before pitching a tent.

Over the last 30 years, a number of national long-distance trails have been developed (a number of them traverse the national parks) and these offer walkers access to the best countryside. They have been created by linking existing public footpaths and often follow routes that have carried travellers for thousands of years.

There are currently 14 national long-distance trails in England and Wales, and three in Scotland created and administered by the relevant Countryside Commissions (who, along with Aurum Press, publish excellent guides). A number of these are mentioned in this chapter. There are also a growing number of regional routes created by county councils, some of which are excellent, well documented and well organised (some aren't). Then there are unofficial long-distance routes, often devised by individuals or groups like the Ramblers' Association. Finally, there are thousands of shorter day walks. TICs will have information about all the possibilities in their locality.

Walkers can choose between walking the entire length of a long-distance trail (or *way*, as they are often called), which might be anything from 40 km (30 miles) to 900 km (560 miles) long, or walking any section they choose. Some of the English long-distance walks, particularly along the coast, and in the Yorkshire Dales and Lakes District, can be very crowded on weekends and in July/August, so if possible choose another time.

The British countryside looks deceptively gentle. Especially in the hills or on the open moors, however, the weather can close in and turn nasty very quickly at any time of the year. It is vital if you're walking in upland areas to carry good maps and a compass and know how to use them – plus of course warm and waterproof clothing.

Ordnance Survey publishes a wide variety of maps, but for walkers their Landranger maps at 1:50,000 or about 1¼ inches to the mile are recommended, unless you're focusing on one small area, in which case the 1:25,000 maps will give you a huge amount of detail. Guidebooks cover every possible walk. Stanford's Bookshop in London stocks an impressive range of books and maps.

For a general introduction look for *Walking in Britain* by John Hillaby. The *Long Distance Trails Almanac* by Colin Elliott (£6.99) gives a brief introduction to 63 of the best known walks. Those intent on a serious walking holiday should contact the Ramblers' Association (☎ 071-582 6878), 1 Wandsworth Rd, London SW8 2XX; their *Yearbook* (£2.99) is widely available and itemises the information available for each walk, the appropriate maps, and nearby accommodation (hostels, B&Bs and bunkhouses).

Skiing

Britain has a growing ski industry based in Scotland. Although convenient, the slopes do not match the Alps, and they are not cheap.

Boating

Even shoestringers should consider the possibility of hiring a canal boat and cruising some of the extraordinary 2000-mile network of canals that has survived the railway era.

Especially if you go outside the high season, prices are quite reasonable. For example, Alvechurch Boat Centres (☎ 021-445 2909) has 33-foot narrow boats that sleep four for between £300 per week in April and £600 in August. All you need after that is food. Other operators you could contact include Blake's Holidays (☎ 0553-460606) or Hoseason's Holidays (☎ 0502-501501) – both have prices starting at £60 per person per week.

The Inland Waterways Association (☎ 071-586 2556), 114 Regent's Park Rd, London NW1 8UQ, can provide mail-order maps and guides, including *The Inland Waterways Guide* (£2.50), a general guide to holiday hire with route descriptions. The *Shell Guide to Inland Waterways* by McKnight (£17.90), a general reference book, is available from bookshops.

Cycling

The scenery changes swiftly, you're never far away from food and accommodation, and there is a great network of backroads and lanes that are comparatively traffic-free. It's cheap and you see more from a bike than any other form of transport.

Most airlines allow you to carry a bicycle as part of your baggage allowance, but if this isn't possible, there are numerous places where you can hire. Prices vary, but you should be able to get a three-speed bike for around £15 per week, a mountain bike for £50. Book ahead if you want a bike in July or August. Hiring is easiest if you have a credit card: a signed slip is used in lieu of a large deposit (ranging from £20 to £100); you will also need ID (a passport will do). Most touring bikes are set up to take panniers, but few shops actually hire them; you'll either have to buy them or bring them with you.

Bicycles are carried free on most Britrail regional services – it is advisable to check in advance, however. In Scotland and on Intercity trains (with the exception of the Gatwick Express) it is necessary to make a reservation, which costs £3. You can make a reservation up to a few minutes before the train leaves, but there's limited space so you could miss out. The major coach operators (National Express, Citylink etc) don't carry bikes, but most local bus lines do.

The Cyclists' Touring Club (☎ 04868-727) Cotterell House, 69 Meadrow, Godalming, Surrey GU7 3HS, is a national cycling association that can provide a great deal of helpful information for visiting cyclists, including a choice of cycle routes. Call or write for a list of its publications. The *CTS Route Guide to Cycling Britain & Ireland* by Christa Gausden & Nick Crane is widely available.

HIGHLIGHTS

Islands
　Orkney, Skye, Lewis and Harris (Scotland)

Coastline
　Beachy Head (East Sussex), Land's End to St Ives (Cornwall), Tintagel (Cornwall), Ilfracombe to Lynton/Lynmouth (Devon), St David's to Cardigan (Dyfed, Wales), around Whitby (North Yorkshire). The entire coastline of Scotland, but particularly the west coast

Museums & Galleries
　British Museum, Victoria & Albert Museum, National Gallery, Tate Gallery (London), Castle Museum (York), HMS Victory (Portsmouth), Ironbridge Gorge (near Shrewsbury)

Historic Towns
　Wells, Salisbury, Winchester, Durham, Oxford, Cambridge, York, Edinburgh, St David's, Whitby, St Andrews

Houses
　Hampton Court Palace (London), Castle Howard (North Yorkshire), Knole House (Kent), Blenheim Palace (Oxfordshire)

Castles
　Dover, Hever, Windsor, Bamburgh, Edinburgh, Conwy, Leeds (near Canterbury), Tower of London

Regions
　Exmoor National Park, Cotswolds, Brecon Beacons National Park, Pembrokeshire National Park, North York Moors National Park, Lake District National Park, Hadrian's Wall, Scottish Highlands and especially the west coast

Other Highlights
　Avebury prehistoric complex

ACCOMMODATION

This will almost certainly be your single largest expense. Even camping – the cheapest option – can be expensive at official sites. For shoestringers, there are really only two options: bed & breakfasts (B&Bs) and some hotels, and youth hostels. With the exception of London, there are few independent backpackers' hostels, although the number is growing, particularly in some of the popular hiking regions.

Hostels

Membership of a Youth Hostels Association (YHA) gives you access to a huge network of hostels throughout England, Wales, Scotland and Ireland.

There are separate, local associations for England/Wales, Scotland, Northern Ireland and Ireland, and each publishes individual accommodation guides. If you are travelling extensively it is *absolutely essential* to get hold of these. Most importantly, they include the (often complicated) days and hours the hostels are open, as well as information on price, facilities and how to reach each place.

Accommodation guides and membership information is available at the YHA Adventure Shop at 14 Southampton St, London WC2 (tube: Covent Garden). The *Accommodation Guide – England & Wales* is £4.99, and the *SYHA Handbook* (for Scotland) is 90p.

All hostels have facilities for self-catering, some have cheap meals (of widely varying quality). Advance booking is advisable, especially on weekends, bank holidays and at any time over the summer months. Booking policies vary: some accept advance payments with Visa or Access (MasterCard) cards; some will accept same-day bookings, although they will usually only hold a bed until 6 pm; some work on a first come, first served basis.

The advantages of hostels are position (they are often well placed for walks), price (although the difference between a cheap B&B and an expensive hostel is not huge), and the chance to meet other travellers. The disadvantages are that some are still run dictatorially (although they are improving), you are usually locked out between 10 am and 5 pm, the front door is locked at 11 pm, you usually sleep in bunks in a single-sex dormitory, and many are closed during winter.

GREAT BRITAIN

Overnight prices are in three tiers: *Young*, from five to 15 years, with prices from £2.80 to £8, but mostly around £4; *Junior*, from 16 to 20 years, with prices from £3.80 to £9.60, but mostly around £5; and *Senior*, from 21 years on, with prices from £4.70 to £16.50, but mostly around £6 or £7. When hostel prices are 'average' they are not shown in this chapter. Bear in mind that when you add £2.30 for breakfast, you can get very close to cheap B&B prices.

Bed & Breakfast (B&B)

B&Bs are a great British institution and the cheapest private accommodation you can find. At the bottom end (£12 to £16 per person) you will get a bedroom in a normal house, a shared bathroom and an enormous cooked breakfast (juice, cereal, bacon, eggs, sausage, baked beans and toast!). Small B&Bs may only have one room to let, and you can really feel like a guest of the family – they may not even have a sign.

More upmarket B&Bs have ensuite bathrooms and TVs in each room. Good showers are rare, however. Double rooms will often have two single beds (twin beds) rather than a double bed so you don't have to be lovers to share a room. On this point, many B&Bs are run by very conservative women (which may explain the twin beds) so it pays to be a little careful what you say and how you act.

Guesthouses, which are often just large converted houses with half a dozen rooms, are an extension of the idea. They range from £12 to £50 a night, depending on the quality of the food and accommodation. In general, they tend to be less personal than B&Bs, and more like small budget hotels (which is what they are really). Local pubs and inns also often have cheap rooms, and place you at the hub of the community.

All these options are promoted and organised by local TICs, which can provide you with a list of nearby possibilities (free), make a local booking for you and, usually, make a booking anywhere in Britain. These services are particularly handy for big cities and over weekends and the summer high season.

Local bookings for accommodation within the next two nights are nearly always free, although some still charge (£5 in the case of London). You do pay a 10% deposit which is subtracted from the nightly price. Don't be embarrassed to ask for the cheapest available option; if you don't, the nice middle-class people that run the TICs will tend to steer you towards nice middle-of-the-road options. Most TICs also participate in the book-a-bed-ahead (BABA) scheme which allows you to book accommodation for the next two nights anywhere in Britain. Most charge a fee, around £2.50, and take a 10% deposit.

The national tourist boards operate a classification and grading system; participating hotels, guesthouses and B&Bs have a plaque at the front door. If you do want to be reasonably confident that your accommodation reaches basic standards of safety and cleanliness, the first classification is 'Listed', denoting clean and comfortable acommodation. The next rungs are shown by one to five crowns – the more crowns the more facilities and, generally, the more expensive. One crown means each room will have a washbasin and there is a public phone. Two crowns means washbasins, public phone, bedside lights and a TV in a lounge or in bedrooms. Three crowns means at least one-third of the rooms have en suite bathrooms and that hot evening meals are available. And so on.

In addition to the classifications there are gradings, and in many ways these are actually more significant. They are 'approved', 'commended' and 'highly commended' and reflect a subjective judgment of quality.

All this sounds as if it will be useful, but in practice there is a wide range within each classification and some of the best B&Bs don't participate at all. A high quality 'listed' B&B can be 20 times nicer than a low quality 'three crown' B&B, and it may or may not be graded. In practice, actually seeing the place, even just from the outside, will give you a better idea of what to expect. Don't be afraid to ask to have a look at your room before you sign up.

Camping

Free camping is rarely possible, except in Scotland. Camping grounds vary widely in quality, most have reasonable facilities, but they're usually ugly, and inaccessible unless you have a car or bike. For an extensive listing, buy *Camping & Caravanning in Britain* published by the Automobile Association (£6.99); local TICs also have lists.

The tourist boards rate caravan and camping grounds with one to five ticks; the more ticks the higher the standard. Don't forget the likely weather.

Self-Catering

There has been a huge upsurge in the number of houses and cottages available for short-term rent. These can easily be within the budget of shoestringers, especially for couples or groups. Staying in one place – preferably an attractive village – gives you an unmatched opportunity to get a real feel for a region and a community. Cottages for four can be as little as £100 per week; they even let for three days.

It is often possible to book through TICs, but there are also a number of excellent agencies who can supply you with glossy brochures to help the decision-making process. Outside weekends and July/August, it is not essential to book a long way ahead. Most have agents in North America and Australasia. Among them, Country Holidays (☎ 0282-445544), Spring Mill, Earby, Colne, Lancashire BB8 6RN, has been highly recommended; English Country Cottages (☎ 0533-460101), Fakenham, Norfolk NR21 9NB, is one of the largest agencies.

The tourist boards rate self-catering accommodation with one to five keys; the more keys, the more facilities. One key indicates a property is clean and comfortable, has adequate heating, lighting and seating, a TV, cooker, fridge and crockery and cutlery.

FOOD

Ordinary British food is poor; the result is an extraordinarily high rate of heart disease and the huge number of overweight, pasty-faced individuals you see waddling around. The native cuisine's most consistent success is with the potato. Baked and mashed potatoes are consistently good, but there's only a 50% success rate with chips/fries.

There are signs of hope. The supply of fresh fruit and vegetables has improved immeasurably. Vegetarianism has taken off in a big way, and in the main towns and cities a cosmopolitan range of cuisines is available. Quality restaurants compete favourably with those in Europe, but their prices are way out of line. If you can afford £25 per head you'll eat well; with rare exceptions however, for under £10 you'll eat shit. Although espresso machines are still rare, it is occasionally possible to buy a decent coffee.

The cheapest and best way to eat in Britain is to cook for yourself. Hopefully, however, you won't be forced to the extremes of an Australian shoestringer who was arrested and jailed for attempting to cook a Canada goose in Hyde Park.

Youth hostels often have cheap meals (for around £3) or cooking facilities. Even if you don't have great culinary skills it is possible to buy very good quality pre-cooked meals from the supermarkets (around £2).

England has a full complement of takeaway chains, including the home-grown and aptly named Wimpy's. You may not be able to avoid them, because they are relatively cheap. The best of the worst is Burger King, which even has a vegetarian beanburger.

On every High St, especially in the bigger towns, you will find a café. These may look pretty seedy, but they're warm and friendly places. They invariably serve cheap breakfasts (eggs, bacon and baked beans) and English tea (the fact that you want milk is assumed; be quick to make sure they don't load in sugar). They also have plain but filling lunches, usually a roast and three veg, or bangers (sausages) and mash (mashed potato).

A step up from there are the pub meals. It's difficult to generalise about these; some are good value. At the cheap end they don't vary significantly from cafés, at the expensive end they're closer to restaurants. A strange brew

GREAT BRITAIN

called *chile con carne* is often the cheapest offering on the menu. There are several excellent reasons for this.

Vegetarians should buy a copy of *The Vegetarian Travel Guide* (£4.25), published annually by the UK Vegetarian Society and covering hundreds of places to eat and stay. Most restaurants have at least a token vegetarian dish, although vegans will find the going tough. Indian restaurants will be your salvation.

DRINKS

English pubs generally serve an impressive range of beers – lagers, bitters, ales and stouts. The drink most people from the New World know as beer is actually lager. Much to the distress of local connoisseurs, lagers (including Fosters and Budweiser) now take a huge proportion of the market. Fortunately, the traditional English bitter has made something of a comeback, thanks to the Campaign for Real Ale (CAMRA) organisation. Look for their endorsement sticker on pub windows.

If you've been raised on lager, a traditional bitter or ale is something of a shock – it's served at room temperature, it's not very gassy, and it can be expensive. Ale is similar to bitter – it's more a regional difference in name than anything else. The best ales and bitters are actually hand-pumped from the cask, because they are not carbonated and under pressure (draught). Stout is a dark, rich, foamy drink; Guinness is the most famous brand.

Don't think of any of these drinks as beers, but as something completely new; you'll discover subtle flavours that a cold and chemical lager cannot match. Beware – potency can vary from around 2% to 8%. The stronger brews are usually 'specials' or 'extras'.

Beers are usually served in pints (around £1.60), but you can also ask for a half pint (around 90p); ask the barkeeper for a pint of your beer of choice, or a half. Pubs are allowed to open for any 12 hours a day they choose from Monday to Saturday. Most maintain the traditional 11 am to 11 pm hours; the bell for last drinks rings out at about 10.45 pm. On Sundays they open from noon to 2 or 3 pm and from 7 to 10.30 or 11 pm.

Continental wines are now more widely available, and are very reasonably priced (except in pubs). Check out the supermarkets; an ordinary, but drinkable, *vin de pays* will cost less than £3.

Take-away alcoholic drinks are sold from *off-licence* shops, not from pubs. Every neighbourhood has one. The best off-licence chain is Oddbins, which has branches throughout the country. Opening hours for off-licences vary, but although some stay open to 8 or 9 pm, Monday to Saturday, many have ordinary shop hours. They all close between 3 and 7 pm on Sundays.

Unfortunately, most restaurants are licensed and their alcoholic drinks, particularly good wines, are always expensive. There are very few BYO restaurants (where you can Bring Your Own bottles for free), although there are a small number in London. Most places charge an extortionate amount of money for 'corkage' – opening your own bottle for you.

Getting There & Away

London is one of the most important transport hubs in Europe and the world. There are an enormous number of travel agents, some of dubious reliability. All the main student travel services have offices in London; they understand shoestringers, are generally competitive, and definitely reliable. You don't have to be a student to use their services. See the London section for details.

As always, buses are the cheapest and most exhausting method of transport, although Interail and BIJ tickets (*Billet International de Jeunesse* – international youth tickets) are competitive and budget flights (especially stand-by and last-minute offers) can be very good value. Shop around. A small saving on the fare may not adequately compensate you for an agonising two days on a bus that leaves you completely exhausted for another two days. When making an assessment don't forget the hidden expenses; getting to and from airports, airport departure taxes, and food and drink consumed en route.

See the Getting There & Away chapter at the beginning of this book for information on long haul flights from Australia, Canada, New Zealand and the USA; the Getting Around chapter for details on Eurail, Interail and other European travel passes; and the Ireland chapter for details of transport to/from Ireland.

Until the opening of the Channel Tunnel, most people going to/from Europe buy combined rail/ferry or coach/ferry tickets between London and European capitals like Paris, Brussels and Amsterdam. At the time of going to press it was unclear how competitive the new rail and bus options via the tunnel will be. The ferry companies were optimistic that they would be able to compete, particularly on the basis of price, if not on time. The increased competition should mean that prices drop.

See the Land section (following) for info on combined tickets and the tunnel. Of course, it is also possible to get to and from the ferry ports under your own steam and just pay for the ferry itself.

AIR

There are international air links with London, Manchester, Newcastle, Edinburgh and Glasgow, but shoestringers will find cheap flights all wind up in one of the four London airports: Heathrow is the largest, followed by Gatwick, Stansted and Luton.

London is an excellent centre for cheap tickets and is a hub for transport to virtually anywhere in the world. For cheap tickets, check *The Sunday Times*, *The Sunday Observer* and *The Sunday Independent*. The best resource, however, is *TNT Magazine*. If you are prepared to shop around and don't mind flying at short notice, you can pick up some interesting bargains.

Excellent discount charter flights are often available to full-time students aged under 30

and all young travellers aged under 26 (you need an ISIC card or an official youth card) and are available through the large student travel agencies. See the London information section.

Typical low season one-way/return flights from London start at: Amsterdam £40/80, Athens £60/90, Frankfurt £60/75, Istanbul £110/140, Madrid £65/100, Paris £50/70, Rome £70/140. Official scheduled flights with carriers like British Airways will cost up to *four* times as much.

LAND

Soon. Just as soon as that tunnel opens... In the meantime, you can still get to Europe by bus or train, it's just that there's a short ferry/hovercraft ride thrown in as part of the deal. The ferries/hovercraft all carry cars and motorbikes.

Channel Tunnel

Two services will operate through the tunnel, when it is finally in full operation. Eurotunnel will operate a rail shuttle service for motorbikes, cars and freight vehicles, using specially designed railway carriages, between terminals at Folkestone in the UK and Calais in France; and the national railway companies of Britain, France and Belgium will operate high-speed passenger trains between London, Paris and Brussels.

At the time of going to press there was no indication of what the ticket prices would be, although they will obviously have to be competitive with existing services. The opening date was being pushed into the distance. At the time this book went to print, Eurotunnel said:

If the contractors meet programmes for installation and commissioning currently under discussion with them, the Tunnel should be able to open at the end of summer 1993 with the launch of Eurotunnel's shuttle services. Through trains operated by the national railways can thereupon be put into service as and when available, so that commercial services are well-established by mid-1994 at which time the phased development of services through the tunnel can be completed.

A number of things are clear: one, they don't know when it will open; two, the shuttle will start service before the trains; and three, it is amazing they have managed to excavate anything more extensive than a sand castle.

Eurotunnel Shuttle Specially designed shuttle trains will run 24 hours a day; they will depart every 15 minutes in each direction at peak times and at least every hour at the quietest periods of the night.

Eurotunnel terminals will be clearly signposted and connected to motorway networks. Both countries' Customs and Immigration formalities will be carried out before you drive on to the shuttle. Inside the shuttle you can stay with your car, listen to the radio, use the toilet facilities or stretch your legs.

Eurotunnel claims the total time from motorway to motorway, including loading and unloading, will be one hour; the shuttle itself will take 35 minutes. This sounds impressive, but the total time if you travel by hovercraft is already under two hours, and ferries only take 2½ hours.

Price will obviously be an important factor. You will be able to buy prepaid tickets or simply pay by cash or credit card at a toll booth. The shuttle will operate on a first come first served basis; reservations for particular services will not be possible.

International Train Services Between 6.30 am and 9 pm there will be at least one train per hour in each direction between London and Paris and London and Brussels. There will be easy onward connections from London to Scotland and Wales and from Brussels to Germany and the Netherlands.

In England, the trains will arrive and depart from the new international terminal at Waterloo Station. Some trains will stop at the planned Ashford International Station in Kent, and at Frethun (near Calais) or Lille. Immigration formalities will be completed on the train, but British Customs will be at Waterloo.

The London to Paris journey will take three hours (dropping to an amazing 2½

hours when the British get it together to build a high-speed track through Kent). From London to Brussels will take three hours and 10 minutes (eventually dropping to two hours and 10 minutes).

Tickets will be widely available from travel agents and major train stations and will include a seat reservation on a particular service.

Bus
Eurolines (☎ 071-730 0202), a division of National Express (the largest UK bus line), has an enormous network of European destinations, including Ireland and Eastern Europe.

You can book through any National Express office, including Victoria Coach Station, which is where they depart and arrive, and at many travel agents. They also have agents all round Europe, including: France (Paris, ☎ 1-40.38.93.93), Netherlands (Amsterdam, ☎ 020-6275 151), Germany (Frankfurt, ☎ 069-79 03 240), Spain (Madrid, ☎ 91-528 11 05), Italy (Rome, ☎ 06-88 40 840), Hungary (Budapest, ☎ 047-26 28 00), Turkey (Istanbul, ☎ 01-25 17 000).

Youth fares are available for passengers up to 25 years old, with the exception of port services where the youth fare is only available for passengers up to 23 years old on presentation of a National Express Coach Card (see the following Getting Around section). In fact, the discount is quite disappointing in most cases.

The following single/return prices and journey times are representative: Amsterdam £30/51 (14 hours), Athens £121/206 (56 hours), Frankfurt £49/83 (18½ hours), Istanbul £104/187 (52 hours), Madrid £76/137 (27 hours), Paris £31/52 (10 hours), Rome £85/136 (36 hours).

Eurolines also have some good-value circuit tickets that are valid up to two months and allow travel between a number of major cities. Their Bus Circuit No 1 allows you to visit Amsterdam, Barcelona, Rome and Paris and return to London for £176.

Rail

Goodness only knows what will happen to the rail/ferry, rail/hovercraft services offered by British Rail when their new tunnel service eventually starts. It's quite likely the most popular services will continue relatively unchanged; with luck they'll be a bit cheaper.

Until the new international station opens at Waterloo, British Rail International's European trains will leave from London's Victoria or Liverpool St; call ☎ 071-834 2345 for enquiries.

For those bound for France, Britrail has a number of different options depending on whether you cross the Channel on a hovercraft or ferry, or from Dover/Folkestone or Newhaven. The cheapest option to Paris is 2nd class via Newhaven and the Sealink ferry; a two-month return from London to Paris is £77; a single is £48.50; and the journey takes nine hours. If you travel via Dover and Hoverspeed the fares jump to £87/54.50, but the journey time drops to six hours.

Direct trains to Rome and Madrid travel via Dover and Sealink. A 2nd class two month return/single to Madrid is £175/109 (34 hours), to Rome is £171/124 (23 hours).

For Holland, Belgium, and Germany you cross the Channel from Harwich. A two-month return/single to Amsterdam is £78.50/44 (13 hours), to Berlin £138/82 (19½ hours).

Eurotrain (☎ 071-730 3402), 52 Grosvenor Gardens, London SW1W 0AG (see the London Student Travel offices), and at Victoria Station, and Wasteels/Route 26 (☎ 071-834 7066), 121 Wilton Rd, London SW1, sell discount BIJ tickets. These offer discounts of up to 40% on single journeys, but for an extensive trip around Europe, the Eurail or Interail tickets are still better value. Eurotrain and Wasteels also Interail tickets.

BIJ tickets are available to anyone under 26, students with ISIC cards and teachers. They allow you to start at any nominated Britrail station (which may be a good saving over normal domestic possibilities), and to break your journey wherever you choose. There are also explorer tickets that string together a number of destinations. BIJ returns/singles to Amsterdam are £48/24, to Athens £246/138, to Brussels £44/29, to Madrid £163/87, Munich £136/70, Paris £68/38, Rome £165/89.

Road

See the Channel Tunnel section for available information on the tunnel shuttle, and the following Sea section for details on ferry charges for cars.

SEA

There are a bewildering array of alternatives between Britain and mainland Europe; it is impossible to list all the services because of space limitations. See the Ireland chapter for details on links between Britain and Ireland. Prices can vary widely depending on the time of year that you travel, and return tickets are often much less than two single fares. There are very cheap day return tickets available (like £8 Dover-Calais), but they are strictly policed; a backpack would definitely give the game away.

To/From France

On a clear day, one can actually see across the Channel. A true shoestringer would obviously swim, but for those who are prepared to compromise their shoestring principles:

To/From Dover & Folkestone The shortest and usually the cheapest ferry link to Europe is from Dover and Folkestone to Calais and Boulogne.

Dover is the most convenient port for those who plan onward travel (in England) by bus or train. P&O (☎ 081-575 8555), Sealink (☎ 0233-647047) and Hoverspeed (☎ 081-554 7061) all operate between Dover and Calais every one to two hours. It is worth checking prices for all three.

Sealink charges adult/student passengers £23/19; cars and drivers from £71 to £108 depending on the date and time, plus £13 for additional passengers; motorcycles and riders from £35 to £43. P&O and Hoverspeed prices are very similar to Sealink's; the hovercraft operated by

Hoverspeed, however, only take 35 minutes to cross the Channel rather than the 90 minutes taken by ferries.

To/From Portsmouth P&O (☎ 0705-827677) operate two or three ferries a day to/from Cherbourg and Le Havre. The day ferries take five to six hours and the night ferries take eight hours. A single is £28; and a car costs from £36 to £78. Brittany Ferries (☎ 0705-827701) has at least one sailing a day to/from Caen and St Malo. Portsmouth-Caen takes six hours; a single is £26 to £33; and a car costs from £53 to £89. Brittany also has a ferry from Plymouth to Roscoff.

To/From Spain
To/From Plymouth Brittany Ferries (☎ 0752-221321) operates at least one ferry a week to Santander on the north coast of Spain. The journey time is 24 hours; a single is from £68 to £98; and a vehicle costs from £70 to £106.

To/From Scandinavia
Until one looks at the ferry possibilities, it's easy to forget how close Scandinavia and Britain are to each other, and why the Vikings found English villages convenient takeaways.

To/From Aberdeen & Shetlands One of the most interesting possibilities is the summer-only link between the Shetlands, Norway, the Faroes, Iceland, and Denmark. The agent is P&O (☎ 0224-571615), but the operator is the Smyril Line.

First you have to get to the Shetlands from the Orkneys, or from Aberdeen, Scotland. P&O (☎ 0224-572615) has daily sailings from Aberdeen to Lerwick (Shetlands) from Monday to Friday. A reclining seat will cost £39.50/44.50 depending on the season.

The Smyril boat operates from 3 June to 28 August. The sailing order is Denmark (Saturday), to the Faroes (Monday), to the Shetlands (Monday), to Norway (Tuesday), to the Shetlands (Wednesday), to the Faroes (Wednesday), to Iceland (Thursday), to the Faroes (Friday), to Denmark (Saturday) and

so on. Depending on the season, one-way couchette fares from Shetland to Norway are £38/50, to the Faroes £45/60, to Denmark £92/122, to Iceland £97/130.

To/From Newcastle The Norwegian Color Line (☎ 091-296 1313) operates ferries all year to Stavanger and Bergen in Norway. They depart on Saturdays and Tuesdays from January to May and September to December, and on Saturdays, Mondays and Wednesdays from mid-May to mid-September. They're overnight trips, and high-season fares for a four-berth cabin are £102; there's a 25% student discount, but not between mid-June and mid-August; a car costs £40.

During summer, Scandinavian Seaways (☎ 091-296 0101) operates ferries to Esbjerg, Denmark and Gothenburg, Sweden.

Esbjerg ferries depart on Fridays and Sundays from mid-June to mid-August; it's an overnight journey taking around 20 hours. A single in a four-berth cabin is £115, a bit less for a couchette, and 50% less for students; a car costs £45.

Gothenburg ferries depart on Sundays from mid-June to mid-August; it's an overnight journey taking around 24 hours. A single in a four-berth cabin is £143, a bit less for a couchette and 50% less for students; a car costs £55.

To/From Harwich Harwich is the major port linking southern England and Scandinavia. Scandinavian Seaways (☎ 0255-240240) has ferries to Esbjerg (Denmark) and Gothenburg (Sweden). In summer ferries leave every two days; the trip to Esbjerg takes 21 hours, to Gothenburg 24 hours. To Esbjerg, a single in a four-berth couchette is from £60 to £105; a car costs from £35 to £55. To Gothenburg, a single in a four-berth couchette is from £88 to £143; a car costs from £35 to £55. There's a 50% reduction for students.

To/From Belgium, Netherlands & Germany
There is only one link direct with Germany;

many people prefer to drive to/from the Dutch ferry ports.

To/From Harwich & Felixstowe Scandinavian Seaways (☎ 0255-240240) has ferries to Hamburg, Germany, every two days; the trip takes 21½ hours. A single in a four-berth couchette is from £52 to £85; a car costs from £35 to £55. There's a 50% reduction for students.

Sealink-Stena Line (☎ 0255-243333) has two ferries a day to the Hook of Holland, Netherlands; the day ferry takes 7½ hours and the night ferry takes 9½ hours. A single is £28 and a car costs from £38 to £64.

P&O (☎ 0304-203388) has two ferries a day from Felixstowe to Zeebrugge, Belgium: the day ferry takes six hours, and the night ferry takes nine hours. A single is £23 (making this one of the cheapest crossing points); and a car costs from £35 to £100.

To/From Dover P&O (☎ 0304- 203388) has six ferries and a number of jet foils to Ostend, Belgium, every day. The ferry takes four hours and the jet foil (passengers only) takes less than two. A single on the ferry costs £23, on the jet foil £29. A car costs from £35 to £100.

LEAVING THE COUNTRY
See the introductory Money section for details on how to reclaim Value Added Tax when you depart. There is no departure tax.

Getting Around

Public transport is generally of a high standard. Unfortunately, most shoestringers are going to want to get to the national parks and small villages where transport is worst. If time is limited, a car becomes a serious temptation, although with a mix of local buses, plenty of time, walking and occasionally hiring a bike, you can get almost anywhere.

Buses are nearly always the cheapest way to get around. Unfortunately, they're also the slowest (sometimes by a considerable margin) and on main routes you are confined to major roads, which screen you from the small towns and landscapes that make travel worthwhile in the first place. With discount passes and tickets (especially APEX), trains can be competitive; they're quicker and often take you through beautiful countryside that is relatively unspoilt by the 20th century.

The British Tourist Authority distributes an excellent brochure, *Getting about Britain for the Independent Traveller*, which gives details of bus, train, plane and ferry transport around Britain and into Europe.

The unsung hero of public transport, Mr Barry Doe, compiles information on routes and timetables. The YHA *Accommodation Guide*, *The National Trust Handbook* and the *Guide to English Heritage Properties* all have detailed transport information thanks to his efforts. Mr Doe also publishes the extremely useful *Doe's Bus/Rail Guide* four times a year. This surprisingly slim volume gives details on public transport to over 300 places of interest. Single copies are £5 (to the UK), £6 (airmail to Europe), £7.50 (airmail to rest of world); payment must be in sterling to BS Doe, 25 Newmorton Rd, Moordown, Bournemouth BH9 3NU (☎ 0202 528707).

See the Scotland and Wales Getting Around sections for information on deals that relate specifically to those countries.

AIR
Most regional centres and islands are linked to London. Prices are high, however, and since train and bus travel is so quick, flying is not a shoestring option.

BUS
National Express (Caledonian Express in Scotland) runs the largest national network – it's almost a monopoly. Long-distance express buses are usually referred to as coaches. Over short distances they're usually more expensive (though quicker) than local buses. A number of counties operate telephone enquiry lines which try to explain the fast-changing and often chaotic situation with timetables; wherever possible, these numbers have been given. Before commenc-

GREAT BRITAIN

ing a journey off the main routes, it is worth phoning to check for changes.

Unless otherwise stated, prices quoted in this chapter are for adult single tickets (which, believe it or not, are the same price as day return tickets). Subtract 30% if you are a young person or student; 20% if you buy a stand-by ticket. When buying a return ticket, discuss the options with the ticket clerk – there are several varieties.

Passes & Discounts

The National Express Britexpress Card allows 30% off standard adult fares on any journey in a 30-day period for £12; it is available to all overseas visitors on presentation of a passport. Its Discount Coach Card is available to young people aged under 24 and all full-time students and gives a 30% discount for a year. It costs £5, and requires a passport photo.

Its Tourist Trail Passes provide unlimited travel on all services for five, eight, 15, 22 and 30 days. A five-day pass for an adult/student is £64/44, a 15-day pass is £133/93, a 30-day pass is £184/128. All these passes can be bought overseas, and in the UK at Victoria Coach Station, Buckingham Palace Rd, SW1. Phone ☎ 071-730 0202 for details on other offices.

Postbus

Many small places can only be reached by postbuses – minibuses that follow postal delivery routes. There are circuitous routes through many of the most beautiful areas of England, Wales and Scotland. For free timetables, write to Postbus Services (☎ 071-250 2040), 148 Old St, London EC1V 9HQ.

TRAIN

Despite the cutbacks of the last decade, Britrail has an impressive service, including a number of beautiful lines through sparsely populated country. Unfortunately, thanks to a classic example of British 'independence' (one could use other words) Eurail passes are not recognised in Britain. There are local equivalents, but they aren't recognised in Europe.

Train buffs will find themselves in seventh heaven, but even those who are spared the obsession should make an effort to use some of the smaller lines. Wales and Scotland have some particularly famous survivors. The AA's *See Britain by Train* describes the most scenic routes. The main routes are served by excellent InterCity trains that travel at speeds of up to 225 km/h and whisk you from London to Edinburgh in just over four hours.

Although recommended, it is not necessary to purchase tickets or make seat reservations in advance, except for some of the main InterCity trains at peak times.

Unless otherwise stated the prices quoted in this chapter are for adult single tickets. Single tickets are generally much the same price as day return tickets, and period return tickets are considerably less than two single tickets. Holders of the Young Person's Railcard (see following section) are eligible for a 30% discount on all quoted prices.

This section will be as boring and painful to read as it was to write, but if you do figure out the system and fully exploit it, you'll save a lot of money. You'll also gain a lasting insight into an insane bureaucracy.

Britrail Passes

The Britrail Passes are the most interesting possibility for visitors, but they are *not available in Britain* and must be bought in your country of origin. A Britrail Pass, which allows unlimited travel, can be bought for four, eight, 15, 22 and 31 days. A four-day pass for an adult/youth is £85/65, a 15-day pass is £170/135, a 31-day pass is £250/200. An even more useful deal is the Flexipass, which allows four days unlimited travel out of eight (£105/85, eight days out of 15 (£150/120), and 15 out of a month (£220/175. Contact the British Tourist Authority in your country for details.

Britrail/Drive

Britrail/Drive combines a Flexipass (see previous section) with the use of a Hertz rental car for side trips. The car rental price is competitive. The package is available in the following combinations: four days out of eight Flexipass plus four days car, eight days out of 15 plus seven days car, and 15 days out of one month plus 10 days car. The following rate is for a Ford Escort (add to Flexipass prices): four days car £125, seven days car £215, 10 days car £310. Contact the British Tourist Authority in your country for details.

Rail Rovers

The domestic version of the passes are Britrail Rovers; a seven-day Rail Rover for unlimited travel costs £210/139. There are also regional rovers and some flexi rovers to Wales, North & Mid Wales, the North Country, the North-West Coast & Peaks, the South West, and Scotland. Details have been given in the appropriate sections.

Young Person's Railcard

The Railcard gives you a third off most tickets and some ferry services. You must be aged 16 to 23 or study at a UK educational establishment for over 15 hours weekly at least 20 weeks a year. The card costs £16 and is valid for one year. It's available from major stations and you'll need two passport photos, and proof of age (birth certificate or passport) or student status.

Network SouthEast

Network SouthEast is a semi-autonomous Britrail operation that covers all of Britrail's London lines and the entire south-east of England – from Dover to Weymouth, Cambridge to Oxford. It has a number of unique tickets and a worthwhile discount card.

Tickets

If the various train passes are complicated enough, try making sense of the different tickets:

Single Ticket – Valid for a single journey at any time on the day specified; expensive

Day Return Ticket – Valid for a return journey at any time on the day specified; relatively expensive

Cheap Day Return Ticket – Valid for a return journey on the day specified on the ticket, but there may be time restrictions and it is usually only available for short journeys; often about the same price as a single

APEX –The cheapest return fare, rivalling National Express prices; you must book seven days in advance

Supersaver – A cheap return ticket with up to 50% savings; not available within Network South-East; cannot be used on Fridays, Saturdays in July and August, nor in London before 9.30 am or between 4 and 6 pm

Saver – Higher priced than the Supersaver, but can be used any day and there are fewer time restrictions

Circular Ticket – Allows you to return by indirect routes, but at a discount similar to the Saver ticket

AwayBreak Ticket – For use on Network SouthEast on journeys over 40 miles. Valid for an outward journey at any time on the day specified with a return journey within five days. From Monday to Friday it may not be used before 9.30 am; about half the price of a straight return ticket

Network Card – For use on Network SouthEast only; £12, or £8 for holders of Britrail's Young Person's Railcard. Discounts apply to up to three adults travelling together providing one of the card holders is a member of the party. It gives 30% off most Network SouthEast tickets after 10 am Mondays to Fridays, and at any time on the weekends. A couple of journeys can pay for the card

CAR & MOTORBIKE

There are five grades of road. Motorways are dual carriageway and deliver you quickly from one end of the country to another. In general, they are an extremely unpleasant experience. You miss the most interesting countryside, and the driving is aggressive and dangerous. Avoid them whenever possible, and be particularly careful if you use them in foggy or wet conditions. The primary routes (main A roads) are often very similar.

Minor A roads are single carriageway and are likely to be clogged with slow-moving trucks. Life on the road starts to look up once you join the B roads and minor roads. Fenced by hedgerows, these wind through the countryside from village to village. You can't travel fast, but you won't want to.

Americans and Australians will find petrol expensive (around 50p per litre), but distances aren't great.

Road Rules

Anyone using the roads should get hold of the *Highway Code* (60p), which is often available in TICs. Briefly, vehicles drive on the left-hand side of the road; front seat belts are compulsory and belts must be worn if they are fitted in the back; the speed limit is 30 mph in built-up areas, 60 mph on single carriageways, and 70 mph on dual carriageways and motorways; you give way to your right at roundabouts (ie traffic already on the roundabout has the right of way); and motorcyclists must wear helmets.

A yellow line painted along the edge of the road indicates there are parking restrictions. The only way to establish the exact restrictions is to find the nearby sign that spells them out. A single line means no parking for at least an eight hour period between 7 am and 7 pm, five days a week; a double line means no parking for at least an eight hour period between 7 am and 7 pm more than five days a week; and a broken line means there are some restrictions.

Hiring

Hire companies often have minimum age limits (usually between 21 and 23 years old) and the process is easiest if you have a credit card. If you're shopping around, check that the contract includes unlimited mileage, full insurance, and a collision damage waiver (usually an additional charge, but it covers you against any insurance excess).

A one-litre, two-door Ford Fiesta, Austin Metro or Vauxhall Nova will carry two in reasonable comfort (three at a pinch) and can be hired from £100 per week. A 1.3-litre, two-door Ford Escort, Austin Maestro or Vauxhall Astra will carry four in reasonable comfort and can be hired from £110 per week. The British Tourist Authority (BTA) can supply lists of hiring companies, and *TNT Magazine* also carries ads from cheap operators.

Two big operators worth trying are Thrifty Car Rental (☎ 0494-442110), 14 Temple End, High Wycombe, Bucks HP13 5DR, and Access Car Hire UK (☎ 0734-452214), Bath Rd, Reading RG3 2HS. Both have vehicles from £135 and will deliver and pick up from Heathrow. Economy Rentals (☎ 081-521 0641) and Lawton Car Hire (☎ 081-203 5151) should have something for around £100 to £120.

Before you leave home, check what sort of deals you can do – sometimes you can get a special rate through your airline. As an example, Driveaway Holidays (Avis) in Australia will hire a Ford Fiesta at the equivalent of £110 per week.

If you're travelling as a couple or a group, a camper van is worth considering. The Campervan Company (☎ 081-960 5747) and Ross Romahome (☎ 081-398 2580) have four-berth and two-berth vans from £200 to £300 per week.

Buying

It is possible to buy a reasonable vehicle for around £1000, a camper van for around £2000. Check *Loot* (weekdays, £1), *Autotrader* (Fridays, 90p, includes photos) and the *Motorists' Guide* (monthly, £1.70, lists models and average prices).

All cars require: an MOT certificate – a Ministry of Transport safety certificate, valid for one year, issued by licensed garages; full third party insurance – shop around but expect £200; registration – a standard form signed by the buyer and seller, with a section to be sent to the Department of Transport; and tax – from main post offices on presentation of valid MOT, insurance and registration documents (£100 for one year, £55 for six months).

You are strongly recommended to buy a vehicle with valid MOT and tax. MOT and tax remain with the car through a change of ownership; third party insurance goes with the driver rather than the car, so you will still have to arrange this (and beware of letting others drive the car). For further information about registering, licensing, insuring and testing your vehicle, contact a post office or Vehicle Registration Office for leaflet V100.

It is worth considering membership of the Automobile Association (AA) or Royal Automobile Club (RAC). Both these organisations offer insurance, including

Europe-wide breakdown services, and can give advice on travelling in Europe. If you are a member of an automobile association in your home country, you will most likely have reciprocal rights in Britain and Europe – contact them before you leave home as you may need a Commonwealth Motoring Conference Card, or Letter of Assistance.

Green Card insurance extends your insurance into other countries; it is issued by insurance companies in Britain and should be validated for each country you plan to visit. Although British insurance will cover you in the EC, check the cover for countries like Turkey, Andorra and Poland. The British AA recommends you have a Green Card wherever you go, since you will need it if you are involved in an accident.

If you plan to drive on the Continent, you'll need a GB sticker to indicate that your car's registered in Great Britain, and you'll have to adapt your headlights to avoid blinding oncoming traffic (cover the triangular section of the headlight lens with tape).

See the Getting Around and Facts for the Visitor chapters at the beginning of this book for further details on private transport and the paperwork involved.

BICYCLE

See the Activities section earlier in this chapter.

HITCHING

Hitching is reasonably easy in the UK, except around the big cities and built-up areas, where you'll need to use public transport. It's against the law to hitch on motorways or the immediate slip roads; make a sign and use approach roads, nearby roundabouts, or the service stations.

HIKING

See the Activities section earlier in this chapter.

BOAT

See the appropriate sections for ferry information, and the Activities section earlier in this chapter for canal boating.

London

Once the capital of the greatest empire the world has ever known, London is still the largest city in Europe. It is embedded in the culture, the vocabulary and the dreams of every English speaker. At times it will be more grand, evocative, beautiful and stimulating than you could have imagined; at others it will be colder, greyer, dirtier and more expensive than you believed possible.

It is a cosmopolitan mixture of the Third World and First World, of chauffeurs and beggars, of the establishment and the avant-garde. There are seven to 12 million inhabitants depending on the count, and 20 million visitors a year. As you will soon discover, an amazing number are extremely wealthy. Fortunately for the shoestringer, however, the majority aren't. It will soon become clear what side of this divide you are on, and you will also discover a London that caters to those who work long hours for lousy wages.

For the shoestring traveller, London is a challenge. Money has a way of mysteriously evaporating every time you move. If you have limited funds it's necessary to plan, to book ahead and to prioritise. There's little point putting up with the crowds, the underground, and the pollution if you can't budget to take advantage of at least some of the theatre, the exhibitions, the shops, the pubs and clubs, the cafés and restaurants. A peg or two above desperation, you can find reasonable value. And some of the very best is free, or very cheap.

History

Although there was a Celtic community around a ford across the River Thames, it was the Romans who first developed the square mile now known as the City of London. They built a bridge and an impressive city wall, and made the city an important port and the hub of their road system.

The Romans left, but trade went on. Few traces of London dating from the Dark Ages can now be found, but London survived the

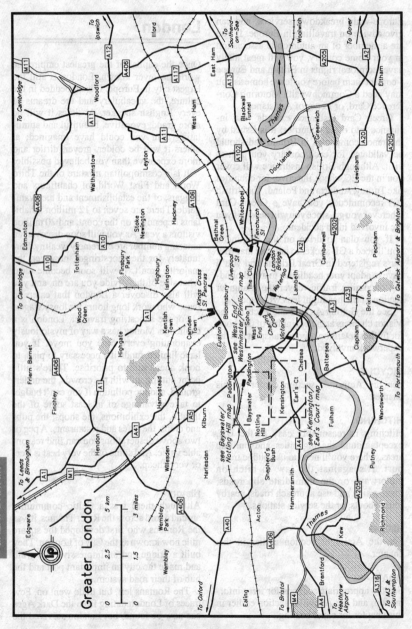

Greater London

To Ipswich
To Cambridge
To Leeds & Birmingham
To Oxford
To Bristol
To M3 & Southampton
To Heathrow Airport
To Portsmouth
To Gatwick Airport & Brighton
To Dover
To Southend-on-Sea

Edgware
Wembley Park
Wembley
Ealing
Acton
Brentford
Kew
Richmond
Putney
Wandsworth
Hammersmith
Shepherd's Bush
Fulham
Chelsea
Battersea
Clapham
Brixton
Camberwell
Peckham
Lewisham
Eltham
Woolwich
Greenwich
Docklands
Blackwall Tunnel
Whitechapel
Bethnal Green
Hackney
Stoke Newington
Leyton
Walthamstow
East Ham
West Ham
Ilford
Woodford
Edmonton
Tottenham
Finsbury Park
Highbury
Islington
Wood Green
Friern Barnet
Finchley
Hendon
Hampstead
Highgate
Kentish Town
Camden Town
Kilburn
Harlesden
Willesden
Kings Cross/St Pancras
Euston
Paddington
Bayswater
Notting Hill
Kensington
Earl's Ct
Bloomsbury
Soho
The City
Liverpool St
Fenchurch St
London Bridge
Waterloo
Lambeth
Victoria
West End
Charing Cross
Westminster/Pimlico
Thames

see West End/Westminster/Pimlico map
see Bayswater/Notting Hill map
see Kensington/Earl's Court map

Thames

GREAT BRITAIN

0   2.5   5 km
0   1.5   3 miles

M11
A12
A406
A117
A13
A102
A11
A10
A106
A10
A1
A406
A41
A5
A40
A406
A205
A316
M4
A4
A205
A3
A23
A2
A202
A2
A20
A205
A2

incursions of the Saxons and Vikings. Fifty years before the Normans arrived, Edward the Confessor built his abbey and palace at Westminster.

William the Conqueror found a city that was, without doubt, the richest and largest in the kingdom. He raised the White Tower (part of the Tower of London) and confirmed the city's independence and right to self-government.

During the reign of Elizabeth I the capital began to expand rapidly – in 40 years to 1603 the population doubled from 100,000 to 200,000. Unfortunately, medieval, Tudor and Jacobean London was virtually destroyed by the Great Fire of 1666. The fire gave Christopher Wren the opportunity to build his famous churches, but did nothing to halt the city's growth.

By 1720 there were 750,000 people, and London, as the seat of Parliament and focal point for a growing empire, was becoming ever richer and more important. Georgian architects replaced the last of medieval London with their imposing symmetrical architecture and residential squares.

The population exploded in the 19th century, creating a vast expanse of Victorian suburbs. As a result of the Industrial Revolution and rapidly expanding commerce, it jumped from 2.7 million in 1851 to 6.6 million in 1901.

Georgian and Victorian London was devastated by the Luftwaffe in WW II – huge swathes of the centre and the East End were totally flattened. After the war, ugly housing and low-cost developments were thrown up on the bomb sites. The docks never recovered – shipping moved to Tilbury, and the Docklands declined to the point of dereliction until they were rediscovered by developers in the 1980s.

Riding on a wave of Thatcherite confidence and deregulation, London boomed in the 1980s. The new wave of property developers proved to be only marginally more discriminating than the Luftwaffe, and their buildings are only slightly better than the eyesores of the 1950s.

Orientation

London's main geographical feature is the Thames, a tidal river that enabled an easily defended port to be established far from the dangers of the Channel. Flowing around wide bends from west to east, it divides the city into northern and southern halves.

London sprawls over an enormous area. Fortunately the underground system, the 'tube', makes most of it easily accessible, and the ubiquitous (though geographically misleading) underground map is easy to use. Any train heading from left to right on the map is designated as eastbound, any train heading from top to bottom is southbound. Each line has its own colour.

Most important sights, theatres, restaurants, and even some cheap places to stay, lie within a reasonably compact rectangle formed by the underground railway's Circle line, just to the north of the river. All the international airports lie some distance from the city centre but transport is easy. See the following Getting Around section for details on airport transport.

Although London's relatively few skyscrapers stick out like sore thumbs, they are not easily accessible to shoestringers. The best and most central lookout to help you orient yourself is, surprisingly, over 300 years old: the Golden Gallery at St Paul's Cathedral.

London blankets mostly imperceptible hills, but there are also good views from Hampstead Heath (north of Regent's Park), and Greenwich Park (pronounced 'Grenitch', downriver, east of central London).

Maps A decent map is vital. First, get a single-sheet map so you can see all of central London at a glance; the BTA produces a good one. Even if you only plan to stay for a night or two, buy a copy of the *'London A-Z'* street directory (black & white £2.25, colour £3.25) as soon as possible. A compass is also handy. It is easy to be totally disoriented when you emerge from a tube station.

Terminology 'London' is an imprecise term used loosely to describe over 2000 sq km of

Greater London enclosed by the M25 ring road, although it is now difficult to see outlying towns like Luton, Reading and Guildford (each around 50 km from the city centre) as anything more than suburbs.

London is not administered as a single unit, but divided into widely differing boroughs governed by local governments with significant autonomy. A borough (or town) with a cathedral was traditionally a city, so traditionally there were two cities in Greater London: Westminster and London! It is the City of London that is known simply as 'the City'.

Boroughs are further subdivided into districts (or suburbs, or precincts if you prefer), which to a large degree tally with the first group of letters and numbers of the postal code. The letter(s) correspond to compass directions from the centre of London, which according to the post office must lie somewhere not too far from St Paul's Cathedral: EC means East Central, WC means West Central, W means West, NW means North West, and so on. The numbering system after the letters is less helpful: 1 is the centre of the zone, further numbers relate to the alphabetical order of the postal district names, which are not always in common use.

Districts and postal codes are often given on street signs, which is obviously vital when names are duplicated (there are 47 Station Rds), or cross through a number of districts. To further confuse visitors, many streets change name (Holland Park Ave becomes Notting Hill Gate, which becomes Bayswater Rd, which becomes Oxford St...), or duck and weave like the country lanes they once were. Street numbering can also bewilder: on big streets the numbers on opposite sides can be way out of kilter (315 might be opposite 520) or, for variation, they can go up one side and down the other.

To add to the confusion, some London suburbs – well within the M25 – do not give London as a part of their addresses, and do not use London postal codes. Instead they're considered part of a county.

The City & the East The City refers to the area that was once the old walled city, before the inexorable colonisation of the surrounding towns and villages had begun. Although it lies in the south-eastern corner of the Circle line, it is regarded as the centre, ground zero. As you may have guessed, the West End (much more the tourist's centre) lies to the west.

The City is still one of the most important financial centres in the world. Full of bankers during the working week, it is deserted outside work hours. The same is not true of its most famous sights: the Tower of London, St Paul's Cathedral and the market at Petticoat Lane.

To the east, beyond the Circle line, is the East End, once the exclusive habitat of the cockney, now a cultural melting pot. This incorporates districts like Smithfields, Hackney, Shoreditch and Bethnal Green. There are some lively corners, and cheap rents, but in general it is blighted by traffic and council estates. Much of the East End was flattened during WW II and it shows.

Farther east again lie the Docklands. Once part of the busiest port in the world, thousands of acres of prime real estate fell into disuse after WW II, mirroring the decline of the empire. In the early 1980s, a light railway (an interesting excursion from Tower Gateway) was built and developers were unleashed.

Across the river (accessible by foot tunnel) is beautiful Greenwich, home to the *Cutty Sark*, superb architecture, open space and the prime meridian.

West West of the City, but before the West End proper, is Holborn and Bloomsbury. Holborn (pronounced 'Hoeburn') is Britain's sedate legal heartland, the home of Rumpole and common law. Bloomsbury is still synonymous with the literary and publishing worlds. There are dozens of specialist shops with lots of lunch-oriented restaurants, and it still has the incomparable British Museum, stuffed to the seams with loot from every age and every corner of the globe.

The West End proper lies west of Tottenham Court Rd and Covent Garden which is trendy and tourist-ridden but fun, and south of Oxford St (an endless succession of department stores packed with vicious, bargain-hunting shoppers). It includes such icons as Trafalgar Square, the restaurants and clubs of not-so-seedy Soho, the famous West End cinemas and theatres around Piccadilly Circus and Leicester Square, and the elegant shops of Regent and Bond Sts – and not to forget Mayfair, the most valuable property on the Monopoly board.

St James and Westminster are south-west, SW1 to be precise. Would this square mile be a nuclear target? Well, in no particular order, it includes Whitehall, No 10 Downing St, the Houses of Parliament, Westminster Abbey and Buckingham Palace.

To the south of Victoria Station, lies Pimlico, not a particularly attractive district, but central, and with a good supply of cheapish, decentish hotels.

Kensington, Earl's Court, South Kensington and Chelsea are in the south-west corner formed by the Circle line.

Earl's Court, once infamous as Kangaroo Valley and home to countless expatriate Australians, now has a strong Middle Eastern influence. It's pretty tacky, and seems to get tackier by the year, but there are still some cheap hotels, a number of backpackers' hostels and a couple of Australian pubs, plus cheap restaurants and travel agents. It is not a bad place to start your visit.

South Kensington is more chic and trendy, and there is a clutch of interesting museums (the Victoria & Albert, Science, Natural History, and Geological). Chelsea has abandoned the bohemian for comfort, and Kings Rd has bid farewell to the punks, but it is still an interesting centre for young fashion.

North Accessible from Notting Hill Gate, but more easily reached from Ladbroke Grove, Notting Hill is a lively, interesting district, with a large West Indian population. It gets trendier by the day, but the Portobello Rd market is still good value and there are pubs, a new crop of wine bars and interesting shops.

North of Kensington Gardens and Hyde Park, Bayswater and Paddington are pretty much tourist ghettos, but there are plenty of hostels, cheap and mid-range hotels, good pubs and interesting restaurants (particularly along Queensway and and Westbourne Grove).

From west to east, the band of suburbs to the north of the Central line include Kilburn, Hampstead, Camden Town, Kentish Town, Highgate and Highbury. Kilburn is London's Irish capital and bedsit land; not a bad place to live. Hampstead, with its great views, is fashionable, quiet and civilised, while Camden Town, although well advanced on the road to gentrification, still has some ordinary people and a gaggle of trendy but very enjoyable weekend markets.

South Cross the Thames from Central London and you could be excused for thinking you've arrived in a different country. This is working-class London and it seems a long way from the elegant, antiseptic streets of Westminster. By contrast, much of South London is very poor, very dirty, but very alive.

For the short-term visitor there may be few pressing reasons to visit, although there are middle-class beachheads like the South Bank Centre (a venue for interesting exhibitions and concerts), Kew with its superb gardens, and Wimbledon with its tennis courts.

If you stay for any length of time, however, there's a fair chance you will end up living in suburbs like Clapham, Brixton and Camberwell, or even farther out.

Brixton was notorious for racial problems in the early 1980s, but it is definitely no Harlem, even though unemployment is estimated at 18% and the crumbling buildings and piles of rubbish may look the part. You'll enjoy its tatty market and arcades whatever your skin colour. Most of the district is as safe as anywhere else, but don't wander too far off the main streets until someone locates the 'front line' for you – an area around Railton Rd which is best left to the locals.

Information

There's no shortage of information; the problem is wading through it to find the nuggets relevant to shoestringers.

Time Out (magazine, issued every Tuesday, £1.30) is a mind-bogglingly complete listing of everything happening and is recommended for every visitor. From the same company, the *Time Out London Guide* (paperback, £9.99) is an excellent practical guide for those planning to spend more than a week or so in London. They also publish the *Time Out Guide to Eating & Drinking in London* (magazine format, £6.99) which lists over 1700 restaurants and bars, although only some are cheap.

If you balk at paying, there are three free magazines available from pavement bins, especially in Earl's Court, Notting Hill and Bayswater: *TNT Magazine*, *Southern Cross* and *Australasian Traveller*. They have Australian and New Zealand news and sports results, but they're invaluable for every budget traveller, with entertainment listings, excellent travel sections, and useful classifieds covering jobs, cheap tickets, shipping services and accommodation. *TNT* is the glossier and most comprehensive of the three; phone ☎ 071-937 3985 for the nearest distribution point.

Loot (90p) is a daily paper made up entirely of classified ads that are placed free by sellers. You can find everything from second-hand wrestling magazines to kitchen sinks and cars, as well as an extensive selection of flats and house-share ads.

Tourist Offices London is a major European travel centre, so aside from information on London there are also offices that deal specifically with England, Scotland, Wales, Ireland and most European countries.

British Travel Centre
    12 Regent St, Piccadilly Circus, SW1Y 4PQ (☎ 071-730 3400, not Sundays). Two minutes' walk from Piccadilly Circus, this is a chaotic and comprehensive information and booking service under one roof: tours; theatre tickets; train, air and car travel; accommodation; map and guidebook shop; American Express; the Wales Tourist

Board; and a telephone information service. It's very busy and open every day.
London Tourist Information Centres
    There are centres in the three Heathrow terminals, and at Gatwick, Luton, and Stansted airports, Harrods and the Tower of London. The main centre on the Victoria Station forecourt has a number of services including accommodation bookings, information, and a book and map shop. They're open every day and can be extremely busy. Written enquiries to 26 Grosvenor Gardens, SW1W 0DU (☎ 071-730 3488).

It is possible to make same-day accommodation bookings at the TICs at Victoria and Heathrow, although they charge £5 for a hotel or B&B booking and £1.50 for hostels.

Alternatively, at Victoria, there are a couple of private hotel reservation centres (one on the main concourse, one outside near the steps to the underground) that charge £3 for a booking. Backpackers can seek out the Accommodation Express, a free service for backpackers to be found outside the station on Buckingham Palace Rd. They have a courtesy bus to the Palace Hotel, London Student Hotel, Westbourne International Residence and Chelsea Hotel (see the following Private Hostels section).

Travel London Regional Transport is responsible for the buses and the underground trains (the 'tube'). It has a number of information centres where you can get free maps, tickets, and information on night buses. Amongst others, there are centres in each Heathrow terminal, and at Victoria, Piccadilly and King's Cross stations; or phone ☎ 071-222 1234.

Britrail has four main enquiry numbers. For services to East Anglia and southern England, ☎ 071-928 5100; to the west and south Wales, ☎ 071-262 6767; for the Midlands, the north-west, and Scotland via the west, ☎ 071-387 7070; for the north-east and Scotland via the east, ☎ 071-287 2477.

Money Whenever possible, avoid using *bureaux de change* to change your money. For more info, see the Facts for the Visitor section at the beginning of this chapter.

There are 24-hour bureaus in each of the four Heathrow terminals. Thomas Cook has a branch at Terminal 1. There's a 24-hour bureau in Gatwick's South Terminal. The airport bureaus are actually reasonable value; they don't charge commission on sterling travellers' cheques, and on other currencies it's 1.5% with a £2 minimum.

At Victoria Railway Station, Thomas Cook has a bureau near the tourist office that's open daily from 6 am to 11 pm.

The main American Express office (☎ 071-930 4411), 6 Haymarket (tube: Piccadilly), is open for currency exchange Monday to Friday from 9 am to 5 pm, Saturdays from 9 am to 7.45 pm, and Sundays from 10 am to 6 pm. Other services are available weekdays from 9 am to 5 pm and Saturdays from 9 am to noon.

The Amex office (☎ 071-839 2682) in the British Travel Centre (see Tourist Offices) has longer hours: 9 am to 6.30 pm from Monday to Friday, and 10 am to 4 pm on Saturday and Sunday.

The main Thomas Cook office (☎ 071-499 4000), 45 Berkeley St (tube: Green Park), is open from 9 am to 5.30 pm Mondays to Fridays, 9 am to 4 pm on Saturdays.

Post & Telecommunications Unless otherwise specified, poste restante mail is sent to London Chief Office (☎ 071-239 5047), King Edward Building, King Edward St, ECI (tube: St Paul's). It's open from 9 am to 6.30 pm, Monday to Friday. It's more convenient to have your mail sent to Poste Restante, Trafalgar Square Branch Office, London WC2N 4DL. The physical address is 24-28 William IV St (tube: Charing Cross). Mail will be held for four weeks; ID is required.

London telephone numbers have two codes (071 or 081) before a seven-digit number. To get a telephone operator, ☎ 100; for London telephone directory enquiries, ☎ 142, outside London, ☎ 192; international, ☎ 153.

For the international operator (for collect/reverse charges) phone ☎ 155.

Remember, directory assistance is only free from a public phone.

Foreign Embassies If you want to visit or do business with a country that doesn't have an embassy, high commission, consulate or information centre in London, the chances are it hasn't existed for a very long time. With a few notable exceptions (Iraq, for instance) London is an excellent place to gather information and visas.

Cultural Centres These are all worth checking out: they'll provide information, often free entertainment, and, of course, a civilised way of escaping the weather.

The ICA (Institute for Contemporary Arts, ☎ 071-930 0493), Nash House, The Mall SW1 (tube: Piccadilly Circus), is an interesting, innovative complex including a bookshop, an art gallery, cinema, bar, café and theatre. There is invariably something worthwhile to see, the bar and restaurant are good value, and there's a young and relaxed crowd. A day pass is £1.50, £1 with any ticket purchase, 50p after 9 pm.

The Barbican Centre (☎ 071-638 4141, or for recorded info, ☎ 071-628 2295) is at Silk St, EC2 (tube: Barbican). On first impressions, the centre is a concrete maze. The good news is that the theatres and galleries are excellent (they are home to the Royal Shakespeare Company and the London Symphony Orchestra, and have many guests) and there are free exhibitions and concerts in the foyer.

South Bank Centre (☎ 071-928 3002), Belvedere Rd, Waterloo SE1, just across the river from Embankment tube station, is London's centre for classical music and includes the Royal Festival Hall, Queen Elizabeth Hall, Purcell Room, Hayward Gallery, the National Film Theatre, the excellent, expensive Museum of the Moving Image, and a range of restaurants and cafés. There are free foyer events every day from 12.30 to 2 pm.

The Riverside Studios complex (☎ 081-748 3354), Crisp Rd W6 (tube: Hammersmith), was originally a TV studio, but it is now an innovative centre with an excellent gallery, an excellent café and restaurant, a bar, two performance spaces (often showing excellent dance or theatre), an art gallery and a bookshop.

Travel Agencies London has always been a centre for cheap travel. Refer to the Sunday papers (especially the *Sunday Times*), *TNT Magazine* and *Time Out* for listings of cheap flights, and watch out for sharks.

The long-standing and reliable firms include:

Trailfinders
194 Kensington High St, W8 (☎ 071-937 5400), tube: High St Kensington. A complete travel service, including a bookshop, information centre, visa service and immunisation centre
STA Travel
74 Old Brompton Rd, SW7 (☎ 071-937 9962), tube: South Kensington. The largest worldwide student/budget agency
Campus Travel
174 Kensington High St, W8 (☎ 071-938 2188), tube: High St Kensington, has offices in large YHA Adventure Shops
Council Travel
28A Poland St, London W1 (☎ 071-437 7767), tube: Oxford Circus. The USA's largest student and budget travel agency

Bookshops All the major chains are good, but Waterstones and Dillons have particularly strong travel sections. There are a number of specialist travel bookshops and several shops that are tourist attractions in their own right:

Stanfords
12 Long Acre, WC2 (☎ 071-836 1321), tube: Covent Garden. This has the largest and best selection of maps and guides in the world
Books for Cooks
4 Blenheim Crescent, W11 (☎ 071-221 1992), tube: Ladbroke Grove. The best collection of cook books in the world
Travel Bookshop
13 Blenheim Crescent, across the road from Books for Cooks, has all the new guides, plus a selection of out of print and antiquarian gems
Foyles
119 Charing Cross Rd, WC2 (☎ 071-437 5660), tube: Leicester Square. The biggest, most disorganised bookshop in the world
Dillons the Bookstore
82 Gower St (☎ 071-636 1577), tube: Euston Square. An enormous bookshop with particularly strong academic sections

Emergency Dial ☎ 999 for fire, police or ambulance. The local police station (see phone book) can advise you of the nearest late-night pharmacy.

Things to See

Walking Tour The centre of London can easily be explored on foot. The following tour could be covered in a day, but it does not allow you the chance to explore any of the individual sights in detail; it will, however, give you an introduction to the West End and Westminster.

Start at **St Paul's Cathedral**, Christopher Wren's masterpiece that was completed in 1710. Entry to the cathedral is free (although a £1 donation is requested). It is worth paying the £2.75 for access to the Golden Gallery and the best view over London. Unless you're feeling very energetic, catch a tube from St Paul's station to Covent Garden (west on the Central line to Holborn, then west on the Piccadilly line).

Covent Garden, once London's fruit and vegetable market, has been restored to a bustling piazza. It's one of the very few places in London where pedestrians rule, and you can watch the buskers for a few coins and the tourists for free. The opera house is on the north-east corner, and the main YHA Adventure Shop is on Southampton St off the south side.

Return to the tube station and turn left into Long Acre (look for Stanfords bookshop on your left) and continue across Charing Cross Rd to **Leicester Square**. This has the greatest concentration of cinemas, franchise food, plastic souvenirs and discos in the world. Note the Leicester Square Theatre Ticket Booth, which sells half-price tickets on the day of performance.

Continue along Coventry St, past the Trocadero and Madame Tussaud's Rock Circus, until you get to **Piccadilly Circus**, with Tower Records, the best music shop in London. Shaftesbury Ave enters the circus at the north-eastern corner, with the cheap kebab/pizza counters. This is the street of theatres and runs back into Soho, with its myriad restaurants. Regent St curves out of the north-west corner.

Continue west along Piccadilly to the

Royal Academy and St James church (with its excellent cheap restaurant). Detour into the extraordinary **Burlington Arcade**, just after the academy; beware the arcade Burties (private 'police') who, amongst other things, are supposed to stop you whistling.

Return to Piccadilly and continue until you get to St James St on your left. This takes you down to **St James' Palace**, the royal home from 1660 to 1837 until it was judged insufficiently impressive. Skirt around its east side and you come onto The Mall.

Trafalgar Square is to the east, **Buckingham Palace** is to the west. From May to July the changing of the guard happens daily at 11.30 am; from August to April it is at 11.30 am on alternate days. The best place to be is by the gates of Buckingham House, but the crowds are awesome. Cross back into St James' Park, the most beautiful in London, and follow the lake to its east end. Turn right onto Horse Guards Rd. This takes you past the **Cabinet War Rooms** (£3.60), which give an extraordinary insight into the dark days of WW II.

Continue along Horse Guards Rd, then turn left on Great George St, which takes you through to beautiful Westminster Abbey, the Houses of Parliament and Westminster Bridge. **Westminster Abbey** is so rich in history you need half a day to do it justice. The coronation chair where all but two monarchs since 1066 have been crowned is behind the altar, and many greats – from Darwin to Chaucer – have been buried here. An admission fee (£3) is charged for the Royal Chapels; alternatively, there are guided tours for £6. The best way to soak in the atmosphere, however, is to attend sung Evensong (5 pm on Monday, Tuesday, Thursday and Friday; 3 pm on Saturday and Sunday).

The **Houses of Parliament** and the clock tower, **Big Ben**, were actually built in the 19th century in mock medieval style. The best way to get into the building is to attend the Commons or Lords visitors' galleries during a Parliamentary debate. Phone ☎ 071-219 4272 to find out if anything is happening.

Walking away from Westminster Bridge, turn right into Whitehall. On your left, Downing St has an ordinary-looking house at **No 10** that offers temporary accommodation to politicians. Farther along on the right is the Inigo Jones-designed Banqueting House, outside which Charles I was beheaded. Continue past the Horse Guards, where you can see a changing of the guard (less crowded than Buck House) at 11 am Monday to Saturday, 10 am on Sundays.

Finally, you reach **Trafalgar Square** and Nelson's Column. The National Gallery and National Portrait Gallery are on the north side.

River Tour If walking doesn't seem like a good idea, consider catching a boat from Westminster Pier (beside Westminster Bridge) down the river to Greenwich (every half hour from 10.30 am, £4). You pass the site of Shakespeare's Globe Theatre, stop at the Tower of London, and continue under Tower Bridge and past many famous docks.

Greenwich can absorb the best part of a day. Start with the **Cutty Sark** (£3), the only surviving tea and wool clipper and one of the most beautiful ships ever built. Wander around the Greenwich market, then visit the **Queen's House**, a masterpiece designed in 1616 by Inigo Jones. If you're interested in boats and naval history, continue to the **National Maritime Museum** (£5.95 for the museum, house and observatory, or £3.25 each). The **Royal Naval College**, beside the river, was designed by Wren; admission is free from 2.30 to 4.30 pm.

Climb the hill behind the museum to the **Old Royal Observatory**. A brass strip in the observatory courtyard marks the prime meridian that divides the world into eastern and western hemispheres. There are great views over Docklands – with the massive and bankrupt Canary Wharf development just over the river – and back to London.

Walk back down the hill and through the Greenwich foot tunnel (near the *Cutty Sark*) to Island Gardens. From the other side of the river there is a superb view of the Naval College and the Queens House – a classic

GREAT BRITAIN

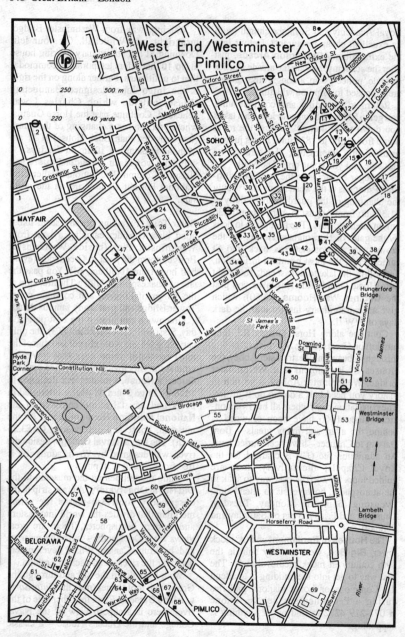

West End/Westminster
Pimlico

■	**PLACES TO STAY**	20	Leicester Square Tube
		23	Hamleys
4	Oxford Street Youth Hostel	24	Museum of Mankind
63	Belgrave House Hotel	25	Burlington Arcade
64	Brindle House Hotel	26	Royal Academy
65	Romany Hotel	28	Piccadilly Circus
66	Victoria Hotel	29	Piccadilly Circus Tube
68	Luna & Simone Hotels	32	Leicester Square
		33	British Travel Centre
▼	**PLACES TO EAT**	34	New Zealand House
		35	American Express
5	Pizza Express	36	National Gallery
6	Mildred's	37	Trafalgar Square Post Office
9	Café Pasta	38	Embankment Tube
10	Neal's Yard	39	Charing Cross Station
11	Food for Thought	40	Charing Cross Tube
12	Diana's Diner	41	South Africa House
13	Café Pacifico	42	Trafalgar Square
21	Poons	43	Canada House
22	La Perla	44	Scottish Tourist Board
27	The Wren at St James	45	Admiralty Arch
30	Wong Kei	46	ICA
31	Stockpot	47	Thomas Cook
62	The Well	48	Green Park Tube
67	Mekong	49	St James Palace
		50	Cabinet War Rooms
	OTHER	51	Westminster Tube
		52	Westminster Pier
1	US Embassy	53	Houses of Parliament
2	Bond Street Tube	54	Westminster Abbey
3	Oxford Circus Tube	55	Home Office
7	Tottenham Court Rd Tube	56	Buckingham Palace
8	British Museum	57	London Student Travel
14	Covent Garden Tube	58	Victoria Station & Tube
15	Rock Garden	59	Westminster Cathedral
16	Covent Garden	60	American Express
17	YHA Adventure Shop	61	Victoria Coach Station
18	Australia House	69	Tate Gallery
19	Stanfords		

arrangement of buildings. The Docklands Light Railway whisks above ground from Island Gardens back to Tower Gateway, and there are good views of the new Docklands developments. Unfortunately it only runs on weekdays; buses run on weekends; Zone 1 & 2 Travelcards are valid.

If you are still raring to go, you could dash in to the **Tower of London**. The Tower dates from the 1070s when William the Conqueror began the White Tower. The castle was turned into an enormous concentric fortress by Henry III; it has been a fortress, royal residence and prison. It now houses the crown jewels and royal armoury, and there are inevitably big crowds (visit during the week); entry is £6/4.50. Or, on Sunday, visit Petticoat Lane market a short walk north up the Minories.

Museums The greatest of them all is the British Museum with its unparalleled Egyptian, Mesopotamian, Greek and Roman collections. The main museum precinct is in Kensington, just north of the South Kensington tube station; the brilliant Victoria &

Albert Museum (decorative arts) and the rejuvenated Science, Natural History and Geological Museums (animated dinosaurs and interactive displays) are all highly recommended.

The **British Museum**, Great Russell St WC1 (tube: Tottenham Court Rd), has the world's greatest collection of antiquities; open from 10 am to 5 pm Monday to Saturday, 2.30 to 6 pm Sunday; free.

The **Victoria & Albert Museum**, Cromwell Rd SW7 (tube: South Kensington), has the world's greatest collection of decorative arts, including clothes; open from 10 am to 5.50 pm Monday to Saturday, 2.30 to 5.50 pm Sunday; £3 donation requested. The V&A has the best café in the Kensington museums.

The **Museum of London**, 150 London Wall EC2 (tube: St Paul's), displays the history of London, from the Romans on; open from 10 am to 6 pm Tuesday to Saturday; £3.

The **Imperial War Museum**, Lambeth Rd SE1 (tube: Lambeth North), has an extraordinary collection and some amazing recreations (the 'Blitz Experience' is recommended, £1); open from 10 am to 6 pm daily; £3.50.

The **Museum of the Moving Image**, South Bank Centre SE1 (tube: Embankment, then cross the foot and rail bridge over the Thames), deals with the history of film and TV with interactive displays; open from 10 am to 8 pm Monday to Saturday, 10 am to 6 pm Sunday; £5.50.

The **Museum of Mankind**, 6 Burlington Gardens W1 (tube: Piccadilly Circus), presents a series of fascinating exhibitions that illustrate non-Western societies and cultures. The collections come from the Americas, Africa, parts of Asia and Europe, and the Pacific; open from 10 am to 5 pm Monday to Saturday, 2.30 to 6 pm Sunday; free.

Galleries A visit to the National and Tate galleries is a must, but there are also likely to be interesting exhibitions at the Hayward Gallery (South Bank Centre), the ICA (see Cultural Centres), Riverside Studios and the Royal Academy of Arts – among many others. Check *Time Out* for current shows.

The **National Gallery**, Trafalgar Square (tube: Charing Cross), covers all leading European schools from the 13th to 20th centuries; open from 10 am to 6 pm Monday to Saturday, 2 to 6 pm Sunday; free.

The **Courtauld Institute Galleries**, Somerset House, The Strand (tube: Temple), has an excellent collection of post-Impressionists (Cézanne, Gauguin, van Gogh); open from 10 am to 6 pm Mondays to Saturdays, 2 to 6 pm Sundays; £3.

The **Tate Gallery**, Millbank SW11 (tube: Pimlico), features the history of British art, especially Turner, and international modern art; open from 10 am to 5.50 pm Monday to Saturday, 2 to 5.50 pm Sunday; free.

Markets The markets are where you see London life at its best; they're bustling, interesting and full of character(s).

Berwick St (tube: Piccadilly) in Soho is one of the last strongholds of real life in the West End. The stall holders are as theatrical as you can find, and the fruit and vegetables are among the best and cheapest in London (stock up for a picnic). There are also some good record shops; visit Quaff, 4 Berwick St, for house music and info about legal raves.

Camden (tube: Camden Town) attracts huge crowds all weekend. It's trendy, but a lot of fun. The Electric Ballroom on High St sells second-hand clothes from 9 am on Sundays, but all you need to do is start at Camden Lock and follow your nose.

Petticoat Lane, Middlesex St (tube: Aldgate), is open from 9 am to 2 pm Sunday. It's the home of the cockney, and has a good selection of fashion (particularly leather) and odds and ends.

Brick Lane (tube: Aldgate East), open from 5 am to 2 pm Sundays, is cheap, chaotic and very East End. It's now dominated by Bengalis, but there are still some fresh bagels to be found (at the north end, away from Whitechapel).

Portobello Rd (tube: Ladbroke Grove) has fruit and vegetables from 8 am to 5 pm Monday to Saturday except Thursday afternoon, and general goods from 8 am to 3 pm Fridays, 8 am to 5 pm Saturdays. There are reasonable second-hand stalls at the Westway end, expensive antiques at the Notting Hill end.

Brixton (tube: Brixton) is open from 9 am to 5.30 pm Monday to Saturday except Wednesday afternoon. Barrows are piled high with fruit and vegetables, and there are lively arcades that *must* be explored – the Caribbean comes to London.

Other Sights A number of London's major sights have been covered in the Walking Tour and River Tour sections. All visitors, but especially shoestringers, should make the most of London's glorious parks. A long walk starting at St James' and continuing through Green, Hyde, Kensington and Holland parks will banish any urban blues.

Harrods, Knightsbridge SW1 (tube: Knightsbridge), is a shop, but not just a shop. Its latest addition is a double-storey Egyptian room on the ground floor that stocks Egyptian merchandise of every kind. The Georgian restaurant on the 4th floor serves an amazing all-you-can-eat buffet tea from 3.45 pm at £8.95 per head.

Hamleys, 188 Regent St (tube: Oxford Circus), is the biggest toy shop in the world, for children aged three months to 90 years.

Hyde Park is central London's largest park. Row a boat on the Serpentine, listen to a military band (on summer Sundays) or heckle the soapbox orators on Sundays at Speakers' Corner (Marble Arch corner).

Hampton Court Palace is the grandest Tudor house in the country. Built by Cardinal Wolsey in 1514 and 'adopted' by Henry VIII, it is a beautiful mixture of architectural styles – from Henry's splendid Great Hall to the State Apartments built for King William III and Queen Mary II by Wren. The superb palace grounds, near the Thames, include deer and a 300-year-old maze.It's open daily from 9.30 am to 6 pm (4.30 pm in winter) and admission is £4.95; the grounds are free. There are trains every half hour from Waterloo (£3.20 return, Zone 4), or you can catch a ferry from Westminster Pier. Ferries sail from April to October at 10.30 and 11.15 am, noon and 12.30 pm, take 3½ hours and cost £6.

Kew Gardens (tube: Kew Gardens, Zone 3), the Royal Botanic Gardens, are a beautiful, restful escape from the real world. Entry is a steep £3. As an alternative to the tube, ferries sail from Westminster Pier every 30 minutes from 10.15 am to 3.30 pm (April to October). They take 1½ hours and cost £3. While you're out here, cross Kew Bridge and walk to the right along the (left) bank of the Thames; there are a number of pleasant riverside pubs.

Tourist Traps If you feel jaded and uninspired by history and culture, perhaps you need to spend money and see the human zoo at Madame Tussaud's and the Rock Circus.

London Zoo (☎ 071-722 3333) in Regent's Park will have closed down by the time you read this, for lack of funding, unless the government coughs up a few extra million. If it is still open – well, it's expensive and the inmates are cramped in tiny cages – it'd be better if they were wax. Give it a miss, unless you want to pay your respects to Bruce, the 40-year-old, Australian lungfish. Admission is £4.30.

Madame Tussaud's (☎ 071-935 6861), Marylebone Rd (tube: Baker St), is permanently crowded, proving that people do want to see wax versions of the royal family and the chamber of horrors. Admission is £6.40. The queues can be horrendous. It opens at 10 am, so get there at 9.30 am.

Rock Circus (☎ 071-734 8025), London Pavilion, Piccadilly Circus, is a high-tech rock'n'roll version of Tussaud's. The robots are remarkable, and it is, after all, as close as you will ever get to John Lennon and Madonna. Admission is £6.25.

Places to Stay

Whichever way you cut it, accommodation in London is ridiculously expensive. In spite of the shoestring ethos, it is worth booking a night or two's accommodation, especially in July and August. The official TICs at the airports and at Victoria Station can arrange last-minute bookings, but they charge £5 for a booking. In summer the Victoria office has enormous queues, but there are also cheaper, less busy, private operators who charge £3 or £4. Outside the station on Buckingham Palace Rd towards the bus station, Accommodation Express (☎ 071-233 8139) has free bookings and a courtesy bus for a number of private hostels (Palace Hotel, London Student Hotel, Westbourne International Residence and Chelsea Hotel).

Hostel dorm accommodation will cost from £8 to £16.50. You can expect to pay £25/30 for very basic singles/doubles without en suite bathrooms, £25/35 with. There are, of course, some superb hotels in London, but they are *very* expensive. If you have enough money for one or two splurges wait until you get into the countryside, where you will get much better value.

The TICs also have a useful booklet on budget accommodation – get it from the BTA before you leave home.

Camping *Tent City* (☎ 081- 743 5708), Old Oak Common Lane W3 (tube: East Acton, Central line), is the cheapest option in London, short of sleeping rough. There are dormitory-style tents with beds for £4. It's only open from June to September and you are advised to book. It also has tent sites but doesn't take caravans or camper vans.

Hackney Camping (☎ 081-985 7656), Millfields Rd E5, is run by the Tent City people, but it's strictly bring-your-own tent. The charge is £2.50 per person, from mid-June to late August. Catch bus No 38 from Victoria.

Lee Valley Park, Picketts Lock Sport & Leisure Centre (☎ 081-803 4756), Picketts Lock Lane, Edmonton N9, has 200 pitches for tents or caravans. It's open all year and the nightly charge for two is £7.20.

YHA Hostels There are seven YHA hostels in London, but they are crowded during summer. Sometimes they can't even accept advance bookings. If they have room, they all take advance bookings by phone (if you pay by Visa or MasterCard). They do hold some beds for those who wander in on the

day, but wander in early, and be prepared to queue. Adults will have to pay £10.30 to £16.50, juniors £8.60 to £14.50.

You can join the association at the YHA London headquarters (☎ 071-240 5236), 14 Southampton St WC2 (tube: Covent Garden), where there's also a bookshop, excellent outdoor equipment, and a branch of Campus Travel.

Rotherhithe (☎ 071-232 2114), Island Yard, Salter Rd SE16 (tube: Rotherhithe), is an impressive, brand new, purpose-built hostel. Unfortunately, it's a bit far out, and the area is not great; transport is fair. On the other hand, the hostel is good; rooms are mainly six-bed, although there are some fours and a few doubles; all have ensuite bathrooms. There's a cheap restaurant as well as kitchen facilities. Rates for seniors/juniors are £16/14; no curfew.

Carter Lane (☎ 071-236 4965), 36 Carter Lane EC4 (tube: St Paul's), is virtually next door to St Paul's Cathedral in an intelligently restored old building, which was the cathedral choir's school. The position and the hostel are excellent, although this end of town does get pretty quiet outside working hours. Rooms are mainly four, three, or two beds. There's a cafeteria and kitchen. Rates are £16/14; no curfew.

Earl's Court (☎ 071-373 7083), 38 Bolton Gardens SW5 (tube: Earl's Court), is an old townhouse in a tacky, though lively, part of town; it is not the best equipped of the hostels, however. Rooms are mainly 10-bed dorms. There's a cafeteria. Rates are £13/12; no curfew.

Hampstead Heath (☎ 081-458 9054), 4 Wellgarth Rd NW11 (tube: Golders Green), is in a beautiful setting with a well-kept garden, although it is a bit isolated. The dorms are comfortable, and each room has a basin with hot and cold water. There's a rather average cafeteria. Rates are £13.50/12.50; no curfew.

Highgate Village (☎ 081-340 1831), 84 Highgate West Hill N6 (tube: Archway), is in a Georgian house not far from Hampstead Heath; once again it is a bit isolated. There are kitchen facilities, but no evening meals.

It's the cheapest YHA option in London with rates at £10.30/8.60; midnight curfew.

Holland House (☎ 071-937 0748), Holland Walk, Kensington W8 (tube: High St Kensington), has a great location in the middle of Holland Park and is close to everything. It's large, very busy, and rather institutional, but the position really can't be beat. There's a cafeteria. Rates are £15.50/13.50; no curfew.

Oxford St (☎ 071-734 1618), 14-18 Noel St W1 (tube: Oxford Circus), is the most basic of the London hostels, but it is right in the centre of town. There's a large kitchen, but no meals. Rates are £16.50/14.50; no curfew.

University Colleges University halls of residence are let to nonstudents during the holidays, usually from June to September. They're a bit more expensive than the youth hostels, but you usually get a single room (there are a small number of doubles) with shared facilities, plus breakfast. Bookings are co-ordinated by the British Universities Accommodation Consortium (BUAC) (☎ 0602-504571) Box 653, University Park, Nottingham NG7 2RD, although you can also contact the colleges direct.

Carr Saunders Hall (☎ 071-580 6338), 18-24 Fitzroy St W1 (tube: Great Portland St), is not the greatest part of town, but it's central enough; open Easter and summer holidays (one week minimum); singles/doubles with breakfast are £17.50 per person.

Imperial College of Science & Technology (☎ 071-589 5111), 15 Princes Garden SW7 (tube: South Kensington), is in a brilliant position near the Kensington museums; open Easter and summer; B&B is £18 to £24.

John Adams Hall (☎ 071-387 4086), 15-23 Endsleigh St WC1 (tube: Euston), is central and facilities include a swimming pool; open Easter and summer; B&B is £19 for more than seven nights, £21.40 for less.

King's Campus Vacation Bureau (☎ 071-351 6011), 552 Kings Rd SW10 0UA, administers bookings for a number of central University of London residence halls. Rates are around £20 per person and include a continental breakfast and access to excellent facilities.

Private Hostels There are a number of hotels/hostels that operate on the simple principle that if you squash six people in a room and charge them £10 each you make more profit than if you have a couple at £20 per person. They are not suitable for fastidious, anti-social claustrophobics.

In terms of facilities offered, most of the hostels don't vary much. Most have three or four small bunk-beds jammed into a room, a small kitchen, and some kind of lounge room. Some have budget restaurants and some even have a bar. They are cheaper and much more relaxed than the official YHA hostels, but the standards are more hit and miss. Problems with theft are relatively unusual, but be careful with your possessions and deposit your valuables in the office safe.

Apart from noise levels and cleanliness, the most important variable is the atmosphere. This can change by the week, as to a certain extent it is dependent on the people who happen to be staying. If you're not happy with your first pick, try somewhere new.

The largest number of private hostels are in Earl's Court (SW5), which consequently has the biggest backpacker scene, but there are some in Paddington and Bayswater (W2), Notting Hill and Holland Park (W11), Bloomsbury (WC1) and Pimlico (SW1). Earl's Court and Paddington seem to get seedier by the year, although there are still some good places. Notting Hill (and around) is recommended.

The hostels all advertise in *TNT Magazine*, and many of them have commission agents (all right – touts) at stations like Victoria and Earl's Court. At Victoria, backpackers can seek out Accommodation Express, a free service to be found outside the station on Buckingham Palace Rd. It has a courtesy bus to the Palace Hotel, London Student Hotel, Westbourne International Residence and Chelsea Hotel (see the following sections).

Notting Hill The pick of the bunch is the *Palace Court Hotel* (☎ 071-727 4412 and 221 9228), 12-14 Pembridge Square W2 (tube: Notting Hill Gate). It's in a good position; and it's all a bit like one big party. Their bar is open late to guests, and there's a budget restaurant. They can usually suggest an alternative if they are full, but arrive early if you can. You'll pay £12 with four others, £16 with one other, £18 for one of the few singles. Prices drop outside summer. Ring for details on their free minibus from Victoria.

The *Palace Hotel* (☎ 071-221 5628), 31 Palace Court W2 (tube: Notting Hill Gate), has dorm beds for £10. It has a pleasant and convenient location and isn't quite as rundown and manic as some of the others. There's a cheap restaurant with meals from £2.50.

The *London Independent Hostel* (☎ 071-229 4238), 41 Holland Park W11 (tube: Holland Park) is on an elegant street and is well positioned. It's also good value (all things being relative) with dorms for £7.50, quads for £8.50, triples for £9, doubles for £9.50 and singles for £12.

The *Holland Park Independent Hostel* (☎ 071- 602 7218), 31 Holland Park Gardens W14 (tube: Holland Park), is a very basic hostel, but acceptably clean and about as cheap as they come. Beds in crowded dorms are £6.

The *Centre Français* (☎ 071-221 8134), 61 Chepstow Place W2 (tube: Notting Hill Gate), is like a cross between a YHA hostel and a college residence. It's immaculately maintained, comfortable in an institutional sort of way, and only about half the clientele are French. A bed in a bright and cheery dorm of eight beds is £12.90, in a three/four bed dorm is £16.40. The singles/doubles (£23/40) are spartan, but do include washbasins and desks.

Bloomsbury The *Museum Inn* (☎ 071-580 5360), 27 Montague St WC1 (tube: Holborn), has an excellent position opposite the British Museum. It's friendly and pretty well organised. There are colour TVs in the four-bed dorms, decent kitchen facilities, and a basic breakfast is included in the price: £16 per person in the one double; £14 in a four-bed dorm; £12.50 in a nine-bed dorm. They also have an annexe that is a pound or two cheaper.

The *International Students House* (☎ 071-631 3223), 229 Great Portland St W1 (tube: Great Portland St), is really in a different class, more like a university residential college. For a start you get singles or doubles; they're ordinary, but clean. There are excellent facilities and a friendly atmosphere – you don't have to be a student. It's open all year. B&B is £20, but there are cheaper weekly rates.

Earl's Court The *Maranton House Hotel* (☎ 071-373 5782), 14 Barkston Gardens (tube: Earl's Court), is a pleasant hotel with a good mix of facilities. They have a couple of civilised dorms that, because they are part of a normal hotel, don't have the same hectic atmosphere as many hostels, and also some pleasant rooms. Four to six-bed dorms are £10, singles are £24/35 without/with facilities, doubles are £28/40, and quads are £60.

The *Curzon House Hotel* (☎ 071-581 2116), 58 Courtfield Gardens SW5 (tube: Gloucester Rd), is one of the best private hostels – much loved by Let's Go researchers, but don't hold that against it. There's a relaxed and friendly atmosphere. Dorms are £13 per person, singles/doubles with facilities are £20/26.

The *Chelsea Hotel* (☎ 071-244 6892), 33 Earl's Court Square SW5 (tube: Earl's Court), is a classic hostel. There's a restaurant with meals for £3, and hundreds of cheery backpackers wandering around. They have some good-value singles and doubles as well as dorms. A dorm bed is £9, a twin is £13 and a single is £15.

Airton House Youth & Student Hotel (☎ 071- 244 7722), 8 Philbeach Gardens SW5 (tube: Earl's Court), is a friendly place, but it's pretty shabby – very basic rooms, small bunks, and a barely adequate kitchen (although it was being worked on when we visited). There's a range of rooms from eight-bed dorms to doubles with prices ranging from £8 per person in a dorm to £10 per person in a double. Continental breakfast.

London Student Hotel (☎ 071-244 6615), 14 Penywern Rd SW5 (tube: Earl's Court), is another pretty rundown hostel, with a tiny kitchen. It would do. Dorms are from £8; doubles from £24. Continental breakfast.

The *Corfu Hotel* (☎ 071-370 4942), 41 Longridge Rd SW5 (tube: Earl's Court), has standard hostel acommodation from £9 per night.

Paddington & Bayswater The *Westbourne International Residence* (☎ 071- 402 0431), 104 Westbourne Terrace W2 (tube: Paddington), is a bit out of the way, which in Paddington is really a blessing. It's a decent hostel in quite a grand row of buildings and you're only a short walk from restaurants. There are kitchen facilities and they have six-bed dorms at £9 per bed.

The *Quest Hotel* (☎ 071-299 7782), 45 Queensborough Terrace W2 (tube: Bayswater), is just around the corner from all the action on Queensway and a minute from Hyde Park. It has a friendly atmosphere, but it's pretty crowded and tacky. There are kitchen facilities, and beds are around £10.

Next door, the *Royal Hotel* (☎ 071-229 7225), 43 Queensborough Terrace W2 (tube: Bayswater), is much like many other hostels, but they do make an effort not to overcrowd the rooms. As a result, many people stay for quite long periods of time. A very basic double is £9 per person, and quads are £8 per person.

Pimlico The *Victoria Hotel* (☎ 071-834 3077), 71 Belgrave Rd SW1 (tube: Victoria), is a 15-minute walk from Victoria station, which makes it ideal if you arrive in London late at night, or have to leave early in the morning. Reception is open 24 hours. It's cheerful and basic and beds are around £10.

Hotels & B&Bs Bloomsbury (WC1), Bayswater (W2), Paddington (W2), Pimlico (SW1) and Earls Court (SW5) are the centres

for budget hotels. Each area has advantages and disadvantages, but the prices remain pretty consistent. If you want an attached bathroom you will be lucky to find anything for less than £25, even in winter.

Outside the high season prices are nearly always negotiable; don't be afraid to ask for the 'best' price and for a discount if you are either staying more than a couple of nights or don't want a cooked breakfast. In July, August and September prices can jump by 25%, and it is definitely worth phoning ahead. Many of the cheapies don't take credit cards.

B&Bs in Londoners' private houses can be good value; double room prices range from £12 to £25 per person per night. At £12 you would be quite a distance out and share a bathroom, at £14 a little closer, at £16 you should be in a central location like Bloomsbury, and from £20 to £25 in a central area with a private bathroom.

Bookings (minimum three days) can be made free in advance through London Homestead Services (☎ 081-949 4455, 24 hours), Coombe Wood Rd, Kingston-upon-Thames, Surrey KT2 7J. Capital Homes (☎ 081-440 7535) can make same-day bookings; they have a two-day minimum. Or contact the BTA or local TICs.

Earl's Court has been a hang out for refugees from the far-flung corners of the empire for a long time. At one stage it was infamous as Kangaroo Valley, but now Australians are less conspicuous than Arabs and Indians. Most people seem to be in transit, and it shows in the grubby, unloved streets. It's relatively convenient, although not quite as convenient as the other districts in this guide – it's not really within walking distance of many places you will want to be, so you're heavily dependent on the tube.

The *Philbeach Hotel* (☎ 071-373 1244), 30 Philbeach Gardens SW5 (tube: Earls Court), is a pleasant hotel popular with a male and female gay clientele. There's a decent restaurant and bar and a nice garden. Singles with/without bathrooms are £35/40; doubles are £45/55.

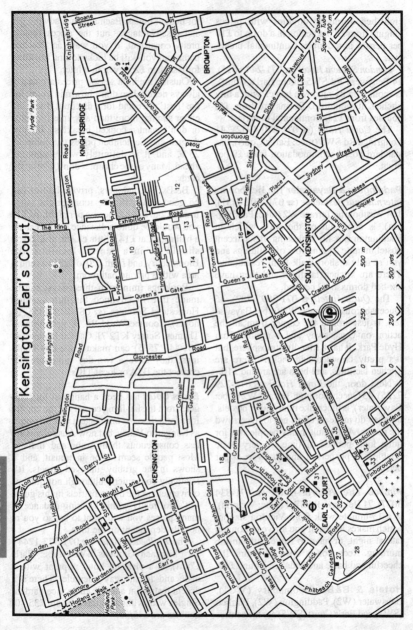

Kensington/Earl's Court

■ PLACES TO STAY

1	Holland House Youth Hostel
8	Imperial College Residence
18	Shellbourne Hotel
21	Corfu Hotel
22	Coronet Hotel
25	Maranton House Hotel
26	Curzon House Hotel
27	Airton House Youth & Student Hotel
30	London Student Hotel
31	London Tourist Hotel
32	Chelsea Hotel
35	Earl's Court Youth Hostel
36	Swiss House Hotel

▼ PLACES TO EAT

16	Spago
20	Bistro Benito
34	La Papardella

OTHER

2	Commonwealth Institute
3	Trailfinders
4	YHA Adventure Shop
5	High Street Kensington Tube
6	Albert Memorial
7	Royal Albert Hall
9	Harrods
10	Imperial College
11	Science Museum
12	Victoria & Albert Museum
13	Geological Museum
14	Natural History Museum
15	South Kensington Tube
17	STA
19	Airbus, Route A1, Stop 6
23	Top Deck Travel
24	Post Office
28	Earl's Court Exhibition Building
29	Earl's Court Tube
33	Troubadour & Encounter Overland

The *York House Hotel* (☎ 071-373 7519), 27 Philbeach Gardens SW5 (tube: Earl's Court), is relatively cheap, but you get what you pay for. The rooms are basic, although some have showers. Singles/doubles without bath are £23.50/36.43; doubles/triples with bath are £50/60.

London Tourist Hotel (☎ 071-370 4356), 15 Penywern Rd SW5 (tube: Earl's Court), is being redecorated, and those rooms that have been through the process are pleasant and a step above many others at the same price. Continental breakfasts are served in the rooms, and there are kitchen facilities you can use. Singles/doubles are £25/35.

The *Shellbourne Hotel* (☎ 071-373 5161), 1 Lexham Gardens W8 (tube: Gloucester Rd), is tatty but clean, and the rooms are well-equipped for their price – TVs, showers, direct dial telephones – and you get a full breakfast (minus the bacon, for reasons that will become obvious). Singles/doubles/triples are £26/35/43.

The *Merlyn Court Hotel* (☎ 071-370 1640), 2 Barkston Gardens SW5 (tube: Earl's Court), is an unpretentious place with a nice atmosphere. The rooms are clean, small and reasonable value. Singles with/without bathrooms are £30/28; doubles with/without £50/40; triples and quads with/without are £60/55.

The *Maranton House Hotel* (☎ 071-373 5782), 14 Barkston Gardens SW5 (tube: Earl's Court), is a pleasant hotel with a good mix of facilities. They have a couple of civilised dorms and a range of pleasant rooms. Dorms with up to six people are £10, singles are £24/35 without/with facilities, doubles are £28/40 and there are quads for £60. Prices vary; recommended.

The *Coronet Hotel* (☎ 071-373 6396), 59 Nevern Square SW5 (tube: Earl's Court), is a well-run place with decent decor and clean rooms. Singles are small, but have everything you need – TV, telephone and hairdryer, and most have en suite bathrooms with showers. It's a cut above most of the nearby choices. Singles with/without are £29/35; doubles are £49. Continental breakfast.

Pimlico is not the most attractive part of London to stay, but you are very close to the action, even if there's not much happening immediately around you. For an area that sees a large transient population, the quality of the hotels is reasonably good. In general the cheap hotels (around £25 per person) are better value than their counterparts in Earl's Court.

If only all London's budget hotels were like the *Luna & Simone Hotels* (☎ 071-834 5897), 47 Belgrave Rd SW1 (tube: Victoria). They're central, spotlessly clean, and comfortable. They don't have offensive decor. Singles without en suite are from £16 to £20; doubles without are £28, with £42. All rooms have TVs and a basin and hot and cold water and a full English breakfast is included. There are storage facilities if you want to leave some bags behind while you go travelling. Highly recommended.

The *Belgrave House Hotel* (☎ 071-828 1563), 32 Belgrave Rd SW1 (tube: Victoria), is another pleasant hotel that doesn't have a doss house atmosphere. Singles/doubles are £25/35 with private showers and TV, £20/30 without, and include a continental breakfast.

The *Romany Hotel* (☎ 071-834 5553), 35 Longmoore St SW1 (tube: Victoria), tucked away off the main streets is a homely place, quite unlike most of the hotels in the area. Parts of the building are 500 years old, and it was in one incarnation a haunt for London's highwaymen. The decor in the rooms is fairly appalling, but they are spotlessly clean. What you get is a basic room and a good breakfast – and that's all right. There's even a small courtyard. A single is £23, doubles are from £32 to £38.

The *Brindle House Hotel* (☎ 071-828 0057), 1 Warwick Place North SW1 (tube: Victoria), is another old building off the main thoroughfares. Although the decor is, once again, a mess, the rooms are much more pleasant than the foyer suggests – they're light and clean. Singles are £25 (shared facilities), doubles are £38/34 (with/without facilities).

A step up in quality and price, *Hamilton House* (☎ 071-821 7113), 60 Warwick Way SW1 (tube: Victoria), has singles/doubles with private bathrooms, TV and telephones for £54/65. The doubles are worth considering.

Chelsea & Kensington are trendy and expensive districts, but they are convenient, especially for museums and shopping, and they don't feel like tourist ghettoes.

The *Magnolia Hotel* (☎ 071-352 0187), 104 Oakley St SW3 (tube: South Kensington), has a good position, and is remarkably good value. The only drawback is a bit of a hike to the nearest tube station. The rooms are pleasant, but if possible get one at the back away from traffic noise. There's colour TV in all rooms, but only some have en suite bathrooms. Singles without are from £25 to £29, doubles are £44/39 with/without, triples are £50 to £55.

The *Swiss House Hotel* (☎ 071-373 2769), 171 Old Brompton Rd is a clean, good-value hotel, on the edge of Earl's Court. Singles/doubles without shower and toilet are £30/46 rising to £43/54 with, which is a bit steep since they only give you a continental breakfast. It is a nice place, however, and you do get a TV and a direct dial phone.

The *Vicarage Private Hotel* (☎ 071-229 4030), 10 Vicarage Gate W8 (tube: Kensington High St), is in a good location near to Hyde Park between Notting Hill and Kensington. It's a pleasant, well-kept place with good showers. Singles/doubles are £28/£50. Book ahead; recommended.

It's stretching the definition to put the *Hillgate Hotel* (☎ 071-221 3433), 6 Pembridge Gardens W2 (tube: Notting Hill Gate), in a shoestring guide, but it is a proper hotel, with a great position. It's not cheap, but if you want real civilisation and don't mind paying, it's worth considering. Singles/doubles are £45/55.

Paddington is even seedier than Earl's Court, and although there are lots of cheap hotels (or is it *because* there are lots of cheap hotels?), single women in particular will probably feel more comfortable elsewhere. It is convenient, however, and there are some decent places at decent prices.

Right in the centre of the action, the *Norfolk Court & St David's Hotel* (☎ 071-723 4963), 16 Norfolk Square W2 (tube: Paddington), is a friendly place with the usual out-of-control decor. It's clean, though, and comfortable. Basic singles/doubles have basins and colour TVs and cost £23/34. With showers and toilets en suite, prices jump to £30/£40.

Sussex Gardens is lined with small hotels and, unfortunately, is also a major traffic route. Most places aren't inspiring, but there are some gems among the dross. The *Balmoral House* (☎ 071-402 0118), 156 Sussex Gardens W2 (tube: Paddington), is an immaculate and very comfortable place with singles/doubles for £25/42. All rooms have TVs, basins and tea-making facilities and some have private facilities. A full English breakfast is served.

The *Albro House Hotel* (☎ 071-724 2931), 155 Sussex Gardens W2 (tube: Paddington), is spartan but OK, and there are some nice rooms. Singles with/without showers are £30/22; doubles with/without are particularly good value at £38/34. A full English breakfast is served.

The *Glynne Court Hotel* (☎ 071-262 4344), 41 Great Cumberland Place W1 (tube: Marble Arch), is not in the main hotel zone at all. In fact, it has a great position behind Marble Arch. Although the hotel has seen better days it is being slowly renovated, and even the old rooms have charm. All have TVs and telephones. Singles/doubles are £30/40, but you only get a continental breakfast.

Bayswater is extremely convenient and some parts feel as if they are under constant invasion. Some of the streets immediately to the west of Queensway – which has an excellent selection of restaurants – are depressingly rundown.

The *Oxford Hotel* (☎ 071-262 9608), 13 Craven Terrace (tube: Lancaster Gate), is very good value, although needless to say it's pretty basic. Still, you get clean rooms (some with private facilities), kitchen facilities and a cheerful welcome. Singles/doubles are £18/30.

Sass House (☎ 071-402 0281), 11 Craven Terrace (tube: Lancaster Gate), is about as basic and threadbare as they come, but, for once, the prices reflect this state of affairs

fairly. Singles range from £12 to £18 and doubles from £20 to £28, depending on your bargaining ability, the weather...

One of the best options in Bayswater is the *Garden Court Hotel* (☎ 071-229 2553), 30 Kensington Gardens Square W2 (tube: Bayswater). It's a well-run, well-maintained family hotel, with well-equipped rooms. They all have telephones and TVs. Breakfasts are good. Singles/doubles without bathrooms are £26/38, with bathrooms £38/51.

Bloomsbury is very convenient, especially for the West End. It's a peculiar mix made up of London University, the British Museum, beautiful squares, Georgian architecture, traffic, office workers, students and tourists. In general, it is a little more expensive than the other areas, but the hotels also tend to be a little better. It's definitely worth considering.

Tucked away to the north of Russell Square, around Cartwright Gardens, there is a group of the most comfortable, attractive and best value hotels in London, and they're still easy walking distance from the West End. They're on a crescent around a leafy garden, and although they aren't the cheapest places in London, they are worth it if you have the money to spend.

Jenkin's Hotel (☎ 071-387 2067), 45 Cartwright Gardens WC1 (tube: Russell Square), has attractive comfortable rooms, with style. All have basins, TVs, telephones and fridges, and prices include English breakfasts. Singles/doubles are £33/46; doubles with private facilities are £56. Guests can even use the tennis courts in the gardens across the road.

The *Crescent Hotel* (☎ 071-387 1515), 49 Cartwright Gardens WC1 (tube: Russell Square), is a bigger place, but it is still a family-owned operation of a high standard, with basically the same prices as Jenkin's. The *Euro & George Hotels* are also good and are around the same price.

There's a row of places along Gower St, and they all seem to be pretty fair value. Not all of them have double glazing on the front

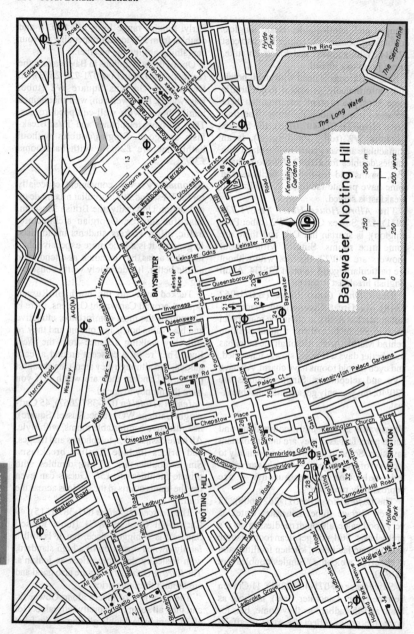

Bayswater/Notting Hill

windows, which is essential if you are sensitive to traffic noise. Otherwise, insist on one of the back rooms overlooking the garden, which happen to be the nicest anyway.

The *Arran House Hotel* (☎ 071-636 2186), 77 Gower St WC1 (tube: Goodge St), is a friendly, welcoming place with a great garden. Singles range from £28 to £35 (with shower and toilet), doubles from £40 to £52, and there are also trebles and quads. They have sound-proofing on their front rooms,

and all have colour TV and telephones. There are also laundry facilities.

The *Hotel Cavendish* (☎ 071-636 9079), at No 75, and the *Jesmond Hotel* (☎ 071-636 3199), at No 63, are both fairly basic, but clean and entirely adequate. They have singles/doubles for £25/36. You share bathrooms, although all rooms have basins and you get a full English breakfast.

The *Repton Hotel* (☎ 071-636 7045), 31 Bedford Place WC1 (tube: Russell Square), is pretty good value considering its position – Bedford Place is not nearly as busy as Gower St. There are TVs and telephones in all rooms; singles/doubles are £28/40 if you share facilities and doubles are £52 if you don't. They also have one dorm with six beds at £12 per person.

If all you want is a room, and you don't mind noise and primitive facilities, you'll be happy with the *Royal Hotel* (☎ 071-636 8401), Woburn Place WC1 (tube: Russell Square). There certainly aren't many cheaper options, and it is clean enough. Singles/doubles are £17.50/30.

Rental Prices for rental accommodation are high and standards are low. At the bottom end of the market there are bedsits – a single furnished room, usually with a shared bathroom and kitchen, although some have basic cooking facilities. Expect to pay £50 to £100 per week. The next step up is a studio, which normally has a separate bathroom and kitchen, for between £75 and £120. One-bedroom flats average between £90 and £135. Shared houses and flats are the best value, with a bedroom for between £40 and £60 plus bills.

Rooms and flats are advertised at the New Zealand News UK office in the Royal Opera Arcade behind New Zealand House, in *TNT Magazine*, *Time Out*, the *Evening Standard* and *Loot*. If you decide to use an agency, check that it doesn't charge fees to tenants.

Places to Eat
It's difficult to eat out in London at a reasonable price, although the situation is gradually improving. In general, eating out is the prov-

GREAT BRITAIN

ince of those with money; you'll be lucky to get a decent meal and a glass of wine for less than £10 per head, except in pubs where the food is usually very average. If you do want to keep your costs down, resist the temptation of alcohol, which is always ridiculously expensive.

Indian restaurants are consistently good value; unfortunately they often tone down their spices for the English palate. There are an increasing number of pasta places, which can be good, especially if they're run by Italians (a lot aren't). Chinese restaurants are also worth considering. It's very difficult to find good-quality English cuisine at a reasonable price.

There's a surprising lack of good guides to London restaurants – the best is the *Time Out – Eating & Drinking in London* (£3.95), but it doesn't have much for shoestringers and it's difficult to wade through. *Just a Bite*, an Egon Ronay Guide (£7.95), is aimed at those eating out on a budget and is a worthwhile purchase if you're planning to spend time in the city. *Cheap Eats in London* by Sandra Gustafson (£5.95) covers a fairly a limited number of places, but the choice is interesting.

There are number of hunting grounds in the West End: around Covent Garden, especially north-east between Endell St and Monmouth St; around Soho, especially north-west of the intersection of Charing Cross Rd and Shaftesbury Ave (including Old Compton St and Frith St); north of Leicester Square on Lisle St and Gerrard St (for Chinese). If you're looking for a peaceful oasis make for Neal's Yard in Covent Garden, a flower-bedecked courtyard surrounded by cheap vegetarian eateries.

Camden Town (NW1) has a cosmopolitan range of restaurants and cafes that can become very crowded on the weekend. Start at Mornington Crescent and wander north-west along Camden High St and its continuation Chalk Farm Rd for a good selection.

The hotel zone around Bayswater (W2) is well served by moderately priced restaurants along Queensway and Westbourne Grove.

There are some interesting possibilities around Notting Hill – a couple of places at the south end of Pembridge Rd and on Hillgate St across Notting Hill Gate, and around Blenheim Crescent and its intersection with Portobello Rd.

Earl's Court (SW5) is full of budget eateries – along Earl's Court Rd, and the streets opposite the tube station (Hogarth Rd for one) and around the intersection of Earl's Court Rd and Old Brompton Rd.

There are a couple of reasonable places in South Kensington (SW7), especially around the tube and on Old Brompton Rd. Further afield, Chiswick High St (W4) has a range of good-value restaurants, many of which spill out on a pleasant tree-lined road – it's hard to believe you're still in London.

There are a number of places to look for Indian food. Brick Lane (E1) in the East End, has a number of cheap, but good, Bangladeshi restaurants; Stoke Newington Church St (N16) has a row of interesting restaurants, a number of which are Indian; and for South Indian menus, which are particularly good for vegetarians, there are some excellent places on Drummond St (NW1).

The main centre for Chinese food is still around Gerrard St, Soho, which has been given the obligatory Chinatown visual effects. There are also a number of good places on Queensway, Bayswater.

Covent Garden *Café Pasta* (☎ 071-379 0198), 184 Shaftesbury Ave (tube: Covent Garden), produces simple but good food at reasonable prices. It's a pleasant little restaurant, not part of an enormous chain. Pastas range from £4 to £5 and are generous in size. A glass of house wine is £1.75.

Diana's Diner (☎ 071-240 0272), 39 Endell St (tube: Covent Garden), is very basic, but it's also very cheap. The food is not inspiring, but it's OK. Spaghetti is from £3 and you'll find a range of grills and roasts from £3.50 to £4.

Café Pacifico (☎ 071-379 7728), 5 Langley St (tube: Covent Garden), serves generous servings of good quality Mexican food. It's a fun and bustling place. Share some dips – guacamole and nachos for £3.75 – then hoe into some enchiladas (two for £5.95, including rice and beans) and you should be safe. Watch out for the margheritas, however. They're very good and very expensive (£3.50 a glass or £24.50 for an eight-glass pitcher). You can blow your mind and your budget very quickly.

Food for Thought (☎ 071-836 0239), 31 Neal St WC2 (tube: Covent Garden), is a small and reliable vegetarian place. The menu features dishes like spinach and mushroom South Indian bake for £2.40, stir-fried vegetables for £2.10. It's nonsmoking, but you can bring your own bottle.

Neal's Yard is a peaceful escape from the West End bustle. There are a number of good-value and healthy takeaway places and a branch of Cranks (part of a well-known vegetarian chain), all grouped around a flower-bedecked courtyard. *Neal's Yard Bakery & Tea Room* (☎ 071-836 5199), 6 Neal's Yard (tube: Covent Garden), is the star performer, however. It has limited, but very good, wholefood vegetarian offerings for between £2 and £5. They're open until 6 pm Monday to Friday and until 4.30 pm on Saturdays. Neal's Yard is signposted from Neal St, and is off Short's Gardens.

Café in the Crypt (☎ 071-839 4342), St Martin-in-the-Fields Church, on Trafalgar Square (tube: Charing Cross), is in a tastefully renovated and atmospheric crypt under the church. The food is good and there are plenty of offerings for vegetarians. Most mains are from £5 to £6. Unfortunately dinner is only served to 8.30 pm, Monday to Saturday, although it is open for lunch on Sundays.

Cheap fuel is available from a number of pizza counters on the north-east corner of Leicester Square. Check the current offers, but you should be able to get a slice of pizza and some salad for £1.

Soho *Poons* (☎ 071-437 4549), 27 Lisle St WC2 (tube: Leicester Square), is where the up-market Poons empire started. It's tiny, with classic laminex tables and fluorescent lights, but it has exceptional food at very good prices. They specialise in superb wind dried meats. The dried duck is heavenly, and the steamed chicken is equally sensational. If you're hungry, start with soup and order perhaps two dishes and rice, you'll pay around £8 per person. Be prepared to queue at busy times, and to be hustled out the door pretty quickly.

Wong Kei (☎ 071-437 8408), 41 Wardour St W1 (tube: Leicester Square), is famous for the rudeness of the waiters. Some find this adds to the experience, but even if you don't you might be tempted by the food, which is cheap and good Cantonese. A set menu starts at £5.30.

Stockpot (☎ 071-839 5142), 40 Panton St SW1 (tube: Piccadilly Circus), is popular with theatre-goers, so it can be very busy in the evenings. The menu is not particularly inspired, but the meals are very good value with casseroles for around £2.50, moussaka for £2.30 and house wine at £1.40 a glass. There are also branches at 6 Basil St, Knightsbridge, 18 Old Compton St, Soho, and 273 King's Rd, Chelsea.

Nusa Dua (☎ 071-437 3559), 11 Dean St, W1 (tube: Tottenham Court Rd), is a rather garish Indonesian restaurant, but the prices are fair. Most main courses are from £4 to £6. The tofu and tempeh are excellent and there are plenty of vegetarian offerings.

Pizza Express (☎ 071-437 9595), 10 Dean St W1 (tube: Tottenham Court Rd), might not sound very appealing, but it is in fact unusually good. At street level you get cheap, good quality pizzas from £3 to £5 and a glass of wine for £1.85; downstairs you get to eat accompanied by excellent jazz (admission downstairs is around £6).

Pasta Fino (☎ 071-722 2282), 27 Frith St W1 (tube: Tottenham Court Rd), is a pleasant restaurant with excellent home-made pasta served with a range of traditional sauces; you'll pay between £4 and £5 for the pasta, £2 for a glass of wine. There's another branch opposite the Chalk Farm tube station.

La Perla (☎ 071-437 2060), 28 Brewer St W1 (tube: Piccadilly Circus), is a classic Italian restaurant, with good service and good quality food. A main course pasta will cost £4.80, but if the budget allows, try something like the fritto misto di mare (including sole, calamari, whitebait and scampi) for £6.80.

Men's Bar Hamine (☎ 071-439 0785), 84 Brewer St W1 (tube: Piccadilly Circus), is a spartan Japanese noodle restaurant – *men* apparently means noodle in Japanese and does not refer to the clientele. The food is very good, with dishes around £6.

Pollo (☎ 071-734 5917), 20 Old Compton St W1 (tube: Leicester Square), attracts an art-student crowd with numerous pastas for around £3. It can be very busy.

Govindas (☎ 071-437 3662), 10 Soho St W1 (tube: Tottenham Court Rd), is run by Radha Krishna followers. There's no attempt to convert. The meals are fairly plain vegetarian, but they are generous in size: vegetable lasagne with salad is £3.80, a large thali is £8.45. It closes at 9 pm.

Stepping into the *New Piccadilly* (☎ 071-437 8530), 8 Denman St (tube: Piccadilly Circus), is like stepping into a time warp – nothing, except the prices, has changed since it first opened in the 1950s. Even the prices haven't changed as much as you would expect: pastas and pizzas are around £2.50, chicken and steaks weigh in around £3.50.

Melati (☎ 071-437 2745), 21 Great Windmill St W1 (tube: Piccadilly Circus), is a highly acclaimed Malaysian restaurant with excellent food and a good range of options for vegetarians. Gado-gado is £4.55, various noodle and rice dishes are under £5. You'll probably spend around £10.

L'Escargot (☎ 071-437 2679), 48 Greek St W1 (tube: Tottenham Court Rd), is a very good French brasserie/restaurant. The restaurant (upstairs) is seriously expensive, but if you are planning a splurge, the brasserie might be within reach. The pre-theatre menu is £12.50; you could spend plenty more. Booking is essential.

Mildred's (☎ 071-494 1634), 58 Greek St W1 (tube: Tottenham Court Rd), is only small, so you may well share a table. The chaos is worth it however, because the vegetarian food is both good and well priced. Expect to pay around £4.50 for a main meal

with delicious fresh flavours, £1.85 for a glass of wine.

St James *The Wren at St James* (☎ 071-437 9419), 35 Jermyn St SW3 (tube: Piccadilly Circus), is the perfect escape from the West End, but it is only open during the day. It adjoins St James church (which often has free lunch-time concerts) and in summer it spills out into the shady churchyard. There are plenty of vegetarian dishes for around £3.50, and excellent homemade cakes.

Bloomsbury & Holborn *The Greenhouse* (☎ 071-637 8038), 16 Chenies St WC1 (tube: Goodge St), is part of the Drill Hall complex; it is not open on Sundays. It's busy, so expect to share a table. The reason it's busy is the excellent vegetarian food, with main courses around £3.50.

The *North Sea Fish Restaurant* (☎ 071-387 5892), 7 Leigh St WC1 (tube: Russell Square), sets out to cook fresh fish and potatoes well. A limited ambition, but one that British fish & chip shops rarely achieve. The North Sea does. The fish (deep-fried or grilled) and a huge serving of chips will set you back from £4 to £5.

Mille Pini (☎ 071-242 2434), 33 Boswell St WC1 (tube: Holborn), is a true Italian restaurant with reasonable prices. You'll waddle out, but you'll only spend about £10 if you have two courses and coffee.

Bayswater There are literally dozens of places on Queensway and Westbourne Grove – from cheap takeaways to good quality restaurants. Surprisingly, there are even some pleasant and popular restaurants on the 2nd floor of Whiteley's shopping centre – although there are not particularly cheap. *Poons* has a set menu for £12, *Santé Brasserie* has a set menu for £9.95, and *Mamma Amalfi* has decent Italian food.

The cheapest pit-stop on Queensway is *Fish & Chips*, opposite the intersection with Moscow Rd, which has fish & chips with salad for £2.50 and pizza with salad for £1. Across the road, there is also a branch of the reliable *Prima Pasta* chain, with good pastas around £5.

For something a little more interesting, you could try the *Rasa Sayang* (☎ 071-229 8417), 38 Queensway W2 (tube: Queensway), which is part of a small but reliable chain – there's another branch in Frith St, Soho. The speciality is Malay/Chinese food, with good-sized portions and plenty of dishes under £5. From noon to 6 pm they have an all-you-can-eat buffet for £5.90.

Micro-Kalamaris (☎ 071-727 9122), 76 Inverness Mews W2 (tube: Queensway), is the cheaper sibling of Mega-Kalamaris in the same mews, parallel to Queensway. Conditions are a bit micro, but the food is macro. Dips are under £2 and main courses are around £4 – you should eat well for around £10.

Khan's (☎ 071-727 5420), 13 Westbourne Grove W2 (tube: Bayswater), is one of the largest and best Indian restaurants – it's authentic, the decor is smart, and it's good value. They have vegetarian dishes and a selection of meat curries £3. A vegetarian thali is £5.25.

Kams (☎ 071-727 8859), 52 Westbourne Park Rd W11 (tube: Ladbroke Grove), has excellent dim sum, popular with Chinese on Sundays, but served here every evening as well. Items on the selection range from £1.50 to £2.50 and you can eat well for around £10 per person. There are set Chinese menus from £9.50 per person.

Nachos (☎ 071-792 0954), 147 Notting Hill Gate W11 (tube: Notting Hill Gate), is a large and popular Mexican joint with all the standards at decent prices. Guacamole dip is £2.75 and most main courses – tacos and nachos and such – are around £5.50.

Notting Hill & Ladbroke Grove *Savvas' Kebab House* (☎ 071-727 9720), 7 Ladbroke Rd W11 (tube: Notting Hill Gate), has unpretentious Greek food at reasonable prices; the best bit is the outdoor eating area. There are all the standards, including moussaka and other main courses for around £4, dips at £1.50.

Costa's Grill (☎ 071-229 3794), 14 Hillgate St W8 (tube: Notting Hill Gate), is another reliable Greek place, a fraction cheaper than Savvas with dips at £1.20 and mains like souvlakia for £4.

Topo D'Oro (☎ 071-727 5813), Farmer St W8 (tube: Notting Hill Gate), is a good-value Italian restaurant, in an area where there are quite a few. Here minestrone costs £2.50, pasta is £3.60. Mouthwatering mains are around £5 – try the petti di pollo topo d'oro (breast of chicken stuffed with ham, parsley, garlic and butter).

Across the road, *Geales* (☎ 071-727 4310), 2 Farmer St W8 (tube: Notting Hill Gate), is a very popular fish restaurant in the old-fashioned English style. The fish is priced according to weight and season, and is always fresh. You should get away with two courses and a glass of wine for under £10.

Portobello Dining Rooms (☎ 071-243 0958), 6-8 All Saints Rd W11 (tube: Ladbroke Grove/Westbourne Park), is a trendy and interesting place with artsy post-apocolyptic decor and eclectic food at reasonable prices. Lentil soup £1.50, and main meals like mandarin chicken with noodles, vegetables and rice for £6. Open lunch Saturday and Sunday, dinner every day.

Pimlico *Manners* (☎ 071- 828 2471), 1 Denbigh St SW1 (tube: Victoria), offers a decent range of dishes at a very good price. Their three-course set dinner is £7.95.

O Sole Mio (☎ 071-976 6887), 39 Churton St SW1 (tube: Victoria), is a standard, decent-value Italian restaurant with pizzas and pastas under £5. Next door, *Grumbles* is a pleasant wine bar with, amongst other things, salad for £2.85, vegetable loaf for £4.45, kebabs for £5.25.

Mekong (☎ 071-834 6896), 46 Churton St SW1 (tube: Victoria), is reputed to be one of the best Vietnamese restaurants in London. It's a bit beyond a shoestring budget, but they do have a set meal for £12.50, and house wine is reasonable at £1.85.

GREAT BRITAIN

Chelsea The *Chelsea Kitchen* (☎ 071-589 1330), 98 King's Rd SW3 (tube: Sloane Square), has some of the cheapest food in London – and it ain't half bad. The surroundings are pretty spartan, however. Minestrone is 60p, spaghetti is £1.80 and apple crumble is 70p.

If the weather is decent make for the Chelsea Farmers Market on Sydney St. There are a number of small stalls that spill out into a pleasant outdoor area. Among them, the *Sydney St Café* has burgers and steak sandwiches around £4.50. The *Il Cappuccino* has coffee for £1.

South Kensington *Spago* (☎ 071-225 2407), 6 Glendower Place SW7 (tube: South Kensington), is the best value restaurant in the vicinity, which can be reflected in queues. The reason? A good range of pastas and pizzas from £3.30 to £5.

La Bouchée, Old Brompton Rd SW7 (tube: South Kensington), is a small but atmospheric bistro with good quality food, including a *menu prix fixe* for £8.95 up until 8 pm.

Earl's Court *La Papardella* (☎ 071-373 7777), 253 Old Brompton Rd SW5 (tube: Earl's Court), is a busy pizzeria opening onto the pavement. The pizzas are good, but cost from £6 to £7.

The *Troubadour*, 265 Old Brompton Rd (tube: Earl's Court), has an illustrious history as a coffee shop and folk venue. Amongst others it has hosted Dylan, Donovan and Lennon. These days they still occasionally have bands, and they also have good-value food. Service is slow, but the wait is worthwhile; order at the counter. Vegetable soup is £1.85; pasta is £4.

Bistro Benito, Earls Court Rd SW5 (tube: Earl's Court), is a fairly typical Italian bistro, but it's friendly and decent value. Pastas are around £4.95, entrees are from £2 to £3, fish and meat main courses are from £5 to £8.

Karyatis (☎ 071-259 2525), 174 Earls Court Rd SW5 (tube: Earls Court), is a moderately priced Greek restaurant with main

meals of moussaka or dolmades for around £5, souvlaki for £6. Dips are £2.15.

Benjy's, Earls Court Rd SW5 (tube: Earls Court), is an institution. It's really nothing more than a fairly traditional café, but it's always busy and although the food is nothing to write home about, it is cheap and filling. Serious breakfasts with as much tea or coffee as you can drink are around £2.50. There are grills for around £4.

China Kitchen (☎ 071-370 2533), 36A Kenway Rd SW5 (tube: Earls Court), is a pleasant Chinese restaurant, a step up from the laminex decor one expects. The prices are reasonable, especially the lunches. There are set lunches for £5 from 12.30 to 4.30 pm.

Camden *Bar Gansa* (☎ 071- 267 8909), 2 Inverness St NW1 (tube: Camden Town), a winner of the Time Out best tapas bar award, is a noisy, trendy, cheerful place with most tapas around £3 (you'll need three each).

A quieter alternative is the *El Parador* (☎ 071-834 8746), 245 Eversholt St (tube: Mornington Crescent). There's an attractive outdoor eating area and the tapas are authentically delicious (around £2 to £2.50). Recommended.

Sanur (☎ 071-388 6905), 31 Camden High St (tube: Mornington Crescent), is a popular Indonesian restaurant with excellent food. They have a budget meal for £3.70, or you can have the vegetarian set menu for £9. Entrees are around £1.80 and mains are around £4.

Ruby in the Dust (☎ 071-485 2744), 102 Camden High St (tube: Camden Town), is an atmospheric bar/café – it's worth a trek across town. There isn't a huge menu, but it's interesting: Mexican snacks, soup for £2.45 and mains like fresh trout for £4.65.

Stoke Newington *Spices* (☎ 071-254 0528), 30 Stoke Newington Church St N16 (tube: Finsbury Park, BR: Stoke Newington), is a good-value Indian restaurant in a street that is full of restaurants. A vegetarian special thali is good value at £5.65. Resist the pressure to drink expensive Indian beer.

Shamsudeen's (☎ 071-254 5696), 119

Stoke Newington Church St N16 (tube: Finsbury Park, BR: Stoke Newington), is a fine institution that has been serving excellent Malay/Indian food at low prices for a long time. It's busy so you may have to wait in the pub across the road, but that's OK. Main courses like curries and nasi goreng are around £4.

Hampstead *Coffee Cup* (☎ 071-435 7565), 74 Hampstead High St NW3 (tube: Hampstead), is a popular cafe with a wide-ranging menu from bacon and eggs to pasta. There's something for every taste and every time of day. Good value.

East End *Ravi Shankar* (☎ 071-833 5849), 422 St John St EC1 (tube: Angel), is a small but inexpensive restaurant favoured by vegetarians – their all-you-can-eat lunch-time buffets for £3.90 are extremely popular. They have another branch at 133 Drummond St NW1 (tube: Warren St).

The Kosher Luncheon Club (☎ 071-247 0039), 13 Greatorex St E1 (tube: Aldgate East), is open from noon to 3 pm from Monday to Friday and Sundays. It's ideally placed if you've worked up an appetite at the Brick Lane or Petticoat Lane markets. The decor is plain, but the food is good-quality and authentic.

Beigel Bake (☎ 071-729 0616), 159 Brick Lane E1 (tube: Whitechapel), is at the Bethnal Green Rd end of Brick Lane – the bagels can't get any fresher (or cheaper, from 10p), and there are fillings like cream cheese and smoked salmon (from 75p). It's very cheap, very delicious and open 24 hours daily.

There are a number of cheap Bangladeshi restaurants on Brick Lane, including *Aladin* (☎ 071-247 8210) at 132 and *Nazrul* at 130 (tube: Aldgate East). Both are unlicensed, but you should eat for around £7.

Bloom's (☎ 081-455 3033), 90 Whitechapel High St E1 (tube: Aldgate East), is a traditional and strict Kosher restaurant, closed Friday and Sunday evenings and all Saturday. Gefilte fish (£2.50), boiled chicken (£5.90), latkes (£1.20), apple strudel

(£2.20) are on the menu. The food is heavy, so make sure you have an appetite.

Entertainment
The essential tool is *Time Out* (£1.30), which is published every Tuesday and covers a week of events. The only danger is that there is so much happening you'll be paralysed with indecision.

The biggest problem is transport. The last trains leave between 11.30 pm and 12.30 am (depending on the station and line), so you either have to figure out the night buses or pay for a minicab. The second-biggest problem is that most pubs close at 11 pm. That's not a misprint. Fortunately, there are clubs where you can continue partying, although you'll have to pay to enter (£5 to £10) and the drinks are always expensive.

Late-night venues often choose to have a 'club' license, which means you have to be a member to enter. In practice, they usually include the membership fee as part of the admission price. Many venues have clubs that only operate one night a week, and have a particular angle – whether it be the style of music they play or the kind of people they attract.

They can change with bewildering speed – and they sometimes use the membership requirement to exclude people they don't think will fit in. In some places you'll be excluded if you wear jeans, runners and a T-shirt, in others you'll be excluded if you don't. It's not a bad idea to phone in advance to get an idea of cost and membership policy.

The major venues for live, contemporary music include the *Brixton Academy* (☎ 071-326 1022), 211 Stockwell Rd SW2 (tube: Brixton); the *Astoria* (☎ 071-434 0403), 157 Charing Cross Rd WC2 (tube: Tottenham Court Rd); the *Hammersmith Odeon* (☎ 081-748 4081), Queen Caroline St W6 (tube: Hammersmith); and the *Wembley Arena* (☎ 081- 900 1234), Empire Way, Middlesex (tube: Wembley Park).

Smaller places with a more 'club-like' atmosphere that are worth checking for interesting bands include the *Borderline* (☎ 071-437 8595), Orange Yard, off Manette

St WC2 (tube: Tottenham Court Rd); the *100 Club* (☎ 071-636 0933), 100 Oxford St W1 (tube: Tottenham Court Rd); the *Town & Country Club* (☎ 071-284 0303), 9-17 Highgate Rd NW5 (tube: Kentish Town); and the *Marquee* (☎ 071-437 6603), 105 Charing Cross Rd WC2 (tube: Leicester Square). Ring ahead to find what kind of band you'll get.

Venues that are usually reliable for club nights and recorded music include: *The Brain Club* (☎ 071-437 7301), 11 Wardour St W1 (tube: Leicester Square); the *Camden Palace* (☎ 071-387 0428), 1 Camden Rd NW1 (tube: Mornington Crescent); *The Fridge*, Town Hall Parade SW2 (tube: Brixton); *The Milk Bar* (☎ 071-439 4655), 12 Sutton Row W1 (tube: Tottenham Court Rd); and the *Electric Ballroom* (☎ 071-485 9006), 184 Camden High St NW1 (tube: Camden Town).

If you're a jazz fan, keep your eye on the *Bass Clef* (☎ 071-729 2476), 35 Coronet St N1 (tube: Old Street); *Ronnie Scott's* (☎ 071-439 0747), 47 Frith St W1 (tube: Leicester Square); and the *Jazz Café* (☎ 071-284 4358), 5 Parkway NW1 (tube: Camden Town).

London theatre and music are extraordinarily diverse, high quality (at their best) and extremely reasonably priced by world standards. Even if you don't normally go to the theatre, you really should have a look at the reviews and organise yourself cheap tickets for one or two of the best productions. The National Theatre (which is actually three theatres: the Olivier, the Lyttleton and the Cottesloe) puts on consistently good performances, often with some of the best young actors and directors around.

The Leicester Square Theatre Ticket Booth, on the south side of Leicester Square sells half-price tickets (plus £1.35 commission) on the day of performance. They open from noon on matinee days for matinee tickets and from 2.30 to 6.30 pm, Monday to Saturday, for evening tickets. The queues can be awesome.

A number of theatres and concert halls have standby tickets 90 minutes before performances. A ticket to the Royal Shakespeare Company ranges from £5 for students to £20 for the best seats. If you're prepared to watch from the highest seats in the house, you can see the opera at Covent Garden for £2.50. The National Theatre on the South Bank sells cheap back-row tickets for each of its theatres from 10 am on the day of performance – get there an hour early to get near the front of the queue, maximum two tickets to each customer. All these offers are advertised in *Time Out*.

Getting There & Away
London is the major gateway to Britain, so Getting There & Away information has been given in the introductory transport sections of this chapter. Look up your proposed British destination for prices and possibilities to/from London.

A number of companies have visa and medical (immunisation) services; a few advertise in TNT. Charges can differ widely. Trailfinders (☎ 071-938 3999), 194 Kensington High St W8, has both a visa service and an immunisation centre. The International Medical Centre (☎ 071-486 3063) has three branches, including one at the Top Deck (Deckers) headquarters, 131 Earl's Court Rd SW5. Top Deck also hosts the Rapid Visa Service (☎ 071-373 3026).

Air See the following Getting Around section for info on transport to/from the airports.

Bus Bus travellers will arrive at Victoria Coach Station, Buckingham Palace Rd, about 10 minutes' walk south of Victoria Railway Station. It is one of the most unpleasant, badly organised bus stations in the world – which is quite an achievement, because the competition is tough. If you do have to wait around, head to *The Well* across Ecclestone Place from the disgusting bus station café – it's a clean, peaceful oasis with cheap food.

Train There are eight major train stations in London, and all are connected by tube. If your train goes via south-east England (to/from France, Belgium, Spain or Italy), Victoria is the station; to/from Harwich or Felixstowe (for Germany, the Netherlands and Scandinavia), Liverpool St is your station; to/from Newcastle (for Scandinavia), King's Cross is your station. A new international terminal is being built at Waterloo for the service that will use the Channel Tunnel.

Britrail has information centres at all its main stations. See the London Information section for phone numbers.

Getting Around
To/From Airports Transport to/from London's four airports is as follows:

Heathrow The airport is accessible by bus and underground, but the underground is the cheapest, most reliable method (between 5 am and 12 pm). The station for Terminals 1, 2 and 3 is directly linked to the terminus buildings; there is a separate station in Terminal 4. Check which terminal your flight uses when you reconfirm. The adult single fare is £2.50, or use an All Zone Travelcard which is £3.40. The journey time from central London is about 50 minutes.

The Airbus (☎ 071-222 1234) services are also useful; there are two routes, the A1 which runs along Cromwell Rd to Victoria, and the A2 which runs along Notting Hill Gate and Bayswater Rd to Russell Square. Buses run every half hour and cost £5. A minicab to central London will cost from around £20; a metered black cab around £35.

Gatwick Express train services run nonstop between the main terminal and Victoria every 15 minutes between 6 am and 11.30 pm, then every hour. Singles are £7.50 and the journey time is around 45 minutes. Gatwick has north and south terminals linked by a monorail; check which terminal your flight uses when you reconfirm. BA customers can check in at Victoria. A minicab to central London will cost around £35, a metered black cab around £60.

Luton Catch the airport-station *Luton Flyer* bus outside the arrivals hall for a 15-minute trip to the train station (single/returns are £1.50/£2.50). The train takes about 45 minutes to King's Cross or St Pancras (£6.40). There are regular services approximately every 20 minutes, starting early and finishing late.

Stansted There is a direct train link to Liverpool St, which takes 45 minutes and costs £9.10. You can change at Tottenham Hale for the West End and other Victoria Line stations, including Victoria. There are trains every half hour.

Bus & Underground London Regional Transport is responsible for the buses and the tube. It has a number of information centres where you can get free maps, tickets, and information on night buses. See the London Information section.

Buses are much more interesting and pleasant to use than the tube, although they can be frustratingly slow. There are four types of tickets: one-journey bus tickets sold on the bus (minimum 50p), weekly bus passes, single or return tube tickets (sold at stations, sometimes from vending machines, minimum 80p), and Travelcards.

Travelcards are the easiest and cheapest option, and they can be used on all forms of transport (Network SouthEast trains in London, buses and tubes) after 9.30 am. London is divided into concentric rings, or zones, and the travelcard you need will depend on how many zones you cross. Most visitors will find that a Zone 1 & 2 card will be sufficient (£2.50). Weekly Travelcards are also available; they require an identification card with a passport photo (Zone 1 & 2 is £10). If you plan to start moving before 9.30 you can buy a Zone 1 & 2 LT Card (London Transport Card) for £3.50.

Times of the last tube trains vary from 11.30 pm to 12.30 am depending on the station and the line. A reasonably comprehensive network of night buses runs from or through Trafalgar Square – get to the Square and ask. London Regional Transport publishes a free timetable, *Buses for Night Owls*, which lists them all. One Day Travelcards cannot be used, but Weekly Travelcards can.

Train Britrail's subsidiary, Network South-East, runs passenger trains in London; most lines interchange with the tube. Travelcards can be used.

Taxi The classic London black cabs (☎ 071-253 5000 or 071-272 0272) are excellent, but not cheap. A cab is available for hire when the yellow sign is lit. Fares are metered and a 10% to 15% tip is expected. They can carry five people.

Minicabs are cheap, freelance competitors to the black cabs; anyone with a car can work, but they can only be hired by phone. Some have a very limited idea of how to get around efficiently (and safely). They don't have meters, so it is essential to get a quote before you start. They can carry four people.

Small minicab companies are based in particular areas – ask a local for the name of a reputable company – or phone one of the large 24-hour operations (☎ 071-272 2612, or 071-602 1234, or 081-340 2450, or 081-560 5346).

Car & Motorbike If you're blessed/cursed with private transport, avoid peak hours (7.30 to 9 am, 4.30 to 7 pm), and plan ahead if you will need to park in the centre. Cars parked illegally will be clamped, which is as agonising as it sounds. A clamp is locked on a wheel and in order to have it removed you have to travel across town, pay an enormous fine, then wait most of the day for someone to come and release you. Phone National Car Parks (☎ 071-499 7050) for car park addresses; rates vary. You're best to forget this option and stick with the public transport – you don't need the aggro.

Boat There is quite a range of services on the river. See the Greenwich, Kew Gardens and Hampton Court Palace sections for two popular trips. The main starting points are at

Westminster Bridge and Charing Cross. For information, phone ☎ 071-730 4812.

Tours A number of companies offer tours around the main sights in double-decker buses. They're all expensive and are really only worth considering if you've either got plenty of money or you're only going to be in London for a day or two. The *Original London Sightseeing Tour* has a 1½ hour tour departing from Victoria St near Victoria Station for £8. *London Plus* has a more extensive route and you can hop on and off the buses at a number of major attractions. They also depart from Victoria St, but they charge £10.

AROUND LONDON
Because of the speed of the train system, a surprisingly large region can be visited on day trips – all of England south-east of an arc drawn through Bournemouth to Bath, Stratford-upon-Avon, Leicester and Norwich.

South-East England

At times, the counties of Kent, Surrey, East and West Sussex, and Hampshire seem like a rural extension of London. Fast, regular trains make it possible for thousands of commuters to work in London, but, equally, make it possible to see much of this region on day trips from London. For this very reason, you'd do best to avoid most of the popular sights on weekends.

While many of the towns and villages are virtual dormitories for London workers, it is still a region exceptionally rich in beauty and history. This has always been Britain's frontline, a mere 35 km (22 miles) from the French coast. Names like Hastings, Dover and Portsmouth inevitably invoke images of invasion and war.

A controversial new invasion will begin sometime in 1993 when the Channel Tunnel finally opens, drawing Britain into an even closer European orbit. Those bold enough to travel underwater from France will pop up

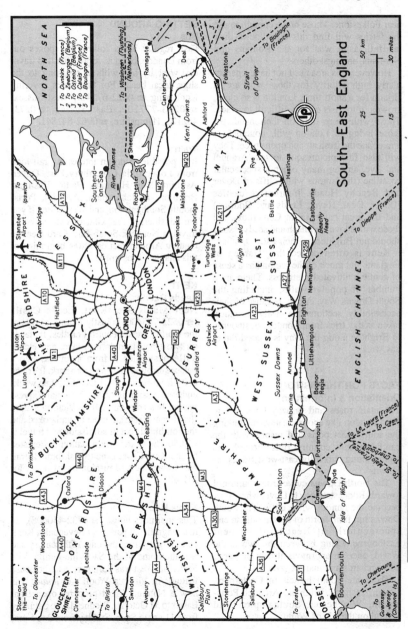

South-East England

1 To Dunkirk (France)
2 To Zeebrugge (Belgium)
3 To Ostend (Belgium)
4 To Calais (France)
5 To Boulogne (France)

NORTH SEA

To Vlissingen (Flushing)/Boulogne (France)

To Boulogne (France)

Ramsgate
Deal
Dover
Folkestone
Strait of Dover

Canterbury
Kent Downs
Ashford
KENT

To Dieppe (France)

Rye
Hastings
Battle
Eastbourne
Beachy Head
Newhaven

EAST SUSSEX
High Weald

M20
Maidstone
Sevenoaks
Tonbridge
Tunbridge Wells
Hever
A21

Southend-on-Sea
Sheerness
Rochester
River Thames
M2
A2

ESSEX
Stansted Airport
To Ipswich
To Cambridge
A12

M11
A10
Hatfield
HERTFORDSHIRE
Luton Airport
Luton
M1

LONDON
GREATER LONDON
M25

A40
Heathrow Airport
Slough
Windsor
Reading

BUCKINGHAMSHIRE
To Birmingham
M40

Oxford
OXFORDSHIRE
Woodstock
A43
Didcot

Stow-on-the-Wold
Cirencester
GLOUCESTERSHIRE
To Gloucester
Lechlade
A40

BERKSHIRE
M4
A4
Swindon
Avebury
WILTSHIRE
Salisbury Plain
Stonehenge
Salisbury
A303
A36

To Bristol

M23
SURREY
Guildford
A3
Gatwick Airport

A23
Brighton
A27
A259
WEST SUSSEX
Sussex Downs
Arundel
Littlehampton
Bognor Regis
Fishbourne

ENGLISH CHANNEL

Portsmouth
Southampton
Winchester
A34
HAMPSHIRE
M3

To Le Havre (France)
To Caen
To St-Malo (France)
To Cherbourg (France)

Ryde
Cowes
Isle of Wight

To Exeter
A31
DORSET
Bournemouth

To Cherbourg

To Guernsey & Jersey (Channel Is)

0   25   50 km
0   15   30 miles

GREAT BRITAIN

near Folkestone. Those brave enough to use the ferries will find this coastline is their landfall, as it was for the Romans and Normans, amongst others.

However, this area need not have a particularly high priority for those who are in Britain for a short time. London is so close, crowds of tourists can be difficult to evade. Those with more time on their hands, or those living in London will, nonetheless, appreciate the fresh air and open space. They will also find picturesque towns (Arundel and Rye, among many others), spectacular coastline (the famous white cliffs of Dover and Beachy Head). impressive castles (Dover, Deal, Hever, Leeds and Bodrum) and the great cathedral at Canterbury. All those with a love for kitsch and seedy resorts should put Brighton on their list.

Kent is often called the 'Garden of England' but much of the region has a sense of gentle, cultivated prettiness. There are a number of popular walks, including the South Downs Way. Again, because of their accessibility, sections can easily be undertaken as day trips from London. Eastbourne to Brighton along the Way is a good three-day walk.

FACTS FOR THE VISITOR
Orientation & Information

The main roads and railway lines radiate from London like spokes in a wheel, linking the south-coast ports and resorts with the capital. Chalk country runs through the region along two hilly east-west ridges, or 'downs'.

The North Downs curve from Guildford towards Rochester, then to Dover where they become the famous white cliffs. The South Downs run from north of Portsmouth to end spectacularly at Beachy Head near Eastbourne. Lying between the two is the Weald, once an enormous stretch of forest, now orchards and market gardens.

There are youth hostels in Canterbury, Dover, Hastings, Brighton, Arundel, Portsmouth, Winchester, Southampton, and several on the Isle of Wight.

GETTING AROUND
Bus

Fast, regular buses follow the spokes out from London, but it is very difficult to travel east-west by bus without resorting to the slow, local buses. For timetables covering Kent, ring ☎ 0622-671411, West Sussex, ☎ 0243-777100, East Sussex, ☎ 0273-482123, Hampshire, ☎ 0962-841841.

Train

It is possible to do an interesting rail loop from London via Canterbury East, Dover, Ashford, Rye, Hastings, Battle, Hastings, Brighton, Littlehampton, Arundel, Portsmouth, Southampton, and Winchester. If you are considering this kind of extensive rail travel, a Network South-East Card (see the Getting Around section at the beginning of this chapter) is essential.

KENT
Leeds Castle

Near Maidstone, Kent, Leeds Castle (☎ 0622-765400) is justly famous as one of the world's most beautiful castles. It stands on two small islands in a lake, and Henry VIII transformed it from a fortress into a palace surrounded by a superb park. It's open daily from Easter to 31 October, then weekends; admission is £5.90. National Express has one bus a day direct from Victoria Station (leaving at 10 am); it must be prebooked and the combined cost of admission and travel is £13.50. The nearest train station is Bearsted on the Kent Coast Line to Ashford. Britrail has a combined admission/travel ticket for £12.60.

Knole House

This enormous house (☎ 0732-450608), set in a magnificent park near Sevenoaks, Kent, dates largely from the mid-15th century and was the home of the Sackville family. Vita Sackville-West was born here, and the house features in Virginia Woolf's *Orlando*. It is now a National Trust property open from Easter to 31 October, Wednesday to Saturday from 11 am to 5 pm, Sunday from 2 to 5 pm;

admission is £3.50. The grounds are open all year.

Hever Castle

Idyllic Hever Castle (☎ 0732-865224) near Edenbridge was the childhood home of Anne Boleyn, mistress to Henry VIII and then his tragic queen. Restored by the Astor family, it also has magnificent gardens. It's open daily from 17 March to 8 November from noon to 6 pm; admission is £4.80. The nearest train station is Hever, a mile from the castle itself (£5.60 from London).

SOUTH-EAST COAST

Dover

Dover has two things going for it: it has the world's busiest passenger harbour and a spectacular castle. The first claim to fame will come under severe pressure with the opening of the Channel Tunnel, although no-one can say what the final impact will be.

Information & Orientation Dover is dominated by the looming profile of the castle to the east. The town itself runs back from the sea along a valley formed by the unimpressive River Dour (in Roman times, this formed a navigable estuary).

Most ferry departures are from the Eastern Docks (accessible by bus) below the castle, but the Hoverport and Western Docks are below the Western Heights. There are two train stations: the first you arrive at is Dover Priory, a short walk to the west of the town centre (best for the hostels and Eastern Docks); the second is at the Western Docks (best for the Hoverport and Western Docks). Not all trains go through to the Western Docks station, but the ferry companies run complimentary buses from Dover Priory. The bus station is in the centre of town.

The TIC (☎ 0304-205108) is on Townwall St near the seafront and is open from 9 am to 6 pm. It has an accommodation and ferry-booking service.

Things to See Dover's main attraction, **Dover Castle** (☎ 0304-201628), is a well-preserved medieval fortress with a beautiful location and spectacular views. To add to its fascination, there are the remains of a Roman lighthouse, or **Pharos**, built in 50 AD, within the fortifications, as well as a restored Saxon church. The excellent tour of **Hellfire Corner** covers the castle's history during WW II, and takes you through the tunnels which burrow through the chalk beneath the castle.

The castle is open daily from 10 am to 6 pm; between October and Good Friday, from 10 am to 4 pm. Entry is £4.50 including Hellfire Corner; there is a worthwhile audio tour for an additional £1.50, and another tour of Hellfire Corner for £1.

Places to Stay & Eat There are two youth hostels, both of which can fill up very quickly in summer; one or other may close during winter. Finding any accommodation at all can be tough in high summer, so making a booking is advisable.

The main hostel, *Dover Central Youth Hostel* (☎ 0304-201314), 306 London Rd, has been recently renovated, but the *Dover Annexe* (☎ 0304-206045), 14 Godwyne Rd, is also comfortable, although a bit cramped.

B&Bs are mainly strung along Folkestone Rd (the A20) but there is another batch on Castle St and Maison Dieu Rd in town. The *Elmo Guest House* (☎ 0304-206236), 120 Folkestone Rd, is good value with a per person rate from £12 to £16.

Tucked under the castle, near the Eastern Docks (ideal if you have an early ferry), the *Cliffe-den* (☎ 0304-202418), 63 East Cliff, Marine Parade, is quiet and pleasant with a per person rate from £13 to £16. Some rooms have showers and TV.

There are a number of restaurants along Cannon St, but you will probably do best with a pub meal. The *Red Lion*, just off Frith St, has excellent, filling meals for around £3, and is convenient to both youth hostels.

Getting There & Away See the Getting There & Away section at the beginning of this chapter for details on ferries, hovercraft and so on to Europe.

GREAT BRITAIN

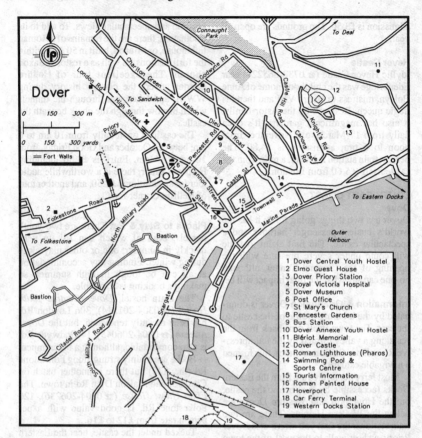

Dover

0   150   300 m

0   150   300 yards

Fort Walls

To Deal

To Sandwich

To Folkestone

Bastion

Bastion

To Eastern Docks

Outer
Harbour

1 Dover Central Youth Hostel
2 Elmo Guest House
3 Dover Priory Station
4 Royal Victoria Hospital
5 Dover Museum
6 Post Office
7 St Mary's Church
8 Pencester Gardens
9 Bus Station
10 Dover Annexe Youth Hostel
11 Blériot Memorial
12 Dover Castle
13 Roman Lighthouse (Pharos)
14 Swimming Pool &
    Sports Centre
15 Tourist Information
16 Roman Painted House
17 Hoverport
18 Car Ferry Terminal
19 Western Docks Station

Bus National Express has numerous buses to Dover, and most stop at Canterbury. London to Dover is £10. Canterbury is the bus hub for the region; there is no direct link, for instance, between Dover and Brighton, which makes an easy bus loop around the coast impossible. There is one bus per day from Canterbury to Brighton.

Train There are over 40 trains a day from Victoria and London's Charing Cross to Dover Priory (two hours, £14.50). Trains that go through to the Western Docks station generally leave from Victoria.

There's an enjoyable hourly service that runs across the rich Romney Marsh farmlands from Ashdown to Rye and Hastings. Ashdown to Hastings takes 45 minutes and costs £15.40. There are hourly trains from Hastings to Battle (15 minutes, £1.80). Hastings to Brighton is another hour and £6.50.

Getting Around Fortunately, the ferry companies run complimentary buses between the docks and train stations. They're a long walk apart, especially if you've got some heavy bags. If you plan to stay overnight and don't have transport, check the timetables. There are East Kent buses to the Eastern Docks that leave on the hour from the Pencester Rd bus station (D25, 15 or 15A for 40p). There are frequent Dover town buses from Pencester Rd to the Western Docks (D2A or D2 for 36p).

Canterbury

Canterbury's greatest treasure is, of course, its magnificent cathedral, the successor to the cathedral St Augustine built after he began converting the English in 597. In 1170 Archbishop Thomas Becket was murdered in the cathedral by four of Henry II's knights, as a result of a dispute over the church's independence. An enormous cult grew up around the martyred Becket and Canterbury became the centre of one of the most important medieval pilgrimages, which was immortalised by Geoffrey Chaucer in the *Canterbury Tales*.

The Archbishop of Canterbury is the 'Primate of All England', the head of the Church of England and the worldwide Anglican Communion. Although he plays an important symbolic and leadership role, he has little direct authority. The cathedral is his 'seat', and is therefore considered to be the most important Anglican cathedral. Although it is not the most beautiful, it is certainly one of the most evocative – the ghosts of saints, soldiers and pilgrims seem to crowd around.

Canterbury was severely damaged during the WW II Blitz, and parts, especially to the south of the cathedral, have been rebuilt insensitively. However, there's still plenty to see and the bustling centre has a good atmosphere. The place crawls with tourists, but that simply means all is well with the world – they've been coming for a very long time.

Orientation & Information The centre of Canterbury is enclosed by a medieval city wall, and a modern ring road. The centre is easy to get around on foot, virtually impossible to get around by car; park by the Wall. There are two railway stations, both a short walk from the centre: East (for the youth hostel) accessible from London's Victoria,

and West accessible from London's Charing Cross and Waterloo. The bus station is just within the city walls at the east end of High St. The TIC (☎ 0227-766567), 34 St Margaret's St, is open seven days from April to October.

Things to See The present **cathedral** (☎ 0227-762897) was built in two stages between 1070 and 1184, and 1391 and 1505. The cathedral complex, including the beautiful cloisters, can easily absorb half a day (suggested donation £1.50). It is a massive rabbit-warren of a building, with treasures tucked away in corners and a trove of associated stories, so a tour is recommended. There are one-hour guided tours at 10 am, noon, 2 and 4 pm for £2.20, or if the crowd looks daunting, you can take a walkman tour for £1.50. On weekdays the cathedral is open from 8.45 am to 7 pm from Easter to September, and from 8.45 am to 5 pm from October to Easter; choral evensong is at 5.30 pm. On Sundays it is open from 12.30 to 2.30 pm, 4.30 to 5.30 pm; choral evensong is at 3.15 pm.

Canterbury Tales (☎ 0227-454888), St Margaret's St, is an entertaining recreation of life in medieval England; recommended if you can part with £3.95 without pain. The **Canterbury Heritage Museum** (☎ 0227-452747), Stour St, in a converted medieval building, gives good coverage of the city's history.

Places to Stay The *youth hostel* (☎ 0227-462911), 54 New Dover Rd, is a km or so from the east railway station. Continue out St George's St (the continuation of High St) which becomes New Dover. The hostel is in an old Victorian villa and is closed from Christmas Eve to the end of January.

Kingsbridge Villa (☎ 0227-766415), 15 Best Lane, in the centre of town just off High St, is a comfortable B&B with colour TVs in rooms, some of which have their own bathrooms. Prices start from £16/30 for singles/doubles. Nearby *Tudor House* (☎ 0227-765650), 6 Best Lane, is also good. It's a bit smaller and in addition to the usual, they have canoes and boats to hire to guests. Singles/doubles are from £15/28.

You can stay right in the heart of the city, right by the cathedral at the *Cathedral Gate Hotel* (☎ 0227-462800), 36 Burgate, which has comfortable facilities from £22, but rising to almost double in high season.

There are quite a number of places on St Dunstan's St (from the West Gate) and on London Rd (its continuation).

Four miles away, the *Thruxted Oast* (☎ 0227-730080), Mystole, Chartham, is an excellent B&B in converted oast houses (where hops were dried). The buildings have loads of character. Rates are around £30 per person.

Places to Eat There's a good range of reasonably priced eating places in Canterbury. If you want to do some window-menu shopping start in St Margaret's St and then walk down High St to West Gate. There are a couple of interesting places outside the gate.

Il Vaticano (☎ 0227-765333), 35 St Margaret's St, has excellent Italian food, in particular a wide range of pastas from £3.95 to £7. *The Teapot* (☎ 0227-456402), 34 St Peter's St, also known as Mother Earth's Vegetarian Restaurant, has good-value vegetarian dishes, a bit more interesting than the usual. Starters are £1.90 (try the ragout of mushrooms in madeira sauce) and main courses are £4.95. They have a huge range of teas, and serve traditional teas with cake and scones from £2.70.

Café des Amis just beyond the West Gate is actually an authentic Mexican restaurant. There's a cheerful atmosphere and the prices are reasonable. For starters – guacamole £2.25, tostada £2.95; for main courses – fajitas (for two) £13.35, burritos £4.95. There are lots of more interesting possibilities. Try mole poblano – roast loin of pork in a sauce made of chillies, spices, nuts, seeds and tomato with rice and salad for £5.95.

Another American connection is the *Front Page* (☎ 0227-761658) 2/3 Iron Bar Lane, which has appetisers (barbecued ribs; tex mex muffins) for around £2 and a good

selection of vegetarian dishes and main meals for around £5 – try the seafood gumbo.

Getting There & Away Canterbury makes a good base for exploring Kent and the High Weald.

Bus East Kent Buses (☎ 0843-581333) has a good network around the region. There are numerous buses from London for £9.35, and Dover for £2.50. During summer there's one bus a day to Brighton (leaving Canterbury at 9.10 am) for £11.75. There's an interesting service to Hastings across an attractive part of Kent – services 400/404 (300 on Sundays) via Ashford and Tenterden. There are four a day Monday to Saturday, two on Sundays.

National Express has regular buses linking Dover, Folkestone, Hythe, Ashford and Canterbury. Canterbury to Dover is £4.50.

Rail There are two railway stations: East (for the youth hostel) accessible from London's Victoria, and West accessible from London's Charing Cross and Waterloo. The journey takes about 1¾ hours and costs £11.40. There are regular trains between Canterbury East and Dover Priory (45 minutes, £3.40).

Rye

Rye was once a Cinque port (a medieval confederation of Channel ports that supplied ships and men for the king's service) but is now isolated from the sea. It's a picturesque medieval town with timbered buildings and cobbled streets. It is sometimes claimed to be the most beautiful town in Britain, and as a result, is inundated with tea and souvenir shops – and tourists. To get away from the hordes, walk down hill and across the bleak Romney Marsh to the sea, or to the bird sanctuary on the wetlands behind the beach.

Brighton

You have to be a true connoisseur of kitsch to have an unreserved love for Brighton, but it does hold a peculiar and undeniable fascination. It's the sort of place where letters disappear leaving gap-toothed signs, but there's a thriving nightlife and good shopping. A visit is definitely worthwhile.

In the first half of the 20th century it catered to millions of working-class families on 'bucket and spade' holidays, and in the 1950s, to Mods and Rockers and other undesirables. Graham Greene's *Brighton Rock* commemorates Brighton at its seediest. Nowadays, of course, the south of Spain provides a stronger lure.

Orientation & Information Brighton Railway Station is a 15-minute walk north of the (loosely described) beach.

When you leave the station, go straight down the hill along Queen's Rd. The interesting part of Brighton lies to the left. When you reach the major intersection at the clock tower, turn left into North St, which will take you down past the Royal Pavilion, then right onto Old Steine (a road) and a large traffic roundabout where you'll find the TIC. Continue a little farther and you'll see the unmistakable Palace Pier.

The bus station is tucked in a small square sandwiched between the beach and Palace Pier (south) and the main traffic roundabout (north) formed by the Old Steine. There's an information/booking office on Old Steine.

The TIC (☎ 0273-23755), Marlborough House, 54 Old Steine, has public transport maps (helpful if you are staying at the youth hostel), restaurant listings, and *14 Days* (30p), an entertainment guide. You may need its accommodation service – the youth hostel is often full.

Things to See The **Royal Pavilion** is an extraordinary fantasy: an Indian palace on the outside, a Chinese brothel on the inside. It was built between 1815 and 1822 for George IV (then Prince Regent). George is said to have cried when he first saw the Music Room, which confirms that he was a very strange man indeed. The whole edifice is over the top in every respect and is not to be missed. It's open from 10 am to 5 pm every day and admission is £3.30.

Nearby, the **Palace Pier** is the very image of Brighton, with its Palace of Fun. In this case, fun is taken to mean takeaway food and 1000 machines, all of which have flashing lights, and all of which take your money. There's quite a good bar and, well, you have to visit.

Up the hill, behind the TIC and the Town Hall, is a charming maze of narrow lanes, known as **The Lanes**, with chic shops, restaurants and bars. Shoppers should also explore **North Laine**, a semicontinuous mall off North St heading north towards the train station (Bond St runs into Gardner St which, with a slight dogleg, runs into Kensington and Sydney Sts). You'll find all sorts of interesting things, including the highest concentration of clairvoyants outside Berkeley.

Places to Stay The *youth hostel* (☎ 0273-556196), Patcham Place, London Rd, is huge but often full, even outside the high season, so call ahead or show up at breakfast time. The hostel is about seven km out; catch bus 5 or 5A from bus stop E on Old Steine along the A23 towards London and get off at the Black Lion Hotel. The hostel is on the other side of the A23.

Since one of the main attractions of Brighton is its nightlife, you may prefer to pay for a B&B. Unfortunately, most are neither cheap nor good value; you won't find anything under about £15.

The main cluster of cheap B&Bs is to the east of the Old Steine roundabout, on the opposite side to the Pavilion and the TIC. Cross the roundabout from the TIC and walk up St James St. There are several streets in on the right with B&Bs, particularly Madeira Place and, on the right, Dorset Gardens.

The *Almara Guest House* (☎ 0273-603186), 11 Madeira Place, is about as good as you'll get with singles/doubles for £15/26. The *Aquarium* (☎ 0273-605761) and the *Alexandra* are all fair. The *Dorset Guest House* (☎ 0273-694646), 17 Dorset Gardens, is recommended and has singles/doubles at £15 per person.

Places to Eat Brighton is jam-packed with good-value and interesting eating places. If you wander around the Lanes or around the cheap accommodation area around St James St, you'll turn up all sorts of interesting, affordable alternatives. Get hold of the TIC's free brochure, *Eating Out in Brighton & Hove*. If you can't eat well for less than £5, buy a hot dog at the pier, or throw yourself off the end.

The best of the lot is *Food for Friends* (☎ 0273-736236), 41 Market St, but as a result it is very busy. Avoid peak times if you want to be sure of a seat. It has a limited but excellent vegetarian menu with main meals for around £3.

Opposite the Palace Pier, *The Hungry Years Gathering Place* has a hungry young crowd hoeing into pub meals of the roast and three veg variety, but cheap.

Entertainment There are plenty of pubs, bars and discos, but as always fashion is fickle – check *14 Days*. The *Concorde Bar*, opposite the pier near the aquarium, is a long-running favourite with reasonable prices and excellent music.

Getting There & Away Transport to and from Brighton is fast and frequent.

Bus National Express has eight buses a day from London (two hours, £8.50). Its coast link west to Cornwall is basically a one-a-day service. It leaves Brighton at 8.20 am. You would get off at Portsmouth 1¾ hours later and £7.75 poorer.

Train There are over 40 trains a day from Victoria and London's King's Cross (one hour, £10.40). There are plenty of trains between Brighton and Portsmouth (1½ hours, £8.90).

Portsmouth

For much of British history, Portsmouth has been the home of the Royal Navy and it is littered with reminders that this was, for hundreds of years, a force that shaped the world.

After 437 years underwater, Henry VIII's favourite ship, the *Mary Rose*, and its time-capsule contents, can be seen. And you can walk the decks of the world's oldest surviving ship, the magnificent HMS *Victory*, Lord Nelson's flagship and shrine. Portsmouth is still a busy naval base and the sleek, grey killing machines of the 20th century are also very much in evidence.

Unfortunately, Portsmouth is not a particularly attractive city, largely due to WW II bombing, so there is no persuasive reason to stay overnight. Consider staying on the Isle of Wight, which is quick and easy to reach.

Orientation & Information The train and bus stations, the harbour, and the ferry terminal for the Isle of Wight are conveniently grouped together a stone's throw from the Naval Heritage Area. When you leave the station, or your bus, you'll immediately see HMS *Warrior*. If you walk around the quay towards her you'll see the TIC and the Victory Gate, the entrance to the heritage area which houses the *Mary Rose*, HMS *Warrior*, HMS *Victory* and the Royal Navy Museum.

The TIC (☎ 0705-826722), The Hard, provides guided tours, an accommodation service and plenty of brochures.

Things to See At various times the navy has shown a fairly flexible attitude to fund-raising techniques, so at the end of a day in Portsmouth you should not be surprised to find you have been separated from many gold coins. Seeing the sights is expensive.

Portsmouth's centrepiece is the **Naval Heritage Area**. Illogically, there is no overall ticket, although you can buy a joint ticket (£6.60) that covers the museum (separately, £1.80), HMS *Victory* (separately, £3.90) and the *Mary Rose* (separately, £3.90). You have to cough up another £3.90 for HMS *Warrior*.

Exploring HMS *Victory*, and walking in the footsteps of Lord Nelson and his multi-cultural crew of ruffians and gentlemen, is about as close as you can get to time travel – an extraordinary experience. The *Mary Rose* is also fascinating. The museum, however, is rather dry and exhausting if you're not a naval buff, and HMS *Warrior* does not have the same magic as the *Victory*.

A tour of the harbour, leaving beside the station (hourly, £2.20), gives you an opportunity to see the modern navy at work, as well as Old Portsmouth, Gosport Town and the **Submarine Museum** with a tour through a large submarine and the chance to look at Britain's first submarine.

Places to Stay The TIC can advise on the numerous B&Bs, although in general they are not particularly cheap. The *youth hostel* (☎ 0705-375661), Old Wymering Lane, Cosham, is about three miles from the main sights. It opens on a restricted basis between December and March.

Getting There & Away Portsmouth is well connected to the rest of the country.

Bus National Express has a daily service between Brighton and Portsmouth (£7.75). There are numerous buses to London, some via Heathrow Airport (2½ hours, £9). One bus a day heads west as far as Penzance in Cornwall (13 hours, £40.50).

Train There are over 40 trains a day from Victoria and Waterloo (1½ hours, £14.40). There are plenty of trains between Brighton and Portsmouth (1½ hours, £8.90). There are two trains a day (departing 9.57 and 10.57 am) to Winchester via Eastleigh.

Sea There are a number of ways of getting to the Isle of Wight, but the most convenient for those without vehicles is from Portsmouth Harbour to Ryde. Ferries connect with trains and buses (15 minutes, singles/returns are £4.10/8.20. Contact Wightlink Ferries (☎ 0705-827744) for more details.

P&O (☎ 0705-827677) has several ferries a day to Cherbourg and Le Havre in France; see the introductory Getting There & Away section.

South-West England

The counties of Avon, Wiltshire, Dorset, Somerset, Devon and Cornwall include some of the most beautiful countryside and spectacular coastline in Britain. They are littered with the evidence of successive cultures and kingdoms that have been swept away by one invader after another.

The region can be divided between Devon and Cornwall in the far west, which are removed culturally and geographically from England, and Dorset, Wiltshire, Avon and Somerset in the east, which are at its very heart.

In the east, the story of English civilisation is signposted by some of its greatest monuments: the Stone Age left Stonehenge and spellbinding Avebury; the Celts left Maiden Castle just outside Dorchester; between them, the Romans and the Georgians created Bath; the legendary King Arthur is supposed to be buried at Glastonbury; the Middle Ages left the great cathedrals at Exeter, Salisbury, Winchester and Wells; and the landed gentry left great houses like Montacute and Wilton.

The east is densely packed with things to see, and the countryside, though varied, is a classic English patchwork of hedgerows, thatched cottages, stone churches, great estates and emerald-green fields.

Parts of Avon and Wiltshire, particularly Bath and Salisbury, are major tourist attractions, but they are still, unquestionably, worth visiting. Dorset and Somerset and North Devon are counties where you can happily wander without too many plans and without stumbling over too many people.

Devon and particularly Cornwall were once Britain's 'wild west', and smuggling was rife. Until the 18th century there were still Celtic speakers in Cornwall. Today, the modern infatuation with sand and sun means that every summer the 'English Riviera' seethes with sunburnt suburbanites. Unless you plan a sociological study, steer clear of the coastal towns in July and August.

The weather is milder in the south-west all

GREAT BRITAIN

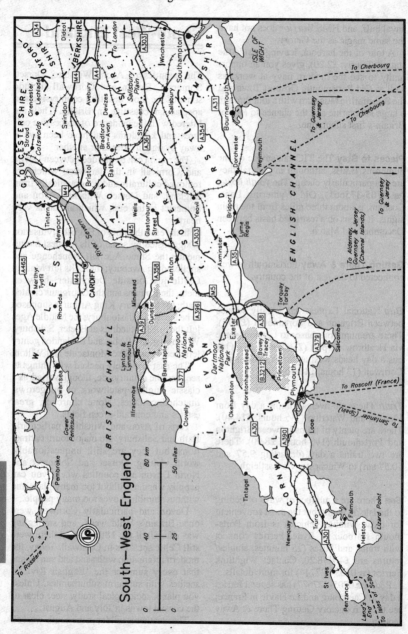

South–West England

year round and, astonishingly, there really are beaches with golden sand and surf. Surfable surf. And then there are the villages tucked into unexpected valleys or overlooking beautiful harbours, and lanes squeezed between high hedges...

Cornwall can be a disappointment, however. You'll certainly feel cheated if you think because you have reached the extreme south-western tip of the island you'll find untouched, undiscovered hideaways. Land's End – a veritable icon – has been reduced to nothing more than a particularly unsavoury tourist trap. Inland, much of the Cornish peninsula has been devastated by generations of tin and china-clay mining, and the coastal villages have either been vandalised or fossilised by/for tourists.

The South West Coast Path, a long-distance walking route, follows the coastline from Poole, near Bournemouth in Dorset, around the peninsula to Minehead in Somerset, and gives spectacular access to the best and most untouched sections. Walkers also head to the Dartmoor and Exmoor National Parks.

FACTS FOR THE VISITOR
Orientation & Information
The chalk downs centred on Salisbury Plain run across Wiltshire, down through the centre of Dorset to the coast. In the west, the granite moors of Ex and Dart dominate the landscape. The railways converge on Exeter, the most important city in the west, then run round the coast, skirting the granite *tors* (outcrops) of Dartmoor to Truro, the uninspiring administrative centre of Cornwall, and Penzance. Bristol and Salisbury are also important crossroads.

Amongst others, there are several youth hostels in Dartmoor and Exmoor National Parks, and at Salisbury, Bath, Bristol, Winchester, Exeter, Plymouth, Falmouth, Penzance, Land's End, Newquay, Tintagel and Ilfracombe.

Activities
Hiking The south-west has plenty of beautiful countryside, but walks in Dartmoor and

Exmoor National Parks, and round the coastline, are the best known. The barren, open wilderness of Dartmoor can be an acquired taste, but Exmoor covers some of the most beautiful countryside in England, and the coastal stretch from Ilfracombe to Minehead is particularly spectacular. See the separate sections on Dartmoor and Exmoor for more information.

The South West Coast Path is not a wilderness walk – villages (with food, beer and accommodation) are generally within easy reach. It is the longest national trail and it follows a truly magnificent coastline. Completing a section of the path should be seriously considered by any keen walker; if possible avoid busy summer weekends.

The South West Way Association publishes an accommodation guide (£3.50) as well as detailed route descriptions. They are available from Mrs M McLeod (☎ 08047-3061), Membership Secretary, 1 Orchard Drive, Kingskerswell, Newton Abbot, Devon TQ12 5DG. The official Countryside Commission (Aurum Press) guides cover Exmouth to Poole, Falmouth to Exmouth, and Minehead to Padstow at £7.95 each.

Another famous walk, the Ridgeway, starts near Avebury and runs north-east for 137 km (85 miles) to Ivinghoe Beacon near Aylesbury. Much of it follows ancient roads over the high open ridge of the chalk downs, then it descends to the Thames Valley before finally climbing into the Chilterns. The western section (to Streatley) can be used by mountain bikes and horses (and unfortunately, 4WDs).

The best guide is *The Ridgeway* by Neil Curtis (Aurum Press). There is an excellent *Information and Accommodation Guide* (£1) available from the Countryside Service, Oxfordshire County Council, Library Headquarters, Holton, Oxford OX9 1QQ. Cyclists should get a copy of *The Mountain Biker's Guide to the Ridgeway* by Andy Bull & Frank Barrett (£5.99, Newspaper Publishing).

Surfing The capital of British surfing is Newquay on the west Cornish coast, and it's complete with surf shops, bleached hair, Kombis, and neon-coloured clothes (for anyone suffering withdrawal symptoms). The surfable coast runs from Porthleven (near Helston) in Cornwall west around Land's End and north to Ilfracombe. The most famous reef breaks are at Porthleven, Lynmouth and Milbrook; though good, they are inconsistent.

Cycling Bikes can be hired in most major regional centres, and the infrequent bus connections make cycling a more than usually attractive proposition. There's no shortage of hills, but the mild weather and quiet back roads make this excellent cycling country.

GETTING AROUND
Bus
National Express buses provide reasonable connections between the main towns, particularly in the east, but the farther west you go the more dire the situation becomes. Transport around Dartmoor and Exmoor is very difficult in summer, nigh on impossible at any other time. This is territory that favours those with their own transport. For timetables covering Dorset, ☎ 0305-204535, Somerset, ☎ 0823-255696, Devon, ☎ 0392-382800, and Cornwall, ☎ 0872-74282.

The Key West bus pass gives unlimited travel in South Devon and Cornwall with a seven-day ticket for £21.50. There are also a number of one-day Explorer passes for around £4; it's always worth asking about them. For example, the Wiltshire Day Rover gives unlimited travel in Wiltshire (Salisbury, Avebury, Bradford-on-Avon etc), but also includes Bath (£4.35, ☎ 0345-090899 for details).

Train
Train services in the east are reasonably comprehensive, linking Bristol, Bath, Salisbury, Weymouth and Exeter. Beyond Exeter a single line follows the south coast as far as Penzance, with spurs to Barnstaple, Gunnislake, Looe, Falmouth, St Ives and Newquay. The line from Exeter to Penzance is one of the most beautiful in Britain. For Britrail information, ☎ 071-262 6767.

The Freedom of the Southwest Rover allows seven days' unlimited travel west of a line drawn through (and including) Portsmouth, Salisbury, Bath, Bristol and Cardiff (£48/32).

WINCHESTER
Winchester is a small, beautiful cathedral city surrounded by rolling chalk downland, crystal clear streams and water meadows. If any one place lies at the centre of English history and embodies the romantic vision of the English heartland, it is Winchester. Despite this it seems to have escaped inundation by tourists – certainly by comparison to nearby Salisbury and to theme parks like Bath and Oxford.

An iron age hill fort overlooks the city. The Romans built a city on the present-day site; part of their defensive wall can still be seen incorporated into a later medieval defence. King Alfred the Great and many of his successors, including Canute and the Danish kings, made Winchester their capital, and William the Conqueror came to the city to claim the crown of England. Much of the present-day city, however, dates from the 18th century by which time Winchester had become a prosperous market centre.

There are lots of good walks in the surrounding countryside. Winchester can be covered in a day trip from London, but it could also be a base for exploring the south coast (Portsmouth, the National Motor Museum at Beaulieu) or the country further west towards Salisbury.

Orientation & Information
The city centre is compact, easily negotiated on foot, and there's a good system of signposts. The train station is a 10-minute walk to the west of the city centre and the bus and coach station is right in the centre directly opposite the Guild Hall and TIC.

The TIC (☎ 0962-840500), The Guildhall, Broadway, is open Monday to Saturday and Sunday afternoons from May to September. They produce an excellent city guide, including info on sights, and places to stay and eat (a must for £1.25). They also have a bureau de change (minimum commission £2) and regular guided walking tours (£1.75) from April to October.

Things to See

Winchester Cathedral is one of the most beautiful in the country, and if you go on the tours (run by enthusiastic local volunteers for 50p), spend some time in the Triforium, explore the cathedral close (the grounds and associated buildings), and go to Evensong (highly recommended; 5.30 pm Monday to Saturday, 3.30 pm Sunday) you'll need a whole afternoon. A £2 donation is requested.

The present cathedral is a mixture of Norman, Early English and Perpendicular styles. The east and west transepts (the arms of the cross) are a magnificent example of pure Norman, and the east transept now houses a fascinating display of medieval sculpture and the 12th century, illuminated Winchester Bible.

Nearby **Winchester College** was founded in 1382 and was the model for the great public (meaning private) schools of England. The chapel and cloisters are open to visitors from 10 am to 5 pm and on Sundays from 2 to 5 pm. From April to September, one-hour guided tours leave at 11 am (not Sundays), 2 and 3.15 pm (£2).

From the college there's a beautiful 1½-km walk to **Hospital St Cross**, which was founded in 1136. It's open Monday to Saturday from 9.30 am to 12.30 pm and 2 to 5 pm; admission is £1.

In town, it's also worth visiting the Great Hall, begun by William the Conqueror, and site of many dramatic moments in English history, including the trial of Sir Walter Raleigh in 1603. It houses **King Arthur's Round Table**, now known to be a fake 'only' 600 years old.

Places to Stay & Eat

The *youth hostel* (☎ 0962-853723), City Mill, 1 Water Lane, is in part of a beautiful 18th century restored water mill; the other part is used by the National Trust. It's close

to the centre of the city; walk down High St, which becomes The Broadway, cross the River Itchen (where you'll see the National Trust section) and take the first left into Water Lane.

There are also camping facilities a 10-minute walk north from the centre of town. The *River Park Leisure Centre* (☎ 0962-869525), Gordon Rd, North Walls, is open from June to September and has tent sites for £3 per person.

There are plenty of B&Bs (the local TIC has a free booking service) but most only have one or two rooms and are in the £15 to £18 bracket. *Mrs B Sullivan* (☎ 0962-862027), 29 Stockbridge Rd, near the railway station has two doubles at £14 per person. *Mrs R Wright* (☎ 0962-855067), 56 St Cross Rd, has one single and two doubles ranging from £14 to £18 per person.

Pubs are a good bet for cheap meals; the *Wykeham Arms* (☎ 0962-853834), 75 Kingsgate St, on the eastern side of the college, has a good range of traditional meals under £5. The ever reliable *Pizza Express* (☎ 0962-841845), 1 Bridge St, near the old mill at the end of The Broadway, serves excellent pizzas (£3 to £5) in a pleasant and efficient environment overlooking the river.

Getting There & Away

Bus There are regular National Express buses to London via Heathrow (two hours, £10.25), less frequent ones to Oxford (2½ hours, £11) and Southampton (30 minutes, £2.75).

Hampshire Bus (☎ 0962-852352) has a good network of local buses linking Salisbury, Portsmouth and Brighton. Their Explorer Ticket (£3.75) is also good on most Wilts and Dorset buses which serve the region further to the west. In summer there are buses to the the National Motor Museum at Beaulieu.

Train There are fast links with London's Waterloo, the south coast and the midlands. To London takes 1½ hours and costs £13.40.

SALISBURY

Salisbury is justly famous for the cathedral and its close, but its appeal lies in the fact that it is still a bustling market town, not just a tourist trap. Markets have been held in the town centre every Tuesday and Saturday since 1361, and the jumble of stalls still draws a large, cheerful crowd.

The town's architecture is a blend of every style since the Middle Ages, including some beautiful, half-timbered black-and-white buildings. It's a good base for visiting the Wiltshire Downs, Stonehenge, Old Sarum, Wilton House and Avebury. Portsmouth and Winchester are also easy day trips if you are travelling by rail. Those who are more interested in the internal combustion engine should not miss the National Motor Museum at Beaulieu, between Bournemouth and Southampton.

Orientation & Information

The town centre is a 10-minute walk from the train station and it's another 15 minutes to the youth hostel. Everything is within walking distance.

From the train station, walk down the hill and turn right at the T-junction into Fisherton St. This leads directly into town (which is well signposted). The bus station is just north of the centre of town; two minutes down Endless St and you're in the thick of things.

The helpful TIC (☎ 0722-334956), Fish Row, is behind the impressive 18th century Guildhall, which stands in the south-east corner of Market Square.

Things to See

The unique St Mary's Cathedral is built in a uniform style known as Early English (or Early Pointed). This period is characterised by the first pointed arches and flying buttresses and a rather austere feel. The cathedral owes its uniformity to the speed with which it was built – between 1220 and 1266, over 70,000 tons of stone were piled up. The spire, at 123 metres (403 feet) the highest in Britain, was an afterthought added between 1285 and 1315. It was undergoing renovation at the time of writing, and was obscured behind scaffolding and plastic. A donation of £1 is requested.

The adjacent Chapter House is one of the most perfect achievements of Gothic architecture. It houses one of the four surviving original versions of the Magna Carta, the agreement made between King John and his barons in 1215, a landmark in the development of human rights.

There is plenty more to see in the Cathedral Close including two houses that have been restored, and two museums. The Salisbury & South Wiltshire Museum (£2.25) is worth visiting.

The TIC has a useful pamphlet, Seeing Salisbury (60p), which gives walks around the town and across the water-meadows for classic views of the cathedral. There are a number of longer walks – the TIC has information. Winchester to Salisbury, for instance, is 42 km (26 miles) and is known as the Clarendon Way.

Places to Stay & Eat

The youth hostel (☎ 0722-327572), Milford Hill, is an attractive old building in two acres of garden, an easy walk from the centre of Salisbury. From the TIC, turn left into Fish Row, then immediately right into Queen St, first left into Milford St, straight for about 400 metres, under the overpass – the youth hostel is on the left.

Ron & Jenny Coats (☎ 0722-327443), 51 Salt Lane, close to the bus station, is an independent hostel-like guesthouse with dorm rooms, but without a curfew. It's a pleasant old house and the Coats are welcoming. A bed only is £7, B&B is £9.

There are plenty of restaurants, but few are cheap. The Pheasant Inn (☎ 0722-327069), an old pub on the corner of Salt Lane and Rollestone St attracts a young crowd with dishes like grilled prawn and chicken kiev for under £5. The Coach & Horses (☎ 0722-336254) is another popular pub with burgers for under £2 and dishes like scotch salmon with coriander sauce under £5.

There's a batch of cheapish and popular restaurants near the railway station. At the Asian on Fisherton St, the Far East on South

Western Rd (to the station) and at *Pinocchio*, left under the railway bridge from the station, you will be able to eat well for around £10.

Entertainment

There is often interesting live entertainment in the *Salisbury Arts Centre* (☎ 0722-321744), Bedwin St, including high quality contemporary music and performances. Get a programme from the TIC.

Getting There & Away

Bus National Express has one bus a day via Salisbury from Portsmouth to Bath and Bristol. It's more expensive than the local bus lines, with the Portsmouth-Salisbury and Salisbury-Bath sectors both costing around £7. Badgerline/Wiltshire buses also run an hourly service (the X4) to Bath via Wilton and Bradford-on-Avon (two hours, £2.80).

Three buses a day run from London via Heathrow to Salisbury (three hours, £10.25). Salisbury would be a nice place to spend your last night in England; if you were heading to Heathrow, buses depart at 7.25 am, 11.10 am and 3.10 pm.

If you plan to spend a day in Wiltshire (Avebury, Lacock) en route to Bath purchase the Wiltshire Day Rover (available on Wiltshire Buses, also the X4 to Bath). This is £4.35; contact the council (☎ 0345-090899) for more details. Wilts & Dorset (☎ 0722-336855) has daily buses to/from Avebury, Stonehenge and Old Sarum – their Explorer Ticket is £3.75.

If you're going through to Bristol or Bath, or plan to spend time exploring Avon, Somerset (Wells, Glastonbury) or Gloucestershire (Cotswolds), get the Badgerline Day Rambler (available on Badgerline buses, also good for the X4 to Bath; £4.10). The first Badgerline X4 leaves at 11 am. Phone ☎ 0225-464446 for more information.

Train Salisbury is linked by rail to Portsmouth (numerous, 1½ hours, £16.60), Bath (numerous, one hour, £8) and Exeter (10 per day, 1¾ hours, £16). There are 30 trains a day from London's Waterloo Station (1½ hours, £16.40).

Getting Around

Bikes can be hired from Haybal's Cycle Shop (☎ 0722-411378) at £5 per day, £25 per week. Local buses are reasonably well organised and link Salisbury with Stonehenge, Old Sarum and Wilton House; phone ☎ 0722-336855 for details.

AROUND SALISBURY
Stonehenge

Stonehenge is the most famous prehistoric site in Europe, a ring of enormous stones (some of which were brought from Wales), built in stages beginning 5000 years ago. Reactions vary; some find that the car park, gift shop and crowds of tourists swamp the monument, which is actually quite small. Avebury, 30 km to the north, is much more impressive in scale and recommended for those who would like to commune with the ley lines in *relative* peace.

Stonehenge is three km west of Amesbury on the junction of the A303 and A344/A360; 15 km from Salisbury (the nearest station); entry is £2.50. Some feel that it is unnecessary to pay the entry fee, because you can get a good view from the road and even if you do enter you are kept at some distance from the stones. There are three buses a day from Salisbury, the first leaving at 11 am; a ticket costs £3.55 return (consider a Wilts/Dorset Explorer for £3.75); phone ☎ 0722-336855 for details.

AVEBURY

Avebury (between Calne and Marlborough just off the A4) stands at the hub of a prehistoric complex of ceremonial sites, ancient avenues and burial chambers dating from 3500 BC. In scale the remains are more impressive than Stonehenge, and if you visit outside of summer weekends it is quite possible to escape the crowds. The impact of Neolithic people on the environment is so dramatic you can almost feel them breathing down your neck.

In addition to an enormous stone circle, there's Silbury Hill, the largest constructed mound in Europe, West Kennet Long Barrow, a burial chamber, and a pretty

GREAT BRITAIN

village with an ancient church. The Avebury Museum (95p) helps explain (as far as this is possible, which is not far) the complex and is a good place to start your exploration.

There are a couple of B&Bs in Avebury's only street, with doubles for £32. The *New Inn* (☎ 06723-240), a mile or two north at Winterbourne Monkton, has singles for £20.

Avebury can be easily reached by frequent buses from Salisbury (Wiltshire bus No 5 or 6) or Swindon. To travel to/from Bath you'll have to change buses at Devizes; check connections with the county enquiry line (☎ 0345-090899).

DORSET

The greater part of Dorset is designated as an area of outstanding natural beauty, but, with the exceptions of Poole and Weymouth, it avoids inundation by tourists.

The coast varies from sandy beaches to shingle banks and towering cliffs. Lyme Regis is a particularly attractive spot, made famous as the setting for John Fowles' book, *The French Lieutenant's Woman*, and the subsequent film.

For those who have read Thomas Hardy, however, Dorset is inextricably linked with his novels. You can visit his birthplace at Higher Bockhampton, or Dorchester (Casterbridge), the unspoilt market town where he lived. Maiden Castle, the largest Celtic fort in England, is three km south of Dorchester.

Orientation & Information

Dorchester makes an ideal base for exploring the best of Dorset, but Bridport will suit those who prefer the coast. One of the reasons for Dorset's backwater status is that no major transport routes cross it. A rail loop runs west from Southampton to Dorchester, then north to Yeovil, and the main westbound InterCity trains stop at Axminster (East Devon).

There is a free county guide available from Dorset Tourism (☎ 0202-201001), Dorset House, 20-22 Christchurch Rd, Bournemouth, Dorset BH1 3NL.

Places to Stay

There is no youth hostel in Dorchester. The nearest hostels are in Bridport (☎ 0308-22655), West Rivers House, West Allington, and Litton Cheney (☎ 0308-482340), but both are closed over winter. For B&Bs, contact the Dorchester TIC (☎ 0305-267992).

Getting There & Away

Dorchester can be reached by train from London (every hour, 2½ hours, £26), Bath (eight per day, 1¾ hours, £8.40), and Weymouth (numerous, 10 minutes, £1.80). There are also buses on these routes but although cheaper they tend to be much slower. The buses from London take four hours! Axminster is also a reasonable transport hub, with hourly buses from the train station to Lyme Regis and Bridport.

Getting Around

There are five buses a day between Dorchester (from Weymouth Ave, a short walk from either the South or West train stations) and Bridport taking 40 minutes and costing £1.90. There are hourly buses between Bridport and Axminster (one hour, £1.90). Lyme Regis is connected to Axminster with an hourly service (20 minutes, £1.25). Contact Southern National (☎ 0308-22080) for more information.

EXETER

Exeter is the largest city in the West Country, with a population of around 100,000. It was devastated during WW II and as a result first impressions are not particularly inspiring; if you get over these, you'll find a livable university city with a thriving nightlife. It's a good starting point for Dartmoor and Cornwall.

The cathedral is one of the most attractive in England, with two massive Norman towers surviving from the 11th century. From 50 AD, when the city was established by the Romans, until the 19th century, Exeter was an important port, and the waterfront (including a large boat museum) is now being restored.

There are a number of highly recommended free tours, both of the cathedral and the town.

Orientation & Information

The old Roman walls enclose a hill in a bend of the River Exe, and the great square towers of the cathedral still dominate the skyline.

There are two train stations, but most InterCity trains use St David's, which is a 20-minute walk west of the city centre and Central Station. From St David's, cross the station forecourt and Bonhay Rd, then climb some steps to St David's Hill and then turn right up the hill for the centre. You'll pass a batch of reasonably priced B&Bs on your right; keep going for another km, then turn left up High St. The centre of the city is well signposted.

The TIC (☎ 0392-265297), Civic Centre, Paris St, is just across the road from the bus station, a short walk north-east of the cathedral; it's not open on Sundays.

Places to Stay & Eat

The *youth hostel* (☎ 0392-873329), 47 Countess Wear Rd, is three km south-east of the city towards Topsham. It's closed in December, and on Tuesdays in November, January and February. From High St, catch minibuses K or T (10 minutes, 80p) and ask for the Countess Wear post office.

There are several reasonable B&Bs on St David's Hill. The *Highbury* (☎ 0392-58288), 85 St David's Hill, is good value with singles/doubles for £14/20. There's another batch on Blackall Rd (near the prison). *Rhona's Guest House* (☎ 0392-77791), 15 Blackall Rd, has TV and coffee-making facilities in all rooms. Singles/doubles are £12/23.

Further out, but easy to reach by bus, *The Old Mill* (☎ 0392-59977), Mill Lane, Alphington, is in a quiet residential suburb and has B&B from £9 – recommended.

For a beer and a decent meal, head to the *Turk's Head Hotel* on High St by the Guildhall. There are a number of busy wine bars on medieval Gandy St which is signposted off High St. *Pizza Piazza*, on Queen St

towards the clock tower, has pizzas for under £5, reasonable drinks and live jazz.

Getting There & Away

Bus Half a dozen buses run between London, Heathrow Airport and Exeter daily (four hours, £24). The daily south coast service between Brighton and Penzance (via Portsmouth, Weymouth, Dorchester, Bridport, Exeter and Plymouth) departs Exeter for Brighton at 12.30 pm (eight hours, £26). Dorchester to Exeter takes two hours and costs £13. Buses for Penzance leave Exeter at 11 am and 4.30 pm (five hours, £17).

Train Exeter is at the hub of lines running from Bristol (numerous, 1½ hours, £14), Salisbury (hourly, two hours, £16), and Penzance (eight per day, three hours, £20.50). There are hourly trains from London's Waterloo and Paddington stations (two hours, £34). The train to/from London is much quicker than the bus.

The 65-km branch line to Barnstaple is promoted as the Tarka Line and gives good views of traditional Devon countryside with its characteristic, deep-sunken lanes. Barnstaple is a useful starting point for North Devon. There are six trains a day, Monday to Saturday, one on Sunday, costing £8.30.

Getting Around

Exeter has an efficient fleet of minibuses (Nippers) and buses. If you are not using the youth hostel, however, you won't need to unravel their mysteries. One possible exception is bus No 55, which links St David's Station, Central Station and the bus and coach station.

DARTMOOR NATIONAL PARK

Although the park is only about 40 km from north to south and east to west, it encloses some of the wildest, bleakest country in England – a suitable terrain for the Hound of the Baskervilles (one of Sherlock Holmes' most famous opponents).

The park covers a granite plateau punctuated by distinctive tors, which can look uncannily like ruined castles, and cut by deep valleys known as *combes*. The high moorland is covered by windswept gorse and heather (there are no trees, apart from some limited plantations), and is grazed by sheep and the semiwild Dartmoor ponies.

Habitation is sparse. There are several small market towns surrounding the table-land, but the only village of any size on the moor is Princetown, which is not a particularly attractive place.

The countryside in the south-east is more conventionally beautiful, with wooded valleys and thatched villages. There are no specific tourist sights of note on Dartmoor. This is hiking country and the attractions are elemental, my dear Watson.

Orientation & Information

Dartmoor is accessible from Exeter and Plymouth, and rare buses run from these regional centres to the surrounding market towns. There are only two roads across the moor and they meet near Princetown.

The National Park Authority has seven information centres in and around the park, but it is also possible to get information in the TICs at Exeter and Plymouth before you set off. The main headquarters (☎ 0626-832093) is open all year and is at Haytor Rd, Bovey Tracey, Devon TQ12 9JQ, at the easternmost tip of the park.

The Ministry of Defence (☎ 0392-70164) has a large training area and three live firing ranges in the north-western section.

Places to Stay

Most of Dartmoor is privately owned, but the owners of unenclosed moorland do not object to backpackers who keep to a simple code: don't camp on moorland enclosed by walls or within sight of roads or houses; don't stay on one site for more than two nights; and leave the site as you found it.

There are youth hostels at Postbridge, bang in the middle, and Steps Bridge, near Dunsford between Moretonhampstead and Exeter, as well as at Exeter, Plymouth and Dartington.

There is a regional booking office

(☎ 0722-337494) or you can phone individual hostels direct.

Bellever Youth Hostel (☎ 0822-88227), Postbridge, is very popular. It closes over winter and on Mondays, except from 1 July to 31 August. *Steps Bridge* (☎ 0647-52435) is open from 27 March to 30 September, except Wednesday.

The larger towns on the edge of the park (like Buckfastleigh, Moretonhampstead, Okehampton and Tavistock) all have plentiful supplies of B&Bs in the £12 to £15 bracket.

Getting There & Away

Exeter is the best starting point for the park and it has good transport connections to the rest of England. Public transport in and around the park is lousy, so consider hiring a bike from Flash Gordon (☎ 0392-213141) in Exeter.

From Exeter, DevonBus 359 follows a circular route through Steps Bridge and Moretonhampstead (Monday to Saturday). The most important bus that actually runs across the moors is the Transmoor Link (DevonBus 82) that runs between Exeter and Plymouth across the moor via Moretonhampstead and Princetown. Unfortunately it only runs in summer, and even then there are only three buses each way. A return ticket that allows you to get on and off as often as you like costs £3.70. Alternatively, you can catch the Transmoor Link in one direction and catch the hourly buses between Plymouth and Exeter (along the A38) the other direction (£4).

Outside summer, life becomes considerably more difficult. There are some buses, but the services change regularly and are infrequent. The best idea is to work out roughly what you want to do, then contact the Devon County Public Transport Help Line (☎ 0392-382800).

SOUTH CORNWALL COAST
Truro

This is Cornwall's uninspiring regional centre; you may need to use it as a transport hub. For bus information, ring Western National (☎ 0872-40404).

Penzance

At the end of the line from London, Penzance is a busy little town that has not yet completely sold its soul to tourists. There's little to entice you to stay, however, because beautiful St Ives is so convenient. That is, unless you are just about to start or finish the section of the Coast Path around Land's End to/from St Ives. This dramatic 40 km section can be broken at the youth hostel at St Just (near Land's End), and there are many other cheap farm B&Bs along the way.

Information The TIC (☎ 0736-62207) is just outside the train station.

Places to Stay The *youth hostel* (☎ 0736-62666), Castle Horneck, Alverton, is an 18th century mansion on the outskirts of town. Walk west through town on the Land's End road (Market Jew St) until you get to a thatched cottage opposite the Pirate Inn, turn right and cross the A30 bypass road until you get to the signposted lane.

Getting There & Away There are three buses a day from Penzance to Bristol via Truro, Plymouth and Exeter; four buses a day to Exeter (five hours, £17); and four buses a day from London and Heathrow (7½ hours, £32.50).

But the train is definitely the civilised way to get to Penzance – a very enjoyable, but expensive, trip. There are 11 trains a day from London's Paddington Station (five hours, £52). There are frequent trains from Penzance to St Ives between 7 am and 8 pm (20 minutes, £2.50).

Land's End

The coast on either side of Land's End is amongst the best in Britain, but the development at Land's End itself is the pits. There is a good nearby *youth hostel* (☎ 0736-788437), Letcha Vean, St Just-in-Penwith, 14 km from Penzance. It's closed over winter.

The coastal hills between St Just and St Ives with its dry stone walling has one of the oldest, most fascinating agricultural landscapes in Britain, still following its Iron Age pattern. There are numerous prehistoric remains and the abandoned engine houses from old tin and copper mines.

WEST CORNWALL COAST
St Ives

St Ives is an exceptionally beautiful little town, but stay clear in July and August. The omnipresent sea, the harbour, the beaches, the narrow alleyways, steep slopes and hidden corners are captivating. It is easily accessible by train from Penzance, there is a swarm of B&Bs in the £12 to £15 bracket, and there are some cheap restaurants and takeaway fish shops.

Information The TIC (☎ 0736-796297), The Guildhall, Street-an-Pol, a short walk downhill from the railway station, is open all year. There are several surf shops on The Wharf (the street edging the harbour) where it is possible to rent boards (seven-foot pop-outs for £5) and wetsuits. Bikes are available from St Ives Mountain Bikes (☎ 0736-796560) on Fore St at £8 per day.

Places to Stay & Eat The main road into St Ives from Penzance, above Carbis Bay, is lined with B&Bs, but the closer you are to the town centre the better. Climb the steep streets immediately behind the harbour (towards Porthmeor Beach) and you'll find several blocks of B&Bs. There are a number of cheap restaurants on The Wharf (around the harbour) and in Fore St behind.

Newquay

This is a brash and tacky tourist town – a schizophrenic cross between a 1970s surf town and a traditional English beach resort. There are numerous sandy beaches, several right in town (including Fistral Beach for board riders).

Information The TIC (☎ 0637-879081) is near the bus station in the centre of town.

There are several surf shops on Fore St and they all hire fibreglass boards and wetsuits, each for around £5 per day. Compare prices; they're competitive. The surfie crowd drinks at the Newquay Arms.

Places to Stay The *youth hostel* (☎ 0637-876381) is on Narrowcliff, the eastern extension of Cliff Rd. It's open daily from 1 July to 31 August, or Mondays to Saturdays from March to November.

A better alternative is the *Towan Beach Backpackers* (☎ 0637-874668), Beachfield Ave, which has dorm beds for £6.50. It has an excellent central position overlooking Towan Beach, there are no curfews, and it's open all day.

Getting There & Away There are four trains a day between Par on the main London-Penzance line, and numerous buses to Truro.

Tintagel

Even the summer crowds and the grossly commercialised village cannot destroy the surf-battered grandeur of Tintagel Head. The scanty ruins are believed to mark the birthplace of King Arthur – anyone born here would have to be wild and wonderful. Entry to the reserve costs £1.80. There is a nearby *youth hostel* (☎ 0840-770334), open in summer. There are irregular buses in summer from Truro (but not on Thursday and Sunday); contact Western National (☎ 0872-40404).

NORTH DEVON

North Devon is one of the most beautiful regions in England with a spectacular, largely unspoilt coastline and the superb Exmoor National Park, which protects the best of it. Hard to beat.

Barnstaple

Barnstaple is a large town and transport hub – a good starting point for North Devon. There are some handsome old buildings, but there's no reason to stay. There's no youth hostel. Contact the TIC (☎ 0271-47172) for B&Bs.

Barnstaple is at the western end of the Tarka Line from Exeter and connects with a number of bus services around the coast. Filer's (☎ 0271-863819) 301 service runs along the A39 south of Bideford where you can connect with a Red Bus (☎ 0271-45444) to Bude. Red Bus' service No 310 runs direct to Lynton (one hour, £1.95, five buses a day, last bus 5 pm), but the most interesting option is the excellent No 300 scenic service that crosses Exmoor from Barnstaple, through Lynton to Minehead (£4 for a one day explorer pass).

Mountain bikes are available from Tarka Trail (☎ 0271-24202) in the train station for £6 per day.

Exmoor National Park

Exmoor is a small national park (400 sq km), but it encloses a wide variety of beautiful landscapes. In the north and along the coast the scenery is particularly breathtaking with dramatic humpbacked headlands giving superb views across the Bristol Channel.

A high plateau rises steeply behind the coast, but is cut by steep, fast-flowing streams. The bare, high hills of heather and grass run parallel to the coast. On the southern side the two main rivers, the Exe and Barle, wind their way south along wooded valleys *(coombes)*. Pony herds descended from ancient hill stock still roam the commons, as do the last herds of wild red deer in England.

There are a number of particularly attractive villages: Lynton/Lynmouth, twin villages joined by a water-operated railway; Porlock at the edge of the moor in a beautiful valley; Dunster, which is dominated by a castle, a survivor from the Middle Ages; and Selworthy, a National Trust village with many classic thatched cottages.

Arguably the best and easiest section of the South West Coast Path is between Minehead and Padstow (sometimes known as the Somerset and North Devon Coast Path). See *South West Coast Path: Minehead to Padstow* by Roland Tarr (paperback, Countryside Commission/Aurum Press, £7.95) for details.

Orientation & Information Exmoor is accessible from Barnstaple (train from Exeter) and Taunton (bus/train from Bristol or London, bus from Wells).

The National Park Authority (NPA) has five information centres in and around the park, but it is also possible to get information in the TICs at Barnstaple, Ilfracombe, Lynton and Minehead. The NPA centres at Dunster (☎ 0643-821835) and Lynmouth (☎ 0598-52509) are open from the end of March to the beginning of November. The main headquarters (☎ 0398-23841) is open all year at Exmoor House, Dulverton, Somerset TA22 9HL (between Bampton and Minehead).

The NPA produces *The Exmoor Visitor*, a free newspaper listing useful addresses, numerous guided walks run by the NPA, accommodation and general information.

Places to Stay In addition to the youth hostel at Ilfracombe, there are hostels at Minehead (☎ 0643-702595), near Lynton (☎ 0598-53237), and Exford (☎ 064383-288) in the centre of the park. All these hostels close over winter and are only fully open in July and August.

The main swarm of B&Bs can be found around Lynton/Lynmouth, but they are scattered throughout the park. They aren't cheap: you're probably looking at £16. Contact the Lynton TIC (☎ 0598-52225) for specific suggestions.

Getting There & Away From Exeter catch the Tarka Line to Barnstaple, from where buses run to Ilfracombe, Lynton and Minehead. See the Exeter and Barnstaple sections for more details.

Alternatively, six buses a day leave Taunton (one hour, £2.90) for Minehead. Contact Southern National (☎ 0823-272033) for details; the last bus leaves after 7 pm. Taunton can be reached from Bristol (Bristol-Plymouth line), Wells and Glastonbury (Badgerline bus No 163), or London (London-Penzance line). An Exmoor Public Transport timetable is available from TICs or you can contact the Devon

County Council's bus enquiry line (☎ 0392-382800).

BATH

For thousands of years, Bath's fortune has been linked to its hot springs and tourism. The Romans developed a complex of baths and a temple to Sulis-Minerva. Today, however, Bath's most important attraction is its Georgian architecture.

Throughout the 18th century, Bath was the most fashionable and elegant haunt of English society. Aristocrats flocked here to gossip, gamble and flirt. Fortunately they had the good sense and fortune to employ a number of brilliant architects who designed the Palladian terrace housing (characterised by simplicity and symmetry) that dominates the city.

Like Florence, Italy, Bath is an architectural jewel. As in Florence, there is a much-photographed, shop-lined bridge, and like Florence, it sometimes seems like nothing more than an exotic shopping mall for wealthy tourists. However, when sunlight brightens the honey-coloured stone, and buskers and strollers fill the streets and line the river, you cannot deny its exceptional beauty.

Orientation & Information

Bath is quite a sprawling town with widely flung suburbs (as you'll discover if you stay at the hostel). Fortunately, the centre is compact and easy to get around, although the tangle of streets, arcades and squares can be confusing. The centre fills a triangle bounded on the east and west sides by the River Avon and a ridge of hills to the north. The train and bus station are at the southern tip of this triangle by the river.

The TIC (☎ 0225-462831), The Colonnades, Bath St, is open all week during summer, not Sundays from October to May. Advance booking for accommodation in July and August is essential. Free walking tours (highly recommended) leave from the Abbey Churchyard at 10.30 am (except Saturdays). The Bath International Festival is

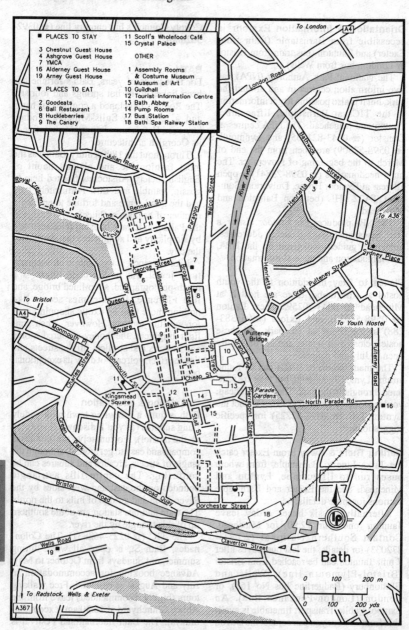

PLACES TO STAY

3 Chestnut Guest House
4 Ashgrove Guest House
7 YMCA
16 Alderney Guest House
19 Arney Guest House

PLACES TO EAT

2 Goodeats
6 Bali Restaurant
8 Huckleberries
9 The Canary

11 Scoff's Wholefood Café
15 Crystal Palace

OTHER

1 Assembly Rooms
  & Costume Museum
5 Museum of Art
10 Guildhall
12 Tourist Information Centre
13 Bath Abbey
14 Pump Rooms
17 Bus Station
18 Bath Spa Railway Station

Bath

held from the last week of May through the first week of June.

Things to See

Bath was designed for wandering around – you need at least a full day. Don't miss the **Covered Market** next to the Guildhall, or the maze of passageways just north of the Abbey Churchyard.

Bath Abbey (donation £1) makes a convenient starting point for a walking tour. Built between 1499 and 1616, it's more glass than stone.

On the south side of the Abbey Churchyard (an open square), the **Pump Room** houses an opulent restaurant that exemplifies the elegant style that once drew the aristocrats.

Nearby, the **Roman Baths Museum** (open all week all year; £3.80, or £4.60 including the Museum of Costume in the Assembly Rooms, a 20-minute walk up the hill) is a series of excavated passages and chambers beneath street level, taking in the sulphurous mineral springs (still flowing after all these years), the ancient central heating system, and the bath itself, which retains its Roman paving and lead base. It can get hopelessly overcrowded in summer.

From the Roman Baths, walk north until you come to the main shopping drag, Milsom St, and finally the **Assembly Rooms** and the **Museum of Costume**, which contains an enormous collection of clothing from 1590 to the present day.

Turn left on Bennet St and walk west to **The Circus**, an architectural masterpiece by John Wood the Elder designed so that a true crescent faces each of its three approaches. Continue to the **Royal Crescent** designed by John Wood the Younger, which is even more highly regarded than his father's effort. No 1 has been superbly restored to its 1770 glory, down to the minutest detail (£2.40, and worth it).

From Royal Crescent, wander back to the Abbey, then keep going east until you find yourself overlooking the formal **Parade Gardens** with their famous view looking up the Avon to Pulteney Bridge. **Pulteney Bridge** was built by Robert Adam and is lined with tiny shops. Continue along Great Pulteney St from the bridge and you reach Sydney Place. Jane Austen lived at No 4 with her parents.

Places to Stay

The *YMCA International House* (☎ 0225-460471) offers the best budget accommodation. It's central, it takes men and women, there's no curfew, and... it's heavily booked. Approaching from the south along Walcot St, keep your eyes peeled on the left about 150 metres past the post office for an archway and steps to the left. Singles/doubles without cooked breakfast are £11.75/20, dorms are £10.

The *youth hostel* (☎ 0225-465674) is out towards the University of Bath, a good 25-minute walk, or catch Badgerline bus No 18 (70p). There are compensatory views. The hostel is open all day, all year, but there is an 11 pm curfew.

The *Ashgrove Guest House* (☎ 0225-421911), 39 Bathwick St, is 10 minutes walk from the centre and has rooms at £16 per person, and it is good value. Also close to the centre, the *Chestnut Guest House* (☎ 0225-425845) on Henrietta Rd is £16 per person, and the *Alderney Guest House* (☎ 0225-312365) on Pulteney Rd is £15 per person. A bit further out (two km) but still good value, the *Avon Guest House* (☎ 0225-423866), 160 Newbridge Rd, is a welcoming place with an en suite double for £15.50 per person, and a couple of other rooms at £13.50 per person.

There are a group of places on Wells Rd, that would do in a pinch, but they're expensive. The *Arney Guest House* (☎ 0225-310020), 99 Wells Rd, charges £20 per person.

Places to Eat

Pubs will probably be your best bet for evening meals. *The Crystal Palace* (☎ 0225-423944), Abbey Green (south of Abbey Churchyard), has a beer garden, traditional ales and meals like lasagne and salad for £3.90.

On Kingsmead Square, the pleasant *Scoff's Wholefood Café* is a pleasant place open during the day from Monday to Saturday. They have takeaway sandwiches, or you can eat in, with soup for £1.50 and tempting possibilities like a tandoori burger with salad and tsatsiki for £2.50.

The Canary (☎ 0225-424846), 3 Queen St, is in one of Bath's most attractive cobbled streets. It has an interesting menu with a range of main dishes for between £4 and £6: for example, vegetarian chestnut and mushroom stroganoff for £5.75, or Somerset rabbit for £4.50.

Huckleberries (☎ 0225-464876), 34 Broad St, is a good-value vegetarian restaurant open during the day, until 9 pm on Thursdays, Fridays and Saturdays. Main courses like spinach roulade and Indian thali are £5.95. *Goodeats* Bartlett St (near the Assembly Rooms), is cheap and and cheerful – a good spot to rest your weary feet and enjoy a real capuccino (90p).

The *Bali Restaurant* (☎ 0225-463341), 2 George St is a pleasant surprise; the prices aren't Balinese, but the food is. Soups are from £1.70, fried noodles are £4.50, chicken curry is £5.

Getting There & Away

Bus There are National Express (☎ 0272-541022) buses every two hours from London (three hours, £16). There's one bus a day between Bristol and Portsmouth via Bath and Salisbury – see the Salisbury section for details. There's also a link with Oxford (3½ hours, £13), and Stratford-on-Avon via Bristol (three hours, £18).

Avon County publishes some excellent map-timetables, available from the bus & coach station (☎ 0225-464446). The Badgerline Day Rover (£4.10) gives you access to a good network of buses in Avon (Bristol), Somerset (Wells, Glastonbury), Gloucestershire (Cotswolds) and Wiltshire (Lacock, Bradford-on-Avon, Salisbury).

See the Salisbury section for information on the Wiltshire Day Rover, if you're planning to spend the bulk of a day in Wiltshire en route to Salisbury.

Train There are numerous trains from London's Paddington Station (1½ hours, £23.50). There are also plenty of trains through to Bristol for onward travel to Cardiff (£9.70), Exeter or the north. There are hourly trains between Portsmouth and Bristol via Salisbury and Bath. Bath to Salisbury is £8; Bath to Portsmouth is £17.

Getting Around

Badgerline has a good service around the city with most trips costing around 50p. Bikes are available from Avon Valley Bike Hire (☎ 0225-461880), Railway Place, from £8 to £16 per day.

AROUND BATH

Lacock

This is a classic, dreamy Cotswolds village with the further attraction of a 13th century abbey (open 30 March to 3 November, daily except Tuesday, 1 to 5.30 pm; £3.75) and a museum of photography. Lacock is accessible by Badgerline, five km south of Chippenham.

Bradford-on-Avon

Nine km east of Bath, this beautiful small town has somehow managed to avoid inundation by tourists. Its narrow streets tumble down a steep bluff overlooking the Avon. There are good bus connections with Bath, and hourly trains (15 minutes), so this could easily be used as a base. There's a reasonable range of B&Bs from £12 up. Contact the TIC (☎ 02216-5797) for more information.

If you can afford a little more, the *Bradford Old Windmill* (☎ 02216-6842) is a beautifully converted windmill overlooking the town. The rates are around £25 per person, but the view, the atmosphere and the friendly welcome are worth it.

WELLS

Wells is a small cathedral city that has kept much of its medieval character; many claim that the cathedral is the most beautiful in England, and it is unquestionably one of the best surviving examples of a full cathedral complex.

Orientation & Information Wells is 34 km south-west of Bath on the edge of the Mendip Hills. The TIC (☎ 0749-672552) is in the Town Hall on the picturesque Market Place. City Cycles (☎ 0749-675096), 80 High St, has bikes for hire – racers at £4.50 per day, mountain bikes at £9 – there are lots of interesting possible routes.

Things to See The cathedral was built in stages from 1180 to 1400 and incorporates a number of styles. The most famous features are the extraordinary west façade, an immense sculpture gallery with over 300 surviving figures, and the interior scissor arches, a brilliant solution to the problem posed by the subsidence of the central tower. You'll need to make several visits to do it justice; if possible, join one of the free tours (Easter to October).

Beyond the cathedral is the moated Bishops Palace, with its beautiful gardens (open Thursday and Sunday summer afternoons only; £1.50), Market Place (markets Wednesdays and Saturdays) and the 14th century Vicars' Close.

Places to Stay & Eat There are plenty of B&Bs with prices around £12. The *Old Poor House* (☎ 0749-75052) is a 14th century cottage just outside the cathedral precincts, with singles from £15. *Richmond House* (☎ 0749-76438), 2 Chamberlain St, is also within a couple of minutes of the centre, with B&B for £13.50. The guesthouse at *17 Priory Rd* (☎ 0749-677300), on the A39 to Glastonbury a short walk from the centre, is a comfortable place with excellent breakfasts, for £15. The nearest youth hostel is at Street near Glastonbury (see following section).

The favourite local watering hole and restaurant is the *Fountain Inn & Boxer's Restaurant* to the east of the cathedral, which has good, though slightly pricey food. There's a wide range of main courses for between £7 and £10. Thank goodness for the ever reliable vegetarian lasagne (£4.75).

Getting There & Away There are hourly buses from Bath and Bristol operated by Badgerline (1¼ hours, £2.10). No 376 from Bristol continues through Wells to Glastonbury and Street. No 163 runs from Wells to Taunton (for Exmoor) via Glastonbury and Street.

GLASTONBURY

Legend and history combine at Glastonbury to produce an irresistible attraction for romantics and nuts of every description. It's a small market town with the ruins of a 14th century abbey, and a nearby hill *(tor)* with superb views.

According to legend, Jesus travelled here with Joseph of Arimathea and the chalice from the Last Supper, it is the burial place of King Arthur and Queen Guinevere, and the tor is either the Isle of Avalon or a gateway to the underworld. Whatever you choose to believe, a climb to the top of the tor is well worthwhile. Turn right at the top of High St (far end from the TIC) into Chilkwell St and then left into Dod Lane; there's a footpath to the tor from the end of the lane.

The TIC (☎ 0458-832954) can supply maps and accommodation information; there are plenty of B&Bs around £12. The nearest *youth hostel* is six km away at Street (☎ 0458-42961) and is open April through October except Sundays, every day in July and August.

There are Badgerline buses from Bristol to Wells, Glastonbury and Street (for the youth hostel, alight at Leigh Rd, and then it's a 1½-km walk). Glastonbury is only 10 km (six miles) from Wells, so walking/hitching is feasible. Bus No 163 from Wells continues to Taunton from where there are buses to Minehead (for Exmoor).

BRISTOL

Bristol is a large city, and if you approach through the unlovely suburbs to the south, you might wonder what the hell you are getting into. The centre, however, has atmospheric old streets and canals, some magnificent architecture, docks and warehouses that are being rescued from ruin, and

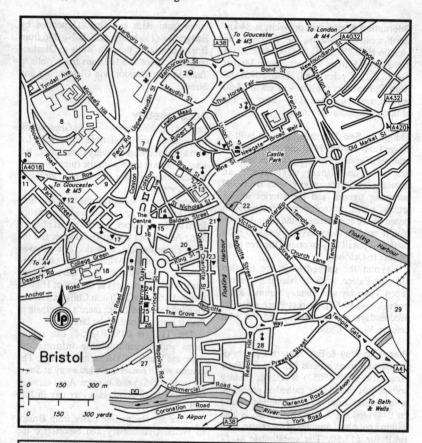

Bristol

1 Bristol Royal Infirmary	16 Prima Pasta
2 Bus & Coach Station	17 Bunch of Grapes
3 John Wesley's Chapel	18 Bristol Cathedral
4 Giovanni Restaurant	19 Watershed
5 Post Office	20 Theatre Royal
6 Bierkeller	21 Ferry
7 Christmas Steps	22 Bristol Bridge
8 University of Bristol	23 Llandoger Trow
9 Red Lodge	24 Tourist Information Centre
10 Museum & Art Gallery	25 Youth Hostel
11 STA	26 Arnolfini Arts Complex
12 Melbourne's Restaurant	27 Bristol Industrial Museum
13 St Nicholas Market	28 St Mary Radcliffe Church
14 American Express	29 Bristol Temple Meads
15 Thomas Cook	Railway Station

a plethora of bars, pubs and restaurants. There is a genuine energy and quite an un-English urban culture.

Although the city definitely has an eye to the tourists, it has not become ossified and Disneyesque in the way of some of the more famous nearby towns and, as a result, some people may well prefer it. There is a lot to see and do and the city has an interesting history that stretches back 1000 years. Bristol is most famous as a port, although it is six miles (10 km) from the Severn estuary, and it grew rich on the 17th century trade with north America and the West Indies (rum, slaves, sugar and tobacco).

It continues to prosper today (although it has had to switch some commodities) and it is an important transport hub with connections north to the Cotswolds and the Midland cities, west to southern Wales, south-west to Devon and Cornwall, and east to Bath (which would be an easy day trip).

Orientation & Information

The city centre is to the north of the Floating Harbour – a system of locks, canals and docks fed by the tidal River Avon. The central area is compact and easy to get around on foot.

The main railway station is Bristol Temple Meads, about one km to the south-east of the centre, although some trains use Bristol Parkway eight km (five miles) to the north, which is accessible from the centre by bus and train. There are also a limited number of suburban train stations. The bus and coach station is to the north of the city centre.

The TIC (☎ 0272-260767), 14 Narrow Quay, faces onto St Augustines Reach, part of the harbour that has now been redeveloped. It's in the same building as the excellent youth hostel, and you can also reach it by walking through the hostel lobby (off Prince St). It's open seven days. The comprehensive Visitors Guide (£1.50) is worth buying, and they also have a good (free) public transport map. American Express (☎ 0272-260427) and Thomas Cook both have offices on Baldwin St.

Things to See

The first thing on a visitors' agenda should be a wander around the twisting streets of the old city centre. Start at the TIC and walk north along Narrow Quay; turn right and walk down King St, with its old buildings, now used as restaurants and clubs and the **Llandoger Trow**, a 17th century pub reputed to be the Admiral Benbow in Robert Louis Stevenson's *Treasure Island*.

Turn left at the harbour reach known as the Welsh Back and turn left again at the **Bristol Bridge**, the site of the Saxon bridge from which the town takes its name. Explore the **St Nicholas Markets**, then continue westwards to the medieval **St John's Church** and cross busy Rupert St to the **Christmas Steps**. Walk south to the College Green flanked by the impressive council offices and **Bristol Cathedral**.

Depending on your level of energy, turn right up the hill, up Park St, with its numerous restaurants, to the suburb of Clifton, which is dominated by fine Georgian architecture. Or you could round off the circuit by visiting the **Arnolfini Centre**, an important contemporary arts complex, or the **Watershed**, on opposite sides of St Augustine's Reach.

There are numerous other important sights, most of which are free: The **New Room**, John Wesley's chapel, the first Methodist church in the world; the 16th century **Red Lodge**; the beautiful **Church of St Mary Redcliffe**; the **Maritime Heritage Centre** and Brunel's **SS *Great Britain*** (£2.50), the first ocean-going iron ship with a screw propeller; the **Bristol Industrial Museum**; the **Theatre Royal**, opened in 1766; and the spectacular **Clifton Suspension Bridge** designed by Brunel to cross the spectacular Avon Gorge.

Places to Stay

Bristol has an excellent *youth hostel* (☎ 0272-253136), 64 Prince St, in a converted warehouse five minutes from the centre of town. The dorms are small, mostly four-bed, and most have en suite facilities. There's also a good, cheap café.

The cheap B&Bs tend to be a fair distance from the centre, although there is a good town bus service. There are a number on Bath Rd (the A4) and Wells Rd (the A37). The *Albany Guest House* (☎ 0272-778710), 500 Bath Rd, about two miles (three km) from the centre, has singles/doubles at £15 per person. The TIC makes free bookings and can suggest other alternatives.

If you want to stay centrally, you'll have to pay around £25. There are quite a few guesthouses/hotels in Clifton, which has a good supply of restaurants and a walking distance to the centre. The *Oakfield Hotel* (☎ 0272-733643) and the *Oakdene Hotel* (☎ 0272-735900) on Oakfield Rd (off Whiteladies Rd) have comfortable, well-equipped rooms for £25/40.

Places to Eat

Bristol is well endowed with restaurants, and most are reasonably priced. The pubs have the best cheap eats. There are a number of restaurants along Park St, which becomes Queen's Rd and Whiteladies Rd.

Whiteladies Rd is a 20-minute walk from the centre; at No 109 the *Latin Quarter* has pasta and pizza dishes for under £4; at 87 the *Malacca Restaurant* (☎ 0272-738930) has Malaysian specialties like gado gado for £3.25, prawns for £7.95.

On Park St, *Melbourne's Restaurant* (☎ 0272-226996), at No 74, is an Australian-style BYO (bring your own bottle of wine) and it packs them in. At lunch, two courses cost £8, at dinner £12.25. The menu features dishes like pan-fried chicken on bed of ratatouille, and vegetable stir-fry with Thai style curry sauce. It's worth the splurge – consider booking, however. At No 28, the *Dionysius* (☎ 0272-279506) has Greek dishes – you should be able to eat well for around £10.

In the centre of town, *Prima Pasta* (☎ 0272-293278), 8 Baldwin St, has a range of fresh pastas with an enormous variety of sauces, with most dishes between £4 and £6. *Giovanni* at 15 Union St is also popular, and has similar prices.

Entertainment

There's plenty going on at night, ranging from high culture to low. Whatever you're looking for, it's worth investing in *Venue* (£1.50), which is a similar listings mag to London's *Time Out* and gives details on theatre, music, the works, for Bath and Bristol. There are three main zones for those looking for the pub/club scene.

There are a number of alternatives on King St, ranging from the *King St Warehouse* (disco) to the *Old Duke* (pub jazz) and *New Vic* (theatre). There's a batch of hot and sweaty pubs, a couple with live bands, near the St Nicholas Market – try the *Bristol Bridge Inn* or the *Crown*. Getting even hotter and sweatier, there's a bunch of pubs in behind Park St and The Centre – the *Bunch of Grapes* and the *Hatchet*.

The legendary *Bierkeller* (☎ 0272-268514), All Saints St, which has played host to luminaries like the Stone Roses, Jane's Addiction and the Stranglers, is a good bet.

Getting There & Away

Bus Bristol has excellent bus connections with an enormous number of places; only a few can be given here. There are hourly National Express (☎ 0272-541022) buses to London via Heathrow Airport (2½ hours, £18). There are frequent buses to Cardiff (1¼ hours, £7) and the 11.30 am bus goes on to Pembroke Docks for the Irish ferry (eight hours, £12.75). There are a couple of buses a day to Barnstaple (4½ hours, £14.50) and regular buses south to Cornwall (Exeter – 1¾ hours, £12). Buses also head north and west to Gloucester and Oxford (2½ hours, £12.50) and Stratford-on-Avon (2½ hours, £15).

The local Badgerline buses have four services a day to/from Bath. There are also services to Salisbury, Weymouth and north to Gloucester. Their Day Rambler ticket is £4.10. For county-wide information ☎ 0272-557013.

Rail Bristol is an important rail hub with fast links to half a dozen interesting cities and regular connections with London's Paddington (1½ hours, £26). Most trains (except those to the south) use both the Temple Meads and Parkway stations. Bath is only 20 minutes and £2.80 away, so it is an easy day trip. There are frequent links to Cardiff (one hour, £7.70), Fishguard (1½ hours, £16), Exeter (one hour, £14), Oxford (1½ hours, £20), and Birmingham (1½ hours, £16). Phone ☎ 0272-294255 for information.

Getting Around

Due to the nature of the nightlife, it's possible a taxi might be a good investment. Phone 0272-264001 or 0272-238128.

There's a good system of local buses – the local council has an enquiry line (☎ 0272-557013). The suspension bridge is quite a walk from the centre of town – catch bus No 8 or 9 (changing to Nos 508 and 509 on weekends) from bus stop 'CU' on the northeast corner of The Centre, or from Temple Meads Station.

The nicest way to get around is the ferry which, from April to September, plies the Floating Harbour. There are a number of stops between Bristol Bridge, the Industrial Museum, the SS *Great Britain* and Hotwell. The ferry runs every 40 minutes and a single fare is 75p, a round trip is £1.50. For details phone the Bristol Ferry Boat Co (☎ 0272-273416).

Southern Midlands

Sometimes known as the Heart of England, this patchwork of small counties contains some of the country's best and worst. The worst can be found in a wide corridor either side of the M1 motorway. Herefordshire, Bedfordshire and Buckinghamshire are a graveyard for modern town planning, exemplified by Milton Keynes, which was founded in 1967.

London's uninspiring suburban sprawl continues to advance into the Chilterns, and Birmingham and Coventry – never famous for their beauty – have struggled to survive

the bombing of WW II and the industrial decline of the 1970s and 1980s.

To the west, however, it's a different story. Oxford is not without modern urban problems, but it is still a very beautiful city. The south-west sections of the Chilterns remain largely unspoilt and are accessible to walkers of the Ridgeway.

The Cotswolds, more than any other region, embodies the popular image of English countryside. The prettiness can be forced, and the villages are certainly not strangers to mass tourism, but there are also moments when you will be transfixed by landscapes that are serenely unreal. The combination of golden stone, flower-draped cottages, church spires, towering chestnuts and oaks, rolling hills and green, stone-walled fields can be too extraordinary to seem anything other than a fantasy.

West again, you reach the Bristol Channel and the wide Severn Valley, a natural border to the county of Hereford and Worcester and the region known as the Welsh Marches. Hereford and Worcester have rich agricultural country with orchards and market gardens. The Wye Valley is a famous beauty spot, popularised by the first Romantic poets in the 18th century. Approaching England from the Welsh plateau, there are wonderful views.

The southern Midlands include some of England's most popular tourist sites – it's something of a toss-up whether they are worth the crowds and costs. There's Blenheim Palace (definitely), Hatfield House, Windsor Castle (definitely), Warwick Castle, Stratford-upon-Avon, and Oxford (definitely).

FACTS FOR THE VISITOR
Orientation & Information

The Midlands is a vague term at best; dividing it between north and south is nothing short of arbitrary. However, the region is cut by two ranges of hills and two major rivers. From east to west, you first meet the chalk ridge of the Chilterns which runs north-east from Salisbury Plain to Hertfordshire, then the Thames Valley, the limestone Cotswolds

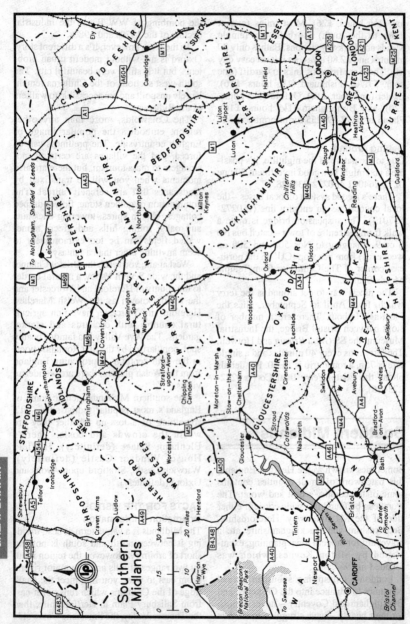

Southern
Midlands

GREAT BRITAIN

which run north from Bath, and finally the Severn Valley.

Major north-bound transport arteries (including the M1) cross the region, so it is highly likely you'll go through it at some stage. There are youth hostels at Windsor, Oxford, Charlbury, Stow-on-the-Wold, Stratford-upon-Avon and Birmingham, amongst others.

Activities
Hiking The best hiking is in the Chilterns and the Cotswolds, although there are a number of other interesting paths in the region.

The Cotswolds Way, with easy accessibility to accommodation, is the best way to discover the Cotswolds. The path follows the western escarpment overlooking the Bristol Channel for 160 km (100 miles) from Chipping Campden to Bath, but it is quite feasible to tackle a smaller section. Bath is obviously easily accessible, but you'll have to contact the Gloucestershire enquiry line (☎ 0452-425543) for information about the infrequent buses between Chipping Campden and Stratford or Moreton-in-Marsh.

Contact the Ramblers Association (☎ 071-582 6878), 1/5 Wandsworth Rd, London SW8 2XX, for copies of the *Cotswold Way Handbook*, which includes accommodation and transport information (£1.50 including local p&p). *The Cotswold Way – a complete walker's guide* by Mark Richards (Penguin) is widely available. You should find both at the Bath TIC.

The Ridgeway starts near Avebury and runs north-east for 137 km (85 miles) to Ivinghoe Beacon near Aylesbury. See the South-Western England section for more information.

HATFIELD HOUSE
Hatfield House (☎ 0707-262823) is the most celebrated Jacobean (meaning built in the reign of James I) house, a graceful red-brick and stone mansion full of treasures. It's open Tuesday to Saturday from noon to 4.15 pm, Sundays from 1.30 pm; admission is £4.30. The entrance is just opposite the Hatfield train station. There are numerous trains from King's Cross en route to Cambridge.

WINDSOR & ETON
Windsor Castle, the home for British royalty for over 900 years, is one of the greatest surviving medieval castles. It was built in stages between 1165 and the 16th century on chalk bluffs overlooking the Thames.

The strategic value of Windsor has long since disappeared, but its symbolic importance has never waned. The current royal family made this connection clear when George V, the current queen's grandfather, changed the family name from the rather too Germanic Saxe-Coburg-Gotha to Windsor.

Inside the castle, St George's Chapel is a masterpiece of perpendicular Gothic architecture (entry £2.50). There is also a collection of royal treasures and the State Apartments. The castle is open daily from 10 am, but it can be closed at short notice. The State Apartments are closed when the royal family are in residence; for opening arrangements, phone ☎ 0753-831118. In summer, the changing of the guard takes place every day at 11 am.

A short walk along Thames St and across the river and you come to yet another enduring symbol of Britain's unpleasant class system, **Eton College**, a famous public (meaning private) school that has educated no less than 19 prime ministers. It is open to visitors from 2.30 to 4.30 pm during term, and from 10.30 am during Easter and summer holidays (admission £2). A number of buildings date from the mid-15th century when the school was founded by Henry VI.

Since it is easily accessible by train and road from London, Windsor crawls with tourists. If at all possible, avoid weekends. There's a *youth hostel* (☎ 0753-861710) two km from the central railway station, open from February through December. There are numerous trains to/from Paddington every day (30 minutes, £4.50); change at Slough (five minutes away on the main line). If you're on your way to Bath or Oxford, return to Slough to pick up the main westbound trains.

OXFORD

It is impossible to pick up any tourist literature about Oxford without reading about its dreaming spires. Like all great clichés it's strikingly apt. Looking across the meadows or rooftops to Oxford's golden spires is one of the most beautiful sights on earth.

These days, however, Oxford battles against a flood of tourists and some typical Midlands social problems. It is not just a university city, but the home of Morris cars, later British Leyland and now the Rover Group, and it has expanded rapidly this century. This has created a city with a congested centre (housing most important university buildings and shops) surrounded by sprawling industrial suburbs.

Oxford University is the oldest university in Britain, but no-one can find an exact starting date. It evolved during the 11th century as an informal centre for scholars and students. The colleges began to appear from the mid-13th century onwards. There are now about 10,000 undergraduates and 35 colleges.

Ninety-two km (57 miles) west of London, Oxford has a population of over 115,000.

Orientation

The city centre is surrounded by rivers and streams on the eastern, southern and western sides and can easily be covered on foot.

The railway station is to the west of the city, with frequent buses to Carfax Tower (in the centre). Alternatively, turn left off the station concourse into Park End St, which becomes New Rd, then Queen St, which at Carfax becomes High St – a 15-minute walk.

The bus station is on Gloucester Green (there's no green). Turn left when you leave the bus station, first right, then almost immediately left into George St. This will bring you out on Cornmarket St, a pedestrian mall on your right. Turn right for the TIC.

Carfax Tower at the intersection of Queen and Cornmarket/St Aldate's is a useful central marker. Coming from the train station, turn right at the tower into St Aldate's St for the TIC. The tower is all that remains of St Martin's Church. There's a fine view from the top, good for orienting yourself. It's open March to October, Monday to Saturday; admission is 75p.

Information

A visit to the hectic TIC (☎ 0865-726871), St Aldate's St, is essential. It's open Monday to Saturday from 9.30 am to 5 pm, Sundays during summer from 10 to 11 am and 3 to 3.30 pm. You need more information than this guide can give if you're going to do the place justice. The *Welcome to Oxford* brochure (50p) has a good map, college opening times, and a walking tour. The TIC has daily two-hour walking tours of the colleges (around 10.30 am and 2 pm daily; £3).

The colleges remain open throughout the year (unlike Cambridge) but their hours vary; many are closed in the morning.

Things to See

You need more than a day to do justice to Oxford, but at a minimum, make sure you visit the following colleges: Christ Church (with Oxford Cathedral), Merton and Magdalen (pronounced 'maudlen').

Starting at the TIC, cross St Aldate's and walk down the hill to **Christ Church**, perhaps the most famous of all Oxford colleges. The main entrance is beneath Tom Tower, which was built by Wren in 1680, but the usual visitor's entrance is farther down the hill via the wrought-iron gates of the War Memorial Gardens and the Broad Walk facing out over Christ Church Meadow. The college chapel is the smallest cathedral in England, but it is a beautiful example of late Norman (1140-80) architecture.

Return to the Broad Walk, follow the stone wall, then turn left up Merton Grove, through wrought-iron gates, then right into Merton St. **Merton** was founded in 1264 and its buildings are amongst the oldest in Oxford. The present buildings mostly date from the 15th to the 17th centuries. The entrance to the 14th century Mob Quad, with its fascinating medieval library, is on your right.

Turn left into Merton St, then first right into Magpie Lane which will take you through to High St with its fascinating mix of architectural styles. Turn right down the hill until you come to **Magdalen** just before the river on your left. Magdalen is one of the richest Oxford colleges and has the most extensive and beautiful grounds with a deer park, river walk, three quadrangles and superb lawns.

Punts and boats are hired at Magdalen Bridge (£5.80 per hour, £20 deposit). There is no better way of letting the atmosphere of Oxford seep in. The seepage can be dramatic: punting is not as easy as it looks. Go left for peace and quiet, right for views back to the colleges across the Botanic Gardens and Christ Church Meadow. Punts are available from Easter to September.

Walk back up High St until you come to **St Mary the Virgin** church on your right (there's a good view from the tower), turn right up Cattle St to the distinctive, circular **Radcliffe Camera**, a reading room for the Bodleian Library. Continue up Cattle St passing the **Bridge of Sighs** on your right, then turn left into Broad St. On your left you pass Wren's **Sheldonian Theatre**, and on your right **Trinity** and **Balliol** Colleges. Turn left at Cornmarket St and you'll be back where you started.

Places to Stay

Unfortunately the *youth hostel* (☎ 0865-62997), Jack Straw's Lane, is not centrally located. Despite this it is booked up very quickly in summer. Catch minibus No 73 outside the post office just down the hill from the TIC (50p).

Alternatively you could catch a train to Charlbury in the Cotswolds (trains every 1½ hours, 15 minutes) where there is another *youth hostel* (☎ 0608-810202). It's open every day from 1 April to 31 August. In 1992 the building was up for sale, so ring ahead and check it is still operating.

B&Bs are expensive and suburban. You're looking at £15 per person rising to £20 in peak season. Perhaps Oxford is a day trip from London after all; the nightlife is nothing to write home about.

The *Athena Guest House* (☎ 0865-243124), 253 Cowley Rd (over Magdalen Bridge and straight on), is easy to reach by bus, and is within walking distance of shops and restaurants. Singles/doubles are £18/36. A bit farther out, the *Earlmont* (☎ 0865-240236) is a large and comfortable B&B with singles/doubles at £25/35.

The *Sportsview Guest House* (☎ 0865-244268), 106 Abingdon Rd (the continuation of St Aldate's St), is a two-star guesthouse for nonsmokers. Singles/doubles are £18/32.

Becket House (☎ 0865-724675) is convenient to the railway station, with singles/doubles at £18/32.

Places to Eat

There's quite a range of places to eat, but most of them aren't cheap. This could mean that college food is so good the students don't eat out, or that the students have plenty of money. Don't be fooled by the *Poor Student* on Ship St – a vegetable lasagne is £5.50! Generally, pubs will be your best bet.

Self-caterers should visit the *Covered Market*, on the north side of High St at the Carfax end, for fruit and vegetables. There's also an excellent bakery, *Oma Bakers*, with pies for £1.35 and slices of pizza for 80p. At lunch time, check the *Convocation Coffee House* in St Mary the Virgin Church (near the Radcliffe Camera); it has a range of hot dishes for around £4 in a pleasant room.

The *Bulldog Hotel* (☎ 0865-250201) is a popular pub with live jazz and a wide range of standards like lasagne and pies for under £4. The *Oxford Brew House* (☎ 0865-727265), 14 Gloucester St, near Gloucester Green bus station, has a wide range of moderately priced dishes and a good atmosphere.

If you're staying in Cowley Rd or the youth hostel, try the *Hi-Lo Jamaican Eating House* (☎ 0865-725984), 70 Cowley Rd, an unusual restaurant with old-fashioned furniture and good Black music. Large portions of healthy food (including vegetarian dishes) are around £7.

Getting There & Away

Bus Oxford is easily and quickly reached from London, and there are a number of competitive bus lines on the route. The Oxford Tube (☎ 0865-772250) starts at Victoria bus station but also stops at Marble Arch, Notting Hill Gate and Shepherd's Bush; a day return from Victoria is £5; the last bus is at 1 am; the journey takes around 1½ hours.

National Express (☎ 0865-791579) has five buses a day that run via Heathrow Airport. There are five services a day to/from Bath (two hours, £11.25), Bristol (2¼ hours, £12.50), and two to/from Gloucester (1½ hours, £7.50) and Cheltenham (one hour, £7). From Bristol there are connections to Wales, Devon and Cornwall. There are five buses a day to Cambridge (three hours, £15). Buses to Shrewsbury and north Wales go via Birmingham, to York and Durham via Birmingham.

Train There are 40 trains a day from London Paddington (50 minutes, £11.60). Windsor and Eton are virtually en route and are easily accessible by train. Network SouthEast cards apply.

There are regular trains north to Coventry and Birmingham (£12), and north-west to Worcester and Hereford (for Moreton-in-Marsh, Gloucester and Cheltenham in the Cotswolds). Birmingham is the main hub for transport farther north.

To connect with trains to the south-west you have to change at Didcot Parkway. There are plenty of connections to Bath; with a bit of luck the whole trip won't take longer than 1½ hours (£18). Change at Swindon for another line running into the Cotswolds (Kemble, Stroud and Gloucester). For train enquiries, ☎ 0865-722333.

Getting Around

There are a number of places where you can hire bicycles: Bee-Line Bicycles (☎ 0865-246615), 33 Cowley Rd, hires bikes at £7 per day or £10.50 per week. Pennyfarthing (☎ 0865-249368), 5 George St, not far from the bus station, has bikes at £5 per day or £10 per week.

Local buses and minibuses leave from the streets around Carfax; most fares are around 50p.

Boat trips and punts are available at Folly Bridge (the bottom of St Aldate's) and at Magdalen Bridge. Salter Bros offers a number of interesting boat trips from Folly Bridge between May and September.

BLENHEIM PALACE

Blenheim Palace (☎ 0993-811325), one of the largest palaces in Europe, was a gift to John Churchill from Queen Anne and Parliament as a reward for his role in defeating Louis XIV. Curiously, the palace was the birthplace for Winston Churchill, who perhaps more than any other was responsible for checking Hitler.

Designed and built by Vanbrugh and Hawksmoor between 1704 and 1722 with gardens by Capability Brown, Blenheim is an enormous Baroque fantasy. It is definitely worth visiting; the house is open between March and October, adults/students £6/4.50; the park is open every day, all year.

Blenheim is just outside the village of Woodstock. Catch a Thames Transit Minibus No 20/A/B/C from Gloucester Green, Oxford (30 minutes, £2.15 return) to the palace's entrance.

STRATFORD-UPON-AVON

Stratford is an ordinary Midlands market town that happened to be William Shakespeare's home. Due to shrewd management of the cult of Bill, it's one of the busiest tourist attractions outside London. There are a number of buildings associated with his life that you can visit.

If you're a serious fan you'll have to visit, but if you're not, don't break a leg. As it's just beyond the northern edge of the Cotswolds, however, Stratford can be a handy stopover on your way to/from the north. The Royal Shakespeare Company has two theatres here, in addition to the Barbican and the Pit in London, and there is nearly always something on.

Information
The TIC (☎ 0789-293127), Bridgefoot, has plenty of information about the numerous B&Bs; you should be able to find something for around £12. Seeing a production by the Royal Shakespeare Company is definitely worthwhile. For information about its current programme call ☎ 0789-295623. Tickets are often available on the day of performance. Get in early; the box office opens at 9.30 am. Stand-by tickets are available to students immediately before performances (£6 to £12).

Place to Stay
The *youth hostel* (☎ 0789-297093), Hemmingford House, Alveston, is four km across town from the railway station. Walk into town along Alcester Rd, which becomes Greenhill, Wood, Bridge and Bridgefoot (with the TIC). Cross Clopton Bridge and follow the B4086. You can take bus No 18 from Wood St near the TIC. It's open from February to December.

Prices for B&Bs have a wild lurch towards ridiculously expensive during summer. There are a number of places on Alcester Rd, although they are a long walk from the centre. *Hunter's Moon Guest House* (☎ 0789-292888), 150 Alcester Rd, has singles and doubles from £12.50 to £17.50 per person. The *Moonlight Guest House* (☎ 0789-298213), 144 Alcester Rd, has singles and doubles from £12.50 to £14.50 per person.

Getting There & Away
Bus National Express (☎ 021-622 4373) buses link Birmingham, Stratford, Warwick, Oxford, Heathrow and London seven times a day (last bus 5 pm). Birmingham is a major hub for all northern buses (York, Chester, Shrewsbury etc). Singles from Stratford are: Birmingham £4.50, Warwick £2.25, Oxford £6.50, and Heathrow/London £12.75.

Train Travelling to/from London, change at

Reading and Leamington Spa. Warwick is on the line between Leamington and Stratford, so you can check the beautiful castle if you feel like dealing with screaming hordes of barbarians. Trains leave from Paddington (2½ hours, £21).

COTSWOLDS
The Cotswolds are a range of limestone hills rising gently from the Thames and its tributaries in the east but forming a steep escarpment overlooking the Bristol Channel in the west. They are characterised by honey-coloured stone villages and a gently rolling landscape. The villages were built on the wealth of the medieval wool trade.

Many of the villages are extremely popular with tourists; it's difficult to escape commercialism unless you have your own transport, or are walking. Some of the small villages worth looking for are Blockley (south of Chipping Campden), Broadwell (near Stow-on-the-Wold), Longborough (between Moreton-in-Marsh and Stow) and Duntisbourne (north-west of Cirencester). The best advice is to get lost!

Orientation
The hills run north from Bath for 160 km to Chipping Campden. The most attractive countryside is bounded in the west by the M5 and Chipping Sudbury, in the east by Stow-on-the-Wold, Burford, Bibury, Cirencester and Chippenham.

There are railway stations at Cheltenham, Kemble (serving Cirencester), Moreton-in-Marsh (serving Stow) and Stroud.

Bath, Cheltenham, Stratford-on-Avon and Oxford are the best starting points for the Cotswolds. Cirencester calls itself the region's capital.

Information
The TICs in surrounding towns all stock information on the Cotswolds, but the TICs dealing specifically with the region are at Cirencester (☎ 0285-654180), Market Place, and Stow-on-the-Wold (☎ 0451-31082), Talbot Court.

Stow-on-the-Wold

Stow is one of the most impressive (and visited) towns in the Cotswolds. It's a terrific base if you don't have a vehicle, because there are a number of beautiful villages in the surrounding area that could easily be reached on a day walk (Longborough, Broadwell, Upper and Lower Slaughter). The *youth hostel* (☎ 0451-30497) is in a 16th century building and it's open from 1 March to 31 October.

Stow can be reached by bus from Moreton-in-Marsh, which is on the main Cotswolds line between Worcester and Oxford. Buses (roughly one an hour; 10 minutes) leave from the town hall, a five-minute walk from the station. Contact Pulham & Sons (☎ 0451-20369) for a timetable.

Cheltenham

Cheltenham is a large, but still elegant, spa town easily accessible by bus and train. The TIC (☎ 0242-522878) is helpful. The *Cleeve Hill Youth Hostel* (☎ 0242-672065) is a wood-panelled ex-golf clubhouse eight km from Cheltenham on the B4362 to Winchcombe. It's open March to October, except Mondays.

If you don't walk, you'll have to catch a bus from the railway to the bus station, and then one of the hourly Castleways C11 buses. Cheltenham is on the main Bristol-Birmingham train line, so it can be easily reached by train from South Wales, Bath and south-west England, and Oxford (changing at Didcot and Swindon).

Places to Stay

The Cotswolds are not particularly well served by youth hostels, but there are countless B&Bs. There are hostels at Charlbury (see the Oxford section), Slimbridge, Wantage and Lechlade, but the most central and most interesting are at Cleeve Hill, Stow-on-the-Wold (both recommended, see the earlier Stow-on-the-Wold section) and Duntisbourne Abbots (which unfortunately has no public transport).

Getting Around

As you may have gathered, it's difficult to use public transport around the Cotswolds. If you're trying anything ambitious, contact the Gloucestershire enquiry line (☎ 0452-425543). Bikes can be hired in Bath, Oxford (see appropriate sections) and Cheltenham. Crabtrees (☎ 0242-515291), 50 Winchcombe St, Cheltenham, rents mountain bikes at £7/30 a day/week.

BIRMINGHAM

Birmingham is the most southerly of the great Midlands industrial cities, and the second largest city in Britain with over one million inhabitants. Although there's plenty of vitality, it's a large industrial complex with no essential sights. It's not beautiful, nor is it particularly accessible to the short-term shoestring traveller. For information contact the Birmingham TIC (☎ 021-643 2514), 2 City Arcade. The *youth hostel* (☎ 021-233 3044) is open from 8 July to 20 September only.

Eastern England

With the exception of Cambridge, most of the eastern counties – Essex, Suffolk, Norfolk and Cambridgeshire – have been overlooked by tourists. East Anglia, as the region is often known, has always been distinct, separated from the rest of England by the fens and the Essex forests.

The fens were a strange water-world that stretched from Cambridge north to the Wash and beyond into Lincolnshire. The marshes were home to people who led an isolated existence amongst the maze of waterways, fishing, hunting and farming scraps of arable land. In the 17th century, however, Dutch engineers were brought in to drain the fens, and the flat open plains with their rich black soil were created. The region is the setting for Graham Swift's excellent recent novel *Waterland*.

To the east of the fens, Norfolk and Suffolk have gentle, unspectacular scenery

1 To Gothenburg (Sweden)
2 To Esbjerg (Denmark)
3 To Hamburg (Germany)
4 To Hook of Holland (Netherlands)
5 To Zeebrugge (Belgium)

Eastern England

that can still be very beautiful. John Constable and Thomas Gainsborough painted in the area known as Dedham Vale, the valley of the River Stour. Villages like East Bergholt (Constable's birthplace), Thaxted and Cavendish are quintessentially English with beautiful churches and thatched cottages.

The distinctive architectural character of the region has been determined by the lack of suitable building stone. Stone was occasionally imported for important buildings, but for humble churches and houses three local materials were used: flint, clay bricks and oak. The most unusual of the three, flint,

can be chipped into usable shape, but a single stone is rarely larger than a fist. Often the flint is used in combination with dressed stone or bricks to form decorative patterns.

More than any other part of England, East Anglia has close links with northern Europe. In the 6th and 7th centuries it was overrun by the Norsemen. From the late Middle Ages, Suffolk and Norfolk grew rich trading wool and cloth with the Flemish; this wealth built scores of churches and helped subsidise the development of Cambridge. The windmills, the long straight drainage canals and even sometimes the architecture (especially in

King's Lynn) call the Low Countries to mind. To this day, Harwich and Felixstowe are major ports for European traffic.

FACTS FOR THE VISITOR
Orientation & Information
East Anglia lies to the west of the main northbound transport arteries. Its southern boundary is the Thames estuary, and its western boundary (now marked by the M1 and A1) was formed by a huge expanse of almost impenetrable marshland – the fens. Norwich is the most important city. Harwich and Felixstowe are the main ports for ferries to Germany, Holland and Denmark.

There are youth hostels at Cambridge, Colchester, Ely, King's Lynn and Norwich, among others. The East Anglia Tourist Board (☎ 0473-822922) can provide further information.

Activities
Hiking The Peddars Way and Norfolk Coast Path runs across the middle of Norfolk (Peddars Way) until it reaches the beautiful north Norfolk coast at Holme next the Sea. It follows this coastline through a number of attractive, untouched villages like Wells-next-the-Sea. The Peddars Way Association, 150 Armes St, Norwich NR2 4EG, publishes a guide for £1.70 and and accommodation list for £1.10 (including local p&p).

Cycling This is ideal bicycling country. Where there are hills, they're gentle. Bicycles can be hired in Cambridge, and the TIC can suggest several interesting routes. The East Anglia Tourist Board has a worthwhile brochure called *Cycling in East Anglia* (£1.50).

Boating The Norfolk Broads, a series of inland lakes (ancient flooded peat diggings) to the east of Norwich, are popular with boat people of every description. Contact Blake's (☎ 0603-782911) for information about hiring narrowboats, cruisers, yachts and houseboats.

GETTING THERE & AWAY
Train
Harwich, Norwich, King's Lynn and Cambridge are all easily accessible from London.

Boat
Sealink (☎ 0255-243333) runs two ferries a day from Harwich to Hook of Holland, Netherlands; Scandinavian Seaways (☎ 0255-240240) runs at least three a week to Esbjerg, Denmark, and Hamburg, Germany, and at least two a week to Gothenburg, Sweden. P&O (☎ 0304-203388) run two ferries a day from Felixstowe to Zeebrugge. See the main Getting There & Away section for more details.

GETTING AROUND
Bus
Bus transport around the region is slow and disorganised. For timetables and information covering Cambridgeshire, ☎ 0223-317740, for Norfolk, ☎ 0603-613613, and for Suffolk, ☎ 0473-265676.

Train
From Norwich you can catch trains to the Norfolk coast and Sheringham, but there's an unfortunate gap between Sheringham and King's Lynn (bus or hitch?) preventing a rail loop back to Cambridge. It may be worth considering the Anglia Flexi Rover, for three days travel out of seven, £18; or an Anglia One Day Ranger, £9.50.

CAMBRIDGE
Cambridge can hardly be spoken of without reference to Oxford – so much so that the term Oxbridge is used to cover them both. The two cities are not just ancient and beautiful university towns; they embody preconceptions and prejudices that are almost mythical in dimension.

An Oxbridge graduate is popularly characterised as male, private-school educated, intelligent and upper-class, but the value judgments attached to the term will very often depend on who is using it. It can be both abusive and admiring: for some it means academic excellence, for others it

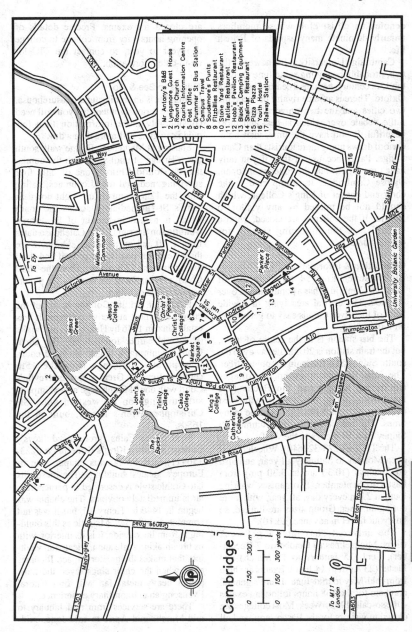

1 Mr Antony's B&B
2 Lyngamore Guest House
3 Round Church
4 Tourist Information Centre
5 Post Office
6 Drummer St Bus Station
7 Campus Travel
8 Scudamore's Punts
9 Fitzbillies Restaurant
10 Stone Yard Restaurant
11 Tatties Restaurant
12 Hobb's Pavilion Restaurant
13 Black's Camping Equipment
14 Shalimar Restaurant
15 Pizza Plaza
16 Youth Hostel
17 Railway Station

Cambridge

0   150   300 m
0   150   300 yards

To M11 &
London

denotes an elitist club whose members unfairly dominate many aspects of British life.

Cambridge University is the newer of the two, probably beginning some time early in the 13th century, perhaps a century later than Oxford. There is a fierce rivalry between the two cities and the two universities, and a futile debate over which is best and most beautiful. If you have the time, visit both. Oxford draws many more tourists than Cambridge. Partly because of this, if you only have time for one and the colleges are open, choose Cambridge. Its trump card is the choir and chapel of King's College, which should not be missed by any visitor to Britain. If the colleges are closed, choose Oxford (see the following section for opening dates).

Orientation & Information

Eighty-seven km (54 miles) north of London, Cambridge has a population of over 100,000. The central area lying in a wide bend of the River Cam is easy to get around on foot or bike.

The bus station is in the centre of town, but the train station is 20 minutes away to the south. Sidney St is the main shopping street. The most important group of colleges (including Kings) and the Backs (the meadows adjoining the Cam) are to the west of Sidney St, which changes its name many times. The bus station is on Drummer St; Sidney St is 50 metres to the west.

The TIC (☎ 0223-322640), Wheeler St, is open Monday to Saturday all year, and also on Sundays (10.30 am to 3.30 pm) from Easter to September. It organises walking tours at 2 pm every day, all year, with more during summer. Group sizes are limited, so buy your ticket in advance (£3.10).

The university has three eight-week terms: Michaelmas (9 October to 7 December), Lent (15 January to 15 March) and Easter (23 April to 14 June). Exams are held from mid-May to mid-June. There's general mayhem for the 168 hours following exams – the so-called May Week. Most colleges are closed to visitors for the Easter term, and all

are closed for exams. Precise details of opening hours vary from college to college and year to year, so contact the TIC for up-to-date information.

Things to See & Do

Cambridge is an architectural treasurehouse. If you are seriously interested you will need considerably more information than this guide can give, and more than a day.

Starting at Magdalene Bridge walk south down Bridge St until you reach the unmistakable **Round Church**, one of only four surviving medieval round churches, dating from the 12th century. Turn right down St John's St (immediately across the road) which is named in honour of **St John's College** (on the right). The Gatehouse dates from 1510 and on the other side there are three beautiful courts, the second and third dating from the 17th century. From the Third Court, you can cross the river by the picturesque Bridge of Sighs.

Next door, **Trinity College** is one of the largest and most attractive colleges. It was established in 1546 by Henry VIII on the site of several earlier foundations. The Great Court, Cambridge's largest enclosed court, incorporates buildings from the 15th century. Beyond Great Court is Nevile's Court with one of Cambridge's most important buildings on its western side: Sir Christopher Wren's library, built in the 1680s.

Next comes Caius (pronounced 'keys') College, and then **King's College** (☎ 0223-350411), and its famous chapel, one of Europe's greatest buildings. The reason its late Gothic style is described as perpendicular is immediately obvious. The chapel was begun in 1446 by Henry VI, but it was not completed until 1545. Majestic as this building is from the outside, it is its interior, with its breathtaking scale and intricate fan vaulting, that makes the greater impact. It comes alive when the choir sings; even the most pagan heavy-metal fan will find Choral Evensong an extraordinary experience.

There are services from mid-January to mid-March, mid-April to mid-June, mid-

July to late July, early October to early December, and 24 and 25 December. Evensong is sung at 5.30 pm Tuesday to Saturday (mens' voices only on Wednesdays) and at 3.30 pm on Sundays.

Continue south on what is now King's Parade and turn right into Silver St (St Catherine's College on the corner) which takes you down to the Cam and the hiring point for punts.

Punting along the Backs (the section of the Cam that runs behind the colleges you have just seen) is at best sublime, but it can also be a wet and hectic experience, especially on a busy weekend. Look before you leap. If you do wimp out, the Backs are also perfect for a walk or a picnic – cross the bridge and walk along the river to the right. Scudamore's rents punts at £6 per hour but requires a £40 deposit. A small number of punts are rented behind Trinity at £4 with a £20 deposit, but they go quickly.

Places to Stay

There's a large *youth hostel* (☎ 0223-354601), 97 Tenison Rd, with small dormitories and a restaurant. It is very popular – book ahead. Seniors/juniors are charged £8.30/7. It's easy walking distance from the train station: go down Station Rd, and Tenison Rd is the first on the right.

There are numerous B&Bs at all times, even more during university vacation from late June to late September. There are a number of B&Bs on Huntingdon Rd, one of the manifestations of Sidney St etc. *Mr Antony* (☎ 0223-357444), 4 Huntingdon Rd, has four singles and four doubles from £13 and £26. A bit further out, *Benson House* (☎ 0223-311594), 24 Huntingdon Rd, has well-equipped rooms, some with en suite bathrooms from £16 to £20 per person.

Turn right into Chesterton Lane when you cross Magdalen Bridge and you reach the most convenient B&B zone. The *Belle Vue Guest House* (☎ 0223-351859), 33 Chesterton Rd, is comfortable and close to the city centre; doubles are £30. A bit further on, the *Lyngamore Guest House* (☎ 0223-312369), 35/37 Chesterton Rd, has rooms from £12 to

£15 per person. *All Seasons Guest House* (☎ 0223-353386), 219 Chesterton Rd, has singles/doubles at £13 per person.

Places to Eat

Market Square is the place for vegetables and budget self-caterers, but for those who like their cooking done for them, Cambridge offers a good selection of reasonably priced choices.

One of the most pleasant is *Hobb's Pavilion* (☎ 0223-67480), Park Terrace, which overlooks cricket ovals on parkland known as Parker's Piece. It specialises in pancakes and has a three-course menu for £7.50. It's open Tuesday to Saturday from noon to 2.30 pm and 7 to 10 pm.

Another budget favourite is *Tatties* (☎ 0223-358478), 26 Regent St, which, as its name suggests, specialises in baked potatoes stuffed with a variety of tempting fillings (from £1.45 to £4).

There are quite a number of reasonably priced restaurants on Regent St, so it's worth going for a wander and looking at the menus. During the day, the *Stone Yard Restaurant*, next door to St Andrew's Baptist Centre, serves cheap cafeteria-style meals at very reasonable prices – some meals are less than £3. The *Shalimar Restaurant* (Indian) and *Pizza Piazza* are both popular and inexpensive.

Fitzbillies (☎ 0223-352500), 52 Trumpington St, is a brilliant bakery/restaurant. The Chelsea buns (50p) are an outrageous experience, and so is the chocolate cake beloved by generations of students, but there are many other temptations in addition to the usual sandwiches and pies – stock up before you go punting.

Getting There & Away

Cambridge can easily be visited as a day trip from London (although it is worth staying at least a night) or en route to the north. It's well served by trains, not so brilliantly by buses.

Bus National Express (☎ 0223-460711) has hourly buses to London (two hours, £8.50). There are four buses a day to/from Bristol

(£25.50); two stop at Bath. There are five buses a day to Oxford (£15). Unfortunately, links to the north aren't very straightforward. To get to Lincoln or York you'll have to change at Peterborough or Nottingham respectively. York via Nottingham is £27. King's Lynn is also only accessible via Peterborough. The county council has an enquiry line (☎ 0223-317740).

Train There are trains every half hour from King's Cross and Liverpool St (one hour, £11). Network SouthEast railcards are valid. If you catch the train at King's Cross you travel via Hatfield (see Hatfield House in the Southern Midlands section) and Stevenage. There are also regular train connections to Bury St Edmunds, Ely (£2.10), and King's Lynn (£6.70). There are connections at Peterborough with the main northbound trains to Lincoln, York (£29.50 and Edinburgh (£66). If you want to head west to Oxford or Bath, you'll have to return to London first. For more information, ☎ 0223-311999.

Getting Around

Cambus (☎ 0223-423554) runs numerous buses around town from Drummer St, including Bus No 1 from the train station to the town centre (60p). It's easy enough to get around Cambridge by foot, but if you're staying out of the centre, or plan to wander into the fens (fine flat country for the lazy cyclist), a bicycle can be hired from Geoff's Bike Hire (☎ 0223-65629), 65 Devonshire Rd, near the youth hostel.

ELY

Ely is a small city set on a low hill that was once an island deep in the watery world of the fens. It is dominated by the overwhelming bulk of Ely Cathedral, a superb example of the Norman Romanesque style, built between 1081 and 1200. There are regular trains from Cambridge (20 minutes, £2.70), and a *youth hostel* (☎ 0353-667423) open from 24 May to 27 August.

NORFOLK
King's Lynn

King's Lynn is an interesting old port with some notable buildings, some of which are distinctly influenced by the trading links with Holland. Contact the TIC (☎ 0553-763044), Saturday Market Place, for further information. The *youth hostel* (☎ 0553-772461), Thoresby College, College Lane, is open fully from 1 July to 31 August and haphazardly outside that time.

Getting There & Away

There are regular trains from Cambridge (one hour, £6.50), but if you're exploring the northern Norfolk coast to the west there are only infrequent buses. Eastern Counties (☎ 0553-772343) has regular buses to Hunstanton on the coast to the west. If you're aiming for Wells, you'll have to go via Fakenham. Contact the Norfolk Bus Information Centre (☎ 0603-613613).

SUFFOLK
Harwich & Felixstowe

These are typically ugly ferry terminals. Contact the TIC (☎ 0255-506139) if you need a B&B. There are numerous trains from Harwich (Parkeston Quay) to London (Liverpool Station); you have to change trains at Manningtree (1¼ hours, £12.80). Alternatively, you could go north to Norwich, or change for Bury St Edmunds and Cambridge at Ipswich. From Felixstowe you catch a train to Ipswich, where you connect with the main Norwich-London line (11 trains per day, 1½ hours, £15.50). See the introductory Getting There & Away section for details on the ferries.

Northern Midlands

The northern Midlands are often dismissed as England's industrial back yard. The density of the network of motorways gives forewarning of the claustrophobic development and the continuing economic

importance of the region, despite the decline of some traditional industries.

In a very real sense this is England's working-class heartland. There is a wide gap between these northern cities and those south of Birmingham. Since the Industrial Revolution created them, life for their inhabitants has often been an uncompromising struggle. The horrific excesses of 19th century capitalism gave birth to a bitter and protracted class struggle that continues today. This is one of the homes of British trade unionism, the Labour Party and soccer; Conservative Party voters are as rare as stockbrokers and French cuisine.

FACTS FOR THE VISITOR
Orientation & Information

The main industrial corridor runs from Merseyside (Liverpool) to the Humber. All the major cities – Doncaster, Sheffield, Nottingham, Derby and Leicester – sprawl into the countryside, burying it under motorways, grim suburbs, power lines, factories and mines.

There are, nonetheless, some important exceptions: Lincoln, one of the great cathedral cities; walled Chester, a starting point for North Wales; and attractive Shrewsbury. On the eastern and western extremes in Shropshire and Lincolnshire (especially the

Wolds) there is beautiful, little-visited countryside, and in the centre there's the Peak District National Park.

There are youth hostels in Ludlow, Shrewsbury, Chester and Lincoln, and many closely spaced hostels in the Peak District National Park (most a day's walk apart).

GETTING AROUND
Bus
Bus transport around the region is fairly efficient, and particularly good in the Peak District.

Train
There's a good network of railway lines; you'll rarely need to resort to buses other than for financial reasons. See Shrewsbury for details on an interesting rail loop around Northern Wales.

SHREWSBURY
Shrewsbury is the attractive regional capital for Shropshire, and is famous for its black-and-white, half-timbered buildings. It's a good base for Ironbridge, Stokesay Castle and Wales. Two famous small railways into Wales terminate here and it's possible to do a fascinating circuit of north Wales – see the Getting There & Away section that follows.

There are no vitally important sights, and because of this, Shrewsbury has been saved from inundation by tourists. Strategically sited within a loop of the River Severn, there are **medieval streets** (including Butcher's Row and Fish St near St Alkmund's Church and around Old St Chads), **Quarry Park** (with a famous flower show in August) and river walks.

Orientation & Information
The station lies across the narrow land bridge formed by the loop of the Severn, a five-minute walk north of the centre of town. The bus station is central and the whole town is well signposted.

There's an efficient TIC (☎ 0743-350761), The Music Hall, The Square, with theatre-booking facilities (including for the Royal Shakespeare Company at Stratford).

There are daily walking tours at 2.30 pm from May to October.

Places to Stay & Eat
The *youth hostel* (☎ 0743-360179), Abbey Foregate, is a two-km walk from the railway and bus stations, 10 minutes after crossing English Bridge. Walk down High St, cross the bridge and veer right when Abbey Foregate splits in two around the abbey.

The *Lucroft Hotel* (☎ 0743-362421), Castlegates, on the way into town from the railway station, is very comfortable and spotlessly clean for £15, but there are some cheaper B&Bs scattered around.

The pubs will probably be your best bet for a meal. *Cromwell's Hotel & Wine Bar* (☎ 0743-361440), 11 Dogpole, has an interesting menu with vegetarian specials. Bar meals are as cheap as £1.50, a main course in the restaurant around £6.

Getting There & Away
Bus National Express (☎ 021-622 4373) has three buses a day to/from London (£16.50); one goes via Birmingham (£4) and Telford/Ironbridge. You change at Birmingham for Oxford and Stratford-on-Avon.

For information on transport in Shropshire, contact the county help line (☎ 0345-056785). Williamsons Motorways (☎ 0743-231010) runs an interesting service, the X96, between Birmingham and Shrewsbury via Ironbridge. There are regular departures in both directions. Enquire about the Wrekin Rambler Ticket. Midland Red West (☎ 0345-212555) has regular buses to/from Ludlow (service No 345) via Craven Arms, for Stokesay Castle.

Train Two fascinating small railways terminate at Shrewsbury, in addition to plenty of main-line connections. It's possible to do a brilliant, highly recommended rail loop from Shrewsbury around north Wales. Timetabling is a challenge, so talk to Britrail in advance (☎ 0743-364041). From Shrewsbury you head due west across Wales to Dovey Junction (1¾ hours, £9.10), where you connect with the famous Cambrian

Coast line, which hugs the beautiful coast on its way north to Porthmadog (1½ hours, £7.30).

At Porthmadog you can pick up the Ffestiniog Railway, a superb restored narrow-gauge steam train that winds up into Snowdonia National Park to Blaenau Ffestiniog (1¼ hours, £5.40) a bleak and strangely lovely slate mining town. From Blaenau another small railway carves its way through the mountains and down the beautiful, tourist-infested Conwy Valley to Llandudno (1¼ hours, £3.50) and Conwy. From there it's a short trip to Chester.

It is possible to do this in a day, although you have to be a bit lucky for everything to run to time. It would be better to allow at least two days; there are certainly plenty of interesting places to stop.

Another famous line, promoted as the Heart of Wales line, runs south-west to Swansea, connecting with the main Fishguard-Cardiff line (five trains a day; 3½ hours, £12.50).

There are numerous trains to/from Euston, London (three hours, £30), and regular links to Chester (one hour, £5). There are also regular trains from Cardiff to Manchester via Bristol, Ludlow and Shrewsbury.

AROUND SHREWSBURY
Ironbridge Gorge
Ironbridge, on the southern edge of Telford, is a monument to the Industrial Revolution. It was the wonder of its age, developing iron smelting on a scale never seen before – easy transport on the Severn, and rich deposits of iron and coal in the gorge itself made it possible.

Things to See There are a number of different sites strung along the gorge. There's Blist's Hill Open Air Museum, which re-creates an entire community, including shops, houses, forges, a mine head and pub; the Coalport China Museum with more than you ever wanted to know about porcelain (someone must love it); the beautiful first iron bridge; the Museum of Iron; and the Museum of the River and Visitor Centre (the

best starting point). A passport ticket allowing entrance to all the museums is £8/5.50 for adults/students.

Places to Stay The *youth hostel* (☎ 0952-433281), Paradise, is fully open from 1 March to 31 October. From the bridge, follow Wellington Rd towards the power station; turn right after one km on the A4169 to Wellington.

Getting There & Away Trains and buses run regularly to Telford from Shrewsbury (see that section), some go on to the Gorge. Otherwise, there are regular buses from Telford town centre. From June to September there's a park-and-ride bus service that calls at Telford bus and railway stations and the museum sites. Outside of this time, you'll need a car or a bike to get around the sites. Appropriately old-fashioned bikes are rented at Monewood House (☎ 0952-883075), Ironbridge Rd, at around £4.50 per day.

CHESTER
Chester proudly proclaims itself a tourist mecca. This honesty may be refreshing, but it's also rather alienating. Your role is clear: stay one night and spend lots of money. Despite this, it's a beautiful town, ringed by an unbroken red sandstone wall that dates back to the Romans. Chester has excellent transport connections, especially to/from North Wales.

The 3.5-km walk along the top of the wall is the best way to see the town – allow a good couple of hours so that you can detour along the river, and perhaps hire a boat.

Information & Orientation
Built in a bow formed by the River Dee, the walled centre is now surrounded by suburbs. The railway station is a 15-minute walk from the city centre: go up City Rd, then turn right into Foregate at the large roundabout. From the bus station, turn left into Northgate St. The TIC (☎ 0244-313126) is in the Town Hall opposite the cathedral. There are excellent guided walks around the city, every day at 10.45 am.

GREAT BRITAIN

Places to Stay & Eat

The recently renovated *youth hostel* (☎ 0244-680056), 40 Hough Green, is over two km from the city centre (on the far side from the railway station). Leave by Grosvenor Rd past the castle on your left, cross the river and turn right at the roundabout.

There are numerous good-value B&Bs for around £12 per person. The *Aplas Guest House* (☎ 0224-312401), 106 Brook St, is very comfortable and only a five-minute walk from the railway station. The *Glen-Garth Guest House* (☎ 0224-310260), 59 Hoole Rd, is a bit farther out (still within walking distance); all rooms have TV. There are plenty of other possibilities on Hoole Rd.

It's not easy to find cheap restaurant food in Chester. Your best bet will certainly be the pubs. The *Red Lion* and the *Pied Bull* on Northgate both have good meals for less than £4. If you're prepared to spend a little more, *No 14* (☎ 0244-318662) is an excellent vegetarian restaurant on Lower Bridge St on the way down to the weir on the Dee. It has an interesting menu (*spanakopita, roulades...*) with main meals from £6 to £7

Getting There & Away

Bus National Express (☎ 061-228 3881) has numerous services (time and prices to/from Chester in brackets): one a day to Glasgow (5½ hours, £24) via Manchester (one hour, £5.75) and Carlisle; one a day from Bristol (three hours, £19) to Liverpool (one hour, £4.25); three a day from Llandudno (1¾ hours, £6) to Birmingham (two hours, £10.25) and on to London (five hours, £20.50); there are one or two connections to Holyhead, for the Irish ferry (3½ hours, £10). For many destinations to the south or east, it will be necessary to change at Birmingham; to the north, at Manchester.

For information on local bus services, which are quite well organised, ring the Cheshire Bus Line (☎ 0244- 602666). Local buses leave from Market Square behind the town hall.

Train There are numerous trains to: Shrews-bury, except Sunday mornings (one hour, £5.60); Manchester (one hour, £5.60) and Liverpool; Holyhead (2¼ hours, £12) via the North Wales coast, for Ireland; Euston, London (2½ hours, £36.50). Contact Britrail (☎ 0244-40170) for details.

MANCHESTER & LIVERPOOL

Manchester and Liverpool were products of the Industrial Revolution and the empire; the postwar years have seen a painful decline. They're still big cities – Liverpool has half a million people, and Manchester is at the centre of an urban conurbation of 3½ million.

The problem is that their charms are not physical, but social and cultural. The down-to-earth people of Liverpool and Manchester are different to their southern cousins – and proud of it. Visitors should use a little caution as there are parts of both Liverpool and Manchester that have degenerated into urban battlegrounds; to those in the cosy home counties, Moss Side in Manchester has become as fearful a symbol as Harlem in New York.

Liverpool was Britain's greatest Atlantic seaport, exporting hundreds of thousands of migrants as well as the cotton fabrics and other manufactured goods produced farther inland. Today it is a shadow of its former glory, abandoned to doctrinaire left-wing politicians who have had little spare time to do anything constructive. Liverpool was the birthplace of the Beatles, and many pilgrims make a journey to Penny Lane and Strawberry Fields. For more information, contact the TIC (☎ 051-709 3631).

Manchester has had more success in surviving the loss of its traditional industries to Asia, and by any standards it is an important cultural centre. However, thanks to several hundred years of nonexistent, then plain bad, planning, it's ugly – not, however, as ugly as it was in the first half of the 19th century, when unchecked capitalism created the hellish working and living (dying, to be more accurate) conditions that were described by Friedrich Engels in *The Condition of the Working Class in England in 1844.*

The famous club scene that spawned The Smiths, New Order and the Stone Roses (amongst others) continues, although in more subdued form that at its peak. The centre for it all is the Hacienda, 11-13 West Whitworth St. For more information, contact the TIC (☎ 061-234 3157). Cheap accommodation is hard to find.

Northern England

Northern England is quite different to the rest of the country, although it is misleading to think of it as a single entity. The three major sections are Yorkshire, bordering the Midlands, to the south; Durham and Northumberland in the north-east; and Cumbria in the north-west. The latter two areas border on Scotland.

As a rule, the countryside is harder and more rugged than in the south and it is as if the history reflects this, because every inch has been fought over. The central conflict has been the long struggle between north and south, with the battle lines shifting over the centuries. The Romans were the first to attempt to delineate a border with Hadrian's Wall, but the struggle continued into the 18th century.

The Danes made York their capital and ruled the Danelaw – all of England north and east of a line between Chester and London. Later, their Norman cousins left a legacy of spectacular fortresses and the marvellous Durham Cathedral. The region prospered on the medieval wool trade, and this sponsored the great cathedral at York, and enormous monastic communities, the remains of which can be seen at Rievaulx and Fountains abbeys.

The countryside is a grand backdrop to this human drama with four of England's best national parks and some spectacular coastline. The Lake District and the Yorkshire Dales are best known and arguably the most beautiful of the parks, but the North York Moors have a great variety of landscapes, and include a superb coastline. All

three parks can be very crowded in summer, but it is easier to escape the masses in the North York Moors park.

FACTS FOR THE VISITOR
Orientation & Information
The dominating geological feature is the Pennine Hills, which form a north-south spine dividing the region into eastern and western halves and provide the source for numerous major rivers (the Mersey, Ribble, Aire, Tees and Tyne, among others).

The major transport routes – both rail and road – basically run either side of the hills from York (which is east of Manchester), to Newcastle (which is east of Carlisle), and Edinburgh (which is east of Glasgow). East-west transport, except between these paired cities, is slow. Newcastle is a ferry port for Scandinavia.

There are youth hostels at York and Newcastle and, even more importantly, dozens scattered about the national parks. Book ahead in summer.

Activities
Hiking There are more great hikes in this region than any other in England. The most famous is the Pennine Way which stretches 400 km from Edale in the Peak District to end in Scotland. Unfortunately, its popularity means that long sections turn into unpleasant bogs. An alternative like the Cumberland Way in the North York Moors National Park (see that section) is likely to be quieter and dryer underfoot.

Alternatively, it is possible to walk sections of Hadrian's Wall, or to tackle sections of the difficult 300-km Coast-to-Coast Walk which crosses the Lake District, Yorkshire Dales and North Moors. Wainwright describes the walk in his inimitable fashion in *A Coast to Coast Walk*.

GETTING AROUND
Bus
Bus transport around the region can be difficult, particularly around the national parks. For timetables and information covering Cumbria, phone ☎ 0228-23456, for

Northern England

Durham, phone ☎ 091-386 4411, and for Northumberland, phone ☎ 0670-514343. There are no central enquiry lines for Yorkshire; phone numbers for individual operators are given in the various Information sections that follow. For onward travel into the Scottish Borders, ☎ 0289-307461.

There are a number of one-day Explorer tickets; always ask if one might be appropriate. The Explorer North East is particularly interesting. It covers a vast area north of York to the Scottish Borders and west to Carlisle and Hawes (in the Yorkshire Dales). The major operator in the scheme is Northumbria

(☎ 091-232 4211) – they'll help plan an itinerary. Unlimited travel for one day is £4.25, and there are also numerous admission discounts for explorers. Tickets are available on the buses.

Train

In addition to the main-line routes running north to Edinburgh and Glasgow there are several useful branch lines, a number of which centre on Carlisle. Travelling to/from the south, it may be necessary to make connections at Leeds or Manchester.

Check whether a North Country Flexi

Rover, the North East Country Flexi Rover, or the North West Country Rover might be appropriate. For example, the North Country Flexi Rover allows unlimited travel throughout the north (not including Northumberland) for any four days out of eight for £43.

Boat

The Norwegian Color Line (☎ 091-296 1313) operates two ferries a week to Stavanger and Bergen in Norway. During summer, Scandinavian Seaways (☎ 091-296 0101) operates two ferries a week to Esbjerg, Denmark, and one a week to Gothenburg, Sweden. See the Getting There & Away section at the beginning of this chapter for details.

YORK

For nearly 2000 years York has been the capital of the north. It existed before the Romans, but entered the world stage under their rule. In 306 AD, Constantine the Great, the first Christian emperor and founder of Constantinople (now Istanbul), was proclaimed emperor here, probably on the site of the cathedral.

Under the Saxons, York became an important centre for Christianity and learning – the first church on the site of the current cathedral was built in 627. Danish invaders captured the city in 867, transforming it into an important trading centre and port – the River Ouse providing the link with the sea – and the capital of the Danelaw.

York continued to prosper as a political and trading centre after William the Conqueror's initial 'pacification'. In the 15th and 16th centuries, however, it lost royal favour and declined economically. Although it remained the social and cultural capital of the north, it was the arrival of the railway in 1839 that gave York a new lease of commercial life, allowing the expansion of Rowntree's and Terry's confectionery factories, and the development of tourism.

The city walls were built during the 13th century and are among the most impressive surviving medieval fortifications in Europe. They enclose a thriving, fascinating centre with medieval streets, grand Georgian town houses, riverside pubs, McDonald's and Marks & Spencer. The crowning glory is the Minster, the largest Gothic cathedral in England. York attracts millions of visitors, and the crowds can get you down, especially in July and August. But it's too old, too impressive, too real, and too convinced of its own importance to be totally overwhelmed by mere tourists.

Orientation

York is not the easiest city to find your way around – signposting leaves something to be desired and the streets are a medieval tangle. Bear in mind that in York, *gate* means street, and *bar* means gate.

There are five major landmarks: the four-km wall that encloses the city centre; the Minster at the northern corner; Clifford's tower, a 13th century castle and mound at the southern end; the River Ouse that cuts the centre in two (the most important part being the north-east two-thirds); and the enormous railway station just outside the western corner.

The main bus station is on Rougier St (off Station Rd, inside the city walls on the west side of Lendal Bridge), but some local buses leave from the train station.

Information

There are small TICs at the railway and bus stations (handy for an introductory map), but the main centre is across the river near Bootham Bar (☎ 0904-621756), De Grey Rooms, Exhibition Square. The main TIC is open Monday to Saturday from 9 am to 5 pm (later during summer) and from June to September on Sundays from 10 am to 1 pm.

Things to See

There's a lot to see in York, and this guide just scratches the surface with an introductory ramble. Before you start, buy a York Visitor Card from the TIC; it costs 90p but it gives significant discounts at all the major sights. It is also worth considering the innovative and excellent Yorspeed Walkman

GREAT BRITAIN

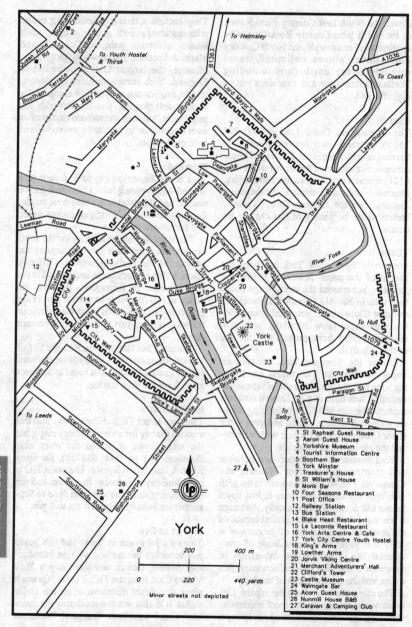

GREAT BRITAIN

York

0   200   400 m

0   220   440 yards

Minor streets not depicted

1 St Raphael Guest House
2 Aaron Guest House
3 Yorkshire Museum
4 Tourist Information Centre
5 Bootham Bar
6 York Minster
7 Treasurer's House
8 St William's House
9 Monk Bar
10 Four Seasons Restaurant
11 Post Office
12 Railway Station
13 Bus Station
14 Blake Head Restaurant
15 La Laconda Restaurant
16 York Arts Centre & Cafe
17 York City Centre Youth Hostel
18 King's Arms
19 Lowther Arms
20 Jorvik Viking Centre
21 Merchant Adventurers' Hall
22 Clifford's Tower
23 Castle Museum
24 Walmgate Bar
25 Acorn Guest House
26 Nunmill House B&B
27 Caravan & Camping Club

Guided Tour – also available from the TIC. For £3 you get an informative tape with atmospheric sound effects, a walkman (if required), and you can wander around at your own speed, with what amounts to a private guide in your pocket.

Starting at the TIC, climb the city wall at **Bootham Bar** (on the site of a Roman gate) and walk north-east along the wall to Monk Bar. There are beautiful views of the Minster.

York Minster took 250 years to complete (from 1220 to 1480), so it incorporates a number of architectural styles. From the wall you can see the nave, which was built in the Decorated style between 1291 and 1350; the central or lantern tower in the perpendicular style, which was the last addition (there are brilliant views from the top; £1.50 admission); the north transept (Early English, 1241-60), the octagonal Chapter House, extending from the north transept, a Decorated masterpiece (1260-1300); and the choir (the eastern end), also in the Decorated style. The cathedral is most famous for its extensive medieval stained glass, particularly the enormous Great Eastern Window (1405-08) which depicts the beginning and end of the world.

By the 1960s the cathedral was in danger of collapse. If you go down to the Undercroft (£1.50) you can see how it was saved: walk through the huge steel and concrete underpinning, with traces in between of earlier buildings on the site, going back as far as the Roman garrison.

The south transept was partly destroyed by fire in 1984 but has been meticulously reconstructed, complete with colourful roof bosses designed by British schoolchildren.

All visitors are asked to donate £1.50; there are worthwhile free guided tours. Evensong is at 5 pm Monday to Friday and at 4 pm on Saturday and Sunday (said, not sung, on Wednesday and Saturday).

Monk Bar is the best preserved medieval gate, with a working portcullis. Leave the walls here, walk along Goodramgate, but take the first right into Ogleforth, then left into Chapter House St. The **Treasurer's House**, on the right, has been restored by the National Trust (open April to October; £2.60). Turn left again into College St (back towards Goodramgate) and pass a 15th century, timber-framed building, **St William's College**, which has an exhibition designed to show the history of the minster.

Turn right onto Goodramgate again, past the ancient Lady Row houses. Cross diagonally over King's Square to the much-photographed **Shambles**, a medieval butcher's street. Walk down the Shambles, then turn left and immediately right into Fossgate, for the **Merchant Adventurers' Hall** (£1.80), which was built in the 14th century by a guild of merchants who controlled the cloth export trade.

Continue down Walmgate to **Walmgate Bar**, the only city gate in England with an intact barbican – an extended gateway designed to make life very difficult for uninvited guests. Follow the wall around to the right and across the River Foss to **Clifford's Tower** and the brilliant York Castle Museum.

The **York Castle Museum** (☎ 0904-653611) is a museum of everyday life and is one of the best in Britain. There are complete streets, but the most fascinating reconstructions are of domestic kitchens and rooms. The extraordinary collection of odds and ends, TVs, washing machines and vacuum cleaners are guaranteed to bring childhood memories flooding back. Admission is £3.50/2 for adults/students; allow at least two hours.

Unless you have a particularly strong interest in archaeology or Vikings, you can spare yourself the queue to the **Jorvik Viking Centre**. It's glitzy and superficial (£3.50). The **National Railway Museum**, adjoining the station, has numerous restored engines and carriages from the 1820s to the present day (£3.80). The **Yorkshire Museum** has the best collection of remnants from the Roman past (adults/students (£2.50/1.50); the grounds are definitely worth visiting for the ruins of St Mary's Abbey and the predominantly Roman Multiangular Tower.

Places to Stay

The *youth hostel* (☎ 0904-653147), Water

GREAT BRITAIN

End, Clifton, is open from early January to December. Seniors/juniors pay £8.30/7. It's large but very busy, so book ahead. It's about 1½ km from the TIC: turn left into Bootham, which becomes Clifton (the A19), then left into Water End. Alternatively, there's a riverside footpath from the station.

The *York City Centre Youth Hostel* (☎ 0904-625904), 11 Bishophill Senior, is equally popular, particularly with school and student parties. There is a range of rooms, from enormous dorms (£7) to doubles (£10.25 per person).

Fortunately the TIC has a free accommodation-booking service, because in summer it can be hard to find a bed. There are quite a few self-catering possibilities, which become economic if you are in a group or plan to stay more than a few days.

There are a number of B&Bs along Bootham Crescent (off the A19). There's another batch around around Scarcroft, Southland and Bishopthorpe Rds. Bishopthorpe is the continuation of Bishopgate which takes off from the southern corner of the wall after Skeldergate Bridge.

On Bishopthorpe itself, *Nunmill House* (☎ 0904-634047), 85 Bishopthorpe, is a good place with rooms from £14 per person. Just in from the corner of Bishopgate and Southland Rd, the *Acorn Guest House* (☎ 0904-620081), 1 Southland Rd, is a decent two-star guesthouse with TV in all rooms and singles from £12 to £15 and doubles from £22 to £32 depending on the season. The next-door *Staymor* (☎ 0904-626935) and *Bishopgarth* (☎ 0904-635220) are similar.

On Bootham Crescent, *Grange Lodge* (☎ 0904-621137), 52 Bootham Crescent is a comfortable nonsmoking place with rooms from £12 per person. The *Aaron* (☎ 0904-625927) at No 42 has pleasant doubles from £12 to £16 per person. On the other side of Bootham, *St Raphael* (☎ 0904-645028) charges from £13 to £15 per person.

The *Caravan & Camping Club* (☎ 0203-694995) is just over Skeldergate Bridge; they charge £3.50 per person.

Places to Eat

There's no shortage of good-value food in York; get hold of the free *Eat Out in York* brochure at the TIC.

There are several decent restaurants along Goodramgate from Monk Bar. *Caesar's Pizzeria & Ristorante* has pasta and pizzas for around £5 and the *Palace of India* (☎ 0904-639886) has thalis for under £8. The *Four Seasons Restaurant* (☎ 0904-633787) is in a half-timbered hall; there are interesting daily specials like hazelnut loaf and goulash for between £5 and £6.

The *King's Arms* on King's Staith is a pub with tables overlooking the river on the south-east side of the Ouse Bridge (the middle of the three main bridges). Nearby, the *Lowther Arms* on the corner of King's Staith and Cumberland has cheap bar meals (under £4) and a reasonable value restaurant, about £2 a dish more expensive. Up Cumberland St, *Plonker's Wine Bar* has specials like beef curry and ratatouille for under £5.

The most acclaimed restaurant in York is *The Blake Head* (☎ 0904-623767), 104 Micklegate, behind a book store with the same name. The emphasis is on simple vegetarian cooking, with soup around £1.50, a main course salad around £4. It is open during the day, but only Friday and Saturday evenings. The *York Art's Centre Café*, *La Laconda* and *The Rise of the Raj* on Micklegate are also recommended. Don't miss *Betty's*, locally famous for cakes, coffee and snacks: the queues are worth it.

Getting There & Away

Bus National Express (☎ 0532- 460011) buses leave from Rougier St. Three National Express buses a day run from Birmingham (4½ hours, £15.50) through to Newcastle (three hours, £12.75) via York – prices and times from York in brackets. Curiously, there are no buses direct to Durham. There are four buses a day to London (4½ hours, £22.50) and two to Edinburgh (six hours, £20.50).

For information on local buses (to Castle Howard, Helmsley, Scarborough, Whitby etc), contact the information office on Rougier St. Yorkshire Coastliner (☎ 0653-

692556) has a useful summer-only service that goes to Whitby via Castle Howard, Malton and Pickering; check its £6.50 Freedom Ticket.

The best deal if you're heading north or east is the Explorer North East ticket (£4.25) which is valid on most bus services and gives unlimited travel for one day – United Auto (☎ 0325-465252) has a bus north to Ripon where you can link into the network.

During summer, Mountain Goat (☎ 05394-45161) has a service between York and Ambleside (Lake District) via Skipton (Yorkshire Dales) on Monday, Wednesday, Friday and Saturday. This costs £16.

Train As the ex-headquarters of North-Eastern Railway, York is well served by rail; it's on the main line through to Edinburgh from London, so many people break their journey here. Contact York Britrail on ☎ 0904-642155. There are numerous trains from London's King's Cross (two hours, £42) and on to Edinburgh (2¾ hours, £35).

North-south trains also connect with Peterborough (1½ hours, £23) for Cambridge and East Anglia, and Lincoln (three hours, £13.50). There are also good connections with south-west England, via Bristol (four hours, £40.50), Cheltenham, Birmingham and Sheffield. Or from Oxford (four hours, £36), also via Birmingham.

Local trains to Scarborough take an hour and cost £6.80. For Whitby it's necessary to change at Middlesborough. Trains to/from the west and north-west go via Leeds.

Getting Around
It's quite possible to get around York on foot, but you'll end up having to cover quite a few miles. Consider hiring a bike from York Cycle Hire (☎ 0904-626064); if you were energetic you could do an interesting loop out to Castle Howard (25 km, 15½ miles), Helmsley and Rievaulx Abbey (another 20 km, 12½ miles) and Thirsk (another 20 km), where you could catch a train back to York.

Yorkshire Cycle Tours & Hire (☎ 0904-

765315) is well set up to suggest longer tours and they hire from £35 per week.

AROUND YORK
Castle Howard
One of the most striking of the great houses turned tourist attractions, Castle Howard should not be missed. The house itself was designed by Vanbrugh (of Blenheim Castle fame) in Baroque style in the early 18th century. It's set in superb grounds with several monumental follies.

Just north of the A64 from York to Scarborough, the castle can be reached by several tours and occasional buses from York. Check with the York TIC for up-to-date schedules; they cost around £5.

Yorkshire Coastliner (☎ 0653-692556) has one bus a day that runs from Leeds to Scarborough via Castle Howard. The castle (☎ 065384-333) is open from April to October; admission is a steep £4.50. Take a picnic and make a day of it.

NORTH YORK MOORS NATIONAL PARK
Only Exmoor and the Lake District rival the North York Moors National Park, but the York Moors are less crowded than the Lake District and more expansive than Exmoor. The coast is superb, with high cliffs backing onto unspoilt countryside. From the ridge-top roads and open moors there are wonderful views, and the dales shelter abbeys, castles and small stone villages.

The 160-km (100-mile) Cleveland Way, a long-distance path, curves around the edge of the park along the western hills (a strenuous walk) from Helmsley to Saltburn-by-the-Sea, then down the coast to Scarborough (a relatively easy, but spectacular, section). For further information, see *The Cleveland Way* by Ian Simpson (Countryside Commission/Aurum Press, £7.95). A leaflet with information on accommodation is available from TICs.

The North Yorkshire Moors Railway, a privately owned steam train, runs up the beautiful wooded Newtondale from Picker-

GREAT BRITAIN

ing to Grosmont (with train connections to Whitby).

Orientation

The western boundary of the park is a steep escarpment formed by the Hambleton and Cleveland Hills; the moors run east-west to the coast between Scarborough and Staithes. Rainwater escapes from the moors down deep, parallel dales – to the Rye and Derwent rivers in the south and the Esk in the north. After the open space of the moors, the dales form a gentler, greener landscape, sometimes wooded, often with a beautiful stone village or two.

The coastline is as impressive as any in Britain, and considerably less spoilt than most; Scarborough and Whitby are both popular resorts, but Whitby retains its charm. Helmsley (near Rievaulx, pronounced 'reevoh') is the centre for the western part of the park.

Information

There's a very useful, tabloid visitors' guide (40p), which is widely available in surrounding towns. There are visitors' centres at Helmsley (**☎** 0439-70173) and Danby (**☎** 0287-660654), but they are open seven days a week only from April to October (weekends from November to March). The TICs in Whitby, Pickering and Scarborough are open all year.

Helmsley

Helmsley is a perfect base for walking a short stretch of the Cumberland Way. There's a picturesque ruined castle just outside the town, and Rievaulx Abbey, Duncombe Park and Nunnington Hall are all within easy walking distance.

Helmsley itself is an attractive market town (Friday market) with excellent short walks in the beautiful surrounding countryside. There's a youth hostel and a number of B&Bs in the £12 to £15 range, a group of them on Ashdale Rd. Contact the TIC (**☎** 0439-70173) for more information. The *youth hostel* (**☎** 0439-70433) is open from

April to October, except Sundays in April, May, September and October.

Everything is grouped around the market place. *Thomas the Baker* is very good and cheap, and it is worth checking out the elegant little shops off Boro Gate, including the Footloose Walking and Outdoor Shop where you can hire bikes; see the following Getting Around section.

There are three buses a day, except Sundays, from Malton Railway Station (on the York-Scarborough line) operated by Yorkshire Coastliner (**☎** 0653-692556); services direct to/from Scarborough (one on Sundays) are operated by Scarborough & District (**☎** 0723-375463).

Rievaulx Abbey A 5½-km (3½-mile) uphill walk from Helmsley, the remains of the 13th century abbey are arguably the most beautiful monastic ruins in England. They lie in a wooded valley, beside a small village and the River Rye. They are open daily from April to September, then from Tuesday to Sunday; admission is £1.80.

Pickering

Pickering is not as attractive as Helmsley, but it is a terminus for the North York Moors Railway (see the following Getting Around section). The TIC (**☎** 0751-73791) will be able to suggest one of the numerous B&Bs. The nearest *youth hostel* is at Lockton (**☎** 0751-60376) about six km north. It's another good walking base – open from mid-April to mid-September, except Sundays.

Pickering can be reached from Malton by hourly buses (only two on Sundays) or Scarborough (seven on Sundays); see the Helmsley section for the operators.

Scarborough

Scarborough is a large, tacky Victorian resort. It's jam-packed with arcades, boarding houses and B&Bs. However, the coastline to the north, especially Robin Hood's Bay, is spectacular. With its ruined castle looming over the harbour, Scarborough must once have been very beautiful itself.

If you do need to stay, contact the TIC (☎ 0723-373333). There's a *youth hostel* (☎ 0723-361176) in Burniston Rd which has an eccentric opening schedule from March to October (sometimes closing on Wednesdays and Thursdays).

Scarborough is a good transport hub connected by rail with York and Kingston-upon-Hull. There are reasonably frequent buses west along the A170 to Pickering and Helmsley; contact Scarborough & District (☎ 0723-375463). Tees & District (☎ 0947-602146) has regular buses to Whitby via Robin Hood's Bay.

Whitby

Somehow Whitby transcends the coaches and fish-and-chip shops – the imposing ruins of the abbey loom over red-brick houses that spill down a headland to a beautiful harbour. Captain James Cook was apprenticed to a Whitby shipowner in 1746, and HMS *Endeavour* was built here, originally to carry coal.

The *youth hostel* (☎ 0947-602878) is beside the abbey and has fantastic views. It has complicated opening hours and is closed on Sundays. There are plenty of B&Bs and a helpful TIC (☎ 0947-602674). It has been claimed that the *Magpie Cafe* on the harbour does the best fish and chips in the world!

Consider attempting the nine-km (5½-mile) cliff-top walk to Robin Hood's Bay; the last Tees & District bus returns to Whitby around 4 pm. There are also some beautiful small fishing villages to the north. James Cook worked in a shop in Staithes as a teenager.

There are buses from Scarborough and York, or you can catch the Esk Valley train from Middlesbrough (four per day, Monday to Saturday, 1½ hours, £4.20).

Getting Around

The excellent free brochure *Moors Connections* is available from TICs and is a must for public transport users. Transport on the A roads is quite good, but beyond them you'll have to find your own way.

The North York Moors Railway (NYMR,

☎ 0751-72508) cuts across an interesting section of the park from Pickering to Grosmont, which is on the Esk Valley line (no Sunday service) between Whitby and Middlesbrough. There are infrequent buses operated by Yorkshire Coastliner, some from Goathland. The NYMR operates from late March to early November (one hour, £3.60), but there are only three trains a day at either end of the season. There are pleasant walks from most of the stations along the line; brochures are available from NYMR shops.

Bicycles are hired by Footloose (☎ 0439-70886) in Helmsley; mountain bikes are expensive at £12.50 per day or £50 per week, 10-speeds are £6 per day.

DURHAM

Durham is the most dramatic cathedral city in Britain; the massive Norman cathedral stands on a high, wooded promontory above a bend in the River Wear. Other cathedrals are more refined, but none have more impact. This extraordinary structure was built to survive to the end of time, with utter confidence in the enduring qualities of faith and stone.

Durham is also home to the third oldest university in England (founded in 1832); the banks of the river and the old town are worth exploring.

Orientation & Information

The marketplace (and TIC), castle and cathedral are all on the teardrop-shaped peninsula surrounded by the River Wear. The railway station is above and to the north-west of the cathedral on the other side of the river. The bus station is also on the western side. Using the cathedral as your landmark, you can't really go wrong. The TIC (☎ 091-384 3720), Market Place, is just a short walk to the north of the castle and cathedral.

Things to See

The **cathedral** dates almost entirely from the 12th century and is the most complete Norman cathedral, with characteristic round arches, enormous columns (over two metres in diameter), and zigzag chevron ornament.

The vast interior is like a cave that is only partly artificial. Don't miss the view from the tower (£1), and make sure you have a look at the beautiful Galilee Chapel at the west end. There are tours in July and August, Monday to Friday at 10 am. Evensong is at 5.15 pm weekdays and at 3.30 pm on Sunday.

The **castle** was begun in 1072 and served as the home for Durham's prince-bishops. These bishops had powers and responsibilities more normally associated with a warrior king than a priest, but this was wild frontier country. It is now a residential college for the university, but it is open to the public on guided tours; weekdays at 10 am, noon, 2 and 4.30 pm from July to September, and at 2 and 4 pm on Monday, Wednesday and Saturday the rest of the year (£1.30).

There are superb views back to the cathedral and castle from the outer bank of the river; walk around the bend between Elvet and Framwelgate bridges, or hire a boat at Elvet Bridge. There are a number of fine 18th century houses to the east of the cathedral.

Places to Stay & Eat
The *youth hostel* (☎ 091-221 2101) is a summer-only hostel (20 July to 30 August) in the Gilesgate Sixth Form College on Providence Row, opposite the ice rink north of Market Place. Several colleges rent their rooms during the university vacations (particularly July to September); inquire at the TIC. The most exciting possibility is Durham Castle (☎ 091-374 3863) which has B&B singles/doubles at £16 per person.

The TIC makes local bookings free, which is useful, since convenient B&Bs are not particularly numerous; the situation is particularly grim during graduation week in late June. There are a number of B&Bs around £15 per person on Gilesgate – leave the market square from its north end, over the freeway onto Claypath, which becomes Gilesgate – *Mrs Koltai* (☎ 091-386 2026) is at No 10, *Mr Nimmins* (☎ 091-384 6485) is at No 14, and *Mrs Foster* (☎ 091-384 1627) is at No 19.

Most of the eating possibilities are around the market square. The *Ristorante San Lorenzo*, just over the old Elvet Bridge is good value with pizzas and pastas for around £4.

Getting There & Away
Bus There are five National Express (☎ 091-261 6077) buses a day to London (4½ hours, £25.50) and three to Edinburgh (five hours, £19) and numerous buses to/from Birmingham (5¾ hours, £28.50) and Newcastle (half an hour, £3.50). Curiously, there seems to be no bus direct to York. There's one bus a day (No 370) between Durham and Edinburgh via Jedburgh and Melrose in the Scottish Borders.

Train There are numerous trains to York (one hour, £14), a good number of which head on to London's King's Cross (three hours, £53) via Peterborough (for Cambridge). Frequent trains from London continue through to Edinburgh (three hours, £24.50).

NORTHUMBERLAND
Taking its name from the Anglo-Saxon kingdom of Northumbria (north of the River Humber), Northumberland is one of the wildest, least spoilt of England's counties. There are probably more castles and battlefield sites here than anywhere else in England, testifying to the long and bloody struggle with the Scots.

The Romans were the first to attempt to draw a line separating north from south: Hadrian's Wall, stretching 118 km (73 miles) from Newcastle to Bowness-on-Solway near Carlisle, was the northern frontier of the empire for almost 300 years. It was abandoned around 410 AD, but enough remains to bring the past dramatically alive.

After the arrival of the Normans, large numbers of castles and fortified houses (or *peles*) were built. Many of them changed hands several times as the Scottish border was pushed back and forth for the next 700 years. Most have now lapsed into peaceful ruin, but others like Bamburgh and Alnwick were converted into great houses, which can be visited today.

The Northumberland National Park lies north of Hadrian's Wall, incorporating the open, sparsely populated Cheviot Hills. The walks can be challenging, and cross some the loneliest parts of England. The most interesting part of Hadrian's Wall is also included (along the southern boundary) – see the Hadrian's Wall section. For more information on the park, contact the National Park Officer, Eastburn, South Park, Hexham, Northumberland NE46 1BS. There are three information centres open from Good Friday to the end of October at Ingram, Rothbury and Once Brewed, plus, in partnership with the National Trust, at Housesteads (☎ 0434-344325) on Hadrian's Wall. All handle accommodation bookings.

Newcastle-upon-Tyne

Newcastle is the largest city in the north-east. It grew famous as a coal exporting port, and in the 19th century it became an important steel, ship-building and engineering centre – all industries that went into serious decline after WWII. Newcastle has retained some 19th century grandeur, but it has had a dour struggle to survive.

There are no major sites, although both **St Nicholas Cathedral** and **Castle Garth** are worth visiting. Shopaholics might be tempted by the Metro Centre, an enormous shopping centre – the largest in Europe – with 350 shops, 50 places to eat (mostly fast food), fairground rides... Needless to say, old Grainger Market in the centre, is *much* more interesting.

It may be necessary to come through on your way to the north; it's also a ferry port for Scandinavia.

Orientation & Information Although Newcastle is dauntingly large, the city centre is easy to get around on foot, and the metro (for the youth hostel and B&Bs) is cheap, efficient and pleasant to use – true! The central railway station is just to the south of the city centre and the coach station is just to the east.

There's a convenient and helpful TIC at the railway station, but the main office is in the Central Library (☎ 091- 261 0691); both

have a free map, guide and accommodations list. The railway station TIC is open Monday to Saturday from 10 am to 5 pm from October to May; and Monday to Friday to 8 pm, Saturday to 6 pm and Sunday to 4 pm Sunday from June to September.

Places to Stay & Eat The *youth hostel* (☎ 091-281 2570), 107 Jesmond Rd, not far from the city centre, is open from February to November (not Mondays or Tuesdays from 1 to 28 February and 1 to 30 November). Catch the metro to Jesmond station (30p), turn left from the station, cross Osborne Rd and continue for five minutes. Call in advance; it can be busy.

There are quite a number of B&Bs within easy walking distance of Jesmond station, mostly along Jesmond and Osborne Rds. The *Chelsea Private Hotel* (☎ 091-281 3469), 66 Jesmond Rd, has a small number of singles and doubles at £16 per person. *Herrons Hotel* (☎ 091-281 4191), 40 Jesmond Rd, is in a Georgian building with a private car park and is also £16 per person.

For interesting restaurants and nightlife walk south down Grey St (lined with beautiful Georgian and Victorian offices), which becomes Dean St and takes you down to the River Tyne and Quayside. *Ristorante Da Paolo* (☎ 091-261 4415), 25 King St, just off Quayside, is a good-value Italian place with minestrone for £1.85 and pastas and pizzas under £5. *Flynns Waterfront Bar* right on Quayside has a beer garden and cheap food and drink.

The *Cooperage* (☎ 091-232 8286), 32 The Close, Quayside, is a popular dance club with a wide-ranging clientele. Not far away at 57 Melbourne St, the *Riverside* (☎ 091-261 4386) is a popular live music venue (indie/alternative).

Getting There & Away Newcastle is a transport hub, so there are many options:

Bus There are numerous National Express (☎ 091-261 6077) connections with virtually every major city in the country (times and prices to Newcastle in brackets). There are

GREAT BRITAIN

buses every two hours to London (5¼ hours, £25.50) and Edinburgh (3¼ hours, £16.50). There are a number of buses each day from York (2¼ hours, £14.50).

For local buses around the north-east, don't forget the excellent value Explorer North East ticket valid on most services (£4.25). The central enquiry bureau (☎ 091-232 4211) has details on services to Berwick and along Hadrian's Wall (see the appropriate sections).

Rail Newcastle (☎ 091-232 6262) is on the main London-Edinburgh line so there are numerous trains; Edinburgh (1¾ hours, £22.50), London's King's Cross (four hours, £53), York (1¼ hours, £15.50). Berwick-upon-Tweed and Alnmouth (for Alnwick) are north on this line. There is also an interesting, scenic line known as the Tyne Valley Line west to Carlisle, roughly every two hours (1½ hours, £6.50).

Boat There are regular ferry links to Stavanger and Bergen. During summer there are ferry links to Esbjerg and Gothenburg. See the Getting There & Away section at the beginning of this chapter for details.

Getting Around There's an excellent, cheap Metro with fares from 30p. For advice and information there's a travel centre in the central railway station (☎ 091-232 5325). Bus No 327 links the ferry (at Tyne Commission Quay), the central railway station and Jesmond Rd (for the youth hostel and B&Bs). The fare is £2, and it leaves the railway station 2½ and 1½ hours before departure time.

Berwick-upon-Tweed

Between the 12th and 15th centuries, Berwick changed hands between the Scots and the English 14 times. This merry-go-round ceased after the construction of massive ramparts that still enclose the town centre. It is beautifully sited at the mouth of the River Tweed. The TIC (☎ 0289-330733) should help you find a B&B for around £13; there's no youth hostel.

There are two superb castles between Newcastle and Berwick: Alnwick (☎ 0665-510777) and Bamburgh (☎ 06684-208).

Getting There & Away Berwick is on the main London-Edinburgh line, so it is easy to get to by train. Northumbria (☎ 091-232 4211) has several services linking Newcastle and Berwick. From Monday to Saturday, Service 505 has four buses a day to Newcastle via Bamburgh and Alnwick.

Berwick is a good starting point if you wish to explore the Scottish Borders. There are buses on to Edinburgh around the coast via Dunbar and west to Coldstream, Kelso and Galashiels; the TIC will be able to advise.

Hadrian's Wall

Hadrian's Wall follows a naturally defensible line along the ridge of hard basalt rock known as Whin Sill (which is bleak and windy, still). The most spectacular section is between Hexham and Brampton, along the southern boundary of the Northumberland National Park, and there are number of fascinating sites set amongst beautiful countryside. A Hadrian's Wall Pass (£6) is a worthwhile investment if you are not a member of English Heritage.

Chesters Roman Fort/Museum (☎ 0434- 681379) in a pleasant valley by the River Tyne is an extensively excavated fort and interesting museum (£1.80).

Housesteads Fort (☎ 0434-344363) is the most popular and dramatic of the ruins. The extraordinarily well-preserved foundations of a fort (and a museum) perch high on a ridge overlooking the Northumbrian countryside (£1.60).

Vindolanda Fort & Museum (☎ 0434-344277), four km to the south, is an extensively excavated fort and civil settlement with a museum that has some unusual artifacts, including shoes and letters (£2.50). A turret and length of wall have been fully reconstructed.

Birdoswald Roman Fort (☎ 06972-602) is in a picturesque valley, and is less inundated with visitors than some of the other sites (£1.80).

Places to Stay Corbridge, Hexham and Haltwhistle are attractive small towns with plentiful B&Bs, although Carlisle is also a good base for exploring the wall. Starting in the east, the *Acomb Youth Hostel* (☎ 0434-602864) is on the edge of a small village about four km north of Hexham and three km south of the wall. Hexham can be reached by bus or train.

Once Brewed Youth Hostel (☎ 0434-344360) is central for both Housesteads Fort (five km) and and Vindolanda (two km). The Northumbria 685 bus (from Hexham or Haltwhistle railway stations) will drop you at Henshaw, three km south, or you could leave the train at Bardon Mill four km to the south-east. Once Brewed is 24 km (15 miles) from Acomb, 11 km (almost seven miles) to Greenhead.

Greenhead Youth Hostel (☎ 06972-401) is five km west of Haltwhistle Railway Station, but is also served by the trusty 685.

Getting There & Away West of Hexham the wall parallels the A69, between Carlisle and Newcastle. The hourly Northumbria 685 bus (☎ 091-232 4211) passes near the youth hostels and three to five km south of the main sites. The Newcastle-Carlisle railway line has stations at Hexham, Haydon Bridge, Bardon Mill, Haltwhistle and Brampton. From mid-April to early September a special hail-and-ride bus runs between Hexham and Haltwhistle stations along the B6318, which runs very close to the wall, calling at the main sites; for further information contact the Hexham TIC (☎ 0434-605225).

The easy option is to take a tour from Carlisle where the TIC organises coach tours on Monday, Thursday and Saturday in June and September, and Monday to Saturday in July and August. The tours depart at 1 pm, take three hours and cost £6; all tours include Birdoswald, but only the Saturday tours in July and August go onto Housesteads.

CARLISLE

For 1600 years, Carlisle defended the north of England, or south of Scotland, depending on who was winning. In 1745 Bonnie Prince Charlie proclaimed his father king at the market cross.

The city's character was spoilt by industrialisation in the 19th century; however, it's an interesting place and its strategic location can be exploited by visitors to Northumberland, Hadrian's Wall, Dumfries & Galloway and Borders (the beautiful Scottish border counties), and the Lake District. It is also the hub for five excellent railway journeys.

Orientation & Information

The city is well signposted. The train station is to the south of the city centre, a 10-minute walk to Greenmarket (the market square) and the TIC. The bus station is on Lowther St, just one block east of the square. The TIC and Visitors' Centre (☎ 0228-512444) is particularly informative, and has a enormous amount of literature. From May to September there are daily guided walks at 1.30 pm (£1).

Things to See

The impressive **castle** is to the north of the cathedral, overlooking the River Eden. It was first built in 1092 and there is a fine Norman keep, but this was definitely a working castle, so there were many alterations and additions (£1.80).

Places to Stay

The *youth hostel* (☎ 0228-23934) is open all year except Sundays and Mondays from 1 January to 30 March, 14 April to 21 May, 29 May to 30 June and 1 September to 21 December. It's about three km north-west of the centre on the banks of the river. From TIC, walk along Scotch St until you get to a major roundabout, cross the Eden Bridge and follow the A7, then left onto Etterby St and left again onto Etterby Rd.

There are plenty of comfortable B&Bs within walking distance of the centre, and you shouldn't need to pay more than £12.

There are a number of reasonable options on Warwick Rd. From the station, cross Butchergate, walk around the crescent and take Warwick Rd on your right. *Cornerways Guest House* (☎ 0228-21733), 107 Warwick Rd, is large and convenient with B&B for £11.50. *Calreena Guest House* (☎ 0228-25020), 123 Warwick Rd, charges £12.

Getting There & Away

Bus There are numerous National Express (☎ 091-261 6077) connections (times and prices to Carlisle in brackets). There are four buses to/from London (5½ hours, £30.50) and many to Glasgow (two hours, £12.75). One service a day comes all the way through from Cambridge (eight hours, £30.50) and Bristol (eight hours, £44); and from York (five hours, £12.75).

There is a Rail Link coach service that runs to Hawick, Selkirk and Galashiels (£13) in the Scottish Borders – six a day from Monday to Saturday, three on Sunday. Contact the council help line (☎ 0228-812812).

Train Carlisle is the terminus for five famous scenic railways; contact Britrail (☎ 0228-44711) for detailed information. There are 18 trains a day to Carlisle from London's King's Cross (3½ hours, £54). Most of the following lines have day ranger tickets that allow you unlimited travel – enquire for details.

The *Leeds-Settle-Carlisle Line* is one of the most famous train journeys in Britain. It cuts south-east across the Yorkshire Dales through beautiful unspoilt countryside. It's one of the great engineering achievements of the Victorian railway age – the Ribblehead Viaduct is 32 metres high. Several stations are good starting points for walks in the Yorkshire Dales National Park. There are trains every two hours from Monday to Saturday, two on Sundays (three hours, £12.50). Alternatively, buy a day ranger for £13. The timetable changes for summer.

The *Lake District Line* branches off the main north-south line between Preston and Carlisle at Oxenholme, just outside Kendal,

for Windermere. The landscape on the main line is beautiful, but you're whisked through pretty quickly. The Windermere branch is only about 10 miles long, but it takes nearly half an hour. There are plenty of trains seven days a week.

The *Tyne Valley Line* follows Hadrian's Wall to/from Newcastle. There are some fine views, and it is useful for visitors to the wall; see the Newcastle and Hadrian's Wall sections.

The *Cumbrian Coast Line* follows the coast in a great arc around to Lancaster with views over the Irish Sea and back to the Lake District. There are five trains a day Monday to Saturday, two on Sundays from Carlisle to Barrow (2½ hours, £13), where you change for a train to Lancaster on the main line (one hour, £5.40). There are bus connections with Windermere from Barrow-in-Furness.

Northwards, the *Glasgow-Carlisle Line* is the main route north to Glasgow, and it gives you a taste of the grand scale of Scottish landscapes. Most trains make few stops (1½ hours, £17).

LAKE DISTRICT

I wandered lonely as a cloud
That floats on high o'er dales and hills
When all at once I saw a crowd...
from *Daffodils*, by William Wordsworth

The Lake District is the most beautiful corner of England: a combination of green dales, so perfect they could almost be parks, rocky mountains that seem to heave themselves into the sky, and lakes that multiply the scenery with their reflections. The Cumbrian Mountains are not particularly high – none reach 1000 metres – but they're much more dramatic than their height would suggest.

This is Wordsworth country, and his houses at Grasmere (Dove Cottage, (☎ 05394-35544) and Rydal between Ambleside and Grasmere (☎ 05394-33002) are shrines.

Unfortunately there are over 10 million visitors a year, and they ain't all daffodils. The crowds are so intense it is questionable whether it is worth visiting on any weekend between May and October, or any time at all from mid-July to the end of August. It is particularly bizarre and horrible to be stuck in a traffic jam in such idyllic surroundings. It is also common. For scenery, weather and crowds the best time to visit is weekdays in May and June, followed by September and October.

Orientation

The two main bases for the Lakes are Keswick in the north (particularly for walkers) and Bowness/Windermere in the south (two contiguous tourist traps). Coniston and Cockermouth are less hectic alternatives. All these towns have youth hostels, plus numerous B&Bs and places to eat.

Ullswater, Grasmere, Windermere, Coniston Water and Derwent Water are often considered to be the most beautiful lakes, but they also teem with boats. Wastwater, Crummock Water and Buttermere are equally spectacular and much less crowded.

In general, the mob stays on the A roads, and the crowds are much thinner west of a line drawn from Keswick to Coniston.

Information

Hundreds of guidebooks and brochures have been produced on this region, and a frightening quantity are available from TICs.

Start at the Windermere or Keswick TICs (both have free local booking services). The Windermere TIC (☎ 05394-46499), Victoria St, is excellent; it's near the railway station at the north end of town. Keswick TIC (☎ 07687-72645), Moot Hall, Market Square, is also helpful.

If you are staying more than a day or so, buy a copy of *The Good Guide to the Lakes* by Hunter Davies (paperback, £3.95), an idiosyncratic guide covering background, practicalities, walks, and where to stay and eat.

The classic walking guides are the seven volumes of Wainwright's *Pictorial Guide to the Lakeland Fells*. Each is a work of art – hand written and hand drawn – and they are still useful despite their age. Cyclists should look for *The Mountain Biker's Guide to the Lake District* by Andy Bull & Frank Barrett (£5.95).

There are numerous walking/climbing shops in the region, particularly in Ambleside and Keswick; they are good sources of local information. Frank Davies (☎ 05394-32297), Compston Rd, Ambleside, and George Fisher (☎ 07687-72484), Lake Rd, Keswick, are both excellent shops that hire equipment (including boots).

There are over 30 youth hostels in the region, many of which can be linked by foot. Look for *Inter Hostel Walks in the Lake District* (£1.50).

Bowness & Windermere

Thanks to the railway, the Bowness/Windermere conglomerate is the largest tourist town in the Lake District. At times it feels like a seaside resort. The town is quite strung out, with Windermere (including the railway station and the TIC) a 20-minute uphill walk from Bowness on the lakeside.

The *youth hostel* (☎ 05394-43543) is open from 15 February to 2 November, a three-km walk from the station. Follow the A591 towards Ambleside until you get to Troutbeck Bridge, then turn right up Bridge Lane. Book in advance. There are a million B&Bs in Windermere particularly, and a stack of restaurants along Lake Rd.

Getting There & Away There are 10 trains a day from London's Euston (four hours, £46). See the Carlisle section for more information on the rail connection. There are two National Express buses a day from Manchester via Preston (three hours, £16) and on to Keswick. There's also a service from London via Birmingham (seven hours, £28.50) and on to Keswick.

During summer, Mountain Goat (☎ 05394-45161) has a service between York and Ambleside (Lake District) via Skipton (Yorkshire Dales) on Monday, Wednesday, Friday and Saturday. This costs £16. Cumberland Motor Services' (☎ 0900-603080) service No 518 runs to Ulverston and Barrow-in-Furness on the Cumbrian

Coast Line. From late June to mid-September there are irregular bus links east to Kirkby Stephen; phone Northumbria on ☎ 091-232 4211.

Keswick

Keswick is very busy, although it is only accessible by bus or private car. It is an important walking centre, but it lacks the green charm of Windermere. The *youth hostel* (☎ 07687-72484) is open from 15 February to November, a short walk down Station Rd from the TIC.

See the Bowness/Windermere section for information on National Express and Mountain Goat buses. Keswick can also be reached from Penrith Railway Station (only one service on Sundays) with Wright's No 888 service. There are plenty of buses linking Windermere, Ambleside and Keswick.

Coniston

This is still very definitely a tourist town, but decidedly smaller and less busy than Keswick or Bowness/Windermere. The TIC (☎ 05394-41533) is open in the summer only.

There are two excellent youth hostels near the town. *Holly How Youth Hostel* (☎ 05394-41323) is just north of Coniston on the Ambleside Rd. It's open from 1 January to 3 November, except Sundays from 21 September. *Coppermines* (☎ 05394-41261) is two km along the minor road between the Black Bull Hotel and Co-op – a good walking base.

CMS (☎ 0900-603080) has a reasonable number of buses from Ambleside, which is easily reached from Keswick or Bowness/Windermere.

Getting Around

Walking or cycling are the two best ways to get around, but bear in mind that conditions can be treacherous, and the going can be very, very steep. Bikes can be hired from Lakeland Leisure near the railway station in Windermere (☎ 05394-44786); mountain bikes are £13 per day.

There are numerous boat trips and a number of steam railways; the TICs have

countless brochures covering the alternatives in detail.

Mountain Goat (☎ 05394-45161) has some interesting minibus services and tours around the district, including a service from Keswick to Buttermere (£20).

YORKSHIRE DALES

Austere stone villages with simple, functional architecture; streams and rivers cutting through the hills; empty moors and endless stone walls snaking over the slopes – this is the region that was made famous by James Herriot and the TV series *All Creatures Great & Small*.

The landscape of the Dales is completely different to the Lakes District. The high tops of the limestone hills are exposed moorland, and the sheltered dales between them range from Swaledale, which is narrow and sinuous, Wensleydale and Wharfedale, which are broad and open, to Littondale and Ribblesdale, which are more rugged.

The Yorkshire Dales are very beautiful, but in summer, like the Lake District, they are extremely crowded. Avoid weekends and the peak summer period, or try to get off the beaten track. The Pennine Way runs through the area, and can be unbelievably busy, while other footpaths are often deserted.

Orientation & Information

The Dales can be broken into northern and southern halves: in the north the two main dales run parallel and east-west. Swaledale, the northernmost, is particularly beautiful. If you have private transport, the B6270 from Kirkby Stephen to Richmond is highly recommended. Parallel and to the south is Wensleydale.

In the southern half, north-south Ribblesdale is the route taken by the Leeds-Settle-Carlisle (LSC) railway line (see the Carlisle section for more information). Wharfedale is parallel to the east.

Skipton is the most important transport hub for the region, although apart from its castle it is not particularly interesting. Richmond is a beautiful town and is handy for the north. For someone without transport, the best bet will be those places accessible on the LSC Line: Kirkby Stephen, Dent and Settle all have nearby youth hostels.

The main National Park Centre (☎ 0756-752774) is at Grassington, 10 km north of Skipton, open daily except Monday to Friday from November to April. It publishes a useful *Visitor* newspaper.

Kirkby Stephen

Kirkby Stephen is a small, little visited market town on the LSC Line. The TIC (☎ 07683-71199) is only open in summer. The *youth hostel* (☎ 07683-71793) is in a converted chapel in the centre of town, just south of Market Square. From late June to mid-September there are irregular bus links east to Windermere – phone Northumbria on ☎ 091-232 4211.

Skipton

Skipton is a major centre for the Dales, but there's little to keep you here once you've raided the TIC (☎ 0756-792809) and stormed the castle. The nearest youth hostel is actually closer to Grassington, which is one of the prettiest and most popular Dales villages.

Apart from being on the LSC Line, there is a National Express bus direct from London. During summer, Mountain Goat (☎ 05394-45161) has a service between York and Ambleside (Lake District) via Skipton (Yorkshire Dales) on Monday, Wednesday, Friday and Saturday. This costs £16. It's £4 to York, £10.80 to Windermere. Bikes are available from Dave Ferguson's Cycles (☎ 0756-795367) at £10 a day.

Grassington

Grassington is home to a National Park Centre and is a good base for walks in Wharfedale. The *Linton Youth Hostel* (☎ 0756-752400) is just south of Grassington and can be reached by the Skipton-Grassington bus. It's open from 31 March to 30 September except Sunday.

From Skipton Railway Station, Keighley & District buses (☎ 0535-603284) depart roughly every hour Monday to Saturday.

There's a Sunday service from April to September. Bikes are available from Pletts Barn (☎ 0756-752266) at £10 a day.

Getting Around

With the exception of the LSC Line, public transport is grim. Bus users need a copy of the *Dales Connections* timetable available from TICs. Cycling is an excellent way to get around; there are some steep climbs, but most of the time the roads follow the bottom of the dales.

Scotland

No visitor to Britain should miss the opportunity to visit Scotland. Despite its official union with England in 1707, it has managed to maintain an independent national identity that extends considerably further than the occasional kilt and bagpipe. There are similarities and close links, but there are also considerable differences.

With very few exceptions the entire country is beautiful; the Highlands, however, are exceptional. You could hardly call it a secret, but for a region that has some of the world's most dramatic and unspoilt scenery, it is curiously underrated. Surprisingly few English realise what an extraordinary neighbour they have.

The Scottish urban culture is also quite different. Edinburgh is one of the most beautiful cities in the world; Glasgow is reinventing itself after the collapse of its traditional industries; St Andrews is Scotland's small version of Cambridge; and prosperous Aberdeen surveys the North Sea with a proprietorial interest.

FACTS ABOUT THE COUNTRY
History

Celts It is believed the earliest settlement of Scotland was undertaken by hunters and fishers 6000 years ago. They were followed by the Celtic Picts, whose loose tribal organisation survived to the 18th century in the clan structure of the Highlands. They

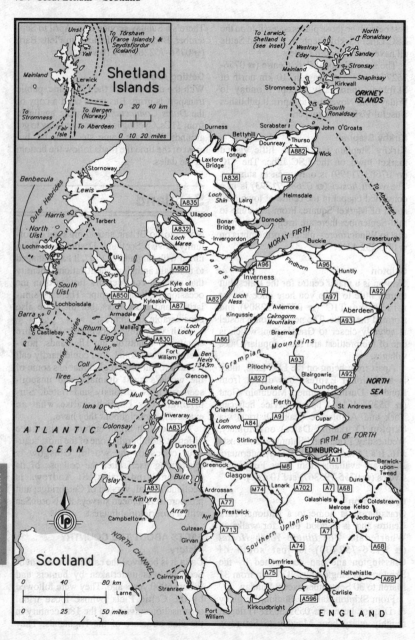

Shetland Islands

To Tórshavn (Faroe Islands) & Seydisfjordur (Iceland)

Unst
Yell
Mainland
Lerwick

To Stromness
To Bergen (Norway)
To Aberdeen

Fair Isle

0   20   40 km
0   10   20 miles

Scotland

0   40   80 km
0   25   50 miles

To Lerwick, Shetland Is (see inset)

North Ronaldsay
Westray
Eday
Sanday
Mainland
Stronsay
Shapinsay
Stromness
Kirkwall
South Ronaldsay

ORKNEY ISLANDS

John O'Groats
Durness
Bettyhill
Scrabster
Thurso
Dounreay
Wick
A882
Tongue
Laxford Bridge
A836
A9
Helmsdale
Stornoway
Lewis
Loch Shin
Lairg
Dornoch
Benbecula
Harris
Tarbert
Ullapool
A835
Bonar Bridge
Invergordon
MORAY FIRTH
Buckie
Fraserburgh
Outer Hebrides
A832
Loch Maree
Findhorn
A96
Huntly
North Uist
Lochmaddy
Uig
A890
A96
Inverness
A97
Aberdeen
A92
Skye
Kyle of Lochalsh
A82
Loch Ness
Aviemore
A93
South Uist
A850
Kyleakin
A87
Cairngorm Mountains
Lochboisdale
Armadale
Kingussie
Braemar
Barra
Rhum
Mallaig
A830
Loch Lochy
A86
Grampian Mountains
A93
Blairgowrie
A92
Castlebay
Eigg
Muck
Fort William
Ben Nevis 1343m
Pitlochry
Dundee
Coll
Inner Hebrides
Glencoe
A827
Dunkeld
NORTH SEA
Tiree
Oban
A85
Crianlarich
Perth
St Andrews
Mull
Iona
A84
A9
Cupar
Colonsay
Inveraray
Loch Lomond
ATLANTIC OCEAN
Jura
Dunoon
Stirling
FIRTH OF FORTH
Greenock
EDINBURGH
Islay
Bute
Glasgow
M8
A1
Berwick-upon-Tweed
A83
Ardrossan
M74
Lanark
A702
A7
A68
Duns
Kintyre
Arran
A77
Galashiels
Coldstream
Campbeltown
Ayr
Prestwick
Melrose
Kelso
NORTH CHANNEL
Culzean
A713
Southern Uplands
Hawick
Jedburgh
A7
Girvan
A74
A68
Cairnryan
Dumfries
Haltwhistle
Stranraer
Larne
A75
A69
Port William
Kirkcudbright
Carlisle
A596

ENGLAND

To Aberdeen

never bowed to the Romans, who retreated and built Hadrian's Wall, defining the north as a separate entity for the first time.

A new Celtic tribe, the Gaels (or Scots), arrived from northern Ireland (Scotia) in the 6th century. They finally united with the Picts in the 9th century in response to the threat posed by the Scandinavians who dominated the northern islands and west coast. By the time the Normans arrived, most of Scotland was loosely united under the Canmore dynasty.

Normans The Normans never conquered Scotland, although they wielded a major influence over several weak kings, and the Lowlands (with the most important arable land) were controlled by French-speaking aristocrats imported from northern England. The Highland clans remained staunchly Gaelic, the islands remained closely linked to Norway, and neither paid much attention to central authority.

Despite almost continuous border warfare, it was not until a dispute over the Canmore succession that Edward I attempted the conquest of Scotland. Beginning in 1296, a series of battles finally ended in 1328 with Robert the Bruce the recognised king of an independent country. Robert, who was more Norman than Scottish in his ancestry, cemented an alliance with France that was to complicate the political map for 400 years.

Stuarts In 1371 the kingship passed to the Fitzalan family. The Fitzalans had served William the Conqueror and his descendants as High Stewards, and Stuart became the name of the dynasty.

In 1503 James IV married the 12-year-old daughter of Henry VII, the first of the Tudor monarchs, linking the two families. This did not prevent the French convincing James to go to war against his in-laws, however; he was killed at the disastrous battle of Flodden Hill along with 10,000 of his subjects.

By the 16th century, Scotland was a nationalistic society, with close links to Europe, and a visceral hatred for the English.

It had universities at St Andrews, Glasgow and Aberdeen (more than the two in England) and a lively intellectual climate that was fertile ground for the ideas of the Reformation – a critique of the medieval Catholic church and the rise of Protestantism.

Mary Queen of Scots In 1542 James V died, leaving his two-week-old daughter Mary to be proclaimed Queen of Scots. Henry VIII of England decided she would make a suitable daughter-in-law, and his armies ravaged the Borders and sacked Edinburgh in a failed attempt to force agreement from the Scots (they called it Rough Wooing). When she was 15, Mary married the French Dauphin and duly became Queen of France as well as Scotland; for good measure she claimed England, on the basis that her Protestant cousin Elizabeth I was illegitimate.

While Catholic Mary was in France, the Scottish Reformation was underway under the leadership of John Knox. In 1560 the Scottish Parliament abolished the Latin mass and the authority of the pope, creating a Protestant church that was independent of Rome and the monarchy.

Eighteen-year-old Mary, one of the most acclaimed beauties of her time, returned to Scotland on the death of her husband. In Edinburgh she married Henry Darnley and gave birth to a son. Domestic bliss did not last, and in a scarcely believable train of events, Darnley was involved in the murder of Mary's Italian secretary (presumably her lover). Then Darnley himself was murdered, presumably by Mary and her next lover and husband, the Earl of Bothwell.

At this point Mary was forced to abdicate in favour of her son James, and imprisoned. She escaped, fleeing to Elizabeth who, recognising a security risk when she saw one, locked her in the Tower of London. Nineteen years later, at the age of 44, she was beheaded for allegedly plotting Elizabeth's death. When the childless Elizabeth died in 1603, Mary's son united the crowns of Scotland and England for the first time.

Revolution The Stuarts have become romantic figures, but their royal skills were extremely suspect. When Charles I began to meddle in religious matters, he provoked the Scots into organising a National Covenant that reaffirmed the total independence of the General Assembly of the Church of Scotland. This led to armed conflict. The civil war between Parliament and the king followed, with the Scottish Covenanters supporting Cromwell in his successful revolution.

In 1660, after Cromwell's death, the Stuart monarchy was restored. The honeymoon was brief, however, and James II, a Catholic, set out determinedly to lose his kingdom. Amongst other poor decisions, he made worshipping as a Covenanter a capital offence.

The prospect of another Catholic king was too much for the English Protestants, so they invited William of Orange, a Dutchman who was James' nephew and married to his oldest Protestant daughter, to take power. In 1689 he landed with a small army; James broke down and fled to France.

When the chief of the MacDonalds of Glencoe failed to take an oath of allegiance to William by a given deadline, the Campbells were ordered to make an example of them – 40 men, women and children were put to the sword, and the massacre at Glencoe became Jacobite (Stuart) propaganda that still resonates today.

Union with England In 1707, after complex bargaining (and buying a few critical votes), England convinced the Scottish Parliament to agree to the union of the two countries under a single parliament and crown. The Scots received trading privileges and retained their independent church and legal system.

The decision was unpopular from the start, and the exiled Stuarts promised to repeal it. The situation was exacerbated when Parliament turned to the house of Hanover to find a Protestant successor to Queen Anne. George, the Elector of Hanover, was James I's great grandson, but he was German and spoke no English.

Scotland was the centre for Jacobitism (Stuart support) and there were two major rebellions – in 1715, when the incompetent Earl of Mar threw away the Stuarts' best chance, and 1745 when Bonnie Prince Charlie failed to extend his support beyond the wild, Catholic Highland clans. The Jacobite cause was finally buried at the Battle of Culloden, and the English set out to destroy the clans, prohibiting tartans, weapons and military service.

The Scottish Enlightenment The old Scotland was already fast disappearing by the mid-18th century. There was considerable economic growth and the beginning of industrialisation. Eighteenth century Scotland was a sceptical, well-educated society and among other figures it produced David Hume the philosopher, Adam Smith the economist and Robert Burns the poet.

The great Highland Clearances began, as the lairds (landowning aristocrats) sought to improve their estates. Sheep were considered more profitable than crofters (subsistence peasants), so the people had to go. They went to the burgeoning slums of the new industrial cities – especially Glasgow and Dundee – and to the four corners of the British empire. By 1870, Glasgow had a population of over 400,000 people, many living in appalling conditions.

Modern Scotland By the end of the 19th century the population was concentrated in the grim industrial towns and cities of the Lowlands. Working-class disillusionment led to the development of fierce left-wing politics. After WW I Scotland's ship, steel, coal, cotton and jute industries began to fail, and though there was a recovery during WW II, since the 1960s they have been in terminal decline.

In the 1970s the economy received a tremendous boost when oil was found in the North Sea – Scottish oil, as many will tell you. Despite the bonanza, Thatcherism failed to impress the Scots. Of the 72 Scottish seats in the House of Commons only 15 are held by the ruling Conservative Party.

Nationalism is still very much a live issue. As the United Kingdom moves ever closer to the European Community, many Scots are looking at the issue again. The most radical are dreaming of a Scottish Parliament within the framework of the EC, but even the Conservatives accept that some changes are inevitable.

Geography

Scotland can be divided into three areas: the south, or southern uplands, with ranges of hills bordering England; the central Lowlands, a triangular slice from Edinburgh and Dundee in the east to Glasgow in the west containing the majority of the population; and the Highlands and Islands in the north. Some two-thirds of the country is mountain and moorland.

The Lowlands is an imprecise, unprepossessing term that is often used to describe everything south of a line from Aberdeen to Loch Lomond. It suggests that mountains and spectacular scenery will only be found in the north. This is incorrect. Just one example: Scotland's highest village is actually in Dumfries in the south-west.

Edinburgh is the capital and financial centre, Glasgow is the industrial centre, and Aberdeen and Dundee are the two largest regional centres.

Population

Scotland has a population of just over five million, around 9% of the total population for the United Kingdom.

Language

Gaelic is now only spoken by some 80,000 people, mainly in the islands and north-west of Scotland. Aye, but the Scottish accent can make English almost impenetrable to the Sassenach and other foreigners, and there are numerous Gaelic and Scots words that linger in everyday speech. Ye ken? Some common terms you might encounter:

aye – yes/always
bairn – child
bap – bread roll
ben – mountain
brae – hill
burn – creek
ceilidh – (pronounced 'kaylee') informal evening entertainment
croft – small farm
firth – estuary
glen – valley
haar – fog off the North Sea
hogmanay – New Year's Eve
ken – know
kirk – church
wynd – lane

FACTS FOR THE VISITOR
Visas & Embassies

No visas are required if you arrive from England or Northern Ireland. If you arrive from the Republic of Ireland or any other country, normal British regulations apply (see the Facts for the Visitor section at the beginning of this chapter). There are numerous diplomatic missions in Edinburgh.

Customs

If you arrive from the Republic of Ireland or any other country, normal British regulations apply (see the Facts for the Visitor section at the beginning of this chapter).

Money

The same currency is valid on both sides of the border; however, the Clydesdale Bank, the Royal Bank of Scotland and the Bank of Scotland have retained the right to issue their own currency. All these banks print pound notes. You may have difficulty trying to change one of these pounds in a *bureau de change* in Greece, but they usually don't present a problem in Britain.

If you have an Access/MasterCard, you can use the cash machines belonging to the Royal Bank of Scotland and Clydesdale Bank; if you have a Visa card you can use the Bank of Scotland, Royal Bank of Scotland, Clydesdale Bank and TSB; if you have an American Express card you can use the Bank of Scotland.

Costs With the exception of Edinburgh,

Scotland is less expensive than England. As a general rule, accommodation and food are around 15% cheaper.

Climate & When to Go

The climate varies widely. The west and east coasts have relatively mild climates, but the Highlands can have extreme weather at any time. Aside from the ski resorts, many facilities (including B&Bs and TICs) are closed between the end of September and the end of March.

The east coast tends to be cool and dry; rainfall averages around 650 mm, and winter temperatures rarely drop below 0°C, although winds off the North Sea can rattle your teeth. The west coast is milder and wetter with over 1500 mm of rain and average summer highs of 19°C.

May and June are generally the driest months, but expect rain at any time. The best time to visit is between May and September – April and October are acceptable weather risks, although many things are closed in October. The Highlands are pretty much off limits during winter, but Edinburgh and Glasgow are still worth visiting. Edinburgh becomes impossibly crowded during the festival which is held in the last two-thirds of August; book a long way ahead if you plan to visit during this time.

The farther north you go in Scotland in summer, the longer the days become; the midsummer sun sets at 10.30 pm in the Shetlands, but even in Edinburgh there are seemingly endless evenings.

Tourist Offices

Outside of Britain, contact the British Tourist Authority for information. The Scottish Tourist Board (☎ 071-930 8661) has an information centre at 19 Cockspur St, London SW1 5BL, just off Trafalgar Square. It can suggest routes, provide detailed information, and make all kinds of reservations. There is a special help line for visitors to the Highlands and Islands, with booking facilities – phone ☎ 0349-65000.

Most towns in Scotland have TICs that are open weekdays from 9 am to 5 pm, some-times extending to weekends during the summer. In small places, particularly in the Highlands, TICs only open from Easter to September.

Useful Organisations

The Scottish Youth Hostels Association (SYHA) markets an Explore Scotland Package that includes a seven-day Citylink Bus Pass, six overnight accommodation vouchers, a bus timetable, a Scotpass Discount Card, free YHA membership and an SYHA handbook, and a Historic Scotland Pass – for £81. The savings are worthwhile, especially if you are not a student. Contact the SYHA headquarters (☎ 0786-51181) at 7 Glebe Crescent, Stirling FK8 2JA.

Business Hours & Holidays

Minimum banking hours are weekdays from 9.30 am to 3.30 pm; a few close between 12.30 and 1.30 pm, but the tendency is to longer hours. Post offices and shops are open from 9 am to 5.30 pm on weekdays; post offices close at 1 pm on Saturdays and shops in small towns sometimes have an early closing day during the week.

In Scotland, bank holidays apply only to banks and some other commercial offices, although in England they are general public holidays. Christmas and New Year's Day are usually taken by everybody, and Scottish towns normally have a Spring and Autumn Holiday. Dates vary.

In 1992, Scottish banks were closed on 1 and 2 January, 17 April, 4 and 25 May, 3 August and 25 and 28 December.

Dangers & Annoyances

Edinburgh and Glasgow are big cities with the usual problems, so normal caution is required. Hikers in the Highlands should be properly equipped and cautious: the weather can become vicious at any time of the year.

The most infuriating and painful problem facing visitors to the west coast and highlands, however, is midges. These are tiny blood-sucking flies, related to mosquitoes (and, again, it's the female that's the problem). Under certain conditions, they can be prolific – it is at least partly thanks to them that much of Scotland remains a wilderness. They are at their worst in the evenings or in cloudy or shady conditions; their season lasts from late May to mid-September, peaking from mid-June to mid-August.

There are a number of possible defensive moves: cover up, particularly in the evening; wear light-coloured clothing (midges are attracted to dark colours); and, most importantly, buy a reliable insect repellent including either DEET or DMP.

Activities

Hiking There are four long-distance hiking routes in Scotland: the Southern Upland Way (see the Stranraer section), the West Highland Way (see the Glasgow section), the Fife Coastal Walk, and the Speyside Way. Beyond this, there is a network of thousands of miles of paths and tracks. Scotland has a long tradition of relatively free access to open country. Numerous guidebooks are available.

The southern Highlands are popular (this does not mean crowded) – the Cairngorms west of Aberdeen, and the Grampians east of Oban and Fort William. The walking and climbing is spectacular, but Scottish mountains can be killers. Caution is required – the climate over 3000 feet is equivalent to that north of the Arctic circle. Bad weather is normal so you must be properly equipped to deal with cold and wet conditions and if necessary to stay put until the weather improves; fogs can descend suddenly at any time so it is essential to be able to use a map and compass. It is also important to notify someone reliable of your plans.

Skiing Scotland has a burgeoning skiing industry. The ski season runs between December and April. Although there is nothing to rival the European Alps, there are several resorts of international standard within a day's drive of London. There are several resorts in the Cairngorm Mountains (near Braemar and Aviemore) and around Ben Nevis (Scotland's highest mountain,

near Fort William). The Scottish Tourist Board can provide details.

Surfing The north coast of Scotland offers some of the best and coldest surfing in Britain.

Accommodation

The two best options for budget travellers are youth hostels and B&Bs. There is also a growing number of independent hostels and bunkhouses, most with prices around £6.

The SYHA is a separate organisation and produces its own handbook (90p), which gives details on around 80 hostels it operates, including transport links. Its hostels are generally cheaper and often better than their English counterparts. In big cities costs are £7.25/6.10 for seniors/juniors; the rest range from £3.45/2.85 to £6.50/5.40.

B&Bs and small hotels are also cheaper than their English counterparts; you are unlikely to have to pay more than £15 per person. The TICs have local booking services (usually free) and a Book-A-Bed-Ahead scheme (£2.50 plus a refundable deposit). This is worth using in July and August, but is not necessary outside this peak time, unless perhaps you plan to arrive in a town after business hours (when the local TIC will be closed).

You can camp free on all public land (unless it is specifically protected). Commercial camping sites are geared to caravans and vary widely in quality. A tent site will cost around £6. If you plan to use a tent regularly, invest in *Scotland: Camping & Caravan Parks* (£3.75), available from most TICs.

Food

Scotland's culinary reputation is as dismal as England's, and the fact that the Scots have the highest rate of heart attacks in Europe is fair warning. In small villages and hotels the alternatives will usually be bleak, although village bakeries are generally excellent.

There are a surprising number of restaurants that cater to vegetarians; look for *The Vegetarian Guide to the Scottish Highlands*

& *Islands* (£2.25), an annual listing of B&Bs, hotels and restaurants.

GETTING THERE & AWAY
Air
There are direct services from a number of European cities to Edinburgh, Glasgow, Dundee, Aberdeen or Inverness, and from North America to Glasgow or Edinburgh. You can also connect with numerous flights to Scotland from London (including to Inverness). New York to Glasgow is around US$500; Oslo to Glasgow is around 1900 kr; London to Glasgow is around £70.

Land
Bus Long-distance buses are usually the cheapest method of getting to Scotland. Citylink (☎ 071-636 9373), the major Scottish operator, and Caledonian Express (☎ 071-730 0202), the Scottish branch of National Express, have numerous regular services from London and other departure points in England (see the Glasgow section).

London to Edinburgh or Glasgow should cost around £35/28 for an adult return/single, £23.50/18.50 for a concessionary return/single. Special offers can be even lower. As in England all return tickets are ridiculously cheap by comparison to singles.

For the sake of brevity in the following sections adult single fares have been shown. Add about 20% for the return fare, and subtract about 30% for concessionary fares. See the following Getting Around section for details.

Train British Rail InterCity services can take you from London's King's Cross (☎ 071-278 2477) to Edinburgh in as little as four hours or to Glasgow in five hours (see those sections). For the sake of brevity, in the following sections adult single fares have been shown; these are the same as day returns. Add around 10% for a low period return (known as a Supersaver Return and not valid on Fridays, public holidays and Saturdays in July and August); subtract around 30% if you hold a Britrail Young Person's Railcard.

Car & Motorbike The main roads are busy and quick. Edinburgh is 597 km (373 miles) from London; Glasgow is 627 km (392 miles) from London. Allow eight hours; of course there are one or two places where you might like to stop on the way, and motorways are horrible...

Hitching It's easy enough to hitch to Scotland along the A68 to Edinburgh, or the A74 to Glasgow. The coastal routes are slow.

Sea
Scotland has ferry links to Larne, near Belfast in Northern Ireland, from Cairnryan (P&O, ☎ 05812-276) and Stranraer (Sealink, ☎ 0776-2262), both south-west of Glasgow. For details, see the Ireland chapter.

From early June to late August there is a fascinating link between the Shetlands, Norway, the Faroe Islands, Iceland and Denmark. The agent is P&O (☎ 0224-572615), but the operator is the Smyril Line. The sailing order is Denmark (Saturday) to the Faroes (Monday), to the Shetlands (Monday), to Norway (Tuesday), to the Shetlands (Wednesday), to the Faroes (Wednesday), to Iceland (Thursday), to the Faroes (Friday), to Denmark (Saturday) and so on. Low/high-season, one-way couchette fares from Shetland to Norway are £40/53, to the Faroes £47/63, to Denmark £96/129, to Iceland £102/136.

GETTING AROUND
If you are not a student, it is worth giving serious consideration to the Scottish Travelpass, which has superseded the excellent Highlands and Islands Travelpass. The Travelpass gives unlimited travel on Scotrail trains and Caledonian MacBrayne ferries to the west coast islands; 33% discount on P&O's Scrabster to Orkney ferry, 20% discount on P&O services from Aberdeen to Shetland, Aberdeen to Orkney and Orkney to Shetland; and 33% on postbuses and most of the important regional bus lines.

Unfortunately Caledonian Express and Citylink, the major coach operators, no longer participate, but they do have explorer tickets and discount cards of their own (see the following Bus section).

A Travelpass for eight days' consecutive travel costs £80; 15 days consecutive travel costs £120. Students get equivalent discounts anyway and could get a seven-day rail Rover ticket much cheaper. For more information contact Scotrail (☎ 031-556 2451), who administer the scheme. Tickets are are available from the Scottish Travel Centre, Victoria and King's Cross railway stations in London, and from the Scotrail stations in Glasgow and Edinburgh.

If you plan to spend any time in the Highlands using public transport, try and get a copy of the brilliant *Getting Around the Highlands & Islands* (£3.50). It gives clear timetables for all available transport, including ferries and postbuses. Unfortunately publication ceased in 1992 so copies are becoming increasingly difficult to find. Hopefully it will be resuscitated if enough people pester the Scottish Travel Centres in London or Edinburgh.

Air

A number of carriers, including Loganair, BA, Air UK and Aberdeen Airways connect the main towns, the Western Isles, Orkney and Shetland. BA has a Highland Rover Ticket that gives you up to eight flights over eight or 21 days.

Bus

Citylink (☎ 041-332 9644) is the major Scottish operator with services to all the major towns; the only gap in their coverage is the northern and western coasts, although Thurso, Ullapool and Kyle of Lochalsh are all served. It has a seven-day Explorer Pass, which gives unlimited travel and a 20% discount on tickets between England and Scotland. The pass costs £45 adult, £35 concession. Phone ☎ 071-636 9373 for the nearest point of sale; they are available at Buchanan Square, Glasgow; St Andrew Square, Edinburgh; and at Victoria, London.

Citylink honours all European under-26 cards, including the Young Scot card which costs £6, but provides discounts all over Scotland and Europe. If they don't have one of these cards, full-time students and people less than 26 years old have to buy the ironically titled Smart Card (more bureaucratic insanity and you can't even blame the government). On presentation of proof of age, or student status (an NUS or ISIC card), a passport photo and a £6 fee you get the Smart Card to add to your collection. All this entitles you to a 30% discount so the chances are you'll be ahead after buying your first ticket.

Caledonian Express (☎ 041-332 4100), the Scottish branch of National Express, also serves most main towns. Again, their coverage of the north-west is weak; they don't go to Ullapool. Their Britexpress Card (discount card) and their Tourist Trail Pass (unlimited travel) are both valid in Scotland (see the introductory Getting Around section for details).

The same privatised mess applies to local buses in Scotland as in England. Companies and services come and go with astonishing rapidity. Regional enquiry telephone numbers have been given throughout the text; you are advised to use them. There are a large number of Royal Mail postbuses, which can be particularly useful for walkers. For a free timetable write to Post Office Public Affairs, 30 St James Square, London SW1Y 4PY. The Citylink and Caledonian Express buses do not carry bicycles, but most of the local buses will.

For the sake of brevity in the following sections adult single fares have been shown. Add about 20% for the return fare, and subtract about 30% for concessionary fares.

Train

Scotland has some fantastic train lines; they are limited and expensive however, so it is quite likely you'll have to turn to alternatives at some point. The routes from Stirling to Inverness, Inverness to Thurso, and Inverness to Kyle of Lochalsh are considered to be among the best in the world.

In addition to the range of Britrail passes, there is a Scotrail pass, all of which have to be bought outside of Britain. There are also a number of Freedom of Scotland Rover tickets that can be bought in Britain, including most railway stations in Scotland. Unlimited travel for four out of eight days is £55, for seven consecutive days is £69, 30% less for holders of the Young Persons Railcard. There are regional Rovers (Heart of Scotland, North Highland and West Highland).

Reservations for bicycles (£3) are compulsory on most services. For the sake of brevity, in the following sections adult single fares have been shown; these are the same as day returns. Add around 10% for a low period return (known as a Supersaver Return and not valid on Fridays, public holidays and Saturdays in July and August); subtract around 30% if you hold a Britrail Young Person's Railcard.

Hitching

Hitching is reasonably good in Scotland, although the north-west is difficult, simply because there is so little traffic. You could easily be stuck for a day or two; even public transport won't necessarily rescue you. Again in the north and west, the Sunday Sabbath is still widely observed, so the traffic is even sparser than usual.

Boat

Caledonian MacBrayne (CalMac) (☎ 0475-33755) is the most important ferry operator on the west coast, with services from Ullapool to the Outer Hebrides, from Kyle of Lochalsh and Mallaig to Skye and on to the Outer Hebrides. Its main west-coast port, however, is Oban, with ferries to virtually all the west-coast islands except Harris and Lewis.

As an example, a single passenger fare from Oban to Lochboisdale, South Uist (Hebrides) is £13.50. They also have Rover tickets offering unlimited travel for eight and 15 days (£31.50/46).

P&O (☎ 0224-572615) has ferries from Aberdeen and Scrabster to the Orkneys and from Aberdeen to the Shetlands. Aberdeen to Lerwick (Shetland) is £46.50, Aberdeen to Stromness (Orkney) is £33.50. There's a 25% student discount.

SOUTH-EASTERN SCOTLAND

There is a tendency to think that the real Scotland doesn't start until you are north of Perth, but the castles, forests and glens of the Borders have a romance of their own. The region survived centuries of war and plunder.

Few people pause in their rush to get to Edinburgh, but if you do stop, you'll find the lovely valley of the Tweed, rolling hills, castles, ruined abbeys and sheltered towns. This is excellent cycling and walking country. It is crossed by the coast-to-coast Southern Upland Way; see the Stranraer section for details.

Orientation & Information

The Borders region lies between the Cheviot Hills along the English border, and the Pentland, Moorfoot and Lammermuir Hills, which form the border with Lothian and overlook the Firth of Forth. The most interesting country surrounds the River Tweed and its tributaries.

Getting Around

Bus There is a Rail Link coach service that runs from Carlisle in north-west Cumbria to Hawick, Selkirk and Galashiels (£7.50); there are six a day from Monday to Saturday, three on Sunday.

Regular buses run between Berwick and Kelso via Coldstream, and from Kelso back to Duns. Another useful service runs from Berwick to Galashiels via Melrose. To get to/from Edinburgh there are regular buses from Duns, via Galashiels. The Waverley Wanderer bus pass allows a day's unlimited travel around the Borders, and includes Carlisle and Edinburgh (£6.50). For further information, ☎ 0835-23301.

National Express has one bus a day (No 370) between Durham and Edinburgh via Newcastle, Jedburgh and Melrose.

Train The main lines from Carlisle and Newcastle/Berwick skirt the region. Buses are the only option.

Bicycle Coldstream would be a good starting point for an expedition, and Coldstream Cycles (☎ 0890-2709) hires bikes from £6 per day.

Jedburgh

Jedburgh Abbey is the most complete of the ruined Border abbeys. After a famous ride to visit her lover, the Earl of Bothwell, at Hermitage Castle, Mary Queen of Scots was nursed back to health in a Jedburgh house (now a museum) that bears her name. The museum is open from Easter to November; £1.50. The TIC (☎ 0835-63435) is the only Borders TIC that stays open all year.

Hermitage Castle, off the B6399 from Hawick, is only accessible if you have transport; its forbidding architecture bears testimony to the Borders' brutal history (open from April to September).

Melrose

Melrose is an attractive small town six km east of Galashiels, and is a popular base for exploring the Borders. This is the only Borders town with a convenient *youth hostel* (☎ 089682-2521). It overlooks the ruined abbey.

Thirlestane Castle (☎ 05782) 430), 16 km north just off the A68, is one of the most fascinating of Scotland's castles. The original keep was built in the 13th century, but was refashioned and added to in the 16th century – with fairy-tale turrets and towers.

It is still very much a family home and as a visitor you feel strangely like you are prying. From May to September it's open Wednesdays, Thursdays and Sundays, plus Mondays and Tuesdays in July and August (£3).

EDINBURGH

Edinburgh is one of the greatest European cities. It has an incomparable location, studded with volcanic hills on the edge of an enormous estuary, and superb architecture, from extraordinary 16th century tenements to monumental Georgian and Victorian masterpieces. Sixteen thousand buildings are listed as architecturally or historically important.

It became the royal capital in the 11th century and since then all the great dramas of Scottish history played at least one act in Edinburgh. Even after the union of 1707 it remained the centre for government administration (now the Scottish Office), the separate Scottish legal system and the Presbyterian Church of Scotland.

In some ways, however, it is the least Scottish of Scotland's cities – partly because of the impact of tourism, partly because of its closeness to England and the links between the two countries' upper classes, partly because of its multicultural population.

History

Edinburgh Castle dominates the city from its rocky crag. This natural defensive position was probably the feature that first attracted settlers; it has been fortified from at least 600.

The old, walled city grew on the east-west ridge (the Royal Mile, which runs from Holyrood Palace to the castle) and south of the castle around Grassmarket. This restricted, defensible zone became a medieval Manhattan, forcing its densely packed inhabitants to build up. Even so, the city was sacked by the English seven times.

In the second half of the 18th century a new city was created across the ravine to the north of the old city. Before it was drained, this valley was the Nor' Loch (more a cesspool than a lake) – it is now a superb park, cut but not spoilt by the railway line.

The population was expanding, defence was no longer a factor, and the thinkers and architects of the Scottish Enlightenment planned to distance themselves from Edinburgh's Jacobite past. Built on a grid, the new city's brilliance lies in the way that it opens onto the castle, the old city and the Firth of Forth, and to the genius of architects like Robert Adams whose gracious, disciplined buildings line the streets. The main street, Princes St, flanks the valley below the castle, running west from Calton Hill.

GREAT BRITAIN

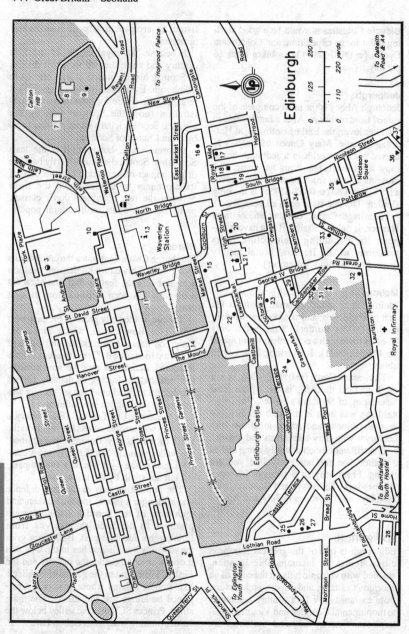

Edinburgh

1 Georgian House
2 American Express
3 Bus Station
4 St James Centre
5 Giuliano's Restaurant
6 Playhouse Theatre
7 City Observatory
8 National Monument
9 Nelson's Monument
10 Café Royal Guest House
11 Scott's Monument
12 GPO
13 Tourist Information Centre
14 National Gallery
15 Edinburgh Festival Office
16 John Knox's House
17 Museum of Childhood
18 High St Hostel
19 The Vaults
20 Fringe Festival Office
21 St Giles' Cathedral
22 Gladstone's Land
23 Preservation Hall
24 Gennaro & Pierre Victoire
    Restaurants
25 Royal Lyceum Theatre
26 HMSO Bookshop
27 Dario's Restaurant
28 Central Cycle Hire
29 Bertie's
30 Greyfriar's Pub
31 Greyfriar's Kirk
32 Campus Travel
33 Negociants Café & Club
34 Edinburgh University
35 Kebab Mahal
36 Seeds Restaurant
37 Pear Tree Hotel

The population exploded in the 19th century – Edinburgh quadrupled in size to 400,000, not much less than it is today – and the tenements of the old city were taken over by refugees from the Irish famines. A new ring of crescents and circuses were built to the south of the new town, then grey Victorian terraces sprung up.

In the 20th century the slums were emptied into new housing estates that now have massive social problems. Modern architecture has failed as totally in Edinburgh as it has elsewhere in Britain.

Orientation

The most important orientation point is Arthur's Seat, the 800-feet-high rocky peak that lies to the south-west of the city. The old and new towns are separated by the valley park (and Waverley Railway Station), and the castle dominates them both.

Princes St is the main shopping street and runs along the north side of the valley. Buildings are restricted to its north side, which has an unattractive selection of High St shops. Princes St runs west from Calton Hill, which is crowned by several monuments – an incomplete war memorial modelled on the Parthenon, and a tower honouring Nelson. The Royal Mile (made up of Lawnmarket, High St and Canongate) is the parallel equivalent in the old town.

The TIC is easily reached from the train station or from Princes St – it's between them, inconspicuously placed on top of the Waverley Market Shopping Centre and is well signposted. The bus station is in the new town and is a little bit more difficult to find, just off the south-east corner of St Andrew Square to the north of Princes St.

Information

Edinburgh and Glasgow's answer to *Time Out* is *The List*, a fortnightly guide to films, theatre, cabaret, music – the works. It's essential if you're staying for a couple of days.

Tourist Office The main TIC (☎ 031-557 1700) is at Waverley Market, Princes St, EH2 2QP. It's busy, but efficient. There is also a branch at Edinburgh Airport. They have information about all of Scotland, and sell a very useful guide to the city (£1.50). They have an accommodation service, but they charge a steep £2.50 fee, so you should consider using their excellent free accommodation brochure and making a booking yourself. It's open seven days a week all year, except Saturday afternoons and Sundays from October to April. In summer it stays open to 8 pm.

Money There's a *bureau de change* at the tourist office, with long opening hours, including 11 am to 3 pm Sundays from May to September. American Express (☎ 031-225 7881) has an office at 139 Princes St, open business hours Monday to Friday, from 9 am to noon on Saturdays.

Emergency Dial ☎ 999 for police, fire or medical emergencies (free call).

Things to See

The best place to start any tour of Edinburgh is **Edinburgh Castle**, which has excellent views overlooking the city.

The castle is still the headquarters for the Scottish Division, and is a complex of buildings that has been altered many times by war and the demands of the military. The smallest and oldest building is **St Margaret's Chapel**, built in the 12th century. The castle was the seat of Scottish kings, and the royal apartments include the tiny room where Mary Queen of Scots gave birth to the boy who became King James VI of Scotland and James I of England. It's open seven days a week (from 11 am on Sundays); admission is £3.40.

The castle is at the western end of the Royal Mile, which runs all the way down to Holyrood Palace. The streetscape is an extraordinarily complete survival from the 16th and 17th centuries, and an exploration of the closes and wynds that run into it evokes the crowded and vital city of that time.

On the left, **Gladstone's Land** and **Lady Stair's House** are restored townhouses that give fascinating insights into urban life. Gladstone's Land was completed in 1620 and has been skilfully restored; it's open from April to October, and costs £2.20. Lady Stair's House contains relics and portraits of Robert Burns, Sir Walter Scott and Robert Louis Stevenson.

Turn right on to George IV Bridge, which crosses Cowgate (an ancient narrow street). Grassmarket, below and to the right, has a number of pubs and restaurants. Continue until you reach the angled intersection with Candlemaker Row and **Greyfriar's Kirk** with a beautiful old churchyard and views

across the roofs to the castle. The National Covenant was signed here.

Return to the Royal Mile and turn right past the much-restored 15th century **St Giles Cathedral**. At the rear of the cathedral is Parliament House, now the seat of the supreme law courts of Scotland. Immediately to the east of St Giles stands the Mercat Cross, which was where public proclamations were made.

Continue down the Royal Mile over North/South Bridge until you come to the **Museum of Childhood** on your right and **John Knox's House** on your left. The Museum of Childhood has a fascinating collection of toys (Monday to Saturday, free). John Knox was the fiery leader of the Scottish religious reformation (open Monday to Saturday, £1.20)

Holyrood Palace lies at the eastern end of the royal mile, a Stuart palace mostly dating from a reconstruction by Charles II in 1671. Holyrood is the official residence of the current royal family, so it can be closed at any time (usually in late May and late June). Normally it is open from Monday to Saturday, and Sundays from late March to late October; admission is £2.50.

From the palace, turn right and climb Abbey Hill (under the railway overpass). Turn left into Regent Rd which takes you back to Princes St. On your right you pass **Calton Hill**, which is worth climbing for its superb views across to the castle.

Continue along Princes St until you get to the extravagant 200-foot spire of the **Sir Walter Scott Monument**. Turn right and walk up the slight hill to **St Andrew Square**, which is home to numerous financial institutions, including the Bank of Scotland. Turn left down George St, the main street of the new town, which is lined with many fine buildings.

If you're a little thirsty at this stage, turn left and then right into Rose St, which is famous for the large number of pubs. Then continue west until you come out on Charlotte Square – the north side is Robert Adam's masterpiece. No 7 is the **Georgian House**, which has been furnished by the

National Trust to bring it back to its full 18th century glory. It's open April to October, seven days a week (Sundays from 2 to 4.30 pm only); admission £2.40.

Festivals

The Edinburgh International Festival was born in 1947 and has established itself as one of the largest, most important arts festivals in the world – the world's premier companies play to packed audiences.

The Fringe Festival has grown up alongside, showcasing the would-be stars of the future. It now claims to be the largest event of its kind in the world with over 500 amateur and professional groups presenting every possible kind of avant-garde performance. Just to make sure that every B&B for 40 miles around is full, the Edinburgh Military Tattoo is held at the same time.

The International and Fringe Festivals run from mid-August to early September. If you want to attend the International Festival, it is necessary to book; the programme is published in April and is available from the Edinburgh Festival (☎ 031-225 5756), 21 Market St, EH1 1BW. The Fringe is less formal, and many performances will have empty seats the day before. Programmes are available from the Fringe Office (☎ 031-226 5257), 180 High St, EH1 1QS. For bookings for the Military Tattoo, contact the Tattoo Office (☎ 031-225 1188), 22 Market St, EH1 1QS.

Booking accommodation months in advance is essential. Contact the Central Reservation Service (☎ 031-557 9655), 3 Princes St, Edinburgh EH2 2QP.

Places to Stay

Edinburgh has numerous accommodation options, but the city can fill up very quickly at Easter and between mid-May and mid-September, particularly August. Book in advance if possible, or use the accommodation service operated by the TIC, or the free accommodation service in the railway station.

Camping The *Little France Caravan Park*

(☎ 031-664 4742), 219 Dalkeith Rd (the A68), is five km south of the city near the Inch Park. Tent sites are £7 and the park is serviced by a number of buses; it's open from April to October.

Hostels & Colleges The most central hostel accommodation is the friendly, good-value, independent *High St Hostel* (☎ 031-557 3984), 8 Blackfriars St. From Princes St, turn right onto North Bridge and walk up the hill until you get to the Royal Mile (High St at this point), turn left and Blackfriars is the second on the right. It's £6.50 per night.

There are two good official youth hostels; Eglington is closed in December, Bruntsfield in January; both have 2 am curfews. *Eglington Youth Hostel* (☎ 031-337 1120), 18 Eglington Crescent, is about two km west of the city near the Haymarket train station; the senior rate is £7.25. Walk down Princes St and continue on Shandwick Place which becomes West Maitland St; veer right at the Haymarket along Haymarket Terrace, then turn right into Coates Gardens which runs into Eglington Crescent. *Bruntsfield Youth Hostel* (☎ 031- 447 2994), 7 Bruntsfield Crescent, is a bit more difficult to get to; it has an attractive location overlooking Bruntsfield Links about four km from Waverley Station; the senior rate is £6.50. Catch bus No 11 or 16 from the garden side of Princes St and alight at Forbes Rd just after the gardens on the left.

During university vacations the *Pollock Halls of Residence* (☎ 031-667 1971), 18 Holyrood Park Rd, has modern accommodation from £15 per person.

B&Bs The best bet will be one of the numerous private houses; book through the TIC. You should have no trouble getting something for around £13, although most will be a bus ride to the centre.

Guesthouses are generally a pound or two more expensive, but they are more likely to be open all year. They don't come more central than the *Cafe Royal Guest House* (☎ 031-556 6894), 5 West Register St, just behind Princes St near Register House.

GREAT BRITAIN

There are 12 doubles, but only one single, from £11 to £18. Parking a car would be impossible; not that you would need one.

The *Ardenlee Guest House* (☎ 031-556 2838), 9 Eyre Place, is reasonably central, north of the new town and 1½ km from the centre; singles/doubles are from £14 to £18 per person. *Blairhaven Guest House* (☎ 031-556 3025) at 5 Eyre Place is a fraction cheaper.

Pilrig St, which is left off Leith Walk (veer left at the eastern end of Princes St), is a happy hunting ground for guesthouses. *Balmoral Guest House* (☎ 031-554 1857), 32 Pilrig St has easy access to the city with singles/doubles from £13.50 to £16. *Glenburn Guest House* (☎ 031- 554 9819), 22 Pilrig St, is similar. *Balquidder Guest House* (☎ 031 554 3377), is a very pleasant two-crown place with rooms from £14 to £20.

There are numerous guesthouses around the suburb of Newington, which is south of the city centre and university on either side of the continuation of North/South Bridge, which continues to change its name about every 400 metres. This is the main traffic artery from the south and carries traffic from the A7 and A68 (both routes are signposted); there are plenty of buses to the centre.

The *Salisbury* (☎ 031-667 1264), 45 Salisbury Rd, is 10 minutes from the centre by bus, and is quiet and very comfortable. Rates are from £16 to £22 per person. *Mrs Birnie* (☎ 031-667 8998), 8 Kilmaurs Rd, has two doubles at £12 per person.

Using the same bus stop as for the Bruntsfield Youth Hostel you can get to the *Bruntsfield Guest House* (☎ 031-228 6458) 55 Leamington Terrace, which has TVs in all bedrooms and singles/doubles for £13 to £18 per person. The next door *Leamington Guest House* (☎ 031 228 3879) charges from £11 to £14.

Places to Eat

For cheap eats, the best areas are Leith Walk, near the Playhouse theatre, around Grassmarket just north of the castle, and near the university around Nicolson St, the extension of North/South Bridge.

From the eastern end of Princes St veer left down Leith St, which becomes Leith Walk. You can take your pick of *Ferris Restaurant* (☎ 031-556 5592), which will feed you pasta or pizza or under £5; *Akash Restaurant* (☎ 031-557 5098), which has curries from £4 to £7; and the *Dragon's Pearl* (☎ 031-556 4547) has a good Chinese menu, including a three-course special lunch for £4. The pick of the bunch, however, is *Giuliano's* (☎ 031-556 6590), opposite the Playhouse Theatre – pastas and pizzas are around £5.

Those staying at Bruntsfield will find a batch of moderately priced Italian and Chinese restaraunts on Leven St (which becomes Bruntsfield Place). You will be able to eat for around £8. The best value, however, is the *Efes* (☎ 031-229 7833), 42 Leven St, which has various kebabs for around £5. There are also some reasonable places around the south end of Lothian Rd and in the streets behind the Royal Lyceum Theatre. *Dario's* (☎ 031-229 9625), 85 Lothian Rd, has pasta and pizzas for under £5. Behind the theatre, *Loon Fung* (☎ 031-229 5757), 32 Grindlay St, has excellent Cantonese food and you should be able to eat well for around £5.

There are some lively pubs and reasonable restaurants on the north side of Grassmarket, catering to a young crowd. *Gennaro* (☎ 031-226 3706) at No 64 has standard Italian fare, with minestrone at £1.60, cannelloni at £5.20 and pizza around £5. *Mamma's Pizzas* is extremely popular. The most interesting possibility is *Pierre Victoire* (☎ 031-226 2442), 38 Grassmarket, which has a relaxed style and an interesting contemporary menu emphasising fresh ingredients. Main meals are from £6 to £8; there are also branches at 8 Union St and 10 Victoria St; all are closed on Sundays.

The university students' budget favourites are between Nicolson St and Bristo Place at the end of George IV Bridge. *Kebab Mahal* (☎ 031-667 5214), on Nicolson Square, is a legendary source of cheap sustenance with kebabs from £2.50.

Vegetarians should also look for *Seeds* (☎ 031-667 8673), on West Nicolson St (west off Nicolson St), which has good inexpensive and healthy food; its only open to 8 pm and is closed all day Sunday and Monday evenings. *Negociant's* (☎ 031-225 6313), 45 Lothian St, is a very hip, but nonetheless comfortable, café and music venue. The food is good value – main courses from £4 to £5 – and the music is often free.

The *Kalpna* (☎ 031-667 9890), 2 St Patrick's Square, is a highly acclaimed Gujarati (Indian) restaurant, that is not only very good, but very reasonable. Thalis are from £6.50 and most main courses are under £4.

Entertainment
There are several rowdy pubs on the north side of Grassmarket, often with live music. For jazz and blues, take the left fork at the eastern end, towards the George IV Bridge, and visit the atmospheric Preservation Hall. The Pear Tree on West Nicolson St has a large outdoor courtyard – pleasant on sunny afternoons and warm evenings.

There are some interesting music/club venues in old vaults under the George IV and South Bridges. Berties, at the end of Merchant St off Candlemaker Row, has good live music, and The Vaults, 15 Niddry St under South Bridge, has a café as well as a variety of club nights.

Getting There & Away
Bus Buses from London are very competitive and you may be able to get cheap promotional tickets. See the Glasgow section; prices are the same and the journey takes half an hour less.

There are numerous links with cities in England. A sample of Citylink's buses follows (National Express is similar): one bus per day from Birmingham (5½ hours, £28); one from Newcastle (five hours, £19), one from York (7½ hours, £25).

National Express has an interesting service (No 370) from Gloucester to Birmingham, Leeds, Durham, Alnwick, Berwick, Melrose and Edinburgh.

As you might expect, Citylink has buses to virtually every major town in Scotland. Most of the west coast towns are reached via Glasgow. There are numerous buses to Glasgow with singles/returns for £3.70/£5.30, and to St Andrews (1¼ hours, £3.60), Aberdeen (3½ hours, £10.70), and Inverness (four hours, £10.30). There's a summer service for Stranraer, for the ferry to Larne, Northern Ireland; £31 will take you all the way to Belfast.

Train There are 20 trains a day from London's King's Cross (☎ 071-278 2477); they're not cheap, but they are much quicker and more comfortable than the bus (4½ hours, £57).

Scotrail (☎ 031-556 2451) has two northern lines from Edinburgh: one that cuts across the Grampians to Inverness (3½ hours, £31.50) and on to Thurso, and another that follows the coast around to Aberdeen (three hours, £20) and on to Inverness.

There are numerous trains to Glasgow (1½ hours, £5.20).

Getting Around
To/From the Airport There are regular bus links with Waverley Railway Station; they take 25 minutes and cost £2.50. A taxi would cost £12.

Bus Bus services are frequent and cheap, but two main companies compete with each other and their tickets are not interchangeable. You can buy tickets when you board buses, but on Lothian Regional Transport buses (with the maroon livery) you have to have exact change. For short trips in the city, fares are 35p or 40p. After midnight there are special night buses. The TIC has a map that shows the most important services, or contact Busline (☎ 031-225 3858), 24 St Giles St, an information service near St Giles Cathedral.

Bicycle Central Cycle Hire (☎ 031-228 6333), 13 Lochrin Place (near Tollcross), hires touring bikes for £6 per day/£40 per week, mountain bikes for £12/50 (£20 deposit and ID required). They also organise half-day, full-day and weekend tours from £8, including the bike. Mountain Sports (☎ 031-229 2233), 134 Lothian Rd, hires mountain bikes for £10 per day.

ST ANDREWS

St Andrews is a beautiful, unusual town – a concoction of medieval ruins, obsessive golfers, windy coastal scenery, tourist glitz, and a schizophrenic university with wealthy English undergraduates rubbing shoulders with Scottish theology students.

For most people, St Andrews is the home of golf. It is the headquarters of the game's governing body, the Royal & Ancient Golf Club, and location for the world's most famous golf course, the Old Course, which was laid out in the 16th century.

Orientation & Information

The most important parts of old St Andrews, lying to the east of the bus station, are easily explored on foot. The TIC (☎ 0334-72021), 78 South St, is open all year. Prospective golf players must either book months in advance or present a handicap certificate or letter of introduction to the Royal & Ancients (☎ 0334-75757), and enter a ballot before 2 pm the day before they wish to play. Green fees are a mere £30.

Places to Stay

The guesthouses and hotels are without exception expensive, but there are numerous private homes with rooms from £12. Book ahead from Edinburgh.

Getting There & Away

Bus Fife Scottish City Liner has four or five buses a day from St Andrew's Square, Edinburgh, to St Andrews (1¾ hours, £3.60) and on to Dundee (¾ hour, £1.60). Its Freedom of Fife Rover Ticket allows unlimited travel for one day for £3.60. From Dundee you can pick up buses for Aberdeen and Inverness.

Train The nearest station to St Andrews is Leuchars (one hour from Edinburgh, £5.60), eight miles away, on the Edinburgh-Dundee-

Aberdeen-Inverness coastal line. There are No 94 or 95 buses every half hour to St Andrews.

EASTERN HIGHLANDS

A great elbow of land juts into the North Sea between Perth and the Firth of Tay in the south and Inverness and Moray Firth in the north. The Cairngorm Mountains are as bleak and demanding as any Scottish mountains; the coastline, especially from Stonehaven to Buckie, is excellent; and the valley of the Dee – the Royal Dee thanks to the Queen's residence at Balmoral – has sublime scenery.

Orientation & Information

The Grampian Mountains march from Oban in a great arc to the north-east, becoming the Cairngorm Mountains in this region. Aberdeen is the main ferry port for the Shetlands, and Inverness is the centre for the northern Highlands. The division between the eastern and western Highlands reflects the transport realities – there are few coast-to-coast links between Perth and Inverness.

Getting Around

The main bus and train routes from Edinburgh to Inverness run directly north through Perth, or around the coast to Aberdeen and then north-west and inland back to Inverness.

Bus Citylink (☎ 0738-26848) and Caledonian Express (☎ 0224-580275) link the main towns. Edinburgh to Inverness via Perth takes four hours (£10.30); to Aberdeen, changing at Dundee, takes 3¾ hours (£10.70). There are also regular buses from both cities to Glasgow for much the same price. Aberdeen to Inverness takes three hours (£8.30). There are hourly buses from Aberdeen to Fraserburgh and from Fraserburgh to Elgin.

For local buses in Tayside, including Perthshire, contact the Transport Unit, Dundee (☎ 0382-23281); for info on the Grampian region, phone Aberdeen (☎ 0224-682222).

Train The train journey from Perth to Inverness is one of the most spectacular in Scotland, with a beautiful climb through the Cairngorms from Dunkeld to Aviemore. There are eight trains a day from Monday to Saturday, three on Sundays (3¼ hours). There are numerous trains from Edinburgh and Glasgow to Aberdeen (from Edinburgh they take three hours) and from Aberdeen to Inverness (two hours).

Perthshire & Cairngorms
On the direct route from Edinburgh to Inverness, Perth, once the capital of Scotland, is an attractive town ringed by castles. Both Dunkeld and Pitlochry to the north are appealing, but touristy, villages. There are youth hostels at Kingussie (☎ 0540-661506) and Aviemore (☎ 0479-810345). The Aviemore youth hostel is open from 20 December to 31 August. Both these towns are touristy and best used as walking bases rather than ends in themselves. Frequent buses and trains service this route.

Grampian Country – coast
Following the coastal route to Aberdeen and Inverness you quickly reach Dundee, one of Scotland's largest cities. Despite its excellent location it has not recovered from (often corrupt) modern development and the loss of its jute and shipbuilding industries.

The Grampian range meets the sea at Stonehaven, with its spectacular Dunnottar Castle. Continuing around the coast from Aberdeen there are long stretches of sand, and on the north coast, some magical fishing villages like Pennan, where the film *Local Hero* was shot.

Old and new hippies should check out the Findhorn Foundation (☎ 0309-73655), Forres IV36 0RD, just west of Inverness. The Foundation is an international spiritual community, founded in 1962. There are 140 members and many more sympathetic souls who have moved into the vicinity. The community has no formal creed, but is dedicated to creating 'a deeper sense of the sacred in every day life, and to dealing with work, relationships and our environment in new and more fulfilling ways'. In many ways the community is very impressive, although it can become a bit outlandish. One recent week-long course was called 'Devas, Fairies and Angels – a practical approach'.

The community is not particularly attractive itself – many members live in caravans – but the nearby fishing village of Findhorn (one km) and town of Forres (four km) are. It is possible to stay in the community caravan park – camping £6, caravans £8 per person. There are also week-long residential programmes for £180, including food and accommodation.

Buses and trains follow the coast to Aberdeen, then the train cuts back directly to Inverness (via Forres). Bus transport around the north-east coast is reasonable.

Grampian Country – inland
The region between Braemar and Huntly and east to the coast is castle country, and includes the Queen's residence at Balmoral. There are more fanciful examples of Scottish baronial architecture, with its turret-capped towers, than anywhere else in the country. The TICs have information on a Castle Trail, but you really need private transport. Balmoral Castle is open Monday to Saturday from May to July, and attracts large numbers of visitors; it can be reached by the Aberdeen-Braemar bus (see following).

Braemar is an attractive small town surrounded by mountains. There is an excellent new regional TIC (☎ 03397- 41600), open every day from Easter to October, and the town makes a fine walking base. There are a number of B&Bs, a *youth hostel* (☎ 03397-41659), and the *Braemar Bunkhouse* (☎ 03397-41242). The bunkhouse has dorm accommodation for £6.75; you need a sleeping bag.

It's a beautiful drive between Perth and Braemar, but unfortunately there are no buses on this route. Braemar can be reached from Aberdeen – there are several buses a day operated by Bluebird Northern (☎ 0224-212266) – along the beautiful valley of the River Dee. In summer there's a limited bus service between Pitlochry and Aviemore. It's known as the Heather Hopper, and Braemar to Pitlochry is £2.80; it runs on Tuesdays and Thursdays from June to September. On the first Saturday in September the town is invaded by 20,000 people for the Braemar Gathering (Highland Games); bookings are essential.

The direct inland route from Aberdeen to Inverness, serviced by bus and train, cuts across rolling agricultural country that, thanks to a mild climate, produces everything from grain to flower bulbs. The grain is turned into a magical liquid known as malt whisky. Aficionados might be tempted by the Malt Whisky Trail (information from TICs) which gives you an inside look and complimentary tastings at a number of famous distilleries (including Cardhu, Glenfiddich and The Glenlivet).

Aberdeen

Aberdeen is an extraordinary symphony in grey. Almost everything is built of grey granite – and the roads are paved with the same granite (crushed). In the sun, especially after a shower of rain, the stone turns silver and shines like a fairy tale, but with low grey clouds and rain scudding in off the North Sea it can all be a bit much.

Aberdeen was a prosperous North Sea trading and fishing port centuries before oil was considered a valuable commodity. Now it services one of the largest oilfields in the world. There are more bars with more marble bar-tops than would seem even remotely viable. Start with 200,000 Scots, add multinational oil workers and a large student population – the result: a thriving nightlife.

Orientation & Information Aberdeen is built on a ridge that runs east-west to the north of the railway and bus stations, and the ferry quay. The bus and railway stations are next to each other off Guild St.

The useful TIC (☎ 0224-632727) is in St Nicholas House, Broad St; in June and September it's open Mondays to Saturdays to 6 pm, Sundays to 4 pm; in July and August it's open to 6 pm on Sundays; from October to May it's open 9 am to 5 pm weekdays, 10 am to 2 pm Saturdays.

Places to Stay & Eat The *youth hostel* (☎ 0224-646988), 8 Queen's Rd, is two km from the railway station. It's open all year except January. Walk east along Union St and take the right fork along Albyn Place until you reach a roundabout; Queen's Rd continues on the east side.

There are batches of B&Bs, which centre on Bon Accord St (close to the centre) and Great Western Rd (the A93, a 20-minute walk); they're a bit more expensive than is usually the case in Scotland. Turn left on Guild St in front of the stations, left at the T-junction onto College St, then take the third right on Wellington Place. Bon Accord St is the second on the right. On Bon Accord St, *Crynoch Guest House* (☎ 0224-582743) at No 164 has singles/doubles for £16/12 per person; the *Stewart Lodge* (☎ 0224-573823) at No 89, and *Trovador* (☎ 0224-596837) at No 158, are similar. There are plenty of other alternatives.

The *Salisbury Guest House* (☎ 0224-590447), 12 Salisbury Terrace, is a very comfortable place with spotless rooms, all with TV, for £15 per person.

Churchill's Lounge Bar, on Bon Accord St opposite the post office, has a range of cheap meals, like lasagne, for around £5. For lots of action and cheap Mexican, burgers and dogs, *Henry J Beans* can't be beat. It's on Windmill Brae below Bridge St. For a classier ambience try *The Wild Boar Gallery & Restaurant* (☎ 0224-624216), 19 Belmont St, with vegetarian dishes under £5, kebabs for £7. There are bars up and down Union St, several in Belmont St and several in Windmill Brae – you should be able to find some live music if you persevere.

Getting There & Away Aberdeen is the main ferry port for the Shetland Islands; there are also boats to the Orkneys. For transport around the region, see the preceding Getting Around section.

Bus & Train Citylink and Caledonian

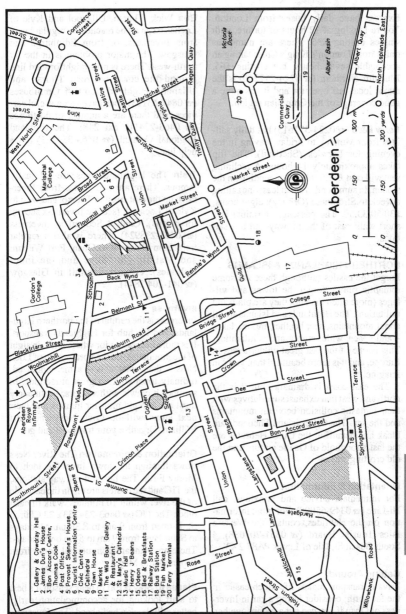

Aberdeen

1 Gallery & Cowdray Hall
2 James Dun's House
3 Bon Accord Centre,
4 Post Office
5 Provost Skene's House
6 Tourist Information Centre
7 Civic Centre
8 Cathedral
9 Town House
10 Market
11 The Wild Boar Gallery
   & Restaurant
12 St Mary's Cathedral
13 Music Hall
14 Henry J Beans
15 Odeon
16 Bed & Breakfasts
17 Railway Station
18 Bus Station
19 Fish Market
20 Ferry Terminal

Express have daily buses from London. You're looking at 12 hours of torture, with singles costing £36. There are numerous trains from London's King's Cross taking an acceptable seven hours, but costing £65. Bluebird Northern (☎ 0224-212266) is the major local bus operator and it has quite a good coverage of the Grampian region.

Ferry P&O (☎ 0224-572615) has daily sailings from Monday to Friday leaving in the evening for Lerwick (Shetland). The trip takes approximately 14 hours. A reclining seat will cost £41.50/46.50 depending on the season. In summer there is at least one sailing a week to Stromness (Orkney); eight hours, £30.50/33.50. The passenger terminal is a short walk east of the railway and bus stations.

NORTHERN HIGHLANDS & ISLANDS

Forget the castles (although there are some romantic ruins), forget the towns and villages (more often than not they are plain and utilitarian). The Highlands and Islands are all about mountains, sea, heather, moors, lakes – and space, wide, empty and exhilarating. This is one of the last great wildernesses in Europe, and it is more beautiful than you can imagine.

The east coast is dramatic, but it is the north and west that exhaust superlatives with their fantastic collision between mountains and the sea. The Orkneys and Shetlands are bleak and beautiful; the Outer Hebrides are the last stronghold of Gaelic culture and the old crofting ways.

Orientation & Information

For immediate advice and bookings, call Hi-Line (☎ 0349-65000). For more information on the Hebrides, contact the Western Isles Tourist Board (☎ 0851-703088), 4 South Beach St, Isle of Lewis PA87 2XY.

Getting Around

Private transport makes life much easier in the far north; consider hiring a car in Inverness or Oban if you can get a group together.

Bus Wick, Thurso, Ullapool and Kyle of Lochalsh can all be reached by regular buses from Inverness, or from Edinburgh and Glasgow. The major problem is in the far north-west. There is no straightforward link around the coast between Thurso and Ullapool. Highland Scottish Omnibuses (☎ 0847-63123) does have some useful services, and there are a number of postbuses (☎ 0463-234111 ext 248). The Highland Regional Council (☎ 0463-234121) has a help line.

Train The Highland lines are all justly famous. There are two routes from Inverness: up the east coast to Thurso, and west to Kyle of Lochalsh (see the Inverness section for details). Contact Scotrail in Inverness (☎ 0463-238924). There is also a regular train from Glasgow to Oban, Fort William and Mallaig (for Skye and the Inner Hebrides). Contact Scotrail in Glasgow (☎ 041-204 2844).

Inverness

Inverness is the capital of the northern Highlands, and the hub for Highlands transport. It is more interesting for where it is – in sight of the mountains, on the northern tip of Loch Ness – than what it is – a medium-sized, ordinary town with no great attractions. In summer it crawls with visitors. Fortunately most are intrepid monster hunters and their next stops will be Loch Ness and Fort William. Organise your transport and go.

Orientation & Information The River Ness flows through the town from the loch to Moray Firth. The bus and railway stations, the TIC and the hostels are all on the east side of the river within 10 minutes' walk of each other. The TIC (☎ 0463-234353), 23 Church St, is open from 9 am to 8.30 pm Mondays to Saturdays, from 9 am to 6 pm on Sundays. There are standard commercial hours from September to May.

Places to Stay & Eat In peak season it's best to start looking for accommodation early; better still, book a bed ahead. The *Inverness*

Student Hotel (☎ 0463-236556), 8 Culduthel Rd, is in the same family as the High St Hostel in Edinburgh – you can make phone bookings from there. It's a friendly, homely place with a great view; it's open all year and doesn't have a curfew; and beds are just £6.40 per night. It's just 10 minutes from the railway station, just past the castle, opposite the youth hostel.

The *youth hostel* (☎ 0453-231771), 1 Old Edinburgh Rd, is open all year except January. Booking is essential during Easter and in July and August.

Within easy walking distance of town (on the east side) there's *Crownleigh Guest House* (☎ 0463-220316), 6 Midmills Rd, and *Leinster Lodge Guest House* (☎ 0463-233311), 27 Southside Rd. Both have rooms for around £13 per person.

There are lots of guesthouses and B&Bs along Old Edinburgh Rd and Kenneth St. *Heathfield Guest House* (☎ 0463-230547, 2 Kenneth St is immaculate; rooms include TV and the rate is £13 per person.

There are two good restaurants in Inverness that make an effort to look after vegetarians: *Dickens Restaurant* (☎ 0463-713111), 77 Church St, and *Vines Food & Wine Bar* (☎ 0463-233648), 10 Bridge St; both have main courses for under £5. The *Castle Restaurant* (☎ 0463-230925), 41 Castle St, near the youth hostel, has steak dinners for under £6.

Hayden's Café Bar (☎ 0463-236969), 37 Queensgate, is a bright and cheery place with good-value food.

Getting There & Away Many people take advantage of the half-day tours of Loch Ness that depart from the TIC; they're good value at £6 or £7. There's a wide range of transport options.

Bus Citylink (☎ 0463- 711000) and National Express have bus connections with a number of major centres in England, including London (12 hours, £36) via Perth and Glasgow. There are numerous buses to/from Glasgow (4¼ hours, £10.60), Edin-

burgh via Perth (four hours, £10.30), and Aberdeen (three hours, £8.30).

There are two buses a day for Ullapool (1½ hours, £7). The 7 am bus connects with the 9.30 am CalMac ferry to Stornoway on Lewis (not Sundays). The 3½-hour trip costs £8.80.

Skye-ways (☎ 0463-710119) has two buses a day between Portree (on Skye), Kyle of Lochailsh, and Inverness. The total journey takes four hours and costs £12. From Portree there are buses to Uig from where there are ferries to Tarbert on Harris and Lochmady on North Uist (both places £6.25).

There are four Citylink buses a day for Thurso and Scrabster (3¾ hours, £7.20) for ferries to the Orkneys.

It's possible, but difficult, to head up to the north-west through Lairg. RGH Rapson of Brora (☎ 0408-21245, evening 21246) has daily services from Lairg to Durness, but you might have to hitch to get to Lairg.

Train The two onward train journeys from Inverness are both famous; the line to Kyle of Lochalsh, however, is one of the greatest scenic journeys in Britain. There are three trains a day on both routes (none on Sundays). The trip to Kyle of Lochalsh (2½ hours, £12) connects with a ferry to Stornoway on Lewis – see the preceding bus section. The trip to Thurso (3¾ hours, £10) connects with the ferry to the Orkneys. London to Inverness costs £65 and takes eight hours.

Car There are quite a number of car rental operators; the TIC has a complete list. In summer, book ahead. The big boys all have branches (and charge around £30 per day), or you could try Sharp's Reliable Wrecks (☎ 0463- 236694), 1st Floor, Highland Rail House, Station Square. They have used cars from £23 per day, and three-berth camper vans from £280 per week.

Bicycle Sharp's (see the previous section) also has mountain bikes at £9 per day. Mountain Bike Hire (**☎** 0463-233231), 32 Crown Drive, will hire and suggest routes.

East Coast

The coast really starts to get interesting when you leave behind the industrial development at Invergordon. Great, heather-covered hills heave themselves out of the wild North Sea. There are several touristy little towns moored precariously at their edge. Helmsdale is quite busy in summer, but it is attractive enough and the location is great. There's a *youth hostel* (**☎** 04312-577) for which you're advised to book early between mid-July and mid-August.

The next major town is Wick, but there's nothing to stop you continuing on to the *hostel* at John O'Groats (**☎** 095581-424) or to Thurso (Scrabster) for the ferry to the Orkneys. By Scottish standards, the coast at the island's north-east tip is understated, and John O'Groats is nothing more than a second-rate tourist trap – but there is something magical about the view across the water to the Orkneys. Thurso is the end of the line, both for the east coast railway and the big bus lines.

Thurso, Scrabster & John O'Groats

Thurso is a largish, bleak town overlooking the north Atlantic – an unlikely surfing centre, but the nearby coast has arguably the best and most regular surf in Britain.

Scrabster, the ferry port, is a three-km walk from the station, or there are buses for 60p. The TIC (**☎** 0847-62371), Riverside, is open every day from Easter to October. Bikes are hired by the Bike & Camping Shop (**☎** 0847-66124), The Arcade, High St.

The nearest *youth hostel*, at John O'Groats (**☎** 095581-424), is open from April to October. There are several buses from Thurso to John O'Groats (the last at 5 pm, £1.95) that pass the hostel (none on Sundays). A Citylink bus to/from Inverness also goes past the hostel.

In July and August it is possible to stay at the *Thurso Youth Club* (**☎** 0847-62964), Old Mill, Millbank, which has dorm accommodation for £7 including breakfast.

In 1992 Thomas & Bews (**☎** 095581-353) operated a free bus to John O'Groats (for Orkney ferry passengers). In Thurso, it connected with the train from Inverness that arrived at 3.40 pm, and departed from the TIC at 3.45 pm for those who had arrived earlier.

There's excellent surf on the east side of town, directly in front of Lord Caithness' castle (a right-hand reef break). There's another shallow reef break eight km west at Brimms Ness.

Orkney

Orkney is only 10 km offshore from Scotland. There are 18 inhabited islands; Kirkwall, with 6000 inhabitants, is the main town, and Stromness, with 2000 inhabitants, is the major port; both are on the major island, which is known as Mainland. The land is treeless, lush and level rather than rugged. The climate, warmed by the Gulf Stream, is surprisingly moderate, with April and May the driest months. Contact the Orkney Tourist Board (**☎** 0856-850716), Ferry Building, Stromness KW16 3AA, for more information.

Places to Stay There's a good selection of cheap B&Bs and six youth hostels, including one on Stromness and a highly recommended hostel on beautiful Papa Westray, the most northerly island. Stromness Youth Hostel (**☎** 0856- 850589), a 10-minute walk from the ferry, is open from April to September; booking is advised from mid-June to August.

There's also an independent hostel in Stromness – *Brown's Hostel* (**☎** 0856-850661), which charges £5.50, and also has bicycles for hire.

The excellent *Papa Westray Hostel* (**☎** 08574-267), Orkney KW17 2BU, is open all year.

Getting There & Away There are car ferries from Scrabster, near Thurso, to Stromness operated by P&O (**☎** 0856-850655). There's at least one departure a day all year, with single fares around £11. P&O also sails from

Aberdeen (see that section). Thomas & Bews (☎ 095581-353) have a passenger ferry from John O'Groats to Burwick on South Ronaldsay from May to September. A one-way ticket is £10, but in 1992 they also had an excellent special deal: a free bus picked up ferry passengers at the railway station (meeting the afternoon train from Inverness) and from the TIC. A return fare on the ferry was £15, providing you left John O'Groats in the afternoon, and Orkney in the morning. A bus for Kirkwall (20 miles away) meets the ferry and from Kirkwall there's a bus for Stromness.

Shetlands

The Shetland Islands remained under Norse rule until 1469, when they were given to Scotland as part of a Danish princess's dowry. Even today these remote, treeless islands are almost as much a part of Scandinavia as of Britain – the nearest mainland town is Bergen, Norway.

The Shetlands are famous for their beautiful coast (the sea is never more than five km away), the birdlife (including puffins), and a 4000-year-old archaeological heritage. They aren't particularly wet and cold, but they are often windy.

There are 20 inhabited islands and a declining population of 23,000. The main town on Mainland Shetland is Lerwick, which is used as a base for the North Sea oilfields. Small ferries connect a handful of smaller islands. Contact the TIC (☎ 0595-3434), Lerwick, Shetland ZE1 0LU, for further information. The *Lerwick Youth Hostel* (☎ 0595-2114) is open from April to October, and there are plenty of B&Bs.

The island's climate is surprisingly mild (thanks to the Gulf Stream) and the conditions for bicycle touring are ideal; there are plenty of places where you can hire bikes.

Getting There & Away Lerwick can be reached by P&O ferries from Aberdeen, some of which call in to Stromness on the Orkneys (see the Aberdeen section). There's also a summer link with Norway, Denmark, the Faroe Islands and Iceland (see the intro-

ductory Scotland Getting There & Away section).

North Coast

From Dounreay, with its nuclear power station, the coast around to Ullapool is mind-blowing. Everything is on a massive scale: vast empty spaces, enormous locks and snow-capped mountains. Unfortunately, public transport is difficult, verging on the impossible. Take your time, hitching may be the only possibility. There are two *youth hostels*: one at Tongue (☎ 084755-301), which has the most spectacular location for any youth hostel I have ever seen, and another at Durness (☎ 0971-511244).

There's a postbus (☎ 0463-234111 ext 248) Monday to Saturday between Lairg and Talmine, via Tongue. During school term, there's a school bus between Thurso and Tongue, leaving Thurso at 3.30 pm; contact Dunnet's Motors (☎ 095583-202). RGH Rapson of Brora (☎ 0408-21245, evening 21246) has daily services from Lairg to Durness. Unfortunately, there's no bus link between Tongue and Durness, and you might have to hitch to get to Lairg.

West Coast

Ullapool is the most northerly town of any significance; it has a youth hostel, a ferry to Stornoway on the Isle of Lewis, and bus connections with Inverness. There's more brilliant coast round to Gairloch, along the incomparable Loch Maree and down to the Kyle of Lochalsh (a short hop from Skye). From here on you are well and truly back in the land of the tour bus; civilisation (or whatever it is you find in Fort William) is a shock.

Ullapool Ullapool is a small fishing village that attracts a fair crowd of visitors, because it is easily accessible along beautiful Loch Broom from Inverness. Everything is strung along the harbour, including the *youth hostel* (☎ 0854-612254) and the TIC (☎ 0854-612135). The hostel is open from April to October; booking is advisable in Easter and summer. See the Inverness section for infor-

GREAT BRITAIN

mation on the ferry to Stornoway on the Isle of Lewis, and bus connections.

Kyle of Lochalsh Kyle, as it is known, is a small village that overlooks the lovely Island of Skye across the narrow Loch Alsh. There's a TIC (☎ 0599-4276) above the ferry ramp, but the nearest youth hostel is just across the loch in Kyleakin on Skye. Frequent ferries shuttle across to Kyleakin (five minutes, free for pedestrians). The Cycle Shop (☎ 0599-4842) hires bikes that can be dropped off at Armadale, Uig or Lochboisdale (South Uist).

Kyle can be reached by bus and train from Inverness (see that section), and by direct Citylink buses from Glasgow (five hours, £12.20), which continue across to Kyleakin and on to Uig (6½ hours, £14.20) for ferries to Tarbert on Harris and Lochmaddy on North Uist.

Skye
Skye is a large, rugged island, 80 km from north to south and east to west. The island is ringed by beautiful coastline and is dominated by the Cuillins, which reach over 1000 metres in height. Tourism is a mainstay of the island economy, so until you get off the main roads, don't expect to escape from the hordes. Contact the TIC (☎ 0478-2137) for more information. Bicycles are hired at Castle Moil Cycle Hire (☎ 0599-4164), Kyleakin, and at the Ferry Filling Station (☎ 04714-249), Ardvasar.

Places to Stay There are six youth hostels on the island and numberless B&Bs. The three hostels most relevant to ferry users are at Kyleakin (☎ 0599-4585) for Kyle of Lochalsh, which is open all year; Uig (☎ 047042-211) for the Western Isles, which is open from Easter to October; and Armadale (☎ 04714-260) for Mallaig, which is also open from Easter to October.

There are also a number of independent hostels. The pick of the pack is the *Skye Backpackers' Guest House* (☎ 0599-4510), Kyleakin, a short walk from the ferry. There's a friendly atmosphere, even some

double rooms. B&B is £6.20. Theres also the nearby *Fossil Bothy* (☎ 0471-822644), Lower Breakish; and on the west coast *Croft Bunkhouse* (☎ 047-842254).

Getting There & Away CalMac (☎ 0599-4482) operates all the ferries to/from Skye. There are at least two ferries a day between Uig and Tarbert on Harris (1¾ hours, £6.25), and to Lochmaddy on North Uist (same). The ferry from Armadale to Mallaig is less dependable; it only operates in summer, and on Sundays only between 30 June and 25 August (£2.30). You *must* book.

The beautiful West Highland railway line runs south from Mallaig to Fort William, Oban and Glasgow. From Mondays to Saturdays, four trains run through to Mallaig, on Sundays, two (five hours, £36). From June to September they're steam-hauled between Fort William and Mallaig (£5.90).

Outer Hebrides
The Outer Hebrides are bleak, remote and treeless. The climate is fierce – they're completely exposed to the gales that sweep in from the Atlantic, and it rains over 250 days a year. Some people find the landscapes mournful, but others find that the stark beauty and the isolated world of the crofters create a unique and strangely captivating atmosphere. Do not forget that the Sabbath is strictly observed – there are no pubs, no buses, no nothing.

See the Skye and Kyle of Lochalsh sections for details of CalMac ferries to Tarbert and Lochmaddy, and the Oban section for ferries to Lochboisdale.

Lewis & Harris Lewis (Stornoway, by ferry from Ullapool) and Harris (Tarbert, by ferry from Uig on Skye) are in fact one island with a border of high hills between them. Lewis has low, rolling hills and miles of untouched moorland and freshwater lochs; Harris is rugged, with stony mountains bordered by meadows and sweeping, sandy beaches.

Stornoway is the largest town, with a population of 8000; there is a reasonable range of facilities including a TIC (☎ 0851-

703088). Book a B&B through the TIC, or stay at the Bayble *Bunkhouse* (☎ 0851-870863), which offers simple facilities for £6. Bayble is 13 km (eight miles) from Stornoway – there are buses. Bicycles are hired by the Sport Shop. There's at least one bus a day between Tarbert and Stornoway (except Sundays).

Tarbert has a bank, a TIC (☎ 0859-2011) and a few shops. The nearest youth hostel is 11 km (almost seven miles) south at Stockinish (no phone); there's one bus a day from Tarbert.

North & South Uist North Uist (Lochmaddy, by ferry from Uig on Skye, and from Tarbert on Harris), Benbecula and South Uist (Lochboisdale, by ferry from Oban) are actually joined by bridge and causeway. These are low, flat, green islands half drowned by sinuous lochs and open to the sea and sky. There's one postbus a day between the two tiny villages – Lochmaddy with a bank, a hotel, a TIC (☎ 08763-321), and a *youth hostel* (☎ 08763-368) open mid-May to September, with hot showers; and Lochboisdale with a TIC (☎ 08784-286). Mrs A McDonald (☎ 0870-2191) hires bikes.

WESTERN HIGHLANDS
This is the Highlands of the tour bus, but there are also some unspoilt peninsulas and serious mountains where you can be very isolated. The scenery is unquestionably dramatic – Ben Nevis is Britain's highest mountain (1343 metres, 4406 feet); brooding Glencoe still seems haunted by the massacre of the MacDonalds; the Cowal and Kintyre peninsulas have a magic of their own; and Loch Lomond may be a tourist cliché but it is still beautiful.

This area provides challenges for the most experienced and well-equipped mountaineers, rock climbers and walkers, but there are also moderate walks that are quite safe if you are properly equipped and take the normal precautions. The West Highland Way runs 147 km (95 miles) between Fort William and Glasgow.

Orientation & Information
Fort William is a major tourist centre, easily reached by bus and train and a good base for the mountains. Oban is the most important ferry port for boats to the Inner Hebrides (Mull, Coll, Tiree, Colonsay, Jura and Islay) and the Outer Hebridean islands of South Uist and Barra. There's a reasonable scattering of youth hostels, including those at Fort William, Glencoe, Oban and Crianlarich.

Getting Around
Although the road network seems more comprehensive, travel around this region is still difficult.

Bus Fort William has connections with Glasgow (three hours, £8.10) and Inverness from Mondays to Saturdays (two hours, £5). Oban has bus links with Glasgow, although Citylink and Caledonian Express only operate this route during summer, from May to mid-October (three hours, £8.50). The same is true of their Inverness to Fort William service, but Highland Scottish Omnibuses (☎ 0397-702373) works all year. Gaelic Bus (☎ 08552-229) has three buses a day, Monday to Saturday, between Fort William and Oban (£4.50). For local buses in the Central region around Stirling, ☎ 0786- 73111.

Train The spectacular west coast railway runs north to Fort William and Mallaig, with a spur to Oban from Crianlarich. There are four trains a day to Oban (three hours, £17.50) from Monday to Saturday, two on Sundays. There are the same number of Glasgow-Fort William trains (3¾ hours, £18.50). If you're travelling from Oban to Fort William, the Gaelic Bus service saves you backtracking to Crianlarich. West Highland Rovers (seven days unlimited travel) cost £28.

Fort William
Fort William has lost any charm it may once have had to modern development. It's an excellent base for the mountains – ski lodges

are amongst the new buildings – but don't plan on hanging around.

The town meanders along the edge of Loch Linnhe for a number of miles. The rather bleak centre and its reasonable selection of shops, takeaways and pubs is easy to get around on foot unless you are staying at a very far-flung B&B. The TIC (☎ 0397-703781) is in the centre of town on Cameron Square, and is open all year. Bikes are available from Off-Beat Bikes (☎ 0397-702663), 4 Inverlochy Place.

The nearest *youth hostel* (☎ 0397-702336) is five km (three miles) from town towards Glen Nevis on the Glen Nevis Rd. There's an independent hostel, the *Inchree Bunkhouse* (☎ 08553-207), and popular *youth hostel* (☎ 08552-219) at beautiful Glencoe, which is particularly favoured by mountain climbing types. The Glencoe hostel is a 1½-mile walk from the main road and the regular Citylink buses that run from Fort William to Glasgow. Booking is advised in July, August and holiday weekends; it's open all year.

Getting There & Away See the preceding Getting Around section for bus and rail information. Fort William is at the northern end of the West Highland Way which runs to Glasgow. This is an excellent walk through some of Scotland's finest scenery. Parts of the way can be tackled, or the whole 147 km (91 miles) could easily be walked in a week. If you do plan to walk the whole route, you are strongly recommended to start in Glasgow and walk north. *The West Highland Way* by Robert Aitken (£9.95) has a complete map and description. The TICs have a free brochure listing accommodation.

Oban

Oban can be inundated by visitors, but as the most important ferry port on the west coast it manages to hold its own. By Highlands standards it's quite a large town, but you can easily get around it on foot. There isn't a great deal to see or do, but it's on a beautiful bay, the harbour is interesting, and there are some lovely coastal and hill walks in the vicinity.

The bus, train, and ferry terminals are all grouped conveniently together by the side of the harbour. The TIC (☎ 0631-63122) on Argyll Square, a block or two behind the harbour, is open all year; during summer it has a *bureau de change* open seven days a week until 9 pm. There are numerous B&Bs and a youth hostel. The *youth hostel* (☎ 0631-62025) is on the Esplanade north of town on the other side of the bay to the terminals.

Getting There & Away See the Scotland introductory Getting Around section for bus and train information. Numerous CalMac (☎ 0631-62285) boats link Oban with the Inner and Outer Hebrides. There are daily ferries to Lochboisdale on South Uist, and return ferries from Lochboisdale on Tuesdays, Thursdays, Fridays and Saturdays. The trip takes four hours and costs £23.20 return.

GLASGOW

Glasgow, with a population of nearly 700,000, is one of Britain's largest and most interesting cities. It doesn't have the beauty of Edinburgh, although it does have a legacy of interesting Victorian architecture and some distinguished suburbs of terraced squares and crescents. What makes it appealing is its vibrancy and energy.

Although influenced by thousands of Irish immigrants, it is the most Scottish of cities – quite different to Edinburgh and completely different to anything south of the border. There's a unique blend of friendliness, urban chaos, black humour and energy. There are some excellent museums, numerous cheap restaurants, countless pubs and bars and a lively arts scene. If the English cities were too bland for your taste, Glasgow should be the antidote.

Glasgow grew up around the cathedral founded by St Mungo in the 6th century. In 1451 the University of Glasgow was founded – the fourth oldest university in Britain. Unfortunately, with the exception of

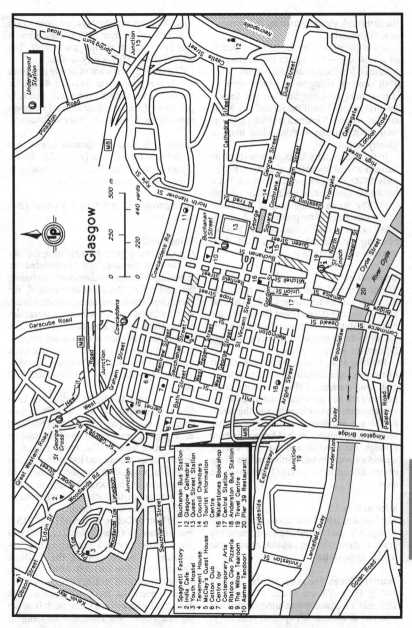

Glasgow

500 m

440 yards

1 Spaghetti Factory
2 India Cafe
3 Youth Hostel
4 Tenement House
5 McClay's Guest House
6 Cotton Club
7 Centre for
  Contemporary Arts
8 Ristoro Ciao Pizzeria
9 The Willow Tearoom
10 Asman Tandoori
11 Buchanan Bus Station
12 Glasgow Cathedral
13 Queen Street Station
14 Council Chambers
15 Tourist Information
   Centre
16 Waterstones Bookshop
17 Central Station
18 Anderston Bus Station
19 Travel Centre
20 Pier 39 Restaurant

Underground
Station

GREAT BRITAIN

the cathedral, virtually nothing of the medieval city remains.

It was swept away by the energetic people of a new age – the age of capitalism, the Industrial Revolution, and the empire. In the 19th century, Glasgow – transformed by cotton, steel, coal, shipbuilding and trade – justifiably called itself the second city of the empire. Grand Victorian public buildings were built, but the working class lived in ghastly slums.

In the 20th century, Glasgow's port and its industries went into terminal decline. By the early 1970s Glasgow looked doomed, but it has fought back by developing service industries. The spooky emptiness of the River Clyde – once one of the greatest shipbuilding ports in the world – and of the soulless housing estates are compensated by a renewed confidence in the city.

Orientation

The city centre is built on a grid system on the north side of the River Clyde. The two railway stations (Central and Queen St), the main bus station (Buchanan St) and the TIC are all within a couple of blocks of George Square, the main city square.

Running along a ridge in the northern part of the city, Sauchiehall St has a pedestrian mall with numerous High St shops at its eastern end, and pubs and restaurants at the western end. The university and the youth hostel are north-west of the city centre around Kelvingrove Park. Motorways bore through the suburbs and the M8 sweeps around the western and northern edges of the centre. The airport is 16 km (10 miles) to the west.

Information

The List, available from newsagents (£1), is Glasgow's and Edinburgh's fortnightly guide to films, theatre, cabaret, music – the works. Invaluable.

Tourist Offices The main TIC (☎ 041-204 4400), 35 St Vincent Place, Glasgow G1 2ER, has a free accommodation service and a *bureau de change*. It's open all year, but to 7 pm Mondays to Saturdays and from 10 am to 6 pm Sundays from May to September. It also has a branch at Glasgow airport. The official guide (75p) is very useful.

The best city maps are available free from the Travel Centre (☎ 041-226 4826), St Enoch Square; the staff there will also help you unravel the complicated local transport possibilities. It's open Monday to Saturday.

Money Full American Express services are available at 115 Hope St (☎ 041-221 4366); it's open commercial hours from Monday to Friday, and to noon on Saturday.

Emergency Dial ☎ 999 on any phone (free call).

Things to See

A good starting point for exploring the city is **George Square**. It's surrounded by imposing Victorian architecture, including the post office, the Bank of Scotland, the Merchants' House and, along its eastern side, the City Chambers. The chambers were built in the 1880s at the high point of the city's wealth; their interior is even more extravagant than their exterior. There are free tours from the main entrance, Monday, Tuesday, Wednesday and Friday at 10.30 am and 2.30 pm.

The current **Glasgow Cathedral** is a direct descendant of St Mungo's simple church. It was begun in 1238 and is regarded as a perfect example of pre-Reformation Gothic architecture. The lower church is reached by a stairway, and its forest of pillars creates a powerful atmosphere around St Mungo's tomb, the focus of a famous medieval pilgrimage that was believed to be as meritorious as a visit to Rome.

The **Burrell Collection** (☎ 041-649 7151) was amassed by a wealthy local before it was given to the city and housed in a prize-winning new museum in the Pollock Country Park, five km south of the city. It's an idiosyncratic collection, including Chinese porcelain, medieval furniture, and paintings by Renoir and Cézanne. It is not so big as to be overwhelming, and the stamp of the individual collector seems to create a weird coherence.

It's open from 10 am to 5 pm Mondays to Saturdays, and 2 to 5 pm on Sundays. Catch a train to Pollokshaws West from Central Station (one every half hour; the second station on the light-blue line to the south) and then walk for 10 minutes through the pleasant park – bring a picnic lunch if the weather allows.

There are a number of superb art nouveau buildings designed by the Scottish architect and designer, Charles Rennie Mackintosh. In particular, check out the **Glasgow School of Art** (☎ 041-332 9797), 167 Renfrew St, which has guided tours Monday to Saturday mornings, and the **Willow Tearoom** (☎ 041-332 0521), 217 Sauchiehall St.

For an extraordinary time-capsule experience, visit the small apartment in the **Tenement House** (☎ 041-333 0183), 145 Buccleuch St. It gives a vivid insight into a middle-class life at the turn of the century, and is open daily from 2 to 5 pm from April to October (£2).

Festivals Not to be outdone by Edinburgh, Glasgow has developed a major festival of its own. Mayfest, in the first three weeks of May, has a strong mix of Scottish and international performers. There is an excellent international jazz festival early in July. Contact the TIC for more information.

Places to Stay
Finding somewhere decent in July/August can be difficult – if you plan to find a B&B, get in to town reasonably early and use the TIC's free booking service. Unfortunately, Glasgow B&Bs are expensive by Scottish standards – you may have to pay up to £15.

Camping There's not much going; the camping grounds are a fair way out, and inaccessible by public transport. *Craigenmuir Caravan Park* (☎ 041-779 4159), Campsie View, Stepps, takes vans and tents for £5.

Hostels & Colleges In summer, it is advisable to book a bed in the excellent *youth hostel* (☎ 041-332 3004), 7 Park Terrace. The hostel has recently moved into what was a hotel, so there are mainly four-bed rooms, many with en suite facilities, as well as a small number of doubles. It's open all day. There is a three-night maximum, but this is usually interpreted fairly flexibly. From the Central Station take bus No 44 and ask for the first stop on Woodlands Rd. Walk left along Lynedoch St which becomes Woodlands Terrace, which becomes Park Terrace...

The *University of Glasgow* (☎ 041-330 5385) has a range of B&B accommodation at £20.50, and self-catering at £9 from mid-March to mid-April, and July, August and September. *McLay Hall* (☎ 041-332 5056) is near the youth hostel on the continuation of Woodlands Terrace. There are 180 rooms, sleeping one to three people.

B&Bs *McClay's Guest House* (☎ 041-332 4796) is labyrinthine, but brilliantly located at 268 Renfrew St, which is behind Sauchiehall St. Considering the location, you can't really quibble at £16.50 per person without bathroom, £18.50 with.

There's a batch of reasonable-value B&Bs to the east of the Necropolis. *Brown's Guest House* (☎ 041-554 6797), 2 Onslow Drive, has singles/doubles from £12.50 per person. *Craigpark Guest House* (☎ 041-554 4160), 33 Circus Drive, charges around £15 per person. *Oakley Guest House* (☎ 041-554 5409), 10 Oakley Terrace, has singles/doubles for £17 per person.

If you don't mind staying a bit farther out of town, *Jordanhill College* (☎ 041-950 3320), Southbrae Drive, has high-quality, university-style accommodation available all year. For £18.35 including breakfast, you're talking luxury. The only hitch will be if it's booked out for a conference. Bus No 44 from Central Station goes to the college gates.

Places to Eat
Glasgow has an excellent range of moderately priced restaurants. Wander along

Sauchiehall or around the city centre and you're certain to find the ethnic cuisine of your choice.

Those staying in the vicinity of Kelvingrove Park will find a scattering of restaurants along Gibson St and Great Western Rd. The *Spaghetti Factory* (☎ 041-334 2665), 30 Gibson St, has delicious pasta main dishes for around £5 and *good* coffee. It has a great-value, three-course student special for £4.85 (from 5 to 7 pm, and 10 pm to midnight). On nearby Woodlands Rd near the corner with Willowbank St, the tiny *India Cafe* has dinners for under £3.

There are a number of interesting choices on Sauchiehall. The *Centre for Contemporary Arts* (☎ 041-332 7521), 346 Sauchiehall St, is an interesting centre for the visual and performing arts – it also has a pleasant café with tapas, sandwiches, salads and drinks. Most tapas are under £2; you should be able to eat for around £6. Check out their gallery and theatre programme. The café is open from 11 am to late, Tuesday to Saturday.

Ristoro Ciao Pizzeria (☎ 041-332 4565), 441 Sauchiehall, is an efficient Italian restaurant in an unusual baroque room. You should be able to eat and drink for around £10, or less. Pizzas and pastas are from £4 to £6. *Loon Fung* (☎ 041-332 1240), 417 Sauchiehall, is one of the best Chinese places in town. There are also a number of Indian restaurants at the west end of Sauchiehall but, relatively speaking, they're expensive.

Paparinos (☎ 041-332 3800), 283 Sauchiehall, is a trendy and popular Italian place with similar prices to Ciao. The *Willow Tearoom* (☎ 041-332 0521), 217 Sauchiehall, above a jewellery shop, was designed as a tea room by Charles Rennie Mackintosh in 1903. This is the place for a light lunch or an old-fashioned cream tea.

There are more restaurants in the area around the intersection with Bath and Renfield Sts. *O Sole Mio* (☎ 041-331 1397), 32 Bath St, is a reliable Italian place with pasta and pizzas around £5. They have some good-value specials, like three courses for £5.95, if you eat between 5 and 6.30 pm. The *Asman Tandoori* (☎ 041-331 2575), 22 Bath St, has pakora at £1.80 and curries from £5 to £6.

Entertainment

There is a good range of rowdy bars, and nightclubs at the west end of Sauchiehall St, and around the intersection of Bath and Renfield Sts. See *The List* for the latest information.

Getting There & Away

Air Glasgow Airport (☎ 041-887 1111) handles domestic traffic, and international flights by Air Canada, Air France, American Airlines, Icelandair, SAS and Lufthansa. Cheap deals are rare.

Bus Buses from London are very competitive and you may be able to get cheap promotional tickets. The standard single ticket with National Express (☎ 041-332 4100) and Citylink (☎ 041-332 9191) is £28, and the journey takes around 7½ hours. The best option is to catch the early morning buses between 9 and 10 am, so that you arrive in good time to organise accommodation. There are direct links with Heathrow and Gatwick.

There are numerous links with other English cities. A sample of Citylink's buses follows (National Express is similar): three buses per day from Birmingham (5¼ hours, £28); one from Cambridge (nine hours, £39.50); numerous from Carlisle (two hours, £12.70), one from Newcastle (five hours, £19), and one from York (7½ hours, £25). There's even a summer link to Salisbury.

As you might expect, Citylink has buses to virtually every major town in Scotland. Most of the east coast towns are reached via Edinburgh. There are numerous buses to Edinburgh with singles/returns for £3.70/£5.30, Inverness (4¼ hours, £10.60), two or three to Oban (2¾ hours, £8.50), Aberdeen (four hours, £10.30), Fort William (three hours, £8.10) and Skye (5¼ hours, £12.20). There's a summer service for Stranraer, connecting with the ferry to Larne in Northern Ireland (five hours, £8).

Train As a general rule, Central Station serves southern Scotland, England and Wales, and Queen St serves the north and east. There are frequent buses between the two (30p). There are 20 trains a day from London's Euston (☎ 071-278 2477); they're not cheap, but they are much quicker and more comfortable than the bus (4¾ hours, £57).

Scotrail (☎ 041-204 2844) has one major line north to Oban and Fort William (see those sections). There are numerous trains to Edinburgh (1½ hours, £5.20).

Getting Around

One of your first stops should be the Travel Centre on St Enoch Square, open Monday to Saturday. If you are staying for a few days, it may be worth considering a Zonecard, which covers all public transport (one week, £11).

To/From the Airport There are buses every half hour from the terminus to Anderston Cross Bus Station; they take 25 minutes and cost £2. A taxi would cost £12.

Bus Bus services are frequent and cheap. You can buy tickets when you board buses, but on some you have to have exact change. For short trips in the city, fares are 45p. After midnight there are special night buses.

Rail There's an extensive suburban network; tickets should be bought before travel if the station is staffed, or from the conductor if it isn't. There's also an underground line that serves 15 stations in the centre, west and south of the city (50p).

SOUTH-WESTERN SCOTLAND

The tourist board bills this region as Scotland's surprising south-west, and it is surprising if you expect magnificent mountain and coastal scenery to be confined to the Highlands. What really is surprising is that you can escape the crowds that flock to the better known Western Highlands.

Ayrshire to the immediate south-west of Glasgow is the least spectacular part of the region, though it was the home of Scotland's national poet, Robert Burns. Dumfries & Galloway covers the southern half of this western elbow, and this is where the coast and mountains really do approach the grandeur of the north. Warmed by the Gulf Stream, this is also the mildest corner of Scotland – there are a number of famous gardens. There are many notable historic and prehistoric attractions linked by the Solway Coast Heritage Trail (information from TICs). Sweetheart Abbey, Caerlaverock Castle and Whithorn Priory are just three of many. Kirkcudbright is a beautiful town, and would make a good base.

This is excellent cycling and walking country, and it is crossed by the coast-to-coast Southern Upland Way (see the Stranraer section).

Orientation & Information

Southern Scotland is divided from east to west by the southern uplands. The western coast from Glasgow to Girvan is quite busy, but south from there, the crowds evaporate. Stranraer is the ferry port to Larne in Northern Ireland; it's the shortest link from Britain to Ireland, taking less than 2½ hours. There are only youth hostels at Ayr, Newton Stewart, Kendoon and Wanlockhead.

Getting Around

Bus Citylink (☎ 0563-25192) has long-distance coaches from London, Birmingham (via Manchester and Carlisle), and Glasgow/Edinburgh to Stranraer. These coaches service the main towns and villages along the A75 (including Ayr, Dumfries, Kirkcudbright and Newton Stewart). Western Scottish (☎ 0387-64105) provides a variety of local bus services.

Train See the Carlisle section for info on the Carlisle-Glasgow rail link, and the Glasgow section for the Glasgow-Stranraer link.

Boat Frequent car and passenger ferries operate between Stranraer and Larne in Northern Ireland (Sealink, (☎ 0776-2262), and between Cairnryan, which is close to

Stranraer, and Larne (P&O, ☎ 05812-276). See the Northern Ireland section in the Ireland chapter for details.

Stranraer & Cairnryan

Stranraer is rather more pleasant than the average ferry port, but there is really no pressing reason to stay. Make for the south coast, or Glasgow. The train station is right on the docks beside the Sealink ferry terminal. Cairnryan is a couple of miles away (linked by bus) on the other side of the bay. The TIC (☎ 0776-2595) is adjacent to the Sealink terminal and can provide the usual information on the region and accommodation.

The Southern Upland Way starts at Portpatrick near Stranraer and runs 340 km (212 miles) to Cockburnspath near Berwick-on-Tweed on the east coast. It offers varied walking country, but includes some very long and demanding stretches – those tackling the whole route should be experienced. The official guide by Ken Andrew is published in two volumes: from Portpatrick to Beattock and Beattock to Cockburnspath.

London to Stranraer by rail is nine hours and £60.

Kirkcudbright

Kirkcudbright with its dignified streets of 17th and 18th century merchants' houses and its lively harbour is the ideal base if you wish to explore the beautiful southern coast. There's no youth hostel but the TIC (☎ 0557-30494) by the harbour can provide all the necessary info about local B&Bs.

Wales

Wales has had the misfortune to be so close to England that it could not be allowed its independence, and yet to be far enough away to be conveniently forgotten. It sometimes feels rather like England's unloved backyard – a suitable place for mines, pine plantations and nuclear power stations. Even the most enduring of its symbols – the grim mining

towns and powerful castles – represent exploitation and colonialism.

It is almost miraculous that anything Welsh should have survived the onslaught of its dominating neighbour. Welsh culture has proved to be remarkably enduring, however, and the language refuses stubbornly to die.

Huge swathes of the countryside have been vandalised by mining, grossly insensitive forestry operations and power lines, but magnificent corners remain. Miles of coastline have been ruined by shoddy bungalows and grotesquely ugly caravan parks, but some of it is still breathtakingly beautiful.

In general, the towns and cities are not particularly inspiring. Wales' appeal lies in its countryside, and the best way to appreciate this is by walking, bicycling, canal boating, hitching, or with some other form of private transport. Simply catching buses or trains from one regional hub to another is not recommended. Instead, base yourself in a small town or farm B&B, and explore the surrounding countryside for a few days. Hay-on-Wye, Brecon, St David's, Pwllheli and Betws-y-coed are possibilities that come to mind.

Much of the most beautiful countryside is now protected by the Pembrokeshire Coast National Park, the Brecon Beacons National Park and the Snowdonia National Park, but the Gower Peninsula and the Llyn Peninsula are also outstanding.

Wales also has an unsurpassed legacy of magnificent medieval castles. All of the following are within a mile of a railway station: Caerphilly, north of Cardiff; Kidwelly, north of Llanelli; Harlech, south of Porthmadog; Caernarfon, in the north west; and Conwy, near Llandudno in the north.

FACTS ABOUT THE COUNTRY
History

The Celts arrived from their European homeland sometime after 500 BC. Little is known about them, although it is to their Celtic forebears that modern Welsh attribute national characteristics like eloquence, warmth and imagination.

The Romans invaded in 43 AD, and for

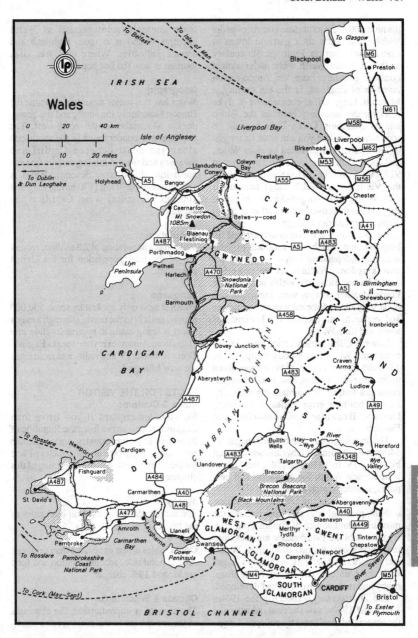

Wales

```
0        20        40 km
0    10      20 miles
```

IRISH SEA

To Belfast

To Isle of Man

To Glasgow

Blackpool

Preston

M6

Liverpool Bay

M61

M58

M62

Liverpool

Birkenhead

M53

Isle of Anglesey

To Dublin
& Dun Laoghaire

Holyhead

A5

Bangor

Llandudno
Conwy

Colwyn
Bay

Prestatyn

A55

M56

Chester

C L W Y D

A41

Caernarfon

Mt Snowdon
1085m

Betws-y-coed

Wrexham

A483

A5

Blaenau
Ffestiniog

G W Y N E D D

Porthmadog

A487

A5

To Birmingham

Llyn
Peninsula

Pwllheli

A470

Snowdonia
National
Park

Shrewsbury

Harlech

A458

E N G L A N D

Barmouth

Ironbridge

CARDIGAN
BAY

C A M B R I A N   M O U N T A I N S

Dovey Junction

A483

Craven
Arms

Aberystwyth

A487

P O W Y S

Ludlow

A49

Builth
Wells

Hay-on-
Wye

River Wye

Hereford

Cardigan

Newport

A483

Llandovery

A484

Talgarth

B4348

Wye
Valley

To Rosslare

D Y F E D

Brecon

Fishguard

Carmarthen

A40

Brecon Beacons
National Park

St David's

A48

Black Mountains

Abergavenny

A477

Amroth

Laugharne

Llanelli

Pembroke

Carmarthen
Bay

To Rosslare

Pembrokeshire
Coast
National Park

Gower
Peninsula

Swansea

W E S T
GLAMORGAN

Merthyr
Tydfil

Rhondda

MID
GLAMORGAN

Caerphilly

Blaenavon

G W E N T

Tintern

Chepstow

A449

Newport

M4

SOUTH
GLAMORGAN

CARDIFF

River Severn

M5

To Cork (May-Sept)

BRISTOL CHANNEL

Bristol

To Exeter
& Plymouth

GREAT BRITAIN

the next 400 years kept close control over the Welsh tribes from their garrison towns at Chester and Caerlon. From the 5th century to the 11th, the Welsh were under almost constant pressure from the Anglo-Saxon invaders of England. In the 8th century, a Mercian king, Offa, constructed a dyke marking the boundary between the Welsh and the Mercians. Offa's Dyke can still be seen today – in fact you can walk its length.

The Celtic princes failed to unite Wales, and local wars were frequent. However, in 927, faced with the destructive onslaught of the Vikings, the Welsh kings recognised Athelstan, the Anglo-Saxon king of England, as their overlord in exchange for an alliance against the Vikings.

By the time the Normans arrived in England, the Welsh had returned to their warring, independent ways. To secure his new kingdom, William set up powerful, feudal barons along the Welsh borders. The Lords Marcher, as they were known, developed virtually unfettered wealth and power and began to advance on the lowlands of south and mid-Wales.

Edward I, the great warrior king, finally conquered Wales in a bloody campaign. In 1302 the title of Prince of Wales was given to the monarch's eldest son, a tradition that continues today. To maintain his authority, Edward built the great castles of Rhuddlan, Conwy, Beaumaris, Caernarfon and Harlech.

The last doomed Welsh revolt began in 1400 under Owain Glyndwr and was crushed by Henry IV. In 1536 and 1543, the Acts of Union made Wales, for all intents and purposes, another region of England.

From the turn of the 18th century, Wales, with its plentiful coal and iron, became the most important source of Britain's pig iron. By the end of the 19th century, almost a third the world's coal exports came from Wales, and an enormous network of mining villages with their unique culture of Methodism, rugby and male-voice choirs had developed.

The 20th century, especially the 1960s, 1970s and 1980s, saw the coal industry and the associated steel industry collapse. Large-scale unemployment persists as Wales attempts to move to more high-tech and service industries. Where coal was king, tourism is now the last hope.

Geography

Wales has two major mountain systems: the Brecon Beacons in the south, and the Snowdonian Mountains in the north-west. The population is concentrated in the south-east along the coast between Cardiff and Swansea and the old mining valleys that run north into the Brecon Beacons. Wales is approximately 270 km (170 miles) long and 100 km (60 miles) wide. Cardiff is the capital.

Population

Wales has a population of 2.8 million, around 5% of the total population for the United Kingdom.

Language

Welsh is now only spoken by some 500,000 people, mainly in the north, although a major effort is being made to reverse its slide into extinction. Almost everyone speaks English. There is Welsh TV and radio, and most signs are now bilingual.

FACTS FOR THE VISITOR
Visas & Customs

No visas are required if you arrive from England. If you arrive from the Republic of Ireland or any other country, normal British regulations apply (see the introductory Facts for the Visitor section at the beginning of this chapter).

Money

The same currency is used on both sides of the border.

Costs Wales is less expensive than England. As a general rule, accommodation and food are around 15% cheaper.

Climate & When to Go

The climate is unpredictable; the closeness of the mountains to the coast creates conditions that can vary widely over a short distance. May/June and September/October are the best months to visit. July/August can be very wet, and very crowded.

Tourist Offices

Outside of Britain, contact the British Tourist Authority for information. The British Travel Centre (☎ 071- 730 3400), 12 Regent St, Piccadilly Circus, London SW1Y 4PQ, can provide information.

Most major towns in Wales have TICs that are open weekdays from 9 am to 5 pm, sometimes extending to weekends during the summer. In small places, TICs only open from Easter to September.

Business Hours & Holidays

Business hours and holidays are the same as in England. In the countryside, shops often close early on Wednesdays.

Activities

Hiking Wales has numerous popular walks; the most challenging are in the rocky Snowdonia National Park (from Betws-y-coed) and the grassy Brecon Beacons National Park (from Brecon). There are seven long-distance walks; the most famous are Offa's Dyke Path and the Pembrokeshire Coast Path.

Offa's Dyke Path follows the English/Welsh border 270 km (168 miles) from Chepstow on the River Severn through the beautiful Wye Valley and Shropshire Hills to end on the north Wales coast at Prestatyn. There are two guides (Chepstow to Knighton, and Knighton to Prestatyn) by Ernie & Kathy McKay & Mark Richards (Aurum Press, £7.95 each). The *Offa's Dyke Path Accommodation & Transport* is available from the Ramblers' Association (☎ 071-582 6878) for £1.20.

Most of the 290-km (180-mile) Pembrokeshire Coast Path is in the Pembrokeshire Coast National Park, an area rich in coastal scenery and historical associations. From Amroth to Cardigan, there are wide, sandy beaches; rocky, windswept cliffs; and picturesque villages. Accommo-

dation is widely available and it is easy to undertake shorter sections. The walk can be crowded, especially on summer weekends. *The Pembrokeshire Coast Path* by Brian John (Aurum Press, £7.95) has maps and information. The National Park people publish an accommodation guide; phone ☎ 0437-764591 for further info.

Surfing The south-west coast of Wales has a number of surf spots. From east to west, try Porthcawl, Oxwich Bay, Rhossili, Manorbier, Freshwater West and Whitesands.

Accommodation

The Youth Hostels Association (England & Wales) publishes a single accommodation guide, available from the YHA Adventure Shop at 14 Southampton St, London WC2.

There are reasonably priced B&Bs everywhere you look. The TICs have local booking services (usually free) and a Book-A-Bed-Ahead scheme allowing you to book 24 hours in advance. This is worth using in July and August, but is not necessary outside this peak time, unless you are going to arrive at your destination late.

Always check with landowners before pitching a tent; this includes in the national parks, which are all privately owned. Commercial camping sites are geared to caravans and vary widely in quality. A tent site will cost around £6. If you plan to use a tent regularly, invest in the AA's *Camping & Caravanning in Britain* (£6.99).

GETTING THERE & AWAY
Land

Bus Long-distance buses are the cheapest method of getting to Wales. National Express (☎ 0222-344751) has routes from London and Bristol along the south coast through Cardiff to Pembroke (for ferries to Ireland), and from Chester and the Midlands along the northern coast to Holyhead (for ferries to Ireland).

London to Cardiff should cost around £29/22.50 for an adult return/single. As in England, all return tickets are ridiculously cheap by comparison to singles. For the sake of brevity in the following sections, adult return fares have been shown. Subtract about 5% for a single fare, and a third for concessionary fares.

London to Pembroke takes six hours and costs £29; Manchester to Holyhead takes 5¼ hours and costs £14.25. Don't ask why.

Train Britrail InterCity services can take you from London's Paddington (☎ 071-262 6767) to Cardiff in as little as 1¾ hours, or to Fishguard (for the Ireland ferry) in four hours. A low-period return ticket from Cardiff to London will cost £31.50 – about the same price as a single. Fast InterCity trains also link south Wales with Birmingham, York and Newcastle.

There are also trains from London's Euston (☎ 071-278 2477) to north Wales and Holyhead via Birmingham, Chester and Llandudno. There are 10 trains a day from Euston to Holyhead; they take 4½ hours and cost £43.50.

Car & Motorbike Motorways bring you into Wales quickly and easily. The M4 travels west across England and deep into south Wales, and the A55 coastal expressway whisks traffic along the north coast. London to Cardiff is 250 km (155 miles) and takes about three hours.

Sea

Wales has five ferry links with Ireland: Holyhead, in the north-west, to Dublin (B&I Line); Holyhead to Dun Laoghaire, near Dublin (Sealink); Pembroke, in the south-west, to Rosslare, in south-east Ireland (B&I Line); Fishguard, in the south-west, to Rosslare (Sealink); and, from May to September, from Swansea to Cork (Swansea-Cork Ferries). See the Ireland chapter for details.

GETTING AROUND

Distances in Wales are small, but with the exception of links around the coast, public transport users have to fall back on infrequent and complicated bus timetables.

Bus

The major operators serving Wales are Crossville Wales (☎ 0492-596969) for the north and west; and South Wales Transport (☎ 0792-475511). There are Rover tickets available that can be very good value. For example, the Crossville Day Rover, covering all points north and west of Shrewsbury, costs £4.70 a day.

Crossville has a particularly useful daily Traws Cambria (west coast) link: Cardiff, Swansea, Carmarthen, Aberystwyth, Porthmadog, Caernarfon, Bangor. Cardiff to Aberystwyth costs £8.35 and takes four hours; Aberystwyth to Porthmadog costs £5.50 and takes two hours.

Bus Gwynedd (☎ 0286-679378) is a council-sponsored network of buses operating in the north-west corner of Wales – from Llandudno to Machynlleth, including all of Snowdonia. Those using a Britrail North and Mid Wales Rover ticket (see the following section) can travel free on these buses as well. Bus Gwynedd pamphlets and maps are available at TICs.

Train

Wales has some fantastic train lines – both Britrail (☎ 0492-585151) and private, narrow-gauge survivors. Apart from the main lines along the north and south coasts to the Irish ferry ports, there are some interesting lines that converge on Shrewsbury (see the Getting There & Away information in the Shrewsbury section). The lines along the west coast, and down the Conwy Valley, are exceptional.

There are several Rover tickets: the North and Mid Wales Rover gives seven days' travel north of Aberystwyth and Shrewsbury – plus Bus Gwynedd services (which means virtually all north-western buses) and the Blaenau Ffestiniog railway – for £33/22; the Freedom of Wales Rover gives seven days' travel for £47/31.50. See also the Getting There & Away information in the Shrewsbury section.

SOUTH WALES

The valleys of the Usk and Wye, with their

castles and Tintern Abbey, are beautiful, but packed with day trippers. The south coast from Newport to Swansea is heavily industrialised, and the valleys running north into the Black Mountains and the Brecon Beacons National Park are still struggling to come to grips with the loss of the coal-mining industry.

Even so, the little villages that form a continuous chain along the valleys have their own stark beauty and the people are very friendly. The traditional market town of Abergavenny is also worth a look. The Big Pit, near Blaenafon, gives you a chance to experience life underground.

The Black Mountains and Brecon Beacons have majestic, open scenery and their northern flanks overlook some of the most beautiful country in Wales.

Cardiff

Cardiff is the capital city, and although it is quite a bustling, friendly place it is neither particularly interesting nor particularly Welsh. If you are planning to explore south Wales, it's worth stopping to stock up on maps and information from the excellent TIC (☎ 0222-227281), 11 Bridge St, which is clearly signposted from the adjacent bus and train stations.

The *youth hostel* (☎ 0222-462303), 1 Wedal Rd, Roath Park, is about three km from the city centre. It operates seven days a week from March to October, opens at 5 pm, and costs £7. See the Getting There & Away section at the beginning of this section for details on transport to/from London.

Swansea

Swansea is the second largest town (it would be stretching the definition to call it a city), and the gateway to the Gower peninsula and its superb coastal scenery (crowded in summer). Dylan Thomas grew up in Swansea and later called it an 'ugly, lovely town'. The town's position is certainly lovely, but there is no pressing reason to stay. For more information, contact the TIC (☎ 0792-468321).

Brecon Beacons National Park

The Brecon Beacons National Park covers over 500 square miles of high bare hills, surrounded on the northern flanks by a number of attractive market towns; Llandovery, Brecon, Talgarth and Hay-on-Wye make good bases. There are a number of National Park information offices including in Brecon (☎ 0874-624437), at the Cattle Market Car Park, and in Llandovery (☎ 0550-20693), 8 Broad St. Both make B&B bookings. The Monmouthshire & Brecon Canal, which runs south-east from Brecon, is popular both with hikers (especially the 33 miles between Brecon and Pontypool) and canal-boaters and cuts through beautiful country.

Brecon Brecon is an attractive, historic market town, with a cathedral dating from the 13th century. The market is on Tuesdays and Fridays. There's a highly acclaimed jazz festival in August. The TIC (☎ 0874-623156) can organise B&Bs. The *Ty'n-y-Caeau youth hostel* (☎ 0874-628 6270) is five km (three miles) from town; ask directions from the TIC. Brecon has no bus or train station, but there are regular bus links. Silverline (☎ 0685-382406) has daily links to Swansea; Red & White (☎ 0633-485118) has regular buses to Hereford, via Hay-on-Wye.

Hay-on-Wye At the north-eastern tip of the Black Mountains, Hay-on-Wye is an eccentric market village that is now known as the world centre for second-hand books – there are 27 shops selling everything from £500 first editions to books by the yard (literally). Contact the TIC (☎ 0497-820144) for info on the excellent restaurants and B&Bs in the neighbourhood.

SOUTH-WESTERN WALES

The coastline north-east of St David's to Cardigan is particularly beautiful, and as it is protected by the National Park, it remains unspoilt. The Pembrokeshire Coast Path begins at Amroth, north of Tenby, on the west side of Carmarthen Bay and continues to St Dogmaels to the west of Cardigan.

Carmarthen Bay is often referred to as Dylan Thomas Country; Dylan's boathouse at Laugharne (☎ 0994-427420), where he wrote *Under Milk Wood*, has been preserved exactly as he left it, and it is a moving memorial. Llanstephan has a beautiful Norman castle overlooking sandy beaches. On west-facing beaches, there can be good surf; the Newgale Filling Station (☎ 0437-721398), Newgale, hires the necessary equipment and has daily surf reports.

B&I Line (☎ 0646-684161) ferries leave Pembroke Dock for Rosslare in Ireland; ferries connect with buses from Cardiff and points east. Sealink (☎ 0348-873523) has ferries to Rosslare from Fishguard; these connect with buses and trains. See the Ireland chapter for more details.

Pembroke Dock is a classically unpleasant ferry port and the surrounding region is not particularly inspiring either, although nearby Pembroke Castle, the home of the Tudors is magnificent. Fishguard is surprisingly pleasant.

Pembrokeshire Coast National Park

The national park protects a narrow band of magnificent coastline, broken only around the denser development around Pembroke and Milford Haven. The only significant inland portion is the Presely Hills to the south-east of Fishguard. There are National Park Information Centres at Tenby (☎ 0834-2402), St David's (☎ 0348-720392) and Newport, amongst others. These centres and the local TICs have an excellent brochure detailing accommodation for those hiking the coast path. Apart from youth hostels, there are loads of B&Bs around £12.

There's quite good public transport in the area, co-ordinated by the Dyfed County Council, who can also help with enquiries (☎ 0267-233333 ext 4333). Around Pembroke the main operator is Silcox (☎ 0267-2459) with buses from Pembroke and Pembroke Dock to Tenby; Richards Bros' (☎ 0437-721428) is the main operator from St David's to Cardigan.

St David's The lynchpin for the south-west is beautiful St David's, one of Europe's smallest cities. There's a web of interesting streets, and concealed in the Vale of Roses, beautiful **St David's Cathedral**. There is something particularly magical about this isolated, secretive, 12th century building. Unfortunately, it's quite a tourist trap.

Contact the TIC (☎ 0437-720392). There are regular Richards Bros' (☎ 0437-721428) buses to/from Fishguard (three a day from Monday to Saturday, one on Sundays). There's an interesting section of the coast path between St David's and Fishguard.

There are three handy *youth hostels*: at St David's (☎ 0437-720345), open from March to October, except Thursdays; at Trevine (☎ 0348-831414), 18 km (11 miles) from St David's; and at Pwll Deri (☎ 03485- 233), 13 km (eight miles) from Trevine and just over seven km (4½ miles) from Fishguard, open March to October except Fridays.

Fishguard Fishguard stands out like a jewel amongst the depressing ranks of bleak and ugly ferry ports. It is on a beautiful bay, and the old part of town – Lower Fishguard – was the location for the 1971 film version of *Under Milk Wood* that starred Richard Burton and Elizabeth Taylor. The railway station and harbour (for Sealink ferries to Rosslare) are a 20-minute walk from the town proper. The TIC (☎ 0348-873484) is open seven days a week from Easter to October.

In Goodwick, *The Beach House* (☎ 0348-872085), above the railway line and over-looking the bay a five-minute walk from the ferry, is remarkably welcoming given the constant flow of visitors – B&B is £13. In Fishguard the *Blair Athol Hotel* (☎ 0348-873147) is also good, although a bit more expensive at £15; their evening meal is £7.

By rail, Fishguard to London is £48, Fishguard to Cardiff is £11.20.

NORTH WALES

North Wales is dominated by the Snowdonia Mountains, which loom over the beautiful coastline. Unfortunately, this is the holiday playground for much of the Midlands, so the coast is marred by tacky holiday villages and the serried ranks of caravan parks.

Heading east from Chester, the country is flat, industrialised and uninteresting until you reach Llandudno. Llandudno is virtually contiguous with Conwy – either spot would make a good base. From Llandudno and Conwy you can catch buses or trains to Betws-y-coed, the main centre for exploring the Snowdonia National Park. From Betws there's a train to the bleak and strangely beautiful mining town of Blaenau Ffestiniog. One of Wales' most spectacular steam railways runs from Blaenau to the bustling coastal market town of Porthmadog. From Porthmadog you can loop back to Shrewsbury, via Harlech with its castle.

The remote Llyn Peninsula in the west, escapes the crowds to a large extent; start from Caenarfon, with its magnificent castle, or Pwllheli. Holyhead is one of the main Irish ferry ports.

The Gwynedd County Council (☎ 0286-679367) coordinates an extensive range of bus links. The Bus Gwynedd Red Rover covers the whole region, including east to Chester and south to Aberystwyth, for £3.50 a day.

Llandudno

Llandudno seethes with tourists, which in this instance seems entirely fitting. It was developed as a Victorian holiday town and it has retained its beautiful architecture and 19th century atmosphere. There's a wonderful pier and promenade – and donkeys on the beach.

Llandudno is on its own peninsula between two sweeping beaches, and is dominated by the spectacular limestone headland – the Great Orme – with the mountains of Snowdonia as a backdrop. The Great Orme, with its Bronze Age mine, tramway, chair lift and superb views, is quite fascinating.

There are literally hundreds of guesthouses, but despite this it can be difficult finding somewhere in the peak July/August season. The TIC (☎ 0492-876413) should be able to rustle something up (free), but to make certain, book ahead.

Getting There & Away There are numerous trains and buses between Llandudno and Chester, and between Llandudno and Holyhead.

Buses and trains run between Llandudno Junction, Betws-y-Coed (for the Snowdonia National Park) and Blaenau Ffestiniog (for the brilliant narrow gauge railway to Porthmadog). There are six trains a day from Monday to Saturday and the journey takes a bit over an hour (£2.40 to Blaenau). See the Shrewsbury section for info on the complete Llandudno, Blaenau, Porthmadog, Dovey Junction, Shrewsbury loop.

Bus Gwynedd (No 5) has a number of morning services between Llandudno, Bangor and Caernarfon; there are plenty of buses from Bangor to Holyhead for the ferry. The Bus Gwynedd Red Rover (£3.50) will probably be your best bet.

Conwy

Conwy has been revitalised since the through traffic on the busy A55 has been consigned to a tunnel that burrows under the estuary of the River Conwy and the town. It is now a picturesque and interesting little town, dominated by the superb Conwy Castle, one of the grandest of Edward I's castles and a medieval masterpiece.

At present, the nearest *youth hostel* (☎ 0492-623476) is at Penmaenmawr, eight km west of Conwy on the main coast road, and accessible by bus; ring for directions. The hostel is right on the cliffs, with a great view, but it is also close to the A55 and would be isolated without transport. A new youth hostel is planned for Conwy itself.

Conwy is just around the bay to the west of Llandudno and is linked to Llandudno by seven buses an hour, and 11 trains a day.

Snowdonia National Park

Although the Snowdonia Mountains are fairly compact, they loom over the coast and are definitely spectacular. The most popular region is in the north around Mt Snowdon, the highest peak in Britain south of the Scottish Highlands. Hikers must be prepared to deal with hostile conditions at any time of the

year. There are National Park Information
Centres at Betws-y-Coed (☎ 0690-710655),
Blaenau Ffestiniog (☎ 0766-830360), and
Harlech (☎ 0766-780658), amongst others;
they're all a wealth of information, and all
make B&B bookings.

Betws-y-Coed Betus (as it is known and
pronounced) is a tourist village in the middle
of the Snowdonia National Park. Despite
busloads of tourists it just can't help being
beautiful. There's nothing to do except to
walk and take afternoon tea, which in this
case is enough.

The TIC (☎ 0690-710426) is useful, but
the National Park Information Centre is
excellent. Both are near the train station.
There's no bank, and you're best off changing money in a larger centre. There are only
two streets of note, so it's easy to find your
way around.

There are plenty of B&Bs, but the nearest
youth hostel (☎ 0690-710225) is at Capel
Curig, nine km (five miles) to the west on the
A5; there's also one at Pen-y-Pas (☎ 0286-
870428), which is particularly well placed
for walks. In Betws, *The Ferns* (☎ 0690-
710587) is a particularly pleasant and comfortable B&B, worth the £17 per person rate.
Plas Derwen Hotel (☎ 0690-710388) has
generous three-course meals for £8.65.

Snowdon Sherpa Buses, who are part of

Bus Gwynedd, run from Llandudno, to
Conwy, Betws-y-Coed, Capel Curig and
Pen-y-Pas (for the youth hostels), then on to
Llanberis for the narrow-gauge train to the
summit of Snowdon (nearly 1100 metres).
Service No 11 goes from Llanberis to
Caernarfon. There are regular services daily
from mid-May to late September. A Rover
ticket (£3.50) can be bought on the bus.

Holyhead
Holyhead is a particularly grey and daunting
ferry port. Both B&I (☎ 0407-760222) and
Sealink (☎ 0407-763031) run ferries to
Ireland. B&I runs direct to Dublin from
Holyhead's Western Dock; there is a short
bus link, or 20-minute walk, from the
railway station. Sealink's car ferry also
leaves from the Western Dock, but its pas-
senger ferry leaves from beside the train
station; it goes to Dun Laoghaire, just outside
Dublin. There are hourly trains east to
Llandudno, Chester, Birmingham and
London.

The TIC (☎ 0407-762622) is near the
Western Dock, and just across the road there
is a batch of B&Bs that are used to dealing
with late ferry arrivals. The *Min-y-don* is
pleasant, with rooms for £12. The Sealink
staff at the railway station also have a list of
B&Bs.

Ireland

This chapter covers the Republic of Ireland and Northern Ireland.

Ireland is one of Western Europe's least densely populated, least industrialised and, in a word, least 'spoilt' countries. It's green, pleasant and relaxed, but behind those smiling faces and noisy pubs lies one of the longest and most tragic histories in Europe.

That long history is easy to trace from Stone Age passage tombs and ringforts, through ancient monasteries and castles, down to great houses and splendid Georgian architecture of the 19th century. The tragic side is equally easy to unearth with frequent reminders of the country's long and difficult relationship with neighbouring England.

What is the Name?
When the distinction between Ireland the island and Ireland the country needs to be made in this chapter then the country is referred to as the Republic of Ireland. Northern Ireland is always referred to as such. You may hear Ireland (the country) referred to as Eire, the Republic, Southern Ireland, the Free State or simply 'the south'. Northern Ireland may be dubbed Ulster or 'the north'. Prior to the division of Ireland, Ulster actually comprised nine counties. Six of these went into Northern Ireland and the other three into the Republic of Ireland.

Facts about the Country

HISTORY
The numerous Stone Age sites are clear indicators of Ireland's long history, and the monastic ruins, round towers and crumbling churches recall the Christian centuries with equal drama. The vivid nature of Irish history continues right up to the present day with frequent reminders of Ireland's long struggle with neighbouring England.

The Romans never got further than

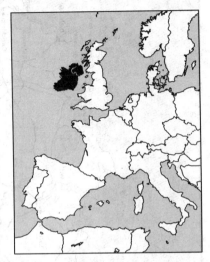

England, but as the Roman Empire declined, Ireland became a beacon of European civilisation. Christianity arrived around the 5th century and the Irish take pleasure in claiming that a raiding party brought St Patrick back from England as a slave. As the Dark Ages submerged Europe, Ireland was the land of saints and scholars with thriving monasteries where hard-working monks illuminated beautiful manuscripts, some of which survive to this day.

From the end of the 8th century the rich monasteries were targets for Viking raids until the Norsemen took to settling in this green, gentle land. At the height of their power they ruled Dublin, Waterford and Limerick, but they were eventually defeated by the legendary hero Brian Boru at the battle of Clontarf in 1014.

In 1168 the Norman conquest of Britain spread to Ireland, when Henry II, fearful of the growing power of the Irish kingdoms, dispatched his forces to Ireland. It was the

IRELAND

Republic of Ireland & Northern Ireland

ATLANTIC OCEAN

IRISH SEA

North Channel

To Stranraer

To Liverpool

0   50   100 km

Rathlin Is
Giant's Causeway
Carrick-a-rede
Bushmills
Portrush
Portstewart
Coleraine
Ballycastle
Cushendall
Cushendun
Larne
Bangor–Newtownards
Strangford Lough
Portaferry
Strangford
Dundrum Bay
Downpatrick
Dundrum
Mountains of Mourne
Lough Foyle
Ballymena
Carrickfergus
BELFAST
Lisburn
Muff
Derry
Strabane
Letterkenny
Cookstown
Omagh
Armagh
Newry
Dundalk
Ardee
Drogheda
Newgrange
Slane
Kells
Navan
Lough Neagh
Donegal
Ardara
Ballyshannon
Belleek
Lower Lough Erne
Upper Lough Erne
Enniskillen
Belturbet
Cavan
Monaghan
Irvinestown
Carrick
Killybegs
Glencolumbkille
Donegal Bay
Sligo Bay
Sligo
Carrick on Shannon
Boyle
Longford
Roscommon
LONGFORD
Killala Bay
Ballina
Charlestown
Castlebar
Westport
Lough Conn
Lough Mask
Belmullet
Bangor
Mulrany
Keel
Achill Island
Clare Is
Cleggan

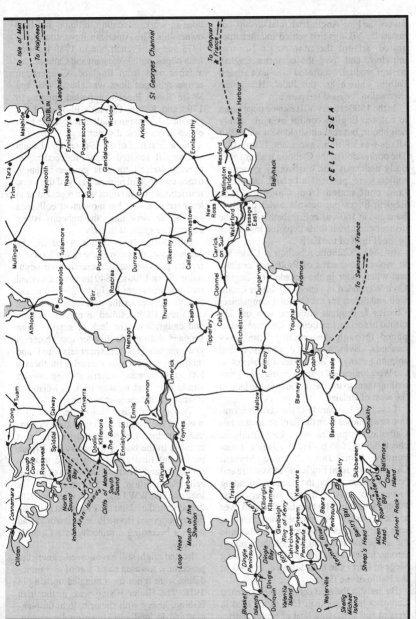

IRELAND

start of the long Anglo-Irish relationship, but just as the Vikings first settled and then integrated, so did the new Anglo-Norman intruders, and over the centuries English control gradually retreated to an area around Dublin known as 'the Pale'. Hence the expression 'beyond the pale'.

In the 1500s Henry VIII moved once again to enforce English control over his unruly neighbour, but real entanglement with Irish affairs was left to his successor, Elizabeth I. The oppression of the Catholic Irish got seriously underway and trustworthy Protestant settlers were 'planted' in Ireland, usually on land confiscated from Catholics. The English forces put down a series of rebellions and in 1607, after Elizabeth's death, the disheartened Irish lords departed for France in the 'Flight of the Earls'.

In 1641 a Catholic rebellion in Ulster led to violent massacres of Protestant settlers, and when, later in the decade, the English Civil War ended in victory for Oliver Cromwell and defeat for the Catholic sympathiser Charles I, English attention was quickly turned to sorting out Ireland. Cromwell rampaged through the country from 1649 onwards, leaving a trail of death behind him, shipping many of the defeated as slaves to the West Indies and dispossessing others and exiling them to the harsh and infertile land in the west of Ireland.

Less than 10 years later the 1660 Restoration saw Charles II on the English throne. His Catholic sympathies were kept firmly in check but in 1685 his brother James II succeeded him. James' more blatant Catholicism raised English Protestant ire and he was forced to flee the country, intending to raise an army in Ireland and regain his throne, which had by then been handed over to the Protestant William of Orange and his wife Mary, James' daughter. Ireland became the stage for the struggle for the English throne. James II was first delayed by the long Siege of Derry and then defeated, in 1690, at the Battle of the Boyne.

By early in the next century, the dispirited Catholics held less than 15% of the land in Ireland and suffered a host of brutal restrictions in work, education, religion and land ownership. The American Revolution from 1775 and the French one in 1789 inspired Irish hopes, both Protestant and Catholic, for a fairer deal from England. Cooperation across religious lines was short-lived, and Wolfe Tone's French-supported uprising in 1798 and Robert Emmet's ill-planned but romantically inspired attempt in 1803 both ended in complete disaster.

In the first half of the 19th century Daniel O'Connell seemed to be succeeding in moving Ireland towards greater independence by peaceful means. Many of the worst restrictions on Catholics were repealed or at least reduced, but his movement collapsed and, at the same time, the unhappy island suffered its greatest tragedy.

Introduced from South America, the easily grown potato was the staple food of a rapidly growing but desperately poor population. From 1800 to 1840 the population had rocketed from four to eight million, but successive failures of the potato crop between 1845 and 1849 resulted in mass starvation and emigration. The lack of support from England during this disaster was shameful and huge numbers of Irish settlers who found their way to America carried with them a lasting bitterness. American-Irish wealth would later find its way back to Ireland to finance the independence struggle.

Two million Irish died or departed as a result of the famine and emigration continued to reduce the population for the next century. In the late 19th century the British parliament finally began to move towards giving Ireland 'Home Rule' and a degree of self-determination, but the process was a long one and WW I and Ulster intervened. In the north of the island the Protestant majority bitterly opposed Home Rule, as it would lead to their becoming a minority in a Catholic country.

Ireland might still have moved, slowly but peacefully, towards some sort of accommodation were it not for a bungled uprising in 1916. The Easter Rising was, in the Irish fashion, heavy with rhetoric, light on planning and decidedly lacking in public support.

The British response, however, was equally ill-planned. After the insurrection had been put down, a long-drawn-out series of executions of the ringleaders converted them from troublemakers to martyrs and roused international support for Irish independence.

From 1918 a guerrilla war took place, pitting the Irish political movement *Sinn Fein* ('Ourselves Alone', or 'We Ourselves') and its military wing, the Irish Republican Army (IRA), against the British. The increasingly harsh responses of the notorious Black & Tans further roused anti-British sentiment, and atrocity was met with atrocity until finally a treaty was signed in 1921.

'I signed my death warrant,' acknowledged IRA leader Michael Collins, for numerous strings were attached to the treaty and the six counties of Northern Ireland were excluded. A bitter civil war followed between those who wanted to accept the agreement as a reasonable compromise and those who wanted to continue the struggle for complete independence for the whole island. Within a year Collins was assassinated.

The Civil War soon ground to an exhausted halt, and for nearly 50 years the Republic of Ireland's history moved slowly and was relatively peaceful. The irksome clauses in the treaty, giving Britain a continuing link to Ireland, were one by one jettisoned and Ireland left the British Commonwealth in 1949. The vision of Ireland as a prosperous agrarian society was also eventually jettisoned and after WW II a century of emigration and declining population finally began to abate. But in the north, problems continued to simmer.

There, the Protestant majority made sure their rule was absolute by systematically excluding Catholics from power, and this 'jobs for the boys' mentality finally provoked an initially non-sectarian Civil Rights Movement in 1967. Violent Protestant opposition to uppity Catholics eventually required a British Army presence in 1969 to keep the sides apart, and soon the long-hibernating IRA had reappeared and the struggle for one Ireland was once more underway.

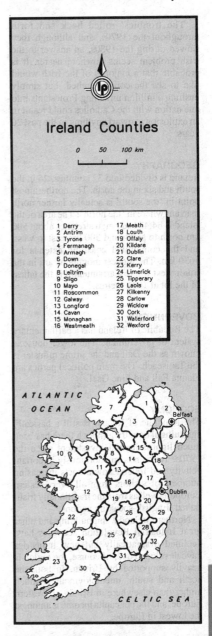

Ireland Counties

0   50   100 km

1 Derry	17 Meath
2 Antrim	18 Louth
3 Tyrone	19 Offaly
4 Fermanagh	20 Kildare
5 Armagh	21 Dublin
6 Down	22 Clare
7 Donegal	23 Kerry
8 Leitrim	24 Limerick
9 Sligo	25 Tipperary
10 Mayo	26 Laois
11 Roscommon	27 Kilkenny
12 Galway	28 Carlow
13 Longford	29 Wicklow
14 Cavan	30 Cork
15 Monaghan	31 Waterford
16 Westmeath	32 Wexford

ATLANTIC OCEAN

Belfast

Dublin

CELTIC SEA

IRELAND

'The troubles' rolled back and forth throughout the 1970s, and although they slowed during the 1980s, an answer to the Irish problem seems nowhere nearer. It is probable that a majority of the Irish would like to see the country united, but simply pushing a million unwilling Protestants into one nation with the Catholics could result in an explosion to dwarf anything of the past 20 years.

GEOGRAPHY

Ireland is divided into 32 counties, 26 in the south and six in the north. The northernmost point in 'the south' is actually farther north than anywhere in 'the north'! The area of the island is 84,404 sq km; it stretches about 500 km north to south and 300 km east to west, and the convoluted coastline extends for 5630 km. The highest mountains are in the south-west where Carrantuohill is the tallest of the lot at 1041 metres.

GOVERNMENT

The Republic of Ireland has a parliamentary system of government. The lower house is known as the Dáil and the prime minister is the Taoiseach. The main political parties are Fianna Fail and Fine Gael.

ECONOMY

The Republic of Ireland is still a basically agricultural country although there has been much light-industrial investment since the 1970s. Tourism is an enormously important activity and Ireland now attracts increasing numbers of visitors from all over Western Europe as well as from the traditionally Irish-linked, English-speaking nations.

Northern Ireland's shipbuilding and other great Industrial Revolution activities have declined dramatically but new industries have developed and, of course, the region is heavily supported by Britain. In both the north and south, unemployment is much higher than elsewhere in Britain or Western Europe, and the per capita income is amongst the lowest in Europe.

POPULATION & PEOPLE

The total population of Ireland is about five million, 3.5 million in the south, 1.5 million in the north. The remarkable thing about this figure is that it is actually less than it was 150 years ago. Prior to the potato famines between 1845 and 1849 the population was probably around eight million. Deaths and huge numbers of emigrants reduced the population to around six million and Irish emigration continued at a high level for the next 100 years. It was not until the 1960s that Ireland's population finally began to increase again.

Major cities are Dublin with nearly one million inhabitants, Belfast with 300,000 and Cork with 175,000.

CULTURE & ARTS

Music

Irish music, with traditional instruments like the flute, the bodhrán and the fiddle, is an aspect of Irish culture which visitors are most likely to encounter. Almost every town and village in Ireland seems to have a pub renowned for its traditional music, and a visit is well worthwhile. The Irish are equally keen on country & western and, more recently, rock music.

Literature

The Irish have probably had the greatest impact on literature, of all the arts. See the Books & Maps section for more on the Irish way with words.

Architecture

Ireland is packed with archaeological sites, prehistoric graves, ruined monasteries, crumbling fortresses and many other solid reminders of its long and often dramatic history. It's necessary to come to terms with some specialist terminology:

Cashel A stone-walled *rath* or *ringfort*.
Dolmen A portal tomb or Stone Age grave consisting of stone 'pillars' supporting an often enormous capstone.
High Cross Tall Christian stone cross with high relief figures usually of Biblical characters and tales.

IRELAND

Ogham Stone Memorial stone of the 4th to 7th century, marked on its edge with groups of straight lines to represent the Latin alphabet.
Passage Graves Megalithic tomb with a narrow stone-walled passage leading into an artificial mound.
Rath or **Ringfort** Circular fort, originally constructed of earth and timber, later of stone.
Round Tower Tall towers constructed as lookouts and as a place of refuge from the Viking marauders who devastated the medieval monasteries.

RELIGION

Religion has always played a major part in Ireland's history. Almost everybody is either Catholic or Protestant with the south 95% Catholic while the north is 70% Protestant. The Catholic church still wields considerable power in the south and there's a curious ambivalence towards it, as it is alternately treated with respect and derision.

LANGUAGE

English is spoken throughout Ireland, but there are still parts of western Ireland known as the *Gaeltacht* where Irish (a Gaelic language) is the native language. Officially the Republic of Ireland is bilingual. Some useful words in Gaelic include *fáilte* – welcome, *gardaí* – police, *fir* – man, *mna* – women, *an lar* – town centre.

Facts for the Visitor

VISAS & EMBASSIES

For citizens of most Western countries no visa is required to visit Ireland. UK nationals born in Great Britain or Northern Ireland do not require a passport. Irish diplomatic offices overseas include:

Australia
    20 Arkana St, Yarralumla, Canberra, ACT 2600 (☎ 06-273 3022)
Canada
    170 Metcalfe St, Ottawa, Ontario K2P 1P3 (☎ 416-745 8624)
UK
    17 Grosvenor Place, London SW1X 7HR (☎ 071-235 2171)

USA
    2234 Massachusetts Ave NW, Washington, DC 20008 (☎ 202-462 3939)

In addition there are consulates in the USA in Boston, Chicago, New York and San Francisco.

Foreign Embassies in Ireland

See the Dublin and Belfast sections for diplomatic offices in those cities.

CUSTOMS

The usual tobacco, alcohol and perfume regulations apply to duty-free imports. Dublin and Shannon airports place great emphasis on their competitive duty-free shopping.

MONEY
Currency

The Irish pound or punt (IR£) is, like the British pound, divided into 100 pence (p). The best exchange rates are obtained at banks, which are usually open from 10 am to 12.30 pm and 1.30 to 3 pm Monday to Friday. In Dublin they stay open until 5 pm on Thursday. The custom of closing for lunch may soon be dropped. *Bureaux de change* and other exchange facilities are usually open longer but the rate and/or commission will be worse.

Pounds sterling (£, see the Britain chapter) are used in Northern Ireland. In Northern Ireland, banks are open from 10 am to 3.30 pm and most stay open until 5 pm on Thursday. Don't confuse Northern Irish pounds (issued by the Bank of Ireland or Allied Irish Banks) with Republic of Ireland pounds (issued by the Central Bank of Ireland). 'Sterling' or 'Belfast' are giveaway words on the Northern Irish notes. The Northern Irish pound sterling is worth the same as the British variety but the notes are not readily accepted in Britain. The pound sterling is worth about 5% less than the Irish pound.

Most major currencies and brands of travellers' cheques are readily accepted in Ireland, but carrying them in pounds sterling has the advantage that in Northern Ireland or Britain you can change them without

IRELAND

exchange loss or commission. Eurocheques can be cashed in Ireland.

Exchange Rates

A$1	=	IR£0.40
C$1	=	IR£0.45
NZ$1	=	IR£0.30
UK£1	=	IR£0.95
US$1	=	IR£0.56

Credit Cards

Major credit cards – particularly Visa and MasterCard (often called Access) – are widely accepted. You can obtain cash advances on these cards from a bank or from Allied Irish Bank (AIB) cash machines in the north or south.

Costs

Costs in Ireland are similar to Britain. Compared to Northern Ireland, the south is sometimes slightly cheaper, sometimes slightly more expensive. Many places to stay, particularly hostels, have different high and low-season prices. Some places may have not just a high-season but a peak-high-season price. In all cases the highest price levels are quoted in this chapter. Entry prices are usually lower for children or students than for adults. Sometimes the student and the child price will differ.

Sightseeing Discounts

Many parks, monuments and gardens in the Republic of Ireland are operated by the Office of Public Works. From any of these sites, for IR£10 (children IR£4) you can get a Heritage Card giving you unlimited access to all these sites for one year.

If you're planning a serious onslaught on Ireland's plentiful supply of castles, monasteries and other sites, this card can be worthwhile. In Northern Ireland the National Trust has a similar deal but it's not so useful for most visitors.

Tipping

Tipping is less prevalent than elsewhere in Europe. Fancy hotels and restaurants usually add a 15% service charge and no additional tip is required. Simpler places usually do not add service, and if you decide to tip, rounding up the bill or adding at most 10% is fine. Taxi drivers do not have to be tipped; if you do, 10% is fine. For porters, 50p per bag is OK.

Consumer Taxes

Value-Added Tax (VAT) applies to most goods and services in Ireland. Visitors can claim back the VAT on large purchases which are subsequently exported outside the European Community (EC).

If you are resident outside the EC and buy something from a Cashback Store, you will be given a Cashback Voucher which can be refunded at Dublin or Shannon airports or can be stamped at ferry ports and mailed back for a refund.

CLIMATE & WHEN TO GO

Ireland has a relatively mild climate. In January and February, average temperatures range from 4°C to 7°C. Average maximums in July and August range from 17 to 20°C. May and June are the sunniest months while December is the most overcast. The sea around Ireland is surprisingly warm for the latitude due to the influence of the North Atlantic Drift, or Gulf Stream.

It does tend to rain in Ireland; even the drier parts of Ireland get rain on 150 days in a typical year and it often rains every day for weeks on end. Annual rainfall is about 100 cm and there's much local terminology and humour about the rain. A 'soft day' is a wet one, and in Northern Ireland amateur weather predictors say that if you can't see Cave Hill outside Belfast it's because it's raining, if you can see the hill then you know it's going to rain. Bring an umbrella.

In July and August the crowds will be greatest and the costs the highest. In the quieter winter months, however, you may get miserable weather and many tourist facilities will be shut.

WHAT TO BRING

The Irish climate is changeable and even at

the height of summer you should be prepared for cold weather and sudden rainfall. A raincoat or an umbrella is a necessity. Walkers should be particularly well prepared if they are crossing exposed country. Otherwise Ireland presents few surprises. Dress is usually casual and you are unlikely to come across many coat & tie-type regulations.

SUGGESTED ITINERARIES
Depending on the length of your stay, you might want to see and do the following things:

Two days
    Visit Dublin and perhaps a couple of places nearby – Powerscourt and Glendalough to the south, or Newgrange, Mellifont and Monasterboice to the north.
One week
    Visit Dublin, Newgrange, Mellifont, Monasterboice, the Burren and Kilkenny.
Two weeks
    As above, plus the Ring of Kerry, Killarney and Cork.
One month
    With your own motorised transport you could cover all the main attractions around the coast but you'd be moving quite fast. This would be more difficult to achieve within a month on public transport.
Two months
    You'd have time to explore Ireland thoroughly with a car or motorcycle, reasonably thoroughly with a bicycle. You could do some walking as well.

TOURIST OFFICES
The Irish Tourist Board, or Bord Fáilte, and the Northern Ireland Tourist Board operate separate tourist offices although they produce some joint brochures and publications.

Local Tourist Offices
Dublin has Irish Tourist Board, Dublin Tourism and Northern Ireland Tourist Board offices. Belfast has Northern Ireland and Irish Tourist Board offices. Elsewhere in Ireland and Northern Ireland there is some sort of tourist office in almost every town big enough to have half a dozen pubs (it doesn't take much population to justify half a dozen

pubs in Ireland). These offices are uniformly friendly, helpful and well informed and will find you a place to stay – a useful service in the busy summer months. Opening hours are usually from 9 am to 6 pm Monday to Friday and 9 am to 1 pm on Saturday, but the hours are often extended in summer.

Tourist Offices Abroad
Overseas offices of the Irish Tourist Board include:

Australia
    5th floor, 36 Carrington St, Sydney, NSW 2000 (☎ 02-299 6177)
Canada
    160 Bloor St East, Suite 934, Toronto, Ontario M4W 1B9 (☎ 416-929 2777)
New Zealand
    Dingwall Building, 87 Queen St, Auckland I (PO Box 279, ☎ 09-379 3708)
UK
    150 New Bond St, London W1Y 0AQ (☎ 071-493 3201)
USA
    757 Third Ave, New York, NY 10017 (☎ 212-418 0800)

Tourist information for Northern Ireland is handled by the British Tourist Board although there are also offices of the Northern Ireland Tourist Board in some locations:

Canada
    111 Avenue Rd, Suite 450, Toronto, Ontario M5P 3J8 (☎ 416-925 6368)
UK
    11 Berkeley St, London W1X 5AD (☎ 071-493 0601)
USA
    Suite 500, 276 5th Ave, New York, NY 10001 (☎ 212-686 6250)

BUSINESS HOURS & HOLIDAYS
Business Hours
Offices are open from 9 am to 5 pm Monday to Friday, shops a little later. On Thursday and/or Friday, shops stay open later. Many are also open on Saturday or Sunday. Tourist attractions are often open shorter hours, fewer days per week or may be shut completely during the winter months.

IRELAND

Public Holidays

Public holidays in Ireland (IR), Northern Ireland (NI) or both are:

New Year – 1 January
St Patrick's Day – 17 March
Good Friday
Easter Monday
May Holiday (NI) – first and last Monday in May
June Holiday (IR) – first Monday in June
The 12th (NI) – 12 July (next day if 12 July is a Sunday)
August Holiday (IR) – first Monday in August
August Holiday (NI) – last Monday in August
October Holiday (IR) – last Monday in October
Christmas Day – 25 December
St Stephen's Day/Boxing Day – 26 December (Monday if 26 December falls on a weekend)

In Northern Ireland the main thing to remember is that many tourist attractions are closed on Sunday morning, rarely opening until around 2 pm, well after church services have finished.

CULTURAL EVENTS

The All Ireland Hurling and Football finals both take place in September. There are some great regional cultural events around the country, like the Galway Arts Festival in late July. In Dublin on Bloomsday (16 June), Leopold Bloom's Joycean journey around the city is followed.

In the north, July is the marching month and every Orangeman in the country hits the streets on the 'glorious 12th'.

POST & TELECOMMUNICATIONS
Postal Services

Post offices in the south are open from 8 am to 5.30 or 6 pm Monday to Saturday – smaller offices close for lunch. Postcards cost 28p to EC countries, 38p outside Europe, while aerograms cost 45p. Post office hours and postal rates in Northern Ireland are as in Britain. Mail can be addressed to poste restante at post offices but is officially only held for two weeks. Writing 'hold for collection' on the envelope may improve things.

Telephone

Old-fashioned pay phones where you rolled coins down ramps and pressed buttons mysteriously labelled A and B are disappearing and phones are becoming modern electronic wonders, in both the north and south. Phonecards, which save fishing for coins and give you a small discount, are worth having. International calls can be dialled directly from pay phones.

See the Telephones appendix in the back of this book for dialling international calls to or from Ireland or Northern Ireland. The one variation is that to call Northern Ireland from Ireland, you do not dial 00-44 as for Britain. Instead you dial 08 and then the Northern Irish area code *without* dropping the leading 0.

TIME

Ireland is on the same time as Britain and, like Britain, advances the clocks by one hour from mid-March to the end of October. During the summer months it stays light until very late at night; you could still just about read by natural light at 11 pm.

ELECTRICITY

Electricity is 220 V, 50 Hz AC, and plugs are usually of the flat three-pin type, as in Britain.

WEIGHTS & MEASURES

As in Britain, progress towards metrication is slow and piecemeal. Meanwhile Ireland mainly uses the Imperial system.

BOOKS & MAPS

English may be an adopted language but the Irish truly have a way with it! A glance in almost any bookshop in Ireland will reveal huge Irish-interest sections whether it's fiction, history and current events, or the numerous local and regional guidebooks. It's definitely worth dipping into Irish writing whether it's by renowned writers like W B Yeats, James Joyce, Oscar Wilde, Sean O'Casey, Samuel Beckett, Flann O'Brien or Brendan Behan; or the many modern writers carrying on the Irish literary tradition.

There are numerous good quality maps of Ireland, and for greater detail, the Ordnance Survey covers the whole island in 25 sheets.

MEDIA
Newspapers & Magazines
English papers and magazines are readily available but the main papers in the south are the *Irish Times* and the *Irish Independent*. The *Irish Times* is noted for its highly opinionated letters page. In the north you will find the *Belfast Telegraph* and the tabloid and staunchly Protestant *News Letter*.

Radio & TV
Ireland has two state-controlled TV channels and three radio stations. British BBC and ITN TV programmes can be picked up in the north-eastern part of the country. Irish radio, AM or FM, is somewhat dreadful.

FILM & PHOTOGRAPHY
Ireland is a photogenic country but often a surprisingly gloomy one, so keen photographers should bring high-speed film. Slide film is not always readily available. Make sure you keep your camera dry.

HEALTH
Apart from the dangers posed by the Irish high-cholesterol diet, Ireland poses no serious health problems. The Irish distaste for contraception does not prevent condoms being sold through pharmacies (that is, if the pharmacist isn't morally opposed!).

WOMEN TRAVELLERS
Although women are in some ways second-class citizens in Ireland (the church influence), they're also generally treated respectfully (the Irish mother influence). Nevertheless the usual care should be taken; see the warning under Hitching in the Getting Around section that follows.

DANGERS & ANNOYANCES
Ireland is probably safer than most countries in Europe but the usual precautions should be observed. Dublin has its fair share of pickpockets and sneak thieves waiting to relieve the unwary of unwatched bags.

If you're travelling by car, do not leave valuables on view inside when the car is parked. Dublin is particularly notorious for car break-ins. Cyclists should always lock their bicycles securely and be cautious about leaving bags on their bikes, particularly in larger towns or more touristy locations.

WORK
With unemployment reaching nearly 20% in the south and well over 10% in the north, this is not a good country for casual work although there is a great deal of seasonal work in the tourist industry.

ACTIVITIES
Ireland is a great place for doing things, and the Tourist Board puts out a wide selection of information sheets covering everything from surfing (there's great surfing along the west coast) to scuba diving, with hang-gliding, birdwatching, fishing, ancestor tracing, horse riding, sailing and canoeing along the way.

Walking is particularly popular although, as usual, you must come prepared for wet weather. The Tourist Board has information on popular long-distance walks like the Wicklow Way, Kerry Way and others. See the Bicycles section under Getting Around for details on bicycle touring in Ireland.

HIGHLIGHTS
Scenery, Beaches & Coastline
The scenery is one of Ireland's major attractions, whether it's those soft green fields, awesome cliffs tumbling into a ferocious Atlantic, or rocky and barren areas in the far west. Highlights include the beautiful scenery around the Ring of Kerry and the Dingle Peninsula, the barren stretches of The Burren, the similarly rocky Aran Islands, and the beautiful lakeland areas south and north.

Favourite stretches of coast include the wildly beautiful Cliffs of Moher, the Connemarra and Donegal coasts, and the wonderful Antrim Coast Road of Northern Ireland. There are some fine beaches (and

IRELAND

marginally warmer water) around the south-east coast and some great surfing around the west and north-west coasts.

Museums, Castles & Houses

Trinity College Library with the ancient Book of Kells is on every visitor's must-see list, but Dublin also has the fine National Museum and National Gallery. Belfast also has an excellent museum and the extensive Ulster Folk Museum just outside the city.

Ireland is littered with castles and forts of various types and in various stages of ruin. The Stone Age forts on the Aran Islands are of particular interest but there are other ancient ringforts all over Ireland. Castles are equally numerous and prime examples include Dublin Castle, Charles Fort at Kinsale and Kilkenny Castle, not forgetting Blarney Castle with its famous stone!

The Anglo-Irish aristocracy left a selection of fine stately homes, many of them now open to the public, like Castletown House, Malahide House, Westport House and the beautiful gardens at Powerscourt.

Religious Sites

Stone rings, portal tombs or dolmens and passage graves are reminders of an earlier, pre-Christian Ireland. The massive passage grave at Newgrange is the most impressive relic of that time. Early Christian churches, many well over 1000 years old, are scattered throughout Ireland, and ruined monastic sites, many of them with round towers still standing, are also numerous. Glendalough, Mellifont Abbey, Grey Abbey, Inch Abbey and Jerpoint Abbey are particularly interesting monastic sites. The rock-top complex at Cashel is one of Ireland's major tourist attractions.

ACCOMMODATION

The Irish Tourist Board's annual *Ireland Accommodation Guide* costs IR£4 and has an awesome list of B&Bs, hotels, camp sites and other accommodation possibilities. It far from exhausts the possibilities, however, as there are also a great many places which are not 'tourist office approved'. This does not

necessarily mean they are in any way inferior to the approved places. In Northern Ireland all accommodation must be inspected and approved, and these places are covered in *Where to Stay in Northern Ireland* (£2.95).

Irish Tourist Board offices will book accommodation for a fee of IR£1 in their locality, IR£2 in another town. All this really involves is phoning a place on their list, but in high summer, when it may take numerous phone calls to find a free room, that can be a pound well spent. The Northern Ireland Tourist Board provides a similar service.

If you're travelling on a tight budget, the numerous hostels offer the cheapest accommodation to be found and are also great centres for meeting fellow travellers and exchanging information. In summer they can be heavily booked but so is everything else.

Camping

Camp sites are not as common as they are on the Continent but there are still plenty of them around Ireland. Some hostels also have camp sites. At commercial camp sites, costs are typically IR£3 to IR£5 for a tent.

Hostels

An Óige, the Irish Youth Hostel Association, has nearly 50 hostels scattered round the country and there are another half-dozen in Northern Ireland. Youth hostels are open to members of the International Youth Hostel Federation (IYHF), members of An Óige (annual membership IR£7.50), or to any overseas visitor for an additional nightly charge of IR£1.25. Pay the additional charge six times (total IR£7.50) and you become an IYHF member. To use a hostel, you must have or rent a sleeping-bag sheet.

Nightly costs vary with the time of year, but in July-August they range from IR£4.50 to IR£5.90 except for the more expensive Dublin Hostel and a few others. Rates are cheaper if you're aged under 18. Prices quoted in this chapter are all high season and for people over 18 years of age.

Nowhere else in Europe have independent hostels popped up like they have in Ireland. The Independent Hostel Owners is a cooperative group who put out a booklet listing nearly 100 hostels all over Ireland. Another 20 or so are members of the Irish Budget Hostels group which carries the additional cachet of being approved by the Irish Tourist Board.

There are still more independent hostels which are members of neither group. Independent hostels are usually a bit cheaper than the An Óige ones. They emphasise their easy-going ambience and lack of rules, but competition from the independents has forced the official hostels to rethink their rule book in recent years.

Bed & Breakfasts

If you're not staying in hostels you will probably stay in a B&B. It sometimes seems every other house in Ireland is a B&B, and you'll stumble upon them in the most unusual and remote locations. Typical cost is IR£12 to IR£15 a night; you rarely pay less or more than that although in the big towns there are some luxurious B&Bs which can cost IR£25 or more a night. B&Bs usually do not have private bathrooms, but where they do, the cost is just a pound or two higher – IR£15 becomes IR£17. At some places costs are higher for a single room. Most B&Bs are very small, just two to four rooms, so in summer they can quickly fill up. With so many to try there's bound to be someone with a spare room, however.

Breakfast at a B&B is almost inevitably cereal followed by 'a fry', which means fried eggs, bacon and sausages. A week of B&B breakfasts exceeds every known international guideline for cholesterol intake, but if you decline fried food, you are left with cereal and toast. If your bloodstream can take it you'll have enough food to last till dinnertime, but it's a shame more places don't offer alternatives like fruit or the delicious variety of Irish breads and scones. In Northern Ireland you may meet the 'Ulster Fry', which adds fried breads, blood sausages, tomatoes and assorted other bits and pieces.

Other Accommodation

Other accommodation possibilities include guesthouses, which are often just like larger and more expensive B&Bs. Farmhouse accommodation usually means it's a B&B on a farm – they are sometimes excellent value and you may get a chance to see how the farm works. Self-catering accommodation is often on a weekly basis and usually means an apartment or house where you look after yourself. Hotels are hotels.

FOOD

It's frequently said that Irish cooking doesn't match up to the ingredients and traditional Irish cooking tends to imitate English – ie cook it until it's dead, dead, dead. Fortunately the Irish seem to be doing a better job than the English in kicking that habit and you can generally eat quite well. Of course, if you want meat or fish cooked until it's dried and shrivelled and vegetables turned to mush, there are plenty of places that can still perform the feat.

Fast food is well established, from traditional fish & chips to more recent arrivals like burgers, pizzas, kebabs and tacos. Apart from the American chains, you'll also find *Abrakebabra* branches around the country. Pubs are often good places to eat, particularly at lunch time when a bowl of the soup of the day (usually vegetable) and some good bread can make a fine and economical meal. Seafood restaurants, long neglected in Ireland, are often very good and there are some superb vegetarian places.

Irish bread has a wonderful reputation and indeed it is very good, but unfortunately there's a tendency to fall back on the infamous white-sliced bread, *pan* in Irish. B&Bs are often guilty of this crime. Irish scones are a delight, however, and tea & scones is a great snack at any time of day. Even pubs will often offer tea & scones. See the previous Bed & Breakfasts section for information on the famous Irish breakfast.

DRINKS

In Ireland a drink means a beer – either lager or stout. Stout usually means Guinness, the famous black beer of Dublin, although in Cork it can mean a Murphy's or a Beamish. If you don't develop a taste for stout (and you should at least try), a wide variety of lager beers are available including Irish Harp or Smithwicks and many locally brewed 'imports' like Budweiser, Foster's or Heineken. Simply asking for a Guinness or a Harp will get you a pint (570 ml, IR£1.70 to IR£2 in a pub). If you want a half pint (90p to IR£1.10), ask for a 'glass' or a 'half'. Children are allowed in pubs until 7 or 8 pm, and in smaller towns this restriction is treated with customary Irish flexibility.

ENTERTAINMENT

A Guinness to go with pub music is the most popular form of entertainment in Ireland. If it's suggested you visit a particular pub for its 'good crack', don't think you've just found the local dope dealer. 'Crack' is Irish for a good time – convivial company, sparkling conversation and rousing music. Theatre is popular, and a 'medieval banquet' (a sort of Irish theatre-restaurant performance in an old castle) finds its way on to many tourist itineraries.

THINGS TO BUY

Clothing, particularly warm woollen sweaters, is probably the most authentically Irish purchase. The Irish produce some high quality outdoor activities gear as they have plenty of experience with wet weather. Jewellery with a Celtic influence, and fine crystal and glassware are other popular buys. There are souvenir and craft shops in all the major towns.

Getting There & Away

Students should contact USIT, the Irish youth and student travel association, for cheap deals to Ireland from the UK. Its London office is at London Student Travel (☎ 071-730 3402), 52 Grosvenor Gardens, London SW1W OAG.

AIR

Aer Lingus is the Irish national airline with international connections to other countries in Europe and to the USA.

To/From the UK

Dublin is linked by a variety of airlines to a variety of cities in the UK including all the major London airports. There are also flights to various regional centres in the Republic of Ireland. The standard one-way economy fare London-Dublin is £70, but advance purchase fares are available offering return tickets for as low as £60 to £70. These must be booked well in advance as seats are often limited.

Belfast is also connected with cities in the UK including the regular British Airways shuttle service from London's Heathrow. Costs on the shuttle range from as high as £99 for a regular one-way to as low as £63 for a one-way stand-by or £111 for an advance purchase return. There's a £74.25 student/youth fare. British Midland Airways offers similar fares, but Britannia Airways flies from Luton to Belfast for just £39. Luton Airport is only 45 minutes north of London.

To/From North America

There are no direct flights to Ireland from Canada and all flights from the USA must put down in Shannon on their way to Dublin. Because competition on flights to London is so much fiercer, it will generally be cheaper to fly to London first.

Shannon Airport

Shannon Airport is a topic of considerable controversy in Ireland. In the early days of trans-Atlantic aviation, flying between the USA and Europe was impossible without a refuelling stop, so Shannon thrived as the first airport on the eastern side of the Atlantic. In the jet age, Shannon is simply an anachronism and the only flights that *have* to stop in Shannon are Aeroflot's Moscow-Havana services. At some point in Irish history, however, it was legislated that all flight between Ireland and North America must put down in Shannon. Since it's only about 200 km from Shannon to Dublin, this is clearly very uneconomic and Aer Lingus loses millions every year by making this unnecessary stop. Apart from Delta, all the US and Canadian operators have simply opted not to fly to Ireland at all. A furious argument rages over whether airlines should be allowed to fly directly to Dublin, but so far local interests (and politicians) have ensured the Shannon stopover remains obligatory.

To/From Australia & New Zealand

Excursion or Apex fares from Australia or New Zealand to Britain (see the Britain chapter) can have a return flight to Dublin tagged on at no extra cost. You can also include Dublin on Round-the-World itineraries.

To/From Other Places

Dublin is connected with major centres in Europe. There are also overseas flights to Cork, Shannon and Belfast. From Paris, one-way fares to Dublin range from 755 to 915 FF one-way, 1205 to 1730 FF return.

SEA

There is a great variety of ferry services from Britain and France to Ireland using modern car ferries. Figures quoted are one-way fares for a single adult, for two adults with a car and for four adults with a car. There are often special deals, return fares and other money savers worth investigating. See the following sections for Britrail Seapass and Eurail pass information.

Want to travel free? On some routes the cost for a car includes up to four or five passengers at no additional cost. If you can hitch a ride in a less than full car, it costs the driver nothing extra.

To/From the UK

There are services from eight ports in England, Scotland and Wales (and from the Isle of Man) to six ports in Ireland. From south to north, interesting possibilities include:

Swansea to Cork The 10-hour crossing costs £26/179/179 at peak times but it operates only from March to November.

Fishguard & Pembroke to Rosslare This popular short crossing takes 3½ hours (Fishguard) or 4½ hours (Pembroke) and costs as much as £23/180/180 on peak season weekends; at other times of year the cost can drop as low as £17/75/75.

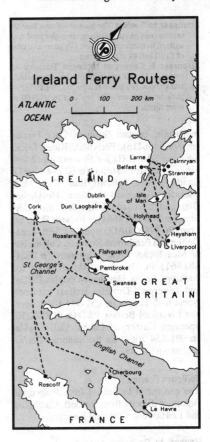

Ireland Ferry Routes

Holyhead to Dublin & Dun Laoghaire The crossing takes 3½ hours and costs £23/180/180 at peak seasons, down to £17/94/94 in the off season.

Liverpool & Heysham to Belfast The Norse Irish overnight service is not heavily promoted but it's easy to get to Liverpool from London. The trip costs £100 for a car and driver, £30 for each additional passenger, including dinner, breakfast and cabin accommodation. There are also the Isle of Man Steam Packet services from Liverpool and Heysham via Douglas (Isle of Man). A small car costs £69 in the peak season, passengers cost £36 each.

IRELAND

Stranraer to Belfast The glamorous new SeaCat service uses an Australian-made high-speed catamaran to race across in just 1½ hours at a cost of £19/126/141 at peak times.

Stranraer & Cairnryan to Larne There are as many as 15 sailings daily on this route which takes about 2½ hours and costs £18/132/132 at peak times, down to as low as £16/100/100 at other times.

In Britain, contact Swansea Cork Ferries (☎ 0792-456116), Ferryport, Kings Dock, Swansea SA1 BRU for Swansea-Cork services. Sealink-Stena (☎ 0233-647047), Charter House, Ashford, Kent TN24 8EZ, operates Fishguard-Rosslare, Holyhead-Dun Laoghaire and Larne-Stranraer. B&I Line (☎ 071-734 4681), 150 New Bond St, London W1Y 0AQ, operates Holyhead-Dublin and Pembroke- Rosslare. Call the Isle of Man Steam Packet Company (☎ 0624-661661) in Douglas, Isle of Man for bookings on its Heysham-Douglas-Belfast and Liverpool-Douglas-Belfast services. Norse Irish Ferries (☎ 051-944 1010) operates Liverpool-Belfast. P&O (☎ 05812-276) operates Cairnryan-Larne. Call SeaCat (☎ 081-554 7061) for the Stranraer-Belfast catamaran service.

To/From France

You can travel to Ireland from France via Britain or directly from Roscoff, Cherbourg and Le Havre to Cork and Rosslare.

Roscoff to Cork This 14-hour service operates from March to October.

Cherbourg to Cork & Rosslare Cherbourg to Cork or Rosslare takes about 17 hours.

Le Havre to Cork & Rosslare Le Havre to Cork or Rosslare takes about 22 hours.

The Cherbourg and Le Havre services are operated by Irish Ferries and can be used by Eurail pass holders. In France, contact Transports et Voyages (☎ 1-42.66.90.90), 8 Rue Auber, 75009 Paris. Fares from Cherbourg or Le Havre to Cork or Rosslare are 625/2410/3660 FF in the peak season.

The Roscoff-Cork service is operated by Brittany Ferries (☎ 1-42.86.03.03), 9 Rue du 4 Septembre, 75002 Paris. The peak-season fares are 836/3140/3140 FF.

A cheaper alternative to these direct routes is to take the Sealink Cherbourg-Southampton and Fishguard-Rosslare ferries, driving from Southampton to Fishguard in Britain. Republique Tours (☎ 1-43.55.39.30), 1bis Ave de la Republique, 75011 Paris, is the agent for Sealink, and the combined fares are 545/2720/2720 FF.

ROAD & SEA

The Bus Éireann/National Express Supabus and Slattery Coach services operate direct from London and other UK centres to Dublin and other cities. For details in London, contact the Coach Travel Centre (☎ 071-730 0202), the Irish Tourist Board (☎ 071-493 3201) or Slattery's Coaches (☎ 071-724 0741). London to Dublin takes about 13 hours and costs £40 one-way or £61 return during the summer and Christmas peak periods.

Citylinking/Ulsterbus (☎ 071-636 9373), Victoria Coach Station, 164 Buckingham Palace Rd, London SW1W 0SH, operates London-Birmingham-Manchester-Stranraer-Belfast services daily. The one-way London-Belfast fare is £38 (students £28) and the trip takes 13 hours.

Getting Around

At a glance, travelling around Ireland looks very simple as the distances are short and there's a dense network of roads and railways. In practice there are a few problems. In Ireland, from A to B is never a straight line and there are always a great many intriguing diversions to make. Public transport is often expensive (particularly train services), infrequent or both. Plus there are many interesting places that public transport simply does not get to. For these reasons, having your own transport can be a major advantage.

DISCOUNT DEALS

Eurail passes are valid for bus and train travel

in the Republic of Ireland but not in Northern Ireland. The Eurail pass can also be used on Irish Ferries' services between Le Havre or Cherbourg in France and Rosslare or Cork in Ireland.

Inter-Rail passes offer free train travel within the Republic of Ireland but only give 34% reduction in Northern Ireland. They also give reductions (percentages vary depending on the company) on ferry services between Le Havre or Cherbourg in France and Rosslare or Cork in Ireland, and between Dun Laoghaire or Rosslare in Ireland and Holyhead or Fishguard in Wales.

For IR£7, full-time students can have a Travelsave Stamp affixed to their ISIC card. This gives up to 50% discount on Irish Rail and Bus Éireann services and on B&I ferries. Enquire at the USIT Office (☎ 071-730 3402) at 52 Grosvenor Gardens, London SW1W OAG, or at the USIT office in Dublin.

There are a variety of unlimited travel tickets for buses and trains, in the north and south. Rambler Tickets are available for bus-only or train-only travel in the Republic of Ireland. They cost IR£26 (three days), IR£60 (eight days) or IR£90 (15 days). A bus and rail version costs IR£78 (eight days) or IR£115 (15 days). Children under 16 years of age pay half fare, and your bicycle can come along for the ride for an additional charge.

An Emerald Card gives you unlimited travel throughout Ireland on all scheduled services of Irish Rail, Northern Ireland Railways, Bus Éireann, Dublinbus, Ulsterbus and Citybus. The card costs IR£105 (or pounds sterling equivalent) for eight days or £180 for 15 days.

These passes can be bought after you arrive in Ireland, but unfortunately they only make economic sense if you're planning a warp-speed circuit of Ireland.

AIR

Ireland is too compact for flying to be necessary, but there are flights between Dublin and some regional centres.

BUS

Bus Éireann is the national bus line with services all over the south and to the north. Standard one-way fares from Dublin include Belfast IR£10, Cork IR£11 or Galway IR£9. These fares are much cheaper than the regular railway fares, return fares are usually only a little more expensive than one-way, and special deals are often available. Details of unlimited-travel Rambler Tickets are given in the previous Discount Deals section.

Ulsterbus is the service in the north. An Ulsterbus Freedom of Northern Ireland Ticket gives you unlimited travel on Ulsterbus and Citybus services for one day for £15, or seven consecutive days for £25.

TRAIN

Iarnród Éireann, the Irish railway system, operates trains on routes which fan out from Dublin. Distances are short in Ireland, and the longest trip you can make by train from Dublin is about three hours to Galway or Killarney. Fares are high: regular fares from Dublin include Belfast IR£13.50, Cork IR£31.50, or Galway IR£24. As with buses, special fares are often available. First-class tickets cost about IR£4 to IR£7 over the standard fare for a single journey. If you're aged under 26 you can get a FairCard for IR£8 which gives you a 50% discount on regular fares.

Northern Ireland Railways has three routes from Belfast and one of them is linked to the system in the south. See the previous Discount Deals section for information on Rambler Tickets for unlimited train travel in the south, or Emerald Cards for unlimited train travel throughout Ireland.

CAR & MOTORBIKE

As in England, driving is on the left. There are no surprises to driving in Ireland, and despite frequent apologies about the roads, there's really little to complain about. Back roads may sometimes be potholed and will often be very narrow, but the traffic is rarely heavy except as you go through popular

IRELAND

tourist towns. In the south speed limits are 70 mph on motorways, 60 mph on other roads and 30 mph or as signposted in towns. Like much else in Ireland, speed limits are treated with some disdain.

The Irish can't seem to make up their minds on metrication – speed limits are in miles per hour, distance signs in km, and most car speedometers are still Imperial rather than metric. In the north, speed limits and other laws are as in Britain.

There are parking meters in Dublin and a handful of other locations, but usually parking is regulated by disk parking or 'pay and display' tickets. It is often loosely enforced in the south. Beware of Control Zones in the north where your car absolutely must not be left unattended. Double yellow lines by the roadside mean no parking at any time, and single yellow lines warn of restrictions. In the north, red, white and blue kerbstones mean you're in a Protestant area; green, white and orange mean it's Catholic!

Unleaded petrol is 15% cheaper in the north.

Rental

Car rental in Ireland is expensive and in high season there can be a shortage of cars, so it's wise to book ahead. Off season some companies simply discount all rates by about 25% and there are often special deals. Some smaller companies make an extra daily charge if you go across the border, north or south.

Typical weekly high-season rental rates with insurance and unlimited distance in the Republic of Ireland are IR£225 for a small car (Ford Fiesta), IR£260 for a middle-size car (Ford Escort) and IR£320 for a larger car (Ford Sierra). In the north, similar cars would cost about £200, £230 and £250 respectively.

Avis, Budget, Hertz, Thrifty and the major local operators, Murrays Europcar and Dan Dooley, are the big rent-a-car companies. There are many smaller and local operators.

BICYCLE

An enormous number of visitors explore Ireland by bicycle. Although the distances are relatively short, the most interesting parts of Ireland can be very hilly and the weather is often wet. Despite these drawbacks it's a great place for bicycle touring, and facilities are good.

You can either bring your bike with you or rent in Ireland. Typical rental costs are IR£7 to IR£10 a day or IR£30 to IR£35 a week. Bags and other equipment can also be rented. Rent-a-Bike has eight offices around the country and offers one-way rentals between its outlets for an extra IR£5. The head office of Rent-a-Bike (☎ 01-725399) is at 58 Lower Gardiner St, Dublin 1. Raleigh Rent-a-Bike agencies can be found all over Ireland, north and south of the border. Contact them at Raleigh Ireland (☎ 01-626 1333), Raleigh House, Kylemore Rd, Dublin 10. There are also many local independent outlets.

Bicycles can be transported by bus on some routes for IR£4. By train the cost is typically IR£6.

There are numerous tourist office publications on cycling, plus Martin Ryle's book *By Bicycle in Ireland*, a guide to 22 routes. Eric Newby's *Round Ireland in Low Gear* is another Newby classic of travel masochism complete with lousy weather, steep hills, high winds and predatory trucks.

HITCHING

Hitching in Ireland is generally quite good. The major exceptions are in heavily touristed areas, where the competition from other hitchers is severe and the cars are usually full to the brim with families. The large number of Irish hitchhikers on the road is indicative that hitching is sometimes the only way to get around the problem of infrequent or non-existent public transport.

The usual hitching rules apply. Try to look like a visitor: put your backpack out on view, ideally with a flag on it. Carry cardboard and a marker pen so you can make a sign showing where you're going. Women should travel with someone else (even though many local women seem to hitch alone and get away with it). If you feel at all doubtful about an offered ride, turn it down. *Sea Legs: Hitch-hiking the Coast of Ireland Alone* by Rosita Boland (New Island Books) tells the tale of an Irishwoman's solo (yes, the Irish are always doing things against the rules) exploration of Ireland by thumb.

BOAT

There are many boat services to outlying islands and across rivers. Some of them make interesting little short cuts, particularly for cyclists.

LOCAL TRANSPORT

There are comprehensive local bus networks in Dublin, Belfast and some other larger towns. The DART (Dublin Area Rapid Transport) line in Dublin and the service from Belfast to Bangor are the only local railway lines. Taxis in Ireland tend to be expensive, but in Belfast and Derry there are share-taxi services operating rather like buses.

Dublin

Ireland's capital and the largest and most cosmopolitan city on the island, north or south, Dublin can swing so rapidly from rich to poor that it's virtually impossible to pin it down. The elegant and prosperous-looking Georgian squares can quickly give way to areas where any elegance has long since faded into decay, and Dublin's long and crowded history has failed to inspire any impressive modern development.

Despite its faults Dublin is a curious and colourful place; it's an easy city to like and a fine introduction to Ireland.

Orientation

Dublin is neatly divided by the Liffey River into more affluent southern and less affluent northern halves. The Viking and medieval city of Dublin first developed south of the river, spread north in the early years of its Georgian heyday and then moved south again as the northern part peaked and declined.

North of the river the important streets for visitors are O'Connell St, the major shopping thoroughfare, and Gardiner St, with its many B&Bs. Most of the hostels are located in this area; Connolly Station is slightly to the east; the main bus station is at the southern end of Gardiner St, which becomes very run-down as it continues north. Immediately south of the river is the intriguing old Temple Bar area and the expanse of Trinity College. Nassau St, along the southern edge of the campus, and pedestrianised Grafton St are the main shopping streets south of the river. As in other Irish towns, there's a tendency for street names to change every few blocks.

Information

Tourist Office There are tourist offices at the airport and on the waterfront at Dun Laoghaire (pronounced 'dun leary'). In the city the Dublin Tourism office (☎ 01-747733) is at 14 Upper O'Connell St. This office is open from 8.30 am to 8 pm Monday to Saturday and 10.30 am to 2 pm Sunday in the summer months, but it can get very crowded with long queues for accommodation bookings and information. The head office of the Irish Tourist Board (☎ 01-765871) at Baggot St Bridge has an information desk and although it is less conveniently situated it is also much less crowded. A new tourist office (☎ 01-770160) opened at 33-34 Essex St in Temple Bar for the summer of 1992 and may be open all year in future.

The head office of An Óige (☎ 01-363111), the Irish Youth Hostel Association, is at the premises of the Dublin International Youth Hostel, 61 Mountjoy St, Dublin 7.

Telephone Numbers By the end of 1994 all Dublin telephone numbers will have been converted to seven digits. Meanwhile, if you have difficulties with a six-digit number, it may have already been converted.

Dublin

0   100   200 m

Map labels:

Hospital
Hospital
Stoney Batter
Grangegorman Street
Constitution Hill
Church Street
Infirmary Road
Brunswick Street
North
King Street
Blackhall Place
Queen Street
Smithfield
Bow Street
Church Street
North Street
Benburb Street
Wolfe Tone Quay
Parkgate St
Heuston Station
Victoria Quay
Ellis Quay
Usher's Island
Arran Quay
Mary's Lane
Chancery Street
Mary's Street
Arran St
To Phoenix Park & the West
Saint James Gate Brewery
Usher's Quay
Inns Quay
Ormond Quay
Steevens' Lane
James Street
Watling Street
Bridgefoot Street
Oliver Bond Street
Usher's Quay
River Liffey
Merchants Quay
Wood Quay
Essex Quay
To Kilmainham Gaol & IMMA
Thomas Street West
St Augustine St
Bridge St
Whitetavern St
Crane St
Meath St
Cornmarket St
High Street
Christ Church Place
Lord
The Liberties
Francis Street
John Dillon Street
Nicholas Street
Werburgh St
Swift's Alley
Dean Street
Patrick Street
Golden Lane
Kevin St Upper
Bride Street
Aungier Street
Kevin St Lower
Bishop Street
Cuffe
Stephen's Green

PLACES TO STAY

2 Dublin International Youth Hostel
4 Young Traveller Hostel
5 Cheap B&Bs
14 Gresham Hotel
19 Cardijn House Hostel
20 More cheap B&Bs
29 Isaacs Hostel (Dublin Tourist Hostel)
35 Kinlay House
53 Avalon House

▼ PLACES TO EAT

3 Joxer Daly's
13 Bewley's Café
18 Kylemore Café
23 Slattery's
25 Sean O'Casey's
31 The Brazen Head
38 Pizza on the Corner
38 Beshoff's Fish & Chips
39 Bewley's Café
41 White House Inn
42 John Mulligan's
43 Buttery Café

OTHER

1 Dublin Zoo
6 Municipal Gallery of Modern Art
7 Dublin Writer's Museum
8 Sinn Fein Bookshop
9 Gate Theatre
10 The Laundry Shop
11 Aer Lingus
12 Telecom Centre
15 Dublin Bus (Bus Átha Cliath) Office
16 Tourist Office
17 St Mary's Pro-Cathedral
21 St Michan's Church
22 St Mary's Abbey
24 Eason Bookshop
26 Irish Rail
27 Abbey Theatre
28 Rent-a-Bike
30 Four Courts
32 Guinness Hop Store
33 St Audoen's Church
34 Christ Church Cathedral
37 USIT Travel Office
40 Bank of Ireland
44 Trinity College Library & Book of Kells
45 City Hall
46 Dublin Castle
47 St Werburgh's Church
48 St Patrick's Cathedral
49 Marsh's Library
50 St Stephen's Green Shopping Centre
51 National Museum
52 National Gallery

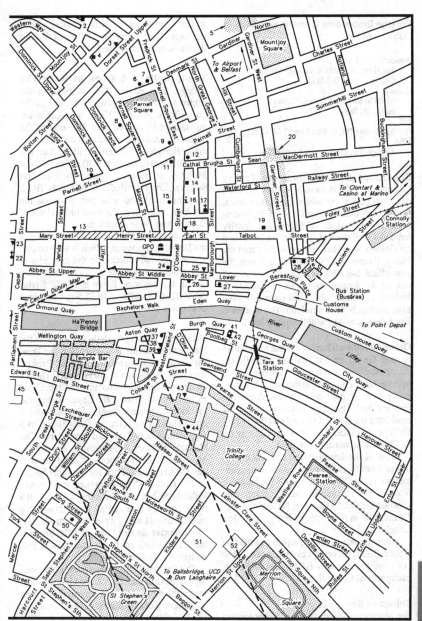

Foreign Embassies Overseas embassies in Dublin include:

Australia
    6th floor, Fitzwilton House, Wilton Terrace, Dublin 2 (☎ 01-761517)
Canada
    65-68 St Stephen's Green, Dublin 2 (☎ 01-781988)
UK
    31 Merrion Rd, Dublin 4 (☎ 01-269 5211)
USA
    42 Elgin Rd, Dublin 4 (☎ 01-688777)

Bookshops Directly opposite Trinity College at 27-29 Nassau St is Fred Hanna's excellent bookshop, while round the corner, facing each other across Dawson St, Waterstone's and Hodges & Figgis are equally large and well stocked. The Dublin Bookshop on Grafton St is also very good. North of the Liffey, Eason, on O'Connell St and near the post office, has a big selection of books and one of the largest ranges of magazines in Ireland. All these bookshops have extensive selections of books on Ireland. The Sinn Fein Bookshop is at 44 Parnell Square West.

Other Facilities There are numerous banks around the centre with exchange facilities. There are also exchange bureaus which operate longer hours than the banks but generally take a bigger commission. American Express and Thomas Cook are across the road from the Bank of Ireland and the Trinity College entrance. The famous GPO is on O'Connell St, north of the river.

Most of the hostel-style accommodation offers laundry facilities at lower than commercial rates. Otherwise there's the Laundry Shop at 191 Parnell St near the centre, the Clothes Line at 53 Clontarf Rd and the Star Laundrette at 47 Upper George St, Dun Laoghaire.

There are left-luggage facilities at the bus station (IR£1.10, backpacks IR£1.60) and at both railway stations (IR£1, but IR£2 for backpacks at Connolly).

Things to See
See Money in the Facts for the Visitor section at the beginning of this chapter about Heritage Card entry to Office of Public Works-administered sites.

Trinity College & Book of Kells The college, founded in 1592, is right in the centre of Dublin. Its prime attraction is the magnificent Book of Kells, an illuminated manuscript of around 800 AD, one of the oldest books in the world. It's on display in the collonades of Trinity College Library. The library is open from 9.30 am to 5.30 pm Monday to Saturday, noon to 5 pm on Sunday. Entry is IR£2.50 (students IR£2, children free) and you can also see the library's long room, the even older Book of Durrow and Brian Boru's harp.

The college's other big tourist attraction is the Dublin Experience, which is a 45-minute audiovisual introduction to the city. Shows take place hourly from 10 am to 5 pm daily during the summer. Entry is IR£2.75 (students IR£2.25, children IR£1.50). Combined tickets are available.

Museums Highlight of the exhibits at the **National Museum** on Kildare St is the Treasury with its superb collection of Bronze, Iron Age and medieval gold objects. There's an interesting audiovisual to go with it. Other exhibits focus on the 1916 Easter Rising and the independence struggle. The museum is open Tuesday to Saturday from 10 am to 5 pm, Sunday from 2 pm, and entry is free. The **Natural History Museum** is nearby on Merrion St, has skeletons, stuffed animals and the like, and is open for the same hours.

The **Dublin Civic Museum** at 58 South William St has exhibits about the city. It's open Tuesday to Saturday from 10 am to 6 pm, Sunday 11 am to 2 pm, and entry is free. The **Chester Beatty Library** at 20 Shrewsbury Rd, south of the centre, has a fine collection of Oriental art.

The **Dublin Writers Museum**, on Parnell Square next to the Hugh Lane Gallery, celebrates the city's long and continuing history as a literary centre. Entry is IR£2 (students IR£1, children 50p).

Galleries The **National Gallery** looks out on to Merrion Square and its excellent collection is particularly strong, of course, in Irish art. Opening hours are from 10 am to 6 pm Monday to Saturday, to 9 pm Thursday, and 2 to 5 pm on Sunday. Entry is free.

On the north side of Parnell Square, north of the river, the **Municipal Gallery of Modern Art**, or Hugh Lane Gallery, has a fine collection of more recent Irish art. It's closed on Mondays.

Churches A casual glance at the Dublin skyline will illustrate what an important part churches play in the city's history. Although you can soon get a surfeit of the experience, some of them are well worth exploring.

Christ Church Cathedral on Christ Church Place was originally built in wood in 1038 and then rebuilt in stone in 1169. In the south aisle is a monument to the legendary Strongbow. Note the precariously leaning north wall of the church. Entry is 50p; like many other fine old Church of Ireland churches in Ireland, making ends meet in an overwhelmingly Catholic country is not easy.

A church stood on the site of **St Patrick's Cathedral** on Patrick St as early as the 5th century but the present building dates from 1190. It's particularly noted for its connections with Jonathan Swift, author of *Gulliver's Travels* and Dean of St Patrick's from 1713 to 1745. Swift and his beloved 'Stella' are both interred here. Other points of interest include the ancient door through which a hole was hacked so a lordly argument could be settled when one 'chanced his arm' through the hole and added the phrase to the English language. Entry is 90p (children 30p). Next to the church is **Marsh's Library**, dating from 1701.

St Michan's Church, on Church St, originally dates from 1095 and contains the organ which Handel played for the first-ever performance of his *Messiah*, but the main attraction is the mummified remains in the subterranean crypts. With more than a little Irish blarney your guide will insist that the vault's special atmosphere accounts for their perfect preservation; in actual fact they're as dried, shrivelled and crumbling as you might expect after the odd few centuries. Tours are conducted regularly Monday to Friday from 10 am to 12.45 pm and 2 to 4.45 pm, Saturday morning only. The cost is IR£1.20 (children 50p).

Dublin Castle The focus of British power in Ireland, the castle dates back to the 13th century although older parts have been successively built over through the centuries. It's behind the City Hall on Dame St and tours run from 10 am to 12.15 pm and 2 to 5 pm Monday to Friday, and in the afternoon only on weekends. The tour costs IR£1 (children 50p) and takes you round the state chambers, which were developed during the heyday of the British but are still used for official state occasions. More interesting are the subterranean excavations which clearly show the development of the castle from its original construction.

Other Central Buildings The finest Georgian architecture and colourful doorways can be found around St Stephen's Green and Merrion Square. The Irish government or Dáil meets in **Leinster House** on Kildare St. **Mansion House** on Dawson St is the residence of the Lord Mayor and was the site for the 1919 Declaration of Independence.

The **GPO building** on O'Connell St is an important landmark physically and historically. It was the focus for the Easter Rising of 1916 when the building was totally destroyed apart from the façade.

The **Four Courts** on the north bank of the River Liffey dates from 1785. One of the best views of the Liffey is from the old pedestrian Ha'penny Bridge, so called as the toll to cross it used to be a halfpenny.

Kilmainham Jail Built in 1792 this grey, solid and threatening old building played a key role in Ireland's struggle for independence, and was the site for the executions following the 1916 Easter Rising. It played an equally fateful part during the civil war although, interestingly, this chapter in the saga is conspicuously played down in the tour which follows an excellent audiovisual introduction to the old building. It's in Inchicore Rd, some way west past Christ Church Cathedral; take bus No 79 from Aston Quay. Hours are 11 am to 6 pm daily in summer, Wednesday and Sunday 2 to 6 pm the rest of the year and entry is IR£1.50 (children 60p).

Guinness Brewery The Guinness Hop Store is the historic brewery's old storehouse for hops (the main ingredient in beer making), where visitors can watch a Guinness audiovisual and inspect an extensive Guinness museum. It is not a tour of the brewery but it does make an interesting visit and your IR£2 entry fee includes a glass of the black stuff. Children pay 50p and don't get a drink! Hours are 10 am to 4 pm Monday to Friday. Take a No 21 bus from College St or a No 78 from Fleet St.

IMMA The Irish Museum of Modern Art at the old Royal Hospital Kilmainham is close to Kilmainham Jail. It only opened in 1991 and the exhibits look puny in comparison to their luxurious surroundings – hopefully it will improve with time. The museum is open from 10 am to 5.30 pm Tuesday to Saturday, noon to 5.30 pm Sunday, and entry is free. Get there on bus No 79 from Aston Quay. There's an excellent restaurant hidden away in the basement.

Other Attractions The Flame on the Hill audiovisual at St Audoen's Church on High St, just west of Christ Church Cathedral, deals with Ireland prior to the Vikings. It operates Monday to Friday from 10 am to 5 pm and costs IR£1.50 (children IR£1).

Dublin Zoo in Phoenix Park is merely OK, a place to take the kids. Entry is IR£5 (children IR£2) and it's open from 9.30 am to 6 pm Monday to Saturday, from 11 am on Sunday. The zoo is in the south-east corner of extensive Phoenix Park.

The Casino at Marino, on the other hand, is not to be missed. This fantasy playhouse was built in the 1770s by a somewhat eccentric member of the nobility. It's by the

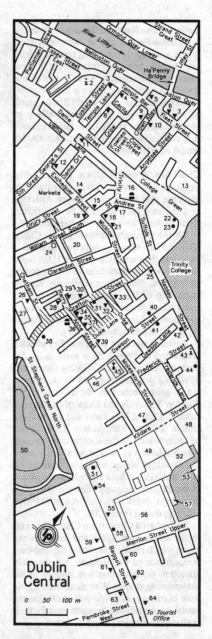

Dublin Central

0   50   100 m

To Tourist Office

IRELAND

■	PLACES TO STAY		61	Baggot Inn
51	Shelbourne Hotel		62	Miller's Pizza Kitchen
			63	James Toner's
▼	PLACES TO EAT		64	Georgian Fare
3	Norseman			OTHER
4	Temple Bar		1	Olympia Theatre
5	Cellary Café		2	Tourist Office
6	Elephant & Castle		13	Bank of Ireland
7	Gallagher's Boxty House		16	Post Office
8	Fat Freddy's Pizza Parlour		20	Powerscourt Shopping Centre
9	Bad Ass Café		22	Thomas Cook
10	Rock Garden Café		23	American Express
11	The Broker's Restaurant		24	Civic Museum
12	Bewley's Café		27	Gaiety Theatre
14	Restaurant Pasta Pasta		31	Dublin Bookshop
15	Old Stand		36	International Post Office
17	Trocadero Restaurant		38	Aer Lingus
18	International Bar		40	Hodges & Figges Bookshop
19	Munchies		41	Waterstone's Bookshop
21	Cornucopia		42	Fred Hanna Bookshop
25	Judge Roy Bean		43	Northern Ireland Tourist Board
26	Pasta Fresca		44	Kilkenny Shop
28	McDaids		45	St Ann's Church
29	Bruxelles		46	Mansion House
30	Bewley's Café		47	Bram Stoker's House
32	Davy Byrne's		48	National Library
33	The Bailey		49	National Museum
34	Eddie Rocket's Diner		50	St Stephen's Green
35	Independent Pizza Company		52	Leinster House
37	John Kehoe's		53	National Gallery
39	Subs n Salad		54	Huguenot Cemetery
55	Galligan's Restaurant		56	Government Building
59	O'Donoghue's		57	Natural History Museum
60	Doheny & Nesbitt		58	Irish Ferries

Malahide Rd, north east of the centre, is open from 9.30 am to 6.30 pm in September, and entry (guided tour only) is IR£1 (children 40p).

Organised Tours Gray Line (☎ 01-619666) has tours around Dublin and farther afield but only in the summer. Dublin Bus (☎ 01-720000) also has a variety of bus tours including Open Deck Tours at IR£7 (children IR£3.50). The Heritage Trail bus does a city tour up to nine times daily, and the IR£5 (children IR£2.50) ticket lets you travel all day, getting on or off at the 10 stops.

In summer there are good walking tours

departing regularly from Trinity College gates (☎ 01-845 0241 for details) and from Bewley's Café on Grafton St (☎ 01-679 4291). Excellent walking tours of Trinity College itself cost IR£3.50 (students IR£3) including entry to the Book of Kells exhibit.

City Cycle Tours (☎ 01-715606) at 1A Temple Lane, Temple Bar, operates bicycle tours of the city which take about three hours and cost IR£10 (students IR£8.50) including use of a bicycle and helmet and entry to Dublin Castle and Kilmainhaim Jail. The summertime Literary Pub Crawl (☎ 01-540228) is another not-to-be-missed tour,

IRELAND

with terrific little theatrical performances leading into each pub along the way. The crawl costs IR£5, the cost of the Guinness consumption is up to you.

Places to Stay

Camping There's no conveniently central camping in Dublin. *Do not* try to camp in Phoenix Park: a German cyclist camping there in 1991 was murdered. The *Shankill Caravan & Camping Park* (☎ 01- 282 0011) is 16 km south of the centre on the N11 Wexford Rd. A site for two costs IR£5 in summer. Other sites are *Donabate* near Swords and *Cromlech* just beyond Dun Laoghaire.

Hostels Despite Dublin's plentiful supply of hostels, they can all be booked out at the height of the summer rush. The *Dublin International Youth Hostel* (☎ 01-301766) is on Mountjoy St and is a big and well-equipped hostel in a restored and converted old building. From Dublin Airport, bus No 41A will drop you in Dorset St Upper, a few minutes' walk from the hostel. It's a longer walk from the bus and train station but it's well signposted. The hostel is in the run-down northern area of the city centre, though not in the worst part of it. The nightly cost is IR£9 and there's an overflow hostel for the height of the summer crush.

Just round the corner from the An Óige hostel is the *Young Traveller Hostel* (☎ 01-305000) on St Mary's Place, just off Upper Dorset St. This is a middle-sized hostel; all the rooms sleep four and have a shower and sink but there are no kitchen facilities. The nightly cost is IR£8.50 including breakfast.

Cardijin House Hostel (☎ 01-788484), subtitled 'Goin' My Way', is a smaller, older hostel centrally located at 15 Talbot St, 400 metres off O'Connell St. The nightly cost is IR£5 plus 50p for a shower.

For convenient transport, you can't beat the big *Dublin Tourist Hostel* (☎ 01-363877), better known as *Isaacs*. It's at 2-5 Frenchman's Lane, a stone's throw from Connolly Station and the bus station, and not far from the popular restaurants and pubs on

either side of the Liffey. In some rooms traffic noise is the penalty for the convenience of being central. The very well equipped hostel is in a converted 18th-century wine warehouse, and costs are IR£5.50 to IR£6.25 in dorms, IR£11.25 each in doubles or IR£15.25 in singles. The restaurant is good value.

South of the Liffey, *Kinlay House* (☎ 01-679 6644) is also centrally located and again some rooms can suffer from traffic noise. It's right beside Christ Church Cathedral at 2-12 Lord Edward St. Kinlay House is big and well equipped and costs from IR£8.50 per person for four-bed dorms, IR£10.50 to IR£13 for the better rooms (some with bathrooms) and IR£17 for a single. A continental breakfast is included.

Finally, *Avalon House* (☎ 01-750001) at 55 Aungier St is nicely positioned just west of St Stephen's Green. Some of the cleverly designed rooms have mezzanine levels (great for families) and it is very well equipped. Basic nightly cost is IR£7 including a continental breakfast. A bed in a room with attached bathroom costs IR£11 in the four-bedded rooms, IR£12.50 in the two-bedded rooms.

Student Accommodation In the summer months (late June to late September) you can stay at Trinity College or at University College Dublin (UCD). Trinity College sometimes has accommodation on campus in the city but it's expensive at IR£25. At *Trinity Hall* (☎ 01-971772), Dartry Rd, Rathmines, rates are IR£14 to IR£17 for singles or IR£12 to IR£15 if you share a twin. If you're aged under 25 and have a student card, the price may drop. There are some family rooms where children aged under 10 can stay free with two adults. To get there, take bus No 14/14A from D'Olier St beside O'Connell St Bridge.

UCD Village (☎ 01-269 7696) is six km south of the centre, en route to Dun Laoghaire. Accommodation here is in apartments with three single rooms sharing a bathroom and kitchen/meals/living area. It's very modern and well equipped but is a little far out and at IR£16.50 (IR£96 a week) rather expensive. For a family, it could be good value. If you've got a car, the ease of parking may compensate for the distance, otherwise bus No 10 departs every 10 minutes from O'Connell St/St Stephen's Green direct to the campus. After 5 pm on Saturday and all day Sunday you have to switch to a No 46A from Fleet St near Trinity College and should ask for the Montrose Hotel stop. Either way the fare is 95p.

B&Bs & Guesthouses Dublin's list of B&Bs is as long as anywhere else in the country and, as elsewhere, the Tourist Board offices will make bookings and direct you to a suitable choice. There are several good hunting grounds. If you want something cheap close to the city, Upper and Lower Gardiner St are the places to look. It's a rather grotty and run-down area, not the prettiest part of Dublin, but it is cheap.

If you're willing to travel farther out, you can find a better price/quality combination on the coast south of the centre at Dun Laoghaire or north of the centre at Clontarf. The seaside suburbs are easy to reach on the DART local train service. The Ballsbridge embassy zone, just south of the centre, offers convenience and quality but you pay for the combination with higher prices. Other suburbs to try are Sandymount and Drumcondra.

At the bottom of Gardiner St there is a large collection of places near the bus and railway stations, and another group farther up near Mountjoy Square. *O'Brien's Hotel* (☎ 01-745203) at 38-39 Gardiner St Lower is a more expensive place with singles at IR£20 to IR£26, doubles at IR£40 to IR£50. The extremely plain *Harvey's Guesthouse* (☎ 01-748384) at 11 Upper Gardiner St, and *Stella Maris* (☎ 01- 740835) next door at No 13 are near Mountjoy Square. Singles are IR£16, doubles IR£28 to IR£30. Hardwicke St is only a short walk from these Upper Gardiner St places and has a number of popular B&Bs like *Waverly House* (☎ 01-746132) at No 4, where singles cost IR£16 to IR£18, doubles IR£28 to IR£32.

There are numerous places along Clontarf Rd, about five km from the centre, including the friendly *Ferryview* (☎ 01-335893) at No 96. Further along there's the slightly more expensive *White House* (☎ 01-333196) at No 125, *San Vista* (☎ 01-339582) at No 237, *Bayview* (☎ 01-339870) at No 265, *Sea-Front* (☎ 01-336118) at No 278 and *Sea Breeze* (☎ 01-332787) at No 312. These Clontarf Rd B&Bs typically cost IR£14 to IR£20 for singles, IR£25 to IR£35 for doubles. Bus No 30 from Abbey St will get you there for 95p.

At Dun Laoghaire, Rosmeen Gardens is packed with B&Bs. To get there, walk south along George's St, the main shopping street; Rosmeen Gardens is the first street after Lower Glenageary Rd, directly opposite People's Park. *Mrs Callanan* (☎ 01-280 6083) is at No 1, *Rathoe* (☎ 01-280 8070) is at No 12, *Rosmeen House* (☎ 01-280 7613) is at No 13, *Mrs McGloughlin* (☎ 01-280 4333) is at No 27, *Annesgrove* (☎ 01-280 9801) is at No 28 and *Mrs Dunne* (☎ 01-280 3360) is at No 30. Prices here are IR£16 to IR£18 for singles, IR£28 to IR£35 for doubles. Dun Laoghaire is easily accessible on the DART or by bus Nos 7, 7A and 8 from central Dublin.

Ballsbridge is a good site for better quality B&Bs like *Morehampton Townhouse* (☎ 01-602106) at 46 Morehampton Rd, directly opposite Sachs Hotel, where singles/doubles are IR£33/50. All rooms are centrally heated and have bathrooms, and the excellent breakfast proves there's more to life than just bacon and eggs. *Mrs O'Donoghue's* (☎ 01-681105), a large, convivial but signless place at 41 Northumberland Rd, costs IR£24/40.

Places to Eat
There are several popular zones for restaurants. North of the river try O'Connell St, south of the river try the Temple Bar area, Dame St, Grafton St and the smaller lanes between those two streets. In general, eating is better to the south of the river than to the north.

Fast Food & Cheap Eats *Isaacs, Kinlay*

House and *Dublin International Youth Hostel* (see Hostels under Places to Stay) all have good cafeteria-style facilities. For fast food ranging from pizzas to *Kentucky Fried, Burger King, McDonald's* and a host of local alternatives like *Abrakebabra*, O'Connell St north of the Liffey and, to a lesser extent, Grafton St to the south are the main hunting grounds. At 1-2 O'Connell St the *Kylemore Café* is a big, fast-food place, or at 5-7 O'Connell St there's the *International Food Court* with a variety of counters including *Beshoff's* for fish & chips. There's another *Beshoff's* at 14 Westmoreland St, just south of the Liffey.

Sandwiches & Cafés *Bewley's Cafés* are a Dublin institution, huge cafeteria-style places offering good quality food from breakfast, to lunch-time sandwiches (IR£1.50 to IR£3) to complete meals (IR£2.50 to IR£3.50). Opening hours vary from branch to branch but you'll find Bewley's at 78 Grafton St, 11-12 Westmoreland St, South Great George's St (all south of the river) and on Mary St (north of the river).

Just beyond Dublin Castle and right across from Christ Church Cathedral on Lord Edward St, Kinlay House's *Refectory* is a good place for lunch-time sandwiches or a quick snack at any time of day.

Subs n Salads is on Anne St South just off Grafton St and turns out filling sandwiches and bread rolls at IR£1.20 to IR£2, snappily and with a smile. Eat there, or even better, if it's a sunny day, take them a couple of minutes south for a park picnic on St Stephen's Green.

Munchies on the corner of Exchequer St and William St South, just west of Grafton St, claims to produce the best sandwiches in Ireland. For IR£1.70 (or IR£1.90 for baps – Irish for bread roll) you can check if it's true. A little closer to Grafton St at 19 Wicklow St is *Cornucopia*, a popular wholemeal café turning out all sorts of healthy goodies for those trying to escape the Irish cholesterol habit. In Temple Bar, *Cellary* offers 'veg and demi-veg' food!

There's a large and excellent café on the 1st floor of the *Kilkenny Shop* on Nassau St. Also hidden away is *Fitzer's*, the slightly pricier but very popular restaurant in the National Gallery. It's open the same hours as the gallery (Thursdays until 8.30 pm) and has meals at IR£4.25 to IR£5.25. Cheaper, but also hidden from view, is the basement *Buttery Café* in Trinity College. It's OK if you like everything with chips. Out from the centre, the *IMMA* at Kilmainham Hospital has an excellent basement café.

Just off St Stephen's Green on Baggot St, *Galligan's Restaurant* is a great place for breakfast. Farther along, *Georgian Fare* is useful for sandwiches.

Restaurants Sandwiched between the south bank of the river and Dame St is Temple Bar, an intriguing old area with numerous good eating places including the very popular *Bad Ass Café*. This cheerful and bright place at 9-11 Crown Alley is just south of the Ha'penny Bridge and offers pretty good pizzas from IR£3 to IR£7.

A block over on Temple Lane is *Fat Freddy's* equally popular pizzeria, although the prices are a bit higher at around IR£5 to IR£9. You can also find pizza at the fancier *Pizza on the Corner*, on the corner of Parliament and Dame Sts.

Recent Temple Bar additions include the techno-sleaze style *Rock Garden Café* (see the following Entertainment section), where you can get a very respectable burger or Mexican dish for IR£6 to IR£9 and get into the show at reduced price. Side by side on Temple Bar are the popular and bustling *Elephant & Castle* (burgers a speciality) and the equally popular *Gallagher's Boxty House*. A *boxty* is a traditional Irish dish which is rather like a stuffed pancake and tastes like an extremely bland Indian *masala dosa*.

If you want something fancier in the restaurant department, Dame St is a good hunting ground. Try *The Broker's Restaurant* on Dame St for truly traditional Irish fare – it even does Irish stew and has three-course meals for around IR£8. Or at 42

Exchequer St, south of Dame St, there's the popular *Restaurant Pasta Pasta* with pasta dishes at around IR£7. At 37 Exchequer St on the corner with St Andrew St is the *Old Stand*, a popular place for pub food at about IR£5. Round the corner is the excellent Italian *Trocadero* on St Andrew St. *Pasta Fresca* (the Irish really like Italian food) is at 3-4 Chatham St just off Grafton St and has very authentic pasta dishes at IR£6.50 to IR£8.50.

Head to Mexico at *Judge Roy Bean's* at 45-47 Nassau St on the corner with Grafton St for popular tacos. *Miller's Pizza*, on Baggot St east of St Stephen's Green, is firmly in pastaland. *Eddie Rocket's* at 7 Anne St South is a genuine 1950s-style American diner ready to dish out anything from breakfast at 7.30 am to a late-night burger from IR£2.85. Next door is the trendy, popular *Independent Pizza Company*.

Entertainment

There are various what's-on publications including *What's On In Dublin*. Dublin has plenty of buskers, and the best of them work busy Grafton St.

Pubs Dublin has a huge selection of pubs so there's no possibility of being unable to find a Guinness should a terrible thirst develop. See the previous Organised Tours section for information on the Literary Pub Crawl.

The Brazen Head on Bridge St, just south of the river, opened in 1666 or 1688 (opinions differ but either way it's the oldest pub in Dublin). In the trendy Temple Bar area the *Norseman* and *Temple Bar* are two very popular small pubs.

Just off Grafton St, *Davy Byrne's* at 21 Duke St, and *The Bailey*, opposite at No 2, both made appearances in *Ulysses* but the former has been extensively yuppified and the latter has been renamed (it was Burton's in Joyce's day). On the other side of Grafton St, the *International Bar* on Wicklow St has entertainment almost every night. *McDaid's* (a Brendan Behan hangout) and *Bruxelles* on Harry St and *John Kehoe's* (with its snugs) on Anne St South are other well-frequented

drinking holes just off Grafton St. A *snug* is a partioned-off table where you can drink in privacy.

Baggott St off St Stephen's Green has a number of notable pubs including *O'Donoghue's*, one of the most renowned music pubs in Ireland. *James Toner's* also has a high reputation for music, and *Dohenny & Nesbitt's*, with its antique snugs, and the trendy *Baggot Inn* are also popular.

At 8 Poolbeg St, between Trinity College and the river, is *John Mulligan's*, long reputed to have the best Guinness in Ireland and even more famous after its appearance in the film *My Left Foot*. Nearby at Burgh Quay is the *White House Inn* with regular rock music. *The Palace* at 21 Fleet St in Temple Bar is a classic example of the Dublin pub.

North of the river, *Slattery's* at 129 Capel St, on the corner of Mary's Lane, and *Sean O'Casey's* at 105 Marlborough St, on the corner of Lower Abbey St, are both busy music pubs where you'll often find traditional Irish music downstairs and loud rock upstairs. *Joxer Daly's* at 103-104 Dorset St Upper is handy for the Young Travellers and An Óige hostels.

Theatre & Concerts Pubs aren't the sole entertainment venues, and Dublin's theatre activity is limited but busy. The famous *Abbey Theatre* is on Abbey St Lower near the river. The *Gate Theatre* is on Parnell Square East, the *Olympia Theatre* is on Dame St and the *Gaiety Theatre* on South King St. The *City Arts Centre* is at 23-25 Moss St.

Concerts take place at the *National Concert Hall* on Earlsfort Terrace just south of St Stephen's Green. For rock concerts, head to the *Point Depot* at East Link Bridge, North Wall Quay by the river, about one km east of the Customs House. The *Rock Garden Café* on Crown Alley in Temple Bar has live music nightly.

Things to Buy

If it's made in Ireland you can probably buy it in Dublin. The wonderful Powerscourt Townhouse Shopping Centre, just west of

Grafton St, is housed in a fine old 1774 building. The Kilkenny Shop on Nassau St has a superb selection of fine Irish crafts. The Tower Design Centre on Pearse St off Grand Canal Quay has studios for a variety of local craftspeople. There are all sorts of weird and wonderful small shops in the Temple Bar area.

Getting There & Away
See the Getting There & Away section at the beginning of this chapter for fares to Dublin from Britain. The USIT Travel Office (☎ 01-679 8833) is at 19 Aston Quay, right by the river and O'Connell Bridge.

Air Dublin is Ireland's major international airport gateway with flights from all over Europe. Flights from North America have to come via Shannon. Aer Lingus offices (☎ 01-377777 for UK enquiries, ☎ 01-377747 for elsewhere) are at 42 Grafton St and 40 Upper O'Connell St.

Bus The Bus Éireann Central bus station, or *Busáras*, is just north of the Customs House and the Liffey. Phone ☎ 01-302222 for details.

Train Rail lines fan out from Dublin around the country. Connolly Station, just north of the Liffey and the city centre, is the station for Belfast, Derry, Sligo, Wexford and other points to the north. Heuston Station, just south of the Liffey and well west of the centre, is the station for Cork, Galway, Killarney, Limerick, Waterford and other points to the west, south and south-west. The Iarnród Éireann Travel Centre (☎ 01-366222) is at 35 Abbey St Lower.

Ferry Sealink-Stena Line (☎ 01- 280 8844) at 15 Westmoreland St operates Dun Laoghaire-Holyhead; B&I Line (☎ 01-679 7977) at 16 Westmoreland St operates Dublin-Holyhead.

Getting Around
To/From the Airport Dublin Airport is 10 km north of the centre and there's an express bus service to the bus station near the river in central Dublin for IR£2.50 (children IR£1.25). Alternatively the slower bus No 41A makes a number of useful stops on the way, terminates across the river on Eden Quay and costs IR£1.10. A taxi to the centre should cost about IR£9, plus additional charges for baggage, extra passengers and 'unsocial hours'. For four people a taxi will probably be cheaper than the bus. There are direct buses between the airport and Belfast.

Local Transport The Dublin Bus company (Bus Átha Cliath) has an information office (☎ 01-734222) at 59 O'Connell St, right across from the tourist office. Buses cost 55p for one to three stages up to a maximum of IR£1.10. Ten-ride tickets are available at a small discount. One-day passes cost IR£2.80 for bus, IR£4 for bus and rail. Other passes include a one-week bus pass for IR£10.50, or bus and rail for IR£14 plus IR£2 for an identity photo. Late-night buses operate from the College St-Westmoreland St-D'Olier St triangle until 3 am on Friday and Saturday night.

The DART provides quick access to the coast as far north as Howth and as far south as Bray. The Pearse station is handy for central Dublin. Taxis in Dublin are expensive, from IR£1.80 flagfall.

Bicycle Rental Rent-a-Bike (☎ 01-725399) at 58 Gardiner St Lower is a popular place just round the corner from Isaacs Hostel. There are a number of Raleigh Rent-a-Bike agencies including C Harding (☎ 732455) at 30 Bachelor's Walk near O'Connell Bridge. All the hostels seem to offer secure bicycle parking areas, but if you're going to have a bike stolen anywhere in Ireland, Dublin is where it would happen.

AROUND DUBLIN
Dun Laoghaire
Dun Laoghaire, only 13 km south of central Dublin, is both a busy harbour with ferry connections to Britain and a popular resort. There are many B&Bs in Dun Laoghaire; they're a bit cheaper than in central Dublin,

and the fast and frequent rail connections make it easy to stay out here. See the Dublin Places to Stay section for some options.

Dun Laoghaire is very popular for sailing, and the **National Maritime Museum** is housed in an old church and is open Tuesday to Sunday from 2.30 to 5.30 pm in summer. Entry is IR£1.20 (children 60p).

On the south side of the harbour is the **Martello Tower** where the action commences in James Joyce's epic novel, *Ulysses*. It now houses a James Joyce Museum. *Ulysses* follows its characters around Dublin during a single day, and many of the places visited on that well-documented journey can still be found. The tourist office's *Ulysses Map of Dublin* locates some of them, but serious Joyce groupies should get a copy of *Joyce's Dublin – A Walking Guide to Ulysses*, or some other Joycean Dublin guide. An annual retracing of the journey takes place on Bloomsday, 16 June. The tower is open April to October Monday to Saturday from 10 am to 1 pm and 2 to 5 pm, Sundays 2.30 to 6 pm. Phone ☎ 01- 280 8571 other times of year. Entry is IR£1.60 (students IR£1.30, children 90p).

Just below the tower is the '40 foot pool' which features in *Ulysses*. The 'wear togs' sign does not apply until 9 am, so until that time it is mainly patronised by '40 foot gentlemen' and brave women.

Bus No 8 or the DART rail service will take you from Dublin to Dun Laoghaire.

Malahide

Despite the vicissitudes of Irish history, the Talbot family managed to keep **Malahide Castle** under their control from 1185 to 1973. The castle is packed with furniture and paintings, and Puck, the family ghost, is still in residence. The extensive Fry Model Railway is in the castle grounds.

In summer the castle is open Monday to Friday from 10 am to 5 pm, Saturday 11 am to 6 pm, Sunday 2 to 6 pm, but shorter hours the rest of the year. Entry is IR£2.45 (students IR£1.85, children IR£1.25).

The railway is open for rather complicated and variable hours but in July-August it's open morning and afternoon (except Sunday morning). Entry is IR£2 (students IR£1.45, children IR£1.15). You can get combined castle and railway tickets for IR£3.90 (IR£2.90, IR£1.95).

To get there, take a bus No 42 from beside the Busáras, or a Drogheda train to the Malahide town station, only a 10-minute walk from the park. Malahide is 13 km north of Dublin.

The South-East

COUNTY WICKLOW

Wicklow, immediately south of County Dublin, has three contenders for the 'best in Ireland' – best garden (at Powerscourt), best monastic site (at Glendalough) and best walk (along the Wicklow Way).

The fine beaches stretching south from Wicklow town to Arklow include Silverstrand, Jack's Hole, Brittas Bay and Arklow Beach. Inland the Wicklow Mountains rise to 927-metre Mt Lugnaquilla, the third-highest mountain in Ireland.

Powerscourt

Near Enniskerry and about 22 km south of Dublin, the house at Powerscourt was accidentally burnt down in 1974, just after a major renovation was completed. The owners now live in one surviving wing but it's the magnificent garden which attracts the crowds. Even with modern power equipment it takes a small army of gardeners to keep the vegetation in line. Stepping down the hill in front of the shell of the house, the gardens are backed by the peak of the Great Sugarloaf, rising to a point on the horizon. The Japanese call it 'borrowed scenery' and Powerscourt also has a small Japanese garden, as well as curiosities like a pets' cemetery.

Opening hours in summer are 9.30 am to 5.30 pm daily, and entry is IR£2.50 (students IR£2, children IR£1). The estate's noted waterfall, the highest in Ireland, is farther south and entry is IR£1.50 (IR£1, 80p).

IRELAND

There's a six-km walking path from the estate to the falls. Bus No 44 runs regularly from Dublin to Enniskerry.

Glendalough

St Kevin may rank as one of Ireland's least friendly hermit monks: he is reputed to have pushed a monastic groupie (who disturbed his isolation) over a cliff edge to her death. The monastery he reluctantly founded has, however, certainly lasted. From its establishment in the 6th century it grew to be one of the most important in Ireland, surviving Viking raids in the 9th and 10th centuries and an English incursion in 1398 before final suppression in the 16th century. The site is entered through the only monastic gateway to survive in Ireland. The ruins include a round tower, the cathedral, a fine high cross and the curious St Kevin's Church. The latter is sometimes referred to as the kitchen due to its chimney-like tower.

Glendalough (pronounced 'glenda-lock') is close enough to Dublin to attract big tourist crowds in summer. Entry to the visitors' centre (not to the site, which is free) is IR£1 (children 40p). The centre has some interesting displays including a model of the monastery in its heyday. A fine audiovisual is regularly shown. It's open from 10 am to 7 pm daily from mid-June to mid-September, and closes earlier for the rest of the year and all day on Monday from November to mid-March.

The *Glendalough International Youth Hostel* (☎ 0404-45342) is near the site and costs IR£5.50 a night. At the village of Laragh, three km west of the monastic site, the *Old Mill Hostel* (☎ 0404-45156) has private rooms, dorm beds at IR£5.30 and camping at IR£3. Laragh has restaurants, pubs and plenty of B&Bs.

St Kevin's Bus Service (☎ 01-281 8119) runs daily between St Stephen's Green in Dublin and the site. Dublin departures are at 11.30 am, Glendalough departures at 4.15 pm, one-way costs IR£5, return IR£8.

The Wicklow Way

Running for 132 km from County Dublin through County Wicklow to County Carlow, this is the longest established and one of the most popular of Ireland's long-distance walks. It's well documented in leaflets and guidebooks. Much of the trail traverses country above 500 metres in altitude, so you should be prepared for Ireland's often rapidly changing weather. If you don't feel up to tackling the whole 10 to 12-day walk, the three-day section from Enniskerry (near Powerscourt) to Glendalough is probably the most attractive and has easy transport at each end.

There are An Óige hostels along the route at *Glencree* (☎ 01-864037), *Knockree* (☎ 01- 864036), *Glendalough*, *Glenmalure* (no phone) and *Aghavannagh* (☎ 0402-36366), as well as numerous B&Bs.

WEXFORD

Rosslare, just 20 km from Wexford, is a popular arrival point for visitors from England and France. Little remains to show the town's Viking origins, apart from the convoluted and rather narrow streets. Cromwell was in one of his most destructive moods when he included Wexford in his 1649 Irish itinerary, and three-quarters of the town's 2000 inhabitants were 'put to the sword'.

Orientation & Information

The Quay Sts run along the waterfront paralleled a block inland by North and South Main Sts. The Tourist Office (☎ 053-23111) is on the waterfront at Crescent Quay. If you need to wash clothes, My Beautiful Laundrette is on St Peter's Square. The Book Centre is on South Main St.

Things to See

Dating from 1300 the huge **Westgate** is the only surviving gate tower to the city although several stretches of wall remain. The ruined state of **Selskar Abbey** is a result of Cromwell's visit. Earlier, Henry II spent 40 days in the abbey as penitence for murdering Thomas Becket in 1170. Bull baiting used to take place at the Bullring, the Cornmarket end of Main St, where today a statue commemorates the 1798 uprising against the English.

About four km out of Wexford, right beside the Dublin-Rosslare N11 road at Ferrycarrig, the **Irish National Heritage Park** is one of those questionable attempts to condense a country's entire history into one theme park. In practice, however, it's quite an interesting place with buildings starting with a Mesolithic camp site and running through to a Norman castle, with dolmens, ringforts, Viking shipyards and other constructions on the way. The tour is excellent. Entry is IR£2.50 (children IR£1.50) and it's open from 10 am to 7 pm from March through October.

Places to Stay
The nearest hostel is the *Rosslare An Óige Hostel* (☎ 053-33399).

There are a number of B&Bs close to the centre with nightly costs from around IR£14 to IR£17 per person. *St Aidan's* (☎ 053-22691) is at 25 Lower John St and *St George's* (☎ 053-23474) is on the corner of John St and George St. John St is a couple of blocks up from Main St. On the other side of John St is Mrs Wallace's *Kilderry* (☎ 053-23848) on St John's Rd, the continuation of George St. Other places can be found along the road into town from the N11.

At the Allen St end of High St, a block back from Main St, *Tara House* is a rock-bottom place with straightforward rooms at IR£13 per person.

The *Ferrybank Camping Park* (☎ 053-44378) is right across the river from the town centre and costs IR£4.50 for a site for two.

Places to Eat
Parallel to the waterfront, North and South Main Sts have something for most tastes including fish & chips (try the *Premier* at No 104), Chinese, pub grub (the *Bohemian Girl* near the Cornmarket has a typical pub-food menu) or even fast food (at *Uncle Sam's* on the corner with Harper's Lane). Good places at lunch time include *Joanne's* at the Cornmarket end of North Main St, *The Wooden Brasserie* on the corner with Rowe St, the

Chapter Coffee Shop under the Book Centre and *Kelly's Deli* at 80 South Main St.

Robertinos has quite good pizzas at IR£4 to IR£5. Try *Abbot's Bistro* near Selskar Abbey for fancier eating.

Entertainment
Even for Ireland, Wexford has a lot of pubs, many of them strung along North and South Main Sts where you'll find *Tim's Tavern,* the *Commodore, Stamp's Store* and the *Bohemian Girl.* Just round the corner on Cornmarket, towards the abbey ruins, is the atmospheric old *Thomas Moore Tavern,* or down on the Quay is the *Wren's Nest.* Music often features. Wexford has a major Opera Festival in October as well as regular live performances in its arts centre and two theatres.

Genuine Irish Music
Finding authentic Irish music isn't always easy despite the plethora of pubs and musicians, so I was pleased when I chanced on a Wexford pub where a fiddler, guitarist and flute player, each with a pint of Guinness in front of them, were getting an enthusiastic reception. 'Good, aren't they?' queried the bartender. 'Certainly are,' I replied. 'They're French,' he said.

Getting There & Away
Wexford is connected to Dublin, and on to Rosslare and Waterford, by train. Bus Éireann services also operate from the railway station near the waterfront, while Ardcavan Coach Company services stop at Crescent Quay by the tourist office.

If you're travelling by bike, it's worth taking the short cut between Wexford and Waterford via Ballyhack/Passage East where you cross the river. Not only is it shorter but there's much less traffic, well worth the IR£1 one-way ferry fare for cyclists (car and passengers IR£3.50).

WATERFORD
Although Waterford is a busy port and commercial centre, it also retains fascinating glimpses of its Viking and Norman history. The legendary Norman Strongbow took the city in 1170, and in later centuries it was the

IRELAND

most powerful centre in Ireland. Today it is famed for its thriving Waterford Crystal factory.

Orientation & Information

Like Wexford, the long riverside quays and narrow lanes behind them are reminders of the town's Viking origins. The tourist office (☎ 051-77388) is at 41 Merchants Quay. If you need to wash clothes, try Washed Ashore, right in the centre, at 36 The Quay, or D's Wash Away, farther out at 109 Barrack St. The Book Centre is on Michael St, the main shopping street which runs back from the quays.

Things to See

There are several handsome chunks of the old city wall still standing, and best known is **Reginald's Tower**, dating from 1003, which now houses a small museum (entry 75p). Next to the ruins of the French Church is a Heritage Centre with more displays (entry 75p). A combined ticket costs IR£1.

Founded in 1240, the **French Church** was used as a hospital in the 16th century, which enabled it to survive the suppression of the monasteries. It takes its name from the Huguenot refugees who used it in the 18th century, after which it fell into ruins. Other important churches include **Christ Church Cathedral**, one of the town's many 18th century buildings constructed by John Roberts. Unfortunately it's rarely open.

Tours of the **Waterford Crystal plant** (☎ 051-73311), on the outskirts of town on the Cork Rd, are free and take about 40 minutes. Officially you're supposed to book in advance but in practice you can generally just turn up. The skilled craftsmen (and they are all men) take about five years' training to become a glass blower or cutter. About 80% of the output is exported to the USA.

City walking tours commence from the Granville Hotel on Meagher Quay at noon and 2 pm daily and cost IR£2.

Places to Stay

Bolton House Hostel (☎ 051-79870) is on Bolton St off Lombard St (the road to Passage East) just past where Lombard St branches off the Mall near Reginald's Tower. The building also bears signs for 'Waterford Protestant YH' and 'Bolton House Student Hostel'. The nightly cost is IR£5 but not all visitors find this hostel a very good place to stay.

Otherwise you can choose from the usual ample supply of B&Bs. Mrs Ryan's *Beechwood* (☎ 051-76677) is wonderfully central at 7 Cathedral Square but only has three rooms at IR£15/24 for a single/double. Mrs O'Brien's *Corlea* (☎ 051-75764) at 2 New St, just off the bottom end of Michael St, is similarly priced.

Rice House (☎ 051-71606), named after the founder of the Christian Brothers, is at 35 Barrack St and is a plain and dull guesthouse, but conveniently situated and well kept. The nightly cost is IR£13, or IR£16 with attached bathroom. The *Portree Guest House* (☎ 051-74574) on Mary St, just off Bridge St, is similarly priced. For more B&Bs, the Mall and its extension, Parnell St, are good places to look, or try farther out along the Cork Rd.

The *Newtown Cove* camp site is at Tramore, 13 km south of Waterford on the coast.

Places to Eat

There's a *Bewley's Café* upstairs in the Broad St Centre on Broad St, the main shopping street. There are various fast-food places along this street including a branch of the popular Irish chain *Abrakebabra*. Once again the Chinese and the Italians dominate the foreign fare, with good pizzas at *Gino's* on Applemarket, just off Michael St.

A number of pubs turn out meals. *T & H Doolan* on Great Georges St is particularly good at lunch times, and *Egan's* does fancier meals. The very popular *Strongbow's* at 124 Quay St features a straightforward chicken, steak and fish menu.

At 11 O'Connell St, *Haricot's* is a delightful wholefood restaurant with superb main courses at IR£3.75 to IR£5. It's good for carnivores or vegetarians, or for a herbal tea and slice of carrot cake at any time. Haricot's is open Monday to Friday to 8 pm, Saturday only to 5.45 pm. More expensive restaurants include the excellent *Poppy's* behind the post office (open Tuesday to Saturday) and the pricier *Reginald's* behind Reginald's Tower.

Entertainment
Yes, there are lots of pubs, many featuring music. The venerable *T & H Doolan* on Great Georges St has one wall which is a remnant of the 1000-year-old city wall! Equally popular are *Geoff's* and *The Pulpit*, side by side on Michael St. Across the road from those two is the *Olde Rogue*, while back towards the river, *Lord's* is just off Broad St, and *Egan's* is by the Cornmarket where Great Georges St turns off. Other popular pubs include the *Metropole* on the corner of Bridge and Mary Sts. *Rorke's* is a rock venue on O'Connell St.

The *Garter Lane* and *Garter Lane Two* arts centres are on O'Connell St. Waterford has a Light Opera Festival in October.

Getting There & Away
The railway and bus stations are across the river from the town centre. There are regular train connections to Dublin, Kilkenny, Limerick and Wexford. There are private as well as Bus Éireann services to Dublin. Waterford has an airport with flights to London. USIT (☎ 051-72601) is at 36/37 Great Georges St.

Getting Around
Wright's on Henrietta St is a Raleigh Rent-a-Bike centre.

WATERFORD TO CORK
Ardmore
A popular seaside resort, Ardmore has a main street of pretty, pastel-coloured buildings. There is, however, an ugly sprawl of caravan parks which spoil the coastal view to the east. It's claimed that St Declan set up shop here well before St Patrick turned up to convert the heathen. On the site of his original monastery stand the ruins of **St Declan's Church** and a fine, rather slender round tower. The outer wall at the west end of the church has some unusual scenes, retrieved from an even older building and placed here. Inside the

church is an old ogham stone. **St Declan's Well** is beyond the Cliff House Hotel, south of the town, and there's a fine cliff walk from there.

Ardmore has B&Bs and camping facilities.

Youghal
Just beyond Ardmore is Youghal (pronounced 'yawl'), a fine little coastal resort with some fascinating reminders of its history. The town's landmark is the curious clock tower which actually bridges Main St. Nearby is a summer-only tourist office. The **Red House** and the sadly decaying **Tyntes Castle** are both on Main St, while **Myrtle Grove**, where Sir Walter Raleigh is said to have resided for a time, is just back from it. In summer, tours of the house are sometimes permitted. The cost is IR£3, phone ☎ 024-92274 for details. St Mary's Church was built in 1220 and is still in use. Above the church there's a fine stretch of the old city wall.

Cobh
Cobh (pronounced 'cove') was for many years the port of Cork and the departure point for countless Irish emigrants. The *Titanic* made its last stop here before its fateful Atlantic voyage, and it was off Cobh that the *Lusitania* was sunk in 1915. There's a *Lusitania* monument by the waterfront of this cheerful little port. Cobh is utterly dominated by the massive, but comparatively recent, St Colman's Cathedral which towers over the town. The return bus fare from Cork is IR£2.20.

CORK
There are no compelling reasons to visit or stay in the Irish Republic's second-largest city, but it's a surprisingly appealing place where it's easy to find a day or two drifting away. This is a fact attested to by the large number of hostels.

The town dates back to the 7th century and survived Cromwell's visit but fell to King William in 1690. It played a key role in Ireland's independence struggle, with one

IRELAND

■ PLACES TO STAY

1   Campus House Hostel
3   An Óige Hostel
5   Jury's Hotel
29 Kinlay House Shandon Hostel
36 Isaacs Hostel (Dublin Tourist Hostel)
37 Sheila's Cork Tourist Hostel
39 Cork International Tourist Hostel

▼ PLACES TO EAT

8   South Quay Co-Op Restaurant
9   An Spailpín Fánach Pub
11 O'Brien's Café
12 Floury Hands Café
15 de Lacy House Pub
17 Bully's Restaurant
20 Bewley's Café
21 An Bodhrán Pub
22 Halpin's Café
25 Gino's Pizzeria
26 Café Kylemore
30 The Lobby, Charlies, An Phoenix &
    Donkey's Ears Pubs

34 Luciano's Pizzeria
35 O'Brien's Café

OTHER

2   Cork Public Museum
4   College Launderette
6   St Fin Barre's Cathedral
7   Elizabeth Fort
10 Tourist Office
13 Waterstone's Bookshop
14 USIT Travel Office
16 St Peter & St Paul's Church
18 Crawford Art Gallery
19 Opera House
23 GPO
24 Holy Trinity Church
27 Shandon Craft Centre/
    Cork Butter Market
28 St Ann's Shandon Church
31 City Hall
32 Bus Station
33 Customs House
38 Kent Railway Station

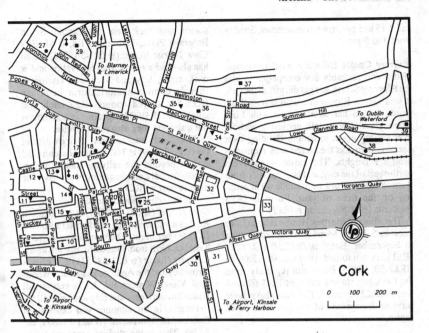

mayor killed by the Black & Tans, his successor dying as a result of a hunger strike and much of the town being burnt down. Today Cork is noted for its fierce rivalry with Dublin.

Orientation & Information

The town centre is an island between two channels of the River Lee. Oliver Plunkett St and the curve of St Patrick's St are the important central streets. The railway station and several hostels are north of the river where MacCurtain St is the main thoroughfare. The Shandon area, also north of the river, is an interesting older area to wander around.

The tourist office (☎ 021-273251) is on Grand Parade at the western end of Oliver Plunkett St. The South Quay Co-op has a good noticeboard. Waterstone's big bookshop runs between St Patrick's and Paul Sts. On Carey's Lane the Collins Bookshop is also good. There's a laundrette at 14 Mac-

Curtain St across from the big Isaacs Hostel, or try the College Laundrette on Western Rd opposite the UCC gates.

Things to See

Around Town Cork's interesting churches include the imposing **St Fin Barre's Cathedral** south of the centre. Nearby are the fragmentary remains of the 17th century Elizabeth Fort. North of the river there's a fine view from the tower of **St Ann's Shandon** (IR£1) and for an additional 50p you can ring the famous Shandon bells. They even provide the notation so you can chime out *Waltzing Matilda* or other favourites. Near the church the **Cork Butter Market** now houses the Shandon Craft Centre.

The **Cork Public Museum** concentrates on Republicanism, Ireland's independence struggle and Cork's part in it. The museum is west of the centre in Fitzgerald Park, near the An Óige Hostel. Entry is free and it's open Monday to Friday from 11 am to 1 pm and 2.15 to 5 pm, to 6 pm in summer, Sunday from 3 to 5 pm.

Blarney Castle Even the most untouristy visitor will probably feel compelled to kiss the **Blarney Stone** and get the gift of the gab. It was Queen Elizabeth I who invented the word, due to her exasperation with Lord Blarney's ability to talk endlessly without ever getting down to action. Bending over backwards to kiss the sacred rock requires a head for heights. The castle is eight km north-west of the city, and is open daily from 9 am to 6.30 or 7 pm, or to sundown depending on the time of year. Entry is IR£3 (students IR£1.50, children IR£1).

The adjacent **Blarney House** is open from noon to 5.30 pm Monday to Saturday, June to September. Entry is IR£2.50 (IR£1.50, IR£1). A combined ticket costs IR£4.50 (IR£2.50, IR£2). Buses run regularly from the Cork bus station and cost IR£1.60 one-way or IR£2.50 return. There are also private services from some of the hostels at IR£2 return.

Places to Stay

Hostels The hostel competition in Cork is fierce. At 48 MacCurtain St, midway between the bus and railway stations and quite close to the centre, *Isaacs* (☎ 021-500011) is a big, new place in a fine old building. A bed costs IR£5.50 in the big dorms, IR£7.50 in the smaller four to six-bed dorms, IR£13.50 in private doubles or IR£18.50 in a single. There are also two-room family suites for IR£44. A light breakfast is included except for the cheapest beds. There's a good cafeteria, kitchen facilities and bicycle hire but the dorms are closed from 11 am to 5 pm.

Also new is *Kinlay House Shandon* (☎ 021-508966) at Bob & Joan Walk in the old Shandon district just north of the river. It's almost as convenient for the centre as Isaacs but a little obscurely located. Dorm beds in rooms for four costs IR£7, twin rooms are IR£10.50 each, or singles are IR£15, and all include a light breakfast.

Beyond Isaacs, towards the railway station and back from MacCurtain St on Belgrave Place, Wellington Rd, is *Sheila's Cork Tourist Hostel* (☎ 021-505562) which has also had a recent total renovation and is neat, clean, tidy and very well equipped; there's even a sauna! Dorm beds are IR£5.50, shared rooms IR£7 each and singles are IR£8. The location is convenient but quiet and they also rent bicycles.

The *Cork International Tourist Hostel* (☎ 021-509089) at 100 Lower Glanmire Rd is just beyond the railway station and is small, friendly and engagingly scruffy. The nightly cost is IR£5.

On the other side of the centre is the *An Óige Hostel* (☎ 021-543289) at 1/2 Western Rd. It's a big, well-organised hostel and costs IR£5.90 per night. There are bikes for rent. Take bus No 8 from the centre, two km away. *Campus House* (☎ 021-343531) is a stone's throw beyond the An Óige Hostel at 3 Woodland View, Western Rd. It's a very small hostel but very neat and tidy and costs IR£5.

Finally, in the summer you can stay at *Castlewhite Apartments* (☎ 021-276871, ext 2479). This is the student accommodation for University College Cork on Western Rd. Rooms range from singles to six-bedroom apartments; each has a kitchen/dining area.

B&Bs On the Dublin side of town, Lower Glanmire Rd beyond the railway station towards Dublin is lined with economical B&Bs. *Tivoli House* (☎ 021-506605) at No 143 is one of the cheapest. Others include *Kent House* (☎ 021-504260), *Oakland* (☎ 021-500578) at No 51 and *Tara House* (☎ 021-500294) at No 52. Singles are IR£14 to IR£20, doubles IR£25 to IR£35.

On the opposite side of town, Western Rd leads towards Killarney and also has plenty of slightly higher priced B&Bs like *St Kildas* (☎ 021-275374). At *Antoine House* (☎ 021-273494) and *Westbourne House* (☎ 021-276153) the rooms all have attached bathrooms and cost around IR£25/35.

Places to Eat

Oliver Plunkett St and pedestrianised streets connecting it with Patrick St have numerous places for a meal, including a fast-food collection which features a *McDonald's* and a *Burger King*. *Bewley's Café* on Cork St is a branch of the popular Dublin-based chain. *Halpin's* at 14/15 Cork St is similar in style with deli and restaurant. Good sandwiches cost from IR£1.25.

Try *O'Brien's* for tea, scones, sandwiches and good, home-made ice cream. There's one on Washington St, near the tourist office and town centre, and one at 39 MacCurtain St near Isaacs and the other hostels north of the river. *Floury Hands* on Grand Parade in the centre also does good sandwiches and coffee.

Between Patrick St and the pedestrian area of Paul St are several narrow lanes with good places for a sandwich or meal. Try *The Gingerbread House* or *Thyme Out* on French Church St for lunch or a coffee or tea. In this same area, *Bully's* at 40 Paul St is a reasonably priced restaurant for pizza and pasta. On French Church St the *Huguenot Bistro* is a fancier place with interesting main courses at IR£5 to IR£6. A block over in Carey's Lane there's *Café Mexicana* and *Paddy Garibaldi's* (yes it's Irish-Italian).

The *South Quay Co-Op Restaurant*, upstairs at 24 Sullivan's Quay, is a delightful vegetarian restaurant with very imaginative starters at IR£1.75 to IR£2.50, and main courses at IR£5.50 to IR£7. *Gino's* at 7 Winthrop St off Oliver Plunkett St, and *Luciano's* on MacCurtain St are two good pizzerias. Finally, if you're out at the museum, try the pleasant little *Museum Tea House*.

Entertainment

The Dublin rivalry even extends to drink. Here a pint of Murphy's is the stout of choice, not Guinness. Or a Beamish, which is lower priced at many pubs. On Union Quay from the corner of Anglesea St, *The Lobby*, *Charlies*, *An Phoenix* and the *Donkey's Ears* are all side by side, and one or other of them will have something on virtually every night. On Oliver Plunkett St, *de Lacy House* at No 74 and *An Bodhrán* at No 42 regularly feature music, or try *An Spailpín Fánach* on South Main St.

Cork prides itself on its cultural pursuits – you can pursue them at the Cork Opera House in Emmet Place or in a number of theatres. The Cork International Jazz Festival takes place in late October and there's an International Film Festival in September.

Getting There & Away

The bus station is on the corner of Merchants Quay and Parnell Place on the central island, while the Kent railway station is across the river on Lower Glanmire Rd. There are frequent bus and train connections to Dublin and other main centres. One-way bus fares include Dublin IR£11, Limerick IR£9, Killarney IR£8 and Waterford IR£9.70. Lower Glanmire Rd, beyond the railway station, is not only lined with cheap B&Bs, it's also often lined with hitchhikers, heading out of town to Dublin.

Cork has an international airport, and there are also ferry connections with the UK and France. USIT (☎ 021-270900) is hidden away at 10/11 Market Parade, an arcade off St Patrick's St near the Grand Parade junction.

Getting Around

A number of the hostels rent bicycles at around IR£5 a day, or try the Cycle Repair Centre (☎ 021-276255) at 6/7 Kyle St or Cycle Scene (☎ 021-301183) at 396 Blarney St. Buses to Cork Airport cost IR£2.20.

KINSALE

If Disney set out to produce a picture-perfect Irish village, they'd end up with Kinsale, minus the traffic jams. There's a small museum in the old courthouse building where the enquiry into the sinking of the *Lusitania* in 1915 was held. Just outside Kinsale are the huge ruins of 17th-century **Charles Fort**, a fine example of a star fort. Entry is IR£1 (children 40p) and it's open from 9 am to 6.30 pm in summer, shorter hours the rest of the year.

Just beyond Kinsale is Ballinaspittle, famed for its 'moving' statue of the Virgin Mary.

Buses connect Kinsale with Cork half a

dozen times a day and cost IR£3.70. Mylie Murphy (☎ 021-772703) on Main St rents bicycles.

Places to Stay & Eat

Kinsale has plenty of B&Bs, an unofficial camping ground close to the waterfront on the edge of town (en route to Summercove and Charles Fort) and two hostels. *Dempsey's Hostel* (☎ 021-772124) is a couple of minutes' walk from the centre of town and costs IR£4 a night plus 50p for showers. The *An Óige Hostel* (☎ 021-772309) is at Summercove near Charles Fort and costs IR£5.50.

Not only is Kinsale impossibly cute, it also lays claim to the title of gourmet centre of Ireland. Fortunately, if your credit card can't stretch to a meal at one of the dozen or so 'Good Food Circle' restaurants, you can still eat well at many more mundane establishments like *Mother Hubbards*. If you want to sample gourmet dining it would be no trouble spending IR£30 a head at some of the fancy restaurants, but you can have a superb three-course lunch plus coffee at *Seasons* for just IR£9.50.

CORK TO BANTRY

Travelling farther west from Kinsale can be tough as bus services are limited and hitching competition can be fierce. Skibbereen does have a bus connection with Cork and it's very scenic from there down to Baltimore from where boats run to Cape Clear Island. *Rolf's Hostel* (☎ 028-20289) in Baltimore is a popular place with a nightly cost of IR£5. There's an *An Óige Hostel* (☎ 028-39144) on Clear Island with a nightly cost of IR£5.50.

West Cork's three peninsulas – Mizen Head, Sheep's Head and the Beara Peninsula – are scenic alternatives to the better known and much more touristy Iveragh (Ring of Kerry) and Dingle peninsulas in Kerry. There's an *An Óige Hostel* (☎ 072-73014) at Allihies on the Beara Peninsula, and independent hostels at Glengarriff, Cahermore and Garranes.

BANTRY

Wedged between mountains and the waters of Bantry Bay, this small town's major attraction is colourful old **Bantry House**, superbly situated overlooking the bay. The gardens are beautifully kept, and the house is noted for its French and Flemish tapestries and the eclectic collection of odds and ends assembled by the 2nd Earl of Bantry during his overseas peregrinations between 1820 and 1850. Entry is IR£2.50 (students IR£1.50, children free with family) and it's open from 9 am to 6 pm daily.

In the grounds of the house is a French Armada exhibit (IR£2.50, students IR£1.50, children IR£1) recounting the sorry saga of the French attempt of 1796 to aid the Irish independence struggle. The exhibit centres around the scuttled French frigate *La Surveillante*, which it is hoped will eventually be raised from Bantry Bay. Bantry also has a small museum just behind the fire station, open odd hours in summer, and an intriguing early Christian stone pillar, on the Cork side of town about half a km inland from the Westlodge Hotel.

There's a tourist office and a laundrette right on the square in town.

Places to Stay & Eat

The *Bantry Hostel* (☎ 027-51050) is off the Glengariff Rd. Take the fork by the Key Properties office and continue uphill almost to the top. The nightly cost is IR£5. There are plenty of B&Bs around including a number around the central square, out along the Glengarriff Rd and at the top end of town, just beyond the bizarrely ugly library building.

Food possibilities include the expensive and highly acclaimed *O'Connor's*, right next to the tourist office, or at the other end of Bridge St *Ó Síocháin* has a standard café-style menu. Try *The Bakehouse*, between the two, for sandwiches, or the excellent café at *Bantry House*. There are plenty of pubs along Bridge St as well, including the popular *Anchor Tavern*.

INLAND

Mitchelstown Caves

These pleasantly uncommercial limestone caves are just off the N8 between Mitchelstown and Cahir, but your exploration is more like 100 metres than the claimed half a mile. Knock at the farmhouse door to get entry tickets at IR£2 (students IR£1, children 50p). Just south of the caves is Ballyporeen with a Ronald Reagan pub to commemorate the ex-president's visit to his ancestral home.

Cahir

Cahir's riverside castle has had numerous later additions, although its basic structure dates back to the 13th or 14th century. It was besieged and taken in 1559, and less than a century later surrendered to Cromwell in 1650. Entry is IR£1 (children 40p) and in summer it's open from 9 am to 7.30 pm.

Cashel

One of Ireland's most spectacular medieval sites, **St Patrick's Rock** (or the Rock of Cashel) is just 18 km north of Cahir. In one handy complex there's a cathedral, a chapel, a round tower, the remains of an unusual high cross, a restored Hall of Vicars and several other structures. If all that isn't enough, there's Hore Abbey and a Dominican Friary at the base of the hill.

The complex is open from 9.30 am to 7.30 pm June to September, to 4.30 or 5.30 pm the rest of the year. Entry is IR£1.50 (children 60p).

Carlow, Castledermot & Moone Abbey

Just east of Carlow beside the R726 road is the massive Browneshill dolmen, the largest in Ireland. Farther north along the N9, the small town of Castledermot has a ruined abbey right by the roadside and, on the opposite side and back from the road, a modern church with two high crosses in the churchyard. A little farther north and just before Timolin an easily missed small sign points to Moone Abbey, almost a km off the main road, where there is a curious and very tall 9th century high cross complete with the 12 apostles, lined up like Lego men at the base of the cross.

Kildare

St Brigid's Church in Kildare has the remains of an ancient fire temple in its grounds, and the second-highest round tower in Ireland. In summer you can climb it between 10 am and 1 pm Monday to Saturday, between 2 and 5 pm any day.

Just south of the town is the National Stud where for IR£2 (students IR£1.50, children IR£1) you can learn all about breeding very expensive racehorses. Adjacent to the stud, and with the same entry charges again, is the curious Japanese Garden. Ireland enjoyed a short-lived mania for building Japanese gardens. The stud and the gardens are open from 10.30 am to 5 pm Monday to Friday, to 6 pm on Saturday, 2 to 6 pm on Sunday.

If you need a meal in Kildare, the very popular *Silken Thomas* pub has middling to average pub food at average to above average prices, and there are numerous other pubs.

Castletown

Castletown House near Maynooth was designed in 1722 and is another fine example of an imposing Anglo-Irish home. The lady of the house had a passion for building follies. There's a curious tower known as the Obelisk, framed in the view to the north, while off to the east, on private property just outside Leixlip, is the even more curious conical Wonderful Barn.

The opening hours vary and the house is closed on Saturday in winter. Entry is IR£2.50 (students IR£2, children IR£1).

KILKENNY

Kilkenny has a long history, some fine reminders of its medieval past and the usual excellent collection of pubs. For a time prior to Cromwell's visit in 1650 Kilkenny was one of the major power centres in Ireland.

Orientation & Information

Most places of interest can be found on or close to High St/Parliament St, parallel to the

IRELAND

river, or John St which runs away from it to the north-east. The tourist office (☎ 056-21755) is in the old Shee Alms House on Rose Inn St, the continuation of John St, just south of the river.

Brett's Laundrette is on Michael St, off John St. The Book Centre is on High St. The Kilkenny Shop, for high quality Irish souvenirs, is opposite the castle.

Things to See

Kilkenny Castle Stronghold of the powerful Butler family, Kilkenny Castle has a history dating back to 1172, although the present castle is a much more recent structure. The Long Gallery with its vividly painted ceiling and extensive portrait collection of Butler family members over the centuries is quite remarkable. In summer the castle is open from 10 am to 7 pm and entry is IR£1 (children 40p). Hours are shorter for the rest of the year and in winter it is closed on Monday.

St Canice's Cathedral At the other end of High St/Parliament St is Irishtown, where St Canice's Cathedral dates from 1251 and has some remarkable tombs and monuments. You can ascend the round tower in the church grounds for 50p (children 30p).

Other Attractions On Parliament St, **Rothe House** is a fine old merchant's house dating from 1594. From April to October it's open from 10.30 am to 5 pm Monday to Saturday, and 3 to 5 pm on Sunday. For the rest of the year it only opens from 3 to 5 pm on Saturday and Sunday. Entry is IR£1 (students 60p, children 40p).

The **Smithwick Brewery,** on Parliament St also, runs tours Monday to Friday at 3 pm from June to September. At other times of year phone ☎ 056-21014 for details. Kilkenny has many other interesting old buildings including the Black Abbey of 1225 and the Shee Alms House of 1582. Walking tours of the town leave from the tourist office several times daily and cost IR£2.50 (students IR£2, children 60p).

Places to Stay

The *Kilkenny Tourist Hostel* (☎ 056- 63541) at 35 Parliament St is very central and has dorm beds at IR£5 plus 50p for sheets. There's an *An Óige Hostel* (☎ 056-67674) at Foulksrath, 13 km north.

In town there are plenty of B&Bs. You'll find *Mrs Dempsey* (☎ 056-21954) and Mrs O'Connell's *St Mary's* (☎ 056-22091) side by side on James St, very close to the centre; they charge IR£13 for a single or IR£12 each in a larger room. On Dean St beside St Canice's Cathedral is Mrs Heffernan's *Kilmore* (☎ 056-64040) where rooms are IR£16/24 for a single/double, or IR£20/30 with attached bathroom. A few doors down is Mrs Brennan's *Bregagh* (☎ 056-22315) with similar prices.

During summer you can camp behind *Mrs Murphy's* at 25 Upper Patrick St for IR£2.50 per person, but the nearest official camp site is the *Nore Valley Park* (☎ 056-27229) about 10 km out of town at Bennettsbridge. Nightly cost there is IR£3 or IR£4 for a small tent.

Places to Eat

On St Kieran St, *Kyteler's Inn*, named after Kilkenny's famous witch, is modern inside and does great hot French bread sandwiches for IR£1.50. On John St, just across the river from the castle, *Flannery's Hotel* is popular for pub food.

Across the road from the castle, the restaurant upstairs in the *Kilkenny Design Centre* (open from 9 am to 5 pm daily) is good for lunch. During the summer the restaurant in the *Kilkenny Castle Kitchen* is another good place for lunch or for delicious home-made scones. It's open from 10 am to 7 pm and you don't have to pay the castle admission charge.

There's a batch of Italian-Irish restaurants at the cathedral end of Parliament St. The *Italian Connection* at No 38 is good value with pizzas and pastas at IR£4 to IR£5.50. Across the road, *Ristorante Melfa* has a similar menu.

Entertainment

At the castle end of High St, *Caisleán uí Cuain* claims to be 'the music pub' in town; it's stylishly old-fashioned and very popular. North of the river on John St there's often music at *Peig's Bar*, while the *Kilford Arms* and *Shems* are other popular pubs along this street. The *Marble City Bar* and the *Metropole* are both on High St, *Daniel Bollard* is on St Kieran St just before the junction with High St. Farther along, High St becomes Parliament St and there's often music at the *Pump House*.

Getting Around

Kilkenny Rent-a-Bike (☎ 056-65409) is at the rear of Avonmore House on Patrick St near the castle end of High St, and has bikes at IR£5 a day. Raleigh Rent-a-Bike centres in Kilkenny are J J Wall at 88 Maudlin St and the Raleigh Cycle Centre at 5 John St.

AROUND KILKENNY

Jerpoint Abbey

Dating from the 12th century, Ireland's finest Cistercian monastery ruins are just south of Thomastown, about 20 km south of Kilkenny. The fragments of the monastery's cloister are particularly notable and there are some fine stone carvings on the church walls and tombs. Entry is 80p (children 55p) and in summer it's open from 9.30 am to 6.30 pm. Winter hours are shorter.

Just north of Thomastown is the small village of **Kilfane** where a small ruined church, well hidden away but signposted, houses the remarkable stone effigy of the *Cantwell Fada* or 'long man', a very tall and thin knight in chainmail armour.

Ahenny

Farther south, almost at Carrick-on-Suir, the graveyard in the small village of Ahenny has two unusual high crosses.

Dunmore Caves

Ancient records related that in 928 AD raiding Vikings killed 1000 people in a cave. Excavations in the caves at Dunmore in 1973 found the remains of at least 44 people and a number of coins, mostly dating from the 920s, none from any later date. It's theorised that the coins were dropped by the Vikings while engaged in the slaughter. Did the Vikings have holes in their pockets? No, pockets had not yet been invented and coins were often carried in your armpits, secured to the hair with wax!

Entry to the caves is IR£1 (children 40p) and it's open from 10 am to 6.30 pm daily in summer. For the rest of the year hours are shorter and it's closed on Monday. In winter it only opens on weekends. The caves are 10 km north of Kilkenny.

The West Coast

KILLARNEY

By the time you reach Killarney you will have seen plenty of heavily touristed Irish towns, but this is the Numero Uno. There are lots of easy escapes if you want to explore the delights of Kerry and avoid the excesses, but Killarney is still more a tourist town than a tourist trap.

Information

Killarney's busy but typically efficient tourist office (☎ 064-31633) is in the Town Hall right in the centre of town. The Four Seasons Laundrette is in the Innisfallen arcade, just a few doors down Main St from the tourist office. Another laundrette lurks behind the Spar Supermarket at the Plunkett St end of College St. The Killarney Bookshop is at 32 Main St.

Things to See

In the Town Killarney's attractions are around the town, not actually in it. **St Mary's Cathedral**, built in 1855, is worth a quick look and the **Transport Museum** has an interesting collection of old cars, bicycles and assorted odds and ends including an 1844 Meteor Stanley Tricycle found in a shop's 'unsold stock' in 1961! The museum is open from 10 am to 8 pm daily in July-

Killarney

0   100   200 m

IRELAND

August, but has shorter hours during the rest of the year. Entry is IR£2.50 (children IR£1).

Knockreer You can walk to the Knockreer Estate, just beyond the cathedral to the west of town. There's fine scenery around Lough Leane, the restored Ross Castle and Innisfallen Island on the lake with its ancient monastery ruins.

Muckross Once you escape the suburbs to the south you can dive into the extensive grounds of the Muckross Estate. Muckross Friary, founded in 1488, had a typically lurid history and was finally put to the torch in 1652. The tombs of the abbey's founder, Kerry chieftains and several noted Gaelic poets are found in the choir.

Muckross House has museum exhibits as well as period-furnished rooms. It's open daily in summer from 9 am to 7 pm, to 5.30 pm in winter. Entry is IR£2 (children IR£1). Continuing east you come to the Meeting of the Waters, Torc Waterfall and finally the road climbs up to Ladies' View, which takes its name from Queen Victoria's ladies in waiting, who apparently liked it.

Places to Stay

Camping Just off Park Rd, the road to Cork, the *Belleville Farm House Hostel* (☎ 064-31482) is on the edge of town but within walking distance of the centre. You can camp in the adjacent field for IR£3 per person.

Hostels Killarney has plenty of hostels but in the summer they're all busy. Newest and one of the biggest is the centrally located *Neptune's Killarney Town Hostel* (☎ 064-35255) just off New St. There are 100 beds, mainly in dorms at IR£6 although there are a couple of private rooms and attached bathroom family rooms at IR£7 per person. This well-equipped hostel has a kitchen area where you can fix your own food, and a free bus which meets arriving buses and trains. *The Súgán* (☎ 064-33104) is also right in the centre on Lewis Rd, by the junction with College St. The nightly cost is IR£5 in this popular small hostel. The *Four Winds*

(☎ 064-33094) is also conveniently central at 43 New St and costs IR£5.50.

Continue beyond the Four Winds and it's about a 15-minute walk to the *Bunrower House Hostel* (☎ 064-33914) on the Ross Rd. It's associated with The Súgán and there's regular free transport between the hostels. The nightly cost is IR£5.

The An Óige *Killarney International Hostel* (☎ 064-31240) is five km west of the centre at Aghadoe House. There's a hostel bus which meets trains from Dublin and Cork. The nightly cost is IR£5.90 in this large (200-plus beds) hostel. The *Fossa Holiday Hostel* (☎ 064-31497) is slightly farther out and costs IR£5 a night.

The *Park Hostel* (☎ 064-32119) is about a km from the railway and bus station on the road to Cork and costs IR£5 a night.

B&Bs Killarney has an awesome number of B&Bs, despite which, finding a room can be difficult in the high season. As usual the answer is to throw yourself upon the tourist office and let them do the looking. Muckross Rd is particularly dense with B&Bs.

Places to Eat

Take care when choosing a restaurant: some places have very ordinary menus at very high prices. For lunch-time sandwiches, try *Grunts Café* on New St or the *Country Kitchen* almost next door. *Dugg's Café* on High St is another possibility, or *Killarney Bakery* across the road.

Near the tourist office on High St, *Stella's* is a straightforward place of the '& chips' variety. Just round the corner on New St, *Caragh* comes out of the same mould. Farther down High St from the tourist office, *Sceilig* has a more up-market menu with pizza, pasta and specials at around IR£4 to IR£5, other dishes at IR£6 to IR£10. A few doors down is *Sheila's*, also at around IR£6 to IR£10.

Up a notch again is the pleasant *Kiwi's Retreat* (closed Sundays) on St Anthony's Place off College St. On Lewis Rd, *The Súgán*, also a popular hostel, has an imaginative menu at IR£5 to IR£9 with some interesting vegetarian dishes. It's closed on Mondays.

Entertainment

Killarney has lots of pubs and even more of them than usual have music although it's often highly tourist oriented. Top of the list in that department would have to be *The Laurels* on Main St – its music pub is actually back behind the main pub, and reached by the side alley. It's *very* touristy with a nightly show in summer from 9.30 to 11 pm and an entry charge of IR£2.50 to IR£3. 'And this is for all the Canadians in the audience,' (or Germans, Scots, Australians, you name it) but it's good-humoured and done well.

Other pubs where there's a good chance of music include *Buckley's Bar* in the Arbetus Hotel on College St; or there's *O'Connor's* on High St, popular with young people who spill out into the side alley on summer nights. *Courtney's*, right across the road on High St, can be good for authentic and enjoyable Irish music. Other pubs to try include *Charlie Foley's* on New St, and *Kiely's Bar*, the *Jug O'Punch*, the *Dunloe Lodge* and the *Tatler Jack Bar*, all on College St.

Getting There & Away

Bus Éireann operates from the railway station. Bus fares include Cork IR£8, Galway IR£13, Kilkenny IR£14 and Limerick IR£9.30.

Getting Around

Bicycles are the ideal way to explore the Killarney area as the sights are somewhat scattered. Additionally, many of them are only accessible by bike or on foot, and the traffic jams on the roads around the town can be horrendous. A number of places hire bikes, typically at around IR£5 a day. They include places in Tuohill's Lane by the tourist office and in Old Market Lane by The Laurels pub. O'Callaghan's on College St is the Raleigh agent. Bikes are also available from some of the hostels.

If you're not on two wheels, Killarney's traditional transport is the horse-drawn jaunting car, complete with a driver known as a *jarvey*.

KENMARE

This pretty little pastel-painted town is a good alternative to Killarney as a base for exploring the Ring of Kerry area. It's still very touristy, but not so big as Killarney. Henry, Main and Shelbourne Sts make a neat triangle defining the town centre. Henry St is almost totally dedicated to tourism, with almost every place a pub, a restaurant or a B&B. The tourist office is on Main St. The Kenmare Bookshop is on Shelbourne St near the Main St corner.

An ancient stone circle is signposted from the park end of Main St, beyond the Henry St junction. You have to pay 50p to walk by somebody's lane to get there.

Places to Stay & Eat

Kenmare Private Hostel (☎ 064-41260) is on Main St, directly opposite the tourist office, or there's the *Fáilte Hostel* (☎ 064-41083) at the junction of Henry and Shelbourne Sts. There's also a place labelled *Private Hostel* with camping space about a km beyond town, on the left side just past the Sneem turn-off. Naturally Kenmare has lots of B&Bs.

For a sandwich or coffee, try the simple *Clifford Café* on Main St, which has an outdoor patio, or *Mickey Ned's* or the *Dunboy Café* on Henry St. There are lots of restaurants like the *Purple Heather Bistro* on Henry St, or the more expensive *An Leath Pingin* on Main St.

Getting Around

If you need a bicycle to ride the Ring of Kerry, Finnegan's at the Fáilte Hostel is a Raleigh Rent-a-Bike agent.

THE RING OF KERRY

The 'Ring of Kerry', the 179-km circuit of the Iveragh Peninsula, is one of Ireland's premier tourist attractions for its stunning views and wonderful scenery. Although it can be 'done' in a day by car or bus, or in three days by bicycle, the more time you spend the more you'll enjoy it.

Getting off the beaten tourist track is also well worthwhile, and the Ballaghbeama Pass cuts across the peninsula's central highlands with some spectacular views and remarkably little traffic. The shorter Ring of Skellig at the end of the peninsula, with fine views of the Skellig islands, is also less touristed.

Anticlockwise is the 'right' way to tackle the ring, but in the high season it's probably worth doing it in the wrong direction in order to avoid the large collection of tourist buses all shuffling round in the same direction from Killarney. You can avoid roads completely by walking the **Kerry Way** which winds through Macgillycuddy's Reeks, past 1041-metre Carrantuohill, the highest mountain in Ireland.

Starting from Killarney, and travelling in the approved anticlockwise direction, highlights of the ring include Killorglin, site of the Puck's Fair on 10-12 August. Glenbeigh offers fine views over Dingle Bay. When the first transatlantic cable reached Ireland at Valentia Island, the town of Cahirciveen was in direct contact with New York, but not with Dublin!

From several ports at this end of the peninsula, boats run to uninhabited **Skellig Michael Island** with its remote monastery ruin. The new **Skellig Experience Centre**, on Valentia Island just across the bridge from ·Portmagee, takes you to the Skellig Island without actually going there. For IR£3 (students IR£2.70, children IR£1.50) you can visit the centre with its displays and interesting audiovisual. For IR£15 (IR£13.50, IR£8) you·can combine the visit with a boat trip which takes you round the islands although it doesn't actually land on them. Noises are being made about completely banning visitors from Skellig Michael.

Beyond the port of Waterville (try the *Villa Maria Hotel/Mick O'Dwyer's* for a bar lunch) is fine old Derrynane House, while a few km farther is the turn inland to **Staigue Fort**. In clear weather the wonderfully situated fort offers sweeping views down to the coast. It's about three km off the main road,

reached by a country lane which gets increasingly narrow as it climbs up to the site. Unfortunately in summer the fort attracts lots of visitors and the road and car park area is the scene for absurd traffic jams!

There are some great beaches and pretty little coves on the stretch from Waterville to Sneem. Sneem is a particularly pretty little picture postcard of a town with a wonderfully rocky river running through the middle of it. It's another good place for a meal or overnight pause on the ring, and the *Village Kitchen* is a pleasant little place for lunch.

Places to Stay

Cycling from hostel to hostel around the ring there's *Hillside House* at Glenbeigh; *Sive Hostel* at Cahirciveen; the *Ring Lyne Hostel*, the *Royal & Pier Hostel* and the An Óige *Valentia Island Hostel* all on Valentia Island; the An Óige *Prior House Hostel* at Ballinskelligs; the *Ring of Kerry Hostel* and *Peter's Place* at Waterville; the *Carrigbeg Hostel* at Caherdaniel; *Willow Hill Farm Hostel* at Sneem; and the An Óige *Black Valley Hostel* in the Macgillycuddy's Reeks. The Black Valley Hostel is a good starting point for walking the Kerry Way or catching the views from the Gap of Dunloe. See the Killarney and Kenmare sections for accommodation in those towns.

THE DINGLE PENINSULA

Less touristed and just as beautiful as the Ring of Kerry, a circuit of the Dingle Peninsula makes a fine substitute. This is the Ireland of *Ryan's Daughter* and is noted for the extraordinary number of ringforts, high crosses and other reminders of ancient history.

Dingle is the main town on the peninsula and has numerous pubs, some good lunch spots (try *Walker's Hole in the Wall Bar* or *An Café Liteártha* with a bookshop in the front) and restaurants noted for their excellent seafood (try *Singing Salmon* by the harbour, or *Greaney's*).

Ferries run to the bleak Blasket Islands, off the tip of the peninsula, from Dunquin. The Dingle Peninsula is nearly as mountainous as the Iveragh Peninsula, and at 953 metres Mt Brandon is the second-highest mountain in Ireland. The Connor Pass which climbs out of Dingle offers spectacular views.

There's an *An Óige Hostel* at Dunquin; *Ballintaggart House Hostel* near Dingle; the *Seacrest Hostel* at Kinard West, Lispole, also near Dingle; the *Tigh-an-Phoist Hostel* at Ballydavid; the *Connor Pass Hostel* at Castlegregory and *Fuchsia Lodge* at Annascaul. As with the Ring of Kerry, bicycles are a fine way to make a circuit of the peninsula. There's a daily bus service between Killarney and Dingle.

LIMERICK

Limerick is an instantly recognisable name, one of the larger cities in Ireland and is becoming a place of interest in its own right, rather than just a convenient crossroads.

Orientation & Information

The main street through town changes name from Patrick St to O'Connell St to O'Connell Ave. The tourist office (☎ 061-317522) is in a new building at Arthurs Quay near the river. There are Speediwash Laundrettes on Ellen St (off Patrick St) and on St Gerard St (off O'Connell Ave).

Things to See

In 1691 Limerick was the site of the final Catholic resistance to the Protestant forces of King William. The riverside **Treaty Stone** marks where the subsequent treaty was signed; soon afterwards the perfidious English reneged on the agreement, a sellout which rankles in Limerick to this day.

Across the river is the 1210 **King John's Castle** and the 1172 **St Mary's Cathedral**. The castle's modern centre has displays and audiovisuals explaining the town and castle's dramatic history, while underground there are fascinating archaeological excavations. The castle is open from 9.30 am to 5.30 pm daily and entry is IR£3 (children IR£1.50).

The **Limerick Museum** is on St John's Square and is open Tuesday to Saturday 10

am to 1 pm and 2.15 to 5 pm. The **Limerick City Gallery of Art** on Pery Square is open Monday to Friday from 10 am to 1 pm and 2 to 6 pm, Saturday just in the morning. The **Hunt Museum** at Plassey House in the University of Limerick has a particularly fine collection. Entry is IR£2 (children 90p)

Places to Stay

The *An Óige Hostel* (☎ 061-31462) is at 1 Pery Square, only a short walk across People's Park from the bus and train station. The nightly cost is IR£5.90. The large independent *Limerick Hostel* (☎ 061-415222) is at Barrington's House on Georges Quay and costs IR£4.90.

There are some cheap B&Bs on Davis St, directly opposite the railway station. *Alexandra* (☎ 061-318472) at 6 Alexandra Terrace, O'Connell Ave, the Cork road, is handily close to the centre and has rooms from IR£15/26. Otherwise the N18 Ennis Rd running out of Limerick to the north is lined with B&Bs and more expensive accommodation for several km.

Places to Eat

For cheap eats, try the modern *Sails Restaurant* in the equally modern Arthurs Quay shopping centre across from the tourist office. Nearby, *Doner Kebabs* on Henry St is open until commendably late at night. *Luigi's* features 15 varieties of burgers and is conveniently located directly opposite the train station on Parnell St. Under the renovated Granary Building on Michael St by Charlotte Quay is *Doc's Bar*, with merely average lunch-time pub food but in a pleasant location.

For a more expensive dinner, the excellent little *Cunningham's Wine Bar* at 3 Ellen St is a shining light. This trendy little place is open Tuesday to Saturday evenings and does good pizzas at IR£4 to IR£7, and some imaginative pasta dishes. Others include *La Piccola Italia* at 55 O'Connell St and *Moll Darby's Restaurant* on Georges Quay near the Limerick Hostel.

Entertainment

The music scene shifts depending on the night but there's often something on at the very popular *Nancy Blake's* on Upper Denmark St. Other good possibilities include the busy *Central Lounge* on Thomas St, *Costello's Tavern* on Dominic St and *South's Pub* at 4 Quinlan St (the short section joining O'Connell Ave and O'Connell St).

Getting There & Away

If you fly to Ireland from the USA, you'll arrive first in Shannon as all flights from North America are required to stop there en route to Dublin. Bus Éireann services operate from the bus and railway station, a short walk south of the centre. There are regular bus connections to Dublin (IR£10), Cork (IR£9), Galway (IR£9.30) and Killarney (IR£9.30) and other centres. By train it costs IR£24 to Dublin. There's a USIT office on O'Connell St.

Getting Around

Buses connect Shannon Airport with the bus and train station for IR£3.40. There are also bus services from Shannon to Dublin. Bicycles can be hired at Emerald Cycles (☎ 061-416983), 1 Patrick St, or at the Bike Shop (☎ 061-315900) on O'Connell Ave.

AROUND LIMERICK

If you're heading south-west from Limerick, pause at Foynes to visit the interesting little **Flying Boat Museum** (entry IR£2), a reminder of Foynes' brief role as the eastern terminus of the first transatlantic airline service. In the 1950s Shannon Airport played an important role as a refuelling stop, when aircraft could not easily cross the Atlantic nonstop.

Just outside Limerick on the N18 road to Ennis is Bunratty with the **Bunratty Castle & Folk Park**, another version of 'Ireland in miniature'. It's open from 9.30 am to 7.30 pm daily in summer and entry is IR£3.60 (students IR£1.70, children IR£1.80). At night Bunratty Castle features 'medieval banquets' where big tourist crowds enjoy Irish songs, corny jokes and truly dreadful

food for IR£28. Phone ☎ 061-360788 as far ahead as possible: these evenings are fun and very popular.

Just east of Ennis, **Knappogue Castle** is open from 9.30 am to 5.30 pm daily and costs IR£2 (children IR£1.20). Nearby is the excellent **Craggaunowen Project** with a restored castle, a ringfort, a crannog (Iron Age lake dwelling) and other interesting reconstructions plus Tim Severin's leather-skinned transatlantic boat, the *Brendan*. It's open from 10 am to 6 pm daily and entry is IR£2.70 (children IR£1.60).

THE BURREN

County Clare's great attraction is the Burren, a harsh and rocky stretch of country which eventually tips precipitously into an often harsh and stormy Atlantic Ocean. Despite its unwelcoming look, the Burren is an area of great interest with many ancient dolmens, ringforts, round towers, high crosses and other reminders of Ireland's long and varied history. There's also some stunning scenery, a good collection of hostels and some of Ireland's best music pubs.

Information

For detailed exploration of The Burren get a copy of Tim Robinson's *The Burren* map. Doolin (see the following section) is a convenient base for exploring the region. The Burren is excellent cycling territory but there are also some good walks.

Doolin

Doolin (Fisherstreet on some maps) is a jumping-off point for boats to Inisheer, the easternmost of the Aran Islands. It's conveniently close to the awesome Cliffs of Moher and renowned for some of the best music pubs in the country. The village comes in three parts: the upper village spread along the road, the compact cluster of the lower village, and the harbour area.

Apart from B&Bs, Doolin also has the *Rainbow Hostel* (☎ 065-74415) at IR£4.50, the *Doolin Hostel* (☎ 065-74006) at IR£5.50 and the *Aille River Hostel* (☎ 065-74260) at

IR£4.50. Down by the harbour you can camp at the *Doolin Caravan & Camping Park*.

McGann's and *O'Connor's* both do good pub food, there's the *Doolin Chipper* next to MacDermott's or the excellent *Bruach na hAille Restaurant* next to McGann's. The *Doolin Café* is a little farther out. Two of the village's three famed music pubs, *McGann's* and *MacDermott's*, are in the upper village, but *O'Connor's Pub* in the lower village is the best known of the three. Note the international collection of police department badges behind the bar.

There are direct buses to Doolin from Limerick and Galway (summer only), making this a good base for exploration of the Burren. See the Aran Islands section for information on ferries to and from the islands. The Aille River and Doolin hostels hire bicycles.

Cliffs of Moher
Eight km south of Doolin are the towering Cliffs of Moher. They're one of the most famous natural features in Ireland, so in season the cars and buses are packed in door to door. Near the car park is O'Brien's Tower, a picturesque lookout point. Walk south or north and the crowds soon disappear. You can walk all the way from Doolin, and at one point a precipitous path leads right down to the base of the cliffs – fine weather only and even then we *do not* recommend it.

Caves, Dolmen & Tombs
The extensive limestone Aillwee Caves are very commercialised, and if you're visiting others in Ireland your life will not be measurably less enriched if you skip them. Entry is IR£2.90 (children IR£1.50).

Heading south from the caves towards Kilfenora, the Gleninsheen passage tomb is right by the road, and just south of that is the huge Poulabrone dolmen, the best known of all the Burren portal dolmens. South again there's a ringfort at Caher Connell.

Kilfenora & Corofin
In Kilfenora, the Burren Display Centre has some exhibits and a video on the Burren,

perhaps not worth the IR£2 (students IR£1.30, children IR£1) entry fee. Behind it is Kilfenora Cathedral with a number of fine old high crosses and some interesting effigies in the ruined building.

The Clare Heritage Centre (adults IR£1.50, children 75p) is a small museum concentrating on the region's often tragic history. The *Corofin Village Hostel* (☎ 065-27683) is right in the centre.

Dunguaire Castle
Just north of the picturesque village of Kinvarra, this small tower house castle is used for 'medieval banquets', a popular tourist attraction in this area. It's worth a visit for the excellent guided tour and the clever way each floor of the castle is set up to reflect a particular period in its history, right down to the last mildly eccentric owner who lived there through the 1960s. Entry is IR£1.80 (children IR£1).

GALWAY
One of Ireland's most enjoyable and energetic cities, Galway has some attractions in its own right and an old-fashioned beach resort nearby, and it's also the jumping-off point for visits to the fascinating Aran Islands.

Orientation & Information
Galway's tightly packed town centre clusters on both sides of the Corrib River. Just south of the river mouth is the historic, but now totally redeveloped, Claddagh area, while slightly farther south-west is the beach resort of Salthill, a popular area for B&Bs.

The tourist office (☎ 091-63081) is just off central Eyre Square. At the height of the season the tourist office is very busy and there can be a delay of an hour or more in making accommodation bookings. There's a branch of the tourist office at the junction of Seapoint Promenade and Upper Salthill Rd at Salthill which is open in June, July and August.

Hawkins House at 14 Churchyard St, right by St Nicholas Collegiate Church, and Sheela na Gig/The Galway Bookshop in the

Cornstore on Middle St are good bookshops. There's also a branch of Eason on Shop St. There's a laundrette on Sea Rd, just off Upper Dominick St on the west side of the river. Others can be found in the centre in the Olde Malte Mall off High St, on Mary St and at Salthill, near the Stella Maris Hostel.

The Eyre Square Centre is a big shopping centre right off Eyre Square by the tourist office. They've cunningly incorporated a reconstructed stretch of the old city wall in this modern centre. Others are Bridge Mills, in an old mill building right by the river, and the Cornstore on Middle St.

Things to See

Galway is a great place to wander, and a copy of the *Medieval Galway* walking guide will point out many curiosities. Right in the centre, the **St Nicholas Collegiate Church** dates from 1320 and has numerous interesting tombs. Across the river, **St Nicholas' Cathedral** is a huge and imposing structure, opened in 1965.

On Shop St, parts of gargoyled **Lynch's Castle**, now a branch of the Allied Irish Banks, date back to the 14th century. Lynch, so the story goes, was a 15th-century mayor of Galway who was so dedicated to upholding justice that when his own son was condemned for murder he personally acted as hangman, since nobody else was willing to do the task. The **Lynch Memorial Window** on Market St tells the tale. Across the road is **Bowling Green**, where James Joyce was a frequent visitor at Nora Barnacle's house.

Little remains of Galway's old city walls, apart from the **Spanish Arch** right by the river. There's a museum in the gateway but it's nothing special. The museum is open from 10 am to 1 pm and 2.15 to 5.15 pm Monday to Saturday.

Follow the pleasant riverside path upriver to the cathedral and the salmon weir. In season you can see salmon leaping the weir, on their way upriver to spawn.

Places to Stay

Camping During summer a blind eye seems to be turned to unofficial camping right by the Corrib River beside the Spanish Arch and farther upstream. Just west of Galway there are several sites on the coast, between Salthill and Barna. They include the *Salthill Caravan & Camping Park* (☎ 091-22479) and *Hunters Silver Strand Caravan & Camping Park* (☎ 091-92452).

Ballyloughane Caravan & Camping Park (☎ 091-55338) is on the Dublin Rd. The *Spiddal Caravan & Camping Park* (☎ 091-83372) is 18 km west of Galway.

Hostels – City Galway has a lot of hostels, despite which it can be hard to find a bed at peak times. *Corrib Villa* (☎ 091-62892) is at 4 Waterside St, near the salmon weir and just north of the centre. The nightly cost is IR£5.90. The glossy new *Wood Quay Hostel* (☎ 091-62618) is well equipped and comfortable and costs IR£6.90. It's also just north of the centre, on Wood Quay by the old Potato Market.

The *Galway City Hostel* (☎ 091-66367) is at 25-27 Lower Dominick St, just across the river from the centre and right on the banks of the Eglington Canal. Beds cost from IR£6.50.

On the other side of the canal is the *Arch View Hostel* (☎ 091-66661), slightly hidden away at the junction of Upper and Lower Dominick Sts, just west of Wolfe Tone Bridge. The nightly cost is IR£6.50. A few steps away on Upper Dominick St is the slightly cheaper *Owen's Hostel.*

Hostels – Salthill Continue north-west from Upper Dominick St through the inevitable name changes (Henry St, St Helens St) to St Mary's Rd and then turn left to find the An Óige *Galway International Youth Hostel* (☎ 091-27411). This summer hostel in St Mary's College is open in July and August and costs IR£8. It's between central Galway and Salthill and on the Salthill bus route.

Salthill is only about 2½ km from the centre, and right on the waterfront promenade the *Grand Holiday Hostel* (☎ 091-21150) has rooms with two or four beds and family rooms, at IR£6 a night. The

IRELAND

Waterside St
Salmon Trap
Waterside St
3
Wood Quay
4
St Vincent's Ave
St Francis Street
To Sligo   To Dublin
Eyre Square
Forster Street
1
2
6
Station Road
Eyre Street
5
Williamsgate St
Eyre Square
8
Eglington Street
7
Eyre Square
Victoria Pl
10
12
Mary Street
13
Eyre Square Centre
9
11
Queen Street
Victoria Road
To Westport
Salmon Weir Bridge
Weir
14
15
City Wall
Smith Street
Abbeygate St Upper
William St
16
To Aran Ferry Pier
17
Kings Gap
Bowling Green
18
Abbeygate St Lower
Dock Rd
19
Shop Street
20
Dock Road
River Corrib
21
22
23
St Augustine Street
24
Corrib Street
25
26
27
Merchants Road
Commercial Road
Nuns Island
Guard St
High Street
Middle Street
28
29
The Cornstore
Nuns Island
Nuns Island Street
30
31
32
34
Mill Street
40
33
35
New Road
William O'Brien Bridge
36
Flood Street
41
37
38
Eglinton
42
Quay Street
39
Dominick St Lower
43
Galway Bay
St Helen's St   Henry Street
Canal
44
45
Raven Terrace
To An Óige Galway International Youth Hostel
47
49
Dominick St Upper
46
48
Fairhill St
Claddagh
Wolfe Tone Bridge
Claddagh Quay
William St West
50
Sea Road
51
52
Grattan Road

Galway

0   50   100 m

To Salthill, Spiddal & Rossaveal

To Salthill

IRELAND

■ PLACES TO STAY		42	Left Bank Café
		45	The Waterfront
3	Wood Quay Hostel	46	Monroe's Tavern
4	Corrib Villa Hostel	47	Taylor's Bar
39	Unofficial Camping	49	The Kebab House
40	St Martin's B&B	50	Galway Shawl Pub
43	Galway City Hostel	51	Crane's Bar
44	Arch View Hostel		
48	Owen's Hostel		OTHER
▼ PLACES TO EAT		6	Kennedy Park
		8	Railway & Bus Station
1	Rabbitt's Bar	10	Tourist Office
2	An Púcán Bar	11	Round the Corner Bicycle Hire
5	MacSwiggan's Pub	12	Launderette
7	Skeffington Arms Pub	13	GPO
9	Sails Café	17	St Nicholas' Cathedral
14	Brannagan's Restaurant	18	Lynch's Castle
15	Cooke's Wine Bar	19	Eason Bookshop
16	Food for Thought Café	20	Augustinian Church
23	Brasserie Restaurant	21	Lynch's Window
26	King's Head Pub	22	St Nicholas Collegiate Church
28	Bewley's Café	24	Nora Barnacle's House
30	Country Basket	25	Hawkins House Bookshop
31	Hungry Grass	27	An Taibhdhearc Theatre
32	Pasta Mista	29	Sheela na Gig/Galway Bookshop
34	Sev'nth Heav'n	33	Druid Theatre
35	Café Nora Crúb	38	Museum & Spanish Arch
36	Fat Freddy's Pizzeria	41	Bridge Mills Shopping Centre
37	Shama Indian Restaurant	52	Launderette

Stella Maris Holiday Hostel (☎ 091-21950) is at 151 Upper Salthill and costs IR£6 or IR£7 per night in two or four bedded rooms.

The *Mary Ryan Hostel* (☎ 091-23303) is at 4 Beechmount Ave, Highfield Park, beyond Salthill to the south of the centre. Phone before you set out as it's about a 20-minute walk from the centre, or a No 2 bus ride from Eyre Square to Taylor Hill Convent. The nightly cost is IR£6 including breakfast.

At Spiddal, about 18 km west of Galway, there's the *Spiddal Village Hostel* (☎ 091-83555).

B&Bs In summer and particularly at peak periods Galway can get very full and you may have to travel some distance to B&Bs in remote suburbs. Salthill and adjacent Knocknacarra and Renmore are good hunting grounds. Upper and Lower Salthill

Rds are packed with places, and you can easily walk into the centre from White-strands Ave in Lower Salthill. There are not so many B&Bs around the town and these are very unlikely to have space in the summer season, but Mrs Sexton's *St Martin's* (☎ 091-68286) at 2 Nuns Island St is delightfully situated backing right on to the river. Costs are from IR£12 per person.

Places to Eat

Galway's choice of restaurants, cafés and pubs is positively overkill compared to many Irish towns. There's a large collection around the river end of Quay St/High St.

Hungry Grass on Upper Cross St has great French bread sub sandwiches from IR£1.50, and lots of other possibilities for less than IR£3. A few doors down, *Country Basket* is an equally appealing lunch spot. *Food for Thought* is another lunch-time sandwich

IRELAND

828 Ireland – The West Coast

possibility with a branch at Abbeygate St Lower, just off Shop St/William St, and another in the tourist office.

There's a *Bewley's Café* in the Cornstore on Middle St, while *Sails*, another popular tea-and-coffee specialist, is in the Eyre Square Centre. Vegetarians can head for the *Sunflower Restaurant* on Quay St, although it also seems to be popular with smokers!

Sev'nth Heav'n is right beside the Druid Theatre on the corner of Courthouse Lane and Flood St and is an excellent place for pasta (around IR£5) and pizza. *Fat Freddy's* on Quay St has a similar menu and likewise is popular. Across the road from Fat Freddy's are the more expensive *Café Nora Crub* and *McDonagh's Fish Shop*.

Other interesting choices include the Indian restaurant *Shama* on Flood St, the *Brasserie* on Middle St, *Cooke's Wine Bar* at 28 Abbeygate Upper and *Brannagan's* a couple of doors down at No 36.

The choice isn't so good on the other side of the river, but the *Left Bank Café* on Dominick St Lower is another good sandwich place, or turn the corner to Upper Dominick St for late-night eats at the *Kebab House*. Out at Salthill there's lots of fast food, pub-style food at the *Galleon Grill*, or there's the restaurant at *Stella Maris*.

Entertainment

There are lots of pubs and lots going on in them. The very popular *Quay's* at the river end of Quay St closed down in 1992 but may reopen. Back from the river on Shop St, the *King's Head* has music most nights in summer. *McSwiggan's* on Eyre St is another busy pub.

There are some slightly glossier pubs around Eyre Square including the popular *Skeffington Arms* ('the Skeff') on the square, *An Púcán Bar* (music most nights) just off the square at 11 Forster St, and *Rabbitt's Bar* at 23 Forster St.

On the west side of the river there are numerous places which feature music. Head for the busy *Monroe's Tavern* on the corner of Upper Dominick and Fairhill Sts, or the *Waterfront* just round the corner on Raven

Terrace. *Taylor's Bar* on Upper Dominick, and the *Galway Shawl* and *Crane's Bar*, both round the corner on Sea Rd, are also worth trying. On Upper Salthill Rd in Salthill, *O'Connor's* is another popular pub with regular live music.

Galway parties with a vengeance at annual events like the late July or early August Galway Arts Festival. There are regular performances at the small Druid Theatre.

Getting There & Away

The railway and bus station is just off Eyre Square in the centre of town. There are four or more Dublin-Galway train services Monday to Saturday, but less on Sunday. Bus Éireann fares include Doolin IR£8, Dublin IR£9, Killarney IR£13, Limerick IR£9.30, Sligo IR£10.50. The Dublin services operate up to five time daily. The USIT travel office is on the university campus.

Getting Around

Round the Corner Bicycle Hire (☎ 091-66606) is on Queen St, just round the corner from the Galway Tourist Office, and at Seapoint, just round the corner from the Salthill Tourist Office, and hires bikes for IR£7 a day.

You can walk to Salthill from the centre but there are regular buses from Eyre Square.

THE ARAN ISLANDS

The bleak, windswept and amazingly atmospheric Aran Islands have become major attractions. This is attributable to the quick and convenient travel connections to the mainland, a plethora of B&B and hostel accommodation, and a veritable armada of mountain bikes waiting to be hired out.

Apart from stunning natural scenery, the islands also have some of the most ancient Christian and pre-Christian remains in Ireland. Inhospitable though the rocky terrain may seem, the islands were settled at a much earlier stage than the mainland, since agriculture was much easier to pursue here than on the densely forested Ireland of the pre-Christian era.

The Irish passion for stone walls is carried

to an absolute fever pitch on the islands, with countless km of stone walls separating off even the most inconsequential little patches of rocky land.

Orientation & Information
There are three major islands in the group. Most visitors head for long (15 km) and narrow (three km at the most) Inishmore, where the land slopes up from the comparatively sheltered northern shores the island, then on the southern side plummets sheer into the often raging turmoil of the Atlantic. Inishmaan and Inisheer are much smaller and less visited. Gaelic is still widely spoken on the islands.

In summer there's a helpful tourist office on the waterfront at Kilronan (Cill Rónáin), the arrival point and major village of Inishmore. You can change money there and at a couple of other places.

J M Synge's *The Aran Islands* is the classic account of life on the islands and is readily available in paperback. For detailed exploration, get a copy of Tim Robinson's *The Aran Islands – a map & guide*. The 1934 film *Man of Aran* (hardworking woman of Aran doesn't rate a title appearance) is regularly shown at the Dance Hall (Halla Rónáin) in Kilronan for IR£2.50.

Although many visitors day trip to the islands, even Inishmore alone is certainly worth a couple of days' exploration. The islands can be very crowded in July and August, a time to avoid.

Things to See
Inishmore has four impressive stone forts of uncertain age, although 2000 years is a good guess. Halfway down the island, semi-circular **Dún Aengus**, perched terrifyingly on the edge of the sheer southern cliff, is the best known. A little beyond Dún Aengus is **Dún Eoghanachta**, while halfway back to Kilronan is **Dún Eochla**, both smaller, perfectly circular ringforts. Directly south of Kilronan and dramatically perched on a promontory is **Dún Dúchathair**.

The ruins of numerous stone churches trace the island's monastic history. The small **St Kieran's** (Teampall Chiaráin), with a high cross in the churchyard, is near Kilronan. Past Kilmurvey are the ruins of the **Seven Churches** (Na Seacht dTeampaill).

On the other islands there are more stone walls, more ruined churches, more ringforts (the magnificent **Dún Conor** on Inishmaan and **Dún Formna** on Inisheer), more *curraghs* (the traditional hide-covered boats) and yet more music pubs.

Places to Stay
The islands have a number of hostels and the usual large collection of B&Bs. The shipping companies will book accommodation for you and often have bargain-priced tickets which include return fare and a night's B&B or hostel accommodation.

In Kilronan the *Aran Islands Hostel* (☎ 099- 61255) is only a few minutes' walk from the pier and has dorm beds at IR£5, breakfast for IR£1.50. It's actually on top of the Joe Mac pub, convenient for a Guinness, but not so good for sleep on party nights. Halfway down the island is the *Mainistir House Hostel* (☎ 099-61159) at IR£6.50 including breakfast. It has a bus which meets incoming boats. Aran Ferries offers special discounts with Aran Islands Hostel, Island Ferries with Mainistir House. Farther down the island the *Dun Aengus Hostel* (☎ 099- 61318) at Kilmurphy costs IR£5.

The numerous B&Bs include the large *Dormer House* (☎ 099-61125) right behind the Joe Mac, with nightly costs of IR£12. *Inishmore Camp Site* (☎ 099-61185) is on the north coast near Kilronan. Elsewhere enquire first before setting up a tent in any old field.

The smaller islands also have B&Bs, and there's a camp site and small hostel on Inisheer.

Places to Eat
In Kilronan there's the *Ould Pier* snack bar, the more restaurant-like *An Tsean Chéibh* and, a little farther from the centre, the excellent *Peig's* snack bar. There's a restaurant in *Dormer House* and a not very good one in the *Bayview B&B*. The fanciest restaurant on

the island is *Dún Aonghasa* but the food is fairly ordinary although there are set meals at IR£8.90 or IR£12.50. Kilronan has a small general store. The *Mainistir Hostel* does excellent vegetarian buffet dinners at 8 pm for IR£5 and non-guests are welcome.

Entertainment

There's music in the Kilronan pubs at night, particularly at *Joe Mac's* or the curiously named *American Bar* or, slightly farther from the harbour, at the *Lucky Star Bar*.

Getting There & Away

Air If speed is important or seasickness a mortal fear, you can fly to the islands with Aer Arann for IR£25 return from Connemara Airport at Inverin near Rossaveal. A connecting bus from Galway costs IR£5.

Sea There are several companies and several routes to the islands. The ferry companies compete fiercely. You'll receive offers of accommodation included, family fares and they all claim impossible speed. They don't like you going with one company and coming back with another, so tickets are mainly on a return basis. There are ferry company desks in the tourist office in Galway. Bicycles usually don't cost extra.

Direct from Galway, Aran Ferries' *Galway Bay* takes about 1½ hours, costs IR£16 return and operates three times daily in summer. The crossing from Rossaveal, 37 km west of Galway, is shorter and cheaper. Also operated by Aran Ferries, the *Aran Flyer* sails from Rossaveal three times a day and claims to take less than 30 minutes to Inishmore. Island Ferries' slightly slower *Aran Seabird* also operates from Rossaveal. The regular adult return fare from Rossaveal is IR£12 and the Galway-Rossaveal bus is IR£3, but there is almost certain to be some sort of special deal worth taking. Car parking at Rossaveal costs IR£1 or IR£2 a day, depending on the car park.

In summer the Island Ferries service from Rossaveal to Inishmore continues on to the smaller islands of Inishman and Inisheer. A service also operates from Doolin to Inisheer

and Inishmore. It's only eight km to Inisheer, taking about 30 minutes and costing IR£7 one-way or IR£13 return.

Inter-island services are not quite so regular but when they do operate in summer the typical inter-island price is IR£6.

Getting Around

Inisheer and Inishmaan are small enough to explore on foot but on larger Inishmore mountain bikes are definitely the way to go. Daily rates are IR£4, but the islands are tough on bikes, so if it's not fairly new, check any bike over carefully before agreeing to rent it. There are a couple of bike hire places at the end of the Kilronan pier and another across from the American Bar. The rocky back roads are definitely mountain bike territory. You can bring your own bike out on the ferries.

There are minibus tours to the main sites for IR£5, usually departing after the arrival of the day-trip hordes on the midday boats. Pony traps are used for local transport around Kilronan.

CONNEMARA

The north-west corner of County Galway is known as Connemara, a bleakly beautiful region where Gaelic is still widely spoken and *poteen*, that well known Irish firewater, is still discreetly brewed. The lack of English signposting can be a little confusing.

Clifden

The port town of Clifden is the main centre in Connemara, and you can stay in *Leo's Hostel* (☎ 095-21429) right by the square for IR£5 a night in the dorms or IR£5.50 a night in private rooms. You can also camp there for IR£3. Right next door is the *Clifden Hostel* (☎ 095-21219). The An Óige *Ben Lettery Hostel* (☎ 095-34636) is 13 km east of Clifden and costs IR£5.50. There's a Galway-Cong-Clifden bus service.

Around Clifden

Several places in Clifden rent bicycles and there's interesting country to explore around the town. Ferries run to Inishbofin Island

(IR£10 return) from Cleggan, about 10 km north-west.

CONG

Drive straight through and this small town would be just another dot on the map, but there's a great deal hidden behind that unremarkable main street. Get a copy of the Heritage Trail brochure from the tourist office in the old court house near the abbey so you can explore the town and discover the fascinating history of the 1123 **Cong Cross**, now residing in the National Museum in Dublin. The locally produced booklets *The Glory of Cong* and *Cong – Walks, Sights, Stories* have even more information on the town.

For John Wayne fans this was the setting for his 1951 movie *The Quiet Man*, and the town also has the evocative ruins of an Augustinian Abbey, originally built in 1120. Note the stone fishing house. The modern Catholic church, in a corner of the abbey site, is a remarkable piece of festering ugliness plonked down with utter disregard for its surroundings.

Cong also has several caves and the remains of an abortive canal-building project to link Lough Mask and Lough Corrib. There are enough interesting sites close to Cong (including a stone ring just beside the road to The Neale) to make a bicycle worth having.

Places to Stay

The *Quiet Man Hostel* (☎ 092-46511) on Abbey St is right in the centre of town and costs IR£5. The same people operate the popular *Cong Hostel* (☎ 092-46089) with nightly costs of IR£5.50. It's two km out of town in Lisloughrey (on the road towards Cross and Galway) and is both an independent hostel and An Óige affiliated. It also has camping for IR£3 per person.

There's also the *Courtyard Hostel* (☎ 092-46203) five km out in Cross. You can camp at the *Hydeout Campsite* a km out of town towards Clonbur.

In and around the town there's a typical collection of B&Bs, or if your American Express gold card will stretch to IR£175, you could try a double at the *Ashford Castle Hotel*. Originally built in 1228, the present fairy-tale castle mainly dates from the 1800s. It's rated as one of the best hotels in Ireland, and prices are lower out of season. If you're not staying there it costs IR£2 (children IR£1) simply to enter the grounds, although sometimes you can just walk in via the village entrance for free.

Places to Eat

The *Rising of the Waters* pub has sandwiches, soup, scones and other straightforward meals. At the other end of the street there's the excellent *Quiet Man Coffee Shop* and *Danagher's Hotel* with a fine old bar, a straightforward eating area and fancier restaurant.

If your credit card didn't stretch to the Ashford Castle, consider unleashing it on *Echoes* on Main St, a restaurant which proves great food can exist in Ireland, but count on IR£50 for two with a bottle of wine.

Getting There & Away

From Monday to Saturday there's at least one daily Bus Éireann connection with Galway (IR£4.80). The service also connects with Clifden.

Getting Around

Hire bicycles from O'Connor's on Main St. It's the combined garage, supermarket, bar and craft shop.

WESTPORT

Westport, in the south of County Mayo, didn't simply acquire its postcard prettiness like so many other small Irish towns. It was designed that way, with the Mall, with the Carrowbeg River running right down the middle of it, is as nice a main street as you could find. There's a tourist office (☎ 098-25711) right on the Mall. There's a laundrette by the clock tower.

Things to See

Just west of town, on the road to Croagh Patrick and Louisburgh, is Westport House, one of the finest stately homes in Ireland. The present house dates from 1730 but commercialisation is taken to the hilt. Name a tacky method of pursuing tourist expenditure and they'll do it, from a hokey 'dungeon' to cheap tourist souvenirs. Entry to the house is a pricey IR£4.50 (children IR£2); but if you're planning to make a day of it and visit the zoo, boat on the lake and picnic in the park, the cost only jumps to IR£5 (IR£2.25), and family tickets are available. It's open from 10.30 am to 6 pm in July-August, shorter hours the rest of the year.

Westport's other major attraction is Croagh Patrick, towering to the west of the town. It was from the top of this mountain that St Patrick performed his snake expulsion act – Ireland has been snake-free ever since. Climbing the 765-metre peak is a holy feat for thousands of pilgrims on the last Sunday of July. The really enthusiastic make the rocky ascent barefoot. If the weather's clear, the two-hour climb (one, if you're in a great hurry) gives fine views at any time of year.

Places to Stay

The new and well equipped *Old Mill Hostel* (☎ 098-27045) is right in the centre on James St and costs IR£5 a night. The equally modern and practical *Club Atlantic* (☎ 098-26644) is on Altamount St across from the railway station. This is another hostel which operates both as an independent and with An Óige affiliation. Nightly cost ranges from IR£5.90 for a dorm bed to IR£7.90 per person in a twin with attached bathroom.

Westport hostels also include the *Granary* (☎ 098-25903) on the Quay, 1½ km from the centre, just before the Westport House entrance. Nightly cost is IR£4.50.

The tourist office will book rooms in the town's plentiful supply of B&Bs.

Places to Eat

Eating places down Bridge St include *Gavin's* for sandwiches and the fancier *Crockery Pot* and *McCormack's*. Round the corner on High St is the excellent *Continental Café* with good pitta bread sandwiches,

soup and cakes. For evening meals, *Café Circe* and *The West* are at opposite ends of Bridge St.

Entertainment

Good music pubs include *Matt Molloy's* on Bridge St, which is actually owned by Matt Molloy of the Chieftains. Or head for *Hoban's* on the Octagon or *McGing's* on High St.

Getting There & Away

There are railway connections with Dublin via Athlone and a variety of bus connections including with Galway.

Getting Around

Bicycles can be hired from the Club Atlantic Hostel or from Breheny Bike Hire on Castlebar St just north of the Mall.

ACHILL ISLAND

Joined to the mainland by a bridge, remote Achill Island combines views, moorland and mountains in one handy package. You can stay at the *Wayfarer Hostel* (☎ 098-43266) in Keel or at *Valley House* (☎ 098-47204) in the Valley.

The North-West

County Sligo and County Donegal make up the north-west, an area of the 'south' which extends farther north than anywhere in the 'north'! The region combines scenery equal of better known regions of Ireland and has sufficient distance from Dublin to deter the worst of the crowds. Perhaps because of this, it's very popular with cyclists.

SLIGO

W B Yeats more or less annexed County Sligo's landscape and there are plentiful reminders of his presence. He was buried at Drumcliff, about seven km north of Sligo and in the shadow of Benbulben Mountain. The tourist office (☎ 071-61201) is on Temple St, just south of the centre. Pam's

Laundrette is in Johnston Court, off O'Connell St. The Washeteria is nearby on Harmony Hill.

Things to See
Sligo town has a **Yeats museum** and a ruined **Dominican Abbey** dating from around 1252, but the two major attractions are a couple of km out of town.

Carrowmore is the site of a megalithic cemetery with a varied assortment of over 60 stone rings, passage tombs and other Stone Age remains. It's the largest Stone Age cemetery in Europe and is open from 9.30 am to 6.30 pm in summer; entry is 80p (children 30p).

A couple of km north-west of Carrowmore is the hilltop cairn grave of **Knocknarea**. About 1000 years younger than Carrowmore (which still makes it quite a venerable age), the huge cairn is popularly suggested to be the grave of the legendary Queen Maeve. Several trails lead to the 20-metre-high bump on top of the hill. The most straightforward trail takes less than a half-hour from the car park on the south-east side of the hill.

Places to Stay
On Pearse Rd the excellent *Eden Hill Holiday Hostel* (☎ 071-43204) is about a 10-minute walk south from the centre on the Dublin road. The nightly cost is IR£5.90. Just north of the town centre on Markievicz Rd, the *White House Hostel* (☎ 071-45160) costs IR£5 per night including breakfast, and has bicycles to rent. The smaller *Yeats County Hostel* (☎ 071-60241) is just west of the centre, opposite the railway station at 12 Lord Edward St, and costs IR£5.

B&Bs can be found all around town including a couple on Temple St just along from the tourist office. *Renaté Central House* (☎ 071-62014) on Upper John St is a traditional B&B costing from IR£16/24.

Places to Eat
Sligo has a couple of *4 Lanterns* and an *Abrakebabra* fast-food outlet in the centre. The *Ritz Restaurant* on O'Connell St is a big place, good for lunch or for tea or coffee and scones at any time. Also on O'Connell St is *Beezies*, a big, old-fashioned place with a very standard Irish menu of almost anything with chips. Round the corner on Grattan St, the popular *Gulliver's* has a similar menu which also features pizza at IR£3.50 to IR£5.

Entertainment
Sligo has the usual phenomenal number of pubs, many of which have music at night, particularly the deservedly popular *D McLynn's* on Old Market St just south of the Courthouse. *TD's* on Hughes Bridge St (the Donegal Rd) has bands most nights. *Hennigan's* on Wine St, *Shoot the Crow* on Castle St at Market Square, and *Feehily's* on the corner of Bridge and Stephen's Sts are other very popular small pubs. *Hargadon Bros* on O'Connell St doesn't have music, but this ancient-looking place is almost a living museum where you can become part of the display.

Getting There & Away
Bus Éireann has three services a day to and from Dublin. There's also a Galway-Sligo-Derry service and other connections. Buses operate from the railway station which is just to the west of the centre.

DONEGAL
Donegal town is not the major centre in County Donegal but it's a pleasant and very popular little place. County Donegal is virtually separated from the rest of the republic by the westward projection of County Fermanagh in Northern Ireland, and it's worth making your way to or from Donegal via Enniskillen and Lough Erne in the north. The triangular Diamond is the centre of Donegal and it's often traffic-choked in summer. Right by the river, mere steps from the Diamond, is the tourist office.

Donegal is principally a jumping-off point for the rest of the county, but the tourist office sells *A Signposted Walking Tour of Donegal Town* guide, and O'Donnell's Castle is worth a look.

IRELAND

Places to Stay

Peter Feely's (☎ 073-22030) is on the Killybegs Rd just across the river from the centre. The nightly cost is IR£5 in this small hostel. Keep going in the same direction and then turn off to the An Óige *Ball Hill Hostel* (☎ 073-21174) in Ball Hill. It's five km out near the bay and has beds at IR£5.50. The cosy *Bosco House & Hostel* (☎ 073-35382) is seven km from Donegal along the Killybegs Rd in Mount Charles. It costs IR£5 and also has a good cafés.

There are plenty of B&Bs within walking distance of the centre, including some right across from the tourist office. *Drumcliffe House* (☎ 073-21200) on the Killybegs Rd is a big, pleasant, old place from IR£17/24.

Places to Eat

There are at least half a dozen places to eat within 100 metres or so of the busy Diamond, quite apart from supermarkets and fast fooderies. The *Atlantic Café*, the *Abbey Hotel* and the slightly fancier *Olde Castle Restaurant* all feature an absolutely standard menu. The Chinese *Midnight Haunt* has surprisingly good Chinese food with main courses at around IR£5 to IR£7.

Numerous pubs can also be found within a stone's throw of the Diamond. *McDyre's Star Bar* is a bit of a yuppie hang-out but often has live music.

Getting Around

The Bike Shop, a couple of doors from the Peter Feely Hostel on Waterloo Place, has bikes for IR£7 a day.

AROUND COUNTY DONEGAL

County Donegal matches anywhere else in Ireland for bleakness, dramatic cliffs and hectares of peat bogs. It can be great if the weather isn't equally bleak and dramatic. West of Donegal town is the hill of Slieve League which drops over 300 metres straight into the sea. You can drive to the cliff edge, but after turning off the Donegal-Killybegs-Glencolumbkille road at Carrick towards Bunglass, continue beyond the narrow track signposted Slieve League to the one sign-

posted Bunglass. Walkers can start from Teelin and walk in a day via Bunglass and the somewhat terrifying One Man's Path to Malinbeg, near Glencolumbkille. The *Hollybush Hostel* (☎ 073-31118) is in Killybegs, the *Derrylahan Hostel* (☎ 073-38079) is between Kilcar and Carrick.

Continue beyond Carrick to Glencolumbkille, where there's a Folk Village open in summer from 10 am to 7 pm Monday to Saturday, noon to 7 pm on Sunday. There's a IR£1 charge (children 50p) for the hourly tour of the site's buildings and for entry to the museum. The café in the complex is good. The *Dooey Hostel* (☎ 073-30130) is about 1½ km beyond the village and offers everything from camping space to private rooms. Buses from Donegal go via Killybegs to Glencolumbkille, from where you can take the scenic road via the Glengesh Pass to Ardara.

In the north of the county, Letterkenny is the county town and is a bustling place which has grown considerably since Derry was effectively cut off from its hinterland by the partition of Ireland. The north-west coast of the county has surfing beaches.

North of Dublin

If you head north from Dublin along the coast, you pass through the counties of Dublin, Meath and Louth before you cross the border into County Down in the north. The main area of interest is around the town of Drogheda where you will find interesting sites dating right back to Celtic times, including the finest passage tomb in the country. Other attractions include Trim with its huge ruined castle, the monastic site of Kells and the ancient Celtic site of Tara. Inland are the less frequented counties of Westmeath, Longford and, farther north, Monaghan and Cavan.

DROGHEDA

Straddling the River Boyne, the interesting little town of Drogheda boasts St Peter's where, in a glass case on the left side of the church, you can see the head of St Oliver Plunkett, executed by the perfidious English in 1681. Lawrence Gate is the finest surviving portion of the city walls, while across the river there are some interesting displays in the Millmount Museum and fine views from the Martello Tower on the museum site.

The museum is open from 2 to 6 pm Tuesday to Sunday in summer and entry is 50p (children 20p).

AROUND DROGHEDA

There are numerous historic markers along the **Boyne Valley**, sites of the Battle of the Boyne, the epic struggle between the forces of the Catholic King James and the Protestant King William of Orange. The defeat of the Catholic forces was to have long-term and tragic consequences for Ireland. Despite their importance, the sites are of limited interest unless you're a student of Irish history, but the fertile valley has other very worthwhile attractions.

Newgrange

The finest Celtic passage tomb in Ireland is a huge flattened mound near the Boyne about 10 km west of Drogheda. It's believed to date from around 4000 to 3000 BC, predating the pyramids of Egypt. The site was extensively restored in the 1970s and you can walk down the narrow passage to the tomb chamber about a third of the way into the colossal mound. At dawn on the mornings of the winter solstice, the rising sun's rays shine directly down the long passage and illuminate the tomb chamber for about 15 minutes.

The site is open from 10 am to 7 pm during the summer months, but for shorter hours during the winter. Entry is IR£1.50 (children 60p) and includes a very good guided tour.

Mellifont Abbey & Monasterboice

Mellifont Abbey, about 10 km north-west of Drogheda, was Ireland's original Cistercian monastery and in its prime was the most magnificent and important centre of this monastic sect. Entry is 80p (children 30p)

and the grounds are open from 10 am to 6 pm during the summer months.

Just off the N1 road, about 10 km north of Drogheda, is Monasterboice with an intriguing little enclosure containing a cemetery, two ancient, though unimportant, church ruins, one of the finest round towers in Ireland and two of the best high crosses.

INLAND
Trim

Few visitors pause here to inspect the ruins of Ireland's largest Anglo-Norman castle, a sprawling construction with a huge keep. There are other interesting ruins around this pleasant little town, and the summer tourist office, right next to the castle entrance, sells a handy little *Trim Tourist Trail* walking tour booklet.

Kells

Almost every visitor to Ireland pays homage to the Book of Kells in Dublin's Trinity College, but far fewer pause to see where it came from in the town of Kells. Little remains of the ancient monastic site but there are some fine high crosses, a 1000-year-old round tower, the perhaps equally ancient St Columba's Oratory and an interesting little exhibit in the gallery of the church.

Tara

Tara, near the Dublin-Navan N3 road, was already a place of legend 1000 years ago when it was held to be the palace and fort of the original High Kings of Ireland. Only mounds and depressions in the grass mark where the Iron Age hill fort and surrounding ringforts once stood.

Northern Ireland

Two decades of bad publicity have resulted in Northern Ireland being far less visited than the Republic of Ireland. In actual fact, and despite the sometimes oppressive military presence, drunken or erratic Irish drivers are probably the biggest danger when visiting

Ireland, north or south. The accent is distinctly different (and less charming) but otherwise the changes from crossing the border are insignificant. The northern Irish are certainly no less friendly than their brethren to the south.

The rewards of a foray to the north, however, are considerable – the Antrim Coast Road is a truly stunning stretch of coastline, there are some fascinating early Christian remains around Lough Erne, and Derry has one of the best preserved old city walls in Europe. Nor should 'the troubles' be ignored – the wall murals in Belfast and Derry, the black taxis and the military roadblocks are as much a part of Ireland as green fields and noisy pubs.

BELFAST

Without the well-publicised troubles, the capital of Northern Ireland would simply be a big industrial city – nicely situated but past its prime. The strife which has torn Belfast since the late 1960s gives it quite another edge, although in recent years it has been comparatively peaceful. When your only view of the city has been through the media's lens it can be surprising to find it's actually quite a busy, bustling and prosperous place with more glossy shopping centres and shiny new cars than Dublin. Black-taxi rides through the strictly divided working-class areas in West Belfast will quickly show you the flip side of the coin.

Orientation & Information

The city centre is a compact area with the imposing City Hall as a convenient central landmark. Great Victoria St runs south from the centre towards Queen's University, the Botanic Gardens and the Ulster Museum, an area known as the Golden Mile. To the east of the city, Samson and Goliath, the giant cranes at the Harland & Wolff shipyards, are a visible landmark across the Lagan River. The good ship *Titanic* was built there. West of the centre the Westlink Motorway divides the city from 'the wrong side of the tracks'. The (Protestant) Shankill Rd and the (Catholic) Falls Rd run west from there with a virtual no-man's-land separating the two roads.

The tourist office (☎ 0232-246609) is at 59 North St and is open Monday to Friday from 9 am to 5.15 pm. The Irish Tourist Board (☎ 0232-327888) is at 53 Castle St. The main post office is on Castle Place, between the two. The Youth Hostel Association of Northern Ireland (☎ 0232-324733) is at 56 Bradbury Place.

Bookshops include Waterstone's on Royal Ave, Dillon's on Fountain St, Eason on Ann St and the Queen's University Bookshop opposite the university on University Rd. American Express is in Hamilton Travel on College St. Due to security concerns, there are no left-luggage facilities at Belfast train and bus stations. In the university area there are laundrettes at 46 and 120 Agincourt St and at 160 Lisburn Rd.

Things to See

Around the City The industrial revolution transformed Belfast, and that rapid rise to muck and brass prosperity shows to this day. The majestic **City Hall**, fronted by a not-amused Queen Vic, is still the symbol of modern Belfast. Not far away, hubby Prince Albert also makes a Belfast appearance with his Pisa-like leaning **clock tower**.

Other reminders of the Victorian era can be found in the narrow alleys known as the Entries off Ann and High Sts, in the wonderful old **Grand Opera House** and in the museum-like **Crown Liquor Saloon**.

Museums & Gardens The **Ulster Museum** is in the poorly kept Botanic Gardens near the university and has excellent displays on Northern Ireland and Belfast plus regular special exhibits. Items from the Spanish Armada wreck of the *Girona* (see the Dunluce Castle section) are a highlight. Entry is free and it's open from 10 am to 5 pm Monday to Friday, from 1 pm Saturday and from 2 pm Sunday. Bus No 69 or 71 will get you there.

Belfast has a **zoo** on the Antrim Rd on the slopes of Cave Hill. It's open from 10 am to

IRELAND

Belfast

0 100 200 m

■ PLACES TO STAY

32 Helga Lodge
34 Botanic Lodge Guesthouse
37 Queen Mary's Hall YWCA
40 Wellesley Hall YWCA
41 Camera Guesthouse
44 Liserin Guesthouse
45 Eglantine Guesthouse

▼ PLACES TO EAT

4   White's Tavern
5   Bewley's Café
12 Morning Star Pub
19 Crown Liquor Saloon
20 The Beaten Docket
21 The Elbow
22 La Belle Epoque
23 Lacey's Restaurant
24 Harvey's
25 Salvo's
26 Jenny's Coffee Shop
27 Chez Delbart (Frogities)
28 Lavery's
31 Bluebell Café
33 Maharaja Restaurant
35 Villa Italia
36 Bob Cratchit's
38 Student's Union Cafeteria
42 The Botanic
43 The Eglantine Inn

OTHER

1   Shankill Rd Black Taxis
2   Albert Memorial Clocktower
3   Northern Ireland Tourist Board
6   Waterstone's Bookshop
7   GPO
8   Irish Tourist Board
9   Falls Rd Black Taxis
10 Aer Lingus
11 Eason Bookshop
13 British Airways
14 USIT/Belfast Student
    Travel Office
15 American Express
16 Dillon's Bookshop
17 Railway Office
18 Grand Opera House
29 Youth Hostel Office Northern
    Ireland YHA
30 Arts Theatre
39 Queen's University Bookshop

5 pm in summer and entry is £3 (children £1.60).

Falls & Shankill Rds The Catholic Falls Rd and the Protestant Shankill Rd have been the battlefronts for 'the troubles', and apart from the occasional bright flash of a wall mural they're still grey and rather dismal places. The ideologically sound way to visit these sectarian zones is by black taxi, recycled London cabs which run a bus-like service up and down their respective roads from terminals in the city.

Ulster Folk & Transport Museum Belfast's biggest tourist attraction is 11 km (seven miles) from the centre beside the A2 Bangor road. The fine collection of old buildings ranges from city terrace houses to thatched farm cottages. Oddities include the Bleach Green Tower, a stone sentry box where a guard would keep watch over linen laid out to bleach. From County Donegal, the displayed tiny byre dwelling sheltered a farming family and their animals. A bridge crosses the A2 to the Transport Museum where you can see a varied collection of Ulster-related transport including the weird SC1 experimental vertical take-off aircraft and, of course, a De Lorean car.

In July-August the museum is open from 10.30 am to 6 pm daily except Sunday when it opens at noon. It still opens daily but the hours are shorter the rest of the year. You can get there on a Route 1 Belfast-Bangor Ulster-bus or on certain Belfast-Bangor trains which stop at Cultra Halt by the museum. Entry is £2.50 (children £1.20) which covers entry to both museums.

Places to Stay
Camping *Belvoir Forest* is just five km (three miles) south of the centre. A Forest Service permit is required to camp here. *Jordanstown Lough Shore Park* (☎ 0232-863133) is 10 km (six miles) north in Newtownabbey and is a more organised camp costing £10 per night, but is mainly intended for caravans.

Hostels The 60-bed *Belfast Youth Hostel* (☎ 0232-647865) is at Ardmore, 11 Saintfield Rd, about four km (2½ miles) south of the centre on the Newcastle road and just inside the inner ring road. Take bus No 38 or 84 from the city centre. The nightly cost is £7.20 at the height of the summer and it's a rather strictly run hostel with curfews and other rules. There are tentative plans to build a new and much larger hostel.

From June to the end of September, *Queen's University Accommodation* (☎ 0232-665938) at 78 Malone Rd offers excellent accommodation possibilities. The rooms are mainly singles and cost £5.40 for UK students, £6.35 for other students and £8.81 for nonstudents. Doubles are £12.69. They often have a take-your-chances price of £4 where you're given the bedding to make your own bed and there's no guarantee that the room has been cleaned. There are cooking and laundry facilities. Rooms may also be available during the one-month vacation at Christmas and at Easter.

There are two YWCAs close to the university; both take either sex. *Queen Mary's Hall* (☎ 0232-240439) is at 70 Fitzwilliam St and has single and shared rooms at £11.50 including breakfast. The other YWCA is *Wellesley House* (☎ 0232-668347) at 3-5 Malone Rd and it costs £12.50 a night, again including breakfast.

B&Bs The tourist office will make bookings at B&Bs. There are many in the university area, with typical prices around £15. This area is conveniently close to the centre, safe and secure and well stocked with restaurants and pubs. Botanic Ave, Malone Rd, Wellington Park and Eglantine Ave are good hunting grounds.

Places to try include the Germanic *Helga Lodge* (☎ 0232-324820) at 7 Cromwell Rd, just off Botanic Ave, which costs £15/29 for singles/doubles. Note the colourful pink frontage and the flowers. Across the road is the *Botanic Lodge Guesthouse* (☎ 0232-327682) at 87 Botanic Ave where rooms are £17/30. Bus No 83, 85 or 86 will get you to these two.

The *Eglantine Guesthouse* (☎ 0232-667585) at 21 Eglantine Ave is £15/28 for singles/doubles. On the same street at No 17 is *Liserin Guesthouse* (☎ 0232-660769), charging £14/26. More expensive places include the well-equipped *Camera Guesthouse* (☎ 0232-660026) at 44 Wellington Park with singles at £16.50 to £27.50, doubles at £31 to £37.50.

Places to Eat

There are plenty of pubs, cafés, sandwich and fast-food places around the centre. There's a branch of the popular Dublin chain *Bewley's Café* in Rosemary St. *White's Tavern* on Winecellar Entry is good for pub lunches, as are several other central city pubs.

Belfast's best eating is found south along the 'Golden Mile'. Here, you'll also find a wide variety of fast food including a *McDonald's*. *Jenny's Coffee Shop* is a pleasant little café-cum-sandwich bar at 81 Dublin Rd. There are a number of bakeries along Botanic Ave, and *Bluebells* is good for a coffee or ice cream. The *Student's Union Cafeteria*, upstairs on University Rd, is OK for lunch-time cheap eats. The *Bookfinders Café* at 47 University Rd is a good little place behind a second-hand bookshop.

There are a number of bright and cheerful Italian places in the area, including *Harvey's*, at 95 Great Victoria St, *Salvos*, nearby at No 119, or *Villa Italia*, at 39 University Rd. *Chez Delbart* (also known as *Frogities*), at 10 Bradbury Place, is very popular. Pricier French cuisine can be sampled in *La Belle Epoque* at 61 Dublin Rd.

Still in the university area the *Maharaja* at 62 Botanic Ave has good Indian food, or in the centre try the *Moghul Restaurant* at 60 Great Victoria St, near the Crown Liquor Saloon and the Europa Hotel.

Entertainment

Belfast has some pubs which are as much museums as drinking places. The wonderful old *Crown Liquor Saloon* opposite the Europa Hotel is a particular example, but there are also places like the *Morning Star* on Pottinger's Entry or *White's Tavern* on Winecellar Entry. Next to the Crown is the much more up-to-date *Beaten Docket*.

In the university area, *Bob Cratchit's* on Lisburn Rd is a trendy, modern pick-up joint. *Lavery's* on Bradbury Place is equally popular though much less trendy. *The Elbow* on Dublin Rd is also worth trying. Farther south, *The Eglantine Inn* and *The Botanic* are popular student hang-outs facing each other across Malone Rd.

Check the *Belfast Telegraph* for pub-music listings. There's often something on at the *Opera House* or at the *Arts Theatre* on Botanic Ave. Concerts from rock to classical take place at the *Ulster Hall* on Bedford St.

Getting There & Away

The USIT/Belfast Student Travel office (☎ 0232-324073) is at 136 Fountain Centre, College St.

Air Flights from some regional airports in Britain arrive at the convenient city airport, but everything else goes to Belfast International Airport at Aldergrove. British Airways (☎ 0345-222111) and British Midland (☎ 0232-325151) are the main operators. See the Getting There & Away section at the beginning of this chapter for airfare details.

Bus Ulsterbus connections to counties Antrim, Down and east Derry operate from the centrally located Oxford St bus station. For everywhere else in Northern Ireland, the Republic, the international airport and the Larne ferries, the equally central Great Victoria St/Glengall St bus station is used. It's right behind the big Europa Hotel. Phone ☎ 0232-320111 for bus information. There are three Belfast-Dublin services daily which take about three hours and cost £10 one-way.

Train Northern Ireland Railways Travel (☎ 0232-230671) is at 28 Wellington Place in the city. Trains to and from Larne operate from the York Rd railway station, directly north of the centre. For all other places, the Central railway station is used and there's a

IRELAND

840 Ireland – Northern Ireland

free (to train passengers) connecting bus every 10 minutes from one station to the other via the city centre. Dublin-Belfast trains run six times a day and take about two hours at a cost of £12.50 one-way. There are half a dozen daily services to Derry, and local services run to Bangor and Portadown.

Ferry See the Getting There & Away section at the beginning of this chapter for more details on the Norse Irish Liverpool-Belfast ferry, the P&O Cairnryan-Larne ferry, the Sealink Stranraer-Larne ferry and the SeaCat Stranraer-Belfast catamaran. In Belfast the dock is reasonably close to the centre, and you can walk, take a taxi or a bus from nearby Great George's St. The ferry service from the Isle of Man docks farther north while the Larne terminal is 30 km (20 miles) north on the Antrim coast. There are trains from Larne to Belfast's York Rd station. Ulsterbus services to and from Belfast's Great Victoria St bus station also connect with the Larne ferries.

Phone numbers in Belfast are Norse Irish ☎ 0232-779191 and SeaCat ☎ 232-312002. Sealink (☎ 0574-273616) and P&O (☎ 0574-274321) both have their offices at Larne Harbour.

Getting Around
To/From the Airport Belfast International Airport is 30 km (20 miles) from the city, and buses connect it with the Oxford St and Great Victoria St/Glengall St bus stations for £3.50. A taxi would cost about £20 but is easy to share. The Belfast City Airport is only six km (four miles) from the centre and you can cross the road from the terminal to the Sydenham Halt railway station.

Local Transport Around the city the standard bus fare is 60p (40p 'short distance fare' in the centre), increasing by zones as you travel farther. An eight-trip ticket costs £4.40. Most local bus services depart from Donegall Square, around the City Hall. Timetables are available from the kiosk on Donegall Square West.

Black taxis operate bus-like services

down the Shankill Rd from North St and down the Falls Rd from Castle St. Fares start from less than 50p. Regular taxis are pricey with a £2 flagfall. If you're driving, be fastidious about where you park. Because of the fear of car bombs, illegally parked cars can expect rough treatment.

Bikeit (☎ 0232-471141) at 4 Belmont Rd is a Raleigh Rent-a-Bike agent. McConvey Cycles (☎ 0232- 238602) at 476 Ormeau Rd, and Coates (☎ 0232-471912) at 108 Grand Parade are other possibilities.

COUNTY DOWN
Giant's Ring & Legananny Dolmen
Just south of the A55 ring road, on the southern side of Belfast, is the **Giant's Ring**, a grassy, 180-metre-diameter circle around a small stone passage tomb. Although its origins are a mystery it's thought to date from 3000 to 2000 BC. Farther south between Castlewellan and Dromore is the **Legananny Dolmen**, one of the finest of these curious three-legged stone constructions in Northern Ireland.

East of Strangford Lough
Bangor is a popular coastal resort 21 km (13 miles) from Belfast and has regular rail connections. The road down the eastern shore of Strangford Lough passes **Mount Stewart**, a wonderfully exotic stately home with a garden noted for its topiary. In summer the gardens are open from noon to 6 pm, the house opens at 1 pm but is closed all Tuesday, the Temple of the Winds opens at 2 pm, closes at 5 pm and is also closed on Tuesday. Entry is £3.30 (children £1.65) to the house, garden and temple.

Farther south are the ruins of **Grey Abbey** which, like Inch Abbey on the other side of the lough and Mellifont Abbey in the republic, is a Cistercian monastery. It dates from 1193. Grey Abbey is open Tuesday to Saturday from 10 am to 7 pm, Sunday 2 to 7 pm, and entry is 50p (children 25p).

Strangford Lough & the Mountains of Mourne
Only the narrow entrance separating Porta-

ferry from Strangford connects Strangford Lough, a favourite with birdwatchers, with the sea. In **Portaferry** the Northern Ireland Aquarium has interesting tanks showing local sea life. It's open from 10.30 am to 5 pm Tuesday to Saturday, and 1 to 6 pm on Sunday. Entry is £1.50 (children 85p). The regular ferry across to Strangford costs 55p per person or £2.30 for a car and driver.

On the west side of the lough **Scrabo Tower** offers great views over the lough and right out to sea. South of the lough is the county's other outstanding natural feature, the **Mountains of Mourne** which, as the song goes, 'run down to the sea'.

Downpatrick & Inch Abbey
West of Strangford Lough, Downpatrick's **Down Cathedral** has gone through the normal Irish cycle of destruction and reconstruction, but is chiefly notable for the large stone slab in its graveyard said to mark the site of the grave of St Patrick himself. In the church, note the enclosed pews, dating from the time when a family literally 'owned' their own row in the church.

Inch Abbey, just north of Downpatrick, is another ruined Cistercian monastery, beautifully situated on the banks of the Quoile River. Its grounds are open at any time.

THE BELFAST-DERRY COAST ROAD
It's easy to spend a couple of days between Belfast and Derry, enjoying the magnificent coastal scenery and historic sites along the coast of Counties Antrim and Derry. **Larne**, just north of Carrickfergus, is the arrival point for ferries from Scotland. You can travel along the coast by the twice daily Ulsterbus Antrim Coaster service which runs from Belfast to Coleraine, just beyond Portstewart. In summer there's an open-top sightseeing bus on the Giant's Causeway-Coleraine stretch.

Carrickfergus
Only 13 km (eight miles) beyond Belfast is Carrickfergus with its fine old Norman castle complete with colourful figures of archers, knights and assorted characters from its

history. Entry is £1.50 (children 75p) and it's open from 10 am to 6 pm Monday to Saturday, and 2 to 6 pm on Sunday.

Glens of Antrim
Between Larne and Ballycastle are the nine Glens of Antrim, picturesque stretches of woodland where streams run down to the sea. Prettily situated Cushendall has been dubbed the 'capital of the glens'. Between Cushenden and Ballycastle, leave the main A2 road for the narrower and more picturesque coastal road and take the turn-off down to beautiful Murlough Bay. The *Cushendall Youth Hostel* (☎ 02667-71344) is about a km north of the village and costs £5.95.

Carrick-a-rede Island
Open from May to September, but closed any time the wind is too high, the 20-metre rope bridge connecting Carrick-a-rede Island to the mainland is a heart-stopper even in the finest weather. The island is the site of a salmon fishery. The car park costs £1.50.

Giant's Causeway
Legends relate that if Finn MacCool had finished the job this would not be a mere pier but a real causeway clear across to Scotland. The bizarre assembly of hexagonal volcanic columns is so artificial-looking it's easy to believe it was a giant's handiwork.

Today it attracts major tourist crowds and boasts a big tourist centre complete with a rather good café, a souvenir shop and an audiovisual show. There are some fine walks along the coast and cliff tops from the causeway. It's eight km (five miles) east along the cliffs to Dunseverick Castle. The car park costs £1.50, the audiovisual is £1 (children 50p).

Dunluce Castle
Abandoned way back in 1641, the ruins of 14th-century Dunluce Castle, dramatically sited overlooking the sea, still bear a hint of historic power. Some of that came from the Spanish armaments conveniently salvaged from the overloaded Spanish ship *Girona*, wrecked just off the coast in 1588 with the

loss of over 1000 crew. The Ulster Museum has interesting exhibits concerning this Spanish Armada shipwreck. Entry to the castle is £1 (children 50p) and it's open from 10 am to 7 pm Tuesday to Saturday, and 2 to 7 pm Sunday. It's between Bushmills and Portrush.

Ballycastle, Portrush & Portstewart

Although the coast itself is the main attraction, there are also several popular resort towns. On the last Monday and Tuesday in August, Ballycastle is the site of the Ould Lammas Fair. Just outside the town are the ruins of Bonamargy Friary. Boats run from Ballycastle to Rathlin Island, just off the coast (population of around 100) for £3 to £5 return.

Between Ballycastle and Portrush is Bushmill's famous whiskey distillery, which has held its licence since 1608. Free tours which include a whiskey sample at the end are operated from 9 am to noon and 1.30 to 3.30 pm on weekdays. Portrush and Portstewart are twin resorts only six km (almost four miles) apart. In May the North-West 200 motorcycle race takes place on a road circuit Portrush-Portstewart-Coleraine and attracts up to 70,000 spectators.

Places to Stay The *Castle Hostel* (☎ 02657-62337) is at 62 Quay Rd in Ballycastle and costs £6 a night. *Whitepark Bay Youth Hostel* (☎ 02657-31745) is at 157 Whitepark Rd, Ballintoy, which is 10 km (just over six miles) west of Ballycastle, and costs £5.95. The *Inverness Hostel* (☎ 0265-833789) is at 4 Victoria Terrace, Atlantic Circle, and costs £4.50 in dorms or £5.50 in private rooms. It has bicycles for hire. There are numerous B&Bs and guesthouses in these resort towns.

Mussenden Temple

The eccentric Bishop of Derry was also the Earl of Bristol, and his fine home at Downhill was built in 1722, burnt down in 1851, rebuilt in 1870 and abandoned after WW II. There are some fine gardens and the ruins of the house, but the major attraction is the curious little Mussenden Temple, perched right on the cliff edge and built by the energetic bishop either to house his library or his mistress, opinions differ! The site is about 20 km (12½ miles) west of Portstewart by road, but much closer as the crow flies.

DERRY

Merely saying the name of the second-largest town of Northern Ireland can be a political statement. Although it's Derry if you're following signs from Dublin, Londonderry if you're driving from Belfast, in practice it's better known as Derry whatever your religion. Doire, the original Irish name, means 'grove of oaks', and the 'London' was appended as a reward for the town's central role in the King William versus King James II struggle. This was the place where 'No surrender' entered the Northern Irish vocabulary.

In 1688 the gates of Derry were slammed shut before the Catholic forces of King James II, and the great Siege of Derry commenced. For 105 days the citizens of Derry withstood bombardment, disease and starvation. By the time a relief ship burst through the boom on the River Foyle and broke the siege, a quarter of the city's 30,000 inhabitants had died. It was not the final victory for the Protestant forces, but the long distraction gave King William time to increase his army's strength and it thus played a central role in his victory at the Battle of the Boyne in 1690.

More recently Derry has been a flashpoint for 'the troubles' when resentment at the long-running and decisively gerrymandered Protestant-dominated council boiled over in the civil rights march of 1968. Attacks on the Catholic Bogside district in 1969 were a major factor in deploying large numbers of British troops, and 'Bloody Sunday' in Derry in 1972 was the definitive clash between the army and Catholic civilians. Although Derry is now a much more peaceful place, there's still a razor-sharp edge to the town's atmosphere.

Orientation & Information

The old centre of Derry is the small walled

city on the west bank of the River Foyle. The Catholic Bogside area is below the walls to the west. Catholic and Protestant areas of Derry are clearly delineated.

The Northern Ireland Tourist Board (☎ 0504-267284) and the Irish Tourist Board (☎ 0504-369501) are together at 8 Bishop St in the old city. The Bookworm, a good local bookshop, is almost next door at No 16-18.

Save your dirty washing for Derry: Duds 'n Suds at 141 Strand Rd is positively the most glamorous laundrette you'll meet anywhere in Europe – it has a pool table, electronic games and snack bar! There's a more conventional laundrette at 147 Spencer Rd, near the railway station on the east bank of the river.

Things to See
Derry may have the finest **city walls** in Europe, but stretches of them are run-down and neglected while other parts are inaccessible or closed because the army uses them. The walls were built between 1613 and 1618.

The fine **Guildhall** was originally built in 1890, rebuilt after a fire in 1908 and bombed by the IRA in 1972. It's just outside the city walls and is noted for its wonderful stained glass windows. **St Columb's Cathedral** dates from 1628 and stands within the walls. The **Foyle Valley Railway Museum** by the bridge is open Tuesday to Saturday 10 am to 4.30 pm, Sunday 2 to 5.30 pm, and entry is £1.25 (children 75p).

Places to Stay
The small *Independent Hostel* (☎ 0504-370011) is at 29 Aberfoyle Terrace, Strand Rd, just north of the centre. There are just 10 beds at £6.50 and it's very anonymous, just a discreet 'H' over the door.

The *Muff Hostel* (☎ 077-84188 in Ireland) is just across the border in Muff, County Donegal. This is only eight km (five miles) from Derry, and Lough Swilly buses run there regularly for £1.10. Nightly cost is IR£5.

In summer you may be able to stay at *Magee University* (☎ 0504-265621) on Northland Rd for £13.75/19.25.

Northland Rd, just north of the centre, has some convenient B&Bs including the slightly officious (but very well run) *Clarence House* (☎ 0504-265342) at No 15 which costs £15/30. A little farther out at No 16 is *Florence House* (☎ 0504-268093) which costs £12/24. Others can be found along the A5 to the south, including some excellent nearby farmhouse accommodation. The helpful tourist office will make bookings.

Places to Eat
There are a couple of *Open Oven* sandwich places in the centre, one just outside the walls, across from the Guildhall. In the pleasant Village Centre, hidden away between Shipquay St and Magazine St, the *Boston Tea Party* is good for snacks or lunch, *Thran Maggies* for dinner as well.

On Victoria St, just across the bridge from the centre, *Brown's* is pleasantly trendy with reasonable food at only moderately expensive prices. Continue on Victoria St – it's the A5 – four km to the big and expensive Bell's Restaurant. Underneath it is *Johnny B's* where good, pub-style food is great value from £4 for main courses.

Entertainment
The *Metro Bar* on Bank St, just inside the walls, is very popular. *Badger's Place*, on the corner of Orchard St and Newmarket St, or the *Castle Bar* and *Dungloe*, both on Waterloo St, are all just outside the walls and worth a look.

Getting There & Away
Eglington Airport has flights from Glasgow and Manchester. The railway station is across the River Foyle from the centre, and a free bus to and from the centre connects with the trains. The bus station is just outside the city walls, beside the Guildhall. Monday to Saturday there are five or six daily buses (£5.20, one hour 40 minutes) and trains (£8, from two hours 20 minutes) between Belfast and Derry. Fewer services operate on Sundays. There are onward connections to Dublin. As well as Ulsterbus there are also

IRELAND

Lough Swilly services from the bus station, which connect to Donegal including Letterkenny for £4.20 one-way. There's a USIT Travel Office on Ferryquay St.

Getting Around

As in Belfast, black taxis operate a bus-like service from the centre to the Bogside.

COUNTY TYRONE

The **Ulster-American Folk Park** at Camphill near Omagh in County Tyrone traces Ulster's numerous connections with the New World. Entry is £2.60 (children £1.30). Also near Omagh is the **Ulster History Park** at Cullion. This display traces the story of Ireland from the Stone Age to the Normans and entry is £1.50 (children £1). East of Omagh are the enigmatic **Beaghmore Stone Circles**, an intriguing Stone Age site near Cookstown.

ENNISKILLEN

Enniskillen is a handy centre for activities on Upper and Lower Lough Erne and the antiquities around them. Enniskillen Castle, in the town, and the mansions of Castlecoole and Florencecourt, outside it, are worth a look.

The town centre is on an island in the waterway connecting the upper and lower loughs. The tourist office (☎ 0365-323110) is near the Lakeland Forum Centre, just south of the town centre. There's a laundrette on the East Bridge St section of the main street.

Places to Stay

The nearest hostel is the *Castle Archdale Hostel* (☎ 03656-28118) 20 km (12½ miles) north of Enniskillen in the Castle Archdale Country Park from where boats run to White Island. The nightly cost is £5.95.

There are no B&Bs right in the centre but plenty on the outskirts, particularly along the A4 Sligo Rd and the A46 up the west shore of Lower Lough Erne. *Willoughby Guest House* (☎ 0365-325275) at 24 Willoughby Rd costs £14/26 and is neat and tidy although there are only baths, no showers. It's just out

of the centre on the Donegal Rd. *Drumcoo House* (☎ 0365-326672) is at 32 Cherryville, Cornagrade Rd, by the roundabout on the road north to Castle Archdale and Omagh. Rooms are £13/23.

Places to Eat

Johnston's Home Bakery on Townhall St, just east of the clock tower in the centre, has good sandwiches, pies and other lunch-time possibilities. *Franco's Pizzeria* on Queen Elizabeth Rd on the north side of town is definitely adventurous – which other restaurant in Ireland would dare to announce on its menu: 'we serve no chips'! Pizzas are £3 to £4.50, pasta dishes £4.50, but there's much more on offer in this very popular restaurant.

The multiple-name main street through town has a number of popular pubs including the resolutely Victorian *William Blake* (Blake's in the Hollow) on Church St, *Crow's Nest* on the High St and *The Vintage* on the Townhall St.

Getting There & Away

There are half a dozen daily Ulsterbus services to Belfast costing £5.20 one-way. It's £2.30 to Omagh, where you change for Londonderry. Express buses also connect with Dublin.

AROUND LOUGH ERNE

There are a number of ancient religious sites on and around Lough Erne, the convoluted stretch of water extending north from Enniskillen. From Enniskillen the MV *Kestrel* operates two-hour tours of the lough including a visit to Devenish Island. It goes three times daily at the height of summer and the cost is £3 (children £1.50).

Boa Island

At the north end of the lough is Boa Island where the Janus figure in Caldragh graveyard could be 2000 years old, one of the oldest stone statues in Ireland. There's just a small sign to the cemetery, about a km from the bridge at the west end of the island, six km (almost four miles) from the east end bridge.

White Island

White Island, close to the east shore of the lough, has the remains of a small 12th-century church containing a line of eight statues thought to date from around the 6th century. Some of them may actually predate the arrival of Christianity in Ireland, but little is known about the origins and purpose of any of these mysteriously mischievous-looking figures.

During the summer a ferry runs across to the island from the Castle Archdale Marina about once an hour from 10 am to 7 pm Tuesday to Saturday, from 2 pm Sunday. The return fare is £2 (children £1) and the crossing takes 10 minutes.

Killadaes

Farther down the lake and right by the road in Killadeas. The church graveyard has another ancient stone statue, known as the Bishop's Stone.

Devenish Island

The most extensive of the ancient sites is Devenish Island. This monastery was sacked by Vikings in 837 AD in just one incident in its colourful history.

There are church and abbey ruins, some fascinating old gravestones, an unusual high cross, an excellent small museum and one of the best round towers in Ireland. The 25-metre-high tower is in perfect condition and you can climb to the top. A ferry runs across to the site from Trory Point landing, about six km (almost four miles) north of Enniskillen. It operates the same hours and for the same fare as the White Island ferry.

Other Attractions

The **Marble Arch Caves** are extensive limestone caverns south of Enniskillen near the border. They're very commercialised and very popular, so it's wise to phone in advance (☎ 036582-8855) and book a tour. The cost is £4 (students £3, children £2) and starts with a boat trip on the river which runs through the caves.

Irvinestown, east of Lough Erne, has the *Hollander Restaurant*, reputedly one of the best restaurants in Northern Ireland.

by Vikings in 837 AD to put one incident in its colourful history.

There are Dublin and abbey ruins, some including old gravestones, an unusual high cross, an excellent small museum and one of the best round towers in Ireland. The 25-metre-high tower is in perfect condition and you can climb to the top. A fairy tale stretches to life one from Tory Point sighting about six km to almost Camerities, north of Enniskillen. It occupies the same house and for the same fare as the White Island ferry.

Other Attractions

The Marble Arch Caves are extensive limestone caverns south of Enniskillen near the border. They are very commercialised and very popular, so it's wise to phone in advance (☎ 01365-348855) and book a tour. The cost is £4 (students £3, children £2) and slate-like a boat trip on the river which runs through the caves.

It is a short way out of Lough Erne, say the Tullahan Restaurant, reputedly one of the best restaurants in Northern Ireland.

White Island

White Island, close to the east shore of the lough, has the remains of a small 12th-century church containing a line of eight statues thought to date from around the 6th century. Some of them may actually predate the arrival of Christianity in Ireland, but little is known about the origins and purpose of any of these mysterious stone figures.

During the summer a ferry runs to the island from the Castle Archdale Marina, once an hour from 10 am to 7 pm Tuesday to Saturday, from 2 pm Sunday. The return fare is £2 (children £1) and the crossing takes 10 minutes.

Killadeas

Farther down the lake and right by the road in Killadeas, the church graveyard has another ancient stone group, known as the Bishop's Stone.

Devenish Island

The most extensive of the ancient sites is Devenish Island. This monastery was sacked

Italy

Since the days of the Grand Tour, travellers to Italy have speculated on the 'fatal spell' of the country. This special charm has been attributed to the women, the art, the history, even the air. What is it that makes Italy so seductive? The Italian writer, Luigi Barzini, had this to say on the question:

It made and still makes unwanted people feel wanted, unimportant people feel important and purposeless people believe that the real way to live intelligently is to have no earnest purpose in life.

This land of vibrant, expressive people has given the world pasta and pizza, da Vinci and Michelangelo, Dante and Machiavelli, Catholicism and a vast array of saints and martyrs, Verdi and Pavarotti, Fellini and Sophia Loren, not to mention the Mafia, a remarkable sense of style and *la dolce vita*. In Italy you can visit Roman ruins, study the art of the Renaissance, stay in tiny medieval hilltowns, go mountaineering in the Alps and Apennines, feel romantic in Venice, participate in traditional festivals and see more beautiful churches than you imagined could exist in one country. Some people come simply to enjoy the food and wine.

Do your research before coming to Italy, but arrive with an open mind and you will find yourself agreeing with Henry James, who wrote on his arrival in Rome: 'At last, for the first time, I live.'

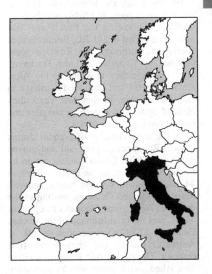

Facts about the Country

HISTORY

Italy's strategic position in the Mediterranean made it a target for colonisers and invaders over thousands of years. But it also gave the Romans an excellent base from which to expand their empire. Italy's history is thus a patchwork of powerful empires and foreign domination, its people have a diverse ethnic background, and, from the fall of the Roman Empire until the Risorgimento (the Italian unification movement) in 1860, the country was never a unified entity.

The traditional date for the founding of Rome by Romulus is 753 BC, but the country was inhabited from 2000 BC, first by the Ligurian and Italic tribes, and from about 900 BC by the mysterious Etruscans, whose origins remain controversial, but who dominated the peninsula between the Arno and Tiber rivers.

After the foundation of Rome, Etruscan civilisation continued to flourish and Etruscan kings, known as the Tarquins, ruled Rome until 509 BC, when the Roman republic was established. By the end of 3rd century BC the Romans had overwhelmed the last Etruscan city.

The new Roman republic, after recovering from the invasion of the Gauls in 390 BC, began its expansion into the south of Italy. The Greeks had colonised this area, which they called Magna Grecia, as early as the 8th century BC, and they had established cities such as Syracuse, which rivalled Athens in power.

By about 265 BC Rome had taken the south from Greece, and Sicily was held by Carthage. Following the First Punic War against Hannibal in 241 BC, Rome claimed Sicily and although the Romans were defeated by Hannibal at Lake Trasimeno after his legendary crossing of the Alps, Rome defeated and destroyed Carthage in 202 BC. Within another few years they claimed Spain and Greece as colonies and had moved into North Africa.

In the first century BC, under Julius Caesar, Rome conquered Gaul and moved into Egypt. After Caesar's assassination by his nephew, Brutus, on the Ides of March, in 44 BC, a power struggle began between Mark Antony and Octavius, leading to the deaths of Antony and Cleopatra in Egypt in 31 BC and the establishment of the Roman Empire in 27 BC. Octavius took the title of Augustus Caesar and became the first emperor. During his rule Roman literature flourished, with great writers including Virgil, Horace and Livy. Augustus was succeeded by Tiberius, Caligula, Claudius and Nero.

By the end of the 3rd century AD, the empire had grown to such an extent that Emperor Diocletian divided it between east and west for administrative purposes. His reign was also noted for the persecution of Christians. His successor, Constantine, declared religious freedom for Christians and moved the seat of the empire to the capital of the Eastern Roman Empire, Byzantium, which he renamed Constantinople. During the 4th century AD, Christianity was declared the official state religion and grew in power and influence; at the same time Rome was under constant threat of barbarian invasion.

By the early 5th century, German tribes had entered Rome, and in 476 the Western Roman Empire ended when the German warrior, Odoacer, deposed the emperor and declared himself ruler of Italy.

While the Eastern Roman Empire contin-ued to exist and even retook part of the country for Byzantium in 553, this was the period of the Dark Ages during which Italy became a battleground of barbarians fighting for control. The south was dominated by the Saracens until the Normans invaded in 1036 and established a kingdom there and in Sicily.

With a view to re-establishing the Western Roman Empire, Pope Leo II crowned Char-lemagne emperor in 800 AD. However, the empire again declined under Charlemagne's successors, culminating in the foundation of the Holy Roman Empire in 962 by the German king Otto I, who also declared himself emperor.

The Middle Ages in Italy were marked by the development of powerful city-states in the north, while in the south the Normans were busily imposing a severe feudal system on their subjects. After the mid-12th century, when Frederick Barbarossa was crowned emperor, conflict between Pope Alexander III and the emperor had reached the point where Italy again became a battleground as cities became either Guelph (supporters of the pope) or Ghibelline (supporters of the emperor). Dante was exiled from Florence during this period, after he sided with the Ghibelline cause. The factional struggles died gradually, but did not prevent a period of great economic, architectural and artistic development. This was the time of Dante, Petrarch and Boccaccio, Giotto, Cimabue and Pisano. The city-states flourished under the rule of powerful families and the papal states were established, even though the French had moved into the country and installed rival popes based in Avignon.

But it was not until the 15th century and the arrival of the Renaissance that Italy redis-covered its former glory. This period was marked by savage intercity wars, internal feuding and French invasions, but the Renaissance, which began in Florence, spread throughout the country, fostering genius of the likes of Brunelleschi, Donatello, Bramante, Botticelli, da Vinci, Masaccio, Lippi, Raphael and, of course, Michelangelo.

By the early 16th century, the Reformation had arrived in Italy, and by 1559 much of the country was under Spanish rule, whose domination lasted until 1713 when, following the War of Spanish Succession, control of Italy passed to the Austrians. The powerful states of the country's north, however, continued to grow in power. It was not until after the invasion of Napoleon in 1796 that a degree of unity was introduced into the country, for the first time since the fall of the Roman Empire. The Congress of Vienna in 1815, which restored power to the nobles and revived the old territorial divisions in Italy, created great discontent among the people and led directly to the Risorgimento.

Under the leadership of Garibaldi, Cavour and Mazzini the unification movement gained momentum until Garibaldi and his Expedition of one Thousand (also known as the Redshirts) took Sicily and Naples in 1860. The Kingdom of Italy was declared in 1861 and Vittorio Emanuele was proclaimed king. Venice was wrested from Austria in 1866 and Rome from the papacy in 1870. However, the new government had great difficulty in achieving actual national unity. As Cavour noted before his death in 1861: 'To harmonise north and south is harder than fighting with Austria or struggling with Rome.'

In the years after WW I, Italy was in turmoil and in 1921 the Fascist Party, formed by Benito Mussolini in 1919, won 35 of the 135 seats in parliament. In October 1921, after a period of considerable unrest and strikes, the king asked Mussolini to form a government, and he became prime minister with only 7% representation in parliament. The Fascists won the 1924 elections, following a campaign marked by violence and intimidation, and by the end of 1925 Mussolini had become head of state, expelled opposition parties from parliament, gained control of the press and trade unions and reduced the voting public by two-thirds. He formed the Rome-Berlin axis with Hitler in 1936 and Italy entered WW II as an ally of Germany in June 1941. After a series of military disasters and the invasion of the Allies in 1943, Mussolini surrendered Italy to the Allies and went into hiding. He was shot, along with his mistress, Clara Petacci, by partisans in April 1945.

In 1946, following a referendum, the constitutional monarchy was abolished and the republic established. In the decades since WW II, Italy's national government has been consistently dominated by the Christian Democrats, usually in coalition with other parties, excluding the Communists. From 1983 to 1986 the Socialists held government, with Bettino Craxi serving as prime minister.

Italy was a founding member of the European Economic Community in 1957 and was seriously disrupted by terrorism in the 1970s, following the appearance of the Red Brigades, who kidnapped and assassinated the Christian Democrat prime minister, Aldo Moro, in 1978. The country enjoyed significant economic growth in the 1980s, although unemployment and inflation rates remain high.

GEOGRAPHY

Italy's boot-shape makes it one of the most recognisable countries in the world. The country, incorporating the islands of Sicily and Sardinia, is bounded by the Adriatic, Ligurian, Tyrrhenian and Ionian seas, which all form part of the Mediterranean Sea. About 75% of the Italian peninsula is mountainous, with the Alps dividing the country from France, Switzerland and Austria, and the Apennines forming a backbone which extends from the Alps into Sicily. There are three active volcanoes: Stromboli (in the Aeolian Islands), Vesuvius (near Naples) and Etna (Sicily). The countryside can be dramatically beautiful, but since Etruscan times, humans have made their mark on the environment. Pollution problems caused by industrial and urban waste exist throughout Italy and most beaches are fouled to some extent, particularly on the Ligurian Coast, in the northern Adriatic (because of algae) and near major cities such as Rome and Naples. However, the western beaches of Sardinia are relatively clean. Air pollution is a problem in the industrialised north.

GOVERNMENT

For administrative purposes Italy is divided into 20 regions which have some degree of autonomy. The regions are then divided into provinces and municipalities.

The country is a parliamentary republic, headed by a president, who appoints the prime minister. The parliament consists of a senate and chamber of deputies, both with equal power. The major parties are the Christian Democrat Party, the Socialist Party and the Communist Party. Although the Communist Party holds considerable power at the municipal and regional level, the Christian Democrats have consistently dominated government at the national level. Italy's electoral system has, however, generally produced unstable coalition governments. Since the declaration of the republic in 1946, there have been 51 governments, each with an average life of one year.

General elections in April 1992 resulted in a major shake-up in the balance of power. The Christian Democrats remained the dominant party, but their share of the vote dropped by just under 5%. A significant feature of the elections was the success of the Northern League, an alliance of regionalist groups to the right of the political spectrum, which won 8.7% of the vote nationwide and more than 20% in Lombardy.

The League's political platform has two fundamental pillars: reaction against corruption in government and against the use of taxes paid by the richer north to support the poorer south. Corruption became an even greater issue after the election, highlighting a political scandal that resulted in the collapse of Milan's municipal government and the arrest of numerous politicians on charges of receiving payoffs in return for favours.

In May 1992, following the elections, Francesco Cossiga announced his resignation, leading to the election of Oscar Luigi Scalfaro as president. Scalfaro, in turn, chose Giuliano Amato, the deputy leader of the Socialist Party, as prime minister.

ECONOMY

Italy has the fifth-largest economy in the world, after enjoying spectacular growth in the 1980s. However, there has been much debate about the ability of the Italian economy to perform efficiently in the context of a unified Europe. It has one of the biggest public sectors in the Western world, also widely known as one of the most inefficient, largely due to the practice of *lottizzazione*, a system of handing out jobs on the basis of political patronage.

Travellers will find that anything to do with banking, telephones and the post office requires considerable patience, particularly in the south. There remains a significant difference between the north and south of Italy, and, though the situation is improving, it is true to say that things generally run more smoothly in the north than in the south. The richest regions are Piedmont, Emilia-Romagna, Lombardy and the poorest are Calabria, Campania and Sicily.

POPULATION & PEOPLE

Foreigners may like to think of Italy as a land of passionate, animated people who gesticulate wildly when speaking, love to eat, drive like maniacs and don't like to work. However, it will take more than a holiday in Italy to understand its vigorous and remarkably diverse inhabitants.

The population of Italy is around 58 million. Overall the people remain fiercely protective of their regional customs, including their dialects and cuisine. Without doubt the country's special charm owes much to its people.

CULTURE

Religious festivals and soccer are the two great passions of the average Italian, followed closely by eating and the traditional August holidays. Normal commerce can be disrupted for an entire day by an important festival or for a few hours by a soccer match. The midday meal is a revered tradition which means that all shops, offices and most institutions close for three to four hours in the afternoon.

In August, particularly during the week around the Feast of the Assumption (August

Regions of Italy

0   150   300 km

- - - = Regional Boundary

AUSTRIA

SWITZERLAND

VALLE
D'AOSTA
• Aosta

TRENTINO-
ALTO
ADIGE
• Trento

FRIULI-
VENEZIA
GIULIA
Trieste •

VENETO
Venice •

LOMBARDY
• Milan

Turin •

PIEDMONT

EMILIA-
ROMAGNA
• Genoa

Bologna •

SLOVENIA

CROATIA

SAN
MARINO

FRANCE

LIGURIAN
SEA

• Florence

TUSCANY

Ancona •

MARCHES

Perugia •

UMBRIA

ADRIATIC
SEA

CORSICA

Pescara •

ABRUZZO

◉ Rome

MOLISE

LAZIO

Campobasso •

CAMPANIA

APULIA

Bari •

TYRRHENIAN
SEA

Naples •

Potenza •

BASILICATA

SARDINIA

Cagliari •

CALABRIA

MEDITERRANEAN
SEA

Catanzaro •

Palermo •

IONIAN
SEA

SICILY

MALTA

TUNISIA

15), known as *ferragosto*, a combination of summer heat and national holidays means that Italians evacuate the cities en masse and head for the hills and beaches. This means that almost *everything* closes down in the big cities during the peak tourist period.

Other than these shared passions, the cultural practices, views and traditions of Italians can vary greatly from region to region. Women should note that light, skimpy clothing which might be acceptable in the north could attract unwanted attention in places such as Sicily and Sardinia. Anyone with bare legs (including men) will find it difficult to get into a church anywhere in Italy.

RELIGION
Some 85% of Italians professed to be Catholic in a census taken in the early 1980s. The remaining 15% included about 500,000 evangelical Protestants and the rest, who professed to have no religion.

LANGUAGE
Although many Italians speak some English, as they study it in school, English is more widely understood in the north, particularly in major centres such as Milan, Florence and Venice, than in the south. Staff at most hotels, *pensioni* and restaurants usually speak a little English, but you will be better received if you at least attempt to communicate in Italian.

Italian is a Romance language which is related to French, Spanish, Portuguese and Romanian. The Romance languages belong to the Indo-European group of languages, which include English. Indeed, as English and Italian share common roots in Latin, you will find many Italian words which you will recognise.

Modern literary Italian began to be developed in the 13th and 14th centuries, predominantly through the works of Dante, Petrarch and Boccaccio, who wrote chiefly in the Florentine dialect. The language drew on its Latin heritage and the many dialects of Italy to develop into the standard Italian of today. Although many and varied dialects are spoken in everyday conversation, standard Italian is the national language of schools, media and literature, and is understood throughout the country.

There are 58 million speakers of Italian in Italy; half a million in Switzerland, where Italian is one of the four official languages; and 1.5 million speakers in France and former Yugoslavia. As a result of migration, Italian is also widely spoken in the USA, Argentina, Brazil and Australia.

Pronunciation
Italian is not difficult to pronounce once you learn a few easy rules. Although some of the more clipped vowels, and stress on double letters, require careful practice for English speakers, it is easy enough to make yourself understood.

Vowels Vowels are generally more clipped than in English.

a	as the second 'a' in 'camera'
e	as the 'ay' in 'day', but without the 'i' sound
i	as in 'see'
o	as in 'dot'
u	as in 'too'

Consonants The pronunciation of many Italian consonants is similar to that of English. The following sounds depend on certain rules:

c	like 'k' before 'a', 'o' and 'u'. Like the 'ch' in 'choose' before 'e' and 'i'
ch	a hard 'k' sound
g	a hard 'g' as in 'get' before 'a', 'o' and 'u'. Before 'e' and 'i', like the 'j' in 'job'
gh	a hard 'g' as in 'get'
gli	as the 'lli' in 'million'
gn	as the 'ny' in 'canyon'
h	always silent
r	a rolled 'rrr' sound
sc	before 'e' and 'i', like the 'sh' in 'sheep'. Before 'h', 'a', 'o' and 'u', a hard sound as in 'school'

ITALY

z   as the 'ts' in 'lights' or as the 'ds' in 'beds'

Note that when 'ci', 'gi' and 'sci' are followed by 'a', 'o' or 'u', unless the accent falls on the 'i', it is not pronounced. Thus the name 'Giovanni' is pronounced 'joh-**vahn**-nee', with no 'i' sound after the 'G'.

Stress Double consonants are pronounced as a longer, often more forceful sound than a single consonant.

Stress often falls on the next to last syllable, as in *spaghetti*. When a word has an accent, the stress is on that syllable, as in *città*, 'city'.

Greetings & Civilities

Hello.	*Buon giorno./Ciao.*
Goodbye.	*Arrivederci./Ciao.*
Yes./No.	*Sì./No.*
Please.	*Per favore./Per piacere.*
Thank you.	*Grazie.*
That's fine./You're welcome.	*Prego.*
Excuse me.	*Mi scusi.*
Sorry. (excuse me, forgive me)	*Mi scusi. Mi perdoni.*
Do you speak English?	*Parla (Parli) inglese?*
Does anyone speak English?	*C'è qualcuno che parla inglese?*
I (don't) understand.	*(Non) Capisco.*
Just a minute.	*Un momento.*
How much is it?	*Quanto costa?*

Signs

Camping Ground	*Campeggio*
Youth Hostel	*Ostello per la Gioventù*
Entrance	*Ingresso/ Entrata*
Exit	*Uscita*
Full/no Vacancies	*Completo*
Guest House	*Pensione*
Hotel	*Albergo*
Information	*Informazione*
No Smoking	*Vietato Fumare*
Open/Closed	*Aperto/Chiuso*
Police	*Polizia/Carabinieri*
Police Station	*Questura*
Telephone	*Telefono*
Toilets	*Gabinetti/Bagni*

Getting Around

What time does ... leave/arrive?	*A che ora parte/arriva ...?*
the boat	*la barca*
the bus	*l'autobus*
the train	*il treno*
first	*il primo*
last	*l'ultimo*
I would like ...	*Vorrei ...*
a one-way ticket	*(un biglietto di) solo andata/ un biglietto semplice*
a return ticket	*(un biglietto di) andata e ritorno*
1st class	*prima classe*
2nd class	*seconda classe*
Where is ...?	*Dov'è ...?*
I want to go to ...	*Voglio andare a ...*
Can you show me (on the map)?	*Me lo puo mostrare (sulla carta/ pianta)?*
far/near	*lontano/vicino*
Go straight ahead.	*Si va (vai) sempre diritto.*
Turn left ...	*Gira a sinistra ...*
Turn right ...	*Gira a destra ...*

Around Town

I'm looking for ...	*Sto cercando ...*
a bank	*un banco*
the church	*la chiesa*
the city centre	*il centro (città)*
the ... embassy	*l'ambasciata di...*
my hotel	*il mio albergo*
the market	*il mercato*
the museum	*il museo*
the post office	*la posta*

a public toilet	*un gabinetto/ bagno pubblico*
the telephone centre	*il centro telefonico/SIP*
the tourist information office	*l'ufficio di turismo/ d'informazione*
beach	*la spiaggia*
bridge	*il ponte*
castle	*il castello*
cathedral	*il duomo/la cattedrale*
church	*la chiesa*
island	*l'isola*
main square	*la piazza principale*
market	*il mercato*
mosque	*la moschea*
old city	*il centro storico*
palace	*il palazzo*
ruins	*le rovine*
sea	*il mare*
square	*la piazza*
tower	*il torre*

Accommodation

Where is ...?	*Dov'è ...?*
a cheap hotel	*un albergo che costa poco*
What is the address?	*Cos'è l'indirizzo?*
Could you write the address, please?	*Può scrivere l'indirizzo, per favore?*
Do you have any rooms available?	*Ha camere libere?/C'è una camera libera?*
I would like ...	*Vorrei ...*
a single room	*una camera singola*
a double room	*una camera matrimoniale/ per due*
a room with a bathroom	*una camera con bagno*
to share a dorm	*un letto in dormitorio*
a bed	*un letto*

How much is it per night/per person?	*Quanto costa per la notte/ciascuno?*
Can I see it?	*Posso vederla?*
Where is the bathroom?	*Dov'è il bagno?*

Food

breakfast	*prima colazione*
lunch	*pranzo/colazione*
dinner	*cena*
I would like the set lunch.	*Vorrei il menu turistico.*
Is service included in the bill?	*È compreso il servizio?*
I am a vegetarian.	*Sono vegetariano/a. Non mangio carne.*

Time & Dates

What time is it?	*Che ora è? Che ore sono?*
today	*oggi*
tomorrow	*domani*
yesterday	*ieri*
in the morning	*di mattina*
in the afternoon	*di pomeriggio*
in the evening	*di sera*
Monday	*lunedì*
Tuesday	*martedì*
Wednesday	*mercoledì*
Thursday	*giovedì*
Friday	*venerdì*
Saturday	*sabato*
Sunday	*domenica*
January	*gennaio*
February	*febbraio*
March	*marzo*
April	*aprile*
May	*maggio*
June	*giugno*
July	*luglio*
August	*agosto*
September	*settembre*
October	*ottobre*
November	*novembre*
December	*dicembre*

ITALY

Numbers

0	*zero*
1	*uno*
2	*due*
3	*tre*
4	*quattro*
5	*cinque*
6	*sei*
7	*sette*
8	*otto*
9	*nove*
10	*dieci*
11	*undici*
12	*dodici*
13	*tredici*
14	*quattordici*
15	*quindici*
16	*sedici*
17	*diciassette*
18	*diciotto*
19	*diciannove*
20	*venti*
21	*ventuno*
22	*ventidue*
30	*trenta*
40	*quaranta*
50	*cinquanta*
60	*sessanta*
70	*settanta*
80	*ottanta*
90	*novanta*
100	*cento*
1000	*mille*
one million	*un milione*

Health

I'm ...	*Sono ...*
diabetic	*diabetico/a*
epileptic	*epilettico/a*
asthmatic	*asmatico/a*
I'm allergic ...	*Sono allergico/a ...*
to antibiotics	*agli antibiotici*
to penicillin	*alla penicillina*
antiseptic	*antisettico*
aspirin	*aspirina*
condoms	*preservativi*
contraceptive	*anticoncezionale*
diarrhoea	*diarrea*

medicine	*medicina*
sunblock cream	*crema solare/latte solare (per protezione)*
tampons	*tamponi*

Emergencies

Help!	*Aiuto!*
Call a doctor!	*Chiama un dottore/un medico!*
Call the police!	*Chiama la polizia!*
Go away!	*Vai via!* (inf) *Mi lasci in pace!*

Facts for the Visitor

VISAS & EMBASSIES

Residents of the USA, Australia, Canada and New Zealand do not need to apply for visas before arriving in Italy. However, at the point of entry to the country, residents of these countries will have their passport stamped with an automatic three-month tourist visa. Theoretically, visitors must go to a *questura* (police headquarters) if they plan to stay at the same address for more than one week to receive a *permesso di soggiorno* – in effect, permission to remain in the country for a nominated period up to the three-month limit. Tourists who are staying in hotels are not required to do this.

It is impossible to extend your visa within Italy and visitors of the nationalities just mentioned must leave the country after three months, even if this means simply crossing a border into France or Switzerland for one day and then re-entering Italy to have their passport restamped.

Foreigners who want to study at a university in Italy must have a student visa, but only Australians and New Zealanders require a visa to study at a language school. This can be obtained from the Italian embassy or consulate in your city, but you must have a letter of acceptance from the university or school you will be attending. This type of visa is renewable within Italy, but you will be required to continue studying and provide proof that you have enough money to support yourself during the period of study. It should be noted that the process to obtain a student visa can take some time.

It is extremely difficult for the nationalities mentioned here to obtain a visa to work in Italy. You must have a promise of a job which is not wanted by an Italian and must apply for the visa in your country of nationality.

The UK is part of the European Community (EC) and Britons are therefore able to travel more freely. After finding a job they must go to the questura with a letter promising employment and can then obtain a work permit for up to two years.

Italian Consulates & Embassies

The following is a selection of Italian diplomatic missions abroad:

Australia
  61-69 Macquarie St, Sydney (☎ 02-247 8442)
  34 Anderson St, South Yarra, Melbourne
  (☎ 03-867 5744)
Canada
  136 Beverley St, Toronto (☎ 416-977 1566)
New Zealand
  34 Grant Rd, Thorndon, Wellington
  (☎ 04-72 9302)
UK
  38 Eton Place, London (☎ 071-235 9371)
USA
  60090 Park Ave, New York (☎ 212-439 8600)
  2590 Webster St, San Francisco
  (☎ 415-931 4925)

Foreign Embassies in Italy

The headquarters of most foreign embassies are in Rome, although there are generally British and US consulates in other major cities. The following addresses and phone numbers are for Rome (the area code is 06):

Australia
  Via Alessandria 215 (☎ 83 27 21)
Austria
  Via Pergolesi 3 (☎ 855 82 41)
Canada
  Via G B de Rossi 27 (☎ 841 53 41)
  Consulate, Via Zara 30 (☎ 440 30 28)

France
  Palazzo Farnese (☎ 68 60 11)
  visas at Via Giulia 251 (☎ 654 21 52)
Germany
  Via Po 25c (☎ 88 47 41)
  Consulate, Via Siacci 2 (☎ 88 47 42 86)
Greece
  Via Mercadante 36 (☎ 855 31 00)
  Consulate, Via Tacchini 6 (☎ 808 20 30)
New Zealand
  Via Zara 28 (☎ 440 29 28)
Spain
  Largo Fontanella Borghese 19 (☎ 687 81 72)
Switzerland
  Via Barnarba Oriani 61 (☎ 808 36 41)
UK
  Via XX Settembre 80a (☎ 482 54 41)
USA
  Via Vittorio Veneto 119a-121 (☎ 46 741)

For a complete list of all foreign embassies in Rome and other major cities throughout Italy, look in the *English Yellow Pages (Pagine Gialle)*, or ask for a list at the tourist office.

DOCUMENTS

A passport is the only important document you will need in Italy if you want to stay as a tourist for up to three months. It is necessary to produce your passport when you register in a hotel or pension in Italy. You will find that many proprietors will want to keep your passport during your stay. This is not a requirement; they only need it long enough to take down the details. If you want to rent a car or motorbike, you will need a valid EC driving licence or an International Driving Permit.

CUSTOMS

People from outside Europe can import two still cameras with 10 rolls of film, a movie or TV camera with 10 cartridges of film, a portable record player with 10 records or a tape recorder with 10 tapes, a CD player, a transistor radio, a pair of binoculars, up to 400 cigarettes, two bottles of wine and one bottle of liquor, without paying duty. Visitors who are residents of a European country and enter from an EC country can import a maximum of 300 cigarettes, one bottle of wine and half a bottle of liquor. There is no limit on the amount of lire you can import; you can export a maximum of L5 million.

MONEY

Anything to do with money and banks is likely to cause significant frustration and time-wasting in Italy. Banks are the most reliable, although not necessarily the fastest, places to exchange money, or to obtain cash advances on your credit card, although some will charge up to L8000 commission on cheques. The dilemma here is that although it is best to exchange large sums at once to save on the commission, it is unwise to carry large amounts of cash throughout Italy.

There are exchange offices at all major airports and railway stations in Italy, but their rates are often poor. You should always check exchange rates for major currencies before deciding which one to bring, but the US dollar and British sterling are a good bet. It is advisable to obtain a small amount of lire before arriving in Italy to avoid problems and queues at the airport and train stations. If you plan to remain in Italy for your entire trip, or for an extended period, investigate the prospect of buying travellers' cheques in lire. By doing this you will avoid paying commission when you cash the cheques in Italy.

Most of the major banks will give cash advances on Visa, but not all will honour MasterCard. The Banca Commerciale Italiana, one of Italy's major banks, *will* give cash advances on MasterCard, as will the Cassa di Risparmio and Credito Italiano. American Express has offices throughout the country, and for sheer convenience their travellers' cheques are a good option.

If you want to have money sent to you in Italy, be prepared for trouble. The procedure can be complicated and it can take weeks to arrive. Money can be sent from the foreign offices of large Italian banks, or through major banks in your own country to a nominated bank in Italy. It is important to have an exact record of all details associated with the money transfer, particularly the exact address of the Italian bank where the money has been sent. This will always be the head

office of the bank in the town to which the money has been sent. It is also important that the money be sent by urgent telex rather than by international draft or other means. Again, the Banca Commerciale is recommended. Another option is to have money sent through American Express, but most offices will require the sender to have an American Express card.

If you plan to remain in Italy for some months, remember that it is possible to open a bank account. If you use one of the larger banks, such as the Banca Commerciale Italiana or the Banca Nazionale del Lavoro, both of which have branches throughout the country, it can be a convenient way to gain easy access to your funds.

Major credit cards, including Visa, MasterCard and American Express are accepted throughout Italy in shops, restaurants and larger hotels. However, many trattorias, pizzerias, most pensioni and one-star hotels do *not* accept credit cards. You will also find that while most stall holders at large flea markets accept credit cards, they will bargain only if you pay cash.

Currency

Italy's currency is the lira (plural: lire). The smallest note is L1000, roughly equivalent to US$1. Other denominations in notes are L2000, L5000, L10,000, L50,000 and L100,000. Coin denominations are L50, L100, L200 and L500. Remember that like other Continental Europeans, Italians indicate decimals with commas and thousands with points.

Exchange Rates

A$1	=	L924
C$1	=	L1036
DM1	=	L877
NZ$1	=	L703
UK£1	=	L2201
US$1	=	L1292

Costs

A reasonable budget per day, covering accommodation, food, public transport and admission fees for galleries and museums, is L50,000. Certainly it is possible to live on less, but even if you find a hostel bed for under L15,000 and eat only one meal a day, you will find entry fees for the major museums cripplingly expensive at around L10,000. Public transport is generally cheap in Italy. Take advantage of the tourist tickets for bus travel within larger cities, which are usually around L2000 for a full day's travel. Italy's railways also offer cut-price options for students, young people and tourists for travel within a nominated period (see the Getting Around section in this chapter for more information). Museums and galleries usually give discounts to students, but you will need a valid student card, which you can obtain from CTS offices if you have documents proving you are a student. A basic breakdown of costs during an average day could be: accommodation L15,000 to L20,000; breakfast (coffee and croissant) L2000; lunch (sandwich and mineral water) L4000 to L5000; public transport (bus or underground railway in a major town) L2000; entry fee for one museum L5000 to L10,000; dinner L15,000.

Tipping & Bargaining

You are not expected to tip on top of restaurant service charges, but it is common practice among Italians to leave a small amount. If there is no service fee, they usually leave 10%, but this is not standard practice. In bars they will leave any small change as a tip, often only L100 or L200.

Bargaining is common throughout Italy in the various flea markets, but not normally in shops. It is quite acceptable to bargain for the price of a room in a pension, particularly if you plan to stay for more than a few days, and it is standard practice to bargain with taxi drivers, but you must agree on the price before you get in the cab.

Consumer Taxes

Whenever you buy an item in Italy you will pay IVA tax. Tourists are able to claim back this tax if the item cost more than a certain amount (L930,000 in 1992). The goods must be for personal use, they must be carried with your luggage and you must keep the fiscal receipt. You have to fill in a form at the point of purchase, have the form checked and stamped by Italian customs and then return it to the vendor within 60 days, who will then make the refund, either by cheque or to your credit card. At major airports and border points, there are places where you can get an immediate cash refund.

CLIMATE & WHEN TO GO

Italy lies in a temperate zone, but the climates of the north and south vary. Summers are uniformly hot, but are often extremely hot and dry in the south. Winters can be severely cold in the north, particularly in the Alps, but also in the Po Valley, whereas they are generally mild in the south and in Sicily and Sardinia. The best time to visit Italy is in the off season, which is from April to June and September to October, when the weather is good, prices are lower and there are fewer tourists. During July and August (the high season) it is very hot, prices are inflated and the country swarms with tourists. Many hotels and restaurants at seaside areas close down for the winter months.

WHAT TO BRING

A backpack is a definite advantage in Italy, but if you plan to use a suitcase and portable trolley, be warned about the endless flights of stairs at train stations and in many of the smaller medieval towns. A small pack for use on day trips and for sightseeing is preferable to a handbag or shoulder bag, particularly in the southern cities where motorcycle bandits are very active. A money belt is absolutely essential in Italy, particularly in the south and in Sicily, but also in the major cities, where groups of dishevelled-looking kids prey on tourists with bulging pockets. While travelling, it is best not to display any valuable jewellery, including rings and expensive watches.

In the more mountainous areas, the weather can change suddenly even in high summer, so remember to bring at least one item of warm clothing. Most importantly, bring a pair of hardy, comfortable walking shoes. In many cities, pavements are uneven and often made of cobblestones.

SUGGESTED ITINERARIES

Depending on the length of your stay, you might want to see and do the following things:

Two days
    Visit Rome to see the Forum, the Colosseum, St Peter's Basilica and the Vatican museums.
One week
    Visit Rome and Florence, with detours to Assisi, Siena and San Gimignano.
Two weeks
    As above, plus Bologna, Verona, Ravenna and at least three days in Venice.
One month
    As above, but go from Sicily to Sardinia for one week at least. Explore the north, including Liguria, and the south, including Puglia.

TOURIST OFFICES

Tourist offices in Italy fall into several categories and go by a variety of names. The EPT (Provincial Tourist Department) usually offers information on a town and its province, but in some areas these offices are now called APT *(Azienda di Promozione Turistica)*. The AAST *(Azienda Autonoma di Soggiorno e Turismo)* offices usually have information only on the town itself. In most of the very small towns and villages the local tourist office is called a Pro Loco.

You should be able to get a map, a list of hotels, and information on the major sights at each tourist office. Most offices have English-speaking staff. You can obtain information on places throughout Italy at the EPT office in Rome, Via Parigi 11, 00185, and at the Rome office of Italy's national tourist office, ENIT *(Ente Nazionale Italiano per il Turismo)*, Via Marghera 2, 00185. This organisation operates abroad under the title of Italian State Tourist Office.

Italian Tourist Offices Abroad

Information on Italy is available from ENIT offices in the following countries:

Australia
    In Australia ENIT operates through Alitalia (Italy's national airline), Orient Overseas Building, suite 202, 32 Bridge St, Sydney. Information is also available from all Alitalia offices. ENIT plans to open an office in Sydney in 1993.
Canada
    1, Place Ville Marie, suite 1914, Montreal, Que H3B 3M9 (☎ 514-866 7667)
UK
    1 Princes St, London W1R 8AY (☎ 071-408 1254)
USA
    630 Fifth Avenue, suite 1565, New York, NY 10111 (☎ 212-245 4822)
    360 Post St, suite 801, San Francisco, CA 94108 (☎ 415-392 5266)
    500 North Michigan Ave, suite 1046, Chicago, IL 60611 (☎ 312-644 0990)

CIT, Italy's national travel agency, has offices in the following countries:

Australia
    123 Clarence St, Sydney 2000 (☎ 02-299 4754) suite 10, 6th floor, 422 Collins St, Melbourne 3000 (☎ 03-670 1322)
Canada
    1450 City Councillors St, suite 750, Montreal, Que H3A 2E6 (☎ 514-845 8781)
    111 Avenue Rd, suite 808, Toronto, Ont M5R 3J8 (☎ 416-927 7712)
UK
    Marco Polo House, 3-5 Lansdown Rd, Croydon, Surrey CR9 1LL(☎ 081-686 0677)
USA
    594 Broadway, suite 307, New York, NY 10006 (☎ 212-27405)
    12400 Wilshire Blvd, Los Angeles, CA 90025 (☎ 310-820 0098)

Italian cultural institutes, in major cities throughout the world, have extensive information on study opportunities in Italy.

USEFUL ORGANISATIONS

The following organisations should be very helpful and cater for many different groups.

CIT *(Compagnia Italiana di Turismo)*
    This is Italy's national tourist agency and has offices throughout the country and abroad (see the Italian Tourist Offices Abroad section). You can book train, bus, air and sea travel and obtain information about guided tours of the cities and package tours of Italy.

CTS *(Centro Turistico Studentesco e Giovanile)*
This agency will have offices all over Italy and
specialises in discounts for students and young
people, but is also useful for travellers of any age
looking for cheap flights and sightseeing discounts. It is linked with the International Student
Travel Confederation. You can get a student card
if you have documents proving that you are a
student.

AIG *(Associazione Italiana Alberghi per la Gioventù)*
(IYHF) The head office (☎ 06-487 11 52) is at
Via Cavour 44, Rome, where you can obtain a list
of all hostels in Italy and buy a membership card
if necessary. There are branch offices throughout
Italy.

CAI *(Club Alpino Italiano)*
This organisation will provide information and
maps for hiking and trekking and phone numbers
for refuges in the Alps. It has offices throughout
Italy which can provide trekking information, but
only for their particular zone. It does not have a
central office for all of Italy.

TCI *(Touring Club Italiano)*
The head office (☎ 02-852 62 44) is at Corso
Italia 10, Milan. It publishes useful trekking
guides and maps (in Italian), and has offices
throughout Italy.

ACI *(Automobile Club d'Italia)*
Tourists driving in Italy used to be able to buy a
package of discounts for autostrade (motorway)
tolls from ACI. Unfortunately, the packages were
scrapped in 1992, but there is talk of their being
reintroduced in 1993. (For more information, see
Car & Motorbike in the Getting There & Away
section that follows.) The club has offices in
Milan (☎ 01-77 451) at Corso Venezia 43, in Rome
(☎ 06-49 981) at Via Marsala 8, and throughout
Italy.

BUSINESS HOURS & HOLIDAYS

Business hours can vary from city to city, but
generally shops and businesses are open
Monday to Saturday from 8 am to 1 pm and
from 5 to 8 pm. Banks are generally open
Monday to Friday from 8.30 am to 1.30 pm
and from 2.30 to 4.30 pm, but hours vary
between banks and cities. Public offices are
usually open Monday to Saturday from 8 am
to 2 pm. Large post offices are open Monday
to Saturday from 8 am to 6 or 7 pm. Most
museums close on Mondays, and restaurants
and bars are required to close for one day each
week. All food outlets close on Thursday afternoons.

National public holidays include: January
6 (Epiphany); Easter Monday; 25 April (Liberation Day); 1 May (Labour Day); 15
August (ferragosto, or the Feast of the
Assumption); 1 November (All Saints' Day);
8 December (the Feast of the Immaculate
Conception); 25 December (Christmas
Day); and 26 December (the Feast of Santo
Stefano).

Individual towns also have public holidays to celebrate the feasts of their patron
saints. Some of these are the Feast of St Mark
in Venice on 25 April; the Feast of St John
the Baptist on 24 June in Florence, Genoa
and Turin; the Feast of Sts Peter and Paul in
Rome on 29 June; the Feast of St Gennaro in
Naples on 19 September; and the Feast of St
Ambrose in Milan on 7 December.

CULTURAL EVENTS

Most towns throughout Italy have a full calendar of religious and cultural festivals. If
you are particularly interested in timing your
visit to coincide with the various festivals,
write to ENIT in Rome, or go to the office in
your city (addresses are listed under the
Tourist Offices section) and ask for the
booklet *An Italian Year*, which lists all cultural events.

Carnevale
During the 10 days before Ash Wednesday, many
towns stage carnivals. The one held in Venice is
the best known, but there are also others, including those at Acireale, near Catania, and Ivrea,
near Turin, where they hold the only carnival in
the world which follows a script.

Festival of the Almond Blossoms
This beautiful festival is held at Agrigento from
10 to 17 February.

Holy Week (the week before Easter)
There are important festivals during this week
everywhere in Italy, in particular the colourful
and sombre traditional festivals of Sicily. In
Assisi the rituals of Holy Week attract thousands
of pilgrims.

Scoppio del Carro (Explosion of the Cart)
This colourful event held in Florence in Piazza
del Duomo on Easter Sunday features the explosion of a cart full of fireworks and dates back to
the Crusades. If all goes well, it is seen as a good
omen for the city.

Corso dei Ceri
One of the strangest festivals in Italy, this is held in Gubbio (Umbria) on 15 May, and features a race run by men carrying enormous wooden constructions called *ceri* in honour of the town's patron saint, Sant'Ubaldo.

Il Palio
On 2 July and on 16 August, Siena stages this extraordinary horse race in the town's main piazza.

POST & TELECOMMUNICATIONS

Italy's postal service is notorious among travellers. Probably the best that can be said is that it is semireliable. Don't expect to receive every letter sent to you, or that every letter you send will reach its destination.

Postal Rates

The cost of sending a letter *via aerea* (air mail) depends on weight, but an average letter to Australia will cost L1500 and around L1000 to the USA. It usually takes 10 days to two weeks for air mail to reach countries outside Europe and approximately one week to reach the UK.

Sending Mail

When sending a letter, print the country of destination in block letters and underline it.

If you want to mail something urgently, you can ask to send the article *espresso* (express). Registered mail is *raccomandato* and insured mail (for valuable items) is *assicurato*. If you want something to reach its destination urgently (within one or two days), use EMS (Express Mail Service), also known as CAI Post. A letter or parcel weighing up to one kg will cost approximately L30,000 within Europe, L50,000 to the USA and Canada, and L70,000 to Australia and New Zealand. Ask at post offices for addresses of EMS outlets. Stamps are available at authorised tobacconists, but any international mail has to be weighed, so it is best to use the post office.

Receiving Mail

The Italian version of poste restante is *fermo posta* and is usually reliable. Tell friends and

relatives to write your surname in block letters.

Telephones

There are several options for making international telephone calls in Italy. At ASST (the national telephone board) offices you can book an international call and pay afterwards. From SIP (the Italian telephone corporation) offices, or any public phone, you can use coins or a *carta telefonica* (telephone card) to dial direct, but remember that it is very expensive to make an international call from Italy. The addresses of both ASST and SIP offices are listed under individual towns throughout this chapter.

You can buy L5000, L10,000 and L50,000 phonecards at tobacconists and newsstands, or from vending machines at SIP offices.

To call Italy from abroad, dial the international access code, 39 (the country code for Italy), the area code (dropping the initial zero) and the number. Important area codes are: 06 (Rome), 02 (Milan), 055 (Florence), 081 (Naples), 070 (Cagliari) and 091 (Palermo).

To make a reverse-charges (collect) call from a public telephone, dial 170. All operators speak English. Another option is to dial 172, the international access code (00 from Italy) and the code for the country you are calling to be connected directly with the operator in that country. (For example, to call the operator in Australia, dial ☎ 172 1061). To make a local call you need L200 or a *gettone*, a special coin for telephones which is legal tender with a value of L200.

TIME

Italy is one hour ahead of GMT/UTC and two hours ahead during summer. Daylight-saving time starts on the last Sunday in March, when clocks are put forward an hour. Clocks are put back an hour on the last Sunday in September. Ensure that you also make allowances for daylight-saving time in your own country. Note that Italy operates on a 24-hour clock.

When it's noon in Rome, it's 11 pm in Auckland, 11 am in London, 6 am in New

York, 3 am in San Francisco and 9 pm in Sydney. European cities such as Paris, Munich, Berlin, Vienna and Madrid are on the same time as Italy. Athens, Cairo and Tel Aviv are one hour ahead.

ELECTRICITY

The electric current in Italy is 220 volts, 50 Hz, but make a point of checking with your hotel management because in some areas, for instance, in Rome, they still use 125 volts. Many appliances have three-round-pin plugs, but, since most power points have only two holes, Italians buy adapters for appliances with three pins. The adapters have two pins and provision for the three-pin plugs.

LAUNDRY

The best place to wash your clothes is in your hotel room. Most laundries in Italy charge by the kg and do the laundry themselves, which makes it an expensive proposition. In some of the larger towns, particularly where there are universities, you can find laundries with coin-operated machines, but a load will still cost around L8000.

WEIGHTS & MEASURES

Italy uses the metric system. Basic terms for weight include: *un etto* (100 grams) and *un chilo* (one kg). Note that Italians indicate decimals with commas and thousands with points.

BOOKS & MAPS

For serious research on Italian history, culture and people try the following books: *The Decline and Fall of the Roman Empire* by Edward Gibbons (three volumes, hardback); *Concise History of Italy* by Vincent Cronin (Cassell, paperback); *Painters of the Renaissance* by Bernard Berenson (Oxford, paperback); and *The Penguin Book of the Renaissance* by J H Plumb (Penguin, paperback).

For lighter reading, you will find many books written by travellers in Italy: *Venice* by James Morris (Faber, paperback); *Venice Observed* and *The Stones of Florence* by Mary McCarthy (Harcourt Brace Jovanovich, paperback); and *A Traveller in Southern Italy* and *A Traveller in Italy* by H V Morton (Methuen London, paperback).

Companion Guides (Collins, paperback) are excellent and include *Rome* by Georgina Masson, *Venice* by Hugh Honour, *Umbria* by Maurice Rowdon, *Tuscany* by Archibald Lyall and *Southern Italy* by Peter Gunn.

For a potted idea of how the great writers saw Italy, it's worth reading *Venice: the Most Triumphant City* compiled by George Bull (Michael Joseph, London, hardback) and *When in Rome: the Humorists' Guide to Italy* (Robson Books, paperback). Italian author Luigi Barzini's classic *The Italians* (Atheneum, paperback) is a must.

Some recommended novels include *The Leopard* by Giuseppe di Lampedusa (Collins & Harvill Press, paperback), *The Agony and the Ecstasy* by Irving Stone (Signet, paperback), *Christ Stopped at Eboli* by Carlo Levi (King Penguin, paperback), and *D H Lawrence and Italy*, which comprises his three books *Twilight in Italy*, *Sea and Sardinia*, and *Etruscan Places* (Penguin, paperback).

For maps of cities, you will generally find those provided by the tourist office adequate. Excellent road and city maps are published by the Istituto Geografico de Agostini and are available in all major bookshops. If you are driving, invest in the De Agostini *Atlante Stradale Italiano* (L32,000).

MEDIA

The major English-language newspapers available in Italy are the *Herald Tribune* (US-based and available Tuesday to Sunday) and the *European* (available Fridays). The *Guardian, The Times* and the *Telegraph* are sent from London, so, outside major cities such as Rome and Milan, they are generally a few days old. *Time* magazine, *Newsweek* and the *Economist* are available weekly. All are expensive, however, ranging from L2200 for the *Herald Tribune* to L6200 for the *Economist*.

RAI, the Italian TV and broadcasting corporation, runs an American news service on Fridays at 11.15 pm on the TV station RAI2.

The American CBS news is broadcast daily at 7.30 and 8 am on the Telemontecarlo (TMC) station. It also broadcasts CNN live from about 2.30 am daily. In Rome there is a radio news service in English every morning at 8am on Vatican Radio.

HEALTH

Residents of EC countries, including the UK, are covered for emergency medical treatment in Italy on presentation of an E111 form (see the Facts for the Visitor chapter at the start of this book). Australia has a reciprocal arrangement with Italy whereby Australian citizens have access to free medical services. If you want to take advantage of this, you should check with Medicare about the exact requirements. The USA, New Zealand and Canada do not have reciprocal health care arrangements with Italy.

Since the quality of public hospital care in Italy can vary dramatically, it is advisable to ensure that health care is covered by your travel insurance policy.

Emergency dental treatment is available in the casualty sections of most public hospitals. It should be noted that the quality of medical treatment in public hospitals varies throughout Italy. Your own doctor and dentist may be able to give you some recommendations or referrals before you leave your own country.

WOMEN TRAVELLERS

Women travellers in Italy will often find themselves plagued by unwanted attention, particularly in Rome and Sicily. Most of the time the attention is annoying but harmless and it is best simply to ignore the catcalls, hisses and whistles. However, some men can be particularly aggressive and insistent.

Women travelling alone should be particularly careful in the south, Sicily and Sardinia. Try to avoid walking around alone at night, especially in Naples, Syracuse and Palermo, and never consider hitchhiking in these areas. Only a minority of Italian men make a habit of harassing foreign women and you will find most men courteous, respectful and helpful.

DANGERS & ANNOYANCES

Theft is the main problem for travellers in Italy. Thieves and pickpockets operate in most major cities, particularly in Rome, Florence and Milan. Watch out for groups of dishevelled-looking women and children. They generally work in groups of four or five and carry paper or cardboard which they use to distract your attention while they swarm around and rifle through your pockets and bag. Never underestimate their skill – they are lightning fast and very adept. The best way to avoid being robbed is to wear a money belt. Never carry a purse or wallet in your pockets and hold on tight to your bag. Pickpockets operate in crowded areas, such as markets and on buses. Motorcycle bandits are particularly active in Rome, Naples, Palermo and Syracuse. If you are using a shoulder bag, make sure that you wear the strap across your body and have the bag on the side away from the road.

Never leave valuables in a parked car – in fact, try not to leave anything in the car if you can help it. It is a good idea to park your car in a supervised car park if you are leaving it for any amount of time. Car theft is a major problem in Rome and Naples. Throughout Italy you can call ☎ 113 (police) or ☎ 112 (carabinieri) in an emergency.

FILM & PHOTOGRAPHY

A roll of normal Kodak film (36 exposures, 100 ASA) costs L8000. It costs up to L20,000 to have 36 exposures developed and L15,000 for 24 exposures. A roll of 36 slides costs L10,000, and L5000 to L7000 for development. Enthusiasts should note that the light changes quite markedly throughout Italy. In the south it is stronger and brighter, whereas the regions of Umbria and Tuscany are noted for their soft light. As you go farther north the atmosphere is generally misty, a combination of natural effect and air pollution.

WORK

It is illegal to work in Italy without a visa, but trying to obtain a work visa is extremely difficult, EC nationals excluded. You will need to have a firm promise of a job which is not wanted by an Italian and then you must apply to the Italian embassy in your own country for a work permit.

Traditionally, the main legal employment for foreigners is to teach English, but even with full qualifications an American, Australian, Canadian or New Zealander will find it difficult to secure a permanent position. Many foreign visitors manage to find illegal, untaxed work in bars and restaurants or as babysitters and housekeepers. The pay and conditions are usually very poor. Many language schools, particularly in remote towns, employ people without permits and there is a high demand for private English lessons. In Rome you can place an advertisement in *Wanted in Rome*, a weekly publication advertising work for English-speakers, and in Milan there is a similar publication entitled *Secondomano*.

If you are seriously looking to work legally in Italy for an extended period, you should seek information from the Italian embassy in your country.

ACTIVITIES

If the churches, museums, galleries and sightseeing are not sufficient to occupy your time in Italy, there are various options if you want to get off the main tourist routes or have specific interests.

Hiking & Trekking

It is possible to go on organised treks in Italy, but if you want to go it alone, you can obtain information and maps from CAI (see the Useful Organisations section). In summer, head for the Alps, particularly the Dolomites and national parks such as the Parco del Gran Paradiso in the Valle d'Aosta and the Parco dello Stelvio in Lombardy. The Apennines, particularly in Abruzzo and Calabria have good trekking routes, as do the Alpi Apuane in Tuscany.

In Sardinia the rugged landscape offers some spectacular hikes, particularly in the eastern mountain ranges, such as Gennar-

gentu, and the gorges near Dorgali (see the Sardinia section for further information).

Skiing

The numerous excellent ski resorts in the Alps and the Apennines usually offer good conditions from December to April (see the Alps section).

Cycling

This is a good option if you can't afford a car but want to see the more isolated parts of the country. A bicycle would be particularly useful in Sardinia to explore the coast between Alghero and Bosa and the area around Dorgali (see the section on Sardinia).

In the south, try cycling along the coast of Apulia, starting from Lecce and continuing down the coast of Salento Province to the tip of the heel, and then up to Gallipoli. Another beautiful area for cycling is the Colle Val d'Elsa in Tuscany, between Florence and Siena, where you can visit towns such as San Gimignano and Volterra.

Courses

Travelling to Italy to study the language is becoming increasingly popular, both for travellers seeking a holiday with a difference and for people who want to study at an Italian university.

There are numerous private schools which offer courses, particularly in Rome, Florence and Siena, but the cheapest option is to study at the Università per Stranieri in Perugia. The average cost of a course in Florence is around L600,000 a month, whereas in Perugia it costs L240,000 a month. Schools in Florence and Rome also offer courses in art, sculpture and architecture.

Italian cultural institutes and embassies in your country will provide information on schools and courses as well as enrolment forms. The university in Perugia and all private schools can arrange accommodation. To do a course it is necessary to obtain a study visa in your own country, for which you will need confirmation of enrolment. Allow four months before your departure to obtain the necessary documents.

ITALY

HIGHLIGHTS
Museums & Galleries
The Vatican museums in Rome and the fabulous Uffizi Gallery in Florence are absolutely not to be missed. The Bargello in Florence, with its excellent sculpture collection, is another must. In Venice visit the Peggy Guggenheim Gallery of Modern Art. The Museo Archeologico Nazionale in Naples is one of the better museums in Italy.

Historic Towns
There are so many fascinating and beautiful medieval towns in Italy that it seems a shame to confine your travels to the major cities. In Tuscany visit San Gimignano and Volterra, and in Umbria take a tour of the medieval hilltowns, many still surrounded by their walls and crowned with ruined castles. The more interesting towns include Assisi, Spoleto, Gubbio and Orvieto, but try to visit the villages of Spello and Narni. Ravenna, with its extraordinary Byzantine churches and mosaics, is one of the great highlights of a visit to Italy.

In Liguria walk along the coast to visit the Cinque Terre, five tiny villages linked by a walking track on the Riviera di Levante. One of the most fascinating towns in Italy is Matera in Basilicata. Wandering through its famous *sassi* (stone houses) is an experience not easily forgotten. Positano is the most beautiful town on the Amalfi Coast, except in summer when it is too crowded.

Churches
The phenomenal number of churches in Italy should satisfy even the most obsessive lover of religious architecture. A few highlights include the cathedrals in Florence, Milan, Siena and Orvieto (considered one of the most beautiful in Italy), and that at Monreale, near Palermo, for its beautiful mosaics. The Basilica of San Vitale in Ravenna is notable both for its mosaics and for the design of the church. The Romanesque cathedral in Otranto (Apulia) is worth a visit to see the extraordinary mosaic of the *Tree of Life*, which covers its floor.

Beaches
Although the water is badly polluted, the beaches along the Riviera di Levante in Liguria are worth visiting. The beach resorts along the Amalfi Coast are particularly scenic, but again, the water is not exactly clean. The cleanest beaches are in Sardinia.

Hotels & Restaurants
The following are hotels which are in characteristic locations. The Pensione Bellavista in Florence has two double rooms with views of the Duomo (cathedral) and the Palazzo Vecchio. Just outside Florence, near Fiesole, is Bencistà, a former villa with a terrace overlooking Florence. In Rome the Albergo Abruzzi is in the same piazza as the Pantheon, and in Venice the Sturion has two rooms with views of the Grand Canal. In Positano the Villa Maria Luisa offers remarkably cheap rooms, some with terraces overlooking the sea. The IYHF youth hostels in Verona and Florence, which are both in renovated villas, are in particularly beautiful settings and are said to be among the best in Europe.

In Naples the best pizzas are at Trianon. If you make it to Syracuse in Sicily be sure to eat at the Trattoria La Foglia, where the risotto is fantastic. Mario's in Florence is a local institution, and Da Maria in Genoa is one of the more unusual eating experiences you will have in Italy. In Perugia try Ubu Re for fantastic Umbrian fare.

General Sights
Italy itself is a virtual museum and in every part of the country you will come across monuments, works of art, views and special places which have the capacity to surprise even the most world-weary traveller. Here are a few of the more renowned ones: Michelangelo's *Pietà* in St Peter's Basilica, Rome; the Grand Canal in Venice; the Pala d'Oro (gold altarpiece) in the Basilica di San Marco (St Mark's Basilica) in Venice; the view of Tuscany from the top of the town hall tower in San Gimignano; the Etruscan sites at Tarquinia, Cerveteri, Saturnia and Sovana; Giotto's frescoes in the Scrovegni Chapel in

Padua; the strange meadow named Piano Grande at Monte Vettore, near Castellucio at the border of Umbria and the Marches; and the Porta Portese market in Rome.

ACCOMMODATION
Camping
Facilities throughout Italy are usually reasonable and vary from those in beautiful locations by the sea, lakes and in the mountains, to camping grounds in the heart of major cities. Prices per person vary from L4000 to L12,000 and from L4000 to L6000 for a small tent. Lists of camping grounds in and near major cities are usually available at tourist information offices. In Sicily and Sardinia the regional tourist boards publish annual booklets listing all facilities throughout the islands.

The TCI (Touring Club Italiano) publishes an annual book on all camping sites in Italy, *Campeggi e Villaggi Turistici in Italia* (L20,000), and the Istituto Geografico de Agostini publishes the annual *Guida di Campeggi in Europa* (L20,000), available in major bookshops in Italy. Free camping is forbidden in many of the more beautiful parts of Italy, although you will find that the authorities pay less attention in the off season.

Hostels
Hostels in Italy are called *ostelli per la gioventù* and are run by the Associazione Italiana Alberghi per la Gioventù (AIG). An IYHF membership card is not always required, but it is recommended that you have one. Membership cards can be purchased at major hostels, from CTS (student and youth travel centre) offices and from AIG offices throughout Italy. Pick up a list of all hostels in Italy, with details of prices, locations etc, from the AIG office (☎ 06-474 67 55) in Rome, Via Cavour 44.

Many Italian hostels are beautifully located in castles and old villas, most have bars and the cost per night often includes breakfast. Many provide dinners, usually for around L12,000. Prices, including breakfast, range from L13,000 to L18,000. Hostels are

generally closed from 10.30 am to 4.30 pm (times vary) and curfew is usually at 11 pm. Note that hostels in major resort areas are often closed in winter.

Pensioni & Hotels
Prices charged by hotels and pensioni in Italy were deregulated by the government in 1992. Previously, all prices had been controlled by provincial boards, which awarded each establishment a classification based on the service and amenities provided. The system was based on stars – a one-star hotel being the most basic and a five-star the most luxurious.

Although the star classification system has been retained, establishments can now set their own prices. This meant that, in early 1992, prices skyrocketed by up to 40% in some cities, particularly Rome, Milan and Florence. Travellers reported that lists of prices set by provincial boards remained posted in some hotels, even though they were no longer adhered to. Tourist offices will continue to publish booklets listing pensioni, hotels and prices, but only those establishments which set their room charges in advance and notify the tourist offices will be included. Once the hotels and pensioni have notified the tourist board of charges for the coming year, they will be required by law to adhere to these prices and tourists can continue to report overcharging to the tourist office. The catch is that proprietors have two legal opportunities annually to increase prices.

The government expects that market forces and common sense will see prices stabilise by the end of 1993. The best advice if you are travelling before then would be to confirm hotel charges before you put your bags down, and shop around to take advantage of the competition that will result from the new deregulated system.

Proprietors still employ various methods of bill padding. These include charges for showers (usually around L2000), a compulsory breakfast (up to L14,000 in the high season) and compulsory half or full board, although this can often be a good deal in some towns.

The cheapest way to stay in a hotel or pension is to share a room with two or more people. In many parts of Italy they will charge no more than 15% of the cost of a double room for each additional person. Single rooms are uniformly expensive in Italy and quite a number of establishments do not even bother to cater for the single traveller.

There is often no difference between an establishment that calls itself a *pensione* and one that calls itself an *albergo* (hotel), in fact, some use both titles. *Locande* (similar to pensioni) and *alloggi*, also known as *affittacamere*, are generally cheaper, but not always. Tourist offices have booklets listing all pensioni and hotels, including prices, and lists of locande and affittacamere.

Rental Accommodation

Finding rental accommodation in the major cities can be difficult and time-consuming and you will often find the cost prohibitive, especially in Rome, Florence, Milan and Venice. For details on rental agencies, refer to the individual city chapters. If you are planning to study in an Italian city, the school or university will help you to find rental accommodation, or a room in the house of a family. Some tourist offices have information on renting flats and villas, otherwise you can obtain information from specialist travel agencies in your own country.

One organisation which publishes booklets on villas and houses in Tuscany, Umbria, Veneto, Sicily and Rome is Cuendet. Write to Signora N Cuendet, 5303 Strove/Monteriggioni, Siena (☎ 0577-30 10 53). Prices, however, are expensive.

In major resort areas, such as the Aeolian Islands and other parts of Sicily, and in the Alps, rental accommodation is reasonably priced and readily available. You can obtain information from local tourist offices.

Agriturismo

This is basically a farm holiday and is becoming increasingly popular in Italy.

However, the number of genuine farms offering rooms and farm work to tourists is decreasing and many establishments are now just hotels in the country. The average cost for a bed is around L32,000 a night and you are supposed to agree on food costs and so on with the farm owner. Recommended areas where you can try this type of holiday are Tuscany, Umbria and Trentino-Alto Adige. Information is available from local tourist offices.

Two national bodies which publish books listing all facilities in Italy are: Agriturist (☎ 651 23 42), Corso Vittorio Emanuele 101, 00186 Rome (the book costs L25,000); and Turismo Verde (☎ 396 33 91), Via Mariano Fortuny 20, 00196 Rome (the book costs L12,000).

Religious Institutions

These institutions offer accommodation in most major cities. The standard is usually good, but prices are no longer low. You can expect to pay about the same as for a one-star hotel, if not more. Information about the various institutions is available at all tourist offices, or you can contact the archdiocese in your city.

Refuges

Before you go hiking in any part of Italy, contact the CAI (see Useful Organisations) for information on Alpine refuges. Local tourist offices in the Alps (see the section on the Alps) will also provide information, including telephone numbers and maps marking the location of refuges.

FOOD

Eating is one of life's great pleasures for Italians. Be adventurous and never be intimidated by eccentric waiters or indecipherable menus and you will find yourself agreeing with the locals, who believe that nowhere in the world is the food as good as in Italy and, more specifically, in their own town.

Cooking styles vary notably from region to region and significantly between the north and south. In the north the food is rich and often creamy, and the regional specialties of

Emilia-Romagna, including spaghetti bolognese (known in Italy as spaghetti al ragù), tortellini, and *mortadella* are perhaps the best known throughout the world.

In Tuscany and Umbria the locals use a lot of olive oil and herbs, and regional specialties are noted for their simplicity, fine flavour and the use of fresh produce. As you go farther south the food becomes hotter and spicier and the *dolci* (cakes and pastries) sweeter and richer. Don't miss the experience of eating a pizza in Naples and don't leave Sicily without trying the rich and very sweet ice cream with almonds known as *cassata*.

Vegetarians will have no problems eating in Italy. Though there are very few restaurants devoted to them (and these few tend to be expensive and on the trendy side), vegetable dishes are a staple of the Italian diet. Most eating establishments serve a selection of *contorni* (vegetables prepared in a variety of ways), and the farther south you go, the more excellent vegetable dishes you'll find.

Restaurants

Eating establishments are divided into several categories. A *tavola calda* (literally hot table) usually offers cheap, preprepared meat, pasta and vegetable dishes in a self-service style. A *rosticceria* usually offers cooked meats, but also often has a larger selection of takeaway food. A pizzeria will of course serve pizza, but usually also a full menu. An *osteria* is likely to be either a wine bar offering a small selection of dishes, or a small trattoria. A trattoria is basically a cheaper version of a *ristorante* (restaurant). The problem is that many of the establishments that are in fact ristoranti call themselves trattorias and vice versa for reasons best known to themselves. It is best to check the menu, which is usually posted by the door, for prices.

Don't panic if you find yourself in a trattoria which has no printed menu as they are often the ones which offer the best and most authentic food and have menus which change daily according to the availability of fresh produce. Just hope that the waiter will patiently explain the dishes and tell you how much they cost.

Most eating establishments charge a *coperto* (cover charge) of around L2000 to L3000, and a service charge *(servizio)* of 10% to 15%. Restaurants are usually open for lunch from 12.30 to 3 pm, but will rarely take orders after 2 pm. In the evening, opening hours vary from north to south. In the north they eat dinner earlier, usually from 7.30 pm, but in Sicily you will be hard-pressed to find a restaurant open before 8.30 pm. Note that very few restaurants stay open after 11.30 pm.

Italians rarely eat a sit-down breakfast. Their custom is to drink a cappuccino, usually *tiepido* (cool), and eat a *brioche*, *cornetto*, or other type of pastry while standing at a bar. Lunch is the main meal of the day, and shops and businesses close for three to four hours each afternoon to accommodate the meal and the siesta which follows.

A full meal will consist of an antipasto, which can vary from *bruschetta*, a type of garlic bread with various toppings, to fried vegetables, or *prosciutto e melone* (ham wrapped around melon). Next comes the *primo piatto*, a pasta dish or risotto, followed by the *secondo piatto* of meat or fish. Italians often then eat an *insalata* (salad) or contorni and round off the meal with dolci and caffè, often at a bar on the way back to work. The evening meal is consequently a less grand affair, but you can certainly eat a full meal if you like.

Numerous restaurants offer tourist menus, at an average price of L18,000 to L24,000. Generally the food is of a reasonable standard, but choices will be limited and you can usually get away with paying less if you want only pasta, salad and wine.

After lunch and dinner, head for the nearest *gelateria* to round off the meal with some excellent Italian *gelati* (ice cream), followed by a *digestivo* (liqueur) at a bar.

Self-Catering

For a light lunch, or a snack, most bars serve *panini* (sandwiches), and there are numerous outlets where you can buy pizza by the slice.

ITALY

Another option is to go to one of the many *alimentari* (grocery stores) and ask them to make a panino with the filling of your choice. At a *pasticceria* you can buy pastries, cakes and biscuits.

If you have access to cooking facilities, you can buy fruit and vegetables at open markets (see the individual towns for information), and salami, cheese and wine at alimentari or *salumerie* (a cross between a grocery store and a delicatessen). Fresh bread is available at a *forno* or *panetteria*.

Remember that as soon as you sit down in Italy, prices go up considerably. A cappuccino at the bar will cost around L1200, but if you sit down, you will pay anything from L2500 to L5000 or more, especially in heavily touristed areas such as Piazza San Marco in Venice and the Spanish Steps in Rome.

DRINKS

Italian wine is justifiably world famous. Few Italians can live without it, and even fewer abuse it, generally drinking wine only with meals. Going out for a drink is considered quite unusual in Italy. Fortunately, wine is reasonably priced so you will rarely pay more than L10,000 for a good bottle of wine and as little as L5000 will still buy good quality. The styles of wine vary throughout the country, so make a point of sampling the local produce in your travels. Try the famous chianti in Tuscany, but also the *vernaccia* of San Gimignano, the *soave* in Verona and the *valpolicella* around Venice. Orvieto's wines are excellent, as are those from Trentino; in Rome try the local *frascati*. In Sicily and Sardinia the wines are sweeter and heavier.

Italians drink wine with lunch and dinner, but prefer to drink beer with pizza, which means that many pizzerias do not serve wine. Beer is known as *birra* and the cheapest local variety is *Peroni*, but a wide range of imported beers are also available, either in bars or at a *birreria*.

ENTERTAINMENT

Whatever your tastes, there should be some form of entertainment in Italy to keep you amused, from the national obsession, *il calcio* (soccer), to the opera, theatre, classical music concerts, rock concerts and traditional festivals. Major entertainment festivals are also held, such as the Festival of Two Worlds in June/July at Spoleto, Umbria Jazz in Perugia in July, and the Venice Biennale in every even-numbered year. Operas are performed in Verona and Rome throughout summer (for details see the Entertainment sections under both cities) and at various times of the year throughout the country, notably at the opera houses in Milan and Palermo.

The main theatre season is during winter, and classical music concerts are generally performed throughout the year. Nightclubs, indoor bars and discotheques are more popular during winter and many close down for the summer months. For up-to-date information on entertainment in each city, buy the local newspaper. Tourist offices will also provide information on important events, festivals, performances and concerts.

THINGS TO BUY

Italy is synonymous with elegant, fashionable and high quality clothing. The problem is that most of the clothes are very expensive. However, if you can manage to be in the country during the summer sales in July and August and the winter sales in December and January, you can pick up incredible bargains. By mid-sale, prices are often slashed by up to 60% or 70%. Generally speaking, Rome, Florence and Milan have the greatest variety of clothing, shoes and accessories.

Italy is renowned for the quality of its leather goods, so plan to stock up on bags, wallets, purses, belts and gloves. At markets such as Porta Portese in Rome and the San Lorenzo leather market in Florence you can find some remarkable bargains.

At San Lorenzo you can still buy excellent quality leather goods for half the price you would pay in a shop. A few price examples are: L70,000 for a bag; L15,000 for a belt; L12,000 for suede gloves; L250,000 for a leather jacket.

Other items of interest include the famous,

but expensive, Venetian glass, and the great diversity of ceramics produced throughout Italy, notably on the Amalfi Coast, at Deruta and Orvieto in Umbria and in Sicily. The beautiful Florentine paper goods also make wonderful gifts and are reasonably priced.

Getting There & Away

AIR

Although paying full fare to travel by plane in Europe is expensive, there are various discount options. Most companies, including Alitalia, offer discount fares for students and people aged under 25 or 26 (depending on the airline). There are also stand-by fares, which are usually around 60% of the full fare. Several airlines, including Alitalia, Qantas, Air France and Philippine Airlines, offer cut-rate fares on legs of international flights between European cities. These can be remarkably cheap, but the catch is that they are usually during the night, or very early in the morning, and the days on which you can fly are severely restricted.

In 1992 the cheapest available one-way fares were: Rome-Paris L180,000; Rome-London L210,000 (L181,000 for students aged under 30); Rome-Amsterdam for people aged under 26 was L198,000. Full-price fares are outrageously expensive: for example, a one-way Alitalia fare Rome-Paris was L711,000, although a return fare with fixed dates was L480,000. In Italy the best option is to go to the CTS or CIT (see the Useful Organisations section) to obtain information on available discount fares.

Few airlines offer discount fares to Russia, but on Polish Airlines you could buy a return Rome-Moscow ticket for L809,000.

A good option is to travel on charter flights. There are several companies throughout Europe which operate these, and fares are significantly cheaper than for normal scheduled flights. Pilgrim Air (☎ 081-748 4999), 227 Shepherd's Bush Rd, London W6 7AS, runs a service called Italy Sky Shuttle, which offers unsold tickets on

Britannia Airways at heavily discounted rates. Pilgrim Air offers charter flights to all major Italian airports, and tickets can be purchased through any travel agency.

Look in the classified pages of the London Sunday newspapers for information on other cheap flights. Within Italy the best information on discount fares is available from CTS and CIT offices.

Details on the numerous charter flights to Italy from London can be obtained from CTS Travel, 44 Goodge St, London W1P 2AD (☎ 071-261 608), or the Charter Flight Centre, 13-15 Gillingham St, London SW1V 1HN (☎ 071-828 1090).

Departure Tax

There is no departure tax on international flights leaving Italy.

LAND

If you are travelling by bus, train or car to Italy, it will be necessary to cross various borders, so remember to check whether you require visas for those countries before leaving home.

Bus

You can obtain detailed information about buses to/from Italy from any CIT office, where you can also make bookings. The most reliable firm is Eurolines and it is linked with International Express in England. The bus companies operating this service in Italy are Lazzi in Florence (☎ 055-36 30 41), Via Mercadante 2, and Rome (☎ 06-841 74 58), Via Tagliamento 27/r; and Sadem in Turin (☎ 011-561 30 19), Corso Siccadi 6, and Milan (☎ 02-80 11 61), Piazza Castello 1. Buses leave from Rome, Florence, Milan, Turin, Venice and Naples, as well as numerous other Italian towns, for major cities throughout Europe, including London, Paris, Barcelona, Amsterdam, Vienna, Prague, Athens and Istanbul.

A guide to the cost of one-way tickets is Rome-Paris L126,000; Rome-London L205,000; Rome-Athens L120,000; Turin-Barcelona L116,000; and Rome-Amsterdam

ITALY

L158,000. Most fares carry a L10,000 to L15,000 supplement in July and August.

Eighteen buses a day link the bus station next to Trieste Railway Station to the combined bus and train station in Koper, Slovenia. In Trieste buy your ticket inside the bus station (US$2); in Koper there's a kiosk next to the stop. All passengers disembark at the border and walk through customs carrying their luggage. In Koper there are frequent bus connections to much of Slovenia and Croatia. This is the cheapest and most interesting way to cross.

Train

From major transport hubs in Italy, such as Naples, Rome, Florence, Bologna and Milan, it is simple to travel by train to most major destinations throughout Europe.

Eurocity trains run from major destinations throughout Europe, including Paris, Geneva, Zürich, Frankfurt, Vienna and Barcelona, directly to major Italian cities. Trains also link up with ferries from Calais to England and from Brindisi to Greece.

Travellers aged under 26 can take advantage of BIGE tickets, sold at Transalpino offices at most train stations and CIT offices in Italy, Europe and overseas. Examples of one-way fares are Rome-London L156,200; Rome-Paris L96,500; Florence-Amsterdam L129,500; and Milan-Munich L43,500.

Examples of normal one-way 2nd-class fares are Rome-London L215,000; Rome-Paris L125,000; and Rome-Amsterdam L250,000. Throughout Europe and in Italy it is worth paying extra for a couchette on night trains. A couchette from Florence to Munich or from Milan to Paris is an extra L18,500.

You can book tickets at train stations or at CTS and CIT offices. Eurocity trains, like the internal intercity trains, carry a supplement.

Car & Motorbike

Europe might be compact, but it can still take a long time to drive to Italy. The distance from London to Rome is 1898 km (about 24 hours), from Paris it is 1449 km (about 20 hours), from Frankfurt 1312 km and from Moscow 3299 km.

Petrol prices have now been deregulated in Italy, so it is not as expensive as it used to be, but you must pay tolls on the autostrade. Foreign tourists, driving their own cars with foreign numberplates, used to be able to buy toll cards for the autostrade from the Italian Automobile Club (ACI). There were four packages, covering northern, central and southern Italy, and Sicily and Sardinia. They also entitled you to free breakdown service and a replacement car if yours was under repair for over 12 hours. The packages were scrapped in 1992, but may be reintroduced in early 1993, when the law will be reviewed.

The main points of entry into Italy are the Mont Blanc tunnel from France at Chamonix, which connects to the A5 for Turin and Milan; the Grand St Bernard tunnel from Switzerland, which also connects to the A5; and the Brenner Pass from Austria, which connects with the A22 to Bologna. Italy has a vast system of autostrade; the main north-south link is the Autostrada del Sole from Milan to Reggio di Calabria (A1 from Milan to Naples and A3 to Reggio di Calabria).

Toll charges can make travelling on the autostrade expensive. The toll from Rome to Bologna, for instance is L27,000. However, south of Naples (including Sicily) some of the autostrade are free. Connecting roads provide access to Italy's major cities from the autostrade system. Rome has a ring road, known as the Grande Raccordo Anulare, and Milan has two tangential roads known as Tangenziali est (east) and ovest (west).

Hitching

The best advice is to make enquiries at youth hostels throughout Europe, where you can often arrange a lift. Otherwise, follow the same advice as for within Italy and stand, with a sign stating your destination, near the entrance to the autostrade.

SEA

Ferry

See Getting There & Away under Brindisi (ferries to/from Greece), Ancona (to/from Greece and Turkey), Venice (to/from Greece and Egypt), Sicily (to/from Malta and Tunis) and Syracuse (to/from Malta).

Adriatica operates a car ferry between Trieste and Durrës, Albania, about nine times a month. The 25-hour journey costs US$100 deck plus L4000 port tax. Tickets are sold by Agenzia Marittima Agemar (☎ 040-363 737), Via Rossini 2, on the old harbour about five blocks from Trieste Railway Station. Three times a month this same ferry calls at Bari on its way to Durrës (42 hours this way) and tickets for the 17-hour crossing from Bari to Albania are US$65 deck plus tax. The agent there is Agestea (☎ 080-331 555), Via Liside 4, Bari. The ferry leaves Trieste around noon and Bari in the evening, and foot passengers should be able to pick up tickets a couple of hours before departure.

Getting Around

AIR
Travelling by plane is expensive within Italy and it makes much better sense to use the efficient and considerably cheaper rail and bus services. The three main domestic airlines are Alitalia, ATI (Alitalia's domestic line) and Alisarda; all have offices in the larger cities. The main airports are in Rome, Pisa, Milan, Naples, Catania and Cagliari, but there are other, smaller airports throughout Italy. Domestic flights can be booked directly with the airlines or through CIT, CTS and other travel agencies.

Various discounts exist, including for families and weekend travel. There is also a 50% discount for Rome-Milan if you take the last flight of the day. Airline fares fluctuate, but the following one-way, economy fares for 1992 will give some idea of the cost: Rome-Cagliari L150,500; Rome-Milan L210,000; and Milan-Palermo L284,000.

BUS
Bus travel within Italy is provided by numerous companies, and services vary from local routes linking small villages (provided for the locals) to major intercity connections. It is generally not necessary to make reservations – just arrive early enough to claim a seat. On major routes the companies will often provide an additional bus if needed. Buses can be a cheaper and faster way to get around if your destination is not on major rail lines, for instance from Umbria to Rome or Florence, and in the interior areas of Sicily and Sardinia. Major companies include Marozzi and Segesta (for the south) and Lazzi (for the north).

You can usually get bus timetables from local tourist offices, and if not, staff will be able to point you in the direction of the main bus companies. In the cities bus services are usually frequent and reliable. You must buy bus tickets before you board the bus and validate them once aboard. Tickets are sold at most tobacconists and at ticket booths at bus terminals (for instance, outside Stazione Termini in Rome where most of the major buses stop). In some smaller towns and villages, tickets are sold in bars – just ask a local where you can get *biglietti per l'autobus* (bus tickets) – but generally tickets are sold on the bus.

Major bus terminals have been listed under the various towns. Note that, unlike trains in Italy, buses almost always leave on time. Some examples of prices for bus travel are Palermo-Rome L65,000; Perugia-Rome L15,000; and Agrigento-Palermo L6500.

TRAIN
Travelling by train in Italy is simple, cheap and generally efficient. The FS *(Ferrovie dello Stato)* is the state railway and there are several private railway services throughout the country.

The FS runs four types of trains: a *locale*, which usually stops at all stations and can be very slow; a *diretto*, which stops less frequently and indicates that you do not need to change trains to reach the final destination; an *espresso*, which stops only at major stations; and a *rapido*, which services only the major cities and is also known as an *intercity*.

Costs & Reservations
To travel on the rapido (intercity) trains, you

ITALY

have to pay a *supplemento*, an additional charge determined by the distance you are travelling. For instance, on the intercity train between Florence and Bologna (about 100 km) you will pay L3800, and between Rome and Perugia (about 250 km) you will pay L7300. Always check whether the train you are about to catch is an intercity, and pay the supplement before you get on the train, otherwise you will pay extra. Note that Eurail pass holders are still required to pay the supplement and that some intercities do not have 2nd-class compartments.

You can catch a Eurocity train (see the previous Getting There & Away section) to travel between major Italian cities, but you must pay a rapido supplement if you do so.

There are left-luggage facilities at all major train stations and at other train stations, except for the smallest, throughout Italy. They are usually open 24 hours a day, seven days a week, and charge L1500 per bag per day.

Discounts

It is not worth buying a Eurail or Inter-Rail pass if you are going to travel only in Italy, since train fares are very cheap. The FS offers its own discount passes for travel within the country. These include the Cartaverde for those aged 26 years and under. It costs L40,000, is valid for one year and entitles you to a 20% discount on all train travel. BTLC tickets, designed specifically for tourists, are valid for a period of eight, 15, 21 or 30 days and entitle you to unlimited travel and exemption from payment of rapido supplements. A ticket for 21 days costs L260,000, or L224,000 for 15 days. You can also buy a *biglietto chilometrico*, which is valid for two months and allows you to cover 3000 km, with a maximum of 20 trips. It costs L183,000 (2nd class) and you must pay the rapido supplement if you catch a rapido. Unless you are on a whirlwind tour of the country, you will probably find it difficult to make a saving.

The FS has just introduced the Italy Flexi Railcard, which offers basically the same advantages as BTLC, but with more flexi-

bility. Some examples of prices for train fares are Rome-Venice L36,000; Rome-Perugia L15,400; Naples-Rome L16,000; Florence-Bologna L8700; and Bologna-Milan L13,000.

TAXI

Try to avoid using taxis in Italy, as they are very expensive, and you can usually catch a bus instead. The shortest taxi ride in Rome will cost around L10,000. If you do need to use a taxi, you can usually find one at train and bus stations or you can telephone for one (radio taxi phone numbers are listed throughout the book in the Getting Around sections of the major cities).

CAR & MOTORBIKE

Trains and buses are fine for travelling through most of Italy, but if you want to get off the beaten track, renting a car or motorbike is a good idea, particularly in Sicily and Sardinia, where some of the most interesting and beautiful places are difficult to reach by public transport. The Istituto Geografico de Agostini publishes detailed road maps for all of Italy. Its book entitled *Atlante Stradale Italiano* has road maps as well as town maps. You can also buy individual maps of the regions you plan to visit.

Road Rules

Italian traffic, particularly in the cities, can appear extremely chaotic, and people drive at high speed on the autostrade (never remain in the left-hand fast lane longer than is necessary to pass a car). Despite this, Italians tend to be quite good drivers.

In Italy as throughout Continental Europe, people drive on the right side of the road and pass on the left. Unless otherwise indicated, you must give way to cars coming from the right. It is compulsory to wear seat belts, and the carabinieri (police) spend a lot of time looking for those who break the law. If caught, you will be required to pay a fine on the spot. Helmets are now compulsory for motorcyclists if the motorcycle is 50 cc or more.

In Rome and Naples you might have difficulty negotiating the extraordinarily chaotic traffic, but remain calm, keep your eyes on the car in front of you and you should be OK. Most roads are well signed and once you arrive in a city or village, follow the *centro* signs to reach the centre of town. Be extremely careful where you park your car. In the major cities it will almost certainly be towed away and you will pay a heavy fine if you leave it in an area marked with a sign reading 'Zona di Rimozione' (Removal Zone) and featuring a tow truck.

Some Italian cities, including Rome, Florence, Milan and Turin, have introduced restricted access to motorists (of both private and rental cars) in their historical centres. The restrictions, however, do not apply to vehicles with foreign registrations, to allow tourists to reach their hotels. If you are stopped by a traffic police officer, you merely need to name the hotel where you are staying. Motorcyclists with large bikes may be stopped, but *motorini* (mopeds) and scooters (such as Vespas) are able to enter the zones without any problems.

Speed limits vary, but are usually 40 km/h in cities and 110 km/h for vehicles up to 1100 cc and 120 km/h for more powerful vehicles.

Expenses
Petrol prices are not as expensive now that they have been deregulated, but you will pay a considerable amount of money to use the autostrade (except in the south, Sicily and Sardinia, where some autostrade are toll-free). Petrol is called *benzina*, unleaded petrol is *benzina senza piombo* and diesel is *gasolio*. If you are driving a car which uses LPG (liquid petroleum gas), you will need to buy a special guide to service stations which have *gasauto*. By law these must be located in nonresidential areas and are usually in the country or on city outskirts.

Rental
It is cheaper to rent a car before you leave your own country. Most major firms, including Hertz, Avis and Budget, will arrange this and you simply pick up the vehicle at a nominated point when in Italy. You will need

to be aged 21 years or over to rent a car in Italy, and it is recommended that you obtain an International Driving Permit before you leave your country if you are not an EC national. Most firms, however, will accept a standard licence with an Italian translation, which can usually be provided by the agencies themselves.

In 1992 Hertz was offering a special weekend rate which compared well with rates offered by other firms. This was L125,000 for a small car from Friday 9 am to Monday 9 am. The cost for a week was L504,000. Other discounts are also offered to tourists.

Rental motorbikes come in two versions: motorini and scooters, such as Vespas. The average cost for a Vespa is L50,000 a day or L300,000 a week. For a motorino you will pay L40,000 a day and L240,000 a week. The cost for a bicycle ranges from L8000 to L15,000 a day and up to L80,000 a week. To rent a Vespa or moped under 120 cc you must be aged 16 years or over and no licence is required. With mopeds and scooters over 120 cc, you need a licence and must be 18 years old.

Rental agencies are listed under the major cities. Most tourist offices have information about where to rent a car or motorbike, or you can look in the Yellow Pages for each town.

Purchase
Car Basically, it is not possible for foreigners to buy a car in Italy, since the law requires that you must be a resident to own and register one. However, if you manage to find a way around this, the average cost of a cheap car is L1,000,000 to L1,500,000, ranging up to around L7,000,000 for a decent second-hand Fiat Uno. The best way to find a car is to look in the classified section of local newspapers in each town or city. If you buy a car in another country and need any assistance or advice in Italy, contact the ACI (see the Useful Organisations section).

Motorbike & Bicycle The same laws apply to owning and registering a motorbike. The

ITALY

cost of a second-hand Vespa ranges from L500,000 to L1,000,000, and a motorino will cost from L200,000 to L1,000,000. Prices for more powerful bikes start at L1,500,000. You can buy a decent second-hand bicycle for L200,000.

BICYCLE

Bikes are available for rent in most Italian towns (see the Getting Around section in each city), but if you are planning to do a lot of cycling, consider buying a bike in Italy (see the previous section). See the Activities section earlier in this chapter for some suggestions on places to cycle.

HITCHING

It is illegal to hitchhike on Italy's autostrade, but quite acceptable to stand near the entrance to the toll booths. It is not often done in Italy, but Italians are friendly people and you will generally find a lift. Women travelling alone should be extremely cautious about hitchhiking, particularly in the south, Sicily and Sardinia. It is preferable to travel with a companion in these areas. Hitching on smaller roads, where there is less traffic, can be very time-consuming.

BOAT

Large ferries (navi) service the islands of Sicily and Sardinia, and smaller ferries (traghetti) and hydrofoils (aliscafi) service areas such as the Aeolian Islands, Capri and Ischia. The main embarkation points for Sicily and Sardinia are Genoa, Livorno, Civitavecchia and Naples. In Sicily the main points of arrival are Palermo and Messina, and in Sardinia they are Cagliari, Arbatax, Olbia and Porto Torres.

Tirrenia Navigazione is the major company servicing the Mediterranean and it has offices throughout Italy. The FS also operates ferries to Sicily and Sardinia. Further information is provided in the Getting There & Away sections under both islands. Most services are overnight and all ferries carry vehicles (you can usually take a bicycle free of charge).

LOCAL TRANSPORT

All of the major cities have good transport systems, including buses and, in Rome, Milan and Naples, underground railways. In Venice, however, your only options are to get around by boat or on foot. Efficient bus services also operate between neighbouring towns and villages. Tourist offices will provide information on urban public transport systems, including bus routes and maps of the underground railway systems.

Bus

Urban buses operate on an honour system. You must buy a ticket beforehand and validate it in the machine on the bus. Tickets generally cost from L700 to L1000, although most cities offer 24-hour tourist tickets for around L2500. Think twice before travelling without a ticket, as in most cities the army of inspectors has been increased along with fines. In Rome you will be fined L50,000 on the spot if caught without a validated ticket.

Underground

On the underground railways (called the metropolitana) in Rome, Milan (where it is referred to as the MM) and Naples, you must buy tickets and validate them before getting on the train. Bus and underground railway tickets are usually sold at tobacconists and newspaper stands.

TOURS

It is less expensive and more enjoyable to do some research and see the sights independently, but if you are in a hurry or prefer guided tours, go to CIT, which has offices in all major cities. It organises city tours for an average price of L25,000 and specialises in package tours of Italy. Offices of CIT abroad (see Useful Organisations under the Facts for the Visitor section) can provide information about and organise package tours to Italy. Tourist offices in Italy sometimes offer cheap guided tours and can usually give you information on local agencies (other than CIT) that offer tours throughout Italy.

Rome

'I now realise all the dreams of my youth,' wrote Goethe on his arrival in Rome in the winter of 1786. Perhaps Rome today is more chaotic, but certainly no less romantic or fascinating. In this city a phenomenal concentration of history, legend and monuments coexists with an equally phenomenal concentration of people busily going about everyday life. It is easy to pick the tourists because they are the only ones to turn their heads as the bus passes the Colosseum.

Some historians believe that Rome (Roma) was founded by the Etruscans. Others, however, are hazy on its origins, so the legend of Romulus and Remus prevails. They were the twin sons of Rhea Silvia and the Roman war god Mars, and were raised by a she-wolf after being abandoned on the Tiber (Tevere). According to the myth, Romulus killed his brother during a battle over who should govern and then established the city on the Palatine (Palatino), one of the famous Seven Hills of Rome. It is said that Romulus disappeared one day, enveloped in a cloud which carried him back to the domain of the gods. From the legend grew an empire which eventually controlled almost the entire world known to Europeans at the time, an achievement described by a historian of the day as being 'without parallel in human history'.

In Rome there is visible evidence of the two great empires of the Western world: the Roman Empire and the Christian Church. On the one hand there are the forum and the Colosseum, and on the other, St Peter's and the Vatican. In between, in almost every piazza, lies history on so many levels, that the saying 'Rome, a lifetime is not enough' must certainly be true. Realistically, at least a week is probably a reasonable amount of time to see Rome, but whatever time you devote to the city, put on your walking shoes, buy a good map and plan your time carefully – the city will seem less chaotic and overwhelming than it first appears.

Orientation

Rome is a vast city, but the historical centre is quite small. Most of the major sights are within walking distance of the central railway station, Stazione Termini. It is, for instance, possible to walk from the Colosseum, through the Forum and the Palatine, up to the Spanish Steps and across to the Vatican in one day, though this is hardly recommended even for the most dedicated tourist. One of the great pleasures of Rome is to allow time for wandering through the many beautiful piazzas (squares), stopping now and again for a caffè and *paste* (cakes). All of the major monuments are to the west and north of the station area, but make sure you use a map. Although it can be enjoyable to get lost in Rome, it can also be very frustrating and time-consuming.

It can be difficult to plan an itinerary if your time is limited, but it is a good idea to head for museums in the morning, as most close by 2 pm. Some sights are open in the afternoon, including the Colosseum, St Peter's Basilica and the Roman Forum (the latter in summer only).

Most new arrivals in Rome will end up at Stazione Termini. It is the terminus for all international and national trains; the main city bus terminus is in Piazza Cinquecento, directly in front of the station, and many intercity buses arrive and depart from the area between Stazione Termini and Piazza della Repubblica.

The main airport is Leonardo da Vinci, at Fiumicino (about an hour by train or car from the centre). For more information, see To/From the Airport under the following Getting Around section.

If you arrive in Rome by car, you can park in one of the numerous small, supervised car parks around the periphery of the historical centre, including between Piazza della Repubblica and Via Parigi (where the tourist office is). For more information, see Car & Motorbike in the following Getting Around section.

The majority of cheap hotels and pensioni are concentrated around Stazione Termini, but if you are prepared to go the extra distance, it is only slightly more expensive and definitely more enjoyable to stay closer to the centre. The area around the station, particularly to the west, is unpleasant, seedy and can be dangerous at night, especially for women, but it is the most popular area for budget travellers.

Although Rome is nowhere near as chaotic as Naples, many drivers, particularly motorcyclists, do not stop at red lights. Don't expect them to stop at pedestrian crossings either: the accepted mode of crossing a road is to step into the traffic and walk at a steady pace. If in doubt, follow a Roman.

Information

Tourist Offices There is a branch office of the EPT (Provincial Tourist Department) opposite platform 2 at Stazione Termini, open from 9 am to 7 pm. The staff will not book accommodation, but will provide a full list of hotels in Rome, a map and other information. In peak periods, queues can be 30 people long. The office has an indecipherable brochure on city bus routes; forget it and invest L4000 in the very good street map and bus guide simply entitled *Roma*, with a red-and-blue cover, which is published by Editrice Lozzi in Rome; it is available at any

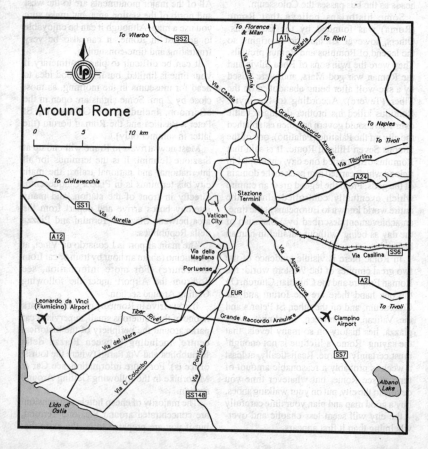

Around Rome

0   5   10 km

To Viterbo

SS2

To Florence
& Milan

A1

To Rieti

To Reti

Via Salaria

Via Flaminia

Via Cassia

To Civitavecchia

SS1

Via Aurelia

A12

Grande Raccordo Anulare

To Naples

To Tivoli

Via Tiburtina

A24

Stazione
Termini

Vatican
City

Via Casilina

SS6

Via della
Magliana

Portuense

Leonardo da Vinci
(Fiumicino) Airport

Tiber River

Via del Mare

Via C Colombo

EUR

Grande Raccordo Annulare

Via Appia

Via Pontina

SS148

Lido di
Ostia

Via Nuova

Ciampino
Airport

To Tivoli

A2

SS7

Albano
Lake

newsstand in Stazione Termini. It lists all streets, with map references, as well as all bus routes, and provides a simple guide in English, French, German and Italian to the major sights.

The main EPT office (☎ 06-488 37 48) is at Via Parigi 11 and is open from 8.15 am to 7.15 pm. Walk directly north from Stazione Termini, through Piazza della Repubblica. Via Parigi runs to the right from the top of the piazza, about five minutes' walk from the station. It has a good range of brochures, including: *Here's Rome*, an excellent introduction to the city, listing important and useful addresses and phone numbers; *Tutta Roma*, a monthly listing of all current events; the *English Yellow Pages* and the *Italian Yellow Pages for Tourists*, which are English-language phone books for Rome; *Carnet di Roma*, a monthly guide to events in Rome, published in English; and individual brochures on most of the major sights. It will also have information on summer festivals and concert seasons.

ENIT (☎ 06-49 711), the national tourist office, is at Via Marghera 2. From here you can pick up information on most towns in Italy.

Money Banks are open Monday to Friday from 8.30 am to 1.30 pm and 2.45 to 3.45 pm. You will find a bank and several exchange offices at Stazione Termini. One exchange office is in the main arrival area and one is near the exit to Piazza Cinquecento. Both are open until late at night. There is also an exchange office (Banco di Santo Spirito) at Fiumicino Airport.

Numerous other exchange offices are scattered throughout the city, including: Credito Italiano, Piazza di Spagna 20, and Piazza Navona 48; Società Rosati, Via Nazionale 186; and American Express in Piazza di Spagna. The Banca Commerciale Italiana, Piazza Venezia, is the most reliable for receiving money transfers.

Post The main post office is at Piazza San Silvestro 28, just off Via del Tritone, and is open Monday to Friday from 8.30 am to 8 pm and Saturday from 8.30 am to midday. Fermo posta (the Italian version of poste restante) is available here. You can send telegrams from the office next door (open 24 hours). There's a post office at the station.

The Vatican post office, in St Peter's Square (Piazza San Pietro), is open Monday to Friday from 8.30 am to 7 pm and Saturday from 8.30 am to 6 pm. The service is supposedly faster and more reliable. The postcode for central Rome is 00100.

Telephone The ASST office is next door to the post office in Piazza San Silvestro, open Monday to Saturday from 8 am to 11.30 pm and Sunday from 9 am to 8.30 pm. There is also a branch of the ASST at Stazione Termini which is open 24 hours a day. The main SIP office is in Corso Vittorio Emanuele 201, near Piazza Navona, open from 8 am to 9 pm. See the Facts for the Visitor section at the start of this chapter for detailed information about making calls and posting mail in Italy.

Rome's telephone code is 06.

Foreign Embassies See Foreign Embassies in the Facts for the Visitor section at the start of this chapter.

Travel Agencies There is a CIT office (Italy's national tourist agency; ☎ 488 16 78) in Stazione Termini, where you can make bookings for planes, trains, buses and ferries. The staff speak English and can provide information on fares and discounts for students and young people. They also arrange tours of Rome and the surrounding areas. CTS (the student tourist centre; ☎ 46 791), Via Genova 16, off Via Nazionale, offers much the same services and will also make hotel reservations, but focuses on discount and student travel. The staff speak English. American Express (☎ 67 641), Piazza di Spagna 38, offers a travel service similar to those just mentioned, as well as a hotel reservation service, and can arrange tours of the city and surrounding areas. A full list of all travel agencies in Rome is available at the EPT office.

ITALY

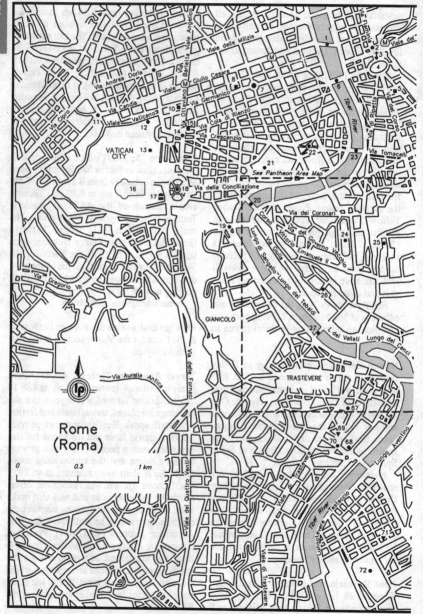

Rome
(Roma)

0   0.5   1 km

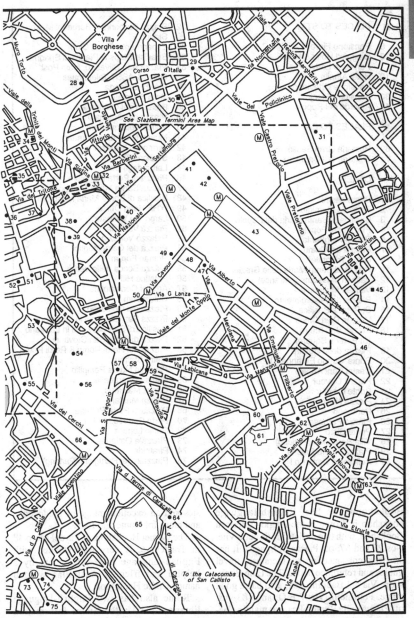

Bookshops The best English-language bookshop in Rome is the Anglo-American Bookshop, with two outlets in Via della Vite, Nos 27 and 57, off Piazza di Spagna. It has an excellent selection of literature, travel guides and reference books. The Lion Bookshop, Via del Babuino 181, also has a good range. Feltrinelli, Via V E Orlando 83, just off Piazza della Repubblica, has mainly classics and an excellent range of guidebooks and maps for Rome and Italy.

The Corner Bookshop, at Via del Moro 48 in Trastevere, is very well stocked with English-language books. It is run by a helpful and friendly Australian woman named Claire Hammond.

Rome also has two English-language libraries: the United States Information

Service (USIS; ☎ 4 67 41), Via Veneto 119a (off Piazza Barberini); and the British Council Library (☎ 482 66 41), Via delle Quattro Fontane 20 (off Via Nazionale).

Emergency Emergency medical treatment is available at the casualty sections (Pronto Soccorso) at public hospitals including: Policlinico Umberto I (☎ 49 971), Via del Policlinico 255, near Stazione Termini; Policlinico A Gemelli (☎ 33 051), Largo A Gemelli 8; and Santo Spirito (☎ 65 09 01), Lungotevere in Sassia. The Rome American Hospital (☎ 25 671), Via E Longoni 69, is a private hospital and you should use its services only if you have health insurance and have consulted your insurance company.

For an ambulance call ☎ 5100, and for first aid call ☎ 115.

There is a pharmacy in Stazione Termini, open from 7 am to 11 pm daily (closed in August). For information on all-night pharmacies in Rome, ring ☎ 1921. The questura (police headquarters; ☎ 4686) is at Via San Vitale 15. The questura's Foreigners' Bureau (Ufficio Stranieri; ☎ 46 86 29 87) is around the corner at Via Genova 2. It is open 24 hours a day and thefts etc can be reported here. For immediate police attendance, call ☎ 112 or 113.

Dangers & Annoyances Thieves are very active in the area around Stazione Termini. Don't be fooled by their 'up-front' approach – they are highly skilled. The best way to avoid being robbed is to remain extremely alert and shout 'Va via!' ('Go away') when approached. Never carry a purse, wallet or documents in your pockets and keep a good grip on any bags you may be carrying. Purse and bag snatchers also use motorcycles in Rome, so if you have a shoulder bag, wear it with the strap across your chest.

Useful Addresses If you need a wash when you arrive, there are public baths (follow the *diurno* signs) downstairs at the station. Showers cost L7000. To wash your clothes there is a Lavasecco a Gettoni at Campo de' Fiori 38 and at Via Castelfidardo 29, near

Stazione Termini. Remember that it is expensive to use a laundry: you will pay around L8000 to L10,000 for a medium load.

The head office of the Italian Youth Hostels Association (☎ 487 11 52) is at Via Cavour 44, 00184 Rome. It will provide information about all the youth hostels in Italy. You can also join the IYHF here.

Things to See & Do
It would take years to explore every corner of Rome, months to begin to appreciate the incredible number of monuments and weeks for a thorough tour of the city. You can, however, cover most of the important monuments in five days, or three at a minimum. If you have even less time, try visiting St Peter's and the Vatican in the morning, and then head for the Roman Forum, Palatine and the Colosseum in the afternoon.

Walking Tour Try to get hold of the book *Strolling around Rome*, published by the Regione Lazio, Assessorato del Turismo, and occasionally available at the EPT office. A good, but rather long walk to help orient yourself in Rome is to start from Piazza della Repubblica and head north-west along Via Vittorio Emanuele Orlando, turning left into Via XX Settembre (which becomes Via del Quirinale) to reach the **Piazza del Quirinale**, which offers one of the best views in Rome. From the piazza walk back down Via del Quirinale and turn left into Via delle Quattro Fontane to get to **Piazza Barberini**. From here you can wander up **Via Veneto**, or take Via Sistina to the **Spanish Steps**.

From Piazza di Spagna go down Via Condotti and turn left on to Via del Corso, crossing over Via del Tritone. Then take the second left (Via delle Muratte) to see the **Trevi Fountain**. Return to Via del Corso and cross into the **Piazza Colonna**. Things get a bit complicated here, but use a good map, follow the tourist signs and you won't get lost. Walk through the piazza into the **Piazza di Montecitorio**, and continue straight ahead along Via degli Uffici del Vicario, where you can buy a gelato at **Giolitti**. Then turn left at Via della Maddalena to get to the **Pantheon**.

ITALY

Take Via Giustiniani from the north-western corner of Piazza della Rotonda to get to **Piazza Navona**. Leave the piazza from Via Cuccagna, cross Corso Vittorio Emanuele II and take Via Cancelleria to reach the **Campo de' Fiori**. From here go down Via Gallo into the **Piazza Farnese** and then walk directly ahead out of the piazza on Via dei Farnesi into **Via Giulia**.

If you still have the energy, you have two choices. Either continue along Via Giulia and cross the Ponte Vittorio Emanuele II to get to **St Peter's Basilica** and the **Vatican**, or cross the **Ponte Sisto** at the southern end of Via Giulia and wander through the streets of **Trastevere**.

Colosseum Construction of the Colosseo, which was originally known as the Flavian Amphitheatre, was started by Emperor Vespasian in 72 AD in the grounds of Nero's Golden House and completed by his son Titus. The massive structure could seat 50,000 people, and the bloody gladiator combat and wild beast shows, when thousands of wild animals were slashed to death, give some insight into Roman people of the day. Historians disagree on whether many early Christian martyrs were fed to lions in the stadium.

In the Middle Ages the amphitheatre became a fortress and was later used as a quarry for travertine and marble for the Palazzo Venezia and other buildings. Opening hours are from 9 am to one hour before sunset, and from 9 am to 1 pm Wednesday and holidays. Entry costs L6000.

Arch of Constantine Next to the Colosseum is the triumphal arch built to honour Constantine following his victory over his rival Maxentius at the battle of Milvian Bridge (near the present-day Zona Olimpica, north-west of the Villa Borghese) in 312 AD. Its decorative reliefs were taken from earlier structures. The arch was recently unveiled after restoration.

Past the Palatine is the **Circus Maximus**. There is not much to see here apart from the few ruins that remain of what was once a chariot racetrack big enough to hold more than 200,000 people.

From the Arch of Constantine, bus No 118, or a 15-minute walk, will take you to the **Baths of Caracalla** (Terme di Caracalla), a huge complex covering 10 hectares. The baths could hold 1600 people and had shops, gardens, libraries and entertainment. Begun by Septimius Severus in 206 AD and completed by his son Antonius Caracalla in 217, the baths were used until the 6th century AD. Today they are an atmospheric venue for opera performances in summer. They are open on weekdays from 9 am to two hours before sunset and on Sundays from 9 am to 1 pm. Entry is L6000.

The Roman Forum & Palatine The commercial, political and religious centre of ancient Rome, the forum stands in a valley between the Capitoline and Palatine hills. Originally marshland, the area was drained during the early Republican era and became a centre for political rallies, public ceremonies and senate meetings. Its importance declined along with the empire after the 4th century AD, and the temples, monuments and buildings constructed by successive emperors, consuls and senators fell into ruin, eventually to be used as pasture land.

The area was excavated in the 18th and 19th centuries. Excavations are continuing even today and you can watch archaeological teams at work in several locations. You can enter the forum from Via dei Fori Imperiali, which leads from Piazza Venezia to the Colosseum. It is open from 9 am to one hour before sunset, and on Sunday and Tuesday from 9 am to 1 pm. Admission costs L10,000 and covers both the forum and the Palatine.

To the right as you you enter the forum is the **Basilica Aemilia**, built as a two-storey portico lined with shops. Next is the **Curia**, once the meeting place of the Roman Senate. It was converted to a Christian church in the Middle Ages, which explains its present well-preserved state. Opposite is the famous **Lapis Niger**, a large piece of black marble which legend says covered the grave of

Romulus. The tomb also contains the oldest known Latin inscription, believed to have been written in the 6th century BC.

To the right of the entrance to the forum is the **Arch of Septimius Severus**, which was erected in 203 AD in honour of this emperor and his sons and is considered one of Italy's major triumphal arches. A recent project to renovate the arch left it exactly half cleaned when the money ran out. To the left is the Rostrum, formerly used by public speakers, which was decorated in ancient times by the rams of captured ships. A circular base stone marks the symbolic centre of ancient Rome, the *umbilicus urbis*. The nearby **Column of Phocus** was erected in 608 AD in the main square of the forum in honour of a Byzantine emperor.

Along Via Sacra lies the **Temple of Saturn**, one of the most important temples in ancient Rome. Eight granite columns remain. The Basilica Julia, opposite, was the seat of justice, and nearby is the Temple of Julius Caesar, which was erected by Octavian in 29 BC on the site where Caesar's body was burned and Antony read his famous speech. The **Temple of Castor & Pollux** was built in 489 BC to mark the defeat of the Etruscan Tarquins and in honour of the 'heavenly twins', or Dioscuri.

The **Church of Santa Maria Antiqua**, near the Palatine, is the oldest Christian church in the forum, and, although badly damaged, still contains frescoes of interest. After walking back to the Arch of Augustus, you will find the **House of the Vestals**, where lived the virgins who tended the sacred flame in the adjoining **Temple of Vesta**. If the flame went out, it was seen as a bad omen. The other major sights are the **Temple of Antoninus & Faustina**, of which six columns remain, and the **Arch of Titus**, at the end of the forum, built in 81 AD in honour of the emperor who conquered Jerusalem.

From here climb the **Palatine**, where wealthy Romans built their homes and where legend says that Romulus founded the city. Cicero lived here and Emperor Augustus built his palace on the hill. His successors

followed suit and built a series of palaces and temples here also. Like the forum, the buildings of the Palatine fell into ruin and in the Middle Ages the hill became the site of convents and churches. During the Renaissance wealthy families established their gardens here. The Farnese villa and gardens were built over the ruins of the Palace of Tiberius.

Worth a look are the **House of Livia**, which is decorated with frescoes; the **Domus Augustana** (House of Augustus) and the **Palace of the Flavians**, both built during the reign of Domitian; the **Temple of Magna Mater**, which was built in 204 BC to house the black stone Cybele; and the impressive ruins of the **Baths of Septimius Severus**. Bring a picnic lunch. Opening hours are the same as for the forum.

Piazza del Campidoglio Designed by Michelangelo in 1538, the piazza is on the Capitoline (Capitolino), the most important of Rome's seven hills, and is bounded by three palaces. It was on this hill, which has always been the seat the Roman government, that Brutus spoke of the death of Julius Caesar and that Nelson hoisted the British flag in 1799 to keep Napoleon out of the city.

In the centre of the piazza is an equestrian statue of Marcus Aurelius, sculpted in the 2nd century AD; it was removed for renovation in 1991.

The Roman Forum is below the piazza and on the way is the **Mamertine Prison**, where prisoners in ancient Rome were put through a hole in the floor to starve to death. The **Chiesa di Santa Maria d'Aracoeli** is between the Campidoglio and the Vittorio Emanuele monument, at the top of a long flight of steps. Built on the site where legend says the Sybil told Augustus of the coming birth of Christ, it features frescoes by Pinturicchio and a statue of the baby Jesus said to have been carved from the wood of an olive tree from the garden of Gethsemane. It is an object of pilgrimage and is placed in a nativity scene at the church each Christmas.

From the Campidoglio walk back past the Forum, down Via della Conciliazione to the piazza of the same name and then along Via San Giovanni Decollato to the Church of Santa Maria in Cosmedin in Piazza Bocca della Verità.

Santa Maria in Cosmedin This is regarded as one of the finest medieval churches in Rome. It has a seven-storey bell tower and its interior is heavily decorated with inlaid marble, including the beautiful floor. The main attraction for the tourist hordes is, however, the **Bocca della Verità** (Mouth of Truth). Legend has it that if you put your right hand into the mouth, while telling a lie, it will snap shut.

Piazza del Quirinale Set on Quirinal Hill, this piazza affords a stunning view of Rome and St Peter's. Italy's president lives at the Quirinal Palace (Palazzo del Quirinale).

The **Piazza Venezia** is overshadowed by one of the world's more unusual monuments, dedicated to Vittorio Emanuele II. This huge, white construction topped with a colonnade stands 70 metres high and incorporates the Museum of the Risorgimento and the Altar of the Fatherland (Altare della Patria). Also in the piazza is the 15th century **Palazzo Venezia**, which was Mussolini's official residence.

The **Piazza del Popolo** is a semicircular piazza designed in the early 19th century by Giuseppe Valadier. It is at the foot of the **Pincio**, a panoramic terrace which affords a stunning view of the city.

Trevi Fountain The high Baroque Fontana di Trevi was designed by Nicola Salvi in 1732. Its water was supplied by one of Rome's earliest aqueducts. Work to clean the fountain and its water supply was completed in 1991. The famous custom is to throw a coin into the fountain (over your shoulder while facing away) to ensure your return to Rome. It is also held that if you throw a second coin you can make a wish.

Baths of Diocletian (Terme di Diocleziano) These baths, built by Emperor Diocletian, were completed in the 4th century. The complex of baths, libraries, concert halls and gardens covered about 13 hectares and could house up to 3000 people. After the aqueduct which fed the baths was destroyed by invaders in 536 AD, the complex fell into decay. Parts of the ruins are now incorporated into the church of Santa Maria degli Angeli, which faces onto Piazza della Repubblica, and the Roman National Museum, facing Piazza dei Cinquecento.

Santa Maria degli Angeli This church was designed by Michelangelo and incorporates what was the tepidarium (lukewarm room) of the original baths. During the following centuries his work was drastically changed and little evidence of his design, apart from the great vaulted ceiling of the church, remains. An interesting feature of the church is a double meridian in the transept, one tracing the polar star and the other telling the precise time of the sun's zenith. The church is open from 7.30 am to 12.30 pm and from 4 to 6.30 pm. Through the sacristy is an entrance to a stairway leading to the upper terraces of the ruins. A plaque near the stairway records the traditional belief that the baths were built by thousands of Christians who were forced to do so.

Roman National Museum The Museo Nazionale Romano houses an important collection of ancient art, the second largest in Rome after the Vatican Museums. It also has a collection of frescoes and mosaics from the Villa of Livia at Prima Porta. The museum is open from 9 am to 2 pm (1 pm on Sundays, closed Monday) and entry is L3000.

Via Vittorio Veneto This was Rome's hot spot in the 1960s, where film stars could be spotted at the expensive outdoor cafés. It is still the city's most fashionable street, but the atmosphere of Fellini's *Roma* is long dead.

Villa Borghese This huge and beautiful park was once the estate of Cardinal Scipione Borghese. His 17th century villa houses the **Galleria Borghese** (entry L8000), and the **National Gallery of Modern Art**. Take a picnic here if the tourist trip starts to wear you down.

Piazza di Spagna & Spanish Steps This piazza, church and famous staircase (Scalinata della Trinità dei Monti) have long provided a major gathering place for foreigners. Built with a legacy from the French in 1725, but named after the Spanish Embassy to the Holy See, the steps lead to the church of Trinità dei Monti, which was built by the French.

In the 18th century the most beautiful men and women of Italy gathered there, waiting to be chosen as artists' models. To the right as you face the steps is the house where Keats spent the last three months of his life, and where he died in 1821. In the piazza is the boat-shaped fountain of the **Barcaccia**, believed to be by Pietro Bernini, father of the famous Gian Lorenzo. One of Rome's most elegant shopping streets, **Via Condotti**, runs off the piazza towards Via del Corso. The famous **Caffè Greco** is at No 86, where artists, musicians and the literati used to meet, including Goethe, Keats, Byron and Wagner.

Pantheon The only building of ancient Rome which remains well preserved, the Pantheon was built by Marcus Agrippa, son-in-law of Emperor Augustus, in 27 BC and dedicated to the most important planetary gods. Although the temple was rebuilt by Emperor Hadrian around 120 AD, Agrippa's name remains inscribed over the entrance.

Over the centuries the temple was consistently plundered and damaged. Pope Gregory III removed the gilded bronze roof tiles, although the original bronze doors remain. The Pantheon's extraordinary dome is considered the most important achievement of ancient Roman architecture. Pagan worship was forbidden by the Christian emperors and in 609 AD the temple was consecrated to the Virgin and to Christian martyrs, supposedly the origin of All Saints' Day.

The Italian kings Vittorio Emanuele II and Umberto I and the painter Raphael are buried

there. The Pantheon is in Piazza della Rotonda and is open from 9 am to 2 pm weekdays and 9 am to 1 pm weekends and holidays. Admission is free.

Piazza Navona This is a vast and beautiful square, lined with Baroque palaces. It was laid out on the ruins of Domitian's stadium and features three fountains, including Bernini's masterpiece, the **Fontana dei Fiumi** (Fountain of the Rivers), in the centre. Take time to relax on one of the stone benches and watch the artists who gather in the piazza to work.

Campo de' Fiori This is a lively piazza where a flower and vegetable market is held every morning except Sunday. Now lined with bars and trattorias, the piazza was a place of execution during the Inquisition.

The **Farnese Palace** (Palazzo Farnese), in the piazza of the same name, is just off Campo de' Fiori. A magnificent Renaissance building, it was started in 1514 by Antonio da Sangello, work was carried on by Michelangelo and it was completed by Giacomo della Porta. Built for Cardinal Alessandro Farnese (later Pope Paul III), the palace is now the French Embassy. The piazza has two fountains, which were enormous granite baths taken from the Baths of Caracalla.

Via Giulia This street was designed by Bramante, who was commissioned by Pope Julius II to create a new approach to St Peter's. It is lined with Renaissance palaces, antique shops and art galleries.

St Peter's Basilica & Square The most famous church in the Christian world, **San Pietro** stands on the site where St Peter was martyred and buried. The first church on the site was built during Constantine's reign in the 4th century, and in 1506 work started on a new basilica, designed by Bramante.

Although several architects were involved in its construction, it is generally held that St Peter's owes more to Michelangelo, who took over the project in 1547 at the age of 72 and was responsible, in particular, for the design of the dome. He died before the church was completed. The cavernous interior contains numerous treasures, including Michelangelo's superb *Pietà*, sculpted when he was only 25 years old and the only work to carry his signature (on the sash across the breast of the Madonna). It has been protected by bulletproof glass since an attack in 1972 by a hammer-wielding Hungarian.

Bernini's huge Baroque *Baldacchino* (a heavily sculpted bronze canopy over the papal altar) stands 29 metres high in the centre of the church, and, though it is an extraordinary work of art, it might not suit all tastes. Another point of note is the red porphyry disc near the central door, which marks the spot where Charlemagne and later emperors were crowned by the pope.

It is forbidden to enter St Peter's if you are wearing shorts or a short skirt.

Bernini's **Piazza San Pietro** (St Peter's Square) is considered a masterpiece. Laid out in the 17th century as a place for Christians of the world to gather, the immense piazza is bounded by two semicircular colonnades, each of which is made up of four rows of Doric columns. In the centre of the piazza is an obelisk that was brought to Rome by Caligula from Heliopolis (in ancient Egypt).

When you stand on the dark paving stones between the obelisk and one of the fountains, the colonnades appear to have only one row of columns. The pope gives a public audience at 11 am every Wednesday, and at 10 am when he is in Castelgandolfo, the pope's summer home, which is just outside Rome. Go to the information office in the piazza for information. To attend a papal audience, you must apply in writing to the Prefettura della Casa Pontificia, 00120 Città del Vaticano.

The Vatican Museums After the Risorgimento the papal states of central Italy became part of the new Kingdom of Italy, which caused a considerable rift between the church and the state. In 1929, Mussolini, under the Lateran Treaty, gave the pope full sovereignty over what is now the Vatican City.

The city has its own postal service, currency, newspaper, radio station, railway station and army of Swiss Guards. From St Peter's follow the wall of the city to the **museums**, which are open Monday to Saturday from 9 am to 1.45 pm (last entry at 1 pm). At Easter and during summer they are open from 9 am to 5 pm. Admission is L10,000. The museums are closed on Sundays and public holidays, but open on the last Sunday of every month from 9 am to 2 pm (free entry).

The Vatican museums contain an incredible collection of art and treasures collected by the popes, and you will need several hours to see the most important areas and museums. One visit is probably not enough to appreciate the full value of the collections. The **Sistine Chapel** (Cappella Sistina) comes towards the end of a full visit, but if you want to spend most of your time in the chapel, you can walk straight there and then work your way back through the museums.

The **Pio-Clementine Museum**, containing Greek and Roman antiquities, is on the ground floor near the entrance. Through the **Tapestry Gallery** and the **Map Gallery** are **Raphael's Rooms** (Stanze di Raffaello), once the private apartments of Pope Julius II, decorated with frescoes by Raphael. Of particular interest is the magnificent **Stanza della Segnatura**, which features Raphael's masterpieces *The School of Athens* and *Dispute over the Sacrament*.

From Raphael's Rooms, go down the stairs to the sumptuous **Borgia Apartments**, painted by Pinturicchio, then go down another flight of stairs to the Sistine Chapel, the private papal chapel, built in 1473 for Pope Sixtus IV. Restoration work on the ceiling has been completed so it is now possible to see Michelangelo's wonderful frescoes, with the *Creation* in the centre, in full, vibrant colour. It took him four years, at the height of the Renaissance, to paint the ceiling. Twenty-two years later he painted the *Last Judgment* on the end wall; this was under renovation in 1992. The other walls of the chapel were painted by Botticelli, Ghirlandaio, Pinturicchio and Signorelli.

Gianicolo Go to the top of the Gianicolo, the hill between St Peter's and Trastevere, for a panoramic view of Rome. At the top of the hill is Piazza Garibaldi, which features an equestrian statue of Garibaldi.

Trastevere You can wander through the narrow medieval streets of this busy and bohemian area. It is especially beautiful at night and one of the more interesting areas for bar-hopping or a meal. The people of this district have always considered themselves separate from the rest of Rome.

Of particular note here is **Santa Maria in Trastevere**, believed to be the oldest church dedicated to the Virgin in Rome. Although the first church was built on the site in the 3rd century AD, the present structure was built in the 12th century and features a Romanesque bell tower and façade, with a mosaic of the Virgin. Its interior was redecorated during the Baroque period.

Catacombs There are several catacombs in Rome, consisting of miles of tunnels carved out of volcanic rock, which were the burial and hiding places of early Christians in Rome. The **Catacombe di San Callisto**, in Via Appia Antica, are the most famous and contain the tomb of the martyred St Cecilia. They are open from 9 am to 1 pm and 3.30 to 6 pm. Entry is with a guide only and costs L6000.

Churches Apart from St Peter's, there are four other basilicas in Rome. **Santa Maria Maggiore**, down Via Cavour from Stazione Termini, was built in the 5th century, but remodelled several times. Its façade is Baroque and its campanile (bell tower) is Romanesque; the interior features 5th century mosaics. **San Giovanni in Laterano** is Rome's cathedral. The original church was built in the 4th century and was the home of the popes until the 14th century. Largely destroyed over the centuries, it was rebuilt in the 17th century. **San Pietro in Vincoli**, just off Via Cavour, is worth a visit because it houses Michelangelo's *Moses* and his unfinished statues of Leah and Rachel. The

Renaissance **Santa Maria del Popolo**, in Piazza del Popolo, contains works of art by Pinturicchio and Caravaggio.

Santa Maria della Concezione, in Via Veneto, is an austere 17th century building; however, the Capuchin cemetery beneath the church (with access on the right of the church steps) features a bizarre display of monks' bones which were used to decorate the walls of a series of chapels.

Organised Tours Carrani Tours (☎ 474 25 01), Via V E Orlando 95, operates half-day tours of the city for L36,000 to L48,000 and a full-day tour for L105,000. It also offers tours to Sorrento, Capri and other historical cities, and gives student discounts. American Express (☎ 6 76 41), Piazza di Spagna, also operates tours of the city. The city bus company, ATAC, operates a daily three-hour bus tour of Rome. Buses leave from Piazza Cinquecento at 3.30 pm and you can purchase tickets at the ATAC information booth. The CIT office at Stazione Termini also offers guided tours.

Places to Stay

Hotels & Pensioni The majority of cheap hotels and pensioni are concentrated to the east and west of Stazione Termini. The area is crowded, noisy and swarms with thieves and pickpockets who prey on newly arrived tourists. It can be unpleasant and dangerous, particularly for women at night, so it is important always to remain extremely alert.

East of Stazione Termini To reach the pensioni in this area, head to the right as you leave the train platforms onto Via Castro Pretorio. One of the cheapest places in the area is *Pensione Katty* (☎ 444 12 16), Via Palestro 35, which has singles/doubles for L34,000/40,000. *Pensione Marini* (☎ 444 00 58), in the same building, has doubles for L40,000 and triples for L18,000 per person (showers included). *Pensione Gexim* (☎ 444 13 11) Via Palestro 34, has singles/ doubles for L35,000/55,000 and triples for L25,000 per person. The *Restivo* (☎ 446 21 72), Via

ITALY

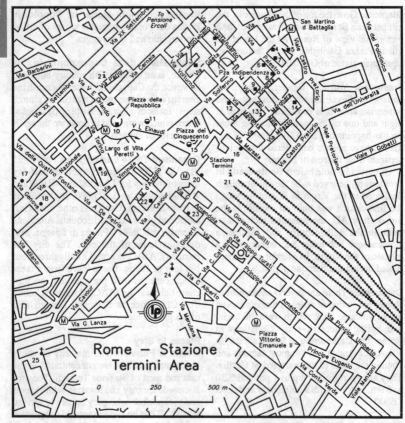

Rome – Stazione
Termini Area

0   250   500 m

Palestro 55 (to the right off Via Castro Pretorio) has doubles only for L60,000, including the cost of showers. A room for three is L25,000 per person. The elderly owner might be reluctant to allow men and women to share a bed without a marriage certificate. There is a midnight curfew. *Hotel Cervia* (☎ 49 10 56) downstairs has clean and pleasant singles/doubles for L35,000/50,000, or L60,000/70,000 with private shower.

The *Hotel Pensione Gabriella* (☎ 445 02 52), Via Palestro 88, is clean but expensive for what you get at L60,000 a double without

bath. *Hotel La Fontanella* (☎ 445 57 70) across the road at No 87 is shabby and pricey, with singles/doubles for 35,000/55,000, but the gregarious owner loves foreigners and if you promise to send a postcard, will probably lower the price. If he doesn't have a room, he is likely to send you to the *Hotel Reatina* (☎ 445 42 79), Via San Martino della Battaglia 11, run by relatives. Its prices (L40,000/80,000 for a single/double without shower) reflect a higher standard. In the same building are several other pensioni. The *Pensione Lachea* (☎ 495 72 56) has doubles/triples for L45,000/60,000. *Hotel*

■ PLACES TO STAY

1 Hotel Castelfidardo
3 Papa Germano
4 Hotel Reatina, Hotel Pensione
   Dolomiti, Pensione Tre Stelle &
   Pensione Lachea
5 Albergo Sandra
6 Hotel La Fontanella
7 Hotel Pensione Gabriella
8 Restivo & Hotel Cervia
9 Pensione Piemonte
10 Pensione Eureka & Pensione
   Arrivederci
12 Pensione Lucy &
   Pensione Giamaica
14 Pensione Katty & Pensione Marini
22 Pensione Argentina &
   Pensione Everest
23 Pensione Terni

OTHER

2 Main EPT Tourist Information
   Office
11 Intercity Bus Terminal
13 ENIT (National Tourist Office)
15 Main City Bus Terminal
16 ASST Telephones
17 Police Headquarters & Office
   for Foreigners
18 CTS (Student & Youth
   Tourist Centre)
19 Teatro dell'Opera
· 20 CIT (National Travel Agency)
21 EPT Tourist Information Office
24 Basilica di Santa Maria Maggiore
25 Basilica di San Pietro in Vincoli

Pensione Dolomiti (☎ 49 10 58) has a helpful management; singles/doubles are L40,000/65,000, breakfast included. A triple is L90,000. Downstairs is *Tre Stelle* (☎ 446 30 95) with singles/doubles for L40,000/55,000 or triples for L75,000. *Papa Germano* (☎ 48 69 19), Via Calatafimi 14a, has singles/doubles for L35,000/47,000, or L40,000/55,000 with bath. It is off Via Volturno, directly in front of the station, to the right.

Around the corner at Via Vicenza 34, is the *Pensione Piemonte* (☎ 445 22 40), with

large, clean rooms and friendly management. Singles/doubles are L40,000/55,000 and triples are L75,000; use of the communal shower is free. *Albergo Sandra* (☎ 495 26 12), Via Villafranca 10 (which runs between Via Vicenza and Via San Martino della Battaglia), is clean, with pleasant rooms and the owner is friendly. Singles/doubles cost L30,000/45,000, including the cost of a shower. Prices go down according to the length of your stay.

Hotel Castelfidardo (☎ 474 28 94), Via Castelfidardo 31, off Piazza Indipendenza, has singles/doubles for L35,000/55,000 and triples for L25,000 per person, or L30,000 per person with private bathroom. Across Via XX Settembre, at Via Collina 48 (a 10-minute walk from the station) is *Pensione Ercoli* (☎ 474 54 54) with singles/doubles for L35,000/45,000 and triples for L65,000. The *Pensione Lucy* (☎ 445 17 40), at Via Magenta 13 (first to the left of Via Vicenza) is a small family-run place and the friendly owner sets prices according to the number of people, how long you stay and which room she gives you. Generally, a single/double will cost up to L35,000/60,000. A triple will cost around L66,000 and can be bargained down. Upstairs is *Pensione Giamaica* (☎ 49 01 21), with average but pricey singles/doubles for L38,000/50,000; the owner will charge more if you stay for only one night.

Behind the station in the San Lorenzo (university) district is the *Albergo del Popolo* (Centro del Giovane; ☎ 446 52 36), at Via degli Apuli 41. Singles are L25,000, or L37,000 with bath. Doubles are L55,000 and triples L75,000, both with bath. Take bus No 492 from in front of the station, along Via Tiburtina and get off near Via dei Sardi, then walk along this street to Via degli Apuli.

West of Stazione Termini This area is decidedly seedier, but prices remain the same. As you exit to the left of the station, follow Via Gioberti to Via G Amendola, which becomes Via F Turati. This street and the parallel Via Principe Amedeo harbour a concentration of budget pensioni, so you shouldn't have any trouble finding a room.

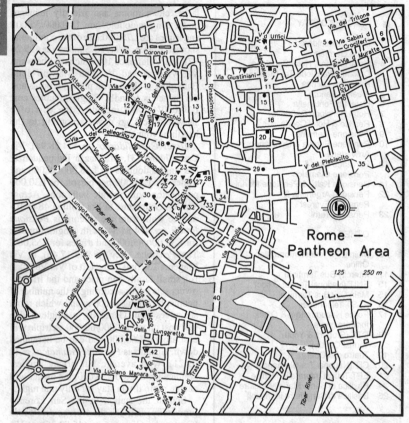

Rome –
Pantheon Area

0   125   250 m

Pensione Terni (☎ 474 54 28) at Via Principe Amedeo 62 is not the best, but it has triples for L75,000. Singles/doubles are L40,000/70,000. *Albergo Onella* (☎ 488 52 57) at No 47 has more presentable singles/doubles for L40,000/70,000.

At Via Cavour 47, the main street running west from the piazza in front of Termini, there are two budget pensioni. The *Argentina* (☎ 488 32 63) is very clean with spacious singles/doubles for L40,000/70,000, shower included. Downstairs is the *Everest* (☎ 488 16 29), which is also clean and simple, and has singles/doubles for L40,000/60,000.

Directly ahead of the station at Piazza della Repubblica 47 are the Pensioni *Eureka* (☎ 488 03 34) and *Arrivederci* (☎ 482 58 06), run by the same management and with singles/doubles for L37,000/62,000, or L39,000/70,000 with shower. Prices include breakfast.

City Centre Prices go up significantly in the areas around the Spanish Steps, Piazza Navona, the Pantheon and Campo de' Fiori, but for the money you have the convenience and pleasure of staying right in the centre of historical Rome. Budget hotels are few and

■ PLACES TO STAY

8	Albergo Abruzzi
19	Pensione Primavera
20	Pensione Mimosa
27	Albergo del Sole
28	Albergo della Lunetta
34	Albergo Pomezia

▼ PLACES TO EAT

4	Giolitti
7	Hosteria l'Angoletto
9	Osteria
10	Bar del Fico & Trattoria
	Pizzeria da Francesco
12	Pizzeria da Baffetto
17	Caffè Gardenia
23	Hosteria Romanesca
24	Café Peru
25	Vineria
26	Toast Modern
32	Il Grottino
33	Filetti di Baccalà
38	D'Augusto
39	Mario's
42	Bar San Callisto
43	Pizzeria Ivo
44	Frontoni

OTHER

1	Ponte V Emanuele II
2	Ponte Sant' Angelo
3	Piazza del Montecitorio
5	Piazza Colonna
6	Trevi Fountain
11	Piazza della Rotonda
13	Piazza Navona
14	Piazza Sant'Eustachio
15	Pantheon
16	Piazza della Minerva
18	SIP
21	Ponte G Mazzini
22	Campo de' Fiori
29	Largo di Torre Argentina
30	Piazza Farnese
31	Palazzo Farnese
35	Piazza Venezia
36	Ponte Sisto
37	Piazza Trilussa
40	Ponte Garibaldi
41	Basilica & Piazza of Santa
	Maria in Trastevere
45	Ponte Palatino

far between, but there are some pleasant surprises. The easiest way to get to the Spanish Steps is on the Metropolitana Linea A to Spagna. To get to Piazza Navona and Pantheon area, take Bus No 64 from Piazza Cinquecento, in front of Termini, to Largo Argentina.

The cheapest and one of the most centrally located hotels is the *Pensione Primavera* (☎ 654 31 09), Piazza San Pantaleo 3 on Via Vittorio Emanuele II, just around the corner from Piazza Navona. A magnificent entrance leads to a shabby and slightly chaotic establishment where there are no singles and doubles or triples cost L37,500 per person. Prices per person go down, so the more there are in a room the cheaper it is and the owner is more than happy to strike a deal. The *Albergo Abruzzi* (☎ 679 20 21), Piazza della Rotonda 69, overlooks the Pantheon. You couldn't find a better location, but it is expensive at L55,000/78,000 singles/doubles. The use of the communal shower is free. Bookings are essential throughout the year at this popular hotel. *Pensione Mimosa* (☎ 654 17 53), Via Santa Chiara 61 (off Piazza della Rotonda), has singles/doubles for L50,000/76,000 with breakfast.

The *Albergo del Sole* (☎ 654 08 73), Via del Biscione 76, off Campo de' Fiori, used to be one of the best bargains in Rome, but it has been renovated and the prices have gone up accordingly. A single is too expensive at around L52,000 (L60,000 with bath) and a double costs L75,000, or up to L96,000 with bath. Around the corner is *Albergo della Lunetta* (☎ 686 10 80), Piazza del Paradiso 68, which charges L30,000/L60,000 for singles/doubles, or L55,000/90,000 with shower. Reservations are essential at both hotels.

The *Albergo Pomezia* (☎ 686 13 71) at Via dei Chiavari 12 (which runs off Via dei Giubbonari from Campo de' Fiori) is reasonably priced given its location, with doubles/triples for L70,000/90,000. Use of the communal shower is free.

Near the Spanish Steps is *Pensione Fiorella* (☎ 361 05 97), Via del Babuino

196; singles/doubles cost L40,000/70,000, breakfast included.

Near St Peter's & the Vatican Bargains do not abound in this area, but it is comparatively quiet and close to the main sights. Bookings are an absolute necessity because rooms are often filled with people attending conferences and so on at the Vatican. The simplest way to reach the area is on the Metropolitana Linea A to Ottaviano. Turn left into Via Ottaviano, and Via Germanico is a short walk away. Bus No 64 from Termini stops at St Peter's – walk away from the basilica along Via di Porta Angelica, which becomes Via Ottaviano after Piazza del Risorgimento, a five-minute walk away. The best bargain in the area is *Pensione Ottaviano* (☎ 38 39 56), Via Ottaviano 6, near Piazza Risorgimento. It has beds in dormitories for L20,000 a person. The owner speaks good English. *Giuggioli Hotel* (☎ 324 21 13), Via Germanico 198, is a delight, but very small. The woman owner, her dog and cats make it seem like home. A double costs L60,000 (no singles). Rooms are beautifully furnished. In the same building is *Hotel Pensione Lady* (☎ 324 21 12), with singles/doubles L45,000/55,000, or L65,000 for a double with shower. *Hotel Amalia* (☎ 31 45 19), Via Germanico 66 (near the corner of Via Ottaviano), has a beautiful courtyard entrance and clean, sunny rooms. Singles/doubles are L50,000/70,000 and include use of the communal shower.

Trastevere The *Pensione Manara* (☎ 581 47 13), Via Luciano Manara 25, is right in the heart of Trastevere and has clean, well-furnished doubles for L52,000.

Rental Apartments near the centre of Rome are expensive, so expect to pay a minimum of L1,500,000 a month. A good way to find a shared apartment is to buy *Wanted in Rome*.

Places to Eat

Of all the Italian cities, Rome hosts the most diverse selection of eating places. This does not mean a diversity of international cuisines – the Italians have regional cooking traditions which are varied enough in themselves. Rather, in Rome it is possible to sample all of the regional cuisines, or, if you prefer, to eat only Roman fare.

Antipasto dishes in Rome are particularly good and many restaurants allow you to make your own mixed selection. Typical pasta dishes include: *fettuccine con panna*, with butter, cream and Parmesan; *penne all'arrabbiata*, which has a hot sauce of tomatoes, peppers and chilli; *spaghetti carbonara*, with *pancetta* (cured bacon), eggs and cheese. Romans eat many dishes prepared with offal. Try the *paiata*, pasta with veal intestines. *Saltimbocca alla Romana*, rolled slices of veal and ham, and veal scallopine, cooked in Marsala, are classic meat dishes, and are followed by a wide variety of vegetables. Drink a bottle of the local frascati wine with your meal. Always remember to check the menu posted outside the establishment for prices, cover and service charges.

A good option for a cheap, quick meal is the hundreds of bars, where panini (sandwiches) cost L2000 to L4000 if taken *al banco* (at the bar), or takeaway pizzerias, where a slice of freshly cooked pizza, sold by weight, can cost as little as L2000. Bakeries are particularly numerous in Piazza Navona and Campo de' Fiori area and are another good choice for a cheap snack. Try a huge piece of *pizza bianca*, a flat bread resembling *focaccia*, costing from around L1000 a slice.

For groceries and supplies of cheese, prosciutto, salami and wine, shop at *alimentari*. For fresh fruit and vegetables there are numerous outdoor markets, notably the lively daily market in Campo de' Fiori. Other, cheaper food markets are held in Piazza Vittorio Emanuele, near the station, and in Via Andrea Doria, near Largo Trionfale, north of the Vatican. The huge wholesale food markets are in Via Ostiense, some distance from the centre, open to the public Monday to Saturday from 10 am to 1 or 2 pm.

Restaurants The restaurants near Stazione Termini are to be avoided if you want to pay reasonable prices for good food. The side streets around Piazza Navona and Campo de' Fiori harbour many budget trattorias and pizzerias, and the areas of San Lorenzo (to the east of Termini, near the university), where you can get the best pizza in Rome, and Testaccio (across the Tiber near Piramide) are popular local eating districts. Trastevere might be among the most expensive places to live in Rome, but it still offers an excellent selection of rustic eating places hidden in tiny piazzas, and pizzerias where it doesn't cost the earth to sit at a table on the street.

City Centre The *Pizzeria da Baffetto*, Via del Governo Vecchio 114, is a Roman institution. Its pizzas are extra large. Expect to join a queue if you arrive after 9 pm and don't be surprised if you end up sharing a table. Pizzas cost around L6000 to L8000, a litre of wine costs L7000 and the coperto is only L1000. A full meal will cost around L16,000. Farther along the street at No 18 is a tiny, nameless *osteria* – a favourite among local workers. There's no written menu, but don't be nervous as this place is very cheap (a full meal at lunch time costs about L15,000) and the food is good. In the evening, however, it is more expensive, with full meals costing from L25,000 to L30,000.

Il Grottino, Vicolo delle Grotte 27, also serves a good pizza for around L5000; a litre of wine costs L4000 and the coperto is L1500. You can get a full meal for around L15,000. *Trattoria Pizzeria da Francesco*, Piazza del Fico 29, has great pasta dishes for L7000 to L9000 and a good range of antipastos and vegetables. It costs about L18,000 for a full meal.

There are several small restaurants in the Campo de' Fiori, notably *Toast Modern*, the best place in Rome to eat a salad (L6000 to L7000). Designer panini cost around L4500, a glass of wine costs L1000 and there is a good range of beers. The coperto is L1000. *Hosteria Romanesca*, also in the Campo de' Fiori, is tiny, so arrive early in winter. In summer there are numerous tables outside. A

dish of pasta will cost around L6000, a full meal around L12,000.

Along Via Giubbonari, off Campo de' Fiori, is *Filetti di Baccalà* in the tiny Largo dei Librari, which serves only deep-fried cod fillets and wine. You can satisfy moderate hunger and thirst for around L3000. *Hosteria l'Angoletto* is tucked into a corner of Piazza Rondanini, between the Pantheon and Piazza Navona. It does cost more than the others, with a full meal costing L20,000 or more, but the food is great.

Near the Trevi Fountain is *Er Buco*, Via del Lavatore 91, where pasta costs L6000 to L8000 and pizza costs from L6000 to L9000. Most of the restaurants in this area are either high class and very expensive, or tourist traps.

West of the Tiber On the west bank of the Tiber, good-value restaurants are concentrated in Trastevere and the Testaccio district, past Piramide. Most of the establishments around St Peter's and the Vatican are geared for tourists and can be very expensive. One decent option, however, is the *Trattoria Marcella*, Via Mascherino 26, which runs off Piazza Risorgimento.

In Trastevere's maze of tiny streets you will find any number of pizzerias and cheap trattorias. The area is beautiful at night and most establishments have outdoor tables. It is very popular, so arrive before 9.30 pm if you don't want to join a queue for a table.

Try *Frontoni*, on Viale di Trastevere, opposite Piazza Mastai, for fantastic panini made with pizza bianca. *Mario's*, Via del Moro 53, is a local favourite for its great pasta dishes (around L6000 each). From Viale di Trastevere walk along Via Lungaretta. *D'Augusto*, Piazza Renzi, just around the corner from the Basilica Santa Maria in Trastevere (turn right as you face the church and walk to Via della Pelliccia), is another great spot for pasta. Try the homemade fettuccine. If you arrive early there is also a good range of contorni. A meal with wine will cost around L15,000. *Pizzeria Ivo*, Via di San Francesco a Ripa 158, has outdoor tables. The pizzas could be bigger for the price (L7500), but they are good. The bruschetta here is an excellent start to the meal. The house wine comes in bottles and is not a bargain at L8000.

From Viale di Trastevere take Via delle Fratte and turn right into Via di San Francesco a Ripa. At the other end of this street, across Viale di Trastevere on the corner of Via San Francesco d'Assisi, is *Hostaria Gran Sasso*, which specialises in dishes from Abruzzo and has excellent food. A meal will cost around L15,000 to L20,000. *Pizzeria da Vittoio*, Via San Cosimato 14a, is tiny and you have to wait if you arrive after 9 pm. A bruschetta, pizza and wine will cost around L13,000.

You won't find a cheaper, noisier, more chaotic pizzeria in Rome than *Pizzeria Remo*, Piazza Santa Maria Liberatrice 44, in Testaccio. *Il Canestro*, Via Maestro Giorgio, Testaccio, specialises in vegetarian food and is relatively expensive, considering that all trattorias serve a good selection of vegetable dishes. In the same street, at the corner of Via Alessandro Volta, is a nameless trattoria which serves Roman food with a legendary reputation. The only problem is that you need to arrive before 8 pm to claim one of the few unreserved tables.

San Lorenzo District You will find typical local fare and good pizzas at prices students can afford at *Pizzeria l'Economica*, Via Tiburtina 44.

If you have no option but to eat near Stazione Termini, try to avoid the tourist traps offering overpriced full menus. The area has many *tavole calde*, particularly to the west of Termini, which offer panini and preprepared dishes for reasonable prices.

Cafés & Bars Remember that prices skyrocket in bars as soon as you sit down, particularly near the Spanish Steps, where a cappuccino *a tavola* (at a table) can cost as much as L5000. The same cappuccino taken at the bar will cost around L1400. There are some exceptions, however. The narrow streets and tiny piazzas in the area between

Piazza Navona and the Tiber offer a good number of popular small cafés and bars.

Number one on the list has to be *Café Peru* in Piazza di Santa Caterina della Rota, just down the street to the right as you face the Palazzo Farnese. Here, serious local drinkers mingle with young bohemians and students and you can buy beer by the bottle at rockbottom prices and sit at a table for no extra charge. The occasional art show brightens the walls of this otherwise seedy, but interesting, bar. Hold on to your bag at all times.

In Piazza del Fico is a small bar of the same name, where you can sit outside and drink at reasonable prices. *Vineria* in Campo de' Fiori, also known as *Giorgio's*, has a wide selection of wine and beers and was once the meeting place of the Roman literati. Though now less glamorous, it's still a good place to drink, but is only cheap if you stand at the bar.

At *Caffè Gardenia*, Via del Governo Vecchio 98, you can listen to live jazz and get snacks for L3500 to L5000. In Trastevere there is the *Bar San Callisto* in the piazza of the same name, with tables outside. Again, this bar is seedy but cheap and interesting, and if you are looking for information on where to sleep out in relative safety, the various homeless young buskers and beggars who gather here to drink away their day's earnings will help you out.

Gelati *Giolitti*, Via degli Uffici del Vicario 40, near the Pantheon, has long been a Roman institution. It was once the gathering place of the local art crowd and writers. Today it remains famous for its fantastic gelati. *Gelateria della Palma*, around the corner at Via della Maddalena 20, has a huge selection of flavours. A cone with three flavours costs L2500 at both places.

Entertainment

Rome's primary entertainment guide is *Trovaroma*, a weekly supplement in the Thursday edition of the newspaper *La Repubblica*. Considered the bible for what is happening in the city, it provides a comprehensive listing, but in Italian only. The newspaper also publishes a daily listing of cinema, theatre and concerts. *Carnet di Roma*, published monthly by the EPT in both English and Italian, gives information on the sights, as well as listing exhibitions and musical and theatrical events. *This Week in Rome* is another excellent guide, in English, to what's happening in the city.

Festivals Although Romans desert their city in summer, particularly in August, when the weather is relentlessly hot and humid, cultural and musical events liven up the place and many performances and festivals are held in the open. A summer festival, organised by the Comune di Roma (Rome City Council) and the EPT, features concerts, dance and folkloric events, including various events held in the city's many piazzas (information is available from the EPT).

The Festa de' Noantri, held in Trastevere in the last two weeks of July in honour of Our Lady·of Mt Carmel, is not much more than a line of street stalls. Some street theatre and music is performed and people eat dinner in the street. The Festa di San Giovanni is held on 23 and 24 June in the San Giovanni district of Rome and features much dancing and eating in the streets. Part of the ritual is to eat stewed snails and suckling pig.

At Christmas the focus is on the many churches of Rome, each setting up its own Nativity scene. Among the most renowned are the 13th century crib at Santa Maria Maggiore and the crib at the Church of Santa Maria d'Aracoeli. During Holy Week, at Easter, the focus is again religious and events include the famous procession of the cross between the Colosseum and the Palatine on Good Friday, and the Pope's blessing of the city and the world in St Peter's Square on Easter Sunday.

The Spanish Steps become a sea of pink azaleas during the Spring Festival in April.

Concerts & Opera During July a series of concerts is held in Piazza del Campidoglio, and in July and August opera is performed at the Baths of Caracalla. Out of season the entertainment moves indoors to the nightclubs, bars, theatres and concert halls. A season of concerts is held in October and November at the *Accademia di Santa Cecilia*, Via della Conciliazione 4, and the *Accademia Filarmonica*, Via Flaminia 18. The opera season at the *Teatro dell'Opera*, Piazza Beniamino Gigli, starts in November. Other musical events in this period feature performances by the RAI Symphonic Orchestra.

Rock concerts are held throughout the year and are advertised on posters plastered all over the city. Concerts by major performers are usually held at the *Palazzo dello Sport* or the *Stadio Flaminia*, two huge sports grounds north of the Villa Borghese, on Viale Tiziano. For information and bookings, contact the ORBIS agency (☎ 475 14 03) in Piazza d'Esquilino near the station.

Nightclubs Nightclubs are popular only during winter. Among the more interesting and popular Roman live music clubs is *Radio Londra*, Via Monte Testaccio, in the Testaccio area. Although entry is free, you might find it hard to get in here because the bouncers tend to pick and choose, but give it a try anyway. There are several other good nightclubs and bars in the same street, including *Caruso Caffè Concerto* at No 36 and *Caffè Latino* at No 96.

Esperimento, Via Rasella 5, near Piazza Barberini, is a rock club which often stages live concerts by young English, and even Australian, bands. Membership costs L10,000. One of Rome's newer nightclubs is *Alpheus*, Via del Commercio 36, near Piramide, which has a variety of music in different rooms. It costs L10,000 to get in and up to L25,000 when there is a concert. The Roman radio station Radio Rock runs a music club of the same name at Via Porta Castello 44.

Roman discos are outrageously expensive. Expect to pay up to L40,000 to get in (although women are often allowed in free of charge), which may or may not include one drink. Hot spots in 1992 included *Alien*, Via Velletri 13; *Hysteria*, Via Giovannelli 3; *Piper '90*, Via Tagliamento 9; and *Uonna Club*, Via Cassia 871. The best gay disco is

L'Alibi, Via di Monte Testaccio 44. Women are allowed in only if accompanied by a man.

Exhibitions & Films During June and July, Tevere Expo, an exhibition of the crafts and products of Italy's regions, is held on the banks of the Tiber. In July at the *Castel Sant'Angelo*, on the Tiber, two huge screens are erected to show films in Italian. Entry is free. Free jazz concerts are also held here, so check daily papers for listings. The cinema *Pasquino* (☎ 580 36 22), Vicolo del Piede 19, in Trastevere, screens films in English. It is just off Piazza Santa Maria in Trastevere. *Alcazar* (☎ 588 00 99), Via Merry del Val 14, Trastevere, shows an English-language film every Monday.

Things to Buy

The first things that come to mind when thinking of shopping in Rome are clothing and shoes. But it can be difficult to find bargains here. The city's main shopping areas are not as compact as Florence, or as impressive as Milan, but, if you have the money, the quality is certainly here.

It is probably advisable to stick to window-shopping in the expensive Ludovisi district, the area around Via Veneto. The major fashion shops are in Via Sistina and Via Gregoriana, heading towards the Spanish Steps. Via Condotti and the parallel streets heading from Piazza di Spagna to Via del Corso are lined with moderately expensive clothing and footwear boutiques, as well as shops selling accessories.

It is cheaper, but not as interesting, to shop along Via del Tritone and Via Nazionale. There are some interesting second-hand clothes shops along Via del Governo Vecchio.

If clothes don't appeal, wander through the streets around Via Margutta, Via Ripetta, Piazza del Popolo and Via Frattina to look at the art galleries, artists' studios and antiquarian shops. You could find some bargain antiques in Via Coronari, between Piazza Navona and Lungotevere di Tor di Nona, while the antique shops along Via del Babuino are expensive.

Everyone flocks to the famous **Porta Portese** market every Sunday morning. Hundreds of stalls selling anything you can imagine line the streets of Porta Portese parallel to Viale di Trastevere, near Trastevere. Here you can pick up a genuine 1960s evening dress for L1000, an antique mirror for L10,000 or a leather jacket for L40,000. Take time to rummage through the piles of clothing and bric-a-brac and you will find some incredible bargains.

The market in Via Sannio, near Porta San Giovanni, sells new and second-hand clothes. For prints, antiques and books, head for the market at Piazza Fontanella Borghese, held every morning except Sunday.

Getting There & Away

Air The main airline offices are in the area around Via Veneto and Via Barberini, north of the station. Qantas, British Airways, Alitalia, Air New Zealand, Lufthansa and Singapore Airlines are all in Via Bissolati.

Bus The main terminal for intercity buses is in Viale delle Terme, between Piazza della Repubblica and Piazza Cinquecento, north of the train station. Buses connect with major cities, including Florence, Milan, Naples and Syracuse, and also with provincial cities throughout Italy. Numerous companies operate these services; as there is no information office at the terminal, contact the CIT office at the station for information. (See Information at the start of this section.)

Train Almost all trains arrive at and depart from Stazione Termini. There are regular connections to all major cities in Italy and throughout Europe, including Florence (four hours), Venice (seven to eight hours), Milan (seven hours) and Naples (three hours). For train timetable information, phone ☎ 4775 (from 7 am to 10.40 pm), or go to the information office at the station (English is spoken). Official timetables are available free of charge, but those listing all services for Italy are usually difficult to come by. Privately produced timetables can be bought at some newsstands. Services at Termini include luggage storage (L1500 per piece per day), a post office, telephones and money exchange (see the Information section). There are eight other stations scattered throughout Rome.

Taxi Taxis are on radio call 24 hours a day in Rome. Phone numbers for the various operators include ☎ 3570 for Cooperativa Radio Taxi Romana and ☎ 4994 for La Capitale. Major taxi ranks are at the airports and Stazione Termini. Remember that there are surcharges on Sundays and for luggage, night service, holidays and travel to/from Fiumicino Airport. The taxi flagfall is L6400 (for the first three km). There is a L7000 supplement from 10 pm to 7 am and L1000 from 7 am to 10 pm on Sundays and holidays. The airport supplement is L15,000.

Car & Motorbike The main road connecting Rome to the north and south is the Autostrada del Sole A1, which extends from Milan to Reggio di Calabria. On the outskirts of the city it connects with the Grande Raccordo Anulare, the ring road encircling Rome. From the Grande Raccordo there are 33 exits into Rome, several of which will take you into the centre, including Via Salaria and Via Nomentana, if you approach from the north. From the south take Via del Mare or Via Pontina. From the Adriatic coast, take Via Appia Nuova. Via del Mare connects Rome to the Lido di Ostia (the beach of Ostia, near Ostia Antica), and the A12 connects the city to Civitavecchia and then goes along the coast to Genoa. Signs from the centre of Rome to the autostrade can be vague and confusing, so invest in a good road map.

Car, Scooter & Bike Rental To rent a car, you will need to be at least 21 years old and have a valid driver's licence. It is cheaper to organise a car from your own country if you want one for a long period. Car rental companies in Rome include: Avis (☎ 167-86 30 63), Piazza Esquilino 1; Hertz (☎ 167-82 20 99), Viale Leonardo da Vinci 421; Europcar (☎ 167-86 80 88), Via Lombardia 7; and

Maggiore (☎ 854 16 20), Via Po 8. All have offices at Stazione Termini and at both airports. For scooters and bicycles, contact Scooters for Rent (☎ 488 54 85), Via della Purificazione 66. For a guide to rental costs, see the general Getting Around section at the start of this chapter.

Hitching It is illegal to hitchhike on the autostrade, and Italians can be very reluctant to stop anyway. To head north, wait for a lift on Via Salaria, near the autostrada exit. To go south to Naples, take the Metropolitana to Anagnina and wait in Via Tuscolana.

Boat Tirrenia and FS (state railway) ferries leave from Civitavecchia, near Rome, for various points in Sardinia (see the Getting There & Away section under Sardinia). Bookings can be made at CIT in Stazione Termini, or directly with Tirrenia (☎ 474 20 41), Via Bissolati 41, Rome, or at the *stazione marittima* (ferry terminal) at the port in Civitavecchia. Bookings can be made at Stazione Termini for FS ferries.

Getting Around
To/From the Airport The main airport is Leonardo Da Vinci (☎ 6 01 21, or 60 12 44 55) at Fiumicino. Access to the city is via the airport-Ostiense train (the station is directly opposite the airport arrivals hall), which costs L5000. The train arrives at Stazione Ostiense, Piramide, from where you catch the Metropolitana Linea B to Stazione Termini. The process is simple, but there is a lot of walking and stair-climbing involved, which can be difficult if you have a lot of luggage (there is a taxi rank outside the station). The airport is connected to Rome by Via del Mare.

Taxis are prohibitively expensive from the airport – expect to pay L60,000 or more and agree on the price *before* you get in the taxi. There is a L15,000 surcharge on taxi rides between the city centre and the airport.

The other airport is Ciampino, which is used for most national and some international flights, including charter flights. Buses connect with the Metropolitana, but if

ITALY

you arrive very late at night you could end up being forced to catch a taxi. The airport is connected to Rome by Via Appia Nuova.

Bus The city bus line is ATAC and most of the main buses terminate in Piazza Cinquecento in front of Stazione Termini. A full timetable is available at the ATAC information booth in the centre of the piazza, otherwise the EPT has a free (but largely indecipherable) timetable.

Another central point for main bus routes in the centre is Largo Argentina, near Piazza Navona. Tickets cost L800 (for two trips within 90 minutes) and must be purchased *before* you get on the bus and then validated in the machine as you enter. Rome has just increased the fine for travelling without a ticket to L50,000 and correspondingly increased its force of inspectors. Tickets are available in Piazza Navona or at any tobacconist. Daily tickets cost L2800 and weekly tickets cost L10,000. If you're staying in Rome for some time, it's worth buying a monthly bus ticket, which costs L22,000. Useful bus numbers to remember are No 64 from Stazione Termini to St Peter's; No 27 from Termini to the Colosseum; and No 44 from Piazza Venezia to Trastevere.

Underground The Metropolitana has two lines, A and B. Both pass through Stazione Termini. Take Linea A for Piazza di Spagna and Flaminio, and Linea B for the Colosseum, Circus Maximus and Piramide. Tickets cost L800, or L7000 for a block of 10, and can be purchased at ticket offices downstairs at Termini, or from tobacconists. Trains run approximately every five minutes. Trains connect Termini with the other suburban railway stations, which include Trastevere, Tiburtina and Ostiense.

Taxi See the preceding Getting There & Away section for information.

Car & Motorbike Negotiating Roman traffic by car is difficult enough, but be aware that you are taking your life in your hands if you ride a motorbike in the city. The rule in Rome

is to watch the vehicles in front and hope that the vehicles behind are watching you.

There are numerous pedestrian zones in the centre of Rome, particularly around the major tourist areas such as Piazza di Spagna, Piazza Navona, the Pantheon etc. Six large areas in the centre are closed to ordinary traffic (except for residents and public transport). Cars with foreign numberplates can enter, to enable tourists to reach their hotels. *Here's Rome* lists these areas in full. Look for the large signs which identify these areas, or ask for information from the *vigili urbani* (traffic police), who wear dark-blue uniforms and white hats.

The major parking area close to the centre is at the Villa Borghese. Entrance is from Piazzale Brasile at the top of Via Veneto. There is a supervised car park at Stazione Termini. Other car parks are at Stazione Tiburtina: these are at Piazza dei Partigiani and Piazza da Verazzano, both of which have easy access to Stazione Ostiense. Small, but expensive, supervised car parks are scattered around the periphery of the historical centre. The EPT office has a list of cheaper car parks on the outskirts of Rome; you can reach the centre by bus or metro. (See the preceding Getting There & Away section for information about car, scooter and bike rental.)

Around Rome

Rome demands so much of your time and concentration that most tourists forget that the city is part of the region of Lazio. There are some interesting places within easy daytrip distance of the city.

TIVOLI
Set on a hill by the Anio River, Tivoli was a resort town of the ancient Romans and again became popular as a summer playground for the rich during the Renaissance. It is famous today for the terraced gardens and fountains of the Villa d'Este and the ruins of the spectacular Villa Adriana, built by the Roman emperor Hadrian.

The local AAST tourist office (☎ 077-42 12 49) is in Largo Garibaldi near the ACOTRAL bus stop.

Things to See & Do

Hadrian built his summer villa, **Villa Adriana**, in the 2nd century AD, influenced by the architecture of the famous classical buildings of the day. It was successively plundered by barbarians and Romans for building materials and many of its original decorations were used to embellish the Villa d'Este. However, enough remains to give an idea of the incredible size and magnificence of the villa. You will need about four hours to wander through the vast ruins. Highlights include La Villa dell'Isola (the Villa of the Island), where Hadrian spent his pensive moments, the Imperil Palace and its Golden Square (Piazza d'Oro) and the floor mosaics of the Hospitalia. The villa is open from 9 am to 7 pm (last entry at 6 pm) in the warmer months and from 9 am to 4 pm in winter. Entry is L8000.

The Renaissance **Villa d'Este** was built in the 16th century for Cardinal Ippolito d'Este on the site of a Franciscan monastery. The villa's beautiful gardens are decorated with numerous fountains, which are its main attraction. Opening hours vary for each season – in summer from 9 am to 6.30 pm and in winter to 4.30 pm. Entry is L5000.

Getting There & Away

Tivoli is about 40 km east of Rome (one hour by car) and accessible by ACOTRAL bus (☎ 591 55 51) which leaves from Via Tiburtina. Take Metropolitana Linea B from Stazione Termini to Rebibbia; the bus leaves from outside the station every half-hour. The bus also stops at the Villa Adriana, about one km from Tivoli.

OSTIA ANTICA

The Romans founded this port city at the mouth of the Tiber in the 4th century BC and it became a strategically important centre of defence and trade. It was populated by merchants, sailors and slaves, and the ruins of the city provide a fascinating contrast to a place

such as Pompeii. After barbarian invasions and the appearance of malaria, it was abandoned, but Pope Gregory IV re-established the city in the 9th century AD.

Information about the town and Roman ruins is available at the EPT office in Rome.

Things to See & Do

Of particular note in the excavated city are the **Terme di Nettuno**; a **Roman theatre** built by Augustus; the **forum** and **temple**, dedicated to Jupiter, Juno and Minerva; and the **Piazzale delle Corporazioni**, where you can see the offices of Roman merchants, distinguished by mosaics depicting their trades.

Getting There & Away

To get to Ostia Antica take the Metropolitana Linea B to Magliana and then the train to Ostia Lido.

ETRUSCAN SITES

Lazio has several important Etruscan archaeological sites, most within easy reach of Rome by car or public transport. These include Tarquinia (one of the most important cities of the Etruscan League), Cerveteri, Veio and Tuscania.

A useful guide to the area entitled *The Etruscans* is published by the Istituto Geografico de Agostini and comes with a map. Free copies are sometimes available at the EPT office in Rome. If you really want to lose yourself in a poetic journey, take along a copy of D H Lawrence's *Etruscan Places* (published by Penguin in the compilation *D H Lawrence & Italy*).

Tarquinia

Believed to have been founded in the 12th century BC and home of the Tarquin kings who ruled Rome before the creation of the republic, Tarquinia was an important economic and political centre of the Etruscan League. The major attractions here are the painted tombs of its necropoli (burial grounds). The AAST tourist information office (☎ 0766-85 63 84) is at Piazza Cavour

1. It is possible to see Tarquinia on a day trip from Rome.

Things to See The 15th century Palazzo Vitelleschi houses the **National Museum** and one of the largest collections of Etruscan treasures, including frescoes removed from the tombs. There are also numerous sarcophagi found in the tombs. The museum is open Tuesday to Sunday from 9 am to 2 pm (closed Monday). Admission costs L8000 and the same ticket admits you to the **necropolis**, a 15 to 20-minute walk away. Ask for directions from the museum. Only a small number of the thousands of tombs have been excavated and only a handful are open on any given day. You must wait until a guide is available to open the tombs and it could be a long wait in summer, when thousands of tourists visit the necropolis daily. The tombs are richly decorated with frescoes, though many are seriously deteriorated. They are are now maintained at constant temperatures to preserve the remaining decorations. This means that it is possible to see them only through glass partitions.

Take the time to wander through the streets of medieval Tarquinia and, if you have a car, ask for directions to the remains of Etruscan Tarquinia, on the crest of the Civita Hill nearby. There is little evidence of the ancient city, apart from a few limestone blocks that once formed part of the city walls. However, a large temple, the Altar of the Queen, was discovered on the hill and has been excavated in this century.

Places to Stay & Eat There is only one budget option in the town if you want to stay overnight and it can be difficult to find a room if you don't book well in advance. *Affittacamere di Benedetti Alessandra* (☎ 85 52 67) has rooms for L20,000 per person. Go to the tabaccheria at Piazza Cavour 12.

There is a camping ground by the sea, *Tusca Tirrenia* (☎ 882 94), Viale Neriedi.

For a good, cheap meal, go to *Cucina Casareccia*, at Via G Mazzii 5, off Piazza Cavour, where a full meal with wine will cost around L17,000.

Getting There & Away Buses leave approximately every hour for Tarquinia from Via Lepanto in Rome, near the Metropolitana Linea A Lepanto stop, arriving at Tarquinia a few steps away from the tourist office. You can also catch a train from Rome, but Tarquinia's station is at Tarquinia Lido (beach), approximately three km from the centre. You will then need to catch one of the regular local buses.

Cerveteri

Ancient Caere was founded by the Etruscans in the 8th century BC and enjoyed a period of great prosperity as a maritime centre from the 7th to 5th centuries BC. The main attractions here are the tombs known as *tumoli*, great mounds with carved stone bases. Treasures taken from the tombs can be seen in the Vatican Museums, the Villa Giulia Museum and the Louvre.

The main necroplis area, Banditaccia, is open daily from 9 am to 4 pm in winter and 9 am to 7 pm in summer and entry is L8000. You can wander freely once inside the area, though it is best to follow the recommended routes in order to see the best preserved tombs. Signs detailing the history of the main tombs are in Italian only.

Banditaccia is accessible by local bus in summer only from the main piazza in Cerveteri; however, it is also a pleasant three-km walk west from the town. There is also a small museum in Cerveteri which contains an interesting display of pottery and sarcophagi. It is located in the Palazzo Ruspoli and is open from 9 am to 2 pm (closed Monday). Entry is free.

The Pro Loco tourist office is at Piazza Risorgimento 19. The town is accessible from Rome by ACOTRAL bus from Via Lepanto, outside the Lepanto stop on Metropolitana Linea A.

Northern Italy

Italy's northern regions are its wealthiest and offer many and varied attractions to travellers. A tour of the north could you take from the beaches of the Italian Riviera in Liguria, to Milan for a shopping spree, into Emilia-Romagna to sample its remarkable *cucina* (cuisine), through countless medieval and Renaissance towns and villages, and into the Alps to ski or trek in the Dolomites, before taking a boat trip down the Grand Canal of timeless Venice.

VENICE

Perhaps no other city in the world has inspired the superlatives heaped upon Venice (Venezia) by great writers and travellers through the centuries. It was, and remains, a phenomenon, *La Serenissima*, the Most Serene Republic.

Forget that Venice is no longer a great maritime republic, that its history has been one of continuous, remorseless decline, and that its buildings are in serious decay and constantly threatened by rising tides. Today Byron would be reluctant to take his daily swim along the now-polluted Grand Canal. But the thoughts of Henry James are as true today as they were a century ago: 'Dear old Venice has lost her complexion, her figure, her reputation, her self-respect; and yet, with it all, has so puzzlingly not lost a shred of her distinction.' In this uniquely splendid city you will have no need of a lover to feel romantic. James wrote: 'Time flows when you rest your elbows on the ledges of Venetian windows'.

The secret to seeing and discovering the romance and beauty of Venice is to *walk*. Parts of Dorsoduro and Castello are empty of tourists even in the high season (July to September). You could become lost for hours in the narrow winding streets between the Accademia and the station, where the signs pointing to San Marco and the Rialto never seem to make any sense, but what a way to pass the time!

After the fall of the Western Roman Empire, as waves of barbarians poured across the Alps, the people of the Veneto cities fled to islands of the coastal lagoon. The waters which once protected the city were safe then, but are a curse today as they threaten its existence. Following years of Byzantine rule, Venice evolved into a republic ruled by a succession of doges (chief magistrates of the republic), a period of independence which lasted 1000 years. It was the point where East met West, and the city eventually grew in power to dominate the entire Mediterranean, the Adriatic and the trade routes to the Levant. It was from here that Marco Polo set out on his voyage to China.

Today, most of Venice is under restoration and this, together with the annual winter floods and soaring property values, make it increasingly unattractive as a place of residence. Most of the 'locals' in fact live in industrial Mestre, which is linked to the city by the four-km-long bridge across the lagoon. The project to save Venice from sinking into the sea is supported by local and international bodies. In January 1992, the Italian government approved a scheme to build tidal barriers at the lagoon's three openings, clean up the canals, which are badly silted up, and repair the foundations of the city's buildings. If all goes as planned, the work should be completed by 2000.

Orientation

Venice is built on 117 small islands, has some 150 canals and more than 400 bridges. Only three bridges cross the Grand Canal (Canale Grande): the Rialto, the Accademia and the one at the station. The city is divided into six *sestieri* (sections): Cannaregio, Castello, San Marco, Dorsoduro, San Polo and Santa Croce. The streets are called *calle* (sometimes shortened to ca') or *salizzada*, a canal is a *rio*, and a quay is a *riva* or *fondamento*. The only square in Venice called a *piazza* is San Marco – all the others are called a *campo*. On maps, you will find the following abbreviations: Cpo for Campo, Sal for Salizzada, cl for Calle and Fond for Fondamenta.

If all that isn't confusing enough, Venice also has its own style of street numbering. Instead of street numbers for each building based on individual streets, there is a long series of numbers for each sestiere.

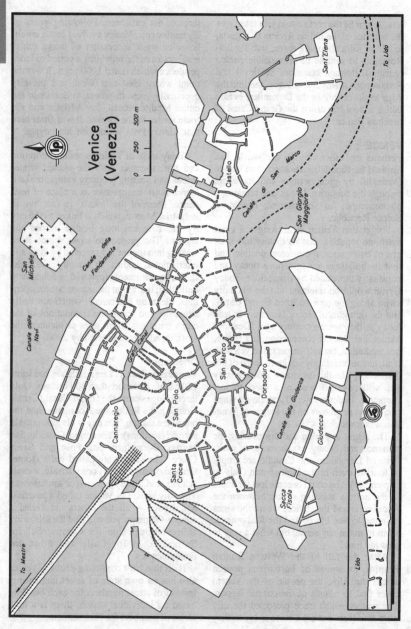

Venice
(Venezia)

0   250   500 m

Sant'Elena

To Lido

Castello

San Michele

Canale della Fondamenta

Canale delle Navi

Grand Canal

Cannaregio

San Polo

San Marco

Dorsoduro

Canale di San Marco

San Giorgio Maggiore

Canale della Giudecca

Santa Croce

Giudecca

Secca Fisola

To Mestre

Lido

There are no cars in the city and all public transport is via the canals, on *vaporetti*. To cross the Grand Canal between the bridges, use a *traghetto* (small ferry) – a cheaper mode of transport than gondolas. Signs will direct you to the various traghetto points. The other mode of transportation is *a piedi* (on foot). To walk from the *ferrovia* (train station) to San Marco, along the main thoroughfare, Lista di Spagna (whose name changes several times), will take a good half-hour – follow the signs to San Marco.

From San Marco the routes to other main areas, such as the Rialto, the Accademia and the ferrovia, are well signed but can be confusing, particularly in the Dorsoduro and San Polo areas. The free map provided by the tourist office (see the following section) provides only a vague guide to the complicated network of streets. Pick up a cheap de Agostini map, simply titled *Venezia*, which lists all street names with map references.

Information

Tourist Offices There is an information office of the APT (Provincial Tourist Department) at the station, open from 8 am to 9.30 pm daily. The staff will give you a map and list of hotels and will book a room for you. The main office (☎ 041-522 63 56) is at the far end of Piazza San Marco, under the porticoes. The staff have little information on the city apart from a brochure listing all the cultural, theatrical and musical events for the year and the useful booklet *Un Ospite di Venezia* (A Guest in Venice), but are helpful if you insist.

Money Banks are always the most reliable places to change money and they offer the best rates. Most of the main banks have branches in the area around the Rialto and San Marco. After hours, the American Express office, Salizzada San Moisè (exit from the western end of Piazza San Marco onto Calle Seconda dell'Ascensione) will exchange money without charging commission. Normal opening hours are from 9 am to 5.30 pm weekdays and to 12.30 pm Saturdays. For card holders the office also has an automatic teller machine.

On the same street, closer to San Marco, is an exchange office open from 9 am to 7 pm Monday to Saturday and 9 am to 1 pm Sundays. Thomas Cook, in Piazza San Marco, is open from 9 am to 7 pm Monday to Saturday. There is also a bank at the train station, or you can change money at the train ticket office from 7 am to 9.30 pm daily.

Post & Telecommunications The main post office is at Salizzada del Fontego dei Tedeschi, just near the Ponte di Rialto (Rialto Bridge) on the main thoroughfare to the station. You can buy stamps at window Nos 11 and 12 in the central courtyard. Another branch of the post office is just off the western end of Piazza San Marco.

The ASST telephone office is next door, open from 8 am to 7.45 pm daily except Sunday. There is another office at the train station. Venice's telephone code is 041 and the postcode is 30100.

Emergency If you need a hospital, the Ospedale Civili Riuniti di Venezia (☎ 520 56 22) is at Campo SS (Santissimi) Giovanni e Paolo. For an ambulance phone ☎ 523 00 00. The municipal police and passport office (☎ 520 32 22), where you can report thefts etc, is at Parrocchia di San Zaccaria, Castello. In an emergency, phone ☎ 113 to contact the police.

Current information on all-night pharmacies is listed in *Un Ospite di Venezia*.

Bookshops A good selection of English-language guidebooks and general books on Venice is available at Studium, on the corner of Calle de la Canonica, on the way from San Marco to Castello. Il Libraio a San Barnaba, in Dorsoduro, between Campo San Barnaba and Campo Santa Margherita, has a good range of English-language books, ranging from the classics to contemporary literature and best sellers.

Things to See & Do
Before you visit the main monuments,

ITALY

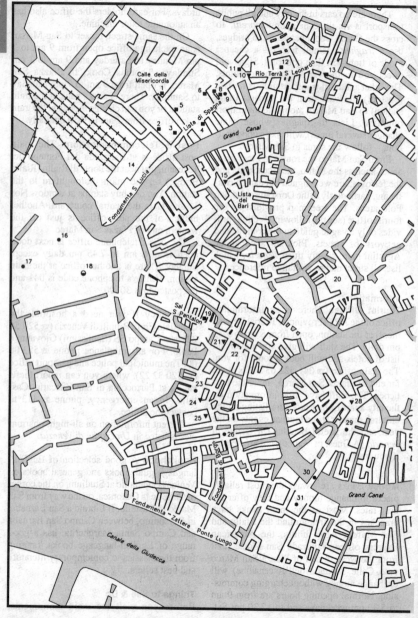

Calle della
Misericordia
1

6
8
9
5
Lista di Spagna
4

2   3

Rio Terrà S Leonardo
11 10   12   13

Grand Canal

14

Fondamenta S. Lucia

15

Lista
dei
Bari

16

17   18

20

Sal
S Pentalon
19

21

22

23
24

25

26

27   28

29

30

31

Grand Canal

Fondamenta – Zattere Ponte Lungo

Fondamenta S Basego

Canale della Giudecca

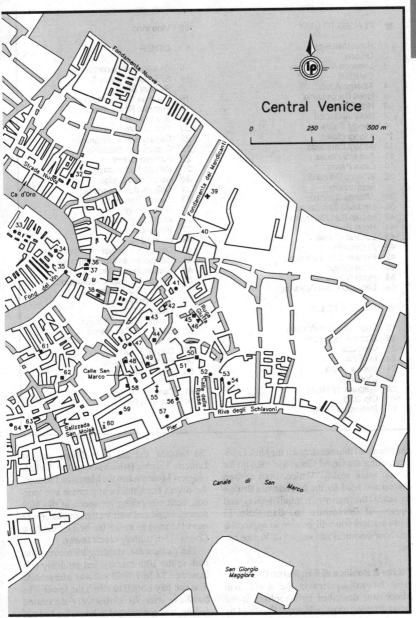

Central Venice

0   250   500 m

Fondamenta Nuove

Strada Nuova

Ca d'Oro

Fond. del Vin

Fondamenta dei Mendicanti

Ruga Giuffa

Calle San Marco

Calle delle Rasse

Riva degli Schiavoni

Salizzada San Moisè

Pier

Canale di San Marco

San Giorgio Maggiore

■ PLACES TO STAY

1 Hotel Villa Rosa
2 Orsaria
3 Locanda Antica Casa Carettoni
4 Albergo Adua
5 Hotel Santa Lucia
6 Hotel Rossi
7 Hotel Al Gobbo
8 Alloggi Calderan
11 Alloggi Biasin
12 Alloggi Smeraldo
13 Archie's House
19 Casa Peron
32 Albergo Bernardi Semenzato
34 Albergo Guerrato
38 Locanda San Salvador
43 Istituto San Giuseppe
44 Hotel Riva
45 Locanda Piave
48 Al Gambero
49 Pensione Al Gazzettino
50 Hotel Bridge
58 Hotel Noemi
62 Locanda Casa Petrarca

▼ PLACES TO EAT

10 Trattoria alla Palazzina
15 Pizzeria all'Anfora
21 Crepizza
22 Da Silvio
24 Bar La Sosta
25 L'Incontro
28 Trattoria da Memi
42 Cip Ciap
46 Ristorante Tucan

63 Vino Vino

OTHER

9 Campo San Geremia
14 APT Tourist Office & Railway Station
16 Piazzale Roma (Parking)
17 Piazzale Roma (Parking)
18 Bus Station
20 Campo San Polo
23 Campo Santa Margherita
26 Campo San Barnaba
27 Palazzo Grassi
29 Campo F Morosini
30 Accademia Bridge
31 Galleria dell'Accademia
33 Campo Beccarie
35 Rialto Bridge
36 ASST Telephones
37 Main Post Office
39 Hospital
40 Campo SS Giovanni e Paolo
41 Campo Santa Maria Formosa
47 Campo San Zulian
51 Campo SS Filippo e Giacomo
52 Campo San Provolo
53 Municipal Police & Passport Office
54 Campo di San Zaccaria
55 Basilica di San Marco
56 Bridge of Sighs
57 Doges' Palace
59 Piazza San Marco
60 APT Tourist Information Office
61 Campo San Luca
64 Teatro la Fenice

churches and museums, catch the No 1 vaporetto along the Grand Canal and then go for a long walk around Venice. Start at **San Marco** and head for the **Accademia Bridge** to reach the narrow, tranquil streets and squares of **Dorsoduro** and **San Polo**. In these sestieri you will be able to appreciate just how beautiful and seductive Venice can be.

Piazza & Basilica di San Marco One of the most famous squares in the world, San Marco was described by Napoleon as the finest drawing room in Europe. Enclosed by the basilica, the old Law Courts and the Libreria Vecchia (which houses the Archaeological Museum and the Marciana Library), the piazza hosts flocks of pigeons and tourists, both competing for space in the high season. Stand and wait for the famous bronze *mori* (Moors) to strike the bell of the Law Courts' 15th century **clock tower**.

The **campanile**, standing 99 metres, was built in the 10th century, but suddenly collapsed on 14 July 1902 and was later rebuilt. You can pay L3000 to climb the tower. The **basilica**, with its elaborately decorated façade, was constructed to house the body of

St Mark, which had been stolen from its burial place in Egypt by two Venetian merchants. The saint has been reburied several times in the basilica (at least twice the burial place was forgotten) and his body now lies under the high altar. The present basilica was built in the Byzantine style in the 11th century and richly decorated during the next five centuries. The famous bronze horses which stood above the entrance have been replaced by replicas. The horses were part of Venice's booty from the famous Sack of Constantinople in 1204. The originals are now in the basilica's museum (entry is L2000). The interior is decorated with marble and Byzantine and Renaissance mosaics.

Don't miss the stunning **Pala d'Oro** (L2000), a gold altarpiece decorated with silver, enamel and precious stones.

Palazzo Ducale The Doges' Palace is next to Piazza San Marco. It was the seat of Venetian power and government, and the residence of the doges, the republic's rulers, who were elected for life. The palace was built in the 12th century. Visit the **Grand Council Chamber** to see the paintings by Tintoretto and Veronese. The palace is open from 8.30 am to 6 pm daily. Admission is L8000. The **Bridge of Sighs** (Ponte dei Sospiri) connects the palace to the old prisons. This bridge now evokes romantic images, probably because of its association with Casanova, a native of Venice who was incarcerated in the prisons. It was, however, the thoroughfare for prisoners being led to their execution.

Galleria dell'Accademia The Academy of Fine Arts contains an important collection of Venetian art, including works by Tintoretto, Titian and Veronese. It is open Monday to Saturday to 2 pm, Sundays from 9 am to 1 pm, and admission is L8000. For a change of pace visit the nearby **Peggy Guggenheim Gallery**, once the home of the American heiress. It contains her collection of modern art, with works by Jackson Pollock, Max Ernst, Salvador Dali and Chagall, and is set in a sculpture garden where Miss Guggenheim and her many pet dogs are buried. It is open daily from 11 am to 6 pm. Admission is L6000.

Churches The Church of the Redeemer (Chiesa del Redentore) on Giudecca Island was built in the 16th century by the architect Palladio and is the scene of the annual *Festa del Redentore* (see the Entertainment section). The Chiesa di Santa Maria della Salute was built at the entrance to the Grand Canal and dedicated to the Madonna after a plague in the 17th century. It contains works by Tintoretto and Titian.

The Lido Easily accessible by the No 1 vaporetto, this thin strip of land, east of the centre, separates Venice from the Adriatic. Once *the* most fashionable beach resort, it is still very popular and it is almost impossible to find a space on its long beach in summer.

Islands The island of **Murano** is the home of Venetian glass. Visit the Glassworks Museum to see the evolution of the famous glassware. **Burano**, despite the constant influx of tourists, is still a relatively sleepy fishing village, renowned for the lace-making of its women residents. **Torcello** remains a favourite among some die-hards, but the island has been in decline for several centuries and it shows. It's worth visiting the cathedral, which features Byzantine mosaics. Excursion boats leave for the three islands from San Marco (L25,000 per person). If you want to go it alone, vaporetto No 12 goes to all three and costs L3300 one-way.

Gondolas These might represent the quint-essential romantic Venice, but at L70,000 (at least) for a 45-minute ride they are very expensive. It is possible to squeeze up to five people into one gondola and still pay the same price, which is less romantic, but more affordable.

Places to Stay
Simply put, Venice is expensive. Following

the liberalisation of hotel prices, many places raised their prices dramatically – some by more than 100%. Unless you choose carefully, you could find yourself paying a lot of money to sleep in very poor conditions. The average cost of singles/doubles without bath is now L40,000/60,000. The hostel and several religious institutions provide some respite for budget travellers.

Hotel proprietors are inclined to inflate the bill by demanding extra for a compulsory breakfast, and, almost without exception, they increase their prices in the high season (usually July to October). It is advisable in Venice, probably more than for any other Italian city, to make a booking before you arrive. In the high season, if you arrive without a booking, you could find yourself backtracking to Padua or Verona. As Venice does not have a traditional street numbering system, the best idea is to ring your hotel when you arrive and ask for specific directions.

Camping There are numerous camping grounds; many with bungalows, at Litorale del Cavallino, the coast along the Adriatic, north-east of the city. The tourist office in Piazza San Marco has a full list, but you could try the *Marina di Venezia* (☎ 96 61 46), Via Montello 6, at Punta Sabbioni. It charges L8000 per person and L22,000 for a space equipped with water and electricity. On the Lido is the cheaper *San Nicolò* (☎ 526 74 15). To get there take bus A as you get off at the Lido vaporetto stop.

Hostels & Institutions The IYHF *Ostello Venezia* (☎ 523 82 11) is on the island of Giudecca, at Fondamenta delle Zitelle 86. It is open to members only, though you can buy a card there. Bed and breakfast is L17,000 and full meals are available for under L12,000. Take vaporetto No 5 sinistra (the left circle line) from the station (L2200 one-way) and get off at Zitelle. The *Istituto San Giuseppe* (☎ 522 53 52), Castello 5402, has dorm beds for L25,000 per person, but it is not the simplest place to find. From Campo San Zulian, near Piazza San Marco, walk

through Campo de la Guerra, go across the bridge and take the first left, where you see the sign.

The *Suore Mantellate* (☎ 522 08 29), Calle Buccari (Castello 10) offers relatively expensive accommodation at L32,000 for bed and breakfast. It is at the far end of Castello, away from San Marco. Take vaporetto No 1 or 2 from the station to Sant'Elena, east of the centre.

Istituto Canosiano (☎ 522 21 57) has beds in large dorms for women only at L14,000 a night. Take vaporetto No 5 sinistra to Sant'Eufemia on Giudecca. It is just near the stop.

Hotels Most of the cheaper hotels are in Cannaregio; places around San Marco and in the Castello, Dorsoduro, San Polo and Santa Croce areas are more expensive. Try the Lido in the low season for some good bargains.

Cannaregio This is the easiest area to find a bed because of the sheer number of pensioni, locande and alloggi. One of the cheapest is *Archie's House* (☎ 72 08 84), Cannaregio 1814B. To find it, follow the Lista di Spagna from the station, through Campo San Geremia, go across the bridge and along Rio Terrà San Leonardo to Campiello Anconetta. It's about a 10-minute walk away. Beds in somewhat dingy dormitories are L18,000 a night, or L20,000 per person for a double.

Closer to the station is the *Locanda Antica Casa Carettoni* (☎ 71 62 31) at Lista di Spagna 130. Singles/doubles cost L26,000/ 46,000 and there is no extra charge for use of the communal shower. The place is full of cats cared for by the pleasant and rather eccentric owner. Just off the Lista di Spagna, at Calle della Misericordia 358, is *Hotel Santa Lucia* (☎ 71 51 80), in a newer building which has rooms for L45,000/65,000.

Hotel Villa Rosa (☎ 71 65 89), Calle della Misericordia 389, has singles/doubles for L40,000/65,000 and triples for L85,000, all with breakfast included. *Orsaria* (☎ 71 52 54) at Calle Priuti 108, just off the Lista di Spagna near the station, has very clean doubles/triples/quads for L55,000/70,000/

88,000. *Albergo Adua* (☎ 71 61 84) is at Lista di Spagna 233a, about 50 metres past Casa Carettoni on the right. It has singles/doubles for L38,000/50,000 and triples for L69,000.

The *Hotel Rossi* (☎ 71 51 64) is also near the station in the tiny Calle de le Procuratie, off Lista di Spagna, and has singles/doubles for L43,000/61,000. Triples/quads cost L90,000/120,000. In the low season singles/doubles are L35,000/55,000, and a double with bathroom is L55,000. At *Al Gobbo* (☎ 71 50 01), in Campo San Geremia, the compulsory breakfast bumps up the prices. Doubles/triples are L69,000/ 79,000. To the left is *Alloggi Calderan* (☎ 71 53 61), with singles/doubles for L33,000/42,000 and a bed in four-bed dorms for L18,000.

Along the Rio Terrà San Leonardo, at No 1333, is the fantastic *Alloggi Smeraldo* (☎ 71 78 38), located in an old palace that retains some signs of its former splendour. Singles/doubles are L35,000/50,000 and triples are L95,000. The Smeraldo plans to close down for renovations at some point in 1993. Run by the same management is *Alloggi Biasin* (☎ 71 72 31), Fondamenta di Cannaregio 1252, just off the Lista di Spagna across the Ponte delle Guglie. Doubles are L50,000 and rooms for three and four are L20,000 a person.

The *Hotel Minerva & Nettuno* (☎ 71 59 68), Lista di Spagna 230, has singles/doubles for L47,000/68,000.

The *Albergo Bernardi Semenzato* (☎ 522 72 57), just off Strada Nova at Campo dei SS Apostoli, has cheap singles/doubles for L28,000/43,000, but many of the rooms are dark and uninviting. If you don't like the idea of a 20-minute walk from the station, catch the No 1 vaporetto to Ca' d'Oro.

San Marco Although this is the most heavily touristed area of Venice, it has some surprisingly good-quality budget pensioni. *Al Gambero* (☎ 522 43 84), Calle dei Fabbri 4685, near Campo San Zulian, has singles/doubles for L35,000/52,000, and triples for L70,200. *Hotel Noemi* (☎ 523 81 44), at Calle dei Fabbri 909, is only a few

steps from the piazza and has clean, basic singles/doubles for L38,000/55,000. A triple is L78,000. *Pensione Al Gazzettino* (☎ 528 65 23) is in Calle Mezzo 4971, off the Calle Sottoportico near Piazza San Marco. It has singles/doubles for L45,000/65,000 and triples for L90,000, breakfast included.

One of the nicest places in this area is *Locanda Casa Petrarca* (☎ 520 04 30), San Marco 4386, which has singles/doubles for L40,000/70,000 and triples for L95,000. Doubles/triples with bath are L100,000/ 120,000. It costs L2000 to use the communal shower. The friendly owner speaks English. To get there, find Campo San Luca, go along Calle dei Fusari, then take the second street on the left and turn right into Calle Schiavone. The *Locanda San Salvador* (☎ 528 91 47), San Marco 5264, is run by the same family and is a bit cheaper. It is just off Campo San Bartolomeo, in Calle del Galliazzo, near the Rialto Bridge.

Castello This area is to the east of Piazza San Marco, and although close to the piazza, is less heavily touristed. The easiest way to get there is to catch the No 1 vaporetto to Castello. *Albergo Casa Verardo* (☎ 528 61 27), Ponte Storto 4765, near Calle dei Mercanti, has singles/doubles for L40,000/ 70,000 and triples/quads for L110,000/ 120,000. *Albergo Corona* (☎ 522 91 74), Calle Corona 4464, has singles/doubles for L34,000/48,000 and triples for L65,000. A shower costs L3000. Catch the vaporetto to San Zaccaria and walk through Campo SS Filippo e Giacomo. It is up four flights of stairs, but there is an electric baggage lift.

The *Hotel Bridge* (☎ 520 52 87), just off Campo SS Filippo e Giacomo, has doubles/triples for L67,000/93,000, breakfast included. The *Locanda Piave* (☎ 528 51 74), Ruga Giuffa 4838/40 (near Campo Santa Maria Formosa), is tucked away in a maze of tiny streets. Doubles are L71,000 including breakfast.

From Campo San Provolo (near Locanda Tiepolo) go through the passageway, cross the bridge and follow Calle Rotta to the end. The *Hotel Riva* (☎ 522 70 34) at Ponte

ITALY

dell'Angelo 5310 is on a lovely side canal. Doubles/triples with breakfast and private bathroom are L70,000/130,000. From San Marco walk along the Calle San Marco and turn left into Calle Angelo to get there.

Dorsoduro, San Polo & Santa Croce The *Albergo Guerrato* (☎ 522 71 31) is just near the Rialto Bridge at Calle drio la Scimia 240a, to the right off Ruga de Speziale. Singles/doubles cost L47,000/65,000 and triples L72,000. *Hotel Al Gallo* (☎ 523 67 61), Calle Amai 197, off Fondamenta Tolentini, has singles/doubles for L40,000/74,000 and triples/quads for L90,000/110,000, all with private shower.

Casa Peron (☎ 528 60 38), Salizzada San Pantalon 84, has rooms for L43,000/70,000 with breakfast and private shower. To get there from the station, cross the bridge (Ponte Scalzi) and follow the signs to San Marco and the Rialto till you reach Rio delle Muneghette, then cross the wooden bridge.

Lido In summer this area is expensive, but there are good bargains in the low season, when the weather is still warm. At *Pensione La Pergola* (☎ 526 07 84), Via Cipro 15, doubles/triples are L64,000/85,000, including breakfast. It is open all year and has a shady terrace. To get there turn left off the Gran Viale Santa Maria Elisabetta into Via Zara, then turn right into Via Cipro. The *Villa Edera* (☎ 526 07 91), Via Negroponte 13, left off Gran Viale Santa Maria Elisabetta, has singles/doubles in the high season for L45,000/65,000, including breakfast. In the low season rooms cost L35,000/50,000 and the owner will be happy to strike a deal.

Mestre Only 15 minutes away on a regular bus No 7, Mestre is an economical alternative to staying in Venice. There are a number of good hotels as well as pleny of cafés and places to eat around the pleasant main square. If you're travelling by car, the saving on car parking charges are considerable.

Places to Eat
Eating in Venice can be an expensive pastime

unless you choose very carefully. Many restaurants, particularly around San Marco, are tourist traps, where prices are high and the quality is poor. Be careful to read the fine print if you want to eat seafood, as most fish is sold by weight.

Many bars serve filling snacks with lunchtime and predinner drinks. Most also have a wide range of Venetian panini, with every imaginable filling. *Tramezzi* (three-pointed sandwiches) and huge bread rolls cost from L3000 to L5000 if you eat them while standing at the bar.

The staples of the Veneto region's cucina are rice and beans. Try the *risotto con piselli* (risotto with peas, also called *risi e bisi*), the *minestra di pasta e fagioli* (pasta and bean soup), and don't miss a risotto or pasta dish with *radicchio trevisano* (red chicory). The rich dessert *tiramisù*, made with *mascarpone* (soft cream cheese), Marsala, sponge and chocolate, is a favourite here.

There are fruit and vegetable stalls lining the main thoroughfare from the station to Piazza San Marco, but the prices are inflated for tourists. The main markets are in the streets around the Rialto Bridge (on the San Polo side). Alimentari, for salami, cheese and bread, are concentrated around Campo Beccarie. There is a *Standa* supermarket on Strada Nova and a *Mega 1* supermarket in Campo Santa Margherita.

Restaurants The best places to look for trattorias and ristoranti (restaurants) are in the side streets of Castello and around Campo San Barnaba and Campo Santa Margherita in Dorsoduro.

Near the Station There are few decent options in this area. *Trattoria alla Palazzina*, Cannaregio 1509, is just over the first bridge after Campo San Geremia. It has a garden at the rear and serves good pizzas for L6000 to L7000. A full meal will cost around L20,000. Otherwise there are numerous bars which serve panini and takeaway pizza by the slice.

Locals say that the best pizza and pasta in Venice is served at *Pizzeria all'Anfora*, across the Scalzi Bridge from the station at

Lista dei Bari 1223. It has a garden at the rear. Try the *pizza Ottombrina*, with Brie and bacon. You can get pizzas from L4000 to L8000, pasta from L4000 to L5000, and a main course from L7000 to L8000. The wine, however, is expensive. To find it walk straight ahead from the bridge, turn left at the second street and follow the signs to Rialto.

Around San Marco & Castello *Vino Vino*, San Marco 2007, is a popular bar/osteria at Ponte Veste near Teatro La Fenice. The menu changes daily and the good-quality food is preprepared. A primo piatto costs L4500, a secondo L10,000, and there is a good selection of vegetables. Wine sold by the glass is L1000. *Trattoria Rivetto*, Salizzada San Provolo, just before Campo San Provolo in Castello, serves typical Venetian food. A pasta dish costs L5000 to L6000 and a main dish L10,000; wine is dear at L9000 a litre.

In this area there are several bars which serve excellent and cheap panini. One is on the corner of Calle delle Rasse, just off Campo SS Filippo e Giacomo, and another is *Al Vecio Penasa*, just around the corner at Calle delle Rasse 4586. Next to the Locanda Piave (follow the directions given for the hotel) is the *Ristorante Tucan*. Pizzas are around L6000 and a full meal will cost close to L20,000. Just off Campo Santa Maria Formosa is *Cip Ciap*, at the Ponte del Mondo Novo. It serves fantastic and filling pizza by the slice for L2000 to L3000. *Il Golosone*, nearby on Salizzada San Lio 5689, is one of the best pasticcerie in Venice.

Another popular place for dolci is *Pasticceria Marchini*, on the other side of Piazza San Marco, just off Campo Santo Stefano, at Calle del Spezier 2769. *Trattoria da Memi*, Campiello Santo Stefano, just off Campo Santo Stefano, has a good tourist menu for L18,000 and pizzas for L5000 to L7000.

Dorsoduro, San Polo & Santa Croce This is the best area for small, cheap trattorias and pizzerias. *L'Incontro*, Rio Terrà Canal, between Campo San Barnaba and Campo Santa Margherita, serves typical food of the region and is one of the better deals in the

city. The menu alters daily and a full meal will cost around L18,000. The *Antica Locanda Montin* (in the hotel of the same name) has good, simple food, and a shady garden. A full meal will cost around L30,000.

In Campo Santa Margherita is *Bar La Sosta*, a student favourite. Panini cost from L1500 to L4000 and you can sit outside at no extra charge. *Crepizza*, Calle San Pantalon 3757, past Campo Santa Margherita, serves pasta for L6000, pizza for L6000 to L7000, and fantastic crêpes for L7000 to L8000. Around the corner at Crosera San Pantalon 3817 is *Da Silvio*, which serves pizzas for L4000 to L7000 in a garden setting. A full meal here will cost under L15,000.

Cafés If you can cope with the idea of paying L10,000 for a cappuccino, spend an hour or so sitting at an outdoor table in Piazza San Marco, listening to the orchestra. *Caffè Florian* is the most famous of San Marco's cafés. Although a bit faded these days, it is still full of atmosphere. Byron, James and friends took breakfast there before crossing the piazza to *Quadri* for lunch. Both cafés have bars where you will pay normal prices for a coffee or drink and still enjoy the elegant surroundings.

Gelati The best ice cream in Venice is at *Gelati Nico*, Fondamenta Zattere 922. The locals take their *passegiata* (evening walk) along the fondamenta, while eating their gelati. *Il Doge*, Campo Santa Margherita, also has excellent gelati.

Entertainment

Exhibitions, theatre and musical events continue throughout the year in Venice. Information is available in the weekly *Un Ospite di Venezia* and the tourist office also has brochures listing events and performances for the entire year.

The major event of the year is the famous Carnevale, held during the 10 days before Ash Wednesday, when Venetians don spectacular masks and costumes for what is literally a 10-day street party.

The Venice Biennale, a major exhibition of international visual arts, is held every even-numbered year, and the Venice International Film Festival is held every September at the *Palazzo del Cinema*, on the Lido.

Concerts and opera are performed throughout the year at *Teatro La Fenice*, and symphony and chamber music concerts are staged in the Church of Santa Maria della Pietà. Major art exhibitions are held at the Palazzo Grassi (at the vaporetto stop of San Samuele), and you will find smaller exhibitions in various venues in the city throughout the year. A Contemporary Music Festival is held annually in October at the *Goldoni Theatre* (Teatro Goldoni), near Campo San Luca.

The most important celebration on the Venetian calendar is the Festa del Redentore (Festival of the Redeemer), on the third weekend in July, which features a spectacular fireworks display. The regatta storica, a gondola race on the Grand Canal, is held on the first Sunday in September.

Things to Buy

Who can think of Venice without an image of its elaborately grotesque Venetian glass coming to mind? There are several workshops and showrooms in Venice, particularly in the area between San Marco and Castello, and on the island of Murano, designed mainly for large tourist groups. If you want to buy Venetian glass, shop around carefully, because quality and prices vary dramatically.

The famous Carnevale masks make a beautiful, though expensive, souvenir of Venice. A small workshop and showroom in a small street off Campo SS Filippo and Giacomo, towards Piazza San Marco, is worth a look. Venice is also famous for its *carta marmorizzata* (marbled paper), sold at many outlets throughout the city.

The main shopping area for clothing, shoes, accessories and jewellery is in the narrow streets between San Marco and the Rialto. Shop hours are roughly the same as throughout Italy, although many outlets open on Sundays during the tourist season.

Getting There & Away

Air Marco Polo Airport is about 20 km from Venice and accessible by regular *motoscafo* (motorboat) from San Marco and the Lido (L15,000). There are also buses from Piazzale Roma. A water taxi from San Marco will cost more than L80,000. The airport services domestic and European flights.

Bus ACTV buses leave from Piazzale Roma for surrounding areas, including Mestre and Chioggia, a fishing port at the southernmost point of the lagoon. Buses also go to Padua and Treviso. Tickets and information are available at the office in the piazza.

Train The Stazione Santa Lucia, known in Venice as the ferrovia, is directly linked to Padua, Verona, Trieste, Milan and Bologna and thus is easily accessible from Florence and Rome. You can also leave from Venice for major points in Germany, Austria and former Yugoslavia.

Boat Ferries run from Venice to Alexandria in Egypt via Bari and stop at Piraeus in Greece. The company operating the ferries is Adriatica (☎ 781861). It has an office at Porto di Venezia, Stazione Marittima Molo 103. The ferries do not have deck class or poltrone (armchairs). Cabins (with four beds) in the 1992 high season (2 July to 9 September) were L335,000 per person to Piraeus and L670,000 to Alexandria.

Getting Around

As there are no cars in Venice, vaporetti are the city's mode of public transport.

Once you cross the bridge from Mestre, cars must be left at one of the huge car parks in Piazzale Roma, or on the island of Tronchetto. They are not cheap and you will pay L30,000 a day at Tronchetto and L18,000 to L25,000 at Piazzale Roma, depending on the size of the car. A cheaper alternative is to leave the car at Fusina, near Mestre, and catch the No 16 vaporetto to Zattere and then the No 5 either to Piazza San Marco or the train station. Ask for information at the tourist information office just before the bridge to Venice.

From Piazzale Roma or Tronchetto, vaporetto No 1 heads along the Grand Canal to San Marco and then the Lido. The No 1 zigzags its way up the canal. There are faster and more expensive alternatives if you are in a hurry. Vaporetti also head from the station to the islands of Murano, Burano and Torcello. A full timetable is available at the tourist office. Tickets cost L2200 for most routes and L2500 for faster vaporetti. A 24-hour ticket costs L10,000 and a three-day ticket costs L17,000.

Water taxis are exorbitant, with a set charge of L28,000 for a maximum of seven minutes, an extra L7000 if you phone for a taxi, and various other surcharges which make a gondola ride seem cheap.

VERONA

Forever associated with Romeo and Juliet, Verona has much more to offer than the relics of a tragic love story. Known as *la piccola Roma* (little Rome) for its importance as a Roman city, its golden era was during the 13th and 14th centuries, under the rule of the Scaligeri family. This was a period noted for the savage family feuding on which Shakespeare based his play.

Information & Orientation

Old Verona is small, but there is much to see and it is a popular base for exploring surrounding towns. The tourist office has two branches: one at Via Dietro Anfiteatro 6b, facing the Roman Arena, and another at Piazza delle Erbe 42. Both offer concise and useful information on the city and its frequent cultural events.

It's easy to find your way around Verona. Buses leave for the centre from outside the train station; otherwise walk to the right, past the bus station, cross the river and walk along Corso Porto Nuovo to Piazza Bra. From there take Via Mazzini and turn left at Via Cappello to reach Piazza delle Erbe.

Verona's telephone code is 045.

Things to See & Do

The pink-marble Roman amphitheatre, known as the **Arena**, in Piazza Bra, was built in the first century AD and is now Verona's opera house. Walk along Via Mazzini to Via Cappello and **Juliet's House** (Casa di Giulietta), its entrance smothered with lovers' graffiti, which is the result of an odd project in 1990. Farther along the street to the right is **Porta Leoni**, one of the gates to the old Roman Verona; **Porta Borsari**, the other gate to the city is north of the Arena at Corso Porta Borsari.

In the other direction is **Piazza delle Erbe**, the former site of the Roman forum. Lined with the characteristic pink-marble palaces of Verona, the piazza today remains the lively centre of the city, but the permanent market stalls in its centre detract from its beauty. In the piazza is the **Fountain of Madonna Verona**. Just off the square are the elegant **Piazza dei Signori**, flanked by the Renaissance **Loggia del Consiglio**; the Scaligeri residence now known as the **Governor's Palace** and partly decorated by Giotto; and the medieval town hall.

Take a look at the **Duomo**, on Via Duomo, for its Romanesque main doors and Titian's **Assumption**.

Throughout the year the city hosts musical and cultural events, culminating in the season of opera and ballet from July to September at the Arena (the cheapest tickets are L25,000). There is a lyric-symphonic season in winter at the 18th century Teatro Filarmonico (on Piazza Bra), and Shakespeare is performed at the Roman Theatre (Teatro Romano) in summer. Information and tickets for these events are available at the Ente Lirico Arena di Verona (☎ 59 01 09), Piazza Bra 28.

Places to Stay & Eat

The beautifully restored IYHF *youth hostel* (☎ 59 03 60), in Villa Francescati, Salita Fontana del Ferro 15, should be your first choice. Bed and breakfast is L14,000 a night and a meal is L12,000. An IYHF card is not necessary. Next door is a camping ground. To reserve a space, speak to the hostel man-

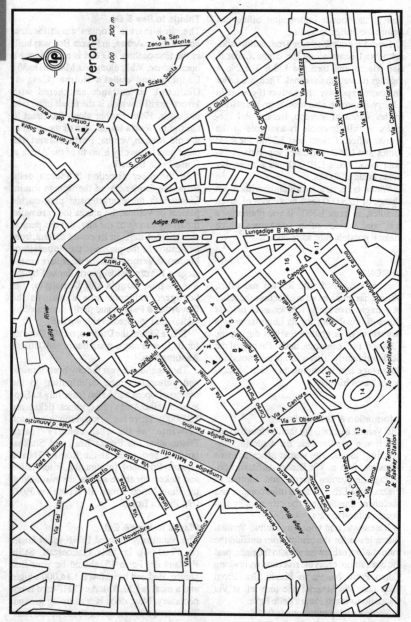

■ PLACES TO STAY

1　IYHF Youth Hostel
3　Casa della Giovane
10　Al Castello
12　Ciopeta

▼ PLACES TO EAT

7　Osteria alle Sgarzarie
8　Bottega dei Vini

　　OTHER

2　Cathedral
4　Piazza dei Signori
5　Piazza delle Erbe
6　Tourist Office
9　Porta Borsari
11　Teatro Filarmonico
13　Piazza Bra
14　Arena
15　Tourist Office
16　Juliet's House
17　Porta Leoni

food. A meal could cost around L20,000. A very cheap, but less filling, alternative is the many osterias in Verona, which are dotted around the historical centre. Their main purpose is to serve wine, but they also offer cheap, and sometimes free, snacks.

Getting There & Away

The Verona-Villafranca Airport (☎ 51 30 39) is just outside the town and accessible by bus and train. Flights from all over Italy, Europe and some international destinations arrive here. Verona is directly linked to Milan, Venice, Florence and Rome.

Verona is also on the Brenner Pass railway line to Austria and Germany. A short distance away by train are Padua, Mantua and Modena.

The main APT bus terminal is in the piazza in front of the station. Buses leave for surrounding areas, including Mantua, Ferrara and Brescia. The city is also at the intersection of the autostrade Serenissima A4 (Milan-Venice) and the Brennero A22.

Getting Around

Bus Nos 2 and 8 leave from outside the station for the centre of Verona, otherwise it's a 15-minute walk along Corso Porto Nuovo. If you arrive by car, you should have no trouble reaching the centre. Simply follow the *centro* signs. There are also signs marking the directions to most hotels.

PADUA

Although famous as the city of St Anthony and for its university, which is one of the oldest in Europe, Padua (Padova) is often merely seen as a convenient and cheap place to stay while visiting Venice. The city, however, offers a rich collection of art treasures and its many piazzas and arcaded streets are a pleasure to explore.

Information

There is a tourist office at the station, open Monday to Saturday from 8 am to 8 pm and Sundays from 8.30 am to 12.30 pm. There you can pick up a map, a list of hotels and

agement. Catch bus No 2 from the station to Piazza Isolo and then follow the signs. The *Casa della Giovane* (☎ 59 68 80), Via Pigna 7, just off Via Garibaldi, is for women only and costs L17,000 a night. Catch bus No 2 and ask the driver where to get off.

The *Volto Cittadella* (☎ 800 00 77), Via Volto Cittadella 8, has doubles/triples for L36,000/55,000. It is off Corso Porta Nuova, just before Piazza Bra. At Corso Cavour 43, *Al Castello* (☎ 800 44 03) offers singles/doubles for L30,000/48,000.

Ciopeta (☎ 800 68 43), Vicolo Teatro Filarmonico 2 near Piazza Bra, has doubles for L60,000.

Known for its fresh produce, its crisp *soave* (a dry white wine) and its boiled meat, Verona offers delicious food at reasonable prices. At the *Osteria alle Sgarzarie*, Corte Sgarzarie 14b, off Corso Porta Borsari near Piazza delle Erbe, you can eat a hearty meal for around L10,000. More expensive, but worth it, is *Bottega dei Vini*, Vicolo Scudo di Francia 3, which serves typical regional the useful booklet *Padova Benvenuti*. The staff will ring to check for hotel vacancies.

The post office is at Corso Garibaldi 25 and the ASST telephone office is next door at No 31. Padua's postcode is 35100 and its telephone code is 049.

Things to See
Thousands of pilgrims arrive in Padua every year to visit the *Basilica del Santo*, in the hope that St Anthony, patron saint of Padua and of lost things, will help them to find whatever it is they are looking for. The saint's tomb is in the church, which also houses important art works, including 14th century frescoes and bronze sculptures by Donatello, which adorn the high altar. A bronze equestrian statue by Donatello is outside the basilica.

The **Scrovegni Chapel** is in the gardens surrounding the **Roman Arena**, off Piazza Eremitani. The interior walls of the chapel were completely covered in frescoes by Giotto in the 14th century. Depicting the life of Christ and ending with the *Last Judgment*, the 36 panels are considered one of the greatest works of figurative art of all time. The **Palazzo della Ragione** (Law Courts) is remarkable for its sloping roof and loggias; inside is the entirely frescoed huge **salon**, containing a huge wooden horse built for a joust in 1466.

Places to Stay & Eat
Padua has no shortage of budget hotels, but they fill up quickly in summer with the overflow from Venice. The non-IYHF *Ostello della Città di Padova* (☎ 875 22 19) is at Via A Aleardi 30. Bed and breakfast is L15,000. Take bus No 3, 8, 12 or 18 from the station to Prato della Valle (about five minutes away) and then ask for directions. The *Verdi* (☎ 66 34 50), Via Dondi dell'Orologio 7, has basic, clean singles/doubles for L30,000/38,000 and is located in the university district off Via Verdi. The *Pavia* (☎ 66 15 58) at Via dei Papafava 11 has singles/doubles for L38,000/54,000. Follow Corso del Popolo until it becomes Via Roma and then turn right into Via Marsala.

Try the café in the small piazza next to the Hotel Verdi or the *Bar Margherita*, Via del Santo 169, near the Basilica del Santo, for good, cheap panini. The *Osteria dei Fabbri*, Via dei Fabbri 13, and *Al Pero*, Via Santa Lucia 38, both near Piazza Dante, serve regional dishes. Al Pero is cheaper and a full meal there will cost around L18,000.

Daily markets are held in the piazzas around the Palazzo Ragione, with fresh produce sold in Piazza delle Erbe and Piazza della Frutta, and bread, cheese and salami sold in the shops under the porticoes.

Getting There & Away
Padua is directly linked by train to Milan, Venice and Bologna and is easily accessible from most other major cities. Regular ATP buses serve Venice, Milan, Trieste and surrounding towns. The terminal is off Via Trieste, near the station. From the station it's a 10-minute walk to reach the centre of town, or you can take bus No 10 along Corso del Popolo, which becomes Corso Garibaldi, to the historic centre.

MILAN
The economic, and some say fashion, capital of Italy, Milan (Milano) has long been an elegant and cultural city. Its origins are believed to be Celtic, but it was conquered by the Romans in 222 BC, after which it became an important trading and transport centre. From the 13th century the city flourished under the rule of two powerful families: the Viscontis and later the Sforzas.

Orientation
If being in Italy means disorganised business and bureaucracy, unreliable public transport and negotiating chaotic traffic, then a visit to Milan is like leaving the country. This major city is geared for workers, not tourists, and, though its air is badly polluted and its winter climate is appalling, the place still functions.

From Milan's central railway station (stazione centrale) it is simple to reach the centre of town and other major points on the Milan underground (known as the MM, or Metropolitana). The city of Milan is huge, but most sights are in the centre. Use the **Duomo** and the **Castello Sforzesco** at the other end of Via Dante as your points of reference. The main shopping areas and sights are around and between the two.

Note that Milan closes down almost completely in August, when most of the city's inhabitants take their annual holidays. You will find few restaurants and and even fewer shops open at this time.

Information
Tourist Office The main branch of the APT (☎ 02-80 96 62) is at Via Marconi 1, in Piazza del Duomo, where you can pick up the useful *Milan is Milano*, one of the most comprehensive city guides in Italy. It is open from 8 am to 8 pm Monday to Saturday and from 9 am to 12.30 pm and 1.30 to 5 pm on Sundays and holidays. There is a branch office at the station which is open from 8 am to 8 pm.

Milan City Council operates an information office in Galleria V Emanuele II, just off Piazza del Duomo.

Money Banks in Milan are open Monday to Friday from 8.30 am to 1 pm and for one hour in the afternoon, usually from 2.45 to 3.45 pm. Exchange offices that open at weekends include: Banca Ponti, Piazza del Duomo 19, from 9 am to 1 pm Saturdays; and Banca delle Comunicazioni, stazione centrale, from 8 am to 7 pm weekdays, 8 am to 6.30 pm Saturdays and 9 am to 1.30 pm on Sundays. There are also weekend exchange offices at both airports.

Post & Telecommunications The main post office is at Via Cordusio 4, off Via Dante, near Piazza del Duomo. *Fermo Posta* is here, open from 8 am to 8 pm Monday to Friday and to 2 pm Saturdays. There are also post offices at the station and at both airports.

ASST telephone offices are at the main post office and at the station (open from 7 am to 7.45 pm daily). The main SIP office is in Galleria V Emanuele II. You will also find a Reuters news service in English here.

Milan's postcode is 20100 and its telephone code is 02. Many telephone numbers in Milan were to be changed in late 1992. Ring the SIP information number (☎ 12) or contact the APT for assistance if the numbers in this section have changed.

Foreign Consulates You will find consulates of the following countries in Milan: Australia (☎ 76 01 33 30), Via Filippo Turati 40; Canada (☎ 669 74 51), Via Vittorio Pisani 19; the UK (☎ 896 34 42), Via San Paolo 7; and the USA (☎ 469 64 51), Via P Amedeo 2/10.

Bookshops The American Bookstore in Largo Cairoli has a great selection of English and American classics and contemporary literature, as well as art books. The English Bookshop, Via Mascheroni 12, west of the Castello Sforzesco, is a popular meeting place for English people visiting or living in Milan.

Emergency The questura centrale (police headquarters; ☎ 6 22 61) is at Via Fatebenefratelli 11. They speak English. In an emergency call the carabinieri on ☎ 112. For an ambulance call ☎ 7733 and for emergency first aid call the Italian Red Cross on ☎ 3883. If you need a hospital, the Ospedale Maggiore Policlinico (☎ 551 35 18) is at Via Francesco Sforza 35, close to the centre. There are all-night pharmacies in the stazione centrale (☎ 669 07 35) and in Piazza del Duomo (☎ 87 22 66). To find out which other pharmacies are open all night, call ☎ 192. For lost property call the Milan City Council on ☎ 87 08 21.

Dangers & Annoyances Milan's main shopping areas are popular haunts for local groups of thieves. They are as numerous here as in Rome and also lightning fast. They use the same technique of waving cardboard or newspaper in your face to distract your attention while they head for your pockets.

Things to See
Start with the extraordinary **Duomo**, commissioned by Gian Galeazzo Visconti in

ITALY

Milan
(Milano)

0   250   500 m

PLACES TO STAY

PLACES TO EAT

OTHER

1386. The first glimpse of this spiky, tumultuous structure is certainly memorable, its marble façade shaped into pinnacles, statues and pillars.

Walk through the graceful **Galleria Vittorio Emanuele II** to **La Scala**, Milan's famous opera house. The theatre's **museum** is open weekdays from 9 am to midday and 2 to 6 pm, and on Sundays from 9.30 am to noon and 2.30 to 6 pm. Admission is L5000. At the end of Via Dante is the huge **Castello Sforzesco**, which was originally a Visconti fortress but was entirely rebuilt by Francesco Sforza in the 15th century. Its museums contain excellent collections of sculpture, including Michelangelo's *Pietà Rondanini*. It is open Tuesday to Sunday from 9.30 am to 12.15 pm and from 2.30 to 5.15 pm. Admission is free.

Nearby in Via Brera is the 17th century **Palazzo di Brera**, which houses the **Pinacoteca di Brera**. This gallery's vast collection of paintings includes Mantegna's masterpiece, the *Dead Christ*. The gallery is open Tuesday to Saturday from 9 am to 5.30 pm and Sundays from 9 am to 12.30 pm. Admission is L8000.

An absolute must is Leonardo da Vinci's *Last Supper*, in the Cenacolo Vinciano, next to the **Chiesa di Santa Maria delle Grazie**, noted for Bramante's tribune. The *Last Supper* has been restored, but centuries of damage from floods, bombing and decay have left their mark. The building is open

Tuesday to Saturday from 9 am to 1.15 pm. Admission is L6000.

Places to Stay

Hostels Fortunately, there is a youth hostel, the IYHF *Ostello Piero Rotta* (☎ 36 70 95), Viale Salmoiraghi 2, north-west of the city centre. Bed and breakfast is L20,000, or L20,000 per bed for family accommodation. Take bus MM1 to the metro stop QT8. The IYHF card is compulsory, but you can buy it there (L20,000). The *Casa Famiglia* (☎ 29 00 01 64), Corso Garibaldi 123, is run by nuns and is only for women aged 29 years and under. Bed and shower is L18,000 a night.

Hotels Milan boasts the most expensive and most heavily booked hotels in Italy. There are numerous one-star hotels and pensioni, but only a minority is located reasonably close to the centre and standards can vary dramatically. Hotel owners in Milan don't mess around with bill-padding techniques – they simply charge higher prices than those set by the tourist board. The tourist offices will make recommendations, but they will not make bookings.

Near Stazione Centrale & Corso Buenos Aires
Most of the cheaper hotels near the station will not take bookings. The *Nettuno* (☎ 29 40 44 81), Via Tadino 27 (turn right off Via D Scarlatti, which is to the left as you leave the station), is a 10-minute walk away. It has singles/doubles for L38,000/53,500. A triple is L83,000.

In Via Vitruvio, to the left off Piazza Duca d'Aosta as you leave the station, there are two good budget options. The *Albergo Salerno* (☎ 204 68 70) at No 18 has doubles with bath for L50,000. The *Italia* (☎ 669 38 26) at No 44 has singles/doubles for L27,000/40,000. The *Due Giardini* (☎ 29 52 10 93), Via Lodovico Settala 46 (which intersects Via Vitruvio), has singles/doubles for L40,000/60,000 and triples for L80,000. Across Corso Buenos Aires at Via Gaspare Spontini 6 is *Del Sole* (☎ 29 51 29 71) with singles/doubles for L38,000/53,000 and

triples for L70,000. The *Verona* (☎ 66 98 30 91), at Via Carlo Tenca 12, near Piazza della Repubblica, has rooms for L40,000/50,000 with telephone and TV.

About halfway between the station and the centre there is a concentration of hotels around Corso Buenos Aires and Viale Tunisia. Take the MM1 and get off at the Porta Venezia stop. *Hotel Casa Mia* (☎ 657 52 49), Viale Vittorio Veneto 30, is a short walk from the MM1 stop. It has singles/doubles for L45,000/60,000. A triple is L80,000.

At Viale Tunisia 6, just off Corso Buenos Aires, there are several hotels. The *Hotel Canna* (☎ 29 52 40 55) is the cheapest, with singles/doubles for L38,000/50,000 and triples with private shower for L28,000 per person. A double with private bathroom is L70,000. The *Hotel Kennedy* (☎ 29 40 09 34) has singles/doubles for L45,000/60,000. A double with private bathroom is L75,000 and triples are L30,000 per person. Bookings are accepted. The *Hotel San Tomaso* (☎ 29 51 47 47) has singles/doubles for L35,000/53,000 and triples for L25,000 per person.

Around the Centre
The *Albergo Commercio* (☎ 86 46 38 80), Via Mercato 1, has singles/doubles with shower for L40,000/50,000. From Piazza Cordusio walk down Via Broletto, which becomes Via Mercato. The entrance to the hotel is around the corner in Via delle Erbe.

Very close to Piazza del Duomo is the *Hotel Speronari* (☎ 86 46 11 25), Via Speronari 4, which is eccentrically decorated but comfortable. Singles/doubles are L38,000/53,000. Triples are L72,000. The *Hotel Nuovo* (☎ 86 46 05 42) at Piazza Beccaria 6 is in a great location just off Corso Vittorio Emanuele II and the Duomo. Singles/doubles cost L40,000/60,000, but the management can be abrasive.

Places to Eat
Italians say that the cucina of Lombardy (Lombardia) is designed for people who don't have time to waste, because they are always in a hurry to work. In Milan tradi-

tional restaurants are being replaced by fast-food outlets and sandwich bars as the favoured eating places.

Bar snacks are an institution in Milan and are more filling and varied than in any other Italian city. Most bars around the centre lay out their fare from 5 pm daily. Via Speronari is the best place to shop for bread, salami, cheese and wine.

Restaurants Avoid the area around the station and head for Corso Buenos Aires and the centre.

Near Corso Buenos Aires *Ciao*, Corso Buenos Aires 7, is part of a chain (there are others in Corso Europa and at Via Dante 5), but the food is first-rate and relatively cheap. Pasta dishes cost around L5000 and excellent salads go for around L3000. *L'Osteria del Treno*, Via San Gregorio 46/48, serves excellent, reasonably priced food. *Trattoria di Polpetta*, on the corner of Via Tadino and Via Panfilo Castaldi (near Viale V Veneto), is a small place with good-quality food which is a favourite with the locals. Pasta costs L6000 to L7000.

In the Centre The first time the Milanese tasted pizza it was cooked at *Di Gennaro*, Via S Radegonda 3, though today there is not much which sets this place above others in the city. You can eat a better pizza at *La Baia*, Via Cellini 3. At *Pizza del Circo*, Via Circo 10, they make a great vegetarian pizza. You can eat there or get takeaway.

Trattoria da Bruno, Via Cavallotti 15, off Corso Europa (near the Duomo), is a popular and cheap local eating place. It has a special set-price lunch for L13,000. *Pizzeria Dogana*, on the corner of Via Capellari and Via Dogana, also near the Duomo, has pasta and pizza for around L7000 and a good selection of contorni for L4000. A full meal will cost around L20,000 and there are tables outside.

Popeye, Via San Tecla 8, near the Duomo, is reputed to have the best pizza in Milan. Pizzas cost around L7000 to L10,000 and a full meal will come to around L15,000 or

more. *San Tomaso*, Via San Tomaso 5 near Via Rovello, is a birreria and bistro which specialises in salads and food for vegetarians. Prices for a salad range from L5000 to L12,000. It also has live jazz music.

Cafés & Sandwich Bars One of Milan's oldest fast-food outlets is *Luini*, Via S Radegonda 16, just off Piazza del Duomo. A popular haunt of teenagers and students, it sells *panzerotti*, similar to *calzone* (a savoury turnover made with pizza dough) but stuffed with tomatoes, garlic and mozzarella. They cost L2000. *Berlin Caffè*, Via G Mora 9 (to the left off Corso Porta Ticinese, near Largo Carrobbio), has a set-price brunch for L10,000 and a small menu at night (L10,000 for one dish). Otherwise it is a pleasant place for a coffee or wine. A few doors down is *Cafe Guarany*, open from 7 am to 7 pm (closed Sunday). It serves pasta from L3000. *Le Tre Marie*, on the corner of Via Cesare Cantù and Via Armorari, off Piazza Cordusio, has great bar snacks.

The best sandwich bars are *Quadronno*, on the corner of Via Quadronno and Porta Vigentina, just south of the centre, which specialises in unusual concoctions – you can have a monkey-ham sandwich, if the mood so takes you. The *Bar Assodi Cuori*, Piazza Cavour, is crowded at lunch time, but the sandwiches are great (for around L3000 to L5000) and you can sit down for no extra charge.

For gourmet takeaway head for *Peck*. Its rosticceria is at Via Cesare Cantù 11, where you can buy cooked meats and vegetables. Another outlet is at Via Spadari 9 (near the Duomo) and is surely the most extraordinary delicatessen in the world. Several other outlets are dotted around the area, including a snack bar and restaurant at Via Victor Hugo 4.

Entertainment
Music, theatre and cinema dominate Milan's entertainment calendar. The opera season at *La Scala* opens on 7 December. For tickets go to the box office (☎ 80 91 20), but don't expect a good seat unless you book well in

advance. There is also a summer season, which features operas, concerts and ballet.

In March/April and October/November organ concerts are performed at the Church of San Maurizio in the Monastero Maggiore, at Corso Magenta 15, the continuation of Via Meravigli. In April/May there is a jazz festival, Città di Milano, and in summer the city stages Milano d'Estate, a series of concerts, theatre and dance performances. This is followed in August by Vacanze a Milano, another special programme of theatre and music.

The main season for theatre and concerts opens in October. Full details of all events are available from the tourist office in Piazza del Duomo. For details on cinema read the listings section in the daily newspaper *Corriere della Sera.*

St Ambrose's Day (7 December) is one of Milan's major festivals, and features a traditional street fair near the Basilica di Sant'Ambrogio, off Via Carducci.

Things to Buy

Every item of clothing you ever wanted to buy, but could never afford, is in Milan. The main streets for clothing, footwear and accessories are behind the Duomo around Corso Vittorio Emanuele II. You can window-shop for high-class fashions in Via Borgospesso and Via della Spiga.

The areas around Via Torino, Corso Buenos Aires and Corso XXII Marzo are less expensive. Markets are held in the areas around the canals (south-west of the centre), notably on Viale Papiniano on Tuesday and Saturday mornings. A flea market is held in Via Calatafimi (between Corso Porta Ticinese and Corso Italia) on Saturdays.

Getting There & Away

Air International flights use Malpensa Airport, about 40 km north-west of Milan. A shuttle bus to the airport leaves from stazione centrale (outside the Doria Agency) daily every half-hour. Tickets cost L8000 from the agency. Extra services are run to coincide with flights. Domestic and European flights use Linate, about 10 km east of the city in the

Forlanini district. Buses to Linate Airport leave from outside the Doria Agency every 20 minutes and cost L2800, or you can take bus No 73 from Piazza San Babila (Corso Europa) for L1000.

Train You can catch a train from stazione centrale to all of the major cities in Italy and Western Europe. Most of the trains from Rome are intercities, for which you pay the rapido supplement. Regular trains go to Venice, Florence (and Bologna), Genoa, Turin and Rome. For train timetable information go to the busy office (they speak English) in the station or call ☎ 6 75 00.

Car & Motorbike Milan is the major junction of Italy's motorways, including the Autostrada del Sole (A1) to Reggio di Calabria, the Milano-Torino (A5) and the Serenissima (A4) for Verona and Venice, and the A8 and A9 north to the lakes (Lago di Como, Lago Maggiore and Lago di Lugano) and the Swiss border.

These roads are connected to Milan by the Tangenziali Est and Ovest (the east and west bypasses). From these and the autostrade, follow the signs which lead into the centre. The A4 in particular is an extremely busy road, where numerous accidents occur and can hold up traffic for hours. In winter all roads in the area become extremely hazardous because of rain, snow and fog.

Getting Around

Bus & Underground Milan's public transport system is extremely efficient. The underground (MM) has three lines. The red MM1 provides the easiest access to the city centre. It is necessary to take the green MM2 from stazione centrale to Loreto metro station to connect with the MM1. The recently opened yellow MM3 also passes through stazione centrale and has a station in Piazza del Duomo.

The city's ATM (Municipal Transport Corporation) buses and trams are cheaper, because you can use your 75-minute ticket as many times as you want within that time, whereas the same ticket is valid for only one use on the MM. However, traffic is generally very heavy in Milan and the MM is faster. Tickets are L1000 for 75 minutes, L3500 for a full day and L6000 for two days. You can buy tickets in the MM stations and, for buses and trams only, at any tobacconist.

Taxi Taxi ranks in Milan all have telephones. A few of the radio taxi companies serving the city are Radiotaxidata (☎ 5353), Esperia (☎ 8388) and Autoradiotaxi (☎ 8585). As with the rest of Italy, taxis are expensive.

Car & Motorbike Traffic is not allowed into the city centre from 7.30 am to 6 pm Monday to Friday. There are numerous supervised car parks in the centre and near the station, but they are expensive. There is an underground car park in Piazza Diaz, near the Duomo. A cheaper alternative is to use one of the supervised car parks at the last stop on each MM line.

Car & Bike Rental Hertz, Avis, Maggiore and Europcar all have offices at stazione centrale. To rent a bicycle try Cooperativa Il Picchio (☎ 837 79 26), Corso San Gottardo 42. To get there go down Via Torino and turn left onto Corso Porta Ticinese, which becomes Corso San Gottardo.

MANTUA

Legend, perpetuated by Virgil and Dante, claims that Mantua (Mantova) was founded by the soothsayer Manto, daughter of Tiresias. Her followers are said to have built a city on the site of her grave and named it Mantova in her honour. Virgil was, in fact, born in a nearby village in 70 AD. Historians believe that the city's origins were Etruscan and later Roman. From the 14th to the 18th century, the city was ruled by the Gonzaga family, who embellished the town with their palaces and employed artists such as Andrea Mantegna and Pisanello to decorate them with their paintings and frescoes. You can easily see the city on a day trip from Verona or Bologna.

The tourist office, Piazza Andrea Mantegna, is a 10-minute walk from the

station, along Corso Vittorio Emanuele, which becomes Corso Umberto 1. Mantua's telephone code is 0376.

Things to See

Start with the **Piazza Sordello**, which is surrounded by impressive buildings including the **cattedrale** (cathedral), a strange building that combines a Romanesque tower, Baroque façade and Renaissance interior. The piazza is dominated by the **Palazzo Ducale** (Ducal Palace), a huge complex of buildings, and seat of the Gonzaga family. There is much to see in the palace, in particular the Gonzaga **apartments** and art collection, and the famous **Camera degli Sposi** (Bridal Chamber), decorated with frescoes by Andrea Mantegna in the 15th century. In the **Sala del Pisanello** (Pisanello's Room) are frescoes by the Veronese painter, depicting the cycle of chivalry and courtly love, which were discovered in 1969 under two layers of plaster. The palace is open Tuesday to Saturday from 9 am to 1 pm, 2.30 to 4 pm, and Sunday and Monday 9 am to 1 pm. Admission is L10,000.

Don't miss the **Palazzo Te**, the lavishly decorated summer palace of the Gonzaga. It is open Tuesday to Sunday from 10 am to 6 pm. Admission is L10,000. Take bus No 5 from the centre to the palace.

Places to Stay & Eat

The IYHF *ostello per la gioventù* (☎ 37 24 65) is just out of town at Lunetta San Giorgio. Take bus No 6 from the town centre. Bed and breakfast is L14,000. There is a camping ground next to the hostel which charges L4000 per person and L3500 for a tent. Both are open from April to October. At the *Rinascita* (☎ 32 06 07), Via Concezione 4, singles/doubles are L25,000/50,000.

For a hearty meal try the *Antica Hosteria Leoncino Rosso*, Via Giustiziati 33. *Nievo*, Via Nievo 8, is a self-service with good food and cheap prices. You could also buy fresh produce from the market in nearby Piazza Broletto and have a picnic in Piazza Virgiliana.

Getting There & Away

Mantua is accessible by train and bus from Verona (about 40 minutes), and by train from Milan and Bologna with a change at Modena.

BOLOGNA

Elegant, intellectual and wealthy, Bologna has an arrogance which makes it stand out among the many beautiful cities of Italy. The regional capital of Emilia-Romagna, Bologna is famous for its porticoes (arcaded streets), its harmonious architecture, its university, which is one of the oldest in Europe and, above all, its gastronomic tradition. The Bolognese have given the world tortellini, lasagne, mortadella and the ubiquitous spaghetti bolognese, hence one of the city's nicknames, *Bologna la Grassa* (Bologna the Fat).

Information

There is an EPT information office (☎ 051-37 22 20) at the train station, open from 9 am to 12.30 pm and from 2 to 5 pm, where you can book accommodation and pick up a map and the useful booklet *A Guest in Bologna*, published monthly in English. More comprehensive information is available at the Centro d'Informazione Comunale in the Palazzo Comunale, Piazza Maggiore, open Monday to Saturday from 9 am to 7 pm and Sundays to 1 pm. If it is closed, there is computerised information in the foyer.

The main post office is in Piazza Minghetti. ASST telephone offices are at Piazza VIII Agosto 24, and the station. Bologna's telephone code is 051.

Things to See

The **Piazza Maggiore**, the adjoining **Piazza del Nettuno** and **Fontana di Nettuno** (Neptune's Fountain), sculpted in bronze by a French artist who became known as Giambologna, and the **Piazza Porta Ravegnana**, with its leaning towers to rival that of Pisa, form the beautiful centre of Bologna.

In Piazza Maggiore is the **Basilica of St Petronius**, dedicated to the city's patron saint. The red-and-white marble of its unfinished façade displays the colours of Bologna. It contains important works of art and it was here that Charles V was crowned emperor by the pope in 1530. The **Palazzo Comunale** (town hall) is a huge building, combining several architectural styles in remarkable harmony. It features a bronze statue of Pope Gregory XIII (a native of Bologna who created the Gregorian calendar), an impressive winding staircase and Bologna's collection of art treasures.

The **Chiesa di Santo Stefano** is in fact a group of four churches in the Romanesque style. In a courtyard is the basin said to have been used by Pontius Pilate to wash his hands after condemning Christ to death.

Places to Stay & Eat

Budget hotels in Bologna are virtually non-existent and it is almost impossible to find a single room. Always book in advance. The best option is the IYHF hostel, *Ostello San Sisto* (☎ 51 92 02), Via Viadagola 14. Take bus No 93, 301 or 20/b from the station and ask the bus driver where to get off, then follow the signs to the hostel. It costs L16,000, including breakfast. Across the road at No 14 is another hostel, *Le Torri-San Sisto 2* (☎ 50 18 10), with bed and breakfast for the same price.

Panorama (☎ 22 18 02), Via Livraghi 1, off Via Ugo Bassi, has doubles/triples for L60,000/80,000. The *Apollo* (☎ 22 39 55), Via Drapperie 5, off Via Rizzoli (an extension of Via Ugo Bassi) has singles/doubles for L36,000/ 60,000 and triples for L81,000. The *Marconi* (☎ 26 28 32), Via G Marconi 22, has doubles/triples for L58,000/75,000.

Fortunately, it is cheaper to eat in Bologna, particularly in the university district north of Via Rizzoli. *Trattoria Belle Arti*, Via delle Belle Arti 14, serves huge pizzas for L6000 to L8000. There is a L2500 cover charge. *Trattoria Da Matusel*, Via Antonio Bertolini 2B, is popular among students and *Sampieri*, Via Sampieri 3B, is notable for its excellent food and good-value tourist menu for around L18,000. A cheaper way to eat is to buy panini (sandwiches) and eat them standing at the bar, or take advantage of the generous bar snacks provided for predinner drinkers in most bars.

Shop at the Mercato Ugo Bassi, Via Ugo Bassi 27, a vast covered market offering all the local fare.

Getting There & Away

Bologna is a major transport junction for northern Italy and trains from virtually all major cities stop here. The only hitch is that many are intercity trains, which means you have to pay the rapido supplement. The city is linked to Milan, Florence and Rome by the A1 (Autostrada del Sole). The A13 heads directly for Venice and Padova, and the A14 goes to Rimini and Ravenna.

Buses to major cities depart from the depot in Via XX Settembre, around the corner from the train station in Piazza delle Medaglie d'Oro.

Getting Around

Traffic is limited in the city centre and major car parks are at Piazza XX Settembre and Via Antonio Gramsci. Bus No 25 will take you from the train station to the historical centre.

RAVENNA

Halfway between East and West, Ravenna has an ancient and legendary history but is now best known for its exquisite mosaics, relics of its period as an important Byzantine city. The town is easily accessible from Bologna and is worth a day trip at the very least.

The APT tourist office (☎ 0544-3 54 04), is at Via Salara 8 and is open daily from 8 am to 1 pm and 3 to 6 pm. Ask for directions from Piazza del Popolo, the centre of town. Ravenna's telephone code is 0544.

Orientation

The train station is in Piazza Farini; Viale Farini, directly in front of the station, becomes Via Diaz and leads to Piazza del Popolo in the centre of town.

Things to See & Do

The main mosaics are in the **Basilica of**
Sant'Apollinare Nuovo, the **Basilica of San Vitale**, the **Mausoleum of Galla Placidia**, which contains the oldest mosaics, and the **Neonian Baptistry**, also known as the Orthodox Baptistry. These are all in the town centre and an admission ticket to the four, as well as to the National and the Archiepiscopal museums, costs L9000 – a bargain given that a ticket to only two monuments costs L5000. The Basilica of Sant'Apollinare Nuovo in Classe is five km from Ravenna and accessible by bus from the station.

Ravenna hosts a music festival from late June to early August, featuring international artists performing in the city's historical churches and at the open-air Rocca di Brancaleone. In winter, opera and dance are staged at the Teatro Alighieri, and an annual theatre and literature festival is held in September in honour of Dante, who spent his last 10 years in the city and is buried there.

Cycling is a popular way to get around the sights. Ask at the tourist office for information on bike rental.

Places to Stay & Eat

The IYHF *Ostello Dante* (☎ 42 04 05) is at Via Aurelio Nicolodi 12. Take bus No 1 from Viale Pallavacini, to the left of the station. Bed and breakfast is L16,000 a night. Family rooms are L18,000 per bed. To the right as you leave the station and across the road on Viale P Maroncelli, is the *Hotel Ravenna* (☎ 21 22 04), with three-star quality for one-star prices. Singles/doubles are L30,000/45,000 or L35,000/55,000 with private shower. *Al Giaciglio* (☎ 3 94 03), Via R Brancaleone 42, has singles/doubles for L25,000/37,000 or L29,000/44,000 with private bath, and triples for L53,000. To find it go straight ahead from the station along Viale Farini and turn right into Via Brancaleone from Piazza Mameli. The *Italia* (☎ 3 56 10), to the left of the station at Viale Pallavacini 4, has singles/doubles for L31,000/50,000.

Getting There & Away

Ravenna is accessible by train from Bologna,

with a change at Castel Bolognese. The trip takes about 1½ hours.

Getting Around

The city has many public car parks and signs give directions from the major entry points to the centre of the city.

FERRARA

A visit to Ferrara is like walking into a fairy tale. The city was the seat of the Este dukes from the 13th century to the end of the 16th century, and its streets are lined with graceful palaces. In its centre is the Castello Estense, surrounded by a moat.

The APT tourist office, open from 9 am to 12.30 pm and from 3 to 7 pm, is in the Piazzetta Municipale. It's a 10-minute walk from the station along Via Cavour, or take bus No 1, 2 or 9 to the castle. The local telephone code is 0532.

Things to See

The historical centre is small, encompassing the medieval Ferrara to the south of the **Castello Estense** and the area to the north, built under Duke Ercole I during the Renaissance. The castello now houses government offices, but certain areas are open to the public. Visit the **medieval prisons**, where in 1425 Duke Nicolò d'Este had his young second wife, Parisina Malatesta, and his son Ugo beheaded after discovering they were lovers, thereby inspiring the poet Robert Browning to write *My Last Duchess*.

The **Corso Ercole I d'Este**, lined with Renaissance palaces, runs off to the north. Worth a look is the **Palazzo del Diamanti**, its façade made up of thousands of diamond-shaped blocks of marble. It houses the national gallery (open from 9 am to 2 pm, entry L8000). The beautiful Romanesque-Gothic **Duomo** has an unusual pink-and-white marble triple façade and houses some important works of art in its museum. The 14th century **Palazzo Schifanoia**, at Via Scandiana 23, another Este palace, houses the Civic Museum and features lively frescoes. It is open daily from 9 am to 7 pm; entry is L6000.

Places to Stay & Eat

Ferrara is a cheap alternative to Bologna, and it can even be used as a base for Padua and Venice. The same woman runs the shabby *Garibaldi*, Via Garibaldi 77 (off Piazza Municipale), and the cleaner *Tre Stelle* (☎ 20 97 48) around the corner at Via Vegri 15. Doubles are L28,000 at both. At the *Alfonsa* (☎ 20 57 26), Via Padiglioni 5 (off Corso Ercole I d'Este), rooms are L26,000/40,000.

For a hearty and delicious meal try *Il Cucco*, Via Voltacasotto 3 (off Via Carlo Mayr). Pasta, wine and the cover charge cost under L10,000 and a full meal costs around L17,000.

Getting There & Away

Ferrara is on the Bologna-Venice train line, with regular trains to both cities. It is 40 minutes from Bologna and 1½ hours from Venice. Regular trains also run directly to Ravenna. Buses run from the train station to Modena (also in Emilia-Romagna).

RIVIERA DI LEVANTE

This area, stretching from Genoa, in the region of Liguria, to La Spezia, on the border with Tuscany, has a spectacular coastline to rival that of Amalfi. It also has several resorts which, despite attracting thousands of summer tourists, manage to remain unspoiled. The region's climate means that both spring and autumn can bring suitable beach weather.

The telephone code is 0185.

Things to See & Do

Santa Margherita Ligure, a pretty resort town noted for its orange blossoms, is a good base from which to visit the area.

From Santa Margherita, the resorts of **Portofino**, a haunt of the rich and famous, and **Camogli**, a fishing village turned major resort town, which still manages to look like a fishing village, are a short bus ride away. Easily accessible by train are the beautiful **Cinque Terre**, literally, Five Lands. These five coastal towns (Monterosso, Vernazza, Corniglia, Manarola and Riomaggiore) are linked by walking tracks along the coast.

Make a point of walking from Monterosso to Riomaggiore (about five hours). Although the track between Manarola and Corniglia has been closed because of landslides, no-one seems to pay any attention and the barricades have been broken down.

There are tourist offices in most of the towns, including at Santa Margherita, Via XXV Aprile, between the station and the sea; at Portofino, Via Roma 35; and at Camogli, Via XX Settembre, just as you leave the station. All of these will advise on accommodation.

Places to Stay & Eat

There are several excellent options in Santa Margherita. The *Albergo Nuovo Riviera* (☎ 28 74 03), in an old villa at Via Belvedere 10, has singles/doubles for L30,000/45,000 or doubles with private shower for L55,000. It also offers half and full board, which is compulsory in the high season. Full board is L65,000 per person, or L75,000 with a private bathroom. The friendly owners impose a strict no-smoking rule in the hotel. The *Albergo Fasce* (☎ 28 64 35), Via L Bozzo 3, has English-speaking owners and you can live there in relative luxury for L50,000 a double or L70,000 with private bathroom (this includes breakfast).

Trattoria San Siso, Corso Matteotti 137 (about 10 minutes from the seafront), has great food at low prices, with a full meal costing around L15,000. Try the *panzotti* (only on Sundays), which are small ravioli in a walnut sauce.

In Camogli try the *Albergo la Camogliese* (☎ 77 14 02), Via Garibaldi 55, on the seafront. Some rooms have balconies and views and prices are graded accordingly. The cheapest singles/doubles cost L35,000/55,000. Full board in the high season is L58,000.

Getting There & Away

The entire coast is served by train and all points are accessible from Genoa. From Santa Margherita, Camogli and the Cinque Terre are both accessible by train. Buses leave from Genoa's Piazza Martiri della

Libertà for Portofino. Boats leave from near the bus stop for Camogli (L16,000 return) and the Cinque Terre (L25,000 return).

GENOA

Travellers who think of Genoa (Genova) as simply a dirty port town and by-pass the city for the coastal resorts don't know what they're missing. This once powerful maritime republic, birthplace of Christopher Columbus (1451-1506) and now capital of the region of Liguria, can still carry the title *La Superba* (the proud). It is a fascinating city that is full of contrasts. Here you can meet crusty old seafarers in the markets and trattorias of the port area, where some of the tiny streets are so narrow it is difficult for two people to stand together. But, go round a corner and you will find young Genoese in the latest Benetton gear strolling through streets lined with grand, black-and-white marble palaces.

Orientation & Information

Most trains stop at both of the main stations in Genoa: Stazione Principe and Stazione Brignole. The area around Brignole is closer to the city centre and offers more pleasant accommodation than does Principe, which is close to the port.

From Brignole walk straight ahead along Via Fiume to get to Via XX Settembre and the *centro storico* (historic centre). It is easier to walk around Genoa than to use the local ATM bus service, but most useful buses stop outside both stations. A one-day tourist ticket for both train and bus costs L4000.

Tourist Offices The best and most helpful tourist office is the EPT at Stazione Brignole, where you can pick up a map and a list of hotels. Others are the AAST office at Via Porta degli Archi 10, and the EPT offices at Via Roma 11 and Stazione Principe.

Post & Telecommunications The main post office is at Via Dante, just off Piazza de' Ferrari. However, it was under renovation in 1992 and a branch office was set up at Via d'Annuncia 34, off Piazza Dante. There is an

SIP office at the post office (Via Dante), and there are numerous booths at Stazione Brignole. Genoa's postcode is 16100 and its telephone code is 010.

Emergency You can call the police on ☎ 113. For an ambulance call ☎ 59 59 51, and for medical attention call the Ospedale San Martino (☎ 3 53 51), Via Benedetto XV. For information about all-night pharmacies call ☎ 192.

Things to See & Do
Start by wandering around the port area, the oldest part of Genoa, to see the huge, 12th century black-and-white marble **Cathedral of San Lorenzo** and the nearby **Palazzo Ducale**, in Piazza Matteotti. In the beautiful, tiny **Piazza San Matteo** are the palaces of the Doria family, one of the most important families of the city in the 14th and 15th centuries. Take a walk along **Via Garibaldi**, which is lined with palaces. Some are open to the public and contain art galleries, including the 16th century **Palazzo Bianco** and the 17th century **Palazzo Rosso**, where the Flemish painter Van Dyck lived. Both are open from 9 am to 7 pm Monday to Saturday and on Sundays from 9 am to 1 pm. Entry is L4000.

Theatre is performed by the acclaimed Genoa Theatre Company throughout the year at three theatres: the *Genovese*, *Duse* and *della Corte*. The company's main season is from January to May. Concerts and opera are performed at the *Politeama Margherita* theatre. For information contact the EPT, or buy the city's daily newspaper *Il Secolo XIX*.

Places to Stay
A new IYHF hostel, *Hostel Genova*, opened in 1992 in Via Costanzi in Righi, just outside of Genoa. Bed and breakfast costs L18,000 and a meal is L12,000. Catch bus No 40 from Stazione Brignole. The *Casa della Giovane* (☎ 20 66 32), Piazza Santa Sabina 4, has beds for women only at L10,000 a night. Turn right as you leave Stazione Brignole and walk up to Piazza Brignole. To your right, at Via Gropallo 4, is a beautiful old

building with several budget pensioni. The best is *Pensione Mirella* (☎ 89 37 22) with singles/doubles for L30,000/45,000. A shower is L2000 extra. The *Valle* (☎ 88 22 57) has singles/doubles for L30,000/35,000. The *Carola* (☎ 89 13 40) is more expensive with rooms at L30,000/46,000. Next door at No 8 is *Albergo Rita* (☎ 87 02 07), with rooms for L22,000/35,000.

Near the port is the *Albergo Riviera Ligure* (☎ 20 19 96), Via Colalanza 2 off Via Santa Luca near Piazza Caricamento, with singles/ doubles for L15,000/30,000. Single women are advised to avoid this area at night.

Places to Eat
Don't leave town without trying *pesto genovese*, pasta with a sauce of basil, garlic and pine nuts, *torta pasqualina*, made with artichokes and eggs, *pansoti* (ravioli), *farinata*, a torte made with chickpea flour and, of course, focaccia. The best deal in town is at *Da Maria*, Vico Testa d'Oro 14, where a full meal is a set L11,000, including wine. Students and old seafarers dine here. *Ristorante San Siro* at Via Cairoli 22 specialises in seafood and offers a set-price lunch for L11,000. The best farinata and pansoti are at *Raggio Alfredo*, Via Galata 35, which specialises in local fare and has a takeaway service. A meal will cost around L20,000.

Getting There & Away
Air Genoa's airport, Christopher Columbus International, is a terminal for domestic and European flights. It is accessible by bus (L4000) from the air terminal in Piazza della Vittoria, just south of Stazione Brignole. Phone ☎ 2411 for information.

Train Genoa is directly connected by train to Turin, Milan, Pisa and Rome, making it reasonably accessible to all other major Italian cities. For train information call ☎ 28 40 81.

Boat The city's busy port is a major embarkation point for ferries to Sicily, Sardinia, Corsica and Tunis. Major companies are: Corsica Ferries (for Corsica and Sardinia), Piazza Dante 5 (☎ 59 33 01); Tirrenia (for

Sicily and Sardinia), Ponte Colombo (☎ 25 80 41); and Grandi Traghetti (for Sardinia), Via Fieschi 17 (☎ 58 93 31). For more information, see the Getting There & Away sections under Sicily and Sardinia, and under Calvi (Corsica) in the France chapter.

The Alps

The Alps sweep across northern Italy from Liguria to the Slovenian border, along the frontiers of France, Switzerland and Austria and through the regions of Valle d'Aosta, Piedmont, Lombardy, Trentino-Alto Adige (which incorporates the Dolomites) and the Veneto.

Information

There are innumerable excellent ski resorts, ranging from the expensive and fashionable Cortina d'Ampezzo to smaller, less pretentious places which still offer excellent skiing and facilities.

The high season is generally from Christmas to early January and from early February to April, when prices go up considerably, but actual dates vary throughout the Alps. A good way to save money is to buy a *settimana bianca* (literally, white week – a package-deal ski holiday) package through CIT, CTS or other travel agencies throughout Italy. This covers accommodation, food and ski passes for seven days.

If you want to go it alone, but plan to do a lot of skiing, invest in a ski pass. Most resort areas offer their own passes for unlimited use of lifts at several resorts for a nominated period. The cost in the 1992-93 high season for a seven-day pass is L195,000. However, the best value is the Superski Dolomiti pass, which allows access to 450 lifts and more than 1100 km of ski runs. In the 1992-93 high season a superski pass for seven days cost L234,000. Ring Superski Dolomiti (☎ 0471-79 53 98) for information. The average cost of ski hire in the Alps is L9000 to L15,000 a day for downhill skis and L7000 to L11,000 for cross country. In an expensive resort like

Cortina, however, the price jumps to L18,000 to L22,000 a day for downhill skis.

Hiking is popular throughout the Alps in summer, particularly in the Dolomites and in the Stelvio National Park (Parco Nazionale dello Stelvio) in Trentino-Alto Adige. You can obtain information about trails and Alpine refuges from CAI offices throughout Italy, but also directly from the tourist offices listed in this section. Another useful organisation is the Associazione Sentiero Italia, with offices in Florence (☎ 055-57 44 57), at Piazza San Gervasio 14, and Turin (☎ 011-33 12 00), at Corso Rosselli 132.

The best idea is to buy a map of the hiking trails, which also shows the locations of Alpine refuges. Recommended maps are published by Tabacco, Kompass and the Istituto Geografico Militare and can be bought in newsagents and bookshops in the area where you plan to hike. They are also often available in major bookshops in larger cities. A useful book is *Grandi Sentieri d'Italia* by Stefano Ardito, published by the Istituto Geografico de Agostini. Although available only in Italian, it is easy to follow and provides details about hiking trails, refuges and the time required for each trek. Also by the same author is *Backpacking & Walking in Italy* (Bradt Publications, 1987), which is in English.

Hiking trails, particularly in more popular areas such as the Dolomites, are generally very well marked.

Remember that even in summer the weather is extremely changeable in the Alps, and, though it might be sweltering when you set off, you should be prepared for very cold and wet weather on even the shortest of walks. Also remember that you might cross borders when skiing or hiking in the Alps, so always carry your passport.

Getting There & Away

You can usually reach resorts by bus and often by train from the nearest large town. Major access points include Turin, Milan, Bologna, Trento and Bolzano; bus services are increased during the winter months.

Sadem Autolinea runs bus services from

Rome, Turin and Milan to most of the resorts listed here. It has offices in Turin (☎ 011-561 30 19) at Corso Siccardi 6, and in Milan (☎ 02-80 11 61) at Piazza Castello 1.

Several bus companies run services from Bologna to Cortina, San Martino di Castrozza, Canazei, Madonna di Campiglio, Courmayeur and various other locations in the Alps. Buses leave from Bologna's Autostazione (main bus station; ☎ 051-24 21 50) in Piazza XX Settembre, where you can also pick up a full timetable.

Getting Around

If you are planning to hike in the Alps during the warmer months, you will find that hitch-hiking is no problem, especially near the resort towns. Tourist offices will also be able to provide information on local bus services. The areas around the major resorts are well serviced by local buses. During winter, most resorts have 'ski bus' shuttle services from the towns to the main ski facilities.

VENETO & TRENTINO-ALTO ADIGE

Trentino-Alto Adige is the Italians' favoured area for skiing, and there is excellent hiking both in the Dolomites near the Veneto and the Stelvio National Park near Lombardy. Information on all ski resorts can be obtained at the APT (Azienda per la Promozione Turistica del Trentino) in Trento (☎ 0461-98 00 00) at Via Sighele 3/5; in Rome (☎ 06-679 42 16) at Via Poli 47; or Milan (☎ 02-87 43 87) at Piazza Diaz 5. For hiking information, contact the APT del Trentino in Trento or the APT of Bolzano (☎ 0471-97 56 56), Piazza Walther-Platz 8. The APT delle Dolomiti Bellunesii (☎ 0473-94 00 83) can provide information on trekking along the Sentiero della Pace (Path of Peace), which traces the Italian/German frontline of WW I.

Cortina d'Ampezzo

The most famous, fashionable and expensive Italian ski resort, Cortina is also one of its best equipped and certainly the most pictur-esque. If you are on a tight budget, the prices for accommodation and food will be prohibitive, even in the low season. However,

camping grounds and Alpine refuges (open only during summer) provide more reasonably priced alternatives.

Situated in the Ampezzo bowl, Cortina is surrounded by the stunning Dolomites, including the Cristallo and Marmarole groups and the Tofane. Facilities for both downhill and cross-country skiing are first class. The area is also very popular for trekking and climbing, with well-marked trails and numerous refuges.

The main tourist information office (APT; ☎ 0436-3231) is at Piazzetta San Francesco 8, in the town centre. It has information on accommodation, ski passes and hiking trails. There is a small information office at Piazza Roma 1.

Things to See & Do The mountains surrounding Cortina are among the best in Italy for hiking and climbing. The scenery is spectacular and the trails are well marked. You can walk for a few hours or head off for a week-long trek. In summer, particularly in August, the trails are packed with Italian and German tourists, but at the beginning and the end of the season it is more peaceful and the weather is still reliable enough for walking.

The CAI will provide information on the best areas, but if you plan to trek for several days, it's worth investing in a good map of the walking trails (see the previous Information section).

By studying your map you can plan each day of walking so as to arrive at a refuge for the night. The tourist office has a brochure with phone numbers of refuges and information on the estimated time needed to complete each trail. Refuges close by the end of September and reopen the following summer, usually in June. Average prices are L15,000 to L20,000 per person per night. Meals at the refuges in this area can be expensive and it is acceptable to eat your own food. Some establishments, however, might require that you pay a cover charge to use a table.

Places to Stay There are not many options for cheap accommodation in Cortina. You could try the *Cavallino* (☎ 2614) or the *Ginestra* (☎ 86 02 55), which charges up to L40,000 per person, including breakfast, in the high season. Camping grounds are open only during the summer. The *Olympia* (☎ 5057) is about five km out of Cortina at Fiames and has a reasonably priced trattoria with the best pizzas north of Naples. A local bus will take you there from Cortina.

Canazei

Set in the Fassa Dolomites, the resort of Canazei has more than 100 km of trails and is linked to slopes in the Val Gardena and Val Bardia. It also offers cross-country skiing and summer skiing on the Marmolada glacier. (At 3342 metres, the Marmolada peak is the highest in the Dolomites.) The *Marmolada* camping ground (☎ 0462-6 16 60) is open all year, or you have a choice of hotels, furnished rooms and apartments. Contact the APT of the Valle di Fassa (☎ 0462-6 24 66), Via Costa, Canazei/Alba for full details. The resort is accessible by bus from Trento and Bolzano and by road from Bolzano.

Madonna di Campiglio

One of the five major ski resorts in Italy and situated in the Brenta Dolomites, Madonna di Campiglio is one of the more beautiful and well-equipped places to ski, but also one of the more expensive. You can also go cross-country skiing there. The resort is accessible by bus or car from Trento. More information is available from the APT office (☎ 0465-4 20 00).

San Martino di Castrozza

Located in a sheltered position beneath the Pale di San Martino, this resort is popular among Italians and offers good facilities and ski runs, as well as cross-country skiing and a toboggan run. Its camping ground, *Sass Maor* (☎ 0439-6 83 47), is open all year.

The APT office (☎ 0439-8101), Via Passo Rolle, will provide a full list of accommodation. Buses travel regularly from Trento and, during the high season, from Milan, Venice, Padua and Bologna. If you are going by car,

exit from the Milan-Venice motorway at Vicenza, or from the Brennero at Ora.

VALLE D'AOSTA
Courmayeur

The resort of Courmayeur, at the base of Mont Blanc (Monte Bianco in Italian), is one of the big five in Italy and one of the more glamorous. Consequently, it is also more expensive. However, its dramatic setting and excellent skiing facilities make it hard to beat. It is possible to ski, with a guide, over Mont Blanc to Chamonix in France. For information call AAST (☎ 0165-84 20 60). The resort is accessible by bus from Turin and on the A5 autostrada from Turin and Milan.

Central Italy

The landscape in central Italy is a patchwork of textures bathed in a beautiful soft light – golden pink in Tuscany, and a greenish gold in Umbria and the Marches. The people remain close to the land, but in each of the regions there is also a strong artistic and cultural tradition – even the smallest medieval hilltown can harbour extraordinary works of art.

FLORENCE

Cradle of the Renaissance, home of Dante, Machiavelli, Michelangelo and the Medici, Florence (Firenze) is overwhelming in its wealth of art, culture and history, and one of the most enticing cities to visit in Italy.

Although its origins are hazy, Florence grew as the major Roman city of Florentia from about 59 BC. In the Middle Ages the city developed a flourishing economy based on banking and commerce, which sparked a period of building and growth previously unequalled in Italy. It was a major focal point for the Guelph and Ghibelline struggle of the 13th century, which saw Dante banished from the city. But Florence truly flourished in the 15th century under the Medici, reaching the height of its cultural, artistic and

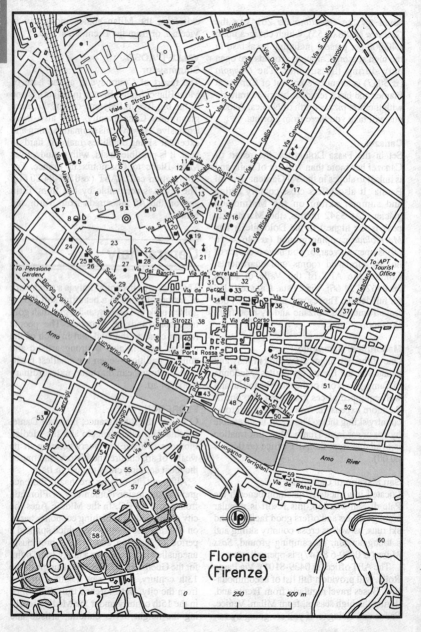

Florence
(Firenze)

0   250   500 m

- **PLACES TO STAY**

7	La Romagnola & La Gigliola
10	Pensione Bellavista, Albergo Ester & Pensione Le Cascine
11	Daniel & Soggiorno Nazionale
12	Pensione Kursaal & Pensione Ausonia & Rimini
20	Pensione Accademia
22	Polo Nord
24	Pensione Montreal
25	Pensione Margaret
26	La Scala
28	La Mia Casa
29	Pensione Ottaviani & Pensione Visconti
30	Pensione Toscana & Pensione Sole
34	Locanda Colore
39	Pensione Maria Luisa de' Medici
42	Soggiorno Davanzati
43	Aily Home
53	Ostello Santa Monica

▼ **PLACES TO EAT**

14	Mario's
15	Café Za Za
35	Osteria Il Caminetto
36	Trattoria Le Mossacce
49	Angie's Pub
50	Trattoria da Benvenuto
54	Trattoria Casalinga
56	La Mangiatora
59	I Tarocchi

OTHER

1	La Fortezza (Parking)
2	Police Headquarters
3	Piazza della Indipendenza
4	Chiesa di San Marco
5	ASST Telephones
6	Central Railway Station
8	SITA Bus Terminal
9	Hotel Information for Tourists
13	Piazza del Mercato Centrale (Parking)
16	Palazzo Riccardi
17	Accademia Gallery
18	Teatro della Pergola
19	Medici Chapels
21	Chiesa di San Lorenzo
23	Chiesa di Santa Maria Novella
27	Piazza Santa Maria Novella
31	Baptistry
32	Duomo
33	Campanile
37	Paperback Exchange Bookshop
38	Piazza della Repubblica
40	Post Office & ASST Telephones
41	Ponte alla Carraia
44	Piazza della Signoria
45	Bargello Palace & National Museum
46	Palazzo Vecchio
47	Ponte Vecchio
48	Uffizi Gallery
51	Piazza Santa Croce
52	Chiesa di Santa Croce
55	Piazza dei Pitti
57	Palazzo Pitti
58	Boboli Gardens
60	Piazzale Michelangelo

political development as it gave birth to the Renaissance.

The Grand Duchy of the Medici was succeeded in the 18th century by the House of Lorraine (related to the Austrian Habsburgs). As a result of the Risorgimento, the Kingdom of Italy was formally proclaimed in March 1861, and Florence was the capital of the new kingdom from 1865 to 1871. During WW II, parts of the city, including all of the bridges except the Ponte Vecchio, were destroyed by bombing, and in 1966 a devastating flood destroyed or severely damaged many important works of art. A worldwide effort helped Florence in its massive restoration works.

Orientation

Whether you arrive by train, bus or car, the central railway station, Santa Maria Novella, is a good reference point. Budget hotels and pensioni are concentrated around Via Nazionale, to the east of the station, and Piazza Santa Maria Novella, to the south. The main thoroughfare to the centre is Via de' Panzani, about a 15-minute walk. You will know that you've arrived when you first glimpse the Duomo.

Once at Piazza del Duomo, you will find Florence easy to negotiate, with most of the major sights within easy walking distance. Think carefully though about how you spend your time. Most important museums close by 2 pm (with the exception of the Uffizi Museum) and virtually all are closed on Mondays. You will need to start your day early, but be careful not to overload your itinerary. Florence is virtually a living art museum and you won't waste your time by just wandering the streets. Take the city ATAF buses for longer distances such as to Piazzale Michelangelo and the nearby suburb of Fiesole which offer panoramic views of the city (see the Getting Around section that follows).

Information

Tourist Offices There is an office at the station where you can pick up a map and hotel guide and sometimes book a hotel room. It is open from 9 am to 9 pm daily. More complete information on the city is available at the main APT office (☎ 055-234 62 84), which is out of the way at Via Manzoni 16, and is open weekdays from 8 am to 1.30 pm and 4 to 6.30 pm, and Saturdays 8.30 am to 1.30 pm.

Also at the station is the Informazioni Turistiche Alberghieri (Hotel Information for Tourists). They will charge a commission to book a hotel room, so use the service only if you're desperate. Bookings can be made only in person. The tourist information office of the Comune di Firenze (Florence City Council) is in Chiasso dei Baroncelli, a tiny street off Piazza della Signoria, open from 8 am to 7.30 pm daily except Sunday. A good map of the city, on sale at newsstands, is the one with the white, red and black cover *(Firenze: Pianta della Città)*, which costs L8000.

Post & Telecommunications The main post office is in Via Pellicceria, off Piazza della Repubblica, open weekdays from 8.15 am to 7 pm and Saturdays to midday. The ASST telephone office is in the same building and is open 24 hours a day. Another ASST office is at the station and is open Monday to Saturday from 8 am to 9.45 pm. The postcode for Florence is 50100 and the telephone code is 055.

Money To change money it is always best to use a bank. Most of the main ones are concentrated around Piazza della Repubblica. You can use the service at the information office in the station but it has bad rates.

Foreign Consulates There is a US Consulate (☎ 239 82 76) at Lungarno Vespucci 38, and a UK Consulate (☎ 28 41 33) at Lungarno Corsini 2.

Bookshops The Paperback Exchange, Via Fiesolana 31r, has a vast selection of new and second-hand books including classics, contemporary literature, reference books and best sellers, as well as travel guides (closed Sunday). Internazionale Seeber, Via de' Tornabuoni 70r, also has a good selection of English and American classics and contemporary literature, as well as a reasonable range of books by Australian authors.

Emergency The questura (☎ 4 97 71) is at Via Zara 2. It has an office for foreigners, where you can report thefts etc. Lost property (☎ 36 79 43) can be collected, if you're lucky, from Via Circondaria 19 (south-west of the centre). Towed-away cars can also be collected here (if you park illegally in Florence, your car *will* be towed away and you risk a large fine, if not getting arrested).

The Tourist Medical Service (☎ 47 54 11), Via Lorenzo il Magnifico 59, is open 24 hours a day and the doctors speak English. All-night pharmacies include the Farmacia Comunale (☎ 21 67 61) inside the station, and Molteni (☎ 21 54 72), in the centre at Via Calzaiuoli 7r. There is also a special volunteer interpreter service (☎ 40 31 26) for foreigners needing hospital treatment.

Laundry One of the cheapest laundrettes is at Via Pietrapiana 34, east of the Duomo, at L3000 a kg.

Things to See & Do

Duomo This beautiful cathedral, with its dome and its pink, white and green marble façade, dominates the skyline of Florence. At first sight, no matter how many times you have visited the city, the Duomo will take your breath away. Called the Cathedral of Santa Maria del Fiore, it was started in 1296 by the Sienese architect Arnolfo di Cambio and took almost two centuries to complete.

The Renaissance architect Brunelleschi won a public competition to design the enormous dome, the first to have been built since antiquity. Although now severely cracked and under restoration, it remains a remarkable achievement of design. The dome was decorated with frescoes by Vasari and Zuccari and stained-glass windows by Donatello, Andrea del Castagno, Paolo Uccello and Ghiberti. The Duomo's marble façade was built in the 19th century to replace the original, uncompleted façade, which was destroyed in the 16th century. Climb to the top of the dome for a magnificent view of Florence (open from 10 am to 5.30 pm, entry L4000).

Giotto designed and began building the **campanile** next to the cathedral, but died before it was completed. This unusual structure is 82 metres high and you can climb its stairs for L4000 (open from 9 am to 7.30 pm).

The Romanesque-style **baptistry**, which is believed to have been built between the 5th and 6th centuries, is famous for its gilded bronze doors, particularly the east doors, facing the cathedral. Designed by Lorenzo Ghiberti, these are known as the **Gates to Paradise**. The south door, by Andrea Pisano, is the oldest. The north door is also by Ghiberti, who won a public competition in 1401 to design it, but the Gates to Paradise remain his consummate masterpiece. Dante was baptised here. The baptistry is open from 1 to 6 pm, free entry.

Uffizi Gallery The Palazzo degli Uffizi, built by Vasari in the 16th century, houses the most important art collection in Italy. The vast collection of paintings dating from the 13th to the 18th centuries represents the great legacy of the Medici family.

You will need more than one visit to appreciate fully the extraordinary number of important works in the Uffizi, which include paintings by Giotto and Cimabue from the 14th century; 15th century masterpieces including Botticelli's *Birth of Venus* and *Allegory of Spring*; and works by Filippo Lippi, Fra Angelico and Paolo Uccello. *The Annunciation* by Leonardo da Vinci is also here. Along the second corridor are 16th century works by Raphael, Michelangelo's *Holy Family* and famous works by Titian, Andrea del Sarto, Tintoretto, Rembrandt, Caravaggio, Tiepolo, Rubens, Van Dyck and Goya. It is open weekdays from 9 am to 7 pm and weekends from 9 am to 1 pm, closed Mondays. Admission is L10,000 (but it's worth it!).

Piazza della Signoria & Palazzo Vecchio Built by Arnolfo di Cambio between 1299 and 1314, the Palazzo Vecchio was, and remains, the seat of the Florentine government. In the 16th century it became the ducal palace of the Medici, before they moved to the Pitti Palace. Visit the beautiful Michelozzi courtyard just inside the entrance and the lavishly decorated apartments upstairs. It is open weekdays from 9 am to 7 pm and Sundays to 1 pm, closed Saturday. Admission is L8000 but is free on Sundays. The palace's turrets, battlements and 94-metre-high bell tower form an imposing and memorable backdrop to Piazza della Signoria, scene of many important political events in the history of Florence, including the execution of the religious and political reformer Savonarola. A bronze plaque marks the spot where he was burned at the stake in 1498. The **Loggia dei Lanzi**, at a right angle to the Palazzo Vecchio, contains important sculptures, including Cellini's *Perseus*.

Ponte Vecchio This famous 14th century bridge, lined with the shops of gold and silversmiths, was the only one to survive Nazi bombing in WW II. Originally, the shops housed butchers. A corridor along the first floor was built by the Medici to link the Pitti Palace and the Uffizi Museum.

Pitti Palace The immense and imposing Palazzo Pitti, housing several museums, was originally designed by Brunelleschi. The **Palatine Gallery** has 16th and 17th century works by Raphael, Filippo Lippi, Tintoretto, Veronese and Rubens, hung in lavishly decorated rooms. The **royal apartments** of the Medici, and later of the Savoy, show the splendour in which these rulers lived. (The apartments were closed for restoration in 1992.) Also worth a look is the **Silver Museum** (Museo degli Argenti). All of the galleries are open weekdays from 9 am to 2 pm and weekends from 9 am to 1 pm, closed Mondays. Admission to the Palatine Gallery is L8000, and admission to the other museums is L6000. After the Pitti Palace visit the beautiful Renaissance **Boboli Gardens** (Giardino di Boboli) and enjoy the view of Florence.

Bargello Palace & National Museum A medieval palace, also known as the Palazzo del Podestà, the Bargello was the seat of the local ruler and, later, of the chief of police. People were tortured at the site of the well in the centre of the courtyard.

The palace now houses Florence's rich collection of sculpture, notably works by Michelangelo, many by Benvenuto Cellini, and Donatello's stunning bronze *David*, the first sculpture since antiquity to depict a fully naked man (open weekdays from 9 am to 2 pm, weekends to 1 pm, closed Mondays; admission is L6000).

Accademia Michelangelo's impressive *David* is in this gallery (the one in Piazza della Signoria is a good copy), as are four of his unfinished *slaves* (or *prisoners*). The gallery upstairs houses many important works of the Florentine primitives. The gallery, at Via Ricasoli 60, is open weekdays from 9 am to 2 pm, weekends to 1 pm, closed Mondays. Entry is L10,000.

Medici Chapels & Church of San Lorenzo The church of San Lorenzo (in the piazza of the same name), rebuilt by Brunelleschi in the early 15th century for the Medici, contains his Old Sacristy, which was decorated by Donatello. It's also worth visiting the

Biblioteca Laurenziana, a huge library designed by Michelangelo to house the Medici collection of some 10,000 manuscripts.

Around the corner, in Piazza Madonna degli Aldobrandini, are the **Medici Chapels**. The **Prince's Chapel**, sumptuously decorated with precious marble and semiprecious stones, was the principal burial place of the Medici grand dukes. The graceful and simple **New Sacristy** was designed by Michelangelo, but he left Florence for Rome before its completion. It contains his beautiful sculptures *Night & Day, Dawn & Dusk* and the *Madonna with Child*, which adorn the Medici tombs. It is open weekdays from 9 am to 2 pm, weekends to 1 pm, closed Mondays. Admission is L8500.

Other Attractions The Dominican church of **Santa Maria Novella** was built during the 13th and 14th centuries, and its white-and-green marble façade was designed by Alberti in the 15th century. The church is decorated with frescoes by Ghirlandaio (who was assisted by a very young Michelangelo) and Masaccio. The **Strozzi Chapel** contains frescoes by Filippo Lippi, and the beautiful **cloisters** feature frescoes by Uccello and his students.

The **Convento di San Marco** (Monastery of St Mark) is a museum of the work of Fra Angelico, who covered its walls and many of the monks' cells with frescoes, and lived here from 1438 to 1455. Also worth seeing are the peaceful cloisters and the cell of the monk Savonarola. It also contains works by Fra Bartolomeo and Ghirlandaio. The monastery is open Tuesday to Friday from 9 am to 2 pm, weekends to 1 pm, closed Monday. Admission is L6000.

Courses Florence has more than 30 schools offering courses in Italian language and culture. Numerous other schools offer courses in art, including painting, drawing and sculpture, as well as art history. While Florence would appear to be the most attractive city in which to study Italian language or art, it is one of the more expensive.

Perugia, Siena and Urbino offer good-quality courses at much lower prices. The cost of language courses in Florence ranges from about L450,000 to L900,000, depending on the school and the length of the course (one month is usually the minimum duration).

Art courses range from one-month summer workshops (costing from L500,000 to more than L1,000,000) to longer term professional diploma courses. These can be expensive, some of them costing more than L6,500,000 a year. Schools will organise accommodation for students, upon request, either in private apartments or with Italian families.

Brochures detailing courses and prices are available at Italian cultural institutes throughout the world. A brief list of schools is included here. You can write in English to request information and enrolment forms – letters should be addressed to the *segretaria*.

Listed here are the addresses of some of the language courses available in Florence:

Dante Alighieri Society Committee of Florence
  Via Gino Capponi 4, 50121 Florence
  (☎ 247 89 81)
Centro Lorenzo de' Medici
  Via Faenza 43, 50122 Florence (☎ 28 31 42)
Centro di Cultura per Stranieri dell'Università di Firenze
  Via V Emanuele 64, 50134 Florence (☎ 47 21 39)

There are also various art courses on offer, including the following:

The Art Institute of Florence
  Via Faenza 43, 50122 Florence (☎ 28 31 42)
Istituto per l'Arte e il Restauro
  Palazzo Spinelli, Borgo Santa Croce 10, 50122 Florence (☎ 24 48 08)

Places to Stay

There are more than 150 budget hotels in Florence, so even in peak season, when the city is packed with tourists, you should be able to find a room. However, it is always advisable to make a booking, and you should arrive by late morning to claim your room.

Always ask for the full price of a room before putting your bags down. Hotels and pensioni in Florence are notorious for bill-padding, particularly in summer. Many require an extra L5000 for a compulsory breakfast and will charge L3000 and more for a shower. The liberalisation of hotel prices had a major impact in Florence, where prices at many establishments skyrocketed. You can complain to the EPT if a hotel overcharges, but don't expect a satisfactory outcome.

Camping The closest camping ground to the centre is *Italiani e Stranieri* (☎ 681 19 77), Viale Michelangelo 80. It is near Piazzale Michelangelo, where the locals take their nightly passeggiata to enjoy the panoramic view of the city. Take bus No 13 from the railway station. *Villa Camerata* (☎ 61 03 00), Viale Augusto Righi 2/4, is next to the IYHF hostel (see the next section), northeast of the centre (take bus 17B from the station, 30 minutes). There is another camping ground at Fiesole, *Campeggio Panoramico* (☎ 59 90 69) at Via Peramonda 1, which also has bungalows. Take bus No 7 to Fiesole from the station.

Hostels The IYHF *Ostello Villa Camerata* (☎ 60 14 51), Viale Augusto Righi 2/4, is widely considered to be the most beautiful in Europe. Take bus No 17B, which leaves from the left of the station (track No 5). The trip takes 30 minutes. Bed and breakfast is L18,000, dinner is L12,000 and there is also a bar. It is open to IYHF members only and reservations can be made by mail (essential in summer).

The private *Ostello Santa Monaca* (☎ 26 83 38), Via Santa Monaca 6, is a 15 to 20-minute walk from the station. Go through Piazza Santa Maria Novella, along Via de' Fossi, across the Ponte alla Carraia and directly ahead along Via de' Serragli. Via Santa Monaca is on the right. A bed costs L15,000, and sheets cost an extra L2000.

Hotels & Pensioni Hotels and pensioni are concentrated in three main areas: near the station, near Piazza Santa Maria Novella, and in the old city from the Duomo to the river. In Florence there is also a large number of private homes which offer rooms for rent, known as *affittacamere*. The APT publishes a full list. They are filled with students during the school year and are generally expensive for short-term stays. It should be noted that prices drop in the low season (September to May), often by L10,000 a room. The prices given here are for the high season.

Around the Station The *Pensione Bellavista* (☎ 28 45 28), Largo Alinari 15 (at the start of Via Nazionale), is small, but a knockout bargain if you manage to book one of the two double rooms with balconies and a view of the Duomo and Palazzo Vecchio. Singles/doubles cost L38,000/52,000, but they will hit you for L3500 to use the bath.

The *Albergo Ester* (☎ 21 27 41) is accessible by the same entrance and offers singles/doubles for L33,000/49,000. A shower costs L2000. Triples are L85,000 with private bath. Also in the same building is the *Pensione Le Cascine* (☎ 21 10 66), a two-star hotel with beautifully furnished rooms, some of which have balconies. Singles/doubles are L48,000/65,000, including use of the communal bathroom. A triple with bathroom is L115,000. There is a midnight curfew.

The cheapest rooms in Florence are at the *Daniel* (☎ 21 12 93), Via Nazionale 22. A double costs L30,000 and rooms for three and four are L15,000 per person, with an extra L1500 to use the shower. The hotel is comfortable, if dark, and one of the rooms has a panoramic view of the Duomo. The owner will not take bookings, so arrive very early. In the same building is *Soggiorno Nazionale* (☎ 238 22 03). Singles/doubles are L42,000/68,000 and triples are L94,500. There is no extra charge to use the communal bathroom.

Next door, at No 24, is the *Pensione Ausonia & Rimini* (☎ 49 65 47), run by a young couple who go out of their way to help travellers. Singles/doubles are L41,000/64,000 and a triple is L88,000. The price includes breakfast and use of the communal bathroom. The same couple also operates *Pensione Kursaal* downstairs.

There are also some options in Via Faenza. The *Pensione Accademia* (☎ 29 34 51), Via Faenza 7, is expensive, but the rooms are very attractive and the hotel incorporates an 18th century palace replete with magnificent stained-glass doors and carved wooden ceilings. Singles/doubles cost L46,000/74,500. A triple, including bathroom and breakfast, is L115,000. Breakfast is L9000 and compulsory in the high season. The *House for Tourists Aglietti* (☎ 28 78 24), on the 4th floor at Via C Cavour 29, has large, comfortable rooms for L31,000/44,000. A shower costs L3000.

Around Piazza Santa Maria Novella *La Mia Casa* (☎ 21 30 61), in the piazza at No 25, is a rambling place, filled with antiques and backpackers. The owner is friendly, helpful and speaks English. Singles/doubles are L29,000/43,000 and triples/quads are L58,000/73,000.

Via della Scala, which runs off the piazza, is lined with pensioni. *La Romagnola* (☎ 21 15 97) at No 40 has large, clean rooms and helpful management. Singles/doubles are L33,000/49,000, or L42,000/62,000 with bathroom. A triple room is a good deal at L65,000, or L81,000 with bathroom. The same family runs *La Gigliola* (☎ 21 15 97) upstairs. *Montreal* (☎ 238 23 31) at No 43 has singles/doubles for L30,000/44,000, or 35,000/52,000 with private shower. *La Scala* (☎ 21 26 29) at No 21 is small and has doubles at L50,000 or L62,500 with bathroom. Rooms for three and four people cost L30,000 per person. There is a midnight curfew. The *Pensione Margaret* (☎ 21 01 38) at No 25 is pleasantly furnished and has singles/doubles for L34,000/50,000 and a triple is L60,000. Use of the communal shower is L2500.

The *Pensione Toscana* (☎ 21 31 56), Via del Sole 8, is an eccentrically decorated place with singles/doubles for L45,000/62,000 and triples/quads for L90,000/110,000. All rooms have a bathroom. In the same building is the *Sole* (☎ 239 60 94), which charges

L33,000/48,000 for singles/doubles, plus L2000 to use the communal shower. A double with bathroom costs L60,000. Triples/quads cost L65,000/ 82,000, or L51,000/87,000 with bathroom. The curfew in summer is 1 am, and midnight in winter. The *Ottaviani* (☎ 239 62 23) at Piazza Ottaviani 1 near Via de' Fossi, has singles/doubles for L37,000/58,000, including breakfast. In the same building is the *Visconti* (☎ 21 38 77) with décor featuring royal blue walls and statues and a pleasant terrace garden where you can have breakfast. Singles/doubles are L33,000/49,000, and a triple is L62,000. Breakfast is optional.

Polo Nord (☎ 28 79 52), Via de' Panzani 7, inflates prices in the high season by charging L9500 for a basic continental breakfast, but from November to April it is not compulsory. Singles/doubles are L37,000/55,000 and use of the communal bathroom is free. Singles/doubles with bathroom are L45,000/ 65,000. At Piazza Vittorio Veneto 8, a five-minute walk west of the station, is the *Garden* (☎ 21 26 69) with singles/doubles for L33,000/49,000. Most rooms overlook a pleasant garden.

From the Duomo to the Arno This area is a 20-minute walk from the station and is right in the heart of old Florence. One of the most central hotels is the *Locanda Colore* (☎ 21 03 01), Via Calzaiuoli 13, right next to the Duomo. One of its double rooms has an evocative view of the church. The clean and basic singles/doubles cost L36,000/49,000. Keep a L100 coin handy for the lift. The *Soggiorno Davanzati* (☎ 28 34 14) at Via Porta Rossa 15 is run down, but the rooms are clean. Singles/doubles are L28,000/ 42,000 and doubles with bathroom are L53,000. Use of the communal shower costs L3000. In 1992 the owners planned to renovate the premises, so check whether it is open before you go there.

The *Maria Luisa de' Medici* (☎ 28 00 48), Via del Corso 1, is in a 17th century palace, and the historically important entrance staircase features a fresco believed to have been painted by Alessandro Gherardini. It has no singles, but with large rooms for up to five people, the management obviously caters for families. All prices include a compulsory L14,000 breakfast. A double is L78,000, a triple L109,500 and a quad L141,000. Prices drop in the low season. The accommodating management speak English.

Overlooking the Ponte Vecchio, at Piazza Santo Stefano 1, is *Aily Home* (☎ 239 65 05), offering rooms for rent (affittacamere) for L20,000 per person. It has only five large rooms, three of which overlook the bridge, and will accept phone bookings.

Fiesole In the hills overlooking Florence is *Bencistà* (☎ 5 91 63), Via Benedetto da Maiano 4, near Fiesole. It is an old villa and from its terrace there is a magnificent view of Florence. Half-pension is compulsory at L80,000 per person, or L100,000 with private bathroom. It might break the budget, but for one or two days it is well worth it.

Rental If you want an apartment in Florence, save your pennies and start looking well before you arrive. They are difficult to come by and can be very expensive. A one-room apartment with kitchenette in the centre will cost from L600,000 to L1,000,000 a month. Florence & Abroad (☎ 48 70 04), Via Zanobi 58, handles rental accommodation (ask for Sally Hood). Alternatively, you can try Florence Housefinding (☎ 247 66 20), which also organises rental accommodation (ask for Carol Webster). Another option is to check the notice board at the university (north-east of the Duomo, off Piazza San Marco) for people looking for someone to share a flat.

Places to Eat
Simplicity and quality appropriately describe the cucina of Tuscany. In a country where the various regional styles and traditions have provided a richly diverse cuisine, Tuscany stands apart for its fine cooking. The region's rich green olive oil, fresh fruit and vegetables, tender meat, and, of course, the classic wine Chianti are the basics of a good meal in Florence.

No meal should begin without bruschetta, a thick slice of toasted bread, rubbed with garlic and soaked with olive oil. Try the *acquacotta* (literally, cooked water), a vegetable soup served with a slice of bread and an egg, topped off with Parmesan, or the deliciously simple *fagiolini alla Fiorentina*, green beans and olive oil. Florence is renowned for its excellent *bistecca* (beefsteak) – thick, juicy and big enough for two people.

The market, open from 7 am to 2 pm Monday to Saturday, and 4 to 8 pm Saturday, offers fresh produce, cheeses and meat at reasonable prices.

Restaurants Eating at a good trattoria can be surprisingly economical, but many tourists fall into the trap of eating at the self-service restaurants which line the streets of the main shopping district between the Duomo and the Arno. Be adventurous and seek out the little eating places in the district of Oltrarno (the other side of the Arno from the centre) and near the Mercato Centrale in San Lorenzo.

In the Oltrarno Just past the Palazzo Pitti is *La Mangiatora*, Piazza San Felice 8-10r. The upstairs section is referred to as a tavola calda and the downstairs as a ristorante, but the prices are the same and downstairs is more pleasant. A primo piatto of pasta will cost L4000 to L5000, a secondo up to L6000 and a pizza from L5000 to L7000. A half-litre of Chianti is L2500 and the coperto is L1500.

Trattoria Casalinga, Via dei Michelozzi 9r, is a bustling place popular with the locals. The food is great and a filling meal of pasta, meat or contorni, and wine will cost you around L15,000. Don't expect to linger over a meal, as there is usually a queue of people waiting for your table.

I Tarocchi, Via de' Renai 12-14r, serves an excellent pizza, ranging from L5500 to L9000, as well as dishes typical of the region, including a good range of pasta from L5000 to L8000, and plenty of salads and vegetable dishes from L3500 to L7000. The coperto is only L1500. Expect to wait for a table at this restaurant.

City Centre *Trattoria da Benvenuto*, Via Mosca 16r, on the corner of Via dei Neri, is considered one of the best trattorias in Florence. Its menu changes regularly and the excellent food is typical of the region. A full meal will cost under L15,000 and a quick meal of pasta, bread and wine will cost around L8000. It is wise to reserve a table. *Osteria Il Caminetto*, Via dello Studio 34, just south of Piazza del Duomo, has a small vine-covered terrace. A pasta dish costs around L6000, and a secondo from L8000 to L10,000. The L2000 coperto, plus a 10% service charge, bumps up the price of a meal.

Trattoria Le Mossacce, Via del Proconsolo 55r, east of the Duomo, serves pasta for around L5000. A full meal with wine will cost up to L18,000. *La Maremmana*, at Via de' Macci 77r, behind the Church of Santa Croce, is a bit out of the way but worth seeking out for its good, hearty food and variously priced menus.

Around San Lorenzo Ask anyone in Florence where they go for lunch and they will answer *Mario's*. This small bar and trattoria at Via Rosina 2r, near the Mercato Centrale, is open only at lunch time and serves pasta dishes for around L4000 to L6000, and a secondo for L5000 to L8000. A few doors down, at Piazza del Mercato Centrale 20, is *Cafè Za Za*, another favourite with the locals. Prices are around the same as at Mario's.

Cafés Among the great undiscovered treasures of Florence is *Angie's Pub*, Via dei Neri 35r, east of Palazzo Vecchio, which offers a vast array of panini and focaccia, as well as hamburgers, served Italian-style with mozzarella and spinach, and hot dogs with cheese and mushrooms. A menu lists the panini, but you can design your own from the extensive selection of fillings. Try one with artichoke, mozzarella and *crema di funghi* (cream of mushroom). Prices range from L3500 to L5000. There is a good range of beers and no extra charge if you sit down. *Caffè* *degl'Innocenti*, Via Nazionale 57, near the famous leather market in the streets around the Mercato Centrale (the covered market), has a great selection of prepared panini and cakes for around L2000 to L3000. However, there is nowhere to sit down. The snack bar *L'Orafo*, Via Por Santa Maria 8, on the way to the Ponte Vecchio, is another good choice for a quick, light and cheap lunch. The streets between the Duomo and the Arno harbour many pizzerias where you can buy pizza by the slice to take away for around L2000 to L3000, depending on the weight.

Gelati The two best outlets for gelati are *Il Triangolo di Bermuda*, Via Nazionale 61, near the leather market, and *Perché No?*, Via dei Tavolini 19r, off Via Calzaiuoli. It would be a toss-up to decide which serves the better ice cream, so alternate between the two.

Entertainment
Several publications list the theatrical and musical events and festivals held in the city and surrounding areas. They include the bimonthly *Florence Today*, the monthly newsletter *Firenze Information*, and the monthly magazine *Firenze Spettacolo*, all available from the tourist information office. Posters at the university and in Piazza della Repubblica advertise current concerts and other events.

Concerts, opera and dance are performed throughout the year at the *Teatro Comunale*, Corso Italia 12, with the main seasons being from September to December and from January to April. In spring there is Maggio Musicale, the Florentine May Music Festival, and in summer a series of classical music concerts is performed at the Teatro Comunale and *Teatro della Pergola* (on Via della Pergola), featuring important musicians from around the world. Estate Fiesoliana (Summer in Fiesole) features films and theatrical and musical performances, many held at the *Roman Theatre* in Fiesole, from June to August. Theatrical events are held in winter at the Teatro Comunale.

In addition to the wealth of art housed permanently in its museums and galleries,

Florence stages a significant number of art exhibitions throughout the year. The major festivals include the Festa del Patrono (the Feast of St John the Baptist) on June 24; the Scoppio del Carro (Explosion of the Cart), held in front of the Duomo on Easter Sunday (see Facts for the Visitor at the start of this chapter); and the lively Calcio Storico (Historical Football), featuring football matches played in 16th century costume, which is held in June.

A more sedate pastime is the nightly passeggiata in Piazzale Michelangelo, overlooking the city (take bus No 13 from the station or the Duomo). One of the more popular nightclubs is *La Dolce Vita*, Piazza del Carmine, in the Oltrarno, which is frequented by both foreigners and Italians.

Things to Buy
It is said that Milan has the best clothes and Rome the best shoes, but Florence without doubt has the greatest variety. The main shopping area is between the Duomo and the Arno, with boutiques concentrated along Via Roma, Via dei Calzaiuoli and Via Por Santa Maria, leading to the goldsmiths lining the Ponte Vecchio. Window-shop along Via de' Tornabuoni, where the top designers, including Gucci, Yves Saint Laurent and Pucci, sell their wares.

The open-air market (open Monday to Saturday) in the streets of San Lorenzo near the Mercato Centrale, offers leather goods, clothing and jewellery at low prices, but quality can vary greatly. You could pick up the bargain of a lifetime here, but check the item carefully before you pay. You can bargain, but not if you want to use a credit card. The flea market at Piazza dei Ciompi, off Borgo Allegri near the Church of Santa Croce (Monday to Saturday), is not as extensive, but there are great bargains.

Florence is famous for its beautifully patterned paper, which is stocked in the many *cartolerie* (stationer's shops) throughout the city and at the markets. One of the better cartolerie is opposite the Pitti Palace in Piazza dei Pitti.

Getting There & Away

Air The local airport is at Pisa, just under an hour away by hourly train connections from Florence's Santa Maria Novella Railway Station. There is an air terminal (☎ 21 60 73) at the station, open daily from 7 am to 8 pm. Passengers can check in there and then catch a train directly to the airport. There are flights to/from major Italian cities, Paris and London.

Bus The SITA bus terminal (☎ 48 36 51), Via Santa Caterina da Siena, is just to the west of the train station. Buses leave for the Colle Val d'Elsa, Poggibonsi (where there is a connecting bus to San Gimignano) and Siena. Full details on other bus services are available at the APT.

Train Florence is on the main Rome-Milan line, which means that most of the trains for Rome, Bologna and Milan are the fast inter-cities, for which you have to pay a rapido supplement. Regular trains also go to/from Venice (three hours) and Trieste. For Verona you will usually need to change at Bologna. To get to Genoa and Turin, a change at Pisa is necessary. For train information ring ☎ 27 87 85, or pick up the handy train timetable booklet which is sometimes available at the station.

Car & Motorbike Florence is connected by the Autostrada del Sole (A1) to Bologna and Milan in the north and Rome and Naples to the south. The motorway to the sea, Autostrada del Mare (A11), joins it to Prato, Lucca, Pisa and the Mediterranean coast, and a superstrada (dual carriageway) joins the city to Siena. Exits from the autostrade into Florence are well signed, and either one of the exits marked 'Firenze nord' or 'Firenze sud' will take you to the centre of town. There are tourist information offices on the A1 both to the north and south of the city.

Getting Around

Bus ATAF buses service the city centre and Fiesole. The terminal for the most useful buses is in a small piazza to the left as you

go out of the station onto Via Valfonda. Bus No 7 leaves from here for Fiesole and also stops at the Duomo. Tickets must be bought before you get on the bus and are sold at most tobacconists, or automatic vending machines at major bus stops (L1000 for 70 minutes, L1300 for two hours). There are good-value tourist tickets, which cost L5000 and are valid for 24 hours.

Taxi You can find taxis outside the station, or call ☎ 4798 or 4390 to book one. As always in Italy, taxis are very expensive.

Car & Motorbike Traffic is restricted in the city centre. The main car parks are in Piazza del Mercato Centrale, which is expensive and only open during the day, and at La Fortezza da Basso, Viale Filippo Strozzi, just behind the station (L1000 an hour for all-night parking). There is also a car park at Piazzale Vittorio Veneto, west of the station.

Car, Scooter & Bike Rental To rent a car, try Hertz (☎ 29 82 05), Via M Finiguerra 17r; Inter-Rent (☎ 21 86 65), Via Borgo Ognissanti 133r; or Avis Autonoleggio (☎ 234 66 68), Lungarno Torrigiani 33. For motorbikes and bicycles try Ciao & Basta (☎ 234 27 26), Costa dei Magnoli 24, near the Ponte Vecchio in the Oltrarno. It also has an office just outside the station at Via Alamanni (☎ 21 33 07).

PISA

Once a maritime power to rival Genoa and Venice, Pisa now seems content to have one remaining claim to fame: its leaning tower. Situated on the banks of the Arno River, near the Ligurian Sea, it was a busy port, the site of an important university and the home of Galileo Galilei (1564-1642). Devastated by Genoa in the 13th century, its history eventually merged with that of Florence. Today Pisa is a pleasant town, but there is not a lot to see after you have explored the main square, Campo dei Miracoli, and taken a walk around the old centre.

Orientation & Information

The EPT tourist office at Piazza del Duomo, just across the grass from the leaning tower, has maps and a list of hotels, but little else to offer. It is open Monday to Saturday from 8 am to 8 pm in summer, and from 9.30 am to midday and 3 to 5.30 pm Monday to Saturday in the off season. It has a branch office at the station, which is open at roughly the same hours. Take bus No 1 from the station, which is across the river from the old town, to Piazza del Duomo.

Pisa's postcode is 56100 and the telephone code is 050.

Things to See & Do

The Pisans can justly claim that their **Campo dei Miracoli** (Field of Miracles) is one of the most beautiful squares in the world. Set in its sprawling lawns are the **cathedral**, the **baptistry** and the **leaning tower**. On any day the piazza is teeming with people – students studying or playing, tourists wandering and Pisan workers eating their lunch.

The Romanesque cathedral, begun in 1064, has a beautiful façade of columns in four tiers and its huge interior is lined with 68 columns. The bronze doors of the transept, facing the leaning tower, are by Bonanno Pisano. The 16th century bronze doors of the main entrance are by Giambologna and were made to replace the original doors, which were destroyed in a fire. The marble baptistry, which was started in 1153 and took almost two centuries to complete, contains a beautiful pulpit by Nicola Pisano.

The famous leaning **bell tower** was in trouble from the start. Its architect, Bonanno Pisano, managed to complete three tiers before the tower started to lean. The problem is generally believed to have been caused by shifting soil, and the tower has continued to lean by an average one mm a year. Galileo climbed its 294 steps to experiment with gravity. Today it is no longer possible to follow in his footsteps. The tower is closed while the Italians try to work out how to stop its inexorable lean towards the ground.

In 1992, there were serious fears that the tower was about to collapse. Emergency action included girdling the tower with steel bands. Earlier in the year, Pisa's mayor threatened to readmit tourists to the tower, claiming that tourism in the town had dropped by 20% since its closure while the Italian government had done nothing about plans to fortify the structure. In response, the government passed a special decree to get work underway, making the end of 1993 the deadline for completion of the project. Few in Italy believe it will be finished by then, and, despite publicity surrounding the mayor's threat, the tower is unlikely to reopen in the foreseeable future.

After seeing the Campo dei Miracoli, take a walk down Via Santa Maria, along the Arno and into the Borgo Stretto to explore the old city.

Places to Stay & Eat

Pisa has a reasonable number of budget hotels for a small town, but many double as residences for students during the school year, so it can be difficult to find a cheap room. The *Albergo E Gronchi* (☎ 56 18 23), Piazza Arcivescovado 1, just near the Campo dei Miracoli, is a great bargain offering singles/doubles for L25,000/40,000, and triples/quads for L54,000/66,000. The *Albergo Giardino* (☎ 56 21 01), Via C Cammeo at the other end of the Campo, has singles/doubles for L28,000/38,000. Near the station is the *Albergo Milano* (☎ 23 162), Via Mascagni 14, with pleasant rooms and a friendly owner. Singles/doubles cost L30,000/44,000, and triples cost L60,000. Down the street at No 24 is the *Albergo Roseto* (☎ 42 596), with a bar, terrace and garden. Singles/doubles are L35,000/50,000 and L17,000 for each additional person.

Being a university town, Pisa hosts a good range of cheap eating places. Head for the area around Borgo Stretto and the university. There is an open-air food market in Piazza delle Vettovaglie, off Borgo Stretto. *Spaghetteria San Francesco*, Vicolo dei Tinti 26, has pasta for around L5000 a plate.

Closer to the Campo, at Piazza Felice Cavalotti 13, is a tavola calda and pizzeria

ITALY

with pasta and vegetable dishes for L4000 and pizzas from L5000 to L7000. In the same area are several alimentari, where you can buy everything you need for a picnic in the campo.

Getting There & Away

The city is linked by direct train to Florence, Rome and Genoa. Local trains head for Lucca and Livorno. The airport, with domestic and international (European), flights is only a few minutes away by train. ACIT buses link Pisa with cities along the coast, including Tirrenia and Livorno.

SIENA

Beautiful, gentle Siena is built on three hills and is still surrounded by its historic ramparts. Its medieval centre has streets lined with majestic Gothic buildings in various shades of the colour known as burnt sienna. According to legend, Siena was founded by the sons of Remus (one of the founders of Rome). In the Middle Ages the city became a free republic, but its success and power led to serious rivalry with Florence. In a famous incident in the 13th century, the Florentines hurled dead donkeys and excrement into Siena, hoping to start a plague.

The city produced important works of art by painters of the Sienese School and was home to St Catherine and St Benedict. Siena is divided into 17 *contrade* (districts) and each year 10 are chosen to compete in *il Palio*, an extraordinary horse race and pageant in the shell-shaped Piazza del Campo on 2 July and 16 August.

Orientation & Information

Siena is well geared for tourism. Signs direct you through the modern town to the medieval city, and within the walls there are easy-to-follow signs to all the major sights.

From the train station catch bus No 2, 4 or 15 to Piazza Matteotti and walk into the centre along Via Piangiani (it takes about five minutes to reach the Campo). From the bus terminal in Piazza San Domenico, it is a five-minute walk along Via Sapienza to the

1	Da Titti
2	Pizzeria Il Riccio
3	Piazza Gramsci
4	Piazza Matteotti
5	Main Post Office
6	Conad Alimentari
7	Albergo Bernini
8	La Chiacciera
9	SIP
10	Albergo La Perla
11	Osteria La Grotta del Fantino
12	APT Tourist Office
13	Piazza del Campo
14	Tre Donzelle
15	Language School
16	Palazzo Comunale
17	Locanda Garibaldi
18	Hostaria Il Carroccio
19	Police Headquarters
20	Museo del Duomo
21	Duomo
22	Palazzo Buonsignori

Campo. No cars, apart from those of residents, are allowed in the medieval centre.

Tourist Office The APT office (☎ 577-28 05 51) is at Piazza del Campo 56 and is open from 8.30 am to 7.30 pm Monday to Saturday.

Post & Telecommunications The main post office is at Piazza Matteotti 1. The SIP office is at Via dei Termini 40. Siena's telephone code is 0577.

Emergency The questura is at Via del Castoro (near the Duomo), or ring the police on ☎ 112 or 113. In a medical emergency ring ☎ 2 99 11, or 28 01 10 for an ambulance. There is a hospital at Via Tufi, near Porta Tufi.

Things to See & Do

The **Piazza del Campo**, known simply as the Campo, is a magnificent shell-shaped, slanting piazza, its paving divided into nine sectors. At the lowest point of the piazza is the imposing **Palazzo Comunale**, considered one of the most graceful Gothic buildings in Italy. Inside the town hall are

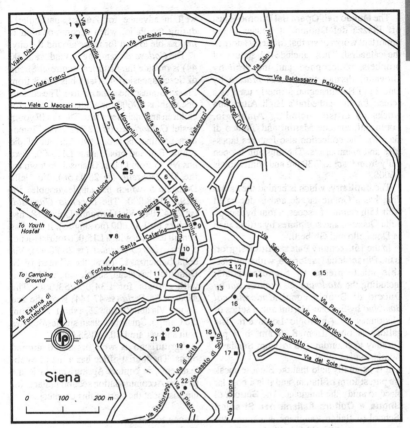

Siena

0   100   200 m

numerous important Sienese works of art, including Simone Martini's *Maestà* and Ambrogio Lorenzetti's frescoes *Effects of Good & Bad Government*. There is also a chapel with frescoes by Taddeo di Bartolo. Entry is L6000, or L3000 for students.

The spectacular **Duomo** is, next to the cathedral in Orvieto, one of the most beautiful in Italy. Its black-and-white striped marble façade has a Romanesque lower section, with carvings by Giovanni Pisano. Its upper section is 14th century Gothic and there are 19th century mosaics at the top. The interior features an inlaid marble floor, with

various works depicting biblical stories. The beautiful **pulpit** was carved in marble and porphyry by Nicola Pisano, the father of Giovanni Pisano. Other important art works include a bronze statue of St John the Baptist by Donatello and statues of St Jerome and Mary Magdalene by Bernini.

Through a door from the north aisle is the **Libreria Piccolomini**, which Pope Pius III (pope during 1503) had built to house the books of his uncle, the former pope Pius II. It features frescoes by Pinturicchio and a Roman statue of the Three Graces. Entry is L2000.

The **Museo dell'Opera del Duomo** is just off Piazza del Duomo. It houses many important works of art that formerly adorned the cathedral. These include 12 statues of prophets, philosophers and the *Sybil* by Giovanni Pisano; the famous *Maestà* by Duccio di Buoninsegna, formerly used as a screen for the cathedral's High Altar; and works by artists including Ambrogio, Lorenzetti, Simone Martini and Taddeo di Bartolo. The collection also features tapestries and manuscripts. The museum is open daily from 9 am to 7.30 pm and admission is L6000.

The **baptistry**, which is behind the cathedral, has a Gothic façade and is decorated with 15th century frescoes, a font by Jacopo della Quercia, and sculptures by artists such as Donatello and Ghiberti.

In the 15th century **Palazzo Buonsignori** is the **Pinacoteca Nazionale**, with innumerable masterpieces by Sienese artists, including the *Madonna dei Francescani* by Duccio di Buoninsegna, *Madonna col Bambino* by Simone Martini and a series of Madonnas by Ambrogio Lorenzetti. The gallery is open from 8.30 am to 7 pm Tuesday to Saturday and to 1 pm Sundays. Admission is L8000.

It is generally held that the Sienese speak the purest form of Italian, and it is a popular place to study the language. The **Scuola di Lingua e Cultura Italiana per Stranieri** (School of Italian Language & Culture for Foreigners; ☎ 4 92 60) is in Piazzetta Grassi 2, 53100 Siena. The school is open all year and the only requirement for enrolment is a high school graduation/pass certificate. There are three areas of study: Italian language and literature; archaeology and history of art; and Italian history and institutions. Courses cost L500,000 for 10 weeks and brochures can be obtained by making a request by letter or telephone to the Secretary, or from the Italian Cultural Institute in your city.

Places to Stay

Although there is good range of budget accommodation in Siena, you should book well in advance for August, particularly during the Palio, when accommodation is impossible to find for miles around the city.

The *Colleverde* camping ground (☎ 28 00 44) is outside the historical centre at Strada di Scacciapensieri 47 (take bus No 8 from Piazza Gramsci near the centre). The cost for one night is L9600 for adults and L4800 for children and includes a tent. The IYHF youth hostel *Guidoriccio* (☎ 52 212), Via Fiorentina, Stellino, is about two km out of the centre. Bed and breakfast is L17,000. Take bus No 15 from Piazza Gramsci. In town try the *Tre Donzelle* (☎ 28 03 58), Via delle Donzelle 5, which has singles/doubles for L29,000/48,000. The *Locanda Garibaldi* (☎ 28 42 04), Via Giovanni Dupré 18, has doubles for L45,000 (no singles). It also has a small trattoria with a L15,000 tourist menu.

The *Albergo Bernini* (☎ 28 90 47), Via della Sapienza 15 (near the Church of St Dominic), has clean, simple singles/doubles with shower for L34,000/53,000. The *Albergo La Perla* (☎ 47 144) is on the 2nd floor at Via delle Terme 25, a short walk from the Campo. Small but clean singles/doubles with shower are L40,000/53,000.

Agriturismo is well organised around Siena. The tourist office has a list of establishments, or contact Agriturismo in Rome (see the Accommodation section in Facts for the Visitor at the start of this chapter).

Places to Eat

Hosteria il Carroccio, Via Casato di Sotto 32, off the Campo, has excellent pasta for around L6000. A bottle of house wine is only L4500, but a full meal will come to around L25,000. *Osteria la Grotta del Fantino*, Via di Fontebranda 5 (off Via di Città) has meals for around the same price.

La Chiacchiera, Costa di Sant'Antonio 4, off Via Santa Caterina, is very small, but it has a good menu with local specialities. Pasta dishes cost from L4500 and a litre of house wine is L4500. A full meal will cost about L15,000.

About 10 minutes' walk from the Campo, in a less frenetic neighbourhood, are several trattorias and alimentari. *Da Titti*, Via di

Camollia 193, is a no-frills establishment with big wooden bench tables where full meals with wine cost around L18,000. *Pizzeria Il Riccio*, nearby at Via Malta 44, has pasta for around L6000 and big pizzas from L5000.

At the local alimentari, near Piazza Matteotti, you can buy panini, as well as preprepared food such as marinated vegetables, salads etc. In the centre near the Campo, head for *Bar Pomo d'Oro* in Piazza Indipendenza and then go next door to the *forno* (bakery) for a piece of *panforte*, Sienese nougat-type cake.

Getting There & Away

Regular SITA buses run from Florence to Siena, arriving at Piazza San Domenico. Buses also go to San Gimignano, Volterra and other points in Tuscany. There is a daily bus to Perugia and another to Rome. Siena is not on a main train line, so from Rome it is necessary to change at Chiusi and from Florence at Empoli, making buses a better alternative.

SAN GIMIGNANO

Few places in Italy rival the beauty of San Gimignano, a town which has barely changed since medieval times. Set on a hill overlooking the misty pink, green and gold patchwork of the Tuscan landscape, the town is famous for its towers (14 of of the original 72 remain), built as a demonstration of power by its prominent families in the Middle Ages.

The town is packed with tourists at weekends, so try to visit during the week. The tourist information office is in Piazza del Duomo in the town centre. San Gimignano's telephone code is 0577.

Things to See

Climb San Gimignano's tallest tower, **Torre Grossa**, also known as the town hall tower, off Piazza del Duomo, for a memorable view of the Tuscan hills. The tower is reached from within the **Palazzo del Popolo**, which houses the **Municipal Museum**, with paintings by Filippo Lippi and Pinturicchio. Also

in the piazza is the **Duomo**, with a Romanesque interior, frescoes by Ghirlandaio in the **Chapel of Santa Fina** and a *Last Judgment* by Taddeo di Bartolo.

The **Piazza della Cisterna**, with a 13th century well, is the most impressive piazza in San Gimignano. It is paved with bricks in a herringbone pattern and lined with towers and palaces.

Places to Stay & Eat

The nearest camping ground is *Il Boschetto di Piemma* (☎ 94 03 52), about three km from San Gimignano at Santa Lucia. It costs L6000 a night and there is a bus service to the site. The non-IYHF hostel, *ostello della gioventù* (☎ 94 19 91), is at Via delle Fonti. Bed and breakfast is L15,000 a night.

Hotels in town are expensive, but there are numerous rooms for rent in private homes. Agriturismo is well organised in this area. For information on both, contact the tourist office or the APT in Siena.

Eating in San Gimignano is very expensive, but there is an outdoor market in Piazza del Duomo and several alimentari in Via San Matteo. For a good cheap meal try *Le Vecchie Mura* at Via Piandornella 15. A pizza costs around L6000 and a full meal will come to around L15,000.

Getting There & Away

Regular SITA buses run from Florence to Poggibonsi, where you need to change for San Gimignano (only 20 minutes away). A direct bus runs from Piazza San Domenico in Siena. Buses arrive in Piazzale dei Martiri Montemaggio at Porta San Giovanni.

PERUGIA

One of Italy's best preserved medieval hilltowns, Perugia has a lively and bloody past. Originally Etruscan, the city is noted for the internal feuding of its families, the Baglioni and the Oddi, and the violent wars against its neighbours during the Middle Ages. Perugia also has a strong artistic and cultural tradition. It was the home of the painter Perugino, and Raphael, his student, also worked here. Its University for Foreign-

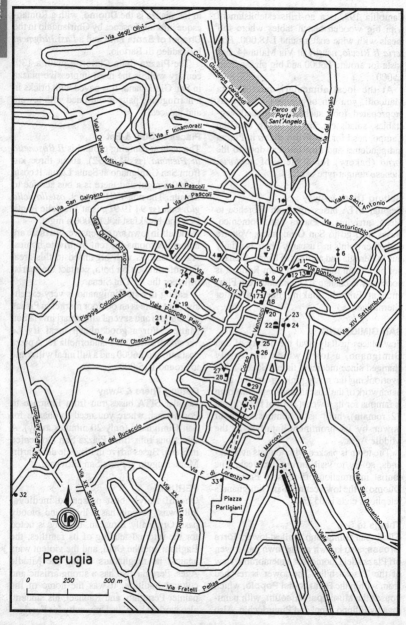

Via degli Olivi

Corso Giuseppe Garibaldi

Parco di
Porta
Sant'Angelo

Via del Bulagaio

Via F. Innamorati

Viale Orazio Antinori

Via San Galigano

Via A. Pascoli

Via A. Pascoli

Viale Sant'Antonio

Viale Orazio Antinori

Via Pinturicchio

1
2

3

4

5

† 6

10
11   Via Bontempi
12 13

9 †

Via del Priori

7
8

15
17 18 16

14

Piaggia Colombata

Viale Pompeo Pellini

19

20

23

22   24

Vannucci

Via Arturo Checchi

21

25

Via XIV Settembre

26

Corso

27

28

29

30
31

Via del Bucaccio

Via del Bucaccio

Via Mario Angeloni

Via G. Marconi

Corso Cavour

34

Via F. di
Lorenzo

32

Via XX Settembre

Via XX Settembre

33

Piazza
Partigiani

Via San Domenico

Viale Roma

Viale Roma

Perugia

Via Fratelli Pellas

0   250   500 m

ers, established in 1925, offers courses in Italian language and attracts thousands of students from all over the world. A full calendar of musical and cultural events make the city even more appealing.

Information

The centre of all activity in Perugia is the Corso Vannucci. The tourist information office is in Piazza IV Novembre, opposite the cathedral at one end of the Corso, and is open daily from 8 am to 2 pm and 4 to 7.30 pm. The main post office is in Piazza Matteotti. For all events and useful information, get a copy of the monthly *Perugia What, Where, When*. Perugia's telephone code is 075.

Things to See & Do

The **Palazzo dei Priori**, on Corso Vannucci, is a rambling 13th century palace housing the impressively frescoed **Notaries Hall** and the **National Gallery of Umbria**, with works by Pinturicchio, Perugino and Fra Angelico. Opposite the palazzo is the **cathedral**, with an unfinished façade in the characteristic Perugian red-and-white marble. Inside are frescoes, decorations and furniture by well-known artists from the 15th to 18th centuries.

Between the two buildings, in Piazza IV Novembre, is the 13th century **Fontana Maggiore**, decorated in marble and bronze by the sculptors Nicola and Giovanni Pisano. Its lower panels feature 50 marble panels depicting in bas-relief the history and trades of Perugia, the sciences and the seasons. At the other end of Corso Vannucci is the **Rocca Paolina**, a massive 16th century fortress built upon the foundations of the palaces and homes of the powerful families of the day, notably the Baglioni. The homes were destroyed and the materials used to build the fortress under the orders of Pope Paul III as a means of suppressing the Baglioni. Destroyed by the Perugians after the declaration of the Kingdom of Italy in 1860, it remains a symbol of their defiance against oppression.

Raphael's Fresco, in a chapel next to the Church of San Severo, in Piazza San Severo, was one of the last works by Raphael in Perugia and was completed by Perugino after Raphael's death in 1520.

Etruscan remains in Perugia include the **Arco Etrusco** (Etruscan Arch), near the university, and the **Pozzo Etrusco** (Etruscan Well), off Piazza Piccinino, near the cathedral. There are Etruscan tombs in the hills just outside the city.

Language Courses Perugia's University for Foreigners offers courses in Italian language and culture for L240,000 a month. Courses are for a minimum of one month and also run for three months and nine months (for advanced students). The quality of the courses is generally good, but there can be up to 70 students in a beginner's class during the summer months. You will need to apply for a study visa in your own country, and to obtain this you must have confirmation of enrolment in a course. Since the process of obtaining the necessary documentation from the university can be lengthy, ensure that you send your enrolment form at least three to four months before your intended departure date.

The university will organise accommodation on request. A room in an apartment (shared with other students), in a private room or with an Italian family will cost around L350,000 to L400,000 a month. Course details can be obtained from Italian cultural institutes in your country, or by writing to the secretary, Università per Stranieri, Palazzo Gallenga, Piazza Forteraccio 4, 06100 Perugia (☎ 57 461).

Places to Stay
Perugia has a good selection of reasonably priced hotels, but if you arrive unannounced during Umbria Jazz in July, or during August, expect problems. The non-IYHF *Centro Internazionale per la Gioventù* (☎ 2 28 80), Via Bontempi 13, charges L10,000 a night. Sheets (for the entire stay) are an extra L1000. Its TV room has a frescoed ceiling and its terrace has one of the best views in Perugia.

Pensione Anna (☎ 6 63 04), Via dei Priori 48, off Corso Vannucci, has singles/doubles for L30,000/40,000. The *Pensione Paola* (☎ 2 38 16), Via della Canapina 5, is five minutes from the centre, down the escalator from Via dei Priori. It has singles/doubles for L30,000/45,000. Just off Corso Vannucci, at Via Bonazzi 25, is the *Piccolo Hotel* (☎ 2 29 87), with doubles for L40,000 (no singles). Showers cost an extra L3000.

The *Hotel Morlacchi* (☎ 20 319), Via

Tiberi 2, north-west of Piazza IV Novembre, has singles/doubles for L35,000/50,000, or a triple with bathroom for L90,000.

The weekly *Cerco e Trovo* (L3000 at newsstands) lists all available rental accommodation.

Places to Eat
Being a student town, Perugia offers many budget eating options. The best places for pizza are *Medio Evo*, just behind the bar on Corso Vannucci, and *Tit-Bit*, Via dei Priori 105. A pizza will cost from L5000 to L6000 at each restaurant.

Another option is the popular *Il Segreto di Pulcinella*, Via Larga 8. It has good pizzas for around L6000 to L8000 and the cover charge is only L1000, but the service charge is 15%.

For a cheap meal try the *tavola calda* in Piazza Danti. For a traditional Umbrian meal and lots of vegetables, try *Ubu Re*, Via Baldeschi 17. A full meal will cost around L25,000, but the food is the best in Perugia. There is a covered market daily (except Sunday) from 7 am to 1.30 pm, downstairs from Piazza Matteotti, which sells fresh produce, bread, cheese and meat.

Sandri in Corso Vannucci near the Palazzo dei Priori is a great meeting place for a quiet coffee and cake.

Getting There & Away
Perugia is not on the main Rome-Florence railway line. There are some direct trains from both cities, but most require a change, either at Foligno (from Rome) or Terontola (from Florence). Buses leave from Piazza Partigiani, at the end of the Rocca Paolina escalators, for Rome (and Fiumicino Airport), Florence, Siena and cities throughout Umbria including Assisi, Gubbio and nearby Lake Trasimeno. The bus to Rome is faster and cheaper than the train. Full timetables for all trains and buses are available at the tourist office.

Getting Around
The central train station is a few km downhill from the historical centre. Catch any bus

heading for Piazza Matteotti or Piazza Italia to get to the centre, which is at the top of the hill. Tickets cost L800 and must be bought before you get on the bus.

If you arrive in Perugia by car, be prepared to be confused. Roads leading to the centre wind around a hill topped by the historical centre, and the normal driving time from the base of the hill to the centre is around 10 to 15 minutes. Signs to the centre are clearly marked 'centro' and by following these signs you should arrive at Piazza Italia, where you can leave the car and walk along Corso Vannucci to the tourist office.

Most of the centre is closed to normal traffic, but tourists are allowed to drive to their hotels. It is probably wiser not to do this, as driving in central Perugia is a nightmare because of the extremely narrow streets, most of which are one-way. To accommodate other traffic, escalators from the historical centre take you to large car parks downhill. The Rocca Paolina escalator leads to Piazza Partigiani, where there is a supervised car park (L10,000 a day), the intercity bus terminal, and escalators to Piazza Italia nearby. The Via dei Priori escalator leads to two major car parks.

ASSISI

Despite the millions of tourists and pilgrims it attracts every year, Assisi, home of St Francis, manages to remain a beautiful and tranquil refuge (as long as you keep away from the main tourist drags). From Roman times its inhabitants have been aware of the visual impact of the city, perched halfway up Mt Subasio. From the valley its pink-and-white marble buildings literally shimmer in the sunlight.

The APT tourist office, Piazza del Comune 12, has all the information you need on hotels, sights and events in Assisi. The local telephone code is 075.

Things to See

Most people visit Assisi to see its religious monuments. **St Francis' Basilica** is composed of two churches, one built on top of the other. The lower church contains the crypt where St Francis is buried. The upper church was decorated by the great painters of the 13th and 14th centuries, including Giotto and Cimabue. Dress rules are applied rigidly – absolutely no shorts, miniskirts or low-cut dresses are allowed.

The 13th century **Basilica di Santa Chiara** contains interesting 14th century frescoes and the remains of St Clare, friend of St Francis and founder of the Order of Poor Clares. The **Cattedrale di San Rufino** is interesting for its impressive Romanesque façade. Its austere interior was altered in the 16th century, but retains the baptismal font where St Francis and St Clare were baptised. The **Piazza del Comune**, in the town centre, was the site of the Roman **forum**, parts of which have been excavated; access is from Via Portico. The piazza also contains the **Temple of Minerva**. It is now a church, but has kept its impressive pillared façade.

Assisi's 'crown' is the **Rocca Maggiore**, a remarkably well-preserved medieval castle. In the valley below Assisi is the **Basilica di Santa Maria degli Angeli**, a huge church built around the first Franciscan monastery and the **Cappella del Transito**, where St Francis died in 1226.

Places to Stay & Eat

Assisi is well geared for tourists and there are numerous budget hotels and rooms for rent (affittacamere). Peak periods, when you will need to book well in advance, are Easter, August and September and the Feast of St Francis on 3 and 4 October. The tourist office has a full list of affittacamere and religious institutions.

The IYHF *Ostello della Pace* (☎ 81 67 67), Via Valecchi, is small and open all year. Bed and breakfast is L16,500. There is a non-IYHF hostel and camping ground (☎ 81 36 36) just out of the town at Fontemaggio. From Piazza Matteotti, at the far end of town from St Francis' Basilica, walk uphill for about two km along Via Eremo delle Carceri till you reach the hostel. *Affittacamere Jole Orbi* (☎ 81 27 42), Vicolo San Lorenzo 2, up Via Porta Perlici from the Cathedral of San Rufino, has doubles for L48,000, or L50,000 with private bathroom. Some rooms open onto a terrace. *La Rocca* (☎ 81 22 84), Via Porta Perlici 27, has singles/doubles for L27,000/38,000 and doubles with bath for L52,000. Half-pension is L42,000 per person, or L45,000 with private bath.

In the same complex as the camping ground at Fontemaggio is *La Stalla*, where you can eat a filling meal under an arbour for less than L15,000. In town try *Il Pozzo Romano*, Via Santa Agnese 10, off Piazza Santa Chiara. The pizzas cost around L6000. The restaurant at the *Albergo La Rocca* has home-made pasta for L5000 to L6000.

Getting There & Away

Buses connect Assisi with Perugia, Foligno and other local towns, leaving from Piazza Santa Chiara. Buses for Rome and Florence leave from Piazza San Pietro. Assisi's train station is in the valley, in the suburb of Santa Maria degli Angeli. It is on the same line as Perugia and there is a shuttle bus service between the town and the station.

AROUND UMBRIA

Umbria is a mountainous region characterised by its many medieval hilltowns. After Perugia and Assisi, visit Orvieto, Spello, Spoleto and Gubbio to appreciate the Romanesque and Gothic architecture, particularly Orvieto's cathedral, considered one of the most beautiful in Italy. Try to time your visit to take in the Festival of Two Worlds at Spoleto in late June and early July, or the weird and wonderful Corsa dei Ceri (see Cultural Events in the Facts for the Visitor section) at Gubbio on 15 May. These hilltowns are accessible by bus or train from Perugia, and the tourist office there has information and timetables.

ANCONA

The main reason to visit Ancona is to catch a ferry to Croatia, Greece or Turkey. This industrial, unattractive port town in the region of the Marches does, however, have an interesting, though small and semi-abandoned, historical centre.

Orientation & Information

The easiest way to get from the train station to the port is by bus No 1. The EPT has an office (☎ 071-4 17 03) at the train station, open Monday to Friday from 8 am to 1 pm and 3.30 to 7 pm and Saturday 8 am to 1 pm. AAST has an office (☎ 071-20 11 83) at the stazione marittima (ferry terminal), open at roughly the same hours. The main AAST office (☎ 071-3 32 49) is at Via Thaon de Revel 4.

The main post office is at Piazza XXIV Maggio, open from 8 am to 7 pm Monday to Saturday. ASST telephones are in the train station, Piazza Rosselli, and the SIP office is in Corso Stamira, near Piazza Roma. The telephone code for Ancona is 071.

Things to See

Walk uphill to the old town and the **Piazza del Duomo** for a view of the port and Adriatic. The town's Romanesque **cathedral** was built on the site of a Roman temple and has Byzantine and Gothic features. The church of **San Francesco delle Scale** has a beautiful Venetian-Gothic doorway, and towards the port are the 15th century **Loggia dei Mercanti** (Merchants' Loggia) and the Romanesque church of **Santa Maria della Piazza**, which has a remarkable, heavily adorned façade.

Places to Stay & Eat

Albergo Fiore (☎ 4 33 90), Piazza Rosselli 24, has singles/doubles for L25,000/40,000 and is just across from the train station. The *Pensione Centrale* (☎ 5 43 88), Via Marsala 10 (near Corso Stamira), has doubles only for L35,500.

The *Mercato Pubblico*, off Corso Mazzini, has fresh fruit and vegetables and alimentari (small grocery stores). *Trattoria da Dina*, Vicolo ad Alto 17 in the old town, has full meals for around L10,000. *Osteria del Pozzo*, Via Bonda 2, just off Piazza del Plebiscito, has good, reasonably priced food. For atmosphere and good fare head for *Osteria Teatro Strabacco*, Via Oberdan 2, near Corso Stamira.

Getting There & Away

Bus & Train Buses link Ancona with towns throughout the Marches Region and also with major cities including Milan (contact Reni on ☎ 20 25 96) and Rome (contact Marozzi on ☎ 06-47 42 801). Most buses depart from in front of the train station or from Piazza Cavour. Ancona is on the Bologna-Lecce train line and thus easily accessible from major towns throughout Italy. It is also directly linked to Rome via Foligno.

Car & Motorbike Ancona is on the A14, which links Bologna and Bari. Tourists can park for free at the port.

Boat All ferry operators have booths at the stazione marittima, off Piazza Kennedy. Here you can pick up timetables and price lists and make bookings. Remember that timetables are always subject to change and that prices fluctuate dramatically with the season. Most lines offer a 10% discount on return fares. Prices listed are for one-way, deck class in the high season.

Minoan Lines (☎ 5 67 89) operates ferries to Igoumenitsa, Corfu, Cephalonia and Patras (Greece) for L96,000 and Kuşadası (Turkey) for L155,000. Karageorgis Lines (☎ 20 10 80) ferries sail to Patras for L96,000. Marlines (☎ 5 00 62) goes to Igoumenitsa, Patras (L69,000), Iraklion (L104,000) and Rhodes (L138,000). Strintzis Lines (☎ 286 44 31) goes to Corfu, Igoumenitsa and Patras (L82,000). Adriatica (☎ 20 49 15) ferries go to Split, Zadar and Dubrovnik in Croatia (L80,000). Jadrolinija (☎ 20 28 05) goes to Zadar and Split (L49,000).

URBINO

This town in the Marches can be difficult to reach, but it is worth the effort to see the birthplace of Raphael and Bramante, which has changed little since the Middle Ages and remains a centre of art, culture and learning.

The AAST tourist information office (☎ 0722-2613) is opposite the Palazzo

Ducale at Piazza del Rinascimento 1. The telephone code for Urbino is 0722.

Things to See & Do

The main sight is the huge **Palazzo Ducale**, designed by Laurana and completed in 1482. The best view is from Corso Garibaldi to the west, from where you can appreciate the size of the building and see its towers and loggias. Enter the palace from Piazza Duca Federico and visit the **National Gallery of the Marches**, featuring works by Raphael, Paolo Uccello and Verrocchio. The palace closes at 2 pm; admission is L7000. Also visit **Raphael's House**, Via Raffaello 57, where the artist was born, and the **Oratorio di San Giovanni Battista**, with 15th century frescoes by the Salimbeni brothers.

There is a concert season at the **Teatro Sanzio** from May to September. Pick up a brochure at the tourist office.

Language Courses Urbino's Università degli Studi (☎ 3051), Via Saffi 2, offers summer language courses for foreigners. There are language courses for beginners, intermediate and advanced students as well as courses in Italian culture. The one-month courses cost L400,000.

Brochures and enrolment forms can be obtained from Italian cultural institutes in your country or by writing to the secretary, Università degli Studi di Urbino, Via Saffi 2, 61029 Urbino (☎ 30 52 26). You can arrange accommodation through the university by writing to Ufficio Alloggi dell'ERSU, Via Saffi 46, 61029 Urbino (☎ 2934). The cost of accommodation is around L250,000 per month.

Places to Stay & Eat

Urbino is a major university town and most cheap beds are taken by students during the school year. The tourist office has a full list of affittacamere. The *Fosca* (☎ 32 96 22), Via Raffaello 67, has doubles/triples for L42,000/55,000. *Albergo Italia* (☎ 2701), Corso Garibaldi 32, is next to the Palazzo Ducale and has singles/doubles for L30,000/40,000.

There are numerous bars around Piazza della Repubblica in the town centre and near the Palazzo Ducale which sell good panini. Try *Il Cortigiano* in Piazza del Rinascimento or *Pizzeria Galli*, Via Vittorio Veneto 19, for takeaway pizza by the slice. *Da Franco*, just off Piazza del Rinascimento, next to the university, has a self-service section with a set price lunch for L8000 in the low season, which jumps to L15,000 in summer.

Getting There & Away

There is no train service to Urbino, but it is connected by bus on weekdays to cities including Ancona, Pesaro and Arezzo. There is a bus link to the train station at Fossato di Vico, on the Rome-Ancona line. There are also buses to Rome twice a day. All buses arrive at Borgo Mercatale, down Via Mazzini from Piazza della Repubblica. The tourist office has timetables for all bus services.

Southern Italy

The land of the *mezzogiorno* (midday sun) will surprise even the most world-weary traveller. Rich in history and cultural traditions, the southern regions are poorer than those of the north, and certainly the wheels of bureaucracy grind increasingly slower as you travel closer to the tip of the boot. The attractions here are simpler and more stark, the people more vibrant and excitable, and myths and legends are inseparable from official history. Campania and Basilicata cry out to be explored and absolutely nothing can prepare you for Naples. Less well known by foreigners, Calabria has beautiful beaches and the striking scenery of the Sila Massif to offer visitors.

NAPLES

Crazy and confusing, but also seductive and fascinating, Naples (Napoli), capital of the Campania Region, has an energy which is palpable. Set on the beautiful Bay of Naples and overshadowed by Mt Vesuvius, it is one of the most densely populated cities in Europe. You will leave Naples with a head full of its classic images – laundry strung across narrow streets, three people and a dog on one Vespa, cars speeding along alleys no wider than a driveway, and the same streets teeming with locals shopping at outdoor markets and drinking wine or caffè with friends.

Naples has its own secret society of criminals, the *Camorra*, which had its golden period of power in the 19th century. Severe anticrime measures by authorities late in that century and again early in this century left the society greatly weakened and many of its members fled to the USA, where the society was eventually absorbed into the Mafia. The Camorra continues to operate in Naples, concentrating its activities on the import and sale of contraband cigarettes. As with the Mafia in Sicily and the *'Ndrangheta* in Calabria, the Camorra is insidious in its impact on the community, its activities interwoven with the everyday life of the locals.

Orientation

Both the stazione centrale (central train station) and the main bus terminal are in the vast Piazza Garibaldi. Don't be distressed by this desolate place – both the Bay of Naples and the famous narrow streets full of hanging laundry and crazy Napoletani (Neapolitans) are close by.

Naples is divided into *quartieri* (quarters). The main thoroughfare into the historic centre, *Spaccanapoli*, is Corso Umberto I, which heads south-west from Piazza Garibaldi. West on the bay are Santa Lucia and Mergellina, both fashionable and picturesque and a far cry from the chaotic, noisy historical centre. South of Mergellina is Posillipo, where the ultra-wealthy live, and in the hills overlooking the bay is the residential Vomero district.

Don't try to hurry in Naples. Although the distances between the main sights and districts are not great, most public transport is slow and unreliable.

Information

Tourist Offices The EPT office at the station will make hotel bookings, but make sure you give specific details on where you want to stay and how much you want to pay. The staff speak English. Ask for *Qui Napoli (Here Naples)*, published monthly in English and Italian and listing events in the city, as well as information about transport and other services. The office (☎ 081-26 87 79) is open daily from 9 am to 2 pm and 2.30 to 8 pm. The main AAST office, inside Palazzo Reale, has a bit more information to offer on Naples. It also has a branch in Piazza del Gesù, near Piazza Dante, open Monday to Saturday from 9 am to 2 pm.

Money Try to change money at banks, where you will get better rates, though many charge a L3000 fee. After banking hours there is a branch of the Banca della Comunicazioni in the station which is open on Saturdays from 8.20 to 11.20 am.

Post & Telecommunications The main post office is in Piazza Matteotti, off Via Armando Diaz at the end of Corso Umberto I. It is open weekdays from 8.30 am to 7.30 pm and Saturdays to midday. There is a branch in the Galleria Umberto I, a shopping mall on Via Toledo.

The ASST telephone office (open 24 hours a day) is at the station, and the SIP office, in Galleria Umberto I, is open from 9 am to 5 pm daily. The postcode for Naples is 80100 and the telephone code is 081.

Emergency For medical services use the Guardia Medica Permanente (☎ 751 31 77), a service of the Municipio di Napoli (Naples City Council) at night or during holidays. It is in the Palazzo Municipale (town hall) on Via Cervantes. For an ambulance phone ☎ 752 06 96. The pharmacy in the central station is open Monday to Saturday from 8 am to 8 pm, or phone ☎ 192 for information about all-night pharmacies.

The questura, Via Medina 75, just off Via Armando Diaz, has an office for foreigners where you can report thefts etc (☎ 79 41 11,

or ☎ 113 for police attendance in an emergency).

Dangers & Annoyances The petty crime rate in Naples is extremely high. Carry your money and documents in a money belt and never carry a bag or purse if you can help it. Thieves on motorbikes and pickpockets are extremely adept in this city. Car and motorbike theft is also a major problem.

Women should be careful if they are walking in the streets at night, particularly near the station and around Piazza Dante. One area *not* to enter at night is the Spanish Quarter, across Via Roma from Piazza Dante. It can be extremely dangerous here, even during the day, and even the Neapolitans are reluctant to go into the quarter.

Take great care when crossing roads. There are few traffic lights and pedestrian crossings, and the Neapolitans never stop at them anyway. The general rule is to drive straight through a red light. When facing a green light, they drive with caution, understanding that those facing the red light will not stop.

Things to See

Start by walking around Spaccanapoli, the historic centre of Naples. From Corso Umberto I turn right into Via Mezzocannone, which will take you to Via Benedetto Croce, the main street of the quarter. To the left is **Piazza del Gesù Nuovo**, with the Neapolitan Baroque **Chiesa del Gesù Nuovo** and the 14th century **Chiesa di Santa Chiara**, restored to its original Gothic-Provençal style after it was severely damaged by bombing during WW II. The beautiful **Chiostro delle Clarisse** (nun's cloisters) should not be missed.

The **Duomo** (Via Duomo) has a 19th century façade but was built by the Angevin kings at the end of the 13th century, on the site of an earlier basilica. Inside is the **Chapel of San Gennaro**, which contains the head of San Gennaro (the city's patron saint) and two vials of his congealed blood. The saint is said to have saved the city from plague, volcanic eruptions and other disas-

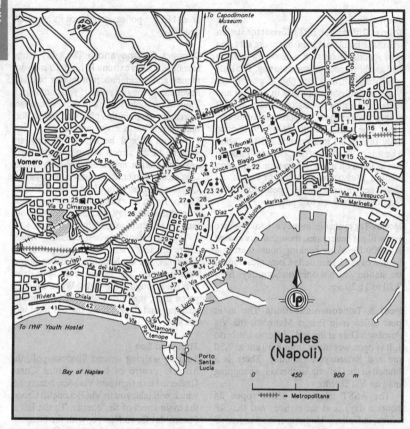

Naples (Napoli)

To Capodimonte Museum

To IYHF Youth Hostel

Bay of Naples

Porto Santa Lucia

Vomero

0   450   900 m

++++ = Metropolitana

ters. Every year the faithful gather in May and September to pray for a miracle, namely that the blood will liquefy and save the city from further disaster.

Turn off Via Duomo into **Via Tribunali**, one of the more characteristic streets of the area, and head for Piazza Dante, through the 17th century **Port'Alba**, one of the gates to the city. Via Roma, the most fashionable street in old Naples, heads to the left (becoming Via Toledo) and ends at Piazza Trento e Trieste and the **Piazza del Plebiscito**.

In the piazza is the **Palazzo Reale**, the former official residence of the Bourbon and

Savoy kings, now a museum. It is open Monday to Saturday from 9 am to 2 pm and to 1 pm Sundays and holidays. Admission is L6000. Just off the piazza is the **San Carlo Opera House**, one of the most famous in the world for its perfect acoustics and beautiful interior.

The 13th century **Castel Nuovo** is in the nearby Piazza del Municipio, at the port. The early Renaissance **triumphal arch** commemorates the entry of Alfonso I of Aragon into Naples in 1443. It is possible to enter the courtyard of the castle, but the building itself is not open to the public. Along the water-

■ PLACES TO STAY

9 Casanova Hotel
10 Albergo Ginevra
11 Hotel Zara
19 Soggiorno Imperia
20 Alloggio Fiamma
25 Pensione Margherita

▼ PLACES TO EAT

4 Ristorante Bellini
6 Trianon
7 Pizzeria Costa Gennaro
15 Trattoria Avellinese
22 La Campagnola
40 L'Osteria

OTHER

1 Piazza Medaglie d'Oro
2 National Archaeological
   Museum
3 Piazza Cavour
5 Duomo
8 Piazza Principe Umberto
12 Piazza Garibaldi
13 Intercity & Urban Bus Terminal
14 Central Railway Station

16 EPT Tourist Information
17 Piazza Montesanto & Stazione
   Cumana
18 Piazza Dante
21 Chiesa del Gesù Nuovo
23 Piazza del Gesù Nuovo
24 Chiesa di Santa Chiara
26 Certosa di San Martino
   (Monastery)
27 Piazza Carità
28 Main Post Office &
   Piazza Matteotti
29 Funicular for Vomero
30 Police Headquarters
31 Piazza Municipio
32 Galleria Umberto I
33 Piazza Trento e Trieste
34 San Carlo Opera House
35 Castel Nuovo
36 Palazzo Reale & AAST Tourist
   Office
37 Piazza del Plebiscito
38 Molo Beverello
39 Port & Ferry Terminal
41 Piazza della Repubblica
42 Villa Comunale
43 Piazza dei Martiri
44 Piazza Vittoria
45 Castel dell'Ovo

front, at Porto Santa Lucia, is the **Castel dell'Ovo**, originally a Norman castle, which is surrounded by a tiny fishing village, the **Borgo Marinaro**.

The **National Archaeological Museum** (Museo Nazionale) is in Piazza Museo, north of Piazza Dante. It contains the collections of the Farnese family, including an important collection of Graeco-Roman art. Art treasures that were discovered at Pompeii and Herculaneum are also exhibited here. It is open Monday to Saturday from 9 am to 2 pm and Sundays to 1 pm. Admission is L8000.

To escape the noise and general chaos of historic Naples, catch the funicular (Funicolare Centrale) to **Vomero** and visit the **Certosa di San Martino**, a monastery built under the Angevins in the 14th century, but completely remodelled in the Baroque style in the 16th and 17th centuries. It contains the **San Martino National Museum**.

The gardens surrounding the monastery are particularly beautiful and afford spectacular views of Naples and the bay.

Places to Stay
Hostel The IYHF *Ostello Mergellina Napoli* (☎ 761 23 46), Salita della Grotta 23 in Mergellina, is modern, safe and the best budget option in the city. Bed and breakfast is L16,000 (L21,000 without an IYHF card). Dinner is L12,000 and there is a bar. It is open all year and imposes a maximum three-night stay in summer. Take bus No 152 from the station, or the Metropolitana to Mergellina, and signs will direct you to the hostel from the waterfront.

Hotels Hotels in Naples can be surprisingly expensive, particularly if you want something safe and clean. Most of the cheap pensioni and hotels are near the station and

Piazza Garibaldi, but many offer a very low standard of accommodation. The area around Piazza Dante is a good alternative, though many budget hotels are filled with students during the school year. Most of the cheaper hotels will not accept bookings by phone and will often say they are tutto completo (full) if you telephone before arriving in the city.

Around the Station The *Hotel Zara* (☎ 28 71 25), Via Firenze 81, is clean and safe with singles/doubles for L25,000/50,000. Doubles with private bath are L60,000. Via Firenze is off Corso Novara, directly to the left as you leave the train station. *Albergo Ginevra* (☎ 28 32 10), Via Genova 116, the second street to the right off Corso Novara, is another reliable and well-kept place with singles/doubles for L30,000/50,000. The *Casanova Hotel* (☎ 26 82 87), Via Venezia 2, through the huge Piazza Garibaldi and past Piazza Principe Umberto in a small side street off Corso Garibaldi, is quiet and safe. Singles are L28,000 and doubles with private shower are L52,000. Triples with shower are L75,000.

Near Piazza Dante *Soggiorno Imperia* (☎ 45 93 47), Piazza Miraglia 386 (at the western end of Via Tribunali), is up an endless flight of stairs and has singles/doubles for L21,000/34,000. Catch bus No 185, CS or CD to Piazza Dante, walk through the archway to the left of the clock tower and walk straight ahead until you reach Piazza Miraglia. *Alloggio Fiamma* (☎ 45 91 87), Via Francesco del Giudice 13, is just around the corner. Take the first right after the Soggiorno Imperia and then the second left to the hotel. Very basic singles/doubles are L20,000/38,000, or L40,000 for a double with private shower.

Out of the Centre Take the metro from Stazione Centrale to Piazza Amedeo and then the Funicolare di Chiaia to Via Domenico Cimarosa. *Pensione Margherita* (☎ 556 70 44), Via D Cimarosa 29, is just near the funicular station. The hotel is more up-market and charges L40,000/72,000 for singles/doubles.

Places to Eat

Naples is the home of pasta and pizza. In fact, once you have eaten a good Neapolitan pizza, topped with fresh tomatoes, oregano, basil and garlic, no other pizza will taste the same. Try a *calzone*, filled with ricotta, prosciutto, mozzarella, egg and Parmesan, or *mozzarella in carozza*, which is mozzarella deep fried in bread. Another famous dish born in Naples is *parmigiana di melanzane*, eggplant (aubergine) layered with tomatoes and mozzarella. The Neapolitans love their dolci and are particularly famous for their mouthwatering *sfogliatelle*, light, flaky pastry filled with ricotta.

City Centre According to the locals the best pizza in Naples is served at *Trianon*, Via Pietro Colletta 46, near Via Tribunali. The pizzas here are fantastic and there is a wide selection, costing from L5000 to L10,000 for the top of the range. There is another Trianon at Via della Principessa Margherita 25-29.

Pizzeria Costa Gennaro, Via Capuana alla Maddalena 1, is near Piazza Capuana; take Via Mancini from Piazza Garibaldi and then turn right onto Via Capuana alla Maddalena. The pizzas are good here and very cheap at around L4000. Nearer the station is *Trattoria Avellinese*, Via Silvio Spaventa 31-35 (third street on the left off Piazza Garibaldi from the train station). It has tables outside and the food is good, particularly the seafood. A full meal will cost around L12,000. *La Campagnola*, Piazzetta Nilo 22 (near Via Benedetto Croce), is a great little trattoria serving traditional Neapolitan food. A full meal with wine could cost you not much more than L10,000. *Ristorante Bellini*, Via Santa Maria di Costantinapoli 79-80, has fantastic seafood. A full meal will cost around L25,000, but it is worth the splurge.

Around Mergellina Neapolitans head for the area around Piazza Sannazzaro, southwest of the centre, for a good meal. *Pizzeria da Pasqualino*, Piazza Sannazzaro 79, has outdoor tables and serves good pizzas and seafood. A meal will cost around L15,000 with wine. *L'Osteria*, Via Santa Maria in Portico 57, has excellent pasta and seafood dishes for under L10,000. A full meal will cost close to L20,000 with wine.

Entertainment

The monthly *Qui Napoli* and the weekly *Posto Unico* are the best guides to what's on in Naples and are available at the tourist office. In July there is a series of free concerts called Luglio Musicale a Capodimonte outside the Capodimonte Museum (in the Capodimonte district north of the centre). Religious festivals are lively occasions in Naples, especially that of San Gennaro, the patron saint of the city, which is held twice a year on the first Sunday in May and on 19 September.

Other important festivals are the Madonna del Carmine on 16 July and the Madonna di Piedigrotta in early September. Join the locals for the nightly passeggiata at the Villa Comunale.

Things to Buy

Naples is famous for its ceramic products and many small shops in the city and surrounding areas sell hand-painted ceramics at reasonable prices. The main shopping areas of central Naples are along Corso Umberto I and Via Roma. The streets east of Piazza dei Martiri, between Santa Lucia and Mergellina, have the best range of clothing and footwear shops. The narrow streets of Naples are full of markets, notably in the area off Via Mancini, off Piazza Garibaldi, and near Piazza Carità, which separates Via Roma and Via Toledo.

Getting There & Away

Air The Capodichino Airport (☎ 780 57 63), Viale Umberto Maddalena, is about half an hour north-east of the city. Take bus No 14 from the station. There are connections to most Italian and some European cities.

Bus Buses leave from Piazza Garibaldi, just outside the station, for Salerno, Benevento, Caserta and Avellino (Campania).

Train Naples is a major rail transport centre for the south, and regular trains for most major Italian cities arrive and depart from the stazione centrale in Piazza Garibaldi, including Rome (three hours), Reggio di Calabria (six hours), Syracuse (10 hours) and Milan (seven hours). The Ferrovia Circumvesuviana, the train line which runs from Naples to Sorrento, leaves for Pompeii and Sorrento from the station downstairs at the stazione centrale. Trains for the Phlegrean Fields (see the Around Campania section that follows) are operated by the Ferrovia Cumana and leave from the station (Stazione Cumana) in Piazza Montesanto.

Car & Motorbike Driving in Naples is not recommended. The traffic is chaotic and car and motorbike theft is rife. The city is easily accessible from Rome on the A2. The Naples-Pompeii-Salerno road connects with the coastal road to Sorrento and the Amalfi Coast.

Boat Traghetti (ferries) and aliscafi (hydrofoils) leave for Capri, Sorrento and Ischia from the Naples port of Molo Beverello, in front of the Castel Nuovo. Operators include Caremar and Libera Navigazione Lauro, and both have offices at the port. Ferries to Capri cost L7500 one-way whereas hydrofoils cost L13,400 one-way, but take only 45 minutes. A hydrofoil from Capri to Sorrento costs L7000 one-way. Services to the islands are regular and timetables are available at the ticket offices at the port. Ferries leave Naples for Sicily, Sardinia and Malta. The main operator is Tirrenia (☎ 551 21 81), at the stazione marittima (see the Getting There & Away sections under Sicily and Sardinia).

Getting Around

There are various ways to make your way around Naples, all of which can be unreliable. Buses leave from Piazza Garibaldi to the main parts of Naples and tickets for one trip cost L1000. A 24-hour ticket, with unlimited trips, costs L3000 and is a better deal.

The Metropolitana (underground) station is downstairs at stazione centrale. Trains head west to Vomero and Mergellina. Trams leave from Piazza Garibaldi for Molo Beverello and Mergellina, travelling along the bay. Funiculars connect the historical centre with Vomero; the main one is the Funicolare Centrale, next to Galleria Umberto I, on Via Toledo.

CAPRI

This beautiful island, an hour by ferry from Naples, retains the mythical appeal which attracted Roman emperors, including Augustus and Tiberius, who built 12 villas here. The town of Capri is packed with tourists in summer, but is more peaceful in the low season. A short bus ride will take you to Anacapri, the town uphill from Capri – a good alternative if rooms are full in Capri. The island is famous for its grottoes, but is also a good place for walking. There is a tourist office at Marina Grande, where all the ferries arrive, and another office in Piazza Umberto I, in the centre of Capri.

Things to See & Do

There are expensive boat tours of the grottoes, including the famous **Blue Grotto**. Boats leave from the Marina Grande and a round trip will cost L25,000. You can walk to most of the interesting points on the island (pick up a walking guide from the tourist office). Sights include the **Gardens of Augustus**, in the town of Capri, and **Villa Jovis**, the ruins of one of Tiberius' villas, along the Via Longano and Via Tiberio. The latter is a one-hour walk uphill from Capri.

Places to Stay & Eat

The *Villa Bianca* (☎ 081-837 80 16), Via Belvedere Cesina 9 in the town of Capri, is not cheap, but is still good value for the price. Some rooms have private terraces and views and cost L100,000/132,000/157,000 for a double/triple/quad (prices include breakfast). The hotel has kitchen facilities which you can use for the price of the gas used. You

will need to book three months in advance for summer. The *Stella Maris* (☎ 837 04 52), Via Roma 27, just off Piazza Umberto I, is cheaper, but right in the noisy heart of town. Singles/doubles are L40,000/75,000 and triples/quads are L90,000/120,000. Prices go down significantly in the off season. Bookings must be made well in advance for summer.

In Anacapri try the *Loreley* (☎ 837 14 40), Via G Orlandi, near the town centre. Singles/doubles are L30,000/60,000, but cost less in the off season.

Another option on the island is affittacamere. The tourist office has a full list, but you could try *Affittacamere d'Angelo* (☎ 837 81 13), Via Lo Palazzo 20, which has singles/doubles for L30,000/50,000.

The *Ristorante San Costanzo*, at Via Marucella 28, about halfway along the road from the Marina Grande to Capri, serves typical *cucina caprese*. A full meal with wine will cost around L25,000, but the food is great. In Anacapri try the *Trattoria il Solitario*, Via G Orlandi 54. It has delicious, cheap food in a beautiful setting. A full meal will cost around L15,000.

Getting There & Away

See the Getting There & Away section under Naples.

Getting Around

From Marina Grande, the funicular directly in front of the port takes you to the town of Capri, which is at the top of a steep hill, some six km from the port up a winding road.

Small local buses leave from the small piazza on Via Roma, just off Piazza Umberto I, for various points around the island, including Anacapri (L1500 for one trip).

SORRENTO

This major resort town is located in a particularly beautiful area, perched on tufa cliffs rising 50 metres above the sea. The town itself, however, is heavily overcrowded in summer with package tourists and traffic. The beaches are small and similarly overcrowded, but Sorrento is a good starting-off point for the Amalfi Coast.

Information & Orientation

The centre of town is Piazza Tasso, a short walk from the train station along Corso Italia. The ASST tourist office (☎ 081-878 22 29) is at Via Luigi de Maio 35, off Piazza Sant'Antonino towards the sea from Piazza Tasso. The staff are helpful and will provide a hotel list and information on buses and hydrofoils. Pick up a copy of the free monthly tourist magazine *Surrentum* for information on local events. The office will also provide information about where to rent a moped or scooter, but you could try Thomas Rent a Car & Scooter (☎ 878 58 61), Piazza Sant'Antonino 4. It has scooters for L35,000 a day or L210,000 a week.

The SIP telephone office is at Piazza Tasso 37 and numerous public telephones are scattered throughout the town. The telephone code is 081 and the postcode is 80067.

Places to Stay

Accommodation prices have increased in Sorrento, along with the rest of Italy, but its saving grace is the IYHF *Ostello Surriento* (☎ 878 17 83), Via Capasso 5, off Corso Italia near the train station. Bed and breakfast is L15,000 and meals are L12,000. It is open from 1 March to 30 November.

There are several camp sites, including *Villaggio Verde* (☎ 807 3258), Via Cesarao 12, off Via degli Aranci, about 10 minutes from the centre, away from the sea. It costs L8500 per person and L8500 for a tent.

At Corso Italia 134 is *Hotel City* (☎ 877 22 10) with doubles for L56,000. *Hotel Elios* (☎ 878 18 12), Via Capo 33, has doubles for L55,000, or L64,000 with private bathroom. It is in the hills above the town and accessible by the SITA bus which leaves from Piazza Tasso for Sant'Agata.

Places to Eat

For a meal try *Le Macine*, Via Atigliana 6, or *Sant'Antonino*, Via Santa Maria delle Grazie 6, both of which are pizzerias with full menus. A meal at both ranges from about

L12,000 for a pizza and wine to L25,000 for a full meal. *Taverna del Curato*, Via Casarlano 10, is in the hills above Sorrento at Casarlano. It is a good 40-minute walk along Via Atigliano. In Via San Cesareo, off Piazza Tasso, there are several alimentari where you can buy food for picnics.

Getting There & Away

Sorrento is easily accessible from Naples on the Circumvesuviana train line. Hourly SITA buses leave from outside the train station for the Amalfi Coast (L3200 for Amalfi). Hydrofoils and ferries leave from the port, along Via de Maio and down the steps from the tourist office, for Capri and Ischia.

If you are driving to Sorrento, be warned about the heavy traffic along the coast in both directions. It is extremely heavy in summer. If you are heading for the Amalfi Coast, avoid the coastal road through Sant'Agnello and take Via Sant'Agata through the hills and the town of Sant'Agata. It eventually reconnects with the road to Positano.

AMALFI COAST

The Amalfi coast swarms with rich tourists in summer and prices are correspondingly high. However, it remains a place of rare and spectacular beauty and if you can manage to get there in spring or autumn, you will be surprised by the reasonably priced accommodation and peaceful atmosphere.

The EPT office (☎ 089-22 43 22) in Salerno, Via Velia 15, has information on the coast, and there are tourist offices in the individual towns, including at Positano (☎ 089-87 50 67), Via Saracino 2, and Amalfi (☎ 089-87 11 07), Corso Roma 19.

The telephone code for the area is 089.

Positano

This is the most beautiful town on the coast, but for exactly this reason it has also become the most fashionable. It is, however, still possible to stay here cheaply.

Villa Nettuno (☎ 87 54 01), Via Pasitea 208, has doubles for L60,000 to L80,000 in the high season, all with private bath, though prices vary according to the length of stay.

ITALY

Half of the rooms are new and have small balconies overlooking the sea. The older rooms are cheaper and open onto a large terrace. Book well in advance for summer.

Villa Maria Luisa (☎ 87 50 23) at Via Fornillo 40 has rooms with terraces for L27,000 per person in the low season. Half-pension (L55,000 per person) is obligatory in the high season. The *Villa delle Palme* (☎ 87 51 62), around the corner in Via Pasitea, is run by the same management and has the same prices. Next door is the pizzeria *Il Saraceno d'Oro*, Via Pasitea 254. The pizzas are fantastic and cost around L6000. A full menu is also available.

Around Positano

The hills behind Positano offer some great walks if you tire of lazing on the beach. The tourist office at Positano has a brochure listing four routes, ranging in length from two to four hours. Once up in the hills, you have spectacular views of the coast. Visit **Nocelle**, a tiny, isolated village above Positano. The only access to the village until 1992 was by a walking track, though a road connection was due for completion by the end of the year. Fortunately, the road will end some 500 metres from the village. Have lunch at *Trattoria Santa Croce* (☎ 87 53 19), which has a terrace with panoramic views. It is open for both lunch and dinner in summer, but at other times of the year it is best to telephone and check in advance. Nocelle is accessible by local bus from Positano, via Montepertuso; buses run roughly every half-hour in summer from 7.50 am to midnight.

On the way from Positano to Amalfi is the town of **Praiano**, which is not as scenic but has more budget options, including the only camping ground on the Amalfi Coast. The *Pensione Aquila* (☎ 87 40 65) at Via degli Ulivi 15 charges L50,000 a double with breakfast, L60,000 with dinner and L80,000 in August. Signs from the coastal road make it easy to find. Farther along the coastal road, but still in Praiano, is *La Tranquillità* (☎ 87 40 84), which has a pensione, bungalows and a small camping ground. It costs L10,000 per head to camp there if you have

your own tent. For a double room or bungalow it is L60,000 (with breakfast) and in June there is compulsory half-pension at L55,000 a head, including room, private bathroom, breakfast and dinner. The SITA bus stops outside the pensione. The entire establishment closes down in winter, reopening at Easter.

Also of interest are the two villages of **Furore**, both accessible by the SITA bus. One is a tiny fishing village and the other, slightly closer to Amalfi, is set in a gorge and is an abandoned fishing village occupied only in summer. It is fascinating to explore this tiny semiabandoned village with its pathway along the clifftop and wander the nearby cliffs overlooking the sea. The fishing village of Furore, which is on the way back to Positano, offers *La Conchiglia*, which is a pension (with double rooms for L50,000) and restaurant. A full meal, on a terrace by the sea, costs around L15,000.

Amalfi

One of the four powerful maritime republics of medieval Italy, Amalfi today is a major tourist resort. Despite this, it manages to retain a tranquil atmosphere. It has an impressive **Duomo**, and nearby is the **Grotto Smeraldo**, which rivals Capri's Blue Grotto.

In the hills behind Amalfi is **Ravello**, accessible by bus and worth a visit if only to see the magnificent 11th century **Villa Rufolo**, once the home of popes and, later, of the German composer Wagner. The **Villa Cibrone**, built in this century, is set in beautiful gardens, which end at a terrace offering a spectacular view of the Gulf of Salerno.

Places to Stay & Eat For a room in Amalfi, try the *Hotel Vittoria* (☎ 87 10 57), Salita Truglio 5, where singles cost L45,000 in the high season and L38,000 in the low season.

The *Hotel Lidomare* (☎ 87 13 32) is at Via Piccolomini 9 (follow the signs from Piazza del Duomo and go left up a flight of stairs). It has doubles for L55,000 in the low season and in summer charges half-pension at L70,000 per person.

Cheaper accommodation can be found at

Atrani, just around the corner from Amalfi towards Salerno, at *A Scalinetta* (☎ 87 14 92), just off Piazza Umberto. It has beds in dorms for two, four and six people for L15,000 per person.

In Amalfi, *Trattoria Pizzeria al Teatro*, Via Mara Francesca Panza 19 (follow the signs to the left from Via Pietro Capuana, the main shopping street of Piazza del Duomo), offers good food in very pleasant surroundings. A pizza costs between L4000 and L7000, pasta costs up to L7000 and fish up to L15,000. *Trattoria da Maria*, Via Genova 14, is good value, with main courses around L8000 to L10,000.

Getting There & Away The coast is accessible by regular SITA buses, which run between Salerno (a 40-minute train trip from Naples) and Sorrento (accessible from Naples on the Circumvesuviana train line). A ticket from Sorrento to Amalfi will cost L3200. Buses stop in Amalfi at Piazza Flavio Gioia, from where you can catch a bus to Ravello. In the same piazza there is a supervised car park, which costs L1000 an hour.

Boat Hydrofoils also service the coast, leaving from Salerno and stopping at Amalfi and Positano. From Positano you can catch a hydrofoil to Capri (L9500 one-way), which leaves at 8.50 am and returns at 4.50 pm.

Car The coastal road is narrow and in summer it is clogged with traffic, so be prepared for long delays. At other times of the year, you should have no problems.

POMPEII & HERCULANEUM

Buried under ash and mud during the devastating eruption of Mt Vesuvius in 79 AD, Pompeii provides a fascinating insight into how the ancient Romans lived. It was a resort town for wealthy Romans, and among the vast ruins are impressive temples, a forum, one of the largest known Roman amphitheatres, and streets lined with shops and luxurious houses, some with frescoes and mosaics.

Most of the houses and shops are locked and you will need to ask one of the ubiquitous guides to let you in. Single women might find that some guides are too willing to take you to the more secluded sights.

The AAST (☎ 081-850 72 55) is at Via Sacra 1, a short walk from the station, where you can pick up a brochure and a vague map of the major sights. The ruins are open from 9 am to one hour before sunset and admission is L10,000. There is no need to stay the night in Pompeii, but if you do, the tourist offices in both Naples and Pompeii have full lists of hotels and camping grounds.

Pompeii is easily accessible from Naples on the Circumvesuviana train. The Naples-Salerno train also stops there.

Herculaneum (Ercolano) is closer to Naples and is also a good point from which to visit Mt Vesuvius. Legend says the city was founded by Hercules. First Greek, then Roman, it was also destroyed by the 79 AD eruption, buried under mud and lava. Unlike Pompeii, most inhabitants of Herculaneum had enough warning and managed to escape. The ruins here are smaller and the buildings, particularly the private houses, are remarkably well preserved. Here you can see better examples of the frescoes, mosaics and furniture that used to decorate Roman houses.

Herculaneum is also accessible on the Circumvesuviana train from Naples. The ruins are open daily from 9 am to one hour before sunset (admission is L8000). Catch the bus from the station to Mt Vesuvius (L3000 return). You can climb to the top for L4000. It only takes 15 minutes from the car park, which costs L2000. You have to pay extra to see the crater.

AROUND CAMPANIA

From Naples it is only a short distance to the **Campi Flegrei** (Phlegraean Fields) of volcanic lakes and mudbaths, which inspired both Homer and Virgil in their writings. The Greek colony of Cuma, and Sophia Loren's home town, Pozzuoli, are in this area. South of Salerno is **Paestum**, with important Greek temples. Farther south again is the less known **Velia**, perhaps the more enjoyable to visit because it is not overrun by tourists.

966 Italy – Southern Italy

Campania is alive with myth and legend. Sirens supposedly used to lure sailors to their deaths off Sorrento. The islands in the Bay of Naples were the domain of mermaids, and Lake Avernus, in the Campi Flegrei, was believed in ancient times to be the entrance to the underworld.

MATERA

This ancient city in the region of Basilicata evokes powerful images of a peasant culture which existed until just over 30 years ago. Its famous **sassi** (stone houses), built in two ravines which slice through the city, were home to more than half of Matera's population until the 1950s, when the local government built a new residential area just out of Matera and relocated the entire population.

The tourist office, Via Viti de Marco 9, off Via Roma (which runs off Piazza V Veneto), will provide you with some information and can organise a professional tour guide (about L20,000 for an hour). An excellent book is *Sassi e Secoli* by R Giura Longo (available in English from the Libreria dell'Arco, Via Ridoli 36, near Sasso Caveoso).

Matera's telephone code is 0835.

Things to See

The two sassi wards, known as **Barisano** and **Caveoso**, had no electricity, running water or sewerage system until well into this century. The oldest sassi are at the top of the ravines, and the dwellings which appear to be the oldest were established in this century. As space ran out in the 1920s, the population started moving into hand-hewn or natural caves, an extraordinary example of civilisation in reverse.

The sassi zones are accessible from Piazza Vittorio Veneto and Piazza del Duomo, at the centre of Matera. Be sure to see the rock churches, **Santa Maria d'Idris** and **Santa Lucia alla Malve**, both with amazingly well-preserved Byzantine frescoes. The 13th century Apulian-Romanesque **cathedral**, overlooking Sasso Barisano, is also worth a visit. In Sasso Caveoso you will be mobbed by young children wanting to act as tour guides. They might be small, but they know their sassi, so pay them a few thousand lire and take up the offer, even if you can't speak Italian.

Some sassi are now being restored and young people have begun to move back into the area.

Places to Stay & Eat

There are not a lot of options for budget accommodation here. Try the *Roma* (☎ 33 39 12), Via Roma 62. Singles/doubles are L22,000/36,000 and a double with private bathroom is L40,000. The local fare is simple and the focus is on vegetables. *Da Aulo*, Via Anza di Lucana, is economical and serves typical cucina of Basilicata. *Trattoria Lucana*, Vico il Lucano, has a good selection of vegetables and the food is excellent, though a full meal will cost around L25,000. There is a fruit and vegetable market near Piazza V Veneto, between Via Lucana and Via A Persio.

Getting There & Away

It is not easy to get to Matera. SITA buses go there from Potenza, Bari and Metaponto (Basilicata), which is on the Taranto-Reggio di Calabria train line. Buses arrive in Piazza Matteotti, a short walk down Via Roma to the town centre. The city is also connected to Bari and Potenza by the private Ferrovia Calabro-Lucane train line. This service can be unreliable and slow. There is also a direct bus from Rome to Matera, which leaves from Piazza della Repubblica twice a day. Contact Marozzi Autolinea (☎ 06-474 28 01) in Rome.

APULIA

Good areas to explore in the region of Apulia (Puglia) are the Gargano Peninsula, for its mountains, and Salento, the area from Lecce to the tip of the heel, with its long beaches and picturesque coastal towns. Also visit Alberobello to see its *trulli*, which are white-washed, conical-shaped buildings, both ancient and modern.

Lecce

Baroque can be grotesque, but never in Lecce. The style here is so refined and particular to the city that the Italians call it *barocco leccese* (Lecce Baroque). A graceful and intellectual city, close to both the Adriatic and Ionian seas, it is a comfortable base from which to explore the region. Its numerous bars and restaurants are a pleasant surprise in such a small city.

There is an EPT office (☎ 0832-30 44 43) in Piazza Sant'Oronzo, the town's main piazza. Take bus No 4 from the station to the town centre.

Lecce's telephone code is 0832.

Things to See & Do The most famous example of Lecce Baroque is the **Basilica di Santa Croce**. Artists worked for 150 years to decorate the building, creating an extraordinarily ornate façade. In the **Piazza del Duomo** are the 12th century **cathedral** (which was completely restored in the Baroque style by the architect Giuseppe Zimbalo of Lecce), and its 70-metre-high **campanile**; the **Palazzo del Vescovo**; and the **Seminario**, with its elegant façade and Baroque well in the courtyard. In Piazza Sant'Oronzo are the remains of a **Roman amphitheatre**.

In summer there are numerous musical and cultural events, notably **Estate Musicale Leccese** in July and August and a series of classical music concerts in August and September. Theatre and music seasons are held throughout the year and information is available at the EPT office.

Places to Stay & Eat Cheap accommodation is not abundant in Lecce, but camping facilities abound in the province of Salento. Near Lecce is *Torre Rinalda* (☎ 65 21 61) at Marina Torre Rinalda in the zone of Litoranea. Tents cost L6700 and it costs L6000 per person per night. In town try *Hotel Cappello* (☎ 30 88 81) at Via Montegrappa 4, near the station. Singles/doubles cost L40,000/60,000 with bath.

Eating in this city is both inexpensive and a pleasure. *Perbacco*, Via delle Bombarde,

serves typical leccese food. A full meal could cost up to L30,000, but it is worth it. *Pizzeria Sonia*, Piazza G Congedo 6, has great pizzas for L5000 to L8000 and is a favourite with the locals. *Creperie*, Via Vittorio Emanuele, off Piazza di Sant'Oronzo, makes great crêpes to your specifications. It is also a popular bar.

Getting There & Away Lecce is directly linked by train to Bari, Brindisi, Rome, Naples and Bologna. The Ferrovie del Sud Est (South-East Railways) runs trains to surrounding areas and major points in Apulia. Intercity buses leave from Via Adua and Viale U Foscolo for towns and cities throughout the region.

Otranto

Without a car it is difficult to tour the picturesque Adriatic coast of Salento, which extends to Italy's southernmost point, the tip of the heel, at Capo Santa Maria di Leuca. However, Otranto is easy to reach by bus and on the Ferrovie del Sud Est.

The tourist office (☎ 0836-80 14 36) is at Lungomare Kennedy. Otranto's telephone code is 0836.

This port town of whitewashed buildings is unfortunately overrun by tourists in summer, but it is worth a visit if only to see the incredible **mosaic** that covers the floor of the Romanesque **cathedral**. The recently restored 12th century mosaic, depicting the tree of life, is a masterpiece unrivalled in southern Italy and is stunning in its simplicity.

The tiny Byzantine **Chiesa di San Pietro** contains some well-preserved Byzantine paintings.

Unfortunately, the town is not geared for budget tourism and has no one-star hotels. *Il Gabbiano* (☎ 0836-80 12 51), Via Porto Craulo 5, has singles/doubles with bath for L35,000/70,000.

Ferries leave from here for Corfu and Igoumenitsa (Greece). For information and reservations, go the stazione marittima at the port. There is a Marozzi bus which runs daily from Rome to Brindisi, Lecce and Otranto.

For information contact Eurojet (☎ 06-474 28 01), Piazza della Repubblica 54, Rome.

Brindisi

Most travellers associate Brindisi with waiting. As the major embarkation point for ferries from Italy to Greece, the city swarms with travellers in transit. There is not much to do here, other than wait, so most back-packers gather at the train station or at the port in the stazione marittima. The two are connected by Corso Umberto I, which becomes Corso Garibaldi, and they are a 10-minute walk from each other; otherwise, you can take bus No 6, 9 or 12.

The old city does offer some points of interest and it is worth taking a few hours out of your waiting time to see them. The EPT tourist information office (☎ 0831-52 19 44) is at Lungomare Regina Margherita 12. Another information office is inside the stazione marittima.

Brindisi's telephone code is 0831.

Things to See & Do From ancient Roman times Brindisi has been Italy's gateway to the east. It was from here that the Crusaders set off for the Holy Land. Tradition has it that Virgil died in a Roman house near the columns marking the end of the **Appian Way** on his return from Greece. In Piazza del Duomo is the 14th century **Palazzo Balsamo**, with a beautiful *loggetta* (small lodge). The town's main monument is **Santa Maria del Casale**, about two km from the centre. Built by Prince Philip of Taranto around 1300, it incorporates Gothic, Roman-esque and Byzantine styles.

Musical and cultural events are held in Brindisi throughout the year, including the **Estate Insieme** (literally, summer together) in July and August. Pick up a brochure from the tourist office if you are in town for any length of time.

Places to Stay & Eat The non-IYHF *ostello per la gioventù* (☎ 41 31 23), Via N Brandi 4, has beds for L11,000 a night. It is about two km out of the centre; take bus No 3 or 4. The *Hotel Venezia* (☎ 2 54 11), Via Pisanelli

4, has singles/doubles for L22,000/36,000. Turn left off Corso Umberto I onto Via S Lorenzo da Brindisi to get there.

If you're after a meal, avoid the tourist traps along the main route between the train and boat stations and head for the side streets. The *Osteria Cucina Casalinga*, Via Mazzini 57, near the station, has good-value meals for L10,000 to L12,000. There is a fruit and vegetable market in Via Battisti, off Corso Umberto I, open from 7 am to 1 pm daily except Sunday.

Getting There & Away Brindisi is directly connected by train to Bologna, and thus to the major cities of the north. It is also easily accessible by train from Rome and Naples. A daily bus runs between Rome and Brindisi. It is operated by Marozzi, which has offices in Piazza Cairoli in Brindisi, and in Rome (☎ 06-474 28 01).

Ferry Ferries depart from Brindisi for Corfu, Igoumenitsa, Patras and Cephalonia in Greece. The major companies operating ferries from Brindisi are: Adriatica (☎ 52 38 25), Viale Regina Margherita 13 (open from 9 am to 1 pm, 4 to 7 pm) and on the 1st floor of the stazione marittima, where you must go to check in; Hellenic Mediterranean Lines (☎ 52 85 31), Corso Garibaldi 8; Fragline (☎ 2 95 61), Corso Garibaldi 88; and Mar-lines (☎ 2 76 84), c/o Il Globo, Corso Garibaldi 97.

Adriatica and Hellenic are the most expensive, but also the most reliable. They are the only lines which can officially accept Eurail passes, which means you travel free but must pay a L25,000 supplement. If you want to use your Eurail pass, it is important to reserve some weeks in advance, particu-larly in summer. Even with a booking in summer, you must still go to the Adriatic or Hellenic embarkation office in the stazione marittima to have your ticket checked. Do not be fooled by the claims of other compa-nies that they accept Eurail passes, or you could find yourself without a booking.

There are numerous other lines, but as the companies regularly change hands and names, it is best to arrive in Brindisi and shop around if you are looking for a cheaper fare.

Discounts are available for travellers under 26 years of age and some companies offer discounts to Inter-Rail pass holders. Note that fares increase by up to 50% in July and August. Ferry services are also increased during this period. Average prices in the 1992 high season for deck class were: Adriatica and Hellenic to Corfu/Igoumenitsa L105,000; Marlines for the same destination L85,000, and L90,000 to Patras (this company offers a 10% discount to students); and Fragline to Corfu/Igoumenitsa L60,000, and L105,000 to Patras.

In cooler weather, deck class can be unpleasant. Prices go up by an average L10,000 for a poltrona (airline-type chair), and for the cheapest cabin accommodation prices jump by L30,000 to L40,000. Bicycles can be taken aboard for free, but the average fare for a motorbike is L45,000 to L60,000 in the high season. Fares for cars are L90,000 in the high season.

CALABRIA

Much of Calabria is still to be discovered by travellers, even though the region's beaches have become popular destinations. Tourist development has begun along the region's Ionian and Tyrrhenian coastlines, but in most areas it is minimal compared to Italy's more touristy regions. The beaches are also among the country's least polluted. This is an area with many small villages in picturesque settings where the pace of life is slow and where things have remained largely unchanged over the years. Market days are still an important local feature and this is when you will find most activity in the villages and towns.

Although the fierce feuding of the 'Ndrangheta, Calabria's version of the Sicilian Mafia, continues to cause havoc and atrocious deaths, tourists travelling in the region should not be concerned.

The Italian government's Southern Italy Development Fund, established in 1950 to invest money in the southern regions and in Sicily and Sardinia (for irrigation, road construction and industrial development), has basically succeeded in dragging the region into the 20th century, but many Calabrians, particularly those in more remote areas, still live in extreme poverty. Despite this, the locals are very hospitable. Few of them, however, speak English and you are more likely to be well received if you at least make an attempt to speak Italian.

The old town of **Catanzaro**, the region's capital, is strikingly set high on a hilltop overlooking the Ionian Sea. Calabria's **riviera**, along the Ionian coast, is overdeveloped and pockmarked with heavy industry, but remains popular among Germans and Italians. **Tropea**, to the north of the region on the Tyrrhenian Sea, was an isolated paradise only a decade ago. Today it too has been affected by tourist development, but is still worth a visit.

If adventure appeals, Calabria's **Sila Massif** is the place to visit. This beautiful wilderness area remains on the verge of major development and incorporates a major national park. The Sila is divided into three areas: the **La Greca**, **La Grande** and **La Piccola**. The best point to start exploring the Sila Massif is **Cosenza**, accessible by train from Paola on the Rome-Reggio di Calabria railway line on the coast. From Cosenza catch a bus to **Camigliatello Silano**, where you can obtain trekking and tourist information from the Pro Loco (☎ 0984-97 80 91), Via del Turismo. Opening hours are extremely irregular.

Reggio di Calabria

The port city of Reggio di Calabria on the Strait of Messina is the capital of the province of Reggio di Calabria and was, until 1971, the capital of the region of Calabria. Founded in approximately 720 BC by Greek colonists, this city was destroyed by an earthquake in 1908, which also razed Messina, and was totally rebuilt. There is a tourist information booth at the station, where you can pick up a map and a list of hotels. The main EPT office is at Via Garibaldi 329, but it has virtually no useful information. Reggio's telephone code is 0965.

Things to See The **lungomare**, the promenade along the port, overlooks Sicily, and in certain atmospheric conditions, such as at dawn, it is possible to see the fabled **mirage of Morgana**, the reflection of Messina in the sea. Reggio's only really impressive sight is the **Museo Nazionale** (National Museum), which houses a remarkable collection documenting Greek civilisation in Calabria. Of particular interest are the **Bronzi di Riace** (Bronze Warriors of Riace), two Greek statues found off the coast of Riace in the Ionian Sea in 1972.

Places to Stay & Eat It is expensive to stay in Reggio and the only decent budget option is the IYHF *Ostello Principessa Paola di Belgio* (☎ 75 40 33), Via Nazionale, in nearby Scilla (about 45 minutes from Reggio by train). If you are coming from Rome, check if your train stops there. The hostel is in a castle overlooking the sea. Bed and breakfast is L13,000 and use of hot water is L1000. The hostel is open only from April to September.

In Reggio try *Albergo San Giorgio* (☎ 9 94 64), Via Gaeta 9, just off Corso Garibaldi to the right of the railway station. Doubles/triples are L50,000/90,000.

There are numerous alimentari along Corso Garibaldi, where you can buy cheese, bread and wine. For a cheap stand-up meal, head for *Cordon Bleu*, Corso Garibaldi 207. *La Pignata*, Via D Tripepi 122, is off Corso Garibaldi. Good pizzas cost around L5000 and a full meal will come to under L15,000.

Getting There & Away Reggio is directly connected by regular trains to Naples and Rome, and also to Metaponto, Taranto and Bari (Apulia). Its two stations are the Lido, at the port, and Centrale, in the town centre at Piazza Garibaldi.

Ferries leave the port of Reggio for Sicily, the Aeolian Islands and Malta, and there are also hydrofoil services to Messina, Milazzo (north-west of Messina) and the Aeolian Islands. It is easier, particularly if you arrive from the north by train, to depart from Villa San Giovanni, 15 minutes north of Reggio

by train. The main lines servicing the route are Tirrenia, FS and Siremar (for hydrofoils) and all have offices in Reggio. You can stay on your train (which is usually taken aboard the ferry), but the trip is short and it is more pleasant to sit on the boat deck. A ticket from Reggio to Messina costs L4000.

Sicily

Think about Sicily (Sicilia) and two things immediately come to mind – beaches and the Mafia. While its beaches are beautiful and the Mafia still manages to assert a powerful influence on the Sicilian economy and way of life, Sicily is remarkably diverse.

The largest island in the Mediterranean, its strategic location made it a prize for successive waves of invaders and colonisers so that it is now a place of Greek temples, Norman castles, Arab and Byzantine domes and Baroque churches. Its landscape ranges from the fertile coast to the mountains of the north and the vast, dry plateau of its centre.

Sicily has a population of about five million. Long neglected by the Italian government after unification, it became a semiautonomous region in 1948, remaining under the control of the central Italian government but with greater powers to legislate on regional matters. Although industry has developed on the island, its economy is still largely based on agriculture and its people remain strongly connected to the land.

Its temperate climate means mild weather in winter. Summers are relentlessly hot and the beaches swarm with holidaying Italians and Europeans. The best times to visit are in spring and autumn, when it is hot enough for the beach, but not too hot for sightseeing.

Sicilian food is hotter, spicier and sweeter than in other parts of Italy. The focus is on seafood, notably swordfish along the coast, and fresh produce. Some say that fruit and vegetables taste better in Sicily. Their dolci can be works of art but are very sweet. Try the *cassata*, both a ricotta cake (traditionally available only in winter) and a rich ice cream with almonds, and the *cannoli*, tubes of pastry filled with cream, ricotta or chocolate.

As mentioned, the Mafia remains a powerful force in Sicily, its main power bases being in Catania, Palermo and the villages of the western hills. The Italian author Luigi Barzini wrote in his novel *The Italians*: 'The phenomenon has deep roots in history, in the character of the Sicilians, in local habits. Its origins disappear down the dim vistas of the centuries.' Mid-1992 saw the assassination by the Mafia of two prominent anti-Mafia judges – Giovanni Falcone and Paolo Borsellino. Falcone died in an explosion on an autostrada outside Palermo together with his wife and three bodyguards, and Borsellino was killed in a car bomb explosion that also killed five police bodyguards and injured 20 others. You are unlikely to be caught in the crossfire of a gang war while in Sicily, but don't expect to be able to have a long discussion about the Mafia phenomenon with a local. On the whole, however, Sicilian people are welcoming and friendly. Female tourists, in fact, might find the local men a little too friendly.

The tourist body responsible for all of Sicily is the Assessorato Regionale del Turismo, delle Comunicazione e dei Trasporti (☎ 091-696 11 11), Via Notarbartolo 11, Palermo.

Getting There & Away

Air There are flights from all major cities in Italy to Palermo and Catania. The two airports are also serviced by flights from major European cities. The easiest way to obtain information is from any CIT or Alitalia office throughout Italy.

Bus & Train Direct bus services from Rome to Sicily are operated by two companies – SAIS and Segesta. In Rome the buses leave from Viale Einaudi, just off Piazza della Repubblica and timetables and tickets are available at Bar Piccarozzi, Piazza della Repubblica 62 (☎ 06-488 59 24). The SAIS bus runs to Agrigento, Catania and Syracuse, with connections to Palermo. A one-way ticket costs L68,000. It leaves daily at 8 pm.

The Segesta bus runs directly to Palermo, leaving Rome at 7.45 am Tuesday, Thursday and Saturday. Tickets cost L65,000.

One of the cheapest ways to reach Sicily is to catch a train to Messina. The cost of the ticket covers the ferry crossing to Messina. Direct trains run from Milan, Florence, Rome, Naples and Reggio di Calabria.

Boat Sicily is accessible by ferry from Genoa, Livorno, Naples, Reggio di Calabria and Cagliari, and also from Malta and Tunisia. The main company servicing the Mediterranean is Tirrenia. Prices are determined by the season and jump considerably in the summer period (Tirrenia's high season varies according to your destination, but is usually from July to September). Timetables change completely each year and it is best to pick up the annual booklet listing all routes and prices at any Tirrenia office.

High-season prices in 1992 for a poltrona were: Genoa-Palermo L102,200 (22 hours); Naples-Palermo L61,900 (10½ hours); Palermo-Cagliari L44,300 (14 hours); Catania-Malta L81,000 (nine hours); and Trapani-Tunisia L84,700 (eight hours). Other main lines servicing the island are Grandi Traghetti for Livorno-Palermo and Gozo Channel for Sicily-Malta. For information on ferries going from the mainland directly to Lipari, see the Getting There & Away section under Aeolian Islands.

Getting Around

Bus is the best mode of public transport in Sicily. Numerous companies run services between Syracuse, Catania and Palermo as well as to Agrigento and towns in the interior. See the Getting Around section under each town for more details. The coastal train service between Messina and Palermo and Messina down to Syracuse is efficient and reliable. However, trains into the interior, especially to Agrigento on the south-western coast, are notoriously slow.

Probably the best way to enjoy Sicily is by car. Some of the autostrade are free of toll charges and roads in the interior are mostly good. It is possible to hitchhike in Sicily, but don't expect a ride in a hurry. Women should not hitchhike alone under any circumstances.

PALERMO
An Arab emirate and later the seat of a Norman kingdom, Palermo was once regarded as the grandest and most beautiful city in Europe. Today it is in a remarkable state of decay, through neglect and heavy bombing during WW II, yet enough evidence remains of its golden days to make Palermo one of the most impressive cities in Italy.

Orientation & Information
Palermo is a large but easily manageable city. The main streets of the historical centre are Via Roma and Via Maqueda, which extend from the stazione centrale to Piazza Castelnuovo, a vast square in the modern part of town.

Tourist Offices The main EPT office (open from 8 am to 8 pm Monday to Saturday and from 8 am to 2 pm Sunday) is at Piazza Castelnuovo 35. The staff speak English. Pick up the monthly calendar of cultural, theatrical and musical events while you're

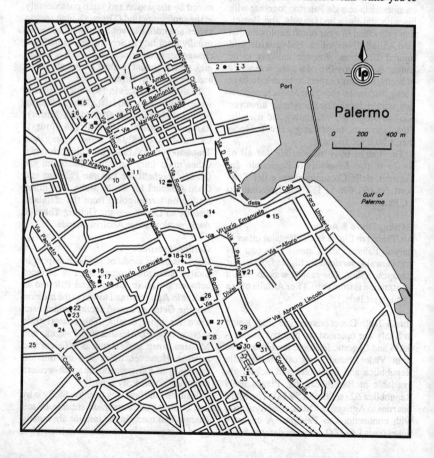

there. There are branch offices at the railway station (open from 8 am to 6.30 pm daily), the stazione marittima at the port and in Piazza San Sepolcro, off Via Maqueda (both open from 8 am to 2 pm Monday to Saturday).

Money There is an exchange office at the stazione centrale, open daily from 7.30 am to 12.30 pm and 2.30 to 8 pm.

■   PLACES TO STAY

5   Hotel Castelnuovo
8   Hotel Petit
9   Hotel Liguria
26 Hotel Sicilia
27 Albergo Rosalia Conca d'Oro
28 Albergo Orientale

▼   PLACES TO EAT

4   Osteria Lo Bianco
21 Trattoria Stella

OTHER

1   Piazza Don Sturzo
2   Port & Ferry Terminal
3   EPT Information Office
6   Main EPT Office
7   Piazza Castelnuovo
10 Teatro Massimo
11 Piazza G Verdi
12 Main Post Office
13 Piazza San Domenico
14 Vucciria Markets
15 Piazza Marina
16 Piazza Pretoria
17 Cathedral
18 Quattro Canti
19 Chiesa di Santa Caterina
20 Piazza Bellini & La Martorana
22 Police Office for Foreigners
23 Piazza della Vittoria
24 Palazzo dei Normanni
25 Piazza Indipendenza
29 ASST Telephones
30 Urban Bus Terminal & Piazza G Cesare
31 Intercity Bus Terminal
32 Central Railway Station
33 EPT Tourist Information

Post & Telecommunications The main post office is at Via Roma 322 and the main ASST telephone office is opposite the station in Piazza G Cesare, open 24 hours a day. The postcode for Palermo is 90100 and the telephone code is 091.

Emergency Call the police on ☎ 113. The police office for foreigners is in Piazza della Vittoria, open only from 8.30 am to 12.30 pm (☎ 651 43 30). For an ambulance call ☎ 30 66 44 or the Guardie Mediche Turistiche on ☎ 53 27 98. There is an all-night pharmacy called Lo Cascio near the train station at Via Roma 1.

Dangers & Annoyances Petty crime is rife in Palermo and highly deft pickpockets and motorcycle bandits prey on tourists. Avoid wearing jewellery or carrying a bag and keep all your valuables in a money belt. Single women should note that it is unsafe to wander through the streets of the historical centre at night, even in the busy Via Roma or Via Maqueda.

Things to See
The intersection of Via Vittorio Emanuele and Via Maqueda marks the **Quattro Canti** (four corners of Palermo). The four 17th century Spanish Baroque façades are each decorated with a statue. Nearby is **Piazza Pretoria**, with a beautiful fountain (Fontana Pretoria), created by Florentine sculptors in the 16th century. Locals used to call it the Fountain of Shame because of its nude figures. Also in the piazza are the Baroque **Chiesa di Santa Caterina** and the **Palazzo del Municipio** (town hall). Just off the piazza is Piazza Bellini and Palermo's most famous church, **La Martorana**, its interior decorated with Byzantine mosaics.

The huge Norman **cathedral** is along Via Vittorio Emanuele, on the corner of Via Bonello. Although modified many times over the centuries, it remains an impressive example of Norman architecture. Opposite Piazza della Vittoria and the gardens is the **Palazzo Reale**, also known as the **Palazzo dei Normanni**, now the seat of the government. Enter from Piazza Indipendenza to see the **Palatine Chapel**, a magnificent example of Arab-Norman architecture, built during the reign of Roger II and decorated with Byzantine mosaics. The **Sala di Ruggero** (King Roger's former bedroom), is decorated with 12th century mosaics. It is only possible to visit the room with a guide (free of charge). Go upstairs from the Palatine Chapel.

Among the strangest sights in Palermo are the **Capuchin Catacombs** in the Convento dei Cappuccini (east of the centre), which contain some 8000 bodies, lined along the walls in various attitudes.

Take bus No 9 from under the trees across the piazza from the train station to the nearby town of **Monreale** to see the mosaics in the famous 12th century cathedral of **Santa Maria la Nuova**.

Places to Stay

The best camping ground is *Trinacria* (☎ 53 05 90), Via Barcarello 25, at Sferracavallo by the sea. It costs L7500 per person, including the cost of a tent. Catch bus No 34 from the Teatro Massimo on Via Maqueda and ask the driver where to get off.

Palermo has numerous budget pensioni and you will have little trouble finding a room. The tourist office at the station will make recommendations, but will not make bookings. Head for Via Maqueda or Via Roma for basic, cheap rooms, some of which are in old palaces. The area around Piazza Castelnuovo offers a higher standard of accommodation, but these places are also more expensive. Catch bus No 7 from the station to Piazza Sturzo.

Near the train station try *Albergo Orientale* (☎ 616 57 27), Via Maqueda 26, in an old and somewhat decayed palace. Singles/doubles are L25,000/40,000 and triples are L60,000. Just around the corner is *Albergo Rosalia Conca d'Oro* (☎ 616 45 43), Via Santa Rosalia 7, with singles/doubles for L22,000/35,000 and triples for L48,000. The *Hotel Sicilia* (☎ 616 84 60), Via Divisi 99, on the corner of Via Maqueda, has rooms of a higher standard and car-parking facilities.

Doubles are L55,000 and triples are L75,000 with private shower.

Near Piazza Castelnuovo is the *Hotel Petit* (☎ 32 36 16), Via Principe di Belmonte 84, with clean and comfortable singles/doubles for L33,000/43,000 with private shower. A single without shower is L25,000. *Hotel Castelnuovo* (☎ 33 40 72), Piazza Castelnuovo 50, has singles/doubles for the same price. The *Hotel Liguria* (☎ 58 15 88), Via Mariano Stabile 128, has better rooms and charges L30,000/45,000 for singles/doubles, or L58,000 for doubles with private bathroom.

Places to Eat

Palermo's cucina takes advantage of the fresh produce of the sea and the fertile Conca d'Oro Valley. One of its most famous dishes is *pasta con le sarde*, pasta with sardines, fennel, peppers, capers and pine nuts. Swordfish is served here sliced into huge steaks. If you can stomach it, head for *Pani Cà Meusa*, at Porta Carbone on the waterfront, to try *panini con milza* (panini with veal innards).

The **Vucciria**, Palermo's famous open-air markets, are held daily (except Sunday) in the narrow streets between Via Roma, Piazza San Domenico and Via Vittorio Emanuele. Here you can buy fresh fruit and vegetables, meat, cheese, seafood and virtually anything else you want.

The Palermitani are late eaters and restaurants rarely open for dinner before 8 pm. *Osteria Lo Bianco*, Via E Amari, off Via Roma at the Castelnuovo end of town, has a menu which changes daily. A full meal will cost around L15,000. *Trattoria Stella*, Via Alloro 104, is in the courtyard of the old Hotel Patria. A full meal will come to around L17,000. *Trattoria dei Vespri*, Piazza Santa Croce dei Vespri, off Via Roma, past the church of St Anna, has outdoor tables and great food. It costs around L15,000 for a full meal.

Getting There & Away

Air The airport is at Punta Raisi, about 30 km west of Palermo, and serves as a terminal for domestic and European flights. Taxis to the airport cost around L50,000. The cheaper option is to catch one of the regular blue buses which leave every 40 minutes from outside the station from 5.25 am to 10 pm (L2500).

Bus The main (intercity) terminal for Agrigento, Catania and Syracuse is in the area around Via Balsamo, to the right as you leave the station. Offices for the various companies are all in this area. SAIS, Via Balsamo 16, runs a daily bus to Rome (L65,000).

Train Regular trains leave from the stazione centrale for Milazzo, Messina, Catania and Syracuse, as well as for nearby towns such as Cefalù. Trains also go to Reggio di Calabria, Naples and Rome.

Ferry Boats leave from the port (Molo Vittorio Veneto) for Sardinia, Naples, Livorno and Genoa (see the Getting There & Away section under Sicily). The Tirrenia office (☎ 602 11 11) is at the port.

Getting Around
Palermo's buses are efficient and most stop outside the train station. Useful numbers to remember are the No 7 along Via Roma from the train station to near Piazza Castelnuovo and the No 39 from the station to the port. You must buy tickets before you get on the bus; they cost L800 for one journey or L2000 for one day.

CEFALÙ
Just over an hour by train from Palermo, Cefalù has one of the most attractive beaches in Sicily and is fast becoming a major tourist destination, though to date it remains unspoiled by development.

The AAST tourist office is at Corso Ruggero 77, the continuation of Via Matteotti. From the train station turn right into Via Moro to reach Via Matteotti and the old town. If you are heading for the beach, turn left and walk along Via Gramsci, which becomes Via V Martoglio.

Cefalù's telephone code is 0921.

Things to See
Visit the Norman **cathedral**, built by Roger II in the 12th century to fulfil a vow to God after his fleet was saved during a violent storm off Cefalù. Inside are interesting Byzantine mosaics. From the old town's main street, Via Matteotti, look for the sign pointing uphill to the **Temple of Diana**; the one-hour climb to the castle is also worthwhile.

Places to Stay & Eat
There are several camping grounds in the area, including *Costa Ponente Internazionale* (☎ 2 00 85), about three km west at Contrada Ogliastrillo. Catch the bus from the station heading for Lasari. It costs L7000 per person and L6500 for a tent. In town you can stay at *Locanda Cangelosi* (☎ 2 15 91), Via Umberto 1, which charges L20,000/30,000 doubles/triples.

Trattoria La Botte, Via Veterani 6, just off Corso Ruggero, serves full meals for around L15,000.

AEOLIAN ISLANDS
The seven islands of this archipelago just north of Milazzo offer great variety and include the well-developed tourist resorts of Lipari and Panarea, the rugged Vulcano, the spectacular scenery of Stromboli and its fiercely active volcano, and the solitude of Alicudi, Filicudi and Salina, which remain relatively undeveloped.

The Aeolian Islands (Isole Eolie) have been inhabited since the Neolithic era, when migrants sought the valuable volcanic glass, obsidian. They are so named because the ancient Greeks believed they were the home of Aeolus, the god of wind. Homer wrote of the islands in the *Odyssey*. They are well known for their rugged coastlines, violent seas, rich colours and volcanic activity.

The main AAST tourist information office (☎ 090-988 00 95) for the islands is on Lipari at Corso Vittorio Emanuele 233. Offices open on Stromboli, Vulcano and

Salina during summer. The telephone code for the islands is 090.

Things to See & Do

On **Lipari** visit the **castello**, with its archaeological park and museum. You can also go on excellent walks on the island. Catch a local bus from the town of Lipari to the hilltop village of **Quattrocchi** for a great view of Vulcano. Boat trips will take you around the island – contact the tourist office for information.

Vulcano, a strange, desolate place, is a short boat trip from Lipari's port. The main volcano (Vulcano Fossa) is still active (though the last recorded period of eruption was from 1888 to 1890) and, though you can do the one-hour hike to the crater, be extremely careful of sudden bursts of sulphurous gas and landslides. In medieval times the crater was believed to be the gateway to hell.

Stromboli is the most spectacular of the islands. Its volcano is the most active in Europe – climb Stromboli at night to see the **Sciara del Fuoco**, lava streaming down the side of the volcano, and the volcanic explosions from the crater. Many people make the trip without a guide, but if you decide to do this, do so with care. Remember to take warm clothes, wear heavy shoes and carry a torch and plenty of water. (Boats leave Lipari every morning for L21,000 return).

Places to Stay & Eat

Lipari provides the best options for a comfortable stay. It has numerous budget hotels, affittacamere and apartments, and the other islands are easily accessible by regular hydrofoils. Even in peak season the tourist office will billet homeless new arrivals in private homes throughout the island. When you arrive on Lipari you are likely to be approached by someone offering accommodation. This is worth checking because the offers are usually genuine.

The island's camping ground, *Baia Unci* (☎ 981 19 09), is at Canneto, about two km out of the Lipari township. It costs L4500 a night and L3600 for a tent. The IYHF *youth hostel* (☎ 981 15 40), Via Castello 17, is inside the walls of the castle. Bed and breakfast costs L13,000 a night, plus L1000 for hot water. A meal costs L12,000 and there are kitchen facilities. *Cassarà Vittorio* (☎ 981 15 23), Vico Sparviero 15, is excellent value at L15,000 per person in the low season and L30,000 in the high season (July to October). There are two terraces with views, and use of the kitchen is L2000. The owner can be found (unless he finds you first) at Via Garibaldi 78, on the way from the port to the centre.

You can eat surprisingly cheaply on Lipari. The best pizzas are at *Zum Willi*, on the corner of Via Vittorio Emanuele and Corso Umberto I, for around L5000. *Al Pescatore*, Via Vittorio Emanuele 214, is a local institution. The food is OK, but the company is great. For an excellent meal eat at *Trattoria d'Oro*, Corso Umberto I. A full meal will come to around L18,000.

Panarea is a beautiful but overdeveloped haunt of the jet set. If you want seclusion, head for Filicudi or Alicudi. Each, however, has only one budget hotel: the *Ericus* (☎ 988 99 02) on Alicudi and the *Locanda la Canna* (☎ 988 99 56) on Filicudi. On Stromboli try the *Locanda Stella* (☎ 98 60 20), and on Vulcano, if you can cope with the sulphurous fumes, try *Casa Sipione* (☎ 985 20 34). Camping facilities are available on Salina and Vulcano. Most accommodation in summer is booked well in advance on the smaller islands, particularly on Stromboli. Most hotels close during winter on the smaller islands.

Getting There & Away

Regular boats leave for the islands from Milazzo (which is easy to reach by train from Palermo and Messina). SNAV runs hydrofoils (L17,000 one-way). Siremar runs ferries for half the price, but they are slower and less regular. SNAV runs hydrofoils from Palermo twice a day in summer and three times a week in the off season. From Catania there are regular SNAV hydrofoils daily, and Alimar runs a ferry once a week.

You can travel directly to the islands from

the mainland. Alimar runs weekly ferries from Livorno, Siremar runs regular ferries from Naples and SNAV runs hydrofoils from Naples and Reggio di Calabria. Note that the sea around the islands can be very rough.

Getting Around

Regular hydrofoil and ferry services operate between the islands. Both Siremar and Aliscafi SNAV have offices at the port on Lipari, where you can get full timetable information.

TAORMINA

Spectacularly located on a hill overlooking the sea and Mt Etna, Taormina was long ago discovered by the European jet set, which has made it one of the more expensive and heavily touristed towns in Sicily. But its magnificent setting, its Greek Theatre and the nearby beaches remain as seductive now as they were for the likes of Goethe and D H Lawrence. The AAST tourist office is in Palazzo Corvaja, just off the main street, Corso Umberto, near Largo Santa Caterina, and has extensive information on the town. The town's telephone code is 0942.

Things to See & Do

The **Greek Theatre** was built in the 3rd century BC and later remodelled by the Romans. Concerts are staged there in summer and it affords a wonderful view of Mt Etna. From the beautiful **public gardens** there is a panoramic view of the sea. Along Corso Umberto is the **Duomo**, with a Gothic façade. The local beach is **Isola Bella**, a short bus ride from Via Pirandello. Concerts and theatre are performed at the Greek Theatre throughout summer. Trips to Mt Etna can be organised through the CIT (☎ 2 33 01), Corso Umberto 101.

Places to Stay & Eat

You can camp near the beach at *Campeggio San Leo* (☎ 2 46 58), Via Nazionale, at Capotaormina. The cost is L6000 per person per night, and tents are L4500 or L7000.

There are numerous affittacamere in Taormina and the tourist office has a full list.

The *Locanda Diana* (☎ 2 38 98), Via di Giovanni 6, is one of the cheapest, with doubles for L30,000 to L40,000. *Il Leone* (☎ 2 38 78), Via Bagnoli Croce 127, near the public gardens, has singles/doubles for L20,000/34,000, or L45,000 per person for half-pension. At *Pensione Svizzera* (☎ 2 37 90), Via Pirandello 26, on the way from the bus stop to the town centre, singles/doubles are L35,000/60,000 and triples L84,000, all with shower and breakfast.

Eating is expensive here. For a light meal head for *Shelter Pub*, Via Fratelli Bandieri 10, off Corso Umberto, for sandwiches and salads from L3000 to L6000. *Osteria Vecchia*, just off the Corso near the post office, in Vico Ebrei, is a wine bar which serves soup, salads and omelettes for around L5000.

Getting There & Away

Taormina is on the main train line between Messina and Catania. The station is on the coast and regular buses will take you to Via Pirandello, near the centre; bus services are heavily reduced on Sundays. You can also catch a bus from outside the train station in either Messina or Catania to go to Taormina.

SYRACUSE

Once a powerful Greek city to rival Athens, Syracuse (Siracusa) is one of the highlights of a visit to Sicily. Founded in 743 BC by colonists from Corinth, it became a dominant sea power in the Mediterranean, prompting Athens to attack the city in 413 BC. In one of the great maritime battles in history, the Athenian fleet was destroyed. Syracuse was conquered by the Romans in 212 BC, and, with the rest of Sicily, fell to a succession of invasions through the centuries. Syracuse was the birthplace of the Greek mathematician and physicist Archimedes, and Plato attended the court of the tyrant Dionysius, who ruled from 405 to 367 BC.

The main sights of Syracuse are in two areas: on the island of Ortygia and the archaeological park two km across town. The main tourist information office (APT; ☎ 0931-6 52 01) is at Via Maestranza 33 on

Ortygia. There is a branch office at the train station and an EPT information office at the archaeological park. The town's telephone code is 0931.

Things to See & Do

The island of Ortygia has always been the spiritual and physical heart of the city. Today its buildings are predominantly medieval, with some Baroque palaces and churches. The 7th century **Duomo** was built on top of the **Temple of Athena**, incorporating most of the original columns in its three-aisled structure. The **Piazza Duomo** is lined with Baroque palaces. Walk down Via Picherali to the waterfront and the **Fonte Aretusa** (Fountain of Arethusa), a natural freshwater spring. According to Greek legend, the nymph Arethusa, pursued by the river god Alpheus, was turned into a fountain by the goddess Diana. Alpheus turned himself into the river which feeds the spring.

To get to the **archaeological park**, catch bus No 1 from Riva della Posta on Ortygia. The main attraction here is the 5th century BC **Greek Theatre**, its seating area carved out of solid rock. Nearby is the **Orecchio di Dionigi**, an artificial grotto in the shape of an ear which Dionysius used as a prison. Its extraordinary acoustics enabled the tyrant to overhear the whispered conversations of his prisoners. The 2nd century AD **Roman Amphitheatre** is impressively well preserved. The park is open daily from 9 am to one hour before sunset. Admission is L2000.

Since 1914, Syracuse has hosted a festival of Greek classical drama in May and June of every even-numbered year. Performances are given in the Greek Theatre.

Places to Stay

Camping facilities are at *Agriturista Rinaura* (☎ 72 12 24), about four km out of the city near the sea. Catch bus No 34 from Corso Umberto. It costs L7000 per person and L7200 for a tent. The non-IYHF *Albergo per la Gioventù* (☎ 71 11 18), Viale Epipoli 45, is eight km out of Syracuse. Catch bus No 11 from Corso Umberto. Beds are L15,000. It is often full of people left homeless after

earthquakes, so check before going there. The *Gran Bretagna* (☎ 6 87 65), Via Savoia 21, just off Largo XXV Luglio, has high-quality rooms, with singles/doubles for L30,000/55,000. At *Hotel Centrale* (☎ 6 05 28), Corso Umberto 141, near the station, small singles/doubles are L18,000/35,000.

Places to Eat

Eating in Syracuse can be expensive. There is an open-air, fresh-produce market in the streets behind the Temple of Apollo, open daily (except Sunday) until 1 pm. You will find several alimentari and supermarkets along Corso Gelone. Try the excellent takeaway pizza and focaccia at the *Casa del Pane*, Corso Gelone 115.

At *Trattoria La Foglia*, Via Capodieci 29, off Largo Aretusa, the eccentric owner/chef and her vegetarian husband serve whatever seafood and vegetables are fresh on the day and cook their own bread. A meal here is one of the best you will eat in Italy. There is no printed menu, but don't be afraid to ask for prices. A full meal could cost around L30,000. *Scugghiu*, Via Scina 11, serves all types of pasta and is cheap at L6000 a dish. *Primus*, opposite the Gran Bretagna Hotel, is a local favourite for its excellent risotto and pasta dishes for L6000 to L7000.

Getting There & Away

Syracuse is easy to reach by train from Messina and Catania. From other destinations buses are faster and more convenient. SAIS buses leave from Piazzale Marconi, near the station, for Catania, Palermo, Enna and surrounding small towns. AST buses also service Palermo from Piazzale Marconi. Tirrenia (☎ 6 69 56) runs ferries to/from Naples three times a week, and also to Reggio di Calabria and Malta. Its office is at Via Mazzini 5.

AGRIGENTO

Founded in approximately 582 BC as the Greek Akragas, it is today a pleasant medieval town, but the Greek temples in the valley below are the real reason to visit. The Italian novelist and dramatist Luigi

Pirandello (1867-1936) was born here, as was the Greek philosopher and scientist Empedocles (circa 490-430 BC). The AAST tourist office (☎ 0922-20 391) is at Via Empedocle 73. Agrigento's telephone code is 0922.

Things to See

The spectacular **Valley of the Temples** is one of the major Greek archaeological sights in the world. Its five main Doric temples were constructed in the 5th century BC and are in various states of ruin because of earthquakes and vandalism by early Christians. The only temple to survive relatively intact is the **Temple of Concord**, which was transformed into a Christian church. The **Temple of Juno**, a five-minute walk uphill to the east, has an impressive sacrificial altar. The **Temple of Hercules** is the oldest of the structures, and across the main road which divides the valley is the massive **Temple of Jupiter**, one of the most imposing buildings of ancient Greece. Although now completely in ruins, it used to cover an area measuring 112 metres by 56 metres, with columns 18 metres high. **Telamoni**, colossal statues of men, were also used in the structure. The remains of one of them are in the **National Museum of Agrigento**. Close by is the **Temple of the Dioscuri**, which was partly reconstructed in the 19th century. The temples are lit up at night until 11.30 pm.

Places to Stay & Eat

The *Bella Napoli* (☎ 2 04 35), Piazza Lena 6, off the main thoroughfare (Via Atenea), has clean and comfortable singles/doubles for L25,000/38,000, or L30,000/45,000 with private bathroom. Opposite is *Akragas da Lillo*, where the ageing owner-chef will prepare you a memorable meal for around L15,000.

Getting There & Away

Never catch a train to/from Agrigento, as it is incredibly slow. Buses are far more efficient and leave from Piazza Roselli, just off Piazza Vittorio Emanuele, for Palermo, Catania and surrounding small towns.

Sardinia

The second-largest island in the Mediterranean, Sardinia (Sardegna) was colonised and invaded by the Greeks, Phoenicians and Romans, followed by the Pisans, Genoese and finally the Spaniards. But, it is often said that the Sardinians, known on the island as *Sardi*, were never really conquered – they simply retreated into the hills.

The Romans were prompted to call the island's eastern mountains *Barbagia* because of their views on the locals' way of life. Today, this area is still known as the 'Barbagia'. Even today the Sardi are a strangely insular people, particularly in the interior, where some women still wear the traditional costume and shepherds still live in almost complete isolation, building enclosures of stone or wood as the ancients did for their sheep and goats. If you venture into the interior, you will find the people incredibly gracious and hospitable, but easily offended if they sense any lack of respect.

The first inhabitants of the island were the Nuraghic people, thought to have arrived here around 2000 BC. Little is known about them, but the island is dotted with thousands of *nuraghi*, their conical-shaped stone houses and fortresses.

Sardinia became a semiautonomous region in 1948, and the Italian government's Sardinian Rebirth Plan of 1962 made some impact on the development of tourism, industry and agriculture.

The island's cucina is as varied as its history. Along the coast most dishes feature seafood and there are many variations of *zuppa di pesce* (fish soup). Inland you will find *porceddu* (roast suckling pig), kid goat with olives, and even lamb's trotters in garlic sauce. The Sardi eat *pecorino* (sheep's milk cheese) and you will rarely find *parmigiano* (Parmesan cheese) here. The preferred bread throughout the island is the paper-thin *carta musica* (literally, music paper), also called *pane carasau*, often sprinkled with oil and salt.

The landscape of the island ranges from the 'savage, dark-bushed, sky-exposed land' described by D H Lawrence, to the incredibly beautiful gorges and valleys near Dorgali, the rugged isolation of the Gennargentu mountain range and the unspoiled coastline between Bosa and Alghero. Although hunters have been traditionally active in Sardinia, some wildlife remains, notably the albino donkeys on the island of Asinara, colonies of griffon vultures on the west coast, and miniature horses in the inland area of Giara di Gesturi, in the south-west. The famous colony of Mediterranean monk seals at the Grotta del Bue Marino, near the beach of Cala Gonone, has not been sighted for some years.

Try to avoid the island in August, when the weather is very hot and the beaches are overcrowded. Warm weather generally continues from May to September.

Getting There & Away

Air Airports at Cagliari, Olbia and Alghero link Sardinia with major Italian and European cities. For information contact Alitalia or the CIT or CTS offices in all major towns.

Boat The island is accessible by ferry from Genoa, Civitavecchia, Naples, Palermo, Trapani, Bonifacio (Corsica) and Tunis. The departure points in Sardinia are Olbia and Porto Torres in the north, Arbatax on the east coast and Cagliari in the south.

The main company is Tirrenia, though FS (Ferrovie dello Stato) runs a slightly cheaper service between Olbia and Civitavecchia. Sardinia Ferries operates ferries from Livorno to Olbia. Timetables change dramatically every year and prices fluctuate according to the season. For full information pick up an annual timetable from any Tirrenia office.

Prices for a poltrona on Tirrenia ferries in the 1992 high season were as follows: Genoa-Cagliari L77,200 (19 hours); Genoa-Porto Torres or Olbia L53,500 (12½ hours); Genoa-Arbatax L56,100 (18 hours); Civitavecchia-Cagliari L47,700 (13½ hours); Civitavecchia-Arbatax L36,400

(nine hours); Civitavecchia-Olbia L27,000 (seven hours); Naples-Cagliari L48,400 (15 hours); and Palermo-Cagliari L44,300 (12½ hours). The cost of taking a small car ranged from L75,000 to L90,000, and L23,000 to L30,000 for a motorbike.

Getting Around

Bus The two main bus companies are ARST, which operates extensive services through-

■	PLACES TO STAY
15	Locanda Firenze
19	Albergo Centrale
22	Locanda Miramare

▼	PLACES TO EAT
20	Trattoria Congera
21	Trattoria Gennargentu
23	Trattoria da Serafino

	OTHER
1	Castle
2	Roman Amphitheatre
3	Tower of San Pancrazio
4	Piazza Indipendenza
5	Piazza Garibaldi
6	Police Headquarters
7	Ferrovie Complementari della Sardegna (Railway Station)
8	Piazza della Repubblica
9	Piazza Palazzo
10	Duomo
11	Bastione di San Remy
12	Piazza Costituzione
13	Piazza dei Martiri
14	AAST & ESIT (Tourist Information)
16	Main Post Office
17	ASST Telephones
18	Piazza del Carmine
24	PANI Bus Terminal
25	Piazza Amendola
26	Piazza Deffenu
27	Railway Station
28	AAST Tourist Information & Piazza Matteotti
29	ARST Bus Terminal
30	Ferry Terminal & EPT Tourist Information

out the island, and PANI, which links the main towns. Buses are generally reliable and faster than trains.

Train The main FS train lines link Cagliari with Oristano, Sassari and Olbia and are generally reliable. The private railways which link smaller towns throughout the island can be very slow. However, the *trenino* (little train), which runs from Cagliari to Arbatax through the Barbagia, is a relaxing way to see part of the interior (See the Getting There & Away section under Cagliari).

Car & Motorbike The only way to explore Sardinia properly is by road. See the Getting Around sections under the individual towns for car rental information.

Hitching You might find hitchhiking laborious once you get away from the main towns because of the light traffic. Women should not hitchhike in Sardinia under any circumstances.

CAGLIARI

This is a surprisingly attractive city, famous for its interesting medieval section, Poetto,

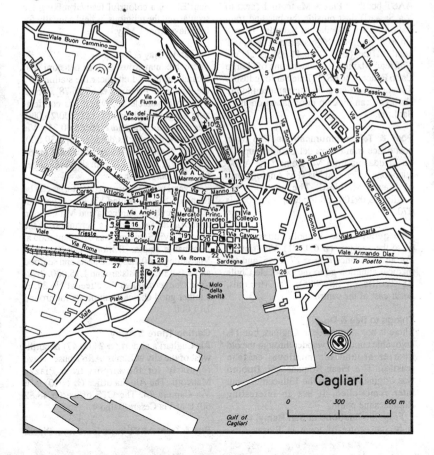

Cagliari

ITALY

its beautiful beach and its population of pink flamingos.

Orientation & Information

If you arrive by bus, train or boat you will find yourself at the port area of Cagliari. The main street along the harbour is Via Roma, and the old city stretches up the hill behind it to the castle. Most of the budget hotels and restaurants are in this area.

Tourist Offices The EPT booth at the airport is open from 8.30 am to 1 pm and 3.30 to 9 pm daily in the high season. There is an AAST booth at Piazza Matteotti 1 (next to Via Sassari), just outside the bus and train stations, open Monday to Saturday from 8 am to 8 pm in the high season. The AAST head office (☎ 070-66 41 95) is at Via Goffredo Mameli 97, which runs off Largo Carlo Felice. The ESIT (Ente Sardo Industrie Turistiche) office is in the same building. Here you can pick up information on all of Sardinia.

Post & Telecommunications The main post office is in Piazza del Carmine, up Via La Maddalena from Via Roma. The ASST telephone office is at Via G M Angioj, north of Piazza Matteotti. The postcode for Cagliari is 09100 and the telephone code is 070.

Emergency Contact the police on ☎ 113, or go to the questura (☎ 6 02 71), Via Amat 9. For an ambulance ring ☎ 27 23 45, and for medical attention go to the Ospedale Civile SS Trinità (☎ 28 19 25), Via Mirrionis, north-east of the centre.

Things to See & Do

There is not a lot to see in Cagliari, but it is enjoyable enough to wander through the old quarter around the medieval **castello** (castle). The Pisan-Romanesque **Duomo** was originally built in the 13th century, but later remodelled. It has an interesting Romanesque pulpit.

From the **Bastione di San Remy**, which is in the centre of town in Piazza Cos-

tituzione and once formed part of the fortifications of the old city, there is a good view of Cagliari and the sea.

The Pisan **Torre di San Pancrazio** (Tower of San Pancrazio), in Piazza Indipendenza, is also worth a look. The **Roman amphitheatre**, on Viale Buon Cammino, is considered the most important Roman monument in Sardinia. Spend a day on the **Spiaggia di Poetto** (east of the centre) and wander across to the salt lakes to see the flamingos.

During summer, opera is performed in the Roman amphitheatre. The Festival of Sant'Efisio, a colourful festival mixing the secular and the religious, is held annually for four days from 1 May.

Places to Stay & Eat

There are numerous budget pensioni and locande in the old city near the station. Try the *Locanda Firenze* (☎ 65 36 78), Corso Vittorio Emanuele 50, which has comfortable singles/doubles for L20,000/26,000. The *Locanda Miramare* (☎ 66 40 21), Via Roma 59, has singles/doubles for L39,000/52,000. Nearby is *Albergo Centrale* (☎ 65 47 83), Via Sardegna 4, with singles/doubles for L25,000/39,000.

Several reasonably priced trattorias can be found in the area behind Via Roma, particularly around Via Sardegna and Via Cavour. *Trattoria da Serafino*, Via Lepanto 6, at the corner of Via Sardegna, has excellent food at reasonable prices. *Trattoria Gennargentu*, Via Sardegna 60, has good pasta and seafood and a full meal costs around L15,000. *Trattoria Congera*, down the street at No 37, is another good choice, with meals for around L15,000.

Getting There & Away

Air Cagliari's airport (☎ 24 00 47) is north-west of the city at Elmas. ARST buses leave regularly for the airport from Piazza Matteotti. The Alitalia office (☎ 6010) is at Via Caprera 14. The CTS office (☎ 48 82 60) is at Via Cesare Balbo 4.

Bus & Train ARST buses leave from Piazza

Matteotti for nearby towns and Nuoro. PANI buses leave from farther along Via Roma at Piazza Darsena for towns such as Sassari and Oristano. The main train station is also in Piazza Matteotti. Regular trains leave for Oristano, Sassari, Porto Torres and Olbia. The private Ferrovie Complementari della Sardegna (railway) station is in Piazza della Repubblica. For information about the trenino, which runs along a scenic route between Cagliari and Arbatax, contact Karalis Viaggi (**☎** 30 69 91), Via della Pineta 199.

Car & Motorbike If you want to rent a car or motorbike try Hertz (**☎** 66 81 05), Piazza Matteotti 1, or Ruvioli (**☎** 65 89 55), Via dei Mille 11.

Boat Ferries arrive at the port just off Via Roma. Bookings for Tirrenia can be made at the stazione marittima (**☎** 66 60 65), or at Via Campidano 1 (**☎** 66 69 10). See the Getting There & Away section under Sardinia for further information.

DORGALI & CALA GONONE
This area, about halfway up the east coast of Sardinia, has unspoiled, isolated beaches, spectacular gorges and trekking routes, as well as important Nuraghic sites.

Although the area is attracting an increasing number of tourists, the locals remain fairly aloof. However, if you befriend a local, you will find them incredibly hospitable and helpful. Major points in the area are accessible by bus and boat, but you will need a car to explore the area. One surprisingly cheap way to see the area is by trekking with an organised guide.

Information
There is a Pro Loco (tourist information) office (**☎** 9 62 43) in Dorgali at Via Lamarmora 106, where you can pick up maps, a list of hotels and information to help you to visit the area. Another tourist information office is at the port in Cala Gonone. The EPT office (**☎** 3 00 83) in Nuoro, Piazza Italia 19, also has information on the area.

For information on trekking, contact Viaggi nel Mondo (**☎** 06-581 63 65), Via Cino da Pistoia 7 in Rome. Otherwise contact one of the local guides directly by ringing **☎** 28 80 24 in Oliena, near Dorgali. Ask for Murena, a local guide who operates a refuge near Tiscali and can take you on a three-day trek from there, through the Gorge of Gorropu (Gola su Gorropu) to the beach at Cala Luna, where you will camp for several days. The cost for the week, including transport from Rome, accommodation and the guide's fee is L310,000. If you prefer, you can stay at the refuge for L10,000 a night and see the area alone. If you do want to do this, it's a good idea to buy a detailed localised map of the area, available at CAI or the Pro Loco office in Dorgali.

CAI also organises trekking tours in Sardinia. Its office (**☎** 070-66 78 77) is at Via Principe Amedeo 25, Cagliari.

The telephone code for the area is 0784.

Things to See & Do
From **Cala Gonone** beach catch a boat to the **Grotta del Bue Marino**, where a guide will take you on a one-km walk to see vast caves with stalagmites, stalactites and lakes. Sardinia's last colony of monk seals lived here, but they have not been sighted in several years. Boats also leave for **Cala Luna**, an isolated beach where you can spend the day by the sea or take a walk along the **Codula di Luna**. Unfortunately, the beach is packed with day-tripping tourists in summer.

A walking track along the coast links the two beaches of Cala Gonone and Cala Luna (about three hours). If you want to walk in the **Gorge of Gorropu**, try hitchhiking from Dorgali, on the road to Cala Gonone.

Places to Stay
At Cala Gonone there is a camping ground (**☎** 96 243) at Via Collodi. It costs L11.900 per person. Free camping is strictly forbidden throughout the area. Hotels include the *Gabbiano* (**☎** 9 30 21) at the port, with singles/doubles for L35,000/45,000.

Getting There & Away

Catch a PANI bus to Nuoro from Cagliari, Sassari or Oristano and then take an ARST bus to Dorgali and Cala Gonone. If you are travelling by car, you will need a detailed road map of the area. One of the best is published by the Istituto Geografico de Agostini. The tourist office has maps which detail the locations of the main sights. Once at Cala Gonone you can catch a boat to Cala Luna (L8000) and the Grotta del Bue Marino (L7500).

ALGHERO

One of the most popular tourist resorts in Sardinia, Alghero is on the island's west coast, in the area known as the Coral Riviera. The Catalan-Aragonese won the town from Genoa in 1354, and even today it is known as the Catalan city of Sardinia. The town is a good base from which to explore the magnificent coastline which links it to Bosa in the south and the famous Grotte di Nettuno (Neptune's Caves) on the Capocaccia, a cape just near Alghero, to the north.

Orientation & Information

The train station is in Via Don Minzoni, some distance from the centre, but there is a free bus to take you to the port.

The main tourist information office (AAST) is at Piazza Porta Terra 9, near the port and just across the gardens from the bus terminal. The staff are extraordinarily reluctant to give out information. The old city and most hotels and restaurants are in the area west of the tourist office.

The main post office is at Via XX Settembre 108. There is a bank of public telephones on Via Vittorio Emanuele at the opposite end of the gardens from the tourist office. The postcode for Alghero is 07041 and the telephone code is 079.

In an emergency ring the police on ☎ 113; for medical attention ring ☎ 95 10 96, or go to the Ospedale Civile (public hospital), Via Don Minzoni.

If you want to rent a bicycle or motorcycle to explore the coast, try Velosport (☎ 97 71 82), Via Vittorio Veneto 90. A bike will cost about L12,000 a day, a moped L25,000 and a scooter L50,000.

Things to See & Do

It's worth wandering through the narrow streets of the old city and around the port. The most interesting church is the **Chiesa di San Francesco**, Via Carlo Alberto. The city's **cathedral** has been ruined by constant remodelling, but its bell tower remains a fine example of Gothic-Catalan architecture. Near Alghero are the **Grotte di Nettuno**, accessible by hourly boats from the port (L15,000), or by the SFS bus from Via Catalogna. For some services you will need to change at Porto Conte (L2000 one-way).

If you have your own means of transport, don't miss the beautiful **Capocaccia** and the **Nuraghe di Palmavera**, about 10 km out of Alghero on the road to Porto Conte.

In summer Alghero stages the **Estate Musicale Algherese** (Alghero's Summer Music Festival) in the cloisters of the church of San Francesco. A festival, complete with fireworks display, is held annually on 15 August for the Feast of the Assumption.

The coastline between **Alghero** and **Bosa** is stunning. Rugged cliffs fall down to isolated beaches, and near Bosa is one of the last habitats of the griffon vulture. It is quite an experience if you are lucky enough to spot one of these huge birds. The only way to see the coast is by car or motorbike, or by hitchhiking.

Places to Stay

It is virtually impossible to find a room in August, unless you book months in advance. At other times of the year you should have little trouble. Camping facilities include *Calik* (☎ 93 01 11) in Fertilia, about seven km out of town, at L12,000 per person. The IYHF *Ostello dei Giuliani* (☎ 93 03 53) is at Via Zara 1, Fertilia. Take bus AF from Via Catalogna to Fertilia. Bed and breakfast costs L14,000, hot water is L1000 and a meal costs L12,000. The hostel is open from April to September.

In the old town is the *Hotel San Francesco* (☎ 97 92 58), Via Ambrogio Machin 2, with doubles/triples for L55,000/72,000. *Pensione Normandie* (☎ 97 53 02), Via Enrico Mattei 6, is out of the centre. To get there follow Via Cagliari, which becomes Viale Giovanni XXIII. It has slightly shabby, but large, singles/doubles for L18,000/30,000.

Places to Eat

One of the best places to eat is *Trattoria il Vecchio Mulino*, Via Don Deroma 3. A full meal will cost around L20,000, but the food is great. A cheaper option is the *pizzeria* just off Via Roma at Vicolo Adami 17. Takeaway pizza by the slice costs about L2000. At Vicolo Adami 25 is *La Posada del Mar*, which serves good pasta for around L7000 and pizzas for L5000 to L8000.

Getting There & Away

Alghero is accessible from Sassari by train. The main bus station is in Via Catalogna, next to the public park. ARST buses leave for Sassari and Porto Torres; FDS buses also service Sassari and there is a special service to Olbia to coincide with ferry departures. Buses also run between Alghero and Bosa.

Liechtenstein

In some ways you could be forgiven for thinking Liechtenstein is merely part of Switzerland. The Swiss franc is the legal currency, all travel documents valid for Switzerland are also valid for Liechtenstein, and the only border regulations are on the Austrian side. Blink and you might miss it, the country measures just 25 km from north to south, and an average of six km from west to east. Switzerland also represents Liechtenstein abroad and in foreign policy, subject to consultation.

But a closer look reveals that Liechtenstein is quite distinct. The ties with Switzerland began only in 1923 with the signing of a customs and monetary union. Before that, it had a similar agreement with Austria-Hungary. It has its own reigning monarch. Prince Franz Josef II was the first ruler to live in the castle above the capital city of Vaduz, which is also the seat of government. He died in 1989 after a reign of 51 years, and was succeeded by his son, Prince Hans-Adam II. There is no military service, the army consists of just a few dozen men.

Although it shares the Swiss telephone and postal system, it issues its own postage stamps. Liechtenstein is a prosperous country and the people are proud of their independence.

Facts about the Country

Liechtenstein was created by the joining together of the domain of Schellenberg and the county of Vaduz in 1719 by the powerful Liechtenstein family. It remained a principality under the Holy Roman Empire until 1806, and after a spell in the German Confederation it achieved full sovereign independence in 1866. The modern constitution was drawn up in 1921. Even today the prince retains the power to dissolve parliament and must approve every act before it

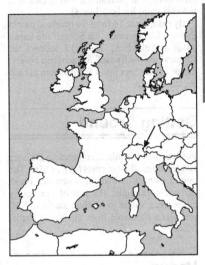

becomes law. Liechtenstein is well known as a tax haven – up to 60% of national income is derived from this status.

Despite its small size, Liechtenstein has two political regions (upper and lower) and three distinct geographical areas: the Rhine valley in the west, the edge of the Tirolean Alps in the south-east, and the northern lowlands. The current population is under 30,000, with a third of that total made up of foreign residents.

See the Switzerland chapter for details on entry regulations, currency etc.

Getting There & Away

There is no airport (the nearest is in Zürich), and only a few trains stop within the country at Schaan. Getting there by postbus is easiest. There are approximately two buses an hour from the Swiss border towns of Buchs and

Sargans which stop in Vaduz (Sfr2 single fare). From the Austrian border town of Feldkirch there are hourly buses, but you must change at Schaan for Vaduz (the Sfr2 ticket is valid for both buses).

By road, route 16 from Switzerland passes through Liechtenstein via Schaan and terminates at Feldkirch. The N13 follows the Rhine along the Swiss/Liechtenstein border; minor roads cross into Liechtenstein at each motorway exit.

Getting Around

Postbus travel within Liechtenstein is cheap and reliable; all fares costs Sfr1 or Sfr2. The only drawback is that some services finish early: for example, the last of the hourly buses from Vaduz to Malbun leaves at 5.10 pm. Get a timetable from the Vaduz tourist office.

Vaduz

The capital of Liechtenstein, with less than 5000 inhabitants, is really no more than a village.

Orientation & Information
Two adjoining streets, Städtle and Äulestrasse, diverge and then rejoin, thereby enclosing the centre of town. Everything of importance is within this small area, including the bus station.

The Vaduz tourist office (☎ 075-2 14 43), Städtle 37, has a free room-finding service and information on the whole country. It is open Monday to Friday from 8 am to noon and 1.30 to 5.30 pm. The office is also open May to September on Saturday from 9 am to noon and 1.30 to 4 pm; and July and August on Sunday from 9 am to noon and 1.30 to 4 pm. The only staff member is kept busy putting souvenir stamps in people's passports (Sfr1).

The main post office, Äulestrasse 38, is open Monday to Friday from 8 am to noon and from 1.45 to 6.30 pm, and on Saturday from 8 to 11 am. Postal rates are the same as for Switzerland. The post office has an adjoining philatelic section that is open similar hours. The telephone code for all Liechtenstein is 075.

Bike rental is available from Hans Melliger (☎ 2 16 06), Kirchstrasse 10, for Sfr20 per day; bikes can be picked up the evening before.

Things to See & Do
Although the **castle** is not open to the public, it is worth climbing up the hill for a closer look. There's a good view of Vaduz and the mountains, and a network of marked walking trails along the ridge. The **National Museum**, Städtle 43, has coins, weapons, folklore exhibits and an informative slide show in English of the history of Liechten-

stein. The museum is open daily (except on Monday from November to March) and entry costs Sfr2 (students Sfr1).

The **State Art Collection** at Städtle 37 has worthwhile, interchanging exhibitions; it is open daily, and entry costs Sfr3 (students Sfr1.50). The **Postage Stamp Museum**, next to the tourist office, contains 300 frames of national stamps issued since 1912. Located in just one room, it is free and open daily. Look out for processions and fireworks on 15 August, Liechtenstein's national holiday.

Places to Stay

The IYHF *Schaan-Vaduz Youth Hostel* (☎ 2 50 22), Untere Ruerrigasse 6, is open from January to mid-November. It's newly renovated, and beds cost from Sfr16.30 including breakfast. Reception is closed from 10 am to 5 pm, when the doors are also locked. It is 20 minutes' walk from Buchs or 10 minutes' walk from Schaan railway stations. Take the road to Vaduz and turn right at Marianumstrasse.

Hotel Falknis (☎ 2 63 77), Landstrasse, is 15 minutes' walk from the centre of Vaduz towards Schaan. Reasonable singles/doubles are Sfr40/80 with a free shower on each floor. *Gasthof Au* (☎ 2 11 17), Austrasse 2, is the only other affordable option in Vaduz. Doubles with shower start at Sfr80, or Sfr60 without.

Places to Eat

Restaurants are expensive in Liechtenstein even by Swiss standards, so look out for lunch-time specials. *Restaurant Seger*, Äulestrasse 32, has dishes for Sfr10.80 and Sfr12.50 and is open daily. Another good place to try is *Café Amann* at No 56 (closed Sunday). Near Restaurant Seger and opposite the car park is *Denner* supermarket, open Monday to Saturday.

MALBUN

Nestled amid the mountains in the southeast, Malbun is Liechtenstein's ski resort. There are some good runs for novices (and two ski schools) as well as more difficult runs. A pass for all ski lifts and chair lifts costs Sfr18 (half a day), Sfr27 (one day) or Sfr100 (one week). Equipment rental costs Sfr33 including skis, shoes and poles – enquire on ☎ 2 26 36, 2 97 70 or 2 37 55.

The road from Vaduz terminates at Malbun. The tourist office (☎ 2 65 77) is open daily (except Thursday and Sunday) from 9 am to noon, and 1.30 to 5pm (4 pm on Saturday). It's closed during the low season from the end of April to early June, and mid-October to mid-December. For snow reports, call ☎ 2 80 80.

There are eight hotels with restaurants in the village; singles/doubles start at Sfr35/60. Some of the cheaper places to try are *Alpenhotel Malbun* (☎ 2 11 81), *Galina* (☎ 2 34 24) and *Turna* (☎ 2 34 21).

Luxembourg

The Grand Duchy of Luxembourg (Luxemburg, Letzeburg) has long been a transit land. For centuries ownership passed from one European superpower to another, and travellers wrote it off as merely an expensive stepping stone to other destinations.

While it's true that this tiny country is more a tax shelter for financial institutions than a budget haven for travellers, many people also miss the best by rushing through. Its countryside is beautiful, dotted with feudal castles, deep river valleys and quaint wine-making towns, while the capital, Luxembourg City, is often described as the most dramatically sited in Europe.

Facts about the Country

HISTORY
Luxembourg's history reads a little like the fairy tale its name conjures. More than 1000 years ago, in 963, a count called Sigefroi (or Siegfried, count of Ardennes) built a castle high up on a promontory, laying the foundation stone of the present-day capital and the beginning of a dynasty which spawned rulers throughout Europe.

By the end of the Middle Ages, the strategically placed fortified city was much sought after – the Burgundians, Spanish, French, Austrians and Prussians all waging bloody battles to conquer and secure it. Besieged, devastated and rebuilt more than 20 times in 400 years, it became the strongest fortress in Europe after Gibraltar, hence its nickname, 'Gibraltar of the North'.

Listed as a French 'forestry department' during Napoleon's reign, it was included in the newly formed United Kingdom of the Netherlands with Belgium and the Netherlands in 1814, only to be cut in half 16 years later when Belgium severed itself from the Netherlands and Luxembourg was split between them. This division is what sparked

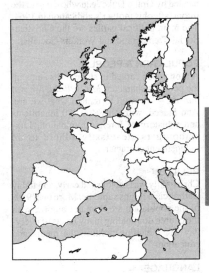

the Grand Duchy's desire for independence, and in 1839, the Dutch portion became present-day Luxembourg. Later, after the country declared itself neutral, the long-contested fort was blown up.

Luxembourg entered the 20th century riding on the wealth of its iron-ore deposits. When this industry slumped in the mid-1970s, the Grand Duchy survived by introducing favourable banking and taxation laws and became a world centre of international finance.

GEOGRAPHY
Only 82 km long and 57 km wide, on maps of Europe Luxembourg usually gets allocated a 'Lux' tag – and even that abbreviation is often too big to fit the space it occupies between Belgium, Germany and France. Riddled with rivers, its 2600 sq km is divided into the forested Ardennes highlands to the north, and farming and mining country to the south.

LUXEMBOURG

GOVERNMENT

One of Europe's smallest sovereign states, Luxembourg is a constitutional monarchy headed by Grand Duke Jean who came to the throne after his mother's abdication in 1964. The main political parties are the Christian-Social, Democratic and Workers-Socialist.

POPULATION & PEOPLE

A motto seen carved in stone walls sums up the people's character: *Mir wëlle bleiwe wat mir sin* – We want to remain what we are. And indeed, with only 400,000 inhabitants and a history of foreign domination, Luxembourgers steadfastly adhere to an independent character.

RELIGION

Christianity was established early, and today Catholicism reigns supreme. More than 95% of the population are Roman Catholic, with the church dominating many facets of everyday life including politics, the media and education.

LANGUAGE

There are three official languages in Luxembourg: French, German and Letzeburgesch, a Germanic language proclaimed as the national tongue in 1985. It's what Luxembourgers speak to each other on the streets and in their homes, a couple of words often overheard being *moien* (good morning/hello) and *äddi* (goodbye). But outside these spheres – such as in the business world, the judiciary or the press – French or German are automatically used. For a rundown on these two languages, see the France and Germany chapters in this book. English is widely spoken in the capital but less so around the countryside.

Facts for the Visitor

VISAS & EMBASSIES

Travellers from Australia, Canada, Israel, Japan, New Zealand, Norway, Sweden and the USA (and 25 other countries) need only a valid passport for a stay of up to three months – no need for a visa. EC and most European nationals, including those from the UK, can enter for three months with just their national identity card or passport. Nationals of all other countries need a visa before entering the country. Applications for extensions to the three-month period (being such a small country, these are usually requested only for work, not travel, reasons) must go through the Ministry of Justice in Luxembourg City.

Luxembourg Embassies & Consulates Abroad

In countries where there is no representative, contact the Belgian or Dutch diplomatic missions. Luxembourg embassies and consulates include:

Australia
    Royal Exchange Building, Level 18, 56 Pitt Street, Sydney, NSW 2000 (☎ 02-241 4322)
Canada
    3877 Ave Draper, Montréal, Que H4A 2N9 (☎ 04-489 6052)
New Zealand
    PO Box 3841, Ambabel, Wellington
UK
    27 Wilton Crescent, London SW1X 8SD (☎ 071-235 6961)
USA
    2200 Massachusetts Ave, NW Washington, DC 20008 (☎ 202-265 4171)

Foreign Embassies in Luxembourg

The nearest Australian, Canadian and New Zealand embassies are in Belgium (see the Belgium Facts for the Visitor section). The following embassies are all in Luxembourg City:

Belgium
    4 Rue des Girondins, L-1626 Luxembourg (☎ 442746)
France
    9 Blvd Prince Henri, L-1724 Luxembourg (☎ 471091)
Germany
    20-22 Ave Emile Reuter, L-2420 Luxembourg (☎ 4534451)
Netherlands
    5 Rue C M Spoo, L-2546 Luxembourg (☎ 227570)

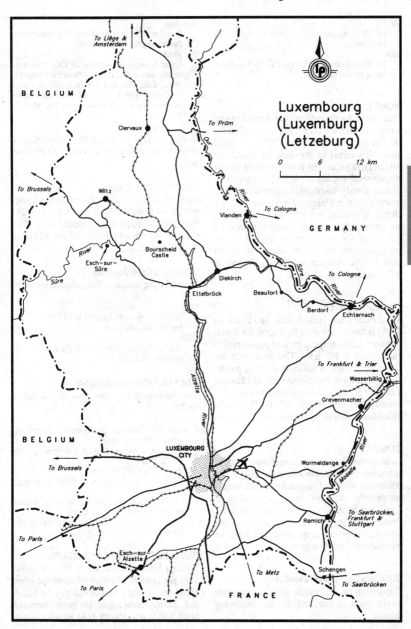

Luxembourg
(Luxemburg)
(Letzeburg)

0   6   12 km

LUXEMBOURG

BELGIUM

Clervaux

To Liège & Amsterdam

To Prüm

To Brussels

Wiltz

Bourscheid Castle

Esch-sur-Sûre

Süre River

Diekirch

Ettelbrück

Beaufort

Berdorf

Echternach

River

To Cologne

Vianden

GERMANY

To Cologne

To Frankfurt & Trier

Wasserbillig

Grevenmacher

BELGIUM

To Brussels

Alzette River

LUXEMBOURG CITY

Wormeldange

Moselle River

To Paris

Remich

To Saarbrücken, Frankfurt & Stuttgart

Esch-sur-Alzette

To Paris

Schengen

To Metz

To Saarbrücken

FRANCE

UK
14 Blvd Roosevelt, L-2450 Luxembourg
(☎ 228964)
USA
22 Blvd Emmanuel Servais, L-2535 Luxembourg (☎ 460123)

MONEY

The unit of currency is the Luxembourg franc – written as 'f' or 'flux' – issued in f1, f5, f20 and f50 coins, and f100 and f1000 notes. It's equal to the Belgian franc (for exchange rates, see the Belgium Facts for the Visitor section), but while Belgian currency is commonly used in Luxembourg, the reverse does not apply. Banks are best for changing money, and all major credit cards are commonly accepted. Prices too are on a par with, or marginally higher than, Belgium, except petrol which is much cheaper (the cheapest in Europe). Tipping is not necessary.

Consumer Taxes

Value-added tax (abbreviated in French as TVA) is calculated at 15%, except for hotel, restaurant and camping ground prices, which enjoy only a 3% levy. The procedure for claiming it back is tedious: a lot of paperwork and a good six-month wait. In addition, you must fly out of Luxembourg to a non-EC country to be eligible for a rebate. The tourist office has a booklet explaining all the details.

CLIMATE

Luxembourg has a temperate climate – warm summers and cold winters, especially in the Ardennes, which often get snow. The sunniest months are May to August, although April and September can be sunny as well. Precipitation is spread pretty evenly over the year. Luxembourg in spring can be a riot of wildflowers and blossoms.

SUGGESTED ITINERARIES

Depending on the length of your stay, you might want to see and do the following things:

Two days
Spend one day in Luxembourg City and another day touring the Moselle Valley.
One week
Spend two days in Luxembourg City, three days in the centre and north (Vianden, Clervaux, Wiltz, Ettelbrück and Diekirch) and two days exploring the Little Switzerland region (Echternach and Beaufort) and the Moselle Valley.

If you're relying on public transport, you might need a few more days to cover all these areas.

TOURIST OFFICES

The Office National du Tourisme headquarters (☎ 400808) is at 77 Rue d'Anvers, or PO Box 1001, L1010, Luxembourg City. This office is not open to the public but will send you information.

Tourist Offices Abroad

Luxembourg tourist offices abroad include:

UK
122-124 Regent St, London W1R 5FE
(☎ 071-434 2800)
USA
801 Second Ave, New York, NY 10017
(☎ 212-370 9850).

USEFUL ORGANISATIONS

The following organisations might prove useful:

Centrale des Auberges de Jeunesse Luxembourgeoises (Youth Hostels)
18 Place d'Armes, L-2013 Luxembourg City
(☎ 225588)
Automobile Club of Luxembourg
54 Route de Longwy, L-8007 Bertrange
(☎ 450045)
Gîtes d'Étape Luxembourgeois (hostel-type houses, see the Accommodation section)
23 Blvd Prince Henri, L-1724 Luxembourg City
(☎ 402131)

BUSINESS HOURS & HOLIDAYS

Trading hours are weekdays from 9 am to 5.30 pm (except Monday when shops open about noon), and a half or full day on Saturday. Many shops close for lunch between noon and 2 pm. Banks hold shorter hours:

weekdays from 9 am to 4.30 pm, and in the capital on Saturday mornings; country branches close for lunch.

Public holidays are: New Year's Day, Easter Monday, May Day (1 May), Ascension Day, Whit Monday, National Day (23 June), Assumption Day (15 August), All Saints' Day (1 November), Christmas Day, Boxing Day.

CULTURAL EVENTS

For a small country, Luxembourg is big on festivals. Pick up the tourist office's *Calendar of Events* brochure for local listings. The biggest national events are carnival, held six weeks before Easter, and Bonfire Day (Bürgsonndeg) one week later.

POST & TELECOMMUNICATIONS

Post offices (except in Luxembourg City) are open similar weekday hours to shops. It costs f14 to send a letter (under 20 grams) within Europe and f22 outside. Expect mail to Australia, Canada, New Zealand and the USA to take at least a week. To the UK and within Europe, it'll take two or three days. There's a f14 fee (often waived) for poste restante.

International phone calls can be made from post office telephone centres or public phones using f250 or f700 phone cards. Local calls cost f5 for an unlimited time – but only for calls within the city/town you're in. Outside that, it's f5 for about three minutes. For making international telephone calls to Luxembourg, the country code is 352. To telephone outside of Luxembourg, the international access code is 00. In the country itself there are no telephone area codes.

TIME

Noon in Luxembourg is 11 am in London, 6 am in New York, 3 am in San Francisco, 6 am in Toronto, 9 pm in Sydney and 11 pm in Auckland. The 24-hour clock is commonly used. Daylight-saving time comes into effect at midnight on the last Saturday in March, when clocks are moved an hour forward; they're moved an hour back again at midnight on the last Saturday in September.

LAUNDRY

While not profuse, you can generally find a self-service *laverie* in larger towns. A five-kg wash costs about f200 – dryers are f15 for five minutes.

WEIGHTS & MEASURES

The metric system is used. Like other Continental Europeans, Luxembourgers indicate decimals with commas and thousands with points.

MEDIA

The only English-language 'newspaper' is the weekly, f80, *Luxembourg News*, which gives a brief rundown on local news and has entertainment listings.

FILM & PHOTOGRAPHY

Processing and developing charges are moderate: about f560/800 for 24/36 prints in a one-hour shop. A 36-exposure Kodak 64 slide film costs f380.

WORK

Seasonal grape picking is available in the Moselle River valley for about six weeks from mid-September. Wages vary: the average is about f1000 a day including accommodation and meals. No permit is needed, but the work is popular with locals, so if possible organise your job in advance directly with a farmer or through a vineyard.

ACTIVITIES

With the world's densest network of marked walking paths, the Grand Duchy is a hiker's haven. National routes are indicated by yellow signposts. Tracks marked by white triangles connect the 12 youth hostels. The youth hostel association headquarters (see the previous Useful Organisations section) is the best place for buying detailed national maps. Local tourist offices have regional walking maps.

ACCOMMODATION

Unless you're camping, there are few cheap alternatives. No-star hotels start at f900/1200 single/double for a basic room with breakfast. In country areas B&Bs are a cheaper, cosy option from f700 per person.

Youth hostels are a good bet, often near castles or overlooking a valley, but sporadically closed in winter. The nightly dorm rate including breakfast is f280 for members under 26 years of age, or f320 for those older (except Luxembourg City which is f40/60 extra).

Camping grounds are profuse, though mainly in the central and northern regions, with rates for one adult per night ranging from f40 in a 'Category 3' ground to between f100 and f160 in the more plentiful 'Category 1'. In general, children are charged half the adult rate, and a camp site is equivalent to an adult rate.

Another option is the Gîtes d'étape: large, hostel-type houses scattered around the countryside but often open only to groups.

The national tourist office has free hotel and camping brochures (local offices have B&B lists), farm-holiday, apartment and cottage lists, and will reserve accommodation free of charge. In summer it's sage to book ahead for all accommodation.

FOOD & DRINK

Luxembourg's cuisine is similar to Belgium's Wallonia region – plenty of pork, river fish and game meat – but with a German influence in local specialities like liver dumplings with sauerkraut. Eating out will rapidly burn your budget as even a *plat du jour* – plate of the day – in the cheapest café will cost f250, and strict vegetarians will find little joy. On a brighter note, beer, both local and Belgian, is plentiful and cheap, and the Moselle Valley white wines are highly drinkable.

Getting There & Away

AIR

The international airport, Findel, is six km east of the capital, connected by frequent buses (see the Luxembourg City Getting Around section). The national carrier,

Luxair, services a pick of European destinations including Amsterdam, Athens and London. It has offices at Findel or in the city centre at Place de la Gare (☎ 481820). Icelandair (☎ 4027 2727) at 59 Rue Glesener has regular flights to the USA. There is no departure tax.

LAND

Train

Eurail and Inter-Rail are valid, as is the 'Benelux Tourrail' pass (see the Belgium Getting Around section), which costs f4810/2770 for a 1st/2nd-class adult ticket and is also valid on Luxembourg Railways' buses. There are hourly trains to Brussels (f822 for a one-way 2nd-class ticket, 2¾ hours) and to Amsterdam via Brussels (f1712, 5½ hours) or less frequently but cheaper via Liège (f1442, six hours). Other destinations include Paris (f1394, four hours, four per day) and Trier in Germany (f234, 40 minutes, 11 per day). For international and national enquiries, the station office (☎ 492424) in Luxembourg City is open from 7 am to 8 pm.

Car & Motorbike

The A4 is the major route to Brussels or Paris, the A31 via Dudelange leads to Metz in France. The main route to Germany is the A48 via Trier.

Getting Around

BUS & TRAIN

Unlike its Benelux partners, Luxembourg does not have an extensive rail system, so getting around, once you leave the main north-south rail line, can take time. The bus network is thorough and the fare system for both train and bus is simple: f30 for a 'short' (about eight km or less) trip, or f120 for a 2nd-class unlimited day ticket, which is also good for travelling on inner-city buses. It's valid from the time of purchase only until 8 am the next day. For information on local buses and trains, ☎ 492424.

In most train stations, you'll find either a luggage room (f60 per article for 48 hours) or luggage lockers which come in an array of sizes and prices – f60, f80 or f100 for 48 hours. If you arrive somewhere by bus, you can expect to lug your stuff with you.

TAXI

Taxis cost f26 per km plus an 11% night surcharge and 25% extra on Sundays.

CAR & MOTORBIKE

Driving is on the right-hand side, wearing seatbelts is compulsory and drink-driving penalties are high. The speed limit is 30 km/h in dense residential areas, 50 km/h in towns, 90 km/h outside towns and 120 km/h on motorways. The maximum permissible blood-alcohol concentration is 0.08%. Fuel is the cheapest in Europe: a litre of super costs f23, lead-free f21, and diesel f15. For other motoring information, contact the Automobile Club de Luxembourg (see the previous Useful Organisations section). Car hire is quite expensive: f900 per day or f5300 per week for a small Citroën.

BICYCLE

Cycling is more a popular pastime than a part of life as elsewhere in the Benelux. Bikes can be hired for about f400 per day – local tourist offices have rental details and cycling maps. It costs f30 to take your bike on a train.

HITCHING

Getting a ride is rarely a problem, but away from the capital city, traffic can be light. It's illegal to hitch on motorways.

Luxembourg City

Strikingly situated high on a promontory overlooking the Pétrusse and Alzette valleys, the Grand Duchy's 1000-year-old capital is a composed blend of old and new. One of Europe's financial leaders, it's a wealthy city with an uncommonly tranquil air and unusually clean streets, probably best typified by its gardeners who dress in business shirts and ties.

Orientation

The city centre has three sections. The main one is the old-town hub, north of the valleys and based around two large pedestrian squares, Place d'Armes and Place Guillaume. The modern commercial centre is across the Pétrusse Valley to the south, connected by two bridges, Pont Adolphe and Passerelle. This area ends dejectedly around the seedy railway station, a 20-minute walk from Place d'Armes along one of two large thoroughfares, Ave de la Gare or Ave de la Liberté. This is where you'll find many of the cheap hotels. The Grund, or lower town, is a picturesque, cobblestoned quarter built well below the fortifications, and home these days to some brisk nightlife. Across the Alzette Valley rise the modern towers of the European Centre (Centre Européen).

Information

Tourist Office The busy city tourist office (☎ 222809) is in the City Hall on Place d'Armes, open weekdays from 9 am to 1 pm and 2 to 6 pm, and from mid-June to mid-September also Saturdays from 9 am to 1 pm, and Sundays from 10 am to noon and 2 to 6 pm. It hands out free city maps, a comprehensive walking tour pamphlet and the handy *Luxembourg Weekly* events guide.

There are two national offices: at the airport (☎ 400808), open daily from 10 am to 6.30 pm, or more centrally at the railway station (☎ 481199), next to the Luxair office on Place de la Gare, open daily from 9 am to noon and 2 to 6.30 pm (closed Sundays from 1 December to 31 March). They provide city and national information and reserve rooms.

Money The Banque de Luxembourg opposite the station has average rates and doesn't charge commission on travellers' cheques. Nor does American Express (☎ 496041) at 6 Rue J Origer, north of the station. Outside

LUXEMBOURG

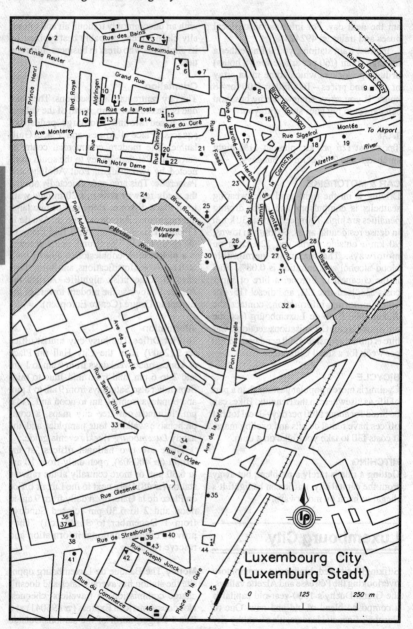

Luxembourg City
(Luxemburg Stadt)

0   125   250 m

bank hours, exchange offices with poorer rates are open daily at the station from 8.30 am to 9 pm, and at the airport from 7 am to 8.30 pm (Sunday from 9 am).

Post & Telecommunications The main post office is two blocks west of Place d'Armes at 25 Rue Aldringen, open Monday to Saturday from 7 am to 7 pm. International telephone calls can be made during opening hours only. Alternatively, there's a post office near the station at 38 Place de la Gare, open daily from 6 am to 8 pm, with phone services weekdays from 6 am to 7.15 pm, Saturdays from noon to 8 pm, and Sundays from 6 am to 8 pm.

Foreign Embassies See the Facts for the Visitor section at the beginning of this chapter.

Travel Agencies Sotours (☎ 461514), 15 Place du Théâtre, specialises in student and youth fares. Nouvelles Frontières (☎ 464140), in the arcade between Rue des Bains and Blvd Royal, has occasional discount airfares.

Bookshops The best place for English-language books is Magasin Anglais, 19 Allée Scheffer, about 15 minutes' walk north-west of Place d'Armes. It's an all round 'English' shop, selling crumpets and pork pies, expensive Penguin novels and a few travel guides.

Laundry The Quick Wash laundrette at 31 Rue de Strasbourg is open weekdays from 8 am to 7 pm, Saturday until 6 pm.

Emergency For urgent 24-hour medical assistance or ambulance, ☎ 012. For police, ☎ 409401.

Things to See & Do

Luxembourg is easily covered by foot. The city seems made for leisurely wandering, with lookouts and serene parks dotting the southern rim of the old town, where you'll find most of the sights.

LUXEMBOURG

Walking Tour From Place d'Armes, head down Rue Chimay to the coach-infested **Place de la Constitution**, where you have excellent views over the green Pétrusse Valley and the spectacular bridges that span it. East along Blvd Roosevelt, the gardens which cover the 17th century **Citadelle du St Esprit** offer superb views up both valleys and over the Grund.

Follow the natural curve north to the **Chemin de la Corniche** – a pedestrian promenade hailed as 'Europe's most beautiful balcony' – which winds up to the **Bock**, the cliff on which Count Sigefroi built his mighty fort. The castle and much of the successive fortifications were blown up over 16 years from 1867 when Luxembourg was declared neutral. There's little left, the main drawing card being the view and the nearby entrance to the **Casemates**, a 21-km network of underground passages spared from destruction because of their delicate position in relation to the town. The **Grund** lies in the valley directly below, accessible from the other side of the Bock or by a free lift dug in the cliff near the citadel at Place du St Esprit.

From the Bock, continue north up Blvd Victor Thorn, past the row of Spanish turrets overlooking the youth hostel, to the 1000-year-old **Three Turrets**. From here it's just a few minutes' walk back to the centre via Marché-aux-Herbes, where you'll find the **Grand Ducal Palace**, built in the 16th and 18th centuries (but closed for restoration until 1995), and **Place Guillaume** with its formal government edifices.

Casemates A honeycomb of damp, rock rooms carved out under the Bock, the Casemates housed bakeries, slaughterhouses and thousands of soldiers in early times, and during WW I and II they were used as a bomb shelter for 35,000 people. Open daily from March to October from 10 am to 5 pm, they cost f50/30 for adults/children.

National Museum Just north of the Grand Ducal Palace on Marché aux Poissons, the Musée National is a blend of Roman and medieval relics, fortification models and art from 13th century to contemporary painters. It's open Tuesday to Friday from 10 am to 4.45 pm, Saturday from 2 to 5.45 pm, and Sunday from 10 to 11.45 am and 2 to 5.45 pm; admission is free.

Market On Wednesday and Saturday mornings there's a food market on Place Guillaume. On the second and fourth Saturday morning of each month, it's bric-a-brac time on Place d'Armes.

Organised Tours The *Pétrusse Express* is a toy train that runs from Constitution Square down through the valleys to the Grund. It goes daily from Easter to October and costs f220/160 for adults/children. Alternatively, Sales-Lentz (☎ 461818) at 26 Rue du Cure operates two-hour city bus trips including the European Centre and nearby war cemeteries, and costs f280/170 for adults/children.

Festivals
Two festivals are worth catching: Octave, a Catholic festival held from late April to early May, climaxing with a street parade headed by the royal family; and Schueberfouer, in which decorated sheep take to the streets during a fortnight-long fun fair from late August.

Places to Stay
The bulk of hotels, particularly the cheap ones, are clustered in the streets north of the station, though most backpackers end up in the scenically sited youth hostel.

Camping There are two sites south of the city. *Kockelscheuer* (☎ 471815) is in Kockelscheuer about four-km away – take bus No 2 from the train station. It's open from Easter to 30 October and charges f90/50 for adults/children; a camp site costs f100. Alternatively, *Bon Accueil* (☎ 367069) on Route de Thionville is about five km south (the bus to Alzingen from the station stops nearby); it's open from 1 April to 30

September and charges f70/40 for adults/children plus f120 for a camp site.

Hostels The *youth hostel* (☎ 226889) at 2 Rue du Fort Olizy is excellently located in a valley below the old city. Bus No 9 from the airport or railway station (last one at 11 pm) will drop you at the door, otherwise it's a 25-minute walk from the station. Open all year, there are doubles and dorms, starting at f320 for members aged under 26, and f380 for those over.

Hotels Directly opposite the station, Rue Joseph Junck has several options, the cheapest being *Hôtel Axe* (☎ 490953) at No 32, with singles/doubles from f900/1400. Next door, the *Zurich* (☎ 491350) has singles/doubles for f1750/1950. By far the most impressive hotel in the street is the *Arcade* (☎ 492496), a modern affair with private parking (f180 per day) and pricey singles/doubles from f2500/3200, more reasonable triples from f3700.

Around the corner on Rue de Strasbourg, the unfriendly *Paradiso* (☎ 484801) has small, dark singles/doubles/triples for f900/1300/1900. Down the street at No 11, *Hôtel Bristol* (☎ 485829) has spotlessly clean singles/doubles from f1350/1750, and parking for f250, but ask to see the rooms first as some are no bigger than walk-in wardrobes.

Three blocks up in a slightly quieter area is *Le Parisien* (☎ 492397) at 46 Rue Sainte Zithe, with decent rooms starting at f1000/1500. The only reasonable alternative in the old centre is the *Schintgen* (☎ 222844) at 6 Rue Notre Dame, where singles/doubles start at f1550/2400.

Places to Eat

There are plenty of restaurants around the station, but surprisingly they are not really cheaper than their old-town counterparts. The one notable exception is the Portuguese-run *As Arcadas* (☎ 491264) at 29 Rue Joseph Junck. It serves an excellent, lunch-time-only, f250 meal which includes your choice of either an entrée plus a main dish, or a main

plus dessert. The menu, which changes daily, is taped to the window.

Up in the old town, one of the best value plats du jour (f280) is at *Chez Mami*, 15 Rue des Bains – a Portuguese family-run café with port straight from the home country. More centrally, *Brasserie Chimay* on Rue Chimay just down from Place d'Armes has a plat du jour for f350 or steaks from f400. *Les Capucins* on Rue Beaumont next to Sotour travel agency serves similarly priced meals, or there's a more modern, arty alternative up the road at *Vis à Vis*.

One of the city's trendiest Italian restaurants is *Bacchus* (☎ 471397) at 32 Rue du Marché-aux-Herbes. Pizzas start at f230 – bookings are advisable. *Scott's Pub* (see the following Entertainment section) overlooks the river and serves snacks. The only vegetarian option, and it's not a cheap one, is *Mesa Verde* (☎ 464126), 11 Rue du St Esprit.

Otherwise, there's a *supermarket* at Place de Strasbourg opposite the laundrette, and another in the basement of the Centre Commercial (next to McDonald's) at 47 Ave de la Gare, open weekdays from 9 am to 7.30 pm, Saturday to 7 pm.

Entertainment

Even on weekends, nightlife is modest, but a few well-patronised watering holes are not hard to find. The Grund area is one of the most popular spots, and when the cliffs are lit up in summer it's a pleasant stroll down to the taverns that huddle here. The *Café des Artistes* at 22 Montée du Grund has live piano music and spontaneous singing until 2 am. Just across the bridge on Bisserweg is *Scott's Pub*, a raucous, weekend live blues and rock venue. Over the road, the calm courtyard atmosphere of *Café Häffchen* – one of the city's oldest meeting spots – has been attracting drinkers since the early 1800s. For more live music on Wednesdays and Fridays, try *Le Bistro Latin* on Rue Laurent near the Vauban Towers.

In the old centre, *Interview* at 19 Rue Aldringen and the nearby *Um Piquet* at 30 Rue de la Poste are popular, trendy bar/cafés. Around the station and along Rue Joseph

Junck there are some interesting biker bars, North African haunts and a few nightclubs. The city's small gay scene revolves around *Beim Menni* and *Café Beim Mike*, just before Place de l'Étoile on Ave Émile Reuter.

Getting There & Away
For information on airlines and international trains, see the Getting There & Away section at the beginning of this chapter. For national destinations, see the Getting There & Away section in each place. Buses to towns within Luxembourg depart from the left as you leave the train station.

Getting Around
To/From the Airport Bus No 9 (three hourly) connects Findel airport with the youth hostel and station and costs f30. There's also a more expensive (f120) but quicker Luxair bus which leaves from outside the Luxair office at the station. For a taxi to Findel, reckon on about f600.

Bus City buses leave from the right out of the train station. In the old town, the main bus terminal is opposite the post office on Ave Monterey.

Car Street parking and car parks are readily available. But while there's little of the traffic congestion which consumes other European capitals, there's also little point in getting around on wheels. Leave the car behind and stroll between the sights in the old-town hub – after all, you may as well leisurely enjoy the sights from 'Europe's most beautiful balcony'.

Most of the large car hire companies have offices at the airport. Head offices are as follows:

Autolux
    33 Blvd Prince Henri, L-1724 Luxembourg (☎ 221181)
Avis
    2 Place de la Gare, L-1616 Luxembourg (☎ 489595)
Budget
    Luxembourg Airport, L-1110 Luxembourg (☎ 4375757)

Lux Rent a Car
    191 Route de Longwy, L-1941 Luxembourg (☎ 440861)

Bicycle The youth hostel hires bikes for f200 per half-day, f400 per day or f1600 per week. *Vélo en Ville* (☎ 4796 2383) at 8 Bisserweg is slightly dearer but gives 20% off for four or more, and for those aged under 26.

Around Luxembourg

MOSELLE VALLEY
Less than half an hour's drive east of the capital, the Luxembourg section of the Moselle River Valley is one of Europe's smallest and most charming wine regions. More than a dozen towns line the *Route du Vin*, or Wine Road, which flows with the Moselle from Wasserbillig, through the region's capital at Grevenmacher, onto the picturesque hillside village of Wormeldange and the popular waterfront playground of Remich, finishing at the small, southern border town of Schengen.

You'll find only two tourist offices along the way. The largest is in Grevenmacher (☎ 758275) at 32 Route de Thionville, open weekdays from 8 am to noon and 2 to 5 pm; the other is in Remich (☎ 698488) in the bus station on the Esplanade, open only in July and August from 10.30 am to 12.30 pm and 3 to 7 pm.

Things to See & Do
Wine-tasting is the obvious attraction and there are about six *caves* ('cellars') en route where you can sample the fruity white vintages. The smaller caves are often the most atmospheric, on Sunday mornings turning into lively meeting spots for the villages' older folk. Try the **Caves Cooperative** at Wormeldange, open weekends only; or in Grevenmacher, the larger **Caves Bernard-Massard**, which are open daily from April to 30 October, and run tours for f70 which end with a 'free' drink. In Remich, **St Martin**

is a similar setup, open the same months; tours here cost f80.

From May to September, it's possible to travel the 'wine river' on board the MS *Princesse Marie-Astrid*, which plies along the Moselle calling in at the major towns between Trier in Germany south to Schengen in Luxembourg. You can get on or off wherever you like. As an example of the prices, Wasserbillig to Wormeldange costs f200/300 for a one-way/return ticket.

In August the **wine festivals** start, with each village celebrating nearly every conceivable stage of wine-making, climaxing with November's 'New Wine' festival in Wormeldange.

Places to Stay

Camping grounds are few and far between in this region. Next to the butterfly garden in Grevenmacher, there's *Camping de la Route Du Vin* (☎ 75234), open from April to September. In Remich, *Camp Europe* (☎ 698018) is 100 metres from the bus station on the main Esplanade, open from Easter to the end of September.

Even the tiniest village has at least one hotel-cum-restaurant, but the only *youth hostel* is in Grevenmacher (☎ 75222), at Gruewereck on the hill behind the town. It's open from mid-February to 31 December.

As for hotels, the *Mosellan* (☎ 75157), 35 Rue de Trèves near the bus station in Grevenmacher, has singles/doubles from f800/1600. In Wormeldange, *La Toque Blanche* (☎ 768121), 87 Rue Principale, has large doubles from f900, serves excellent river trout and can sometimes help find vineyard work. Remich has several riverfront choices, the cheapest being *Beau Séjour* (☎ 698126), 30 Quai de la Moselle, which has singles/doubles from f1050/1800.

Getting There & Away

The region is difficult to explore by train, the line to Germany only going through the northern tip at Wasserbillig. Otherwise, there are twice-daily buses from Luxembourg to Grevenmacher with frequent connections to the smaller towns farther south. Alternatively, there's the boat (see the previous Things to See & Do section).

CENTRAL LUXEMBOURG

While there's not much to keep you in central Luxembourg, the area can make a good exploration base. The most conveniently sited town is Ettelbrück, the nation's central road and rail junction, while nearby Diekirch is home to the region's main wartime museum.

Both towns have tourist offices: in Ettelbrück (☎ 82068) at the railway station, open weekdays from 8.30 am to noon and 1.30 to 5 pm (in July and August also on weekends); in Diekirch (☎ 803023) at Place Guillaume, eight minutes' walk from the station, open weekdays from 9 am to noon and 2 to 5 pm (in July and August it's weekdays from 9 am to 6 pm, and weekends from 10 am to noon and 2 to 4 pm).

Things To See & Do

A hand-painted 'Welcome to our Liberators' sign marks the entrance to the **Diekirch Historical Museum**, where showrooms detail the 1944 Battle of the Bulge and the US liberation. It's open from May to October, daily from 10 am to noon and 2 to 6 pm.

With a car, it's well worth the winding drive north-west of Diekirch to the 1000-year-old **Bourscheid Castle**, high on a plateau overlooking fertile farm lands and the Sûre River way below. The castle is open from March to September, daily from 10 am to 7 pm.

Places to Stay

If you're camping in Ettelbrück, there's *Kalkesdelt* (☎ 82185) on Chemin du Camping, 2.5 km from the station. In Diekirch, *de la Sûre* (☎ 809425) is on Route de Gilsdorf. Both camping grounds are open from 1 April to 30 September.

The Ettelbrück *youth hostel* (☎ 82269) is at Rue G D Joséphine-Charlotte, about 20 minutes' walk from the station. It's closed at various times during the year – ring before you go. Otherwise, B&Bs are the best bet, or there's *Hôtel du Marché* at 5 Rue de Bastogne (☎ 82244) with doubles for f1440.

In Diekirch, there are a couple of reasonable hotels: *de la Gare* (☎ 803305) or *Au Bon Accueil* (☎ 803476) near the station.

Getting There & Away

Hourly trains from Luxembourg City to Ettelbrück take 30 minutes; to Diekirch, 40 minutes.

LITTLE SWITZERLAND

Centred around the old Christian town of Echternach in a small pocket of wooded land north-east of the capital, the Little Switzerland (Petite Suisse) region is where outdoor enthusiasts go on retreat – though rarely a solitary one. Hiking, cycling and rock climbing make it one of Luxembourg's prime tourist areas.

There's an information office in Echternach (☎ 72230) at Porte St Willibrord, open weekdays from 9 am to noon and 2 to 5 pm (in July and August also on weekends). When closed, ask at Hôtel Regina opposite the bus station. There are smaller offices in the two other main towns in the region: at Berdorf (☎ 79643) in the Town Hall, open weekdays from 9 am to noon and 2 to 6 pm, and in Beaufort (☎ 86081) at 9 Rue de l'Église, open weekdays from 1 to 4 pm.

Things to See & Do

If you're in Echternach on Whit Sunday, look out for the handkerchief pageant in honour of St Willibrord, a missionary who died in the town centuries ago. If not, you can visit the **Basilica** where St Willibrord's remains lie in a white marble sarcophagus. Behind the Basilica hides a Benedictine **Abbey**.

You can also head west to the walking paths which wind through rocky chasms and waterfalls to **Berdorf** on the tableland six km away, or farther to the crumbling castle of **Beaufort**, open daily from 1 April to 25 October from 9 am to 6 pm.

Places to Stay

Camping grounds are abundant all through-

out this region, the loveliest ones of course being away from the towns. But if you're stuck, *Camp Officiel* (☎ 72272) is about 200 metres from the bus station in Echternach.

There are two *youth hostels* – one in Echternach (☎ 72158), 9 Rue André Duchscher, and the other at Beaufort (☎ 86075), 6 Rue de l'Auberge. Both close irregularly throughout the year – ring ahead.

Hotels are plentiful in Echternach: try *Bon Accueil* (☎ 72052) on 3 Rue des Merciers, or *Hôtel de l'Abbaye* (☎ 729184) at No 2. In Berdorf, *Hôtel Herber* (☎ 79188) at 53 Rue d'Echternach has singles/doubles from f1300/1800 (closed December and January). In Beaufort, there's the more affordable *Hôtel Rustique* (☎ 86086) at 55 Rue du Château with rooms from f900/1300 (closed from January to mid-February).

Getting There & Away

There are no trains, only buses from the capital city to Echternach which take 40 minutes. From Echternach, buses connect to the other towns.

THE NORTH

Known as the Luxembourg Ardennes, the Grand Duchy's northern region is its most spectacular. Winding valleys with fast-flowing rivers cut deep through high, green plateaus crowned by castles. Of the three main towns, Clervaux to the far north is the most easily accessible, while Vianden in the east, with its famous chateau, is arguably Luxembourg's most touristic town. To the west, the town of Wiltz holds no special appeal, though the tiny nearby hamlet of Esch-sur-Sûre attracts a staggering number of tourists simply because of its location.

Clervaux's tourist office (☎ 92072) is ensconced in its castle, open weekdays from Easter to 30 June from 2 to 5 pm, and from 1 July to 31 October from 10 am to noon and 2 to 6 pm. Outside these hours, the town hall, also in the castle, has local information. The slick Vianden office (☎ 84257), 37 Rue de la Gare, is open daily from 1 April to 30 October from 9.30 am to noon and 2 to 6 pm. Outside these months, it's closed on Wednesday. In Wiltz, the office (☎ 957444) is also in the castle, open from mid-June to mid-September weekdays from 10 am to noon and 1.30 to 5.30 pm.

Things to See & Do

Clervaux This town has two main sights: its feudal **castle** which sits down amongst the town, and the turreted Benedictine **abbey** high in the forest above. The castle houses several exhibits including the famous photography collection, *Family of Man*, assembled in the 1950s by Luxembourg-born photographer Edward Steichen. It's open daily in June from 1 to 5 pm, and from 1 July to mid-September from 10 am to 5 pm. The rest of the year it's open Sunday afternoons only.

Vianden Though little more than a village, Vianden's attractions are considerable. Besides its 9th century charm, the town's most noted feature is its impeccably restored, but now somewhat atmosphere-lacking, **chateau**. It's open daily from March to September, weekends only in January and February. The chateau's striking position can be photographed from the **chair lift** which climbs the nearby hill daily from March to September.

Vianden's other ace is the former home, now museum-cum-tourist office, of the French poet Victor Hugo, who lived here during exile from his homeland in the 1860s.

Wiltz Built on the side of a small plateau, Wiltz has a feel of infinitely more space and air than either the above towns, but perhaps that's what makes it less picturesque. It's divided in two: the Ville Haute (High Town) sits up on a crest and is where most of the sights are located, while down below is the Ville Basse and the railway station. The rather sterile **chateau** sits on the edge of the Ville Haute and is home to an exhibition on the Battle of the Bulge in 1944 (also known as the Ardennes Offensive), open from mid-June to mid-September.

Esch-sur-Sûre The tiny village of Esch-sur-Sûre is what draws most people to this neck of the woods. About 12 km south of Wiltz (off the main road to Ettelbrück), it's built up on a rocky peninsula, draped around by the Sûre River, and lorded over by steep cliffs. To top it off, it's even crowned by a ruined castle – the whole effect being one which lures hordes of tourists, evident by the disproportionate number of hotels that exist here.

Places to Stay

Clervaux In Clervaux, the nearest camping is *Reuler* (☎ 92160) about 1.5 km from the train station. There's no youth hostel, the nearest being six km up the railway line in Troisvierges (☎ 98018) at 24 Rue de la Gare (closed from mid-October to 30 November).

However, there are a few cheap hotels: try *des Nations* (☎ 91018) opposite the station, or *Auberge des Ardennes* (☎ 92254), 22 Grand Rue. Alternatively, there's *Hôtel du Parc* (☎ 91068) at 2 Rue du Parc, a beautiful old chateau with singles/doubles from f1450/2100.

Vianden There are three camping grounds in Vianden. The closest to the centre is *Op dem Deich* (☎ 84375) on the river to the south, open from Easter to mid-October. Vianden's *youth hostel* (☎ 84177) is at 3 Montée du Château, in the shadow of the chateau and open all year except December.

There are heaps of hotels but most are pricey and many are open from Easter to October only. The most expensive of them line the Grand Rue, the cheapies run along Rue de la Gare – for the latter, try *Petry* (☎ 84122) at No 15, or *de l'Our* (☎ 84675) at No 35.

Wiltz In Wiltz, the spic *youth hostel* (☎ 958039) at Rue de la Montagne is a good km's climb from the train station – up the hill and then behind the Ville Haute. Just below the youth hostel is *Camping du Château* (☎ 957444) at Rue de la Fontaine. In the Ville Basse, *Hôtel du Pont* (☎ 958103) at 11 Rue du Pont has decently priced rooms.

LUXEMBOURG

Getting There & Away

To Clervaux, there are trains every two hours from Luxembourg City; the journey takes one hour. To Vianden, take the Luxembourg City-Ettelbrück train and then jump on a connecting bus. To Wiltz, take the Luxembourg City-Clervaux train and change trains in Kautenbach. The total journey time is about 1½ hours.

The Netherlands

A small country with a big reputation for liberalism, the Netherlands (Nederland, or Holland as it's commonly but incorrectly known) swims in a sea of familiar images. A land of bikes and dykes, of blazing flower fields, and mills but few hills – these are all quintessential Netherlands, and largely true outside the major cities and the once-radical, still exuberant, capital of Amsterdam.

While topping most travellers' itineraries, there is plenty to entice you away from the 'anything goes' capital. The countryside's endlessly flat landscape, broken only by slender church steeples in scenes which inspired the nation's early artists, is a cyclist's nirvana. And while you may be pressed to find wide-open spaces and solitude, you'll discover a hard-fought-for land, with proud people and farmers who, yes, still wear traditional clogs.

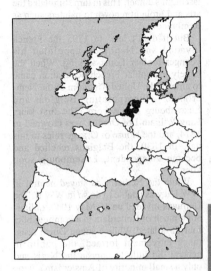

Facts about the Country

HISTORY

The Netherlands' early history is linked with Belgium and Luxembourg, the three known as the 'Low Countries' until the 16th century when the present-day Netherlands' boundaries were roughly drawn. Originally inhabited by tribal groups, the Germanic Batavi drained the sea lagoons while the Frisii lived on mounds in the remote north.

In the late-16th century, the region's northern provinces united to fight the Spanish (see the Belgium History section). The most powerful of these provinces was Holland with its main city of Amsterdam, and to the outside world, Holland became synonymous with the independent country that was to emerge in this corner of Europe (a bit like saying England when you mean Britain).

Led by Prince William I of Orange, nicknamed William the Silent for his refusal to enter into religious arguments, the Revolt of the Netherlands lasted 80 years, ending in 1648 with a treaty that recognised the 'United Provinces' as an independent republic. As part of the deal, the Scheldt River was closed to all non-Dutch ships. This destroyed the trade of the largest port in that time, Antwerp, but ensured the prosperity of its rival, Amsterdam.

Amsterdam stormed onto the European scene in what was the province of Holland's most glorified period: the Golden Age from about 1580 to about 1740, after which the British began dominating the world seas. The era's wealth was generated by the Dutch East India Company, which sent ships to the Far East in search of spices and other exotic goods, while colonising the Cape of Good Hope and Indonesia and establishing trading posts throughout Asia. Later the West Indies Company sailed to West Africa and the Americas, creating colonies in Suriname, the Antilles and New Amsterdam (today's New York).

Meanwhile Amsterdam's bourgeoisie indulged in fine, gabled canal houses and paintings of themselves and the remains of last night's dinner. This in turn stimulated the arts and brought renown to painters such as Rembrandt.

But it didn't last. In 1795 the French invaded and Napoleon appointed his younger brother Louis as king. When the largely unpopular French occupation came to an end, the United Kingdom of the Netherlands – incorporating Belgium and Luxembourg – was born. The first king, King William I of Orange, was crowned in 1814, and the House of Orange rules to this day. In 1830, the Belgians rebelled and became independent, Luxembourg soon after.

While the Netherlands stayed neutral in WW I, it was unable to do so in WW II. The Germans invaded on 10 May 1940, obliterating much of Rotterdam in a bombing blitz four days later. While a sound Dutch resistance movement formed, the public in general did little to oppose the Nazis and only a small minority of Amsterdam's large Jewish population survived the war.

In 1949, despite military attempts to hold onto Indonesia, the colony won independence. Suriname followed much later with a peaceful handover of sovereignty in 1975. The Antilles are still a colony, with a large degree of self-rule.

In 1953 one of the country's worst disasters hit when a high spring tide coupled with a severe storm breached the dykes in Zeeland, drowning 1835 people. To ensure the tragedy would never be repeated, the Delta Plan was conceived (see the Delta Region section later in this chapter).

The 1960s' social consciousness found fertile ground in the Netherlands, especially in Amsterdam which became the radical heart of Europe. The riotous squatter's movement stopped the demolition of much cheap inner-city housing, the lack of which is a problem that has lasted into the 1990s.

GEOGRAPHY
Bordered by the North Sea, Belgium and Germany, the Netherlands is largely artificial, its lands reclaimed from the sea over many centuries and the drained polders protected by dykes. More than half of the country lies below sea level. Only in the south-east Limburg province will you find hills.

The south-west province of Zeeland is the combined delta area of the Scheldt, Meuse, Lek and Waal rivers; the Lek and Waal are branches of the Rhine, carrying most if its water to the sea – the mighty Rhine itself peters out in a pathetic little stream (the Oude Rijn, or Old Rhine) at the coast near Katwijk.

GOVERNMENT
Against the European trend, the Netherlands developed from a republic to a constitutional monarchy, headed today by Queen Beatrix who took over from her mother, Juliana, in 1980. Coalition governments pursue policies of compromise. The three main parties are the Catholic-Protestant CDA, the socialist PvdA and the Liberal VVD.

The country consists of 12 provinces, one of which, Flevoland, belonged to the sea less than 50 years ago. The province of Holland was split into North Holland (capital: Haarlem) and South Holland (capital: The Hague) during the Napoleonic era. The Catholic half of the population lives mainly in the south-eastern provinces of North Brabant and Limburg. The province of Zeeland gave New Zealand its name (Australia used to be known as New Holland).

POPULATION & PEOPLE
Western Europe's most densely populated country, there are 15 million people, and a lot of Frisian cows, in its 34,000 sq km. This concentration is intensified in the Randstad – the western hoop of cities including Amsterdam, The Hague and Rotterdam – which is one of the most densely populated conurbations on earth.

ARTS
Over the centuries the Netherlands has spawned a realm of famous painters. Rembrandt, Frans Hals and Jan Vermeer led the

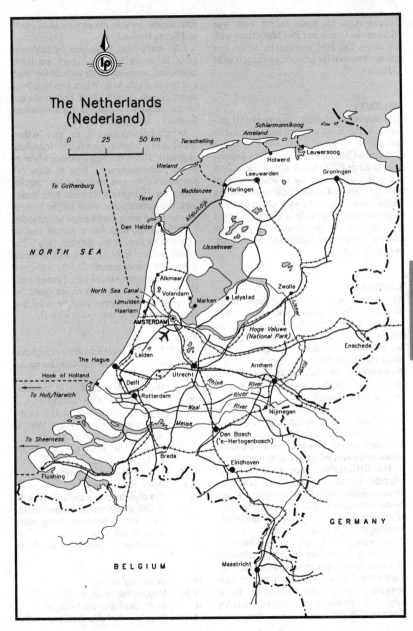

The Netherlands
(Nederland)

0   25   50 km

To Gothenburg

NORTH SEA

Schiermonnikoog
Ameland
Terschelling
Lauwersoog
Vieland
Holwerd
Leeuwarden
Groningen
Waddenzee
Harlingen
Texel
Afsluitdijk
Den Helder
IJsselmeer
Alkmaar
Volendam
Zwolle
IJmuiden
Marken
Lelystad
North Sea Canal
Haarlem
AMSTERDAM
Hoge Veluwe
(National Park)
Enschede
Leiden
The Hague
Arnhem
Hook of Holland
Utrecht
To Hull/Harwich
Delft
Rhine   River
Rotterdam
Waal   River
River
Nijmegen
Meuse
Den Bosch
('s-Hertogenbosch)
To Sheerness
Breda
Eindhoven
Flushing
IJssel
River

GERMANY

BELGIUM

Maastricht

NETHERLANDS

Golden Age. Of more recent note was Vincent van Gogh, and Piet Mondriaan with his cubic De Stijl movement, while this century has seen the perplexing designs of M C Escher.

RELIGION
The number of churches that house art galleries is the most obvious sign of today's attitude to religion – and art. The Dutch Reformed Church, to which half the population belonged 100 years ago, attracts 20% today though it's still the official church of the royal family. Catholicism remains strong in the south-east, in theory if not in practice. The independent attitude of Dutch Catholics is evidenced by the many who insist on calling themselves 'Catholic' without the prefix 'Roman'.

LANGUAGE
Most English speakers use the term 'Dutch' to describe the language spoken in the Netherlands, and 'Flemish' for that spoken in the northern half of Belgium and a tiny northwestern corner of France. Both are in fact the same language, the correct term for which is Netherlandic, or *Nederlands*, a West Germanic language that is spoken by about 25 million people worldwide.

The people of the northern Friesland province speak their own language. Although Frisian is actually the nearest relative of the English language, you won't be able to make much sense of it when you hear it spoken.

The differences between Dutch and Flemish, in their spoken as well as written forms, are similar to those between UK and North American English: despite some differences they're very much the same language, with a shared literature. The Flemish might call their tongue *Vlaams* to distinguish themselves from their Walloon (French-speaking) compatriots. But the Dutch don't have a specific name for their language apart from *Nederlands*; some might call it *Hollands* ('Hollandic'), but only when they're not thinking about their many compatriots outside the provinces of North and South Holland.

Like many other languages, Netherlandic gives its nouns genders. There are three: masculine, feminine (both with *de* for 'the') and neuter (with *het*). When you're talking about people, you'll often find male and female versions: *student* is a male student, *studente* a female student.

Where English uses 'a' or 'an', Netherlandic uses *een* (pronounced *ern*), regardless of gender. This is the only instance where **ee** is not pronounced as a long **e**, since *een* pronounced as *ayn* indicates the number 'one'. To distinguish between both meanings, the Netherlandic word for the number 'one' is often written with acute accents: *één*.

Netherlandic also has a formal and an informal version of the English 'you'. The formal version is *U* (written with a capital letter and pronounced *ü*), the informal version is *je* (pronounced *yer*). Netherlandic has become less formal in recent years, but as a general rule, people who are older than you, should still be addressed with *U*.

Pronunciation
Vowels Single vowels are pretty straightforward, with long and short sounds for each:

a	short, as the second 'a' in 'camera'
aa	long, like the 'a' in 'father'
au, ou	both are pronounced the same, somewhere between the 'ow' in 'how' and the 'ow' in 'glow'
e	short, as the 'e' in 'bet', or the 'er' in 'fern'
e, ee	long, as the 'ay' in 'day'
ei, ij	as the 'ey' in 'they'
eu	this combination sounds the way the British queen would pronounce the *o* in 'over' if she were exaggerating
i	short, as the 'i' in 'in'
ie	as the 'ee' in 'meet', but not drawn out
o	short, as 'pot'
oe	as the 'oo' in 'zoo'
o, oo	long, as the 'o' in 'note'
u	short, similar to the 'u' in 'urn'
u, uu	long, like the 'u' in the German *über*

ui   there's no equivalent sound in English. For those who speak French, the *eui* in *'fauteuil'* comes pretty close, if you leave out the slide towards the 'l'.

Consonants These, too, are pretty straightforward, except for the 'ch' and 'g' which make (northern) Netherlandic sound so harsh:

ch & g   in the north, a hard 'kh' sound as in the Scottish *loch*. In the south, a softer, lisping sound.

j   a 'y' sound. Occasionally, especially with borrowed words, a 'j' or 'zh' sound, as in 'pleasure'.

r   in the south, a trilled sound. In the north it varies, often occurring as a back-of-the-throat sound as in French or German.

s   usually the 's' in 'sample'. Sometimes a 'zh' sound as in 'pleasure'.

w   a clipped sound, almost like a 'v', when at the beginning of a word. At the end of a word it is like the English 'w'.

Greetings & Civilities

Hello.	*Dag/hallo.*
Goodbye.	*Dag.*
Yes.	*Ja.*
No.	*Nee.*
Please.	*Alstublieft/ alsjeblieft.*
Thank you.	*Dank U/je (wel).*
You're welcome.	*Geen dank.*
Excuse me.	*Pardon.*
Sorry.	*Sorry.*

Some Useful Phrases

Do you speak English?	*Spreekt U/spreek je Engels?*
Does anyone speak English?	*Spreekt iemand Engels?*
I (don't) understand.	*Ik begrijp het (niet).*
Just a minute.	*Een ogenblikje.*

Please write that down.	*Kunt U/Kun je het alstublieft/alsje- blieft opschrij- ven?*
How much is it?	*Hoeveel kost het?*

Useful Signs

Camping Ground	*Camping*
Entrance	*Ingang*
Exit	*Uitgang*
Full/No Vacancies	*Vol*
Guesthouse	*Pension*
Hotel	*Hotel*
Information	*Informatie, Inlichtingen*
Open/Closed	*Open/Gesloten*
Police	*Politie*
Police Station	*Politiebureau*
Prohibited	*Verboden*
Rooms Available	*Kamers Vrij*
Toilets	*WC's/Toiletten*
Youth Hostel	*Jeugdherberg*

Getting Around

What time does... leave/arrive?	*Hoe laat ver- trekt/arriveert...?*
What time is the...?	*Hoe laat is de...?*
next	*volgende*
first	*eerste*
last	*laatste*

the boat	*de boot*
the bus/tram	*de bus/tram*
the train	*de trein*

I would like...	*Ik wil graag...*
a one-way ticket	*een enkele reis*
a return ticket	*een retour*
1st class	*eerste klas*
2nd class	*tweede klas*

Where is the bus/tram stop?	*Waar is de bus/tramhalte?*
I want to go to...	*Ik wil naar...gaan.*
Can you show me (on the map)?	*Kunt U/kun je het (op de kaart) aanwijzen?*

far/near	*ver/dichtbij*
Go straight ahead.	*Ga rechtdoor.*

NETHERLANDS

Turn left...	*Ga linksaf...*
Turn right...	*Ga rechtsaf...*

Around Town

I'm looking for...	*Ik zoek...*
a bank	*een bank*
the city centre	*het centrum*
the...embassy	*de...ambassade*
the hospital	*het ziekenhuis*
my hotel	*mijn hotel*
the market	*de markt*
the police	*de politie*
the post office	*het postkantoor*
a public toilet	*een openbare WC/openbaar toilet*
the telephone centre	*de telefooncentrale*
the tourist information office	*de VVV (in the Netherlands)/ het toeristenbureau*

beach	*strand*
bridge	*brug*
castle	*kasteel, burcht*
cathedral	*kathedraal*
church	*kerk*
island	*eiland*
lake	*meer*
main square	*plein/grote markt*
market	*markt*
monastery	*klooster*
mosque	*moskee*
old city	*oude stad*
palace	*paleis*
opera house	*operagebouw*
quay/bank	*kade, oever*
ruins	*ruïne*
sea	*zee*
square	*plein*
tower	*toren*

Accommodation

Where is a cheap hotel?	*Waar is een goedkoop hotel?*
What is the address?	*Wat is het adres?*
Could you write the address, please?	*Kunt U/kun je het adres opschrijven, alstublieft/alsjeblieft?*
Do you have any rooms available?	*Heeft U kamers vrij?*
I would like (a)...	*Ik wil graag (een)...*
single room	*eenpersoonskamer*
double room	*tweepersoonskamer*
room with a bathroom	*kamer met badkamer*
to share a room bed	*een kamer delen bed*
How much is it per night/per person?	*Hoeveel is het per nacht/per persoon?*
Can I see it?	*Kan ik het zien?*
Where is the bathroom?	*Waar is de badkamer?*

Food

bakery	*bakkerij*
grocery/delicatessen	*kruidenier/ delicatesse*
restaurant	*restaurant*
breakfast	*ontbijt*
lunch	*middageten/lunch*
dinner	*avondeten/diner*
I would like the set lunch, please.	*Ik wil graag het toeristenmenu, alstublieft.*
Is service included?	*Is bediening inbegrepen?*
I am a vegetarian.	*Ik ben vegetariër.*

Time & Dates

today	*vandaag*
tomorrow	*morgen*
in the morning	*'s-morgens*
in the afternoon	*'s-middags*
in the evening	*'s-avonds*
Monday	*maandag*
Tuesday	*dinsdag*

Wednesday	*woensdag*
Thursday	*donderdag*
Friday	*vrijdag*
Saturday	*zaterdag*
Sunday	*zondag*
January	*januari*
February	*februari*
March	*maart*
April	*april*
May	*mei*
June	*juni*
July	*juli*
August	*augustus*
September	*september*
October	*oktober*
November	*november*
December	*december*

Numbers

0	*nul*
1	*één*
2	*twee*
3	*drie*
4	*vier*
5	*vijf*
6	*zes*
7	*zeven*
8	*acht*
9	*negen*
10	*tien*
11	*elf*
12	*twaalf*
13	*dertien*
14	*veertien*
15	*vijftien*
16	*zestien*
17	*zeventien*
18	*achttien*
19	*negentien*
20	*twintig*
21	*éénentwintig*
22	*tweeëntwintig*
30	*dertig*
40	*veertig*
50	*vijftig*
60	*zestig*
70	*zeventig*
80	*tachtig*
90	*negentig*

100	*honderd*
1000	*duizend*
one million	*één miljoen*

Health

I'm...	*Ik ben...*
diabetic	*suikerziek*
epileptic	*epileptisch*
asthmatic	*astmatisch*

I'm allergic to antibi-otics/penicillin.	*Ik ben allergisch voor antibiotica/penicilline.*

antiseptic	*antisepticum*
aspirin	*aspirine*
condoms	*condooms*
constipation	*verstopping*
contraceptive	*voorbehoedsmiddel*
diarrhoea	*diarree*
medicine	*medicijn*
nausea	*misselijkheid*
sunblock cream	*zonnebrandolie*
sunburn	*zonnebrand*
tampons	*tampons*

Emergencies

Help!	*Help!*
Call a doctor!	*Haal een dokter!*
Call the police!	*Haal de politie!*
Go away!	*Ga weg!*

Facts for the Visitor

VISAS & EMBASSIES

Travellers from Australia, Canada, Israel, Japan, New Zealand, Norway, Sweden, the USA and 33 other countries need only a valid passport – no visa – for a stay of up to three months. EC nationals and most other Europeans can enter for three months with just their national identity card or a passport expired for not more than five years. After three months, extensions can be applied for through the Vreemdelingendienst (Foreigners' Service) department of the police. Nationals of all other countries need

NETHERLANDS

to get a Netherlands visa before entry – allow at least three months for the paperwork.

Dutch Embassies

Dutch embassies abroad include:

Australia
> 120 Empire Circuit, Yarralumla, Canberra, ACT 2600 (☎ 06-273 3111)

Canada
> 3rd floor, 275 Flater St, Ottawa, Ontario (☎ 613-237 5030)

New Zealand
> 10th Floor, Ballance & Featherston St, or PO Box 840, Wellington (☎ 04-738 652)

UK
> 38 Hyde Park Gate, London SW7 5DB (☎ 071-584 5040)

USA
> 4200 Linnaan Ave, NW Washington, DC 20008 (☎ 202-244 5300)

Foreign Embassies in the Netherlands

Embassies (in The Hague) and consulates (in Amsterdam) of other countries in the Netherlands include:

Australia
> Carnegielaan 12, 2517 KH The Hague (☎ 070-310 82 00)

Belgium
> Embassy: Lange Vijverberg 12, 2513 AC The Hague (☎ 070-364 49 10)
> Consulate: Drentestraat 11, 1083 HK Amsterdam (☎ 020-642 97 63)

Canada
> Parkstraat 25, 2514 JD The Hague (☎ 070-364 48 25)

France
> Embassy: Smidsplein 1, 2514 BT The Hague (☎ 070-356 06 06)
> Consulate: Vijzelgracht 2, 1017 HR Amsterdam (☎ 020-624 83 46). Visas are issued at the crowded side office on Weteringdwarsstraat. Apply between 9 and 11.30 am, pick up after 4 pm.

Germany
> Embassy: Groot Hertoginnelaan 18, 2517 EG The Hague (☎ 070-342 06 00)
> Consulate: De Lairessestraat 172, 1075 HM Amsterdam (☎ 020-673 62 45)

New Zealand
> Mauritskade 25, 2514 HD The Hague (☎ 070-346 93 24)

UK
> Embassy: Lange Voorhout 10, 2514 ED The Hague (☎ 070-364 58 00)
> Consulate: Koningslaan 44, 1075 EJ Amsterdam (☎ 020-676 43 43)

USA
> Embassy: Lange Voorhout 102, 2514 EJ The Hague (☎ 070-362 49 11)
> Consulate: Museumplein 19, 1071 DJ Amsterdam (☎ 020-679 03 21)

MONEY

Overall, banks have the best exchange rates for travellers' cheques or cash, charging f5 commission. The national exchange organisation, De Grenswisselkantoren ('The Border Exchange Offices', GWK), has similar rates and fees. You'll find branches at all major border posts, train stations and Schiphol airport, open Monday to Saturday from 8 am to 8 pm, Sunday 10 am to 4 pm. With a student card there's no commission. In larger cities there are exchange services (mainly for cash) at the post office, as well as many private exchange bureaus that close late but generally demand exorbitant fees. All major credit cards are accepted.

Currency

The currency is the guilder, divided into 100 cents and symbolised as 'Dfl' or 'f' (originally 'florin'). There are 5c, 10c, 25c, f1, f2.50 and f5 coins, and f5, f10, f25, f50, f100, f250 and f1000 notes.

Exchange Rates

A$1	=	f1.19
Bf1	=	f0.05
C$1	=	f1.33
DM1	=	f1.13
NZ$1	=	f0.90
UK£1	=	f2.83
US$1	=	f1.66

Costs

Living in hostels and eating in cheap restaurants, you'll be looking at spending roughly f45 a day. Travelling costs little due to the country's size. Tipping is not expected, but 'rounding up' the bill is always appreciated in taxis, restaurants and pubs with table or pavement service.

Avid museum goers should consider the yearly Museumcard, which gives free entry into 400 museums and art galleries. It costs f40 for adults (f15 for those aged under 19) and is issued at museums or tourist information (VVV) offices. Unless stated otherwise, all the museums and art galleries mentioned in this chapter are free with the Museumcard.

Consumer Taxes

The value-added tax (BTW in Dutch) is calculated at 18.5%, but travellers from non-EC countries don't have to pay it on goods over f300. To claim the tax back, ask the shop owner to provide an export certificate (form OB90) when you make the purchase. When you leave, get the form endorsed by the Dutch customs, who will send the certificate to the supplier, who in turn refunds you the tax by cheque or money order. If you want the tax before you leave the country, it's best to buy through shops displaying the 'Holland Tax Free Shopping' sign (but because of red tape, you won't get the full refund). In this case the shopkeeper will give you a stamped cheque which can be cashed at the border.

CLIMATE & WHEN TO GO

The Netherlands has a temperate maritime climate with cool winters and mild summers. Spring is the ideal time as there's less chance of rain and the bulbs are in bloom – April for daffodils, tulips in May. The wettest months are July and August, though precipitation is spread pretty evenly over the year. The sunniest months are May to August, and the warmest are June to September. Because it's such a flat country, wind has free reign – something you'll soon notice if you take to cycling.

SUGGESTED ITINERARIES

Depending on the length of your stay, you might want to see and do the following things:

Two days
Visit Amsterdam.

One week
Spend two days in Amsterdam, one day each in Haarlem (make sure you visit the Keukenhof gardens), Leiden, The Hague and the Hoge Veluwe national park, and the remaining day visiting Rotterdam, the Kinderdijk windmills and the Delta Expo (see the Delta Region section).

Two weeks
Spend three days in Amsterdam, two days each in Haarlem (Keukenhof), The Hague and Schiermonnikoog, one day each in Leiden, Delft, Rotterdam (Kinderdijk), the Delta Region (Delta Expo and Middelburg) and the Hoge Veluwe national park, and if you have any time left over you can throw in Maastricht or Den Bosch.

One month
This should give you enough time to have a look around the whole country.

TOURIST OFFICES

The ubiquitous VVV – the national tourist organisation – sells brochures on everything and maps on everywhere. Its offices are generally open Monday to Friday from 9 am to 5 pm, Saturday 10 am to noon, and will book accommodation for a f4 fee. In larger cities, and during the summer months of July and August, opening hours are extended. The Netherlands Board of Tourism (NBT) head office (☎ 070-370 57 05) is at Vlietweg 15, 2266 KA Leidschendam.

NBT Offices Abroad

The NBT has offices in:

Australia
5 Elizabeth St, Sydney, NSW 2000 (☎ 02-247 6921)
Belgium
68 Rue Ravenstein, 1000 Brussels (☎ 02-511 6445)
Canada
25 Adelaide St East, Suite 710, Toronto, Ont M5C 1Y2 (☎ 416-363 1577)
UK
25-28 Buckingham Gate, London, SW1E 6LD (☎ 071-630 0451)
USA
355 Lexington Ave (21st floor), New York, NY 10017 (☎ 212-370 7367)
Suite 305, 90 New Montgomery St, San Francisco, CA 94105 (☎ 415-543 6772)
225 N Michigan Ave, Suite 326, Chicago, IL 60601 (☎ 312-819 0300)

NETHERLANDS

USEFUL ORGANISATIONS

Some useful organisations include:

COC – gay and lesbian information service – Rozenstraat 14, 1016 NX Amsterdam (☎ 020-623 40 79 or 626 30 87)

Dutch Touring Association (ANWB) – motoring and cycling club – Wassenaarseweg 22, 2596 EC The Hague (☎ 070-314 71 47), or Museumplein 5, 1071 DJ Amsterdam (☎ 020-673 08 44)

Eurail Aid Office, PO Box 2025, 3500 HA Utrecht (☎ 030-35 44 80)

Mobility International Nederland – travels for handicapped people – Postbus 165, 6560 AD Groesbeek (☎ 08891-7 17 44 Wednesday only)

Nederlandse Jeugdherberg Centrale (NJHC) – youth hostel association – Prof Tulpplein 4, 1018 GX Amsterdam (☎ 020-551 31 55)

Vrouwenhuis ('Women's House') – feminist centre – Nieuwe Herengracht 95, 1011 RX Amsterdam (☎ 020-625 20 66)

BUSINESS HOURS & HOLIDAYS

The working week starts leisurely at lunch time Monday. For the rest of the week, shops open at 8.30 or 9 am and close at 5.30 or 6 pm, except Thursday or Friday when many close at 9 pm, and on Saturday, at 4 pm. Banks are generally open Monday to Friday from 9 am to 4 or 5 pm. Most museums are closed Monday.

Public holidays are: New Year's Day, Good Friday (but most shops stay open), Easter Monday, Queen's Birthday (30 April), Ascension Day, Whit Monday, Christmas Day, Boxing Day.

CULTURAL EVENTS

There are many local, but few national, festivals. Religious celebrations like carnival are confined to the Catholic south. For Amsterdam, one of the biggest events is Koninginnedag ('Queen's Day'), the 30 April national holiday held on the former Queen Juliana's birthday. On this day the whole central city becomes a huge street market/party where people sell whatever they've dug out of their attics.

POST & TELECOMMUNICATIONS

Post offices are open Monday to Friday from 8.30 am to 5 pm, Saturday to noon. Letters cost 80 cents for up to 20 grams within Europe, f1.60 outside, and will take about a week to the USA and Canada, six to 10 days to Australia and New Zealand, and two to three days to the UK.

Local phone calls cost 25 cents for roughly five minutes. Telephones take 25-cent, f1 and f2.50 coins, or f5, f10 and f25 phone cards. International calls can be made from public phones, post offices or telephone kiosks, and unlike its Benelux (BElgium-NEtherlands-LUXembourg) partners, the Netherlands has cheaper rates for late-night calls to Australia and New Zealand.

For making international telephone calls to the Netherlands, the country code is 31. To telephone abroad, the international access code is 09. Telephone codes for some of the cities and towns within the Netherlands include Amsterdam 020, Arnhem 085, Delft 015, Den Bosch 073, Haarlem 023, Leiden 071, Maastricht 043, Middelburg 01180, Rotterdam 010, The Hague 070 and Utrecht 030.

TIME

The Netherlands is in the Central European Time zone. Noon is 11 am in London, 6 am in New York, 3 am in San Francisco, 6 am in Toronto, 9 pm in Sydney, and 11 pm in Auckland. The 24-hour clock is commonly used. Daylight-saving time comes into effect at midnight on the last Saturday in March, when clocks are moved an hour forward, and ends at midnight on the last Saturday in September, when they're moved an hour back again.

LAUNDRY

If you can push past all the piles of clothes in a typical Dutch *wassalon*, you're lucky – at least you're in the front door. Generally, self-service laundrettes are no more than a few machines put aside for do-it-yourselfers in staffed laundries (which are often closed on Wednesday). In large cities, you'll also find the traditional unattended laundrette. A five-kg wash costs an average of f10 including drying.

WEIGHTS & MEASURES

The metric system is used. In shops, 100 grams is referred to as an *ons* and 500 grams is a *pond*. EC directives have prohibited the use of *ons* in pricing and labelling, but the term is so ingrained it will take a while to disappear. Like other Continental Europeans, the Dutch indicate decimals with commas and thousands with points.

BOOKS

The Diary of Anne Frank movingly describes life in hiding in Nazi-occupied Amsterdam (paperback). For a humorous look at Dutch ways, pick up *The UnDutchables* by Colin White & Laurie Boucke (paperback).

MEDIA

There's no English-language newspaper, but international papers are easy to find and London's BBC radio World Service can be tuned to on 648 kHz medium wave.

HEALTH

The Netherlands has reciprocal health arrangements only with other EC countries (bring your formula E111 card).

WOMEN TRAVELLERS

The women's movement has long had a strong foothold and you'll find *vrouwen* (women's) cafés, bookshops and help centres in many cities.

DANGERS & ANNOYANCES

The number of tales of travellers in Amsterdam having their wallets swiped could fill a book. Basically, keep your hands on your valuables especially at Centraal Station in Amsterdam, the post office, telephone centres and tourist strongholds. Cyclists too should be warned: the stolen bicycle racket is rife. Locals use two chains to lock up their bikes, and even that's no guarantee.

Despite popular belief to the contrary, drugs are illegal. Possession of more than 30 grams of marijuana or hash can, strictly speaking, get you a f5000 fine and/or land you in jail – hard drugs can definitely land you in jail. Small amounts of 'soft' drugs for personal use are generally, though not officially, tolerated, but could complicate matters if you're already in trouble with the police over something else.

FILM & PHOTOGRAPHY

Films and developing are expensive. A Kodak 64 (36-exposure) slide film costs f27. Film developing is f5.50 plus f1 per print. In red-light districts, 'No photo' stickers often adorn windows and should be taken seriously.

WORK

It's illegal for non-EC nationals to work, but jobs in the bulb fields (June to October) around Leiden are relatively easy to pick up. Many travellers' hotels in Amsterdam use touts to drum up business.

HIGHLIGHTS

The Keukenhof gardens (see the Haarlem section) are a must for flower aficionados, while anyone into a bit of dirt should investigate *wadlopen* – mud-flat-walking (see the Frisian Islands section). Museum and cycling buffs will be in their glory throughout – a visit to the Kröller-Müller Museum (see the Hoge Veluwe section) can superbly combine the two.

ACCOMMODATION

Rarely cheap and often full, budget accommodation in peak times is best booked ahead. This applies to summer and public holidays, but also if you're going to be in the Randstad during the Keukenhof season.

The cheapest alternative is the 43 official youth hostels, which generally charge members f20.50 a night with breakfast (f5 more if you're not a member). In large cities you'll find similarly priced unofficial hostels and cheaper 'sleep-ins'.

Camping grounds are copious but prices vary – on average f4.50/1.50/3 per adult/tent/car. The NBT has a selective list of sites or there's the ANWB's annual camping guide (f16.95), both available from the VVV or bookshops. Hotels start at f55/75 single/double for basic rooms that are rarely flash, with continental breakfast thrown in. B&Bs are a good f30 alternative – local VVVs have lists.

You can book ahead (no deposit required) either in writing or by telephone or fax to the Netherlands Reservation Centre (NRC) (see the previous Useful Organisations section). You must supply all the relevant details and allow time for them to confirm the booking with you (in writing or by fax).

FOOD

While gastronomical delights are not a Dutch forte, you won't go hungry. What the cuisine lacks in taste sensation, it makes up for in quantity. And thanks to the sizeable Indonesian, Chinese, Surinamese, Turkish and Italian communities there are plenty of spicy alternatives. Vegetarians will find that many restaurants have at least one meat-free dish.

Snacks

On the savoury side, the national fast-food habit is *frites* – chips or French fries. *Kroketten*, or croquettes (crumbed fried concoctions), are sold hot from vending machines; *broodjes* (open sandwiches) are everywhere; and mussels, raw herrings and deep-fried fish are popular coastal snacks.

As for sweets, *appelgebak* (apple pie) ranks up there with frites, while *poffertjes* (fried doughy balls sprinkled with icing sugar) are sure-fire tourist food, as are *pannekoeken* (pancakes) and *stroopwafels* (hot wafers glued together with syrup).

Main Dishes

Dinner traditionally comprises thick soups and meat, fish or chicken dishes fortified with potatoes. Most restaurants have a *dagschotel* (dish of the day) for about f14, while *eetcafés* ('eating pubs') serve meals or cheap snacks. Everywhere you'll see signs for the f21.50, three-course 'Tourist Menu'. Otherwise, the Indonesian *rijsttafel* ('rice table') of boiled rice with oodles of side dishes is pricey but worth a try, as are Zeeland mussels, best during months with an 'r' in their name (or so local tradition has it).

Self-Catering

For the very basics, like bread and cheese, you'll find Hema stores on the main street of most towns. If fruit and vegies etc are also on the shopping list, try the yellow-and-black Vroom & Dreesmann (V & D) department stores, which often have a basement supermarket.

DRINKS

Beer is the staple, served cool and topped by a two-finger-thick head of froth – a sight which can horrify Anglo-Saxon drinkers. According to the Heineken tour guide, it's not to 'rip off English uninitiates' but to 'capture the flavour bubbles which would otherwise fly away!' Apparently it's reason enough for bar staff to coolly respond to requests of 'no head please'.

Dutch gin *(genever)* is made from juniper berries; a common combination, known as a *kopstoot* ('head butt'), is a glass of genever with a beer chaser – two or three of those is all most people can handle. There are plenty of indigenous liqueurs, including *advocaat* (a kind of eggnog) and the herb-based *Beerenburg*.

ENTERTAINMENT

You'll rarely have to search for nightlife. In summer, parks come alive with festivals while city squares reverberate with the sounds of street musicians. Bars and cafés abound, from pavement terraces filled with sun-seekers to old brown cafés thick with conversation and smoke. Movies screen in their original language with Dutch subtitles, and are often cheaper on Wednesdays.

THINGS TO BUY

Diamonds and flowers are the specialities, the latter cheap and plentiful all year. For flower bulbs it's easiest to buy through one of the specialist mail-order companies. They'll handle all the red tape including the 'health certificate' many countries require for importing bulbs. As for diamonds, if you've got the budget to buy them, you probably don't need advice.

Getting There & Away

AIR

The Netherlands has just one main international airport, Schiphol, about 10 km south-west of Amsterdam. One of Western Europe's major international hubs, it services flights from airlines worldwide as well as the national carrier, KLM Royal Dutch Airlines. Most foreign airlines have offices in Amsterdam (see the Amsterdam Getting There & Away section) but KLM also has an airport office (☎ 020-649 91 23).

The airport is connected by frequent train services to the nearby Randstad cities including Amsterdam (20 minutes), The Hague (40 minutes) and Rotterdam (45 minutes). There is no departure tax when flying out. For other general information, telephone Schiphol, ☎ 020-601 09 66.

LAND
Bus

Eurolines and Hoverspeed Citysprint are the two international bus companies servicing the Netherlands. Tickets can be bought in most travel agencies as well as at NS (Dutch Railways) Reisburos ('Travel Bureaus') at large train stations. Both offer reduced fares for those aged under 26.

Eurolines has regular buses to a crop of Western, Eastern, Mediterranean and central European destinations as well as Scandinavia and North Africa. Hoverspeed Citysprint buses run only between London, Belgium and the Netherlands. Depending on the service, there are stops in Breda, Maastricht, Rotterdam, The Hague and Utrecht as well as Antwerp, Bruges and Brussels in Belgium. Citysprint buses all go via Calais in France, using either the SeaCat or Hovercraft to cross the Channel. Travellers using Hoverspeed's service should check whether French visas are required to enter France.

For more detailed information on both companies, see the Amsterdam (or other relevant city) Getting There & Away section.

Train

Eurail and Inter-Rail tickets are valid for use on Netherlands Railways (NS), which operates regular and efficient services to all its neighbouring countries from Amsterdam, the country's international hub. For all international train information and reservations, you'll find NS Reisburos in all large train stations. These offices are generally open weekdays from 8 am to 7 pm and Saturday from 9 am to 5 pm. In peak periods, it's wise to reserve all seats in advance.

There are two main lines south from Amsterdam. One passes through The Hague and Rotterdam and on to Antwerp (f42, 2¼ hours, hourly trains), Brussels (f50, three hours, hourly trains), Paris (f115, six hours, seven per day) and eventually Spain. The other goes via Utrecht and Maastricht to Luxembourg City (f77, six hours, six per day) and on to France and Switzerland. The line south-east runs via Utrecht and Arnhem to Cologne (f66, three hours, every two hours) and farther into Germany. The line east goes to Berlin, with a branch north to Hamburg. All these fares are one-way in 2nd class; people aged under 26 get a 20% discount.

To/From the UK To London, there are three train/ferry routes. The basic one-way fare for all from Amsterdam is f145 – reservations are strongly recommended. One service goes via Hook of Holland (Hoek van Holland) on the coast near Rotterdam to Harwich in England and on to London's Liverpool Street station. The daytime run takes 10½ hours, the overnight service, 13 hours.

The second service is via Flushing (Vlissingen) to Sheerness and on to Victoria Station in London. The daytime service takes 12½ hours, the overnight one, 14½ hours.

The third goes via Ostend in Belgium to Dover and on to Victoria Station. There are four services per day but journey lengths vary greatly depending on whether a jetfoil or ferry is used to cross the Channel. Using the jetfoil, the total trip takes about 7¼ hours but you must pay a f28 jetfoil supplement.

With the overnight ferry, it's a 12½-hour journey.

SEA

Several companies operate car/passenger ferries between the Netherlands and England, and one company to Sweden. For information on train/ferry services, see the previous Train section.

Sealink-Stena Line sails from Hook of Holland to Harwich. It has day (6½ hours) and night (eight hours) boats – fares for a car (including up to six people) start at f295/395 for the day/night service. An adult one-way passenger ticket costs f100. Sealink-Stena has an office (☎ 020-620 20 11) at Vijzelgracht 17, 1017 HM Amsterdam.

North Sea Ferries operates an overnight boat (12 hours) between Europoort (near Rotterdam) and Hull. Basic rates for cars start at f192, while adult tickets are from f151 (including dinner and breakfast). The North Sea Ferries office (☎ 01819-5 55 00) is at the Europoort terminal.

Olau Line sails between Flushing and Sheerness. The daytime ferry takes six hours, the overnight one, 8½ hours. Car rates vary depending on the ferry – starting prices are f105/176 for the day/night services. Passenger tickets start at f99. Olau has an office (☎ 01184-8 80 00) at the Flushing ferry terminal.

Scandinavian Seaways sails two or three times a week from Amsterdam to Gothenburg (Göteborg) in Sweden. The voyage takes 24 hours. Rates for cars start at f160; for passengers, they vary depending on the season, with low/high season prices starting at f190/230. Future Line Travel (see the Amsterdam Travel Agents section) has information and tickets.

Getting Around

The only thing that takes time in the Netherlands is getting used to the country's small size. The public transport system is excellent, particularly the trains, and relatively cheap. For all national train/bus/tram information, there is one central telephone number: ☎ 06-92 92.

BUS, TRAM & METRO

Buses are used for city and regional transport rather than for long distances, and are much slower than trains. Trams operate in most cities, and Amsterdam and Rotterdam also have metros.

Costs

Fares operate nationally. You buy a *strippenkaart* (strip card) valid throughout the country, and stamp off a number of strips depending on how many zones you cross. The ticket is then valid on any bus, tram, metro or city train for an hour, or longer depending on the number of strips you've stamped. Around central Amsterdam for example, you'll use two strips – one for the journey plus one for the zone. A zone farther will cost three strips, and so on. It's an honesty system backed by spot checks, and fare dodgers get f100 on-the-spot fines. The buses are more conventional, with drivers stamping the strips as you get on. Bus and tram drivers sell two-strip cards for f2.25, three-strip for f3.25 and 10-strip for f10.25. More economical are 15-strip cards for f10.25 or 45-strip ones for f29 which you purchase in advance at railway stations, post offices and tobacconists.

TRAIN

Netherlands Railways (NS) trains are fast and efficient, with at least one InterCity train every 15 minutes between major cities, and half-hourly trains on branch lines. Most train stations have either luggage lockers (small/large cost f1/2 for 36 hours) or a luggage room (f1.40 per bag for 24 hours). In Amsterdam, these prices are slightly higher.

Costs

The national strip card is valid on trains only within city limits. Outside, you should buy a normal train ticket. Fares are calculated per kilometre – on average, 100 km will cost f25/42 single/return. If you're returning on the same day, it's cheaper to buy a return ticket rather than two singles.

There's a mélange of discount fares but you'd have to live on the trains to make most of them worthwhile. A One-Day Rover gives unlimited 2nd-class travel for f54, or there's a Seven-Day Rover for f129. The 'Meermans Kaart', or Multi Rover, gives two to six people (f82 to f138) unlimited travel all day on weekends but only after 9 am on weekdays. For longer distances, the 'Holland Rail Pass' gives three days' travel within 10 days for f79. From June to August there's an alternative 'Summer Tour' pass which gives three days' travel in 10 for two people for f99. For the full list, get the *Touring Holland by Rail* brochure, which also details discount 'Day Excursions'.

TAXI

Usually booked by phone, taxis also hover outside railway stations and hotels and cost roughly f17.50 for five km.

CAR & MOTORBIKE

Foreign drivers need a Green Card as proof of insurance. Road rules are basically stick to the right and give way to the right (except at major crossroads and roads with right of way). Speed limits are 50 km/h in towns, 80 km/h outside and 120 km/h on motorways. Fuel prices per litre are f2 for super, f1.84 for lead-free ('Euro loodvrij') and f1.15 for diesel. The maximum permissible blood alcohol concentration is 0.05%. For other motoring information, contact the ANWB (see the previous Useful Organisations section).

BICYCLE

With 10,000 km of cycling paths, a *fiets* (bicycle) is *the* way to go. The VVV has a *Cycling in Holland* brochure which details scenic routes, while the ANWB publishes a complete cycling map. Major roads have separate bike lanes, and except for motorways there's virtually nowhere bicycles can't go. That said, in places such as the Delta region and along the coast you'll often

need muscles to combat the North Sea headwinds. It costs f8 to put a bicycle on a train (not in peak hours).

While about 85% of the population own bikes and there are more bikes than people, they're also abundantly available for hire. Private operators charge f10 to f12 per day, f50 per week, with f50 deposit. Railway station hire shops uniformly charge f7.50 per day, f30 per week and demand f200 deposit. You must also return the bike to the same station.

Alternatively, it can work out much cheaper to buy a 'second-hand' bike from a street market for upwards of f25, bearing in mind it's probably part of the stolen bike racket (see the previous Dangers & Annoyances section).

HITCHING

Hitching is usually effortless, but illegal on motorways.

Amsterdam

For many travellers, Amsterdam is a city of preconceived ideas. Personal freedom, liberal drug laws, the gay centre of Europe – they're images synonymous with the Dutch capital since the heady 1960s and 1970s when it led as Europe's most radical city. While the exuberance dimmed somewhat during the 1980s, it wasn't extinguished. Tolerance still holds pride of place although it's being increasingly tested with a chronic housing shortage, growing numbers of homeless and signs of racial tension.

More obvious, however, are the rich historical and lively contemporary airs that meld here, as you'll feel when exploring the myriad art galleries and museums, relaxing in the canalside cafés or enjoying the open-air entertainment that beats through the heart of summer.

Orientation

By capital-city standards, Amsterdam (population 700,000) is small. Its major sights,

NETHERLANDS

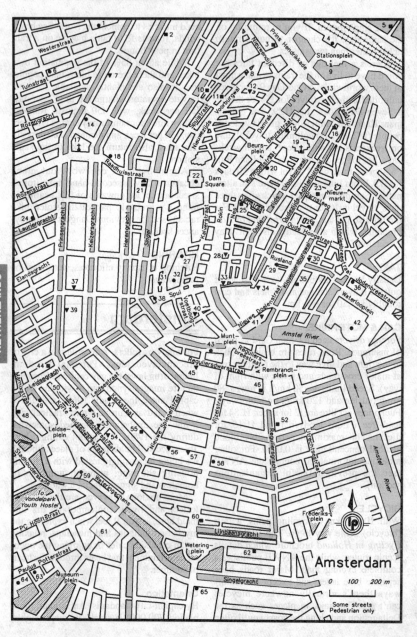

Amsterdam

0   100   200 m

Some streets
Pedestrian only

■ PLACES TO STAY

2	Keizersgracht Hotel
3	Hotel Beaux Arts
5	*Amstel*
10	Hotel Brian
11	Bob's Youth Hostel
15	Hotel Beursstraat
16	The Crown
23	The Shelter
25	RHO Hotel
35	Stadsdoelen Youth Hostel
44	International Budget Hotel
46	The Veteran
48	Hotel King
52	Seven Bridges
55	Hotel Hans Brinker
60	Euphemia Budget Hotel
62	Hotel Sphinx

▼ PLACES TO EAT

7	Pancake Bakery
8	De Keuken van 1870
12	Egg Cream
28	Sisters
30	De Engelbewaarder
31	Haesje Claes
33	La Margarita
34	Atrium
37	Miramare
39	Library Café
40	Friture
41	Café de Jaren
45	Rose's Cantina
53	Bojo

54	Piccolino
56	Françcoise
57	Hollandse Glorie

OTHER

1	Laundry
4	Centraal Station (CS)
9	Tourist Office
13	In den Olofspoort
14	Anne Frank's House
17	Westerkerk
18	Telephone Centre
19	Oude Kerk
20	Condomerie
21	Main Post Office
22	Royal Palace
24	Pie
26	Goa
27	Historical Museum
29	Rusland
32	Begijnhof
36	Rembrandt's House
38	Hoppe
42	City Hall/Music Theatre ('Stopera')
43	Flower Market
47	Laundry
49	Milky Way
50	Tourist Office
51	Easy Times
58	Supermarket
59	Paradiso
61	Rijksmuseum
63	van Gogh Museum
64	Stedelijk Museum
65	Heineken Brewery

NETHERLANDS

accommodation and nightlife are scattered around a web of concentric canals *(grachten)* known as the canal belt, which gives the city an initially confusing, yet ultimately orderly and unique feel.

The centre, easily and enjoyably covered on foot, has two main parts: the old, medieval core and the 'newer', 17th century canal-lined quarters which surround it. Corked to the north by Centraal Station (CS), the old city centre is encased by the Kloveniers-burgwal and Singel canals. After Singel come Herengracht, Keizersgracht and Prinsengracht, the newer canals dug to cope with Amsterdam's Golden Age expansion. The city's central point is Dam Square, five

minutes' walk straight down Damrak from Centraal Station. Main streets bisect the canal belt like spokes in a wheel.

Information
The VVV has two offices. The busiest, outside CS at Stationsplein 10 (☎ 020-626 64 44), is open from Easter to September daily from 9 am to 11 pm, in winter week-days to 6 pm, Saturdays to 5 pm, and Sundays from 10 am to 1 pm and 2 to 5 pm. The office at Leidsestraat 106 is open from Easter to September daily from 9 am to 10.30 pm, in winter weekdays from 10.30 am to 5.30 pm and Saturdays to 9 pm.

Money There are 24-hour GWK offices at CS and Schiphol airport; otherwise, there's a throng of midnight-trading change bureaus along Damrak and Leidsestraat. Check Change Express at Damrak 86 (☎ 020-624 66 82) or Leidsestraat 106: its rates are often comparable to banks and commissions surprisingly low.

American Express' main office is at Amstelkade 166, but more convenient is the branch at Damrak 66 (☎ 020-520 77 77) open from 9 am to 5 pm; to report lost or stolen cards, ☎ 020-642 44 88, or travellers' cheques, ☎ 06-022 01 00. Thomas Cook's main offices are at Damrak 1-5 (☎ 020-620 32 36), open daily until 7 pm, and at Leidseplein 31a (☎ 020-626 70 00), until 6 pm.

Post & Telecommunications The main post office is at Singel 250 near Dam Square, open weekdays from 8.30 am to 6 pm, Thursday until 8.30 pm, Saturday from 9 am to noon. International phone calls can be made all hours nearby at Telehouse, Raadhuisstraat 48-50, or from Tele Talk Centre, Leidsestraat 101.

Amsterdam's telephone code is 020.

Foreign Embassies See the Facts for the Visitor section earlier in this chapter.

Travel Agencies Amsterdam is a major European centre for cheap fares to anywhere in the world. A few of the better known budget agencies are:

NBBS – nationwide 'student' travel agency – Rokin 38 (☎ 624 0989) or Leidsestraat 53 (☎ 638 17 36)
Malibu Travel – long-time, cheap flight specialists – Damrak 30 (☎ 623 68 14)
Amber Reisbureau – cheap flights to outside Europe and often no queues – Da Costastraat 77 (☎ 685 11 55)
Future Line Travel – reduced ferry fares to Sweden for youth hostel members – Prof Tulpstraat 2 (☎ 622 28 59)
ILC Reizen (☎ 620 51 21 for flights, ☎ 622 43 42 for other queries), NZ Voorburgwal 256 – flights, train and bus tickets and paid car lifts to other European capitals
Budget Air, Rokin 34 (☎ 627 12 51)

Budget Bus – for Eurolines (Europabus) tickets – Rokin 10 (☎ 627 51 51)

Bookshops English-language books are plentiful but horribly expensive. Try the following:

American Discount Book Centre – good travel guide section, cheaper than competitors, extra 10% off for students – Kalverstraat 185 (☎ 625 55 37)
De Slegte – Amsterdam's specialist in remaindered novels and coffee-table books – Kalverstraat 48-52 (☎ 622 59 32)
W H Smith – strong on guides, maps and novels – Kalverstraat 152 (☎ 638 38 21)
Allert de Lange – long established with new separate travel section two doors up – Damrak 60 (☎ 624 67 44)
Pied à terre – huge range of travel literature, hiking and trekking information – Singel 393 (☎ 627 44 55)
A la carte – guides and maps, near Frederiksplein – Utrechtsestraat 110-112 (☎ 625 06 79)
The Book Exchange – rabbit warren of second-hand books – Kloveniersburgwal 58 (☎ 626 62 66)

Laundry The Clean Brothers have a laundrette near Leidseplein at Kerkstraat 52, and another to the north at Westerstraat 26, both open daily from 7 am to 9 pm (last wash 8 pm). In the red-light district there's Happy Inn at Warmoesstraat 30, open Monday to Saturday from 9 am to 6 pm.

Emergency For police, ambulance and fire brigade, the national number is ☎ 06 11. The main police station (☎ 559 91 11) is at Elandsgracht 117. For medical emergencies, phone the 24-hour Central Doctor and Dental Service (☎ 664 2111/679 18 21). The closest hospitals to the centre are VU Ziekenhuis (☎ 548 91 11), de Boelelaan 1117, or Onze Lieve Vrouwe Gasthuis (☎ 599 91 11), 1e Oosterparkstraat 197. In the event of rape or attack, *Tegen haar wil* ('Against her will') (☎ 625 34 73) is a 24-hour crisis line.

Things to See & Do

With more than 141 art galleries and 40 museums, Amsterdam is justly famed for its cultural proliferation. The Rijksmuseum (honouring Rembrandt) and the Vincent van

Gogh Museum are the two top attractions – as you'll see by the queues.

Walking Tour The best place to start is **Dam Square** (the 'Dam'), where the Amstel River was dammed in the 13th century, giving the city its name. Today it's the crossroads for the crowds surging along the pedestrianised Kalverstraat and Nieuwendijk shopping streets, and the pivotal point to interesting outer quarters.

Heading west along Raadhuisstraat, you'll cross the main canals to the towered **Westerkerk** in whose shadow stands a statue of **Anne Frank**, the young Jewish diarist who hid for years with her family in a nearby house only to be tragically discovered near the end of WWII. Across Prinsengracht from here spreads the **Jordaan**, an area built up in the 17th century to house the city's lower class. Revived in the 1960s as a student ghetto, today its many renovated gabled houses sit atop canal-front cafés in Amsterdam's trendiest quarter.

South from the Dam along NZ Voorburgwal, the quaint **Spui** square acts as a façade to hide one of the inner city's most tranquil spots, the **Begijnhof**. Such *hofjes*, or groupings of almshouses, where built throughout the Low Countries in the Middle Ages to house Catholic women, the elderly and poor. Around the corner on Kalverstraat is Amsterdam's **Historical Museum**.

Continuing south, Leidsestraat ends where the city's nightlife takes off at **Leidseplein**. From here it's just a few minutes' walk south-east past **Vondelpark** – a summer-long entertainment venue – to the ever-inundated Museumplein where you'll find the Rijksmuseum, van Gogh Museum and Stedelijk Museum (see the following section). Follow Singelgracht two blocks east to the **Heineken Brewery**.

Back across the canals, the **Muntplein** tower denotes the colourful **floating flower market**. Farther north, the sleaze of the **red-light district** extends along the parallel OZ Voorburgwal and OZ Achterburgwal canals, past **Oude Kerk**, the city's oldest church, to **Zeedijk**, once the heroin nerve centre and *the*

street not to go. It's recently been given a face-lift but plenty of drugs still are going down in the alleys leading to the stark **Nieuwmarkt**.

East of here is the city's Jewish quarter or **Jodenhoek**. It was from here, in a small park opposite the **Jewish Historical Museum**, that 425 young Jewish men were rounded up and sent to their deaths in concentration camps in retaliation for the killing of a Nazi collaborator. The nearby **Rembrandthuis** and **Waterlooplein market** attract hordes. Farther east, the **Hortus Botanicus** (Botanical Garden) is home to the world's oldest potplant, to the north near the harbour is the **Scheepvaart Museum** (Dutch Maritime Museum), while at the end of Plantage Middenlaan is the excellent **Tropenmuseum** (Museum of the Tropics).

Museums & Art Galleries If you intend visiting more than a few museums, it can be worth buying the Museumcard (see Money in the Facts for the Visitor section earlier in this chapter). Alternatively, there's the Museum Boat's f25 'combi-ticket' which gives entry into three of 20 museums between which the boat plies.

The **Rijksmuseum** on Stadhouderskade 42 is the Netherlands' largest art collection, concentrating on Dutch artists from the 15th to 19th centuries and housing Rembrandt's famous *Night Watch*. It's open Tuesday to Saturday from 10 am to 5 pm, Sunday 1 to 5 pm, and costs f6.50/3.50 for adults/children.

Despite a recent failed theft attempt, the **van Gogh Museum** at Paulus Potterstraat 7 (same hours as the Rijksmuseum) has 200 or so of his works; admission costs f10/5 for adults/children. Next door, the **Stedelijk Museum** has contemporary Dutch art, open daily from 11 am to 5 pm, admission f7/3.50 for adults/children.

Excerpts from **Anne Frank's** diary movingly describe the Jewish teenager's last years in the house at Prinsengracht 263, now also the Antifascist Movement centre. Open Monday to Saturday from 9 am to 5 pm and Sunday from 10 am, it costs f6/3 for adults/children; Museumcards are not accepted.

For a wider picture, the **Jewish Historical Museum** at Jonas Daniël Meijerplein 2 details Jewish society and the Holocaust. It's open daily from 11 am to 5 pm, and costs f7/3.50 for adults/children; take tram No 9 or the metro to Waterlooplein.

The **Verzetsmuseum** (Resistance Museum) at Lekstraat 63 gives another angle, telling the story of Dutch resistance. There's an excellent English guide for f3.50. Open Tuesday to Friday from 10 am to 7 pm, weekends 1 to 5 pm, it costs f3.50/1.75 for adults/children; take tram No 4 or 25.

The **Rembrandthuis** at Jodenbreestraat 4-6 displays sketches by the master in his former home, open Monday to Saturday from 10 am to 5 pm, Sunday 1 to 5 pm; it costs f4/2.50 for adults/children; take the metro to Waterlooplein.

Considering the Netherlands' role in seafaring history, the **Scheepvaart Museum** at Kattenburgerplein 1 comes as no surprise. A complete collection of everything maritime, it's lorded over by the superbly restored, 18th century, United East India Company rig, *Amsterdam*. Open Tuesday to Saturday from 10 am to 5 pm, Sunday from 1pm, admission costs f10/7.50 for adults/children and includes entry to the *Amsterdam*. It's about 15 minutes' walk east of CS, or take bus No 22 or 28.

The **Tropenmuseum** at Linnaeusstraat 2 realistically depicts African, Asian and Latin American lifestyles including historical and contemporary problems. It's open weekdays from 10 am to 5 pm, weekends noon to 5 pm, and costs f6/3 for adults/children; take tram No 9.

Royal Palace Occasionally used by the royal family who opt more for their residences in The Hague, the Dam Square palace is open for guided tours in summer only, but hours are irregular. Check at the palace or the VVV.

Heineken Brewery Closed for beer production in early 1988, the 120-year-old brewery at Stadhouderskade 78 still coerces beer buffs to its twice-daily (10 am and 2 pm)

tours. Tickets (f2) go on sale at 9.30 am but come early, as even first thing Monday there are plenty of takers.

Markets There's a profusion of street markets. Most open daily except Sunday, from 9 or 10 am to 5 pm. The biggest flea market is **Waterlooplein**, good for cheap bikes and locks. The **Bloemenmarkt** on Singel is a floating flower market popular with tourists and pickpockets.

Bike Tours Several companies will put you on a bike. Try the following:

Ena's Bike Tour (☎ 015-14 37 97) – cheese factories and working windmills for f37.50 (f5 off for Vondelpark YHA stayers). It's a Delft telephone number but tours depart daily at 10 am from the bicycle depot in the basement of Amstel Station

Dunn's (☎ 664 74 00), Meerhuizenstraat 1 – takes in the waterland reserve to the north in a seven-hour cycle for f58 including lunch

Yellow Bike (☎ 620 69 40), NZ Voorburgwal 66 – same as above, f39 and bring your own food. City tours for f25

Lindbergh (☎ 622 27 66), Damrak 26 – large company with the same tours and prices as Yellow Bike.

Around Amsterdam Nearby sights are easily reached by public transport or guided tours – get brochures from the VVV or the NZH Travel kiosk (☎ 625 07 72) on Damrak.

The world's biggest flower auction is held daily (except weekends) at **Aalsmeer** south of Amsterdam, in a complex the size of 100 football fields. Bus No 172 from CS takes an hour and drops you at the back – from there you'll need a compass and your own lunch. Either walk the perimeter or take a short cut through the complex (up the spiral stairs just before the loading docks 100 metres to the right once through the back gate). Bidding starts early, so arrive by 9 am. Admission costs f4 for anyone aged 14 and over (free for those under).

To get to the once typical, now tourist-filled, fishing village of **Volendam**, take bus No 110 from CS (35 minutes). To the similar village and former island of **Marken**, now connected to the mainland by a dyke, get bus

No 111 (45 minutes) or go to Volendam and take the ferry (summer only, f4.50/7 single/return).

The **Alkmaar cheese market**, staged at 10 am every Friday in summer on the town's main market square, attracts droves. Arrive early if you want to get more than a fleeting glimpse of the famous round cheeses being whisked away. There are two trains per hour from CS (30 minutes) and it's a 10-minute walk at the other end.

Places to Stay

Amsterdam is popular all year but in peak times it's overrun – bookings are essential.

Camping Backpackers are generally directed to 'the two 'youth camps'. The closest is *Vliegenbos* (☎ 636 88 55) at Meeuwenlaan 138, across the harbour from CS, open from April to September, charging f4.50 for those aged under 15 years, f5.50 for those between 15 and 30 years old, and f6.50 for those older than 30. There are no site fees, but a motorbike/car/camper van costs f2/3/13.50. Take bus No 32 or 39.

The other, *Zeeburg* (☎ 694 44 30), is at Zuider IJdijk 44, open as above with a flat rate of f6, plus f1.25/2/2.50/7.50 per tent/motorbike/car/camper van; take bus No 22. Otherwise, *De Badhoeve* (☎ 02904-2 94) at Uitdammerdijk 10, or *Gaaspercamping* (☎ 696 73 26) at Loosdrechtdreef 7 are open all year.

Hostels & Youth Hotels There are many official or private hostels and youth hotels, but facilities, atmosphere and breakfast menus vary greatly. Most don't take advance bookings, so turn up early.

Old City Centre Accurately advertised as the 'cheapest B&B in town', *The Shelter* (☎ 625 32 30) at Barndesteeg 21 is a Christian youth hostel in the red-light district just over 10 minutes' walk from CS. It has huge, single-sex dorms, a fusion of nationalities, midnight curfews and the odd undesirable in the alley outside, but at f13.50 there are few

complaints. Follow the signs from CS or get the metro to Nieuwmarkt.

Five minutes' walk south is one of the city's two official NJHC youth hostels, *Stadsdoelen* (☎ 624 68 32) at Kloveniersburgwal 97. Open from March to November, it's on one of the city's oldest canals, charges f20 and has a 2 am curfew; the closest metro is Nieuwmarkt. Right in the heart of the red-light district, the lively *Kabul* (☎ 623 71 58) at Warmoesstraat 38 is big and friendly and has frequent bands, singles/doubles/triples for f65/75/110 or dorms from f21; breakfast is f6 extra.

To the right out of the back entrance of CS is the popular *'t Ancker* (☎ 622 95 60) at de Ruyterkade 100, with harbour views, dorms/doubles for f30/80 and an assortment of other rooms. It accepts telephone reservations.

A short walk west of CS is *Hotel Beaux Arts* (☎ 638 19 41) at Martelaarsgracht 12. It has a laid-back bar with soft rules on soft drugs and dorms/singles for f25/50. Farther at NZ Voorburgwal 92 is *Bob's Youth Hostel* (☎ 623 00 63), with a 3 am curfew that doesn't apply to the loud rock that permeates from its basement café. A bunk in a clean dorm costs f20. It's 10 minutes' walk from CS or take tram No 1, 2 or 5. North-west of CS is *Bill's 'Happy Hour' Youth Hostel* (☎ 625 52 59) at Binnen Wieringerstraat 8, with dorms/doubles from f25/60.

Beyond Old City Centre The main official youth hostel, *Vondelpark* (☎ 683 17 44), is at Zandpad 5, open all year, popular with teenage school groups, and charges f20.50. Get tram No 1, 2 or 5 to Leidseplein, cross Singelgracht, turn left into Stadhouderskade and right into Zandpad.

Ideally sited in a colourful canal house near Leidseplein, the *International Budget Hotel* (☎ 624 27 84) at Leidsegracht 76 is a great choice. It's calm and friendly, there's no curfew and there's 24-hour security. A bed in a four-person room costs f30, doubles are from f80. From CS, take tram No 1, 2 or 5 to Leidseplein. If it's full, it also runs the larger *Euphemia Budget Hotel* (☎ 622 90 45) at

Fokke Simonszstraat 1 – same prices; take tram No 16, 24 or 25 from CS and get off at Prinsengracht. Closer to Leidseplein is the huge, newly renovated *Hotel Hans Brinker* (☎ 622 06 87) at Kerkstraat 136. It's popular with well-off visiting students and has singles/doubles/dorms from f67/103/35.

A Christian hostel similar to The Shelter, but in a more urbane area than its red-light counterpart, is *Eban Haëzer* (☎ 624 47 17) at Bloemstraat 179; you'll find the same prices, rules and big dorms as in The Shelter – get tram No 13 or 17 to Marnixstraat. For even bigger dorms, try the legendary *Sleep-In* at 's-Gravesandestraat 51 (☎ 694 74 44). A 1960s survivor, it's still the haunt of dope and Doors fans and regularly has live bands. There's no curfew but it's closed from noon until 4 pm. A bunk in a 100-bed, mixed-sex dorm costs f13.50. Breakfast is f5 extra. Take the metro to Weesperplein, then walk, or jump on tram No 6.

Near the Jordaan, the *Keizersgracht Hotel* (☎ 625 13 64) at Keizersgracht 15-17 has light security, a big bar and 3 am curfew; singles/triples/dorms cost f60/105/24 without breakfast.

Hotels There is a glut of hotels, mainly in the sky-high category. The following rates are for rooms without shower and toilet but, unless stated, including breakfast.

Old City Centre The closest option to CS is Amsterdam's only remaining 'botel': the *Amstel* (☎ 626 42 47) at de Ruyterkade pier No 5 behind CS. Spotlessly clean doubles/triples/quads start at f86/108/128.

Hotel Beursstraat (☎ 626 37 01), at Beursstraat 9 just up from the 'Beurs' (Stock Exchange), is ordinary but secure and clean, and there's public parking nearby. Singles/doubles cost f55/75 without breakfast. Two streets over on one of the main red-light canals is *The Crown* (☎ 626 96 64) at OZ Voorburgwal 21. There's plenty of space, a lively bar, and singles/doubles start at f65/100 without breakfast.

Just off Dam Square, *RHO Hotel* (☎ 620 73 71) at Nes 11-23 has three-star comfort,

private parking (f35 per day) and singles/doubles for f125/175. At the other end of the spectrum, *Hotel Brian* (☎ 624 46 61) at Singel 69 is small, semi-secluded and wrapped in a permanent smoke haze. Singles/doubles cost f40/80.

Beyond Old City Centre A sage choice is *Seven Bridges* (☎ 623 13 29) at Reguliersgracht 31. A spiral staircase leads up to lofty rooms sparsely decorated with wicker chairs and Tiffany lamps. Singles/doubles/triples start at f85/120/140, but it's already been discovered so book well ahead. Note the interesting eagle gable on the house across the canal. Two blocks away, *The Veteran* (☎ 620 26 73) on the canal at Herengracht 561 is another good option. Cheery and welcoming, single/double rooms start at f100/135, but out of season the owner, Lida, enjoys a good haggle.

Not far from the Heineken brewery is the more affordable and friendly *Hotel Sphinx* (☎ 627 36 80) on Weteringschans 82 with singles/doubles from f55/75. Near the museum stronghold, the *Hotel P C Hooftstraat* (☎ 662 71 07) at P C Hooftstraat 63 is a reasonable option in a district free of dog turds. Singles/doubles start at f60/90.

Close to Leidseplein, *Hotel King* ☎ 624 96 03) at Leidsekade 85 has a country-cottage atmosphere and singles/doubles from f80/110. Just around the curve, at No 77, *Impala* (☎ 623 47 06) has cheaper doubles from f90.

Places to Eat
Restaurants abound: try the neon-lit streets off Leidseplein for a veritable diner's market, the Jordaan for discreet eetcafés or the city centre for fast-food factories, student cafeterias and vegetarian hideaways.

Old City Centre Not far from CS, at St Jacobsstraat 19, the vegetarian *Egg Cream* (☎ 623 05 75) serves a f15.50 special from 5.30 to 8 pm – come early. Nearby, *De Keuken van 1870* (☎ 624 89 65) on Spuistraat 4 is an unpretentious Dutch diner, open until 8 pm, offering hearty soups for f3 and 'half a young cock' for f13. For classier Dutch, try *Haesje Claes* (☎ 624 99 98) on NZ Voorburgwal 320 near Spui – a dark, refined basement restaurant with traditional fare like salted herrings for f6.50, seafood and other main courses from f15 to f30.

Nearby, the city's favourite friture, *Anno Vleminckx Sausmeesters* at Voetboogstraat 33, is a must for chip fans. In a seemingly age-old tradition, young and old queue for a f2 paper cone of 'Amsterdam's best' sauce-smothered frites which they then stand and eat in an air of camaraderie in the dimly lit alley. Even if you don't like frites, it's a great sight.

Just before the red-light district, *Sukasari* (☎ 624 00 92) on Damstraat 26 has Indonesian mains from f18, or there are more serene options tucked away in the Nes – the easily missed lane off Dam Square's south-east corner. *Café Frascati* (☎ 624 13 24) at Nes 59 is modernly spacious with mains from f18, while farther along, *Sisters* (☎ 626 39 70) is a slightly cheaper vegetarian haunt with a diverse menu including guacamole and curries.

A block farther south, *La Margarita* (☎ 624 05 29) at Langebrugsteeg 6 serves huge Mexican nachos for f12.50. Follow Langebrugsteeg east to the university's student cafeteria *Atrium* at OZ Achterburgwal 237 for f6.50 meals weekdays only, from noon to 2 pm and 5 to 7 pm.

Beyond Old City Centre Indonesian, Greek and Italian cuisine compete fiercely with steak houses and Dutch fare in the streets off Leidseplein. Here you'll find *Bojo* (☎ 622 37 59) at Lange Leidsedwarsstraat 51, a great value Indonesian restaurant and one of the few late-night or early-morning options. On the next corner, *Piccolino* (☎ 623 14 95) at Lange Leidsedwarsstraat 63 has pizzas from f9 and comes highly recommended.

Back towards Singel, *Hollandse Glorie* (☎ 624 47 64) at Kerkstraat 222 is laced and intimate, with Dutch mains from f23. Continuing to Singel, *Rose's Cantina* (☎ 625 97 97) at Reguliersdwarsstraat 38 is a big Mexican restaurant with even bigger pitchers of sangria.

In the Jordaan, the amiable *Miramare* (☎ 625 88 95) pizzeria at Runstraat 6 has pizzas from f8, while the *Pancake Bakery* (☎ 625 13 33), in the basement of an old warehouse at Prinsengracht 191, serves platter-sized pancakes from f7 to f15. To the east of the city, the Tropenmuseum's *Soeterijn* (☎ 568 83 92) has a menu to match its international exhibitions – Cambodian and Moroccan dishes (average f17), for a start.

Cafés & Eetcafés Amsterdam has a plethora of cafés where you can have a coffee or a snack, and an increasing number of pubs that also serve meals. As a rule, if it looks good, go in.

Spaciousness – rather than a wall of smoke – is the first thing that hits you about *Café de Jaren* (☎ 625 57 71) at Nieuwe Doelenstraat 20 near Muntplein. There's a large, popular sun deck out the back and English newspapers. Just up the canal at Kloveniersburgwal 59, *De Engelbewaarder* (☎ 625 37 72) is a pleasant, one-time literary café, or for the contemporary real thing, try the *Central Library* coffee shop (closed Sundays) at Prinsengracht 587, where there are racks of English magazines and papers.

Françoise (☎ 624 01 45) at Kerkstraat 176 is a serene coffee shop-cum-art-and-plant gallery, not far from the trendy antique enclave around Nieuwe Spiegelstraat, open only until 6 pm. Opposite the Tropenmuseum, the terraced *East of Eden* café with its huge tusker mural is a fitting finale to an afternoon in the museum.

Self-Catering In the old city centre, there's a *Mignon* supermarket at Nieuwendijk 175. Outside the old city centre, *Albert Heijn* is at Vijzelstraat 119. There are many other small supermarkets hidden away around town.

Entertainment
While the infamous youth clubs, 'smoking' coffee shops and red-light district live on, the radical air is largely gone. These days you'll

NETHERLANDS

see groups of elderly tourists herded en masse past the windowed women while the younger set head for the music cafés, designer bars and nightclubs dotted throughout the city.

Classical music, theatre and ballet are high on the priorities, as are African and world music. Pick up the fortnightly, f2.75 'What's On' guide from the VVV (or free from the Amsterdam Uit Buro (AUB) ticket shop on the corner of Leidseplein and Marnixstraat).

Gay nightlife centres on Reguliersdwarsstraat and Kerkstraat and the streets off Rembrandtplein. The COC (see the Useful Organisations section earlier in this chapter) has a list of homosexual and lesbian clubs and bars.

Pubs Pubs, bars, brown cafés, cafés – call them what you like, but places to drink abound. For the intimate atmosphere of the old brown café, try *Hoppe* at Spui 18 – it's been enticing drinkers behind its thick curtain for more then 300 years (the entrance is to the right of the pub-with-terrace of the same name). In the Jordaan, *Tuin* at 2e Tuindwarsstraat 13 has an impressive view of the Westerkerk tower, especially when it's backed by an azure evening sky. At the top end of the red-light district, *In den Olofspoort* at Nieuwebrugsteeg 13 is a typical genever-tasting house.

There's a throng of gay bars and cafés, although not nearly as many options for lesbians. *Saarein* at Elandsstraat 119 and *Vive la vie* at Amstelstraat 7 are two of the most popular women's bars, while *CO2* at Rozenstraat 14 is a daytime men's café.

Live Music The Dutch favour live jazz, and Amsterdam's no exception. There are plenty of venues. *Café Alto* (☎ 626 32 49) at Korte Leidsedwarsstraat 15 has nightly sessions from 9.30 or 10 pm. A more mellow, blues and folk scene can be found at *The String* (☎ 625 90 15), Nes 98. Another blues stronghold is *Maloe Melo* (☎ 625 33 00) on Lijnbaansgracht 160.

The legendary *Melkweg* (Milky Way) (☎ 624 17 77), behind Leidseplein on Lijnbaansgracht 234a, moves from late until early with live rock, reggae and African rhythm. The equally hallowed *Paradiso* (☎ 626 45 21) at Weteringschans 6 these days has everything from Turkish theatre to heavy rock or classical. *Soeterijn* (☎ 568 83 92), downstairs at the Tropenmuseum, is a leading venue for music, film and theatre, often in English, from developing countries.

'Smoking' Coffee Shops Although the once omnipresent hemp leaf stickers have largely come unstuck, you'll have little difficulty pinpointing the coffee shops whose trade is marijuana, hash and spacecakes rather than tea, coffee and cookies. The most famous is *The Bulldog*, now with four branches around town, the chief one at Leidseplein 13-17. *Goa* at Kloveniersburgwal 42 sells spacecake for f7.50; more discreet is *Rusland* at Rusland 16. *Easy Times* at Prinsengracht 476, next to the modern African art gallery, is a favoured Surinamese haunt, while in the Jordaan, the canalside *Pie* on Lauriergracht is the pick of the crop.

Nightclubs For discoing, there's the *Roxy* at Singel 465, or *Mazzo* at Rozengracht 114 in the Jordaan. Two of the many gay nightclubs are *Havana* at Reguliersdwarsstraat 17 and *De Club* at Amstel 178.

Cinema Cafés and the like have posters stuck to their windows listing what's screening at the mainstream cinemas. For foreign and art films, try *Desmet* (☎ 627 34 34) on Plantage Middenlaan 4a.

Theatre English-speaking performances are held at the *Stalhouderij* theatre (☎ 626 22 82) on Eerste Bloemdwarsstraat 4.

Things to Buy
Amsterdam is a shopper's city, and there are exclusive outlets everywhere. Here's a random selection of some interesting shops:

Terra
    Reestraat 21 (☎ 638 59 13) – specialises in sun-baked Spanish pots
De Witte Tandenwinkel
    Runstraat 5 (☎ 623 34 43) – toothbrush trader
Musiques du Monde
    Singel 281 (☎ 624 13 54) – world music
The Headshop
    On the corner of Nieuwe Hoogstraat and Kloveniersburgwal (☎ 624 90 61) – all kinds of drug devices
Flying Objects
    Tweede Tuindwarsstraat 8 (☎ 626 84 25) – getting high on kites
Condomerie
    Warmoesstraat 141 (☎ 627 41 74) – well situated for its trade
De Klompenboer
    NZ Voorburgwal 20 (☎ 623 06 32) – clog specialist

Getting There & Away

Air Schiphol airport is one of Western Europe's major international hubs, and Amsterdam is long known for its cheap bucket-shop tickets (see Travel Agents in the Amsterdam Orientation & Information section). Airline offices in Amsterdam include:

American Airlines
    WTC, Stravinskylaan 1019 (☎ 664 86 86)
British Airways
    Stadhouderskade 4 (☎ 685 22 11)
Canadian Airlines International
    Stadhouderskade 2 (☎ 685 17 21)
KLM
    Gabriël Metsustraat 2-6, on the corner of Museumplein (☎ 649 36 33, or ☎ 06-874 77 47 for 24-hour reservations and information)
Qantas
    Stadhouderskade 6 (☎ 683 80 81)

Bus Eurolines (☎ 694 17 91) operates from Amstel Station, connected to CS by metro. Tickets can be bought from Budget Bus on Rokin 10. It has services to many European and Scandinavian destinations, including two or three buses per day to London – a one-way ticket for those aged over/under 26 years costs f95/85. The overnight bus takes about 12½ hours and goes via The Hague and Rotterdam, crossing the Channel from Ostend in Belgium, and arriving at London's Victoria Coach Station at about 6 am the next

day. The daytime service (11½ hours) runs via Utrecht and Breda, Antwerp and Bruges in Belgium, and crosses the Channel from Calais in France (check whether you need a French visa), arriving in London at about 7.30 pm. On Friday and Saturday nights (or every night during the peak holiday and summer seasons), an extra service leaves Amsterdam at about 10 pm, goes via The Hague, Rotterdam and Ostend, arriving at London at 11.30 am the next day. Other services include Brussels (f35, five hours), Cologne (f45, 4½ hours), Copenhagen (f115, 12 hours) and Paris (f70, 8½ hours).

Hoverspeed Citysprint (☎ 664 66 26) buses to London leave from Van Tuyll van Serooskerkenweg 125 – tram No 24 from CS. Arrivals from London are dropped more centrally at Leidseplein. A one-way ticket for those aged over/under 26 years costs f95/80. All Hoverspeed buses cross the Channel with the SeaCat or Hovercraft from Calais in France (check whether you need a French visa), ending at London's Victoria Station.

The departure times and frequency of Citysprint services vary depending on the season. But basically, all year there is a daily daytime bus (11 hours) which goes via The Hague, Rotterdam and Breda, Antwerp and Bruges in Belgium, to Calais, arriving in London in the early evening. From Easter to the end of September, there's an additional, quicker daytime run (10 hours) which goes via Utrecht, Breda and Antwerp, arriving in London about 10 pm. And in the peak season (June to September), there are another two services: a daytime bus (10 hours) via Utrecht, Breda and Antwerp, and an overnight bus (11½ hours) which takes the same route (minus Antwerp), arriving in London at 7 am.

Train There's an international information and reservations office (☎ 620 22 66) at CS, open weekdays until 10 pm, weekends 8 pm. For national information, ☎ 06-92 92, or ask at the ticket windows. Luggage lockers at CS cost f1.50/3 for small/large; the luggage room, f2 per item. In peak times there are queues for both.

For fares and journey times to other destinations in the Netherlands, check the Getting There & Away sections in those places. For prices and times of trains to neighbouring countries, as well as information on the train/ferry services to London, see Train in the Getting There & Away section at the beginning of this chapter.

Car & Motorbike Local companies have the cheapest car rental – about f60 per day, plus km fees. Try the following in Amsterdam:

Diks Autohuur
    Gen Vetterstraat 51-55, 1059 BT Amsterdam
    (☎ 662 33 66)
Kuperus BV
    Middenweg 175, 1098 AM Amsterdam
    (☎ 693 87 90)
Kaspers en Lotte
    Van Ostadestraat 232, 1073 TT Amsterdam
    (☎ 671 70 66)
Budget
    Overtoom 121, 1054 HE Amsterdam
    (☎ 612 60 66)
Europcar
    Wibautstraat 224a, 1097 BN Amsterdam
    (☎ 590 91 43)
Hertz
    Overtoom 333, 1054 JM Amsterdam
    (☎ 612 24 41)
Avis
    Nassaukade 380, 1054 AD Amsterdam
    (☎ 683 60 61)

For motorbikes, Selling (☎ 644 83 69) at Amsteldijk 161 (closed Tuesdays) rents machines for f100/450 per day/week.

Hitching For Groningen and northern Germany, take the metro to Amstel Station and get onto Gooiseweg; for Utrecht, Belgium and central/southern Germany, take tram No 25 to Nieuwe Utrechtseweg; for Schiphol, Leiden and The Hague, get tram No 6, 16 or 24 to Stadionplein and head out on Amstelveenseweg; for Haarlem and Alkmaar, get tram No 12 or bus No 15 to Haarlemmerweg.

Ferry For details on train/ferry services to London and ferries to Sweden, see the Getting There & Away section at the beginning of this chapter.

Getting Around
To/From the Airport There are trains every 15 minutes to Amsterdam CS (20 minutes), costing f5 one-way. Taxis cost about f50.

Bus, Tram & Metro CS is the hub of Amsterdam's comprehensive network of public transport, run by the Gemeentevervoerbedrijf (GVB), which has an information office next to the VVV on Stationsplein, open weekdays from 7 am to 10.30 pm and weekends from 8 am. It has free transport maps and night-bus timetables.

Buses, trams and metros use strip cards (see Getting Around in the Facts for the Visitor section earlier in this chapter), or you can buy a one/two/three-day unlimited ticket for f10.25/13.60/16.80 from the GVB (one-day tickets are also sold by bus/tram drivers).

All services run from about 5 am until midnight when the more limited night buses take over. For all information, call the national public transport number (☎ 06-92 92).

Car & Motorbike A 17th century city enmeshed by waterways is hardly the place for motorised transport. Traffic, particularly parking, is a major problem, and anti-car feelings are strong: in 1992, the city's inhabitants voted in a landmark referendum to restrict parking even further. The *Parking and Roadmap* leaflet, free from the VVV, pinpoints parking areas and dircly warns of penalties – usually a wheel clamp – for nonconformists.

Parking spaces within the central canal zone either have meters or a system where you buy a ticket from a central 'parking pole'. Parking garages charge about f3 per hour. A large and central one that often has space is under the modern City Hall/Music Theatre (the 'Stopera') on Waterlooplein. Motorcycles can usually be parked on pavements (sidewalks) so long as they don't obstruct pedestrians, but security is a big problem with any parked vehicle, irrespective of the time of day. For any queries, contact the Parking Department (☎ 626 69 11) at Prins Hendrikkade 108.

Bicycle Tram tracks and the other 550,000 bikes are the only real obstacle to cycling. It's advisable to book rental bikes ahead in summer. Try the following places:

Take a Bike (☎ 624 83 91), Stationsplein 33 – f7.50/30 per day/week
Amstel Stalling (☎ 692 35 84), Amstel Station – f7.50/30 per day/week
Macbike (☎ 620 09 85), Nieuwe Uilenburgerstraat 116 – f10/50 per day/week
Holland Rent-a-Bike (☎ 622 32 07), Damrak 247 – f12.50/50 per day/week
Damstraat Rent-a-Bike (☎ 625 50 29), Pieter Jacobszdwarsstraat 11 – f12.50/50 per day/week

Canal Boat, Bus & Bike A horde of operators sell canal cruises for about f10 per hour, leaving from in front of CS, along Damrak and Rokin near the Rijksmuseum. The Canal Bus (☎ 623 98 86) (day ticket f12.50) stops at the tourist enclaves between CS and the Rijksmuseum. In summer, canal 'bikes' can be hired at Amstel 57 (☎ 626 55 74), with two/four-seaters costing f19.50/29.50 per hour.

Taxi & Watertaxi Both are expensive, but watertaxis, with their f2 or f3-per-minute rates, prohibitively so. For watertaxi information and bookings, ☎ 622 21 81; for road taxis, ☎ 677 77 77.

The Randstad

The Netherlands' most densely populated region, the Randstad (literally, 'Urban Agglomeration') spreads in a circle from Amsterdam, incorporating The Hague, Rotterdam and Utrecht, and smaller towns like Haarlem, Leiden and Delft. A compact area, its many sights are highlighted by the bulb fields, which explode in intoxicating colours between March and May. They're best viewed between Haarlem and Leiden; even from the window of a train, they're a spectacular sight.

HAARLEM
Less than 15 minutes by train from Amsterdam, Haarlem is close to the spectacular colours of the Keukenhof and the wealthy seaside resort of Zandvoort. It's a small but vibrant town, home to the country's oldest museum as well as one dedicated to the city's favourite son, Frans Hals.

Orientation & Information
The train and bus stations are 10 minutes' walk, straight up Kruisweg, from the Grote Markt, Haarlem's central square. Zandvoort is 10 minutes down the railway line. The post office is at Gedempte Oude Gracht 2. The telephone code is 023.

For washing clothes, My Beautiful Laundrette is at Botermarkt 20, open daily from 7 am to 9 pm (Sunday from 9 am).

Tourist Offices The Haarlem VVV (☎ 31 90 59), at Stationsplein 1 to the right outside the train station, sells city brochures and has the weekly *Uitloper* entertainment guide. It's open Monday to Saturday from 9 am to 5.30 pm (from 1 October to 30 March on Saturday from 10 am to 4 pm).

The Zandvoort office (☎ 02507-1 79 47) is at Louis Davidsstraat 18.

Things to See & Do
Haarlem's main attractions are its museums, which can be covered in a day if you're not planning on visiting the nearby Keukenhof and Zandvoort as well.

Museums The **Frans Hals Museum** at Groot Heiligland 62 showcases many of the 17th century artist's portraits. It's open Monday to Saturday from 11 am to 5 pm, Sunday from 1 pm, and costs f4.50/2 for adults/children.

Close to the town centre, the **Tylers Museum** at Spaarne 16 is the country's oldest, housing a curious collection including drawings by Michelangelo and Raphael.

It's open Tuesday to Saturday from 10 am to 7 pm, Sunday 1 to 5 pm, and costs f6.50/3 for adults/children.

One of the town's most modest sights is the **Corrie Ten Boom House**, otherwise known as 'The Hiding Place', at Barteljorisstraat 19. In an old clock shop, it was the home of the Ten Boom family, who hid Jews and resistance workers during WW II. Eventually betrayed, Corrie Ten Boom was the only member to survive the concentration camps. It's open in summer Monday to Saturday from 10 am to 4.30 pm, November to March from 11 am to 3.30 pm; entry is free.

St Bavo Churches There are two St Bavos in Haarlem: the cathedral to the north-west of the train station, and the more popular Grote Kerk or St Bavokerk on the Grote Markt. This voluminous latter church is home to the equally grand Müller organ which a young Mozart played, and which you can hear in summer on Tuesday at 8.15 pm and Thursday at 3 pm.

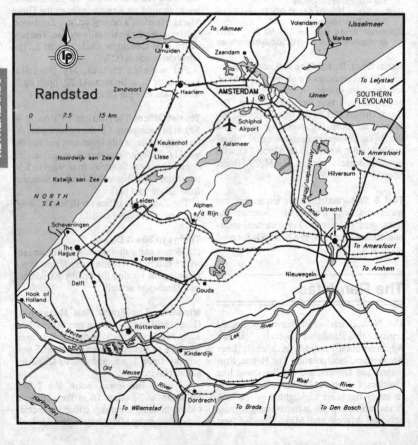

Around Haarlem Near the town of Lisse between Haarlem and Leiden, the world's largest garden, the **Keukenhof**, attracts a staggering 800,000 people for a mere eight weeks every year. Its beauty is something of an enigma, combining nature's talents with artificial precision to create a garden where millions of tulips and daffodils bloom every year, perfectly in place and exactly on time. It's open from late March to May but dates vary slightly, so check with the VVV or Keukenhof (☎ 02521-1 90 34). Take bus No 50 or 51 from Haarlem station. The Keukenhof costs f14/6.50 for adults/children.

The beach is all that will draw you to **Zandvoort**, Haarlem's seaside suburb. Recently awarded the Blue Flag of Europe for its 'clear water and clean environment', it's a fanciful claim, considering that the water is murky and the droning from the nearby motor racing track is nothing short of pollution.

Places to Stay

There are a few reasonably priced hotels in Haarlem, or else try the pensions at Zandvoort.

Camping *De Liede* (☎ 33 23 60) at Liewegje 17 is open all year – take bus No 5 to the end and walk 15 minutes. Alternatively, summer-only sites dot the dunes near Zandvoort.

Hostels The *youth hostel* (☎ 37 37 93) at Jan Gijzenpad 3 is out of town, but bus No 2 stops at the front door, or get the train to Santpoort Zuid and walk 10 minutes. It's open from March to October.

Hotels The *Waldor* (☎ 31 26 22) at Jansweg 40 has singles/doubles for f65/75; the *Carillon* (☎ 31 05 91) at Grote Markt 27 and *Stadscafé* (☎ 32 52 02) at Zijlstraat 56 have singles/doubles from f50/75.

In Zandvoort, the Hogeweg is littered with places – try *Pension Zilvermeeuw* (☎ 1 72 86) at No 32 with singles/doubles for f40/70, or if you're game, *Fawlty Towers* (☎ 1 53 26) at Dr Smitstraat 5 has singles/doubles for f65/150.

Places to Eat

The vegetarian *Eko* (☎ 32 65 68) at Zijlstraat 39 has a dagschotel for f15.50 with complimentary herb bread, or closer to Grote Markt there's the tavern-like *Stadscafé* (see Hotels in the previous Places to Stay section). To the side of the Markt at Rivier Vismarkt 1, *Piccolo* (☎ 32 68 49) is a popular pizza haunt, or there's slightly more expensive Mexican at *Santa Fe* (☎ 31 01 13), Gedempte Oude Gracht 33. Just up the road at No 58, there's a *Deka Markt* supermarket.

Entertainment

The *Café 1900* on Barteljorisstraat 10 has rock several nights a week, while the *Jazz & Blues Eetcafé* at Jansweg 21 near the station has nightly sessions. If it's a Belgian beer you're after, try the laid-back *Café het Melkwoud* at Zijlstraat 63, open until 2 am.

Getting There & Away

InterCity trains run every 15 minutes to/from Amsterdam CS (f5, 15 minutes) and Leiden (f7.50, 30 minutes).

LEIDEN

Home to the country's oldest university, Leiden is an effervescent town, bubbling with canalside cafés and with an aura of intellect generated by the 20,000 students who make up a sixth of the population. The university was a present from William the Silent for withstanding a long Spanish siege in 1574. A third of the townsfolk starved before the Spaniards retreated on October 3, now the date of Leiden's biggest festival.

Orientation & Information

Arriving by train, first impressions can be deceiving. The area around the railway and bus stations is being modernised, making it one of the least appealing parts. Most of the sights lie within a slightly confusing network of central canals, about a 10-minute walk from the station.

The main post office is north-east of the station at Schipholweg 130, or there's a central branch at Breestraat 46. There's a

NETHERLANDS

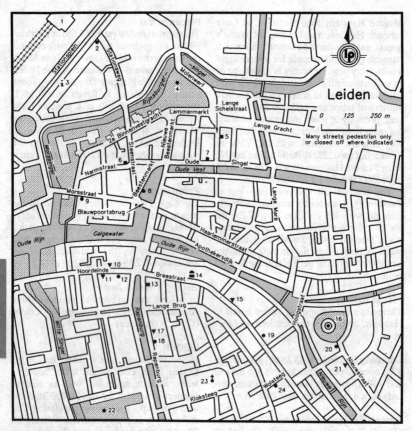

Leiden

0   125   250 m

Many streets pedestrian only
or closed off where indicated

wassalon at Morsstraat 50, open weekdays
from 8 am to 9 pm.

Leiden's telephone code is 071.

Tourist Office The VVV (☎ 14 68 46) is at
Stationsplein 210, open weekdays from 9 am
to 5.30 pm, Saturday until 4 pm. It has
walking-tour pamphlets and the monthly
Agenda entertainment booklet.

Things to See & Do
You can pick from a dozen museums, or in
summer, canal cruises leave from near the
bridge at Beestenmarkt.

Museums The **Rijksmuseum van Oudheden** (National Museum of Antiquities) at
Rapenburg 28 tops the list. Its striking
entrance hall contains the Temple of Taffeh,
a gift from Egypt for the Netherlands' help
in saving ancient monuments from inundation when the Aswan High Dam was built.
It's open Tuesday to Saturday from 10 am to
5 pm, Sunday from noon, and costs f3.50/2
for adults/children.

The 17th century **Lakenhal** (Cloth Hall)
at Oude Singel 28 houses an assortment of
works by old masters, period rooms and
temporary exhibitions. It's open the same

■ PLACES TO STAY

5 Lits-Jumeaux Youth Hostel
6 Helvoort Pension
13 Hotel de Doelen

▼ PLACES TO EAT

10 Splinter Eethuis
11 Topolobampo
15 Foen Food
17 Augustinus
21 Blonks Café

OTHER

1 Centraal Station
2 Supermarket
3 Tourist Office
4 De Valk Museum
7 Lakenhal Museum
8 Canal Cruises
9 Laundry
12 Fandangos
14 Post Office
16 Burcht
18 Rijksmuseum van Oudheden
19 Supermarket
20 De Burcht Café
22 Hortus Botanicus
23 Pieterskerk
24 Café de WW

hours as the Museum of Antiquities (except Sundays from 1 to 5 pm), and costs f2.50/1.25 for adults/children.

The **Valk** (Falcon), Leiden's landmark windmill, is a museum that will blow away notions that windmills were a Dutch invention. It's at Binnenvestgracht 1, open Tuesday to Saturday from 10 am to 5 pm, Sunday from 1 pm, and costs f3/1.50 for adults/children.

Hortus Botanicus Europe's oldest botanical garden, dating back 400 years, is at Rapenburg 73, and open daily from 9 am to 5 pm (from 10 am on Sundays), but closed Saturdays in winter.

Burcht This is a 12th century citadel built high on an artificial mound in the town centre. It's good for a view of Leiden's red roofs and steepled skyline. Enter off Nieuwstraat or Oude Rijn.

Around Leiden The **Keukenhof** (see the Things to See section in Haarlem) is about 10 km north of Leiden. It can be reached by NZH bus No 54 (20 minutes, two per hour), which runs directly there (during the flower season only) and leaves from the train station.

Places to Stay
There is a dearth of budget options, with only one central youth hotel and several pensions.

Camping The closest seaside grounds are *De Zuidduinen* at Zuidduinseweg 1 (☎ 01718-1 47 50) and *De Noordduinen* at Campingweg 1 (☎ 01718-2 52 95), both at Katwijk aan Zee and open from April to October. *Koningshof*, at Elsgeesterweg 8, Rijnsburg, is open all year – bus No 40 stops nearby.

Hostels The *Lits-Jumeaux Youth Hotel* (☎ 12 84 57) at Lange Scheistraat 9 has lofty dorms, a cosy bar and costs f20 a night with breakfast for f6. It's 10 minutes' walk from the station – head up Stationsweg, after the canal turn left into Binnenvestgracht, continue to the windmill, then it's two streets on your right. The nearest *youth hostel* (☎ 02523-7 29 20) is 45 minutes away near Noordwijk. It charges f21 – take bus No 60 (two per hour; last bus at 11 pm) to Sancta Maria hospital and walk 10 minutes.

Hotels & Pensions The closest to the station is *Helvoort* (☎ 13 23 74) at Narmstraat 1b with rooms for f35 a head. The canal-front *Witte* (☎ 12 45 92) at Witte Singel 80, or *Bik* (☎ 12 26 02) at No 92, both have singles/doubles for f40/75 – take bus No 43. The cheapest hotel is *Haas* (☎ 17 47 87) at Mariënpoelstraat 1a, with singles/doubles for f65/125, and parking. Alternatively, on the canal near the Rijksmuseum is the plush *Hotel de Doelen* (☎ 12 05 27) at Rapenburg

NETHERLANDS

2; all rooms have a shower and toilet, and start at f80/110.

Places to Eat

The best value in town is *Augustinus*, a student mensa on Rapenburg 24 with ultra-cheap meals from f5.25, open weekdays from 5.30 to 7.15 pm. *Blonks Café* (☎ 12 20 39) at Nieuwstraat 13 has a diverse menu plus vegetarian meals from f13.50 to f16.

The *Splinter Eethuis* (☎ 14 95 19) at Noordeinde 30 has a dagschotel with free soup for f11.75 (closed Monday), or across the road at No 27 is the pricier Mexican *Topolobampo* (☎ 13 19 14), which serves a combination of dishes for f16.50. *Foen Food* (☎ 12 61 78) at Breestraat 56 is an unpretentious Surinamese eatery (closed Sunday), or there are several well-priced shoarma (pitta-bread) cafés along Morssstraat.

With guilders to burn, there's a lane of candle-lit restaurants behind Pieterskerk on Kloksteeg. For self-caterers, there's a *supermarket* in the basement of the V & D department store on Breestraat.

Entertainment

Evenings revolve around the canalside cafés. The VVV has a list of current films, or for more alternative happenings, check the notice board at the entrance to *De Burcht*, a literary bar next to the citadel. *Café de WW* at Wolsteeg 6 has live music late Wednesdays. For cocktails, try *Fandangos* on Noordeinde 49.

Getting There & Away

Trains every 15 minutes connect with Amsterdam (f10.75, 35 minutes), Haarlem (f7.50, 30 minutes), The Hague (f4.25, 10 minutes) and Schiphol (f7.50, 17 minutes).

THE HAGUE

Officially known as 's-Gravenhage ('the Count's Domain') because a count built a castle here in the 13th century, The Hague – Den Haag in Dutch – is the country's seat of government and residence of the royal family, though the capital city is Amsterdam. It has a refined air, created by the many stately mansions and palatial embassies that line its green boulevards.

It's known for its prestigious art galleries, a huge jazz festival held annually near the seaside suburb of Scheveningen, and the miniature town of Madurodam. There is a poorer side to all the finery, though, and the area south of the centre is far removed from its urbane neighbours to the north.

Orientation & Information

Trains stop at Station HS (Hollands Spoor), 20 minutes' walk south of the city, or CS (Centraal Station), five minutes from the centre – head straight up Herengracht.

Tourist Offices The main VVV (☎ 070-354 62 00) is at Koningin Julianaplein 30 to the right out of CS; the other is in Scheveningen, at Gevers Deynootweg 1134 near the Kurhaus. Both are open from mid-April to mid-September, Mondays to Saturdays from 9 am to 9 pm (to 6 pm the rest of the year) and Sundays from 10 am to 5 pm. They stock the free monthly events booklet and f1.50 city guides.

Money Besides the GWK office in the station, there's an American Express (☎ 070-34 65 15) at Venestraat 20.

Post & Telecommunications The main post office is on Kerkplein next to the Grote Kerk. The Hague's telephone code is 070.

Laundry There's a wassalon to the east behind CS at Theresiastraat 250.

Emergency For police, fire or ambulance, the national emergency number is ☎ 06 11. For general medical information, ☎ 345 53 00; for an after-hours doctor, ☎ 346 96 69; for an emergency dentist, ☎ 397 44 91.

Things to See & Do

The Hague has a good selection of galleries and historical edifices. Scheveningen has the beach, dominated by the only real sight, the highbrow Kurhaus casino.

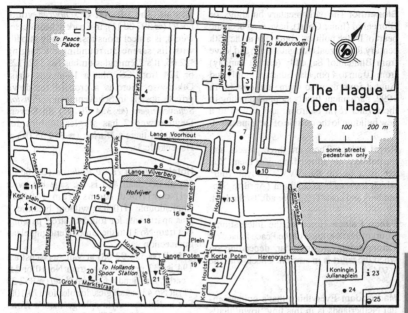

The Hague
(Den Haag)

0   100   200 m

some streets
pedestrian only

Museums & Art Galleries The showpiece is
the **Mauritshuis**, an exquisite 17th century
mansion housing a superb collection of
Dutch and Flemish masterpieces and a touch
of contemporary with Andy Warhol's *Queen
Beatrix*. On Korte Vijverberg between the
Binnenhof and the Plein, it's open Tuesday
to Saturday from 10 am to 5 pm, Sunday
from 11 am, and costs f6.50/3.50 for
adults/children.

Fans of *de Stijl*, and in particular of Piet
Mondriaan, will want to see the **Gemeente
Museum** at Stadhouderslaan 41. Open
Tuesday to Sunday from 11 am to 5 pm, it
costs f7/6 for adults/children – take tram No
10 or bus No 14.

Near the Binnenhof, the **Gevangenpoort**
(Prison Gate museum) on Buitenhof has
hourly tours showing how justice was dispensed in early times. It's open weekdays
from 10 am to 4 pm, in summer also weekends from 1 to 4 pm, and costs f5/2.50 for
adults/children.

1	Haags Filmhuis
2	Theatre PePijn
3	De Dageraad
4	Canadian Embassy
5	Royal Palace
6	British Embassy
7	Royal Palace
8	Belgian Embassy
9	US Embassy
10	French Embassy
11	Post Office
12	Gevangenpoort
13	Schlemmer Café
14	Grote Kerk
15	Hotel Corona
16	Mauritshuis
17	American Express
18	Binnenhof
19	Le Perroquet
20	Supermarket
21	De Paraplu
22	De Sax
23	Tourist Office
24	Centraal Station (CS)
25	Buses to London

Binnenhof The parliamentary buildings, or Binnenhof (Inner Court), have long been the heart of Dutch politics. Tours take in the 13th century Ridderzaal (Knight's Hall) and leave from Binnenhof 8a, daily (except Sunday) from 10 am to 4 pm, also Sundays in July and August from noon to 4 pm, and cost f4. In 1992, parliament finally stopped meeting in the former royal ballroom and moved to a new building to the outside of the Binnenhof.

Royal Palace There are three palaces and the public is not allowed in any of them. You can pass by on the VVV's 'Royal Tour' which leaves CS at 1.30 pm (April to September) and costs f19/15 for adults/children.

Peace Palace Home of the International Court of Justice, tours of the Peace Palace on Carnegieplein are irregular, depending on when the court is in session. Check with the VVV.

Madurodam Everything that's quintessential Netherlands is in this tiny 'town' that's big with tourists. It opens at 9 am daily from late March to early January, and costs f11/6 for adults/children. Take tram No 1 or bus No 22.

Places to Stay
While diplomats and royalty may call The Hague home, few budget travellers will. The handful of budget hotels tend to be clustered near Station HS, hidden somewhere in the sprawl towards Scheveningen, or in the coastal town itself.

Camping There are sites in the dunes either side of Scheveningen. *Duinhorst* (☎ 324 22 70) at Buurtweg 135, or to the south, *Ockenburgh* (☎ 325 23 64) at Wijndaelerweg 25, are open summer only. Ockenburgh lays claim to being Europe's largest camping ground, and is often packed with German tourists who come to sample the delights of Holland's continuous beach – a unique feature of the coast from Hook of Holland all the way up to the Frisian Islands.

Hostels The official *Ockenburgh* youth hostel (☎ 397 00 11), in a park at Monsterseweg 4, is a steel monstrosity totally at odds with its serene surroundings. Charging f22.65, it's 25 minutes on bus No 122, 123 or 124 from CS, plus a 10-minute walk. Otherwise, there is a crop of run-down private hostels in Scheveningen – *Pension Scheveningen* (☎ 354 70 03) on Gevers Deynootweg 2 has singles/doubles for f35/50, or there's *Marion* (☎ 354 35 01) at Havenkade 3a.

Hotels *Pension Huize Bellevue* (☎ 360 55 52) at Beeklaan 415 is the sage bet, with self-contained rooms from f60/100 single/double (f10 less without breakfast), plus apartments for four and street parking. Get tram No 11 to the Groot Hertoginnelaan intersection.

Jodi (☎ 355 92 08) at Van Aerssenstraat 194 is f33 per person – tram No 10 or 11. Nearby, the friendly *Esquire Hotel* (☎ 352 23 41) at No 43 has singles/doubles for f70/100. For a diplomat-style splurge there's *Hotel Corona* (☎ 363 79 30) at Buitenhof 39, with rooms from f245/310.

Alternatively, on the other side of town in front of Station HS, *Hotel Arista* (☎ 389 08 47) at Stationsweg 164 has singles/doubles from f45/75. *Astoria* (☎ 384 04 01) across the road, has rooms from f65. Farther along, near the reptile pet shop, is the cheaper *Hotel Bristol* (☎ 384 00 73).

In Scheveningen, a row of mid-price options overlook the sea at Zeekant. If you can forgo the view, *Hotel Duinhorst* (☎ 350 69 99) at Alkmaarsestraat 6 is friendly with singles/doubles with shower for f60/97, and parking. Similarly priced is *Hotel Patria* (☎ 354 22 37) on Harstenhoekweg 6.

Places to Eat
Fortunately you get a more versatile outlook on eating than sleeping. The cobbled streets off Denneweg, north of the Lange Voorhout royal palace, are one of the livelier areas with canalside cafés, intimate restaurants, theatres and bars. Here you find *De Dageraad* (☎ 364 56 66) at Hooikade 4, a vegetarian

place with cheese fondues for f25; it's open daily until 9 pm.

Le Perroquet (☎ 363 97 86), on the corner of Lange Poten and Korte Houtstraat, serves huge satay specials for f12.50. It's also good for the ubiquitous 'koffie met appelgebak' (coffee with apple pie). *Schlemmer Café* (☎ 360 85 80) at Lange Houtstraat 17 is tastefully decorated and frequented by similarly dressed people; a lunch-time dagschotel costs f15. In Bagijnestraat, a tiny alley off Lange Poten, you'll find a gourmet's UN as well as the music café *De Paraplu* (☎ 364 71 34). The V & D on Grote Markt Straat has a basement *supermarket*.

Entertainment

Although it's more a city for fine dining than raging, there are a few lively cafés, and in mid-July the week-long North Sea Jazz Festival considerably invigorates the music scene. If you're into ballet, be sure to catch a performance by the innovative and renowned Nederlands Danstheater in its theatre off the Spui (casual dress will do).

On a daily level, there's the happening little bar *De Sax* (☎ 346 67 55) on Korte Houtstraat 14a just off the Plein, or *Theatre PePijn* (☎ 346 03 54) on Nieuwe Schoolstraat 21, with a solid live jazz lineup. Just up the street at No 1 and 2, *Boko* and *Stairs* are two gay bars/discos, and at Denneweg 56 there's the *Haags Filmhuis* (☎ 365 60 30), which screens non-mainstream movies.

The *Paard van Troje* (☎ 360 18 38), Prinsengracht 12, is The Hague's answer to Amsterdam's Melkweg and Paradiso 'cultural activity centres', with bands often performing on Thursday, Friday and Saturday, and theatre on Wednesday or Sunday – otherwise, there's film or disco. Admission costs f5 to f25 depending on what's happening. It's usually closed Monday and Tuesday, but it's under threat of permanent closure after more than 20 years with talk of cutbacks in municipal subsidies.

Getting There & Away

Bus Eurolines and Hoverspeed buses stop at Anna van Bueren Straat to the east behind CS. Tickets for both can be bought at Broere Reizen (☎ 382 40 51) travel agent inside the Babylon Centre next to the VVV. London services all originate in Amsterdam, arriving in The Hague about 50 minutes later. For details, see the Amsterdam Getting There & Away section.

Train Trains to Amsterdam (f14, 45 minutes), Delft (f3.25, five minutes), Leiden (f4.25, 10 minutes) and Rotterdam (f6, 15 minutes) depart from Station HS, though the line that takes in Schiphol airport (40 minutes) via Leiden on its way to Amsterdam leaves from CS. Trains to Utrecht (f14, 45 minutes) leave from CS. For all rail, bus and tram enquiries, ☎ 06-92 92.

Tram Just nine km away, Delft can be reached by tram No 1 (30 minutes), which departs from next to CS.

Getting Around

Buses leave from above CS, trams take off from the side. Tram Nos 7 and 8 go to Scheveningen via the Peace Palace, while tram Nos 1 and 9 follow Nieuwe Parklaan past Madurodam to the coast.

DELFT

Had the potters who lived in Delft long ago not been such accomplished copiers, today's townsfolk would probably live in relative peace. But the distinctive blue-and-white pottery which the 17th century craftsmen duplicated from Chinese porcelain became famous worldwide as delftware. If you're here in summer you'll probably wish you weren't; in winter its old-world charm and narrow, canal-lined streets make a pleasant day trip from nearby Rotterdam or The Hague. Delft is home to the country's technical university, which explains the high proportion of young males.

Orientation & Information

The train and neighbouring bus station are a 10-minute stroll south of the central Markt. The post office is on Hippolytusbuurt. There's a laundry at Koornmarkt 68, open

NETHERLANDS

NETHERLANDS

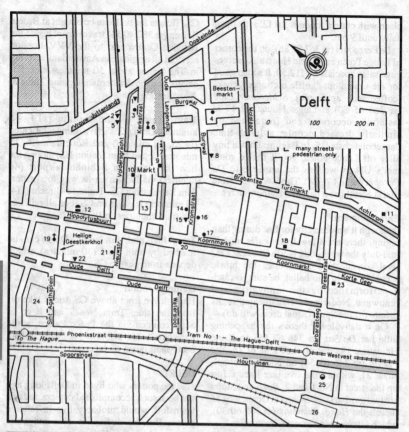

Delft

0   100   200 m

many streets
pedestrian only

PLACES TO STAY

9   Les Compagnons Hotel
10 Hotel Monopole
11 Van Leeuwen Pension
18 Hotel Leeuwenbrug
23 De Vos Pension

PLACES TO EAT

1   De Ruif Café
2   Shinta
5   Calasapone
8   De Kleine Uitspanning
15 De Kurk
22 Uit de Kunst

OTHER

3   Atelier de Candelaer
4   Kobus Kuch
6   Nieuwe Kerk
7   Tourist Office
12 Post Office
13 Town Hall
14 Filmhuis
16 Bepop Jazzcafé
17 Laundry
19 Oude Park
20 Canal Boats
21 Café de Joffer
24 Prinsenhof
25 Bus Station
26 Train Station

weekdays (closed Wednesday) from 8 am to 6 pm, Saturday to 2 pm. Delft's telephone code is 015.

Tourist Office The VVV (☎ 12 61 00) at Markt 85 sells Delft booklets for f2.50. It's open Monday to Friday from 9 am to 6 pm, Saturday until 5 pm, and in summer Sunday from 11 am to 3 pm.

Things to See & Do
Buying pottery tops most visitors' priorities. There are three factories where you can watch working artists while being set straight on identifying genuine from fake. Armed with the difference, it'll be the last thing you'll discuss with Riet, the 73-year-old owner of the delftware shop at Markt 50. An avid adventurer with an infectious, raspy laugh, her shop will be open if she's back from her travels.

Alternatively, a smattering of museums and churches attract passers-by, and canal boats cruise around in summer.

Delftware The most central and modest outfit is **Atelier de Candelaer** at Kerkstraat 12, a small operation going since 1975. The other two factories sit poles apart outside the centre. **De Delftse Pauw** at Delftweg 133 is the smaller, employing 35 painters who work mainly from their homes; take tram No 1 to Pasgeld, walk up Broekmolenweg to the canal and turn left; it has daily tours but you won't see the painters on weekends. **De Porceleyne Fles**, south at Rotterdamseweg 196, is the only original factory, operating since the 1650s. It's slick and pricey; bus No 60 from Burgwal stops nearby, or it's a 25-minute walk.

Churches The 14th century **Nieuwe Kerk** houses the crypt of the Dutch royal family as well as the mausoleum of William the Silent. Open daily except Sunday, it costs f2/1 for adults/children. The Gothic **Oude Kerk**, with 140 years' seniority and a two-metre tilt in its tower, is at Heilige Geestkerkhof. A combination ticket costs f3/1.50 for adults/children.

Prinsenhof Across from Oude Kerk at St Agathaplein 1, the Prinsenhof is where William the Silent held court until assassinated here in 1584. It now has historical and contemporary art, is open Tuesday to Saturday from 10 am to 5 pm, Sunday from 1 pm, and costs f3.50/1.75 for adults/children.

Places to Stay
There's a camping ground, *Delftse Hout* (☎ 13 00 40), at Korftlaan 5, closed from November to April – get bus No 60 from the station.

Unless you want to part with plenty of guilders for rooms often resembling wardrobes, the best bets are the pensions near the station. *Van Leeuwen* (☎ 12 37 16) at Achterom 143 is welcoming, with plenty of rooms for f35 per person – from the station, cross the canal and head straight along Barbarasteeg. *De Vos* (☎ 12 32 58) at Breestraat 5 has doubles for f60. Alternatively, on the Markt, *Hotel Monopole* (☎ 12 30 59) at No 48a has doubles for f95, or the slightly cheaper *Les Compagnons Hotel* (☎ 14 01 02) at No 61 has parking.

For a bit more, you'll get old-world charm and some space at *Hotel Leeuwenbrug* (☎ 14 77 41), Koornmarkt 16. Rooms start at f115/145.

Places to Eat
Delft's restaurants and cafés are proportional to its tourist trade. *De Ruif Café* (☎ 14 22 06) at Kerkstraat 23 has well-priced and sized meals served in the shadow of the Nieuwe Kerk. *De Kleine Uitspanning* (☎ 14 21 07) at Burgwal 11 is the place for iced coffees after Saturday's nearby street market. *Uit de Kunst* at Oude Delft 140 has tables amongst a modern art gallery and a relaxing ambience.

Pizzeria Calasapone (☎ 13 65 96) at Voldergracht 29 has pizzas from f12, while two doors along, *Shinta* (☎ 13 09 46) at No 31 is a little Indonesian eatery with rijsttafel for f27 (closed Wednesday). Otherwise, there's great local cuisine with a tropical flavour at *De Kurk* (☎ 14 14 74), Kromstraat 20.

Entertainment

Delft is no raving metropolis. The *Bepop Jazzcafé* (☎ 13 52 10) on Kromstraat is probably the liveliest spot, while nearby, the *Filmhuis* (☎ 14 02 26) at No 27 has an alternative film circuit. The local crowds at *Café de Joffer* (☎ 13 60 83) inevitably spill out onto Nieuwstraat, or for a slightly quieter haunt, try *Kobus Kuch* (☎ 12 42 80) on Beestenmarkt 1.

Getting There & Away

It's 10 minutes by train to Rotterdam, less to The Hague. Tram No 1 leaves every 15 minutes from in front of the train station for The Hague (30 minutes).

ROTTERDAM

The world's largest port, Rotterdam's catastrophic bombardment on 14 May 1940 left it crippled then and soulless today. Its centre is modern, dominated by mirrored skyscrapers, the air lacking Amsterdam's frivolity or The Hague's refinement.

Orientation & Information

Searching for a city 'centre' is fruitless – there is no real hub. The budget accommodation and sights are scattered over a large area, accessible by determined foot-slogging, metro or tram.

Tourist Office There are two offices. The main VVV (☎ 06-3403 40 65), at Coolsingel 67, is open Monday to Saturday from 9 am to 5.30 pm, and from April to September also Sundays from 10 am to 4 pm. The other office is at Centraal Station (CS), open from 9 am (10 am on Sundays) until 10 pm. Both have the weekly *Uit Journaal* or the monthly *Punt Uit* entertainment guides, and public-transport maps.

Money Besides the GWK at the station, American Express (☎ 010-433 03 00) has an office at Meent 92, along the street to the right of the post office.

Post & Telecommunications The post office is at Coolsingel 42, opposite the main tourist office. Rotterdam's telephone code is 010.

Laundry The wassalon at Proveniersssingel 35, along the canal to the right out the back entrance of CS, is open weekdays (closed Wednesday) from 8 am to 6 pm.

Emergency For police, ambulance and fire brigade, the national number is ☎ 06 11.

Things to See & Do

Rotterdam's sights lie within a region bordered by the old town of Delfshaven, the Meuse River (Maas in Dutch) and the Blaak district.

Museums Free on Wednesdays, the city's museums are lorded over by the **Boymans van Beuningen**, a rich gallery of 14th century to contemporary art at Mathenesserlaan 18. It's open Tuesday to Saturday from 10 am to 5 pm, Sunday from 11 am, and costs f3.50 for adults (free for those aged under 16).

The **Schielandshuis** museum on Korte Hoogstraat 31, the only 17th century central building to survive the German blitz, gives insight on that tragic day. Same entry costs and hours apply as with the Boymans (except that it's open from 1 pm on Sunday).

Cruises Spido (☎ 413 54 00) runs daily, 75-minute harbour cruises which cost f11.50/5.75 for adults/children, and day trips from f35 to the harbour heart at Europoort, or through the northern part of the Delta works (f37.50), taking in Kinderdijk (see Around Rotterdam) and Willemstad (see the Delta Region section) but not the Delta Expo on the Eastern Scheldt.

Euromast This 185-metre tower pricks the skyline at Parkhaven 20. There are good views on clear days but prices match the height: f13/8 for adults/children. Take tram No 4 or 9, or the metro to Dijkzigt.

Kijk-Kubus With Escher-like design, the 'cube houses' offer a new angle to modern living. They're open from April to December, Tuesday to Friday from 10 am to 5 pm, weekends from 11 am, and from January to March on Friday, Saturday and Sunday from 11 am to 5 pm. Adults/children pay f2.50/1.50; take the metro to Blaak.

Delfshaven Rotterdam's old town is most famed for its **Oude Kerk** at Aelbrechtskolk 20, where the Pilgrim Fathers set sail to the New World. Understandably popular with Americans, even Australian nostalgia rises when the church carillon surprisingly chimes *Waltzing Matilda*! Take the metro to Delfshaven.

Around Rotterdam The **Delta Expo** (see Middelburg Things to See in the Delta Region section) can be reached from CS by taking the metro to Spijkenisse, then an hour on NZH bus No 104.

The **Kinderdijk**, the Netherlands' picture-postcard string of 19 working windmills, sits between Rotterdam and Dordrecht near Alblasserdam. On Saturday afternoons in July and August the mills' sails are set in motion. One windmill is open daily from May to September – get the metro to Zuidplein, then bus No 154.

Places to Stay
A modest selection of cheap hotels gives nothing to rave about.

Camping The *camping ground* at Kanaalweg 84 (☎ 415 97 72) is about 40 minutes' walk north-west of the station, or take bus No 33.

Hostels The *youth hostel* (☎ 436 57 63) on Rochussenstraat 107 is 20 minutes' walk from the station, or get the metro to Dijkzigt. The newly renovated, summer-only *Sleep-In* (☎ 412 14 20) is at Mauritsweg 29, a few minutes' walk straight down from the station, and charges f10 including breakfast; check in after 4 pm.

Hotels The best options are out the back entrance of CS. *Bienvenue* (☎ 466 93 94) at

Spoorsingel 24, two blocks straight up the canal, is true to its name, with nice singles/doubles, all with TV, from f95/125. Alternatively, the friendly *Bagatelle* (☎ 467 63 48) at Provenierssingel 26, along the canal to the right, has singles/doubles for f37.50/60 without breakfast.

Otherwise, south of CS, *Metropole* (☎ 436 03 19) at Nieuwe Binnenweg 13a, about 10 minutes' walk straight down from the station's front entrance, has ordinary rooms for f38/75 including breakfast. On the busy 's-Gravendijkwal, *Rox-Inn* (☎ 436 61 09) at No 14 (a 15-minute walk from CS, or take tram No 1 or 7 to 'Tiendplein') has singles/doubles from f40/65 without breakfast, or there's the preferable *Traverse* (☎ 436 40 40) at No 70, a few hundred metres on, with rooms from f75 including breakfast.

Places to Eat
De Wagon (☎ 433 17 28), a train carriage-cum-restaurant at Geldersekade 10, has good views of the cube houses. Near the youth hostel, *Jazzcafé Dizzy* (☎ 477 30 14) at 's-Gravendijkwal 127 buzzes with live jazz and has snacks or pricey meals. Across the road, the *Congo Bongo* (☎ 436 63 16) tropical cookery is equally as atmospheric and expensive. For cheaper fare, *de Djoek Eetcafé* (☎ 436 15 80) up the road at No 100 is candle-lit with meals and vegetarian plates from f11.

In Delfshaven, *Het Eethuisje* at Mathenesserdijk 436a is a humble café with f8.75 meals, Monday to Friday nights until 9 pm.

At Mauritsweg 28 near the Sleep-In, *De Eend* (☎ 412 98 08) has unpretentious meals from f10.95, but is open weekdays only from 4.30 to 8 pm. Along at No 46a, *La Clé Café* (☎ 433 45 75) caters for carnivores, with steaks from f12. Opposite the station entrance, *Mallejan BV* (☎ 433 38 58) at Kruisplein 1 has a dagschotel for f12.95 and vegetarian dishes from f15. Self-caterers will find a *supermarket* in the basement of V & D on Beursplein two blocks south of the main VVV.

Entertainment

Rotterdam is home to one of the country's biggest music venues, the *Ahoy* – check the *UitJournaal* for listings. On a local level, try the *Jazzcafé Dizzy* (see Places to Eat). On Saturday nights *De Kandelaar* (☎ 476 16 26) at Nieuwe Binnenweg 326, at the Delfshaven end of the road, screens films for f5.

Getting There & Away

Bus Eurolines and Hoverspeed buses stop at Conradstraat to the right as you leave the station. Tickets can be bought from NBBS Reizen (☎ 414 98 22) at Meent 126 near the main VVV. Services to London leave from Amsterdam (for details, see Bus in the Amsterdam Getting There & Away section) and generally arrive in Rotterdam 1¼ hours later.

Train There are trains every 15 minutes to Amsterdam (f21, one hour), Delft (f4.25, 10 minutes), The Hague (f6, 15 minutes) and Utrecht (f12.25, 40 minutes). Half-hourly services run to Middelburg (f27.50, 1½ hours) and Hook of Holland.

Ferry For information on the ferries from Hook of Holland and Europoort to England, see the main Getting There & Away section at the beginning of his chapter. North Sea Ferries has a bus (f10) which leaves daily at 4 pm from CS to connect with the awaiting ferry at Europoort.

Getting Around

Trams leave from in front of the train station; the metro, underneath. Both run until about 1 am; on Fridays and Saturdays, night buses then take over.

UTRECHT

Lorded over by the Dom, the country's tallest tower, Utrecht is an antique frame surrounding an increasingly modern interior. Its 14th century sunken canals, once-bustling wharfs and cellars now brim with chic shops and cafés. Also home to the country's largest university, its student population adds spice to a once largely church-oriented community.

Orientation & Information

A compact city, the most appealing quarter lies between Oudegracht and Nieuwegracht and the streets around the Dom. Unfortunately, none of the past character is evident when arriving at the train station, which lies behind Hoog Catharijne, the Netherlands' largest indoor shopping centre and a modern-day monstrosity.

The post office is at Neude 11. There's a laundry at Wittevrouwenstraat 13 (at the end of Voorstraat a few blocks from the Sleep-In), open weekdays from 8 am to 6 pm, Saturday to 1 pm. Utrecht's telephone code is 030.

Tourist Office The VVV (☎ 403 40 85) is five minutes from the station at Vredenburg 90, open weekdays from 9 am to 6 pm, Saturday until 4 pm, and has a free *Uit in Utrecht* guide.

Things to See & Do

The 102-metre Dom tower and some unusual museums can elevate your visit. Canal cruises leave from Oudegracht.

Dom Tower The 465 steps give way to excellent views. In winter the tower is open only on weekends from noon to 5 pm; from 1 April to 31 October, it opens weekdays from 10 am to 4 pm and weekends from noon to 4 pm.

Museums There are about 15 museums, but many are little more than bizarre hideaways for particular paraphernalia – an insurance museum is one example.

The **Grocery Museum** on Hoogt 6 is worth 10 minutes. In a tiny 1800s grocery store, the one-roomed museum sits above a sweet shop filled with the popular Dutch *drop* (a sweet or salted liquorice). It's open Tuesday to Saturday from 12.30 to 4.30 pm, and entry is free.

The **Van Speelklok tot Pierement** ('From Musical Clock to Street Organ') museum has a colourful collection including 18th century instruments demonstrated with gusto during hourly tours. It's at Buurkerkhof 10, open Tuesday to Saturday from 10 am to 5 pm, Sunday from 1 pm, and costs f6/4/3 for adults/students/children.

For religious and medieval art buffs, **Het Catharijneconvent** museum winds through a 15th century convent at Nieuwegracht 63 and has the country's largest collection of medieval Dutch art. Open Tuesday to Friday from 10 am to 5 pm, weekends from 11 am, it costs f3.50/2 for adults/students and children.

Places to Stay
Central options are sparse, the budget hotels all out from the hub and the youth hostel miles away.

Camping *De Berekuil* (☎ 71 38 70) at Ariënslaan 5 is easily reached by bus No 57 from the station, but is closed from early November to 31 March.

Hostels The *Snurkhuis* (Sleep-In) (☎ 31 53 26) at Jansveld 51 is 10 minutes' walk from the station – head straight up Vredenburg to the post office, take Voorstraat to the left and it's two streets on your right; it costs f7.50 with breakfast, and you can only book in between 9 pm and 1 am. Alternatively, the *Rhijnauwen Youth Hostel* (☎ 03405-6 12 77) on Rhijnauwenselaan 14 is eight km east, 20 minutes on bus No 40 or 43.

Hotels The *Domstad* (☎ 31 01 31) at Parkstraat 5, 15 minutes' walk from the station, or bus No 3, has singles/doubles for f50/70. For a few guilders more, there's *Hotel Oowi* (☎ 71 63 03) at F C Dondersstraat 12 – get bus No 4. The *Park Hotel* (☎ 51 67 12) at Tolsteegsingel 34 has rooms from f50/70 single/double, and parking; it's 25 minutes' walk from the station, or take bus No 2.

Places to Eat
The Oudegracht is lined with outdoor cafés but their prices generally match their prime location. Near the Sleep-In in Voorstraat, there are cheaper pizza and shoarma (pittabread) places. Follow it until it changes name to Wittevrouwenstraat, and you'll find *Pomo* (☎ 31 92 72) at No 22, a Surinamese restaurant with mains from f16.

For pasta, join the crowds at *Toque Toque* (☎ 31 87 87) on the corner of Oudegracht and Vinkenburgstraat. The terrace tables overlook the Dom and buskers often set up shop nearby. *De Werfkring* (☎ 31 17 52) at wharf No 123 on Oudegracht is a very reasonable vegetarian haunt, or there's a *Veritas* student mensa at Kromme Nieuwe Gracht 54, open weeknights from 5 pm.

For self-caterers, there's a *supermarket* in the V & D in Hoog Catharijne, or another at Albert Heijn on Voorstraat 38 near the Sleep-In.

Entertainment
The *Café Rio* on Bilstraat 23 has late live music. For jazz, try *SJU-huis* on Kroonstraat 9. *De Roze Wolk* is a gay and lesbian bar/disco at Oudegracht 45.

Getting There & Away
Bus Eurolines and Hoverspeed buses stop at Jaarbeursplein out the back of the train station; tickets can be bought from the NS Reisburo or NBBS (☎ 31 43 44) at Oud Kerkhof 27.

Eurolines has two services a day to London: one in the morning originating from Amsterdam (see the Amsterdam Getting There & Away section), and another starting in Utrecht in the evening and arriving London about 6 am the next day. For information on Hoverspeed services, see the Amsterdam Getting There & Away section.

Train As Utrecht is the national rail hub, there are frequent trains to Amsterdam (f9.25, 30 minutes), Arnhem (f14, 40 minutes), Den Bosch (f10.75, 30 minutes), Maastricht (f33.50, two hours), Rotterdam (f12.25, 40 minutes) and The Hague (f14, 45 minutes).

Getting Around
Buses leave from underneath Hoog Catha-

NETHERLANDS

rijne, and in summer, canal bikes can be hired on Oudegracht.

Arnhem & the Hoge Veluwe

About an hour's' drive east of Amsterdam, the Hoge Veluwe is the Netherlands' largest national park and home of the prestigious Kröller-Müller museum. Literally meaning 'High' Veluwe, it's little more than a bump on the flat lands around it, but here it is possible to touch on a sense of isolation and wilderness found nowhere else.

To the south, the town of Arnhem was the site of fierce fighting between the Germans and British and Polish airborne troops during the failed Operation Market Garden in WW II. Today it's a peaceful town, the closest base to the nearby war museum and the park.

Orientation & Information

The VVV (☎ 085-42 03 30) is at Stationsplein, to the left out of Arnhem's station, open weekdays from 9 am to 5.30 pm, Saturday to 4 pm. Buses leave from the right. The town's pedestrianised centre, based around the well-hidden Korenmarkt, is five minutes' walk away – head down Utrechtsestraat, cross over Willemsplein and cut through Korenstraat.

The post office is at Jansplaats 56. There's a laundry at Spykerstraat 193, out of the centre to the east over the main Velperbinnensingel, open weekdays from 8 am to 6 pm, Saturday to noon. Arnhem's telephone code is 085.

Things to See & Do

There's little to see within Arnhem itself, but outside there are several museums including Oosterbeek's wartime **Airborne Museum** at Utrechtseweg 232. It's open weekdays from 11 am to 5 pm and Sundays from noon – get bus No 1.

Hoge Veluwe Stretching for nearly 5500 hectares, the Hoge Veluwe is a strange mix of forests and woods, shifting sands and heathery moors. It's home to red deer, wild boar, moufflon (a Mediterranean goat) and the Kröller-Müller Museum with its vast collection of van Goghs.

A year-round retreat, the Hoge Veluwe is most inviting from mid-August to mid-September when ablaze with heather, or during the red deer's rutting season in September and October. It's best seen on foot or bicycle – 400 of the latter are available free of charge from the visitor's centre.

There are three entrances, but if you're using public transport the easiest route is with a special hourly bus (No 12) from Arnhem station to the visitor's centre. Running daily from 1 June to 1 September (and on Sundays in May), the bus costs f6.85/3.35 return for adults/children. Alternatively, catch the hourly bus No 107 from Arnhem to Otterlo and follow the signs to the entrance one km away. From here it's another four-km walk to the visitor's centre. The park is open daily from 8 am to sunset and costs f7/3.50/7 for adults/children/cars. The yearly Museumcard is not valid.

Kröller-Müller Museum Near the Hoge Veluwe visitor's centre, the museum's 278 van Goghs are only a start. There are works by Picasso and Mondriaan, and out the back is Europe's largest sculpture garden. Once in the park, the museum is free. It's open Tuesday to Saturday from 10 am to 5 pm, and Sunday from 11 am.

Places to Stay

Camping There are grounds on the outside perimeter of the Hoge Veluwe, but closer to Arnhem try *Kampeercentrum* (☎ 43 16 00) at Kemperbergerweg 771 – it's 25 minutes on bus No 11 and a one-km walk.

Hostels The *Alteveer Youth Hostel* (☎ 42 01 14) at Diepenbrocklaan 27 is 10 minutes on bus No 3. The cheapest male-only option is the *Slaaphuis* (☎ 51 46 05) on Rijnkade 25; a converted car park, it's f10 with breakfast, open from 9 am to noon and 5 to 11 pm.

Hotels For a room with a rare view, *Hotel Rosorum* (☎ 45 53 66) on Amsterdamseweg 233 charges f35 per person and there's parking. From the station it's a 10-minute uphill walk or get bus No 107. *Hotel Pension Parkzicht* (☎ 42 06 98) at Apeldoornsestraat 16 is 10 minutes downhill from the station and has singles/doubles with TV for f42.50/75. Nearby, the similarly priced *Hotel Rembrandt* (☎ 42 01 53) is at Paterstraat 1.

Places to Eat
The *Old Inn* (☎ 42 06 49) on Stationsplein has standard Dutch fare and a f17 vegetarian menu. In the centre, *Ark van Noach* (☎ 51 55 82) on the corner of Rijnstraat and Nieuweplein is a tranquil pizza restaurant, or even cheaper is the mainly takeaway fare at *Picolino Pizza House* (☎ 43 81 23) nearby on Hoogstraat 4.

Getting There & Away
Trains to Amsterdam (f22.50, 65 minutes) and Rotterdam (f25.50, 75 minutes) go via Utrecht (f14, 40 minutes), while the line south passes Den Bosch (f14, 45 minutes) and continues to Maastricht (f27.50, two hours).

The Delta Region

The Netherlands' aptly named province of Zeeland ('Sea Land') makes up most of the Delta region. Spreading out over the southwest corner of the country, it was until recent decades a solitary place, where isolated islands were battered by howling winds and white-capped seas, and where little medieval towns, nestled somewhere in a protected groove, were seemingly lost in time.

But after the 1953 flood (see the History section at the beginning of this chapter) came the decision to defend Zeeland from the sea – and thus bring it into the present day. One by one the islands were connected by causeways and bridges, and the Delta Project (see Things to See in the Middelburg section that follows) became a reality.

These days, despite there being traffic lights at each intersection of an otherwise deserted 'island', there's still a sense of a wild land, interspersed with quaint towns like Middelburg and Zierikzee, the busy port of Flushing (Vlissingen in Dutch), and farther east, the fortified village of Willemstad.

Without a car, the region can be difficult to explore, although local buses do connect towns and villages. If the wind's not up, biking is fine – if it is, you may as well swap your wheels for a sailboard and join those on the water.

MIDDELBURG
The long-time capital of Zeeland and the province's largest town, Middelburg's attractions are threefold. Historically, there are the lingering visions from its medieval past; contemporarily, there's its proximity to the Delta Expo; and unquestionably, it's more likeable then the nearby town of Flushing where cross-Channel ferries ply between England and back.

Orientation & Information
On street maps, Middelburg looks distinctly floral. Its outer flanks are bordered on three sides by a wide, frilly moat while a second canal more tightly ensconces the centre. The heart of the town is ringed by a circle of streets including the pedestrianised Lange Delft, the main shopping thoroughfare, which leads onto the Markt, the town's central hub.

Here at Markt 65a is the VVV (☎ 01180-1 68 51), open weekdays from 9 am to 5 pm, Saturday to 2 pm. In July and August it's open until 6 pm. About a five-minute walk from the train station, to get there head straight across the two bridges, turn left along the canal and then immediately the first right into Herenstraat. Follow this to Lange Delft, turn left and the VVV is diagonally across the square.

Middelburg's telephone code is 01180.

Things to See
Dating back to the mid-1400s, the Gothic

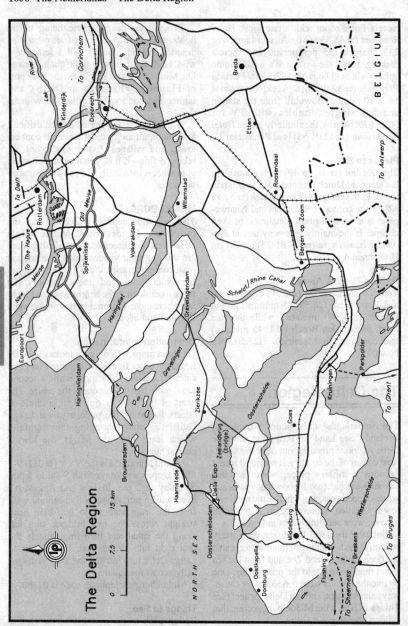

The Delta Region

0   7.5   15 km

To Delft

To The Hague

New Meuse

Lek River

To Gorinchem

Kinderdijk

Dordrecht

Rotterdam

Europoort

Spijkenisse

Old Meuse

Haringvliet

Volkerakdam

Haringvlietdam

Brouwersdam

Grevelingen

Grevelingendam

Haamstede

Zierikzee

's Delta Expo

Oosterscheldedam

Zeelandbrug
(bridge)

Oosterschelde

Goes

NORTH SEA

Ooskapelle

Domburg

Middelburg

Flushing

Breskens

Westerschelde

To Sheerness

To Bruges

Scheldt/Rhine Canal

Bergen op Zoom

Kruiningen

Perkpolder

To Ghent

Willemstad

Roosendaal

Etten

Breda

BELGIUM

To Antwerp

Town Hall was destroyed (like much of the central district) during the 1940 German blitz which flattened Rotterdam. Convincingly restored, it's open for guided visits only between mid-April and 30 October. Times of the tours, which cost f3/2 for adults/children, are posted on the notice board at the entry.

A few streets away is **Lange Jan**, the town's other distinctive tower, which rises from the former 12th century **Abdij** (Abbey) complex, later converted to Protestant churches. The tower can be climbed from mid-April to 31 October, daily (except Sunday) from 10 am to 5 pm. The charge is f2/1.30 for adults/children.

For insight into the province's history, the **Zeeuws Museum** (Zeeland Museum) inside the Abbey is open Tuesday to Friday from 10 am to 5 pm, Monday and Saturday from 1.30 pm. Admission is f3.50/1 for adults/children.

Around Middelburg

The disastrous 1953 flood was the impetus for the Delta Project in which the south-west river deltas were blocked using a network of dams, dykes and a remarkable 3.2-km storm surge barrier. Lowered only in rough conditions, this barrier was built following environmental opposition to plans to dam the Eastern Scheldt (Oosterschelde). It can be dropped during abnormally high tides but generally remains open to allow normal tidal movements and the survival of the region's shellfish.

Finished in 1986, the project is exhibited at the **Delta Expo** (☎ 01115-27 02) which sits steadfastly on top of the barrier, defying the gale-force winds which play with the stick windmills lined up nearby. Open daily from 10 am to 5 pm (closed Monday and Tuesday from 1 November to 31 March), it costs f13/10 for adults/children, and is free with Museumcards. To get there from Middelburg, take the ZWN bus No 104 (30 minutes, buses every hour) to the stop 'Neeltje Jans'. By car or hitching, head onto the N57 in the direction of 'Burgh-Haamstede'.

Places to Stay & Eat

Between mid-April and mid-October, campers can try *Camping Middelburg* (☎ 2 53 95) to the west over the moat at Koninginnelaan 55.

The nearest youth hostel, *Westhove* (☎ 01188-12 54), is in a medieval castle about 15 km west between the villages of Domburg and Oostkapelle. It's open from mid-March to mid-October – from Middelburg station, take ZWN bus No 54.

Alternatively, in town there's a smattering of reasonable hotels. Near the Abbey, *Pension Bij de Abdij* (☎ 2 71 35) at Bogaardstraat 14 has singles from f35, doubles from f70. Two blocks from the VVV, *De Geere* (☎ 1 30 83) at Langeviele 51 is a popular café/pension with rooms from f30/60. Slightly closer to the station, *Pension Huize Orliëns* (☎ 2 75 29) at Nieuwstraat 23 charges f32.50/70 for a single/double.

As for food, there are plenty of restaurants and tearooms lining the Markt, and down Vlasmarkt opposite the tourist office.

Getting There & Away

Train For all national information, ☎ 06-92 92. Major destinations north-east include Amsterdam (f36.50, 2½ hours) and Rotterdam (f27.50, 1½ hours).

Ferry Middelburg is just six kilometres up the train line from Flushing, where boats leave for Sheerness in England. For ferry details, see Ferry in the main Getting There & Away section at the beginning of this chapter.

WILLEMSTAD

Sitting on the edge of the Delta region but officially part of Brabant province, Willemstad is a tiny picturesque medieval village with a big place in Dutch hearts and on their day-tripping calender.

Built in the mid-16th century, the village was given to the nation's saviour, William the Silent, as compensation for his expenses in leading the Revolt of the Netherlands. He renamed it Willemstad ('William's City') and, because of its strategic position at the

NETHERLANDS

entrance to the main inland rivers, had it heavily fortified. Ramparts in the shape of a seven-point star were built, a moat was dug – both still remain – and Willemstad was written into the Netherlands' history books.

Information
The VVV (☎ 01678-35 55) is at Voorstraat 2a, open daily from 10.30 am to 5 pm.

Places to Stay
Overnighters will find only two pricey choices: *Willemstad Hotel* (☎ 01687-37 00) at Voorstraat 42, which has just eight rooms starting at f100/120 for a single/double (breakfast f12.50 extra), or there's the slick, harbour-front *Het Wapen van Willemstad* (☎ 01687-24 75) at Benedenkade 12, which has rooms overlooking the nearby 18th century windmill from f100/140 including breakfast.

Getting There & Away
Without a car, it's up to your thumb or the BBA bus (one every hour) from Roosendaal or Breda. Rotterdam is about 25 km north on the A29 highway.

Frisian Islands

Known as the Frisian or Wadden Islands, the country's five northern isles are an escape for stressed southerners wanting to touch roots with nature and walk in the mud. Stretching in an arc from Texel to Schiermonnikoog, they are important bird-breeding grounds, their shores washed by the shallow Waddenzee which is home to a small number of seals and the unique Dutch sport of wadlopen.

Ferries connect the islands to the mainland, and there are (mainly summer) youth hostels on all except Vlieland. Bikes are a good way to get around and can be hired for about f7.50 a day.

TEXEL
The largest and most populated island,

Texel's 24 km of beach can seem overrun all summer but even more so in June when the world's largest catamaran race is staged here. The largest village is Den Burg where you'll find the VVV (☎ 02220-1 28 47) on Groeneplaats 9.

Things to See
For information on the island's ecology, visit **Ecomare** at Ruyslaan 92. Set up 40 years ago to protect the tourist-inundated environment, it's also a hospital for sick seals from the pollution-embattled Waddenzee population.

Places to Stay
If you're after isolated camping, head to *Loodsmansduin* (☎ 02220-1 92 03) at Rommelpot 19 near Den Hoorn. *De Krim* camping (☎ 02220-1 62 75) at Roogeslootweg 6 in Cocksdorp is open all year.

There are two youth hostels on opposite sides of Den Burg. *De Eyercoogh* (☎ 02220-1 29 07) at Pontweg 106 is 10 minutes' walk from town, or get bus No 27 or 28 from the ferry. The more pleasant *Panorama* (☎ 02220-1 54 41) is at Schansweg 7 – bus No 29.

The VVV has a list of cheap B&Bs. Otherwise, try *Hotel De Merel* (☎ 02220-1 31 32) at Warmoesstraat 22 with doubles for f120, or *'t Koogerend* (☎ 02220-1 33 01) at Kogerstraat 94 with singles/doubles for f37.50/75.

Getting There & Away
Trains from Amsterdam to Den Helder (1½ hours) are met by a bus that whips you to the awaiting, hourly car ferry. The voyage takes 20 minutes, and costs f10.70/5.40 return for adults/children; cars/bicycles are charged f47/6.50.

VLIELAND & TERSCHELLING
Both connected by ferry to the mainland town of Harlingen, Vlieland is one of the two car-free isles, while Terschelling is the group's longest. A popular family island, Vlieland has one village: Oost-Vlieland; its

western sister drowned in the 1700s. The VVV (☎ 05621-11 11) is on Havenweg 10.

Thirty-km-long Terschelling is known as a good-time isle. Its main village is West-Terschelling, where the VVV (☎ 05620-30 00) is at Willem Barentszkade 19.

Places to Stay

On Vlieland there's *De Stortemelk* camping ground (☎ 05621-12 25) at Kampweg 1, while the 'cheapest' hotel is *De Herbergh van Flielant* (☎ 05621-14 00) at Dorpsstraat 105 with doubles for f125.

On Terschelling, *Dellewal* camping ground (☎ 5620-26 02) is next to the *youth hostel* (☎ 05620-23 38) on Burg van Heusdenweg 39. Along the same road, *Dellewal Hotel* (☎ 05620-23 05) at No 44 charges f47.50 per person, or there's *De Holland* (☎ 05620-23 02) at Molenstraat 5.

Getting There & Away

From Amsterdam, trains run regularly to Leeuwarden (1½ hours) with connections to Harlingen. In summer, three boats a day make the 90-minute voyage to Vlieland; two do so in winter. A return costs f33.40/16/14.45 for adults/children/bicycles. The trip to Terschelling takes the same time and costs the same – cars can be taken but that's expensive. There's also a faster ferry to Terschelling – f7.50 extra each way.

AMELAND

Ameland has no real notable features except the number of tourists who explode onto the scene in summer. There are four villages; the main one, Nes, is home to the VVV (☎ 05191-20 20) at Rixt van Doniaweg 2.

Places to Stay

Five minutes' walk north of the village of Hollum is *Koudenburg* camping (☎ 05191-43 67). The *youth hostel* (☎ 05191-41 33) is at Oranjeweg 59 near Hollum – get bus No 130 from Nes. Back in Nes, *Hotel de Jong* (☎ 05191-20 16) across from the VVV has singles/doubles from f45/90. At Strandweg 11 is the slightly cheaper *Hotel Pension Töben* (☎ 05191-21 63).

Getting There & Away

From Amsterdam, get the train to Leeuwarden (1½ hours), then bus No 66 to the port at Holwerd. On weekdays there are six boats a day, weekends four. Returns cost f13.55/7.30/6.30 for adults/children/bikes, and cars start at f70.

SCHIERMONNIKOOG

With one of the nation's most tongue-tying names, Schiermonnikoog is the smallest island, off limits to cars and distinct for the sport of wadlopen (organised from the mainland). In the only village, about three km from the ferry, you'll find the VVV (☎ 05195-12 33) at Reeweg 2.

Things to Do

While it may sound strange to the uninitiated, **wadlopen** is a serious pastime – strenuous and at times dangerous – involving kilometre-long, low-tide walks in mud that can come up to your thighs. Walks have to be arranged beforehand – contact the Wadlopen Centrum (☎ 05952-3 00) or Dijkstra Wad Walking Tours (☎ 05952-3 45), both at Pieterburen, north of Groningen.

Places to Stay

Any bus will drop you at the *youth hostel* (☎ 05195-3 12 57) at Knuppeldam 2. Alternatively, there's *Seedune* camping (☎ 05195-3 13 98) at Seeduneweg 1, or *Hotel Zonneweelde* (☎ 05195- 3 13 04) at Langestreek 94 with singles for f45.

Getting There & Away

There are four ferries a day (less on weekends) from the village of Lauwersoog, between Leeuwarden and Groningen. To get there from Leeuwarden, take bus No 50; from Groningen, bus No 63. The voyage takes 45 minutes and costs f13.30/7.40/5.90 for adults/children/bikes.

NETHERLANDS

The South-East

Sprinkled with woods, heather and the odd incline, the Netherlands' south-eastern corner is a world apart from everything up north. Best described in art terms, it's the Burgundian Netherlands of Hieronymus Bosch and Peter Paul Rubens (the latter from neighbouring Antwerp), rather than the Netherlands which inspired northerners like Frans Hals and Rembrandt. Made up of the North Brabant and Limburg provinces, its two main towns, Den Bosch and Maastricht, are intimate and alive, and easily able to win you to the ways of the south.

DEN BOSCH

Capital of the province of North Brabant, Den Bosch (officially known as 's-Hertogenbosch, 'The Count's Forest') is one of the gateways to the south, and as such, already has a different air. Possibly that's what causes northern Protestants to make jokes about the Catholics from Brabant, but if so, it's unneeded. For while only a small town, there are several rich museums and a lovely carillon. As for the name, it's the townsfolk of long ago you can thank for shortening it from the official version to the more pronounceable Den Bosch.

Orientation & Information

Nearly enclosed by a triangle of waterways, the town's pedestrianised centre is based around the Markt, an unusually triangular central 'square'. It's about a 10-minute walk east of the train station – to get there, head straight up Stationsweg and along Visstraat; at the end, turn right into Hogesteenweg which leads down to the Markt, on the way passing the town's oldest building, now home to the VVV (☎ 073-12 30 71) at Markt 77. It's open weekdays from 9 am to 5.30 pm, Saturday to 4 pm.

Things to See

The **Noordbrabants Museum** housed in the elegant, former governor's residence at Ver-wersstraat 41 is one of the city's premier sights. An extensive showcase of Brabant life and art from earlier times, it's open Tuesday to Friday from 10 am to 5 pm, weekends from noon.

The other main attraction is **St Jan's Cathedral**, one of the most ornate churches in the Netherlands. It's a few minutes' walk from the Markt at the end of Kerkstraat, the main shopping thoroughfare.

Back on the Markt, the **Stadhuis** (Town Hall) has a 35-bell carillon whose half-hourly chimes are the signal for the clockwork horsemen to ride into view. And if you keep craning your neck, you'll see some of Den Bosch's less obvious sights: the decorative gables and carved doorways which adorn many edifices.

Places to Stay & Eat

Regional camping grounds are profuse. One of the closest is *De Wildhorst* (☎ 04139-14 66) at Meerstraat 30 in Heeswijk-Dinther about 12 km to the east. It's open all year; take bus No 158 to 'Heeswijk' and then it's one km. There's a *youth hostel* (☎ 073-57 90 02) at Boxtelseweg 48 in Vught, about eight km south, but it's open July and August only; take bus No 154.

As for hotels, at the station, the *Terminus* (☎ 073-13 77 77) at Stationsplein 19 has decent singles/doubles from f45/85. In the centre, *Hotel All In* (☎ 073-13 40 57) at Gasselstraat 1 has rooms for the same price, but it's rougher around the edges and breakfast is f10 extra – note the gold elephant gable across the street.

There's no shortage of atmospheric cafés and restaurants – try Korte Putstraat or Molenstraat. At No 4 on the latter is *van Puffelen*, a spacious eetcafé (closed Monday) with excellent, good-value local cuisine.

Getting There & Away

Trains run regularly to Amsterdam via Utrecht (f10.75, 30 minutes), and to Arnhem (f14, 45 minutes) and Maastricht (f27.50, 1½ hours).

MAASTRICHT

The Netherlands' oldest city, Maastricht sits at the bottom end of the thin finger of land which juts down between Belgium and Germany – and which is influenced by them both. Capital of the largely Catholic Limburg province, its history stretches back to 50 BC when the Romans set up camp on the bank of the River Meuse.

Today spanning both banks, this lively city with its small student population has a reputation even in its own country as being something a little 'foreign'. For here you can pay for a beer in Belgian francs or German marks; you can sample the distinct tastes of neighbouring cuisines; and, before Lent, party with the rest of the revellers in the Netherlands' largest carnival festival.

Orientation & Information

Divided by the Meuse River, the city centre has two parts. The west bank is the hub, where you'll find the old, now largely pedestrianised, centre with its trendy Stokstraat quarter. Directly across the river on the east bank there's the Wyck, an area of 17th century houses and slightly less modern cafés and bars. Farther on, 10 minutes' walk from the VVV, are the train and bus stations. To the south of the Wyck a new commercial area, Céramique, is being developed on a site long occupied by the pottery industry.

The main post office is at Grote Staat 5. There's a laundry just up from the Markt at Boschstraat 82, open Monday to Friday from 8.30 am to 5 pm. Maastricht's telephone code is 043.

Tourist Information The VVV (☎ 25 21 21) is housed in Het Dinghuis ('The Thing House') on the corner of Kleine Staat and Jodenstraat. It's open Monday to Saturday from 9 am to 6 pm. In July and August, hours are extended until 7 pm and it's also open on Sundays from 11 am to 3 pm.

NETHERLANDS

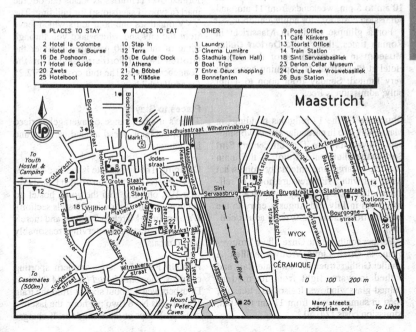

PLACES TO STAY	PLACES TO EAT	OTHER	
2 Hotel la Colombe	10 Stap In	1 Laundry	9 Post Office
4 Hotel de la Bourse	12 Terra	3 Cinema Lumière	11 Café Klinkers
16 De Poshoorn	15 De Gulde Clock	5 Stadhuis (Town Hall)	13 Tourist Office
17 Hotel le Guide	19 Athena	6 Boat Trips	14 Train Station
20 Zwets	21 De Bóbbel	7 Entre Deux shopping	18 Sint Servaasbasiliek
25 Hotelboot	22 't Klöôske	8 Bonnefanten	23 Derlon Cellar Museum
			24 Onze Lieve Vrouwebasiliek
			26 Bus Station

Maastricht

Money The GWK office at the train station is open Monday to Saturday from 8 am to 8.30 pm, Sunday from 9 am to 5 pm.

Emergency For police, fire and ambulance, the national emergency number is ☎ 06 11.

Things to See & Do
Besides what's mentioned below, the VVV has a brochure on a walk around the fortification walls which still partly surround the city.

Museums The premier museum is the **Bonnefanten**, presently housed above the Entre Deux shopping centre at Dominikanerplein 5, but is due to move to a purpose-built complex across the river in Céramique in 1994 (it's expected to be closed for some months in 1993). An impressive showcase of art and architecture from the Limburg area, it also often has temporary contemporary exhibitions. It's open Tuesday to Friday from 10 am to 5 pm, weekends from 11 am, and admission costs f5/3 for adults/children.

For a glimpse of life in Maastricht in Roman times, there's the **Derlon Cellar Museum** in the basement of the Derlon Hotel at Plankstraat 21. Opening hours are very limited: Sunday from noon to 4 pm only; admission is free.

Churches Of the 17 religious buildings in Maastricht, two in particular attract worshippers and visitors alike. The 10th century **Sint Servaasbasiliek** on Vrijthof is the main basilica – large and internally somewhat stark, but with a rich treasure house of religious artefacts. Open daily from 10 am to 5 pm (6 pm in July and August), entry to the treasure trove costs f3.50/1 for adults/children.

Farther south, on the Onze Lieve Vrouweplein, is **Onze Lieve Vrouwebasiliek**, a smaller Gothic structure – intimate, dark and bathed in warm light from its modern stained-glass windows. It also has a treasury, open in summer only from 11 am to 5 pm; admission costs f2/0.50.

Casemates Eight metres deep, lit by kerosine lamps and rather cold and damp, this 10-km labyrinth of tunnels on the city's western outskirts was started in the late 1500s to keep pace with the defence network. One-hour tours cost f4.25/2.25 for adults/children, but unless you speak Dutch, they can be a little dull. The VVV has details on the irregular tour times. Real underground buffs should better consider the Mount St Peter caves (see the Around Maastricht section that follows).

Boat Trips Stiphout Cruises (☎ 25 41 51) operates a handful of trips along the Meuse. There's a one-hour jaunt costing f7/4.25 for adults/children; a three-hour tour (f11/7) including a visit to the Mount St Peter caves; and a day cruise to Liège in Belgium. Trips leave from Maaspromenade 27.

Around Maastricht A few kilometres south of the city, the **Mount St Peter Caves** were formed over centuries as locals cut out the marl (a type of sandstone) for building. The VVV organises one-hour tours which leave from the city and which take you through some of the 20,000 passages in either the Grotten Nord (Northern Caves) or the Zonneberg Caves. The tour costs f4.25/2.25 for adults/children.

Places to Stay
There's a small range of averagely priced hotels, but book ahead around carnival and in summer.

Camping The closest site is the five-star *De Dousberg* (☎ 43 21 71) on a hill at Dousbergweg 102, one km from the youth hostel (to get there, see the following Hostels section). It's open from March to October, and there's an on-site restaurant serving reasonably priced meals.

Hostels Part of a large, modern sporting complex, the *youth hostel* (☎ 43 44 04) is at Dousbergweg 4, about six km from the train station. Bus No 8 (two per hour, the last one at 11 pm) stops at the front door. It charges f21.25 for a bed in a dorm, or f47.50 for a double room – check in after 3 pm.

Hotels One block from the station, *Hotel le Guide* (☎ 21 61 76) at Stationsstraat 17a is friendly and clean, with singles/doubles/triples starting at f60/90/120. Two blocks along at No 47, *De Poshoorn* (☎ 21 73 34) has decent rooms from f48/92. The best central option is B&B *Zwets* (☎ 21 64 82) at Brede Straat 41. It has four rooms and charges f30 per person.

Alternatively, just downstream from the centre is the *Hotelboot* (☎ 21 90 23) at Maasboulevard 95. It has singles/doubles from f55/70, but is moored beside the main thoroughfare into town so could get noisy.

Otherwise, the only two reasonable hotels are on the Markt. *Hotel la Colombe* (☎ 21 57 74) at Markt 30 has singles/doubles from 75/95, or there's the fractionally dearer *Hotel de la Bourse* (☎ 21 81 12) at No 37.

Places to Eat
Thanks mainly to the gastronomic influences of its Belgian and German neighbours, Maastricht ranks high among the Dutch where cuisine is concerned.

In the centre, Platielstraat is lined with restaurants and cafés. Nearby, there's *De Bóbbel* (☎ 21 74 13) at Wolfstraat 32, a brown café with snacks or decent meals from f10. Another cheap option is the popular *Stap In* (☎ 21 97 10) at Kesselkade 61; spaghetti dishes start at f12, or there's a f17, three-course menu.

For averagely priced Greek cuisine, *Athena* (☎ 21 58 79) at Achter het Vleeshuis 13 has the regular plates as well as an almighty 'Olympusschotel' ('Olympus Dish') for f22.50. *Hotel la Colombe* (see the previous Hotels section) serves satays for f15, or there are slightly pricier ones at *De Gulde Clock* (☎ 25 27 09), Wycker Brugstraat 54.

If you're into a local cuisine splurge, *'t Kläöske* (☎ 21 81 18) at Plankstraat 20 has sumptuous three-course menus starting from f50. The tranquil *Terra* (☎ 25 54 13) at

Brusselsestraat 47 is a leafy vegetarian restaurant with a dagschotel for f12.20 (closed Sunday and Monday).

For self-caterers, there's a small *Van Sint Fiet* supermarket at Rechtstraat 26, or food shops in the Entre Deux shopping centre on Helmstraat. Wednesdays and Fridays are market mornings on the Markt.

Entertainment
If the weather's good, Vrijthof and Onze Lieve Vrouweplein are taken over by people-watching terrace cafés. For a drink in a 'modernly classical' atmosphere, try *Café Klinkers* (☎ 25 56 33) at Rechtstraat 12 (closed Monday). Cinema *Lumière* (☎ 21 40 80) at Bogaardenstraat 40 screens non-mainstream films. To find out what's on, pick up the free *Week IN Week UIT* pamphlet at the VVV.

Getting There & Away
Bus Hoverspeed's daily daytime bus to London leaves from Stationsplein just to the left out of the train station. The bus goes via Calais in France (check whether you need a French visa) and takes 10 hours. A one-way ticket costs f100/85 for adults/those aged under 26, and can be bought from the NS Reisburo in the station.

Train Within the Netherlands, major lines include those to Amsterdam (f38.50, 2½ hours) and Den Bosch (f27.50, 1½ hours). Major international connections include those to Liège in Belgium (f10.10, 30 minutes, one train per hour), Cologne in Germany (f30, 1½ hours, every two hours), and Luxembourg City (f40.40, three hours, every two hours). For national information, ☎ 06-92 92; international information, ☎ 25 62 70.

Getting Around
Yellow VSL buses run the local routes until about midnight, leaving from the bus station to the right out of the train station. Bikes can be hired to the left.

Portugal

Simultaneously spirited and unassuming, Portugal is a dusty patina of faded grandeur: the quiet remains of a far-flung colonialist realm. Even as it flows towards the economic mainstream of the European Community (EC), it still seems to gaze over its shoulder and out to sea.

For visitors, this far side of Europe offers more than beaches and port wine. Beyond the crowded Algarve, one finds wide appeal: a simple but hearty cuisine based on seafood and lingering conversation, an enticing architectural blend that wanders from the Manueline to Moorish and Surrealist styles, and a changing landscape that occasionally lapses into Impressionism. Like the *emigrantes*, economically inspired Portuguese vagabonds who eventually find their way back to their grass roots, *estrangeiros*, or foreigners (literally 'strange people'), who have had a taste of the real Portugal can only be expected to return.

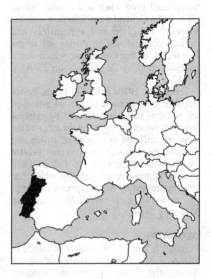

Facts about the Country

HISTORY

The early history of Portugal is traced back to the Celts who settled in the Iberian Peninsula around 700 BC. A subsequent pattern of invasion and reinvasion was established by the Phoenicians, Greeks, Romans and Visigoths who marched through in succession.

In the 8th century, the Moors crossed the Strait of Gibraltar and commenced a long occupation which introduced their culture, architecture, and agricultural techniques to Portugal. Resistance to the Moors culminated in their ejection during the 12th century.

In the 15th century, Portugal entered a phase of conquest and discovery under the rule of Henry the Navigator. Famous explorers such as Vasco da Gama, Ferdinand Magellan and Bartolomeu Diaz set off to discover new trade routes and assisted in creating a huge empire that, at its peak, extended to India, the Far East, Brazil and Africa.

This period of immense power and wealth faded towards the end of the 16th century when Spain occupied Portugal. Although the Portuguese regained their country within a few decades, the momentum of the empire steadily declined over the following centuries.

At the close of the 18th century, Napoleon sent several expeditions to invade Portugal, but was eventually trounced by the troops of the Anglo-Portuguese alliance.

During the 19th century, Portugal's economy fell apart and there was a general muddle of civil war and political mayhem which culminated in the abolition of the monarchy in 1910 and the founding of a democratic republic.

The brief democratic phase lasted until a

military coup in 1926 set the stage for a long period of dictatorship under Antonio de Oliveira Salazar, who clung tenaciously to power until 1968 when he died after falling off a chair! General dissatisfaction with the repressive regime and a pointless and ruinous colonial war in Africa led to the Revolution of the Carnations, which was a peaceful coup by the military on 25 April 1974.

During the 1970s and early 1980s, Portugal went through some painful adjustments: the political scene was marked by extreme swings between the right and the left; and the economy suffered as a result of strikes and disputes over government versus private ownership. Entry into the EC in 1986 secured a measure of stability which has been buttressed by the acceptance of Portugal as a full member of the European Monetary System in 1992.

GEOGRAPHY

Portugal is one of the smaller countries in Europe – approximately twice the size of Switzerland. From north to south it's 560 km and from east to west 220 km.

The northern and central regions are densely populated, particularly near the coast, and characterised inland by lush vegetation and mountains – the highest range is Serra da Estrela which peaks at Torre (1991 metres). The south is less populated, and apart from the mountains forming a backdrop to the Algarve, it is much flatter and drier.

GOVERNMENT

Portugal has a Western-style democracy based on the *Assembleiada República*, a single-chamber parliament with 230 members and an elected president. The two main parties are the Social Democratic Party (Partido Social Democrata, or PSD) and the Socialist Party (Partido Socialista, or PS). There are several other parties, including the Monarchist Popular Party (Partido Popular Monárquico, or PPM) and the Green Party (Partido Ecologista Os Verdes, or PEV). Members of the latter party are occasionally

referred to as 'watermelons' – green on the outside and red on the inside!

ECONOMY

After severe economic problems and rampant inflation in the 1980s, Portugal has tamed the inflation rate to hover around 10%. The previous tight grip of the state on ownership has been relaxed and privatisation is being implemented. Agriculture plays a major role in the economy and tourism is rapidly increasing in importance. Membership in the EC has provided vital funding for improving the country's infrastructure and, in addition, Portugal looks set to benefit from its low labour costs, young population (40% are under 25 years old), and traditional trading links with South America and Africa.

POPULATION & PEOPLE

The population of 10 million in Portugal does not include an estimated three million Portuguese who live abroad as migrant workers. In general, the southerners have features showing a darker, Moorish influence, whereas northerners tend to be more Celtic in appearance.

CULTURE & THE ARTS
Music

The most well-known form of Portuguese music is *fado*. Fado songs are a blend of melancholic and nostalgic feelings and are popularly considered to have originated in the yearnings of sailors during the 16th century. In its pure form, fado is generally sung in intimate surroundings to a small audience. Much of what is offered in tourist shows in Lisbon is overpriced and far from authentic. Amália Rodrigues is *the* star – and household name – in Portuguese fado circles; her recordings can be bought in just about any record shop in Portugal.

Literature

During the 16th century, Gil Vicente, who excelled at writing farces and religious dramas, set the stage for Portuguese dramatic tradition. Later in the same century, Luís de Camões wrote *The Lusiads*, an epic poem

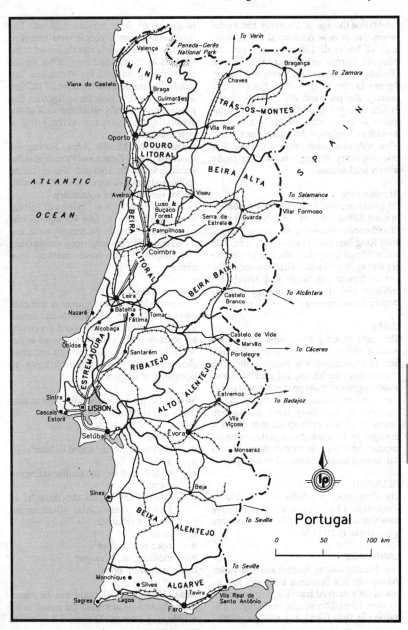

PORTUGAL

celebrating the age of discovery and exploration. He is now considered the national poet of Portugal. The romantic dramatist Almeida Garrett and the novelist Eça de Queiroz were the leading Portuguese literary figures in the 19th century. Early in this century the poet and dramatist Fernando Pessoa emerged as one of the finest Portuguese writers. Some of his works were written in English; others have been translated and, as a result, he is one of the few contemporary Portuguese writers to be widely read abroad.

Architecture

Of special architectural interest is the development during the 16th century of the style of architecture known as *Manueline*, named after King Manuel I (1495-1521). The style is considered to represent the zest for discovery during that era and is characterised by the use of boisterous twists and spirals for columns and the application of nautical themes for decoration.

Crafts

The most striking Portuguese craft is the making of decorative tiles, known as *azulejos*. The technique was learnt in the 15th century from the Moors, and the Portuguese soon progressed from producing blue *(azul)* tiles – hence azulejos – to creating multi-coloured ones. Today there are superb examples of this craft to be seen all over Portugal in churches, public parks, on house façades, and even in train stations. Lisbon has its own museum devoted to azulejos.

RELIGION

The Portuguese population is 99% Roman Catholic. The Protestant community numbers less than 120,000, and there are approximately 5000 Jews.

LANGUAGE

Like French, Italian, Spanish and Romanian, Portuguese is a Romance language, that is, one closely derived from Latin. It is spoken by over 10 million people in Portugal, 130 million in Brazil, and it is also the official language of five African nations. The obscure indigenous people who inhabited the Iberian Peninsula before the arrival of the Romans are considered responsible for the most striking traits of the Portuguese language. Roman domination from 27 BC saw Vulgar Latin take over the indigenous languages, more slowly so in the west of the Peninsula, the Lusitanian territory that is now Portugal.

During the Middle Ages, Portuguese absorbed mostly French and Provençal influences; later, in the 16th and 17th centuries, Italian and Spanish were above all responsible for innovations in vocabulary.

In large cities such as Oporto and Lisbon, it's generally easy to find Portuguese who speak English, but in the remoter areas few locals speak foreign languages – unless they are emigrants who have returned from abroad.

Pronunciation

Pronunciation of Portuguese is difficult, given that, like English, vowels and consonants have more than one sound depending on position in the syllable and word stress. Moreover, there are nasal vowels and diphthongs in Portuguese which have no equivalent in English.

Vowels Single vowels should present relatively few problems:

a	as the 'u' in 'cut'
a	similar to the 'ur' sound in 'hurt'
e	as in 'bet'
e	as in French *été*, and similar to English 'laird'
e	silent final 'e', as the final 'e' in English 'these'. Also silent in unstressed syllables
i	as in 'see'
o	open o, as in 'pot'
o	closed o, as in 'caught'
o, u	'oo', as in 'good'

Nasal Vowels Nasalisation can be represented by an **n** or an **m** after the vowel, or by a tilde, (~) over it. The nasal **i** exists in

English as the 'ing' in 'sing'. For other vowels, try to pronounce a long **a**, 'ah', or **e**, 'eh', holding your nose, as if you had a head cold.

Diphthongs Double vowels are relatively straightforward:

au	as in 'now'
ai	as in 'pie'
ei	as in 'day'
eu	pronounced together
oi	similar to 'boy'

Nasal Diphthongs Try the same technique as for nasal vowels. To say *não* (no), pronounce 'now' through your nose.

ão	nasal 'now' (nowng)
ãe	nasal 'day' (eing)
õe	nasal 'boy' (oing)
ui	similar to the 'uing' in 'ensuing'

Consonants The following consonants are specific to Portuguese:

c	before **a**, **o** or **u**
c	before **e** or **i**, as in 'see'
ç	as in 'see'
g	before **a**, **o** or **u**, as in 'garden'
g	before **e** or **i**, as in 'treasure'
gu	before **e** or **i**, as in 'get'
h	is never pronounced at the beginning of a word
nh	as in 'onion'
lh	as in 'million'
j	as in 'treasure'
m	in final position is not pronounced, it simply nasalises the previous vowel: *um* (oong), *bom* (bõ)
qu	before **e** or **i**, as the 'k' in 'key'
qu	before **a** or **o**, as the 'q' in 'quad'
r	at the beginning of a word, or **rr** in the middle of a word, is a harsh, guttural sound similar to the French *rue*, or to the Scottish *loch*, or the German *Bach*. In some areas of Portugal this **r** is not guttural, but strongly rolled.
r	in the middle or at the end of a word is a rolled sound stronger than the English 'r'

s	at the beginning of a word, or **ss** in the middle of a word, is pronounced as the 's' in 'see'
s	between vowels is pronounced as the 'z' in 'zeal'
s	before another consonant, or at the end of a word, is pronounced 'sh', as in 'she'
x	*taxa*, a 'sh' sound, as in 'ship'
x	*exame*, as in 'zeal'
x	*taxi*, both in English and in Portuguese

Word stress is important in Portuguese, as it can change the meaning of the word. Many Portuguese words have a written accent. The stress must fall on that syllable when you pronounce it.

Greetings & Civilities

Hello./Goodbye.	*Olá./Adeus.*
Yes./No.	*Sim./Não.*
Please.	*Se faz favor.*
Thank you.	*Obrigado/a.*
That's fine. You're welcome.	*De nada.*
Excuse me.	*Desculpe./Com licença.*
Sorry. (excuse me, forgive me)	*Desculpe.*
Do you speak English?	*Fala Inglês?*
Does anyone speak English?	*Há aqui alguém que fale Inglês?*
I (don't) understand.	*(Não) Percebo/ Entendo.*
Just a minute.	*Um momento.*
Please write that down.	*Pode escrevê-lo por favor.*
How much is it?	*Quanto custa?*

Signs

Camping Ground	*Parque de Campismo*
Entrance	*Entrada*
Exit	*Saída*
Free Admission	*Entrada Grátis*
Guest House	*Pensão*
Hotel	*Hotel*
Information	*Informações*

PORTUGAL

Open/Closed	*Aberto/Encerrado (or: fechado)*	far/near	*longe/perto*
Police	*Polícia*		
Police Station	*Esquadra da Polícia*	**Around Town**	
Prohibited	*Proibido*	I'm looking for ...	*Ando à procura ...*
Toilets	*WC*	a bank	*dum banco*
Train Station	*Estação de Comboios*	the city centre	*do centro da cidade/da baixa*
Youth Hostel	*Albergue de Juventude*	the ... embassy	*da embaixada de ...*
		my hotel	*do meu hotel*

Getting Around

		the market	*do mercado/da praça*
What time does ... leave/arrive?	*A que horas chega/parte ...?*	the police	*da polícia*
What time is the ... ?	*A que horas é o ... ?*	the post office	*dos correios*
next	*próximo*	a public toilet	*duma casa de banho pública*
first	*primeiro*		
last	*último*	the telephone centre	*da central de telefones*
		the tourist information office	*do turismo/do serviço de informações para turistas*
boat	*barco*		
bus	*autocarro*		
train	*combóio*		
tram	*eléctrico*		
		beach	*a praia*
I would like ...	*Queria ...*	bridge	*a ponte*
a one-way ticket	*um bilhete simples/de ida*	castle	*o castelo*
		cathedral	*a catedral/sé*
a return ticket	*um bilhete de ida e volta*	church	*a igreja*
		hospital	*o hospital*
two tickets	*dois bilhetes*	island	*a ilha*
tickets for all of us	*bilhetes para todos nós*	lake	*o lago*
		main square	*a praça principal*
a student's fare	*bilhete de estudante*	market	*o mercado*
		mosque	*a mesquita*
1st class	*primeira classe*	old city	*a cidade velha*
2nd class	*segunda classe*	palace	*o palácio*
		ruins	*os escombros/as ruinas*
Where is the bus/tram stop?	*Onde é a paragem do autocarro/do eléctrico?*	sea	*o mar*
		square	*a praça*
I want to go to ...	*Quero ir para ...*	tower	*a torre*
I am looking for ...	*Ando à procura de ...*	**Accommodation**	
Can you show me (on the map)?	*Pode-me mostrar (no mapa)?*	Where is a cheap hotel?	*Onde há um hotel barato?*
Go straight ahead.	*Siga sempre a direito/sempre em frente.*	What is the address?	*Qual é a morada/direcção?*
Turn left ...	*Vire à esquerda ...*	Could you write the address, please?	*Podia escrever a morada/direcção?*
Turn right ...	*Vire à direita ...*		

Do you have any rooms available?	*Tem quartos livres?*
I would like ...	*Queria ...*
a single room	*um quarto individual*
a double room	*um quarto duplo/um quarto de casal*
a room with a bathroom	*um quarto com casa de banho*
to share a dorm	*ficar num dormitório*
a bed	*uma cama*
How much is it per night/per person?	*Quanto é por noite/por pessoa?*
Can I see it?	*Posso ver?*
Where is the bathroom?	*Onde é a casa de banho?*

Food

breakfast	*pequeno almoço*
lunch	*almoço*
afternoon tea	*lanche*
dinner	*jantar*
I would like the set lunch.	*Queria o almoço da casa.*
Is service included in the bill?	*O serviço está incluído na conta?*
I am a vegetarian.	*Sou vegetariano/a.*

Time & Dates

today	*hoje*
tomorrow	*amanhã*
in the morning	*de manhã*
in the afternoon	*de tarde/à tarde.*
in the evening	*ao fim da tarde/ à noite*
Monday	*segunda-feira*
Tuesday	*terça-feira*
Wednesday	*quarta-feira*
Thursday	*quinta-feira*
Friday	*sexta-feira*
Saturday	*sábado*
Sunday	*domingo*

January	*Janeiro*
February	*Fevereiro*
March	*Março*
April	*Abril*
May	*Maio*
June	*Junho*
July	*Julho*
August	*Agosto*
September	*Setembro*
October	*Outubro*
November	*Novembro*
December	*Dezembro*

Numbers

0	*zero*
1	*um/uma*
2	*dois/duas*
3	*três*
4	*quatro*
5	*cinco*
6	*seis*
7	*sete*
8	*oito*
9	*nove*
10	*dez*
11	*onze*
12	*doze*
13	*treze*
14	*catorze*
15	*quinze*
16	*dezasseis*
17	*dezassete*
18	*dezoito*
19	*dezanove*
20	*vinte*
21	*vinte e um/uma*
22	*vinte e dois/duas*
100	*cem*
1000	*mil*
one million	*um milhão (de)*

Health

I'm ...	*Sou ...*
diabetic	*diabético/a*
epileptic	*epiléptico/a*
asthmatic	*asmático/a*
I'm allergic to...	*Sou alérgico/a a...*
antibiotics	*antibióticos*
penicillin	*à penicilina*

PORTUGAL

antiseptic	*antisséptico*
condoms	*preservativos*
contraceptive	*anticoncepcional*
diarrhoea	*diarreia*
medicine	*remédio/medicamento*
nausea	*náusea/vómitos*
tampons	*tampões*

Emergencies

Help!	*Socorro!*
Call a doctor!	*Chame um médico!*
Call the police!	*Chame a polícia!*
Go away!	*Deixe-me em paz!*

Facts for the Visitor

VISAS & EMBASSIES

Nationals of the UK are allowed to stay up to 90 days and must take a passport; nationals of other EC countries can use their national identity cards.

Nationals of Australia and New Zealand do not require a visa for stays of up to three months, and nationals of the USA and Canada do not require a visa unless they are staying over 60 days, but they must carry a passport.

Portuguese Embassies

Portuguese embassies abroad include:

Australia
    6 Campion Street, 1st floor, Deakin, ACT 2600
    (☎ 062-85 2084)
Canada
    645 Island Park Drive, Ottawa, Ont K1Y OB8
    (☎ 613-729 0883)
Spain
    Calle del Pinar 1, Madrid 6 (☎ 91-261 7808)
UK
    11 Belgrave Square, London SW1X 8PP
    (☎ 071-235 5331)
USA
    2125 Kalorama Rd, NW Washington, DC 20008
    (☎ 202-328 8610)

Visa Extensions & Re-Entry Visas

Outside Portugal, information is supplied by Portuguese consulates. Inside Portugal,

contact the Foreigners' Registration Service, Rua Conselheiro José Silvestre Ribeiro, 22, Lisbon 1600 (☎ 01-7141027 or 7155268).

Foreign Embassies in Portugal

The following foreign embassies can be found in Lisbon:

Australia
    Avenida da Liberdade, 244, 1200 Lisbon
    (☎ 01-523350)
Canada
    Edifício MCB, Avenida da Liberdade, 144, 1200
    Lisbon (☎ 01-3474892)
Spain
    Rua do Salitre, 1, Lisbon (☎ 01-3472792)
UK
    Rua São Domingos á Lapa, 37, 1200 Lisbon
    (☎ 01-3961191)
USA
    Avenida das Forças Armadas, 1600 Lisbon
    (☎ 01-7266600)

The UK Embassy is the proxy embassy for New Zealand citizens.

CUSTOMS

Visitors entering the country have no limit on the importation of currency. However, when leaving the country there is a limit of 100,000$00 escudos (the Portuguese currency), and a limit of 500,000$00 in foreign currency. If you are exporting more, you will have to prove that an equal amount or more was originally imported.

The duty-free allowance is 200 cigarettes (or 250 grams of tobacco or 50 cigars or 150 cigarillos); one litre of alcoholic drinks over 22% volume or two litres of alcoholic drinks not over 22% volume; two litres of still table wine; 50 grams of perfume; and 0.25 litres of toilet water.

MONEY

Providing you have half an hour or so at your disposal, changing money at banks in Portugal should run smoothly. Travellers' cheques or foreign currency (major European currencies or US dollars) are equally acceptable.

In large cities such as Lisbon, Oporto, Évora and in the main Algarve resorts, there are automatic exchange machines to change an amazing variety of European currencies, US dollars and even Japanese yen. The machines operate day and night and give an excellent rate of exchange with a minimal commission.

If you change travellers' cheques or foreign currency in the bank rather than by using an exchange machine, expect to pay up to 1000$00 commission plus about 70$00 as a government tax.

All major credit cards are accepted in most cities and large towns – Visa and MasterCard are especially widespread. The major banks in Portugal have grouped together and now provide a system of automatic machines, known as 'Multibanco', which operates 24 hours a day. Visa cards can be used with those machines which display an MB-Visa sign.

Having money cabled to Portugal is not advisable unless you have a few weeks to spare and can make it absolutely clear where the money is to be sent – otherwise you and your money could spend considerable time floating around the labyrinthine banking system without making contact.

Currency

The unit of currency used in Portugal is the escudo, which is further divided into 100 centavos. The standard practice for writing prices is to place a $ sign between the number of escudos and the number of centavos. So, for example, a price of 25 escudos and 50 centavos is written 25$50.

Coins are available for 200$00, 100$00, 50$00, 20$00, 10$00, 5$00, 2$50 and 1$00. Notes currently in circulation include 10,000$00, 5000$00, 2000$00, 1000$00 and 500$00. Portuguese frequently refer to 1000$00 as a *conto*.

Exchange Rates

A$1	=	93$44
C$1	=	104$79
DM1	=	88$70
NZ$1	=	71$06
1 pta	=	1$24
UK£1	=	222$53
US$1	=	130$63

Costs

Portugal is still one of the least expensive places to travel in Europe and offers excellent value in transport, accommodation, and food. On a rock-bottom budget – using youth hostels or camp sites and eating only occasionally in restaurants – you can squeeze by with US$12 a day. If you move up a bracket to stay in bottom-end accommodation and occasionally eat in inexpensive restaurants, daily costs will hover around US$18. If you travel with a companion and time your trip to take advantage of discounts outside the high season (see the Climate & When to Go section), it's quite feasible to eat and sleep in real style for US$50 for two. Once you leave the major tourist areas such as Lisbon and the Algarve, prices dip appreciably.

Tipping

In general, the rate for tipping in restaurants varies between 5% and 10%. If you've merely had a snack at a *cervejaria, pastelaria* (see the Food section that follows) or café, a bit of loose change is sufficient. Taxi drivers appreciate a tip of between 5% and 10% of the fare. At petrol stations, tips for the attendant vary between 20$00 and 50$00.

Consumer Taxes

A 16% sales tax, referred to as IVA, is levied on bills for hotels, restaurants, car hire, etc.

Providing they are resident outside the EC, foreign tourists and Portuguese citizens can claim an IVA refund on goods purchased at shops which are members of Portugal Tax-Free Shopping. The minimum purchase amount is 11,600$00. The shop assistant will fill in a cheque for the amount of the refund – minus an administration fee. When leaving Portugal, the goods, cheque, and purchaser's passport should be presented at customs where there is a tax refund counter, which can then return the money in cash, or refund via mail or credit card. At present, this service is available at the airports in Lisbon, Oporto, and Faro; and at Lisbon harbour (customs section). Further details are available from Portugal Tax-Free Shopping

PORTUGAL

(☎ 01-4188703), Avenida Forte, 3, Carnaxide, 2795 Linda-a-Velha.

CLIMATE & WHEN TO GO

The climate in Portugal is temperate and it's only searingly hot in midsummer in the Algarve and Alentejo. The tourist season in the Algarve lasts from late February to November – the peak season extends from June to September and prices for accommodation outside this season can be discounted by as much as 50%. Prices quoted in this chapter are mid-season prices.

During winter, the north receives plenty of rain and temperatures can be chilly. Snowfall is common in the mountainous parts, particularly Serra da Estrela, which has basic ski facilities. The tourist season in the north extends from approximately May to September.

To take advantage of low tourist numbers and seasonal discounts while enjoying spectacular scenery and foliage, spring (late March/April) or late summer (September/early October) would be optimum times to visit.

SUGGESTED ITINERARIES

Depending on the length of your stay you might want to see the following places:

Two days
    Visit Lisbon.
One week
    Visit Lisbon, Sintra and Óbidos, spending three days in Lisbon and two days each in the other two cities.
Two weeks
    As above, plus a trip to the Algarve, including Tavira, Lagos and Sagres, spending two days in each of these three cities.
One month
    As above, plus Oporto, Serra da Estrela, Peneda-Gerês, Évora, spending two days in each place with leisurely travel time from one place to the next.
Two months
    All of the above but spending twice as much time in each place.

TOURIST OFFICES
Local Tourist Offices

Local tourist offices are known as *postos de turismo*, often abbreviated to 'turismos'. These can be found throughout Portugal, even in the smallest towns, and will provide brochures and varying degrees of help. See the Orientation & Information sections under individual places for further details.

Portuguese Tourist Offices Abroad

The following countries have Portuguese tourist offices:

Canada
    Portuguese National Tourist Office, 60 Bloor Street West, Suite 1005, Toronto, Ont M4W 3B8 (☎ 416-921 7376)
Spain
    Oficina de Turismo de Portugal, Gran Via 27, 1st floor, 28013 Madrid (☎ 91-5229354)
UK
    Portuguese National Tourist Office, 22-25a Sackville St, London W1X 1DE (☎ 071-4941441)
USA
    Portuguese National Tourist Office, 590 Fifth Ave, 4th floor, New York, NY 10036-4704 (☎ 212-354 4403)

BUSINESS HOURS & HOLIDAYS

Banks are open from 8.30 am to 3 pm Monday to Friday. Museums and other tourist attractions are usually open from 10 am to 5 pm during the week, but are often closed on Mondays. Shopping hours generally extend from 9 am to 7 pm on weekdays, and from 9 am to 1 pm on Saturdays. Lunch is given serious and lingering attention between noon and 3 pm.

Public Holidays

Public holidays in Portugal are as follows:

1 January
    New Year's Day
February
    Carnival & Shrove Tuesday (dates variable)
March
    Good Friday (date variable)
25 April
    Anniversary of the Revolution

1 May
    May Day
May
    Corpus Christi (date variable)
10 June
    National Day (Camões Day)
15 August
    Day of the Assumption
5 October
    Republic Day
1 November
    All Saints' Day
1 December
    Independence Day
8 December
    Day of the Immaculate Conception
25 December
    Christmas Day

CULTURAL EVENTS

The most interesting cultural events in Portugal include:

Holy Week Festival
    This is celebrated at Braga during Easter week and features a series of colourful processions of which the most famous is the Ecce Homo procession.
Festas das Cruzes (Festival of the Crosses)
    Held in Barcelos in May, this festival is noted for its processions, performances of folk arts, and exhibitions of regional handicrafts.
Feira Nacional da Agricultura (National Agricultural Fair)
    In June, Santarém holds a grand country fair with bullfighting, folk singers and dancers.
Festa do Santo António (Festival of Saint Anthony)
    This street festival is held in Lisbon (mainly in the Alfama district) on June 13.
Festas de São João (St John's Festival)
    From 16 to 24 June, Oporto parties – the night of the 23rd sees virtually all the townsfolk out on the streets amicably bashing each other over the head with plastic hammers or leeks.
Festas da Nossa Senhora da Agonia (Agonia Fair & Festival)
    This is held on the first Sunday after 15 August and is famed for its folk arts, parades, fireworks, and handicrafts fair.
Feira de São Martinho (National Horse Festival)
    Equine enthusiasts will want to gallop off to Golegã between 3 and 11 November to see all manner of horses, riding contests and bullfights.

POST & TELECOMMUNICATIONS
Postal Rates

Postcards and letters up to 20 grams cost 120$00 to destinations outside Europe, and 65$00 to EC destinations. For delivery to the USA or Australia, allow eight to 10 days; delivery times for Europe average four to six days.

Sending Mail

If you're sending a parcel, Economy Air (or SAL – Surface Airlift) costs about a third less than air mail, but usually arrives just a week or so later. If you plan on sending large parcels, bear in mind that postal regulations can tie both you and the counter clerk in a frustrating knot – patience is advised. The main post offices in Lisbon and Oporto are open daily until 11 pm.

Receiving Mail

Most major towns have a post office with a *posta restante* service, but it can take time to find out exactly which post office feels responsible. Sometimes a charge of about 35$00 is levied for each item of mail received.

Telephones

The largest coin accepted by standard pay phones is 50$00. This makes them impractical for international calls, although the operating instructions are courteously provided in the booth in several languages. Local calls cost a minimum of 15$00.

Much more useful for both domestic and international calls are the increasingly common pay phones known as 'Credifone' which accept plastic telephone cards available from newsagents or tobacconists. Two cards are currently available: 750$00 (50 units) or 1750$00 (120 units). Prices for international calls average 300$00 for one minute to Europe; your call to Australia or the USA will cost about 600$00 per minute during the peak rate. Unit charges from private phones are about a third cheaper than those for public phones. A new phonecard system, T-SETE, has also been introduced for use in Lisbon and Oporto only.

If you make calls from your hotel room, you will probably be charged about 25$00 per unit – almost double the standard rate.

PORTUGAL

Post offices also provide phone services, but you often have to wait ages before being assigned a booth. It's generally cheaper to phone between 8 pm and 8 am, and on Saturday and Sunday.

To call Portugal from abroad, dial the international access code, 351 (the country code for Portugal), the area code and the number. Important area codes include 01 (Lisbon) and 02 (Oporto).

If you want to call abroad from Portugal, the international access code is 00.

Fax

The post offices are now operating a domestic and international fax service known as CORFAX. Prices for transmission to Europe start at 1900$00 for the first page; prices for transmission to the USA start at 2700$00 for the first page.

TIME

The time in Portugal is GMT/UTC. Portugal no longer applies seasonal time changes.

ELECTRICITY

The electric current is 220 volts, 50 Hz, and plugs are normally of the two-round-pin variety.

BOOKS & MAPS

They Went to Portugal (paperback) and *They Went to Portugal Too* (hardback) are two books by Rose Macaulay which provide a romp through the experiences of a wide variety of travellers in Portugal from medieval times to the 19th century.

For a general overview of Portugal and its place in the modern world, try *The Portuguese: the Land and Its People* (paperback) by Marion Kaplan.

For a look at Portuguese literature in translation, you could dip into *The Lusiads* (paperback) by Luis de Camões, which is considered the classical cornerstone of Portuguese literature. Translations are also available of works by other major Portuguese writers such as Eça de Queiroz *(The Maias)*, Fernando Pessoa *(Selected Poems)*, Fernando Namora *(Mountain Doctor)*, and

Mario Braga. For a recent Portuguese 'whodunnit' – close to the political bone – you could pick up a copy of *The Ballad of Dog's Beach* (paperback) by José Cardoso Pires.

The Michelin map of Portugal is accurate and extremely useful even if you are not using a car. The maps produced by the Automóvel Club de Portugal (ACP) provide slightly more up-to-date, but less detailed, coverage.

Those interested in walking in Portugal should pick up copies of the walking booklets available in the tourism offices in the Algarve (Faro) and Serra da Estrela (Covilhã).

MEDIA

Newspapers & Magazines

Major Portuguese-language newspapers include *Diário de Notícias*; daily newspapers such as *Público* and *Jornal de Notícias*; and the gossip tabloid *Correio da Manhã*, which may lack finesse, but easily licks all the others in terms of circulation. Weeklies include *O Independente* and *Expresso*. For entertainment listings, the most useful publication is the weekly *SE7E* (in Portuguese). An English-language weekly which aims to serve all of Portugal is the *Portugal Post*.

English-language newspapers and magazines from abroad are widely available in Lisbon, Oporto and the Algarve. The Algarve also has at least half a dozen of its own English-language newspapers and magazines which mostly cater to expatriate tastes, but are perhaps worth a look for entertainment listings or small advertisements.

Radio & TV

Portuguese radio is represented by the state-owned stations, *Antenna Um* and *Antenna Dois*, and by *Rádio Renascença* and a clutch of recently founded local radio stations. Sadly, *Radio Caos* made a promising start with its anarchic name but was unable to stay in one piece, and folded after only a few months.

Portuguese TV is expanding from two state-run channels (RTP1 and RTP2) to include two private channels (SIC and TV1). Sports programmes and soaps (known as *telenovelas*) take up the lion's share of broadcasting time – and some wits believe that the only time the Portuguese stop talking is when one or other of these items is on TV.

HEALTH

There is little to worry about in Portugal. Avoid swimming on beaches which are not marked out as safe – Atlantic currents are notoriously dangerous. Take the usual precautions for sunburn and sunstroke. If you are an EC national, make sure you get an E111 or similar form a few weeks before your departure. This will entitle you to free emergency medical treatment in Portugal. Considering the relatively small investment required, travel insurance is advisable as a backup.

For minor health problems you can pop into a local chemist (just ask directions to a *farmácia*). If you experience more serious health problems, you can usually ask your embassy or the local tourist office to refer you to the nearest hospital with an English-speaking doctor. The number to dial in any emergency is ☎ 115.

WOMEN TRAVELLERS

Women travelling around Portugal on their own or in a small group will be accorded attention by males who have the curious habit of hissing. The attention is wearisome, but generally unfocused and best ignored.

DANGERS & ANNOYANCES

Crime against foreigners in Portugal usually involves pickpocketing, theft from cars or pilfering from camp sites. It is mostly prevalent in heavily touristed parts of the country such as the Algarve, specific parts of Lisbon and a couple of the other major cities. Providing you take the usual simple precautions (use a money belt or something similar, don't leave valuables in a car or tent), there should be little cause for worry. For peace of mind you should definitely take out travel insurance.

FILM & PHOTOGRAPHY

It's best to take film and camera equipment with you, especially if you hanker after Kodachrome, which is very expensive. Other brands of slide film are widely available and represent good value at the *hipermercados* (hypermarkets). Print film processing is as fast and inexpensive as anywhere else in Europe.

WORK

The Portuguese have a long tradition of emigrating to look for work, so it seems logical to assume that the scope for foreigners seeking work in Portugal is strictly limited. The only exception is the teaching of English, for which it's best to have a specific qualification. Unless you happen to work for an organisation such as the British Council, which is backed by the British government, you will probably land up at a local language school which may provide enough to cover your living expenses, but little else. This isn't a problem providing you know this from the outset and consider the job as a means of dipping into Portuguese life rather than acquiring riches. For work in this and other fields (bar and restaurant work etc) it's worth scanning the English-language papers in Portugal which usually have a page or two devoted to personal advertisements.

For information about obtaining temporary or holiday work, contact the following organisations:

Intercultura
    Avenida Almirante Reis, 219, r/c Esq, Apartado 1395, Lisbon 1011 (☎ 01-895056)
International Friendship League
    Calçada da Baleia, 9, Ericeira 2655

ACTIVITIES

See the Algarve section for information on water sports and hiking. For walking, hiking and pony-trekking, see Serra da Estrela in the Central Portugal section and Peneda-Gerês National Park in the North section.

HIGHLIGHTS

The following are some of the highlights of Portugal:

Scenery
>Serra da Estrela; Alto Douro; Peneda-Gerês National Park; Alentejo in the spring

Beaches & Coastlines
>Eastern Algarve (Cacela Velha, Olhão, Tavira); Western Algarve (Carrapateira, Sagres, Lagos); Minho coast; São Pedro de Moel; Nazaré

Museums
>Gulbenkian (Lisbon); Museu dos Azulejos (Lisbon)

Palaces
>Palácio da Pena and Seteais (Sintra); Buçaco (Buçaco Forest); Estói (Estói, Algarve); Paço Ducal (Vila Viçosa)

Religious Sites
>Bom Jesus (Braga); Jerónimos Monastery (Belém, Lisbon); Santa Luzia Church (Viana do Castelo); Santa Maria Monastery (Alcobaça); Batalha Monastery (Batalha)

Walled Cities
>Óbidos; Marvão; Monsaraz; Monsanto; Évora

Hotels
>Buçaco Palace (Buçaco Forest); Sul Americano (Bom Jesus, Braga), Santa Luzia (Viana do Castelo); Casa do Poço (Óbidos); União (Tomar)

Restaurants
>Nazaré seafood restaurants away from the main tourist drag; Tulhas (Sintra); O Pátio (Tavira); Alcaide (Óbidos)

Literary Cafés
>Majestic (Oporto); Brasileira do Chiado (Lisbon); Aliança (Faro); Brasileira (Braga)

Walks & Hikes
>Serra da Estrela; Peneda-Gerês National Park; Serra de Monchique (Fóia)

ACCOMMODATION

Most *turismos* have lists of accommodation to suit a wide range of budgets, and can help you to locate a place to stay and make reservations. Although the government uses a system of stars ranging from one to five to grade some types of accommodation in Portugal, the criteria for awarding stars seem erratic. Also, it's worth remembering that the mandatory price list hanging on the door of your room shows the *maximum* price permitted by the government – the price is usually only applicable at the peak of the high season. If you want a room with a double bed, ask for a *quarto de casal*; for a room

with twin beds, ask for a *duplo*; and for a single room, ask for a *quarto individual*.

Camping

Camping is widespread and popular in Portugal. The *Roteiro Campista* (400$00), published annually in April and sold in most large bookshops, is an excellent multilingual guide which gives details of camp sites in Portugal and regulations for camping outside these sites. Depending on the facilities offered and the season, prices per night average 300$00 for an adult (over 10 years old), and 300$00 for a tent smaller than three sq metres. Considerably lower prices apply in less touristed regions or in the low season. This makes camping easily the cheapest option for accommodation.

Youth Hostels

There is a small network of about 17 youth hostels *(Pousadas de Juventude)* in Portugal. Although the overnight costs are low, the financial advantage is offset by restrictions such as an 11 pm (or earlier) curfew and exclusion from the hostel for part of the day. Prices for a dorm bed range from 800$00 in the low season to 1200$00 in the high season. Some hostels also offer private rooms at prices around 1750$00 per person per night. If you don't already possess a membership card from your national youth hostel association – recommended – you can purchase a guest card for 2500$00. The usual limit for a stay is three nights, but this rule may be negotiable in the low season. Breakfast is included in the price, and lunch or dinner costs 650$00. Demand for places at hostels is high, so advance reservations (100$00 charge) are essential. For more information, contact the Associação Portuguesa das Pousadas de Juventude (☎ 01-3559081), Avenida Duque d'Ávila, 137, 1000 Lisbon.

Cheap Rooms

One of the cheapest options for accommodation, apart from camping or youth hostels, is simply to look for *quartos particulares* (private rooms), also known in abbreviated form as *quartos*, which are usually just a room in a private house. The home-owners may approach you in the street or at the bus or train station; otherwise you can look out for a sign advertising 'quartos'. Tourist offices sometimes have relevant lists. The rooms are often a great bargain – they are clean, cheap and free from the restrictions of hostels, and the home owners can be interesting characters. A more commercial variation on this theme is provided by *dormidas*, normally rooming houses. Prices for a quarto in a dormida generally hover around 2000$00 for a double in the high season. Low-season prices drop depending on the willingness of the owner to bargain for trade. Breakfast isn't always included, and hot water may or may not be forthcoming. If you want to be assured of both, you should expect to pay more or upgrade to a guesthouse (see next section).

Guesthouses

The most common types of guesthouses which are the Portuguese equivalent of B&B are the *residencial* and the *pensão*. Both types are graded from one to three stars, and the top rated establishments are often cheaper and better run than some hotels which are clinging to their last star(s). During the high season, rates for a double room in the cheapest pensão start around 4500$00; for a residencial, expect to pay slightly more. During the low season, rates drop by at least a third. Breakfast is usually included in the price.

Hotels

Hotels are graded from one to five stars. Generally, you may be able to find a better deal in a residencial or pensão which earns its single star or couple of stars than in the hotels rated with two stars or less. At the top end of the scale, you can expect to pay between 15,000$00 and 25,000$00 for a double in the high season. At the lower end of the scale, anticipate paying around 6000$00 for a double in the high season. Prices in the low season drop spectacularly. This makes it possible to take a double room

in a spiffy four-star hotel for as little as 7000$00. Breakfast is usually included in the price.

First-Class Accommodation & Private Houses

Apart from hotels, there is a wide selection of more opulent accommodation in Portugal. *Pousadas* are establishments such as castles, monasteries or palaces which the government has turned into hotels. Full details for the pousadas are provided by tourist offices, and a leaflet is available from Portuguese National Tourist offices abroad.

The private counterparts of pousadas are mostly operated under a scheme called *Turismo de Habitação*, which allows you to stay in classy mansions, with or without the attention of the owner or occupier. Information on this private network is available from Direcção-Geral do Turismo, Turismo de Habitação (☎ 01-681174), Rua Alexandre Herculano, 51-3\o, Dto, 1200 Lisbon, or from Portuguese National Tourist offices abroad. In the same category, but more similar to up-market inns, are the *estalagem* and *albergaria*.

Prices for all these types of accommodation usually include breakfast, and are graded according to categories and high or low-season occupancy. As a rule of thumb, for a double room in the high season you can expect to pay a minimum of 9000$00 in a pousada, 6000$00 when staying in a house which belongs to the Turismo de Habitação scheme, and around 6000$00 for an estalagem or albergaria. The real bargains are to be found in the low season, when prices drop by as much as 50% and you can literally stay in a palace for the price of an average B&B elsewhere in Europe.

FOOD

Eating and drinking are given serious attention in Portugal, where hearty portions and excellent value for money are the norm. It's also heartening to find that Portugal has solidly ignored the fast-food era in favour of leisurely dining and devotion to wholesome ingredients.

PORTUGAL

The line between snacks and full-scale meals is not drawn too precisely. Bars and cafés often sell snacks or even offer a small menu. Full-scale meals are offered in establishments such as a *restaurante*, *cervejaria* (a type of bar and restaurant), or *marisqueira* (restaurant with an emphasis on seafood). The *prato do dia* (dish of the day) is often reasonably priced and may include three courses for about 900$00. In more touristed regions, restaurants may advertise an *ementa turística* (tourist menu). In contrast to the prato do dia, these are not real bargains.

The titbits offered at the start of a meal *(couvert)* often include bread rolls, cheese and butter – you will generally be charged an additional amount for this. A full portion of a complete meal, which is ample to feed two decent appetites, is known as a *dose*. If you want a smaller portion or need to adjust your budget, ask for a *meia dose* (half-portion) which is about a third cheaper. Lunch time moves at a leisurely pace from noon to 3.30 pm; evening meals are taken between 7 and 10.30 pm.

Snacks

Typical snacks include *sandes* (sandwiches); *prego em pão* (slab of meat with egg sandwiched in a roll); *pastéis de bacalhau* (cod fishcakes); and *tosta mista* (toasted cheese-and-ham sandwich). Prices for these items start at around 150$00. Soups are also cheap and filling.

Main Dishes

Traditional soups such as *caldo verde* (kale, potatoes and a slice of sausage) and *açorda* (bread soup, usually with seafood and strong herbal seasoning) are excellent starters.

Seafood in Portugal offers exceptional value, especially for fish dishes such as *linguado grelhado* (grilled sole), *bife de atúm* (tuna steak), and the omnipresent *bacalhau* (cod) which is cooked in dozens of different ways. Meat is somewhat hit-and-miss in Portugal; definitely worth sampling are *presunto* (ham) from the Chaves region; lamb, which is usually roasted, and known as *borrego* by the gourmets of Alentejo; and

cabrito, kid. Prices for main dishes start at around 800$00.

Desserts

In most cafés, *salões de chá* (teahouses) and *pastelarias* (pastry shops), you will be able to gorge yourself on some of the sweetest desserts *(sobremesas)* and cakes *(bolos)* imaginable – sugar reigns supreme! As a welcome change, you should ask what is in season and try local fruit which ranges from oranges, pears and grapes, to melons, figs and peaches. The cheeses from Serra da Estrela, Serpa and the Azores are also worth sampling although they are relatively expensive at about 2200$00 a kg.

Self-Catering

Apart from local shops and supermarkets, self-caterers should try to get an early start and visit local markets where seafood, vegetables and fruit are excellent value. A visit to the markets not only provides a feel for the priorities of locals, but in addition there are often market stalls selling inexpensive drinks or snacks.

DRINKS

Nonalcoholic Drinks

Surprisingly, fresh fruit juices are a rarity. The local mineral water *(água mineral)* is excellent and is consumed either carbonated *(com gás)* or still *(sem gás)*.

Coffee is a hallowed institution which comes complete with its own convoluted nomenclature. As a rule of thumb, the small black espresso is called a *bica* in central and southern Portugal, and *cimbalino* in the north. For coffee with milk, you can ask for a *galão* (more milk than coffee). In the north, if you want half coffee and half milk, you should ask for a *meia de leite*; elsewhere, you can achieve a similar result by asking for a *café com leite*. Tea drinkers can ask for tea *(chá)* with lemon *(com limão)* or with milk *(com leite)*.

Alcohol

Beer *(cerveja)* is popular in Portugal. Local brands include Sagres, Super Bock and

Tuborg (produced under licence). To order draught beer, ask for a *fino* or an Imperial.

Portuguese wine *(vinho)* offers excellent value in any of its three forms: red *(tinto)*, white *(branco)* and sparkling (or green-tinted) wine *(vinho verde)*. The red wines from Dão, Reguengos, Colares and Bairrada are especially good.

Port, synonymous with Portugal, is produced in the Douro Valley near Oporto and is drunk in three forms: ruby, tawny and white. While in Portugal, you should definitely try the dry tawny and dry white ports.

Restaurants often have *vinho da casa* (house wine) for as little as 250$00 for a bottle or jug, and for less than 700$00 you can buy a bottle to please some of the most discerning taste buds.

A recent lowering of duty on imported spirits has made foreign brands more affordable. Even so, local brands of brandy *(aguardente)* are worth a try. If you fancy a go at some rough stuff that tries hard to destroy your throat, ask for a *bagaço* (grape marc)! Bartenders in Portugal have the pleasant habit of serving large measures: a single brandy often contains almost the equivalent of a triple in the UK or the USA.

ENTERTAINMENT

Football (soccer) dominates the sporting scene – literally everything stops for a big match. The football season lasts from August to May and virtually every village or town even in the remotest parts of Portugal finds enough players for a team. The three main teams are Benfica and Sporting in Lisbon, and FC Porto in Oporto. Ask at the tourist office about forthcoming matches.

Bullfighting takes place between late April and October. The rules for a Portuguese *tourada* (bullfight) do not allow for the bull to be killed during the event, but the hapless beast endures more than enough wear and tear to make it necessary sometimes to dispatch it in private afterwards. In Lisbon, bullfights are held at the Campo Pequeno on Thursdays. Ribatejo is the major centre for breeding bulls; major fights are staged during the season in Ribatejo (Vila Franca da Xira and Santarém).

Cinemas in Portugal are inexpensive, and, in a bid to counter the audience erosion caused by video rental, some even reduce prices on a certain day at the beginning of the week. Foreign films are never dubbed: they are normally shown in the original language with Portuguese subtitles.

For details on current dance, music (rock, jazz and classical) and other cultural events, ask at the tourist offices or pick up a copy of *SE7E*, a cultural 'what's on' magazine published weekly in Lisbon.

Discos abound in Lisbon, Oporto and the Algarve where the town of Albufeira has a reputation as *the* hot spot of Portugal.

Perhaps the most original forms of entertainment are found at the local festivals (see the Cultural Events section). And, of course, for the price of a coffee you can sit outside a café and watch everyone else on their evening stroll!

THINGS TO BUY

Leather goods, especially shoes and bags, are good value, as are textiles such as embroidered linen or lace. Handicrafts range from inexpensive pottery or basketwork to really substantial purchases, such as rugs from Arraiolos, filigree jewellery in gold or silver, and sets of azulejos made to order.

Getting There & Away

AIR

Direct flights between London and Lisbon are operated by British Airways and TAP (Air Portugal). The same airlines also provide direct services to Oporto and Faro. Fare categories are extremely complicated and seem to change every six months.

As a rule of thumb, low-season tickets between London and Lisbon cost around £130, and high-season tickets are priced around £165. However, it's sometimes possible to get 'cheapie' deals as low as £90 for charter or package return flights between

London and Faro. For a general idea of prices from England to Portugal, phone the following airlines or agencies in London: TAP (Air Portugal, ☎ 071-839 1031), BA (British Airways, ☎ 081-897 4000), Abreu (travel agency, ☎ 071-229 9905) and Latitude 40 (travel agency, ☎ 071-581 3104), or ask the Portuguese National Tourist Office for its full listing, entitled *Tour Operators' Guide: Portugal.*

For similar price ideas from Portugal to England, you can phone the following airlines or travel agencies in Lisbon: TAP (☎ 01-544080), BA (☎ 01-3460931), Jumbo (youth travel agency, ☎ 01-7932645), and Abreu (☎ 01-3476441).

Since France, and Paris in particular, has a huge population of Portuguese immigrants, there are also frequent flights at reasonable prices between the two countries. For more details you can phone the following airlines in Paris: Air France (☎ 1-42.99.20.75) and TAP (☎ 1-42.96.15.65). Air France has been offering discounted prices for people aged under 26.

Madeira and the Azores are both served by direct flights from Lisbon. There are also direct flights to Madeira from London; and to the Azores from New York and Montreal. The standard fare for a return flight with TAP from Lisbon to Madeira is 29,000$00 (US$211); and the fare for a return flight with TAP from Lisbon to the Azores is 46,000$200 (US$337). For a return trip which leaves from Lisbon and takes in Madeira and the Azores before returning to Lisbon, the price is 77,400$00 (US$565). It is often cheaper to book package deals (flight and accommodation) from Lisbon – a return flight between Lisbon and Madeira plus seven nights' accommodation costs around 50,000$00 (US$365). Package deals offered by travel agents in England for the direct flights from England sometimes provide even better value.

Departure Tax

There is no airport departure tax in Portugal.

LAND

To/From Neighbouring Countries

Bus Eurolines operates regular bus services at least once a day between Madrid (Estación Sur de Autobuses) and Lisbon (Avenida Casal Ribeiro). The trip takes about 11 hours and tickets cost 10,280$00 one-way. Eurolines also operates bus services between other major towns in Portugal and Spain. For information and reservations in Madrid, call ☎ 09-2281105; in Lisbon, call ☎ 01-547300.

Train The main rail route between Spain and Portugal runs from Madrid to Lisbon via Valencia de Alcántara in about seven hours. Other popular train routes are the one from northern Spain which runs from Corunna to Oporto; and in southern Spain, the route from Seville to Ayamonte, which is opposite the Portuguese town of Vila Real de Santo António in the Algarve.

Car & Motorbike The major border posts – Elvas/Badajoz, Vilar Formoso/Fuentes de Oñoro and Valença do Minho/Tuy – are open round the clock. Other border posts are usually open from 7 am to midnight, but between November and March, they are generally only open from 8 am to 8 pm.

To/From Major Transport Hubs

Bus Eurolines operates regular bus services between Portugal (Lisbon, Oporto and other cities) and Spain, France and England.

The journey from England (Victoria Coach Station in London) runs via Paris where you change buses to continue the journey to Portugal. Allow about 22 hours for the trip; a standard ticket costs about £75. For more information from Eurolines in England, call ☎ 0582-40 4511. If you're in Portugal and require information on the Eurolines services, the number to call in Lisbon is ☎ 547300.

Train In general, it's only worth taking the train if you can take advantage of special tickets for people under 26. See the Getting Around chapter at the beginning of this book for details on Inter-Rail, Eurail etc.

Services from London to Lisbon and other destinations in Portugal run via Paris, where you will need to change trains. There are two standard routes: the Sud Express runs from Paris via Irún and then across Spain to Pampilhosa in Portugal (connections for Oporto) before continuing to Lisbon; the other route runs from Paris to Madrid, where you can catch the Lisboa Express via Entroncamento (connections for Oporto) to Lisbon. Allow about 40 hours for the trip from London to Lisbon, and expect to pay about £140 for a one-way ticket if you're over 26.

Car & Motorbike From England there are two standard routes. Those who favour spending less time driving can take the ferry from Plymouth to Santander (Spain) and then continue to Portugal via northern Spain. For information on the Plymouth-Santander ferry in England, phone Brittany Ferries (☎ 0752-22 1321). For a much longer drive, you can take the ferry to France and then motor down the coast via Bordeaux before crossing into Spain and continuing via Burgos and Salamanca to Portugal. One option to reduce driving time on this route would be to use Motorail for all or part of the trip from Paris to Lisbon. Information on Motorail is available in England from French Railways (☎ 071-493 9731).

SEA
To/From Neighbouring Countries
Ferry For details of the ferry connection between Faro and Tangier (Morocco), see Getting There & Away in the Algarve section.

Getting Around

AIR
Local Air Services
Flights inside Portugal are extremely expensive and hardly worth considering for the short distances involved.

LAR (Linhas Aéreas Regionais) operates flights to/from Lisbon, Oporto, Bragança, Chaves, Coimbra, Covilhã, Faro, Portimão, Vila Real and Viseu. The cheapest fares for a flight between Lisbon and Faro (50 minutes) cost 13,000$00/25,000$00 one-way/return. For further information, phone LAR at Lisbon Airport (☎ 01-8488509).

BUS
The state-run RN (Rodoviária Nacional), and private companies such as Mundial Turismo and Resende, operate a dense network of bus services which are divided into two types: *expressos* provide comfortable, fast and direct connections between major cities or towns; the *carreiras*, on the other hand, chug into eternity and stop at every crossroad. Timetables are a rare commodity: make a point of stocking up on information at tourist offices or bus stations in major towns.

Private bus companies also operate express services on the routes to major cities and the Algarve, with luxury buses used on some routes.

Express buses run from Lisbon to Faro in just under five hours and the fare is 1400$00; from Lisbon to Oporto, express buses take four hours and the fare is 1400$00.

TRAIN
CP (Caminhos de Ferro Portugueses) is the state railway company, which operates three main types of train service: *rápido, intercidade* and *regional*. Tickets for the first two types cost at least double the price for a trip on a regional service, and reservations are either mandatory or highly recommended. If you can match your itinerary and pace to that of a regional service, travel by rail is even cheaper, if slower, than by bus. Allow plenty of time before the departure of your train to queue for your ticket.

When in Lisbon, you should pop into Santa Apolónia Station to purchase a copy of the *Guia Horário Oficial* (200$00) from counter No 2. This has instructions in English and provides both international and domestic timetables.

Tourist tickets *(bilhetes turísticos)* are

available for seven (15,200$00), 14 (24,200$00) or 21 (34,500$00) days. The expense can only be justified if you plan to spend a great deal of your visit whizzing around on trains.

Most major train and bus stations have luggage storage facilities. If you ask politely, Turismo offices in small towns are also often willing to keep an eye on your belongings.

TAXI

Taxis offer good value – especially if you're travelling as a pair or in a larger group – and are usually plentiful in towns. The flagfall rate starts around 200$00, and 350$00 is often enough for a short zip across town.

CAR & MOTORBIKE
Road Rules

There is indeed a set of rules, but the two guiding principles for Portuguese drivers seem to be: first, to find the fastest route between two points; and second, to defy the law of mortality in doing so. Although city driving (and parking) is hectic, minor roads out in the countryside are surprisingly good with very little traffic. Recent injections of EC subsidies have ensured that the road system has been upgraded and there are now several long stretches of motorway – some of which require toll payment.

Petrol is decidedly pricey at 146$00 for a litre of super. Unleaded petrol (sem chumbo) is available, but not in the remoter regions. ACP (Automóvel Clube de Portugal, ☎ 01-3563931), Rua Rosa Araújo, 24, Lisbon, can provide more information and maps for driving in Portugal.

Speed limits in Portugal are as follows: 60 km/h in cities and public centres, unless otherwise indicated; 90 km/h on normal roads; and 120 km/h on motorways. The maximum permissible blood alcohol concentration is 0.05%. Driving is on the right, and front passengers are required by law to wear seat belts.

Rental

There are dozens of local car-hire firms in Portugal, but the best deals are often those arranged from abroad, either with one of the large travel companies as part of a package with the flight, or through an international car-hire firm. For the smallest category of car, expect to pay around US$160 for seven days in the high season, and about US$100 for the same deal in the low season. The minimum age for driving a hire car in Portugal is 23 and you must have held your licence for over a year.

HITCHING

Thumbing a ride can take considerable time in Portugal because drivers in the remoter regions tend to be going short distances. You get to meet some interesting characters, but you may only advance from one field to the next! You'll make more dependable progress when hitching from town to town on major roads.

LOCAL TRANSPORT
Bus

Most towns have adequate bus services, but timetables are hard to track down. Rural services tend to pass through once in a blue moon or on market days – whichever comes sooner. You can buy tickets from the driver or at kiosks in the town centre.

Train

In many rural regions, trains pass through magnificent scenery, but they seem to be moving in reverse and stopping at every second blade of grass. This is a frustrating option if your time is limited, but a delightful dawdle if it isn't.

Underground

Lisbon's underground system, the Metropolitano (commonly known as the metro), is handy for the core area of the city, but doesn't extend much farther. (See Getting Around in the Lisbon section.)

Trams & Other Mechanical Contrivances

If you are an enthusiast for stately progress, don't miss a ride on the trams. Both Lisbon and Oporto have extensive tram networks. Also worth trying are the funiculars and ele-

vadores (elevators) in Lisbon, Bom Jesus (Braga), Nazaré and elsewhere.

Taxi
Taxis are available in almost all towns and are an inexpensive and efficient way to run short distances. Remember, once the taxi leaves the town or city limits, you may have to pay the return trip – whether you take it or not.

Lisbon

Although it bustles with the crowds, noise and traffic that befit a capital city, Lisbon's low skyline, breezy position beside the River Tagus (Rio Tejo), and friendly nature lend it a small and manageable feel. Its unpretentious atmosphere and pleasant blend of architectural styles conspire with diverse attractions – and a few unique quirks – to make it a favourite with a wide range of visitors. Furthermore, Lisbon (Lisboa) is one of Europe's most economical destinations, offering excellent returns (yes, you'll be back!) for very modest prices.

Orientation
Apart from the puff required to negotiate the hills in Lisbon, orientation is straightforward. Activity centres on the lower part of the city, known as the Baixa district, where the focal point is the Rossio. Just north of the Rossio is the Praça dos Restauradores which is at the bottom of the Avenida da Liberdade. West of the Rossio, it's a steep climb to the Bairro Alto district where one section, known as Chiado, is still waiting for renovation after a huge fire in 1988. East of the Rossio, it's another steep climb to the Castelo de São Jorge and the adjacent Alfama district, which is a convoluted maze of tiny streets. Several km to the west is Belém with its cluster of attractions.

Information
Tourist Offices The main tourist office, Turismo (☎ 3425231), Palácio Foz, Praça dos Restauradores near Restauradores metro station, has stacks of literature and will make reservations for accommodation in Lisbon. It's open from 9 am to 8 pm Monday to Saturday, and from 10.30 am to 5.30 pm on Sunday. There are also tourist offices at the airport (☎ 893689) and at Santa Apolónia Station (☎ 867848), but expect long queues for all offices during the high season.

Maps The best maps are those published by *Falk* (these also show the direction of one-way streets) and *Lisbon City Map – Vista Aérea Geral*. The tourist office provides an adequate city map free of charge.

Theft & Security There's no need to be paranoid, but take the usual precautions, particularly in the Rossio and the Alfama and Bairro Alto districts. Use a money belt, keep cameras out of sight when not in use, and avoid unlit or unfamiliar streets at night. The Tourist Police Office (☎ 3466141) is at Rua Capelo, 13, in Bairro Alto, a connecting street between Rua Serpa Pinto and Rua Garrett. It's a friendly office and they speak a variety of languages – useful for dealing with any loss or theft reports, which you'll need if you want to claim insurance.

Money There are useful banks and exchange machines (for foreign cash) at the airport, Santa Apolónia Station, and on Rua Augusta (at the far end, close to the massive arch leading into Praça do Comércio). The automats operate 24 hours a day, give an excellent rate, save you waiting ages inside at the requisite bank counters, and charge less commission and tax than banks. Banco Borges e Irmão (☎ 3476838) at Avenida da Liberdade, 9A, is open from 6 am to 11 pm Monday to Friday.

Post & Telecommunications The general post office (☎ 01-3463231) is at Praça do Comércio. If you want to save frustration running from office to office, address your poste restante items: Posta Restante, Terreiro do Paço, 1100 Lisboa. This should direct your mail to counter 20 at the general post

PORTUGAL

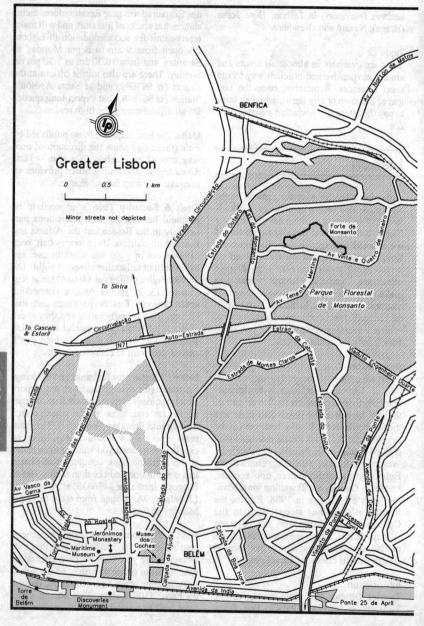

Greater Lisbon

0   0.5   1 km

Minor streets not depicted

BENFICA

Forte de Monsanto

To Sintra

Parque Florestal de Monsanto

To Cascais & Estoril

Circunvalação

Auto-Estrada   N7

Estrada da Cabreста

Viaduto Engenheiro Duarte

Estrada de Circunvalação

Estrada do Outeiro

EL Monsanto

Av Vinte e Quatro de Janeiro

Av Tenente Martins

Estrada de Montes Claros

Estrada do Aviño

Av G Norton de Matos

Estrada de

Av Vasco da Gama

Avenida das Descobertas

Avenida J Madeira

Calçada do Galvão

Calçada da Ajuda

Calçada de Boa Hora

Viaduto da Ponte

Acesso à Ponte

Av E do Rosteiro

Av da Torre de Belém

Jerónimos Monastery

Maritime Museum

Museu dos Coches

BELÉM

Torre de Belém

Discoveries Monument

Avenida da India

Ponte 25 de April

PORTUGAL

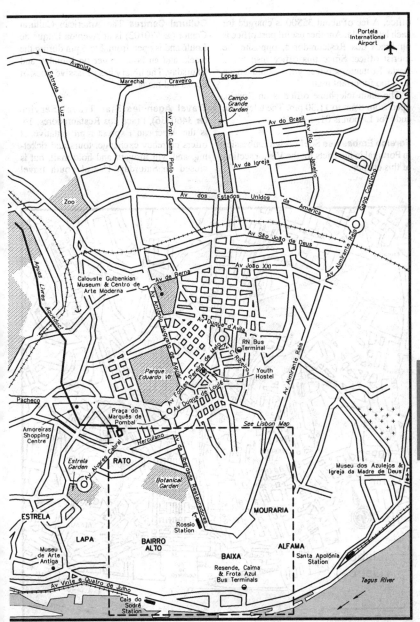

office. A fee of about 35$00 is charged for each letter held. Another useful post office is on Praça dos Restauradores, opposite the tourist office. Since this office also has a Posta Restante service, you should check here too for errant mail.

The main telephone office is on Rossio, open from 8 am to 11.30 pm. The telephone code for Lisbon is 01.

Foreign Embassies See Foreign Embassies in Portugal in the Facts for the Visitor section of this chapter.

Cultural Centres The American Cultural Center (☎ 570102) is at Avenida Duque de Loulé and is open from 2 to 6 pm during the week, and an hour longer on Monday and Thursday. The library has a massive stock of books and magazines.

Travel Agencies Star Travel Service (☎ 3460336), Praça dos Restauradores, 14, is the American Express representative. It offers currency exchange, tours and ticketing, and will forward and hold mail, but is closed on Saturday. Useful youth travel

agencies include Jumbo (☎ 7932645), Avenida da República, 96 R/C, and Turismo Juvenil (☎ 8484957), Praça de Londres, 9B.

Bookshops The Livraria Editora in Praça dos Restauradores, virtually next to the tourist office, is an excellent source of foreign-language maps and guides for Portugal. For second-hand travel guides and other dusty volumes, pop into Livraria Antiga do Carmo, Calçada do Carmo, 50, a few minutes' climb behind Rossio Station.

Laundry The Lavacentro (☎ 667394) at Rua Saraiva Carvalho, 117-B, is open from 8 am to 7.30 pm Monday to Saturday. Services include dry cleaning, washing, ironing and self-service.

Emergency The British Hospital (☎ 602020, night number 603785), Rua Saraiva Carvalho, 49, has English-speaking staff and doctors. The national number for an emergency is ☎ 115.

Things to See
Baixa The Baixa district is ideal for strolling through the ordered network of streets lined with colourful, gently crumbling buildings. You can strike out from the Rossio until you reach the foot of the hills surrounding the Baixa, and then save sweat and shoe leather by ascending at the stately pace of a funicular or elevator to explore higher levels.

Castelo de São Jorge From its Visigothic high times, the castle has gracefully declined into ruin, but it still commands a superb view of Lisbon – particularly early or late in the day. Take bus No 37, or, even better, tram No 28, which clanks up steep gradients and incredibly narrow streets.

Alfama It's best to wander at random through this ancient district below the castle, where the mazes of streets and alleys contain superb architecture. The terrace at the **Largo de Santa Luzia** provides a great viewpoint. The nearby **Museu de Arte Decorativa**

PLACES TO STAY		
5	Pensão Monumental	
6	Hotel Suisso-Atlântico	
10	Pensão o Globo	
21	Pensão Ninho das Aguias	

PLACES TO EAT		
4	A Petisqueira da Glória	
8	Odeon	
16	O Pinóquio	
18	Nicola	
24	Restaurante O Sol	
25	Cervejaria Trindade	
26	Café a Brasileira do Chiado	
27	Porto de Abrigo	
28	Mercado da Ribeira	
34	Martinho da Arcada	

OTHER		
1	Avenida Metro Station	
2	Hot Club	
3	Fábrica de Cerâmica Viúva Lamego	

7	Gloria Elevator	
9	Restauradores Post Office	
11	Main Tourist Office	
12	Praça dos Restauradores	
13	Restauradores Metro Station	
14	Star Travel Service (American Express)	
15	Rossio Railway Station	
17	Main Telephone Office	
19	Rossio Metro Station	
20	Praça da Figueira	
22	Castelo de São Jorge	
23	Museu de Arte Decorativa	
29	Cais do Sodré Station	
30	Tourist Police Office	
31	Casa das Cortiças	
32	Santa Justa Elevator	
33	General Post Office	
35	Resende, Caima & Frota Azul Bus Terminals	
36	Casa dos Bicos	
37	Sé (Cathedral)	
38	Ferries to Cacilhas	

PORTUGAL

(Museum of Portuguese Decorative Arts) is worth a look. There are guided tours (50 minutes), and it's open from 10 am to 1 pm and from 2.30 to 5 pm, closed on Monday. Restaurants, bars and nightclubs abound in Alfama. Rua da Graça is renowned for its taverns.

Belém This quarter, about six km west of the Rossio, has several sights which survived the Lisbon earthquake in 1755. **Jerónimos Monastery** is a clear choice for the finest sight in Lisbon – do not miss it. Constructed in 1496, it is a magnificent, soaring extravaganza of Manueline architecture. It's closed on Mondays and public holidays.

A 10-minute walk from the monastery is **Torre de Belém**, a tower also built in Manueline style, which sits obligingly in the river as *the* tourist image of Portugal – shutters click like gunfire! Admission into the tower costs 400$00. It's open from 10 am to 6.30 pm Tuesday to Saturday, and 10 am to 2 pm on Sunday. It's closed on Monday, and closes earlier between October and May.

Coach fans will make a beeline for the sumptuous display of hundreds of carriages at the **Museu dos Coches** (Coach Museum). It's open Tuesday to Friday from 10 am to 1 pm and from 2.30 to 6 pm, and closed on Monday and public holidays. Admission costs 400$00.

Just beside Jerónimos Monastery, the **Museu da Marinha** (Maritime Museum) houses a collection of nautical paraphernalia. It's open daily from 9 am to 5 pm, but closed on Monday. Admission costs 200$00.

To reach Belém, take the train from Cais do Sodré for a 10-minute ride; or the bus (No 43, 27 or 14); or, for some classy transport, the tram (No 17, 16 or 15).

Museums One of the most attractive museums in Lisbon is the **Museu dos Azulejos** inside the precincts of the Madre de Deus Church, west of Santa Apolónia Station in the Xabregas district. It contains superb displays of azulejos tastefully integrated into the elegant buildings. The restaurant provides light meals in a bright,

traditional kitchen – tiled with azulejos of course – or you can eat in a covered garden. Take tram No 17, 16 or 3. It's open Tuesday to Friday from 10 am to 1 pm and from 3 to 5 pm. Admission costs 300$00.

Calouste Gulbenkian Museum is considered the finest museum in Portugal and requires several hours to view a wide range of paintings, sculptures, carpets and much more, from Europe, Asia and beyond. The most convenient metro stations are São Sebastião and Palhavã. It's open Tuesday to Sunday from 10 am to 5 pm. Admission costs 400$00, but is free on Sundays.

If your feet aren't too tired, you can then visit the adjacent **Centro de Arte Moderna** which displays a cross section of modern Portuguese art.

The **Museu de Arte Antiga**, Rua das Janelas Verdes, houses the national collection of works of art by Portuguese painters. It is being completely renovated. Opening times are Tuesday to Sunday from 10 am to 5 pm. Admission costs 400$00 and is free on Sundays. Take bus No 40 or tram No 19 from the centre.

Mercado da Ribeira This is *the* Lisbon market, diagonally opposite Cais do Sodré Station. Get there early in the day to see vegetables, fruit, seafood and more being sold by feisty vendors.

Places to Stay
Camping There's a *Parque de Campismo Municipal* (municipal camping ground) (☎ 2430380) at Oeiras. Take the train from Cais do Sodré Station towards Estoril and get off at Oeiras.

The *Parque de Turismo e Campismo* (☎ 704413) in Monsanto Park is 12 km north-west of the city. Take bus no 14 from the centre of town. See the Facts for the Visitor section in this chapter for camping prices.

Youth Hostels Close to the centre is the *Pousada da Juventude* (☎ 532696), Rua Andrade Corvo, 46. It's closed during the day from 10 am to 6 pm, and the doors are locked at midnight. The closest metro station is Picoas, or take bus No 46 from Santa Apolónia Station and get off at 'Marquês de Pombal'. It's very popular, so reservations are essential.

The *Pousada da Juventude de Catalazete* (☎ 4430638) is at Estrada Marginal (next to Inatel), 2780 Oeiras. This is a very pleasant beachside hostel, but it is 12 km west of central Lisbon. To get there from the centre, take the train from Cais do Sodré Station and get off at Oeiras. It's open during the day from 2 to 6 pm and the doors are locked at 11 pm, which means you can forget nighttime pursuits if you stay there. Reservations are also essential.

Hotels & Guesthouses The tourist office in Restauradores will make reservations for accommodation, but only for Lisbon. During the high season there's strong competition for accommodation near the centre, so reservations are imperative.

Baixa At Rua da Glória, 21, the *Pensão Monumental* (☎ 3469807) has functional rooms at a budget price (doubles from 2500$00) but the street noise can be annoying.

Hotel Suisso-Atlântico (☎ 3461713), Rua da Glória, 13-19, is a solid choice with well-maintained rooms and is close to the tourist office. Doubles start at around 7000$00.

Bairro Alto At Rua do Teixeira, 37, close to the Restauradores metro station, the *Pensão Globo* (☎ 3462279) makes a pleasant base, and has doubles from 3500$00.

Casa de São Mamede (☎ 3963166), Escola Politécnica, is a stylish hotel in an elegant old house, with doubles from 7500$00.

Castelo de São Jorge Pensão Ninho das Aguias (☎ 867008), Costa do Castelo, 74, is perched in a green jungle below the castle and offers amazing views, after a very steep climb. Reservations are essential; reception can be vague or distant (perhaps it's living

with the view that does it). Doubles start at around 4000$00.

Places to Eat
Restaurants Most of the city's restaurants are also in the Baixa and Bairro Alto districts.

Baixa The *Odeon*, close to the Condes cinema on Rua dos Condes, has friendly waiters and inexpensive main dishes, including some from Trás-os-Montes. *O Pinóquio* (☎ 3465106), Praça dos Restauradores, is more expensive, but good value, especially for seafood. *Restaurante o Sol*, Calçada do Duque, 23, is an inexpensive vegetarian option (set meals 770$00).

Bairro Alto The *Cervejaria Trindade* (☎ 3468251), Rua Nova da Trindade, 20-C, is a converted convent and the cavernous interior is decorated with azulejos. Main dishes start at around 800$00. It stays open until 2 am.

A Petisqueira da Glória, Rua da Glória, 27, close to the tourist office, is friendly and totally unpretentious and offers delicious food.

Porto de Abrigo (☎ 3460873) is at Rua dos Remolares, 18, close to Cais do Sodré Station. The seafood dishes are recommended and main dishes cost 800$00 or more.

Cafés Most of the cafés are in the Baixa and Bairro Alto districts.

Baixa Nicola, Praça Dom Pedro IV, is the celebrated *grande dame* of Lisbon's turn-of-the-century cafés. Pop in for a coffee or a meal – elderly locals weave through shoals of tourists and home in on their habitual tables. It closes on Sunday. *Martinho da Arcada*, Praça do Comércio, was once a haunt of the literary set, including Fernando Pessoa, but has lost a little of its integrity after recent renovation. It closes at 8 pm and on Sundays.

Bairro Alto A Brasileira do Chiado, Rua Garrett, 120, is another venerable institution with strong literary traditions. Take a look at Fernando Pessoa glued to his chair on the street outside.

Entertainment

For listings of current cultural events and entertainments, pick up a copy of *SE7E* or *Público*. Staff at the tourist office are also a good source of information.

Music In its authentic form, fado is a fascinating form of music. However, the sad truth in Lisbon is that many of the *casas de fado* produce pale tourist imitations, often at prices which may make you feel like groaning as much as the fado singer. Even the simplest places now demand a cover charge of around 2000$00. The tourist office has lists of fado clubs. In the Bairro Alto you could try *Vieira*, Rua das Taipas, 14. In the Alfama district, *Parreirinha d'Alfama* (☎ 868209), Beco do Espírito, 1, provides a reasonable show for a moderate charge.

Hot Club, Praça da Alegria, 39, is the centre for a thriving Lisbon jazz scene with a friendly, intimate atmosphere for jazz fans of all ages. You can listen to live music there on weekends. It's open from 10 pm to 2 am, closed on Monday.

Discos boom and bust at lightning speed. Try *Skylab* (☎ 658955), Rua Artilharia, 1, 69-B, which raves from 10 pm until 3.30 am.

The African music scene (predominantly Cape Verdean) bops in numerous bars in the area around Rua São Bento.

Cinemas Lisbonites are avid film-goers and there are plenty of cinemas dotted around the city. The Amoreiras Shopping Centre, for example, has a multiscreen cinema (☎ 692558) which shows almost a dozen different films every night. Cinema tickets average 350$00 and represent excellent value compared with the rest of Europe.

Spectator Sports Football fans might like to see a match. The local teams are Benfica and Sporting. The tourist office can advise on dates and ticket purchase. Between April and October, bullfights are staged at Campo Pequeno.

Things to Buy

For azulejos, try Fábrica de Cerâmica Viuva Lamego (☎ 3152401), Largo do Intendente, 25. The Museu dos Azulejos also has a small selection on sale. Cork enthusiasts will find everything imaginable made from the stuff at Casa das Cortiças (☎ 3425858), Rua Ivens, 30-34. On Tuesday and Saturday morning, the Feira da Ladra, a type of flea market, is held in the Alfama district. Keen shoppers will head for the Amoreiras Shopping Centre, one of the latest and biggest of its kind in Europe. For considerably more atmosphere, just wander the backstreets of Baixa and Bairro Alto.

Getting There & Away

Air Lisbon's airport is just 20 minutes from the city centre. For airport information phone ☎ 802060. For information on international and domestic connections, see the Getting There & Away and Getting Around sections at the beginning of this chapter.

Bus The state-run RN has its main bus station (☎ 577715) at Avenida Casal Ribeiro, 18, not far from Picoas metro station. Private bus companies operating from other terminals include Resende (☎ 870497) at Rua dos Bacalhoeiros, 20-A; Caima (☎ 875061) at Rua dos Bacalhoeiros, 16-C; and Frota Azul ☎ 879324) at Campo das Cebolas. For information on domestic and international connections, see the Getting There & Away and Getting Around sections at the beginning of this chapter.

Train Santa Apolónia Station (☎ 876025 for information) is the terminus for trains from north and central Portugal, and for international services. Cais do Sodré Station provides the rail service westwards to Cascais and Estoril. Rossio Station is centrally placed and serves Sintra and Estremadura. Barreiro Station lies across the river and is the terminus for rail services for the south of Portugal and the Algarve – a ferry connection leaves frequently from the pier at Praça do Comércio. For information on international and domestic connections, see the Getting There and Away and Getting Around sections at the beginning of this chapter.

Car & Motorbike
The new Lisbon-Oporto expressway provides a four-hour link between the two cities. Fill up your petrol tank before you leave though, as service stations are few and far between. The toll is 2565$00 for cars travelling between Lisbon and Oporto on the expressway.

Getting Around
To/From the Airport Bus No 90, more commonly known as the Linha Verde (Green Line), is a special bus service (20 minutes, 250$00) running between the city centre and the airport from 7 am to 11 pm. Local bus Nos 5, 8, 22, 44 and 45 also run to the centre. Taxis are a good bargain for two or more people. Expect to pay about 1000$00 to the centre; you may have to pay an extra 50% of the fare if your luggage exceeds 30 kg.

Bus & Tram Individual bus tickets are expensive at 135$00 each; a cheaper option is a *modulo*, which is a block of 10 tickets costing 600$00. Tickets, passes, and a map *(Mapa: Rede de Transportes)* for bus and tram services is available from Cais do Sodré Station, Praça da Figueira and kiosks in the city centre. If you plan to spend more than four days of intensive sightseeing in Lisbon, tourist passes valid for all trams and buses are available daily (140$00), for four days (1200$00) or one week (1700$00). Buses and trams run from 4 am to 2 am – the map has details for night services.

The clattering, antediluvian trams *(eléctricos)* are an essential and endearing component of Lisbon. Don't leave Lisbon without having taken at least one ride on tram No 28. Fares start at 95$00.

Underground The underground system isn't extensive, but useful for short hops

across the centre of town. Individual tickets cost 50$00, and a modulo of 10 tickets is cheaper at 425$00. The metro operates from 6.30 am to 11 pm. Pickpockets can be a nuisance.

Taxi Compared with rest of Europe, Lisbon taxis are fast, cheap and plentiful. Either flag taxis down on the street or go to a rank. The flagfall rate is 200$00, and a short zip across town costs about 400$00.

Around Lisbon

SINTRA
If you make only one side trip from Lisbon, Sintra should receive top priority. Long favoured by Portuguese royalty and English nobility (Lord Byron was dotty about the place), the thick forests and surrealist architecture of Sintra provide a complete change from urban Lisbon. The tourist office (☎ 9231157), on the ground floor of the local museum on Praça da República, has maps which provide orientation for hikes in the hills. During weekends expect droves of visitors. Even during the week, accommodation seems to be permanently tight, so reservations will be essential.

The telephone code for Sintra is 01.

Things to See
The **Palácio Nacional de Sintra** (Sintra National Palace) dominates the town with its twin kitchen chimneys. From its Moorish origins, the palace has been developed into a synthesis of Manueline and Gothic architectural styles. Inside, the highlights include the **Magpie Room** and the **Swan Room**. It's closed on Wednesday but open during the rest of the week from 10 am to 5 pm. Admission costs 300$00.

A steep climb of three km from the town centre leads to the **Palácio da Pena**, which was built in 1839 in exuberant Romantic style complete with every conceivable embellishment within and without. The grounds are also ideal for botanical forays.

PORTUGAL

The palácio is open from 10 am to 5 pm and closed on Monday. Admission costs 400$00.

The nearby castle ruins of **Castelo dos Mouros** provide a magnificent view over the town and its surroundings. Open daily from 10 am to 5 pm.

Places to Stay

Camping Capuchos (☎ 862350) is nine km from Sintra, but there are no bus connections. *Camping Praia Grande* (☎ 9290581) is on the coast 11 km from Sintra, and a much better bet for travellers without their own transport because it is linked by frequent bus service with Sintra.

The new youth hostel, *Pousada da Juventude* (☎ 9241210), is at Santa Eufémia, four km from the town centre. Apart from the usual dormitory beds, the hostel has double rooms which are good value at 3000$00. Advance reservations are essential.

Pensão Adelaide (☎ 9230873), Rua Guilherme Gomes Fernandes, 11, is a 10-minute walk from the station. It offers friendly reception and comfortable rooms; doubles without bath start at around 2500$00. *Pensão Economica* (☎ 9230229), Avenida Heliodoro Salgado, 6, has functional doubles for 2000$00 and is just five minutes on foot from the station. For a real splurge, the *Hotel Tivoli Sintra* (☎ 9233505), Praça da República, fully deserves its four stars. A sumptuous double costs 11,000$00 in the low season.

Places to Eat

Tulhas (☎ 9232378), Rua Gil Vicente, 4-6, is an excellent restaurant, close to the tourist office. Closed on Wednesdays. *Fonte da Pipa* (☎ 9234437), Rua Fonte da Pipa, 11-13, is a cosy bar with light snacks and inexpensive drinks. If you're lucky, you'll get to hear Mário Elias, the local sultan of swing, having a crack at everything from the Beatles to Springsteen.

Getting There & Away

The bus and train stations are together in the north of the town on Avenida Dr Miguel Bombarda, about two km from the Royal Palace. Trains from Lisbon take about an hour (145$00). Bus services run from Sintra to Estoril, Cascais and Mafra.

Getting Around

Taxis are a convenient way to reach the sights. For a two-hour trip to the major sights, expect to pay around 2000$00. There is also an infrequent bus service linking the sights, or give yourself time to enjoy the lush forests to the full by hiking.

ESTORIL

Estoril is a beach resort with a balmy climate favoured by the rich and famous. The tourist office (☎ 4680113) is on Arcadas do Parque. Attractions are limited to the beach and strolls in the public gardens.

The telephone code for Estoril is 01.

Places to Stay

For gently fading elegance, try the *Pensão Residencial Continental* (☎ 4684026) at Rua Joaquim Santos, 2. The *Hotel Londres* (☎ 4684245), Avenida Fausto Figueiredo, 7, is popular as a budget place to stay, and reservations are imperative.

Getting There & Away

From Cais do Sodré Station in Lisbon it's a half-hour trundle by train (185$00).

CASCAIS

Cascais has attractions similar to those in Estoril, but has become more popular as an 'in' beach resort. Cascais tourist office (☎ 4868204), Rua Visconde de Luz, 14, has lists for accommodation and timetables for bus services.

The telephone code for Cascais is 01.

Things to See & Do

Two km west of the town centre is **Boca do Inferno** (Mouth of Hell), where the sea roars into the coast. **Cabo da Roca**, the western-most point of Europe, is a spectacular and often very windy spot about 16 km from Cascais and Sintra (bus services from both towns) – pop into the tiny windswept post office for a commemorative certificate.

Those who like their beach wild, long and dangerous, will want to visit **Guincho**, which is three km from Cascais, and was the venue for the World Surfing Championships in 1991.

Places to Stay
Camping Orbitur do Guincho, seven km from Cascais on the way to Sintra, is useful if you have your own transport.

Getting There & Away
From Cais do Sodré Station in Lisbon it's a 25-minute train trip (115$00).

QUELUZ
Things to See
The **Royal Palace** (Palácio Nacional de Queluz) constructed in the 17th century and later enlarged with inspiration derived from Versailles, has sumptuous rooms and fine gardens. The Throne Room and the gargantuan kitchen (now a restaurant) are highlights. It's open Wednesday to Monday from 10 am to 1 pm and 2 to 5 pm. Admission costs 400$00, or half-price during the low season (October to May).

Getting There & Away
There are frequent trains from Rossio Station for the 20-minute ride (90$00) to Queluz.

MAFRA
Things to See
The *big* – and only – attraction is the colossal **Palace & Convent** (Palácio Nacional de Mafra), which tops the league for size on the Iberian Peninsula. The dimensions (an estimated 4500 doors!) and austere atmosphere make the tour rather depressing. It's open from 10 am to 5 pm, closed on Tuesday and public holidays. Admission costs 250$00.

Getting There & Away
Buses from Lisbon take 1½ hours (500$00), and from Sintra it's a 45-minute bus ride (350$00).

The Algarve

Loud, boisterous and strongly influenced by foreigners, the stereotypical Algarve is about as far from quintessential Portugal as one can go. While sun and sand are the major draws

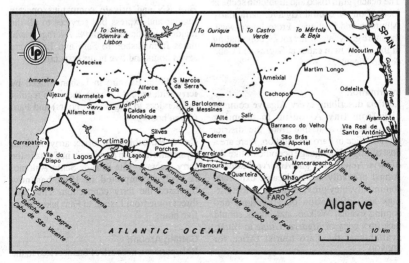

PORTUGAL

– the region boasts over 3000 hours of sunshine annually compared with 2500 hours in Majorca – the tourist warrens of the central Algarve are surrounded by other attractions. West of Lagos are wild and all but deserted beaches, whereas the coastline east of Faro is dotted with enticing and colourful fishing villages. Finally, for those who've filled up on seascapes, there are such attractions as the forested slopes of Monchique, the fortified village of Silves and the past glory of Estoi Palace tucked away in the mountain backdrop.

Orientation

The southernmost slice of Portugal, the Algarve divides neatly into four sections: the windward coast, or *Sotavento*, extending from Amoreira to Lagos; the central coast from Lagos to Faro; the leeward coast, or *Barlavento*, from Faro to Vila Real de Santo António; and the interior.

The largest town, and the district capital, is Faro. The easternmost town, Vila Real de Santo António, is a border crossing to Ayamonte, Spain. The towns are linked by a car ferry and a recently completed highway bridge across the Guadiana River mouth. The beach, golf, disco and nightclub scene is focused on the central Algarve, particularly Albufeira and Portimão. From Lagos west, the shore grows steep and rocky, culminating in the windy twin capes at Sagres and Cabo de São Vicente.

Information

Leaflets describing every Algarve community from tiny Alcoutim to booming Albufeira are available from the district tourist office in Faro. In addition, there are a host of English-language periodicals like the *Algarve News*, *APN* and *Algarve Resident*. Aimed primarily at the sizeable expatriate community, they provide entertainment listings and information on attractions and coming events. Walkers and hikers should pick up a copy of *Algarve: Guide to Walks*, available at the Faro tourist office for 300$00.

Dangers & Annoyances

Because of the presence of individuals tempted by cameras, watches and holiday funds, it's a good idea to take extra security precautions in the Algarve. Although paranoia is unwarranted, don't leave anything of value in your vehicle or unattended on the beach.

Swimmers should beware of dangerous currents. Beaches are marked by coloured flags: red means the beach is closed to bathing, yellow means swimming is prohibited but wading is fine. When the flag is green, anything goes.

Things to Buy

Few souvenir goodies are actually made in the Algarve, but Moorish-influenced ceramics and local woollens (cardigans and fishing pullovers) are good value. You may also want to try a bottle of Algarviana, a local amaretto (bitter liqueur), or the salubrious bottled waters of Monchique, which are on sale everywhere.

Getting There & Away

Air The only airport for domestic and international connections is in Faro.

Bus RN and private companies operate regular and express bus services to all the major towns on the Algarve. Average travel times from Lisbon to Faro and Lagos are seven hours and five hours respectively.

Train From Barreiro in Lisbon (linked by ferry with central Lisbon), there are regular rail services to Lagos (6½ hours) and Faro (seven hours).

Car & Motorbike Motorists arriving from Ayamonte in Spain previously had to take the ferry across to Vila Real de Santo António. A bridge completed in 1991 has now bypassed the ferry connection. The most direct route from Lisbon to Faro takes about five hours.

Getting Around

RN operates a network of bus services to the

major towns along the Algarve. Via Infante, the super-highway planned to run the length of the coast to Spain, is only partially completed.

FARO

The capital of the Algarve, Faro is also the main transport hub and a thriving commercial centre. Since it lacks interest, most visitors use it only as a brief staging point.

The tourism office (☎ 089-803604), Rua da Misericórdia, can provide a wide range of tourist literature.

The telephone code for Faro is 089.

Things to See & Do

The waterfront area around Praça de Dom Francisco Gomes has pleasant gardens and cafés nearby. Faro's beach, **Praia de Faro**, is six km south-west of the city. Take bus No 16 from the stop in front of the tourist office. Another option between May and September is to take a ferry ride to the beach from Arco da Porta Nova, close to Faro's port.

At Estói, about 12 km north of Faro, is the wonderful crumbling wreck of **Estói Palace**, which is sinking into a surreal garden of statues, balustrades and azulejos – a highly recommended visit. The bus from Faro to São Brás de Alportel goes via Estói.

Places to Stay & Eat

There are moderate camping facilities at Faro beach. Conveniently close to the port and the train station is *Pensão O Faraó* (☎ 823356), Largo da Madalena, 4, with singles/doubles for around 3000$00/5000$00. *Residencial Avenida* (☎ 823347) at Avenida da República, 150 has singles/doubles at similar prices.

The *Snack Bar Ramires*, Rua Filipe Alistão, 19, serves excellent seafood. *Café Aliança* on Rua Dom Francisco Gomes is a turn-of-the century gem and certainly worth visiting for a coffee.

Getting There & Away

The airport is six km from the city centre. Bus No 18 runs to the airport, but the service stops around 8 pm. The average price for a taxi is 1000$00.

The bus station is in the centre of town, close to the harbour. There are at least three daily buses to Lisbon (1800$00), and frequent buses to other coastal Algarve towns.

The train station is just a few minutes on foot west of the bus station. At least six services go to Lisbon daily (1800$00), and a similar number to Vila Real de Santo António, Albufeira and Portimão.

TAVIRA

Tavira is one of the oldest and most beautiful towns in the Algarve. Graceful bridges cross the Gilão River which divides the town. Like all good tourist offices, Tavira's (☎ 081-22511), on Praça da República, provides detailed maps.

The telephone code for Tavira is 081.

Things to See & Do

In the old part of town is the **Igreja da Misericórdia** church, which has a striking Renaissance doorway. From there, it's a short climb to the **castle** which dominates the town.

Two km from Tavira is **Ilha da Tavira**, an attractive island beach which is connected to the mainland by a ferry. Take the bus from Praça da República to the ferry terminal at Quatro Águas.

For a look at the way the Algarve used to be, take the bus to **Cacela Velha**, an unspoilt fishing village eight km from Tavira. Another worthwhile day trip would be to see the colourful quay and brilliant white church at **Olhão**. If you go, drop in for a delicious seafood lunch at *Papy's*, just opposite the park, where the main course is as fresh as it comes.

Places to Stay & Eat

There's a camp site on Ilha da Tavira, but night owls should remember that the ferry stops running at 11 pm. *Pensão Residencial Lagoas* (☎ 22252), Rua Almirante Cândido dos Reis, 24, has singles/doubles for 2000$00/3000$00. *Princesa do Gilão* (☎ 325171), Rua Borda d'Água de Aguiar,

PORTUGAL

10, is right beside the river. Singles/doubles cost 3000$00/4000$00, but avoid the street-side rooms which can be very noisy.

Restaurante O Pátio (☎ 23008) at Rua António Cabreira, 30 serves excellent seafood – tuna steak *(bife de atum)* is a speciality.

Getting There & Away
There is regular bus service along the 45-minute run between Faro and Tavira.

VILA REAL DE SANTO ANTÓNIO
The only cogent reason to visit this town is to use the ferry to leave or enter Portugal via Spain. The tourist office (☎ 081-43272) opposite the ferry pier is not particularly helpful.

The telephone code for Vila Real de Santo António is 081.

Places to Stay
Pousada de Juventude de Vila Real de Santo António (☎ 44565), Rua Dr Sousa Martins, 40, is a pleasant youth hostel in the centre of town – a bright spot in an otherwise rather dingy scene.

Getting There & Away
From Vila Real de Santo António, a ferry crosses to Ayamonte in Spain where there are two rail services daily to Huelva and further connections to Seville.

The ferry operates daily from 8 am to 7.30 pm and the crossing takes 10 minutes. The cost for a car plus driver is 650$00; and car passengers or pedestrians pay 130$00 each.

From the bus station close to the ferry pier in Vila Real de Santo António, direct buses depart for Lisbon. There are also train services to Lisbon (2500$00), via Faro.

LAGOS
Lagos is a major tourist resort and offers some of the best and most picturesque beaches on the Algarve. The tourist office (☎ 763031), Largo Marquês de Pombal, is in the centre of town.

The telephone code for Lagos is 082.

Things to See & Do
In the old part of town is the **Municipal Museum**, which houses an odd assortment of ecclesiastical treasures, handicrafts and preserved animal fetuses. The adjacent **Chapel of Santo António** contains some extraordinarily intricate Baroque wood-work.

The beach scene around Lagos includes **Praia da Luz; Meia Praia**, a vast strip of sand to the east; and the more secluded **Praia do Pinhão** to the west.

Places to Stay & Eat
A good camp site is *Valverde de Praia da Luz* (☎ 789211). The *Residencial Marazul* (☎ 769749), Rua 25 de Abril, 13, has singles/doubles for 4000$00/5000$00.

For standard food at reasonable prices, try *A Muralha*, Rua da Atalaia. *Navegador Jazz Club* (☎ 62622), Rua Vasco da Gama, 2, features live music and a friendly, folksy atmosphere. Prices for snacks and drinks are reasonable and navigation continues until 2 am.

Getting There & Away
Bus and train services each depart up to five times daily to Lisbon.

MONCHIQUE
Monchique, a quiet highland town in the forested Serra de Monchique, offers an Algarve alternative, which is in complete contrast to the discos and lazy beach life on the coast.

The telephone code for Monchique is 082.

Things to See & Do
In Monchique itself, the **Igreja Matriz** church has an amazing Manueline portal – about the closest you'll get to seeing stone tied in knots!

Six km south of Monchique is the drowsy hot-spring community of **Caldas de Monchique**. Have a soak in the spa or try the bottled water.

The best excursion from Monchique is to drive or hike eight km through thick forest to the rooftop of the Algarve at **Fóia**. If you can ignore the forests of radio masts, the views are terrific.

Places to Stay & Eat

The *Residencial Miradouro* (☎ 92163), Rua dos Combatentes do Ultramar, has singles/doubles for 2500$00/3000$00. *Restaurante Charette*, Rua Samora Gil, is friendly, unpretentious and inexpensive. *Barlefante* (☎ 92822), Travessa da Guerreira, a very popular local bar which serves reasonably priced drinks, stays open until 1 am.

Getting There & Away

Eight daily buses run between Lagos and Monchique, travelling via Portimão.

SILVES

Silves was once the Moorish capital of the Algarve and even rivalled Lisbon in its influence. Times are a great deal quieter in the backstreets now, but the huge castle dominating the town is a reminder of past grandeur and well worth a visit.

The tourist office, Rua 25 de Abril, has information leaflets and can help with finding accommodation.

The telephone code for Silves is 082.

Places to Stay & Eat

The *Residencial Sousa* (☎ 442502), Rua Samoura Barros, 17, has singles/doubles for 1500$00/3000$00. *Restaurante Rui*, Rua C Vitarinho, 23, is a bit touristy, but prices are reasonable.

Getting There & Away

Silves Railway Station is two km from town – either walk or wait for the connecting bus service which runs every 30 minutes. Another bus service connects Silves with Portimão.

SAGRES

Sagres is a small.fishing port perched on the cliffs at the south-western extremity of Europe amid dramatic, windswept scenery.

The telephone code for Sagres is 082.

Things to See & Do

The **fort** stands on a wide, windy promontory. This is where Henry the Navigator founded his school of navigation and primed the explorers who later contributed to the founding of the Portuguese empire. The fort contains the tourist office (☎ 64125).

There are several beaches close to Sagres. A particularly pleasant one is at the fishing village of **Salema**, 17 km east.

No visit to Sagres would be complete without a trip to precipitous **Cabo de São Vicente** (Cape St Vincent), six km from Sagres. A solitary lighthouse stands on this barren cape which proclaims itself the south-westernmost point of Europe.

Places to Stay & Eat

Camping Sagres (☎ 64351) is two km from town and a short distance just off the road towards Lisbon. The site has well-maintained facilities, and scooters are available for hire. Some of the locals in Sagres let out private rooms for around 1250$00/2000$00 for a single/double. *Café Atlântico*, on the main street near the turnoff to the pousada, prepares cheap, filling meals.

Getting There & Away

There are 10 buses daily between Sagres and Lagos; two connect Sagres to Faro.

Central Portugal

Central Portugal, good for weeks of desultory rambling, deserves more attention than it receives. From the varied beaches of the Costa de Prata to the lofty Serra da Estrela and the sprawling Alentejo plains, it is a landscape of scenic extremes.

From the Dão region come some of Portugal's finest wines, while farther south, the hills and plains are studded with the country's equally famous cork oaks. To literally top it all off, the centre is graced with scores of fortresses and walled cities. In these hilltop eyries, you can wander through ancient cobbled streets, breathe the clean air,

PORTUGAL

and contemplate the awe-inspiring nature of
the broad expanses below.

ÉVORA
One of the architectural gems of Portugal,
the walled town of Évora is the capital of
Alentejo province – a vast district with surprisingly varied landscapes composed of
olive groves, vineyards and wheat fields.
The flowers in the spring would make an
Impressionist painter suffer seizures of
desire. Évora's charm lies in the typically
narrow one-way streets (mind those wing

mirrors!) of the inner town, which is remarkably well preserved.

Orientation & Information
The focal point for orientation is Praça do
Giraldo. From there you can wander off
through the backstreets until you meet the
city walls. The tourist office (☎ 066-22671),
Praça do Giraldo, 73, has maps which outline
walking routes through the town. Nazareth,
Praça do Giraldo, 46, has books in English.

Money Outside the tourist office is a foreign

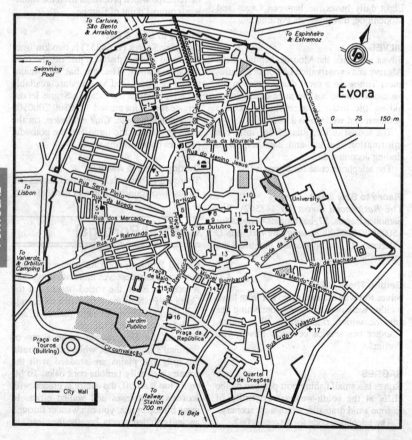

currency exchange machine which changes a wide range of currencies from US dollars to Swiss francs.

Post & Telecommunications The post office is on Rua de Olivença. The telephone code for Évora is 066.

Emergency The hospital (☎ 22132) is on Rua do Valasco.

Things to See

Inside **Sé** cathedral, on Largo do Marquês de Marialva, is a museum with a choice display of ecclesiastical treasures and interesting cloisters. Admission to the museum, closed on Monday, costs 200$00.

The **Museu de Évora**, opposite the Sé, contains a selection of Roman and Manueline sculptures, and paintings by Portuguese artists from the 16th century. Opposite the museum is the Roman-era **Temple of Diana**, the subject of Évora's top-selling postcard.

The **Igreja de São Francisco**, a few blocks south of Praça do Giraldo, is a church with a distinctly ghoulish attraction. Inside, the Capela dos Ossos (Ossuary Chapel) has been constructed with the bones and skulls of several thousand people.

1	Pastelaria Mimosa
2	Restaurant Martinho
3	O Garfo
4	Post Office
5	Casa Portalegre
6	Nazareth Bookshop
7	Tourist Office
8	Dom João Cafetaria
9	Residencial Riviera
10	Temple of Diana
11	Évora Museum
12	Sé Cathedral
13	Pensão Eborense
14	Casa de Pasta
15	Igreja d São Francisco
16	Bus Terminal
17	Hospital

Places to Stay

Accommodation gets very tight in Évora, which is popular with Spanish tourists. The tourist office can help with accommodation lists and reservations, but definitely book ahead.

Camping *Orbitur* (☎ 25190) is about two km south of the town – take a bus in the direction of Alcaçovas.

Guesthouses The *Pensão O Eborense* (☎ 22031), Largo da Misericórdia, 1, is a minipalace with leafy surroundings which provides fading singles/doubles from 6400$00/7900$00. The *Casa Portalegre* (☎ 22326), Travessa do Barão, 18, is another architectural charmer. Singles/doubles are good value at 1500$00/3000$00, breakfast not included. The *Residencial Riviera* (☎ 23304), Rua 5 de Outubre, 49, is run like a quality hotel and its singles/doubles are good value at 6000$00/7000$00.

Places to Eat

Casa de Pasto, Rua Miguel Bombarda, 56, is a cheery, simple and inexpensive eatery. It's closed on Monday, and last orders are taken at 9 pm, so arrive early. *O Garfo* (☎ 29256), Santa Catarina, 17, is close to the Praça do Giraldo. Its large dining hall is in traditional style. Here you'll find large portions for small prices and it stays open until 11 pm; closed on Monday. *Restaurante Martinho* (☎ 23057), Largo Luis de Camões, 24-25, is a specialist restaurant for *borrego* (lamb) dishes.

Entertainment

A popular student hang-out that stays open late is *Dom João Cafétaria*, Rua Vasco da Gama, 10. There are numerous pubs and discos in the centre of town. *Pastelaria Mimosa*, Praça Joaquim António d'Aguiar, is worth a visit in the early morning for a coffee and a chance to see the guy serving behind the counter, who must rate as the fastest coffee slinger in Alentejo.

The Feira de São João is Évora's big bash,

PORTUGAL

held from 22 June to 2 July, and renowned as one of Alentejo's biggest country fairs.

Getting There & Away

Bus There are frequent bus services from the terminal (☎ 22121) on Praça da República to Lisbon, the Algarve, and regional destinations such as Elvas, Estremoz and Monsaraz.

Train Train connections include those to Lisbon (frequent departures for the 3½-hour trip), the Algarve (tedious and indirect), Coimbra (changes required), and regional chug-a-lug services to Beja.

MONSARAZ

Monsaraz, a magical walled town, perched high above the plain, affords wonderful views. This place is well worth the effort spent getting there.

Things to See

Monsaraz is small and easily covered on foot in a couple of hours. The major buildings of architectural note are the **Misericórdia** hospital and the former **tribunal**. Clamber up onto the parapets of the castle for the best views. This isn't a place to tick off sights – just enjoy the clear light and eerie medieval atmosphere.

Places to Stay & Eat

The tourist office on the main square has a brief list of places, including private rooms and Turismo de Habitação, and can help with reservations. There are a couple of restaurants near the main square. Eat before 8 pm, as the town goes to bed early.

Getting There & Away

Monsaraz is a convenient side trip by bus from Évora. It's best considered as a two-day trip: take the bus to Monsaraz one day, stay the night, then return on the bus the next day. There is also an infrequent bus service from Reguengos de Monsaraz which has more frequent connections with Évora.

ESTREMOZ

The region around Estremoz is dominated by

marble, huge mounds of which are extracted in quarries and piled up above. The architectural appeal of Estremoz lies in the elegant, gently deteriorating buildings which are liberally embellished with marble, of course.

Information

The tourist office (☎ 22538), Largo da República, 26, has maps and lists of accommodation.

Things to See & Do

Estremoz is an attractive town divided into upper and lower sections. The upper section is crowned by the castle's tower, **Torre de Menagem**. At the foot of the castle is a former palace, which has been converted into a pousada. The focal point of the lower section is the main square, known as the Rossio, and two interesting sights nearby are the **Igreja de São Francisco** church, and **Misericórdia** hospital.

The Saturday market is the major event of the week and renowned for its colourful character.

Vila Viçosa is 17 km from Estremoz and within easy reach by bus. The major attraction is the **Palácio Ducal** (Ducal Palace) – the ancestral home of the Dukes of Bragança – which contains a large collection of carpets, furniture, and works of art. The mandatory guided tour (in Portuguese) is perhaps too thorough; you may be distracted by shrieking peacocks ambushing swans in the carefully tended gardens. It's open from 9.30 am to 1 pm, and from 2 to 5.30 pm; closed Mondays and on public holidays. Admission costs 400$00 and an additional 100$00 to the adjoining coach museum.

Places to Stay & Eat

The *Pensão-Restaurante Mateus* (☎ 22226), Rua Almeida, 41, has singles/doubles at 2000$00/4000$00. These are good-value rooms with lofty ceilings, but the door locks are a bit dodgy – you can easily lock yourself in! Prices include breakfast in the restaurant which is also good for other meals.

Getting There & Away
Bus services are frequent from Évora, but infrequent from Lisbon, Elvas, and Arraiolos.

CASTELO DE VIDE & MARVÃO
From Portalegre (near the Spanish border north-east of Lisbon) it's a short hop to Castelo de Vide, a town noted for its mineral water and picturesque houses clustered round a castle. The tourist office (☎ 045-91361), Rua de Bartolomeu Álvares da Santâ, 81, has lists of accommodation and a good town map.

Marvão, 12 km from Castelo de Vide, is a magnificent walled village tucked away on a mountaintop – literally in the clouds – and highly recommended. The tourist office (☎ 045-93226), Rua Dr Matos Magalhães, has lists of accommodation. The telephone code for Castelo de Vide and Marvão is 045.

Things to See & Do
In Castelo de Vide, the highlights are the **Judiaria** (Old Jewish Quarter) in the very well-preserved network of medieval back-streets, and the view from the castle.

While you're ambling around Marvão, have a look at the castle, the equally well-preserved medieval streets, and the grand views which encompass large chunks of both Spain and Portugal.

Places to Stay & Eat
The tourist office in Castelo de Vide can help with accommodation, but you should try to spend at least one night in Marvão, where the tourist office provides a selection of private rooms and Turismo de Habitação.

Getting There & Away
Bus services connect Portalegre with Castelo de Vide and Marvão. There are only two or three services daily; change at Portagem for Marvão. The train station for Castelo de Vide is four km from the town. Infrequent train services from Portalegre to Spain run via Castelo de Vide.

ALCOBAÇA
Alcobaça's big attraction is the immense **Santa Maria Monastery** (Mosteiro), which was founded in 1178. The original Gothic style has undergone Manueline, Renaissance and Baroque additions. Of particular interest are the tombs of Pedro I and Inês de Castro, the Cloisters, the Kings' Room and the kitchens. It's open from 9 am to 7 pm, and admission costs 400$00.

Alcobaça is an easy day trip from Nazaré. The tourist office (☎ 062-42377) is opposite the monastery. The telephone code for Alcobaça is 062.

Getting There & Away
There are frequent buses to Nazaré, Batalha and Leiria. The closest train station is five km north-west of Alcobaça at Valado dos Frades, where you can get a bus into town.

BATALHA
Batalha's single highlight is **Batalha Monastery** (Mosteiro de Santa Maria de Vitória), a colossal Gothic masterpiece which was constructed between 1388 and 1533. Earthquakes and vandalism by French troops caused considerable damage over the subsequent centuries, but a full restoration was completed in 1965. Highlights within the monastery include the Founder's Chapel, which contains the tomb of Henry the Navigator, the Royal Cloisters, Chapter House and the Unfinished Chapels. It's open from 9 am to 5 pm daily and admission costs 400$00.

The tourist office (☎ 044-96180) is in a nearby shopping complex. The telephone code for Batalha is 044.

Getting There & Away
There are frequent bus connections to Alcobaça, Nazaré, Tomar and Leiria, and up to three direct buses to Lisbon daily.

NAZARÉ
Nazaré originated as a fishing village in the 17th century and went its peaceful way until it was 'discovered' by tourism, which rapidly awarded it the title of Portugal's 'Most Pic-

turesque Fishing Village'. Today, the old techniques of fishing and the distinctive local dress have more or less gone overboard, and in the high season the whole place resembles a tourist circus. Providing you aren't expecting pristine authenticity, a visit to Nazaré is still worthwhile for the beauty of the coastline and the superb seafood.

The tourist office (☎ 062-561194) is on Avenida da República. The telephone code for Nazaré is 062.

Things to See & Do
Nazaré is composed of two parts. The lower part along the beach has retained a core district of narrow streets where many of the houses, shops and restaurants cater to the tourist trade. The upper section, known as O Sítio, sits on the cliffs overlooking the beach and is accessed by a vintage funicular railway from the lower town. The far-ranging clifftop view along the coastline is superb.

The beaches attract huge crowds in the summer and pollution is an increasing problem. Beware of dangerous and changeable currents. Enquire at the tourist office if you are unsure which beaches are safe for swimming.

Places to Stay & Eat
The locals derive useful income from letting private rooms, and you will probably receive offers when you arrive at the bus station. Prices for singles/doubles start at around 1000$00/1300$00. *Camping Golfinho* (☎ 553680) is an inexpensive camp site at Pederneira, three km from Nazaré. There are also dozens of pensões, but prices can be inflated during the high season when accommodation is tight and reservations are essential.

One compelling reason to visit Nazaré is the superb seafood served in a large number of restaurants. In general, the restaurants on the seafront are more expensive than those in the centre of the village. *Restaurante Maria Matos* (☎ 551069), Travessa do Elevador, 7, serves a superb *açorda de mariscos*

(bread soup with seafood) for 1200$00 – more than enough for two.

Getting There & Away
The nearest railway station is six km away at Valado, connected by a frequent bus service with Nazaré. There are numerous bus connections to Lisbon, Alcobaça, Óbidos and Coimbra.

ÓBIDOS
Óbidos is an impressive walled town which has retained or preserved its medieval network of streets and alleys almost too perfectly. The friendly staff at the tourist office (☎ 062-959231), Rua Direita, can assist with information not only for Óbidos, but also for the whole region.

The telephone code for Óbidos is 062.

Things to See
The best plan is to climb up onto the town walls and do a circuit to admire the views and get your bearings. Then wander at random through the back alleys before popping into **Igreja de Santa Maria** church, which has fine azulejos, and finishing with a look at the **Museu Municipal**.

Places to Stay & Eat
Accommodation in Óbidos is nearly twice as expensive as elsewhere in the region. The town is small and easily covered in a day, so there's no real reason to stay. For Turismo de Habitação, the *Casa do Poço* (☎ 959358), Travessa da Mouraria, is recommended. It has excellent singles/doubles grouped round an inner courtyard at prices starting around 5000$00/6000$00.

Restaurants in Óbidos are not cheap either. The modest supermarket just inside the entrance gate would suit self-caterers. *Restaurante Alcaide* (☎ 959220) at Rua Direita has excellent food and you can eat on the terrace in warm weather. Main dishes start around 900$00. It's closed on Monday and during November when the owners pop off to the Azores to search out new recipes.

Getting There & Away

There are excellent bus connections for Lisbon, Oporto, Coimbra, Tomar and the surrounding region. From the railway station, which is outside the walls at the foot of the hill, there are fairly frequent rail services to Lisbon.

COIMBRA

Coimbra is famed for its university, which dates back to the 13th century, and its traditional role as a centre of culture and art, which has been complemented in more recent times by industrial development.

The tourist office (☎ 039-238 86) on Largo da Portagem provides an accurate map of the city and information on cultural events.

The telephone code for Coimbra is 039.

Things to See

The town consists of two parts. In the lower part, the most interesting sight is the **Santa Cruz Monastery** with its ornate pulpit, medieval tombs and intricate sacristy.

In the upper part, the two main attractions are the **Old University** with its Baroque library and Manueline chapel; and the **Machado de Castro Museum**, which houses a fine collection of sculptures and paintings. Once you've seen these, it's best to explore the back alleys of this university quarter, which has all the hang-outs and the exuberant atmosphere suited to student life.

At **Conimbriga**, 16 km south of Coimbra, are the excavated remains of a large Roman city. On display are some impressive mosaic floors, baths and fountains. The site museum is worth visiting to see a wide variety of Roman artefacts – epicures will head for the museum restaurant. Admission costs 100$00 to the museum and the same again for the ruins – no charge on Sundays and public holidays. The museum is open daily, except Monday, from 9 am to 6 pm. The ruins are open daily from 9 am to 8 pm. The easiest way to reach Conimbriga is to take the AVIC bus (210$00) which leaves daily in the morning at 9.05 am (9.35 am on Saturday and Sunday) from outside the Hotel Astoria

in Coimbra, and returns from Conimbriga at 12.50 pm (5.50 pm on Saturday and Sunday).

Places to Stay & Eat

The *Pousada de Juventude de Coimbra* (☎ 22955), Rua Henriques Seco, 12-14, is Coimbra's youth hostel. Take bus No 46, 29, 8 or 7 and ask the driver where to get off. *Pensão Antunes* (☎ 23048), Rua Castro Matoso, 8, has singles/doubles at 3900$00/4900$00.

There are numerous student eateries around the Praça do Comércio. *Diligência Bar*, Rua Nova, 30, is both a restaurant and bar, and a popular place for amateur and professional fadistas to perform. For a complete change, try the cosy *Restaurante Ticino* (☎ 35989), Rua Bernardo de Albuquerque, 120, Olivais, which serves good Italian food. Main dishes start around 750$00.

Getting There & Away

Buses run frequently to Lisbon, Oporto, Évora and Faro. Train services to these destinations are also frequent, but don't be confused by Coimbra's two stations: Coimbra A is for local services, and Coimbra B is for international services and destinations in the north. The two stations are linked by a shuttle train.

LUSO & BUÇACO FOREST

Anyone who likes forest trails will want to make at least a day trip to the Buçaco Forest, which was chosen by monks as a retreat in the 6th century and has managed to escape serious harm up to the present day. The forest is a couple of km from the spa resort of Luso, where the tourist office (☎ 031-939133) on Avenida Emídio Navarro has maps of the forest trails. These will help with orientation past numerous wayside shrines and gateways, and through more than 700 different species of trees and shrubs.

The telephone code for Luso is 031.

Places to Stay & Eat

The Luso tourist office has accommodation lists. *Pensão Central* (☎ 939254), Avenida

Emídio Navarro, has bright singles/doubles at around 2000$00/3000$00. Close to the *Hotel Eden* – which is in the central praça, and has a restaurant that's best avoided – there's an extraordinary café built like an American diner.

For a real touch of class, you can eat at the *Palace Hotel* (☎ 93101), a former hunting lodge for royalty which lies in the centre of the forest. It is as zany and beautiful an expression of Manueline style as any found elsewhere in Portugal and is certainly worth a visit. If you just eat in the palace restaurant, expect to pay at least 1500$00 per head for a modest meal, but if you want to stay in this positively elegant five-star establishment, expect to pay from 14,000$00/18,000$00 singles/doubles.

Getting There & Away

There are frequent bus services from Coimbra and Viseu which run via Luso – some also make the detour into the park to the Palace Hotel.

SERRA DA ESTRELA

Serra da Estrela, the highest mountain range in Portugal, stretches between Guarda and Castelo Branco. With its steep valleys, forests and mountain streams, it offers superb scope for hiking. The highest peak, known as Torre (1991 metres), is snow-covered for much of the year.

Orientation & Information

The best bases for information are at the tourist offices in quirky Covilhã (☎ 075-322170), Manteigas (☎ 075-981129) and Guarda (☎ 071-212251). Covilhã is an uninteresting industrial hub, but it is a good base for excursions into the mountains.

The youth hostel at Penhas da Saúde (see the North section) is also a good choice for a base. The tourist administration for Serra da Estrela has published a walking guide in Portuguese entitled *À Descoberta da Estrela*, which has detailed hiking maps and descriptions of walks. The Covilhã tourist office has copies on sale for 400$00.

Places to Stay

The *Pousada de Juventude das Penhas da Saúde* (☎ 075-25375), Penhas da Saúde, high on the mountain, is nine km from Covilhã and has full facilities for meals and accommodation. Bus connections are infrequent, so a taxi ride may be a better option.

Getting There & Away

Bus and train connections from Coimbra to Guarda, Manteigas and Covilhã operate several times a day.

Getting Around

Bus connections between Guarda and Covilhã operate daily but infrequently.

The North

Most visitors are surprised by Portugal's northern tier. With considerable tracts of forest, rich viticultural countryside, the peaks of Peneda-Gerês National Park, and a strand of underattended beaches, it is Portugal's new tourism horizon. The north's urban scene focuses on Oporto with its magnificent vantage point on the River Douro. Beyond Oporto but within easy reach are a trio of stately historical cities: Braga, Portugal's religious centre; beautifully situated Viana do Castelo; and Guimarães, which proudly declares itself the birthplace of Portugal.

OPORTO

Oporto (Porto) is the second-largest city in Portugal and despite its reputation as the country's industrial hub, with its fair share of grime, it has considerable charm beyond the imbibing of port wine.

Orientation

The city is divided by the River Douro, which is spanned by four bridges named Ponte Dom Luís, Ponte Arrábida, Ponte São João and Ponte Maria Pia. On the north bank is central Oporto; on the south bank is Vila

Oporto (Porto)

PORTUGAL

Nova da Gaia with its concentration of port wine lodges.

The focus for central Oporto is Avenida dos Aliados. To the east is the major shopping area around Rua de Santa Catarina; to the west is a similar commercial district around Rua dos Clérigos. Praça da Liberdade marks the southern end of Avenida dos Aliados and is close to São Bento Station and its cavernous booking hall covered with superb azulejos. The picturesque Ribeira district lies below Ponte Dom Luís, which is several streets south of São Bento.

Information

Tourist Offices The main turismo (☎ 02-312740) is at Rua Clube dos Fenianos, 25, close to the town hall. It's open from 9 am to 7 pm Monday to Friday, closing at 4 pm on Saturday. Between July and September it's also open from 10 am to 1 pm on Sunday. A smaller, national tourist office (☎ 02-317514) is found at Praça Dom João, 1.

Money Several banks line Avenida dos Aliados, one with a currency exchange machine. The bank inside the Brasilia Shopping Centre stays open until 10 pm Monday to Friday.

Post & Telecommunications The main post office, also responsible for poste restante, is on Praça General Humberto Delgado, directly opposite the tourist office. It's open from 8 am to 10 pm Monday to Friday. The main telephone office is at Praça da Liberdade, 62, and is open every day from 8 am to 11 pm. There are plans to move this post office in 1993. Plenty of Credifone booths have popped up in the city centre.

The telephone code for Oporto is 02.

Foreign Consulates The US Consulate (☎ 6063094) is at Praça Conde Samodãeas, 66, and open from 8.30 am to 5.30 pm (closes from 1 to 2 pm) Monday to Friday. The UK Consulate (☎ 684789), Avenida da Boavista, 3072, is open from 9.30 am to 5 pm (closes from 12.30 to 3 pm) Monday to Friday.

Emergency The Santo António Hospital (☎ 2005241 day; 2007354 night) has some English-speaking staff. The national emergency number is ☎ 115.

Things to See & Do

The **Torre dos Clérigos** on Rua dos Clérigos is the highest tower in Portugal. If you feel fit, climb its 200-plus steps for the best panorama of the city. It's open from 9 am to noon and from 2 to 5 pm (closed on Wednesday). Admission costs 80$00.

The formidable **Sé** cathedral dominates central Oporto, even more so at night when it is illuminated. It's worth a visit for its mixture of architectural styles and ornate interior. It's open daily from 8 am to noon, and from 2.30 to 5 pm.

The **Soares dos Reis National Museum**, on Rua Dom Manuel II, displays masterpieces of Portuguese painting and sculpture. It's open Tuesday to Friday from 10 am to 5 pm. Admission costs 200$00.

In Vila Nova da Gaia you can visit some of the numerous **port wine lodges** for a tour of the cellars and a sample of the goods. A couple of the larger lodges include Porto Sandeman (☎ 304081), Largo Miguel Bombarda, 3, and Ferreira (☎ 3700010), Avenida Diogo Leite, 70.

The **Solar do Vinho do Porto** (☎ 697793) is at Rua de Entre Quintas, 220. Sample a glass of port chosen from a huge list in stylish surroundings, with a terrace offering an excellent view across the city. It is closed on Sundays and public holidays.

Bolhão is a fascinating market, just east of Avenida dos Aliados. A cheery band of strapping market ladies offer everything from seafood to herbs and honey. It's open from 7 am to 5 pm Monday to Friday and from 7 am to 1 pm Saturday.

Trips can be made up the valley of the **River Douro** to see the spectacular scenery. Highly recommended is the train trip from Oporto to Peso da Régua (four trains daily; 2½ hours one-way) – the last 50 km of this route clings dramatically to the bank of the river. There are also infrequent trains continuing inland along the river valley as far as Pocinho (5½ hours).

If you fancy boating up the river, *Endouro* (☎ 324236) organises cruises which depart from Oporto and last several days. Travellers with private transport can spend a pleasant day or so driving along the twisting, narrow roads beside the river.

Places to Stay
Camping *Camping da Prelada* (☎ 812616) is at Rua Monte dos Burgos, about five km from the city centre. From Praça de Liberdade, take bus No 6.

Camping Marisol (☎ 7115942) is at Madalena, about 10 km south of Oporto. Take bus No 57.

Hostels *Pousada de Juventude do Porto* (☎ 6065535), Rua Rodrigues Lobo, 98, has a convenient central location and only 50 beds – reservations are essential. The doors are locked at midnight. Take bus No 52, 20 or 3 from Praça da Liberdade.

Guesthouses The *Pensão Mondariz* (☎ 2005600), Rua Cimo de Vila, 147, is grubby and loud, but is one of the cheapest places in the city. It's close to São Bento Station.

The *Pensão Pão de Açúcar* (☎ 2002425) is at Rua do Almada, 262. Prices start around 5000$00/6000$00 for a single/double with bathroom and spacious terrace. It's popular, so bookings are essential.

Pensão Aviz (☎ 320722) at Avenida Rodrigues de Freitas, 451 provides good value. Prices for rooms without bath start around 2500$00/4200$00 single/double; for rooms with bath expect to pay 4450$00/5750$00.

Places to Eat
Restaurants *A Tasquinha* (☎ 322145), Rua do Carmo, 23, is close to the university and popular with students.

The Ribeira district harbours dozens of restaurants. *Filha da Mãe Preta* (☎ 315515), Cais Ribeira, 39-40, serves inexpensive seafood; and *Pesa Arroz*, (☎ 310291), Cais

Ribeira, 41-42, has a congenial atmosphere and prices.

Café *Café Majestic* is at Rua de Santa Catarina, 112. It's a wonderful Art-Nouveau relic, constantly under threat of demolition, and definitely worth a visit for a cimbalino (black espresso) or a snack. It's closed on Sunday.

Entertainment
The *Pinguim Café* (☎ 323100), Rua de Belomonte, 67, is a cultural and musical meeting spot close to the Ribeira.

In the same area, there are several lively pubs: try *Mercado*, or test your competitive skills at the curiously named *O Meu Mercedes é Melhor que O Teu* (My Mercedes is Better than Yours).

The big festival in Oporto is the Festas de São João (St John's Festival) held in June.

Things to Buy
Port, of course, is a favourite purchase. Casa Oriental, Rua dos Clérigos, 111, has a good selection of port interspersed with dangling bacalhau (cod). Casa Januário, Rua do Bonjardim, 352, is also a specialist in port. Other good buys are shoes and gold filigree jewellery. For handicrafts, there's the Centre for Traditional Arts & Crafts at Rua da Reboleira, 37 in the Ribeira.

Getting There & Away
Air International and domestic flights serve Oporto's airport, Pedras Rubras Aeroporto (☎ 9482141), 20 km outside the city. During peak traffic time, allow an hour from the city centre. Take bus No 44 or 56 or a taxi (1500$00).

Bus RN has two terminals. The northern terminal on Praça Filipa de Lancastre serves Braga and other destinations in the north. The southern terminal (Garagem-Atlântico) at Rua Alexandre Herculano is for services to Coimbra and destinations in the south. Resende (☎ 310401), Rua das Carmelitas, 7, is recommended for its express services to Lisbon – reserve tickets at least a day ahead.

PORTUGAL

Several private bus companies are also based around the RN north terminal.

Train Oporto is a rail hub for northern Portugal and has three major train stations. Campanhã Station (☎ 564141) is the largest station, serving routes throughout the country. São Bento Station (☎ 2002722) concentrates on regional destinations, and Trindade Station (☎ 2005224) provides services to Póvoa de Varzim and Guimarães only.

Trains to Spain depart from both Campanhã and São Bento stations, which are connected by frequent services.

Car & Motorbike Driving in the city centre can be a real pain – the traffic seems to spend more time gridlocked than on the move, and parking spaces are limited.

Getting Around

Bus An extensive bus system operates around focal points at Cordoaria and Praça Dom João I. If you plan to make frequent use of the buses, it's cheaper to buy a *caderneta* (book of 20 tickets) or a four-day or one-week *Passe Turístico* (Tourist Pass), sold at kiosks near the bus stops or from the newsagent next to the Café Imperial on Avenida dos Aliados.

Tram Oporto's trams are one of the delights of a visit to the city. Take a ride on tram No 1, which trundles from Infante out to Foz – best at sunset. On Sundays, the tram service is replaced by a bus service.

Taxi Taxis are good value. For a quick zip across town, expect to pay about 500$00. An additional charge is made if you cross the Dom Luís Bridge to Vila Nova da Gaia; or for any destination outside the city limits.

VIANA DO CASTELO

This port, in an attractive setting at the mouth of the Lima River, is renowned for its historic buildings in the old part of the city and for its active promotion of folk traditions.

The tourist office (☎ 058-822620) on Praça da Erva has exceptionally helpful staff and a large stock of tourist literature for the region. The telephone code for Viana do Castelo is 058.

During August, the town hosts the *Festas de Nossa Senhora da Agonia* (Agonia Fair & Festival). See the Facts for the Visitor section at the start of this chapter for more details.

Things to See & Do

The focal point of the town is the splendid Praça da República with its delicate fountain and several elegant buildings, such as the **Misericórdia** church.

Four km above the town rises the steep hill of **Santa Luzia**. At the top of the hill, enter the church and climb the steps at the back for a grand panorama across the coast. A funicular railway runs every 30 minutes (from 9 am to 8 pm) from behind the station to the top of the hill.

Places to Stay & Eat

The tourist office has extensive listings for accommodation, and can make reservations for Turismo de Habitação – the cheapest category starts at 4300$00 for a single. The *Pensão Guerreiro* (☎ 822099), Rua Grande, 14 (1st floor), has clean singles/doubles for 1500$00/2800$00. The *Residencial Magalhães* (☎ 823293), Rua Manuel Espregueira, 24, has comfortable doubles around 3500$00.

Run by a friendly family, the *Restaurante Minho* (☎ 823261), Rua Gago Coutinho, 103-5, serves wholesome and inexpensive dishes and stays open until midnight. *Os Três Potes* (☎ 829928), Rua Beco dos Fornos, 9, is decorated in folksy style and even has dancers skipping between the tables during the summer! Seafood dishes start around 750$00. It's closed on Monday.

Getting There & Away

There are frequent bus connections to Oporto (two hours) and Braga (one hour). Train services run north to Spain and south to Oporto.

PORTUGAL

BRAGA

Braga is crammed with churches and, not surprisingly, it's considered the religious capital of Portugal. During Easter week, Braga attracts huge crowds to its Holy Week Festival.

The tourist office (☎ 053-22550), Avenida da Liberdade, 1, provides town maps and can help reserve accommodation. The telephone code for Braga is 053.

Things to See & Do

At **Bom Jesus do Monte**, a pilgrimage site perched on a hill seven km from the city, there's the extraordinary **Escadaria do Bom Jesus** (Stairway of the Five Senses), with sculpted representations of the five senses, and a superb view. Buses run from Braga to the site, where you can either follow the steep path to the top, or take a short ride on a funicular railway.

In the centre of Braga is the **Sé**, a massive cathedral which contains an interesting treasury and several tomb chapels. Admission costs 200$00.

From Braga it's only a short bus ride to **Guimarães**, which is considered the cradle of Portugal and is of interest for its medieval town centre and the **Palace of the Dukes of Bragança**. Guimarães is easily visited on a day trip from Braga.

Places to Stay & Eat

The *Pousada de Juventude de Braga* (☎ 616163), Rua de Santa Margarida, 6, is a friendly hostel in the city centre. The *Pensão Residencial Avenida* (☎ 22955), Avenida da Liberdade, 738, provides good value with doubles around 3000$00.

For a room with a stunning view, try the *Hotel Sul-Americano* (☎ 676615) at Bom Jesus do Monte. Prices for singles/doubles start at 3500$00/4500$00. It's very popular, so reserve a place.

Café Brasileira is a turn-of-the-century special. Order a coffee and watch the world pass by. At *Primavera* (☎ 72482), Rua Gabriel Pereira Castro, 100, the prato do dia is probably the best value meal in town.

Getting There & Away

The completion of an expressway between Oporto and Braga has put it within easy day-trip reach of Oporto. The toll is 300$00. Train services connect Braga with Viana do Castelo and Spain to the north, and with Oporto and Coimbra to the south. There are excellent bus services to Oporto and Lisbon, and local bus lines run to Guimarães and Bom Jesus.

PENEDA-GERÊS NATIONAL PARK

This park in a superb wilderness area close to the Spanish border has spectacular scenery and has managed to retain a wide variety of fauna and flora. Although it's a favourite destination for Portuguese holidaymakers, they tend to crowd around the camping areas and leave the rest of the park to small numbers of hikers.

Orientation & Information

The main centre for the park is Caldas do Gerês, a sleepy, hot-spring village, where you can obtain information from the tourist office. The Peneda-Gerês National Park administration has a small office here (☎ 053-391181), and a head office (☎ 053-613166) in Braga, Rua de São Geraldo, 29. Both these offices sell good hiking maps and interesting publications about the region's fauna and flora.

The telephone code for Caldas do Gerês is 053.

Things to Do

The main activities are camping, hiking and pony-trekking (ask at the park office for information). There are no facilities for hikers, so you need to be self-sufficient.

Places to Stay

The *Pousada de Juventude de Vilarinho das Furnas* (☎ 053-35339) is at São João do Campo, 4840 Terras de Bouro. This youth hostel, in the heart of the park, less than 20 km north-west of Caldas do Gerês, is a good base for hikes. From Braga, take the bus to Lindoso (which bypasses Caldas do Gerês), and then walk 30 minutes to the hostel.

PORTUGAL

In Caldas do Gerês there are several pensões, and a camping site at Vidoeiro, one km from the village.

Places to Eat

Caldas do Gerês has several restaurants and cafés. You can stock up on provisions for picnics or long hikes at small local shops.

Getting There & Away

Bus services connect Caldas do Gerês with Braga, and some of these services continue to Oporto.

Getting Around

Unless you have your own transport, you will have to rely on infrequent local bus services to remote villages, or take your time walking. For an organised spin through the major sights in the park, a bus company in Caldas do Gerês runs tours during the summer.

Spain

Spaniards approach life with such exuberance and inspiration that most foreigners have to stop and stare. The rich heritage of the Spanish people gives the nation an inimitable reputation for an exciting and varied social and cultural life. When most northerners are turning in for the night, Spain awakens, spilling its people onto the streets in the early hours of the morning. In almost every town in the country, the nightlife will outlast the foreigners. Then just when they think they are coming to terms with the frenetic pace, they are surrounded by the beating drums of a festival – Carnival, Las Fallas, Semana Santa, San Fermines, Semana Grande – with day and night turning into a blur of dancing, laughing, eating and drinking.

Spain can also proudly hold its own in the world of culture and the arts, with some exciting museums spread throughout the country. The Prado in Madrid and the Museo de Bellas Artes in Bilbao contain fabulous collections of fine arts, and Cuenca's Museum of Abstract Art is bound to arouse your imagination, as is the wacky Dali Museum in Figueras. In Barcelona, Picasso and Miró compete for praise, and back in Madrid Picasso's *Guernica* is presented with mind-boggling security.

Then, of course, there is the weather. From April to October the sun shines with uncanny predictability on the Mediterranean coast and the Balearic Islands. Elsewhere you can enjoy the weather on the more secluded coves of Galicia, or the surf beaches of western Andalusia or the Basque Country. If you prefer, you can also soak up the rays in one of the many beautiful squares around the country – in Salamanca, Santiago de Compostela, Mojácar, to name just a few – and simply watch Spain happen.

A wealth of history also awaits the visitor to Spain. It begins with the extraordinary 20,000-year-old cave paintings at Altamira near Santander, passes through prehistoric times so carefully presented by the archaeological museums in Teruel and Madrid, and

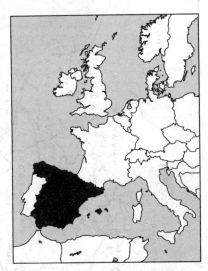

eventually leads to Roman times. The city of Numáncia near Soria, the world's oldest lighthouse in Corunna and the aqueduct in Segovia, are all remnants of this long-gone era. After Roman times, and for many centuries, there was the Moorish occupation of the peninsula. They left behind a cultural and artistic legacy more powerful than that of any other civilisation – Granada's Alhambra, Cordova's mosque, the Alcázar in Seville and Almería's Alcazaba.

Images of bullfighting and twirling flamenco dancers may be enough for some, but don't forget that there is so much more. *Que viva España!*

Facts about the Country

HISTORY
Although Romans, Etruscans, Phoenicians, Celts, Iberians and many others have left

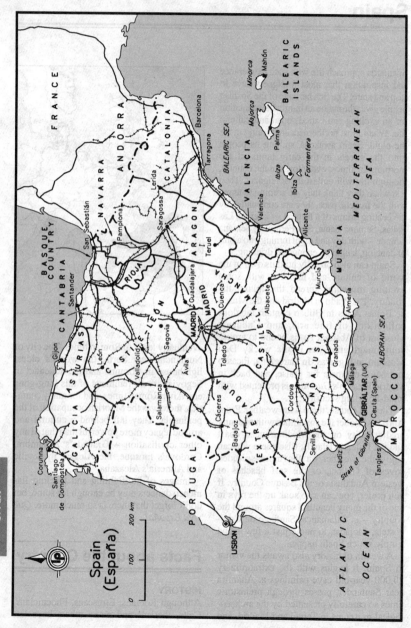

Spain
(España)

0   100   200 km

FRANCE

BALEARIC ISLANDS

Minorca
Mahón

BALEARIC SEA

Majorca
Palma

Ibiza   Formentera
Ibiza

MEDITERRANEAN SEA

ANDORRA

CATALONIA
Barcelona
Tarragona

NAVARRA
Pamplona
Lerida
Saragossa

San Sebastián

BASQUE COUNTRY

ARAGON
Teruel

VALENCIA
Valencia

Alicante

Santander

CANTABRIA

RIOJA

Guadalajara
MADRID
Cuenca

LA MANCHA

MURCIA
Murcia

ASTURIAS

Gijón

MADRID

Almería

ALBORAN SEA

GALICIA

León

CASTILE-LEON
Valladolid
Segovia

Ávila

Toledo

CASTILE-LA MANCHA
Albacete

Granada

ANDALUSIA
Málaga

Corunna

Santiago
de Compostela

Salamanca

Cáceres

EXTREMADURA

Cordova

GIBRALTAR (UK)
Ceuta (Spain)

Badajoz

Seville

Cadiz

Strait of Gibraltar

Tangiers

MOROCCO

PORTUGAL

LISBON

ATLANTIC OCEAN

their mark on Spain, none has had such an indelible effect as the Moors and the Christians. The Moorish invaders ruled the peninsula for 700 years until they were driven out by King Ferdinand and Queen Isabel in 1492.

The expulsion of the Moors also signalled the unification of the various kingdoms in the peninsula, which was completed in 1512. The 'discovery' of the Americas by Columbus in 1492 turned Spain into the wealthiest country in Europe. This monumental event 500 years ago shaped Spain, and indeed the rest of Europe, into what it is today. During the following centuries, all the wealth which was brought back from the New World was spent on armies, lavish buildings, great explorative journeys and the good life. The money landed in the coffers of northern Europe, while Spain became a victim of its own success.

The 19th century was not kind to Spain. Napoleon ransacked the country, taking with him much of what still remained from the good times. He even tried to blow up the Alhambra, but was thwarted thanks to a soldier with a conscience. The rest of the century was sorely marked by the loss of an empire in the Americas.

The loss of Cuba at the end of last century, and a colonial war in Morocco early this century, acted as a poor introduction to the 20th century. Military rule did not help to stabilise the country. In the 1931 elections, Spain became a republic and the king went into exile. In 1936 the country erupted into civil war. At the end of three years of bloodshed, General Francisco Franco proclaimed himself dictator. He ruled with an iron fist and maintained an isolationist policy until his death in 1975. Within seven years of his death, Spain moved from fascism under Franco to democratic socialism under Felipe González. Aside from a nervous hiccup in early 1981, when there was an attempted military coup, Spain has adopted democracy with a passion.

GEOGRAPHY

Covering around 80% of the Iberian Penin-sula, Spain has a total area of 504,788 sq km. The image of Spain as a low, flat country is only partly true. In fact, within Europe, only Switzerland has a higher average altitude. The major mountain range in Spain is the Pyrenees, which marks the country's northern borders with France and Andorra. There are, however, four other important mountain ranges in Spain, the best known being the Sierra Nevada in Andalusia. The Cordillera Central starts to the west of Madrid in northern Extremadura and passes Madrid to the north. The Cordillera Ibérica runs parallel to the Central Cordillera from the region around Burgos to southern Aragon. Finally, the Cordillera Cantábrica, along the north Atlantic coast, is home to the Picos de Europa, which offer some of Europe's best hiking.

GOVERNMENT

Spain is a constitutional monarchy. The head of state, King Juan Carlos, is a highly respected international figure whose role is, nevertheless, primarily that of a figurehead. The prime minister, Felipe González, became Europe's longest serving head of government with the resignation of Margaret Thatcher in 1991. His socialist party, PSOE, has been in power since 1982, when it became the first political party in Spanish history to rule democratically with an absolute majority.

ECONOMY

Spaniards have long known economic hardship. Theirs is one of the poorest countries in Europe, and yet life is almost as expensive as in France or Germany. Unemployment rates officially at over 16%, but in some areas levels higher than 20% are evident. Poverty is a serious problem, especially in the interior, and the gap between the haves and the have-nots is depressingly wide.

On the plus side, the downward trend of the early 1980s made a sharp turn in 1986, when Spain became a provisional member of the European Community (EC). It now has the fastest growing economy in the developed world. The service industry employs

SPAIN

over six million people and accounts for close to 60% of the GNP. Agriculture, on the other hand, accounts for only 4% or 5% as opposed to 23% in 1960.

POPULATION & PEOPLE

Spain has around 40 million inhabitants. In recent years there has been a growing tendency for people to shift out of the centre of the country (with Madrid as the notable exception) to the coastal regions. The most heavily populated regions, per sq km, are Madrid, with over three million inhabitants, the Basque Country and Catalonia, in that order. At the other end of the scale are Extremadura, Aragon and Castile-León.

ARTS

Wherever you go in Spain, you will be confronted by art. It may be in the form of a museum or a gallery, it may be in the architecture of the modernist Antonio Gaudí, it may be in the music and traditional dance of flamenco, or it may be in the fine handicrafts of the Toledan metalsmiths. Spanish history is so finely intertwined with its art world that the two are inseparable, and to appreciate Spain fully, you must take the time to absorb some of this history. Among the artists who have helped to shape Spain and the way it is perceived are such illustrious names as El Greco, Goya, Velázquez, Ribera, Murillo, Zurbarán, Picasso, Miró and Dali. Works by these and many other artists can be found in museums all over the country.

Art

Spain is home to some of the finest art galleries in the world. The Prado in Madrid has very few rivals, and some even consider it to be better than the Louvre in Paris. Barcelona has one of the most important collections of Picasso's work, as well as the wonderful Miró museum, among others. In the north of Catalonia is a museum dedicated to the work of Spain's most eccentric artist, Salvador Dali, and the museum of Spanish Abstract Art in Cuenca is one of the best museums of its kind in Europe.

Literature

Spain's contribution to the world of literature has been considerable. Who hasn't heard of *Don Quixote de la Mancha* by Miguel de Cervantes? Other significant works of that era and earlier, include *Fuente ovejuna* by Lope de Vega, and *Cantar de mío Cid*, an epic poem whose author is unknown to this day. The latter describes the social, political and religious tensions that existed between the Iberian Christians and their Moorish overlords in the Middle Ages.

Among the most important 20th century writers is a group known as the 'Generation of the 98'. The best known member is the existentialist writer Miguel de Unamuno, whose work *Abel Sánchez*, a study of envy as a destructive force, has been standard text for students of Spanish ever since. Camilo José Cela is one of Spain's most important postwar writers. In particular, his novel, *La colmena*, has been praised for its detailed portrait of artists living during Franco's reign.

Of all the authors who were forced into exile during General Franco's dictatorship, none has won such wide international acclaim as García Lorca. His plays, *Yerma* and *La casa de Bernada Alba* highlight the anguish of women in a traditional society. Ramón José Sender, powerfully portrayed the injustices of war and fascism with his easy reading novel *Requiem por un campesino Español*.

There has been a proliferation of women writers in the last 20 to 25 years, and particularly of feminist writings. One of the earliest and most influential works in this genre is *El balneario* by Carmén Martín Gaite. Modern-day women writers include Adelaide Morales, who wrote *El sur*, a story of the pain of a girl growing up surrounded by adult bitterness, and Ana Maria Matute, whose work *Los hijos muertos* is a fine example of contemporary feminist literature.

CULTURE
Avoiding Offence

If you want to offend a Spanish man, say something unpleasant about his mother. Otherwise, Spaniards are pretty thick-skinned, though perhaps you should think twice about nude sunbathing on family beaches. Topless bathing is so commonplace now that even the most conservative oldies have become used to it.

Sport

Spectator sports are very popular. If you want to get actively involved in sport, the local tourist office can always tell you where to go. The tourist office in Madrid even publishes a map highlighting all the major sporting facilities. For information on spectator sports, see Entertainment in the Facts for the Visitor section.

RELIGION

Catholicism is the predominant religion in Spain, with many centres of worship and pilgrimage throughout the country.

LANGUAGE

Spanish, or Castilian, as it is often and more precisely called, is the most widely spoken of the Romance languages. Outside Spain, it is the language of much of South and Central America, the West Indies, and, to some extent, of the Philippines and Guam, as well as of some areas of the African coast. In Spain itself, three Romance languages are spoken: Castilian, the main one, is spoken in the north, centre and south; Catalan, in the east and south-east; and Galician (a dialect of Portuguese), in the north-west. Another language, of obscure, non-Latin origin – Basque – is spoken in the north-east. Castilian, or Spanish, covers by far the largest territory.

Within Spanish there are three dialectal divisions (Castilian-Andalusian, Leonese-Asturian, and Navarro-Aragonese), but these mainly involve differences in pronunciation. Spanish is the neo-Latin language derived from the Vulgar Latin which Roman soldiers and merchants brought to the Iberian Peninsula during the period of the Roman conquest (3rd to 1st centuries BC). With Columbus' discovery of the New World in 1492 began an era of Spanish expansion in America, which naturally is reflected in the language, too. *Patata, tomate, cacao* and *chocolate* are a few examples of accretions from the American Indian languages. But, fundamentally, Spanish lexicon, syntax, phonology and morphology always remained neo-Latin.

Pronunciation

Pronunciation of Spanish is not difficult, given that many Spanish sounds are similar to their English counterparts, and there is a clear and consistent relationship between pronunciation and spelling. If you stick to the following rules you should have very few problems in being understood.

Vowels Unlike English, each of the vowels in Spanish has a uniform pronunciation which does not vary. For example, the Spanish 'a' has one pronunciation rather than the numerous pronunciations we find in English, such as the 'a' in 'cake', 'art' and 'all'. Vowels are pronounced clearly even if they are in unstressed positions or at the end of a word.

a	as the 'u' in 'nut', or a shorter sound than the 'a' in 'art'
e	as the 'e' in 'met'
i	similar to the 'i' sound in 'marine' but not so drawn out or strong; between that sound and that of the 'i' in 'flip'
o	similar to the 'o' in 'hot'
u	as the 'oo' in 'fool'

Consonants Some Spanish consonants are the same as their English counterparts. The pronunciation of other consonants varies according to which vowel follows and also according to which part of Spain you happen to be in. The Spanish alphabet also contains three consonants which are not found within the English alphabet: 'ch', 'll' and 'ñ'.

b	as the 'b' in 'book' when initial, or preceded by a nasal, ; elsewhere, and most often in Spanish, a much softer 'b' than the English one

SPAIN

c	a hard 'c' as in 'cat' when followed by 'a', 'o', 'u' or a consonant; as the 'th' in 'thin' before 'e' or 'i'
ch	as the 'ch' in choose
d	in an initial position, as the 'd' in 'dog'; elsewhere as the 'th' in 'then'
g	in an initial position, as the 'g' in 'gate' before 'a', 'o' and 'u'; everywhere else, the Spanish 'g' is much softer than the English one. Before 'e' or 'i' it is a harsh, breathy sound, similar to the 'h' in 'hit'
h	never pronounced, silent
j	a harsh, guttural sound similar to the 'ch' in Scottish 'loch'
ll	as the 'll' in 'million'; some people pronounce it rather like the 'y' in 'yellow'
ñ	this is a nasal sound like the 'ni' in 'onion'
q	as the 'k' in 'kick'; 'q' is always followed by a silent 'u' and is only combined with 'e' as in *que* and 'i' as in *qui*
r	a rolled 'r' sound; a longer and stronger sound when it is a double 'rr' or when a word begins with 'r'
s	as the 's' in 'send'
v	the letters 'b' and 'v' represent the same sound in Spanish, so 'v' is pronounced like the 'b' in 'book' when in initial position; elsewhere, as a much softer 'b' than the English one
x	as the 'ks' in 'taxi', when between two vowels; as the 's' in 'say' when the 'x' precedes a consonant
z	as the 'th' in 'thin'

Semiconsonant Spanish also has a semi-consonant:

y	This is pronounced as the Spanish 'i' when it's at the end of a word or when it stands alone as a conjunction. As a consonant, its sound is somewhere between 'y' in 'yonder' and 'g' in 'beige', depending on the region.

Greetings & Civilities

Hello./Goodbye.	¡Hola!/ ¡Adiós!
Yes./No.	Sí./No.
Please.	Por favor.

Thank you.	Gracias.
That's fine./You're welcome.	De nada.
Excuse me.	Permiso.
Sorry. (excuse me, forgive me)	Lo siento/ Discúlpeme.
Do you speak English?	¿Habla inglés?
Does anyone speak English?	¿Hay alguien que hable inglés?
I (don't) understand.	(No) Entiendo.
Just a minute.	Un momento.
Please write that down.	¿Puede escribirlo, por favor?
How much is it?	¿Cuánto cuesta?/ Cuánto vale?

Signs

Camping Ground	Terreno de Camping
Entrance	Entrada
Exit	Salida
Full	Ocupado/Completo
Guesthouse	Pensión/Casa de Huespedes
Hotel	Hotel
Information	Información
Open/Closed	Abierto/Cerrado
Police	Policía
Police Station	Estacion de Policía
Prohibited	Prohibido
Rooms Available	Habitaciones Libres
Toilets	Servicios/Aseos
Train Station	Estación (de Ferrocarril)
Youth Hostel	Albergue Para Jovenes

Getting Around

What time does the ... leave/arrive?	¿A qué hora sale/llega el ...?
next	próximo
first	primer
last	último
the boat	el buque/barco
the bus (city)	el autobús, el bus
the bus (intercity)	el autocar

the train	*el tren*
the tram	*el tranvía*
I would like ...	*Quisiera ...*
a one-way ticket	*un billete sencillo*
a return ticket	*un billete de ida y vuelta*
1st class	*primera clase*
2nd class	*segunda clase*

Where is the bus/tram stop?	*¿Dónde está la parada de autobús/tranvía?*
I want to go to ...	*Quiero ir a ...*
Can you show me (on the map)?	*¿Me puede mostrar/indicar (en el mapa)?*
far/near	*lejos/cerca*
Go straight ahead.	*Siga/Vaya todo derecho.*
Turn left.	*Doble a la izquierda.*
Turn right.	*Doble a la derecha.*

Around Town

I'm looking for ...	*Ando buscando ...*
a bank	*un banco*
the city centre	*el centro de la ciudad*
the ... embassy	*la embajada ...*
my hotel	*mi hotel*
the market	*el mercado*
the police	*la policía*
the post office	*correos*
a public toilet	*servicios/aseos públicos*
the telephone centre	*la central telefónica*
the tourist information office	*la oficina de turismo*

beach	*la playa*
bridge	*el puente*
castle	*el castillo*
cathedral	*la catedral*
church	*la iglesia*
hospital	*el hospital*
lake	*el lago*

main square	*Plaza Mayor*
market	*el mercado*
mosque	*la mezquita*
old city	*la ciudad antigua*
palace	*el palacio*
ruins	*las ruinas*
sea	*el mar*
square	*la plaza*
tower	*el torre*

Accommodation

Where is a cheap hotel?	*¿Dónde está un hotel barato?*
What is the address?	*¿Cuál es la dirección?*
Could you write the address, please?	*¿Puede escribir la dirección, por favor?*
Do you have any rooms available?	*¿Tiene habitaciones libres?*
I would like ...	*Quisiera ...*
a single room	*una habitación individual*
a double room	*una habitación doble*
a room with a bathroom	*una habitación con baño*
to share a dorm	*compartir un dormitorio*
a bed	*una cama*
How much is it per night/per person?	*¿Cuánto cuesta por noche/por persona?*
Can I see it?	*¿Puedo verla?*
Where is the bathroom?	*¿Dónde está el baño?*

Food

breakfast	*desayuno*
lunch	*almuerzo/comida*
dinner	*cena*
I would like the set lunch.	*Quisiera el almuerzo a precio fijo/ almuerzo corriente.*

| Is service included in the bill? | ¿El servicio está incluido en la cuenta? |
| I am a vegetarian. | Soy vegetariano/a. |

Time & Dates

| What time is it? | ¿Qué hora es? ¿Qué horas son? |

today	hoy
tomorrow	mañana
in the morning	de la mañana
in the afternoon	de la tarde
in the evening	de la noche

Monday	lunes
Tuesday	martes
Wednesday	miércoles
Thursday	jueves
Friday	viernes
Saturday	sábado
Sunday	domingo

January	enero
February	febrero
March	marzo
April	abril
May	mayo
June	junio
July	julio
August	agosto
September	setiembre/ septiembre
October	octubre
November	noviembre
December	diciembre

Numbers

0	cero
1	uno, una
2	dos
3	tres
4	cuatro
5	cinco
6	seis
7	siete
8	ocho
9	nueve
10	diez
11	once
12	doce
13	trece
14	catorce
15	quince
16	dieciséis
17	diecisiete
18	dieciocho
19	diecinueve
20	veinte
30	treinta
40	cuarenta
50	cincuenta
60	sesenta
70	setenta
80	ochenta
90	noventa
100	cien/ciento
1000	mil
one million	un millón

Health

I'm ...	Soy ...
diabetic	diabético/a
epileptic	epiléptico/a
asthmatic	asmático/a

| I'm allergic to antibiotics/penicillin. | Soy alérgico/a a los antibióticos/la penicilina. |

antiseptic	antiséptico
aspirin	aspirina
condoms	preservativos/condones
contraceptive	anticonceptivo
diarrhoea	diarrea
medicine	medicamentos/remedios
nausea	náusea
sunblock cream	crema protectora contra el sol
tampons	tampones

Emergencies

Help!	¡Socorro! ¡Auxilio!
Call a doctor!	¡Llame a un doctor!
Call the police!	¡Llame a la policía!
Go away!	¡Váyase!

SPAIN

Facts for the Visitor

VISAS & EMBASSIES

US citizens, Canadians, Australians and New Zealanders may enter Spain as tourists without a visa. US citizens, Canadians and New Zealanders are allowed an initial stay of 90 days, and Australians are given 30 days. EC passport holders can come and go as they please.

Spanish Embassies

To apply for visas, or for other consular information, Spanish embassies can be found at the following addresses. Cities in which consulates can be found are also listed.

Australia
Arkana St, PO Box 66, Deakin, ACT
(☎ 06-273 3555)
Consulates in Sydney & Melbourne
Canada
350 Sparks St, suite 802, Ottawa
(☎ 613-237 2193)
Consulates in Toronto and Montreal
France
13 Ave George V, 75301 Paris (☎ 1-47.23.61.83)
Consulates in Marseille, Bayonne, Hendaye, Pau, etc
New Zealand
Represented in Australia
Portugal
Rua do Salitre 1, 1296 Lisbon (☎ 01-372381)
Consulates in Oporto and Valencia
USA
277 15th St, Washington 20009
(☎ 202-265 0190)
Consulates in NYC, LA, San Francisco, Chicago, Miami, etc
UK
24 Belgrave Square, London SW1X 8KA
(☎ 071-235 5555)
Consulates in Edinburgh and Manchester

Visa Extensions

To extend your stay in Spain, simply turn up at a police station with your passport before the original entry stamp expires. They will either extend your permit for 30 days or tell you where you can get it done. It varies from town to town and according to the duty officer's mood. If you are having trouble getting an extension for any reason, the best thing you can do is to leave the country and come back 12 hours later – to ensure that the same border guards are not on duty.

Foreign Embassies in Spain

Some 70 countries now have embassies in Madrid, including:

Australia
Paseo de la Castellana 143 (☎ 279 8504)
Canada
Calle Nuñez de Balboa 35 (☎ 431 4300)
France
Calle Salustiano Olózoga 9 (☎ 435 5560)
Ireland
Calle Claudio Coello 73 (☎ 276 4500)
Japan
Calle Joaquin Costa 29 (☎ 262 5546)
Morocco
Calle Velázquez 90 (☎ 563 1090)
Portugal
Calle Pinar 1 (☎ 261 7800)
UK
Calle Fernando el Santo 16 (☎ 319 0336)
USA
Calle Serrano 75 (☎ 576 3400)

DOCUMENTS

To enter Spain you need a valid passport or, for EC nationals, travel documents. If you are coming from an area with a preponderance of exotic diseases, bring a health card too.

CUSTOMS

Theoretically, EC internal borders are customs-free as of 1 January 1993. This does not mean that customs officers will not be in action. Think twice about smuggling across the 'free borders'.

MONEY
Currency

The currency in Spain is the peseta. It is freely convertible with all major currencies, and forms a part of the European monetary system. In the early 1990s there was a major overhaul of the currency and banking system in Spain, apparently bringing Spain into line with European Currency Unit (ECU) specifications. Among the coins, and to a lesser extent the notes, you will often find two or even three different forms for one value, so you should be careful when parting with your money that you have read its face value correctly. Among the legal denominations in Spain are coins of 1, 5, 10, 25, 100 and 500 pta. There are notes of 1000, 2000, 5000 and 10,000 pta. It is often difficult to break 10,000 pta notes, so avoid them if you can.

Exchange Rates

As this book went to press, the exchange rates were as follows:

A$1	=	71.0 pta
C$1	=	84.2 pta
DM1	=	71.3 pta
1FF	=	20.9 pta
P100$00	=	80.4 pta
Sfr	=	66.6 pta
UK£1	=	178.9 pta
US$1	=	105.0 pta
100 Yen	=	86.7 pta

All major foreign currencies can be exchanged for pesetas in Spain. All the same, Deutschmarks, US dollars and UK pounds are the safest currencies to travel with. Thomas Cook and American Express travellers' cheques are the best known. Visa and MasterCard are the most widely accepted credit cards.

Costs

Spain is not cheap! Prices jumped by 30% the day Spain joined the EC and they haven't stopped climbing since. If you are particularly frugal outside the big cities, and you stick to camp sites, you can scrape by on as little as 1000 to 1500 pta a day. Add around 33% if you're spending your time in the cities. Here are some sample prices to give you an idea of what you're in for:

Youth hostel	880 pta
Cheap hotel (single)	1000 pta
Cheap restaurant	750 pta
Big Mac	345 pta
Loaf of bread	60 pta

Beer (glass)	125 pta
Local telephone call	15 pta
Time magazine	350 pta
100 km bus trip	550 pta
100 km train trip	600 pta
1 litre petrol	94 pta

Tipping

Wages in Spain are still pretty low, so waiters and taxi drivers should be tipped around 10% if you can afford it. The only places in Spain where you are likely to bargain are in markets, and occasionally, in cheap hotels. You can always get lucky, but don't push it.

Consumer Taxes

In Spain, VAT (value-added tax) is known as IVA, which is the abbreviation of *impuesto sobre el valor añadido*. On most goods there is a flat rate of 6% IVA. Many hotels do not include IVA on their advertised room rates, so if every peseta counts, you should ask if the price is *con IVA* (with VAT) or *sin IVA* (without VAT).

As of 1 January 1993, there are no more duty-free allowances within the EC. This means that if you want a rebate on anything, you must declare it on departing from Europe. From Spain this effectively means flying, unless you live in Morocco. Simply present your receipts with the goods you are exporting at the customs office at your port of departure.

CLIMATE & WHEN TO GO

In July and August the sun in Spain is at its strongest. In southern Andalusia the temperature has been known to climb to 45°C in the shade. Madrid is unbearable at this time of year, and as such the city is almost deserted. In the north, and on the Balearic Islands, temperatures of up to 35°C are standard. In winter the rains never seem to stop in the north, except in the backlands of Galicia and the Pyrenees, where they turn into snow. If you want to escape the northern European freeze, Andalusia is the place to be. It doesn't often drop below 10°C in Granada, and yet you can ski in the Sierra Nevada nearby.

During the summer season Spain is overflowing with north Europeans in search of a better tan. In some respects this is the time to be in Spain: there are never-ending festivals, including the Running of the Bulls in Pamplona, and Semana Grande all along the north coast. On the other hand, there are excellent festivals during the rest of the year, and the crowds are more bearable.

If you have complete freedom in deciding when to visit Spain, there is no doubt that the best time to be there is either directly before or directly after the mad summer rush. By mid-April the weather is predictably magnificent in the south, and the rains are letting up in the far north. The weather is pretty good until mid-October in the south, and it is still quite possible to swim in the Mediterranean at that time of year.

WHAT TO BRING
You can buy anything you need in Spain, but some articles are more expensive here than elsewhere. Suntan cream, for instance, is a rip-off here. It can be difficult to find books in English, though in big cities and tourist ghettos there are always some bright spark making a killing. Spanish condoms were given pretty bad press in a 1991 Europe-wide study – apparently they break four times as often as their English and German counterparts. Things may well have changed since that report was written.

SUGGESTED ITINERARIES
Depending on the length of your stay, you might want to see the following places:

Two days
Visit Madrid or Barcelona for two days if flying. If you're travelling by train or car, spend two days in Barcelona.
One week
Spend two days each in Barcelona and Madrid, and one day each in Toledo and San Sebastián, allowing one day for travel.
Two weeks
Visit Barcelona, Madrid, Toledo, Granada, Costa del Sol and Seville.
One month
Visit Barcelona, Mallorca, Valencia, Madrid, Toledo, Seville, Costa del Sol, Granada, Cordova, Salamanca, Picos de Europa and San Sebastián.

Two months
As for one month, with side trips from most destinations, plus Santiago de Compostela, Ávila, Cuenca, Guadalajara, Trujillo, Pyrenees, Pamplona and Gerona.

TOURIST OFFICES
Most towns of any consequence have a local tourist office. Exceptions, such as Ciudadela in Minorca, are serviced by the police or, in really small places such as Castrojeriz in Castile-León, the mayor or one of his assistants will help you. In large towns and important cities, there are usually a number of offices, one of them generally in a convenient, central location.

Local Tourist Offices
The head office of the Spanish National Tourist Office is on Plaza de España in Madrid. For region-specific information, you should first try the regional capital. If the information is too specialised, you should go directly to the tourist office for the town (or nearest town) in question.

Spanish Tourist Offices Abroad
The Spanish National Tourist Office has representatives in the following countries:

Australia
203 Casterleagh St, suite 21, Sydney, NSW 2000 (☎ 02-264 7966)
France
43 Avenue Pierre 1er de Serbie, 75381 Paris (☎ 1-47.20.90.54)
Portugal
Rua Camilo Costelo Branco 34, 1000 Lisbon (☎ 01-541992)
UK
57-58 St James Street, London SW1 A1LD (☎ 071-499 1169)
USA
665 Fifth Ave, New York, NY 10022 (☎ 212-759 8822)

USEFUL ORGANISATIONS
Most useful organisations have their headquarters in Madrid. If you are in another part of the country and are in need of advice or help, the various Madrid-based organisations listed here will often be able to supply

SPAIN

you with more convenient names, addresses or phone numbers.

The Spanish Youth Hostel Association (☎ 521 4427) has its head office at Calle Sagasta 13 (metro Bilbao). The Instituto de la Juventud (☎ 347 7776) at Calle Ortega y Gasset 71 (metro Lista) looks after youth affairs in general. One of the best sources of information for young people is the Centro de Información Juvenil (☎ 521 3960) at Calle Caballero de Gracia 32. They have another office (☎ 521 9511) inside the Sol metro station. In both cases it is best to go in person, as the phone tends to be very busy.

An organisation which deals specifically with the affairs of young women is the Asociación de Mujeres Jovenes (☎ 308 3294), Calle Almagro 28. For women's affairs in general, contact the Instituto de la Mujer (☎ 410 5112), a few doors down at Calle Almagro 36.

For families or elderly travellers in need of help, you should contact the Ministério de Asuntos Sociales (☎ 441 8100) at Calle José Abascal 39. Another organisation which deals specifically with the elderly is INSERSO (☎ 733 3600) at Calle Agustín Foxá s/n. Disabled people requiring advice or help in their travels should contact Auxilia (☎ 445 5300) at Calle Santa Isabel 15, 1st floor Centro B, near metro Atocha.

Gay travellers wanting information or help relating specifically to their requirements should call Gai-Inform on 523 0070. The number is only in service Monday to Friday from 5 to 9 pm. Another organisation which may be able to help is COGAM (colectivo Gai de Madrid; ☎ 532 5929).

Finally, motorists who are members of an automobile club in their home country should carry proof of membership with them, as there are fairly broad reciprocal arrangements with RACE (☎ 447 3200), the Spanish automobile club. The head office is at Calle José Abascal 10. For 24-hour on-road emergency service throughout the country, call ☎ 01-593 33 33.

BUSINESS HOURS & HOLIDAYS

Business hours are fairly uniform throughout the country. Generally, people work from 9 am to 2 pm and then again from 4.30 or 5 pm for another three hours. Banks close an hour later for lunch and do not open up again in the afternoon. Museums tend to follow the same hours as most other businesses, with a long lunch break, but the majority of museums close on Mondays. Unless otherwise stated, it can be assumed that museums and businesses mentioned in this chapter do just that.

Any excuse will do for a holiday in Spain. As such, every region has its own public holidays. There are also over a dozen national holidays: 1 January (New Year's Day), 6 January (Epiphany), the day before Good Friday, Good Friday, Easter Monday, 1 May (Labour Day), Corpus Christi, 24 June (Feast of St John), 25 July (Feast of St James – Santiago), 15 August (Feast of the Assumption), 12 October (National Day), 1 November, 8 December (Feast of the Immaculate Conception), 25 December. Although these are national holidays, they are not all celebrated in every province every year.

CULTURAL EVENTS

Cultural events are almost inevitably celebrated with a wild party and a holiday to boot. Among the festivals to look out for are *La Tamborada* in San Sebastián in February, when the whole town dresses up and goes berserk. Carnival takes place throughout the country in late February; the wildest is said to be in Sitges. In April, Valencia has a week-long party known as *Las Fallas*; it is marked by all-night dancing and drinking, first-class fireworks displays and colourful processions. *Semana Santa* (Holy Week) is the week before Easter Sunday; if you can get accommodation, Seville is the place to be, as it is for the *Feria de Abril*, which is a kind of counter-reaction to the religious fervour of Easter. The *Running of the Bulls* in Pamplona in July is Spain's most famous festival, while all along the north coast, some time in the first half of August, is *Semana Grande*, another week of heavy drinking and hangovers.

POST & TELECOMMUNICATIONS

Post and telecommunications are run by two separate bodies in Spain: Telecom and Correos.

Postal Rates

The costs involved in sending a standard airmail letter weighing 20 grams are as follows: Australia and New Zealand 100 pta; USA and Canada 83 pta; Europe 45 pta; and Spain (surface) 27 pta.

Sending Mail

It can sometimes take a long time for a letter to get from Spain to anywhere. If you have birthday cards to send, it is a good idea to allow three or four weeks. They may arrive early, but it's better to be safe than sorry.

Receiving Mail

Poste restante is called *lista de correos*. It is a pretty reliable system, although you must be prepared for mail to arrive late. American Express card or travellers' cheque holders are entitled to use the clients' mail-holding service free of charge. For more information, see the Facts for the Visitor chapter at the beginning of this book.

Common abbreviations used in Spanish addresses are 1\o, 2\o, 3\o etc, which mean 1st/2nd/3rd floor, and s\n *(sin numero)*, which means the building has no number.

Telephones

The ease with which you can make a reverse-charges call out of Spain is astonishing, if you come from the right country. For Australians, US citizens and Britons it is truly a dream. Simply find a blue public phone, a private phone or a Telecom phone centre and dial direct. The magic number is 900 9900 followed by 61 for Australians, 44 for Brits and either 11 or 14 for the USA, depending on whether you are with MCI or AT&T. The system is being expanded, so it may be worthwhile giving it a go for other countries too, before you go through the nightmare of an operator-connected call.

To call Spain from abroad, dial the international access number, 34 (the country code

for Spain), the area code and the number. Area codes in Spain begin with the number 9; if you are calling from abroad do not dial the initial 9.

Important area codes include 1 (Madrid), 3 (Barcelona), 6 (Valencia) and 54 (Seville).

TIME

Spain is one hour ahead of GMT/UTC during winter, and two hours ahead from the last Sunday in March to the last Sunday in September.

ELECTRICITY

The electric current in Spain is 220 V, 50 Hz, but some places are still on 125 V. In fact, the voltage sometimes differs in the same house. Plugs have two round pins.

LAUNDRY

Self-service laundrettes are a rarity in Spain, and when you do find one, they are expensive. It is generally only marginally more expensive to leave it in a normal laundrette, and in that case it may come back ironed. A laundrette is called a *lavandería* or, sometimes, a *tintorería*.

WEIGHTS & MEASURES

The metric system is used in Spain. Like other Continental Europeans, the Spanish indicate decimals with commas and thousands with points.

BOOKS & MAPS

The *APA Insight Guide to Spain* is full of colour photos and has a very readable historical introduction.

Spain off the Beaten Track, by the Moreland Publishing Company, has 16 interesting articles, most of them about lesser known regions of the country.

Time off in Spain & Portugal, by Teresa Tinsley, has comprehensive information on courses and work in Spain, in addition to the general touristy stuff. The *Cadogan Guide to Spain* is a well-researched guide aimed at the middle to upper-middle budget range.

The head office of IGN Spain (Instituto Geográfico Nacional; ☎ 533 24 00) is at

SPAIN

Calle General Ibañez de Ibero 3, in Madrid, but you should try to purchase your maps from a retailer before contacting IGN.

MEDIA

The major daily newspapers in Spain are *El País* and *Diario 16*. There are also regional dailies, the best being in Barcelona and the Basque Country. In summer there is an English-language daily in Majorca, but the rest of the year it comes out once a week. The *International Herald Tribune* and *USA Today* can be bought in Madrid and Barcelona, sometimes on the day of publication; in heavily touristed areas it can usually be found the day after publication. *The European* can be purchased in most important centres every Friday.

HEALTH

Apart from the obvious dangers of contracting STDs in Europe's number-one holiday destination, the only thing you have to be a little wary of is the drinking water. It's nowhere as bad as Asian, African or South American water, but sometimes it is a little brownish. Bottled water is available everywhere, generally for less than 100 pta per litre.

WOMEN TRAVELLERS

The best way to approach Spain is simply to be ready to ignore stares, cat calls and unnecessary comments. However, Spain has one of the lowest incidences of reported rape in the developed world, and even physical harassment is much less frequent than you might expect.

DANGERS & ANNOYANCES

Don't park a car with French number plates anywhere in the Basque Country. The odds are high on it getting burned! Elsewhere, it is a good idea to take your car radio and any other valuables with you any time you leave your car. In youth hostels, don't leave any belongings unattended for even a moment – there is a disgracefully high incidence of theft among travellers. Beware of pickpockets in cities and tourist resorts. There is

also a relatively high incidence of mugging in such places, so keep your wits about you.

Drugs

In early 1992 Spain's liberal drug laws were quite severely tightened. No matter what anyone tells you, it is not legal to smoke dope in public bars. There is a reasonable degree of tolerance when it comes to people having a smoke in their own home, but if your hotel owner or another guest complains to the police about the smell coming from your room, something will be done about it.

FILM & PHOTOGRAPHY

The EC has ensured that there is not too much discrepancy in the price of film from one country to the next. All major brand names are available in Spain. Don't take photos of anything which might be militarily sensitive. Before taking photos of people, ask if it is OK.

WORK

Residents of the EC are allowed to work in Spain without a visa. You still have to register, but it is just a formality. Everyone else needs a work visa, which you must apply for from your home country. Before you can apply, you must have a job in Spain. Although it is not legal, many people teach English on the sly. See the Costa del Sol section for other pertinent information.

ACTIVITIES

Surfing

For the longest left you've ever seen, go to Mundaka on the Basque Coast (see the Basque Country section). Elsewhere in the Basque Country, there are good waves in San Sebastián and Zarautz, among others. There is also some good surfing on the north coast of Galicia (see the Foz section). On the south coast, Tarifa (west of Algeciras), is another surfies' hang-out with long, empty beaches.

Skiing

Skiing in Spain is cheap, and the best value skiing is to found in the Pyrenees. The Sierra Nevada, however, comes a close second, and has the advantage of being very close to Granada – great for day trips. The tourist office in Granada has maps of the ski fields and information on organised day trips. For the Pyrenees, ask in Pamplona, Jaca or Barcelona.

Trekking
Spain is a trekker's paradise, so much so that Lonely Planet has published a guide to some of the best treks in the country, *Trekking in Spain* by Marc Dubin. See also the Majorca and Picos de Europa sections for brief information.

Language Courses
The best place to take a language course in Spain is generally at a university. Those with the best reputations are Salamanca, Santiago de Compostela and Santander. The University of Barcelona also offers excellent courses, but only in Catalan. Spanish embassies and consulates can help you with more detailed information.

HIGHLIGHTS
Beaches
Yes, it is still possible to have a beach to yourself in Spain. In summer, it may be a little tricky, but spots where things are bound to be quiet are such gems as the beaches of Cabo Favoritx in Minorca, and some of the secluded coves around Cabo de Gata on the Costa de Almería. On the Galician coast, between Noya and Pontevedra, are literally hundreds of beaches where, even in mid-August, you will not feel claustrophobic. In Tarifa near Algeciras, and Mundaka near Bilbao, you are in for the best surfing in Europe.

Museums & Galleries
The Archaeological Museum in Teruel, Aragon, is one of the best of its kind. Don't miss the Abstract Art Museum in Cuenca's hanging houses. See also Arts in the Facts about the Country section.

Castles
The fairy-tale Alcázar in Segovia has to be seen to be believed. For even more exciting views, and loads of medieval ghosts, don't dare miss the ruins of the castle in Morella, Valencia Province.

Historic Towns
Many of the most interesting historic towns are totally unknown to tourists. Medinaceli in Castile-León is one of the jewels in the Spanish crown. Other towns to look for on the map are Castrojeriz, Saldaña, Arévalo and Toro, which are all small, yet fascinating, historical towns.

Hotels & Restaurants
You are unlikely to forget Teruel's *Fonda Tozal* with its enormous rooms, cast iron beds and wacky owner. The most romantically located hotel in Spain is undoubtedly *Hostal América* in Granada. It isn't cheap, but what would you expect from a hotel situated on the grounds of the Alhambra?

For unbeatable value in restaurants, you can't go past the *Restaurante Sarasate* in Pamplona for a first-class vegetarian meal, or the *Mesón Restaurante As Brasas* in Foz (northern Galicia) for enormous servings of juicy spare ribs.

ACCOMMODATION
Camping
Most city camp sites in Spain are a fair distance from the cities to which they are attached. They also vary drastically in quality. In general, you can expect to pay around 200 to 250 pta per person, tent, and vehicle.

Hostels
The Spanish youth hostel system is terribly overloaded. Hostels are more often than not booked out by school groups from all over Spain. If you do manage to get in, many of them have midnight curfews, which means that you can forget about taking part in Europe's best nightlife. Although they are cheap (juniors/seniors pay around 770/1100 pta), they cannot be highly recommended, particularly for senior members who can often get an equivalent deal in a pensión.

SPAIN

'Juniors' are people aged under 27 and 'seniors' are those over 27.

Cheap Hotels

The Spanish hotel classification system is complicated. In theory at least, the cheapest places to stay are *fondas*, followed by *casas de huéspedes*, various kinds of *hostales*, *pensiones* with star ratings, and finally *hoteles* rated from one to five stars. This final category is always expensive, and as such it cannot seriously be considered a form of budget accommodation.

The other classifications, usually referred to by the generic term pensiones, overlap with each other to the extent that it is usually impossible to differentiate between the different kinds of accommodation. In general the range covered by this chapter runs from around 800/1300 to 2000/3500 pta singles/doubles, and as such includes all classifications apart from hoteles.

FOOD

You could easily put food under entertainment in a guidebook about Spain, as eating out here is a most enjoyable experience.

Cafés & Bars

Cafés and bars are the main ingredient of entertainment in Spain. Cafés do good business early in the evening and at weekends. There is a relatively quiet period between around 8 pm and 11 pm. After that, the real nightlife begins.

Snacks

In almost any bar in the country you will find bite-sized snacks, varying from a calamari ring or a baby squid to a spoonful of potato salad or a small serving of tripe. *Tapas*, or *pinchos*, as these snacks are known, are a part of the Spanish way of life.

The other popular snacks are sandwiches, or *bocadillos*. Spaniards eat so many bocadillos that there are cafés which sell nothing else. Don't leave Spain without eating a *bocadillo de tortilla de patata*, which is a potato omelette sandwich.

Breakfast

A breakfast that you will only find in Spain is *churros con chocolate*. Churros are something like long, deep-fried doughnuts, and the chocolate is the thickest hot chocolate you have ever seen. Dipped in the chocolate, the churros are delicious. Some people prefer to dip them in coffee.

Vegetarian Food

Finding vegetarian fare in Spain can be a real headache. It is not uncommon (although less common than it used to be) for vegetarian food to be flavoured with beef or chicken stock. Fortunately, in the larger cities, and in important student centres, there is a growing awareness of just what you can do with vegetables, so that if there is not a vegetarian restaurant, there are often vegetarian items on the menu. A favourite vegetarian snack which you can get almost anywhere where sandwiches are available, is a *sandwich de vegetal*, which is usually a hot salad sandwich with a fried egg (*sin huevo* means without egg).

Menus, Platos Combinados & Main Dishes

Spanish menus are the budget traveller's best friend. For as little as 500 pta in some restaurants, you get an entrée, a main course, dessert, bread and wine. In many cases you have a choice of two or three dishes for each course. Even in the best restaurants there is often a menu costing no more than 1000 pta.

The *plato combinado* is a near relative of the menu. It is a single-course meal consisting of any number of possible foods. It may be a steak and egg with chips and salad, or it may be squid in its own ink with potato salad and vegetables. Prices start as low as 300 pta in some restaurants.

If you choose your meal from the menu, you can expect it to be considerably more expensive than the budget specials mentioned here. All the same, you can often have an excellent main course for around 600 or 700 pta. A full meal with an entrée, main course, dessert and drinks is unlikely to cost less than 1000 to 1200 pta.

SPAIN

Fruit

If you have spent any time in northern Europe, you have probably already tasted Spanish fruit. The oranges around Valencia and the western Andalusian strawberries are heavenly. Olives are a national favourite and are often given in bars as a free tapa when you order a drink.

Self-Catering

Every town of any substance has a *mercado*, or food market. They are loads of fun and great value. Even big eaters should be able to put together a filling meal of bread, mortadella, cheese, fruit and a drink for 250 pta or less. If you shop really carefully you can eat three healthy meals a day for as little as 550 pta.

DRINKS
Nonalcoholic Drinks

Soft drinks, orange juice, strong coffee (*con leche*, with milk, or *solo*, for black coffee), you name it, you can have it in Spain.

Alcohol

The perfect evening out in Spain requires a combination of music, movement, good conversation and just the right amount of alcohol. Of course there are regional specialities – for example, sherry in Jerez de la Frontera, *cava* (like champagne) in Barcelona – but you can't go beyond good old beer or a glass of red wine. A glass of beer is simply known as *una cerveza*, while a *doble* is twice as big. A small beer is generally known as *un corto*, although in the Basque Country it is called *un zurrito*. Wine is *vino*. If you want it red, ask for *tinto*. For white, the word is *blanco*.

ENTERTAINMENT

Entertainment is an important part of life in Spain and the people really mean it when they go out to have a good time. In acknowledgement of this fact, you will find information on entertainment in every town in this chapter.

Cinemas

In general, Madrid is the best place to see films in their original language. Tickets are cheap (sometimes as low as 300 pta), so keep an eye on the programmes as you pass by. See the Madrid and Barcelona sections for more information.

Discos

Even if you are not a disco fan, don't leave Spain without going to at least one. It is nothing like a disco back home and is simply a part of the Spain experience. You will be alone if you go to a disco before 2 am. Watch out for hefty cover charges.

Spectator Sports

Without a doubt, Spain's national sport is football (or soccer, as some of us call it). If you have the opportunity to see a football game in Spain, don't pass it up. The best places to see a game are generally Madrid, Barcelona and Santander, though the atmosphere is electric anywhere.

Talk of Spain often conjures up images of bulls being murdered in front of bloodthirsty crowds. Bullfighting is still very popular in many parts of the country, even though it has become a controversial subject in recent years. If you really want to see a bullfight, try Seville, Madrid or Pamplona.

In the Basque Country there are a few unusual sports which you will probably only see during festivals. People here are keen wood choppers, and love to point out that their only real rivals are the Australian champions. Jai alai is a Basque sport which has had some success outside Europe as well. It is vaguely reminiscent of squash, with a ball being bounced off walls. Instead of a racket, however, a kind of scoop is used to catch the ball. It is the fastest ball game in the world. Finally, there is one bizarre sport where the object appears to be to carry enormous rocks around.

SPAIN

Getting There & Away

AIR

Spain has many international airports: Madrid, Barcelona, Bilbao, Santiago de Compostela, Seville, Granada, Málaga, Almería, Alicante, Valencia, Palma de Mallorca, Ibiza and Mahón (in Minorca), among others. In general, the cheapest destinations are Málaga, the Balearic Islands, Barcelona and Madrid, with Málaga and Palma de Mallorca a nose ahead of the rest. Spain itself is not a good place to buy international airfares. In the event that you have no choice, see the Madrid section for more information on this subject.

To/From Australia

There are no special deals on flights from Australia to Spain. In general, the best thing to do is to fly to London, Paris, Frankfurt or Rome, and then make your way overland. Many flights to London also include one short-haul return trip within Europe. In most cases, Madrid or Barcelona are acceptable destinations on these flights. Some round-the-world (RTW) fares include possible stops in Spain. STA Travel should be able to help you out with a good price. Generally speaking, a return fare to Europe for under A$1700 is too good to pass up. For RTW fares, the same can be said when the total drops below A$2000.

To/From North America

There are some pretty good prices available on flights from the USA to Madrid. From New York, fares go as low as US$533 return with Delta. From Miami, fares on Iberia and TWA drop to US$499 return in the low season, and the rest of the year you can still pick up a TWA ticket for as little as US$529. From Chicago, you should be able to pick up a Delta flight from around US$584 return. On the west coast, agencies such as Adventure Center Travel in Oakland can put together return fares as low as US$723.

To/From London

London's bucket shops are no longer what they used to be, but you can still get some knockout fares if you hunt around. Big name agencies such as STA and Trailfinders are hard to beat, but it is possible. Check the *Evening Standard* travel section or *Time Out* for world-beating fares.

Many of the agencies are telephone-only operations, and the offers are laden with restrictions, however, a good deal of them are kosher, and it certainly can't hurt to ring around. Some examples on return fares from London are:

Destination	Fare	Agent	Phone
Alicante	£69	The Flight Company	081-977 9455
Barcelona	£75	Springways	071-976 5833
Bilbao	£89	STA	071-730 3402
Lanzarote	£80	Flight Dealers	071-630 9494
Las Palmas	£84	Flight Dealers	071-630 9494
Madrid	£59	Apex Travel	071-437 9561
Mahón	£65	Flight Club	0903-23 1857
Málaga	£69	Flight Club	0903-23 1857

LAND

Spain has land borders with three countries: Portugal, France and Andorra. From Andorra, there are buses to Barcelona and to Pyrenean towns such as Jaca. From Portugal there are a number of options. There are three official land borders with Galicia in the north. The border crossing by Tui, near the coast, is the most frequently used of these, as it is on the main Oporto-Santiago-Corunna train line. Be warned that the train is very slow, but that the road is even slower.

There are some 10 or 12 places where you can officially cross between Spain and Portugal on the north-south border. The most commonly used are Fuentes de Oñoro to the west of Salamanca on the Madrid-Coimbra train line; Badajoz, on the second line connecting Madrid with Lisbon; and Ayamonte to the west of Seville, connecting the Algarve with the Costa de la Luz.

The most frequently used border crossings between France and Spain are by Irún, near San Sebastián, and Port Bou, to the north of Barcelona. Both are on train lines connected with Paris. Drivers headed for Barcelona tend to cross at La Jonquera, a little way inland from Port Bou, while Hondarribia on the coast a few km from Irún is a popular crossing point because there is less traffic, good scenery and no freeway.

The other crossing points from France are in the Pyrenees and are accessible from Pau, Tarbes, Toulouse, Foix and Perpignan in France. On the Spanish side, a train runs to Canfranc north of Jaca, but the French side of this route has been discontinued. Some claim that this was done to damage the Spanish ski industry (or at least to help the French ski industry). There is also a train service to Puigcerda from Barcelona. The nearby Spanish town of Llivia is only accessible through France, an interesting anomaly which has been used by smugglers for many years.

SEA
To/From the UK
The Santander-Plymouth ferry timetable is horribly complicated. There is a ferry almost every Thursday from Santander. It leaves sometime between 11 am and 3 pm depending on the season. From mid-March to the end of May, there are generally two more ferries per week which usually leave on Saturday and Monday. From June to September, in addition to the Thursday sailing, there is a ferry on Tuesday. In October and November the timetable is similar to that of March to May, and in December the extra ferry leaves on Saturday. There are no ferries between 22 December and 9 January.

Sailing times out of Plymouth work on a similar system. Simply subtract one day from the Spanish departure times and you've got the British departure times. The basic one-way passenger fare is 13,100 pta (£65). For cars, the fares start at 13,500 pta (£68) and vary according to car size. Motorbikes start at 5400 pta (£27). Motorbikes over five years old are supposedly not allowed on the ferry. All fares are subject to seasonal variation, costing as much as 50% more in the high season (August and September). Bicycles are free most of the year, but cost up to

1300 pta (£7) between late June and late September.

To/From Morocco
The most popular destination is Tangier on the Moroccan side of the strait. Ferries leave Algeciras every two hours or so and cost 2700/5400 pta one-way/return. Cars cost 8500 pta and motorbikes 2400 pta one-way. You can buy a ticket at the harbour, but it is more convenient to go to one of the numerous agencies along the waterfront. The price does not vary from shop to shop, so just look for the place with the shortest queue. A word of advice – don't buy your Moroccan currency until you arrive in Morocco, as you will get ripped off something shocking in Algeciras.

LEAVING SPAIN
Departure Tax
There is no airport departure tax in Spain. There has been talk of an 800 pta departure tax for some years, and it appears that to some extent it has been included in the price of tickets purchased in Spain, but there are, at present, no plans to begin collecting the tax from those who purchased their tickets outside the country.

Getting Around

AIR
The only time that you might seriously consider flying within Spain is to get out to the islands. From Barcelona, Valencia or Alicante, there are often good deals available on charter flights. The difference in price between the ferry and some of these flights is minimal, particularly when you consider the time saved. If you do buy a return ticket for an internal flight, try to ensure that there is a Sunday between the flights as it makes it considerably cheaper.

Local Air Services
There are two major airlines which fly internally in Spain: Iberia and Aviaco. They tend

SPAIN

to alternate on routes and timetables and work together as much as possible. As a result their prices are much the same. Iberia has offices all over the world and also acts as the international agent for Aviaco.

BUS

There are numerous independent bus companies in Spain. They generally operate out of one town, with a limited number of destinations. Prices are very slightly cheaper than train fares, and, if a train runs the same route, the bus tends to be faster, though that depends on the roads.

Reservations

On most routes, the only way to make a reservation is to go in person to the bus station and seek out the bus company which plies the route of your choice. Exceptions to this are the major routes, such as Madrid to Barcelona, Málaga, Seville and so on. In such cases you may get lucky at a travel agency, though that too depends on the time of year, the bus company and the price.

Costs

Bus fares change frequently in Spain. Very approximately, you should expect to pay around 50 pta for the first 50 km and then 50 pta for every 10 km thereafter. Based on this formula, 500 km by bus should cost around 2300 pta. Variations are usually of the upward variety.

TRAIN

The Spanish train system has improved beyond imagination in the last 10 years. Even so, you must learn to live with late arrivals, though these days more than a couple of hours is fairly uncommon, and often can lead to partial refunds.

Classes

On Spanish trains there are two basic classes – 1st and 2nd. There are, however, numerous different kinds of train. As a rule of thumb, the cheapest trains are the ones which stop most frequently.

Talgo Travelling with the Talgo is travelling in luxury. It is considerably faster than the other types of train and has such extras as TV and excellent, though expensive, food. If you have a rail pass, make the most of it and use the Talgo as often as possible. Everyone else has to pay a hefty supplement, which may be up to double in some cases.

Super Fast Train This is the Spanish version of the French TGV and the German ICE. At present there is only one line, from Madrid to Seville (often stopping in Cordova, among other cities). See the Seville Getting There & Away section for further details.

Reservations

You can make reservations for any RENFE train at any RENFE station – in theory. Most major towns have a central RENFE (Spain's national railway) office where you can make reservations and avoid the unpleasantries of train station queuing.

Costs

The intricacies of the Spanish fare system could fill a book, and indeed RENFE has written a 500 page fare guide. Unfortunately, to understand fully what is inside you need a PhD in cryptography. The long and the short of it is that, for any one route, there are up to 24 different fares per class.

There are, however, a few tips which may help you get on to the best value fares. First and foremost are the so-called *Dias Azules* (Blue Days). On these days you can travel for as little as half the basic fare – only basic fares are quoted on train journeys in this chapter. You can get a list of Dias Azules at any RENFE station. To take advantage of Dias Azules, you must mention it when you buy your ticket.

CAR & MOTORBIKE

With a good road map, you can't really go wrong driving in Spain. European and national routes are marked E- and N- respectively. These are most direct routes between points and are generally of high quality. Other routes, marked by C-, or not at all, vary enormously in quality and can often be very slow going, though they are usually more scenic. On many freeways, particularly in the north, you have to pay a hefty toll. San Sebastián to Bilbao, for example, costs around 1000 pta.

Road Rules

A general disrespect for road rules has given Spain the dubious honour of having one of the highest road-death tolls in the developed world. For those who need to know, speed limits are 120 km/h on freeways, 100 km/h on other country roads and 50 or 60 km/h in built-up areas. The maximum allowable blood alcohol level is 0.08%. Safety belts must be worn on country roads and freeways, and motorcyclists must always wear a helmet.

Trying to find a parking spot can be a nightmare in larger towns and cities. Spanish drivers just park anywhere to save themselves the hassle of a half-hour search. Although it is fun to park the Spanish way, be warned that the *gruás* (tow trucks) will tow your car away if given the chance. The cost of bailing out a car hovers around the 6000 pta mark.

Rental

Of the major companies, Atesa is the best value. Others, such as Europcar, Avis and Budget, are to be found all over the country. There are always a couple of agents in any airport. Prices start at around 8500 pta a day (insurance and kms included) if you take a car for a few days.

Local companies in touristy spots such as the Balearic Islands, Costa del Sol and Costa de Almería leave the major companies for dead on price. The cars must always be returned to the same place, and a day's hire is often from 9 am to 5 pm, but the prices are unbeatable. Finding something for under 5000 pta a day should not be a problem. See also Majorca for the car rental deal of a lifetime.

BICYCLE

Cycling in the south of Spain is becoming ever more popular. By the end of October there are swarms of Canadians and Germans pedalling their way along the coast. The same can be said for the Balearic Islands, particularly Majorca. Unfortunately, mapping material for cyclists is nonexistent and you'll have to make do with walking maps. The German publishing company, Cyklos, has a good guide on cycling in Majorca called *Majorca Per Rad.*

HITCHING

Solo hitchhiking by women is not recommended. Two women hitching together should be able to choose the car they want to ride in. A man and a woman together will usually not have to wait for longer than 15 minutes for a ride. A man, whether hitching alone or with a male companion or two, will often be left standing on the roadside for an hour or more.

There is, of course, regional variation. In the Basque Country there is a mortal fear of terrorists. I have seen people get a lift in five minutes, but I have also heard of people giving up after eight hours. In Andalusia and Castile, rides can be sparse, but to reward your patience they can be wonderfully long.

WALKING

If you have time to spare, walking is the best way to meet the locals. In Extremadura, Galicia and southern Aragon, in particular, you will be greeted with unending curiosity. Unfortunately, most of the detailed mapping material available is pretty old. IGN Spain has published reasonably up-to-date maps on a scale of 1:25,000 for most of the coast, the Balearic Islands and some of the national parks, and they can supply you with a catalogue free of charge. For 1:50,000 and 1:100,000 maps, you are better off buying military maps – ask in any travel bookshop.

For information on trekking, see Lonely Planet's *Trekking in Spain* by Marc Dubin, in which specialist mapping material is discussed for the most important trekking centres in the country.

If you are interested in a really long walk, there is the Camino de Santiago. This route,

SPAIN

which has been followed by Christian pilgrims for centuries, can be started at various places in France. It then crosses the Pyrenees into Spain and runs via Pamplona, Logroño, Burgos, León and Lugo all the way to the cathedral in Santiago de Compostela. There are numerous guidebooks explaining the route, and among the maps published the best is by IGN Spain.

BOAT
Inter-Island Ferry
For information on ferries to and between the Balearic Islands, see the relevant section of this book.

LOCAL TRANSPORT
In most Spanish towns you will not need to use the public transport systems, as accommodation is centralised and generally within comfortable walking distance of all tourist attractions.

Bus
Most cities in Spain have a local bus system. In cases where the train or bus stations are out of town, there is almost always a bus which runs to the centre. In other cases, such as in Murcia, you may have to take a bus from the train station to the bus station, then another to the centre of town. In larger cities, the bus systems can be horribly complicated, and there is usually no bus map available.

Underground
Barcelona and Madrid both have efficient underground systems. They are cheaper, faster and easier to use than the bus systems. See the Barcelona and Madrid sections for more information.

Taxi
Taxis are still pretty cheap in Spain. If you split a cross-town fare between three or four people, it can be a decidedly good deal. With slight variations from city to city, the rates are around 110 pta per km and 35 pta per minute, with a flagfall of 210 pta. There are supplements for luggage, airport and railway station pick-ups, and dogs.

Madrid

Whatever apprehensions you may have about Madrid when you first arrive, Spain's capital city is sure to grow on you as you get to know it. It takes time as there is a seemingly unending list of things to see, places to visit and people to meet. It also takes energy, as keeping up with the Madrileños may seem like hard work during the day, but just wait until it gets dark! Furthermore, it takes patience – Spain's bureaucracy is infamous. Use your imagination.

Orientation
The centre of Madrid, and the point from which all distances in Spain are measured, is Puerta del Sol. Although Madrid is an enormous metropolis, the region which is of interest to tourists is confined by Campo del Moro in the west and Parque del Buen Retiro (also known as Parque del Retiro, or simply El Retiro) in the east. These two parks are more or less connected by Calle de Alcalá, which forms the northern boundary of Parque del Buen Retiro, and runs south-west to Puerta del Sol, continuing from there as Calle Mayor, past Plaza Mayor, to the Royal Palace in front of Campo del Moro.

The Paseo del Prado marks the beginning of Madrid's main north-south thoroughfare, Paseo de la Castellana. Starting at Atocha Railway Station in the south, it runs (with a couple of name changes), all the way to Madrid's other big station, Chamartín.

Information
Tourist Office The main tourist office in Madrid is in the Torre de Madrid on Plaza de España. It is open Monday to Friday from 9 am to 7 pm, and Saturday from 9.30 am to 1.30 pm. There is another office at Calle Duque de Medinaceli 2, open Monday to Friday from 9 am to 3 pm, and on Plaza Mayor, open Monday to Friday from 10 am to 1.30 pm and 4 to 7 pm, and Saturday 10 am to 1.30 pm. The offices in Chamartín

Railway Station and Barajas Airport are open seven days a week.

There is an excellent youth tourist information office in the underground station at Puerta del Sol. It has an ever-growing computer database of youth-related information: cheap accommodation, jobs, courses, personal ads, travel agents, bookshops and much more. To find the office you have to go through the underground entrance closest to Calle de San Jerónimo, and pass through the ticket barrier. It is on the upper level to the left.

There are laundrettes on Calle Infantes and Calle Cervantes, both near Plaza de Santa Ana. You will find another one at Calle Palma 2 near metro Tribunal.

Money Apart from the usual array of banks, you can also change money at El Corte Inglés department store. American Express charges a flat rate of 1% which is good for small amounts. For after hours and Sunday exchange, try Cambios Uno at Calle Alcalá 20. It charges a minimum commission of 250 pta and advertises a special deal for students. Its hours are Monday to Saturday from 9 am to 9 pm, and Sunday from 9 am to 3 pm.

Post The main post office is on Plaza de Cibeles. Poste restante (lista de correos) is through the main entrance at window 37. American Express is not too far away for those using the clients' mail service, at Plaza de las Cortes 2. It does not close for lunch, so hours are Monday to Friday from 9 am to 5.30 pm and Saturday from 9 am to noon.

Telephone There is a Telecom telephone centre at Gran Via 30. Remember the magic number for reverse-charge calls (blue phones only): 900 9900 plus your country code. See the Facts for the Visitor section for more information.

In Madrid, more so than anywhere else in the country, it is normal to make phone calls from a bar. Most bars have a counter, so you can make intercity or even international calls at almost any time of the day. Madrid's telephone code is 91.

Foreign Embassies See the Facts for the Visitor section earlier in this chapter for information.

Travel Agencies For cheap travel arrangements in Madrid you can't go beyond TIVE, the local student travel organisation. It is at Calle José Ortega y Gaset 71 (☎ 401 1300), and Calle Fernando el Católico 88 (☎ 243 0208).

Bookshops There are a number of travel bookshops in Madrid. Most of them have a reasonable English-language selection. Años Luz Libros, Calle Francisco de Ricci 8, is one of the better known shops, while Librería la Tienda Verde, Calle Maudes 38, has an excellent selection of maps, including many IGN and military 1:25,000, 1:50,000 and 1:100,000 maps.

There are two women's bookshops in Madrid. Librería de Mujeres, Calle San Cristóbal 17, is a well-known feminist meeting place. Librería Bookshop at Calle José Abascal 48 sells English-language women's titles.

For general English and other foreign language books, your best bet is Librería Turner, at Calle Genova 3. Another shop worth trying is Booksellers, at Calle José Abascal 48.

To see an amazing selection of second-hand books, take a walk along Cuesta de Claudio Mollano, which runs from Paseo del Prado to the south-west corner of the Parque del Buen Retiro. There are 30 bookstalls along this street selling almost any Spanish-language book you can imagine. There are also quite a number of English-language books for sale. For a more conventional selection, Librería Carmelo Blazquez, at Calle Alfonso XII 66, is Madrid's largest second-hand bookshop. Though it primarily deals in Spanish-language books, it will buy foreign-language books and has a small selection of English novels in stock.

Emergency The police headquarters is at Puerta del Sol 7. If you need a police officer ring ☎ 091 or ☎ 092. In a medical emergency

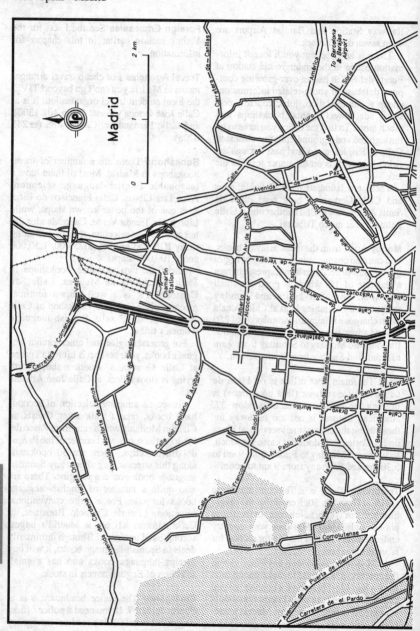

Madrid

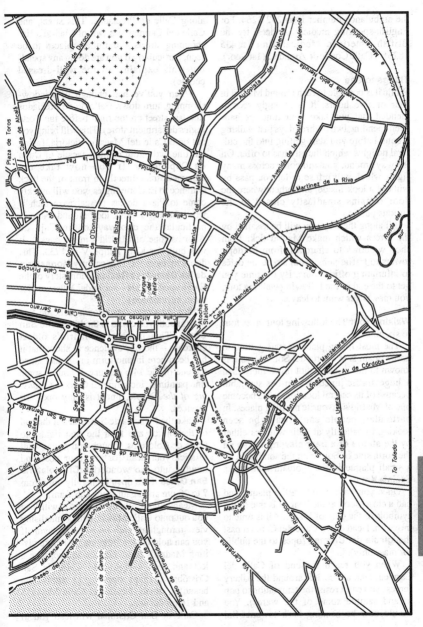

the ambulance number is ☎ 252 3264. For English-speaking medical services, try the British-American Medical Unit (☎ 435 1823) at Calle Conde de Aranda 1 (1st floor).

Things to See

While it is possible to rush around Madrid in four or five hours, it is strongly recommended that you take your time, perhaps even spending two or three days just walking around before you start getting into the cultural delights which the city has to offer. On the way around, you will come across many sights which will refuse to let you pass by without a look inside, and others where the door remains steadfastly closed to the curious public.

All along the way you will be assailed by the forces which make Madrid tick: from shop windows to churches, from Mudéjar towers to traffic jams, from streetside cafés to infuriating office hours. By the time you get to the end of the following walking tour, you may never want to leave.

Walking Tour The following tour takes four to six hours.

The most fitting place to start getting to know Spain is at Puerta del Sol. Sol, as it is known to the locals, is not much more than a huge traffic-junction-cum-bus-stop, but because of its central location, it has become one of Madrid's favourite meeting places. In particular, people can always be seen looking impatiently at their watches either by the **statue of a bear clawing a tree** on the north side of Sol, or on the south side by a small plaque in the footpath that marks Spain's **Km 0**.

Once you have stood on the plaque and had a closer look at the bear (it is one of the symbols of the City of Madrid), it is time to move on. Head down Calle del Carmen past the **Iglesia del Carmen** (open to the public for mass only).

When you reach the end of Calle del Carmen, take a hard left around the bakery (unless you can't resist the temptation to pop in and sample some of the wares). You should now be heading back towards Sol along Calle de Preciados. This street, and Calle del Carmen, are two of Madrid's 'in' shopping streets – definitely places to be seen, particularly if you are doing any spending (this explains all the well-dressed people).

When you've had enough of window-shopping, turn down Callejon de Preciados (the last street on the right before the Corte Inglés department store). This will bring you out onto Calle del Maestro Victoria, facing the fine early 20th century façade of **Casa de Capellanes**. If you now take the unnamed street directly in front of the back entrance to El Corte Inglés, you will quickly come to Plaza de las Descalzas, which is worth having a quick look around. Note in particular the **doorway** to the Caja de Ahorros (one of Madrid's many banks). It was built for King Felipe V in 1733. This doorway faces the 16th century **Monastério de las Descalzas Reales** (Monastery of the Barefooted Royals – see under Museums for more information).

Moving along, head down Calle de San Martín until you come to the **Iglesia de San Ginés**. This is one of Madrid's oldest churches – there is evidence to show that it has been here in one form or another since the end of the 14th century. It houses some fine paintings, including El Greco's *Cleansing of the Temple*, but it is only open for services.

Take the Plazuela de San Ginés at the end of the church and then the first right into Calle de Coloreros, though you might want to stick your head (or just your nose and mouth) into the wonderful **Chocolatería San Ginés** if it's open (generally only from 7 to 10 pm and again from 1 to 7 am).

Meanwhile, Calle de Coloreros will lead you out onto Calle Mayor, with a tantalising view through an arch into Plaza Mayor. If you can hold back a little longer before visiting Madrid's most famous square, take a left and then a right into Calle de San Cristóbal, perhaps stopping to admire the beautiful, ornate façades at Calle Mayor 5 and 16 on the way.

Calle de San Cristóbal will lead you to

Plaza de la Provincia, with the 16th century **Palacio de Santa Cruz**, now home to the Ministry of Foreign Affairs. Almost next door, at the end of Calle Atocha, is the **Iglesia de la Santa Cruz** with its 60-metre-high neo-Mudéjar tower. There is said to be a *lignum crucis* (piece of the Cross) inside.

Once again Plaza Mayor beckons through another archway. No need to hold back any longer. On a sunny day the cafés on Plaza Mayor do a roaring trade, with some 500 tables in the square – definitely a place to be seen, as the prices indicate.

In the middle of the early 17th century square is a **statue of Felipe III**, who was responsible for the building of the square. The building on the north side of the square is the **Real Casa de la Panadería** (Royal Bakers' Guild).

Leaving Plaza Mayor, take the arch in the north-west corner (Calle de Ciudad Rodrigo) out onto Cava de San Miguel. With the **Mercado de San Miguel** on your left, you could always stock up on food for a cheap lunch in one of the squares or parks later in the day. If not, then head west along Calle Mayor. You'll soon come to the historic **Plaza de la Villa**, with Madrid's 17th century **town hall** (note its late 18th century balcony on Calle Mayor). Also on Plaza de la Villa is the 16th century **Casa de Cisneros** and the Gothic-Mudéjar **Torre de Los Lujánes**, one of the city's oldest buildings, dating from the Middle Ages.

Take the street down the side of Casa de Cisneros, cross the road at the end, go down the stairs and follow the cobbled Calle del Cordón out onto Calle de Segovia. Almost directly in front of you is the Mudéjar tower of **Iglesia de San Pedro**. Heading down the hill on the busy Calle de Segovia isn't much fun, so turn right when you come to Plaza de la Cruz Verde. A little way up the hill behind you is the domed **Iglesia de San Andres**. The decoration inside the dome is rather unusual and worth a peek if you're not in a hurry. Also note the beautiful tiling on the liquor store on Plaza de San Andres.

Back on Plaza de la Cruz Verde now, walk up Calle de la Villa and follow the traffic flow up past the military church, back onto Calle Mayor, where you will see the **National Military Headquarters** on your left. Walk down Calle de la Almudena (the street opposite the main entrance to the military HQ), where the secretary to the Austrian king was murdered at Easter in 1578. This street will bring you out onto Calle de Bailén.

As you walk northward along Calle de Bailén towards Plaza de Oriente, you will pass **Madrid's Cathedral**, or **Iglesia de la Almudena** as it is also known. It was finally completed and opened to the public in mid-1992, after being more than 110 years under construction. A little farther along is the **Royal Palace** (see the Museums section).

Walk across Plaza de Oriente past the **statue of Felipe IV**, down Calle de Felipe V, and around to the front of the **Royal Theatre** on Plaza de Isabel II. You'll have to back away from the theatre a little to appreciate fully the frescoes at the top. Calle del Arenal gives you the best view.

From Plaza de Isabel II walk up Calle de Campomanes, across the intersection and along Calle de Fomento, turning left at Calle de la Bola. This will lead you to the **Monastério de la Encarnación** on Plaza de la Encarnación. The monastery was founded in 1611 by Queen Margarita of Austria. After being destroyed by fire, it was rebuilt in 1767 (though the façade is still the original).

Walk along Calle de la Encarnación and you will come to the **National Senate**. Turn left and head back down to Calle de Bailén. Turn right on Calle de Bailén and make your way onto **Plaza de España**.

There are a few things worth noting once you reach the square. Firstly, just off the south-eastern end of the square is the strange **Basílica de Santa Teresa de los Padres Carmelitas** with its rainbow dome. Inside, it isn't much to speak of, although Mary's position above the altar is rather impressive, and the series of confessional boxes, crowded into a corner known as the Chapel of Penitence, is certainly different.

On the Plaza de España itself is a **statue of Cervantes** dating from 1927. Note also the imposing **Edificio de España** and Madrid's tallest building, the **Torre de Madrid** (which, incidentally, houses a tourist information office). The square itself has, in recent years, become rather seedy, perhaps even dangerous. The police presence is at times nothing short of astounding. All the same, coming here is a must: Plaza de España marks the beginning of Madrid's main street – Gran Via.

The Gran Via is not known for outstanding monuments, historic buildings or fine art. It is a place where money is made and spent. From luxury hotels to cheap hostales, pinball parlours to jewellery shops, high fashion to fast food, sex shops, shoe shiners, cinemas, airline offices, banks and car-rental agencies, Gran Via is the number one place to watch Madrid and Madrileños in action. You can walk the full length in 15 minutes, but take your time – wander into cafés, enjoy the window displays (do some shopping?) – do as the locals do and just enjoy it.

When you finally reach the end of Gran Via, note the superb dome of the **Metropolis Building**. Now take a left into Calle del Marqués de Valdeiglesias and right into Calle de las Infantas which will lead you to **Plaza del Rey**, a peaceful square with a nice mixture of buildings and very photogenic views back across the rooftops towards Gran Via.

Take a left at the north-eastern corner of the square into Calle del Barquillo and then first right into Calle del Prim. At the end of this street turn left into Paseo de Recoletos and walk down the middle of the tree-lined promenade. On your left you will pass some of the city's best known cafés, including Gran Café de Gijon, Café Espejo and El Gran Pabellón del Espejo which, surprisingly, was built in 1990!

When you reach this last café, try to cross the road to the enormous 19th century **National Library** on the right. If you're not keen on such a life-threatening stunt, there is an underpass a little farther on.

By now you will see the **statue of Colón** (Columbus) in the Plaza de Colón. At the far end of the square is the impressive **Monu-ment to the Discovery of America**. Sculpted in the mid-1970s, it is covered in text and images commemorating the event.

From here walk around the back of the National Library where the **Archaeological Museum** is housed (see the Museums section). Walk south along Calle del Serrano until you reach Plazuela de Independencia, with the **Puerta de Alcalá** in the middle of the busy intersection. The gate was built to celebrate the arrival of Charles III in Madrid in 1778. On the south-eastern corner of the square is one of the entrances to the **Parque del Buen Retiro** (see the Parks section).

Looking down the hill through the gate, you will see Plaza de Cibeles, marked by a fountain. When you arrive at the square you will see the beautiful **General Post Office** on the south-eastern corner, which was opened at the end of WW I. The **Bank of Spain** building on the south-western corner was built at the end of last century.

Following the Paseo del Prado, another beautiful tree-lined boulevard, you will come to (you guessed it) the museum after which it is named. On the way you pass the **Naval Museum** (for naval history freaks only) before reaching Plaza de la Lealtad, with an **obelisk** erected in 1840 in memory of the martyrs of 2 May 1808 (see also the Prado under the Museums section).

The **Prado** itself was built in the late 18th century as a science academy. In 1819 Fernando VII turned it into the museum that you're so dying to visit.

After contemplating (or visiting) the museum, cross over Paseo del Prado and walk up Calle de las Huertas until you reach the early 17th century **Convento de las Trinitarias**, where Cervantes is buried (closed to the public). Walk down Costanilla de las Trinitarias, cross Calle Lope de Vega into Calle de San Agustín and turn left at Calle de Cervantes. On your right you will pass **Lope de Vega's House**, at No 11. It has been closed for some time but may be open to the public again in 1993.

At the end of Calle Cervantes, take a right turn then a left, then first right, first left. You should now be on Calle Manuel Fernandez

Gonzalez. You should also have noticed that the area is pretty thick on the ground with bars. As you cross Calle Echegaray, notice the beautiful interior of **Bar los Gabrieles** on the corner. You are now in the heart of one of Madrid's top nightlife areas.

Follow Calle Manuel Fernandez Gonzalez to the end. Take a left, then turn right into Plaza de Santa Ana. Turn right at Calle Nuñez de Arce, and after noting the beautiful tiling on the **façade** (see also the Places to Stay & Places to Eat section) at No 15, it's into the home stretch. Follow the street to the end then zig-zag left, first right, first left, right, then left again. If you're not back in Puerta del Sol now, you must have made a mistake somewhere on the way. Use the accompanying map.

Museums Make sure you set aside a substantial part of your visit to Madrid for its museums. Many of them, including the Sorolla Museum, the Archaeological Musuem, Cáson del Buen Retiro and, of course, the internationally renowned Prado, are simply too good to miss and must be seen as an integral part of any visit to Spain.

El Prado This is one of the greatest art galleries in the world. Although the main emphasis is on Spanish art, the collection gives the visitor a comprehensive overview of the works of many of the most important European artists from the 15th to the 19th centuries. Certainly there are other European museums which can make the same claim, but somehow the Prado stands out.

Entry to the museum costs 400 pta or is free if you have an international student card. It is free for all on 18 May every year. Opening hours are Tuesday to Saturday from 9 am to 7 pm, and Sunday from 9 am to 2 pm. Renovation and modernisation of the Prado has been going on in phases for a number of years. It will probably still be underway at the end of the century. For this reason, the Prado no longer produces giveaway maps, though you can buy expensive, nonillustrated guides to the museum in the bookshop. It is best to enter the museum

through the northern end and start with the ground floor. In this way you will see the collection in an approximately chronological order.

The following description of the museum's contents was up to date at the time of printing. Allowing for the slow pace of modernisation, it should be reasonably accurate.

In rooms 48, 49 and 50 you will find 14th and 15th century Spanish art. This period was very heavily dominated by religious themes. Look out for works by Fernando Gallego. Rooms 53, 55, 55B, 55C, 56, 56B and 57 contain 16th century Spanish art. Juan de Juanes (room 53) was undoubtedly the most outstanding artist of the period. Note the way Judas is depicted in *The Last Supper*.

Flemish art dating from the 15th and 16th centuries is housed in rooms 55A, 56A and 57A. In particular don't miss the single painting by Pieter Brueghel, Jan Brueghel's father *(El Triunfo de la Muerte)* and Van Hemesen's *El Cirujano* (The Surgeon). It makes you shiver, doesn't it? Still more Flemish art is to be found in rooms 60 to 65 and 75, including works by De Vos, van Eyck, Jordaens, Van Dyck and a wonderful collection of Rubens. Note the latter's original interpretation of the Milky Way *(La Via Láctea)* and his powerful mythological imagery in *George & the Dragon* and *Saturn*. There are also some paintings by Jan Brueghel and a few which Brueghel and Rubens painted together.

The 17th century Dutch school is represented in rooms 64 and 65. Included in the selection are two Rembrandts, one of them a rather peeved-looking self-portrait.

Rooms 66 and 67 are dedicated entirely to Goya. The works in room 67 in particular have the wonderfully distorted faces that are Goya's trademark. Compare his rendition of *Saturn* with that of Rubens.

Then it's upstairs (unless you stop for a smoko in the café. Rooms 19 to 23, and 34 to 38, are also dedicated solely to Goya. Look out for an interesting pair in *Maja desnuda* and *Maja vestida* at the southern end of the 1st floor. Legend has it that she was the Duchess of Alba. Goya was supposedly commissioned to paint her for her husband and somehow ended up becoming romantically involved with her. As such he painted one portrait for the Duke and one for himself. Sadly, the legend probably isn't true, but the paintings attract a lot of attention anyway.

In room 39 is yet more Goya. *El dos de Mayo 1808* and *Los fusilamientos de Moncloa* (also known as *El tres de mayo 1808*) are among the most prized paintings of El Prado. It is often quite impossible to see past the crowds.

Rooms 16A, 16B, 17, 17A, 18 and 18A contain works from the 17th century Spanish school. Outstanding artists of the time include Francisco Zurbarán and José de Ribera, who used people off the street as his models. His painting of San Andrés is considered his greatest masterpiece.

You'll find a wealth of Velázquez in rooms 12 to 14, 15A, 16 and 27. In his painting of Felipe IV (room 15A) you can see that he made changes to the painting – note the shadows and lines of the original cape. *Las Meninas* (room 12) is Velázquez' most famous painting. The painter in the painting is the artist himself. He is painting a portrait of the king and queen, who can be seen in the mirror in the backgound of Las Meninas.

Room 11 is the only place where you'll find French art, and in the small annexe off that room is a strange painting depicting the delivery of the head of John the Baptist. All the other characters are dressed for the 16th century (thereabouts).

Italian artists including Titian, Tintoretto and Veronese are in rooms 7, 7A, 8, 8A, 8B, 9A and 10. Tintoretto's *El Paraiso* is mindboggling in its detail. Note also Titian's depiction of the Titan having his liver eaten by the eagle.

The works of Domenikos Theotocopoulos, the Cretan-born artist, better known as El Greco, are sublime. Thirty-four of his outstanding works are to be found in rooms 9B and 10B.

Rooms 2 to 6 are dedicated to 15th and 16th century Italian artists, including a number of works by Raphael. Rooms 24 to 29 have been closed for some time, but it is thought that they will be filled with 16th and 17th century Spanish art.

Casón del Buen Retiro This museum is run under the auspices of El Prado. As such, your ticket to the Prado will get you in here at no extra cost. It lies between the Prado itself and the main entrance to the Parque del Buen Retiro and contains what must surely be one of Europe's artistic highlights – Picasso's *El Guernica*.

Before being confronted by the showpiece itself, you pass through a security check reminiscent of Tel Aviv Airport. Once you have that behind you, there is a collection of preliminary sketches and paintings which Picasso put together in May 1937, shortly before painting his masterpiece. *El Guernica* itself was painted in Paris. Picasso insisted that the painting not be moved to Spain until Franco and his cronies were gone and democracy had been restored. It was not until 1981 that the painting was secretly brought into Spain.

Even today the painting causes heated discussion and bitter feelings in Spain. It was painted to protest the German bombing of the Basque town of Guernica during the Spanish Civil War (1936-39). Twenty-six April 1937 was a typical market day in the town of 5000 people. Because of the market there were another 5000 visitors from the surrounding region selling their wares or doing their weekly shopping. The bombs started to drop at 4 pm. By the time they stopped three hours later, the town, its population and the visitors had been annihilated.

In the same building is a collection of 18th and 19th century Spanish art. If you haven't run out of puff after El Prado and *El Guernica*, it is worth a look. *Niños en la Playa* by Sorolla is one of the more highly acclaimed pieces in the collection. If this painting appeals to you, you may be interested in the separate gallery dedicated solely to his work (see the Sorolla Museum section in this chapter).

Royal Palace The nearest metro station to the palace is Opera. Entry is free on Wednesdays, otherwise it costs 325 pta for foreign students and 400 pta for everyone else. A guided tour of the palace (in English or Spanish) is included in the price, if you wish to join a group.

The palace was built in the 18th century and took 26 years to build. It has not been used as a royal residence for some time and today it is only used for official receptions and, of course, tourism.

Most of the tapestries in the palace were made in the Royal Tapestry Factory, though there are a number of French tapestries scattered throughout the rooms.

There are 2800 rooms in the palace. All the chandeliers are original and no two are the same. Electricity was connected in 1904. The chapel is still used today by the Royal Family – note the mummified body of St Felix under the altar.

Among the collections in the palace is a good selection of Goyas, 215 absurdly ornate clocks from the Royal Clock Collection, and five Stradivarius violins, which are still used in concerts and balls. There are copies of all the Goyas in El Prado (don't worry, the copies are by Goya).

Archaeological Museum The museum contains an excellent collection tracing the history of the peninsula, from the earliest prehistoric cave paintings to the Iberian, Roman, Punic, Greek, Visigoth, Moorish and Christian eras. Exhibits include mosaics, pottery, fossilised bones and a reconstructed prehistoric burial site. Entry is free to students, but is 200 pta for everyone else.

Centro de Arte Reina Sofía The centre has been home to the complete collection of the **Museum of Contemporary Art** since late 1992. It is also used for high-quality temporary exhibitions. The old modern art museum is still marked on many maps as being way out by the university. Don't be fooled. Today the premises are used to house a rather strange and cluttered collection of copies of Greek and Roman statues.

Sorolla Museum This museum is on Paseo de General Martinez Campos 37, metro Rubén Dario. Entry is free to ISIC holders, otherwise it will cost you 200 pta. The museum is in the house in which the artist once resided and contains the most comprehensive collection of his work in Spain. If you liked his paintings in the Casón del Buen Retiro, don't miss this museum.

Museo de la Castellana This is an interesting open-air collection of abstract sculptures. The works were donated to the city by 15 artists, who include some of Spain's better known modern sculptors, such as Serrano, Sempere, Martí and Miró. The sculptures can be found under the flyover near the Paseo Castellana exit to the Rubén Dario metro station. There is no charge and the collection can be visited 24 hours a day, seven days a week.

Panteón de Goya The nearest metro is Norte. When you come out of the station, turn right down Paseo de Florida and follow it until you come to two small churches on the right. Inside the first one is one of Goya's greatest works – the entire ceiling and dome beautifully painted with religious scenes. Much needed restoration work was started in early 1990 and will not be completed until well into 1993, at least. All the same, it is open to the public to allow people to appreciate the excellent work being done by the restorers. As an added attraction, the master's tomb is directly in front of the altar. Entry is free (at least until restoration is completed).

Monastério de las Descalzas Reales (Monastery of the Barefooted Royals) This monastery was awarded the title of European Museum of the Year in 1987. Built in 1559, it contains 33 shrines in all. On the obligatory guided tour you will see a number of tapestries based on works by Rubens. You will also be confronted by a wonderful painting entitled (equally wonderfully) *The Voyage of the 11,000 Virgins*. Empress María of Austria, the royal in question, is entombed

SPAIN

here. She was not a religious member of the order.

Other Museums There are a number of other museums worth visiting in Madrid. The **Museo Municipal**, by metro Tribunal, includes works by Bayeu and Goya, an interesting 20th century collection, and some beautiful old maps, scale models, silver, porcelain and period furniture. The scale model of Madrid in 1830 is most impressive.

The **Collection of the Musical Library** is a fascinating display of musical instruments – a must for music buffs.

Museo Casa de la Moneda is numismatic heaven. It contains a first-class collection of coins, dating back to the 7th century BC. It follows the history of coinage and minting in great detail from its inception through to the present day. The collection of paper money is just as mind-boggling.

Market If you get up early on a sunny Sunday morning you'll find the city almost deserted, until you get to El Rastro. The Rastro is one of the biggest flea markets you are ever likely to see. If you are prepared to hunt around, you can find almost anything at all for sale here. The market begins near metro Tirso Molina, at the corner of Calle San William and Calle de los Estudios. From there it quickly spreads out and down the hill, before converging for a final fling in Plaza del Campilla del Mundo Nuevo and petering out in Calle Gasómetro, just across Ronda de Toledo. This is said to be the street to go to if you want to buy your car stereo back.

Parque del Buen Retiro This is a truly beautiful, thoughtfully landscaped park. On a warm spring day there is no better way to escape the hustle and bustle of the city than to walk among the flower beds and hedgerows or just to sprawl out on one of the lawns.

In the park itself are a number of interesting sights. In particular you should take a stroll along the **Paseo de las Estatuas**, a path lined with statues originally from the Royal Palace. The Paseo ends at a lake where a **statue of Alfonso XII** overlooks carefree

rowers from a pedestal on the other side. There are rowing boats for rent at the northern end when the weather is good.

Aside from the Paseo de las Estatuas, there are fountains and monuments scattered throughout the park. Perhaps the most important, and certainly the most controversial, is the **Monument to the Fallen Angel**. First-prize winner at an international exhibition in Paris in 1878, it is said to be the first statue in the world dedicated to the devil.

While in the park you should also visit some of the small, but beautifully tended, gardens, such as the exquisite **Rose Garden** (la Roselada) or the **Chinese Garden** on a tiny island near the Fallen Angel.

Finally, there is the **Crystal Palace** in the middle of the park. This all-glass building occasionally has exhibitions of modern art. Generally it costs 100 pta to get in to see the exhibits. Look through the walls from the outside first to see if you really want to pay for it.

Campo del Moro This serene and stately garden is set directly behind the Royal Palace in such a way that the one-time regal residence is visible through the trees from just about all points. It is one of the few places in the city where the roar of the traffic is reduced to no more than a whisper. As such, it is quite a haven for local birdlife; on a warm day you can easily hear five or six different species singing together. There are a couple of fountains and statues, and a thatch-roofed pagoda and a **Carriage Museum** (200 pta entry) if you're looking for artificial diversions, but basically nature is the greatest attraction here.

Activities
Language Courses There are numerous private language schools in Madrid. Although some such as Berlitz, Inlingua and International House are very well known, it is recommended that you go through the university. For more information contact either of the following:

Español para Extranjeros,
Secretaría de Cursos de Lenguas Extranjeras,
Facultad de Filosofía y Letras,
Edificio A,
Ciudad Universitaria,
28003 Madrid
(☎ 549 6500, from 9 am to 2 pm)

Escuela Oficial de Idiomas,
Departamento de Español para Extranjeros,
Calle Jesus Maestro s/n,
28003 Madrid
(☎ 554 4492, from 9 am to 2 pm)

Festivals

Madrid's patron saint is San Isidro Labrador. Although the day of his festival is 15 May, the festival continues to take place in typical Spanish fashion for a number of days either side. Malasaña has its biggest party on 2 May, and the Festival of San Juan is still celebrated in the Parque del Buen Retiro for the seven days leading up to 24 June, even though the saint appears to have been decanonised. The last week of September is Chamartín's Festival de Otoño (Autumn Festival), and is about the only time you would go to Chamartín without going there to catch a train.

Places to Stay

Finding a place to stay in Madrid is never really a problem. Pensiones tend to be clustered around three or four regions of the city and the price-to-quality ratio tends to be fairly standard, plus or minus a couple of hundred pesetas, depending on where you are looking.

In summer the city is drained of people, thanks to the horrific heat, so if you are mad enough to be here then, you may well be able to make a hot deal on the price. The rest of the year it is still worth trying to bargain if you intend to stay a while, otherwise you can forget it.

Camping There are only two camp sites which are relatively close to the city. Both are open all year. *Camping Madrid* (☎ 302 2835) is a few km to the north. To get there take bus No 129 from Plaza de Castilla.

Camping Osuna (☎ 741 0510) is on Avenida de Logroño near the airport. The site is of better quality than Camping Madrid, but keep the proximity of the airport in mind before you pitch your tent.

To get there take Interbus No 151 or 154 from Plaza de Castilla and get off at Iglesia de los Domenicos at Km 11 on the road to Burgos (Carretera de Burgos). If you are driving, leave the highway at exit No 12.

Hostels & Colleges Madrid has two youth hostels. The most centrally located, at Calle Santa Cruz de Marcenado 28 (☎ 247 4532), is about a five-minute walk from the Argüelles metro station. The second one, *Hostel Richard Schirmann*, is at Casa de Campo. The nearest metro is Lago, about a 15-minute walk through the forest from the hostel. The hostels are almost always full, do not take reservations, and have midnight curfews. For two people, the saving on a double room does not make up for missing out on the nightlife (particularly for senior members).

Madrid's university has numerous colleges. Trying to get a room there during term time is a complete waste of time. In summer chances are slim, unless you are taking a language course. All the same, if you persevere you may get lucky.

Pensiones Spain's absurdly complicated hotel classification system is at its most impressive in Madrid. Suffice it to say that if a place is a pensión or hostal of some kind, it may be in the budget traveller range. Any other sort of hotel will almost certainly be disgracefully expensive. As no-one seems to be able to explain the difference between a pensión and hostal, the generic term pensión is used to refer to any such potential budget accommodation.

Around Plaza de Santa Ana Santa Ana is well on the way to becoming one of the in places to be in Madrid. It is well situated, being close to Sol, and within walking distance of the Prado and Atocha Railway

SPAIN

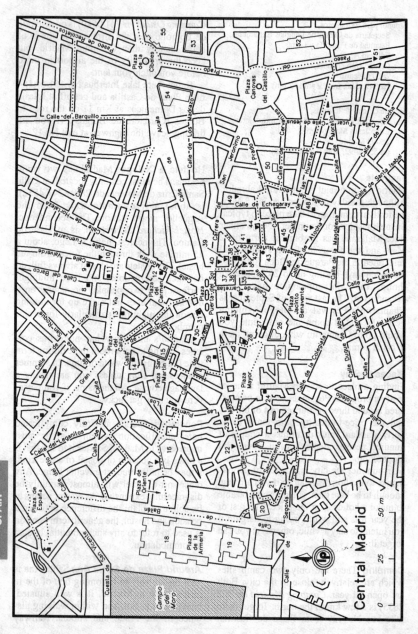

Central Madrid

0   25   50 m

■	**PLACES TO STAY**	38	Hostal Gibert	47	Cafetería Atocha 47
		41	Hostal La Rosa	49	Restaurante Integral
3	Hostal Residencia	43	Pensión Poza & Social		Artemisa
	Amberes		Club	51	Restaurante Museo
4	Hostal Besaya	45	Hostal Vetusta		del Jamón
5	Hostal Gago	46	Hostal Persal		
6	Hostal El Pinar	48	Hostal Eureka		**OTHER**
7	Hostal Canoa				
8	Hotel Laris	▼	**PLACES TO EAT**	1	Basílica de Santa
9	Hostal América				Teresa de los
11	Hostal Flores	2	Cafetería Cantania		Padres Carmelitas
12	Hotel Montesol	10	Bar Restaurante	15	Monastério de las
13	Hostal Infanta Isabel		Cochifrito		Descalzas Reales
14	Hostal Conchita	17	Taberna del Alabardero	16	Teatro Real
23	Hostal Leonesa	21	Restaurante La Villa III	18	Royal Palace
24	Hostal Los Gallegos	22	Cafetería Los Alpes	19	Iglesia de la Almudena
27	Hostal La Perla	30	Cafeteria-Restaurante	20	National Military
	Asturiana		Virginia		Headquarters
28	Hostal Soledad	33	Restaurante Casa	25	Ministry of Foreign
29	Hostal Sanz		Antón		Affairs
31	Hostal Cosmopolitan	36	Restaurante Mesón	26	Iglesia de la Santa
32	Hostal Los Arcos		Asturias		Cruz
34	Casa de Huéspedes	39	Restaurante El Club	50	Lope de Vegas' House
	Lartosa	40	Cafetería Elitesse	52	Museo del Prado
35	Hostal La Torre	42	Pizzería Il Sorriso	53	Museo Naval
37	Hostal Residencia	44	Bar Cervecería La	54	Banco de España
	Tineo		Plaza	55	Post Office

Station. It is about as close as you would want to stay to Atocha Station, and is much the same pricewise as Sol. To top it all off, it is one of Madrid's nightlife areas and there is a growing number of budget restaurants serving up quality food.

Hostal Eureka (☎ 531 9460), Calle Montera 7 (3rd floor), has singles/doubles from 1800/2700 pta. There are a number of very popular pensiones on Calle Nuñez de Arce. *Pensión Poza* (☎ 522 4871) at No 9 (1st floor), is one of the cheapest, with singles/doubles from 1000/1800 pta. *Hostal La Rosa* (☎ 532 7046) at No 15, 3rd floor l has singles/doubles from 2000/3300 pta (see also the Walking Tour and Places to Eat sections). *Hostal Vetusta* (☎ 429 6404), Calle de las Huertas 3 (1st floor), is a little more up-market and very well priced with singles/doubles from 2000/4000 pta. The *Hostal Gibert* (☎ 522 4214), Calle Victoria 6 (2nd floor), is also a good deal with singles/doubles from 2200/3200 pta. If all

these are full, don't despair. Just about every street in the area has a budget household or two to suit almost all tastes.

Around Puerta del Sol This area begins a little to the east of Puerta del Sol. It almost connects with Santa Ana on one side, and Gran Via on the other side, and continues west to Plaza Mayor. *Hostal Residencia Tineo* (☎ 521 4943), Calle Victoria 6, has singles/doubles from 2000/3500 pta. There are quite a number of pensiones in Calle Espoz y Mina; among them is *Hostal La Torre* (☎ 522 2150) at No 8, 3rd floor D, one of the cheapest with singles/doubles from 1500/2500 pta. *Casa de Huéspedes Lartosa* (☎ 521 1845), Calle Carretas 13, 5th floor D, also has singles/doubles from 1700/2800 pta. This is another pensión-filled street. *Hostal Los Arcos* (☎ 522 5976) at Calle Marqués Viudo de Pontejos 3 (2nd floor) has good-value singles/doubles from 1600/2000 pta. Farther along towards Plaza Mayor is

SPAIN

Hostal Soledad (☎ 521 2210), at Calle San Cristóbal 11. Singles/doubles cost from 1500/3000 pta. For one of the best positions in the city, you can't go beyond *Hostal Los Gallegos* (☎ 266 5884) at Calle Toledo 4, 1st floor D, which has singles/doubles from 1100/2500 pta. The *Hostal Leonesa* (☎ 248 8185), Calle Costanilla de Santiago 2, 2nd floor Centro, has singles/doubles from 1800/2800 pta. For something a little more up-market, there is *Hostal Sanz* (☎ 266 4415) on Calle Mayor at No 14 (3rd floor), with singles/doubles from 2000/3500 pta. Finally, if you don't mind the traffic, *Hostal Cosmopolitan* (☎ 522 6651) is at Puerta del Sol 9, 3rd floor D, with singles/doubles from 1500/2800 pta.

Around Gran Vía The pensiones on and around Gran Via tend to be a little more expensive than those in the Sol area. All the same, it is undoubtedly one of the more popular areas to stay in. The following pensiones are listed with the first being the closest to Plaza de España, the second being the second-closest and so on.

Hostal Residencia Amberes (☎ 247 61 00) at Gran Via 68 has good doubles, some overlooking Gran Via, for 6996 pta. Triples with bath cost 9328 pta.

Hostal El Pinar (☎ 247 3282), Calle Isabel la Católica 19, has singles/doubles from 2000/3300 pta. For 4000/5500 pta you can rent a room at *Hostal Besaya* (☎ 541 3206/7), Calle San Bernardo 13. *Hostal Gago* (☎ 521 2275), Calle de la Estrella 5, 2nd floor I, is better value with singles/doubles from 1600/2700 pta. *Hostal Canoa* (☎ 429 5756/6808) at Calle de Silva 18 (1st floor), is a women-only pensión which has singles/doubles from 950/1500 pta; however, short-term rental is generally not possible.

At Calle Preciados 33, 2nd floor D, right stairway, is *Hostal Conchita* (☎ 522 4923), with doubles from 2700 pta. *Hostal Infanta Isabel* at Gran Via 33, 8th floor I, is a quality splurge with great rooms, friendly owners and mouthwatering smells emanating from the kitchen. Doubles go for 4000 pta. *Hostal*

Flores (☎ 522 8152), just a little farther along at Gran Via 30 (entrance at Calle G Jiménez Quesada 2, 8th floor D), has singles/doubles from 2200/3200 pta.

Hotel Laris (☎ 521 4680), Calle del Barco 3, is a good middle-range hotel with singles/doubles for 4500/7400 pta. All of the rooms have air-con and colour TV. Garage space is available to guests. For similar standards try *Hotel Montesol* (☎ 531 7600) at Calle de la Montera 25. Singles/doubles cost 4664/7314 pta, and breakfast costs 375 pta per person.

There are loads of places to stay on Calle Valverde. *Hostal América* (☎ 522 2614) at No 9 (4th floor), is excellent value, with singles/doubles from 1500/2900 pta.

Around Argüelles A lot of people end up in the area around Argüelles hoping to get into the youth hostel. Very often it is full, and rather than go through the hassle of lugging your bags halfway across town, it is good to know that there are a few reasonably priced pensiones nearby. Especially good value is the friendly *Fonda Princesa* (no phone) at Calle Princesa 45 (5th floor), which has singles/doubles from an amazing 900/1400 pta. Of course, it is usually full. On the same street at No 84, 5th floor I, is the *Hostal Princesa Universal* (☎ 543 9454), with singles/doubles from 2600/3300 pta. The *Pensión Nuestra Señora de la Esperanza* (☎ 549 4402), Calle Hilarión Eslava 14, lower C, has singles/doubles from 2000/3000 pta. At No 12, lower C, is *Hostal María Teresa* (☎ 543 5640), which has rooms from 2500/3000 pta.

Rental Many of the hostals listed previously will do a deal on long stays. This may include a considerable price reduction, meals and laundry. It is simply a matter of asking.

Of course, if you intend to stay a while in Madrid, be it for work, play or study, there are other more attractive options. *Hostal Canoa* (☎ 429 5756/6808) at Calle Silva 18 (1st floor), the women-only pensión mentioned previously, rents rooms by the month as well, with a starting price of 21,000 pta per month per person.

Places to Eat

Around Santa Ana If you are staying around Santa Ana, there is no reason to look elsewhere for good-value eats. *Restaurante Mesón Asturias* in Calle Alvarez Gato s/n has a menu for 800 pta, and at the nearby *Pizzería Il Sorriso*, Calle Nuñez del Arce 14, you can have a pizza from 650 pta. *Restaurante El Club*, at Calle de la Victoria, has a menu for 900 pta. It has great paella and is simply too good to miss.

Bar Cervecería La Plaza at Plaza Santa Ana 2 has a good selection of platos combinados, starting at 425 pta. *Restaurante Integral Artemisa* on Calle Ventura de la Vega is an excellent vegetarian restaurant, with a lunch-time menu for 950 pta (not at weekends). At Calle Nuñez de Arce 15, on the 1st floor, is a social club with an exceptionally cheap restaurant that is too good to pass up. It is open to the general public for lunch (menu 650 pta).

Other Areas Just about anywhere you go in central Madrid, you can find cheap restaurants with good food. The menu del día is often posted outside, particularly when a few places are competing with each other – just look around. For those who don't have time to look, here are a few suggestions. *Cafetería Atocha 47* at Calle Atocha 47 has a menu for 600 pta. They do platos combinados from 400 pta. *Restaurante La Villa III*, Calle de la Villa 3 (metro Opera), has a menu for 599 pta. They have a money-back guarantee if you eat better somewhere else. *Restaurante Museo del Jamón*, Paseo del Prado 44 (near Atocha), is decked out with more kinds of ham than you've ever seen. They also have a great menu for 700 pta.

For a really first-class meal in a cosy atmosphere try *Taberna del Alabardero* at Calle Felipe V 6. You should expect to pay somewhere between 3500 and 5000 pta per person. If this is a bit steep, consider trying a couple of the mouthwatering tapas at the bar in the same restaurant.

On the other side of town, *Bar Mesón O'Barquino*, Calle Francisco de Ricci 15 (metro Argüelles), has a menu for 700 pta. Not far away is a Chinese restaurant, *Palacio del Mar* at Calle de Meléndez Valdés 64, with a menu for 675 pta. *Restaurante Mas Madera*, Calle Blasco de Garay 12, and *Mesón Al-Andalus* at No 7 in the same street, have menus for 695 and 700 pta respectively. *Cafetería Cantania* on Calle Flor de la Baja (metro Plaza de España) has a menu for 750 pta at the bar, 800 pta at the table. Closer to metro Callao is *Bar Restaurante Cochifrito*, Calle Valverde 9, with a menu for 750 pta.

For cheap platos combinados try *Cafetería Elitesse* on Carrera San Jerónimo (opposite No 3). *Cafetería Los Alpes*, Calle Mayor s/n (next to No 56), has particularly large platos combinados from 800 pta, and great tapas. Not far away at *Restaurante Casa Antón*, Calle Marqués Viudo de Pontejos next to No 15, has a menu for 800 pta. *Cafetería Restaurante Virginia*, Calle Tetuan near No 2 (metro Sol), has an excellent menu for 900 pta.

Entertainment

Cinemas Cinemas have had a definite revival of late in Madrid. They are very reasonably priced, often with tickets costing no more than 350 pta. On Mondays, tickets are often especially cheap. If you want to see a film in its original language (with Spanish subtitles), check the film pages of *El País* – it lists such films under the heading *Version Original*. The following are some of the cinemas which frequently show films in their original language: *Cines Renoir* in Calle Martín de los Heros, *Cines Alphaville* next door to the Renoir, *Cines Lumiere, Cine Rosales* in Calle Ferraz – all these are near Plaza de España. In other parts of town you will find: *Cine California* in Calle Andrés Mellado (metro Moncloa), *Cines Renoir* and *Cine Alexandra* on Calle San Bernardo (metro Lavapiés) among others.

Discos Discos are outrageously expensive in Madrid. It is not uncommon to pay over 2000 pta just to get in and then 1500 pta

SPAIN

minimum per drink. On the other hand, good-looking women (determined by the public relations people) and their male companions very rarely have to pay to get in. For the truly beautiful (again to be decided by the PR people) drinks are also free. This actually appears to be official policy!

Madrid's best known discos are *Pacha*, at Calle Barceló 11, and *Joy Eslava*, at Puerto de Santa María (near Sol). Both fit snugly into the previously mentioned price range. Other popular places to flaunt your money are *Archy* (Calle Marqués de Riscal/Fortuny) and *Zenith* at Calle Conde de Xiquena 12.

Bars Centred around Plaza Dos de Mayo and encircled by the metro stations of Tribunal, Bilbao and Noviciado, the area known as Malasaña is the epicentre of Madrid when it comes to nightlife. Among the bars which are absolutely not to be missed are *La Vía Láctea*, at Calle Velarde 18, and *King Creole*, at Corredera Alta de San Pablo 17. For great music you can't go past them. *La Pollaza*, Calle San Andrés 11, gets crowded after 1 am and is yet another place with great music. *Jaque Mate* at Calle del Dos de Mayo 6 has some of the cheapest drinks in the area.

Café de Manuela, at Calle de Vicente Ferrer 29, and *Palmanegra*, at Calle Palma 11, both have a cosy atmosphere and there is often live music. Palmanegra also has a pool table. Another place for a game of pool is *El Sol de Mayo*, in the heart of it all on Plaza Dos de Mayo, and *Ellas* at Calle San Dimas 3 is a lesbian's pub.

Madrid's gay scene is in Chueca, an area approximately bordered by metros Banco and Chueca. *Rimel*, at Calle Luis de Góngora 4, and *Cruising*, at Calle Perez Galdos 5, are among the best known gay bars. *Catacumbas*, at Calle Augusto Figueroa 17, has good music and a varied crowd. *Bar el Poseidon*, Calle San Gregorio 42, is a cosy bar with varied music. Calle Pelayo has loads of gay bars as well.

Another area with a great atmosphere is Santa Ana. Most of the bars in this area are on Calle Manuel Fernandez Gonzalez, Calle Echegaray and Calle Ventura de la Vega.

Because of the high concentration of bars in a small area, it is not necessary to focus on any one bar, though *Bar Los Gabrieles*, on the corner of Echegaray and Manuel Fernandez Garcia, has outstanding décor and is a very popular place for a drink. For live jazz, you could try *Café Central* at Plaza del Angel 10.

Concerts, Theatre & Opera Madrid's most important theatre, the *Teatro Real*, is undergoing a major overhaul, and could well be closed until the end of the century. That said, the city's other cultural offerings more than compensate. The *Teatro Lírico Nacional de la Zarzuela* (☎ 429 8225), Calle Jovellanos 4, has pretty much stepped in to fill the gap left by the Teatro Real as Madrid's top opera venue. At the *Teatro Monumental* (☎ 429 1281), Calle Atocha 65, there are often classical concerts by the Spanish Radio & Television Orchestra, while at the private *Juan March Foundation* (☎ 435 4240), Calle Castelló 77, classical concerts by Spanish and international performers are the norm.

At the *Centro Cultural de la Villa* (☎ 575 6080) under the waterfall on Plaza Colón, there is an ever-changing array of offerings varying from classical concerts and opera to dramatic and comic theatre. Other places for comedy are the *Teatro Cómico* (☎ 527 4537) at Paseo de las Delicias 41, and *Teatro de la Comedia* (☎ 521 4931), Calle Príncipe 14, which is also home to the National Classical Theatre Company. Madrid's avant-garde theatre scene is at its best in the *Centro Nacional de Nuevas Tendencias* (☎ 527 4622) at Plaza de Lavapiés.

To find out what is on at these venues and others, buy a copy of *Guia de Ocio* from any news kiosk. Prices vary from show to show, but there are often very reasonably priced tickets available (from 700 pta for certain seats at some performances at the Teatro Lírico Nacional de la Zarzuela).

Spectator Sports A football (soccer) match in Spain is a definite highlight of any visit to the country. You don't need to be an aficionado to get a buzz out of the atmosphere. If you get the chance to see a match between

Madrid's two main teams, Real Madrid and Atlético Madrid, don't pass it up. Tickets can be bought on the day of the match, at either of the stadiums, with the cheapest tickets going for only 500 pta. Real Madrid's home stadium is Bernabeu. To get there, take a northbound bus No 5 from the centre. Atlético Madrid plays at Vicente Calderón south-west of the centre. Bus Nos 23, 34 and 35 will get you there.

Bullfighting is the other spectator sport most commonly associated with Spain. If you have sadistic tendencies you may even enjoy seeing the poor animals tortured and frightened before being murdered. If that is the case, Madrid and Seville are the best places to satiate your thirst for blood. There are two bullrings in Madrid – one near metro Ventas and the other by metro Vista Alegre.

Things to Buy

For general shopping needs, the best places to start at are either the markets or the large department stores. The most famous market is El Rastro, described separately in this chapter. Another market worth looking at is the Mercado Puerta de Toledo (by the metro of the same name). There are over 150 shops dedicated to design, antiques, jewellery, fashion and so on.

The best known department store is El Corte Inglés. You can find branches at Calle Preciados 3, Calle Goya 76, Calle Princesa 40 and Calle Raimundo Fernández Villaverde 79. The other big name in department stores is Galerias Preciados. There are branches at Plaza del Callao 2, Calle Goya 85, Calle Arapiles 10 and Calle Jose Ortega y Gasset 3.

For specialist purchases you have to go elsewhere. For guitars and other musical instruments, hunt around the area near the Royal Palace. For leather the best shops are on Calle Príncipe and Gran Via, and also Calle Fuencarral for shoes. For souvenirs of Madrid, try on Plaza Mayor, Puerta del Sol, Gran Via or Paseo del Prado.

Getting There & Away

Air Internal one-way fares out of Madrid are fixed throughout the year. Return fares vary according to the season. If you make sure that there is a Sunday between your flights, then a special fare applies, again with seasonal variation. The fares quoted here are low-season fares with the necessary Sunday in between. The fares apply for both Iberia and Aviaco, Spain's two domestic airlines.

Destination	One-way	Return
Málaga	12,300 pta	16,000 pta
Palma de Mallorca	14,300 pta	17,150 pta
Barcelona	13,150 pta	15,775 pta
Seville	11,475 pta	13,775 pta
Santander	10,850 pta	13,025 pta
Santiago de Compostela	13,250 pta	15,900 pta

If there is any way you can avoid it, don't buy international tickets in Spain. In the event that you have no choice, a one-way fare to London costs 57,600 pta in the low season. If you are under 25 you may be eligible for a discount of up to 65%. Ask at Iberia direct. You can also get discounted tickets from Iberojet at the airport (it works a little like stand-by).

Most of the major airline offices are on Gran Via. Following are some useful addresses:

Iberia
    Plaza Canovas 4 (☎ 587 8787)
Aviaco
    Calle Mandes 51 (☎ 534 4200)
British Airways
    Calle Serrano 60, 5th floor (☎ 900 177777; toll-free)
Continental
    Gran Via 59 (☎ 559 2520)
American Airlines
    Calle Pedro Teisera 8, 5th floor (☎ 900 100566; toll-free within Spain)

Bus There are so many bus companies, and even more possible destinations from Madrid, that there are eight bus stations in the city. The tourist office has comprehensive timetable information and can tell you which station to go to for your destination. See the Facts for the Visitor section for further information on fares.

Train Trains will take you from Madrid to

just about anywhere that is worth going to. There are three major train stations in the city. If you are headed for Salamanca, Galicia or Extremadura, your train will probably leave from Príncipe Pío Railway Station (behind the Royal Palace). If you are going north, the train will definitely pass through Chamartín Railway Station, though they often start at Atocha. If you are going south, the train almost always passes through Atocha, and often starts at Chamartín.

For information on fares, see the Getting There & Away section under the city you are going to. There is always the same number of trains per day going from Madrid to any destination as there is arriving in Madrid from that destination. For detailed timetabling or other relevant information, call the RENFE information line on ☎ 429 0202. You can also get information and buy tickets from RENFE's head office at Calle Alcalá 44.

Car & Motorbike All the major car rental companies have offices in Madrid. Atesa (☎ 241 5004), the Spanish company, is generally the best value. It is at Calle Princesa 25. Europcar (☎ 448 8706) is at Calle García de Paredes 12. There are other companies with offices along Gran Via.

You can get a good deal on motorbike rental from Moto Alquiler (☎ 242 0657), Calle Conde Duque 13. Prices start at 1200 pta a day for a 49 cc Vespino and go through to 5000 pta a day for a Yamaha 400. A fully refundable deposit is required. They also rent bicycles.

For route information see the next section.

Car Pooling A good alternative to hitching, and cheaper than buses and trains, is to pre-organise a ride to your destination. You can do this through Compartecoche (☎ 265 6565), Calle Colegiata 12.

Hitching To hitch out of Madrid you need to get well out of the centre on public transport. To Andalusia you need to get onto route E-05. Once you get south of Aranjuez, your chances of long rides improve dramatically.

Route N-401, also southbound, tends to be good for shorter rides only, particularly to Toledo. For Cuenca, Valencia and Alicante, take route E-901 and for Catalonia route E-90. Be sure to look out for the northbound road just past Medinaceli if you are heading for Soria or beyond to the Basque Country.

Route E-90 runs in the other direction, to Extremadura and Portugal. If you are heading north, route E-05 cuts the city in half and runs to Burgos, where you can branch off to Santander. This is also another option if you are bound for the Basque Country or even Paris.

Getting Around
To/From the Airport A taxi to the airport from the centre of Madrid should cost around 2000 to 3000 pta. A better option is the airport bus which leaves from under Plaza de Colón every 10 minutes. The trip takes 30 minutes and costs 250 pta.

Bus In general, you are better off using the underground (metro) to get around in Madrid, as it is faster and easier to use. There is no map of the bus routes in Madrid, and just about the only way to find out where a bus is going is to get on it – the streetside officials from the bus company don't usually know! For those destinations where bussing is the best option or a viable alternative, the bus number has been given.

Underground Madrid has a very efficient and simple underground system. Single rides cost 75 pta, but you can buy a ticket which is valid for 10 rides for 450 pta. The direction of travel is always determined by the end station on the line you are travelling on.

Taxi As always in big cities, taxis are good to have around late at night. Shared by three or four people, they can be very good value indeed. You can always find a taxi on Puerta del Sol, Gran Via and Paseo del Prado, as well as at Atocha and Chamartín stations.

Around Madrid

EL ESCORIAL

About one hour north-east of Madrid by train is the town of San Lorenzo del Escorial, or El Escorial, as it is more popularly known. The town's name has become synonymous with the monastery it is home to. El Escorial is, in fact, a part of the Community of Madrid, one of Spain's autonomous communities, and not a part of Castile as you might expect.

The monastery itself was founded by Phillip II, King of Naples, Sicily, Milan, the Netherlands and Spain. He began searching for a site to bury his father, Emperor Charles V in 1558, deciding on San Lorenzo in 1562. The last stone was placed in 1584, and the next 11 years were spent on decoration and other finishing touches. It is said to be the monument which best exemplifies the ideological and cultural ambitions of the Spanish Golden Age.

Information

The best place to collect brochures and other

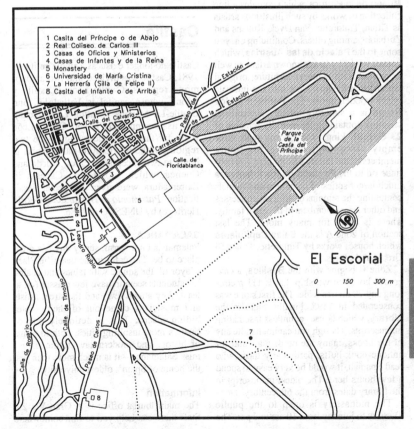

1 Casita del Príncipe o de Abajo
2 Real Coliseo de Carlos III
3 Casas de Oficios y Ministerios
4 Casas de Infantes y de la Reina
5 Monastery
6 Universidad de María Cristina
7 La Herrería (Silla de Felipe II)
8 Casita del Infante o de Arriba

El Escorial

0   150   300 m

SPAIN

tourist information on El Escorial is at one of the tourist offices in Madrid. If you are already in El Escorial when you read this, then there is an information office of sorts (more like a desk) at the monastery. Be warned, however, that you will have to pay for all but the most basic of the printed information which they can supply you with. Almost all visitors to El Escorial make it a day trip from Madrid.

Things to See & Do

The monastery at El Escorial is divided into two zones. Zone A and zone B. Starting with zone A, the first section you come to is the **Museo de la Pintura**, which contains a fine collection of works by such illustrious artists as Titian, Tintoretto, Van Dyck, Rubens and Zurbarán, among others. Continuing on, you come to the **Palacio de las Austrias**, which houses works by lesser known artists as well as period (15th century) furniture, original tapestries and maps. Note also the intricate inlaid wooden doors. The **Panteón de los Reyes** is a superbly ornate subterranean chamber containing the worldly remains of 23 Spanish kings and queens (and three empty sarcophagi waiting for future members of the family). From here you continue on to the **Panteón de los Infantes**, a much larger series of chambers and tunnels containing the remains of princes, princesses and other lesser members of the royal family. There is room for many more. The last section of zone A is the **Salas Capitulares** which houses works by Tintoretto, Titian, El Greco, and others.

Zone B begins with the **Basilica**, a cavernous house of worship that is 111 metres long and 70 metres wide. The first stone was consecrated in 1595. Finally, there is the **Library**, which houses countless fascinating manuscripts. Though you cannot handle any of the books, many are on display, and for antique book buffs, particularly those who read Spanish, it would be very easy to spend a few hours here. The oldest manuscript in the library dates from the 6th century.

The monastery is open to the public Tuesday to Sunday from 10 am to 7 pm. The general entry fee is 500 pta. Students and handicapped visitors pay 350 pta. On Wednesdays, EC citizens are admitted free on presentation of their passport. You should allow at least 2½ hours to visit the entire complex.

Getting There & Away

There are hourly buses from Madrid (metro Moncloa) to El Escorial. The trip takes around one hour, costs 600 pta return, and the bus drops you off near the monastery. Trains run with similar frequency from Madrid's Atocha Station, also taking around one hour.

Castile

Castile no longer exists as a single entity. In 1981, Castile was divided into two autonomous regions, Castile-León (Castilla y Léon), whose capital is Valladolid, and Castile-La Mancha (Castilla La Mancha), with its government in Toledo. Castile-León is by far the more interesting of the two regions, although Castile-La Mancha is home to two exceptional cities, Toledo and Cuenca, which, along with Cáceres in Extremadura, were given the special classification 'Patrimonio de Humanidad' (World Heritage) by UNESCO in 1986.

SALAMANCA

Salamanca on a warm, sunny day is a great place to be. The cafés in the beautiful Plaza Mayor fill the square with tables and chairs, the students seem to have few classes (or, at least, they attend few) and the street artists and musicians come out of their winter hiding places. This is definitely one of Spain's most inspiring cities, both in terms of history and modern-day culture. Don't miss Salamanca – it is much more than just the home of Spain's oldest university.

Information

The main tourist office is at Gran Via 29. Staff there can help you to find somewhere

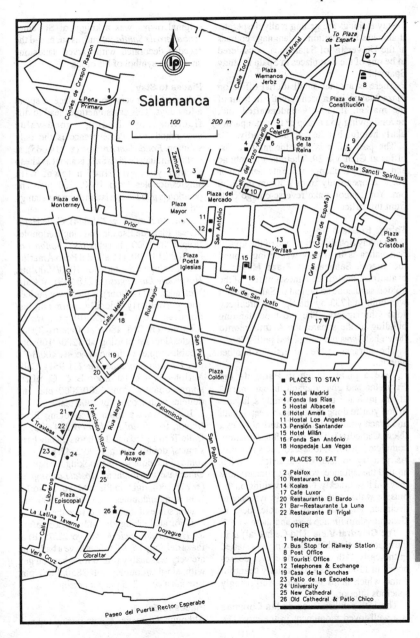

Salamanca

0   100   200 m

■ PLACES TO STAY

3   Hostal Madrid
4   Fonda las Rías
5   Hostal Albacete
6   Hotel Amefa
11 Hostal Los Angeles
13 Pensión Santander
15 Hotel Milán
16 Fonda San António
18 Hospedaje Las Vegas

▼ PLACES TO EAT

2   Palafox
10 Restaurant La Olla
14 Koalas
17 Cafe Luxor
20 Restaurante El Bardo
21 Bar–Restaurante La Luna
22 Restaurante El Trigal

OTHER

1   Telephones
7   Bus Stop for Railway Station
8   Post Office
9   Tourist Office
12 Telephones & Exchange
19 Casa de las Conchas
23 Patio de las Escuelas
24 University
25 New Cathedral
26 Old Cathedral & Patio Chico

SPAIN

to stay if things are getting really desperate. It also has information on language courses at the University of Salamanca, considered to be one of the best places in Spain to study Spanish.

There is another small tourist office on Plaza Mayor, in an arch directly in front of the market. It is very understaffed and, beyond giving you a map or two, not particularly helpful, but the staff are friendly.

The post office is near the main tourist office on Gran Via 39. There is a telephone and currency exchange office at Plaza Mayor 10. It is open daily from 9.30 am to 11.30 pm. You cannot make reverse-charge calls from this office.

Things to See & Do

As in many Spanish cities, one of the joys of Salamanca is in simply wandering around the streets. Salamanca's **Plaza Mayor** is beautiful. Constructed almost entirely of the golden sandstone so typical of Salamanca, it was built in 1733 by the Spanish architect, José Churriguera. The most outstanding building in the square, the **Ayuntamiento** (town hall) was not completed until 1755.

The entrance to the university is another wonder.

Take a picnic lunch to **Patio de las Escuelas** and give yourself time to marvel at the intricacy of the university's façade. When you're done there, take a deep breath and brace yourself for the **Catedral Nueva** (New Cathedral). This incredible structure, completed in 1733, took 220 years to build. As you try to take in the detailed relief around the entrance, you'll ask yourself how they did it so quickly. Note the writing on the outside walls. Although not always easy to decipher, you can make out references to Generalissimo Franco here and there.

The **Catedral Vieja** (Old Cathedral) is in the nearby Patio Chico. Building was started in the early 11th century and it was consecrated in 1160. It has a particularly beautiful dome which helps to create a surprisingly spacious interior.

The 15th century **Casa de las Conchas** is a well-loved monument in the city. The original owner was a knight of St James (*caballero de Santiago*) and, as such, had the façades decorated with carved sandstone shells, the symbol of his order.

Places to Stay

Salamanca is a very popular place to spend a few days. This can sometimes lead to difficulties in finding good-value accommodation. Perseverance is the only solution. *Fonda San António* (☎ 214 065), at Calle San Juan de la Cruz 9, is about as cheap as any you will find in town, with singles/doubles from 1000/1500 pta. The position is good, but it is a little on the scungy side.

Pensión Europa (☎ 221 844), Calle Heras 3, near Plaza de España, has singles/doubles from 1200/1900 pta (plus tax). *Fonda Las Rias* (☎ 213 339), at Calle del Pozo Amarillo 19, has singles/doubles for 1000/1900 pta. *Hospedaje Las Vegas* (☎ 218 749), at Calle Melendez 13 (1st floor), is pretty well priced and particularly friendly, with singles/doubles from 1000/2000 pta. *Hostal Albacete* (☎ 218 480), at Caleros 3, has singles/doubles starting at 1200/2100 pta. Doubles/triples with shower cost 2400/3400 pta. *Pensión Santander* (☎ 211 961), Calle Varillas 17-19, 1st floor B & C, offers singles/doubles from 1200/2000 pta, and doubles with shower for 2800 pta.

If you want a room overlooking Plaza Mayor, try *Hostal Madrid* (☎ 214 296), at Calle Toro 1 (2nd and 3rd floors). They have singles/doubles from 1590/2545 pta, with some of the doubles overlooking the square. Otherwise, you might try *Hostal Los Angeles* (☎ 218 166), right on Plaza Mayor at No 10, with singles/doubles from 1500/2500 pta. Again, some of their rooms face the square.

If you are looking for a little extra comfort, try *Hotel Residencia Milán* (☎ 21 7518) at Plaza del Angel 5. All rooms have a bath, and are very reasonably priced for what you get, with singles/doubles for 2850/4400 pta. Breakfast costs 275 pta per person.

Places to Eat

Although Salamanca is a university town, it

is not very easy to find cheap eats. The best place to start, for those on a really low budget, is at the excellent food market. This is conveniently situated right by Plaza Mayor, on Plaza del Mercado.

At *Palafox* on Calle de Zamora, just outside Plaza Mayor as well, there is a good selection of bocadillos with an equally wide range of prices. You can fill up on a pretty good lunch-time menu for only 700 pta at *Snack-Bar Samir* at Cuesta Sancti Spiritus 1 – a real bargain!

In the evenings you might want to try *Restaurante el Bardo*, inside the Casa de las Conchas, for a vegetarian menu at 800 pta. Another vegetarian restaurant with similar prices is *Restaurante el Trigal* at Calle Libreros 20. For a choice of carnivorous menus try *Bar Restaurante La Luna* just down the road at Calle Libreros 4. They have menus for 750, 1300 and 1900 pta. For a slightly more expensive treat try *Restaurante la Olla* near Plaza Mayor at Plaza del Mercado 2. The menu costs 2200 pta and you can eat well à la carte from around 3000 pta.

Entertainment

When the university is in session, the nightlife in Salamanca is bound to please. Most of the places to be seen at are on or around Gran Via. Among the spots worth going to are *Koalas* at Gran Via 63. It is, of course, a must for homesick Aussies, and as the day grows old, this place really begins to move. Nearby is *Cafe Bar Leonardo* at Gran Via 64 which is good for late-night bocadillos. Opposite Leonardo is the very laid-back *Cafe Moderno*.

If you want to get off Gran Via, make sure you see the amazing décor at *Cafe Luxor*, a little way to the east up Calle de San Justo from Gran Via. Also try the unnamed, rather 'aromatic' bar at Calle Varillas 15, which has an interesting mix of punk and rockabilly clientele.

Getting There & Away

Among the numerous destinations with direct train or bus connections to Salamanca, are Madrid (usually via Ávila), Santiago de Compostela, Santander, and Cáceres.

Bus There are up to 25 buses to Madrid every day, with the first one running at 6 am. They take between 2½ and 3½ hours to complete the journey, depending on the route and the type of bus. The fare is 1455/2630 pta one-way/return. Express buses are around 20% more expensive.

The easiest way to get to Santiago is by bus. Departures for the seven-hour-plus trip are at 5.05 and 10 am and 4.30 pm. The fare is 2540/4845 pta one-way/return.

There is a bus to Cáceres at 9.30 am every morning. On weekdays there are also buses at 6.40 and 11.30 am, 3.30 and 5.30 pm. On Friday there is an additional bus at 7 pm, and on Sunday there is a bus at 5 pm. The Cáceres trip takes three to four hours. The fare is 1455/2625 one-way/return.

Train The basic train fare to Madrid (Príncipe Pio Station) is 1470/2325 pta one-way/return. There are only four trains a day, all taking 3½ hours or more.

If you really want to take the long train trip to Santiago, change in León or Venta de Baños. To get to Santander you need to change trains in Valladolid. Departures from Salamanca are at 7 and 8.49 am, 4.25 and 10.10 pm. The basic fare is 1785/3770 pta one-way/return.

Getting Around

The only time you will need public transport in Salamanca is for getting to or from the train or bus station. Bus No 1 stops on Gran Via, near the post office and has its terminus at the train station.

The bus station is at Avenida Filiberto Villalobos 85. To get there, take bus No 4 from the corner where Plaza Mayor, Plaza del Mercado and Plaza Poeta Iglesias meet. There is a bus stop directly opposite the bus station.

The fixed price for bus rides is 60 pta.

LEÓN

León is far too often left off travellers' itin-

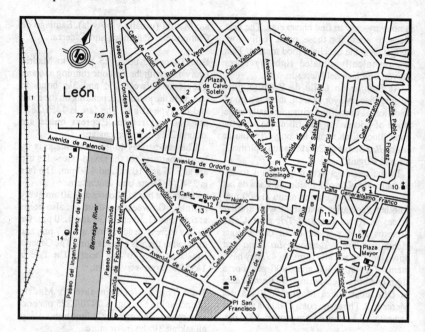

León

0   75   150 m

1   RENFE Railway Station
2   Churreria
3   Camas Florez
4   Pensión Oviedo
5   Hotel Riosol
6   Pensión Americana
7   Casa de Botines
8   Restaurante Bodega Regia
9   Tourist Office
10   Cathedral of Santa Maria
11   Market
12   Telephone Office
13   Restaurante del Fuero
14   Long-Distance Bus Station
15   Post Office
16   Restaurante La Cepedana
17   Pensión Puerta del Sol

eraries. For those who make the effort to get here, a surprisingly fresh and pleasant city awaits. It's a city of long, wide boulevards, open squares, an excellent nightlife and,

among the monuments, even some Gaudí architecture.

There are very friendly staff at the tourist office, which is under the arcades, directly in front of the main entrance to the cathedral. The telephone office, open from 9 am to 2 pm and 4.30 to 9.30 pm is at Burgo Nuevo 15. León's telephone code is 987.

Things to See & Do

León's **cathedral**, built primarily in the 13th and 14th centuries, is a wonder of Gothic architecture. The most outstanding feature of the cathedral is its breathtaking stained glass. Make sure you look at them from the inside, as from outside it is difficult to appreciate their beauty fully. Opening hours are from 9 am to 1 pm and 4 to 6 pm.

Plaza Mayor in the old town, a short distance to the south of the cathedral, is a little run-down, but this is part of its romance. It is also the heart of León's buzzing nightlife. Just head down the side streets toward the music – south is more alternative and west is the mainstream.

Antonio Gaudí's most famous works are, of course, in Barcelona. He left his mark in very few places outside that city, and León is one of the few places to be so blessed. His work is immediately recognisable in **Casa de Botines** on Plaza San Marcelo, although it is almost conservative by his Catalonian standards. Sadly, it is also closed to the public.

There is more of Gaudí's work in the nearby town of Astorga, south-west of Léon. The **Episcopal Palace**, which he built there in 1889, is now home to the museum of the pilgrims' route to Santiago. This building is much more typical of Gaudí as he is known in Barcelona. To visit the interior, you must pay the 200 pta museum entry fee. Even if the museum doesn't interest you, the interior is too good to miss.

Places to Stay

There is plenty of budget accommodation to be found in León. Most of the cheaper places are on or around Avenida de Ordoño II. In addition, there are a few places on Avenida de Roma and a couple of others down around Plaza Mayor in the old town. *Pensión Americana* (☎ 251 654), Avenida de Ordoño II 25, is run by two very modern old women. Singles/doubles go for 1200/2200 pta. *Pensión Oviedo* (☎ 222 236), at Avenida de Roma 26 (2nd floor), has singles/doubles from 1400/2500 pta. *Pensión Puerta del Sol* (☎ 211 966), at Calle Puerta del Sol 1 (2nd floor), is about as cheap as León gets with singles/doubles from 1000/1900 pta.

Accommodation outside the lower budget range is hard to come by, unless you want to splurge and stay at the magnificent 15th century *Parador de San Marcos* (☎ 237 300) at Plaza de San Marcos 7. With the most basic singles/doubles costing 14,000/20,000 pta, however, this is out of reach for many tourists. A slightly better option is the three-star *Hotel Riosol* (☎ 216 650) near the railway station at Avenida de Palencia 3. Singles/doubles/triples/quads go for 5300/8300/11,205/14,006 pta.

Places to Eat

You shouldn't have too much trouble finding cheap eats in León either. If you are in the old town, a couple of no-frills places worth looking out for are *La Cepedana* and *Casa Lorenzo*. Both are at Calle Mariano Dominguez, Berrueta 9, and both have menus for 700 pta. La Cepedana has a considerably larger choice. At the other end of town, *Meson Restaurante El Fuero*, at Calle del Fuero 7, is excellent value with a menu for 650 pta. A good place for breakfast is the *Churreria* at Calle Colón 8.

For a really good meal in a cosy atmosphere, you can't go past *Restaurante Bodega Regia* (☎ 213 173) at Calle General Mola 5. They have a menu for 1500 pta, and you can eat really well à la carte from around 2500 pta. The restaurant has won a number of national and international awards for quality and presentation of food. It is very popular, so it might be a good idea to reserve a table in advance.

Getting There & Away

Bus To get to León's bus station from the city centre, cross the river and turn left. It is about five minutes' walk along the river bank. Nonexpress buses for the 4½-hour bus ride to Madrid leave at 8 and 10.15 am, 3.30 and 6 pm. The fare is 2120 pta one-way. The fare to Astorga is 325 pta one-way, with the first bus leaving León at 9 am, the last at 8.30 pm and six buses in between.

Train There are numerous trains connecting León to Madrid every day. The trip takes around five hours and the basic fare is 2625/4160 pta one-way/return. The only direct connection to a major coastal city is with Gijon. There are eight trains a day which cover the distance in around three hours. The basic fare is 1070/1695 pta one-way/return.

Car For drivers and hitchhikers, León is situated on a major intersection. Route N-630 runs all the way from Gijon to Seville, via León, Salamanca and Cáceres. Route N-601 runs from Madrid to León, via Segovia and Valladolid. Finally, León is on the Camino de Santiago, the ancient pilgrims' route which runs all the way from southern France (and, theoretically, from Jerusalem) to Santiago de Compostela.

ÁVILA

Ávila is an extremely well-preserved walled city. In all, the walls are almost three km long with 90 turrets. The city has nine gates, the most beautiful of which are the gates of San Vicente and the gate of the Alcázar.

The telephone code for Ávila is 918.

Things to See & Do

Inside the walls, the most interesting monument is undoubtedly the 12th century **cathedral**, constructed from stone of an unusual, almost pink, colouring. Note the 14th century baptismal font to the left as you come through the main entrance.

A short distance outside the walls is the 16th century **Casa de los Deanes**. Today this is in use as the provincial museum and is well worth a visit. It contains an interesting ethnological collection and a number of regional archaeological finds. The real attractions here, however, are the temporary exhibitions. Unfortunately, they only occur two or three times a year, but if you're lucky you will be treated to a display of some very high-quality work by modern local artists. Keep your fingers crossed. Either way, the museum is worth the 200 pta entry fee.

For the best view of the city and its perfectly preserved walls, you have to head out of town on the Salamanca road. There is an observation platform around 2½ km from the city gates, along this road.

In the province of Ávila there are a number of towns well worth visiting. Of particular interest are **Arévalo** and **Mombeltrán**. In Arévalo, among other monuments, are two ancient churches, San Martín and Santa María (on the verge of collapse), both with Mudéjar towers.

Finally, if you are in the region in October, don't miss the Festival of Santa Teresa (October 8 to 15). This is particularly fun in the capital itself. Semana Santa is also a hot tip in Ávila.

Places to Stay & Eat

Most people make Ávila a day trip from Madrid, but there is no reason not to stay longer. *Hostal Las Cancelas* (☎ 212 249), at Calle Cruz Vieja 6, has singles/doubles from 2120/3710 pta. The two-star *Hostal El Rastro* (☎ 211 218), at Plaza del Rastro 1, is a great deal with doubles from 3710 pta. Unfortunately, there are no singles.

Restaurante Los Leales, at Plaza de Italia 4, has a good menu for only 725 pta, though downstairs doesn't always smell too good. *El Zamorano*, at Calle El Tostado 10, is only slightly more expensive and just as tasty, with a menu for 650 pta.

Getting There & Away

There are around 40 trains a day to Madrid. The basic fare is 795/1260 pta one-way/return, and the trip takes less than two hours.

The bus to Segovia leaves at 7.10 and 11.30 am, 12.45, 4.15 and 6.30 pm every weekday. The 11.30 am bus also runs on weekends.

SEGOVIA

Segovia is one of the precious few cities in Spain to have been classified on the UNESCO World Heritage list. The city has been inhabited for literally thousands of years. It was conquered by the Romans a number of years before Christ was born. The Visigoths and the Moors also left their mark on Segovia before the city finally ended up in Christian hands in the 11th century. Segovia's most awesome symbol is its enormous and magnificently preserved aqueduct, left by the Romans all those years ago.

The telephone code for Segovia is 911.

Things to See & Do

You can't help but see the aqueduct. It is over 800 metres long with 165 arches. The dates are a little hazy, but it was probably built around the end of the 2nd century BC.

The aqueduct is by no means all that Segovia has to offer. The 16th century

Gothic **cathedral** is in the very pretty main square. The first thing that catches your attention when you go inside is how bright it is. As it has a very high ceiling and no transepts, the sheer volume is quite overwhelming.

Perched on a craggy clifftop, Segovia's **Alcázar**, with its turrets, towers and spires, is a fairy-tale castle. While it has been there for many centuries, the Alcázar was severely damaged by fire last century, leaving only the towers fully intact. All the same, it is a beautiful building with magnificent views. A number of the rooms in the castle are open to the public, and there is a guided tour included in the entry fee of 200 pta. Particularly interesting, for some, will be the collection of medieval weapons. There is also a number of superb stained-glass windows, but above all, it is just plain fun to be wandering around in a castle just like the ones you imagined when you were a child.

If you have wheels, or hitching time, consider a side trip to the **Castillo de Coca** in Coca, north-west of Segovia. One of the best known castles in Spain, this pink-granite building dates from the 15th century. It is now in use as a forestry school. Guided tours are conducted on demand by the students, providing they do not have class at the time. Keeping this in mind, the best time to visit is during lunch or after 5 pm. The tours cost as much or as little as you want to pay (but please be generous).

Places to Stay

Finding somewhere to stay in Segovia is no mean feat. However, if you get lucky, it is certainly not expensive. *Pension Aragón* (☎ 433 527), right on the main square (Plaza Mayor) at No 4, has singles/doubles, with the going rate starting at 1000/2000 pta. *Casa de Huéspedes Ferri* (☎ 430 544), at Calle Escuderos 10, attracts a young clientele and has singles/doubles from 1000/1800 pta. A little way out of Segovia, on the road to La Granja, is *Camping Acueducto*. The price is a standard 475 pta per person, car and tent. In the event that you can't find anywhere to stay in Segovia, it may be worth your while driving past the camp site and on to La Granja. It has a few cheap pensiones, and the nightlife is considerably better than that in Segovia.

Getting There & Away

There are around 10 trains a day to Madrid. The trip takes about two hours, with a basic fare of 675/1070 pta one-way/return. There are also nine buses a day to Madrid, the first one leaving at 6.45 am. To Ávila, there are buses at 7.45 am, 1.30 and 5.30 pm.

CUENCA

Cuenca's setting is hard to believe. The old town, which is the city's real attraction, is cut off from the rest of the city by the Jucar and Huecar rivers. There are about half a dozen bridges across the Huecar, and a road running around the base of the steep rise on which the old city is built. By the time you come to the last of these bridges, you'll find Cuenca sitting at the top of a deep gorge, with its most famous monuments teetering on the edge – a photographer's delight.

Cuenca's tourist office is quite difficult to find. Persevere, as it is there. The address is Calle Dalmacio García Izcara 8 (1st floor), and the building is on the corner of Calle Fermín Caballero.

The telephone code for Cuenca is 966.

Things to See & Do

The so-called **Casas Colgadas**, or Hanging Houses, are Cuenca's number one attraction. These houses are precariously positioned on a clifftop, with their balconies literally hanging over the gorge. They were originally built in the 15th century, and after the original owner died, they served as Cuenca's town hall for over two centuries. They have since been through various renovations, the last in 1978, when the balconies were fully rebuilt so as to resemble the original façade. The fame of these spectacular buildings is such that a footbridge across the gorge was built especially to allow visitors to gain a better view from the other side.

Inside the Casas Colgadas is the **Museo de Arte Abstracto Español**. The collection

SPAIN

is made up of works by the Spanish 'abstract generation', a group of artists who were particularly active in the 1950s. The museum was set up by one of these artists, and later donated to a private organisation which still runs it today. Credited both nationally and internationally, it's an exciting collection not to be missed. Opening hours are Tuesday to Friday from 11 am to 2 pm and 4 to 6 pm, Saturday 11 am to 2 pm and 4 to 8 pm, and Sunday 11 am to 2.30 pm. The entry fee is 200 pta (100 pta for ISIC holders).

Nearby is a very different museum, the **Museo Diocesano**. The contrast to its wild neighbour is too much for some to handle in one day, but it is also well worth visiting. It contains a beautiful collection of textiles, tapestries and religious art and artefacts dating as far back as the 13th century. Among the works exhibited are two by El Greco. The entry fee is 100 pta.

As you wander around the beautiful streets of the old town, there are a few other monuments and attractions to look out for. Among these are the **Torre de Mangana**, the remains of a **Moorish fortress** in a square overlooking the plain below, and the **Archaeological Museum**.

Thirty-five km from Cuenca is the bizarre **Ciudad Encantada**, or Enchanted City. This 'city' is the result of a geological phenomenon which left unusually shaped rocks strewn around what is today a private property. Many of the rocks have names which refer to their shape – crocodile and elephant fighting, mushrooms, roller coaster, and many more. If you have a car, it is worth the trip; the scenery on the way is great and the Ciudad Encantada itself makes a wonderful playground – a must if you are with kids. The only other way to get there is to hitch. It could be slow going on the way up, as there is not much traffic, but on the way back it shouldn't be too difficult. Either way, make sure you take your own food and drink with you, as the café up there is a first-class rip-off.

Places to Stay & Eat
Most of the cheaper accommodation is in the new town. The best place to start looking is

on and around Calle Ramón y Cajal, which runs from very near the train station to the edge of the old town. *Hospedaría San Isidro* (☎ 211 163), at Calle Ramón y Cajal 33 and *Hostal del Pilar* (☎ 211 684) at No 35, have singles/doubles from 1500/2000 pta. *Hostal Alaska* (☎ 212 323), at Calle Hurtado de Mendoza 3 (1st floor), has singles/doubles from 1375/2135 pta.

For good-value eats try *Bar El Tata* at Calle del 18 de Julio 4. They have a menu for 700 pta, as well as some good, cheap main courses. Otherwise, you might have luck on and around Calle Fermín Caballero near the train and bus stations.

Entertainment
Nightlife is a little limited, but if you want to rage, all is not lost. Go for a late evening walk along Avenida de la República Argentina and you'll stumble across most of the nightspots. There are also a few bars in Calle San Francisco, off Calle Ramón y Cajal.

Getting There & Away
The easiest way to get to Madrid is by bus, because if you go by train you will have to change in Aranjuez. There are buses at 8 am, 2.30, 4.30 and 6.30 pm every day. There is also an extra bus at 10.30 am on weekdays, and 8 pm every day except Saturday.

There is one bus a day to Teruel, departing at 7 am, and one to Barcelona at 9.30 am. You can take a bus to Valencia half an hour later.

TOLEDO
Toledo is magnificent. It is also expensive. Tourism has hurt Toledo as it has no other inland town. Although there is no doubt that the city must be visited, it can be most frustrating trying to avoid the busloads which arrive from Madrid every morning. It is strongly recommended that you spend at least a couple of days here, as, after the buses have headed north in the evening, you can enjoy the street and café life without continually being assailed by batteries of 'My God! Martha, isn't that beautiful!', 'This way

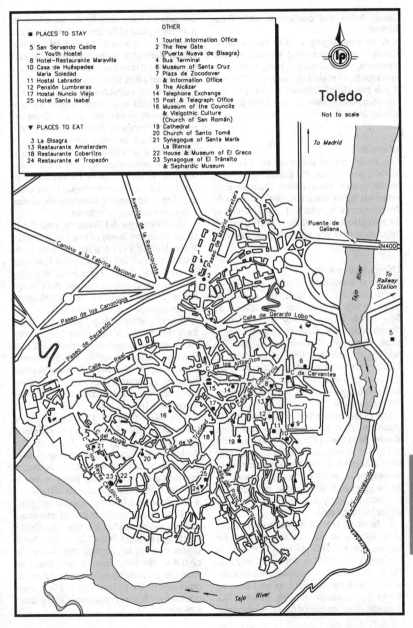

■ PLACES TO STAY

5 San Servando Castle
  – Youth Hostel
8 Hotel–Restaurante Maravilla
10 Casa de Huéspedes
   Maria Soledad
11 Hostal Labrador
12 Pensión Lumbreras
17 Hostal Nuncio Viejo
25 Hotel Santa Isabel

▼ PLACES TO EAT

3 La Bisagra
13 Restaurante Amsterdam
18 Restaurante Cobertizo
24 Restaurante el Tropezón

OTHER

1 Tourist Information Office
2 The New Gate
  (Puerta Nueva de Bisagra)
4 Bus Terminal
6 Museum of Santa Cruz
7 Plaza de Zocodover
  & Information Office
9 The Alcázar
14 Telephone Exchange
15 Post & Telegraph Office
16 Museum of the Councils
   & Visigothic Culture
   (Church of San Román)
19 Cathedral
20 Church of Santo Tomé
21 Synagogue of Santa María
   La Blanca
22 House & Museum of El Greco
23 Synagogue of El Tránsito
   & Sephardic Museum

Toledo

Not to scale

To Madrid

Puente de
Galiana

N400

To
Railway
Station

Tajo River

Paseo de Madrid Carretera

Avenida de la Reconquista

Camino a la Fabrica Nacional

Paseo de los Canonigos

Paseo de Recaredo

Calle Real

Calle de Gerardo Lobo

C. de los Alfileritos

Calle Comercio

C. de Cervantes

Calle de la Trinidad

C. del Angel

Calle de los Reyes Catolicos

Calle de la Circunvalación

Calle de la podra amarga

Tajo River

SPAIN

please, ladies and gentlemen' and 'Wunderschön!'.

A warning: if you wish to take in all of Toledo's most interesting monuments and museums, you will need to budget carefully. You should set aside a minimum of 2000 pta. If you can afford it, make it 3000 pta. In a few places, discounts are available to ISIC holders but this is not the rule.

Information

The main tourist office is on Paseo de Madrid, just outside the Bisagra gate at the northern end of the old town. Far more convenient is the information booth on Plaza de Zocodover, in the centre of town. Neither of the two places is particularly useful, though they can supply you with adequate maps.

Things to See & Do

Toledo is absolutely jammed with sights. Apart from the city itself, the undoubted highlight is to be found inside the **Iglesia de San Tomé**. This otherwise inconspicuous church contains El Greco's greatest masterpiece, *Burial of the Conde de Orgaz*. The painting depicts the burial of the count in 1322, by Sts Stephen and Augustin. They are observed by a heavenly entourage including such personages as Noah, St Peter, Jesus and the Virgin Mary.

One of the most important collections of El Greco's work in Spain can be viewed in the **Museo de la Santa Cruz**. *La Asunción* is the undisputed masterpiece of the collection. Note also *La Sagrada Familia*. During cleaning of the painting in the 1980s, San José appeared in the background to the surprise and delight of all concerned. Entry is free to ISIC holders, 200 pta for everyone else.

El Greco's House & Museum is trumpeted as one of the city's highlights. Be warned that the 200 pta entry fee (free to foreigners under 21) is not really worth it. The house contains a small selection of some of the artist's minor works, as well as some works by Bassano, among others. The museum, in an annexe of the same premises, contains 14 fairly sketchy works, which are not very typical of El Greco. To top it all off, the house is rumoured to be a fake: it was simply decorated in the style of El Greco's era. At best it may have belonged to the man who rented other premises to the artist.

Entry to the **cathedral** is free to all. Unfortunately, there is a catch. There are nine minimuseums in various annexes. To see any of the collections in these so-called private rooms, which include, among others, a number of works by El Greco, you have to pay an all-encompassing entry fee of some 350 pta. While you're in the cathedral, be sure to note the souvenir market in the cloisters. Someone seems to have forgotten Jesus' attitude to markets in temples.

The **Sinagoga del Tránsito**, near the El Greco Museum, is one of two left in Toledo. It was built in 1357 and handed over to the Catholic church in 1492, when the Jews were expelled from Spain. There is an interesting museum that examines the history of Jewish culture in Spain prior to 1492. Entry to the synagogue and museum costs 200 pta.

Toledo's other synagogue, **Santa María de la Blanca**, dates back to the 12th century. Although it is considerably smaller than the first synagogue, it is architecturally the more interesting of the two, with arches and columns supporting the roof in a fashion reminiscent of the Mezquita in Cordova. The entry fee is 100 pta.

The **Museum of the Councils & Visigoth Culture** is a haven for anthropology and archaeology buffs. The interior of the building, which is a total smorgasbord of architectural and artistic styles, is at least as interesting as the exhibits. Entry is free to ISIC holders, otherwise it costs 100 pta.

The **Alcázar** is Toledo's number one landmark. It has been the scene of numerous military sieges and battles, from the Middle Ages right through to the 20th century, when it was overrun by Republicans during the civil war. The best views of the Alcázar are from the grounds of the youth hostel on the other side of the river. Inside is a very comprehensive military museum. Entry costs 125 pta.

Places to Stay

The nearest camp site is *Circo Romano*, at Calle Circo Romano 21. It is quite reasonably priced but, unlike at the youth hostel, there is a charge for use of the swimming pool.

Toledo's *youth hostel* is one of the few in Spain which deserves a special mention. It is in San Servando Castle, to the east of the city across the Tajo River (up the hill from the train station). It is open all year except for a one-week break either before or after Semana Santa (the Easter week).

Cheap accommodation in the city itself is not easy to come by, and is usually full. All the same, there are a few places worth trying. Among them, *Casa de Huéspedes Maria Soledad* on Calle de Pascuales s/n, must be close to the best value in Toledo with singles/doubles from 950/1500 pta. The *Hostal Nuncio Viejo* (☎ 228 178), at Calle Nuncio Viejo 19, has singles/doubles from 1700/2100 pta. *Pensión Lumbreras* (☎ 221 571), Calle Juan Labrador 7, and *Hostal Labrador* (☎ 222 620), Calle Juan Labrador 16, have singles/doubles from 1300/1800 pta and 1750/2100 pta respectively.

Hotel Santa Isabel (☎ 253 136), Calle Santa Isabel 24, is well situated near the cathedral, and yet away from the tourist masses – finally a quiet spot! Pleasant singles/doubles cost 3500/5250 pta. Parking space is available for 585 pta a day. *Hotel Maravilla* (☎ 223 300), in a similar category, is right in the thick of it at Plaza de Barrio Rey 7 only a few metres from Plaza de Zocodover. It has air-conditioned rooms for 2512/4388 pta in the low season, 3657/6249 pta in the high season, and 3042/5326 pta the rest of the year.

Places to Eat

When you get hungry, look out for *Bar El Tropezón* at Travesía de Santa Isabel 2, with two delicious menus for 875 and 950 pta. *Restaurante Amsterdam* at Plaza de la Magdalena 5, has a menu for 1300 pta, and *La Bisagra* at Calle Arrabal 14, does platos combinados for under 600 pta and a menu for 800 pta.

The restaurant in Hotel Maravilla has an excellent reputation for seafood. They have a menu for 1700 pta. À la carte should cost around 3000 pta. Another place to go for quality eating is *Restaurant El Cobertizo*, Calle Hombre de Palo 9, which also specialises in seafood. The menu costs 1600 pta, but if you eat à la carte expect to pay around 3500 pta.

Getting There & Away

Almost everyone using public transport to get here arrives here from Madrid. There are around 10 trains every day from Atocha, with most of them starting at Chamartín. The trip takes a little over an hour, with a basic fare of 570/900 pta one-way/return.

There is a freeway under construction (route N-401) which will link Toledo directly with Madrid. Until that is completed, you will have to follow the N-400 as far as Aranjuez, before turning off to Madrid. The N-400 continues on to Cuenca. Route N-403 runs to Ávila, where you can turn off to Salamanca. If you're headed for Andalusia, route N-401 southbound is well and truly completed, and will take you as far as Ciudad Real.

Catalonia

Catalonia (Catalunya in Catalan, Cataluña in Spanish) is the wealthiest autonomous region in Spain. The Catalans speak a distinct language, Catalan, and do not consider themselves Spanish. Their region has so much to offer the visitor that you could easily spend your entire trip to Spain here, without ever entering a Spanish-speaking region. Apart from Barcelona, there are cities such as Tarragona, with its fine archaeological museum and Roman ruins, and Sitges, with Spain's most forthright gay community and a carnival to challenge Rio de Janeiro's. Figueras in the north has the Salvador Dali Museum, surely one of the most bizarre art galleries in Europe.

SPAIN

BARCELONA

Barcelona has always had the advantage over Madrid in that it lies closer to France and is on the coast. For all the problems associated with the Olympic Games in 1992, Barcelona has finally taken its rightful place on the list of the world's great cities. Barcelona's most famous son, Antonio Gaudí, has left his mark all over the city with his inspiring and unique architecture: the Sagrada Familia church and Güell park, among others, but there is so much more to Barcelona – world-class museums such as the Picasso and Miró museums, a fine old quarter in the Barri Gotic and a night scene as good as anywhere in the country. If you only visit one city in Spain, it probably should be Barcelona.

Orientation

Barcelona's main street, Las Ramblas, runs north-east from the harbour to Plaça de Catalunya, the most important square in the city. On the east side of Las Ramblas is the old town, or Barri Gotic, while in the streets on the west side are numerous budget restaurants. Continuing north-west from Plaça de Catalunya on Rambla de Catalunya or Passeig de Gràcia, you cross Gran Via de les Corts Catalanes (often referred to simply as Gran Via), where the main tourist office is, and then continue on to Avinguda Diagonal, the main east-west thoroughfare. To the north is the suburb of Gracia, and to the west Eixample, with the main train station, Barcelona Sants, still farther west.

Information

The main tourist office in Barcelona is at Gran Via 658, open from 9 am to 7 pm, with no lunch break (Saturday 9 am to 2 pm). The staff there are extremely helpful and have at hand a great deal of useful information on just about any aspect of the city. There is a smaller office at Barcelona Sants, the main train station. It can supply you with maps and hotel lists when you first arrive. There is another small information booth at the airport, but apart from the most basic services, it is not much use. There is a youth

tourist office (☎ 302 0682) at Carrer Gravina 1. It is pretty good on budget travel and accommodation information, but you can expect long queues.

There is a 24-hour pharmacy at Passeig de Gràcia 71. It also has a bar and billiard tables, should you have an early morning urge.

Money Most banks charge a commission of around 200 to 500 pta when changing travellers' cheques. Note that the charge is per transaction and not per cheque. American Express charges a flat rate of 2%. The rates are often pretty good at El Corte Inglés department store on Plaça de Catalunya and on Avinguda Diagonal, by metro María Cristina. The exchange office there is also open later than the banks.

Post & Telecommunications The main post office is on Plaça d'Antoni López. It is open Monday to Friday from 9 am to 2 pm and 5 to 8 pm, Saturday from 9 am to 2 pm. Poste restante is called lista de correos.

There is an international telephone centre on Plaça de Catalunya, on the corner of Carrer Fontanella. There are telephones in the Corte Inglés department stores on Plaça de Catalunya and Avinguda Diagonal, by metro María Cristina. You cannot make reverse-charge calls from these. For information on making reverse-charge calls, see the Facts for the Visitor section in this chapter. Barcelona's telephone code is 93.

Emergency The police presence in Spain is, at times, a little disconcerting. However, when you do need assistance it can be an advantage, as there may be an officer nearby. In the event that you cannot find one, call ☎ 019. In spring and summer there is a tourist police number as well: ☎ 317 6016.

Dangers & Annoyances The section of Las Ramblas, between the port and Plaça Reial, does not feel safe, and the closer you get to the harbour, the seedier it gets. The streets to the south of this section of Las Ramblas are known as the Barrio Xinés. This area has a reputation for violence, so the best thing to do is keep away late at night.

Among the annoyances specific to Barcelona are the drug dealers on Plaça Reial. It is all very well if you want to do some shopping, but the incessant hissing of 'hachís' can drive you to distraction. Also be very wary of street gambling, in particular the ball and three-cup game. The guys making money out of this racket are first-class sleight-of-hand merchants.

Things to See

Barcelona is well known for the modernist architecture of Antonio Gaudí and others. Although this period has made Barcelona truly unique, there is much more on offer. Some of the most exciting modern art in Spain, a beautiful old Gothic quarter and a fine waterfront promenade by the 1992 Olympic village, not to mention a nonstop night scene, have all helped to secure Barcelona's place among Europe's great cities.

Sagrada Familia Construction on Gaudí's principal work and Barcelona's most famous attraction (at metro Sagrada Familia) was started in 1882. Building is still underway today, and most estimates do not reckon on completion for another 20 years. Many feel that it should never be completed but rather left as a monument to the master, whose career was cut short when he was hit by a tram in 1926.

Today there are eight towers, all over 100 metres high. Gaudí had intended to build 18, representing the 12 Apostles, the four Evangelists and the mother of God, with the tallest tower (170 metres) standing for her son. Although there is still much work to do, the awesome dimensions and extravagant, yet well-proportioned, sculpting of the towers and outer walls make the Sagrada Familia one of Barcelona's highlights.

You can climb a spiral staircase right up into the towers (400 steps) for an overview of the interior and good views to the sea, or you can opt out and take a lift some of the way up, for 100 pta. There is a small museum

under the building with models, plans and photos, showing various stages of the building from the early days through to the present and, of course, the completed version. Entry to the Sagrada Familia compound is 400 pta with no exceptions. It is open from 9 am to 8 pm.

Parc Güell This park represents Gaudí at his best. The perfect combination of architecture and art with nature leads one to feel that the park grew here. As you pass through the gate you enter a fantasy land.

The main gate, which has the appearance of Hansel and Gretel's gingerbread house, sets the mood of the entire park, with winding paths and carefully tended flower beds, skewed tunnels with rough stone arches and the famous lizard of broken glass and tiles. The house in which Gaudí lived from 1906 until his untimely death in 1926 is in the grounds of the park, and is open to the public Sunday to Friday from 10 am to 2 pm and 4 to 6 pm. If you miss Parc Güell, you will have missed a part of the essence of Barcelona.

To get to the park, take a metro to Vallarca, then walk to Baixada de la Gloria. There is an escalator right to the top – a real breath saver, and in itself a very strange sight. From the escalator, it is an easy five to 10-minute walk to the park.

More Modernism The Passeig de Gràcia and its surrounds is a veritable modernist heaven. Though the best known examples of modernist work are by Gaudí, he was by no means the only talented exponent. Places to look for are **Casa Batló**, **La Pedrera**, and **Casa Vicens**, all on Passeig de Gràcia. Any of the sugar candy houses around Casa Batló are bound to please your sense of the unexpected. **Casa Calvet** on Carrer de Carp is another fine building, and the **Palau de Música** on Carrer d'Amadeu (by Domenic Montaner) is one of the most imposing modernist buildings in the city. **Palau Güell**, on Carrer Nou de la Rambla, just off Las Ramblas at the harbour end, was Gaudí's first major work, built from 1886 to 1888.

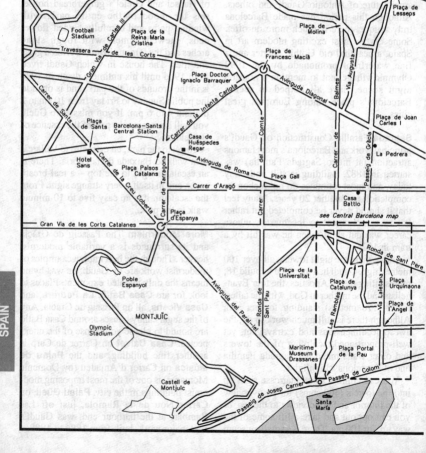

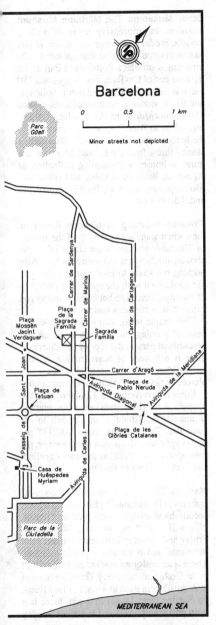

Barcelona

0   0.5   1 km

Minor streets not depicted

Parc Güell

Plaça Mossèn Jacint Verdaguer

Plaça de la Sagrada Família

Sagrada Família

Carrer de Sardenya

Carrer de Marina

Carrer de Cartagena

Avinguda de la Meridiana

Carrer d'Aragó

Plaça de Pablo Neruda

Plaça de Tetuan

Avinguda Diagonal

Plaça de les Glòries Catalanes

Sant Joan

Passeig de Sant Joan

Avinguda de Carles I

Casa de Huéspedes Myriam

Parc de la Ciutadella

MEDITERRANEAN SEA

Gaudí also left his mark in a few places outside the centre. The **Collegi de les Teresianes**, on Carrer de Ganduxer (Les Tres Torres Station), is less eccentric than a lot of his other works, but is still one of the city's architectural masterpieces. It is open to the public on Saturday mornings only. In **Finca Güell**, on Avinguda de Pedralbes and Passeig dels Tiller (metro Palau Reial), Gaudí has combined Catalan Gothic with Oriental architecture in his own unique fashion. A few blocks away on Passeig de Manuel Girona is a wall built by Gaudí.

Picasso Museum The museum on Carrer de Montcada houses the most important collection of Picasso's work in Spain. Many of the works in the collection were donated to the museum by the artist in 1970, and although there are plans to extend the collection to include some of his better known works, little has been done in that respect to date.

Among the works displayed are a number of rare ceramics. The precubist era is well represented and includes fine miniatures, self portraits and even a cut-out dog and dove behind glass. There is an interesting variety of works from the blue period (1901 to 1904), when Picasso began to be a little more experimental with his work, and there is an all-too-small selection of wonderful cubist work.

The museum is open Tuesday to Saturday from 9 am to 2 pm and 4 to 8.30 pm, and Sunday from 9 am to 2 pm. Entry is always free to ISIC holders and to the general public on Sunday. The rest of the time the entry fee is 400 pta. Don't take any photos unless you want to give one of the guards a heart attack.

Montjuïc Once the home to Barcelona's largest Jewish community, the hill of Montjuïc is now jammed with museums, convention and exposition centres, the 1992 **Olympic Stadium**, a castle containing a **military museum**, and an entire life-size **model of a Spanish village**. The Fira de Barcelona, built for the 1929 International Fair, consists of a number of enormous buildings primarily used for expositions. They line the Avinguda de la Reina María Cristina, which leads from Plaça de Espanya directly to the **Museu d'Art de Catalunya**.

There are three distinct sections to this museum. The smallest of them contains Renaissance, Baroque and neoclassical art, and includes works by El Greco, Velázquez and Tintoretto, among others. The Gothic collection contains a good selection of work from all over Spain, and the Romanesque selection is considered to be among the best and largest of its kind in the world. The museum is undergoing major renovations, and many rooms will not be accessible to the public for some time (possibly years). What the entry fee will be then is anyone's guess.

The **Ethnological Museum** has interesting displays from Africa, Asia and South America. As usual you need to be able to read Spanish or Catalan to get the most out of it. Opening hours are Tuesday to Saturday from 9 am to 8.30 pm and Sunday from 9 am to 2 pm. Entry is free.

For archaeology buffs the **Archaeological Museum** is a must. It contains an excellent selection of finds from the region and the Balearic Islands. Opening hours are the same as in the Ethnological Museum except that they have a lunch break from noon to 2 pm. Entry costs 200 pta but is free on Sundays.

The **Fundació Joan Miró**, open Tuesday to Saturday from 11 am to 8 pm and Sunday from 11 am to 2 pm, is one of the best modern art museums in Spain. Aside from many works by Miró and his contemporaries, there is a large and permanently changing exhibition of lesser known modern artists. Entry to the museum costs 400 pta, or 200 pta for students.

To get to Montjuïc you can either walk or take a bus from Plaça de Espanya. Bus No 61 will take you past the Olympic Stadium and right up to the cable car which leads to the castle. The other way up or down from Montjuïc is to take the funicular which goes from Plaça Raquel Meller (metro Parallel) to the bottom of the cable car to the castle.

Other Museums The **Maritime Museum** contains an impressive array of sailing vessels, models, paintings and more. If you like boats you won't be disappointed. The museum is on Plaça Portal de la Pau at the harbour end of Las Ramblas. Entry costs 150 pta; it is free on Sundays and public holidays, and free to students. Also look for the replica of the *Santa María*, the ship in which Columbus sailed to America, near the museum in the harbour. Barcelona's **Textile Museum**, a stone's throw from the Picasso Museum, is a must. It houses a fascinating collection of tapestries, items of clothing and other textiles. Opening hours are from 9 am to 2 pm and 4.30 to 7 pm.

Tibidabo You can go no higher in Barcelona than when standing at the top of the temple of Tibidabo, with only the statue of Christ above you; the sea is 561 metres below. With nothing but smog to hinder your view, you are confronted with the sprawling enormity of the city. There is no better view unless you can afford to charter a helicopter.

The temple itself, completed in 1968, is only of passing interest. There is an old amusement park at the foot of the church. If there is a history of heart trouble in your family, don't ride on the roller coaster – it almost hangs over the side of the mountain.

From metro Avinguda Tibidabo, take the Tranvía Azul (blue tram) or a bus marked 'Funicular de Tibidabo' up the hill to the funicular. The funicular costs 200/375 pta one-way/return. Keep your eyes open on the way up in the funicular, as there are excellent but fleeting views of the city.

Markets There are a number of open-air markets in Barcelona. **Els Encants** is a good second-hand market on Plaça de les Glòries. You will find it on Monday, Wednesday, Friday and Saturday between 8 am and 7 pm in winter, and 8 am and 8 pm in summer. There is an **antiques market** on Plaça del Pi in the Gothic quarter every Thursday (except in August) from 9 am to 8 pm. In Plaça Reial, on Sunday from 10 am to 2 pm, there is a **coin and stamp market**. On the last Sunday of every month (except in July and August) there is an **art market** on Plaça del Roser from 10 am to 3 pm.

Activities
Courses The best value language courses for foreigners, whether they are Catalan or Spanish, are offered in summer by the University of Barcelona. Contact the Secretaria General, (☎ 318 4266) at Gran Via de les Corts Catalans 585. As the dates and costs vary considerably, the best thing to do is get in touch with the youth tourist organisation a few months before you intend to take a course.

Organised Tours The best organised tour is a self-guided tour, which you follow at your own pace. Bus No 100, which starts at Plaça de Catalunya, is a special tourist bus which operates from June to September. It leaves every half-hour and does a city circuit, passing many of the most important monuments and points of interest in town. You can get on or off anywhere along the route. Each time you get on, you have to pay 100 pta, or you can pay 800 pta for a whole day. This beats the other tours hands down on price.

Places to Stay
Thanks to the Olympic Games in Barcelona in 1992, accommodation has become outrageously expensive. Fortunately, the city weathered the storm somewhat better than Seville did with EXPO '92, but you will be hard pushed to find singles for less than 1000 pta.

Camping The nearest camp site to Barcelona is *Camping Barcino* (☎ 372 8501), Carrer Laureà Miró 50. It is only two km from the city, but with only 150 sites it is often full. *Camping Cala Gogó* (☎ 379 4600), on Carretera de la Platja, is nine km south of the city. With 1500 sites you have a much better chance here. There are another 8000 sites spread among seven camping grounds between Km 11 and Km 17 on route N-246 to the south of the city.

Hostels Apart from the IYHF hostels, there is a handful of private places in Barcelona providing dormitory-style accommodation. The best known, most popular and most revolting are in Plaça Reial. They are certainly good places to meet other foreigners, as no Spaniard would stay in them. It has to be said that they are cheap. *Hostal Kabul* (☎ 318 5190), Plaça Reial 17, has 160 beds which go for 825 pta a night. *Hostal de Joves* near metro Arc de Triomf at Passeig Pujades 29, has 68 beds at 850 pta a night.

There are two IYHF hostels in Barcelona. They have curfews, are somewhat inconveniently located, and if you don't have a booking you probably won't get in. But then, if you don't give it a go you will never know. *Hostal Verge de Montserrat* (☎ 213 8633), at Carrer Maré de Déu del Coll 41-51, is the largest with 200 beds and charges 770 pta for junior members and 1120 pta for seniors. The nearest metro station is Vallcarca. *Hostal Pere Tarrés*, (☎ 410 2309), Carrer Numancia 149-151, has 60 beds at 800/1100 pta for juniors/seniors.

Pensiones Generally speaking, pensiones are a better deal than hostels. They may be more expensive, but they are usually cleaner and they don't have the problem of curfews.

Pensión Galerias Malda (☎ 317 3002), Carrer del Pi 5 (1st floor), is a clean and friendly family-run establishment with singles/doubles from an unbelievable 750/1500 pta. *Pensión Palácio* (☎ 319 3609), Passeig d'Isabel II, 10, is friendly but very noisy, with singles/doubles from 1200/2100 pta. *Casa de Huéspedes Fernando* (☎ 301 7993), Carrer Arco del Remedio 4, has rooms from 1300/2500 pta. It is very clean, but be warned that the tiled floors in the bedrooms and bathrooms are excruciatingly cold.

Hostal Paris (☎ 310 3785) at Carrer Cardenal Casañas 4 has large singles/doubles from 2200/2800 pta. *Casa de Huéspedes Myriam* (☎ 345 4415), at Carrer Trafalgar 80 (3rd floor), has singles/doubles from 1500/2500 pta. If you want to stay longer, they also have a monthly rate of 17,000 pta

Gran Via de les Corts Catalanes

Plaça de la Universitat

▼ 1

i 2

La Rambla

Carrer de Pau Claris

Carrer de Casp

Carrer del Bruc

Ronda Universitat

Carrer de Pelai

Plaça de Castella

Carrer Bergara

3

Carrer del

Plaça de Catalunya

Ⓜ 6

Plaça Urquinaona

Carrer dels Tallers

Carrer Fontanella

Ronda de Sant Pere

Avinguda Portal de l'Angel

Via Laietana

Carrer Jonqueres

Ⓜ 4

7 ▼

Carrer d'Ortigosa

Plaça Vicenç Martorell

8

Carrer de Santa Ana

5

10

9 ▼

Carrer Sant Pere Més Alt

Carrer Pintor Fortuny

La Rambla

Plaça Vila de Madrid

Carrer del Carme

Carrer Portaferrissa

Carrer Sant Pere Mes Baix

11

13 Ⓜ

15

Av Catedral

Plaça Antoni Maura

Av F Cambó

Carrer de Hospital

12

Carrer del Pi

23

14

16

Via Laietana

Pau

22

21

Carrer Boqueria

Carrer de la Princesa

24 25

30 31

17

Sant

28

29

Carrer Jaume I

20

27

Carrer de Ferran

Ⓜ

Carrer Argenteria

Carrer Montcada

26

Carrer La Unió

32

Plaça Sant Miquel

Plaça de l'Angel

18

33

Plaça Reial

35

19

34

36

37

Plaça Santa Maria

Carrer dels Escudellers

Plaça del Teatre

Carrer Nou de Sant Francesc

38

Plaça d'Antoni López

41 Ⓜ

Carrer de Fusteria

Via Laietana

Passeig d'Isabel II

Carrer Ample

39

Central Barcelona

Plaça Portal de la Pau

0   125   250 m

Passeig de Colom

40 Ⓜ

SPAIN

■ PLACES TO STAY	▼ PLACES TO EAT	37	Bar El Ascensor
3 Casa Calvet	1 Bar Estudiantil		OTHER
15 Pensión Galerias Malda	7 Restaurante Tallers		
17 Casa de Huéspedes	8 Self Naturista	2	Tourist Information
Princesa	9 Restaurant Raco de la	4	Urquinaona Metro
21 Hostal Paris	Poma		Station
23 Hotel San Augustín	10 Biocenter	5	Palau de la Música
25 Hotel Peninsular	12 Bocatta	6	Catalunya Metro
30 Pension Europa	14 Sandvitxería Entrepaipa		Station
31 Casa de Huéspedes	19 Bar Champañería	11	Market
Fernando	22 Restaurante Moderno	13	Liceu Metro Station
33 Hostel de Joves	24 Restaurante Els Tres	16	Cathedral
34 Hostal Kabul	Bots	18	Picasso Museum
35 Hotel Roma	26 Kashmir Restaurant	20	Jaume Metro Station
39 Pensión Palácio	Tandoori	28	Gran Teatre del Liceu
	27 Restaurante Pollo Rico	38	Post Office
	29 Restaurant Casa	40	Barceloneta Metro
	Culleretes		Station
	32 Cervessería Glaciar	41	Drassanes Metro
	36 Buén Bocadl		Station

per person. *Casa de Huéspedes Princesa* (☎ 319 5031), Carrer de la Princesa 7, is a friendly family house with singles/doubles from 1300/2000 pta.

Hostal Residencia Europa (☎ 318 7620), Carrer Boquería 18, is a friendly place with basic but clean rooms and above average security. Singles/doubles cost 1500/3000 pta. Doubles with shower cost 3300 pta.

Higher up the scale, but still with very reasonable prices, is *Hotel Roma* (☎ 302 0366) at Plaça Real 11. Singles/doubles cost 2750/4000 pta. In the high season expect to pay around 25% extra. *Hotel Peninsular* (☎ 302 31 38), Carrer de Sant Pau 34, has quite spacious singles/doubles from 2620/4600 pta. *Hotel San Agustín* (☎ 318 1658) at Plaça San Agustín 3, in a quiet square close to Las Ramblas, offers singles/doubles for 5247/7870 pta. All of the rooms have air-con and colour TV.

Accommodation near Barcelona Sants Railway Station is pretty limited and not really recommended. However, if you arrive late at night there are a couple of budget options. *Casa de Huéspedes Regar* (☎ 321 0440), at Avinguda de Roma 5, has singles/doubles from 2500/4000 pta. *Hotel*

Sans (☎ 331 3700), at Carrer Antoni de Campmany 82, has singles/doubles from 1950/2950 pta without bath, 2950/4500 pta with bath.

Rental There are a couple of organisations which cater for young people who are looking for reasonably priced medium to long-term accommodation. Servipark (☎ 301 3676), Passeig de Gracia 7 (4th floor), open from 10 am to 2 pm, is said to be the most helpful but, of course, it charges a fee for the service. Another place where you can get advice is the Oficina de Turisme Juvenil (☎ 302 0682) at Carrer Gravina 1.

Places to Eat
If you are willing to hunt around, you will find plenty of cheap eats in Barcelona. The greatest concentration of these establishments is within walking distance of Las Ramblas.

There are a few extremely good-value restaurants on Carrer de Sant Pau (also known as Carrer de Sant Pablo). *Kashmir Restaurant Tandoori* at Carrer de Sant Pau 39 does very tasty curries from around 550 pta. At *Restaurante Pollo Rico*, Carrer de Sant Pau

31, you can have a quarter of a chicken with chips, bread and wine, for 350 pta, or half a chicken with the same extras for 525 pta. *Restaurante Els Tres Bots* at Carrer de Sant Pau 42 has a menu for 650 pta or main courses from 275 pta.

Restaurante Tallers, Carrer dels Tallers 6, has a menu for 850 pta. *Bar Estudiantil* on Plaça de la Universitat, has excellent platos combinados from 450 pta. All the restaurants in Plaça Reial have menus for around 650 pta. There is a self-service vegetarian restaurant, *Self Naturista*, on Carrer de Santa Ana, with menus from around 650 pta. Another vegetarian option is the very small *Biocenter* at Carrer Pintor Fortuny 24.

Restaurante Moderno at Carrer de Hospital 5, just off Las Ramblas, has something to suit all budgets. They offer three menus (890/1690/2100 pta) or you can eat very well á la carte from around 2500 pta. *Restaurante Casa Culleretes*, Carrer de Quintana 5, one of the oldest restaurants in Barcelona (founded in 1786), offers a good mix of regional and international cuisine with a menu for 1800 pta. For à la carte you should expect to pay around 2500 to 3000 pta. It is closed on Sunday evening and all day Monday.

For cheaper fare, you will have to go for a sandwich. *Cervessería Glaciar* on Plaça Reial, has bocadillos from 125 pta, and a large glass of coñac will set you back only 250 pta. *Sandvitxería Entrepaipa*, Carrer Cardenal Casañas 5, has filling bocadillos from 225 pta. *Bocatta* on Las Ramblas near the market is very popular and also has bocadillos from 225 pta. *Buén Bocadí* on Carrer dels Escudellers, near the corner of Carrer Nou de Sant Francesc, is Barcelona's best known felafel joint.

Entertainment

Bars Barcelona has a seemingly endless variety of nightspots. The best way to get into the bar scene is to try three or four of the most popular places and try to join in with some of the locals. If you speak Spanish this shouldn't be too difficult. If you speak Catalan, you're in. *Bar El Ascensor* on Carrer Bellafila is relaxed, with very cool music. *Bar Champañería* on Carrer Moncada, opposite a pizzeria near the Picasso Museum, is a place you might well overlook – the name is not written anywhere on the outside – but it is too good to miss. The tapas are out of this world and they specialise in cava, the local champagne.

Bar Pastis, in Carrer Santa Mónica in Barri Xinés, very close to Las Ramblas, is an institution among young locals in the know. Another institution which you shouldn't miss is *Café de l'Opéra* on Las Ramblas. More a coffee shop than a bar, and best in the early evening, it must be the most famous café in Barcelona. The crowd is generally about half local and half foreign.

Discos Barcelona's disco owners never thought about budget travellers and backpackers when they opened up. They are expensive and dress codes are pretty strict. The same scam with good-looking women seems to be operating here as in Madrid – if the bouncers like her looks, she's in for free and so is her male companion (usually). Some of the places to be seen (if you can afford it) are *Up & Down* on Avinguda Diagonal, *Otto Zutz* at Carrer Lincoln 15, *KGB* at Carrer Algre de Dalt 55, *Jimmy's* on Plaça Pio XII and *Ars* on Carrer Atenas.

For the affordable disco range, the best area to look is around Carrer de Balmes. In particular, keep an eye open for *Latinos* and *Discoteca Coco*, both on Carrer de Balmes itself, quite close to the Gran Via end on the west side of the road.

Theatre One of the great treats in Barcelona is a night at the Teatre Liceu on Las Ramblas. You can forget the first two or three nights of any production, but after that there are almost always very cheap tickets available at the door, shortly before the performance begins. Ballet tickets cost 350 pta and symphony and opera tickets 550 pta. The seats are not generally very good, but once the lights go out it is often possible to move down a little way.

Cinema For up-to-date cinema information, get yourself a copy of *Guía de Ocio* from one of the numerous newsstands on Las Ramblas. One cinema worth going to is *Cine Malda*, at Carrer del Pi 5. On Monday, tickets cost only 300 pta and the films are usually up to date.

Getting There & Away
Air You can fly to Madrid for 13,150 pta one-way with Iberia. A return ticket, with a Sunday between flights, can cost as little as 17,100 pta. To Seville, the equivalent fares are 18,025 and 23,425 pta, to Málaga 17,550 and 22,825 pta, and to Palma de Mallorca and Ibiza 7975 and 10,375 pta. Iberia offers a basic one-way fare to London at 46,100 pta. Those under 25 may be eligible for a reduction of up to 65% by booking tickets one day before flying. Check with Iberia direct.

Train On the international front, the most common destinations from Barcelona are Paris and London. The standard train fare to Paris is 10,350 pta one-way and to London, 19,800 pta. If you are under 26, you can get a 40% discount by purchasing a Eurotrain ticket from the youth tourist office at Carrer Gravina 1.

The main internal destinations from Barcelona are Madrid and Valencia. There are also trains to Málaga and Pamplona, among many others. There are seven trains a day to Madrid, one of them via Valencia, the rest via Saragossa. The basic fare is 4215/6675 pta one-way/return. To Valencia there are up to 10 trains a day. The basic fare is 2260/3585 pta. Trains for the 14-hour trip to Málaga leave at 7.30 am and 5.30 pm and cost 6230/9860 pta one-way/return. Pamplona-bound trains leave Barcelona Sants at 7.25 am, noon and 10.30 pm. The basic fare is 3300/5225 pta one-way/return.

Car & Motorbike If you are coming from or heading to France, the main road is route E-15. As this is an expressway, you must pay a toll. Route N-11 follows a somewhat longer route to the same border post at La Jonquera, but it is toll-free. The French side of the border is La Perthus. If your destination is Andorra or Toulouse, route N-152 is more convenient, though it can be pretty slow going in the Pyrenees.

Route E-15 continues south from Barcelona, staying close to the coast and passing through Tarragona, Valencia, and Alicante. It will soon be extended to Murcia and eastern Andalusia. The other option for this route is to follow route N-340, which runs more or less parallel to the E-15.

The best route to Madrid is route E-90 to Saragossa, then onto route N-11. The E-90 splits off the E-15 about 30 km north of Tarragona, with Saragossa clearly signposted. If freeways really turn you off, then you will need to continue on the N-340 to Tarragona, before getting onto the N-240 to Lérida, then onto the N-11 which will take you through Saragossa to Madrid. Another option to Madrid is to take route N-420 from Tarragona, and then use your road map very carefully to pick your way through the back roads of Aragon and Castile-La Mancha. It looks more direct than the other routes, and the distance is definitely less, but it is a long, slow slog. Good luck.

Getting Around
To/From the Airport Barcelona's international airport is some 12 km from the city centre. There is a train every 30 minutes from the airport to Barcelona Sants (platform 4), starting at 6.12 am, with the last departure at 10.42 pm. A bus leaves the airport, bound for Plaça d'Espanya, every 80 minutes or so from 6.35 am to 8.35 pm. In addition, there are four buses between 10.15 pm and 2.40 am. A taxi from the airport to Las Ramblas should cost 1500 to 2000 pta depending on the traffic.

Bus A single ride on a bus costs 80 pta. If you are staying any amount of time and intend to use the bus frequently, you are better off with a T-1 ticket. This is valid for 10 rides on bus or metro and costs 550 pta. In general, the metro is a more convenient transport system. Bus information will be given for points of interest not accessible by metro. Also, note bus No 100 under Organised Tours earlier in this section. Here's a hot tip: if you want to get to the centre of town, any red bus will take you there.

Underground Barcelona's metro system spreads its tentacles around the city in such a way that most places of interest are within 10 minutes' walk of a station. Exceptions will be noted as they arise. A single ride on the metro costs 70 pta. A much better deal is the so-called T-2 ticket, which is valid for 10 rides and costs only 400 pta. See also under the Bus section for the T-1 ticket. In summer you can buy one-day, three-day and five-day tickets for 450, 1000 and 1300 pta respectively.

Taxi Taxis are pretty reasonably priced, and are a viable option for late-night transport. Typically you might expect to pay 600 or 700 pta from Barcelona Sants to Plaça de Catalunya. Finding a taxi is no problem. On Plaça de Catalunya, Gran Via, Plaça d'Espanya, Passeig de Gràcia, Avinguda Diagonal and Las Ramblas, it should take no more than a few minutes for an empty taxi to come by. If you aren't having any luck, call ☎ 322 2222 or ☎ 212 2222.

COSTA BRAVA
The Costa Brava ranks with the Costa Blanca and the Costa del Sol as one of Europe's popular holiday spots. It stands alone, however, thanks to spectacular scenery and its proximity to northern Europe, both of which have sent prices skyrocketing to make this the most exclusive of Spain's mainland coasts.

Orientation & Information
The main entry point to the Costa Brava is Gerona. Those coming by car from the north sometimes use Figueras as their jumping off point, particularly if they are bound for one of the northernmost resorts, such as Cadaqués. Both Figueras and Gerona are on the A-7 freeway (toll-paying traffic) and the

N-II highway (toll-free) which connect Barcelona with the south of France. Along the coast, coming from the north, the most appealing resorts are Cadaqués, Ampurias, El Estartit and Palafrugel.

Things to See
The Costa Brava is all about beaches, picturesque inlets and coves. There are some longer beaches at places like El Estartit and Ampurias which are worth visiting out of season, but there has been a tendency to build tall buildings where building engineers think it can be done. Fortunately, there are many places on the Costa Brava, with its rugged coastline, where such building simply could not happen.

Perhaps the most picturesque of all Spanish resort towns is **Cadaqués**, about one hour's drive from Figueras at the end of an agonising series of hairpin bends. Cadaqués is very short on beaches, so people tend to spend a lot of time sitting at waterfront cafés or wandering along the beautiful rocky coast.

About 10 km from Cadaqués is **Cabo Creus**, a rocky peninsula with a single restaurant set at the top of a craggy cliff. This is paradise for anyone who likes to scramble around rocks risking life and limb with every step.

Farther down the coast, past Ampurias and El Estartit (see the Activities section for more on El Estartit), you eventually come to the town of Palafrugell. Palafrugell itself is a few km inland and has very little to offer, but the three nearby beach towns have to be seen to be believed. From the north, the first of these is **Tamariu**, the smallest, least crowded and most relaxed of them all. **Llafranc** is the largest and the busiest, and has the longest beach, while the picture postcard setting of **Calella de Palafrugell** has ensured that it is the most exclusive, never overly crowded, very relaxed, and definitely one of the places to be seen. If you are driving down this coast, it is worth making the effort to have a look at some of these places, particularly out of season.

· When you have had enough beach for a

while, make sure that you put Figueras at the top of your list. Figueras itself is a fairly unexciting town, with one attraction that is a notable exception: the **Salvador Dali Museum**. This museum was purposely built to hold the largest collection of the artist's work in the world, and must not be missed. Among the many works of genius is the incredible holographic interpretation of Velazquéz' *Meninas* (the original, non-holographic version is in the Prado in Madrid).

Activities

For a spectacular stretch of coastline, take a drive from Tossa de Mar to San Feliu de Guixols. There are 360 curves in these 20 km of road, which, with brief stops to take in the scenery, can take at least two hours to drive along. The road is too treacherous for buses, so you will need a car.

One of the most exciting, and least known, attractions on the Costa Brava are the Medas Islands, off the coast from El Estartit and Torroella de Montgri. These seven islets and their surrounding coral reefs, which cover a total land area of only 21.5 hectares, have been declared a natural park in order to protect their extraordinarily diverse flora and fauna. To date, almost 1500 different life forms have been identified on and around the islands. If you are interested in visiting them, ask at the tourist office in Torroella. They can also help to arrange snorkelling and diving trips to the islands.

Places to Stay

Most visitors to the Costa Brava rent apartments or stay inland in Figueras or Gerona in order to make day trips to the beach. If you are interested in renting an apartment for a week or so, contact local tourist offices in advance for information.

There are 29 youth hostels in Cataluña, four of which are on or near the Costa Brava. All youth hostels in Cataluña charge 850/1275 pta for junior/senior members per night, breakfast included.

Figueras The two-star *Hotel Los Angeles*

(☎ 510 661) at Carrer Barceloneta 10 is excellent value, particularly in the low season when roomy singles/doubles cost 2100/3800 pta. In the high season the rates climb to 2500/4500 pta. As an alternative, there is a *Youth Hostel* (☎ 501 213) at Carrer Anicet Pagès 2.

Gerona Gerona's modern *Youth Hostel* (☎ 201 554 or 218 003) is perfectly situated in the middle of the old town at Carrer dels Ciutadans 9. It is often full with groups but is large enough to make it worth a try. Nearby, *Pensión Viladomat* (☎ 203 176) at Carrer Ciutadans 5 is basic but can be recommended if you don't mind sharing a bathroom. It has singles/doubles for 1650/2900 pta.

Cadaqués The camp site in Cadaqués is up the top of the town as you head towards Cabo de Creus. The cost of a site is 1800 pta, and you pay 400 pta per person on top of the site cost. At these prices, a single person is better off staying in town near the waterfront. *Hostal Marina* (☎ 258 199) at Carrer Riera 3 has singles/doubles for 1800/3500 pta in the low season and 2000/4000 pta in the high season.

Palafrugell There are camp sites at all three of Palafrugell's satellites. In Calella try *Camping a Siesta* (☎ 300 016). The charges are 525 pta per adult, 420 pta per child, 550 pta per tent and 525 pta per car in the high season. In the low season the rates are about 20% lower. In Llafranc *Kim's Camping* (☎ 301 156) is about 15% cheaper, and in Tamariu *Camping Tamariu* is a little cheaper again.

Hotel rooms are relatively thin on the ground here, particularly in Calella, as most people tend to come on package deals and stay in apartments. In Calella, the cheapest place to stay is *Pensión Calella* (☎ 300 599), at Carrer Lladó 6, which has doubles for 3400/4800 pta in the low/high season price. *Pensión Montana* (☎ 301 291) at Carrer Cesàrea 2 in Llafranc is well positioned near the beach and has doubles for 3200/3600 pta in the low/high season. In Tamariu try *Pensión Vora La Mar* (☎ 300 553), Passeig del Mar 6, which has doubles for 3922/4452 pta in the low/high season.

Other Areas The other youth hostels in the Costa Brava region are in Camps I Armet (☎ 972-630 185, Carrer Monells) and Empúries (☎972-771 200, Carrer Les Coves 41). Local tourist offices on the coast can give you information on medium to long-term rentals.

Getting There & Away
Gerona and Figueras are both on the train line connecting Barcelona to France. All trains running from Barcelona to Port Bou at the border stop in Gerona on the way, and the vast majority also make a stop in Figueras. The fare from Barcelona to Gerona is 570/900 pta one-way/return. To Figueras it is 890/1405 pta one-way/return.

Getting Around
There are three or four buses a day from Figueras to Cadaqués at a cost of 600 pta one-way. You must buy tickets before getting on the bus when you return from Cadaqués. It is a good idea to buy your tickets a couple of days in advance, particularly in the high season, as you may not get out of town at all if the bus is full.

Palafrugell can be reached by bus from Gerona. To Calella and Llafranc there are buses from Palafrugell all year. Tamariu is only served by public transport from around May to October. The rest of the year you have to hitch or walk (said to take about one hour from Palafrugell). Most other coastal towns (south of Cadaqués) can be reached by bus from Gerona.

MONASTERIO DE MONTSERRAT
Unless you are on a pilgrimage, Montserrat's prime attraction is its setting. The monastery sits high above the plain, below a spectacular craggy mountain, in some of Spain's wildest countryside (although tourism has tamed it somewhat). The monastery was originally built towards the end of the 1st millennium

AD to commemorate an apparition on this site of the Virgin Mary in the 9th century. Pilgrims still come from all over Christendom to pay homage to the Black Virgin, a 12th century wooden sculpture of Mary, which is high above the altar in the basilica, the only part of the monastery proper open to the public.

Orientation & Information
The best place to get tourist information on Montserrat is at the tourist office in Barcelona. Once you are there, it is just a matter of following the signs. If you need specific information while you are at the monastery, try asking at the three-star hotel. Sometimes they have information pamphlets to give away and the staff are generally pretty friendly.

The Montserrat Boys' Choir sings in the basilica every day at 1 pm. Be warned that it fills up quickly, and you may be left standing at the back craning your neck to see anything. If you can, try to arrive a little earlier so as to get a seat close to the front.

If you are making a day trip to Montserrat, it is wise to take the earliest train from Barcelona. Although you don't need very much time to see what the monastery has to offer, there are a number of truly beautiful walks which start on the grounds. For the best views of the monastery and the surrounding area, you need to climb to the summit – a pretty solid walk by any standards.

Places to Stay & Eat
It is possible to spend the night in the monastery. There are monastic cells for rent at very reasonable prices, with singles/doubles available from 1500/2150 pta. For more information call *Despatx de Celdas* on ☎ 835 0251, ext 230.

There is a restaurant of sorts in the monastery car park. It is not the most inspiring place to eat, but their 900 pta menu will fill most stomachs. They have bocadillos for 400 pta but they may be a little stale. There is also a supermarket up there if you don't want to face the sterile atmosphere of the restaurant.

Getting There & Away

There is a train from Plaça d'Espanya in Barcelona. Rail passes are not valid for the trip, which takes a little over an hour. Trains leave Barcelona every two hours at 10 past the hour, starting at 9.10 am and ending at 3.10 pm.

If the cable car is running from Montserrat Railway Station to the monastery, you can buy a return ticket in Barcelona which includes the cable-car ride for 850 pta. If the cable car is not running, the price is 600 pta return. The bus trip from Montserrat Railway Station to the monastery costs 750 pta return.

TARRAGONA

A wealth of history awaits the visitor to Tarragona. The city was founded by the Romans in 218 BC. Many of the structures built by the Romans, including parts of the city walls and the forum, figure among Tarragona's most important attractions. Other periods of history are also well represented, including the medieval cathedral and 17th century British additions to the old city walls. The city's archaeological museum is one of the most interesting in Spain. Today, aside from its historical interest, Tarragona is a modern city with a large student population, and a pretty lively beach scene. It makes the perfect day trip if you need a break from the smog of Barcelona.

Orientation & Information

Tarragona's main street is Rambla Nova, which runs approximately north-west from a clifftop overlooking the Mediterranean. A couple of blocks to the east, running parallel to Rambla Nova, is Rambla Vella, which marks the beginning of the old town. The Roman Forum is a few blocks down the hill to the west of Rambla Nova. To the south-west, on the coast, is the train station.

Tarragona's tourist information office is at Rambla Nova 46. Telephones are on Carrer Fortuny at the corner of Rambla Nova. The telephone code for Tarragona is 977.

Things to See & Do

Tarragona's **Archaeological Museum**, on Plaça del Rei, is the best place to start a visit to this city, as it gives you an insight into its rich and fascinating history. The carefully presented exhibits include frescoes, mosaics, sculptures, statues and pottery dating back to the 2nd century BC. The museum is open all day from Tuesday to Sunday. Entry is free to all on Tuesdays, and all week to students and EC passport holders under the age of 21, otherwise it costs 100 pta.

The **cathedral** sits grandly at the highest point of Tarragona, overlooking the old town. Some parts of the cathedral date back to the 12th century AD. Try to visit the cathedral at around 10 am on a Sunday when the organist gets in some practice for mass: the acoustics are wonderful – music from heaven, so to speak. The cathedral is open to the public daily from 10 am to 2 pm.

The **Passeig Arqueològic** is a peaceful walk along and within the old city walls, which are a combination of Roman, Iberian and 17th century British efforts.

A few blocks to the west of Rambla Nova are the ruins of a once grand **Roman Forum**. Even in its state of decay, it is considered to be one of the finest outside Italy. If you head north from the forum to Avenida Ramon y Cajal and then turn east, you will come to the **Necropolis**. Archaeologists have uncovered a number of Christian and pagan burial sites here, and there are fine examples of sculpture dating from the 3rd to the 6th centuries AD.

If you are here in summer, Platja Miracles is the main city beach. It is reasonably clean but can get terribly crowded. If you walk north along the coast out of town, you may find the beaches a little more isolated, though it must be stressed that in summer you will never be alone. By the way, don't waste your time walking south in search of beaches, as there is a petrochemical plant not too far away.

Places to Stay

If you are intending to spend the night in Tarragona, it would be wise to call ahead to book a room. For one of the best positions in town you can't go past the one-star *Hotel España* (☎ 232 707) at Rambla Nova 49.

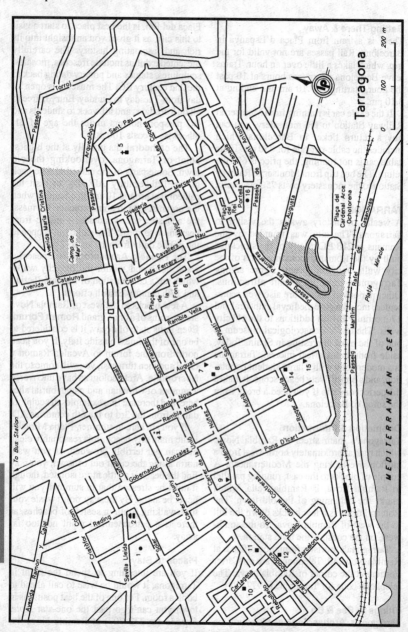

1	Roman Forum
2	Post & Telegraph Office
3	Telephone Office
4	Tourist Office
5	Cathedral
6	Pensión Marsal
7	Restaurante Delicias
8	Hotel España
9	Restaurant Buffet el Tiberí
10	Pensión Carmen
11	Hostal Catalònia
12	Hostal Residencia Abella
13	RENFE Station
14	Hotel Lauria
15	Restaurant La Rambla
16	Archaeological Museum

With singles/doubles for 3000/5000 pta, it is a worthwhile splurge. If this is out of your budget range, try *Hostal Residencia Catalònia* (☎ 211 008) at Carrer Apadoca 7. Singles/doubles cost only 1000/1500 pta. With a shower in the room, the going rate is 1200/2000 pta.

Some other places worth trying are *Hostal Residencia Abella* (☎ 234 224) at Apodaca 26 which has singles/doubles for 1100/1800 pta, and *Pensión Marsal* (☎ 224 069), in the old town at Plaça de la Font 26, with singles/doubles for 1100/2200 pta. As a last resort, *Pensión Carmen* (☎ 223 387) at Cartagena 10 has a limited number of clean singles/doubles for 1000/2000 pta. The nearest camp site, *Camping Tamarit* (☎ 650 128) is four km south of town, on the beach.

Places to Eat

For a taste of traditional Catalan food, *Restaurant Bufet El Tiberi* is one of the better options. They offer an all-you-can-eat buffet for 1200 pta per person. It is open daily from 1 to 4 pm and again from 8 to 11 pm. You will find it on the corner of Carrer Martí d'Ardenya and Carrer Arquitecte Rovira. Two highly recommended restaurants on Rambla Nova are *La Rambla* at No 10 and, almost directly opposite, *Restaurant Mirador*. La Rambla has a menu for 1350 pta

and you can eat well á la carte for around 3000 pta. The Mirador is marginally cheaper. For somewhat cheaper fare try *Restaurant Delicias*, Carrer Apodaca 10, which has a menu for 750 pta.

Getting There & Away

There are almost 40 trains a day from Barcelona Sants to Tarragona. The trip takes anywhere from 55 minutes to almost two hours depending on which train you take. The basic fare (for the slow trains) is 510/810 pta one-way/return. Many of these trains stop in Sitges on the way, home to Spain's most outspoken gay community, and supposedly the wildest carnival in the country.

The other major destination from Tarragona is Valencia. About 10 trains, most of them originating in Barcelona, run the route every day, taking from around three to five hours. The basic fare is 1710/2710 pta one-way/return. A number of these trains continue on to Madrid (4655/7365 pta one-way/return). A cheaper way to Madrid is via Mora and Saragossa (3545/5610 one-way/return). Saragossa itself is around three hours from Tarragona, with tickets costing 1590/2520 one-way/return (via Mora).

If you are driving, route N-340, which runs from Barcelona to Valencia and beyond, also passes through Tarragona.

Balearic Islands, Valencia & Murcia

MAJORCA

Majorca (Mallorca) is the largest of the Balearic Islands (Islas Baleares). Most of the five million annual visitors to the island are here for the three S's: sun, sand and sea. There are, however, other reasons for coming to Majorca. Palma, the main population centre, is in itself worth visiting, and the island offers a number of noncoastal attractions.

SPAIN

Palma de Mallorca

1 Hospital
2 Bus Stop
3 Tourist Office
4 Plaça Espanya
5 Santa Magdalena Church
6 Market
7 Tourist Office
8 Bus Stop
9 Teatre Principal
10 Restaurante Fonda España
11 Casa de Huéspedes Garrido
12 Hostal Goya
13 Hostal Ritzi
14 Telephone Office
15 Post Office
16 Tourist Office
17 Town Hall
18 Rincón del Artista
19 Maritime Museum
20 Casa Regional de Murcia
21 Almudaina Palace
22 Cathedral
23 Desbrull Palace
24 Arab Baths

0   150   300 m

Orientation & Information

The capital, Palma de Mallorca, is at the southern end of the island, in a bay famous for its brilliant sunsets. To the north are the mountains of the Serra de Tramuntana, a trekker's heaven, which lead to the spectacular Cape Formentor with the most exciting beaches on the island. South-east of the cape is the Bay of Alcudia, with some of the more crowded beaches outside Palma.

The main tourist office in Palma is on Avinguda Jaume III. This office is good for information on all the Balearic Islands. There are also two smaller tourist offices in town: one on Plaça Espanya and the other on Carrer Santo Domingo, near the port. The post office and the international telephone office are both on Carrer de la Constitució. The *Majorca Daily Bulletin* speaks for itself. It is available free from the tourist offices in Palma, until they run out. Thereafter it can be bought for 75 pta from many newsstands.

Palma's telephone code is 971.

Things to See & Do

Palma itself is a very pleasant town, and is well worth spending a day or so exploring. The enormous **cathedral** is the first landmark you will see as you approach the island by ferry. Some of the interior features were designed by Antonio Gaudí.

In front of the cathedral is the **Palau de Almudaina**, the one-time residence of the Majorcan monarchs. The kings are gone but you can still take an interesting guided tour.

The **Banys Arabs**, or Arab Baths, are at Carrer de Can Sera 7. These delicate structures, dating back to the 10th century AD, represent the only monument to the Moorish domination of the island.

Heading east along the coast from Palma, you come to **Colonia San Jordi**. This resort town is very popular with Germans. Although it is not a very exciting spot, there are some good quiet beaches nearby, particularly Ses Arenes and Es Trenc, both a few km back up the coast towards Palma.

Just by Porto Cristo are the **Cuevas del Drach**. Every hour, on the hour, except at 1 pm, there is a guided tour through these

stalagmite and stalactite-filled caves. The only way in is with a group and the fee is 600 pta. The town of Porto Cristo itself has a good beach in a sheltered bay.

Around the coast beyond Alcudia is **Cape Formentor**. The road along the peninsula to the cape is amazing, and at the highest point is a plaque dedicated to the engineer who built it. Very close to the end of the peninsula is the very secluded beach of Formentor. There is also a hotel out there, but the prices are exorbitant.

Sóller on the north-west coast is one of the few places on that side of the island with good beaches. It is also the best place to base yourself for trekking.

Detailed information on trekking is not covered in this book. If you are interested in what the island has to offer in this respect, have a look at Lonely Planet's *Trekking in Spain* by Marc Dubin. For inexperienced trekkers who want to know what all the excitement is about, the walk from **Sóller to Deía** is bound to get you hooked.

Places to Stay

The days of budget travel in Majorca are numbered. The local tourist authority has been on a crusade for some time now, aimed at stamping out as many cheap pensiones and hostals as possible. The places listed here were all pretty stable at the time of writing, and the owners were confident of another few years before being run out of town. We can only hope.

In Palma, *Pensión Pons* (no telephone), at Carrer del VI 6, has singles/doubles from 850/1800 pta. *Hostal Goya* (☎ 726 986), Carrer Estanco 7, has singles/doubles from 1000/1500 pta. For amazing value try *Pensión Costa Brava* (☎ 711 729), Carrer Feliu 16, which has singles/doubles from 1000/2000 pta. *Hostal Ritzi* (☎ 714 610), as its name suggests, offers a little more style. It is at Carrer Apuntadors 6, and has singles/doubles from 1500/2600 pta. *Casa de Huéspedes Garrido*, Carrer Ca'n Espanya 4, is dingy, unhelpful and unfriendly, but cheap (doubles from 1500 pta).

In Colonia San Jordi, *Hostal Colonia* at

Carrer Gabriel Roca has singles/doubles from 1200/1800 pta and full board from 2550 pta. About the only really cheap eats in town are to be found at *Hamburguesería D2* on Carrer Pou D'en Verdera, near Avenida Primavera.

There is a youth hostel and a camp site (both in summer only) near Alcudia. To get there, take a bus to the Museo Arqueológico, then hitch or walk up towards Victoria. The hostel is about five km from the turn-off.

If you are here for the trekking, you'll probably want to base yourself in Sóller. *Hotel El Guía* (☎ 630 227), near the train station, has singles/doubles from 2000/4000 pta. It is one of the better places to meet other trekkers.

Places to Eat

Fortunately, the tourist authorities haven't touched this aspect of budget travel yet. As such, it is still quite easy to fill up on good food, at very reasonable prices, on Majorca. In Palma, the *Casa Regional de Murcia* at Avinguda Antoní Maura 24 has a great menu for 600 pta. *Restaurante La Viña* at Carrer del VI 6, also does a menu for the same price, while *Restaurante Fonda España* at Plaça Major 7, is a little more expensive with a menu for 825 pta. Excellent value is *Rincón del Artista* at Carrer de Can Malla 2 (alongside the Santa Eulalia Church). It has a tasty menu for 650 pta and bocadillos from an unbelievable 90 pta.

Getting There & Away

Inter-island flights are excellent value. Palma to Mahón, and Palma to Ibiza can cost as little as 3750 pta one-way. A return flight can cost as little as 4500 pta if you have a Sunday between flights. Palma de Mallorca to Barcelona fares start at 7650/9200 pta one-way/return and Palma to Valencia fares start at 8700/10450 pta one-way/return.

There are six or seven ferries a week from Barcelona to Palma. The fare is the same as the Barcelona to Ibiza fare. For information on ferries between the islands, see the Ibiza and Minorca sections.

Getting Around

A taxi from Palma Airport into the centre of town should cost around 1700 pta. Bus No 17 passes by the airport on the way into town every half-hour. If you don't mind the wait, the nine-km journey will only set you back 200 pta.

The best way to get around the island is by car. If you are intending to rent for a week or more, there are some fantastic deals around. For example, Garage Segui (☎ 260 252), will rent you a car for seven days (delivered to you at the airport) from 10,000 pta (16,000 pta in the high season) all-inclusive. You will need to book some time ahead. Another company, Hasso Rent A Car (☎ 260 219), Carrer Bartolomé Ruitort 160 in C'an Pastilla near Palma, rents cars from a daily rate of 1008 pta including the first 100 km free – surely the cheapest rental cars in Spain. For motorbike rental try Rent A Bike (☎ 401 821), Carrer Joan Miró 330 D.

There are two train lines on Majorca. One goes to the inland town of Inca and the other goes to Sóller. If you are headed for Sóller for the beaches or the trekking, the train is the best and most enjoyable way of making the trip.

MINORCA

Minorca (Menorca) is still the gem of the Balearic Islands. The local government is moving to put limits on tourism, although with over 500,000 visitors each year, there is a general feeling among conservationists that it is too little too late.

Orientation & Information

The capital, and most important port, Mahón, is at the eastern end of the island. A road runs down the middle of the island to the Ciudadela, Minorca's second town. Almost exactly halfway between the two is the 357-metre-high Monte Toro, near the town of Mercadal.

There are two tourist offices in Mahón: one on Plaza de la Conquista and the other on Plaza de la Explanada. In Ciudadela you can get 24-hour information (in summer only) from the police on the main square.

The post office in Mahón is by the port at the bottom of Parc Rochina. Finally, for your laundry, (telephone, supermarket, exchange, boat rental and many other needs), the company known as 215 (also by the port of Mahón) is most helpful.

Things to See & Do

For a great view of the island, climb or drive to the top of Monte Toro. On a clear day you can see the whole island and even as far as Majorca. There is a monastery and some kind of military installation at the top, so be careful what you photograph.

The town of **Cala Galdana** on the south coast has a nice beach in a protected cove. **Cala Morell** north of Ciudadela also has a good, calm beach. The town itself leaves much to be desired, though there is some beautiful clifftop walking to be done in the area.

If you are looking for really quiet beaches, there are a few options. South of Ciudadela is the beach of **Torre Saura**. It is a private beach, so without your own wheels you haven't got a hope of getting there. Assuming you do have transport, follow the signs from Ciudadela towards the coast, then turn off to Son Saura. Make sure you close any gates behind you.

There are no beaches in the town of **Fornells** on the north coast, but there is a very appealing looking spot across the bay. For a price, one of the local fishers will take you. If the price isn't right, then try the beach of Binimella to the west of Fornells. Another option is the tantalising Cala Pregonda, which is visible from Binimella but inaccessible by car.

Quiet beaches near Mahón are rare. Your best chance is to drive across the lunar landscape to the lighthouse at **Favoritx**. If you park just before the gate to the lighthouse and climb up the rocks behind you, you'll see a couple of the eight beaches that are just waiting for scramblers like yourself to grace their sands.

Finally, if you're looking for nightlife, don't come to Minorca in winter. In summer, on the other hand, the port in Mahón should provide you with all the hangovers you need for a first-class holiday.

Places to Stay

The best choice of Minorca's limited budget accommodation is in Mahón. The *Hostal España* (☎ 363 686), above Buscas Bar at Cami D'es Castell 203, is probably the cheapest place in town, with singles/doubles from 1200/2000 pta. The well-located *Hostal Orsi* (☎ 364 751), at Carrer Infanta 19, is owned by a young English couple who are a mine of information about the island. With singles/doubles ranging from 1500/2500 to 1850/2900 pta, it is highly recommended. *Hostal La Isla* (☎ 366 492) at Carrer Santa Catalina 4, offers singles/doubles from 1600/2900 pta.

In Ciudadela, the options are far more restricted, but also considerably cheaper. *Pensión Casa Juana* (☎ 383 054), at Carrer Ibiza 8, has very clean singles/doubles from 700/1400 pta. Nearby, at No 4, is an unnamed *pensión* (☎ 383 905), belonging to another Juana, with singles/doubles from 650/1300 pta.

Other options on the island are limited. On Plaza S'Algaret, in the picturesque town of Fornells, is *Hostal La Palma* (☎ 376 634), with singles/doubles from 2200/3400 pta. For a longer stay in Fornells, you can get information on apartments for rent by phoning ☎ 376 572.

There is a camp site near the town of Cala Galdana. It is only open in summer. The bus to Cala Galdana will drop you off in front of the camp site.

Places to Eat

Buscas Bar, below Hostal España in Mahón, is owned by four Britons who became tired of England a few years back. A plate of the day costs 500 pta. The *Cafetería Bar La Bombilla*, in Plaza Bastió, with a menu at the same price, is somewhat more traditional.

In Ciudadela, *Bar Triton* by the port has platos combinados from 375 pta. You can have a pizza for 600 pta at *Restaurante Las Voltes* on Carrer de Jose María Quadrado in the old town.

Getting There & Away

There is only one weekly ferry from Valencia to Mahón. It leaves Valencia at 11 pm on Saturday evening and arrives in Mahón at 3.30 pm on Sunday. The minimum fare is 4830 pta. The same ferry makes a stop in Palma to drop off and pick up passengers (departs from Palma at 9 am on Sunday). The minimum fare from Palma to Mahón is 3480 pta. The fare from Barcelona to Mahón is the same as that from Valencia to Mahón, but you have to change ferries in Palma, as the Sunday ferry is the only one which runs to Mahón.

Getting Around

There is a bus which runs down the middle of the island, connecting the two main towns and those in between. However, if you want to get to some of the more remote beaches, you will need your own transport. Motos Ramos (☎ 366 813), at Andén de Levante 21, by the port in Mahón, rents bicycles from 1300 pta a day. They also have motorised two-wheelers from 2000 and 2800 pta a day, depending on the cc's.

You can rent a car from Autos Gaviota for 6656/8475 pta a day in the low/high season. They have a booth at the airport (☎ 366 400), which is open daily. They also have an office at Plaza Explanada 8 (☎ 360 620) in Mahón and at Carrer Conquistador 59 (☎ 382 998) in Ciudadéla. For a really great deal you can rent a car from Autos San Clemente (☎ 366 857), 300 metres from the airport, for 18,000 pta a week in the low season. They also rent sailboards.

IBIZA

The island of Ibiza receives over a million visitors a year, half of them from the UK and a quarter of them from Germany. That is almost 5000 people per km of coastline! Of course, they don't all arrive in Ibiza at the same time, but at times it can seem like it. To be fair, there are a few out-of-the-way beaches on the island which are among the most picturesque in Spain.

Orientation & Information

The capital, Ibiza (or Eivissa as it is known to the locals), is at the southern end of the island. Whether you fly in or arrive by sea, this is where you will arrive. The big resorts are scattered along both the south coast and the north coast. Budget travellers generally have to make do with Ibiza as a base unless they decide to camp.

The island's main tourist office is at Carrer Vara de Rey 13. There is also a small booth at the airport. There are telephones on Avenida Santa Eulalia by the port which are open until midnight in summer. The telephone code for Ibiza is 971.

There is a laundrette, Lavandería Master Clean, at Carrer Felipe II 12D.

Things to See

There are plenty of crowded beaches on Ibiza. Most of the few quiet beaches worth seeking out are on the north coast. Cala Benirras is one of the most attractive. Set in a beautiful bay, and with minimal development, it is not yet well known by the tourist crowd. It is signposted from the Ibiza to San Juan road, a few km before San Juan. Cala d'Eubaroa, near San Mateo, is a favourite with the locals. Cala Xarraca, near Portinatx, is in a picturesque, semiprotected bay. In Cala Portinatx itself, there is a so-called hippie market on Sunday evening.

Places to Stay

Among Ibiza's camp sites are *Es Cana* (☎ 332 117), and *Florida* (☎ 331 154), both near Santa Eulalia. The first is the more appealing of the two, but both are well positioned for excursions to the more secluded northern beaches

It is surprising just how cheap some of the pensiones in Ibiza are. *Pensión Mar* (☎ 303 405), Carrer Historiador José Clapés 9 (1st floor), has clean singles/doubles from only 700/1400 pta (low season), 1000/1900 pta (high season). *Casa de Huéspedes Navarro* (☎ 310 825), at Carrer de la Cruz 20 (3rd floor), is also reasonably priced, with singles/doubles from 800/1800 pta (low season), 1100/2200 pta (high season). The friendly *Hostal Sol y Brisa* (☎ 310 818), Avenida Bartolomé V Ramón 15, has singles/doubles from 900/1600 pta (low season), 1200/2200 pta (high season). For a youth hostel atmosphere, try *Hostal Estrella del Mar* (☎ 312 212), Carrer Felipe II 28 (3rd floor), with singles/doubles from 1100/2000 pta without bath, 2200/3000 pta with bath or, for the same price, *Hostal La Marina* (☎ 310 172), at Andenes del Puerto 4.

Places to Eat

The cheapest meals in Ibiza can be put together in the market, which is on Plaça de la Constitució. There is another market at the eastern end of Carrer Catalunya. There are also a few restaurants in Ibiza with good-value platos combinados. At *Bar Mariano*, Carrer D'Enmig s/n, the starting price is 470 pta. *Cafe Nuevo Centro* starts at 400 pta. It is in a passage between Carrer Pere de Portugal and Carrer de Joan d'Austria. Pizzas start at 650 pta at *Pizzería Da Franco En Romano* (below Hostal Sol y Brisa).

Entertainment

Ibiza's nightlife is renowned. The gay scene is wild and the dress code expensive. Of course, you don't have to take part in the frivolities, but then why else would you choose Ibiza over other areas of Spain?

The infamous *Ku* is about six km out of Ibiza, on the road to San António. It is also seriously in debt, but such institutions die hard. *Amnesia* and *Pacha* are the other big-name discos. Be warned that all three are big on price too. *La Ánfora* in the old town is the only all-gay disco. *Space*, yet another disco, is still open when all the others have shut up shop.

Getting There & Away

Most people coming to Ibiza arrive on package deals from northern Europe. There are also reasonable nonpackage fares available from the peninsula and from Palma. Often the convenience of flying outweighs the relatively small price difference – if you can manage to get a seat.

There are ferries to Ibiza every week from Valencia (two), Denia (variable), Barcelona (six) and Palma (two). The minimum fare from the mainland is 4830 pta, and from Palma it is 3480 pta.

Getting Around

A taxi from the airport to Ibiza costs 1250 pta. There is also a bus every hour on the half-hour, which costs 80 pta.

Buses to other parts of the island leave from Avenida Isidoro Macabich. Timetables and prices change frequently. Check the local papers *Diario de Ibiza* or the *Prensa de Ibiza* for the latest timetables.

If you are intent on getting to some of the more secluded beaches you will need to rent wheels. There is no shortage of rental agencies on the island. Among the cheapest is Casa Rubí (☎ 310 821), at Avenida Bartolomé V Ramón 16, where you can rent a car from 3800 pta a day in the low season.

FORMENTERA

Formentera is the smallest of the four Balearic Islands. It is also the least developed and least crowded. On this idyllic island it is still possible to find yourself a strip of sand out of sight of tourist colonies and out of earshot of other tourists. If you're looking for an island atmosphere without the luxury and expense associated with Ibiza and Majorca, Formentera may well be for you.

Orientation & Information

Formentera's port is in the settlement of La Sabina, which is around three km north of the administrative capital, San Francisco Javier. From San Francisco, the road runs south some five km towards Cabo de Barbería. There are a couple of tracks leading to the coast on the way. The road to the east of San Francisco runs down the middle of the island, with the main beaches of Mitjorn and Es Caló south and north of the road respectively. At the far eastern point of the island is the Formentera lighthouse.

For information on Formentera, you should go to the tourist office in Ibiza. If you are already in Formentera when you read this suggestion, go to the capital, San Francisco

SPAIN

Javier. The Patronat Municipal de Turisme (☎ 322 057) is at Plaça Sa Constitució 1. Staff there may be able to help you, but they are chronically short-staffed, and out of season the office is only sporadically run by friendly people who don't have much information.

Things to See & Do

Es Caló and Mitjorn are the two main stretches of beach on Formentera, both made up of numerous coves. Mitjorn is the one to go to if you are looking for your own stretch of beach.

There is a particularly beautiful stretch of white, sandy beach jutting out from Es Pujols towards Ibiza. There are a couple of bars out on the promontory, so it can get quite lively at times. If you keep on walking past the bars, you will come to the end of the island. A short wade across a narrow strait brings you to Isla Espalmador, a tiny islet with beautiful, quiet beaches. If you come a little out of season, you could well have the islet to yourself.

Places to Stay & Eat

Camping is strictly not allowed on Formentera and you will promptly be thrown off the island if caught in the act.

Formentera's only nightlife to speak of is in the town of Es Pujols. As such it is quite a popular place to shack up for the night. A couple of places worth trying there are *Hostal Tahiti*, (☎ 328 122), which has singles/doubles, including breakfast, from 2835/4600 pta in the low season, 3000/5000 pta in the high season, and *Hostal Los Rosales* (☎ 328 123).

If you prefer peace and quiet you would be better off in Es Caló. Both *Fonda Can Rafalet* and *Casa de Huéspedes Miramar* are good value. Neither has a telephone (at least not one they want to make public). In both cases the address is simply Es Caló.

Getting There & Away

Most people arrive at Formentera by ferry from Ibiza. Departures from Ibiza for the 30-minute crossing are at 9 am, 1, 5 and 6 pm every day except Sunday. You can return to Ibiza at 8 and 10.30 am, 4 and 5.30 pm. On Sundays, ferries leave Ibiza at 9.30 and 11.30 am and 5.30 pm. Departures from Formentera are at 9 am, 10.30 am and 5 pm. The fare for a one-way journey is 1200 pta. A return costs double.

The other option is to take the 4½-hour ferry trip from Denia on the mainland (between Valencia and Alicante). The ferry leaves Denia at 10.30 pm on Saturday and the return ferry leaves Formentera at 11 am on Sunday. The one-way fare is 4970 pta per person. For a car you have to pay 12,400 pta, motorbikes cost 3900 pta and bicycles cost 1800 pta.

Getting Around

There are two or three car rental agencies by the harbour, but the island is too small to justify the cost. Your best bet is to rent a bicycle in the port town of La Sabina. The going rate is around 500 pta a day, though this is tipped to double as Formentera becomes more popular.

VALENCIA

Spain's third-biggest city, and capital of the province of Valencia, comes as a pleasant surprise to many. Home to paella and the Holy Grail, it is also blessed with great weather and *Las Fallas* (in March), one of the wildest parties in the country.

Orientation & Information

Plaza del Ayuntamiento marks the centre of Valencia. With the exception of the train station, most points of interest lie to the north of the square and are generally within easy walking distance. The Turia River cuts the central region of the city from the northern and eastern suburbs. This once mighty river is now almost dry since being diverted after serious flooding last century. The old river bed is slowly being turned into a city-length park.

The tourist office is at Plaza del Ayuntamiento. The staff can supply you with an accommodation list if you are having trouble finding somewhere to stay. The post office and the telephone centre (open until 11 pm) are in the square as well.

A small selection of English-language novels is available at The English Book Centre at Calle Pascual y Genis 16. There is a self-service laundrette at Calle Pelayo 11 (near the station), where a load of washing costs 300 pta and drying costs 250 pta.

Things to See & Do

One of Valencia's most raved about attractions is the Baroque **Palacio de Marqués de dos Aguas**. The façade is extravagantly sculpted and the inside is just as outrageous. It contains the **Museo de Cerámica** (200 pta entry), which houses a big and impressive collection of ceramic art.

The **Museo de Bellas Artes** ranks among the best museums in the country, after the Prado and Bilbao. It contains a beautiful collection, including works by El Greco, Goya, Velázquez and a number of Valencian impressionists. Entry to the museum costs 200 pta (free to ISIC holders). You can reach it on bus No 11 if you think it is too far to walk. Another museum with works by El Greco, among others, is in the **Colegio de la Patriarca** on Plaza de la Patriarca. Entry costs 100 pta and it is only open to the public from 11 am to 1 pm.

Valencia's **cathedral** is also worth a visit. Climb to the top of the tower for a great view of the sprawling city. Unbeknown to many Christians, this cathedral is also home to the **Holy Grail** (Santo Cáliz). It is in a small chapel in an annexe of the cathedral.

Places to Stay

The nearest camp site is 10 km south of Valencia at El Saler (☎ 367 041). There is a youth hostel (☎ 359 0152) at Avenida del Puerto 69, but it is usually full.

The price and quality of accommodation in Valencia varies enormously. Among the cheaper places worth considering are the very well-situated *Hospedaría del Pilar* (☎ 331 6600), at Plaza del Mercado 19, with singles/doubles from 800/1500 pta or *Pensión San Martín* (☎ 392 2616), Calle Chofrens 8 (3rd floor), with singles/doubles

from 1200/2000 pta. Places in this price range are hard to come by unless you head into the red-light district (not recommended). Otherwise, the best prices you are likely to find are in places such as *Hostal Alicante* (☎ 351 2296), Calle Ribera 8, with singles/doubles from 2800/3300 pta, or *Hostal Castelar* (☎ 351 3199), nearby at No 1, with singles/doubles from 1590/2968 pta. There are a few places in Calle Bailén and Calle Pelayo near the station, but they are not very good deals and tend to be noisy.

Places to Eat

There is an excellent food market on Plaza del Mercado. If you are looking for a more civilised, knife-and-fork type meal, there is no shortage of good-value establishments in Valencia. *Mos Cafetería*, Plaza Porchets 1, has a menu for 750 pta. For the same price you can have an excellent menu, which often includes a Valencian paella, at *Cafetería Escocia* on Calle de Caballeros near the cathedral. *Cervecería Bar La Ceu* on Plaza Miracle del Mocadoret, off Plaza de la Reina, has a menu for 1000 pta, as does *Restaurante La Rolonda* at Plaza Redonda 6. For a great splurge you can't go wrong at *Restaurante Don Ramón*, Calle Salva 2, with a menu for 900 pta and à la carte from 3000 pta. One of the best places for breakfast or tapas is *Barrachina* at Plaza del Ayuntamiento 2.

Entertainment

The best area for Valencia's excellent nightlife is on and around Plaza Xuquer and Avenida Blasco Ibañez, near the university. It is quite a way from the centre of town – you'll have to walk for around 45 minutes or take a taxi or a bus (No 81 from Plaza del Ayuntamiento). Unfortunately, by the time it is worth being there, the buses have stopped running.

There is also nightlife in the old town, but the area has a pretty bad reputation and may not be very safe. All the same, there is a never-ending selection of bars to choose from, and the best streets to start on are Calle Serranos or Calle Quart.

SPAIN

Calle San Pío
1

Calle Pintor

Calle de Caballeros
2
Plaza de la Virgen

Calle Micalet
3

Calle Cabillars
5

Calle Bolsería
4

Plaza del Mercado
6

Plaza de la Reina

Calle San Martín
7
8
9

Calle de la Paz

Av. María Cristina
Calle San Fernando

10

Calle Poeta Querol
Plaza de la Patriarca
11
13

To Plaza Xuquer

Calle Pintor Sorolla
12

Plaza los Pinazo

Calle Pérez Bayer
Calle Barcas

Avenida Barón de Cárcer
Calle Garrigues
Calle en Sanz
Calle Padilla
Calle Periodista Azzati
Calle Martín
Calle de la Sangre
Calle en Vicente

Plaza del Ayuntamiento

Calle Correos

Calle Roger de Lauria

14
15 16
17

18
19
21
20

Calle de Ribera

Calle de Colón

Avenida Marqués de Sotelo

San Vicente Mártir

Calle de Játiva

22

23

Plaza de Toros

Cirilo Amorós

Gran Via Marqués del Turia

Valencia

0   100   200 m

■ PLACES TO STAY

4 Hospedería del Pilar
8 Pensión San Martín
9 Hotel Bristol
19 Hotel Europa
20 Hostal Alicante
21 Hostal Castelar

▼ PLACES TO EAT

2 Cafetería Escocia
5 Cervecería Bar La Ceu
6 Central Market
7 Restaurante La Rolonda
11 Restaurante Don Ramón
12 Restaurante Austria 7
13 Mos Cafetería
14 Barrachina

OTHER

1 Museo de Bellas Artes
3 Cathedral
10 Museo Nacional de Cerámica
15 Town Hall
16 Tourist Information
17 Post Office
18 Telephones
22 Tourist Information
23 Railway Station

After you've had your fill of bars and you feel like dancing, *Distrito 10* can be highly recommended. For more information on nightlife, buy a copy of *Turia* from any newsstand (100 pta).

Getting There & Away

The best way to get from Valencia to Madrid is by train. The trip, which generally takes a little over four hours, costs 2995/4740 pta one-way/return (via Albacete to Atocha). There are trains at 7 and 9 am, noon, 4.30, 5.30, 5.45, 7 and 11.10 pm. Via Cuenca, the trip is considerably cheaper, but it can take almost twice as long and there are only three trains a day (8.30 and 11.10 am and 3.30 pm).

There are nine trains a day to Barcelona. The trip takes four to six hours and the basic fare is 2260 pta one-way. Seven trains a day ply the route to Alicante, taking anywhere

from two to four hours. The basic fare is 1120 pta one-way. Most of these trains stop in Xàtiva on the way to Alicante.

A major freeway, the E-15, runs all the way from Alicante through Valencia to Barcelona, and on into France. For a slower, cheaper (no toll gates) and more picturesque coastal route, you can follow the N-340, which runs alongside the freeway for most of the distance.

See the Ibiza section for information on transport from Valencia to the Balearic Islands.

Getting Around

Although Valencia is a big city, most of the attractions are within walking distance of the city centre. Notable exceptions can all be reached by bus. Valencia's beach, Malvarrosa, is serviced by bus No 19, which leaves from Plaza del Ayuntamiento. The same bus will take you to the Balearic Islands' terminal. Bus No 81 goes to the university and the best nightlife in town, and bus No 11 will drop you off at the Museo de Bellas Artes. Both these buses also leave from Plaza del Ayuntamiento.

MORELLA

The fairy-tale town of Morella, in the north of Valencia Province, is an outstanding example of a medieval fortress. Perched on a hilltop, crowned by a castle and completely enclosed by a wall over two km long, it is one of Spain's oldest continually inhabited towns.

The closest thing to a tourist office in Morella is in the town hall. The staff are very friendly and will help you as much as they can, but they don't have much information. They will also supply you with ridiculously oversized maps of the town. The telephone code for Morella is 964.

Things to See & Do

Morella's wonderful castle is the town's most exciting monument. Although it is in ruins it is still most imposing. You can almost hear the clashing of swords and clip-clop of horses that were once a part of everyday life

SPAIN

in the fortress. The views are breathtaking and there are so many intriguing nooks and crannies to explore that you could easily spend a couple of hours up in the castle grounds. Just watch out for ghosts. Entry to the castle is free. It opens at 9 am and closes at 2 pm on the dot – if you are not out by then, you will have to spend the night.

Places to Stay & Eat

Hostal El Cid (☎ 160 125), Puerta San Mateo 2, is the town's best known hotel. They have singles/doubles from 1100/1900 pta, doubles with shower 3300 pta. *Fonda Moreno* (☎ 160 105), Calle San Nicolas 12, is considerably cleaner and cheaper, with doubles from 1400 pta. Full board costs 2200 pta per person. *Hotel La Muralla* (☎ 160 243), Calle Muralla 12, has singles/doubles from 2200/2800 pta.

All three of these places have restaurants of sorts, with *Fonda Moreno* offering the best value at 850 pta for a menu. The three-star *Hotel Rey Don Jaime* (☎ 160 911), Calle Juan Giner 6, has singles/doubles from 4000/6500 pta.

Getting There & Away

There is one bus every day to/from Villaroz on the coast. Twice a week there is a service to/from Alcañiz in Aragon. These are the only public transport services, and departure times are not particularly fixed. Your best bet for such information is to ask at Hostal El Cid.

If you are driving or hitching to Morella in winter, check the weather forecast first, as the town is sometimes snowed in for days. If all is well, you will need to get onto route N-232, which runs from Saragossa to Villaroz, passing Morella on the way.

ALICANTE & THE COSTA BLANCA

The coast as far as the border of Murcia is no less popular with package-deal tourists than the Costa del Sol. Who hasn't heard of such best avoided nightmares as Benidorm and Torrevieja? Inland, however, there are one or two surprises and Alicante itself is large enough to absorb the tourists admirably.

Alicante and the surrounding coastal area, the Costa Blanca, is one of Europe's most heavily touristed regions. If you want to find a secluded beach in midsummer, you should keep well away from here. If, however, you are looking for a lively social life, white, sandy beaches and a suntan...

Orientation & Information

You will find a tourist office in any town of consequence on the Costa Blanca. In Alicante the main information office (☎ 520 0000) is on Plaza del Ayuntamiento. There is another tourist office next door to the bus station on Calle Portugal. Alicante's telephone code is 965.

There is a laundrette near the bus station at Calle Reyes Católicos 16. In summer, the English-language *Costa Blanca News* is published weekly in Alicante and can be bought at most newsstands along the Costa Blanca.

In Santa Pola, the tourist office is at Plaza de la Diputación s/n (☎ 541 5911) near the edge of town as you come in from Alicante. In Torrevieja the tourist office (☎ 571 5936) is centrally located at Plaza Capdepont s/n. Be warned that they have a very long lunch break at this office: it is closed from 1 to 5 pm.

Benidorm's tourist office (☎ 585 3224) is on the edge of the old town, not far from the waterfront, at Calle Martinez Alejos 16. The small information office in Altea is on the waterfront directly opposite Paseo Joaquín Mirallas 33. It is open from 10 am to 1 pm, and again from 5 to 8 pm (more or less).

Things to See

Alicante Alicante is a surprisingly refreshing town, with wide boulevards, long, white, sandy beaches, and a number of attractions beyond the standard coastal offerings of Benidorm, Torrevieja and others. The most obvious attraction in Alicante is the **Castillo de Santa Barbara**, a 16th century fortress overlooking the city. There is a lift shaft deep inside the mountain which will take you right to the castle. The entrance to the lift is on Paseo Juan Bautista at Playa Postiguet. It is

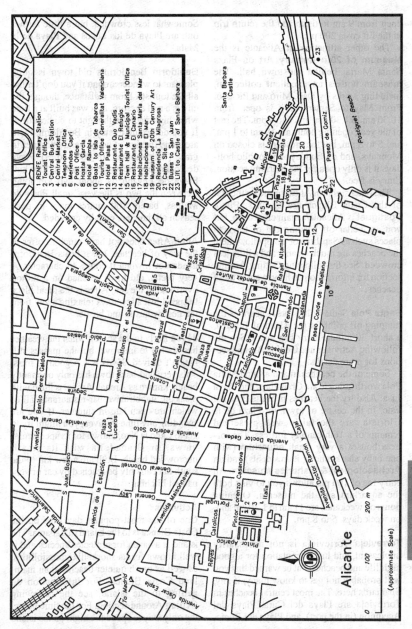

1 RENFE Railway Station
2 Tourist Office
3 Central Bus Station
4 Central Market
5 Telephone Office
6 Meriendas Capri
7 Post Office
8 Hostal Garcia
9 Hotel Rambla
10 Boats to Isla de Tabarca
11 Tourist Office Generalitat Valenciana
12 Hotel Palas
13 Restaurante Quo Vadis
14 Restaurante El Refugio
15 Town Hall & Municipal Tourist Office
16 Restaurante El Canario
17 Habitaciones Santa Maria del Mar
18 Habitaciones El Mar
19 Museum of 20th Century Art
20 Residencia La Milagrosa
21 Camp Site
22 Buses to San Juan
23 Lift to Castle of Santa Barbara

Alicante

0   100   200 m

(Approximate Scale)

open from 9 am to 6 pm and the return trip in the lift costs 200 pta.

The other attraction in Alicante is the **Museum of 20th Century Art** on Plaza Santa Maria, behind the town hall. The museum houses an excellent collection, including works by Dali, Miró and Picasso. From May to September it is open from 10.30 am to 1.30 pm, and 6 to 9 pm. The rest of the year, opening hours are 10 am to 1 pm, and 5 to 8 pm, but the museum is closed on Mondays, and on Sundays and public holidays it is only open for the morning session. Entry is free.

The other sights in Alicante and on the rest of the Costa Blanca are beaches. **Playa Postiguet** is Alicante's main city beach, but you are better off heading out of town to places such as San Juan or Campello, where the beaches are much cleaner and a little less crowded. See the following Getting Around section for information on how to get to these beaches.

Santa Pola Santa Pola is best known as the jumping off point for the island of Tabarca, a short 30-minute ferry trip away. See the following Activities and Getting Around sections for more details.

Some of the beaches in and around Santa Pola worth going to are Gran Playa and Playa Lisa. Also try the beaches in Santa Pola del Este. In the centre of town, on Plaza de la Glorieta, are the fairly well preserved remains of a 16th century fortress. The fortress houses a very small **aquarium** (with one baby shark among its residents) and an **Archaeological & Fisheries Museum**. An entry fee of 100 pta allows you to visit both the aquarium and the museum. Opening hours on weekends are 11 am to 1.30 pm and, on week days, 5 to 8 pm.

Torrevieja Torrevieja is not necessarily unpleasant, and has a reputation for a good nightlife and beaches, but be warned that you will probably not get to know many, if any, Spaniards here. The most central beaches in Torrevieja are Playa del Cura, Playa del Acequión (in the port), and Playa del Rocío.

Somewhat less crowded, but a little farther out, are Playa de los Locos and Playa de la Mata.

Benidorm Benidorm's old town is quite pleasant to wander around if you don't mind all the tourists. From a distance, though, the city is a real eyesore, as it was built at a time when high-rise was thought to be beautiful. If you do decide to stay in Benidorm, there are some five km of white, sandy beaches to grace (with another 100,000 bodies). Playa de Poniente is the longest beach at three km. Playa de Levante is about two km long. Between the two is the very small Playa de Malpas, barely 100 metres long. In peak season all three are equally crowded.

Altea Altea does not have much to offer in the way of beaches, but it beats Benidorm hands down when it comes to character. A very pretty, old town perched on a hilltop overlooking the sea, Altea is the ideal place to spend just a few days relaxing away from the nearby hustle and bustle.

Jávea Early in the season when the weather has started to improve, but the masses still haven't arrived, Jávea is too good to miss. This very laid-back town has only one sandy beach, known as Arenal. Arenal is lined with pleasant, unobtrusive bar-restaurants, all of which are open late in summer. If you are spending any time in Jávea, you might try to get to Cabo la Nao, known for its spectacular views, or Granadella with its small, uncrowded beach. Both are a few km to the south but can only be reached by car or very patient hitching.

Activities

One of the most popular day trips on the Costa Blanca is to the island of Tabarca. The island is a haven for protected species and is well known for its snorkelling possibilities, as well as much quieter beaches than mainland Costa Blanca. For information on getting to the island, see the following Getting Around section. For the time being, the only way to spend the night on the island is to camp. However, there are plans afoot to build a hotel in the next few years, and when this happens, camping will probably be banned.

Places to Stay & Eat

Alicante One of the cheapest places to stay in Alicante is *Habitaciones Santa María del Mar* (☎ 521 3230), Calle Lonja de Caballeros 4, which has singles/double for 900/1500 pta in the low season and 1100/2200 pta in the high season. *Habitaciones El Mar* (☎ 521 4156), Calle Jorge Juan 23, has the same price all year with singles/doubles for 1500/3000 pta. *Residencia la Milagrosa* (☎ 521 6918), Calle Villavieja 8, is a budget bargain with singles/doubles for 1000/2000 pta. If you are looking for a little more comfort, try the three-star *Hotel Palas* (☎ 520 6690) on Plaza Puerta del Mar, which has singles/doubles for 4730/7590 pta in the low season, and 5830/9355 pta in the high season. It is questionable whether it earns the three stars, but it is pleasant enough and well placed for the beach and the old town.

For a varied menu and prices to suit most budgets, try *Cafeteria Capri*, Calle San Ildefonso 6, which has 22 different platos combinados costing from 550 to 1300 pta. They also have a menu for 750 pta. *El Canario*, Calle Maldonado 25, is a no-frills local eating house which does a hearty menu for 580 pta. The restaurant attached to Hotel Palas has quite a good reputation. They have a menu for 1800 pta, or you can eat á la carte for around 3000 pta. Another place in a similar price and quality range is *Quo Vadis*, Plaza Santisima Faz 3, which is known for its seafood.

Santa Pola The most convenient camp site to Santa Pola is *Camping Bahia* (☎ 541 1012). It is about 15 minutes' walk from the tourist office at Calle Partida Rural de Valverde Bajo 9. *Hostal Manolita* (☎ 541 3542), by the market on Plaza Maestro Quislant, has singles or doubles for 3000 pta. The attached restaurant does a menu for 650 pta.

Mesón Los Arcos at Calle San António 46,

offers a good-value menu of local fare for 800 pta. For something a little more up-market, try *Restaurante Patilla*, Calle Elche 29, which has a menu for 2300 pta, or you can eat á la carte from around 3000 pta.

Torrevieja *Hostal Belén* (☎ 670 1635, Calle Apolo 45, has singles/doubles with bathroom for 1250/2450 pta low season and 1500/2700 pta high season. Rooms without bathroom cost 900/1000 pta per bed, in both the high and low seasons. The attached restaurant has a reasonable menu for 700 pta. *Pensión Leandro* (☎ 571 0100) at Calle Huerto 2 offers basic singles/doubles for 1000/2000 pta low season and 1200/2400 pta high season. Full board costs 2500/2600 pta per person, high and low seasons. If you don't want to eat in your hotel, try *Mes'n Restaurante Puerto Bello*, Calle Ramble Juan Mateo 6, which has a fairly reasonable menu for 850 pta.

Benidorm The most accessible of Benidorm's camp sites for those without their own transport is *Camping Vilasol* on Camino Viejo de Valencia (the old road to Valencia). If you are looking for a hotel or pensión, the tourist office has a list of available beds which is updated daily. They can also give you information on appartments for rent. If you want to try your luck at booking a room before you arrive, try the two-star *Hotel Internacional* (☎ 585 0271), Paseo de la Carretera 40. In the low season the rooms are excellent value with singles/doubles going for a song at 2500/3000 pta. In the high season, they are not such a bargain at 4000/5500 pta. Another interesting option is *Hostal Jardín* (☎ 585 0620), Calle Tomas Ortuño 10, which offers full board at 1800/3000 pta per person in the low/high season.

Finding somewhere to eat in Benidorm is not an issue. There are countless places covering the full spectrum of prices and tastes. The level of competition seems to keep the quality reasonably high.

Altea *Hotel San Miguel* (☎ 584 0400) on the

waterfront at Calle La Mar 65, has pleasant singles/doubles for 2000/3800 pta low season, and 2800/5000 pta high season.

Jávea Though you can stay in the main town of Jávea, it is about three km from the beach. There is a camp site, *Camping Naranjal* (☎ 579 2989), about 10 minutes' walk from Arenal beach. You pay 1100 pta for a site, 400 pta for a tent, and 350 pta per person. If you are not interested in camping, follow the coastal road north from Arenal for about one km until you reach the port, where there are a number of reasonably priced pensions and guesthouses. Try *Fonda Pachanca* (☎ 579 0510) at Calle Cristo del Mar 6, with singles/doubles for 1500/3000 pta, or *Hotel Miramar* (☎ 579 1000) at Plaza Almirante Bastarreche 12, with singles/doubles for 2000/3400 pta low season and 2250/4240 pta high season.

The best place for food is at one of the bar-restaurants along Playa Arenal. Both pensions mentioned here have restaurants with menus for around 1000 pta.

Getting There & Away

Alicante is the gateway to the Costa Blanca. There are at least 10 trains to Madrid every day, taking anywhere from four hours for the fastest Talgo to eight hours for the night train. The basic fare is 2810/4450 pta one-way/return. There are three direct trains to Barcelona every day, all of which make a stop in Valencia on the way. The basic fare is 3420/5420 pta one-way/return (1195/1890 pta one-way/return to Valencia).

There are a number of buses every day to Almería (2135 pta one-way), Granada (2790 pta one-way), Valencia (1600 pta one-way), Barcelona (3790 pta one-way), Madrid (2500 pta one-way) and others.

You can fly to Alicante from most major airports in Spain. There are also flights from many European cities, including London, Amsterdam, Paris and Frankfurt. Very often you can arrange a package deal which includes flight and one week's accommodation at a Costa Blanca resort. Check with a travel agent.

Getting Around

There are two possibilities for those who wish to visit Isla de Tabarca. From Alicante there are a number of boats going each direction every day in summer. The rest of the year the boats run on a demand basis. The trip takes 50 minutes each way and the return fare is 1000 pta. For information on timetables, call Kontiki on ☎ 521 6396 or after 8 pm on ☎ 526 0922, or simply go to the boats on La Espalanada.

The other point of departure to Tabarca is Santa Pola. Boats leave from the port almost every day of the year; the trip takes 30 minutes each way and costs 700 pta return. Timetables vary, so call in advance to check departure times (☎ 541 2338).

To get to Campello and San Juan, you can either take bus No C1 or C2 from Plaza Puerta del Mar in Alicante, or you can take the *trenete* (little train) along the coast towards Denia. Rail passes are not accepted on this train as it is run by the private FEVE line.

Benidorm is on the Alicante-Denia FEVE line. Bus No 1 runs from Plaza Triangular to the train station on Calle Estación. If you prefer to travel by bus, Benidorm's bus station is on Avenida de Jaime I, and is best reached on bus No 8 from Plaza Triangular.

Jávea is most easily reached by bus from the town of Gata, which in turn is on the Alicante-Denia FEVE line.

MURCIA

The Murcian coast, beyond Cartagena, has some of the least developed beaches on the Mediterranean coast, and towns in the interior, such as Lorca, have a flavour unique to this part of the country.

The best known and most touristed beaches in the area are in the so-called Mar Menor, just south of the Valencian Murcian border. You are better off passing them by and heading on to Mazarrón to the west of Cartagena, or even farther to the golden beaches at Águilas. Both Mazarrón and Águilas have camp sites and it is possible to swim here without dying of hypothermia as early as the beginning of March.

Andalusia

The stronghold of the Moors for seven centuries and the pride of the Christians for many more thereafter, Andalusia (Andalucía) is home to two of Spain's most treasured monuments: the Alhambra in Granada and the Mezquita in Cordova. Among the other beautiful cities in Andalusia are Seville; the town of Ronda, set in the hills inland from the Costa del Sol; and Jerez de la Frontera, the home of sherry and Spain's finest horses.

Andalusia has the longest coastline of any of the Spanish regions, stretching from the quiet beaches of the Costa de Almería to the mayhem of the Costa del Sol, then beyond to Gibraltar. It comes within 14 km of the African coast before opening up to the Atlantic Ocean on the Costa de la Luz, which sweeps by Cadiz and the beautiful, isolated Doñana National Park, and on to the Portuguese border.

SEVILLE

Seville (Sevilla) is one of the most exciting cities in Spain. EXPO '92 plunged the city into the international limelight with mixed results. It is now a very expensive city, so it is worth planning your visit carefully; there is no point spending lots of money and not enjoying yourself. In summer, Seville is stiflingly hot and not a fun place to be in. In midwinter, the nightlife and general entertainment is not up to scratch. If you really want to experience Seville at its best, you should try to come for a festival – a truly unforgettable experience.

Orientation

Seville's main thoroughfare, Avenida de la Constitución, runs more or less north-south with the city's most important monuments, the cathedral and the Alcazar, close by on the east side. The Guadalquivir River meanders through the city to the west of the centre, separating it from the main nightlife areas in the south and the EXPO '92 grounds in the

north. The new train station is a few km east of the cathedral and the bus station, near the beautiful Plaza de España, is just a few hundred metres south-east of the Alcazar.

Information

The main tourist office is on Avenida de la Constitución, very close to the cathedral. Staff there are very knowledgeable about their city, but as a result it is often extremely full and you may find yourself waiting half an hour for information. Seville's telephone code is 954.

One of Seville's few self-service laundrettes is at Calle Castellar 2. There is a second-hand bookshop with a small selection of English books at Pasaje de la Vila 2 (Barrio de Santa Cruz).

Things to See

Cathedral The Cathedral of Santa María de la Sede is listed in the *Guiness Book of Records* as having an area greater than any other in the world. It is 126 metres long, 82 metres wide and 30 metres high. Its structure is primarily Gothic (1401 to 1507), though there are substantial Baroque and neoclassical (1618 to 1929) additions. The tower, known as the Giralda, is Moorish and dates from the 12th century. The climb to the top of the Giralda is well worth the effort for the great views of the city. It is also quite an easy climb, as there are no stairs but a ramp all the way up the inside.

Christopher Columbus' remains are proudly displayed in the main entrance of the cathedral. The four crowned bearers represent the four kingdoms of Spain at the time of Columbus' sailing.

Entry to the cathedral costs 250 pta, which includes the Giralda. The cathedral is open Monday to Friday from 11 am to 5 pm, Saturday from 11 am to 4 pm and Sunday from 2 to 4 pm.

Alcázar Though the Alcázar is undoubtedly a magnificent monument to the Moorish occupation of Spain, it is really just the poor cousin of Granada's Alhambra. The Christian restorations helped to create a classical

SPAIN

Seville
(Sevilla)

0   125   250 m

SPAIN

Mudéjar building, with beautiful and extensive gardens which are still immaculately tended today. If you haven't been to the Alhambra yet, you will certainly be taken aback by the incredible detail in which the Moorish architects worked. It is open Tuesday to Saturday from 10.30 am to 6 pm, Sunday and public holidays from 10 am to 2 pm. On Monday, as is usual in Spain, it is closed. Entry is free to students, but everyone else has to fork out 300 (justifiable) pta.

Archivo de las Indias This museum houses one of the most important archives in the world. It contains over 40 million documents, dating from 1492 through to the decolonisation of the Americas. Most of the

documents are in files which can only be consulted with special permission. There are, however, a number of beautiful and well-preserved original maps on display, dating from the late 16th century. Entry is free, but you must present your passport at the door.

Places to Stay

The first thing you will notice about accommodation in Seville is that it is very expensive. It has always been among the most expensive cities in Spain and EXPO '92 settled it once and for all. The best area to look for cheap accommodation is in the streets beyond Plaza Nueva, about 10 minutes' walk from the cathedral. *Casa Saes* (☎ 441 6753), Plaza de Curtidores 6, is a real bargain with singles/doubles from 1700/3000 pta. *Huéspedes La Montera* (☎ 412 407), Calle San Clemente 12, is even better, with singles/doubles from 1100/2200 pta. *Hostal Pino* (☎ 421 2810), Calle Tarifa 6, is small but must be about the cheapest place in town with rooms from 1500/2400 pta, 3000/4000 pta with shower.

There are a few mid-range pensions worth considering. *Pensión Lis* (☎ 421 3088) at Calle Escarpín 10 has doubles for 3500 pta. *Pensión Lis II* (☎ 456 0228), in a beautiful house at Calle Olavide 5, charges 1700/3500 pta for singles/doubles. *Hostal Monsalves* (☎ 421 6853), Calle Monsalves 29, has doubles only for 3500 pta, and *Hostal Generalife* (☎ 224 638) at Calle Fernán Caballero 4, has singles/doubles for 1500/3000 pta.

Hotel Simón (☎ 422 6660), at Calle García de Vinuesa 19, in a typical 18th century Sevillian house, has pleasant singles/doubles for 4300/6000 pta. Another hotel in a similar class is *Hotel Residencia Amefa* (☎ 218 189) at Calle Pozo Amarillo 18. Singles/doubles are a little dearer at 5500/7975 pta.

The Barrio de Santa Cruz, behind the cathedral, is one of the most beautiful parts of the city. It is also a popular area to spend the night, though in general it is more expensive than the area beyond Plaza Nueva. *Pensión Cruces* (☎ 422 6041), at Plaza de las

SPAIN

Cruces 10, with singles/doubles from 2000/3000 pta and dorm beds for 1300 pta, is in one of the quietest spots in Seville, and *Pensión San Pancracio* (☎ 441 3104), at Plaza de las Cruces 9, is probably the best deal in Barrio de Santa Cruz with singles/doubles for 1500/2400 pta, or doubles with bath for 3000 pta. The *Hostal Monreal* (☎ 421 4166) at Calle Rodrigo Caro 8 has rooms from 2120/3180 pta. *Hostal Toledo* (☎ 421 5335), Calle Santa Teresa 15, has rooms from 3180/5300 pta. *Huéspedes Sweet Dreams* (☎ 419 393), may have a corny name but it is well positioned at Calle Santa María la Blanca 21. It has singles/doubles from 2000/4000 pta.

Places to Eat

The cheapest way to eat in Seville is to buy your food from the market. Mercado del Arenal, on Calle Arenal and Calle Pastor Hilandero, is the biggest market in town.

It's difficult to find a restaurant meal for less than 1000 pta. There is no need to panic, however, as there are a few well-kept secrets in town. *Cafe Bar El Callejon*, Calle Adriano 24, for example, has a selection of menus, each costing 700 pta. *Cafe Bar Nipal* in Pasaje de las Delicias has a menu for 700 pta, and at *Bar Restaurante El Solomillo*, Calle Santas Patronas s/n (off Calle Reyes Católicos), you can have a menu for 2000 pta.

For a delicious seafood meal in a beautiful little restaurant right in the heart of Barrio Santa Cruz, try *Restaurante La Cueva* at Calle Rodrigo Caro 18. They have a menu for 1500 pta, and you can eat á la carte for around 3000 pta.

Often your best bet is to forget about full menus and go for platos combinados. *Cafe Bar Guadalquivir*, Calle García de Vinuesa 21, has a good selection with some platos as cheap as 550 pta. *Cafe Restaurante Alianza*, Plaza Romero Morube, in Barrio de Santa Cruz, has medium-sized platos from 650 pta. *Restaurante Punta del Diamante* on the corner of Alemanes and Constitución, has platos from 700 pta.

Entertainment

Seville is entertainment city. Its most famous festival happens during the *Semana Santa*, the week leading up to Easter Sunday. Although the festival culminates in a religious fervour which you would be hard pushed to see elsewhere, it is also an excuse for a really wild party. The other big festival here is the *Feria de Abril*. This festival takes place at the end of April and lasts around 10 days. It has been suggested that the festival is needed to counter the pious feelings that arise from Semana Santa, but then, Sevillians don't really need an excuse to party.

Even if you cannot be here for a festival, you should have no trouble filling in time in the evenings in Seville. Most of the night spots are concentrated on the south-east bank of the Guadalquivir River. On Calle Betis, which runs right alongside the river, there are numerous discos and noisy but atmospheric bars. Names and trends change so often that it is really just a matter of following the locals. *Discoteca B-60*, Calle Betis 60, is one of the few hangers-on. It is outrageously crowded and great fun.

When you have lost enough weight in the discos, there are plenty of places to cool off with a drink. Along Calle Asunción, the southern extension of Calle Betis, are a number of very with-it places, and farther south-east is the area known as Los Remedios, bordered by Calle Fernando and Calle Ramón de Carranza. Los Remedios is totally jammed with bars and music spots, and has something for everyone. Don't come until at least midnight, unless you are looking for deserted streets.

On the west side of the river, there is plenty of action earlier on. It is considerably more staid, but it is where most people start out after dinner. Calle San Eloy has a number of good, cheap bars with great tapas. One of the best known bars in Seville is the very cheap *Patio de San Eloy* at Calle San Eloy 7. The early evening atmosphere here is simply too good to miss. One place on this side of the river which does stay open late is *La Carbonería*, in Calle Lesies in Barrio de

Santa Cruz. It often has live music after 11 pm during the week. It is pretty hard to find, and is often full with foreigners, but is definitely worth the effort.

Seville is Spain's flamenco capital. Unfortunately, flamenco has become big business. Unless you get lucky at La Carbonería or wandering around in Los Remedios, or come to Seville for the Feria de Abril, you will have to pay at least 2000 to 3000 pta to get into a club where you will sit with another 500 foreigners. The best and most touristy club is *El Gallo* in Barrio de Santa Cruz.

Sevillian bullfights are said to be the best in the country. During the Feria de Abril, they take place every day at 5.30 pm. Although bullfighting has a long tradition in Andalusia, young Sevillians are starting to realise that no matter how 'brave' the *torero* (bullfighter) might be, it is still a horrific, frightening and painful death for the poor animal.

Getting There & Away

Train To go by train from Seville to Granada, Algeciras and Málaga, you have to change in Bobadilla. Departures are at 7.45 am, 12.05 and 5.05 pm, with reasonable connections in Bobadilla to all three towns.

Trains for Barcelona leave Seville at 8.53 am, 6.12 and 8 pm; the trip takes 12 to 15 hours. Trains bound for Barcelona all make a stop in Cordova, between one and two hours after leaving Seville. Basic fares are as follows: Seville to Barcelona, 5975/9455 pta one-way/return, and Seville to Cordova, 795/1260 pta one-way/return.

In the other direction, you can head to Huelva and on to the Portuguese border at Ayamonte. The train station in Ayamonte is about one km from the ferry across the Guadiana River into Portugal. There is no bus from the station to the river, so you either have to walk or hitch (which tends to be difficult). There are seven trains a day to Huelva, with reasonable connections from there on to Ayamonte.

In addition to the train services mentioned here, there is a super-fast service to Madrid called AVE. This is the Spanish version of the French TGV and the German ICE. At present the only line is between Madrid and Seville (often stopping in Cordova, among other cities). It began carrying paying passengers the day after EXPO '92 opened, in order to make it feasible for visitors to make a day trip down. Rail passes are not valid for the train, and it could be years before this situation changes. The fare varies according to the departure time and the number of stops the train makes between Madrid and Seville. There are six AVEs a day in each direction and the trip takes from 2½ to three hours. Fares start at 6000 pta and vary upwards to 16,500 pta one-way. Seville-Cordova fares start at 1500 pta one-way, and Cordova-Madrid fares start at 4400 pta one-way. The return fare is always double the one-way fare.

Bus There are buses to Madrid at 10 am, and 3 and 11 pm. The eight-hour trip costs 2090/3400 pta one-way/return. Málaga is around three hours away, with some 10 buses plying the route daily for 1615 pta one-way. There are four to six buses a day to Salamanca, at a cost of 3380 pta one-way, and the trip takes eight hours. Although many other destinations are served by train, it is generally faster and cheaper to go by bus.

Car Compartecoche (☎ 4214895) at Calle Amparo 22 (2nd floor), is an intercity carpooling service. Some of their recommended one-way prices from Seville are: Madrid 1950 pta, Málaga 800 pta, Barcelona 3700 pta, Paris 6870 pta. Their service is free to drivers. Office hours are Monday to Friday 11 am to 1.30 pm and 4 to 6 pm.

Getting Around

The only time you are likely to use public transport in Seville is to get to and from the new train station. Bus No 70 stops on Avenida Kansas City, right next to the station, and runs to the bus station. Bus No 27 runs directly to the tourist office from Avenida Kansas City.

If you are having trouble finding a taxi, there is a stand on Plaza Nueva at the northern end of Avenida de la Constitución.

SPAIN

GRANADA

During the period of Moorish domination of Spain, Granada was the finest city on the peninsula. Today it is still home to the greatest Moorish legacy in Europe, and one of the most exciting and inspiring attractions on the continent – the Alhambra.

Orientation & Information

Granada's main street, Gran Via de Colón, runs east to west, with the cathedral and the central Plaza Bib-Rambla to the south, at the eastern end. Running north to south at this end of the city is Calle Reyes Católicos, with Plaza Nueva at the northern end. From Plaza Nueva, Cuesta de Gomerez runs north-east to the Alhambra, while north from the square is the Albaicín, Granada's Arab quarter.

The most conveniently located tourist office is in Arco de Cucharas, a small street off the south side of Plaza Bib-Rambla. If you need more detailed information, try the offices on Plaza de Mariana Pineda or Plaza del Padre Suárez. The first one is particularly good for information about other parts of Andalusia.

Granada's telephone code is 958.

Things to See

The Alhambra One of the greatest accomplishments of Islamic art and architecture, the Alhambra is simply breathtaking. Much has been written about the fortress, the palace, its patios and gardens, but somehow nothing can really prepare you for what you will see. A brief introduction to the various parts of the Alhambra, however, may help you to appreciate it a little more.

The Alcazaba is a Moorish fortress dating from the 11th to the 13th centuries. The views of the city from the tops of the towers are great. The Palácio de Nazaries is the centrepiece of the Alhambra. The intricacy of the stonework, epitomised by the Patio de los Leones (Patio of the Lions) and Sala de las Dos Hermanas (Chamber of the Two Sisters), is somehow unreal, and is clearly the highlight of the Alhambra. Finally, there is the Generalife. This was the summer palace of the sultans. It is set in the soulsoothing Alhambra gardens. The gardens and the Generalife make a great place to relax and contemplate the rest of the Alhambra complex from afar.

Other Attractions Granada's biggest attraction after the Alhambra is the city itself. Simply wandering around the narrow streets of the **Albaicín** district (not too late at night) or the area around **Plaza Bib-Rambla** is a real pleasure. On your wanderings, stop by the **Archaeological Museum** in the Albaicín and the **Capilla Real** (Royal Chapel) in which Ferdinand and Isabella, the liberators of Granada in 1492, are buried along with their daughter and son-in-law. Next door to the chapel is Granada's **cathedral**, which dates in part from the early 16th century. The Gypsy caves of **Sacromonte** are another popular attraction. See the Entertainment section in this chapter for more information.

■ PLACES TO STAY

1 Hostal Viena
3 Hostal Residencia Gomerez
13 Pensión Muñoz
14 Huéspedes Romero
15 Huéspedes Capuchinas
16 Hostal Zurita
17 Pensión Europa
18 Pensión Marquez

▼ PLACES TO EAT

2 Restaurante Morillo
4 Restaurante La Riviera
5 La Nueva Bodega

OTHER

6 Telephones
7 Royal Chapel & Cathedral
8 Tourist Information
9 Tourist Information
10 Post Office
11 Laundrette
12 Tourist Information
19 University

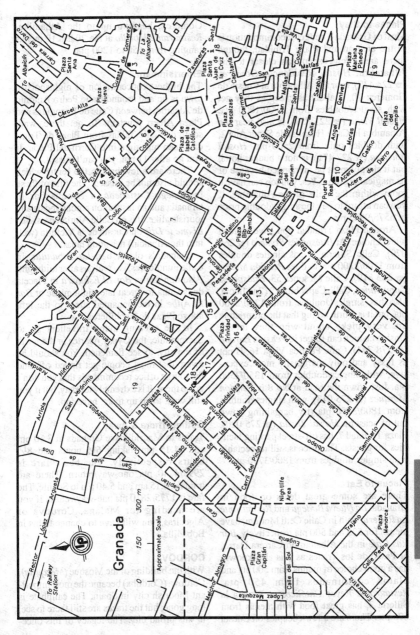

Granada

Approximate Scale

0   150   300 m

To Railway Station

Places to Stay

Most of Granada's budget accommodation is in the area around Plaza Trinidad, though there are a few exceptions closer to the Alhambra. *Hostal Residencía Gomérez* (☎ 224 437), near the Alhambra at Cuesta de Gomérez 10, is about as cheap as they get with singles/doubles from 1000/1800 pta. *Hostal Viena* (☎ 221 859), is also near the Alhambra in Calle Hospital de Santa Ana 2, with doubles only from 2500 pta. *Hostal América* (☎ 227 471), is not a budget hotel, but it simply must be mentioned because of its magical position. Yes, you too can have a room within the walls of the Alhambra, if you can afford to pay the single/double price of 6575/9965 pta.

Around Plaza Trinidad you have a much wider choice. At *Huéspedes Romero* (☎ 266 079), Calle Sílleria 1, has singles/doubles from 1100/2200 pta, as does *Pensión Muñoz* (☎ 263 819), Calle Mesones 53. *Huéspedes Capuchinas*, Calle Capuchinas 2 (2nd floor), also has singles/doubles from 1200/2400 pta, but it is worth noting that the proprietors are very picky about who they let in. Unshaven men can forget it. *Pensión Europa* (☎ 278 744), Calle Fábrica Vieja 16, is not as fussy and only marginally more expensive, with singles/doubles from 1350/2500 pta. Just down the road at No 8 is *Pensión Marquez* (☎ 275 013), with singles/doubles from 1800/3750 pta (try bargaining down out of season). *Hostal Zurita* (☎ 275 020), Plaza Trinidad 7, has off-street parking facilities for guests. The price is still respectable with singles/doubles from 1800/3750 pta.

Places to Eat

There are some great deals on food in Granada. *La Nueva Bodega* and *Restaurante La Riviera*, both in Calle Cetti Meriém, have menus for 525 and 500 pta respectively. *Bar Ras Café* in the Albaicín on Carrera Darro, or Paseo de los Tristes as it is also known, has a good choice of menus from 500 pta and platos combinados from 450 pta. *Restaurante Reyes Católicos* at Placeta la Sílleria 3, has great food with menus from 675 pta. There are a few cheapies on Cuesta Gomerez, heading up to the Alhambra. *Restaurante Morillo* at No 20 has 10 menus ranging from 650 to 1200 pta.

Entertainment

The highest concentration of nightspots in town is on and around Calle Pedro António de Alcarón, between Calle de Recogidas and Plaza Albert Einstein. To get there, walk south on Calle Tablas from Plaza de Trinidad, then turn right into Carril del Picón. If you go after 11 pm, you can't miss it.

There are a few bars in the centre which should also not be missed. The first of these is *Bodega Castañeda*, a famous bar in Granada and an institution among locals and tourists alike. It is on Calle Almireceros. *Bar El que te Dije* on Cuesta de la Victoria (well into the Albaicín) has good tapas.

Granada's oldest bar, *La Sabanilla*, in Calle Fundidores, is a real gas after midnight. Also don't miss *Bar El Eshavira* in Placeta de la Cuna for great late-night music or *Bar El Ajibe* in the unnamed street to the left, above Plaza de Cuchilleros.

In the evening many travellers go to Sacromonte, the Gypsy quarter in the north of the city, to see flamenco. You should be aware that most people get ripped off, and the tourist office recommends that you don't go up there. It is extremely touristy, but if you still want to go up there, have fun.

Getting There & Away

Trains to Madrid leave Granada at 3.10 pm and 11.15 pm, taking 6½ hours and 8½ hours respectively. The basic fare is 2995/4740 pta one-way/return. There are trains at 8.15 am and 5.40 pm to Seville. The fare is 1775/2810 pta one-way/return. If you are heading for Málaga, Cordova or Algeciras, you will have to change trains in Bobadilla.

CORDOVA

With the building of the Mosque *(Mezquita)*, Cordova (Córdoba) became the most important Moorish city in Spain. The caliphate is long gone, but the traces are still there to see, in this proud city. The legacy of this once-great civilisation makes Cordova one of the most interesting and important historical centres in Spain.

Orientation & Information

Cordova centres on and around the Mezquita, which lies near the banks of the Guadalquivir River. The Mezquita is surrounded by the Jewish and Muslim quarters, which make up the old town. The commercial centre of modern Cordova is Plaza Tendillas, a few hundred metres to the north-east of the Mezquita. From here streets run north, which is approximately towards the train station, north-west to the new suburbs, and south-east to Plaza de Corredera and the workers' suburbs.

The tourist office in Cordova is on Plaza de Juda Levi in the Jewish quarter near the Mezquita. The main post office is on Calle José Cruz Conde, north of Plaza Tendillas. There is a public telephone office on Calle Cardenal Herrero by the Mezquita. For late-night calls there are a number of phones on Plaza Tendillas.

Cordova's telephone code is 957.

The nearest laundry to the centre is on Calle Maestro Prieto Lopez, off Camino de los Sastres, about 1500 metres north-west of the Mezquita.

Things to See & Do

After Granada and Seville, Cordova seems almost provincial. It is quite a laid-back town, and a pleasant place to spend a couple of days just relaxing. Its most important attraction is the **Mezquita**. Built by the Emir of Cordova, Abd ar-Rahman in the 8th century AD, and enlarged by following generations, it became the largest mosque in the Islamic world. In 1236 it was converted into a cathedral, but it was not until the 16th century that the choir and high altar were built, adding to the staggering proportions of the mosque. Opening hours are 8.30 am to 1.30 pm, and 4 to 7 pm daily. Entry is free from 8.30 to 10 am and on Sunday mornings, otherwise it will cost you 500 pta.

If you can manage it, try to visit the Mezquita on a Sunday morning. There are sometimes as many as five masses going on at the one time (up to 25 in a day!). Search out a mass in one of the smaller chapels – they often have Baroque singers accompanying the priest.

Cordova's **Archaeological Museum** on Plaza Jerónimo de Paez is also worth a visit, though it is often closed for renovations. On the other side of the Guadalquivir River, across the **Roman Bridge**, is the Tower of Calahora, which houses the **Museum of Three Cultures**. Although some aspects of the museum are rather kitsch, it contains an excellent model of Granada's Alhambra and some of the commentary in the light-and-sound display is interesting.

Places to Stay

Cordova's youth hostel (☎ 290 166) probably has the best position of any youth hostel in Spain. It is a little sterile, but as it has no curfew and is cheap (610/795 pta for juniors/seniors), it is well worth considering. It is on Plaza Juda Levi, by the tourist office.

Most people tend to look for lodgings in the area around the Mezquita. There are a few very well positioned places which are worth trying out. *Hostal Martinez Rücker* (☎ 472 562), Calle Martinez Rücker 14, with singles/doubles from 1200/2400 pta, is particularly friendly and only a stone's throw from the Mezquita. *Hostal El León* (☎ 473 021), Calle Céspedes 6, has singles/doubles from 1200/2400 pta. *Hostal Nieves* (☎ 475 139), Calle La Cara 12, also has doubles from 2200 pta (no singles). The *Fonda Agustina* (☎ 470 872), Calle Zapatería Vieja 5, is unbeatable on value with singles/doubles from 1000/2000 pta.

For those with a little extra to spend, *Hostal El Triunfo* (☎ 47 55 00), Calle Cardenal González 79 by the mosque, is a real treat. Comfortable singles/doubles/triples cost 3286/5194/6254 pta.

If you want to keep away from the tourist masses as much as possible, there are a few pensiones on and around the Plaza Corredera, a little farther from the centre. *Hostal Plaza Corredera* (☎ 470 581), Calle Rodriguez Marín 15, has singles/doubles

Paseo de la Victoria
Concepción
Avenida del Gran Capitán
Cruz Conde
Conde de Torres
Rua Casas Deza
Morano
Eduardo Dato
Pérez
Calle Morería
Calle José Cruz
Plaza San Miguel
Calle Carboneli y
Calle Alfaros
Lope de Hoces
San Felipe de Castro
Conde de Gondomar
Calle de Alfonso XIII
Calle de San Pablo
Tesoro
Homo Trinidad
Calle de Sevilla
Plaza Tendillas
Claudio Marcelo
Plaza Trinidad
Plaza San Juan
Rua Sánchez
Jesús María
Leiva Aguilar
Calle Barroso
Saavedra
Juan de Mena
Conde Cárdenas
Reloj
Pastor
Almanzor Romero
Buen
Deanes
Ángel Saavedra
Alfa San Ana
Juan Valera
Pompeyos
Morales
Diario Córdoba
C Pedro López
Blanco Belmonte
Fernando Colón
C Rodríguez Marín
2
3
4
Manríquez
Calle Cardinal Herrero
Encarnación
11
Eulogio Ambrosio de Morales
12
Calle Maese Luis Tarrillo
Plaza Cañas
Plaza de Juda Leví
Calle de Torrijos
6
10
Calle de Oslo
Heredia
Julio Romero de Torres
Calle de San Fernando
San Francisco
Calle de San Francisco
Calle de la Candelaría
Carlos Rubio
13
14
15
5
Magistral Glez Francés
9
8
Altayabas
Calderéres
Calle Lineros
Lucano
Don Rodrigo
Mucho Trigo
16
17
Amparo
Paseo de la Ribera
7
Ronda de Isasa
Guadalquivir River
Roman Bridge
18
Acera Mira al Río
Acera Homos Gitanos
Cordova (Córdoba)
Avenida de la Confederación
Acera Arrecife
Acera Pintada
Calle del Santo Cristo

0   100   200 m

SPAIN

```
■  PLACES TO STAY

 2   Youth Hostel
 4   Hostal León
 7   Hostal El Triunfo
 8   Hostal Trinidad
 9   Hostal Martinez Rucker
12   Pensión San Francisco
13   Hostal Plaza Corredera
16   Fonda Agustina
17   Hostal Nieves

▼  PLACES TO EAT

 3   Restaurante Self-Service Los Patios
10   Taberna Santa Clara
15   Casa Paco

     OTHER

 1   Post Office
 5   Regional Tourist Office
 6   Mezquita
11   Archaelogical Museum
14   Plaza de la Corredera
18   Tower of Calahorra
```

from 1500/2500 pta and *Pensión San Francisco* (☎ 472 716), Calle de San Fernando 24, has singles/doubles from 1150/2300 pta.

Places to Eat
You shouldn't have too much trouble finding somewhere to eat in Cordova. *Restaurante Self-Service Los Patios*, right by the Mezquita on Calle Cardenal Herrero, has a good choice of filling main courses with nothing costing over 500 pta. *Taberna Santa Clara* at Calle de Oslo 2 has a menu for 750 pta, as do the two restaurants in the city walls on Calle de la Luna, *Mesón de la Luna* and *Mesón de la Muralla*.

For a really first-class meal you can't go past *Restaurante Bandolero*, Calle de Torrijos 6 by the Mezquita. You should expect to pay around 4000 pta per person for an excellent seafood meal. If you are looking for one big splurge in Spain, this place would have to go high on the list of possibilities.

There is an excellent and cheap market in Plaza de la Corredera, a still relatively unknown part of town which is as much a place to see as a place to eat. The market gets going at around 9.30 am. For a great breakfast, come along at 9 am and have some *churros con chocolate* at *Casa Paco* (at No 47 in the square). You have to buy the churros outside from a street vendor.

Entertainment
As you might expect, Cordova has pretty good nightlife. If you start at Plaza Tendillas, most of the activity is to the north-east. In particular, try Calleja Barqueros, Plaza San Miguel, Calle Ramirez de Arellano, Calle María de Arjona and Calle del Caño. If you are getting peckish in the early hours, a really hot tip is *Bar Colombia* at Calle Conde de Cardenal 5, which must have the cheapest bocadillos in Spain.

Getting There & Away
Buses to Málaga, Granada and Seville leave from the south side of Avenida de Medina de Azahara. Buses to Madrid leave from Avenida de Cervantes near the corner of Calle Alhaken II. The train station is another 100 metres to the north of this corner.

There are over a dozen trains a day from Cordova to Seville. The trip takes under two hours and the basic fare is 795/1260 pta one-way/return. There are around six or seven trains to Bobadilla every day. Most of them continue on to Málaga, or allow for good connections to Granada and Almería from Bobadilla. All trains from Málaga to Madrid stop in Cordova on the way. The basic fare from Cordova to Madrid is 2750/4355 pta one-way/return.

COSTA DE ALMERÍA
The Costa de Almería is perhaps the last section of Spain's Mediterranean coast where you can have a beach completely to yourself. If you come in high summer, you can forget it, but Almería is Spain's hottest region, so even in late March or early April it is often warm enough to take in some rays and try out your new swimsuit.

Orientation & Information
The Costa de Almería begins in the Gulf of

SPAIN

Almería in the south-eastern corner of Andalusia. After rounding Cabo de Gata, the coast runs north-east to the border of Murcia. The city of Almería, which is the provincial capital, and Mojácar, a short distance south of Murcia, are the only population centres of any great interest to travellers. Mojácar, in particular, makes a good base for exploring the most secluded beaches.

The tourist office in Almería is at Calle Jesús Durban 1. They have reasonable maps of the city and basic information on the rest of the province. If you want information on some of the more remote places, you're better off asking in Mojácar. The tourist office there is in a small shopping mall off the main square in the old town.

The telephone code for Costa de Almería is 951.

Things to See & Do

Mojácar has a very large population of English pensioners. If you can accept them as a part of the landscape, and ignore the souvenir shops, it wouldn't be too hard to spend some time in town. In winter it is one of the great escapes from the cold of northern Europe.

Along the coast from Mojácar, towards Almería, are some of the most beautiful **beaches** on the Mediterranean coast. It is hard to believe, but many of these could almost be considered undiscovered, particularly those towards Cabo de Gata, such as **Playa de Monsul**. You will need your own transport to explore the coast effectively and find your own private paradise. The best thing to do when you do find it, is keep it to yourself.

A little way inland, between Mojácar and Almería, near the town of Tabernas on route N-340, is Mini Hollywood. This, and a number of other sites in the Almerian desert, have been the sets for a number of Westerns. The most famous production on this set has been *A Fistful of Dollars*. It's quite fun to see the place if you happen to be passing by.

The enormous **Alcazaba** is certainly the highlight of any visit to Almería itself. This 10th century Moorish fortress is the largest of its kind in Spain and, in its heyday the city it dominated was more important than

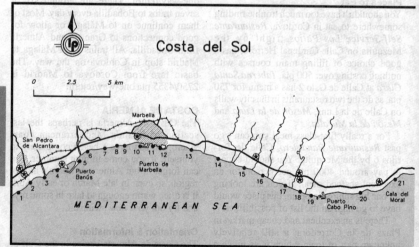

Costa del Sol

MEDITERRANEAN SEA

Granada. Entry to the Alcazaba is free for EC nationals, and 250 pta for others.

Places to Stay

Mojácar is not cheap, but there are still some pretty good prices around. The only budget option down at the beach is the camp site, El Cantal (☎ 478 204), which charges 450 pta per person, tent and car.

As a splurge, you might consider *Pensión Rio Abajo* (☎ 478 928), Playa de Mojácar, with singles/doubles from 3000/4500 pta, including breakfast. The cheaper places are all up in the old town. *Pensión La Justa* (☎ 478 372), Calle Morote 7, and *Pensión La Esquinica* (☎ 475 009), Calle Cano 1, both have singles/doubles from 1200/2300 pta. *Pensión El Torreon* (☎ 475 259), Calle Jazmín s/n, which has singles/doubles from 2700/3500 pta, is in one of the most beautiful houses in town.

If you want to rent a house inland from Mojácar, get in touch with Neinca (☎ 478 407) or Valle del Sol (☎ 478 362). With a little luck you should be able to find a fully furnished house from around 8500/10,000 pta a week in the low/high season.

Places to Eat

Cheap eats are pretty hard to find in Mojácar. In summer, *Restaurante La Ermita* has a menu for around 900 pta, otherwise they have platos combinados starting at around the same price. Down along the beach you can pick up a pizza for about 750 pta.

Getting There & Away

Almería is accessible by train from Madrid and Granada. From Almería to Mojácar, you will either have to go by bus or by thumb. There is also a bus service from Murcia via Lorca and Mojácar to Almería.

If you want to explore some of the more out-of-the-way beaches near Mojácar you will need a car. Alméricar down by the beach rents mokes or more civilised cars if you prefer.

COSTA DEL SOL

Twenty years ago the Costa del Sol was very much a place to be seen. Today it is still incredibly popular with package-deal tourists from Britain and Germany as well as with the time-share crowd. As a result, independent budget travellers do not tend to

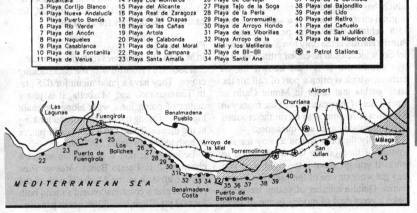

1 Playa Guadalmina	12 Playa de la Bajadilla	24 Playa de los Boliches	35 Playa del Saltillo
2 Playa San Pedro de Alcántara	13 Playa del Pinillo	25 Playa de las Gaviotas	36 Playa de Montemar
3 Playa Cortijo Blanco	14 Playa Los Monteros	26 Playa de Carvajal	37 Playa de la Carihuela
4 Playa Nueva Andalucía	15 Playa del Alicante	27 Playa Tajo de la Soga	38 Playa del Bajondillo
5 Playa Puerto Banús	16 Playa Real de Zaragoza	28 Playa de la Perla	39 Playa del Lido
6 Playa Río Verde	17 Playa de las Chapas	29 Playa de Torremuelle	40 Playa del Retiro
7 Playa del Ancón	18 Playa de las Cañas	30 Playa de Arroyo Hondo	41 Playa del Cañuelo
8 Playa Nagueles	19 Playa Artola	31 Playa de las Viborillas	42 Playa de San Julián
9 Playa Casablanca	20 Playa de Calabonda	32 Playa Arroyo de la Miel y los Melilleros	43 Playa de la Misericordia
10 Playa de la Fontanilla	21 Playa de Cala del Moral	33 Playa de Bil–Bil	
11 Playa de Venus	22 Playa de la Campana	34 Playa Santa Ana	✹ = Petrol Stations
	23 Playa Santa Amalia		

MEDITERRANEAN SEA

spend very long here. Many people pass through out of curiosity: Torremolinos, for example, has acquired such a bad reputation that it has been dubbed 'Terrible Torre'.

Orientation & Information
The Costa del Sol begins at Málaga and runs south-west towards Gibraltar and ever closer to the African coast. The main resorts along the coast are Torremolinos, Benalmadena, Fuéngirola, Marbella and, much closer to Gibraltar, Estepona. From Marbella onwards, you can see the Rif Mountains in Morocco on a clear day.

The telephone code for this area is 952.

Things to See & Do
The great attractions of the Costa del Sol are the weather, the beach and the warm Mediterranean water. It is true that the resort towns were originally characterful Spanish fishing villages, but that aspect has all but disappeared in most cases. **Torremolinos** and **Fuéngirola** are a high-rise continuum designed to allow as many people as possible to squeeze into the smallest possible area. This is mass tourism at its worst. It has gone so far that you will be surprised every time you hear someone speaking Spanish. For what it is worth, there is a ruined castle of sorts in Fuéngirola.

Marbella is much more inviting than Torremolinos and Fuéngirola. In the old town, which has managed to retain some of its original character, there is a well-preserved 15th century castle. The nearby town of **Puerto Banus** is the only town on the Costa del Sol which could be called attractive. It is also exorbitant. It is best known for its harbour, which is often a port of call for the same yachts that moor in Monte Carlo at other times of the year. A lot of the money in this town is rumoured to be on the crooked side, but nobody asks any questions.

Probably the only reason to stay for any amount of time on the Costa del Sol is to work. If you go about it the right way, you may get work on one of the yachts in Puerto Banus. Quite a number of young travellers make a great deal of money (some of them

bringing in over US$1000 a week) in Marbella, Fuéngirola and Torremolinos. You will probably notice them swarming all over middle-aged Europeans on the beach front promenades trying to sell them time-share properties.

Places to Stay
Surprisingly, there are some good accommodation deals on the Costa de Sol. In Málaga try *Hostal Lampérez* (☎ 2219 484), Calle Santa María 6 (2nd floor), which has singles/doubles from 1200/2000 pta, or *Pensión Córdoba* (☎ 2214 469), Calle Bolsa 7, with doubles from 2000 pta (no singles). In terrible Torre (molinos) *Pensión Minerva* (☎ 382 084), at Calle Cruz 10, is hard to beat with singles/doubles from 1300/2200 pta, and *Pensión Pedro* (☎ 380 536), Calle Bulto 1, also has good budget prices, with rooms for 1200/2000 pta.

Farther down the coast at Fuéngirola, there are singles/doubles from as little as 1000/2000 pta at *Hostal Paris Roma* (☎ 2471 149), Avenida de Santa Amalia 4. *Hostal Lido* (☎ 472 085), Calle Lorenzo Ramirez s/n, is another place worth trying.

Marbella has a great *youth hostel*, (☎ 2771 491), Calle Trapiche 2; juniors/seniors pay 715/883 pta without breakfast, 850/1150 pta with breakfast. If the hostel is full, don't panic, as there are also a couple of good-value pensiones in town. *Pensión Isabel de Pacheco* (☎ 2771 978), Calle Luna 24, for example, has doubles for 2400 pta.

Places to Eat
In Málaga, the *El Tormes* restaurant, on Calle San José is a favourite with the backpacking crowd. They have a good menu for 875 pta. In Torremolinos and Marbella, it is just a matter of going for a walk along the main highway or along the beachfront and looking at the menus. There are a number of places in both towns for under 1000 pta.

Believe it or not, it is possible to get a cheap meal in Puerto Banus. *Mamas Fast Food Cafetería* at the Marbella end of the port has platos combinados and a menu both for 600 pta. Their bocadillos are expensive.

Getting There & Away

Hundreds of thousands of tourists arrive at Málaga International Airport from all over Europe every year. As a result, there are some very good deals on flights, particularly from Britain and Germany. If you want to buy a ticket in Málaga, a one-way flight to London with Iberia costs around 59,100 pta. If you are under 25, you can get a reduction of up to 65% if you book your ticket directly through Iberia the day before you fly.

Getting Around

A local train leaves Málaga's main train station at least every 30 minutes from 6.03 am to 10.33 pm, bound for Fuéngirola. It stops at Málaga International Airport 11 minutes later, Torremolinos 20 minutes later and Fuéngirola 38 minutes later. The fare from the airport is 90 pta to Málaga, 165 pta to Fuengirola. From Fuéngirola, there is a frequent bus service to Marbella which continues as far as Algeciras, from where the ferries cross to Morocco. Fuéngirola-Algeciras is 785 pta.

Gibraltar

The British colony of Gibraltar sits on a narrow peninsula at the mouth of the Mediterranean Sea. It is about five km long and just over one km wide. It has had a rather rocky history, beginning with the Moorish invasion of Spain in 711 AD, when Tariq ibn Ziyad landed here with an army of some 7000 men. The rock has held his name ever since – Gebal Tariq, or Tariq's Mountain.

Between 1309 and 1506 Gibraltar changed hands on numerous occasions between Moorish and Spanish rulers. In 1704 an Anglo-Dutch fleet captured Gibraltar after a one-week siege. Spain attempted on more than one occasion to recapture the stronghold, giving in in 1713, when, in the Treaty of Utrecht, Spain ceded Britain 'the full and entire ownership of Gibraltar to be held and enjoyed for ever'. Although Spain tried again to recapture the rock, and Hitler

had his eyes on it as well, it has been sturdily in British hands ever since.

Today Gibraltar is a self-governing entity dependent on Britain only for defence. During the Franco years, Gibraltar was an extremely sore point between Britain and Spain, and the border was closed for many years. However, the Spanish socialists, under Felipe González, opened the border and have since made diplomatic attempts to change the colony's status. An overwhelming majority of Gibraltarians want to remain with Britain, so it seems unlikely that any major changes will occur in the near future. With the freeing of border and trade restrictions in the European community in 1993, many observers hope that the issue will be defused for ever.

Information

Gibraltar's main tourist information office is in the Gibraltar Museum opposite the corner of Bomb House Lane and Baker's Passage. The tourist office is open Monday to Friday from 10 am to 6 pm and Saturday from 10 am to 2 pm.

Gibraltar is probably the best place in the Mediterranean to stock up on your English-language reading material. Of the three bookshops on the rock, Gibraltar Bookshop at 300 Main St is the best.

The currency in Gibraltar is the Gibraltar pound or pound sterling. You can use pesetas here but you are better off using pounds as you get a better exchange rate. If you're from the UK, you should change any unspent Gibraltar pounds into UK pounds before you leave.

To call Gibraltar from abroad, dial the international access number, 350 (the code for Gibraltar) and the local number.

Things to See & Do

Gibraltar's anomalous status as the only colony on the European mainland is perhaps its greatest tourist drawcard. It is quite a pleasant city with a few unique attractions, and if you are in the region it is well worth visiting for a day or two. First and foremost of the rock's attractions is its small colony of

SPAIN

1 Tour Africa
2 Wun Tun Laundrette
3 Star Bar
4 Brass House
5 Continental Hotel
6 Telephones
7 Montarik Hotel
8 The Clipper
9 Miss Seruya Guesthouse
10 The Three Owls
11 Corks
12 The English Tearoom
13 Viceroy of India
14 Museum & Tourist
    Information Office
15 Gibralter Bookshop
16 The Angry Friar
17 Queens Hotel
18 Cable–Car Station

Gibraltar

0   75   150 m

Approximate Scale

Barbary Macaques, the only primates (apart from Homo sapiens) in Europe. There are two packs of apes in Gibraltar. Visitors can see one of the packs every day at **Apes' Den**, but the other lives wild on the slopes of the rock and is not often seen, even by local residents. The cheapest and most interesting way to get to the Apes' Den is to take the cable car (see the following Getting Around section), and follow the signs (and tourists).

The cable car continues up the rock from the Apes' Den to the imaginatively named **Top of the Rock**, from where there are spectacular views of Gibraltar, the nearby Andalusian coast, and the north coast of Morocco.

St Michael's Cave, 20 minutes' walk from the Apes' Den, is a natural grotto some 300 metres above sea level. It is best known for its stalagmites and stalactites. During WW II the cave was used as a hospital. Today, apart from attracting tourists in droves, the cave is used to host concerts, plays and even fashion shows. Ask at the tourist office about a guided tour through some of the many subterranean tunnels which lead off from the main chambers.

The **Upper Galleries** are an artificially made series of caves near the summit of the rock. They were excavated during the siege of 1779-83 in order to give better protection to the British troops, and more importantly, to protect their cannons from enemy fire.

Down in the town itself is the **Gibraltar Museum**, opposite the corner of Bomb House Lane and Baker's Passage. It contains an interesting historical, architectural and military collection as well as a most impressive model of the rock (completed in 1865). It also has a small collection of paintings, mainly by local artists. The museum is open Monday to Friday from 10 am to 6 pm and Saturday from 10 am to 2 pm. Entry is £1.

Places to Stay

Cheap accommodation and Gibraltar do not go together. The only true budget option on the rock is *Miss Seruya Guest House* (☎ 73220), 92/1a (1st floor) Irish Town (the street that runs parallel to Main St at the bottom end). Singles cost from £10 to £16 and doubles cost from £12 to £18. Beds are very limited, so you should book ahead, particularly in summer.

Your next best bet is *Queen's Hotel* (☎ 74000) at 1 Boyd St. Singles/doubles with communal bathroom facilities cost £24/33. Singles with bath or shower cost £33 and doubles with bath cost from £38 to £50, depending on the view you have from the room. Triples with bath cost £50. The *Continental Hotel* (☎ 76900) at 1 Engineer Lane is also worth considering. Singles/doubles cost £38/50. For around the same prices you can also rent a room at the very pleasant *Montarik Hotel* (☎ 77065) on Main St (the entrance to the hotel is on Bedlam Crt).

If these prices don't grab you, consider staying in the Spanish border town of La Linea. *Pensión La Perla* (☎ 76 9513) at Calle Clavel 10 has singles/doubles for 1500/2500 pta.

Places to Eat

Fish and chips, steak and kidney pie, eels and mash, roast beef and Yorkshire pudding – you can have them all in Gibraltar. Most pubs in town do counter meals with all sorts of British goodies on the menu. Try the *Star Bar* in Parliament Lane, which is said to be the oldest pub in Gib. Fish and chips and a pint of beer will only set you back around five quid. Another pub worth stopping at for a meal is the *Angry Friar* at 287 Main St. You'll find lots of pubs in Irish Town.

For great Indian food you can't go past the *Viceroy of India* at Horse Barrack Lane, Main St. You can eat à la carte for around £8 to £15, and the chef insists that he can do a curry to blow your socks off.

For a no-frills break, try the *English Tearooms* at 9 Market Lane (open from 9 am to 7 pm). The place isn't much to look at, but it is always full of local ladies, and they whip up the best scones, jam and cream this side of the English Channel/Bay of Biscay. At only £1.60 a serving, you can't go wrong. They also do daily lunch-time specials with prices from £2.50 to £4.

Getting There & Away

Bus Most tourists who do not fly to Gibraltar directly from the UK arrive on foot from La Linea in Spain. La Linea's bus station is only a five-minute walk from Gibraltar's passport control. Buses run from the bus station in La Linea to Málaga at 7 and 10.30 am and at 1.45 and 5.15 pm. There is also an 8.45 pm departure on Sundays. The trip takes around three hours and costs 975 pta one-way. Among the stops on the way are Marbella (1½ hours, 530 pta), Fuéngirola (two hours, 740 pta) and Torremolinos (2½ hours, 855 pta).

Buses leave La Linea for Algeciras every 30 minutes or so. It takes 45 to 50 minutes and costs 185 pta. Seville is a little over four hours away, with direct buses from La Linea at 7 am and 4 pm. The one-way fare is 2080 pta. There are also buses from La Linea to Madrid (12 hours, 3285 pta) and Barcelona via Valencia (8485 pta).

Ferry At present there is a ferry twice a week in each direction between Gibraltar and Tangier in Morocco. Departures from Gibraltar are on Monday and Fridays. From Tangier the ferry leaves on Sunday and Friday. The fare is £14/28 one-way/return. In Gibraltar the best place to buy your tickets is from Tourafrica International (☎ 79140) in Unit G10 of the International Commercial Centre at 2a Main St.

Getting Around

The bus from the frontier and the airport into town costs 30p.

Gibraltar can be covered on foot, but there are other options worth considering. The most obvious is the cable car, which is a tourist attraction in itself. Weather permitting, the cable car leaves from the lower station on Red Sands Rd every 10 minutes between 9.30 am and 5.15 pm. For the Ape's Den, you should disembark at the middle station. If you continue on to the top station (£4 for the round trip), you will be treated to one of the best views on the rock and a very expensive restaurant. From the top station it is a 20-minute walk down the hill to St Michael's Cave.

If you're in a hurry, you can take a taxi-driven tour of the rock. The tour will take you to St Michael's Cave, the Apes' Den, the Top of the Rock and the Upper Galleries. All taxi drivers charge the same fee of £20.

Extremadura

Extremadura is probably Spain's least known region – and yet it has much to offer the visitor. From the conquistador towns of Cáceres and Trujillo to the prehistoric dolmens of Valencia de Alcántara, and from the Virgin of Guadalupe to the stunning Monastery at Yuste, Extremadura is full of some of the most pleasant surprises that Spain has in store for the visitor. It can still be difficult, if not impossible, to get to some of the most memorable places without your own wheels, but it is worth the effort a thousand times over.

CÁCERES

No matter where you're coming from, the naturally attractive city of Cáceres is a breath of fresh air. The beautiful monuments, many of them capped with storks' nests, combine wonderfully with a young population and an active nightlife to make this one of Spain's most underrated cities.

Information

The tourist information office is on Plaza Mayor. It is open Monday to Friday from 10 am to 1.30 pm and 5 to 8 pm. If you decide to stay a while, you may find getting your clothes washed a real hassle. The nearest laundrette is quite a way from the centre on Avenida António Hurtado (off Plaza de América).

Things to See & Do

Cáceres was included on UNESCO's World Heritage list in 1986. As you pass through the 18th century **Estrella Arch** from Plaza Mayor into the walled old town, it becomes clear why. The road leads straight ahead to the **Iglesia de Santa María**, a magnificent 15th century building which is now the city's cathedral.

The **Archaeological Museum** in Plaza de San Mateo houses Cáceres' most important Moorish ruin, a 12th century reservoir with intricate horseshoe arches.

When the sun is shining, the real attraction of Cáceres is in simply walking around the old town. Among the numerous monuments worth looking out for are the **Arco de Cristo**, a gateway dating back to Roman times, the **Iglesia de San Mateo** which took over three centuries to build (it was completed in the 18th century), and the 15th century **Casa de los Pereros**, which is today the provincial museum of paintings, sculpture and religious art. The **Jewish quarter** around the hermitage of San António is also particularly interesting.

Places to Stay

The cheapest place to stay in town is *Pensión Marquez* (☎ 244 960), Calle Gabriel y Galán 2 (2nd floor), with doubles for 2000 pta (no singles). *Hostal Castilla* (☎ 244 404), at Calle Rio Verde 3, with singles/doubles for 1200/2400 pta is less likely to be full. *Fonda Soraya* (☎ 244 310), Plaza Mayor 20 (3rd floor), has doubles for 2400 pta. *Hostal Residencia Goya* (☎ 249 950), Plaza Mayor 11, is a little more up-market with singles/ doubles for 3600/3900 pta, although it will often be cheaper out of season.

Places to Eat

Cafetería Lux at Calle Pintores 32, just off Plaza Mayor, has platos combinados from 375 pta. *Cafetería Norba*, a little out of the centre (five minutes' walk from Plaza Mayor) has filling platos combinados from as little as 300 pta. *Mesón Cali* at Calle Santa Polonia 5, has a good vegetarian selection to go with very reasonable prices. If you're looking for a full menu, you need go no farther than *El Pato* right on Plaza Mayor. You'll know the place by the picture of Donald Duck above the entrance.

For a special treat, head for the *Bodega Medieval* (☎ 245 458) at Calle Orellana 1, at the top of the old town. A meal with a drink should set you back 2500 to 5000 pta. To get there, follow the signs in the old town to the parador, then follow the signs from the parador to the Bodega Medieval.

Entertainment

Nightlife in Cáceres revolves around Plaza Mayor. On weekends it is already bopping by 8 pm, though this early on the crowd is pretty young. The later you go out, the better it gets.

Getting There & Away

The bus and train stations are both some way out of town, more or less opposite each other. If you're coming out of the train station, turn right onto the highway, and cross the road to the bus stop. Bus No 1 will take you into town (or back again).

If you're headed for Trujillo, there are buses at 12.30, 1.30, 4.30 and 6.30 pm at a cost of 400/770 pta one-way/return. Buses to Salamanca leave at 7, 9 and 10.30 am, and 2 and 6 pm every day. There is a bus at 5 pm daily except Sunday, and there is an extra bus at 11.15 am on Sunday only. The fare is 1455 pta one-way.

There are seven trains a day to Madrid and six a day from Madrid. The general tariff is 2140 pta one-way. Lisbon is less than two hours away, with trains leaving at 5.37 pm and 3.51 am.

If you're driving, there are three major routes to look out for. To Trujillo and Madrid take route N-521. The same route runs west to Valencia de Alcántara and on to the Portuguese border. If you're headed for Coimbra or Oporto, this is the way to go. To Lisbon, take route N-523 via Badajoz. Route N-630 runs south to Andalusia and north to Plasencia and on towards Salamanca.

TRUJILLO

Trujillo is best known as the birthplace of Francisco Pizarro, the conquistador who led Spain to a bloody victory over the Incas. Several others of his genre were also born here, most notably Francisco de Orellana,

SPAIN

who was the first European to explore the Amazon.

The town is in many ways similar to Cáceres. Here too, the Plaza Mayor, with its **statue of Pizarro**, is the town's heart and soul (and home to the tourist office). Unfortunately, tourism has taken a more obvious toll here than in Cáceres, with scores of souvenir shops selling 'original, handmade' conquistador clothing. All the same, if you are spending some time in Extremadura, don't miss Trujillo. Once you get into the back streets, you'll quickly forget the tacky souvenirs.

Things to See & Do

The most dominant feature of Trujillo is its **castle**. Primarily of Arabic origin and dating to the 11th century, there are also signs of Roman and Christian influence. The **Iglesia de Santa María** is undoubtedly Trujillo's most beautiful church. It is an interesting hotchpotch of 13th, 15th and 16th century architecture. Inside are a number of magnificent paintings by Fernando Gallego of the Flemish school.

There are numerous convents in Trujillo, among them the 15th century **Convento de las Jerónimas** and the 16th century Franciscan **Convento de San Pedro**. Ironically, the town's most important monument, the **Monastery of San Francisco**, where Pizarro and his brothers are buried, is one of the less pleasing to the eye.

Places to Stay & Eat

Trujillo is not cheap, and as such, finding affordable accommodation can be a problem. *Pensión Pizarro* (☎ 320 255), right on Plaza Mayor at No 13, has singles/doubles from 1600/3200 pta. *Hostal Boni* (☎ 321 604), Calle Domingo Ramos 7, is slightly better value with singles/doubles from 1500/2500 pta.

Cheap food is even harder to find. Both of the places to stay just mentioned have restaurants offering reasonably priced meals, though they're nothing to write home about. *Restaurante La Troya* in Plaza Mayor, has some of the best food in town and, if you

select your food with care, it shouldn't break your budget. They have hefty main courses beginning at around 600 pta.

Getting There & Away

Buses from Cáceres to Madrid pass through Trujillo about an hour after leaving Cáceres. The bus station is on the Carretera de Badajoz (route N-V) which runs from the Portuguese border through Badajoz and Trujillo and then all the way to Madrid.

Getting Around

Trujillo is small and the centre of town is the only area of particular interest to tourists. If you drive into town, park your car in Plaza Mayor and give your feet some exercise. Many of the streets in this part of town are too narrow for cars anyway.

LAS HURDES

There is probably nowhere in Europe which has been left completely untouched by tourism. With barely 50 beds to let in the entire area, Las Hurdes comes about as close to pure as you'll find. It also happens to be extremely beautiful. It gets very hot in summer, but in spring and autumn it is a wonderful place in which to forget about the hassles of city life. Time has not quite stood still, but it has certainly slowed down, and many people still live in the traditional stone houses that are quite unique to this corner of Spain.

Orientation & Information

Las Hurdes are more or less bordered by Pinofranqueado in the south and Castile-León in the north and west. To all intents and purposes anything to the east of route N-512 is outside Las Hurdes as well.

The tourist offices in Cáceres and Plasencia can supply you with pamphlets about Las Hurdes. However, the maps which they have of the region are pitiful. The best map available of the region is a Spanish military map on a scale of 1:25,000. For the casual visitor though, our map is more than enough.

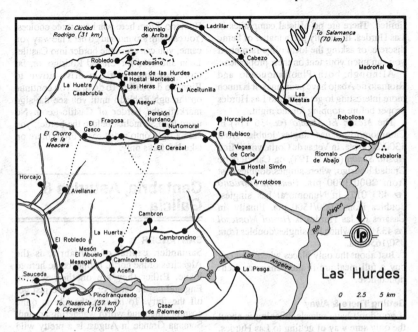

Things to See & Do

In Las Hurdes the things to see are villages and the thing to do is marvel at the scenery and simply walk along the trails and hillsides. Some of the more interesting places to stop at are described here.

Horcajada is a hamlet with a population of around 10 people. The turn-off is a poorly signposted road on the right as you enter El Rubiaco. There are plans to open a historical museum in Horcajada sometime this century.

From Nuñomoral you can make a side trip to El Gasco, from where there is a beautiful walk to a waterfall known as **El Chorro de la Meacera**. Back on the main road, a little past Nuñomoral, is Asegur, which has many traditional stone houses, and a little beyond that is Casares de las Hurdes, which is almost cosmopolitan. From here there is another side trip to the stunningly set Casabrubia, which also makes a great starting point for walks.

If you continue on to **Riomalo de Arriba**,

you will no doubt notice the isolation of this picturesque village. From here the road leads back towards route N-512. Make sure you stop in **Cabezo** and take a walk around the beautiful little town. Even the locals know they live in a special place, though they are quick to tell you that living and farming here is another story.

Finally there is **Las Mestas**. Quite a lively place in the evenings (everything is relative), it helps to ease you back into Spain as you knew it before you came to Las Hurdes. There is also a secondary road with great views which leads to Salamanca from here. If the weather is good, this road is worth keeping in mind. As you cross the border into Castile-León, you enter an area known as **Las Batuecas**. With a little luck and good timing you may be treated to one of the most extraordinary sunsets you've ever seen.

Places to Stay & Eat

Accommodation in Las Hurdes is extremely

limited. There are no official camp sites in
Las Hurdes. It is really just a matter of being
discrete, or asking the local olive farmers if
you can pitch your tent on their properties.

Although both Pinofranqueado and
Riomalo de Abajo have pensiones, it is much
more interesting to get right into Las Hurdes
proper before stopping for the night.

The *Mesón El Abuelo* (☎ 436 114) in
Caminomorisco has singles/doubles from
1300/2600 pta. In Vegas de Coria, you'll find
Hostal Simón (☎ 433 193), on Carretera de
Ciudad Rodrigo, where singles/doubles cost
from 2000/3500 pta. *Pensión Hurdano*
(☎ 433 012) in Nuñomoral has singles/
doubles from 1000/1500 pta. Finally, in
Casares de las Hurdes is *Hostal Montesol*
(☎ 433 025), which has singles/doubles from
950/1650 pta.

Just about the only places where you can
buy a full meal are in the pensiones mentioned here.

Getting There & Away

If you don't have wheels, hitching is about
the only sure way of getting to Las Hurdes.
There are rumours of an occasional bus
service from Plasencia to Pinofranqueado,
but no-one in Las Hurdes is willing to
commit themselves.

If you are driving, the easiest way is on
route N-512, which runs through north-
western Extremadura and on to Salamanca.
If you're coming from the south, this road is
rather complicated to find. Take the turn-off
from Plasencia to Carcaboso and follow that
road on to Montehermoso, Pozuelao de
Zarzón and Villanueva de la Sierra.
Pinofranqueado is signposted from this last
town.

Getting Around

Be warned that hitching can be painfully
slow, particularly out of season when there
is almost no traffic. If you're driving around
the region, the main gateway is Vegas de
Coria. The road to Nuñomoral will take you
into the heart of Las Hurdes.

Once you reach the Nuñomoral turn-off,
it is pretty straightforward until you reach

Robledo. From here you have three choices.
You can turn around and go back the way you
came, you can cross the border into Castile-
León and head for Ciudad Rodrigo, or, far
more exciting, you can drive down to
Riomalo de Arriba. To do this, you continue
on through Robledo until you see the sign
marking the border of Castile-León. No
more than 50 metres before the border, you
take a right onto a dirt road. From there on
take left forks only.

Cantabria, Asturias & Galicia

SANTANDER

Santander, capital of Cantabria, is the
Algeciras of the north. People come here to
leave. Either they are on their way to
England on the ferry, or they have just got
off the ferry. To be fair, the city is quite
cosmopolitan and worth wandering around.
Semana Grande in August is a pretty wild
party, but you won't find any accommodation here, or anywhere else on the north coast
at that time, without booking well in
advance.

Things to See & Do

Santander's main attractions are the nightlife
and El Sardinero beach. As you come around
to El Sardinero on bus Nos 1 or 2, there is an
uncanny resemblance to Bondi Beach in
Australia, with surfers out in force by mid-
March, despite the cold. The streets back
from the sea near El Sardinero are lined with
beautiful houses. This is some of Spain's
most expensive real estate.

Nightlife in Santander is centred around
Calle Santa Lucía. It is particularly good
between Calle Santa Lucía and the waterfront. In summer, there is also quite a good
scene in El Sardinero along the main drag.

Places to Stay

The most convenient camp site is less than
one km from El Sardinero. To get there from

the train stations, take the bus marked 'Cueto'. It stops directly in front of the site, but it is probably safest to ask the driver to let you know when to get off.

Santander has a reputation for overblown prices. That considered, *Fonda Perla de Cuba* (☎ 210 041), Calle Hernán Cortés 8 (1st floor), must be the best deal in town with singles/doubles from 800/1400 pta. *Hostal La Corza* (☎ 212 950), down the same street at No 25 (3rd floor), has pleasant rooms from 1800/3000 pta. *Pensión de Europa* (☎ 225 374), very near the bus station at Calle Calderón de la Barca 5 (3rd floor), is also reasonably priced with singles/doubles from 2500/3200 pta.

If you have just got off the ferry from England, you might be looking for a little more luxury. In that case, don't go past *Hotel Mexico* (☎ 212 450) at Calle Calderón de la Barca 3. Out of season the rooms are very reasonably priced with singles/doubles for 3300/5600 pta. In summer, the rates increase substantially, with singles/doubles going for 4600/7800 pta.

Places to Eat
The best place to look for cheap eats is on and around Calle Santa Lucía. *Bar Restaurante Cantabria*, Calle Rio de la Pila s/n, has a menu for 900 pta. At *Restaurante Fradejas* on Plaza Cañadio, you can sit at an outdoor table and catch a glimpse of the sea while you savour an 850 pta menu.

Bar Iguña at Calle Daoiz y Velarde 18, has a menu for 800 pta. It is not very exciting, but the food is edible and you would be pushing it to find cheaper in Santander.

For first-class regional specialties, try *Restaurante Cañadio* on Plaza Cañadio. Prices range from 800 to 2500 pta per dish. The squid in its own ink *(chipirones en su tinta)* is highly recommended.

Getting There & Away
Santander is one of the major entry points to Spain, thanks to the ferry link with Plymouth in England. For more information on this service, see the introductory Getting There & Away section.

Trains to Bilbao and Oviedo are run by FEVE, a private line which, unfortunately, does not accept rail passes. There are three trains a day to Bilbao (8.30 am, 2 and 6.30 pm). The trip, which takes just under three hours, costs 750 pta one-way. The fare to Oviedo is 1350 pta. There are two trains a day (8.35 am and 4 pm) and the trip takes over four hours.

Trains to Madrid are run by RENFE, so rail passes are valid. There are four trains a day (8.30 am, 3.45, 7.50 and 11.10 pm) which run via Ávila. The first three take around six hours to reach Madrid, while the last one takes almost nine hours and continues on to Málaga. The basic fare to Madrid is 3175/5030 pta one-way/return.

There are also hourly buses with Turitrans to Bilbao. It takes 2¼ hours and costs 790 pta.

SANTILLANA DEL MAR
The beautiful village of Santillana del Mar, also in Cantabria, has a wonderful feeling of timelessness. Cobblestone streets lined with well-preserved old houses give it a character all its own. When it rains in Santillana, the water pours off the overhanging roofs in a powerful torrent, somehow adding to the unusual charm of the town.

Things to See & Do
Santillana's fame lies as much in the nearby **Cuevas de Altamira** as it does in the town itself. The prehistoric paintings inside the Altamira caves reduce many people to tears, and all those lucky enough to gain entry are deeply moved by what they see. A maximum of 25 people a day are allowed into the caves free of charge.

If you want to be one of the few, you must request permission at least 10 months in advance, listing three or four preferred dates, by writing to: Centro de Investigación y Museo de Altamira, 39330-Santillana del Mar, Cantabria, Spain. Some people turn up on the day in the hope that someone has cancelled and they can get lucky. There is also a very impressive stalactite cave and a

SPAIN

museum on the grounds, to which there are no entry restrictions.

Places to Stay & Eat

Santillana is mainly a day-trippers' stop, so there is not much choice when it comes to staying overnight. There is a camp site a little way to the north of the town on the main highway. The very friendly González family runs a nameless *pensión* (☎ 818 199) of sorts at Plaza Las Arenas 4, with singles/doubles from 1500/2000 pta. Most of the other places are considerably more expensive. In an emergency, *Hostal Montañes* (☎ 818 177), Calle L'Dorat 8, has singles/doubles from 2500/4000 pta.

The only restaurant which even comes close to catering for budget travellers is *Casa Cossío*, Plaza Abad Francisco Navarro 12. If you exercise restraint, you can fill up on a couple of entrées and a drink for under 1000 pta. There's a menu for 950 pta.

Getting There & Away

There are four buses a day (six in summer) each way between Santander and Santillana del Mar.

If you are driving from Santander, take route E-70 towards Oviedo (east) and turn off to Comillas at Torrelavega. You will pass through a lot of ugly industrial territory, but don't worry, it stops well before Santillana.

PICOS DE EUROPA

This small mountainous region bordering Cantabria, Asturias and Castile-León, is considered to be some of the finest trekking country in Spain. Spectacular scenery, combined with unique flora and fauna, ensures a continual and growing flow of visitors from all over Europe and beyond.

Orientation & Information

The Picos are 25 km from the coast, and are only around 40 km long and 40 km wide. They are comprised of three limestone massifs. In the south-east is the Andara Massif, with a highest point of 2441 metres. In the west is the Cornión Massif, with a highest point of 2596 metres. In the centre is

the best known and largest, the Uriello Massif. The highest point in the Picos is here, soaring to 2648 metres.

If you want to do some serious trekking in the Picos de Europa, you would be well advised to buy a copy of Lonely Planet's *Trekking in Spain*. If you want to buy detailed topographical maps of the area before coming to Spain, Stanfords Maps in London (12-14 Long Acre, London WC2E 9 LP) can send you a list of all the maps available. Try getting hold of the *Mapa Excursionista del Macizo Central de los Picos de Europa* by Miguel Andrade (1:25,000) and *Mapa del Macizo del Cornión* by José Ramón Lueje (1:25,000).

Activities

Serious trekkers should allow plenty of time for the Picos. If you are not quite that adventurous, there are other options. Perhaps the least strenuous way to get a feel for the place is to drive up to Lago La Ercina from Covadonga in the west of the Picos or to Sotres in the east of the Picos. From either of these places you can set out on well-marked walking trails and into the heart of the Picos de Europa.

Places to Stay & Eat

On short trips into the Picos, Lago Ercina and Sotres are the best places to head for. At Lago Ercina, and at the nearby Lago Enol, there is a refuge and a restaurant. If you want a little pampering, then you could try one of the pensiones in Covadonga. In Sotres, *Pensión Cipriano* is both the place to stay and the place to eat.

Getting There & Away

If you don't have a car or much time, Covadonga and the lakes are more accessible than Sotres. There are four buses a day from Oviedo to Covadanga, with one of them continuing on to the two lakes. If you are driving, look out for the signpost to Covadonga on route N-634, a few km before it meets route N-632 at Ribadasella.

Most people heading for Sotres start off in Santander. There is no bus service, so you will have to hitch or drive. Follow route N-632 west from Santander to the intersection with route N-621. Follow this road the short distance to the town of Panes, then turn off (west) to Arenas de Cabrales. Sotres is signposted (south) from Arenas.

GALICIA

The region of Galicia has been spared the horrors of mass tourism that have affected many other parts of Spain. It is a land of hidden coves, rolling green hills, picturesque farm houses, potholed roads and pilgrims. In

winter, it can be freezing, with snow falling in the hills around Lugo. In summer, it has one of the most agreeable climates in Europe, although you must expect a little rain.

Orientation & Information

Galicia is roughly square in shape, with a rugged coastline that resembles the fjords of Norway. The Rias Gallegas, as these many inlets are known, hide some of the prettiest and least known beaches in Spain. In the centre-west of Galicia is its best known and

1 Casa Manolo
2 University Language School
3 Hospedaje Recarey
4 Tourist Office
5 Hospedaje Santa Cruz
6 Bar Azul
7 Hospedaje Ramos
8 Restaurante Camilo
9 Post Office
10 Cathedral
11 Plaza do Obradoiro

Santiago de Compostela

0   125   250 m

(Approximate Scale)

most important city, Santiago de Compostela, some 35 km from the coast. Around 60 km to the north on the coast is Corunna (the regional capital), famous for its wonderful waterfront promenade. Around the coast to the east, nearing the border of Asturias, are numerous little-known coves, which protect the cleanest beaches in Europe.

The tourist office in Santiago (☎ 548 081) is at Rúa del Villar 43.

Things to See & Do

Santiago de Compostela's old town is a work of art. The locals realised this long ago, which is why they come out in droves when the weather is good and simply wander around the streets and the beautifully landscaped Paseo de la Herredura park.

Santiago de Compostela is the end of the pilgrims' route to Santiago. This route was supposedly followed by St James in the 1st century AD. Many thousands of Christian pilgrims come to this beautiful city every year to pay homage to the bones of St James, which are inside the magnificent 11th to 13th century twin-towered **Cathedral** on **Plaza do Obradoiro**. The square itself is awe-inspiring.

The most important religious festivals in Santiago are the Festival of St James, which takes place in the second half of July, and the Festival of the Ascensión, which takes place at a different time every year.

Corunna's most interesting and most popular attraction is the **Torre de Hercules**. This 104-metre-high tower was built by the Romans as a lighthouse in the 2nd century AD. It is still in use!

If you are looking for the beach in Galicia, it is very difficult to decide where to go. One town worth serious consideration is **Foz**, to the east of Corunna, close to the border with Asturias. Foz itself is not the most exciting place you've ever been to. It does, however, have a pleasant atmosphere, good food, reasonable prices and, most important of all, lots of inviting beaches nearby.

If you don't have a car, there is a very beautiful beach, **Playa de San Cosmé**, across the river, which is accessible by ferry unless you want to paddle across on your surfboard. Otherwise there is Playa de Rapadoira in town and a little farther, for some really clean swimming, Playa de Llás.

If you have your own transport, you can get to some great beaches to the east. Starting at Ribadeo on the border and heading back along the coast towards Foz, make sure you stop off at Playa dos Castros, Playa Reinante and the wonderful long, white beach of Benquerencia, before you arrive at Playa de San Cosmé.

Santiago is also a university town. It is highly regarded for the Spanish-language courses offered throughout the year.

Places to Stay

Finding somewhere to stay in Santiago can be a real pain. It is true that the city is jammed with cheap pensiones, but more often than not they are full with local students when the university is in session, and with foreign students throughout the summer. There are several places worth trying. *Hospedaje Santa Cruz* (☎ 582 815), Rúa del Villar 42 (1st floor), has singles at 1200 pta and doubles at 1700 and 2000 pta. *Hospedaje Recarey* (☎ 588 194), Patio de Madres 15, offers singles/doubles from 1000/1500 pta. *Hospedaje Ramos* (☎ 581 859), at Calle Raíña 18 (3rd floor), is only a little more expensive with singles/doubles from 1200/2000 pta.

If you are looking for a little more comfort, one of your best options is *Hotel Gelmirez* (☎ 561 100). It is well located about halfway from the train station to the old town at Calle Horreo 92. All rooms have a bathroom, telephone, TV and a minibar. Singles/doubles cost 5700/8000 pta from April to October, and 4570/6400 pta the rest of the year.

If you decide to stay in Santiago for a course (or any other reason), your best option would be to look for a room in an apartment with local students. There are notice boards in the university building on Plaza del Instituto, as well as in various shop windows in Rúa das Casas Reales, at the north-eastern end of the old town.

Most of the budget hotels in Corunna are in the streets parallel to Avenida de la Marina. *Fonda María Pita* (☎ 221 187), Calle Riego de Agua pta 38 (3rd floor), is great value with singles/doubles from 900/1700 pta. *Hospedaje Soto* (☎ 225 813), on the same street at No 12 (2nd floor), has singles/doubles from 1200/2200 pta. If the places in the new town are full, you might try *Hospedaje Paris* (☎ 205 038), Calle Zapatería 5 (2nd floor), in the old town. It also has singles/doubles from 1200/2200 pta in winter, 1700/3400 pta in summer.

Foz is a little short on budget pensiones. *Fonda Morymar* (☎ 140 035), Calle Ramón Rodriguez 7, is a notable exception, with singles/doubles from 800/1600 pta in winter, 1100/2200 in summer.

Places to Eat

Casa Manolo, Calle San Agustin 1, in Santiago, is an institution. An excellent menu for 500 pta ensures that the place is always full of foreigners and local students alike. The new town, Calle Santiago de Chile, is lined with restaurants serving up menus from around 500 pta as well. There are also a couple of very good-value places on Calle del Cardenal Payá.

Restaurante Camilo (☎ 584 593), Calle Raíña 24, is one of the best seafood restaurants you are likely to find, unless you want to pay US$100 per head. The restaurant has been awarded prizes for quality and presentation of food, and all sorts of impressive people have eaten there (including François Mitterand, as the owner so proudly informs clients). Anyway the food is great and the menu only costs 1700 pta. If you can afford it, don't miss it.

In Corunna, *Mesón O'Calexo*, Calle de la Franja 32, has a menu for 625 pta. *Cafetería Tala*, at Calle de la Galera 32, has platos combinados from 475 pta.

The *Mesón Restaurante As Brasas*, at the bottom of Rúa Illa Novain in Foz, is fantastic. It serves a mouthwatering *churrasco* (barbecued spare-ribs) at 800 pta per portion. One portion should be more than enough for two or even three people.

Entertainment

As is to be expected of a university town, Santiago has a good social scene. One of the better bars in the old town is *Metate* in Callejon de San Payo. It serves a delicious hot chocolate if you've had your fill of harder drinks. Earlier in the day, *Bar Azul* at Rúa do Franco 83, serves great coffee.

Getting There & Away

Train There are two trains a day (at 1 and 9.15 pm) from Santiago de Compostela to Madrid. The day train takes nine hours and the night train takes almost 12 hours to reach Madrid. The basic fare is 4155/6575 pta one-way/return.

Santiago's railway station is south-east of the old town at the end of Calle Horreo (also known as Calle General Franco).

From Corunna to León, there are three trains a day. The basic fare is 2750/4355 pta and the trip takes between five and seven hours, depending on the train.

Bus Buses to Salamanca leave Santiago at 8 am, 3 and 7 pm. The morning bus costs 3790 pta, while the other two cost 2540 pta one-way. The trip takes around nine hours.

Buses to Oporto take five hours and cost 1600 pta one-way.

The bus station is a 10 to 15-minute walk to the north of the cathedral on Calle San Caetano.

The Basque Country, Navarre & Aragon

SAN SEBASTIÁN

The capital of the Basque province of Guipúzcoa, San Sebastián is famed as a ritzy resort for wealthy Spaniards who want to get away from the hordes in the south. It has long been a stronghold of Basque separatist feeling, well before El Generalísimo Franco banned the use of the complicated Basque language, Euskera, in the 1930s.

Donostia, as the city is known in Euskera,

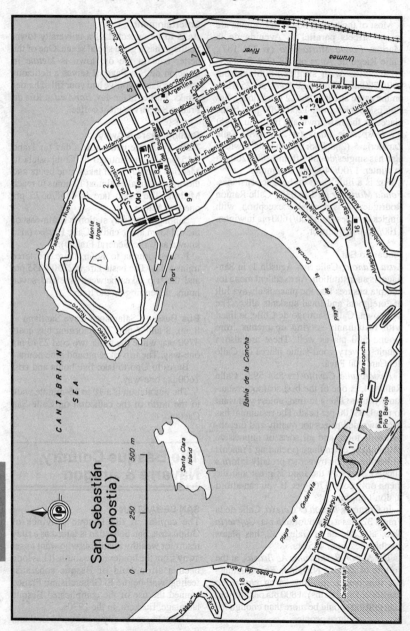

San Sebastián
(Donostia)

CANTABRIAN SEA

Monte Urgull

Old Town

Port

Santa Clara Island

Bahía de la Concha

Playa de la Concha

Playa de Ondarreta

Paseo Nuevo

Paseo Nuevo

Paseo del Peine

Paseo de Miraconcha

Paseo Pío Baroja

Urumea River

Avenida de Zurriola

Paseo República Argentina

Oyendo

Legazpi

Echaide

Santa Catalina

Camino

Idiaquez

Vergara

General

Prim

Aldamar

Alameda del Boulevard

Elcano

Churruca

Fuenterrabía

Garibay

Hernani

Euskadi

San Martín

Avenida de la Libertad

Urbieta

Easo

Urbieta

Easo

Miracruz

San Martín

Prim

J Urbieta

Loyola

Arrase

Guetaria

San Bartolomé

Paseo de la Concha

Alkolea

Paseo Miraconcha

Avenida Satrustegui

Avenida Zumalacárregui

Ondarreta

Zubieta

Matía

0   250   500 m

1 Castill de la Mota
2 Museo San Telmo
3 Pensión San Lorenzo
4 Tourist Information
5 Puente Zurriola
6 Hotel Maria Cristina
7 Puente Santa Catalina
8 Pensión Arsuaga
9 Town Hall
10 Telephones
11 San Martin Market
12 Catedral de Buen Pastor
13 Post Office
14 Railway Station
15 Pension Añorga
16 Hostal Eder
17 Palacio da Miramar
18 Plaza del Funicular

is a surprisingly relaxed town with a population approaching 170,000. Those who live here consider themselves the luckiest people in Spain and will not hesitate to tell you so. After spending a few days on the beaches in preparation for the wild evenings, you may well begin to appreciate their unbashful claim.

Information
The main tourist office (☎ 481 166/7), is on the corner of Avenida de la República Argentina and El Boulevar. It has good maps of the city and can help you with just about any other information you care to ask for. If you are coming in summer, make sure you book ahead. There is a Basque Government tourist office (☎ 426 282) on Avenida de la Libertad.

The main post office is on Calle San Martín, behind the cathedral. They have unpredictable opening hours and also have to cope with the problem of occasional bomb threats. There are telephone centres on Avenida de la Libertad near Calle Hernani, and at San Marcial 29. The telephone code for San Sebastián is 943.

Things to See
San Sebastián is stunning. The beach of La

Concha, and its continuation at Ondarreta, makes up one of the most beautiful city centre beaches in Spain. If you intend to spend your evenings as the Basques do, you won't be up to much more than sitting on the beach during the day. However, there is some worthwhile sightseeing to be done in and around San Sebastián.

The most obvious tourist attraction is **Monte Urgull**, with a statue of Christ on the top. Although it is possible to drive up, it only takes around half an hour to walk up. To find the path, head for the back of the old town and then simply work your way up the hill.

On the far side of the bay is **Monte Igueldo**. The view of La Concha is even better from the top of this peak. A funicular runs from the base right up to the four-star hotel Monte Igueldo and the Ku discotheque (which has a sister in Ibiza).

In the middle of the bay is Isla de Santa Clara. You can get out there by boat from the port, but it is more exciting to swim. In summer, a number of rafts are anchored about halfway from Ondarreta to the island to serve as rest stops for the daring. You should figure on around 20 minutes' slow breaststroking to get out there.

The **Playa de Gros** has a bad reputation because of its severe pollution problem. It is, on the other hand, a very fine surf beach at times. Just make sure you have a good shower after swimming there.

Places to Stay & Eat
There are no great deals on accommodation in San Sebastián. There are, however, a few places which will not break the average budget overnight. *Pensión San Lorenzo* (☎ 425 516), Calle San Lorenzo 2, 1st floor D, is small and eminently friendly, with both singles and doubles going from 2000 pta. *Pensión La Perla* (☎ 428 123), Calle Loyola 10 (1st floor), has singles/doubles from 2000/3000 pta. *Pensión Arsuaga* (☎ 420 681) at Calle Narrica 3 (3rd floor), has singles/doubles from 2000/3500 pta. If you are having trouble finding somewhere to stay, pop into the expensive *Hostal Eder* at Calle San Bartolomé 33. The woman who

SPAIN

runs the place can probably help you to find a room in a *casa particular* (private house).

Another very friendly place worth considering is *Pensión Añorga* (☎ 467 945) at Calle Easo 12. Singles/doubles go for 2500/4000 pta in summer, and 2000/3000 pta during the rest of the year. Doubles with a shower cost 5000 pta all year round.

Eating in San Sebastián is a pleasure. It is almost a shame to sit down in a restaurant when there are such wonderful tapas, or *pinchos*, as they are known here. Basque cuisine is reputed to be the best in Spain, so if you do want to appreciate a full meal, just go for a walk around the old town or the suburb of Gros. Both are jammed with great restaurants, though they are not cheap. The market is on El Boulevar, just past the eastern end of the old town.

Entertainment
San Sebastián's nightlife is great. The old town comes alive at around 8 pm pretty much every night of the week. The Spanish habit of bar-hopping has been perfected here and there are surely around 200 bars in the compact old town. One street alone has 28 bars in a 300-metre stretch! Typical drinks are a *zurrito* (a very small, cheap beer) and *txacolí* (a Basque wine, not to everyone's liking).

Once the old town begins to quieten down, the crowd heads for the area behind the cathedral. Things are usually pretty quiet in this area until a couple of hours after midnight. Incidentally, a good place when you need a break is a bar called *Bocata*. Everyone knows it.

Getting There & Away
Train San Sebastián is on the train line which connects Paris to both Madrid and Lisbon. As such, an awful lot of travellers pass through here. Trains to Madrid leave at 2.22 and 8.26 am, 3.27, 4.07 and 11.17 pm. The trip takes anywhere from seven to 10 hours and the basic fare is 3665/5805 pta one-way/return. Trains to Barcelona leave at 9.55 am and 10.32 pm, taking eight to 10 hours. The basic fare is 4155/6575 pta one-

way/return. The train to Paris leaves at 9.12 am and, with a change at the border, arrives at Paris Austerlitz at 7 pm.

Bus The bus station is about a 15-minute walk upstream from the train station. If you're headed for Bilbao, there are buses with Pesa and Turytrans every hour. The trip, which takes a little over an hour, costs 880 pta with Pesa and 785 pta with Turitrans. Pamplona is around two hours away and costs 1050 pta.

BASQUE COAST
Although the Spanish Basque coast (Costa Vasca) is very close to the French border, it is one of the least touristed coastal regions in Spain. A combination of cool weather, rough seas and terrorism tends to put some people off.

Orientation & Information
The Basque coast actually starts in southern France. There are some beautiful beaches on both sides of the border which are very popular with Spaniards and French alike. Starting at Saint Jean de Luz and Hendaye in France, then across the border to Fuenterrabia (Hondarribia, in Euskera) are some very much family-oriented resorts which have calm waters by Atlantic standards. Farther along is the idyllic village of Pasajes de San Juan, around seven km before San Sebastián. On the other side of San Sebastián, the coast extends to Bilbao, passing through some of the finest surfing territory in Europe. Keep your wet suit handy, though, as the water here can be pretty chilly.

Things to See & Do
A short way west of San Sebastián is the town of Zarautz. There is an international surfing competition here in summer, when all the big names turn up for one of Europe's greatest surfing spectacles.

A little way beyond Zarautz is the picturesque village of Guetaria. There is a small beach in the town, but the main attraction is just in wandering around the narrow streets and the fishing harbour. If you are driving along the coast, it is well worth stopping here.

Mundaka, a little way north of Guernica, is a surfing town. For much of the year, professional surfers and beachbums can be seen sitting on their boards waiting for the right wave. Ecstatic surfies will tell you of the biggest 'left' they have ever seen. If you are lucky enough to catch the right wave at the right time, you could literally be in for the ride of your life. To rent a surfboard, ask the locals to direct you to Craig's shop (Craig is an Aussie who came here to surf some years ago and never managed to leave).

Finally, there is Bilbao. The **Museo de Bellas Artes** is excellent, with an impressive collection, including works by El Greco, Ribera, Zurbarán, Velázquez and Goya. It also contains an important collection of Basque art and an interesting international selection of 20th century art.

Places to Stay & Eat

San Sebastián and Bilbao are the most obvious places to base yourself for excursions along the Basque coast. In Bilbao you might try *Hostal Jofra* (☎ 421 2949), at Calle Elcano 34, which has singles/doubles from 1350/2400 pta.

In the smaller towns the easiest option is camping. The camp site in Zarautz is very close to the beach, and in Mundaka it is at Calle Potuondo 1 (☎ 687 6368). As you arrive in Zarautz from San Sebastián, ask the driver to let you off at Apartamentos Talaimendi. From there the camp site is a 10-minute walk away. In Mundaka the site is about one km out of town on the road to Guernika.

Guetaria is well known for its excellent seafood. There are a couple of harbourside restaurants where you can sit outside and watch the fishing boats unload. In Mundaka, you will pretty much be limited to sandwiches or camp site food, as anything else is prohibitively expensive. There is an excellent market in nearby Bermeo, where you should have no trouble putting cheap meals together.

Getting Around

The coastal road is best discovered by car. There are buses from San Sebastián to Zarautz and Guetaria, and from Bilbao to Guernica. From Guernica you can take a bus to Bermeo which will drop you off in Mundaka. Be warned that hitching can be painstakingly slow in the Basque Country, as people are worried about picking up terrorists.

PAMPLONA

Pamplona, capital of the region of Navarre, is home to Spain's most infamous festival. This fact alone gives the city an aura which affects the first-time visitor even six months before the event. There is always an air of something about to happen in Pamplona. You may even hear talk of a tenfold increase in population during San Fermines, or the Running of the Bulls, as it is also known. This is perhaps a slightly inflated estimate, but the population of Pamplona certainly doubles.

Things to See & Do

Although Pamplona became a household name in Europe thanks to San Fermines, the festival is not to everyone's taste. The madcap festivities run from 5 to 16 July. They are characterised by nonstop partying, out-of-control drunkenness and, of course, the bulls being set free in the streets of the old town. Every year there are injuries, and occasionally deaths, as the frenzied crowd runs through the streets in front of, behind and around the frightened and angry bulls. Inevitably someone gets a little too close, with predictable, gory consequences.

The safest place to watch the *corrida* is on TV. If this is too tame for you, see if you can sweet-talk your way onto a balcony in one of the streets where the bulls are to run. You might have to pay for it, but it is well worth the cost if you can afford it. The other places to watch from are in Plaza Santo Domingo where the action begins, or near the entrance to the bullring (inside if you want to see the killing, outside if you don't).

If you are staying out of town, you will

1222 Spain – The Basque Country, Navarre & Aragon

have to get up early to be there in time for the day's beginning. The bulls are let into the street at 8 am, but if you want to get a good vantage point you will have to be there around 6 am.

Places to Stay & Eat

The camp site nearest Pamplona is *Camping Ezcaba*, seven km north of the city. During San Fermines this fills up a couple of days before the festival. To get to the camp site, take a bus from Calle Teovaldos in the centre of town, towards Oricain. Let the driver know you are going to Camping Ezcaba.

If you arrive in Pamplona for San Fermines hoping to find somewhere to stay, forget it. The general estimate is that you will need to make a reservation two years in advance. Occasionally, there is floor space to rent in student households, but you can expect to pay 5000 pta plus for that luxury. If you really want to sleep in a bed, you'll probably have to make a daily trip to San Sebastián. If you miss your train or bus in the evening, just do what everyone else does and sleep in one of the squares or shopping malls. You can lock your bags up at the bus station for 150 pta a day.

During the rest of the year, you should have no trouble finding somewhere to stay. *Casa García* (☎ 223 893), Calle San Gregorio 12, is a bargain with doubles from 2500 pta. Prices for singles are negotiable. *Hostal Velate* is also reasonably priced with rooms from 2500/4000 pta.

The best way to eat cheaply in Pamplona is to fill up on tapas. If you are intent on a restaurant meal, *Restaurante Sarasate*, Calle San Nicolás 19 (1st floor), dishes up a truly first-class vegetarian menu for 750 pta.

Getting There & Away

Trains to/from San Sebastián are excruciatingly slow. Take a bus. They only take a couple of hours and cost 600 pta. Departures are at 8.30, 9.30 and 11.15 am, and 5.30, 7.45 and 9 pm. Buses for the seven-hour trip to Madrid leave at 8.30 am and 3.30 pm. The bus station is on Calle Conde de Oliveto. There is an overnight train to Barcelona.

SARAGOSSA

Saragossa (Zaragoza), capital of Aragon, is often said to be the most Spanish city in Spain. The city's appeal lies in the fact that it has been left relatively untouched by tourism: most travellers know it only as a train station on the way from Barcelona to Madrid. Those who take the time to get off the train are rarely disappointed. The old town is full of authentic Spanish restaurants – Aragonese cooking is superb. Saragossa's other big plus is its fine main square, completely remodelled in 1990-91.

Orientation & Information

Saragossa straddles the Ebro River, with most points of interest on the south side of the river. If you arrive at the train station, head across Calle Jose Anselmo Clave, down Calle Mayandia until you reach Paseo María Agustín, one of the main thoroughfares through the city. To the south-east along this road are two of the city's most important north-pointing streets: Avenida Cesar Augusto, which heads into the old town and down to the river, and Paseo Independencia, which runs from Plaza de Aragón to Plaza de España, the main entrance to the old town. The main square, Plaza de Nuestra Señora del Pilar, is at the northernmost end of the old town, separated from the river by the city's cathedral.

Saragossa's main tourist information office (☎ 297 582) is at Calle Don Jaime I, very close to Plaza de España. There is another, ultramodern tourist information office on Plaza de Nuestra Señora del Pilar between Hotel Las Torres and Hostal Plaza. It is a large, rather surreal-looking cube made of deep-blue glass, so you probably won't miss it. The telephone code for Saragossa is 976.

Things to See & Do

The *Aljafería*, Saragossa's erstwhile major tourist attraction is undergoing a major overhaul. As such, 70% of the complex is off limits to the public (including travel writers), and it seems unlikely that this state of affairs will change before 1997. However, if you

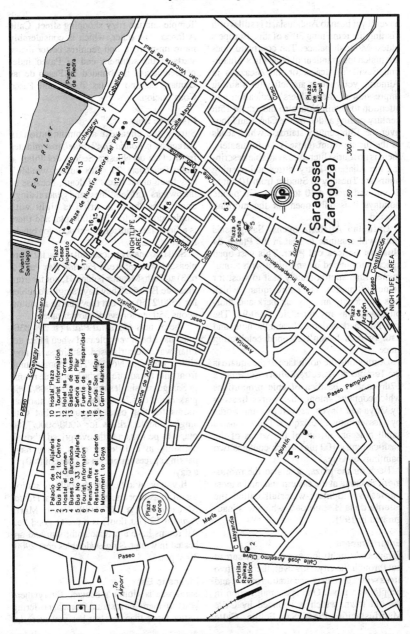

Saragossa (Zaragoza)

1 Palacio de la Aljafería
2 Bus No 22 to Centre
3 Hostal el Carmen
4 Buses to Barcelona
5 Bus No 33 to Aljafería
6 Tourist Information
7 Pensión Rex
8 Restaurante el Caserón
9 Monument to Goya
10 Hostal Plaza
11 Tourist Information
12 Hotel las Torres
13 Basílica de Nuestra
   Señora del Pilar
14 Fuente de la Hispanidad
15 Churrería
16 Fonda San Miguel
17 Central Market

SPAIN

haven't yet been to Andalusia, it is still worth visiting the remaining 30% of this, Europe's oldest Moorish palace. The courtyard does not match the grandeur of Granada's Alhambra, Seville's Alcázar or the Alcazaba in Almeria, yet visitors are left with a strong impression of the builders' dedication and attention to detail. Note also the ornate 15th century ceiling added by the Christian kings over the 13th century staircase which leads to the throne room (closed). Unfortunately, there is no tourist literature available describing the Aljafería. Entry is free and opening hours are Tuesday to Sunday from 10 am to 2 pm, and from 4.30 to 6 pm. On public holidays it is only open for the morning session.

Until the Aljafería opens, Saragossa's heart will continue to beat in the **Plaza de Nuestra Señora del Pilar**. This vast open space, surrounded by and filled with monuments, runs approximately east to west for some 500 metres. The entire square, which was previously an ugly car park and thoroughfare, was revamped in 1990-91. The cars now park underneath, and the hotel and café owners haven't stopped celebrating since.

Dominating the north face of the square is the **Templo de Nuestra Señora del Pilar**, a 17th century basilica of epic proportions which contains, among other works, frescoes by Goya and Bayeu, as well as some works by a lesser known Velázquez. There is also a small museum in one of the wings of the basilica (entry 100 pta) which contains two paintings by Goya.

Back on the plaza, note also the **monument to Goya** at the eastern end, and a most impressive fountain-waterfall called the **Fuente de la Hispanidad**, which was inaugurated in 1991.

Entertainment

Saragossa's nightlife spots are pretty spread out through the city. However, there are two areas with a greater concentration of bars and people than most. One is a small region in the old town, which is bounded by Calle Manifestación, Plaza San Felipe, Calle Temple and the ritzy shopping street, Calle Alfonso. The other, which is considerably more up-market, and requires better dress, starts at the southern end of Paseo Independencia and is bounded by Paseo de las Damas, Camino de las Torres and Paseo Constitución.

Places to Stay

Surely the cheapest accommodation in Saragossa is *Fonda San Miguel*, just minutes from Plaza de Nuestra Señora del Pilar, at Calle Prudencia 23. This author wouldn't stay there under threat of death, because of the owners' unfriendliness and general dingy conditions, but the price is right with singles/doubles for 750/1000 pta, and there is a first-class churreria next door for breakfast.

Still reasonably priced, but with a far more pleasant atmosphere is *Pensión Rex* (☎ 392 633) at Casto Méndez Núñez 31, not far from Plaza de España. They have singles/doubles for 1500/2750 pta, but they charge an outrageous 350 pta for every shower taken.

The owners of *Hostal Plaza* (☎ 294 830) must have been very pleased when Plaza del Pilar was pedestrianised. Business is now sitting pretty at No 14. The rooms which front onto the square are the best value rooms in Saragossa (singles/doubles for 1908/2968 pta). *Hotel Las Torres* (☎ 394 254) also has rooms fronting onto the square, but with singles/doubles/triples for 4000/5000/7500 pta, it is perhaps a little overpriced, though certainly in a different class. They have parking spaces for guests at a cost of 800 pta a day.

If you want to be near the railway station for one reason or another, the two-star *Hostal El Carmen* (☎ 211 100), Paseo María Agustín 13 (1st floor) is a pretty good bet. All rooms have a private bathroom and are heated in winter. Singles/doubles cost 2900/3000 pta.

Places to Eat

Saragossa is glutton's heaven. Everywhere you turn there is a restaurant or a bar offering tastier tapas than the last bar you were in.

Restaurante El Caserón has to be seen to be believed. The décor is out of this world, and the quality and variety of the food is up there with it. They proudly advertise the fact that they have 137 different items on their menu (to suit all budgets and tastes). It is in a tiny lane called Blasón Aragones, off Plaza de Sas, which in turn is off Calle Alfonso.

Once you have tried all 137 dishes at El Caserón, keep an eye out for *Parrilla Albarracín* at Plaza del Carmen 1. The bar is lined with a mouthwatering array of tapas, there are main courses from 600 pta, and a filling, and delicious, menu for 1500 pta.

For those on a tighter budget, *Cafeteria Restaurante Fiesta*, Calle Zurita 15, has seven menus ranging in price from 700 to 2100 pta. *Restaurante Mayor Uno* at Calle Mayor 1, has a menu for 900 pta and another for 1300 pta. A few doors away at Calle Mayor 9 is *Restaurante El Mejillon de Oro*. They offer a number of platos combinados for 500 pta and have a few dishes for as little as 350 pta. These two places on Calle Mayor don't look up to much from the outside, but you won't be disappointed with the food.

Getting There & Away

There are about 15 trains a day in each direction between Zarragoza and Madrid, taking from three to 4½ hours, depending on the train. The basic fare is 2080/3290 pta one-way/return. To Barcelona there are 11 trains a day taking four to five hours. A number of these trains make a stop in Tarragona on the way. The basic fare to Barcelona is 2200/3485 pta one-way/return.

There are two direct trains a day to Valencia leaving Saragossa's Portillo Station at 9.05 am and 3.35 pm. The trip takes 6½ to seven hours, with a stop in Teruel (among numerous other stops) after about 3½ hours. The basic fare is 1130/1795 pta one-way/return.

There are daily trains at 2.38 am and 4 pm to San Sebastián, with a stop in Pamplona on the way. Both these trains continue on to Irún, from where you can make connections to Bordeaux and Paris. Travelling time to San Sebastián is about six hours on the

morning train, and just under four hours on the afternoon train. The basic fare to San Sebastián is 1955/3100 pta one-way/return.

Getting Around

The centre of town is a good 15-minute walk from the train station, on Calle José Anselmo Clave. If you prefer to take a bus into town, cross the road when you leave the train station and you will see a bus stop on Calle José Anselmo Clave, near the corner of Calle Mayandia. Bus No 22 is the one to take.

To get to the Aljafería from the centre, you can walk (about 20 minutes) or you can take bus No 33 from Plaza de España.

TERUEL

In the deep south of Aragon, Teruel is a world apart from the Pyrenees, for which the region is better known. You won't hear the locals speaking Catalan or Basque here, in country which is culturally much closer to Castile-La Mancha or the backlands of Valencia. And yet, Teruel has an atmosphere all its own. It is best known for its Mudéjar architecture and the general flavour left by the many centuries of Moorish domination.

Things to See & Do

Teruel's best known attractions are its Mudéjar towers. In all, there are four of these structures: the cathedral of **Santa María** and the churches of **El Salvador** (13th century), **San Martín** and **San Pedro** (14th century). These magnificent examples of Mudéjar architecture are among the best in Spain. Note the inlaid stones and colourful tiles which are so typical of the style. A further example of Moorish influence in Teruel can be seen in the flight of stairs which leads down to the train station from Paseo de Ovalo, on the edge of the old town

The **Museo Provincial de Teruel** is too good to miss. It contains a small selection of local *artisanía* such as basketwork and pottery, but the real attraction is the archaeological collection. Although the authorities in Madrid would not like to hear it, this collection is far more palatable than that in the National Archaeological Museum. It contains fascinating and well-presented pre-historic displays going back to the days of Homo erectus. The other collections are also beautifully presented. Entry is free, but you need a ticket to get in.

Places to Stay & Eat

Most of the budget accommodation in town is in the streets around the main square, Plaza Carlos Castell. *Fonda Tozal* (☎ 601 022) at Calle Rincon 5 is good value. It is in an amazing rickety old house run by a wonderful, wacky old couple, and most of the rooms have cast-iron beds, enamelled chamber pots and running water. Singles/doubles cost 1000/2000 pta! *Fonda Moderna* (☎ 601 280), Calle Tomás Nogués 3, is also pretty reasonable with singles/doubles from 1000/2000 pta.

Unfortunately, eating cheaply is not so easy in Teruel. At *Restaurante La Parilla*, Calle San Estebán 2, you can eat quite well for around 1000 pta. Beyond that, it is just a matter of checking the menus before you sit down.

Getting There & Away

Bus The bus station is on Ronda Anabeles. There is a daily bus (except Sunday) to Barcelona. The bus leaves Teruel at 12.30 pm

and arrives in Barcelona at 6.30 pm. The one-way fare is 2650 pta. In the other direction, the bus leaves Barcelona at 6 am and arrives in Teruel at noon. The bus to Cuenca leaves at 1.30 pm, takes three hours and costs 925 pta one-way. For information on these two bus routes (Barcelona and Cuenca), call ☎ 602 004. Five buses ply the two-hour route to Valencia every day (two on Sunday) for a one-way fare of 1000 pta. There are buses to Madrid at 8 am and 2 and 5 pm. The five-hour trip costs 2025 pta. Departures from Madrid to Teruel are at 8 am and 1 and 5 pm. For information on these bus routes (Valencia and Madrid), call ☎ 603 450.

Train There are five trains a day to Valencia which take about an hour longer than the bus and cost 40 pta extra. The train to Valencia costs 1040 pta and is agonisingly slow.

Car If you are driving or hitching, Teruel is at the intersection of routes N-234 and N-420. The first runs from Burgos, through Soria and Teruel, to Sagunto on the coast a little north of Valencia. The second road leads to Cuenca and on to Andalusia (almost to Cordova) and would also be the best road to take if you are headed for Madrid or Toledo.

Switzerland

Think of Switzerland and you think of chocolates, cuckoo clocks and mountains. These are here in abundance but there's a lot more to it than that. Switzerland (Schweiz, Suisse, Svizerra) is almost a byword for efficiency – the country runs as smoothly as one of its own watches. Getting around couldn't be easier, everything works, it is almost unnervingly civilised, and unemployment and poverty are negligible. Yet Switzerland's great asset is its countryside; despite ever-expanding tourism, much of it remains stunningly beautiful with endless vistas of mountains, forests and lakes.

Of the cities, Bern has a charming small-town feel, Geneva an international flavour and Zürich a no-nonsense prosperity. All have sufficient diversions to occupy the visitor for several days. Smaller towns like St Gallen and Lucerne have delightful old-town centres and a well-preserved historical heritage. Away from the towns, scenic highlights include the Matterhorn and the locality round Interlaken. Resorts such as St Moritz offer a bewildering choice of sports as well as the expected skiing and hiking. The canton of Ticino shows a glimpse of Switzerland wearing a Mediterranean disguise. Unfortunately, high costs may prompt you to rush through the whole landscape faster than you would like.

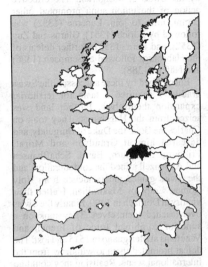

Facts about the Country

HISTORY

The first inhabitants of the region were a Celtic tribe, the Helvetii. The Romans appeared on the scene in 107 BC by way of the St Bernard Pass, but owing to the difficulty of the terrain their attempted conquest of the area was never decisive. They were gradually driven back by Germanic tribes who settled in the 5th century. Burgundians and Franks also settled the area, and Christianity was gradually introduced.

The territory was united under the Holy Roman Empire in 1032 but central control was never very tight, allowing neighbouring nobles to contest each other for local influence. That was all changed by the Habsburg family of Aargau, to the east of Zürich, who gradually extended their power throughout central Europe. Habsburg expansion was spearheaded by Rudolph I, who gradually brought the squabbling dynasties west of Zürich to heel.

Upon his death in 1291, local leaders saw a chance to gain independence. The forest communities of Uri, Schwyz and Nidwalden formed an alliance on 1 August 1291. Their pact of mutual assistance is seen as the origin of the Swiss Confederation and the inaugural document is still preserved in the canton of Schwyz. Thanks to the exploits of people such as the legendary William Tell, they undermined the sphere of influence of th

Habsburgs. Duke Leopold responded by dispatching a powerful Austrian army in 1315 which was nevertheless thoroughly defeated by the Swiss at Morgarten. The effective action of the union soon prompted other communities to join. Lucerne (1332) was followed by Zürich (1351), Glarus and Zug (1352), and Bern (1353). Further defeats of the Habsburgs followed at Sempach (1386) and Näfels (1388).

Encouraged by these successes, the Swiss gradually acquired a taste for territorial expansion themselves. Further land was seized from the Habsburgs. They took on Charles the Bold, the Duke of Burgundy, and defeated him at Grandson and Morat. Fribourg, Solothurn, Basel, Schaffhausen and Appenzell joined the confederation, and the Swiss gained independence from Holy Roman Emperor Maximilian I after their victory at Dornach in 1499. Finally the Swiss over-reached themselves. They took on a superior combined force of French and Venetians at Marignano in 1515 and lost. The defeat prompted them to withdraw from the international scene. Realising they could no longer compete against larger powers with better equipment, they renounced expansionist policies and declared their neutrality. Even so, Swiss mercenaries continued to serve in other armies for centuries to come, and earned an unrivalled reputation for their skill and courage.

The Reformation in the 17th century caused upheaval throughout Europe. Many Swiss urban areas succumbed to the Protestant teachings of Luther, Zwingli and Calvin, although the rural cantons remained Catholic. This caused some local unrest but the Swiss did at least manage to avoid international disputes, and at the end of the Thirty Years' War in 1648 they were recognised in the Treaty of Westphalia as a neutral state. Although domestic disputes continued intermittently, Switzerland gradually prospered as a financial and intellectual centre.

During his quest for European domination, Napoleon invaded Switzerland in 1798 and established the Helvetic Republic. The Swiss did not take too kindly to such cen-

tralised control, and internal fighting prompted Napoleon to restore the former confederation of cantons in 1803, although France retained overall jurisdiction. Further cantons also joined the confederation: Aargau, St Gallen, Graubünden, Ticino, Thurgau and Vaud. Napoleon was finally sent packing following his defeat by the British and Prussians at Waterloo. The Congress of Vienna established Switzerland as a federation in 1815, and guaranteed its independence and permanent neutrality, as well as adding the cantons of Valais, Geneva, and Neuchâtel.

Civil war followed in 1847 when the Protestant army led by General Dufour quickly crushed the Catholic cantons who had formed a separatist league. Throughout the gradual move towards one nation, each canton remained fiercely independent, even to the extent of controlling their own coinage and postal services. They lost these powers in 1848 when a new federal constitution was agreed, which is largely still in place today. Bern was established as the capital and the federal assembly was set up to take care of national issues. Cantons nevertheless retained legislative (Grand Council) and executive (State Council) powers to deal with local matters. In 1874 the constitution was revised to enable citizens to partake in direct democracy (see the following Government section).

Having achieved political stability, Switzerland was able to concentrate on economic and social matters. Relatively poor in mineral resources, it developed industries predominantly dependent on highly skilled labour. A network of railways and roads was built, opening up previously inaccessible Alpine regions and helping the development of tourism. The international Red Cross was founded in Geneva in 1863 by Henri Dunant, and compulsory free education was introduced.

The Swiss have carefully guarded their neutrality in the 20th century. Their only involvement in WW I lay in the organising of Red Cross units. Switzerland joined the League of Nations after peace was won,

Switzerland
(Schweiz)
(Suisse)
(Svizzera)

0   25   50 km

GERMANY

AUSTRIA

LIECHTENSTEIN

Lake Constance
(Bodensee)

Vaduz

Swiss
National Park

Zernez

Zuoz

Bernina
Pass

Klosters

Davos

St Moritz

Maloja

Arosa

Chur

GRAUBÜNDEN

San
Bernardino
Pass

Lake
Lugano

Bellinzona

THURGAU

Frauenfeld

St Gallen

Appenzell

Herisau

Buchs

Sargans

Rhine

Locarno

Lugano

Schaffhausen

Winterthur

ZÜRICH

Baden

Zürich

Lake
Zürich

Glarus

GLARUS

ST GALLEN

SCHWYZ

Schwyz

Oberalp
Pass

Lake
Maggiore

Rhine

Zug

ZUG

Rigi

Altdorf

St Gotthard

TICINO

AARGAU

Aarau

Limmat
River

Stans

Mt
Titlis
3239m

Engelberg

Meiringen

Simplon
Pass

Olten

LUCERNE

Lucerne

Lake
Vierwaldstätter

Sarnen

Brienz

Lake
Brienz

Grindelwald

Jungfraujoch

Brig

Simplon
Rail Tunnel

Basel

BASEL

Délémont

Solothurn

River
Aare

Beatenberg

Interlaken

Thun

Wengen

Mürren

Visp

Saas
Fee

Mt Rosa
4554 m

Rhine

Moutier

JURA

Biel

Lake
Neuchâtel

Bern

BERN

Spiez

Lake
Thun

Leukerbad

Täsch

Zermatt

Matterhorn
4478 m

ITALY

Fribourg

FRIBOURG

Gruyères

Lenk

Crans/
Montana

Sion

VALAIS

Verbier

La Chaux-
de-Fonds

Le Locle

Neuchâtel

NEUCHÂTEL

Montreux

Rhône

Martigny

Great
St Bernard Pass

FRANCE

Lausanne

VAUD

Lake Geneva
(Lac Léman)

GENEVA

Geneva

FRANCE

SWITZERLAND

SWITZERLAND

under the proviso that its involvement would be purely financial and economic rather than entailing any possible military sanctions. World War II also left Switzerland largely unscathed, barring some accidental bombing in 1940 and 1944, and its territory proved to be a safe haven for escaping Allied prisoners.

While the rest of Europe underwent the painful process of rebuilding from the ravages of war, Switzerland was able to expand from an already powerful commercial, financial and industrial base. Zürich developed as an international banking and insurance centre. The World Health Organisation and the World Council of Churches based their headquarters in Geneva. Social reforms were also introduced, such as old-age pensions in 1948.

Afraid that its neutrality would be compromised, Switzerland declined to become a member of the United Nations, NATO or the EEC. It did, however, join UNESCO (the United Nations Educational, Scientific and Cultural Organisation) and EFTA (the European Free Trade Association). In the face of other EFTA nations applying for EC (European Community) membership, Switzerland finally made its own application in 1992. Full membership is expected to be granted in 1996.

Despite the fact that Switzerland has managed to avoid international conflicts for over 400 years, every able-bodied male undergoes two years' national service at age 19. Even when this is finished, he remains in the reserves for 30 years and keeps his rifle and full kit at home. During this time, he must serve regular refresher courses and be ready for recall if the country is threatened. Since national service began, there has never been a complete recall, not even during the nervous days of WW II.

In the last 40 years, Switzerland has made comprehensive preperations against attack. Besides the civilian army, a whole infrastructure is in place to repel any invasion. Roads and bridges have built-in recesses at key points so that they can be primed for explosion without delay. All new buildings must have a substantial air-raid capacity, and underground car parks can be instantly converted to bunkers. Fully equipped emergency hospitals, unused yet maintained, await underneath ordinary hospitals. It's a sobering thought, as you explore the countryside, to realise that those apparently undisturbed mountains and lakes hide a network of military installations and storage depots. The message that comes across today is the same as that dealt out by the country's fearless mercenaries of centuries ago: don't mess with the Swiss.

GEOGRAPHY

Mountains make up 60% of Switzerland's 41,295 sq km. The land is 45% meadow and pasture, 24% forest and 6% arable. Farming of cultivated land is intensive and cows graze on the upper slopes in the summer as soon as the retreating snow line permits.

The Alps occupy the central and southern regions of the country. The Dufour summit at 4634 metres is the highest point, although the Matterhorn (4478 metres) is more well known. A series of high passes in the south provide overland access into Italy. Glaciers account for an area of 2000 sq km, most notably the Aletsch Glacier which at 169 sq km is the largest valley glacier in Europe.

The St Gotthard Massif in the centre of Switzerland is the source of many lakes and rivers, such as the Rhine and the Rhône. The Jura Mountains straddle the northern border with France. These mountains peak at 1723 metres and are less steep and less severely eroded than the Alps.

Between the two mountain systems is the Mittelland, also known as the Swiss Plateau, a region of hills crisscrossed by rivers, ravines and winding valleys. This area has spawned the most populous cities and is also where much of the agricultural activity takes place.

GOVERNMENT

The modern Swiss Confederation is made up of 23 cantons; three are subdivided bringing the total to 26. Each has its own constitution and legislative body for dealing with local issues. Bern achieved full cantonal status as late as 1979.

National legislative power is in the hands of the Federal Assembly which consists of two chambers. The lower chamber, the National Council, is elected by proportional representation with one member per 22,000 people. The upper chamber, the States Council, is composed of 46 members, two per canton. The Federal Assembly elects seven members to form the Federal Council, which holds executive power. All elections are for a four year term except the posts of president and vice-president of the Confederation, which are decided annually from a roster. The vice-president always succeeds the president. In this way the Swiss avoid their governing body being dominated by any one individual.

Laws can actually be influenced directly by the Swiss people, provided enough signatures can be collected from active citizens: 50,000 to force a full referendum on proposed laws, and 100,000 to initiate legislation. Surprisingly for such a democratic people, women only won the right to vote in federal elections in 1971. In some cantons women gained a local vote only in the last few years. A few cantons still vote by a show of hands in an open-air parliament called the *Landsgemeinde*.

ECONOMY

Switzerland has a mixed economy with the emphasis on private ownership. The only industries nationalised outright are telephone, telegraph, post and some railways. Other than municipal enterprises, everything else is in private hands and operates according to free-market principles, with the occasional subsidy thrown in. A good proportion of the wealth generated is channelled back into the community via social welfare programmes. The overall result is incredibly efficient. Unemployment is virtually nonexistent and strikes are rare.

In the absence of other raw materials, hydro-electric power has become the main source of energy. Chemicals, machine tools and watches and clocks are the most import-

ant exports. Silks and embroidery, also important, are produced to a high quality. Swiss banks are a magnet for foreign funds attracted by political and monetary stability. Tourism is an important industry and the Swiss aim to make things as easy as possible for visitors. Swiss breakthroughs in science and industry include vitamins, DDT, gas turbines and milk chocolate. They also, for their sins, developed the modern formula for life insurance.

POPULATION & PEOPLE

With a population of 6.8 million, Switzerland averages 164 inhabitants per sq km. The Alpine districts are sparsely populated, meaning that the Mittelland is densely settled, especially round the shores of the larger lakes. Zürich is the largest city with 410,000 inhabitants, next comes Basel (212,000), Geneva (175,000) and Bern (150,000). Most of the people are of Germanic origin as indicated by the breakdown of languages spoken in Switzerland. German speakers account for 66% of the population, French 18%, Italian 10% and Romansch just 1%. As many as 11% of people living in the country are residents but not Swiss citizens.

ARTS

Switzerland does not have a very strong tradition in the arts, even though many foreign writers and artists have visited and settled, attracted by the beauty and tranquillity of the mountains and lakes. Among them were Voltaire, Byron and Shelley. Paul Klee is the best known native painter. He created abstract works which used colour, line and form to evoke a variety of sensations. The 18th century writings of Rousseau in Geneva played an important part in the development of democracy. Carl Jung, with his research in Zürich, was instrumental in developing modern psychoanalysis.

Arthur Honegger is the only Swiss composer of note. Despite that, music is strongly emphasised with a full symphony orchestra in every main city. Gothic and Renaissance architecture are evident in urban areas, especially Bern. Rural Swiss houses vary

SWITZERLAND

according to region, but are generally characterised by ridged roofs with wide, overhanging eaves, and balconies and verandahs which are usually enlivened by colourful floral displays.

CULTURE
Traditional Lifestyle

In a few mountain regions such as Valais, people still wear traditional rural costumes, but dressing up is usually reserved for festivals. Every spring hardy herders climb to Alpine pastures with their cattle and live in summer huts while tending their herds. They gradually descend back to village level as the grassland is grazed. Both the departure and the return is a cause for celebrations and processions. Yodelling and playing the alp horn are also part of the Alpine tradition.

Avoiding Offence

In general the Swiss are a law-abiding nation; even minor transgressions such as littering can cause offence. Always shake hands when being introduced to a Swiss, and again when leaving. Formal titles should also be used (*Herr* for men and *Frau* for women). It is also customary to greet shopkeepers when entering their shops. Public displays of affection are OK, but are more common in French Switzerland than in the slightly more formal German-speaking parts. Attitudes to homosexuality are reasonably tolerant.

Sport

Shooting and gymnastic clubs are popular with male adults. The interest in shooting is a spillover from the need to maintain a minimum standard with service weapons while in the reserves. Mountaineering, hiking and fishing are also favourite pastimes.

RELIGION

Just over 50% of the population are Protestant. Nearly all the rest are Roman Catholic based predominantly in the cantons of Fribourg, Valais, Ticino and Lucerne. Some churches are supported entirely by donations from the public, others receive state subsidies.

LANGUAGE

Located in the corner of Europe where the German, French and Italian language areas meet, the linguistic melting pot which is Switzerland has three official federal languages: German (spoken by about two-thirds of the population), French (18%) and Italian (10%). A fourth language, Rhaeto-Romanic, or Romansch, is spoken by 1% of the population, mainly in the canton of Graubünden. Derived from Latin, it's a linguistic relic which, along with Friulian and Ladin across the border in Italy, has survived in the isolation of mountain valleys. In 1938, Romansch was recognised as an official national (though not federal) language by referendum.

For a rundown on German, French and Italian, turn to the Language sections in the relevant country chapters in this book. Though German-speaking Swiss have no trouble with standard High German, they use Swiss German, or *Schwyzerdütsch*, in private conversation and in most nonofficial situations. Swiss German covers a wide

Language Areas

- German
- French
- Italian
- Romansh

variety of melodic dialects that can differ quite markedly from High German. Visitors will probably note the frequent use of the suffix *-li* to indicate the diminutive, or as a term of endearment.

You will have few problems being understood in English in the German-speaking parts of Switzerland. However, it is simple courtesy to greet people with *guten Tag* (good day) and to enquire *sprechen Sie Englisch?* (do you speak English?) before launching into English. In French Switzerland you shouldn't have too many problems either, though the locals' grasp of English is likely to be less complete than that of German speakers. Italian Switzerland is where you will have the greatest difficulty. Most locals speak some French and/or German in addition to Italian, but English has a lower priority. Even so, you will find that the majority of restaurants have at least one English-speaking staff member.

Facts for the Visitor

VISAS & EMBASSIES
Visas are not required for passport holders of the UK, the USA, Canada, Australia or New Zealand. A maximum three-month stay applies although passports are rarely stamped. The few Third World and Arab nationals who require visas should have a passport valid for at least six months after their intended stay.

Swiss Embassies
Swiss embassies abroad include:

Australia
    7 Melbourne Ave, Forrest, Canberra, ACT 2603 (☎ 06-273 3977)
Canada
    5 Ave Marlborough, Ottawa, Ont K1N 8E6 (☎ 613-235 1837/8)
New Zealand
    22 Panama St, Wellington (☎ 04-721 593/4)
UK
    16-18 Montague Place, London W1H 2BQ (☎ 071-723 0701)

USA
    2900 Cathedral Ave NW, Washington, DC 20008-3499 (☎ 202-745 7900)

Foreign Embassies in Switzerland
These are located in Bern and Zürich. See the Bern and Zürich Information sections for details. Consulates can be found in many other towns.

DOCUMENTS
British citizens may travel on a one-year British Visitors' passport. If you're driving, an EC driving licence is OK but other nationals should have an International Driving Permit.

CUSTOMS
Visitors from Europe may import 200 cigarettes, 50 cigars or 250 grams of pipe tobacco. Visitors from non-European countries may import twice as much. The allowance for alcohol is the same for everyone: one litre of spirits plus two litres below 15% vol. Tobacco and alcohol may only be brought in by people aged 17 or over.

MONEY
Currency
Swiss francs are divided into 100 centimes (centimes are often called *Rappen* in German-speaking Switzerland). There are notes for 10, 20, 50, 100, 500 and 1000 francs, and coins for five, 10, 20 and 50 centimes, as well as for one, two and five francs.

All major travellers' cheques and credit cards are equally acceptable. Virtually all train stations have money exchange facilities which are open daily, and many offer Visa card cash advances. There is never a commission charge for exchanging travellers' cheques; rates hardly vary from place to place and are about 1% better than those for cash. To get money sent to Switzerland, a direct transfer of funds through a bank is possible but an international money order is cheaper.

If you're driving to Switzerland and intend to use the motorways, you'll have to

SWITZERLAND

pay a one-year motorway tax of Sfr30. Have this money ready, since there may not always be an exchange facility at the border.

Exchange Rates

A$1	=	Sfr0.93
C$1	=	Sfr1.04
DM1	=	Sfr0.88
NZ$1	=	Sfr0.71
UK£1	=	Sfr2.21
US$1	=	Sfr1.30

Costs

Some people can scrimp by on as little as Sfr40 a day but that is hard work. Average costs are: youth hostel Sfr16, cheap hotel Sfr40, cheap restaurant Sfr10, loaf of bread Sfr2, glass of draught beer Sfr2.50 (0.3 litre), Big Mac Sfr5.50, petrol Sfr1.10 per litre, 100 km by train Sfr29, local bus Sfr0.80 to Sfr2.40, local telephone call Sfr0.40, and Time magazine Sfr4.50. Tipping is rarely necessary as hotels, restaurants and bars are required by law to include a 15% service charge in bills. Even taxis normally have a charge included. Bargaining is nonexistent.

Consumer Taxes

A 6.2% 'turnover' tax is levied on all goods. Nonresidents are eligible for a refund but a form must be signed at the time of purchase. Depending on the shop, a refund will be given immediately or else sent to your home address. Swiss customs will need to see this form upon departure.

CLIMATE & WHEN TO GO

Ticino in the south has a hot, Mediterranean climate, and Valais in the south-west is noted for being dry. Elsewhere the temperature is typically 20° to 25°C in summer and 2° to 6°C in winter, with spring and autumn hovering around the 7° to 14°C mark. Summer tends to bring a lot of sunshine, and most rain falls in the spring and autumn. You will need to be prepared for a range of temperatures dependent on altitude.

Look out for the *Föhn*, a hot, dry wind that sweeps down into the valleys and can be oppressively uncomfortable. It can strike at any time of the year. Daily weather reports covering 25 resorts are displayed in major train stations. Barring November, which is the wettest month, Switzerland is visited throughout the year – December to April for winter sports, and May to October for general tourism.

WHAT TO BRING

Take a sturdy pair of boots if you intend to walk in the mountains, and warm clothing for those cold nights at high altitude. Youth hostel membership is invaluable, and it's cheaper to join before you get to Switzerland.

SUGGESTED ITINERARIES

Depending on the length of your stay, you might want to see and do the following things:

Two days
Visit the sights in Geneva and take a trip on the lake. Don't miss Chillon Castle in Montreux.
One week
Visit Geneva and Montreux, and take an Interlaken day trip to the Jungfraujoch. Spend two days in Zürich.
Two weeks
As above, but add Basel, St Gallen, Appenzell and two days in Bern.
One month
As above, but after Appenzell head south to Liechtenstein, Graubünden and Ticino.
Two months
As above, but take your time. Detour to Neuchâtel and the Jura on your way to Geneva. Stay in Lucerne. Spend some time hiking.

TOURIST OFFICES

The Swiss National Tourist Office (SNTO) abroad and local tourist offices (*Verkehrsbüro*) in Switzerland are extremely helpful and have plenty of literature to give out, including maps (nearly always free). Somebody invariably speaks English. Local offices can be found everywhere tourists are likely to go, and will often book hotel rooms and organise excursions.

Local tourist offices in some resorts organise a Visitor's Card. The aim is to entice tourists to stay those extra couple of days. Cards are issued by the tourist office or by hotels, but they must be stamped by your hotel in order to be valid. Visitor's cards are good for various discounts, but entitlement sometimes depends on a minimum stay of several nights.

Tourist Offices Abroad
SNTO offices outside Switzerland include:

Australia
 Swiss Consulate General, 3 Bowen Crescent, Melbourne 3004 (☎ 03-867 2266)
 SNTO, PO Box 82, Edgecliff, NSW 2027 (☎ 02-328 7925)
Canada
 SNTO, 154 University Ave, Toronto, Ont M5H 3Z4 (☎ 416-971 9734)
UK
 SNTO, Swiss Centre, Swiss Court, London W1V 8EE (☎ 071-734 1921)
USA
 SNTO, Swiss Center, 608 Fifth Ave, New York, NY 10020 (☎ 212-757 59 44)

The SNTO also has offices in Los Angeles, San Francisco, Chicago, Paris, Rome, Munich and Vienna.

USEFUL ORGANISATIONS
Useful organisations in Switzerland include:

Youth Hostel Association
 Schweizerischer Bund für Jugendherbergen, Neufeldstrasse 9, CH-3012 Bern (☎ 031-24 55 03)
Swiss Hotel Association
 Schweizer Hotelier-Verein (SHV), Monbijoustrasse 130, CH-3001 Bern (☎ 031-50 71 11)
Swiss Camping and Caravanning Association
 Schweizerischer Camping- und Caravanning-Verband (SCCV), Habsburgerstrasse 35, CH-6004 Lucerne (☎ 041-23 48 22)
Swiss Automobile Club
 Automobil-Club der Schweiz (ACS), Wasserwerkgasse 39, CH-3000 Bern 13 (☎ 031-22 47 22)
Swiss Alpine Club
 Schweizer Alpenclub (SAC), Helvetiaplatz 4, CH-3005 Bern (☎ 031-43 36 11)
Swiss Invalid Association
 Schweizerischer Invalidenverband, Froburgstrasse 4, CH-4600 Olten (☎ 062-32 12 62)

BUSINESS HOURS & HOLIDAYS
Most shops are open from 8 am to 6.30 pm, Monday to Friday, with a 90-minute break for lunch at noon. Some are closed on Monday morning. Banks are open Monday to Friday from 8.30 am to 4 pm with some local variations. National holidays are 1 January, Good Friday, Easter Monday, Ascension Day, Whit Monday, 25 and 26 December. Some cantons observe 2 January, 1 May (Labour Day), Corpus Christi and 1 August (National Day).

CULTURAL EVENTS
Numerous events take place at a local level throughout the year, so it's worth checking with the tourist office. Most dates vary from year to year. This is just a brief selection:

January
 Costumed sleigh-rides in the Engadine
February
 Carnival time in Basel
March
 Engadine Skiing Marathon, Graubünden
April
 Meetings of the Landsgemeinde in Appenzell, Hundwil, Sarnen and Stans (last Sunday of the month)
May
 May Day celebrations, especially in St Gallen and Vaud
June
 Geneva Rose Week, cow fighting (yes, the cows fight each other!) in lower Valais, and the International June Festival of the Arts in Zürich
July
 Montreux Jazz Festival
August
 National Day celebrations and fireworks, Swiss wrestling in the Emmental, and the Geneva Festival
September
 Knabenschiessen shooting contest
October
 Vintage festivals in wine-growing regions such as Morges, Neuchâtel and Lugano
November
 Open-air markets including the Onion Market in Bern
December
 St Nicholas Day celebrations on 6 December, and the Escalade festival in Geneva

SWITZERLAND

POST & TELECOMMUNICATIONS

Postcards and letters to Europe cost Sfr0.70 and Sfr0.90, letters within Switzerland cost Sfr0.50 2nd class. The term 'poste restante' is widely understood although you might prefer to use the German term, *Postlagernde Briefe*. Mail can be sent to any town with a post office and is held for 30 days, but you need to show your passport in order to collect it. American Express also holds mail for one month for people who use its cheques or cards.

Post office opening times vary but typically are Monday to Friday from 8 am to noon and 2 pm to 6.30 pm, and Saturday from 8 am to 11 am. The larger post offices offer services outside normal hours (daily lunch time and evening), but transactions are subject to a Sfr1 to Sfr2 surcharge.

Nearly all post offices have telephones. Hotels can charge as much as they like for telephone calls, so avoid using their switchboards to make calls. Calls within Switzerland are 60% cheaper on weekdays between 5 pm and 7 pm and between 9 pm and 8 am, and throughout the weekend. International calls to Europe are cheaper from 9 pm to 8 am on weekdays, and throughout the weekend. You can direct-dial to just about anywhere worldwide. Phone cards (*Taxcard*) are available for Sfr10 and Sfr20.

TIME

Swiss time is GMT/UTC plus one hour. If it's noon in Bern it is 11 am in London, 6 am in New York and Toronto, 3 am in San Francisco, 9 pm in Sydney and 11 pm in Auckland. Daylight-saving time comes into effect at midnight on the last Saturday in March, when the clocks are moved forward one hour; they go back again on the last Saturday in September.

LAUNDRY

There is no shortage of coin-operated or service laundrettes in cities. Expect to pay around Sfr10 to wash and dry a five kg load. Many youth hostels also have washing machines, and prices are usually slightly cheaper.

WEIGHTS & MEASURES

The metric system is used. Like other Continental Europeans, the Swiss indicate decimals with commas and thousands with points.

ELECTRICITY

The electric current is 220 volts, 50Hz. Plugs are of the standard Continental type, with two round pins.

BOOKS & MAPS

The SNTO sells camping and hiking guides in English, and other books and maps on Switzerland. A useful guide for hikers is *On Foot Through Europe – Austria, Switzerland and Liechtenstein* by Craig Evans (paperback). *Off the Beaten Track – Switzerland* (various authors, paperback) concentrates, as the name suggests, on lesser known destinations. *Living and Working in Switzerland* by David Hampshire (paperback) is an excellent practical guide for those contemplating a long stay in the country.

Michelin covers the whole country with four maps. The *Landeskarte der Schweiz* (Topographical Survey of Switzerland) series is larger in scale and especially useful for hiking. These maps are widely available in Switzerland.

MEDIA

The BBC World Service broadcasts on medium wave (1296 and 648 kHz), and American Forces Network is on the FM band (101.8 MHz). Swiss radio Channel 1 broadcasts British news daily at 7 pm. English-language newspapers are widely available and cost around Sfr3.

HEALTH

No inoculations are required for entry to the country. There is no state health service in Switzerland and all treatment must be paid for. Medication and consultations are expensive, so travel insurance is recommended, especially if you intend to indulge in winter sports. Remember that the air is thinner at high altitude. Take things easy above 3000 metres, and if you start feeling light-headed, come down to a lower altitude.

WOMEN TRAVELLERS
Women travellers should experience no special problems. Swiss men generally believe that a woman's place is in the home (under Swiss marriage laws, wives weren't granted equal rights until 1988!), but the independence of female travellers is respected.

DANGERS & ANNOYANCES
Emergency telephone numbers are police, ☎ 117, fire brigade, ☎ 118, motoring assistance, ☎ 140, and ambulance, ☎ 144 (most areas). Take special care in the mountains: helicopter rescue is extremely expensive (make sure you have good travel insurance).

FILM & PHOTOGRAPHY
You may photograph anything anywhere you're allowed to go. Film is cheaper than in Austria at around Sfr7 for Kodak Gold and Sfr16 for Kodachrome (36 exposures).

WORK
Officially, only foreigners with special skills can work legally but people still manage to find work in ski resorts. Potentially all sorts of jobs are available during the season, ranging from snow clearing to washing dishes. Hotel work has the advantage of including meals and accommodation. In theory, jobs and work permits should be sorted out before arrival, but in practice if you find a job by asking around the resort, the employer may well have unallocated work permits. The seasonal 'A' permit (Permis A, Saisonbewilligung) is valid for up to nine months, and the elusive and much sought-after 'B' permit (Permis B, Aufenthaltsbewilligung) is renewable and valid for a year.

ACTIVITIES
Water Sports
Water-skiing, sailing and surfing are possible on most lakes. Courses are usually available, especially in Graubünden and central Switzerland. There are over 350 beaches. Anglers should contact the local tourist office for a fishing permit valid for lakes and rivers. The Rotsee near Lucerne is a favourite place for rowing. Rafting is possible on many Alpine rivers including the Rhine and the Rhône. Canoeing is mainly centred on the Muota in Schwyz canton and on the river Doubs in the Jura.

Skiing
There are dozens of ski resorts throughout the Alps, the Pre-Alps and the Jura, incorporating some 200 ski schools. Those resorts favoured by the package-holiday companies do not necessarily have better skiing facilities, but they do tend to have more diversions off the slopes, in terms of sightseeing and nightlife.

Equipment can always be hired at resorts; charges average about Sfr35/20 per day for downhill/cross-country gear. You can buy new equipment at reasonable prices. It's also worth looking around for ski dumps, as the Swiss are so affluent they tend to throw away perfectly usable equipment.

Ski passes (around Sfr40 per day) provide transport to the slopes, but it might be cheaper for beginners to buy ski coupons where available if they only want to try a couple of experimental runs. Most resorts are fairly dead in May and November.

Hiking & Mountaineering
There are 50,000 km of designated footpaths with regular refreshment stops en route. Bright yellow signs marking the trail make it difficult to get lost; each gives an average walking time to the next destination. Zermatt is a favourite destination for mountaineers, but you should never climb on your own. For information contact the Swiss Alpine Club (see the Useful Organisations section earlier in this chapter).

ACCOMMODATION
Camping
There are about 450 camp sites, which are

classified from one to five stars depending upon their amenities and convenience of location. Charges per night are around Sfr5 per person plus Sfr3 to Sfr5 for a tent. Many sites offer a slight discount if you have a Camping Carnet. Free camping is not actively encouraged and should be discrete.

Hostels

Youth hostel in German is *Jugendherberge*. There is a good network of IYHF hostels spread throughout the country. Membership cards must be shown, and precedence is given to those aged under 25. Prices are in the range of Sfr10 to Sfr20. Nonmembers pay a Sfr7 'guest fee', but that's not as bad as it sounds, as six guest fees add up to a full membership card. However, you're better off paying a one-off fee of Sfr30 for international membership, and becoming a member in your country of residence is even cheaper. Sheets are nearly always provided in hostels at no extra cost.

Hostels do get full, and telephone reservations are not accepted. Write, or use the excellent telefax service. Under this system, Swiss hostels will reserve ahead to the next hostel for you but you must give specific dates. The cost is only Sfr1 plus a Sfr9 refundable deposit, and you must claim your bed by 7 pm. Hostels sell a worthwhile guide to Switzerland (around Sfr2.50), which includes an excellent map giving full details of all hostels on the reverse, including fax numbers.

Cheap Hotels

Swiss accommodation is geared towards value for money rather than low cost, so even bottom-of-the-range rooms are fairly comfortable. High-season prices can be 10% to 40% higher than in the low season, but exactly when the high season occurs varies from region to region. Hotels are star rated. Prices start at around Sfr60 for a basic double room. Count on at least Sfr10 more for a room with a shower.

Other

The classification 'Country Inn' denotes a smaller scale establishment, usually in a scenic location. 'Hotel Garni' means bed and breakfast without any extra meals being available. Private houses in rural areas sometimes offer inexpensive rooms: look out for signs saying *Zimmer frei* ('room(s) vacant'). Some farms also take paying guests. Self-catering accommodation is available in holiday chalets, apartments or bungalows. Local tourist offices have full lists of everything on offer in the area. The Swiss Alpine Club maintains around 150 mountain huts at higher altitudes.

FOOD

The Swiss emphasis on quality extends to meals. Basic restaurants provide simple but well-cooked food although prices are generally high. Many budget travellers rely on picnic provisions from supermarkets, but even here prices can be a shock with cheese costing Sfr20 a kg! The main supermarket chains are Migros and Coop. The larger stores have good quality self-service restaurants, which typically open to around 6.30 pm on weekdays and to mid-afternoon on Saturdays. These are usually the cheapest places for hot food, with dishes starting at around Sfr7.

University restaurants (mensas) are a real bargain, and when mentioned in this chapter they are open to everyone. Buffet-style restaurant chains, like Manora and Inova, offer good food at low prices. Don't be put off by the description 'self-service' – they are comfortable inside, the food is freshly cooked in front of you, and you can sometimes select the ingredients yourself.

In restaurants the best value is a fixed-menu dish of the day (*Tagesteller, plat du jour,* or *piatto del giorno*). Fast-food joints are proliferating. Some wine bars *(Weinstübli)* and beer taverns *(Bierstübli)* serve meals. Main meals are eaten at noon. Cheaper restaurants tend to be fairly rigid in when they serve. Go to a hotel or more up-market restaurant for more flexible, later eating. Dedicated vegetarian restaurants can be hard to come by.

Swiss food borrows characteristics from

its larger neighbours. Breakfast is of the continental variety. *Müsli* was invented in Switzerland at the end of the 19th century but nobody seems to eat it in its country of origin. Soups are popular and often very filling. Cheeses form an important part of the Swiss diet. Emmentaler and Gruyère are combined with white wine to create *fondue*, which is served up in a vast pot and eaten with bread cubes. *Raclette* is another cheese dish, served with potatoes. *Rösti* (crispy, fried, shredded potatoes) is German Switzerland's national dish. A wide variety of *Wurst* (sausage) is available. Veal is highly rated throughout Switzerland. In Zürich it is thinly sliced and served in a cream sauce (*Geschnetzeltes Kalbsfleisch*). *Bündnerfleisch* is dried beef, smoked and thinly sliced. Swiss chocolate, excellent by itself, is often used in desserts and cakes.

DRINK

Mineral water is readily available but tap water is fine to drink. The health-conscious should be aware that milk from Alpine cows contains a high level of fat.

There are no restrictive alcohol licensing laws in Switzerland but you may find you haven't the financial resources to take full advantage of this fact. Fortunately, beer and wine prices in supermarkets aren't too bad. In bars, lager beer comes in half-litre bottles or on draught (*vom Fass*) with measures ranging from 0.2 to 0.5 litre.

Wine is considered an important part of the meal even though it is rather expensive. Local wines are generally good but you may not have heard of them before, as output can not even meet domestic demand so they are rarely exported. The main growing region is the French-speaking part of the country, particularly in Valais and by Lake Neuchâtel and Lake Geneva (Lac Léman in French). Both red and white wines are produced, and each region has its own speciality. There is also a choice of locally produced fruit brandies, often served with or in coffee.

ENTERTAINMENT

In German Switzerland, cinemas nearly always show films in the original language. In French Switzerland, look for *VO*, which signifies 'original version'. Nightlife is not all it could be in the cities, and where it does exist, it is expensive. Geneva is the best place for late nightclubs (*boîtes*), although Zürich is also lively. In ski resorts the 'après ski' atmosphere can keep things lively until late. Listening to music is popular. Classical, folk, jazz and rock concerts can be found in all major cities.

THINGS TO BUY

Watches, penknives, textiles and embroidery are all popular buys. Swiss knives range from simple blades (Sfr10) to mini toolboxes (Sfr100). Interlaken and Geneva have a good choice. A grotesquely tacky cuckoo clock with a girl bouncing on a spring will set you back at least Sfr20, a musical box anything upwards of Sfr25. Should you want a cowbell to warn people of your arrival, one with a decorative band will cost Sfr14 to Sfr25.

Getting There & Away

AIR

The main entry points for flights are Zürich and Geneva. Each has several nonstop fights a day to major transport hubs such as London, Paris and Frankfurt. Both airports are linked directly to the Swiss rail network. Basel airport is another busy centre, even though it is actually on the French side of the border at Mulhouse. Dan Air flies direct to Bern from the UK. There are Swissair luggage check-in facilities at many Swiss train stations. There is no airport departure tax to pay when flying out of Switzerland.

LAND

Bus

The international bus service to Switzerland is minimal, although four buses a week go to both Zürich and Geneva from London's Victoria Coach Station. The journey takes 21 hours and there are discount fares available for those aged under 26.

Train

Located at the heart of Europe, it is not surprising that Switzerland has excellent and frequent train connections to the rest of the continent. Zürich is the busiest international terminus. It has five trains daily to Vienna, journey time is eight hours. There are several trains a day to both Geneva and Lausanne from Paris, and journey time is three to four hours by super-fast TGV. Paris to Bern takes 4½ hours by TGV. Most connections from Germany pass though Zürich or Basel. Nearly all connections from Italy pass through Milan before branching off to Zürich, Lucerne, Bern or Lausanne. Reservations on InterCity or EuroCity trains are subject to a surcharge of Sfr4 to Sfr22.

Car & Motorbike

Roads into Switzerland are good despite the difficulty of the terrain, but special care is needed when negotiating mountain passes. Some, such as the N5 route from Morez (in France) to Geneva are not recommended if you have not had previous experience. Upon entering Switzerland you will need to decide whether you wish to use the motorways. There is a one-off charge of Sfr30 if you do (organise this money beforehand, since you might not always be able to change money at the border). The sticker you receive is valid for a year and must be displayed on the windscreen. Some Alpine tunnels incur additional tolls.

BOAT

Basel can be reached by Rhine steamer from Amsterdam or any other stops along the way. The total journey time is more than four days. Switzerland can also be reached by steamer from several lakes: from Germany via Lake Constance (Bodensee in German); from Italy via Lake Maggiore; and from France via Lake Geneva.

Getting Around

Swiss public transport is a fully integrated and comprehensive system incorporating trains, buses, boats and funiculars. Various special tickets are available to the tourist to make the system even more attractive.

The best deal for people planning to travel extensively is the Swiss Pass, entitling the holder to unlimited travel on Swiss Federal Railways, boats, most Alpine postbuses and also on trams and buses in 30 towns. Reductions of 25% apply on funiculars and mountain railways. Passes are valid for four days (Sfr180), eight days (Sfr220), 15 days (Sfr260) and one month (Sfr360) – prices are for 2nd-class tickets.

The Swiss Card allows a free return journey from your arrival point to any destination in Switzerland, 50% off rail, boat and bus excursions, and reductions on mountain railways. The cost is Sfr110 (2nd class) or Sfr140 (1st class) and it is valid for a month. The Half-Fare Card is a similar deal minus the free return trip. The cost is Sfr85 for one month or Sfr125 for one year. The Swiss Flexi Pass allows free, unlimited trips for three days out of 15. The cost is Sfr180 for 2nd class. A Day Card allows free travel on specified days within the validity period, but only if used in conjunction with a Swiss Card or a Half-Fare Card. All these cards can be purchased before arrival in Switzerland from SNTO, or after arrival in major transport centres.

Regional passes are available for free travel on certain days and for half-price travel on other days within a seven or 15-day period, but they are only valid within that particular region. Swiss Pass and Swiss Card holders can get free Family cards from SNTO or Swiss train stations for free travel for minors accompanied by at least one parent.

AIR

Internal flights are not of great interest to the visitor, owing to the excellent ground transport. Cross Air, a branch of Swissair, is the local carrier, and links major towns and cities several times daily.

BUS
Yellow postbuses are a supplement to the rail network, following postal routes and linking towns to the more inaccessible regions in the mountains. In all, routes cover some 8000 km of terrain. They are extremely regular, and departures tie in with train arrivals. Postbus stations are next to train stations.

TRAIN
The Swiss rail network covers 5000 km and is a combination of state-run and private lines. Trains are clean, reliable, frequent and as fast as the terrain will allow. The drawback is that they are expensive. All fares quoted are for 2nd class. In general, Eurail passes are not valid for private lines and Inter-Rail gets 50% off. All major stations are connected to each other by hourly departures, but services stop from around midnight to 6 am.

Train stations invariably offer luggage storage, either at a counter (Sfr2) or in 24-hour lockers (Sfr2 or Sfr3). They also have excellent information counters which give out free timetable booklets and advice on connections. Single train tickets are often valid for two days and it is possible to break the journey on the same ticket, but tell the conductor of your intentions. Train schedules are revised yearly, so double-check all times that are quoted in this chapter.

CAR & MOTORBIKE
Be prepared for winding roads, high passes and long tunnels. Speed limits are 50 km/h in towns, 120 km/h on motorways and 80 km/h on other roads. Mountain roads are good but stay in low gear whenever possible. Snow chains are recommended in winter. Some minor Alpine passes are closed from November to May. The tourist office can provide details and you can ring ☎ 163 for road reports. Cars and occupants can be carried by train through some rail tunnels.

The Swiss Touring Club operates a 24-hour breakdown service on ☎ 022-3 58 00. Switzerland is tough on drink-driving, so don't risk it; the BAC limit is 0.08%, and if caught exceeding this limit, you face a fine or imprisonment.

Rental
Sixt is one of the cheapest rental agencies. A group-A Lancia Y10 costs Sfr135 per day or Sfr90 per day for a week, both with unlimited km. A low weekend rate of Sfr155 applies from noon on Friday to 9 am on Monday, also with unlimited mileage. See the Geneva and Zürich sections for more details. Hertz, Avis and Budget rates are about 50% higher.

BICYCLE
Despite the hilly countryside, cycling is popular in Switzerland. Cycles can be hired from most train stations and returned to any station with a rental office. Cost is Sfr16 per day or Sfr64 per week. Bikes can be transported on normal trains but not on InterCity or EuroCity trains. The SNTO issues three free, useful booklets on cycling holidays, concentrating on the Pre-Alps, the Midlands, and from the Rhine to Ticino.

HITCHING
Although illegal on motorways, hitching is allowed on other roads and can be fairly easy. At other times it can be quite slow. Indigenous Swiss are not all that sympathetic towards hitchers, and you'll find that most of your lifts will come from foreigners. A sign is helpful. Make sure you stand in a place where vehicles can stop. To try to get a ride on a truck, ask around the customs post at border towns.

WALKING
The SNTO shows the way with its *Switzerland Step by Step* booklets detailing 100 walks to mountain lakes, over mountain passes, and from town to town.

BOAT
All the larger lakes are serviced by steamers operated by Swiss Federal Railways. Rail passes are valid for these services. A Swiss

SWITZERLAND

Navigation Boat Pass costs Sfr30 and entitles the bearer to 50% off fares. It is valid from 1 April to 31 October.

MOUNTAIN TRANSPORT

There are five main modes of transport used in steep Alpine regions. A funicular (*funiculaire* or *Standseilbahn*) is a pair of counter-balancing cars drawn by cables. A cable car (*téléphérique* or *Luftseilbahn*) is dramatically suspended from a cable high over a valley. A gondola (*télécabine* or *Gondelbahn*) is a smaller version of a cable car except that the gondola is hitched onto a continuously running cable once the passengers are inside. A cable chair (*télésiège* or *Sesselbahn*) is likewise hitched onto a cable but is unenclosed. A ski lift (*téléski* or *Schlepplift*) is a T-bar hanging from a cable, which the skiers hold onto while their feet slide along the snow.

LOCAL TRANSPORT
Public Transport

All local city transport is linked together on the same ticketing system. You should buy tickets before boarding. In some towns tickets are valid for one hour's travel, or one-day passes are even better value. There are regular checks for people travelling without tickets; those found wanting, pay an on-the-spot fine of Sfr40 to Sfr50.

Taxi

Taxis are always metered and tend to wait around train stations. Beware – they are expensive!

TOURS

Tours are booked through local tourist offices. The country is so compact that excursions to the major national attractions are offered from most towns. A trip up to Jungfraujoch, for example, is available from Zürich, Geneva, Bern, Lucerne and Interlaken. Most tours represent reasonable value.

Bern

Founded in 1191, Bern (Berne in French) is Switzerland's capital and fourth-largest city. The story goes that the city was named after the first animal killed by the founder, Berchtold V, when hunting in the area. That animal was a bear, and even today the bear remains the heraldic mascot of the city. Despite playing host to the nation's politicians, Bern retains a relaxed, small-town charm. A picturesque Old Town contains six km of covered arcades and 11 historic fountains, as well as the descendants of the city's first casualty who perform tricks for tourists. The world's largest Paul Klee collection is housed in the Museum of Fine Arts.

Orientation

The compact centre of town is contained within a sharp U-bend of the River Aare. Much of it is pedestrian access only. The main train station is in the mouth of this 'U' and is within easy reach of all the main sights. The station has luggage lockers (Sfr2), bicycle rental (daily from 6.10 am to 11.45 pm) and Swissair check-in.

Most shops are shut on Monday morning and have extended hours on Thursday.

Information

Tourist Office The Offizielles Verkehrsbüro Bern (☎ 031-22 76 76) is in the train station and is open daily from 9 am to 8.30 pm. From 1 November to 30 April it shuts two hours earlier and Sunday hours are from 10 am to 5 pm. Services include hotel reservations (Sfr3 service charge) and excursions. Its free booklet, *This Week in Bern*, contains much practical and recreational information.

Money Exchange facilities can be found at the train station, open daily from 6.10 am to 10 pm, except from January to March when it closes at 9 pm.

Post & Telecommunications The main post office (Schanzenpost 1) is at Schanzenstrasse; it is open Monday to Friday from 7.30 am to 6.30 pm and on Saturday from 7.30 am to 11 am. The telephone code for Bern is 031.

Foreign Embassies The British Embassy (☎ 44 50 21) is south of Kirchenfeldbrücke at Thunstrasse 50. The US Embassy (☎ 43 70 11) is at Jubiläumsstrasse 93. The Canadian Embassy (☎ 44 63 81) is at Kirchenfeldstrasse 88. The Australian Embassy (☎ 43 01 43) is at Alpenstrasse 29. The French Embassy (☎ 43 24 24) is at Schosshaldenstrasse 46. The German Embassy (☎ 44 08 31) can be found at Willadingweg 83. As Bern is Switzerland's capital city, most other embassies are also here. The tourist office has a full list.

Travel Agencies American Express (☎ 22 94 01) is at Bubenbergplatz 11; it is open Monday to Friday from 8.30 am to 6 pm and Saturday from 9 am to noon. The Swiss budget travel agency SSR has two offices: a branch at Falkenplatz 9 (☎ 24 03 12), and one at Rathausgasse 64 (☎ 21 07 22). Both are open Monday to Friday only.

Bookshops Stauffacher AG (☎ 22 14 23), Neuengasse 25, has a section on English-language books.

Emergency There is a police station (☎ 68 41 11) and a chemist in the train station. For medical emergencies, ☎ 22 92 11.

Dangers & Annoyances There is a drug problem in this otherwise idyllic town, which the authorities try to contain within one area. The location changes periodically, but it's not a pleasant thing to stumble upon: you find youngsters openly injecting themselves, and the area littered with needles and bloody swabs. Not a pretty sight.

Things to See & Do
Walking Tour The city map from the tourist office details a picturesque walk through the old town. The core of the walk is Marktgasse and Kramgasse with their covered arcades

and colourful fountains. Dividing the two streets is the **Zeitglockenturm**, a clock tower on which revolving figures herald the chiming hour. Congregate a few minutes before the hour on the east side to see them twirl. Originally a city gate, the clock was installed in 1530.

The unmistakably Gothic, 15th century **cathedral** *(Münster)*, Münstergasse, is noted for its stained-glass windows and elaborate main portal. Just over the river Aare are the **bear pits** *(Bärengraben)*. Bears have been at this site since 1857, although records show that as far back as 1441 the city council bought acorns to feed the ancestors of these overgrown pets. Up the hill is the **Rose Garden**, which has 200 varieties of roses and an excellent view of the city.

Parliament Well worth a visit is the Bundeshäuser, home of the Swiss Federal Assembly. There are free daily tours when the parliament is not in session. Arrive early and reserve a place for later in the day. A multilingual guide takes you through the impressive chambers, and highlights the development of the Swiss constitution.

Museums There is no shortage of museums. The **Museum of Fine Arts** *(Kunstmuseum)*, Hodlerstrasse 8-12, holds the Klee collection and an interesting mix of Italian masters, Swiss and modern art. It is open Tuesday from 10 am to 9 pm, and Wednesday to Sunday from 10 am to 5 pm; entry costs Sfr4 (students Sfr3).

Worth a few minutes is the **Einstein House**, Kramgasse 49, where the physicist developed his special theory of relativity (free entry).

Many museums are grouped together on the south side of the Kirchenfeldbrücke. The best here is the **Bern Historical Museum** *(Bernisches Historisches Museum)*, Helvetiaplatz, open Tuesday to Sunday from 10 am to 5 pm (admission Sfr3). Highlights include the original sculptures from the Münster doorway depicting the Last Judgement, Niklaus Manuel's macabre *Dance of Death*

Bern
(Berne)

0   200   400 m

Some Streets Pedestrian Only

panels, and the ridiculous codpiece on the William Tell statue upstairs.

Also worthwhile is the **Natural History Museum** (*Naturhistorisches Museum*) on Bernastrasse, with animals depicted in realistic dioramas. It is open Monday from 2 pm to 5 pm, Tuesday to Saturday from 9 am to 5 pm, and Sunday from 10 am to 5 pm. Entry is Sfr3, or Sfr1.50 for students.

Market An open-air vegetable, fruit and flower market can be found at Bärenplatz or Bundesplatz in the morning on Tuesday and Saturday.

Organised Tour
There is a daily two-hour city tour by coach, costing Sfr19, which goes nowhere you can't walk yourself. Get details from the tourist office.

Places to Stay
Camping To get to *Camping Eymatt* (☎ 901 15 01), take postbus No 3 or 4 from the train station to Eymatt. Open all year, reception is shut from 1 pm to 4 pm and the gates close at 11 pm. Cost is Sfr6 per person, Sfr7 per car and Sfr4 per tent. Near the river but to the south of town is *Camping Eichholz* (☎ 961

■ PLACES TO STAY

1 Marthahaus Garni
10 Hospiz zur Heimat
18 Hotel Krebs
29 National
31 Youth Hostel

▼ PLACES TO EAT

3 Mensa
6 Kornhauskeller
12 Ratskeller
14 Menuetto
17 Migros & GD Restaurant
23 Vegi
24 Della Casa
25 Gfeller
27 Manora

OTHER

2 Kursaal (Entertainment/
   Gambling Centre)
4 Museum of Fine Arts
5 Aarbergerhof
7 Kornhausplatz
8 Rathaus
9 Rathausplatz
11 Bear Pits
13 Cathedral
15 Theaterplatz
16 Zeitglockenturm
19 Bahnhofplatz
20 Tourist Office
21 Bus Station
22 Post Office
26 Bundesplatz
28 Bubenbergplatz
30 Parliament
32 Helvetiaplatz
33 Bern Historical Museum
34 Natural History Museum

26 02), Strandweg 49. Take tram No 9 from the station. The site is open from late April to the end of September, and costs are Sfr4.80 per person, tents Sfr3, cars Sfr2, and vans Sfr8. It also has two-bed rooms for Sfr12 plus Sfr4.80 per person.

Hostel The IYHF *youth hostel* (☎ 23 63 16), Weihergasse 4, is in a good location below Parliament. The paths down the hill are signposted to the hostel. It is usually full in summer, when a three-day maximum stay applies. Reception is shut from 9.30 am to 4 or 5 pm, but bags can be left in the common room during the day. Beds are Sfr14, breakfast Sfr5, and lunch and dinner are Sfr9 each. There are free lockers, a midnight curfew, and washing machines at Sfr3 per load.

Hotels There's a limited choice of budget rooms in Bern. *Bahnhof-Süd* (☎ 56 51 11), Bümplizstrasse 189, to the west of town beyond the autobahn, has singles/doubles from Sfr50/80 without breakfast (shower and WC out in the corridor). To get there, take bus No 13 from the city centre. Convenient for the train station is *National* (☎ 25 19 88), Hirschengraben 24. It has adequate singles/doubles without shower from Sfr47/84, or Sfr 85/110 with shower and WC; breakfast is included.

Right in the middle of the Old Town in an 18th century building is *Hospiz zur Heimat* (☎ 22 04 36), Gerechtigkeitsgasse 50. Features include clean, spacious rooms and a wonderfully rude and impatient Basil Fawltyesque proprietor. Singles/doubles are Sfr58/84, and triples/quads are Sfr111/148, all with breakfast. Rooms with shower are around Sfr20 more expensive, otherwise there are showers in the hall. The hotel also has a restaurant with a cheap lunch-time menu.

Opposite is the more up-market *Goldener Adler* at No 50, which has doubles from Sfr100. Another good choice for mid-price accommodation is *Hotel Krebs* (☎ 22 49 42), Genfergasse 8, near the train station. Singles with shower, WC, TV and breakfast buffet are expensive at Sfr112, but the corresponding doubles are a much better deal at Sfr138; the family room for four costs Sfr235. Take bus No 20 from Bahnhofplatz for *Martha-haus Garni* (☎ 42 41 35), Wyttenbachstrasse 22A. It's a friendly place with comfortable rooms and two TV lounges. Singles/doubles/triples with breakfast start from Sfr55/85/120, although prices go up slightly in the summer.

SWITZERLAND

Places to Eat

Migros supermarket at Marktgasse 46 is open Monday from 2 to 6.30 pm, Tuesday, Wednesday and Friday from 8 am to 6.30 pm, Thursday from 8 am to 9 pm and Saturday from 7 am to 4 pm. It has a cheap self-service restaurant on the 1st floor. On the same floor is *G D Restaurant* with a good selection of local dishes from Sfr9, open Monday to Friday from 8.30 am to 7.30 pm (closes 9.30 pm on Thursday), and Saturday from 8 am to 4 pm.

The best value in town is at the university *Mensa*, Gesellschaftsstrasse 2, on the 1st floor. Menus cost around Sfr6, and there are reductions for students. It is open Monday to Friday from 11.30 am to 1.45 pm and 5.45 to 7.30 pm (it closes at 1.45 pm on Friday). The café downstairs keeps longer hours for drinks and snacks.

Apero, on the 1st floor in the train station, has daily specials from Sfr8 to Sfr15, and terraced seating overlooking the square. *Manora* (☎ 22 37 55), Bubenbergplatz 5a, is a busy and sometimes hectic self-service restaurant. Meals are Sfr8.80 to Sfr16, and the pile-it-on-yourself salad is Sfr4.50 to Sfr9.50 per plate. Nearby is *Café Bubenberg Vegi* (☎ 22 75 76), Bubenbergplatz 8, which has terrace seating and good vegetarian food for Sfr11 to Sfr18. It is open Monday to Friday from 7 am to 10 pm and Saturday from 7 am to 5 pm. Slightly more expensive but also recommended for vegetarian food is *Menuetto* (☎ 22 14 48), Münstergasse 47, open daily except Sunday from 9 am to 10 pm.

Several pleasant restaurants with outside seating line Bärenplatz. There's little to choose between them although *Gfeller* has the advantage of a cheaper self-service section upstairs. The dingy exterior of *Della Casa* (☎ 22 21 42), Schauplatzgasse 16, hides a good-quality restaurant within. The local speciality, *Bärner Platte* (a selection of meats with sauerkraut and beans), is served here but it is expensive. If you're lucky, you can find it on the excellent three-course daily menu for Sfr18 (different menu lunch and dinner). It is open Monday to Friday from 8.30 to 11.30 pm but the menu stops at 9 pm.

Kornhauskeller (☎ 22 11 33), Kornhausplatz 17, is a traditional beer hall with live music nightly (entry is free but the music can yield more pain than pleasure, depending on the band) and a jazz matinée on Sunday (entry Sfr15 to Sfr20). Food can get pricey, but the well-prepared, two-course menu (lunch and evening) is good value at Sfr14.50. It is open Tuesday to Saturday from 6 am to around midnight, and Sunday from 11.15 am to 11 pm.

Around the corner, the *Restaurant Brasserie Anker* (☎ 22 11 13) at Zeughausgasse 1 has fondues from Sfr17.50. Its relaxed atmosphere is as popular with drinkers as its low beer prices – just Sfr3.40 for half a litre.

For good-quality fish and meat dishes (Sfr15 to Sfr40) in a calm setting, try the *Ratskeller* at Gerechtigkeitsgasse 81 (open daily). More lively and atmospheric is *Klötzlikeller* (☎ 22 74 56), a wine cellar at Gerechtigkeitsgasse 62. It has interesting dishes ranging from snails to tripe (Sfr15 to Sfr25), and is open Tuesday to Saturday from 4 pm till after midnight.

Entertainment

On Mondays, cinemas cost Sfr9 instead of the usual Sfr12. The *Kursaal*, Schänzlistrasse 71-77 (take tram No 9 from Kornhausplatz), has mini golf, gambling from 9 pm, and a disco and live music (the cover charge is Sfr5 to Sfr12, or free for women). There are a few late venues in the city centre which shut around 3 am (except Sunday) but they can get expensive. *Babalu*, Gurtengasse 3, is a nightclub with live music and different themes each night, including a gay night on Wednesday. Cover charge is Sfr13 to Sfr23.

Places popular with young people are the bright bar/café *Aarbergerhof*, Aarbergergasse 40, and the rather noisier and darker *Interview*, down the Ryffligässchen passage between Neuengasse and Spitalgasse.

Getting There & Away

Air There are daily flights to/from London and Paris, and frequent services to other destinations such as Lugano, Florence and Venice.

Bus Postbuses depart from the Schanzenstrasse side of the train station.

Train There are at least hourly connections to the following towns and cities: Geneva trains depart at 18 minutes past the hour and take 1¾ hours; Basel departures leave at 48 minutes past the hour and take 70 minutes; Interlaken Ost departures leave at 28 minutes past the hour and take 50 minutes; trains to Zürich depart at 45 minutes past the hour and take 1½ hours.

Car & Motorbike There are three motorways which intersect at the northern part of the city. The N1 is the route from Neuchâtel in the west and Basel and Zürich in the north-east. The N6 connects Bern with Thun and the Interlaken region in the south. The N12 is the route from Geneva and Lausanne in the south-west.

Getting Around
To/From the Airport The small airport is 10 km south-east of the city centre. A bus links the airport to the train station. The fare is Sfr9 to Sfr 12 depending on the size of the bus; it takes 20 minutes and is coordinated with flight arrivals and departures.

Bus Getting around on foot is easy enough if you're staying near the city centre, although buses and trams are reliable. Tickets cost Sfr1.10 to Sfr1.70, but you're better off buying daily tourist cards valid for unlimited travel. One, two or three-day passes cost Sfr3, Sfr5 or Sfr7. A 24-hour card costs Sfr4 and is valid from first use. Buy single-journey tickets at stops and daily cards from the tourist office or the public transport office (☎ 22 14 44) at Bubenbergplatz 59.

Taxi Many taxis wait by the station. The cost is Sfr6 plus Sfr2.20 to Sfr2.80 per km depending on the number of passengers.

Car & Motorbike There are several underground parking spots in the city centre, including one at the train station. The tourist office map lists locations.

Neuchâtel

Neuchâtel is just inside the French-speaking region of Switzerland, on the north-west shore of the lake that shares its name. A relaxing town where locals unhurriedly kiss each other on the cheeks upon meeting, it is relatively untouristed and offers easy access to the mountain areas of the Jura.

Orientation & Information
The train station (Gare CFF) changes money daily from 5.30 am to 10 pm. The main post office is just opposite (Poste, 2002 Neuchâtel 2, open daily). The old part of town is less than one km away down the hill along Ave de la Gare. The commercial centre is the pedestrian-only Rue de l'Hôpital.

The tourist office (☎ 038-25 42 42) is between Place Pury and the port, at Rue de la Place d'Armes 7, and is open Monday to Friday from 9 am to noon and 1.30 to 5.30 pm, and Saturday from 9 am to noon (hours are extended in summer). Pick up a copy of its walking tour of the town centre.

Things to See & Do
The centrepiece of the old town is the **castle** and the adjoining **Collegiate Church**. The castle dates from the 12th century and now houses cantonal offices. The church contains a striking cenotaph of 15 statues dating from 1372. Nearby, the **Prison Tower** (entry Sfr0.50) offers a good view of the area and has interesting models showing the town as it was in the 15th and 18th centuries.

One of the town's several museums, the **Musée d'Art et d'Histoire**, 2 quai Léopold Robert, is especially noted for three 18th century clockwork figures. Unfortunately they are only activated on the first Sunday of each month. Entry is Sfr7, or Sfr4 for students, and the museum is shut on Mondays.

Six km to the east of town at Marin (take bus No 1 from Place Pury) is a **Papiliorama**, open daily in the Marin Centre, with over 1000 butterflies of all sizes and hues. The tourist office has information on nearby walking trails and boat trips on the lake.

Places to Stay & Eat

The IYHF *youth hostel* (☎ 038-31 31 90) is two km from the town centre; take bus No 3 to Vanseyon and then follow the signs. It is a small, pleasant, family-run place with good evening meals and a laundry service. Beds are Sfr16 per night with breakfast.

Marché (☎ 038-24 58 00) is ideally placed in the town centre at Place des Halles 4. Ask for a room overlooking the square. Rooms vary in size, each has a TV but no shower. Singles/doubles are Sfr 60/85 including breakfast. An extra bed in the room costs Sfr20. *Hôtel du Poisson* (☎ 038-33 30 31), Ave Bachelin 7, Marin, has singles/doubles for Sfr36/68, with breakfast.

The *Buffet de la Gare* at the station is not too expensive with daily menus for Sfr10 to Sfr14.50. In the town centre there are two *Coops* with self-service restaurants at Rue de la Treille 4 and Portes-Rouges 55. There is also a *Migros* supermarket on Rue de l'Hôpital. Opposite Migros is the *Crêperie*, which is reasonably priced, highly rated and popular with locals.

Getting There & Around

There are hourly fast trains to Geneva (70 minutes, Sfr37), Bern (35 minutes, Sfr16) and many other destinations. Postbuses leave from outside the station. Local buses cost Sfr1.20 to Sfr2, or Sfr6 for a 24-hour ticket.

JURA MOUNTAINS

Less visited by tourists, this area to the north and west of Lake Neuchâtel is slightly cheaper than the rest of Switzerland. The mountains are less rugged than the Alps and are ideal for hikers, with over 2000 km of maintained and marked footpaths. Horse riding is also a popular activity. In the winter, hiking gives way to cross-country skiing, for which some of the groomed trails are lit. It is

also an important area for watch-making and there are several museums devoted to this industry, most notably in La Chaux de Fonds and Le Locle (both museums shut on Mondays).

Orientation & Information

The largest town in the region and also the highest in Switzerland (1000 metres) is La Chaux de Fonds, 20 km north-west of Neuchâtel. The tourist office (☎ 039-28 13 13) is at Rue Neuve 11. Opening hours are similar to Neuchâtel. For snow reports, ring ☎ 039-28 75 75.

Places to Stay & Eat

There is winter camping at Le Locle. In La Chaux de Fonds, the IYHF *youth hostel* (☎ 039-28 43 15), has beds for Sfr16 including breakfast. It's 10 minutes' walk from the station, at Rue de Doubs 34. Opposite the station, on Rue Daniel Richard, is *Garni de France* (☎ 039-23 11 16), with singles/doubles from Sfr25/50.

Also in La Chaux de Fonds, restaurant *La Pinte Neuchâteloise* on Rue du Grenier has menus from Sfr10, as well as meat, fish and cheese specialities (closed Tuesday).

Getting There & Away

La Chaux de Fonds and Le Locle are connected to each other, as well as to Neuchâtel and Basel, by rail. A network of postbuses connects the smaller towns and villages in the region, although departures can be infrequent.

Geneva

Geneva (Genève, Genf, Ginevra) is Switzerland's third-largest city. Comfortably encamped on the southern shore of Lake Geneva (Lac Léman), it is surrounded by France on nearly all sides. French influence encompasses the language and the cuisine, yet it is undeniably an international city. One in three residents are non-Swiss and many world organisations are based here, not least the United Nations, the European headquarters of which is in the former League of Nations building. Unfortunately, the presence of so many businesspeople, bankers and diplomats means that prices for food and accommodation can be high.

After gaining independence from the Duke of Savoy in 1530, Geneva was ripe for the teachings of John Calvin two years later, and soon became known as the 'Protestant Rome', during which time fun became frowned upon. Thankfully this legacy barely lingers and today Geneva has the best nightlife in Switzerland. In 1798 Napoleon annexed the city and held it for 16 years before it was admitted to the Swiss Confederation as a canton in 1815.

Orientation

The city centre forms a crescent round the edge of Lake Geneva and is split down the middle by the westward progress of the Rhône. Conveniently in the centre of town on the north side of the river is the main train station, Gare de Cornavin. To the south of the river lies the old part of town, where many important buildings are located. Geneva's most visible landmark is the Jet d'Eau, a 140-metre-high fountain spouting water into the lake from a pier on the southern shore.

Information

Tourist Office The busy tourist office (☎ 022-738 52 00) is in the train station, and is open Monday to Saturday from 9 am to 6 pm. From mid-June to mid-September, opening hours are extended and become Monday to Friday from 8 am to 8 pm, and Saturday and Sunday from 8 am to 6 pm. Hotel reservations cost Sfr5.

The Centre d'Accueil et de Recontres (CAR) (☎ 022-731 46 47) has tourist and accommodation information. It is based in a yellow bus at the entrance to the Gare de Cornavin and is open daily between 8.30 am and 11 pm, but only between 15 June and 15 October.

Money Exchange counters in Gare de Cornavin are open daily from 6 am to 9.45 pm. Banque Migros at 16 Rue du Mont Blanc is open Monday to Friday from 8.30 to 6.30 pm, and Saturday from 8 am to 5 pm.

Post & Telecommunications There is a post office (☎ 022-739 24 58) by the Gare de Cornavin at Cornavin Dépôt, 16 Rue des Gares, 1211 Genève 2. Look for the yellow PTT signs. It is open Monday to Friday from 6 am to 10.45 pm, Saturday from 6 am to 8 pm, and Sunday from 9 am to 12.30 pm and 3 to 10 pm. There is also a large post office at 18 Rue du Mont Blanc, 1211 Genève 1. It is open Monday to Friday from 7.30 am to 6 pm, and Saturday from 7.30 am to 11 am. Both post offices will accept poste restante, but unless you specify the office, it will end up at Mont Blanc.

The telephone code for Geneva is 022.

Consulates The British Consulate (☎ 734 38 00) is at 37-39 Rue de Vermont. The US Consulate (☎ 738 76 13) is by the United Nations at 1-3 Ave de la Paix. The Canadian Consulate (☎ 733 90 00) is at 1 Pré de la Bichette. The Australian Consulate (☎ 734 62 00) is at 56-58 Rue de Moillebeau. The New Zealand Consulate (☎ 734 95 30) is at 28A Chemin du Petit-Saconnex. The French Consulate (☎ 29 62 11) is at 11 Rue J Imbert Galliox. The Italian Consulate (☎ 46 47 44) is at 14 Rue Charles Galland.

Travel Agencies American Express (☎ 731 76 00) is at 7 Rue du Mont Blanc, open Monday to Friday from 8.30 am to 5.30 pm and Saturday from 9 am to noon. Budget travel agency SSR (☎ 29 97 33), 3 Rue Vignier, is open Monday to Friday from 9 am to 5.30 pm. Many other travel agents and airline offices are concentrated along Rue Chantepoulet and Rue du Mont Blanc.

Bookshops Elm Book Shop (☎ 36 09 45), 5 Rue Versonnex, sells English-language books and has lists of city restaurants. Librairie des Amateurs, 15 Grand Rue, sells second-hand books at around Sfr2 to Sfr4 for a paperback.

SWITZERLAND

Geneva
(Genève)

0   250   500 m

1

Botanical
Gardens

Avenue de Ferney

Avenue de la Paix

2
3

Rue de Lausanne

Avenue Giuseppe-Motta

Rue de Montbrillant

Rue du Vidollet

Rue de Monthoux

Avenue de

Parc
Mon Repos

Rue de France

Rue de Valais

Lake Geneva

Rue du Grand Pré

5

Rue Rothschild

Rue de la Servette

To Airport

15

Rue de la Prairie

Rue de Lyon

Rue des Gares

Gare de Cornavin

13   12
i

14

Rue de la Môle

Rue de Berne

6

Quai Wilson

Rue du
L'Ancien-Port

7

8   9

Rue Philippe-Plantamour

Rue des Alpes

10
11

20

Jetée des Pâquis

Rue Voltaire

16

23

17

18

19

Rue du Mont-Blanc

21

Quai du Mont-Blanc

Pont de la
Couloverrière

Rue de Cornavin

22   Pont
de la
Machine

24

Rousseau

Jet d'Eau

Pont du
Mont-Blanc

Quai du Seujet

Pont
de l'Ile

Pont des
Bergues

Rhône River

Rue du Stand

25

Quai des
Forces
Motrices

Boulevard de Saint-Georges

Quai du Général Guisan

26

27

Promenade
du Lac

28

Quai Gustave-Ador

30

31

35

32

29

Rue du Rhône

Rue de la
Confédération

Rue de Rive

Rue de la
Croix-d'Or

Rue
Pierre-Fatio

Rue
Versonnex

34

33

Grand-Rue

37

36

Rue Gourgas

Rue du Vieux-Billard

Boulevard Jacques-Dalcroze

Rue de la
Croix-Rouge

Rond-Point
de Rive

Avenue
de Sainte-
Clotilde

38

Rond-Point
de Plainpalais

Cours des Bastions

Boulevard

39

Rue
Ferdinand-
Hodler

40   41

Rue Lefort

Rue G–
Leschot

43

des Philosophes

44

45

Rue F–D'Ivernois

Rue des Voisins

42

Boulevard des Tranchées

Route de Malagnou

Route de Florissant

Arve River

■ **PLACES TO STAY**

3   Centre Masaryk
4   Auberge de Jeunesse
9   Hôtel de la Cloche
10 International Terminus
15 Pension de la Servette
32 Hôtel le Chandelier
37 Hôtel le Grenil
42 Hôtel Saint Victor
44 Centre Universitaire
    Zofingen
45 Hôtel le Prince

▼ **PLACES TO EAT**

6   Migros
7   Le Blason
8   Auberge de Savièse
14 Restaurant Sinbad
17 La Siesta
22 Miyako
24 Restaurant Manora
25 l'Usine
29 Café du Centre
31 Le Potager
35 Cave Valaisanne et
    Chalet Suisse
36 Le Bleu Nuit

OTHER

1   Palais des Nations
2   Place des Nations
5   Post Office (Genève 2)
11 Place de Cornavin
12 Tourist Office
13 Place du Reculet
16 Notre-Dame
18 Post Office (Genève 1)
19 Place Dorcière
20 Place des Alpes
21 International Bus Terminal
23 Place des Cantons
26 Place du Lac
27 Jardin Anglais
28 CGN Boat Station
30 Place de la Synagogue
33 Cathedral St Pierre
34 Place Neuve
38 Reformation Monument
39 Museum of Art and History
40 Place Emile Guyénot
41 Museum of Natural History
43 Place des Philosophes
46 Place Edouard Claparède

Emergency Permanence Médicale is open 24 hours a day with branches at 21 Rue de Chantepoulet (☎ 731 21 20) and 7 Rue des Pâquis (☎ 731 21 80). Also open 24 hours is Hôpital de la Tour (☎ 780 01 11), 3 Ave J D Maillard. Dental treatment (☎ 733 98 00) can be obtained between 7.30 am and 8 pm at 60 Ave Wendt. Ring ☎ 735 81 83 for a legal advice service.

Things to See & Do
Walking Tour The centre of the city is so compact that it is easy to see most of the main sights on foot. Start a scenic walk through the Old Town at the **Île Rousseau**. It is noted for a statue in honour of the celebrated free thinker, who formulated his seminal thoughts on democracy whilst, in his own words, a 'citizen of Geneva'.

Turn right along the south side of the Rhône until you reach the 13th century **Tour d'Île**, once part of the medieval city fortifications. Walk south down the narrow, cobbled Rue de la Cité until it becomes Grand Rue. On each side are a variety of interesting buildings, including Rousseau's birthplace at no 40. Grand Rue terminates at **Place du Bourg-de-Four**, the site of a medieval marketplace which now has a fountain and touristy shops.

The centre of town is dominated by the partially Gothic **Cathedral St Pierre**. John Calvin preached here from 1536 to 1564. There is a good view from the tower, which is open daily to 5.30 pm (entry Sfr2). The cathedral is on an important archaeological site which is of only limited general appeal (entry Sfr5, students Sfr3, closed Monday).

Nearby, the **Promenade des Bastions** is a pleasant park which contains a massive monument to the Reformation. The giant figures of Bèze, Calvin, Farel and Knox are flanked by smaller statues of other important figures and carved depictions of events instrumental in the spread of the movement.

Perhaps the best walk is along the shores of the lake. At weekends in the summer the water is alive with the bobbing white sails of sailing boats. On the lakefront near the old town, the **Jardin Anglais** features a large clock composed of flowers. Close by is the **Jet d'Eau**, the waters of which shoot up with incredible force (200 km/h, 1360 horsepower) and, according to the whims of the wind, spray spectators who venture out on the pier. Colourful flower gardens and the occasional statue line the promenade on the north shore of the lake leading to two relaxing parks. Well worth a visit is the **Botanical Gardens** (Jardin Botanique) which, among other attractions, features exotic plants, llamas and an aviary. Entry is free and it is open daily from 7 am to 7.30 pm.

Museums Geneva is not a bad place to get stuck on a rainy day as there are plenty of museums, many of which are free. The most important is the **Museum of Art and History** (Musée d'Art et d'Histoire), 2 Rue Charles Galland, with a vast and varied collection including paintings, sculpture, weapons and archaeology. It is open Tuesday to Sunday from 10 am to 5 pm and entry is free. The nearby **Museum of Natural History** (Musée d'Histoire Naturelle), Route de Malagnou, has dioramas, minerals and anthropological displays. It is also free, and open Tuesday to Sunday from 10 am to 5 pm. In the old town, **Maison Tavel**, 6 Rue du Puits Saint Pierre, is notable for a detailed relief map of Geneva covering 35 sq metres. Once again, entry is free, and it is open Tuesday to Sunday from 10 am to 5 pm.

United Nations The Palais des Nations at the Place des Nations is the home of the UN and is the base for a resident population of 3000 international civil servants. Interesting but not essential is the hour-long tour of the interior, a touch expensive at Sfr8 (students Sfr6). There is no charge to walk around the gardens. Among other attractions is a towering grey monument coated with heat-resistant titanium, donated by the USSR to commemorate the conquest of space.

The gardens are open Monday to Friday from November to March and daily from April to October. Guided tours are from 10 am to noon and 2 to 4 pm, and from 9 am to noon and 2 to 6 pm during July and August. You need to show your passport to gain admittance.

Excursions A popular outing is the cable car up **Mont Salève** for an excellent view of the city and Lake Geneva. Take bus No 8 to Veyrier and walk across the border into France. It's just a few minutes to the cable car which costs Sfr14.30 return, Sfr7.90 for students, and operates daily from May to September, Tuesday to Sunday during April, October and early November, and only weekends and holidays during winter.

Places to Stay

Camping The most central camp site, *Sylvabelle* (☎ 47 06 03), 10 Chemin de Conches, has rather eccentric management. When you phone up they try to give you the impression that you've got the wrong number. Four-person bungalows are available and camping is Sfr4 per person, Sfr3 per tent and Sfr3 per car. It is open from 1 April to 31 October. To get there, take bus No 8 from Gare de Cornavin or Rond-Point de Rive.

Seven km east of city the centre on the south side of the lake is *Camping Pointe a la Bise* (☎ 752 12 96), 1222 Vesenaz. It's open from 1 April to 30 September, and costs Sfr5 per person, tents from Sfr5. Take bus E from Rive. Reception shuts at 10 pm. Seven km farther away from the city in the same direction and five minutes' walk from the last stop on bus E is *Camping D'Hermance* (☎ 751 14 83), Chemin des Glerrets. It is open from 1 April to 30 September and costs Sfr6 per person, Sfr2.50 per tent and Sfr0.50 for showers. People without tents are accepted, and there is free entry to the beach and free car parking outside the site. Reception shuts at midnight.

Camping du Val de l'Allondon (☎ 753 15 15), Route des Granges, Peissy Satigny, is 15 km west of the city centre and only accessible by private transport. It's open from 1 April to 30 October and charges are Sfr3.20 per person (Sfr4 in July and August), tent Sfr2, motorcycle Sfr1, car Sfr6 and parking Sfr2 (free outside the camp). There is a 20%

reduction with a Camping Carnet. Reception shuts at 10 pm and facilities include a grocery shop on site.

Hostels A good selection of dormitory beds is listed in the *Young People Info* leaflet issued by the tourist office.

North of the Rhône The IYHF *youth hostel* (☎ 732 62 60), 28-30 Rue Rothschild, is big, modern and busy with helpful and knowledgeable staff. Dorms are Sfr18 and there are a few family rooms and doubles (Sfr66) for couples. Breakfast is included; dinners are reasonable (Sfr9.50) even if they are served with all the grace of a decapitated ballerina. A TV room, laundry and kitchen facilities are all available. The hostel is closed from 10 am to 5 pm (to 4 pm from 15 June to 15 September) and there is a midnight curfew. If you tire of eating at the hostel, try the cheap university café next door on the other side of Rue des Buis.

Centre Masaryk (☎ 733 07 72), 11 Ave de la Paix, has dorms for Sfr24.50 with an 11 pm curfew. Singles/doubles/triples cost Sfr36/62/87 and you can get your own key for late access. Breakfast is included. Get there by bus No 5 or 8 from Gare de Cornavin.

South of the Rhône Cité Universitaire (☎ 46 23 55), 46 Ave Miremont, has 500 beds available. Take bus No 3 from Cornavin to the terminus at Champel, south of the city centre. Dorms cost Sfr13 without breakfast. Rooms are subject to a three-night minimum stay: singles/doubles cost Sfr34/47 or Sfr28/41 for students, likewise without breakfast. A double studio with kitchen, WC and shower costs Sfr56. Reception is open from 8 am to noon and 2 pm (6 pm on weekends) to 10 pm.

Centre Universitaire Zofingen (☎ 29 11 40), 6 Rue des Voisins, has well-equipped rooms which are excellent value even if they are slightly cramped. Each room has a WC, shower, sink and small cooker. Singles/doubles/triples are Sfr48/72/90 with breakfast included. The very cheap restau-

rant downstairs, *Le Zofage*, has a choice of plats du jour for Sfr9.50 (Sfr8 for students) and is open daily from 7 am to midnight.

Hotels As befits an international city that receives many important visitors on unlimited expense accounts, there is no lack of high-class, high-cost hotels. Some of the more affordable options are as follows:

North of the Rhône Hôtel de la Cloche (☎ 732 94 81), 6 Rue de la Cloche, is small, friendly, and liable to be full unless you call ahead. Singles/doubles without shower or breakfast start at Sfr40/65; breakfast and hall showers cost a couple of francs each. *Pension de la Servette* (☎ 734 02 30), 31 Rue de la Prairie, is a touch old and dilapidated but the rooms are spacious enough. Singles/doubles /triples are Sfr35/50/75 with breakfast.

The three-star *International Terminus* (☎ 732 80 95), 20 Rue des Alpes, is ideally situated. Singles/doubles without shower are Sfr75/105, but these cheaper doubles are usually booked out by companies. Rooms with shower cost around Sfr45 extra. Breakfast is included.

South of the Rhône To get to *Hôtel Saint Victor* (☎ 46 17 18), 1 Rue Lefort, take bus No 8 or 3 from Cornavin. The entrance is opposite the hairdresser's at the far end of the square from the Russian church. It's convenient for the museums, in a building that's a little bit past its prime. Singles/doubles with breakfast are available from Sfr43/70.

Hôtel le Grenil (☎ 28 30 55) is at 7 Ave Sainte Clotilde. Singles are overpriced at Sfr85 upwards but there are also doubles/ triples/quads for Sfr110/115/130. Dormitory beds at Sfr25 are only for people 25 years old or less. Breakfast is included. Night owls will appreciate the reception being open 24 hours.

Hôtel le Prince (☎ 29 84 44/5), 16 Rue des Voisins, has comfortable if smallish rooms with a TV, telephone and shower. Singles/doubles are Sfr65/95, and breakfast costs Sfr6. The restaurant is open Monday to

Saturday from 7 pm to 10 pm and has meals from Sfr12 to Sfr16.

Mid-Range Hotels There's not much to choose between the tourist-class hotels clustered round the train station. *Bernina* (☎ 731 49 50), *Astoria* (☎ 732 10 25) and *Excelsior* (☎ 732 09 45) all have reasonably comfortable singles/doubles with shower and WC for around Sfr100/130. *Hotel Suisse* (☎ 732 66 30), 10 Place de Cornavin, is the pick of them, with a nice swirling staircase and better appointed rooms, but it's also more expensive, starting at Sfr125/165 for singles/doubles.

Hôtel le Chandelier (☎ 21 56 88), 23 Grand Rue, has all the same amenities plus the added character of a 300-year-old building. Singles are Sfr80 to Sfr140, doubles Sfr130 to Sfr190, and it's Sfr30 for an extra bed. The more expensive rooms are very spacious. It's just in the pedestrian area of the old town, so parking can be a bit of a problem.

Places to Eat

Eating is generally cheaper north or west of Gare de Cornavin, or south of the old town in the vicinity of the university. Fondue and raclette are widely available. Also popular is perch caught from the river, but it is likely to set you back around Sfr20 unless you can find it as a plat du jour. There is a small fruit-and-vegetable market open daily on Rue de Coutance. Migros supermarket on the corner of Rue des Pâquis and Rue du Môle has a self-service restaurant. The previous Places to Stay section also mentions some places where you can eat.

North of the Rhône *La Siesta*, opposite the station on the corner of Place de Cornavin and Rue de Chantepoulet, has a good range of Italian (Sfr8 to Sfr13) and local (Sfr12 to Sfr26) dishes, and a lunch-time plat du jour for Sfr11.50. It is open daily for food from 11.30 am to 11.30 pm. Round the back of the station is *Restaurant Sinbad* (☎ 738 38 28), 4 Place de Montbrillant, open daily from 9 am to midnight. Ideal for a quick snack

between trains, it is self-service with Egyptian food, vegetarian specialities and snacks.

Two informal and intimate bistro-style restaurants face each other on Rue des Pâquis. *Le Blason* (☎ 731 91 73) at No 23 has plats du jour for Sfr12 and Sfr14 and a wide selection of salads. It is open from noon to 11 pm Monday to Friday. *Auberge de Savièse* at No 20 has lunch-time plats du jour from Sfr13, and Swiss specialities such as fondue from Sfr16.50. Opening hours are Monday to Friday from 8.30 am to midnight, and Saturday from 5.30 to midnight. *Restaurant Manora*, 4 Rue de Cornavin, is self-service with tasty daily dishes from Sfr9 and salad from Sfr1.50. Always popular, it is open daily to 9 pm.

Take advantage of the international flavour of Geneva to vary your diet. Rue Chaponnière, off Rue du Mont Blanc, is a good street to explore for cheapish Mexican, Chinese and Oriental food. *Miyako* (☎ 738 01 20), 11 Rue de Chantrepoulet, is expensive but the quality is excellent. This Japanese restaurant has three-course business lunches from Sfr26, and a full evening meal will cost around Sfr50.

South of the Rhône *Café du Centre* (☎ 21 85 86), 5 Place du Molard, has outside seating in a pleasant square near the old town. Office staff relax here after work over a coffee or a beer. The lunch-time plat du jour costs around Sfr14 and the café is open daily from 6 am to 2 am. *Le Potager* (☎ 21 85 86), 2 Place de la Synagogue, has plats du jour from Sfr14. It has a new owner and specialises in creative salad concoctions. The restaurant is closed on Sunday.

More up-market is the large and popular *Cave Valaisanne et Chalet Suisse* (☎ 28 12 36), 23 Blvd Georges Favon. It's an excellent place to try fondue (starting at Sfr16.90); the scent of bubbling cheese inside could give a mouse palpitations at 20 paces. It's open from 7 am to 1 am daily.

Another good place for those with slightly larger budgets is *l'Amiral* (☎ 735 18 08), 24 Quai Gustave Ador, near the Jet d'Eau. Try the fillets of perch here. For cheaper eating in the old town, make for the restraurant in the EPA department store on Rue de la Croix d'Or, opposite Place du Molard. Meals are Sfr8 to Sfr10.

Entertainment

Geneva has a good selection of nightclubs but they are expensive. Popular with the money-to-burn brigade are *Arthur's* (☎ 788 16 00), 20 Route de Pré Bois, and *Le Milliardaire* (☎ 788 21 22), 26 Voie de Moëns. *Midnight Rambler* (☎ 21 41 98), 21 Grand Rue, has alternating theme evenings ranging from Gothic and rock to soul and rap.

The only 'alternative' place in town and highly recommended is *l'Usine* (☎ 781 34 90), 4 Place de Volontaires. A converted old factory, it is now a centre for cinema, cabaret, theatre, concerts and impromptu art objects. It has a good restaurant with menus for Sfr10, Sfr12 and Sfr14 which are available daily from noon to 2 pm and from 7.30 pm to 10.30 pm. There is also a cheap bar open to 2 am, with beer at around Sfr3 for half a litre.

Another lively place is *le Bleu Nuit* (☎ 28 34 44), 4 Rue des Vieux Billard. Lunch and evening plats du jour are Sfr13 and Sfr14. Open from 7 am weekdays and 6 pm weekends, it closes around 1 am or later. *Au Chat Noir* (☎ 43 49 98), 13 Rue Vautier, is a jazz club with interesting murals and music every night. A good British/Irish meeting place is *Post Café*, 7 Rue de Berne. It's the only place in town with draught cider.

There are several sports centres in the city. *Geneva Sports des Vernets* (☎ 43 88 50), 4 Rue Hans Wilsdorf, has swimming (Sfr3) and ice skating and is open daily except Monday from 9 am. Swimming in the lake is possible at Genève Plage on the south shore and Pâquis Plage on the north shore.

Getting There & Away

Air Geneva airport is an important transport hub and has frequent connections to every major city. Youth-fare bargains are possible on Swissair but only if you are flexible enough to buy tickets the day before. On this basis, the one-way fare for people aged 24 years or less to Amsterdam is Sfr252 and to Zürich is Sfr85. Enquire at the Swissair office (☎ 799 59 99) in Gare de Cornavin (closed Sunday). Fares may be higher depending on the time of the year.

Bus International buses depart from Place Dorcière (☎ 732 02 30), off Rue des Alpes. There are three buses a week to both London (Sfr150) and Barcelona (Sfr99). There are several buses a day to Chamonix (Sfr30).

Train There are more-or-less hourly connections to most Swiss towns. To Zürich via Bern takes 3½ hours and costs Sfr69. To Interlaken Ost takes three hours and 20 minutes by fast train. There are regular international trains to Paris (Sfr74), Hamburg (Sfr230), Milan (Sfr66) and Barcelona (Sfr95). Gare des Euax-Vives is the station for Annecy and Chamonix. To get there from Gare de Cornavin, take bus No 8 or 1 to Rond-Point de Rive and then tram No 12.

Car & Motorbike Lyons is 130 km by motorway to the west. The N1/E4 from Lausanne and the north, and the E21 from the southeast, also lead directly into Geneva. Toll-free main roads follow the course of these motorways.

Sixt (☎ 738 13 13), 1 Place de la Navigation, offers one-way car rentals to Zürich (see the Getting Around section at the beginning of this chapter for rates). Also cheap is Alsa (☎ 732 90 90), at 22-24 Rue des Pâquis. Special all-inclusive weekend rates on a Lancia Y10 are Sfr155 (rental period from noon on Friday to 9 am on Monday).

Boat Compagnie Générale de Navigation (CGN) (☎ 21 25 21) by the Jardin Anglais operates a steamer service to all towns and major villages bordering Lake Geneva, including those in France. Most boats only operate between May and September, such as those to Lausanne (3½ hours, Sfr24 one-way or Sfr38 return) and Montreux (4½ hours, Sfr29 one-way or Sfr47 return). CGN also has excursions on the lake lasting one hour (Sfr13) and two hours (Sfr20), operating from the end of March to the end of September. Both Eurail and Swiss passes are valid on these trips.

Getting Around

To/From the Airport Getting from Cointrin Airport couldn't be easier. There are 100 trains a day into Gare de Cornavin. The trip takes six minutes and costs Sfr4. Alternatively, take bus No 10 to Gare de Cornavin for Sfr2.

Bus A combination of buses, trolley buses and trams makes getting around just as easy. There are ticket dispensers at bus stops. A ticket for multiple rides within one hour costs Sfr2; a book of six such tickets costs Sfr11; and a book of 12 tickets costs Sfr20. Day passes are also available for the city and country network. One, two or three-day passes cost Sfr8.50, Sfr15 or Sfr19. Passes are available from the tourist office or from Transports Publics Genevois at the lower level of Gare de Cornavin (by the yellow escalators) or at Rond-Point de Rive.

Taxi The cost for taxis is Sfr5 per person plus Sfr2.50 per km.

Bicycle The bike rental office at Gare de Cornavin is open daily from 6.20 am to 8 pm. It has a leaflet showing cycle routes in and around the city.

Boat In addition to CGN (see the previous Getting There & Away section) smaller companies operate excursions on the lake between April and October but no passes are valid. Ticket offices and departures are along Quai du Mont Blanc in front of the Grand Casino. Trips range from half an hour (Sfr8, several departures a day) to two hours (Sfr22), with commentary in English.

AROUND LAKE GENEVA
Lausanne

This hilly city is Switzerland's fifth-largest, with 127,000 inhabitants. Water sports and

1	Musée d'Art Brut
2	Migros
3	Musée cantonal des Beaux-Arts
4	Cathedral
5	Manora
6	PTT-Saint François
7	Couscous
8	Gare CFF
9	Musée de l'Elysée
10	Office du Tourisme
11	Hôtel d'Angleterre

Alpine scenery are big attractions, as well as one of Europe's most unusual art collections.

Orientation & Information Lausanne, at the crown of the crescent of Lake Geneva, is the capital of the canton of Vaud. There is a tourist office in the train station, open daily between 1 May and 30 June from 2 to 8 pm, between 1 July to 15 October from 10 am to 9 pm, and between 16 October and 30 April from 3 to 7 pm. Bicycle rental in the station is open from 6.30 am to 10.30 pm. The main post office is opposite the station. The cathedral and steep, winding shopping streets are up the hill from Place de la Gare.

Down towards the lake in the opposite direction is the picturesque harbour of Ouchy. The main tourist office (☎ 021-617 73 21), 2 Ave de Rhodanie, is by the harbour. Opening hours are: Easter to 15 October, Monday to Saturday from 8 am to 7 pm, and Sunday from 9 am to noon and 1 to 6 pm; 16 October to Easter, Monday to Friday from 8 am to 6 pm, and Saturday from 8.30 am to noon and 1 to 5 pm. Pick up a free copy of the excellent *Lausanne Official Guide*, which lists everything from consulates to local walking tours.

Things to See & Do The Gothic **cathedral** was built in the 12th and 13th centuries and has an impressive main portal and attractive stained-glass windows. The church and tower are open daily.

The **Musée de l'Art Brut**, 11 Ave de Bergières, is a fascinating amalgam of art created by the mentally unhinged and by

Lausanne

0   200   400 m

Port d'Ouchy

Lake Geneva

incarcerated criminals. Some of the images created are startling. Explanations are in English and the collection is open Tuesday to Friday from 10 am to noon and 2 to 6 pm, and on Saturday and Sunday from 2 to 6 pm. Entry costs Sfr5, or Sfr3 for students.

Lausanne is the headquarters of the International Olympic Committee, so it is perhaps inevitable that there's a museum devoted to the games. The **Musée Olympique**, 18 Ave Louis-Ruchonnet, is free and open daily.

The large **Musée cantonal des Beaux-Arts** on Place de la Riponne has many works by Swiss artists, and temporary exhibitions. Parts of the collection are free (closed Monday).

The lake provides plenty of sporting opportunities. Vidy Sailing School (☎ 021-617 90 00) offers courses on windsurfing, water-skiing and sailing, as well as equipment rental. For less athletic entertainment, try a tour of the nearby wine-growers' cellars, centering on Lavaux and Chablais to the east and La Côte to the west. Simply turn up and sample the produce.

Places to Stay Year-round lakeside camping is possible at *Camping de Vidy* (☎ 021-24 20 31), just to the west of the Vidy sports complex. The IYHF *youth hostel* (☎ 021-26 57 82), 1 Chemin du Miguet, Ouchy, can be reached by bus No 1 from the train station, or it's a 15-minute walk if you get on the lake side of the station and head right down Ave Mont d'Or. Dorms cost Sfr16.75 per night including breakfast. Dinners cost Sfr9. Reception is closed from 9 am to 5 pm and a curfew comes into effect at 11.30 pm. *Villa Cherokee* (☎ 021-37 57 20), 4 Charmilles, Presbytère, has singles/doubles from Sfr30/50 without breakfast. To get there, take bus No 2 from the train station.

The pick of the hotels is *Hôtel d'Angleterre* (☎ 021-617 21 11) on the Quai d'Ouchy. It's a stately old building and has large, comfortable rooms with TV and views of the lake. Singles/doubles start at Sfr90/120 with shower or Sfr55/85 without. Byron wrote the *Prisoner of Chillon* here in

1816. *Du Marché* (☎ 021-37 99 00), Pré du Marché 42, has singles/doubles from Sfr45/65, and studios available for longer stays. It's OK if you don't mind rude staff.

Places to Eat There is a *Migros* restaurant below Place de la Riponne at Rue Chaucrau, but you're better off heading for the buffet-style *Manora*, 17 Place St François, open daily to 10.30 pm. There's a good choice of vegetables, salad and fruit, and main dishes are around Sfr10. Restaurant *Au Couscous* (☎ 021-312 20 17), 2 Rue Enning, on the 1st floor, has a wide menu including Tunisian, vegetarian and macrobiotic food. Specials start at Sfr11.50 and it's open daily to 1 am. The vivid red curtains and screens may make you think you've stumbled into some sultan's harem by mistake, although the obsequious waiters probably aren't eunuchs.

Café de l'Everche (☎ 021-23 93 23), 4 Rue Louis Curtat, by the cathedral, has a lunch and evening two-course menu for Sfr12 and a pleasant garden round the back. It is open daily from 7 am to midnight.

Getting There & Away There are three trains an hour from Geneva, the journey takes 40 to 50 minutes and costs Sfr18. Most trains from Bern to Geneva go via Lausanne. For boat services, see the Geneva section. Trains to Interlaken-Ost go either via Bern (Sfr44) or the scenic route via Montreux (Sfr48).

Montreux

Centrepiece of the so-called Swiss Riviera, Montreux offers marvellous lakeside walks and access to the ever-popular Château de Chillon.

Orientation & Information Montreux is at the eastern end of Lake Geneva. The train station and main post office are on Ave des Alpes, which down to the left leads to Place de la Paix and the main streets of Grand Rue and Ave du Casino. The tourist information office (☎ 021-963 12 12) is a few minutes away on the lakefront to the west of Place du Marché; it is open Monday to Friday from 9 am to noon and 2 to 6 pm, and on Saturday from 9 am to noon. Hours are extended in the summer, when the place is open daily.

Things to See & Do Montreux is known for the **Château de Chillon** (Chillon Castle), which receives more visitors than any other historical building in Switzerland. Occupying a stunning position right on Lake Geneva, the fortress caught the public imagination when Lord Byron wrote about the fate of Bonivard, a follower of the Reformation, who was chained to the fifth pillar in the dungeons for four years in the 16th century. Byron etched his own name on the third pillar.

The castle, still in excellent condition, dates from the 11th century and has been much modified and enlarged since then. Allow at least two hours to view the tower, courtyards, dungeons and numerous rooms containing weapons, utensils, frescoes and furniture. Entry costs Sfr5.50 for adults, Sfr4.50 for students and Sfr2 for children, and the castle opens daily at 10 am (9 am from April to September). The closing time varies through the year: it is 4.45 pm from November to February; 5.30 pm in March and October; 6.30 pm in April, May, June and September; and 7 pm in July and August. The castle is a pleasant 45-minute walk along the lakefront from Montreux (15 minutes from the youth hostel), or it's also accessible by train or bus No 1.

Montreux's other claim to fame is the **Jazz Festival** in early July. The programme is announced in mid-May and tickets are available shortly afterwards from the Montreux tourist office or from branches of the Swiss Bank Corporation throughout Switzerland.

Places to Stay The IYHF *youth hostel* (☎ 021-963 49 34) is at 8 Passage de l'Auberge, Territet, 30 minutes' walk along the lake to the east from the tourist office. It's nicely situated near the waterfront although the trains clattering overhead will ensure you won't sleep in. Unfortunately it is closed for renovations until some time in 1993.

Near the train station in Montreux, the *Élite* (☎ 021-963 67 33), 25 Ave du Casino,

has singles/doubles from Sfr45/70, or Sfr60/100 with shower. *Hostellerie du Lac* (☎ 021-963 10 71), 12 Rue du Quai, has rooms with high ceilings, big balconies and views of the lake. Singles/doubles start from Sfr45/60, or Sfr 70/90 with shower.

Most hotels raise their prices for the summer season. An exception is *Villa Germaine* (☎ 021-963 15 28), 3 Ave de Collonge, Territet. Singles/doubles start at Sfr45/75.

Places to Eat The tourist office has a list of restaurants, giving culinary specialities but not price ranges. *Restaurant City*, 37 Ave des Alpes, is also self-service with meals for around Sfr12. The main advantage of this place is the sunny terrace overlooking the lake (open daily).

L'Apollo, 2 Place du Marché, has a reasonable three-course menu for Sfr14. Around the corner on the lake along Rue de Quay, check *Restaurant le Palais*, decked out in ceramic inlays like a low-budget version of the Taj Mahal. It's fairly pricey, with Oriental and vegetarian food for around Sfr20 to Sfr30, but the weird patio and posey patrons make up for the expense.

Migros supermarket on Ave du Casino has a self-service restaurant, open Monday to Friday until 6.30 pm, and Saturday until 5 pm.

Getting There & Away Hourly trains depart from Geneva at 39 minutes past the hour and take one hour 10 minutes. The fare is Sfr26. From Lausanne, there are three trains an hour (Sfr8) which take 19 to 35 minutes. Slow local trains continue eastwards from Montreux to stop at Territet for the youth hostel and Chillon for the castle. Interlaken can be reached via a scenic rail route, with changeovers at Zweisimmen and Spiez. The track winds its way up the hill for an excellent view over Lake Geneva. For boat services, see Getting There & Away in the Geneva section.

Valais

The dramatic Alpine scenery of Valais (Wallis in German) once made it one of the most inaccessible regions of Switzerland. Nowadays the mountains and valleys have been opened up by an efficient (if expensive) network of roads, railways and cable cars. It is an area of great natural beauty, and naturally enough, each impressive panorama has spawned its own resort. Skiing (47 listed centres) in the winter and hiking in the summer are primary pursuits, but angling, swimming, mountaineering, even tennis, are widely enjoyed.

Aside from skiing, Valais is also known for its *Combats des Reines*, cow fights organised in villages to determine which beast is most suited to lead the herd up to the summer pastures. They usually take place on selected Sundays through the summer from April, accompanied by much celebration and pageantry. The combatants rarely get hurt. There is a grand final in Aproz on Ascension Day and at the Martigny Fair in October. Get details from the regional tourist office in Sion (☎ 027-22 31 61), 16 Rue Pré-Fleuri, Sion.

ZERMATT

Skiing and mountaineering are the main attractions in this resort, all overseen by the Matterhorn, the most famous peak in the Alps.

Orientation & Information

The massive Matterhorn stands sentinel at the end of the valley. Zermatt is car-free except for electric taxis, and there are no street names. The centre of the resort is to the right of the train station.

The post office is on the main street, and there are money-exchange facilities in the train station. The tourist office (☎ 028-66 11 81), opposite the train station, is open Monday to Friday from 8.30 am to noon and 1.30 to 6.30 pm, and Saturday from 8.30 am to noon. During the high season (Christmas, and February to mid-April) it is open Monday to Friday from 8.30 am to noon and 2 to 7 pm, Saturday from 8.30 am to 7 pm, and Sunday from 4 to 7 pm. Some hotels and restaurants close during the low season which falls in May, June, and mid-September to mid-November.

Activities

Zermatt has many demanding slopes to test the experienced skier; beginners have less possibilities. Spring is the most popular time as the higher runs are opening up, but in early summer the snow is still good and the lifts are much less busy. There are excellent views of mountain panoramas, including Mt Rosa and the Matterhorn, from the network of cable cars and gondolas.

The cog-wheel railway to Gornergrat (3100 metres) is a particular highlight. The Klein Matterhorn tramway is the highest tramway in Europe, at 3820 metres, and provides access to summer skiing slopes. It is possible to ski into Italy from here along the Ventina route but don't forget to take your passport. There are footpaths to and from many of the cable-car terminals. A day pass for all rides costs Sfr54, and ski coupons are available. Ski shops open daily for rental – allow Sfr30 per day for skis and sticks and Sfr14 per day for boots.

A walk in the cemetery is a sobering experience for would-be mountaineers, as numerous monuments tell of deaths on Mt Rosa and the Matterhorn. On a slightly different theme, there is a pool hall by the Coop in the shopping arcade, where tables cost Sfr14 per hour.

Places to Stay & Eat

Camping Matterhorn Zermatt, to the left of the train station, is open from June to September and charges Sfr7 per day, including showers. The IYHF *youth hostel* (☎ 028-67 23 20) is very rule-orientated but has an excellent view of the Matterhorn. Cross the river to the left of the church and take the second right. Dorm beds including breakfast and compulsory dinner or lunch packet cost Sfr29. Laundry loads cost Sfr8. The doors stay open during the day, but a curfew comes into effect at 11.30 pm. The hostel is shut during May, and from the beginning of November to mid-December.

Opposite the train station and popular with mountaineers is *Hotel Bahnhof* (☎ 028-67 24 06), with dorms from Sfr20 to Sfr22 and singles/doubles for around Sfr38/66. Guests have use of a communal kitchen and there is no curfew or daytime closing. Hotel prices vary about 40% depending upon the season, but the price difference at the Hotel Bahnhof is minimal.

Hotel Garni Malva (☎ 028-67 30 33), overlooking the east side of the river, costs from Sfr33 per person or from Sfr44 with private shower. *Cima* (☎ 028-67 62 79), in front of the station and half-way to the river, is the same price.

North Wall Bar, near the youth hostel, is the cheapest and best bar in the village, and popular with resort workers. It has ski videos, music, good pizzas from Sfr8 and beer at Sfr3.50 for half a litre. The bar is closed during the low season, otherwise it's open daily from 6.30 pm to midnight. Just down the hill, the more expensive *Papperla Pub* is also popular.

Beyond the church on the main street, *Restaurant Weisshorn* and the *Café du Pont* next door are both good places for food. Also recommended is *Walliser Kanne*, by the post office, which has pizzas, fondue, fish dishes and Valais specialities from Sfr9 to Sfr18.

Getting There & Away

Hourly trains depart from Brig at 23 minutes past the hour up to 8.23 pm, calling at Visp en route. The steep and scenic journey takes 80 minutes and costs Sfr33 one way, or Sfr55 return. It is a private railway; Eurail passes are not valid, Inter-Rail earns 50% off and the Swiss Card is good for free travel. The only way out is back, but if you're going to Saas Fee you can divert there from Stalden-Saas.

As Zermatt is car-free, you need to park cars at Täsch (Sfr4.50 per day) and take the train from there (Sfr5.60). Parking is free in Visp if you take the Zermatt train (for details, ☎ 028-23 13 33).

SAAS FEE

In the valley adjoining Zermatt, Saas Fee may not have the Matterhorn, but there are plenty of other towering peaks to keep you occupied.

Orientation & Information

The village centre and ski lifts are to the left of the bus station, which contains a post office. High season is from mid-December to mid-April. The tourist office (☎ 028-57 14 57), opposite the bus station, is open in the high season Monday to Friday from 8.30 am to noon and from 2 to 6.30 pm, Saturday from 8.30 am to 7 pm, and Sunday from 4 to 6 pm. During the low season, weekend opening is reduced depending on demand.

Activities

Saas Fee is surrounded by an impressive panorama of 4000-metre peaks and rivals Zermatt as a summer skiing centre. There is also ski mountaineering along the famous Haute Route to Chamonix. The highest metro in the world operates all year to Mittelallalin at 3500 metres.

A general lift pass costs Sfr48 for one day. Ski rental prices are as for Zermatt. The tourist office has a map of summer walking trails. Even in winter, 20 km of marked footpaths remain open.

Places to Stay & Eat

The summer *camp site* in the resort costs Sfr4 per person plus Sfr3 for a tent. The *Albana* has dorm beds from Sfr32 to Sfr45 including dinner and breakfast; there's no curfew or daytime closure. It shuts at the end of April and reopens in early July. It's a good idea to book in advance in winter. Reception is in the adjoining *Hotel Mascotte* (☎ 028-57 27 24), which has singles/doubles for Sfr60/114 with private WC and shower as well as breakfast. In the south of the village, convenient for the ski lifts, is *Garni Feehof* (☎ 028-57 33 44), with reasonable singles/doubles for around Sfr40/80 including breakfast.

Eat pizza at *Boccalino* near the ski lifts. *Restaurant Vieux Chalet* in the main street is good for snacks of raclette and ravioli. In the extreme north of the village, *Restaurant Alp Hitta* (☎ 028-57 10 50) has a relaxed atmosphere, raclette for Sfr5, fondue from Sfr17 and other dishes from Sfr9. It is open daily from 8 am to 1.30 am, except between 20 April and 20 June, when it closes down. Despite this break, the restaurant manages two to four-person apartments, each with a small kitchen, which are available all year. The price of Sfr35 per person includes breakfast. Visitor's cards provided by hotels entitle the bearer to discounts (see Tourist Offices in the Facts for the Visitor section at the beginning of this chapter).

Getting There & Away
Saas Fee cannot be reached by train. Hourly buses depart from Brig via Visp, take one hour and cost Sfr30 for a one-month return.

Like Zermatt, Saas Fee is car-free. Park at the entrance to the village, where charges are Sfr10 for the first 24 hours and Sfr6 per day thereafter, of Sfr12 and Sfr8 respectively to park in the garage.

OTHER RESORTS
The best known resort in west Valais is Verbier, with 350 km of ski runs. Ski passes cost Sfr52 for one day or Sfr1168 for the season. Lesser known resorts can have comparable skiing yet be much cheaper. Ski passes in Leukerbad, for example, north-east of Verbier, are Sfr32 (students Sfr26) for one day or Sfr410 (students Sfr320) for the season. Leukerbad has the added attraction of hot springs.

Ticino

Situated south of the Alps and enjoying a Mediterranean climate, Ticino (Tessin in German) gives more than just a taste of Italy. Indeed, it belonged to Italy until the Swiss Confederation seized it in 1512. The people are darker skinned, and the cuisine, architecture and vegetation reflect that found farther south. Italian is the official language of the canton. Many people also speak French and German but you will find English less widely spoken than in the rest of Switzerland. The region offers mountain hikes and dramatic gorges in the north; water sports and relaxed, leisurely towns in the south.

LOCARNO
Locarno lies at the northern end of Lake Maggiore. Switzerland's lowest town, at 205 metres above sea level, it enjoys the country's best climate.

Orientation & Information
The centre of town is the Piazza Grande where the main post office can be found. The tourist office (☎ 093-31 03 33) is nearby at Largo Zorzi, adjoining the Kursaal. It has brochures on many parts of Switzerland. From April to October, it's open Monday to Friday from 8 am to 7 pm, and Saturday and Sunday from 9 am to noon and 1 to 5 pm. From November to March, opening hours are Monday to Friday from 8 am to noon, and 2 to 6 pm.

Five minutes' walk away is the train station, where money exchange counters are open daily from 5.10 am to 9.30 pm, and bike rental and left-luggage are available daily from 5.10 am to 11.30 pm.

Things to See & Do
The principal attraction is the **Madonna del Sasso**, up on the hill with a good view of the lake and the town. The sanctuary was built after the Virgin Mary appeared in a vision in 1480. It contains some 15th century paintings, a small museum and several distinctive statue groups. There is a funicular from the town centre, but the 20-minute walk up is not demanding (take Via al Sasso off Via Cappuccini) and you pass some 15th century shrines on the way.

In the town, as well as exploring the Italianate piazzas and arcades, there are a couple of churches worth a look, including the 17th century **Chiesa Nuova** on Via Cittadella, with an ornate roof complete with frolicking angels.

Locarno has more hours of sunshine than anywhere else in Switzerland, just right for strolls round the lake. **Giardini Jean Arp** is a small lakeside park off Lungolago Gius Motta, where sculptures by the surrealist artist are scattered among the palm trees and tulips.

Places to Stay

Delta Camping (☎ 093-31 60 81) is expensive at Sfr16 minimum per site, rising to Sfr39 from 1 June to 31 August. *Pensione Città Vecchia* (☎ 093-31 45 54), Via Toretta 13, off Piazza Grande (head up the hill by the sign for 'Innovazione'), is a friendly, private hostel without curfew or daytime closing. Beds are Sfr20 with your own sleeping bag, or Sfr24 if you need sheets. Dorms vary in size but the price doesn't change. Hall showers are free, and breakfast is Sfr4 including refills. It is only open from 1 March to 31 October.

Convenient for the station is *Garni Montaldi* (☎ 093-33 02 22), Piazza Stazione, with singles/doubles from Sfr40/80, breakfast included. Reception is also here for *Stazione*, an older, noisier building to the rear where singles/doubles start at Sfr36/72 with shower. Both hotels are open from mid-March. Stazione closes again at the end of October, and Garni Montaldi at the beginning of January.

Hotel Ristorante Zurigo (☎ 093-33 16 17), Via Verbano 9, offers comfortable accommodation overlooking the lake. Gold-coloured metal bedsteads, tastefully arranged pictures and patterned tiled floors give the rooms some style. Prices including breakfast buffet start at Sfr75/105 for a single/double in winter, rising to Sfr130/160 in summer. All rooms have cable TV and private shower/WC. The restaurant serves good, mid-price food.

Places to Eat

For a good, gastronomic feast, where the food is served on sparkling silver salvers,

wander down the road to *Ristorante Centenario* (☎ 093-33 82 22), Lungo Lago 17. It's widely acknowledged as the best restaurant in Ticino, but the prices might make you flavour its French cuisine with the salt of your own tears. Three small courses in the business lunch cost Sfr48, the eight-course evening menu is Sfr128, and à-la-carte eating is around Sfr38 to Sfr48. The restaurant is closed on Sunday and Monday.

Both the *Migros* and *Coop* supermarkets on Piazza Grande have a self-service restaurant. *Inova*, Via Stazione 1, by the train station, has good self-service dishes from Sfr6.90 and help-yourself salad plates from Sfr3.80 to Sfr9.50. It is open daily to 10 pm. The popular *Trattoria Campagna Ristorante* (☎ 093-31 99 47), Via Castelrotto near St Antonio church, has *piatti del giorno* (dishes of the day) from Sfr11.50, and pizza and pasta from Sfr9. It is open every day until midnight.

Getting There & Away

The St Gotthard pass provides the road link (N2) to central Switzerland. There are trains every two hours from Brig, passing through Italy en route. The cost is Sfr47 and it takes around three hours. You change trains at Domodossola across the border, so bring your passport.

One-day travel passes for boats on Lake Maggiore cost Sfr9 to Sfr17 depending upon the area they're valid for on the lake. For more information, contact Navigazione Lago Maggiore on ☎ 093-31 18 65. There is a regular boat and hydrofoil service from Italy.

BELLINZONA

The capital of Ticino is a city of castles. It is set in a valley of lush mountains, and stands at the southern side of two important Alpine passes, San Bernardino and St Gotthard.

Orientation & Information

Postbuses arrive one block in front of the train station on Via C Molo. The money-exchange counter in the station is open daily from 5.20 am to 9.40 pm. The tourist office

(☎ 092-25 21 31), Via Camminata 2, Palazzo Civico, is open Monday to Friday from 8 am to noon and 1.30 to 6.30 pm, and, from 1 March to 30 November, Saturday from 9 am to noon. To get there, turn left out of the station and walk for 10 minutes, passing the main post office (6500 Bellinzona 1) on the way.

Things to See & Do

The three medieval castles which dominate the town are testimony to Bellinzona's historical importance, based on its key location at the crossroads of the major routes through the Alps. All the castles are well preserved and offer marvellous views of the town and surrounding mountains. The central **Castel Grande** dates from around the 6th century. Entry is free and it's open daily for visits to the grounds. The **Archaeological Museum** in the castle is closed on Monday (admission Sfr2, students Sfr1).

Castello di Montebello, slightly above the town, is open daily from 8 am to 6 pm with free entry. It houses a small museum which is closed on Monday and costs Sfr2 (students Sfr1) for admission. Quite a trek up the hill is the smaller **Castello di Sasso Corbaro**, open from 1 April to 31 October from 9 am to noon and 2 to 5 pm, except on Monday when it's closed. It also has a small museum in the dungeon, which costs Sfr2 (students Sfr1) to get in. There are no buses up there but it's easy to beg a lift back down again from the car park. Combined museum tickets for the three castles cost Sfr4 (students Sfr2).

The **Santa Maria delle Grazie** church in the town features an impressive 15th century fresco of the Crucifixion, similar to that in Lugano.

Places to Stay

The *camp site* (☎ 092-29 11 18), Bosco di Molinazzo, costs from Sfr4.60 per person, Sfr4 per tent and Sfr8 for a camper van. The budget hotels in town fill quickly. Two places to try near the city centre are *Ticino* (☎ 092-25 33 83), Viale Portone 5, with singles/doubles from Sfr32/64, and *San Giovanni* (☎ 092-25 19 19), Via San Giovanni 7, with singles/doubles for Sfr35/64. All rooms are without a private shower and with breakfast. Ideally situated is *Croce Federale* (☎ 092-25 16 67), Viale Stazione 12, with singles/doubles/triples for Sfr80/110/140. All rooms have shower, WC and TV.

Places to Eat

The food is good in *Ristorante l'Arcada*, Piazza Collegiata 1. Pasta starts at Sfr10, salads at Sfr4.50, and meat and fish dishes are Sfr18 to Sfr30. Similarly priced and also good is *Birreria Corona*, opposite the tourist office at Via Camminata 5. There is a supermarket and the cheap, self-service *Ristorante Inova* downstairs in the Innovazione department store on Viale Stazione. All these restaurants are closed on Sunday.

Getting There & Away

Bellinzona is on the train route connecting Locarno (Sfr7, takes 18 to 25 minutes) and Lugano (Sfr10, takes 26 to 36 minutes). It is also on the Zürich-Milan route. Postbuses head north-east to Chur. You need to reserve your postbus seat the day before on ☎ 092-25 77 55. There is a good cycling track along the Ticino River to Lake Maggiore and Locarno.

LUGANO

Switzerland's southernmost tourist town offers an excellent combination of lazy days, watery pursuits and hillside hikes.

Orientation & Information

Postbuses leave from the front of the train station; just beyond, down the hill, lies the old town. The money-exchange office in the station is open daily from 6 am to 10 pm. Less than 15 minutes' walk away, the tourist office (☎ 091-21 46 64) overlooks Lake Lugano, on Riva G Albertolli 5. Opening hours are Monday to Friday from 9 am to 6 pm (6.30 pm between 1 July and 30 September). On Saturday, it is open from 9 am to 5 pm. These hours are subject to change depending on demand.

The main post office is in the centre of the old town on the corner of Contrada di Verla and Via della Posta. The Italian Consulate (☎ 091-22 05 13) is at Via Monte Ceneri 16.

Things to See & Do

Winding alleyways, pedestrian-only piazzas and colourful parks make Lugano an ideal town for walking around. The **Cathedral Santa Maria degli Angioli**, Piazza Luini, has a vivid fresco of the Crucifixion by Bernardino Luini dating from 1529. The **Thyssen-Bornemisza Gallery**, Villa Favorita, Castagnola, is a well-known private art collection, but admission is expensive at Sfr12 for adults or Sfr8 for students. It's due to reopen after Easter 1993 following a period of closure, although some of the collection will have been transferred to Spain.

For people who want a more affordable taste of art, the **Cantonal Art Museum**, Via Canova 10, has a worthwhile modern selection. It only costs Sfr5 (students Sfr1) to get in, and it's also closed on Monday.

The **Lido**, west of the Cassarate River, offers a swimming pool and sandy beaches for Sfr4 a day, and it's open daily from 1 May to mid-September. A tourist fishing permit for Lake Lugano costs Sfr50 and is valid for 10 days. There are boat and bus departures approximately every 90 minutes to nearby Melide, where **Swiss Miniatur** (☎ 091-68 79 51) displays 1:25 scale models of national attractions.

The tourist office has free guides detailing walks of up to three hours' duration heading south along the lake or north towards Locarno. There are good hikes and views from Monte San Salvatore and Monte Brè. The funicular from Paradiso up Monte San Salvatore operates from March to November only and costs Sfr10 to go up or Sfr14 return. To get up Monte Brè, you can take the year-round funicular from Cassarate which costs Sfr10 to go up or Sfr15 return.

Places to Stay

The relaxed IYHF *youth hostel* (☎ 091-56 27 28), Via Cantonale 13, is a hard 20 minutes' walk uphill from the train station (signposted), or take bus No 5 to Crocifisso (Sfr1.50). Beds are Sfr12 plus Sfr2 for sheets and Sfr5 for breakfast. Reception is shut from 1 to 3 pm and curfew is at 10 pm. The hostel closes from 31 October to 20 March.

Around the back of the train station is *Hotel Montarina* (☎ 091-56 72 72), Via Montarina 1, which has beds in large dorms for Sfr16, singles/doubles for Sfr42/70 and triples/quads for Sfr96/120, all without breakfast. It's a nice building but watch out for the resident ants. Reception is open from 9 am to 9 pm and there is no daytime closing or curfew. The hotel is closed from 31 October to about a week before Easter. *Hotel Rex* (☎ 091-22 76 08), Viale C Cattaneo 11, offers standard singles/doubles from Sfr36/70. Rooms with shower cost just Sfr4 extra, and breakfast is included. It's closed during January.

The hotel *Felix au Lac* (☎ 091-23 97 33), Piazza Rezzonico 6, is very centrally situated near Piazza Riforma. Singles/doubles with shower start at Sfr60/110. Around the bay in Paradiso is *Victoria au Lac* (☎ 091-54 20 31), Via General Guisan 3, which sometimes has space when places in town are full. It's slightly ageing but comfortable enough and very atmospheric; singles/doubles start at around Sfr40/70, or Sfr60/90 with shower. Parking is no problem, and it's open from April to October.

Places to Eat

Any number of restaurants around town offer pizza and pasta from about Sfr10. *Ristorante Cantinone* (☎ 091-23 10 68) on Piazza Cioccaro has a vast selection of good-sized pizzas from Sfr9.50 and is open daily from 7 am to midnight. Up the stairs alongside is *Ristorante Inova*, which has good, cheap self-service food. It's open daily to 10 pm. Also good and cheap for Italian and vegetarian food is *Pestalozzi* on Piazza Indipendenza, open daily from 6 am to 11 pm.

Across Piazza Cioccaro from Ristorante Cantinone is the large *Sayonara*. It has the usual pizza/pasta, and, in season, a strangely comprehensive selection of asparagus (Sfr10 to Sfr30). There is a large *Migros* supermarket and restaurant on Via Pretorio opposite Via Emilio Bossi.

Getting There & Away

Lugano is on the same road and rail route as Bellinzona. There is a daily postbus service direct to St Moritz (one in winter, two in summer), which costs Sfr53 and takes four hours. You need to reserve your seat the day before at the train information counter in the station, or by phoning ☎ 091-21 95 20. A seven-day regional holiday ticket costs Sfr78 and is valid for all regional public transport including funiculars and boats on Lake Lugano.

Graubünden

Once upon a time, tourists in Switzerland were a summer phenomenon. Then, in 1864, the owner of the Engadiner Kulm Hotel in St Moritz offered four English summer guests free accommodation if they returned for the winter. He told them they were missing the best time of the year. Although dubious, the English were unable to refuse a free offer. They returned, enjoyed themselves, and winter tourism was born.

Today Graubünden (Grisons, Grigioni, Grishun) has some of the most developed and best known winter sports centres in the world, including Arosa, Davos, Klosters, Flims, and, of course, St Moritz. Away from the international resorts, Graubünden is a relatively unspoiled region of rural villages, Alpine lakes and hilltop castles. The people speak German, Italian or Romansch.

CHUR

Chur is the cantonal capital, yet retains a small-town feel. It has been continuously inhabited since 3000 BC.

Orientation & Information

Money exchange is possible in the train station daily from 5.45 am to 9.15 pm. Five minutes' walk straight ahead down Bahnhofstrasse is Postplatz. To the left is the post office (PTT 7002, Chur 2) and to the right is the tourist office (☎ 081-22 18 18), Grabenstrasse 5, open Monday to Friday from 8 am to noon and 1.30 to 6 pm, and Saturday from 9 am to noon. Pick up a free copy of the walking tour of the centre of town. The regional tourist office (☎ 081-22 13 60), Alexanderstrasse 24, has information on the whole canton but it's only open on weekdays.

Things to See & Do

Chur has an attractive old town with 16th century buildings, fountains, alleyways and amusing murals of ordinary people painted on various façades by Robert Indermaur. Augusto Giacometti designed three of the windows in the 1491 **Church of St Martin**. In the impressive **cathedral**, built from 1150, take note of the crypt, the high altar and the carved heads on the choir stalls. The **Kunstmuseum** on Postplatz contains modern art, including a generous gathering of stuff by the three Giacomettis. Note also the sci-fi work by local artist, HR Giger, who created the monsters in the *Alien* films. Entry costs Sfr5 (students Sfr3), and the place is closed Monday.

At night the hectic, crowded *Churchill Pub* on Grabenstrasse is where the local youth go to drink, pose and play pool.

Places to Stay

Camp Au (☎ 081-24 22 83), to the north of town by the sports centre, costs Sfr5 per person and from Sfr4 for a tent. The IYHF *youth hostel* (☎ 081-22 65 63), Berggasse 28, is up the hill to the east, 15 minutes' walk from the tourist office. This rustic hostel is very intimate: each bunk comprises at least five mattresses side by side! Beds cost Sfr16.40 including breakfast. Curfew is at 10 pm, and reception shuts from 10 am to 5 pm during which time the doors are locked. The hostel is closed at Christmas and during January and February.

There are no particularly cheap hotels in town. *Franziskaner* (☎ 081-22 12 61), Untere Gasse, has adequate singles/doubles including breakfast for Sfr40/80, with free use the hall shower; doubles with shower and WC are Sfr100. Greater comfort can be found at *Hotel Drei Könige* (☎ 081-22 17 25), Reichsgasse 18. Singles/doubles are Sfr85/135 with shower or Sfr60/100 without. Garage parking is available and it also stages occasional concerts.

Places to Eat
For well-prepared food in a wooden environment (the décor, not the company), go to *Hotel Stern*, opposite Drei Könige on Reichsgasse. Main dishes are around Sfr30, or you can splash out on the eight-course gourmet menu at Sfr130 for two. Lunch-time eating is cheaper, with three menus (one vegetarian) from Sfr14 including soup. Opposite the train station on Steinbockstrasse there's one of the always reliable *Manora* buffet restaurants. Main dishes are Sfr8 to Sfr11. Both places are open daily.

Calanda Restaurant on Postplatz has a variety of cheap menus from Sfr12.50, including vegetarian choices. It's also popular with evening drinkers. There is a *Coop* with a restaurant on the intersection of Bahnhofstrasse and Alexanderstrasse.

Getting There & Away
Postbuses leave from in front of the train station, including the express service to Bellinzona. There are rail connections to Davos, Klosters and Arosa, and fast trains to Sargans (the station for Liechtenstein, only 22 minutes away) and Zürich (85 minutes, Sfr36). Chur can be visited on the Glacier Express route (see Getting There & Away in the following St Moritz section).

ST MORITZ
This resort needs little introduction. Playground of today's international jet-setters, the curative properties of its waters have been known for 3000 years.

Orientation & Information
St Moritz exudes health and wealth. The train station near the lake rents bikes and changes money from 6.45 am to 7.45 pm

daily. Just up the hill is the post office and five minutes farther on is the tourist office (☎ 082-3 31 47) at Via Mistra 12. It's open Monday to Friday from 9 am to noon and 2 to 6 pm, on Saturday morning, and also on Saturday afternoon during the high season. To the south-west, around the lake from the main town, St Moritz Dorf, lies St Moritz Bad. Not much stays open during November, May and early June.

Activities
In the St Moritz region there are 350 km of downhill runs, although the choice for beginners is limited. A one-day ski pass costs Sfr45, and ski and boot rental is about Sfr39 per day. There are also 160 km of cross-country trails (equipment rental Sfr18) and 120 km of marked hiking paths.

Numerous other sporting activities are on offer: golf (including on the frozen lake in winter), tennis, squash, fishing, horse riding, sailing, windsurfing and river rafting, to mention just a few. Inevitably, however, they are expensive. The tourist office has a price list. Buying a health treatment in the spa is another way to spend money.

Places to Stay
The *Olympiaschanze* camp site (☎ 082-3 40 90) is one km south-west of St Moritz Bad; it is open from early June to mid-September.

The IYHF *Stille Youth Hostel* (☎ 082-3 39 69), Via Surpunt 60, St Moritz Bad, is 30 minutes' walk round the lake from the tourist office. It's in a new building with excellent facilities. Beds in four-bed dorms are Sfr30.30, and double rooms are Sfr40.30 per person. That sounds expensive but the price does include breakfast and dinner. Laundry costs Sfr4 per load. Reception is closed from 9 am to 4 pm, curfew is 10 pm and the hostel closes from May to mid-June, and from early September to the end of December.

Hotel prices fluctuate according to the season, and reach a peak from around mid-December to mid-February. The summer high season, July and August, isn't quite so expensive. The nearest thing to a budget hotel is *Bellaval* (☎ 082-3 32 45), right by the train station on the south side of the tracks. Singles/doubles start at Sfr50/90, including breakfast.

Staying right in the centre of St Moritz Dorf involves spending at least Sfr100 per person in a four or five-star hotel. The best three-star deal is *Soldanella* (☎ 082-3 36 51), with rooms starting at Sfr85 per person. It's a few minutes' walk south from the centre of town at Via Somplaz 17.

Places to Eat

The cheapest restaurants are in St Moritz Bad. There is a *Coop* with a restaurant in Via dal Bagn. Next door are two restaurants, *Bellevue* and *Al Tavolo*, with menus including soup starting at Sfr9. The popular *Hotel Sonne*, Via Sela 11, close to the youth hostel, serves pasta, salads and tasty pizzas from Sfr10.50. It is open daily from 7 am to midnight.

Try an expensive taste of the highlife at the top of the Corviglia funicular by sampling the truffles, caviar and desserts at *la Marmite* (☎ 082-3 63 55). Queue or reserve ahead in season.

Getting There & Away

To Lugano, two postbuses run daily in summer, one in winter. A train-and-bus combination will get you to Landeck in Austria for Sfr45. In summer there is also a direct bus. Nine daily trains travel south to Tirano in Italy with connections to Milan. The famous Glacier Express connects St Moritz to Zermatt via the 2033-metre Oberalp Pass. The wonderful, scenic route takes 7½ hours to cover the 290 km and crosses 291 bridges. Drink glasses in the dining car have sloping bases to compensate for the hills – but you must remember to keep turning them around!

OTHER RESORTS & ATTRACTIONS

In the Davos/Klosters region there are 450 km of ski runs, mostly medium to difficult, including one of the hardest runs in the world, the Gotschnagrat. The other ski resorts have predominantly easy to medium runs. Ski passes average Sfr42 per day. The annual cross-country ski marathon between Maloja and Zuoz takes place on the second Sunday in March. The route crosses ice-covered lakes and passes near St Moritz.

Flora and fauna abound in the 169 sq km of the Swiss National Park. The park information centre (☎ 082-8 13 78), Zernez, has details of hiking facilities. Trains to Zernez from St Moritz cost Sfr14. The canton is dotted with youth hostels. Private rooms, around Sfr18 to Sfr50 per person, are another cheap option.

Zürich

Zürich started life as a Roman customs post until it graduated to the status of a free city under the Holy Roman Empire in 1218. Today, Switzerland's most populous city offers an ambience of affluence and plenty of cultural diversions. Banks and art galleries will greet you at every turn, in a strange marriage of finance and aesthetics.

The city's reputation as a cultural and intellectual centre began after it joined the Swiss Confederation in 1315. Zwingli helped things along with his teachings during the Reformation. The city's intellectual and artistic tradition continued during WW I with the influx of luminaries such as Lenin, Trotsky, Tristan Tzara, Hans Arp and James Joyce. On the financial side, Zürich's status as an international industrial and business centre is thanks in no small part to the efforts of the energetic administrator and railway magnate, Alfred Escher, in the 19th century.

Orientation

Zürich is 409 metres above sea level at the northern end of Lake Zürich. The city centre is on both sides of the Limmat River which heads north from the lake before sweeping round to the west. Like many Swiss cities, it is compact and conveniently laid out. The main train station (Hauptbahnhof) is on the west bank of the river.

Information

Tourist Office The main tourist office (☎ 01-211 40 00) is at the Hauptbahnhof, Bahnhofplatz 15, and arranges hotel reservations (Sfr5 commission), car rentals and excursions. Opening hours change depending upon the season. During March to October it is open Monday to Friday from 8 am to 10 pm, and Saturday and Sunday from 8 am to 8.30 pm. During November to February it is open Monday to Friday from 8 am to 8 pm, and Saturday and Sunday from 9 am to 6 pm. There is an airport branch in Terminal B (☎ 01-816 35 11), open daily from 7 am to 8 pm. Tourist offices charge Sfr1 to Sfr3 for maps of Zürich and lists of hotels.

The Swiss National Tourist Office headquarters (☎ 01-288 11 11) is at Bellariastrasse 38, and has information on the whole of Switzerland. It's open Monday to Friday from 8 to 11.45 am and 1 to 5 pm.

Money There's no shortage of choice when exchanging money in this banking city. Banks are open Monday to Friday from 8.15 am to 4.30 pm, except Thursday when they are open until 6 pm. Union Bank of Switzerland, Credit Suisse and Swiss Bank Corporation are all open until at least 6.30 pm on weekdays. Various exchange offices around the city, including the one in the Hauptbahnhof, are open daily from 6.15 am to 10.45 pm.

Post & Telecommunications The main post office is Sihlpost (☎ 01-245 41 11), Kasernenstrasse 95-99. It is open Monday to Friday from 7.30 am to 6.30 pm, and Saturday from 7.30 to 11 am. Like many other Swiss post offices, it also has extended trading hours but transactions are subject to a small surcharge during these times. The post office in the Hauptbahnhof is open Monday to Friday from 7.30 am to 6.30 pm and Saturday from 7.30 to 11 am.

The telephone code for Zürich is 01.

Consulates The British Consulate (☎ 47 15 20) is at Dufourstrasse 56. The US Consulate (☎ 363 06 44) is at Riedtilstrasse 15. The South African Consulate (☎ 911 06 60) is south-east of Zürich at Seestrasse 221 in Küsnacht. The German Consulate (☎ 265 65 65) is at Kirchgasse 48, and the Austrian Consulate (☎ 252 72 00) is at Minervastrasse 116.

Travel Agents SSR (☎ 261 29 56), Leonhardstrasse 5 and 10, is a specialist in student and youth fares. The SSR administration headquarters (☎ 242 30 00) is at Bäckerstrasse 52; there's another branch at Bäckerstrasse 40. Globetrotter (☎ 211 77 80), Rennweg 35, concentrates on non-European destinations; it's open Monday to Friday from 9 am to 12.30 pm and 1.30 to 6 pm. American Express (☎ 211 83 70) is at Bahnhofstrasse 20; it's open Monday to Friday from 8.30 am to 5.30 pm and Saturday from 9 am to noon.

Bookshops Buchhandlung Stäheli (☎ 201 33 02), Bahnhofstrasse 70, has many English-language books: fiction, nonfiction, travel, and old stock (during May only) from Sfr1. It is open Monday to Friday from 9 am to 6.30 pm and Saturday from 9 am to 4 pm. English and French-language books are also available at Librairie Poyot, Bahnhofstrasse 11. The Travel Book Shop (☎ 252 38 83), Rindermarkt 20, has a huge selection of English-language travel books and can order anything you want (expect to pay Sfr2 to Sfr10 above the cover price). It also runs the map shop next door.

Emergency For medical help, ring ☎ 261 61 00; for dental help, ☎ 257 32 69. The Cantonal University Hospital (☎ 255 11 11), Schmelzbergerstrasse 8, has a casualty department. There is a 24-hour chemist at Bellevue Apotheke (☎ 252 56 00), Theaterstrasse 14. The police (☎ 216 71 11) are at Bahnhofquai 3.

Dangers & Annoyances Zürich's drug casualties congregate in the Platzpromenade behind the Schweizerisches Landesmuseum. You're liable to be hassled if you wander

Zürich

0 250 500 m

Zürichberg

Bergstrasse
Kraftstrasse
Freudenberg-strasse
Süsenbergstrasse
Germaniastrasse
Gladbachstrasse
Toblerstrasse
Gloriastrasse
Plattenstrasse
Freiestrasse
Rigiplatz
Universitätstrasse
Rämistrasse
Winterthurer Strasse
Sonneggstrasse
Scheuchzerstrasse
Künstlergasse
Leonhardstrasse
Hirschengraben
Seiler Graben
Rindermarkt
Neumarkt
Münster-gasse
Riedtlistrasse
Central
Zähringer-str
Mühlegasse
Niederdorf
Limmatquai
Weinbergstrasse
Schaffhauser Strasse
Nordstrasse
Bahnhofquai
Oetenbachgasse
Rennweg
Limmat River
Sihlquai
Platz-promenade
Museumstrasse
Bahnhofplatz
Bahnhofstrasse
Urania-str
Augustiner Gasse
Wasserwerkstrasse
Kornhausstrasse
Hauptbahnhof
Gessneralle
Löwenstrasse
Sihlstrasse
Uraniastr
Sihlquai
Landstrasse
Neugasse
Kasernenstrasse
Lagerstrasse
Militärstrasse
Gessneralle
Sihl River
Limmatstrasse
Sihlquai
Röntgenstrasse
Zeughausstrasse
Kanzleistrasse
Müllerstrasse
Brauerstrasse
Langstrasse
Badener Strasse
Staufbach Quai

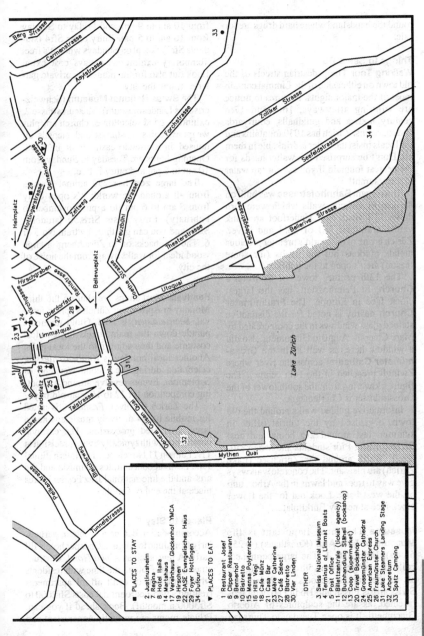

PLACES TO STAY

2 Justinusheim
7 Regina
8 Hotel Italia
14 Martahaus
17 Vereinshaus Glockenhof YMCA
19 Hirschen
22 OASE Evangelisches Haus
29 Foyer Hottingen
34 Dufour

▼ PLACES TO EAT

1 Restaurant Josef
6 Clipper Restaurant
9 Bernerhof
10 Bistretto
15 Mensa Polyterrace
16 Hiltl Vegi
18 Cafe Münz
21 Casa Bar
23 Wäre Catherine
27 Café Select
28 Bistretto
30 Vier Linden

OTHER

3 Swiss National Museum
4 Terminus of Limmat Boats
5 Post Office
11 Billettzentrale (ticket agency)
12 Buchhandlung Stähell (bookshop)
13 Coop (supermarket)
20 Travel Bookshop
24 Grossmünster Cathedral
25 American Express
26 Fraumünster Church
31 Lake Steamers Landing Stage
32 Arboretum
33 Spatz Camping

round the bandstand where hard drugs are for sale.

Things to See & Do
Walking Tour The pedestrian streets of the old town on either side of the Limmat contain most of the major sights. Features to notice are winding alleyways, 16th and 17th century houses and guildhalls, courtyards and fountains. Zürich has 1030 fountains and the locals insist the water is drinkable in them all. Don't be surprised if a waiter heads for the nearest fountain if you ask for tap water in a restaurant!

The elegant **Bahnhofstrasse** was built on the site of the city walls which were torn down 150 years ago. Underfoot are bank vaults crammed full of gold and silver. Zürich is one of the world's premier precious metals markets but the vaults (for some reason) aren't open to the public.

The 13th century tower of **St Peter's Church**, St Peterhofstatt, has the largest clock face in Europe. The **Fraumünster Church** nearby is noted for the distinctive stained glass windows in the choir created by Marc Chagall. Augusto Giacometti also did a window here, as well as in the **Grossmünster Cathedral** across the river where Zwingli preached in the 16th century. The figure glowering from the south tower of the Grossmünster is Charlemagne.

Informative guided walks around the old town, organised by the tourist office in summer, last around 2½ hours and cost Sfr16 (or Sfr14 for students and senior citizens). Walks around the Zürichsee (Lake Zürich) are pleasant. The concrete walkways give way to trees and lawns in the Arboretum on the west bank. Look out for the flower clock face at nearby Bürkliplatz.

Museums The most important is the **Museum of Fine Arts** (Kunsthaus) (☎ 251 67 65), Heimplatz 1. The large permanent collection ranges from 15th century religious art to the various schools of modern art. Swiss artists Füssli and Hodler are well represented, as are the sculptures of Alberto Giacometti. It is open Tuesday to Thursday

from 10 am to 9 pm, and Friday to Sunday from 10 am to 5 pm. Entry costs Sfr4 (students Sfr3) except on Sundays when it's free. Temporary exhibitions always cost extra. Look out also for the numerous private galleries round the city.

The **Swiss National Museum** (Schweizerisches Landesmuseum), Museumstrasse 2, exhibits a good selection of church art, plus weapons, coins, costumes and utensils all housed in a pseudo-castle built in 1898. Opening hours are Tuesday to Sunday from 10 am to 5 pm and entry is free.

The large **zoo** has 250 animal species from all around the world; it's open daily from 8 am to 6 pm (to 5 pm November to February). Entry costs Sfr8.50 (students Sfr4) and you can get there by tram No 5 or 6. The zoo backs on to Zürichberg, a large wood ideal for walks away from the noise of the city.

Festivals Most shops are shut on the third Monday in April when Zürich's spring festival, *Sechseläuten*, is held. Guild members parade down the main streets in historical costume and then adjourn to the local pubs. Another local holiday is *Knabenschiessen*, celebrated during the second weekend of September. Events revolve around a shooting competition for 12 to 16-year-old boys.

The Zürich Carnival, *Fasnacht*, is noted for mobile bands of lively musicians and a large, costumed procession. The carnival commences with typically Swiss precision at 11.11 am on 11 November. The International June Festival concentrates on music and the arts, and the International Jazz Festival takes place at the end of October.

Places to Stay
Accommodation can be a problem, particularly from June to August. Cheaper hotels fill early. A few, such as *Alpha Hotel*, Gertrudstrasse 48, are full all the time with residents who can't find or can't afford apartments (renting a two-bedroom flat costs Sfr2000 to Sfr3000 a month!). Book ahead if you can. Private rooms are virtually nonexistent and

boarding houses generally require a stay of at least a week.

Camping *Camping Seebucht* (☎ 482 16 12) is on the west shore of the lake, four km from the city centre, at Seestrasse 559. It is well signposted and can be reached by bus No 161 or 165 from Bürkliplatz. It has good facilities including a shop and café, although it is only open from 1 May to 30 September. Prices are Sfr5 per person (20% discount with Camping Carnet), tent Sfr8 and camper van Sfr10.

For camping and trekking equipment, go to Spatz Camping (☎ 53 43 00/1), Hedwigstrasse 25. Take tram No 11 from the Hauptbahnhof. It is closed on Sunday.

Hostels Near the Centre *Vereinhaus Glockenhof YMCA* (☎ 221 36 73), Sihlstrasse 33, takes men only, and singles cost from Sfr35 without breakfast. Reception closes at 7.45 pm weekdays, 3.45 pm Saturday and 1.30 pm Sunday. It has a cheap café open to all, with daily menus, and breakfast for Sfr5.50. You have your best chance (almost your *only* chance) of getting a room here from June to September, when students are on holiday.

Foyer Hottingen (☎ 261 93 15), Hottingerstrasse 31, is run by nuns. The sisters of the cloth believe that single men always cause problems, so they only accept women, married couples and families. Such people reckon this is a very nice place to stay, an opinion that is probably not totally uninfluenced by the absence of noisy young men. Reception hours are from 8 am to midnight. Singles/doubles are Sfr42/70, and triples/quads are Sfr76/84. Dorms (with lockers) start from Sfr18. Breakfast is included but showers cost Sfr1. Telephone reservations are accepted.

OASE Evangelisches Haus (☎ 252 39 81) is at Freiestrasse 38, off Hottingerstrasse. It's mainly geared towards students and those between 18 and 28 years old, although older people can stay. Expect a not-so-subtle purveying of Christian faith and values, but at

least it's cheap: singles/doubles for Sfr59/98, and dorms for Sfr25.

Hostels Away From the Centre The IYHF *youth hostel* (☎ 482 35 44) is at Mutschellenstrasse 114, Wollishofen, in a 25-year-old building with a faded pink paint job. Take tram No 6 or 7 to the Morgental stop. Reception is closed from noon to 12.30 pm, but the doors are always open during the day – check in from 10.30 am. Curfew is at 1 am and beds are Sfr22 including breakfast and lockers. Dinner costs Sfr9 and there are laundry facilities available (Sfr8 to wash and dry).

Justinusheim (☎ 361 38 06), Freudenbergstrasse 146, is a student home which has up to 30 beds available from mid-July to mid-October and during March and April. The rest of the year there are only a few vacancies. The staff are friendly and you get your own key for returning late at night. Singles/doubles vary in size and price, starting at Sfr35/65 with breakfast included. Just a few paces away from the woods of Zürichberg, it's an attractive old building with balconies, a terrace and good views of Zürich and the lake. Take tram No 10 from the Hauptbahnhof to Rigiplatz and then the Seilbahn to the top (it runs every few minutes and city network tickets are valid).

If all the places in Zürich are full, consider the IYHF *youth hostel* in Winterthur (☎ 052-27 38 40), Schloss Hegi, Hegifeldstrasse 125. It's an intimate, friendly place in a 15th century castle and receives no school groups, so it invariably has spaces. Reception is closed from 10 am to 2 pm (5 pm Monday and Friday) and the hostel is open from 1 March until 31 October. Winterthur is just 20 minutes by train from Zürich and there are four to five departures an hour. From Winterthur, take bus No 1 to Oberwinterthur and then it's 10 to 15 minutes' walk to the castle. Beds are just Sfr10 without breakfast.

Budget Hotels *Martahaus* (☎ 251 45 50), Zähringerstrasse 36, is in an excellent location in the old town. Singles/doubles cost Sfr60/90, and Sfr30 gets you a place in a six-bed dorm which is separated into individual cubicles by partitions and curtains. Breakfast is included in the price. There is a comfortable lounge and breakfast room, and a shower on each floor. Book ahead (telephone reservations OK), particularly for single rooms.

Hirschen (☎ 51 42 52), Niederdorfstrasse 13, is in a 600-year-old building. Low ceilings and sloping floors add character (except when you're inebriated!). It's also in an ideal central location. Newly renovated singles/doubles/triples are Sfr60/100/120 with breakfast. Rooms with private shower are available, and the reception is open 24 hours a day. *Regina* (☎ 242 65 50), Hohlstrasse 18, is in a noisy and lively area of the red-light district. The reception is open 24 hours. Singles/doubles start from Sfr40/60, although the cheaper rooms in the decaying old wing are usually full, so expect to pay Sfr60/100, or more if you want a room with shower. *Dufour* (☎ 55 36 55), Seefeldstrasse 188, has acceptable singles/doubles for Sfr55/70. Reception in the bar downstairs is open daily from 8 am to midnight. Get there by tram No 2 or 4.

Hotel Italia (☎ 241 05 55), Zeughausstrasse 61, is welcoming, if ageing, and has singles/doubles for Sfr60/80 with free hall showers. Prices rise by Sfr5 in the summer.

Mid-Range Hotels As even budget hotels are in effect mid-range in Zürich, the following two-star hotels are only slightly more expensive than those listed previously. In the city centre, *Hotel Limmathof* (☎ 261 42 20), Limmatquai 142, has modern fittings but it's a bit stingy with space. Singles/doubles with bath or shower are 90/120, and triples/quads are Sfr170/190. Nearby is *Leonhard* (☎ 251 30 80), Limmatquai 136, with singles/doubles from Sfr99/140. The rooms are better but the staff aren't as solicitous as they should be.

Goldenes Schwirt (☎ 252 59 40), Marktgasse 14, has singles/doubles from Sfr80/120, or Sfr55/100 without shower. The staff thoughtfully (and significantly) lay out ear plugs in each room. Reception is opposite in the *Hotel Rothus*, which is mar-

ginally cheaper. The three-star *Hotel Scheuble* (☎ 251 87 95), also in the old town at Mühlegasse 17, has singles/doubles starting at Sfr110/140.

Places to Eat
Zürich has hundreds of restaurants serving all types of local and international cuisine. The Zürich speciality, *Geschnetzeltes Kalbsfleisch* (thinly sliced veal in a cream sauce), will probably set you back at least Sfr20. Fast-food stands offer Bratwurst and bread from around Sfr4.50. There is a large *Coop* opposite the Hauptbahnhof, open Monday to Friday from 7 am to 6.30 pm and Saturday from 7 am to 4 pm.

East Bank *Mensa Polyterrace*, Leonhardstrasse 34, is next to the Seilbahn (cable car) exit, overlooking the city. Large and busy, it has good meals for around Sfr9 (Sfr5 for students) including vegetarian options. The self-service counters are open Monday to Friday from 11.15 am to 1.30 pm and 5.30 to 7.15 pm, and every second Saturday from 11.30 am to 1 pm. From mid-July to the end of September, the mensa is open for lunch only. There is a café upstairs which is also popular. Just along the road, there is another mensa in the universiy building, Rämistrasse 71, open Monday to Friday from 7.30 am to 8 pm, and alternative Saturdays to the Polyterrace.

Mère Catherine (☎ 262 22 50), Nägelhof 3, is a popular French restaurant in a small courtyard. The food is good quality but not cheap unless you choose the lunch-time menus for Sfr12.50 or Sfr13.50. Also popular is *Café Select*, Limmatquai 16, with outside tables overlooking the square. The service is not the swiftest but the food is fine. It serves Italian and Swiss dishes, and there is a games area upstairs.

Vier Linden, Gemeindestrasse 48, has a wide choice of vegetarian food including menus from Sfr13.70. It is open Monday to Friday from 11.30 am to 8.30 pm. Sample quality Spanish fare (Sfr17 to Sfr38) at *Bodega Española* (☎ 251 23 10), on the 1st floor at Münstergasse 15. It has a good selection of Spanish wines from Sfr31 a bottle.

West Bank *Clipper Restaurant* (☎ 242 63 20), Lagerstrasse 1, is basic and busy with good value if simple food. Seating opens on to the pavement making it nice and cool in the summer. Most main dishes cost as little as Sfr9 to Sfr12.50. The cheap beer (Sfr4 for half a litre) attracts many local drinkers. It is open daily from 10 am to 11.30 pm.

Bernerhof (☎ 241 73 06), Zeughausstrasse 1, has satisfying, filling food in an unpretentious environment. Several daily menus from Sfr10.80 (including soup) are available midday and evening. The restaurant is open daily from 8 or 9 am to midnight, except on Saturday when it only opens after 3 pm. Food stops around 9 pm, after which time you will find the locals sitting around drinking and playing board and card games.

Bistretto, Schweizergasse 6, has spaghetti and pasta dishes from Sfr9.30 to Sfr12.80 which must be ordered at the counter. Build salad tower blocks at the help-yourself salad bar where different plate sizes cost from Sfr4.30 to Sfr9.30. Opening hours are Monday to Saturday from 6.30 am to 9.30 pm (11 pm Thursday) and Sunday from 9 am to 8 pm. There is another branch with the same prices and setup on the corner of Schifflände and Kruggasse; this one closes at 11.30 pm daily.

Vegetarians will have a field day in the meat-free environment of *Hiltl Vegi* (☎ 221 38 71), Sihlstrasse 28, on two floors. It has a wide menu including tofu steak, curry (from Sfr15.20), wholemeal *(Vollkorn)* spaghetti bolognese for Sfr13.90, salads from Sfr8.90 and varying lunch-time specials. It is open Monday to Saturday from 6.30 am to 9 pm, and Sunday from 11 am to 9 pm.

Splurge on French food amid the mirrors and gleaming metal of *Brasserie Lipp Restaurant* (☎ 211 11 55), Uraniastrasse 9, opposite the Billettzentrale (see the following Entertainment section). Its elegant clientele are attracted by a wide choice of sumptuous dishes in the Sfr20 to Sfr35 range (open daily). *Restaurant JOSEF* (☎ 271 65

95), Gasometerstrasse 24, is yuppie territory. It offers German food prepared in interesting styles (from Sfr20 to Sfr30). Reservations are usually necessary in this small place, and it's closed Sunday.

Zürich also has numerous cafés where you can linger over a coffee. Try the entertaining *Café Münz* (☎ 221 30 27), Münzplatz 3, where Jean Tinguely mobiles hang from the ceiling. It is open Monday to Friday from 6.30 am to 7 pm (9 pm on Thursday), and Saturday from 8 am to 5 pm.

Entertainment

Many late-night pubs, clubs and discos are in Niederdorfstrasse and adjoining streets in the old town. This area is also a red-light district. On Sundays you might come across devout parishioners parading through the sin-sodden streets chanting hymns to anyone who can't avoid listening. Another red-light district is south-west of the Hauptbahnhof around Brauerstrasse. The *Casa Bar*, Münstergasse 30, is a lively pub with live jazz from 8 pm. During summer, the *Comedy Club* performs plays in English – get information and tickets from the Jelmoli department store on Bahnhofstrasse.

Cinema prices are reduced to Sfr9.90 every Monday from their normal price of around Sfr15. Films are nearly always in the original language.

Alternative arts are centred in *Rote Fabrik* (☎ 481 65 64), Seestrasse 395, not far from the youth hostel. It has concerts most nights ranging from rock and jazz to avant-garde (Sfr15 to Sfr20), original-language films (Sfr10), plus theatre and dance. It's worth going along simply to enjoy the laid-back atmosphere in the bar area.

If you're making a night of it in Niederdorfstrasse, kick off with a few cheap beers (Sfr3.60 for half a litre) at *Rheinfelder Bierhalle* at No 76. The food isn't bad either, with all-day menus including soup starting from Sfr12.50. Opening hours are 9 am to midnight daily.

Tickets for most events in the city can be obtained from the *Billettzentrale* (☎ 221 22 83), Werdmühleplatz, off Bahnhofstrasse;

it's open Monday to Friday from 10 am to 6.30 pm, Saturday to 4 pm. It is a government agency, so there are no commission charges. It's closed in July and August when activities in the arts die down.

Getting There & Away
Air The major gateway of Kloten Airport is 10 km north of the city centre and has several daily flights to/from all important destinations. Swissair has an office in the Hauptbahnhof (☎ 258 33 11) which is open Monday to Friday from 8 am to 6 pm, Saturday to 4 pm. For Swissair reservations around the clock, ☎ 251 34 34.

Train The busy Hauptbahnhof has direct trains to Stuttgart (Sfr52), Munich (Sfr75), Innsbruck (Sfr55) and Milan as well as to many other international destinations. There are also hourly departures to most Swiss towns, eg Lucerne (50 minutes, Sfr16.60), Bern (70 minutes, Sfr38) and Basel (65 minutes, Sfr26).

Car & Motorbike The N3 approaches Zürich from the south along the shore of Lake Zürich. The N1 is the fastest route from Bern and Basel and the main entry point from the west. The N1 also services routes to the north and east of Zürich. Sixt AG car rental (☎ 201 12 12) is at Tödistrasse 9; one-way rentals to Geneva are possible (see the Getting Around section at the beginning of this chapter for rates).

Hitching Zürich's Mitfahrzentrale (☎ 261 68 93) is at Leonhardstrasse 15. This agency links drivers and hitchers; hitchers end up paying about half the equivalent train fare.

Getting Around
To/From the Airport Don't take a taxi if you can help it. Trains cost about 10% of the price at Sfr4.20 and are fast and frequent. The service goes direct to the Hauptbahnhof.

Public Transport There is a comprehensive and unified bus, tram and S-Bahn service in the city. Tickets are also valid for boats on the Limmat River and should be bought in advance from dispensers at stops. The variety of tickets and zones available can be confusing. Short trips cost Sfr1.70, but it's worth getting a 24-hour pass for Sfr6 (press the blue key and return symbol). A two-zone, 24-hour pass for Sfr8.40 extends to trips to the airport *or* (the zones are different) for short tours of the lake. A 24-hour pass valid for unlimited travel within the whole canton of Zürich costs Sfr22.40, including extended tours of the lake.

Lake steamers leave from Bürkliplatz, departing hourly between 29 March and 20 October. There are only limited services in winter. For boat information, ☎ 482 10 33.

Other Transport Taxis in Zürich are expensive even by Swiss standards, at Sfr6 plus Sfr2.80 per km. Bicycle rental in the Hauptbahnhof is open from 6 am to 11.30 pm. The tourist office has a list of car-parking spaces near the central pedestrian zone.

Central Switzerland

This is the region which many visitors think of as the 'true' Switzerland. Not only is it rich in typical Swiss features – mountains, lakes, tinkling cowbells, Alpine villages and ski resorts – but it is also where Switzerland began as a nation 700 years ago. The original pact of 1291, signed by the communities of Uri, Schwyz and Nidwalden, can be viewed today in the Bundesbriefarchiv hall in Schwyz town centre.

LUCERNE
Ideally situated in the historic and scenic heart of Switzerland, Lucerne (Luzern in German) is an excellent base for a variety of excursions, yet it also has a great deal of charm in its own right, particularly the medieval town centre.

Orientation & Information
Lucerne is on the edge of Vierwaldstätter Lake, on both sides of the River Reuss. The

train station is on the south bank close to the medieval town centre. Extensive station facilities below ground level include daily bike rental (from 7 am to 7.45 pm) and money exchange.

Exit left for the tourist office (☎ 041-51 71 71), Frankenstrasse 1, which is open Monday to Friday from 8.30 am to 6 pm and Saturday from 9 am to 5 pm between April and October; and Monday to Friday from 8.30 am to noon and 2 to 6 pm, and Saturday from 9 am to 1 pm, between November and March.

In front of the train station is the boat landing stage, and alongside it is the main post office (Luzern 2, Bahnhof). Across the river is American Express (☎ 041-50 11 77) at Schweizerhofquai 4, open Monday to Friday from 8.30 am to 6 pm, Saturday to noon.

Things to See & Do

The picturesque old-town centre offers 15th century buildings with painted façades and the towers of the city walls. Some of these towers can be climbed for good views of the town and the lake. Be sure to walk along the two covered bridges, **Kapellbrücke** (built in

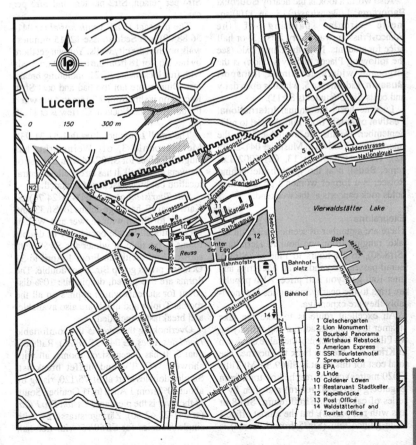

1 Gletschergarten
2 Lion Monument
3 Bourbaki Panorama
4 Wirtshaus Rebstock
5 American Express
6 SSR Touristenhotel
7 Spreuerbrücke
8 EPA
9 Linde
10 Goldener Löwen
11 Restaruant Stadtkeller
12 Kapellbrücke
13 Post Office
14 Waldstätterhof and Tourist Office

1333) with its water tower that appears in just about every photograph of Lucerne, and **Spreuerbrücke**. Both contain a series of pictorial panels under the roof.

The poignant **Lion Monument**, carved out of natural rock in 1820, is dedicated to the Swiss soldiers who died in the French Revolution. Next to it is the fascinating **Gletschergarten** (Glacier Garden), Denkmalstrasse 4, where giant glacial potholes prove that 20 million years ago Lucerne was a subtropical palm beach. The potholes can be perused from Tuesday to Sunday, and admission costs Sfr6.50 (students 4.50).

Also worth a look is the nearby **Bourbaki Panorama**, Löwenstrasse 18, an 1100-sq-metre circular painting of the Franco-Prussian war. Entry is Sfr 3, or half price for students. Near the Camp Lido (see the following Places to Stay section) is the large and widely acclaimed **Transport Museum**, Lidostrasse 5, which is open daily and costs Sfr15 (students Sfr11).

Lucerne hosts the annual **International Festival of Music** from mid-August to mid-September. Details are available from the International Festival of Music (☎ 041-23 35 62), Hirschmattstrasse 13, CH-6002 Lucerne. **Sedel**, near the youth hostel behind Rotsee, is a former women's prison which holds rock concerts at the weekend.

Excursions

There are a number of scenic cruises on the lake, ranging from one hour to Hermitage (Sfr8.80), to six hours to Flüelen (Sfr36). Eurail passes are valid on all boat trips and Inter-Rail gets you half price. Also popular are trips to the nearby mountains but inevitably they are expensive.

An excellent route is to take the lake steamer to Alpnachstad, the cog railway up Mt Pilatus (2100 metres), the cable car down to Kriens and the bus back to Lucerne. The total cost for this jaunt is Sfr69.80. Mt Titlis (3020 metres) can be reached by train from Engelberg (Sfr24.40 return) and then by a series of cable cars (Sfr60 return, Sfr48 or less with rail passes), but the tourist office's all-in guided tour (Sfr75 from Lucerne) is

cheaper. A combination steamer, cog railway and cable car excursion up Mt Rigi (1800 metres) costs Sfr62.80 but there are reductions with rail passes.

Places to Stay

Get your hotel to stamp your Visitor's Card to entitle you to various discounts (see Tourist Offices in the Facts for the Visitor section at the beginning of this chapter for details).

Camp Lido (☎ 041-31 21 46), Lidostrasse 8, is on the north shore of the lake and east of the town. It is open all year and charges Sfr4 per person, Sfr2 per tent and Sfr3 per car.

The pleasant IYHF *youth hostel* (☎ 041-36 88 00) is at Sedelstrasse 12, 15 minutes' walk north of the city walls. You can get there by bus No 1 or 18 from the train station. Beds with free lockers are Sfr21, including breakfast. Dinners are not too bad and cost Sfr9. Reception is shut from 9.30 am to 4 pm when the doors are also locked. Curfew is at 11.30 pm.

The small *Linde* hotel (☎ 041-51 31 93), Metzgerrainle 3, off Weinmarkt, has singles/doubles for Sfr37/74 with free use of showers in the hall. It has an excellent central location but breakfast is not included.

SSR Touristenhotel (☎ 041-51 24 74), St Karli Quai 12, has large dorms for Sfr33, and doubles for Sfr98 with shower and WC, or Sfr76 without. Single occupancy of double rooms is possible in winter for Sfr59 with shower, Sfr48 without. From 1 April to 31 October, prices go up Sfr20 per double. The dorms are overpriced, despite the 10% discount for students which applies on all the rooms. Triples and quads are also available, and breakfast is included.

Overlooking the river is the comfortable *Hotel des Alpes* (☎ 041-51 58 25), Rathausquai 5. It has decent-sized rooms, all with shower, WC, TV and buffet breakfast. Singles/doubles start at Sfr75/120, rising by about 20% from 1 April to 31 October. South of the river is the pleasant *Pension Pro Filia*, (☎ 041-22 42 80), Zäringerstrasse 24, with singles/doubles for Sfr50/85 with free hall

shower, and doubles with shower for Sfr95.
Extra beds are Sfr30 each.

Places to Eat
Tagesmenus in town are in the range of Sfr13
to Sfr15. *Goldener Löwen*, Eisengasse 1, is
small, intimate, fairly untouristy and open
daily. Main courses, including Swiss specialities, start at around Sfr12. At the other
extreme, *Restaurant Stadtkeller* (☎ 041-51
47 33), Sternenplatz 3, has two folklore
shows a day to allow you to yodel with your
mouth full. A full meal with a show will cost
around Sfr50 per person, and reservations
are usually necessary. From November to
mid-March, live music replaces the full
show.

The only vegetarian place in town is *Hotel
Restaurant Waldstätterhof* (☎ 041-23 54
93), Zentralstrasse 4, next to the tourist
office. It has a daily menu for Sfr14.50 and
also serves meat dishes. *Migros* supermarket
and restaurant is at Hertensteinstrasse 44.
EPA department store, Mühlenplatz, has an
excellent self-service restaurant with unbelievable prices for Switzerland: soup
Sfr1.50, salad buffet Sfr4.50 and Sfr5.80,
lunch-time specials from Sfr6, and tea or
coffee for Sfr1.60.

Wirtshaus Rebstock (☎ 041-51 35 81), St
Leodegar Platz, is popular mainly with
younger people. It has daily specials from
Sfr10 to Sfr25, various vegetarian dishes,
and a sociable café area. *Hotel-Restaurant
Schiff* (☎ 041-51 38 51), Unter der Egg 8,
overlooks the river. There are cheap lunch
specials with soup from Sfr13, but it's also a
good place to shed some francs on quality
evening dining. Cuisine from different
nationalities is featured on a regular basis,
and it has a five-course gourmet menu for
Sfr63.

Getting There & Away
Hourly trains connect Lucerne to Interlaken
Ost (Sfr23), Bern (Sfr29), Zürich (Sfr17),
Lugano (Sfr54) and Geneva (via Interlaken
or Langnau). The N2/E9 motorway connecting Basel and Lugano passes by Lucerne,
and the N14 provides the road link to Zürich.

INTERLAKEN
Interlaken, flanked by Lake Thun and Lake
Brienz and within striking distance of the
mighty peaks of the Jungfrau, Mönch and
Eiger, is an ideal centre from which to
explore the surrounding delights. It is the
centre of the Bernese Oberland, where the
scenic wonders of Switzerland come into
their own. People nearly always end up
staying longer than they planned.

Orientation & Information
Most of Interlaken is coupled between its
two train stations. Each station offers bike
rental and daily money exchange facilities,
and behind each is a boat landing for boat
services on the lakes. The main shopping
street, Höheweg, runs between the two stations. You can walk from one to the other in
20 minutes.

The tourist office (☎ 036-22 21 21),
Höheweg 37, is nearer to Interlaken West and
it's open Monday to Friday from 8 am to
noon and 2 to 6 pm, and Saturday from 8 am
to noon. During July and August, hours are
extended. The office charges Sfr5 for hotel
reservations and has lists of private rooms
from Sfr30 per night, but the minimum stay
for these is three days; the minimum for
apartments is one week. The main post office
(Interlaken 3800, Postplatz) is near the Interlaken West station at Marktgasse 1.

Things to See & Do
Numerous hiking trails dot the area surrounding Interlaken, all with signposts
giving average walking times. The funicular
up to Harder Kulm (Sfr18.40) yields an
excellent panorama and further prepared
paths. There are worthwhile boat trips to
several towns and villages round the lakes.
Eurail passes are valid on all boats and Inter-
Rail is good for 50% off the fare. On Lake
Thun, both the towns of Spiez (Sfr17.60
return by steamer or train) and Thun
(Sfr24.40 return by steamer or train) have a
castle.

A short, Sfr4.60 boat ride from Interlaken
are the **St Beatus Höhlen** (St Beatus Caves),
with some impressive stalagmite formations

and a small museum. Combined entry is Sfr8.50, or Sfr7.50 for students. The department-store dummies in a 'realistic reconstruction of a prehistoric settlement' are a laugh. Photography is prohibited in the caves as it holds up the guided tour – not that that stops anybody. The caves can also be reached from Interlaken by bus or a 90-minute walk, and are open daily from 9.30 am to 5 pm.

Lake Brienz has a more rugged shoreline than its neighbour. Brienz itself (Sfr18.80 return by steamer, or Sfr11.20 return by train) is the centre of the Swiss woodcarving industry and close to the **Freilichtmuseum Ballenberg**, a huge open-air park displaying typical Swiss crafts and houses. The park is open daily from mid-April to the end of October, and admission costs Sfr12 (students Sfr10).

Evening entertainment in Interlaken encompasses the casino with its folklore show, and several discos round town. Good places for a drink are *Buddy's Pub*, Höheweg 33, and *Mr Pickwick* on Postgasse.

Places to Stay

Ask your hotel for the Visitor's Card, which is valid for useful discounts (see Tourist Offices in the Facts for the Visitor section at the beginning of this chapter).

There are five camp sites close together north-west of Interlaken West. *Camp Alpenblick* (☎ 036-22 77 57), on Seestrasse by the Lombach River, costs Sfr4.50 per person, from Sfr3 per tent and Sfr4 for a car. Just along the road by the lake is *Manor Farm* (☎ 036-22 22 64), which is more expensive in the high season. Both are open all year.

The IYHF *youth hostel* (☎ 036-22 43 53), Aareweg 21, am See, Bönigen, is 25 minutes' walk round the lake from Interlaken Ost, or you can take bus No 1. It has an excellent location by the lake, with swimming facilities, but it's not the best run hostel and there are lots of petty regulations to contend with. Beds in large dorms are Sfr11.60, breakfast is Sfr5, a lunch packet is Sfr8.50 and dinner is Sfr9. The reception

shuts between 9.30 am and 5 pm, there is an 11 pm curfew, and the hostel is closed from 1 November to 31 January.

More central and much more sociable is *Balmer's Herberge* (☎ 036-22 19 61), Hauptstrasse 23, 15 minutes' walk (signposted) from either station. Excellent communal facilities include a reading room, games room, music room and videos every night. The staff also organises various excursions and rents bikes. There's a great atmosphere and it's a refreshing change of style from youth hostels. Somebody even escorts you to your dorm! Beds are Sfr15 including breakfast, showers are Sfr1, optional sheet rental is Sfr4, and there is a choice of dinners nightly in the price range of Sfr5 to Sfr10. Sign for a bed during the day and check in at 5 pm. During busy periods, people aged over 30 are charged Sfr18 in dorms. It is open all year.

A few metres on the right from Interlaken West is *Touriste Garni* (☎ 036-22 28 31); average singles/doubles start at Sfr35/60, including breakfast. Prices are Sfr10 higher in the high season.

Hotel Splendid (☎ 036-22 76 12), Höheweg 33, and the next-door *Hotel Europe* (☎ 036-22 71 41) both offer three-star comfort with singles/doubles from around Sfr60/80 with shower. Hotel Europe's prices come down in winter. *Hotel Garni Bären* (☎ 036-22 76 76) on Marktgasse has singles/doubles for Sfr40/80 with free hall shower. Doubles are especially spacious and have a sofa. All these hotels include breakfast.

The *Bellevue Garden Hotel* (☎ 036-22 47 48), also on Marktgasse, has some cheap rooms (from Sfr35) in what they call the 'Alp Lodge'.

Places to Eat

Anker Restaurant, Marktgasse 57, has a wide menu including vegetarian dishes from Sfr11, and it's open daily except Thursday evening. There is a games room around the back. More up-market is the restaurant in the *Hotel Metropole*, by the tourist office, which has a lunch-time budget menu of the day for

Sfr13. In the plusher inner sanctum of the restaurant, there is a three-course menu for around Sfr36 (lunch time only), and à-la-carte dishes start at around Sfr25. The hotel also has the *Panoramic Bar/Café* on the 15th floor – it's worth going up for a beer or a coffee to admire the view and to walk round the balcony.

A good place for cheap Italian food is *Pizzeria Mercato*, off Höheweg round the back of Chalet Hotel, open to at least midnight (closed Tuesday). The *Migros* restaurant, above the supermarket on Bahnhofstrasse by Interlaken West, is open Monday to Friday from 7.30 am to 6.30 pm, Saturday to 4 pm.

The *Hotel Europe* (see the previous section) has tasty two-course menus for Sfr12, and a three-course vegetarian menu for Sfr17; other dishes cost Sfr15 to Sfr25. A good place for traditional food in comfortable surroundings is *Gasthof Hirschen*, on the corner of Hauptstrasse and Parkstrasse; it's closed on Wednesday.

Getting There & Away
Trains to Lucerne depart hourly from Interlaken Ost. Trains to Brig (Sfr33, via Lötschberg) and to Montreux (via Bern or Zweisimmen) depart from Interlaken West or Ost. Main roads go to Lucerne, Bern and to the west via Zweisimmen. For vehicles, the only way south through the mountains without a big detour is to take the car-carrying train from Kandersteg, south of Spiez.

AROUND INTERLAKEN
Grindelwald
Only 40 minutes by train from Interlaken Ost (Sfr8.40 one-way, Sfr16.80 return) is Grindelwald, a busy resort under the north face of the Eiger. Scenically striking, it is a great base for hiking, especially in the First region where there are 90 km of paths above 1200 metres. Of these, 48 km stay open in winter. The cable car up here is the longest in Europe (Sfr23 up, Sfr39 return). In winter, the First is also the main skiing area, with a variety of runs stretching from Oberjoch at 2486

metres, right down to the village at 1050 metres. Grindelwald can be reached by road.

The tourist office (☎ 036-53 12 12) is in the centre by the Sportzentrum; it's open daily in summer, and weekdays and Saturday morning from October to June. It is 200 metres up from the train station – only follow the more visible Information sign down the hill if you speak Japanese.

Places to Stay & Eat Grindelwald has several camp sites and an IYHF *youth hostel* (☎ 036-53 10 09), which is at Terrassenweg, 20 minutes' climb from the train station. Dorm beds are Sfr18.50 with breakfast, or Sfr13.50 in summer when breakfast is optional. Kitchen facilities are available. Reception is shut from 9 am to 5 pm and the hostel closes completely from one week after Easter for five weeks, and from the end of October to mid-December. Close to the youth hostel is the *Naturfreundehaus* (☎ 036-53 13 33), which has dorms from Sfr16.50. Other dorms are listed in the tourist office leaflet.

In the centre of the village on the main street, the best place to stay is *Hotel Tschuggen* (036-53 17 81), with attractive singles/doubles for Sfr50/100 with hall shower or Sfr60/100 with private bath/shower. Next door is the Hotel Spinne which has the *Ristorante Mercado*, about the cheapest place to eat in this pricey village. Pizza and pasta start from Sfr10 and lunch specials are around Sfr14. Along the road, *Restaurant Rendez-vous* also has decent daily specials (closed Tuesday). There's a *Coop* supermarket opposite the tourist office.

Gimmelwald Valley
This valley is the other fork branching from Interlaken into the mountains. The first village reached by car or rail is **Lauterbrunnen**, known mainly for the Staubbach Falls cascading down outside the village, and the more impressive and farther Trümmelbach Falls, spitting its spray inside a glacier (Sfr8 entry, open April to Novem-

ber). Find out more from the tourist office (☎ 036-55 19 55) near the train station.

Above the village (via funicular, Sfr7.80) is the car-free **Mürren**, a skiing and hiking resort. Its efficient tourist office (☎ 036-55 16 16) is in the sports centre. Forty minutes' walk down the hill from Mürren is tiny **Gimmelwald**, virtually undisturbed by tourists. There are tremendous views across the valley to the Jungfrau, Mönch and Eiger peaks.

Gimmelwald and Mürren can also be reached from the valley floor by the Stechelberg cable car, which runs all the way up to **Schilthorn** at 2971 metres (Sfr64 return). From the top there's a fantastic 360° panorama, and film shows will remind you that James Bond performed his stunts here in *On Her Majesty's Secret Service*.

Places to Stay & Eat Lauterbrunnen and Grimmelwald are bargains for accommodation, but Mürren is more touristy and therefore more expensive.

Lauterbrunnen *Camping Schützenbach* (☎ 036-55 12 68) and *Matratzenlager Stocki* (☎ 036-55 17 54) both have kitchen facilities and dorms for around Sfr10. *Chalet im Rohr* has singles/doubles for around Sfr20 per person. Eating is more of a problem. Go to the *Coop*, or try the *Hotel Jungfrau* for salads (Sfr4 to Sfr6.50), spaghetti bolognese (Sfr9.50) and three-course specials from Sfr13.

Gimmelwald The diminutive, decaying, regulation-free *Mountain Hostel* (☎ 036-55 17 04) has dusty dorms for Sfr7, with kitchen facilities. It's by the cable-car station. Up the hill a bit is *Mittaghorn* (☎ 036-55 24 55), with singles/doubles for Sfr54/59 and triples/quads for Sfr78/96, including breakfast. The food is great in the café there, but you must preorder unless you just want beer (Sfr3.60 for an 0.6-litre bottle). There's another café by the Mountain Hostel, and an adjoining shop open just a few mornings a week.

Mürren Staying in the village costs around Sfr80 per person, the only cheaper pensions being 20 or 30 minutes' walk up the hill. If you stay for five days or more, you do at least get 10% off the Jungfrau Region ski pass (but you can get this by staying in Gimmelwald, too).

One of the cheapest places to stay in the village is *Hotel Edelweiss* (☎ 036-55 26 12), which also has reasonable food from Sfr12, and good views from the south-facing terrace (closed Tuesday). The small *Staeger-stübli*, next to the Coop supermarket, has daily specials from Sfr10, salad plates for Sfr11 and fondue from Sfr17.50. It's open daily.

Jungfraujoch

The trip to Jungfraujoch by railway (the highest in Europe) is excellent. Unfortunately, the price is as steep as the track and is hardly worth it unless you have good weather – call ☎ 036-55 10 22 for forecasts in German, French and English. From Interlaken Ost, trains go via Grindelwald or Lauterbrunnen to Kleine Scheidegg. From here, the line is less than 10 km long but took 16 years to build. Opened in 1912, the track powers through both the Eiger and the Mönch with wonderful views from two windows blasted in the mountain side, before terminating at 3454 metres at Jungfraujoch.

On the summit, there is free entry to the **ice palace** (a maze cut in a glacier). From the terrace of the Sphinx Research Institute (a weather station) the panorama of peaks is unforgettable, including the Aletsch Glacier to the south, and mountains as distant as the Jura and the Black Forest. Take warm clothing and your own food to cut costs.

Journey time is 2½ hours each way and the fare is Sfr140 (Eurail no reduction, Inter-Rail Sfr70, Swiss Pass Sfr97). If you depart at 6.34 am or 7.37 am, the fare is reduced to Sfr97 (rail cards no reduction, Swiss Pass Sfr74). From 1 May to 31 October these reductions (so-called 'excursion fares') apply only on the first train and you must return from the summit by noon. The last train back in the summer is at 6 pm. Allow at least three hours at the site.

Other Destinations

Marvellous views and hikes compete for attention from various other vantage points near Interlaken, such as **Schynige Platte**, **Wengen** and **Kleine Scheidegg**. Many of the funiculars in the region only operate in the summer.

Skiing is a major activity in the winter months, with a good variety of intermediate runs plus the demanding run down from the Schilthorn. Ski passes cost Sfr43 or Sfr45 per day, or Sfr118 for a minimum three days in the whole Jungfraujoch region.

Northern Switzerland

This part of the country is important for industry and commerce, yet it is by no means lacking in tourist attractions. Take time to explore Lake Constance, the Rhine and the picturesque town centres of the region.

BASEL

Basel (Bâle in French) joined the Swiss Confederation in 1501. Although an industrial city, it retains an attractive old town and offers many interesting museums. The famous Renaissance Humanist, Erasmus of Rotterdam, was associated with the city and his tomb rests in the cathedral.

Orientation & Information

Basel's strategic position on the Rhine at the dual border with France and Germany has been instrumental in its development as a commercial and cultural centre. On the north bank of the Rhine is Klein (Little) Basel, surrounded by German territory. The old town and most of the sights are on the south bank in Grosser (Greater) Basel.

The main tourist office (☎ 061-261 50 50) is by the Mittlere bridge at Blumenrain 2, Schifflände. It has good free city maps and is open Monday to Friday from 8.30 am to 6 pm, and Saturday from 8.30 am to 1 pm. One

km south is the main SBB Bahnhof which has bike rental (6 am to 10 pm daily), money exchange (6 am to 9.45 pm daily) and another tourist office (☎ 061-271 36 84), open Monday to Friday from 8.30 am to 6 pm, and Saturday from 8.30 am to 12.30 pm. This tourist office is open additional hours during parts of the year: between April and September, it is open to 7 pm weekdays and from 1.30 to 6 pm Saturdays; between June and September, it is also open on Sunday from 10 am to 2 pm.

The main post office is just outside the station. Address poste restante to: Basel 2, Gartenstrasse, CH-4002 Basel.

Things to See & Do

The tourist office has free guides to walks through the old town, taking in cobbled streets, colourful fountains and 16th century buildings. The restored **Rathaus** is very impressive and has a frescoed courtyard. The 12th century **Münster** (cathedral) is also worth a look with its Gothic spires and Romanesque St Gallus doorway.

Of the many museums, the most important is the **Kunstmuseum**, St Albangraben 16, with a good selection of religious, Swiss and modern art. It is open Tuesday to Saturday from 10 am to 5 pm, and costs Sfr3 (students Sfr2) except on Sunday when it's free. It has an excellent collection of Picassos. The artist was so gratified when the people of Basel paid a large sum for two of his paintings that he donated a further four from his own collection.

Be sure to take a look at the **Tinguely Fountain** on Theaterplatz. It's a typical display by the Swiss sculptor of the same name, with madcap machinery playing water games with hoses – art with a juvenile heart.

Basel is also a carnival town. At the end of January, *Vogel Gryff* is when winter is chased away. On the Monday after Ash Wednesday, three days of festivities begin. Known as *Fasnacht*, it's a spectacle of parades, masks, music and costumes, all starting at 4 am!

For evening entertainment, try *Atlantis* (☎ 061-272 20 38), Klosterbergstrasse 13. It

1 Drei Könige
2 Information Office
3 Rathaus
4 Weinstube Gifthüttli
5 Café Zum Roten Engel
6 Hasenburg Château Lapin
7 Restaurant Wilhelm Tell
8 EPA
9 Kunsthotel Teufelhof
10 Stadthof
11 Münster
12 Kunstmuseum
13 Youth Hostel
14 Tinguely Fountain
15 Mr Wong
16 Steinenschanze
17 Atlantis
18 Information Office
19 Bahnhof SBB
20 Post Office

Feldbergstrasse
Johanniterbrücke
Schanzenstrasse
Blumenrain
Mittlere Brücke
Rhine River
Spalenvorstadt
Schützengraben
Gerbergasse
Leonhardsgraben
Freie Strasse
Wettsteinbrücke
Münster
Laimenstrasse
Sternengraben
Heuwaage-Viadukt
Aeschenvorstadt
Dufourstrasse
St Alban-Vorstadt
St Alban-Anlage
St Alban-Strasse
Viaduktstrasse
Aeschengraben
St Jakobs-Strasse
Engelgasse
St Jakobs-Strasse
Nauenstrasse
Grosspeterstrasse

Basel

0   200   400 m

SWITZERLAND

has live music daily (mainly rock, jazz and R&B), and entry costs between Sfr5 and Sfr25.

Places to Stay

Hotels are expensive and liable to be full during numerous trade fairs and conventions. Be sure to book ahead. The tourist office in the SBB Bahnhof reserves rooms for Sfr5 commission.

Six km south of the train station is *Camp Waldhort* (☎ 061-711 64 29) at Heideweg 16, Reinach.

The IYHF *youth hostel* (☎ 061-272 05 72) is conveniently near the centre of town at St Alban Kirchrain 10. Beds cost Sfr20 per night with breakfast. Reception is shut from 10 am to 2 pm (3 pm in winter), when the doors are also locked. The 1 am curfew is brought forward to midnight in winter.

In the old town, *Stadthof* (☎ 061-261 87 11), Gerbergasse 84, has singles/doubles from Sfr50/90 without breakfast. Not far from SBB Bahnhof is *Steinenschanze* (☎ 061-272 53 53), Steinengraben 69, which has singles/doubles with breakfast for Sfr60/90. The price for students is reduced to Sfr40 per person.

If you can afford to splash out on accommodation, there are two unique possibilities. The best hotel in Basel is the *Drei Könige* (☎ 261 52 52), Blumenrain 8. It has welcomed luminaries through its portals since 1026 – royals such as Princess (later Queen) Victoria, and the likes of Napoleon, Voltaire and Dickens. You can join them, but only if you can afford the king's ransom of at least Sfr220/360 for a single/double. Breakfast buffet is Sfr27 extra.

The most interesting hotel in Basel is the *Kunsthotel Teufelhof* (☎ 261 10 10), Leonhardsgraben 47. Each of the rooms was assigned to a different artist to create a piece of environmental art. All rooms will stay intact for just two years before being reassigned to a new artist. The shock of waking up in a piece of art is quite something. The rooms have bath and shower, and prices start at Sfr140/170 for a single/double. Some rooms are more elaborately kitted out than others, but all are a welcome respite from standard hotel fixtures.

Places to Eat

Restaurant Wilhelm Tell, Spalenvorstadt 38, by the Spalentor city gate, is small and busy. In other words it's claustrophobic, but it's still worth paying a visit for tasty local and Italian dishes from Sfr8.90. Opening hours are Monday to Saturday from 7 am to midnight. The *EPA* department store, Gerbergasse 4, near the Rathaus, has a cheap self-service restaurant with soup for Sfr1.50 and main dishes from Sfr7. *Mister Wong*, Steinenvorstadt 1a, also self-service, offers a reasonable choice of Asian dishes with good portions from Sfr6.50. It has a salad bar and is open daily to 10 pm except on Friday and Saturday when it closes at 11 pm.

For Basel specialities in a typical ambience, try *Weinstube Gifthüttli* (☎ 061-25 16 56), Schneidergasse 11. It has daily menus from Sfr11 to Sfr30. Opposite is the slightly more down-to-earth *Hasenburg Château Lapin*. Vegetarians should check the environmentally sound *Café Zum Roten Engel* in the adjoining courtyard (outside tables). It serves only organic vegetarian food (plus some fish dishes) for around Sfr12.50 to Sfr14. Good breakfasts are available.

Getting There & Away

Basel is a major European rail hub. All trains to France go from SBB Bahnhof where you pass the border controls in the station. There are three to four trains a day to Paris (Sfr65) and connections to Brussels and Strasbourg. Trains to Germany (border controls on the train) stop at BBF Bahnhof on the north bank although they originate at SBB. Main destinations along this route are Frankfurt (Sfr70), Cologne, Hamburg and Amsterdam. Services within Switzerland go from SBB: there are fast trains to Geneva via Bern (one minute past the hour) and Zürich (27 and 54 minutes past). By motorway, the E9 heads down from Strasbourg and passes by Mulhouse Airport, and the E4 hugs the German side of the Rhine.

Getting Around

Buses and trains run every six to 12 minutes. Tickets cost Sfr1 for up to four stops, or Sfr1.80 for the whole central zone. Multi-journey cards are available, but you're better off with a day card for Sfr6. Cars are no use for exploring the central pedestrian area – park in one of the spots indicated on the tourist office map.

SCHAFFHAUSEN

The capital of the canton that bears its name, this communications and arms centre was accidently bombed by the USA in 1944. Thankfully, however, its medieval town centre remains intact. The largest waterfall in Europe, the Rheinfall, is three km down the Rhine.

Orientation & Information

Schaffhausen is in a bulge of Swiss territory surrounded by Germany on the north bank of the Rhine. The train station is adjacent to the old town, where you'll find the tourist office (☎ 053-25 51 41) at Vorstadt 12. It is open Monday to Friday from 9 am to 6 pm, and to noon Saturday. Postbuses depart from the rear of the station and local buses from the front. The main post office is also opposite the station.

The telephone code for Schaffhausen is 053.

Things to See & Do

The attractive old town is bursting with oriel windows, painted façades and ornamental fountains. The best streets are Vordergasse, which has the 16th century **Haus zum Ritter** with its painted historical scenes, and Vorstadt, which intersect at Fronwagplatz. Get an overview of the town from the **Munot** castle up on the hill (open daily, free). The **Allerheiligen Museum**, by the cathedral in Klosterplatz, houses a collection ranging from ancient bones to modern art (free, closed Monday).

The **Rheinfall** can be reached by a 40-minute stroll westward along the river, or by bus Nos 1 and 9 to Neuhausen. The largest waterfall in Europe drops 23 metres and makes a tremendous racket as 700 cubic metres of water crashes down every second. The 45 km of the Rhine from Schaffhausen to Constance is one of the river's most beautiful stretches, passing by meadows, castles and ancient villages, not least the picturesque **Stein am Rhein**, 20 km to the east.

Places to Stay

The IYHF *youth hostel* (☎ 25 88 00) is 20 minutes' walk west of the train station (or take bus No 3), at Randenstrasse 65. Dorms cost Sfr16 with breakfast, and the reception is closed from 9 am to 5.30 pm. The cheapest deal in the town centre is *Steinbock* (☎ 25 42 60), Webergasse 47, with singles/doubles for Sfr38/65. It's above a fairly noisy café but the rooms are clean, reasonably sized, and there are free hall showers.

Tanne (☎ 25 41 79), Tanne 3 off Fronwagplatz, has singles/doubles from Sfr40/76. Mid-price comfort and amenities are found at *Hotel Bahnhof* (☎ 24 19 24), Bahnhofstrasse 46.

Places to Eat

Eat for under Sfr10 at either the *Migros* supermarket and restaurant at Vorstadt 39, or the *EPA* department store restaurant at Vordergasse 69. A better ambience, despite the glowering masks on the wall, can be found at *Walliser Kanne*, Webergasse 27, which specialises in fondues (from Sfr17.50) and other cheese concoctions; it's closed Tuesday.

For a taste treat, go to *Rheinhotel Fischerzunft* (☎ 25 32 81), Rheinquai 8. It has been voted one of the top restaurants in Switzerland, a justification for spending around Sfr50 per main dish. It serves Oriental and Swiss food, particularly fish dishes.

Getting There & Away

There are hourly direct trains to Zürich (Sfr13.80) and Constance (via Singen, Sfr12.60). Basel can be reached by either Swiss or German trains. Steamers travel to Constance several times a day in summer, and the trip takes four hours; they depart from Freier Platz (call ☎ 25 42 82 for information). Schaffhausen has excellent road connections radiating out in all directions.

ST GALLEN

In 612 AD, an itinerant Irish monk called Gallus fell into a briar. Relying on a peculiar form of Irish logic, the venerable Gallus interpreted this clumsy act as a sign from God and decided to stay put and build a hermitage. From this inauspicious beginning the town of St Gallen evolved and developed into an important medieval cultural centre.

Orientation & Information

The main post office (Bahnhofplatz, CH-9001 St Gallen) is opposite the train station. Two minutes away is the tourist office (☎ 071-22 62 62), Bahnhofplatz 1a, which is open Monday to Friday from 9 am to noon and 1 to 6 pm, and on Saturday from 9 am to noon. It has good free city maps. A few minutes to the east is the pedestrian-only old town.

Things to See & Do

St Gallen has one of the best old-town centres in Switzerland. It's full of interesting buildings with colourful murals, carved balconies and relief statues. Some of the best are on Gallusplatz, Spisergasse and Kugelgasse. The twin-tower **cathedral** cannot and should not be missed. Completed in 1766, it's immensely impressive and impressively immense. Forget the Sistine Chapel in Rome – a lot more paint went onto this ceiling! Look out also for the pulpit, arches, statue groups and woodcarvings around the confessionals.

Adjoining the church is the **Stiftsbibliothek** (Collegiate Library), containing some beautifully etched manuscripts from the Middle Ages and a splendidly opulent Rococo interior. There's even an Egyptian mummy (dating from 700 BC and as well preserved as the average grandparent). Entry is Sfr3, students Sfr2, and it's closed on Sunday.

The *Grabenhalle* (☎ 071-22 82 11), Blumenberg Platz, is a major venue for rock and jazz concerts.

Places to Stay

The IYHF *youth hostel* (☎ 071-25 47 77) is a signposted, 15-minute walk east of the old town at Jüchstrasse 25 (once you get into Linsebühlstrasse, follow only the hostel signs with the adult and child – turning right with the other hostel signs makes the walk much longer). Beds are Sfr18 in a dorm or Sfr28 in a double room, with breakfast included. Reception is closed from 9 am to 5 pm during which time the doors are locked. This is one of the few hostels in Switzerland where chores are given out: the last person to leave has the pleasure of sweeping the dorm. Curfew is at 10 pm but there is a key available for late entry. The hostel closes for two weeks at Christmas and from 1 February to the end of March.

Weisses Kreuz (☎ 071-23 28 43) on Engelgasse has reasonable singles/doubles for Sfr38/72 with free use of the hall shower. There are also four good-sized doubles with shower for Sfr86. The reception is in the cosy bar downstairs. *Touring Garni* (☎ 071-22 58 01) is virtually opposite. Rooms are of varying quality, so ask to see several; those with a proper *en suite* bathroom are a good deal. Singles/doubles are around Sfr55/95, and there are cheaper rooms with no shower facilities available. *Elite Garni* (☎ 071-22 21 77), Metzgergasse 9-11, is a similar standard but slightly more expensive.

Places to Eat

Eating can be pretty good in St Gallen. The best mid-price place is *Wirtschaft Zur Alten Post* (☎ 071-22 66 01), Gallusstrasse 4. The food is typically Swiss, with meat and fish dishes starting at Sfr25. Small and cosy, this restaurant fills quickly, so reserve ahead. It's closed on Sunday and Monday.

Hörni, Marktplatz 5, has a wide selection of beers available on the ground floor. Upstairs, daily specials (lunch and evening) start at Sfr10. *Bistretto*, off Marktplatz on Augustinergasse, has good, cheap pasta and pizzas, and a self-service salad bar with plates from Sfr4.30. Both restaurants are open daily. *Merkur Restaurant*, on the corner of Gutenbergstrasse and St Leonhardstrasse, offers vegetarian specials from Sfr10.50. On the other side of the road is *Migros* supermarket and restaurant. Look out for various fast-food stalls selling St Gallen sausage and bread for around Sfr3.50.

Getting There & Away

St Gallen is a short train ride from Lake Constance (Bodensee), upon which boats sail to Bregenz in Austria, and to Constance and Lindau in Germany. There are also regular trains to Bregenz (Sfr12), Constance (Sfr15), Chur (Sfr32) and Zürich (Sfr24.20).

APPENZELL

If you ever hear a joke in Switzerland, the inhabitants of Appenzell are likely to be the butt. They are known for their parochialism and are considered (rather unkindly) to be several stages lower on the evolutionary ladder than the rest of humanity. Women were finally allowed to vote in local affairs in 1991, and then only after the supreme court ruled their exclusion by the men unconstitutional.

Such resistance to change has its advantages for the tourist. The village is a delight to wander around, with traditional old houses, painted façades and lush surrounding countryside. The streets are bedecked with flags and flowers on the last Sunday in April when the locals vote on cantonal issues by a show of hands in the open-air parliament *(Landsgemeinde)*. Everyone wears traditional dress for the occasion and many of the men carry swords or daggers as proof of citizenship.

Getting There & Away

There are hourly connections from St Gallen by a narrow-gauge train which careers along following the course of the road and takes 40 minutes (Sfr9.10 one-way, Sfr18.20 return).

Appendix I – International Country Abbreviations

The following is a list of official country abbreviations that you may encounter on vehicles in Europe. Other abbreviations are likely to be unofficial, often referring to a particular region, province or city. A motorised vehicle entering a foreign country must carry a sticker identifying its country of registration, though this rule is not always enforced.

A	–	Austria
AL	–	Albania
AND	–	Andorra
AUS	–	Australia
B	–	Belgium
BG	–	Bulgaria
CC	–	Consular Corps
CD	–	Diplomatic Corps
CDN	–	Canada
CH	–	Switzerland
CS	–	Czechoslovakia
CY	–	Cyprus
D	–	Germany
DDR	–	German Democratic Republic (the former East Germany)
DK	–	Denmark
DZ	–	Algeria
E	–	Spain
ET	–	Egypt
F	–	France
FL	–	Liechtenstein
GB	–	Great Britain
GBA	–	Alderney
GBG	–	Guernsey
GBJ	–	Jersey
GBM	–	Isle of Man
GBZ	–	Gibraltar
GR	–	Greece
H	–	Hungary
HKJ	–	Jordan
HR	–	Croatia

I	–	Italy
IL	–	Israel
IND	–	India
IR	–	Iran
IRL	–	Ireland
IRQ	–	Iraq
IS	–	Iceland
J	–	Japan
KWT	–	Kuwait
L	–	Luxembourg
LAR	–	Libya
M	–	Malta
MA	–	Morocco
MC	–	Monaco
MEX	–	Mexico
N	–	Norway
NA	–	Netherlands Antilles
NL	–	Netherlands
NZ	–	New Zealand
P	–	Portugal
PAK	–	Pakistan
PL	–	Poland
RIM	–	Mauritania
RL	–	Lebanon
RO	–	Romania
RSM	–	San Marino
S	–	Sweden
SCV	–	Vatican City
SF	–	Finland
SLO	–	Slovenia
SME	–	Surinam
SN	–	Senegal
SU	–	Soviet Union
SYR	–	Syria
TN	–	Tunisia
TR	–	Turkey
USA	–	United States
VN	–	Vietnam
WAN	–	Nigeria
YU	–	Yugoslavia
ZA	–	South Africa

Appendix II – Alternative Place Names

The following abbreviations are used:

(B) Basque
(C) Catalan
(D) Dutch (and Flemish)
(E) English
(F) French
(Fl) Flemish (and Dutch)
(G) German
(Ir) Irish
(I) Italian
(L) Luxembourgian
(I) Italian
(P) Portuguese
(Rh) Romansch
(S) Spanish

AUSTRIA
Österreich

Carinthia (E) – Kärnten (G)
Danube (E) – Donau (G)
East Tirol (E) – Osttirol (G)
Lake Constance (E) – Bodensee (G)
Lower Austria (E) – Niederösterreich (G)
Upper Austria (E) – Oberösterreich (G)
Styria (E) – Steiermark (G)
Tirol (E, G) – Tyrol (E)
Vienna (E) – Wien (G)
Vienna Woods (E) – Wienerwald (G)

BELGIUM
België (Fl), Belgique (F)

Alost (E, F) – Aalst (Fl)
Antwerp (E) – Antwerpen (Fl), Anvers (F)
Bruges (E, F) – Brugge (Fl)
Brussels (E) – Bruxelles (F), Brussel (Fl)
Courtrai (E, F) – Kortrijk (Fl)
Ghent (E) – Gent (Fl), Gand (F)
Liège (E, F) – Luik (Fl), Lüttich (G)
Louvain (E, F) – Leuven (Fl)
Mechlin (E, F) – Mechelen (Fl), Malines (F)
Meuse (River) (E, F) – Maas (Fl)
Mons (E, F) – Bergen (Fl)
Namur (E, F) – Namen (Fl)
Ostend (E) – Oostende (Fl), Ostende (F)
Scheldt (River) (E) – Schelde (Fl), Escaut (F)
Tournai (E, F) – Doornik (Fl)
Ypres (E, F) – Ieper (Fl)

FRANCE

Alps (E) – les Alpes (F)
Basque Country (E) – Pays Basque (F)
Burgundy (E) – Bourgogne (F)
Brittany (E) – Bretagne (F)
Corsica (E) – la Corse (F)
French Riviera (E) – Côte d'Azur (F)
Dunkirk (E) – Dunkerque (F)
Guernsey (Channel Islands) (E) – Guernesey (F)
Channel Islands (E) – Îles Anglo-Normandes (F)
English Channel (E) – La Manche (F)
Lake Geneva (E) – Lac Léman (F)
Lyons (E) – Lyon (F)
Marseilles (E) – Marseille (F)
Normandy (E) – Normandie (F)
Pyrenees (E) – Pyrénées (F)
Rheims (E) – Reims (F)
Rhine (River) (E) – Rhin (F) Rhein (G)
Sark (Channel Islands) (E) – Sercq (F)

GERMANY
Deutschland

Aachen (E, G) – Aix-la-Chapelle (F)
Baltic Sea (E) – Ostsee (G)
Bavaria (E) – Bayern (G)
Bavarian Alps (E) – Bayerische Alpen (G)
Bavarian Forest (E) – Bayerischer Wald (G)
Black Forest (E) – Schwarzwald (G)
Cologne (E) – Köln (G)
Constance (E) – Konstanz (G)
Danube (E) – Donau (G)
East Friesland (E) – Ostfriesland (G)
Federal Republic of Germany (FRG) (E) –
    Bundesrepublik Deutschland (BRD) (G)
Franconia (E) – Franken (G)
Hamelin (E) – Hameln (G)
Hanover (E) – Hannover (G)
Harz Mountains (E) – Harzgebirge (G)
Heligoland (E) – Helgoland (G)
Hesse (E) – Hessen (G)
Lake Constance (E) – Bodensee (G)
Lower Saxony (E) – Niedersachsen (G)
Lüneburg Heath (E) – Lüneburger Heide (G)
Mecklenburg-Pomerania (E) –
    Mecklenburg-Vorpommern (G)
Munich (E) – München (G)
North Friesland (E) – Nordfriesland (G)
North Rhine-Westphalia (E) –
    Nordrhein-Westfalen (G)
Nuremberg (E) – Nürnberg (G)
Pomerania (E) – Pommern (G)
Prussia (E) – Preussen (G)

Rhine (E) – Rhein (G)
Rhineland-Palatinate (E) – Rheinland-Pfalz (G)
Romantic Road (E) – Romantische Strasse (G)
Saxon Switzerland (E) –
   Sachsische Schweiz (G)
Saxony (E) – Sachsen (G)
Swabia (E) – Schwaben (G)
Thuringia (E) – Thüringen (G)
Thuringian Forest (E) – Thüringer Wald (G)

IRELAND
Eire

Aran Islands (E) – Oileáin Árainn (Ir)
Athlone (E) – Baile Átha Luain (Ir)
Bantry (E) – Beanntraí (Ir)
Belfast (E) – Bealfeirste (Ir)
Belmullet (E) – Béal an Mhuirthead (Ir)
Cork (E) – Corcaigh (Ir)
Derry (E) – Doire (Ir)
Dingle (E) – Daingean (Ir)
Donegal (E) – Dún na nGall (Ir)
Dublin (E) – Baile Átha Cliath (Ir)
Galway (E) – Gaillimh (Ir)
Kerry (E) – Ciarraighe (Ir)
Kilkenny (E) – Cill Chainnigh (Ir)
Killarney (E) – Cill Áirne (Ir)
Kilronan (E) – Cill Ronáin (Ir)
Limerick (E) – Luimneach (Ir)
Rossaveal (E) – Ros an Mhíl (Ir)
Shannon (E) – Sionann (Ir)
Tipperary (E) – Tiobrad Árann (Ir)
Waterford (E) – Port Láirge (Ir)
Wexford (E) – Loch Garman (Ir)

ITALY
Italia

Aeolian Islands (E) – Isole Eolie (I)
Alps (E) – le Alpi (I)
Apulia (E) – Puglia (I)
Florence (E) – Firenze (I)
Genoa (E) – Genova (I)
Herculaneum (E) – Ercolano (I)
Lombardy (E) – Lombardia (I)
Mantua (E) – Mantova (I)
Milan (E) – Milano (I)
Naples (E) – Napoli (I)
Padua (E) – Padova (I)
Rome (E) – Roma (I)
Sicily (E) – Sicilia (I)
Sardinia (E) – Sardegna (I)
Syracuse (E) – Siracusa (I)
Tiber (River) (E) – Tevere (I)
Venice (E) – Venezia (I)

LUXEMBOURG
Letzeburg (L), Luxembourg (F), Luxemburg (G)

THE NETHERLANDS
Nederland

Den Bosch (E, D) – 's-Hertogenbosch (D)
Europoort (D) – Europort (E)
Flushing (E) – Vlissingen (D)
Hook of Holland (E) – Hoek van Holland (D)
Meuse (River) (E, F) – Maas (D)
Rhine (River) (E) – Rijn (D)
The Hague (E) – Den Haag or 's-Gravenhage (D)

PORTUGAL

Cape St Vincent (E) – Cabo de São Vicente (P)
Lisbon (E) – Lisboa (P)
Oporto (E) – Porto (P)

SPAIN
España

Andalusia (E) – Andalucía (S)
Balearic Islands (E) – Islas Baleares (S)
Basque Country (E) – Euskardi (B), País Vasco (S)
Castile-Léon (E) – Castilla y Léon (S)
Castile-La Mancha (E) – Castilla La Mancha (S)
Catalonia (E) – Catalunya (C), Cataluña (S)
Cordova (E) – Córdoba (S)
Corunna (E) – La Coruña (S)
Majorca (E) – Mallorca (S)
Minorca (E) – Menorca (S)
Navarre (E) – Navarra (S)
San Sebastián (E, S) – Donostia (B)
Seville (E) – Sevilla (S)

SWITZERLAND
Schweiz (G), Suisse (F), Svizzera (I), Svizra (Rh)

Basel (E, G) – Basle (E), Bâle (F), Basilea (I)
Bern (E, G) – Berne (E, F), Berna (I)
Fribourg (E, F) – Freiburg (G), Friburgo (I)
Geneva (E) – Genève (F), Genf (G), Ginevra (I)
Graubünden (E, G) – Grisons (F), Grigioni (I),
   Grishun (Rh)
Lake Constance (E) – Bodensee (G)
Lake Geneva (E) – Lac Léman (F)
Lake Maggiore (E) – Lago Maggiore (I)
Lucerne (E, F) – Luzern (G), Lucerna (I)
Neuchâtel (E, F) – Neuenburg (G)
Ticino (E, I) – Tessin (G, F)
Valais (E, F) – Wallis (G)
Zürich (E, G) – Zurich (F), Zurigo (I)

Appendix III – Climate Charts

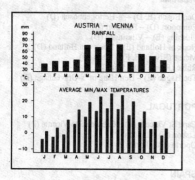

AUSTRIA – VIENNA
RAINFALL

AVERAGE MIN/MAX TEMPERATURES

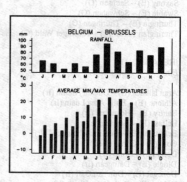

BELGIUM – BRUSSELS
RAINFALL

AVERAGE MIN/MAX TEMPERATURES

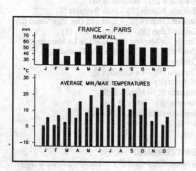

FRANCE – PARIS
RAINFALL

AVERAGE MIN/MAX TEMPERATURES

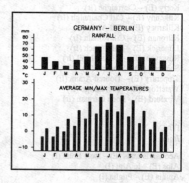

GERMANY – BERLIN
RAINFALL

AVERAGE MIN/MAX TEMPERATURES

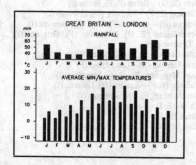

GREAT BRITAIN – LONDON
RAINFALL

AVERAGE MIN/MAX TEMPERATURES

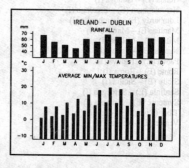

IRELAND – DUBLIN
RAINFALL

AVERAGE MIN/MAX TEMPERATURES

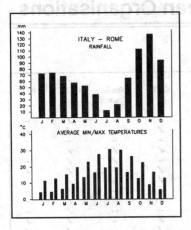

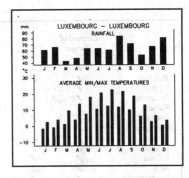

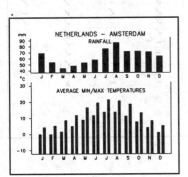

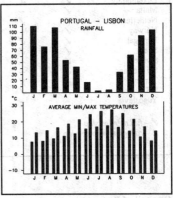

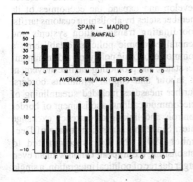

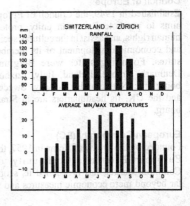

Appendix IV – European Organisations

	Council of Europe	EC	EFTA	NATO	Nordic Council	OECD	WEU
Austria	✓	–	✓	–	–	✓	–
Belgium	✓	✓	–	✓	–	✓	✓
Cyprus	✓	–	–	–	–	–	–
Denmark	✓	✓	–	✓	✓	✓	–
Finland	–	–	✓	–	✓	✓	–
France	✓	✓	–	✓	–	✓	✓
Germany	✓	✓	–	✓	–	✓	✓
Greece	✓	✓	–	✓	–	✓	–
Iceland	✓	–	✓	✓	✓	✓	–
Ireland	✓	✓	–	–	–	✓	–
Italy	✓	✓	–	✓	–	✓	✓
Luxembourg	✓	✓	–	✓	–	✓	✓
Malta	✓	–	–	–	–	–	–
Netherlands	✓	✓	–	✓	–	✓	✓
Norway	✓	–	✓	✓	✓	✓	–
Portugal	✓	✓	–	✓	–	✓	✓
Spain	✓	✓	–	✓	–	✓	–
Sweden	✓	–	✓	–	✓	✓	–
Switzerland	✓	–	✓	–	–	✓	–
Turkey	–	✗	–	✓	–	✓	–
UK	✓	✓	–	✓	–	✓	✓
Yugoslavia	–	–	✗	–	–	✗	–

✓ – full membership
✗ – associate membership

Council of Europe

Established in 1949, the Council of Europe aims to promote European unity, protect human rights, and assist in the cultural, social and economic development of its member states. Founding states were Belgium, Denmark, France, Ireland, Italy, Luxembourg, the Netherlands, Norway, Sweden and the UK. Its headquarters are in Strasbourg.

European Community (EC)

Founded by the Treaty of Rome in 1957, the European Economic Community, or Common Market, has broadened its scope far beyond mere economic measures and is now generally referred to as the European Community. Its original aims were to develop and expand the economies of its member states by abolishing customs tariffs, coordinating transportation systems and general economic policies, establishing a common economic policy towards nonmember states, and promoting the free movement of labour and capital within its borders. Further measures included streamlining of telecommunications, abolishment of border controls and linking of currency exchange rates. Since the Maastricht treaty of December 1991, the EC is committed to establishing a European Union with an even larger degree of political integration, a single currency and one central bank. The EEC's founding states were Belgium, France, (West) Germany, Italy, Luxembourg and the Netherlands (the Treaty of Rome was an extension of the European Coal and Steel Community founded by these six states in 1952). Full economic union was achieved in 1969. Denmark, Ireland and the UK joined in 1973, Greece in 1981, and Spain and Portugal in 1986; Greenland, a self-governing member of the Kingdom of Denmark, voted by referendum to leave the Community in 1982. The main EC organisations are the European Parliament (elected by direct universal suffrage, with growing powers), the European Commission (the daily 'government'), the Council of Ministers (ministers of member states who make the important decisions), and the Court of Justice. The European Parliament meets in Strasbourg, Luxembourg is home to the Court of Justice, and the other EC organisations are based in Brussels.

European Free Trade Association (EFTA)

Established in 1960, EFTA aims to eliminate trade tariffs on industrial products between member states, though each member retains the right to its own commercial policy towards nonmembers. EFTA is in effect a watered-down version of the EC, without supranational powers. The two are working towards a European Economic Area, which links them in economic matters and will create a single market. Denmark and the UK left EFTA to join the EC in 1973. Its headquarters are in Geneva.

North Atlantic Treaty Organisation (NATO)

This is a defence alliance established in 1949 between the USA, Canada and several European countries to safeguard their common political, social and economic systems against external threats (read: against the powerful Soviet military presence in Europe after 1945). An attack against any member state would be considered an attack against them all. Greece and Turkey joined in 1952,

West Germany in 1955, and Spain in 1982; France withdrew from NATO's integrated military command in 1966 and Greece did likewise in 1974, though both remain members. NATO's Soviet counterpart, the Warsaw Pact founded in 1955, has collapsed with the democratic revolutions of 1989 and the subsequent disintegration of the Soviet Union. NATO's headquarters are in Brussels.

Nordic Council

Established in 1952, the Nordic (or 'Norden') Council aims to promote economic, social and cultural cooperation among its member states. Since 1971, the Council has acted as an advisory body to the Nordic Council of Ministers, a meeting of ministers from the member states responsible for the subject under discussion. Decisions taken by the Council of Ministers are usually binding, though member states retain full sovereignty. Environmental, tariff, labour and immigration policies are often coordinated.

Organisation for Economic Cooperation and Development (OECD)

The OECD was set up in 1961 to supersede the Organisation for European Economic Cooperation, which allocated US aid under the Marshall Plan and coordinated the reconstruction of postwar Europe. Sometimes seen as the club of the world's rich countries, the OECD aims to encourage economic growth and world trade. Its 24 member states include most of Europe, as well as Australia, Canada, Japan and the USA. Its headquarters are in Paris.

Western European Union (WEU)

Set up in 1955, the WEU was designed to coordinate the military defences between member states, to promote economic, social and cultural cooperation, and to encourage European integration. Social and cultural tasks were transferred to the Council of Europe in 1960, and these days the WEU is sometimes touted as a future, more 'European', alternative to NATO. Its headquarters are in London.

Appendix V – Telephones

Dial Direct

You can dial directly from public phone boxes from almost anywhere in Europe to almost anywhere in the world. This is usually cheaper than going via the operator, and you don't even need a pocketful of coins if you use one of the phonecards which have become increasingly common in recent years.

To call overseas you simply dial the overseas access code (OS) for the country you are calling from, the country code (CC) for the country you are calling to, the local area code (dropping the leading zero if there is one) and then the number. If, for example, you are in Italy (overseas access code 00) and want to make a call to the USA (country code 1), San Francisco (area code 415), number 123 4567, then you dial 00-1-415-123 4567. To call from the UK (010) to Australia (61), Sydney (02), number 123 4567, you dial 010-61-2-123 4567.

Home Direct

If you would rather have somebody else pay for the call, you can, from many countries, dial directly to your home country operator and then reverse charges, charge the call to a phone company credit card or perform other credit feats. To do this, simply dial the relevant Home Direct number to be connected to your own operator. For the US there's a choice of AT&T, MCI or Sprint home direct services. Home direct numbers vary from country to country – check with your telephone company before you leave, or with the international operator in the country you're ringing from.

In some places, you may find dedicated Home Country Direct phones where you simply press the button labelled USA, Australia, Hong Kong or whatever for direct connection to the relevant operator. Note that the Home Direct service does not operate to and from all countries. You cannot phone Australia home direct from Germany, for example.

Dialling Tones

In some countries, after you've dialled the overseas access code, you have to wait for a dialling tone before dialling the code for your target country. Often the same applies when you ring from one city to another within these countries: wait for a dialling tone after you've dialled the area code for your target city. If you're not sure what to do, simply wait three or four seconds after dialling a code – if nothing happens, you can probably keep dialling.

Phone Cards

In major locations you may find phones which accept credit cards: simply swipe your card through the slot and the call is charged to the card. Phone company credit cards can be used to charge calls via your home country operator.

Stored-value phone cards are becoming increasingly common all over Europe. You buy a card from a post office, phone office, newsagent or other outlet and simply insert the card into the phone each time you make a call. The card saves the problem of finding the correct coins for calls (or lots of correct coins for international calls) and sometimes gives you a small discount.

Call Costs

Avoid ringing from a hotel room, unless you really don't care what it's going to cost. The cost of making an international call varies widely from one country to another. A US$10 call from Germany or Switzerland would cost you US$15 from France or US$20 from Italy. Choosing where you call from can make a big difference to the budget. The countries listed below are rated from * to *** in ascending order of cost – * is cheap, *** is expensive. Reduced rates are available at certain times, though these vary from country to country and should make little difference to relative costs – check the local phone book or ask the operator.

TELEPHONE CODES	CC	cost (see text)	OS	IO
Andorra (via Spain)	34738	***	0	19
Andorra (via France)	33628	**	0	19
Austria	43	*	00	09
Belgium	32	**	00	1324
Cyprus	357		00	
Cyprus (Turkish)	905			
Czechoslovakia	42		00	0131
Denmark	45	*	009	0015
Faroe Islands	298		009	0017
Finland	358	*	990	92022
France	33	**	19(w)	19(w)33
Germany †	49	*	00	0010
Gibraltar	350		00	100
Greece	30	**	00	161
Hungary	36		00(w)	09
Iceland	354		90	09
Ireland	353	*	00	114
Italy	39	***	00	15
Liechtenstein	41		00	114
Luxembourg	352		00	0010
Malta	356		00	94
Morocco	212		00(w)	12
Netherlands	31	**	09(w)	060410
Norway	47	**	095	091
Poland	48		0(w)0	900
Portugal	351	**	00	099
Romania	40			071
Spain	34	***	07(w)	91389
Sweden	46	***	009(w)	0018
Switzerland	41	*	00	114
Tunisia	216		00	
Turkey	90		9(w)9	248888
UK	44	*	010	155
Yugoslavia	38	**	99	901

CC – Country Code (to call that country)
OS – Overseas Access Code (to call abroad from that country)
(w) – wait for dialling tone
IO – International Operator (to make enquiries)

Other country codes: Australia 61, Canada 1, Hong Kong 853, India 91, Indonesia, 62, Japan 81, Macau 853, Malaysia 60, New Zealand 64, Singapore 65, South Africa 27, Thailand 66, USA 1

† The eastern part of Germany is still being amalgamated with the western German phone system. The old East Germany country code was 37, the old overseas access code 06 or 000.

Appendix VI – Clothing Size Conversions

CONVERSIONS APPROXIMATE ONLY – TRY BEFORE YOU BUY

Women's Clothing

Australia, NZ	8	10	12	14	16	18	20
France	34	36	38	40	42	44	46
Germany	32	34	36	38	40	42	44
Italy	36	38	40	42	44	46	48
Japan	5	7	9	11	13	15	17
UK	6	8	10	12	14	16	18
USA	4	6	8	10	12	14	16

Women's Shoes

Aust, NZ, USA	5.5	6	6.5	7	7.5	8	8.5
Continental Europe	37	38	38	39	39	40	41
UK	4	4.5	5	5.5	6	6.5	7

Men's Shoes

Aust, NZ, USA	7.5	8	8.5	9.5	10.5	11.5	12
Continental Europe	40	41	42	43	44	45	46
UK	6-6.5	7	7.5	8.5	9.5	10.5	11

Men's Clothing (Collar Size)

Italy, UK, USA (inches)	14	14.5	15	15.5	16	16.5	17
Aust, France, Germany, Japan (cm)	36	37	38	39	40	41	42

Men's Clothing (Chest Size)

Aust, NZ, France, Italy	42	44	46	48	50	52	54
Japan			S	M	L	XL	
UK, USA	32	34	36	38	40	42	44
Metric	81	86	91	97	102	107	112

Sweaters & T-Shirts

Aust, Germany, USA	S	M	L	XL
France	1	2-3	4	5
Italy	44	46-48	50	52
Japan		S-M	L	XL
UK	34	36-38	40	42-44

Index

TEXT

Map references are in **bold** type.

Keep in touch!

We love hearing from you and think you'd like to hear from us.

The Lonely Planet Newsletter covers the when, where, how and what of travel. (AND it's free!)

When...is the right time to see reindeer in Finland?
Where...can you hear the best palm-wine music in Ghana?
How...do you get from Asunción to Areguá by steam train?
What...should you leave behind to avoid hassles with customs in Iran?

To join our mailing list just contact us at any of our offices. (details below)

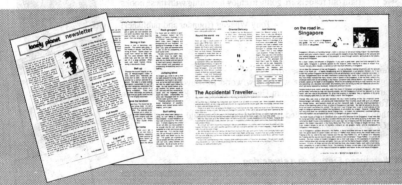

Every issue includes:

* *a letter from Lonely Planet founders Tony and Maureen Wheeler*
* *travel diary from a Lonely Planet author - find out what it's really like out on the road*
* *feature article on an important and topical travel issue*
* *a selection of recent letters from our readers*
* *the latest travel news from all over the world*
* *details on Lonely Planet's new and forthcoming releases*

Also available Lonely Planet t-shirts. 100% heavy weight cotton (S, M, L, XL)

LONELY PLANET PUBLICATIONS

Australia: PO Box 617, Hawthorn, 3122, Victoria (tel: 03-819 1877)
USA: Embarcadero West, 155 Filbert Street, Suite 251, Oakland, CA 94607 (tel: 510-893 8555)
UK: Devonshire House, 12 Barley Mow Passage, Chiswick, London W4 4PH (tel: 081-742 3161)

Lonely Planet guides to Europe

Twenty years ago Maureen and I set out on the trip across Asia which led to the very first Lonely Planet guidebook. Since then our reputation has been built on boldly going where no guidebook publisher had gone before. Now after all these years it has been a delight to return to Europe; culminating with the launch of our Europe series.

We deliberately didn't try to produce one monster Europe volume. Instead we've divided Europe into regions, sometimes overlapping, which has enabled us to include more maps and information – all the detail you've come to expect from a Lonely Planet book.

We're certain our readers are going to enjoy travelling with these books just as much as we enjoyed researching, writing and publishing them.

– Tony Wheeler (founder and publisher)

Eastern Europe on a shoestring
This guide has opened up a whole new world for travellers - Albania, Bulgaria, Czechoslovakia, eastern Germany, Hungary, Poland, Romania and Yugoslavia.
'...a thorough, well-researched book. Only a fool would go East without it.' – *Great Expeditions*

Mediterranean Europe on a shoestring
Details on hundreds of galleries, museums and architectural masterpieces and information on outdoor activities including hiking, sailing and skiing. Information on travelling in Albania, Andorra, Cyprus, France, Greece, Italy, Malta, Morocco, Portugal, Spain, Tunisia, Turkey and former republics of Yugoslavia.

Scandinavian & Baltic Europe on a shoestring
A comprehensive guide to travelling in this region including details on galleries, festivals and museums, as well as outdoor activities, national parks and wildlife. Countries featured are Denmark, Estonia, the Faroe Islands, Finland, Iceland, Latvia, Lithuania, Norway and Sweden.

Finland – a travel survival kit
Finland is an intriguing blend of Swedish and Russian influences. With its medieval stone castles, picturesque wooden houses, vast forest and lake district, and interesting wildlife, it is a wonderland to delight any traveller.

Iceland, Greenland & the Faroe Islands – a travel survival kit
Iceland, Greenland & the Faroe Islands contain some of the most beautiful wilderness areas in the world. This practical guidebook will help travellers discover the dramatic beauty of this region, no matter what their budget.

USSR – a travel survival kit
Invaluable advice on getting around and beating red tape for individual and group travellers alike. This comprehensive guide includes an unsanitised historical background and complete information on art and culture. Over 130 reliable maps, and all place names are given in Cyrillic script. (includes the independent states)

Trekking in Spain
Aimed at both overnight trekkers and day hikers, this guidebook includes useful maps and full details on hikes in some of Spain's most beautiful wilderness areas.

Also available:
Eastern Europe phrasebook
Discover the most enjoyable way to get around and make friends in Bulgarian, Czech, Hungarian, Polish, Romanian and Slovak.

Mediterranean Europe phrasebook
Ask for directions to the galleries and museums in Albanian, Greek, Italian, Macedonian, Maltese, Serbian & Croatian and Slovene.

Scandinavian Europe phrasebook
Find your way around the ski trails and enjoy the local festivals in Danish, Finnish, Icelandic, Norwegian and Swedish.

Western Europe phrasebook
Show your appreciation for the great masters in Basque, Catalan, Dutch, French, German, Irish, Portuguese and Spanish (Castilian).

Russian phrasebook
This indispensable phrasebook will help you get information, read signs and menus, and make friends along the way. Includes phonetic transcriptions and Cyrillic script.

Also:
Look out for **Lonely Planet travel survival kits** to the Baltic states, France, Greece, Hungary, Ireland, Italy, Poland and Switzerland.

Lonely Planet Guidebooks

Lonely Planet guidebooks cover every accessible part of Asia as well as Australia, the Pacific, South America, Africa, the Middle East, Europe and parts of North America. There are five series: *travel survival kits*, covering a country for a range of budgets; *shoestring guides* with compact information for low-budget travel in a major region; *walking guides*; *city guides* and *phrasebooks*.

Australia & the Pacific
Australia
Bushwalking in Australia
Islands of Australia's Great Barrier Reef
Fiji
Micronesia
New Caledonia
New Zealand
Tramping in New Zealand
Papua New Guinea
Papua New Guinea phrasebook
Rarotonga & the Cook Islands
Samoa
Solomon Islands
Sydney
Tahiti & French Polynesia
Tonga
Vanuatu

South-East Asia
Bali & Lombok
Bangkok
Burma
Burmese phrasebook
Cambodia
Indonesia
Indonesia phrasebook
Malaysia, Singapore & Brunei
Philippines
Pilipino phrasebook
Singapore
South-East Asia on a shoestring
Thailand
Thai phrasebook
Vietnam, Laos & Cambodia

North-East Asia
China
Mandarin Chinese phrasebook
Hong Kong, Macau & Canton
Japan
Japanese phrasebook
Korea
Korean phrasebook
North-East Asia on a shoestring
Taiwan
Tibet
Tibet phrasebook

West Asia
Trekking in Turkey
Turkey
Turkish phrasebook
West Asia on a shoestring

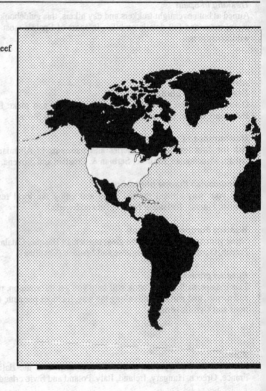

Middle East
Egypt & the Sudan
Egyptian Arabic phrasebook
Iran
Israel
Jordan & Syria
Yemen

Indian Ocean
Madagascar & Comoros
Maldives & Islands of the East Indian Ocean
Mauritius, Réunion & Seychelles

Mail Order

Lonely Planet guidebooks are distributed worldwide. They are also available by mail order from Lonely Planet, so if you have difficulty finding a title please write to us. US and Canadian residents should write to Embarcadero West, 155 Filbert St, Suite 251, Oakland CA 94607, USA; European residents should write to Devonshire House, 12 Barley Mow Passage, Chiswick, London W4 4PH; and residents of other countries to PO Box 617, Hawthorn, Victoria 3122, Australia.

Indian Subcontinent
Bangladesh
India
Hindi/Urdu phrasebook
Trekking in the Indian Himalaya
Karakoram Highway
Kashmir, Ladakh & Zanskar
Nepal
Trekking in the Nepal Himalaya
Nepal phrasebook
Pakistan
Sri Lanka
Sri Lanka phrasebook

Africa
Africa on a shoestring
Central Africa
East Africa
Kenya
Swahili phrasebook
Morocco, Algeria & Tunisia
Moroccan Arabic phrasebook
Zimbabwe, Botswana & Namibia
West Africa

Mexico
Baja California
Mexico

Central America
Central America on a shoestring
Costa Rica
La Ruta Maya

North America
Alaska
Canada
Hawaii

Europe
Eastern Europe on a shoestring
Eastern Europe phrasebook
Finland
Iceland, Greenland & the Faroe Islands
Mediterranean Europe on a shoestring
Mediterranean Europe phrasebook
Scandinavian & Baltic Europe on a shoestring
Scandinavian Europe phrasebook
Trekking in Spain
USSR
Russian phrasebook
Western Europe on a shoestring
Western Europe phrasebook

South America
Argentina, Uruguay & Paraguay
Bolivia
Brazil
Brazilian phrasebook
Chile & Easter Island
Colombia
Ecuador & the Galápagos Islands
Latin American Spanish phrasebook
Peru
Quechua phrasebook
South America on a shoestring
Trekking in the Patagonian Andes

The Lonely Planet Story

Lonely Planet published its first book in 1973 in response to the numerous 'How did you do it?' questions Maureen and Tony Wheeler were asked after driving, bussing, hitching, sailing and railing their way from England to Australia.

Written at a kitchen table and hand collated, trimmed and stapled, *Across Asia on the Cheap* became an instant local bestseller, inspiring thoughts of another book.

Eighteen months in South-East Asia resulted in their second guide, *South-East Asia on a shoestring*, which they put together in a backstreet Chinese hotel in Singapore in 1975. The 'yellow bible' as it quickly became known to backpackers around the world, soon became *the* guide to the region. It has sold well over half a million copies and is now in its 7th edition, still retaining its familiar yellow cover.

Today there are over 100 Lonely Planet titles – books that have that same adventurous approach to travel as those early guides; books that 'assume you know how to get your luggage off the carousel' as one reviewer put it.

Although Lonely Planet initially specialised in guides to Asia, they now cover most regions of the world, including the Pacific, South America, Africa, the Middle East and Europe. The list of *walking guides* and *phrasebooks* (for 'unusual' languages such as Quechua, Swahili, Nepalese and Egyptian Arabic) is also growing rapidly.

The emphasis continues to be on travel for independent travellers. Tony and Maureen still travel for several months of each year and play an active part in the writing, updating and quality control of Lonely Planet's guides.

They have been joined by over 50 authors, 48 staff – mainly editors, cartographers, & designers – at our office in Melbourne, Australia and another 10 at our US office in Oakland, California. In 1991 Lonely Planet opened a London office to handle sales for Britain, Europe and Africa. Travellers themselves also make a valuable contribution to the guides through the feedback we receive in thousands of letters each year.

The people at Lonely Planet strongly believe that travellers can make a positive contribution to the countries they visit, both through their appreciation of the countries' culture, wildlife and natural features, and through the money they spend. In addition, the company makes a direct contribution to the countries and regions it covers. Since 1986 a percentage of the income from each book has been donated to ventures such as famine relief in Africa; aid projects in India; agricultural projects in Central America; Greenpeace's efforts to halt French nuclear testing in the Pacific and Amnesty International. In 1991 $68,000 was donated to these causes.

Lonely Planet's basic travel philosophy is summed up in Tony Wheeler's comment, 'Don't worry about whether your trip will work out. Just go!'